Small Business Sourcebook

ISSN 0883-3397

Small Business Sourcebook

The Entrepreneur's Resource

TWENTY-NINTH EDITION

Volume 1

Specific Small Business Profiles

(Entries 1-7780)

Sonya D. Hill
Project Editor

GALE
CENGAGE Learning

Detroit • New York • San Francisco • New Haven, Conn • Waterville, Maine • London

Small Business Sourcebook, 29th edition

Project Editor: Sonya D. Hill

Editorial Support Services: Charles Beaumont

Composition and Electronic Prepress: Gary Leach

Manufacturing: Rita Wimberley

Gale
27500 Drake Rd.
Farmington Hills, MI, 48331-3535

ISBN-13: 978-1-4144-6919-5 (set)
ISBN-10: 1-4144-6919-5 (set)
ISBN-13: 978-1-4144-6920-1 (vol. 1)
ISBN-10: 1-4144-6920-9 (vol. 1)
ISBN-13: 978-1-4144-6921-8 (vol. 2)
ISBN-10: 1-4144-6921-7 (vol. 2)
ISBN-13: 978-1-4144-6986-7 (vol. 3)
ISBN-10: 1-4144-6986-1 (vol . 3)
ISBN-13: 978-1-4144-6987-4 (vol . 4)
ISBN-10: 1-4144-6987-X (vol . 4)
ISBN-13: 978-1-4144-6988-1 (vol . 5)
ISBN-10: 1-4144-6988-8 (vol . 5)
ISBN-13: 978-1-4144-7694-0 (vol . 6)
ISBN-10: 1-4144-7694-9 (vol . 6)

ISSN 0883-3397

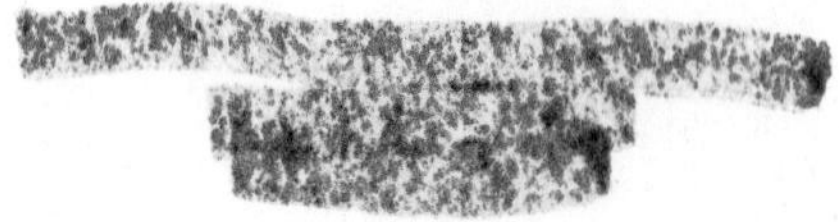

Printed in the United States of America
1 2 3 4 5 16 15 14 13 12

FD109

Contents

Introduction

The appeal of small business ownership remains perpetually entrenched in American culture as one of the most viable avenues for achieving the American Dream. To many entrepreneurs going into business for themselves represents financial independence, an increased sense of identity and self-worth, and the fulfillment of personal goals. Small business owners strive to make their mark in today's competitive marketplace by establishing healthy businesses that can, over time, become legacies handed down from one generation to the next. Entrepreneurs from each generation tackle the obstacles and adversities of the current business and economic climate to test their business savvy and generate opportunities. Today's entrepreneurs face many of the problems of their predecessors, as well as some distinctly new challenges.

With the rightsizing, downsizing, and reorganization of-corporate America, many individuals have decided to confront the risks of developing and operating their own businesses. Small business ownership is rapidly becoming a viable alternative to what is perceived as an equally unstable corporate environment. These entrepreneurs, many of whom have firsthand experience with the problems and inefficiencies inherent in today's large corporations, seek to improve upon an archaic business model and to capitalize on their own ingenuity and strengths. Led by their zeal, many would-be entrepreneurs let their desire, drive, and determination overshadow the need for business knowledge and skill. Ironically, aids in obtaining these components of entrepreneurial success are widely available, easily accessible, and often free of charge.

Small Business Sourcebook (*SBS*) is a six-volume annotated guide to more than 21,199 listings of live and print sources of information designed to facilitate the start-up, development, and growth of specific small businesses, as well as over 26,073 similar listings on general small business topics. An additional 8,679 state-specific listings and over 1,997 U.S. federal government agencies and offices specializing in small business issues, programs, and assistance are also included. *SBS* covers 340 specific small business profiles and 99 general small business topics.

Features of This Edition

This edition of *Small Business Sourcebook* has been revised and updated, incorporating thousand of changes to names, addresses, contacts, and descriptions of listings from the previous edition.

Contents and Arrangement

The geographical scope of *SBS* encompasses the United States and Canada, with expanded coverage for resources pertaining to international trade and for resources that have a U.S. or Canadian distributor or contact. Internet sites that are maintained outside of the U.S. and Canada are also included if they contain relevant information for North American small businesses. Resources that do not relate specifically to small businesses are generally not included.

The information presented in *SBS* is grouped within four sections: Specific Small Business Profiles, General Small Business Topics, State Listings, and Federal Government Assistance. Detailed outlines of these sections may be found in the Users' Guide following this Introduction. Also included is a Master Index to Volumes 1 through 6.

Specific Small Business Profiles This section includes the following types of resources: start-up information, associations and other organizations, educational programs, directories of educational programs, reference works, sources of supply, statistical sources, trade periodicals, videocassettes/audiocassettes, trade shows and conventions, consultants, franchises and business opportunities, computerized databases, computer systems/software, Internet databases, libraries, and research centers-all arranged by business type. Entries range from Accounting Service to Word Processing Service, and include such businesses as Airbag Replacement Service Centers, Computer Consulting, Damage Restoration Service, and Web Site Design.

General Small Business Topics This section offers such resources as associations, books, periodicals, articles, pamphlets, educational programs, directories of educational programs,videocassettes/audiocassettes, trade shows and conventions, consultants, computerized databases, Internet databases, software,libraries, and research centers, arranged alphabetically by business topic.

State Listings Entries include government, academic, and commercial agencies and organizations, as well as select coverage of relevant state-specific publications; listings are arranged alphabetically by state, territory, and Canadian province. Some examples include small business development consultants, educational programs, financing and loan programs, better business bureaus, and chambers of commerce.

Federal Government Assistance Listings specializing in small business issues, programs, assistance, and policyare arranged alphabetically by U.S. government agency or office; regional or branch offices are listed alphabetically by state.

Master Index All entries in Volumes 1 through 6 are arranged in one alphabetic index for convenience.

Entries in *SBS* include (as appropriate andavailable):

- Organization, institution, or product name
- Contact information, including contact name, address and phone, toll-free, and fax numbers
- Author/editor, date(s), and frequency
- Availability, including price
- Brief description of purpose, services, or content
- Company and/or personal E-mail addresses
- Web site addresses

SBS also features the following:

Guide to Publishers—An alphabetic listing of 2,425 companies, associations, institutions, and individuals that publish the periodicals, directories, guidebooks, and other publications noted in the Small Business Profiles and General Topics sections. Users are provided with full contact information, including address, phone, fax,and e-mail and URL when available. The Guide to Publishers facilitates contact with publishers and provides a one- stop resource for valuable information.

Method of Compilation

SBS was compiled by consulting small business experts and entrepreneurs, as well as a variety of resources, including direct contact with the associations, organizations, and agencies through telephone surveys, Internet research, or through materials provided by those listees; government resources; and data obtained from other relevant Gale directories. *SBS* was reviewed by a team of small business advisors, all of whom have numerous years of expertise in small business counseling and identification of small business information resources. The last and perhaps most important resource we utilize is direct contact with our readers, who provide valuable comments and suggestions to improve our publication. *SBS* relies on these comprehensive market contacts to provide today's entrepreneurs with relevant, current, and accurate informationon all aspects of small business.

Available in Electronic Formats

Licensing. *Small Business Sourcebook* is available for licensing. The complete database is provided in a fielded format and is deliverable on such media as disk or CD-ROM. For more information, contact Gale's Business Development Group at1-800-877-GALE, or visit our website at www.gale.com/bizdev.

Comments and Suggestions Welcome

Associations, agencies, business firms, publishers, and other organizations that provide assistance and information to the small business community are encouraged to submit material about their programs, activities, services, or products. Comments and suggestions from users of this directory are also welcomed and appreciated. Please contact:

Project Editor
Small Business Sourcebook
Gale, Cengage Learning
27500 Drake Rd.
Farmington Hills, MI 48331-3535
Phone: (248) 699-4253
Fax: (248) 699-8070
E-mail: BusinessProductsgale.com
URL: www.gale.com

Small Business Sourcebook (*SBS*) provides information in a variety of forms and presentations for comprehensive coverage and ease of use. The directory contains four parts within two volumes:

- Specific Small Business Profiles
- General Small Business Topics
- State Listings
- Federal Government Assistance

Information on specific businesses is arranged by type of business; the many general topics that are of interest to the owners, operators, or managers of all small businesses are grouped in a separate section for added convenience. Users should consult the various sections to benefit fully from the information *SBS* offers. For example, an entrepreneur with a talent or interest in the culinary arts could peruse a number of specific small business profiles, such as Restaurant, Catering, Cooking School, Specialty Food/Wine Shop, Bakery/Doughnut Shop, Healthy Restaurant, or Candy/Chocolate Store. Secondly, the General Small Business Topics section could be consulted for any applicable subjects, such as Service Industry, Retailing, Franchising, and other relevant topics. Then, the appropriate state within the State Listings section would offer area programs and offices providing information and support to small businesses, including venture capital firms and small business development consultants. Finally, the Federal Government Assistance section could supply relevant government offices, such as procurement contacts.

Features Included in Volumes 1 through 3

List of Small Business Profiles. This list provides an alphabetic outline of the small businesses profiled, with cross-references for related profiles and for alternate names by which businesses may be identified. The page number for each profile is indicated.

Standard Industrial Classification (SIC) Codes for-Profiled Small Businesses. This section lists four-digit SIC codes and corresponding classification descriptions for the small businesses profiled in this edition. The SIC system, which organizes businesses by type, is a product of the Statistical Policy Division of the U.S. Office of Management and Budget. Statistical data produced by government, public, and private organizations is usually categorized according to SIC codes, thereby facilitating the collection, comparison, and analysis of data as well as providing a uniform method for presenting statistical information. Hence, knowing the SIC code for a particular small business increases access and the use of a variety of statistical data from many sources.

Guide to Publishers. This resource lists alphabetically the companies, associations, institutions, and individuals that publish the periodicals, directories, guidebooks, and other publications noted in the "Small Business Profiles" and "General Topics" sections. Users are provided with full contact information, including address, phone, fax, and e-mail and URL when available. The "Guide" facilitates contact with publishers and provides a one-stop resource for valuable information.

Glossary of Small Business Terms. This glossary defines nearly 400 small business terms, including financial, governmental, insurance, procurement, technical, and general business definitions. Cross-references and acronyms are also provided.

Small Business Profiles A-Z. A total of 340 small businesses is represented in volumes 1 through 3. Profiles are listed alphabetically by business name. Entries within each profile are arranged alphabetically by resource type, within up to 17 subheadings.These subheadings are detailed below:

- ***Start-up Information***—Includes periodical articles, books, manuals, book excerpts, kits, and other sources of information. Entries offer title; publisher; address; phone, fax, toll-free numbers; company e-mail and URL addresses; and a description. Bibliographic data is provided for cited periodical articles whenever possible.
- ***Associations and Other Organizations***—Includes trade and professional associations whose members gather and disseminate information of interest to small business owners. Entries offer the association's

name; address; phone, toll-free and fax numbers; company e-mail address; contact name; purpose and objective; a description of membership; telecommunication services; and a listing of its publications, including publishing frequency.

- ***Educational Programs***—Includes university and college programs, schools, training opportunities, association seminars, correspondence courses, and other educational programs.Entries offer name of program or institution, sponsor name, address, phone, toll-free and fax numbers, e-mail and URL addresses; and description of program.
- ***Directories of Educational Programs***—Includes directories and other publications that list educational programs. Entries offer name of publication; publisher name, address, and phone, toll-free and fax numbers; editor; frequency or date of publication; price; and description of contents, including directory arrangement and indexes.
- ***Reference Works***—Includes handbooks, manuals, textbooks, guides, directories, dictionaries, encyclopedias, and other published reference materials. Entries offer name of publication; publisher name, address, and phone, toll-free and fax numbers; e-mail and URL addresses; and, when available, name of author or editor, publication year or frequency, and price. A brief description is often featured.
- ***Sources of Supply***—Includes buyer's guides,directories, special issues of periodicals, and other publications that list sources of equipment, supplies, and services related to the operation of the profiled small business. Entries offer publication name; publisher name, address, and phone, toll-free and fax numbers; e-mail and URL addresses; and, when available, editor's name, frequency or publication year, and price. A brief description of the publication, including directory arrangement and indexes, is often provided.
- ***Statistical Sources***—Includes books, reports, pamphlets, and other sources of statistical data of interest to an owner, operator or manager of the profiled small business, such as wage, salary, and compensation data; financial and operating ratios; prices and costs; demographics; and other statistical information. Entries offer publication/data source name; publisher (if applicable); address; phone, toll-free and fax numbers of data source; publication date or frequency; and price. A brief description of the publication/data source is often provided.
- ***Trade Periodicals***—Includes trade journals, newsletters, magazines, and other serials that offer information about the management and operation of the profiled small business. Such periodicals often contain industry news; trends and developments; reviews; articles about new equipment and supplies; and other information related to business operations. Entries offer publication name; publisher name, address, phone, toll-free and fax numbers, and e-mail and URL addresses; editor name; publication frequency; andprice. A brief description of the publication's content is also included, when known.
- ***Videocassettes/Audiocassettes***—Includes videocassettes, audiocassettes, and other audiovisual media offering information on the profiled small business. Entries offer program title; distributor name, address, phone, toll-free and fax numbers, and e-mail and URL addresses; description of program; release date; price; and format(s).
- ***Trade Shows and Conventions***—Includes tradeshows, exhibitions, expositions, conventions, and other industry meetings that provide prospective and existing business owners with the opportunity to meet and exchange information with their peers, review commercial exhibits, establish business or sales contacts, and attend educational programs. Entries offer event name; sponsor or management company name, address, phone, toll-free and fax numbers, and e-mail and URL addresses; a description of the event, including audience, frequency, principal exhibits, and dates and locations of event for as many years ahead as provided by the event's sponsor.
- ***Consultants***—Includes consultants and consulting organizations that provide services specifically related to the profiled small business. Entries offer individual consultant or consulting organization name, address, and phone, toll-free and fax numbers; company and individual e-mail addresses; and a brief description of consulting services. (For e-mail and URL addresses, see the Small Business Development Consultants subheadings in the State Listings section in Volume 2.)
- ***Franchises and Business Opportunities***—Includes companies granting franchise licenses for enterprises falling within the scope of the profiled small business, as well as other non-franchised business opportunities that operate within a given network or system. Entries offer franchise name, address, phone, toll-free and fax numbers, and e-mail and URL addresses, as well as a description of the franchise or business opportunity, which has been expanded whenever possible to include the number of existing franchises, the founding date of the franchise, franchise fees, equity capital requirements, royalty fees, any managerial assistance offered, and available training.
- ***Computerized Databases***—Includes diskettes, magnetic tapes, CD-ROMs, online systems, and other computer-readable databases. Entries offer database name; producer name, address, phone, toll-free and fax numbers, e-mail and URL addresses; description; and available format(s), including vendor name.

(Many university and public libraries offer online information retrieval services that provide searches of databases, including those listed in this category.)

- ***Computer Systems/Software***—Includes softwareand computerized business systems designed to assist in the operation of the profiled small business. Entries offer name of the software or system; publisher name, address, phone, toll-free and fax-numbers; price; and description.
- ***Libraries***—Includes libraries and special collections that contain material especially applicable to the profiled small business. Entries offer library or collection name; parent organization (where applicable); address; phone, toll-free and fax numbers; e-mail and URL addresses; contact name and title; scope of collection; and description of holdings, subscriptions, and services.
- ***Research Centers***—Includes university-related and independently operated research institutes and information centers that generate, through their research programs, data related to the operation of the profiled small business. Also listed are associations and other business-related organizations that conduct research programs. Entries offer name of organization; address; phone, toll-free and fax numbers; company web site address; contact name and personale-mail; a description of principal fields of research or services; publications, including title and frequency; and related conferences.

Features Included in Volumes 2 through 6

General Small Business Topics. This section offers chapters on different topics in the operation of any small business, for example, venture capital and other funding, or compensation. Chapters are listed alphabetically by small business topic; entries within each chapter are arranged alphabetically, within up to 14 subheadings, by resource type:

- ***Associations and OtherOrganizations***—Includes trade and professional associations that gather and disseminate information of interest to small business owners. Entries offer the association's name; address; phone, toll-free and fax numbers; organization e-mail and URL addresses; contact name;purpose and objectives; a description of membership; telecommunication services; and a listing of its publications, including publishing frequency.
- ***Educational Programs***—Includes university and college programs, schools, training opportunities, association seminars, correspondence courses, and other educational programs. Entries offer name of program or institution, sponsor name, address, phone, toll-free and fax numbers, e-mail and URL addresses, and description of program.
- ***Directories of Educational Programs***—Includes directories and other publications that list educational programs. Entries offer name of publication; publisher name, address, phone, toll-free and fax numbers, and e-mail and URL addresses; editor; frequency or date of publication; price; and description of contents, including arrangement and indexes.
- ***Reference Works***—Includes articles, handbooks, manuals, textbooks, guides, directories, dictionaries, encyclopedias, and other published reference materials. Entries offertitle of article, including bibliographic information; name of publication; publisher name, address, phone, toll-free and fax numbers, and e-mail and URL addresses; and, when available, name of author oreditor, publication year or frequency, and price. A brief descriptionis often featured.
- ***Sources of Supply***—Includes buyer's guides,directories, special issues of periodicals, and other publications that list sources of equipment, supplies, and services. Entries offer publication name; publisher name, address, phone, toll-free and fax numbers, and e-mail and URL addresses; editor's name, frequency or publication year, price, and a brief description of the publication, when available.
- ***Statistical Sources***—Includes books, reports, pamphlets, and other sources of statistical data of interest to an owner, operator, or manager of a small business, such as wage, salary, and compensation data; financial and operating ratios; prices and costs; demographics; and other statistical information. Entries offer publication/data source name; publisher (if applicable); address; phone, toll-free and fax numbers of data source; publication date or frequency; and price. A brief description is often provided.
- ***Trade Periodicals***—Includes journals, newsletters, magazines, and other serials. Entries offer name of publication; publisher name, address, phone, toll-free and fax numbers, and e-mail and URL addresses; and name of editor, frequency, and price.A brief description of the periodical's content is included when known.
- ***Videocassettes/Audiocassettes***—Includes videocassettes, audiocassettes, and other audiovisual media. Entries offer program title; distributor name, address, phone, toll-free and fax numbers, and e-mail and URL addresses; price; description of program; release date; and format(s).
- ***Trade Shows and Conventions***—Includes tradeshows, exhibitions, expositions, seminars, and conventions. Entries offer event name; sponsor or management company name, address, phone, toll-free and fax numbers, and e-mail and URL ad-

dresses; frequency of event; and dates and locations of the event for as many years ahead as known.

- ***Consultants***—Includes consultants and consulting organizations. Entries offer individual consultant or-consulting organization name, address, and phone, toll-free and fax numbers; company and individual e-mail addresses; and a brief description of consulting services. (See also Consultants in the State Listings section.)

- ***Computerized Databases***—Includes diskettes, CD-ROMs, magnetic tape, online systems and other computer-readable databases. Entries offer database name; producer, address, phone, toll-free and fax numbers, and e-mail and URL addresses; description; and available format(s), including vendor name. (Many university and public libraries offer online information retrieval services that provide searches of databases, including those listed in this category.)

- ***Computer Systems/Software***—Includes software and computerized business systems. Entries offer name of the software or system; publisher name, address, phone, toll-free and fax numbers, and e-mail and URL addresses; price; and description.

- ***Libraries***—Includes libraries and special collections that contain material applicable to the small business topic. Entries offer library or collection name, parent organization (where applicable), address, phone and fax numbers, e-mail and URL addresses, scope of collection, and description of holdings and services.

- ***Research Centers***— Includes university-related and independently operated research institutes and information centers that generate, through their research programs, data related to specific small business topics. Entries offer name of organization, address, phone, toll-free and fax numbers, e-mail and URL addresses, a description of principal fields of research or services, and related conferences.

State Listings. This section lists various sources of information and assistance available within given states, territories, and Canadian provinces; entries include governmental, academic, and commercial agencies, and are arranged alphabetically within up to 15 subheadings by resource type:

- ***Small Business Development Center Lead Office***— Includes the lead small business development center (SBDC) for each state.

- ***Small Business Development Centers***—Includes any additional small business development centers (SBDC) in the state, territory, or province. SBDCs provide support services to small businesses, including individual counseling, seminars, conferences, and learning center activities.

- ***Small Business Assistance Programs***—Includes state small business development offices and other programs offering assistance to small businesses.

- ***SCORE Offices***—Includes SCORE office(s) for each state. The Service Corps of Retired Executives Association (SCORE), a volunteer program sponsored by the Small Business Administration, offers counseling, workshops, and seminars across the U.S. for small business entrepreneurs.

- ***Better Business Bureaus***—Includes various better business bureaus within each state. By becoming a member of the local Better Business Bureau, a small business owner can increase the prestige and credibility of his or her business within the community, as well as make valuable business contacts.

- ***Chambers of Commerce***—Includes various chambers of commerce within each state. Chambers of Commerce are valuable sources of small business advice and information; often, local chambers sponsor SCORE counseling several times per month for a small fee, seminars, conferences, and other workshops to its members. Also, by becoming a member of the local Chamber of Commerce, a small business owner can increase the prestige and credibility of his or herbusiness within the community, as well as make valuable business contacts.

- ***Minority Business Assistance Programs***—Includes minority business development centers and other sources of assistance for minority-owned business.

- ***Financing and Loan Programs***—Includes venture capital firms, small business investment companies (SBIC), minority enterprise small business investment companies (MESBIC), and other programs that provide funding to qualified small businesses.

- ***Procurement Assistance Programs***—Includes state services such as counseling, set-asides, and sheltered-market bidding, which are designed to aid small businesses in bidding on government contracts.

- ***Incubators/Research and Technology Parks***—Includes small business incubators, which provide newly established small business owners with work sites, business services, training, and consultation; also includes research and technology parks, which sponsor research and facilitate commercialization of new technologies.

- ***Educational Programs***—Includes university and college programs, as well as those sponsored by other organizations that offer degree, nondegree, certificate, and correspondence programs in entrepreneurship and in small business development.

- ***Legislative Assistance***—Includes committees, subcommittees, and joint committees of each state's senate and house of representatives that are concerned with small business issues and regulations.

- ***Consultants***—Includes consultants and consulting firms offering expertise in small business development.
- ***Publications***—Includes publications related to small business operations within the profiled state.
- ***Publishers***—Includes publishers operating in or for the small business arena within the profiled state.

Federal Government Assistance. This section lists federal government agencies and offices, many with additional listings for specific offices, as well as regional or district branches. Main agencies or offices are listed alphabetically; regional, branch, ordistrict offices are listed after each main office or agency.

Master Index. This index provides an alphabetic listing of all entries contained in Volumes 1 throgh 6. Citations are referenced by their entry numbers. Publication titles are rendered in italics.

Acknowledgements

The editors would like to extend sincere thanks to the following members of the Small Business Sourcebook advisory board for their expert guidance, recommendations, and suggestions for the ongoing development of this title:

Susan C. Awe
Assistant Director,
William J. Parish Memorial Business Library

Jill Clever
Business Technology Specialist,
Toledo-Lucas County Public Library

Jules Matsoff
District Manager,
Service Corps of Retired Executives (SCORE) Milwaukee Chapter

Ken MacKenzie
President,
Southeast Business Appraisal

The editors would also like to thank the individuals from associations and other organizations who provided information for the compilation of this directory.

List of Small Business Profiles

This list is an outline of the 341 small businesses profiled in this edition of Small Business Sourcebook. The beginning page number of each profile is provided. For convenience, this index also provides cross-references to small businesses known by alternate names, businesses contained within other small business profiles, and synonymous or related businesses.

Standard Industrial Classification (SIC) Codes for Profiled Small Businesses

Included here are the four-digit SIC codes and corresponding classification descriptions for the businesses profiled in this edition. The SIC system, which organizes businesses by type, is a product of the Statistical Policy Division of the U.S. Office of Management and Budget. Statistical data produced by government, public, and private organizations usually are categorized according to SIC codes, thereby facilitating the collection, comparison, and analysis of data as well as providing a uniform method for presenting statistical information. Hence, knowing the SIC code for a particular small business increases the access to, and the use of, a variety of statistical data from many sources. The following SIC codes were obtained from the 1987 edition of the Standard Industrial Classification Manual, the most recent version available. (The term "nec" stands for "not elsewhere classified.")

Accounting Service

7291 Tax return preparation services

8721 Accounting, auditing, and bookkeeping services

Adult Day Care Center

8322 Individual and family social services (includes adult day carecenters)

Advertising Service

7311 Advertising agencies (includes advertising consultants)

7312 Outdoor advertising agencies

7313 Radio, television, and publishers' advertising representatives

7319 Advertising, nec

7331 Direct mail advertising services

8999 Services, nec (includes advertising copywriters)

Airbag Replacement Service Centers

7538 General automotive repair shops

7539 Automotive repair shops, nec

Air Charter Service

4512 Air transportation, scheduled (includes air cargo and passenger carriers)

4513 Air courier services

4522 Air transportation, nonscheduled (includes charter service)

Air-conditioning/Heating and Cooling Contractor

1711 Plumbing, heating, and air-conditioning contractors

Air Purification/Cleaning Service

7699 Repair shops and related services, nec (includes furnace cleaning service)

Ambulance Service

4119 Local passenger transportation, nec (includes ambulance service, road)

4522 Air transportation, nonscheduled (includes ambulance service, air)

Amusement Arcade

7993 Coin-operated amusement devices

Amusement/Water Park

7996 Amusement parks

7999 Amusement and recreation services, nec (includes waterslides and wave pools)

Animal Breeder

0279 Animal specialties, nec (includes kennels, breeding and raising own stock)

0752 Animal specialty services, except veterinary (includes breeding of animals other than farm animals)

Animal Clinic

0742 Veterinary service for animal specialties (includes animal hospitals for pets and other animals)

Antique Shop

5932 Used merchandise stores (includes retail antique stores)

7641 Reupholstery and furniture repair (includes antique furniture repair and restoration)

7699 Repair shops and related services, nec (includes antique repair and restoration, except furniture)

Apartment Locating Service

6531 Real Estate Agents and Managers

Appliance Store

5722 Household appliance stores

Appraisal Service

7389 Business services, nec (includes appraisers, except real estate)

6531 Real estate agents and managers (includes appraisers, realestate)

Aquarium Maintenance/Leasing Service

7359 Equipment rental and leasing, nec

8999 Services, nec

Archery/Target/Shooting Range

7999 Amusement and recreation services, nec (includes archery ranges, shooting galleries, shooting ranges, and trap-shooting facilities, except membership)

Architectural Restoration/Conservation

8712 Architectural Services

Art Gallery

5932 Used merchandise stores (includes retailers of art objects)

5999 Miscellaneous retail stores, nec (includes art dealers)

8412 Museums and art galleries (includes noncommercial art galleries)

Art Supplies Store

5999 Miscellaneous retail stores, nec (includes retail artists' supplies and materials stores)

Assisted Living Facilities

8051 Skilled nursing care facilities (includes extended care facilities and skilled nursing homes)

8052 Intermediate care facilities (includes intermediate care nursing homes)

8059 Nursing and personal care facilities, nec (includes rest homeswith health care)

Association Management Service

8611 Business associations

8621 Professional membership organizations

8631 Labor unions and similar labor organizations

8641 Civic, social, and fraternal associations

8699 Membership organizations, nec

8741 Management services (does not include operating staff)

Auctioneer

5154 Livestock (includes wholesale livestock auctioning)

5999 Miscellaneous retail stores, nec (includes retail general merchandise auction rooms)

7389 Business services, nec (includes auctioneering services)

Auto Supply Store

5531 Auto and home supply stores

Automobile Detailing/Painting Service

7532 Automotive paint shops

7542 Carwashes (includes detailing, cleaning and polishing, new autos on a contract or fee basis; washing and polishing, automotive; waxing and polishing, automotive)

Automobile/Truck Leasing Service

7513 Truck rental and leasing, without drivers

7514 Passenger car rental, without drivers

7515 Passenger car leasing, without drivers

Baby Store

5999 Miscellaneous retail stores, nec (includes retail baby)

Bagel Shop

2051 Bread and other bakery products, except cookies and crackers (includes bagels)

5461 Retail bakeries (includes retail bagel stores)

Bait and Tackle Shop

5941 Sporting goods stores and bicycle shops (includes bait and tackle shops and fishing equipment, retail)

Bakery/Doughnut Shop

5461 Retail bakeries

Bar/Cocktail Lounge

5813 Drinking places alcoholic beverages (includes bars, cocktail lounges, saloons, tap rooms, taverns, and like establishments)

Beauty Supply Center

5087 Service establishment equipment and supplies (includes wholesale barber shop and beauty parlor equipment and supplies)

Bed and Breakfast Operation

7011 Hotels and motels (includes bed and breakfast inns)

Beekeeping

0279 Animal specialties, nec (includes apiaries and bee farms)

Beeper/Paging Service

4812 Radiotelephone communications (includes beeper and paging services)

Bicycle Shop

5941 Sporting goods stores and bicycle shops

7699 Repair shops and related services, nec (includes bicycle repair shops)

Billiards Hall

7999 Amusement and recreation services, nec (includes billiard parlors)

Blacktop Surfacing Business

1771 Concrete work (includes blacktop work: private driveways and private parking areas contractors)

Blind Cleaning/Installation

2431 Millwork (includes wood blinds and shutters)

2591 Drapery hardware and window blinds and shades

Body Care Shop

5999 Miscellaneous retail stores, nec (includes cosmetics stores)

Book Publishing

2731 Books; publishing or publishing and printing

Bookbinder

2789 Bookbinding and related work

Bookkeeping

8721 Accounting, auditing, and bookkeeping services

Bookstore

5932 Used merchandise stores (includes used book retailers)

5942 Bookstores

Bottled Water Service

5149 Groceries and related products, nec (includes natural spring and mineral water bottling and distribution services)

5499 Miscellaneous food stores (includes mineral water, retail)

Bowling Alley

7933 Bowling centers

Brewery Operation

2082 Malt beverages

Bridal Shop/Bridal Consultant

5621 Women's clothing stores (includes retail bridal shops, exceptcustom designers)

Building/Home Inspection

7389 Business services, nec (includes safety inspection, except automotive)

Building Maintenance/Custodial Service

7349 Building cleaning and maintenance services, nec (includes interior building cleaning services, contract janitorial services, and like enterprises)

Bulletin Board Service

4822 Telegraph and other message communications (includes electronic mail services)

7379 Computer related services, nec

Business Broker Service

7389 Business services, nec (includes business brokers buying andselling business enterprises)

Business Consulting Service

8748 Business consulting services, nec

Business Services Operation

8744 Facilities support management services (includesbasemaintenance, providing personnel on continuing basis)

Butcher Shop

5423 Meat and fish (seafood) markets, including freezer provisioners

5499 Miscellaneous food stores (includes retail poultry dealers)

Cable Network

1623 Water, Sewer, Pipeline, and Communications and Power Line Construction (includes cable television line construction-contractors)

1731 Electrical Work (includes cable television hookup-contractors)

4841 Cable and Other Pay Television Services

Calligraphy Service

7389 Business services, nec (includes lettering services)

Camera Shop

5946 Camera and photographic supply stores

7699 Repair shops and related services, nec (includes camera repair shops)

Campground Management

7033 Recreational vehicle parks and campsites

Candy/Chocolate Shop

5441 Candy, nut, and confectionery stores

Car Alarm and Stereo Store

5531 Auto and home supply stores (includes automobile accessorydealers, retail)

5731 Radio, television, and consumer electronics stores (includesautomotive stereo equipment, retail)

Car Inspection Service

7549 Automotive services, except repair services and car washes(includes inspection service, automotive)

Car Towing Service

7549 Automotive services, except repair services and car washes(includes automotive towing and wrecker services)

Car Wash

7542 Car washes

Career Counseling

7389 Business services, nec (includes career counseling service)

Carpentry Service

1751 Carpentry work

Catering Service

5812 Eating places (includes caterers)

CD-ROM Developer/Producer

7372 Prepackaged software (includes pre-packaged computer software publishers)

7379 Computer related services, nec (includes database developers)

Cellular Phone/Telephone Business

4812 Radiotelephone communications

5999 Miscellaneous retail stores, nec (includes telephone stores, retail)

Charter Boat Service

4499 Water transportation service, nec (includes boat rental, commercial)

Check Cashing Service

6099 Functions related to depository banking, nec (includes check cashing agencies)

Children's Apparel Shop

5611 Men's and boys' clothing stores

5641 Children's and infants' wear stores

5651 Family clothing stores

5699 Miscellaneous apparel and accessory stores (includes children's wear)

5932 Used merchandise stores (includes retail second hand clothing stores)

Children's Day Care Center

8351 Child day care services

Chimney Sweeping Business

7349 Building cleaning and maintenance services, nec (includeschimney cleaning service)

Christmas Decoration Store

5999 Miscellaneous retail stores, nec

Christmas Tree Farm

0811 Timber tracts (includes Christmas tree growing)

Clipping Service

7389 Business services, nec (includes press clipping service)

Clothing Designer

2311 Men's and boys' suits, coats, and overcoats

2325 Men's and boys' separate trousers and slacks

2329 Men's and boys' clothing, nec

2331 Women's, misses', and juniors' blouses and shirts

2335 Women's, misses', and juniors' dresses

2337 Women's, misses', and juniors' suits, skirts, and coats

2361 Girls', children's, and infants' dresses, blouses, and shirts

Clothing Store

5611 Men's and boys' clothing and accessory stores

5621 Women's clothing stores

5632 Women's accessory and specialty stores

5641 Children's and infants' wear stores

5651 Family clothing stores

5699 Miscellaneous apparel and accessory stores

5932 Used merchandise stores (includes retail secondhand clothing stores)

Coffee Service

5149 Groceries and related products, nec (includes coffee, wholesale)

Coin/Stamp Dealer

5961 Catalog and mail order houses (includes retail mail order coinand stamp businesses)

5999 Miscellaneous retail stores, nec

Comedy Club

5813 Drinking placesMalcoholic beverages (includes nightclubs)

Comic Book/Collectibles Store

5999 Miscellaneous retail stores, nec

Commercial/Graphic Art Business

7336 Commercial art and graphic design

Commercial Mail Receiving Agency

7389 Business services, nec (includes post office contract stations)

Compact Disc/Record Store

5735 Recorded and prerecorded tape stores

Computer Consulting

7379 Computer related services, nec (includes computer consultants

Computer Data Storage Company

3572 Computer storage devices

Computer Learning/Training Center

8243 Data processing schools

Computer Maintenance and Repair Service

7378 Computer maintenance and repair

Computer Programming and Data Processing Service

7374 Computer processing and data preparation services

Computer Store

5734 Computer and computer software stores

Computer System Integrators

7371 Computer programming services

7373 Computer integrated systems design

7379 Computer related services, nec (includes computer consultants and database developers)

Computerized Billing Service

7374 Computer processing and data preparation and processing services

Computerized Matching Service

7299 Miscellaneous personal services, nec (includes dating services)

7375 Information retrieval services

Concession Stand Business

5812 Eating places (includes concession stands in airports and sports arenas, and refreshment stands)

7999 Amusement and recreation services, nec (concession operators andamusement concessions)

Consignment Shop

5932 Used merchandise stores (includes clothing stores, secondhand retail; furniture stores, secondhand retail; home furnishing stores, secondhand retail)

Construction Company

1521 General contractors—single family houses

1522 General contractors—residential buildings other than single-family

Consumer Electronics Store

5731 Radio, television, and consumer electronics stores

Convenience Store

5411 Grocery stores (includes retail convenience food stores)

Cooking School

8299 Schools and educational services, nec (includes cooking schools)

Copy Shop

7334 Photocopying and duplicating services

Cosmetics Business

2844 Perfumes, cosmetics, and other toilet preparations

5122 Drugs, drug proprietaries, and druggists' sundries (includes cosmetics—wholesale)

5963 Direct selling establishments (includes canvassers , headquarters for retail sale of merchandise, and direct selling organizations—retail)

5999 Miscellaneous retail stores, nec (includes cosmeticss-tores—retail)

Costume Shop

7299 Miscellaneous personal services, nec (includes costume rental)

7922 Theatrical producers and miscellaneous theatrical services(includes theatrical costume design)

Craft Artisan

3269 Pottery products, nec (includes art and ornamental ware; pottery; ceramic articles for craft shops; cookware; crockery; china, earthenware and stoneware figures; kitchen articles; coarse earthenware; lamp bases; and vases)

Craft/Hobby Shop

5945 Hobby, toy, and game shops (includes retail hobby stores and craft kit and supply retailers)

5947 Gift, novelty, and souvenir shops pottery; ceramic articles for craft shops; cookware; crockery; china, earthenware and stoneware figures; kitchen articles; coarse earthenware; lamp bases; and vases)

Create Your Own...Store

3269 Pottery Products, nec

5947 Gift, Novelty, and Souvenir Shops

5999 Micellaneous Retail Stores, nec

Credit Card Issuing Service

6153 Short-Term Business Credit Institutions, Except Agricultural (includes credit card service, collection by central agency)

7389 Business Services, nec (includes credit card service collection by individual firms)

Credit Repair Service

7299 Miscellaneous personal services, nec (includes debt counseling and adjustment services)

Credit Reporting and Collection Service

7322 Adjustment and collection services

7323 Credit reporting services

Damage Restoration Service

1790 Special trade contractors, nec (includes cleaning building exteriors, dampproofing buildings, dewatering, fireproofing buildings, steam cleaning of building exteriors, and waterproofing)

Dance School

7911 Dance studios, schools, and halls

Delicatessen/Sandwich Shop

5812 Eating places (includes sandwich bars or shops and submarine sandwich shops)

Desktop Publishing Company

2711 Publishing, or publishing and printing newspapers

2721 Publishing, or publishing and printing periodicals

2731 Publishing, or publishing and printing books

2741 Miscellaneous publishing

Dial-it Services

4813 Telephone communications, except radio-telephone

Diaper Service

7219 Laundry and garment services, nec

Disc Jockey Service

8999 Services, nec

Domestic Help/Maid Service

7349 Building cleaning and maintenance services, nec (includes housekeeping and office cleaning services)

8811 Private households (includes private households employing cooks, maids, and other domestic help)

Driving School

8249 Vocational schools, nec (includes truck driving schools)

8299 Schools and educational services, nec (includes automobile driving instruction)

Drug Store/Pharmacy

5912 Drug stores and proprietary stores

Dry Cleaning Service/Coin-Operated Laundry

7215 Coin-operated laundries and dry cleaning services

7216 Dry cleaning plants, except rug cleaning

Editorial/Freelance Writing Business

8999 Services, nec (includes writing and ghostwriting services)

Electrical Contractor

1731 Electrical work (includes trade contractors engaged in on-site electrical work)

Electrical Lighting Supply Store

5719 Miscellaneous home furnishings stores (includes retail lamp and shade shops)

Employee Leasing Service

7363 Help supply services

Employment Agency

361 Employment agencies

Engraving/Monogramming Service

3479 Coating, engraving, and allied services, nec (includes jewelryand silverware engraving)

7389 Business services, nec (includes advertising embroidery services, embossing services, and identification engraving services)

Environmental Consultant

8748 Business consulting services, nec

Environmental Store

5999 Miscellaneous retail stores, nec

Estate Planning

8811 Private Households

Estate Sales Business

6530 Real estate agents and managers

Executive Recruiting Agency

7361 Employment agencies (includes executive placement)

Fashion Accessories Business

3961 Costume jewelry and costume novelties, except precious metal

5137 Women's, children's, and infants' clothing and accessories

5632 Women's accessory and specialty stores

Fax Service

4822 Telegraph and other message communications (includes facsimile transmission services)

Film and Video Production Operation

7812 Motion picture and videotape production services

Financial Planning Service

282 Investment Advice

Fish and Seafood Store

5421 Meat and fish (seafood) markets, including freezer provisioners

Fish Farm

0273 Animal aquaculture (includes fish farms except hatcheries)

Floor Covering/Restoration Business

5713 Floor covering stores—retail

Florist

5992 Florists

Food Delivery Service

5812 Eating places

5963 Direct selling establishments (includes door-to-door selling organizations and mobile lunch wagons)

5999 Miscellaneous retail stores, nec

Formalwear Rental Business

7299 Miscellaneous personal services, nec (includes tuxedo rental)

Freight Forwarding Service

4731 Arrangement of transportation of freight and cargo (includes freight forwarding services)

Fund Raising Consultant

7389 Business services, nec (includes fund raising on a contract or fee basis)

Funeral Service

7261 Funeral services and crematories

Fur Farm

0271 Fur-bearing animals and rabbits

Fur Store

5632 Women's accessory and specialty stores (includes fur shops and furriers)

Furniture Restoration Service

7641 Reupholstery and furniture repair

Gambling Organizations/Service

7011 Hotels and Motels (includes casino hotels)

7993 Coin-Operated Amusement Devices

7999 Amusement and Recreation Services, nec (includes gambling establishments not primarily operating coin-operated machines and lotteries, operation of)

9311 Public Finance Taxation, and Monetary Policy (includes gambling control boards-government and lottery control boards-government)

Genealogy Service

7299 Miscellaneous personal services, nec (includes genealogical investigation service)

Gift Basket Service

5961 Catalog and mail-order houses

Gift/Card Shop

5943 Stationery stores

5947 Gift, novelty, and souvenir shops (includes card shops)

Glass Repair and Replacement Service

1751 Carpentry work (includes prefabricated window and door installation)

7536 Automotive glass replacement shops

Golf Shop

5941 Sporting goods stores and bicycle shops (includes retail golf goods and equipment stores)

Gourmet Coffee/Tea House

5499 Miscellaneous food stores (includes coffee stores, retail)

5812 Eating places (includes coffee shops)

Greenhouse/Garden Center/Nursery Business

0181 Ornamental floricultural and nursery products (includes greenhouses for floral products, growing of nursery stock, growing of potted plants)

5261 Retail nurseries, lawn and garden supply stores (includes nursery stock, seeds, and bulbs, retail)

Greeting Card Publishing

2771 Greeting card publishing and printing

8999 Services, nec (includes hand painting of greeting cards)

Grocery Store

5411 Grocery stores

Gunsmith/Gun Shop

5941 Sporting good stores and bicycle shops (includes firearms,retail)

7699 Repair shops and related services, nec (includes gunsmith shops)

Hair Replacement/Electrolysis Clinic

7299 Miscellaneous personal services, nec (includes depilatory salons, electrolysis, and hair weaving or replacement services)

Hair Salon/Barber Shop

7231 Beauty shops (includes beauty and barber shops combined)

7241 Barber shops

Handwriting Analysis Consultant

7389 Business services, nec (includes handwriting analysis)

Hardware Store

5251 Hardware stores

Hat Store

5611 Men's and boys' clothing and accessory stores (includes retail hat stores)

5621 Women's accessory and specialty stores (includes retail millinery stores)

Hazardous Waste Disposal Business

4953 Refuse systems (includes hazardous waste material disposal sites)

Healthy Restaurants

5812 Eating Places

Health Food Store

5499 Miscellaneous food stores (includes health food stores)

Hearing Aid Testing and Fitting Service

5999 Miscellaneous retail stores, nec (includes hearing aids, retail)

8099 Health and allied services, nec (includes hearing testing service)

Herb Farm

0191 General farms, primarily crop

2833 Medical chemicals and botanical products (includes herb grinding, grading, and milling)

5499 Miscellaneous food stores (includes spice and herb stores)

Home Accessory Store

5714 Drapery, curtain, and upholstery stores

5719 Miscellaneous home furnishings stores

Home Furnishings Store

5712 Furniture stores

5719 Miscellaneous home furnishings stores

5932 Used merchandise stores (including antique and secondhand retail furniture stores)

Home Health Care Service

8082 Home health care services

Horse Riding Academy

752 Animal specialty services, except veterinary (includes boarding and training horses)

Hotel/Motel/Resort Operation

7011 Hotels and motels (includes resort hotels)

Housesitting Service

8999 Services, nec

Ice Cream/Frozen Yogurt Shop

5451 Dairy products stores (includes retail packaged ice cream stores)

5812 Eating places (includes retail dairy bars)

563 Direct selling establishments (includes ice cream wagons)

Image Consultant

8299 Schools and educational services, nec (includes personal development schools)

8743 Public relations services

Import/Export Service

4731 Arrangement of the transportation of freight and cargo

Incubator

7389 Business services, nec

8748 Business consulting services, nec

Information Broker

7375 Information retrieval services

Insulation Contractor

1742 Plastering, dry wall, acoustical, and insulation work (includes insulation installation contractors)

Insurance Agency

6411 Insurance agents, brokers, and services

Interior Design Service

7389 Business services, nec (includes interior decoration consulting services and interior design services)

Internet/Online Service Provider

4822 Telegraph and other message communications (includes electronicmail services)

7379 Computer related services, nec

Investment/Securities Broker

6211 Security brokers, dealers, and flotation companies

Jewelry Store

5632 Women's accessory and specialty stores (includes costume jewelry stores)

5944 Jewelry stores

7631 Watch, clock, and jewelry repair

Job Training/Retraining

8331 Job training and vocational rehabilitation services (includesjob training)

Kiosk/Pushcart/Vendor Business

5812 Eating places (includes box lunch stands, concession stands,food bars, hamburger and hot dog stands, ice cream stands, refreshment stands, and soft drink stands)

Landscaping Service

0781 Landscape counseling and planning services

0782 Lawn and garden services

0783 Ornamental shrub and tree services

Lawn Maintenance Service

0782 Lawn and garden services

0783 Ornamental shrub and tree services

Limousine Service

4119 Local passenger transportation, nec (includes hearse and limousine rental, with drivers)

7514 Passenger car rental (includes limo rental, w/o drivers)

Lingerie Shop

5632 Lingerie storesMretail

Liquor Store

5921 Liquor stores

Literary Agency

7389 Business services, nec (includes agents and brokers for authors and non-performing artists)

Locksmith

7699 Repair shops and related services, nec (includes locksmith shops and made-to order lock parts)

Luggage and Leather Goods Business

5948 Luggage and leather goods stores

Lumberyard

5211 Lumber and other building materials dealers

Machine Shop/Metalorking Shop

3541 Machine tools, metal cutting types

3542 Machine tools, metal forming types

3544 Special dies and tools, die sets, jigs and fixtures, and industrial molds

3545 Cutting tools, machine tool accessories, and machinists' precision measuring devices

3549 Metalworking machinery, nec

Mail Order Business

5961 Catalog and mail order houses

Management Consulting Service

8742 Management consulting services

Manufacturer's Representative

7389 Business services, nec

Marine Shop

5551 Boat dealers (includes retail marine supply dealers)

Market Research and Analysis

8732 Commercial, economic, sociological, and educational research

8742 Management consulting services

Martial Arts Studio

7999 Amusement and recreation services, nec (includes Judo and Karate instruction)

Masonry, Stonework, and Plastering Contractors

1741 Masonry, stone setting, and other stonework

1742 Plastering, dry wall, acoustical, and insulation work

Massage Therapist

7299 Massage parlor 8049 Offices and clinics of health practitioners,nec

Mediation Service

7389 Business services, nec (includes arbitration and conciliationservices)

Medical and Dental Instrument Manufacturing

3841 Surgical and medical instruments and apparatus

3843 Dental equipment and supplies

Medical Claims Service

6411 Insurance agents, brokers, and service (includes processing ofmedical claims on a contract or fee basis)

Medical Laboratory Service

8071 Medical laboratories

Medical Supplies Store

5047 Medical, dental, and hospital equipment and supplies

Medical Transcription Service

7374 Computer processing and data preparation and processing services

Messenger/Delivery/Subpoena Service

4215 Courier services, except by air (includes letter, mail, package,and parcel delivery services)

4822 Telegraph and other message communication (includes cablegrams, mailgrams, electronic mail, and other message services)

7389 Business services, nec (includes process serving services)

Miniature Golf Course Operation

7999 Amusement and recreation services, nec (includes miniature golf course operations)

Modeling School/Agency

7363 Help supply services (includes modeling services)

8299 Schools and educational services, nec (includes modeling schools)

Mortgage Broker

6162 Mortgage bankers and loan correspondents (includes mortgage brokers using own money)

6163 Loan brokers (includes mortgage brokers arranging for loans but using money of others)

6211 Security brokers, dealers, and flotation companies (includes buying and selling mortgages)

Motorcycle/Moped Store

5571 Motorcycle dealers

Movie Theatre Operation

7832 Motion picture theatres, except drive-ins

7833 Drive-in motion picture theatres

Moving Service

4212 Local trucking, without storage (includes furniture and other moving services)

4214 Local trucking, with storage (includes furniture and household goods moving services)

Music School

8299 Schools and educational services, nec (includes music schools)

Music Shop

5736 Musical instrument stores

5932 Used merchandise stores (includes retailers of secondhand musical instruments)

7699 Repair shops and related services, nec (includes musical instrument repair shops)

Musical Instrument Repair/Piano Tuning Service

7699 Repair shops and related services, nec (includes musical instrument repair shops and piano tuning and repair)

Nail Salon

7231 Beauty shops (includes manicure and pedicure salons)

Nanny Service

7299 Miscellaneous personal services, nec (includes babysitting bureaus)

New Age Services and Supplies

5999 Miscellaneous retail stores, nec

8999 Services, nec

New and Used Car Dealer

5511 Motor vehicle dealers (new and used)

5521 Motor vehicle dealers (used only)

Newsletter Publishing

2721 Periodicals; publishing or publishing and printing

2741 Miscellaneous publishing (includes business service newsletterspublishing and/or printing)

Novelty Items Business

2499 Wood products, nec (includes wood and wood fiber novelties)

2514 Metal household furniture (includes metal novelty furniture)

2679 Converted paper and paperboard products, nec (includes papernovelties)

3199 Leather goods, nec (includes leather novelties)

3229 Pressed and blown glass and glassware, nec (includes novelty glassware made in glassmaking plants)

3231 Glass products, made of purchased glass (includes glassnovelties)

3499 Fabricated metal products, nec (includes metal novelties and specialties, except advertising novelties)

3961 Costume jewelry and costume novelties, except precious metal andgems

3999 Manufacturing industries, nec (includes bone, beaded and shell novelties)

Nursing Home/Long-Term Care Center

8051 Skilled nursing care facilities

8052 Intermediate care facilities (includes intermediate care nursing homes)

8059 Nursing and personal care facilities, nec (includes convalescent homes, rest homes, and like facilities)

Nutritional Consultant/Diet Planner

7299 Miscellaneous personal services, nec (includes diet workshops)

8049 Offices and clinics of health practitioners, nec (includes offices of nutritionists and offices of dietitians)

Office Design Service

7389 Business services, nec (includes interior decorating and design services)

Office Supply/Equipment Store

5943 Stationery stores (includes retail office forms and supplies stores)

Online Store

5734 Computer and computer software stores

7375 Information retrieval services

Paint/Wall Covering Center

5231 Paint, glass, and wallpaper stores

Painting Contractors

1721 Painting and paperhanging contractors

Party Entertainment Services

7929 Bands, orchestras, actors, and other entertainers and entertainment groups

Party/Reunion Planning Service

7359 Equipment rental and leasing, nec (includes party supplies rental and leasing)

8999 Services, nec

Pawnbroker

5932 Used merchandise stores (includes pawnshops)

Payroll Preparation Service

8721 Accounting, auditing, and bookkeeping services (includes payrollaccounting service)

Periodical/Newspaper Publishing

2721 Periodicals; publishing or publishing and printing

Personal Shopping Service

7299 Miscellaneous personal services, nec (includes shopping servicesfor individuals)

Pest Control Service

0851 Forestry services (includes forest pest control)

7342 Disinfecting and pest control services

Pet Boarding/Grooming Service

0279 Animal specialties, nec (includes breeding kennels)

0752 Animal specialty services (includes boarding kennels, doggrooming services, and related services)

Pet Cemetery

0782 Lawn and garden services (includes independent cemetery upkeep services)

6531 Real estate agents and managers (includes cemetery management services)

6553 Cemetery subdividers and developers (includes animal cemetery operations)

Pet Obedience School

0752 Animal specialty services, except veterinary (includes training of pets and other animal specialties)

Pet Shop

5999 Miscellaneous retail stores, nec (includes pet shops)

Pet Sitting Service

0752 Animal specialty services, except veterinary

Photo Finishing Center

7384 Photo finishing laboratories

7819 Services allied to motion picture production (includes motion picture film processing)

Photographer, Commercial

7335 Commercial photography

Photographic Studio

7221 Photographic studios, portrait

Physical Fitness Center

7991 Physical fitness facilities

Physical Therapy Clinic/Practice

8049 Offices and clinics of health practitioners, nec (includes offices of physical therapists)

Pizzeria

5812 Eating places (includes pizza parlors and pizzerias)

Plant Leasing Service

7359 Equipment rental and leasing, nec (includes plants)

Plumbing Service

1711 Plumbing, heating, and air-conditioning contractors

Porcelain Refinishing Service

1799 Special trade contractors, nec

Power Washing Service

1799 Special trade contractors, nec (includes cleaning of building exteriors)

7349 Building cleaning and maintenance services, nec (includes cleaning of building interiors)

7542 Car washes (includes automotive washing and polishing)

Prepaid Phone Card Business

4812 Radiotelephone communications

4813 Telephone communications, except radiotelephone

Print/Frame Shop

7699 Repair shops and related services, nec (includes custom picture framing services)

Printing Business

2752 Commercial printing, lithographic

2754 Commercial printing, gravure

2759 Commercial printing, nec

2761 Manifold business form printers

Private Investigation/Personal Security Service

7381 Detective, guard, and armored car services

Private Label Product Manufacturer/ Retailer

3999 Manufacturing industries, nec

5399 Miscellaneous general mer chandise stores

5499 Miscellaneous food stores 5699 Miscellaneous apparel and accessory stores

5999 Miscellaneous retail stores, nec

Professional Organizer

7299 Miscellaneous personal services, nec

7389 Business services, nec

Property Management

6531 Real estate agents and managers

Public Relations Consultant

8743 Public relations services

Public Warehousing/Ministorage Operation

4221 Farm product warehousing and storage

4222 Refrigerated warehousing and storage

4225 General warehousing and storage

4226 Special warehousing and storage, nec (includes fur storage, household goods warehousing and storage, whiskey warehousing, and like enterprises)

Quick Oil Change Service

5541 Gasoline service stations (includes automobile servicestations—retail)

7538 General automotive repair shops

Radio Station

4832 Radio broadcasting stations

Radon Testing Service

1799 Special trade contractors, nec

8734 Testing laboratories

Real Estate Agency

6531 Real estate agents and managers

Real Estate Investment Service

6798 Real estate investment trusts

Recording Studio

7399 Business services, nec (includes recording studios operating on a contract or fee basis)

Recreational Vehicle Dealer

5561 Recreational vehicle dealers

Recycling Business

5093 Scrap and waste materials

Rental Service

7299 Miscellaneous personal services, nec (includes clothing rental)

7352 Medical equipment rental and leasing

7353 Heavy construction equipment and leasing

7359 Equipment rental and leasing, nec

7377 Computer rental and leasing

7999 Amusement and recreation services, nec (includes pleasure boat rental, canoe and rowboat rental, bicycle, motorcycle and moped rental, and sporting goods rental)

Restaurant

5812 Eating places (includes sitdown, carry-out, and fast food)

Resume Service

7338 Secretarial anc court reporting services (includes resumewriting services)

Roofing Contractor

1761 Roofing, siding, and sheet metal work

Satellite Dish Service

4841 Cable and other pay television services (includes directbroadcast satellite services and satellite master antenna systems services)

Screen Printing Business

2261 Finishers of broadwoven fabrics of cotton (includes printing andfinishing of cotton broadwoven fabrics)

2262 Finishers of broadwoven fabrics of manmade fiber and silk(includes printing manmade fiber and silk broadwoven fabrics)

2759 Commercial printing, nec (includes screen printing on glass, plastics, paper, and metal, including highway signs)

Security Systems Service

7382 Security systems services

Seminar Planner/Lecturer

8999 Services, nec (including lecturers)

Service Station/Auto Repair and Service Shop

5541 Gasoline service stations

7532 Top, body, and upholstery repair shops and paint shops

7533 Automotive exhaust system repair shops

7534 Tire retreading and repair shops

7536 Automotive glass replacement shops

7537 Automotive transmission repair shops

7538 General automotive repair shops

7539 Automotive repair shops, nec

Sewer and Drain Cleaning Business

7699 Repair shops and related services, nec (includes sewer cleaning and rodding and septic tank cleaning) Sewing Center 5722 Household appliance stores (includes retail sewing machine stores)

5949 Sewing, needlework, and piece goods stores

7699 Repair shops and related services, nec (includes sewing machine repair shops)

Shoe Repair Shop

7251 Shoe repair shops and shoeshine parlors

Shoe Store

5661 Shoe stores

Sign Shop

3993 Signs and advertising specialties

7389 Business services, nec (includes sign painting shops)

Silk Plant Shop

5999 Miscellaneous retail stores, nec (includes artificial flowers—retail)

Skating Rink Operation

7999 Amusement and recreation services, nec (includes ice and rollerskating rink operations)

Ski Shop

5941 Sporting goods stores and bicycle shops

Software Publishing

7372 Packaged software

Solar Energy Design/Contracting Business

1711 Plumbing, heating, and airconditioning contractors (includes solar heating apparatus contractors)

1742 Plastering, dry wall, acoustical, and insulation work (includes solar reflecting insulation film contractors)

Specialized Staffing

7361 Employment Agencies

7363 Help Supply Services

Specialty Foods/Wine Shop

5499 Miscellaneous food stores

5921 Liquor stores (includes packaged wine—retail)

Sports Promotional Services

7941 Professional Sports Clubs and Promoters

Sporting Goods Store

5941 Sporting goods stores and bicycle shops

Surveying Service

8713 Surveying services (includes surveying: land, water, and aerial)

Swimming Pool/Hot Tub Business

1799 Special trade contractors, nec (includes swimming pool construction contractors)

5999 Miscellaneous retail stores, nec (includes hot tubs, retail)

7389 Business services, nec (includes swimming pool cleaning and maintenance services)

7999 Amusement and recreation services, nec (includes swimming pooloperations)

Tailor Shop

5699 Miscellaneous apparel and accessory stores (includes customtailor shops) 7219 Laundry and garment services, nec (includes tailorshops, except custom or merchant tailors)

Talent Agency

7922 Theatrical producers and miscellaneous theatrical services (includes agents)

Tanning Parlor/Sauna

7299 Miscellaneous personal services (includes steam baths and tanning salons)

Tattoo Parlor

7299 Miscellaneous personal services, nec (includes tattoo parlors)

Tax Preparation Business

7291 Tax return preparation services

8721 Accounting, auditing, and bookkeeping services

Taxicab/Van Shuttle Service

4121 Taxicabs

Taxidermy Service

7699 Repair shops and related services, nec (includes taxidermy)

Teacher Supply Store

5999 Miscellaneous retail stores, nec

Telemarketing Service

7389 Business services, nec (includes telemarketing services operating on a contract or fee basis)

Telephone Answering Service

7389 Business services, nec (includes answering services)

Television/Radio Repair Service

7622 Radio and television repair shops

Television Station

4833 Television broadcasting stations

Temporary Employment Agency

7363 Help supply services (includes temporary help services

Tennis Court/Racquet Club Operation

7997 Membership sports and recreation clubs (includes racquetball and tennis clubs)

7999 Amusement and recreation services, nec (includes nonmembership racquetball and tennis court operations)

Tire Dealer

5531 Auto and home supply stores (includes retail tire dealers) 7534 Tire retreading and repair shops

Tobacco Shop

5993 Tobacco stores and stands

Tour Guide Operation/Adventure Service

4725 Tour operations

7999 Amusement and recreation services, nec (includes tour guides)

Toy Business

5945 Hobby, toy, and game shops

Trade Show/Conference Management Service

7389 Business services, nec (includes trade show arrangement)

Translating/Interpreting Service

7389 Business services, nec (includes translation service)

Travel Agency

4724 Travel agencies

Trucking Business

4212 Local trucking, without storage services

4213 Trucking, except local

4214 Local trucking, with storage services

Tutoring Service

8299 Schools and educational services, nec (includes tutoring services)

Typesetting Business

2791 Typesetting

Typing/Stenographic Service

7338 Secretarial and court reporting services (includes stenographic and typing services)

Upholstery/Carpet Services

1752 Floor laying and other floor work, nec (includes carpet laying and removing services)

5714 Drapery, curtain, and upholstery stores (includes upholstery materials stores)

7217 Carpet and upholstery cleaning

Vending Machine Merchandising and Service Business

5962 Automatic merchandising machine operators (includes retail sale of products through vending machines)

7359 Equipment rental and leasing services, nec (includes vending machine rental businesses)

Videocassette Rental Store

5735 Recorded and prerecorded tape stores (includes retail videotape stores)

7841 Videotape rental establishments

Vision Center

5995 Optical goods stores

Voice Mail Service

4813 Telephone communications, except radiotelephone (includes voice telephone communications)

Water Conditioning Service

7389 Business services, nec (includes water softener services)

Web Site Design

7371 Computer programming services (includes custom computer programsor systems software development and computer software systems analysis and design)

Weight Reduction/Control Center

7991 Physical fitness facilities (includes reducing facilities and slenderizing salons)

Welcome Service

7389 Business service, nec (includes welcoming service)

Window Dressing Business

3993 Signs and advertising specialties (includes advertising displays, except printed, and window and lobby cutouts and displays)

7319 Advertising, nec (includes display advertising services, exceptoutdoor)

Word Processing Service

7338 Secretarial and court reporting services (includes wordprocessing services)

Licensing Assistance Programs

Included here are state offices that provide information and assistance to small business owners and entrepreneurs concerning business licensing requirements and regulations.

ALABAMA

Dept. of Revenue—Business Licensing
50 N. Ripley
Montgomery, AL 36132
334-242-1170
URL: http://www.revenue.alabama.gov/licenses/index.html

ALASKA

Corporations, Business and Professional Licensing
PO Box 110806
Juneau, AK 99811-0806
907-465-2534
Fax: 907-465-2974
Email: businesslicense@alaska.gov
URL: http://www.dced.state.ak.us/occ/home.htm

ARIZONA

Arizona Dept. of Commerce
1700 W. Washington, Ste. 600
Phoenix, AZ 85007
602-771-1100
Toll-Free: 800-528-8421
URL: http://www.azcommerce.com/BusAsst/SmallBiz

CALIFORNIA

Consumer Affairs Dept
1625 N. Market Blvd., Ste. 112
Sacramento, CA 95814
916-445-1254
Toll-Free: 800-952-5210
URL: http://www.dca.ca.gov
URL: http://www.2dca.ca.gov/licensee/shtml

COLORADO

Dept. of Regulatory Agencies
1560 Broadway, Ste. 1550
Denver, CO 80202
303-894-7855
Fax: 303-894-7885
URL: http:// www.dora.state.co.us

CONNECTICUT

Dept. of Consumer Protection—DCP License Services Division
165 Capitol Ave.
Hartford, CT 06106
800-842-2649
Fax: 860-713-7239
Email: license.services@po.state.ct.us
URL: http://www.ct.gov/dcp/site/default.asp
URL: http://www.ct-clic.com

DELAWARE

Dept. of State — Professional Regulation Division
Cannon Bldg.
861 Silver Lake Blvd., Ste. 203
Dover, DE 19904
302-744-4500
Fax: 302-739-2711
URL: http://dpr.delaware.gov

DISTRICT OF COLUMBIA

Dept. of Consumer and Regulatory Affairs
1100 4th St., SW
Washington, DC 20024
202-442-4400
URL: http://dcra.dc.gov/drca/site/default.asp

FLORIDA

Business & Professional Regulation Dept.
1940 N. Monroe St.
Tallahassee, FL 32399
850-487-1395
http://www.myfloridalicense.com/dbpr

GEORGIA

Georgia Secretary of State— Professional Licensing Boards Division
237 Coliseum Dr.
Macon, GA 31217-3858
478-207-2440
Fax: 877-588-0446
URL: http://www.sos.georgia.gov/plb/
URL: http://www.georgia.gov

HAWAII

State Dept. of Commerce and Consumer Affairs—Professional and Vocational Licensing
Street Address:
335 Merchant St. 3rd Fl, Rm. 301
Honolulu, HI 96813

Mailing Address:
PO Box 3469
Honolulu, HI 96801
808-587-3295
URL: http:// hawaii.gov/dbedt/business

IDAHO

Occupational Licenses Bureau
Owyhee Plaza
1109 Main St., Ste. 220
Boise, ID 83702-5642
208-334-3233
Fax: 208-334-3945
Email: ibol@ibol.idaho.gov
URL: http://wwwv.secure.ibol.idaho.gov/IBOL/home.aspx

ILLINOIS

Illinois Professional Regulation Dept
320 W. Washington St.
Springfield, IL 62786
217-785-0800
URL: http://www.idfpr.com

INDIANA

Professional Licensing Agency
302 W. Washington St., Rm. EO-34
Indianapolis, IN 46204
317-232-2980

Fax: 317-232-231
URL: http://www.in.gov/pla/

IOWA

Professional Licensing Division
1920 SE Hulsizer Rd.
Ankeny, IA 50021
515-281-7393
Fax: 515-281-7411
URL: http://www.state.ia.us/government/com/prof/home.html

KENTUCKY

Secretary of State—One-Stop Business Licensing Program
700 Capital Ave., Ste. 152
State Capitol Frankfurt, KY 40601
502-564-3490
Fax: 502-564-5687
URL: http://sos.ky.gov/business/onestop.htm

LOUISIANA

Secretary of State—Commercial Div.
URL: http://www.sos.louisiana.gov

MAINE

URL: http://www.maine.gov/portal/business/licensing.html

MARYLAND

Labor, Licensing and Regulation Dept— Division of Occupational and Professional Licensing
500 N. Calvert St., 3rd. Fl.
Baltimore, MD 21202
410-230-6020
Email: op@dllr.state.md.us
URL: http://www.dllr.state.md.us/license/

MASSACHUSETTS

Division of Professional Licensure
239 Causeway
Boston, MA 02114
617-727-3074
Fax: 517-727-2197
URL: http://www.mass.gov/dpl

MICHIGAN

Dept. of Energy, Labor and Economic Growth
525 W. Ottawa
PO Box 30004
Lansing, MI 48909
517-373-1820
Fax: 517-373-2129
URL: http://www.michigan.gov/dleg

MINNESOTA

Commerce Dept.
85 7th Place East, Ste. 500
St Paul, MN 55101
651-296-6319
Toll-Free: 800-657-3978
Email: licensing.commerce@state.mn.us
URL: http://www.state.mn.us/

MISSISSIPPI

Mississippi Secretary of State— Business Services
PO Box 136
Jackson, MS 39205
601-359-1350
Fax: 601-359-1633
Email: Wthompson@sos.state.ms.us
URL: http://www.sos.ms.gov/business_services.aspx
URL: http://www.ms.gov

MISSOURI

Dept. of Economic Development—Professional Registration Division
3605 Missouri Blvd.
Jefferson City, MO 65102 PO Box 1335
573-751-0293
Email: profreg@pr.mo.gov
URL: http://www.pr.mo.gov/

MONTANA

Department of Labor and Industry
PO Box 1728
Helena, MT 59624
406-841-2300
URL: http:// dli.mt.gov

NEBRASKA

See Nebraska Online for more information
Toll Free: 800-747-8177
URL: http://www.nol.org/business/
URL: http://www.sos.ne.gov

NEVADA

Nevada Secretary of State
101 North Carson St.
Carson City, NV 89701-4786
775-684-5708
URL: http://www.nvsos.gov

NEW HAMPSHIRE

Joint Board of Licensure & Certification
57 Regional Dr.
Concord, NH 03301
603-271-2219
Fax: 603-271-6990
Email: llavertu@nhsa.state.nh.us
URL: http://www.nh.gov/jtboard/

NEW JERSEY

New Jersey Dept. of Law and Public Safety—Consumer Affairs Division
124 Halsey St.
Newark, NJ 07102
973-504-6534
URL: http://www.state.nj.us/lps/ca/boards.htm

NEW MEXICO

Regulation & Licensing Dept
2550 Cerrillos Rd
Santa Fe, NM 87505
505-476-4500
URL: http://www.rld.state.nm.us/

NEW YORK

New York State Dept. of State, Division of Licensing Services
99 Washington Ave.
Albany, NY 12231
518-474-4752
Fax: 518-474-4597
Email: licensing@dos.state.ny.us
URL: http://www.dos.state.ny.us/lcns/licensing.html

NORTH CAROLINA

Dept. of the Secretary of State—Busirof/ ness License Information Office (BLIO)
301 N. Wilmington St.
Raleigh, NC 27601
919-733-4151
Toll-Free: 800-228-8443
URL: http://www.nccomerce.com/en/BusinessServices/startyourbusiness

NORTH DAKOTA

Secretary of State—Business Information and Registration
600 E. Boulevard Ave., Dept. 108
Bismarck, ND 58505-0500
701-328-4284
800-352-0867 ext. 4284
Fax: 701-328-2992
Email: sosbir@nd.gov
URL: http://www.nd.gov/sos/Businessserve/

OHIO

Commerce Dept.
77 S. High St.
Columbus, OH 43215
614-466-4100
URL: http://www.com.ohio.gov/

OKLAHOMA

Dept. of Commerce—Oklahoma Business Licensing System
877-879-6552
URL: http://www.okonestop.com

OREGON

Secretary of State—Corporate Division
255 Capitol St. NE, Ste. 151
Salem, OR 97310-1327
503-986-2200
URL: http://www.oregon.gov/lic

Portland Bureau of Licenses
111 SW Columbia St., Ste. 600
Portland, OR 97201
503-823-5157
Fax: 503-823-5192
URL: http://www.pdxbl.org

PENNSYLVANIA

Professional & Occupational Affairs Bureau
Secretary of Commonwealth (State Dept.)
302 North Office Bldg.
Harrisburg, PA 17120
717-787-8503
URL: http://www.mylicense.state.pa.us/

RHODE ISLAND

Office of the Secretary of State
82 Smith St., Rm. 217
Providence, RI 02903
401-222-2357
Fax: 401-222-1356
URL: http://www.state.ri.us/

SOUTH CAROLINA

Dept. of Labor, Licensing and Regulation Dept.
PO Box 11329
Columbia, SC 29211
803-896-4300
Email: contactllr@mail.llr.state.sc.us
URL: http://www.llr.state.sc.us/pol.asp

SOUTH DAKOTA

Dept. of Labor Boards, Commissions and Councils
700 Governors Dr.
Pierre, SD 57501
605-773-3101
Fax: 605-773-6184
URL: http://www.state.sd.us
URL: http://dol.sd.gov/bdcomm/

TENNESSEE

State of Tennessee
500 James Robertson Pkwy.
Nashville, TN 37243-0572
615-741-3449
URL: www.state.tn.us/
URL: http://www.tennesseeanytime.org/business

TEXAS

Licensing and Regulation Dept.
PO Box 12157
Austin, TX 78711
512-463-6599
Toll-Free: 800-803-9202
Fax: 512-475-2854
URL: http://www.license.state.tx.us

UTAH

Occupational & Professional Licensing Div.—Commerce Dept.
PO Box 146741
Salt Lake City, UT 84114-6741
801-530-6628
Toll-Free: 866-275-3675
Fax: 801-530-6511
URL: http://www.commerce.state.ut.us/

VERMONT

Office of Professional Regulation
26 Terrace St.
Montpelier, VT 05609
802-828-2363
URL: http://www.sec.state.vt.us/
URL: http://vtprofessionals.org

VIRGIN ISLANDS

Licensing & Consumer Affairs Dept.
Golden Rock Shopping Ctr.
Christiansted
340-773-2226
Fax: 340-778-8250
URL: http:// dlca.vi.gov/links/

VIRGINIA

Professional and Occupational Regulations Dept.
9960 Maryland Dr., Ste. 400
Richmond, VA 23233
804-367-8500
Email: dpor@dpor.state.va.us
URL: http://www.state.va.us/dpor/

WASHINGTON

Dept. of Licensing
405 Black Lake Blvd., Bldg. 2
Olympia, WA 98502
360-664-1400
URL: http://www.dol.wa.gov/business

WISCONSIN

Regulation and Licensing Dept.
PO Box 8935
Madison, WI 53708-8935
URL: http://www.drl.state.wi.us/

This Guide lists alphabetically by name the companies, associations, institutions, and individuals who publish the periodicals (magazines, journals, etc.), directories, guide books, and other publications noted in the "Small Business Profiles" and "General Topics" sections. In these two sections, you will see "Pub:" (publisher) noted following publication names. This note provides the name of the entity that publishes the work.

If you should need to directly contact the publisher, you can locate the contact information in this Guide. Note that some publications listed provide the specific name and e-mail address of an individual to be contacted regarding the publication; this information can be found in the text of the entry. Please use that contact information when available. Listings in this Guide provide full publisher name, address, phone and fax numbers, and e-mail and URL when available.

NUMERICS

101 Communications
9121 Oakdale Ave., Ste. 101
Chatsworth, CA, USA 91311
Ph: (818) 814-5200
E-mail: info@ats1105media.com
URL: http://www.1105media.com/

1105 Media Inc.
9121 Oakdale Ave., Ste. 101
Chatsworth, CA, USA 91311
Ph: (818) 734-1520
E-mail: info@ats1105media.com
URL: http://www.1105media.com/

1105 Media, Inc.
14901 Quorum Dr., Ste. 425
Dallas, TX, USA 75254
Ph: (972) 687-6700
E-mail: http://www.stevenspublishing.com/home.html

124 S Mercedes Rd.
Fallbrook
CA, , USA 92028
E-mail: http://www.encorepublishers.com

360 Youth L.L.C.
151 W 26th St., 9th Fl.
New York, NY, USA 10001
Ph: (212) 244-4307
E-mail: marketing@ats360youth.com
URL: http://www.360youth.com/

A

A & C Black
38 Soho Sq.
London, , GBR W1D 3HB
E-mail: http://www.acblack.com

The A.I. Root Co.
PO Box 706
Medina, OH, USA 44256
Ph: (330) 725-6677
E-mail: http://www.rootcandles.com

A.M. Best Co.
Ambest Rd.
Oldwick, NJ, USA 8858
Ph: (908) 439-2200
E-mail: customer_service@atsambest.com
URL: http://www.ambest.com

A/N Group Inc.
17 Scott Dr.
Melville, NY, USA 11747
Ph: (631) 549-4090
E-mail: angroup@atspb.net
URL: http://www.smbiz.com

AACSB--American Assembly of Collegiate Schools of Business
777 South Harbour Island Blvd., Ste. 750
Tampa, FL, USA 33602-5730
Ph: (813) 769-6500

Abbeyfield Houses Society of Canada
427 Bloor St. W, Box 1
Toronto, ON, CAN M5S 1X7
Ph: (416) 920-7483
E-mail: info@atsabbeyfield.ca
URL:

ABC Book Publishing
20609 NE Lakeside Dr.
Fairview, OR, USA 97024
Ph: (503) 780-7322

ABC-CLIO
PO Box 1911
Santa Barbara, CA, USA 93102-1911
Ph: (805) 968-1911
E-mail: customerservice@atsabc-clio.com
URL: http://www.abc-clio.com

The ABWA Company Inc.
9100 Ward Pky.
PO Box 8728
Kansas City, MO, USA 64114-0728
E-mail: abwa@atsabwa.org
URL: http://www.abwa.org/

ACA International
4040 W 70 St.
Minneapolis, MN, USA 55435
Ph: (952) 926-6547
E-mail: aca@atsacainternational.org
URL: http://www.acainternational.org

Academic Press
525 B St., Ste. 1900
San Diego, CA, USA 92101-4495
Ph: (619) 231-0926
E-mail: http://www.elsevierdirect.com/imprint.jsp?iid=5

Academy of Doctors of Audiology
3493 Lansdowne Dr., Ste. 2
Lexington, KY, USA 40517
Ph: (859) 271-0607
E-mail: http://www.audiologist.org

Academy of Management
Pace University
PO Box 3020
Briarcliff Manor, NY, USA 10510-8020
Ph: (914) 923-2607

Access Intelligence
110 William St.
New York, NY, USA 10038
Ph: (212) 621-4900

Access Intelligence L.L.C.
4 Choke Cherry Rd., 2nd Fl.
Rockville, MD, USA 20850-4024
Ph: (301) 354-2000
E-mail: info@atsaccessintel.com
URL: http://www.accessintel.com

Accordionists and Teachers Guild, International
2312 W 71st Ter.
Prairie Village, KS, USA 66208-3322

Accrediting Commission of Career Schools and Colleges of Technology
2101 Wilson Blvd., Ste. 302
Arlington, VA, USA 22201
Ph: (703) 247-4212
E-mail: info@atsaccsc.org
URL: http://www.accsc.org

Accudata America
5220 Summerlin Commons Blvd., Ste. 200
Fort Myers, FL, USA 33907
Ph: (239) 425-4400

E-mail: info@atsaccudata.com
URL:

Accuity Inc.
4709 Golf Rd.
Skokie, IL, USA 60076
Ph: (847) 676-9600
E-mail: custserv@atsaccuitysolutions.com
URL: http://www.accuitysolutions.com

Accurate Writing & More
16 Barstow Ln.
Hadley, MA, USA 1035
Ph: (413) 586-2388
E-mail: http://www.principledprofit.com

Achill River Corp.
PO Box 1409
Arden, NC, USA 28704
Ph: (828) 687-0011
E-mail: circulations@atsaquaculturemag.com
URL: http://www.aquaculturemag.com

Acoustic Guitar
PO Box 767
San Anselmo, CA, USA 94979
Ph: (415) 485-6946
E-mail: acousticguitar@atspcspublink.com
URL: http://www.acousticguitar.com/

ACTA Press
Bldg. B6, Ste. 101
2509 Dieppe Ave. SW
Calgary, AB, CAN T3E 7J9
Ph: (403) 288-1195
E-mail: journals@atsactapress.com
URL: http://www.actapress.com/

Action Communication Inc.
135 Spy Ct.
Markham, ON, CAN L3R 5H6
Ph: (905) 477-3222

Active Interest Media
300 Continental Blvd., Ste. 650
El Segundo, CA, USA 90245-5067
Ph: (310) 356-4100
E-mail: http://www.aimmedia.com

Adams Business Media
833 W Jackson, 7th Fl.
Chicago, IL, USA 60607
Ph: (312) 846-4600
E-mail: http://www.adamsbusinessmedia.com

Adams Business Media
50 Washington St., 10th Fl.
Norwalk, CT, USA 6854
Ph: (203) 855-8499

Adams Media Corp.
57 Littlefield St.
Avon, MA, USA 02322-1944
Ph: (508) 427-7100
E-mail: rights@atsadamsmedia.com
URL: http://www.adamsmedia.com

Advanced Medical Technology Association
701 Pennsylvania Ave. NW, Ste. 800
Washington, DC, USA 20004-2654
Ph: (202) 783-8700
E-mail: info@atsadvamed.org
URL: http://www.advamed.org

Advanced Research Press Inc.
690 Rte. 25A, Ste. 150
Setauket, NY, USA 11733
Ph: (631) 751-9696
E-mail: http://www.fitnessrxmag.com

Advanstar Communications
6200 Canoga Ave., 2nd Fl.
Woodland Hills, CA, USA 91367
Ph: (818) 593-5000
E-mail: info@atsadvanstar.com
URL: http://web.advanstar.com/advanstar/v42/index.cvn

Advanstar Communications Inc.
641 Lexington Ave., 8th Fl.
New York, NY, USA 10022
Ph: (212) 951-6600
E-mail: info@atsadvanstar.com
URL: http://web.advanstar.com

Advantage Business Media
100 Enterprise Dr., Ste. 600
Box 912
Rockaway, NJ, USA 07866-0912
Ph: (973) 920-7000
E-mail: advantagecommunications@atsadvantagemedia.com
URL: http://www.advantagebusinessmedia.com/

Adventure Cycling Association
150 E Pine St.
PO Box 8308
Missoula, MT, USA 59807
Ph: (406) 721-1776
E-mail: info@atsadventurecycling.org
URL: http://www.adventurecycling.org

Adventure Publishing Group Inc.
286 5th Ave., 3rd Fl.
New York, NY, USA 10001
Ph: (212) 575-4510
E-mail: http://www.adventurepublishinggroup.com/

Advertising Research Foundation
432 Park Ave. S, 6th Fl.
New York, NY, USA 10016-8013
Ph: (212) 751-5656
E-mail: info@atsthearf.org
URL: http://www.thearf.org

Adweek L.P.
100 Boylston St., Ste. 210
Boston, MA, USA 2116
E-mail: http://www.adweek.com

Agate Publishing
1045 Westgate Dr.
Saint Paul, MN, USA 55114
Ph: (847) 475-4457
E-mail: seibold@atsagatepublishing.com
URL: http://www.agatepublishing.com

Agate Publishing, Incorporated
1501 Madison St.
Evanston, IL, USA 60202

AGCD Brandspa Books
215 Glenridge Ave.
Montclair, NJ, USA 7042
Ph: (973) 509-2728
E-mail: inquiry@atsbrandspa.net
URL: http://www.brandspa-llc.com

Agricore United
CanWest Global Pl.
201 Portage Ave.
PO Box 6600
Winnipeg, MB, CAN R3C 3A7
Ph: (204) 944-5411
E-mail: rcarter@atsagricoreunited.com
URL: http://www.agricoreunited.com

Agricultural Resources & Communications Inc.
4210 Wam-Teau Dr.
Wamego, KS, USA 66547
Ph: (785) 456-9705
E-mail: chris@atsagresources.com
URL: http://www.agresources.com

Aha! House
1519 Oakmoor Pl.
Marietta, GA, USA 30062-2745
Ph: (770) 565-1231

Aiken Standard
326 Rutland Dr. NW
Aiken, SC, USA 29801
Ph: (803) 648-2311

Air Age Publishing Inc.
20 Westport Rd.
Wilton, CT, USA 6897
Ph: (203) 431-9000
E-mail: production@atsairage.com
URL: http://www.airage.com

Air Conditioning Contractors of America
2800 Shirlington Rd., Ste. 300
Arlington, VA, USA 22206
Ph: (703) 575-4477
E-mail: http://www.acca.org

Air-Conditioning and Refrigeration Institute
4100 N Fairfax Dr., Ste. 200
Arlington, VA, USA 22203-1627
Ph: (703) 524-8800
E-mail: http://ari.org

AKTRIN Furniture Research
2267 Daffodil Ct.
Oakville, ON, CAN L6J 5Y2
Ph: (905) 845-3474
E-mail: aktrin@atsaktrin.com
URL: http://www.aktrin.com

Alan B. Lancz & Associates Inc.
2400 N Reynolds Rd.
Toledo, OH, USA 43615
Ph: (419) 536-5200
E-mail: abl@atsablonline.com
URL:

Alaska Business Publishing Company
501 W Northern Lights Blvd., Ste. 100
Anchorage, AK, USA 99503
Ph: (907) 276-4373

Alberta Association of Optometrists (AAO)
10724-113 St.
Edmonton, AB, CAN T5H 3H8
Ph: (780) 451-6824
E-mail: alberta.association@atsoptom-etrists.ab.ca
URL:

Alberta Veterinary Medical Association (AVMA)
Weber Centre, No. 950
5555 Calgary Trl.. NW
Edmonton, AB, CAN T6H 5P9
Ph: (780) 489-5007
E-mail: avma@atsavma.avma.ab.ca
URL:

Alcuin Society
PO Box 3216
Vancouver, BC, CAN V6B 3X8
Ph: (604) 937-3293
E-mail: info@atsalcuinsociety.com
URL: http://www.alcuinsociety.com

Alexander Communications Group Inc.
712 Main St., Ste. 187B
Boonton, NJ, USA 7005
Ph: (973) 265-2300
E-mail: info@atsalexcommgrp.com
URL: http://www.alexcommgrp.com

Alexander Communications Group Inc.
28 W. 25th St., 8th Fl.
New York, NY, USA 10010
Ph: (212) 228-0246
E-mail: info@atsalexcommgrp.com
URL: http://www.alexcommgrp.com

Alexander Graham Bell Association for the Deaf and Hard of Hearing
3417 Volta Pl. NW
Washington, DC, USA 20007
Ph: (202) 337-5220
E-mail: info@atsagbell.org
URL: http://www.agbell.org

Alexander Hamilton Institute Inc.
70 Hilltop Rd.
Ramsey, NJ, USA 07446-1119
Ph: (201) 825-3377
E-mail: editorial@atsahipubs.com
URL: http://www.ahipubs.com

Algonquin Publishing
PO Box 2225
Chapel Hill, NC, USA 27515
Ph: (919) 967-0108
E-mail: inquiry@atsalgonquin.com
URL: http://www.algonquin.com

Alive Publishing Group Inc.
100-12751 Vulcan Way
Richmond, BC, CAN V6V 3C8
E-mail: editorial@atsalive.com
URL: http://www.alive.com

All American Crafts Inc.
7 Waterloo Rd.
Stanhope, NJ, USA 07874-2621
Ph: (973) 347-6900
E-mail: http://www.allamericancrafts.com

Allen & Unwin
PO Box 8500
Saint Leonards, NW, AUS 1590
E-mail: http://www.allenandunwin.com

Allen & Unwin Pty., Limited
83 Alexander St.
Crows Nest, NW, AUS 2065

Allen-Reed Publishing Company
160 W Foothill Pkwy., Ste. 105-125
Corona, CA, USA 92882
Ph: (951) 340-9024

Allied Distribution Inc.
PO Box 607
Eagle River, WI, USA 54521
Ph: (715) 479-3530
E-mail: info@atswarehousenetwork.com
URL: http://www.warehousenetwork.com/

Allured Publishing Corp.
336 Gundersen Dr., Ste. A
Carol Stream, IL, USA 60188-2403
Ph: (630) 653-2155
E-mail: customerservice@atsallured.com
URL: http://www.allured.com

Allworth Press
10 E 23rd St., Ste. 510
New York, NY, USA 10010
Ph: (212) 777-8395

Allyear Tax Guides
20484 Glen Brae Dr.
Saratoga, CA, USA 95070
Ph: (408) 867-2628

ALM
120 Broadway, 5th Fl.
New York, NY, USA 10271
Ph: (212) 457-9400

ALM Media Inc.
1 SE 3rd Ave., Ste. 900
Miami, FL, USA 33158
Ph: (305) 377-3721

Alpha Forum Inc.
104 Enterprise Dr.
Kingston, NY, USA 12401-7002

Alpha Publishing House
411 Eagleview Blvd., Ste. 100
Exton, PA, USA 19341
E-mail: http://www.alphapub.com

Alternative Aquaculture Association
630 Independent Rd.
Breinigsville, PA, USA 18031
Ph: (610) 398-1062
E-mail: altaqua@atsptd.net
URL:

Altitude Publishing
1500 Railway Ave.
Canmore, AB, CAN T1W 1P6
Ph: (403) 678-6888

AMACOM
1601 Broadway
New York, NY, USA 10019
Ph: (212) 586-8100
E-mail: customerservice@atsamanet.org
URL: http://www.amanet.org

Amber Books
1334 E Chandler Blvd., Ste. 5-D67
Phoenix, AZ, USA 85048
Ph: (480) 460-1660

AMC Institute
100 N 20th St., 4th Fl.
Philadelphia, PA, USA 19103
Ph: (215) 564-3484
E-mail: info@atsamcinstitute.org
URL: http://www.amcinstitute.org

American Academy of Sleep Medicine
2510 North Frontage Rd.
Darien, IL, USA 60561
Ph: (630) 737-9700
E-mail: publications@atsaasmnet.org
URL: http://www.aasmnet.org

American Accounting Association
5717 Bessie Dr.
Sarasota, FL, USA 34233-2399
Ph: (941) 921-7747
E-mail: office@atsaaahq.org
URL: http://aaahq.org

American Advertising Federation
1101 Vermont Ave. NW, Ste. 500
Washington, DC, USA 20005-6306
Ph: (202) 898-0089
E-mail: aaf@atsaaf.org
URL:

American Alliance for Health, Physical Education, Recreation & Dance
1900 Association Dr.
Reston, VA, USA 20191-1598
Ph: (703) 476-3400
E-mail: info@atsaahperd.org
URL: http://www.aahperd.org/

American Animal Hospital Association
12575 W Bayaud Ave.
Lakewood, CO, USA 80228
Ph: (303) 986-2800
E-mail: info@atsaahanet.org
URL: http://www.aahanet.org

American Arbitration Association
1633 Broadway, Fl. 10
New York, NY, USA 10019
Ph: (212) 716-5800
E-mail: websitemail@atsadr.org
URL: http://www.adr.org

American Association for Career Education
2900 Amby Pl.
Hermosa Beach, CA, USA 90254-2216
Ph: (310) 376-7378

American Association for Counseling and Development
5999 Stevenson Ave.
Alexandria, VA, USA 22304
Ph: (703) 823-6862
E-mail: http://www.counseling.org

American Association for Employment in Education
3040 Riverside Dr., Ste. 117
Columbus, OH, USA 43221
Ph: (614) 485-1111
E-mail: office@atsaaee.org
URL: http://www.aaee.org

American Association for Homecare
2011 Crystal Dr., Ste. 725
Arlington, VA, USA 22202
Ph: (703) 836-6263
E-mail: info@atsaahomecare.org
URL:

American Association for Laboratory Accreditation
5301 Buckeystown Pke, Ste. 350
Frederick, MD, USA 21704-8307
Ph: (301) 644-3248
E-mail: info@atsa2la.org
URL: http://www.a2la.org/

American Association of Bioanalysts (AAB)
906 Olive St., Ste. 1200
Saint Louis, MO, USA 63101-1434
Ph: (314) 241-1445
E-mail: aab@atsaab.org
URL:

American Association of Cereal Chemists
3340 Pilot Knob Rd.
Saint Paul, MN, USA 55121-2097
Ph: (651) 454-7250
E-mail: aacc@atsscisoc.org
URL: http://www.aaccnet.org

American Association of Clinical Chemistry
1850 K St. NW, Ste. 625
Washington, DC, USA 20006-2215
Ph: (202) 857-0717
E-mail: info@atsaacc.org
URL: http://www.aacc.org

American Association of Fund-Raising Counsel Inc.
4700 W Lake Ave.
Glenview, IL, USA 60025
Ph: (847) 375-4709
E-mail: info@atsaafrc.org
URL: http://www.aafrc.org

American Association of Individual Investors
625 N Michigan Ave.
Chicago, IL, USA 60611
Ph: (312) 280-0170
E-mail: techsupport@atsaaii.com
URL: http://www.aaii.com

American Association of Insurance Services (AAIS)
1745 S. Naperville Rd.
Wheaton, IL, USA 60189-8132
Ph: (630) 681-8347
E-mail: info@atsAAISonline.com
URL: http://www.aaisonline.com/

American Association of Meat Processors
1 Meating Pl.
PO Box 269
Elizabethtown, PA, USA 17022-2883
Ph: (717) 367-1168
E-mail: info@atsaamp.com
URL: http://www.aamp.com

American Association of Medical Assistants
20 N Wacker Dr., Ste. 1575
Chicago, IL, USA 60606
Ph: (312) 899-1500
E-mail: http://www.aama-ntl.org/index.aspx

American Bar Association
321 N Clark St.
Chicago, IL, USA 60654-7598
Ph: (312) 988-5522
E-mail: service@atsabanet.org
URL: http://www.abanet.org

American Beekeeping Federation Inc.
115 Morning Glory Cir.
Jesup, GA, USA 31546
Ph: (404) 760-2875
E-mail: info@atsabfnet.org
URL:

American Board of Family Medicine
1648 McGrathiana Pky., Ste. 550
Lexington, KY, USA 40511-1247
Ph: (859) 269-5626
E-mail: help@atstheabfm.org
URL: http://www.theabfm.org/

American Boat & Yacht Council Inc.
613 3rd St., Ste. 10
Annapolis, MD, USA 21403
Ph: (410) 990-4460
E-mail: info@atsabycinc.org
URL: http://www.abycinc.org

American Booksellers Association
200 White Plains Rd., Ste. 600
Tarrytown, NY, USA 10591
Ph: (914) 591-2665
E-mail: info@atsbookweb.org
URL: http://www.bookweb.org

American Business Women's Association
PO Box 8728
Kansas City, MO, USA 64114
E-mail: http://www.abwa.org/

American Business Women's Association
11050 Roe Ave., Ste. 200
Overland Park, KS, USA 66211

American Camp Association
5000 State Rd. 67 N
Martinsville, IN, USA 46151-7902
Ph: (765) 342-8456
E-mail: http://www.acacamps.org

American Cat Fanciers Association Inc.
PO Box 203
Point Lookout, MO, USA 65726
Ph: (417) 334-5430
E-mail: info@atsacfacat.com
URL:

The American Ceramic Society
600 N Cleveland Ave., Ste. 210
Westerville, OH, USA 43082
E-mail: customerservice@atsceramics.org
URL: http://ceramics.org

American Chain of Warehouses
156 Flamingo Dr.
Beecher, IL, USA 60401
Ph: (708) 946-9792
E-mail: bjurus@atsacwi.org
URL: http://www.acwi.org

American Chamber of Commerce Researchers Association
PO Box 407
Arlington, VA, USA 22210
Ph: (703) 522-4980
E-mail: sam@atsaccra.org

URL:

American Chemical Society
1155 16th St., NW
Washington, DC, USA 20036
Ph: (202) 872-4600
E-mail: service@atsacs.org
URL: http://www.chemistry.org

American City Business Journals
1 E Pratt St., Ste. 205
Baltimore, MD, USA 21202
Ph: (410) 576-1161
E-mail: baltimore@atsbizjournals.com
URL: http://baltimore.bizjournals.com

American City Business Journals
1233 West Loop S, Ste. 1300
Houston, TX, USA 77027
Ph: (713) 688-8811
E-mail: Houston@atsbizjournals.com
URL: http://http://ouston.bizjournals.com/

American City Business Journals
825 N Jefferson St., Ste. 200
Milwaukee, WI, USA 53202
Ph: (414) 278-7788
E-mail: Milwaukee@atsbizjournals.com
URL: http://milwaukee.bizjournals.com/milwaukee

American City Business Journals
255 S Orange Ave., Ste. 700
Orlando, FL, USA 32801
Ph: (407) 649-8470
E-mail: Orlando@atsbizjournals.com
URL: http://Orlando.bizjournals.com/orlando

American City Business Journals
801 Second Ave., Ste. 210
Seattle, WA, USA 98104
Ph: (206) 876-5500

American City Business Journals
4890 W Kennedy Blvd., Ste. 850
Tampa, FL, USA 33609
Ph: (813) 873-8225
E-mail: tampabay@atsbizjournals.com
URL: http://tampabay.bizjournals.com/tampabay/

American City Business Journals Inc.
111 Congress Ave., Ste. 750
Austin, TX, USA 78701
Ph: (512) 494-2500

American City Business Journals Inc.
400 Market St., Ste. 1200
Philadelphia, PA, USA 19106
Ph: (215) 238-1450

American City Business Journals Inc.
851 SW 6th Ave., Ste. 500
Portland, OR, USA 97204
Ph: (503) 274-8733
E-mail: http://portland.bizjournals.com

American City Business Journals, Inc.
160 Federal St., 12th Fl.
Boston, MA, USA 2110
Ph: (617) 330-1000

American City Business Journals, Inc.
465 Main St.
Buffalo, NY, USA 14203
Ph: (716) 541-1600

American City Business Journals, Inc.
120 W Morehead St.
Charlotte, NC, USA 28202
Ph: (704) 973-1000

American City Business Journals, Inc.
303 W Nationwide Blvd.
Columbus, OH, USA 43215
Ph: (614) 461-4040

American City Business Journals, Inc.
1100 Main St., Ste. 210
Kansas City, MO, USA 64105-5123
Ph: (816) 421-5900

American City Business Journals, Inc.
40 British American Blvd.
Latham, NY, USA 12110
Ph: (518) 640-6800

American City Business Journals, Inc.
600 Virginia Ave., Ste. 500
Milwaukee, WI, USA 53204
Ph: (414) 278-7788

American City Business Journals, Inc.
101 N 1st Ave., Ste. 2300
Phoenix, AZ, USA 85003
Ph: (602) 230-8400

American College of Apothecaries
Research & Education Resource Center
PO Box 341266
Memphis, TN, USA 38184
Ph: (901) 383-8119
E-mail: aca@atsacainfo.org
URL: http://www.americancollegeofapothecaries.com

American College of Healthcare Executives
1 N Franklin St., Ste. 1700
Chicago, IL, USA 60606-3529
Ph: (312) 424-2800
E-mail: geninfo@atsache.org
URL: http://www.ache.org/

American College of Physician Executives
400 N Ashley Dr., Ste. 400
Tampa, FL, USA 33602-4322
Ph: (813) 287-2000
E-mail: acpe@atsacpe.org
URL: http://www.acpe.org

American Counseling Association
5999 Stevenson Ave.
Alexandria, VA, USA 22304
Ph: (703) 823-6862
E-mail: cwelch@atscounseling.org
URL: http://www.counseling.org

American Craft Council
1224 Marshall St. NE, Ste. 200
Minneapolis, MN, USA 55413-1036
Ph: (612) 206-3100
E-mail: council@atscraftcouncil.org
URL: http://www.craftcouncil.org

American Culinary Federation Inc.
180 Center Pl. Way
Saint Augustine, FL, USA 32095-8859
Ph: (904) 824-4468
E-mail: acf@atsacfchefs.net
URL: http://www.acfchefs.org

American Edged Products Manufacturers Association
21165 Whitfield Pl., No. 105
Potomac Falls, VA, USA 20165
Ph: (703) 433-9281
E-mail: info@atsaepma.org
URL: http://www.aepma.org

American Farm Bureau Federation
600 Maryland Ave. SW, Ste. 800
Washington, DC, USA 20024
Ph: (202) 406-3600
E-mail: fbnews@atsfborg
URL:

American Financial Services Association (AFSA)
Legal Department
919 18th St. NW, Ste. 300
Washington, DC, USA 20006
Ph: (202) 296-5544
E-mail: afsa@atsafsamail.org
URL:

American Fisheries Society
5410 Grosvenor Ln.
Bethesda, MD, USA 20814-2144
Ph: (301) 897-8616
E-mail: main@atsfisheries.org
URL: http://www.fisheries.org

American Fitness
15250 Ventura Blvd., Ste. 200
Sherman Oaks, CA, USA 91403
E-mail: lpafaa@atsaol.com
URL: http://www.americanfitness.com

American Foundry Society
1695 N Penny Ln.
Schaumburg, IL, USA 60173-4555
Ph: (847) 824-0181
E-mail: info@atsafsinc.org
URL: http://www.afsinc.org

American Furniture Manufacturers Association
317 W High Ave. 10th Fl.
PO Box HP-7
High Point, NC, USA 27261
Ph: (336) 884-5000
E-mail: info@atsahfa.us
URL: http://www.ahfa.us

American Health Assistance Foundation
22512 Gateway Center Dr.
Clarksburg, MD, USA 20871
Ph: (301) 948-3244
E-mail: http://www.ahaf.org

American Health Care Association
1201 L St. NW
Washington, DC, USA 20005
Ph: (202) 842-4444
E-mail: http://www.ahcancal.org

American Health Consultants Inc.
PO Box 105109
Atlanta, GA, USA 30374
Ph: (404) 262-7436
E-mail: ahc.management@atsthomson.com
URL: http://www.ahcpub.com/

American Horse Council
1616 H St. NW, 7th Fl.
Washington, DC, USA 20006-4903
Ph: (202) 296-4031
E-mail: ahc@atshorsecouncil.org
URL: http://www.horsecouncil.org

American Horticultural Society
7931 East Blvd. Dr.
Alexandria, VA, USA 22308-1300
Ph: (703) 768-5700
E-mail: editor@atsahs.org
URL: http://www.ahs.org

American Hospital Association
1 N Franklin
Chicago, IL, USA 60606-3421
Ph: (312) 422-3000
E-mail: storeservice@atsaha.org
URL: http://www.aha.org

American Hotel & Lodging Association
1201 New York Ave. NW, Ste. 600
Washington, DC, USA 20005-3931
Ph: (202) 289-3100
E-mail: informationcenter@atsahla.com
URL: http://www.ahla.com

American Humane
63 Inverness Dr. E
Englewood, CO, USA 80112-5117
Ph: (303) 792-9900
E-mail: info@atsamericanhumane.org
URL: http://www.americanhumane.org

American Institute for Economic Research
250 Division St.
PO Box 1000
Great Barrington, MA, USA 01230-1000
Ph: (413) 528-1216
E-mail: info@atsaier.org
URL: http://www.aier.org/

American Institute of Baking
PO Box 3999
1213 Bakers Way
Manhattan, KS, USA 66505-3999
Ph: (785) 537-4750
E-mail: http://www.aibonline.org

The American Institute of Certified Public Accountants
1211 Ave. of the Americas
New York, NY, USA 10036-8775
Ph: (212) 596-6200
E-mail: http://www.aicpa.org/

American Institute of CPAs
1211 Ave. of the Americas
New York, NY, USA 10036
Ph: (212) 596-6200

American Institute of Food Distribution Inc.
1 Broadway
Elmwood Park, NJ, USA 7407
Ph: (201) 791-5570
E-mail: foodl@atsfoodinstitute.com
URL: http://www.foodinstitute.com

American Institute of Graphic Arts
164 5th Ave.
New York, NY, USA 10010
Ph: (212) 807-1990
E-mail: comments@atsaiga.org
URL: http://www.aiga.org

American International Automobile Dealers Association (AIADA)
211 N Union St., Ste. 300
Alexandria, VA, USA 22314-1538
Ph: (703) 519-7800
E-mail: goaiada@atsaiada.org
URL:

American Law Institute-American Bar Association
4025 Chestnut St.
Philadelphia, PA, USA 19104-3099
E-mail: http://www.ali-aba.org

American Lighting Association
2050 Stemmons Fwy., Ste. 10046
PO Box 420288
Dallas, TX, USA 75342-0288
Ph: (214) 698-9898
E-mail: skelley@atsamericanlightingassoc.com
URL: http://www.americanlightingassoc.com

American Lock Collectors Association
8576 Barbara Dr.
Mentor, OH, USA 44060
Ph: (440) 257-2346
E-mail: dixlock@atsaol.com
URL:

American Management Association
1601 Broadway
New York, NY, USA 10019
E-mail: customerservice@atsamanet.org
URL: http://www.amanet.org/books

American Marketing Association
311 S Wacker Dr., Ste. 5800
Chicago, IL, USA 60606
Ph: (312) 542-9000
E-mail: http://www.marketingpower.com

American Massage Therapy Association
500 Davis St., Ste. 900
Evanston, IL, USA 60201-4695
Ph: (847) 864-0123
E-mail: info@atsamtamassage.org
URL: http://www.amtamassage.org/

American Medical Association
515 N State St.
Chicago, IL, USA 60654
E-mail: http://www.ama-assn.org

American Motorcyclist Association
13515 Yarmouth Dr.
Pickerington, OH, USA 43147
Ph: (614) 856-1900
E-mail: ama@atsama-cycle.org
URL: http://www.ama-cycle.org

American Musicological Society Inc.
6010 College Sta.
Brunswick, ME, USA 04011-8451
Ph: (207) 798-4243
E-mail: ams@atsams-net.org
URL: http://www.ams-net.org/

American Numismatic Association
818 N Cascade Ave.
Colorado Springs, CO, USA 80903-3208
Ph: (719) 632-2646
E-mail: ana@atsmoney.org
URL: http://www.money.org

American Numismatic Society
96 Fulton St.
New York, NY, USA 10038
Ph: (212) 571-4470
E-mail: info@atsnumismatics.org
URL: http://www.numismatics.org

American Nurseryman Publishing Co.
223 W Jackson Blvd., Ste. 500
Chicago, IL, USA 60606-6904
Ph: (312) 427-7339
E-mail: admin@atsamerinursery.com
URL: http://www.amerinursery.com/

American Optometric Association
243 N Lindbergh Blvd.
Saint Louis, MO, USA 63141
Ph: (314) 983-4133
E-mail: rabrauns@atsaoa.org
URL: http://www.aoa.org/

American Pharmacists Association
2215 Constitution Ave. NW
Washington, DC, USA 20037-2985
Ph: (202) 429-7557
E-mail: pt@atsaphanet.org
URL: http://www.aphanet.org

American Philatelic Society
100 Match Factory Pl.
PO Box 8000
Bellefonte, PA, USA 16823
Ph: (814) 933-3803
E-mail: flsente@atsstamps.org
URL: http://www.stamps.org/

American Physical Therapy Association
1111 N Fairfax St.
Alexandria, VA, USA 22314-1488
Ph: (703) 684-2782
E-mail: apta@atsapta.org
URL: http://www.apta.org

American Polygraph Association
PO Box 8037
Chattanooga, TN, USA 37414-0037
Ph: (423) 892-3992
E-mail: manager@atspolygraph.org
URL: http://www.polygraph.org

American Public Health Association
800 I St. NW
Washington, DC, USA 20001-3710
Ph: (202) 777-2742
E-mail: comments@atsapha.org
URL: http://www.apha.org

American Public Human Services Association
1133 19th St., NW, Ste. 400
Washington, DC, USA 20036-3631
Ph: (202) 682-0100
E-mail: pubs@atsaphsa.org
URL: http://www.aphsa.org

American Publishing Co.
85 Canisteo St.
Hornell, NY, USA 14843-1544
E-mail: http://oaspub.epa.gov/

American Purchasing Society
8 E Galena Blvd., Ste. 203
Aurora, IL, USA 60506
Ph: (630) 859-0250
E-mail: propurch@atsmgci.com
URL:

American Quarter Horse Association
1600 Quarter Horse Dr.
Amarillo, TX, USA 79104
Ph: (806) 376-4811
E-mail: http://www.aqha.com

American Quilt Study Group
1610 L St.
Lincoln, NE, USA 68508-2509
Ph: (402) 477-1181
E-mail: aqsg2@atsamericanquiltstudygroup.org
URL: http://www.americanquiltstudygroup.org

American Rental Association
1900 19th St.
Moline, IL, USA 61265-4179
Ph: (309) 764-2475
E-mail: http://www.ararental.org

American Riding Instructors Association
28801 Trenton Ct.
Bonita Springs, FL, USA 34134-3337
Ph: (239) 948-3232
E-mail: aria@atsriding-instructor.com
URL: http://www.riding-instructor.com

American Salers Association
19590 E Main St., Ste. 202
Parker, CO, USA 80138
Ph: (303) 770-9292
E-mail: http://www.salersusa.org/

American School Health Association
7263 State Route 43
PO Box 708
Kent, OH, USA 44240
Ph: (330) 678-1601
E-mail: asha@atsashaweb.org
URL: http://www.ashaweb.org

American Self-Protection Association (ASP)
825 Greengate Oval
Sagamore Hills, OH, USA 44067
Ph: (330) 467-1750
E-mail: ebaltazzi@atsaol.com
URL:

American Society for Clinical Pathology
33 W Monroe, Ste. 1600
Chicago, IL, USA 60603
Ph: (312) 541-4999
E-mail: info@atsascp.org
URL: http://www.ascp.org

American Society for Nutrition
9650 Rockville Pke.
Bethesda, MD, USA 20814
Ph: (301) 634-7050
E-mail: info@atsnutrition.org
URL: http://www.nutrition.org/

American Society for Public Administration
1301 Pennsylvania Ave. NW, Ste. 840
Washington, DC, USA 20004-1735
Ph: (202) 393-7878
E-mail: info@atsaspanet.org
URL: http://www.aspanet.org

American Society for Quality
PO Box 3005
Milwaukee, WI, USA 53201-3005
Ph: (414) 272-8575
E-mail: help@atsasq.org
URL: http://www.asq.org

American Society for Training & Development
1640 King St.
PO Box 1443
Alexandria, VA, USA 22313-2043
Ph: (703) 683-8100
E-mail: customercare@atsastd.org
URL: http://www.astd.org

American Society of Agricultural and Biological Engineers
2950 Niles Rd.
Saint Joseph, MI, USA 49085
Ph: (269) 429-0300
E-mail: hq@atsasae.org
URL: http://www.asabe.org

American Society of Andrology
1100 E Woodfield Rd., Ste. 520
Schaumburg, IL, USA 60173
Ph: (847) 619-4909
E-mail: info@atsandrologysociety.com
URL: http://www.andrologysociety.com/

American Society of Artists
PO Box 1326
Palatine, IL, USA 60078-1326
Ph: (312) 751-2500
E-mail: asoaartists@atsaol.com
URL: http://www.americansocietyofartists.org

American Society of Association Executives
The ASAE Bldg.
1575 I St. NW
Washington, DC, USA 20005-1103
Ph: (202) 626-2723
E-mail: infocentral@atsasaenet.org
URL: http://www.asaecenter.org/

American Society of Association Executives (ASAE)
1575 Eye St. NW
Washington, DC, USA 20005-1168
Ph: (202) 626-2723
E-mail: asaeservice@atsasaecenter.org
URL: http://www.asaecenter.org

American Society of Civil Engineers
1801 Alexander Bell Dr.
Reston, VA, USA 20191-4400
Ph: (703) 295-6300
E-mail: marketing@atsasce.org
URL: http://www.asce.org

American Society of Consultant Pharmacists
1321 Duke St.
Alexandria, VA, USA 22314-3563
Ph: (703) 739-1300
E-mail: info@atsascp.com
URL: http://www.ascp.com/

American Society of Consulting Arborists
15245 Shady Grove Rd., Ste. 130
Rockville, MD, USA 20850
Ph: (301) 947-0483
E-mail: asca@atsmgmtsol.com
URL:

American Society of Consulting Arborists
9707 Key W Ave., Ste. 100
Rockville, MD, USA 20850
Ph: (301) 947-0483
E-mail: asca@atsmgmtsol.com
URL: http://www.asca-consultants.org

American Society of Electroneurodiagnostic Technologists Inc.
402 E Bannister Rd., Ste. A
Kansas City, MO, USA 64131-3019
Ph: (816) 931-1120
E-mail: info@atsaset.org
URL: http://www.aset.org/i4a/pages/index.cfm?pageid=1

American Society of Furniture Designers
c/o Christine Evans, Exec. Dir.
144 Woodland Dr.
New London, NC, USA 28127
Ph: (910) 576-1273
E-mail: info@atsasfd.com
URL: http://www.asfd.com

American Society of Journalists & Authors
1501 Broadway, Ste. 302
New York, NY, USA 10036
Ph: (212) 997-0947
E-mail: http://www.asja.org

American Society of Landscape Architects
636 Eye St., NW
Washington, DC, USA 20001-3736
Ph: (202) 898-2444
E-mail: email@atsasla.org
URL: http://www.asla.org/

American Society of Mechanical Engineers
3 Park Ave.
New York, NY, USA 10016-5990
Ph: (973) 882-1170
E-mail: infocentral@atsasme.org
URL: http://www.asme.org

American Society of Media Photographers Inc.
150 N 2nd St.
Philadelphia, PA, USA 19106-1912
Ph: (215) 451-2767
E-mail: info@atsasmp.org
URL: http://www.asmp.org

American Society of Plant Biologists
15501 Monona Dr.
Rockville, MD, USA 20855-2768
Ph: (301) 251-0560
E-mail: info@atsaspb.org
URL: http://www.aspb.org/index.cfm

American Society of Professional Estimators
2525 Perimeter Place Dr., Ste. 103
Nashville, TN, USA 37214
Ph: (615) 316-9200
E-mail: info@atsaspenational.org
URL: http://www.aspenational.org

American Society of Safety Engineers
1800 E Oakton St.
Des Plaines, IL, USA 60018-2100
Ph: (847) 699-2929
E-mail: customerservice@atsasse.org
URL: http://www.asse.org

American Society of Women Accountants
1760 Old Meadow Rd., Ste. 500
McLean, VA, USA 22102
Ph: (703) 506-3265
E-mail: aswa@atsaswa.org
URL: http://www.aswa.org

American Society on Aging
833 Market St., Ste. 511
San Francisco, CA, USA 94103
Ph: (415) 974-9600

American Sociological Association
1430 K St. NW, Ste. 600
Washington, DC, USA 20005
Ph: (202) 383-9005
E-mail: executive.office@atsasanet.org
URL: http://www.asanet.org

American Solar Energy Society
4760 Walnut St., Ste. 106
Boulder, CO, USA 80301-2843
Ph: (303) 443-3130
E-mail: ases@atsases.org
URL: http://www.ases.org

American String Teachers Association with National School Orchestra Association--Michigan Chapter (MASTA w/NSOA)
4153 Chain Bridge Rd.
Fairfax, VA, USA 22030
Ph: (703) 279-2113
E-mail: http://www.astaweb.com/

American Supply Association
222 Merchandise Mart Plz., Ste. 1400
Chicago, IL, USA 60654
Ph: (312) 464-0090
E-mail: info@atsasa.net
URL: http://www.asa.net

American Tort Reform Association
1101 Connecticut Ave. NW, Ste. 400
Washington, DC, USA 20036
Ph: (202) 682-1163

American Trade Magazines
360 N Michigan Ave.
Chicago, IL, USA 60601-3806
Ph: (312) 649-5200
E-mail: http://www.crain.com/index.html

American Translators Association
225 Reinekers Ln., Ste. 590
Alexandria, VA, USA 22314
Ph: (703) 683-6100
E-mail: ata@atsatanet.org
URL: http://www.atanet.org

American Trucking Associations Inc.
950 N. Glebe Rd., Ste. 210
Arlington, VA, USA 22203-4181
Ph: (703) 838-1700
E-mail: orders@atstrucking.org
URL: http://www.truckline.com

American Typecasting Fellowship
PO Box 263
Terra Alta, WV, USA 26764
Ph: (304) 789-2455
E-mail: wvtypenut@atsaol.com
URL:

American Veterinary Medical Association
1931 N Meacham Rd., Ste. 100
Schaumburg, IL, USA 60173-4360
Ph: (847) 925-8070
E-mail: avmainfo@atsavma.org
URL: http://www.avma.org

American Water Works Association (AWWA)
6666 W Quincy Ave.
Denver, CO, USA 80235
Ph: (303) 347-6272

American Wholesale Marketers Association
2750 Prosperity Ave., Ste. 530
Fairfax, VA, USA 22031
Ph: (703) 208-3358

E-mail: info@atsawmanet.org
URL: http://www.awmanet.org

American Wind Energy Association
1101 14th St. NW, Ste. 1000
Washington, DC, USA 20005
Ph: (202) 383-2500
E-mail: windmail@atsawea.org
URL: http://www.awea.org

American Window Cleaner Magazine
750-B NW Broad St.
Southern Pines, NC, USA 28387
Ph: (910) 693-2644
E-mail: info@atsawcmag.com
URL: http://www.awcmag.com/information.htmlstaff

American Woman's Society of Certified Public Accountants
136 S Keowee St.
Dayton, OH, USA 45402
Ph: (937) 222-1872
E-mail: info@atsawscpa.org
URL:

Americana Unit
PO Box 127
New Britain, CT, USA 6050

American-International Charolais Association
11700 NW Plz. Cir.
Kansas City, MO, USA 64153
Ph: (816) 464-5977
E-mail: http://www.charolaisusa.com/

AMIDEAST Publications
1730 M St. NW, Ste. 1100
Washington, DC, USA 20036-4505
Ph: (202) 776-9600
E-mail: inquiries@atsamideast.org
URL: http://www.amideast.org

Amos Press Inc.
911 Vandemark Rd.
Sidney, OH, USA 45365-0150
E-mail: http://www.amospress.com

Anchor Press
77 Accord Park Dr., Unit C4
Norwell, MA, USA 2061
Ph: (781) 982-9510
E-mail: info@atsanchorpress.com
URL: http://www.anchorpress.com

Andersen Horticultural Library
University of Minnesota Landscape
3675 Arboretum Dr.
Chaska, MN, USA 55318
Ph: (952) 443-1405
E-mail: hortlib@atsumn.edu
URL: http://www.arboretum.umn.edu/library.aspx

Animal Health Institute
1325 G St. NW, Ste. 700
Washington, DC, USA 20005
Ph: (202) 637-2440
E-mail: rphillips@atsahi.org
URL:

Animal Rights Network Inc.
3500 Boston St., Ste. 325
Baltimore, MD, USA
Ph: (410) 675-4566

Annex Publishing & Printing Inc.
105 Donly Dr. S
PO Box 530
Simcoe, ON, CAN N3Y 4N5
Ph: (519) 429-3966
E-mail: http://www.annexweb.com

Antique Bottle and Glass Collector
PO Box 180
East Greenville, PA, USA 18041
Ph: (215) 679-5849
E-mail: glswrk@atsenter.net
URL: http://www.glswrk-auction.com

AOCS Press
2710 S Boulder
PO Box 17190
Urbana, IL, USA 61802-6996
Ph: (217) 359-2344
E-mail: general@atsaocs.org
URL: http://www.aocs.org

APA--The Engineered Wood Association
7011 S 19th
Tacoma, WA, USA 98466
Ph: (253) 565-6600
E-mail: help@atsapawood.org
URL:

Apartment News Publications Inc.
15502 Graham St.
Huntington Beach, CA, USA 92649
Ph: (714) 893-3971
E-mail: aptmags@atsaptmags.com
URL: http://www.aptmags.com

Apex Publications Inc.
185 St. Paul
Quebec, QC, CAN G1K 3W2
E-mail: info@atsphotolife.com
URL: http://www.photolife.com/

Apparel News Group
110 E 9th St., Ste. A-777
Los Angeles, CA, USA 90079-1777
Ph: (213) 627-3737
E-mail: info@atsapparelnews.net
URL: http://www.apparelnews.net

Appendx
PO Box 382806
Cambridge, MA, USA 2238
Ph: (617) 495-4115
E-mail: appendx@atsgsd.harvard.edu
URL: http://www.appendx.org

Applied Arts Inc.
18 Wynford Dr., Ste. 411
Toronto, ON, CAN M3C 3S2
Ph: (416) 510-0909
E-mail: http://www.appliedartsmag.com

The Appraisal Institute of American Inc.
386 Park Ave. S, Ste. 2000
New York, NY, USA 10016
Ph: (212) 889-5404
E-mail: aaa@atsappraisersassoc.org
URL:

Appraisal Institute of Canada
403-200 rue, Catherine St.
Ottawa, ON, CAN K2P 2K9
Ph: (613) 234-6533
E-mail: info@atsaicanada.org
URL: http://www.aicanada.ca

Appraisers Association of America Inc.
386 Park Ave. S, Fl. 20, Ste. 2000
New York, NY, USA 10016-8804
Ph: (212) 889-5404
E-mail: aaa@atsappraisersassoc.org
URL: http://www.appraisersassoc.org

Apress
2855 Telegraph Ave., Ste. 600
Berkeley, CA, USA 94705
Ph: (510) 549-5930
E-mail: info@atsapress.com
URL: http://www.apress.com/

Apress L.P.
2560 9th St., Ste. 219
Berkeley, CA, USA 94710
Ph: (510) 549-5930

Aquarian Research Foundation
5620 Morton St.
Philadelphia, PA, USA 19144
Ph: (215) 848-2292
E-mail: judyrosenblum@atsjuno.com
URL: http://www.aquarian.cjb.net/

The Arc of Carroll County Inc.
180 Kriders Church Rd.
Westminster, MD, USA 21158
Ph: (410) 848-4124

Architectural Designs Inc.
57 Danbury Rd., Ste. 203
Wilton, CT, USA 6897
E-mail: info@atsarchitecturaldesigns.com
URL: http://www.architecturaldesigns.com/

Arizona Daily Star
4850 S Park Ave.
Tucson, AZ, USA 85714

Arizona Farm Bureau Federation
325 S Higley Rd.
PO Box 9000
Higley, AZ, USA 85236-9000
Ph: (480) 635-3604

Arkansas Business Publishing Group
122 E 2nd St.
Little Rock, AR, USA 72201
Ph: (501) 372-1443

Art Dealers Association of America Inc.
205 Lexington Ave., Ste. 901
New York, NY, USA 10016
Ph: (212) 488-5550
E-mail: http://www.artdealers.org

Art News L.L.C.
48 W 38th St.
New York, NY, USA 10018
Ph: (212) 398-1690
E-mail: info@atsartnews.com
URL: http://artnews.com

Art Now Inc.
601 W 26th St., Ste. 410
PO Box 5541
New York, NY, USA 10001
Ph: (212) 447-9555
E-mail: northamericapress@atsartinfo.com
URL: http://www.artinfo.com/galleryguide/

The Art of Eating
PO Box 242
Peacham, VT, USA 5862
E-mail: http://www.artofeating.com/

Artech House, Incorporated
685 Canton St.
Norwood, MA, USA 2062
Ph: (781) 769-9750

Artificial Language Laboratory
405 Computer Ctr.
East Lansing, MI, USA 48824-1042
Ph: (517) 353-0870
E-mail: artlang@atspilot.msu.edu
URL: http://www.msu.edu/@tldartlang/CommOut.html

ARTnews
48 W 38th St.
New York, NY, USA 10018
Ph: (212) 398-1690
E-mail: info@atsartnews.com
URL:

Arts & Media Inc.
PO Box 678
Richboro, PA, USA 18954
Ph: (215) 968-4655
E-mail: info@atsglasscraftsman.com
URL: http://www.glasscraftsman.com

ARTWEEK
PO Box 52100
Palo Alto, CA, USA 94303-0751
E-mail: info@atsartweek.com
URL: http://www.artweek.com

Ascend Integrated Media
7015 College Blvd., Ste. 600
Overland Park, KS, USA 66211
Ph: (913) 469-1110
E-mail: info@atsascendmedia.com
URL: http://www.ascendmedia.com/

Ascend Media
7015 College Blvd., Ste. 600
Overland Park, KS, USA 66211
Ph: (913) 469-1110
E-mail: info@atsascendmedia.com
URL: http://www.ascendintegratedmedia.com

ASIS International
1625 Prince St.
Alexandria, VA, USA 22314-2818
Ph: (703) 519-6200
E-mail: asis@atsasisonline.org
URL: http://www.asisonline.org

ASM International
9639 Kinsman Rd.
Novelty, OH, USA 44073-0001
Ph: (440) 338-5151
E-mail: customerservice@atsasminternational.org
URL: http://asmcommunity.asminternational.org/portal/site/www/

ASM Journals
1752 North St. NW
Washington, DC, USA 20036-2904
Ph: (202) 737-3600
E-mail: journals@atsasmusa.org
URL: http://www.journals.asm.org

Aspatore Books, Incorporated
264 Beacon St., 2nd Fl.
Boston, MA, USA 2116
Ph: (617) 369-7007

Aspen Publishers
Wolters Kluwer Law & Business
76 Ninth Ave., 7th Fl.
New York, NY, USA 10011
Ph: (212) 771-0786
E-mail: aspen-internationals@atswolterskluwer.com
URL: http://www.aspenpublishers.com

Aspen Publishers Inc.
7201 McKinney Circ.
PO Box 990
Frederick, MD, USA 21705
Ph: (800) 638-8437
E-mail: http://www.aspenpublishers.com

Aspen Publishers Inc.
76 9th Ave., 7th Fl.
New York, NY, USA 10011-5201
Ph: (212) 771-0600
E-mail: http://www.aspenpublishers.com

Aspen Publishers, Inc. (Frederick, Maryland)
7201 McKinney Cir.
Frederick, MD, USA 21704
E-mail: customerservice@atsaspenpublisher.com
URL: http://www.aspenpublishers.com

The Asphalt Contractor
1233 Janesville Ave.
Fort Atkinson, WI, USA 53538-0803
Ph: (920) 563-6388
E-mail: http://www.forconstructionpros.com

Asphalt Emulsion Manufacturers Association
3 Church Cir.
PMB 250
Annapolis, MD, USA 21401
Ph: (410) 267-0023
E-mail: krissoff@atsaema.org
URL: http://www.aema.org

Asphalt Recycling & Reclaiming Association
Church Cir., Ste. 3
PO Box 250
Annapolis, MD, USA 21401
Ph: (410) 267-0023
E-mail: krissoff@atsarra.org
URL: http://www.arra.org

Asset International Inc.
1055 Washington Blvd.
Stamford, CT, USA 6901
E-mail: http://www.globalcustodian.com

Associated Builders and Contractors Inc.
4250 N Fairfax Dr., 9th Fl.
Arlington, VA, USA 22203-1607
Ph: (703) 812-2000
E-mail: gotquestions@atsabc.org
URL: http://www.abc.org

Associated Equipment Distributors Inc.
600 Hunter Dr., Ste. 220
Oak Brook, IL, USA 60523
Ph: (630) 574-0650
E-mail: info@atsaednet.org
URL: http://www.aednet.org

Associated General Contractors of America
2300 Wilson Blvd., Ste. 400
Arlington, VA, USA 22201
Ph: (703) 548-3118
E-mail: info@atsagc.org
URL: http://www.agc.org

Associated Humane Societies
124 Evergreen Ave.
Newark Airport
Newark, NJ, USA 7114
Ph: (973) 824-7080
E-mail: associatedhumane@atsaol.com
URL:

Associated Locksmiths of America
3500 Easy St.
Dallas, TX, USA 75247
Ph: (214) 819-9733
E-mail: http://www.aloa.org

Associated Plumbing Heating & Cooling
PO Box 36972
Birmingham, AL, USA 35236-6972
Ph: (205) 985-9488
E-mail: dconsult1@atsbellsouth.net
URL: http://www.alphccapprentice.org/

Associated Press
1120 John St.
PO Box 70
Seattle, WA, USA 98111
Ph: (206) 464-2111

Associated Warehouses Inc.
1740 W Katella Ave., Ste. M
Orange, CA, USA 92867
Ph: (973) 539-1277
E-mail: barb@atsawilogistics.com
URL: http://www.awilogistics.com/

Association de la construction du Quebec
7400, Blvd. les Galeries d'Anjou, Bureau 205
Montreal, QC, CAN H1M 3M2
Ph: (514) 354-0609
E-mail: info@atsprov.acq.org
URL: http://www.acq.org

Association for Childhood Education International
17904 Georgia Ave., Ste. 215
Olney, MD, USA 20832
Ph: (301) 570-2111
E-mail: headquarters@atsacei.org
URL: http://www.acei.org/

Association for Computing Machinery
1515 Broadway, 17th Fl.
New York, NY, USA 10036
Ph: (212) 626-0500
E-mail: acmhelp@atsacm.org
URL: http://www.acm.org

Association for Computing Machinery
2 Penn Plz., Ste. 701
PO Box 30777
New York, NY, USA 10121-0701
Ph: (212) 869-7440
E-mail: acmhelp@atsacm.org
URL: http://www.acm.org

Association for Computing Machinery
Editorial Offices
Baylor University, Hankamer School of Business
PO Box 98005
Waco, TX, USA 76798-8005

Association for Educational Communications and Technology
1800 N Stonelake Dr., Ste. 2
PO Box 2247
Bloomington, IN, USA 47402-2447
Ph: (812) 335-7675
E-mail: aect@atsaect.org
URL: http://www.aect.org

Association For Manufacturing Technology AMT
7901 Westpark Dr.
Mc Lean, VA, USA 22102-4206
Ph: (703) 893-2900
E-mail: amt@atsamtonline.org
URL: http://www.amtonline.org

Association for Technology in Music Instruction (ATMI)
312 E Pine St.
Capital University
2199 E Main St.
Missoula, MT, USA 59802
Ph: (614) 236-6236

Association for the Advancement of Medical Instrumentation
1110 N Glebe Rd., Ste. 220
Arlington, VA, USA 22201-4795
Ph: (703) 525-4890
E-mail: publications@atsaami.org
URL: http://www.aami.org

Association for the Advancement of Medical Instrumentation
4301 N Fairfax Dr., Ste. 301
PO Box 1211
Arlington, VA, USA 22203
Ph: (703) 525-4890
E-mail: customerservice@atsaami.org
URL: http://www.aami.org

Association of American Publishers Inc.
50 F St. NW, Ste. 400
Washington, DC, USA 20001
Ph: (202) 347-3375

Association of American University Presses
28 W 36th St., Ste. 602
New York, NY, USA 10018
Ph: (212) 989-1010
E-mail: info@atsaaupnet.org
URL: http://www.aaupnet.org

Association of Asphalt Paving Technologists
6776 Lake Dr., Ste. 215
Lino Lakes, MN, USA 55014
Ph: (651) 293-9188
E-mail: aaptinfo@atsgmail.com
URL: http://www.asphalttechnology.org

Association of Bridal Consultants
56 Danbury Rd., Ste. 11
New Milford, CT, USA 6776
Ph: (860) 355-7000
E-mail: office@atsbridalassn.com
URL: http://www.bridalassn.com/

Association of Directory Marketing
One Thorn Run Ctr., Ste. 630
1187 Thorn Run Rd.
Moon Township, PA, USA 15108-3198
Ph: (412) 269-0663
E-mail: adm@atsadmworks.org
URL:

Association of Machinery and Equipment Appraisers
315 S Patrick St.
Alexandria, VA, USA 22314
Ph: (703) 836-7900
E-mail: amea@atsamea.org
URL: http://www.amea.org/

Association of Millwork Distributors
10047 Robert Trent Jones Pkwy.
New Port Richey, FL, USA 34655-4649
Ph: (727) 372-3665
E-mail: mail@atsamdweb.com
URL:

Association of Ontario Land Surveyors
1043 McNicoll Ave.
Toronto, ON, CAN M1W 3W6
Ph: (416) 491-9020
E-mail: admin@atsaols.org
URL: http://www.aols.org/

Association of Professional Genealogists
PO Box 350998
Westminster, CO, USA 80035-0998
Ph: (303) 465-6980
E-mail: admin@atsapgen.org
URL: http://www.apgen.org/

Association of Registered Interior Designers of Ontario
717 Church St.
Toronto, ON, CAN M4W 2M5
Ph: (416) 921-2127
E-mail: adminoffice@atsarido.ca
URL:

Association of Retail Travel Agents
73 White Bridge Rd., Box 238
Nashville, TN, USA 37205
Ph: (800) 969-9069
E-mail: info@atsartaonline.com
URL:

Association of Schools & Colleges of Optometry
6110 Executive Blvd., Ste. 420
Rockville, MD, USA 20852
Ph: (301) 231-5944
E-mail: carmstrong@atsopted.org
URL: http://www.opted.org

Association of the Wall and Ceiling Industries International
513 W Broad St., Ste. 210
Falls Church, VA, USA 22046
Ph: (703) 538-1600
E-mail: info@atsawci.org
URL: http://www.awci.org

Association of Writers & Writing Programs
George Mason University
PO Box 1E3
Fairfax, VA, USA 22030-4444
Ph: (703) 993-4301
E-mail: awp@atsawpwriter.org
URL: http://www.awpwriter.org

Athletic Business Publications Inc.
4130 Lien Rd.
Madison, WI, USA 53704
Ph: (608) 249-0186
E-mail: http://www.athleticbusiness.com

Atlanta Journal Constitution
223 Perimeter Center Pkwy.
Atlanta, GA, USA 30346
Ph: (404) 526-5151

Atlantic Boating Almanac
3 Church Cir., Ste. 109
Annapolis, MD, USA 21401
E-mail: editor@atsprostarpublications.com
URL: http://www.prostarpublications.com

Atlantic Monthly Press
841 Broadway, 4th Fl.
New York, NY, USA 10003
Ph: (212) 614-7850
E-mail: http://www.groveatlantic.com/

Atlantic Publishing Company
1210 SW 23rd Pl.
Ocala, FL, USA 34474
Ph: (352) 622-1825
E-mail: sales@atsatlantic-pub.com
URL: http://www.atlantic-pub.com

Atlantic Publishing Company
1405 SW 6th Ave.
Ocala, FL, USA 34471
E-mail: http://www.atlantic-pub.com

Atlantic Publishing Company
1405 SW 7th Ave.
Ocala, FL, USA 34474-7014

Atlantic Publishing Group, Inc.
1405 SW 6th Ave.
Ocala, FL, USA 34471
E-mail: sales@atsatlantic-pub.com
URL: http://www.atlantic-pub.com

Atlantic Spinners & Handweavers
1747 Summer St.
Halifax, NS, CAN B3H 3A6
Ph: (902) 865-3641

Auction Marketing Institute
8880 Ballentine
Overland Park, KS, USA 66214
Ph: (913) 541-8084
E-mail: info@atsusaweb.com
URL:

Audio Engineering Society Inc.
60 E 42nd St., Rm. 2520
New York, NY, USA 10165-2520
Ph: (212) 661-8528
E-mail: hq@atsaes.org
URL: http://www.aes.org

Audiotex News
2362 Hempstead Tpke., 2nd Fl.
East Meadow, NY, USA 11554

August Home Publishing
2200 Grand Ave.
Des Moines, IA, USA 50312
Ph: (515) 875-7000
E-mail: http://www.augusthome.com

Austin & Company, Incorporated
104 S Union St., Ste. 202
Traverse City, MI, USA 49684
Ph: (231) 933-4649

Austrian Press and Information Service
3524 International Ct.
Washington, DC, USA 20008-3027
Ph: (202) 895-6775
E-mail: austroinfo@atsaustria.org
URL: http://www.austria.org

AuthorHouse
1663 Liberty Dr.
Bloomington, IN, USA 47407
E-mail: authorsupport@atsauthorhouse.com
URL: http://www.authorhouse.com

Automotive Body Parts Association
1510 Eldridge Pky., Ste. 110-168
Houston, TX, USA 77077
Ph: (281) 531-0809
E-mail: autobpa@atsinfohwy.com
URL: http://www.autobpa.com

Automotive Engine Rebuilders Association
500 Coventry Lane Ste 180
Buffalo Grove, IL, USA 60014
Ph: (847) 541-6550
E-mail: info@atsaera.org
URL:

Automotive Fleet and Leasing Association
21061 S Western Ave.
Torrance, CA, USA 90501
Ph: (651) 203-7247

Automotive Parts International
PO Box 5950
Bethesda, MD, USA 20824-5950
Ph: (301) 229-2077

Automotive Service Association
PO Box 929
1901 Airport Fwy.
Bedford, TX, USA 76095-0929
Ph: (817) 283-6205
E-mail: asainfo@atsasashop.org
URL: http://www.asashop.org/

Automotive Warehouse Distributors Association
7101 Wisconsin Ave., Ste. 1300
Bethesda, MD, USA 20814-4866
Ph: (301) 654-6664
E-mail: aaia@atsaftermarket.org
URL: http://www.aftermarket.org/Segments/awda.aspx

Awards and Recognition Association
4700 W Lake Ave.
Glenview, IL, USA 60025
Ph: (847) 375-4800
E-mail: info@atsara.org
URL:

Axios Press
PO Box 118
Mount Jackson, VA, USA 22842
Ph: (540) 984-3829
E-mail: http://www.axiospress.com

Azure Publishing Inc.
460 Richmond St. W, Ste. 601
Toronto, ON, CAN M5V 1Y1
Ph: (416) 203-9674
E-mail: azure@atsazureonline.com
URL:

B

The B&B and Country Inn Marketplace
926 Lenoir Rhyne Blvd. SE
Hickory, NC, USA 28602
Ph: (828) 324-7291
E-mail: innsales@atscharter.net
URL: http://www.innmarketing.com

Babcox
3550 Embassy Pky.
Akron, OH, USA 44333
Ph: (330) 670-1234
E-mail: bbabcox@atsbabcox.com
URL: http://www.babcox.com/

Back Bay/Little, Brown
PO Box 8828
Boston, MA, USA 2114
E-mail: http://www.hachettebookgroupusa.com/publishing_back-bay-books.aspx

Baker & Taylor
1120 Rte. 22 E
Bridgewater, NJ, USA 8807
Ph: (908) 541-7000
E-mail: btinfo@atsbtol.com
URL: http://www.btol.com

Bale Publications
5121 St. Charles Ave., Ste. 13
New Orleans, LA, USA 70115

Ball Publishing
622 Town Rd.
PO Box 1660
West Chicago, IL, USA 60186
Ph: (630) 231-3675
E-mail: info@atsballpublishing.com
URL: http://www.ballpublishing.com

Ballantine/Random House
1745 Broadway
New York, NY, USA 10019
Ph: (212) 782-9000
E-mail: customerservice@atsrandom-house.com
URL:

Baltimore Business Journal
1 E Pratt St., Ste. 205
Baltimore, MD, USA 21202
Ph: (410) 576-1161

Bangor Daily News
491 Main St.
Bangor, ME, USA 4402
Ph: (207) 990-8000

Bantam Books
Front Porch Institute
964 17th St.
Astorta, OR, USA 97103
Ph: (503) 338-6218
E-mail: http://patrickoverton.com

Bantam Books
1745 Broadway
New York, NY, USA 10019
Ph: (212) 782-9000
E-mail: http://www.randomhouse.com/bantamdell/

Barbara Wallraff
1010 E Missouri Ave.
Phoenix, AZ, USA 85014
Ph: (602) 395-5850

Bard Press
5275 McCormick Mt. Dr.
Austin, TX, USA 78734
Ph: (512) 266-2112
E-mail: info@atsbardpress.com
URL: http://www.bardpress.com

Barger & Wolen
633 W 5th St., Ste. 4700
Los Angeles, CA, USA 90017
Ph: (213) 680-2800

Barnard Enterprises Inc.
17 Kenneth Rd.
Upper Montclair, NJ, USA 7043
Ph: (973) 655-8888

Barron's Editorial & Corporate Headquarters
Dow Jones & Company
1211 Ave. of the Americas
New York, NY, USA 10036
Ph: (212) 416-2000

Barron's Educational Series Inc.
250 Wireless Blvd.
Hauppauge, NY, USA 11788-3924
Ph: (631) 434-3311
E-mail: barrons@atsbarronseduc.com
URL: http://www.barronseduc.com

Basic Books
387 Park Ave. S
New York, NY, USA 10022-5299
E-mail: http://www.basicbooks.com

Basic Books/Perseus Books Group
387 Park Ave. S, 12th Fl.
New York, NY, USA 10016
Ph: (212) 340-8100

BASS/ESPN
5845 Carmichael Rd.
Montgomery, AL, USA 36117-2329
Ph: (334) 272-9530
E-mail: customerservice@atsbassmaster.com
URL: http://espn.go.com/

Baum Publications Ltd.
201 - 2323 Boundary Rd.
Vancouver, BC, CAN V5M 4V8
Ph: (604) 291-9900
E-mail: http://www.baumpub.com

Bay Area Independent Publishers Association (BAIPA)
PO Box E
Corte Madera, CA, USA 94976
Ph: (415) 257-8275
E-mail: info@atsbaipa.net
URL:

Bay Area Poets Coalition Inc.
PO Box 11435
Berkeley, CA, USA 94712-2435
E-mail: poetalk@atsaol.com
URL:

Baylor University
1 Bear Pl.
Waco, TX, USA 76798
Ph: (254) 710-4290
E-mail: sharon_k_johnson@atsbaylor.edu
URL: http://www.baylor.edu

Baywood Publishing Company Inc.
26 Austin Ave.
PO Box 337
Amityville, NY, USA 11701
Ph: (631) 691-1270
E-mail: info@atsbaywood.com
URL: http://www.baywood.com

Beacon Health Corp.
12308 N Corporate Pkwy., Ste. 100
Mequon, WI, USA 53092-3380
Ph: (262) 243-6100
E-mail: info@atsbeaconhealth.org
URL:

Beacon Press
25 Beacon St.
Boston, MA, USA 02108-2892
Ph: (617) 742-2110

The Beauty Industry Report
22287 Mulholland Hwy.
PMB 403
Calabasas, CA, USA 91302-5157
Ph: (818) 225-8353
E-mail: mike@atsbeautyindustryreport.com
URL:

Bee Publishing Company Inc.
PO Box 5503
Newtown, CT, USA 06470-5503
Ph: (203) 426-3141
E-mail: http://newtownbee.com/

Bell Springs Publishing
106 State St.
PO Box 1240
Willits, CA, USA 95490
Ph: (707) 459-6372

Bellingham Herald
1155 N State St., Ste. 200
Bellingham, WA, USA 98225
Ph: (360) 676-2660

BenBella Books
6440 N Central Expy., Ste. 617
Dallas, TX, USA 77459
Ph: (214) 750-3600
E-mail: http://www.benbellabooks.com

Benzinga.com
160 Greentree, Ste. 101
Dover, DE, USA 19904

Berens & Tate, P.C.
10050 Regency Cir., Ste. 400
Omaha, NE, USA 68114
Ph: (402) 391-1991
E-mail: berens@atsberenstate.com
URL:

Berkley Trade
Penguin Group
375 Hudson St.
New York, NY, USA 10014

Ph: (212) 366-2372
E-mail: http://us.penguingroup.com/static/html/aboutus/adult.berkley.html

Berkley Trade/Penguin Group (USA) Inc.
375 Hudson St.
New York, NY, USA 10014
Ph: (212) 366-2000
E-mail: fran.corea@atsus.penguingroup.com
URL: http://www.penguin.com

Berlitz International Inc.
400 Alexander Park
Princeton, NJ, USA 8540
Ph: (609) 514-3400

Bermuda Department of Tourism
675 3rd Ave., 20th Fl.
New York, NY, USA 10017-5706
Ph: (212) 818-9800
E-mail: http://www.bermudatourism.com

Berrett-Koehler Publishers, Inc.
235 Montgomery St., Ste. 650
San Francisco, CA, USA 94104
Ph: (415) 288-0260
E-mail: http://www.bkconnection.com

Best-Met Publishing Company Inc.
5537 Twin Knolls Rd., Ste. 438
Columbia, MD, USA 21045
Ph: (410) 730-5013
E-mail: office@atsbest-met.com
URL: http://www.best-met.com

Beverage Information Group
17 High St., 2nd Fl.
Norwalk, CT, USA 6851
Ph: (203) 855-8499
E-mail: http://www.bevinfogroup.com

Beverage Marketing Corp.
PO Box 126
Mingo Junction, OH, USA 43938
Ph: (740) 598-4133
E-mail: consulting@atsbeveragemarketing.com
URL: http://www.beveragemarketing.com

Beverage World
200 E Randolph St., 7th fl.
Chicago, IL, USA 60601
Ph: (646) 708-7300
E-mail: info@atsbeverageworld.com
URL: http://www.beverageworld.com

Beverage World
90 Broad St., Ste. 402
New York, NY, USA 10004-3312
Ph: (646) 708-7300
E-mail: info@atsbeverageworld.com
URL: http://www.beverageworld.com

BIA Financial Network Inc.
15120 Enterprise Ct., Ste. 100
Chantilly, VA, USA 20151
Ph: (703) 818-2425
E-mail: info@atsbia.com
URL: http://www.bia.com

Bibliographical Center for Research, Rocky Mountain Region Inc.
14394 E Evans Ave.
Aurora, CO, USA 80014-1478
Ph: (303) 751-6277
E-mail: admin@atsbcr.org
URL:

Bibliotheca Press
c/o Prosperity & Profits Unltd.
PO Box 416
Denver, CO, USA 80201-0416
Ph: (303) 575-5676

Bicycling
135 N Sixth St.
Emmaus, PA, USA 18049-2441
E-mail: http://www.bicycling.com/

Bill Communications Inc.
1115 Northmeadow Pkwy.
Roswell, GA, USA 30076
Ph: (770) 569-1540

Billian Publishing Inc. and Trans World Publishing Inc.
2100 Powers Ferry Rd. SE
Atlanta, GA, USA 30339
Ph: (770) 955-5656
E-mail: info@atsbillian.com
URL: http://www.billian.com

Billiards and Bowling Institute of America
615 Six Flags Dr.
Arlington, TX, USA 76011
Ph: (817) 385-8120
E-mail: bbia@atsbilliardandbowling.org
URL: http://www.billiardandbowling.org/

Billings Gazette
PO Box 36300
Billings, MT, USA 59107-6300
Ph: (406) 657-1200

Bio-Integral Resource Center
PO Box 7414
Berkeley, CA, USA 94707
Ph: (510) 524-2567
E-mail: birc@atsigc.apc.org
URL:

Bissett Communications Corp.
12844 Berkhamsted St.
Cerritos, CA, USA 90703
Ph: (562) 809-8917
E-mail: bbissett@atsmfpreport.com
URL:

Black Book Marketing Group
740 Broadway, Ste. 202
New York, NY, USA 10003
Ph: (212) 979-6700
E-mail: eryder@atsblackbook.com
URL: http://www.blackbook.com

Black Tennis Magazine
PO Box 210767
Dallas, TX, USA 75211
Ph: (214) 339-7370
E-mail: marcus.freeman.tennis@atsair-mail.net
URL: http://www.btmag.com/

Blackwell Publishers Ltd.
111 River St.
Hoboken, NJ, USA 7030
Ph: (201) 748-6000

Blackwell Publishing Limited
350 Main St.
Malden, MA, USA 2148
Ph: (781) 388-8200

Blackwell Publishing, Inc.
Commerce Place
350 Main St.
Malden, MA, USA 2148
Ph: (781) 388-8200

Bloomberg Press
731 Lexington Ave.
New York, NY, USA 10022
E-mail: press@atsbloomberg.com
URL: http://www.bloomberg.com

Bloomsbury USA
175 5th Ave.
New York, NY, USA 10010
E-mail: http://www.bloomsburyusa.com

Blue Dolphin Publishing Inc.
13340-D Grass Valley Ave.
PO Box 8
Grass Valley, CA, USA 95945
Ph: (530) 477-1503
E-mail: bdolphin@atsbluedolphinpublishing.com
URL: http://www.bluedolphinpublishing.com

Bluestocking Press
3333 Gold Country Dr.
PO Box 1014
Placerville, CA, USA 95667
Ph: (530) 622-8586
E-mail: customerservice@atsbluestocking-press.com
URL: http://www.bluestockingpress.com

BNA Tax and Accounting
9435 Key West Ave.
Rockville, MD, USA 20850
Ph: (800) 372-1033
E-mail: tm@atsbna.com
URL: http://www.bnatax.com

BNP Media
1050 Illinois Rte. 83, Ste. 200
Bensenville, IL, USA 60106
Ph: (630) 694-4353

BNP Media
155 Pfingsten Rd., Ste. 205
Deerfield, IL, USA 60015
Ph: (847) 405-4000
E-mail: info@atsstagnito.com
URL: http://www.myfoodandpackaging.com/

BNP Media
2401 W Big Beaver Rd., Ste. 700
Troy, MI, USA 48084
Ph: (248) 362-3700
E-mail: privacy@atsbnpmedia.com
URL: http://www.bnpmedia.com

Boat Owners Association of The United States
880 S Pickett St.
Alexandria, VA, USA 22304
Ph: (703) 461-4666
E-mail: mail@atsboatus.com
URL: http://www.boatus.com/

Bobit Business Media
3520 Challenger St.
Torrance, CA, USA 90503
Ph: (310) 533-2400
E-mail: webmaster@atsbobit.com
URL: http://www.bobit.com

Body Positive
250 W 57th St.
New York, NY, USA 10107
E-mail: bodypositive@atsbodypos.org
URL: http://www.bodypos.org

Bohman Industrial Traffic Consultants Inc.
116 Deer Meadow Lane
Chatham, MA, USA 2633
Ph: (508) 945-2272

Bollinger Capital Management Inc.
PO Box 3358
Manhattan Beach, CA, USA 90266
Ph: (310) 798-8855
E-mail: bbands@atsbollingerbands.com
URL:

Bonnier Corp.
460 N Orlando Ave., Ste. 200
Winter Park, FL, USA 32789
Ph: (407) 628-4802
E-mail: http://www.bonniercorp.com/

Book Industry Study Group, Inc.
370 Lexington Ave., Ste. 900
New York, NY, USA 10017
Ph: (646) 336-7141
E-mail: info@atsbisg.org
URL: http://www.bisg.org

Booklocker.com Inc.
PO Box 2399
Bangor, ME, USA 04402-2399
E-mail: http://booklocker.com

BookSurge LLC
7290 B Investment Dr.
Charleston, SC, USA 29418
Ph: (843) 789-5000
E-mail: customerservice@atsbooksurge.com
URL: http://www.booksurge.com

Booksurge, LLC
5341 Dorchester Rd., Ste. 16
North Charleston, SC, USA 29418
Ph: (843) 579-0000

Boston Business Journal
160 Federal St., 12th Fl.
Boston, MA, USA 02110-1700
Ph: (617) 330-1000

Bowes Publishers Ltd.
1540 N Routledge Pk.
London, ON, CAN N6H 5L6
Ph: (519) 471-8520
E-mail: bowes@atsbowesnet.com
URL: http://www.quebecor.com

Bowhunters of North America
1811 E Thayer Ave.
Bismarck, ND, USA 58501-4780

BowTie Inc.
PO Box 6050
Mission Viejo, CA, USA 92690-6040
Ph: (949) 855-8822

BPS Communications
PO Box 340
Willow Grove, PA, USA 19090-0340
Ph: (215) 830-8467
E-mail: info@atsnatclo.com
URL: http://www.natclo.com

Bradenton Herald
102 Manatee Ave. W
Bradenton, FL, USA 34205-8810
Ph: (941) 748-0411

Brain Brew Books
Eureka Institute
3849 Edwards Rd.
Cincinnati, OH, USA 45244
Ph: (513) 271-9911
E-mail: Doug@atsDougHall.com
URL: http://www.DougHall.com

Brant Publications Inc.
575 Broadway, 5th Fl.
New York, NY, USA 10012-3230
Ph: (212) 941-2800
E-mail: http://www.artinamericamagazine.com

Brazilian-American Chamber of Commerce Inc.
509 Madison Ave., Ste. 304
New York, NY, USA 10022
Ph: (212) 751-4691
E-mail: info@atsbrazilcham.com
URL: http://www.brazilcham.com

Brewers Publications
736 Pearl St.
PO Box 1679
Boulder, CO, USA 80302
Ph: (303) 447-0816
E-mail: info@atsbrewersassociation.org
URL: http://www.beertown.org

Brewery Collectibles Club of America
747 Merus Ct.
Fenton, MO, USA 63026-2092
Ph: (636) 343-6486
E-mail: bcca@atsbcca.com
URL: http://www.bcca.com/

Brick Industry Association
1850 Centennial Park Dr., Ste. 301
Reston, VA, USA 20191
Ph: (703) 620-0010
E-mail: brickinfo@atsbia.org
URL: http://www.gobrick.com

Brick Tower Press
1230 Park Ave., No. 10A
New York, NY, USA 10128
Ph: (212) 427-7139

Briefings Media Group
2807 N Parham Rd., Ste. 200
Richmond, VA, USA 23294
Ph: (570) 567-1982
E-mail: briefingsweborders@atspublishersserviceassociates.com
URL: http://www.briefingsmediagroup.com

Briefings Publishing Group
2807 N. Parham Rd., Ste. 200
Richmond, VA, USA 23294
Ph: (800) 791-8699
E-mail: customerservice@atsdouglaspublications.com
URL: http://www.briefings.com

Broadcast Cable Financial Management Association
550 W Frontage Rd., Ste. 3600
Northfield, IL, USA 60093
Ph: (847) 716-7000
E-mail: info@atsmediafinance.org
URL: http://www.bcfm.com

Broadcast Education Association
1771 North St. NW
Washington, DC, USA 20036-2891
Ph: (202) 429-3935
E-mail: beamemberservices@atsnab.org
URL: http://www.beaweb.org

Broadcast Interview Source Inc.
2233 Wisconsin Ave. NW, Ste. 301
Washington, DC, USA 20007-4132
Ph: (202) 333-5000
E-mail: editor@atsyearbook.com
URL: http://www.expertclick.com

Broadway Books
1745 Broadway
New York, NY, USA 10019
Ph: (212) 572-6066
E-mail: bwaypub@atsrandomhouse.com
URL: http://www.randomhouse.com/broadway/

Broadway Books
Crown Publishing Group
1745 Broadway
New York, NY, USA 10019
Ph: (212) 782-9000
E-mail: http://www.randomhouse.com/crown/broadway-books/

Broadway Books, a Division of Random House
1745 Broadway
New York, NY, USA 10019
Ph: (212) 782-9000
E-mail: ddaypub@atsrandomhouse.com
URL: http://www.broadwaybusinessbooks.com

Brookings Institution Press
1775 Massachusetts Ave. NW
Washington, DC, USA 20036-2188
Ph: (202) 797-6252

Brooklyn Botanic Garden
1000 Washington Ave.
Brooklyn, NY, USA 11225
Ph: (718) 623-7200
E-mail: http://www.bbg.org

Brown Books Publishing Group
16200 N Dallas Pkwy., Ste. 170
Dallas, TX, USA 75248
Ph: (972) 381-0009

Brownstone Publishers Inc.
149 Fifth Ave., 16th Fl.
New York, NY, USA 10010
Ph: (212) 473-8200
E-mail: custserv@atsbrownstone.com
URL: http://www.brownstone.com

Bruce Mooney Associates Inc.
PO Box 749
Marlton, NJ, USA 8053
Ph: (856) 797-9164
E-mail: remgro@atsbrucemooney.com
URL:

Bryan Sadoff
250 W Coventry Ct., No. 109
Milwaukee, WI, USA 53217-3961
Ph: (414) 352-8460
E-mail: info@atssadoffinvestments.com
URL:

BUC International Corp.
1314 NE 17th Ct.
Fort Lauderdale, FL, USA 33305-3318
Ph: (954) 565-6715
E-mail: info@atsbuc.com
URL: http://www.buc.com

The Buffalo News
1 News Plaza
Buffalo, NY, USA 14240
Ph: (716) 856-5555

Building Green Inc.
122 Birge St., Ste. 30
Brattleboro, VT, USA 05301-3206
Ph: (802) 257-7300
E-mail: info@atsbuildinggreen.com
URL:

Building Industry Association of Southeastern Michigan
2075 Walnut Lake Rd.
West Bloomfield, MI, USA 48323
Ph: (248) 737-4477
E-mail: bia@atsbuilders.org
URL: http://www.builders.org/index.php

Building Service Contractors Association Int'l.
401 N Michigan Ave., Ste. 2200
Chicago, IL, USA 60611
Ph: (312) 321-5167
E-mail: info@atsbscai.org
URL: http://www.bscai.org

Bureau of Business & Economic Research
University of Montana
Gallagher Business Bldg., Ste. 231
32 Campus Dr., Ste. 6840
Missoula, MT, USA 59812
Ph: (406) 243-3113

Bureau of Labor Statistics
2 Massachusetts Ave. NE, PSB Ste. 2850
Washington, DC, USA 20212-0001
Ph: (202) 691-5200

Bureau of National Affairs Inc.
9435 Key West Ave.
Rockville, MD, USA 20850
Ph: (703) 341-3000
E-mail: customercare@atsbna.com
URL: http://www.bna.com

BurrellesLuce
75 E Northfield Rd.
Livingston, NJ, USA 7039
Ph: (973) 992-6600
E-mail: inquiry@atsburrellesluce.com
URL: http://www.burrelles.com

Business & Legal Reports Inc.
141 Mill Rock Rd. E
Old Saybrook, CT, USA 6475
Ph: (860) 510-0100
E-mail: service@atsblr.com
URL: http://www.blr.com

Business and Professional Women/USA
1718 M St. NW, Ste. 148
Washington, DC, USA 20036
Ph: (202) 293-1100
E-mail: foundation@atsbpwusa.org
URL: http://www.bpwusa.org

Business Communications Co., Inc.
70 New Canaan Ave.
Norwalk, CT, USA 6850
Ph: (203) 750-9783
E-mail: info@atsbccresearch.com
URL: http://wwww.bccresearch.com

Business Communications Company Inc.
35 Walnut St., Ste 100
Wellesley, MA, USA 2481
Ph: (781) 489-7301
E-mail: sales@atsbccresearch.com
URL: http://www.bccresearch.com

Business Courier
101 W 7th St.
Cincinnati, OH, USA 45202
Ph: (513) 621-6665

Business Ethics
55 W 39th St., Ste. 800
New York, NY, USA 10018
Ph: (646) 688-3620
E-mail: info@atsbusiness-ethics.com
URL: http://business-ethics.com/

Business First
303 W Nationwide Blvd.
Columbus, OH, USA 43215
Ph: (614) 461-4040

Business Information Group
12 Concorde Pl., Ste. 800
Toronto, ON, CAN M3C 4J2
Ph: (416) 442-5600
E-mail: customercare@atsbizinfogroup.ca
URL: http://www.businessinformation-group.ca

Business Insurance
360 N Michigan Ave.
Chicago, IL, USA 60601-3806
Ph: (312) 649-5200
E-mail: biweb@atscrain.com
URL: http://www.businessinsurance.com

Business Intelligence Program
333 Ravenswood Ave.
Menlo Park, CA, USA 94025
Ph: (650) 859-4600
E-mail: E-mail: info@atssric-bi.com

URL:

Business Journals Inc.
50 Day St.
Norwalk, CT, USA 6854
Ph: (203) 853-6015
E-mail: stunifoo@atsbusjour.com
URL: http://www.busjour.com

Business Marketing & Publishing Inc.
PO Box 7457
Wilton, CT, USA 6897
Ph: (203) 834-9959
E-mail: info@atsepnweb.com
URL:

Business Marketing Association
1833 Centre Point Cir., Ste. 123
Naperville, IL, USA 60563
Ph: (630) 544-5054
E-mail: info@atsmarketing.org
URL: http://www.marketing.org

Business News Publishing Company II L.L.C.
22801 Ventura Blvd., No. 115
Woodland Hills, CA, USA 91364
Ph: (818) 224-8035
E-mail: http://www.bnpmedia.com

Business North Carolina
5435 77 Center Dr., Ste. 50
Charlotte, NC, USA 28217-0711
Ph: (704) 523-6987

Business Plus
PO Box 8828
Boston, MA, USA 2114
E-mail: http://www.hachettebookgroupusa.com

Business Plus/Warner Business Books
PO Box 8828
Boston, MA, USA 2114
E-mail: http://www.hachettebookgroupusa.com

Business Publications Inc.
93 High St.
Portsmouth, NH, USA 3801
Ph: (603) 436-9401

Business Research Services Inc.
7720 Wisconsin Ave., Ste. 213
Bethesda, MD, USA 20814
Ph: (301) 229-5561
E-mail: brspubs@atssba8a.com
URL: http://www.sba8a.com

The Business Review
40 British American Blvd.
Latham, NY, USA 12110
Ph: (518) 640-6825

Business Service Corp.
PO Box 60762
San Diego, CA, USA 92166-8762
E-mail: boj@atsboj.com
URL: http://www.boj.com/

Business Success Systems, Incorporated
49 Cliffwood Ave., Ste. 200
Cliffwood, NJ, USA 7721
Ph: (732) 566-3660

Business Technology Association
12411 Wornall Rd., Ste. 200
Kansas City, MO, USA 64145
Ph: (816) 941-3100
E-mail: info@atsbta.org
URL: http://www.bta.org

Business Trend Analysts
38 E 29th St., 6th Fl.
New York, NY, USA 10016
Ph: (212) 807-2629
E-mail: customerservice@atsmarketresearch.com
URL: http://www.marketresearch.com

Business Trend Analysts, Inc.
2171 Jericho Tpke., Ste. 200
Commack, NY, USA 11725
Ph: (631) 462-5454
E-mail: sales@atsbta-ler.com
URL: http://www.businesstrendanalysts.com

Business Vision Group
4914 Country Club Dr.
Highland, UT, USA 84003
Ph: (801) 420-2838

The Business Word
11211 E Arapahoe Rd., Ste. 101
Centennial, CO, USA 80112-3851
Ph: (303) 290-8500
E-mail: thebusinessword@atsyahoo.com
URL: http://www.businessword.com

Butterworth-Heinemann
225 Wildwood Ave.
Woburn, MA, USA 1801
Ph: (781) 904-2500

Buyers Laboratory Inc.
20 Railroad Ave.
Hackensack, NJ, USA 07601-4130
Ph: (201) 488-0404
E-mail: info@atsbuyers-lab.com
URL: http://www.buyerslab.com

C

C.E. Publications Inc.
PO Box 3006
Bothell, WA, USA 98041-3006
Ph: (425) 806-5200
E-mail: staff@atscjhunter.com
URL: http://www.cjhunter.com

Cabletelevision Advertising Bureau
830 3rd Ave., 2nd Fl.
New York, NY, USA 10022
Ph: (212) 508-1200
E-mail: http://www.onetvworld.org

Cadmus Journal Services
8621 Robert Fulton Dr., Ste. 100
Columbia, MD, USA 21046
Ph: (410) 850-0500
E-mail: http://www.cadmus.com/locations.htm

Cahners Publishing Co.
360 Pk. Ave. S
New York, NY, USA 10010
Ph: (646) 746-6400
E-mail: corporatecommunications@atsreedbusiness.com
URL: http://www.reedbusiness.com/index.asp?layout=cahnerscom

California Builder & Engineer Inc.
1200 Madison Ave., LL20
Indianapolis, IN, USA 46225
Ph: (317) 423-7080
E-mail: http://www.acppubs.com

California Trucking Association
3251 Beacon Blvd.
West Sacramento, CA, USA 95691
Ph: (916) 373-3500
E-mail: cta@atscaltrux.org
URL:

The California Wine Club
2175 Goodyear Ave., Ste. 102
PO Box 3699
Ventura, CA, USA 93006-3699
Ph: (805) 650-4330
E-mail: info@atscawineclub.com
URL:

California Women's Caucus
2900 Amby Pl.
Hermosa Beach, CA, USA 90254-2216
Ph: (310) 376-7378

Calorie Control Council
1100 Johnson Ferry Rd., Ste. 300
Atlanta, GA, USA 30342
Ph: (404) 252-3663
E-mail: ccc@atskellencompany.com
URL:

Cambridge Scientific Abstracts
7200 Wisconsin Ave., Ste. 601
Bethesda, MD, USA 20814
Ph: (301) 961-6700
E-mail: sales@atscsa.com
URL: http://www.csa.com/

Cambridge University Press
32 Ave. of the Americas
New York, NY, USA 10013-2473
Ph: (212) 924-3900
E-mail: newyork@atscambridge.org

URL: http://www.cambridge.org/us

Cambridge University Press
40 W 20th St.
New York, NY, USA 10011-4211
Ph: (212) 924-3900

Campground Data Resource
1004 Tequesta Trl.
Lake Wales, FL, USA 33898
Ph: (863) 676-0009
E-mail: db@atscampground-data.com
URL:

Camping Programs
101 N Wacker Dr.
Chicago, IL, USA 60606
Ph: (312) 977-0031
E-mail: fulfillment@atsymca.net
URL: http://www.ymca.net

Canada Wide Magazines & Communications Ltd.
4180 Lougheed Hwy., 4th Fl.
Burnaby, BC, CAN V5C 6A7
Ph: (604) 299-7311
E-mail: cwm@atscanadawide.com
URL: http://www.canadawide.com

Canadian Apparel Federation
124 O'Connor St., Ste. 504
Ottawa, ON, CAN K1P 5M9
Ph: (613) 231-3220
E-mail: info@atsapparel.ca
URL: http://www.apparel.ca

Canadian Association of Moldmakers (CAMM)
2000 Talbot Rd. W
PO Box 16
Windsor, ON, CAN N9A 6S4
Ph: (519) 255-7863
E-mail: info@atscamm.ca
URL: http://www.camm.ca

Canadian Co-Operative Wool Growers Ltd.
c/o Ontario Stockyards Inc.
Box 1051, 3807 Hwy. No. 89
Cookstown, ON, CAN L0L 1L0
Ph: (705) 458-4800
E-mail: ccwgosy@atsbellnet.ca
URL: http://www.seregonmap.com/SCM/index.htm

Canadian Council for Small Business and Entrepreneurship
Faculty of Administration
University of Regina
Regina, SK, CAN S4S 0A2
Ph: (306) 585-4728

Canadian Federation of Chefs & Cooks
582 Somerset St. W
Ottawa, ON, CAN K1R 5K2
Ph: (613) 562-0123
E-mail: cfcc@atscfcc.ca
URL:

Canadian Honey Council
234-5149 Country Hills Blvd. NW, Ste. 236
Calgary, AB, CAN T3A 5K8
Ph: (403) 208-7141
E-mail: editor@atshoneycouncil.ca
URL:

Canadian Innovation Centre
490 Dutton Dr., Unit 1A
Waterloo, ON, CAN N2L 6H7
Ph: (519) 885-5870
E-mail: moreinfo@atsinnovationcentre.ca
URL:

Canadian Institute of Geomatics
900 Dynes Rd., Ste. 100 D
Ottawa, ON, CAN K2C 3L6
Ph: (613) 224-9851
E-mail: http://www.Cig-acsg.ca

Canadian Medical Association
1867 Alta Vista Dr.
Ottawa, ON, CAN K1G 5W8
Ph: (613) 520-7685
E-mail: cmamsc@atscma.ca
URL: http://www.cma.ca

Canadian Pharmacists Association
1785 Alta Vista Dr.
Ottawa, ON, CAN K1G 3Y6
Ph: (613) 523-7877
E-mail: info@atspharmacists.ca
URL: http://www.pharmacists.ca/flash.cfm

Canadian Public Health Association
400-1565 Carling Ave.
Ottawa, ON, CAN K1Z 8R1
Ph: (613) 725-3769
E-mail: info@atscpha.ca
URL: http://www.cpha.ca

Canadian Restaurant and Foodservices Association (CRFA)
316 Bloor St. W
Toronto, ON, CAN M5S 1W5
Ph: (416) 923-8416
E-mail: info@atscrfa.ca
URL:

Canadian Society of Cinematographers
3007 Kingston Rd., Ste. 131
Toronto, ON, CAN M1M 1P1
Ph: (416) 266-0591
E-mail: admin@atscsc.ca
URL: http://www.csc.ca

Canadian Society of Respiratory Therapists
102-1785 Alta Vista Dr.
Ottawa, ON, CAN K1G 3Y6
Ph: (613) 731-3164
E-mail: adminasst@atscsrt.com
URL: http://www.csrt.com/

Canadian Veterinary Medical Association
339 Booth St.
Ottawa, ON, CAN K1R 7K1
Ph: (613) 236-1162
E-mail: admin@atscvma-acmv.org
URL: http://canadianveterinarians.net

Canadian Wood Council
99 Bank St., Ste. 400
Ottawa, ON, CAN K1P 6B9
Ph: (613) 747-5544
E-mail: info@atscwc.ca
URL: http://www.cwc.ca

Canola Council of Canada
167 Lombard Ave., Ste. 400
Winnipeg, MB, CAN R3B 0T6
Ph: (204) 982-2100
E-mail: admin@atscanola-council.org
URL: http://www.canola-council.org/

Canon Communications L.L.C.
11444 W Olympic Blvd., Ste. 900
Los Angeles, CA, USA 90064
Ph: (310) 445-4200
E-mail: info@atscancom.com
URL: http://www.ubmcanon.com

Cape Cod Media Group
319 Main St.
Hyannis, MA, USA 2601
Ph: (508) 775-1200

Cape Cod Times
319 Main St.
Hyannis, MA, USA 2601
Ph: (508) 775-1200

Cape Project Management Inc.
12 Remington Ln.
Plymouth, MA, USA 02360-1424

Capital Newspapers
1901 Fish Hatchery Rd.
Madison, WI, USA 53713
Ph: (252) -6200

Capitol Information Group Inc.
PO Box 9070
McLean, VA, USA 22102

Career Planning & Adult Development Network
543 Vista Mar Ave.
Pacifica, CA, USA 94044
Ph: (650) 359-6911
E-mail: admin@atscareernetwork.org
URL:

Career Press
3 Tice Rd.
PO Box 687
Franklin Lakes, NJ, USA 7417
Ph: (201) 848-0310
E-mail: contact@atscareerpress.com
URL: http://www.careerpress.com

Career Press, Inc.
220 W Parkway, Unit 12
Pompton Plains, NJ, USA 7417
Ph: (201) 848-0310
E-mail: sales@atscareerpress.com
URL: http://www.careerpress.com

Career Recruitment Media
2 LAN Dr., Ste. 100
Westford, MA, USA 1886
Ph: (978) 692-5092
E-mail: information@atsalloyeducation.com
URL: http://www.alloyeducation.com/request.htm

Career Steps
4112 Park Blvd.
Oakland, CA, USA 94602
Ph: (510) 531-2071

Carpet Cleaners Institute of the Northwest
PMB 366
2661 N Pearl St.
Tacoma, WA, USA 98407
Ph: (253) 759-5762
E-mail: info@atsccinw.org
URL: http://www.ccinw.org/

Carstens Publications Inc.
108 Phil Hardin Rd.
PO Box 700
Newton, NJ, USA 07860-5223
Ph: (973) 383-3355
E-mail: carstens@atscarstens-publications.com
URL: http://www.carstens-publications.com

Carswell
One Corporate Plz.
2075 Kennedy Rd.
Toronto, ON, CAN M1T 3V4
Ph: (416) 609-8000
E-mail: carswell.customerrelations@atsthomson.com
URL: http://www.carswell.com

Casket & Funeral Supply Association of America
49 Sherwood Ter., Ste. Y
Lake Bluff, IL, USA 60044
Ph: (847) 295-6630
E-mail: brussell@atscfsaa.org
URL:

Castle Publications Ltd.
PO Box 580
Van Nuys, CA, USA 91408
Ph: (818) 708-3208
E-mail: info@atscastlepublications.com
URL:

Cat Fanciers' Association Inc.
1805 Atlantic Ave.
PO Box 1005
Manasquan, NJ, USA 08736-0805
Ph: (732) 528-9797
E-mail: cfa@atscfa.org
URL: http://www.cfainc.org/Client/home.aspx

Catawba County Chamber of Commerce
1055 Southgate Corporate Pk. SW
PO Box 1828
Hickory, NC, USA 28602
Ph: (828) 328-6111
E-mail: info@atscatawbachamber.org
URL: http://www.catawbachamber.org

Catholic Charities USA
66 Canal Center Pl., Ste. 600
Alexandria, VA, USA 22314-1583
Ph: (703) 549-1390
E-mail: info@atscatholiccharitiesusa.org
URL: http://www.catholiccharitiesusa.org

CBA Service Corporation Inc.
CBA International
PO Box 62000
Colorado Springs, CO, USA 80962-2000
Ph: (719) 265-9895
E-mail: publications@atscbaonline.org
URL:

CCH Canadian Ltd.
90 Sheppard Ave. E, Ste. 300
Toronto, ON, CAN M2N 6X1
Ph: (416) 224-2224
E-mail: cservice@atscch.ca
URL: http://www.cch.ca/Products/

CCH Inc.
4025 W Peterson Ave.
Chicago, IL, USA 60646-6085
Ph: (847) 267-7000
E-mail: http://www.cch.com

CCH, Inc.
2700 Lake Cook Rd.
Riverwoods, IL, USA 60015
Ph: (347) 267-7000
E-mail: http://www.cch.com

CCIM Institute
430 N Michigan Ave.
Chicago, IL, USA 60611-4092
Ph: (312) 321-4460
E-mail: magazine@atsccim.com
URL: http://www.ccim.com

CD Publications
8204 Fenton St.
Silver Spring, MD, USA 20910
Ph: (301) 588-6380
E-mail: info@atscdpublications.com
URL: http://www.cdpublications.com/

CDG Books Canada, Incorporated
99 Yorkville Ave., Ste. 400
Toronto, ON, CAN M5R 3K5
Ph: (416) 963-8830

Ceilings and Interior Systems Construction Association
405 Illinois Ave., Ste. 2B
Saint Charles, IL, USA 60174-2963
Ph: (630) 584-1919
E-mail: cisca@atscisca.org
URL: http://www.cisca.org/i4a/pages/index.cfm?pageid=1

Celestial Arts Publishing Company
999 Harrison St.
PO Box 7123
Berkeley, CA, USA 94707
Ph: (510) 559-1600

Cenflo Inc.
PO Box 44040
Rio Rancho, NM, USA 87174
Ph: (505) 771-8841
E-mail: info@atscenflo.com
URL: http://www.cenflo.com

Cengage Gale
27500 Drake Rd.
Farmington Hills, MI, USA 48331-3535
Ph: (248) 699-4253

Cengage Learning
PO Box 6904
Florence, KY, USA 41022-6904
E-mail: esales@atscengage.com
URL: http://www.cengage.com

Cengage South-Western
5191 Natorp Blvd.
Mason, OH, USA 45040
Ph: (513) 229-1000
E-mail: http://www.cengage.com

Center for Ethics and Social Policy
Graduate Theological Union
2400 Ridge Rd.
Berkeley, CA, USA 94709
Ph: (510) 649-2560
E-mail: cesp@atsgtu.edu
URL:

Center for Health, Environment and Justice
PO Box 6806
Falls Church, VA, USA 22040
Ph: (703) 237-2249
E-mail: chej@atschej.org
URL:

Center for Hearing and Communication
50 Broadway, 6th Fl.
New York, NY, USA 10004
Ph: (917) 305-7700
E-mail: http://www.chchearing.org/

Center for Labor Research and Education
Box 951478
Los Angeles, CA, USA 90095-1478
Ph: (510) 642-0323
E-mail: osmer@atsvclink.berkley.edu

URL:

Center for Science in the Public Interest
1875 Connecticut Ave. NW, Ste. 300
Washington, DC, USA 20009
Ph: (202) 332-9110
E-mail: cspi@atscspinet.org
URL: http://www.cspinet.org

Centers for Disease Control and Prevention
1600 Clifton Rd.
Atlanta, GA, USA 30329-4018
E-mail: cdcinfo@atscdc.gov
URL: http://www.cdc.gov

CFA Institute
560 Ray C. Hunt Dr.
PO Box 3668
Charlottesville, VA, USA 22903
Ph: (434) 951-5499
E-mail: info@atscfainstitute.org
URL: http://www.cfainstitute.org

CFO Publishing Corporation
111 W 57th St., 12th Fl.
New York, NY, USA 10019
Ph: (212) 698-9787

Chain Store Age
425 Park Ave.
New York, NY, USA 10022
Ph: (212) 756-5257

Chain Store Guide
3922 Coconut Palm Dr.
Tampa, FL, USA 33619
Ph: (813) 627-6800
E-mail: info@atscsgis.com
URL: http://www.chainstoreguide.com

Chain Store Guide Information Services
3922 Coconut Palm Dr.
Tampa, FL, USA 33619
Ph: (813) 627-6800
E-mail: info@atscsgis.com
URL: http://www.csgis.com

Chamber Music America
305 7th Ave.
New York, NY, USA 10001
Ph: (212) 242-2022
E-mail: http://www.chamber-music.org

Charles River Media
10 Downer Ave.
Hingham, MA, USA 2043
Ph: (781) 740-0400

Charlotte Business Journal
1100 S Tryon St., Ste. 100
Charlotte, NC, USA 28203
Ph: (704) 973-1100

Chart Your Course International
2814 Hwy. 212 SW
Conyers, GA, USA 30094-3349
Ph: (770) 860-9464

Chartcraft Inc.
30 Church St.
PO Box 1747
New Rochelle, NY, USA 10802-1747
Ph: (914) 632-0422

Chase Online Marketing Strategies,Inc
29 John St. No.102
New York, NY, USA 10038
Ph: (212) 619-4780
E-mail: me@atslarrychase.com
URL:

Chattanooga Publishing Company
400 E 11th St.
Chattanooga, TN, USA 37403
Ph: (423) 756-6900

Chattanooga Times/Free Press
400 E 11th St.
Chattanooga, TN, USA 37403
Ph: (423) 756-6900

The Cheese Reporter Publishing Company Inc.
2810 Crossroads Dr., Ste. 3000
Madison, WI, USA 53718
Ph: (608) 246-8430
E-mail: http://www.cheesereporter.com/

Chelsea Green Publishing
85 N Main St., Ste. 120
White River Junction, VT, USA 5001
Ph: (802) 295-6300
E-mail: http://www.chelseagreen.com

Chelsie Communications Inc.
61 Alness St., Ste. 216
North York, ON, CAN M3J 2H2
Ph: (416) 663-9229
E-mail: cantoymag@atsbellnet.ca
URL: http://www.toysandgamesmag.com

The Chemical Educator
1910 University Dr.
Boise, ID, USA 83725
Ph: (208) 440-1866
E-mail: chemeducator@atsgmail.org
URL: http://chemeducator.org/

Chemical Week Associates
110 Williams St., 11th Fl.
New York, NY, USA 10038
Ph: (212) 621-4900
E-mail: webmaster@atschemweek.com
URL: http://www.chemweek.com/

The Chemists' Club Library
3 W. 51st St.
New York, NY, USA 10019
Ph: (212) 626-9300
E-mail: info@atsthechemistsclub.com
URL: http://www.thechemistsclub.com

Chicago Home & Garden
435 N Michigan Ave., Ste. 1100
Chicago, IL, USA 60611
Ph: (312) 222-8999
E-mail: chicagohome@atschicagomag.com
URL: http://www.chicagohomeandgarden.com

Child Welfare League of America Inc.
1726 M St. NW, Ste. 500
Washington, DC, USA 20036
Ph: (202) 688-4200
E-mail: order@atscwla.org
URL: http://www.cwla.org

Children of Aging Parents
1609 Woodbourne Rd., Ste. 302A
PO Box 167
Richboro, PA, USA 18954-0167
E-mail: info@atscaps4caregivers.org
URL: http://www.caps4caregivers.org

Children's Apparel Manufacturers' Association
6900 Decarie, Ste. 3110
Montreal, QC, CAN H3X 2T8
Ph: (514) 731-7774
E-mail: cama@atscama-apparel.org
URL: http://www.cama-apparel.org

Children's Book Insider
901 Columbia Rd.
Fort Collins, CO, USA 80525
Ph: (970) 495-0056
E-mail: mail@atswrite4kids.com
URL:

Christian Camp and Conference Association
405 W Rockrimmon Blvd.
PO Box 62189
Colorado Springs, CO, USA 80962-2189
Ph: (719) 260-9400
E-mail: info@atsccca.org
URL: http://www.ccca.org

Chronicle Books LLC
680 2nd St.
San Francisco, CA, USA 94107
Ph: (415) 537-4200

Chronicle Books LLC
85 2nd St., 6th Fl.
San Francisco, CA, USA 94105
Ph: (415) 537-4200
E-mail: frontdesk@atschroniclebooks.com
URL: http://www.chroniclebooks.com

The Chronicle of Philanthropy
1255 23rd St. NW, Ste. 700
Washington, DC, USA 20037
Ph: (202) 466-1200
E-mail: help@atsphilanthropy.com
URL: http://philanthropy.com/

Cincinnati Magazine Inc.
441 Vine St., Ste. 200
Cincinnati, OH, USA 45202-2039
Ph: (513) 421-4300
E-mail: cmletters@atscintimag.emmis.com
URL: http://www.cincinnatimagazine.com/

CIO
PO Box 9208
Framingham, MA, USA 1701
Ph: (508) 872-0080

Cisco Press
800 E 96th St.
Indianapolis, IN, USA 46240-3770

Cision Canada
1100-150 Ferrand Dr.
Toronto, ON, CAN M3C 3E5
E-mail: http://ca.cision.com

Cision US Inc.
332 S Michigan Ave., Ste. 900
Chicago, IL, USA 60604
Ph: (312) 363-9793
E-mail: info.us@atscision.com
URL: http://us.cision.com

CITA International
5331 W Montebello Ave.
Glendale, AZ, USA 85301
Ph: (602) 447-0480
E-mail: esammorsy@atsqwestoffice.net
URL: http://www.citainternational.com/contact.htm

Citadel Press
119 W 40th St.
New York, NY, USA 10018
E-mail: http://www.kensingtonbooks.com

The City Centre Business Association of Windsor
474 Oullette Ave.
Windsor, ON, CAN N9A 1B2
Ph: (519) 252-5723
E-mail: ccba@atswindsordowntown.ca
URL:

Clayton-Fillmore Ltd.
125 Dorset Ct.
PO Box 480894
Denver, CO, USA 80248
Ph: (303) 663-0606
E-mail: ht@atsclayfil.com
URL: http://www.clayfil.com

CLB Media Inc.
240 Edward St.
Aurora, ON, CAN L4G 3S9
Ph: (905) 727-0077

Clearbridge Publishing
PO Box 33772
Seattle, WA, USA 98133
Ph: (206) 533-9357

Clement Communications Inc.
3 Creek Pky.
PO Box 2208
Upper Chichester, PA, USA 19061
Ph: (800) 253-6368
E-mail: customerservice@atsclement.com
URL: http://www.clement.com/

Clinical Laboratory Management Association
401 N Michigan Ave., Ste. 2200
Chicago, IL, USA 60611
Ph: (312) 321-5111
E-mail: info@atsclma.org
URL: http://www.clma.org

Clintron Publishers
PO Box 30998
Spokane, WA, USA 99223-3016
Ph: (509) 458-3924
E-mail: info@atsagpowermag.com
URL: http://www.agpowermag.com

Close-Up Media
13400 Sutton Park Dr., S, Ste. 1504
Jacksonville, FL, USA 32224
Ph: (904) 223-3377
E-mail: http://closeupmedia.com/

Closing the Gap Inc.
526 Main St.
PO Box 68
Henderson, MN, USA 56044
Ph: (507) 248-3294
E-mail: info@atsclosingthegap.com
URL: http://www.closingthegap.com

Clothing Manufacturers Association of the U.S.A.
1330 Ave. of the Americas, 19th Fl.
New York, NY, USA 10019-5400

The Clute Institute for Academic Research
PO Box 620760
Littleton, CO, USA 80162
Ph: (303) 904-4750
E-mail: staff@atscluteinstitute.com
URL: http://www.cluteinstitute.com/

CN Publishing
PO Box 5084
Costa Mesa, CA, USA 92628-5084
Ph: (714) 751-7433
E-mail: editor@atscyclenews.com
URL: http://www.cyclenews.com

CNW Group
WaterPark Pl.
20 Bay St., Ste. 1500
Toronto, ON, CAN M5J 2N8

CNW Publishing, Editing, & Promotion Inc.
Main St.
PO Box A
North Stratford, NH, USA 3590
Ph: (603) 922-8338
E-mail: info@atswriters-editors.com
URL: http://www.writers-editors.com

Coastal Communications Corp.
2700 N Military Trl., Ste. 120
Boca Raton, FL, USA 33431-6394
Ph: (561) 989-0600
E-mail: ccceditor2@atsatt.net
URL: http://www.themeetingmagazines.com/index/Default.aspx?tabid=197

Coin Laundry Association
1 S 660 Midwest Rd., Ste. 205
Oakbrook Terrace, IL, USA 60181
Ph: (630) 953-7920
E-mail: info@atscoinlaundry.org
URL: http://www.coinlaundry.org

Collectors Club Inc.
22 E 35th St.
New York, NY, USA 10016-3806
Ph: (212) 683-0559
E-mail: collectorsclub@atsverizon.net
URL: http://www.collectorsclub.org

Collectors' Information Bureau
506 2nd St.
PO Box 306
Grundy Center, IA, USA 50638
Ph: (319) 824-6981
E-mail: cib@atsthepioneergroup.com
URL: http://www.collectorsinfo.com

College Art Association (CAA)
275 7th Ave.
New York, NY, USA 10001
Ph: (212) 691-1051
E-mail: nyoffice@atscollegeart.org
URL:

College of Veterinarians of Ontario (CVO)
2106 Gordon St.
Guelph, ON, CAN N1L 1G6
Ph: (519) 824-5600
E-mail: inquiries@atscvo.org
URL:

Collins Publications
3233 Grand Ave., Ste. N-294C
Chino Hills, CA, USA 91709
Ph: (909) 590-2471
E-mail: Collins@atscollinspub.com
URL: http://www.collinspub.com

Color Association of the United States (CAUS)
315 W 39th St., Studio 507
New York, NY, USA 10018
Ph: (212) 947-7774
E-mail: caus@atscolorassociation.com
URL:

Colorado Calligraphers' Guild
Box 6746
Denver, CO, USA 80206
E-mail: info@atscoloradocalligrahers.com
URL:

Colorado Municipal League
1144 Sherman St.
Denver, CO, USA 80203
Ph: (303) 831-6411
E-mail: cml@atscml.org
URL:

Colorado Society of Certified Public Accountants
7979 E Tufts Ave., Ste. 500
Denver, CO, USA 80237-2845
Ph: (303) 773-2877
E-mail: jturner@atscocpa.org
URL:

Colorado Springs Fine Arts Center
30 W Dale St.
Colorado Springs, CO, USA 80903
Ph: (719) 634-5581
E-mail: info@atscsfineartscenter.org
URL:

Columbia Books & Information Services
8120 Woodmont Ave., Ste. 110
Bethesda, MD, USA 20814
Ph: (202) 464-1662
E-mail: info@atscolumbiabooks.com
URL: http://www.columbiabooks.com

The Columbian
701 W 8th St.
PO Box 180
Vancouver, WA, USA 98666
Ph: (360) 694-3391

Columbus Times
2230 Buena Vista Rd.
Columbus, GA, USA 31902
Ph: (706) 324-2404
E-mail: columbustimes@atsknology.net
URL: http://www.columbustimes.com

Commercial Appeal
495 Union Ave.
Memphis, TN, USA 38103
Ph: (901) 529-2345
E-mail: http://www.commercialappeal.com/

Commercial Finance Association
370 7th Ave., Ste. 1810
New York, NY, USA 10001
Ph: (212) 792-9390
E-mail: info@atscfa.com
URL: http://www.cfa.com/

Commonwealth Business Media
400 Windsor Corporate Park
50 Millstone Rd., Ste. 200
East Windsor, NJ, USA 8520
Ph: (609) 371-7701

Communications Concepts Inc.
7481 Huntsman Blvd., No. 720
Springfield, VA, USA 22153-1648
Ph: (703) 643-2200
E-mail: concepts@atswritingthatworks.com
URL:

Community Information & Referral Inc.
2200 N Central Ave., Ste. 601
Phoenix, AZ, USA 85004
Ph: (602) 263-8856
E-mail: http://www.cirs.org

Compliance Action
PO Box 1632
Doylestown, PA, USA 18901
Ph: (215) 230-8661
E-mail: milner@atsbankersonline.com
URL: http://www.BankersOnline.com/

Computer Industry Almanac Inc.
PO Box 53
Arlington Heights, IL, USA 60006
Ph: (847) 758-3687
E-mail: ej@atsc-i-a.com
URL: http://www.c-i-a.com

ComputerTalk Associates Inc.
492 Norristown Rd., Ste. 160
Blue Bell, PA, USA 19422
Ph: (610) 825-7686
E-mail: wal@atscomputertalk.com
URL: http://www.computertalk.com

Computing Technology Industry Association
1815 S Meyers Rd., Ste. 300
Oakbrook Terrace, IL, USA 60181-5228
Ph: (630) 678-8300
E-mail: http://www.comptia.org

Comtex
625 N Washington St., Ste. 301
Alexandria, VA, USA 22314
Ph: (703) 820-2000

Comtex News Network Inc.
625 N Washington St., Ste. 301
Alexandria, VA, USA 22314
Ph: (703) 820-2000

Comtex News Network Inc.
950 3rd Ave., 9th Fl.
New York, NY, USA 10022
Ph: (212) 688-6240

Concepts Travel Media Ltd.
282 Richmond St. E, Ste. 100
Toronto, ON, CAN M5A 1P4
Ph: (416) 365-1500
E-mail: travelweek@atstravelweek.ca
URL: http://www.travelweek.ca

Conde Nast Publications Inc.
4 Times Sq.
New York, NY, USA 10036
Ph: (212) 286-2860
E-mail: http://www.condenet.com

Consensus Inc.
PO Box 520526
Independence, MO, USA 64052-0526
Ph: (816) 373-3700
E-mail: editor@atsconsensus-inc.com
URL:

Conservative Publishing Corp.
751 W Camelback Rd.
Phoenix, AZ, USA 85013
Ph: (602) 390-3391

Consolidated Marketing Services, Inc.
PO Box 7838
New York, NY, USA 10150
Ph: (212) 688-8797
E-mail: nschneel@atsdrop-shipping-news.com
URL:

Construction Financial Management Association
100 Village Blvd., Ste. 200
Princeton, NJ, USA 8540
Ph: (609) 452-8000
E-mail: http://www.cfma.org/

Construction Management Association of America Inc.
7926 Jones Branch Dr., Ste. 800
Mc Lean, VA, USA 22102
Ph: (703) 356-2622
E-mail: info@atscmaanet.org
URL: http://cmaanet.org

The Construction Specifications Institute
110 S Union St., Ste. 100
Alexandria, VA, USA 22314
Ph: (800) 689-2900
E-mail: csi@atscsinet.org
URL: http://www.csinet.org

Consumer Electronics Association
2500 Wilson Blvd.
Arlington, VA, USA 22201-3834
Ph: (703) 907-7600
E-mail: cea@atsce.org
URL: http://www.ce.org

Contact Lens Manufacturers Association
PO Box 29398
Lincoln, NE, USA 68529
Ph: (402) 465-4122
E-mail: http://www.clma.net

Contact Lens Society of America
441 Carlisle Dr.
Herndon, VA, USA 20170
Ph: (703) 437-5100
E-mail: clsa@atsclsa.info
URL:

Contemporary A Cappella Society of America
325 Sharon Park Dr. Ste. 110
Menlo Park, CA, USA 94025-6805
Ph: (415) 358-8067
E-mail: casa@atscasa.org
URL:

Continental Records Company Ltd.
2665 Thomas St., Ste. 37
PO Box 7
Mississauga, ON, CAN L5M 6G4
Ph: (905) 813-9544
E-mail: conrecs@atsgocontinental.com
URL: http://www.gocontinental.com

Continuing Education of the Bar-California
300 Frank H. Ogawa Plz., Ste. 410
Oakland, CA, USA 94612
Ph: (510) 302-0770

Continuus
PO Box 416
Denver, CO, USA 80201-0416
Ph: (303) 575-5676
E-mail: mail@atscontentprovidermedia.com
URL:

Conway Data Inc.
6625 The Corners Pkwy., Ste. 200
Norcross, GA, USA 30092-2901
Ph: (770) 446-6996
E-mail: http://www.conway.com

COR Healthcare Resources
PO Box 50507
Santa Barbara, CA, USA 93150
Ph: (805) 564-2177
E-mail: info@atscorhealth.com
URL:

Corbin Manufacturing & Supply Inc.
600 Industrial Cir.
PO Box 2659
White City, OR, USA 97503
Ph: (541) 826-5211
E-mail: sales@atscorbins.com
URL: http://www.corbins.com

CoreNet Global
260 Peachtree St. NW, Ste. 1500
Atlanta, GA, USA 30303-1237
Ph: (404) 589-3200

Cornell Feline Health Center
College of Veterinary Medicine
Cornell University
PO Box 13
Ithaca, NY, USA 14853-6401
Ph: (607) 253-3414
E-mail: cvmerm@atscornell.edu
URL:

Cornell University Press
Box 6525
750 Cascadilla St.
Ithaca, NY, USA 14851
Ph: (607) 277-2211
E-mail: cupressinfo@atscornell.edu
URL: http://www.cornellpress.cornell.edu

Cornell University School of Hotel Administration
537 Statler Hall
Ithaca, NY, USA 14853
Ph: (607) 255-9780
E-mail: hosp_research@atscornell.edu
URL: http://www.hotelschool.cornell.edu/research/chr/

Corporation for Public Broadcasting
401 9th St. NW
Washington, DC, USA 20004-2129
Ph: (202) 879-9600
E-mail: oigemail@atscpb.org
URL: http://www.cpb.org

Cosmic Awareness Communications
PO Box 115
Olympia, WA, USA 98507
E-mail: cosmiccomm@atsaol.com
URL:

Council for Exceptional Children
1110 N Glebe Rd., Ste. 300
Arlington, VA, USA 22201-5704
Ph: (703) 620-3660
E-mail: http://www.cec.sped.org/

Council of Residential Specialists
430 N Michigan Ave., Ste. 300
Chicago, IL, USA 60611
Ph: (312) 321-4400
E-mail: crshelp@atscrs.com
URL: http://www.crs.com

Council on Foundations
2121 Crystal Dr., Ste. 700
Arlington, VA, USA 22202
E-mail: info@atscof.org
URL: http://www.cof.org

The Counselor
33 Irving Pl.
New York, NY, USA 10003
Ph: (212) 460-1400

Country Dance and Song Society
132 Main St.
PO Box 338
Haydenville, MA, USA 01039-0338
Ph: (413) 268-7426
E-mail: office@atscdss.org
URL: http://www.cdss.org/

Country Sampler Group
707 Kautz Rd.
Saint Charles, IL, USA 60174-5302
Ph: (630) 377-8000
E-mail: http://www.sampler.com

Country Skier L.L.C.
PO Box 550
Cable, WI, USA 54821
Ph: (715) 798-5500
E-mail: http://www.crosscountryskier.com

Course Technology
20 Channel Center St.
Boston, MA, USA 02210-3402
Ph: (617) 757-7900
E-mail: http://www.coursetechnology.com

Cox Publishing Company Inc.
105 N Vermont Ave.
PO Box 1477
Glendora, CA, USA 91740-1477
Ph: (626) 914-3916
E-mail: pcnmagazine@atsaol.com
URL: http://www.pacificcoastnurseryman.com

CP Publishing, Inc.
PO Box 267
Fond du Lac, WI, USA 54936-0267
Ph: (920) 923-3700
E-mail: comments@atscookingforprofit.com
URL: http://www.cookingforprofit.com/home.html

CQ Roll Call
1255 22nd St. NW
Washington, DC, USA 20037
Ph: (202) 419-8500

Craft Council of Newfoundland and Labrador
Devon House Craft Ctr.
59 Duckworth St.
Saint John's, NL, CAN A1C 1E6
Ph: (709) 753-2749
E-mail: info@atscraftcouncil.nl.ca
URL: http://www.craftcouncil.nl.ca/

The Crafts Center
8601 Georgia Ave., Ste. 800
Silver Spring, MD, USA 20910
Ph: (301) 587-4700
E-mail: craftscenter@atschfhq.org
URL: http://www.craftscenter.org

Crafts Fair Guide
PO Box 39429
Downey, CA, USA 90239-0429
Ph: (415) 924-3259
E-mail: info@atscraftsfairguide.com
URL: http://www.craftsfairguide.com

The Crafts Report
PO Box 5000
Iola, WI, USA 54945
Ph: (715) 445-5000
E-mail: jonespub@atsjonespublishing.com
URL: http://www.craftsreport.com/

Crain Communications Inc.
77 Franklin St., Ste. 809
Boston, MA, USA 02110-1510
Ph: (617) 292-3385
E-mail: info@atscrain.com
URL: http://www.crain.com

Crain Communications Inc.
360 N Michigan Ave.
Chicago, IL, USA 60601
Ph: (312) 649-5200
E-mail: http://www.crain.com/

Crain Communications Inc.
700 W Saint Clair Ave., Ste. 300
Cleveland, OH, USA 44113
Ph: (216) 522-1383

Crain Communications Inc.
1155 Gratiot Ave.
Detroit, MI, USA 48207-2997
Ph: (313) 446-6000
E-mail: info@atscrain.com
URL: http://www.crain.com

Crain Communications Inc.
711 3rd Ave.
New York, NY, USA 10017
Ph: (212) 210-0100

Crain Communications Inc.
811 3rd Ave.
New York, NY, USA 10017
Ph: (212) 210-0100

Crain Communications Inc. - Detroit
1400 Woodbridge
Detroit, MI, USA 48207-9987
Ph: (313) 446-6000

CRC Press L.L.C.
6000 Broken Sound Pkwy, Ste. 300
Boca Raton, FL, USA 33487
Ph: (561) 994-0555

Creative Book Publishers
PO Box 1421
Ridgefield, WA, USA 98642
Ph: (360) 887-8356
E-mail: creativebookpublishers@atsyahoo.com
URL: http://www.creativebookpublishers.com

Crittenden Research Inc.
PO Box 1150
Novato, CA, USA 94948
Ph: (619) 393-1814
E-mail: market@atscrittendenonline.com
URL: http://www.crittendenonline.com

Crossing Press, Incorporated
PO Box 7123
Berkeley, CA, USA 94707
Ph: (510) 559-1600

Crown Business
1745 Broadway
New York, NY, USA 10019
Ph: (212) 782-9000
E-mail: crownpublicity@atsrandomhouse.com
URL: http://www.randomhouse.com/crown/crownbusiness.html

Crown Publishing Company
1745 Broadway
New York, NY, USA 10019
Ph: (212) 751-2600

Crown Publishing Group
1745 Broadway
New York, NY, USA 10019
Ph: (212) 782-9000
E-mail: crownpublicity@atsrandomhouse.com
URL:

The Croydon Group Ltd.
833 Featherstone Rd.
Rockford, IL, USA 61107-6302
Ph: (815) 399-8700
E-mail: info@atsthefabricator.com
URL: http://www.fmanet.org

CSIRO Publishing
PO Box 1139
Collingwood, VI, AUS 3066
E-mail: http://www.publish.csiro.au

CTE Publications Inc.
40 Skokie Blvd., Ste. 450
Northbrook, IL, USA 60062
Ph: (847) 498-9100
E-mail: info@atsctemag.com
URL: http://www.ctemag.com

CTVglobemedia Publishing Inc.
444 Front St. W
Toronto, ON, CAN M5V 2S9
Ph: (416) 585-5000

Currency/Doubleday Broadway Publishing Group
1745 Broadway
New York, NY, USA 10019
Ph: (212) 782-9000

Custom Tailors and Designers Association of America Inc.
42732 Ridgeway Dr.
Broadlands, VA, USA 20148
E-mail: http://www.ctda.com

Cutler Publishing Inc.
4500 Campus Dr., Ste. 480
Newport Beach, CA, USA 92660-1872
Ph: (949) 852-1990
E-mail: http://www.building-products.com/

Cutter Information Corp.
37 Broadway, Ste. 1
Arlington, MA, USA 2474
Ph: (781) 648-8700
E-mail: service@atscutter.com
URL: http://www.cutter.com

Cygnus Business Media
1233 Janesville Ave.
Fort Atkinson, WI, USA 53538
Ph: (920) 563-6388
E-mail: http://www.cygnusb2b.com

Cygnus Business Media
3 Huntington Quad., Ste. 301N
Melville, NY, USA 11747
Ph: (631) 845-2700

D

Dadant & Sons Inc.
51 S 2nd St.
Hamilton, IL, USA 62341
Ph: (217) 847-3324
E-mail: dadant@atsdadant.com
URL: http://www.dadant.com

Daily Journal Corp.
915 E 1st St.
Los Angeles, CA, USA 90012
Ph: (213) 229-5300
E-mail: http://www.dailyjournal.com

Daily News
724 Bell Fork Rd.
Jacksonville, NC, USA 28546
Ph: (910) 353-1171

The Daily Record Corp.
6 Century Dr.
Parsippany, NJ, USA 7054
E-mail: http://www.dailyrecord.com/

Dale Ennis
5540 Loyalist Pkwy.
PO Box 370
Bath, ON, CAN K0H 1G0
Ph: (613) 352-7448
E-mail: moneyinfo@atscanadianmoney-saver.ca
URL:

Dan Kiedrowski Co.
PO Box A
La Honda, CA, USA 94020
Ph: (650) 747-0549

Dan Newman Co.
1051 Bloomfield Ave.
Clifton, NJ, USA 7012

Dana Chase Publications Inc.
PO Box 3247
Oak Brook, IL, USA 60522-3247
E-mail: http://www.appliance.com

Dance Magazine Inc.
333 7th Ave., 11th Fl.
PO Box 678
New York, NY, USA 10001
Ph: (646) 459-4800
E-mail: dancemag@atsdancemagazine.com
URL: http://www.dancemagazine.com

Dance Research Foundation Inc.
37 W 12th St., No. 7/J
New York, NY, USA 10011
Ph: (212) 924-5183
E-mail: info@atsballetreview.com
URL: http://www.balletreview.com/

Dark Horse, Incorporated
22331 Mandarin Ln.
Saugus, CA, USA 91390

Dartnell Publications
PO Box 12038
Durham, NC, USA 27709
Ph: (800) 477-4030
E-mail: customerservice@atsdartnellcorp.com
URL: http://www.dartnellcorp.com

Data & Analysis Center for Software
775 Daedalian Dr.
Rome, NY, USA 13441-4909
Ph: (315) 334-4905
E-mail: dacs@atsdtic.mil
URL:

Data Conversion Laboratory
61-18 190th St., 2nd Fl.
Fresh Meadows, NY, USA 11365
Ph: (718) 357-8700
E-mail: convert@atsdelab.com
URL:

Data Driven Publishing, LLC
PO Box 340
Newburyport, MA, USA 1950
Ph: (603) 969-5020

Data Storage Systems Center
Carnegie Mellon University
ECE Dept.
Pittsburgh, PA, USA 15213
Ph: (412) 268-6600
E-mail: dssc@atsece.cmu.edu
URL:

David Hall Rare Coins
PO Box 6220
Newport Beach, CA, USA 92658
Ph: (949) 567-1325
E-mail: info@atsdavidhall.com
URL: http://www.davidhall.com

David W. Wood
503 E Deering Rd.
Deering, NH, USA 3244
Ph: (603) 529-2355
E-mail: woody@atswordsfromwoody.com
URL:

The Davlin Report Inc.
PO Box 60040
Boulder City, NV, USA 89006-0040
Ph: (702) 293-6400

Days Communications
1208 Juniper St.
Quakertown, PA, USA 18951-1520
Ph: (215) 538-1240
E-mail: subscriptions@atspoliceandsecuritynews.com
URL: http://policeandsecuritynews.com

DC & D Technologies Inc.
PO Box 948
Valrico, FL, USA 33595-0948
Ph: (813) 662-6830
E-mail: info@atsdcd.com
URL: http://www.dcd.com

Dearborn Trade Publishing Inc.
30 S Wacker Dr. Ste. 2500
Chicago, IL, USA 60606
Ph: (312) 836-4400
E-mail: Trade@atsdearborn.com
URL: http://www.dearborn.com

Decatur Daily
201 1st Ave. SE
Decatur, AL, USA 35609
Ph: (256) 353-4612

Delahaye Medialink
195 New Hampshire Ave., Ste. 225
Portsmouth, NH, USA 03801-2875

Denver Post
101 W Colfax Ave.
Denver, CO, USA 80202
Ph: (303) 954-1010

Department of Economic and Community Development
William Snodgrass Tennessee Twr., 11th Fl.
31 Rosa L. Parks Ave., 11th Fl.
Nashville, TN, USA 37243-0405
Ph: (615) 741-1888
E-mail: http://www.state.tn.us/ecd/

Desktop Wings Inc.
,

The Destin Log
PO Box 339
Destin, FL, USA 32540
Ph: (850) 837-2828

Destiny Productions for Print, Radio & Cable Promotions
3395 S Jones Blvd., No. 217
Las Vegas, NV, USA 89146-6729
Ph: (702) 438-1470
E-mail: destinymag@atsaol.com
URL:

Diamond Research Corp.
530 W Ojai Ave., Ste. 108
Ojai, CA, USA 93023-2471
Ph: (805) 640-7177
E-mail: drc@atswest.net
URL: http://www.imagingnews.com

DIANE Publishing Co.
601 Upland Ave.
Upland, PA, USA 19015
Ph: (610) 499-7415
E-mail: dianepub@atserols.com
URL: http://www.dianepublishing.com

DIANE Publishing Company
330 Pusey Ave., Unit 3 Rear
PO Box 1428
Collingdale, PA, USA 19023-8428
Ph: (610) 461-6200

DIANE Publishing Company
PO Box 617
Darby, PA, USA 19023-0617
Ph: (610) 461-6200

Dickinson Press
1815 1st St. W
Dickinson, ND, USA 58602
Ph: (701) 225-8111

Diesel & Gas Turbine Publications
20855 Watertown Rd., Ste. 220
Waukesha, WI, USA 53189
E-mail: storeadmin@atsdieselpub.com
URL: http://storefront.dieselpub.com

Dietary Managers Association
406 Surrey Woods Dr.
Saint Charles, IL, USA 60174
Ph: (630) 587-6336
E-mail: http://www.dmaonline.org

Dietitians of Canada
480 University Ave., Ste. 604
Toronto, ON, CAN M5G 1V2
Ph: (416) 596-0857
E-mail: centralinfo@atsdietitians.ca
URL: http://www.dietitians.ca

Direct Marketing Association of Washington, DC
11709 Bowman Green Dr.
Reston, VA, USA 20190
Ph: (703) 689-3629
E-mail: Info@atsdmaw.org
URL:

Direct Marketing Club of New York
54 Adams St.
Garden City, NY, USA 11530
Ph: (516) 746-6700
E-mail: info@atsdmcny.org
URL:

Direct Marketing Club of New York
55 Adams St.
Garden City, NY, USA 11530
Ph: (516) 746-6700
E-mail: info@atsdmcny.org
URL:

Direct Marketing Club of New York
56 Adams St.
Garden City, NY, USA 11530
Ph: (516) 746-6700
E-mail: info@atsdmcny.org
URL:

Direct Marketing Club of New York
57 Adams St.
Garden City, NY, USA 11530
Ph: (516) 746-6700
E-mail: info@atsdmcny.org
URL:

Directors Guild of America Inc.
7920 Sunset Blvd.
Los Angeles, CA, USA 90046
Ph: (310) 289-2000
E-mail: darrellh@atsdga.org
URL: http://www.dga.org

Discovery Publications Inc.
1501 Burlington, Ste. 207
Kansas City, MO, USA 64116
Ph: (816) 474-1516
E-mail: dispub@atsdiscoverypub.com
URL: http://www.discoverypub.com/contacts.htm

Distance Education & Training Council
1601 18th St. NW, Ste. 2
Washington, DC, USA 20009
Ph: (202) 234-5100
E-mail: detc@atsdetc.org
URL: http://www.detc.org

Diversity Information Resources Inc.
2105 Central Ave. NE
Minneapolis, MN, USA 55418
Ph: (612) 781-6819
E-mail: info@atsdiversityinforesources.com
URL: http://www.diversityinforesources.com

Divibest Inc.
3111 Cole Ave.
Dallas, TX, USA 75204-1138
Ph: (214) 871-2930
E-mail: info@atsbuilderinsider.com
URL: http://www.builderinsider.com

DK Publishing/Penguin Group
375 Hudson St.
New York, NY, USA 10014
Ph: (212) 366-2679

DL Perkins Company
PO Box 700570
Tulsa, OK, USA 74170

DM News
114 W 26th St., 4th Fl.
New York, NY, USA 10001
Ph: (646) 638-6000
E-mail: news@atsdmnews.com
URL: http://www.dmnews.com

DNA Press
Pottstown, PA, USA
E-mail: editor@atsdnapress.com
URL: http://www.dnapress.com

Doane Agricultural Services
77 Westport Plz., Ste. 250
Saint Louis, MO, USA 63146-4193
Ph: (314) 569-2700
E-mail: doane@atsdoane.com
URL: http://www.doane.com

Doctorow Communications Inc.
180 Phillips Hill Rd. No. 1B
New City, NY, USA 10956
Ph: (973) 779-1600
E-mail: email@atshomelighting.com
URL: http://www.homelighting.com

Document Center
111 Industrial Rd., Ste. 9
Belmont, CA, USA 94002
Ph: (650) 591-7600
E-mail: info@atsdocument-center.com
URL:

Doggone
PO Box 1846
Estes Park, CO, USA 80517
Ph: (303) 449-2527

Dogwise Publishing
403 S Mission
Wentachee, WA, USA 98801
Ph: (509) 663-9115
E-mail: http://www.dogwise.com

Dohmen Capital Research Institute
PO Box 49-2433
Los Angeles, CA, USA 90049
Ph: (310) 476-6933
E-mail: client@atsdohmencapital.com
URL:

Dolan Company
11 Saratoga St.
Baltimore, MD, USA 21202
Ph: (443) 524-8100

Dolan Media
31 E Platte Ave., Ste. 300
Colorado Springs, CO, USA 80903
Ph: (719) 634-5905

Dolan Media
921 SW Washington St., Ste. 210
Portland, OR, USA 97205
Ph: (503) 226-1311

Dolan Media Co.
222 S 9th St., Ste. 2300
Minneapolis, MN, USA 55402
Ph: (405) 808-6825
E-mail: http://www.dolanmedianewswires.com/

Dolan Media Newswires
855 W Broad St., Ste. 103
Boise, ID, USA 83702
Ph: (208) 336-3768

Dolan Media Newswires
U.S. Trust Bldg., Ste. 100
730 2nd Ave. S
Minneapolis, MN, USA 55402
Ph: (612) 333-4244

Dolan Media Newswires
2150 Smithtown Ave., Ste. 7
Ronkonkoma, NY, USA 11779
Ph: (631) 737-1700

Dolan Media Newswires
401 S Boston Ave., Ste. 105
Tulsa, OK, USA 74103
Ph: (918) 295-0098

Dominion Enterprises
150 Granby St.
Norfolk, VA, USA 23510
Ph: (757) 351-7000
E-mail: mediainfo@atsdominionenterprises.com
URL: http://www.dominionenterprises.com/

Donald H. Rowe
8830 S. Tamiami Trl., Ste. 110
2 N Tamiami Trl.
Sarasota, FL, USA 34238-3130
Ph: (941) 954-5500
E-mail: subscribe@atswallstreetdigest.com
URL:

Donrey Media Group
700 Brookside Ave.
Redlands, CA, USA 92373
Ph: (909) 793-3221
E-mail: http://www.redlandsdailyfacts.com

Double Storey Books
PO Box 24309
Cape Town, , SAF 7779
E-mail: http://www.doublestorey.com/

Doubleday
Random House/Doubleday
1745 Broadway
New York, NY, USA 10019
Ph: (212) 782-9000
E-mail: ddaypub@atsrandomhouse.com
URL: http://www.randomhouse.com/publishers/pub_double_broad.html

Doubleday
Random House/Doubleday Business
1745 Broadway
New York, NY, USA 10019
Ph: (212) 782-9000
E-mail: ddaypub@atsrandomhouse.com
URL: http://www.randomhouse.com/

Doubleday
Random House/Doubleday/Currency
1745 Broadway
New York, NY, USA 10019
Ph: (212) 782-9000
E-mail: ddaypub@atsrandomhouse.com
URL: http://www.randomhouse.com/doubleday/currency

Doubleday Broadway Publishing Group
1745 Broadway
New York, NY, USA 10019
Ph: (212) 782-9000
E-mail: ddaypub@atsrandomhouse.com
URL: http://www.randomhouse.com/publishers/pub_double_broad.html

Doubleday Canada, Limited
1 Toronto St., Unit 300
Toronto, ON, CAN M5C 2V6
Ph: (416) 364-4449
E-mail: http://www.randomhouse.ca

Doubleday, a Division of Random House
1745 Broadway
New York, NY, USA 10019
Ph: (212) 782-9000
E-mail: ddaypub@atsrandomhouse.com
URL: http://www.randomhouse.com

Dow Jones & Co., Inc.
1 World Financial Center
200 Liberty St.
New York, NY, USA 10281
Ph: (212) 416-2000

Dow Jones & Company Inc.
1 World Financial Ctr.
200 Liberty St.
New York, NY, USA 10281
Ph: (212) 416-2000
E-mail: http://www.dowjones.com

Dow Jones & Company Inc.
1211 Ave. of the Americas
New York, NY, USA 10036
Ph: (212) 416-2000

Dow Jones & Company, Inc.
1 World Financial Center
200 Liberty St.
New York, NY, USA 10281
Ph: (212) 416-2000

DP Group, Incorporated
30 S Wacker, No. 2500
Chicago, IL, USA 60606
Ph: (312) 894-0361

Dreamscape Productions
510 Woodhaven
Aptos, CA, USA 95003-5522
E-mail: info@atssfdreamscape.com
URL: http://www.sfdreamscape.com/

Driving School Association of Americas
3090 E Gause Blvd., Ste. 425
Slidell, LA, USA 70461
Ph: (800) 270-3722
E-mail: info@atsthedsaa.org
URL:

Drug Store News
425 Park Ave.
New York, NY, USA 10022

Drycleaning & Laundry Institute
14700 Sweitzer Ln.
Laurel, MD, USA 20707
Ph: (301) 622-1900
E-mail: techline@atsifi.org
URL: http://www.ifi.org/

Dun & Bradstreet Corp.
103 JFK Pky.
Short Hills, NJ, USA 7078
Ph: (973) 921-5500
E-mail: custserv@atsdnb.com
URL: http://www.dnb.com

Dundren Press Limited
3 Church St., Ste. 500
Toronto, ON, CAN M5E 1M2
Ph: (416) 214-5544

Dundurn Group
8 Market St., Ste. 200
Toronto, ON, CAN M5E 1M6
Ph: (416) 214-5544

Dundurn Press
3 Church St., Ste. 500
Toronto, ON, CAN M5E 1M2
Ph: (416) 214-5544
E-mail: http://www.dundurn.com/

duPont Publishing Inc.
3051 Tech Dr.
Saint Petersburg, FL, USA 33716
Ph: (727) 573-9339
E-mail: info@atsnet.dupontregistry.com
URL: http://www.dupontregistry.com

Dustbooks
PO Box 100
Paradise, CA, USA 95967
Ph: (530) 877-6110
E-mail: info@atsdustbooks.com
URL: http://www.dustbooks.com

E

E.W. Williams Publications Co.
2125 Center Ave., Ste. 305
Fort Lee, NJ, USA 07024-5898
Ph: (201) 592-7007
E-mail: philpl@atsewwpi.com
URL: http://www.williamspublications.com

Eagle Newspapers
4901 Indian School Rd. NE
PO Box 12008
Salem, OR, USA 97305
Ph: (503) 393-1774
E-mail: http://www.eaglenewspapers.com/

Eagle Publications Inc.
42400 Grand River, Ste. 103
Novi, MI, USA 48375
Ph: (248) 347-3486
E-mail: joan@atsfiltnews.com
URL: http://www.filtnews.com

Earl G. Graves Publishing Co. Inc.
130 5th Ave.
New York, NY, USA 10011
Ph: (212) 242-8000

Earth Action Network
1536 Crest Dr.
Los Angeles, CA, USA 90035
E-mail: eanla@atsaol.com
URL: http://www.emagazine.com/view/?289&printview

Earth Island Institute
2150 Allston Way, Ste. 460
Berkeley, CA, USA 94704-1375
Ph: (510) 859-9100
E-mail: http://www.earthisland.org/

Earthscan
Dunstan House
14a St. Cross St.
London, , GBR EC1N 8XA
Ph: (440) 2078411930
E-mail: http://www.earthscan.co.uk

East Coast Publications
PO Box 55
Accord, MA, USA 02018-0055
Ph: (781) 878-4540
E-mail: nyrej@atsrejournal.com
URL: http://www.rejournal.com

Eastern Perishable Products Association Inc.
PO Box 4878
Colts Neck, NJ, USA 7722
Ph: (973) 831-4100
E-mail: eppa@atseppainc.org
URL: http://www.eppainc.org

Eating Well Inc.
823A Ferry Rd.
PO Box 1010
Charlotte, VT, USA 5445
Ph: (802) 425-5700
E-mail: eatingwell@atsemailcustomerservice.com
URL: http://www.eatingwell.com

Eaton Publishing
1 Research Dr. Sui 400A
PO Box 1070
Westborough, MA, USA 01581-6070
Ph: (508) 614-1414
E-mail: info@atsbiotechniques.com
URL: http://www.biotechniques.com

Eaton-Moghannam Publishing
696 San Ramon Valley Blvd., Ste. 214
Danville, CA, USA 94526
Ph: (925) 743-1083

EBSCO Publishing Inc.
10 Estes St.
Ipswich, MA, USA 1938
Ph: (978) 356-6500
E-mail: information@atsebscohost.com
URL: http://www.ebscohost.com

Ebury Press
c/o Random House
1745 Broadway
New York, NY, USA 10019
Ph: (212) 782-9000
E-mail: customerservice@atsrandom-house.com
URL:

Ecco
10 E 53rd St.
New York, NY, USA 10022
Ph: (212) 207-7000
E-mail: http://www.harpercollins.com/imprints/index.aspx?imprintid=517997

Ecco/HarperCollins
10 E 53rd St.
New York, NY, USA 10022
Ph: (212) 207-7000
E-mail: http://www.harpercollins.com/imprints/index.aspx?imprintid-517997

eCompany Now
One California St., 29th Fl.
San Francisco, CA, USA 94111
Ph: (415) 293-4800
E-mail: http://www.business2.com

Economic Development Institute
760 Spring St. NW
Atlanta, GA, USA 30332-0640
Ph: (404) 894-3475

Economics Dept.
1201 15th St. NW
Washington, DC, USA 20005
Ph: (202) 266-8200

Economist Intelligence Unit
111 W 57th St.
New York, NY, USA 10019
Ph: (212) 554-0600
E-mail: newyork@atseiu.com
URL:

The Economist Newspaper Inc.
90 New Montgomery St., Ste. 201
San Francisco, CA, USA 94105
Ph: (415) 278-0880

Economist Newspaper Ltd.
90 New Montgomery St., Ste. 201
San Francisco, CA, USA 94105
Ph: (415) 278-0880

ECRI Institute
5200 Butler Pke.
Plymouth Meeting, PA, USA 19462-1298
Ph: (610) 825-6000
E-mail: info@atsecri.org
URL: http://www.ecri.org

Ed Varney
PO Box 3655
Vancouver, BC, CAN V6B 3Y8
Ph: (604) 266-8289

Edgell Communications Inc.
4 Middlebury Blvd., Ste. 1
Randolph, NJ, USA 07869-1121
Ph: (973) 607-1300
E-mail: gedgell@atsedgellmail.com
URL: http://www.edgellcommunications.com

Editorial Freelancers Association Inc.
71 W 23rd St., 4th Fl.
New York, NY, USA 10010-4102
Ph: (212) 929-5400
E-mail: info@atsthe-efa.org
URL: http://www.the-efa.org

Editorial Projects in Education Inc.
6935 Arlington Rd., Ste. 100
Bethesda, MD, USA 20814-5287
Ph: (301) 280-3100
E-mail: ads@atsepe.org
URL: http://www.edweek.org

Educational Technology Publications
700 Palisade Ave.
Englewood Cliffs, NJ, USA 07632-0564
Ph: (201) 871-4007
E-mail: edtecpubs@atsaol.com
URL: http://www.bookstoread.com/etp

Edward Elgar Publishing, Inc.
9 Dewey Ct.
Northampton, MA, USA 01060-3815
Ph: (413) 584-5551
E-mail: elgarinfo@atse-elgar.com
URL: http://www.e-elgar-business.com

Edward Elgar Publishing, Incorporated
136 West St., Ste. 202
Northampton, MA, USA 1060
Ph: (413) 584-5551

Edwin Mellen Press
PO Box 450
Lewiston, NY, USA 14092-0450
Ph: (716) 754-2266

EGW.com Inc.
4075 Papazian Way No. 208
Fremont, CA, USA 94538
Ph: (510) 668-0268
E-mail: support@atsegw.com
URL: http://www.egw.com

ELF Publications Inc.
5285 W Louisiana Ave.
Lakewood, CO, USA 80232-5976
Ph: (303) 975-0075
E-mail: elfedit@atsqwest.net
URL: http://www.elfpublications.com/

Elsevier
1600 John F. Kennedy Blvd., Ste. 1800
Philadelphia, PA, USA 19103-2899
Ph: (215) 239-3900
E-mail: healthpermissions@atselsevier.com
URL: http://www.elsevier.com

Elsevier Advanced Technology Publications
Kelly School of Business
Indiana University
1309 E 10th St.
Bloomington, IN, USA 47405
Ph: (812) 855-6342

Elsevier Business Intelligence
5635 Fishers Ln., Ste. 6000
Rockville, MD, USA 20852
Ph: (212) 633-3648
E-mail: fdc.customer.service@atsfdcreports.com
URL: http://www.elsevierbi.com/contactus.html

Elsevier Science
PO Box 945
New York, NY, USA 10159-0945
Ph: (212) 989-5800
E-mail: usinfo@atssciencedirect.com
URL: http://www.elsevierscience.com/

Elsevier Science & Technology Books
200 Wheeler Rd., 6th Fl.
Burlington, MA, USA 1803
Ph: (781) 313-4700
E-mail: http://www.elsevier.com

Elsevier Science & Technology Books
11830 Westline Industrial Dr.
Saint Louis, MO, USA 63146
Ph: (314) 453-7010

Elsevier Science & Technology Books
525 B St., Ste. 1900
San Diego, CA, USA 92101
Ph: (781) 313-4700

Elsevier Science B.V.
Radarweg 29
Amsterdam, , NLD NL-1043
E-mail: http://www.elsevier.com/wps/find/homepage.cws_home

Elsevier Science Inc.
360 Park Ave. S
New York, NY, USA 10010-1710
Ph: (212) 633-3730
E-mail: usinfo-ehelp@atselsevier.com
URL: http://www.elsevier.com/wps/find/homepage.cws_home

Elsevier Technology Publications
360 Park Ave. S
New York, NY, USA 10010
Ph: (212) 633-3730

Elton Stephens Investments
PO Box 476
South Bend, IN, USA 46614
Ph: (574) 291-3823

Emerald Group Publishing Inc.
Brickyard Office Park
84 Sherman St.
Cambridge, MA, USA 2140
Ph: (617) 945-9130

Emerald Inc.
Harvard Square
1 Mifflin Place, Ste. 400
Cambridge, MA, USA 2138
Ph: (617) 576-5782

Emmis Books
The Old Firehouse, 2nd Fl.
1700 Madison Rd.
Cincinnati, OH, USA 45206
Ph: (513) 861-4045

Employee Benefit Research Institute
1100 13th St. NW, Ste. 878
Washington, DC, USA 20005
Ph: (202) 659-0670
E-mail: info@atsebri.org
URL: http://www.ebri.org/

Employee Relocation Council
4401 Wilson Blvd., Ste. 510
Arlington, VA, USA 22203
Ph: (703) 842-3400
E-mail: webmaster@atsworldwideerc.org
URL: http://www.erc.org/

Employer Resource Institute Inc.
1819 Polk St. No. 290
San Francisco, CA, USA 94109
E-mail: custserv@atsemployeradvice.com
URL:

Enfield Publishing
217 W 2nd St.
PO Box 612
Whitefish, MT, USA 59937
Ph: (406) 862-1233

Engineering Contractors Association
8310 Florence Ave.
Downey, CA, USA 90240
E-mail: info.eca@atsverizon.net
URL: http://www.ecaonline.net/ECA_Homex.html

Enterprise Magazines Inc.
5555 N Port Washington Rd., Ste. 305
Milwaukee, WI, USA 53217
Ph: (414) 882-2878
E-mail: info@atsfranchisehandbook.com
URL: http://www.franchisehandbook.com

Enterprise Technology Corp.
6 Hemlock Dr.
Greenwich, CT, USA 06831-5218

Entree Travel
695 Olive Rd.
Santa Barbara, CA, USA 93108
Ph: (805) 969-5848
E-mail: wtomicki@atsaol.com
URL:

Entrepreneur Media Inc.
2445 McCabe Way, Ste. 400
Irvine, CA, USA 92614
Ph: (949) 261-2325
E-mail: http://www.entrepreneur.com

Entrepreneur Press
2445 McCabe Way, Ste. 400
Irvine, TX, USA 92614-6244
Ph: (949) 261-2325

Entrepreneur Press
McGraw-Hill
55 Francisco St., Ste. 200
San Francisco, CA, USA 94133
Ph: (415) 433-2821

Entrepreneurial Press
2445 McCabe Way, Ste. 400
Irvine, CA, USA 92614-6244
Ph: (949) 261-2325

Environmental News Network
402 N B St.
Fairfield, IA, USA 52556
Ph: (319) 217-2362
E-mail: http://www.enn.com/

EPM Communications Inc.
19 W 21st St., Ste. 303
New York, NY, USA 10010
Ph: (212) 941-0099
E-mail: info@atsepmcom.com
URL: http://www.epmcom.com

EPM Communications, Inc.
160 Mercer St., 3rd Fl.
New York, NY, USA 10012
Ph: (212) 941-0099

EPRI
3420 Hillview Ave.
PO Box 10412
Palo Alto, CA, USA 94304
Ph: (650) 855-2121
E-mail: askepri@atsepri.com
URL: http://www.epri.com

Equipment Marketing & Distribution Association
PO Box 1347
Iowa City, IA, USA 52244
Ph: (319) 354-5156
E-mail: pat@atsemda.net
URL: http://www.emda.net

Erie Times-News
205 W 12th St.
Erie, PA, USA 16534
Ph: (814) 878-1943

Escapees, Inc.
100 Rainbow Dr.
Livingston, TX, USA 77351
Ph: (936) 327-8873
E-mail: editor@atsescapees.com
URL:

ESM Association
568 Spring Rd., Ste. D
Elmhurst, IL, USA 60126-3896
E-mail: esmahq@atsesmassn.org
URL: http://www.esmassn.org

ETA International
5 Depot St.
Greencastle, IN, USA 46135
Ph: (765) 653-8262
E-mail: eta@atseta-i.org
URL: http://www.eta-i.org

Ethics Resource Center Inc.
2345 Crystal Dr., Ste. 201
Washington, DC, USA 22202
Ph: (202) 647-2185
E-mail: ethics@atsethics.org
URL: http://www.ethics.org

Everton Publishers Inc.
PO Box 442
Garden City, UT, USA 84028
Ph: (435) 752-6022
E-mail: cs@atseverton.com
URL: http://www.everton.com

Executive Business Media Inc.
825 Old Country Rd.
Westbury, NY, USA 11590-0812
Ph: (516) 334-3030
E-mail: ebm-mail@atsebmpubs.com
URL: http://www.ebmpubs.com

Executive Protection Institute
16 Penn Plz., Ste. 1570
New York, NY, USA 10001
Ph: (212) 268-4555
E-mail: info@atspersonalprotection.com
URL: http://www.personalprotection.com

Exhibit Builder Magazine
22900 Ventura Blvd., Ste. 245
PO Box 4144
Woodland Hills, CA, USA 91364
Ph: (818) 225-0100
E-mail: jillb@atsexhibitbuilder.net

URL: http://www.exhibitbuilder.net

EXPO Magazine Inc.
7015 College Blvd., Ste. 600
Overland Park, KS, USA 66211
Ph: (913) 469-1110
E-mail: http://www.expoweb.com

Export Institute
6901 W 84th St., Ste. 301
Minneapolis, MN, USA 55438
Ph: (952) 943-1505
E-mail: jrj@atsexportinstitute.com
URL: http://www.exportinstitute.com

Eye Contact Media
1344 Disc Dr., No. 105
Sparks, NV, USA 89436

F

F & W Publications, Incorporated
4700 E Galbraith Rd.
Cincinnati, OH, USA 45236
Ph: (513) 531-2690

Faber & Faber, Inc.
19 Union Sq. W
New York, NY, USA 10003
Ph: (212) 741-7900
E-mail: http://us.macmillan.com/faberandfaber.aspx

Fabricare Canada
PO Box 968
Oakville, ON, CAN L6J 5E8
Ph: (905) 337-0516
E-mail: http://www.fabricarecanada.com

Fabricators & Manufacturers Association, International
833 Featherstone Rd.
Rockford, IL, USA 61107
Ph: (815) 399-8700
E-mail: info@atsfmanet.org
URL:

Fahy-Williams Publishing Inc.
171 Reed St.
PO Box 1080
Geneva, NY, USA 14456
Ph: (315) 789-0458
E-mail: kfahy@atsfwpi.com
URL: http://www.fwpi.com

Fairchild Publications Inc.
750 Third Ave., 8th Fl.
New York, NY, USA 10017
Ph: (212) 630-4600
E-mail: nicole_doucette@atscondenast.com
URL: http://www.fairchildpub.com

Fairchild Tropical Botanic Garden
10901 Old Cutler Rd.
Coral Gables, FL, USA 33156
Ph: (305) 667-1651
E-mail: webmaster@atsfairchildgarden.org
URL:

Family Enterprise Publishers
1220-B Kennestone Cir.
Marietta, GA, USA 30061
Ph: (770) 421-0110
E-mail: info@atsefamilybusiness.com
URL:

Family Firm Institute Inc.
200 Lincoln St., Ste. 201
Boston, MA, USA 2111
Ph: (617) 482-3045

Family History World
PO Box 129
Tremonton, UT, USA 84337-0129
E-mail: genealogy@atsutahlinx.com
URL:

Fandata Publications
7614 Cervantes Ct.
Springfield, VA, USA 22153-1608
Ph: (703) 913-5575
E-mail: email@atsfandata.com
URL: http://www.fandata.com

Fantagraphics Books Inc.
7563 Lake City Way NE
Seattle, WA, USA 98115
Ph: (206) 524-1967
E-mail: fbicomix@atsfantagraphics.com
URL: http://www.fantagraphics.com

Farm & Ranch News
PO Box 160
Lithia, FL, USA 33547-0160
Ph: (813) 737-6397
E-mail: farmranchnews@atsaol.com
URL: http://www.farmandranchnews.com/

Farrar, Straus and Giroux
18 W 18th St.
New York, NY, USA 10011
E-mail: http://www.fsgbooks.com

Fastline
4900 Fox Run Rd.
PO Box 248
Buckner, KY, USA 40010
Ph: (502) 222-0146
E-mail: custcare@atsfastline.com
URL: http://www.fastline.com

Faulkner Information Services
116 Cooper Ctr.
7905 Browning Rd.
Pennsauken, NJ, USA 08109-4319
Ph: (856) 662-2070
E-mail: faulkner@atsfaulkner.com
URL: http://www.faulkner.com

FCW
50 Charles Lindbergh Bldg., Ste. 100
Uniondale, NY, USA 11553
Ph: (516) 229-3600
E-mail: http://www.floorcoveringweekly.com

FDA News
300 N Washington St., Ste. 200
Falls Church, VA, USA 22046-3431
Ph: (703) 538-7600
E-mail: customerservice@atsfdanews.com
URL:

F-D-C Reports Inc.
5635 Fishers Ln., Ste. 6000
Rockville, MD, USA 20852
Ph: (800) 332-2181
E-mail: fdc.customer.service@atsfdcreports.com
URL: http://www.fdcreports.com

Feature Publishing Ltd.
1800 McGill College Ave., Ste. 1600
Montreal, QC, CAN H3A 3J6
Ph: (514) 939-5024
E-mail: editor@atsfeature.ca
URL: http://www.movieentertainment.ca/

Federal Jobs Digest
326 Main St.
Emmaus, PA, USA 18049
E-mail: webmaster@atsjobsfed.com
URL: http://www.jobsfed.com

Federal Library and Information Network
Library of Congress
101 Independence Ave., SE
Adams Bldg., Rm. 217
Washington, DC, USA 20540-4935
Ph: (202) 707-4800
E-mail: fliccfpe@atsloc.gov
URL:

Federal Reserve Bank of Dallas
PO Box 655906
Dallas, TX, USA 75265-5906
Ph: (214) 922-5254

Federick News-Post
351 Ballenger Center Dr.
Frederick, MD, USA 21703
Ph: (301) 662-1177

Feed-Lot Magazine
PO Box 850
116 E Long
Dighton, KS, USA 67839
E-mail: http://www.feedlotmagazine.com/contact.html

FERA Inc.
1810 Warrington Cir.
Ann Arbor, MI, USA 48103
Ph: (734) 994-9060
E-mail: jskiff@atsferaonline.com
URL:

Ferdic Inc.
PO Box 28
Camp Hill, PA, USA 17011
Ph: (717) 731-1426
E-mail: ferdic@atsix.netcom.com
URL:

Ferney Scribes Inc.
PO Box 1118
Mill Valley, CA, USA 94942

Fiction Writer's Connection
PO Box 72300
Albuquerque, NM, USA 87195
Ph: (505) 352-9490

Fifth Estate
PO Box 201016
Ferndale, MI, USA 48220
E-mail: fe@atsfifthestate.org
URL: http://www.fifthestate.org

Film Society of Lincoln Center
70 Lincoln Center Plz.
New York, NY, USA 10023-6595
Ph: (212) 875-5367
E-mail: custsvc_fc@atsfulcoinc.com
URL: http://www.filmlinc.com

Finan Publishing Company Inc.
15 W Moody Ave.
Saint Louis, MO, USA 63119-3776
Ph: (314) 961-6644
E-mail: http://www.finan.com/

Financial Executives International
PO Box 303
Uxbridge, MA, USA 1569
Ph: (502) 278-8006

Financial Planning Association
4100 E. Mississippi Ave., Ste. 400
Denver, CO, USA 80246-3053
Ph: (800) 322-4237
E-mail: http://www.fpanet.org

Financial Research Associates Inc.
203 A Ave., NW, Ste. 202
Winter Haven, FL, USA 33881-4540
Ph: (863) 299-3969
E-mail: sales@atsfrafssb.com
URL:

Financial Times/Prentice Hall
1 Lake St.
Upper Saddle River, NJ, USA 7458
Ph: (201) 236-7000
E-mail: http://www.prenhall.com/

Find/SVP
17 Oxford St.
Rochester, NY, USA 14607
Ph: (212) 645-4500
E-mail: infoadvisor@atsfindsvp.com
URL:

Fireside Publishing
Rockefeller Center
1230 Ave. of the Americas
New York, NY, USA 10020

Fitch IPCA Inc.
1 State St. Plz.
New York, NY, USA 10004
Ph: (212) 908-0500
E-mail: usaclientservices@atsfitchratings.com
URL:

Fleisher Fine Arts Inc.
15 McMurrich St., Ste. 706
Toronto, ON, CAN M5R 3M6
Ph: (416) 925-5564
E-mail: http://www.fleisher.org/

Floor Covering Installation Contractors Association (FCICA)
7439 Millwood Dr.
West Bloomfield, MI, USA 48322-1234
Ph: (248) 661-5015
E-mail: info@atsfcica.com
URL:

Floor Focus Inc.
3001 S Broad St., Ste. 100
Chattanooga, TN, USA 37408
Ph: (423) 752-0400
E-mail: info@atsfloorfocus.com
URL: http://www.floordaily.net/

Florida Department of Agriculture and Consumer Services
The Capitol
Tallahassee, FL, USA 32399-0800
Ph: (850) 488-3022
E-mail: http://www.doacs.state.fl.us/

Florida International University
3000 NE 151st St.
North Miami, FL, USA 33181
Ph: (305) 919-4500
E-mail: http://hospitality.fiu.edu/

Florida Publishers Association
PO Box 430
Highland City, FL, USA 33846-0430
Ph: (863) 647-5951
E-mail: fpabooks@atsaol.com
URL:

Florida Times-Union
1 Riverside Ave.
Jacksonville, FL, USA 32202
Ph: (904) 359-4324

Florist's Review Enterprises Inc.
PO Box 4368
Topeka, KS, USA 66604
Ph: (785) 266-0888
E-mail: mail@atsfloristsreview.com
URL: http://www.floristsreview.com/main/contactus.html

FM Atlas Publishing
PO Box 336
Esko, MN, USA 55733-0336
Ph: (218) 879-7676
E-mail: fmatlas@atsaol.com
URL: http://members.aol.com/fmatlas/home.html

Foodservice Consultants Society International
144 Parkedge Str.
Rockwood, ON, CAN N0B 2K0
Ph: (519) 856-0783
E-mail: info@atsfcsi.org
URL: http://www.fcsi.org

Forbes Inc.
90 5th Ave.
New York, NY, USA 10011
Ph: (212) 366-8900

Forbes Magazine
60 5th Ave.
New York, NY, USA 10011
Ph: (212) 366-8900
E-mail: http://www.forbes.com

Ford Dealers Alliance
401 Continental Plz.
Hackensack, NJ, USA 7601
Ph: (201) 342-4542

Ford Investor Services Inc.
11722 Sorrento Valley Rd., Ste. I
San Diego, CA, USA 92121
Ph: (858) 755-1327

Forensic Drug Abuse Advisor Inc.
PO Box 5139
Berkeley, CA, USA 94705-5139
Ph: (510) 849-0923
E-mail: info@atsfdaa.com
URL:

Forum Publishing Co.
383 E Main St.
Centerport, NY, USA 11721
Ph: (631) 754-5000
E-mail: forumpublishing@atsaol.com
URL: http://www.forum123.com

Foundation Center
79 5th Ave.
16th St.
New York, NY, USA 10003-3076
Ph: (212) 620-4230
E-mail: communications@atsfoundation-center.org
URL: http://foundationcenter.org/newyork

Foundation for American Communications FACS
85 S Grand Ave.
Pasadena, CA, USA 91105
Ph: (626) 584-0010
E-mail: http://www.facsnet.org

Foundation of Flexographic Technical Association
900 Marconi Ave.
Ronkonkoma, NY, USA 11779-7212
Ph: (631) 737-6020
E-mail: memberinfo@atsflexography.org
URL: http://www.flexography.org

Fourth Seacoast Publishing Company Inc.
25300 Little Mack Ave.
Saint Clair Shores, MI, USA 48081
Ph: (586) 779-5570
E-mail: http://www.fourthseacoastonline.com

The Fragrance Foundation Inc.
545 5th Ave., Ste. 900
New York, NY, USA 10017
Ph: (212) 725-2755
E-mail: info@atsfragrance.org
URL: http://www.fragrance.org

Frances Lincoln Limited
4 Torriano Mews
Torriano Ave.
London, , GBR NW5 2RZ
Ph: (440) 2072844009
E-mail: http://www.franceslincoln.com

Franchise News
PMB 240
540 S Mendenhall Rd., Ste. 12
Memphis, TN, USA 38117-4245
E-mail: franmark@atsmsn.com
URL:

Fraud & Theft Information Bureau
9770 S Military Trl., Ste. 380
Boynton Beach, FL, USA 33436
Ph: (561) 737-8700
E-mail: sales@atsfraudandtheft.com
URL: http://www.fraudandtheft.com

Free Press
1230 Avenue of the Americas
New York, NY, USA 10020

Free Press Media Group Inc.
PO Box 362
Hendersonville, TN, USA 37075
Ph: (615) 822-1186

Free Press/Simon & Schuster Inc.
Simon & Schuster Bldg.
1230 Avenue of the Americas
New York, NY, USA 10020
Ph: (212) 698-7000
E-mail: http://www.simonsays.com

FreeBridge Publishing, Inc.
8105 Pinehurst Harbour Way
Pasadena, MD, USA 21122
Ph: (231) 933-0445

Freedom Communications
2 Eglin Pkwy. NE
Fort Walton Beach, FL, USA 32548
Ph: (850) 863-1111

Freedom Communications Inc.
521 Pile St.
Clovis, NM, USA 88101
Ph: (575) 763-3431

Freedom Communications Inc.
3200 Wellons Blvd.
New Bern, NC, USA 28562
Ph: (252) 638-8101

French-Canadian Genealogical Society of Connecticut Inc.
Box 928
Tolland, CT, USA 06084-0928
Ph: (860) 872-2597

Fresh Produce & Floral Council
16700 Valley View Ave., Ste. 130
La Mirada, CA, USA 90638
Ph: (714) 739-0177
E-mail: info@atsaol.com
URL: http://www.fpfc.org

Frontline Publishers, Incorporated
8268 Streamwood Dr.
PO Box 32674
Baltimore, MD, USA 21208-8674
Ph: (410) 922-4903

FSBO Publishing
Livonia, MI, USA
Ph: (734) 629-7222
E-mail: info@atsfsbo-cd.com
URL: http://www.fsbo-cd.com

FT Press
800 E 96th St.
Indianapolis, IN, USA 46240
E-mail: http://www.ftpress.com

FT Press
1 Lake St.
Upper Saddle River, NJ, USA 37458
E-mail: http://www.ftpress.com/index.asp

FundWorks, Inc.
186 Crescent Rd.
Needham, MA, USA 2494
Ph: (781) 433-0909
E-mail: jimlowell@atsfidelityinvestor.com
URL:

Funeral Consumers Alliance
33 Patchen Rd.
South Burlington, VT, USA 5403
Ph: (802) 865-8300
E-mail: fca@atsfunerals.org
URL: http://www.funerals.org

Future Network USA
4000 Shoreline Ct., Ste. 400
South San Francisco, CA, USA 94080
Ph: (650) 872-1642
E-mail: http://www.futureus.com/contact/

Futures Magazine
222 S Riverside Plz., Ste. 620
Chicago, IL, USA 60606
Ph: (312) 846-4600
E-mail: gszala@atsfuturesmag.com
URL: http://www.futuresmag.com

FW Media Inc.
4700 E Galbraith Rd.
Cincinnati, OH, USA 45236
Ph: (513) 531-2690
E-mail: contact_us@atsfwmedia.com
URL: http://www.fwmedia.com/

FXC Investors Corp.
PO Box 1366
Selden, NY, USA 11784
Ph: (800) 392-0992
E-mail: fxcmgt@atsaol.com
URL:

G

G.I.E. Media, MC
4020 Kinross Lakes Pkwy., Ste. 201
Richfield, OH, USA 44286
Ph: (330) 523-5400
E-mail: http://www.giemedia.com

G.R. Leonard & Co.
181 N Vermont Ave.
Glendora, CA, USA 91741
Ph: (626) 914-3200
E-mail: http://www.leonardsguide.com

G2 Computer Intelligence Inc.
11 Danis Ave.
Glen Cove, NY, USA 11542
Ph: (516) 759-7025
E-mail: news@atsg2news.com
URL: http://www.g2news.com/

Gale
PO Box 6904
Florence, KY, USA 41022-6904
E-mail: investors@atscengage.com
URL: http://www.gale.cengage.com

Gallup
Gallup Bldg.
901 F St. NW
Washington, DC, USA 20004
Ph: (202) 715-3030

Gallup Press
1251 Avenue of the Americas, 23rd Fl.
New York, NY, USA 10020

Gannett Co.
PO Box 357
Granville, OH, USA 43023-0357
Ph: (740) 587-3397
E-mail: cpeterson@atsnncogannett.com
URL: http://www.granvillesentinel.com

Gardner Publications
6915 Valley Ave.
Cincinnati, OH, USA 45244-3029
Ph: (513) 527-8800

Gasoline and Automotive Service Dealers Association (GASDA)
18 Liberty St 2nd FL
Stamford, CT, USA 6902
Ph: (203) 327-4773
E-mail: info@atsgasda.org
URL:

Gay-Lesbian History Stamp Club
PO Box 190842
Dallas, TX, USA 75219-0842

Gazette
500 3rd Ave. SE
Cedar Rapids, IA, USA 52401
Ph: (319) 398-8333

The Gazette
30 S Prospect St.
Colorado Springs, CO, USA 80903
Ph: (719) 632-5511

GC Publishing Company Inc.
744 Main St., Rte. 6A
PO Box 2010
Dennis, MA, USA 2638
Ph: (508) 385-7700
E-mail: sgriffin@atsgccomm.net
URL: http://www.gccomm.net/contact/index.asp

Gearhead Communications, LLC
Three Research Ctr.
Marion, IA, USA 52302
Ph: (319) 447-5550
E-mail: http://www.premierguitar.com/Privacy.asp

Gebbie Press Inc.
143 Glford Schoolhouse Rd
PO Box 1000
New Paltz, NY, USA 12561
Ph: (845) 255-7560
E-mail: gebbiepress@atspipeline.com
URL: http://www.gebbiepress.com

GemStone Press
Sunset Farms Offices
Rte. 4
PO Box 237
Woodstock, VT, USA 5091
Ph: (802) 457-4000
E-mail: persmissions@atsgemstonepress.com
URL: http://www.gemstonepress.com/

Genealogical Publishing Company Inc.
3600 Clipper Mill Rd., Ste. 260
Baltimore, MD, USA 21211
Ph: (410) 837-8271
E-mail: info@atsgenealogical.com
URL: http://www.genealogical.com

General Books LLC
PO Box 29000, NAS485
Miami, FL, USA 33102
E-mail: http://www.general-books.net

General Learning Communications
900 Skokie Blvd., Ste. 200
Northbrook, IL, USA 60062
Ph: (847) 205-3000
E-mail: http://glcedu.com/

The Generations Network
360 W 4800 N
Provo, UT, USA 84604
Ph: (801) 705-7000
E-mail: pr@atsmyfamilyinc.com
URL: http://www.myfamilyinc.com

George Brooks
7925 Looking Glass Ct.
Raleigh, NC, USA 27612-7346

George K. Schweitzer
407 Ascot Ct.
Knoxville, TN, USA 37923
Ph: (865) 690-7831
E-mail: http://www.gensources.com/gensources/Prattsite.htm

George W. Southerland
PO Box 4254
Chattanooga, TN, USA 37405-0254
Ph: (423) 886-1628

Georgia Tech University
Center for Sports Performance
Atlanta, GA, USA 30332-1009

GIE Media, Inc.
4020 Kinross Lakes Pky., Ste. 201
Richfield, OH, USA 44286
E-mail: http://www.giemedia.com/

Gift and Decorative Accessories Center Association
360 Park Ave. S
New York, NY, USA 10010
Ph: (646) 746-6400
E-mail: gdacustserv@atscdsfulfillment.com
URL: http://www.giftsanddec.com

Gilston-Kalin Communications, LLC
P.O. Box 5325
Rockville, MD, USA 20848-5325
Ph: (202) 463-1250
E-mail: info@atswttlonline.com
URL:

Glass Patterns Quarterly Inc.
8300 Hidden Valley Rd.
PO Box 69
Westport, KY, USA 40077-9797
Ph: (502) 222-5631
E-mail: info@atsglasspatterns.com
URL: http://www.glasspatterns.com/

Glaucoma Research Foundation
251 Post St., Ste. 600
San Francisco, CA, USA 94108
Ph: (415) 986-3162
E-mail: jrulon@atsglaucoma.org
URL:

Global Health Council (White River Junction, Vermont)
15 Railroad Row
White River Junction, VT, USA 5001
Ph: (802) 649-1340
E-mail: ghc@atsglobalhealth.org
URL: http://www.globalhealth.org

Global Sports Productions Ltd.
16810 Crystal Dr. E
Enumclaw, WA, USA 98022-8044
Ph: (310) 454-9480
E-mail: globalnw@atsearthlink.net
URL: http://www.sportsbooksempire.com

Globe Pequot Press
246 Goose Ln.
PO Box 480
Guilford, CT, USA 6437
Ph: (203) 458-4500
E-mail: info@atsglobepequot.com
URL: http://www.globepequot.com

Gloucester Publishers
108 E Main St.
Gloucester, MA, USA 1930
Ph: (978) 283-3200
E-mail: info@atsoldhouseinteriors.com
URL: http://www.oldhouseinteriors.com

Gold Leaf Publishing
PO Box 800041
Roswell, GA, USA 30075
Ph: (678) 248-3558

Gold Pen Publishing
PO Box 70057
Sunnyvale, CA, USA 95054
E-mail: info@atsgoldenpress.com
URL: http://www.goldenpress.com

Golden Bell Press
2403 Champa St.
Denver, CO, USA 80205
Ph: (303) 296-1600
E-mail: basusan@atsgoldenbellpress.com
URL: http://www.goldenbellpress.com

Gom Publishing, LLC
6052 Coventry Hurst Ln.
Hilliard, OH, USA 43026
Ph: (614) 876-7097

Gotham
375 Hudson St.
New York, NY, USA 10014-3657
Ph: (212) 366-2933
E-mail: academics@atsus.penguingroup.com
URL: http://us.penguingroup.com

Gotham/Penguin Group Incorporated
375 Hudson St.
New York, NY, USA 10014
Ph: (212) 366-2000
E-mail: customerservice@atspenguinputnam.com
URL: http://www.penguinputnam.com

Government Data Publications Inc.
2300 M St. NW
Washington, DC, USA 20037
E-mail: gdp@atsgovdata.com
URL: http://www.govdata.com

Government Development Bank for Puerto Rico
PO Box 42001
San Juan, PR, USA 00940-2001
Ph: (787) 728-9200
E-mail: gdbcomm@atsbgf.gobierno.pr
URL:

Government Institutes
15200 NBN Way, Bldg. B
Blue Ridge Summit, PA, USA 17214-0191
Ph: (717) 794-3800
E-mail: custserv@atsrowman.com
URL: http://www.govinstpress.com/

Government Printing Office
732 N Capitol St. NW
Washington, DC, USA 20401
Ph: (202) 512-1800

Government Relations Section
1575 I St. NW
Washington, DC, USA 20005-1103
Ph: (202) 371-0940

Graham & Whiteside
PO Box 9187
Harrogate
Farmington Hills, MI, USA 48333-9187
Ph: (248) 699-4253
E-mail: gale.customerservice@atscengage.com
URL: http://www.gale.cengage.com/graham&whiteside/

Graham Communications
40 Oval Rd., Ste. 2
Quincy, MA, USA 02170-3813
Ph: (617) 328-0069
E-mail: info@atsgrahamcomm.com
URL: http://www.grahamcomm.com/

Grand Central Publishing
1271 Ave. of the Americas
New York, NY, USA 10020
Ph: (212) 364-1200
E-mail: http://www.hachettebookgroup.com

Grand Central Publishing
237 Park Ave.
New York, NY, USA 10017

Grand Circle Corporation
85 Main St., Ste. 101
Watertown, MA, USA 2472
E-mail: http://odysseys-unlimited-catalog.com

Grandich Publications
PO Box 243
Perrineville, NJ, USA 8535
Ph: (732) 642-3992
E-mail: peter@atsgrandich.com
URL:

Graphic Arts Center Publishing Company
PO Box 10306
Portland, OR, USA 97296-0306
Ph: (503) 226-2402

Graphic Communication Conference of the International Brotherhood of Teamsters
25 Louisiana Ave. NW
Washington, DC, USA 20001
Ph: (202) 624-6800
E-mail: webmessenger@atsgciu.org
URL: http://www.gciu.org/index.shtml

Graphic Dimensions
9065 Taverna Way
Boynton Beach, FL, USA 33472
Ph: (585) 381-3428
E-mail: mkleper@atsprinterport.com
URL: http://www.printerport.com/kdp

Graphico Publishing Company
1601 W 5th Ave., Ste. 123
Columbus, OH, USA 43212-2303
Ph: (614) 801-9977

Great American Publishing Co.
PO Box 128
75 Applewood Dr. Ste. A
Sparta, MI, USA 49345
Ph: (616) 887-9008
E-mail: http://www.fruitgrowersnews.com

Great Lakes Publishing Co.
1422 Euclid Ave., No. 730
Cleveland, OH, USA 44115
Ph: (216) 771-2833
E-mail: webmaster@atsglpublishing.com
URL: http://www.glpublishing.com

Great Lakes Publishing Company
1422 Euclid Ave., Ste. 730
Cleveland, OH, USA 44115
Ph: (216) 771-2833

Greater Phoenix Chamber of Commerce
201 N Central Ave., 27th Fl.
Phoenix, AZ, USA 85004
Ph: (602) 495-2195
E-mail: info@atsphoenixchamber.com
URL: http://www.phoenixchamber.com

Green Mountain Coffee
33 Coffee Ln.
Waterbury, VT, USA 05676-1529
Ph: (888) 879-4627

Greenleaf Book Group Press
4425 S Mo Pac Expy., Ste. 600
Austin, TX, USA 78735
Ph: (512) 891-6100
E-mail: http://www.greenleafbookgroup.com

The Greenmoney Journal
PO Box 67
Santa Fe, NM, USA 87504
Ph: (505) 988-7423
E-mail: info@atsgreenmoneyjournal.com
URL:

Greenpeace USA
702 H St. NW, Ste. 300
Washington, DC, USA 20001
Ph: (202) 462-1177
E-mail: info@atswdc.greenpeace.org
URL: http://usactions.greenpeace.org/

Greenwood Publishing Group Inc.
Praeger Publishers
88 Post Rd. W
Westport, CT, USA 6881
Ph: (203) 226-3571
E-mail: http://www.greenwood.com/praeger.aspx

Greenwood Publishing Group, Inc.
214 Bald Eagle Ln.
Cary, NC, USA 27518-9681
Ph: (203) 226-3571

Greenwood Publishing Group, Inc.
PO Box 6926
Portsmouth, NH, USA 3802
Ph: (603) 431-2214
E-mail: http://www.greenwood.com/

Greeting Card Association
1133 Westchester Ave., Ste. N136
White Plains, NY, USA 10604-3547
Ph: (914) 421-3331
E-mail: gca@atsgcamail.org
URL: http://www.greetingcard.org/

Greg and Pat Williams
750 Black Lick Rd.
Gravel Switch, KY, USA 40328
Ph: (859) 332-7606

Grey House Publishing
4919 Rte. 22
PO Box 56
Amenia, NY, USA 12501
Ph: (518) 789-8700
E-mail: customerservice@atsgreyhouse.com
URL: http://www.greyhouse.com

Grey House Publishing
185 Millerton Rd.
Millerton, NY, USA 12546
Ph: (518) 789-8700
E-mail: http://www.greyhouse.com

Grey House Publishing Canada Inc.
555 Richmond St. W, Ste. 301
PO Box 1207
Toronto, ON, CAN M5V 3B1
Ph: (416) 644-6479
E-mail: info@atsgreyhouse.ca
URL: http://www.greyhouse.ca

Griffin Publishing Group
18022 Cowan, Ste. 202
Irvine, CA, USA 92614-6811

Grimes and Associates
24 Daisy St.
Ladera Ranch, CA, USA 92694
Ph: (949) 388-4848
E-mail: info@atsvowsmagazine.com
URL: http://www.vowsmagazine.com

Group C Communications Inc.
44 Apple St., Ste. 3
Tinton Falls, NJ, USA 7724
Ph: (732) 842-7433
E-mail: lconnor@atsgroupc.com
URL: http://www.groupc.com

Grove Atlantic
841 Broadway
New York, NY, USA 10003
Ph: (212) 614-7850
E-mail: http://www.groveatlantic.com

Gruner & Jahr USA
350 Fifth Ave., Ste. 4610
New York, NY, USA 10118
Ph: (212) 268-3344
E-mail: dustin.guzowski@atshusonmedia.com
URL: http://www.gujmedia.de/en/

Gruner & Jahr USA Publishing
375 Lexington Ave., 42nd St.
New York, NY, USA 10017-5514
Ph: (212) 499-2000
E-mail: http://www.meredith.com

Guild of Book Workers Inc.
521 5th Ave.
New York, NY, USA 10175-0038
Ph: (212) 757-6454
E-mail: secretary@atsguildofbookworkers.org
URL: http://www.guildofbookworkers.org

H

H.H. Backer Associates Inc.
18 S Michigan Ave., Ste. 1100
Chicago, IL, USA 60603
Ph: (312) 578-1818
E-mail: hhbacker@atshhbacker.com
URL: http://www.hhbacker.com/

The H.W. Wilson Co.
950 University Ave.
Bronx, NY, USA 10452
Ph: (718) 588-8400
E-mail: custserv@atshwwilson.com
URL: http://www.hwwilson.com

Hachette Filipacchi Media U.S. Inc.
1633 Broadway
New York, NY, USA 10019-6708
Ph: (212) 767-6000
E-mail: http://www.hfmus.com

Hagedorn Communications
PO Box 680
New Rochelle, NY, USA 10801
Ph: (914) 636-7400
E-mail: http://www.rew-online.com

Halle House Publishing
5966 Halle Farm Dr.
Willoughby, OH, USA 44094-3076
Ph: (216) 486-2000

Halper Publishing Co.
210 Skokie Valley Rd., Ste. 4
Highland Park, IL, USA 60035
E-mail: info@atshalper.com
URL: http://www.halper.com/

Hanley-Wood L.L.C.
1 Thomas Cir. NW, Ste. 600
Washington, DC, USA 20005-5803
Ph: (202) 452-0800
E-mail: http://www.hanleywood.com

Happy About
20660 Stevens Creek Blvd., Ste. 210
Cupertino, CA, USA 95014
Ph: (408) 257-3000
E-mail: questions@atshappyabout.com
URL: http://www.happyabout.com

Happy About
21265 Stevens Creek Blvd., Ste. 205
Cupertino, CA, USA 95014
Ph: (408) 257-3000

Hardwood Plywood & Veneer Association
1825 Michael Faraday Dr.
Reston, VA, USA 20190
Ph: (703) 435-2900
E-mail: hpva@atshpva.org
URL: http://www.hpva.org

Harper Associates Inc.
PO Box 50
Sun Valley, ID, USA 83353-0050
Ph: (208) 622-3183
E-mail: harper@atsandrewharpertravel.com
URL:

Harper Business
10 E 53rd St.
New York, NY, USA 10022
Ph: (212) 207-7969
E-mail: harperbiz@atsharpercollins.com
URL: http://www.harpercollins.com

Harper Press
10 E 53rd St.
New York, NY, USA 10022
Ph: (212) 207-7000
E-mail: orders@atsharpercollins.com
URL: http://www.harpercollins.com

HarperAudio
10 E 53rd St.
New York, NY, USA 10022
Ph: (212) 207-7000
E-mail: harperaudio@atsharpercollins.com
URL: http://www.harperaudio.com

HarperCollins
10 E 53rd St.
New York, NY, USA 10022
Ph: (212) 207-7000
E-mail: orders@atsharpercollins.com
URL: http://www.harpercollins.com

HarperCollins Publishers Inc.
10 E 53rd St.
New York, NY, USA 10022
Ph: (212) 207-7791
E-mail: http://www.harpercollins.com

HarperInformation
10 E 53rd St.
New York, NY, USA 10022-5299
Ph: (212) 207-7000

HarperOne
10 E 53rd St.
New York, NY, USA 10022
Ph: (212) 207-7000
E-mail: orders@atsharpercollins.com
URL: http://www.harpercollins.com

HarperStudio/HarperCollins
10 E 53rd St.
New York, NY, USA 10022
Ph: (212) 207-7000
E-mail: http://www.harpercollins.com

Harris InfoSource
2057 E Aurora Rd.
Twinsburg, OH, USA 44087-1999
Ph: (330) 425-9000
E-mail: customerservice@atsharrisinfo.com
URL: http://www.harrisinfo.com

Harris Publications Inc.
1115 Broadway
New York, NY, USA 10010-3450
Ph: (212) 807-7100
E-mail: subscriptions@atsharris-pub.com
URL: http://www.harris-pub.com

Harris Publishing Inc.
360 B St.
Idaho Falls, ID, USA 83402
Ph: (208) 524-7000
E-mail: info@atsharrispublishing.com
URL: http://www.harrispublishing.com

Harrison Scott Publications Inc.
5 Marine View Plz., Ste. 400
Hoboken, NJ, USA 7030
Ph: (201) 659-1700
E-mail: info@atshspnews.com
URL:

Harvard Business Press
300 N Beacon St.
Watertown, MA, USA 2472
Ph: (617) 783-7600
E-mail: custserv@atshbsp.harvard.edu
URL: http://hbsp.harvard.edu

Harvard Business School
Soldiers Field Rd.
Boston, MA, USA 2163
Ph: (617) 495-1003

Harvard Business School Press
60 Harvard Way
Boston, MA, USA 2163
E-mail: permissions@atshbsp.harvard.edu
URL: http://www.harvard.edu

Harvard Business School Press
300 N Beacon St.
Watertown, MA, USA 2472
Ph: (617) 783-7500
E-mail: corpcustserv@atshbsp.harvard.edu
URL: http://www.hbsp.harvard.edu

Harvard Business School Publishing
60 Harvard Way
Boston, MA, USA 2163
Ph: (617) 783-7400
E-mail: corpcustserv@atshbsp.harvard.edu
URL: http://www.hbsp.harvard.edu

Harvard Business School Publishing
300 N Beacon St.
Watertown, MA, USA 2472
Ph: (617) 783-7500
E-mail: corpcustserv@atshbsp.harvard.edu
URL: http://www.hbsp.harvard.edu

Harvey W. Watt & Company Inc.
PO Box 20787
Atlanta, GA, USA 30320
Ph: (404) 767-7501
E-mail: pilot@atsharveywatt.com
URL:

Hatton-Brown Publishers Inc.
225 Hanrick St.
PO Box 2268
Montgomery, AL, USA 36102
Ph: (334) 834-1170
E-mail: dianne@atshattonbrown.com
URL: http://www.hattonbrown.net

Hawaii Business Publishing
1000 Bishop St., Ste. 405
Honolulu, HI, USA 96813
Ph: (808) 537-9500

Haymarket Group Ltd.
12 W 37th St., 9th fl.
New York, NY, USA 10018
Ph: (212) 239-0855
E-mail: http://www.pastryartanddesign.com/

Haymarket Media Inc.
114 W 26th St., 4th Fl.
New York, NY, USA 10001
Ph: (646) 638-6000

Haymarket Media, Inc.
25 Philips Pkwy., Ste. 105
Montvale, NJ, USA 7645
Ph: (201) 505-9730

Hazelden Foundation
PO Box 176
Center City, MN, USA 55012-0011
Ph: (651) 213-4000

HCM Publishing
c/o Mapletree Publishing
6233 Howard Ln.
Highland Ranch, CO, USA 80130-3773
Ph: (303) 791-9024

Healing Ministry of Catholic Health Care
4455 Woodson Rd.
Saint Louis, MO, USA 63134
Ph: (314) 427-2500
E-mail: servicecenter@atschausa.org
URL: http://www.chausa.org

Health Administration Press
1 N Franklin, Ste. 1700
Chicago, IL, USA 60606-3529
Ph: (312) 424-2800
E-mail: geninfo@atsache.org
URL: http://www.ache.org

Health Care Financing Administration
200 Independence Ave. SW
Washington, DC, USA 20201
Ph: (202) 619-0257
E-mail: http://www.os.dhhs.gov/about/opdivs/hcfa.html

Health Communications, Inc.
3201 SW 15th St.
Deerfield Beach, FL, USA 33442
Ph: (954) 360-0909
E-mail: http://www.hcibooks.com

Health Forum L.L.C.
155 N Wacker Dr., Ste. 400
Chicago, IL, USA 60606
Ph: (312) 893-6800
E-mail: http://www.healthforum.com

Health Resources Publishing
1913 Atlantic Ave., Ste. F4
PO Box 456
Manasquan, NJ, USA 8736
Ph: (732) 292-1100
E-mail: hrp@atshealthrespubs.com
URL: http://www.healthrespubs.com

Healthcare Convention & Exhibitors Association
1100 Johnson Ferry Rd., Ste. 300
Bldg. G, Ste. 500
Atlanta, GA, USA 30342
Ph: (404) 252-3663
E-mail: hcea@atskellencompany.com
URL:

Hearst Business Communications/ Electronics Group
50 Charles Lindbergh Blvd., Ste. 100
Uniondale, NY, USA 11553
Ph: (516) 227-1383
E-mail: http://www.electronicproducts.com

Hearst Magazines
300 W 57th St.
New York, NY, USA 10019-3741
Ph: (212) 649-4115
E-mail: jdeval@atshearst.com
URL: http://www.hearst.com/

Heart of America Genealogical Society
PO Box 481727
Kansas City, MO, USA 64148-1727
Ph: (816) 701-3445

Heartland Communications Group Inc.
1003 Central Ave.
PO Box 1052
Fort Dodge, IA, USA 50501
Ph: (515) 955-1600
E-mail: http://www.hlipublishing.com

Heavy Duty Representatives Association
c/o Wade & Partners
160 Symphony Way
Elgin, IL, USA 60120
Ph: (847) 760-0067
E-mail: kholliday@atswade-partners.com
URL: http://www.hdra.org/

Heldref Publications
325 Chestnut St., Ste. 800
1319 18th St. NW
Philadelphia, PA, USA 19106
Ph: (215) 625-8900
E-mail: heldref@atssubscriptionoffice.com
URL: http://www.heldref.org

Hemmings Motor News
PO Box 100
Bennington, VT, USA 5201
Ph: (802) 442-3101
E-mail: hmnmail@atshemmings.com
URL: http://www.hemmings.com

Hemophilia Ontario
45 Charles St. E, Ste. 802
Toronto, ON, CAN M4Y 1S2
Ph: (416) 972-0641
E-mail: info@atshemophilia.on.ca
URL:

Henry Holt & Company
115 W 18th St., 5th Fl.
New York, NY, USA 10011
Ph: (212) 886-9200
E-mail: info@atshholt.com
URL: http://www.henryholt.com

Henry Holt and Company
175 5th Ave.
New York, NY, USA 10010
Ph: (646) 307-5095
E-mail: http://us.macmillan.com/http://en-ryhttp://olt.aspx

The Herb Growing & Marketing Network
PO Box 245
Silver Spring, PA, USA 17575-0245
Ph: (717) 393-3295
E-mail: herbworld@atsaol.com
URL: http://www.herbworld.com

Herb Society of America Inc.
9019 Kirtland Chardon Rd.
Kirtland, OH, USA 44094
Ph: (440) 256-0514
E-mail: herbs@atsherbsociety.org
URL: http://www.herbsociety.org

Heritage Books Inc.
100 Railroad Ave., Ste. 104
Westminster, MD, USA 21157-4826
Ph: (410) 876-6101
E-mail: info@atsheritagebooks.com
URL: http://www.heritagebooks.com

Hiaring Co.
1800 Lincoln Ave.
San Rafael, CA, USA 94901-1298
Ph: (415) 453-9700
E-mail: info@atswinesandvines.com
URL: http://www.winesandvines.com

Hideaways International
767 Islington St.
Portsmouth, NH, USA 3801
Ph: (603) 430-4433
E-mail: info@atshideaways.com
URL: http://hideaways.com

HighBeam Research
c/o Cengage Learning
1 N State St., Ste. 900
Chicago, IL, USA 60602

Highway Safety Research Center
CB No. 3430
CB 3430
Chapel Hill, NC, USA 27599
Ph: (919) 962-2202

Hispanic Business Inc.
425 Pine Ave.
Santa Barbara, CA, USA 93117-3709
Ph: (805) 964-4554
E-mail: http://www.hispanicbusiness.com

Historical Trends Corp.
69A 7th Ave.
Brooklyn, NY, USA 11217
Ph: (718) 636-0788
E-mail: htcstaff@atstraditional-building.com
URL:

Hobby Publications Inc.
207 Commercial Ct.
Morganville, NJ, USA 07751-1070
Ph: (732) 536-5160
E-mail: info@atshobbymerchandiser.com
URL: http://www.hobbypub.com/

Hoke Communications Inc.
224 7th St.
Garden City, NY, USA 11530
Ph: (516) 746-6700
E-mail: frmmag@atsaol.com
URL: http://www.directmarketingmag.com/

Home Furnishings Retailer
3910 Tinsley Dr., Ste. 101
High Point, NC, USA 27265
Ph: (336) 886-6100
E-mail: info@atsnhfa.org
URL: http://www.nhfa.org/

The Home Shop Machinist
PO Box 629
Traverse City, MI, USA 49685
E-mail: http://www.homeshopmachinist.net/

Home-Based Working Moms
PO Box 500164
Austin, TX, USA 78750-0164
Ph: (281) 757-2207
E-mail: hbwm@atshbwm.com
URL:

Homeworkers Organized for More Employment
PO Box 10
Orland, ME, USA 4472
Ph: (207) 469-7961
E-mail: info@atshomecoop.net
URL:

Horizon Publishing Company L.L.C.
7412 Calumet Ave.
Hammond, IN, USA 46324
Ph: (219) 852-3200
E-mail: http://www.horizonpublishing.com/

The Horn Book Inc.
56 Roland St., Ste. 200
Boston, MA, USA 2129
Ph: (617) 628-0225
E-mail: info@atshbook.com
URL: http://www.hbook.com

Horticultural Data Processors
PO Box 489
New York, NY, USA 10028

Horticultural Research Institute
1000 Vermont Ave. NW, Ste. 300
Washington, DC, USA 20005
Ph: (202) 789-2900

Hot To Books Ltd.
3 Newtec Pl.
Magdalen Rd.
Oxford, , GBR OX4 1RE
E-mail: info@atshowtobooks.co.uk
URL: http://www.howtobooks.co.uk

Hotel & Travel Index International Edition
100 Lightning Way
Secaucus, NJ, USA 07094-3626
Ph: (201) 902-2000
E-mail: tweditorial@atsntmllc.com
URL: http://www.travelweekly.com/ManualPages.aspx?id=4834

Houghton Mifflin
222 Berkeley St.
Boston, MA, USA 2116
Ph: (617) 351-5000
E-mail: http://www.hmco.com/

Houghton Mifflin College Division
222 Berkeley St.
Boston, MA, USA 02116-3764
Ph: (617) 351-5000

Houghton Mifflin Company
222 Berkeley St.
Boston, MA, USA 02116-3764
Ph: (617) 351-5000

Houghton Mifflin Harcourt
222 Berkeley St.
Boston, MA, USA 2116
Ph: (617) 351-5000
E-mail: http://www.hmco.com

House of White Birches
306 E Parr Rd.
Berne, IN, USA 46711-1138
Ph: (260) 589-4000
E-mail: http://drgnetwork.com

Houston Chronicle
PO Box 4260
Houston, TX, USA 77210-4260
Ph: (713) 362-7171

How To Books
Spring Hill House
Spring Hill Rd.
Oxford, , GBR 0X5 1RX
Ph: (440) 1865375794
E-mail: http://www.howtobooks.co.uk

Hubbard Marketing & Publishing Ltd.
15 Wertheim Ct., Ste. 710
Richmond Hill, ON, CAN L4B 3H7
Ph: (905) 771-7333
E-mail: info@atspoolspamarketing.com
URL: http://www.poolspamarketing.com

Hudson River Sloop Clearwater Inc.
112 Little Market St.
Poughkeepsie, NY, USA 12601
Ph: (845) 454-7673
E-mail: office@atsclearwater.org
URL:

Hulbert Financial Digest
PO Box 300
Princeton, NJ, USA 8543
Ph: (866) 428-6568
E-mail: orders@atsmarketwatch.com
URL:

Human Factors and Ergonomics Society
PO Box 1369
Santa Monica, CA, USA 90406-1369
Ph: (310) 394-1811
E-mail: info@atshfes.org
URL: http://www.hfes.org/

Hunt Personnel Ltd.
1050 Wall St. W, Ste. 330
Lyndhurst, NJ, USA 07071-3615
Ph: (201) 438-8200

Hunterdon County Historical Society
114 Main St.
Flemington, NJ, USA 8822
Ph: (908) 782-1091

Huntington Press
3687 S Procyon Ave.
Las Vegas, NV, USA 89103-1907
Ph: (702) 252-0655
E-mail: customerservice@atshuntington-press.com
URL: http://www.huntingtonpress.com

Hyperion
114 5th Ave.
New York, NY, USA 10011
E-mail: http://www.hyperionbooks.com

Hyperion Books
77 W 66th St., 11th Fl.
New York, NY, USA 10023
Ph: (212) 633-4400

Hyperion Press
77 W 66th St., 11th Fl.
New York, NY, USA 10023-6298
Ph: (212) 456-0100

Hyperion Special Markets
77 W 66th St., 11th Fl.
New York, NY, USA 10023
Ph: (212) 456-0100

I

IAPMO
4755 E Philadelphia St.
Ontario, CA, USA 91761-2816
Ph: (909) 472-4100
E-mail: iapmo@atsiapmo.org
URL: http://www.iapmo.org

IAPMO
5001 E Philadelphia St.
Ontario, CA, USA 91761-2816
Ph: (909) 472-4100
E-mail: iapmo@atsiapmo.org
URL: http://www.iapmo.org

IBM Corp.
One New Orchard Rd.
Armonk, NY, USA 10504-1722
Ph: (914) 945-3836
E-mail: ews@atsus.ibm.com
URL: http://www.ibm.com

ICD Publications
45 Research Way, Ste. 106
East Setauket, NY, USA 11733
Ph: (631) 246-9300
E-mail: info@atshotelbusiness.com
URL: http://www.homeworldbusiness.com

Ice Cream Reporter
7 Hilton Terr.
Willsboro, NY, USA 12996
Ph: (518) 963-4333

Ice Skating Institute
6000 Custer Rd., Bldg. 9
Plano, TX, USA 75023
Ph: (972) 735-8800
E-mail: pubs@atsskateisi.org
URL: http://www.skateisi.org/

ICON Inc.
211 S 45th St.
Philadelphia, PA, USA 19104
Ph: (215) 349-6500
E-mail: wasterec@atsaol.com
URL:

Idaho Business Review
855 W Broad St., Ste. 103
Boise, ID, USA 83702
Ph: (208) 336-3768

Idea Group Publishing
701 E Chocolate Ave.
Hershey, PA, USA 17033-1240
Ph: (717) 533-8845
E-mail: cust@atsidea-group.com
URL: http://www.igi-pub.com/

IDEA Inc.
10455 Pacific Center Ct.
San Diego, CA, USA 92121-4339
Ph: (858) 535-8979
E-mail: contact@atsideafit.com
URL: http://www.ideafit.com

Ideal Media
90 Broad St., Ste. 402
New York, NY, USA 10004
Ph: (646) 708-7327

IGI Global
701 E Chocolate Ave., Ste. 200
Hershey, PA, USA 17033
Ph: (717) 533-8845
E-mail: http://www.igi-global.com

Illinois Landscape Contractor Association
2625 Butterfield Rd., Ste. 204-W
Oak Brook, IL, USA 60523
Ph: (630) 472-2851
E-mail: information@atsilca.net
URL: http://www.ilca.net

Illinois State Genealogical Society
PO Box 10195
Springfield, IL, USA 62791-0195
Ph: (217) 789-1968
E-mail: isgsoffice@atsa5.com
URL: http://www.rootsweb.ancestry.com/@tldilsgs/

Illuminating Engineering Society of North America
120 Wall St., 17th Fl.
New York, NY, USA 10005-4001
Ph: (212) 248-5000
E-mail: ies@atsies.org
URL: http://www.iesna.org

IMAS Publishing Inc.
810 7th Ave., 27th Fl.
New York, NY, USA 10019
Ph: (212) 378-0400
E-mail: http://www.imaspub.com

iMoneyNet Inc.
One Research Dr., Ste. 400A
Westborough, MA, USA 01581-5193
Ph: (508) 616-6600
E-mail: info@atsimoneynet.com
URL:

Impact Publications
9104 Manassas Dr., Ste. N
Manassas Park, VA, USA 20111-5211
Ph: (703) 361-7300
E-mail: http://www.impactpublications.com

Imperial College Press
Imperial College
London, , GBR SW7 2BT

Inc. Magazine
477 Madison Ave.
New York, NY, USA 10022
Ph: (212) 326-2600

Incisive Media
120 Broadway, 5th Fl.
New York, NY, USA 10271
Ph: (212) 457-9400
E-mail: customerservices@atsincisivemedia.com
URL: http://www.incisivemedia.com

Incisive Media Ltd.
120 Broadway
New York, NY, USA 10271
Ph: (212) 457-9400

Independent Book Publishers Association
627 Aviation Way
Manhattan Beach, CA, USA 90266
Ph: (310) 372-2732
E-mail: info@atspma-online.org
URL: http://www.pma-online.org

Independent Computer Consultants Association
11131 S Towne Sq., Ste. F
Saint Louis, MO, USA 63123
Ph: (314) 892-1675
E-mail: info@atsicca.org
URL:

Independent Electrical Contractors Inc.
4401 Ford Ave., Ste. 1100
Alexandria, VA, USA 22302-1432
Ph: (703) 549-7351
E-mail: info@atsieci.org
URL: http://www.ieci.org

Independent Lubricant Manufacturers Association
400 N. Columbus St., Ste. 201
Alexandria, VA, USA 22314-2259
Ph: (703) 684-5574
E-mail: ilma@atsilma.org
URL: http://www.ilma.org/publications/compoundings.cfm

Indiana Association of Plumbing Heating Cooling Contractors Inc.
9595 Whitley Dr., Ste. 208
Indianapolis, IN, USA 46240
Ph: (317) 575-9292
E-mail: http://www.iaphcc.com

Indiana Historical Society Press
450 W Ohio St.
Indianapolis, IN, USA 46202-3269
Ph: (317) 232-1882
E-mail: ihspress@atsindianahistory.org
URL: http://www.indianahistory.org/

Indiana University Press
601 N Morton St.
Bloomington, IN, USA 47404
Ph: (812) 855-7931
E-mail: http://iupress.indiana.edu

Indianapolis Business Journal Corporation
41 E Washington St., Ste. 200
Indianapolis, IN, USA 46204-3592
Ph: (317) 634-6200

Industrial Fabrics Association International
1801 County Rd. B W
Roseville, MN, USA 55113
Ph: (651) 222-2508
E-mail: generalinfo@atsifai.com
URL: http://www.ifai.com

Industrial Relations Center (IRC)
Gregg M. Sinclair Library
2425 Campus Rd.
Honolulu, HI, USA 96822
Ph: (808) 956-8132
E-mail: uhirc@atshawaii.edu
URL:

Industry Publications Inc.
3621 Hill Rd.
Parsippany, NJ, USA 7054
Ph: (973) 331-9545

Industry Shopper Publishing Inc.
1521 Church St.
Gardnerville, NV, USA 89410
Ph: (775) 782-0222
E-mail: cycle@atsmimag.com
URL: http://www.mimag.com/

Infinity Publishing
1094 New Dehaven St., Ste. 100
West Conshohocken, PA, USA 19424
Ph: (610) 941-9999
E-mail: http://www.infinitypublishing.com

Infocom Group
124 Linden St.
Oakland, CA, USA 94607
Ph: (510) 596-9300
E-mail: http://www.bulldogreporter.com/

Informa Healthcare
52 Vanderbilt Ave., 7th Fl.
New York, NY, USA 10017-3846
E-mail: healthcare.enquiries@atsinforma.com
URL: http://informahealthcare.com

Informa Publishing Group
BioTechniques
One Research Dr. Ste. 400A
PO Box 1070
Westborough, MA, USA 1581
Ph: (508) 614-1414
E-mail: http://www.informa.com

Information Age Publishing
PO Box 79049
Charlotte, NC, USA 28271-7047
Ph: (704) 752-9125
E-mail: http://www.infoagepub.com

Information Gatekeepers Inc.
1340 Soldiers Field Rd., Ste. 2
Brighton, MA, USA 2135
Ph: (617) 782-5033
E-mail: info@atsigigroup.com
URL: http://www.igigroup.com

Information Gatekeepers Inc.
320 Washington St., Ste. 302
Brighton, MA, USA 2135
Ph: (617) 782-5033
E-mail: info@atsigigroup.com
URL: http://www.igigroup.com

Information Today Inc.
143 Old Marlton Pke.
Medford, NJ, USA 08055-8750
Ph: (609) 654-6266
E-mail: custserv@atsinfotoday.com
URL: http://www.infotoday.com

infoUSA Inc.
5711 S 86th Cir.
PO Box 27347
Omaha, NE, USA 68127-0347
Ph: (402) 593-4500
E-mail: internet@atsabii.com
URL: http://www.infousa.com

InfoWorld Media Group
501 2nd St.
San Francisco, CA, USA 94107
E-mail: feedback@atsinfoworld.com
URL: http://www.infoworld.com/

Inn Room Visitors Magazine
1400 Quail St., Ste. 138
Newport Beach, CA, USA 92660
Ph: (949) 833-2550

Inside Mortgage Finance Publications Inc.
7910 Woodmont Ave., Ste. 1000
Bethesda, MD, USA 20814
Ph: (301) 951-1240
E-mail: service@atsimfpubs.com
URL: http://www.imfpubs.com/

Inside Washington Publishers
1225 S. Clark St., Ste. 1400
Ben Franklin Sta.
Arlington, VA, USA 22202
Ph: (703) 416-8500

E-mail: custsvc@atsiwpnews.com
URL: http://www.iwpnews.com

Inside Washington Publishers
1919 S Eads St., Ste. 201
Arlington, VA, USA 22202
Ph: (703) 416-8500
E-mail: custsvc@atsiwpnews.com
URL: http://www.iwpnews.com

INSIGHT Into Diversity
c/o Potomac Publishing, Inc.
225 Meramec Ave., Ste. 400
Saint Louis, MO, USA 63105
Ph: (314) 863-2900
E-mail: info@atsaarjobs.com
URL: http://www.insightintodiversity.com/

Institute for Supply Management
PO Box 22160
Tempe, AZ, USA 85285-2160
Ph: (480) 752-6276
E-mail: http://www.napm.org

Institute of Business Appraisers
6950 Cypress Rd.
PO Box 17410
Plantation, FL, USA 33317-2370
Ph: (954) 584-1144
E-mail: hqiba@atsgo-iba.org
URL: http://www.go-iba.org

Institute of Electrical and Electronics Engineers Inc.
3 Park Ave., 17th Fl.
New York, NY, USA 10016-5997
Ph: (212) 419-7900
E-mail: http://www.comsoc.org/pubs/commag/index.html

Institute of Governmental Studies
109 Moses Hall No. 2370
Berkeley, CA, USA 94720-2370
Ph: (510) 642-6723
E-mail: igspress@atsuclink4.berkeley.edu
URL:

Institute of Industrial Engineers
3577 Pkwy. Ln., Ste. 200
Norcross, GA, USA 30092
Ph: (770) 449-0460
E-mail: cs@atsiienet.org
URL: http://www.iienet.org/

Institute of Management & Administration
1 Washington Park, Ste. 1300
Newark, NJ, USA 07102-3130
Ph: (973) 718-4700

Institute of Museum & Library Services
1800 M St. NW, 9th Fl.
Washington, DC, USA 20036-5802
Ph: (202) 653-4657
E-mail: imlsinfo@atsimls.gov
URL: http://www.imls.gov

Institute of Public Administration of Canada
1075 Bay St., Ste. 401
Toronto, ON, CAN M5S 2B1
Ph: (416) 924-8787
E-mail: http://www.ipac.ca

Institute of Real Estate Management
430 N Michigan Ave.
Chicago, IL, USA 60611
E-mail: custserv@atsirem.org
URL: http://www.irem.org

Institute of Scrap Recycling Industries Inc.
1615 L St. NW, Ste. 600
Washington, DC, USA 20036-5610
Ph: (202) 662-8500
E-mail: isri@atsisri.org
URL: http://www.isri.org

Institutional Investor
225 Park Ave. S, 8th Fl.
New York, NY, USA 10003-1604
Ph: (212) 224-3300
E-mail: http://www.institutionalinvestor.com/

Institutional Real Estate Inc.
2274 Camino Ramon
San Ramon, CA, USA 94583
Ph: (925) 244-0500
E-mail: http://www.irei.com

Instrumentalist Co.
200 Northfield Rd.
Northfield, IL, USA 60093
Ph: (847) 446-5000
E-mail: advertising@atstheinstrumentalist.com
URL: http://www.instrumentalistmagazine.com

Insurance Forum Inc.
PO Box 245
Ellettsville, IN, USA 47429-0245
Ph: (812) 876-6502

Insurance Institute of Southern Alberta
833 4th Ave. SW, Ste. 1110
Calgary, AB, CAN T2P 3T5
Ph: (403) 266-3427
E-mail: iisamail@atsinsuranceintitute.ca
URL:

Insurance Marketing and Management Services
17280 Newhope St., Ste. 15
Fountain Valley, CA, USA 92708
Ph: (800) 753-4467
E-mail: sales@atsimms.com
URL: http://www.imms.com/

Integrated Research Services Inc.
66 Club Rd., Ste. 370
Eugene, OR, USA 97401
Ph: (541) 683-9278

International Advertising Association
275 Madison Ave., Ste. 2102
New York, NY, USA 10016
Ph: (212) 557-1133
E-mail: membership@atsiaaglobal.org
URL: http://www.iaaglobal.org

International Association of Assembly Managers
635 Fritz Dr., Ste. 100
Coppell, TX, USA 75019-4442
Ph: (972) 906-7441
E-mail: mike.meyers@atsiaam.org
URL: http://www.iaam.org

International Association of Electrical Inspectors (IAEI)
901 Waterfall Way, Ste. 602
Richardson, TX, USA 75083
Ph: (972) 235-1455
E-mail: iaei@atsiaei.org
URL: http://www.iaei.org

International Association of Exhibitions and Events
12700 Park Central Dr., Ste. 308
PO Box 802425
Dallas, TX, USA 75251-1313
Ph: (972) 458-8002
E-mail: info@atsiaee.com
URL: http://www.iaee.com

International Association of Financial Crimes Investigators
1020 Suncast Ln., Ste. 102
El Dorado Hills, CA, USA 95762
Ph: (916) 939-5000
E-mail: admin@atsiafci.org
URL: http://www.iafci.org

International Bottled Water Association
1700 Diagonal Rd., Ste. 650
Alexandria, VA, USA 22314
Ph: (703) 683-5213
E-mail: ibwainfo@atsbottledwater.org
URL: http://www.bottledwater.org

International Brotherhood of Magicians
13 Point West Blvd.
Saint Charles, MO, USA 63301-4431
Ph: (636) 724-2400
E-mail: office@atsmagician.org
URL: http://www.magician.org/

International Cinematographers Guild
7755 Sunset Blvd.
Los Angeles, CA, USA 90046
Ph: (323) 876-0160
E-mail: http://www.cameraguild.com

International City/County Management Association
777 N Capitol St. NE, Ste. 500
Washington, DC, USA 20002-4201
Ph: (202) 289-4262
E-mail: customerservices@atsicma.org
URL: http://www.icma.org

International Code Council
5360 Workman Mill Rd.
Whittier, CA, USA 90601
Ph: (562) 699-0543
E-mail: http://www.icbo.org

International Code Council (Washington, District of Columbia)
500 New Jersey Ave., NW, 6th Fl.
Washington, DC, USA 20001-2070
Ph: (202) 370-1800
E-mail: members@atsiccsafe.org
URL: http://www.iccsafe.org

International Commission for the Prevention of Alcoholism and Drug Dependency
12501 Old Columbia Pke.
Silver Spring, MD, USA 20904
Ph: (301) 680-6719
E-mail: landlessp@atsgc.adventist.org
URL:

International Council on Hotel, Restaurant & Institutional Education
2810 N Parham Rd., Ste. 230
Richmond, VA, USA 23294
Ph: (804) 346-4800
E-mail: publications@atschrie.org
URL: http://www.chrie.org

International Dairy-Deli-Bakery Association
636 Science Dr.
PO Box 5528
Madison, WI, USA 53711
Ph: (608) 238-7908
E-mail: iddba@atsiddba.org
URL:

International Data Corp.
5 Speen St.
Framingham, MA, USA 1701
Ph: (508) 872-8200

International Directory of Importers
1741 Kekamek NW
Poulsbo, WA, USA 98370
Ph: (360) 779-1511
E-mail: helpdesk@atsexport-leads.com
URL: http://www.export-leads.com

International Economic Development Council
734 15th St. NW, Ste. 900
Washington, DC, USA 20005
Ph: (202) 223-7800
E-mail: kbielen@atsiedconline.org
URL: http://www.iedconline.org

International Federation of Accountants
545 5th Ave., 14th Fl.
New York, NY, USA 10017
Ph: (212) 286-9344
E-mail: mariahermann@atsifac.org
URL:

International Formalwear Association
401 N Michigan Ave.
Chicago, IL, USA 60611
Ph: (312) 321-5139
E-mail: admin@atsformaltimes.com
URL:

International Foundation of Employee Benefit Plans
18700 W Bluemound Rd.
PO Box 69
Brookfield, WI, USA 53008-0069
Ph: (262) 786-6700
E-mail: books@atsifebp.org
URL: http://www.ifebp.org

International Franchise Association
1501 K St. NW, Ste. 350
Washington, DC, USA 20005
Ph: (202) 628-8000
E-mail: ifa@atsfranchise.org
URL: http://www.franchise.org

International Graphoanalysis Society
842 5th Ave.
New Kensington, PA, USA 15068
Ph: (724) 472-9701
E-mail: http://www.igas.com

International Hearing Society
16880 Middlebelt Rd., Ste. 4
Livonia, MI, USA 48154
Ph: (734) 522-7200
E-mail: pwilson@atsihsinfo.org
URL: http://www.ihsinfo.org

International Home Furnishings Center
210 E Commerce Ave.
PO Box 828
High Point, NC, USA 27260-5238
Ph: (336) 888-3700
E-mail: marketing@atsihfc.com
URL: http://www.ihfc.com

International Informatics Institute
405 4th St.
Brooklyn, NY, USA 11215
Ph: (718) 499-1884

International Labour Office
1828 L St. NW, Ste. 600
Washington, DC, USA 20036-5121
Ph: (202) 653-7652

International Life Sciences Institute
1 Thomas Cir., 9th Fl.
Washington, DC, USA 20005-5802
Ph: (202) 659-0074
E-mail: ilsi@atsilsi.org
URL: http://www.ilsi.org

International Midas Dealers Association
14 W 3rd St., Ste. 200
Kansas City, MO, USA 64105
Ph: (816) 472-6632

International Personnel Management Association
1617 Duke St.
Alexandria, VA, USA 22314
Ph: (703) 549-7100
E-mail: publications@atsipma-hr.org
URL: http://www.ipma-hr.org/

International Risk Management Institute Inc.
12222 Merit Dr., Ste. 1450
Dallas, TX, USA 75251-2276
Ph: (972) 960-7693
E-mail: info@atsirmi.com
URL: http://www.irmi.com

International Schizophrenia Foundation
16 Florence Ave.
Toronto, ON, CAN M2N 1E9
Ph: (416) 733-2117
E-mail: centre@atsorthomed.org
URL: http://www.orthomed.org/

International Scientific Communications Inc.
30 Controls Dr.
Shelton, CT, USA 06484-0870
Ph: (203) 926-9300
E-mail: iscpubs@atsiscpubs.com
URL: http://www.iscpubs.com

International Self-Counsel Press, Limited
1481 Charlotte Rd.
North Vancouver, BC, CAN V7J 1H1
Ph: (604) 986-3366

International Society for Technology in Education
1710 Rhode Island Ave. NW, Ste. 900
Washington, DC, USA 20036
Ph: (202) 861-7777
E-mail: iste@atsiste.org
URL: http://www.iste.org

International Society for Terrain-Vehicle Systems
US Army Cold Reg. Researchlab
Applied Research Division
Hanover, NH, USA 03755-1290
Ph: (603) 646-4362
E-mail: rliston@atscrrel.usace.army.mil
URL: http://www.istvs.org/

International Society for Vehicle Preservation
PO Box 50046
Tucson, AZ, USA 85703-1046
Ph: (520) 622-2201
E-mail: isvp@atsearthlink.net
URL: http://www.aztexcorp.com/root/isvp.html

International Society of Certified Employee Benefit Specialists
18700 W Bluemound Rd.
PO Box 209
Brookfield, WI, USA 53008-0209

Ph: (262) 786-8771
E-mail: iscebs@atsiscebs.org
URL: http://www.iscebs.org

International Specialized Book Services, Inc.
5602 NE Hassalo St.
Portland, OR, USA 97213-3640

International Textile & Apparel Association
c/o Nancy Rutherford, PhD, Exec. Dir.
PO Box 70687
Knoxville, TN, USA 37938-0687
Ph: (865) 992-1535
E-mail: info@atsitaaonline.org
URL: http://www.itaaonline.org

International Trumpet Guild (ITG)
241 E Main St., No. 247
Westfield, MA, USA 01086-1633
Ph: (413) 568-1239
E-mail: info@atstrumpetguild.org
URL:

International Warehouse Logistics Association
2800 S River Rd., Ste. 260
Des Plaines, IL, USA 60018
Ph: (847) 813-4699
E-mail: email@atsiwla.com
URL: http://www.iwla.com

International Wealth Success, Inc. IWS
PO Box 186
Merrick, NY, USA 11566-0186
Ph: (516) 766-5850
E-mail: admin@atsiwsmoney.com
URL: http://www.iwsmoney.com

International Wealth Success, Incorporated
24 Canterbury Rd.
Rockville Centre, NY, USA 11570-1310
Ph: (516) 766-5850

International Women's Writing Guild
PO Box 810, Gracie Sta.
New York, NY, USA 10028-0082
Ph: (212) 737-7536
E-mail: dirhahn@atsaol.com
URL: http://www.iwwg.org

International Wood Products Association
4214 King St.
Alexandria, VA, USA 22302
Ph: (703) 820-6696
E-mail: info@atsiwpawood.org
URL: http://www.iwpawood.org

Internet/Media Strategies Inc.
Old City Hall
625 Commerce St., Ste. 330
Tacoma, WA, USA 98402

The Intrepid Traveler
371 Walden Green Rd., Box 531
Branford, CT, USA 6405

The Intrepid Traveler
PO Box 531
Branford, CT, USA 6405
Ph: (203) 469-0214
E-mail: admin@atsintrepidtraveler.com
URL: http://www.intrepidtraveler.com

Investment Adviser Association
1050 17th St. NW, Ste. 725
Washington, DC, USA 20036-5514
Ph: (202) 293-4222
E-mail: info@atsinvestmentadviser.org
URL: http://www.investmentadviser.org

Investment Advisor Group
33-41 Newark St., 2nd Fl.
Hoboken, NJ, USA 7030
Ph: (732) 389-8700
E-mail: http://www.advisorone.com

Investment Div.
409 3rd St. SW
Washington, DC, USA 20416
Ph: (202) 205-9984
E-mail: http://www.sba.gov/

Investment Media Inc.
909 3rd Ave., 27th Fl.
New York, NY, USA 10022
Ph: (212) 370-3700
E-mail: info@atsglobalinv.com
URL: http://www.globalinv.com

Investment Weekly News
2727 Paces Ferry Rd. SE, Ste. 2-440
Atlanta, GA, USA 30339
Ph: (770) 435-8286
E-mail: phil@atsnewsrx.com
URL: http://verticalnews.com/

Investor's Business Daily
12655 Beatrice St.
Los Angeles, CA, USA 90066
Ph: (310) 448-6747

Iowa Grocery Industry Association
2540 106th St., Ste. 102
Des Moines, IA, USA 50322
Ph: (515) 270-2628
E-mail: info@atsiowagrocers.com
URL: http://www.iowagrocers.com

Irish Genealogical Foundation
Dept. HPA
PO Box 7575
Kansas City, MO, USA 64116
Ph: (816) 454-2410
E-mail: http://www.irishroots.com

Irving Levin Associates Inc.
268 1/2 Main Ave.
Norwalk, CT, USA 6851
Ph: (203) 846-6800
E-mail: general@atslevinassociates.com
URL: http://www.levinassociates.com

Island Press
1718 Connecticut Ave. NW, Ste. 300
Washington, DC, USA 20009-1148
Ph: (202) 232-7933
E-mail: info@atsislandpress.org
URL: http://www.islandpress.org

Islands Publishing Co.
6267 Carpinteria Ave., Ste. 200
Carpinteria, CA, USA 93013
Ph: (805) 745-7100
E-mail: info@atsresortsgreathotels.com
URL:

ISSA
7373 N Lincoln Ave.
Lincolnwood, IL, USA 60712-1799
Ph: (847) 982-0800
E-mail: info@atsissa.com
URL: http://www.issa.com

IT Financial Management Association
PO Box 30188
Santa Barbara, CA, USA 93130
Ph: (805) 687-7390
E-mail: info@atsitfma.com
URL: http://www.isfma.com

Italy-America Chamber of Commerce Inc.
730 5th Ave., Ste. 600
New York, NY, USA 10019
Ph: (212) 459-0044
E-mail: info@atsitalchamber.org
URL: http://www.italchamber.org

iUniverse
1663 Liberty Dr.
Bloomington, IN, USA 47403
E-mail: http://www.iuniverse.com

iUniverse, Incorporated
2021 Pine Lake Rd., Ste. 100
Lincoln, NE, USA 68512
Ph: (402) 323-7800

Ivan Levison & Associates
14 Los Cerros Dr.
Greenbrae, CA, USA 94904
Ph: (415) 461-0672

Ivy Sea, Inc.
3701 Sacramento St., No. 199
San Francisco, CA, USA 94118-1705
Ph: (415) 752-6317
E-mail: info@atsivysea.com
URL: http://www.ivysea.com

J

J.R. O'Dwyer Company Inc.
271 Madison Ave., No. 600
New York, NY, USA 10016
Ph: (212) 679-2471

E-mail: http://www.odwyerpr.com

Jack Erickson
PO Box 2184
Reston, VA, USA 20195-0184
E-mail: http://www.realbeer.com/redbrick-press/jack.html

James H. Schmidt
PO Box 1688
Greenwich, CT, USA 6836
Ph: (203) 629-3503
E-mail: contact@atstimerdigest.com
URL:

James Lorimer & Company Ltd.
35 Britain St.
Toronto, ON, CAN M5A 1R7

James R. Tolliver
, , USA

Jason Kelly
11032 Moorpark St., No. 17
North Hollywood, CA, USA 91602

Jay Conrad Levinson
PO Box 1336
Mill Valley, CA, USA 94942
Ph: (415) 381-8361

Jenkins Group Inc.
1129 Woodmere Ave., Ste. B
Traverse City, MI, USA 49686
Ph: (231) 933-0445
E-mail: publish@atsjenkinsgroupinc.com
URL: http://www.jenkinsgroupinc.com/

Jet Airtransport Exchange Inc.
52 W Main St.
Milford, CT, USA 06460-3310
Ph: (203) 301-0255
E-mail: editor@atsjaxfax.com
URL: http://www.jaxfaxmagazine.com

JL Com Publishing Company L.L.C.
26 Hawthorn Dr.
Succasunna, NJ, USA 07876-2112
Ph: (973) 252-7552
E-mail: lawpublish@atsaol.com
URL:

JMS Publishing L.L.C.
323 Lincoln St.
Roseville, CA, USA 95678-2229
Ph: (916) 784-3880
E-mail: http://www.bamagazine.com

Joan Stewart
3434 County KK
Port Washington, WI, USA 53074
Ph: (262) 284-7451
E-mail: jstewart@atspublicityhound.com
URL:

John Baer's Sons
PO Box 328
Lancaster, PA, USA 17608
Ph: (717) 392-0733
E-mail: info@atsjohnbaer.com
URL:

John Wiley & Sons Inc.
111 River St.
Hoboken, NJ, USA 07030-5773
Ph: (201) 748-6000
E-mail: info@atswiley.com
URL: http://www.wiley.com

John Wiley & Sons Inc.
350 Main St., Commerce Pl.
Malden, MA, USA 02148-5089
Ph: (781) 388-8200
E-mail: http://as.wiley.com/WileyCDA

John Wiley & Sons, Inc.
10475 Crosspoint Blvd.
Indianapolis, IN, USA 46256
Ph: (877) 762-2974
E-mail: consumers@atswiley.com
URL: http://www.wiley.com

John Wiley and Sons Canada Ltd.
22 Worcester Rd.
Etobicoke, ON, CAN M9W 1L1
E-mail: info@atswiley.com
URL: http://www.wiley.com

John Wiley and Sons, Inc.
Winthrop Group
111 River St.
Hoboken, NJ, USA 7030
Ph: (201) 748-6000

The Johns Hopkins University Press
2715 N Charles St.
Baltimore, MD, USA 21218-4363
Ph: (410) 516-6900
E-mail: webmaster@atsjhupress.jhu.edu
URL: http://www.press.jhu.edu

The Joint Commission Journal on Quality Improvement
1 Renaissance Blvd.
Oakbrook Terrace, IL, USA 60181
Ph: (630) 792-5453
E-mail: sberman@atsjcrinc.com
URL: http://www.jcrinc.com

Jola Publications
2933 N 2nd St.
Minneapolis, MN, USA 55411
Ph: (612) 529-5001
E-mail: medical@atsjolapub.com
URL: http://www.jolapub.com

Jones Publishing Inc.
N7450 Annstad Rd.
PO Box 5000
Iola, WI, USA 54945-8229
Ph: (715) 445-5000
E-mail: jonespub@atsjonespublishing.com
URL: http://www.jonespublishing.com

Jordans Publishing Limited
21 St. Thomas St.
Bristol, , GBR BS1 6JS

Joseph Schlussel
580 5th Ave., Ste. 806
New York, NY, USA 10036
Ph: (212) 575-0444
E-mail: diamond58@atsaol.com
URL:

Jossey Bass
c/o John Wiley and Sons, Inc.
111 River St.
Hoboken, NJ, USA 7030
Ph: (201) 748-6000

Jossey-Bass
111 River St.
Hoboken, NJ, USA 07030-5774
Ph: (201) 748-6000
E-mail: info@atswiley.com
URL: http://www.josseybass.com

Jossey-Bass
989 Market St.
San Francisco, CA, USA 94103
Ph: (415) 433-1740
E-mail: jbsubs@atsjbp.com
URL: http://www.joseybass.com

Jossey-Bass Publishers
989 Market St.
San Francisco, CA, USA 94103-1741
Ph: (415) 433-1740
E-mail: jbsubs@atsjbp.com
URL: http://www.josseybass.com

Journal of the Canadian Economics Association
CP 35006
1221 Fleury E
Montreal, QC, CAN H2C 3K4
Ph: (646) 257-5906

Journal Publications Inc.
4343 Sonoma Hwy.
Santa Rosa, CA, USA 95409
Ph: (707) 566-9734
E-mail: ewalsh@atsfbworld.com
URL: http://www.fbworld.com

Journal Publishing Inc.
PO Box 909
Tupelo, MS, USA 38802
Ph: (662) 678-1536

Journal Register Ohio
7085 Mentor Ave.
Willoughby, OH, USA 44094
Ph: (440) 951-0000

Journal Star
1 News Plaza
Peoria, IL, USA 61643
Ph: (309) 686-3000

Journeywoman
50 Prince Arthur Ave.
Toronto, ON, CAN M5R 1B5
Ph: (416) 929-7654
E-mail: editor@atsjourneywoman.com
URL: http://www.journeywoman.com

Junior Achievement Inc.
One Education Way
Colorado Springs, CO, USA 80906-4449
Ph: (719) 540-8000
E-mail: newmedia@atsja.org
URL:

K

KAL Publications Inc.
559 S Harbor Blvd., Ste. A
Anaheim, CA, USA 92805-4525
Ph: (714) 563-9300
E-mail: http://www.kalpub.com

Kalmbach Publishing Co.
21027 Crossroads Cir.
PO Box 1612
Waukesha, WI, USA 53187-1612
Ph: (262) 796-8776
E-mail: customerservice@atskalmbach.com
URL: http://www.kalmbach.com

Kane Communications Inc.
10 E Athens Ave., Ste. 208
Ardmore, PA, USA 19003
Ph: (610) 645-6940
E-mail: sounovmag@atsaol.com
URL: http://www.kanec.com

Kaplan Books
1230 Avenue of the Americas, 1st Fl.
New York, NY, USA 10020
Ph: (856) 824-2289

Kaplan Publishing
30 N Wacker Dr., No. 2500
Chicago, IL, USA 60606-7481
Ph: (312) 836-4400

Kaplan Publishing
1 Liberty Plz., 24th Fl.
New York, NY, USA 10006
E-mail: http://www.kaplanpublishing.com

Kaplan Publishing
1230 Avenue of the Americas
New York, NY, USA 10020
Ph: (212) 632-4973
E-mail: kaplanpubsales@atskaplan.com
URL: http://www.kaplanpublishing.com

Katydid Press
4736 Meadowview Blvd.
Sarasota, FL, USA 34233
Ph: (941) 924-4142

Kazak Communications
16 Ottawa St.
Toronto, ON, CAN M4T 2B6

Keith Key
2451 Cumberland Pkwy., Ste. 3374
Atlanta, GA, USA 30339
Ph: (404) 419-6701
E-mail: info@atsfertiltyweekly.com
URL:

Kennedy Information
1 Phoenix Mill Ln., 3rd Fl.
Peterborough, NH, USA 3458
Ph: (603) 924-1006
E-mail: bookstore@atskennedyinfo.com
URL: http://www.kennedyinfo.com

Kensington Publishing Corporation
850 3rd Ave.
New York, NY, USA 10022
E-mail: http://www.kensingtonbooks.com

The Kerner Group Inc.
1319 Howard Ln.
Palmer, PA, USA 18045-2153

Key Communications Inc.
385 Garrisonville Rd.
PO Box 569
Stafford, VA, USA 22554
Ph: (540) 720-5584
E-mail: info@atsglass.com
URL: http://www.key-com.com

Kiplinger Books and Tapes
1729 H St. NW
Washington, DC, USA 20006
Ph: (202) 887-6680
E-mail: books@atskiplinger.com
URL: http://www.kiplinger.com

Kluwer Academic/Plenum Publishing Corp.
101 Philip Dr.
Norwell, MA, USA 2061
Ph: (781) 871-6600
E-mail: kluwer@atswkap.com
URL: http://www.springeronline.com

Knight-Ridder/Tribune Business News
600 S Tryon St.
Charlotte, NC, USA 28202-1880
Ph: (704) 358-5000

Knopf Publishing/Random House
1745 Broadway
New York, NY, USA 10019
Ph: (212) 782-9000
E-mail: customerservice@atsrandom-house.com
URL:

Knowledge Technology Inc.
PO Box 30130
Phoenix, AZ, USA 85046-0130
Ph: (602) 971-1869
E-mail: info@atspcai.com
URL: http://www.pcai.com

Knoxville News Sentinel
2332 News Sentinel Dr.
Knoxville, TN, USA 37921
Ph: (865) 521-8181

Kodaly Society of Canada
198 Davenport Rd.
Toronto, ON, CAN M5R 1J2
E-mail: http://www.kodalysocietyof-canada.ca

Kogan Page, Limited
120 Pentonville Rd.
London, , GBR N1 9JN
E-mail: kpinfo@atskogan-page.co.uk
URL: http://www.kogan-page.co.uk/

Kogan Page, Ltd.
525 S 4th St., No. 241
Philadelphia, PA, USA 19147
Ph: (215) 928-9112
E-mail: info@atskoganpage.com
URL: http://www.koganpageusa.com

Kona Communications Inc.
707 Lake Cook Rd.
Deerfield, IL, USA 60015
Ph: (847) 498-3180
E-mail: truckbooks@atskonacommunica-tions.com
URL: http://www.truckpartsandservice.com/

Kon-Lin Research & Analysis Corp.
5 Water Rd.
Rocky Point, NY, USA 11778
Ph: (631) 744-8536

Korean Chamber of Commerce & Industry in USA Inc.
460 Park Ave., Ste. 410
New York, NY, USA 10022
Ph: (212) 644-0140
E-mail: webmaster@atskocham.org
URL: http://www.kocham.org

Kostuch Publications Ltd.
101-23 Lesmil Rd., Ste. 101
Toronto, ON, CAN M3B 3P6
Ph: (416) 447-0888
E-mail: http://www.foodserviceworld.com/

Krause Publications Inc.
700 E State St.
Iola, WI, USA 54945-9642
Ph: (715) 445-2214
E-mail: http://www.krause.com

L

L.C. Clark Publishing Company Inc.
840 U.S. Hwy., 1 Ste. 330
North Palm Beach, FL, USA 33408
Ph: (561) 627-3393

E-mail: info@atsdwconline.com
URL: http://www.dwconline.com/

L/L Research
PO Box 5195
Louisville, KY, USA 40255-0195
Ph: (502) 245-6495

La Crosse Tribune
401 3rd St. N
La Crosse, WI, USA 54601
Ph: (608) 782-9710
E-mail: http://www.lacrossetribune.com/

La Leche League International Inc.
957 N Plum Grove Rd.
PO Box 4079
Schaumburg, IL, USA 60173
Ph: (847) 519-7730
E-mail: fdassociate@atsllli.org
URL: http://www.llli.org

Lafayette Instrument Co.
3700 Sagamore Pkwy. N
PO Box 5729
Lafayette, IN, USA 47904
Ph: (765) 423-1505
E-mail: lic@atslicmef.com
URL:

Landscape Communications Inc.
14771 Plaza Dr., Ste. M
Tustin, CA, USA 92780
Ph: (714) 979-5276
E-mail: http://www.landscapeonline.com

Landscape Ontario Horticultural Trades Association
7856 5th Line S
Milton, ON, CAN L9T 2X8
Ph: (905) 875-1805
E-mail: stevemoyer@atslandscapeontario.com
URL: http://www.landscapeontario.com/

Lapidary Journal
300 Chesterfield Pky., Ste. 100
Malvern, PA, USA 19355
Ph: (610) 232-5700
E-mail: ljeditorial@atsinterweave.com
URL: http://www.jewelryartistmagazine.com/

Lark Books
67 Broadway St.
Asheville, NC, USA 28801-2919

Las Vegas Insider
PO Box 1185
Chino Valley, AZ, USA 86323
E-mail: amchb@atsprimnet.com
URL:

Latest Scoop Publishing
PO Box 7477
Loveland, CO, USA 80537-0477
Ph: (970) 686-6155
E-mail: SCOOPautovents@atsaol.com
URL:

Laughing Bear Press
PO Box 613322
Dallas, TX, USA 75261-3322
E-mail: editor@atslaughingbear.com
URL: http://www.laughingbear.com

Lawrence Oakly
5 Savage Ct.
Bluffton, SC, USA 29910-4430
Ph: (843) 705-5591
E-mail: up415@atsaol.com
URL:

Lawrence Ragan Communications Inc.
111 E. Wacker Dr., Ste. 500
Chicago, IL, USA 60601
Ph: (312) 960-4100
E-mail: cservice@atsragan.com
URL: http://www.ragan.com

Lawrence/Erlbaum Associates
10 Industrial Ave.
Mahwah, NJ, USA 07430-2262
Ph: (201) 258-2200

Le Chef D.S.A. Inc.
252, Rte. St. Andre
Saint-Etienne-de-Lauzon, QC, CAN G6J 1E8
Ph: (418) 831-5317
E-mail: lechef@atsmagazinelechef.com
URL: http://www.magazinelechef.com/FR/NousJoindre/index.html

Learning House Publishing, Inc.
110 1st Ave.
Charlestown, MA, USA 2629
E-mail: info@atspracticalactionlearning.com
URL: http://www.practicalactionlearning.com

Lebhar-Friedman Inc.
425 Park Ave.
New York, NY, USA 10022
Ph: (212) 756-5000
E-mail: info@atslf.com
URL:

Lee Enterprises
501 Commercial St.
Waterloo, IA, USA 50704
Ph: (319) 291-1400

Lee Enterprises Inc.
201 N Harrison St.
Davenport, IA, USA 52801-1932
Ph: (563) 383-2100
E-mail: information@atslee.net
URL: http://www.lee.net

Leisure Publications Inc.
4160 Wilshire Blvd.
Los Angeles, CA, USA 90010-3500
Ph: (323) 964-4800

Lessons Professional Publishing
Fitzroy House
11 Chenies St.
London, , GBR WC1E 7EY
Ph: (440) 2076364777

Lewis and Renn Associates
4860 E Main St., No. A128
Mesa, AZ, USA 85205
Ph: (231) 275-7287

Lexington Books
4501 Forbes Blvd., Ste. 200
Lanham, MD, USA 20706
Ph: (301) 459-3366

LexisNexis
1018 W. 9th Ave., 3rd Fl.
King of Prussia, PA, USA 19406-1225
Ph: (610) 768-7800
E-mail: info@atsmealeys.com
URL: http://www.lexisnexis.com/mealeys/

LexisNexis Group
9443 Springboro Pike
Dayton, OH, USA 45342
E-mail: customer.support@atslexisnexis.com
URL: http://www.lexisnexis.com

LFB Scholarly Publishing LLC
24 W 27th St., No. 1108
New York, NY, USA 10010
Ph: (212) 337-3487

Lightner Publishing Corp.
1006 S Michigan Ave.
Chicago, IL, USA 60605

LIMS/Letter
PO Box 935
Kenwood, CA, USA 95452
Ph: (707) 526-6885
E-mail: webmaster@atslimsletter.com
URL:

Linn's Stamp News
911 Vandemark Rd.
PO Box 926
Sidney, OH, USA 45365-0926
Ph: (937) 498-0801
E-mail: cuserv@atsamospress.com
URL: http://www.linns.com

Lippincott Williams & Wilkins
16522 Hunters Green Pky.
Hagerstown, MD, USA 21740
Ph: (301) 233-2300
E-mail: orders@atslww.com
URL: http://www.lww.com/

Lippincott Williams & Wilkins
PO Box 1620
Hagerstown, MD, USA 21741
Ph: (215) 521-8300
E-mail: lww@atslww.com
URL: http://www.lww.com/

Lippincott Williams & Wilkins
530 Walnut St.
Philadelphia, PA, USA 19106-3603
Ph: (215) 521-8300
E-mail: customerservice@atslww.com
URL: http://www.lww.com

Lippincott Williams & Wilkins Vision-Care Group
323 Norristown Rd., Ste. 200
Ambler, PA, USA 19002
Ph: (215) 646-8700
E-mail: http://www.boucher1.com

Little Brown & Company
1271 Avenue of the Americas
New York, NY, USA 10020
Ph: (212) 522-8700
E-mail: http://www.twbookmark.com

Little Mountain Corp.
PO Box 178
Westpoint, TN, USA 38486-0178
Ph: (931) 766-6066
E-mail: moneychanger@atscompuserve.com
URL:

Little, Brown and Company
237 Park Ave.
New York, NY, USA 10017
E-mail: http://www.HachetteBookGroup.com

LLM Publications Inc.
8201 SE 17th Ave.
Portland, OR, USA 97202
Ph: (503) 445-2220
E-mail: erin@atsllm.com
URL: http://www.llm.com

Lockwood Trade Publications Inc.
26 Broadway, Fl. 9M
New York, NY, USA 10004-1703
Ph: (212) 391-2060
E-mail: sales@atslockwoodpublications.com
URL: http://www.lockwoodpublications.com

Loeb Associates Inc.
PO Box 1155
New York, NY, USA 10018
E-mail: loeb@atsidt.net
URL:

Lovejoy Corp.
PO Box 1442
Palmer Sq.
Princeton, NJ, USA 8542
Ph: (609) 989-9484

LRP Publications
747 Dresher Rd., Ste. 500
PO Box 980
Horsham, PA, USA 19044-0980
Ph: (215) 784-0860
E-mail: custserve@atslrp.com
URL: http://www.lrp.com

LRP Publications
360 Hiatt Dr.
Palm Beach Gardens, FL, USA 33418
Ph: (561) 622-6529
E-mail: custserve@atslrp.com
URL: http://www.lrp.com

LRP Publications
PO Box 24668
West Palm Beach, FL, USA 33416-4668
Ph: (800) 341-7874
E-mail: custserve@atslrp.com
URL: http://www.lrp.com

Luby Publishing
122 S Michigan Ave., Ste. 1506
Chicago, IL, USA 60604
Ph: (312) 341-1110
E-mail: email@atslubypublishing.com
URL: http://www.lubypublishing.com

Luce Press Clippings
42 S. Ctr. St.
Mesa, AZ, USA 85210
Ph: (480) 834-4884
E-mail: clip@atslucepress.com
URL:

Lucis Trust
120 Wall St., 24th Fl.
New York, NY, USA 10005
Ph: (212) 292-0707
E-mail: newyork@atslucistrust.org
URL:

Lulu.com
860 Aviation Pkwy., Ste. 300
Morrisville, NC, USA 27560

M

M. Evans & Company Inc.
4501 Forbes Blvd., Ste. 200
Lanham, MD, USA 20706-4346
Ph: (301) 459-3366
E-mail: custserv@atsnbnbooks.com
URL: http://www.rlpgtrade.com

M. Evans and Company, Incorporated
216 E 49th St.
New York, NY, USA 10017
Ph: (212) 688-2810

M. Shanken Communications Inc.
387 Park Ave. S
New York, NY, USA 10016
Ph: (212) 684-4224
E-mail: caonline@atsmshanken.com
URL: http://www.cigaraficionado.com

M.E. Sharpe Inc.
80 Business Park Dr.
Armonk, NY, USA 10504
Ph: (914) 273-1800
E-mail: info@atsmesharpe.com
URL: http://www.mesharpe.com

Mac Publishing
501 2nd St.
San Francisco, CA, USA 94107
Ph: (415) 243-0500

Macfadden Communications Group L.L.C.
333 7th Ave., 11th Fl.
New York, NY, USA 10001
Ph: (212) 979-4800
E-mail: http://www.macfad.com/

Machinery Dealers National Association
315 S Patrick St.
Alexandria, VA, USA 22314-3501
Ph: (703) 836-9300
E-mail: office@atsmdna.org
URL: http://www.mdna.org

Macmillan Publishers Limited
2 Penn Plz., 5th Fl.
New York, NY, USA 10121-2298
Ph: (212) 904-3834
E-mail: international_school@atsmcgraw-hill.com
URL: http://www.mmhschool.com

Macmillan Reference USA
12 Lunar Dr.
Woodbridge, CT, USA 6525
Ph: (203) 397-2600
E-mail: gale.galeord@atscengage.com
URL: http://www.gale.cengage.com/macmillan

Macon Telegraph
120 Broadway
Macon, GA, USA 31201
Ph: (478) 744-4200

Magazines/Creative Inc.
31 Merrick Ave.
Merrick, NY, USA 11566
Ph: (516) 378-0800
E-mail: info@atscreativemag.com
URL: http://www.creativemag.com/homepage.html

Magill's Choice
2 University Plz., Ste. 121
Hackensack, NJ, USA 7601
Ph: (201) 968-9899
E-mail: csr@atssalempress.com
URL: http://www.salempress.com

Maher Publications Inc.
102 N Haven Rd.
Elmhurst, IL, USA 60126
Ph: (630) 941-2030

E-mail: http://www.downbeat.com/

Mail Tribune
111 N Fir St.
Medford, OR, USA 97501
Ph: (541) 776-4411

Making Waves, Publishers
7 Ripley Rd.
Montague, MA, USA 1351
Ph: (800) 267-6388
E-mail: info@atschangingcourse.com
URL:

MANA
16 A Journey, Ste. 200
Aliso Viejo, CA, USA 92656
Ph: (949) 859-4040
E-mail: http://www.manaonline.org/

Management Accounting Quarterly
10 Paragon Dr., Ste. 1
Montvale, NJ, USA 7645
Ph: (201) 573-9000

Manitoba Beekeepers' Association
204-545 University Crescent
Winnipeg, MB, CAN R3T 5S6
Ph: (204) 945-3861
E-mail: lsimpson@atsmb.sympatico.ca
URL:

Manitoba Child Care Association
2nd Fl., 2350 McPhillips St.
Winnipeg, MB, CAN R2V 4J6
Ph: (204) 586-8587
E-mail: info@atsmccahouse.org
URL:

Mansueto Ventures LLC
7 World Trade Center
New York, NY, USA 10007
Ph: (212) 389-5377

Manufacturers' Agents National Association
16 A Journey, Ste. 200
Aliso Viejo, CA, USA 92656-3317
Ph: (949) 859-4040
E-mail: mana@atsmanaonline.org
URL: http://www.manaonline.org

Manufacturers' Mart Publications
PO Box 310
Georgetown, MA, USA 1833
E-mail: info@atsmanufacturesmart.com
URL: http://www.manufacturersmart.com

Manufacturing Confectioner Publishing Corp.
711 W Water St.
Princeton, WI, USA 54968
Ph: (920) 295-6969
E-mail: mcinfo@atsgomc.com
URL: http://www.gomc.com

Manufacturing Jewelers & Suppliers of America
45 Royal Little Dr.
Providence, RI, USA 02904-1861
Ph: (401) 274-3840
E-mail: mjsa@atsmjsainc.com
URL:

Maria C. Smith
PO Box 75064
Houston, TX, USA 77234
Ph: (281) 857-6571
E-mail: tp@atsglobalwaterintel.com
URL:

Marine Business Journal Inc.
330 N Andrews Ave.
Fort Lauderdale, FL, USA 33301
Ph: (954) 522-5515
E-mail: mbj@atsmarinebusinessjournal.com
URL: http://www.marinebusinessjournal.com/

Maritime Activity Reports Inc.
118 E 25th St., 2nd Fl.
New York, NY, USA 10010
Ph: (212) 477-6700
E-mail: jomalley@atsmarinelink.com
URL: http://www.marinelink.com

Market Search Inc.
2727 Holland Sylvania Rd., Ste. A
Toledo, OH, USA 43615
Ph: (419) 535-7899
E-mail: jb@atscbrief.biz
URL:

Marketing & Technology Group
1415 N Dayton St.
Chicago, IL, USA 60622
Ph: (312) 266-3311
E-mail: http://www.meatingplace.com

Marketing Research Association
110 National Dr., 2nd Fl.
Glastonbury, CT, USA 06033-1212
Ph: (860) 682-1000
E-mail: email@atsmra-net.org
URL: http://www.mra-net.org

MarketResearch.com
38 E 29th St.
New York, NY, USA 10016
Ph: (800) 298-5699
E-mail: http://www.marketresearch.com

MarketResearch.com
38 E 29th St., 6th Fl.
New York, NY, USA 10016
Ph: (212) 807-2629
E-mail: customerservice@atsmarketresearch.com
URL: http://www.marketresearch.com

MarketResearch.com
641 Avenue of the Americas
New York, NY, USA 10011
Ph: (212) 807-2629
E-mail: http://www.marketresearch.com

MarketResearch.com
11200 Rockville Pke., Ste. 504
Rockville, MD, USA 20852
Ph: (240) 747-3093
E-mail: customerservice@atsmarketresearch.com
URL: http://www.marketresearch.com

The Markets Directory
320 E 42 St., Ste. 2018
New York, NY, USA 10017
Ph: (212) 490-1212
E-mail: jimroxton@atsmarketsdirectory.com
URL: http://www.focusgroups.com

Marketwire
48 Yonge St., 8th Fl.
Toronto, ON, CAN M5E 1G6
Ph: (416) 362-0885
E-mail: http://www.marketwire.com

Marketwire Canada
25 York St., Ste. 900
PO Box 403
Toronto, ON, CAN M5J 2V5
Ph: (416) 362-0885

Markkula Center for Applied Ethics
Santa Clara University
500 El Camino Real
Santa Clara, CA, USA 95053-0633
Ph: (408) 554-5319
E-mail: ethics@atsscu.edu
URL:

Marquis Who's Who L.L.C.
300 Connell Dr., Ste. 2000
Berkeley Heights, NJ, USA 7922
Ph: (908) 673-1000
E-mail: info@atsmarquiswhoswho.com
URL: http://www.marquiswhoswho.com

Martha Stewart Living Omnimedia
11 W 42nd St., 25th Fl.
New York, NY, USA 10036
Ph: (212) 827-8000
E-mail: http://www.marthastewart.com

Martindale-Hubbell Inc.
121 Chanlon Rd.
New Providence, NJ, USA 7974
Ph: (908) 464-6800
E-mail: info@atsmartindale.com
URL: http://www.martindale.com

Martineau Corp.
7910 Woodmont Ave., No. 1150
Bethesda, MD, USA 20814-3088
Ph: (301) 652-8666

E-mail: associationtrends@atsassociation-trends.com
URL: http://www.associationtrends.com

Mary Ann Liebert Incorporated Publishers
140 Huguenot St., 3rd Fl.
New Rochelle, NY, USA 10801-5215
Ph: (914) 740-2100
E-mail: info@atsliebertpub.com
URL: http://www.liebertpub.com

The Masonry Society
3970 Broadway, Ste. 201-D
Boulder, CO, USA 80304-1135
Ph: (303) 939-9700
E-mail: info@atsmasonrysociety.org
URL: http://www.masonrysociety.org

Mass Market Retailers
220 5th Ave.
New York, NY, USA 10001
Ph: (212) 213-6000

Master Associates
PO Box 116
Livingston Manor, NY, USA 12758-0116
Ph: (845) 439-8177

Masthead Publishing Ltd.
8-1606 Sedlescomb Dr.
Mississauga, ON, CAN L4X 1M6
Ph: (905) 625-7070
E-mail: circulation@atsgraphicmonthly.ca
URL: http://www.mastheadonline.com

Mavora Publications Inc.
86 Kingsway Cres.
Toronto, ON, CAN M8X 2R6
Ph: (416) 233-5490
E-mail: info@atscanadian-charities.com
URL: http://www.canadian-charities.com/

Maximum Press
605 Silverthorn Rd.
Gulf Breeze, FL, USA 32561
Ph: (850) 934-0819
E-mail: http://www.maxpress.com/

McClatchy Company
124 Main St.
Fort Mill, SC, USA 29715
Ph: (803) 547-2353

McClatchy Company
150 W Brambleton Ave.
Norfolk, VA, USA 23510
Ph: (757) 446-2000

McClatchy Company
315 S Boulder Ave.
Tulsa, OK, USA 74103
Ph: (918) 581-8418

McClatchy Tribune Information Services
120 S Lawler
Mitchell, SD, USA 57301
Ph: (605) 996-5514

McClatchy-Tribune Information Services
800 S Main St.
Burlington, IA, USA 52601
Ph: (319) 754-8461

McClatchy-Tribune Information Services
435 N Michigan Ave., Ste. 1500
Chicago, IL, USA 60611
Ph: (847) 635-6550

McClatchy-Tribune Regional News
1320 SW Broadway
Portland, OR, USA 97123
Ph: (503) 648-1131

McClatchy-Tribune Regional News
345 Cedar St.
Saint Paul, MN, USA 55101
Ph: (651) 222-1111

McClathcy-Tribune
333 W Canal Dr.
Kennewick, WA, USA 99336
Ph: (509) 582-1500

McCollum Spielman Worldwide
1111 Marcus Ave, Ste. MZ 200
Lake Success, NY, USA 11042
Ph: (516) 394-6000
E-mail: mail@atsmswresearch.com
URL:

McEntee Media Corp.
9815 Hazelwood Ave.
Cleveland, OH, USA 44149
Ph: (440) 238-6603
E-mail: ken@atsrecycle.cc
URL: http://www.recycle.cc

McFarland & Company Inc., Publishers
960 NC Hwy. 88 W
PO Box 611
Jefferson, NC, USA 28640
Ph: (336) 246-4460
E-mail: info@atsmcfarlandpub.com
URL: http://www.mcfarlandpub.com

McGraw-Hill
PO Box 545
Blacklick, OH, USA 43004
Ph: (800) 262-4729
E-mail: http://www.mcgrawhill.com

McGraw-Hill
160 Spear St., 7th Fl.
San Francisco, CA, USA 94105
Ph: (415) 357-8000
E-mail: customer.service@atsmcgraw-hill.com
URL: http://www.mcgraw-hill.com/

McGraw-Hill
55 Francisco St., Ste. 200
San Francisco, CA, USA 94133
Ph: (415) 433-2821

The McGraw-Hill Companies
860 Taylor Station Rd.
Blacklick, OH, USA 43004
Ph: (800) 352-3566
E-mail: http://www.mcgraw-hill.com

McGraw-Hill Companies
PO Box 182604
Columbus, OH, USA 43272
E-mail: http://www.mcgraw-hill.com/

McGraw-Hill Companies
1221 Avenue of the Americas
New York, NY, USA 10020-1095
Ph: (212) 904-2000
E-mail: customer.service@atsmcgraw-hill.com
URL: http://www.mcgraw-hill.com

McGraw-Hill Education
Shoppenhangers Rd.
Maidenhead, , GBR SL6 2QL
Ph: (999) 44 16 28502500
E-mail: http://www.mheducation.com

McGraw-Hill Higher Education
1333 Burr Ridge Pkwy., 3rd Fl.
Burr Ridge, IL, USA 60527
Ph: (630) 789-5302
E-mail: jim_kelly@atsmcgraw-hill.com
URL: http://www.mhhe.com

McGraw-Hill Inc.
PO Box 182604
Columbus, OH, USA 43272
Ph: (614) 430-4000
E-mail: customer.service@atsmcgraw-hill.com
URL: http://www.mcgraw-hill.com

McGraw-Hill Inc.
1221 Avenue of the Americas
New York, NY, USA 10020
Ph: (212) 512-2000
E-mail: customer.service@atsmcgraw-hill.com
URL: http://www.mcgraw-hill.com

McGraw-Hill Ryerson Ltd.
300 Water St.
Whitby, ON, CAN L1N 9B6
Ph: (905) 430-5000
E-mail: orders@atsmcgrawhill.ca
URL: http://www.mcgrawhill.ca

McIlvaine Co.
191 Waukegan Rd., Ste. 208
Northfield, IL, USA 60093
Ph: (847) 784-0012
E-mail: editor@atsmcilvainecompany.com

URL: http://www.mcilvainecompany.com/

McMillan Analysis Corp.
PO Box 1323
Morristown, NJ, USA 07962-1323
Ph: (973) 328-1674
E-mail: info@atsoptionsstrategist.com
URL:

MD Publications Inc.
3057 E Cairo St.
PO Box 2210
Springfield, MO, USA 65802
Ph: (417) 866-3917
E-mail: http://www.mdpublications.com

Meadow Books
Three Rivers
Minions
Liskeard, , GBR 44 15 7936

Mechanical Contractors Association of America Inc.
1385 Piccard Dr.
Rockville, MD, USA 20850
Ph: (301) 869-5800
E-mail: abreedlove@atsmcaa.org
URL: http://www.mcaa.org

Media Enterprises L.P.
155 S El Molino Ave, Ste. 100
Pasadena, CA, USA 91101
Ph: (626) 396-0250
E-mail: editorial@atsboxoffice.com
URL:

Mediacorp Canada Inc.
21 New St.
Toronto, ON, CAN M5R 1P7
Ph: (416) 964-6069
E-mail: info@atsmediacorp.ca
URL: http://www.mediacorp.ca

Meister Media Worldwide
37733 Euclid Ave.
Willoughby, OH, USA 44094-5992
Ph: (440) 942-2000
E-mail: info@atsmeistermedia.com
URL: http://www.meistermedia.com

Meister Publishing Co.
37733 Euclid Ave.
Willoughby, OH, USA 44094-5992
Ph: (440) 942-2000
E-mail: info@atsmeistermedia.com
URL: http://www.meistermedia.com

Membership Section
The ASAE Bldg. 1575 I St. NW
Washington, DC, USA 20005-1103
Ph: (202) 371-0940
E-mail: mbrshpsec@atsasaenet.org
URL:

MENC: The National Association for Music Education
1806 Robert Fulton Dr.
Reston, VA, USA 20191
Ph: (703) 860-4000
E-mail: michaelb@atsmenc.org
URL: http://www.menc.org

The Mercier Press, Ltd.
16 Hume St.
Dublin, CK, IRL
Ph: (353) 1 6615299
E-mail: http://www.mercierpress.ie/

Mercor Media
IBM Plz., 330 N Wabash, Ste. 3201
Chicago, IL, USA 60611
Ph: (312) 628-5870
E-mail: info@atszweigwhite.com
URL: http://www.mercormedia.com

Meredith Corp.
125 Park Ave.
New York, NY, USA 10017-5529
Ph: (212) 557-6600
E-mail: http://www.meredith.com

Merriman Market Analyst
PO Box 250012
West Bloomfield, MI, USA 48325-0012
Ph: (248) 626-3034
E-mail: mmacycles@atsmsn.com
URL:

Messenger Courier Association of America
1156 Fifteenth St. NW, Ste. 900
Washington, DC, USA 20005
Ph: (202) 785-3298
E-mail: bdecaprio@atskellencompany.com
URL: http://www.mcaa.com

Messenger-Inquirer
1401 Frederica St.
Owensboro, KY, USA 42301
Ph: (270) 926-0123

Metropolitan Books
175 5th Ave.
New York, NY, USA 10010
Ph: (212) 982-9300
E-mail: http://us.macmillan.com/Metropolitan.aspx

Meyers Publishing
799 Camarillo Springs Rd.
Camarillo, CA, USA 93012-8111
Ph: (805) 445-8881
E-mail: len@atsmeyerspublishing.com
URL: http://www.meyerspublishing.com

Michigan Association of CPAs
PO Box 5068
Troy, MI, USA 48007-5068
Ph: (248) 267-3700
E-mail: macpa@atsmichcpa.org
URL: http://www.michcpa.org

Michigan Department of Consumer and Industry Services
7150 Harris Dr.
PO Box 30643
Lansing, MI, USA 48909-8143
Ph: (517) 322-1791

Michigan Floral Association
1152 Haslett Rd.
Haslett, MI, USA 48840
Ph: (517) 575-0110
E-mail: http://www.michiganfloral.org

Michigan Hospital Association
6215 W St. Joseph Hwy.
Lansing, MI, USA 48917-4852
Ph: (517) 323-3443
E-mail: http://www.mha.org/mha/aboutmha

MicroDesign Resources
298 S Sunnyvale Ave. Ste. 101
Sunnyvale, CA, USA 94086-6245
Ph: (408) 483-4440
E-mail: cs@atsmdr.cahners.com
URL:

Microsoft Press
1 Microsoft Way
Redmond, WA, USA 98052-6399
Ph: (425) 882-8080

Mid-America Lumbermens Association
638 W 39th St.
PO Box 419264
Kansas City, MO, USA 64111
Ph: (816) 561-5323
E-mail: mail@atsthemla.com
URL: http://www.themla.com

Midwest Travel Writers Association
PO Box 83542
Lincoln, NE, USA 68501-3542
Ph: (402) 438-2253
E-mail: glhinz@atswindstream.net
URL: http://www.mtwa.org

Mid-West Truckers Association
2727 N Dirksen Pkwy.
Springfield, IL, USA 62702
Ph: (217) 525-0310
E-mail: info@atsmid-westtruckers.com
URL:

Mike French Publishing
1619 Front St.
Lynden, WA, USA 98264
Ph: (360) 354-8326

Millennium Publishing Inc.
1170 Ridge Rd., Ste. 217
Webster, NY, USA 14580
Ph: (585) 797-4399
E-mail: http://www.techny.com/

Miller Publishing Company
12400 Whitewater Dr., Ste. 160
Minnetonka, MN, USA 55343
Ph: (952) 931-0211

Miller Publishing Company, Inc.
1235 Sycamore View Rd.
Memphis, TN, USA 38134
Ph: (901) 372-8280

Miller Publishing Group L.L.C.
1918 Main St., 3rd Fl.
Santa Monica, CA, USA 90405
Ph: (310) 893-5300
E-mail: http://www.tennis.com/

Miller Sports Group L.L.C.
79 Madison Ave., 8th Fl.
New York, NY, USA 10016-7802
Ph: (212) 636-2700
E-mail: http://www.tennis.com

Milwaukee Business Journal
825 N Jefferson St., Ste. 200
Milwaukee, WI, USA 53202
Ph: (404) 278-7788

Mini-Storage Messenger
2531 W. Dunlap Ave.
Phoenix, AZ, USA 85021
Ph: (602) 678-3579
E-mail: info@atsminico.com
URL: http://www.ministoragemessenger.com/

Minneapolis Business Journal
120 S 6th St., Ste. 900
Minneapolis, MN, USA 55402
Ph: (612) 288-2100

Minnesota Center for Book Arts
1011 Washington Ave. S, Ste. 100
Minneapolis, MN, USA 55415
Ph: (612) 215-2520
E-mail: mcba@atsmnbookarts.org
URL: http://www.mnbookarts.org

Minnesota Department of Transportation, Office of Aeronautics
222 E Plato Blvd.
Saint Paul, MN, USA 55107-1618
Ph: (651) 234-7200
E-mail: aeroinfo@atsdot.state.mn.us
URL: http://www.dot.state.mn.us/aero

Minority Business Entrepreneur
3528 Torrance Blvd., Ste. 101
Torrance, CA, USA 90503
Ph: (310) 540-9398
E-mail: gconrad@atsmbemag.com
URL: http://www.mbemag.com

Mint Publishing
10532 Los Vaqueros Cir.
Los Alamitos, CA, USA 90720
Ph: (562) 252-4010
E-mail: support@atshatlife.com
URL: http://www.hatlife.com

MIS Research Center
University of Minnesota
Carlson School of Management
321 19th Ave. S, Ste. 3-306
Minneapolis, MN, USA 55455-0438
Ph: (612) 624-0862
E-mail: misrc@atsumn.edu
URL: http://www.misrc.umn.edu/

Missouri Botanical Garden Press
PO Box 299
Saint Louis, MO, USA 63166-0299
Ph: (314) 577-9594
E-mail: http://www.mbgpress.info/

Missouri Municipal League
1727 Southridge Dr.
Jefferson City, MO, USA 65109
Ph: (573) 635-9134
E-mail: info@atsmocities.com
URL: http://www.mocities.com

Missouri State Genealogical Association
PO Box 833
Columbia, MO, USA 65205-0833
E-mail: mosga@atsmosga.org
URL: http://www.mosga.org/

MIT Press
55 Hayward St.
Cambridge, MA, USA 2142
Ph: (617) 253-5641
E-mail: http://mitpress.mit.edu

Mobile Air Conditioning Society Worldwide
225 S Broad St.
PO Box 88
Lansdale, PA, USA 19446
Ph: (215) 631-7020
E-mail: info@atsmacsw.org
URL:

Moby Press
5375 SW Humphrey Blvd.
Portland, OR, USA 97221
Ph: (503) 292-6504

Modern Drummer Publications Inc.
12 Old Bridge Rd.
Cedar Grove, NJ, USA 07009-1288
Ph: (973) 239-4140
E-mail: info@atsmoderndrummer.com
URL: http://www.moderndrummer.com

Modern Trade Communications Inc.
7450 Skokie Blvd.
Skokie, IL, USA 60077
Ph: (847) 674-2200
E-mail: boneill@atsmoderntrade.com
URL: http://www.moderntrade.com

Montana Standard
25 W Granite St.
Butte, MT, USA
Ph: (406) 496-5500

The Mood Disorders Association of Ontario
36 Eglinton West Ste 603
Toronto, ON, CAN M4R1A1
Ph: (416) 486-8046
E-mail: info@atsmooddisorders.on.ca
URL:

Morehouse Publishing
4775 Linglestown Rd.
Harrisburg, PA, USA 17112-8509
Ph: (212) 545-2614
E-mail: http://www.morehousegroup.com

Morgan & Claypool Publishers
1537 4th St., Ste. 228
San Rafael, CA, USA 94901
Ph: (415) 462-0004
E-mail: http://www.cled.biz/books/intedition.htm

Morgan James Publishing LLC
1225 Franklin Ave., Ste. 325
Garden City, NY, USA 11530
Ph: (516) 620-2528
E-mail: http://publishing.morgan-james.com

Morning Sentinel
31 Front St.
Waterville, ME, USA 4901
Ph: (207) 873-3341

Morris Animal Foundation
10200 E Girard Ave Ste B430
Denver, CO, USA 80231
Ph: (303) 790-2345

Morrow/HarperCollins
10 E 53rd St.
New York, NY, USA 10022
Ph: (212) 207-7000
E-mail: http://www.harpercollins.com

Mortgage Bankers Association
1331 L St. NW
Washington, DC, USA 20005
Ph: (202) 557-2700
E-mail: info@atsmbaa.org
URL: http://www.mbaa.org/

Mortgage Bankers Association of America
1717 Rhode Island Ave., NW, Ste. 400
Washington, DC, USA 20036
Ph: (202) 557-2700
E-mail: http://www.mbaa.org/

Mosby
1600 John F. Kennedy Blvd., Ste. 1800
Philadelphia, PA, USA 19103-2899
Ph: (215) 239-3275

E-mail: h.licensing@atselsevier.com
URL: http://www.us.elsevierhealth.com/article.jsp?pageid=368

Mosby Inc.
10801 Executive Center Dr., Ste. 509
Little Rock, AR, USA 72211
Ph: (501) 223-5165
E-mail: http://www.mosbysdrugconsult.com/HS/Help/officesUS.html

Mosby Inc.
11830 Westline Industrial Dr.
Saint Louis, MO, USA 63146-3313
Ph: (314) 872-8370
E-mail: custserv.ehs@atselsevier.com
URL: http://us.elsevierhealth.com

Motion Picture Enterprises Publications Inc.
PO Box 276
Tarrytown, NY, USA 10591-0276
Ph: (212) 245-0969
E-mail: info@atsmpe.net
URL: http://www.mpe.net

Motor & Equipment Manufacturers Association
10 Laboratory Dr.
Research Triangle Park, NC, USA 27709-3966
Ph: (919) 549-4800
E-mail: info@atsmema.org
URL: http://www.mema.org

Motor Information Systems
1301 W Long Lake Rd., Ste. 300
Troy, MI, USA 48098
E-mail: motormagazine@atsmotor.com
URL: http://www.motor.com/

The Motorcyclist's Post
c/o Leo Castell
11 Haven Ln.
Huntington, CT, USA 6484
E-mail: lcastell@atssnet.net
URL: http://www.motorcyclistspost.com

Mountain Bike Magazine
33 E Minor St.
Emmaus, PA, USA 18098-0099
E-mail: http://www.bicycling.com

Mountain Publishing Company
PO Box 1747
Hillsboro, OR, USA 97123-1747
Ph: (503) 628-3995
E-mail: info@atsmountainpublishingusa.com
URL: http://www.mountainpublishingusa.com

Moyer Bell
549 Old North Rd.
Kingston, RI, USA 02881-1220
Ph: (401) 783-5480

MPL Communications Inc.
133 Richmond St. W, Ste. 700
Toronto, ON, CAN M5H 3M8
Ph: (416) 869-1177
E-mail: customers@atsmplcomm.com
URL: http://www.adviceforinvestors.com

Multicultural Marketing Resources Inc.
101 Fifth Ave., Ste. 10B
New York, NY, USA 10003
Ph: (212) 242-3351
E-mail: lisa@atsmulticultural.com
URL:

Multimed Inc.
66 Martin St.
Milton, ON, CAN L9T 2R2
Ph: (905) 875-2456
E-mail: order@atsmulti-med.com
URL: http://www.multi-med.com

Municipal Art Society
457 Madison Ave.
New York, NY, USA 10022
Ph: (212) 935-3960
E-mail: info@atsmas.org
URL:

Municipal World Inc.
42860 Sparta Line
PO Box 399
Union, ON, CAN N0L 2L0
Ph: (519) 633-0031
E-mail: mwadmin@atsmunicipalworld.com
URL: http://www.municipalworld.com

Music Teachers National Association
441 Vine St., Ste. 3100
Cincinnati, OH, USA 45202-2811
Ph: (513) 421-1420
E-mail: mtnanet@atsmtna.org
URL: http://www.mtna.org

Music Trades Corp.
80 West St.
Englewood, NJ, USA 7631
Ph: (201) 871-1965
E-mail: music@atsmusictrades.com
URL: http://www.musictrades.com

MyFamily.com Inc.
360 W. 4800 N
Provo, UT, USA 84604
Ph: (801) 705-7000
E-mail: pr@atsmyfamilyinc.com
URL: http://www.myfamilyinc.com/

N

NACE International
1440 S Creek Dr.
Houston, TX, USA 77084-4906
Ph: (281) 228-6200
E-mail: firstservice@atsnace.org
URL: http://www.nace.org

NACOMEX USA Inc.
PO Box 394
Tivoli, NY, USA 12583
Ph: (212) 808-3062
E-mail: info@atsnacomex.com
URL:

NAGMR Consumer Products Sales Agencies
766 W Algonquin Rd.
Arlington Heights, IL, USA 60005
Ph: (312) 644-6610
E-mail: nagmr@atssba.com
URL:

NAPL
75 W Century Rd.
Paramus, NJ, USA 7652
Ph: (201) 634-9600
E-mail: perc@atsnapl.org
URL: http://www.napl.org

NARSA
300 Village Run Rd., Ste. 103, No. 221
Wexford, PA, USA 15090-6315
Ph: (412) 847-5747
E-mail: info@atsnarsa.org
URL: http://www.narsa.org/

National Accrediting Agency for Clinical Laboratory Sciences
8410 W Bryn Mawr Ave., Ste. 670
Chicago, IL, USA 60631-3415
Ph: (773) 714-8880
E-mail: info@atsnaacls.org
URL:

National Agricultural Aviation Association
1005 East St. SE
Washington, DC, USA 20003-2847
Ph: (202) 546-5722
E-mail: information@atsagaviation.org
URL: http://www.agaviation.org

National Agri-Marketing Association
11020 King St., Ste. 205
Overland Park, KS, USA 66210
Ph: (913) 491-6500
E-mail: agrimktg@atsnama.org
URL: http://www.nama.org

National Air Transportation Association
4226 King St.
Alexandria, VA, USA 22302
Ph: (703) 845-9000
E-mail: http://www.nata.aero/

National Antique & Art Dealers Association of America Inc.
220 E 57th St.
New York, NY, USA 10022
Ph: (212) 826-9707
E-mail: paulh@atsnaada.org
URL: http://www.naadaa.org

National Appliance Parts Suppliers Association
c/o Appliance Parts Co.
4015 W Marshall Ave.
Longview, TX, USA 75604
E-mail: board06@atsnapsaweb.org
URL: http://www.napsaweb.org

National Arbor Day Foundation
100 Arbor Ave.
Nebraska City, NE, USA 68410
Ph: (402) 474-5655
E-mail: info@atsarborday.org
URL: http://www.arborday.org

National Association for Drama Therapy
44365 Premier Plz., Ste. 220
Ashburn, VA, USA 20147
Ph: (571) 333-2991
E-mail: nadt.office@atsnadt.org
URL: http://www.nadt.org

National Association for Healthcare Quality
4700 W Lake Ave.
Glenview, IL, USA 60025
Ph: (847) 375-4720
E-mail: info@atsnahq.org
URL: http://www.nahq.org/

National Association for Home Care
228 Seventh St. SE
Washington, DC, USA 20003
Ph: (202) 547-7424
E-mail: http://www.nahc.org

National Association for Home Care & Hospice
228 Seventh St. SE
Washington, DC, USA 20003
Ph: (202) 547-7424
E-mail: http://www.nahc.org/

National Association for Printing Leadership
75 W. Century Rd., Ste. 100
Paramus, NJ, USA 07652-1408
Ph: (201) 634-9600
E-mail: Information@atsnapl.org
URL: http://www.napl.org

National Association for the Education of Young Children
1313 L St. NW, Ste. 500
PO Box 97156
Washington, DC, USA 20005
Ph: (202) 232-8777
E-mail: naeyc@atsnaeyc.org
URL: http://www.naeyc.org

National Association of Attorneys General
2030 M St. NW, 8th Fl.
Washington, DC, USA 20036
Ph: (202) 326-6000
E-mail: http://www.naag.org/

National Association of Black Accountants Inc.
7249-A Hanover Pkwy.
Greenbelt, MD, USA 20770
Ph: (301) 474-6222
E-mail: http://www.nabainc.org/

National Association of Black Accountants Inc.
7474 Greenway Ctr. Dr., Ste. 1120
Greenbelt, MD, USA 20770
Ph: (301) 474-6222
E-mail: customerservice@atsnabainc.org
URL: http://www.nabainc.org/

National Association of Black Journalists
University of Maryland
8701-A Adelphi Rd.
Adelphi, MD, USA 20783-1716
Ph: (301) 445-7100
E-mail: nabj@atsnabj.org
URL:

National Association of Colleges and Employers
62 Highland Ave.
Bethlehem, PA, USA 18017-9085
Ph: (610) 868-1421
E-mail: amcewen@atsnaceweb.org
URL: http://www.naceweb.org

National Association of Concessionaires
35 E Wacker Dr., Ste. 1816
Chicago, IL, USA 60601
Ph: (312) 236-3858
E-mail: info@atsnaconline.org
URL: http://https:www.b-online.com/secure/nac/

National Association of Convenience Stores (NACS)
1600 Duke St.
Alexandria, VA, USA 22314
Ph: (703) 684-3600
E-mail: nacs@atsnacsonline.com
URL: http://www.nacsonline.com

National Association of Educational Procurement
5523 Research Pk. Dr., Ste. 340
Baltimore, MD, USA 21228
Ph: (443) 543-5540
E-mail: http://www.naepnet.org

National Association of Electrical Distributors Inc.
1181 Corporate Lake Dr.
Saint Louis, MO, USA 63132
Ph: (314) 991-9000
E-mail: customerservice@atsnaed.org
URL: http://www.naed.org

National Association of Floor Covering Distributors
401 N Michigan Ave. Ste. 2400
Chicago, IL, USA 60611-4267
Ph: (312) 321-6836
E-mail: info@atsnafcd.org
URL:

National Association of Home and Workshop Writers (NAHWW)
c/o Richard Day
3131 Tori Trl.
Templeton, CA, USA 93465-5906
E-mail: writer@atsdanramsey.com
URL:

National Association of Home Builders
1201 15th St. NW
Washington, DC, USA 20005
Ph: (202) 266-8200
E-mail: 76176.2456@atscompuserve.com
URL: http://www.nahb.org/

National Association of Independent Fee Appraisers
401 N Michigan Ave., Ste. 2200
Chicago, IL, USA 60611
Ph: (312) 321-6830
E-mail: info@atsnaifa.com
URL: http://www.naifa.com

National Association of Insurance Commissioners
2301 McGee St., Ste. 800
Kansas City, MO, USA 64108-2662
Ph: (816) 842-3600
E-mail: prodserv@atsnaic.org
URL: http://www.naic.org/

National Association of Insurance Women (International)
9343 E 95th Ct. S
Tulsa, OK, USA 74133
Ph: (918) 294-3700
E-mail: joinnaiw@atsnaiw.org
URL: http://www.naiw.org/

National Association of Investors Corp.
711 W 13 Mile Rd.
Madison Heights, MI, USA 48071
Ph: (248) 583-6242
E-mail: service@atsbetterinvesting.org
URL: http://www.betterinvesting.org/Public/ContactUs/ContactUs/default.htm

National Association of Jewelry Appraisers Inc.
PO Box 18
Rego Park, NY, USA 11374-0018
Ph: (718) 896-1536
E-mail: office@atsNAJAappraisers.com
URL: http://www.najaappraisers.com/

National Association of Marine Surveyors Inc.
PO Box 9306
Chesapeake, VA, USA 23321-9306
Ph: (757) 638-9638

E-mail: office@atsnams-cms.org
URL:

National Association of Music Merchants (NAMM)
5790 Armada Dr.
Carlsbad, CA, USA 92008
Ph: (760) 438-8001
E-mail: info@atsnamm.com
URL:

National Association of Pizza Operators
908 S 8th St., Ste. 200
Louisville, KY, USA 40203
Ph: (502) 736-9500
E-mail: plachapelle@atspizzatoday.com
URL: http://www.pizzatoday.com

National Association of Realtors
430 N Michigan Ave.
Chicago, IL, USA 60611-4087
Ph: (312) 329-8458
E-mail: narpubs@atsrealtors.org
URL: http://www.realtor.org

National Association of Schools of Music
11250 Roger Bacon Dr., Ste. 21
Reston, VA, USA 20190-5248
Ph: (703) 437-0700
E-mail: info@atsarts-accredit.org
URL: http://nasm.arts-accredit.org

National Association of State Boards of Accountancy
150 Fourth Ave. N Ste. 700
Nashville, TN, USA 37219-2417
Ph: (615) 880-4200

National Association of State Procurement Officials
201 East Main St., Ste. 1405
Lexington, KY, USA 40507
Ph: (859) 514-9159
E-mail: lpope@atsamrinc.net
URL: http://www.naspo.org

National Association of Tax Professionals
720 Association Dr.
PO Box 8002
Appleton, WI, USA 54912-8002
Ph: (920) 749-1040
E-mail: natp@atsnatptax.com
URL: http://www.natptax.com/contact_us.html

National Association of Wholesaler-Distributors (NAW)
1325 G St. NW, Ste. 1000
Washington, DC, USA 20005
Ph: (202) 872-0885
E-mail: naw@atsnawd.org
URL:

National Association of Women Artists Inc.
80 Fifth Ave., Ste. 1405
New York, NY, USA 10011
Ph: (212) 675-1616
E-mail: office@atsnawanet.org
URL:

National Association of Women in Construction (NAWIC)
327 S Adams St.
Fort Worth, TX, USA 76104
Ph: (817) 877-5551
E-mail: nawic@atsnawic.org
URL:

National Auctioneers Association
8880 Ballentine St.
Overland Park, KS, USA 66214
Ph: (913) 541-8084
E-mail: support@atsauctioneers.org
URL: http://www.auctioneers.org

National Auto Auction Association
5320 Spectrum Dr., Ste. D
Frederick, MD, USA 21703
Ph: (301) 696-0400
E-mail: naaa@atsnaaa.com
URL: http://www.naaa.com

National Automotive Radiator Service Association (NARSA)
15000 Commerce Pkwy., Ste. C
Mount Laurel, NJ, USA 8054
Ph: (856) 439-1575
E-mail: info@atsnarsa.org
URL: http://www.narsa.org/

National Bicycle Dealers Association
777 W19th St., Ste. 0
Costa Mesa, CA, USA 92627
Ph: (949) 722-6909
E-mail: info@atsnbda.com
URL:

National Burglar and Fire Alarm Association
2300 Valley View Ln., Ste. 230
Irving, TX, USA 75062
Ph: (214) 260-5970
E-mail: staff@atsalarm.org
URL: http://www.alarm.org

National Bus Trader Inc.
9698 W Judson Rd.
Polo, IL, USA 61064-9049
Ph: (815) 946-2341
E-mail: info@atsbusmag.com
URL: http://www.busmag.com/

National Business Media Inc.
2800 W Midway Blvd.
Broomfield, CO, USA 80020-7174
Ph: (303) 469-0424
E-mail: http://www.nbm.com

National Career Development Association
305 N Beech Cir.
Broken Arrow, OK, USA 74012
Ph: (918) 663-7060
E-mail: dpenn@atsncda.org
URL: http://www.ncda.org

National Catholic Office for Persons with Disabilities
415 Michigan Ave., NE, Ste. 95
Washington, DC, USA 20017-4501
Ph: (202) 529-2933
E-mail: ncpd@atsncpd.org
URL:

National Chamber of Commerce for Women
10 Waterside Plz., Ste. 6H
New York, NY, USA 10010
Ph: (212) 685-3454
E-mail: commerce-for-women@atsjuno.com
URL:

National Christmas Tree Association
16020 Swingley Ridge Rd., Ste. 300
Chesterfield, MO, USA 63017
Ph: (636) 449-5070
E-mail: info@atsrealchristmastrees.org
URL: http://www.christmastree.org/home.cfm

National Community Pharmacists Association
100 Daingerfield Rd.
Alexandria, VA, USA 22314
Ph: (703) 683-8200
E-mail: info@atsncpanet.org
URL: http://www.ncpanet.org

National Community Pharmacists Association
205 Daingerfield Rd.
Alexandria, VA, USA 22314
Ph: (703) 683-8200
E-mail: info@atsncpanet.org
URL:

National Concrete Masonry Association
13750 Sunrise Valley Dr.
Herndon, VA, USA 20171-4662
Ph: (703) 713-1900
E-mail: ncma@atsncma.org
URL: http://www.ncma.org/

National Conference of State Liquor Administrators
6183 Beau Douglas Ave.
Gonzales, LA, USA 70737
Ph: (225) 473-7209
E-mail: pamsalario@atscox.net
URL: http://www.ncsla.org/

The National Consumer Voice for Quality Long-Term Care
1828 L St. NW, Ste. 801
Washington, DC, USA 20036
Ph: (202) 332-2275
E-mail: nccnhr@atsnccnhr.org
URL: http://www.nursinghomeaction.org

National Council for Geocosmic Research Inc.
c/o Liane Thomas Wade
531 Main St., No. 1612
New York, NY, USA 10044-0114
Ph: (212) 838-6247
E-mail: execsec@atsgeocosmic.org
URL: http://www.geocosmic.org

National Council of Acoustical Consultants
9100 Purdue Rd., Ste. 200
Indianapolis, IN, USA 46268
Ph: (317) 328-0642
E-mail: info@atsncac.com
URL: http://www.ncac.com

National Council on the Aging (NCOA)
409 3rd St. SW, Ste. 200
Washington, DC, USA 20024
Ph: (202) 479-1200
E-mail: http://www.ncoa.org

National Customs Brokers & Forwarders Association of America
1200 18th St. NW, Ste. 901
Washington, DC, USA 20036
Ph: (202) 466-0222
E-mail: staff@atsncbfaa.org
URL: http://www.ncbfaa.org/

National Cutting Horse Association
260 Bailey Ave.
Fort Worth, TX, USA 76107
Ph: (817) 244-6188
E-mail: http://www.nchacutting.com/ag/contact/contacthome.php

National Dance Association
1900 Association Dr.
Reston, VA, USA 20191-1598
Ph: (703) 476-3400
E-mail: nda@atsaahperd.org
URL: http://www.aahperd.org

The National Dipper
1028 W Devon Ave.
Elk Grove Village, IL, USA 60007
Ph: (847) 301-8400
E-mail: http://www.nationaldipper.com/

National Electrical Contractors Association
3 Bethesda Metro Ctr., Ste. 1100
Bethesda, MD, USA 20814-5372
Ph: (301) 657-3110
E-mail: http://www.necanet.org

National Electrical Manufacturers Representatives Association
28 Deer St., Ste. 302
Portsmouth, NH, USA 10591-1504
Ph: (914) 524-8650
E-mail: nemra@atsnemra.org
URL: http://www.nemra.org

National Electronic Distributors Association
1111 Alderman Dr., Ste. 400
Alpharetta, GA, USA 30005-4175
Ph: (678) 393-9990
E-mail: admin@atsnedassoc.org
URL: http://www.nedassoc.org

National Federation of Community Broadcasters (NFCB)
1970 Broadway, Ste. 1000
Oakland, CA, USA 94612
Ph: (510) 451-8200
E-mail: newsletter@atsnfcb.org
URL:

National Federation of Independent Business
1201 F St. NW, Ste. 200
Washington, DC, USA 20004
Ph: (615) 82-5800

National Fisherman
PO Box 7438
Portland, ME, USA 04112-7437
Ph: (207) 842-5608
E-mail: info@atsnationalfisherman.com
URL: http://www.nationalfisherman.com

National Foundation for Credit Counseling
801 Roeder Rd., Ste. 900
Silver Spring, MD, USA 20910
Ph: (301) 589-5600
E-mail: nfcc@atsnfcc.org
URL: http://www.debtadvice.org/

National Frozen & Refrigerated Foods Association Inc.
4755 Linglestown Rd., Ste. 300
PO Box 6069
Harrisburg, PA, USA 17112-8547
Ph: (717) 657-8601
E-mail: info@atsnfraweb.org
URL: http://www.nfraweb.org

National Funeral Directors Association
13625 Bishop's Dr.
Brookfield, WI, USA 53005-6607
Ph: (262) 789-1880
E-mail: nfda@atsnfda.org
URL: http://www.nfda.org

National Funeral Directors Association NFDA
13625 Bishop's Dr.
Brookfield, WI, USA 53005-6607
Ph: (262) 789-1880
E-mail: nfda@atsnfda.org
URL: http://www.nfda.org

National Genealogical Society
3108 Columbia Pike, Ste. 300
Arlington, VA, USA 22204-4304
Ph: (703) 525-0050
E-mail: ngs@atsngsgenealogy.org
URL: http://www.ngsgenealogy.org

National Geographic
1145 17th St. NW
Washington, DC, USA 20036
Ph: (202) 857-7027
E-mail: pressroom@atsngs.org
URL: http://www.ngsp.com

National Glass Association
8200 Greensboro Dr., Ste. 302
McLean, VA, USA 22102-3881
Ph: (703) 442-4890
E-mail: administration@atsglass.org
URL: http://www.glass.org

National Guild of Community Schools of the Arts
520 8th Ave., Ste. 302
New York, NY, USA 10018
Ph: (212) 268-3337
E-mail: info@atsnationalguild.org
URL: http://www.nationalguild.org

National Guild of Decoupeurs
1017 Pucker St.
Stowe, VT, USA 5672
Ph: (802) 253-3903
E-mail: mdpeer@atsaol.com
URL: http://www.decoupage.org

National Hardwood Lumber Association
6830 Raleigh LaGrange
PO Box 34518
Memphis, TN, USA 38184-0518
Ph: (901) 377-1818
E-mail: info@atsnhla.com
URL: http://www.natlhardwood.org

National Health Association
12115 Wasatch Ct.
PO Box 30630
Tampa, FL, USA 33624
E-mail: lgrudnik@atshealthscience.org
URL: http://healthscience.org

National Health Council Inc.
1730 M St. NW, Ste. 500
Washington, DC, USA 20026-4561
Ph: (202) 785-3910
E-mail: info@atsnhcouncil.org
URL: http://www.nationalhealthcouncil.org

National Highway Carriers Directory Inc.
PO Box 6099
Buffalo Grove, IL, USA 6099
Ph: (847) 634-0606
E-mail: nhcd2@atsaol.com
URL:

National Hispanic Council on Aging
734 15th St., NW, Ste. 1050
Washington, DC, USA 20005
Ph: (202) 347-9733
E-mail: nhcoa@atsnhcoa.org
URL:

National Independent Automobile Dealers Association
2521 Brown Blvd.
Arlington, TX, USA 76006
Ph: (817) 640-3838
E-mail: http://www.niada.com

National Information Standards Organization
1 N Charles St., Ste. 1905
Baltimore, MD, USA 21201
Ph: (301) 654-2512
E-mail: nisohq@atsniso.org
URL: http://www.niso.org

National Institute for Automotive Service Excellence
101 Blue Seal Dr. SE, No. 101
Leesburg, VA, USA 20175
Ph: (703) 669-6600

National Institute of Business Management
1750 Old Meadow Rd., Ste. 302
Mc Lean, VA, USA 22102
Ph: (703) 905-8000
E-mail: customer@atsnibm.net
URL:

National Insulation Association
12100 Sunset Hills Rd., Ste. 330
Reston, VA, USA 20190
Ph: (703) 464-6422
E-mail: http://www.insulation.org

National League for Nursing
61 Broadway, 33rd Fl.
New York, NY, USA 10006-2701
Ph: (212) 363-5555
E-mail: generalinfo@atsnln.org
URL: http://www.nln.org

National Marine Fisheries Service
1315 EW Hwy.
Silver Spring, MD, USA 20910
E-mail: st1help@atsnoaa.gov
URL: http://www.st.nmfs.gov/st1/

National Marine Manufacturers Association (NMMA)
200 E Randolph Dr. Ste. 5100
Chicago, IL, USA 60601
Ph: (312) 946-6200

National Marine Representatives Association
1333 Delany Rd., No. 500
PO Box 360
Gurnee, IL, USA 60031
Ph: (847) 662-3167
E-mail: info@atsnmraonline.org
URL: http://www.nmraonline.org

National Meat Association
1970 Broadway, Ste. 825
Oakland, CA, USA 94612
Ph: (510) 763-1533
E-mail: staff@atsnmaonline.org
URL: http://www.nmaonline.org/

National Minority Business Council Inc.
120 Broadway, 19th Fl.
New York, NY, USA 10271
Ph: (212) 693-5050
E-mail: nmbc@atsmsn.com
URL:

National Opera Association
2403 Russell Long Blvd.
PO Box 60869
Canyon, TX, USA 79016-0869
Ph: (806) 651-2857
E-mail: rhansen@atsnoa.org
URL: http://www.noa.org

National Publishing Company Inc.
1533 Burgundy Pkwy.
Streamwood, IL, USA 60107
Ph: (630) 837-2044
E-mail: natllock@atsaol.com
URL: http://www.thenationallocksmith.com/index.asp

National Recreation and Park Association
22377 Belmont Ridge Rd.
Ashburn, VA, USA 20148
Ph: (703) 858-0784
E-mail: info@atsnrpa.org
URL: http://www.nrpa.org

National Research Council Canada, NRC Research Press
1200 Montreal Rd., Bldg. M-58
Ottawa, ON, CAN K1A 0R6
Ph: (613) 993-9101
E-mail: info@atsnrc-cnrc.gc.ca
URL: http://www.nrc-cnrc.gc.ca

National Rifle Association of America
11250 Waples Mill Rd.
Fairfax, VA, USA 22030
E-mail: info@atsnraila.org
URL: http://www.nrahq.org

National Roofing Contractors Association
10255 W Higgins Rd., Ste. 600
Rosemont, IL, USA 60018-5607
Ph: (847) 299-9070
E-mail: llewis@atsnrca.net
URL: http://www.nrca.net

National Sculpture Society
c/o ANS
75 Varick St., 11th Fl.
New York, NY, USA 10013
Ph: (212) 764-5645
E-mail: nss1893@atsaol.com
URL: http://www.nationalsculpture.org/nss/default.asp

National Shoe Retailers Association
3037 W Ina Rd., Ste. 101
Tucson, AZ, USA 85741
Ph: (520) 209-1710
E-mail: info@atsnsra.org
URL: http://www.nsra.org

National Skeet Shooting Association
5931 Roft Rd.
San Antonio, TX, USA 78253
Ph: (210) 688-3371
E-mail: nssa@atsnssa-nsca.com
URL: http://www.mynssa.com

National Ski & Snowboard Retailers Association
1601 Feehanville Dr., Ste. 300
Mount Prospect, IL, USA 60056-6035
Ph: (847) 391-9825
E-mail: info@atsnssra.com
URL:

National Sporting Goods Association
1601 Feehanville Dr., Ste. 300
Mount Prospect, IL, USA 60056
Ph: (847) 296-6742
E-mail: info@atsnsga.org
URL: http://www.nsga.org

National Strength & Conditioning Association (NSCA)
1885 Bob Johnson Dr.
Colorado Springs, CO, USA 80906-4000
Ph: (719) 632-6722
E-mail: nsca@atsnsca-lift.org
URL: http://www.nsca-lift.org/contact.shtml

National Tank Truck Carriers Inc.
950 N Glebe Rd., Ste. 520
Arlington, VA, USA 22203-4183
Ph: (703) 838-1960
E-mail: nttcstaff@atstanktruck.org
URL: http://www.tanktruck.org

National Taxpayers Union
108 N Alfred St.
Alexandria, VA, USA 22314
Ph: (703) 683-5700
E-mail: ntu@atsntu.org
URL:

National Technical Information Service
5285 Port Royal Rd.
Springfield, VA, USA 22161
Ph: (703) 605-6585
E-mail: helpdesk@atsntis.gov
URL: http://www.ntis.gov/

National Tour Association
546 E Main St.
Lexington, KY, USA 40508
Ph: (859) 226-4444

E-mail: questions@atsntastaff.com
URL:

National Trade Publications Inc.
13 Century Hill Dr.
Latham, NY, USA 12110-2113
Ph: (518) 783-1281
E-mail: hstyler@atsntpinc.com
URL: http://www.ntpinc.com

National Truck Equipment Association
37400 Hills Tech Dr.
Farmington Hills, MI, USA 48331-3414
Ph: (248) 489-7090
E-mail: info@atsntea.com
URL: http://www.ntea.com

National Vehicle Leasing Association
1199 N Fairfax St., Ste. 400
Alexandria, VA, USA 22314
E-mail: http://www.nvla.org/

National Venture Capital Association
1655 N Fort Myer Dr., Ste. 850
Arlington, VA, USA 22209
Ph: (703) 524-2549
E-mail: http://www.nvca.org

National Wellness Institute Inc.
1300 College Ct.
PO Box 827
Stevens Point, WI, USA 54481
Ph: (715) 342-2969
E-mail: nwi@atsnationalwellness.org
URL: http://www.nationalwellness.org

National Wood Carvers Association
PO Box 43218
Cincinnati, OH, USA 45243
Ph: (513) 561-0627
E-mail: nwca@atschipchats.org
URL: http://www.chipchats.org

The National Writers Association
10940 S Parker Rd., No. 508
Parker, CO, USA 80134
Ph: (303) 841-0246
E-mail: natlwritersassn@atshotmail.com
URL: http://www.nationalwriters.com

NATSO
1737 King St., Ste. 200
Alexandria, VA, USA 22314
Ph: (703) 549-2100
E-mail: tpmembership@atsnatso.com
URL: http://www.natso.com

Natural Hazards Research and Applications Information Center
482 UCB
Institute of Behavioral Science, No. 6
University of Colorado
Boulder, CO, USA 80309-0482
Ph: (303) 492-6818
E-mail: hazctr@atscolorado.edu
URL: http://www.colorado.edu/hazards/

Navellier-MPT Review Inc.
1 E Liberty, 3rd Fl.
Reno, NV, USA 89501
Ph: (775) 785-2300
E-mail: info@atsnavellier.com
URL:

Neal-Schuman Publishers Inc.
100 William St., Ste. 2004
New York, NY, USA 10038-5018
Ph: (212) 925-8650
E-mail: info@atsneal-schuman.com
URL: http://www.neal-schuman.com

Ned Davis Research Inc.
600 Bird Bay Dr.
Venice, FL, USA 34285
Ph: (941) 484-6107
E-mail: http://www.ndr.com

The Needlecraft Shop L.L.C.
23 Old Pecan Rd.
Big Sandy, TX, USA 75755-2200
E-mail: privacy@atsdrgnetwork.com
URL: http://www.needlecraftshop.com

Nelson Business
PO Box 141000
Nashville, TN, USA 37214-1000

Nelson Information
c/o Thomson Financial
195 Broadway
New York, NY, USA 10007-3100
E-mail: nelson.support@atsthomson.com
URL:

Nelson Publishing Inc.
2500 Tamiami Trl. N
Nokomis, FL, USA 34275
Ph: (941) 966-9521
E-mail: http://www.nelsonpub.com/

Nelson Thomson Learning
1120 Birchmount Rd.
Scarborough, ON, CAN M1K 5G4
Ph: (416) 752-9100

New American Library/Penguin Group
375 Hudson St.
New York, NY, USA 10014-3657
E-mail: insidesales@atsus.penguingroup.com
URL: http://us.penguingroup.com/static/pages/publishers/adult/nal.html

New Bay Media, LLC
810 7th Ave., 27th Fl.
New York, NY, USA 10019
Ph: (212) 378-0400
E-mail: http://www.nbmedia.com/

New England Appraisers Association
5 Gill Ter.
Ludlow, VT, USA 5149
Ph: (802) 228-7444
E-mail: llt44@atstds.net
URL: http://www.newenglandappraisers.net/

New England Bride Inc.
29 Durham Dr.
Lynnfield, MA, USA 1940
Ph: (978) 535-4186
E-mail: http://www.nebride.com/

New England Connexion
PO Box 621
Goshen, NY, USA 10924-0621
Ph: (845) 294-6867
E-mail: nhsip@atsfrontiernet.net
URL:

New England Historic Genealogical Society
101 Newbury St.
Boston, MA, USA 02116-3007
Ph: (617) 536-5740
E-mail: administration@atsnehgs.org
URL: http://www.americanancestors.org

New Hope Natural Media
1401 Pearl St., Ste. 200
Boulder, CO, USA 80302
Ph: (303) 939-8440
E-mail: http://www.deliciouslivingmag.com

New Jersey Law Journal
PO Box 20081
Newark, NJ, USA 7101
Ph: (973) 642-0075

New Orleans Lettering Arts Association Inc.
PO Box 4117
New Orleans, LA, USA 70178
Ph: (504) 861-1807
E-mail: nolaa@atsgnofn.org
URL: http://www.gnofn.org/@tldnolaa/

New Paradigm Media
11661 W 14th Ave.
Golden, CO, USA 80401
E-mail: http://holistic-books.ning.com

New Road Publishing
3650 Rogers Rd., Ste. 328
Wake Forest, NC, USA 27587
Ph: (919) 453-2850
E-mail: info@atsnewroadpublishing.com
URL: http://www.newroadpublishing.com

New Society Publishers
PO Box 189
Gabriola Island, BC, CAN V0R 1X0
Ph: (250) 247-9737
E-mail: info@atsnewsociety.com
URL: http://www.newsociety.com/

New Writer's Magazine
PO Box 5976
Sarasota, FL, USA 34277
Ph: (941) 953-7903
E-mail: newriters@atsaol.com

URL: http://www.pspcom.com/

New York AMA Communication Services Inc.
116 E 27th St., 6th Fl.
New York, NY, USA 10016
Ph: (212) 849-2752
E-mail: info@atsgreenbook.org
URL: http://www.greenbook.org

The New York Review of Books
435 Hudson St., Ste. 300
New York, NY, USA 10014
Ph: (212) 757-8070
E-mail: http://www.nybooks.com

New York State Society of CPAs
3 Park Ave., 18th Fl.
New York, NY, USA 10016-5991
Ph: (212) 719-8300
E-mail: http://www.nysscpa.org/

The New York Times Co.
620 Eighth Ave.
New York, NY, USA 10018
Ph: (212) 556-1234
E-mail: http://www.nytimes.com

New York Times Co./Globe Newspaper Co.
135 Morrissey Blvd.
PO Box 2378
Boston, MA, USA 02107-3310
Ph: (617) 929-2935

The New York Times Company
229 W 43rd St.
New York, NY, USA 10036-3913
Ph: (212) 556-7652

Newmarket Press
18 E 48th St.
New York, NY, USA 10017
Ph: (212) 832-3575
E-mail: http://www.newmarketpress.com

Newport Communications
38 Executive Pk., Ste. 300
Irvine, CA, USA 92614
Ph: (949) 261-1636
E-mail: http://www.newportcommunicationsgroup.com

News & Observer
215 S McDowell St.
Raleigh, NC, USA 27602
Ph: (919) 829-4500

News Media Directories
PO Box 316
Mount Dora, FL, USA 32757
Ph: (352) 589-9020
E-mail: newsmedia@atscomcast.net
URL: http://www.newsmediadirectories.info

News RX
2727 Paces Ferry Rd. SE, Ste. 2-440
Atlanta, GA, USA 30339
Ph: (770) 435-8286

New-Sentinel
600 W Main St.
Fort Wayne, IN, USA 46802
Ph: (260) 461-8298

News-Herald
7085 Mentor Ave.
Willoughby, OH, USA 44094
Ph: (440) 951-0000

The Newsletter Factory
1775 The Exchange, Ste. 300
Atlanta, GA, USA 30339
Ph: (770) 955-1600

Newsletter on Newsletters
20 W Chestnut St.
PO Box 348
Rhinebeck, NY, USA 12572
Ph: (845) 876-5222
E-mail: newsonnews@atsnewsletterbiz.com
URL:

Newsletter Publishing Corp.
117 Mercer St., Ste. 200
Seattle, WA, USA 98119-3960
Ph: (206) 281-9609

NewsLinc
15115 S 76th Ave.
Bixby, OK, USA 74008

NewYorkAncestry.com
PO Box 4311
Boise, ID, USA 83711
Ph: (208) 469-0673
E-mail: newyorkancestry@atsaol.com
URL: http://www.newyorkancestry.com

Nielsen Business Media
770 Broadway
New York, NY, USA 10003-9595
E-mail: http://www.nielsen.com

Nielsen Business Media
90 Broad St., Rm. 402
New York, NY, USA 10004-3312
Ph: (646) 654-5000
E-mail: http://www.nielsenbusinessmedia.com/

Nielsen Company
VNU Business Media Inc.
770 Broadway, 7th Fl.
New York, NY, USA 10003
Ph: (818) 487-4596

The Ninety-Nines Inc.
4300 Amelia Earhart Rd.
Oklahoma City, OK, USA 73159
Ph: (405) 685-7969
E-mail: president@atsninety-nines.org
URL:

NOLO
950 Parker St.
Berkeley, CA, USA 94710-2524
Ph: (510) 549-1976

NOLO Publications
950 Parker St.
Berkeley, CA, USA 94710
E-mail: http://www.nolo.com

Nomis Publications Inc.
8570 Foxwood Ct.
PO Box 5159
Youngstown, OH, USA 44514-4301
Ph: (330) 965-2380
E-mail: info@atsnomispublications.com
URL: http://www.nomispublications.com

NorlightsPress.com
2323 State Rd. 252
Martinsville, IN, USA 46151-7401
E-mail: info@atsnorlightspress.com
URL: http://NorlightsPress.com

North American Association of Floor Covering Distributors
401 N Michigan Ave., Ste. 1900
Chicago, IL, USA 60611
Ph: (312) 321-6836
E-mail: info@atsnafcd.org
URL: http://www.nafcd.org/

North American Bookdealers Exchange
PO Box 606
Cottage Grove, OR, USA 97424
Ph: (541) 942-7455
E-mail: nabe@atsbookmarketingprofits.com
URL: http://www.bookmarketingprofits.com

North American Building Material Distribution Association
401 N Michigan Ave.
Chicago, IL, USA 60601
Ph: (312) 321-6845
E-mail: info@atsnbmda.org
URL: http://www.nbmda.org

North American Die Casting Association
241 Holbrook Dr.
Wheeling, IL, USA 60090-5809
Ph: (847) 279-0001
E-mail: nadca@atsdiecasting.org
URL: http://www.diecasting.org/

North American Publishing Co.
1500 Spring Garden St., Ste. 1200
Philadelphia, PA, USA 19130-4069
Ph: (215) 238-5300
E-mail: customerservice@atsnapco.com
URL: http://www.napco.com

North American Retail Dealers Association
222 S Riverside Plz., Ste. 2160
Chicago, IL, USA 60606
Ph: (312) 648-0649
E-mail: nardasvc@atsnarda.com
URL: http://www.narda.com/

North American Retail Hardware Association
6325 Digital Way, No. 300
Indianapolis, IN, USA 46278
Ph: (317) 290-0338

North County Times
207 E Pennsylvania Ave.
Escondido, CA, USA 92025
Ph: (760) 745-6611

North Island Publishing
1606 Sedlescomb Dr., Unit 8
Mississauga, ON, CAN L4X 1M6
Ph: (905) 625-7070
E-mail: http://www.northisland.ca/

North Jersey Media Group
150 River St.
Hackensack, NJ, USA 7601
Ph: (201) 646-4000

Northeast Mississippi Daily Journal
1242 S Green St.
Tupelo, MS, USA 38804
Ph: (662) 842-2611

Northeastern Lumber Manufacturers Association
272 Tuttle Rd.
PO Box 87A
Cumberland Center, ME, USA 4021
Ph: (207) 829-6901
E-mail: info@atsnelma.org
URL: http://www.nelma.org/

Northeastern Retail Lumber Association
585 N Greenbush Rd.
Rensselaer, NY, USA 12144
Ph: (518) 286-1010
E-mail: http://www.nrla.org

Northern Arizona Genealogical Society
Box 695
Prescott, AZ, USA 86302
E-mail: sunshinegirl@atsisp.com
URL:

Northern Lights Internet Solutions Ltd.
438 - 5th St.
Saskatoon, SK, CAN S7H 1E9
Ph: (306) 931-0020
E-mail: info2@atslights.ca
URL: http://www.lights.ca

North-South Center Press at the University of Miami
1320 S Dixie Hwy.
Coral Gables, FL, USA 33146-3027
Ph: (305) 284-2211
E-mail: nscenter@atsmiami.edu
URL: http://www6.miami.edu

Northstar Travel Media
100 Lighting Way, 2nd Fl.
Secaucus, NJ, USA 7094
Ph: (201) 902-2000
E-mail: http://www.northstartravelmedia.com

NorthStar Travel Media LLC
116 W 32nd St., 14th Fl.
New York, NY, USA 10001
Ph: (646) 380-6240

Northwest Fuchsia Society
Box 33071, Bitter Lake Sta.
Seattle, WA, USA 98133
Ph: (253) 588-4541

Northwestern Lumber Association
5905 Golden Valley Rd., Ste. 110
Minneapolis, MN, USA 55422
Ph: (763) 544-6822
E-mail: nlassn@atsnlassn.org
URL: http://www.nlassn.org

Nouveau Connoisseurs Corporation
, , USA
Ph: (503) 590-4329
E-mail: Monique@atsnouveauconnoisseurs.com
URL: http://moniquehayward.com

Nova Publishing Company
1103 W College
Carbondale, IL, USA 62901
Ph: (618) 457-3521

Nova Science Publishers, Inc.
400 Oser Ave., Ste. 1600
Hauppauge, NY, USA 11788
Ph: (631) 231-7269
E-mail: http://www.novapublishers.com

Novicom Inc.
6100 Center Dr., Ste. 1000
Los Angeles, CA, USA 90045
Ph: (310) 642-4400
E-mail: http://www.ptproductsonline.com

NPT Publishing Group Inc.
201 Littleton Rd., 2nd Fl.
Morris Plains, NJ, USA 7950
Ph: (973) 401-0202
E-mail: http://www.nptimes.com/

NPTA Alliance
401 N Michigan Ave., Ste. 2200
Chicago, IL, USA 60611
Ph: (312) 321-4092
E-mail: npta@atsgonpta.com
URL: http://www.gonpta.com

NRF Enterprises Inc.
325 7th St. NW, Ste. 1100
Washington, DC, USA 20004
Ph: (202) 783-7971
E-mail: http://www.nrf.com

NSBE Publications
205 Daingerfield Rd.
Alexandria, VA, USA 22314
Ph: (703) 549-2207
E-mail: publications@atsnsbe.org
URL: http://www.nsbe.org/

NSC Press
1121 Spring Lake Dr.
Itasca, IL, USA 60143-3201
Ph: (630) 285-1121
E-mail: info@atsnsc.org
URL: http://www.nsc.org

Numismatic Counseling Inc.
PO Box 38
Plainview, NY, USA 11803
Ph: (516) 433-5800
E-mail: mauricerosen@atsaol.com
URL:

Nurre Ink
PO Box 670705
Dallas, TX, USA 75367-0705
Ph: (972) 243-1356

Nursecom Inc.
100 N 20th St., 4th Fl.
Philadelphia, PA, USA 19103
Ph: (215) 545-7222
E-mail: info@atsnursecominc.com
URL: http://www.nursecominc.com

NVST Inc.
1100 Dexter Ave. N
Seattle, WA, USA 98109
E-mail: info@atsnvst.com
URL: http://www.nvst.com

NYFEA--The Association for Educating Agricultural Leaders
PO Box 20326
Montgomery, AL, USA 36120
Ph: (334) 288-0097
E-mail: natloffice@atsnyfea.org
URL:

NYU Press
838 Broadway, 3rd Fl.
New York, NY, USA 10003
Ph: (212) 998-2575
E-mail: information@atsnyupress.org
URL: http://nyupress.org

O

O Books
46A West St.
Alresford, , GBR SO24 9AU
E-mail: http://www.obooks.com

OAG Worldwide
3025 Highland Pky., Ste. 200
Downers Grove, IL, USA 60515-5561
Ph: (630) 515-5300
E-mail: custsvc@atsoag.com
URL: http://www.oag.com

Obsidian Launch LLC
239 Myrtle Ave.
Boonton, NJ, USA 7005
Ph: (973) 453-4534
E-mail: info@atsobsidianlaunch.com
URL: http://www.obsidianlaunch.com

Ocala Star-Banner
2121 SW 19th Ave.
Ocala, FL, USA 34471
Ph: (352) 867-4010

Office for History of Science and Technology
543 Stephens Hall, Ste. 2350
Berkeley, CA, USA 94720-2350
Ph: (510) 642-4581
E-mail: ohst@atsberkeley.edu
URL: http://www.ohst.berkeley.edu

Office of Advocacy
409 3rd St. SW
Washington, DC, USA 20416
Ph: (202) 205-6533

Office of Product Management
5285 Port Royal Rd.
Springfield, VA, USA 22161
Ph: (703) 605-6515
E-mail: info@atsntis.gov
URL: http://www.ntis.gov

Office of Research and Creative Activity
207 Montana Hall
PO Box 172460
Bozeman, MT, USA 59717-2460
Ph: (406) 994-5607
E-mail: research@atsmontana.edu
URL:

Ohara
24715 Rockefeller
PO Box 918
Santa Clarita, CA, USA 91355
E-mail: rainbow@atsrsabbs.com
URL:

Ohio State University
Enarson Hall
154 W 12th Ave.
Columbus, OH, USA 43210
Ph: (614) 292-6446
E-mail: http://www.osu.edu/

Ohio United Way
88 E Broad St., Ste. 620
Columbus, OH, USA 43215-3506
Ph: (614) 224-8146
E-mail: oh_unitedway@atsouw.org
URL:

Oildom Publishing Company of Texas Inc.
1160 Dairy Ashford Rd., Ste. 610
Houston, TX, USA 77079
Ph: (281) 558-6930

Oklahoma Genealogical Society
PO Box 12986
Oklahoma City, OK, USA 73157
Ph: (405) 286-1190
E-mail: okgensoc@atsaol.com
URL:

OMB Watch
1742 Connecticut Ave. NW
Washington, DC, USA 20009-1171
Ph: (202) 234-8494
E-mail: ombwatch@atsombwatch.org
URL:

Omnigraphics Inc.
PO Box 31-1640
Detroit, MI, USA 48231
E-mail: info@atsomnigraphics.com
URL: http://www.omnigraphics.com

Online, A Division of Information Today Inc.
143 Old Marlton Pke.
Medford, NJ, USA 08055-8750
Ph: (609) 654-6266
E-mail: custserv@atsinfotoday.com
URL: http://www.infotoday.com

Ontario Accommodation Association
347 Pido Rd., Unit 2
RR 6
Peterborough, ON, CAN K9J 6X7
Ph: (705) 745-4982
E-mail: info@atsontarioaccommodation.com
URL:

Ontario Beekeepers' Association
Bayfield, ON, CAN N0M 1G0
Ph: (519) 674-1007
E-mail: info@atsontariobee.com
URL:

Ontario Long Term Care Association
345 Renfrew Dr., 3rd Fl.
Markham, ON, CAN L3R 9S9
Ph: (905) 470-8995
E-mail: info@atslotca.com
URL: http://www.oltca.com/

Ontario Public Buyers Association
Ste. 361, 111 4th Ave., Ridley Sq.
Ridley Sq.
Saint Catharines, ON, CAN L2S 3P5
Ph: (905) 682-2644
E-mail: info@atsopba.ca
URL:

Ontario Safety League
2595 Skymark Ave Ste. 212
Mississauga, ON, CAN L4W 4L4
Ph: (905) 625-0556

Open Horizons
PO Box 2887
Taos, NM, USA 87571
Ph: (641) 472-6130
E-mail: info@atsbookmarket.com
URL: http://www.bookmarket.com

Optical Society of America
2010 Massachusetts Ave., NW
Washington, DC, USA 20036-1023
Ph: (202) 223-8130
E-mail: info@atsosa.org
URL: http://www.osa.org

Orange County Multi-Housing Service Corp.
12822 Garden Grove Blvd., Ste. D
Garden Grove, CA, USA 92843
Ph: (714) 638-5550
E-mail: info@atsaaoc.com
URL: http://www.aaoc.com/

Orban Communications Inc.
25 Washington St., 4th Fl.
Morristown, NJ, USA 7960
Ph: (973) 605-2442
E-mail: http://www.e-travelnews.com/

Oregon Genealogical Society Inc.
PO Box 10306
Eugene, OR, USA 97440-2306
Ph: (541) 345-0399

Oregon Newspaper Publishers Association
7150 SW Hampton St., Ste. 111
Portland, OR, USA 97223
Ph: (503) 624-6397
E-mail: onpa@atsorenews.com
URL: http://www.orenews.com

The Oregonian
1320 SW Broadway
Portland, OR, USA 97201
Ph: (503) 221-8327

Organization of American Kodaly Educators
1612 29th Ave., S.
Moorhead, MN, USA 56560
Ph: (218) 227-6253
E-mail: oakeoffice@atsoake.org
URL: http://oake.org

Orion Research Corp.
14555 N Scottsdale Rd., Ste. 330
Scottsdale, AZ, USA 85254-3457
E-mail: support@atsusedprice.com
URL: http://www.usedprice.com/

Oryx Press
88 Post Rd. W
PO Box 5007
Westport, CT, USA 6881
E-mail: http://www.greenwood.com

Out Your Backdoor
4686 Meridian Rd.
Williamston, MI, USA 48895
Ph: (517) 347-1689
E-mail: jeff@atsoutyourbackdoor.com
URL: http://www.outyourbackdoor.com/list_articles.php?catid=20

Outskirts Press, Incorporated
10940 S Parker Rd., No. 515
Parker, CO, USA 80134

Owl Books
1021 Rte. 109
Farmingdale, NY, USA 11735
Ph: (631) 249-9803
E-mail: http://www.owlbooks.com

Owner-Operator Independent Drivers Association Inc.
1 NW OOIDA Dr.
Grain Valley, MO, USA 64029
Ph: (816) 229-5791
E-mail: webmaster@atsooida.com
URL: http://www.ooida.com/

Oxbridge Communications Inc.
186 5th Ave.
New York, NY, USA 10010-5202
Ph: (212) 741-0231
E-mail: info@atsoxbridge.com
URL: http://www.oxbridge.com

Oxford University Press
198 Madison Ave.
New York, NY, USA 10016-4314
Ph: (212) 726-6000

P

Pace Communications Inc.
1301 Carolina St.
Greensboro, NC, USA 27401
Ph: (336) 378-6065
E-mail: http://www.pacecommunications.com

Pace Law School
78 North Broadway
White Plains, NY, USA 10603
Ph: (914) 422-4210

Pacific Northwest Christmas Tree Association
PO Box 3366
Salem, OR, USA 97302-1741
Ph: (503) 364-2942
E-mail: http://www.nwtrees.com

Pacific Resource Development Group, Inc.
1651 NE, 185th St.
Seattle, WA, USA 98155
E-mail: pacres@atsshadesofgray.com
URL:

PageFree Publishing, Incorporated
109 S Farmer St.
Otsego, MI, USA 49078
Ph: (269) 692-3926

Paint and Decorating Retailers Association
1401 Triad Ctr. Dr.
Saint Peters, MO, USA 63376-7353
Ph: (636) 326-2636
E-mail: info@atspdra.org
URL: http://www.pdra.org

Painting & Decorating Contractors of America
1801 Park 270 Dr., Ste. 220
Saint Louis, MO, USA 63146
Ph: (314) 514-7322
E-mail: http://www.pdca.org

Paisano Publications L.L.C.
28210 Dorothy Dr.
Agoura Hills, CA, USA 91301
Ph: (818) 889-8740
E-mail: bulkmagazines@atspaisanopub.com
URL: http://www.easyriders.com

Palgrave Macmillan
175 5th Ave.
New York, NY, USA 10010
Ph: (212) 982-9300

Palm Beach County Genealogical Society Inc.
PO Box 17617
West Palm Beach, FL, USA 33416
Ph: (561) 616-3455
E-mail: ancestry@atspbcgensoc.org
URL: http://www.pbcgensoc.org/

Palm Beach Post
2751 S Dixie Hwy.
West Palm Beach, FL, USA 33416
Ph: (561) 820-4100

Pan American Health Organization
Publications Program, PAHO
525 23rd St. NW
Washington, DC, USA 20037
Ph: (202) 974-3000
E-mail: http://www.paho.org

Panoptic Enterprises
6055 Ridge Ford Dr.
PO Box 11220
Burke, VA, USA 22015-3653
Ph: (703) 451-5953
E-mail: panoptic@atsfedgovcontracts.com
URL: http://www.fedgovcontracts.com

The Pantagraph
301 W Washington St.
Bloomington, IL, USA 61702
Ph: (309) 829-9000

Pantheon Books
1745 Broadway
New York, NY, USA 10019
Ph: (212) 782-9000
E-mail: http://pantheon.knopfdoubleday.com

Para Publishing
530 Ellwood Ridge Rd.
Santa Barbara, CA, USA 93117-1047
Ph: (805) 968-7277
E-mail: info@atsparapublishing.com
URL: http://www.parapublishing.com

Para Publishing
PO Box 8206-240
Santa Barbara, CA, USA 93118
Ph: (805) 968-7277
E-mail: info@atsparapublishing.com
URL: http://www.parapublishing.com

Parkwest Publications, Incorporated
PO Box 310251
Miami, FL, USA 33231
Ph: (305) 256-7880

PartiLife Publications
65 Sussex St.
Hackensack, NJ, USA 7601
Ph: (201) 441-4224
E-mail: info@atsballoonsandparties.com
URL: http://www.balloonsandparties.com/

Paul Turok
Old Chelsea Sta.
PO Box 202
New York, NY, USA 10113-0202
Ph: (212) 691-9229
E-mail: tcpublication@atsverizon.net
URL:

PBI Media L.L.C.
2700 Westchester Ave., Ste. 107
Purchase, NY, USA 10577
Ph: (914) 251-4705
E-mail: clientservices@atspbimedia.com
URL:

PC Magazine
28 E 28th St.
New York, NY, USA 10016
Ph: (212) 503-3500

PCS Mailing List Company
39 Cross St.
Peabody, MA, USA 01960-1628
Ph: (978) 532-7100
E-mail: info@atspcslist.com
URL:

Peachpit Press
1249 8th St.
Berkeley, CA, USA 94710
Ph: (510) 524-2178

Peanut Butter and Jelly Press LLC
PO Box 590239
Newton, MA, USA 2459
E-mail: info@atspbjpress.com
URL: http://www.pbjpress.com

Pearson Education
1 Lake St.
Upper Saddle River, NJ, USA 7458
Ph: (201) 236-7000

Pearson Education, Ltd.
Magna Park
3 Castle Mound Way
Harlow, WW, GBR CV23 0WB
E-mail: http://www.pearsoned.co.uk

Pearson Technology Group Canada
10 Alcorn Ave., Ste. 304
Toronto, ON, CAN M4V 3B2

Penguin Group
375 Hudson St.
New York, NY, USA 10014-3757
Ph: (212) 366-2000
E-mail: customerservice@atspenguinput-nam.com
URL: http://www.penguinputnam.com

Penguin Group USA Inc.
375 Hudson St.
New York, NY, USA 10014
Ph: (212) 366-2000
E-mail: http://us.penguingroup.com

Penner Publishing
PO Box 926
Hightstown, NJ, USA 8520
Ph: (609) 443-0038

Pennsylvania State University
116 Deike Bldg.
University Park, PA, USA 16802
Ph: (814) 865-6546
E-mail: http://www.ems.psu.edu

Pennsylvania State University Press
820 N University Dr., USB-1, Ste. C
University Park, PA, USA 16802
Ph: (814) 865-1327

PennWell Corp.
1421 S Sheridan Rd.
Tulsa, OK, USA 74112
Ph: (918) 835-3161
E-mail: http://www.pennwell.com

PennWell Publishing Co.
98 Spit Brook Rd.
Nashua, NH, USA 3062
Ph: (603) 891-0123
E-mail: http://www.ils.pennet.com

Penton Business Media Inc.
7900 International Dr., Ste. 300
Minneapolis, MN, USA 55425
Ph: (952) 851-9329

Penton Media
249 W 17th St.
New York, NY, USA 10011-5390
Ph: (212) 204-4200
E-mail: corporatecustomerservice@atspenton.com
URL: http://www.penton.com

Penton Media Inc.
2100 West Loop S, Ste. 900
Houston, TX, USA 77027
Ph: (713) 300-0674

Penton Media Inc.
9800 Metcalf Ave.
Overland Park, KS, USA 66212
Ph: (913) 341-1300
E-mail: http://www.penton.com

Percussive Arts Society
110 W Washington St., Ste. A
Indianapolis, IN, USA 46294
Ph: (317) 974-4488
E-mail: percarts@atspas.org
URL: http://www.pas.org

Perkins Communications L.L.C.
1513 Reserve Ln.
DeKalb, IL, USA 60115
Ph: (815) 758-1914
E-mail: http://www.greenhousebiz.com

Perseus Books Group
387 Park Ave. S, 12th Fl.
New York, NY, USA 10016
Ph: (212) 340-8100

Personal Care Products Council
1101 17th St. NW, Ste. 300
Washington, DC, USA 20036-4702
Ph: (202) 331-1770
E-mail: publications@atsctfa.org
URL: http://www.personalcarecouncil.org

Personal Selling Power Inc.
1140 International Pkwy.
PO Box 5467
Fredericksburg, VA, USA 22406
Ph: (540) 752-7000
E-mail: editorial@atssellingpower.com
URL: http://www.sellingpower.com

The Pet Care Services Association
2760 North Academy Blvd.
Colorado Springs, CO, USA 80917
Ph: (719) 667-1600
E-mail: webmaster@atsPetCareServices.org
URL: http://www.petcareservices.org/

Pet Industry Distributors Association (PIDA)
2105 Laurel Bush Rd., Ste. 200
Bel Air, MD, USA 21015
Ph: (443) 640-1060
E-mail: pida@atsksgroup.org
URL:

Peter Baylies
61 Brightwood Ave.
Durham, NC, USA 27707
Ph: (978) 685-7931
E-mail: athomedad@atsaol.com
URL:

Peter Glenn Publications
235 SE 5th Ave., Ste. R
Delray Beach, FL, USA 33483
Ph: (561) 404-4685
E-mail: http://www.pgdirect.com/About.asp

Peter Katz Productions Inc.
9 Romar Ave.
White Plains, NY, USA 10605
Ph: (914) 949-7443
E-mail: http://www.aviationmonthly.com

Pfingsten Publishing, LLC
6000 Lombardo Center Dr., Ste. 420
Seven Hills, OH, USA 44131
Ph: (216) 328-8926

PG Publishing Company
34 Blvd. of the Allies
Pittsburgh, PA, USA 15222
Ph: (412) 263-1100

Pharmacy Week
7780 Elmwood Ave, Ste. 210
Madison, WI, USA 53562
Ph: (608) 251-1112
E-mail: info@atspharmacyweek
URL:

Pheasant Meadow Farm
1338 Hughes Shop Rd.
Westminster, MD, USA 21158
E-mail: http://www.qis.net/@tldminidonk/donktext.htm

Philadelphia Inquirer
400 N Broad St.
Philadelphia, PA, USA 19130
Ph: (215) 854-2000

Philadelphia Media Network
400 N Broad St.
Philadelphia, PA, USA 19130
Ph: (215) 854-2000

Phillips Business Information Inc.
4 Choke Cherry Rd., 2nd Fl.
Rockville, MD, USA 20850
Ph: (301) 354-2101

Phoenix Business Journal
101 N 1st Ave., Ste. 2300
Phoenix, AZ, USA 85003
Ph: (602) 230-8400

Phoenix Media Corporation
100 Cummings Center, Ste. 211-C
Beverly, MA, USA 1915
Ph: (978) 338-6545

The Photo Review
140 E Richardson Ave., Ste. 301
Langhorne, PA, USA 19047
E-mail: info@atsphotoreview.org
URL: http://www.photoreview.org

The Photograph Collector
140 E Richardson Ave., Ste. 301
Langhorne, PA, USA 19047-2824
Ph: (215) 891-0214
E-mail: info@atsphotoreview.org
URL:

Photographic Society of America
3000 United Founders Blvd., Ste. 103
Oklahoma City, OK, USA 73112
Ph: (405) 843-1437
E-mail: hq@atspsa-photo.org
URL: http://www.psa-photo.org

PhotoSource International
Pine Lake Farm
1910 35th Rd.
Osceola, WI, USA 54020-5602
Ph: (715) 248-3800
E-mail: info@atsphotosource.com
URL: http://www.photosource.com

Pi Yee Press
4855 W Nevso Dr.
Las Vegas, NV, USA 89103
Ph: (702) 579-7711
E-mail: info@atsbj21.com
URL: http://www.bj21.com

Piano Today
PO Box 58629
Boulder, CO, USA 80323
E-mail: http://www.pianotoday.com/

Picador USA
175 5th Ave.
New York, NY, USA 10010
Ph: (212) 674-5151
E-mail: academic@atshholt.com
URL: http://www.picadorusa.com

Pictorial Photographers of America
PO Box 2234
Ogunquit, ME, USA 03907-2234

Pierian Press
3196 Maple Dr.
Ypsilanti, MI, USA 48108-1416
Ph: (734) 434-4074
E-mail: mew_42strat@atsyahoo.com
URL: http://www.pierianpress.com

Pinnacle Publishing Group
8205-F Estates Pky.
Plain City, OH, USA 43064
E-mail: http://www.midwestfoodnetwork.com/

Pinnacle Publishing Inc.
316 N Michigan Ave., Ste. 300
Chicago, IL, USA 60601
Ph: (312) 960-4100
E-mail: pinpub@atsragan.com
URL:

Pioneer Communications Inc.
218 6th Ave., Ste. 610
Des Moines, IA, USA 50309
Ph: (515) 246-0402
E-mail: kroberson@atsthepioneergroup.com
URL: http://www.thepioneergroup.com/aboutus.htm

Pitney-Bowes
1 Elmcroft Rd.
Stamford, CT, USA 06926-0700
Ph: (203) 356-5000
E-mail: webmaster@atspb.com
URL: http://www.pb.com

Pittsburgh-Post Gazette
34 Blvd. of the Allies
Pittsburgh, PA, USA 15222
Ph: (412) 263-1100

Planning Shop
555 Bryant St., No. 180
Palo Alto, CA, USA 94301
Ph: (650) 289-9120

Polar Bear Alumni Association (PBAA)
165 Morse Rd.
Columbus, OH, USA 43214
Ph: (614) 263-8317
E-mail: lfaust@atscolumbus.rr.com
URL:

Polaris International
9200 S Dadeland Blvd., Ste. 510
Miami, FL, USA 33156
Ph: (305) 670-0580
E-mail: info@atsaccountants.org
URL: http://www.accountants.org

Polish Genealogical Society of America Inc.
984 N Milwaukee Ave.
Chicago, IL, USA 60622
Ph: (773) 384-3352
E-mail: pgsamerica@atsaol.com
URL: http://www.pgsa.org/

Portbook Publications Inc.
PO Box 462
Belfast, ME, USA 4915
Ph: (207) 338-1619
E-mail: info@atsportbook.net
URL: http://www.portbook.net

Porter Sargent Publishers Inc.
11 Beacon St., Ste. 1400
Boston, MA, USA 02108-3099
Ph: (617) 523-1670
E-mail: http://www.portersargent.com

Portfolio
375 Hudson St.
New York, NY, USA 10014-3657
Ph: (212) 366-2372
E-mail: info@atsus.penguingroup.com
URL: http://us.penguingroup.com

Portfolio Hardcover
375 Hudson St.
New York, NY, USA 10014-3657
Ph: (212) 366-2372
E-mail: info@atsus.penguingroup.com
URL: http://us.penguingroup.com

Portfolio Publishing
375 Hudson St.
New York, NY, USA 10014
Ph: (212) 366-2372
E-mail: http://www.penguingroup.com

Portland Business Journal
851 SW 6th Ave., Ste. 500
Portland, OR, USA 97204
Ph: (503) 274-8733

Portland Press Herald
PO Box 1460
Portland, ME, USA 4101
Ph: (207) 791-6920

Postcard History Society
1795 Kleinfeltersvil Rd.
Stevens, PA, USA 17578
Ph: (717) 721-9273

Potomac Books
PO Box 605
Herndon, VA, USA 20172
E-mail: pbimail@atspresswarehouse.com
URL: http://www.potomacbooksinc.com/

Power Trade Media L.L.C.
4742 N 24th St., Ste. 340
Phoenix, AZ, USA 85016
Ph: (602) 265-7600
E-mail: friend@atsbusride.com
URL: http://www.powertrademedia.com

Powerboat Magazine
2575 Vista Del Mar
Ventura, CA, USA 93001
Ph: (805) 667-4100
E-mail: edit-dept@atspowerboatmag.com
URL: http://www.powerboatmagazine.com

Powershift Communications Inc.
245 Fairview Mall Dr., 5th Fl.
Toronto, ON, CAN M2J 4T1
Ph: (416) 494-1066
E-mail: dbm@atspowershift.ca
URL: http://www.powershift.ca

Poynter Center for the Study of Ethics and American Institutions
618 3rd St.
Bloomington, IN, USA 47405
Ph: (812) 855-0261
E-mail: poynter@atsindiana.edu
URL:

PR Newswire
350 Hudson St., Ste. 300
New York, NY, USA 10014

Practitioners Publishing Company
PO Box 966
Fort Worth, TX, USA 76101-0966

Precision Metalforming Association
6363 Oak Tree Blvd.
Independence, OH, USA 44131-2500
Ph: (216) 901-8800
E-mail: http://www.metalforming.com/

Precision Shooting Inc.
222 McKee St.
Manchester, CT, USA 6040
Ph: (860) 645-8776
E-mail: http://www.precisionshooting.com

Premiere Publications
14531 Jefferson St.
Midway City, CA, USA 92655
Ph: (714) 893-0053
E-mail: editor@atsthe-royal-spaniels.com
URL: http://www.the-royal-spaniels.com/

Prentice Hall
375 Hudson St.
New York, NY, USA 10014
E-mail: http://www.pearsonhighered.com

Prentice Hall Business Publishing
1 Lake St.
Upper Saddle River, NJ, USA 7458
Ph: (201) 236-7000

Prentice Hall Higher Education
75 Arlington St.
Boston, MA, USA 2116

Prentice Hall Press
240 Frisch Ct.
Paramus, NJ, USA 7652
Ph: (201) 909-6200

Prentice Hall Press
1 Lake St.
Upper Saddle River, NJ, USA 7458
Ph: (201) 236-7000

Prentice Hall PTR
1 Lake St.
Upper Saddle River, NJ, USA 7458
Ph: (201) 236-7676
E-mail: http://phbusiness.prenhall.com

Prentiss Publishing
PO Box 1257
Prentiss, MS, USA
Ph: (601) 792-4221

Presidential Families of America
10939 West 59th Pl.
Arvada, CO, USA 80004-4732
Ph: (305) 493-0003

Preston Publications
6600 W Touhy Ave.
Niles, IL, USA 60714-4588
Ph: (847) 647-2900
E-mail: tpreston@atsprestonpub.com
URL: http://www.prestonpub.com

Prima Publishing
3875 Atherton Rd.
Rocklin, CA, USA 95765
Ph: (916) 632-4400

Primedia
261 Madison Ave., 6th Fl.
New York, NY, USA 10016
E-mail: power&motoryacht@atspalm-coastd.com
URL: http://www.powerandmotoryacht.com/contacts/

Primedia Business
PO Box 603
Indianapolis, IN, USA 46206
Ph: (317) 297-5500
E-mail: atmarketing@atsprimediabusiness.com
URL: http://www.primediabusiness.com

Primedia Business
3585 Engineering Dr., Ste. 100
Norcross, GA, USA 30092
Ph: (678) 421-3000
E-mail: inquiries@atsprimediabusiness.com
URL:

Primedia Business Magazines
PO Box 66010
Houston, TX, USA 77266
Ph: (713) 523-8124
E-mail: inquiries@atsprismb2b.com
URL: http://www.primediabusiness.com

Primedia Business Magazines & Media
3585 Engineering Dr., Ste 100
Norcross, GA, USA 30092
Ph: (678) 421-3000
E-mail: http://www.primedia.com/contact-us.aspx

Primedia Consumer Media and Magazine Group
3585 Engineering Dr., Ste. 100
Norcross, GA, USA 30092
Ph: (678) 421-3000
E-mail: nbigley@atsprimedia.com
URL: http://www.primedia.com/

PRIMEDIA Los Angeles
3585 Engineering Dr., Ste. 100
Norcross, GA, USA 30092-2891
Ph: (678) 421-3494
E-mail: http://www.primedia.com

Primedia Special Interest Publications
3585 Engineering Dr., Ste. 100
Norcross, GA, USA 30092
Ph: (678) 421-3000
E-mail: http://www.primedia.com/

Princeton University Press
41 William St.
Princeton, NJ, USA 8540
Ph: (609) 258-4900
E-mail: orders@atscpfs.pupress.princeton.edu
URL:

Print It Design and Publishing, Inc.
191 Blossom Ct.
Paso Robles, CA, USA 93446
Ph: (805) 237-7906
E-mail: trq@atsprintitdesign.com
URL: http://printitdesign.com/contact_me.html

Print Services & Distribution Association
433 E Monroe Ave.
Alexandria, VA, USA 22301-1645
Ph: (703) 836-6232
E-mail: psda@atspsda.org
URL: http://www.psda.org

Print Services & Distribution Association
401 N Michigan Ave., Ste. 2200
Chicago, IL, USA 60611
E-mail: psda@atspsda.org
URL: http://www.psda.org

PrintImage International
2250 East Devon Ave., Ste. 245
Chicago, IL, USA 60018
Ph: (800) 234-0040
E-mail: info@atsprintimage.org
URL: http://www.naqp.com

Printing Industries of America Inc.
200 Deer Run Rd.
Sewickley, PA, USA 15143
Ph: (412) 741-6861
E-mail: printing@atsprinting.org
URL: http://www.printing.org/

Printworld International Inc.
937 Jefferson Way
PO Box 1957
West Chester, PA, USA 19380
Ph: (610) 431-6654
E-mail: sales@atsprintworlddirectory.com
URL: http://www.printworlddirectory.com/printworld

Product News Network
5 Penn Plz., 14th Fl.
New York, NY, USA 10001

Productive Publications
Entrepreneurship Institute of Canada
75 King St. S
PO Box 40043
Waterloo, ON, CAN N2J 4V1
Ph: (519) 885-1559
E-mail: entinst@atssympatico.ca
URL: http://www.entinst.ca/Business 20Prod.Pub.htm

Professional and Technical Consultants Association
PO Box 2261
Santa Clara, CA, USA 95055
Ph: (408) 971-5902
E-mail: info@atspatca.org
URL: http://www.patca.org

Professional Association of Canadian Theatres
215 Spadina Ave., Ste. 555
Toronto, ON, CAN M5T 2C7
Ph: (416) 595-6455
E-mail: info@atspact.ca
URL: http://www.pact.ca

Professional Association of Innkeepers International
207 White Horse Pke.
Haddon Heights, NJ, USA 08035-1703
E-mail: info@atspaii.org
URL:

Professional Grounds Management Society
720 Light St.
Baltimore, MD, USA 21230
Ph: (410) 223-2861
E-mail: pgms@atsassnhqtrs.com
URL: http://www.pgms.org

Professional Landcare Network
950 Herndon Pky., Ste. 450
Herndon, VA, USA 20170
Ph: (703) 736-9666
E-mail: info@atslandcarenetwork.org
URL: http://www.landcarenetwork.org

Professional Photographers of America Inc.
229 Peachtree St. NE, Ste. 2200
Atlanta, GA, USA 30303
Ph: (404) 522-8600
E-mail: csc@atsppa.com
URL: http://www.ppa.com/

Professional School Photographers of America
3000 Picture Pl.
Jackson, MI, USA 49201
Ph: (517) 788-8100

Professional Writers Association of Canada
215 Spadina Ave., Ste. 123
Toronto, ON, CAN M5T 2C7
Ph: (416) 504-1645
E-mail: info@atspwac.ca
URL: http://www.pwac.ca

Profile Books Limited
Exmouth Market
3A Exmouth House
Pine St.
London, , GBR EC1R 0JH
Ph: (440) 2078416300
E-mail: http://www.profilebooks.com

Program for Art on Film Inc.
c/o Pratt Sils
200 Willoughby Ave.
New York, NY, USA 11205
Ph: (718) 399-4506
E-mail: info@atsartfilm.org
URL: http://www.artfilm.org

Progressive Business Publications
370 Technology Dr.
Malvern, PA, USA 19355
Ph: (610) 695-8600
E-mail: customer_service@atspbp.com
URL: http://www.pbp.com

Project HOPE
255 Carter Hall Ln.
Millwood, VA, USA 22646
E-mail: hope@atsprojecthope.org
URL: http://www.projecthope.org/

Project Management Institute
14 Campus Blvd.
Newtown Square, PA, USA 19073
Ph: (610) 356-4600
E-mail: customercare@atspmi.org
URL: http://www.pmi.org/

Promociones Tyson S.A. de C.V.
7770 Regents Rd., No. 113-387
San Diego, CA, USA 92122
Ph: (858) 569-0172
E-mail: tyson@atstysonpromotions.com
URL: http://promocionestyson.com/

Promotion Marketing Association Inc.
257 Park Ave. S, Ste. 1102
New York, NY, USA 10010
Ph: (212) 420-1100
E-mail: pma@atspmalink.org
URL:

Promotional Products Association International
3125 Skyway Cir. N
Irving, TX, USA 75038-3526
E-mail: http://www.ppa.org/default

Property Management Association
7508 Wisconsin Ave., 4th Fl.
Bethesda, MD, USA 20814
Ph: (301) 657-9200
E-mail: info@atspma-dc.org
URL: http://www.pma-dc.org/

Prosperity & Profits Unlimited, Distribution Services
PO Box 416
Denver, CO, USA 80201-0416
Ph: (303) 575-5676
E-mail: mail@atsprosperityandprofitsunlimited.com
URL: http://www.gumbomedia.com

Prostar Publications Inc.
3 Church Cir., Ste. 109
Annapolis, MD, USA 21401
Ph: (310) 280-1010
E-mail: editor@atsprostarpublications.com
URL: http://www.prostarpublications.com

The PRS Group
6320 Fly Rd., Ste. 102
PO Box 248
East Syracuse, NY, USA 13057
Ph: (315) 431-0511
E-mail: custserv@atsprsgroup.com
URL:

Public Affairs
250 W 57th St., Ste. 1321
New York, NY, USA 10107
E-mail: http://www.perseus.com/

Public Relations Society of America
33 Maiden Ln., 11th Fl.
New York, NY, USA 10038-5150
Ph: (212) 460-1400
E-mail: ppc@atsprsa.org
URL: http://www.prsa.org

Publicom, Inc.
2800 E Fort Lowell Rd.
Tucson, AZ, USA 85716
Ph: (520) 323-6144
E-mail: info@atswcponline.com
URL: http://www.wcponline.com

PublishAmerica, Incorporated
111/113 E Church St.
Frederick, MD, USA 21701
Ph: (301) 695-1707

Publishers & Producers
PO Box 36
Annandale, VA, USA 22003
Ph: (703) 750-2664
E-mail: subscriptions@atsmanufacturing-news.com
URL:

Publishers Communication Group
875 Massachusetts Ave., 7th Fl.
Cambridge, MA, USA 2139
Ph: (617) 497-6514

Publishers Development Corp.
12345 World Trade Dr.
San Diego, CA, USA 92128
E-mail: subs@atsexpressionartmagazine.com
URL: http://www.shootingindustry.com/Pages/ADClass.html

Publishers Media
PO Box 1295
El Cajon, CA, USA 92022-1295
E-mail: rvhmedia@atsaol.com
URL: http://www.rvhfreegate.com

Publishers Weekly
71 W 23 St., No. 1608
New York, NY, USA 10010
Ph: (212) 377-5500
E-mail: http://www.publishersweekly.com/

The Pueblo Chieftain
825 W 6th St.
Pueblo, CO, USA 81003
Ph: (719) 544-3520

Pulsus Group Inc.
2902 S Sheridan Way
Oakville, ON, CAN L6J 7L6
Ph: (905) 829-4770
E-mail: pulsus@atspulsus.com
URL: http://www.pulsus.com

Purchasing Management Association of Canada (PMAC)
2 Carlton St., Ste. 1414
Toronto, ON, CAN M5B 1J3
Ph: (416) 977-7111
E-mail: info@atspmac.ca
URL:

Purdue University Press
504 W State St.
West Lafayette, IN, USA 47907-2058
E-mail: order@atsbookmasters.com
URL: http://www.thepress.purdue.edu

Q

Qualitative Research Consultants Association
1000 Westgate Dr., Ste. 252
Saint Paul, MN, USA 55114
Ph: (651) 290-7491
E-mail: inquiries@atsqrca.org
URL: http://www.qrca.org

Que
201 W 103rd St.
Indianapolis, IN, USA 46290-1094
Ph: (317) 581-3500

Quebec Dans Le Monde
PO Box 8503
404-1001, Rte. de l'Eglise
Sainte-Foy, QC, CAN G1V 4N5
Ph: (418) 659-5540
E-mail: info@atsquebecmonde.com
URL: http://www.quebecmonde.com

Queens Chamber of Commerce
75-20 Astoria Blvd., Ste. 140
Jackson Heights, NY, USA 11372-1131
Ph: (718) 898-8500
E-mail: queenschamber@atsworldnet.att.net
URL:

Questex Media Group
275 Grove St., 2-130
Newton, MA, USA 2466
Ph: (617) 219-8300
E-mail: http://www.questex.com

Quigley Publishing Company Inc.
64 Wintergreen Ln.
Groton, MA, USA 01450-4129
Ph: (978) 448-0272
E-mail: quigleypub@atsquigleypublishing.com
URL: http://www.quigleypublishing.com

Quinlan Publishing Co.
610 Opperman Dr.
Eagan, MN, USA 55123
Ph: (651) 687-7000
E-mail: http://west.thomson.com/quinlan/

Quirk Enterprises Inc.
4662 Slater Rd.
Eagan, MN, USA 55122
Ph: (651) 379-6200
E-mail: info@atsquirks.com
URL: http://www.quirks.com

R

R & R Publishing
446 N Wells St., Ste. 254
Chicago, IL, USA 60610
Ph: (312) 952-4900
E-mail: info@atsrnrpublishing.com
URL: http://www.rnrpublishing.com

R I D Publications
333 Commerce St.
Alexandria, VA, USA 22314
Ph: (703) 838-0030
E-mail: views@atsrid.org
URL:

R. Max Bowser
PO Box 6278
Newport News, VA, USA 23606
Ph: (757) 877-5979
E-mail: ministocks@atsaol.com
URL:

R. S. Means Co., Inc.
63 Smiths Ln.
Kingston, MA, USA 2364
Ph: (800) 334-3509
E-mail: http://www.rsmeans.com

R.R. Bowker L.L.C.
630 Central Ave.
New Providence, NJ, USA 7974
Ph: (908) 286-1090
E-mail: http://www.bowker.com

Racher Press Inc.
220 5th Ave., Ste. 18
New York, NY, USA 10001
Ph: (646) 763-8268

Radio-Television News Directors Association
1025 F St. NW, Ste. 700
Washington, DC, USA 20004
Ph: (202) 467-5214
E-mail: membership@atsrtnda.org
URL: http://www.rtnda.org

Raising Capital
1729 H St. NW
Washington, DC, USA 20006
Ph: (202) 887-6400
E-mail: books@atskiplinger.com
URL: http://www.kiplinger.com

RAM Research Group
Rockefeller Ctr.
1230 Ave. of the Americas, 7th Fl.
New York, NY, USA 10020
Ph: (212) 745-1362
E-mail: cardstaff@atsramresearch.com
URL:

RAND Corporation
1776 Main St.
PO Box 2138
Santa Monica, CA, USA 90407-2138
Ph: (310) 393-0411

Randall Publishing Inc.
PO Box 1426
Elk Grove Village, IL, USA 60009
Ph: (847) 437-6604
E-mail: publisher@atsgeartechnology.com
URL: http://www.geartechnology.com

Randall-Reilly Publishing Co.
3200 Rice Mine Rd. NE
Tuscaloosa, AL, USA 35406
E-mail: http://www.randallpub.com/

Random House
1745 Broadway
New York, NY, USA 10019
Ph: (212) 782-9000
E-mail: customerservice@atsrandomhouse.com
URL:

Random House Information Group
1745 Broadway
New York, NY, USA 10010
Ph: (212) 751-2600
E-mail: bwaypub@atsrandomhouse.com
URL: http://www.randomhouse.com

Random House Publishing Group
1745 Broadway
New York, NY, USA 10019
Ph: (212) 751-2600
E-mail: bwaypub@atsrandomhouse.com
URL: http://www.randomhouse.com

Random Lengths Publications Inc.
450 Country Club Rd., Ste. 240
PO Box 867
Eugene, OR, USA 97401-6053
Ph: (541) 686-9925
E-mail: rlmail@atsrandomlengths.com
URL: http://www.randomlengths.com/

The Rangefinder Publishing Company Inc.
6059 Bristol Pky., Ste. 100
Culver City, CA, USA 90230
Ph: (310) 846-4770
E-mail: http://www.rangefindermag.com

Rayve Productions, Inc.
PO Box 726
Windsor, CA, USA 95492
Ph: (707) 838-6200

RB Publishing Co.
2901 International Ln.
Madison, WI, USA 53704
E-mail: http://www.rbpub.com/ME2/Default.asp

ReadHowYouWant.com, Ltd.
1201 11871 Horseshoe Way
Richmond, BC, CAN V7A 5H5
E-mail: http://Readhttp://owYouWant.com

Reading Eagle/Reading Times
345 Penn St.
Reading, PA, USA 19603
Ph: (610) 371-5000

Realtor Magazine
430 N Michigan Ave.
Chicago, IL, USA 60811

Realtors Land Institute
430 N Michigan Ave.
Chicago, IL, USA 60611
Ph: (800) 441-5263
E-mail: rli@atsrealtors.org
URL:

Realty Publications Inc.
PO Box 20069
Riverside, CA, USA 92516
Ph: (951) 781-7300
E-mail: customerservice@atsfirsttuesday.us
URL: http://www.firsttuesdayonline.com/

Record
150 River St.
Hackensack, NJ, USA 7601
Ph: (201) 646-4000

Recreation Vehicle Dealers Association of North America
3930 University Dr.
Fairfax, VA, USA 22030-2515
Ph: (703) 591-7130
E-mail: info@atsrvda.org
URL: http://www.rvda.org

Recreation Vehicle Industry Association
1896 Preston White Dr.
PO Box 2999
Reston, VA, USA 20191
Ph: (703) 620-6003
E-mail: rvia@atsrvia.org
URL: http://www.rvia.org

Rector Press, Ltd.
130 Rattlesnake Gutter Rd.
Leverett, MA, USA 01054-9926
Ph: (413) 367-0303
E-mail: info@atsrectorpress.com
URL: http://www.rectorpress.com

Recycling Council of Ontario
51 Wolseley, 2nd Fl.
Toronto, ON, CAN M5T 1A4
Ph: (416) 657-2797
E-mail: rco@atsrco.on.ca
URL:

RedCoat Publishing Inc.
900 Cummings Center, Ste. 222-T
Beverly, MA, USA 1915
Ph: (978) 232-9494

RedCoat Publishing, Inc.
900 Cummings Ctr., Ste. 222-T
Beverly, MA, USA 1915
Ph: (978) 232-9494
E-mail: http://www.redcoatpublishing.com/

Reed Business Geo, Inc.
100 Tuscanny Dr., Ste. B-1
Frederick, MD, USA 21702
Ph: (301) 682-6101
E-mail: psm@atsprofsurv.com
URL: http://www.profsurv.com/reedbusinessgeo.aspx

Reed Business Information
360 Park Ave. S
New York, NY, USA 10010-1710
Ph: (646) 746-6400
E-mail: corporatecommunications@atsreedbusiness.com
URL: http://www.reedbusiness.com

Reed Business Information
2000 Clearwater Dr.
Oak Brook, IL, USA 60523
Ph: (630) 288-8000

Reed Construction Data
30 Technology Pky. S, Ste. 100
Norcross, GA, USA 30092
Ph: (770) 417-4000
E-mail: http://www.reedconstructiondata.com

Reed Elsevier Reference Publishing
125 Park Ave., 23rd Fl.
New York, NY, USA 10017
Ph: (212) 309-8100

Reed Reference Publishing
125 Park Ave., 23rd Fl.
New York, NY, USA 10017
Ph: (212) 309-8100

Reed Travel Group
3025 Highland Pky., Ste. 200
Downers Grove, IL, USA 60515-5561
Ph: (630) 515-5300
E-mail: custsvc@atsoag.com
URL: http://www.oag.com

Reflector Publishing
1150 Sugg Pky.
PO Box 1967
Greenville, NC, USA 27834
Ph: (252) 329-9500
E-mail: http://www.reflector.com

The Register-Guard
3500 Chad Dr.
Eugene, OR, USA 97408
Ph: (541) 485-1234

Rehabilitation Research and Training Center on Blindness and Low Vision
PO Box 6189
Mississippi State, MS, USA 39762
Ph: (662) 325-2001
E-mail: rrtc@atsra.msstate.edu
URL:

Reilly Communications Group
16 E Schaumburg Rd.
Schaumburg, IL, USA 60194-3536
Ph: (847) 882-6336
E-mail: info@atsrcgpubs.com
URL: http://new.reillycomm.com/contact.php

Rent-A-Wreck of America Inc.
Licensee Service Center
105 Main St.
Laurel, MD, USA 20707
E-mail: http://www.rentawreck.com

RePlay Magazine
18757 Burbank Blvd., No. 105
Tarzana, CA, USA 91356
Ph: (818) 776-2880
E-mail: editor@atsreplaymag.com
URL: http://www.replaymag.com/

Research Institute of America
395 Hudson St.
New York, NY, USA 10014
Ph: (212) 367-6300 FAX
E-mail: http://ria.thomson.com/

Resort and Commercial Recreation Association
PO Box 1564
Dubuque, IA, USA 52004-1564
E-mail: info@atsrcra.org
URL: http://www.rcra.org

Resource Recycling
PO Box 42270
Portland, OR, USA 97242-0270
Ph: (503) 233-1305
E-mail: info@atsresource-recycling.com
URL: http://www.resource-recycling.com

Restoration Industry Association
12339 Carroll Ave.
Rockville, MD, USA 20852
Ph: (301) 231-6505
E-mail: executiveoffice@atsrestorationindustry.org
URL: http://www.ascr.org

The Retailer's Bakery Association
8201 Greensboro Dr., Ste. 300
McLean, VA, USA 22102
Ph: (703) 610-9035
E-mail: info@atsrbanet.com
URL:

Retired Persons Services Inc.
500 Montgomery St.
Alexandria, VA, USA 22314
Ph: (703) 684-0245

RIA
195 Broadway
New York, NY, USA 10007
Ph: (212) 807-2298
E-mail: http://ria.thomsonreuters.com

RIA
395 Hudson St., 4th Fl.
New York, NY, USA 10014-3669
Ph: (212) 367-6300
E-mail: ria@atsthomson.com
URL: http://www.ria.thomson.com

Rich Publishing LLC
4330 N Civic Center Plz., Ste. 100
Scottsdale, AZ, USA 85251
E-mail: customerservice@atsrichdad.com
URL: http://www.richdad.com

Richard Barovick
5523 Brige Dr
Bethesda, MD, USA 20817
Ph: (301) 907-8647

Richard T. Scofield
PO Box 476
New Albany, OH, USA 43054
Ph: (614) 855-9315

Rick Chapman
34 Sugar Hill Rd.
Killingworth, CT, USA 6419
Ph: (860) 663-0552

E-mail: customer@atssoftletter.com
URL:

Ridgewood Press
728 Glendale Dr.
Jefferson City, MO, USA 65109
Ph: (573) 636-7472

Rimbach Publishing Inc.
St. 8650 Babcock Blvd.
Pittsburgh, PA, USA 15237
Ph: (412) 364-5366
E-mail: info@atsrimbach.com
URL: http://www.rimbach.com/RimPub/PandS/ProdandServ.htm

Riverhead Booksk
375 Hudson St.
New York, NY, USA 10014
Ph: (212) 366-2000
E-mail: riverhead.web@atsus.penguingroup.com
URL: http://www.riverheadbooks.com

Roanoke Times
201 W Campbell Ave.
Roanoke, VA, USA 24010
Ph: (540) 981-3211

Robert M. Parker, Jr.
PO Box 311
Monkton, MD, USA 21111
Ph: (410) 329-6477
E-mail: wineadvocate@atserobertparker.com
URL:

Robert Morris Associates (RMA)
1801 Market St., Ste. 300
Philadelphia, PA, USA 19103-7398
Ph: (215) 446-4000
E-mail: http://www.rmahq.org

The Robert Wood Johnson Foundation (RWJF 2003)
College Rd. E Rte. 1
PO Box 2316
Princeton, NJ, USA 08543-2316
Ph: (877) 843-7953

Robotic Industries Association
900 Victors Way
PO Box 3724
Ann Arbor, MI, USA 48106
Ph: (734) 994-6088
E-mail: webmaster@atsrobotics.org
URL:

Rodale Inc.
33 E Minor St.
Emmaus, PA, USA 18098
Ph: (610) 967-5171
E-mail: info@atsrodale.com
URL: http://www.rodale.com

Rodale Press, Inc.
400 S 10th St.
Emmaus, PA, USA 18098
Ph: (610) 967-8775
E-mail: http://www.rodale.com

RO-EL Productions Inc.
550 W Old Country Rd., Ste. 204
Hicksville, NY, USA 11801
Ph: (516) 932-7860
E-mail: http://www.floorcoveringnews.net/contactus.asp

Rogers Media
1 Mt. Pleasant Rd., 11th Fl.
Toronto, ON, CAN M4Y 2Y5
Ph: (416) 764-1200

Rogers Media Publishing
Box 860
Markham, ON, CAN L3P 8H8
Ph: (905) 946-0084
E-mail: rmpublishing@atsindas.ca
URL: http://www.rogersmagazines.com

Rogers Media Publishing
One Mount Pleasant Rd., 7th Fl.
Toronto, ON, CAN M4Y 2Y5
Ph: (416) 764-2000
E-mail: http://www.rogers.com

Rogers Publishing Ltd.
333 Bloor St. E, 6th Fl.
Toronto, ON, CAN M4W 1G9
Ph: (416) 764-2000

Roll Call CQ
1255 22nd St. NW
Washington, DC, USA 20037
Ph: (202) 419-8500

Ron Mader
12345 SW 18th St., No. 417
Miami, FL, USA 33175

RosettaBooks LLC
200 W 57th St., Ste. 904
New York, NY, USA 10019
Ph: (646) 274-1970
E-mail: editor@atsrosettabooks.com
URL: http://www.rosettabooks.com

Ross Periodicals
42 Digital Dr., No. 5
Novato, CA, USA 94949
E-mail: http://www.sci-mag.com/

Roswell Park Cancer Institute
Elm and Carlton Sts.
Buffalo, NY, USA 14263
Ph: (716) 845-8182
E-mail: askrpci@atsroswellpark.org
URL:

Routledge
270 Madison Ave., Ste. 3
New York, NY, USA 10016
Ph: (212) 216-7800

E-mail: http://www.routledge.com

Routledge
711 3rd Ave., 8th Fl.
New York, NY, USA 10017
Ph: (212) 216-7800

Routledge Journals
270 Madison Ave.
New York, NY, USA 10016-0601
Ph: (212) 216-7800
E-mail: http://www.routledge.com/

Rowman and Littlefield Publishers, Inc.
4501 Forbes Blvd., Ste. 200
Lanham, MD, USA 20706
Ph: (301) 459-3366

Royal Historical Society
University College London
Gower St.
London, , GBR WC1E 6BT

Royal Publishing Inc.
PO Box 398
Glendora, CA, USA 91740-0398
Ph: (626) 335-8069
E-mail: http://www.speakandgrowrich.com

RSVP: The Directory of Illustration and Design
PO Box 050314
Brooklyn, NY, USA 11205-4266
E-mail: info@atsrsvpdirectory.com
URL: http://www.rsvpdirectory.com

Rubber Division
PO Box 499
Akron, OH, USA 44309-0499
Ph: (330) 972-7814
E-mail: http://www.rubber.org

Rug News Magazine
5 Hanover Sq., 21st Fl.
New York, NY, USA 10004
Ph: (212) 269-2016
E-mail: rugnews@atsmuseumbooks.com
URL: http://www.museumbooks.com

Runzheimer International
Runzheimer Pk.
Rochester, WI, USA 53167
Ph: (262) 971-2200
E-mail: cls@atsrunzheimer.com
URL:

Russell Sage Foundation Publications
112 E 64th St.
New York, NY, USA 10065
Ph: (212) 750-6000

Ruth Finley
153 E 87th St.
New York, NY, USA 10128
Ph: (212) 289-0420
E-mail: http://www.fashioncalendar.net/

Rutledge Books Inc.
107 Mill Plain Rd., Ste. 302
Danbury, CT, USA 6811
Ph: (203) 778-5925
E-mail: info@atsrutledgebooks.com
URL:

S

S. Harman & Associates Inc.
PO Box 1129
Sykesville, MD, USA 21784-1129
Ph: (410) 795-9296
E-mail: sharmaninc@atsaol.com
URL:

Sacramento Bee
2100 Q St.
Sacramento, CA, USA 95816
Ph: (916) 321-1000

Sacramento Business Journal
1400 X St.
Sacramento, CA, USA 95818
Ph: (916) 447-7661

Saddle & Bridle Inc.
375 Jackson Ave.
Saint Louis, MO, USA 63130-4243
Ph: (314) 725-9115
E-mail: editor@atssaddleandbridle.com
URL: http://www.saddleandbridle.com

SAGE Publications, Inc.
2455 Teller Rd.
Thousand Oaks, CA, USA 91320-2218
Ph: (805) 499-9774

Saint Louis Business Journal
815 Olive St., Ste. 100
Saint Louis, MO, USA 63101
Ph: (314) 421-6200

Salesforce Training & Consulting Inc.
2005 Sheppard Ave. E, Ste. 109
Toronto, ON, CAN M2J 5B4
Ph: (800) 461-7355
E-mail: info@atssalesforcetraining.com
URL: http://www.salesforcetraining.com

San Diego Business Journal
4909 Murphy Canyon Rd., Ste. 200
San Diego, CA, USA 92123
Ph: (858) 277-6359

San Diego Community Newspaper Group
4645 Cass St., 2nd Fl.
San Diego, CA, USA 92109
Ph: (858) 270-3103
E-mail: sales@atssdnews.com
URL: http://www.sdnews.com

San Diego Floral Association
1650 El Prado, Rm. 105
San Diego, CA, USA 92101-1684
Ph: (619) 232-5762
E-mail: info@atssdfloral.org
URL: http://www.sdfloral.org

San Diego Union-Tribune
350 Camino de la Reina
San Diego, CA, USA 92108

San Fernando Valley Association for the Retarded
15725 Parthenia St.
North Hills, CA, USA 91343
Ph: (818) 894-9301
E-mail: hrasey@atsnhsfvar.org
URL:

San Francisco AIDS Foundation
995 Market St., Ste. 200
San Francisco, CA, USA 94103
Ph: (415) 487-3000
E-mail: feedback@atssfaf.org
URL: http://www.sfaf.org/

San Jose Mercury News
750 Ridder Park Dr.
San Jose, CA, USA 95190
Ph: (408) 288-8060

Sandow Media Corp.
3731 NW 8th Ave.
Boca Raton, FL, USA 33431
Ph: (561) 750-0151
E-mail: sandowinfo@atssandowmedia.com
URL: http://www.sandowmedia.com

Sara Wyant
191 S Gary Ave.
Carol Stream, IL, USA 60188
Ph: (630) 462-2266
E-mail: swyant@atsfarmprogress.com
URL:

Saskatchewan Pulse Corp.
PO Box 516
Regina, SK, CAN S4P 3A2

Scandinavian Collectors Club
PO Box 13196
El Cajon, CA, USA 92022
E-mail: sccwebman@atsgmail.com
URL: http://www.scc-online.org/

Scarecrow Press Inc.
4501 Forbes Blvd., Ste. 200
Lanham, MD, USA 20706
Ph: (301) 459-3366
E-mail: customercare@atsrowman.com
URL: http://www.scarecrowpress.com

Scentouri
PO Box 416
Denver, CO, USA 80201
Ph: (303) 575-5676
E-mail: mail@atscontentprovidermedia.com
URL:

Schaeffer's Investment Research Inc.
5151 Pfeiffer Rd., Ste. 250
Cincinnati, OH, USA 45242
Ph: (513) 589-3800
E-mail: service@atssir-inc.com
URL:

Schiffer Publishing
4880 Lower Valley Rd.
Atglen, PA, USA 19310
E-mail: http://www.schifferbooks.com/

Schneider Publishing Company Inc.
11835 W Olympic Blvd., 12th Fl.
Los Angeles, CA, USA 90064
Ph: (310) 577-3700
E-mail: info@atsschneiderpublishing.com
URL: http://www.schneiderpublishing.com/

Schofield Media Group
200 E Randolph St., 70th Fl.
Chicago, IL, USA 60601
Ph: (312) 236-4090

ScholarOne, Inc.
275 Greenbriar Dr., Ste. 200
Charlottesville, VA, USA 22901
Ph: (434) 817-2040

Schonfeld & Associates Inc.
1931 Lynn Cir.
Libertyville, IL, USA 60048
E-mail: saiinfo@atssaibooks.com
URL: http://www.saibooks.com

School of Labor and Industrial Relations
Michigan State University
404 S Kedzie Hall
East Lansing, MI, USA 48823
Ph: (517) 355-1800
E-mail: shrm@atslir.msu.edu
URL:

Schoolhouse Press
6899 Cary Bluff
Pittsville, WI, USA 54466
Ph: (715) 884-2799
E-mail: info@atsschoolhousepress.com
URL: http://www.schoolhousepress.com/

Scotsman Community Publications
PO Box 4970
Syracuse, NY, USA 13221-4970
Ph: (315) 472-7825
E-mail: pennysaver@atsscotsmanpress.com
URL: http://www.scotsmanonline.com

Scott American Corp.
PO Box 88
West Redding, CT, USA 06896-0088
Ph: (203) 938-2955
E-mail: service@atstravelpublicityleads.com
URL:

Scott Publications
30595 8th Mile
Livonia, MI, USA 48152
Ph: (248) 477-6650
E-mail: polymercafe@atsscottpublications.com
URL: http://www.scottpublications.com

Scott Publishing Co.
911 Vandemark Rd.
PO Box 926
Sidney, OH, USA 45365-0828
E-mail: cuserv@atsamospress.com
URL: http://www.linns.com

Scott's Directories
12 Concorde Pl., Ste. 800
Toronto, ON, CAN M3C 4J2
Ph: (416) 442-2122
E-mail: customercare@atsscottsdirectories.com
URL: http://www.scottsdirectories.com

SCP Journal
PO Box 4308
Berkeley, CA, USA 94704
Ph: (510) 540-0300
E-mail: scp@atsscp-inc.org
URL: http://www.scp-inc.org/

Screenprinting and Graphic Imaging Association International
10015 Main St.
Fairfax, VA, USA 22031-3489
Ph: (703) 385-1335
E-mail: sgia@atssgia.org
URL: http://www.sgia.org

Scribner Educational Publishers
1230 Ave. of the Americas
New York, NY, USA 10020
Ph: (212) 698-7000
E-mail: http://www.simonsays.com

Seahorse Financial Advisers Inc.
359 Shunpike
Millbrook, NY, USA 12545
Ph: (845) 677-6865

Seal Press
Perseus Books Group
1700 4th St.
Berkeley, CA, USA 94710
Ph: (212) 340-8100

Securities Industry and Financial Markets Association
1101 New York Ave. NW, 8th Fl.
Washington, DC, USA 20005
Ph: (202) 962-7300
E-mail: http://www.sifma.org/

Security Letter Inc.
166 E 96th St.
New York, NY, USA 10128
Ph: (212) 348-1553

Sedgwick Publishing
PO Box 328
Boyds, MD, USA 20841-0328
Ph: (301) 528-0011
E-mail: support@atspnmsi.com
URL: http://www.businessmailersreview.com

Seed Savers Exchange
3094 N Winn Rd.
Decorah, IA, USA 52101
Ph: (563) 382-5990
E-mail: john@atsseedsavers.org
URL: http://www.seedsavers.org

Self-Counsel Press Inc.
1704 N State St.
Bellingham, WA, USA 98225
Ph: (360) 676-4530
E-mail: orderdesk@atsself-counsel.com
URL: http://www.self-counsel.com

Self-Counsel Press, Incorporated
1481 Charlotte Rd.
North Vancouver, BC, CAN V7J 1H1
Ph: (604) 986-3366
E-mail: service@atsself-counsel.com
URL: http://www.self-counsel.com

Self-Help Publishers
3-445 Pioneer Dr.
Kitchner, ON, CAN N2P 1L8
E-mail: http://www.selfhelppublishers.com

SER-Jobs for Progress National Inc.
100 E Royal Ln., Ste. 130
Irving, TX, USA 75039
Ph: (469) 549-3600
E-mail: info@atsser-national.org
URL: http://www.ser-national.org

Serves You Right!, Incorporated
6105 E Osborn Rd.
Scottsdale, AZ, USA 85251
Ph: (480) 994-1918

Service Directions Inc.
PO Box 380
Pelham, NY, USA 10803
Ph: (914) 738-3800
E-mail: SDIWECARE@atsaol.com
URL:

Sexuality Information and Education Council of the United States
90 John St., Ste. 704
New York, NY, USA 10038
Ph: (212) 819-9770
E-mail: pmalone@atssiecus.org
URL: http://www.siecus.org/

SGC Horizon LLC
3030 W Salt Creek Ln., Ste. 201
Arlington Heights, IL, USA 60005
Ph: (847) 391-1000
E-mail: http://www.sgchorizon.com/

Shane Downing
PO Box 7939
Torrance, CA, USA 90504
Ph: (310) 515-7369
E-mail: orders@atsgreysheet.com
URL:

SHARE
1501 Broadway, Ste. 704A
between W. 43rd & W. 44th Sts.
New York, NY, USA 10036
Ph: (212) 719-0364

Shelby Publishing Company Inc.
517 Green St. NW
Gainesville, GA, USA 30501
Ph: (770) 534-8380
E-mail: editor@atsshelbypublishing.com
URL: http://www.shelbypublishing.com

Sheltie Pacesetter
9428 Blue Mound Dr.
Fort Wayne, IN, USA 46804
Ph: (260) 434-1566
E-mail: sheltiepacesetter@atscharter.net
URL: http://www.sheltie.com

Shoe Trades Publishing Co.
241 Senneville Rd.
Senneville, QC, CAN H9X 3X5
Ph: (514) 457-8787
E-mail: books@atsshoetrades.com
URL: http://www.shoetrades.com

Shrimp World Inc.
417 Eliza St.
New Orleans, LA, USA 70114
Ph: (504) 368-1571

Shugar's Publishing
15873 Hartwell St.
PO Box 38665
Detroit, MI, USA 48238-0665
Ph: (313) 836-8600
E-mail: purfuneral@atsaol.com
URL: http://www.purpledirectory.com

Siefer Consultants Inc.
525 Cayuga St.
Storm Lake, IA, USA 50588
Ph: (712) 660-1026
E-mail: info@atssiefer.com
URL: http://www.siefer.com

Signcraft Publishing Company Inc.
10271 Deer Run Farms Rd.
PO Box 60031
Fort Myers, FL, USA 33966
Ph: (239) 939-4644
E-mail: signcraft@atssigncraft.com
URL: http://www.signcraft.com

SIGS Publications & Conferences
1250 Broadyway, 19th Fl.
New York, NY, USA 10001-3701
Ph: (212) 242-7447
E-mail: info@atssigs.com
URL:

Silver Lake Publishing
1119 N Broadway St.
Aberdeen, WA, USA 98520-2433

SIMBA Information Inc.
11200 Rockville Pk., Ste. 504
Rockville, MD, USA 20852
Ph: (240) 747-3096
E-mail: customerservice@atssimbainformation.com
URL: http://www.simbanet.com/

Simon & Schuster
1230 Ave. of the Americas
New York, NY, USA 10020
Ph: (212) 698-7000
E-mail: http://www.simonandschuster.com

Simon & Shuster
135 S Mt. Zion Rd.
Lebanon, IN, USA 46052
E-mail: http://www.simonandschuster.com

Simon and Schuster
100 Front St.
Riverside, NJ, USA 8075
Ph: (800) 223-2348

The Simon Foundation for Continence
PO Box 815
Wilmette, IL, USA 60091
Ph: (847) 864-3913

Singles in the Suburbs Inc.
PO Box 952
Winchester, MA, USA 01890-8252
Ph: (781) 721-4220
E-mail: singlessuburbs@atsyahoo.com
URL:

SK Publications
PO Box 6983
Huntington Beach, CA, USA 92615
Ph: (714) 963-1558
E-mail: sk_publishing@atsyahoo.com
URL: http://skinnedknuckles.net/pages/index.htm

Skilled Learning Incorporated
20 Townsite Rd., 2nd Fl.
Nanaimo, BC, CAN V9S 5T7
Ph: (250) 244-2937

Small Business Advisors Inc.
11 Franklin Ave.
PO Box 436
Hewlett, NY, USA 11557
Ph: (516) 374-1387
E-mail: letters@atssmallbusinessadvice.com
URL: http://www.smallbusinessadvice.com/

Small Business Council of America Inc.
4800 Hampton Lane 7th FL
Bethesda, DE, USA 20814
Ph: (301) 656-7603

Small Farm Center
University of California
One Shields Ave.
Davis, CA, USA 95616-8699
Ph: (530) 752-8136
E-mail: sfcenter@atsucdavis.edu
URL:

Smaller Business Association of New England
1601 Trapelo Rd., Ste. 212
Waltham, MA, USA 2451
Ph: (781) 890-9070
E-mail: info@atssbane.org
URL: http://www.sbane.org

Snips Magazine
2401 W Big Beaver Rd., Ste. 700
Troy, MI, USA 48084-3333
Ph: (248) 362-3700
E-mail: http://www.bnpmedia.com

SNL Financial L.C.
1 SNL Plz.
PO Box 2124
Charlottesville, VA, USA 22902
Ph: (434) 977-1600
E-mail: CustomerService@atssnl.com
URL:

SnowSports Industries America
8377-B Greensboro Dr.
McLean, VA, USA 22102-3587
Ph: (703) 556-9020
E-mail: siamail@atssnowsports.org
URL: http://www.snowsports.org/

Society for Business Ethics
University of New Brunswick
PO Box 4400
Fredericton, NB, CAN E3B 5A3

Society for Calligraphy
PO Box 64174
Los Angeles, CA, USA 90064-0174
E-mail: president@atssocietyforcalligraphy.org
URL: http://www.societyforcalligraphy.com

Society for Human Resource Management
1800 Duke St.
Alexandria, VA, USA 22314
Ph: (703) 548-3440
E-mail: shrm@atsshrm.org
URL: http://www.shrm.org

Society for Scholarly Publishing
10200 W 44th Ave., Ste. 304
Wheat Ridge, CO, USA 80033-2840
Ph: (303) 422-3914
E-mail: info@atssspnet.org
URL: http://www.sspnet.org

Society for the Preservation and Advancement of the Harmonica Inc.
PO Box 865
Troy, MI, USA 48099-0865
E-mail: HarpSPAH@atsspah.org
URL:

Society of Actuaries
475 N Martingale Rd., Ste. 600
Schaumburg, IL, USA 60173-2226
Ph: (847) 706-3500
E-mail: bhaynes@atssoa.org
URL: http://www.soa.org

Society of American Travel Writers
7044 S 13th St.
Oak Creek, WI, USA 53154
Ph: (414) 908-4949
E-mail: satw@atssatw.org
URL:

Society of Architectural Historians
1365 N Astor St.
Chicago, IL, USA 60610-2144
Ph: (312) 573-1365
E-mail: info@atssah.org
URL: http://www.sah.org/

Society of Automotive Engineers, Inc.
400 Commonwealth Dr.
Warrendale, PA, USA 15096
Ph: (724) 776-4970
E-mail: sae@atssae.org
URL: http://www.sae.org

Society of Environmental Toxicology & Chemistry
1010 N 12 Ave.
Pensacola, FL, USA 32501-3370
Ph: (850) 469-1500
E-mail: setac@atssetac.org
URL: http://www.setac.org

Society of Financial Service Professionals
17 Campus Blvd., Ste. 100
Newtown Square, PA, USA 19073-3230
Ph: (610) 526-2500
E-mail: custserv@atsfinancialpro.org
URL: http://www.financialpro.org

Society of Financial Service Professionals
19 Campus Blvd., Ste. 100
Newtown Square, PA, USA 19073
Ph: (610) 526-2500
E-mail: custserv@atsfinancialpro.org
URL: http://www.financialpro.org

Society of Industrial and Office Realtors
1201 New York Ave. NW, Ste. 350
Washington, DC, USA 20005-6126
Ph: (202) 449-8200
E-mail: admin@atssior.com
URL: http://www.sior.com

Society of Manufacturing Engineers
1 SME Dr.
PO Box 930
Dearborn, MI, USA 48121
Ph: (313) 425-3000
E-mail: service@atssme.org
URL: http://www.sme.org

Society of Professional Audio Recording Services
9 Music Sq. S, Ste. 222
Nashville, TN, USA 37203
Ph: (800) 771-7727
E-mail: spars@atsspars.com
URL:

Society of Satellite Professionals International
55 Broad St., 14th Fl.
New York, NY, USA 10004
Ph: (212) 809-5199

Software & Information Industry Association
1090 Vermont Ave. NW, 6th Fl.
Washington, DC, USA 20005-4095
Ph: (202) 289-7442
E-mail: info@atssiia.net
URL: http://www.siia.net

Solar Rating & Certification Corp.
400 High Point Dr., Ste. 400
Cocoa, FL, USA 32926
Ph: (321) 213-6037
E-mail: srcc@atssolar-rating.org
URL: http://www.solar-rating.org

SoloDining.com
PO Box 2664
Carlsbad, CA, USA 92018
Ph: (760) 720-1011
E-mail: editor@atssolodining.com
URL:

Sortis Publishing
2193 E Claxton Ave.
Gilbert, AZ, USA 85296
E-mail: info@atssortispublishing.com
URL: http://www.sortispublishing.com

Sosland Publishing Co.
4800 Main St., Ste. 100
Kansas City, MO, USA 64112-2504
Ph: (816) 756-1000
E-mail: web@atssosland.com
URL: http://www.sosland.com

Sound Publishing Inc.
1321 King St., Ste. 4
Bellingham, WA, USA 98229
Ph: (360) 647-8805
E-mail: editor@atsbbjtoday.com
URL: http://bbjtoday.com/

Soundings Publications L.L.C.
10 Bokum Rd.
Essex, CT, USA 6426
Ph: (860) 767-3200
E-mail: info@atssoundingspub.com
URL: http://www.soundingsonline.com/about-us

Source Book Publications
1814 Franklin St., Ste. 820
PO Box 12488
Oakland, CA, USA 94612
Ph: (510) 839-5471
E-mail: http://www.sourcebookpublications.com

Source Interlink Media L.L.C.
261 Madison Ave., 6th Fl.
New York, NY, USA 10016
Ph: (212) 915-4000
E-mail: webmastersim@atssourceinterlink.com
URL: http://www.sourceinterlinkmedia.com/contact/

Sourcebooks Mediafusion
1935 Brookdale Rd., Ste. 139
Naperville, IL, USA 60563
Ph: (630) 961-3900
E-mail: http://www.sourcebooks.com/content/books_mediafusion.asp

Sourcebooks, Inc.
1935 Brookdale Rd., Ste. 139
Naperville, IL, USA 60563
Ph: (630) 961-3900

SourceMedia Inc.
1 State St. Plaza, 27th Fl.
New York, NY, USA 10004
Ph: (212) 803-8200

SourceMedia Inc.
55 Broadway, 6th Fl.
New York, NY, USA 10006
Ph: (212) 803-8200

South Carolina Department of Natural Resources
1000 Assembly St.
Columbia, SC, USA 29201
Ph: (803) 734-3886
E-mail: http://www.dnr.sc.gov/

South Carolina Poultry Federation
1921-A Pickens St.
Columbia, SC, USA 29201
Ph: (803) 779-4700
E-mail: martyg@atsscpoultry.com
URL: http://www.scpoultry.org/contact/

Southern California Genealogical Society & Family Research Library
417 Irving Dr.
Burbank, CA, USA 91504
Ph: (818) 843-7247
E-mail: scgs@atsearthlink.net

URL:

Southern Festivals
PO Box 390
Blakely, GA, USA 39823
E-mail: jimtaylor@atsalltel.net
URL: http://www.southfest.com/festival-_list/georgia.html

Southern Oregon Media Group
111 N Fir St.
Medford, OR, USA 97501
Ph: (541) 776-4411

Southwest Farm Press
7900 International Dr., Ste. 300
Minneapolis, MN, USA 55425-1510
Ph: (952) 851-4631
E-mail: http://southwestfarmpress.com

South-Western
5191 Natorp Blvd.
Mason, OH, USA 45040
Ph: (513) 229-1000

Special Events Magazine
17383 Sunset Blvd., Ste. A220
Pacific Palisades, CA, USA 90272
Ph: (310) 230-7160

Special Interest Group on Data Communication
1515 Broadway, 17th Fl.
New York, NY, USA 10036

Special Interest Group on Programming Languages
Department of Computer Science
151 Engineer's Way
Charlottesville, VA, USA 22904
Ph: (212) 869-7440
E-mail: acmhelp@atsacm.org
URL: http://www.acm.org/sigplan

Specialized Carriers & Rigging Association
2750 Prosperity Ave., Ste. 620
Fairfax, VA, USA 22031-4312
Ph: (703) 698-0291
E-mail: info@atsscranet.org
URL: http://www.scranet.org/

Specialty Equipment Market Association
PO Box 4910
Diamond Bar, CA, USA 91765-0910
Ph: (909) 396-0289
E-mail: info@atssema.org
URL: http://www.sema.org

The Speedy Bee
PO Box 1317
Jesup, GA, USA 31598
Ph: (912) 427-4018
E-mail: speedybee@atsbellsouth.net
URL: http://thespeedybee.com

Sphinx Publishing
1935 Brookdale Rd. Ste. 139
Naperville, IL, USA 60563
Ph: (630) 961-3900

Spiegel & Grau
1745 Broadway
New York, NY, USA 10019
Ph: (212) 782-9000
E-mail: http://www.randomhouse.com/spiegelandgrau/

SPIN
408 Broadway, 4th Fl.
New York, NY, USA 10013
Ph: (515) 242-0297

Spiritual Massage Healing Ministry
6907 Sherman St.
Philadelphia, PA, USA 19119
Ph: (215) 842-0265
E-mail: aschatz@atsunix.temple.edu
URL: http://www.healingandlaw.com/

Splash Magazine
8033 Sunset Blvd., No. 841
Los Angeles, CA, USA 90046
Ph: (323) 650-0084
E-mail: contact@atslasplash.com
URL: http://www.lasplash.com

Spokesman Review
999 W Riverside
Spokane, WA, USA 99201
Ph: (509) 459-5000

Spoon River Press
2319-C West Rohmann Ave.
PO Box 3676
Peoria, IL, USA 61604-5072
Ph: (309) 672-2665

Springer
233 Spring St.
New York, NY, USA 10013
Ph: (212) 460-1500

Springer
Assinippi Pk.
101 Philip Dr.
Norwell, MA, USA 2061
Ph: (781) 681-0537
E-mail: http://www.springer-sbm.com

Springer Netherlands
Van Godewijckstraat 30
Dordrecht, , NLD 3311 GX
E-mail: permissions.dordrecht@atsspringer.com
URL: http://www.springer.com

Springer Publishing Co.
11 W 42nd St., 15th Fl.
New York, NY, USA 10036
Ph: (212) 431-4370
E-mail: cs@atsspringerpub.com
URL: http://www.springerpub.com

Springer Publishing Company
233 Spring St.
New York, NY, USA 10013
Ph: (212) 460-1500
E-mail: http://www.springerpub.com

Springer-Verlag New York Inc.
233 Spring St.
New York, NY, USA 10013-1578
Ph: (212) 460-1500
E-mail: service-ny@atsspringer.com
URL: http://www.springer.com/

Springfield Resources
205 Ash Ln.
Lafayette hill, PA, USA 19444
Ph: (610) 278-7550
E-mail: jdl@atsmaintrainer.com
URL:

SRDS
1700 Higgins Rd.
Des Plaines, IL, USA 60018-5605
Ph: (847) 375-5000
E-mail: http://www.srds.com

ST Media Group International Inc.
11262 Cornell Park Dr.
Cincinnati, OH, USA 45242
Ph: (513) 421-2050
E-mail: customer@atsstmediagroup.com
URL: http://stmediagroup.com

St. James Press
PO Box 9187
Farmington Hills, MI, USA 48333-9187
Ph: (248) 699-4253
E-mail: gale.galeord@atscengage.com
URL: http://www.gale.cengage.com/stjames

St. Louis Post-Dispatch
900 N Tucker Blvd.
Saint Louis, MO, USA 63101
Ph: (314) 340-8000

St. Martin's Press
175 5th Ave.
New York, NY, USA 10010
E-mail: publicity@atsstmartins.com
URL: http://us.macmillan.com/SMP.aspx

St. Martins Press/Macmillan
175 5th Ave.
New York, NY, USA 10010
Ph: (646) 307-5151
E-mail: customerservice@atsmpsvirginia.com
URL: http://us.macmillan.com/smp.aspx

Staffing Industry Analysts Inc.
1975 W El Camino Real, Ste. 304
Mountain View, CA, USA 94040
Ph: (650) 232-2350
E-mail: subservices@atssireport.com
URL: http://www.staffingindustry.com

Stagewrite Publishing Inc.
6220 Stevenson Way
Las Vegas, NV, USA 89120-2722
Ph: (702) 798-0099
E-mail: editor@atsmagicmagazine.com
URL: http://www.magicmagazine.com/contacts.html

Standard & Poor's
55 Water St.
New York, NY, USA 10041-0004
Ph: (212) 438-2000
E-mail: questions@atsstandardandpoors.com
URL: http://www.standardandpoors.com

Standard Publishing Corp.
155 Federal St., 13th Fl.
Boston, MA, USA 02110-9637
Ph: (617) 457-0600
E-mail: customerservice@atsspcpub.com
URL: http://www.spcpub.com/

Standard-Examiner
332 Standard Way
Ogden, UT, USA 84412
Ph: (801) 625-4234

Stanford University Press
11030 S Langley Ave.
Chicago, IL, USA 60628
Ph: (773) 702-7000

Stanford University Press
1450 Page Mill Rd.
Palo Alto, CA, USA 94304
Ph: (650) 723-9434
E-mail: info@atswww.sup.org
URL: http://www.sup.org/

Star-News
1003 S 17th St.
Wilmington, NC, USA 28401
Ph: (910) 343-2000

StartingUp Now
, , USA

State Bar of California
180 Howard St.
San Francisco, CA, USA 94105
Ph: (415) 538-2590

State Service Systems Inc.
10405-B E 55th Pl.
Tulsa, OK, USA 74146
Ph: (918) 627-8000

State University of New York Press
90 State St., Ste. 700
Albany, NY, USA 12207
Ph: (518) 472-5000

Step-By-Step Publishing
6000 N Forest Park Dr.
Peoria, IL, USA 61614
E-mail: ddnservice@atsdgusa.com
URL:

Stevens Publishing Corp.
5151 Beltline Rd., 10th Fl.
Dallas, TX, USA 75254
Ph: (972) 687-6700
E-mail: http://www.pollutiononline.com/storefronts/stevenspub.html

Stoddart Publishing Company, Ltd.
895 Don Mills Rd.
Toronto, ON, CAN M3C 1W3
Ph: (416) 445-3333

Storey Publishing LLC
210 Mass Moca Way
North Adams, MA, USA 1247
Ph: (413) 346-2100
E-mail: http://www.storey.com

Stork Technimet Inc.
662 Cromwell Ave.
St. Paul, MN, USA 55114
Ph: (651) 645-3601
E-mail: info.tct@atsstork.com
URL:

Strafford Publications Inc.
590 Dutch Valley Rd. NE
PO Drawer 13729
Atlanta, GA, USA 30324-0729
Ph: (404) 881-1141
E-mail: custserv@atsstraffordpub.com
URL: http://www.straffordpub.com

Successful Meetings
770 Broadway
New York, NY, USA 10003-9595
Ph: (646) 654-5000
E-mail: http://www.mimegasite.com/

Successful Publishing
7933 Glacier Club Dr.
Washington, MI, USA 48094
Ph: (586) 786-1897
E-mail: http://marksaid.com/_wsn/page2.html

Summit Business Media
5081 Olympic Blvd.
Erlanger, KY, USA 41018
Ph: (859) 692-2100
E-mail: http://www.summitbusinessmedia.com/

Summit Business Media
33-41 Newark St., 2nd Fl.
Hoboken, NJ, USA 7030
Ph: (201) 526-1230

The Sun News
PO Box 406
Myrtle Beach, SC, USA 29578
Ph: (843) 626-8555

Sun News Inc.
1321 King St., Ste. 4
Bellingham, WA, USA 98229
Ph: (360) 647-8805

Sunshine Group Worldwide Ltd.
770 Broadway, 7th Fl.
New York, NY, USA 10003-9595
Ph: (646) 654-7680
E-mail: robert.sunshine@atsnielsen.com
URL: http://www.filmjournal.com/filmjournal/index.jsp

Survey Research Laboratory
505 E Green St., Ste. 3
Champaign, IL, USA 61820-5723
Ph: (217) 333-7109
E-mail: info@atssrl.uic.edu
URL:

Suzuki Association of Americas
PO Box 17310
Boulder, CO, USA 80308
Ph: (303) 444-0948
E-mail: info@atssuzukiassociation.org
URL: http://www.suzukiassociation.org/

Swedish-American Chamber of Commerce
570 Lexington Ave.
New York, NY, USA 10022
Ph: (212) 838-5530
E-mail: business.services@atssaccny.org
URL:

Sybex
111 River St.
Hoboken, NJ, USA 7030
Ph: (201) 748-6000
E-mail: http://www.wiley.com/WileyCDA/Brand/id-23.html

SYS-CON Media
577 Chestnut Ridge Rd.
Woodcliff Lake, NJ, USA 7677
Ph: (201) 802-3000
E-mail: subscribe@atssys-con.com
URL: http://www.sys-con.com

T

T.E. Smith Inc.
PO Box 14-2096
Coral Gables, FL, USA 33114
Ph: (305) 740-7170
E-mail: http://www.thewinenews.com/

T.F.H. Publications Inc.
PO Box 427
Neptune, NJ, USA 7754
E-mail: info@atstfh.com
URL: http://www.tfh.com

T.T. Publications Inc.
203 W SR 434
Winter Springs, FL, USA 32708
Ph: (407) 327-4817
E-mail: news@atstowtimes.com
URL: http://www.towtimes.com

TAB Computer Systems, Incorporated
31 Beechwood Ln.
South Windsor, CT, USA 6074
Ph: (860) 289-8850

Talcott Communication Corp.
20 W Kinzie St., Ste. 1200
Chicago, IL, USA 60654
Ph: (312) 849-2220
E-mail: talcottpub@atstalcott.com
URL: http://www.talcott.com

Tampa Bay Business Journal
4890 W Kennedy Blvd., Ste. 850
Tampa, FL, USA 33609
Ph: (813) 873-8225

Target Communications Corp.
7626 W Donges Bay Rd.
Mequon, WI, USA 53097
Ph: (262) 242-3990
E-mail: judy@atsdeerinfo.com
URL: http://www.deerinfo.com

Target Publishing Company Inc.
2470 E Main St.
Columbus, OH, USA 43209
Ph: (614) 235-1022
E-mail: rinksider@atsrinksider.com
URL: http://www.rinksider.com

Target Research
PO Box 1345
Wheaton, MD, USA 20915
Ph: (301) 452-1105

Targetmark Books
PO Box 421428
Atlanta, GA, USA 30342
Ph: (404) 705-9093

Tate Publishing and Enterprises, LLC
127 E Trade Center Terr.
Mustang, OK, USA 73064
Ph: (405) 376-4900

Taunton Press Inc.
63 S Main St.
PO Box 5506
Newtown, CT, USA 06470-2355
Ph: (203) 426-8171
E-mail: booksales@atstaunton.com
URL: http://www.taunton.com

Tax Analysts
400 S Maple Ave., Ste. 400
Falls Church, VA, USA 22046
Ph: (703) 533-4400
E-mail: cservice@atstax.org
URL: http://www.tax.org

Tax Executives Institute Inc.
1200 G St. NW, Ste. 300
Washington, DC, USA 20005
Ph: (202) 638-5601
E-mail: http://www.tei.org/

Tax Management Inc.
9435 Key West Ave.
Rockville, MD, USA 20850
Ph: (800) 372-1033
E-mail: tm@atsbna.com
URL: http://www.bnatax.com

Taxicab, Limousine & Paratransit Association
3200 Tower Oaks Blvd., Ste. 200
Rockville, MD, USA 20852
Ph: (301) 984-5700
E-mail: info@atstlpa.org
URL: http://www.tlpa.org

Taylor & Francis Group
325 Chestnut St.
Philadelphia, PA, USA 19106
Ph: (215) 625-8900

Taylor & Francis Group Ltd.
270 Madison Ave.
New York, NY, USA 10016-0601
Ph: (212) 216-7800
E-mail: info@atstaylorandfrancis.com
URL: http://www.routledge-ny.com

Taylor and Francis Group Ltd
2 Park Sq., Milton Park
Abingdon, , GBR OX14 4RN
E-mail: http://www.taylorandfrancis.com

TEACH Magazine
87 Barford Rd.
Toronto, ON, CAN M9W 4H8
Ph: (416) 537-2103
E-mail: info@atsteachmag.com
URL: http://www.teachmag.com

Technical Insights/M John Wiley & Sons Inc.
111 River St.
Hoboken, NJ, USA 07030-5774
Ph: (201) 748-6000
E-mail: insights@atswiley.com
URL: http://www.wiley.com

Technology Marketing Corp.
800 Connecticut Ave, 1st Fl. E.
Norwalk, CT, USA 6854
Ph: (203) 852-6800
E-mail: tmc@atstmcnet.com
URL: http://www.tmcnet.com

Technology Student Association (TSA)
1914 Association Dr.
Reston, VA, USA 20191-1540
Ph: (703) 860-9000
E-mail: general@atstsaweb.org
URL:

Technomic Information Services
300 S. Riverside Plz., Ste. 1200
Chicago, IL, USA 60606
Ph: (312) 876-0004
E-mail: foodinfo@atstechnomic.com
URL: http://www.technomic.com/

Telecommunications Industry Association
2500 Wilson Blvd., Ste. 300
Arlington, VA, USA 22201
Ph: (703) 907-7700
E-mail: tia@atstia.eia.org
URL:

Teleflora
11444 W Olympic Blvd.
Los Angeles, CA, USA 90064
Ph: (310) 966-3517
E-mail: http://www.teleflora.com

The Telegraph
111 E Broadway
Alton, IL, USA 62002
Ph: (618) 463-2500

Ten Speed Press
PO Box 7123
Berkeley, CA, USA 94707

Tennessee Municipal League
226 Capitol Blvd., Ste. 710
Nashville, TN, USA 37219
Ph: (615) 255-6416
E-mail: http://www.tml1.org

Tennis Week
304 Park Ave. S, 8th Fl.
New York, NY, USA 10010
Ph: (646) 871-2431
E-mail: http://www.tennisweek.com

Testa Communications
25 Willowdale Ave.
Port Washington, NY, USA 11050
Ph: (516) 767-2500
E-mail: testa@atstesta.com
URL: http://testa.com/index.htm

Teton Media Inc.
20917 Higgins Ct.
Torrance, CA, USA 90501
E-mail: http://www.cableyellowpages.com/

Theatre Communications Group
520 8th Ave., 24th Fl.
New York, NY, USA 10018-4156
Ph: (212) 609-5900
E-mail: tcg@atstcg.org
URL: http://www.tcg.org

Theta Corp. Reports
38 E 29th St., 6th Fl.
New York, NY, USA 10016
Ph: (212) 807-2629
E-mail: customerservice@atsmarketresearch.com
URL: http://www.marketresearch.com

Thin Book Publishing Company
86 SW Century Dr., No. 446
Bend, OR, USA 97702

Think Services
600 Harrison St., 6th Fl.
San Francisco, CA, USA 94017
Ph: (415) 947-6224

Thomas Nelson Inc.
501 Nelson Pl.
PO Box 141000
Nashville, TN, USA 37214-1000

Thomas Nelson Inc.
PO Box 141000
Nashville, TN, USA 37214-1000
Ph: (615) 889-9000
E-mail: http://www.thomasnelson.com

Thomas Publishing Company
5 Penn Plz., 14th Fl.
New York, NY, USA 10001

Thompson Publishing Group Inc.
805 15th St. NW, 3rd Fl.
Washington, DC, USA 20005
Ph: (202) 872-4000
E-mail: service@atsthompson.com
URL: http://www.thompson.com

Thomson CompuMark
500 Victory Rd.
North Quincy, MA, USA 02171-3145
Ph: (617) 479-1600
E-mail: support@atst-t.com
URL: http://www.thomson-thomson.com

Thomson Financial
195 Broadway, 4th Fl.
New York, NY, USA 10007
Ph: (212) 953-3570
E-mail: tfonlinerequests@atsthomson.com
URL: http://www.thomsonreuters.com/business_units/financial

Thomson South-Western
5191 Natorp Blvd.
Mason, OH, USA 45040
Ph: (513) 229-1000
E-mail: swinformation@atsthomsonlearning.com
URL: http://www.swlearning.com

Thomson South-Western/Texere
10650 Toebben Dr.
Independence, KY, USA 41051
E-mail: http://www.swlearning.com

Thomson West
610 Opperman Dr.
PO Box 64833
Eagan, MN, USA 55123
Ph: (651) 687-7000
E-mail: west.customerservice@atsthomson.com
URL: http://www.andrewsonline.com/

Thomson-Shore Inc.
7300 W. Joy Rd.
Dexter, MI, USA 48130
Ph: (734) 426-3939
E-mail: questions@atstshore.com
URL: http://www.thomsonshore.com/

Thorsons
HarperCollins Publishers Inc.
10 E 53rd St.
New York, NY, USA 10022
Ph: (212) 207-7791
E-mail: http://www.thorsons.com

Three Rivers Press
1745 Broadway
New York, NY, USA 10019
Ph: (212) 782-9000
E-mail: http://www.randomhouse.com/crown/three-rivers-press

Tilden Press Inc.
Six Hillwood Pl.
Oakland, CA, USA 94610
Ph: (510) 451-3100
E-mail: gbl@atsgreenbiz.com
URL: http://www.greenbizletter.com

Tile and Stone Inc.
18 E 41st St.
New York, NY, USA 10017
Ph: (212) 376-7722
E-mail: publisher@atsashlee.com
URL:

Timber Framers Guild
PO Box 60
Becket, MA, USA 1223
E-mail: info@atstfguild.org
URL: http://www.tfguild.org

Time Inc.
1271 Ave. of the Americas
New York, NY, USA 10020
Ph: (212) 522-1212
E-mail: information@atstimeinc.com
URL: http://www.timeinc.com

Time Warner Paperbacks
1 Time Warner Center
New York, NY, USA 10019-8016
Ph: (212) 484-8000
E-mail: http://www.timewarner.com

Time4 Media Inc.
1271 Avenue of the Americas
New York, NY, USA 10020-1300
Ph: (212) 522-1212
E-mail: http://www.timeinc.com/home

The Times
3410 Delta Dr.
Portage, IN, USA 46368
Ph: (219) 762-4334

The Times and Democrat
1010 Broughton St.
Orangeburg, SC, USA 29115
Ph: (803) 533-5500
E-mail: http://www.thetandd.com/

Times Publishing Co.
490 1st Ave. S
PO Box 1121
Saint Petersburg, FL, USA 33701
Ph: (727) 893-8111
E-mail: http://www.sptimes.com/connect/corporate/history/

Times-News
707 S Main St.
Burlington, NC, USA 27215
Ph: (336) 227-0131

Tire Guides Inc.
1101 S Rogers Cir., Ste. 6
Boca Raton, FL, USA 33487-2748
Ph: (561) 997-9229
E-mail: http://tireguides.com

Tire Industry Association
1532 Pointer Ridge Pl., Ste. G
Bowie, MD, USA 20716-1883
Ph: (301) 430-7280
E-mail: info@atstireindustry.org
URL: http://www.tireindustry.org

TKG Publishing
1800 S Robertson Blvd., Ste. 125
Los Angeles, CA, USA 90035
Ph: (310) 827-9060

TKO/Real Estate Advisory Group Inc.
PO Box 2630
Mercerville, NJ, USA 8690
Ph: (609) 587-6200
E-mail: aoneal@atsspecialtyretail.net
URL:

TL Enterprises Inc.
2575 Vista Del Mar
Ventura, CA, USA 93001
Ph: (805) 667-4100
E-mail: info@atsaffinitygroup.com
URL: http://www.affinitygroup.com

TMB Publishing Inc.
1838 Techny Ct.
Northbrook, IL, USA 60062
Ph: (847) 564-1127
E-mail: http://www.plumbingengineer.com

TMR Publications
PO Box 381822
Cambridge, MA, USA 02238-1822
Ph: (617) 489-9120
E-mail: customer.service@atstmreview.com
URL:

Toastmasters International Inc.
23182 Arroyo Vista
PO Box 9052
Rancho Santa Margarita, CA, USA 92688-2620
Ph: (949) 858-8255
E-mail: http://www.toastmasters.org

Tobacco Merchants Association of the U.S. Inc.
PO Box 8019
Princeton, NJ, USA 08543-8019
Ph: (609) 275-4900
E-mail: tmg@atstma.org
URL: http://www.tma.org/

Toledo Times
541 N Superior St.
Toledo, OH, USA 43660
Ph: (419) 724-6000

Tom Hendricks
4000 Hawthorne Ave., No. 5
Dallas, TX, USA 75219
E-mail: tomHendricks474@atscs.com
URL:

Toolkit Media Group
2700 Lake Cook Rd.
Riverwoods, IL, USA 60015
Ph: (847) 267-7000

TORO
PO Box 427
Bronx, NY, USA 10458

Touchpoint Publishing
505 N Hwy. 169 Ste. 465
Minneapolis, MN, USA 55441
Ph: (763) 595-0808
E-mail: info@atstouchpointpublishing.com
URL: http://www.tpgsports.com

Touchstone/Simon & Schuster Inc.
1230 Ave. of the Americas
New York, NY, USA 10020
E-mail: business@atssimonandschuster.com
URL:

Towing & Recovery Association of America
2121 Eisenhower Ave., Ste. 200
Alexandria, VA, USA 22314-4677
Ph: (703) 684-7713
E-mail: towservice@atsaol.com
URL:

Towse Publishing Co.
1333A North Ave.
New Rochelle, NY, USA 10804
Ph: (914) 235-3095
E-mail: russ@atsfurninfo.com
URL: http://www.furninfo.com/

Toy Industry Association Inc.
1115 Broadway, Ste. 400
New York, NY, USA 10010
Ph: (212) 675-1141
E-mail: info@atstoyassociation.org
URL: http://www.toyassociation.org

Trade Dimensions
55 Greens Farms Rd.
Westport, CT, USA 06880-6149
Ph: (203) 222-5750
E-mail: info@atstradedimensions.com
URL:

Trade Press Media Group
2100 W Florist Ave.
Milwaukee, WI, USA 53209
Ph: (414) 228-7701
E-mail: info@atstradepress.com
URL: http://www.tradepress.com

Trade Show Exhibitors Association
McCormick Pl.
2301 S Lake Shore Dr., Ste. 1005
Chicago, IL, USA 60616-1419
Ph: (312) 842-8732
E-mail: tsea@atstsea.org
URL: http://www.tsea.org/

Trader Media Corp.
15 Apex Rd.
Toronto, ON, CAN M6A 2V6
Ph: (416) 781-5516

Tradeshow Week Inc.
5900 Wilshire Blvd., Ste. 3100
Los Angeles, CA, USA 90036-5804
Ph: (323) 617-9100
E-mail: http://www.tradeshowweek.com

Trafford Publishing
2333 Government St., Ste. 6E
Victoria, BC, CAN V8T 4P4
Ph: (250) 383-6864
E-mail: sales@atstrafford.com
URL: http://www.trafford.com/

Trafford Publishing
2657 Wilfert Rd.
Victoria, BC, CAN V9B 5Z3
Ph: (250) 383-6864
E-mail: http://www.trafford.com

Training Education Management
1874 S Pacific Coast Hwy.
Redondo Beach, CA, USA 90277
Ph: (310) 316-2240
E-mail: info@atstrainingeducationmanagement.com
URL: http://www.trainingeducationmanagement.com

Trajan Publishing Corp.
PO Box 28103, Lakeport PO
St. Catharines, ON, CAN L2N 7P8
Ph: (905) 646-7744
E-mail: office@atstrajan.ca
URL: http://trajan.com/

Transitions Abroad Publishing
18 Hulst Rd.
Amherst, MA, USA 1002
Ph: (413) 253-4924
E-mail: info@atstransitionsabroad.com
URL: http://www.transitionsabroad.com

Transportation Consumer Protection Council Inc.
120 Main St.
Huntington, NY, USA 11743
Ph: (631) 549-8984
E-mail: tcpc@atstransportlaw.com
URL:

Travel Goods Association
301 N Harrison St., No. 412
Princeton, NJ, USA 08540-3512
Ph: (877) 842-1938
E-mail: info@atstravel-goods.org
URL: http://www.travel-goods.org/

Travel Industry Network Inc.
28 Knight St.
Norwalk, CT, USA 06851-4719
Ph: (203) 286-6679
E-mail: http://www.travelworldnews.com

Travel Trade
122 E 42nd St.
New York, NY, USA 10168
Ph: (212) 730-6600
E-mail: http://www.traveltrade.com/index.htm

Travelers Aid Society of Rhode Island
177 Union St.
Providence, RI, USA 2903
Ph: (401) 521-2255
E-mail: http://riroads.com/links/listdetail.cgi?Lookup=378039

Traveling Times Inc.
25061 Ave. Stanford, Ste. 10
Valencia, CA, USA 91355-4551
Ph: (661) 295-1250

Tree Care Industry Association
136 Harvey Rd., Ste. 101
Londonderry, NH, USA 3053
Ph: (603) 314-5380
E-mail: tcia@atstreecareindustry.org
URL: http://www.treecareindustry.org

Tree Publishers Inc.
PO Box 107
Lecompton, KS, USA 66050-0170
Ph: (785) 887-6324
E-mail: ctreesmag@atsaol.com
URL: http://www.christmastreesmagazine.com/

Tri-M Music Honor Society
1806 Robert Fulton Dr.
Reston, VA, USA 20191-4348
Ph: (703) 860-4000
E-mail: mbrserv@atsmenc.org
URL:

Truck Frame and Axle Repair Association
3741 Enterprise Dr. SW
Rochester, MN, USA 55902
E-mail: w.g.reich@atsatt.net
URL: http://www.taraassociation.com

Truck Renting and Leasing Association
675 N Washington St., Ste.410
Alexandria, VA, USA 22314
Ph: (703) 299-9120
E-mail: http://www.trala.org

Trucker's Connection Inc.
5960 Crooked Creek Rd., Ste. 15
Norcross, GA, USA 30092
E-mail: http://www.truckersconnection.com

Tufts University
P.O Box 420235
Palm Coast, FL, USA 32142
Ph: (800) 829-5116

Tulsa World
315 S Boulder Ave.
Tulsa, OK, USA 74103
Ph: (918) 582-0921
E-mail: http://www.tulsaworld.com/

Tulsa World
PO Box 1770
Tulsa, OK, USA 74102
Ph: (918) 581-8400

Turley Publications
24 Water St.
Palmer, MA, USA 1069
E-mail: http://www.turley.com

Turnaround Associates
1120 Avenue of the Americas, 4th Fl.
New York, NY, USA 10036
Ph: (212) 626-6940
E-mail: info@atsturnaroundassociates.com
URL: http://www.turnaroundassociates.com

Tuscarora Inc.
PO Box 1125
Maywood, NJ, USA 7607

TV Guide Magazine
100 Matsonford Rd., Bldg. 4
Radnor, PA, USA 19088
Ph: (610) 293-8433
E-mail: http://www.tvguidemediasales.com

Twelve Books/Hachette Book Group USA
PO Box 8828
Boston, MA, USA 2114
E-mail: http://www.hachettebookgroupusa.com

Twelve/Hatchette Book Group
237 Park Ave.
New York, NY, USA 10017
E-mail: http://www.hatchettebookgroup.com

U

U.S. Bureau of Labor Statistics
2 Massachusetts Ave. NE Ste. 2135
Washington, DC, USA 20212-0001
Ph: (202) 691-5200
E-mail: feedback@atsbls.gov
URL: http://www.bls.gov

U.S. Chamber of Commerce
1615 H St. NW
Washington, DC, USA 20062-2000
Ph: (202) 659-6000
E-mail: http://www.uschamber.com

U.S. Department of Agriculture
2202 Monterey St., Ste. 104-F
Fresno, CA, USA 93721-3129
Ph: (559) 487-5178

U.S. Economic Development Administration
111 N Canal St., Ste. 855
Chicago, IL, USA 60606-7208
Ph: (312) 353-8143
E-mail: http://www.eda.gov

U.S. Food and Drug Administration
10903 New Hampshire Ave.
Rockville, MD, USA 20857
Ph: (301) 594-1086
E-mail: http://www.fda.gov

U.S. Government Printing Office and Superintendent of Documents
Mail Stop: IDCC
732 N Capitol St. NW
Washington, DC, USA 20401
Ph: (202) 512-1800
E-mail: contactcenter@atsgpo.gov
URL: http://www.gpoaccess.gov

UBM Global Trade
400 Windsor Corporate Pk.
50 Millstone Rd., Ste. 200
East Windsor, NJ, USA 08520-1415
Ph: (609) 371-7700
E-mail: customerservice@atscbizmedia.com
URL: http://www.cbizmedia.com

Underwriters Laboratories Inc.
2600 N.W. Lake Rd.
Camas, WA, USA 98607-8542
E-mail: cec@atsus.ul.com
URL: http://www.ul.com

UNICOL Inc.
PO Box 260550
Pembroke Pines, FL, USA 33026
Ph: (954) 430-7271
E-mail: customerservice@atsunicol-publishing.com
URL: http://www.unicol-publishing.com

United Association of Manufacturers' Representatives (UAMR)
PO Box 784
Branson, MO, USA 65615
Ph: (417) 779-1575
E-mail: info@atsuamr.com
URL:

United Brotherhood of Carpenters and Joiners of America, AFL-CIO
101 Constitution Ave. NW
Washington, DC, USA 20001
Ph: (202) 546-6206
E-mail: http://www.carpenters.org/

United Business Media
245 Blackfriars Rd.
London, , GBR SE1 9UY
E-mail: http://www.ubm.com/ubm/aboutus/contactus/

United Business Media
350 Hudson St., Ste. 300
New York, NY, USA 10014

United Communications Group
11300 Rockville Pike, Ste. 1100
Rockville, MD, USA 20852-3030
Ph: (301) 287-2700
E-mail: webmaster@atsucg.com
URL: http://www.ucg.com

United Empire Loyalists' Association of Canada
50 Baldwin St., Ste. 202
Toronto, ON, CAN M5T 1L4
Ph: (416) 591-1783
E-mail: uelac@atsuelac.org
URL: http://www.uelac.org

United Nations Publications
2 United Nations Plaza
New York, NY, USA 10017
Ph: (212) 963-8302

United Press International-USA
1133 19th St. NW
Washington, DC, USA 20036
Ph: (202) 898-8000

United Publications Inc.
106 Lafayette St.
PO Box 995
Yarmouth, ME, USA 4096
Ph: (207) 846-0600
E-mail: http://www.unitedpublications.com

United States Government Printing Office
USGPO Stop SSMB
Washington, DC, USA 20401
Ph: (202) 512-1800

United Way of New York City
2 Park Ave.
New York, NY, USA 10016
Ph: (212) 251-2500
E-mail: info@atsdorlandhealth.com
URL: http://www.uwnyc.org

University Film and Video Association
PO Box 1777
Edwardsville, IL, USA 62026
Ph: (914) 761-1187
E-mail: ufvahome@atsaol.com
URL: http://www.ufva.org

University of California Press
2120 Berkeley Way
Berkeley, CA, USA 94704-1012
Ph: (510) 643-8465
E-mail: foundation@atsucpress.edu
URL: http://www.ucpress.edu

University of Chicago Graduate School of Business
5807 S Woodlawn Ave.
Chicago, IL, USA 60637
Ph: (773) 702-7743
E-mail: helpdesk@atschicagobooth.edu
URL: http://www.chicagobooth.edu/

University of Chicago Press
1427 E 60th St.
Chicago, IL, USA 60637
Ph: (773) 702-7700
E-mail: custserv@atspress.uchicago.edu
URL: http://www.press.uchicago.edu

University of Georgia Press
330 Research Dr., Ste. B100
Athens, GA, USA 30602-4901
Ph: (706) 369-6130

University of Illinois
1 University Plz.
Springfield, IL, USA 62703
Ph: (217) 206-6600
E-mail: http://www.uis.edu/index.html

University of Illinois Press
1325 S Oak St.
Champaign, IL, USA 61820-6903
Ph: (217) 333-0950
E-mail: uipress@atsuillinois.edu
URL: http://www.press.uillinois.edu

University of Montana
634 Eddy Ave.
Missoula, MT, USA 59812-6696
Ph: (406) 243-6355
E-mail: schoonen@atsselway.umt.edu
URL:

University of Nebraska
PO Box 880407
Lincoln, NE, USA 68588-0407
Ph: (402) 472-7931
E-mail: qjbe@atsunlnotes.unl.edu
URL: http://www.qjbe.unl.edu

University of North Carolina Press
108 Battle Ln., CB3410
Chapel Hill, NC, USA 27599-3410
Ph: (919) 962-3074

University of Toronto Press
Black Rose Books
5201 Dufferin St.
Downsview, ON, CAN M3H 5T8
E-mail: utpbooks@atsgpu.utcc.utoronto.ca
URL: http://www.blackrosebooks.net

University of Toronto Press
10 St. Mary St., Ste. 700
Toronto, ON, CAN M4Y 2W8
Ph: (416) 978-2239

University of Toronto Press-Journal Div.
5201 Dufferin St.
Toronto, ON, CAN M3H 5T8
Ph: (416) 667-7810
E-mail: journals@atsutpress.utoronto.ca
URL: http://www.utpjournals.com

University of Wisconsin Press
1930 Monroe St., 3rd Fl.
Madison, WI, USA 53711-2029
Ph: (608) 263-1110
E-mail: uwiscpress@atsuwpress.wisc.edu
URL: http://www.wisc.edu/wisconsinpress/

University of Wisconsin-Eau Claire
405 Hibbard Hall
Eau Claire, WI, USA 54702-4004
Ph: (715) 836-2639
E-mail: engl.contact@atsuwec.edu
URL: http://www.uwec.edu/english/graduate/admissionqualifications.htm

University Press of America Inc.
4501 Forbes Blvd., Ste. 200
Lanham, MD, USA 20706
Ph: (301) 459-3366
E-mail: customercare@atsrowman.com
URL: http://unity3.rowman.com/Page/Contact

Uniworld Business Publications Inc.
6 Seward Ave.
Beverly, MA, USA 1915
Ph: (978) 927-0219
E-mail: info@atsuniworldbp.com
URL: http://www.uniworldbp.com

Update Publicare Co.
c/o Prosperity & Profits Unlimited
PO Box 416
Denver, CO, USA 80201-0416
Ph: (303) 575-5676
E-mail: mail@atscontentprovidermedia.com
URL: http://www.gumbomedia.com

Urban Land Institute
1025 Thomas Jefferson St., NW, Ste. 500 W
Washington, DC, USA 20007
Ph: (202) 624-7000
E-mail: customerservice@atsuli.org
URL: http://www.uli.org/

Urner Barry Publications Inc.
PO Box 389
Toms River, NJ, USA 8754
Ph: (732) 240-5330
E-mail: mail@atsurnerbarry.com
URL: http://www.urnerbarry.com

USA International Business Publications
1466 Broadway, No. 910
New York, NY, USA 10036
Ph: (212) 490-3999

USA Table Tennis
One Olympic Plaza
Colorado Springs, CO, USA 80909-5769
Ph: (719) 866-4583
E-mail: usatt@atsusatt.org
URL: http://www.usatt.org

Utah Department of Workforce Services
140 E 300 S.
PO Box 45249
Salt Lake City, UT, USA 84145-0249
Ph: (801) 526-9675
E-mail: dwscontactus@atsutah.gov
URL:

V

Valley Calligraphy Guild
278 Hambletonian Dr.
Eugene, OR, USA 97401
Ph: (503) 343-9094

Valuation Research Corp.
330 E Kilbourn Ave., Ste. 1020
Milwaukee, WI, USA 53202-3141
Ph: (414) 271-8662

Vance Publishing Corp.
400 Knightsbridge Pky.
Lincolnshire, IL, USA 60069
Ph: (847) 634-2600
E-mail: info@atsvancepublishing.com
URL: http://www.vancepublishing.com

Vancouver Ballet Society
Scotiabank Dance Ctr.
677 Davie St., Level 6
Vancouver, BC, CAN V6B 2G6
Ph: (604) 681-1525
E-mail: vbs@atstelus.net
URL: http://www.vancouverballetsociety.ca/

Vanguard Press
425 Madison Ave., 3rd Fl.
New York, NY, USA 10017
Ph: (212) 223-2969
E-mail: http://www.vanguardpressbooks.com

VBM Printers Inc.
2115 NE McDonald Ln.
PO Box 449
McMinnville, OR, USA 97128
Ph: (503) 434-5386
E-mail: ron@atsoldstuffnews.com
URL: http://www.oldstuffnews.com

The Vegetarian Resource Group
PO Box 1463
Baltimore, MD, USA 21203
Ph: (410) 366-8343
E-mail: vrg@atsvrg.org
URL: http://www.vrg.org/

Vending Times Inc.
55 Maple Ave., Ste. 102
Rockville Centre, NY, USA 11570
Ph: (516) 442-1850
E-mail: subscriptions@atsvendingtimes.net
URL: http://www.vendingtimes.com

Venice Family Clinic
604 Rose Ave.
Venice, CA, USA 90291
Ph: (310) 392-8630
E-mail: vfcinfo@atsmednet.ucla.edu
URL: http://www.venicefamilyclinic.org/

Ventura County Star
550 Camarillo Center Dr.
Camarillo, CA, USA 93011
Ph: (805) 437-0000

Venture Economics Inc.
195 Broadway
New York, NY, USA 10007
Ph: (646) 822-2000
E-mail: ve.cs@atstfn.com
URL: http://www.vcjnews.com/

VerticalNews
2727 Paces Ferry Rd. SE, Ste. 2-440
Atlanta, GA, USA 30339
Ph: (770) 435-8286

Veterinary Learning Systems
780 Township Line Rd.
Yardley, PA, USA 19067
Ph: (913) 322-1643
E-mail: info@atsvetlearn.com
URL: http://www.veterinarylearningsystems.com

Vickers Stock Research Corp.
98 Pratt Oval
Glen Cove, NY, USA 11542
Ph: (516) 945-0020
E-mail: sales@atsvickers-stock.com
URL: http://www.vickers-stock.com

Video Watchdog
PO Box 5283
Cincinnati, OH, USA 45205-0283
Ph: (513) 297-1855
E-mail: orders@atsvideowatchdog.com
URL: http://www.videowatchdog.com

Viking Press/Penguin Group
375 Hudson St.
New York, NY, USA 10014
Ph: (212) 366-2679

Village Press Publications
2779 Aero Park Dr.
PO Box 968
Traverse City, MI, USA 49685
Ph: (231) 946-3712
E-mail: info@atsvillagepress.com
URL: http://www.villagepress.com

Vindicator
107 Vindicator Sq.
Youngstown, OH, USA 44503
Ph: (330) 747-1471

Virgin Books/Random House
20 Vauxhall Bridge Rd.
London, , GBR SW1V 2SA
E-mail: editorial@atsvirgin-books.co.uk
URL: http://www.virginbooks.co.uk

Virginia Food Dealers Association Inc.
5937 Hopkins Rd., Ste. 201 1/2
Richmond, VA, USA 23234-5412
Ph: (804) 271-5964
E-mail: vfda@atsmindspring.com
URL:

Virginia Native Plant Society
400 Blandy Farm Ln., Unit 2
Boyce, VA, USA 22620
Ph: (540) 837-1600
E-mail: vnpsofc@atsshentel.net
URL:

Virginian-Pilot
150 W Brambleton Ave.
Norfolk, VA, USA 23510
Ph: (757) 446-2000

The Virginia-Pilot
Box 449
150 W Brambleton Ave.
Norfolk, VA, USA 23510
Ph: (757) 446-2000

Visionaire Publishing
11 Mercer St.
New York, NY, USA 10013
Ph: (212) 274-8959
E-mail: info@atsvisionaireworld.com
URL: http://www.visionaireworld.com

VNU Business Media, Inc.
770 Broadway, 4th Fl.
New York, NY, USA 10003
Ph: (646) 654-5000

VNU Business Publications
770 Broadway
New York, NY, USA 10003
Ph: (646) 654-5000
E-mail: http://www.vnubusinessmedia.com

VNU eMedia Inc.
770 Broadway
New York, NY, USA 10003
E-mail: http://www.vnuemedia.com/index.html

The Voice of Florida
PO Box 030397
Fort Lauderdale, FL, USA 33303-0397
Ph: (954) 463-5556

Voyageur Magazine
PO Box 8085
Green Bay, WI, USA 54308-8085
Ph: (920) 465-2446
E-mail: voyageur@atsuwgb.edu
URL: http://www.uwgb.edu/voyageur/index2.html

W

W.W. Norton & Company
500 5th Ave.
New York, NY, USA 10110
Ph: (212) 354-5500
E-mail: http://wwnorton.com

Waco Tribune-Herald
900 Franklin Ave.
Waco, TX, USA 76702
Ph: (254) 757-5757

Wakeman/Walworth Inc.
PO Box 7376
Alexandria, VA, USA 22307-7376
Ph: (703) 768-9600
E-mail: newsletters@atsstatecapitals.com
URL: http://statecapitals.com/

Walker & Company
104 5th Ave.
New York, NY, USA 10011
Ph: (212) 727-8300
E-mail: http://www.walkerbooks.com

Ward's Communications
3000 Town Ctr., Ste. 2750
Southfield, MI, USA 48075
Ph: (248) 357-0800

E-mail: wards@atswardsauto.com
URL: http://wardsauto.com

Warner Books Inc.
PO Box 8828
Boston, MA, USA 2114
E-mail: http://www.hachettebookgroupusa.com

Warner Books, Incorporated
1271 Avenue of the Americas
New York, NY, USA 10020
Ph: (800) 759-0190
E-mail: marcy.haggag@atstwgb.com
URL: http://www.twbookmark.com/

Warner Business Books
1271 Avenue of the Americas
New York, NY, USA 10020-1300
Ph: (212) 522-7200
E-mail: rick.wolff@atstwbg.com
URL: http://www.twbookmark.com/

Warren Communications News
2115 Ward Ct. NW
Washington, DC, USA 20037-1209
Ph: (202) 872-9200
E-mail: info@atswarren-news.com
URL: http://www.warren-news.com

Washington Business Information Inc.
300 N Washington St., Ste. 200
Falls Church, VA, USA 22046
Ph: (703) 538-7600

Washington Independent Writers
1001 Connecticut Ave. NW, Ste. 701
Washington, DC, USA 20036
Ph: (202) 775-5150
E-mail: info@atswashwriter.org
URL: http://www.amerindywriters.org/home/

Washington Information Source
6506 Old Stage Rd., Ste. 100
Rockville, MD, USA 20852-4326
Ph: (703) 779-8777
E-mail: wis@atsfdainfo.com
URL: http://www.fdainfo.com

Waste Equipment Technology Association
4301 Connecticut Ave. NW, Ste. 300
Washington, DC, USA 20008-2304
Ph: (202) 244-4700
E-mail: wastecinfo@atswastec.org
URL: http://www.wastec.org

Water Environment Federation
601 Wythe St.
Alexandria, VA, USA 22314-1994
Ph: (703) 684-2400
E-mail: pubs@atswef.org
URL: http://www.wef.org

Water Quality Association
4151 Naperville Rd.
Lisle, IL, USA 60532-3696
Ph: (630) 505-0160
E-mail: info@atswqa.org
URL: http://www.wqa.org

Waterways Journal Inc.
319 N 4th St., Ste. 650
Saint Louis, MO, USA 63102
Ph: (314) 241-7354
E-mail: http://www.waterwaysjournal.net/

Wayfarer Publications
PO Box 39938
Los Angeles, CA, USA 90039
Ph: (323) 665-7773
E-mail: taichi@atstai-chi.com
URL: http://www.tai-chi.com

Wedding & Portrait Photographers International
1312 Lincoln Blvd.
PO Box 2003
Santa Monica, CA, USA 90406-2003
Ph: (310) 451-0090

Weekly Reader Corp.
3001 Cindel Dr.
Delran, NJ, USA 8075
E-mail: customerservice@atsweeklyreader.com
URL: http://www.weeklyreader.com

Weidenbum Center
Washington University
1 Brookings Dr.
Campus Box 1027
St. Louis, MO, USA 63130-4899
Ph: (314) 935-5630
E-mail: http://www.wustl.edu

Weider Publications
21100 Erwin St.
Woodland Hills, CA, USA 91367-3712
Ph: (818) 884-6800
E-mail: http://www.muscleandfitness.com/

Wells Publishing Inc.
3570 Camino del Rio N, Ste. 200
San Diego, CA, USA 92108
Ph: (619) 584-1100
E-mail: http://www.wellspublishing.com

West Group
19 Corbin Pl.
Brooklyn, NY, USA 11235
Ph: (718) 646-0932

Western Association of Venture Capitalists
3000 Sand Hill Rd., Ste. 2-290
PO Box 1221
Menlo Park, CA, USA 94025-7156
Ph: (650) 854-1322
E-mail: kimyatesgrosso@atswavc.org
URL: http://www.wavc.net

Western English Retailers Association
451 E 58th Ave., Ste. 4781
Denver, CO, USA 80216
E-mail: wera@atsfrii.com
URL:

Western League of Savings Institutions
9841 Airport Blvd., Ste. 418
Los Angeles, CA, USA 90045-5416
E-mail: http://www.westernleague.org

Western Retail Implement and Hardware Association
638 W 39th St.
PO Box 419264
Kansas City, MO, USA 64141-6264
Ph: (816) 561-5323
E-mail: http://www.southwesternassn.com/

Westminster John Knox Press
100 Witherspoon St.
Louisville, KY, USA 40202-1396
Ph: (502) 569-5052
E-mail: annie.mcclure@atspcusa.org
URL: http://www.wjk.org

Westview Press
5500 Central Ave.
Boulder, CO, USA 80301
Ph: (303) 444-3541
E-mail: westview.orders@atsperseusbooks.com
URL: http://www.perseusbooks.com

Wet Feet, Incorporated
101 Howard St., Ste. 300
San Francisco, CA, USA 94105-1619
Ph: (415) 284-7900

WFC Inc.
4041 G Hadley Rd., Ste. 101
South Plainfield, NJ, USA 7080
Ph: (908) 769-1160
E-mail: info@atswfcinc.com
URL: http://www.wfcinc.com

Wharton School Publishing
Pearson Technology Group
800 E 96th St.
Indianapolis, IN, USA 46240
Ph: (317) 428-3341
E-mail: http://www.whartonsp.com

Wharton School Publishing
1 Lake St.
Upper Saddle River, NJ, USA 7458
Ph: (201) 236-7113

Wheatmark
610 E Delano St., Ste. 104
Tucson, AZ, USA 85705
Ph: (520) 798-0888

White Publishing Co.
Box 3343
Jackson, TN, USA 38303-0343

Wholesale Florists & Florist Supplier Association
105 Eastern Ave., Ste. 104
Annapolis, MD, USA 21403
Ph: (410) 940-6580
E-mail: info@atswffsa.org
URL: http://www.wffsa.org

Wilen Media Corp.
5 Wellwood Ave.
Farmingdale, NY, USA 11735
Ph: (631) 439-5000
E-mail: info@atswilengroup.com
URL: http://www.wilengroup.com

Wiley Publishing
111 River St.
Hoboken, NJ, USA 07030-5774
Ph: (317) 572-3993
E-mail: http://www.dummies.com

Wiley-Blackwell
111 River St.
Hoboken, NJ, USA 07030-5773
Ph: (201) 748-6000
E-mail: info@atswiley.com
URL: http://www.wiley.com

Wilkes-Barre Publishing Company
15 N Main St.
Wilkes-Barre, PA, USA 18711
Ph: (570) 829-7101

William Morrow
10 E 53rd St.
New York, NY, USA 10022
Ph: (212) 207-7000
E-mail: http://www.harpercollins.com

WindStar Wildlife Institute
10072 Vista Ct.
Myersville, MD, USA 21773
Ph: (301) 293-3351
E-mail: wildlife@atswindstar.org
URL:

Wine & Spirits Magazine Inc.
2 W 32nd St., Ste. 601
New York, NY, USA 10001
Ph: (212) 695-4660
E-mail: info@atswineandspiritsmagazine.com
URL: http://www.wineandspiritsmagazine.com

Wine Appreciation Guild, Ltd.
360 Swift Ave., Unit 30-40
South San Francisco, CA, USA 94080
Ph: (650) 866-3020
E-mail: info@atswineappreciation.com
URL: http://www.wineappreciation.com

Wine Enthusiast Co.
333 N Bedford Rd.
Mount Kisco, NY, USA 10549
Ph: (914) 345-8463
E-mail: http://www.wineenthusiast.com

Winston J. Brill & Associates
12529 237th Way, NE
Redmond, WA, USA 98053
Ph: (425) 898-1077
E-mail: office@atswinstonbrill.com
URL:

Wireless Week
100 Enterprise Dr., Ste. 600
Rockaway, NJ, USA 7866
Ph: (973) 920-7783
E-mail: http://www.wirelessweek.com

Wisconsin State Journal
1901 Fish Hatchery Rd.
Madison, WI, USA 53713
Ph: (608) 252-6200

Wisconsin Taxpayers Alliance
401 N. Lawn Ave.
Madison, WI, USA 53704-5033
Ph: (608) 241-9789
E-mail: wistax@atswistax.org
URL: http://www.wistax.org

Wizards of the Coast Inc.
PO Box 707
Renton, WA, USA 98057
Ph: (425) 226-6500
E-mail: corporateinfo@atswizards.com
URL: http://www.wizards.com

Wm. K. Walthers Inc.
5601 W Florist Ave.
Milwaukee, WI, USA 53218-1622
Ph: (414) 527-0770
E-mail: custserv@atswalthers.com
URL: http://www.walthers.com

Wolf Rinke Associates,Inc.
PO Box 350
Clarksville, MD, USA 21029-0350
Ph: (410) 531-9280
E-mail: marcela@atswolfrinke.com
URL: http://www.wolfrinke.com/MIWL-NEWSLETTER/miwlnl.html

Wolfe Publishing Co.
2180 Gulfstream, Ste. A
Prescott, AZ, USA 86301
Ph: (928) 445-7810
E-mail: circ@atsriflemagazine.com
URL: http://www.riflemagazine.com

Woman's Missionary Union
100 Missionary Ridge
Birmingham, AL, USA 35242
Ph: (205) 991-8100

Women's Council of Realtors
430 N Michigan Ave.
Chicago, IL, USA 60611
Ph: (312) 329-8483
E-mail: wcr@atswcr.org
URL:

Women's National Book Association
2166 Broadway, No.9-E
New York, NY, USA 10024
Ph: (212) 208-4629
E-mail: sandy@atsskpassociates.com
URL:

Woodall Publications Corp.
2575 Vista Del Mar Dr.
Ventura, CA, USA 93001-3920
E-mail: info@atswoodallpub.com
URL: http://www.woodalls.com

WoodenBoat Publications Inc.
41 WoodenBoat Ln.
Brooklin, ME, USA 04616-0078
Ph: (207) 359-4651
E-mail: woodenboat@atswoodenboat.com
URL: http://www.woodenboat.com

Woodhead Publishing Limited
Abington Hall
Cambridge, , GBR CB21 6AH
Ph: (441) 223891358
E-mail: http://www.woodheadpublishing.com

Wordstar Processing Users' Group Inc.
PO Box 16-1443
Miami, FL, USA 33116-1443

Workman Publishing Company
225 Varick St.
New York, NY, USA 10014
Ph: (212) 254-5900
E-mail: info@atsworkman.com
URL: http://www.workman.com

World Organization of China Painters
2641 NW 10th St.
Oklahoma City, OK, USA 73107-5400
Ph: (405) 521-1234
E-mail: wocporg@atstheshop.net
URL: http://www.theshop.net/wocporg/

World Proof Numismatic Association
PO Box 4094
Pittsburgh, PA, USA 15201
Ph: (412) 782-4477

World Publishing
324 S Main St.
Tulsa, OK, USA 74103

World Publishing Co.
990 Grove St., Ste. 400
Evanston, IL, USA 60201-4370
Ph: (847) 491-6440
E-mail: cs@atscenturysports.net
URL: http://www.cruisetravelmag.com

World Scientific Publishing
27 Warren St., Ste. 401-402
Hackensack, NJ, USA 7601
Ph: (201) 487-9655
E-mail: wspc@atswspc.com
URL: http://www.wspc.com

World Trade Press
800 Lindberg Ln., Ste. 190
Petaluma, CA, USA 94952
Ph: (707) 778-1124
E-mail: accounting@atsworldtradepress.com
URL: http://www.worldtradepress.com

World Wide Gun Report Inc.
PO Box 38
Aledo, IL, USA 61231
Ph: (309) 582-5311
E-mail: contactus@atsthegunreport.com
URL:

WorldatWork
14040 N Northsight Blvd.
Scottsdale, AZ, USA 85260
Ph: (480) 922-2020
E-mail: customerrelations@atsworldat-work.org
URL:

Worldprofit Inc.
No. 205, 17505 - 107 Ave.
Edmonton, AB, CAN T5S 1E5
Ph: (780) 444-7477

Worldwide Videotex
PO Box 3273
Boynton Beach, FL, USA 33424-3273
Ph: (561) 738-2276
E-mail: markedit@atsjuno.com
URL:

Worm Digest
1455 E 185th St.
Cleveland, OH, USA 44145
Ph: (216) 531-5374
E-mail: mail@atswormdigest.org
URL: http://www.wormdigest.org/

Writers' Union of Canada
90 Richmond St. E., Ste. 200
Toronto, ON, CAN M5C 1P1
Ph: (416) 703-8982
E-mail: info@atswritersunion.ca
URL: http://www.writersunion.ca

Y

Yakima Herald-Republic
114 N 4th St.
Yakima, WA, USA 98901
Ph: (509) 248-1251

Yale University Press
302 Temple St.
New Haven, CT, USA 6511
Ph: (203) 432-0960
E-mail: http://www.yale.edu/yup/

Yale University Press
PO Box 209040
New Haven, CT, USA 06520-9040
Ph: (203) 432-0960
E-mail: http://yalepress.edu/yup

The Yamamoto Forecast
PO Box 573
Kahului, HI, USA 96733
Ph: (808) 877-2690

Yarn Tree Design Inc.
117 Alexander Ave.
PO Box 724
Ames, IA, USA 50010
Ph: (515) 232-3121
E-mail: info@atsyarntree.com
URL: http://yarntree.com

Ye Olde Genealogie Shoppe
PO Box 39128
Indianapolis, IN, USA 46239
Ph: (317) 862-3330
E-mail: yogs@atsiquest.net
URL: http://www.yogs.com

York Publishing Inc.
1350 E 9th St.
PO Box 4591
Chico, CA, USA 95928-5932
Ph: (530) 891-8410
E-mail: customerservice@atsvideomaker.com
URL: http://www.videomaker.com

Yuill & Associates
Box 11373
Ottawa, ON, CAN K2H 7V1
Ph: (613) 265-1997
E-mail: info@atsyuill-associates.com
URL: http://www.yuill-associates.com

The Yuma Sun
2055 Arizona Ave.
Yuma, AZ, USA 85364
Ph: (928) 783-3333

Y-Visionary Publishing L.P.
265 S Anita Dr., Ste. 120
Orange, CA, USA 92868
E-mail: http://www.bowhunting.net/bow&arrow/default.htm

Z

Zackin Publications Inc.
PO Box 2180
Waterbury, CT, USA 6722
Ph: (203) 262-4670
E-mail: info@atszackin.com
URL: http://www.zackin.com

Zen-Do Kai Martial Arts Association
12 W Main St., 2nd Fl.
PO Box 186
Johnstown, NY, USA 12095
Ph: (518) 762-4723
E-mail: zendokai@atssuperior.net
URL:

Ziff Davis Enterprise
28 E 28th St.
New York, NY, USA 10016
Ph: (212) 503-5900

Ziff Davis Inc.
28 E 28th St.
New York, NY, USA 10016

GLOSSARY

Absolute liability ▮ Liability that is incurred due to product defects or negligent actions. Manufacturers or retail establishments are held responsible, even though the defect or action may not have been intentional or negligent.

ACE ▮ See Active Corps of Executives.

Accident and health benefits ▮ Benefits offered to employees and their families in order to offset the costs associated with accidental death, accidental injury, or sickness.

Account statement ▮ A record of transactions, including payments, new debt, and deposits, incurred during a defined period of time.

Accounting system ▮ System capturing the costs of all employees and/or machinery included in business expenses.

Accounts payable ▮ *See* Trade credit.

Accounts receivable ▮ Unpaid accounts which arise from unsettled claims and transactions from the sale of a company's products or services to its customers.

Active Corps of Executives (ACE) ▮ (*See also* Service Corps of Retired Executives) A group of volunteers for a management assistance program of the U.S. Small Business Administration; volunteers provide one-on-one counseling and teach workshops and seminars for small firms.

ADA ▮ *See* Americans with Disabilities Act.

Adaptation ▮ The process whereby an invention is modified to meet the needs of users.

Adaptive engineering ▮ The process whereby an invention is modified to meet the manufacturing and commercial requirements of a targeted market.

Adverse selection ▮ The tendency for higher-risk individuals to purchase health care and more comprehensive plans, resulting in increased costs.

Advertising ▮ A marketing tool used to capture public attention and influence purchasing decisions for a product or service. Utilizes various forms of media to generate consumer response, such as flyers, magazines, newspapers, radio, and television.

Age discrimination ▮ The denial of the rights and privileges of employment based solely on the age of an individual.

Agency costs ▮ Costs incurred to insure that the lender or investor maintains control over assets while allowing the borrower or entrepreneur to use them. Monitoring and information costs are the two major types of agency costs.

Agribusiness ▮ The production and sale of commodities and products from the commercial farming industry.

America Online ▮ (*See also* Prodigy) An online service which is accessible by computer modem. The service features Internet access, bulletin boards, online periodicals, electronic mail, and other services for subscribers.

Americans with Disabilities Act (ADA) ▮ Law designed to ensure equal access and opportunity to handicapped persons.

Annual report ▮ (*See* also Securities and Exchange Commission) Yearly financial report prepared by a business that adheres to the requirements set forth by the Securities and Exchange Commission (SEC).

Antitrust immunity ▮ (*See* also Collective ratemaking) Exemption from prosecution under antitrust laws. In the transportation industry, firms with antitrust immunity are permitted—under certain conditions—to set schedules and sometimes prices for the public benefit.

Applied research ▮ Scientific study targeted for use in a product or process.

Asians ▮ A minority category used by the U.S. Bureau of the Census to represent a diverse group that includes Aleuts, Eskimos, American Indians, Asian Indians, Chinese, Japanese, Koreans, Vietnamese, Filipinos, Hawaiians, and other Pacific Islanders.

Assets ▮ Anything of value owned by a company.

Audit ▮ The verification of accounting records and business procedures conducted by an outside accounting service.

Average cost ▮ Total production costs divided by the quantity produced.

Balance Sheet ▮ A financial statement listing the total assets and liabilities of a company at a given time.

Bankruptcy ▮ (*See* also Chapter 7 of the 1978 Bankruptcy Act; Chapter 11 of the 1978 Bankruptcy Act) The condition in which a business cannot meet its debt obligations and petitions a federal district court either for reorganization of its debts (Chapter 11) or for liquidation of its assets (Chapter 7).

Basic research ▮ Theoretical scientific exploration not targeted to application.

Basket clause ▮ A provision specifying the amount of public pension funds that may be placed in investments not included on a state's legal list (*see* separate citation).

BBS ▮ *See* Bulletin Board Service.

BDC ▮ *See* Business development corporation.

Benefit ▮ Various services, such health care, flextime, day care, insurance, and vacation, offered to employees as part of a hiring package. Typically subsidized in whole or in part by the business.

BIDCO ▮ *See* Business and industrial development company

Billing cycle ▮ A system designed to evenly distribute customer billing throughout the month, preventing clerical backlogs.

Birth ▮ *See* Business birth.

Blue chip security ▮ A low-risk, low-yield security representing an interest in a very stable company.

Blue sky laws ▮ A general term that denotes various states' laws regulating securities.

Bond ▮ (*See also* General obligation bond; Taxable bonds; Treasury bonds) A written instrument executed by a bidder or contractor (the principal) and a second party (the surety or sureties) to .assure fulfillment of the principal's obligations to a third party (the obligee or government) identified in the bond. If the principal's obligations are not met, the bond assures payment to the extent stipulated of any loss sustained by the obligee.

Bonding requirements ▮ Terms contained in a bond (*see* separate citation).

Bonus ▮ An amount of money paid to an employee as a reward for achieving certain business goals or objectives.

Brainstorming ▮ A group session where employees contribute their ideas for solving a problem or meeting a company objective without fear of retribution or ridicule.

Brand name ▮ The part of a brand, trademark, or service mark that can be spoken. It can be a word, letter, or group of words or letters.

Bridge financing ▮ A short-term loan made in expectation of intermediate-term or long-term financing. Can be used when a company plans to go public in the near future.

Broker ▮ One who matches resources available for innovation with those who need them.

Budget ▮ An estimate of the spending necessary to complete a project or offer a service in comparison to cash-on-hand and expected earnings for the coming year, with an emphasis on cost control.

Bulletin Board Service (BBS) ▮ An online service enabling users to communicate with each other about specific topics.

Business birth ▮ The formation of a new establishment or enterprise. The appearance of a new establishment or enterprise in the Small Business Data Base (*see* separate citation).

Business conditions ▮ Outside factors that can affect the financial performance of a business.

Business contractions ▮ The number of establishments that have decreased in employment during a specified time.

Business cycle ▮ A period of economic recession and recovery. These cycles vary in duration.

Business death ▮ The voluntary or involuntary closure of a firm or establishment. The disappearance of an establishment or enterprise from the Small Business Data Base (*see* separate citation).

Business development corporation (BDC) ▮ A business financing agency, usually composed of the financial institutions in an area or state, organized to assist in financing businesses unable to obtain assistance through normal channels; the risk is spread among various members of the business development corporation, and interest rates may vary somewhat from those charged by member institutions. A venture capital firm in which shares of ownership are publicly held and to which the Investment Act of 1940 applies.

Business dissolution ▮ For enumeration purposes, the absence of a business that was present in the prior time period from any current record.

Business entry ▮ *See* Business birth.

Business ethics ▮ Moral values and principles espoused by members of the business community as a guide to fair and honest business practices.

Business exit ▮ *See* Business death.

Business expansions ▮ The number of establishments that added employees during a specified time.

Business failure ▮ Closure of a business causing a loss to at least one creditor.

Business format franchising ▮ (*See also* Franchising) The purchase of the name, trademark, and an ongoing business plan of the parent corporation or franchisor by the franchisee.

Business and industrial development company (BIDCO) ▮ A private, for-profit financing corporation chartered by the state to provide both equity and long-term debt capital to small business owners (*see* separate citations for equity and debt capital).

Business license ▮ A legal authorization issued by municipal and state governments and required for business operations.

Business name ▮ (*See also* Business license; Trademark) Enterprises must register their business names with local governments usually on a "doing business as" (DBA) form. (This name is sometimes referred to as a "fictional name.") The procedure is part of the business licensing process and prevents any other business from using that same name for a similar business in the same locality.

Business norms ▮ *See* Financial ratios.

Business permit ▮ *See* Business license.

Business plan ▮ A document that spells out a company's expected course of action for a specified period, usually including a detailed listing and analysis of risks and uncertainties. For the small busi-ness, it should examine the proposed products, the market, the industry, the management policies, the marketing policies, produc-tion needs, and financial needs. Frequently, it is used as a pros-pectus for potential investors and lenders.

Business proposal ▮ *See* Business plan.

Business service firm ▮ A business primarily engaged in rendering services to other businesses on a fee or contract basis.

Business start ▮ For enumeration purposes, a business with a name or similar designation that did not exist in a prior time period.

Cafeteria plan ▮ *See* Flexible benefit plan.

Capacity ▮ Level of a firm's, industry's, or nation's output corresponding to full practical utilization of available resources.

Capital ▮ Assets less liabilities, representing the ownership interest in a business. A stock of accumulated goods, especially at a specified time and in contrast to income received during a specified time period. Accumulated goods devoted to production. Accumulated possessions calculated to bring income.

Capital expenditure ▮ Expenses incurred by a business for improvements that will depreciate over time.

Capital gain ▮ The monetary difference between the purchase price and the selling price of capital. Capital gains are taxed at a rate of 28% by the federal government.

Capital intensity ▮ (*See also* Debt capital; Equity midrisk venture capital; Informal capital; Internal capital; Owner's capital; Secondhand capital; Seed capital; Venture capital) The relative importance of capital in the production process, usually expressed as the ratio of capital to labor but also sometimes as the ratio of capital to output.

Capital resource ▮ The equipment, facilities and labor used to create products and services.

Caribbean Basin Initiative ▮ An interdisciplinary program to support commerce among the businesses in the nations of the Caribbean Basin and the United States. Agencies involved include: the Agency for International Development, the U.S. Small Business Administration, the International Trade Administration of the U.S. Department of Commerce, and various private sector groups.

Catastrophic care ▮ Medical and other services for acute and long-term illnesses that cost more than insurance coverage limits or that cost the amount most families may be expected to pay with their own resources.

CDC ▮ *See* Certified development corporation.

CD-ROM ▮ Compact disc with read-only memory used to store large amounts of digitized data.

Certified development corporation (CDC) ▮ A local area or statewide corporation or authority (for profit or nonprofit) that packages U.S. Small Business Administration (SBA), bank, state, and/or private money into financial assistance for existing business capital improvements. The SBA holds the second lien on its maximum share of 40 percent involvement. Each state has at least one certified development corporation. This program is called the SBA 504 Program.

Certified lenders ▮ Banks that participate in the SBA guaranteed loan program (*see* separate citation). Such banks must have a good track record with the U.S. Small Business Administration (SBA) and must agree to certain conditions set forth by the agency. In return, the SBA agrees to process any guaranteed loan application within three business days.

Champion ▮ An advocate for the development of an innovation.

Channel of distribution ▮ The means used to transport merchandise from the manufacturer to the consumer.

Chapter 7 of the 1978 Bankruptcy Act ▮ Provides for a court-appointed trustee who is responsible for liquidating a company's assets in order to settle outstanding debts.

Chapter 11 of the 1978 Bankruptcy Act ▮ Allows the business owners to retain control of the company while working with their creditors to reorganize their finances and establish better business practices to prevent liquidation of assets.

Closely held corporation ▮ A corporation in which the shares are held by a few persons, usually officers, employees, or others close to the management; these shares are rarely offered to the public.

Code of Federal Regulations ▮ Codification of general and permanent rules of the federal government published in the Federal Register.

Code sharing ▮ *See* Computer code sharing.

Coinsurance ▮ (*See also* Cost sharing) Upon meeting the deductible payment, health insurance participants may be required to make additional health care cost-sharing payments. Coinsurance is a payment of a fixed percentage of the cost of each service; copayment is usually a fixed amount to be paid with each service.

Collateral ▮ Securities, evidence of deposit, or other property pledged by a borrower to secure repayment of a loan.

Collective ratemaking ▮ (*See also* Antitrust immunity) The establishment of uniform charges for services by a group of businesses in the same industry.

Commercial insurance plan ▮ *See* Underwriting.

Commercial loans ▮ Short-term renewable loans used to finance specific capital needs of a business.

Commercialization ▮ The final stage of the innovation process, including production and distribution.

Common stock ▮ The most frequently used instrument for purchasing ownership in private or public companies. Common stock generally carries the right to vote on certain corporate actions and may pay dividends, although it rarely does in venture investments. In liquidation, common stockholders are the last to share in the proceeds from the sale of a corporation's assets; bondholders and preferred shareholders have priority. Common stock is often used in first-round start-up financing.

Community development corporation ▮ A corporation established to develop economic programs for a community and, in most cases, to provide financial support for such development.

Competitor ▮ A business whose product or service is marketed for the same purpose/use and to the same consumer group as the product or service of another.

Computer code sharing ▮ An arrangement whereby flights of a regional airline are identified by the two-letter code of a major carrier in the computer reservation system to help direct passengers to new regional carriers.

Consignment ▮ A merchandising agreement, usually referring to secondhand shops, where the dealer pays the owner of an item a percentage of the profit when the item is sold.

Consortium ▮ A coalition of organizations such as banks and corporations for ventures requiring large capital resources.

Consultant ▮ An individual that is paid by a business to provide advice and expertise in a particular area.

Consumer price index ▮ A measure of the fluctuation in prices between two points in time.

Consumer research ▮ Research conducted by a business to obtain information about existing or potential consumer markets.

Continuation coverage ▮ Health coverage offered for a specified period of time to employees who leave their jobs and to their widows, divorced spouses, or dependents.

Contractions ▮ *See* Business contractions.

Convertible preferred stock ▮ A class of stock that pays a reasonable dividend and is convertible into common stock (*See* separate citation). Generally the convertible feature may only be exercised after being held for a stated period of time. This arrangement is usually considered second-round financing when a company needs equity to maintain its cash flow.

Convertible securities ▮ A feature of certain bonds, debentures, or preferred stocks that allows them to be exchanged by the owner for another class of securities at a future date and in accordance with any other terms of the issue.

Copayment ▮ *See* Coinsurance.

Copyright ▮ A legal form of protection available to creators and authors to safeguard their works from unlawful use or claim of ownership by others. Copyrights may be acquired for works of art, sculpture, music, and published or unpublished manuscripts. All copyrights should be registered at the Copyright Office of the Library of Congress.

Corporate financial ratios ▮ (*See also* Industry financial ratios) The relationship between key figures found in a company's financial statement expressed as a numeric value. Used to evalu-ate risk and company performance. Also known as Financial averages, Operating ratios, and Business ratios.

Corporation ▮ A legal entity, chartered by a state or the federal government, recognized as a separate entity having its own rights, privileges, and liabilities distinct from those of its members.

Cost containment ▮ Actions taken by employers and insurers to curtail rising health care costs; for example, increasing employee cost sharing (*see* separate citation), requiring second opinions, or preadmission screening.

Cost sharing ▮ The requirement that health care consumers contribute to their own medical care costs through deductibles and coinsurance (*see* separate citations). Cost sharing does not include the amounts paid in premiums. It is used to control utilization of services; for example, requiring a fixed amount to be paid with each health care service.

Cottage industry ▮ (*See also* Home-based business) Businesses based in the home in which the family members are the labor force and family-owned equipment is used to process the goods.

Credit Rating ▮ A letter or number calculated by an organization (such as Dun & Bradstreet) to represent the ability and disposition of a business to meet its financial obligations.

Customer service ▮ Various techniques used to ensure the satisfaction of a customer.

Cyclical peak ▮ The upper turning point in a business cycle.

Cyclical trough ▮ The lower turning point in a business cycle.

DBA ▮ *See* Business name.

Death ▮ *See* Business death.

Debenture ▮ A certificate given as acknowledgment of a debt (*see* separate citation) secured by the general credit of the issuing corporation. A bond, usually without security, issued by a corporation and sometimes convertible to common stock.

Debt ▮ (*See also* Long-term debt; Mid-term debt; Securitized debt; Short-term debt) Something owed by one person to another. Financing in which a company receives capital that must be repaid; no ownership is transferred.

Debt capital ▮ Business financing that normally requires periodic interest payments and repayment of the principal within a specified time.

Debt financing ▮ *See* Debt capital.

Debt securities ▮ Loans such as bonds and notes that provide a specified rate of return for a specified period of time.

Deductible ▮ A set amount that an individual must pay before any benefits are received.

Demand shock absorbers ▮ A term used to describe the role that some small firms play by expanding their output levels to accommodate a transient surge in demand.

Demographics ▮ Statistics on various markets, including age, income, and education, used to target specific products or services to appropriate consumer groups.

Demonstration ▮ Showing that a product or process has been modified sufficiently to meet the needs of users.

Deregulation ▮ The lifting of government restrictions; for example, the lifting of government restrictions on the entry of new businesses, the expansion of services, and the setting of prices in particular industries.

Desktop Publishing ▮ Using personal computers and specialized software to produce camera-ready copy for publications.

Digital cash ▮ A system that allows a person to make financial transactions over the Internet. This system allows a person to purchase goods or services by transmitting a number from one computer to another.

Disaster loans ▮ Various types of physical and economic assistance available to individuals and businesses through the U.S. Small Business Administration (SBA). This is the only SBA loan program available for residential purposes.

Discrimination ▮ The denial of the rights and privileges of employment based on factors such as age, race, religion, or gender.

Diseconomies of scale ▮ The condition in which the costs of production increase faster than the volume of production.

Dissolution ▮ *See* Business dissolution.

Distribution ▮ Delivering a product or process to the user.

Distributor ▮ One who delivers merchandise to the user.

Diversified company ▮ A company whose products and services are used by several different markets.

Doing business as (DBA) ▮ *See* Business name.

Dow Jones ▮ An information services company that publishes the Wall Street Journal and other sources of financial information.

Dow Jones Industrial Average ▮ An indicator of stock market performance.

Earned income ▮ A tax term that refers to wages and salaries earned by the recipient, as opposed to monies earned through interest and dividends.

E-commerce ▮ *See* Electronic commerce.

Economic efficiency ▮ The use of productive resources to the fullest practical extent in the provision of the set of goods and services that is most preferred by purchasers in the economy.

Economic indicators ▮ Statistics used to express the state of the economy. These include the length of the average work week, the rate of unemployment, and stock prices.

Economically disadvantaged ▮ *See* Socially and economically disadvantaged.

Economies of scale ▮ *See* Scale economies.

EEOC ▮ *See* Equal Employment Opportunity Commission.

8(a) Program ▮ A program authorized by the Small Business Act that directs federal contracts to small businesses owned and operated by socially and economically disadvantaged individuals.

Electronic mail (e-mail) ▮ The electronic transmission of mail via phone lines.

Electonic commerce (e-commerce) ▮ Buying and selling goods and services through the Internet.

E-mail ▮ *See* Electronic mail.

Employee leasing ▮ A contract by which employers arrange to have their workers hired by a leasing company and then leased back to them for a management fee. The leasing company typically assumes the administrative burden of payroll and provides a benefit package to the workers.

Employee tenure ▮ The length of time an employee works for a particular employer.

Employer identification number ▮ The business equivalent of a social security number. Assigned by the U.S. Internal Revenue Service.

Enterprise ▮ An aggregation of all establishments owned by a parent company. An enterprise may consist of a single, independent establishment or include subsidiaries and other branches under the same ownership and control.

Enterprise zone ▮ A designated area, usually found in inner cities and other areas with significant unemployment, where businesses receive tax credits and other incentives to entice them to establish operations there.

Entrepreneur ▮ A person who takes the risk of organizing and operating a new business venture.

Entry ▮ *See* Business entry

Equal Employment Opportunity Commission (EEOC) ▮ A federal agency that ensures nondiscrimination in the hiring and firing practices of a business.

Equal opportunity employer ▮ An employer who adheres to the standards set by the Equal Employment Opportunity Commission (*see* separate citation).

Equity ▮ (*See also* Common Stock; Equity midrisk venture capital) The ownership interest. Financing in which partial or total ownership of a company is surrendered in exchange for capital. An investor's financial return comes from dividend payments and from growth in the net worth of the business.

Equity capital ▮ *See* Equity; Equity midrisk venture capital.

Equity financing ▮ *See* Equity; Equity midrisk venture capital.

Equity midrisk venture capital ▮ An unsecured investment in a company. Usually a purchase of ownership interest in a company that occurs in the later stages of a company's development.

Equity partnership ▮ A limited partnership arrangement for providing start-up and Seed capital to businesses.

Equity securities ▮ *See* Equity.

Equity-type ▮ Debt financing subordinated to conventional debt.

Establishment ▮ A single-location business unit that may be independent (a single-establishment enterprise) or owned by a parent enterprise.

Establishment and Enterprise Microdata File ▮ *See* U.S. Establishment and Enterprise Microdata File.

Establishment birth ▮ *See* Business birth.

Establishment Longitudinal Microdata File ▮ *See* U.S. Establishment Longitudinal Microdata File.

Ethics ▮ *See* Business ethics.

Evaluation ▮ Determining the potential success of translating an invention into a product or process.

Experience rating ▮ *See* Underwriting.

Exit ▮ *See* Business exit.

Export ▮ A product sold outside of the country.

Export license ▮ A general or specific license granted by the U.S. Department of Commerce required of anyone wishing to export goods. Some restricted articles need approval from the U.S. Departments of State, Defense, or Energy.

Extranet ▮ (*See also* Intranet) An intranet that provides various levels of accessibility to outsiders. Access to an extranet can only be obtained if you have a valid username and password.

Failure ▮ *See* Business failure.

Fair share agreement ▮ (*See also* Franchising) An agreement reached between a franchisor and a minority business organization to extend business ownership to minorities by either reducing the amount of capital required or by setting aside certain marketing areas for minority business owners.

Feasibility study ▮ A study to determine the likelihood that a proposed product or development will fulfill the objectives of a particular investor.

Federal Trade Commission (FTC) ▮ Federal agency that promotes free enterprise and competition within the U.S.

Federal Trade Mark Act of 1946 ▮ *See* Lanham Act.

Fictional name ▮ *See* Business name.

Fiduciary ▮ An individual or group that hold assets in trust for a beneficiary.

Financial analysis ▮ The techniques used to determine money needs in a business. Techniques include ratio analysis, calculation of return on investment, guides for measuring profitability, and break-even analysis to determine ultimate success.

Financial intermediary ▮ A financial institution that acts as the intermediary between borrowers and lenders. Banks, savings and loan associations, finance companies, and venture capital companies are major financial intermediaries in the United States.

Financial ratios ▮ *See* Corporate financial ratios; Industry financial ratios.

Financial statement ▮ A written record of business finances, including balance sheets and profit and loss statements.

Financing ▮ *See* First-stage financing; Second-stage financing; Third-stage financing.

First-stage financing ▮ (*See also* Second-stage financing; Third-stage financing) Financing provided to companies that have expended their initial capital, and require funds to start full-scale manufacturing and sales. Also known as First-round financing.

Fiscal year ▮ Any twelve-month period used by businesses for accounting purposes.

504 Program ▮ *See* Certified development corporation.

Flexible benefit plan ▮ A plan that offers a choice among cash and/or qualified benefits such as group term life insurance, accident and health insurance, group legal services, dependent care assistance, and vacations.

FOB ▮ *See* Free on board

Format franchising ▮ *See* Business format franchising; Franchising.

401(k) plan ▮ A financial plan where employees contribute a percentage of their earnings to a fund that is invested in stocks, bonds, or money markets for the purpose of saving money for retirement.

Four Ps ▮ Marketing terms: Product, Price, Place, and Promotion.

Franchising ▮ A form of licensing by which the owner—the franchisor—distributes or markets a product, method, or service through affiliated dealers called franchisees. The product, method, or service being marketed is identified by a brand name, and the franchisor maintains control over the marketing methods employed. The franchisee is often given exclusive access to a defined geographic area.

Free on board (FOB) ▮ A pricing term indicating that the quoted price includes the cost of loading goods into transport vessels at a specified place.

Frictional unemployment ▮ *See* Un-employment.

FTC ▮ *See* Federal Trade Commission.

Fulfillment ▮ The systems necessary for accurate delivery of an ordered item, including subscriptions and direct marketing.

Full-time workers ▮ Generally, those who work a regular schedule of more than 35 hours per week.

Garment registration number ▮ A number that must appear on every garment sold in the U.S. to indicate the manufacturer of the garment, which may or may not be the same as the label under which the garment is sold. The U.S. Federal Trade Commission assigns and regulates garment registration numbers.

Gatekeeper ▮ A key contact point for entry into a network.

GDP ▮ *See* Gross domestic product.

General obligation bond ▮ A municipal bond secured by the taxing power of the municipality. The Tax Reform Act of 1986 limits the purposes for which such bonds may be issued and establishes volume limits on the extent of their issuance.

GNP ▮ *See* Gross national product.

Good Housekeeping Seal ▮ Seal appearing on products that signifies the fulfillment of the standards set by the Good Housekeeping Institute to protect consumer interests.

Goods sector ▮ All businesses producing tangible goods, including agriculture, mining, construction, and manufacturing businesses.

GPO ▮ *See* Gross product originating.

Gross domestic product (GDP) ▮ The part of the nation's gross national product (*see* separate citation) generated by private business using resources from within the country.

Gross national product (GNP) ▮ The most comprehensive single measure of aggregate economic output. Represents the market value of the total output of goods and services produced by a nation's economy.

Gross product originating (GPO) ▮ A measure of business output estimated from the income or production side using employee compensation, profit income, net interest, capital consumption, and indirect business taxes.

HAL ▮ *See* Handicapped assistance loan program.

Handicapped assistance loan program (HAL) ▮ Low-interest direct loan program through the U.S. Small Business Administration (SBA) for handicapped persons. The SBA requires that these persons demonstrate that their disability is such that it is impossible for them to secure employment, thus making it necessary to go into their own business to make a living.

Health maintenance organization (HMO) ▮ Organization of physi-cians and other health care professionals that provides health services to subscribers and their dependents on a prepaid basis.

Health provider ▮ An individual or institution that gives medical care. Under Medicare, an institutional provider is a hospital, skilled nursing facility, home health agency, or provider of certain physical therapy services.

Hispanic ▮ A person of Cuban, Mexican, Puerto Rican, Latin American (Central or South American), European Spanish, or other Spanish-speaking origin or ancestry.

HMO ▮ *See* Health maintenance organization.

Home-based business ▮ (*See also* Cottage industry) A business with an operating address that is also a residential address (usually the residential address of the proprietor).

Hub-and-spoke system ▮ A system in which flights of an airline from many different cities (the spokes) converge at a single airport (the hub). After allowing passengers sufficient time to make connections, planes then depart for different cities.

Human Resources Management ▮ A business program designed to oversee recruiting, pay, benefits, and other issues related to the company's work force, including planning to determine the optimal use of labor to increase production, thereby increasing profit.

Idea ▮ An original concept for a new product or process.

Import ▮ Products produced outside the country in which they are consumed.

Income ▮ Money or its equivalent, earned or accrued, resulting from the sale of goods and services.

Income statement ▮ A financial statement that lists the profits and losses of a company at a given time.

Incorporation ▮ The filing of a certificate of incorporation with the secretary of state, thereby limiting the business owner's liability.

Incubator ▮ A facility designed to encourage entrepreneurship and minimize obstacles to new business formation and growth, particularly for high-technology firms, by housing a number of fledgling enterprises that share an array of services, such as meeting areas, secretarial services, accounting, research library, on-site financial and management counseling, and word processing facilities.

Independent contractor ▮ An individual considered self- employed (*see* separate citation) and responsible for paying Social Security taxes and income taxes on earnings.

Indirect health coverage ▮ Health insurance obtained through another individual's health care plan; for example, a spouse's employer-sponsored plan.

Industrial development authority ▮ The financial arm of a state or other political subdivision established for the purpose of financing economic development in an area, usually through loans to nonprofit organizations, which in turn provide facilities for manufacturing and other industrial operations.

Industry financial ratios ▮ (*See also* Corporate financial ratios) Corporate financial ratios averaged for a specified industry. These are used for comparison purposes and reveal industry trends and identify differences between the performance of a specific company and the performance of its industry. Also known as Industrial averages, Industry ratios, Financial averages, and Business or Industrial norms.

Inflation ▮ Increases in volume of currency and credit, generally resulting in a sharp and continuing rise in price levels.

Informal capital ▮ Financing from informal, unorganized sources; includes informal debt capital such as trade credit or loans from friends and relatives and equity capital from informal investors.

Initial public offering (IPO) ▮ A corporation's first offering of stock to the public.

Innovation ▮ The introduction of a new idea into the marketplace in the form of a new product or service or an improvement in organization or process.

Intellectual property ▮ Any idea/work that can be considered proprietary in nature and thus protected from infringement by others.

Internal capital ▮ Debt or equity financing obtained from the owner or through retained business earnings.

Internet ▮ A government-designed computer network that contains large amounts of information and is accessible through various vendors for a fee.

Intranet ▮ (*See also* Extranet) A web site belonging to an organization or a corporation, that is accessible only to employees, members, or others that have authorization.

Intrapreneurship ▮ The state of employing entrepreneurial principles to nonentrepreneurial situations.

Invention ▮ The tangible form of a technological idea, which could include a laboratory prototype, drawings, formulas, etc.

IPO ▮ *See* Initial public offering.

Job description ▮ The duties and responsibilities required in a particular position.

Job tenure ▮ A period of time during which an individual is continuously employed in the same job.

Joint marketing agreements ▮ Agree-ments between regional and major airlines, often involving the coordination of flight schedules, fares, and baggage transfer. These agreements help regional carriers operate at lower cost.

Joint venture ▮ Venture in which two or more people combine efforts in a particular business enterprise, usually a single transaction or a limited activity, and agree to share the profits and losses jointly or in proportion to their contributions.

Keogh plan ▮ Designed for self-employed persons and unincorporated businesses as a tax-deferred pension account.

Labor force ▮ Civilians considered eligible for employment who are also willing and able to work.

Labor force participation rate ▮ The civilian labor force as a percentage of the civilian population.

Labor intensity ▮ (*See also* Capital intensity) The relative importance of labor in the production process, usually measured as the capital-labor ratio; i.e., the ratio of units of capital (typically, dollars of tangible assets) to the number of employees. The higher the capital-labor ratio exhibited by a firm or industry, the lower the capital intensity of that firm or industry is said to be.

Labor surplus area ▮ An area in which there exists a high unemployment rate. In procurement (*see* separate citation), extra points are given to firms in counties that are designated a labor surplus area; this information is requested on procurement bid sheets.

Labor union ▮ An organization of similarly-skilled workers who collectively bargain with management over the conditions of employment.

Laboratory prototype ▮ *See* Prototype.

LAN ▮ *See* Local Area Network.

Lanham Act ▮ Refers to the Federal Trade Mark Act of 1946. Protects registered trademarks, trade names, and other service marks used in commerce.

Large business-dominated industry ▮ Industry in which a minimum of 60 percent of employment or sales is in firms with more than 500 workers.

LBO ▮ *See* Leveraged buy-out.

Leader pricing ▮ A reduction in the price of a good or service in order to generate more sales of that good or service.

Legal list ▮ A list of securities selected by a state in which certain institutions and fiduciaries (such as pension funds, insurance companies, and banks) may invest. Securities not on the list are not eligible for investment. Legal lists typically restrict investments to high quality securities meeting certain specifications. Generally, investment is limited to U.S. securities and investment-grade blue chip securities (*see* separate citation).

Leveraged buy-out (LBO) ▮ The purchase of a business or a division of a corporation through a highly leveraged financing package.

Liability ▮ An obligation or duty to perform a service or an act. Also defined as money owed.

License ▮ (*See also* Business license) A legal agreement granting to another the right to use a technological innovation.

Limited partnerships ▮ *See* Venture capital limited partnerships

Liquidity ▮ The ability to convert a security into cash promptly.

Loans ▮ *See* Commercial loans; Disaster loans; SBA direct loans; SBA guaranteed loans; SBA special lending institution categories.

Local Area Network (LAN) ▮ Computer networks contained within a single building or small area; used to facilitate the sharing of information.

Local development corporation ▮ An organization, usually made up of local citizens of a community, designed to improve the economy of the area by inducing business and industry to locate and expand there. A local development corporation establishes a capability to finance local growth.

Long-haul rates ▮ Rates charged by a transporter in which the distance traveled is more than 800 miles.

Long-term debt ▮ An obligation that matures in a period that exceeds five years.

Low-grade bond ▮ A corporate bond that is rated below investment grade by the major rating agencies (Standard and Poor's, Moody's).

Macro-efficiency ▮ (*See also* Economic efficiency) Efficiency as it pertains to the operation of markets and market systems.

Managed care ▮ A cost-effective health care program initiated by employers whereby low-cost health care is made available to the employees in return for exclusive patronage to program doctors.

Management and technical assistance ▮ A term used by many programs to mean business (as opposed to technological) assistance.

Management Assistance Programs ▮ *See* SBA Management Assistance Programs

Mandated benefits ▮ Specific treatments, providers, or individuals required by law to be included in commercial health plans.

Market evaluation ▮ The use of market information to determine the sales potential of a specific product or process.

Market failure ▮ The situation in which the workings of a competitive market do not produce the best results from the point of view of the entire society.

Market information ▮ Data of any type that can be used for market evaluation, which could include demographic data, technology forecasting, regulatory changes, etc.

Market research ▮ A systematic collection, analysis, and reporting of data about the market and its preferences, opinions, trends, and plans; used for corporate decision-making.

Market share ▮ In a particular market, the percentage of sales of a specific product.

Marketing ▮ Promotion of goods or services through various media.

Master Establishment List (MEL) ▮ A list of firms in the United States developed by the U.S. Small Business Administration; firms can be selected by industry, region, state, standard metropolitan statistical area (*see* separate citation), county, and zip code.

Maturity ▮ (*See also* Term) The date upon which the principal or stated value of a bond or other indebtedness becomes due and payable.

Medicaid (Title XIX) ▮ A federally aided, state-operated and administered program that provides medical benefits for certain low-income persons in need of health and medical care who are eligible for one of the government's welfare cash payment programs, including the aged, the blind, the disabled, and members of families with dependent children where one parent is absent, incapacitated, or unemployed.

Medicare (Title XVIII) ▮ A nationwide health insurance program for disabled and aged persons. Health insurance is available to insured persons without regard to income. Monies from payroll taxes cover hospital insurance and monies from general revenues and beneficiary premiums pay for supplementary medical insurance.

MEL ▮ *See* Master Establishment List.

Metropolitan statistical area (MSA) ▮ A means used by the government to define large population centers that may transverse different governmental jurisdictions. For example, the Washington, D.C., MSA includes the District of Columbia and contiguous parts of Maryland and Virginia because all of these geopolitical areas comprise one population and economic operating unit.

Mezzanine financing ▮ *See* Third-stage financing.

MESBIC ▮ *See* Minority enterprise small business investment corporation.

MET ▮ *See* Multiple employer trust.

Micro-efficiency ▮ (*See also* Economic efficiency) Efficiency as it pertains to the operation of individual firms.

Microdata ▮ Information on the characteristics of an individual business firm.

Mid-term debt ▮ An obligation that matures within one to five years.

Midrisk venture capital ▮ *See* Equity midrisk venture capital.

Minimum premium plan ▮ A combination approach to funding an insurance plan aimed primarily at premium tax savings. The employer self-funds a fixed percentage of estimated monthly claims and the insurance company insures the excess.

Minimum wage ▮ The lowest hourly wage allowed by the federal government.

Minority Business Development Agency ▮ Contracts with private firms throughout the nation to sponsor Minority Business Development Centers which provide minority firms with advice and technical assistance on a fee basis.

Minority Enterprise Small Business Investment Corporation (MESBIC) ▮ A federally funded private venture capital firm licensed by the U.S. Small Business Administration to provide capital to minority-owned businesses (*see* separate citation).

Minority-owned business ▮ Businesses owned by those who are socially or economically disadvantaged (*see* separate citation).

Mom and Pop business ▮ A small store or enterprise having limited capital, principally employing family members.

Moonlighter ▮ A wage-and-salary worker with a side business.

MSA ▮ *See* Metropolitan statistical area.

Multi-employer plan ▮ A health plan to which more than one employer is required to contribute and that may be maintained through a collective bargaining agreement and required to meet standards prescribed by the U.S. Department of Labor.

Multi-level marketing ▮ A system of selling in which you sign up other people to assist you, and they, in turn, recruit others to help them. Some entrepreneurs have built successful companies on this concept because the main focus of their activities is their product and product sales.

Multimedia ▮ The use of several types of media to promote a product or service. Also refers to the use of several different types of media (sight, sound, pictures, text) in a CD-ROM (*see* separate citation) product.

Multiple employer trust (MET) ▮ A self-funded benefit plan generally geared toward small employers sharing a common interest.

NAFTA ▮ *See* North American Free Trade Agreement.

NASDAQ ▮ *See* National Association of Securities Dealers Automated Quotations.

National Association of Securities Dealers Automated Quotations ▮ Provides price quotes on over-the-counter securities as well as securities listed on the New York Stock Exchange.

National income ▮ Aggregate earnings of labor and property arising from the production of goods and services in a nation's economy.

Net assets ▮ *See* Net worth.

Net income ▮ The amount remaining from earnings and profits after all expenses and costs have been met or deducted. Also known as Net earnings.

Net profit ▮ Money earned after production and overhead expenses (*see* separate citations) have been deducted.

Net worth ▮ (*See also* Capital) The difference between a company's total assets and its total liabilities.

Network ▮ A chain of interconnected individuals or organizations sharing information and/or services.

New York Stock Exchange (NYSE) ▮ The oldest stock exchange in the U.S. Allows for trading in stocks, bonds, warrants, options, and rights that meet listing requirements.

Niche ▮ A career or business for which a person is well-suited. Also, a product which fulfills one need of a particular market segment, often with little or no competition.

Nodes ▮ One workstation in a network, either local area or wide area (*see* separate citations).

Nonbank bank ▮ A bank that either accepts deposits or makes loans, but not both. Used to create many new branch banks.

Noncompetitive awards ▮ A method of contracting whereby the federal government negotiates with only one contractor to supply a product or service.

Nonmember bank ▮ A state-regulated bank that does not belong to the federal bank system.

Nonprofit ▮ An organization that has no shareholders, does not distribute profits, and is without federal and state tax liabilities.

Norms ▮ *See* Financial ratios.

North American Free Trade Agreement (NAFTA) ▮ Passed in 1993, NAFTA eliminates trade barriers among businesses in the U.S., Canada, and Mexico.

NYSE ▮ *See* New York Stock Exchange

Occupational Safety & Health Administration (OSHA) ▮ Federal agency that regulates health and safety standards within the workplace.

Optimal firm size ▮ The business size at which the production cost per unit of output (average cost) is, in the long run, at its minimum.

Organizational chart ▮ A hierarchical chart tracking the chain of command within an organization.

OSHA ▮ *See* Occupational Safety & Health Administration.

Overhead ▮ Expenses, such as employee benefits and building utilities, incurred by a business that are unrelated to the actual product or service sold.

Owner's capital ▮ Debt or equity funds provided by the owner(s) of a business; sources of owner's capital are personal savings, sales of assets, or loans from financial institutions.

P & L ▮ *See* Profit and loss statement.

Part-time workers ▮ Normally, those who work less than 35 hours per week. The Tax Reform Act indicated that part-time workers who work less than 17.5 hours per week may be excluded from health plans for purposes of complying with federal nondiscrimination rules.

Part-year workers ▮ Those who work less than 50 weeks per year.

Partnership ▮ Two or more parties who enter into a legal relationship to conduct business for profit. Defined by the U.S. Internal Revenue Code as joint ventures, syndicates, groups, pools, and other associations of two or more persons organized for profit that are not specifically classified in the IRS code as corporations or proprietorships.

Patent ▮ A grant by the government assuring an inventor the sole right to make, use, and sell an invention for a period of 17 years.

PC ▮ *See* Professional corporation.

Peak ▮ *See* Cyclical peak.

Pension ▮ A series of payments made monthly, semiannually, annually, or at other specified intervals during the lifetime of the pensioner for distribution upon retirement. The term is sometimes used to denote the portion of the retirement allowance financed by the employer's contributions.

Pension fund ▮ A fund established to provide for the payment of pension benefits; the collective contributions made by all of the parties to the pension plan.

Performance appraisal ▮ An established set of objective criteria, based on job description and requirements, that is used to evaluate the performance of an employee in a specific job.

Permit ▮ *See* Business license.

Plan ▮ *See* Business plan.

Pooling ▮ An arrangement for employers to achieve efficiencies and lower health costs by joining together to purchase group health insurance or self-insurance.

PPO ▮ *See* Preferred provider organization

Preferred lenders program ▮ *See* SBA special lending institution categories

Preferred provider organization (PPO) ▮ A contractual arrangement with a health care services organization that agrees to discount its health care rates in return for faster payment and/or a patient base.

Premiums ▮ The amount of money paid to an insurer for health insurance under a policy. The premium is generally paid periodically (e.g., monthly), and often is split between the employer and the employee. Unlike deductibles and coinsurance or copayments, premiums are paid for coverage whether or not benefits are actually used.

Prime-age workers ▮ Employees 25 to 54 years of age.

Prime contract ▮ A contract awarded directly by the U.S. Federal Government.

Private company ▮ *See* Closely held corporation. Private placement A method of raising capital by offering for sale an investment or business to a small group of investors (generally avoiding registration with the Securities and Exchange Commis-sion or state securities registration agencies). Also known as Private financing or Private offering.

Pro forma ▮ The use of hypothetical figures in financial statements to represent future expenditures, debts, and other potential financial expenses.

Proactive ▮ Taking the initiative to solve problems and anticipate future events before they happen, instead of reacting to an already existing problem or waiting for a difficult situation to occur.

Procurement ▮ (*See also* 8(a) Program; Small business set asides) A contract from an agency of the federal government for goods or services from a small business.

Prodigy ▮ (*See also* America Online) An online service which is accessible by computer modem. The service features Internet access, bulletin boards, online periodicals, electronic mail, and other services for subscribers.

Product development ▮ The stage of the innovation process where research is translated into a product or process through evaluation, adaptation, and demonstration.

Product franchising ▮ An arrangement for a franchisee to use the name and to produce the product line of the franchisor or parent corporation.

Production ▮ The manufacture of a product.

Production prototype ▮ *See* Prototype.

Productivity ▮ A measurement of the number of goods produced during a specific amount of time.

Professional corporation (PC) ▮ Organized by members of a pro-fession such as medicine, dentistry, or law for the purpose of con-ducting their professional activities as a corporation. Liability of a member or shareholder is limited in the same manner as in a business corporation.

Profit and loss statement (P & L) ▮ The summary of the incomes and costs of a company's operation during a specific period of time. Also known as Income and expense statement.

Proposal ▮ *See* Business plan.

Proprietorship ▮ The most common legal form of business ownership; about 85 percent of all small businesses are proprietorships. The liability of the owner is unlimited in this form of ownership.

Prospective payment system ▮ A cost-containment measure included in the Social Security Amendments of 1983 whereby Medicare payments to hospitals are based on established prices, rather than on cost reimbursement.

Prototype ▮ A model that demonstrates the validity of the concept of an invention (laboratory prototype); a model that meets the needs of the manufacturing process and the user (production prototype).

Prudent investor rule or standard ▮ A legal doctrine that requires fiduciaries to make investments using the prudence, diligence, and intelligence that would be used by a prudent person in making similar investments. Because fiduciaries make investments on behalf of third-party beneficiaries, the standard results in very conservative investments. Until recently, most state regulations required the fiduciary to apply this standard to each investment. Newer, more progressive regulations permit fiduciaries to apply this standard to the portfolio taken as a whole, thereby allowing a fiduciary to balance a portfolio with higher-yield, higher-risk invest-ments. In states with more progressive regulations, practically every type of security is eligible for inclusion in the portfolio of investments made by a fiduciary, provided that the portfolio investments, in their totality, are those of a prudent person.

Public equity markets ▮ Organized markets for trading in equity shares such as common stocks, preferred stocks, and warrants. Includes markets for both regularly traded and nonregularly traded securities.

Public offering ▮ General solicitation for participation in an investment opportunity. Interstate public offerings are supervised by the U.S. Securities and Exchange Commission (*see* separate citation).

Quality control ▮ The process by which a product is checked and tested to ensure consistent standards of high quality.

Rate of return z ▮ (*See also* Yield) The yield obtained on a security or other investment based on its purchase price or its current market price. The total rate of return is current income plus or minus capital appreciation or depreciation.

Real property ▮ Includes the land and all that is contained on it.

Realignment ▮ *See* Resource realignment.

Recession ▮ Contraction of economic activity occurring between the peak and trough (*see* separate citations) of a business cycle.

Regulated market ▮ A market in which the government controls the forces of supply and demand, such as who may enter and what price may be charged.

Regulation D ▮ A vehicle by which small businesses make small offerings and private placements of securities with limited disclosure requirements. It was designed to ease the burdens imposed on small businesses utilizing this method of capital formation.

Regulatory Flexibility Act ▮ An act requiring federal agencies to evaluate the impact of their regulations on small businesses before the regulations are issued and to consider less burdensome alternatives.

Research ▮ The initial stage of the innovation process, which includes idea generation and invention.

Research and development financing ▮ A tax-advantaged partnership set up to finance product development for start-ups as well as more mature companies.

Resource mobility ▮ The ease with which labor and capital move from firm to firm or from industry to industry.

Resource realignment ▮ The adjustment of productive resources to interindustry changes in demand.

Resources ▮ The sources of support or help in the innovation process, including sources of financing, technical evaluation, market evaluation, management and business assistance, etc.

Retained business earnings ▮ Business profits that are retained by the business rather than being distributed to the shareholders as dividends.

Revolving credit ▮ An agreement with a lending institution for an amount of money, which cannot exceed a set maximum, over a specified period of time. Each time the borrower repays a portion of the loan, the amount of the repayment may be borrowed yet again.

Risk capital ▮ *See* Venture capital.

Risk management ▮ The act of identifying potential sources of financial loss and taking action to minimize their negative impact.

Routing ▮ The sequence of steps necessary to complete a product during production.

S corporations ▮ *See* Sub chapter S corporations.

SBA ▮ *See* Small Business Administration.

SBA direct loans ▮ Loans made directly by the U.S. Small Business Administration (SBA); monies come from funds appropriated specifically for this purpose. In general, SBA direct loans carry interest rates slightly lower than those in the private financial markets and are available only to applicants unable to secure private financing or an SBA guaranteed loan.

SBA 504 Program ▮ *See* Certified development corporation.

SBA guaranteed loans ▮ Loans made by lending institutions in which the U.S. Small Business Administration (SBA) will pay a prior agreed-upon percentage of the outstanding principal in the event the borrower of the loan defaults. The terms of the loan and the interest rate are negotiated between the borrower and the lending institution, within set parameters.

SBA loans ▮ *See* Disaster loans; SBA direct loans; SBA guaranteed loans; SBA special lending institution categories.

SBA Management Assistance Programs ▮ (*See also* Active Corps of Executives; Service Corps of Retired Executives; Small business institutes program) Classes, workshops, counseling, and publications offered by the U.S. Small Business Administration.

SBA special lending institution categories ▮ U.S. Small Business Administration (SBA) loan program in which the SBA promises certified banks a 72-hour turnaround period in giving its approval for a loan, and in which preferred lenders in a pilot program are allowed to write SBA loans without seeking prior SBA approval.

SBDB ▮ *See* Small Business Data Base.

SBDC ▮ *See* Small business development centers.

SBI ▮ *See* Small business institutes program.

SBIC ▮ *See* Small business investment corporation.

SBIR Program ▮ *See* Small Business Innovation Development Act of 1982.

Scale economies ▮ The decline of the production cost per unit of output (average cost) as the volume of output increases.

Scale efficiency ▮ The reduction in unit cost available to a firm when producing at a higher output volume.

SCORE ▮ *See* Service Corps of Retired Executives.

SEC ▮ *See* Securities and Exchange Commission.

SECA ▮ *See* Self-Employment Contribu-tions Act.

Second-stage financing ▮ (*See also* First-stage financing; Third-stage financing) Working capital for the initial expansion of a com-pany that is producing, shipping, and has growing accounts receiv-able and inventories. Also known as Second- round financing.

Secondary market ▮ A market established for the purchase and sale of outstanding securities following their initial distribution.

Secondary worker ▮ Any worker in a family other than the person who is the primary source of income for the family.

Secondhand capital ▮ Previously used and subsequently resold capital equipment (e.g., buildings and machinery).

Securities and Exchange Commission (SEC) ▮ Federal agency charged with regulating the trade of securities to prevent unethical practices in the investor market.

Securitized debt ▮ A marketing technique that converts long-term loans to marketable securities.

Seed capital ▮ Venture financing provided in the early stages of the innovation process, usually during product development.

Self-employed person ▮ One who works for a profit or fees in his or her own business, profession, or trade, or who operates a farm.

Self-Employment Contributions Act (SECA) ▮ Federal law that governs the self-employment tax (*see* separate citation).

Self-employment income ▮ Income covered by Social Security if a business earns a net income of at least $400.00 during the year. Taxes are paid on earnings that exceed $400.00.

Self-employment retirement plan ▮ *See* Keogh plan.

Self-employment tax ▮ Required tax imposed on self-employed individuals for the provision of Social Security and Medicare. The tax must be paid quarterly with estimated income tax statements.

Self-funding ▮ A health benefit plan in which a firm uses its own funds to pay claims, rather than transferring the financial risks of paying claims to an outside insurer in exchange for premium payments.

Service Corps of Retired Executives (SCORE) ▮ (*See also* Active Corps of Executives) Volunteers for the SBA Management Assistance Program who provide one-on-one counseling and teach workshops and seminars for small firms.

Service firm ▮ *See* Business service firm.

Service sector ▮ Broadly defined, all U.S. industries that produce intangibles, including the five major industry divisions of transportation, communications, and utilities; wholesale trade; retail trade; finance, insurance, and real estate; and services.

Set asides ▮ *See* Small business set asides.

Short-haul service ▮ A type of transportation service in which the transporter supplies service between cities where the maximum distance is no more than 200 miles.

Short-term debt ▮ An obligation that matures in one year.

SIC codes ▮ *See* Standard Industrial Classification codes.

Single-establishment enterprise ▮ *See* Establishment.

Small business ▮ An enterprise that is independently owned and operated, is not dominant in its field, and employs fewer than 500 people. For SBA purposes, the U.S. Small Business Administration (SBA) considers various other factors (such as gross annual sales) in determining size of a business.

Small Business Administration (SBA) ▮ An independent federal agency that provides assistance with loans, management, and advocating interests before other federal agencies.

Small Business Data Base ▮ (*See also* U.S. Establishment and Enterprise Microdata File; U.S. Establishment Longitudinal Microdata File) A collection of microdata (*see* separate citation) files on individual firms developed and maintained by the U.S. Small Business Administration.

Small business development centers (SBDC) ▮ Centers that provide support services to small businesses, such as individual counseling, SBA advice, seminars and conferences, and other learning center activities. Most services are free of charge, or available at minimal cost.

Small business development corporation ▮ *See* Certified development corporation.

Small business-dominated industry ▮ Industry in which a minimum of 60 percent of employment or sales is in firms with fewer than 500 employees.

Small Business Innovation Development Act of 1982 ▮ Federal statute requiring federal agencies with large extramural research and development budgets to allocate a certain percentage of these funds to small research and development firms. The program, called the Small Business Innovation Research (SBIR) Program, is designed to stimulate technological innovation and make greater use of small businesses in meeting national innovation needs.

Small business institutes (SBI) program ▮ Cooperative arrangements made by U.S. Small Business Administration district offices and local colleges and universities to provide small business firms with graduate students to counsel them without charge.

Small business investment corporation (SBIC) ▮ A privately owned company licensed and funded through the U.S. Small Business Administration and private sector sources to provide equity or debt capital to small businesses.

Small business set asides ▮ Procurement (*see* separate citation) opportunities required by law to be on all contracts under $10,000 or a certain percentage of an agency's total procurement expenditure.

Smaller firms ▮ For U.S. Department of Commerce purposes, those firms not included in the Fortune 1000.

SMSA ▮ *See* Metropolitan statistical area.

Socially and economically disadvantaged ▮ Individuals who have been subjected to racial or ethnic prejudice or cultural bias without regard to their qualities as individuals, and whose abilities to compete are impaired because of diminished opportunities to obtain capital and credit.

Sole proprietorship ▮ An unincorporated, one-owner business, farm, or professional practice.

Special lending institution categories ▮ *See* SBA special lending institution categories.

Standard Industrial Classification (SIC) codes ▮ Four-digit codes established by the U.S. Federal Government to categorize businesses by type of economic activity; the first two digits correspond to major groups such as construction and manufacturing, while the last two digits correspond to subgroups such as home construction or highway construction.

Standard metropolitan statistical area (SMSA) ▮ *See* Metropolitan statistical area.

Start-up ▮ A new business, at the earliest stages of development and financing.

Start-up costs ▮ Costs incurred before a business can commence operations.

Start-up financing ▮ Financing provided to companies that have either completed product development and initial marketing or have been in business for less than one year but have not yet sold their product commercially.

Stock ▮ (*See also* Common stock; Convertible preferred stock) A certificate of equity ownership in a business.

Stop-loss coverage ▮ Insurance for a self-insured plan that reimburses the company for any losses it might incur in its health claims beyond a specified amount.

Strategic planning ▮ Projected growth and development of a business to establish a guiding direction for the future. Also used to determine which market segments to explore for optimal sales of products or services.

Structural unemployment ▮ *See* Un-employment.

Sub chapter S corporations ▮ Corpora-tions that are considered noncorporate for tax purposes but legally remain corporations.

Subcontract ▮ A contract between a prime contractor and a subcontractor, or between subcontractors, to furnish supplies or services for performance of a prime contract (*see* separate citation) or a subcontract.

Surety bonds ▮ Bonds providing reimbursement to an individual, company, or the government if a firm fails to complete a contract. The U.S. Small Business Administration guarantees surety bonds in a program much like the SBA guaranteed loan program (*see* separate citation).

Swing loan ▮ *See* Bridge financing.

Target market ▮ The clients or customers sought for a business' product or service.

Targeted Jobs Tax Credit ▮ Federal legislation enacted in 1978 that provides a tax credit to an employer who hires structurally unemployed individuals.

Tax number ▮ (*See also* Employer identification number) A number assigned to a business by a state revenue department that enables the business to buy goods without paying sales tax.

Taxable bonds ▮ An interest-bearing certificate of public or private indebtedness. Bonds are issued by public agencies to finance economic development.

Technical assistance ▮ *See* Management and technical assistance

Technical evaluation ▮ Assessment of technological feasibility.

Technology ▮ The method in which a firm combines and utilizes labor and capital resources to produce goods or services; the application of science for commercial or industrial purposes.

Technology transfer ▮ The movement of information about a tech-nology or intellectual property from one party to another for use.

Tenure ▮ *See* Employee tenure.

Term ▮ (*See also* Maturity) The length of time for which a loan is made.

Terms of a note ▮ The conditions or limits of a note; includes the interest rate per annum, the due date, and transferability and convertibility features, if any.

Third-party administrator ▮ An outside company responsible for handling claims and performing administrative tasks associated with health insurance plan maintenance.

Third-stage financing ▮ (*See also* First-stage financing; Second-stage financing) Financing provided for the major expansion of a company whose sales volume is increasing and that is breaking even or profitable. These funds are used for further plant expansion, marketing, working capital, or development of an improved product. Also known as Third-round or Mezzanine financing.

Time deposit ▮ A bank deposit that cannot be withdrawn before a specified future time.

Time management ▮ Skills and scheduling techniques used to maximize productivity.

Trade credit ▮ Credit extended by suppliers of raw materials or finished products. In an accounting statement, trade credit is referred to as "accounts payable."

Trade name ▮ The name under which a company conducts business, or by which its business, goods, or services are identified. It may or may not be registered as a trademark.

Trade periodical ▮ A publication with a specific focus on one or more aspects of business and industry.

Trade secret ▮ Competitive advantage gained by a business through the use of a unique manufacturing process or formula.

Trade show ▮ An exhibition of goods or services used in a particular industry. Typically held in exhibition centers where exhibitors rent space to display their merchandise.

Trademark ▮ A graphic symbol, device, or slogan that identifies a business. A business has property rights to its trademark from the inception of its use, but it is still prudent to register all trade marks with the Trademark Office of the U.S. Department of Commerce.

Translation ▮ *See* Product development.

Treasury bills ▮ Investment tender issued by the Federal Reserve Bank in amounts of $10,000 that mature in 91 to 182 days.

Treasury bonds ▮ Long-term notes with maturity dates of not less than seven and not more than twenty-five years.

Treasury notes ▮ Short-term notes maturing in less than seven years.

Trend ▮ A statistical measurement used to track changes that occur over time.

Trough ▮ *See* Cyclical trough.

UCC ▮ *See* Uniform Commercial Code. UL *See* Underwriters Laboratories.

Underwriters Laboratories (UL) ▮ One of several private firms that tests products and processes to determine their safety. Although various firms can provide this kind of testing service, many local and insurance codes specify UL certification.

Underwriting ▮ A process by which an insurer determines whether or not and on what basis it will accept an application for insurance. In an experience-rated plan, premiums are based on a firm's or group's past claims; factors other than prior claims are used for community-rated or manually rated plans.

Unfair competition ▮ Refers to business practices, usually unethical, such as using unlicensed products, pirating merch-andise, or misleading the public through false advertising, which give the offending business an unequitable advantage over others.

Unfunded accrued liability ▮ The excess of total liabilities, both present and prospective, over present and prospective assets.

Unemployment ▮ The joblessness of individuals who are willing to work, who are legally and physically able to work, and who are seeking work. Unemploy-ment may represent the temporary joblessness of a worker between jobs (frictional unemployment) or the joblessness of a worker whose skills are not suitable for jobs available in the labor market (structural unemployment).

Uniform Commercial Code (UCC) ▮ A code of laws governing commercial transactions across the U.S., except Louisiana. Their purpose is to bring uniformity to financial transactions.

Uniform product code (UPC symbol) ▮ A computer-readable label comprised of ten digits and stripes that encodes what a product is and how much it costs. The first five digits are assigned by the Uniform Produce Code Council, and the last five digits by the individual manufacturer.

Unit cost ▮ *See* Average cost.

UPC symbol ▮ *See* Uniform product code.

US Establishment and Enterprise Microdata (USEEM) File ▮ A cross-sectional database containing information on employment, sales, and location for individual enterprises and establishments with employees that have a Dun & Bradstreet credit rating.

US Establishment Longitudinal Microdata (USELM) File ▮ A database containing longitudinally linked sample microdata on establishments drawn from the U.S. Establishment and Enterprise Microdata file (*see* separate citation).

US Small Business Administration 504 Program ▮ *See* Certified development corporation.

USEEM ▮ *See* U.S. Establishment and Enterprise Microdata File.

USELM ▮ *See* U.S. Establishment Longitudinal Microdata File.

VCN ▮ *See* Venture capital network.

Venture capital ▮ (*See also* Equity; Equity midrisk venture capital) Money used to support new or unusual business ventures that exhibit above-average growth rates, significant potential for market expansion, and are in need of additional financing to sustain growth or further research and development; equity or equity- type financing traditionally provided at the commercialization stage, increasingly available prior to commercialization.

Venture capital company ▮ A company organized to provide seed capital to a business in its formation stage, or in its first or second stage of expansion. Funding is obtained through public or private pension funds, commercial banks and bank holding companies, small business investment corporations licensed by the U.S. Small Business Administration, private venture capital firms, insurance companies, investment management companies, bank trust departments, industrial companies seeking to diversify their investment, and investment bankers acting as intermediaries for other investors or directly investing on their own behalf.

Venture capital limited partnerships ▮ Designed for business development, these partnerships are an institutional mechanism for providing capital for young, technology-oriented businesses. The investors' money is pooled and invested in money market assets until venture investments have been selected. The general partners are experienced investment managers who select and invest the equity and debt securities of firms with high growth potential and the ability to go public in the near future.

Venture capital network (VCN) ▮ A computer database that matches investors with entrepreneurs.

WAN ▮ *See* Wide Area Network.

Wide Area Network (WAN) ▮ Computer networks linking systems throughout a state or around the world in order to facilitate the sharing of information.

Withholding ▮ Federal, state, social security, and unemployment taxes withheld by the employer from employees' wages; employers are liable for these taxes and the corporate umbrella and bankruptcy will not exonerate an employer from paying back payroll withholding. Employers should escrow these funds in a separate account and disperse them quarterly to withholding authorities.

Workers' compensation ▮ A state-mandated form of insurance covering workers injured in job-related accidents. In some states, the state is the insurer; in other states, insurance must be acquired from commercial insurance firms. Insurance rates are based on a number of factors, including salaries, firm history, and risk of occupation.

Working capital ▮ Refers to a firm's short-term investment of current assets, including cash, short-term securities, accounts receivable, and inventories.

Yield ▮ (*See also* Rate of return) The rate of income returned on an investment, expressed as a percentage. Income yield is obtained by dividing the current dollar income by the current market price of the security. Net yield or yield to maturity is the current income yield minus any premium above par or plus any discount from par in purchase price, with the adjustment spread over the period from the date of purchase to the date of maturity.

ASSOCIATIONS AND OTHER ORGANIZATIONS

1 ■ American Society for Indexing
10200 W 44th Ave., Ste. 304
Wheat Ridge, CO 80033
Ph:(303)463-2887
Fax:(303)422-8894
Co. E-mail: info@asindexing.org
URL: http://www.asindexing.org/i4a/pages/index.cfm?pageid=1
Contact: Richard Shrout, Pres.

Description: Professional indexers, librarians, editors, publishers, and organizations employing indexers. Works to improve the quality of indexing and adherence to indexing standards; to encourage members to increase their professional indexing capabilities and performance; to advise authors, editors, and publishers on the qualifications and remuneration of indexers; to protect the professional interests of indexers; to facilitate communication among members concerning methods and developments in the field; to maintain liaison with related organizations. Members' activities include indexing books, databases, and periodicals, teaching indexing courses, and conducting research on indexing problems. **Publications:** *A Guide to Indexing Software*; *Generic Markup of Electronic Index Manuscripts*; *The Indexer* (semiannual); *Indexing from A to Z*; *Key Words: American Society of Indexers* (bimonthly).

2 ■ Indexing Society of Canada–Societe Canadienne D'indexation
PO Box 664, Sta. P
Toronto, ON, Canada M5S 2Y4
Co. E-mail: mary.newberry@rogers.com
URL: http://www.indexers.ca
Contact: Mary Newberry, Co-Pres.

Description: Indexing and abstracting services; corporations; institutions; interested individuals. Works to: promote production and use of indexes and abstracts; further the recognition of indexers and abstracters; develop improvements in indexing and abstracting techniques; facilitate communication among members. **Publications:** *ISC/SCI Bulletin* (3/year); *Register of Indexers* (annual).

REFERENCE WORKS

3 ■ "IRS Announces New Standards for Tax Preparers" in *Bellingham Business Journal* (Vol. February 2010, pp. 9)
Pub: Sound Publishing Inc.

Ed: Isaac Bonnell. **Description:** A new oversight plan was announced by the Internal Revenue Services (IRS) that will require tax professionals to pass a competency test and register with the government in order to ensure greater accountability in the industry.

Accounting Service

START-UP INFORMATION

4 ■ *The 100 Best Businesses to Start When You Don't Want To Work Hard Anymore*
Pub: Career Press Inc.
Ed: Lisa Rogak. **Price:** $16.99. **Description:** Author helps burned-out workers envision a new future as a small business owner. Systems analysis, adventure travel outfitting, bookkeeping, food delivery, furniture making, and software development are among the industries examined.

5 ■ *Start and Run a Bookkeeping Business*
Pub: Self-Counsel, Incorporated
Ed: Angie Mohr. **Released:** October 2005. **Price:** $17.95 (US), $22.95 (Canadian). **Description:** Advice for starting and running a bookkeeping service business. Includes MS Word and PDF formats for use in Windows-based PC.

6 ■ *Working for Yourself: An Entrepreneur's Guide to the Basics*
Pub: Kogan Page, Limited
Ed: Jonathan Reuvid. **Released:** September 2006. **Description:** Guide for starting a new business venture, focusing on raising financing, legal and tax issues, marketing, information technology, and site location.

ASSOCIATIONS AND OTHER ORGANIZATIONS

7 ■ Accountants Global Network
2851 S Parker Rd., Ste. 850
Aurora, CO 80014
Ph:(303)743-7880
Free: 800-782-2272
Fax:(303)743-7660
Co. E-mail: rhood@agn.org
URL: http://www.agn-na.org
Contact: Rita J. Hood, Exec. Dir.
Description: Represents and promotes the fields of separate and independent accounting and consulting firms serving business organizations. .

8 ■ Accounting and Finance Benchmarking Consortium
4606 FM 1960 W, Ste. 250
Houston, TX 77069-9949
Free: 800-324-4685
URL: http://www.afbc.org
Description: Accounting and finance managers of corporations with an interest in benchmarking. Promotes the use of benchmarking, wherein businesses compare their processes with those of their competitors, as a means of improving corporate efficiency and profitability. Facilitates exchange of information among members; conducts target operations, procurement, development, and maintenance studies; identifies model business practices. .

9 ■ AGN International North America
2851 S Parker Rd., Ste. 850
Aurora, CO 80014
Ph:(303)743-7880
Fax:(303)743-7660
Co. E-mail: rhood@agn.org
URL: http://www.agn-na.org
Contact: Rita Hood, Exec. Dir.
Description: Certified public accounting firms. Provides networking resources, technical and marketing assistance, and staff training programs to members. Compiles statistics. Maintains networking share groups. **Publications:** *Client Newsletter* (quarterly); *Tax Brochures* .

10 ■ American Accounting Association
5717 Bessie Dr.
Sarasota, FL 34233-2330
Ph:(941)921-7747
Fax:(941)923-4093
Co. E-mail: info@aaahq.org
URL: http://aaahq.org
Contact: Tracey Sutherland, Exec. Dir.
Description: Professors and practitioners of accounting. Promotes worldwide excellence in accounting education, research and practice. **Publications:** *Accounting Horizons* (quarterly); *Issues in Accounting Education* (quarterly).

11 ■ American Association of Attorney-Certified Public Accountants
3921 Old Lee Hwy., Ste. 71A
Fairfax, VA 22030
Ph:(703)352-8064
Free: 888-288-9272
Fax:(703)352-8073
Co. E-mail: info@attorney-cpa.com
URL: http://www.attorney-cpa.com
Contact: Nicole E. Ratner CAE, Exec. Dir.
Description: Represents persons who are licensed both as attorneys and as certified public accountants (CPAs). Promotes high professional and ethical standards; seeks to safeguard and defend the professional and legal rights of attorney-CPAs. Conducts research on dual licensing and dual practice; maintains speakers' bureau, placement service. Has compiled a list of attorney-CPAs in the United States; conducts biennial economic and practice survey. Maintains liaison with bar associations and accounting groups and offers referral service of potential clients. State groups conduct extensive self-education programs. **Publications:** *The Attorney-CPA* (quarterly); *Attorney-CPA Directory* (annual).

12 ■ American Institute of Certified Public Accountants
1211 Ave. of the Americas
New York, NY 10036-8775
Ph:(212)596-6200
Free: 888-777-7077
Fax:(212)596-6213
Co. E-mail: service@aicpa.org
URL: http://www.aicpa.org/Pages/Default.aspx
Contact: Barry C. Melancon, Pres./CEO
Description: Professional society of accountants certified by the states and territories. Responsibilities include establishing auditing and reporting standards; influencing the development of financial accounting standards underlying the presentation of U.S. corporate financial statements; preparing and grading the national Uniform CPA Examination for the state licensing bodies. Conducts research and continuing education programs and oversight of practice. Maintains over 100 committees including Accounting Standards, Accounting and Review Services, AICPA Effective Legislation Political Action, Auditing Standards, Taxation, Consulting Services, Professional Ethics, Quality Review, Women and Family Issues, and Information Technology. **Publications:** *The CPA Letter* (bimonthly); *The Tax Adviser* (monthly).

13 ■ American Society of Women Accountants
1760 Old Meadow Rd., Ste. 500
McLean, VA 22102
Ph:(703)506-3265
Free: 800-326-2163
Fax:(703)506-3266
Co. E-mail: aswa@aswa.org
URL: http://www.aswa.org
Contact: Lee K. Lowery, Exec. Dir.
Description: Professional society of women accountants, educators and others in the field of accounting dedicated to the achievement of personal, professional and economic potential. Assists women accountants in their careers and promotes development in the profession. Conducts educational and research programs. .

14 ■ American Taxation Association
9201 University City Blvd.
Charlotte, NC 28223
Ph:(704)687-7696
Co. E-mail: americantaxationassociation@aaahq.org
URL: http://aaahq.org/ata/index.htm
Contact: Hughlene Burton, Pres.
Description: Membership comprises primarily university professors teaching federal income tax, federal estate, and/or gift tax courses; other members are practitioners, including certified public accountants. Seeks to further taxation education. Researches the impact of the tax process, particularly tax code sections, on the social and economic structure of the U.S. Maintains speakers' bureau. .

15 ■ American Woman's Society of Certified Public Accountants
136 S Keowee St.
Dayton, OH 45402
Ph:(937)222-1872
Free: 800-297-2721
Fax:(937)222-5794
Co. E-mail: info@awscpa.org
URL: http://www.awscpa.org
Contact: Wendy S. Lewis, Pres.
Description: Citizens who hold Certified Public Accountant certificates as well as those who have passed the CPA examination but do not have certificates. Works to improve the status of professional women and to make the business community aware of the professional capabilities of the woman CPA. Conducts semiannual statistical survey of members; offers specialized education and research programs. **Publications:** *Membership Roster* .

16 ■ Association for Accounting Administration
136 S Keowee St.
Dayton, OH 45402
Ph:(937)222-0030
Fax:(937)222-5794
Co. E-mail: aaainfo@cpaadmin.org
URL: http://www.cpaadmin.org
Contact: Kimberly A. Fantaci, Exec. Dir.
Description: Promotes the profession of accounting administration and office management in accounting firms and corporate accounting departments. Sponsors activities, including consulting and placement services, seminars, salary and trends surveys, and speakers' bureau. Provides a forum for representation and exchange. Offers group purchasing opportunities. **Publications:** *AAA Report* (bimonthly).

17 ■ Association of Chartered Accountants in the United States
1050 Winter St., Ste. 1000
Waltham, MA 02451
Ph:(508)395-0224
Co. E-mail: admin@acaus.org
URL: http://www.acaus.org
Contact: Lindi Jarvis, Pres.
Description: Chartered accountants from England, Wales, Scotland, Ireland, Canada, Australia, New Zealand and South Africa in commerce and public practice. Represents the interests of chartered accountants; promotes career development and international mobility of professionals. Offers educational and research programs. Maintains speakers' bureau and placement service. **Publications:** *Member's Directory and Handbook* (annual).

18 ■ BKR International
19 Fulton St., Ste. 306
New York, NY 10038
Ph:(212)964-2115
Free: 800-BKR-INTL
Fax:(212)964-2133
Co. E-mail: bkr@bkr.com
URL: http://www.bkr.com
Contact: Maureen M. Schwartz, Exec. Dir.
Description: Accounting firms in the U.S. and abroad. Seeks to create an international group of competent professional firms, which will provide full services in major markets of the world and enable member firms to send and receive referrals. Helps reduce operating costs of member firms by: developing consolidated purchasing arrangements for services and supplies at the lowest possible cost; developing recruiting programs, marketing materials, and advertising to reduce the collective recruiting effort of group members; expanding the group to reduce the burden on individual member firms and increase their potential scope of services. Compiles statistics to provide member firms with data helpful to sound management decisions. Organizes clinical and administrative peer reviews to insure quality and provide management with professional counsel. Develops forms, procedures, and manuals to provide guidance and accommodate the needs of partners. Conducts 12 continuing education programs per year in all areas of expertise. **Publications:** *Worldwide Bulletin* (bimonthly).

19 ■ Canadian Academic Accounting Association–Association Canadienne des Professeurs de Comptabilite
3997 Chesswood Dr.
Toronto, ON, Canada M3J 2R8
Ph:(416)486-5361
Fax:(416)486-6158
Co. E-mail: admin@caaa.ca
URL: http://www.caaa.ca
Contact: Vaughan Radcliffe, Pres.
Description: Post-secondary school accounting professors and students, accounting organizations, accountants, and accounting firms. Seeks to advance the study, teaching, and practice of accounting, broadly defined to include many related areas and disciplines of study. **Publications:** *Accounting Perspective* (quarterly); *Canadian Accounting Education and Research News* (quarterly); *Contemporary Accounting Research* (quarterly).

20 ■ Canadian Institute of Chartered Accountants–Institut Canadien des Comptables Agrees
277 Wellington St. W
Toronto, ON, Canada M5V 3H2
Ph:(416)977-3222
Fax:(416)977-8585
Co. E-mail: jan.burns@cica.ca
URL: http://www.cica.ca
Contact: Nigel Byars, Exec. VP
Description: Sets national accounting, auditing, and financial reporting standards. Maintains an active professional development program for its members. Represents the profession's viewpoint on federal legislation issues and matters of national concern. Confers with other national organizations to achieve worldwide harmonization of accounting and auditing standards. **Publications:** *Directory of Canadian Chartered Accountants* (periodic).

21 ■ Canadian Institute of Quantity Surveyors–Institut Canadien des Economistes en Construction
90 Nolan Ct., Unit 19
Markham, ON, Canada L3R 4L9
Ph:(905)477-0008
Free: (866)345-1168
Fax:(905)477-6774
Co. E-mail: info@ciqs.org
URL: http://www.ciqs.org
Contact: Roy Lewis, Pres.
Description: Quantity surveyors and construction estimators. Establishes and maintains standards for certification and provides through advice to members relating to construction costs, management and administration of construction projects. Conducts continuing professional development programs for members. **Publications:** *The Construction Economist* (quarterly). **Telecommunication Services:** electronic mail, president@ciqs.org.

22 ■ Canadian Insurance Accountants Association–Association Canadienne du Comptables d'Assurance
2175 Sheppard Ave. E, Ste. 310
Toronto, ON, Canada M2J 1W8
Ph:(416)971-7800
Fax:(416)491-1670
Co. E-mail: ciaa@ciaa.org
URL: http://www.ciaa.org
Contact: Terri Martin, Pres.
Description: Accountants employed in the insurance industry. Promotes excellence in the practice of insurance accounting; seeks to insure continuing professional development among members. Serves as a forum for the exchange of information among members; sponsors educational programs. **Telecommunication Services:** electronic mail, sandrat@osbie.on.ca.

23 ■ Canadian Tax Foundation–Association Canadienne d'Etudes Fiscales
595 Bay St., Ste. 1200
Toronto, ON, Canada M5G 2N5
Ph:(416)599-0283
Free: 877-733-0283
Fax:(416)599-9283
Co. E-mail: lchapman@ctf.ca
URL: http://www.ctf.ca
Contact: FCA Larry Chapman, Exec. Dir./CEO
Description: Individuals and organizations with an interest in taxation. Promotes increased awareness of the Canadian Tax Code and the social ramifications of taxation. Serves as a clearinghouse on taxation; sponsors research and educational programs. **Publications:** *Canadian Tax Journal* (quarterly).

24 ■ Community Banking Advisory Network
624 Grassmere Park Dr., Ste. 15
Nashville, TN 37211
Ph:(615)377-3392
Free: 800-231-2524
Fax:(615)377-7092
Co. E-mail: info@bankingcpas.com
URL: http://www.bankingcpas.com
Contact: Patrick Pruett, Exec. Dir.
Description: Certified Public Accounting (CPA) firms providing financial and consulting services to community banks. Seeks to advance CPA services to the community banking industry. Sponsors continuing education and training courses; conducts industry and member surveys; facilitates formation of joint ventures; makes available marketing assistance; facilitates resource sharing among members. **Publications:** *Community Banking Advisor* (quarterly).

25 ■ Construction Industry CPAs/Consultants Association
15011 E Twilight View Dr.
Fountain Hills, AZ 85268
Ph:(480)836-0300
Free: 800-864-0491
Fax:(480)836-0400
Co. E-mail: jcorcoran@cicpac.com
URL: http://www.cicpac.com
Contact: John J. Corcoran CPA, Exec. Dir.
Description: Certified Public Accounting (CPA) firms providing financial and consulting services to construction companies. Seeks to advance CPA services to the construction industries. Sponsors continuing education and training courses; conducts industry and member surveys; facilitates formation of joint ventures; makes available marketing assistance; facilitates resource sharing among members. .

26 ■ CPA Associates International
Meadows Office Complex
301 Rte. 17 N
Rutherford, NJ 07070
Ph:(201)804-8686
Fax:(201)804-9222
Co. E-mail: homeoffice@cpaai.com
URL: http://www.cpaai.com
Contact: James F. Flynn, Pres.
Description: Independent firms of Certified Public Accountants (CPAs) offering professional accounting, auditing, tax, and management advisory services. Fosters exchange of ideas and information among members; works to improve the profitability and practice of the accounting profession. **Publications:** *Client Newsletter Tax Outlook* (quarterly).

27 ■ CPA Auto Dealer Consultants Association
624 Grassmere Park Dr., Ste. 15
Nashville, TN 37211
Ph:(615)377-3392
Free: 800-231-2524
Fax:(615)377-7092
Co. E-mail: info@autodealercpas.net
URL: http://www.autodealercpas.net
Contact: Patrick Pruett, Exec. Dir.
Description: Certified Public Accounting (CPA) firms providing financial and consulting services to automobile dealers. Seeks to advance CPA services to automobile dealers. Sponsors continuing education and training courses; conducts industry and member surveys; facilitates formation of joint ventures; makes available marketing assistance; facilitates resource sharing among members. **Publications:** *Auto Focus* (quarterly).

28 ■ CPA Manufacturing Services Association
624 Grassmere Park Dr., Ste. 15
Nashville, TN 37211
Ph:(615)377-3392
Free: 800-231-2524
Fax:(615)377-7092
Co. E-mail: info@manufacturingcpas.com
URL: http://www.manufacturingcpas.com
Contact: Patrick Pruett, Exec. Dir.
Description: Certified Public Accounting (CPA) firms providing financial and consulting services to the manufacturing industries. Seeks to advance CPA services to manufacturers. Sponsors continuing education and training courses; conducts industry and member surveys; facilitates formation of joint

ventures; makes available marketing assistance; facilitates resource sharing among members. **Publications:** *Client* (periodic);Membership Directory (periodic).

29 ■ Educational Foundation for Women in Accounting
136 S Keowee St.
Dayton, OH 45402
Ph:(937)424-3391
Fax:(937)222-5749
Co. E-mail: info@efwa.org
URL: http://www.efwa.org
Contact: Gail Anikouchine CPA, Pres.
Description: Women in the accounting field. Supports the advancement of women in the accounting profession through funding of education, research, career literature, publications, and other projects. **Publications:** *The Educator* (semiannual).

30 ■ IGAF Worldwide
3235 Satellite Blvd., Bldg. 400, Ste. 300
Duluth, GA 30096
Ph:(678)417-7730
Fax:(678)999-3959
Co. E-mail: kmead@igafworldwide.org
URL: http://www.igaf.org
Contact: Kevin Mead, Pres./Exec. Dir.
Description: Works to ensure that the standard for accounting, auditing, and management services are maintained. .

31 ■ Institute of Management Accountants
10 Paragon Dr., Ste. 1
Montvale, NJ 07645-1774
Ph:(201)573-9000
Free: 800-638-4427
Fax:(201)474-1600
Co. E-mail: ima@imanet.org
URL: http://www.imanet.org
Contact: Jeffrey C. Thomson, Pres./CEO
Description: Management accountants in industry, public accounting, government, and academia; other persons interested in internal and management uses of accounting. Conducts research on accounting methods and procedures and the management purposes served. Established Institute of Certified Management Accountants to implement and administer examinations for the Certified Management Accountant (CMA) program and the Certified in Financial Management (CFM) program. Annually presents chapter medals for competition, manuscripts and for the highest scores on the CMA Examination. Offers continuing education programs comprising courses, conferences, and a self-study program in management accounting areas. Offers ethics counseling services for members by telephone. Sponsors the Foundation for Applied Research. **Publications:** *Management Accounting Quarterly* (quarterly); *Strategic TechNotes* (semimonthly).

32 ■ Interamerican Accounting Association
275 Fountainebleau Blvd., Ste. 245
Miami, FL 33172
Ph:(305)225-1991
Fax:(305)225-2011
Co. E-mail: oficina@contadoresaic.org
URL: http://www.contadoresaic.org
Contact: Victor Manuel Abreu Paez, Exec. Dir.
Description: National associations representing 1,100,000 accountants in the Americas. Objectives are to maintain high technical and ethical standards for the accounting profession; further accounting as a scientific discipline by fostering contacts between members and institutions of higher learning; provide members with information on current accounting practices and concepts; encourage members to establish ties with accounting groups worldwide; assure that professional services rendered by members contribute to the social and economic development of their community. Operates speakers' bureau. **Publications:** *IAA Directory* (biennial); *Interamerican Accounting Magazine* (quarterly); *Interamerican Bulletin* (monthly).

33 ■ International Budget Partnership
820 1st St. NE, Ste. 510
Washington, DC 20002
Ph:(202)408-1080
Fax:(202)408-8173
Co. E-mail: info@internationalbudget.org
URL: http://www.internationalbudget.org
Contact: Warren Krafchik, Dir.
Description: Works to assist civil society organizations globally to improve budget policies and decision-making processes. **Publications:** *A Guide to Budget Work for NGOs*; *Budgeting for the Future, Building another Europe*; *IBP Newsletter* (bimonthly).

34 ■ Moore Stephens North America
Park 80 West
Plaza II, Ste. 200
Saddle Brook, NJ 07663
Ph:(201)291-2660
Fax:(201)368-1944
Co. E-mail: theteam@msnainc.org
URL: http://www.msnainc.com
Contact: Steven E. Sacks CPA, Exec. Dir.
Description: North American public accounting and consulting firms. Aids certified public accounting firms in increasing, expanding, and diversifying their practices. Capitalizes on diversity of resources resident throughout the network to build a stronger revenue base for all members. Sponsors training programs in areas such as industry niche development, service niche development tax, staff, and computer auditing; conducts tax and management seminars. Compiles statistics. Offers networking forums, marketing assistance, and technology consulting to member firms. **Publications:** *MSNA Membership Directory* (annual); *MSNA Networker* (monthly).

35 ■ National Association of Black Accountants
7474 Greenway Center Dr., Ste. 1120
Greenbelt, MD 20770
Ph:(301)474-6222
Free: 888-571-2939
Fax:(301)474-3114
Co. E-mail: customerservice@nabainc.org
URL: http://www.nabainc.org
Contact: Gregory Johnson, Exec. Dir./Chief Operating Off.
Description: Minority students and professionals currently working, or interested in the fields of accounting, finance, technology, consulting or general business. Seeks, promotes, develops, and represents the interests of current and future minority business professionals. **Publications:** *Achieve* (3/year); *Spectrum* (annual).

36 ■ National Association of State Boards of Accountancy
150 4th Ave. N, Ste. 700
Nashville, TN 37219-2417
Ph:(615)880-4200
Free: (866)MY-NASBA
Fax:(615)880-4290
Co. E-mail: cpaexam@nasba.org
URL: http://www.nasba.org
Description: Comprises 54 state boards of accountancy. Serves as a forum for the boards, which administer the Uniform CPA Examination, license certified public accountants, and regulate the practice of public accountancy in the United States. Sponsors committee meetings, conferences, programs and services designed to enhance the effectiveness of its member boards. **Publications:** *State Board Report* (monthly); *State Boards of Accountancy of the United States* (periodic).

37 ■ National Association of Tax Professionals
PO Box 8002
Appleton, WI 54914-8002
Free: 800-558-3402
Co. E-mail: natp@natptax.com
URL: http://www.natptax.com
Contact: Michael D. Whittle EA, Pres.
Description: Serves professionals who work in all areas of tax practice, including individual practitioners, enrolled agents, certified public accountants, accountants, attorneys and certified financial planners. **Publications:** *TAXPRO Quarterly Journal* (quarterly); *TAXPRO Weekly E-Mail* (weekly).

38 ■ National Conference of CPA Practitioners
22 Jericho Tpke., Ste. 110
Mineola, NY 11501
Ph:(516)333-8282
Free: 888-488-5400
Fax:(516)333-4099
URL: http://www.nccpap.org
Contact: Andrew Hult CPA, Pres.
Description: Represents the interests of CPA regional and local accounting firms. Works to enhance the professionalism of local firms. Works with the IRS and local and national government. .

39 ■ National Society of Accountants
1010 N Fairfax St.
Alexandria, VA 22314
Ph:(703)549-6400
Free: 800-966-6679
Fax:(703)549-2984
Co. E-mail: members@nsacct.org
URL: http://www.nsacct.org
Contact: John G. Ams, Exec. VP
Description: Professional organization and its affiliates represent 30,000 members who provide auditing, accounting, tax preparation, financial and estate planning, and management services to approximately 19 million individuals and business clients. Most members are sole practitioners or partners in small to mid-size accounting firms. **Publications:** *National Society of Accountants Technology Advisor* (8/year); *NSAlert* (biweekly).

40 ■ National Society of Accountants for Cooperatives
136 S Keowee St.
Dayton, OH 45402
Ph:(937)222-6707
Fax:(937)222-5794
Co. E-mail: info@nsacoop.org
URL: http://www.nsacoop.org
Contact: Russell D. Watson, Pres.
Description: Employees of cooperatives, certified public accountants, auditors, chief financial officers, attorneys and bankers. Unites persons performing accounting, auditing, financial and legal services for cooperative and non-profit associations. Holds technical sessions annually. Compiles statistics. **Publications:** *The Cooperative Accountant* (quarterly).

41 ■ National Tax Association
725 15th St. NW, No. 600
Washington, DC 20005-2109
Ph:(202)737-3325
Fax:(202)737-7308
Co. E-mail: natltax@aol.com
URL: http://www.ntanet.org
Contact: Ms. Charmaine J. Wright, Sec.
Description: Government and corporate tax officials, accountants, consultants, economists, attorneys, and others interested in the field of taxation. Promotes nonpartisan academics, study of taxation; encourages better understanding of the common interests of national, state, and local governments in matters of taxation and public finance; and disseminates higher quality research through publications and conferences. **Publications:** *National Tax Journal* (quarterly); *Proceedings of the Annual Conference on Taxation* (annual).

42 ■ Society of Depreciation Professionals
347 5th Ave., Ste. 703
New York, NY 10016
Ph:(646)417-6378
Co. E-mail: admin@depr.org
URL: http://www.depr.org
Contact: Rob Pierce CDP, Pres.
Description: Accountants and other individuals with an interest in the depreciation of assets. Promotes "professionalism and ethics within the art of depreciation." Serves as a forum for the discussion of issues affecting depreciation; sponsors continuing professional development courses for members. .

43 ■ Society of Management Accountants of Canada
1 Robert Speck Pkwy., Ste. 1400
Mississauga, ON, Canada L4Z 3M3
Ph:(905)949-4200

Free: 800-263-7622
Fax:(905)949-0888
Co. E-mail: info@cma-canada.org
URL: http://www.cma-canada.org
Description: Certified Management Accountants (CMAs). Provides business advice and direction to improve organizational decisions. Offers educational and research programs. **Publications:** *CMA Management Magazine* (9/year).

44 ■ Society of Professional Accountants of Canada–La societe des comptables professionnels du Canada
250 Consumers Rd., Ste. 1007
Toronto, ON, Canada M2J 4V6
Ph:(416)350-8145
Free: 877-515-4447
Fax:(416)350-8146
Co. E-mail: president@professionalaccountant.org
URL: http://www.professionalaccountant.org
Contact: Mr. John Singer RPA, VP
Description: Professional accountants and individuals working to pass qualifying accountancy examinations. Promotes ongoing professional education among accountants; encourages students to enter the accounting field; works to advance the profession of accounting. Gathers and disseminates information on accounting; sponsors educational programs; conducts professional accountancy qualifying examinations. **Publications:** *Professional Accountant* (quarterly).

DIRECTORIES OF EDUCATIONAL PROGRAMS

45 ■ *Directory of Private Accredited Career Schools and Colleges of Technology*
Pub: Accrediting Commission of Career Schools and Colleges of Technology
Contact: Michale S. McComis, Exec. Dir.
Released: On web page. **Price:** Free. **Description:** Covers 3900 accredited post-secondary programs that provide training programs in business, trade, and technical fields, including various small business endeavors. Entries offer school name, address, phone, description of courses, job placement assistance, and requirements for admission. Arrangement is alphabetical.

REFERENCE WORKS

46 ■ "2011 Tax Information of Interest" in *Business Owner* (Vol. 35, November-December 2011, No. 6, pp. 10)
Pub: DL Perkins Company
Description: Compilation of 2011 tax information to help small business take advantage of all tax incentives.

47 ■ "Accountants Get the Hook" in *Canadian Business* (Vol. 80, October 22, 2007, No. 21, pp. 19)
Pub: Rogers Media
Ed: John Gray. **Description:** Chartered Accountants of Ontario handed down the decision on Douglas Barrington, Anthony Power and Claudio Russo's professional misconduct case. The three accountants of Deloitte & Touche LLP must pay C$100,000 in fines and C$417,000 in costs. Details of the disciplinary case are presented.

48 ■ *Accounting and Finance for Your Small Business*
Pub: John Wiley & Sons, Incorporated
Ed: Steven M. Bragg; E. James Burton. **Released:** April 2006. **Price:** $49.00. **Description:** Financial procedures and techniques for establishing and maintaining a profitable small company are outlined.

49 ■ "Accrual vs. Cash Accounting, Explained" in *Business Owner* (Vol. 35, July-August 2011, No. 4, pp. 13)
Pub: DL Perkins Company
Description: Cash method versus accrual accounting methods are examined, using hypothetical situations.

50 ■ "Adler Blanchard & Freeman Reports New SmartKeeper Bookkeeping Service" in *Professional Services Close-Up* (March 24, 2011)
Pub: Close-Up Media
Description: Profile of Adler Blanchard & Freeman (AB&F) accountants and business advisors. The firm has expanded its client offerings to include their new SmartKeeper Business and Personal Bookkeeping Service for small to mid-sized companies and individuals.

51 ■ *American Society of Women Accountants—Membership Directory*
Pub: American Society of Women Accountants
Contact: Stacey L. Craig, President
E-mail: slcraig@drhorton.com
Released: Annual. **Covers:** Approximately 5,000 members in accounting and accounting-related fields. **Entries Include:** Name, address, phone, fax, e-mail. **Arrangement:** Classified by chapter, then alphabetical.

52 ■ "Bar Hopping: Your Numbers At a Glance" in *Inc.* (January 2008, pp. 44-45)
Pub: Gruner & Jahr USA Publishing
Ed: Michael Fitzgerald. **Description:** Software that helps any company analyze data include Crystal Xcelsius, a program that takes data from Excel documents and turns them into animated gauges, charts and graphs; CashView, a Web-based application that tracks receivables and payables; iDashboards, a Web-based programs that produces animated gauges, maps, pie charts and graphs; Corda Human Capital Management, that transforms stats like head count, productivity, and attrition into graphs and dials; NetSuite, a Web-based application that tracks key indicators; and Cognos Now, that gauges, dials, and graphs data.

53 ■ "Battling Back from Betrayal" in *Harvard Business Review* (Vol. 88, December 2010, No. 12, pp. 130)
Pub: Harvard Business School Publishing
Ed: Daniel McGinn. **Description:** Stephen Greer's scrap metal firm, Hartwell Pacific, lost several million dollars due to a lack of efficient and appropriate inventory audits, accounting procedures, and new-hire reference checks for his foreign operations. Greer believes that balancing growth with control is a key component of success.

54 ■ "A Bigger Deal" in *Crain's Cleveland Business* (Vol. 28, November 12, 2007, No. 45, pp. 1)
Pub: Crain Communications, Inc.
Ed: Shawn A. Turner. **Description:** In an attempt to boost its revenue CBiz Inc., a provider of accounting and business services, is looking to balance its acquisitions of smaller companies with larger ones as part of its overall growth strategy.

55 ■ "Book of Lists 2010" in *Philadelphia Business Journal* (Vol. 28, December 25, 2009, No. 45, pp. 1)
Pub: American City Business Journals
Description: Rankings of companies and organizations within the banking, biotechnology, economic development, healthcare, hospitality, law and accounting, marketing and media, real estate, and technology industries in the Philadelphia, Pennsylvania area are presented. Rankings are based on sales, business size, and more.

56 ■ "Bookkeeping Service Opens First Sacramento Franchise" in *Sacramento Bee* (April 13, 2011)
Pub: Sacramento Bee
Ed: Mark Glover. **Description:** Franchise bookkeeping service called BookKeeping Express opened its new office in Roseville, California; its first shop in the area.

57 ■ "Businesses Balk at 1099 Provision in Health Reform Law" in *Baltimore Business Journal* (Vol. 28, August 13, 2010, No. 14, pp. 1)
Pub: Baltimore Business Journal
Ed: Scott Dance. **Description:** Small business advocates and accountants have criticized the Internal Revenue Service Form 1099 provision in the health care reform law as not worth the cost of time and money. Critics believe the policy would create a deluge of the documents that is too much for the companies or the IRS to handle. Details of the provision are also discussed.

58 ■ "Cautions On Loans With Your Business" in *Business Owner* (Vol. 35, July-August 2011, No. 4, pp. 5)
Pub: DL Perkins Company
Description: Caution must be used when borrowing from or lending to any small business. Tax guidelines for the borrowing and lending practice are also included.

59 ■ "Changing the Rules of the Accounting Game" in *Canadian Business* (Vol. 81, December 8, 2008, No. 21, pp. 19)
Pub: Rogers Media Ltd.
Ed: Al Rosen. **Description:** Interference from world politicians in developing accounting standards is believed to have resulted in untested rules that are inferior to current standards. European lawmakers have recently asked to change International Financial Reporting Standards.

60 ■ "Channeling for Growth" in *The Business Journal-Serving Greater Tampa Bay* (Vol. 28, July 11, 2008, No. 29, pp. 1)
Pub: American City Business Journals, Inc.
Ed: Margie Manning. **Description:** HSN Inc., one of the largest employers in Tampa Bay, Florida, is expected to spend an additional $9.7 million annually as it plans to hire more accounting, internal audit, legal, treasury and tax personnel after its spin-off to a public company. Details on the company's sales growth are provided.

61 ■ *Computer Accounting Essentials with Microsoft Office Accounting 2010*
Pub: McGraw-Hill Higher Education
Ed: Carol Yacht, Susan Crosson. **Released:** March 10, 2010. **Description:** Step-by-step guide to using Microsoft's Office Professional 2007 Accounting program.

62 ■ "Convergence Collaboration: Revising Revenue Recognition" in *Management Accounting Quarterly* (Vol. 12, Spring 2011, No. 3, pp. 18)
Pub: Management Accounting Quarterly
Ed: Jack T. Ciesielski, Thomas R. Weirich. **Description:** While revenue recognition is critical, regulations have been developed on an ad hoc basis until now. The joint FASB/IASB proposed accounting standard on revenue recognition is a meaningful convergence of standards that will require a major adjustment for financial statement preparers. The proposal is a radical departure from the way revenue has been recognized by the U.S. GAAP. For industries such as consulting, engineering, construction, and technology, it could dramatically change revenue recognition, impacting the top line. The new proposed standard, its potential impact, and the critical role that contracts play is examined thoroughly.

63 ■ *Deduct It!: Lower Your Small Business Taxes*
Pub: NOLO
Ed: Stephen Fishman. **Released:** November 2009. **Price:** $34.99. **Description:** Ways to make the most of tax deductions for any small business are covered. The book is organized into categories featuring common deductions, start-up expenses, health deductions, entertainment, travel, inventory, equipment and more. Current tax laws and numbers for 2008 are included.

64 ■ "DHS Finalizes Rules Allowing Electronic I-9s" in *HR Specialist* (Vol. 8, September 2010, No. 9, pp. 5)
Pub: Capitol Information Group Inc.
Description: U.S. Department of Homeland Security issued regulations that give employers more flexibility to electronically sing and store I-9 employee verification forms.

65 ■ "Different Aspects of Project Management" in *Contractor* (Vol. 57, February 2010, No. 2, pp. 30)
Pub: Penton Media, Inc.
Ed: H. Kent Craig. **Description:** There are differences when managing a two-man crew as a foreman and a 2,000 employee company as a corporate president. A project manager should have good skills in human psychology, accounting, and the knowledge of a mechanical engineer, architect, civil engineer, and also the meditative skills of a Zen master.

66 ■ *Directory of Global Professional Accounting and Business Certifications*
Pub: John Wiley & Sons, Incorporated
Ed: Lal Balkaran. **Released:** February 9, 2007. **Price:** $35.00. **Description:** Resource for international accounting, auditing, and business professions.

67 ■ "Do Fair Value Adjustments Influence Dividend Policy?" in *Accounting and Business Research* (Vol. 41, Spring 2011, No. 2, pp. 51)
Pub: American Institute of CPAs
Ed: Igor Goncharov, Sander van Triest. **Description:** The impact of positive fair value adjustments on corporate distributions is examined using a Russian setting that requires disclosure of unrealized fair value adjustments in income. It was found that there is no rise in dividends due to positive fair value adjustments and that on the contrary, a negative relationship exists between adjustments and dividend changes.

68 ■ "Economic Crisis and Accounting Evolution" in *Accounting and Business Research* (Vol. 41, Summer 2011, No. 3, pp. 2159)
Pub: American Institute of CPAs
Ed: Gregory Waymire, Sudipta Basu. **Description:** Financial reporting changes at the face of economic crises are studied using a punctuated equilibrium evolution. Findings show that financial reporting has a minor impact but may amplify economic crises. Attempts to enhance accounting amid economic crises may not be as beneficial as planned.

69 ■ *Electronic Commerce: Technical, Business, and Legal Issues*
Pub: Prentice Hall PTR
Ed: Oktay Dogramaci; Aryya Gangopadhyay; Yelena Yesha; Nabil R. Adam. **Released:** August 1998. **Description:** Provides insight into the goals of using the Internet to grow a business in the areas of networking and telecommunication, security, and storage and retrieval; business areas such as marketing, procurement and purchasing, billing and payment, and supply chain management; and legal aspects such as privacy, intellectual property, taxation, contractual and legal settlements.

70 ■ *Employer Legal Forms Simplified*
Pub: Nova Publishing Company
Ed: Daniel Sitarz. **Released:** August 2007. **Price:** $24.95. **Description:** Business reference containing the following forms needed to handle employees in any small business environment: application, notice, confidentiality, absence, federal employer forms and notices, and many payroll forms. All forms are included on a CD that comes in both PDF and text formats. Adobe Acrobat Reader software is also included on the CD. The forms are valid in all fifty states and Washington, DC.

71 ■ "Ethics Commission May Hire Collection Agency" in *Tulsa World* (August 21, 2010)
Pub: World Publishing
Ed: Barbara Hoberock. **Description:** Oklahoma Ethics Commission is considering a more to hire a collection agency or law firm in order to collect fees from candidates owing money for filing late financial reports.

72 ■ "Finally, Justice" in *Canadian Business* (Vol. 82, April 27, 2009, No. 7, pp. 12)
Pub: Rogers Media
Ed: John Gray. **Description:** Former investment adviser Alex Winch feels that he was vindicated with the Canadian Court's ruling that Livent Inc. founders Garth Drabinsky and Myron Gottlieb were guilty of fraud. Drabinsky filed a libel case on Winch over Winch's letter that complained over Livent's accounting procedures. Winch also criticized the inconsistent accounting during Drabinsky's term as chief executive of another firm.

73 ■ *Finance & Accounting: How to Keep Your Books and Manage Your Finances with an MBA, a CPA, or a Ph.D*
Pub: Adams Media Corporation
Ed: Suzanne Caplan. **Price:** $19.95.

74 ■ "The Finance Function In A Global Corporation" in *Harvard Business Review* (Vol. 86, July-August 2008, No. 8, pp. 108)
Pub: Harvard Business School Press
Ed: Mihir A. Desai. **Description:** Designing and implementing a successful finance function in a global setting is discussed. Additional topics include the internal capital market, managing risk and budgeting capital internationally.

75 ■ *Financial Management 101: Get a Grip on Your Business Numbers*
Pub: Self-Counsel Press, Incorporated
Ed: Angie Mohr. **Released:** November 2007. **Price:** $16.95. **Description:** An overview of business planning, financial statements, budgeting and advertising for small businesses. s.

76 ■ *Financial Times Guide to Business Start Up 2007*
Pub: Pearson Education, Limited
Ed: Sara Williams; Jonquil Lowe. **Released:** November 2006. **Price:** $52.50. **Description:** Guide for starting and running a new business is presented. Sections include ways to get started, direct marketing, customer relations, management and accounting.

77 ■ *The Flaw of Averages: Why We Underestimate Risk in the Face of Uncertainty*
Pub: John Wiley & Sons, Inc.
Ed: Sam L. Savage. **Released:** June 3, 2009. **Price:** $22.95. **Description:** Personal and business plans are based on uncertainties on a daily basis. The common avoidable mistake individuals make in assessing risk in the face of uncertainty is defined. The explains why plans based on average assumptions are wrong, on average, in areas as diverse as finance, healthcare, accounting, the war on terror, and climate change.

78 ■ "Function Over Forms?" in *Barron's* (Vol. 88, June 30, 2008, No. 26, pp. 17)
Pub: Dow Jones & Co., Inc.
Ed: Eric Savitz. **Description:** Securities and Exchange Commission (SEC) chairman Christopher Cox wants the SEC to consider an overhaul of the forms used to meet the agency's disclosure requirements. Cox also said that the U.S. Generally Accepted Accounting Standards has too many rules with exceptions and alternative interpretations.

79 ■ "Getting More Out of Retirement" in *Agency Sales Magazine* (Vol. 39, November 2009, No. 10, pp. 48)
Pub: MANA
Ed: Joshua D. Mosshart. **Description:** Overview of the Tax Increase Prevention and Reconciliation Act, which lets employees convert to a Roth IRA in 2010. The benefits of conversion depend on age and wealth and it is best to consult a tax advisor to determine the best strategy for retirement planners.

80 ■ *Getting Rich In Your Underwear: How To Start and Run a Profitable Home-Based Business*
Pub: HCM Publishing
Ed: Peter I. Hupalo. **Released:** April 1, 2005. **Price:** $17.95. **Description:** Book offers insight into starting a home-based business. Entrepreneurs will learn about business models and the home business; distribution and fulfillment of product or service; marketing and sales; how to overcome the fear of starting a business; personal success characteristics; naming a business; zoning and insurance; intellectual capital; copyrights, trademarks, and patents; limited liability companies and S-corporations; business expenses and accounting; taxes; fifteen basic steps for starting a home-based business, state resources for starting a home company; and seven home-based business ideas.

81 ■ "Give Until It Works" in *Hispanic Business* (Vol. 30, March 2008, No. 3, pp. 26)
Pub: Hispanic Business
Ed: Rick Munarriz. **Description:** Donating to qualified charities and non-profit organizations for maximizing tax advantage to be availed on the income tax bill is examined. The amount that can be deducted from the total taxable amount is usually less then the actual amount donated and must be made during that calendar year.

82 ■ "Growing Strong" in *Entrepreneur* (Vol. 35, November 2007, No. 11, pp. 36)
Pub: Entrepreneur Media Inc.
Ed: Nichole L. Torres. **Description:** Amy Langer founded Salo LL with partner John Folkestad. The company is growing fast since its 2002 launch, with over $40 million in projections for 2007. The finance and accounting staffing company tops the list of the fastest-growing women-led companies in North America.

83 ■ "Handle With Care" in *Hawaii Business* (Vol. 53, October 2007, No. 5, pp. 66)
Pub: Hawaii Business Publishing
Ed: Kenneth Sheffield. **Description:** Discusses a fiduciary, who may be a board member, business owner, or a trustee, and is someone who supervises and manages the affairs and the resources of a principal. Fiduciary duties, which include accounting, cost review and risk management, must be served with the benefit of the principal as the priority. Ways of breaching fiduciary duties and how to avoid them are discussed.

84 ■ "The Hidden Tax" in *Canadian Business* (Vol. 81, April 14, 2008, No. 6, pp. 28)
Pub: Rogers Media
Ed: Al Rosen. **Description:** Accounting fraud could take out a sizable sum from one's retirement fund when computed over a long period of time. The much bigger tax on savings is the collective impact of the smaller losses that do not attract the attention they deserve. Ensuring that investors are not unnecessarily taxed 2 percent of their total investments every year outweighs the benefit of a 2 percent reduction in personal tax rates.

85 ■ *How to Start an Internet Sales Business*
Pub: Lulu.com
Ed: Dan Davis. **Released:** August 2005. **Price:** $19. 95. **Description:** Small business guide for launching an Internet sales company. Topics include business structure, licenses, and taxes.

86 ■ *How to Start and Run a Small Book Publishing Company: A Small Business Guide to Self-Publishing and Independent Publishing*
Pub: HCM Publishing
Ed: Peter I. Hupalo. **Released:** August 30, 2002. **Price:** $18.95. **Description:** The book teaches all aspects of starting and running a small book publishing company. Topics covered include: inventory accounting in the book trade, just-in-time inventory management, turnkey fulfillment solutions, tax deductible costs, basics of sales and use tax, book pricing, standards in terms of the book industry, working with distributors and wholesalers, cover design and book layout, book promotion and marketing, how to select profitable authors to publish, printing process, printing on demand, the power of a strong backlist, and how to value copyright.

87 ■ "How To: Manage Your Cash Better" in *Inc.* (Volume 32, December 2010, No. 10, pp. 69)
Pub: Inc. Magazine
Description: A monthly guide to policies, procedures and practices for managing cash for a small business.

88 ■ "IFRS Monopoly: the Pied Piper of Financial Reporting" in *Accounting and Business Research* (Vol. 41, Summer 2011, No. 3, pp. 291)
Pub: American Institute of CPAs
Ed: Shyam Sunder. **Description:** The disadvantages of granting monopoly to the international financial reporting standards (IFRS) are examined. Results indicate that an IFRS monopoly removes the chances for comparing alternative practices and learning from them. An IFRS monopoly also eliminates customization of financial reporting to fit local differences in governance, business, economic, and legal conditions.

89 ■ "Internal Auditor Wants Ethics Review of City's Casper Golf Contract" in *Business Courier* (Vol. 27, September 10, 2010, No. 19, pp. 1)
Pub: Business Courier
Ed: Dan Monk. **Description:** Mark Ashworth, an internal auditor for Cincinnati, Ohio is pushing for an ethics review of management contract for seven city-owned golf courses. Ashworth wants the Ohio Ethics Commission to investigate family ties between a superintendent for the Cincinnati Recreation Commission and Billy Casper Golf.

90 ■ "Kaboom!" in *Canadian Business* (Vol. 81, November 10, 2008, No. 19, pp. 18)
Pub: Rogers Media Ltd.
Ed: Al Rosen, Mark Rosen. **Description:** International Financial Reporting Standards (IFRS) is a good idea in theory but was implemented in a hurry and had poor quality standards from the beginning.

91 ■ "Know Your Numbers" in *Inc.* (Volume 32, December 2010, No. 10, pp. 39)
Pub: Inc. Magazine
Ed: Norm Brodsky. **Description:** Ways to maximize profit and minimize tax burden are presented.

92 ■ "Lifesavers" in *Black Enterprise* (Vol. 41, December 2010, No. 5, pp. 38)
Pub: Earl G. Graves Publishing Co. Inc.
Ed: Tamara E. Holmes. **Description:** Profile of Interventional Nephrology Specialists Access Center and founders Dr. Omar Davis and Dr. Natarsha Grant; the center generated $5.5 million in revenue for 2009. Details on how they run their successful center are included.

93 ■ "Living in a 'Goldfish Bowl'" in *WorkingUSA* (Vol. 11, June 2008, No. 2, pp. 277)
Pub: Blackwell Publishers Ltd.
Ed: John Lund. **Description:** Recent changes in laws, regulations and even the reporting format of labor organization annual financial reports in both the U.S. and Australia have received surprisingly little attention, yet they have significantly increased the amount of information available both to union members and the public in general, as reports in both countries are available via government Websites. While such financial reporting laws are extremely rare in European countries, with the exception of the UK and Ireland, the U.S. and Australian reporting systems have become among the most detailed in the world. After reviewing these changes in financial reporting and the availability of these reports, as well as comparing and contrasting the specific reporting requirements of each country, this paper then examines the cost-benefit impact of more detailed financial reporting.

94 ■ "May I Handle That For You?" in *Inc.* (March 2008, pp. 40, 42)
Pub: Gruner & Jahr USA Publishing
Ed: Taylor Mallory. **Description:** According to a recent survey, 53 percent of all companies outsource a portion of their human resources responsibilities. Ceridian, Administaff, Taleo, KnowledgeBank, and CheckPoint HR are among the companies profiled.

95 ■ *MBA In a Day*
Pub: John Wiley and Sons, Inc.
Ed: Steven Stralser, PhD. **Released:** 2004. **Price:** $34.95. **Description:** Management professor presents important concepts, business topics and strategies that can be used by anyone to manage a small business or professional practice. Topics covered include: human resources and personal interaction, ethics and leadership skills, fair negotiation tactics, basic business accounting practices, project management, and the fundamentals of economics and marketing.

96 ■ "Merger Mania: Regional Snaps Up HVS" in *The Business Journal-Serving Greater Tampa Bay* (Vol. 28, September 26, 2008, No. 40, pp. 1)
Pub: American City Business Journals, Inc.
Ed: Alexis Muellner. **Description:** It was reported that Harper Van Scoik & Co. LLP has finalized a merger with Carr Riggs & Ingram LLC. The agreement, effective October 1, 2008, is a merger of HVS assets into CRI. Bill Carr, a managing partner, revealed that HVS' $5 million in revenue will take CRI from $78 million to $82 million in revenue.

97 ■ *Mergers and Acquisitions from A to Z*
Pub: Amacom
Ed: Andrew J. Sherman, Milledge A. Hart. **Released:** January 2006. **Price:** $35.00. **Description:** Guide for the entire process of mergers and acquisitions, including taxes, accounting, laws, and projected financial gain.

98 ■ *Microfinance*
Pub: Palgrave Macmillan
Ed: Mario La Torre; Gianfranco A. Vento; Philip Molyneux. **Released:** October 2006. **Price:** $80.00. **Description:** Microfinance involves the analysis of operational, managerial and financial aspects of a small business.

99 ■ *Minding Her Own Business, 4th Ed.*
Pub: Sphinx Publishing
Ed: Jan Zobel. **Released:** January 1, 2005. **Price:** $16.95. **Description:** A guide to taxes and financial records for women entrepreneurs is presented.

100 ■ "My Favorite Tool for Managing Expenses" in *Inc.* (Volume 32, December 2010, No. 10, pp. 60)
Pub: Inc. Magazine
Ed: J.J. McCorvey. **Description:** Web-based service called Expensify is outlined. The service allows companies to log expenses while away from the office using the service's iPhone application.

101 ■ "A Necessary Balancing Act: Bookkeeping" in *Contractor* (Vol. 56, November 2009, No. 11, pp. 22)
Pub: Penton Media, Inc.
Ed: Al Schwartz. **Description:** Pros and cons of getting a bookkeeper or a certified public accountant for the subcontractor are discussed. A bookkeeper can help a subcontractor get new accounting software up and running while an accountant will more than likely keep after the books at regular intervals throughout the year.

102 ■ "New Century's Fall Has a New Culprit" in *Barron's* (Vol. 88, March 31, 2008, No. 13, pp. 20)
Pub: Dow Jones & Company, Inc.
Ed: Jonathan R. Laing. **Description:** Court examiner Michael Missal reports that New Century Financial's auditor contributed to New Century's demise by its negligence in permitting improper and imprudent practices related to New Century's accounting processes. New Century's bankruptcy filing is considered the start of the subprime-mortgage crisis.

103 ■ "New Institutional Accounting and IFRS" in *Accounting and Business Research* (Vol. 41, Summer 2011, No. 3, pp. 309)
Pub: American Institute of CPAs
Ed: Peter Wysocki. **Description:** A new framework for institutional accounting research is presented. It has five fundamental components – efficient versus inefficient results, interdependencies, causation, level of analysis, and institutional structure. The use of the framework for evaluation accounting institutions such as the international financial reporting standards is discussed.

104 ■ "New Money" in *Entrepreneur* (Vol. 36, February 2008, No. 2, pp. 62)
Pub: Entrepreneur Media Inc.
Ed: C.J. Prince. **Description:** Tips on how to handle business finance, with regard to the tightened credit standards imposed by leading institutions, are provided. These include: selling receivables, margining blue chips, and selling purchase orders.

105 ■ "Olympus is Urged to Revise Board" in *Wall Street Journal Eastern Edition* (November 28, 2011, pp. B3)
Pub: Dow Jones & Company Inc.
Ed: Phred Dvorak. **Description:** Koji Miyata, once a director on the board of troubled Japanese photographic equipment company, is urging the company to reorganize its board, saying the present group should resign their board seats but keep their management positions. The company has come under scrutiny for its accounting practices and costly acquisitions.

106 ■ *The One Minute Entrepreneur*
Pub: Doubleday
Ed: Ken Blanchard; assisted by Don Hutson and Ethan Willis. **Released:** 2008. **Price:** $19.95. **Description:** Four traditional business ideas are covered including: revenue needs to exceed expenses, bill collection, customer service, and employee motivation in order to be successful.

107 ■ *Open Source Solutions for Small Business Problems*
Pub: Charles River Media
Ed: John Locke. **Released:** May 2004. **Price:** $35. 95. **Description:** Open source software provides solutions to many small business problems such as tracking electronic documents, scheduling, accounting functions, managing contact lists, and reducing spam.

108 ■ *Outfoxing the Small Business Owner*
Pub: Adams Media Corporation
Ed: Gene Marks. **Released:** January 2005. **Description:** Special skill sets are required to sell, service or deal with small business customers.

109 ■ "Paperless Bookkeeping Program" in *Fleet Owner Online* (February 15, 2011)
Pub: Penton Business Media Inc.
Description: TruckTax launched its new paperless bookkeeping system to help manage bookkeeping tasks, accounting and business tax information and filings for truckers.

110 ■ "Pick and Save" in *Entrepreneur* (Vol. 36, April 2008, No. 4, pp. 66)
Pub: Entrepreneur Media, Inc.
Ed: C.J. Prince. **Description:** Business owners can purchase the needed big equipment to offset this year's expected profit. They can also switch to annualized computing of quarterly income and estimated tax payments to pay less estimated taxes for the first half of the year. Other tips on tax planning are provided.

111 ■ "Piece of Health Law 'A Goner'" in *Baltimore Business Journal* (Vol. 28, November 19, 2010, No. 28, pp. 1)
Pub: Baltimore Business Journal
Ed: Kent Hoover. **Description:** Montana Senator Max Baucus, a Democrat who heads the Senate Finance Committee, has revealed his plan to push legislation that would repeal the 1099 IRS provision that was created by the health care reform law and will result in more paperwork for small businesses when it goes into effect in 2012.

112 ■ "Place Restrictions on Your Stock Shares" in *Business Owner* (Vol. 35, July-August 2011, No. 4, pp. 14)
Pub: DL Perkins Company
Description: It is critical for any small business owner to be certain that the buyer or recipient of any part of the company represents that the stock is being acquired or given for investment purposes only.

113 ■ "Privacy Concern: Are 'Group' Time Sheets Legal?" in *HR Specialist* (Vol. 8, September 2010, No. 9, pp. 4)
Pub: Capitol Information Group Inc.
Description: Under the Fair Labor Standards Act (FLSA) employers are required to maintain and preserve payroll or other records, including the number of hours worked, but it does not prescribe a particular order or form in which these records must be kept.

114 ■ "Proposed Accounting Changes Could Complicate Tenant's Leases" in *Baltimore Business Journal* (Vol. 28, July 2, 2010, No. 8, pp. 1)
Pub: Baltimore Business Journal
Ed: Daniel J. Sernovitz. **Description:** The Financial Accounting Standards Board has proposed that companies must indicate the value of real estate leases as assets and liabilities on balance sheets instead of expenses. The proposals could cause some companies to document millions of dollars in charges on their books or find difficulty in getting loans.

115 ■ "Prosecutors Dish Sordid AIPC Story" in *The Business Journal-Serving Metropolitan Kansas City* (Vol. 27, September 19, 2008, No. 1)
Pub: American City Business Journals, Inc.
Ed: Suzanna Stagemeyer. **Description:** Prosecutors in the American Italian Pasta Co.'s accounting fraud case have revealed evidence on the schemes used by then-officers of the company to commit fraud. District attorney John Wood has dubbed the case as the largest corporate fraud lawsuit in the history of the district of Missouri. How AIPC fell from being an industry leader is also discussed.

116 ■ *QuickBooks All-in-One Desk Reference for Dummies*
Pub: John Wiley & Sons, Incorporated
Ed: Stephen L. Nelson. **Released:** January 2007. **Price:** $29.99 (US), $42.99 (Canadian). **Description:** Compilation of nine self-contained minibooks to get the most from QuickBooks accounting software. Companion Web site with sample business plan workbook and downloadable profit-volume cost analysis workbook included.

117 ■ *QuickBooks for the New Bean Counter: Business Owner's Guide 2006*
Pub: Wheatmark
Ed: Joseph L. Catallini. **Released:** July 2006. **Price:** $21.95. **Description:** Profile of QuickBooks software, offering insight into using the software's accounting and bookkeeping functions.

118 ■ *QuickBooks Simple Start for Dummies*
Pub: John Wiley & Sons, Incorporated
Ed: Stephen L. Nelson. **Released:** October 2004. **Price:** $21.99. **Description:** Profile of Intuits new accounting software geared to micro businesses. Advice is offered on daily, monthly, and yearly accounting activities covering records, sales tax, and reports.

119 ■ *QuickBooks X on Demand*
Pub: Que
Ed: Gail Perry. **Released:** December 2006. **Price:** $34.99. **Description:** Step-by-step training for using various small business financial software programs; includes illustrated, full color explanations.

120 ■ *QuickBooks X for Dummies*
Pub: John Wiley & Sons, Incorporated
Ed: Stephen L. Nelson. **Released:** November 2006. **Price:** $21.99. **Description:** Key features of QuickBooks software for small business are introduced. Invoicing and credit memos, recoding sales receipts, accounting, budgeting, taxes, payroll, financial reports, job estimating, billing, tracking, data backup, are among the features.

121 ■ "Quicken Starter Edition 2008" in *Black Enterprise* (Vol. 38, March 2008, No. 8, pp. 54)
Pub: Earl G. Graves Publishing Co. Inc.
Ed: Sonya A. Donaldson. **Description:** Profile of Quicken Starter Edition 2008 offering programs that track spending; it will also categorize tax deductible expenses.

122 ■ *Reading Financial Reports for Dummies*
Pub: John Wiley and Sons, Inc.
Ed: Lita Epstein. **Released:** January 2009. **Price:** $21.99. **Description:** This second edition contains more new and updated information, including new information on the separate accounting and financial reporting standards for private/small businesses versus public/large businesses; updated information reflecting 2007 laws on international financial reporting standards; new content to match SEC and other governmental regulatory changes over the last three years; new information about how the analyst-corporate connection has changed the playing field; the impact of corporate communications and new technologies; new examples that reflect the current trends; and updated Websites and resources.

123 ■ "Reform or Perish" in *Canadian Business* (Vol. 82, April 27, 2009, No. 7, pp. 20)
Pub: Rogers Media
Ed: Al Rosen. **Description:** It is believed that Canada needs to fix its financial regulatory framework in order to provide more oversight on accounting procedures that is often left up to auditors. While the U.S. has constantly rebuilt its regulatory framework, Canada has not instituted reforms on its regulations. Canada entered the recession with a strong system but needs to build more substance into it.

124 ■ *Running Your Small Business on a MAC*
Pub: Peachpit Press
Ed: Doug Hanley. **Released:** November 2007. **Price:** $29.99. **Description:** Information to effectively start and run a small business using a MAC, including setting up a network and accounting.

125 ■ *Sarbanes-Oxley for Dummies, 2nd Ed.*
Pub: John Wiley and Sons, Inc.
Ed: Jill Gilbert Welytok. **Released:** February 2008. **Price:** $21.99. **Description:** Provides the latest Sarbanes-Oxley (SOX) legislation with procedures to safely and effectively reduce compliance costs. Topics include way to: establish SOX standards for IT professionals, minimize compliances costs for every aspect of a business, survive a Section 404 audit, avoid litigation under SOX, anticipate future rules and trends, create a post-SOX paper trail, increase a company's standing and reputation, work with SOX in a small business, meet new SOX standards, build a board that can't be bought, and to comply with all SOX management mandates.

126 ■ *Schaum's Outline Financial Management, Third Edition*
Pub: McGraw-Hill
Ed: Jae K. Shim; Joel G. Siegel. **Released:** May 2007. **Price:** $22.95 (CND). **Description:** Rules and regulations governing corporate finance, including the Sarbanes-Oxley Act are discussed.

127 ■ "Scottsdale Bank Plans 4Q Opening" in *The Business Journal - Serving Phoenix and the Valley of the Sun* (Vol. 28, August 15, 2008, No. 50)
Pub: American City Business Journals, Inc.
Ed: Chris Casacchia. **Description:** Arizona's Department of Financial Institutions has approved Scottsdale Business Bank, a community bank which plans to open in the fourth quarter of 2008. The bank, which is to be located near McCormick Ranch in Scottsdale, Arizona, will cater to small business owners in the professional sector, such as accountants and doctors.

128 ■ "SEC Extends Small Business Deadline for SOX Audit Requirement" in *HRMagazine* (Vol. 53, August 2008, No. 8, pp. 20)
Pub: Society for Human Resource Management
Description: Securities and Exchange Commission has approved a one-year extension of the compliance date for smaller public companies to meet the Section 404(b) auditor attestation requirement of the Sarbanes-Oxley Act.

129 ■ *Self-Employed Tax Solutions: Quick, Simple, Money-Saving, Audit-Proof Tax and Recordkeeping Basics*
Pub: The Globe Pequot Press
Ed: June Walker. **Released:** January 1, 2009. **Price:** $17.95. **Description:** A simple system for maintaining tax records and filing tax forms for any small business is explored.

130 ■ *Six SIGMA for Small Business*
Pub: Entrepreneur Press
Ed: Greg Brue. **Released:** October 2005. **Price:** $19.95 (US), $26.95 (Canadian). **Description:** Jack Welch's Six SIGMA approach to business covers accounting, finance, sales and marketing, buying a business, human resource development, and new product development.

131 ■ "Small is Bountiful for Intuit" in *Barron's* (Vol. 90, September 13, 2010, No. 37, pp. 22)
Pub: Barron's Editorial & Corporate Headquarters
Ed: Mark Veverka. **Description:** Finance software maker Intuit wants to tap the underserved small business market. One analyst sees Intuit's shares rising 25 percent to 55 percent in the next 12 months from September 2010.

132 ■ *The Small Business Bible: Everything You Need to Know to Succeed in Your Small Business*
Pub: John Wiley & Sons, Incorporated
Ed: Steven D. Strauss. **Released:** September 2008. **Price:** $19.95 (US), $28.99 (Canadian). **Description:** Comprehensive guide to starting and running a successful small business. Topics include bookkeeping and financial management, marketing, publicity, and advertising.

133 ■ *Small Business Desk Reference*
Pub: Penguin Books (USA) Incorporated
Ed: Gene Marks. **Released:** December 2004. **Description:** Comprehensive guide for starting or running a successful small business, focusing on buying a business or franchise, writing a business plan, financial management, accounting, legal issues, human resources management, operations, marketing, sales, customer service, taxes, insurance, and ethics. Information for launching a restaurant, property management firm, retail outlet, consulting firm, and service business is included.

134 ■ *Small Business for Dummies, 3rd Ed.*
Pub: John Wiley and Sons, Inc.
Ed: Eric Tyson; Jim Schell. **Released:** March 2008. **Price:** $21.99. **Description:** Guidebook for anyone wanting to start or grow a small business; topics include information financing, budgeting, marketing, management and more.

135 ■ *The Small Business Owner's Manual: Everything You Need to Know to Start Up and Run Your Business*
Pub: Career Press, Incorporated
Ed: Joe Kennedy. **Released:** June 2005. **Price:** $19.99 (US), $26.95 (Canadian). **Description:** Comprehensive guide for starting a small business, focusing on twelve ways to obtain financing, business plans, selling and advertising products and services, hiring and firing employees, setting up a Web site, business law, accounting issues, insurance, equipment, computers, banks, financing, customer credit and collection, leasing, and more.

136 ■ *Small Business Survival Guide*
Pub: Adams Media Corporation
Ed: Cliff Ennico. **Price:** $12.95. **Description:** Small business expert provides strategies to start a company and survive in the 21st Century. He shows small business owners how to succeed despite challenges that can defeat any firm. His advice covers suppliers; customers and contractors; competitors and creditors; spouses, family and friends; as well as the ways lawyers, accountants and other can steal an entrepreneur's success. Ennico also describes how startups can comply with local regulations.

137 ■ *Small Business Survival Guide: Starting, Protecting, and Securing Your Business for Long-Term Success*
Pub: Adams Media Corporation
Ed: Cliff Ennico. **Released:** September 2005. **Price:** $12.95 (US), $17.95 (Canadian). **Description:** Entrepreneurship in the new millennium. Topics include creditors, taxes, competition, business law, and accounting.

138 ■ *Smart Tax Write-Offs, 5th Ed.*
Pub: Rayve Productions, Inc.
Ed: Norm Ray. **Released:** February 2008. **Price:** $15.95. **Description:** Guidebook to help small business owners take advantage of legitimate tax deductions for home-based and other entrepreneurial businesses.

139 ■ "Smart Year-End Tax Moves" in *Business Owner* (Vol. 35, November-December 2011, No. 6, pp. 8)
Pub: DL Perkins Company
Description: Managing small business and individual taxes is more important in a bad economy. It is imperative to seek all tax incentives that apply to your business.

140 ■ "Spotlight on Pensions" in *Business Horizons* (Vol. 51, March-April 2008, No. 2, pp. 105)
Pub: Elsevier Advanced Technology Publications
Ed: Laureen A. Maines. **Description:** Perceptions of pension burden and risk among financial statement users is likely to increase with changes in pension accounting. These perceptions might affect decisions on pension commitments and investments.

141 ■ "Spotlight on Principles-based Financial Reporting" in *Business Horizons* (September-October 2007, pp. 359)
Pub: Elsevier Technology Publications
Ed: Laureen A. Maines. **Description:** Employment of principles-based standards in order to generate reliable financial reporting and to reduce misrepresentations is discussed. Rules-based standards are distinguished from principles-based standards.

142 ■ "Staffing Firm Grows by Following Own Advice-Hire a Headhunter" in *Crain's Detroit Business* (Vol. 24, October 6, 2008, No. 40, pp. 1)
Pub: Crain Communications, Inc.
Ed: Sherri Begin. **Description:** Profile of Venator Holdings L.L.C., a staffing firm that provides searches for companies in need of financial-accounting and technical employees; the firm's revenue has increased from $1.1 million in 2003 to a projected $11.5 million this year due to a climate in which more people are exiting the workforce than are coming in with those particular specialized skills and the need for a temporary, flexible workforce for contract placements at companies that do not want to take on the legacy costs associated with permanent employees. The hiring of an external headhunter to find the right out-of-state manager for Venator is also discussed.

143 ■ *Streetwise Finance and Accounting for Entrepreneurs: Set Budgets, Manage Costs, Keep Your Business Profitable*
Pub: Adams Media Corporation
Ed: Suzanne Caplan. **Released:** November 2006. **Price:** $25.95. **Description:** Book offers a basic understanding of accounting and finance for small businesses, including financial statements, credits and debits, as well as establishing a budget. Strategies for small companies in financial distress are included.

144 ■ *Streetwise Small Business Book of Lists: Hundreds of Lists to Help You Reduce Costs, Increase Revenues, and Boost Your Profits!*
Pub: Adams Media Corporation
Ed: Gene Marks. **Released:** September 2006. **Price:** $25.95. **Description:** Strategies to help small business owners locate services, increase sales, and lower expenses.

145 ■ "Surviving an IRS Audit: Tips for Small Businesses" in *Agency Sales Magazine* (Vol. 39, July 2009, No. 7, pp. 52)
Pub: MANA
Ed: Joshua D. Mosshart. **Description:** It is a good idea to enlist the services of a tax professional even if an audit is expected to go smoothly since the IRS is likely to scrutinize the unreported income and personal as well as business expenses of a small business during an audit.

146 ■ "Technology and Returnable Asset Management" in *Canadian Electronics* (Vol. 23, February 2008, No. 1, pp. 6)
Pub: CLB Media Inc.
Ed: Mark Borkowski. **Description:** Peter Kastner, president of Vestigo Corporation, believes that public companies without an asset track, trace, and control system in place could face Sarbanes-Oakley liability if error-prone processes result to misstatements of asset inventory positions. He also thinks that the system can improve return on assets by increasing the utilization of returnables.

147 ■ "Test Your Structural Integrity" in *Entrepreneur* (Vol. 37, August 2009, No. 8, pp. 60)
Pub: Entrepreneur Media, Inc.
Ed: Jennifer Lawler. **Description:** Tax considerations can be important when choosing a business structure. For example, profits are taxed to the corporation in a C corp while profits are taxed only once at an S corp or a limited liability company. Meeting a tax professional should be done prior to switching to a different structure.

148 ■ "The File On...Skoda Minotti" in *Crain's Cleveland Business* (Vol. 28, October 8, 2007, No. 40, pp. 26)
Pub: Crain Communications, Inc.
Ed: Kimberly Bonvissuto. **Description:** Overview of Skoda Minotti, the accounting and financial services firm located in Mayfield Village; the company has 140 employees and an expanded slate of services.

149 ■ "Throughput Metrics Meet Six Sigma" in *Management Accounting Quarterly* (Vol. 12, Spring 2011, No. 3, pp. 12)
Pub: Management Accounting Quarterly
Ed: Shaun Aghili. **Description:** Throughput accounting (TA) metrics can be combined with six sigma's DMAIC methodology and various time-tested analysis and measurement tools for added effectiveness in resolving resource constraint issues. The goal is to optimize not only the output of a specific department but that of the entire system, by implementing a cost accounting system that is conducive to system optimization while increasing product quality, process integrity, or ideally, both.

150 ■ "ValienteHernandez Acquired" in *The Business Journal-Serving Greater Tampa Bay* (Vol. 28, September 12, 2008, No. 38, pp. 1)
Pub: American City Business Journals, Inc.
Ed: Alexis Muellner. **Description:** Minnesota accounting firm LarsonAllen LLP has acquired Florida-based ValienteHernandez PA, creating a company with 35 employees to be based in ValienteHernandez's newly built office in Tampa Bay Area. Other details about the merger are provided.

151 ■ "Welcome Back" in *Canadian Business* (Vol. 82, April 27, 2009, No. 7, pp. 25)
Pub: Rogers Media
Ed: Sarka Halas. **Description:** Some Canadian companies such as Gennum Corporation have taken advantage of corporate sale-leasebacks to raise money at a time when credit is hard to acquire. Corporate sale-leasebacks allow companies to sell their property assets while remaining as tenants of the building. Sale-leasebacks allow firms to increase capital while avoiding the disruptions that may result with moving.

152 ■ "Where Women Work" in *Marketing to Women* (Vol. 21, April 2008, No. 4, pp. 8)
Pub: EPM Communications, Inc.
Description: According to the U.S. Census Bureau, 60 percent of America's professional tax preparers are women. Also features additional trends concerning women in the workplace. Statistical data included.

153 ■ *Working Papers, Chapters 1-14 for Needles/Powers/Crosson's Financial and Managerial Accounting*
Pub: Cengage South-Western
Ed: Belverd E. Needles, Marian Powers, Susan V. Crosson. **Released:** May 10, 2010. **Price:** $62.95. **Description:** Appropriate accounting forms for completing all exercises, problems and cases in the text are provided for financial management of a small company.

STATISTICAL SOURCES

154 ■ *RMA Annual Statement Studies*
Pub: Robert Morris Associates (RMA)
Released: Annual. **Price:** $175.00 2006-07 edition, $105.00. **Description:** Contains composite balance sheets and income statements for more than 360 industries, including the accounting, auditing, and bookkeeping industries. Also contains five years of comparative historical data for discerning trends. Includes 16 commonly used ratios, computed for most of the size groupings for nearly every industry.

TRADE PERIODICALS

155 ■ *The Accounting Review*
Pub: American Accounting Association
Contact: Prof. Steven J. Kachelmeier, Sen. Ed.
Ed: Shannon W. Anderson, Editor. **Released:** Quarterly. **Price:** $340 print; $340 online from volume 74 through current issue; $380 online and print. **Description:** Accounting education, research, financial reporting, and book reviews.

156 ■ *Auditing*
Pub: American Accounting Association
Ed: Dan A. Simunic, Editor, dan.simunic@sauder.ubc.ca. **Released:** Semiannual. **Price:** $120 print only; $160 online only; $175 online and print. **Description:** Trade journal covering the practice and theory of auditing for accounting professionals.

157 ■ *AWSCPA Newsletter*
Pub: American Woman's Society of Certified Public Accountants
Contact: Kimberly Fantaci
Released: 3/year. **Description:** Concerned with future developments within the accounting profession for women CPA's. Carries items on new accounting methods, member profiles, and other topics of interest.

158 ■ *Behavioral Research in Accounting*
Pub: American Accounting Association
Ed: Prof. Theresa Libby, Editor, tlibby@wlu.ca. **Released:** Semiannual. **Price:** $150 print; $160 electronic from volume 13 to current issue; $175 print & electronic. **Description:** Academic journal covering research in accounting.

159 ■ *CFO & Controller Alert*
Pub: Progressive Business Publications
Contact: John Hiatt
Ed: John Hiatt, Editor, hiatt@pbp.com. **Released:** Semimonthly. **Price:** $299, individuals. **Description:** Assists busy financial executives to boost cash flow, control expenses, manage resources, and comply with changing regulations. Recurring features include case studies, success stories, financial and tax developments, cost-saving ideas and columns titled Management and Sharpen Your Judgment.

160 ■ *CPA Client Bulletin*
Pub: The American Institute of Certified Public Accountants
Ed: Maria Luzarraga Albanese, Editor. **Released:** Monthly. **Price:** $195, members $174/year for members only; $243.75, nonmembers. **Description:** Discusses business-related topics, including taxes, management, and government regulation. Recurring features include news briefs on personal financial planning and taxes.

161 ■ *CPA Client Tax Letter*
Pub: The American Institute of Certified Public Accountants
Ed: Maria Luzarraga Albanese, Editor. **Released:** Quarterly. **Price:** $119, members; $148.75, nonmembers. **Description:** Covers tax planning, including laws and legislation.

162 ■ *The CPA Journal*
Pub: New York State Society of CPAs
Contact: Joanne S. Barry, Publisher
E-mail: jbarry@nysscpa.org
Released: Monthly. **Price:** $42; $135 other countries 3 years; $98 other countries 2 years; $54 other countries; $74 two years; $99 3 years. **Description:** Refereed accounting journal.

163 ■ *IFAC News*
Pub: International Federation of Accountants
Released: Quarterly. **Price:** Included in membership. **Description:** Focuses on the activities of the Federation, whose goal is to coordinate efforts to achieve international, technical, ethical, and educational guidelines for the accountancy profession. Also reports on member accounting bodies and on regional groups with similar goals. Recurring features include news of research, a calendar of events, and reports of meetings.

164 ■ *Journal of Accountancy*
Pub: The American Institute of Certified Public Accountants
Contact: Joanne E. Fiore, Ed.-in-Ch./Publisher
E-mail: jfiore@aicpa.org
Released: Monthly. **Price:** $75; $60 members. **Description:** Accounting journal.

165 ■ *Journal of Accounting Research*
Pub: University of Chicago Graduate School of Business
Contact: Lisa M. Johnson, Managing Editor
Released: Semiannual, 5/yr. **Description:** Trade journal covering all areas of accounting research.

166 ■ *Journal of the American Taxation Association*
Pub: American Accounting Association
Contact: Jay Soled, Assoc. Ed.
E-mail: jaysoled@andromeda.rutgers.edu
Ed: Richard C. Sansing, Editor. **Released:** Semiannual, with a third conference supplement. **Price:** $120 print; $160 online from volume 21 to current issue; $175 online and print. **Description:** Academic journal covering accounting and taxation.

167 ■ *Journal of Management Accounting Research*
Pub: American Accounting Association
Contact: Thomas Hemmer, Assoc. Ed.
Ed: Prof. Ramji Balakrishnan, Editor, ramji-balakrishnan@uiowa.edu. **Released:** Annual. **Price:** $125 print; $160 online only (vol. 12 through current issue); $175 online and print. **Description:** Academic journal covering the theory and practice of management accounting by promoting applied and theoretical research.

168 ■ *Leader's Edge*
Pub: Michigan Association of CPAs
Ed: Marla Janness, Editor, mjanness@ix.netcom.com. **Released:** Bimonthly, 10/year. **Price:** $20. **Description:** Contains professional and technical information for certified public accountants.

169 ■ *NACOMEX Insider*
Pub: NACOMEX USA Inc.
Contact: Robert Zises
Ed: Robert Zises, Editor, zises@nacomex.com. **Released:** Quarterly. **Price:** $199, U.S.. **Description:** Provides information on historical values, current tactics, and residual value forecasting for ad valorem tax, bankruptcy, loss compensation, and related purposes. Recurring features include news of research and a column titled Industry Round-up.

170 ■ *National Association of Black Accountants—News Plus*
Pub: National Association of Black Accountants Inc.
Released: Quarterly. **Price:** Included in membership; $20, nonmembers. **Description:** Addresses concerns of black business professionals, especially in the accounting profession. Reports on accounting education issues, developments affecting the profession, and the Association's activities on the behalf of minorities in the accounting profession. Recurring features include member profiles, job listings, reports of meetings, news of research, and a calendar of events.

171 ■ *NewsAccount*
Pub: Colorado Society of Certified Public Accountants
Contact: Liz Julin, Publisher
Released: 6/year. **Description:** Relays information on issues and trends affecting the Society, its members, and the accounting profession. Recurring features include letters to the editor, job listings, a calendar of events and columns titled Committees in Action, Student Corner, SEC Corner, and Technical Update.

172 ■ *Polaris International*
Pub: Polaris International
Ed: Jonathan Hume, Editor, jon@accountants.org. **Released:** Monthly. **Price:** Included in membership. **Description:** Advises independent accounting firms worldwide on management of accounting practices. Covers topics such as marketing, employee training, and office products and equipment. Provides news of research, and information about educational opportunities. Recurring features include meeting reports and a calendar of events.

173 ■ *The Practical Accountant*
Pub: SourceMedia Inc.
Contact: Howard Wolosky, Assoc. Publisher/Exec. Ed.
E-mail: howard.woloskly@amspubs.com
Released: 12/yr. **Price:** $89; $158 two years; $109 other countries; $218 other countries two years. **Description:** Magazine for accountants covering every aspect of accounting, financial planning, practice development, consulting, technology, and taxation.

174 ■ *Practical Tax Strategies*
Pub: RIA Group
Contact: Irving Evall, Editorial Advisory Board
Released: Monthly. **Price:** $250 print; $385 online/print; $280 online. **Description:** Magazine covering taxes and accounting.

175 ■ *The Practicing CPA*
Pub: The American Institute of Certified Public Accountants
Contact: John von Brachel
Ed: William Moran, Editor, wmoran@aicpa.org. **Released:** Monthly. **Price:** Included in membership. **Description:** Focuses on accounting practice management and the practical application of professional standards. Recurring features include letters to the editor, announcements of seminars and conferences, and bizsites.

176 ■ *Public Accounting Report*
Pub: CCH Inc.
Contact: Whitney Greer
Ed: Jon McKenna, Editor. **Released:** Bimonthly. **Price:** $449, U.S.. **Description:** Provides public accounting firms and other interested parties with authoritative news and analysis of developments in the accounting profession today and emerging trends for the future. Reports mergers, acquisitions, auditor changes, and related events.

177 ■ *Single Audit Information Service*
Pub: Thompson Publishing Group Inc.
Contact: Denise Lamoreaux, Sr. Pub. Mgr.
Ed: Lisa Hayes, Editor, lisa_hayes@thompson.com. **Released:** Monthly. **Price:** $399. **Description:** Covers single audit developments.

178 ■ *Spectrum*
Pub: National Association of Black Accountants Inc.
Released: Annual. **Price:** $20 nonmembers. **Description:** Professional magazine of the National Association of Black Accountants, Inc.

179 ■ *State Board Report*
Pub: National Association of State Boards of Accountancy
Ed: Louise Dratler Haberman, Editor. **Released:** Monthly. **Price:** $85, individuals. **Description:** Describes the activities and concerns of the National Association of State Boards of Accountancy. Recurring features include reports of meetings.

180 ■ *Taxes—The Tax Magazine*
Pub: CCH Inc.
Released: Monthly. **Price:** $349. **Description:** Magazine on tax laws and regulations.

VIDEOCASSETTES/ AUDIOCASSETTES

181 ■ *The Accountant as a Business Advisor*
SmartPros LTD
12 Skyline Dr.
Hawthorne, NY 10532
Ph:(914)345-2620
Free: 800-621-0043
Co. E-mail: admin@smartpros.com
URL: http://www.smartpros.com
Released: 1988. **Price:** $449.00. **Description:** Independent public accountancy can also include management and financial consulting, this video claims, and then provides information to help accountants lay claim to this new field of endeavor. **Availability:** VHS.

182 ■ *Accounting & Auditing Update: Implementation of Recent Developments*
Bisk Education
9417 Princess Palm Ave.
Tampa, FL 33619
Free: 800-874-7877
Co. E-mail: info@bisk.com
URL: http://www.bisk.com
Price: $179.00. **Description:** Details techniques for implementing the latest changes in accounting principles and auditing. Provides information on post-retirement benefits, market value, income taxes, and GAAP. Includes workbook and quizzer. **Availability:** VHS.

183 ■ *Accounting Library*
Moonbeam Publications, Inc.
PO Box 5150
Traverse City, MI 49696
Ph:(616)922-0533
Free: 800-445-2391
Fax:800-334-9789
Co. E-mail: custserv@moonbeampublications.com
URL: http://www.moonbeampublications.com
Released: 1992. **Price:** $229.65. **Description:** Covers accounting software Quicken, Peachtree, DacEasy Accounting, and DacEasy Payroll for IBM and IBM-compatible computers. Each of the seven tapes is available individually. **Availability:** VHS.

184 ■ *Basic Accounting Video Series*
Cambridge Educational
c/o Films Media Group
132 West 31st Street, 17th Floor
Ste. 124
New York, NY 10001
Free: 800-257-5126
Fax:(609)671-0266
Co. E-mail: custserve@films.com
URL: http://www.cambridgeol.com
Released: 1988. **Price:** $98.00. **Description:** The four parts of this tape cover all pertinent information about learning accounting. Worksheets are included. The tapes can be purchased individually or as a set. **Availability:** VHS.

185 ■ *CPE Network: Accounting and Auditing Report*
Bisk Education
9417 Princess Palm Ave.
Tampa, FL 33619
Free: 800-874-7877
Co. E-mail: info@bisk.com
URL: http://www.bisk.com
Released: 1994. **Price:** $799.00. **Description:** Outlines informaton on current industry issues, pronouncements, new standards, recent decisions, insider reports on exposure drafts, and other early indicators of upcoming changes in the accounting and auditing areas. Video newsletter published 11 times per year. **Availability:** VHS.

186 ■ *CPE Network: Tax & Accounting Report*
Bisk Education
9417 Princess Palm Ave.
Tampa, FL 33619
Free: 800-874-7877
Co. E-mail: info@bisk.com
URL: http://www.bisk.com
Price: $1200.00. **Description:** Provides information on current tax regulations and current accounting and auditing changes. Video newsletter published 11 times per year. **Availability:** VHS.

187 ■ *FMN (Financial Management Network)*
SmartPros LTD
12 Skyline Dr.
Hawthorne, NY 10532
Ph:(914)345-2620
Free: 800-621-0043
Co. E-mail: admin@smartpros.com
URL: http://www.smartpros.com
Released: 1993. **Price:** $4320.00. **Description:** This monthly video magazine keeps accountants up-to-date on the latest occurances in their field, and helps them earn continuing education CPE credits. The price given is for a yearly subscription. **Availability:** VHS.

TRADE SHOWS AND CONVENTIONS

188 ■ American Accounting Association Annual Meeting
American Accounting Association
5717 Bessie Dr.
Sarasota, FL 34233-2399
Ph:(941)921-7747
Fax:(941)923-4093
Co. E-mail: info@aaahq.org
URL: http://aaahq.org/index.cfm
Released: Annual. **Principal Exhibits:** Accounting equipment, supplies, and services.

189 ■ American Association of Attorney-Certified Public Accountants Annual Meeting and Educational Conference
American Association of Attorney-Certified Public Accountants
24196 Alicia Pky., Ste. K
Mission Viejo, CA 92691
Ph:(949)768-0336
URL: http://www.attorney-cpa.com
Released: Annual. **Principal Exhibits:** Exhibits for persons licensed both as attorneys and CPAs.

190 ■ Association of Insolvency and Restructuring Advisors Conference
Association of Insolvency Accountants
132 W. Main, Ste. 200
Medford, OR 97501
Ph:(541)858-1665
Fax:(541)858-9187
Released: Annual. **Principal Exhibits:** Exhibits for CPAs and licensed public accountants, attorneys, examiners, trustees and receivers involved in insolvency accounting. **Dates and Locations:** 2011 Jun 08-11, Boston, MA.

191 ■ Business & Technology Solutions Show
Illinois Certified Public Accounting Society
550 W. Jackson, Ste. 900
Chicago, IL 60661
Ph:(312)933-0407
Free: 800-993-0407
Fax:(312)993-9954
URL: http://www.icpas.org
Released: Annual. **Audience:** Certified public accountants and their clients, business owners and managers, and others from the financial and business community. **Principal Exhibits:** Computers, office equipment, software publishing and educational supplies, and financial services.

192 ■ Institute of Internal Auditors - USA International Conference
Institute of Internal Auditors (Altamonte Springs, Florida)
247 Maitland Ave.
Altamonte Springs, FL 32701-4201
Ph:(407)937-1100
Fax:(407)937-1101
URL: http://www.theiia.org
Released: Annual. **Audience:** All levels of internal auditors from every industry. **Principal Exhibits:** Internal auditing equipment, supplies, and services, software, computer related equipment.

193 ■ National Society of Public Accountants Annual Convention
National Society of Public Accountants
1010 N. Fairfax St.
Alexandria, VA 22314-1574
Ph:(703)549-6400
Free: 800-966-6679
Fax:(703)549-2984
Co. E-mail: NSA@wizard.net
URL: http://www.nsa.org
Released: Annual. **Principal Exhibits:** Exhibits related to public accounting.

194 ■ New Jersey Accounting, Business & Technology Show & Conference
Flagg Management, Inc.
353 Lexington Ave.
New York, NY 10016
Ph:(212)286-0333
Fax:(212)286-0086
Co. E-mail: flaggmgmt@msn.com
URL: http://www.flaggmgmt.com
Released: Annual. **Audience:** CPAs, accounting professionals, business and financial executives of New Jersey, Fortune 1000 corporations, business owners and managers, IT managers. **Principal Exhibits:** Information and technology, financial and business services, computer accounting systems, software, tax preparation, accounting, audit, practice management software - windows, and computer and business systems. Banking, insurance, financial and business software. Internet, online systems and middle market software and investment services. **Dates and Locations:** 2011 May 18-19, Secaucus, NJ.

CONSULTANTS

195 ■ Accounting Systems
PO Box 1720
Santa Monica, CA 90402
Ph:(310)393-5887
Fax:(310)393-5887
Co. E-mail: debabe@earthlink.net
Contact: Deborah Peters, Principle
Scope: Trains companies on bookkeeping procedures and consults on selecting appropriate accounting systems. Installs accounting software and trains on system usage. Teaches how to interpret financial statements. Also offers a variety of accounting and bookkeeping services.

196 ■ Achieve Management Inc.
2215 E Henry Ave.
Tampa, FL 33610
Ph:(813)239-1179
Free: 800-749-5155
Fax:(813)237-3091
Co. E-mail: kryals@achievemanagement.com
URL: http://www.achievemanagement.com
Contact: Brandi Reeves, Mgr of Bus Devel
E-mail: breeves@atsachievemanagement.com
Scope: Firm's management services organization provides customized direct services, focused consultation, and strategic planning. These services include general management (strategic planning, sustainability planning, contract management, quality improvement, policies/procedures development, partnership development); accounting; human resources (hiring process, performance management, compliance, payroll, benefit coordination training); and information technology.

197 ■ ARC Analytics L.L.C.
20960 Blanca Terr.
Boca Raton, FL 33434
Ph:(561)852-1936
Fax:(561)807-0084
Co. E-mail: arc@arcmg.com
URL: http://www.arcmg.com
Contact: Coletta L. Dorado, Partner
E-mail: cdorado@atsarcmg.com
Scope: A consulting firm specializing in investment related disputes. Litigation support services include forensic accounting in securities litigation, portfolio analysis, and damage calculations. Brokerage firm experts in compliance, operations and trading.

198 ■ Arnold S. Goldin & Associates Inc.
5030 Champion Blvd., Ste. G-6231
Boca Raton, FL 33496
Ph:(561)994-5810
Fax:(561)994-5860
Co. E-mail: arnold@goldin.com
URL: http://www.goldin.com
Contact: Arnold S. Goldin, Principle
E-mail: arnold@goldin.com
Scope: An accounting and management consulting firm. Serves clients worldwide. Provides management services. Handles monthly write-ups and tax returns.

199 ■ Automated Accounting
23325 Gerbera St.
Moreno Valley, CA 92553
Ph:(951)653-5053
Co. E-mail: autoacc@earthlink.net
Contact: Gary Capolino, Owner
Scope: A business management consulting firm that caters to small businesses. Offers software installation services, tax preparation services and business plan advisory services. **Publications:** "Inflated Real Estate Prices. . .How Did This Happen," Moreno Valley Magazine, Aug, 2005.

200 ■ Avery, Cooper & Co.
4918-50th St.
PO Box 1620
Yellowknife, NT, Canada X1A 2P2
Ph:(867)873-3441
Free: 800-661-0787
Fax:(867)873-2353
Co. E-mail: gerry@averyco.nt.ca
URL: http://www.averyco.nt.ca
Contact: Theresa Slator, Mgr
E-mail: theresa@atsaveryco.nt.ca
Scope: Accounting and management consulting firm. **Seminars:** Sage Software Training. **Special Services:** ACCPAC Plus; Sage Accpac ERP.

201 ■ BAPTurnkey
12 Greenway Plz., Ste. 1100
Houston, TX 77046
Ph:(281)705-0427
Fax:(281)398-8886
Co. E-mail: customercare@bapturnkey.com
URL: http://www.bapturnkey.com
Contact: Greg Businelle, Mgr
Scope: A "turnkey" hardware, internet, and software best practices company. Provides partners and direct hire candidates. Specializes in several industries: industrial, information technology, engineering, finance, and accounting. Turnkey hardware solutions include maintenance and evaluation and support of hardware/network infrastructure. Suggest solutions to supplement current set-up. Turnkey internet solutions incorporate solid design principles. Turnkey software solutions include updating and patching software.

202 ■ Bowie Decimal Systems
719 N 81st St.
Seattle, WA 98103
Ph:(206)715-5261
Fax:(206)783-4236
Co. E-mail: paulinebowie@mac.com
Contact: Pauline Bowie, Principle
Scope: Assists with accounting system installation, conversion, set-up, training, and support for businesses. Works closely with clients' CPA s. Offers continuing on-site support as well as telephone assistance.

203 ■ BRB Business Solutions
80 Washington St.
Barre, VT 05641-4448
Ph:(802)479-0999
Contact: Richard Barton Jr., Principle
Scope: Consultant offers book keeping and management assistance to businesses, including how to use MYOB accounting software.

204 ■ The Business Advisor
6 Main st.
Hamilton, ON, Canada L9S 1M8
Ph:(705)431-0511
Fax:(705)431-0522
Contact: Jacob M. Hoeppner, President
Scope: Assists in the preparation and implementation of efficient systems and procedures. Advises on business and management methods and procedures. Provides temporary interim management solutions for businesses requiring leadership to re-evaluate business direction and operations. Offers accounting and tax advice. Prepares for business succession.

205 ■ Capital Balance L.L.C.
1105 Berea Dr.
Boulder, CO 80305
Ph:(303)579-8893
Fax:(303)554-1555
Co. E-mail: toni@capitalbalance.com
URL: http://www.capitalbalance.com
Contact: Toni Frank, Principle
E-mail: toni@capitalbalance.com
Scope: Accounting system consultant specializing in MYOB installation and proper company set up; training; support by phone, email, or on site; month end and year end procedures, including tax prep; payroll, quarterly reports, and filing of federal and state taxes; implementation of safety programs for workman's compensation; and consulting for new business start up.

206 ■ Century Business Services Inc.
6050 Oak Tree Blvd. S, Ste. 500
Cleveland, OH 44131-6951
Ph:(216)525-1947
Fax:(216)447-9007
Co. E-mail: info@cbiz.com
URL: http://www.cbiz.com
Contact: Steven L. Gerard, CEO
E-mail: gdufour@cbiz.com
Scope: A business consulting and tax services firm providing financial, consulting, tax and business services through seven groups: Financial management, tax advisory, construction and real estate, health-care, litigation support, capital resource and CEO outsource. **Publications:** "FAS 154: Changes in the Way We Report Changes," 2006; "Equity-Based Compensation: How Much Does it Really Cost Your Business," 2006; "Preventing Fraud - Tips for Nonprofit Organizations"; "Today's Workforce and Nonprofit Organizations: Meeting a Critical Need"; "IRS Highlights Top Seven Form 990 Errors". **Seminars:** Health Care - What the Future Holds; Consumer Driven Health Plans; Executive Plans; Health Savings Accounts; Healthy Wealthy and Wise; Legislative Update; Medicare Part D; Retirement Plans.

207 ■ CFO Service
112 Chester Ave.
Saint Louis, MO 63122
Ph:(314)757-2940
Contact: John D. Skae, President
E-mail: jds217@aol.com
Scope: A group of professional executives that provide upper management services to companies that cannot support a full time COO or CFO. Provides clients in the areas of business planning, company policies, contract negotiations, safety policies, product and service pricing, loans management, taxes, cost analysis, loss control and budgeting.

208 ■ CheckMark Software Inc.
724 Whalers Way, Bldg. H, Ste. 101
Fort Collins, CO 80525-7578
Ph:(970)225-0522
Free: 800-444-9922
Fax:(970)225-0611
Co. E-mail: info@checkmark.com
URL: http://www.checkmark.com
Contact: Terry Stone, Dir of Sales
E-mail: rgilmore@checkmark.com
Scope: Developer of accounting software tools for small businesses and provides fast, easy to use, affordable accounting and payroll solutions to small and medium sized businesses. Provides payroll software and multiledger integrated accounting software. **Special Services:** MultiLedger™; Payroll.

209 ■ DacEasy Inc.
1715 N Brown Rd.
Lawrenceville, GA 30043
Ph:(770)492-6414
Free: 800-322-3279
Fax:(770)724-2874
Co. E-mail: sales@daceasy.com
URL: http://www.daceasy.com
Contact: Marchell Gillis
E-mail: marchell.gillis@sage.com
Scope: Develops an accounting system for small businesses that integrates accounting, invoicing, payroll, communications, and management software into a single package. **Seminars:** DacEasy Training. **Special Services:** DacEasy.

210 ■ Emerald Alliance L.L.C.
3170 N Federal Hwy., Ste. 205B
Lighthouse Point, FL 33064
Ph:(954)608-4302
Fax:(954)839-6213
Co. E-mail: info@myob-accounting.com
URL: http://www.myob-accounting.com
Contact: Julie Fitzpatrick, Principle
Scope: Performs business planning, accounting, and tax preparation for companies and individuals. Specializes in MYOB and Netsuite programs. Services include new business set up, conversion to MYOB from another accounting system, training, troubleshooting services, streamlining services and bookkeeping assistance.

211 ■ Fiscal Management Associates L.L.C.
440 Park Ave. S, 3rd Fl.
New York, NY 10016
Ph:(646)403-8040
Fax:(212)630-9922
Co. E-mail: info@fmaonline.net
URL: http://www.fmaonline.net
Contact: Henry Lopez, Mgr
E-mail: jcampayne@atsfmaonline.net
Scope: Firm provides a range of fiscal consulting services to clients in the not-for-profit sector. Services include accounting, bookkeeping, audit preparation; budgeting, cost analysis, grants management; accounting software, FUND E-Z; defining fiscal staff roles and responsibilities; fiscal policies and procedures, internal controls; and fiscal training and coaching for staff and boards. Also provides fiscal management services to New York City charter schools. Supports school leaders through a training and audit support program in partnership. **Publications:** "The Evolution of Human Resources Directors' Responsibilities," The CPA Journal, Jul, 2009; "The Yin and the Yang of Strong Fiscal Infrastructures and Sound Programs," Apr, 2009; "A Countywide Non-profit Call to Action," The Register Star, Feb, 2009; "Fiscal Management: How Do Nonprofits Do It," New York Nonprofit Press, Sep, 2008; "What is the proper role of a nonprofit Chief Financial Officer," CPA Journal, Feb, 2008. **Seminars:** Building on Quality, Strengthening Financial Management Initiative Launch, Jul, 2009; Hands- On Tools for Managing through Tough Times, New York, May, 2009; Creating Investment Policies For Your Nonprofit, May, 2009; Seminars In Nonprofit Excellence, Apr, 2009; The Wallace Foundation Bidders Conference, Chicago, IL, Jan, 2009; The 2009 Nonprofit Economic Climate, Jan, 2009.

212 ■ Gates, Moore & Co.
3340 Peachtree Rd. NE, Tower Pl. 100, Ste. 600
Atlanta, GA 30326
Ph:(404)266-9876
Fax:(404)266-2669
Co. E-mail: postmaster@gatesmoore.com
URL: http://www.gatesmoore.com
Contact: Lori Foley, Principle
E-mail: lfoley@atsgatesmoore.com
Scope: Firm provides management consulting and accounting services to medical practices, hospital owned practices, staff model managed care organizations, IPAs, MSOs, PO, and PHOs. Services include comprehensive operational assessments, managed care negotiations, practice start-ups and expansion, development of MSOs, strategic planning, mergers, cost accounting analysis, practice valuations, income division plans, medical record documentation and coding reviews, expert witness testimony, patient satisfaction surveys and corporate compliance planning. **Publications:** "Practicing Medicine in the 21st Century"; "Physicians, Dentists and Veterinarians"; "Insurance Portability and Accountability Act Privacy Manual"; "How To Guide for your Medical Practice and Health Insurance Portability and Accountability Act Security Manual"; "A How To Guide for your Medical Practice"; "Cost Analysis Made Simple: A Step by Step Guide to Using Cost Accounting to Ensure Practice Profitability"; "Cost Cutting Strategies for Medical Practices"; "Cost Cutting Strategies for Medical Practices"; "Getting the Jump on Year-End Tax Planning"; "New 401(k) Safe Harbor Option: Increased Opportunities for the Physician and Practice"; "Not All Tax News is Bad News"; "Shareholder Agreements: Identifying and Addressing Five Risk Areas"; "Surprise - Your Practice has a Deferred Income Tax Liability". **Seminars:** Documenting and Billing High Risk Codes, 2010; Current Challenges in Ob/Gyn Recruiting, 2010; Planning for Physician Wind-down & Retirement, 2010; HITECH "How To" - Opportunities & Risks, 2010; Pediatric Coding and Audits; Recruiting and Retaining Physicians; How to Prepare for the Recovery Audit Contractors - RAC, 2010; Meaningful Use Rule, 2010; The Revenue Stream in Practice, Apr, 2008; Improving Efficiencies in a Small Family Medicine Practice, Oct, 2007; Using Compensation Models to Improve Performance, Sep, 2007; The Financial Side of Personnel Management, Sep, 2007; Pay for Performance-Is it Really Contracting for Quality?, New York State Ophthalmological Society, Sep, 2007; Beyond the Class Action Settlement Payments-Looking Prospectively at Managed Care Companies Behavior, New York State Ophthalmological Society, Sep, 2007; Protecting your clients from Embezzlement, Jun, 2007; What P4P Means to Your Medical Practice, May, 2007; Finance for the Practicing Physician, May, 2007; Trashing, Dipping and Ghosts in Medical Practices: Protecting your clients from Embezzlement, Apr, 2006.

213 ■ Goldstein & Associates
8380 Waring Ave., Ste. 108
Los Angeles, CA 90069
Ph:(310)657-7161
Fax:(323)658-1034
Co. E-mail: dg90210@aol.com
Contact: David Goldstein, Owner
Scope: Firm provides temporary and permanent employment placement services. Offers career guidance and resume writing for job applicants. Also provides computer consulting to clients in the area of database applications, installation, training and support for small and medium business accounting systems.

214 ■ JLA Consulting
1013 N Causeway Blvd., Ste. 202
Metairie, LA 70001
Ph:(504)835-9639
Fax:(504)835-7850
Co. E-mail: jleonard@jlaconsulting.net
URL: http://www.jlaconsulting.net
Contact: John P. Leonard, Principle
E-mail: jleonard@jlaconsulting.net
Scope: Firm provides implementation of accounting software solutions for small to medium-size businesses. Helps companies evaluate, select and implement computer hardware and software solutions. Provides training and continuing support. Also offers Crystal Report writing and FRx Financial report writing consulting services.

215 ■ Job Finders Employment Service
1729 W Broadway, Ste. 4
Columbia, MO 65203-1190
Ph:(573)446-4250
Fax:(573)446-4257
URL: http://www.jobfindersusa.com
Contact: Ashley Winter, Principle
E-mail: sarahsw@atsjobfindersusa.com
Scope: Firm places professional, para professional and temporary associates. Offers direct, temp to hire, temporary, and contract positions. Placements range from administrative assistants to accounting personnel, to sales support, engineering, and software or web designers.

216 ■ John N. Zaremba
1314 N State St.
Bellingham, WA 98225
Ph:(360)671-1023
Fax:(360)671-3458
Co. E-mail: jackie@zarembacpa.com
URL: http://www.zarembacpa.com
Contact: Brian Paxton, Principle
E-mail: brian@atszarembacpa.com
Scope: A full service public accounting office providing tax preparation services for individuals and businesses, financial statement preparation, and consultation regarding retirement planning and estate and gift tax issues. Also staffs certified MYOB software consultants and provides support services for many accounting software products.

217 ■ Kroll Zolfo Cooper L.L.C.
777 S Figueroa St., 24th Fl.
Los Angeles, CA 90017
Ph:(212)561-4000
Fax:(212)948-4226
Co. E-mail: mwyse@krollzolfocooper.com
URL: http://www.krollzolfocooper.com
Contact: Stephen F. Cooper, Principal
E-mail: scooper@kroll.com
Scope: Firm provides accounting consulting services to businesses. Specializes in restructuring and turnaround consulting; interim and crisis management; performance improvement; creditor advisory; cross-border restructuring and corporate finance.

218 ■ Mary T. Rice
5623 Sugar Ridge Rd.
Crozet, VA 22932
Ph:(434)823-1882
Fax:(434)953-5788
Co. E-mail: ricebooks@cville.net
Contact: Frederick T. Williamson, Owner
E-mail: f1w2@cville.net
Scope: Consultant assists nonprofits with QuickBooks accounting software setup, ongoing accounting operations and financial statements. Also offers training in office administration and management.

219 ■ McCallum & Kudravetz P.C.
250 E High St.
Charlottesville, VA 22902-5178
Ph:(434)293-8191
Fax:(434)296-9641
Co. E-mail: sreid@mkpc.com
URL: http://www.mkpc.com
Contact: Stacie H. Reid, Principle
E-mail: sreid@atsmkpc.com
Scope: Certified Public Accountant provides nonprofit tax preparation and general consulting on nonprofit accounting issues.

220 ■ Midwest Computer Group L.L.C.
6060 Franks Rd.
House Springs, MO 63051-1101
Ph:(636)677-0287
Fax:(636)677-0287
Co. E-mail: sales@mcgcomputer.com
URL: http://www.mcgcomputer.com
Contact: Jeffrey A. Sanford, Mgr
E-mail: jeffrey@atsmcgcomputer.com
Scope: Firm specializes in helping businesses create accounting, marketing and business information systems; software development; and database design and management.

221 ■ Nelson & Pickens
18383 Preston Rd., Ste. 350
Dallas, TX 75252
Ph:(972)380-4096
Fax:(972)380-4096
Contact: Mark Pickens, President
Scope: A full service certified public accounting firm focused on selling, training, and supporting accounting software.

222 ■ Network Telecommunications Consultants
57 Pickering Wharf
Salem, MA 01970
Ph:(978)745-9671
Fax:(978)745-0681
Co. E-mail: psantore@ntcconsultants.com
E-mail: psantore@ntcconsultants.com
Scope: Provides assistance in the planning, selection, and account maintenance of their telecommunications services. Services in telecommunications account planning, management, and auditing.

223 ■ Nonprofit Center of Milwaukee Inc.
2819 W Highland Blvd.
Milwaukee, WI 53208-3217
Ph:(414)344-3933
Fax:(414)344-7071
Co. E-mail: info@nonprofitcentermilwaukee.org
URL: http://www.nonprofitcentermilwaukee.org
Contact: Ylonda Glover, Mgr
E-mail: rsanchez@atsnonprofitcentermilwaukee.org
Scope: Mission is to promote excellence in financial management, offering a comprehensive mix of training, consulting, and contracted services. Consultation and administrative and management services include conference planning, conflict resolution, executive searches, nonprofit accounting, personnel policy review, and retreat and meeting facilitation. **Seminars:** Administrative Support Professionals Round table; Orientation to Starting a Nonprofit: To Be or Not To Be; Triad Leadership: How the Best Fund raising Teams Work; ED Leaders Circle; Learning Circle for Supervisors; Retirement Plans for 501(c)(3) Organizations: Maximizing the Value & Benefits-Minimizing the Costs and Administration.

224 ■ On-Q Software Inc.
13764 SW 11th St.
Miami, FL 33184
Ph:(305)553-2400
Free: 800-553-2862
Fax:(305)220-2666
Co. E-mail: info@on-qsoftware.com
URL: http://www.on-qsoftware.com
Contact: Terry Cajigas, Principle
E-mail: hcajigas@on-qsoftware.com
Scope: Provides the small business community with simple to use, feature rich software. Provides software solutions including time and fixed fee billing, due date tracking and practice manager.

225 ■ Penny & Associates Inc.
166 Water St., Ste. 3
Port Perry, ON, Canada L9L 1C4
Ph:(905)985-0712
Free: 800-699-6190
Fax:(905)985-9461
Co. E-mail: mail@pennyinc.com
URL: http://www.pennyinc.com
Contact: Tracey Hepburn, Principle
E-mail: sbaylis@atspennyinc.com
Scope: Accounting and management firm that offers accounting and business solutions. Assistance in preparation of financial reports, reconciliation of inter company accounts, foreign currency transactions, investment trades and auditor working paper files and assistance in developing accounting policies and procedures. Provides part-time controllers to prepare financial statements, cash flow management, credit negotiations and give financial management advice or oversee accounting staff. **Seminars:** Quick Books, Aug, 2001; How to Stand Up to People Without Being a Jerk; How to Build Influence and Rapport With Almost Anyone; Dealing With Dissatisfied, Different and Difficult People; Effective Public Speaking; How to Incorporate Yourself; Company Perks: Attracting & Retaining Good People; FIRST AID. **Special Services:** Quickbooks[R].

226 ■ Professionals for NonProfits Inc.
515 Madison Ave., Ste. 1100
New York, NY 10022
Ph:(212)546-9091
Fax:(212)546-9094
Co. E-mail: info@nonprofitstaffing.com
URL: http://www.nonprofitstaffing.com
Contact: Gayle A. Brandel, CEO & Pres
E-mail: gbrandel@atsnonprofitstaffing.com
Scope: Firm provides temporary and permanent staff exclusively to non profits, including arts, social service and healthcare organizations, museums, universities, independent schools, cultural institutions, and international organizations. The Perm Division provides permanent staff on a contingency fee basis for senior executive and mid-level management positions as well as administrative and support positions. The Temp Division provides temporary staff and consultants with nonprofit experience in fundraising and special events, grants writing, accounting and book keeping, finance, information technology, administration and office support.

227 ■ R. Shane Chance
1000 W Aztec Blvd.
PO Box 341
Aztec, NM 87410-1867
Ph:(505)334-4375
Fax:(505)334-1850
Co. E-mail: shanechancecpa@qwestoffice.net
URL: http://www.chancecpa.com
Contact: R. Shane Chance, Owner
E-mail: shanechancecpa@qwest.net
Scope: Firm's services include accounting, tax preparation, financial statements and training on MYOB accounting software. Offers installation, setup and on-site customer support for software.

228 ■ RAFFA P.C.
1899 L St. NW, Ste. 900
Washington, DC 20036
Ph:(202)822-5000
Fax:(202)822-0669
Co. E-mail: info@raffa.com
URL: http://www.raffa.com
Contact: Dennis Shine, Partner
E-mail: kraffa@atsraffa.com
Scope: Firm provides a range of accounting, tax, technology, outsourcing, and business advisory services. Specific services include financial projections and forecasts; business valuations; budgeting and cash management; strategic planning; due diligence procedures; investment analysis, products and services; evaluation and structuring of business transactions, mergers, dispositions and reorganizations; establishment of new organizations, charter organizations, affiliates and for-profit and not-for-profit subsidiaries and ventures; grant and contract applications and administration; applications for the Combined Federal and United Way Campaigns; assistance in audits by granting, contracting and taxing authorities; establishment and reevaluation of indirect cost rates. Also provides high-level talent for short term emergencies or long term assignments with CFO, human resource directors, human resource consultants, benefit managers, controllers or bookkeepers, network administrators and web masters.

229 ■ Richard Ditzler
58 W Portal Ave., Ste. 138
San Francisco, CA 94122
Ph:(415)661-6652
Co. E-mail: rditzler@pon.net
E-mail: rditzler@pon.net
Scope: Consultant specializes in providing installation, setup, training, support for MYOB accounting systems, and bookkeeping services.

230 ■ Sphere Consulting Group L.L.C.
12901 Jefferson Hwy., Ste. 922
Baton Rouge, LA 70816

Ph:(225)751-0898
Co. E-mail: info@getsphere.com
URL: http://www.getsphere.com
Contact: Dennis J. Savoie, Managing Partner
E-mail: dennis.savoie@cox.net

Scope: A management consulting firm that provides management consulting in sales and marketing, engineering, information systems, finance, management, research and operations by combining strategies with products, services and technology. The firm's range of consulting services support products, services and technology include general management, finance and accounting, information systems, operations, engineering, research and technology, sales, marketing and customer service.

231 ■ Sterling Management Systems
350 W Arden Ave.
Glendale, CA 91203-1110
Ph:(818)241-1144
Free: 800-933-7538
Fax:(818)241-0271
Co. E-mail: info@sterling.us
URL: http://www.sterling-management.com
Contact: Jerry Alangen, Principle

Scope: Offers business consulting and management training for accountants and healthcare professionals. Offers on-site training and consulting. Designs an individualized program for clients to help them achieve their goals for their practice and to improve quality of life through precise application of Hubbard technology. Creates an organization and an environment that promotes, supports and rewards people for their contribution and productivity. **Seminars:** How to Achieve Your Goals; How Staff Can Increase Sales in the Workplace; Handling Emotions in the Workplace; Successful Team Building; How to Be Happy, Winning and Successful as an Executive; The Secrets to Getting Great Products; Honesty and Integrity in the Workplace; How to Sell More Using the Tone Scale; Improving Business Through Communication; Successful Time Management; How to Be Happy, Winning and Successful; Increasing Productivity and Job Satisfaction.

232 ■ Steve Burns Inc.
Landmark Sq. II, 1708 Dolphin Ave., Ste. 806
Kelowna, BC, Canada V1Y 9S4
Ph:(250)763-4706
Free: 877-763-4022
Fax:877-353-8608
Co. E-mail: steve@burnsinnovation.com
Contact: Steve Burns, Principle
E-mail: steve@burnsinnovation.com

Scope: A full-service accounting firm with experience in advising technology companies on a broad range of financing, accounting, and taxation issues. **Publications:** "Entrepreneurialism Okanagan Style," 2005; "Burns Business Builder Beyond the Box," 2005; "Overhauling Your Sales Effort," 2005; "The Inside/Outside Marketing Measurement System," 2005; "Overhauling Your Marketing Efforts," 2005. **Seminars:** Performance Management Seminar; Marketing Intelligence Part 1; Human Resource Planning/Policies; Four Ways To Grow Your Business; How To Effectively Recruit High Technology Personnel; How To Interview, Select And Hire High Technology Personnel; Making Your Business Really Fly.

233 ■ Steven E. Kramer C.P.A.
8282 University Ave.
La Mesa, CA 91941-3821
Ph:(619)464-8183
Fax:(619)463-6256
Co. E-mail: talltax@ix.netcom.com
E-mail: talltax@ix.netcom.com

Scope: Provides accounting and management services in the following areas: Estate and tax planning, income tax preparation, expert witness services, small business development, professional liability insurance, and professional practice management. **Seminars:** Starting Your Own CPA Firm; Protecting the Small CPA Firm Against Malpractice; Sole Practitioner's Conference; Loss Prevention Conference.

234 ■ The Stillwater Group
920 E Shore Dr.
PO Box 168
Stillwater, NJ 07875
Ph:(973)579-7080
Fax:(973)579-7970
Co. E-mail: education@stillwater.com
URL: http://www.stillwater.com
Contact: David Woodward, COO
E-mail: gfinch@atsstillwater.com

Scope: Provides strategic planning, budget and financial management, process improvement, organizational design and assessment, and college student services operations. **Publications:** "Integrated Resource Planning (Irp)," Business Officer Magazine, 2005; "The Economic Risk Conundrum," University Business Magazine; "Revenue Analysis and Tuition Strategy"; "Managing Advancement Services: Processes and Paper".

235 ■ T. L. Cramer Associates L.L.C.
1788 Broadstone Rd.
Grosse Pointe Woods, MI 48236
Ph:(313)332-0182
Co. E-mail: info@tlcramerassociates.com
URL: http://www.tlcramerassociates.com
Contact: Terry L. Cramer, Principle
E-mail: tlcramer@tlcramerassociates.com

Scope: Firm provides management advisory services to small and mid-sized businesses. Sessions include corporate structure; strategic and operational focus; financial management and issues, including accounting and cash flow; marketing and business development; business planning and implementation; human resources and administrative issues; key management; information technology; and growth and profitability. **Publications:** "Biz Journals"; "Business Week for Small Business"; "Trade Pub".

FRANCHISES AND BUSINESS OPPORTUNITIES

236 ■ Accountants, Inc.
Select Appointments
111 Anza Blvd., No. 400
Burlingame, CA 94010
Ph:(650)579-1111
Free: 800-491-9411

No. of Franchise Units: 16. **No. of Company-Owned Units:** 22. **Founded:** 1986. **Franchised:** 1994. **Description:** Placement for accounting & finance candidates. **Equity Capital Needed:** $144,400-$193,700 + franchise fee. **Franchise Fee:** $30,000. **Financial Assistance:** Yes. **Training:** Yes.

237 ■ CFO Today Inc.
545 E Tennessee St.
Tallahassee, FL 32308
Ph:(850)681-1941
Free: 888-643-1348
Fax:(850)561-1374
URL: http://www.cfotoday.com

No. of Franchise Units: 103. **No. of Company-Owned Units:** 1. **Founded:** 1989. **Franchised:** 1990. **Description:** Offers regional franchise program through which a regional owner solicits local franchisees. Local franchisees operate an accounting and tax practice, utilizing special marketing techniques, in addition to operational and computer systems, to provide tax, record keeping and other services to clients. **Equity Capital Needed:** $24,400-$40,000. **Franchise Fee:** $24,000. **Royalty Fee:** Varies. **Financial Assistance:** No. **Training:** Provides 5 days training at corporate headquarters and 1 day onsite, with ongoing support.

238 ■ Ledgerplus
259 E 7th Ave.
Tallahassee, FL 32303
Ph:(850)561-1374
Free: 888-643-1348

No. of Franchise Units: 156. **No. of Company-Owned Units:** 5. **Founded:** 1989. **Franchised:** 1991. **Description:** Accounting, tax & consultation. **Equity Capital Needed:** $29,000. **Franchise Fee:** $16,000. **Financial Assistance:** Yes. **Training:** Yes.

239 ■ Liquid Capital Canada Corp.
5734 Yonge St., Ste. 400
Toronto, ON, Canada M2M 4E7
Ph:(416)342-8199
Free: (866)272-3704
Fax:(866)611-8886
Co. E-mail: birnbaum@liquidcapitalcorp.com
URL: http://www.lcfranchise.com

No. of Franchise Units: 27. **No. of Company-Owned Units:** 1. **No. of Operating Units:** 63. **Founded:** 1999. **Franchised:** 2000. **Description:** Operation of home-based B2B providing account receivable financing to small business. **Equity Capital Needed:** $200,000. **Franchise Fee:** $50,000. **Training:** Yes.

240 ■ Padgett Business Services
400 Blue Hill Dr., Ste. 201
Westwood, MA 02090
Free: 877-729-8725
Co. E-mail: padgett@smallbizpros.com
URL: http://www.smallbizpros.com

No. of Franchise Units: 400. **Founded:** 1966. **Franchised:** 1975. **Description:** Padgett provides an array of services to small businesses, such as consulting, financial reporting, government compliance, payroll and tax preparation services. Padgett also offers credit card processing, pension and 125 plan administration, equipment financing and workers' compensation payment service. **Equity Capital Needed:** Total investment and net worth &105,955; liquid or cash $78,750. **Franchise Fee:** $56,000. **Financial Assistance:** Third party financing up to $75,000. Also enrolled in the SBA registry. **Training:** Initial training 12 days + field visits, covering marketing, operations, and software. Ongoing training and support is provided through regular seminars in marketing, operations, tax, etc. Support is delivered through toll-free telephone and a wide range of information and material is provided via the company's web site.

241 ■ Sareen & Associates
10702 Vandor Ln.
Manassas, VA 20109
Ph:(703)366-3444
Fax:(703)366-3417

No. of Company-Owned Units: 5. **Founded:** 1993. **Franchised:** 2006. **Description:** Accounting, bookkeeping, taxes and payroll services. **Equity Capital Needed:** $75,800-$145,000. **Franchise Fee:** $20,000. **Royalty Fee:** 15%. **Financial Assistance:** Inhouse equipment financing available.

242 ■ Webber Consulting Group, Inc.
3506 SW Sawgrass Pky.
Ankeny, IA 50023
Ph:(515)419-6122
Fax:(253)679-4351

Description: Franchise development and accounting service.

COMPUTERIZED DATABASES

243 ■ *AICPA Online*
American Institute of Certified Public Accountants
1211 Ave. of the Americas
New York, NY 10036-8775
Ph:(212)596-6200
Free: 888-777-7077
Fax:(212)596-6213
Co. E-mail: service@aicpa.org
URL: http://www.aicpa.org
Contact: Barry C. Melancon, Pres./CEO
E-mail: bmelancon@aicpa.org

Entries Include: Contact information. Principal content of publication is a searchable collection of accounting information, including AICPA news and product information, a site tutorial with navigation tips, links to sites of interest to CPAs, and a students section offering information about the profession and research tips. **Database Includes:** Organizations, colleges, and universities with accounting degree programs.

244 ■ *Daily Tax Report*
The Bureau of National Affairs Inc.
1801 S Bell St.
Arlington, VA 22202
Free: 800-372-1033
Co. E-mail: customercare@bna.com
URL: http://www.bna.com
Description: Contains the complete text of the *Daily Tax Report.* Covers U.S. tax and pension legislation; pertinent court and agency rulings; accounting standards; pension rules; agency personnel charges; federal budget activity; International Revenue Service (IRS) and treasury policy; Congressional deliberations; and executive policy-making. Includes such sections as the following: Today's Summaries—contains a brief overview and summary of the day's most important news and developments in tax law and policy. Congressional and Presidential Calendars—contains the Summary of Congressional actions and a schedule of Presidential activities including bills introduced, scheduled for hearings, and enacted. Taxation, Budget, and Accounting—contains news reports of legislative and regulatory developments affecting tax policy including reports of federal budget developments, coverage of policy, personnel, and administrative changes in the IRS and Treasury Department, and developments in pension rules, policies, and legislation. Court Decisions—provides reports of federal court decisions including summaries of facts and holdings and partial text of options. rulings, revenue procedures, notices, and other announcements arranged by Internal Revenue Code Section. Court Decisions—provides reports of federal court decisions including summaries of facts and holdings and partial text of options. **Availability:** Online: Thomson Reuters, The Bureau of National Affairs Inc. **Type:** Full text.

245 ■ *e-JEP*
American Economic Association
2014 Broadway, Ste. 305
Nashville, TN 37203
Ph:(615)322-2595
Fax:(615)343-7590
Co. E-mail: aeainfo@vanderbilt.edu
URL: http://www.vanderbilt.edu/AEA
Description: Contains the full text of the *Journal of Economic Perspectives.* Includes articles, reports, and other material for economists and economics professionals. Features analysis and critiques of recent research findings and developments in public policy. Includes coverage of global economics issues and developments. Features articles on education in economics, employment issues for economists, and other issues of concern to professional economists. **Availability:** Online: American Economic Association, Thomson Reuters; CD-ROM: American Economic Association. **Type:** Full text.

246 ■ *ProQuest Accounting & Tax*
ProQuest LLC
789 E Eisenhower Pky.
PO Box 1346
Ann Arbor, MI 48106-1346
Ph:(734)761-4700
Free: 800-521-0600
Fax:(734)761-6450
Co. E-mail: info@proquest.com
URL: http://www.proquest.com
Description: Contains citations and abstracts to more than 2300 key publications in accounting, financial management, taxation, and auditing worldwide. Also provides citations to articles in more than 800 newspapers, business journals, dissertations and news magazines. Titles include *The Internal Auditor, Inside Public Accounting, Journal of Accounting and Finance Research, Journal of the American Taxation Association*, and the *National Tax Journal.* **Availability:** Online: ProQuest LLC, ProQuest LLC, ProQuest LLC. **Type:** Bibliographic.

247 ■ *State Tax Notes*
Tax Analysts
400 S Maple Ave., Ste. 400
Falls Church, VA 22046
Ph:(703)533-4400
Free: 800-955-2444
Co. E-mail: cservice@tax.org
URL: http://www.taxanalysts.com
Description: Follows tax developments in every state, and keeps track of interstate trends. Covers multi-state Organizations, state tax conferences, tax decisions from courts nationwide, rulings and regulations from revenue departments, and legislation from all 50 states each week. **Availability:** Online: LexisNexis Group. **Type:** Full text.

248 ■ *State Tax Today*
Tax Analysts
400 S Maple Ave., Ste. 400
Falls Church, VA 22046
Ph:(703)533-4400
Free: 800-955-2444
Co. E-mail: cservice@tax.org
URL: http://www.taxanalysts.com
Description: Covers tax news and documents from every state, the District of Columbia, and all U.S. possessions, complete with summaries and full text of legislation. Includes proposed and finalized regulations, *Revenue Rulings & Procedures*, supreme, appellate, and tax court opinions, and private letter rulings. **Availability:** Online: Tax Analysts. **Type:** Full text.

249 ■ *The Tax Directory*
Tax Analysts
400 S Maple Ave., Ste. 400
Falls Church, VA 22046
Ph:(703)533-4400
Free: 800-955-2444
Co. E-mail: cservice@tax.org
URL: http://www.taxanalysts.com
Description: Contains information on more than 20,000 tax professionals. Vol. One Government Officials Worldwide including state and federal officials, including taxwriting committees U.S. Department of Treasury and IRS, Tax Court Judges, International Financial Specialists, Tax and Business Journalists, Professional Associations, and Tax Groups and Coalitions. Vol. Two Corporate Tax Managers including names and contact information for tax managers in largest U.S corporations. Entries including industry description derived from the Securities and Exchange Commission's four-digit Standard Industry Classification code used by the listed companies for filing purposes. **Availability:** Online: LexisNexis Group; CD-ROM: Tax Analysts. **Type:** Directory.

250 ■ *Tax Notes Today*
Tax Analysts
400 S Maple Ave., Ste. 400
Falls Church, VA 22046
Ph:(703)533-4400
Free: 800-955-2444
Co. E-mail: cservice@tax.org
URL: http://www.taxanalysts.com
Description: Provides daily tax news coverage, including the complete text of items to be published in *Tax Notes.* Includes news items and feature articles on tax developments, tax policy issues, and congressional developments. Also provides the complete text of all Internal Revenue Service (IRS) regulations and selected relevant court opinions, summaries of tax-related correspondence between the U.S. Treasury and the tax bar, IRS letter rulings and Technical Advice Memoranda, *Congressional Record* items, IRS manual changes, and public comments on IRS regulations. Also provides the complete text of such documents as the IRS General Counsel Memoranda, Technical Memoranda, and Actions on Decisions; IRS revenue rulings and revenue procedures; the House-Senate Conference Committee Report on the Tax Reform Act of 1986; and tax-related news releases and reports from the IRS, U.S. Treasury, General Accounting Office, Congressional Budget Office, and other sources. Also contains the complete text of IRS publications for taxpayers' use in preparing tax returns, and references to individuals and organizations involved in tax-related issues from *The Federal Tax Directory.* Beginning with September 1985, the complete text of federal court decisions affecting taxation is available. **Availability:** Online: ProQuest LLC, LexisNexis Group, PricewaterhouseCoopers LLP. **Type:** Full text.

251 ■ *Weekly Report*
The Bureau of National Affairs Inc.
1801 S Bell St.
Arlington, VA 22202
Free: 800-372-1033
Co. E-mail: customercare@bna.com
URL: http://www.bna.com/tax-accounting-t5000
Description: Contains the complete text of *Tax Management Weekly Report*, a newsletter covering legislative, regulatory, judicial, and policy actions related to taxation and accounting. Provides summaries of selected cases, Internal Revenue Service (IRS) rulings and procedures, private letter rulings by code section, and general counsel and technical memoranda. **Availability:** Online: The Bureau of National Affairs Inc., Thomson Reuters. **Type:** Full text.

COMPUTER SYSTEMS/ SOFTWARE

252 ■ Accountant's Relief
AccountantsWorld
140 Fell Ct.
Hauppauge, NY 11788
Ph:888-999-1366
Free: 800-829-7354
Fax:800-927-1283
Co. E-mail: contactus@accountantsworld.com
URL: http://www.accountantsworld.com
Description: Available for IBM computers and compatibles. System prepares 53 tax forms and schedules and calculates various personal and business taxes.

253 ■ BNA Estate and Gift Tax Planner
BNA Software Inc.
1801 S Bell St.
Arlington, VA 22202
Ph:800-424-2938
Free: 800-424-2938
Fax:(703)341-2938
Co. E-mail: software@bna.com
URL: http://www.bnasoftware.com
Price: Contact BNA. **Description:** Available for IBM computers. System calculates federal and state taxes for the estates of spouses.

254 ■ BNA Fixed Asset Management System
BNA Software Inc.
1801 S Bell St.
Arlington, VA 20037
Ph:800-424-2938
Free: 800-424-2938
Fax:(703)341-2938
Co. E-mail: software@bna.com
URL: http://www.bnasoftware.com
Price: Contact BNA. **Description:** Available for IBM computers and compatibles. System provides depreciation calculations for state and federal purposes.

255 ■ BNA Income Tax Planner
BNA Software Inc.
1801 S Bell St.
Arlington, VA 20037
Ph:800-424-2938
Free: 800-424-2938
Fax:(703)341-2938
Co. E-mail: software@bna.com
URL: http://www.bnasoftware.com
Price: Contact BNA. **Description:** Available for IBM computers and compatibles. Calculates federal and state individual income taxes.

256 ■ CPA Client Master
Management Systems, Inc.
2629 Redwing Rd.
Ft. Collins, CO 80527
Ph:(970)223-1530
Fax:(970)223-3004
URL: http://www.msifc.com
Description: Available for IBM computers and compatibles. System maintains client information for CPAs.

257 ■ FAS Fixed Asset Programs–Sage Software SB, Inc.
Best Software, Inc.
2325 Dulles Corner Blvd., Ste. 800
Herndon, VA 20171
Ph:(703)793-2700
Free: 800-368-2405
Fax:(703)793-2770
URL: http://www.sagenorthamerica.com
Price: Description: Windows based. System calculates taxes and provides comparisons of tax liability over a certain number of years.

258 ■ TAX/PACK: Professional 1040
Alpine Data, Inc.
Division of Analytical Processes Corp.
737 S Townsend Ave.
Montrose, CO 81401
Ph:(805)525-1040
Free: 800-525-1040
Fax:(970)249-8511
Co. E-mail: info@taxpack.com
URL: http://www.alpinedata.com
Price: $410 (with laser), $245 (without laser). **Description:** Available for IBM computers and compatibles. Provides tax form preparation.

259 ■ Tax$imple
AJV Computerized Data Management, Inc.
8 Emery Ave.
Randolph, NJ 07869
Ph:(973)989-8955
Free: 800-989-8955
Fax:(973)366-5877
Co. E-mail: support@taxsimple.com
URL: http://www.taxsimple.com/
Price: Contact TaxSimple for Pricing. **Description:** Available for IBM computers and compatibles. System for tax professionals offering tax form input, calculations, tables, schedules, and printing options.

LIBRARIES

260 ■ Brooklyn Public Library Business Library
280 Cadman Plaza, W.
Tillary St.
Brooklyn, NY 11201
Ph:(718)623-7000
Co. E-mail: busref@brooklynpubliclibrary.org
URL: http://www.brooklynpubliclibrary.org/business
Contact: Dionne Mack-Harvin, Exec.Dir.
Scope: Accounting, advertising, business management, business procedure, career development and employment, finance, insurance, investment, public relations, small business, real estate. **Services:** Copying; Library open to the public. **Holdings:** 133,000 books; 730,000 microfiche; 22,000 reels of microfilm; 1000 directories; 120 videocassettes and DVDs; selective U.S. government documents depository. **Subscriptions:** 700 journals and other serials; 5 newspapers.

261 ■ Caixa Geral do Depositos SA CGD Mediateca e Centro de Informacao Europeia
Edificio-Sede da CGD, Av Joao XXI, 63
P-1000 Lisbon, Portugal
Co. E-mail: ana.monteiro@cgd.pt
URL: http://www.cgd.pt
Scope: Finance. **Services:** Centre open to the public. **Holdings:** 40,000 volumes. **Subscriptions:** 1000 journals and other serials.

262 ■ Canada Office of the Auditor General Knowledge Centre Library
240 Sparks St., 11th Fl. W.
Ottawa, ON, Canada K1A 0G6
Ph:(613)952-0213
Fax:(613)943-5485
Co. E-mail: deborah.maclean@oag-bvg.gc.ca
URL: http://www.oag-bvg.gc.ca/
Contact: Deb MacLean, Mgr.
Scope: Accounting, auditing, public administration, finance, management. **Services:** Interlibrary loan; copying; SDI; Library open to the public by appointment. **Holdings:** 20,000 books; AV items. **Subscriptions:** 400 journals and other serials.

263 ■ CMA Ontario–Member Services Centre
70 University Ave., Ste. 101
Toronto, ON, Canada M5J 2M4
Ph:(416)204-3142
Fax:(416)977-1365
Co. E-mail: msc@cma-ontario.org
Contact: Patricia Black, Mgr., Member Svcs.Ctr.
Scope: Accounting, management, finance, strategy, taxation, investments. **Services:** Copying; SDI; Library not open to the public. **Holdings:** 2069 books; 267 videocassettes; 184 audiocassettes; 6 videodiscs. **Subscriptions:** 53 journals and other serials; 2 newspapers.

264 ■ Deloitte & Touche LLP Library
350 S. Grand Ave., Ste. 200
Two California Plaza
Los Angeles, CA 90071-3462
Ph:(213)688-0800
Fax:(213)688-0100
URL: http://www.deloitte.com
Contact: Elizabeth Carranza, Hd.Libn.
Scope: Auditing, taxation, management consultation, actuarial services, employee benefits, valuation consultation. **Services:** Library not open to the public. **Holdings:** Figures not available.

265 ■ Ernst & Young Center for Business Knowledge
1 Victory Pk., Ste. 2000
2323 Victory Ave.
Dallas, TX 75219
Ph:(214)969-8000
Fax:(214)969-8587
URL: http://www.ey.com
Contact: Tommy M. Yardley, Reg.Res.Mgr.
Scope: Consulting, accounting, tax accounting, auditing. **Services:** Center open to the public at librarian's discretion.

266 ■ Ernst & Young Center for Business Knowledge Libraries
1220 Skylight Office Twr.
1660 W. 2nd St.
Cleveland, OH 44113
Ph:(216)737-1355
Fax:(216)622-0199
Scope: Accounting, auditing, management, consulting. **Services:** Interlibrary loan; copying; Center not open to the public. **Holdings:** 1000 volumes. **Subscriptions:** 500 journals and other serials; 15 newspapers.

267 ■ Ernst & Young Library
875 E. Wisconsin Ave.
Milwaukee, WI 53202
Ph:(414)273-5900
URL: http://www.ey.com
Contact: Julie Porter, Sr.Mgr.
Scope: Taxation, tax law, accounting, auditing. **Services:** Performs searches on fee basis for clients only. **Holdings:** 1200 books. **Subscriptions:** 35 journals and other serials.

268 ■ Ernst & Young LLP Center for Business Knowledge
5 Times Sq.
New York, NY 10019
Ph:(212)773-3000
Fax:(212)773-6350
Co. E-mail: center_for_business_knowledge@ey.com
URL: http://www.ey.com/cbk
Scope: Accounting and auditing, taxation, finance. **Services:** Interlibrary loan; Library open to clients and SLA members. **Holdings:** 3500 books. **Subscriptions:** 500 journals and other serials.

269 ■ Illinois CPA Society–Information & Research Center
550 W. Jackson, Ste. 900
Chicago, IL 60661-5716
Ph:(312)601-4613
Free: 800-993-0407 (Illinois
Fax:(312)906-8045
Co. E-mail: research@icpas.org
URL: http://www.icpas.org
Contact: Michele Courtney, Asst.Dir.
Scope: Accounting; auditing; taxation; business. **Services:** Library open to the public with restrictions. **Holdings:** 5500 books; 50 bound periodical volumes; 225 microfilms. **Subscriptions:** 120 journals and other serials.

270 ■ Institute of Management Accountants–McLeod Information Center
10 Paragon Dr., Ste. 1
Montvale, NJ 07645-1718
Ph:(201)573-9000, x1535
Free: 800-638-4427
URL: http://www.imanet.org
Scope: Management and financial accounting, management and financial management. **Services:** Library open to members only. **Holdings:** 5000 books; 450 bound periodical volumes; 30 VF drawers. **Subscriptions:** 30 journals and other serials.

271 ■ KPMG–Research Centre
777 Dunsmuir St.
PO Box 10426
Vancouver, BC, Canada V7Y 1K3
Ph:(604)691-3000
Fax:(604)691-3031
URL: http://www.kpmg.ca
Contact: Julian Richards, Libn.
Scope: Accounting, tax, general business, stocks. **Services:** SDI; Library not open to the public. **Holdings:** 1000 books; 70 bound periodical volumes. **Subscriptions:** 50 journals and other serials; 6 newspapers.

272 ■ KPMG Resource Centre
160 Elgin St., Ste. 2000
Ottawa, ON, Canada K2P 2P8
Ph:(613)212-2844
Fax:(613)212-2896
Co. E-mail: hopebell@kpmg.ca
URL: http://www.kpmg.ca/en/
Contact: Hope A. Bell, Mgr.Rsrc.Ctr.
Scope: Economics, accounting, government. **Services:** Interlibrary loan; copying; Performs searches on fee basis. **Holdings:** 2000 books. **Subscriptions:** 20 journals and other serials; 5 newspapers.

273 ■ PricewaterhouseCoopers–Research Centre
1250 Boul Rene-Levesque O
Bureau 2800
Montreal, QC, Canada H3B 2G4
Ph:(514)205-5105
Fax:(514)876-1502
Co. E-mail: dany.lessard@ca.pwc.com
URL: http://www.pwc.com/ca
Contact: Dany Lessard, Mgr.
Scope: Accounting, tax, management, business, finance. **Subscriptions:** 200 journals and other serials.

274 ■ Protape, Inc. Library
1540 Broadway
New York, NY 10036
Contact: Richard Sobelsohn
Scope: Accounting, law, real estate, English, math, insurance, travel, taxation, stock broker, medical billing, claims adjusting, private investigation, paralegal. **Services:** Library not open to the public. **Holdings:** 25,000 books; 250 bound periodical volumes. **Subscriptions:** 65 journals and other serials; 20 newspapers.

275 ■ U.S. Dept. of the Treasury–Treasury Library
1500 Pennsylvania Ave. NW, Rm. 1428
Washington, DC 20220
Ph:(202)622-0990
Co. E-mail: library.reference@do.treas.gov
URL: http://www.ustreas.gov/offices/management/privacy-records
Contact: Judy Lim-Sharpe, Chf.Libn.
Scope: Taxation, public finance, law, domestic and International economics, economic conditions and management. **Services:** Interlibrary loan within D.C.; copying; Library open to the public by appointment

for reference use only. **Holdings:** 70,000 books and bound periodical volumes; 500,000 microforms. **Subscriptions:** 300 journals and other serials; 6 newspapers.

276 ■ U.S. Tax Court Library
400 2nd St., NW
Washington, DC 20217
Ph:(202)521-4585
Fax:(202)521-4574
Co. E-mail: tclib@ustaxcourt.gov
Contact: Elsa B. Silverman, Libn.
Scope: Federal tax law - income, estate, and gift. **Services:** Interlibrary loan; Library not open to the public. **Holdings:** 60,000 books; 9000 bound periodical volumes; Congressional Record, Federal Register, and federal tax legislation. **Subscriptions:** 200 journals and other serials.

277 ■ University of Kentucky–Business & Economics Information Center
B&E Info. Ctr., Rm. 116
335-BA Gatton College of Business & Economics
Lexington, KY 40506-0034
Ph:(859)257-5868
Fax:(859)323-9496
Co. E-mail: mrazeeq@pop.uk.edu
URL: http://www.uky.edu//Provost/academicprograms.html
Contact: Michael A. Razeeq, Bus.Ref.Libn.
Scope: Business, economics, business management, marketing, finance, accounting. **Services:** Library open to the public for reference use only.

Adult Day Care Center

START-UP INFORMATION

278 ■ "Caring Concern" in *Small Business Opportunities* (September 2010)
Pub: Harris Publications Inc.
Description: Profile of Joshua Hoffman, founder and CEO of HomeWell Senior Care, Inc., provider of non-medical live-in and hourly personal care, companionship and homemaker services for seniors so they can remain in their own homes.

279 ■ *There's Someplace Like Home: Developing an Adult Day Care Center in Your Church*
Pub: Westminster John Knox Press
Ed: Donna T. Lott. **Released:** 1999. **Price:** $4.50.

ASSOCIATIONS AND OTHER ORGANIZATIONS

280 ■ Assisted Living Federation of America
1650 King St., Ste. 602
Alexandria, VA 22314-2747
Ph:(703)894-1805
Fax:(703)894-1831
Co. E-mail: rgrimes@alfa.org
URL: http://www.alfa.org
Contact: Richard Grimes MEd, Pres./CEO
Description: Providers of assisted living, state associations of providers, and others interested or involved in the industry. Promotes the interests of the assisted living industry and works to enhance the quality of life for the population it serves. Provides a forum for assisted living providers to unite, exchange information, and interact. Encourages the development of high standards for the industry. Promotes the concept of assisted living facilities with public and private agencies and other professionals. Works to educate providers and the public and increase national awareness of assisted living. Sponsors speakers' bureau, conferences, educational opportunities, trade show, research & training products. **Publications:** *ALFA Alert* (weekly); *ALFA Executive Portfolio: Inside the Minds of the Leaders in Assisted Living and Senior Housing*; *Assisted Living Executive* (9/year); *Guide to Choosing an Assisted Living Residence* .

281 ■ Little Brothers - Friends of the Elderly
28 E Jackson Blvd., Ste. 405
Chicago, IL 60604
Ph:(312)829-3055
Fax:(312)829-3077
Co. E-mail: national@littlebrothers.org
URL: http://www.littlebrothers.org
Contact: Elisa T. Drew, Natl. Exec. Dir.
Description: Seeks to combat the isolation and loneliness often experienced by elderly people by providing friendship and special assistance. Sponsors visitation programs, holiday and birthday parties, and summer vacations. Provides transportation for shopping and doctor's visits, food packages, and other "special touches." Also offers information, referrals, and contacts with other public or private agencies. **Publications:** *Little Brothers Bulletin* (3/year).

282 ■ National Adult Day Services Association
1421 E Broad St., Ste. 425
Fuquay Varina, NC 27526
Free: 877-745-1440
Fax:(919)552-0254
Co. E-mail: nadsanews@gmail.com
URL: http://www.nadsa.org
Contact: Linda Alexander-Lieblang, Chair
Description: Adult daycare practitioners; health and social service planners; individuals involved in planning and providing services for older persons. (Daycare centers offer services in a group setting ranging from active rehabilitation to social and health care.) Promotes and enhances adult daycare programs; provides services and activities for disabled older persons on a long-term basis; provides training and technical assistance and consultation services for daycare personnel; organizes funding; develops standards and guidelines for adult daycare programs; encourages adult daycare centers to participate in local area health planning activities to heighten the effectiveness of adult daycare. Plans and conducts training events for annual meeting and related conferences; maintains annotated bibliography; lobbies for approved public policy positions; surveys state adult daycare regulations and legislation. .

283 ■ National Council on Aging
1901 L St. NW, 4th Fl.
Washington, DC 20036
Ph:(202)479-1200
Free: 800-373-4906
Fax:(202)479-0735
Co. E-mail: info@ncoa.org
URL: http://www.ncoa.org
Contact: Dr. James P. Firman EdD, Pres./CEO
Description: Serves as a national voice and powerful advocate on behalf of older Americans. Has developed programs such as Benefits CheckUp, Foster Grandparents and Family Friends. Works with thousands of its community organization members nationwide to provide needed services to the elderly. Members include senior centers, area agencies on aging, employment services, congregate meal sites, faith congregations, health centers and senior housing. Accredits senior centers nationally; provides consumer information for older Americans on health care and related programs and insurance; directs an intergenerational volunteer program that matches mature men and women with children and families at risk; Best Practices encompasses a series of research projects that have provided best practices for senior centers and other community based organizations in health care and other areas; administers two federal programs (Senior Community Service Employment Service and Senior Environmental Program), and the Maturity Works partnership that provide employment and training opportunities for mature adults through offices nationwide. **Publications:** *Abstracts in Social Gerontology* (quarterly).

REFERENCE WORKS

284 ■ "$20M Aimed at Affordable Los Angeles Seniors Housing" in *Commercial Property News* (March 17, 2008)
Pub: Nielsen Company
Description: Grand Plaza Apartments in Los Angeles, California will be renovated in order to maintain housing for over 400 low-income seniors. Details of plans are included.

285 ■ "Advancing the Ball" in *Inside Healthcare* (Vol. 6, December 2010, No. 7, pp. 31)
Pub: RedCoat Publishing Inc.
Ed: Michelle McNickle. **Description:** Profile of Medicalodges an elder-care specialty company that provides both patient care and technology development. President and CEO of the firm believes that hiring good employees is key to growth for any small business.

286 ■ "Big Sell-Off At Sunwest" in *The Business Journal-Portland* (Vol. 25, July 25, 2008, No. 20, pp. 1)
Pub: American City Business Journals, Inc.
Ed: Robin J. Moody. **Description:** Oregon's largest operator of assisted living facilities Sunwest Management Inc. is expected to sell 132 of its properties. The planned sale, which is believed to be worth more than $1 billion, will help Sunwest pay creditors and investors. Other views and information on the planned sale, as well as on Sunwest's services which include adult day care, are presented.

287 ■ "Connecting the Dots Between Wellness and Elder Care" in *Benefits and Compensation Digest* (Vol. 47, August 2010, No. 8, pp. 18)
Pub: International Foundation of Employee Benefit Plans
Ed: Sandra Timmermann. **Description:** Employees caring for aged and infirm parents deal with time and financial issues and other stresses. The connection between health status of caregivers and employers' health care costs could be aided by linking programs and benefits with wellness and caregiving.

288 ■ "Elder Care Costs Surge" in *National Underwriter Life & Health* (Vol. 114, November 8, 2020, No. 21, pp. 25)
Pub: Summit Business Media
Ed: Trevor Thomas. **Description:** Nursing home and assisted living rates rose from 2009 to 2010, according to MetLife Mature Market Institute. Statistical data included.

289 ■ "Elder Care, Rx Drugs Reforms Top Zoeller's Agenda" in *Times* (December 21, 2010)
Pub: The Times
Ed: Sarah Tompkins. **Description:** Indiana Attorney General Greg Zoeller is hoping to develop a program in the state that will help regulate care for the elderly; freeze medical licenses for doctors involved in

criminal investigations; address illegal drug use; and to establish a program to help individuals dispose of old prescription medications easily at pharmacies.

290 ■ "Elder-Care Seminar to Teach Ways to Avoid Falls" in *Virginian-Pilot* (November 25, 2010)
Pub: Virginian-Pilot
Ed: Amy Jeter. **Description:** ResCare HomeCare, a home health services firm, offers free seminars on helping to make residences safer for seniors prone to falling.

291 ■ "EVMS Gets Grant to Train Providers for Elder Care" in *Virginian-Pilot* (October 29, 2010)
Pub: Virginian-Pilot
Ed: Elizabeth Simpson. **Description:** Eastern Virginia Medical School received a federal grant to train health providers in elder care. Details of the program are provided.

292 ■ "Face Issues if Elder Care, Unemployment Collide" in *Atlanta Journal-Constitution* (December 26, 2010, pp. G1)
Pub: Atlanta Journal-Constitution
Ed: Amy Lindgren. **Description:** More issues arise during holiday for families with older members requiring care, including the issue of employment for those doing the caregiving.

293 ■ "GeckoSystems Reduces Sensor Fusion Costs Due to Elder Care Robot Trials" in *Internet Wire* (December 14, 2010)
Pub: Comtex
Description: GeckoSystems International Corporation has been able to reduce the cost of its sensor fusion system while maintaining reliability and performance. The firm's ongoing first in-home elder care robot trials have sparked interest regarding its business model, technologies available for licensing, and joint domestic and international ventures.

294 ■ *How to Start a Home-Based Senior Care Business: Check-in-Care, Transportation Services, Shopping and Cooking*
Pub: The Globe Pequot Press
Ed: James L. Ferry. **Released:** January 1, 2010. **Price:** $18.95. **Description:** Information is provided to start a home-based senior care business.

295 ■ *National Directory of Adult Day Care Centers*
Pub: Health Resources Publishing
Released: Irregular, latest edition 2002, 3rd edition. **Price:** $39.95, individuals print; $995, individuals database on CD. **Covers:** Over 3,200 centers and programs providing adult day care; 1,100 are described in detail. **Entries Include:** Center or program name, address, phone, director or coordinator name; detailed listings include programs, providing sponsor information, geographic area served, fees, number of clients and staff, hours and days of operation, client eligibility criteria, services and activities offered. **Arrangement:** Geographical. **Indexes:** Executive director, Alphabetical county, social models, medicals models.

296 ■ "New Elder Care Center to Focus on Residents with Failing Memories" in *Tulsa World* (November 30, 2010)
Pub: World Publishing
Ed: Robert Evatt. **Description:** People with Alzheimer's disease and other mental disorders require specialized care. Constant Care Management Company runs 'memory care' centers designed for the elderly with such conditions.

297 ■ "Renewed Vision" in *Hawaii Business* (Vol. 54, August 2008, No. 2, pp. 49)
Pub: Hawaii Business Publishing
Ed: Jason Ubay. **Description:** Saint Francis Healthcare System of Hawaii, ranked 81 in Hawaii's top 250 companies for 2008, has been rebranding to focus on senior community healthcare and sold some of its operations, which explains the decline in gross sales from $219.5M in 2006 to $122.7M in 2007. The system's senior services and home hospice service expansion are provided.

298 ■ "Silver Dollars" in *Small Business Opportunities* (September 2008)
Pub: Entrepreneur Media Inc.
Description: Profile of Always Best Care Senior Services, a franchise created by Michael Newman, which offers non-medical In-Home Care, Personal Emergency Response Systems, and Assisted Living Placement Services to seniors; the company offers franchisees the opportunity to fill what is oftentimes a void for the seniors and their families in the community.

299 ■ "State Budget Woes Hurt Many Vendors, Senior Services" in *Sacramento Business Journal* (Vol. 25, August 15, 2008, No. 24, pp. 1)
Pub: American City Business Journals, Inc.
Ed: Melanie Turner. **Description:** Delays in the passage of the California state budget have adversely affected the health care industry. The Robertson Adult Day Health Care had taken out loans to keep the business afloat. The state Legislature has reduced Medi-Cal reimbursement to health care providers by 10 percent.

STATISTICAL SOURCES

300 ■ *Adult Day Care in America: Summary of a National Survey*
Pub: National Council on the Aging (NCOA)
Ed: Ruth Van Behren. **Released:** 1986. **Price:** $5.95 (paper).

301 ■ *Adult Day Care: Findings From a National Survey*
Pub: Johns Hopkins University Press
Ed: William G. Weissert, Jennifer M. Elston, Elise J. Bolda, William N. Zelman, Elizabeth Mutran and Anne B. Magnum. **Released:** 1990.

TRADE PERIODICALS

302 ■ *Adult Day Services Letter*
Pub: Health Resources Publishing
Contact: Beth-Ann Kerber, Managing Editor
Released: Monthly. **Price:** $97, individuals. **Description:** Provides crucial management information and serves as a link between adult day programs across the country.

303 ■ *Clinical Gerontologist*
Pub: Routledge Journals
Contact: Daniel L. Segal PhD, Assoc. Ed.
Released: Quarterly. **Price:** $108 online; $113 print & online. **Description:** Contains practical information and research on assessment and intervention of mental health needs of aged patients.

304 ■ *Homecare Administrative HORIZONS*
Pub: Beacon Health Corp.
Contact: Diane J. Omdahl RN, MS, Editor-in-Chief
Released: Monthly. **Price:** $347, individuals. **Description:** Provides homecare agency management information on all kinds of business and personnel topics. Incorporates comprehensive how-to information, current regulatory requirements, and documentation strategies. Runs a series of articles, including how to move into managed care, how to manage and measure outcomes, how to survive scrutiny by medicare's fraud squad, strengthening agency/physician relationships, and personnel issues. Recurring features include columns titled Peaks & Valleys, Fine-tuning the Fundamentals, Clearing the Fog, and Higher Ground.

305 ■ *Homecare DIRECTION*
Pub: Beacon Health Corp.
Contact: Diane J. Omdahl RN, MS, Editor-in-Chief
Released: Monthly. **Price:** $337. **Description:** Delivers timely regulatory information with how-to elements to apply to everyday care delivery. Equips agency patient care personnel with knowledge they need to deliver quality care and comply with medicare certification and reimbursement requirements. Offers valuable tips on interpreting medicare rules to justify care; how to create policies that reduce survey surprises, and documentation tips and examples. Recurring features include columns titled Documenting with Impact, Survey Sense, Looking for Direction, and From the Lamp Room.

VIDEOCASSETTES/ AUDIOCASSETTES

306 ■ *Aging Population: Caring for the Family*
American Society for Training and Development (ASTD)
1640 King St.
Box 1443
Alexandria, VA 22313-2043
Ph:(703)683-8100
Free: 800-628-2783
Fax:(703)683-8103
URL: http://www.astd.org
Released: 1987. **Price:** $250.00. **Description:** A program for professional caregivers about the growing elderly population and its impact on our society. Covers the problems of nostlagia involved in caring for the elderly and the many misconceptions about them. **Availability:** VHS; 3/4U.

307 ■ *Alzheimer's Disease: Effects on Communication*
American Society for Training and Development (ASTD)
1640 King St.
Box 1443
Alexandria, VA 22313-2043
Ph:(703)683-8100
Free: 800-628-2783
Fax:(703)683-8103
URL: http://www.astd.org
Released: 1986. **Price:** $250.00. **Description:** A program for professionals about the signs and symptoms of Alzheimer's disease and how to determine the nature of communicative changes in patients. **Availability:** VHS; 3/4U.

308 ■ *Art with the Elders in Long-Term Care*
Filmakers Library, Inc.
124 E. 40th St.
New York, NY 10016
Ph:(212)808-4980
Free: 800-555-9815
Fax:(212)808-4983
URL: http://www.filmakers.com
Released: 1985. **Description:** Filmed at Hillhaven Convalescent Hospital, this film describes the art program developed for people over 80 years old. **Availability:** VHS; 3/4U.

309 ■ *Assessment & Intervention: The Confused Elderly*
Kinetic Film Enterprises Ltd.
255 Delaware Ave.
Buffalo, NY 14202
Ph:(716)856-7631
Free: 800-466-7631
Fax:(716)856-7838
Co. E-mail: info@kineticvideo.com
URL: http://www.kineticvideo.com
Released: 1986. **Price:** $295.00. **Description:** Two different ways of dealing with older people who have grown confused are suggested for health care pros. **Availability:** VHS; 3/4U.

TRADE SHOWS AND CONVENTIONS

310 ■ Senior Housing South
Merchandise Mart Properties Inc.
222 Merchandise Mart, Ste. 470
Chicago, IL 60654
Free: 800-677-6278
URL: http://www.merchandisemart.com
Released: Annual. **Principal Exhibits:** Equipment, supplies, and services for the planning, building, design and management of long-term care facilities.

FRANCHISES AND BUSINESS OPPORTUNITIES

311 ■ Aging Excellence
115 Middle St., Ste. 100
PO Box 8660
Portland, ME 04104
Ph:(207)771-0991
Fax:(207)771-0958
No. of Franchise Units: 8. **Founded:** 1999. **Franchised:** 2003. **Description:** Non-medical senior care services. **Equity Capital Needed:** $61,600-$89,600 total investment. **Franchise Fee:** $35,000. **Royalty Fee:** 5%. **Financial Assistance:** Third party financing available. **Training:** Provides 1 week at headquarters, 2 days onsite with ongoing support.

312 ■ AristoCare
698 E Wetmore Rd., Ste. 200
Tucson, AZ 85715
Ph:(520)577-4825
Fax:(520)721-1915
No. of Franchise Units: 2. **No. of Company-Owned Units:** 3. **Founded:** 1999. **Franchised:** 2003. **Description:** Senior care services. **Equity Capital Needed:** $148,900-$259,400. **Franchise Fee:** $36,000. **Royalty Fee:** 5-6%. **Financial Assistance:** No. **Training:** Yes.

313 ■ CareMinders Home Care Inc.
11625 Rainwater Dr., Ste. 350
Alpharetta, GA 30004
Ph:(770)973-6400
Free: 877-264-6337
Fax:(770)973-6425
No. of Franchise Units: 21. **Founded:** 2004. **Franchised:** 2004. **Description:** Non-medical personal care for seniors & convalescing adults. **Equity Capital Needed:** $75,500-$123,900. **Franchise Fee:** $39,000. **Royalty Fee:** 3.75-5%. **Financial Assistance:** No. **Training:** 1 week training provided at headquarters, 2 days onsite and ongoing support.

314 ■ Caring Senior Service
3940 Laurel Canyon Blvd., No. 1214
Studio City, CA 91604
Ph:(206)781-1047
Free: 800-314-9494
No. of Franchise Units: 9. **No. of Company-Owned Units:** 23. **Franchised:** 2002. **Description:** Cares for health and nutrition services to senior people. **Equity Capital Needed:** $50,000-$80,000. **Franchise Fee:** $32,500. **Financial Assistance:** No. **Training:** Yes.

315 ■ ComForcare Senior Services
ComForcare Healthcare Holdings Inc.
2510 Telegraph Rd., Ste. 100
Bloomfield Hills, MI 48302
Ph:(248)745-9700
Free: 800-886-4044
Fax:(248)745-9763
URL: http://www.ComForcare.com
No. of Franchise Units: 150. **No. of Company-Owned Units:** 1. **Founded:** 1996. **Franchised:** 2001. **Description:** Franchise provides home health care for seniors. **Equity Capital Needed:** $80,000-$115,000 includes franchise fee. **Franchise Fee:** $39,500. **Financial Assistance:** No. **Training:** 1 week onsite training program, and ongoing support available.

316 ■ Homewatch CareGivers
7100 E Belleview Ave., Ste. 303
Greenwood Village, CO 80111
Ph:(303)953-6871
Free: 800-472-2290
Fax:(303)758-1724
Co. E-mail: franchise@homewatchcaregivers.com
URL: http://www.homewatchcaregivers.com
No. of Franchise Units: 193. **No. of Company-Owned Units:** 3. **Founded:** 1980. **Franchised:** 1997. **Description:** Offers services to elderly people who want to stay at home. **Equity Capital Needed:** $58,500-$90,000 initial investment. **Franchise Fee:** $35,000. **Financial Assistance:** No. **Training:** Offers pre-training, initial training, and post training program.

317 ■ Passport Health, Inc.
921 E Fort Ave., Ste. 100
Baltimore, MD 21230
Ph:(410)727-0556
Fax:(410)727-0696
No. of Franchise Units: 180. **No. of Company-Owned Units:** 8. **Founded:** 1997. **Franchised:** 1997. **Description:** Offers health and nutrition services along with senior care facilities. **Equity Capital Needed:** $100,000. **Franchise Fee:** $35,000. **Financial Assistance:** No. **Training:** Yes.

318 ■ Personal Training Institute
Personal Training Institute Franchises, LLC
500 N Broadway
Jericho, NY 11753
Ph:(516)342-9064
Fax:(516)342-9067
No. of Franchise Units: 7. **No. of Company-Owned Units:** 7. **Founded:** 1987. **Franchised:** 2005. **Description:** Weight loss and fitness center. **Equity Capital Needed:** $19,500. **Franchise Fee:** $50,000 liquid; $350,000 net worth. **Financial Assistance:** Yes. **Training:** Yes.

COMPUTERIZED DATABASES

319 ■ *AgeLine*
EBSCO Publishing
10 Estes St.
Ipswich, MA 01938
Ph:(978)356-6500
Free: 800-653-2726
Fax:(978)356-6565
Co. E-mail: information@ebscohost.com
URL: http://www.ebscohost.com
Description: Contains more than 90,000 abstracts including books, research reports, and articles from more than 200 journals and magazines, as well as videos related to issues of aging and life at 50 and up. Includes English-language publications from many publishers and organizations worldwide. **Type:** Bibliographic.

320 ■ *Consumer InSite*
Thomson Reuters
610 Opperman Dr.
Eagen, MN 55122
Free: 800-477-4300
Co. E-mail: gale.contentlicensing@cengage.com
URL: http://www.insite2.gale.com
Description: Focuses on consumer behavior, political opinion, contemporary lifestyles, leisure activities, and trends in popular culture. Provides the full text and summaries from more than 350 widely read North American newsstand titles and specialty magazines; derived from Magazine Database. Contains approximately 600,000 articles, including entertainment reviews of books, films, video, theatre, concerts, musical recordings, hotels, and restaurants, consumer buyer's guides, columns, editorials, product evaluations, biographies, speeches, interviews, and obituaries. **Availability:** Online: Thomson Reuters. **Type:** Full text.

321 ■ *Health & Wellness InSite*
Thomson Reuters
610 Opperman Dr.
Eagen, MN 55122
Free: 800-477-4300
Co. E-mail: gale.contentlicensing@cengage.com
URL: http://www.insite2.gale.com
Description: Contains complete information about health, medicine, fitness, and nutrition. Provides access to 170 of the world's leading professional and consumer health publications, including *The Lancet* and *Nutrition Today*, 550 health and medical pamphlets; 200,000 health-related articles from more than 3000 other publications; and 1800 overviews of different diseases and medical conditions published by Clinical Reference Systems, Ltd. Includes six medical reference books: *Columbia University College of Physicians & Surgeons Complete Home Medical Guide; Mosby's Medical, Nursing, and Allied Health Dictionary; Consumer Health Information Source Book; The People's Book of Medical Tests; USP DI-Vol. II Advice for the Patient; Drug Information in Lay Language;* and *The Complete Directory for People With Chronic Illness.*. Allows searches by article title, article type, author, company name, person discussed in the article, publication name, publication date range, publication type, target audience, ticker symbol, words in the title, and words that appear anywhere in the article. **Availability:** Online: Thomson Reuters. **Type:** Full text.

322 ■ *State Health Care Regulatory Developments*
The Bureau of National Affairs Inc.
1801 S Bell St.
Arlington, VA 22202
Free: 800-372-1033
Co. E-mail: customercare@bna.com
URL: http://www.bna.com
Description: Contains information on health care regulatory news and developments in the United States. Subjects include community-based care, home care, emergency care, infectious diseases, managed care, insurance, laboratories, Medicaid, mental health, medical waste, nursing homes, pharmaceuticals, physician services, professional licensing, provider relationships, worker protection and compensation. Entries are organized by state, topic, and register citation. **Availability:** Online: The Bureau of National Affairs Inc., Thomson Reuters. **Type:** Full text.

LIBRARIES

323 ■ American College of Health Care Administrators–ACHCA Information Center
12100 Sunset Hills Rd., Ste. 130
Reston, VA 20190
Ph:(703)739-7900
Fax:(866)874-1585
Co. E-mail: info@achca.org
URL: http://www.achca.org
Contact: Anita Bell, Off.Coord.
Scope: Long-term care, gerontology. **Services:** Center open to ACHCA members only. **Holdings:** 100 books; governmental statistical reports. **Subscriptions:** 125 journals and other serials.

324 ■ Arkansas Aging Foundation Information Center
706 S. Pulaski St.
Little Rock, AR 72201-3927
Ph:(501)376-6083
Contact: Ed Doman, Pres.
Scope: Health promotion; seniors - enhancing independent living, health issues, activities. **Services:** Copying. **Holdings:** Monthly newspaper. **Subscriptions:** 1 newspaper.

325 ■ Benjamin Rose Library
11900 Fairhill Rd.
Cleveland, OH 44120
Ph:(216)373-1682
Fax:(216)373-1813
Co. E-mail: kbensing@benrose.org info@benrose.org
URL: http://www.benrose.org/Library/Library.cfm
Contact: Karen McNally Bensing, Libn.
Scope: Aged - research, home care, long-term care, nursing homes, social work, nursing, elder abuse. **Services:** Interlibrary loan; copying; Library open to the public by appointment on a limited schedule. **Holdings:** 1500 books; 4 lateral file drawers of reports, papers, manuscripts. **Subscriptions:** 80 journals and other serials.

326 ■ Philadelphia Corporation for Aging Library
642 N. Broad St.
Philadelphia, PA 19130
Ph:(215)765-9000
Fax:(215)765-9066
Co. E-mail: sspencer@pcaphl.org
URL: http://www.pcacares.org/
Contact: Scott Spencer, Libn.
Scope: Gerontology, gerontological literature, health and social services for the aging. **Services:** Interlibrary loan; copying; Library open to the public for

reference use only; collection of proposals for services to elderly available for review by appointment only (photocopies not permitted). **Holdings:** 3700 books and reports; 154 periodical volumes on microfiche; 300 videos; 16 VF drawers of pamphlets and reports. **Subscriptions:** 100 journals and other serials.

327 ■ Pima Council on Aging Library
8467 E. Broadway Blvd.
Tucson, AZ 85710
Ph:(520)790-7262
Fax:(520)790-7577
Co. E-mail: help@pcoa.org
URL: http://pcoa.org/
Contact: Melissa S. Morgan, Libn.
Scope: Aging programs and services, gerontology, long-term care, public policy related to the elderly. **Services:** Interlibrary loan; copying; SDI; Library open to the public by appointment. **Holdings:** 2000 books; 24 VF drawers; 20,000 other cataloged items. **Subscriptions:** 30 journals and other serials; 350 newsletters; 6 newspapers.

328 ■ United Way 2-1-1–Information & Referral Service
PO Box 7548
Madison, WI 53707-7548
Ph:(608)246-4350
Fax:(608)246-4349
Co. E-mail: sandye@uwdc.org
URL: http://www.unitedwaydanecounty.org
Contact: Sandy Erickson, Dir.
Scope: Geriatrics, medical care. **Services:** Community resource telephone line providing information and referral services for Dane County.

329 ■ Virginia Commonwealth University–Virginia Center on Aging–Information Resources Center (730 E)
730 E. Broad St.
Theatre Row Building
Richmond, VA 23219
Ph:(804)828-1525
Fax:(804)828-7905
Co. E-mail: eansello@vcu.edu
URL: http://www.vcu.edu/vcoa
Contact: Dr. Edward F. Ansello, Dir.
Scope: Gerontology, mental health, sociology and the politics of aging, geriatrics, family relationships, long-term care, lifelong learning. **Services:** Library open to the public with restrictions. Audiovisual materials available to Virginia residents only. **Holdings:** 1500 books; 4 archives; 120 AV items. **Subscriptions:** 6 journals and other serials.

330 ■ Western Illinois Area Agency on Aging–Greta J. Brook Elderly Living and Learning Facility
729 34th Ave.
Rock Island, IL 61201
Ph:(309)793-6800
Free: 800-322-1051
Fax:(309)793-6807
Co. E-mail: firststopforseniors@wiaaa.org
URL: http://www.wiaaa.org
Contact: Janice Stille, Exec.Dir.
Scope: Gerontology, Senior Housing, Family Caregiving, Medicare, Medicaid, Social Security, Retirement Planning, Intergenerational Programs, Program Development. **Services:** Interlibrary loan; Center open to the public (Senior Computer Center open to those fifty years of age or older; classes on Tuesdays 10am to noon or 1pm to 3pm). **Holdings:** 1108 books; 260 videotapes; 130 audio/visual materials; 35 DVDs and CDs. **Subscriptions:** 3 journals and other serials, 13 periodicals.

RESEARCH CENTERS

331 ■ Brown University–Center for Gerontology and Health Care Research
121 S Main St., S-6
Providence, RI 02912
Ph:(401)863-3211
Fax:(401)863-3489
Co. E-mail: richard_besdine@brown.edu
URL: http://www.chcr.brown.edu
Contact: Dr. Richard W. Besdine, Dir.
E-mail: richard_besdine@brown.edu
Scope: Aging, chronic disease, and long-term care with particular emphasis on the assessment of function and health status and its application to diagnosis, prognosis and monitoring of long-term care. **Services:** Data collection, database development and training. **Publications:** Monograph Series. **Educational Activities:** Biology of Aging Conference. **Awards:** Medical Student Gerontology Prize.

332 ■ Case Western Reserve University–Elderly Care Research Center
231B Mather Memorial Bldg.
10900 Euclid Ave.
Cleveland, OH 44106-7124
Ph:(216)368-2704
Fax:(216)368-1078
Co. E-mail: exk@case.edu
URL: http://www.case.edu/artsci/soci/ecrc
Contact: Dr. Eva Kahana, Dir.
E-mail: exk@case.edu
Scope: Aging, health, and mental health, including public policy issues, predictors of wellness and vulnerability, environmental and social influences on well-being of the elderly, cross-national and cross-cultural comparisons, and health and mental health outcomes of stress, coping, and adaptation. **Publications:** Brochure.

START-UP INFORMATION

333 ■ *The Small Business Owner's Manual: Everything You Need to Know to Start Up and Run Your Business*
Pub: Career Press, Incorporated
Ed: Joe Kennedy. **Released:** June 2005. **Price:** $19.99 (US), $26.95 (Canadian). **Description:** Comprehensive guide for starting a small business, focusing on twelve ways to obtain financing, business plans, selling and advertising products and services, hiring and firing employees, setting up a Web site, business law, accounting issues, insurance, equipment, computers, banks, financing, customer credit and collection, leasing, and more.

ASSOCIATIONS AND OTHER ORGANIZATIONS

334 ■ Advertising Club of New York
235 Park Ave. S, 6th Fl.
New York, NY 10003-1450
Ph:(212)533-8080
Fax:(212)533-1929
Co. E-mail: gina@theadvertisingclub.org
URL: http://www.theadvertisingclub.org
Contact: Gina Grillo, Pres./CEO
Description: Professionals in advertising, publishing, marketing and business. Sponsors educational and public service activities, promotional and public relations projects and talks by celebrities and advertising persons. Conducts annual advertising and marketing course, which offers classes in copywriting, special graphics, verbal communication, advertising production, sale promotion, marketing and management. Sponsors competitions and charitable programs. **Publications:** *ACNY Membership Roster* (annual); *Auction Catalogue and Program* (annual).

335 ■ Advertising Council
815 2nd Ave., 9th Fl.
New York, NY 10017
Ph:(212)922-1500
Free: 800-933-7727
Fax:(212)922-1676
Co. E-mail: info@adcouncil.org
URL: http://www.adcouncil.org
Contact: Peggy Conlon, Pres./CEO
Description: Founded and supported by American business, media, and advertising sectors to conduct public service advertising campaigns. Encourages advertising media to contribute time and space and advertising agencies to supply creative talent and facilities to further timely national causes. Specific campaigns include: Drug Abuse Prevention; AIDS Prevention; Teen-Alcoholism; Child Abuse; Crime Prevention; Forest Fire Prevention. **Publications:** *PSA Bulletin* (bimonthly).

336 ■ Advertising and Marketing International Network
3587 Northshore Dr.
Wayzata, MN 55391
Ph:(952)457-1116
Fax:(952)471-7752
Co. E-mail: jsundby@aminworldwide.com
URL: http://www.aminworldwide.com
Contact: Janna Sperry Sundby, Membership Mgr.
Description: Comprised of cooperative worldwide network of non-competing independent advertising agencies organized to provide facilities and branch office services for affiliated agencies. .

337 ■ Advertising Standards Canada–Normes Canadiennes de la Publicite
S Tower
175 Bloor St. E, Ste. 1801
Toronto, ON, Canada M4W 3R8
Ph:(416)961-6311
Fax:(416)961-7904
Co. E-mail: info@adstandards.com
URL: http://www.adstandards.com/en
Contact: Linda J. Nagel, Pres./CEO
Description: Committed to ensuring the integrity and viability of advertising through industry self-regulation. Administers the Canada Code of Advertising Standards, accepts and reviews complaints about advertising, and provides advertising pre-clearance services. **Publications:** *Ad Complaints Report* (annual).

338 ■ Advertising Women of New York
25 W 45th St., Ste. 403
New York, NY 10036
Ph:(212)221-7969
Fax:(212)221-8296
Co. E-mail: awny@awny.org
URL: http://www.awny.org
Contact: Ms. Liz Schroeder MS, Exec. Dir.
Description: Women in advertising and related industries that provides a forum for professional growth, serves as catalyst for enhancement and advancement of women; promotes philanthropic endeavors. Conducts events of interest and benefit to members and non-members involved in the industry. Membership concentrated in the metropolitan New York area. .

339 ■ American Academy of Advertising
24710 Shaker Blvd.
Beachwood, OH 44122
Ph:(786)393-3333
Free: (866)607-8512
Co. E-mail: director@aaasite.org
URL: http://www.aaasite.org
Contact: Patricia B. Rose, Exec. Dir.
Description: Serves as a professional organization for college and university teachers of advertising and for industry professionals who wish to contribute to the development of advertising education. **Publications:** *Journal of Advertising* (quarterly); *Journal of Interactive Advertising* (semiannual); *Proceedings of the Conference of the American Academy of Advertising* (annual); *Roster of Members* (annual).

340 ■ American Advertising Federation
1101 Vermont Ave. NW, Ste. 500
Washington, DC 20005-6306
Ph:(202)898-0089
Free: 800-999-2231
Fax:(202)898-0159
Co. E-mail: aaf@aaf.org
URL: http://www.aaf.org
Contact: James Edmund Datri, Pres./CEO
Description: Works to advance the business of advertising as a vital and essential part of the American economy and culture through government and public relations; professional development and recognition; community service, social responsibility and high standards; and benefits and services to members. Operates Advertising Hall of Fame, Hall of Achievement, and National Student Advertising Competition. Maintains speakers' bureau. **Publications:** *Communicator* (monthly); *Newsline* (monthly).

341 ■ American Association of Advertising Agencies
405 Lexington Ave., 18th Fl.
New York, NY 10174-1801
Ph:(212)682-2500
Fax:(212)682-8391
Co. E-mail: nhill@aaaa.org
URL: http://www.aaaa.org
Contact: Nancy Hill, Pres./CEO
Description: Fosters development of the advertising industry; assists member agencies to operate more efficiently and profitably. Sponsors member information and international services. Maintains 47 committees. Conducts government relations. **Publications:** *AAAA Publications Catalog* (periodic); *The Reporter* (bimonthly); *Roster of Members* (annual).

342 ■ American Photographic Artists
PO Box 725146
Atlanta, GA 31139
Free: 888-889-7190
Co. E-mail: ceo@apanational.com
URL: http://www.apanational.org
Contact: Stephen Best, CEO
Description: Enhances dialogue among professional photographers and their clients. Suggests standards and business practices to improve the quality of professional photography; and acts as a forum for discussion of problems and solutions. Conducts discussion groups. **Publications:** *1999 APA National Photographer's Survey Report* .

343 ■ Association of National Advertisers
708 3rd Ave., 33rd Fl.
New York, NY 10017-4270
Ph:(212)697-5950
Fax:(212)687-7310
Co. E-mail: bliodice@ana.net
URL: http://www.ana.net
Contact: Robert D. Liodice, Pres./CEO
Description: Serves the needs of members by providing marketing and advertising industry leadership in traditional and e-marketing, legislative leadership, information resources, professional development and industry-wide networking. Maintains offices in New York City and Washington, DC. **Publications:** *The Advertiser* (bimonthly).

344 ■ Canadian Advertising Research Foundation–La Fondation Canadienne de Recherche en Publicite
160 Bloor St. E, Ste. 1005
Toronto, ON, Canada M4W 1B9
Ph:(416)413-3864
Fax:(416)413-3879
Co. E-mail: tjames@tvb.ca
URL: http://www.carf.ca
Contact: Tiffany James, Admin.
Description: Advertisers, advertising agencies, media outlets, research companies, and other firms with an interest in advertising and advertising research. Promotes growth and development in the fields of advertising research and media evaluation. Develops and publishes guidelines for communications research and studies; stimulates creation of new research techniques; serves as a forum for exchange of information on advertising and media research. Makes available services including media research and executive appraisals; offers reduced subscription rates to national and international advertising and media research publications. **Publications:** *CARF Newsletter* (bimonthly); *CARF Update* (periodic).

345 ■ Canadian Marketing Association–Association Canadienne du Marketing
1 Concorde Gate, Ste. 607
Don Mills, ON, Canada M3C 3N6
Ph:(416)391-2362
Fax:(416)441-4062
Co. E-mail: info@the-cma.org
URL: http://www.the-cma.org
Contact: John Gustavson, Pres./CEO
Description: Information-based marketing firms. Promotes growth and development in the information-based marketing industry. Facilitates communication and cooperation among members; serves as a clearinghouse on information-based marketing. **Publications:** *Annual Fact Book* (annual); *E-Communicator* (10/year).

346 ■ Concerned Children's Advertisers
885 Don Mills Rd., Ste. 301
Toronto, ON, Canada M3C 1V9
Ph:(416)484-0871
Fax:(416)484-6564
Co. E-mail: info@cca-arpe.ca
URL: http://www.cca-kids.ca
Contact: Bev Deeth, Pres.
Description: Companies marketing their products to children. Seeks to combine effective children's advertising with the "social responsibility of caring for children". Promotes adherence by members to the Broadcast Code for Advertising for Children. Creates alliances between members, advertising producers, and government agencies to ensure creation of effective and socially responsible children's advertising. Conducts research and educational programs; produces television public service announcements on topics including substance abuse and healthy lifestyles.

347 ■ Intermarket Agency Network
5307 S 92nd St.
Hales Corners, WI 53130
Ph:(414)425-8800
Fax:(414)425-0021
Co. E-mail: ekleban@juicecoms.com
URL: http://www.intermarketnetwork.com
Contact: Ed Ekleban, Pres.
Description: An active network of high-powered marketing/communications agencies in the United States, Canada, Central and South America, and Europe. .

348 ■ International Advertising Association
275 Madison Ave., Ste. 2102
New York, NY 10016
Ph:(212)557-1133
Fax:(212)983-0455
Co. E-mail: membership@iaaglobal.org
URL: http://www.iaaglobal.org
Contact: Michael Lee, Exec. Dir.
Description: Global network of advertisers, advertising agencies, the media and related services, spanning 99 countries. Demonstrates to governments and consumers the benefits of advertising as the foundation of diverse, independent media. Protects and advances freedom of commercial speech and consumer choice, encourages greater practice and acceptance of advertising self-regulation, provides a forum to debate emerging professional marketing communications issues and their consequences in the fast-changing world environment, and takes the lead in state-of-the-art professional development through education and training for the marketing communications industry of tomorrow. Conducts research on such topics as restrictions and taxes on advertising, advertising trade practices and related information, and advertising expenditures around the world. Sponsors IAA Education Program. Has compiled recommendations for international advertising standards and practices. **Publications:** *The Case for Advertising Self-Regulation*; *IAA Annual Report* (annual); *IAA Membership Directory* (annual).

349 ■ International Communications Agency Network
PO Box 490
Rollinsville, CO 80474-0490
Ph:(303)258-9511
Fax:(303)484-4087
Co. E-mail: info@icomagencies.com
URL: http://www.icomagencies.com
Contact: Mr. Gary Burandt, Exec. Dir.
Description: Network of non-competing advertising agencies. Provides an interchange of management information, international facilities, and branch office service for partner agencies. Provides discounts on syndicated services and access to 1,000 computer databases. **Publications:** *Agency Client Lists* (monthly); *The Globe* (monthly); *Membership Roster* (annual).

350 ■ Mailing and Fulfillment Service Association
1421 Prince St., Ste. 410
Alexandria, VA 22314-2806
Ph:(703)836-9200
Free: 800-333-6272
Fax:(703)548-8204
Co. E-mail: mfsa-mail@mfsanet.org
URL: http://www.mfsanet.org
Contact: Ken Garner, Pres./CEO
Description: Commercial direct mail producers, letter shops, mailing list houses, fulfillment operations, and advertising agencies. Conducts special interest group meetings. Offers specialized education; conducts research programs. **Publications:** *MFSA Wage Salary, and Fringe Benefit Survey* (semiannual); *Performance Profiles: The Financial Ratios for the Mailing Service Industry* (annual); *Postscripts* (monthly); *Who's Who: MASA's Buyers' Guide to Blue Ribbon Mailing Services* (annual).

351 ■ Marketing and Advertising Global Network
1017 Perry Hwy., Ste. 5
Pittsburgh, PA 15237
Ph:(412)366-6850
Fax:(412)366-6840
Co. E-mail: mxdirector@verizon.net
URL: http://www.magnetglobal.org
Contact: Cheri D. Gmiter, Exec. Dir.
Description: Cooperative network of non-competing advertising, marketing, merchandising, and public relations agencies. Aims to bring about, through mutual cooperation, greater accomplishment and efficiency in the management of member advertising agencies. Other goals are: to raise standards of the advertising agency business through the exchange of information relative to agency management and all phases of advertising; to exchange information on all common problems, such as management, sales development, market studies, agency functions, and operations. Aims to inform the general public of current global marketing trends. **Publications:** *MAGNET Matters* (3/year); *This Week at MAGNET* (weekly).

352 ■ National Advertising Review Board
70 W 36th St., 13th Fl.
New York, NY 10018
Ph:(212)705-0114
Co. E-mail: bhopewell@narc.bbb.org
URL: http://www.narbreview.org
Contact: Howard Bell, Chm.
Description: Individuals from industry and the public. Sponsored by the National Advertising Review Council for the purpose of sustaining high standards of truth and accuracy in national advertising. Aims to maintain a self-regulatory mechanism that responds constructively to public complaints about national advertising and which significantly improves advertising performance and credibility. **Publications:** *NARB Panel Reports* .

353 ■ Sign Association of Canada–Association Canadienne de l'enseigne
216 Chrislea Rd., Ste. 301
Woodbridge, ON, Canada L4L 8S5
Ph:(905)856-0000
Free: 877-470-9787
Fax:(905)856-0064
Co. E-mail: fred.elkins@ndgraphics.com
URL: http://www.sac-ace.ca
Contact: Fred Elkins, Pres.
Description: Manufacturers of advertising signs; suppliers of sign components and services. Promotes increased use of signs in advertising. Represents members' interests. Facilitates communication and cooperation among members; conducts research and studies on advertising, sign technologies, and human resources. Sponsors competitions. **Publications:** *Signs Canada* (bimonthly).

354 ■ Traffic Audit Bureau for Media Measurement
271 Madison Ave., Ste. 1504
New York, NY 10016
Ph:(212)972-8075
Fax:(212)972-8928
Co. E-mail: inquiry@tabonline.com
URL: http://www.tabonline.com
Contact: Joseph C. Philport, Pres./CEO
Description: Advertisers, advertising agencies, operators of outdoor advertising plants, bus shelter advertising companies, and backlighted display and painted bulletin companies. Sets standard practices for the evaluation of circulation and visibility of outdoor advertising; issues statements on the circulation values of outdoor advertising plants. Encourages standardization of terminology and practices in the industry. Seeks to educate those involved in out-of-home media on ways of developing circulation data for advertising sites. Compiles statistics. **Publications:** *Building Accountability for Out of Home Media*; *TAB Eyes On Out of Home*; *TABBriefs*; *What You Should Know About the New TAB Audit* .

355 ■ Transworld Advertising Agency Network
814 Watertown St.
Newton, MA 02465
Ph:(617)795-1706
Fax:(419)730-1706
Co. E-mail: peterg@taan.org
URL: http://www.taan.org
Contact: Peter Gerritsen, Pres.
Description: Independently owned advertising agencies that cooperate for exchange of management education and information, reciprocal service, and personal local contact. Allows members to seek aid of other members in campaign planning, creative services, merchandising, public relations, publicity, media, research, and test facilities. Conducts annual expertise audit. .

DIRECTORIES OF EDUCATIONAL PROGRAMS

356 ■ *Who's Who in the Media and Communications*
Pub: Marquis Who's Who L.L.C.
Covers: More than 18,500 professionals in print journalism, broadcasting, publishing, television, public relations, advertising, radio, telecommunications, interactive multimedia, and education. **Entries Include:** Biographical data.

REFERENCE WORKS

357 ■ "10 Trends That Are Shaping Global Media Consumption" in *Advertising Age* (Vol. 81, December 6, 2010, No. 43, pp. 3)
Pub: Crain Communications, Inc.
Ed: Ann Marie Kerwin. **Description:** Ad Age offers the statistics from the TV penetration rate in Kenya to the number of World Cup watchers and more.

358 ■ "A&E Networks" in *Brandweek* (Vol. 49, April 21, 2008, No. 16, pp. SR9)
Pub: VNU Business Media, Inc.
Ed: Anthony Crupi. **Description:** Provides contact information for sales and marketing personnel for the A&E Networks as well as a listing of the station's top programming and an analysis of the current season and the target audience for those programs running in the current season. A&E has reinvented itself as a premium entertainment brand over the last five years and with its $2.5 million per episode acquisition of The Sopranos, the station signaled that it was serious about getting back into the scripted programming business. The acquisition also helped the network compete against other cable networks and led to a 20 percent increase in prime-time viewers.

359 ■ "Abacast, Citadel Strike Radio Ad Deal" in *Business Journal Portland* (Vol. 27, December 31, 2010, No. 44, pp. 3)
Pub: Portland Business Journal
Ed: Erik Siemers. **Description:** Software firm Abacast Inc. has partnered with Citadel Media to aid the latter's advertising sales. Citadel provides radio networks and syndicated programs to 4,200 affiliate stations.

360 ■ "ABC" in *Brandweek* (Vol. 49, April 21, 2008, No. 16, pp. SR6)
Pub: VNU Business Media, Inc.
Ed: John Consoli. **Description:** Provides contact information for sales and marketing personnel for the ABC network as well as a listing of the station's top programming and an analysis of the current season and the target audience for those programs running in the current season.

361 ■ "Ad Firms Stew Over Lost Car Biz; Diversifying Business Is Uphill Battle" in *Crain's Detroit Business* (Vol. 23, July 30, 2007, No. 31)
Pub: Crain Communications, Inc.
Ed: Jean Halliday. **Description:** Struggling Detroit automakers are breaking their tradition of loyalty and moving their advertising accounts to agencies in Los Angeles, San Francisco, and Boston; This has Detroit's advertising community very worried.

362 ■ "Advertisers Don't Party With CBS's Swingers" in *Advertising Age* (Vol. 79, July 7, 2008, No. 26, pp. 1)
Pub: Crain Communications, Inc.
Ed: Brian Steinberg. **Description:** Broadcast networks that are trying to air edgier programming such as CBS's "Swingtown" but are running into problems with advertisers who are fearful of consumer complaints and backlash when running commercials during such fare.

363 ■ "Advertisers Hooked on Horns, their Playground" in *Austin Business JournalInc.* (Vol. 28, July 25, 2008, No. 19, pp. A1)
Pub: American City Business Journals
Ed: Sandra Zaragoza. **Description:** Renovation of the D.K. Royal-Texas Memorial Stadium has increased its advertising revenue from $570,000 in 1993 to $10 in 2008. Sponsorship has grown in the past years due to the revenue-sharing agreement, a ten-year contract through 2015 between the University of Texas and IMG College Sports.

364 ■ *Advertising Age—Agencies Ranked by Gross Income Issue*
Pub: Crain Communications Inc.
Contact: Craig Endicott, Datacenter Ed.
Released: Annual. **Covers:** More than 600 advertising agencies. **Entries Include:** For agencies with gross income over three million dollars: agency name, rank for two years, billing, gross income, and number of employees.

365 ■ "Advertising May Take a Big Hit in Southwest/AirTran Merger" in *Baltimore Business Journal* (Vol. 28, October 1, 2010, No. 21, pp. 1)
Pub: Baltimore Business Journal
Ed: Gary Haber. **Description:** Advertising on television stations and the publishing industry in Baltimore could drop as a result of the merger between rival discount airlines Southwest Airlines and AirTran Airways. Southwest is among the top advertisers in the U.S., spending $126 million in 2009. No local jobs are expected to be affected because neither airline uses a local advertising firm.

366 ■ "Africa Rising" in *Harvard Business Review* (Vol. 86, September 2008, No. 9, pp. 36)
Pub: Harvard Business School Press
Ed: John T. Landry. **Description:** Review of the book entitled, "Africa Rising: How 900 Million African Consumers Offer More Than You Think" provides advice for marketing to those on the African continent.

367 ■ "The Agency Model Is Bent But Not Broken" in *Advertising Age* (Vol. 79, July 7, 2008, No. 26, pp. 17)
Pub: Crain Communications, Inc.
Ed: Stephen Fajen. **Description:** In the new-media environment, advertising agencies must change the way in which they do business and receive payment.

368 ■ "The Agency-Selection Process Needs Fixing Now" in *Advertising Age* (Vol. 79, July 7, 2008, No. 26, pp. 18)
Pub: Crain Communications, Inc.
Ed: Avi Dan. **Description:** Marketers are facing increased challenges in this sagging economic climate and must realize the importance of choosing the correct advertising agency for their company in order to benefit from a more-stable relationship that yields better business results. Advice for marketers regarding the best way to choose an agency is included.

369 ■ "The AHA Moment" in *Hispanic Business* (December 2010)
Pub: Hispanic Business
Ed: Rebecca Vallaneda. **Description:** An interview with Gisela Girard on how competitive market conditions push buttons. Girard stepped down from her 18-month position as chairwoman the Association of Hispanic Advertising Agencies. She has more than 20 years of experience in advertising and research marketing.

370 ■ "All Bundled Up" in *Entrepreneur* (Vol. 35, November 2007, No. 11, pp. 104)
Pub: Entrepreneur Media Inc.
Ed: Kim T. Gordon. **Description:** Bundling is a marketing strategy that combines a variety of features to present products and services as a whole. Tips on how to handle bundling are outlined.

371 ■ *All You Need Is a Good Idea!: How to Create Marketing Messages that Actually Get Results*
Pub: John Wiley and Sons, Inc.
Ed: Jay Heyman. **Released:** May 2008. **Price:** $24. 95. **Description:** Advertising guru Jay Heyman offers advice to successfully market products and services. Heyman uses his years of experience and case histories to become creative with advertising campaigns.

372 ■ "Alliance Atlantis Takes a Cheekier Attitude to Life" in *Globe & Mail* (March 5, 2007, pp. B5)
Pub: CTVglobemedia Publishing Inc.
Ed: Keith McArthur. **Description:** Alliance Atlantis Communications Inc. is re-branding its human life ministry Life Network specialty channel as Slice. The new channel is being promoted with an advertising campaign.

373 ■ "Ampm Focus Has BP Working Overtime; New Convenience-Store Brand Comes to Chicago" in *Crain's Chicago Business* (April 28, 2008)
Pub: Crain Communications, Inc.
Ed: John T. Slania. **Description:** Britian's oil giant BP PLC is opening its ampm convenience stores in the Chicago market and has already begun converting most of its 78 Chicago-area gas stations to ampms. The company has also started to franchise the stores to independent operators. BP is promoting the brand with both traditional and unconventional marketing techniques such s real or simulated 3D snacks embedded in bus shelter ads and an in-store Guitar Hero contest featuring finalists from a recent contest at the House of Blues.

374 ■ "Anja Carroll; Media Director-McDonald's USA" in *Advertising Age* (Vol. 79, November 17, 2008, No. 34, pp. 6)
Pub: Crain Communications, Inc.
Ed: Emily Bryson York. **Description:** Profile of Anja Carroll who is the media director for McDonald's USA and has the challenge of choosing the right mix of media for the corporation.

375 ■ "App Time: Smartphone Applications Aren't Just for Fun and Games Anymore" in *Inc.* (Volume 32, December 2010, No. 10, pp. 116)
Pub: Inc. Magazine
Ed: Jason Del Rey. **Description:** Smart phone technology can help any small business market their products and services.

376 ■ "Apparel Apparatchic at Kmart" in *Barron's* (Vol. 88, March 17, 2008, No. 11, pp. 16)
Pub: Dow Jones & Company, Inc.
Description: Kmart began a nationwide search for women to represent the company in a national advertising campaign. Contestants need to upload their photos to Kmart's website and winners will be chosen by a panel of celebrity judges. The contest aims to reverse preconceived negative notions about the store's quality and service.

377 ■ "Are Offline Pushes Important to E-Commerce?" in *DM News* (Vol. 31, September 14, 2009, No. 23, pp. 10)
Pub: Haymarket Media, Inc.
Description: With the importance of Internet marketing and the popularity of ecommerce increasing experts debate the relevance of more traditional channels of advertising.

378 ■ "Art Attack 2007 Comes to Minneapolis" in *Art Business News* (Vol. 34, November 2007, No. 11, pp. 11)
Pub: Pfingsten Publishing, LLC
Description: Overview of Art Attack 2007, an open studio and gallery crawl in the Northeast Minneapolis Arts District which featured artists working in glass, ceramics, jewelry, mosaics, mixed media, photography, painting, pottery, sculpture, textiles and wood.

379 ■ "Ask Inc." in *Inc.* (October 2007, pp. 74)
Pub: Gruner & Jahr USA Publishing
Description: Promoting a new comedy club using television, radio and print advertising and tracking results is discussed.

380 ■ "At 5-Year Mark, News 9 Makes Presence Felt in Competition for Ad Dollars" in *Business Review, Albany New York* (October 5, 2007)
Pub: American City Business Journals, Inc.
Ed: Barbara Pinckney. **Description:** The 24-hour news channel Capital News 9 can be watched live by viewers on their cell phones beginning late 2007 or early 2008 as part of a deal between Time Warner Cable and Sprint Nextel Corporation to bring Sprint's Pivot technology. News 9 marked its fifth year and plans to continue expanding coverage and provide better services to viewers.

381 ■ "Attention, Please" in *Entrepreneur* (Vol. 36, April 2008, No. 4, pp. 52)
Pub: Entrepreneur Media, Inc.
Ed: Andrea Cooper. **Description:** Gurbaksh Chahal created his own company ClickAgents at the age of 16, and sold it two years later for $40 million to ValueClick. He then founded BlueLithium, an online advertising network on behavioral targeting, which Yahoo! Inc. bought in 2007 for $300 million. Chahal, now 25, talks about his next plans and describes how BlueLithium caught Yahoo's attention.

382 ■ *Authenticity: What Consumers Really Want*
Pub: Harvard Business School Press
Ed: James H. Gilmore. **Released:** September 24, 2007. **Price:** $26.95. **Description:** In today's marketplace, consumers tend to buy based on how authentic a company's offer appears. A company's identity is explored through case studies and advertising slogans. The authors write from the theory that most everything is artificial, manmade, and fake.

383 ■ "avVaa World Health Care Products Rolls Out Internet Marketing Program" in *Health and Beauty Close-Up* (September 18, 2009)
Pub: Close-Up Media
Description: avVaa World Health Care Products, Inc., a biotechnology company, manufacturer and distributor of nationally branded therapeutic, natural health care and skin products, has signed an agreement with Online Performance Marketing to launch of an Internet marketing campaign in order to broaden its presence online. The impact of advertising on the Internet to generate an increase in sales is explored.

384 ■ "Being all a-Twitter" in *Canadian Business* (Vol. 81, December 8, 2008, No. 21, pp. 22)
Pub: Rogers Media Ltd.
Ed: Andrew Wahl. **Description:** Marketing experts suggest that advertising strategies have to change along with new online social media. Companies are advised to find ways to incorporate social software because workers and customers are expected to continue its use.

385 ■ "Better ROI Or Your Money Back, Says Buzz Agency" in *Advertising Age* (Vol. 79, July 14, 2008, No. 7, pp. 1)
Pub: Crain Communications, Inc.
Ed: Michael Bush. **Description:** Word-of-mouth marketing is discussed as well as the impact on the advertising industry. Although many firms specializing in this form of marketing have opened over the past few years, many marketers are reluctant to try this route.

386 ■ "Better Than New" in *Bellingham Business Journal* (Vol. February 2010, pp. 16)
Pub: Sound Publishing Inc.
Ed: Ashley Mitchell. **Description:** Profile of family owned Better Than New clothing store that sells overstock items from department stores and clothing manufacturers. The stores location makes it easy to miss and its only advertising is a large sign posted outside. This is the sixth store owned by the couple, Keijeo and Sirba Halmekanqas.

387 ■ "Blue Bell Touts Non-Shrinkage" in *Ice Cream Reporter* (Vol. 21, July 20, 2008, No. 8, pp. 1)
Pub: Ice Cream Reporter
Description: Blue Bell Ice Cream is promoting its decision to keep their ice cream products in a full half-gallon container rather than downsizing the package. Thirty-second television ads contrast the move by other ice cream makers to offer less for the same money.

388 ■ *BOOM: Marketing to the Ultimate Power Consumer-The Baby-Boomer Woman*
Pub: American Management Association
Ed: Mary Brown; Carol Orsborn. **Released:** 2006. **Price:** $24.00.

389 ■ "Branding Your Way" in *Canadian Business* (Vol. 80, February 12, 2007, No. 4, pp. 31)
Pub: Rogers Media
Ed: Erin Pooley. **Description:** The trend in involving consumers in brand marketing by seeking their views through contests or inviting them to produce and submit commercials through Internet is discussed.

390 ■ "Brands' Mass Appeal" in *ADWEEK* (Vol. 51, June 14, 2010, No. 24)
Pub: Nielsen Business Media Inc.
Ed: Lisa Thorell, James Sherret. **Description:** Engineering/science crowdsourced projects tend to result from posting and/or publishing interim results as well as from other talents building upon those results to produce even better results. However, the author does not see the same results in the creative world.

391 ■ "Brewing Up a Brand" in *Canadian Business* (Vol. 80, February 26, 2007, No. 5, pp. 68)
Pub: Rogers Media
Ed: Clavin Leung. **Description:** The marketing strategies adopted by Molson Coors Brewing Company, to improve customer loyalty to the Coors Light brand, are presented.

392 ■ *Briefs for Building Better Brands: Tips, Parables and Insight into Market Leaders*
Pub: AGCD Brandspa Books
Ed: Allan Gorman. **Released:** September 2004. **Description:** In today's marketplace, a company needs to gain consumer trust in order to build a brand. By gaining trust, the brand gets sold by word-of-mouth publicity. The author calls this type of marketing: guerrilla marketing, and he believes it to be more effective than traditional advertising.

393 ■ "Bright Lights, Big Impact: Why Digital Billboards are Growing in Popularity" in *Inc.* (March 2008, pp. 61-62)
Pub: Gruner & Jahr USA Publishing
Ed: Sarah Goldstein. **Description:** Clear Channel provides high tech digital billboards which allow companies to change advertising as often as necessary during a contract period. The Outdoor Advertising Association of America predicts the growth of digital billboards at several hundred per year over the next few years. CEO of Magic Media believes all billboards will eventually go digital.

394 ■ "Broadcast Commercial Acceptance" in *MarketingMagazine* (Vol. 115, September 27, 2010, No. 13, pp. 29)
Pub: Rogers Publishing Ltd.
Description: Advertising rules for the broadcast commercial industry in Canada are reviewed.

395 ■ "Business Forecast: Stormy and Successful" in *Women In Business* (Vol. 62, June 2010, No. 2, pp. 12)
Pub: American Business Women's Association
Ed: Kathleen Leighton. **Description:** Stormy Simon, vice president of customer service at Overstock.com is a self-made career woman who started out as a temporary employee in the company in 2001. She was not able to attend college because she had two sons to care for after her divorce. Simon got involved in advertising and media buying and shares her love for business.

396 ■ "Buying In" in *Harvard Business Review* (Vol. 86, September 2008, No. 9, pp. 36)
Pub: Harvard Business School Press
Ed: Andrew O'Connell. **Description:** Review of the book entitled, "Buying In: The Secret Dialogue between What We Buy and Who We Are" which offers tips that those in the field of marketing will find useful.

397 ■ *Buying In: The Secret Dialogue Between What We Buy and Who We Are*
Pub: Random House
Ed: Rob Walker. **Released:** 2008. **Price:** $25.00. **Description:** The book offers a look at the state of advertising today and shows why even those who feel like they see through marketing feel attached to specific brands as a way to both project and foster their identities.

398 ■ "Buzz Marketing for Movies" in *Business Horizons* (September-October 2007, pp. 395)
Pub: Elsevier Technology Publications
Ed: Iris Mohr. **Description:** Application of buzz marketing through the context of movie differentiation strategies such as cosmetic movie features, differentiation to reach market segments, growing a movie segment, positioning to support the movie image, positioning to extend the movie image, and differentiation via non-traditional channels are all discussed.

399 ■ *Call Me Ted*
Pub: Grand Central Publishing
Ed: Ted Turner. **Released:** 2008. **Price:** $30.00. **Description:** Media mogul, Ted Turner's biography is full of personal and business details from his careers in advertising and broadcasting.

400 ■ "Canadian Market Data" in *MarketingMagazine* (Vol. 115, September 27, 2010, No. 13, pp. 6)
Pub: Rogers Publishing Ltd.
Description: Canadian marketing statistics are outlined.

401 ■ "CBS" in *Brandweek* (Vol. 49, April 21, 2008, No. 16, pp. SR6)
Pub: VNU Business Media, Inc.
Ed: John Consoli. **Description:** Provides contact information for sales and marketing personnel for the CBS network as well as a listing of the station's top programming and an analysis of the current season and the target audience for those programs running in the current season.

402 ■ "CBS Television Distribution" in *Brandweek* (Vol. 49, April 21, 2008, No. 16, pp. SR13)
Pub: VNU Business Media, Inc.
Ed: Marc Berman. **Description:** Provides contact information for sales and marketing personnel for CBS Television Distribution as well as a listing of the station's top programming and an analysis of the current season and the target audience for those programs running in the current season. Due to the unprecedented, decade-plus advantage of first-run leaders such as Wheel of Fortune, Oprah, Judge Judy and Entertainment Tonight, CBS is poised to remain a leader among the syndicates.

403 ■ "Change Agent; What Peter Francese Says You Need to Know" in *Advertising Age* (Vol. 79, July 7, 2008, No. 26, pp. 13)
Pub: Crain Communications, Inc.
Ed: Peter Francese. **Description:** Advice for marketers on how to deal effectively with a changing consumer base is given.

404 ■ "Charlotte Pipe Launches Satirical Campaign" in *Contractor* (Vol. 57, January 2010, No. 1, pp. 6)
Pub: Penton Media, Inc.
Description: Charlotte Pipe and Foundry Co. launched an advertising campaign that uses social media and humor to make a point about how it can be nearly impossible to determine if imported cast iron pipes and fittings meet the same quality standards as what is made in the U.S. The campaign features 'pipe whisperers' and also spoofs pipe sniffing dogs.

405 ■ "Cheese Spread Whips Up a Brand New Bowl" in *Brandweek* (Vol. 49, April 21, 2008, No. 16, pp. 17)
Pub: VNU Business Media, Inc.
Ed: Mike Beirne. **Description:** Mrs. Kinser's Pimento Cheese Spread is launching a new container for its product in order to attempt stronger brand marketing with a better bowl in order to win over the heads of households as young as in their 30s. The company also intends to begin distribution in Texas and the West Coast. Mrs. Kinser's is hoping that the new packaging will provide a more distinct branding and will help consumers distinguish what flavor they are buying.

406 ■ "Chief Boo Boo Officer" in *Marketing to Women* (Vol. 21, February 2008, No. 2, pp. 1)
Pub: EPM Communications, Inc.
Ed: Ellen Neuborne. **Description:** Pharmaceutical companies are reaching out to women through innovative marketing techniques.

407 ■ "Clicks For Cash: Earning More From Your Website" in *Inc.* (December 2007, pp. 64-65)
Pub: Gruner & Jahr USA Publishing
Ed: Michael Fitzgerald. **Description:** Ways to use a company's Website to generate revenue are discussed. Free services for placing ads include Google

AdSense, AdBrite, AuctionAds, Chitkia eMiniMalls, Vizu Answers, and Value Click; profiles of each service are presented.

408 ■ "CMO Nicholson Exits Pepsi as Share Declines" in *Advertising Age* (Vol. 79, July 7, 2008, No. 26, pp. 4)
Pub: Crain Communications, Inc.
Ed: Natalie Zmuda. **Description:** Cie Nicholson, the chief marketing officer at Pepsi-Cola UK, is leaving the company at a time when its market share is down; the brand, which was known for its dynamic marketing, has diverted much of its attention from its core brands and shifted attention to the ailing Gatorade brand as well as Sobe Life Water and Amp.

409 ■ "Comcast Networks" in *Brandweek* (Vol. 49, April 21, 2008, No. 16, pp. SR9)
Pub: VNU Business Media, Inc.
Ed: Anthony Crupi. **Description:** Provides contact information for sales and marketing personnel for the Comcast networks as well as a listing of the station's top programming and an analysis of the current season and the target audience for those programs running in the current season. Experts believe Comcast will continue to acquire more stations into their portfolio.

410 ■ "Commensurate with Experience" in *Entrepreneur* (Vol. 37, October 2009, No. 10, pp. 84)
Pub: Entrepreneur Media, Inc.
Ed: Carol Tice. **Description:** RingRevenue, a firm that specializes in pay-per-call technology that allows affiliate networks and advertising agencies to track purchases, began a funding round in June 2009 which it closed quickly after obtaining $3.5 million in venture capital. The round was closed earlier than the projections of its owners due to their track record.

411 ■ "Commercials Make Us Like TV More" in *Harvard Business Review* (Vol. 88, October 2010, No. 10, pp. 36)
Pub: Harvard Business School Publishing
Ed: Leif Nelson. **Description:** Research indicates that people prefer commercial interruption over uninterrupted shows due to the break creating a reactivation of the initial pleasure when beginning a desirable activity.

412 ■ *The Complete Guide to Google Adwords: Secrets, Techniques, and Strategies You Can Learn to Make Millions*
Pub: Atlantic Publishing Company
Released: December 1, 2010. **Price:** $24.95. **Description:** Google AdWords, when it launched in 2002 signaled a fundamental shift in what the Internet was for so many individuals and companies. Learning and understanding how Google AdWords operates and how it can be optimized for maximum exposure, boosting click through rates, conversions, placement, and selection of the right keywords, can be the key to a successful online business.

413 ■ "Congress Targets Ad Tracking" in *Inc.* (Vol. 33, November 2011, No. 9, pp. 30)
Pub: Inc. Magazine
Ed: Issie Lapowsky. **Description:** Congressional bills dealing with behavioral tracking whereby advertising networks monitor people's online behavior and use the date to tailor ads to people's interest propose Do Not Track measures which would allow consumers to turn off online behavior tracking by clicking a button.

414 ■ "Connie Ozan; Founder, Design Director, Twist Creative, 37" in *Crain's Cleveland Business* (Vol. 28, November 19, 2007, No. 46)
Pub: Crain Communications, Inc.
Ed: John Booth. **Description:** Profile of Connie Ozan, design director and founder of Twist Creative, an advertising agency that she runs with her husband, Michael; Ms. Ozan credits her husband's business sense in bringing a more strategic side to the company in which to complement her art direction.

415 ■ "Contest Produce Ad Designs on a Dime" in *San Diego Business Journal* (Vol. 31, August 23, 2010, No. 31, pp. 1)
Pub: San Diego Business Journal
Ed: Mike Allen. **Description:** San Diego-based Prova.fm runs design contests for clients such as the U.S. Postal Service. The client then chooses the best entry from the contest. Prova.fm relies on the Internet to deliver a range of possible graphic solutions and allowing the customer to make the right selection for its business through a process called crowdsourcing.

416 ■ "Conversations Need to Yield Actions Measured in Dollars" in *Advertising Age* (Vol. 79, July 7, 2008, No. 26, pp. 18)
Pub: Crain Communications, Inc.
Ed: Jonathan Salem Baskin. **Description:** New ways in which to market to consumers are discussed.

417 ■ "Crain's Makes Ad Sales, Custom Marketing Appointments" in *Crain's Chicago Business* (Vol. 34, October 24, 2011, No. 42, pp. 13)
Pub: Crain Communications Inc.
Description: Crain's Chicago Business announced key appointments in its sales department: David Denor has been named first director of custom marketing services and Kate Van Etten will succeed Denor as advertising director.

418 ■ *The Creative Business Guide to Running a Graphic Design Business*
Pub: W.W. Norton & Company, Incorporated
Ed: Cameron S. Foote. **Released:** April 2004. **Price:** $23.10. **Description:** Advice for running a graphic design firm, focusing on organizations, marketing, personnel and operations.

419 ■ "The CW" in *Brandweek* (Vol. 49, April 21, 2008, No. 16, pp. SR8)
Pub: VNU Business Media, Inc.
Ed: John Consoli. **Description:** Provides contact information for sales and marketing personnel for the CW network as well as a listing of the station's top programming and an analysis of the current season and the target audience for those programs running in the current season. Purchases of advertising feel that Warner Bros. and CBS made a mistake merging The WB and UPN into the new CW rather than folding UPN into the more-established WB; compared to last season ratings are down more than 20 percent across the board.

420 ■ "Dana Anderson's Celebrity Rules for Digital Marketing" in *Advertising Age* (Vol. 81, December 6, 2010, No. 43, pp. 4)
Pub: Crain Communications, Inc.
Ed: Kunur Patel. **Description:** Things that can be learned from Hollywood in terms of marketing strategy and communications are outlined.

421 ■ "Datran Media Executives to Lead Industry Debates Across Q1 Conferences" in *Internet Wire* (January 22, 2010)
Pub: Comtex News Network, Inc.
Description: Datran Media, an industry-leading digital marketing technology company, will be sending members of its management team to several conferences in the early part of the first quarter of 2010; discussions will include Internet marketing innovations, e-commerce and media distribution.

422 ■ "Dear Customer: Managing E-Mail Campaigns" in *Inc.* (March 2008, pp. 58-59)
Pub: Gruner & Jahr USA Publishing
Ed: Ryan Underwood. **Description:** Internet services that help firms manage their online business including email marketing, to manage subscriber lists, comply with spam regulations, monitor bouncebacks, and track potential customers are profiled. Constant Contact, MobileStorm Stun, Campaign Monitor, Pop Commerce, Emma, and StrongMail E-mail Server are among software and services highlighted.

423 ■ *Design and Launch Your Online Boutique in a Week*
Pub: Entrepreneur Press
Ed: Melissa Campanelli. **Released:** June 26, 2008. **Price:** $17.95. **Description:** Tips for starting an online boutique in a short amount of time are given. The books shows how to build the online boutique with designer goods or your own product, ways to create eye-catching content, online tools to handle payments and accept orders, marketing and advertising techniques, and customer service.

424 ■ "Designer is Walking Ad for TIBI Line" in *Charlotte Observer* (February 5, 2007)
Pub: Knight-Ridder/Tribune Business News
Ed: Crystal Dempsey. **Description:** Profile of Amy Smilovic, mother of two children, and clothing designer. Smilovic wears what she designs, making her a great marketing tool for her clothing line TIBI.

425 ■ "A Direct Approach" in *Business Journal-Portland* (Vol. 24, November 9, 2007, No. 36, pp. 1)
Pub: American City Business Journals, Inc.
Ed: Matthew Kish. **Description:** Respond 2 LLC's annual revenue has increased from $14.2 million in 2004 to almost $50 million in 2007. The growth is attributed to a $100 million contract with Vonage. The role of the popularity of infomercials on the success of the Portland-based marketing company is evaluated.

426 ■ "Direct Marketing" in *MarketingMagazine* (Vol. 115, September 27, 2010, No. 13, pp. 74)
Pub: Rogers Publishing Ltd.
Description: Direct marketing data is shared covering provinces in Canada.

427 ■ "Discovery Networks" in *Brandweek* (Vol. 49, April 21, 2008, No. 16, pp. SR9)
Pub: VNU Business Media, Inc.
Ed: Anthony Crupi. **Description:** Provides contact information for sales and marketing personnel for the Discovery networks as well as a listing of the station's top programming and an analysis of the current season and the target audience for those programs running in the current season. The networks flagship station returned to the top 10 in 2007, averaging 1.28 million viewers.

428 ■ "Disney-ABC Domestic Television Distribution" in *Brandweek* (Vol. 49, April 21, 2008, No. 16, pp. SR13)
Pub: VNU Business Media, Inc.
Ed: Marc Berman. **Description:** Provides contact information for sales and marketing personnel for Disney-ABC Domestic Television Distribution as well as a listing of the station's top programming and an analysis of the current season and the target audience for those programs running in the current season.

429 ■ "Doyle: Domino's New Pizza Seasoned with Straight Talk" in *Crain's Detroit Business* (Vol. 26, January 11, 2010, No. 2, pp. 1)
Pub: Crain Communications, Inc.
Ed: Nathan Skid. **Description:** Interview with J. Patrick Doyle, the CEO of Domino's Pizza, Inc.; the company has launched a new marketing campaign that focuses on its bold new vision.

430 ■ "Dramatic Results: Making Opera (Yes, Opera) Seem Young and Hip" in *Inc.* (October 2007, pp. 61-62)
Pub: Gruner & Jahr USA Publishing
Description: Profile of Peter Gelb, who turned New York's Metropolitan Opera into one of the most media-savvy organizations in the country, using a multifaceted marketing strategy through the media. Gelb used streaming audio and simulcasts on satellite radio and movie theaters to promote a message that opera is hip.

431 ■ *Duct Tape Marketing: The World's Most Practical Small Business Marketing Guide*
Pub: Thomas Nelson Inc.
Ed: John Jantsch. **Released:** May 2008. **Price:** $14.99. **Description:** Small business owners are provided the tools and tactics necessary to market and grow a business.

432 ■ *e-Riches 2.0: Next-Generation Marketing Strategies for Making Million Online*
Pub: AMACOM
Ed: Scott Fox. **Released:** May 27, 2009. **Price:** $25.00. **Description:** Beginner's guide to using the Internet to help grow business, including the best ways to

use email lists and newsletters, RSS feeds, online viral marketing, social networking, microblogging, online video and radio/podcasts, tele-seminars and webinars, search engine keyword advertising and affiliate program advertising.

433 ■ *EBay Income: How ANYONE of Any Age, Location, and/or Background Can Build a Highly Profitable Online Business with eBay (Revised 2nd Edition)*
Pub: Atlantic Publishing Company
Released: December 1, 2010. **Price:** $24.95. **Description:** A complete overview of eBay is given and guides any small company through the entire process of creating the auction and auction strategies, photography, writing copy, text and formatting, multiple sales, programming tricks, PayPal, accounting, creating marketing, merchandising, managing email lists, advertising plans, taxes and sales tax, best time to list items and for how long, sniping programs, international customers, opening a storefront, electronic commerce, buy-it now pricing, keywords, Google marketing and eBay secrets.

434 ■ "Economic Crises Calls For Better Marketing Plans" in *Entrepreneur* (October 1, 2008)
Pub: Entrepreneur Media Inc.
Ed: Tim Berry. **Description:** Revising one's business plan is essential, especially during times of economic crisis; sales and marketing plans should be reviewed, analyzed and changed in an attempt to survive the economic downturn.

435 ■ "Economy Should Play Big Role When Presidential Spotlight Returns" in *Business First-Columbus* (November 9, 2007, pp. A1)
Pub: American City Business Journals, Inc.
Ed: Jeff Bell. **Description:** Ohio leaders, including the president of Columbus Chamber, Ty Marsh, suggests that Ohio has benefited from past campaigns as candidates spend money on advertising along with the media exposure the state received. The significance of Ohio in determining the winner in the 2008 presidential elections is discussed.

436 ■ "Elanco Challenges Bayer's Advantage, K9 Advantix Ad Claims" in *Pet Product News* (Vol. 64, November 2010, No. 11, pp. 11)
Pub: BowTie Inc.
Description: Elanco Animal Health has disputed Bayer Animal Health's print and Web advertising claims involving its flea, tick, and mosquito control products Advantage and K9 Advantix. The National Advertising Division of the Council of Better Business Bureaus recommended the discontinuation of ads, while Bayer Animal Health reiterated its commitment to self-regulation.

437 ■ "Entrepreneur Column" in *Entrepreneur* (September 24, 2009)
Pub: Entrepreneur Media, Inc.
Ed: Allen Moon. **Description:** In an attempt to compete with Google, Microsoft and Yahoo have entered a partnership to merge their search services; advice on the best ways to get noticed on this new search engine entitled Bing, is provided.

438 ■ "Every Little Bit Helps" in *Black Enterprise* (Vol. 38, November 2007, No. 4, pp. 102)
Pub: Earl G. Graves Publishing Co. Inc.
Ed: Tennille M. Robinson. **Description:** After a career in the cosmetics industry, Tricialee Riley is marketing and advertising her new venture, the Polish Bar, a salon offering manicures, pedicures, makeup application, and waxing.

439 ■ "Everyone Has a Story Inspired by Chevrolet" in *Automotive News* (Vol. 86, October 31, 2011, No. 6488, pp. S003)
Pub: Crain Communications Inc.
Ed: Keith E. Crain. **Description:** Besides being a great ad slogan, 'Baseball, Hot Dogs, Apple Pie and Chevrolet', the brand conjures up memories for most everyone in our society. Louis Chevrolet had a reputation as a race car driver and lent his name to the car that has endured for 100 years.

440 ■ "Far Out: Satellite Radio Finds New Way to Tally Listeners" in *Globe & Mail* (March 14, 2007, pp. B14)
Pub: CTVglobemedia Publishing Inc.
Ed: Grant Robertson. **Description:** The marketing strategy adopted by satellite radio broadcasting firm XM Satellite Radio Inc. in Canada for increasing its subscriber based is discussed.

441 ■ *Financial Management 101: Get a Grip on Your Business Numbers*
Pub: Self-Counsel Press, Incorporated
Ed: Angie Mohr. **Released:** November 2007. **Price:** $16.95. **Description:** An overview of business planning, financial statements, budgeting and advertising for small businesses. s.

442 ■ "First Mariner's New Ads No Passing Fancy" in *Boston Business Journal* (Vol. 29, September 16, 2011, No. 19, pp. 1)
Pub: American City Business Journals Inc.
Ed: Gary Haber. **Description:** Baltimore, Maryland-based First Mariner Bank replaced Ed Hale, the bank's CEO and founder, as the pitchman for its television ads with Ravens quarterback Joe Flacco. Hales' exit from the advertisements is the result of First Mariner's struggle to raise money for recapitalization.

443 ■ "First the Merger: Then, The Culture Clash. How To Fix the Little Things That Can Tear a Company Apart" in *Inc.* (January 2008)
Pub: Gruner & Jahr USA Publishing
Ed: Elaine Appleton Grant. **Description:** Ways three CEOs handled the culture classes that followed after company mergers; companies profiled include Fuel Outdoor, an outdoor advertising company; Nelson, an interior design and architecture firm; and Beber Silverstein, an ad agency.

444 ■ "Fitter from Twitter" in *Boston Business Journal* (Vol. 30, December 17, 2010, No. 47, pp. 1)
Pub: Boston Business Journal
Ed: Lisa van der Pool. **Description:** Small businesses are increasing their use of the Twitter microblogging platform to attract and retain customers. Lisa Johnson, who owns Modern Pilates studios, managed to raise awareness of her personal brand nationally through the social media platform.

445 ■ "Fox" in *Brandweek* (Vol. 49, April 21, 2008, No. 16, pp. SR3)
Pub: VNU Business Media, Inc.
Ed: John Consoli. **Description:** Provides contact information for sales and marketing personnel for the Fox network as well as a listing of the station's top programming and an analysis of the current season and the target audience for those programs running in the current season. In terms of upfront advertising dollars, it looks as if Fox will be competing against NBC for third place due to its success at courting the 18-49-year-old male demographic.

446 ■ "Fox Cable Entertainment Networks" in *Brandweek* (Vol. 49, April 21, 2008, No. 16, pp. SR10)
Pub: VNU Business Media, Inc.
Ed: Anthony Crupi. **Description:** Provides contact information for sales and marketing personnel for the Fox Cable Entertainment networks as well as a listing of the station's top programming and an analysis of the current season and the target audience for those programs running in the current season.

447 ■ "A Framework for Conceptual Contributions in Marketing" in *Journal of Marketing* (Vol. 75, July 2011, No. 4, pp. 136)
Pub: American Marketing Association
Ed: Deborah J. MacInnis. **Description:** A look at a new framework for thinking about conceptualization in marketing is presented. Conceptual advances are essential to the vitality of the marketing discipline but recent writings indicate that advancement is slowing. The types of conceptual contributions are described, including their similarities and difference, and their importance to the field of marketing.

448 ■ "Friendly" in *Ice Cream Reporter* (Vol. 21, August 20, 2008, No. 9, pp. 8)
Pub: Ice Cream Reporter
Description: Advertising Age presented Friendly's with the award, "Ad of the Day" for its television commercial depicting a Norman Rockwell-esque family transported to a psychedelic wonderland.

449 ■ "From OTC Sellers to Surgeons, Healthcare Marketers Target Women to Achieve Growth" in *Marketing to Women* (February 2008)
Pub: EPM Communications, Inc.
Description: Healthcare companies are targeting women with ad campaigns, new product development and new technology in order to reach and develop brand loyalty.

450 ■ "FTC Takes Aim At Foreclosure 'Rescue' Firm" in *The Business Journal-Serving Greater Tampa Bay* (Vol. 28, September 19, 2008, No. 39)
Pub: American City Business Journals, Inc.
Ed: Michael Hinman. **Description:** United Home Savers LLP has been ordered to halt its mortgage foreclosure rescue services after the Federal Trade Commission accused it of deceptive advertising. The company is alleged to have charged customers $1,200 in exchange for unfulfilled promises to keep them in their homes.

451 ■ "Funeral Directors Get Creative As Boomers Near Great Beyond" in *Advertising Age* (Vol. 79, October 13, 2008, No. 38, pp. 30)
Pub: Crain Communications, Inc.
Ed: Lenore Skenazy. **Description:** Despite the downturn in the economy, the funeral business is thriving due to the number of baby boomers who realize the importance of making preparations for their death. Marketers are getting creative in their approach and many companies have taken into consideration the need for a more environmental friendly way to dispose of bodies and thus have created innovative businesses that reflect this need.

452 ■ "Funny Business" in *Canadian Business* (Vol. 82, April 27, 2009, No. 7, pp. 27)
Pub: Rogers Media
Ed: Rachel Pulfer. **Description:** Companies are advised to use humor in marketing to drive more revenue. IBM Canada, for example, commissioned Second City Communications for a marketing campaign that involved humor. While IBM Canada declined to give sales or traffic figures, firm executives rank the marketing campaign as an overall success.

453 ■ "General Motors Can't Kick Incentives-But They Work" in *Advertising Age* (Vol. 79, July 7, 2008, No. 26, pp. 3)
Pub: Crain Communications, Inc.
Ed: Jean Halliday. **Description:** General Motors Corp. was able to maintain their market share just as Toyota Motor Corp. was beginning to pass the manufacturer; GM lured in customers with a sales incentive that they heavily advertised and subsequently helped build demand; investors, however, were not impressed and GM shares were hammered to their lowest point in 50 years after analysts speculated the company might go bankrupt.

454 ■ "Get Real" in *Entrepreneur* (Vol. 36, April 2008, No. 4, pp. 86)
Pub: Entrepreneur Media, Inc.
Ed: Kim T. Gordon. **Description:** Selling points of a product or service must show real benefits to women. Provide detailed information as women look at details more deeply before purchasing. Other tips on how to market products designed for women consumers are provided.

455 ■ "Giants Now Admit They Roam Planet Earth; Time To Buy?" in *Barron's* (Vol. 88, March 31, 2008, No. 13, pp. 39)
Pub: Dow Jones & Company, Inc.
Ed: Eric J. Savitz. **Description:** Oracle's third-quarter results showed that top-line growth fell short of expectations but the company is expected to fare

better than most applications companies in the downturn. Google had a flat growth in the number of people who click their online ads. The time for investors in the tech sector with a long-term horizon has arrived.

456 ■ "Global Imagery in Online Advertisements" in *Business Communication Quarterly* (December 2007, pp. 487)
Pub: Sage Publications USA
Ed: Geraldine E. Hynes, Marius Janson. **Description:** Respondents from six countries were interviewed about their reactions to two online ads to determine cultural differences in understanding advertising elements. Universal appeals and cultural values determine the effectiveness of symbols in online advertising.

457 ■ "Go Beyond Local Search With Hyper-Local" in *Women Entrepreneur* (October 30, 2008)
Pub: Entrepreneur Media Inc.
Ed: Lena West. **Description:** According to Forrester Research, as much as $500 billion in local spending in 2007 was influenced by the Internet and industry analysts report that consumers spend approximately 80 percent of their income within 50 miles of their home. Discussion of ways in which to capitalize on the hyper-local trend that is being driven by greater Internet connectivity and use of the web to find information is provided.

458 ■ "Google, MySpace Deal Hits Snag" in *Globe & Mail* (February 7, 2007, pp. B11)
Pub: CTVglobemedia Publishing Inc.
Ed: Julia Angwin; Kevin J. Delaney. **Description:** MySpace's intention to partner with eBay which is delaying the finalization of its $900 million online advertising deal signed with Google Inc. is discussed.

459 ■ "Got Slogan? Guidelines for Creating Effective Slogans" in *Business Horizons* (September-October 2007, pp. 415)
Pub: Elsevier Technology Publications
Ed: Chiranjeev Kohli, Lance Leuthesser, Rajneesh Suri. **Description:** Relevant case studies of industry publications are considered to determine the creation and utilization of effective slogans. The importance of branding as well as factors that contribute to memory and recall are discussed.

460 ■ *Guerrilla Marketing During Tough Times*
Pub: Morgan James Publishing, LLC
Ed: Jay Conrad Levinson. **Released:** November 2005. **Price:** $14.00. **Description:** Ways to market a small business during slow economic times.

461 ■ *Guerrilla Marketing for the New Millennium*
Pub: Morgan James Publishing, LLC
Ed: Jay Conrad Levinson. **Released:** September 2005. **Price:** $14.00. **Description:** Steps to successfully market a small business on the Internet.

462 ■ *Guerrilla Marketing: Put Your Advertising on Steroids*
Pub: Morgan James Publishing, LLC
Ed: Jay Conrad Levinson. **Released:** December 2005. **Price:** $14.00. **Description:** Marketing concepts to successfully advertise any Internet business, featuring the ten most successful advertising campaigns of the 20th Century.

463 ■ "Half of Canadian Firms to Boost Marketing Budgets" in *Globe & Mail* (January 22, 2007, pp. B1)
Pub: CTVglobemedia Publishing Inc.
Ed: Keith McArthur. **Description:** The advertising and marketing spending plans of different companies are presented.

464 ■ "Harley-Davidson Moves to Unconventional Marketing Plan" in *Business Journal-Milwaukee* (Vol. 28, November 26, 2010, No. 8, pp. A1)
Pub: Milwaukee Business Journal
Ed: Rich Rovito. **Description:** Harley Davidson Inc. hired Boulder, Colorado-based Victors & Spoils, an agency that specializes in crowdsourcing, to implement a new creative marketing model. Under the plan, Harley Davidson will draw on the ideas of its brand enthusiasts to help guide the brand's marketing direction.

465 ■ "Headwinds From the New Sod Slow Aer Lingus" in *Barron's* (Vol. 88, March 10, 2008, No. 10, pp. M6)
Pub: Dow Jones & Company, Inc.
Ed: Sean Walters; Arindam Nag. **Description:** Aer Lingus faces a drop in its share prices with a falling US market, higher jet fuel prices, and lower long-haul passenger load factors. British media companies Johnston Press and Yell Group are suffering from weaker ad revenue and heavier debt payments due to the credit crunch.

466 ■ "'Help Wanted' Meets 'Buy It Now': Why More Companies Are Integrating Marketing and Recruiting" in *Inc.* (November 2007, pp. 50-52)
Pub: Gruner & Jahr USA Publishing
Ed: Ryan McCarthy. **Description:** Five tips to merge marketing and recruiting together include: thinking every help wanted ad as a marketing opportunity, treating every job candidate as a potential customer, involving the youngest employees in the interview process, look for way to promote recruiting events, and to sponsor community-oriented events.

467 ■ "Herrell's Launches New Corporate Identity at Fancy Food Show" in *Ice Cream Reporter* (Vol. 23, July 20, 2010, No. 8, pp. 3)
Pub: Ice Cream Reporter
Description: Herrell's ice cream introduced a new corporate branding at the Summer 2010 Fancy Food Show last summer. Slightly Mad Communications advertising agency developed the new brand to reflect the era of the early 1970s.

468 ■ "High-Tech, Niche Options Change Sports Marketing" in *Crain's Detroit Business* (Vol. 24, March 17, 2008, No. 11, pp. 14)
Pub: Crain Communications, Inc.
Ed: Leah Boyd. **Description:** Sports advertisers have an ever-increasing menu of high-tech or niche marketing options such as interactive campaigns through cell phones and electronic banners which can span arenas.

469 ■ *How to Advertise a Small Business: Step by Step Guide to Starting Your Own Business*
Pub: Lewis and Renn Associates
Ed: Leslie D. Renn; Jerre G. Lewis. **Released:** 2007. **Price:** $21.95. **Description:** Step-by-step guide to help small business owners advertise products and services.

470 ■ "How to Attract Big-City Talent to Small Towns" in *Advertising Age* (Vol. 79, July 7, 2008, No. 26, pp. 24)
Pub: Crain Communications, Inc.
Ed: Joe Erwin. **Description:** Advice concerning ways in which to attract talent to mid-market agencies is given and innovative techniques that have worked for some firms are discussed.

471 ■ "How to Boost Your Super Bowl ROI" in *Advertising Age* (Vol. 80, December 7, 2009, No. 41, pp. 3)
Pub: Crain's Communications
Ed: Abbey Klaassen. **Description:** Internet marketing is essential, even for the corporations that can afford to spend $3 million on a 30-second Super Bowl spot; last year, Super Bowl advertising reached an online viewership of 99.5 million while 98.7 million people watched the game on television validating the idea that public relations must go farther than a mere television ad campaign. Social media provides businesses with a longer shelf life for their ad campaigns. Advice is also given regarding ways in which to strategize a smart and well-thought plan for utilizing the online marketing options currently available.

472 ■ *How to Get Rich on the Internet*
Pub: Morgan James Publishing, LLC
Ed: Ted Ciuba. **Released:** August 2004. **Price:** $19.95. **Description:** Interviews with successful Internet entrepreneurs provide insight into marketing products and services online using minimal investment. The importance of a sound marketing ad campaign using the Internet is discussed; maintaining a database and Website will automatically carry out business transactions daily. Suggestions for various types of businesses to run online are given.

473 ■ "How to Improve Your Mobile Marketing" in *Contractor* (Vol. 56, October 2009, No. 10, pp. 54)
Pub: Penton Media, Inc.
Ed: Matt Michel. **Description:** Plumbers can improve their mobile advertising by making their logos as large as possible and positioning their logo on top of the truck so people can see it over traffic. They should also make the phone numbers small because people only take note of these when the truck is parked.

474 ■ "How to Ramp Up Marketing in a Downturn" in *Entrepreneur* (Vol. 37, July 2009, No. 7, pp. 55)
Pub: Entrepreneur Media, Inc.
Ed: Jeff Wuorio. **Description:** How businesses can save money while boosting their marketing efforts during a down economy is discussed. Using price-driven marketing, online social networks, and cause-driven marketing are among the suggested ways companies can attract more customers. Guarantees and warrantees, as well as contests, can also be used as marketing tools.

475 ■ *How to Start a Faux Painting or Mural Business, Second Edition*
Pub: Allworth Press
Ed: Rebecca Pittman. **Released:** October 1, 2010. **Price:** $24.95. **Description:** Updated and expanded to cover better ways to advertise, innovative supplies (such as Venetian plasters and stained cements), unique bidding and studio setups required for new plasters and varnishes.

476 ■ *How to Use the Internet to Advertise, Promote, and Market Your Business or Web Site: With Little or No Money*
Pub: Atlantic Publishing Company
Released: December 1, 2010. **Price:** $24.95. **Description:** Information is given to help build, promote, and make money from your Website or brick and mortar store using the Internet, with minimal costs.

477 ■ *Hug Your Customers*
Pub: Hyperion Books
Ed: Jack Mitchell. **Price:** $19.95. **Description:** The CEO of Mitchells/Roberts, two very successful clothing stores, professes his belief in showering customers with attention. His secrets for long-term business success include advice about attracting a good staff, lowering marketing costs, and maintaining higher gross margins and revenues.

478 ■ "An Ice Boost in Revenue; Wings Score With Expanded Corporate Sales" in *Crain's Detroit Business* (Vol. 25, June 1, 2009, No. 22)
Pub: Crain Communications Inc. - Detroit
Ed: Bill Shea. **Description:** Stanley Cup finals always boost business for the Detroit area, even during a recession. The Red Wings corporate office reported corporate sponsorship revenue luxury suite rentals, Legends Club seats and advertising were up 40 percent this year over 2008.

479 ■ *Instant Income*
Pub: McGraw-Hill Inc.
Ed: Janet Switzer. **Released:** February 2007. **Price:** $30.95 (CND). **Description:** Book covers small business advertising techniques, marketing, joint ventures, and sales.

480 ■ "Insurers No Longer Paying Premium for Advertising" in *Brandweek* (Vol. 49, April 21, 2008, No. 16, pp. SR3)
Pub: VNU Business Media, Inc.
Ed: Eric Newman. **Description:** Insurance companies are cutting their advertising budgets after years of accelerated double-digit growth in spending due to the economic downturn, five years of record-breaking ad spend and a need to cut expenditures as claims costs rise and a competitive market keeps premiums in place. Statistical data included.

481 ■ "Internet Marketing Agency .Com Marketing Wins National Awards for Web Design and SEO" in *Marketing Weekly News* (Jan. 2, 2010)
Pub: Investment Weekly News
Description: Internet marketing agency .Com Marketing has won two bronze awards for its exceptional quality web services; the company is a full-service interactive marketing and advertising agency that specializes in a variety of online services including web design, social media marketing and press releases.

482 ■ "Internet Marketing and Social Media Knowledge Vital for SMBs" in *Internet Wire* (November 24, 2009)
Pub: Comtex News Network, Inc.
Description: Small and medium-size businesses must learn to market themselves over the Internet in order to succeed and grow in today's marketplace. Web Marketing Today offers the largest source of the most important information concerning doing business on the Internet including e-commerce, email marketing and social networking opportunities.

483 ■ "Irene Rosenfeld; Chairman and CEO, Kraft Foods Inc." in *Crain's Chicago Business* (Vol. 31, May 5, 2008, No. 18, pp. 31)
Pub: Crain Communications, Inc.
Ed: David Sterrett. **Description:** Profile of Irene Rosenfeld who is the chairman and CEO of Kraft Foods Inc. and is entering the second year of a three-year plan to boost sales of well-known brands such as Oreo, Velveeta and Oscar Mayer while facing soaring commodity costs and a declining market-share. Ms. Rosenfeld's turnaround strategy also entails spending more on advertising and giving managers more control over their budgets and product development.

484 ■ "Israeli Spam Law May Have Global Impact" in *Information Today* (Vol. 26, February 2009, No. 2, pp. 28)
Pub: Information Today, Inc.
Ed: David Mirchin. **Description:** Israels new law, called Amendment 40 of the Communications Law, will regulate commercial solicitations including those sent without permission via email, fax, automatic phone dialing systems, or short messaging technologies.

485 ■ "It's Back to Business for the Ravens" in *Boston Business Journal* (Vol. 29, July 29, 2011, No. 12, pp. 1)
Pub: American City Business Journals Inc.
Ed: Scott Dance. **Description:** The Baltimore Ravens football team has been marketing open sponsorship packages following the end of the National Football League lockout. Team officials are working to get corporate logos and slogans on radio and television commercials and online advertisements.

486 ■ *It's Not Who You Know - It's Who Knows You!: The Small Business Guide to Raising Your Profits by Raising Your Profile*
Pub: John Wiley & Sons, Inc.
Ed: David Avrin. **Released:** November 9, 2010. **Price:** $24.95. **Description:** When it comes to promoting a small business or a brand, it is essential to know how valuable high-profile attention can be. But for most small companies, the cost of hiring an outside firm to increase attention can be too expensive.

487 ■ "Johnson's Taps Online Animation" in *Marketing to Women* (Vol. 21, April 2008, No. 4, pp. 3)
Pub: EPM Communications, Inc.
Description: Johnson's has launched a new integrated campaign for its baby lotion in an effort to appeal to the growing number of moms online.

488 ■ "Kawasaki's New Top Gun" in *Brandweek* (Vol. 49, April 21, 2008, No. 16, pp. 18)
Pub: VNU Business Media, Inc.
Description: Discusses Kawasaki's marketing plan which included designing an online brochure in which visitors could create a video by building their own test track on a grid and then selecting visual special effects and musical overlay. This engaging and innovative marketing technique generated more than 166,000 unique users within the first three months of being launched.

489 ■ *The King of Madison Avenue: David Ogilvy and the Making of Modern Advertising*
Pub: Palgrave Macmillan
Ed: Kenneth Roman. **Released:** 2009. **Price:** $27.95. **Description:** The rise and fall of David Ogilvy, once the leader on Madison Avenue, is discussed.

490 ■ *Lateral Marketing: New Techniques for Finding Breakthrough Ideas*
Pub: John Wiley & Sons, Incorporated
Ed: Philip Kotler, Fernando Trias de Bes. **Released:** September 2003. **Price:** $34.95. **Description:** Lateral marketing complements traditional marketing by allowing marketers develop a new product for a wider audience.

491 ■ "LatinWorks Cozies Up to Chevy in Detroit" in *Austin Business Journal* (Vol. 31, August 12, 2011, No. 23, pp. A1)
Pub: American City Business Journals Inc.
Ed: Sandra Zaragoza. **Description:** Hispanic marketing agency LatinWorks opened an office in Detroit to better serve its client Chevrolet and to potentially secure more contracts from its parent company General Motors, whose offices are located nearby.

492 ■ "Leading Ohio Internet Marketing Firm Announces Growth in September" in *Marketing Weekly News* (September 26, 2009, pp. 24)
Pub: Investment Weekly News
Description: Despite a poor economy, Webbed Marketing, a leading social media marketing and search engine optimization firm in the Midwest, has added five additional professionals to its fast-growing team. The company continues to win new business, provide more services and hire talented employees.

493 ■ "Leapin' Lizards, Does SoBe Have Some Work To Do On Life Water" in *Brandweek* (Vol. 49, April 21, 2008, No. 16, pp. 32)
Pub: VNU Business Media, Inc.
Ed: Amy Shea. **Description:** Discusses the competing marketing campaigns of both Vitaminwater, now owned by Coca-Cola, and SoBe Life Water which is owned by Pepsi; also looks at the repositioning of Life Water as a thirst-quencher, rather than a green product as well as the company's newest advertising campaign.

494 ■ "LED Screen Technology Takes Centre Stage" in *Canadian Electronics* (Vol. 23, June-July 2008, No. 4, pp. 17)
Pub: Action Communication Inc.
Ed: Ed Whitaker. **Description:** Display technologies based on light emitting diodes are becoming more popular due to their flexibility, versatility and reproducibility of displays. These are being increasingly used in different applications, such as advertising and concerts.

495 ■ "Lifetime Networks" in *Brandweek* (Vol. 49, April 21, 2008, No. 16, pp. SR10)
Pub: VNU Business Media, Inc.
Ed: Anthony Crupi. **Description:** Provides contact information for sales and marketing personnel for the ABC network as well as a listing of the station's top programming and an analysis of the current season and the target audience for those programs running in the current season. Lifetime will still produce its original signature movies but will now focus its emphasis more clearly on series development in order to appeal to a younger, hipper female demographic.

496 ■ "Local Firm Snaps up 91 Area Pizza Huts" in *Orlando Business Journal* (Vol. 26, January 8, 2010, No. 32, pp. 1)
Pub: American City Business Journals
Ed: Alexis Muellner, Anjali Fluker. **Description:** Orlando, Florida-based CFL Pizza LLC bought the 91 Orlando-area Pizza Hut restaurants for $35 million from parent company Yum! Brands Inc. CFL Pizza plans to distribute parts of the business to Central Florida vendors and the first business up for grabs is the advertising budget.

497 ■ "Looking Out for the Little Guys" in *Black Enterprise* (Vol. 38, October 2007, No. 3, pp. 58)
Pub: Earl G. Graves Publishing Co. Inc.
Ed: Kaylyn Kendall Dines. **Description:** Biz Tech-Connect is a Web portal that offers free online and social networking, along with four modules that help small businesses with marketing and advertising, communications and mobility, financial management, and customer relationship management.

498 ■ "Lotteries Scratch Their Way to Billions" in *Saint Louis Business Journal* (Vol. 31, August 19, 2011, No. 52, pp. 1)
Pub: Saint Louis Business Journal
Ed: Kelsey Volkmann. **Description:** Missouri Lottery reported $1 billion in sales in 2011. A six-fold increase in the lottery's advertising budget is seen to drive the revenue increase; a 4.5 percent rise in its scratch-off tickets and new sponsorships has also contributed to the development.

499 ■ "Macy's Seeks Balance in All Things Ad-Related" in *Crain's Chicago Business* (Vol. 31, March 31, 2008, No. 13, pp. 19)
Pub: Crain Communications, Inc.
Ed: Natalie Zmuda. **Description:** Macy's Inc. is seeking to balance its national television campaign with locally tailored promotions and products.

500 ■ *Made To Stick: Why Some Ideas Survive and Others Die*
Pub: Random House
Ed: Chip Heath; Dan Heath. **Released:** 2007. **Price:** $26.00. **Description:** Eight principles marketers can use to make their ideas and branding efforts resonate with consumers.

501 ■ *MadScam: Kick-Ass Advertising Without the Madison Avenue Price Tag*
Pub: McGraw-Hill Ryerson Ltd.
Ed: George Parker. **Released:** November 2006. **Price:** $24.95. **Description:** Effective advertising strategies for small companies on a budget are presented.

502 ■ *Mail Order in the Internet Age*
Pub: Morgan James Publishing, LLC
Ed: Ted Ciuba. **Released:** May 2004. **Price:** $19.95. **Description:** Direct response market, or mail order, for marketing and selling a product or service is discussed, with emphasis on how direct marketing compares favorably to other methods in terms of speed, ease, profitability, and affordability. Advice is given for writing ads; seminars to attend; and newsletters, mailing lists and magazines in which to subscribe.

503 ■ "Making Sense of Ambiguous Evidence" in *Harvard Business Review* (Vol. 86, September 2008, No. 9, pp. 53)
Pub: Harvard Business School Press
Ed: Lisa Burrell. **Description:** Documentary filmmaker Errol Morris emphasizes the role of perception in portraying objective reality, and how investigation and analysis enhance the accuracy of that portrayal.

504 ■ "Marketers Push for Mobile Tuesday as the New Black Friday" in *Advertising Age* (Vol. 79, December 1, 2008, No. 44, pp. 21)
Pub: Crain Communications, Inc.
Ed: Natalie Zmuda. **Description:** Marketers are using an innovative approach in an attempt to stimulate business on the Tuesday following Thanksgiving by utilizing consumer's cell phones to alert them of sales or present them with coupons for this typically slow retail business day; with this campaign both advertisers and retailers are hoping to start Mobile Tuesday, another profitable shopping day in line with Black Friday and Cyber Monday.

505 ■ "Marketing in the Digital World: Here's How to Craft a Smart Online Strategy" in *Black Enterprise* (Vol. 40, July 2010, No. 12, pp. 47)
Pub: Earl G. Graves Publishing Co. Inc.
Ed: Sonya A. Donaldson. **Description:** Social media is an integral part of any small business plan in addressing marketing, sales, and branding strategies.

506 ■ *Marketing Outrageously: How to Increase Your Revenue by Staggering Amounts*
Pub: Bard Press
Ed: Jon Spoelstra. **Released:** July 25, 2001. **Price:** $24.95. **Description:** Creative marketing strategies are defined. The book shows how considering marketing problems as outrageously but consistently can benefit any small business. The author talks about his own experience when there were not adequate funds for marketing and advertising and the outrageous approach he created to promote sports teams.

507 ■ "Marketing: 'Twill Be the Season" in *Entrepreneur* (Vol. 35, October 2007, No. 10, pp. 108)
Pub: Entrepreneur Media Inc.
Ed: Kim T. Gordon. **Description:** Entrepreneurs should plan ahead in order to promote products for the holiday season, since it is peak sales time. They can unify their business theme, use customer incentives, advertise early using TV or radio, and reorganize the company Website. Other ways to market for the holiday season are provided.

508 ■ *Marketing in a Web 2.0 World - Using Social Media, Webinars, Blogs, and More to Boost Your Small Business on a Budget*
Pub: Atlantic Publishing Company
Ed: Peter VanRysdam. **Released:** June 1, 2010. **Price:** $24.95. **Description:** Web 2.0 technologies have leveled the playing field for small companies trying to boost their presence by giving them an equal voice against larger competitors. Advice is given to help target your audience using social networking hubs.

509 ■ *Marketing Without Money for Small and Midsize Businesses: 300 FREE and Cheap Ways to Increase Your Sales*
Pub: Halle House Publishing
Ed: Nicholas E. Bade. **Released:** July 2005. **Price:** $16.95. **Description:** Three hundred practical low-cost or no-cost strategies to increase sales, focusing on free advertising, free marketing assistance, and free referrals to the Internet.

510 ■ *Marketing Works: Unlock Big Company Strategies for Small Business*
Pub: Morgan James Publishing, LLC
Ed: Chris Lee; Daniele Lima. **Released:** May 2006. **Price:** $19.95. **Description:** Marketing strategies for any small business are outlined.

511 ■ *Marketing Your Small Business for Big Profits*
Pub: Morgan James Publishing, LLC
Released: September 2006. **Price:** $12.95. **Description:** Successful marketing tip to grow a small business are presented.

512 ■ "Mars Advertising's Orbit Grows as Other Ad Segments Fall" in *Crain's Detroit Business* (Vol. 25, June 1, 2009, No. 22, pp. 10)
Pub: Crain Communications Inc. - Detroit
Ed: Bill Shea. **Description:** An electrical fire burned at Mars Advertising's headquarters in Southfield, Michigan. The company talks about its plans for regrouping and rebuilding. The family firm specializes in in-store marketing that targets consumers already in the buying mode.

513 ■ "McD's Warms Up For Olympics Performance" in *Advertising Age* (Vol. 79, July 7, 2008, No. 26, pp. 8)
Pub: Crain Communications, Inc.
Ed: Description: Overview of McDonald's marketing plans for the company's sponsorship of the Olympics which includes a website, an alternate-reality game, names featured on U.S. athletes and on-the-ground activities.

514 ■ "Medicine Men" in *Canadian Business* (Vol. 80, February 12, 2007, No. 4, pp. 19)
Pub: Rogers Media
Ed: Joe Castaldo. **Description:** The effort of HPI Health Products' owners Dong Pedersen and Kent Pedersen to popularize their pain reliever product 'Lakota' is discussed.

515 ■ "Mobile Marketing Grows With Size of Cell Phone Screens" in *Crain's Detroit Business* (Vol. 24, January 14, 2008, No. 2, pp. 13)
Pub: Crain Communications Inc. - Detroit
Ed: Bill Shea. **Description:** Experts are predicting increased marketing for cell phones with the inception of larger screens and improved technology.

516 ■ "Moet, Rivals Pour More Ad Bucks Into Bubbly" in *Advertising Age* (Vol. 88, September 3, 2007, No. 35, pp. 4)
Pub: Crain Communications, Inc.
Ed: Jeremy Mullman. **Description:** In an attempt to revive sluggish sales, champagne companies are raising their advertising budgets, transforming themselves from light-spending seasonal players to year-round heavyweights in the advertising world.

517 ■ "Moms Dis Super Bowl Ads" in *Marketing to Women* (Vol. 21, March 2008, No. 3, pp. 6)
Pub: EPM Communications, Inc.
Description: According to a survey by the Marketing to Moms Coalition, although 80 percent of moms tune into the Super Bowl most complain that the advertisements are not appropriate for a family sports viewing experience.

518 ■ "Moms Rely on Coupons, Specials to Lower Grocery Bills" in *Marketing to Women* (Vol. 23, November 2010, No. 11, pp. 8)
Pub: EPM Communications, Inc.
Description: Eighty-four percent of moms surveyed reported using coupons when grocery shopping in order to lower costs. They are also purchasing less snack foods, fewer brand name items, alcoholic beverages, organic items, meat and fresh fruits and vegetables.

519 ■ "Moosylvania Releases Latest XL Marketing Trends Report" in *Wireless News* (October 6, 2009)
Pub: Close-Up Media
Description: Moosylvania, a digital promotion and branding agency that also has an on-site research facility, has released its 2nd XL Marketing Trends Report which focuses on digital video; the study defines the top digital video trends marketers must focus on now and well into the future and notes that in 2010, Mobile Web Devices, such as smart phones will outnumber computers in this country. Statistical data included.

520 ■ "More Ad Shops Link Payment to Results" in *Boston Business Journal* (Vol. 30, November 12, 2010, No. 42, pp. 1)
Pub: Boston Business Journal
Ed: Lisa van der Pool. **Description:** A growing number of advertising firms are proposing a 'value-based' payment scheme where they are paid a base fee plus a bonus if certain sales goals or other targets are met. The proposed shift in payment scheme is seen as reminiscent of the dot-com boom about ten years ago. Advertising firms are traditionally paid by the hour.

521 ■ "More Leading Retailers Using Omniture Conversion Solutions to Boost Sales and Ecommerce Performance" in *Internet Wire* (Sept. 22,2009)
Pub: Comtex News Network, Inc.
Description: Many retailers are utilizing Omniture conversion solutions to improve the performance of their ecommerce businesses; recent enhancements to Omniture Merchandising and Omniture Recommendations help clients drive increased conversion to their Internet ventures.

522 ■ "More Sales Leads, Please: Or, What Happened When Frontline Selling Started Practicing What It Preaches" in *Inc.* (November 2007)
Pub: Gruner & Jahr USA Publishing
Description: Frontline Selling located in Oakland, New Jersey helps train sales teams to generate and convert sales leads. The consulting firm doubled their marketing budget to increase their own sales.

523 ■ "MTV Networks" in *Brandweek* (Vol. 49, April 21, 2008, No. 16, pp. SR10)
Pub: VNU Business Media, Inc.
Ed: Anthony Crupi. **Description:** Provides contact information for sales and marketing personnel for the MTV networks as well as a listing of the station's top programming and an analysis of the current season and the target audience for those programs running in the current season. MTV networks include MTV, VH1, Nickelodeon and Comedy Central.

524 ■ "Navigate to Better Direct Response Messaging Through Search Marketing" in *DM News* (Vol. 32, January 18, 2010, No. 2, pp. 26)
Pub: Haymarket Media, Inc.
Ed: Mark Simon. **Description:** Important lessons to apply when utilizing Internet marketing schemes include telling your customers you have what they want to buy, provide them with discounts or ways to save additional money and drive them to a customized destination like an Online store.

525 ■ "NBC" in *Brandweek* (Vol. 49, April 21, 2008, No. 16, pp. SR6)
Pub: VNU Business Media, Inc.
Ed: John Consoli. **Description:** Provides contact information for sales and marketing personnel for the NBC network as well as a listing of the station's top programming and an analysis of the current season and the target audience for those programs running in the current season. NBC also devised a new strategy of announcing its prime-time schedule 52 weeks in advance which was a hit for advertisers who felt this gave them a better opportunity to plan for product placement. Even with the station's creative sales programs, they could face a challenge from Fox in terms of upfront advertisement purchases.

526 ■ "NBC Universal Cable" in *Brandweek* (Vol. 49, April 21, 2008, No. 16, pp. SR11)
Pub: VNU Business Media, Inc.
Ed: Anthony Crupi. **Description:** Provides contact information for sales and marketing personnel for the NBC Universal Cable networks as well as a listing of the station's top programming and an analysis of the current season and the target audience for those programs running in the current season. The network's stations include USA, Sci Fi and Bravo. Ad revenue for the network grew 30 percent in the first quarter.

527 ■ "NBC Universal Domestic Television Distribution" in *Brandweek* (Vol. 49, April 21, 2008, No. 16, pp. SR13)
Pub: VNU Business Media, Inc.
Ed: Marc Berman. **Description:** Provides contact information for sales and marketing personnel for NBC Universal Domestic Television Distribution as well as a listing of the station's top programming and an analysis of the current season and the target audience for those programs running in the current season.

528 ■ "Never Boring: Ad Agencies' Big Changes" in *Business Courier* (Vol. 24, February 8, 2008, No. 44, pp. 1)
Pub: American City Business Journals, Inc.
Ed: Dan Monk. **Description:** Many changes are occurring in Cincinnati's advertising industry, including new clients, acquisitions, and market leaders, and an increase in employment. Bridge Worldwide passed Northlich LLC as the city's largest advertising agency.

529 ■ "The New Basics of Marketing" in *Inc.* (February 2008, pp. 75-81)
Pub: Gruner & Jahr USA Publishing
Ed: Leigh Buchanan. **Description:** New tools for marketing a business or service include updating or upgrading a Website, using email or texting, or advertising on a social Internet network.

530 ■ "New King Top the Charts" in *The Business Journal-Portland* (Vol. 25, August 8, 2008, No. 22, pp. 1)
Pub: American City Business Journals, Inc.
Ed: Andy Giegerich. **Description:** Spanish-language KRYP-FM station's spring 2008 ratings soared to 6.4

from 2.8 for the previous year. The station timing is flawless given the fact that one of every three new Portland-area residents between 2002 and 2007 were Latino.

531 ■ "New Sony HD Ads Tout Digital" in *Brandweek* (Vol. 49, April 21, 2008, No. 16, pp. 5)
Pub: VNU Business Media, Inc.
Description: Looking to promote Sony Electronics' digital imaging products, the company has launched another campaign effort known as HDNA, a play on the words high-definition and DNA; originally Sony focused the HDNA campaign on their televisions, the new ads will include still and video cameras as well and marketing efforts will consist of advertising in print, Online, television spots and publicity at various venues across the country.

532 ■ "New TurnHere Survey Reveals Online Video Trends" in *Internet Wire* (October 22, 2009)
Pub: Comtex News Network, Inc.
Description: TurnHere, Inc., the leading online video marketing services company, released the findings of its recent survey regarding current and future trends in online video among marketing agencies and brand recognition; the report found that online video has and will continue to play a prominent role in the realm of marketing edging out both search and email marketing campaigns. Additional highlights and statistical data included.

533 ■ "A Nice Consistency" in *Inc.* (Vol. 31, January-February 2009, No. 1, pp. 94)
Pub: Mansueto Ventures LLC
Ed: Jason Del Rey. **Description:** PJ Madison spent almost a quarter of its revenue promoting its latest product, organic ice cream. The Texas-based firm saw sales increase dramatically.

534 ■ "No, Those Casino Rama Ads Aren't Running in NYC" in *Globe & Mail* (March 15, 2006, pp. B1)
Pub: CTVglobemedia Publishing Inc.
Ed: Keith McArthur. **Description:** The reason Casino Rama did not advertise on New York Cabs is discussed.

535 ■ "Nortel Makes Customers Stars in New Campaign" in *Brandweek* (Vol. 49, April 21, 2008, No. 16, pp. 8)
Pub: VNU Business Media, Inc.
Ed: Mike Beirne. **Description:** Nortel has launched a new television advertising campaign in which the business-to-business communications technology provider cast senior executives in 30-second TV case studies that show how Nortel's technology helped their businesses innovate.

536 ■ "Nowspeed and OneSource to Conduct Webinar" in *Internet Wire* (December 14, 2009)
Pub: Comtex News Network, Inc.
Description: OneSource, a leading provider of global business information, and Nowspeed, an Internet marketing agency, will conduct a webinar titled "How to Develop Social Media Content That Gets Results" in order to provide marketers insight into how to develop and optimize effective social media content to get consumer results that translate into purchases and lead generation.

537 ■ "Nowspeed's David Reske to Speak at SolidWorks World 2010 in Anaheim" in *Internet Wire* (January 7, 2010)
Pub: Comtex News Network, Inc.
Description: David Reske, managing director at Nowspeed, an Internet marketing agency based in the Boston area, will be presenting at SolidWorks World 2010; the convention's presentation will focus on proven methodologies, practical tips and real-world case studies in order to help attendees leverage the powerful Internet marketing innovations that are proving effective for businesses.

538 ■ *Obsessive Branding Disorder: The Illusion of Business and the Business of Illusion*
Pub: Public Affairs
Ed: Lucas Conley. **Released:** 2008. **Price:** $22.95. **Description:** The implications of brand-centric marketing shows how defenseless consumers are against advertising because they are assaulted with 3,000 to 5,000 ads and branding stratagems that subtly dictate all aspects of their lives.

539 ■ "Old Spice Guy (Feb.-July 2010)" in *Canadian Business* (Vol. 83, August 17, 2010, No. 13-14, pp. 23)
Pub: Rogers Media Ltd.
Ed: Andrew Potter. **Description:** Old Spice Guy was played by ex-football player and actor Isaiah Mustafa who made the debut in the ad for Old Spice Red Zone body wash that was broadcast during Super Bowl XLIV in February 2010. Old Spice Guy has become one of social marketing success but was cancelled in July when online viewership started to wane.

540 ■ "Omniture's Next Version of SearchCenter Delivers Landing Page Optimization" in *Internet Wire* (September 24, 2009)
Pub: Comtex News Network, Inc.
Description: Omniture, Inc., a leading provider of online business optimization software, has announced a new release of Omniture SearchCenter; this latest version will allow search engine marketers to test landing pages across campaigns and ad groups.

541 ■ "The One Thing You Must Get Right When Building a Brand" in *Harvard Business Review* (Vol. 88, December 2010, No. 12, pp. 80)
Pub: Harvard Business School Publishing
Ed: Patrick Barwise, Sean Meehan. **Description:** Four uses for new media include: communicating a clearly defined customer promise, creating trust via delivering on the promise, regularly improving on the promise, and innovating past what is familiar.

542 ■ "Online Marketing: Puppy Power: Using a New Tool Called a Widget To Boost Your Brand" in *Inc.* (November 2007, pp. 55-56)
Pub: Gruner & Jahr USA Publishing
Ed: Dan Brody. **Description:** Widgets look like small television screens posted on Websites, blogs or desktops with a company's brand or logo. It can display any type of information or image, including sports scores, news headlines, weather reports, animated graphics, or a slide show. Profiles of CarDomain Network, Babystrology, DailyPuppy.com, AnchorBank and more are included.

543 ■ "Our World with Black Enterprise" in *Black Enterprise* (Vol. 37, February 2007, No. 7, pp. 145)
Pub: Earl G. Graves Publishing Co. Inc.
Description: Our World with Black Enterprise is a television broadcast that features roundtable discussions and interviews with important African American figures.

544 ■ "Out to Draw Work, Talent" in *Crain's Detroit Business* (Vol. 24, April 14, 2008, No. 15, pp. 3)
Pub: Crain Communications, Inc.
Ed: Bill Shea. **Description:** Profile of Southfield-based Kinetic Post Inc., a growing post-production house that offers video, audio, animation, print, online and related services to corporations and advertising agencies.

545 ■ "Out-Of-Home and Transit" in *MarketingMagazine* (Vol. 115, September 27, 2010, No. 13, pp. 53)
Pub: Rogers Publishing Ltd.
Description: Out-of-home and transit marketing data covering Canada is presented.

546 ■ "Paper Tigers" in *Conde Nast Portfolio* (Vol. 2, June 2008, No. 6, pp. 84)
Pub: Conde Nast Publications, Inc.
Ed: Roger Lowenstein. **Description:** Newspapers are losing their advertisers and readers and circulation today is equal to that of 1950, a time when the U.S. population was half its present size.

547 ■ "Pet-Food Crisis a Boon to Organic Players" in *Advertising Age* (Vol. 78, April 9, 2007, No. 15, pp. 3)
Pub: Crain Communications, Inc.
Ed: Jack Neff. **Description:** In the wake of the pet-food recall crisis, the natural-and-organic segment of the market is gaining recognition and sales; one such manufacturer, Blue Buffalo, has not only seen huge sale increases but also has witnessed a 50-60 percent increase in traffic to the brand's website which has led to the decision to move up the timetable for the brand's first national ad campaign.

548 ■ "Planning Your Next Move in Ad Land" in *Advertising Age* (Vol. 81, January 4, 2009, No. 1, pp. 1)
Pub: Crain's Communications
Description: Overview of the challenges that ad agencies face today and will face in the years to come; highlights include problems occurring in various industries, Internet marketing innovations and the social media landscape.

549 ■ "Play By Play: These Video Products Can Add New Life to a Stagnant Website" in *Black Enterprise* (Vol. 41, December 2010, No. 5)
Pub: Earl G. Graves Publishing Co. Inc.
Ed: Marcia Wade Talbert. **Description:** Web Visible, provider of online marketing products and services, cites video capability as the fastest-growing Website feature for small business advertisers. Profiles of various devices for adding video to a Website are included.

550 ■ "Play It Safe" in *Entrepreneur* (Vol. 35, November 2007, No. 11, pp. 26)
Pub: Entrepreneur Media Inc.
Ed: Gwen Moran. **Description:** U.S.-based toy manufacturers find opportunity from concerns regarding the recent recalls of toys that are made in China. The situation can provide better probability of parents buying toys made in the U.S. or Europe, where manufacturing standards are stricter.

551 ■ "Political Ads Big Boost to Local Media" in *Baltimore Business Journal* (Vol. 28, October 22, 2010, No. 24, pp. 1)
Pub: Baltimore Business Journal
Ed: Scott Dance. **Description:** Information about the intense demand for advertising time from political campaigns in Baltimore, Maryland is provided. The surge in political advertisement spending would mean big money for local broadcasters, because they see a surging demand for local advertising time for virtually any time of day.

552 ■ "PopCap Games Achieves Significant Increase in Return on Ad Spend With Omniture SearchCenter" in *Internet Wire* (September 15, 2009)
Pub: Comtex News Network, Inc.
Description: PopCap Games, a leading computer games provider, is using Omniture SearchCenter together with Omniture SiteCatalyst to increase revenue from its search engine marketing campaign. Omniture, Inc. is a leading provider of Internet business optimization software.

553 ■ *The Power of Nice: How to Conquer the Business World with Kindness*
Pub: Doubleday
Ed: Linda Kaplan Thaler; Robin Koval. **Released:** September 19, 2006. **Price:** $17.95. **Description:** The key principles to running a business through thoughtfulness and kindness are exhibited with the use of success stories.

554 ■ "Prime-Time Exposure" in *Inc.* (March 2008, pp. 66, 68)
Pub: Gruner & Jahr USA Publishing
Ed: Adam Bluestein. **Description:** Product placement in television shows has increase sales for many companies. Tips for placing products or services into TV shows are explained: consider hiring an agency, target efforts, dream up a plot point, be ready to go on short notice, and work the niches.

555 ■ "Pro Teams Shift Ad Budgets; Naming Rights Deals Near $1 Billion" in *Brandweek* (Vol. 49, April 21, 2008, No. 16, pp. 18)
Pub: VNU Business Media, Inc.
Ed: Barry Janoff. **Description:** More and more professional sports marketers are spending less of their advertising budgets on traditional media outlets such as television, print and radio; the growing trend in sports marketing is in utilizing new media venues such as the Internet in which innovative means are used to encourage interaction with fans.

556 ■ "Promotions Create a Path to Better Profit" in *Pet Product News* (Vol. 64, December 2010, No. 12, pp. 1)
Pub: BowTie Inc.
Ed: Joan Hustace Walker. **Description:** Pet store retailers can boost small mammal sales by launching creative marketing and promotions such as social networking and adoption days.

557 ■ "Psst...Spread the Word" in *Boston Business Journal* (Vol. 27, November 23, 2007, No. 43, pp. 1)
Pub: American City Business Journals Inc.
Ed: Lisa van der Pool. **Description:** More and more Boston companies are using word-of-mouth marketing to boost sales, and spending on it rose to $981 million in 2006. It is projected that spending on word-of-mouth marketing will reach $1.4 billion in 2007, and marketing companies using this type of method are getting higher funding. Trends in word-of-mouth marketing are discussed.

558 ■ "Put Power in Your Direct Mail Campaigns" in *Contractor* (Vol. 56, September 2009, No. 9, pp. 64)
Pub: Penton Media, Inc.
Ed: Matt Michel. **Description:** Advice on how members of the United States plumbing industry should manage direct mail marketing campaigns are offered. Determining the purpose of a campaign is recommended. Focusing on a single message, product or service is also encouraged.

559 ■ "Quantivo Empowers Online Media Companies to Immediately Expand Audiences and Grow Online Profits" in *Internet Wire* (Nov. 18, 2009)
Pub: Comtex News Network, Inc.
Description: Quantivo, the leader in on-demand Behavioral Analytics, has launched a new solution that includes 22 of the most critical Internet audience behavior insights as out-of-the-box reports; Internet marketers need to understand their audience, what they want and how often to offer it to them in order to gain successful branding and campaigns online.

560 ■ "Quebecor Inc. Takes Hit on Slipping Ad Revenue" in *Globe & Mail* (February 21, 2007, pp. B7)
Pub: CTVglobemedia Publishing Inc.
Ed: Catherine McLean. **Description:** Canada-based Quebecor Inc. has reported fourth quarter losses of $97.1 million with revenues of $847.8 million. Decreased advertisement revenues are said to be the key reason behind the loss.

561 ■ "Reply! Grows at Unprecedented Rate, Rips Beta Off Its Marketplace" in *Marketing Weekly News* (September 19, 2009, pp. 149)
Pub: Investment Weekly News
Description: Profile of Reply.com, a leader in locally-targeted Internet marketing, announced significant growth in terms of revenue, enhanced features and services and new categories since launching its beta Reply! Marketplace platform. Even in the face of an economic downturn, the company has posted over 50 percent revenue growth in the Real Estate and Automotive categories.

562 ■ "Reportlinker Adds Report: Social Networks: Five Consumer Trends for 2009" in *Wireless News* (October 23, 2009)
Pub: Close-Up Media
Description: "Social Networks: Five Consumer Trends for 2009," a new market research report by Reportlinker.com found that in the countries of Italy and Spain lag behind their European neighbors in Internet development. Since large numbers of consumers in these two countries remain offline, only a minimal portion of total advertising spending goes into Internet marketing, and those advertising campaigns are directed at the relatively young, affluent users. Statistical data included.

563 ■ "Research and Markets Adds Report: The U.S. Mobile Web Market" in *Entertainment Close-Up* (December 10, 2009)
Pub: Close-Up Media
Description: Highlights of the new Research and Markets report "The U.S. Mobile Web Market: Taking Advantage of the iPhone Phenomenon" include: mobile Internet marketing strategies; the growth of mobile web usage; the growth of revenue in the mobile web market; and a look at Internet business communications, social media and networking.

564 ■ "Research and Markets Adds Report: USA - Internet Market - Analysis, Statistics and Forecasts" in *Wireless News* (January 15, 2010)
Pub: Close-Up Media
Description: According to Research and Markets new report concerning the United State's Internet market, e-commerce and Online advertising are expected to recover strongly in 2010.

565 ■ "Retailers Pull Out All Stops to Combat Poor Projections" in *Austin Business JournalInc.* (Vol. 28, November 21, 2008, No. 36, pp. 1)
Pub: American City Business Journals
Ed: Jean Kwon. **Description:** Report from Wachovia Economics Group reports that holiday sales for 2008 are expected to decline by 2 percent and local retailers are planning to boost holiday sales through marketing efforts, which include giving freebies to early shoppers. Details on marketing strategies of several retailers are provided.

566 ■ "The Return of the Infomercial" in *Canadian Business* (Vol. 83, September 14, 2010, No. 15, pp. 19)
Pub: Rogers Media Ltd.
Ed: James Cowan. **Description:** Infomercials or direct response ads have helped some products succeed in the marketplace. The success of infomercials is due to the cheap advertising rates, expansion into retail stores and the products' oddball appeal. Insights into the popularity of infomercial products on the Internet and on television are given.

567 ■ "Rich Returns: Media Master" in *Entrepreneur* (Vol. 35, October 2007, No. 10, pp. 42)
Pub: Entrepreneur Media Inc.
Ed: Robert Kiyosaki. **Description:** Advertising is a powerful way of reaching clients, however, public relations is a less expensive method which is just as effective as advertising. Entrepreneurs must also be ready to try something new to be noticed by the public. Insights on how to master the use of media are given.

568 ■ "Rise Interactive, Internet Marketing Agency, Now Offers Custom Google Analytics Installation" in *Internet Wire* (September 29, 2009)
Pub: Comtex News Network, Inc.
Description: In order to optimize a client's return of investment, Rise Interactive, a full-service Internet marketing agency, now offers custom Google Analytics installation to its customers; the installation process includes identifying an Internet marketing campaign's unique key performance indicators, translating them to actions one will perform o n a website and configuring the analytical tool to ensure the customized advertising campaign goals are set and properly tracked.

569 ■ "Rock Hall Shifts Advertising to 'Significant Markets' in Region" in *Crain's Cleveland Business* (Vol. 28, July 23, 2007, No. 29, pp. 6)
Pub: Crain Communications, Inc.
Ed: John Booth. **Description:** Cleveland's Rock and Roll Hall of Fame and Museum is attempting a different marketing strategy this year with aims of reaching a broader audience in the Midwest and Great Lakes regions.

570 ■ "ROIonline Announces Streaming Video Products" in *Marketing Weekly News* (December 5, 2009, pp. 155)
Pub: Investment Weekly News
Description: ROIonline LLC, an Internet marketing firm serving business-to-business and the industrial marketplace, has added streaming video options to the Internet solutions it offers its clients; due to the huge increase of broadband connections, videos are now commonplace on the Internet and can often convey a company's message in a must more efficient, concise and effective way that will engage a website's visitor thus delivering a high return on a company's investment.

571 ■ "Ronald Taketa" in *Hawaii Business* (Vol. 54, September 2008, No. 3, pp. 28)
Pub: Hawaii Business Publishing
Ed: Shara Enay. **Description:** Interview with Ronald Taketa of the Hawaii Carpenters Union who states that the economic downturn has affected the construction industry as 20 percent of the union's 7,800 members are unemployed. He shares his thoughts about the industry's economic situation, the union's advertisements, and his role as a leader of the union.

572 ■ "Scripps Networks" in *Brandweek* (Vol. 49, April 21, 2008, No. 16, pp. SR12)
Pub: VNU Business Media, Inc.
Ed: Anthony Crupi. **Description:** Provides contact information for sales and marketing personnel for the Scripps networks as well as a listing of the station's top programming and an analysis of the current season and the target audience for those programs running in the current season. Scripps networks include HGTV and the Food Network. HGTV boasts on of the industry's best commercial-retention averages, keeping nearly 97 percent of its viewers during advertising breaks.

573 ■ "Search and Discover New Opportunities" in *DM News* (Vol. 31, December 14, 2009, No. 29, pp. 13)
Pub: Haymarket Media, Inc.
Ed: Chantal Tode. **Description:** Although other digital strategies are gaining traction in Internet marketing, search marketing continues to dominate this advertising forum. Companies like American Greetings, which markets e-card brands online, are utilizing social networking sites and affiliates to generate a higher demand for their products.

574 ■ *The Secrets of Spiritual Marketing: A Complete Guide for Natural Therapists*
Pub: O Books
Ed: Lawrence Ellyard. **Released:** November 1, 2009. **Price:** $24.95. **Description:** Strategies for marketing and advertising a natural therapy business are examined.

575 ■ "Seed Funding" in *Saint Louis Business Journal* (Vol. 31, July 29, 2011, No. 49, pp. 1)
Pub: Saint Louis Business Journal
Ed: Kelsey Volkmann. **Description:** Monsanto kicked off a new campaign, 'St. Louis Grown' to show its commitment to the St. Louis, Missouri region after spending millions of dollars in recent years on national advertising campaigns. Monsanto had a marketing budget totaling $839 million in 2010 for both brand and corporate marketing.

576 ■ *The Seven Principles of WOM and Buzz Marketing: Crossing the Tipping Point*
Pub: Springer
Ed: Panos Mourdoukoulas, George J. Siomkos. **Released:** October 9, 2010. **Price:** $119.00. **Description:** An examination into the reasons for some word-of-mouth marketing campaigns being effective while other fail, with a discussion about which group of consumers should be targeted, and how to turn a word-of-mouth campaign into buzz.

577 ■ "Shoestring-Budget Marketing" in *Women Entrepreneur* (January 5, 2009)
Pub: Entrepreneur Media Inc.
Ed: Maria Falconer. **Description:** Pay-per-click search engine advertising is the traditional type of e-marketing that may not only be too expensive for certain kinds of businesses but also may not attract

the quality customer base a business looking to grow needs to find. Social networking websites have become a mandatory marketing tool for business owners who want to see growth in their sales; tips are provided for utilizing these networking websites in order to gain more visibility on the Internet which can, in turn, lead to the more sales.

578 ■ "Show Me the Love" in *Canadian Business* (Vol. 79, November 6, 2006, No. 22, pp. 77)
Pub: Rogers Media
Ed: Jeannette Hanna. **Description:** The strategies to improve brand image with relation to success of Tim Horton's brand are presented.

579 ■ "Sick of Trends? You Should Be" in *Brandweek* (Vol. 49, April 21, 2008, No. 16, pp. 22)
Pub: VNU Business Media, Inc.
Ed: Eric Zeitoun. **Description:** Eric Zeitoun, the president of Dragon Rouge, a global brand consultancy, discusses the importance of macrotrends as opposed to microtrends which he feels are often irrelevant, create confusion and cause marketers to lose site of the larger picture of their industry. Macrotrends, on the other hand, create a fundamental, societal shift that influences consumer attitudes over a long period of time.

580 ■ "Sign, Sign, Everywhere a Sign: How I Did It: Richard Schaps" in *Inc.* (October 2007, pp. 128)
Pub: Gruner & Jahr USA Publishing
Ed: Stephanie Clifford. **Description:** Richard Schaps shares the story of selling his outdoor-advertising firm, Van Wagner for $170 million and sharing the wealth with his employees. Schaps then started another outdoor-sign company.

581 ■ *The Small Business Bible: Everything You Need to Know to Succeed in Your Small Business*
Pub: John Wiley & Sons, Incorporated
Ed: Steven D. Strauss. **Released:** September 2008. **Price:** $19.95 (US), $28.99 (Canadian). **Description:** Comprehensive guide to starting and running a successful small business. Topics include bookkeeping and financial management, marketing, publicity, and advertising.

582 ■ *The Social Media Bible: Tactics, Tools, and Strategies for Business Success*
Pub: John Wiley & Sons, Inc.
Ed: Lon Safko, David Brake. **Released:** June 17, 2009. **Price:** $29.95. **Description:** Information is given to build or transform a business into social media, where customers, employees, and prospects connect, collaborate, and champion products and services in order to increase sales and to beat the competition.

583 ■ "Sony Pictures Television" in *Brandweek* (Vol. 49, April 21, 2008, No. 16, pp. SR13)
Pub: VNU Business Media, Inc.
Ed: Marc Berman. **Description:** Provides contact information for sales and marketing personnel for Sony Pictures Television Distribution as well as a listing of the station's top programming and an analysis of the current season and the target audience for those programs running in the current season.

584 ■ "Sorrell Digs Deep to Snag TNS" in *Advertising Age* (Vol. 79, July 14, 2008, No. 7, pp. 1)
Pub: Crain Communications, Inc.
Ed: Michael Bush. **Description:** Martin Sorrell's strategic vision for expansion in order to become the largest ad-agency holding company in the world is discussed.

585 ■ *Start Your Own Fashion Accessories Business*
Pub: Entrepreneur Press
Released: March 1, 2009. **Price:** $17.95. **Description:** Entrepreneurs wishing to start a fashion accessories business will find important information for setting up a home workshop and office, exploring the market, managing finances, publicizing and advertising the business and more.

586 ■ "Staying Power" in *Canadian Business* (Vol. 79, November 6, 2006, No. 22, pp. 73)
Pub: Rogers Media
Ed: John Gray. **Description:** The effects on brand image on customer choices are analyzed. The need of maintaining brand image is also emphasized.

587 ■ "Strength In Numbers" in *Black Enterprise* (Vol. 38, January 2008, No. 6, pp. 53)
Pub: Earl G. Graves Publishing Co. Inc.
Description: According to recent studies geared to advertisers, African Americans represent a demographic that drives style and consumer trends. The African American buying power is expected to increase to $1.1 trillion by 2011. Beyond Demographics helps clients identify ways to value and measure investments within the black community.

588 ■ "Stretch Your Advertising Dollars" in *Women Entrepreneur* (January 27, 2009)
Pub: Entrepreneur Media Inc.
Ed: Rosalind Resnick. **Description:** During such poor economic times, most businesses are having to cut their advertising budgets; tips for targeting your advertising dollars toward the customer base most likely to buy your product are given.

589 ■ "Success a Big Seller: N. Carolina, Duke Coaches Cash in as Marketers' Dreams" in *Charlotte Observer* (February 7, 2007)
Pub: Knight-Ridder/Tribune Business News
Ed: Ken Tysiac. **Description:** North Carolina sporting coaches are marketing goods and services in television commercials and print media.

590 ■ *Success Secrets of Social Media Marketing Superstars*
Pub: Entrepreneur Press
Ed: Mitch Meyerson. **Released:** June 1, 2010. **Price:** $21.95. **Description:** Provides access to the playbooks of social media marketers who reveal their most valuable strategies and tactics for standing out in the new online media environment.

591 ■ "Suits Keep Flying in Wireless Service Marketing Wars" in *Globe & Mail* (March 22, 2007, pp. B3)
Pub: CTVglobemedia Publishing Inc.
Ed: Catherine McLean. **Description:** The suit filed by Telus Corp. against BCE Mobile Communications Inc. over the latter's alleged misleading advertisement in the press is discussed.

592 ■ "Survey: More Buyers Expect to Spend Less in Most Media" in *Advertising Age* (Vol. 79, July 7, 2008, No. 26, pp. 3)
Pub: Crain Communications, Inc.
Ed: Megan McIlroy. **Description:** Marketers are decreasing their budgets for advertising in television, radio, newspaper and outdoor due to the economic downturn. Statistical data concerning advertising agencies and marketers included.

593 ■ "Survey Points to Big Jump in 2006 Ad Budgets" in *Globe & Mail* (January 23, 2006, pp. B3)
Pub: CTVglobemedia Publishing Inc.
Ed: Keith McArthur. **Description:** The findings of ICA Survey of Marketing Budgets on the advertising budgets of marketing executives, in 2006, are presented.

594 ■ "T3 Grows, Recovers Well After Losing Dell" in *Austin Business JournalInc.* (Vol. 28, September 19, 2008, No. 27)
Pub: American City Business Journals
Ed: Sandra Zaragoza. **Description:** T3 Inc. an Austin, Texas-based advertising company is recovering from losing its Dell Inc. account with the addition of new clients, such as Taco Bell, ConocoPhillips, Robbins Brothers, and Intel. The country is projected to earn capitalized billings of $313 million for 2008. Details on the company's plans to consolidate its offices are discussed.

595 ■ "Taco Bell; David Ovens" in *Advertising Age* (Vol. 79, November 17, 2008, No. 43, pp. S2)
Pub: Crain Communications, Inc.
Ed: Emily Bryson York. **Description:** Due to the addition of new products such as a low-calorie, low-fat Fresco menu; a fruity iced beverage; and a value initiative, Taco Bell now accounts for half of Yum Brands' profits. The chain has also benefited from a new chief marketing officer, David Ovens, who oversees ad support.

596 ■ "Telemundo" in *Brandweek* (Vol. 49, April 21, 2008, No. 16, pp. SR8)
Pub: VNU Business Media, Inc.
Ed: John Consoli. **Description:** Provides contact information for sales and marketing personnel for the Telemundo network as well as a listing of the station's top programming and an analysis of the current season and the target audience for those programs running in the current season.

597 ■ "That Canadian Tire Couple Won't Be Annoying You Anymore" in *Globe & Mail* (March 10, 2006, pp. B3)
Pub: CTVglobemedia Publishing Inc.
Ed: Keith McArthur. **Description:** The details pertaining to the rolling out of new advertisements by Canadian Tire Corp. Ltd. are presented. The commercials have been made by Taxi Advertising and Design, which has redesigned the previous ad of the tire maker.

598 ■ "This Week: McD's Eyes Ad Plan, Shifts Breakfast Biz" in *Crain's Chicago Business* (Vol. 30, February 2007, No. 6, pp. 1)
Pub: Crain Communications, Inc.
Ed: Kate MacArthur. **Description:** McDonald's is moving its national breakfast ad account from DDB Chicago to Arnold Worldwide of Boston and Moroch of Dallas in an attempt to change its marketing strategy. It is also doing a study to keep abreast of consumer trends.

599 ■ "Thomas Morley; President, The Lube Stop Inc., 37" in *Crain's Cleveland Business* (Vol. 28, November 19, 2007, No. 46, pp. F-12)
Pub: Crain Communications, Inc.
Ed: David Bennett. **Description:** Profile of Thomas Morley, president of The Lube Stop Inc., who is dedicated to promoting the company's strong environmental record as an effective way to differentiate Lube Stop from its competition. Since Mr. Morley came to the company in 2004, Lube Stop has increased sales by 10 percent and has boosted its operating profits by 30 percent.

600 ■ "Ticket Tiff Erupts Over Fund Ads" in *Globe & Mail* (January 31, 2007, pp. B1)
Pub: CTVglobemedia Publishing Inc.
Description: The opposition of Cineplex Entertainment LP to Mackenzie Financial Corp.'s advertisement about high cost of movie ticket is discussed.

601 ■ "Tim Armstrong" in *Canadian Business* (Vol. 81, July 21, 2008, No. 11, pp. 10)
Pub: Rogers Media Ltd.
Ed: Calvin Leung. **Description:** Interview with Tim Armstrong who is the president of advertising and commerce department of Google Inc. for North America; the information technology company executive talked about the emerging trends and changes to YouTube made by the company since its acquisition in 2006.

602 ■ "Titan to Become New York's Largest Provider of Phone Kiosk Advertising" in *Marketing Weekly News* (September 11, 2010, pp. 150)
Pub: VerticalNews
Description: Titan will acquire from Verizon 1,900 payphones at 1,300 phone kiosk locations in New York City, New York. This transaction will triple the firm's inventory of New York Phone Kiosk media to over 5,000 advertising faces. Details are included.

603 ■ "To Catch Up, Colgate May Ratchet Up Its Ad Spending" in *Advertising Age* (Vol. 81, December 6, 2010, No. 43, pp. 1)
Pub: Crain Communications, Inc.
Ed: Jack Neff. **Description:** Colgate-Palmolive Company has been losing market share in the categories of toothpaste, deodorant, body wash, dish soap and pet food.

604 ■ "The Top Mistakes of Social Media Marketing" in *Agency Sales Magazine* (Vol. 39, November 2009, No. 9, pp. 42)
Pub: MANA
Ed: Pam Lontos; Maurice Ramirez. **Description:** One common mistake in social media marketing is having more than one image on the Internet because this ruins a business' credibility. Marketers need to put out messages that are useful to their readers and to keep messages consistent.

605 ■ *TRUTH: The New Rules for Marketing in a Skeptical World*
Pub: AMACOM
Ed: Lynn B. Upshaw. **Released:** August 8, 2007. **Price:** $24.95. **Description:** Because consumers are more informed today, small business owners must find new ways to market products and services.

606 ■ "Turner Broadcasting System" in *Brandweek* (Vol. 49, April 21, 2008, No. 16, pp. SR13)
Pub: VNU Business Media, Inc.
Ed: Anthony Crupi. **Description:** Provides contact information for sales and marketing personnel for the Turner Broadcasting System networks as well as a listing of the station's top programming and an analysis of the current season and the target audience for those programs running in the current season. Recent acquisitions are also discussed.

607 ■ "Twentieth Television" in *Brandweek* (Vol. 49, April 21, 2008, No. 16, pp. SR16)
Pub: VNU Business Media, Inc.
Ed: Marc Berman. **Description:** Provides contact information for sales and marketing personnel for Twentieth Television as well as a listing of the station's top programming and an analysis of the current season and the target audience for those programs running in the current season.

608 ■ "The Twittering Class" in *Entrepreneur* (Vol. 37, September 2009, No. 9, pp. 40)
Pub: Entrepreneur Media, Inc.
Ed: Mikal E. Belicove. **Description:** Advice on how entrepreneurs can use online social networks to promote their businesses is presented. Facebook offers applications and advertising solutions to promote Websites, products and services. Twitter, on the other hand, provides instant messaging, which can be done through computer or cell phone.

609 ■ *Twitterville: How Businesses Can Thrive in the New Global Neighborhoods*
Pub: Portfolio Hardcover
Ed: Shel Israel. **Price:** $23.95. **Description:** Twitter is the most rapidly adopted communication tool in history, going from zero to ten million users in just over two years. On Twitter, word can spread faster than wildfire. Companies no longer have the option of ignoring the conversation. Unlike other hot social media spaces, Twitterville is dominated by professionals, not students. And despite its size, it still feels like a small town. Twitter allows people to interact much the way they do face-to-face, honestly and authentically.

610 ■ *Ultimate Guide to Project Management*
Pub: Entrepreneurial Press
Ed: Sid Kemp. **Released:** October 2005. **Price:** $29.95 (US), $39.95 (Canadian). **Description:** Project management strategies including writing a business plan and developing a good advertising campaign.

611 ■ *The Ultimate Small Business Marketing Toolkit: All the Tips, Forms, and Strategies You'll Ever Need!*
Pub: McGraw-Hill Inc.
Ed: Beth Goldstein. **Released:** July 2007. **Price:** $27.95. **Description:** An all-in-one sales and marketing resource for entrepreneurs to grow a business.

612 ■ "Univision" in *Brandweek* (Vol. 49, April 21, 2008, No. 16, pp. SR8)
Pub: VNU Business Media, Inc.
Ed: John Consoli. **Description:** Provides contact information for sales and marketing personnel for the Univision network as well as a listing of the station's top programming and an analysis of the current season and the target audience for those programs running in the current season. Univision is the No. 1 network on Friday nights in the 18-34 demographic, beating all English-language networks.

613 ■ "Unleashing the Power of Marketing" in *Harvard Business Review* (Vol. 88, October 2010, No. 10, pp. 90)
Pub: Harvard Business School Publishing
Ed: Beth Comstock, Ranjay Gulati, Stephen Liguori. **Description:** Chronicle of the development of General Electric's marketing framework that focused on three key factors: Principles, people and process. GE determined that successful marketing fulfills four functions: instigating, innovating, implementing, and integrating.

614 ■ "Use Social Media to Enhance Brand, Business" in *Contractor* (Vol. 56, December 2009, No. 12, pp. 14)
Pub: Penton Media, Inc.
Ed: Elton Rivas. **Description:** Advice on how plumbing contractors should use online social networks to increase sales is presented including such issues as clearly defining goals and target audience. An additional advantage to this medium is that advertisements can easily be shared with other users.

615 ■ "Utah Technology Council: Social Media Is Here to Stay; Embrace It" in *Wireless News* (December 14, 2009)
Pub: Close-Up Media
Description: Social media outlets such as Facebook and Twitter are blurring the lines between advertising, public relations, branding and marketing; businesses must stop thinking in terms of traditional marketing versus Internet marketing if they want to succeed in today's marketing climate.

616 ■ "Warner Bros. Domestic Television Distribution" in *Brandweek* (Vol. 49, April 21, 2008, No. 16, pp. SR16)
Pub: VNU Business Media, Inc.
Ed: Marc Berman. **Description:** Provides contact information for sales and marketing personnel for Warner Bros. Domestic Television Distribution as well as a listing of the station's top programming and an analysis of the current season and the target audience for those programs running in the current season.

617 ■ "Web-Based Marketing Excites, Challenges Small Business Use" in *Colorado Springs Business Journal* (January 20, 2010)
Pub: Dolan Media Co.
Ed: Becky Hurley. **Description:** Business-to-business and consumer-direct firms alike are using the fast-changing Web technologies to increase sales, leads and track consumer behavior but once a company commits to an Online marketing plan, experts believe, they must be prepared to consistently tweak and overhaul content and distribution vehicles in order to keep up.

618 ■ "Web Traffic Numbers Facing Scrutiny" in *Boston Business Journal* (Vol. 27, November 2, 2007, No. 40, pp. 1)
Pub: American City Business Journals Inc.
Ed: Jesse Noyes. **Description:** Interactive Advertising Bureau (IAB) held a summit meeting with major industry players in an effort to create more transparent standards for measuring Internet traffic. The terms at issue were registered users, unique visitors, time spent and retention.

619 ■ "Webadvertising" in *MarketingMagazine* (Vol. 115, September 27, 2010, No. 13, pp. 70)
Pub: Rogers Publishing Ltd.
Description: Website advertising in Canada is examined.

620 ■ "Web.Preneuring: How Local TV Ads and Online Marketing Can Help You Win Big" in *Small Business Opportunities* (January 2008)
Pub: Harris Publications Inc.
Ed: David Waxman. **Description:** Spot Runner, an Internet-based advertising agency offers low-cost local business television ads. The company secures the ad buy, places and tracks the ads, and analyzes viewership and demographics for clients.

621 ■ "Welch's Uses Taste Strips in Ads" in *Marketing to Women* (Vol. 21, April 2008, No. 4, pp. 3)
Pub: EPM Communications, Inc.
Description: Welch's is positioning its 139-year-old brand in a new and inventive way with a new marketing campaign in which print ads will feature a tamper-evident flavor pouch that contains a dissolving taste strip flavored with Welch's grape juice.

622 ■ "What Players in the Midmarket Are Talking About" in *Mergers & Acquisitions: The Dealmaker's Journal* (March 1, 2008)
Pub: SourceMedia, Inc.
Description: Sports Properties Acquisition Corp. went public at the end of January; according to the company's prospectus, it is not limiting its focus to just teams, it is also considering deals for stadium construction companies, sports leagues, facilities, sports-related advertising and licensing of products, in addition to other related segments.

623 ■ "What Women Watch on TV" in *Marketing to Women* (Vol. 21, February 2008, No. 2, pp. 6)
Pub: EPM Communications, Inc.
Description: According to BIGresearch, women are more likely to watch sports than they are soap operas. Statistical data included.

624 ■ "Why Some Get Shaften By Google Pricing" in *Advertising Age* (Vol. 79, July 14, 2008, No. 7, pp. 3)
Pub: Crain Communications, Inc.
Ed: Abbey Klaassen. **Description:** Google's search advertising is discussed as well as the company's pricing structure for these ads.

625 ■ "Why You Need a New-Media 'Ringmaster'" in *Harvard Business Review* (Vol. 88, December 2010, No. 12, pp. 78)
Pub: Harvard Business School Publishing
Ed: Patrick Spenner. **Description:** The concept of ringmaster is applied to brand marketing. This concept includes integrative thinking, lean collaboration skills, and high-speed decision cycles.

626 ■ "With Traffic Jam in Super Bowl, Can Any Auto Brand Really Win?" in *Advertising Age* (Vol. 81, December 6, 2010, No. 43, pp. 1)
Pub: Crain Communications, Inc.
Ed: Rupal Parekh, Brian Steinberg. **Description:** Car marketers are doubling down for Super Bowl XLV in Arlington, Texas and asking their ad agencies to craft commercials unique enough to break through the clutter and to capture viewers' attention.

627 ■ "Women See Special Interest, Review Sites as Most Brand-Friendly" in *Marketing to Women* (Vol. 23, November 2010, No. 11, pp. 4)
Pub: EPM Communications, Inc.
Description: Rather focusing on specific demographics, marketing and ad agencies should focus on women's core needs such as mom versus mom or Gen X versus Baby Boomer.

628 ■ *Work at Home Now*
Pub: Career Press, Inc.
Ed: Christine Durst, Michael Haaren. **Released:** October 9, 2010. **Price:** $14.99. **Description:** There are legitimate home-based jobs and projects that can be found on the Internet, but trustworthy guidance is scarce. There is a 58 to 1 scam ratio in work at-home advertising filled with fraud.

629 ■ "XM Burning Through Cash to Catch Sirius" in *Globe & Mail* (April 17, 2007, pp. B5)
Pub: CTVglobemedia Publishing Inc.
Ed: Grant Robertson. **Description:** The effort of XM Satellite Radio Holdings Inc. to spend about $45 million to increase sale of its radio in Canada is discussed.

630 ■ "Yahoo! - Microsoft Pact: Alive Again?" in *Barron's* (Vol. 89, July 27, 2009, No. 30, pp. 8)
Pub: Dow Jones & Co., Inc.
Ed: Mark Veverka. **Description:** Yahoo! reported higher than expected earnings in the second quarter of 2009 under CEO Carol Bartz who has yet to articulate her long-term vision and strategy for turning around the company. The media reported that Yahoo! and Microsoft are discussing an advertising-search partnership which should benefit both companies.

631 ■ "You Lost Me at Hello" in *Entrepreneur* (Vol. 35, November 2007, No. 11, pp. 136)
Pub: Entrepreneur Media Inc.
Ed: John Jantsch. **Description:** Managing your marketing materials by making them more informational is an effective tool to educate consumers about your product. Information that should be included in your marketing kit are outlined.

632 ■ "Your Big Give" in *Small Business Opportunities* (September 2008)
Pub: Entrepreneur Media Inc.
Ed: Michael Guld. **Description:** Cause related marketing is beneficial to businesses as well as the communities they inhabit; three small businesses that are elevating their standing in the community while at the same time increasing their customer base are profiled.

633 ■ *YouTube and Video Marketing: An Hour a Day*
Pub: Sybex
Ed: Greg Jarboe. **Released:** August 10, 2009. **Price:** $29.99. **Description:** The importance of online video marketing for businesses is stressed. Tips for developing and implementing video marketing are outlined.

SOURCES OF SUPPLY

634 ■ *Business Marketing Association—Membership & Resource Directory*
Pub: Business Marketing Association
Contact: Rick Kean
Released: Annual, January. **Covers:** Over 4,500 member business communications professionals in fields of advertising, marketing communications, and marketing; their service and supply companies are listed in the "Marketing Resources" section. **Entries Include:** For individuals—Name, title, company with which affiliated, address, phone. For companies—Name, address, phone, contact, description of products or services. **Arrangement:** Individuals are alphabetical within chapter; companies are classified by product or service. **Indexes:** Alpha, company, chapter.

STATISTICAL SOURCES

635 ■ *RMA Annual Statement Studies*
Pub: Robert Morris Associates (RMA)
Released: Annual. **Price:** $175.00 2006-07 edition, $105.00. **Description:** Contains composite balance sheets and income statements for more than 360 industries, including the accounting, auditing, and bookkeeping industries. Also contains five years of comparative historical data for discerning trends. Includes 16 commonly used ratios, computed for most of the size groupings for nearly every industry.

636 ■ *Standard & Poor's Industry Surveys*
Pub: Standard & Poor's Corp.
Released: Annual. **Price:** $3633.00. **Description:** Two-volume book that examines the prospects for specific industries, including trucking. Also provides analyses of trends and problems, statistical tables and charts, and comparative company analyses.

TRADE PERIODICALS

637 ■ *AAF Government Report*
Pub: American Advertising Federation
ULS http://www.aaf.org/. **Ed:** Bob Kohlmeyer, Editor. **Released:** 10/year. **Description:** Supplies information on federal and state legislative and regulatory issues that affect the advertising industry. Remarks: Available online only.

638 ■ *Advertising Compliance Service*
Pub: JL Com Publishing Company L.L.C.
Contact: John Lichtenberger, Editor-in-Chief
Released: Semimonthly. **Price:** $595, individuals. **Description:** Functions as the only comprehensive reference source for information regarding advertising compliance requirements and issues. Subscription includes: 24 issues annually, 6 special reports, and a three- volume based volume (1,500 plus pages) for initial subscribers only.

639 ■ *Adweek/New England*
Pub: Adweek L.P.
Released: Weekly. **Price:** $299 print and online; $149 digital access only; $24.95 monthly, print + online; $19.95 monthly, online only. **Description:** News magazine serving the advertising, marketing, and media industries in New England.

640 ■ *IAA National & World News*
Pub: International Advertising Association
Ed: Pamela Yaeger, Editor, pamela@iaaglobal.org. **Released:** Quarterly. **Price:** $50, Included in membership. **Description:** Supplies information on Association policies and activities. Includes reviews of publications and reports from the 62 chapters worldwide.

641 ■ *Journal of Advertising Research*
Pub: Advertising Research Foundation
Ed: Geoffrey Precourt, Editor. **Released:** Quarterly. **Price:** $171 print & online; $108 print & online. **Description:** Journal of advertising, marketing, and media research.

642 ■ *PROMO*
Pub: Penton Media Inc.
Contact: Leslie Bacon, Gp. Publisher
E-mail: leslie.bacon@penton.com
Released: Monthly. **Description:** Trade publication covering information, trends, and how-to features relating to consumer and trade promotion marketing.

643 ■ *Promotional Products Business*
Pub: Promotional Products Association International
Contact: Audrey Sellers, Assoc. Ed.
Ed: Tina Berres Filipski, Editor, tinaf@ppa.org. **Released:** Monthly. **Price:** $48 members; $60 Canada and Mexico members; $65 other countries members; $62 members for prospective members in U.S.; $74 Canada and Mexico for prospective members in Canada and Mexico; $79 other countries for prospective members in and other countries. **Description:** Magazine covering news, trends, new products and business issues affecting the promotional products industry. Official magazine of the Promotional Products Assoc. International.

644 ■ *Topline*
Pub: McCollum Spielman Worldwide
Ed: Paula Kay Pierce, Editor. **Released:** Quarterly. **Price:** Free. **Description:** Contains advertising research findings and analysis. Covers trends in advertising.

VIDEOCASSETTES/ AUDIOCASSETTES

645 ■ *Ad Campaigns That Work*
Instructional Video
2219 C St.
Lincoln, NE 68502
Ph:(402)475-6570
Free: 800-228-0164
Fax:(402)475-6500
Co. E-mail: feedback@insvideo.com
URL: http://www.insvideo.com
Price: $89.95. **Description:** Three successful ad agency executives furnish information on successful ad campaigns and why they were successful. Covers principles of successful advertising. **Availability:** VHS.

646 ■ *Advertising: The Hidden Language*
First Light Video Publishing
2321 Abbot Kinney Blvd., Top Fl.
Venice, CA 90291
Ph:(310)577-8581
Free: 800-262-8862
Fax:(310)574-0886
Co. E-mail: sales@firstlightvideo.com
URL: http://www.firstlightvideo.com
Description: Features Dr. Phillip Bell as he demostrates how successful ads grab the consumer and make them want to purchase the product. **Availability:** VHS.

647 ■ *Advertising Tricks Without the Gimmicks*
Instructional Video
2219 C St.
Lincoln, NE 68502
Ph:(402)475-6570
Free: 800-228-0164
Fax:(402)475-6500
Co. E-mail: feedback@insvideo.com
URL: http://www.insvideo.com
Price: $79.00. **Description:** Offers an overview and practical hints on the basics of advertising. **Availability:** VHS.

648 ■ *Promotion: Polishing the Apple*
RMI Media
1365 N. Winchester St.
Olathe, KS 66061-5880
Ph:(913)768-1696
Free: 800-745-5480
Fax:800-755-6910
Co. E-mail: actmedia@act.org
URL: http://www.actmedia.com
Released: 1991. **Price:** $89.95. **Description:** Presents promotional mixes developed by Apple Computers for the Apple IIc, the Macintosh, and the Macintosh Office to demonstrate successful uses of print and television advertising. **Availability:** VHS.

CONSULTANTS

649 ■ Black Eagle Consulting 2000 Inc.
451 Barclay Cres.
Oakville, ON, Canada L6J 6H8
Ph:(905)842-3010
Fax:(905)842-9586
Co. E-mail: info@blackeagle.ca
URL: http://www.blackeagle.ca
Contact: Richard L. Simms, President
E-mail: rsimms@blackeagle.ca
Scope: Business firm offers services in outplacement and career counseling career review and personal assessment, Myers-Briggs type instrument practitioner, resume review and revision, interview coaching, job search techniques, job offer counsel, strategic planning and corporate reviews business plan analysis, corporate vision, mission and values definition, goals and objectives, strengths, weaknesses, opportunities, threats (swot) analysis, merger and acquisition strategy; facilitator, strategic planning meetings (agenda preparation, on topic/on time, meeting assessment); organizational structure review (requirements for growth, succession planning); executive coaching; and marketing and sales (analysis of the company's product line, pricing, packaging, merchandising, and advertising programs, market research, assessment of current sales organization/ compensation issues). **Special Services:** Myers-Briggs Type Instrument[R].

650 ■ The Center for Technical Communication
590 Delcina Dr.
River Vale, NJ 07675
Ph:(201)505-9451

Fax:(201)385-1138
Co. E-mail: rwbly@bly.com
URL: http://www.bly.com
Contact: Bob Bly, President
E-mail: rwbly@bly.com
Scope: An independent consultant and copywriter specializing in business-to-business, industrial, hi-tech, and direct response advertising, marketing, publicity, and promotion. Writes marketing plans, ad campaigns, sales brochures, publicity materials, direct response ads, sales letters, and direct mail packages for clients nationwide. Industries served: publishing, business-to-business products or services, software or computers, electronics, financial, healthcare, medical equipment, industrial equipment, chemicals, consulting, and professional services. **Publications:** "The Bulletproof Book Proposal "; "Finding A Good Idea For Your Book"; "A Fine Position to Be In"; "What to Do When Your Book Goes Out of Print"; "How To Write a Good Advertisement"; "31 -derfully Simple Ways To Make Your Ads Generate More Inquiries"; "On Target Advertising"; "How to Write More Effective Product Brochures "; "Classy Outfit...Classy Brochure?"; "Improving Your Listening Skills"; "Improving Your Interpersonal Skills"; "10 Ways To Get More Done in Less Time"; "How to Give a Successful Presentation". **Seminars:** Active Listening; Become an Instant Guru; Get More Done In Less Time: How To Double Your Personal Productivity; How To Write A Nonfiction Book And Get It Published; How To Succeed as a Freelance Writer; The 1-Hour E-Zine Writing Formula; World's Best-Kept Copywriting Secrets; What's Working in Direct Mail Today; What's Working in E-Mail Marketing Today; Copywriting for Non-Copywriters; Effective Business Writing; Effective Technical Writing; How To Write Copy That Sells; Selling Your Services.

651 ■ Ideas To Go Inc.
10 N Park Pl., Ste. 520
Morristown, NJ 07960
Ph:(612)331-1570
Fax:(612)331-1602
Co. E-mail: inquiries@ideastogo.com
URL: http://www.ideastogo.com
Contact: Susan Wandell, Principal
E-mail: swandell@ideastogo.com
Scope: Offers creative process consultation and facilitation, in the context of creative problem-solving, long-range planning, new product development, team building, marketing and advertising issues. Serves private industries as well as government agencies. **Seminars:** Pennsylvania Manufacturing Confectioners' Association, Feb, 2010; Custom-designed creativity training; Creative Problem Solving Institute facilitator training; Received focus group moderator training, RIVA Institute. **Special Services:** Forness[R]; E-deation[R]; Concentrated Concept Development; Claimstorming; Creative Ethnography.

652 ■ IMC Consulting & Training
901 McHenry Ave., Ste. A
Modesto, CA 95350
Ph:(209)572-2271
Fax:(209)572-2862
Co. E-mail: info@imc-1.net
URL: http://www.imc-1.net
Contact: Ed Stout, Principle
E-mail: michael@imc-1.net
Scope: Firm helps businesses and professionals identify, develop and market their selling proposition to increase profits. Services include B-to-B surveys, direct marketing, media relations, planning and strategy, sales management, training and leadership coaching. **Publications:** "Consultant Earns Advanced Certificate," Hccsc Business Review, Dec, 2004; "Adapting to Change - the New Competitive Advantage," Business Journal, Jul, 2004; "Loyalty Marketing Can Divide New Business," Jun, 2004; "Eleven Major Marketing Mistakes," Jul, 2003; "Planning to Win or Racing to Fail," Jun, 2003. **Seminars:** Negotiating High Profit Sales; How to Write Winning Proposals, Modesto Chamber of Commerce, Oct, 2007; Winning the 2nd Half: A 6-month Plan to Score New Customers and Profits.

653 ■ The K.S. Giniger Company Inc.
1045 Park Ave.
New York, NY 10028
Ph:(212)369-6692
Fax:(212)269-6692
Co. E-mail: bernicecullinan@verizon.net
Contact: Kenneth Seeman Giniger, President
Scope: Consultants on book publishing to publishers of books, magazines and newsletters, direct sales organizations, government agencies, educational organizations, financial and investment institutions; public relations and advertising agencies. Clients in the United States, Canada, Mexico, England, Denmark, France, Spain, Switzerland, Germany, Israel, Singapore and Australia.

654 ■ ReCourses Inc.
6101 Stillmeadow Dr.
Nashville, TN 37211-6518
Ph:(615)831-2277
Free: 888-476-5884
Fax:(615)831-2212
Co. E-mail: info@recourses.com
URL: http://www.recourses.com
Contact: David C. Baker, Principle
E-mail: david@recourses.com
Scope: A management consulting firm that works exclusively with small service providers in the communications industry, including public relations firms, advertising agencies, interactive companies and design studios. Services include Total Business Review, a complete examination of your business starting with an on site examination or discussion, followed by written recommendations and then supplemented with six months of implementation guidance. Areas reviewed include positioning, marketing, management, personnel, structure, finance, retirement, technology and specific growth issues. **Publications:** "Managing (Right) for the First Time". **Seminars:** Managing Client Relationships; Research and Strategy; Financial Management: Measuring and Enhancing Performance in a Marketing Firm, Sep, 2009; Building and Leading a Staff: The When, How, and What of Growth and Culture, Sep, 2009; Doing Effective Work: Adding Significance to the Strategic Portion of Your Work for Clients, Sep, 2009; Resourcing the Creative Process: Managing Pricing, Deadlines, Budgets, Quality, and Capacity, Apr, 2009. **Special Services:** ReCourses[R].

FRANCHISES AND BUSINESS OPPORTUNITIES

655 ■ AllOver Media
6901 E. Fish Lake Rd., Ste. 180
Maple Grove, MN 55369
Ph:(763)488-4030
Fax:(763)424-1836
No. of Franchise Units: 27. **No. of Company-Owned Units:** 1. **Founded:** 2002. **Franchised:** 2002. **Description:** Indoor print, gas pump and electric LCD advertising. **Equity Capital Needed:** $37,300-$124,800 total investment; $75,000 net worth, $35,000 liquidity. **Franchise Fee:** $30,000. **Royalty Fee:** 6%. **Financial Assistance:** Third party financing available. **Training:** Provides 40 hours at headquarters and 40 hours onsite with ongoing support.

656 ■ American Town Mailer
4638 E Ingram
Mesa, AZ 85205
Ph:(480)649-0344
Fax:(480)641-9988
No. of Franchise Units: 3. **Founded:** 1976. **Franchised:** 2000. **Description:** Direct-mail advertising. **Equity Capital Needed:** $23,900-$37,200 total investment; $25,000 net worth, $25,000 cash liquidity. **Franchise Fee:** $20,000. **Financial Assistance:** No. **Training:** Provides 1 week at headquarters, 1 week onsite with ongoing support.

657 ■ AmeriCare Franchise Ltd.
225 Laura Dr.
Addison, IL 60101
Ph:(630)458-1990
Free: 800-745-6191
Fax:(630)458-1994
No. of Franchise Units: 20. **No. of Company-Owned Units:** 5. **Founded:** 1964. **Franchised:** 1968. **Description:** Offers restroom sanitation and air-freshening services. **Equity Capital Needed:** $90,000. **Franchise Fee:** $50,000. **Royalty Fee:** 15%. **Financial Assistance:** No. **Training:** Provides 2 weeks at headquarters, 1 week+ ongoing support.

658 ■ Best Coupon Book
260 Maitland Ave., Ste. 2000
Altamonte Springs, FL 32701
Ph:(407)571-3713
No. of Franchise Units: 3. **No. of Company-Owned Units:** 1. **Founded:** 1997. **Franchised:** 2005. **Description:** Direct mail advertising. **Equity Capital Needed:** $50,000. **Franchise Fee:** $35,000. **Financial Assistance:** No. **Training:** Yes.

659 ■ Billboard Connection
2121 Vista Pky.
West Palm Beach, GA 33416
Ph:(561)868-1497
Free: (866)257-6025
Fax:(561)478-4340
Co. E-mail: franchise@billboardconnection.com
URL: http://www.billboardconnection.com
No. of Franchise Units: 89. **Founded:** 1997. **Franchised:** 2003. **Description:** Advertising agency specializing in out-of-home media. We consult with clients & place their ads on billboards, buses, taxis, airport dioramas, mall kiosks, movie theaters and more. **Equity Capital Needed:** $41,000. **Franchise Fee:** $24,500. **Financial Assistance:** Yes. **Training:** Offers 2 week training program and ongoing support.

660 ■ Bride and Groom Planner
Bride & Groom Planner Licensing Corp.
5330B Wooster Pike
Cincinnati, OH 45227
Free: 888-515-3095
Founded: 2001. **Franchised:** 2005. **Description:** Wedding Planner Book. **Equity Capital Needed:** $49,000-$86,000, includes franchise fee. **Franchise Fee:** $15,000-$30,000. **Financial Assistance:** No. **Training:** Yes.

661 ■ City Publications
City Publications Franchise Group, Inc.
Interstate North Pky. SE
Atlanta, GA 30339
Ph:(770)951-0441
Fax:(770)951-0437
No. of Franchise Units: 54. **Founded:** 2002. **Description:** Sale of advertising for direct mail. **Equity Capital Needed:** $100,000. **Franchise Fee:** $89,000. **Financial Assistance:** Yes. **Training:** Yes.

662 ■ Kwik Kopy Business Centers
Kwik Kopy Business Centers, Inc.
12715 Telge Rd.
Cypress, TX 77429
Free: 888-638-8722
Fax:(281)256-4178
Co. E-mail: franchisedevelopment@iced.net
URL: http://www.iced.net
No. of Franchise Units: 16. **No. of Company-Owned Units:** 1. **Founded:** 2001. **Franchised:** 2001. **Description:** Offers business advertisement aids and printing and copying services. **Equity Capital Needed:** $65,000 liquid capital; $250,000 net worth. **Franchise Fee:** $35,000. **Financial Assistance:** Conventional bank and SBA loans, and through in-house financing with sufficient collateral. **Managerial Assistance:** Provide business support, advertising, and marketing materials. **Training:** Owners attend classroom and field training, as well as ongoing training through workshops and conferences.

663 ■ Money Mailer, Inc.
12131 Western Ave.
Garden Grove, CA 92841
Free: 800-508-6663
No. of Franchise Units: 183+. **Founded:** 1979. **Franchised:** 1980. **Description:** Offers direct mail advertising services to local and national businesses and professionals, whose ads are combined and mailed in the same envelope to residences in the franchisees exclusive market between regions, local

franchisees, and the corporate office with regional conferences and newsletters. **Equity Capital Needed:** $20,000 above franchise fee. **Franchise Fee:** $37,500. **Financial Assistance:** Yes. **Training:** 5 weeks of classroom and in-field training is provided for regional owners. Local franchisees receive a mandatory 2 week training course that includes 1 week of classroom training and 1 week of field training in their local areas.

664 ■ Monthly Coupons Franchising
Monthly Coupons Franchising, Inc.
7231 Boulder Ave.
Highland, CA 92346
Ph:(909)386-0550
Fax:(909)425-5989
No. of Franchise Units: 45. **No. of Company-Owned Units:** 6. **Founded:** 2001. **Franchised:** 2007. **Description:** Advertising/direct mail coupons. **Equity Capital Needed:** $33,700. **Franchise Fee:** $25,000. **Financial Assistance:** Yes. **Training:** Yes.

665 ■ Our Town America, A Franchising Corp.
Our Town, Inc.
3845 Gateway Centre Blvd., Ste. 300
Pinellas Park, FL 33782
Ph:(727)345-0811
Free: 800-497-8360
Fax:(727)345-0338
No. of Franchise Units: 43. **Founded:** 1972. **Franchised:** 2004. **Description:** Direct mail. **Equity Capital Needed:** $74,800-$105,450. **Franchise Fee:** $47,500. **Financial Assistance:** No. **Training:** Offers classroom training at headquarters followed with up to 2 weeks field training with a Franchise Training Manager who will be your ongoing sales support.

666 ■ RSVP Publications
6730 W Linebaugh Ave., Ste. 201
Tampa, FL 33625
Ph:(813)960-7787
Free: 800-360-7787
Co. E-mail: rsvp@publications.com
URL: http://www.rsvpublications.com
No. of Franchise Units: 96. **Founded:** 1985. **Franchised:** 1986. **Description:** "Direct mail to the upscale," is ideal for sales or marketing professionals. **Equity Capital Needed:** $49,499-$180,599. **Franchise Fee:** $30,000-$120,000. **Royalty Fee:** 7%. **Financial Assistance:** No. **Training:** Offers 7 days training and ongoing support.

667 ■ Sign Biz, Inc.
24681 La Plaza, Ste. 270
Dana Point, CA 92629
Ph:(949)234-0408
Free: 800-633-5580
Fax:(949)234-0426
URL: http://www.signbiz.com
No. of Franchise Units: 185. **Founded:** 1989. **Franchised:** 1990. **Description:** Visual communication stores developing digital sign making. **Equity Capital Needed:** $45,000-$50,000 liquid. **Franchise Fee:** None. **Financial Assistance:** SBA registered. **Training:** 2 weeks initial training at corporate office and 1-2 week home study program.

668 ■ SuperCoups
Valassis
350 Revolutionary Dr.
East Taunton, MA 02718
Ph:(508)977-2000
Free: (866)855-2525
Fax:(508)977-0644
No. of Franchise Units: 136. **No. of Company-Owned Units:** 22. **Founded:** 1982. **Franchised:** 1983. **Description:** Cooperative direct mail. **Equity Capital Needed:** $50,000. **Franchise Fee:** $17,000-$26,000. **Royalty Fee:** Varies. **Financial Assistance:** No. **Training:** Provides 1 week training at headquarters, 1 week at franchisee's location, and ongoing support.

669 ■ Valpak Direct Marketing Systems Inc.
8065 Largo Lakes Dr.
Largo, FL 33773
Ph:(727)399-3091
Free: 800-237-6266
Fax:(727)392-0049
Co. E-mail: todd_leiser@valpak.com.com
URL: http://www.valpakfranchising.com
No. of Franchise Units: 7. **No. of Company-Owned Units:** 2. **Founded:** 1968. **Description:** Valpak is a direct mail franchisor and contains money-savings coupons from a variety of businesses, which are mailed via Canada post. **Equity Capital Needed:** $75,000 and up Canadian. **Franchise Fee:** $15,000 Canadian. **Training:** Offers 3 weeks training and ongoing.

COMPUTERIZED DATABASES

670 ■ *Advertising Age*
Crain Communications Inc.
1155 Gratiot Ave.
Detroit, MI 48207
Ph:(313)446-6000
Free: 800-678-2427
Fax:(313)446-1616
Co. E-mail: info@crain.com
URL: http://www.crain.com
Description: Contains the complete text of *Advertising Age, The International Newspaper of Marketing,* covering developments and trends in advertising, marketing, media communications, and public relations. **Availability:** Online: Crain Communications Inc., ProQuest LLC, ProQuest LLC. **Type:** Full text.

671 ■ *Advertising Red Books*
LexisNexis Group
9443 Springboro Pike
Dayton, OH 45342
Ph:(937)865-6800
Free: 800-227-4908
Fax:(937)847-3090
URL: http://www.lexisnexis.com
Description: Contains information on 24,300 of the world's leading advertisers, plus 18,000 domestic and international advertising agencies and branch offices. Contains the names and positions of more than 50,000 key corporate executives and individuals. Provides detailed information on 27,000 corporate advertising programs, including sales volume, budgets, and media usage as well as descriptions and cross-references to some 138,000 products and services handled by entrants. For each agency, provides company name, address, telephone number, executive name and position, number of employees, year founded, specialization, billings and advertising budget, gross billings and sales, media type, classification, account title, product, U.S. Standard Industrial Classification (SIC) code, monthly agency budget, trade name, description, and agency title. Corresponds to the print versions of the NRP Advertising Red Books : *Standard Directory of Advertisers, Standard Directory of Advertising Agencies,* and *Standard Directory of International Advertisers and Agencies.* **Availability:** Online: LexisNexis Group; CD-ROM: LexisNexis Group. **Type:** Directory; Numeric.

672 ■ *Big Yellow: Yellow Pages on the Web*
SuperMedia LLC
2200 W Airfield Dr.
DFW Airport, TX 75261
Free: 800-555-4833
URL: http://www.supermedia.com
Description: Provides all Business listings for the U.S., including current advertising information. Ability to search by Business name, location, heading, zip code, person, email and more. Also provides categories and hierarchies of listings for browsing. Allows creation of customized directory for personal usage. **Availability:** Online: SuperMedia LLC. **Type:** Directory.

673 ■ *MultiAd Builder*
MultiAd Inc.
1720 W Detweiller Dr.
Peoria, IL 61615
Ph:(309)692-1530
Fax:(309)692-6566
Co. E-mail: info@multiad.com
URL: http://www.multiad.com
Description: Contains illustrations, clip art, and sample designs and layouts for retail advertising. Includes headings, borders, seasonal images, promotional art, and suggested layouts for ad campaigns, as well as sample financial, grocery, newspaper, and other retail display ads. All images can be exported as encapsulated PostScript (EPS) files to Apple Macintosh page layout or desktop publishing programs where they can be edited or manipulated. Also includes a printed index of all images and materials. **Availability:** Online: MultiAd Inc; CD-ROM: MultiAd Inc. **Type:** Image.

LIBRARIES

674 ■ Advertising Research Foundation Information Center
432 Park Ave., S.
New York, NY 10016
Ph:(212)751-5656
Fax:(212)319-5265
Co. E-mail: mihui@thearf.org
URL: http://www.thearf.org
Contact: Mi hui Pak
Scope: Market research, advertising, research methods, media research. **Services:** Library open to members. **Holdings:** 3000 volumes; 2000 vertical files of clippings, reports, surveys. **Subscriptions:** 110 journals and other serials.

675 ■ Chemistri Information Center
3310 W. Big Beaver, Ste. 107
Troy, MI 48084
Ph:(248)458-8535
Fax:(248)458-8520
URL: http://www.chemistri.com/
Contact: Beth Callahan, Dir.
Scope: Marketing, advertising. **Services:** Copying (limited). **Holdings:** 3000 books; 200,000 pictures. **Subscriptions:** 150 journals and other serials; 8 newspapers.

676 ■ DDB Chicago Library
200 E. Randolph
Chicago, IL 60601
Ph:(312)552-6934
Fax:(312)552-2370
Co. E-mail: eileen.claybough@chi.ddb.com
URL: http://www.ddb.com
Contact: Eileen Claybough, Dir.
Scope: Advertising, marketing research, business. **Services:** Interlibrary loan; SDI; full reference service; Center not open to the public except for prearranged student group tours. **Holdings:** 5000 books; 200 VF drawers of pictures and print advertisements; 300 VF drawers of subject clippings; 150 VF drawers of corporation files and Annual reports; 100 pamphlet boxes of consumer analysis material. **Subscriptions:** 450 journals and other serials; 6 newspapers.

677 ■ DDB Worldwide Information Center
437 Madison Ave.
New York, NY 10022
Ph:(212)415-2000
Fax:(212)415-3414
Co. E-mail: pat.sloan@ddb.com
URL: http://www.ddb.com
Contact: Pat Sloan, Sr.VP
Scope: Advertising, marketing. **Services:** Interlibrary loan; Center not open to the public. **Holdings:** 9000 books; 100 bound periodical volumes; 50 VF drawers of pictures; 150 VF drawers of subject files. **Subscriptions:** 304 journals and other serials.

678 ■ Draft/FCB Worldwide Information Center
101 E. Erie
Chicago, IL 60611
Ph:(312)425-5000
Co. E-mail: info@draftfcb.com
URL: http://www.draftfcb.com/
Contact: Mark Modesto, Pres.
Scope: Advertising and marketing. **Services:** Library not open to the public. **Holdings:** 1000 books; 100 subject files. **Subscriptions:** 20 journals and other serials; 6 newspapers.

679 ■ Hanley-Wood, LLC Library
426 S. Westgate St.
Addison, IL 60101-4546
Ph:(630)543-0870
Fax:(630)543-3112
URL: http://www.hanleywood.com
Contact: Kimberly Last, Libn.

Scope: Concrete, cement, masonry, construction, home building. **Services:** Interlibrary loan; copying. **Holdings:** 3000 books; 120 bound periodical volumes. **Subscriptions:** 100 journals and other serials.

680 ■ International Advertising Association–World Service Center
275 Madison Ave., Ste. 2102
New York, NY 10016
Ph:(212)557-1133
Fax:(212)983-0455
Co. E-mail: iaa@iaaglobal.org
URL: http://www.iaaglobal.org
Contact: Nubia Martinez, Educ.Adm.

Scope: Advertising and marketing. **Services:** Service Center open to members only. **Holdings:** General reference books; foreign advertising and marketing periodicals; reports; archives. **Subscriptions:** 25 journals and other serials; 10 newspapers.

681 ■ J. Walter Thompson Canada–Information Services
160 Bloor St., E.
Toronto, ON, Canada M4W 3P7
Ph:(416)926-7300
Fax:(416)926-7375
Co. E-mail: susan.varney@jwt.com
URL: http://www.jwt.com/
Contact: Susan Varney, Mgr.Info.Svcs.

Scope: Marketing, advertising, economics, industry, communication, mass media, finance. **Services:** Services not open to the public. **Holdings:** Information and picture file. **Subscriptions:** 33 journals and other serials; 3 newspapers.

682 ■ McCann-Erickson Advertising of Canada Ltd. Information Centre
10 Bay St., Ste. 1012
Toronto, ON, Canada M5J 2S3
Ph:(416)594-6400
Fax:(416)594-6272
Co. E-mail: contact@mccann.com
URL: http://www.mccann.com/
Contact: Valerie Walton, Info.Ctr.Mgr.

Scope: Advertising, marketing, business, industry. **Services:** Center not open to the public. **Holdings:** 1000 books. **Subscriptions:** 90 journals and other serials.

683 ■ Noble and Associates Library
2155 W. Chesterfield Blvd.
Springfield, MO 65807
Ph:(417)875-5000
Co. E-mail: julie.tumy@noble.net
URL: http://www.noble.net
Contact: Julie Tumy, Pres.

Scope: Food, food service, advertising, construction, agriculture. **Services:** Interlibrary loan; copying; SDI; Library not open to the public. **Holdings:** 500 books; 1000 reports. **Subscriptions:** 300 journals and other serials; 5 newspapers.

684 ■ Television Bureau of Canada Library
160 Bloor St. E., Ste. 1005
Toronto, ON, Canada M4W 1B9
Ph:(416)923-8813
Fax:(416)413-3879
Co. E-mail: tvb@tvb.ca
URL: http://www.tvb.ca
Contact: Duncan Robertson, Mgr., Rsrc.Ctr.

Scope: Television, advertising. **Services:** Copying; Library open to members of the advertising industry. **Holdings:** 50 books; 500 bound periodical volumes; 500 reports; 2 archives. **Subscriptions:** 50 journals and other serials; 4 newspapers.

ASSOCIATIONS AND OTHER ORGANIZATIONS

685 ■ Automotive Service Association
PO Box 929
Bedford, TX 76095-0929
Ph:(817)283-6205
Free: 800-272-7467
Fax:(817)685-0225
Co. E-mail: asainfo@asashop.org
URL: http://www.asashop.org
Contact: Ron Pyle, Pres./Chief Staff Exec.

Description: Automotive service businesses including body, paint, and trim shops, engine rebuilders, radiator shops, brake and wheel alignment services, transmission shops, tune-up services, and air conditioning services; associate members are manufacturers and wholesalers of automotive parts, and the trade press. Represents independent business owners and managers before private agencies and national and state legislative bodies. Promotes confidence between consumer and the automotive service industry, safety inspection of motor vehicles, and better highways. **Publications:** *AutoInc* (monthly).

REFERENCE WORKS

686 ■ *Air Bag Technology, 1999*
Pub: Society of Automotive Engineers, Inc.

Ed: Powell. **Released:** 1999. **Price:** $95.00.

687 ■ *SAE Online Roster*
Pub: Society of Automotive Engineers International

Released: Continuous. **Publication Includes:** List of 121,000 members concerned with self-propelled ground, air, and space vehicles worldwide. **Entries Include:** For members—Member name, company name, address, job title. **Arrangement:** Alphabetical by member name. **Indexes:** Members by company name, product.

TRADE PERIODICALS

688 ■ *The Auto Parts Report*
Pub: Automotive Parts International

Ed: Ron Demarnes, Editor, itsron@bellatlantic.net. **Released:** Semimonthly. **Description:** Provides news and information on auto parts.

689 ■ *AutoInc.*
Pub: Automotive Service Association
Contact: Levy Joffrion, Assoc. Ed.
E-mail: levyj@asashop.org

Ed: Leona Dalavai Scott, Editor, leonad@asashop.org. **Released:** Monthly. **Price:** $35; $65 two years; $95 other countries; $175 other countries two years; $40 Canada and Mexico; $70 Canada and Mexico two years. **Description:** Automotive service industry magazine serving independent mechanical, collision, and transmission repair shop owners.

690 ■ *Automotive Litigation Reporter*
Pub: Thomson West

Ed: Nick Sullivan, Editor. **Released:** Semimonthly. **Price:** $2,683.56, individuals. **Description:** Covers significant federal and state lawsuits, including pretrial, trial, and appeal proceedings, settlements, and class action suits. Offers complete texts of key decisions and pleadings.

691 ■ *Motor Vehicle Regulation*
Pub: Wakeman/Walworth Inc.

Ed: Keyes Walworth, Editor. **Released:** 48/year. **Price:** $245, individuals. **Description:** Covers state laws and regulations regarding vehicle safety, inspections, tages, fees and taxes, emissions standards, drunken driving laws, motorist licensing, insurance and education, and school bus regulation.

TRADE SHOWS AND CONVENTIONS

692 ■ Dayton Auto Show
Hart Productions, Inc.
2234 Bauer Rd., Ste. B
Batavia, OH 45103
Ph:(513)797-7900
Free: 877-704-8190
Fax:(513)797-1013
URL: http://www.hartproductions.com

Released: Annual. **Audience:** General public. **Principal Exhibits:** Automobiles and automotive equipment, supplies, and services.

693 ■ Massachusetts International Auto Show
Expo Management Group
69 Milk St., No. 206
PO Box 785
Westborough, MA 01581
Ph:(508)836-2222
Co. E-mail: info@expomanage.com
URL: http://www.worcestershows.com

Released: Annual. **Audience:** General public and trade professionals. **Principal Exhibits:** New automobiles, trucks, vans, and related equipment, supplies, and services.

694 ■ Montreal International Auto Show
Montreal International Auto Show, Ltd.
Palais des congres de Montreal
1001, De Bleury (place Jean-Paul-Riopelle)
Montreal, QC, Canada H2Z 1M2
Ph:(514)331-6571
Fax:(514)331-7818
Co. E-mail: communications@ccam.qc.ca
URL: http://www.ccam.qc.ca/en/salon-de-lauto-de-montreal/

Released: Annual. **Audience:** General public. **Principal Exhibits:** New cars, light trucks, and vehicle accessories/services.

COMPUTERIZED DATABASES

695 ■ *ALLDATA Online*
ALLDATA L.L.C.
9650 W Taron Dr., Ste. 100
Elk Grove, CA 95757
Ph:(916)684-5200
Free: 800-859-3282
Fax:(916)684-5225
Co. E-mail: marketing@alldata.com
URL: http://www.alldata.com

Description: Contains engine-specific automotive diagnostic and repair information, electrical diagrams, maintenance schedules and tables, daily technical service bulletins and recalls, and parts and labor for estimating. Offers alphabetized component and systems listings, manufacturer TSBs and recall data, original manufacturer's wiring diagrams with connector, ground, power distribution, and splice information, maintenance tables, and more. **Availability:** Online: ALLDATA L.L.C. **Type:** Image; Full text.

LIBRARIES

696 ■ U.S. National Highway Traffic Safety Administration–Technical Information Services
1200 New Jersey Ave., SE
Washington, DC 20590
Ph:888-327-4236
Fax:(202)493-2833
Co. E-mail: tis@nhtsa.dot.gov
URL: http://www.nhtsa.dot.gov/cars/problems/trd/?name=
Contact: Kevin M. Ball

Scope: Motor vehicle safety, highway traffic safety, alcohol countermeasures for driving safety, vehicle occupant protection, emergency medical services. **Services:** Copying; TIS open to the public. **Holdings:** 200 books; 52,000 agency and related publications and reports; 920,000 microfiche. **Subscriptions:** 40 journals and other serials.

RESEARCH CENTERS

697 ■ Center for Auto Safety
1825 Connecticut Ave. NW, Ste. 330
Washington, DC 20009-5708
Ph:(202)328-7700
Fax:(202)387-0140
URL: http://www.autosafety.org
Contact: Clarence Ditlow, Exec.Dir.

Scope: Automobile defects, fuel economy, gasoline quality, consumer complaints, automobile recalls, sudden acceleration, crash tests, lemon laws, fuel volatility, child safety seats, "secret warranties", and access to government information on automobile safety. **Services:** Safety research service. **Publications:** Impact (bimonthly); Lemon Times (quarterly).

698 ■ Insurance Institute for Highway Safety
1005 N Glebe Rd., Ste. 800
Arlington, VA 22201

Ph:(703)247-1500
Fax:(703)247-1588
Co. E-mail: permissions@iihs.org
URL: http://www.iihs.org
Contact: Adrian Lund, Pres.
E-mail: permissions@iihs.org
Scope: Highway safety, including studies on seat belt use, air bags, alcohol and drugs in highway crashes, property damage from vehicle crashes, vehicle crashworthiness, child restraint devices, and radar detectors. Seeks to reduce deaths, injuries, and property damage resulting from crashes on the nation's highways. **Publications:** Annual Report; Status Report.

ASSOCIATIONS AND OTHER ORGANIZATIONS

699 ■ Air Line Pilots Association International - Canada–Association Canadienne des Pilotes de Ligne Internationale
155 Queen St., Ste. 1301
Ottawa, ON, Canada K1P 6L1
Ph:(613)569-5668
Fax:(613)569-5681
Co. E-mail: humanresources@alpa.org
URL: http://www.alpa.org
Contact: Captain John Prater, Pres.
Description: Commercially licensed pilots. Promotes safety and efficiency in air transportation. Collects and distributes information on professional problems and concerns. Negotiates collective employment agreements with airlines. **Publications:** *Air Line Pilot* (quarterly).

700 ■ Air Transport Association of America
1301 Pennsylvania Ave. NW, Ste. 1100
Washington, DC 20004-7017
Ph:(202)626-4000
Co. E-mail: ata@airlines.org
URL: http://www.airlines.org
Contact: Nicholas E. Calio, Pres./CEO
Description: Airlines engaged in transporting persons, goods and mail by aircraft between fixed terminals on regular schedules. **Publications:** *Air Transport* (annual); *Economic* (annual).

701 ■ Air Transport Association of Canada
255 Albert St., Ste. 700
Ottawa, ON, Canada K1P 6A9
Ph:(613)233-7727
Fax:(613)230-8648
Co. E-mail: atac@atac.ca
URL: http://www.atac.ca
Contact: Mr. Mark Williams, Chm.
Description: Air transport companies. Promotes a business climate beneficial to members. Represents' members interests before government agencies. Conducts research and educational programs; compiles industry statistics. **Publications:** *Flightplan* (semiannual).

702 ■ Aircraft Owners and Pilots Association
421 Aviation Way
Frederick, MD 21701
Ph:(301)695-2000
Free: 800-872-2672
Fax:(301)695-2375
Co. E-mail: aopahq@aopa.org
URL: http://www.aopa.org
Contact: Craig Fuller, Pres.
Description: Represents general aviation pilots and owners, 60 percent of U.S. are members, as are three-quarters of the nation's general aviation aircraft owners. Works to make flying safer, less expensive, and more fun. **Publications:** *AOPA Flight Training Magazine* (monthly); *AOPA Pilot* (monthly); *AOPA's Airport Directory*; *AOPA's Aviation U.S.A.* (semiannual).

703 ■ Airport Minority Advisory Council
2345 Crystal Dr., Ste. 902
Arlington, VA 22202
Ph:(703)414-2622
Fax:(703)414-2686
Co. E-mail: amac.info@amac-org.com
URL: http://www.amac-org.com
Contact: Gene Roth, Exec. Dir.
Description: Advocates for equal opportunity for minorities and women in airport contracting and employment. **Publications:** *AMACESP Informational Brochure* .

704 ■ Canadian Business Aviation Association
55 Metcalfe St., Ste. 430
Ottawa, ON, Canada K1P 6L5
Ph:(613)236-5611
Fax:(613)236-2361
Co. E-mail: info@cbaa.ca
URL: http://www.cbaa-acaa.ca
Contact: Mr. Sam Barone, Pres./CEO
Description: Companies operating or supporting business aviation. Promotes business aviation; encourages safety and efficiency; makes recommendations to regulatory agencies. **Publications:** *News Brief* (bimonthly); Membership Directory (annual).

705 ■ Flight Safety Foundation
801 N Fairfax St., Ste. 400
Alexandria, VA 22314
Ph:(703)739-6700
Fax:(703)739-6708
Co. E-mail: wahdan@flightsafety.org
URL: http://flightsafety.org
Contact: William R. Voss, Pres./CEO
Description: Aerospace manufacturers, domestic and foreign airlines, insurance companies, fuel and oil companies, schools and miscellaneous organizations having an interest in the promotion of safety in flight. Sponsors safety audits. Compiles statistics. **Publications:** *Accident Prevention* (monthly); *Flight Safety Digest* (monthly); *Human Factors and Aviation Medicine* (bimonthly).

706 ■ Helicopter Association International
1635 Prince St.
Alexandria, VA 22314-2818
Ph:(703)683-4646
Free: 800-435-4976
Fax:(703)683-4745
Co. E-mail: questions@rotor.com
URL: http://www.rotor.com
Contact: Matthew S. Zuccaro, Pres.
Description: Owners, operators, helicopter enthusiasts, and affiliated companies in the civil helicopter industry. Receives and disseminates information concerning the use, operation, hiring, contracting, and leasing of helicopters. Maintains a collection of current helicopter service bulletins and technical data; organizes safety seminars, continuing education courses, and helicopter operator management courses; and maintains a maintenance malfunction information database. **Publications:** *Helicopter Annual* (annual); *Heliport Directory* (biennial); *Heliport/Vertiport Development Guide* (periodic); *Operations Update* (monthly); *Rotor: By the Industry - For the Industry* (quarterly).

707 ■ International Business Aviation Council
999 Rue University, Ste. 16-33
Montreal, QC, Canada H3C 5J9
Ph:(514)954-8054
Fax:(514)954-6161
Co. E-mail: info@ibac.org
URL: http://www.ibac.org
Contact: Donald D. Spruston, Dir. Gen.
Description: International business aircraft associations; national and regional business aviation organizations or subgroups. Aims to provide information on all aspects of international business aircraft operations; ensure that the interests of international business aviation are brought to the attention of and understood by authorities; improve the safety, efficiency and economic use of business aircraft operating internationally. Stresses the importance of business aviation to the economy and to the well-being of all nations. Maintains liaison with international aviation organizations to ensure safe and orderly growth of international business aviation throughout the world. Compiles statistics. **Publications:** *IBAC Update* (quarterly). **Telecommunication Services:** electronic mail, dspruston@ibac.org; electronic mail, plessard@ibac.org.

708 ■ International Civil Aviation Organization–Organisation de l'Aviation Civile Internationale
999 University St.
Montreal, QC, Canada H3C 5H7
Ph:(514)954-8219
Fax:(514)954-6077
Co. E-mail: icaohq@icao.int
URL: http://www.icao.int
Contact: Mr. Roberto Kobeh Gonzalez, Pres.
Description: National government representatives. Seeks to develop the standards and procedures in international air navigation and to foster the planning and development of international air transport so as to insure safe and orderly growth of international civil aviation. Carries out activities in air navigation, air transport, and legal matters. Provides advice, assistance, and training. Compiles statistics. **Publications:** *ICAO Journal* (9/year).

709 ■ National Air Carrier Association
1000 Wilson Blvd., Ste. 1700
Arlington, VA 22209
Ph:(703)358-8060
Fax:(703)358-8070
Co. E-mail: obrooks@naca.cc
URL: http://www.naca.cc
Contact: A. Oakley Brooks, Pres.
Description: Represents U.S. certificated airlines specializing in low-cost scheduled and air charter operations. Assists members in the promotion of air transportation and serves as a liaison between members and U.S. government bodies that regulate air transportation. .

710 ■ National Air Transportation Association
4226 King St.
Alexandria, VA 22302
Ph:(703)845-9000
Free: 800-808-6282
Fax:(703)845-8176
Co. E-mail: rmulholland@nata.aero
URL: http://www.nata.aero
Contact: James K. Coyne, Pres./CEO
Purpose: Represents the interests of aviation businesses nationwide. Provides vital aviation services to the airlines, the military, and business/corporate/individual aircraft owners and operators; services includes fueling, maintenance, and flight instruction. **Publications:** *NATAnews* (monthly); *Wage and Salary Handbook* (annual);Membership Directory (annual).

711 ■ National Business Aviation Association
1200 18th St. NW, Ste. 400
Washington, DC 20036-2527
Ph:(202)783-9000
Fax:(202)331-8364
Co. E-mail: info@nbaa.org
URL: http://www.nbaa.org
Contact: Edward M. Bolen, Pres./CEO
Description: Companies owning and operating aircraft for business use, suppliers, and maintenance and air fleet service companies. Compiles statistics; provides literature for researchers and students. **Publications:** *Maintenance and Operations Bulletin* (semiannual); *Management Guide*; *National Business Aircraft Association—Membership Directory* (periodic); *NBAA Update* (weekly).

712 ■ World Airlines Clubs Association
PO Box 113
Montreal, QC, Canada H4Z 1M1
Ph:(514)874-0202
Fax:(514)874-1753
Co. E-mail: info@waca.org
URL: http://www.waca.org
Contact: Maga Ramasamy, Pres.
Description: Airline/interline clubs in 50 countries representing 3,000 employees of the civil and commercial airline industry. Promotes airline transportation as a mode of travel and works to provide better service to the traveling public. Seeks to increase public awareness of the contribution of the airlines to world of the contribution of the airlines to world understanding and to extend, promote, and publicize the airline/interline clubs movement; advises on and coordinates the activities of member clubs worldwide. Promotes economic and social programs for the betterment of airlines and the community and country that the club serves. Fosters discussion on civil and commercial aviation; organizes annual and ongoing projects in the field; sponsors charitable programs and conducts sports tournaments. **Publications:** *Airline/Interline Club Newsletter* (3/year).

DIRECTORIES OF EDUCATIONAL PROGRAMS

713 ■ *Directory of Private Accredited Career Schools and Colleges of Technology*
Pub: Accrediting Commission of Career Schools and Colleges of Technology
Contact: Michale S. McComis, Exec. Dir.
Released: On web page. **Price:** Free. **Description:** Covers 3900 accredited post-secondary programs that provide training programs in business, trade, and technical fields, including various small business endeavors. Entries offer school name, address, phone, description of courses, job placement assistance, and requirements for admission. Arrangement is alphabetical.

REFERENCE WORKS

714 ■ *Minnesota Airport Directory & Travel Guide*
Pub: Minnesota Department of Transportation, Office of Aeronautics
Contact: Jenny Olson
E-mail: jenny.olsen@dot.state.nm.us
Released: Annual. **Price:** Free. **Covers:** Airports and public seaplane bases in Minnesota. **Entries Include:** Address and telephone number.

715 ■ *National Air Transportation Association—Aviation Resource and Membership Directory*
Pub: National Air Transportation Association
Released: Annual, Latest edition 2008. **Price:** $50, nonmembers; $25, members. **Covers:** More than 1,000 regular, associate, and affiliate members; regular members include airport service organizations, air taxi operators, and commuter airlines. **Entries Include:** Company name, address, phone, fax number, name and title of contact. **Arrangement:** Regular members are classified by service; associate and affiliate members are alphabetical in separate sections. **Indexes:** Geographical.

STATISTICAL SOURCES

716 ■ *RMA Annual Statement Studies*
Pub: Robert Morris Associates (RMA)
Released: Annual. **Price:** $175.00 2006-07 edition, $105.00. **Description:** Contains composite balance sheets and income statements for more than 360 industries, including the accounting, auditing, and bookkeeping industries. Also contains five years of comparative historical data for discerning trends. Includes 16 commonly used ratios, computed for most of the size groupings for nearly every industry.

717 ■ *Standard & Poor's Industry Surveys*
Pub: Standard & Poor's Corp.
Released: Annual. **Price:** $3633.00. **Description:** Two-volume book that examines the prospects for specific industries, including trucking. Also provides analyses of trends and problems, statistical tables and charts, and comparative company analyses.

TRADE PERIODICALS

718 ■ *99NEWS Magazine*
Pub: The Ninety-Nines Inc.
Contact: Lu Hallender
Released: Bimonthly. **Price:** $20, nonmembers within the U.S.; $30, nonmembers in Canada and other countries; Included in membership. **Description:** Includes material of interest to the members of The Ninety-Nines, Inc., an international organization of women pilots. Recurring features include interviews, news of research, letters to the editor, news of educational opportunities, a calendar of events, and columns titled President's and Careers.

719 ■ *Air Medical Journal*
Pub: Mosby Inc.
Ed: Jacqueline C. Stocking, Editor, jackie.stocking@yahoo.com. **Released:** Bimonthly. **Price:** $119; $169 Canada and Mexico; $169 other countries. **Description:** Journal for air medical transport professionals.

720 ■ *Aviation Medical Bulletin*
Pub: Harvey W. Watt & Company Inc.
Contact: Cindy Burch
Ed: Released: Monthly. **Price:** $19.95, U.S. and Canada. **Description:** Provides the latest medical information for those working in the aviation field. Recurring features include news of research.

721 ■ *Aviation Monthly*
Pub: Peter Katz Productions Inc.
Contact: Peter Katz, Editor & Publisher
Released: Monthly. **Price:** $39; $20 air mail. **Description:** Magazine on aviation safety. Includes accident reports.

TRADE SHOWS AND CONVENTIONS

722 ■ AOPA Aviation Summit - Aircraft Owners and Pilots Association
Aircraft Owners and Pilots Association
421 Aviation Way
Frederick, MD 21701
Ph:(301)695-2000
Fax:(301)695-2375
URL: http://www.aopa.org
Released: Annual. **Audience:** Pilots, aircraft owners, suppliers, and used aircraft trade. **Principal Exhibits:** Single-engine and multi-engine aircraft, avionics, airframes, power plant and equipment, financing information, and related equipment, supplies, and services. **Dates and Locations:** 2011 Nov 11-13, Long Beach, CA.

723 ■ Aviation Industry Expo
Cygnus Business Media
801 Cliff Rd., Ste. 201
Burnsville, MN 55337
Ph:(952)894-8007
Free: 800-827-8009
Fax:(952)894-8252
Co. E-mail: info@farmshows.com
URL: http://www.cygnusb2b.com
Released: Annual. **Audience:** Air cargo dealers, aircraft dealers, flight schools, ground handlers, manufacturers, military. **Principal Exhibits:** General aviation products and services; fixed base operation and air charter products and services.

724 ■ HELI-EXPO - Helicopter Association International Annual Meeting and Industry Exposition
Helicopter Association International
1635 Prince St.
Alexandria, VA 22314
Ph:(703)683-4646
Free: 800-435-4976
Fax:(703)683-4745
Co. E-mail: questions@rotor.com
URL: http://www.rotor.com
Released: Annual. **Audience:** Helicopter operators. **Principal Exhibits:** Helicopter airframes, engines, accessories, avionics, communications equipment, and insurance information.

CONSULTANTS

725 ■ AVITAS Inc.
14520 Avion Pky., Ste. 300
Chantilly, VA 20151
Ph:(703)476-2300
Fax:(703)860-5855
Co. E-mail: info@avitas.com
URL: http://www.avitas.com
Contact: Stephen R. Jarvis, Managing Director
E-mail: stephen.jarvis@atsavitas.com
Scope: A full service consulting company providing advisory and technical services to airlines, aircraft manufacturers, industry suppliers, maintenance providers, aircraft lessors and financiers, legal council and government entities. **Publications:** "Bluebook of Jet Aircraft Values"; "Bluebook of Commercial Turboprop Aircraft Values"; "Bluebook of Jet Engine Values"; "BlueBook of Flight Simulator Values"; "Aircraft Block Hour Operating Costs and Operations Guide"; "SAVI - Scenario Analysis & Value Index". **Special Services:** AVITAS Analyst; Online Aircraft Appraisal Service; Online Portfolio Monitoring Service; Online Engine Appraisal Service; Online Flight Distance Calculator.

726 ■ CAROPAM Corp.
20125 Stewart Airlines Hangar X37
PO Box 60166
Spring, TX 77379
Ph:(281)355-8182
Free: 888-926-7645
Fax:(281)355-8182
Co. E-mail: caropamcorp@caropam.com
URL: http://www.caropam.com
Contact: William Jordan, Vice President
E-mail: williamjordan@atscaropam.com
Scope: Firm offers services to the aviation industry including industrial relations, flight training and airline management.

COMPUTERIZED DATABASES

727 ■ *AvData Air Carrier File*
Jetnet LLC
101 First St., 2nd Fl.
Utica, NY 13501
Ph:(315)797-4420
Free: 800-553-8638

Fax:(315)797-4798
URL: http://www.avdatainc.com
Description: Contains up-to-date information on the status of air carrier fleets, providing inventories by carrier or aircraft model. Includes aircraft model, aircraft serial number, aircraft registration mark, date aircraft acquired by current operator, aircraft year of manufacturer, owner name and address, operator name and address, chief executive name and phone (where available), engines, airframe hours and cycles (most jets), and first delivery date and country. **Availability:** Online: McGraw-Hill Companies Inc. **Type:** Directory.

728 ■ *Aviation Daily*
McGraw-Hill Companies Inc.
1200 G St. NW, Ste. 922
Washington, DC 20005
Ph:(202)383-2403
Free: 800-525-5003
Fax:(202)383-2346
URL: http://www.aviationweek.com
Description: Contains the complete text of *Aviation Daily*, a newsletter covering the commercial aviation industry, including relevant government activities, key issues and trends, and personnel developments. Provides news and market intelligence such as US and International air carrier route and fare changes, suppliers, cargo, mergers and acquisitions, and more. Major markets covered include expanded coverage of Brussels, London, Taipei, Mumbai, Tokyo, Amsterdam, Singapore, and Beijing. **Availability:** Online: LexisNexis Group, ProQuest LLC, Dow Jones & Company Inc., McGraw-Hill Companies Inc. **Type:** Full text.

729 ■ *History of Aviation*
MultiEducator Inc.
244 North Ave.
New Rochelle, NY 10801
Ph:(914)235-4340
Free: 800-866-6434
Fax:(914)235-4367
Co. E-mail: multied@multied.com
URL: http://www.multieducator.net
Description: Covers the evolution of manned flight. Presents more than 100 video clips and more than 1000 photos of aircraft and aviators throughout history. **Availability:** CD-ROM: MultiEducator Inc. **Type:** Full text; Image; Video.

730 ■ *Jane's Aero-Engines*
IHS Global Ltd.
Sentinel House
163 Brighton Rd.
Surrey
Coulsdon CR5 2YH, United Kingdom
Ph:44 20 8700 3700
Fax:44 20 8763 1006
Co. E-mail: info.uk@janes.com
URL: http://www.janes.com
Description: Contains the complete text of *Jane's Aero-Engines*, providing profiles of all gas turbine engines for civil and military aircraft, helicopters, and cargo carriers in Service, under development, and in production. Includes a full market Analysis, covering technological issues such as engine cycles, fuel, and combustion, materials, design, and Environmental concerns. **Availability:** Online: IHS Global Ltd. **Type:** Full text; Directory; Image.

731 ■ *Jane's Aircraft Upgrades*
IHS Global Ltd.
Sentinel House
163 Brighton Rd.
Surrey
Coulsdon CR5 2YH, United Kingdom
Ph:44 20 8700 3700
Fax:44 20 8763 1006
Co. E-mail: info.uk@janes.com
URL: http://www.janes.com
Description: Contains the complete text of *Jane's Aircraft Upgrades*, providing the latest information on aircraft that are no longer manufactured, but are still in Service today, identifying what upgrades are available on almost every civil or military aircraft. Describes 700 aircraft from military airplanes to passenger and cargo carriers. Includes specifications on weight, dimensions, performance data, and loadings for each aircraft in addition to range of variants available. **Availability:** Online: IHS Global Ltd. **Type:** Full text; Directory; Image.

732 ■ *Jane's Airports and Handling Agents Library*
IHS Global Ltd.
Sentinel House
163 Brighton Rd.
Surrey
Coulsdon CR5 2YH, United Kingdom
Ph:44 20 8700 3700
Fax:44 20 8763 1006
Co. E-mail: info.uk@janes.com
URL: http://www.janes.com
Description: Contains the complete text of *Jane's Airports and Handling Agents*, covering more than 2200 airports and 4000 handling agents/FBOs worldwide. Includes customs and immigration requirements, fuellers, and caterers. Covers the following regions (each available separately): Europe. USA and Canada. Middle East and Africa. Far East, Asia, and Australasia. Central and Latin America (incl. the Caribbean). **Availability:** Online: IHS Global Ltd. **Type:** Directory; Full text.

733 ■ *Jane's Helicopter Markets and Systems*
IHS Global Ltd.
Sentinel House
163 Brighton Rd.
Surrey
Coulsdon CR5 2YH, United Kingdom
Ph:44 20 8700 3700
Fax:44 20 8763 1006
Co. E-mail: info.uk@janes.com
URL: http://www.janes.com
Description: Contains the complete text of *Jane's Helicopter Markets and Systems*, providing technical information on every civil and military helicopter flying. Features sales history, forecasts, fleet inventories, and prices; details of manufacturers, suppliers, and major operators; and design features and performance. Includes current status of the helicopter fleets of armed forces, paramilitary agencies, and commercial operators country-by-country. **Availability:** Online: IHS Global Ltd. **Type:** Full text; Directory; Image.

734 ■ *Jane's Unmanned Aerial Vehicles and Targets*
IHS Global Ltd.
Sentinel House
163 Brighton Rd.
Surrey
Coulsdon CR5 2YH, United Kingdom
Ph:44 20 8700 3700
Fax:44 20 8763 1006
Co. E-mail: info.uk@janes.com
URL: http://www.janes.com
Description: Contains the complete text of *Jane's Unmanned Aerial Vehicles and Targets*, covering more than 180 unmanned aerial vehicles (UAVs), their guidance and tracking systems, engines, airframe structure and materials, dimensions, speed, and range. Also includes coverage of 120 aerial targets and 240 sub-systems. Includes information on the civil and military organizations using UAVs and their manufacturers. Profiles UAV subsystems and support systems and reviews 69 different payloads, including infra-red sensors, thermal imagers, TV systems, optical cameras, datalinks, and launch and recovery systems. **Availability:** Online: IHS Global Ltd. **Type:** Full text; Directory; Image.

735 ■ *Jane's World Airlines*
IHS Global Ltd.
Sentinel House
163 Brighton Rd.
Surrey
Coulsdon CR5 2YH, United Kingdom
Ph:44 20 8700 3700
Fax:44 20 8763 1006
Co. E-mail: info.uk@janes.com
URL: http://www.janes.com
Description: Contains the complete text of *Jane's World Airlines*, monitoring the performance of more than 500 airlines worldwide. Provides the latest data on each airline including its structure, operations, fleet, financial performance, routes operated, traffic statistics, and cargo capacity. Topics covered include: fleet composition; maintenance; summary of equity holdings; airline alliance summaries; financial data; traffic statistics; destinations; key personnel; contact details. **Availability:** Online: IHS Global Ltd. **Type:** Directory; Full text.

LIBRARIES

736 ■ Aircraft Technical Publishers Library
101 S. Hill Dr.
Brisbane, CA 94005
Ph:(415)330-9500
Free: 800-227-4610
Fax:(415)468-1596
URL: http://www.atp.com
Contact: Thomas P. Tantillo, Dir. of Prod.
Scope: Aviation maintenance, avionics, aviation regulations. **Services:** Center not open to the public. **Holdings:** 4 million pages of aviation information.

737 ■ Boeing Company–Integrated Defense Systems–Business Information Center (2201)
2201 Seal Beach Blvd., 110-SB72
Seal Beach, CA 90740
Ph:(562)797-2534
Fax:(562)797-5030
Co. E-mail: sandra.tung@boeing.com
URL: http://www.boeing.com/bds/
Contact: Sandra Tung, Bus.Info.Mgr.
Scope: Military/aircraft, defense electronics, space, communications, marketing. **Services:** Library not open to the public. **Holdings:** Figures not available.

738 ■ British Columbia Institute of Technology–Aerospace and Technology Campus Library
3800 Cessna Dr.
Richmond, BC, Canada V7B 0A1
Ph:(778)333-3708
Fax:(604)207-8437
Co. E-mail: bill_nadiger@bcit.ca
URL: http://www.lib.bcit.ca/
Contact: Bill Nadiger, Libn.
Scope: Aeronautics. **Services:** Interlibrary loan; Library open to the public with restrictions (upon purchase of a membership card). **Holdings:** 4000 books; 900 videos. **Subscriptions:** 50 journals and other serials.

739 ■ Canada - Transport Canada–Aircraft Services Directorate–Technical Library, AAFBAA (275 S)
275 Slater St., 6th Fl.
Ottawa, ON, Canada K1A 0N5
Ph:(613)998-5128
Fax:(613)954-4731
Co. E-mail: library-bibliotheque@tc.gc.ca
URL: http://www.tc.gc.ca/eng/corporate-services/library-menu.htm
Scope: Transportation. **Services:** Library open to the public. **Holdings:** 100,000 books; 2000 technical manuals; 8000 technical drawings. **Subscriptions:** 300 journals and other serials.

740 ■ Flight Safety Foundation Library
601 Madison St., Ste. 300
Alexandria, VA 22314
Ph:(703)739-6700
Fax:(703)739-6708
Co. E-mail: setze@flightsafety.org
URL: http://www.flightsafety.org/home.html
Contact: Patricia Setze, Libn.
Scope: Aviation safety. **Services:** Library open to the public for reference use only. **Holdings:** 1000 books, audio/visuals, periodicals, and archival materials. **Subscriptions:** 150 journals and other serials.

741 ■ Honeywell, Inc.–Air Transport Systems Engineering Library
21111 N. 19th Ave.
Phoenix, AZ 85027
Ph:(602)436-2311

Fax:(602)436-2252
URL: http://www51.honeywell.com/honeywell/
Contact: Kay Heiberg

Scope: Electronic engineering, computer sciences, flight instrumentation. **Services:** Interlibrary loan; copying. **Holdings:** 3000 books; 1000 technical reports. **Subscriptions:** 150 journals and other serials.

742 ■ International Association for Air Travel Couriers Library

PO Box 31279
Omaha, NE 68132
Ph:(402)218-1982
Co. E-mail: inforeq@iaatc.org
URL: http://www.courier.org
Contact: Kathy Craig, Pres.

Scope: Air courier industry. **Services:** Library open to the public for reference use only. **Holdings:** 2100 books and maps. **Subscriptions:** 18 journals and other serials.

743 ■ U.S. Federal Aviation Administration–Mike Monroney Aeronautical Center Library

Academy Bldg. Rm. 114
6500 S. MacArthur Blvd.
Oklahoma City, OK 73169
Ph:(405)954-2665
Fax:(405)954-4742
Co. E-mail: 9amcmmaclibrary@faa.gov
URL: http://www.academy.faa.gov/library/
Contact: Virginia C. Hughes, Libn.

Scope: Aeronautics, airplanes, mathematics, avionics, electronics, management. **Services:** Interlibrary loan; Library open to the public with restrictions. **Holdings:** 12,000 volumes; books; periodicals; 15,000 technical reports. **Subscriptions:** 65 journals and other serials.

ASSOCIATIONS AND OTHER ORGANIZATIONS

744 ■ Air Conditioning Contractors of America
2800 Shirlington Rd., Ste. 300
Arlington, VA 22206
Ph:(703)575-4477
Fax:(703)575-4449
Co. E-mail: info@acca.org
URL: http://www.acca.org
Contact: Paul T. Stalknecht, Pres./CEO
Description: Contractors involved in installation and service of heating, air conditioning, and refrigeration systems. Associate members are utilities, manufacturers, wholesalers, and other market-oriented businesses. Monitors utility competition and operating practices of HVAC manufacturers and wholesalers. Provides consulting services, technical training, and instructor certification program; offers management seminars. Operates annual educational institute. **Publications:** *ACCA Technical Bulletin* (monthly); *Air Conditioning Contractors of America Membership Directory* (annual); *Air Conditioning Contractors of America Quality Contractor's Catalog of Products and Services* (annual).

745 ■ Air-Conditioning Heating and Refrigeration Institute
2111 Wilson Blvd., Ste. 500
Arlington, VA 22201
Ph:(703)524-8800
Fax:(703)562-1942
Co. E-mail: ahri@ahrinet.org
URL: http://www.ahrinet.org
Contact: Ray Hoglund, Chm.
Description: Manufacturers of air conditioning, refrigeration and heating products and components. Develops and establishes equipment and application standards and certifies performance of certain industry products; provides credit and statistical services to members. Provides representation and technical assistance to government entities in federal, state and local legislative matters; provides public relations, consumer education and promotional programs for the industry. **Publications:** *ARI Curriculum Guide*; *Minuteman* (monthly).

746 ■ American Society of Heating, Refrigerating and Air-Conditioning Engineers
1791 Tullie Cir. NE
Atlanta, GA 30329
Ph:(404)636-8400
Free: 800-527-4723
Fax:(404)321-5478
Co. E-mail: ashrae@ashrae.org
URL: http://www.ashrae.org
Contact: Thomas Watson PE, Pres.-Elect
Description: Represents Technical society of heating, ventilating, refrigeration, and air-conditioning engineers. Sponsors numerous research programs in cooperation with universities, research laboratories, and government agencies on subjects such as human and animal environmental studies, effects of air-conditioning, quality of inside air, heat transfer, flow, and cooling processes. Conducts professional development seminars. Writes method of test standards and other standards addressing energy conservation in buildings, indoor air quality, and refrigerants. Publishes extensive literature and electronic products. **Publications:** *ASHRAE Insights* (monthly); *IAQ Applications* (quarterly); *International Journal of HUAC&R Research* (quarterly);Journal (monthly).

747 ■ Associated Specialty Contractors
3 Bethesda Metro Ctr., Ste. 1100
Bethesda, MD 20814
Co. E-mail: dgw@necanet.org
URL: http://www.assoc-spec-con.org
Contact: Daniel G. Walter, Pres./COO
Description: Works to promote efficient management and productivity. Coordinates the work of specialized branches of the industry in management information, research, public information, government relations and construction relations. Serves as a liaison among specialty trade associations in the areas of public relations, government relations, and with other organizations. Seeks to avoid unnecessary duplication of effort and expense or conflicting programs among affiliates. Identifies areas of interest and problems shared by members, and develops positions and approaches on such problems. **Publications:** *Contract Documents* .

748 ■ Evaporative Cooling Institute
MSC 3ECI - NMSU
PO Box 30001
Las Cruces, NM 88003-8001
Ph:(505)646-1846
Fax:(505)646-3841
Co. E-mail: moreinfo@evapcooling.org
URL: http://www.evapcooling.org
Contact: Robert Foster
Description: Represents manufacturers of evaporative apparatus; designers, specifiers, and users of heating, ventilating, and air conditioning systems; sales representatives; representatives of educational and governmental agencies; interested individuals. Seeks to advance the art and science of evaporative air cooling and air conditioning by: promoting the technology and industry; collecting and publishing information on applying, installing, operating, and maintaining evaporative systems; disseminating information on codes, standards, and certification programs; identifying and encouraging research; maintaining contact with related trade associations, professional societies, government agencies, and customers. **Publications:** *Evaporative Air-conditioning Applications for Environmentally Friendly Cooling*; *Membership Services Directory* (annual).

749 ■ Heating, Refrigeration and Air Conditioning Institute of Canada
2800 Skymark Ave., Bldg. 1, Ste. 201
Mississauga, ON, Canada L4W 5A6
Ph:(905)602-4700
Free: 800-267-2231
Fax:(905)602-1197
Co. E-mail: hraimail@hrai.ca
URL: http://www.hrai.ca
Contact: Warren Heeley, Pres.
Description: Corporations engaged in the heating, refrigeration, air-conditioning, ventilation, and related industries. Seeks to advance the techniques and technologies available to members, and the heating and cooling industries as a whole. Conducts educational programs; compiles statistics.

750 ■ Home Ventilating Institute
1000 N Rand Rd., Ste. 214
Wauconda, IL 60084
Ph:(847)416-7257
Fax:(480)559-9722
Co. E-mail: hvi@hvi.org
URL: http://www.hvi.org
Description: Aims to serve consumers and members by advancing residential ventilation. Provides a forum for industry to meet and discuss common issues. **Publications:** *Home Ventilating Guide* (periodic).

751 ■ International Association of Plumbing and Mechanical Officials
4755 E Philadelphia St.
Ontario, CA 91761
Ph:(909)472-4100
Free: 800-854-2766
Fax:(909)472-4150
Co. E-mail: iapmo@iapmo.org
URL: http://www.iapmo.org
Contact: Mr. Dwight Perkins, Sr. Dir. of Field Services
Description: Government agencies, administrative officials, plumbing officials, mechanical officials, plumbing and mechanical product manufacturers, trade associations, and members of associations related to the plumbing field. Sponsors and writes uniform plumbing codes, uniform mechanical code, uniform solar energy code and uniform swimming pool, spa and hot tub code. Sponsors speakers' bureau. **Publications:** *Directory of Listed Plumbing Products* (weekly); *Directory of Listed Plumbing Products for Mobile Homes and Recreational Vehicles* (bimonthly); *Official* (bimonthly); *Uniform Mechanical Illustrated Training Manual* (periodic); *Uniform Plumbing Code Illustrated Training Manual* .

752 ■ International District Energy Association
24 Lyman St., Ste. 230
Westborough, MA 01581-2841
Ph:(508)366-9339
Fax:(508)366-0019
Co. E-mail: idea@districtenergy.org
URL: http://www.districtenergy.org
Contact: Robert P. Thornton, Pres.
Description: Suppliers of space heating by means of steam and hot water, and air conditioning by means of steam and chilled water, via piping systems from a central station to groups of buildings. **Publications:** *District Energy* (quarterly); *District Energy Now* (quarterly); *International District Energy Association—Membership Directory* (annual); *Manual of District Heating* .

753 ■ International Ground Source Heat Pump Association
374 Cordell S
Stillwater, OK 74078-8018
Ph:(405)744-5175
Free: 800-626-4747
Fax:(405)744-5283
Co. E-mail: igshpa@okstate.edu
URL: http://www.igshpa.okstate.edu
Contact: Jim Bose PhD, Exec. Dir.
Description: Manufacturers, distributors, and contractors in the ground source heat pump systems and products industry. Seeks to educate the public about ground source heat pump systems and promote their use as economical energy saving systems. (The system consists of a water source heat pump connected to a plastic pipe buried in the ground in which the earth supplies energy for space heating, domestic water heating, and a place to waste excess heat during cooling cycles.) Sponsors teleconferences, exhibits at trade show, and conducts training workshops. **Publications:** *Closed-Loop Ground-Source Heat Pump Systems Installation Guide*; *Grouting Procedures for Ground Source Heat Pump Systems*; *Installation Guide*; *The Source* (bimonthly).

754 ■ Masonry Heater Association of North America
2180 S Flying Q Ln.
Tucson, AZ 85713
Ph:(520)883-0191
Fax:(480)371-1139
Co. E-mail: execdir@mha-net.org
URL: http://www.mha-net.org
Contact: Richard Smith, Exec. Dir.
Description: Represents builders, manufacturers and retailers of masonry heaters. Seeks to promote the industry, sponsor research and development, shape regulations, standards and codes, inform and educate the public and further the expertise and professionalism of its membership. **Publications:** *Masonry Heaters - The Intelligent Choice* .

755 ■ Mechanical Contractors Association of America
1385 Piccard Dr.
Rockville, MD 20850-4340
Ph:(301)869-5800
Fax:(301)990-9690
Co. E-mail: mcaainfo@mcaa.org
URL: http://www.mcaa.org
Contact: John R. Gentille, Exec. VP/CEO
Description: Represents firms involved in heating, air conditioning, refrigeration, plumbing, piping, and mechanical service. Provides educational materials and programs to help members attain the highest level of managerial and technical expertise. **Publications:** *MCAA Membership Directory and Buyers' Guide* (annual); *MCAA National Update* (weekly); *MCAA Reporter* (bimonthly).

756 ■ Mobile Air Conditioning Society Worldwide
PO Box 88
Lansdale, PA 19446
Ph:(215)631-7020
Fax:(215)631-7017
Co. E-mail: macsworldwide@macsw.org
URL: http://www.macsw.org
Contact: Elvis Hoffpauir, Pres./COO
Description: Distributors, service specialists, installers, manufacturers, and suppliers of automotive and truck air conditioners and parts. Works to disseminate information and develop specialized education. **Publications:** *Action* (8/year); *MACS Service Reports* (monthly).

757 ■ National Environmental Balancing Bureau
8575 Grovemont Cir.
Gaithersburg, MD 20877
Ph:(301)977-3698
Fax:(301)977-9589
Co. E-mail: karen@nebb.org
URL: http://www.nebb.org
Contact: Steve Johnson PE, Exec. VP
Description: Qualified heating, ventilation, and air-conditioning contractors specializing in the fields of air and hydronic systems balancing, sound vibration measuring, testing of heating and cooling systems, building systems commissioning, and testing of clean rooms. Seeks to establish and maintain industry standards, procedures, and specifications for testing, adjusting, and balancing work; certify those firms that meet the qualification requirements; establish educational programs to provide competent management and supervision of Testing and Balancing (TAB) work. Establishes professional qualifications for TAB supervisors. Maintains chapters in Australia and Canada. **Publications:** *Procedural Standards for TAB Environmental Systems*; *Procedural Standards for the Measurement and Assessment of Sound and Vibration* .

758 ■ Plumbing-Heating-Cooling Contractors Association
PO Box 6808
Falls Church, VA 22046
Ph:(703)237-8100
Free: 800-533-7694
Fax:(703)237-7442
Co. E-mail: naphcc@naphcc.org
URL: http://www.phccweb.org
Contact: Gerard J. Kennedy Jr., Exec. VP
Description: Federation of state and local associations of plumbing, heating, and cooling contractors. Seeks to advance sanitation, encourage sanitary laws, and generally improve the plumbing, heating, ventilating, and air conditioning industries. Conducts apprenticeship training programs, workshops, seminars, political action committee, educational and research programs. .

759 ■ Refrigerating Engineers and Technicians Association
PO Box 1819
Salinas, CA 93902
Ph:(831)455-8783
Fax:(831)455-7856
Co. E-mail: info@reta.com
URL: http://www.reta.com
Contact: Don Tragethon, Exec. Dir.
Description: Focuses on the professional development of industrial refrigeration operators and technicians. Offers self-study and on-line training courses on industrial refrigeration. Offers a nationally-recognized certification program for operators and technicians on two levels of understanding and knowledge. **Publications:** *RETA Breeze* (bimonthly).

760 ■ Refrigeration Service Engineers Society
1666 Rand Rd.
Des Plaines, IL 60016-3552
Ph:(847)297-6464
Free: 800-297-5660
Co. E-mail: bruceirma@aol.com
URL: http://www.rses.org
Contact: Robert J. Sherman CM, Intl. Pres.
Description: Persons engaged in refrigeration, air-conditioning and heating installation, service, sales and maintenance. Conducts training courses and certification testing. Maintains a hall of fame and a speakers' bureau. **Publications:** *Service Application Manuals* .

761 ■ Sheet Metal and Air Conditioning Contractors' National Association
4201 Lafayette Center Dr.
Chantilly, VA 20151-1209
Ph:(703)803-2980
Fax:(703)803-3732
Co. E-mail: info@smacna.org
URL: http://www.smacna.org
Contact: Vincent R. Sandusky, CEO
Description: Ventilation, air handling, warm air heating, architectural and industrial sheet metal, kitchen equipment, testing and balancing, siding, and decking and specialty fabrication contractors. Prepares standards and codes; sponsors research and educational programs on sheet metal duct construction and fire damper (single and multi-blade) construction. Engages in legislative and labor activities; conducts business management and contractor education programs. **Publications:** *SMACNews* (monthly)-;Membership Directory (annual).

DIRECTORIES OF EDUCATIONAL PROGRAMS

762 ■ *Directory of Private Accredited Career Schools and Colleges of Technology*
Pub: Accrediting Commission of Career Schools and Colleges of Technology
Contact: Michale S. McComis, Exec. Dir.
Released: On web page. **Price:** Free. **Description:** Covers 3900 accredited post-secondary programs that provide training programs in business, trade, and technical fields, including various small business endeavors. Entries offer school name, address, phone, description of courses, job placement assistance, and requirements for admission. Arrangement is alphabetical.

REFERENCE WORKS

763 ■ "Burner Handles Everything From 2 to B100" in *Indoor Comfort Marketing* (Vol. 70, May 2011, No. 5, pp. 24)
Pub: Industry Publications Inc.
Description: A new oil burner being offered by AMERIgreen Energy is profiled.

764 ■ "A Quick Guide to NATE" in *Indoor Comfort Marketing* (Vol. 70, February 2011, No. 2, pp. 12)
Pub: Industry Publications Inc.
Description: Guide for training and certification in the North American Technician Excellence award.

765 ■ "Adventures at Hydronicahh" in *Contractor* (Vol. 56, September 2009, No. 9, pp. 52)
Pub: Penton Media, Inc.
Ed: Mark Eatherton. **Description:** Installation of the heating system of a lakeview room are described. The room's radiant windows are powered by electricity from a solar PV array and a propane-powered hydrogen fuel cell. The system will be programmed to use the most energy available.

766 ■ *Air Conditioning Contractors of America—Membership Directory*
Pub: Air Conditioning Contractors of America
Contact: Chris Hoelzel, Vice President
E-mail: chris.hoezel@acca.org
Released: Annual, summer. **Covers:** Member air conditioning and heating contractors, manufacturers, vocational technical schools. **Entries Include:** Company name, address, phone, fax, names and titles of key personnel, description of fields, and types of work performed. **Arrangement:** Geographical. **Indexes:** Alphabetical.

767 ■ *Air Conditioning, Heating & Refrigeration News—Directory Issue*
Pub: BNP Media
Contact: Mary Wray
E-mail: wraym@bnpmedia.com
Released: Annual, Latest edition 2011. **Publication Includes:** Lists of about 2,086 manufacturers, 4,383 wholesalers and factory outlets, 1,667 HVACR products, exporters specializing in the industry; related trade organizations; manufacturers representatives, consultants, services; videos and software. **Entries Include:** For manufacturers—Company Name, address, phone, fax, e-mail, URL, names of key personnel, brand names, list of products; similar information for other categories. **Arrangement:** Manufacturers and exporters are alphabetical; wholesalers and representatives are geographical. **Indexes:** Product, trade name.

768 ■ "Alternative Energy Calls for Alternative Marketing" in *Indoor Comfort Marketing* (Vol. 70, June 2011, No. 6, pp. 8)
Pub: Industry Publications Inc.
Ed: Richard Rutigliano. **Description:** Advice for marketing solar energy products and services is given.

769 ■ *American Supply Association—Membership Directory*
Pub: American Supply Association
Released: Annual. **Price:** $25, members; $299, nonmembers; $1,125, individuals electronic; $225, nonmembers diskette. **Covers:** 4,000 member wholesalers handling plumbing, heating, and cooling materials and supplies. **Entries Include:** Company name, address, phone, names of executives, list of products or services, fax numbers, email and website. **Arrangement:** Geographical and alphabetical. **Indexes:** Special interest divisions.

770 ■ "AREE Meets in Atlantic City" in *Indoor Comfort Marketing* (Vol. 70, June 2011, No. 6, pp. 28)
Pub: Industry Publications Inc.
Description: Highlights of the Atlantic Region Energy Expo are provided.

771 ■ "Art Institute of Chicago Goes Green" in *Contractor* (Vol. 56, July 2009, No. 7, pp. 1)
Pub: Penton Media, Inc.
Ed: Candace Roulo. **Description:** Art Institute of Chicago's Modern Wing museum addition will receive a certification that makes them one of the most environmentally sound museum expansions in the U.S. A modified variable-air-volume system is being used to meet temperature and humidity requirements in the building and it also has a double curtain wall to capture summer heat.

772 ■ "Be Proactive - Closely Review Contracts" in *Contractor* (Vol. 56, July 2009, No. 7, pp. 19)
Pub: Penton Media, Inc.
Ed: Al Schwartz. **Description:** Contract disputes can make subcontractors suffer big financial losses or even cause a new subcontractor to fail. Subcontractors should scour the plans and specifications for any references to work that might remotely come under their scope and to cross out any line in the contract that does not accurately reflect the work that they agreed to.

773 ■ "Be Wary of Dual-Flush Conversion Kits" in *Contractor* (Vol. 56, September 2009, No. 9, pp. 66)
Pub: Penton Media, Inc.
Ed: John Koeller; Bill Gauley. **Description:** Recommendation of untested dual-flush conversion devices for tank-type toilets in the United States have been questioned. The products are being advertised as having the ability to convert single-flush to a dual-flush toilet. No evidence of water conservation from using such devices has been recorded.

774 ■ "Bigger is Definitely Not Better When It Comes to Cooling" in *Indoor Comfort Marketing* (Vol. 70, May 2011, No. 5, pp. 49)
Pub: Industry Publications Inc.
Ed: Eugene Silberstein. **Description:** Efficiency is more important when installing air conditioning equipment over size of the unit. Details are provided.

775 ■ "Bioheat – Alternative for Fueling Equipment" in *Indoor Comfort Marketing* (Vol. 70, May 2011, No. 5, pp. 14)
Pub: Industry Publications Inc.
Ed: Gary Hess. **Description:** Profile of Worley and Obetz, supplier of biofuels used as an alternative for fueling industry equipment.

776 ■ "Bold Goals Will Require Time" in *Contractor* (Vol. 56, October 2009, No. 10, pp. S2)
Pub: Penton Media, Inc.
Ed: Ted Lower. **Description:** Offering a broad range of courses is the Radiant Panel Association (RPA), an organization that holds education as its top priority. The RPA must lead the industry by raising the educational bar for future installers.

777 ■ "Canadian Hydronics Businesses Promote 'Beautiful Heat'" in *Indoor Comfort Marketing* (Vol. 70, September 2011, No. 9, pp. 20)
Pub: Industry Publications Inc.
Description: Canadian hydronics companies are promoting their systems as beautiful heat. Hydronics is the use of water as the heat-transfer medium in heating and cooling system.

778 ■ "Cash for Appliances Targets HVAC Products, Water Heaters" in *Contractor* (Vol. 56, October 2009, No. 10, pp. 1)
Pub: Penton Media, Inc.
Ed: Candace Roulo. **Description:** States and territories would need to submit a full application that specifies their implementation plans if they are interested in joining the Cash for Appliances program funded by the American Recovery and Reinvestment Act. The Department of Energy urges states to focus on heating and cooling equipment, appliances and water heaters since these offer the greatest energy savings potential.

779 ■ "Certified Technicians can Increase Bottom Line" in *Contractor* (Vol. 56, September 2009, No. 9, pp. 37)
Pub: Penton Media, Inc.
Ed: Ray Isaac. **Description:** Certified technicians increase the value of HVAC firms, a survey by Service Round Table has reported. The increased value has been attributed to fewer callbacks, less warranty work and greater ability to educate consumers. Meanwhile, consumers are willing to pay more for the services of certified technicians.

780 ■ "The Challenges of Commercial Work" in *Indoor Comfort Marketing* (Vol. 70, May 2011, No. 5, pp. 14)
Pub: Industry Publications Inc.
Ed: Matt Spink. **Description:** The challenges faced by heating, ventilation, cooling small businesses expanding into commercial accounts are discussed.

781 ■ "Changing Fuel Compositions: What It Means To You and Your Business" in *Indoor Comfort Marketing* (Vol. 70, June 2011, No. 6, pp. 30)
Pub: Industry Publications Inc.
Ed: Paul Nazzaro. **Description:** Biofuels are outlined and the way it is changing the HVAC/R industry are discussed.

782 ■ "Chicago Public School District Builds Green" in *Contractor* (Vol. 56, October 2009, No. 10, pp. 5)
Pub: Penton Media, Inc.
Ed: Candace Roulo. **Description:** Chicago Public Schools district has already built six U.S. Green Building Council LEED certified schools and one addition in five years and will continue to build new green buildings. The district has an Environmental Action Plan that strives to reduce energy usage, improve indoor air quality, and reduce contribution to climate change.

783 ■ "Climate Right Systems Provides Pre-Assembled Equipment Packages" in *Contractor* (Vol. 56, July 2009, No. 7, pp. 1)
Pub: Penton Media, Inc.
Description: Climate Right Systems offers completely engineered, assembled, and tested equipment packages for hydronic heating and cooling. This package does away with the need to custom fabricate on-site and lets mechanical and plumbing contractors expand their offerings without added overhead and risk.

784 ■ "Combo Dorm-Field House Built to Attain LEED Gold" in *Contractor* (Vol. 56, September 2009, No. 9, pp. 1)
Pub: Penton Media, Inc.
Ed: Candace Roulo; Robert P. Mader. **Description:** North Central College in Illinois has built a new dormitory that is expected to attain Leadership in Energy and Environmental Design Gold certification from the United States Green Building Council. The structure features a geo-exchange heat pump system and radiant floor heat. A description of the facility is also provided.

785 ■ "Contractors Can't Do It Alone, PHCC's Pfeffer Says" in *Contractor* (Vol. 56, October 2009, No. 10, pp. 3)
Pub: Penton Media, Inc.
Ed: Robert P. Mader. **Description:** President Herbert "Skip" Pfeffer of the Plumbing-Heating-Cooling Contractors National Association says lobbying and education are the services that the association offers that a contractor cannot do individually. Pfeffer says the dues for the association are set up in a manner that allows members to pay monthly.

786 ■ "A Day Late and a Dollar Short" in *Indoor Comfort Marketing* (Vol. 70, March 2011, No. 3, pp. 30)
Pub: Industry Publications Inc.
Ed: Philip J. Baratz. **Description:** A discussion involving futures options and fuel oil prices is presented.

787 ■ "Design Programs for HVAC Sizing Solutions" in *Contractor* (Vol. 57, January 2010, No. 1, pp. 44)
Pub: Penton Media, Inc.
Ed: William Feldman; Patti Feldman. **Description:** Rhvac 8 is an HVAC design program that lets users calculate peak heating and cooling load requirements for rooms, zones, systems, and entire buildings. The HVAC Pipe Sizer software for the iPhone enables quick sizing of a simple piping system.

788 ■ *Directory of Certified Unitary Air-Conditioners, Unitary Air-Source Heat Pumps and Sound-Rated Outdoor Unitary Equipment*
Pub: Air-Conditioning and Refrigeration Institute
Contact: David Martz
Released: Semiannual, January and July. **Price:** $10 plus $5 shipping; payment with order.. **Publication Includes:** List of about 65 manufacturers of air- and coil-heating and cooling units, and air-to-air heat pumps. **Entries Include:** Manufacturer name, address. **Arrangement:** Alphabetical. **Indexes:** Trade name.

789 ■ "Do the Right Thing" in *Contractor* (Vol. 56, December 2009, No. 12, pp. 16)
Pub: Penton Media, Inc.
Ed: Robert P. Mader. **Description:** Applewood Plumbing, Heating and Electric has won Contractor magazine's 2009 Contractor of the Year Award. The company has ranked eighth among more than 300 service companies in the United States. A brief history of the company is also provided.

790 ■ "DOE Proposes New Water Heater Efficiency Standards" in *Contractor* (Vol. 57, January 2010, No. 1, pp. 3)
Pub: Penton Media, Inc.
Ed: Robert P. Mader. **Description:** U.S. Department of Energy is proposing higher efficiency standards for gas and electric water heaters which will not take effect until 2015. The proposal calls for gas-fired storage water heaters less than 60 gallons to have an Energy Factor of 0.675 and those larger than 60 gallons to have an Energy Factor of 0.717.

791 ■ "Eco Smart Home Will Showcase Green Technology" in *Contractor* (Vol. 56, September 2009, No. 9, pp. 3)
Pub: Penton Media, Inc.
Ed: Steve Spaulding. **Description:** Eco Smart World Wide is building the Eco Smart Demonstration House to promote the latest in sustainable, renewable and high-efficiency practices and products. The company will use insulated concrete forms in the construction of the building. Features and dimensions of the structure are also presented.

792 ■ "Energy Is Put to Good Use in Antarctica" in *Contractor* (Vol. 56, July 2009, No. 7, pp. 32)
Pub: Penton Media, Inc.
Ed: Carol Fey. **Description:** Recapturing waste heat is an important part of the heating system at the McMurdo Station in Antarctica. The radiators of generators are the heat source and this is supplemented by modular boilers when seasonal demands for heat increase. Waste heat is also used to make 55,000 gallons of fresh water a day.

793 ■ "EPA to Tighten Energy Star Standards for 2011" in *Contractor* (Vol. 56, September 2009, No. 9, pp. 6)
Pub: Penton Media, Inc.
Description: United States Environmental Protection Agency will tighten standards for its Energy Star for Homes program in 2011. The green trend in the

construction industry has been cited as reason for the plan. The agency is adding requirements for energy-efficient equipment and building techniques.

794 ■ "Expect Action on Health Care and the Economy" in *Contractor* (Vol. 57, January 2010, No. 1, pp. 30)
Pub: Penton Media, Inc.
Ed: Kevin Schwalb. **Description:** The Plumbing-Heating-Cooling Contractors National Association is working to solidify its standing in the public policy arena as the legislative agenda will focus on health care reform, estate tax and immigration reform, all of which will impact the industries.

795 ■ "Explore New Avenues to Success...Boldly!" in *Indoor Comfort Marketing* (Vol. 70, May 2011, No. 5, pp. 18)
Pub: Industry Publications Inc.
Ed: Rich Rutigliano. **Description:** Strategies to help fuel companies succeed in today's market are explored.

796 ■ "Fix-It Career: Jobs in Repair" in *Occupational Outlook Quarterly* (Vol. 54, Fall 2010, No. 3, pp. 26)
Pub: U.S. Bureau of Labor Statistics
Ed: Elka Maria Torpey. **Description:** Auto mechanics and HVAC technician occupations require repair skills. Advantages for individuals with proper skills are outlined.

797 ■ "Get Online Quick in the Office Or in the Field" in *Contractor* (Vol. 56, October 2009, No. 10, pp. 47)
Pub: Penton Media, Inc.
Ed: William Feldman; Patti Feldman. **Description:** Contractors can set up a web site in minutes using the www.1and1.com website. Verizon's Novatel MIFI 2372 HSPA personal hotspot device lets contractors go online in the field. The StarTech scalable business management system helps contractors manage daily operations.

798 ■ "Getting the Bioheat Word Out" in *Indoor Comfort Marketing* (Vol. 70, September 2011, No. 9, pp. 32)
Pub: Industry Publications Inc.
Description: Ways to market advanced liquid fuels to the public are outlined.

799 ■ "Gray, Gray, & Gray: a Difficult Year for Oilheat" in *Indoor Comfort Marketing* (Vol. 70, September 2011, No. 9, pp. 30)
Pub: Industry Publications Inc.
Description: According to the 20th Annual Oilheat Industry Survey, 2011 will be another dismal year for the industry sector.

800 ■ "Growing Your Business Through BPI Certification" in *Indoor Comfort Marketing* (Vol. 70, May 2011, No. 5, pp. 12)
Pub: Industry Publications Inc.
Ed: Scott Vadino. **Description:** Profile of the Building Performance Institute and the ways BPI certification will help grow a heating, ventilation, cooling firm.

801 ■ "Harness the Internet to Boost Equipment Sales" in *Indoor Comfort Marketing* (Vol. 70, July 2011, No. 7, pp. 24)
Pub: Industry Publications Inc.
Ed: Richard Rutigliano. **Description:** Advice is given to increase HVAC/R equipment sales using the Internet.

802 ■ "Help Customers Choose Full Service Over Discount" in *Indoor Comfort Marketing* (Vol. 70, September 2011, No. 9, pp. 10)
Pub: Industry Publications Inc.
Ed: Richard Rutigliano. **Description:** Marketing strategies for HVAC/R firms to use in 2011 and 2012 heating seasons are outlined, focusing on oil heat.

803 ■ "Housing Slide Picks Up Speed" in *Crain's Chicago Business* (Vol. 31, April 21, 2008, No. 16, pp. 2)
Pub: Crain Communications, Inc.
Ed: Eddie Baeb. **Description:** According to Tracy Cross & Associates Inc., a real estate consultancy, sales of new homes in the Chicago area dropped 61 percent from the year-earlier period which is more bad news for homebuilders, contractors and real estate agents who are eager for an indication that market conditions are improving.

804 ■ "How Good Advice 'Online' Can Attract Customers" in *Indoor Comfort Marketing* (Vol. 70, August 2011, No. 8, pp. 20)
Pub: Industry Publications Inc.
Ed: Richard Rutigilano. **Description:** Online marketing tips for heating and cooling small businesses are explained.

805 ■ "How to Keep a US Naval Destroyer Warm" in *Indoor Comfort Marketing* (Vol. 70, April 2011, No. 4, pp. 34)
Pub: Industry Publications Inc.
Ed: George R. Carey. **Description:** Boiler facts regarding US Naval destroyers are discussed.

806 ■ *HPAC Engineering—Info-Dex*
Pub: Penton Media Inc.
Released: Annual, Latest edition 2008-2009. **Publication Includes:** Listing of over 2,000 manufacturers in the heating/piping/air conditioning industry, and associations and government agencies concerned with standards for the industry. **Entries Include:** Company or organization name, address, phone, fax, URL and product codes. Listings for advertisers also show key personnel and branch and representatives' offices. **Arrangement:** Separate alphabetical sections for manufacturers, associations, and advertisers. **Indexes:** Product, trade name.

807 ■ "HVAC/R Evolution" in *Indoor Comfort Marketing* (Vol. 70, March 2011, No. 3, pp. 14)
Pub: Industry Publications Inc.
Ed: Gene Bartholomew. **Description:** Tools and techniques for heating, ventilation, air conditioning and refrigeration are examined.

808 ■ "IAPMO Seeks Group Participants" in *Contractor* (Vol. 56, September 2009, No. 9, pp. 37)
Pub: Penton Media, Inc.
Description: International Association of Plumbing and Mechanical Officials is accepting applications for task groups that will develop its Uniform Plumbing Code and Uniform Mechanical Code. The codes are developed using American National Standards Institute accredited consensus process. Task groups are assigned to address a specific topic or problem.

809 ■ "If the Opportunity is There, Move Boldly" in *Indoor Comfort Marketing* (Vol. 70, March 2011, No. 3, pp.)
Pub: Industry Publications Inc.
Ed: Rich Rutigliano. **Description:** Suggestions are offered to help improve air conditioning sales.

810 ■ "Illinois Residential Building Legislation Includes New HVAC Requirements" in *Contractor* (Vol. 56, July 2009, No. 7, pp. 3)
Pub: Penton Media, Inc.
Ed: Candace Roulo. **Description:** Illinois' Energy Efficient Building Act will require all new buildings and houses to conform to the International Energy Conservation Code. The code includes a duct leakage requirement followed by a post-construction test to verify leakage rates and requires programmable thermostats on all houses.

811 ■ "Independence Station Utilizes Sustainable Technologies" in *Contractor* (Vol. 56, September 2009, No. 9, pp. 3)
Pub: Penton Media, Inc.
Ed: Candace Ruolo. **Description:** Independence Station building in Oregon is seen to receive the most LEED points ever awarded by the United States Green Building Council. The building will use an ice-based cooling storage system, biofuel cogeneration system and phovoltaic system. Other building features and dimensions are also supplied.

812 ■ "Indoor Air Quality – a Tribute to Efficiency" in *Indoor Comfort Marketing* (Vol. 70, August 2011, No. 8, pp. 8)
Pub: Industry Publications Inc.
Ed: Matthew Maleske. **Description:** Efficiency of new HVAC/R equipment has helped improve indoor air quality.

813 ■ "Interested in 12 Billion Dollars?" in *Indoor Comfort Marketing* (Vol. 70, March 2011, No. 3, pp. 18)
Pub: Industry Publications Inc.
Ed: Matthew Maleske. **Description:** Trends in the indoor quality industry are cited, with insight into expanding an existing indoor heating and cooling business.

814 ■ "It's Always 55 Degrees F" in *Contractor* (Vol. 56, September 2009, No. 9, pp. 38)
Pub: Penton Media, Inc.
Ed: Carol Fey. **Description:** Geothermal-exchange heating and cooling systems can save businesses up to 60 percent on energy costs for heating and cooling. Geothermal systems get heat from the earth during winter. Design, features and installation of geothermal systems are also discussed.

815 ■ "It's New or Improved, But Does It Work?" in *Contractor* (Vol. 57, January 2010, No. 1, pp. 22)
Pub: Penton Media, Inc.
Ed: Al Schwartz. **Description:** There is a place for skepticism in the HVAC and plumbing industry as not all new products that are specified may not always perform. The tradesman has the responsibility of integrating new technology into the field.

816 ■ "Know the Facts About Natural Gas!" in *Indoor Comfort Marketing* (Vol. 70, August 2011, No. 8, pp. 26)
Pub: Industry Publications Inc.
Description: AEC Activity Update is presented on the American Energy Coalition's Website.

817 ■ "Large Homes can be Energy Efficient Too" in *Contractor* (Vol. 56, October 2009, No. 10, pp. 5)
Pub: Penton Media, Inc.
Ed: Candace Roulo. **Description:** Eco Estate at Briggs Chaney subdivision in Silver Spring, Maryland has model houses that use sustainable technologies and products and the homes that will be built on the subdivision will feature some of the technologies featured on the model home. The energy efficient HVAC system of the model homes are discussed.

818 ■ "The Latest on E-Verify" in *Contractor* (Vol. 56, September 2009, No. 9, pp. 58)
Pub: Penton Media, Inc.
Ed: Susan McGreevy. **Description:** United States government has required federal contractors to use its E-Verify program to verify the eligibility of incoming and existent employees. The use of the program is seen to eliminate Social Security mismatches.

819 ■ "Legislation Introduced" in *Indoor Comfort Marketing* (Vol. 70, July 2011, No. 7, pp. 6)
Pub: Industry Publications Inc.
Description: New industry legislation is examined by the National Oilheat Research Alliance.

820 ■ "Manufacturers Become Part of Coalition" in *Contractor* (Vol. 56, July 2009, No. 7, pp. 40)
Pub: Penton Media, Inc.
Description: Bradford White Water Heaters, Rheem Water Heating, Rinnai America Corp., and A.O. Smith Water Heaters have joined the Consortium for Energy Efficiency in the Coalition for Energy Star Water Heaters. The coalition seeks to increase the awareness of Energy Star water heaters.

821 ■ "The Many Hats and Faces of NAOHSM" in *Indoor Comfort Marketing* (Vol. 70, May 2011, No. 5, pp. 8)
Pub: Industry Publications Inc.
Description: Profile of the National Association of Oil Heating Service Managers, and its role in the industry, is presented.

822 ■ "Minnesota State Park Building Exemplifies Sustainability" in *Contractor* (Vol. 56, November 2009, No. 11, pp. 5)
Pub: Penton Media, Inc.
Ed: Candace Roulo. **Description:** Camden State Park's newly remodeled information/office building in Lynd, Minnesota features a 10 kw wind turbine which

is capable of offsetting most of the facility's electricity and a geothermal heat pump system. The heat pump is a 4-ton vertical closed-loop ground source heat pump by ClimateMaster.

823 ■ "A Necessary Balancing Act: Bookkeeping" in *Contractor* (Vol. 56, November 2009, No. 11, pp. 22)
Pub: Penton Media, Inc.
Ed: Al Schwartz. **Description:** Pros and cons of getting a bookkeeper or a certified public accountant for the subcontractor are discussed. A bookkeeper can help a subcontractor get new accounting software up and running while an accountant will more than likely keep after the books at regular intervals throughout the year.

824 ■ "A New Day is Dawning" in *Indoor Comfort Marketing* (Vol. 70, August 2011, No. 8, pp. 18)
Pub: Industry Publications Inc.
Ed: Paul Nazzaro. **Description:** New trends in the HVAC/R industry regarding biofuels and bioheat are explored.

825 ■ "New Hydronic Heating Technologies Work" in *Contractor* (Vol. 57, January 2010, No. 1, pp. 58)
Pub: Penton Media, Inc.
Ed: Carol Fey. **Description:** Technology behind hydronic heating systems is reviewed. These technologies include radiant and geothermal hydronic heating. System requirements for installing these greener forms of heating are discussed.

826 ■ "Nexstar Super Meeting Breaks Business Barriers" in *Contractor* (Vol. 56, November 2009, No. 11, pp. 3)
Pub: Penton Media, Inc.
Ed: Candace Roulo. **Description:** Around 400 Nexstar members met to discuss the trends in the HVAC industry and the economic outlook for 2010. Former lead solo pilot John Foley for the Blue Angels made a presentation on how a business can increase overall productivity based on the culture of the Blue Angels. Some breakout sessions tackled how to optimize workflow and marketing.

827 ■ "OHC Aids Long Island Family" in *Indoor Comfort Marketing* (Vol. 70, May 2011, No. 5, pp. 45)
Pub: Industry Publications Inc.
Ed: Judy Garber. **Description:** Ways Community Oil Heat helped a customer living in Long Island heat their home during desperate times.

828 ■ "Oilheating Delivery Issues" in *Indoor Comfort Marketing* (Vol. 70, September 2011, No. 9, pp. 14)
Pub: Industry Publications Inc.
Ed: John Levey. **Description:** Tools and techniques for delivery heating oil to customers this season are discussed.

829 ■ "Overheating Taking Place? Pay Attention to Details..." in *Indoor Comfort Marketing* (Vol. 70, March 2011, No. 3, pp.)
Pub: Industry Publications Inc.
Ed: George R. Carey. **Description:** Boiler facts are outlined to help the small HVAC company when servicing customers.

830 ■ "PHCC Convention, Show Gets High Marks" in *Contractor* (Vol. 56, December 2009, No. 12, pp. 1)
Pub: Penton Media, Inc.
Ed: Robert P. Mader. **Description:** Plumbing-Heating-Cooling Contractors National Association has held its first convention and trade show in New Orleans, Louisiana. Attendees were treated to a variety of seminars and exhibitors during the event. Comments from event organizers are also given.

831 ■ "Phoenix Conference Reveals Opportunities are Coming" in *Indoor Comfort Marketing* (Vol. 70, March 2011, No. 3, pp. 24)
Pub: Industry Publications Inc.
Ed: Paul J. Nazzaro. **Description:** Advanced liquid fuels were spotlighted at the Phoenix conference revealing the opportunities for using liquid fuels.

832 ■ "Plumbing, Heating Products Shine at Greenbuild Expo" in *Contractor* (Vol. 56, December 2009, No. 12, pp. 1)
Pub: Penton Media, Inc.
Ed: Robert P. Mader. **Description:** Greenbuild Show held in Phoenix, Arizona has showcased the latest in plumbing and heating products. Zurn displayed its EcoVantage line of fixtures and valves during the event. Meanwhile, Sloan Valve offered its washdown 1-pint/flush Alphine urinal.

833 ■ *PM Directory & Reference Issue*
Pub: BNP Media
Contact: Jim Olsztynski, Editorial Dir.
E-mail: wrdwzrd@aol.com
Ed: Steve Smith, Editor, smiths@bnpmedia.com. **Released:** Annual, Latest edition 2010. **Covers:** Manufacturers, wholesalers, products, consultants, and manufacturers' representatives in the industries of plumbing, piping, and hydronic heating. **Entries Include:** Contact name, company, address, phone, fax, and product descriptions. **Arrangement:** Alphabetical. **Indexes:** By products.

834 ■ "Portland Home Is First in U.S. to Use Variable Speed 'Inverter' Technology" in *Contractor* (Vol. 56, December 2009, No. 12, pp. 5)
Pub: Penton Media, Inc.
Description: Daikin Altherma heat pump with inverter drive has been installed in a Portland, Oregon home. The heat pump provides a high coefficient of performance while delivering hydronic and domestic hot water functionality. Other product features and dimensions are also supplied.

835 ■ "Positive Transformational Change" in *Indoor Comfort Marketing* (Vol. 70, April 2011, No. 4, pp. 30)
Pub: Industry Publications Inc.
Ed: Blaine Fox. **Description:** Management changes taking place at Shark Bites HVAC firm are discussed.

836 ■ "PPC's Major Commitment to Biofuel Infrastructure" in *Indoor Comfort Marketing* (Vol. 70, April 2011, No. 4, pp. 6)
Pub: Industry Publications Inc.
Description: Petroleum Products Corporation's commitment to the biofuel infrastructure is outlined.

837 ■ "Programs Provide Education and Training" in *Contractor* (Vol. 56, September 2009, No. 9, pp. 56)
Pub: Penton Media, Inc.
Ed: William Feldman; Patti Feldman. **Description:** Opportunity Interactive's Showroom v2 software provides uses computer graphics to provide education and training on HVAC equipment and systems. It can draw heat pump balance points for a specific home. Meanwhile, Simutech's HVAC Training Simulators provide trainees with 'hands-on' HVACR training.

838 ■ "Proposal Ruffles Builders" in *Austin Business JournalInc.* (Vol. 29, November 20, 2009, No. 37, pp. 1)
Pub: American City Business Journals
Ed: Jacob Dirr. **Description:** A proposal that requires heating, ventilation and cooling equipment checking for a new commercial building having an area of at least 10,000 square feet might cost 25 cents to 50 cents per square foot for the owners. This may lead to higher housing costs. Both the Building and Fire Code Board of Appeals and the Mechanical Plumbing and Solar Board have recommended the plan.

839 ■ "Put Your Heating Cap On..." in *Indoor Comfort Marketing* (Vol. 70, September 2011, No. 9, pp. 26)
Pub: Industry Publications Inc.
Ed: George Carey. **Description:** Tools and techniques for HVAC/R technicians servicing boilers are outlined.

840 ■ "Radiant – the Hottest Topic in ... Cooling" in *Indoor Comfort Marketing* (Vol. 70, February 2011, No. 2, pp. 8)
Pub: Industry Publications Inc.
Description: Examination of radiant cooling systems, a new trend in cooling homes and buildings.

841 ■ "Rehab Center Slashes Energy Bills By Going Tankless" in *Contractor* (Vol. 56, December 2009, No. 12, pp. 3)
Pub: Penton Media, Inc.
Description: Melburne Health and Rehabilitation Center in Florida has reduced its energy bills by installing a tankless hot water system. Sun Plumbing was selected to install the system. The system was installed on a mechanical room that housed the old tank-type heaters.

842 ■ "Route Optimization Impacts the Bottom Line" in *Contractor* (Vol. 56, November 2009, No. 11, pp. 48)
Pub: Penton Media, Inc.
Ed: Dave Beaudry. **Description:** Plumbing and HVAC businesses can save a significant amount of money from route optimization. The process begins with gathering information on a fleet and a routing software tool can determine the effectiveness of current route configurations and identify preferable route plans.

843 ■ "RPA Preps for Building Radiant Conference, Show" in *Contractor* (Vol. 57, January 2010, No. 1, pp. 5)
Pub: Penton Media, Inc.
Description: Radiant Panel Association is accepting registrations for its Building Radiant 2010 Conference and Trade Show. The conference will discuss radiant heating as well as insurance and other legal matters for mechanical contractors.

844 ■ "Safety Managers Need to Be Safety Experts" in *Indoor Comfort Marketing* (Vol. 70, May 2011, No. 5, pp. 10)
Pub: Industry Publications Inc.
Ed: Mike Hodge. **Description:** It is imperative to have a good safety manager in place for all heating and cooling firms.

845 ■ "Selling a Job When There's Buyer's Remorse" in *Contractor* (Vol. 56, December 2009, No. 12, pp. 37)
Pub: Penton Media, Inc.
Ed: H. Kent Craig. **Description:** Advice on how contractors should manage low-profit jobs in the United States are presented. Efforts should be made to try and find at least one quality field foreman or superintendent. Contractors should also try to respectfully renegotiate the terms of the job.

846 ■ "Software Solutions from Trane and Carrier" in *Contractor* (Vol. 56, July 2009, No. 7, pp. 38)
Pub: Penton Media, Inc.
Ed: William Feldman; Patti Feldman. **Description:** Trane Trace 700 software helps HVAC contractors optimize the design of a building's HVAC system and aids in the evaluation of various key energy-saving concepts, including daylighting, high-performance glazing, and other optimization strategies. Carrier's E20-II family of software programs lets contractors increase the accuracy of an HVAC system estimate.

847 ■ "Solar Choices" in *Contractor* (Vol. 56, October 2009, No. 10, pp. 32)
Pub: Penton Media, Inc.
Ed: Tom Scheel. **Description:** Price, performance, and ease of installation of a flat plate versus an evacuated tube collector for a plumbing and heating job are compared. The better choice with regards to weight, aesthetics, efficiency in warm or cool climates, year round load, and space heating is discussed.

848 ■ "Start Connecting Today" in *Indoor Comfort Marketing* (Vol. 70, May 2011, No. 5, pp. 34)
Pub: Industry Publications Inc.
Ed: Paul Nazzaro. **Description:** An in-depth discussion regarding the use of biofuels on bioheat use and dealership.

849 ■ "Tracking Your Fleet Can Increase Bottom Line" in *Contractor* (Vol. 56, November 2009, No. 11, pp. 26)
Pub: Penton Media, Inc.
Ed: Candace Roulo. **Description:** GPS fleet management system can help boost a contractor's profits, employee productivity, and efficiency. These are

available as a handheld device or a cell phone that employees carry around or as a piece of hardware installed in a vehicle. These lets managers track assets and communicate with employees about jobs.

850 ■ "Trade Craft: Take Pride in Your Trade, Demand Excellence" in *Contractor* (Vol. 56, October 2009, No. 10, pp. 24)
Pub: Penton Media, Inc.
Ed: Al Schwartz. **Description:** There is a need for teaching, developing, and encouraging trade craft. An apprentice plumber is not only versed in the mechanical aspects of the trade but he also has a working knowledge of algebra, trigonometry, chemistry, and thermal dynamics. Contractors should be demanding on their personnel regarding their trade craft and should only keep and train the very best people they can hire.

851 ■ "Two Field Service Management Solutions" in *Contractor* (Vol. 56, November 2009, No. 11, pp. 37)
Pub: Penton Media, Inc.
Ed: William Feldman; Patti Feldman. **Description:** Bella Solutions Field Service Software v. 4.2 is a web based solution for HVAC service contractors that enables scheduling of emergency, one-time, multi-visit or periodically recurring jobs with drag and drop appointments. VaZing is another web based solution that costs $99 per month for contractors. It can handle line-item discounting and invoices aside from scheduling.

852 ■ "UA Turns Ann Arbor Green" in *Contractor* (Vol. 56, September 2009, No. 9, pp. 5)
Pub: Penton Media, Inc.
Ed: Robert P. Mader. **Description:** Instructors at the United Association of Plumbers and Steamfitters have studied the latest in green and sustainable construction and service at the Washtenaw Community College in Michigan. Classes included building information modeling, hydronic heating and cooling and advanced HVACR troubleshooting. The UA is currently focusing on green training.

853 ■ "The Ultimate Comfort System" in *Contractor* (Vol. 56, July 2009, No. 7, pp. 30)
Pub: Penton Media, Inc.
Ed: Mark Eatherton. **Description:** Retrofitting of a hydronic heating system to an existing home is presented. The project approaches near net-zero energy production.

854 ■ "Ultra Green Energy Services Opens NJ Biodiesel Transload Facility" in *Indoor Comfort Marketing* (Vol. 70, June 2011, No. 6, pp. 35)
Pub: Industry Publications Inc.
Description: Profile of Ultra Green Energy Services and the opening of their new biodiesel facility in New Jersey is discussed.

855 ■ "Ultra Low Sulfur Diesel: The Promise and the Reality" in *Indoor Comfort Marketing* (Vol. 70, July 2011, No. 7, pp. 22)
Pub: Industry Publications Inc.
Ed: Ed Kitchen. **Description:** Impacts of ultra low sulfur diesel are examined.

856 ■ "University Data Center Goes Off-Grid, Is Test Bed" in *Contractor* (Vol. 57, February 2010, No. 2, pp. 1)
Pub: Penton Media, Inc.
Ed: Candace Roulo. **Description:** Syracuse University's Green Data Center has gone off-grid through the use of natural gas fired turbines. It is expected to use 50 percent less energy than a typical computer center. The center's heating and cooling system setup is also discussed.

857 ■ "Warm Floors Make Warm Homes" in *Contractor* (Vol. 56, October 2009, No. 10, pp. S18)
Pub: Penton Media, Inc.
Ed: Lisa Murton Beets. **Description:** Three award winning radiant floor-heating installations are presented. The design and the equipment used for these systems are discussed.

858 ■ "Water Efficiency Bill Move Through Congress" in *Contractor* (Vol. 56, July 2009, No. 7, pp. 20)
Pub: Penton Media, Inc.
Ed: Kevin Schwalb. **Description:** National Association, a plumbing-heating-cooling contractor, was instrumental in drafting the Water Advanced Technologies for Efficient Resource Use Act of 2009 and they are also backing the Water Accountability Tax Efficiency Reinvestment Act. The first bill promotes WaterSense-labeled products while the other promotes water conservation through tax credits.

859 ■ "Web-Based Solutions Streamline Operations" in *Contractor* (Vol. 56, December 2009, No. 12, pp. 28)
Pub: Penton Media, Inc.
Ed: William Feldman; Patti Feldman. **Description:** Sage Project Lifecycle Management is a Web-based service platform for plumbing and HVAC contractors. It enables effective workflow and document management. Projectmates, on the other hand, is a Web-based enterprise-wide solution for managing both commercial plumbing and HVAC projects.

860 ■ "What Is a Geothermal Heat Pump" in *Indoor Comfort Marketing* (Vol. 70, August 2011, No. 8, pp. 14)
Pub: Industry Publications Inc.
Ed: George Carey. **Description:** Examination of geothermal heat pumps is provided, citing new trends in the industry.

861 ■ "Where the Future is Made" in *Indoor Comfort Marketing* (Vol. 70, May 2011, No. 5, pp. 48)
Pub: Industry Publications Inc.
Description: Research being performed at Brookhaven National Laboratory, located in Upton, New York, is discussed, focusing on new energy sources for our nation.

862 ■ "Yates Helps Turn Log Home Green" in *Contractor* (Vol. 56, December 2009, No. 12, pp. 40)
Pub: Penton Media, Inc.
Description: Upgrading and greening of a log home's HVAC system in Pennsylvania is discussed. F. W. Behler Inc. president Dave Yates was chosen to manage the project. A large coil of R-flex was used to connect the buffer tank to the garage's radiant heat system.

863 ■ "Yates Turns Log Home Green - Part Three" in *Contractor* (Vol. 57, January 2010, No. 1, pp. 5)
Pub: Penton Media, Inc.
Description: Dave Yates of F.W. Behler Inc. discusses remodeling a log home's HVAC system with geo-to-radiant heat and thermal-solar systems. The solar heater's installation is discussed.

864 ■ "You Can't Fix It If You Don't Face It!" in *Indoor Comfort Marketing* (Vol. 70, June 2011, No. 6, pp. 14)
Pub: Industry Publications Inc.
Ed: John Levey. **Description:** Tips for avoiding repeat customer calls when installing or servicing HVAC/R equipment are provided.

SOURCES OF SUPPLY

865 ■ *Appliance—Appliance Industry Purchasing Section Issue*
Pub: Dana Chase Publications Inc.
Ed: David Chase, Editor, david@appliance.com. **Released:** Annual, January. **Publication Includes:** Suppliers to manufacturers of consumer, commercial, and business appliances. Membership directories for the following associations: Air-Conditioning and Refrigeration Institute, Association of Home Appliance Manufacturers, Commercial Refrigerator Manufacturers Association, Computer and Business Equipment Manufacturers Association, Consumer Electronics Group/Electronic Industries Association, Gas Appliance Manufacturers Association, Cookware Manufacturers Association, National Association of Food Equipment Manufacturers, National Housewares Manufacturers Association, Power Tool Institute, and Vacuum Cleaner Manufacturers Association. **Entries Include:** Company name, address, phone, fax, and products. **Arrangement:** Classified by product. **Indexes:** Manufacturer, product heading.

866 ■ *The Wholesaler—Directory of Manufacturers Representatives Issue*
Pub: TMB Publishing Inc.
Contact: James Schaible, Managing Editor
E-mail: jim@thewholesaler.com
Released: Annual, Latest edition 2009. **Price:** $50, individuals hardcopy or CD-ROM. **Publication Includes:** 2,000 manufacturers' representatives handling plumbing, heating, piping, air conditioning, and refrigeration products. **Entries Include:** Representative's name or firm name, address, phone, fax, territory, and lines carried. **Arrangement:** Geographical by territory (Central States, North Pacific, etc.).

STATISTICAL SOURCES

867 ■ *RMA Annual Statement Studies*
Pub: Robert Morris Associates (RMA)
Released: Annual. **Price:** $175.00 2006-07 edition, $105.00. **Description:** Contains composite balance sheets and income statements for more than 360 industries, including the accounting, auditing, and bookkeeping industries. Also contains five years of comparative historical data for discerning trends. Includes 16 commonly used ratios, computed for most of the size groupings for nearly every industry.

TRADE PERIODICALS

868 ■ *Alabama Contractor*
Pub: Associated Plumbing Heating & Cooling
Released: Annual. **Description:** Trade and technical magazine for plumbing, heating, and cooling contractors.

869 ■ *Contracting Business*
Pub: Penton Media Inc.
Contact: Joseph A. Fristik, Gp. Publisher
E-mail: joe.fristik@penton.com
Released: Monthly. **Price:** $72 U.S.; $108 U.S. 2 years; $95 Canada; $113 Canada 2 years; $180 out of country 2 years; $108 out of country. **Description:** Serves those contractors engaged in the design, new construction and/or service of mechanical systems in residential, commercial and industrial buildings. The mechanical systems field includes: air conditioning, warm air heating, hydronic heating, refrigeration, ventilation, sheet metal and glass fiber duct fabrication, piping, electrical, ice makers, airhandling, solar energy systems and energy management. Also included are organizations which maintain/operate the mechanical systems or equipment in commercial, institutional and industrial buildings; manufacturers' representatives and wholesalers (including executives and salesmen).

870 ■ *Heating/Piping/Air Conditioning Engineering HPAC*
Pub: Penton Media Inc.
Contact: Scott Arnold, Exec. Ed.
E-mail: scott.arnold@penton.com
Released: Monthly. **Price:** $115 other countries; $180 two years and other countries. **Description:** Business magazine serving the growing mechanical engineered systems market in the areas of building construction, renovation, and retrofit.

871 ■ *Heating-Plumbing-Air Conditioning Magazine HPAC*
Pub: Rogers Media Publishing
Contact: Kim Rossiter, Sales, Mktg. Coord.
E-mail: kim.rossiter@rci.rogers.com
Released: 7/yr. **Price:** Free to qualified subscribers. **Description:** Plumbing, heating, air conditioning, refrigeration, and insulation trade magazine.

872 ■ *Indiana Contractor*
Pub: Indiana Association of Plumbing Heating Cooling Contractors Inc.
Contact: Brenda A. Dant
E-mail: brenda@iaphcc.com
Released: Quarterly. **Description:** Official publication of the Indiana Association of Plumbing, Heating, Cooling Contractors, Inc.

873 ■ *MACS Service Reports*
Pub: Mobile Air Conditioning Society Worldwide
Ed: Elvis Hoffpauir, Editor, elvis@macsw.org. **Released:** Monthly. **Price:** $70. **Description:** Serves as the technical information publication of the Mobile Air Conditioning Society Worldwide. Recurring features include news of research, news of educational opportunities, and How to and technical articles.

874 ■ *MCAA Reporter*
Pub: Mechanical Contractors Association of America Inc.
Contact: Stephanie Mills, Managing Editor
Ed: Adrienne Breedlove, Editor. **Released:** Monthly, except in February and August. **Price:** Included in membership; $50, nonmembers. **Description:** Covers labor issues and government affairs as they affect mechanical contractors in the plumbing, pipefitting, air conditioning, refrigeration, fire protection, and high-purity piping industries. Recurring features include reports on the activities of the Association and notices of pertinent seminars and meetings.

875 ■ *Snips Magazine*
Pub: Snips Magazine
Contact: Sally Fraser, Publisher
E-mail: frasers@bnpmedia.com
Ed: Michael McConnell, Editor, mcconnellm@bnpmedia.com. **Released:** Monthly. **Description:** Magazine for the sheet metal, warm-air heating, ventilating, and air conditioning industry. Provides helpful hints for contractors.

TRADE SHOWS AND CONVENTIONS

876 ■ AHR Expo - International Air-Conditioning, Heating, Refrigerating Exposition
International Exposition Co., Inc.
15 Franklin St.
Westport, CT 06880-5958
Ph:(203)221-9232
Fax:(203)221-9260
Co. E-mail: info@chemshow.com
URL: http://www.chemshow.com
Released: Annual. **Audience:** Air conditioning, heating, refrigeration, and ventilation industry and related industries professionals; contractors, engineers, distributors, reps, OEMs. **Principal Exhibits:** Industrial, commercial, and residential heating, refrigeration, air conditioning, and ventilation equipment and components.

877 ■ North Carolina Association of Plumbing, Heating, and Cooling Contractors Annual Trade Show
North Carolina Association of Plumbing, Heating, and Cooling Contractors
5540 McNeely Dr. Ste. 202
Raleigh, NC 27612
Ph:(919)532-0522
Fax:(919)532-0523
Co. E-mail: carlagilbert@phccnc.org
URL: http://www.ncaphcc.org
Released: Annual. **Audience:** Plumbing, heating, and cooling contractors; architects; engineers; and general public. **Principal Exhibits:** Plumbing, heating, and cooling equipment, supplies, and services.

878 ■ Sheet Metal and Air-Conditioning Contractors National Association Convention/Exhibition Forum
Sheet Metal and Air-Conditioning Contractors National Association
4201 Lafayette Center Dr.
Chantilly, VA 20151-1219
Ph:(703)803-2980
Fax:(703)803-3732
Co. E-mail: info@smacna.org
URL: http://www.smacna.org
Released: Annual. **Audience:** Owners of sheet metal and air-conditioning contracting firms. **Principal Exhibits:** Limited to table tops only.

879 ■ Southeast Roofing and Sheet Metal Spectacular Trade Exposition
Florida Roofing, Sheet Metal, and Air Conditioning Contractors Association FRSA
4111, Metric Dr., Ste. 6
Winter Park, FL 32792
Ph:(407)671-3772
Fax:(407)679-0010
Co. E-mail: frsa@floridaroof.com
URL: http://www.floridaroof.com
Released: Annual. **Audience:** Roofing, and sheet metal, contractors, architects, specifiers, and building officials. **Principal Exhibits:** Roofing and sheet metal supplies, products and services. **Dates and Locations:** 2011 Jun 23-25, Orlando, FL.

CONSULTANTS

880 ■ Ben Briskin Associates Inc.
5434 Claridge Ln.
West Bloomfield, MI 48322-3862
Ph:(248)851-2114
Fax:(248)851-8489
Contact: Ben Briskin, Principal
E-mail: bbriskin@hotmail.com
Scope: Consultants in the design and analysis of heating, air conditioning, ventilating and piping systems. Emphasis is on air conditioning design, energy use, and energy audit studies. Additional expertise in areas of research and development labs and paint spray booths. Industries served: Construction, pharmaceutical laboratories, research labs and government agencies.

881 ■ Calmac Manufacturing Corp.
3-00 Banta Pl.
Fair Lawn, NJ 07410
Ph:(201)797-1511
Fax:(201)797-1522
Co. E-mail: info@calmac.com
URL: http://www.calmac.com
Contact: Brian Silvetti, VP of Engr
E-mail: jwilliams@atscalmac.com
Scope: Offers facility evaluation, product design, manufacture and installation of off-peak cooling systems to air condition buildings. provides services to laboratories, airlines, hotels, schools, universities, medical centers and ice rinks throughout the world. Other solutions include clever designs of heating pads for hospitals. **Seminars:** Thermal Storage and Ice Rinks to Utilities.

882 ■ Environmental & Engineering Services Inc.
687 NW 5th St.
Corvallis, OR 97330
Ph:(541)754-1062
Fax:(541)753-3948
Co. E-mail: kelly.guenther@eesinet.com
URL: http://www.eesinet.com
Contact: Ron Anderson, Principle
E-mail: fred.shaub@atseesinet.com
Scope: Provides mechanical, electrical engineering and commissioning services, with a special emphasis in renovation and energy upgrades. Offers a wide range of HVAC, electrical and controls engineering services including feasibility assessments, master planning, budgeting, cost analysis, design, computer aided drafting, energy use modeling, facility management and construction management.

883 ■ Fanning, Fanning & Associates Inc.
2555 74th St.
Lubbock, TX 79423-1405
Ph:(806)745-2533
Fax:(806)745-3596
Co. E-mail: nfanning@fanningfanning.com
URL: http://www.fanningfanning.com
Contact: William White, Principle
E-mail: bwhite@atsfanningfanning.com
Scope: Firm specializes in engineering services including mechanical, electrical, plumbing design and plant layout, HVAC, energy conservation and management, utilities, fire protection and alarms, central heating and cooling plants and communications for institutional, commercial and industrial buildings. Offers design services for drawings, specifications and bid documents, master planning, engineering reports, estimates, analysis, feasibility studies and construction phase services.

884 ■ GHT Ltd.
1010 N Glebe Rd., Ste. 200
Arlington, VA 22201-4749
Ph:(703)243-1200
Fax:(703)276-1376
Co. E-mail: ght@ghtltd.com
URL: http://www.ghtltd.com
Contact: Robert M. Menuet Jr., Principle
E-mail: rmenuet@ghtltd.com
Scope: Provides design services in mechanical engineering. Offers telecommunications and security engineering services. Provides life safety engineering services and utilities planning services. Provides estimates of life expectancy and replacement or upgrade costs for mechanical and electrical equipment and systems. **Publications:** "Critical spaces keep the pace of business humming," May, 2004; "To avoid staticlater, hire right telecom consultant," Oct, 2007. **Special Services:** LEED[R].

885 ■ GPD P.C.
524 First Ave. S
Great Falls, MT 59401
Ph:(406)452-9558
Fax:(406)727-9720
Co. E-mail: gpd-info@gpdinc.com
URL: http://www.gpdinc.com
Contact: Kevin Wilkerson, Vice President
E-mail: kwilkerson@atsgpdinc.com
Scope: Mechanical and electrical engineers offering counsel on heating; ventilation; air conditioning; refrigeration; air pollution control; plumbing; construction management; site, design and build utilities; fire protection; temperature control; incineration; lighting; power distribution; communications; airports; energy conservation; and lifecycle costing.

886 ■ Greacen Consulting Engineers Inc.
919 Old Hwy. 8 NW, Ste. 200
Saint Paul, MN 55112
Ph:(651)633-1318
Fax:(651)633-1885
Contact: Ed Greacen, Principle
Scope: Specializes in plumbing, heating, ventilating, air conditioning and project management. Designs domestic water and water treatment systems, fire protection, fuel and gas piping, humidification and de-humidification systems, variable air volume (VAV), fan-powered VAV, and retrofit systems for Indoor Air Quality (IAQ).

887 ■ Lawrence G. Spielvogel Inc.
190 Presidential Blvd., Ste. 310
Bala Cynwyd, PA 19004-1151
Ph:(610)783-6350
Fax:(610)783-6349
Co. E-mail: spielvogel@comcast.net
URL: http://www.lspielvogel.com
Contact: Lawrence G. Spielvogel, President
E-mail: spielvogel@comcast.net
Scope: Technical consultant in energy management and mechanical and electrical engineering for buildings. Areas of activities include energy procurement, heating, ventilating, and air conditioning and plumbing, system design, energy studies, feasibility studies, reports, appraisals, trouble-shooting, heat recovery and computer applications. Serves consulting engineers, contractors, government agencies, architects and owners. Provides expert legal testimony in relevant cases.

888 ■ Lundquist, Killeen, Potvin and Bender Inc.
1935 W County Rd. B2, Ste. 300
Saint Paul, MN 55113-2722
Ph:(651)633-1223
Fax:(651)633-1355
Co. E-mail: nbart@lkpb.com
URL: http://www.lkpb.com
Contact: Stephen J. Gentilini, Principle
E-mail: sgent@atslkpb.com
Scope: Provides services in heating, ventilation, plumbing, piping, refrigeration, air conditioning, fire protection, lighting design and fixture selection, com-

munications, electrical power distribution, security, life safety system design, energy conservation analysis, design and implementation.

889 ■ Robert G. Thomas Jr.
1417 Sadler Rd., Ste. 269
Fernandina Beach, FL 32034
Ph:(904)343-2365
Co. E-mail: rgt@rgthomas.com
URL: http://www.eifs.com
E-mail: rgt@rgthomas.com
Scope: Provides insulation, weatherproofing and a finished surface in a single integrated product. **Publications:** "EIFS Design Handbook"; "EIFS New Construction Inspection Guide"; "EIFS Existing Construction Inspection Maintenance and Repair Guide"; "EIFS Homeowners Guide".

890 ■ Stueven Engineering Consultants
140 W 3rd Ave.
Escondido, CA 92025
Ph:(760)735-8577
Fax:(760)735-8578
Co. E-mail: sb@stueven-engineering.com
URL: http://www.stueven-engineering.com
Contact: Steve Balderrama, Principle
E-mail: sb@atsstueven-engineering.com
Scope: Provides services in professional engineering, planning, design, and construction support services for mechanical and plumbing systems.

FRANCHISES AND BUSINESS OPPORTUNITIES

891 ■ Aire Serv Heating and Air Conditioning
The Dwyer Group
1020 N University Parks Dr.
Waco, TX 76707
Free: 800-583-2662
Fax:800-378-9480
No. of Franchise Units: 91. **No. of Company-Owned Units:** 101. **Founded:** 1992. **Franchised:** 1992. **Description:** National heating, ventilating and air conditioning franchise organization, focused on the residential and light commercial service and replacement market. Franchisees typically professional, state-licensed HVAC contractors. **Equity Capital Needed:** Minimum $36,095-$136,500. **Franchise Fee:** $22,000/$100,000 population. **Financial Assistance:** Yes. **Training:** training is provided throughout the year with 4 national conferences, each focused on a topic of concern to the HVAC contractor.

892 ■ One Hour Heating & Air
50 Central Ave., Ste. 920
Sarasota, FL 34236
Ph:(941)552-5100
Free: (866)370-8302
Fax:(941)552-5130
No. of Franchise Units: 223. **No. of Company-Owned Units:** 48. **Founded:** 1999. **Franchised:** 2003. **Description:** HVAC replacement & services. **Equity Capital Needed:** $42,015-$535,870. **Franchise Fee:** $58,265-$535,870. **Royalty Fee:** 5%. **Financial Assistance:** Limited inhouse and third party financing available. **Training:** Provides 3 days training at headquarters, 3 days at franchisee's location, at model centers & training school, Internet training and ongoing support.

LIBRARIES

893 ■ International Union of Operating Engineers - Training Center–Local 68, 68A, 68B Library
14 Fairfield Pl.
West Caldwell, NJ 07006
Ph:(973)227-6426
URL: http://www.iuoe-68.org/index1.cfm
Contact: Thomas P. Giblin
Scope: Refrigeration, welding, heating, ventilation, air conditioning, labor, occupational health and safety. **Services:** Copying; SDI; Library open to the public by appointment. **Holdings:** 1000 books; 2000 VF materials; 15 operator's manuals; 40 equipment manuals; 95 AV programs. **Subscriptions:** 15 journals and other serials.

894 ■ Refrigeration Service Engineers Society Library
1666 Rand Rd.
Des Plaines, IL 60016-3552
Ph:(847)297-6464
Free: 800-297-5660
Fax:(847)297-5038
Co. E-mail: mlowry@rses.org
URL: http://www.rses.org
Contact: Mark Lowry
Scope: Refrigeration, air conditioning, heating, heat pumps, HVAC controls, ventilation, indoor air quality, electricity. **Services:** Copying; Library open to members. **Holdings:** 500 books; 1000 bound periodical volumes; reports; manuscripts. **Subscriptions:** 35,000 journals and other serials.

RESEARCH CENTERS

895 ■ American Society of Heating, Refrigerating and Air-Conditioning Engineers Research Program
1791 Tullie Cir. NE
Atlanta, GA 30329
Ph:(404)636-8400
Free: 800—527-4723
Fax:(404)321-5478
Co. E-mail: ashrae@ashrae.org
URL: http://www.ashrae.org
Contact: Jeff Littleton, Exec.VP
E-mail: ashrae@ashrae.org
Scope: Sponsors research projects at colleges, universities, and private research firms on technical subjects dealing with heating, refrigeration, air conditioning, and ventilation and their effects on humans and the environment. Projects include air pollution sources in HVAC systems, evaluation of service hot water system distribution losses in residential and commercial installations, investigation and identification of indoor allergens and biological toxins that can be moved by filtration, computer algorithms for moisture loss and latent heat loads in bulk storage of fruits and vegetables, and modeling of reflected solar heat gain from neighboring structures in building energy simulation programs. **Publications:** ASHRAE Handbook (annually); ASHRAE Transactions (semiannually); HVAC&R RESEARCH (bimonthly).

896 ■ University of California–California Institute for Energy and Environment
2087 Addison St., 2nd Fl.
Berkeley, CA 94704-1103
Ph:(510)643-1440
Fax:(510)643-9324
Co. E-mail: blumstei@berkeley.edu
URL: http://uc-ciee.org
Contact: Dr. Carl Blumstein, Dir.
E-mail: blumstei@berkeley.edu
Scope: Building energy efficiency, including integrated lighting systems, commercial cooling systems, HVAC distribution systems, residential cooling systems, improved building HVAC controls; building commissioning, operations, and maintenance; air quality effects of energy efficiency, including emission reduction strategies, gas combustion systems, and alternative transportation systems. Institute seeks to secure sustainable, affordable energy for California while improving the state's economy and resources and remaining sensitive to climate change issues. **Publications:** Technical reports. **Educational Activities:** Project workshops (annually), on global climate change, demand response, and transmission research.

ASSOCIATIONS AND OTHER ORGANIZATIONS

897 ■ Allergy/Asthma Information Association–Association d'information sur l'allergie et l'asthme
295 The West Mall, Ste. 118
Toronto, ON, Canada M9C 4Z4
Ph:(416)621-4571
Free: 800-611-7011
Fax:(416)621-5034
Co. E-mail: admin@aaia.ca
URL: http://www.aaia.ca
Contact: Mary Allen, CEO
Description: Seeks to develop societal awareness of the seriousness of allergic disease, including asthma, and to enable allergic individuals, their families, and caregivers to increase control over allergy symptoms. Provides leadership in information, education, and advocacy through partnership with healthcare professionals, businesses, industry, and government. Maintains speakers' bureau. **Publications:** *Awareness and Info Allergie* (quarterly).

REFERENCE WORKS

898 ■ "Chicago Public School District Builds Green" in *Contractor* (Vol. 56, October 2009, No. 10, pp. 5)
Pub: Penton Media, Inc.
Ed: Candace Roulo. **Description:** Chicago Public Schools district has already built six U.S. Green Building Council LEED certified schools and one addition in five years and will continue to build new green buildings. The district has an Environmental Action Plan that strives to reduce energy usage, improve indoor air quality, and reduce contribution to climate change.

899 ■ "San Diego Museum Receives LEED Certification" in *Contractor* (Vol. 57, January 2010, No. 1, pp. 14)
Pub: Penton Media, Inc.
Description: San Diego Natural History Museum received an LEED certification for existing buildings. The certification process began when they committed to displaying the Dead Sea Scrolls in 2007 and they had to upgrade their buildings' air quality and to control for air moisture, temperature, and volume. They reduced their energy consumption by upwards of 20 percent.

TRADE PERIODICALS

900 ■ *The Air Pollution Consultant*
Pub: Aspen Publishers, Inc. (Frederick, Maryland)
Contact: Vicki A. Dean, Managing Editor
Released: Bimonthly, 6/yr. **Description:** Journal covering air pollution issues.

901 ■ *Air Pollution Monitoring and Sampling Newsletter*
Pub: McIlvaine Co.
Contact: Marilyn McIlvaine
Ed: Christine Hennig, Editor, chennig@mail.mcilvaine.com. **Released:** Monthly. **Price:** $270, U.S.; $300. **Description:** Provides current information on air pollution monitoring and sampling equipment and service. Includes "product comparisons, trends, conference reports, coverage of new products, new orders, a calendar of events, and informed analysis."

VIDEOCASSETTES/ AUDIOCASSETTES

902 ■ *Air Pollution: Indoor*
Films for the Humanities & Sciences
132 West 31st Street
New York, NY 10001
Ph:(609)671-1000
Free: 800-257-5126
Fax:(609)671-0266
Co. E-mail: custserv@films.com
URL: http://www.films.com
Released: 1989. **Description:** This tape explores indoor air pollution, particularly pollutants introduced in homes from painting, thermal insulation and other energy saving improvements, and water-proofing devices. **Availability:** VHS; 3/4U.

CONSULTANTS

903 ■ Pathogen Control Associates Inc.
270 Scientific Dr., Ste. 3
Norcross, GA 30092
Ph:(770)446-0540
Fax:(770)446-0610
Co. E-mail: info@pathcon.com
URL: http://www.pathcon.com
Contact: Brad Fox, Principal
E-mail: bfox@atspathcon.com
Scope: Applied microbiology problems: microbiological/air quality issues, sick building syndrome, Legionella and air quality testing, prevention and control of food-related pathogens diseases, hazard analysis, prevention strategies, medical, epidemiological, public health evaluations, seminars, courses, laboratory evaluations and expert witness testimony. Industries served: buildings indoor air quality, heating/air conditioning, poultry industry and government agencies. **Publications:** "Microbes in the Indoor Environment"; "Legionellosis: Is there a National Preventing Strategy". **Seminars:** Micro Organisms in Indoor Air: Health Complaints Associated With Environmental and Occupational Settings; Environmental Hazards in HealthCare Settings.

FRANCHISES AND BUSINESS OPPORTUNITIES

904 ■ Coit Cleaning and Restoration Services
897 Hinckley Rd.
Burlingame, CA 94010
Free: 800-243-8797
Fax:(650)692-8397
Co. E-mail: franchise@coit.com
URL: http://www.coit.com
No. of Franchise Units: 42. **No. of Company-Owned Units:** 8. **Founded:** 1950. **Franchised:** 1962. **Description:** Coit is a multi-service cleaning company, offering drapery cleaning, carpet cleaning, upholstery cleaning, area rug cleaning, air duct cleaning and more. **Equity Capital Needed:** $50,000-$145,000. **Franchise Fee:** $24,000-$40,000. **Financial Assistance:** Limited financing available. **Training:** Includes 10 days in corporate office.

905 ■ Ductmedic
Ductmedic International, Inc.
2939 Cornhusker Hwy., Ste. A
Lincoln, NE 68504
Ph:(402)435-3828
Free: 800-700-9877
Fax:(402)467-2561
No. of Franchise Units: 2. **No. of Company-Owned Units:** 1. **Founded:** 1994. **Franchised:** 2004. **Description:** Air duct cleaning/indoor air quality. **Equity Capital Needed:** $50,000-$90,000; $10,000-$20,000 area fee. **Franchise Fee:** $9,500. **Financial Assistance:** Yes. **Training:** Yes.

LIBRARIES

906 ■ Cadwalader, Wickersham & Taft Library
700 6th St., N.W.
Washington, DC 20001
Ph:(202)862-2200
Fax:(202)862-2400
Co. E-mail: jane.platt-brown@cwt.com
URL: http://www.cadwalader.com
Contact: Jane Platt-Brown, Lib.Hd.
Scope: Law - antitrust, corporate, securities, taxation, business fraud. **Services:** Interlibrary loan; Library open to the public by appointment (with restrictions). **Holdings:** 15,000 volumes; microforms; CD-ROM.

907 ■ California Environmental Protection Agency Library
PO Box 2815
Sacramento, CA 95812-2815
Ph:(916)327-0635
Fax:(916)322-7060
Co. E-mail: calepalibrary@arb.ca.gov
URL: http://www.calepa.ca.gov/Library/
Contact: John Hoffman, Supv.Libn. II
Scope: The environment, air and water pollution, climate change, solid hazardous waste management, pesticide application. **Services:** Interlibrary loan; copying; Library open to the public. **Holdings:** 30,000 books, reports, documents, journals, and other reference materials. **Subscriptions:** 310 journals and other serials; 13 newspapers.

908 ■ URS Library
Crown Corporate Center
2870 Gateway Oaks Dr., Ste. 150
Sacramento, CA 95833-4324
Ph:(916)679-2000
Fax:(916)679-2900
URL: http://www.urscorp.com
Scope: Environment, air quality, hazardous waste. **Services:** Interlibrary loan; Library not open to the public. **Holdings:** 5000 books; technical and government reports; government agency rules and regulations. **Subscriptions:** 75 journals and other serials.

909 ■ Washington University–Center for Air Pollution Impact and Trend Analysis Library
Campus Box 1124
St. Louis, MO 63130
Ph:(314)935-6099
Fax:(314)935-6145
Co. E-mail: rhusar@me.wustl.edu
URL: http://capita.wustl.edu/capita/people/sfalke/SFalkeCV.htm
Contact: Rudolf B. Husar, Dir.
Scope: Air pollution. **Holdings:** 1000 reports. **Subscriptions:** 10 journals and other serials; 2 newspapers.

RESEARCH CENTERS

910 ■ Northeastern University–Center for Nano and Microcontamination Control
Egan Research Ctr.
360 Huntington Ave.
Boston, MA 02115-5000
Ph:(617)373-6012
Fax:(617)373-3266
Co. E-mail: busnaina@coe.neu.edu
URL: http://www.cmc.neu.edu
Contact: Prof. Ahmed A. Busnaina, Dir.
E-mail: busnaina@coe.neu.edu
Scope: Microcontamination and particulate control applied to process equipment and manufacturing. Specific areas of research include nanoparticle transport, deposition, adhesion, and removal from silicon and other substrates; modeling of particle and mass transport in semiconductor processing; particle deposition and generation in semiconductor manufacturing processes, micro and nanofabrication of interconnects and the development of Cu physically enhanced electroplating. **Services:** Consulting. **Publications:** Newsletter; Research conference report (biennially). **Educational Activities:** Short courses (annually); Technical conference (annually).

911 ■ University of California, Davis–Air Quality Group
Crocker Nuclear Laboratory
1 Shields Ave.
Davis, CA 95616
Ph:(530)752-1460
Fax:(530)752-0952
Co. E-mail: flocchini@crocker.ucdavis.edu
URL: http://crocker.ucdavis.edu/research_aqg.php
Contact: Robert G. Flocchini PhD, Dir.
E-mail: flocchini@crocker.ucdavis.edu
Scope: Air quality, including chemical size-analysis and source identification of air pollutants, particulate monitoring, and development of sampling equipment.

ASSOCIATIONS AND OTHER ORGANIZATIONS

912 ■ American Ambulance Association
8400 Westpark Dr., 2nd Fl.
McLean, VA 22102
Ph:(703)610-9018
Free: 800-523-4447
Fax:(703)610-0210
Co. E-mail: jjohnson@lifeemsinc.com
URL: http://www.the-aaa.org
Contact: Jimmy Johnson, Pres.-Elect
Description: Represents private suppliers of ambulance service. Aims to: aid in developing private enterprise pre-hospital emergency medical treatment and medical transportation services as a viable cost-effective alternative to publicly-operated services; promote improved patient care; develop efficient medical transportation at a reasonable cost; improve personnel and equipment standards; work with organizations offering medical transportation; encourage high standards of ethics and conduct. Acts as an information clearinghouse; informs members of developments in the industry. Offers advice on federal statutes and regulations related to the medical transportation industry, such as insurance and antitrust regulations. Holds four regional seminars per year on topics such as training requirements, insurance systems, Medicare reimbursement, and local, state, and federal legislation and regulations. Conducts quarterly emergency medical services management seminar. **Publications:** *Medicare Reference* (annual).

TRADE PERIODICALS

913 ■ *Emergency Medicine Alert–Practical Summary and Accute Care Report*
Pub: American Health Consultants Inc.
Ed: Richard A. Harrigan, M.D., Editor. **Released:** Monthly. **Price:** $299, U.S. **Description:** Provides information on developments and improvements in emergency medicine.

VIDEOCASSETTES/ AUDIOCASSETTES

914 ■ *Advanced Skills for the EMT*
Emergency Training
PO Box 13896
Emory University
Dobbs University Center - 5th Floor
Fairlawn, OH 44334
Ph:(404)727-3853
Fax:(404)727-5667
Released: 1988. **Price:** $620.00. **Description:** A video series desinged to supplement the teachings of an EMT Intermediate course. **Availability:** VHS.

915 ■ *AIDS, Hepatitis and the Emergency Responder*
Commonwealth Films, Inc.
223 Commonwealth Ave.
Boston, MA 02116
Ph:(617)262-5634
Fax:(617)262-6948
Co. E-mail: info@commonwealthfilms.com
URL: http://www.commonwealthfilms.com
Released: 1988. **Price:** $250.00. **Description:** The tape shows how an emergency worker can better help victims and reduce his own risk of getting a disease. **Availability:** VHS; 3/4U; Special order formats.

916 ■ *Anonymous Hero*
Pyramid Media
PO Box 1048/WEB
Santa Monica, CA 90406
Ph:(310)398-6149
Free: 800-421-2304
Fax:(310)398-7869
Co. E-mail: info@pyramedia.com
URL: http://www.pyramidmedia.com
Released: 1989. **Price:** $195.00. **Description:** This program teaches emergency medical dispatchers about anxious callers, medical interrogation, and telephone treatment sequences for common emergencies. **Availability:** VHS; 3/4U.

COMPUTERIZED DATABASES

917 ■ *State Health Care Regulatory Developments*
The Bureau of National Affairs Inc.
1801 S Bell St.
Arlington, VA 22202
Free: 800-372-1033
Co. E-mail: customercare@bna.com
URL: http://www.bna.com
Description: Contains information on health care regulatory news and developments in the United States. Subjects include community-based care, home care, emergency care, infectious diseases, managed care, insurance, laboratories, Medicaid, mental health, medical waste, nursing homes, pharmaceuticals, physician services, professional licensing, provider relationships, worker protection and compensation. Entries are organized by state, topic, and register citation. **Availability:** Online: The Bureau of National Affairs Inc., Thomson Reuters. **Type:** Full text.

RESEARCH CENTERS

918 ■ University of California, San Francisco–San Francisco Injury Center
San Francisco General Hospital
Department of Surgery, Ward 3A, Box 0807
1001 Potrero Ave.
San Francisco, CA 94110
Ph:(415)206-4623
Fax:(415)206-5484
Co. E-mail: pknudson@sfghsurg.ucsf.edu
URL: http://sfic.surgery.ucsf.edu
Contact: Prof. M. Margaret Knudson MD, Dir.
E-mail: pknudson@sfghsurg.ucsf.edu
Scope: Acute trauma care, injury prevention and surveillance.

Amusement Arcade

ASSOCIATIONS AND OTHER ORGANIZATIONS

919 ■ American Amusement Machine Association
450 E Higgins Rd., Ste. 201
Elk Grove Village, IL 60007
Ph:(847)290-9088
Co. E-mail: information@coin-op.org
URL: http://www.coin-op.org
Contact: John Schultz, Pres.
Description: Manufacturers and distributors of coin machines; parts suppliers and others interested in promoting and protecting the amusement machine industry. Seeks solutions to the problem of copyright infringement by foreign manufacturers, and legislative and regulatory problems facing the industry and manufacturers. Works to improve the image of the coin-operated amusement industry. Presents views to governmental decision-makers. Operates American Amusement Machine Charitable Foundation. **Publications:** *Loose Change* (monthly);Membership Directory (annual).

REFERENCE WORKS

920 ■ "Boots Treat Street Rolls Out Trolley Dash App on Androis and iPhone OS" in *Entertainment Close-Up* (October 24, 2011)
Pub: Close-Up Media
Description: Shoppers using Boots Treat Street can now download the Trolley Dash app game, available from the Apple Store and the Android Market, and enjoy the pastel colored street featuring favorite retailers such as eBay, New Look and Play.com collecting prizes while avoiding hazards.

921 ■ "Boxing, Tech Giants Team to Help Teens" in *Hispanic Business* (January-February 2009, pp. 44)
Pub: Hispanic Business
Ed: Daniel Soussa. **Description:** Microsoft and Oscar de la Hoya are providing teens a head start for careers in the sciences by offering a competition in the categories of photography, short films or Web-based games.

922 ■ "Cineplex Sees Past the Big Picture" in *Globe & Mail* (February 8, 2007, pp. B9)
Pub: CTVglobemedia Publishing Inc.
Ed: Shirley Won. **Description:** Cineplex Entertainment LP reported $4.6 million profit in the final quarter of 2006. The movie chain is introducing video-game tournaments and live rock concerts to improve sales.

923 ■ "Game Changer" in *Canadian Business* (Vol. 83, June 15, 2010, No. 10, pp. 52)
Pub: Rogers Media Ltd.
Ed: Jordan Timm. **Description:** Ubisoft chose Ontario to be the site for its new development studio and it has appointed Jade Raymond as its managing director. Raymond was born in Montreal in 1975 and studied computer science at McGill. Raymond is said to possess the understanding of the game industry's technical, art, and business components.

924 ■ *The Game Makers*
Pub: Harvard Business School Press
Ed: Philip E. Orbanes. **Released:** November 2003. **Price:** $29.95. **Description:** Profile of game expert and president of a specialty game company, author of books about games, Monopoly championship judge, senior vice president of research and development at Parker Brothers, and inventor of board and card games in highlighted.

925 ■ "Games Gone Wild: City's Newest Public Company Aims for the Sky" in *Business Courier* (Vol. 27, September 24, 2010, No. 21, pp. 1)
Pub: Business Courier
Ed: Dan Monk. **Description:** Video game company Zoo Entertainment Inc., which is based in Norwood near Cincinnati, Ohio aims to build a strong company and to position itself for future growth. The company reported $27.6 million in revenue for the first half of 2010 and analysts project $100 million in sales for 2011.

926 ■ "Great Canadian's President Folds His Cards" in *Globe & Mail* (February 21, 2006, pp. B4)
Pub: CTVglobemedia Publishing Inc.
Ed: Peter Kennedy. **Description:** The reasons behind the resignation of Anthony Martin as president of Great Canadian Gaming Corp. are presented.

927 ■ *How to Get Rich*
Pub: Ebury Press
Ed: Felix Dennis. **Released:** 2008. **Price:** $25.95. **Description:** Publisher of Maxim, The Week, and Stuff magazines, discusses the mistakes he made running his companies. He didn't understand that people who buy computer gaming magazines wanted a free game with each copy, as one of his rivals was offering. And he laments not diversifying into television and exploiting the Internet.

928 ■ "Kiosk Outfit ecoATM Now Recycling Video Games" in *San Diego Union-Tribune* (October 7, 2010)
Pub: San Diego Union-Tribune
Ed: Mike Freeman. **Description:** ecoATM makes automated kiosks to buy back cell phones will now include video games as part of their recycling business.

929 ■ "Lighter Than Air" in *Game Developer* (Vol. 18, November 1, 2011, No. 10, pp. 38)
Pub: Think Services
Ed: Andy Firth. **Description:** Floating point performance tips and tricks are outlined. Floating point allows freedom of representation when implementing algorithms and is both intuitive to set up and simple to work with; hardware is also improved so that it is faster to use floating point math as opposed to integer in many environments.

930 ■ "Our Gadget of the Week: Balancing Act" in *Barron's* (Vol. 88, March 31, 2008, No. 13, pp. 40)
Pub: Dow Jones & Company, Inc.
Ed: Naureen S. Malik. **Description:** Wii Fit gives users the experience of a virtual personal trainer and workouts that become progressively harder. The device turns the typical fitness regimes into fun exercises and users can choose workouts in four categories including yoga, balance, strength-training and, low impact aerobics.

931 ■ "Public Media Works to Launch DVD Kiosk Operations in Toronto, Canada" in *Internet Wire* (November 15, 2010)
Pub: Comtex
Description: Public Media Works Inc. along with its EntertainmentXpress Inc., have partnered with Spot Venture Distribution Inc. and Signifi Solutions Inc., both headquartered in Toronto, Canada, to manage and expand the Spot DVD movie and game kiosk business in greater Toronto and other Canadian locations.

932 ■ *The Race for a New Game Machine: Creating the Chips Inside the Xbox 360 and the PlayStation 3*
Pub: Citadel Press
Ed: David Shippy, Mickie Phipps. **Released:** 2009. **Price:** $21.95. **Description:** The story of Microsoft and Sony's race to deliver the goods for the Xbox 360 and Playstation 3 is explored.

933 ■ "Silverdome Bidders Bring New Proposals" in *Crain's Detroit Business* (Vol. 24, March 17, 2008, No. 11, pp. 23)
Pub: Crain Communications, Inc.
Ed: Daniel Duggan. **Description:** Discusses the seven plans which have been proposed as part of the third round of bidding for the Pontiac Silverdome; proposals range from Global Baseball Inc., a baseball league that would pit a team from every country against one another, to an Indian casino, a musical "hall of fame", a convention center, a horse track, a hotel and an indoor water park.

934 ■ "Tony Hawk Carves a New Niche" in *Entrepreneur* (Vol. 37, October 2009, No. 10, pp. 26)
Pub: Entrepreneur Media, Inc.
Ed: Gary Cohn. **Description:** Professional skateboarder Tony Hawk discusses the growth of Birdhouse, the skateboard company he founded. He is excited about the release of Tony Hawk Ride, a videogame with a skateboard controller.

935 ■ *Vending Times—Buyers Guide and Directory Issue*
Pub: Vending Times Inc.
Contact: Alicia Lavay-Kertes, Pres./Publisher
E-mail: alicia@vendingtimes.net
Released: Annual, Latest edition 2009. **Price:** $40, individuals includes shipping and handling. **Publication Includes:** Lists of manufacturers and suppliers of equipment and products used by vending machine industry operators, including product venders, juke

boxes, pinball and other games; industry trade associations. **Entries Include:** Company name, address, phone, names of key personnel, description of products. **Arrangement:** Classified by product or service.

936 ■ "Work for Play: Careers in Video Game Development" in *Occupational Outlook Quarterly* (Vol. 55, Fall 2011, No. 3, pp. 2)
Pub: U.S. Bureau of Labor Statistics

Ed: Drew Liming, Dennis Vilorio. **Description:** Game developers make a living creating the games the public enjoys playing. The video gaming industry reported sales over $10 billion in 2009 and employed 32,000 people in 34 states. Career options in video game development are featured.

TRADE PERIODICALS

937 ■ *RePlay Magazine*
Pub: RePlay Magazine
Contact: Barry Zweben, Advertising Mgr
E-mail: barry@replaymag.com

Ed: Steve White, Editor, steve@replaymag.com. **Released:** Monthly. **Price:** $65; $90 Canada and Mexico; $230 other countries airmail. **Description:** Trade magazine covering the coin-operated amusement game industry.

TRADE SHOWS AND CONVENTIONS

938 ■ Amusement and Music Operators Association Convention
Amusement and Music Operators Association
600 Spring Hill Ring Rd., Ste. 111
West Dundee, IL 60010
Ph:(847)428-7699
Free: 800-937-2662
Fax:(847)428-7719
Co. E-mail: amoa@amoa.com
URL: http://www.amoa.com

Released: Annual. **Audience:** Trade professionals. **Principal Exhibits:** Coin-operated arcade, video and gaming machines, games, jukeboxes, stuffed toys, records, and jewelry. **Dates and Locations:** 2011 Mar 01-03, Las Vegas, NV.

939 ■ FUN Expo
Reed Exhibitions North American Headquarters
383 Main Ave.
Norwalk, CT 06851
Ph:(203)840-4800
Fax:(203)840-5805
Co. E-mail: export@reedexpo.com
URL: http://www.reedexpo.com

Released: Annual. **Principal Exhibits:** Amusement and recreation products for family and location based entertainment centers, small amusement parks and family oriented businesses such as bowling centers, skating rinks, sports parks, miniature golf courses, golf driving ranges, family restaurants, resorts and other entertainment/recreation businesses. **Dates and Locations:** 2011 Mar 01-03, Las Vegas, NV.

940 ■ Pinball Expo
Pinball Expo / Flip Out Pinball Tournament
c/o Robert Berk
1085 Eagle Trace Rd.
Warren, OH 44484
Ph:(330)369-1192
Free: 800-323-3547
Fax:(330)369-1087
Co. E-mail: brkpinball@aol.com
URL: http://www.pinballexpo.net

Released: Annual. **Audience:** Trade personnel, collectors, distributors and suppliers of related products. **Principal Exhibits:** Pinball machines and related supplies. **Dates and Locations:** 2011 Oct 19-23, Wheeling, IL.

CONSULTANTS

941 ■ Erin Services Inc.
111 Travelers Way
PO Box 1048
Saint Simons Island, GA 31522-5632
Ph:(912)638-9916
Free: 800-862-5361
Fax:(912)638-5701
Co. E-mail: dennisd@ns.technonet.com
Contact: Dennis J. Donnelly III, President
E-mail: dennis179@yahoo.com
Scope: Offers assistance in technical proposal production, marketing, and research. Industries served: Food service, janitorial, landscaping, hospitality and lodging, parks, and recreational.

FRANCHISES AND BUSINESS OPPORTUNITIES

942 ■ Monkey Joe's Party And Play
Raving Brands
1718 Peachtree St. NW, Ste. 1070
Atlanta, GA 30309
Ph:(404)351-3500
URL: http://www.monkeyjoes.com
No. of Franchise Units: 56. **No. of Company-Owned Units:** 1. **Founded:** 2004. **Franchised:** 2005. **Description:** Interactive indoor party center filled with an array of giant air-filled play structures, jumps, slides, thrilling obstacle courses, development games and fun party rooms. For the parents, there's comfortable seating, flatscreen TVs and high-speed internet. **Equity Capital Needed:** $500,000 net worth; $150,000 liquid. **Franchise Fee:** $25,000. **Financial Assistance:** Relationships with multiple financial institutions with experience assisting franchisees as they start their business. **Training:** Raving Brands University classroom and onsite training provided. From register operation to food preparation, from hiring staff to accounting procedures, you'll improve your management skills, setup back office and develop a sales and marketing plan.

Amusement/Water Park

START-UP INFORMATION

943 ■ "Noah's Park: $150M Project Eyed in Ky." in *Business Courier* (Vol. 27, November 19, 2010, No. 29, pp. 1)
Pub: Business Courier
Ed: Lucy May. **Description:** Grant County, Kentucky has been abuzz with speculation about a $150M Noah's Ark-themed project being planned for Williamstown, Kentucky. The theme park's planned location is halfway between Cincinnati, Ohio and Louisville, Kentucky and about 40 minutes south of the Answers in Genesis Creation Museum in Petersburg.

ASSOCIATIONS AND OTHER ORGANIZATIONS

944 ■ Amusement Industry Manufacturers and Suppliers International
3026 S Orange
Santa Ana, CA 92707
Ph:(714)425-5747
Fax:(714)276-9666
Co. E-mail: info@aimsintl.org
URL: http://www.aimsintl.org
Description: Represents manufacturers and suppliers of amusement riding devices and equipment used by amusement parks, carnivals, and traveling amusement companies. Exchanges information on safety, maintenance, state laws, transportation, and credit. Works to develop safety programs and codes at the federal and state levels; carries out public relations activities; and cooperates with the ASTM to develop voluntary standards for amusement rides and devices. .

945 ■ Canadian Association of Fairs and Exhibitions–Association Canadienne des Foires et Expositions
43 Eccles St.
Ottawa, ON, Canada K1R 6S3
Ph:(613)233-0012
Free: 800-663-1714
Fax:(613)233-1154
Co. E-mail: info@canadian-fairs.ca
URL: http://www.canadian-fairs.ca
Contact: Mavis Hanna, Exec. Dir.
Description: Exhibition and fair operators. Seeks to advance the exhibition industry. Represents members' interests before trade organizations, government agencies, and the public.

946 ■ International Association of Amusement Parks and Attractions
1448 Duke St.
Alexandria, VA 22314
Ph:(703)836-4800
Fax:(703)836-6742
Co. E-mail: ccleary@iaapa.org
URL: http://www.iaapa.org
Contact: Chip Cleary, Pres./CEO
Description: Operators of amusement parks, theme parks, tourist attractions, water parks, zoos, aquariums, museums, miniature golf courses and family entertainment centers; manufacturers and suppliers of amusement equipment and services. Conducts research programs; compiles statistics; hosts annual convention and trade show; publishes periodicals. **Publications:** *Funworld* (11/year); *Year in Review* (annual).

947 ■ Outdoor Amusement Business Association
1035 S Semoran Blvd., Ste. 1045A
Winter Park, FL 32792
Ph:(407)681-9444
Free: 800-517-OABA
Fax:(407)681-9445
Co. E-mail: oaba@oaba.org
URL: http://www.oaba.org
Contact: Robert W. Johnson, Pres.
Description: Represents executives and employees of carnivals and fairs; ride owners; independent food and games concessionaires; manufacturers and suppliers of equipment. Promotes and lobbies on behalf of the interests of the outdoor amusement industry; provides a center for dissemination of information. **Publications:** *Midway Marquee* (annual).

948 ■ World Waterpark Association
8826 Santa Fe Dr., Ste. 310
Overland Park, KS 66212
Ph:(913)599-0300
Fax:(913)599-0520
Co. E-mail: memberservices@waterparks.org
URL: http://www.waterparks.org
Contact: Rick Root, Pres.
Description: Water leisure amusement facilities; suppliers of products and services. Provides a forum for the discussion of information related to the water amusement park industry. Furthers safety and profitability in the water leisure industry through educational conferences and publications. Maintains placement service; compiles statistics. **Publications:** *Considerations for Operating Safety*; *Splash & Spray* (9/year); *World Waterpark* (10/year).

REFERENCE WORKS

949 ■ "Cedar Fair to Solicit Bids for Geauga Lake" in *Crain's Cleveland Business* (Vol. 28, October 8, 2007, No. 40, pp. 1)
Pub: Crain Communications, Inc.
Ed: Stan Bullard. **Description:** Cedar Fair Entertainment Co. plans to seek sealed bids for the redevelopment of nearly 540 acres of their amusement park site in southwest Geauga County and northwest Portage County.

950 ■ "Legoland Florida Theme Park Construction to Start in May" in *Orlando Business Journal* (Vol. 26, January 29, 2010, No. 35, pp. 1)
Pub: American City Business Journals
Ed: Richard Bilbao. **Description:** Merlin Entertainments Group purchased the closed Cypress Garden theme park in Winter Haven, Florida for $22.3 million and plans to spend a reported $100 million or more to begin transforming it into the world's largest Legoland. Winter Haven businesses are expecting a windfall from the theme park's constructions workers.

951 ■ "Legoland Plans Could Tumble After State's Modesa Denial" in *Business Journal-Serving Metropolitan Kansas City* (November 16, 2007)
Pub: American City Business Journals, Inc.
Ed: Jim Davis. **Description:** RED Development LLC's officials are not giving up after the Missouri Department of Economic Development said RED could not exploit the Missouri Downtown and Rural Economic Stimulus Act (Modesa) for the Legoland theme park development in Lee's Summit. Legoland's proposed site southeast of Interstate 470 and U.S. Highway 50 does not fit the Modesa because it is outside Lee's Summit.

952 ■ *Promising Practices: Progress Toward the Goals (1998): Lessons from the States*
Pub: DIANE Publishing Co.
Ed: Emily Wurtz. **Released:** 1999. **Price:** $15.00.

953 ■ "Schlitterbahn Broadens" in *Austin Business JournalInc.* (Vol. 28, September 19, 2008, No. 27, pp. A1)
Pub: American City Business Journals
Ed: Kate Harrington. **Description:** Schlitterbahn is planning to introduce a Christmas-themed event this winter 2008 in its water amusement park that will keep it open from November to January. The company is also constructing its first out-of-Texas park, which is a $170 million, 376-acre project in Kansas City, Missouri. Other details about Schlitterbahn's expansion are discussed.

954 ■ "Silverdome Bidders Bring New Proposals" in *Crain's Detroit Business* (Vol. 24, March 17, 2008, No. 11, pp. 23)
Pub: Crain Communications, Inc.
Ed: Daniel Duggan. **Description:** Discusses the seven plans which have been proposed as part of the third round of bidding for the Pontiac Silverdome; proposals range from Global Baseball Inc., a baseball league that would pit a team from every country against one another, to an Indian casino, a musical "hall of fame", a convention center, a horse track, a hotel and an indoor water park.

955 ■ "Theme Park Sale has Vendor Upside" in *Tampa Bay Business Journal* (Vol. 29, October 23, 2009, No. 44, pp. 1)
Pub: American City Business Journals
Ed: Margie Manning. **Description:** Private equity firm The Blackstone Group has concluded its $2.7 billion purchase of Busch Entertainment Corporation. Aside from enhanced business opportunities in Florida's Tampa Bay area, new attractions might be built in the Busch Gardens and Adventure Island properties that will be acquired by Blackstone. Blackstone's other plans are also discussed.

956 ■ "Up In the Air" in *The Business Journal-Serving Greater Tampa Bay* (Vol. 28, July 18, 2008, No. 30, pp. 1)
Pub: American City Business Journals, Inc.
Ed: Margie Manning. **Description:** Views and information on Busch Gardens and on its future, are

presented. The park's 3,769 employees worry for their future, after tourism industry experts have expressed concerns on possible tax cuts and other cost reductions. The future of the park, which ranks number 19 as the most visited park in the world, is expected to have a major impact on the tourism industry.

957 ■ "Water Park, Convention Center Plan Matures" in *Austin Business JournalInc.* (Vol. 28, July 18, 2008, No. 18, pp. 1)
Pub: American City Business Journals
Ed: Kate Harrington. **Description:** Plans for the proposed water park in Cedar Park in Austin, Texas is moving forward as it grows in size from 40 to 90 acres, with first phase of construction to begin in early 2009.

STATISTICAL SOURCES

958 ■ *The Amusement and Theme Parks Industry Market*
Pub: Rector Press, Ltd.
Contact: Lewis Sckolnick, Pres
Released: 2009. **Price:** Contact Rector Press.

959 ■ *RMA Annual Statement Studies*
Pub: Robert Morris Associates (RMA)
Released: Annual. **Price:** $175.00 2006-07 edition, $105.00. **Description:** Contains composite balance sheets and income statements for more than 360 industries, including the accounting, auditing, and bookkeeping industries. Also contains five years of comparative historical data for discerning trends. Includes 16 commonly used ratios, computed for most of the size groupings for nearly every industry.

TRADE PERIODICALS

960 ■ *Splash Magazine*
Pub: Splash Magazine
Contact: Lawrence Davis, Publisher/Ed.-in-Ch.
Ed: Barbara Keer, Editor. **Released:** Monthly. **Description:** Online trade magazine covering the water leisure industry. Targets owners, managers, suppliers, and developers of private and community owned water leisure facilities, in addition to hotels and resorts with these facilities.

TRADE SHOWS AND CONVENTIONS

961 ■ FUN Expo
Reed Exhibitions North American Headquarters
383 Main Ave.
Norwalk, CT 06851
Ph:(203)840-4800
Fax:(203)840-5805
Co. E-mail: export@reedexpo.com
URL: http://www.reedexpo.com
Released: Annual. **Principal Exhibits:** Amusement and recreation products for family and location based entertainment centers, small amusement parks and family oriented businesses such as bowling centers, skating rinks, sports parks, miniature golf courses, golf driving ranges, family restaurants, resorts and other entertainment/recreation businesses. **Dates and Locations:** 2011 Mar 01-03, Las Vegas, NV.

962 ■ International Association of Amusement Parks and Attractions Annual Convention and Trade Show
International Association of Amusement Parks and Attractions
1448 Duke St.
Alexandria, VA 22314
Ph:(703)836-4800
Fax:(703)836-6742
Co. E-mail: convention@iaapa.org
URL: http://www.iaapa.org
Released: Annual. **Audience:** Trade professionals. **Principal Exhibits:** Amusement, leisure, recreation, and family entertainment-related products and services.

963 ■ International Association of Fairs and Expositions Trade Show
International Association of Fairs and Expositions
3043 E. Cairo
Springfield, MO 65802
Ph:(417)862-5771
Free: 800-516-0313
Fax:(417)862-0156
Co. E-mail: iafe@fairsandexpos.com
URL: http://www.fairsandexpos.com
Released: Annual. **Audience:** Fair managers, staffs, and board members; carnival owners and staffs; concessionaires; talent and other agencies related to the fair industry. **Principal Exhibits:** Talent agencies, concessionaires, novelties, amusement devices, insurance, ribbons, plaques, attractions, and equipment. Products and services for the fair industry.

CONSULTANTS

964 ■ Dennis G. Glore Inc.
120 S Virginia Eureka
PO Box 200
Eureka, MO 63025-2003
Ph:(636)938-7887
Fax:(636)938-6590
Co. E-mail: dgginc@inlink.com
URL: http://www.dgg-inc.com
Contact: Margaret Glore, Mgr
E-mail: mike.key@atsdgg-inc.com
Scope: Offers counsel on the design of food service facilities for hotels, motels, hospitals, office buildings, restaurants, cafeterias, amusement parks and any commercial operation.

965 ■ Erin Services Inc.
111 Travelers Way
PO Box 1048
Saint Simons Island, GA 31522-5632
Ph:(912)638-9916
Free: 800-862-5361
Fax:(912)638-5701
Co. E-mail: dennisd@ns.technonet.com
Contact: Dennis J. Donnelly III, President
E-mail: dennis179@yahoo.com
Scope: Offers assistance in technical proposal production, marketing, and research. Industries served: Food service, janitorial, landscaping, hospitality and lodging, parks, and recreational.

966 ■ Frank Barnes & Associates
PO Box 241806
Los Angeles, CA 90024-9606
Ph:(213)388-5800
Fax:(213)388-2221
Co. E-mail: frank-barnes@santa-monica.org
Contact: Edgar Tom, President
E-mail: frank-barnes@santa-monica.org
Scope: Provides transit, park-and-ride, traffic control, and parking operations planning for special events and activities involving the movement of large numbers of people and vehicles at stadiums, theaters, convention centers, arenas, shopping centers and amusement parks. Services are provided to both government and private clients.

967 ■ KZF Design Inc.
700 Broadway St.
Cincinnati, OH 45202-6010
Ph:(513)621-6211
Fax:(513)621-6530
Co. E-mail: natascha.grody@kzf.com
URL: http://www.kzf.com
Contact: Michael Mcinturf, Director
E-mail: michael.mcinturf@atskzf.com
Scope: Provides design and counsel in the fields of architecture, engineering, space planning, interior design and planning. Skilled in all aspects of design and planning for industry, institutions, commercial, corporations and public sector. Offers civil and transportation engineering for highways, bridges and storm and waste water systems. Also offers city, regional and land development planning. **Publications:** "The art of grieving," Oct, 2008; "Cincinnati Enquirer," 2008; "KZF Design moving Downtown," Feb, 2008; "Cincinnati Business Courier," Feb, 2008; "Tampa Bay Business Journal," Feb, 2008; "Work life strategy". **Special Services:** LEED[R].

968 ■ Lougheed Resource Group Inc.
17608 Deer Isle Cir.
Winter Garden, FL 34787
Ph:(407)654-1212
Fax:(407)654-5419
Co. E-mail: info@lrgconstruction.com
URL: http://www.lrgconstruction.com
Contact: Karen Lougheed, Owner
E-mail: karen@lrgmanagement.com
Scope: Construction consultants specializing in project strategies, scope preparation, contract negotiation, project management, document and code evaluation, peer reviews, scheduling/estimates, dispute resolution, and forensic analysis expert testimony.

969 ■ Nikki Safety Consultants
333 Elmer St.
Trenton, NJ 08611-1512
Ph:(609)599-1345
Contact: T.J. Valli, Principle
Scope: Inspects amusement rides and consults on codes governing amusement rides. Also involves in the area of fire protection, crime prevention, and security inspection. Industries served: manufacturing, investigations, accidents, safety and security, crime prevention, amusement rides, hotel and restaurant management, engineering, and electrical.

970 ■ Nyikos Associates Inc.
18219A Flower Hill Way
Gaithersburg, MD 20879-5331
Ph:(240)683-9530
Fax:(240)683-9532
Co. E-mail: nyikassoc@aol.com
URL: http://www.nyikosassociates.com
Contact: Robert M. Nyikos, President
E-mail: rnyikos@atsnyikos.com
Scope: Independent professional design/consulting organization specializing in commercial food service and laundry facilities for hospitals, hotels, restaurants, schools, universities, employee cafeterias, correctional facilities, convention centers, nursing homes, ski resorts, amusement parks and sports stadiums. Firm also offers management consulting for marketing and feasibility purposes. **Publications:** "Maryland State Department of Education School Food and Nutrition Design Manual," Jan, 1995.

971 ■ Turner Consulting Group Inc.
306 Florida Ave. NW
Washington, DC 20001-1804
Ph:(202)986-5533
Fax:(202)986-5532
Co. E-mail: talktous@tcg.com
URL: http://www.tcg-inc.com
Contact: Maureen Sullivan, Principle
Scope: Offers the expertise needed to take advantage of the web. Specialization includes e-government, egrants innovation, grants gov connector, grants gov readiness assessment, web enablement, systems integration, knowledge management, project and program management, IV and V and CMMI mentoring.

Animal Breeder

ASSOCIATIONS AND OTHER ORGANIZATIONS

972 ■ Alpaca Breeders of the Rockies
PO Box 1965
Estes Park, CO 80517
Ph:(970)586-5589
Free: 888-993-9898
Co. E-mail: president@alpacabreeders.org
URL: http://www.alpacabreeders.org
Contact: Denise Haines, Pres.

Description: Breeders of Alpacas (an Alpaca is a close relative of the Llama); processors and distributors of Alpaca products. Promotes public awareness of Alpacas; seeks to advance the Alpaca industries. Facilitates communication and cooperation among members; conducts marketing campaigns. Participates in agricultural fairs; sponsors parades and other social activities. .

973 ■ American Border Leicester Association
PO Box 500
Cuba, IL 61427
Ph:(309)785-5058
Co. E-mail: ads.banner@sybertech.net
URL: http://www.ablasheep.org
Contact: Greg Deakin, Pres.

Description: Owners and admirers of Border Leicester sheep. Promotes Border Leicesters as a source of wool and meat. Sets breed standards and confers certification; maintains breed registry. Sponsors competitions; conducts educational programs. **Publications:** *American Border Leicester Association Quarterly News* (quarterly).

974 ■ American Brahmousin Council
PO Box 88
Whitesboro, TX 76273
Ph:(903)564-3995
Co. E-mail: info@brahmousin.org
URL: http://www.brahmousin.org
Contact: Bob Cummins, Interim Dir.

Description: Breeders of Brahmousin cattle. **Publications:** *Brahmousin Connection* (quarterly).

975 ■ American Cat Fanciers Association
PO Box 1949
Nixa, MO 65714-1949
Ph:(417)725-1530
Fax:(417)725-1533
Co. E-mail: acfa@aol.com
URL: http://www.acfacat.com
Contact: Jim Mendenhall, Pres.

Description: Breeders and exhibitors of purebred cats; individuals interested in educating the public regarding the health and welfare of domesticated cats. Maintains studbook registry and licenses cat shows and cat judges. Registers pedigreed cats. Sponsors charitable program; compiles statistics. **Publications:** *ACFA Bulletin* (7/year); *AFCA Parade of Royalty* (annual); *Clerking Manual*; *Robinson's Genetics for Cat Breeders and Veterinarians* (periodic).

976 ■ American Kennel Club
260 Madison Ave.
New York, NY 10016
Ph:(212)696-8200
Fax:(212)696-8299
Co. E-mail: info@akc.org
URL: http://www.akc.org
Contact: Dennis B. Sprung, Pres./CEO

Description: All-breed, specialty breed, obedience, and field trial dog clubs. Maintains stud book registry and pedigree records; approves standards for judging breeds eligible for registration; adopts and enforces rules governing shows, obedience trials, hunting tests, and field trials. Supervises a public and children's education program promoting responsible dog ownership. Provides free information to the public. Offers judging education; compiles statistics. **Publications:** *AKC Dog Care and Training*; *AKC Family Dog* (bimonthly); *Complete Dog Book*; *Puppies* (annual); *Pure-Bred Dogs - American Kennel Gazette* (monthly); *The Stud Book Register* (monthly).

977 ■ Ayrshire Breeders' Association of Canada–Association des Eleveurs Ayrshire du Canada
4865, boul. Laurier O
St.-Hyacinthe, QC, Canada J2S 3V4
Ph:(450)778-3535
Fax:(450)778-3531
Co. E-mail: info@ayrshire-canada.com
URL: http://www.ayrshire-canada.com
Contact: Linda Ness, Exec. Dir.

Description: Breeders of Ayrshire cattle. Promotes improvement of the Ayrshire breed; seeks to advance the dairy industry. Maintains breed registry; provides support and assistance to Ayrshire breeders. **Publications:** *Canadian Ayrshire Review* .

978 ■ Canadian Cat Association–Association Feline Canadienne
5045 Orbitor Dr., Bldg. 12, Ste. 102
Mississauga, ON, Canada L4W 4Y4
Ph:(905)232-3481
Fax:(289)232-9481
Co. E-mail: office@cca-afc.com
URL: http://www.cca-afc.com
Contact: Ken McGill, Pres.

Description: Cat breeders and fanciers. Promotes responsible pet care; seeks to improve the bloodlines of purebred cats. Serves as a clearinghouse on purebred cats; maintains breed registries; sponsors competitions.

979 ■ Canadian Kennel Club–Club Canin Canadien
200 Ronson Dr., Ste. 400
Etobicoke, ON, Canada M9W 5Z9
Ph:(416)675-5511
Free: 800-250-8040
Fax:(416)675-6506
Co. E-mail: information@ckc.ca
URL: http://www.ckc.ca
Contact: Sonny Allinson

Description: Dog owners, breeders, and enthusiasts. Promotes responsible pet ownership; seeks to improve the bloodlines of pedigreed dogs. Sponsors educational programs for dogs and dog owners; maintains breed registries; sets breed standards; holds competitions. **Publications:** *Dogs in Canada* (monthly).

980 ■ Canadian Thoroughbred Horse Society
PO Box 172
Rexdale, ON, Canada M9W 5L1
Ph:(416)675-3602
Fax:(416)675-9405
Co. E-mail: cthsont@idirect.com
URL: http://www.cthsont.com
Contact: R. Glenn Sikura, Pres.

Description: Owners and breeders of thoroughbred horses; providers of services to horse racing and the thoroughbred horse industry. Promotes a viable future for the thoroughbred industry in Canada. Serves as a clearinghouse on thoroughbred breeding, provides support and services to members including remote naming and live foal reporting. Lobbies government agencies to secure tax legislation more favorable to the industry. Operates Thoroughbred Improvement Programs, in conjunction with the provincial governments. Sponsors stakes races; compiles statistics. **Publications:** *Breeders' News* (quarterly).

981 ■ Cat Fanciers' Association
1805 Atlantic Ave.
Manasquan, NJ 08736
Ph:(732)528-9797
Fax:(732)528-7391
Co. E-mail: cfa@cfa.org
URL: http://www.cfainc.org
Contact: Jerold Hamza, Pres.

Description: Federation of all-breed and specialty cat clubs. Promotes the welfare of cats, register pedigrees, and license shows held under association rules. **Publications:** *CFA Complete Cat Book*; *Show Rules*; *Show Standards Booklet* .

982 ■ Cat Fanciers' Federation
PO Box 661
Gratis, OH 45330
Ph:(937)787-9009
Fax:(937)787-9009
Co. E-mail: lcestee@aol.com
URL: http://www.cffinc.org
Contact: Linda Neilsen, Pres.

Description: Federation of local clubs of persons who own, breed, and exhibit cats and who are interested in the general welfare of cats. Maintains records on the ancestry of cats; encourages the holding of shows; trains judges; creates and promulgates rules and standards for judging cats, holding shows, and recording ancestry. Local clubs hold annual cat shows under federation rules, usually for the benefit of humane organizations. **Publications:** *CFF Newsletter* (quarterly).

983 ■ Field Spaniel Society of America
351 E Kerley Corners Rd.
Tivoli, NY 12583

Ph:(845)756-2595
Co. E-mail: maxinereed@frontiernet.net
URL: http://fieldspaniels.org
Contact: Ms. Maxine Reed, Membership Chair/Sec.
Description: Owners and admirers of field spaniels. Promotes responsible breeding and pet ownership; seeks to increase public awareness and appreciation of field spaniels. Maintains breed registry; conducts educational and public relations activities. **Publications:** *Field Spaniel Fancier* (quarterly).

984 ■ International Generic Horse Association
PO Box 6778
San Pedro, CA 90734-6778
Co. E-mail: volunteer@equinerescue.net
URL: http://www.igha.org/index1.html
Description: Owners and breeders of horses. Promotes "a better understanding, appreciation, and development of all equine types and breeds without prejudice or fault due to any known or unknown origin, lineage or breeding." Maintains registry of horses of unknown or crossbreeding; collects data relevant to the well-being of crossbred horses. **Publications:** *IGHA/HA Catalog* (periodic); *IHG/HA Informational Brochure* (periodic).

985 ■ International Jumper Futurity
PO Box 1445
Georgetown, KY 40324
Ph:(502)535-6787
Fax:(502)535-4412
Co. E-mail: yjcoffice@youngjumpers.com
URL: http://www.youngjumpers.com
Description: Owners, breeders, and trainers of sport horses. Promotes interest and participation in show jumping and other equestrian events; seeks to improve sport horse bloodlines. Serves as a clearinghouse on North American sport horses; recognizes outstanding equestrian riders, trainers, and breeders.
.

986 ■ International Sporthorse Registry
517 DeKalb Ave.
Sycamore, IL 60178
Ph:(815)899-7803
Fax:(815)899-7823
Co. E-mail: isreg@aol.com
URL: http://www.isroldenburg.org
Description: Owners and breeders of sport horses. Seeks to improve sport horse bloodlines. Formulates and enforces standards of breed conformance; maintains breed registry. **Publications:** *Breeders Guide* (annual);Newsletter (quarterly).

987 ■ International Spotted Horse Registry Association
PO Box 412
Anderson, MO 64831-0412
Ph:(417)475-6273
Free: (866)201-3098
Co. E-mail: ishrppa@aol.com
URL: http://spottedhorses.tripod.com/index.html
Contact: Rebecca Rogers, Founder/Pres.
Description: Color registry for any/all types of spotted horses. Drafts to miniatures, grade to purebred, champion to family pet. Spots from Paints to Pintaloosas; each horse gets a permanent registration number. Conducts several programs for members and horses for year-end awards and rewards. **Publications:** *Foundation Stallions, Foundation Broodmares* (annual); *Rainbow Connection* (3/year).

988 ■ National Chincoteague Pony Association
2595 Jensen Rd.
Bellingham, WA 98226
Ph:(360)671-8338
Fax:(360)671-7603
Co. E-mail: gfreder426@aol.com
URL: http://www.pony-chincoteague.com
Contact: Gale Park Frederick
Description: Admirers of Chincoteague ponies, a rare breed of horse which developed on Chincoteague Island off the coast of Virginia. Promotes responsible horse ownership; seeks to improve the Chincoteague pony. Facilitates communication and cooperation among members; maintains breed registry; establishes standards required for breed conformation; arranges Chincoteague pony sales. .

989 ■ Navajo-Churro Sheep Association
PO Box 1994
El Prado, NM 87529
Ph:(575)751-3767
Co. E-mail: churrosheep@mac.com
URL: http://www.navajo-churrosheep.com
Contact: Connie Taylor, Registrar
Description: Owners and breeders of Navajo-Churro sheep; fiber artists and collectors of textiles. Promotes preservation the Navajo-Churro breed of sheep. Facilitates breeding of Navajo-Churro sheep and maintains breed registry. **Publications:** *Catch Pen* (quarterly); *Flockbook* (annual).

990 ■ Norwegian Forest Cat Breed Council
260 E Main St.
Alliance, OH 44601
Ph:(330)680-4070
Co. E-mail: dawn@skogeier.com
URL: http://www.nfcbc.org
Contact: Dawn M. Shiley, Sec.
Description: Breeders and owners of Norwegian Forest Cats. Works to promote healthy and beautiful cats. .

991 ■ Oldenburg Registry N.A.
517 DeKalb Ave.
Sycamore, IL 60178
Ph:(815)899-7803
Fax:(815)899-7823
Co. E-mail: isreg@aol.com
URL: http://www.isroldenburg.org
Description: Owners and breeders of modern sport horses used as dressage, hunter/jumpers, and performance horses. Seeks to improve sport horse bloodlines. Maintains breed registry; formulates and enforces standards of breed conformance. .

992 ■ Professional Handlers' Association
17017 Norbrook Dr.
Olney, MD 20832-2623
Ph:(301)924-0089
Co. E-mail: kathy@phadoghandlers.com
URL: http://www.phadoghandlers.com
Contact: Kathleen Bowser, Exec. VP
Description: Seeks to promote the interests of individuals who show purebred dogs at dog shows as a profession. Enhances the stature of professional dog handling. Provides information on purebred dogs to interested persons. Sponsors seminars and lectures. .

993 ■ Traditional Cat Association
PO Box 178
Heisson, WA 98622-0178
Co. E-mail: info@traditionalcats.com
URL: http://www.traditionalcats.com
Contact: Diana Fineran, Founder
Description: Breeders and fanciers of traditional cats. Promotes, preserves, protects, and perpetuates the traditional cat. Operates kitten referral services. Conducts educational, charitable, and research programs. Sponsors competitions and shows; compiles statistics. Maintains registry, placement services, hall of fame, and museum. **Publications:** Newsletter (monthly).

994 ■ United Kennel Club
100 E Kilgore Rd.
Portage, MI 49002-0506
Ph:(269)343-9020
Fax:(269)343-7037
Co. E-mail: registration@ukcdogs.com
URL: http://www.ukcdogs.com
Contact: Wayne R. Cavanaugh, Pres.
Description: Registry for purebred dogs. Maintains records and pedigrees and establishes rules for events. Promotes improvement of dog breeds; sponsors events to test merit and quality of individual dogs. Awards championships for outstanding dogs. Conducts seminars for show judges, masters of hounds, and for training and handling of dogs. Compiles statistics. Maintains computerized services. **Publications:** *Bloodlines* (monthly); *Coonhound Bloodlines* (monthly); *Hunting Retriever Magazine* (bimonthly).

REFERENCE WORKS

995 ■ *Cat Fanciers' Association—Yearbook*
Pub: Cat Fanciers' Association Inc.
Released: Annual, Latest edition 2010. **Price:** $40, individuals. **Publication Includes:** List of cat clubs, cat breeders. **Entries Include:** Name, address.

996 ■ "No-Shed Dogs Lead the Way to Big Growth" in *Business Courier* (Vol. 26, January 8, 2010, No. 38, pp. 1)
Pub: American City Business Journals, Inc.
Ed: Lucy May. **Description:** Ed Lukacevic of Grant County, Kentucky is developing Dinovite, a dietary supplement that minimizes shedding and scratching in dogs. Statistical data included.

997 ■ *QuickBooks for the New Bean Counter: Business Owner's Guide 2006*
Pub: Wheatmark
Ed: Joseph L. Catallini. **Released:** July 2006. **Price:** $21.95. **Description:** Profile of QuickBooks software, offering insight into using the software's accounting and bookkeeping functions.

998 ■ "Shear Profit" in *Crain's Cleveland Business* (Vol. 28, October 29, 2007, No. 43, pp. 3)
Pub: Crain Communications, Inc.
Ed: David Bennett. **Description:** Alpaca farms are becoming a very profitable business for a number of Northeast Ohio entrepreneurs due to the high return on initial investments, tax incentives and the rise in demand for the animals. Ohio leads the country in the number of alpaca farms with roughly one-third located in Northeast Ohio.

999 ■ "VC Boosts WorkForce; Livonia Software Company to Add Sales, Marketing Staff" in *Crain's Detroit Business* (March 24, 2008)
Pub: Crain Communications, Inc.
Ed: Tom Henderson. **Description:** WorkForce Software Inc., a company that provides software to manage payroll processes and oversee compliance with state and federal regulations and with union rules, plans to use an investment of $5.5 million in venture capital to hire more sales and marketing staff.

TRADE PERIODICALS

1000 ■ *ACFA Bulletin*
Pub: American Cat Fanciers Association Inc.
Released: 7/year. **Description:** Contains Association news, show schedules, news about the officers and judges, and articles of interest to cat fanciers.

1001 ■ *American Salers*
Pub: American Salers Association
Contact: Dean Pike, Field Rep.
E-mail: dcssalers@actcom.net
Released: Quarterly. **Description:** Trade magazine for the livestock industry. Represents Salers cattle breed. Official publication of the American Salers Association.

1002 ■ *Charolais Journal*
Pub: American-International Charolais Association
Released: Monthly. **Price:** $75 U.S.; $100 1st class; $125 other countries first class; $100 other countries. **Description:** International magazine on Charolais cattle, including special interest articles, show/sale reports, and association news.

1003 ■ *Feed-Lot*
Pub: Feed-Lot Magazine
Contact: Robert Strong, Pres./Publisher/Ed.
E-mail: rstrong@st-tel.net
Released: Bimonthly. **Price:** $50 other countries. **Description:** Trade magazine covering feedlot and cattle feeder information.

1004 ■ *Miniature Donkey Talk*
Pub: Pheasant Meadow Farm
Ed: Bonnie Gross, Editor. **Released:** Bimonthly. **Price:** $32 by mail 1st class; $60 two years mailed 1st class; $35 Canada; $65 Canada 2 years; $55 other countries. **Description:** Trade magazine covering animal health care, management, and training.

1005 ■ *Palmetto Poultry Life*
Pub: South Carolina Poultry Federation
Released: Quarterly. **Price:** $20 Free to qualified subscribers; $20. **Description:** Trade magazine for the poultry industry.

1006 ■ *The Rottweiler Quarterly*
Pub: Print It Design and Publishing, Inc.
Released: Quarterly. **Price:** $40; $60 first class; $75 two years; $55 outside U.S.; $100 via airmail. **Description:** Magazine covering the training, breeding, health, and showing of rottweilers.

1007 ■ *The Royal Spaniels*
Pub: Premiere Publications
Contact: John Garrison
Ed: Holly Cornwell, Editor. **Released:** Quarterly. **Price:** $45; $55 Canada; $80 other countries airmail. **Description:** Consumer magazine covering the breeding and exhibiting of show dogs of the breeds, Cavalier King Charles Spaniels and King Charles Spaniels.

1008 ■ *Sheltie Pacesetter*
Pub: Sheltie Pacesetter
Contact: Nancy Lee Cathcart, Editor & Publisher
Released: Quarterly. **Price:** $61.95; $109.20 first class mail; $77.70 Canada and Mexico; $124.95 Canada and Mexico first class mail; $82.95 other countries surface mail; $145.95 other countries first class mail; $21 single issue; $25.73 single issue first class mail; $22.05 single issue Canada. **Description:** Trade magazine covering Shetland Sheepdogs (Shelties).

1009 ■ *Terrier Type*
Pub: Dan Kiedrowski Co.
Contact: Shawn Nichols, Editor & Publisher
E-mail: editor@terriertype.com
Released: Monthly. **Price:** $45 regular/surface; $75 first class; $75 Canada first/class airmail. **Description:** Trade magazine covering show dogs for breeders, handlers, and owners.

VIDEOCASSETTES/ AUDIOCASSETTES

1010 ■ *Breeding by Artificial Insemination*
Phoenix Learning Group
2349 Chaffee Dr.
St. Louis, MO 63146-3306
Ph:(314)569-0211
Free: 800-221-1274
Fax:(314)569-2834
URL: http://www.phoenixlearninggroup.com
Released: 1990. **Price:** $39.95. **Description:** Discusses how to breed horses by using the technique of artificial insemination. **Availability:** VHS.

1011 ■ *Dog Showmanship: The Winning Edge*
ESPN Home Video
ESPN Plz., 935 Middle St.
Bristol, CT 06010
Ph:(860)766-2000
Fax:(860)585-2213
URL: http://www.espn.go.com
Released: 198?. **Price:** $39.95. **Description:** Is your dog good enough to show? This video demonstrates grooming and nutrition, as well as gaiting, ring patterns, and stacking. Also includes advice from top breeders. **Availability:** VHS.

1012 ■ *The Inaugural Purina/CFA International Cat Show*
Bergwall Productions, Inc.
1 DIckinson Drive, Brandywine BUilding 5, Ste. 105
PO Box 1481
Chadds Ford, PA 19317
Ph:(610)361-0334
Free: 800-934-8696
Fax:(610)361-0092
URL: http://www.bergwall.com
Released: 1990. **Description:** This video documents the largest pedigreed cat show ever held in North America, which took place in St. Louis, November 19 and 20 of 1988. **Availability:** VHS.

1013 ■ *Maintenance and Show Grooming*
Aspen Publishers
7201 McKinney Circ.
Frederick, MD 21704
Ph:(301)698-7100
Free: 800-234-1660
Fax:800-901-9075
URL: http://www.aspenpublishers.com
Released: 1990. **Description:** This tape features a complete visual text on the basics of daily show horse care. **Availability:** VHS.

1014 ■ *The Westminster Kennel Club Dog Care Guide*
Paramount Home Video
5555 Melrose Ave.
Los Angeles, CA 90038
Ph:(323)956-5000
URL: http://www.paramount.com
Released: 1989. **Price:** $19.95. **Description:** A high-pedigree instructional tape explaining how to select, care for and properly train a dog. **Availability:** VHS.

LIBRARIES

1015 ■ American Kennel Club Library
260 Madison Ave., 4th Fl.
New York, NY 10016
Ph:(212)696-8245
Fax:(212)696-8281
Co. E-mail: library@akc.org
URL: http://www.akc.org/about/library/index.cfm
Contact: Barbara Kolk, Libn.
Scope: Dogs - breeds, training, health, literature, art. **Services:** Copying; Library open to the public by appointment. **Holdings:** 18,000 volumes; VF drawers of clippings; videocassettes; fine art collection; 5 dissertations. **Subscriptions:** 300 journals and other serials.

1016 ■ Bloodstock Research Information Services, Inc. Library
801 Corporate Dr., 3rd Fl.
PO Box 4097
Lexington, KY 40544-4097
Ph:(859)223-4444
Free: 800-354-9206
Fax:(859)223-7024
Co. E-mail: brisinfo@brisnet.com
URL: http://www.brisnet.com
Contact: Becky Seabrook
Scope: Thoroughbred horses, horse breeding, horse racing, horse and farm management. **Services:** Library not open to the public. **Holdings:** 1000 bound volumes. **Subscriptions:** 20 journals and other serials.

1017 ■ Cleveland Public Library–Science and Technology Department
Louis Stokes Wing, 3rd Fl.
325 Superior Ave.
Cleveland, OH 44114-1271
Ph:(216)623-2932
Co. E-mail: scitech@cpl.org
URL: http://www.cpl.org/TheLibrary/SubjectsCollections/ScienceTechnology.aspx
Contact: Maureen Mullin, Mgr.
Scope: Engineering, science, metallurgy, aeronautics, mechanics, chemistry, geology, environment, agriculture, history of science and technology, natural history, handicrafts, photography. **Services:** Interlibrary loan; copying; department open to the public. **Holdings:** 347,249 volumes; 380 VF drawers; 1239 CD-ROMs; 21,322 microfiche; 795 reels of microfilm.

1018 ■ Glendale Public Library Special Collections Room
222 E. Harvard St.
Glendale, CA 91205
Ph:(818)548-2037
Fax:(818)548-7225
Co. E-mail: centlibref@ci.glendale.ca.us
URL: http://glendalepubliclibrary.org
Contact: Cindy Cleary, Dir. of Libs.
Scope: Glendale and area history, California history, cats and cat genealogy. **Services:** Copying; room open to the public for reference use only (call for open hours or appointments). **Holdings:** 400 bound periodical volumes; city departmental reports; archives; microfilm, clippings file. **Subscriptions:** 11 current journals and other serials.

1019 ■ National Animal Control Association–Research Library
PO Box 480851
Kansas City, MO 64148
Ph:(913)768-1319
Fax:(913)768-1378
Co. E-mail: naca@nacanet.org
URL: http://www.nacanet.org
Contact: John Mays, Exec.Dir.
Scope: Animal control, bites and attacks, rabies, euthanasia, humane education, officer training. **Services:** Copying; Library open to the public. **Holdings:** 85 books; 50 bound periodical volumes; 10,000 reports; videocassettes. **Subscriptions:** 15 journals and other serials; 1 newspaper.

1020 ■ Oregon Thoroughbred Breeders Association Library
PO Box 17248
Portland, OR 97217
Ph:(503)285-0658
Fax:(503)285-0659
Co. E-mail: info@oregontoba.com
URL: http://www.oregontoba.com
Contact: Wendie Hayes-Pounds, Exec.Dir.
Scope: Thoroughbreds - life, breeding, racing. **Services:** Copying; Library open to the public. **Holdings:** 200 books; 3 bound periodical volumes; 50 reports; microfiche; CD-ROMs. **Subscriptions:** 15 journals and other serials; 2 newspapers.

1021 ■ Second Chance Animal Center Library
PO Box 620
Shaftsbury, VT 05262-0620
Ph:(802)375-2898
Fax:(802)375-0235
Co. E-mail: secondch@sover.net
URL: http://www.2ndchanceanimalcenter.org/
Scope: Animals - welfare, rights, farm, dog and cat care. **Services:** Library open to the public. **Holdings:** 600 books; videocassettes. **Subscriptions:** 14 journals and other serials; 3 newspapers.

1022 ■ U.S. Dept. of Defense–Central Repository for Military Working Dog Records–Archives (DOD D)
DOD Dog Center
Lackland AFB, TX 78236-5000
Ph:(512)671-3402
Scope: Military working dogs - training, working assignments, veterinary records.

1023 ■ Voice for Animals, Inc. Library
PO Box 120095
San Antonio, TX 78212
Ph:(210)737-3138
Co. E-mail: voice@voiceforanimals.org
URL: http://www.voiceforanimals.org/
Scope: Animal rights; vegetarianism. **Services:** Library not open to the public. **Holdings:** 200 books; newsletters; videocassettes.

RESEARCH CENTERS

1024 ■ University of California, Davis–Veterinary Genetics Laboratory
School of Veterinary Medicine
1 Shields Ave.
Davis, CA 95616-8744

Ph:(530)752-2211
Fax:(530)752-3556
Co. E-mail: karnelson@ucdavis.edu
URL: http://www.vgl.ucdavis.edu
Contact: Karen Nelson, Mgr.
E-mail: karnelson@ucdavis.edu
Scope: Genetics, genomic and forensic research of domestic and wildlife animal species, including horses, cattle, sheep, goats, camelids, dogs, cats, wild felids and canids, bears, birds and primates. Activities include DNA genotyping and mitochondria sequencing for applications in animal identification, parentage verification, forensic analyses, population structure and genetic diversity.

Animal Clinic

START-UP INFORMATION

1025 ■ "Elanco Challenges Bayer's Advantage, K9 Advantix Ad Claims" in *Pet Product News* (Vol. 64, November 2010, No. 11, pp. 11)
Pub: BowTie Inc.

Description: Elanco Animal Health has disputed Bayer Animal Health's print and Web advertising claims involving its flea, tick, and mosquito control products Advantage and K9 Advantix. The National Advertising Division of the Council of Better Business Bureaus recommended the discontinuation of ads, while Bayer Animal Health reiterated its commitment to self-regulation.

ASSOCIATIONS AND OTHER ORGANIZATIONS

1026 ■ American Animal Hospital Association
12575 W Bayaud Ave.
Lakewood, CO 80228
Ph:(303)986-2800
Free: 800-883-6301
Fax:(303)986-1700
Co. E-mail: info@aahanet.org
URL: http://www.aahanet.org
Contact: Kate S. Knutson, VP

Description: Represents veterinary care providers who treat companion animals. Accredits veterinary hospitals throughout the U.S. and Canada. Conducts stringent accreditation process that covers patient care, client service and medical protocols. **Publications:** *Journal of the American Animal Hospital Association* (bimonthly); *NEWStat* (biweekly); *TRENDS Magazine* (bimonthly);Membership Directory (annual).

1027 ■ American Veterinary Medical Association
1931 N Meacham Rd., Ste. 100
Schaumburg, IL 60173-4340
Ph:(847)925-8070
Free: 800-248-2862
Fax:(847)925-1329
Co. E-mail: avmainfo@avma.org
URL: http://www.avma.org
Contact: Dr. Larry Kornegay DVM, Pres.

Description: Professional society of veterinarians. Conducts educational and research programs. Provides placement service. Sponsors American Veterinary Medical Association Foundation and Educational Commission for Foreign Veterinary Graduates. Compiles statistics. Accredits veterinary medical education programs and veterinary technician education programs. **Publications:** *American Journal of Veterinary Research* (monthly); *AVMA Convention Notes* (annual); *AVMA Disaster Preparedness and Response Guide*; *AVMA Membership Directory and Resource Manual* (annual); *Economic Report on Veterinarians and Veterinary Practices* (semiannual); *Journal of the American Veterinary Medical Association* (semimonthly); *U.S. Pet Ownership and Demographic Sourcebook* (semiannual).

1028 ■ Animal Health Institute
1325 G St. NW, Ste. 700
Washington, DC 20005-3127
Ph:(202)637-2440
Fax:(202)393-1667
Co. E-mail: rphillips@ahi.org
URL: http://www.ahi.org
Contact: Alexander S. Mathews, Pres./CEO

Description: Represents manufacturers of animal health products (vaccines, pharmaceuticals, and feed additives used in modern food production; and medicines for household pets). Works with government agencies and legislators; prepares position papers; and compiles and disseminates information. Sponsors AHI Foundation. .

1029 ■ Canadian Veterinary Medical Association–Association Canadienne des Medecins Veterinaires
339 Booth St.
Ottawa, ON, Canada K1R 7K1
Ph:(613)236-1162
Fax:(613)236-9681
Co. E-mail: admin@cvma-acmv.org
URL: http://canadianveterinarians.net/index.aspx
Contact: Mr. Jost Am Rhyn, Exec. Dir.

Description: Veterinarians in Canada. Encourages excellence in the field of veterinary medicine; seeks to increase awareness of the importance of animals; represents the interests of members. **Publications:** *Canadian Journal of Veterinary Research* (quarterly); *Canadian Veterinary Journal* (monthly); *CVMA Directory* (annual). **Telecommunication Services:** electronic mail, jamrhyn@cvma-acmv.org.

1030 ■ Cornell Feline Health Center
Cornell University
College of Veterinary Medicine
PO Box 13
Ithaca, NY 14853-6401
Ph:(607)253-3414
Free: 800-548-8937
Fax:(607)253-3419
Co. E-mail: kmm8@cornell.edu
URL: http://www.vet.cornell.edu/fhc
Contact: Dr. Colin R. Parrish PhD, Dir.

Description: Professionals devoted to cats. Seeks to unravel the mysteries of feline health, nutrition, and behavior. Works to educate veterinarians and cat owners, and to aid veterinarians when new or unknown diseases occur. Provides educational programs. **Publications:** *CatWatch* (monthly); *The Cornell Book of Cats, Second Edition*; *Dog Watch*; *Pre-Veterinary* (bimonthly).

1031 ■ Vaccine and Infectious Disease Organization - International Vaccine Centre
University of Saskatchewan
120 Veterinary Rd.
Saskatoon, SK, Canada S7N 5E3
Ph:(306)966-7465
Fax:(306)966-7478
Co. E-mail: info@vido.org
URL: http://www.vido.org
Contact: Dr. Andrew Potter, CEO/Dir.

Description: Promotes animal health through diagnosis and prevention of production-limiting diseases. Conducts research focusing on development of new vaccines to better treat infectious diseases and the discovery and application of biotechnologies. Serves as a clearinghouse on commercial veterinary diagnosis and treatment techniques; makes available laboratory and field study services. Makes available educational and extension services.

REFERENCE WORKS

1032 ■ *American Veterinary Medical Association—Directory and Resource Manual*
Pub: American Veterinary Medical Association

Released: Annual, January; Latest edition 2008-2009. **Price:** $150, nonmembers in USA and their territories; $175, nonmembers other countries. **Covers:** AVMA members; code of ethics, AVMA bylaws. **Entries Include:** Name, spouse's name, address, email, phones and codes for practice activity, type of employer, institution granting degree, and year received. **Arrangement:** Geographical and alphabetical. **Indexes:** Alphabetical.

1033 ■ "Best In Show" in *Pet Product News* (Vol. 64, November 2010, No. 11, pp. 20)
Pub: BowTie Inc.

Ed: Lizett Bond. **Description:** Cherrybrook Premium Pet Supplies offers an expanded array of quality holistic products and is staffed by people who possess wide knowledge of these products. Aside from receiving the Outstanding Holistic Approach award, Cherrybrook has opened three stores in New Jersey. How a holistic approach to service kept customers coming back is discussed.

1034 ■ "Capture New Markets" in *Pet Product News* (Vol. 64, December 2010, No. 12, pp. 12)
Pub: BowTie Inc.

Ed: Ethan Mizer. **Description:** Flea and tick treatments are among the product categories that can be offered in order to clinch new markets. With the help of manufacturers, pet store retailers are encouraged to educate themselves about these products considering that capturing markets involves variations in customer perceptions. Retailers would then be deemed as resources and sources for these products.

1035 ■ "Experts Strive to Educate on Proper Pet Diets" in *Pet Product News* (Vol. 64, November 2010, No. 11, pp. 40)
Pub: BowTie Inc.

Ed: John Hustace Walker. **Description:** Pet supply manufacturers have been bundling small mammal food and treats with educational sources to help retailers avoid customer misinformation. This action has been motivated by the customer's quest to seek proper nutritional advice for their small mammal pets.

1036 ■ "Food as Nature Intended" in *Pet Product News* (Vol. 64, November 2010, No. 11, pp. 30)
Pub: BowTie Inc.
Ed: Nikki Moustaki. **Description:** Dog owners have been extending their health-consciousness to their pets by seeking natural products that will address their pets' raw food diet. Retailers response to this trend are outlined.

1037 ■ "Must Work for Food" in *Pet Product News* (Vol. 64, November 2010, No. 11, pp. 24)
Pub: BowTie Inc.
Ed: Wendy Bedwell-Wilson. **Description:** Pet supply retailers can benefit from stocking foods and treats that address obesity, which according to the American Veterinary Medical Association, has become the most prevalent nutritional disorder in dogs. With the rise in dog obesity, products like work-for-their food toys have been sought by dog owners.

1038 ■ "No-Shed Dogs Lead the Way to Big Growth" in *Business Courier* (Vol. 26, January 8, 2010, No. 38, pp. 1)
Pub: American City Business Journals, Inc.
Ed: Lucy May. **Description:** Ed Lukacevic of Grant County, Kentucky is developing Dinovite, a dietary supplement that minimizes shedding and scratching in dogs. Statistical data included.

1039 ■ "Online Pet Medication Store Supports Free Vaccinations for Cats" in *Internet Wire* (August 31, 2010)
Pub: Comtex
Description: Pethealth Inc., The Petango Store will help to support The Humane Society of Tampa Bay's efforts by offering free feline vaccinations for the cat's entire lifetime that is adopted between September 1, 2010 and February 28, 2010. The cat must be one year or older at time of adoption.

1040 ■ "Pet Kiosk Offers Search Options" in *Times-News* (October 14, 2010)
Pub: Times-News Publishing Company
Ed: Roselee Papandrea. **Description:** Chameleon Pet Kiosk located at the Spay and Neuter Clinic of Alamance County in Burlington, North Carolina allows users to see and read about animals available for adoption at the center.

1041 ■ "Solutions for the Frustrating Feline" in *Pet Product News* (Vol. 64, November 2010, No. 11, pp. 46)
Pub: BowTie Inc.
Ed: Lori Luechtefeld. **Description:** Products that can help customers deal with problematic cat behaviors, such as out-of-the-box urination and scratching are described. Information on such products including litter box deodorants and disposable scratchers is provided. Feline territorial behaviors can also be addressed by pheromone products that can calm hyperactive cats.

1042 ■ "Supplements Mix Nutrition With Convenience" in *Pet Product News* (Vol. 64, November 2010, No. 11, pp. 44)
Pub: BowTie Inc.
Ed: Karen Shugart. **Description:** Pet supply manufacturers have been making supplements and enhanced foods that improve mineral consumption, boost bone density, and sharpen appetite in herps. Customers seem to enjoy the convenience as particular herps demands are being addressed by these offerings. Features of other supplements and enhanced foods for herps are described.

1043 ■ "Sustaining Health" in *Pet Product News* (Vol. 64, November 2010, No. 11, pp. 28)
Pub: BowTie Inc.
Ed: Angela Pham. **Description:** How pet supply retailers have responded to dog owners' interest in health supplements and their ingredients is discussed. Dog owners are showing interest in the ingredients inside the supplements and are reading labels. Retailers must now prove the beneficial effects of these ingredients in order to make the sale.

1044 ■ "Tapping the 'Well' in Wellness" in *Pet Product News* (Vol. 64, November 2010, No. 11, pp. 1)
Pub: BowTie Inc.
Ed: Wendy-Bedwell Wilson. **Description:** Healthy food and treats are among the leading wellness products being sought by customers from specialty retailers to keep their pets healthy. With this demand for pet wellness products, retailers suggest making sure that staff know key ingredients to emphasize to customers. Other insights into this trend and ways to engage customers are discussed.

TRADE PERIODICALS

1045 ■ *AHI Newsletter*
Pub: Animal Health Institute
Ed: Released: 4/year. **Price:** Free. **Description:** Discusses developments of significance to animal health, livestock, and veterinary industries. Includes legislative and regulatory updates and news of research.

1046 ■ *American Journal of Veterinary Research*
Pub: American Veterinary Medical Association
Contact: Gussie J. Tessier PhD, Asst. Ed.
Released: Monthly. **Price:** $245; $255 other countries; $35 single issue; $40 single issue other Country. **Description:** Veterinary research on nutrition and diseases of domestic, wild, and furbearing animals.

1047 ■ *Animal News*
Pub: Morris Animal Foundation
Contact: C. Lester
Ed: Carissa Lester, Editor, clester@morrisanimalfoundation.org. **Released:** 3/year. **Price:** Included in membership; Free. **Description:** Contains articles about Morris Animal Foundation's work to ensure a healthier tomorrow for animals.

1048 ■ *AVMA Members' Magazine*
Pub: Alberta Veterinary Medical Association (AVMA)
Ed: Midge Landals, Editor, midge.landals@avma.ab.ca. **Released:** Bimonthly. **Price:** Included in membership. **Description:** Features, letters to the editor, a calendar of events, reports of meetings, news of educational opportunities, and job listings.

1049 ■ *Canadian Veterinary Journal*
Pub: Canadian Veterinary Medical Association
Contact: Heather Broughton, Managing Editor
Released: Monthly. **Price:** $170 Canada; $180 other countries. **Description:** Professional journal for veterinarians.

1050 ■ *Compendium on Continuing Education for the Practicing Veterinarian*
Pub: Veterinary Learning Systems
Contact: Tracey Giannouris, Exec. Ed.
E-mail: tgiannouris@vetlearn.com
Released: Monthly. **Description:** Refereed journal reviewing and updating topics in medicine and surgery for the veterinarian in practice.

1051 ■ *CVO Update*
Pub: College of Veterinarians of Ontario (CVO)
Contact: Beth Ready, Assistant to Editor
E-mail: bready@cvo.org
Released: Quarterly. **Price:** Free. **Description:** Covers veterinary-related issues.

1052 ■ *Feline Health Topics*
Pub: Cornell Feline Health Center
Contact: Dr. James Richards, Director
Released: Quarterly. **Price:** $30, U.S.; $1, single issue; $35. **Description:** Focuses on diseases of cats, examining particular diseases in depth in each issue. Provides news of disease outbreaks, recommendations for treatment, and news of research. Publishes news and activities of the Center, and social issues pertaining to veterinarians.

1053 ■ *Humane News*
Pub: Associated Humane Societies
Ed: Roseann Trezza, Editor. **Released:** Monthly. **Price:** Included in membership. **Description:** Reports on news of the programs and activities of humane societies seeking to assist wild and domestic animals. Provides legislative updates on bills supporting animal welfare.

1054 ■ *Journal of the American Animal Hospital Association*
Pub: American Animal Hospital Association
Contact: Dr. Lisa Fulton, Editorial Review Board
Released: Bimonthly. **Price:** $107 institutions and non-members; $107 institutions, Canada and non-members; $107 institutions, other countries and non-members. **Description:** Scientific and educational journal that publishes information for the practice of small animal medicine and surgery.

1055 ■ *Journal of the American Veterinary Medical Association*
Pub: American Veterinary Medical Association
Contact: Dr. Kurt J. Matushek, Editor-in-Chief
Released: Semimonthly. **Price:** $210 nonmembers; $230 other countries; $25 single issue; $30 single issue foreign. **Description:** Trade journal for veterinary medical professionals.

1056 ■ *Miniature Donkey Talk*
Pub: Pheasant Meadow Farm
Ed: Bonnie Gross, Editor. **Released:** Bimonthly. **Price:** $32 by mail 1st class; $60 two years mailed 1st class; $35 Canada; $65 Canada 2 years; $55 other countries. **Description:** Trade magazine covering animal health care, management, and training.

1057 ■ *Protecting Animals*
Pub: American Humane
Released: Quarterly. **Description:** Covers animal control and sheltering issues. Reports on ideas, technologies, and procedures to enhance and expand shelter programs and animal care.

1058 ■ *TRENDS Magazine*
Pub: American Animal Hospital Association
Contact: Stephanie Pates, Advertising Mgr
E-mail: stephanie.pates@aahanet.org
Ed: Constance Hardesty, Editor. **Released:** 6-8/yr. **Price:** $60 U.S. and Canada; $70 other countries; $20 single issue. **Description:** Professional magazine covering the management of small animal veterinary practices.

1059 ■ *Veterinary Clinics*
Pub: Elsevier
Contact: Prof. Simon A. Turner, Consulting Ed.
Released: 3/yr. **Price:** $466 institutions, other countries; $320 other countries; $159 students, other countries; $373 institutions; $117 students; $277 Canada; $238; $159 students, Canada; $466 institutions, Canada. **Description:** Journal reviewing current techniques, drugs, and diagnostic and treatment techniques in veterinary medicine.

1060 ■ *Your Dog*
Pub: Tufts University
Contact: Linda Ross D.V.M., Editor-in-Chief
Ed: Gloria Parkinson, Editor. **Released:** Monthly. **Price:** $20, individuals. **Description:** Publishes medical and behavioral advice and tips on dogs by veterinarians. Recurring features include columns titled My Dog and Chewing It Over.

TRADE SHOWS AND CONVENTIONS

1061 ■ American Veterinary Medical Association Annual Convention
American Veterinary Medical Association
1931 N. Meacham Rd., Ste. 100
Schaumburg, IL 60173-4360
Ph:800-248-2862
Fax:(847)925-1329
Co. E-mail: avmainfo@avma.org
URL: http://www.avma.org
Released: Annual. **Audience:** Veterinarians. **Principal Exhibits:** Products, materials, equipment, data, and services for veterinary medicine. **Dates and Locations:** 2011 Jul 16-19, St. Louis, MO; 2012 Aug 04-07, San Diego, CA; 2013 Jul 20-23, Chicago, IL.

1062 ■ Florida Veterinary Medical Association Annual Meeting
Florida Veterinary Medical Association
7131 Lake Ellenor Dr.
Orlando, FL 32809
Ph:(407)851-3862
Free: 800-992-3862
Fax:(407)240-3710
Co. E-mail: info@fvma.com
URL: http://www.fvma.com
Released: Annual. **Audience:** Veterinarians and technicians. **Principal Exhibits:** Scientific drugs and equipment related to veterinary medicine. **Dates and Locations:** 2011 Apr 29 - May 01, Orlando, FL.

1063 ■ GEOTECH EXPO 2011
Artenergy Publishing
Via Antonio Gramsi, 57
20032 Cormano, Italy
Ph:39 2 66306866
URL: http://www.artenergy.it/
Released: Biennial. **Audience:** Energy, water, and utility companies; mining companies; contractors; engineers; government agencies; environmental and civil protection agencies. **Principal Exhibits:** Platforms and equipment for onsite geotechnical investigations, perforation for deep foundations and horizontal directions, instrumentation and equipment for environmental analysis, land monitoring and restoration.

1064 ■ Missouri Veterinary Medical Association Annual Convention
Missouri Veterinary Medical Association
2500 Country Club Dr.
Jefferson City, MO 65109
Ph:(573)636-8612
Fax:(573)659-7175
Co. E-mail: mvma@mvma.us
URL: http://www.mvma.us
Released: Annual. **Audience:** Veterinarians; veterinary medicine students, spouses, and veterinary technicians. **Principal Exhibits:** Veterinary instruments, surgical equipment, pharmaceuticals, dog food, publications, and animal care products.

1065 ■ Ohio Veterinary Medical Association/ Midwest Veterinary Conference
Ohio Veterinary Medical Association
3168 Riverside Dr.
Columbus, OH 43221
Ph:(614)486-7253
Free: 800-662-OVMA
Fax:(614)486-1325
Co. E-mail: ohiovma@ohiovma.org
URL: http://www.ohiovma.org
Released: Annual. **Audience:** Veterinarians, technicians, students, and suppliers of veterinary medicine, hospital staff, spouses, hospital managers. **Principal Exhibits:** Veterinary supplies.

1066 ■ Western Veterinary Conference
Western Veterinary Conference
2425 E Oquendo Rd.
Las Vegas, NV 89120-2406
Ph:(702)739-6698
Fax:(702)739-6420
Co. E-mail: info@westernveterinary.org
URL: http://www.wvc.org
Released: Annual. **Audience:** Veterinarians, veterinary technicians, and veterinary hospital management. **Principal Exhibits:** Veterinary equipment, supplies, and services, including drugs. **Dates and Locations:** 2011 Feb 20-24, Las Vegas, NV.

1067 ■ Wisconsin Veterinary Medical Association Annual Convention
Wisconsin Veterinary Medical Association
301 N Broom St.
Madison, WI 53703
Ph:(608)257-3665
Fax:(608)257-8989
Co. E-mail: wvma@wvma.org
URL: http://www.wvma.org
Released: Annual. **Audience:** Veterinarians, certified veterinary technicians, veterinary students, veterinary practice managers, spouses. **Principal Exhibits:** Veterinary supplies, pharmaceuticals, pet food, business systems, and record-keeping equipment. **Dates and Locations:** 2011 Oct 20-23, Madison, WI.

CONSULTANTS

1068 ■ Thinnes & Dutton P.C.
121 W Locust St., Ste. 304
Davenport, IA 52803-2827
Ph:(563)323-6622
Fax:(563)323-1232
Contact: Teresa A. Thinnes, President
Scope: Practice management consultant for physicians, dentists, osteopathic physicians, and veterinarians. Services are adapted to each client's individual needs and desires.

COMPUTER SYSTEMS/ SOFTWARE

1069 ■ DentalWare
Data Strategies, Inc.
9645 Granite Ridge Dr., Ste. 230
San Diego, CA 92123
Ph:(858)514-0300
Free: 800-875-0480
Fax:(858)514-1210
Co. E-mail: sale@e-dsi.com
URL: http://www.e-dsi.com/
Description: Available for IBM computers and MS-DOS compatibles. Software contains a series of programs for veterinary office management, including billing, posting payments and charges, and statements and insurance forms.

1070 ■ VetLogic
Data Strategies, Inc.
9645 Granite Ridge Ste. 230
San Diego, CA 92123
Ph:(858)514-0300
Free: 800-875-0480
Fax:(858)514-0318
Co. E-mail: sale@e-dsi.com
URL: http://www.e-dsi.com/
Price: $2000.00. **Description:** Available for IBM computers and MS-DOS compatibles. System providing management reports, accounts receivable, patient data storage, and other functions.

LIBRARIES

1071 ■ Animal Medical Center Library
510 E. 62nd St.
New York, NY 10021
Ph:(212)838-8100
Co. E-mail: info@amcny.org
URL: http://www.amcny.org
Scope: Veterinary medicine, medicine. **Services:** Interlibrary loan; medical editing; Library open to the public by appointment. **Holdings:** 1000 books; 1000 bound periodical volumes; 500 periodical volumes on microfiche. **Subscriptions:** 75 journals and other serials.

1072 ■ Auburn University–Charles Allen Cary Veterinary Medical Library
College of Veterinary Medical Complex
Greene Hall, Rm. 101
Auburn University, AL 36849
Ph:(334)844-1749
Fax:(334)844-1758
Co. E-mail: vmedlib@auburn.edu
URL: http://www.lib.auburn.edu/vetmed/
Contact: Bob Buchanan, Libn.
Scope: Veterinary medicine. **Services:** Interlibrary loan; copying; Library open to the public. **Holdings:** 30,000 volumes. **Subscriptions:** 120 active paper serials; 7000 online journals and other serials.

1073 ■ District of Columbia Public Library–Technology and Science Division
Martin Luther King Memorial Library
901 G St., NW, Rm. 107
Washington, DC 20001
Ph:(202)727-1175
Fax:(202)727-1129
Co. E-mail: commentssuggestions.dcpl@dc.gov
URL: http://dclibrary.org
Contact: Lessie O. Mtewa, Asst.Libn.
Scope: Automobile and appliance repair, botany, cookery, general science, geology, genetics, manufacturing, nutrition, paleontology, pet care, printing, zoology, mathematics, computer science, biology, domestic arts, earth science, chemistry and chemical technology, physics, engineering, agriculture, gardening, medicine, psychiatry, astronomy, consumer information, health, veterinary science, physical anthropology. **Services:** Interlibrary loan; copying; Library open to the public. **Holdings:** 92,127 books; 2500 bound periodical volumes; 5755 microforms; 65 VF drawers. **Subscriptions:** 300 journals and other serials.

1074 ■ Massachusetts Society for the Prevention of Cruelty to Animals MSPCA–Angell Memorial Animal Hospital Veterinary Library
350 S. Huntington Ave.
Boston, MA 02130-4803
Ph:(617)522-7282
Fax:(617)522-4885
Co. E-mail: angellquestions@mspca.org
URL: http://www.mspca.org/site/PageServer
Contact: Judi Beland, Libn.
Scope: Veterinary medicine, conservation, zoology, pet care, humane education, animal welfare, animal rights. **Services:** Library open to the public by appointment. **Holdings:** 2000 volumes. **Subscriptions:** 50 journals and other serials.

1075 ■ National Animal Control Association–Research Library
PO Box 480851
Kansas City, MO 64148
Ph:(913)768-1319
Fax:(913)768-1378
Co. E-mail: naca@nacanet.org
URL: http://www.nacanet.org
Contact: John Mays, Exec.Dir.
Scope: Animal control, bites and attacks, rabies, euthanasia, humane education, officer training. **Services:** Copying; Library open to the public. **Holdings:** 85 books; 50 bound periodical volumes; 10,000 reports; videocassettes. **Subscriptions:** 15 journals and other serials; 1 newspaper.

1076 ■ Ross University–School of Veterinary Medicine–Stanley Mark Dennis Veterinary Library (499 T)
499 Thornall St., Ste. 1101
Edison, NJ 08837-2285
Ph:(869)465-4161
Contact: Cheryle Cumberbath, Lib.Dir.
Scope: Veterinary medicine. **Services:** Interlibrary loan; copying; Library open to the public with restrictions (closed weekends and two weeks prior to finals). **Holdings:** 6000 volumes. **Subscriptions:** 107 journals and other serials.

1077 ■ Second Chance Animal Center Library
PO Box 620
Shaftsbury, VT 05262-0620
Ph:(802)375-2898
Fax:(802)375-0235
Co. E-mail: secondch@sover.net
URL: http://www.2ndchanceanimalcenter.org/
Scope: Animals - welfare, rights, farm, dog and cat care. **Services:** Library open to the public. **Holdings:** 600 books; videocassettes. **Subscriptions:** 14 journals and other serials; 3 newspapers.

1078 ■ Voice for Animals, Inc. Library
PO Box 120095
San Antonio, TX 78212
Ph:(210)737-3138
Co. E-mail: voice@voiceforanimals.org
URL: http://www.voiceforanimals.org/
Scope: Animal rights; vegetarianism. **Services:** Library not open to the public. **Holdings:** 200 books; newsletters; videocassettes.

RESEARCH CENTERS

1079 ■ Cornell University–Baker Institute for Animal Health
College of Veterinary Medicine
Hungerford Hill Rd.
Ithaca, NY 14853
Ph:(607)256-5600
Fax:(607)256-5608
Co. E-mail: jaa2@cornell.edu
URL: http://bakerinstitute.vet.cornell.edu
Contact: Judith A. Appleton PhD, Dir.
E-mail: jaa2@cornell.edu
Scope: Improvement of animal/human health through 2 major areas: 1. Immunology and Infectious Diseases; 2. Genetics and Reproduction. Research includes: infectious diseases, reproductive immunology, genetics/genomics, development, and reproductive and cancer biology with emphasis on the dog, cat and horse, often using a mouse model. **Publications:** Annual report; Brochures on Research Topics (periodically). **Educational Activities:** Scientific conference (annually); Tuesday Noon Seminar Series, Thaw lecture theater.

1080 ■ Cornell University–Cornell Feline Health Center
College of Veterinary Medicine
Hungerford Hill Rd.
Ithaca, NY 14853
Ph:(607)253-3414
Free: 800—548-8937
Fax:(607)253-3419
URL: http://www.vet.cornell.edu/fhc
Contact: Colin R. Parrish, Dir.
Scope: Basic and clinical research on diseases of domestic and non-domestic cats, designed to help prevent or cure cat diseases and to aid veterinarians when new or unknown diseases occur. Performs multidisciplinary studies on antiviral substances (including interferon); cardiovascular, respiratory, urinary tract, reproductive, nutritional, neurological, fungal, and hormonal diseases; infectious peritonitis; leukemia; panleukopenia (enteritis); feline immunodeficiency virus; and vaccines. **Services:** Camuti Consultation and Diagnostic Service, which aids veterinarians and cat owners. **Publications:** Annual report; Cat Watch (monthly); Feline Health Topics for Veterinarians (quarterly); Feline Information Bulletin (periodically). **Educational Activities:** Continuing Education Program, on feline diseases for feline practitioners and cat owners; Feline Specialist Seminar (annually), for veterinarians.

1081 ■ Iowa State University of Science and Technology–Institute for International Cooperation in Animal Biologics
2160 College of Veterinary Medicine
Ames, IA 50011
Ph:(515)294-7189
Fax:(515)294-8259
Co. E-mail: iicab@iastate.edu
URL: http://www.cfsph.iastate.edu/IICAB
Contact: James A. Roth PhD, Dir.
E-mail: iicab@iastate.edu
Scope: Improvement of animal health and productivity through the effective use of biologics (vaccines) to control animal disease. **Services:** Technology transfer, from the Center to industry. **Publications:** IICAB Annual Report (annually). **Educational Activities:** Veterinary Biologies Training Program (annually), for biologics industry and government regulatory officials; every May.

1082 ■ Iowa State University of Science and Technology–Veterinary Diagnostic Laboratory
College of Veterinary Medicine
1600 S 16th St.
Ames, IA 50011-1250
Ph:(515)294-1950
Fax:(515)294-3564
Co. E-mail: isuvdlv@iastate.edu
URL: http://vetmed.iastate.edu/diagnostic-lab
Contact: Patrick G. Halbur PhD, Exec.Dir.
E-mail: isuvdlv@iastate.edu
Scope: Infectious diseases of animals, veterinary chemistry, and toxicology. Characterizes infectious diseases as well as chemical toxicants by means of pathology, bacteriology, virology, serology, chemistry, and toxicology studies. Serves as a reference laboratory for veterinary diagnostic procedures. **Services:** Diagnostic services and consultation, to livestock and pet owners. **Publications:** Scientific journal articles (30/year); Annual Reports. **Educational Activities:** Continuing education and scientific presentations, 8-15 per year.

1083 ■ Oklahoma State University–Surgical Laser Laboratory
Department of Veterinary Clinical Sciences
Veterinary Teaching Hospital
College of Veterinary Medicine
Stillwater, OK 74078
Ph:(405)744-8689
Fax:(405)744-6265
Co. E-mail: kebart@okstate.edu
Contact: Dr. Kenneth E. Bartels, Dir.
E-mail: kebart@okstate.edu
Scope: Lasers in veterinary medicine, focusing on selective ablation of tissue, photodynamic therapy, and diode lasers. **Services:** Clinical treatment using laser modalities for large and small animals (weekly). **Educational Activities:** Didactic classes (occasionally), on basic laser surgery.

1084 ■ University of California, Davis–Center for Companion Animal Health
School of Veterinary Medicine
1 Shields Ave.
Davis, CA 95616-8782
Ph:(530)752-7295
Fax:(530)752-7701
Co. E-mail: ncpedersen@ucdavis.edu
URL: http://www.vetmed.ucdavis.edu/ccah
Contact: Niels C. Pedersen DVM, Dir.
E-mail: ncpedersen@ucdavis.edu
Scope: Health problems in companion animals, including studies on cancer, infectious diseases, congenital diseases, eye diseases, skin diseases, kidney diseases, animal population control, behavior problems, nutrition, medicine, and surgery (including laser surgery and therapies). **Educational Activities:** Annual Canine or Feline Health Seminars; Research Educational Meeting (annually).

1085 ■ University of Wyoming–Wyoming State Veterinary Laboratory
1174 Snowy Range Rd.
Laramie, WY 82070
Ph:(307)766-9925
Free: 800—442-8331
Fax:(307)721-2051
Co. E-mail: montgome@uwyo.edu
URL: http://wyovet.uwyo.edu
Contact: Prof. Donald L. Montgomery PhD, Dir.
E-mail: montgome@uwyo.edu
Scope: Animal disease problems, including experimental control measures of animal diseases; etiology of animal diseases; and diseases of food-providing animals, wildlife, and companion animal species. **Publications:** Annual report; Newsletter.

1086 ■ Utah State University–Central Utah Veterinary Diagnostic Laboratory
PO Box 80
Nephi, UT 84648-0080
Ph:(435)623-1402
Fax:(435)623-1548
URL: http://www.usu.edu/uvdl/
Contact: Dr. Jane Kelly
Scope: Animal diseases and parasites. Conducts field experiments in support of studies conducted by members of the staff at the Experiment Station.

1087 ■ Virginia Polytechnic Institute and State University–Marion Du Pont Scott Equine Medical Center
PO Box 1938
Leesburg, VA 20177
Ph:(703)771-6800
Free: 800—436-2911
Fax:(703)771-6810
Co. E-mail: nawhite2@vt.edu
URL: http://equinemedicalcenter.net
Contact: Prof. Nathaniel A. White II, Dir.
E-mail: nawhite2@vt.edu
Scope: Equine research, including colic, shock, neurologic diseases, tendon and ligament injury and lameness. **Services:** Clinical service to horses. **Educational Activities:** Continuing education programs; Veterinary professional curriculum, residency training programs, graduate studies program.

Antique Shop

ASSOCIATIONS AND OTHER ORGANIZATIONS

1088 ■ American Hatpin Society
2505 Indian Creek Rd.
Diamond Bar, CA 91765-3307
Co. E-mail: info@americanhatpinsociety.com
URL: http://www.americanhatpinsociety.com
Contact: Jodi Lenocker, Pres.
Description: Collectors of hatpins. Promotes collection, preservation, and restoration of hatpins and related fashion accessories. Serves as a clearinghouse on hatpins and their history; facilitates exchange of information among members; conducts educational programs. .

1089 ■ Antiquarian Booksellers' Association of Canada–Association de la Librairie Ancienne du Canada
783 Bank St.
Ottawa, ON, Canada K1S 3V5
Co. E-mail: info@abac.org
URL: http://www.abac.org
Contact: Liam McGahern, Pres.
Description: Bookselling firms and dealers in rare books and manuscripts. Promotes adherence to high standards of ethics and practice in the trade of antiquarian books. Serves as liaison between members and book collectors and as a clearinghouse on antiquarian books and their trade.

1090 ■ Appraisers Association of America
386 Park Ave. S, 20th Fl., Ste. 2000
New York, NY 10016
Ph:(212)889-5404
Fax:(212)889-5503
Co. E-mail: aaa@appraisersassoc.org
URL: http://www.appraisersassoc.org
Contact: Beth G. Weingast, Pres.
Description: Professional society of appraisers of personal property such as: Americana; antiques; armor; art objects; bibelot; books; bronzes; china and porcelain; clocks and watches; coins; crystal and glass; curios; diamonds and jewelry; enamels; etchings; fine art; firearms; furniture; furs; graphic art; guns; household furnishings; ivories; leather goods; lighting fixtures; linens and lace; miniatures; music; musical instruments; oriental art; paintings; pewter; pianos; primitive art; prints; rugs; sculpture; Sheffield plate; silver and silverware; stamps; steins and tankards; taxes; and woodcarvings. **Publications:** *The Appraiser* (quarterly); *Appraisers Association of America—Membership Directory* (biennial).

1091 ■ Art and Antique Dealers League of America
PO Box 2066
Lennox Hill Sta.
New York, NY 10021
Ph:(212)879-7558
Fax:(212)772-7197
Co. E-mail: secretary@artantiquedealersleague.com
URL: http://www.artantiquedealersleague.com
Contact: Clinton Howell, Pres.
Description: Represents retailers and wholesalers of antiques and art objects. Convention/Meeting: none.
.

1092 ■ Cracker Jack Collectors Association
4908 N Holborn Dr.
Muncie, IN 47304
Co. E-mail: lindajfarris@comcast.net
URL: http://www.crackerjackcollectors.com
Contact: Nancy Schultz, Pres.
Description: Collectors of Cracker Jack prizes and related items. Promotes collection and preservation of Cracker Jack memorabilia. Gathers and disseminates information on Cracker Jack collectibles and their availability; facilitates exchange of information and promotes good fellowship among members.
.

1093 ■ Fostoria Glass Collectors
PO Box 826
Moundsville, WV 26041
Ph:(304)845-9188
URL: http://www.fostoriacollectors.org
Contact: Jim Davis, Pres.
Description: Collectors and admirers of handmade American glassware. Promotes appreciation of handmade American glass products. Serves as a clearinghouse on handmade American glassware and its collection; sponsors research and educational programs; participates in charitable activities; maintains museum. **Publications:** *The Glass Works* (bimonthly).

1094 ■ Foundation for the Study of the Arts and Crafts Movement at Roycroft
46 Walnut St.
East Aurora, NY 14052
Ph:(716)652-3333
Fax:(716)655-0562
Co. E-mail: info@roycroftshops.com
URL: http://www.roycroft.org
Contact: Kitty Turgeon, Exec. Dir.
Description: Represents individuals interested in getting information about and collecting mission, prairie, and other arts and crafts pieces from the arts and crafts era (1895-1930). Studies the works of William Morris, Elbert Hubbard and Roycrofters, furniture designer Gustav Stickley, and architects Frank Lloyd Wright and Greene & Greene. Encourages the collecting of antiques from the Craftsman era and the Roycroft shops. Operates speakers' bureau. Sponsors educational programs. Group is currently expanding with Elderhostel and higher visibility. **Publications:** *Annual Issue* (annual); *Craftsman Homeowner* .

1095 ■ International League of Antiquarian Booksellers
35 W Maple Ave.
Merchantville, NJ 08109-5141
Ph:(856)665-2284
Fax:(856)665-3639
Co. E-mail: mail@betweenthecovers.com
URL: http://www.ilab.org
Contact: Arnoud Gerits, Pres.
Description: Represents national associations of antiquarian booksellers around the world. Organizes professional training courses for members. Sponsors book fairs. .

1096 ■ International Paperweight Society
761 Chestnut St.
Santa Cruz, CA 95060
Ph:(408)427-1177
Free: 800-538-0766
Co. E-mail: lselman@got.net
URL: http://www.paperweight.com
Contact: Wibarine Favre, Pres.
Description: Promotes paperweight collecting. Conducts educational programs. Runs a speakers' bureau. .

1097 ■ National Antique and Art Dealers Association of America
220 E 57th St.
New York, NY 10022
Ph:(212)826-9707
Fax:(212)832-9493
URL: http://www.naadaa.org
Contact: James McConnaughy, Pres.
Description: Art and antique dealers who handle antiques and works of art of the highest quality. Safeguards the interests of those who buy, sell, and collect antiques and works of art. Sponsors periodic exhibitions; maintains speakers' bureau. .

1098 ■ National Shaving Mug Collectors Association
366 Lake Shore Dr.
Hewitt, NJ 07421
URL: http://www.nsmca.net
Contact: Don Allain, Treas.
Description: Collectors of shaving mugs and other shaving equipment. Promotes collection of shaving paraphernalia as a hobby. Facilitates communication and trading among members; gathers and disseminates information on shaving mugs and related equipment. .

REFERENCE WORKS

1099 ■ *Appraisers Association of America—Membership Directory*
Pub: Appraisers Association of America Inc.
Contact: Aleya Lehmann Bench, Exec. Dir.
Released: Biennial, Even years. **Covers:** 1,000 member appraisers of fine art, antiques, and personal property. **Entries Include:** Name, address, phone, specialties. **Arrangement:** Geographical. **Indexes:** Alphabetical, specialty.

1100 ■ "Echo Vintage Clothing Fundraiser Set July 24" in *Tri-City Herald* (July 22, 2010)
Pub: McClathcy-Tribune
Description: Bicentennial Echo Vintage Clothing Show and Tea was held July 24, 2010 at the Echo City Hall Ballroom in Echo, Oregon. The event is held every two years to fund project in Echo and to maintain the vintage clothing collection.

1101 ■ *How to Buy and Sell Antiques*
Pub: Parkwest Publications, Incorporated
Ed: Fiona Shoop. **Released:** August 2006. **Price:** \$28.50. **Description:** Fiona Shoop shares twenty years experience to train individuals to become successful antiques dealers.

1102 ■ *National Antique & Art Dealers Association of America—Membership Directory*
Pub: National Antique & Art Dealers Association of America Inc.
Contact: Mark Schaffer, Director
Released: Continuous. **Covers:** 46 member dealers. **Entries Include:** Firm name, address, phone, names of one or more principal executives, cable address, specialties, and areas of expertise. **Arrangement:** Alphabetical.

1103 ■ *Old-Stuff—Directory of Shops Section*
Pub: VBM Printers Inc.
Contact: Donna Miller, Editor & Publisher
E-mail: donna@oldstuffnews.com
Released: 6 times a year. **Price:** $20, individuals yearly subscription; $5.50, single issue; $35, two years; $35, Canada. **Publication Includes:** List of approximately 900 antiques shops in the northwestern United States. **Entries Include:** Shop name, address, phone. **Arrangement:** Geographical. **Indexes:** Shops, alphabetical by city.

1104 ■ "Prime Time for Vintage" in *Daily Variety* (Vol. 308, August 23, 2010, No. 35, pp. 12)
Pub: Reed Business Information Inc.
Ed: Cynthia Littleton. **Description:** The week of August 23 starts the busy season for owners of Los Angeles' vintage couture shops due to Emmy-related events.

1105 ■ "Shop Around" in *Houston Chronicle* (December 7, 2010, pp. 3)
Pub: Houston Chronicle
Ed: Tara Dooley. **Description:** Profile of Diana Candida and Maria Martinez who partnered to open Beatniks, a shop carrying vintage clothing, art from various artists, dance shoes, and jewelry.

1106 ■ *Warman's Antiques & Collectibles Price Guide*
Pub: Krause Publications Inc.
Contact: Mark F. Moran, Author
Released: Annual, latest edition 45th; 2012. **Price:** $16.19, individuals Paperback. **Covers:** Over 50,000 antiques and collectibles, plus listings for collector's clubs. **Entries Include:** Description, price.

SOURCES OF SUPPLY

1107 ■ *Collectibles Market Guide & Price Index*
Pub: Collectors' Information Bureau
Released: Annual, latest edition 19th; February, 2005. **Price:** $24.95, individuals suggested retail; $19.96, individuals sales price. **Publication Includes:** List of manufacturers of limited edition collectible plates, figurines, bells, graphics, ornaments, dolls, and steins; related associations and museums; price guide to secondary market values of limited edition collectibles. **Entries Include:** Company name and address, history, current projects, values of retired editions. **Arrangement:** Membership organization. Editorial restricted to member companies. **Indexes:** Price index of collectibles. Biographies of collectibles artists; collectibles price index; feature articles; glossary; directory of secondary market dealers.

TRADE PERIODICALS

1108 ■ *Antique Bottle and Glass Collector*
Pub: Antique Bottle and Glass Collector
Released: Monthly. **Price:** $32 2nd class; $47 Canada; $57 other countries by airmail; $95 other countries by airmail; $54 1st class. **Description:** Trade magazine for antique bottle and glass collectors.

1109 ■ *Antique & Collectibles Showcase*
Pub: Trajan Publishing Corp.
Contact: Shari Szeplaki, Advertising Contact
E-mail: sharis@trajan.ca
Released: Bimonthly. **Price:** $27 Canada; $48 two years Canada; $49 other countries; $28; $51 two years. **Description:** Magazine providing helpful information for antique lovers, including book reviews, show calendars, museum exhibitions and acquisitions, and news about upcoming trends.

1110 ■ *Antique Trader Weekly*
Pub: Krause Publications Inc.
Contact: Sandra Sparks, Assoc. Ed.
E-mail: sandra.sparks@fwpubs.com
Released: Weekly. **Price:** $24.98; $115.98 Canada; $165.98 other countries. **Description:** Magazine featuring stories, auction and show listings, and classified and display advertising for antiques and collectibles.

1111 ■ *Antiques and the Arts Weekly*
Pub: Bee Publishing Company Inc.
Contact: Scudder R. Smith, Editor & Publisher
Released: Weekly. **Price:** $81 print & web access; $143 two years print & web access. **Description:** Magazine featuring antiques.

1112 ■ *Antiques & Collecting Magazine*
Pub: Lightner Publishing Corp.
Contact: Gregory K. Graham, Gen Mgr
Released: Monthly. **Price:** $38; $66 two years. **Description:** Magazine for antique and hobby collectors.

1113 ■ *Art & Antiques*
Pub: Billian Publishing Inc. and Trans World Publishing Inc.
Contact: Bill Besch, Publisher
E-mail: billb@curtco.com
Released: 12/yr. **Price:** $80; $120 two years; $105 Canada; $170 Canada 2 years; $120 other countries; $200 other countries 2 years. **Description:** Consumer magazine for those interested in the fine and decorative arts and their settings.

1114 ■ *Collectors News*
Pub: Pioneer Communications Inc.
Ed: Linda Kruger, Editor, lkruger@pioneermagazines.com. **Released:** Monthly. **Price:** $26.95. **Description:** Magazine covering antiques and collecting for pleasure and profit.

1115 ■ *Country Home*
Pub: Meredith Corp.
Released: Monthly, 10/yr. **Price:** $4.95 newstand; $21.97 two years. **Description:** Magazine furnishing information on American interior design, architecture, antiques and collectibles, gardening, art, and culinary endeavor.

1116 ■ *Discover Mid-America*
Pub: Discovery Publications Inc.
Contact: Bruce Rodgers, Exec. Ed./Publisher
E-mail: publisher@discoverypub.com
Released: Monthly. **Description:** Trade magazine covering antiques, arts, crafts, regional history, and events.

1117 ■ *The Magazine Antiques*
Pub: Brant Publications Inc.
Released: Monthly. **Price:** $29.95; $79.95 Canada; $95 other countries. **Description:** Magazine featuring articles on the fine and decorative arts and architecture: furniture, ceramics, glass, paintings, prints, sculpture, textiles, preservation, and private collections.

1118 ■ *The New England Antiques Journal*
Pub: Turley Publications
Contact: John Fiske, Editor-in-Chief
E-mail: johnfiske@verizon.net
Released: Monthly. **Price:** $15.95; $25.95 two years; $15.95 gift subscription; $25.95 two years two years gift subscription; $32 Canada; $63 European (surface price); $142 European (air mail); $54 Canada two years. **Description:** Magazine covering antiques, arts, historic preservation, restoration, artisanship and more.

1119 ■ *Uncoverings*
Pub: American Quilt Study Group
Contact: Judy Brott Buss PhD, Exec. Dir.
Ed: Lauren Horton, Editor. **Released:** Annual. **Price:** $20 single issue. **Description:** Scholarly journal covering quilts, textiles and quilt makers.

VIDEOCASSETTES/ AUDIOCASSETTES

1120 ■ *Hidden Treasures: A Collector's Guide to Antique and Vintage Jewelry of the 19th and 20th Centuries*
S.I. Video Sales Group
PO Box 63745
Philadelphia, PA 19147
Ph:(267)519-2222
Co. E-mail: stann@sivideo.com
URL: http://www.sivideo.com
Released: 1992. **Price:** $24.95. **Description:** A tour through the decades highlights the popular jewelry of the day and how to distinguish the real articles through workmanship, materials, motif, and other signs of authenticity, age, and value. Also provides a visual price guide. **Availability:** VHS.

1121 ■ *Inside Tips on Discovering Antiques*
Curtis, Inc.
1105 Western Ave.
Cincinnati, OH 45203
Ph:(513)621-8895
Free: 800-733-2878
Fax:(513)621-0942
Co. E-mail: info@curtisinc.com
URL: http://www.curtisinc.com
Released: 1992. **Price:** $19.95. **Description:** Learn how to buy and sell antiques with confidence and discover secrets on finding treasures in the trash, reviving old wood without stripping, and finding antiques at affordable prices. **Availability:** VHS.

TRADE SHOWS AND CONVENTIONS

1122 ■ The Winter Olympia Fine Art and Antiques Fair
Clarion Events Ltd.
Earls Court Exhibition Centre
Warwick Rd.
London SW5 9TA, United Kingdom
Ph:44 20 7370 8139
URL: http://www.clarionevents.com
Released: Annual. **Audience:** Trade and general public. **Principal Exhibits:** Antiques including fine, oak, garden, and country furniture; rugs; paintings; ceramics; clocks; sculptures; jewelry, silver, and bronzes.

LIBRARIES

1123 ■ Bayard Taylor Memorial Library
216 E. State St.
P.O. Box 730
Kennett Square, PA 19348-3112
Ph:(610)444-2702
Fax:(610)444-1752
Co. E-mail: dmurray@ccls.org
URL: http://www.bayardtaylor.org
Contact: Donna Murray, Lib.Dir.
Scope: Antiques, arts, social sciences, history, gardening. **Services:** Interlibrary loan; copying; Library open to the public. **Holdings:** 50,000 fiction and nonfiction books; 1000 books on tape; 2000 feature films; 150 periodical titles. **Subscriptions:** 150 journals and other serials; 8 newspapers.

1124 ■ California University of Pennsylvania–Louis L. Manderino Library I Special Collections
250 University Ave., Rm. 435
California, PA 15419
Ph:(724)938-5926
Fax:(724)938-5901
Co. E-mail: nolf@cup.edu
URL: http://www.library.calu.edu
Contact: Alber Pokol, Libn.
Scope: Rare books, art, music. **Services:** Library open to the public by appointment.

1125 ■ Dunham Tavern Museum Library
6709 Euclid Ave.
Cleveland, OH 44103
Ph:(216)431-1060
Co. E-mail: dunhamtavern@sbcglobal.net
URL: http://www.dunhamtavern.org/
Contact: William Ruper, Interim Pres.
Scope: Antique collecting; history of Cleveland and Ohio. **Services:** Library open to members only. **Holdings:** 1000 books.

1126 ■ Hope Foundation Inc.–Margaret L. Tyler Library
132 Hope House Rd.
Windsor, NC 27983
Ph:(252)794-3140
Fax:(252)794-5583
Co. E-mail: hopeplantation@coastalnet.com
URL: http://www.hopeplantation.org
Contact: Gregory Tyler, Cur.
Scope: Rare books 18th and 19th centuries; North Carolina; decorative arts; genealogy; plantation - management, law. **Services:** Copying; Library open to the public by appointment. **Holdings:** 1400 books; 100 reports; 40 cubic ft. archival materials. **Subscriptions:** 4 journals and other serials; 1 newspaper.

1127 ■ Houston Museum of Decorative Arts Library
201 High St.
Chattanooga, TN 37403
Ph:(423)267-7176
Fax:(423)267-7177
Co. E-mail: houston@chattanooga.net
URL: http://www.thehoustonmuseum.com
Contact: Amy H. Frierson, Dir.
Scope: Hand-blown antique glass, porcelain, pottery, ceramics, early American furniture, decorative art. **Holdings:** 300 books; 750 unbound reports; unbound periodical volumes; archival files of articles pertaining to the collection.

1128 ■ Hunter Museum of American Art Library
10 Bluff View St.
Chattanooga, TN 37403-1197
Ph:(423)267-0968
Fax:(423)267-9844
Co. E-mail: esimak@huntermuseum.org
URL: http://www.huntermuseum.org
Contact: Ellen Simak, Chf.Cur.
Scope: American art, antiques, architecture, biography, abstract art, arts and crafts. **Services:** Library not open to the public. **Holdings:** 800 books; 13 VF drawers of sales and auction catalogs; 17 VF drawers of museum and exhibition catalogs. **Subscriptions:** 38 journals and other serials.

1129 ■ Karpeles Manuscript Library–Buffalo Museum
Porter Hall, 453 Porter Ave.
North Hall, 220 North St.
Buffalo, NY 14201
Ph:(716)885-4139
Co. E-mail: kmuseumbuf@aol.com
URL: http://www.rain.org/IAtkarpeles/
Contact: Christopher Kelly, Dir.
Scope: Special manuscripts. **Services:** Library open to the public. **Holdings:** 30,000 books; 1.1 million manuscripts.

1130 ■ Karpeles Manuscript Library–Charleston Museum
68 Spring St.
Charleston, SC 29403
Ph:(843)853-4651
Co. E-mail: kmuseumchr@aol.com
URL: http://www.rain.org/IAtkarpeles/
Contact: Dr. Stephen J. White, Dir.
Scope: Special manuscripts. **Services:** Library open to the public. **Holdings:** Figures not available.

1131 ■ Karpeles Manuscript Library–Collections
21 W. Anapamu St.
Santa Barbara, CA 93101
Ph:(805)962-5322
Co. E-mail: kmuseumsb@aol.com
URL: http://www.karpeles.org
Scope: Historical manuscripts from all periods in world history. **Holdings:** 1 million manuscripts.

1132 ■ Karpeles Manuscript Library–Jacksonville Museum
101 W. 1st St.
Jacksonville, FL 33206
Ph:(904)356-2992
URL: http://www.rain.org/IAtkarpeles/jax.html
Contact: Richard Minor, Dir.
Scope: Rare manuscripts. **Services:** Library open to the public. **Holdings:** 200 books; manuscripts.

1133 ■ Karpeles Manuscript Library–Santa Barbara Museum
21 W. Anapamu St.
Santa Barbara, CA 93101
Ph:(805)962-5322
Co. E-mail: kmuseumsba@aol.com
URL: http://www.rain.org/IAtkarpeles/sb.html
Contact: Norman Cohan, Dir.
Scope: Special manuscripts. **Services:** Library open to the public. **Holdings:** 1 million manuscripts; patents; archives.

1134 ■ Karpeles Manuscript Library–Tacoma Museum
407 S. G St.
Tacoma, WA 98405
Ph:(253)383-2575
Co. E-mail: kmuseumtaq@aol.com
URL: http://www.rain.org/IAtkarpeles/taqfrm.html
Contact: Thomas M. Jutilla, Dir.
Scope: Rare manuscripts. **Services:** Library open to the public. **Holdings:** Figures not available.

1135 ■ Miami University–Southwest Ohio Regional Depository
4200 E. University Blvd.
Middletown, OH 45052
Ph:(513)727-3475
Fax:(513)727-3478
Co. E-mail: lipscope@muohio.edu
URL: http://www.sword.org
Contact: Pam Lipscomb, Depository Mgr.
Scope: Rare books. **Services:** Interlibrary loan; copying; Library open to the public by appointment. **Holdings:** 1,990,618 volumes.

1136 ■ Niagara University Library–Rare Book Room Collection
Lewiston Rd.
Niagara Falls, NY 14109
Ph:(716)286-8001
Fax:(716)286-8006
Co. E-mail: schoen@niagara.edu
URL: http://library.niagara.edu/about/special-collections/rare-book-collection/
Contact: David Schoen, Dir. of Libs.
Scope: Rare books, 1473-1800. **Services:** Library open to the public by appointment. **Holdings:** 2000 books; manuscripts.

1137 ■ Ohio Wesleyan University–L.A. Beeghly Library–Archives/Special Collections (43 Ro)
43 Rowland Ave.
Delaware, OH 43015
Ph:(740)368-3250
Fax:(740)368-3222
Co. E-mail: aoum@owu.edu
URL: http://lis.owu.edu/spcindex.htm
Contact: Carol Holliger, Archv.
Scope: Ohio Wesleyan University history, Methodism in Ohio, rare books. **Services:** Interlibrary loan; Library open to the public by appointment. **Holdings:** 480,000 items. **Subscriptions:** 1000 journals and other serials.

1138 ■ Shelburne Museum, Inc.–Research Library
U.S. Rte. 7
PO Box 10
Shelburne, VT 05482-0010
Ph:(802)985-3346
Fax:(802)985-2331
Co. E-mail: curators@shelburnemuseum.org
URL: http://shelburnemuseum.org
Contact: James Pizzagalli, Chm.
Scope: American folk art, decorative arts, fine art, and design. **Services:** Library open to the public by appointment. **Holdings:** 5000 books; 400 lin.ft. archives; 400 manuscript items. **Subscriptions:** 30 journals and other serials.

1139 ■ Society of Inkwell Collectors Library
PO Box 447
Fort Madison, IA 52627-0447
Ph:(319)372-0881
Fax:(319)372-0882
Co. E-mail: sam@pendemonium.com
URL: http://www.soic.com/Library.html
Contact: Sam Fiorella, Libn.
Scope: Inkwells, bottles, and pens; history of writing; repair and cleaning techniques. **Services:** Library open to the public for reference use only. **Holdings:** 75 books; periodicals; clippings; audio/visuals.

1140 ■ Villanova University–Falvey Memorial Library I Special Collections
Villanova, PA 19085
Ph:(610)519-4290
Fax:(610)519-5018
Co. E-mail: bente.polites@villanova.edu
URL: http://www.library.villanova.edu
Contact: Bente Polites, Spec.Coll.Libn.
Scope: Augustiniana, early printed books and general rare books, Irish history, James Joyce. **Services:** Interlibrary loan; copying; Library open to the public. **Holdings:** 15,000 items.

1141 ■ Western Maryland Public Libraries–Regional Library
100 S. Potomac St.
Hagerstown, MD 21740
Ph:(301)739-3250
Fax:(301)739-5839
Co. E-mail: jthompson@washcolibrary.org
URL: http://www.westmdlib.info
Contact: Joe Thompson, Assoc.Dir.
Scope: Small business; antiques and collectibles; Civil Service and vocational tests; small scale farming. **Services:** Interlibrary loan; copying; Library open to the public with restrictions. **Holdings:** 62,000 books; 2500 audiovisuals. **Subscriptions:** 3 newspapers.

1142 ■ Winfred L. and Elizabeth C. Post Foundation–Post Memorial Art Reference Library
300 Main St.
Joplin, MO 64801-2384
Ph:(417)782-7678
Co. E-mail: lsimpson@postlibrary.org
URL: http://www.postlibrary.org
Contact: Leslie Simpson, Libn./Dir.
Scope: Visual arts, antiques, architecture, photography, historic preservation, heraldry. **Services:** Copying; monthly art exhibits; Library open to the public. **Holdings:** 3600 books; 245 bound periodical volumes; 16 VF drawers of pictures, articles, pamphlets; 1000 slides. **Subscriptions:** 31 journals and other serials.

TRADE PERIODICALS

1143 ■ *Apartment Management Magazine*
Pub: Apartment News Publications Inc.
Contact: Donn R. Smeallie Jr., Publisher/Pres.
Released: Monthly. **Price:** $15 Southern California only; $24 out of area; $69 out of area. **Description:** Trade magazine serving owners, builders, and managers of apartment buildings.

1144 ■ *Apartment News*
Pub: Orange County Multi-Housing Service Corp.
Released: Monthly. **Price:** $36. **Description:** Magazine for apartment managers, owners, and builders.

1145 ■ *Building Business & Apartment Management*
Pub: Building Industry Association of Southeastern Michigan
Contact: Irvin H. Yackness, Exec. Ed.
Ed: Susan Adler Shanteau, Editor. **Released:** Monthly. **Price:** $48. **Description:** Construction and apartment industry magazine.

VIDEOCASSETTES/ AUDIOCASSETTES

1146 ■ *Apartment For Rent*
Cambridge Educational
c/o Films Media Group
132 West 31st Street, 17th Floor
Ste. 124
New York, NY 10001
Free: 800-257-5126
Fax:(609)671-0266
Co. E-mail: custserve@films.com
URL: http://www.cambridgeol.com
Released: 1991. **Price:** $89.00. **Description:** Follows three individuals on their quests for apartments. Introduces terms and questions that should be asked before signing a lease. Outlines basic considerations to be explored by the individual, including size needs, cost effectiveness, etc. **Availability:** VHS.

1147 ■ *Finding That First Apartment*
Cambridge Educational
c/o Films Media Group
132 West 31st Street, 17th Floor
Ste. 124
New York, NY 10001
Free: 800-257-5126
Fax:(609)671-0266
Co. E-mail: custserve@films.com
URL: http://www.cambridgeol.com
Released: 1991. **Price:** $79.00. **Description:** Outlines the basic needs that should be considered when apartment hunting, explains what to look for in ads, how to make a budget, and deposit fees. Also debates buying and renting furniture. **Availability:** VHS.

TRADE SHOWS AND CONVENTIONS

1148 ■ American Real Estate Society Annual Meeting
American Real Estate Society
5353 Parkside Dr.
Cleveland State Univ.
Coll. of Bus.
Dept. of Finance, UC513
Jupiter, FL 33458
Ph:(561)799-8664
Fax:(561)799-8535
Co. E-mail: dcooper@fau.edu
URL: http://www.aresnet.org
Released: Annual. **Audience:** College and university professors; high-level practicing professionals involved in all aspects real estate. **Principal Exhibits:** Exhibits relating to decision-making within real estate finance, real estate market analysis, investment, valuation, development, and other areas related to real estate in the private sector. Data providers, book publishers, etc.

1149 ■ Canadian Real Estate Association Annual Conference and Trade Show
Canadian Real Estate Association
Canada Bldg.
200 Catherine St.
Ottawa, ON, Canada K2P 2K9
Ph:(613)237-7111
Free: 800-842-2732
Fax:(613)234-2567
Co. E-mail: info@crea.ca
URL: http://www.crea.ca
Released: Annual. **Audience:** Real estate professionals, brokers, managers, corporate representatives from real estate boards across the country. **Principal Exhibits:** Real Estate, financial, printing, and computer business equipment.

1150 ■ GMC Philadelphia Home Show
dmg world media (USA) inc. (Philadelphia, Pennsylvania)
200 Haddonfield-Berlin Rd., Ste. 302
High Ridge Commons
Gibbsboro, NJ 08026
Ph:(856)784-4774
Free: 800-756-5692
Fax:(856)435-5920
URL: http://www.dmgworldmedia.com
Released: Annual. **Audience:** Home owners and apartment dwellers. **Principal Exhibits:** House and apartment products, supplies, and services.

1151 ■ Old House/New House Home Show
Kennedy Productions, Inc.
1208 Lisle Pl.
Lisle, IL 60532-2262
Ph:(630)515-1160
Fax:(630)515-1165
Co. E-mail: kp@corecomm.net
URL: http://www.kennedyproductions.com
Released: Semiannual. **Audience:** Trade professionals and general public. **Principal Exhibits:** Products and services for home remodeling, improvement, enhancement, decorating, landscaping and more. Hundreds of ideas to improve and beautify every home.

1152 ■ South Dakota Association of Realtors Convention
South Dakota Association of Realtors
204 N. Euclid Ave.
Pierre, SD 57501
Ph:(605)224-0554
Fax:(605)224-8975
Co. E-mail: sdar@sdrealtor.org
URL: http://www.sdrealtor.org
Released: Annual. **Audience:** Industry professionals. **Principal Exhibits:** Real estate. **Dates and Locations:** 2011 Sep 14-16, Pierre, SD.

1153 ■ Texas Apartment Association Annual Education Conference and Lone Star Expo
Texas Apartment Association, Inc.
1011 San Jacinto Blvd., Ste. 600
Austin, TX 78701-1951
Ph:(512)479-6252
Fax:(512)479-6291
URL: http://www.taa.org
Released: Annual. **Audience:** Owners and management company reps of multi-housing communities from Texas. **Principal Exhibits:** Goods and services geared to multi-housing professionals, including software, soft goods, and property supplies.

CONSULTANTS

1154 ■ Rental Relocation Inc.
281 S Atlanta St.
Roswell, GA 30075
Ph:(770)641-8393
Free: 800-641-7368
Fax:(770)641-8607
Co. E-mail: ahlsinfo@rentalrelocation.com
URL: http://www.rentalrelocation.com
Contact: Christopher Bliss, President
E-mail: cbliss@atsrentalrelocation.com
Scope: Relocation firm offering services in corporate housing, rentals, free metro Atlanta apartment locating service, property management, house and condo rental relocation tours.

COMPUTERIZED DATABASES

1155 ■ *Claritas Update Demographics*
The Nielsen Co.
770 Broadway
New York, NY 10003-9595
URL: http://www.claritas.com/sitereports/default.jsp
Description: Contains 2000 data, current-year estimates, and five-year projections of key demographics, including data on households, populations,

families, income, age, and race. **Availability:** Online: The Nielsen Co; CD-ROM: The Nielsen Co; Diskette: The Nielsen Co;Magnetic Tape: The Nielsen Co. **Type:** Statistical.

1156 ■ *Colorado Economic and Demographic Information System*
Colorado Department of Local Affairs
1313 Sherman St., Rm. 500
Denver, CO 80203
Ph:(303)866-4904
Fax:(303)866-4077
Co. E-mail: dola.helpdesk@state.co.us
URL: http://dola.colorado.gov
Description: Contains demographic, financial, and employment time series data on Colorado local governments and all 50 U.S. states. Includes population data; housing unit and household data; employment data; financial, tax base, and tax rate data; and income and earnings data. **Availability:** Online: Colorado Department of Local Affairs. **Type:** Time series.

1157 ■ *Psychoanalytic Dialogues*
Taylor & Francis Group
27 Church Rd.
Hove
East Sussex BN3 2FA, United Kingdom
Ph:44 20 7017 7747
Fax:44 20 7017 6717
URL: http://www.psychoanalysisarena.com
Description: Contains articles covering interpersonal psychoanalysis, including British object relations theories; self psychology; the empirical traditions of infancy research and child development; and certain currents of contemporary Freudian thought for theoreticians and clinicians. Enables users to search abstracts and table of contents. **Availability:** Online: Taylor & Francis Group. **Type:** Full text.

RESEARCH CENTERS

1158 ■ Harvard University–Joint Center for Housing Studies
1033 Massachusetts Ave., 5th Fl.
Cambridge, MA 02138
Ph:(617)495-7908
Fax:(617)496-9957
Co. E-mail: laurel_gourd@harvard.edu
URL: http://www.jchs.harvard.edu
Contact: Chris Herbert, Res.Dir.
E-mail: laurel_gourd@harvard.edu
Scope: Policy research in housing and construction, demographics, and related topics. Seeks to develop scholars, policy makers, and practitioners. Provides a forum for academics, business and labor leaders, and government officials. **Publications:** Newsletter (semiannually); State of the Nation's Housing Report (annually); Working Papers (10/year). **Educational Activities:** John T. Dunlop lecture in Housing Studies (annually); Lunchtime lecture series.

1159 ■ National Housing Law Project
614 Grand Ave., Ste. 320
Oakland, CA 94610
Ph:(510)251-9400
Fax:(510)451-2300
Co. E-mail: nhlp@nhlp.org
URL: http://www.nhlp.org
Contact: Gideon Anders, Exec.Dir.
E-mail: nhlp@nhlp.org
Scope: Legal and policy research in area of low-income housing, including community development, displacement and relocation, landlord-tenant relationship, Housing and Urban Development-subsidized multifamily housing, rural housing, public housing and Section 8, single-family housing, state housing finance agencies, syndication, and housing management. **Services:** Case assistance, to legal services lawyers and housing development corporations. **Publications:** Housing Law Bulletin (bimonthly).

1160 ■ San Francisco Planning and Urban Research Association
654 Mission St.
San Francisco, CA 94105-4015
Ph:(415)781-8726
Fax:(415)781-7291
Co. E-mail: rmandel@rci.rutgers.edu
URL: http://www.spur.org
Contact: Ruth B. Mandel, Dir.
E-mail: rmandel@rci.rutgers.edu
Scope: Public policy issues of concern to San Francisco, including studies on housing, transportation, regional affairs, city planning, urban design and open space, city finance and operations. Recent activities include a study of an evaluation of how to improve service on the municipal railway and a ballot measure; a study of ways to increase housing supply in San Francisco and proposed legislation; car sharing; policy recommendation to improve operations of the city parks, and two proposed ballot measures; and ballot analysis of city propositions for each election. **Publications:** SPUR Newsletter (11/year). **Educational Activities:** Annual conference; Forums, 12 per month, on topics including transportation, housing, urban planning, etc.. **Awards:** Silver SPUR Awards (annually), for long-term contribution to the civic life of the city.

1161 ■ University of California at Berkeley–Fisher Center for Real Estate and Urban Economics
Gerson Baker Faculty Bldg., F602
Haas School of Business, MC 6105
Berkeley, CA 94720-6105
Ph:(510)643-6105
Fax:(510)643-7357
Co. E-mail: creue@haas.berkeley.edu
URL: http://groups.haas.berkeley.edu/realestate
Contact: Nancy Wallace PhD, Co-Ch.
E-mail: creue@haas.berkeley.edu
Scope: Policy research in commercial real estate development and finance, housing finance and construction, and urban and regional development. Activities focus on improving understanding and encouraging innovation in the housing and mortgage finance systems and providing detailed study and analysis of the urban and regional economy of California, including studies on the demand for housing, affordability, alternative mortgage instruments, restructuring the housing finance system, land use regulations, property taxation and housing production, rental housing, housing revitalization and the change in national policy, housing and energy conservation, commercial real estate, real estate investment analysis, and international housing. Communicates research findings to both the public and private sectors, particularly to those concerned with allocation of urban land resources. **Publications:** Newsletter; Reprints; Working papers. **Educational Activities:** Executive education conferences (annually); Professional conferences; Public lectures; Seminars.

START-UP INFORMATION

1162 ■ "Stockerts Open Repair Business" in *Dickinson Press* (July 13, 2010)
Pub: Dickinson Press
Ed: Ashley Martin. **Description:** Ed Stockert is opening his new appliance repair firm in Dickinson, North Dakota with his wife Anna.

ASSOCIATIONS AND OTHER ORGANIZATIONS

1163 ■ Appliance Parts Distributors Association
3621 N Oakley Ave.
Chicago, IL 60618
Ph:(773)230-9851
Fax:888-308-1423
Co. E-mail: ro@apda.com
URL: http://www.apda.com
Contact: Kirk Coburn, Pres.
Description: Wholesale distributors of appliance parts, supplies and accessories. Promotes the sale of appliance parts through independent parts distributors. .

1164 ■ Association of Home Appliance Manufacturers
1111 19th St. NW, Ste. 402
Washington, DC 20036
Ph:(202)872-5955
Fax:(202)872-9354
Co. E-mail: info@aham.org
URL: http://www.aham.org
Contact: Joseph M. McGuire, Pres.
Description: Companies manufacturing major and portable appliances; supplier members provide products and services to the appliance industry. Major areas of activity include: market research and reporting of industry statistics; development of standard methods for measuring appliance performance and certification of certain characteristics of room air conditioners, refrigerators, freezers, humidifiers, dehumidifiers, and room air cleaners; public relations and press relations. Represents the appliance industry before government at the federal, state, and local levels. **Publications:** *AHAM Major Home Appliance Industry Factbook*; *AHAM Membership Directory* (annual); *Directory of Certified Dehumidifiers* (semiannual); *Directory of Certified Humidifiers* (semiannual); *Directory of Certified Refrigerators and Freezers* (semiannual).

1165 ■ International Housewares Association
6400 Shafer Ct., Ste. 650
Rosemont, IL 60018
Ph:(847)292-4200
Fax:(847)292-4211
Co. E-mail: pbrandl@housewares.org
URL: http://www.housewares.org
Contact: Philip J. Brandl, Pres.
Description: Manufacturers and distributors of housewares and small appliances. Conducts annual market research survey of the housewares industry. Manages the international housewares show. **Publications:** *BusinessWatch* (monthly); *Housewares MarketWatch* (quarterly); *IHA Reports* (bimonthly); *January Exhibitors Directory* (annual); *NHMA Reports Newsletter* (bimonthly).

1166 ■ National Appliance Parts Suppliers Association
4015 W Marshall Ave.
Longview, TX 75604
Co. E-mail: board11@napsaweb.org
URL: http://www.napsaweb.org
Contact: Jim Bossman, Pres.
Description: Wholesale distributors of replacement parts for major home appliance. Promotes and supports good relations among groups in the supply and distribution of appliance service parts. Sponsors Young Executives Society of NAPSA to prepare younger generations for leadership in the appliance parts wholesale and distribution industry and to handle problems characteristic of family businesses. **Publications:** *National Appliance Parts Suppliers Association—Results* (quarterly).

1167 ■ National Appliance Service Association
PO Box 2514
Kokomo, IN 46904
Ph:(765)453-1820
Fax:(765)453-1895
Co. E-mail: nasahq@sbcglobal.net
URL: http://www.nasa1.org
Contact: Carrie Giannakos, Exec. Dir.
Description: Owners of factory-authorized portable appliance repair centers servicing small electrical appliances and commercial food equipment. Promotes the interests and welfare of the commercial-domestic appliance service industry. **Publications:** *NASA News* (monthly);Membership Directory (annual).

REFERENCE WORKS

1168 ■ *Appliance—Appliance Industry Purchasing Section Issue*
Pub: Dana Chase Publications Inc.
Ed: David Chase, Editor, david@appliance.com. **Released:** Annual, January. **Publication Includes:** Suppliers to manufacturers of consumer, commercial, and business appliances. Membership directories for the following associations: Air-Conditioning and Refrigeration Institute, Association of Home Appliance Manufacturers, Commercial Refrigerator Manufacturers Association, Computer and Business Equipment Manufacturers Association, Consumer Electronics Group/Electronic Industries Association, Gas Appliance Manufacturers Association, Cookware Manufacturers Association, National Association of Food Equipment Manufacturers, National Housewares Manufacturers Association, Power Tool Institute, and Vacuum Cleaner Manufacturers Association. **Entries Include:** Company name, address, phone, fax, and products. **Arrangement:** Classified by product. **Indexes:** Manufacturer, product heading.

1169 ■ "A Call for Common Sense with WaterSense" in *Contractor* (Vol. 56, July 2009, No. 7, pp. 42)
Pub: Penton Media, Inc.
Ed: Dave Yates. **Description:** Instillation of a shower that is supposed to protect bathers from being scalded is presented. Plumbers should be aware that the WaterSense shower heads still have a 50/50 chance of scalding their users.

1170 ■ "Cash for Appliances Targets HVAC Products, Water Heaters" in *Contractor* (Vol. 56, October 2009, No. 10, pp. 1)
Pub: Penton Media, Inc.
Ed: Candace Roulo. **Description:** States and territories would need to submit a full application that specifies their implementation plans if they are interested in joining the Cash for Appliances program funded by the American Recovery and Reinvestment Act. The Department of Energy urges states to focus on heating and cooling equipment, appliances and water heaters since these offer the greatest energy savings potential.

1171 ■ "Consumers Like Green, But Not Mandates" in *Business Journal-Milwaukee* (Vol. 28, December 10, 2010, No. 10, pp. A1)
Pub: Milwaukee Business Journal
Ed: Sean Ryan. **Description:** Milwaukee, Wisconsin consumers are willing to spend more on green energy, a survey has revealed. Respondents also said they will pay more for efficient cars and appliances. Support for public incentives for homeowners and businesses that reduce energy use has also increased.

1172 ■ *Electrical Appliance and Utilization Equipment Directory*
Pub: Underwriters Laboratories Inc.
Released: Annual, latest edition 2010. **Price:** $150, individuals. **Covers:** Companies that have qualified to use the UL listing mark or classification marking on or in connection with products that have been found to be in compliance with UL's requirements. Coverage includes foreign companies that manufacture for distribution in the United States. **Entries Include:** Company name, city, ZIP code, UL file number, and type of product. **Arrangement:** Classified by type of product. **Indexes:** Company name.

1173 ■ "The Final Piece; Lowe's to Fill Last Big Parcel Near Great Lakes Crossing" in *Crain's Detroit Business* (March 10, 2008)
Pub: Crain Communications, Inc.
Ed: Daniel Duggan. **Description:** Silverman Development Co. is developing a Lowe's home-improvement store on the last major retail parcel near the intersection of I-75 and Joslyn Road, an area which was once desolate but is now home to several restaurants and other retail facilities.

1174 ■ "Life's Work" in *Harvard Business Review* (Vol. 88, July-August 2010, No. 7-8, pp. 172)
Pub: Harvard Business School Publishing
Ed: Alison Beard. **Description:** The founder of appliance company Dyson Ltd. discusses the role of mak-

ing mistakes in learning and innovation, and emphasizes the importance of hands-on involvement to make a company successful.

1175 ■ *National Appliance Parts Suppliers Association—Membership Roster*
Pub: National Appliance Parts Suppliers Association
Released: Annual. **Covers:** Over 100 wholesale distributors of appliance parts operating in 250 locations, about 80 manufactures of replacement parts for major home appliances and service providers, over 20 manufacturer's representatives. **Entries Include:** Company name, address, phone, name of principal executive. **Arrangement:** Alphabetical. **Indexes:** Geographical.

1176 ■ "A Switch in the Kitchen" in *Barron's* (Vol. 88, March 24, 2008, No. 12, pp. 17)
Pub: Dow Jones & Company, Inc.
Description: Men are doing more kitchen duties, with 18 percent of meals at home being made by men in 2007 compared to 11 percent four years previously. Young wives, however, choose to forgo work and stay at home.

1177 ■ "War Veteran Hit Payoff with Repair Business" in *Tulsa World* (July 28, 2010)
Pub: Tulsa World
Ed: Tim Stanley. **Description:** Profile of Sam Melton, Korean War veteran and retired Air Force staff sergeant, launched appliance repair stores in the Tulsa, Oklahoma area 50 years ago.

1178 ■ "A Wireless Makes 8 Store-In-Store Kiosk Acquisitions" in *Wireless News* (October 16, 2010)
Pub: Close-Up Media Inc.
Description: A Wireless, a retailer for Verizon Wireless has acquired eight of Verizon's retail kiosks that are positioned in home appliance and electronics stores.

1179 ■ "Your Turn in the Spotlight" in *Inc.* (Volume 32, December 2010, No. 10, pp. 57)
Pub: Inc. Magazine
Ed: John Brandon. **Description:** Examples of three video blogs created by entrepreneurs to promote their businesses and products are used to show successful strategies. Wine Library TV promotes a family's wine business; SHAMA.TV offers marketing tips and company news; and Will It Blend? promotes sales of a household blender.

STATISTICAL SOURCES

1180 ■ *RMA Annual Statement Studies*
Pub: Robert Morris Associates (RMA)
Released: Annual. **Price:** $175.00 2006-07 edition, $105.00. **Description:** Contains composite balance sheets and income statements for more than 360 industries, including the accounting, auditing, and bookkeeping industries. Also contains five years of comparative historical data for discerning trends. Includes 16 commonly used ratios, computed for most of the size groupings for nearly every industry.

1181 ■ *Standard & Poor's Industry Surveys*
Pub: Standard & Poor's Corp.
Released: Annual. **Price:** $3633.00. **Description:** Two-volume book that examines the prospects for specific industries, including trucking. Also provides analyses of trends and problems, statistical tables and charts, and comparative company analyses.

TRADE PERIODICALS

1182 ■ *Appliance*
Pub: Dana Chase Publications Inc.
Ed: Tim Somheil, Editor, tim.somheil@cancom.com. **Released:** Monthly. **Price:** $30 print copy domestic; $35 print copy foreign; $40; $45 print copy; $85 print copy domestic; $95 print copy foreign; $137 print copy domestic; $154 print copy foreign; $190 print copy domestic; $214 print copy foreign. **Description:** Trade magazine focusing on appliances: commercial, consumer, medical and business.

1183 ■ *Appliance Design*
Pub: BNP Media
Contact: Lindsay Nagy, Production Mgr
E-mail: nagyl@bnpmedia.com
Released: Monthly. **Description:** Magazine on appliance technology, design for manufacturing, and design trends.

TRADE SHOWS AND CONVENTIONS

1184 ■ National Appliance Parts Suppliers Association Annual Convention
National Appliance Parts Suppliers Association
16420 Se McGillivray, Ste. 103-133
Vancouver, WA 98687
Ph:(360)834-3805
Fax:(360)834-3507
Co. E-mail: info@napsaweb.org
Released: Annual. **Principal Exhibits:** Exhibits for wholesale distributors of replacement parts of major home appliances.

FRANCHISES AND BUSINESS OPPORTUNITIES

1185 ■ Corbeil Appliances
6783 blvd. Leger
Montreal Nord, QC, Canada H1G 6H8
Ph:(514)322-7726
Fax:(514)322-8051
Co. E-mail: claude.deluca@corbeilelectro.com
URL: http://www.corveilelectro.com
No. of Franchise Units: 19. **No. of Company-Owned Units:** 11. **Founded:** 1949. **Franchised:** 1997. **Description:** Specialty retailer of quality and innovative home appliance products and services. **Equity Capital Needed:** $150,000-$200,000. **Franchise Fee:** $35,000-$85,000. **Training:** Provides 3 weeks training.

COMPUTERIZED DATABASES

1186 ■ *Consumer Buying Power*
The Nielsen Co.
770 Broadway
New York, NY 10003-9595
URL: http://www.claritas.com/sitereports/default.jsp
Description: Contains current-year estimates and 5-year projections of total household expenditures for more than 350 product categories, including goods and services, and 73 summary categories. Provides estimated potential consumer expenditures by store types for 41 retail store types, such as eating places; furniture; grocery; shoes; and sporting goods; as well as a breakdown of average household expenditures, such as apparel; education; electronic devices; food at home; furniture; major appliances; medical expenses; and personal care. Also includes average household expenditures for 53 Yellow Page headings. **Availability:** Online: The Nielsen Co. **Type:** Statistical.

ASSOCIATIONS AND OTHER ORGANIZATIONS

1187 ■ American Society of Appraisers
555 Herndon Pkwy., Ste. 125
Herndon, VA 20170
Ph:(703)478-2228
Free: 800-ASA-VALU
Fax:(703)742-8471
Co. E-mail: asainfo@appraisers.org
URL: http://www.appraisers.org/ASAHome.aspx
Contact: Jane Grimm, Exec. VP
Description: Professional appraisal educator, testing, and accrediting society. Sponsors mandatory recertification program for all members. Offers a consumer information service to the public. **Publications:** *ASA Professional Magazine* (quarterly); *Business Valuation Review* (quarterly); *Directory of Professional Appraisal Services* (annual); *Personal Property Journal* (quarterly); *Real Property Journal* (3/year).

1188 ■ Appraisal Institute
550 W Van Buren St., Ste. 1000
Chicago, IL 60607
Ph:(312)335-4100
Free: 888-756-4624
Fax:(312)335-4400
Co. E-mail: aiceo@appraisalinstitute.org
URL: http://www.appraisalinstitute.org
Contact: Fred Grubbe, CEO
Description: General appraisers who hold the MAI designation, and residential members who hold the SRA designation. Enforces Code of Professional Ethics and Standards of Professional Appraisal Practice. Confers one general designation, the MAI, and one residential designation, the SRA. Provides training in valuation of residential and income properties, market analysis, and standards of professional appraisal practice. Sponsors courses in preparation for state certification and licensing; offers continuing education programs for designated members. **Publications:** *The Appraisal Journal* (quarterly); *Appraiser News in Brief* (8/year); *The Dictionary of Real Estate Appraisal, 4th Edition* .

1189 ■ Appraisers Association of America
386 Park Ave. S, 20th Fl., Ste. 2000
New York, NY 10016
Ph:(212)889-5404
Fax:(212)889-5503
Co. E-mail: aaa@appraisersassoc.org
URL: http://www.appraisersassoc.org
Contact: Beth G. Weingast, Pres.
Description: Professional society of appraisers of personal property such as: Americana; antiques; armor; art objects; bibelot; books; bronzes; china and porcelain; clocks and watches; coins; crystal and glass; curios; diamonds and jewelry; enamels; etchings; fine art; firearms; furniture; furs; graphic art; guns; household furnishings; ivories; leather goods; lighting fixtures; linens and lace; miniatures; music; musical instruments; oriental art; paintings; pewter; pianos; primitive art; prints; rugs; sculpture; Sheffield plate; silver and silverware; stamps; steins and tankards; taxes; and woodcarvings. **Publications:** *The Appraiser* (quarterly); *Appraisers Association of America—Membership Directory* (biennial).

1190 ■ International Society of Appraisers
303 W Madison St., Ste. 2650
Chicago, IL 60606
Ph:(312)981-6778
Fax:(312)265-2908
Co. E-mail: isa@isa-appraisers.org
URL: http://www.isa-appraisers.org
Contact: Judith M. Martin, Pres.
Description: Represents personal property appraisers. Seeks to provide the public with a network of appraisal specialists who have been pre-screened by ISA. Conducts educational opportunities for members, the consumer public and other affinity groups. Offers Certified Appraiser of Personal Property Program, education, testing and certification program. Compiles statistics; maintains speakers' bureau. Offers free appraisal referral service in the U.S. and Canada. **Publications:** *ISA Professional Appraisers Information Exchange* .

1191 ■ Jewelers' Security Alliance
6 E 45th St.
New York, NY 10017
Free: 800-537-0067
Fax:(212)808-9168
Co. E-mail: jsa2@jewelerssecurity.org
URL: http://www.jewelerssecurity.org
Contact: John J. Kennedy, Pres.
Description: Advocates for crime prevention in the jewelry industry. Provides crime information and assistance to the jewelry industry and law enforcement. **Publications:** *Annual Report on Crime Against the Jewelry Industry in U.S.* (annual); *JSA Manual of Jewelry Security* (biennial); *JSA Newsletter* (quarterly);Bulletins (periodic).

1192 ■ National Association of Independent Fee Appraisers
401 N Michigan Ave., Ste. 2200
Chicago, IL 60611
Ph:(312)321-6830
Fax:(312)673-6652
Co. E-mail: info@naifa.com
URL: http://www.naifa.com
Contact: Kevin Hacke, Exec. VP
Description: Appraisers for real estate groups, savings and loan associations, title insurance groups, governmental agencies, and related industries. Raises the standards of the appraisal profession. Sponsors career training and professional development programs. Conducts general and applied research in real estate and related fields. **Publications:** *Appraiser-Gram* (quarterly); *National Convention Proceedings* (annual); *Technical Manual* (periodic);Membership Directory (annual).

1193 ■ National Association of Jewelry Appraisers
PO Box 18
Rego Park, NY 11374-0018
Ph:(718)896-1536
Fax:(718)997-9057
Co. E-mail: office@najaappraisers.com
URL: http://www.najaappraisers.com
Contact: Ms. Gail Brett Levine GG, Exec. Dir.
Description: Gem and jewelry appraisers, jewelers, importers, brokers, manufacturers, gemological students, and others professionally interested in jewelry appraisal. Seeks to recognize and make available to the public the services of highly qualified, experienced, independent, and reliable jewelry appraisers. Conducts seminars on jewelry appraisal techniques, methods, and pricing for members and the public. Supports legislation to establish minimum standards of competency and licensing of jewelry appraisers; maintains code of professional ethics. Operates appraiser referral program; sponsors ongoing public relations campaign. Offers equipment discounts, new appraisal forms, travel discounts, insurance, and professional aids for members only. Compiles statistics. **Publications:** *National Association of Jewelry Appraisers—Membership Directory* (annual).

1194 ■ National Association of Real Estate Appraisers
PO Box 879
Palm Springs, CA 92263
Ph:(760)327-5284
Free: 877-815-4172
Fax:(760)327-5631
Co. E-mail: support@assoc-hdqts.org
URL: http://www.narea-assoc.org
Contact: Dave Ehrnstein
Description: Real estate appraisers. Aims to make available the services of the most highly qualified real estate appraisers. Offers certification to members. **Publications:** *NAREA Real Estate Appraisal Newsletter* (bimonthly).

REFERENCE WORKS

1195 ■ *Appraisers Association of America—Membership Directory*
Pub: Appraisers Association of America Inc.
Contact: Aleya Lehmann Bench, Exec. Dir.
Released: Biennial, Even years. **Covers:** 1,000 member appraisers of fine art, antiques, and personal property. **Entries Include:** Name, address, phone, specialties. **Arrangement:** Geographical. **Indexes:** Alphabetical, specialty.

1196 ■ *Directory of the Association of Machinery and Equipment Appraisers*
Pub: Association of Machinery and Equipment Appraisers
Ed: Mary Flynn Boener, Editor, mary.boener@amea.org. **Released:** Annual, January. **Price:** Free. **Covers:** Nearly 300 member certified machinery appraisers. **Entries Include:** Firm name, address, phone, name and title of contact, geographic territory covered, professional designation. **Arrangement:** Alphabetical. **Indexes:** Geographical.

1197 ■ *Gems & Jewelry Appraising: Techniques of Professional Practice*
Pub: GemStone Press
Ed: Anna M. Miller; Gail Brett Levine. **Released:** August 28, 2008. **Price:** $39.99 paperback. **Description:** Comprehensive book for practicing appraisers, would-be appraisers; provides extension information about the profession.

1198 ■ *Institute of Business Appraisers—Directory*
Pub: Institute of Business Appraisers
Price: $20, members; $20, nonmembers. **Covers:** Listing of members and certified business appraisers.

1199 ■ *National Association of Independent Fee Appraisers—National Membership Directory*
Pub: National Association of Independent Fee Appraisers
Contact: Kevin Hacke, Exec. VP
Released: Annual, January. **Covers:** 4,300 independent real estate appraisers. **Entries Include:** Name, address, phone, level of membership. **Arrangement:** Geographical.

TRADE PERIODICALS

1200 ■ *The Appraiser*
Pub: The Appraisal Institute of American Inc.
Ed: Hermine Chivian-Cobb, Editor. **Released:** Quarterly. **Price:** $90. **Description:** Covers topics of interest to personal property appraisers. Recurring features include a calendar of events, book reviews, and news of educational opportunities.

1201 ■ *The Appraisers Standard*
Pub: New England Appraisers Association
Released: Quarterly. **Price:** $20; $25 Canada; $30 other countries. **Description:** Trade magazine for personal property appraisers.

1202 ■ *Canadian Property Valuation*
Pub: Appraisal Institute of Canada
Contact: Kris Fillion, Sales Mgr
E-mail: kfillion@kelman.ca
Released: Quarterly. **Price:** $20. **Description:** Magazine on the certification of real property appraisers and techniques regarding real estate appraising.

1203 ■ *IBA News*
Pub: Institute of Business Appraisers
Ed: Raymond C. Miles, Editor. **Released:** Bimonthly. **Price:** Included in membership. **Description:** Directed toward business appraising and supplies news of the Institute. Recurring features include news of research, a calendar of events, reports of meetings, book reviews, and notices of publications available.

1204 ■ *The Jewelry Appraiser*
Pub: National Association of Jewelry Appraisers Inc.
Ed: Gail Breit Leving, Editor. **Released:** Quarterly. **Price:** Included in membership. **Description:** Provides information on jewelry and gem appraising. Carries items on current appraisal practices and standards, and a wholesale price guide titled the Price Reporter. Recurring features include editorials, news of research, letters to the editor, news of new products, news of members, book reviews, a calendar of events, and columns titled News and Views, Industry News, and Association News.

TRADE SHOWS AND CONVENTIONS

1205 ■ American Society of Appraisers - International Appraisal Conference
American Society of Appraisers
555 Herndon Pkwy., Ste. 125
Herndon, VA 20170
Ph:(703)478-2228
Free: 800-ASA-VALU
Fax:(703)742-8471
Co. E-mail: asainfo@appraisers.org
URL: http://www.appraisers.org
Released: Annual. **Principal Exhibits:** Exhibits for professional appraisers.

1206 ■ Appraisal Institute Annual Meeting
Appraisal Institute
550 W. Van Buren St., Ste. 1000
Chicago, IL 60607
Ph:(312)335-4100
Fax:(312)335-4400
Co. E-mail: aiservice@appraisalinstitute.org
URL: http://www.appraisalinstitute.org
Released: Annual. **Audience:** Real estate appraisers, and valuation professionals. **Principal Exhibits:** Exhibits for general appraisers who hold the MAI, SRPA or designations and residential members who hold the SRA or RM designations.

CONSULTANTS

1207 ■ Artemis Inc.
4715 Crescent St.
Bethesda, MD 20816
Ph:(301)229-2058
Fax:(301)229-2186
Contact: Sandra J. Tropper, Owner
E-mail: sjtropper@aol.com
Scope: Fine art appraiser, consultation on art purchases decoration, framing and presentation.

FRANCHISES AND BUSINESS OPPORTUNITIES

1208 ■ Auto Appraisal Network Inc.
17845 Sky Park Cir., Ste. F
Irvine, CA 92614
Ph:(949)387-7774
Fax:(949)387-7775
No. of Franchise Units: 24. **No. of Company-Owned Units:** 3. **Founded:** 1989. **Franchised:** 2007. **Description:** Vehicle appraisal services. **Equity Capital Needed:** $16,700-$64,275. **Franchise Fee:** $12,000-$30,000. **Royalty Fee:** $95/appraisal. **Financial Assistance:** Limited in-house financial assistance. **Training:** Offers 5-6 days training and ongoing support.

1209 ■ Business America
Business America Assoc., Inc.
2120 Greentree Rd.
Pittsburgh, PA 15220
Ph:(412)276-7701
No. of Franchise Units: 4. **Founded:** 1984. **Franchised:** 1985. **Description:** Sells businesses and franchise appraisal. **Equity Capital Needed:** $10,000. **Franchise Fee:** $7,995. **Financial Assistance:** No. **Training:** Yes.

1210 ■ Property Damage Appraisers, Inc.
PO Box 471909
Ft. Worth, TX 76147
Ph:(817)731-5555
Free: 800-749-7324
Fax:(817)731-5550
No. of Franchise Units: 256. **Founded:** 1963. **Franchised:** 1963. **Description:** Appraising company. Automobile damage appraising experience is a prerequisite. Provides automobile and property appraisal services for insurance companies and the self-insured. **Equity Capital Needed:** $9,250-$24,050. **Franchise Fee:** None. **Financial Assistance:** No. **Managerial Assistance:** National marketing support, a computerized office management system, training and ongoing management assistance are provided. **Training:** Yes.

COMPUTER SYSTEMS/ SOFTWARE

1211 ■ Building Cost Analysis
Datamatics, Inc.
330 New Brunswick Ave.
Fords, NJ 08863
Ph:(732)738-8500
Free: 800-673-0366
Fax:(732)738-9603
Co. E-mail: info@datamaticsinc.com
URL: http://www.datamaticsinc.com

LIBRARIES

1212 ■ Appraisal Institute–Y.T. and Louise Lee Lum Library
550 W. Van Buren St., Ste. 1000
Chicago, IL 60607
Ph:(312)335-4467
Fax:(312)335-4486
Co. E-mail: ailibrary@appraisalinstitute.org
URL: http://www.appraisalinstitute.org/profession/lumlibry.aspx
Contact: Eric B. Goodman, Sr.Mgr.
Scope: Real estate appraisal, real estate market analysis, real estate finance. **Services:** Library open to members, nonmember appraisers, and allied real estate professionals. **Holdings:** 2500 books. **Subscriptions:** 35 journals and other serials.

START-UP INFORMATION

1213 ■ "Add Aquatics to Boost Business" in *Pet Product News* (Vol. 64, December 2010, No. 12, pp. 20)
Pub: BowTie Inc.

Ed: David Lass. **Description:** Pet stores are encouraged to add aquatics departments to increase profitability through repeat sales. This goal can be realized by sourcing, displaying, and maintaining high quality live fish. Other tips regarding the challenges associated with setting up an aquatics department are presented.

1214 ■ "Aquatic Medications Engender Good Health" in *Pet Product News* (Vol. 64, November 2010, No. 11, pp. 47)
Pub: BowTie Inc.

Ed: Madelaine Heleine. **Description:** Pet supply manufacturers and retailers have been exerting consumer education and preparedness efforts to help aquarium hobbyists in tackling ornamental fish disease problems. Aquarium hobbyists have been also assisted in choosing products that facilitate aquarium maintenance before disease attacks their pet fish.

1215 ■ "Foods for Thought" in *Pet Product News* (Vol. 64, December 2010, No. 12, pp. 16)
Pub: BowTie Inc.

Ed: Maddy Heleine. **Description:** Manufacturers have been focused at developing species-specific fish foods due to consumer tendency to assess the benefits of the food they feed their fish. As retailers stock species-specific fish foods, manufacturers have provided in-store items and strategies to assist in efficiently selling these food products. Trends in fish food packaging and ingredients are also discussed.

ASSOCIATIONS AND OTHER ORGANIZATIONS

1216 ■ Canadian Association of Aquarium Clubs
908-373 Front St. W
Toronto, ON, Canada M5V 3R7
Ph:(416)883-0571
Co. E-mail: robert.j.l.wright@sympatico.ca
URL: http://www.caoac.ca
Contact: Bob Wright, Pres.
Description: Represents aquarium owners and other aquaculture hobbyists in Canada. Promotes effective care and breeding of aquatic plants and animals; encourages participation in the hobby of aquaculture. Conducts educational programs. **Publications:** *CAOAC Newsletter* (10/year).

1217 ■ World Pet Association
135 W Lemon Ave.
Monrovia, CA 91016-2809
Ph:(626)447-2222
Free: 800-999-7295
Fax:(626)447-8350
Co. E-mail: info@wpamail.org
URL: http://www.wwpia.org
Contact: Doug Poindexter CAE, Pres.
Description: Manufacturers, retailers and distributors of pet food and services and of avian, aquarium and companion animal care products, equipment and services. Seeks to advance the economic interests of members; promotes responsible pet ownership. Conducts trade shows, certificate training courses and seminars for pet shop retailers, grooming establishments and veterinary clinics. .

TRADE PERIODICALS

1218 ■ *Tropical Fish Hobbyist*
Pub: T.F.H. Publications Inc.
Released: Monthly. **Price:** $28; $48 Canada; $53 other countries; $49 two years. **Description:** Tropical fish magazine for biologists, naturalists, schools, libraries, and commercial and non-commercial keepers and breeders of aquarium fish and plants.

RESEARCH CENTERS

1219 ■ Auburn University–International Center for Aquaculture and Aquatic Environments
203 Swingle Hall
Department of Fisheries & Allied Aquacultures
Auburn, AL 36849
Ph:(334)844-4786
Fax:(334)844-9208
Co. E-mail: fish@auburn.edu
URL: http://www.ag.auburn.edu/fish/international/academic-exchanges/
Contact: Prof. Bryan L. Duncan PhD, Dir.
E-mail: fish@auburn.edu
Scope: Provides technical assistance to developing countries on use of inland fisheries and aquaculture to enhance the production of food and income. Conducts in-country surveys, prepares project proposals for international funding agencies, helps establish pond culture research and development stations, and assists in the implementations of research, training, and extension programs in the following areas: aquacultural economics, aquacultural extension, inventory of fish species, fish taxonomy, fish nutrition and feeding, fish diseases, fish culture, hatchery management, chemical and biological aquatic weed control, limnological surveys, water pollution control and abatement, pond engineering and facility design, and fish technology, processing and preservation. **Services:** Provides information on relevant technical subjects. **Publications:** Abstracts; Newsletter (quarterly).

Archery/Target/Shooting Range

ASSOCIATIONS AND OTHER ORGANIZATIONS

1220 ■ Archery Range and Retailers Organization
156 N Main, Ste. D
Oregon, WI 53575
Ph:(608)835-9060
Free: 800-234-7499
Fax:(608)835-9360
Co. E-mail: lynn@archeryretailers.com
URL: http://www.archeryretailers.com
Contact: Lynn Stiklestad, Exec. Sec./Admin. Dir.
Description: Owners of archery retail shops and/or indoor archery lanes. Functions as a cooperative buying group. Sanctions indoor archery leagues; provides national cash awards. .

1221 ■ National Field Archery Association
800 Archery Ln.
Yankton, SD 57078
Ph:(605)260-9279
Free: 800-811-2331
Fax:(605)260-9280
Co. E-mail: nfaarchery@aol.com
URL: http://www.NFAAarchery.com
Contact: Bruce Cull, Pres.
Description: Field archers and bowhunters. Sponsors field archery schools, three national tournaments, and 16 sectional tournaments; works toward conservation of game and its natural habitat. **Publications:** *Archery* (bimonthly); *Constitution and By-Laws of Field Archery* (annual).

1222 ■ National Rifle Association of America
11250 Waples Mill Rd.
Fairfax, VA 22030
Ph:(703)267-1600
Free: 800-672-3888
Co. E-mail: membership@nrahq.org
URL: http://home.nra.org
Description: Target shooters, hunters, gun collectors, gunsmiths, police officers, and others interested in firearms. Promotes rifle, pistol, and shotgun shooting, hunting, gun collecting, home firearm safety, and wildlife conservation. Encourages civilian marksmanship. Educates police firearms instructors. Maintains national and international records of shooting competitions; sponsors teams to compete in world championships. Also maintains comprehensive collection of antique and modern firearms. Administers the NRA Political Victory Fund. Compiles statistics; sponsors research and education programs; maintains speakers' bureau and museum. Lobbies on firearms issues. **Publications:** *American Rifleman* (monthly).

1223 ■ National Sporting Clays Association
5931 Roft Rd.
San Antonio, TX 78253
Ph:(210)688-3371
Free: 800-877-5338
Fax:(210)688-3014
Co. E-mail: mhampton@nssa-nsca.com
URL: http://www.mynsca.com
Contact: Michael Hampton, Exec. Dir.
Description: Promotion of shooting sports. Acts as the governing body of sporting clays and has an Advisory Council composed of range owners, shooters, and industry persons. Sanctions registered tournaments for member clubs, and uses registered scores to create an impartial classification system for competition. Operates national league and sweepstakes. Conducts championship competitions. Offers Instructor Certification Program to members. **Publications:** *Rule Book*; *Sporting Clays Magazine* (monthly).

REFERENCE WORKS

1224 ■ *Guns Illustrated*
Pub: Krause Publications Inc.
Contact: Dan Shideler, Author
Released: Annual, Latest edition 43rd; 2011. **Price:** $17.81, individuals softcover. **Publication Includes:** Lists of national and international firearms associations; manufacturers, importers, and distributors of firearms, shooting equipment, and services. **Entries Include:** For associations—Name, address, phone, area of interest. For manufacturers and distributors—Name, address, phone, product or service provided. Principal content of publication is articles on hunting, handloading, ammunition, ballistics, collecting, gunsmithing, and customizing, as well as other related information. **Arrangement:** Alphabetical.

TRADE PERIODICALS

1225 ■ *American Rifleman*
Pub: National Rifle Association of America
Contact: Brian Sheetz, Sen. Exec. Ed.
Released: Monthly. **Price:** $10. **Description:** Magazine covering firearms ownership and use.

1226 ■ *Bow and Arrow Hunting*
Pub: Y-Visionary Publishing L.P.
Contact: Kevin Kaiser, Advertising Mgr
Ed: Joe Bell, Editor. **Released:** 9/yr. **Price:** $21.95. **Description:** Magazine for bow hunters and archery enthusiasts.

1227 ■ *Guns & Ammo*
Pub: PRIMEDIA Los Angeles
Ed: Richard Venola, Editor. **Released:** Monthly. **Price:** $12; $20 two years; $25 Canada; $46 Canada 2 years; $27 other countries; $50 other countries 2 years. **Description:** Magazine on firearms for beginners and experts. Features articles on target shooting, defensive techniques, plinking, hunting, law enforcement.

1228 ■ *Precision Shooting*
Pub: Precision Shooting Inc.
Released: Monthly. **Price:** $70 two years; $37; $62 Canada; $70 Europe; $75 other countries. **Description:** Magazine on rifle accuracy.

1229 ■ *Rifle*
Pub: Wolfe Publishing Co.
Contact: Mark Harris, Assoc. Publisher
Released: Bimonthly. **Price:** $19.97; $51 combo; $11.99 military; $19.95 online. **Description:** Covers all types of rifles-centerfires, rimfires, air rifles and muzzle loaders.

1230 ■ *Shooting Industry*
Pub: Publishers Development Corp.
Contact: Anita Carson, Sales Mgr
E-mail: anita@shootingindustry.com
Ed: Russ Thurman, Editor, russ@shootingindustry.com. **Released:** Monthly. **Price:** $45 other countries. **Description:** Magazine serving the firearms industry.

1231 ■ *Shooting Times*
Pub: PRIMEDIA Los Angeles
Contact: Matt Johnson, Gen Mgr
E-mail: matt.johnson@imoutdoors.com
Ed: Joseph von Benedikt, Editor, shootingtimes@imoutdoors.com. **Released:** Monthly. **Price:** $12; $22 two years; $25 Canada; $27 other countries. **Description:** Magazine focusing on guns and shooting sports.

1232 ■ *Skeet Shooting Review*
Pub: National Skeet Shooting Association
Ed: Susie Fluckiger, Editor, sfluckiger@nssa-nsca.com. **Released:** Monthly. **Price:** $24; $60 Canada and Mexico; $92 other countries; $45 two years. **Description:** Official magazine of the National Skeet Shooting Association; including shooting news, schedules of tournaments, shotgun tests and evaluations, shooting tips, new products, and coverage of major tournaments.

1233 ■ *The Tab*
Pub: Bowhunters of North America
Ed: Adrian Jacobs, Editor. **Released:** 2/year. **Price:** Included in membership. **Description:** Provides articles intended to promote the sport of bowhunting. Discusses such topics as improving hunter-landowner relations and increasing the understanding of bowhunting among the non-hunting public. Recurring features include news of members, announcements of new products, and articles on bowhunting techniques.

TRADE SHOWS AND CONVENTIONS

1234 ■ JAGEN UND FISCHEN - International Exhibition for Hunters, Fishermen and Marksmen
Kallman Worldwide, Inc.
4 North St., Ste. 800
Waldwick, NJ 07463-1842
Ph:(201)251-2600
Fax:(201)251-2760
Co. E-mail: info@kallman.com
URL: http://www.kallman.com
Principal Exhibits: Equipment, supplies, and services for hunters, fishermen, and marksmen.

1235 ■ The Shooting, Hunting, and Outdoor Trade Show
Reed Exhibitions Contemporary Forums
11900 Silvergate Dr.
Dublin, CA 94568
Ph:(925)828-7100
Fax:800-329-9923
Co. E-mail: info@cforums.com
URL: http://www.contemporaryforums.com
Audience: Federally licensed firearms dealers and legitimate sporting goods dealers. **Principal Exhibits:** Shooting and hunting equipment and products; sports accessories, clothing, and supplies.

LIBRARIES

1236 ■ National Rifle Association of America–NRA Technical Library
11250 Waples Mill Rd.
Fairfax, VA 22030
Ph:(703)267-1000
Fax:(703)267-3971
Co. E-mail: mbussard@nrahq.org
Contact: Michael Bussard, Tech.Ed.
Scope: Firearms, ammunition, military ordnance, antique arms, ballistics, handloading, collecting, history. **Services:** Library not open to the public. **Holdings:** 1700 books. **Subscriptions:** 25 journals and other serials.

Architectural Restoration/Conservation

ASSOCIATIONS AND OTHER ORGANIZATIONS

1237 ■ Blair Society for Genealogical Research
726 Falling Oaks Dr.
Medina, OH 44256-2778
URL: http://www.blairsociety.org
Contact: Brenda Weeks, Pres.
Description: Individuals with the surname Blair and its variants; others with an interest in Blair family genealogy. Promotes interest in, and study of, Blair family genealogy; seeks to preserve family records and artifacts. Conducts educational programs; assists Blair family genealogists.

1238 ■ Canadian Centre for Architecture–Centre Canadien d'Architecture
1920, rue Baile
Montreal, QC, Canada H3H 2S6
Ph:(514)939-7026
Co. E-mail: info@cca.qc.ca
URL: http://www.cca.qc.ca/en
Contact: Mr. Mirko Zardini, Dir.
Description: Study center and museum devoted to the art of architecture, past and present. Provides access to research collections, exhibitions, publications, colloquia, educational and cultural programs, as well as family programs. **Publications:** *Money Matters: A Critical Look at Bank Architecture*; *Sense of the City* .

1239 ■ Royal Architectural Institute of Canada–Institut Royal d'Architecture du Canada
330-55 rue Murray St.
Ottawa, ON, Canada K1N 5M3
Ph:(613)241-3600
Fax:(613)241-5750
Co. E-mail: info@raic.org
URL: http://www.raic.org
Contact: Ranjit K. Dhar, Pres.
Description: Registered architects in Canada united to further develop the quality of architecture. **Publications:** *Building the West*; *RAIC Bulletin* (monthly); *Update* (bimonthly).

1240 ■ Royal Oak Foundation
35 W 35th St., Ste. 1200
New York, NY 10001-2205
Ph:(212)480-2889
Free: 800-913-6565
Fax:(212)785-7234
Co. E-mail: general@royal-oak.org
URL: http://www.royal-oak.org
Contact: Mr. Sean E. Sawyer PhD, Exec. Dir.
Description: Professionals, students, and laypeople who are interested in architecture, nature conservation, and historic preservation areas. Seeks to further the preservation and understanding of Anglo-American cultural and architectural heritage. Conducts symposia; presents lecture series and special lectures given by foreign speakers visiting the U.S.; sponsors exhibits emphasizing historic preservation. Maintains charitable program. .

DIRECTORIES OF EDUCATIONAL PROGRAMS

1241 ■ *The Encyclopedia of Associations and Information Sources for Architects, Designers, and Engineers*
Pub: M.E. Sharpe Inc.
Contact: David Kent Ballast, Author
Price: $176.95, individuals available to all countries. **Covers:** 5,000 U.S. and Canadian resources such as journals, online databases, CD-ROMs, testing laboratories, government sources, web sites and more for architects, designers, and engineers. **Entries Include:** Contact information, web addresses.

REFERENCE WORKS

1242 ■ "$100 Million Plan for Jefferson Arms" in *Saint Louis Business Journal* (Vol. 32, October 14, 2011, No. 7, pp. 1)
Pub: Saint Louis Business Journal
Ed: Evan Binns. **Description:** Teach for America is planning a $100 million renovation project of the former Jefferson Arms hotel in St. Louis, Missouri. The organization has signed a letter of intent to occupy the space. Financing of the project will be mainly through tax credits.

1243 ■ "2010: Important Year Ahead for Waterfront" in *Bellingham Business Journal* (Vol. March 2010, pp. 2)
Pub: Sound Publishing Inc.
Ed: Isaac Bonnell. **Description:** A tentative timeline has been established for the environmental impact statement (EIS) slated for completion in May 2010. The plan for the Waterfront District includes detailed economic and architectural analysis of the feasibility of reusing remaining structures and retaining some industrial icons.

1244 ■ "Advertisers Hooked on Horns, their Playground" in *Austin Business JournalInc.* (Vol. 28, July 25, 2008, No. 19, pp. A1)
Pub: American City Business Journals
Ed: Sandra Zaragoza. **Description:** Renovation of the D.K. Royal-Texas Memorial Stadium has increased its advertising revenue from $570,000 in 1993 to $10 in 2008. Sponsorship has grown in the past years due to the revenue-sharing agreement, a ten-year contract through 2015 between the University of Texas and IMG College Sports.

1245 ■ "Annapolis Seeks City Market Vendors" in *Boston Business Journal* (Vol. 29, June 10, 2011, No. 5, pp. 3)
Pub: American City Business Journals Inc.
Ed: Daniel J. Sernovitz. **Description:** The city of Annapolis, Maryland is planning to revive the historical landmark Market House and it is now accepting bids from vendors until June 10, 2011. The city hopes to reopen the facility by July 2011 for a six-month period after which it will undergo renovations.

1246 ■ "Bridging the Ingenuity Gap" in *Canadian Business* (Vol. 79, November 6, 2006, No. 22, pp. 12)
Pub: Rogers Media
Ed: Rachel Pulfer. **Description:** The views of Patrick Whitney, director of Illinois Institute of Technology's Institute of design, on globalization and business design methods are presented.

1247 ■ "Can This Duo be Saved? Renovating 2 Tallest Edifices Downtown Will Be Costly, Owner Says" in *Charlotte Observer* (February 4, 2007)
Pub: Knight-Ridder/Tribune Business News
Ed: Jefferson George. **Description:** Gastonia, North Carolina city leaders are making plans to renovate the Lawyers Building and the Commercial Building in an effort to revitalize the downtown area.

1248 ■ "Firm Takes 'Local' Worldwide" in *Hispanic Business* (July-August 2007, pp. 48)
Pub: Hispanic Business
Ed: Keith Rosenblum. **Description:** Willy A. Bermello tells how he has expanded his architectural, engineering and construction firm globally.

1249 ■ "First the Merger: Then, The Culture Clash. How To Fix the Little Things That Can Tear a Company Apart" in *Inc.* (January 2008)
Pub: Gruner & Jahr USA Publishing
Ed: Elaine Appleton Grant. **Description:** Ways three CEOs handled the culture classes that followed after company mergers; companies profiled include Fuel Outdoor, an outdoor advertising company; Nelson, an interior design and architecture firm; and Beber Silverstein, an ad agency.

1250 ■ "'Groundhog Day' B & B Likely Will Be Converted Into One In Real Life" in *Chicago Tribune* (October 21, 2008)
Pub: McClatchy-Tribune Information Services
Ed: Carolyn Starks. **Description:** Everton Martin and Karla Stewart Martin have purchased the Victorian house that was featured as a bed-and-breakfast in the 1993 hit move "Groundhog Day"; the couple was initially unaware of the structure's celebrity status when they purchased it with the hope of fulfilling their dream of owning a bed-and-breakfast.

1251 ■ "Historic Glenview Homes Could Be Torn Down" in *Chicago Tribune* (September 25, 2008)
Pub: McClatchy-Tribune Information Services
Ed: Courtney Flynn. **Description:** Leaders of the Glenview New Church would like to see a buyer emerge who would move and restore two historic homes sitting on the church's property. If a buyer does not come forward the church plans to demolish the homes to make room for condominiums and the expansion of their school.

1252 ■ "Historic Tax Credit Plan Gains Support" in *Baltimore Business Journal* (Vol. 27, January 8, 2010, No. 36, pp. 1)
Pub: American City Business Journals
Ed: Heather Harlan Warnack. **Description:** Maryland Governor Martin O'Malley plans to push legislation in the General Assembly to extend for three more years

the tax credit program for rehabilitation of obsolete buildings. The Maryland Heritage Structure Rehabilitation Tax Credit Program has declined from almost $75 million in expenses in 2001 to roughly $5 million in 2010 fiscal year. Details on the projects that benefited from the program are explored.

1253 ■ "Honcoop Honored as BIAWC's Builder of the Year" in *Bellingham Business Journal* (Vol. February 2010, pp. 17)
Pub: Sound Publishing Inc.
Description: Gary Honcoop, co-owner and president of Roosendaal-Honcoop Construction Inc. was honored by the Building Industry Association of Whatcom County as Builder of the Year. The construction company was founded in 1979.

1254 ■ "Hospital to Get $72M Makeover" in *Austin Business Journallnc.* (Vol. 29, January 15, 2010, No. 45, pp. 1)
Pub: American City Business Journals
Ed: Sandra Zaragoza. **Description:** St. David's South Austin Medical Center, formerly St. David's South Austin Hospital, is undertaking an expansion and renovation project worth $72 million. Meanwhile, CEO Erol Akdamar has resigned to serve as CEO of Medical City Hospital in Dallas, Texas. A new CEO and a general contractor for the project are yet to be chosen by the hospital.

1255 ■ *How to Open and Operate a Financially Successful Redesign, Redecorating, and Home Staging Business: With Companion CD-ROM*
Pub: Atlantic Publishing Group, Inc.
Ed: Mary Larsen; Teri B. Clark. **Released:** January 2008. **Price:** $39.95 paperback. **Description:** Questions are asked to help individuals determine if they should launch their own redesign or real estate staging firm.

1256 ■ "Innovation Can Be Imperative for Those in Hands-On Trades" in *Crain's Cleveland Business* (Vol. 28, November 12, 2007, No. 45)
Pub: Crain Communications, Inc.
Ed: Harriet Tramer. **Description:** Discusses the importance of networking and innovative marketing concerning those in art and restoration trades.

1257 ■ "Investors Eye Old Buildings" in *Business Journal-Portland* (Vol. 24, October 19, 2007, No. 34, pp. 1)
Pub: American City Business Journals, Inc.
Ed: Wendy Culverwell. **Description:** Office vacancy rates in downtown Portland has dipped to around five percent, causing brokers and investors to search for older buildings in the Class B and Class C categories where the rent is also cheaper. Some notable older and cheaper buildings will be renovated for use.

1258 ■ "Muirhead Farmhouse B & B Owners Get Hospitality Right" in *Chicago Tribune* (July 31, 2008)
Pub: McClatchy-Tribune Information Services
Ed: Glenn Jeffers. **Description:** Profile of the Muirhead Farmhouse, a bed-and-breakfast owned by Mike Petersdorf and Sarah Muirhead Petersdorf; Frank Lloyd Wright designed the historic farmhouse which blends farm life and history into a unique experience that is enhanced by the couple's hospitality.

1259 ■ "N.H. Near the LEED in Green Space" in *New Hampshire Business Review* (Vol. 33, March 25, 2011, No. 6, pp. 30)
Pub: Business Publications Inc.
Description: New Hamphire's architects, contractors and suppliers are among the leaders with LEED-certified space per capita.

1260 ■ "Not Enough Room" in *Austin Business Journallnc.* (Vol. 29, November 13, 2009, No. 36, pp. A1)
Pub: American City Business Journals
Ed: Jacob Dirr. **Description:** Hotel and convention business in downtown Austin, Texas lost nearly $5.3 million when Dell Inc. relocated its annual convention to Las Vegas. However, lack of capital caused the postponement of various hotel projects which need to be finished in order to attract well-attended conventions. Makeover projects on Austin's Waller Creek and Sixth Street are discussed.

1261 ■ "P&L Building Owner Nears Start of $157M Condo Plan" in *Business Journal-Serving Metropolitan Kansas City* (November 23, 2007)
Pub: American City Business Journals, Inc.
Ed: Jim Davis. **Description:** The owner of Power and Light Building is ready to begin a $157 million plan to refurbish the Kansas City landmark and redevelop a property right next to it after receiving tax increment refinancing for the project.

1262 ■ "The Power of Fun" in *Canadian Business* (Vol. 79, November 6, 2006, No. 22, pp. 58)
Pub: Rogers Media
Ed: Zena Olijnyk. **Description:** The creative efforts of Phillippe Starck in designing condos are analyzed.

1263 ■ "Restoring Grandeur" in *Business Courier* (Vol. 26, December 4, 2009, No. 32, pp. 1)
Pub: American City Business Journals, Inc.
Ed: Dan Monk. **Description:** Eagle Realty Group intends to spend more than $10 to restore the historic 12-story Phelps apartment building in Lytle Park in Cincinnati. Its president, Mario San Marco, expressed the need to invest in the building in order to maintain operations. The building could be restored into a hotel catering to executives and consultants.

1264 ■ "Stone Company Slated to Expand Here" in *Austin Business Journallnc.* (Vol. 28, September 12, 2008, No. 26, pp. 1)
Pub: American City Business Journals
Ed: Jean Kwon. **Description:** Architectural Granite & Marble Inc. has a $6 million investment that moved the company from 2,500 square feet of space to a 10,000 square foot office in Southwest Austin, Texas. The investment will also provide for the company's expansion in Nashville, Tennessee and San Antonio, Texas.

1265 ■ "Texas State Poised for Boom" in *Austin Business Journallnc.* (Vol. 29, January 29, 2010, No. 47, pp. 1)
Pub: American City Business Journals
Ed: Sandra Zaragoza. **Description:** Texas State University, San Marcos has seen its student population grow to 30,800 and the university is set for $633 million in construction projects to address demand for student housing and building expansions and renovations. Details on the buildings and student housing plans for the projects are provided.

1266 ■ "This Just In" in *Crain's Detroit Business* (Vol. 25, June 22, 2009, No. 25, pp. 1)
Pub: Crain Communications Inc. - Detroit
Description: Yamasaki Associates, an architectural firm has been sued for non payment of wages to four employees. Yamasaki spokesperson stated the economy has affected the company and it is focusing marketing efforts on areas encouraged by recovery funding.

1267 ■ "USF Plans $30M Sports Complex" in *Tampa Bay Business Journal* (Vol. 29, October 23, 2009, No. 44, pp. 1)
Pub: American City Business Journals
Ed: Jane Meinhardt. **Description:** University of South Florida (USF) is going to build a new sports complex with the aid of a $30 million loan from BB&T. The project, which is also comprised of new and renovated athletic facilities on USF's Tampa campus, is projected to create more than $37 million in revenue in its first year. Revenues from the said facilities are expected to achieve an annual growth of at least four percent.

1268 ■ "Vegas in the D; Local Architects Collaborate On MGM Grand" in *Crain's Detroit Business* (Vol. 23, October 1, 2007, No. 40, pp. 1)
Pub: Crain Communications Inc. - Detroit
Ed: Daniel Duggan. **Description:** Local Detroit architects, Smith Group and Hamilton Anderson Associates are among the contractors vying for subcontracted architecture, construction and consulting contracts for the new MGM Grand Detroit casino and hotel.

1269 ■ "Vernon Revamp" in *Business Courier* (Vol. 26, October 9, 2009, No. 24, pp. 1)
Pub: American City Business Journals, Inc.
Ed: Dan Monk. **Description:** Al Neyer Inc. will redevelop the Vernon Manor Hotel as an office building for the Cincinnati Children's Hospital Medical Center. The project will cost $35 million and would generate a new investment vehicle for black investors who plan to raise $2.7 million in private offerings to claim majority ownership of the property after its renovations.

TRADE PERIODICALS

1270 ■ *AppendX*
Pub: Appendx
Released: Annual. **Description:** Professional journal covering architecture criticism.

1271 ■ *Azure Magazine*
Pub: Azure Publishing Inc.
Contact: Sergio Sgaramella, Publisher
Ed: Nelda Rodger, Editor. **Released:** 8/yr. **Price:** $32. 95; $54.95 two years; $32.95; $54.95 two years; $48 other countries; $78 other countries 2 years. **Description:** Trade magazine covering art, design and architecture.

1272 ■ *Downtown Idea Exchange*
Pub: Alexander Communications Group Inc.
Contact: Margaret DeWitt, Publisher
Ed: Paul Felt, Editor. **Released:** Monthly. **Price:** $227, individuals; $227, elsewhere. **Description:** Focuses on revitalizing central business districts, including planning, design, development, preservation, parking, transit, traffic, funding, and organization.

1273 ■ *Journal of the Society of Architectural Historians JSAH*
Pub: Society of Architectural Historians
Contact: Prof. Hilary Ballon, Founding Ed.
E-mail: hilary.ballon@nyu.edu
Released: Quarterly. **Description:** Professional magazine devoted to architectural history.

1274 ■ *Municipal Art Society Newsletter*
Pub: Municipal Art Society
Ed: Released: 6/year. **Price:** Included in membership. **Description:** Provides updates on advocacy efforts, exhibitions, and programming on urban issues. Recurring features include a calendar of events and tour schedule.

1275 ■ *Timber Framing*
Pub: Timber Framers Guild
Ed: Ken Rower, Editor. **Released:** Quarterly. **Price:** $25 Free with membership; $25 nonmembers. **Description:** Trade magazine covering timber frame design home construction, history, restoration, and preservation.

VIDEOCASSETTES/ AUDIOCASSETTES

1276 ■ *The California Capitol Restoration Series*
PBS Home Video
Catalog Fulfillment Center
PO Box 751089
Charlotte, NC 28275-1089
Ph:800-531-4727
Free: 800-645-4PBS
Co. E-mail: info@pbs.org
URL: http://www.pbs.org
Price: $399.00. **Description:** Three-part series that covers the seven-year effort to restore California's State Capitol back to its look at the turn-of-the-century. Also features historical information on the building itself. Includes footage of the actual restoration. **Availability:** VHS; 3/4U; Special order formats.

CONSULTANTS

1277 ■ ALSA Architecture L.L.C.
570 7th Ave., Ste. 1206
New York, NY 10018-1603
Ph:(212)302-2180
Fax:(212)391-2148
Co. E-mail: mail@alsaarchitecture.com
URL: http://www.alsaarchitecture.com
Contact: Roy Sokoloski, President
E-mail: roy@alsaarchitecture.com
Scope: Architectural and engineering design firm that provides consulting expertise in construction contract documents, construction administration and facilities management. The firm has a preservation department specializing in exterior and interior building rehabilitation, including landmark properties restoration. Offers comprehensive services including architectural, mechanical, plumbing, electrical, fire and life safety design. Industries served: Academic, industrial, financial, government, health care, housing, corporate and retail.

1278 ■ Architerra Inc.
1516 Hepburn Ave.
Louisville, KY 40204
Ph:(502)585-1800
Fax:(502)584-9414
Co. E-mail: architerra@yahoo.com
Contact: Moseley L. Putney AIA, President
E-mail: architerra@yahoo.com
Scope: Specializes in downtown revitalization, historic preservation and urban planning.

1279 ■ Beckett and Raeder Inc.
535 W William St., Ste. 101
Ann Arbor, MI 48103
Ph:(734)663-2622
Fax:(734)663-6759
Co. E-mail: info@bria2.com
URL: http://www.bria2.com
Contact: Deb Cooper, Partner
E-mail: coop@atsbria2.com
Scope: Provides exceptional and innovative professional service to a variety of municipal governments, state and federal agencies, institution and private sector clients.

1280 ■ Brenda Spencer
10150 Onaga Rd.
Wamego, KS 66547-9584
Ph:(785)456-9857
Fax:(785)456-9857
Co. E-mail: spencer@wamego.net
Contact: Mike Boatwright, Mgr
Scope: Specializes in main street revitalization and historic preservation.

1281 ■ Building Conservation Associates Inc.
158 W 27th St.
New York, NY 10001
Ph:(212)777-1300
Fax:(212)777-1606
Co. E-mail: info@bcausa.com
URL: http://www.bcausa.com
Contact: Claudia Kavenagh, Director
E-mail: bbailly@atsbcausa.com
Scope: A consulting firm that specializes in both the technical and historical aspects of restoring buildings and works of art. Assists clients in the preparation of federal rehabilitation tax credit applications. Combines field documentation, archival research, materials testing and scientific research. **Publications:** "Journal of the American Institute foe Conservation".

1282 ■ Cox Graae Spack Architects
2909 M St. NW
Washington, DC 20007-3714
Ph:(202)965-7070
Fax:(202)965-7144
Co. E-mail: info@cgsarchitects.com
URL: http://www.cgsarchitects.com
Contact: William Spack, Principle
E-mail: bspack@atscgsarchitects.com
Scope: Services include architecture, historic preservation, planning, programming, space planning, interior design, building codes, design guidelines, ADA, waterfront development, rehabilitation technology, restoration and public transportation.

1283 ■ Cropsey and Associates Inc.
800 W Taylor St.
PO Box 1006
Griffin, GA 30224-2722
Ph:(770)229-1100
Fax:(770)229-1326
Contact: Paul A. Cropsey, President
Scope: General practice architectural design firm experienced in rehabilitating historic buildings in accordance with the Secretary of the Interior's guidelines for Historic Preservation and ISTEA funding.

1284 ■ DANTH Inc.
83-85 116th St., Ste. 3D
Kew Gardens, NY 11418
Ph:(718)805-9507
Fax:(718)805-2656
Co. E-mail: danth@danth.com
URL: http://www.danth.com
Contact: N. David Milder, President
E-mail: danthinc@yahoo.com
Scope: Provides economic revitalization consulting to downtown, commercial district and local government organizations. Focuses on the development of comprehensive retail and office revitalization policies and programs. **Publications:** "MAKING MEMBERSHIP BUY-INS EASY," Downtown Idea Exchange, Oct, 2004. **Seminars:** Niche Development and Marketing; Reconnaissance and Action Plan; Retail Revitalization Strategy and Action Plan.

1285 ■ Glenn Acomb Associates Inc.
1024 NE 5th St.
Gainesville, FL 32601
Ph:(352)392-6098
Fax:(352)372-6233
Co. E-mail: ufadvisor06@flasla.org
Contact: Glenn A. Acomb, President
E-mail: gaafl@aol.com
Scope: Offers planning and design services for downtown revitalization, CRA/development, master plans, historic design, waterfronts, parks and plazas. **Publications:** "Implications of the Physical Plan," 2006; "Low Impact Design and Development Techniques," May, 2005; "New Towns and New Urbanism: A Critique from a Landscape Perspective," 2000. **Seminars:** Downtown Revitalization; Planning Your Streetscape; Livable Communities; Sustainable Communities.

1286 ■ Gove Lumber Co.
80 Colon St.
Beverly, MA 01915
Ph:(978)922-0921
Fax:(978)921-4522
Co. E-mail: info@govelumber.com
URL: http://www.govelumber.com
Contact: Sandy Gove, Principle
Scope: Specializes in wood doors and windows for historic preservation. Supplies mill work in mahogany, cypress, oak and ships in the United States and abroad. Areas of expertise include: Adaptive reuse, architectural historic preservation, design guidelines, rehabilitation technology, and restoration.

1287 ■ Halstead Architects
207 S Washington St.
Marion, IN 46952
Ph:(317)684-1431
Fax:(317)684-1433
Co. E-mail: mikeh@halstead-architects.com
URL: http://www.halstead-architects.com
Contact: Steve Schubert, Principal
E-mail: steves@halstead-architects.com
Scope: Offers architectural expertise in planning, libraries, community based projects, historic preservation, residential, entertainment, religious, educational, and interiors in the United States. **Publications:** "Coffee, snacks ahead for canal walkers," Indianapolis Star, Oct, 2003; "Canal-side Church Building to Get Makeover," Indiana Business Journal.

1288 ■ Hemmler Camayd Architects
409 Lackawanna Ave., Ste. 400
Scranton, PA 18503-1432
Ph:(570)961-1302
Fax:(570)961-3919
Co. E-mail: info@hc-architects.com
URL: http://www.hc-architects.com
Contact: Richard J. Leonari, Partner
E-mail: bdoran@atshc-architects.com
Scope: Provides comprehensive architectural, interior design and planning services to corporate, government, education, health/elderly care and religious sectors in the mid-Atlantic states, primarily Pennsylvania. Offers services for creative design of new buildings, renovation and alteration of existent buildings and adaptive reuse, restoration and preservation of historic structures. Also provides feasibility studies, existing conditions evaluations, master planning, facility planning, interior space planning and FF and E (furniture, fixtures, and equipment)planning and construction observation services.

1289 ■ Historic Exterior Paint Colors Consulting
3661 Waldenwood Dr.
Ann Arbor, MI 48105
Ph:(734)668-0298
Co. E-mail: robs@umich.edu
URL: http://www.historichousecolors.com
Contact: Robert Schweitzer, Owner
E-mail: robs@umich.edu
Scope: Provides exterior paint color consulting services. Provides services for historic, contemporary, new, commercial and residential services; museums. **Publications:** "Proof that Paint Color Lends Detail," Arts and Crafts Homes, 2006; "Bungalow Colors-Exteriors," Gibbs-Smith Publishers, 2002; "Color Scheming," Design NJ, 2002; "Colonial Revival Homes," Victorian Homes, Feb, 2003; "America's Favorite Homes"; "Color a New World," 60s Ranch Color Makeover, Romantic Homes, Aug, 2001; "How Shall I Paint my House," American Bungalow, 1999; "Color Concepts and Bungalow Basics," Cottages & Bungalows.

1290 ■ Hoisington Koegler Group Inc.
123 N 3rd St., Ste. 100
Minneapolis, MN 55401
Ph:(612)338-0800
Fax:(612)338-6838
Co. E-mail: blc@hkgi.com
URL: http://www.hkgi.com
Contact: Judith Guy, Office Mgr
E-mail: jguy@atshkgi.com
Scope: Planners and landscape architects provide the technical and strategic expertise needed to develop innovative solutions that respond to the natural environment and to the needs of the community. Emphasizes sustainability and integration of the natural landscape and historic resources. Areas of expertise include city planning, landscape architecture, urban planning, community development, and group facilitation.

1291 ■ Howard L. Zimmerman Architects P.C.
11 W 30th St.
New York, NY 10001
Ph:(212)564-9393
Fax:(212)564-9032
Co. E-mail: info@hlzimmerman.com
URL: http://www.hlzimmerman.com
Contact: Howard L. Zimmerman, President
E-mail: howard@hlzimmerman.com
Scope: Offers evaluation of building restoration and preventive maintenance to building owners. Services include exterior restoration, historic preservation, capital improvement, forensic investigation and interior design services. Technical services include facade investigation, materials testing, analysis and evaluation, due diligence evaluations, building systems analysis, pre-purchase inspections, inspection reports, local law reports, CAD services, building code analysis and interpretation, building alteration reviews and peer reviews. Provides expert legal testimony. Specializes in the design of commercial spaces, restaurants, luxury apartments and adaptive re-use of buildings. **Publications:** "Forensic Architecture: The Art of Understanding a Buildings Unwritten History".

1292 ■ Integrated Conservation Resources Inc.
41 E 11th St., 3rd Fl.
New York, NY 10003-4602
Ph:(212)947-4499
Fax:(212)947-7766
Co. E-mail: info@icr-icc.com
URL: http://www.icr-icc.com
Contact: Tina Paterno, Principle
E-mail: atrienens@atsicr-icc.com
Scope: Assists design professionals by providing specialized expertise on historic building materials. Services span the full spectrum of architectural conservation services.

1293 ■ Jan Rubin Associates Inc.
2022 Chandler St.
Philadelphia, PA 19103-5605
Ph:(215)564-5956
Fax:(215)564-1939
Co. E-mail: jra@jragroup.com
URL: http://www.jragroup.org
Contact: Jan Rubin, Owner
E-mail: janrubin@jragroup.org
Scope: Firm specializes in structuring and developing low income housing and historic tax credits, HOPE VI, CDBG or HOME transactions for public and private organizations.

1294 ■ John Leeke
26 Higgins St.
Portland, ME 04103
Ph:(207)773-2306
Fax:(207)773-2306
Co. E-mail: johnleeke@historichomeworks.com
URL: http://www.historichomeworks.com
Contact: John Leeke, Principle
Scope: Assists owners, trades people, contractors and professionals understand and maintain their historic and older buildings. **Publications:** "Window Restoration". **Seminars:** Save Your Wood Windows; Exterior Wood and Paint; Restore Omaha, Nov, 2006; The Business Side of Preservation Vermont, Nov, 2006; Save Your Wood Windows, May, 2007; Exterior Woodwork: Repairs and Painting, Jun, 2007; Windows: Small Shop Business, 2007. **Special Services:** Historic HomeWorks™.

1295 ■ Jonathan Cohen and Associates, Architects and Planners
65 Acacia Ave.
Berkeley, CA 94708-1201
Ph:(510)558-8154
Fax:(510)558-8054
Co. E-mail: info@jcarchitects.com
URL: http://www.jcarchitects.com
Contact: Peter W. Tsugawa, Principle
E-mail: jonathan@jcarchitects.com
Scope: Firm offers a full range of architectural, planning and urban design services including programming, master planning, feasibility studies; design, rehabilitation and restoration; materials research; working drawings and specifications; construction administration; post construction evaluation; and seismic and disabled access retrofit. Expertise in the application of information technology used in the design, construction, and operations of buildings. Expert testimony and dispute consultation is also provided to the construction and design industries. **Publications:** "The New Architect: Keeper of Knowledge and Rules," The Architect's Handbook of Professional Practice, John Wiley and Sons, 2004; "Participatory Design with the Internet," Architectural Record, Aug, 2003; "Communication and Design with the Internet"; "Secrets to a Fulfilling Life". **Seminars:** Project Information Managers: The New Master Builders, Zweig White AEC Technology Strategies, Washington, DC, Jun, 2003; Web-based Design Communication, Fisher Center for Information Technology & Marketplace Transformation, Haas School of Business, UC Berkeley, Apr, 2003; Web Development for Architects, AIA Minnesota annual convention, Nov, 2002; Geographic Information Systems for Architects, AEC Systems, Anaheim, CA, Jun, 2002; The Internet in Architectural Practice and Web Authoring for Architects; Ontario Association of Architects annual convention: Changing Practice, Practicing Change, Niagara Falls, Ontario, Canada, May, 2002; Architect at the Center: A Radical Proposal for the Building Industry, AIA Professional Practice Conference, Washington, DC, Apr, 2002; Networked Design Organizations and the Project Information Manager, Build Boston Nov, 2001; Architecture in the Net Economy, Form, Function, Future, AIA Professional Practice Conference, Portland, OR, Oct, 2000; Healing a Fragmented Industry: New Opportunities for the Architectural Profession, Association of Collegiate Schools of Architecture Technology Conference, MIT, Jul, 2000; Owning the Project Information: An Opportunity for Architects, Greenwich 2000 Symposium on Digital Creativity, Virtual Design/Build Organizations and the Project Information Manager; University of Greenwich, London, UK, Jan, 2000; Intra nets and Web Portals for Collaboration and Knowledge Management; Virtual Design/Build Organizations and the Project Information Manager; Web Sites for Participatory Programming and Design; Geographic Information Systems; Cool Software Tools for Designers; Participatory Design and Planning with the Internet Case Study; Intra nets and Web Portals for Collaboration and Knowledge Management; Virtual Design/ Build Organizations and the Project Information Manager.

1296 ■ Karl Kardel Consultancy
4926 E 12th St.
Oakland, CA 94601
Ph:(510)261-4149
Fax:(510)436-7486
Co. E-mail: karl@kardelconsultancy.com
URL: http://www.kardelconsultancy.com
Contact: Aaron Atnip, Managing Director
E-mail: aaron@atskardelconsultancy.com
Scope: Provides consultation in water invasion in windows, wall systems and membranes. Offers problem resolution in finishes and coatings and forensic analysis in building failures. Specializes in historic conservation, architectural finishes, water invasion, windows, curtain walls and stucco. Gives analysis for managed case cost controls.

1297 ■ Karn Charuhas Chapman & Twohey
1120 Connecticut Ave. NW, Ste. 1250
Washington, DC 20036
Ph:(202)659-5600
Fax:(202)659-5605
Co. E-mail: info@kcct.com
URL: http://www.kcct.com
Contact: Christopher Peoples, Mgr
E-mail: cpeoples@atskcct.com
Scope: Consultants for architecture, urban design and planning. Specialists in transportation design, building renovation, and historic preservation.

1298 ■ Kartiganer Associates P.C.
555 Blooming Grove Tpke.
Newburgh, NY 12553-7843
Ph:(845)562-4499
Fax:(845)562-4395
Contact: Drew A. Kartiganer, Owner
Scope: Offers architectural design services in residential and commercial areas, along with interior design and specializes in the corporate and retail fields. Also designs master plan development for subdivisions, commercial and residential user. Involves in historic renovations, housing and site plan analysis for commercial and residential use. Industries served include commercial, residential, and interior designers in the mid-Hudson region.

1299 ■ Leeds Clark Inc.
3010 Shady Grove Rd.
Midlothian, TX 76065
Ph:(972)775-3843
Fax:(972)725-3263
Co. E-mail: info@leedsclark.com
URL: http://www.leedsclark.com
Contact: Tom Clark, Owner
E-mail: tomclark@atsleedsclark.com
Scope: Provides historic preservation consulting, condition assessment and inspections, proforma cost estimating, historic window surveys, duplication and retrofit. **Seminars:** Historic Building Condition Assessment; Main Street Training and Lead Paint Abatement on Windows; selecting and working with contactors; specification writing and code compliance; project planning.

1300 ■ Richard Sharpe Associates P.C.
30 Connecticut Ave.
Norwich, CT 06360-1502
Ph:(860)889-7314
Fax:(860)889-3940
Co. E-mail: rsa-arch@snet.net
Contact: William C. Clapet, Mgr
Scope: Design consultants providing architectural design, interior design, urban and regional design, project analysis, space analysis and planning, and graphic design services. Special expertise in historic rehabilitation, industrial, corporate planning, courthouses, and schools. Industries served: state, federal government, municipalities, and the private sector in the northeast region U.S. **Seminars:** Local Fire Code; Americans with Disabilities Act (ADA); Innovations in Lighting; Various Window Solutions; Standing Seam Metal Roofs. **Special Services:** Auto CAD Release 2000.

1301 ■ Roger du Toit Architects Ltd.
50 Park Rd.
Toronto, ON, Canada M4W 2N5
Ph:(416)968-7908
Fax:(416)968-0687
Co. E-mail: admin@dtah.com
URL: http://www.dtah.com
Contact: Adam Nicklin, Principal
E-mail: brent@atsdtah.com
Scope: Architects, landscape architects, urban designers, and planners specializing in facilities for educational, institutional, recreation land commercial/ retail uses; barrier-free design, design for the elderly; housing; renovation/restoration; streets-capes; and waterfronts. Services: include master plans, feasibility studies, site analysis, design, working drawings, specifications, and contract administration. **Publications:** "Designs for second Bow Bridge unveiled," Sep, 2009; "Waterfront on a roll with classy Wave Deck," Jun, 2009; "Skate parks, promenades and plazas," Jun, 2009; "Evergreen Brick Works"; "Toronto Central Waterfront".

1302 ■ Schrager Lighting Design L.L.C.
412 Main St., Ste. H
Ridgefield, CT 06877
Ph:(203)438-1188
Fax:(203)438-2299
Co. E-mail: sspublic@schragerlightingdesign.com
URL: http://www.schragerlightingdesign.com
Contact: Sara Schrager, Principle
Scope: Provides consulting services in architectural lighting design, with experience in lighting museums, academic and religious institutions, historic preservation, public atriums, corporate interiors, exterior lighting for landscapes and hard capes, art collections, restaurants and fine homes and estates.

1303 ■ Shakespeare Composites & Electronics
19845 US Hwy. 76
PO Box 733
Newberry, SC 29108
Ph:(803)276-5504
Free: 800-800-9008
Fax:(803)276-8940
Co. E-mail: composites@skp-cs.com
URL: http://www.skp-cs.com
Contact: J. Wayne Merck, Principal
E-mail: jprochak@atsskp-cs.com
Scope: Specializes in fiberglass reinforced composites design, engineering and manufacturing.

1304 ■ Uptown Shelby Association Inc.
211 S Trade St.
Shelby, NC 28150
Ph:(704)484-3100
Fax:(704)484-3934
Co. E-mail: info@uptownshelby.org
URL: http://www.uptownshelby.org
Contact: Allison Gragg, Mktg Mgr
E-mail: agragg@atsuptownshelby.org
Scope: Consults on a number of downtown issues addressing virtually any aspect of design, organization, promotion, economic restructuring and historic preservation, board training, strategic planning,

technical assistance or resource teams and problem solving on specific issues. **Publications:** "Help Save Historic Rogers Theatre".

1305 ■ Vertical Systems Analysis Inc.
307 W 36th St., 8th Fl.
New York, NY 10018
Ph:(212)989-5525
Free: 800-989-5525
Fax:(212)989-6860
Co. E-mail: bisufi@vsaconsulting.com
URL: http://www.vsaconsulting.com
Contact: Jose Romero, President
E-mail: mmottola@atsvsaconsulting.com
Scope: Elevator and escalator engineering and consulting firm. Works with residential and commercial buildings of all sizes. Firm evaluates elevators and escalators for modernization and restoration projects. Prepares and creates specifications and plans for all elevator and escalator applications. Also evaluates elevators to ensure that proper maintenance is being provided. Industries served: real estate, hospital, hotel, engineering, legal, universities and schools, cooperatives and condominiums, architectural and state facilities, and government agencies. **Publications:** "Owners Guide to Better Elevator Service".

1306 ■ Walter Sedovic Architects
1 Bridge St., Ste. 1
Irvington, NY 10533
Ph:(914)591-1900
Fax:(914)591-1999
Co. E-mail: wsa@modernruins.com
URL: http://www.modernruins.com
Contact: Shelley Smith, Principle
E-mail: gibrwalter@atsmodernruins.com
Scope: Dedicated to all aspects of historic preservation and contextual design. Specializes in acquisition planning, condition assessments and problem solving and scope of work recommendation. **Publications:** "What Replacement Windows Can't Replace," Association for Preservation Technology International, 2005; "Helping Main Street Thrive," Traditional Building, May, 2002; "Traditional Bldgs," Feb, 2002.

1307 ■ W.J. Whatley Inc.
3550 Odessa Way, Ste. A
Aurora, CO 80011
Ph:(303)287-8053
Free: 877-959-7678
Fax:(303)286-7216
Co. E-mail: sales@whatley.com
URL: http://www.whatley.com
Contact: Chris Gomez, Human Resources Mgr
E-mail: sdrake@atswhatley.com
Scope: A composite lamp post company offering coordinated luminaries and accessories. Specialist in custom designs and historic replicas. **Special Services:** XTREME™.

LIBRARIES

1308 ■ City College of City University of New York–Art Visual Resources Library
Compton-Goethals, Rm. 245A
160 Convent Ave.
New York, NY 10031
Ph:(212)650-7175
Fax:(212)650-7604
Co. E-mail: artimage@ccny.cuny.edu
URL: http://www1.ccny.cuny.edu/library/art_resources/index.cfm
Contact: Ching-Jung Chen, Cur.
Scope: Art, architecture, design. **Services:** Library not open to the public. **Holdings:** 100,000 slides.

1309 ■ Tri-County Heritage Society Reference Library
PO Box 352
Morgantown, PA 19543
Ph:(610)286-7477
Co. E-mail: tchs@dejazzd.com
URL: http://www.tricountyheritage.org/reflibrary.html
Contact: Rebecca Leamy, Libn.
Scope: History - state, local; architectural research; genealogy. **Services:** Library open to the public for reference use only. **Holdings:** 1500 books; 500 bound periodical volumes; 70 cubic feet archival materials; 25 reels of microfilm; maps; warrants; surveys; magazines; journals; photographs. **Subscriptions:** 12 journals and other serials; 4 newspapers.

1310 ■ University of Nevada, Las Vegas–Architecture Studies Library
Box 454049
4505 Maryland Pkwy.
Las Vegas, NV 89154-4049
Ph:(702)895-1959
Fax:(702)895-1975
Co. E-mail: jeanne.brown@unlv.edu
URL: http://www.library.unlv.edu/arch/index.html
Contact: Jeanne M. Brown, Hd., Arch.Stud.
Scope: Architecture - history, design, theory, and criticism; landscape architecture; interior design; construction; urban planning. **Services:** Interlibrary loan; copying; scanners; Library open to the public. **Holdings:** 25,000 volumes; 600 videos/DVDs; archives; microfiche and microfilm. **Subscriptions:** 150 journals and other serials.

RESEARCH CENTERS

1311 ■ College of William and Mary–Center for Archaeological Research
PO Box 8795
Williamsburg, VA 23187-8795
Ph:(757)221-1581
Fax:(757)221-2564
Co. E-mail: jbjone@wm.edu
URL: http://web.wm.edu/wmcar
Contact: Joseph B. Jones, Dir.
E-mail: jbjone@wm.edu
Scope: Performs historic and prehistoric archaeological and architectural research services, including cultural resource management studies, archaeological testing and excavation of historic properties, architectural survey and evaluation, preservation planning, and historical research and interpretation. **Services:** Artifact identification and analysis, zooarchaeological analysis, and material excavation of archaeological ceramics; Preparation of cultural resource planning overviews and reports for inclusion in Environmental Impact Statements; Professional assistance to both public and private agencies and organizations in the area of cultural resource management. **Publications:** Occasional Papers in Archaeology; Technical Report Series. **Educational Activities:** Internships in public archaeology for graduate and undergraduate students of anthropology, history, and American studies.

1312 ■ Cornell University–Program in International Studies in Planning
106 W Sibley Hall
Ithaca, NY 14853-3901
Ph:(607)255-4331
Fax:(607)255-1971
Co. E-mail: wwg2@cornell.edu
URL: http://www.aap.cornell.edu/crp/programs/grad/mrp.cfm
Contact: Prof. William Goldsmith, Ch.
E-mail: wwg2@cornell.edu
Scope: Analysis of the regional and spatial dimensions of development issues with a focus—although by no means exclusive—on the Third World, including political economy of regional and national development; planning and the global economy; critical development theory; project planning and administration; political ecology and international environmental planning; community economic development; gender and development; infrastructure; and NGOs and social movements. Areas of research include Latin America, Caribbean, Africa, Europe, and Southeast Asia. **Educational Activities:** Annual one-semester lecture series; Courses abroad; Seminars, held Fridays with visiting lecturers in the spring; Seminars; Student travel grants.

1313 ■ Frank Lloyd Wright Preservation Trust–Research Center
931 Chicago Ave.
Oak Park, IL 60302
Ph:(708)848-1976
Fax:(708)848-1248
Co. E-mail: research@gowright.org
URL: http://www.gowright.org/research.html
Contact: Brian Reis, Pres./CEO
E-mail: research@gowright.org
Scope: Frank Lloyd Wright, Prairie style of architecture, and architectural preservation and restoration. **Publications:** Journal (quarterly); Newsletter (monthly).

1314 ■ The Getty Conservation Institute
1200 Getty Center Dr., Ste. 700
Los Angeles, CA 90049-1684
Ph:(310)440-7325
Fax:(310)440-7702
Co. E-mail: gciweb@getty.edu
URL: http://www.getty.edu/conservation
Contact: Timothy P. Whalen, Dir.
E-mail: gciweb@getty.edu
Scope: Created to enhance the quality of conservation practice. Addresses the conservation needs of cultural property, including fine art collections, historic buildings and archeological sites. Also undertakes research in conservation and documentation methods and technologies. Maintains laboratories at the Getty Center in Los Angeles, where scientific research is conducted in the following areas: museum environment, conservation materials and techniques, analytical techniques, and archaeological and architectural conservation. **Publications:** Conservation Perspectives Newsletter (semiannually); Research in Conservation Series, Tools for Conservation Series; Symposium proceedings and preprints. **Educational Activities:** Conservation Guest Scholars Program (annually); Seminars, meetings, and workshops.

1315 ■ Mississippi State University–Carl Small Town Center
College of Architecture, Art, & Design
PO Box AQ
Mississippi State, MS 39762
Ph:(662)325-2207
Fax:(662)325-0723
Co. E-mail: cstcinfo@caad.msstate.edu
URL: http://www.carlsmalltowncenter.org
Contact: Prof. John Poros, Dir.
E-mail: cstcinfo@caad.msstate.edu
Scope: Problems of small towns in America and the solutions of these problems, ranging from location and growth to the concept of the small town as an art object. Research focuses on community development, town planning, land use analysis, town zoning strategies, socio-political surveys, ecological design, market analysis, downtown revitalization strategies, affordable housing, historical architecture evaluation, architectural presentation, and graphic design.

1316 ■ University of Florida–Research and Education Center for Architectural Preservation
331 ARCH Bldg.
College of Design, Construction & Planning
PO Box 115701
Gainesville, FL 32611-5701
Ph:(352)392-4836
Fax:(352)392-7266
Co. E-mail: peprugh@ufl.edu
URL: http://www.dcp.ufl.edu/hp/hp_recap.aspx
Contact: Prof. Peter E. Prugh, Co-Dir.
E-mail: peprugh@ufl.edu
Scope: Architectural preservation, conservation, and historic content, including initiation, coordination, and supervision of projects in Florida, Nantucket, the greater Caribbean region, and Vicenza, Italy. Develops secondary education programs in preservation. **Services:** Historic Preservation and Community Redevelopment Assistance. **Publications:** Project Documentation; Varies. **Educational Activities:** Preservation Institute: Nantucket (annually), summer program in historic preservation on Nantucket open to students and professionals nation-wide.

1317 ■ University of Mary Washington–Center for Historic Preservation
1301 College Ave.
Fredericksburg, VA 22401
Ph:(540)654-1041

Fax:(540)654-1068
Co. E-mail: dsanford@umw.edu
URL: http://centerforhistoricpreservation.org
Contact: Dr. Douglas Sanford, Dir.
E-mail: dsanford@umw.edu

Scope: Archeological, architectural, and landscape studies focusing primarily on the Chesapeake region and Piedmont, Virginia from the 17th to the early 20th century. **Services:** Cultural resource management. **Publications:** Cultural resource management reports; Historic Preservation at Mary Washington College Newsletter. **Educational Activities:** Lectures, conferences, workshops.

1318 ■ University of Texas at Austin–Center for American Architecture and Design
Battle Hall, Ste. 100
School of Architecture
1 University Station, B7500
Austin, TX 78712-0222
Ph:(512)471-9890
Fax:(512)471-7033
Co. E-mail: caad@austin.utexas.edu
URL: http://soa.utexas.edu/caad
Contact: Prof. Michael L. Benedikt, Dir.
E-mail: caad@austin.utexas.edu

Scope: Architecture for the emerging American city, architectural history of all the Americas, historic preservation, design, work of twentieth century American architects, the dwelling, placemaking in American cities, and architecture and media. **Publications:** CENTER: Architecture and Design in America. **Educational Activities:** Exhibitions and symposia, open to the public.

Art Gallery

ASSOCIATIONS AND OTHER ORGANIZATIONS

1319 ■ Art Dealers Association of America
205 Lexington Ave., Ste. 901
New York, NY 10016
Ph:(212)488-5550
Fax:(646)688-6809
Co. E-mail: lmitchem@artdealers.org
URL: http://www.artdealers.org
Contact: Lucy Mitchell-Innes, Pres.
Description: Art dealers united to promote the highest standards of connoisseurship, scholarship, and ethical practice within the profession and to increase public awareness of the role and responsibilities of reputable art dealers. Works with museums and scholars on activities and problems of mutual concern; cooperates with domestic and international government agencies on art matters and offers assistance and expertise to these agencies; advises on legislation and other governmental activity regarding the fine arts; seeks to identify and remove fake works of art from the marketplace. Appraises, for tax purposes only, works of art donated to nonprofit institutions. **Publications:** *Art Dealers Association of America Directory* (annual).

1320 ■ Association of International Photography Art Dealers
2025 M St. NW, Ste. 800
Washington, DC 20036
Ph:(202)367-1158
Fax:(202)367-2158
Co. E-mail: info@aipad.com
URL: http://www.aipad.com
Contact: Ms. Meredith Young, Exec. Dir.
Description: Galleries and private dealers in fine art and photography, who have been in business for at least 5 years. Promotes a greater understanding of photography as an art form. Fosters communication within the photographic community. Encourages public support of art photography. Seeks to increase the public's confidence in responsible photography dealers. **Publications:** *AIPAD Membership Directory and Illustrated Catalogue* (annual); *On Collecting Photographs* .

1321 ■ Inuit Art Foundation
2081 Merivale Rd.
Ottawa, ON, Canada K2G 1G9
Ph:(613)224-8189
Free: 800-830-3293
Fax:(613)224-2907
Co. E-mail: iaf@inuitart.org
URL: http://www.inuitart.org
Contact: Marybelle Mitchell, Exec. Dir.
Description: Promotes appreciation of and demand for Inuit art. Offers professional development opportunities to Canadian Inuit artists. Organizes research and educational programs; operates Inuit artists' shop. **Publications:** *Canadian Arctic Multimedia Information Kit*; *Inuit Art Quarterly* (quarterly).

REFERENCE WORKS

1322 ■ "Arario Gallery Opens First American Space" in *Art Business News* (Vol. 34, November 2007, No. 11, pp. 14)
Pub: Pfingsten Publishing, LLC
Description: Opening a new space in New York's Chelsea gallery district is Arario Gallery, a leader in the field of Asian contemporary art; the gallery will feature new works by Chinese artists at its opening.

1323 ■ *Art Dealers Association of America—Directory*
Pub: Art Dealers Association of America Inc.
Contact: Gilbert S. Edelson, Admin. VP
Released: Annual, Fall. **Covers:** About 160 members of the ADAA. **Entries Include:** Company name, address, phone, fax, names and titles of key personnel, and descriptions of areas of specialization. **Arrangement:** Alphabetical.

1324 ■ "Art Miami Comes to Miami's Wynwood Art District" in *Art Business News* (Vol. 34, November 2007, No. 11, pp. 18)
Pub: Pfingsten Publishing, LLC
Description: In December, The Art Group will hold its Art Miami fair in the Wynwood Art District; the exhibitors range from painting, sculpture, video and works on paper.

1325 ■ *Art Now Gallery Guides*
Pub: Art Now Inc.
Contact: Gail Mading, Subscriptions & Circulation
E-mail: gail@galleryguide.org
Released: Monthly, 10/year. **Price:** $35, individuals. **Covers:** in 'M Art Now Gallery Guide—International Edition' current exhibitions in over 1,800 museums and galleries. Separate regional editions cover metropolitan New York, Boston and New England, the Philadelphia area, the southeast, Chicago and the midwest, the southwest, California and the northwest, Latin America, and Europe. Listings are paid. **Entries Include:** Gallery or museum name, address, phone, days and hours of operation, artist's name or name of the exhibit, medium, and dates of showing. **Arrangement:** International and regional editions are geographical.

1326 ■ "Artexpo Celebrates 30th Anniversary" in *Art Business News* (Vol. 34, November 2007, No. 11, pp. 18)
Pub: Pfingsten Publishing, LLC
Description: In honor of its 30th anniversary Artexpo New York 2008 will be an unforgettable show offering a collection of fine-art education courses for both trade and consumer attendees and featuring a variety of artists working in all mediums.

1327 ■ "An Artwork in Progress" in *Hawaii Business* (Vol. 53, March 2008, No. 9, pp. 45)
Pub: Hawaii Business Publishing
Ed: Jolyn Okimoto Rosa. **Description:** Art galleries in Honolulu, Hawaii holds the First Friday Gallery Walk and other special events, which draw crowd to and increase sales activities in the city's downtown. The district also advocates for the reintroduction of Honolulu's Chinatown to the people. Details regarding the art galleries' Chinatown revival and its local economic impact are discussed.

1328 ■ "Creative Cluster Paints Business Success" in *Business Journal Serving Greater Tampa Bay* (Vol. 30, October 29, 2010, No. 45, pp. 1)
Pub: Tampa Bay Business Journal
Ed: Jane Meinhardt. **Description:** How Tom Gaffney, a cofounder of the private equity firm The Anderson Group realized the great return on investment in the 600 block of Central Avenue in St. Petersburg, Florida is discussed. Focusing on long-term value rather than short-term profitability and exit, Gaffney purchased this block in 2008 for $2.3 million and cultivated arts businesses at tenants.

1329 ■ "Gallery Street Launches ArtCandy" in *Art Business News* (Vol. 34, November 2007, No. 11, pp. 8)
Pub: Pfingsten Publishing, LLC
Description: Fine-art reproduction house Gallery Street recently launched its new division, ArtCandy Editions; the division was created in order to help a network of artists expand the distribution of their work.

1330 ■ *How to Market and Sell Your Art, Music, Photographs, and Handmade Crafts Online*
Pub: Atlantic Publishing Group, Inc.
Ed: Lee Rowley. **Released:** May 2008. **Price:** $24. 95. **Description:** The book provides all the basics for starting and running an online store selling arts, crafts, photography or music. There are more than 300 Websites listed to help anyone market and promote their arts and/or crafts online.

1331 ■ *Institute of Museum & Library Services—Annual Report*
Pub: Institute of Museum & Library Services
Ed: Mamie Bittner, Editor, mbittner@imls.gov. **Released:** Annual, fall; Latest edition 2006. **Covers:** more than 1,000 museums and libraries receiving federal support. **Entries Include:** Museum or library name, city, state, grant amount. **Arrangement:** Classified by type of funding received. **Indexes:** Institution name, museum discipline, size of budget.

1332 ■ "Let the Light Shine" in *Retail Merchandiser* (Vol. 51, July-August 2011, No. 4, pp. 74)
Pub: Phoenix Media Corporation
Description: For over 25 years, The Thomas Kinkade Company has been producing art that is collected by both old and young, and is the only company that publishes Thomas Kinkade art.

1333 ■ *Rogues' Gallery: The Secret Story of the Lust, Lies, Greed, and Betrayals That Made the Metropolitan Museum of Art*
Pub: Crown Business Books
Ed: Michael Gross. **Released:** May 11, 2010. **Price:** $16.99. **Description:** Michael Gross, leading chronicler of the American rich, looks at the saga of the nation's largest museum, the Metropolitan Museum of Art.

1334 ■ *Seven Days in the Art World*
Pub: W.W. Norton & Company
Ed: Sarah Thornton. **Released:** 2009. **Price:** $24.95. **Description:** A sociologist renders the interplay among buyers, critics, curators and makers of contemporary art.

1335 ■ "Show Dates" in *Art Business News* (Vol. 34, November 2007, No. 11, pp. 18)
Pub: Pfingsten Publishing, LLC
Description: Listing of conferences, trade shows and gallery openings for artists and those in the art industry.

1336 ■ "A Vegas Sensation Inaugural Artexpo Las Vegas" in *Art Business News* (Vol. 34, November 2007, No. 11, pp. 1)
Pub: Pfingsten Publishing, LLC
Ed: Jennifer Dulin. **Description:** Overview of the first Artexpo Las Vegas which featured exhibitors, artists and buyers and was a wonderful place for networking.

TRADE PERIODICALS

1337 ■ *ARTnews Magazine*
Pub: Art News L.L.C.
Contact: Milton Esterow, Editor & Publisher
Released: Monthly. **Price:** $39.95 Canada; $99.95 other countries; $19.95. **Description:** News magazine reporting on art, personalities, issues, trends, and events that shape the international art world.

1338 ■ *The ARTnewsletter*
Pub: ARTnews
Ed: Eileen Kinsella, Editor. **Released:** Semimonthly. **Price:** $279, individuals $279/year, U.S.; $309 elsewhere; $309 Canada and other countries. **Description:** Presents reviews of forthcoming auctions, analyses of prices, attribution controversies, ownership squabbles, and case histories of thievery, forgery, and fraud. Discusses the impact of museum exhibitions on the art market, the latest IRS rulings, import and export regulations, legislative hearings, debates and acts, print tax shelters, art insurance, and appraisals. Recurring features include interviews with dealers, auctioneers, curators, and collectors.

1339 ■ *Artsfocus*
Pub: Colorado Springs Fine Arts Center
Ed: Released: Quarterly. **Price:** Included in membership. **Description:** Notifies of upcoming art exhibitions and other related events. Covers museum acquisitions. Gives updates on traveling exhibitions. Visual art exhibitions, live theatre performances and Bemis school of Art classes for adults and children. Lectures, tours, permanent collection and pre collection of Southwestern and Native American art. a calendar of events, reports of meetings, news of educational opportunities, and notices of publications available.

1340 ■ *ARTWEEK*
Pub: ARTWEEK
Ed: Laura Richard Janku, Editor. **Released:** Monthly. **Price:** $64 two years; $38 institutions; $60 Canada; $80 other countries. **Description:** Magazine containing contemporary West Coast art reviews, commentary, features and interviews.

1341 ■ *Azure Magazine*
Pub: Azure Publishing Inc.
Contact: Sergio Sgaramella, Publisher
Ed: Nelda Rodger, Editor. **Released:** 8/yr. **Price:** $32. 95; $54.95 two years; $32.95; $54.95 two years; $48 other countries; $78 other countries 2 years. **Description:** Trade magazine covering art, design and architecture.

1342 ■ *CAA News*
Pub: College Art Association (CAA)
Contact: Rachel Ford
Ed: Christopher Howard, Editor. **Released:** Bimonthly. **Price:** Included in membership. **Description:** Features news of the Association as well as activities, achievements, funding opportunities, conferences, programs, exhibitions, and legislation in the arts field. Recurring features include news of research, a calendar of events, reports of meetings, news of educational opportunities, notices of publications available, and columns titled From the Executive Director, People in the News, Grants, Awards & Honors, Conferences & Symposia, and Opportunities.

1343 ■ *CityArt Magazine*
Pub: Fleisher Fine Arts Inc.
Contact: Pat Fleisher, Publisher
E-mail: info@artfocus.com
Released: 3/yr. **Price:** $15 Canada 7%GST. **Description:** Magazine on the contemporary arts scene, including overview articles and reviews of exhibits, artbooks, and an annual summer art school directory.

1344 ■ *Country Home*
Pub: Meredith Corp.
Released: Monthly, 10/yr. **Price:** $4.95 newstand; $21.97 two years. **Description:** Magazine furnishing information on American interior design, architecture, antiques and collectibles, gardening, art, and culinary endeavor.

1345 ■ *Musea*
Pub: Tom Hendricks
Ed: Art S. Revolutionary, Editor. **Released:** Monthly. **Price:** $10, individuals; Free. **Description:** A zine opposed to the Corporate Art 10, and for the best of 'indie' arts.

1346 ■ *National Association of Women Artists, Inc. News*
Pub: National Association of Women Artists Inc.
Contact: Marcelle Harwell Pachnowski, President
Released: Semiannual. **Price:** Included in membership. **Description:** Presents news of women in the art field. Recurring features include a calendar of events, news of educational opportunities, juried shows, workshops, exhibits, and a column titled President's Letter. (This is a members only newsletter).

1347 ■ *NSS News Bulletin*
Pub: National Sculpture Society
Contact: Patricia Delahanty
Ed: Patricia, Delahanty, Editor. **Released:** Bimonthly. **Price:** Included in membership. **Description:** Covers sculpture competitions, awards, grants, exhibitions, and commissions. Reports members' works and activities. Recurring features include news of research, a calendar of events, reports of meetings, news of educational opportunities, job listings, notices of publications available, and Seeking and Offering.

1348 ■ *The Photograph Collector*
Pub: The Photograph Collector
Ed: Stephen Perloff, Editor, sperloff@libertynet.org. **Released:** Monthly. **Price:** $149.95, individuals in North America; $169.95, elsewhere. **Description:** Carries in-depth coverage of topics such as print prices, archival techniques, dealer activities, major acquisitions, and the international photography market. Recurring features include statistics, book reviews, news of research, and columns titled Gallery Row, Auction News, and Publishers Row.

VIDEOCASSETTES/ AUDIOCASSETTES

1349 ■ *David Armstrong Paints*
Karol Media
Hanover Industrial Estates
375 Stewart Rd.
PO Box 7600
Wilkes Barre, PA 18773-7600
Ph:(570)822-8899
Free: 800-526-4773
Co. E-mail: sales@karolmedia.com
URL: http://www.karolmedia.com
Released: 1997. **Price:** $29.95. **Description:** Portrays the artist and his work. **Availability:** VHS.

1350 ■ *Maya Collection*
Tapeworm Video Distributors
25876 The Old Road 141
Stevenson Ranch, CA 91381
Ph:(661)257-4904
Fax:(661)257-4820
Co. E-mail: sales@tapeworm.com
URL: http://www.tapeworm.com
Description: Ten volume collection documents the art and philosophy of Mayan Culture. **Availability:** VHS.

1351 ■ *Windows to a View: Chris Reis*
Karol Media
Hanover Industrial Estates
375 Stewart Rd.
PO Box 7600
Wilkes Barre, PA 18773-7600
Ph:(570)822-8899
Free: 800-526-4773
Co. E-mail: sales@karolmedia.com
URL: http://www.karolmedia.com
Released: 1997. **Price:** $29.95. **Description:** Portrays the artist and his work. **Availability:** VHS.

TRADE SHOWS AND CONVENTIONS

1352 ■ The Winter Olympia Fine Art and Antiques Fair
Clarion Events Ltd.
Earls Court Exhibition Centre
Warwick Rd.
London SW5 9TA, United Kingdom
Ph:44 20 7370 8139
URL: http://www.clarionevents.com
Released: Annual. **Audience:** Trade and general public. **Principal Exhibits:** Antiques including fine, oak, garden, and country furniture; rugs; paintings; ceramics; clocks; sculptures; jewelry, silver, and bronzes.

CONSULTANTS

1353 ■ Lawrence Jeppson Associates
9004 Honeybee Ln.
Bethesda, MD 20817-6927
Ph:(301)365-7400
Fax:(301)365-7409
Contact: Lawrence S. Jeppson, Owner
Scope: Provides counseling service to artists, galleries, museums and business on exhibition, sales and promotion of fine art.

COMPUTERIZED DATABASES

1354 ■ *Art on Screen Database*
Program for Art on Film Inc.
200 Willoughby Ave.
Brooklyn, NY 11205-3817
Ph:(718)399-4506
Fax:(718)399-4507
Co. E-mail: info@artfilm.org
URL: http://www.artfilm.org
Description: Contains bibliographic information on more than 25,000 videos, films, multimedia, and CD-ROM productions about the visual arts. For each product, provides title, credits, length, year, country, language, synopsis, production date, distributors, formats, awards, reviews, and in many cases evaluations. Includes entries for more than 5000 distribution sources, providing name, address, telephone, and fax numbers for each entry. Users may perform searches by artist name, style or period, materials, techniques, genre or by associated concepts. **Availability:** Online: Program for Art on Film Inc. **Type:** Directory.

1355 ■ *Bibliography of the History of Art*
J. Paul Getty Trust
1200 Getty Center Dr.
Los Angeles, CA 90049-1679
Ph:(310)440-7300
Fax:(310)440-7716
Co. E-mail: info@getty.edu
URL: http://www.getty.edu
Description: Abstracts and indexes current publications in the history of art, with more than 481,000 bibliographic citations. Sources include more than 4300 journals, books, reviews, conference proceedings, Festschriften, essays, exhibition catalogs, dis-

sertations, and electronic publications. Corresponds to *Bibliography of the History of Art.* **Availability:** Online: Wolters Kluwer Health, ProQuest LLC, J. Paul Getty Trust. **Type:** Bibliographic.

1356 ■ *The Getty Provenance Index Databases*
J. Paul Getty Trust
1200 Getty Center Dr.
Los Angeles, CA 90049-1679
Ph:(310)440-7300
Fax:(310)440-7716
Co. E-mail: info@getty.edu
URL: http://www.getty.edu
Description: Contains indexed transcriptions of material from auction catalogs and archival inventories of western European works of art. Includes nearly 1 million records covering the period from the late 16th century to the early 20th century. Archival documents include works or art from private collections in France, Italy, the Netherlands, and Spain from 1550 to 1840. Sale catalogs cover auction sales in Belgium, France, Germany, Great Britain, the Netherlands, and Scandinavia from 1650 to 1840. Public collections include descriptions and provenance of paintings by artists born before 1900, and cover American and British public institutions between 1500 and 1990. **Availability:** Online: J. Paul Getty Trust; CD-ROM: J. Paul Getty Trust. **Type:** Directory.

1357 ■ *Gordon's Print Prices Database*
LTB Gordonsart Inc.
610 E Bell Rd., Ste. 2-163
Phoenix, AZ 85022
Ph:(602)253-6948
Free: 800-892-4622
Fax:(602)253-2104
Co. E-mail: office@gordonsart.com
URL: http://www.gordonsart.com
Description: Provides information on more than 1 million transactions involving art prints sold at major auction houses worldwide. Covers artists ranging from famous to the obscure. Includes a list of *catalogues raisonnes*, monographs, articles, advertiser information, auction house information, and more. For each print, provides the artist name, description of the work, medium, auction house handling the sale, address, auction date, lot number, and price realized. Includes a calendar of auctions and a directory of auction houses, print dealers, and photography dealers. Includes a print term lexicon in three languages (English, German, and French). Corresponds to the print version of *Gordon's Print Price Annual.* **Availability:** Online: LTB Gordonsart Inc; CD-ROM: LTB Gordonsart Inc. **Type:** Directory.

1358 ■ *A Survey of Western Art*
Technology Dynamics Corp.
1601 N Sepulveda Blvd., Ste. 374
PO Box 219
Manhattan Beach, CA 90267
Ph:(310)406-1803
Fax:(310)406-0833
Co. E-mail: contact@tdcinteractive.com
URL: http://www.tdcinteractive.net
Description: Contains a basic encyclopedia of more than 1000 photographs of art works from ancient Egypt to contemporary America. Images are accompanied by detailed data cards, many with associated explanatory text on the subject, as well as artist biographies. Covers painting, sculpture, architecture, photography, design, and theater. **Availability:** CD-ROM: Technology Dynamics Corp. **Type:** Full text; Image.

LIBRARIES

1359 ■ Abbaye Saint-Benoit–Bibliotheque
1 Main St.
St. Benoit du Lac, QC, Canada J0B 2M0
Ph:(819)843-4080
Fax:(819)868-1861
Co. E-mail: abbaye@st-benoit-du-lac.com
URL: http://www.st-benoit-du-lac.com/
Scope: Religion, theology, philosophy, history, art, church science. **Services:** Bibliotheque open to the public at librarian's discretion to men only. **Holdings:** Figures not available.

1360 ■ Allen Sapp Gallery Archives
1 Railway Ave.
PO Box 460
North Battleford, SK, Canada S9A 2Y6
Ph:(306)445-1760
Fax:(306)445-1694
Co. E-mail: sapp@accesscomm.ca
URL: http://www.allensapp.com
Contact: Dean Bauche, Dir.
Scope: Cree artist Allan Sapp. **Services:** Library open to the public with restrictions. **Holdings:** Graphic materials; moving images; textual records; reports; archives; film videos.

1361 ■ Andy Warhol Museum–Archives Study Center
117 Sandusky St.
Pittsburgh, PA 15212-5890
Ph:(412)237-8300
Fax:(412)237-8340
Co. E-mail: wrbicanm@warhol.org
URL: http://www.warhol.org/collections/archives.html
Contact: Matt Wrbican, Archv.
Scope: Andy Warhol, pop art movement, journalism, rock music, celebrity culture, fashion. **Services:** Archives is open to researchers by appointment. **Holdings:** Business records; scrapbooks; photographs; audiocassettes; videotapes; published materials; books; art work; clothing; posters; correspondence; personal objects; 4000 audio tapes.

1362 ■ Art Gallery of Greater Victoria Library
1040 Moss St.
Victoria, BC, Canada V8V 4P1
Ph:(205)384-4101
Fax:(250)361-3995
Co. E-mail: mjhughes@aggv.bc.ca
URL: http://www.aggv.bc.ca
Contact: Mary Jo Hughes, Chf.Cur.
Scope: Art - Canadian, Asian; British Columbia artists. **Services:** Library currently only available to in-house staff and volunteers due to lack of staff. **Holdings:** 10,000 volumes.

1363 ■ Beaverbrook Art Gallery Library
703 Queen St.
Fredericton, NB, Canada E3B 5A6
Ph:(506)458-8545
Fax:(506)459-7450
Co. E-mail: bag@beaverbrookartgallery.org
URL: http://beaverbrookartgallery.org
Contact: Laura Ritchie, Reg.
Scope: Art, humanities, culture. **Services:** Copying; Library open by permission only. **Holdings:** 4000 books and videos. **Subscriptions:** 15 journals and other serials; 2 newspapers.

1364 ■ California University of Pennsylvania–Louis L. Manderino Library I Special Collections
250 University Ave., Rm. 435
California, PA 15419
Ph:(724)938-5926
Fax:(724)938-5901
Co. E-mail: nolf@cup.edu
URL: http://www.library.calu.edu
Contact: Alber Pokol, Libn.
Scope: Rare books, art, music. **Services:** Library open to the public by appointment.

1365 ■ Carnegie Library of Pittsburgh–Music Department
4400 Forbes Ave.
Pittsburgh, PA 15213
Ph:(412)622-3105
Fax:(412)687-8982
Co. E-mail: musicdept@carnegielibrary.org
URL: http://www.clpgh.org/locations/music
Contact: Kathryn Logan, Dept.Hd.
Scope: Music, art, architecture, interior design, collectibles, dance. **Services:** Reference and reader's assistance; department open to the public. **Holdings:** 110,000 music books and scores; 63,000 art books; 1500 dance books; 30,000 sound recordings; 1200 videocassettes; 280,000 mounted pictures; 54,000 slides; 69 VF drawers; 1700 videos and DVDs. **Subscriptions:** 320 journals and other serials.

1366 ■ Colby College–Bixler Art and Music Library
Box 5660 Mayflower Hill
Waterville, ME 04901
Ph:(207)859-5660
Fax:(207)859-5105
Co. E-mail: mericson@colby.edu
URL: http://libguides.colby.edu/bixler
Contact: Margaret D. Ericson, Mus. & Art Libn.
Scope: Art, Music, Photography. **Services:** Interlibrary loan; copying; Apple computer lab; in-house listening and video viewing stations; Library open to the public for reference use only. **Holdings:** 33,000 books and bound periodical volumes; 10,000 music scores; 11,000 sound recordings; 1200 videos; 450 CD-ROMs. **Subscriptions:** 90 journals and other serials.

1367 ■ Craigdarroch Castle
1050 Joan Crescent
Victoria, BC, Canada V8S 3L5
Ph:(250)592-5323
Fax:(250)592-1099
Co. E-mail: info@thecastle.ca
URL: http://www.thecastle.ca
Contact: Bruce Davies, Cur.
Scope: Nineteenth Century European and North American domestic material. **Services:** Library open by appointment to serious researchers only. **Holdings:** Photographs; documents; memorabilia; electronic records; graphic materials; microforms; moving images; sound recordings; textual records.

1368 ■ Drury University–F.W. Olin Library–Art & Architecture Slide Library (900 N)
900 N. Benton Ave.
Springfield, MO 65802
Ph:(417)873-7337
Fax:(417)873-7432
Co. E-mail: jtygart@drury.edu
URL: http://library.drury.edu/library/index.php/services-info/slide-library/
Contact: Jacqueline Tygart, Slide Cur.
Scope: Architecture, art, photography, textiles, ceramics. **Services:** Library open to the public. **Holdings:** 60,000 35mm slides.

1369 ■ Edinboro University–Baron-Forness Library I Special Collections
200 Tartan Rd., 7th Fl.
Edinboro, PA 16444
Ph:(814)732-2415
Fax:(814)732-2883
Co. E-mail: obringer@edinboro.edu
URL: http://www.edinboro.edu/departments/library
Contact: Prof. David Obringer, Archv. & Ref.Libn.
Scope: Music, art, education, Pennsylvania history, Civil War regimental history, rare books. **Services:** Interlibrary loan; tutoring; Library open to the public with restrictions. **Holdings:** 3000 volumes; prints.

1370 ■ Emmanuel College–Cardinal Cushing Library
400 The Fenway
Boston, MA 02115
Ph:(617)735-9927
Co. E-mail: tholl@emmanuel.edu
URL: http://www1.emmanuel.edu/library/
Contact: Dr. Susan von Daum Tholl, Dir.
Scope: Theology, pastoral ministry, religious history, women's studies, arts, humanities, education. **Services:** Interlibrary loan; Library open to the public. **Holdings:** 130,000 volumes. **Subscriptions:** 1000 journals and other serials.

1371 ■ Hardin-Simmons University–Rupert and Pauline Richardson Library
2341 Hickory St.
Abilene, TX 79698
Ph:(325)670-1236
Fax:(325)677-8351
Co. E-mail: aspecht@hsutx.edu
URL: http://hsutx.edu/library
Contact: Alice Specht, Dean
Scope: Hardin-Simmons University history, government records. **Holdings:** 150 online databases.

1372 ■ Hillwood Museum & Gardens–Art Research Library
4155 Linnean Ave., NW
Washington, DC 20008
Ph:(202)243-3953
Fax:(202)966-7846
Co. E-mail: plynagh@hillwoodmuseum.org
URL: http://www.hillwoodmuseum.org/resources/library.html
Contact: Pat Lynagh, Asst.Libn.

Scope: Art - decorative, French, Russian; Russian imperial history; interior design. **Services:** Copying; Library open to the public by appointment. **Holdings:** 30,000 volumes; 16,000 auction catalogs; pamphlets. **Subscriptions:** 30 journals and other serials.

1373 ■ Institute for Unpopular Culture Library
1592 Union St., Ste. 226
San Francisco, CA 94123
Ph:(415)786-5003
Fax:(815)717-7790
Co. E-mail: admin@ifuc.org
URL: http://www.ifuc.org

Scope: Art, censorship, political dissidence, literature, subversive culture. **Services:** Copying; Library open to the public. **Holdings:** 5000 books. **Subscriptions:** 20 journals and other serials.

1374 ■ Juilliard School–Lila Acheson Wallace Library
60 Lincoln Center Plaza
New York, NY 10023-6588
Ph:(212)799-5000, x-265
Fax:(212)724-6421
Co. E-mail: library@juilliard.edu
URL: http://www.juilliard.edu/libraryarchives/general.html
Contact: Jane Gottlieb, Assoc. VP, Lib.Info.Rsrcs.

Scope: Music, drama, dance. **Services:** Interlibrary loan; Library open to public for reference use by arrangement only. **Holdings:** 22,000 books; 70,000 music performance, study scores; 25,000 sound recordings; 2000 videos. **Subscriptions:** 200 journals and other serials.

1375 ■ Kenyon College–Olin Library–Visual Image Collection (Kenyo)
Kenyon College
103 College Dr.
Gambier, OH 43022-9623
Ph:(740)427-5193
Co. E-mail: zhouy@kenyon.edu
URL: http://lbis.kenyon.edu
Contact: Yan Zhou, Vis.Rsrcs.Cur.

Scope: Painting, sculpture, architecture, furniture, theater, history, music, religion, psychology, historical biography, sociology. **Services:** Collection not open to the public. **Holdings:** Slides. **Subscriptions:** 2 journals and other serials.

1376 ■ Menil Collection Library
1515 Sul Ross St.
Houston, TX 77006
Ph:(713)525-9400
Fax:(713)525-9444
Co. E-mail: info@menil.org
URL: http://www.menil.org/home.html
Contact: Phillip T. Heagy, Libn.

Scope: Modern art, medieval art, classical antiquities, tribal art. **Services:** Interlibrary loan; copying; Library open to the public by appointment. **Holdings:** 15,000 books; 3000 bound periodical volumes; 10,000 auction sales catalogs. **Subscriptions:** 100 journals and other serials.

1377 ■ Musee McCord d'histoire Canadienne–Archives and Documentation Centre
690, rue Sherbrooke ouest
Montreal, QC, Canada H3A 1E9
Ph:(514)398-7100, x249
Fax:(514)398-5045
Co. E-mail: info@mccord.mcgill.ca
URL: http://www.musee-mccord.qc.ca/en/services/archives/
Contact: Dr. Nicole Vallieres, Dir., Coll.Res. and Prog.

Scope: Art, Canadian history, photography, ethnology. **Services:** Copying; Library open to the public by appointment. **Holdings:** 9108 books; 2000 rare books; 200 meters of archives; 95 reels of microfilm; 1 million photographs; electronic records; graphic materials; textual records. **Subscriptions:** 180 journals and other serials.

1378 ■ Museum of Classical Chinese Furniture Library
PO Box 100
Renaissance, CA 95962
Ph:(916)692-3142
Fax:(916)692-1596
Contact: Brian Flynn, Musm.Cur.

Scope: Oriental Art, Chinese furniture and porcelains. **Services:** Library open to the public with permission of the museum director. **Holdings:** 1000 books. **Subscriptions:** 150 journals and other serials.

1379 ■ St. Cloud State University–Learning Resource Services–University Archives and Special Collections (720 4)
720 4th Ave., S.
Miller Center 314
St. Cloud, MN 56301-4442
Ph:(320)308-4755
Fax:(320)308-5623
Co. E-mail: archives@stcloudstate.edu
URL: http://lrts.stcloudstate.edu/library/special/archives/default.asp
Contact: Tom Steman, Univ.Archv.

Scope: Art, theater, literature, Sinclair Lewis.

1380 ■ St. Norbert Arts Centre Archives
PO Box 175
Winnipeg, MB, Canada R3V 1L6
Ph:(204)269-0564
Fax:(204)261-1927
Co. E-mail: snac@snac.mb.ca
URL: http://www.snac.mb.ca
Contact: Gerry Atwell, Dir.

Scope: Art - visual art, music, theater, and dance. **Services:** Archives open to the public. **Holdings:** Graphic materials; textual records.

1381 ■ San Francisco Public Library–Bernard Osher Foundation–Art, Music & Recreation Center (100 L)
100 Larkin St.
San Francisco, CA 94102
Ph:(415)557-4525
Fax:(415)557-4524
Co. E-mail: info@sfpl.org
URL: http://www.sfpl.org/librarylocations/main/art/art.htm
Contact: Mark Hall, Fl.Mgr.

Scope: Arts - visual, graphic; sports and recreation; photography; architecture; arts and crafts; performing arts; music - orchestral, chamber, opera, popular, folk, jazz. **Services:** Center open to the public. **Holdings:** Books; serials; scores.

1382 ■ Santa Clara University–de Saisset Museum Library
500 El Camino Real
Santa Clara, CA 95053-0550
Ph:(408)554-4528
Fax:(408)554-7840
Co. E-mail: rnadel@scu.edu
URL: http://www.scu.edu/deSaisset
Contact: Rebecca Schapp, Dir.

Scope: Art publications. **Services:** Library not open to the public. **Holdings:** Art magazines, art catalogs from the de Saisset Museum and other institutions. **Subscriptions:** 9 journals and other serials.

1383 ■ Sculptors' Society of Canada–Canadian Sculpture Centre–Archives (500 C)
500 Church St.
Toronto, ON, Canada M4Y 2C8
Ph:(647)435-5858
Fax:(416)214-0389 (please c
Co. E-mail: gallery@cansculpt.org
URL: http://www.cansculpt.org
Contact: Judi Michelle Young, Pres.

Scope: Sculpture. **Services:** Archive open to the public by appointment. **Holdings:** Photographs; slides; files.

1384 ■ Sweet Briar College–Martin C. Shallenberger Book Arts Library
134 Chapel Rd.
Sweet Briar, VA 24595
Ph:(434)381-6139
Fax:(434)381-6173
Co. E-mail: jgjaffe@sbc.edu
URL: http://www.cochran.sbc.edu
Contact: John Jaffe, Dir., Lib. & Integ.Lrng.Rsrcs.

Scope: Book arts, rare books, archives. **Services:** Interlibrary loan. **Holdings:** 14,000

1385 ■ Tom Thomson Art Gallery Archives
840 1st Ave. W.
Owen Sound, ON, Canada N4K 4K4
Ph:(519)376-1932
Fax:(519)376-3037
Co. E-mail: ttag@e-owensound.com
URL: http://www.tomthomson.org
Contact: Virginia Eichhorn, Dir./Cur.

Scope: Art. **Services:** Library open to the public by appointment. **Holdings:** Textual records; archives. **Subscriptions:** 1 journal.

1386 ■ University of California, San Diego–The Arts Libraries
Geisel Bldg.
9500 Gilman Dr., 0175Q
La Jolla, CA 92093-0175
Ph:(858)534-4811
Fax:(858)534-0189
Co. E-mail: labrams@ucsd.edu
URL: http://libraries.ucsd.edu/locations/arts/
Contact: Leslie Abrams, Hd.

Scope: Western art history from prehistory to contemporary with strength in post 1950 art movements; art criticism and aesthetics; art and literature; ethnic and tribal arts; Latin American, pre-Columbian and Asian art; photography as fine art; documentary photography; landscape architecture; architectural history and theory; decorative arts; music theory; folk music; jazz music. **Services:** Library open to the public. **Holdings:** 101,000 volumes; 4900 CDs; 308,000 slides; 5000 factual film archive; 64,000 sound recordings; 49,000 pieces of music. **Subscriptions:** 305 journals and other serials.

1387 ■ University of North Carolina School of the Arts–Semans Library
UNC School of the Arts
1533 S. Main St.
Winston-Salem, NC 27127
Ph:(336)770-3270
Fax:(336)770-3271
Co. E-mail: rebeccab@uncsa.edu
URL: http://www.uncsa.edu/library
Contact: Rebecca Brown, Hd. of Access Svcs.

Scope: Music, art and design, theater, film, dance, humanities. **Services:** Interlibrary loan; Library open to the public. **Holdings:** 111,000 books; 9000 bound periodical volumes; 50,000 music scores; 45,000 sound recordings; 5200 DVDs and videos. **Subscriptions:** 470 journals and other serials; 25 newspapers.

1388 ■ University of Saskatchewan Art Collection–Kenderdine Art Gallery–Archive (Unive)
University of Saskatchewan
2nd Level, Agriculture Bldg.
51 Campus Dr.
Saskatoon, SK, Canada S7N 5A8
Ph:(306)966-6816

Fax:(306)978-8340
Co. E-mail: kent.archer@usask.ca
URL: http://www.usask.ca/kenderdine
Contact: Kent Archer, Dir./Cur.
Scope: Art. **Services:** Library open to the public with restrictions. **Holdings:** Graphic materials; textual records.

1389 ■ Watkins College of Art, Design, & Film Library
2298 Rosa L. Parks Blvd.
Nashville, TN 37228
Ph:(615)277-7427
Fax:(615)383-4849
Co. E-mail: library@watkins.edu
URL: http://www.watkins.edu/library
Contact: Lisa Williams, Libn.
Scope: Film, fine arts, interior design, graphic design, photography. **Services:** Library open to the public for reference use only. **Holdings:** 11,600 books; 1200 videotapes and films. **Subscriptions:** 50 journals and other serials; 11 newspapers.

RESEARCH CENTERS

1390 ■ New York University–Conservation Center
Stephen Chan House
14 E 78th St.
New York, NY 10075
Ph:(212)992-5848
Fax:(212)992-5851
Co. E-mail: conservation.program@nyu.edu
URL: http://www.nyu.edu/gsas/dept/fineart/conservation/index.htm
Contact: Hannelore Roemich PhD, Actg.Chm.
E-mail: conservation.program@nyu.edu
Scope: Deterioration, preservation, and restoration of works of art, including research and development of methods of examination to determine identity of materials and extent of alteration of works of art, preservation of stone, prevention of degradation, causes of deterioration in frescos, neutron activation analysis of art materials, and metal technology of antiquity. **Services:** Consultation, to museums. **Publications:** Newsletter. **Educational Activities:** Lecture series; Summer sessions, for museum professionals; Symposia; Workshops.

ASSOCIATIONS AND OTHER ORGANIZATIONS

1391 ■ Art and Creative Materials Institute
PO Box 479
Hanson, MA 02341-0479
Ph:(781)293-4100
Fax:(781)294-0808
Co. E-mail: debbief@acminet.org
URL: http://www.acminet.org
Contact: Deborah M. Fanning CAE, Exec. VP
Description: Manufacturers of art and creative materials; sponsors certification program to ensure that art materials are non-toxic or affixed with health warning labels where appropriate. Works with ASTM International and the American National Standards Institute to develop and maintain chronic hazard labeling standards and performance standards. Sponsors annual Youth Art Month in March to emphasize the value of art education for all children and to encourage public support for quality school art programs; publicizes value of art and art education in newspapers and magazines. **Publications:** *What You Need to Know About the Safety of Art and Craft Materials* .

1392 ■ National Art Materials Trade Association
20200 Zion Ave.
Cornelius, NC 28031
Ph:(704)892-6244
Fax:(704)892-6247
Co. E-mail: info@namta.org
URL: http://www.namta.org
Contact: Sid Smith, Exec. Dir.
Description: Domestic and international retailers, distributors, manufacturers, publishers, and importers of fine art and creative materials. Provides useful business education and services, including research programs. Maintains the art materials industry's Hall of Fame. **Publications:** *Art Materials Retailer* (quarterly); *NAMTA's Annual Convention Directory*; *National Art Materials Trade Association—News and Views* (monthly); *Who's Who in Art Materials* (annual).

REFERENCE WORKS

1393 ■ "Creative Cluster Paints Business Success" in *Business Journal Serving Greater Tampa Bay* (Vol. 30, October 29, 2010, No. 45, pp. 1)
Pub: Tampa Bay Business Journal
Ed: Jane Meinhardt. **Description:** How Tom Gaffney, a cofounder of the private equity firm The Anderson Group realized the great return on investment in the 600 block of Central Avenue in St. Petersburg, Florida is discussed. Focusing on long-term value rather than short-term profitability and exit, Gaffney purchased this block in 2008 for $2.3 million and cultivated arts businesses at tenants.

TRADE PERIODICALS

1394 ■ *CityArt Magazine*
Pub: Fleisher Fine Arts Inc.
Contact: Pat Fleisher, Publisher
E-mail: info@artfocus.com
Released: 3/yr. **Price:** $15 Canada 7%GST. **Description:** Magazine on the contemporary arts scene, including overview articles and reviews of exhibits, artbooks, and an annual summer art school directory.

1395 ■ *Country Home*
Pub: Meredith Corp.
Released: Monthly, 10/yr. **Price:** $4.95 newstand; $21.97 two years. **Description:** Magazine furnishing information on American interior design, architecture, antiques and collectibles, gardening, art, and culinary endeavor.

1396 ■ *Needlework Retailer*
Pub: Yarn Tree Design Inc.
Released: Bimonthly. **Description:** Trade magazine for the needlework industry, especially small, independent needlework retailers.

VIDEOCASSETTES/ AUDIOCASSETTES

1397 ■ *Piet Mondrian: Mr. Boogie-Woogie Man*
Home Vision Cinema
c/o Image Entertainment
20525 Nordhoff St., Ste. 200
Chatsworth, CA 91311
Co. E-mail: inquiries@image-entertainment.com
URL: http://www.homevision.com
Released: 1998. **Price:** $39.95. **Description:** Details the painter's development of a new art and his experiments with Symbolism, Fauvism, and Cubism. **Availability:** VHS.

1398 ■ *Vermeer: Light, Love, and Silence*
Home Vision Cinema
c/o Image Entertainment
20525 Nordhoff St., Ste. 200
Chatsworth, CA 91311
Co. E-mail: inquiries@image-entertainment.com
URL: http://www.homevision.com
Released: 1998. **Price:** $39.95. **Description:** Explores the social, economic, scientific, and political context of the painter's work. **Availability:** VHS.

TRADE SHOWS AND CONVENTIONS

1399 ■ The Winter Olympia Fine Art and Antiques Fair
Clarion Events Ltd.
Earls Court Exhibition Centre
Warwick Rd.
London SW5 9TA, United Kingdom
Ph:44 20 7370 8139
URL: http://www.clarionevents.com
Released: Annual. **Audience:** Trade and general public. **Principal Exhibits:** Antiques including fine, oak, garden, and country furniture; rugs; paintings; ceramics; clocks; sculptures; jewelry, silver, and bronzes.

FRANCHISES AND BUSINESS OPPORTUNITIES

1400 ■ Marad Fine Art International
66 Glenbrook Rd., Ste. 3327
Stamford, CT 06902
Ph:(203)912-8402
Fax:(203)539-6001
No. of Franchise Units: 3. **No. of Company-Owned Units:** 1. **Founded:** 1938. **Franchised:** 2000. **Description:** Artwork supplies business. **Equity Capital Needed:** $49,000-$70,000. **Franchise Fee:** $39,000. **Financial Assistance:** No. **Training:** Yes.

Assisted Living Facilities

ASSOCIATIONS AND OTHER ORGANIZATIONS

1401 ■ American College of Health Care Administrators
1321 Duke St., Ste. 400
Alexandria, VA 22314
Ph:(202)536-5120
Fax:(866)874-1585
Co. E-mail: mgrachek@achca.org
URL: http://www.achca.org
Contact: Marianna Kern Grachek, Pres./CEO
Description: Persons actively engaged in the administration of long-term care facilities, such as nursing homes, retirement communities, assisted living facilities, and sub-acute care programs. Administers professional certification programs for assisted living, sub-acute and nursing home administrators. Works to elevate the standards in the field and to develop and promote a code of ethics and standards of education and training. Seeks to inform allied professions and the public that good administration of long-term care facilities calls for special formal academic training and experience. Encourages research in all aspects of geriatrics, the chronically ill, and administration. Maintains placement service. Holds special education programs; facilitates networking among administrators. **Publications:** *ACHCA E-News* (biweekly).

1402 ■ Assisted Living Federation of America
1650 King St., Ste. 602
Alexandria, VA 22314-2747
Ph:(703)894-1805
Fax:(703)894-1831
Co. E-mail: rgrimes@alfa.org
URL: http://www.alfa.org
Contact: Richard Grimes MEd, Pres./CEO
Description: Providers of assisted living, state associations of providers, and others interested or involved in the industry. Promotes the interests of the assisted living industry and works to enhance the quality of life for the population it serves. Provides a forum for assisted living providers to unite, exchange information, and interact. Encourages the development of high standards for the industry. Promotes the concept of assisted living facilities with public and private agencies and other professionals. Works to educate providers and the public and increase national awareness of assisted living. Sponsors speakers' bureau, conferences, educational opportunities, trade show, research & training products. **Publications:** *ALFA Alert* (weekly); *ALFA Executive Portfolio: Inside the Minds of the Leaders in Assisted Living and Senior Housing*; *Assisted Living Executive* (9/year); *Guide to Choosing an Assisted Living Residence* .

REFERENCE WORKS

1403 ■ "Advancing the Ball" in *Inside Healthcare* (Vol. 6, December 2010, No. 7, pp. 31)
Pub: RedCoat Publishing Inc.
Ed: Michelle McNickle. **Description:** Profile of Medicalodges an elder-care specialty company that provides both patient care and technology development. President and CEO of the firm believes that hiring good employees is key to growth for any small business.

1404 ■ "Big Sell-Off At Sunwest" in *The Business Journal-Portland* (Vol. 25, July 25, 2008, No. 20, pp. 1)
Pub: American City Business Journals, Inc.
Ed: Robin J. Moody. **Description:** Oregon's largest operator of assisted living facilities Sunwest Management Inc. is expected to sell 132 of its properties. The planned sale, which is believed to be worth more than $1 billion, will help Sunwest pay creditors and investors. Other views and information on the planned sale, as well as on Sunwest's services which include adult day care, are presented.

1405 ■ "Connecting the Dots Between Wellness and Elder Care" in *Benefits and Compensation Digest* (Vol. 47, August 2010, No. 8, pp. 18)
Pub: International Foundation of Employee Benefit Plans
Ed: Sandra Timmermann. **Description:** Employees caring for aged and infirm parents deal with time and financial issues and other stresses. The connection between health status of caregivers and employers' health care costs could be aided by linking programs and benefits with wellness and caregiving.

1406 ■ "Elder Care Costs Surge" in *National Underwriter Life & Health* (Vol. 114, November 8, 2020, No. 21, pp. 25)
Pub: Summit Business Media
Ed: Trevor Thomas. **Description:** Nursing home and assisted living rates rose from 2009 to 2010, according to MetLife Mature Market Institute. Statistical data included.

1407 ■ "Elder Care, Rx Drugs Reforms Top Zoeller's Agenda" in *Times* (December 21, 2010)
Pub: The Times
Ed: Sarah Tompkins. **Description:** Indiana Attorney General Greg Zoeller is hoping to develop a program in the state that will help regulate care for the elderly; freeze medical licenses for doctors involved in criminal investigations; address illegal drug use; and to establish a program to help individuals dispose of old prescription medications easily at pharmacies.

1408 ■ "Elder-Care Seminar to Teach Ways to Avoid Falls" in *Virginian-Pilot* (November 25, 2010)
Pub: Virginian-Pilot
Ed: Amy Jeter. **Description:** ResCare HomeCare, a home health services firm, offers free seminars on helping to make residences safer for seniors prone to falling.

1409 ■ "EVMS Gets Grant to Train Providers for Elder Care" in *Virginian-Pilot* (October 29, 2010)
Pub: Virginian-Pilot
Ed: Elizabeth Simpson. **Description:** Eastern Virginia Medical School received a federal grant to train health providers in elder care. Details of the program are provided.

1410 ■ "Face Issues if Elder Care, Unemployment Collide" in *Atlanta Journal-Constitution* (December 26, 2010, pp. G1)
Pub: Atlanta Journal-Constitution
Ed: Amy Lindgren. **Description:** More issues arise during holiday for families with older members requiring care, including the issue of employment for those doing the caregiving.

1411 ■ "GeckoSystems Reduces Sensor Fusion Costs Due to Elder Care Robot Trials" in *Internet Wire* (December 14, 2010)
Pub: Comtex
Description: GeckoSystems International Corporation has been able to reduce the cost of its sensor fusion system while maintaining reliability and performance. The firm's ongoing first in-home elder care robot trials have sparked interest regarding its business model, technologies available for licensing, and joint domestic and international ventures.

1412 ■ "New Elder Care Center to Focus on Residents with Failing Memories" in *Tulsa World* (November 30, 2010)
Pub: World Publishing
Ed: Robert Evatt. **Description:** People with Alzheimer's disease and other mental disorders require specialized care. Constant Care Management Company runs 'memory care' centers designed for the elderly with such conditions.

1413 ■ "Prime Site Lands Retirement Center" in *Business Courier* (Vol. 24, November 2, 2008, No. 29, pp. 1)
Pub: American City Business Journals, Inc.
Ed: Laura Baverman. **Description:** Erickson Retirement Communities plans to build a $220 milllion campus on 65 acres of land between Evendale and Glendale. The project will depend on votes casted by village councils in Evendale and Glendale, expected to take place in December 2007. Both areas must sign on and alter zoning rules before the development can proceed.

1414 ■ "Silver Dollars" in *Small Business Opportunities* (September 2008)
Pub: Entrepreneur Media Inc.
Description: Profile of Always Best Care Senior Services, a franchise created by Michael Newman, which offers non-medical In-Home Care, Personal Emergency Response Systems, and Assisted Living Placement Services to seniors; the company offers franchisees the opportunity to fill what is oftentimes a void for the seniors and their families in the community.

1415 ■ "Small Is Best, Says Housing Officials" in *Business First Buffalo* (November 16, 2007, pp. 1)
Pub: American City Business Journals, Inc.
Ed: Tracey Drury. **Description:** Nonprofit organizations in some parts of the U.S. are moving senior citizens from larger institutions into smaller housing. The benefits of smaller housing for the elderly are evaluated.

1416 ■ "Sunwest Vies To Stave Off Bankruptcy" in *The Business Journal-Portland* (Vol. 25, August 15, 2008, No. 23, pp. 1)
Pub: American City Business Journals, Inc.
Ed: Robin J. Moody. **Description:** Sunwest Management Inc. is teetering on the edge of bankruptcy as creditors start foreclosure on nine of their properties. This could potentially displace residents of the assisted living operator. Sunwest is trying to sell smaller packages of properties to get a $100 million bridge loan to maintain operations.

1417 ■ "They've Fallen, But They Can Get Up" in *Barron's* (Vol. 88, March 10, 2008, No. 10, pp. 43)
Pub: Dow Jones & Company, Inc.
Ed: Kopin Tan. **Description:** Shares of senior housing companies present buying opportunities to investors because of their low prices. Companies such as Brookdale Senior Living are not as dependent on housing prices but have suffered declines in share prices.

TRADE PERIODICALS

1418 ■ *AHCA Notes*
Pub: American Health Care Association
Ed: Nathan Childs, Editor, nchilds@ahca.org. **Released:** Monthly, 12/year. **Price:** Included in membership. **Description:** Presents information on nursing homes, assisted living, and residential care facilities. Covers legislation on prescription drug prices, nurse assistant training, certification enforcement, Medicare/Medicaid and long term care requirements, and legal activities.

1419 ■ *The Capsule Newsletter*
Pub: Children of Aging Parents
Contact: Lorraine Sailor
Ed: Lorraine Sailor, Editor. **Released:** Bimonthly. **Price:** Included in membership; Free; $100. **Description:** Contains articles and informational notices on the concerns and issues of elderly persons and those who care for them. Provides organizations, resources, and services to help caregivers of elderly.

1420 ■ *Home Health Care Services Quarterly*
Pub: Routledge Journals
Contact: William T. Wake MD, Editorial Board
Ed: Maria Aranda, PhD, Editor. **Released:** Quarterly. **Price:** $118 online; $124 print & online. **Description:** Professional journal.

1421 ■ *Housing for Seniors Report*
Pub: CD Publications
Contact: Carol Solomon
Ed: Marcella Kogan, Editor. **Released:** Monthly. **Price:** $297/year. **Description:** Provides news and practical suggestions concerning the production, management, marketing and other business aspects of housing for the elderly. Coverage includes nursing homes, apartment projects, and retirement communities; also government-operated programs. Recurring features include news of research.

1422 ■ *National Hispanic Council on Aging —News*
Pub: National Hispanic Council on Aging
Contact: Luis Acevedo
E-mail: luisacevedo@att.net
Ed: Released: Quarterly. **Price:** Included in membership; Free. **Description:** Publicizes the activities of the Council, which fosters the well-being of the Hispanic elderly through research, policy analysis, projects, development of educational resources, and training. Also provides a network for organizations and community groups interested in the Hispanic elderly. Recurring features include a calendar of events, legislative updates, and notices of publications available.

TRADE SHOWS AND CONVENTIONS

1423 ■ California Association of Homes and Services for the Aging Annual Meeting and Exhibition
California Association of Homes and Services for the Aging
1315 "I" St., Ste. 100
Sacramento, CA 95814
Ph:(916)392-5111
Fax:(916)428-4250
Co. E-mail: aburnsjohnson@aging.org
URL: http://www.aging.org
Released: Annual. **Audience:** Administrators of retirement homes, nurses, executives of multihome corporations (nonprofit), activities directors, and dieticians. **Principal Exhibits:** Food services, medical and financial record systems, industrial cleaning and maintenance equipment, architectural services, interior design materials, medical equipment, computers, software, insurance services, employee benefit services and accounting services.

LIBRARIES

1424 ■ Albany Medical College–Schaffer Library of Health Sciences
43 New Scotland Ave.
Albany, NY 12208
Ph:(518)262-5586
Co. E-mail: library@mail.amc.edu
URL: http://www.amc.edu/Academic/Schaffer/index.html
Contact: Enid Geyer, Dir.
Scope: Medicine, pre-clinical sciences, nursing. **Services:** Interlibrary loan; copying; Library open to allied health personnel. **Holdings:** 150,000 volumes; 98,597 bound periodical volumes; 2700 audio/visual programs. **Subscriptions:** 4950 journals and other serials.

1425 ■ American Association of Occupational Health Nurses Library
7794 Grow Dr.
Pensacola, FL 32514
Ph:(850)474-6963
Free: 800-241-8014
Fax:(850)484-8762
Co. E-mail: aaohn@aaohn.org
URL: http://www.aaohn.org
Contact: Jon Dancy, Exec.Dir.
Scope: Occupational and environmental health nursing, occupational medicine. **Services:** Library not open to the public. **Holdings:** 1200 books; 24 bound periodical volumes; 1050 pamphlets. **Subscriptions:** 54 journals and other serials; 6 newspapers.

1426 ■ American Nurses Association–Library Information Center
8515 Georgia Ave., Ste. 400
Silver Spring, MD 20910-3492
Ph:(301)628-5143
Fax:(301)628-5008
Co. E-mail: richard.barry@ana.org
URL: http://www.nursingworld.org/
Contact: Richard J. Barry, MSLS, AHIP
Scope: Nurses, nursing, healthcare. **Services:** Library not open to the public. **Holdings:** 180 books; 1275 reports. **Subscriptions:** 30 journals and other serials.

1427 ■ Arkansas Aging Foundation Information Center
706 S. Pulaski St.
Little Rock, AR 72201-3927
Ph:(501)376-6083
Contact: Ed Doman, Pres.
Scope: Health promotion; seniors - enhancing independent living, health issues, activities. **Services:** Copying. **Holdings:** Monthly newspaper. **Subscriptions:** 1 newspaper.

1428 ■ Deaconess Hospital Health Science Library
600 Mary St.
Evansville, IN 47747
Ph:(812)450-3384
Fax:(812)450-7255
Co. E-mail: julia_esparza@deaconess.com
URL: http://www.deaconess.com/body.cfm?id=81
Contact: Julia Esparza, Hea.Sci.Libn
Scope: Nursing, clinical medicine, consumer health, healthcare management, business management, allied health sciences, clinical pastoral care. **Services:** Interlibrary loan; copying; current awareness; Library open to laypersons. **Holdings:** 2000 books; 200 audio/visual programs. **Subscriptions:** 135 journals and other serials; 2 newspapers.

1429 ■ El Camino Hospital–Health Library and Resource Center
Main Bldg., 1st Fl.
2500 Grant Rd.
Mountain View, CA 94040
Ph:(650)940-7210
Fax:(650)940-7174
Co. E-mail: healthlib@elcaminohospital.org
URL: http://www.elcaminohospital.org/Patient_Services/Health_Library
Contact: Jack Black, Sr.Libn.
Scope: Medicine, nursing, healthcare administration, caregiving, elder care. **Services:** Interlibrary loan; copying; Library open to the public. **Holdings:** 5500 books and videotapes. **Subscriptions:** 150 journals and other serials; 3 newspapers.

1430 ■ Health Occupations Center–Learning Resource Center
9368 Oakbourne Rd.
Santee, CA 92071
Ph:(619)596-3676
Fax:(619)579-4779
Co. E-mail: johnsonk@guhsd.net
Contact: Kathleen A. Johnson
Scope: Nursing, medicine, dentistry. **Services:** Copying; Center open to the public for reference use only. **Holdings:** 2100 books. **Subscriptions:** 30 journals and other serials.

1431 ■ Jefferson College of Health Sciences Learning Resource Center
920 S. Jefferson St.
Roanoke, VA 24016
Ph:(540)985-8273
Co. E-mail: jelacate@jchs.edu
URL: http://www.jchs.edu/page.php/prmID/611
Contact: Jennifer Flint, Lib.Dir.
Scope: Nursing, allied health, respiratory care, physical therapy assistant, occupational therapy assistant, emergency health services, physicians' assistant, radiologic science, biology. **Services:** Interlibrary loan; copying; Center open to the public for reference use only. **Holdings:** 11,000 books; 1704 bound periodical volumes. **Subscriptions:** 370 journals and other serials.

1432 ■ Kaiser-Permanente Medical Center Health Sciences Library
2425 Geary Blvd.
San Francisco, CA 94115
Ph:(415)202-3835
Fax:(415)202-3257
URL: http://www.kaiserpermanente.org
Scope: Clinical sciences. **Services:** Interlibrary loan; Library not open to the public. **Holdings:** 3800 books; 11,000 bound periodical volumes; 50 pamphlets. **Subscriptions:** 190 journals and other serials.

1433 ■ Loma Linda University–Del E. Webb Memorial Library
11072 Anderson St.
Loma Linda, CA 92350-1704
Ph:(909)558-4550
Fax:(909)558-4188
Co. E-mail: cdrake@llu.edu
URL: http://www.llu.edu/llu/library
Contact: Carlene Drake, Dir.
Scope: Medicine, nursing, dentistry, religion, health, allied health professions. **Services:** Interlibrary loan; copying; Library open to qualified users. **Holdings:** 186,719 books; 121,609 bound periodical volumes; 62,318 microforms; 6265 tapes and phonograph records; 8130 filmstrips, films, slides; 1160 feet of archival materials. **Subscriptions:** 1411 journals and other serials; 7 newspapers.

1434 ■ Los Angeles County/Harbor-UCLA Medical Center–A.F. Parlow Library of the Health Sciences
1000 W. Carson St.
Box 18
Torrance, CA 90502
Ph:(310)222-2372

Fax:(310)212-5542
Co. E-mail: libref@labiomed.org
URL: http://www.humc.edu
Contact: Mary Ann Berliner, Dir., Lib.Svc.
Scope: Medicine, nursing, patient education, administration. **Services:** Interlibrary loan; copying; Library open to the public with restrictions. **Holdings:** 35,000 books; 45,000 bound periodical volumes; 1700 AV programs. **Subscriptions:** 866 journals and other serials.

1435 ■ McMaster University Health Sciences Library
1200 Main St., W.
Hamilton, ON, Canada L8N 3Z5
Ph:(905)525-9140
Fax:(905)528-3733
Co. E-mail: bayleyl@mcmaster.ca
URL: http://hsl.mcmaster.ca
Contact: Liz Bayley, Dir.
Scope: Basic medical sciences, clinical medicine, nursing, allied health sciences, history of medicine. **Services:** Interlibrary loan; copying; Library open to the public for reference use only. **Holdings:** 61,777 (volumes) books; 93,330 bound periodical volumes; 1717 multimedia resources, including 879 videotapes; 828 audiocassettes; 284 computer software programs. **Subscriptions:** 2600 journals and other serials.

1436 ■ Spectrum Health Sciences Libraries
A-level, West Bldg.
100 Michigan St., NE
Grand Rapids, MI 49503-2560
Ph:(616)391-1655
Fax:(616)391-3527
Co. E-mail: diane.hummel@spectrum-health.org
URL: http://www.spectrum-health.org
Contact: Diane Hummel, Mgr.
Scope: Medicine, surgery, medical/surgical specialties, nursing. **Services:** Copying; document delivery; Library open to the public. **Holdings:** 6000 books; bound periodical volumes; audio and videocassettes; microfiche; microfilm. **Subscriptions:** 500 periodicals.

ASSOCIATIONS AND OTHER ORGANIZATIONS

1437 ■ AMC Institute
100 N 20th St., 4th Fl.
Philadelphia, PA 19103-1443
Ph:(215)564-3484
Fax:(215)564-2175
Co. E-mail: info@amcinstitute.org
URL: http://www.amcinstitute.org
Contact: Francine Butler PhD, Exec. VP
Description: Management companies serving a number of associations on a professional basis (but not executives serving more than one association in an employee relationship). Membership employs nearly 3,000 association management professionals and serves over 1,200 associations with annual budgets exceeding 960 million dollars and serving nearly 1.7 million members. .

1438 ■ American Society of Association Executives
1575 I St. NW
Washington, DC 20005
Ph:(202)371-0940
Free: 888-950-2723
Fax:(202)371-8315
Co. E-mail: asaeservice@asaecenter.org
URL: http://www.asaecenter.org
Contact: John H. Graham IV, Pres./CEO
Description: Professional society of paid executives of international, national, state, and local trade, professional, and philanthropic associations. Seeks to educate association executives on effective management, including: the proper objectives, functions, and activities of associations; the basic principles of association management; the legal aspects of association activity; policies relating to association management; efficient methods, procedures, and techniques of association management; the responsibilities and professional standards of association executives. Maintains information resource center. Conducts resume, guidance, and consultation services; compiles statistics in the form of reports, surveys, and studies; carries out research and education. Maintains ASAE Services Corporation to provide special services and ASAE Foundation to do future-oriented research and make grant awards. Offers executive search services and insurance programs. Provides CEO center for chief staff executives. Conducts Certified Association Executive (CAE) program. **Publications:** *Association Management* (monthly); *Journal of Association Leadership*; *Leadership: The Magazine for Volunteer Association Leaders* (annual); *Who's Who in Association Management* (annual).

1439 ■ Canadian Society of Association Executives–Societe Canadienne des Directeurs d'Association
10 King St. E, Ste. 1100
Toronto, ON, Canada M5C 1C3
Ph:(416)363-3555
Free: 800-461-3608
Fax:(416)363-3630
Co. E-mail: csae@csae.com
URL: http://www.csae.com
Contact: Michael Anderson CAE, Pres./CEO
Description: CEO, presidents, executive directors and managers working for non-profit associations operating in Canada. Promotes efficient operation of non-profit associations; facilitates continued professional advancement of members. Serves as a forum for exchange of ideas and information among members; conducts educational and training programs. **Publications:** *Association* (bimonthly); *The Association Agenda* (periodic).

1440 ■ DMA Nonprofit Federation
1615 L St. NW, Ste. 1100
Washington, DC 20036
Ph:(202)861-2410
Co. E-mail: cquinn@the-dma.org
URL: http://www.nonprofitfederation.org
Contact: Christopher Quinn, Exec. Dir.
Description: Trade and lobbying group for non-profit organizations that use direct and online marketing to raise funds and communicate with members. Sponsors professional development conferences and seminars, lobbies on state and federal legislation, regulation, and standards related to direct marketing and related issues. Provides information about and participants in litigation affecting non-profits. Promotes the overall welfare of non-profits. Represents health care charities, social service agencies, religious groups, colleges and universities and fraternal organizations. **Publications:** *Journal of the DMA Nonprofit Federation* (quarterly); *News Update* (biweekly).

1441 ■ Society for Nonprofit Organizations
5820 Canton Center Rd., Ste. 165
Canton, MI 48187-2683
Ph:(734)451-3582
Fax:(734)451-5935
Co. E-mail: info@snpo.org
URL: http://www.snpo.org
Contact: Katie Burnham-Laverty, Co-Founder/Pres./CEO
Description: Brings together those who serve in the nonprofit world in order to build a strong network of professionals throughout the country; provides a forum for the exchange of information, knowledge, and ideas on strengthening and increasing productivity within nonprofit organizations and among their leaders. Mission is accomplished through the publication of Nonprofit World magazine, educational programs offered by the Learning Institute, and other communications with its members. **Publications:** *Funding Alert* (monthly); *Nonprofit World* (bimonthly).

REFERENCE WORKS

1442 ■ *Association Management Companies Institute—Directory*
Pub: AMC Institute
Contact: Suzanne C. Pine, Exec. VP
E-mail: spine@amcinstitute.org
Released: Latest edition 2010-2011. **Covers:** 200 members representing 4,000 associations. **Entries Include:** Management company name, address, phone, fax, e-mail, URL address, member and title. **Arrangement:** Alphabetical. **Indexes:** Association name, member name, city, state.

1443 ■ *Association Management—Convention Center & Convention Bureau Directory*
Pub: American Society of Association Executives
Contact: Keith C. Skillman
Ed: Debra Popovich, Editor. **Released:** Annual, February. **Price:** Free. **Publication Includes:** List of convention halls, centers, auditoriums, arenas, and convention and visitors bureaus in the United States, Canada, and abroad. **Entries Include:** Name of hall or CVB, phone, fax, and exhibit space available. **Arrangement:** Geographical.

1444 ■ *Encyclopedia of Associations*
Pub: Gale
Released: Annual. **Price:** $778, individuals. **Covers:** Approximately 25,000 nonprofit U.S. Membership organizations of national scope divided into 18 classifications: trade, business, and commercial; environmental and agricultural; legal, governmental, public administration, and military; engineering, technological, and natural and social science; educational; cultural; social welfare; health and medical; public affairs; fraternal, nationality, and ethnic; religious organizations; veterans, hereditary, and patriotic; hobby and avocational; athletic and sports; labor unions, associations, and federations; chambers of commerce and trade and tourism; Greek and non-Greek letter societies, associations, and federations; fan clubs. **Entries Include:** Organization name, address, phone, fax, name of executive officer, staff size, date founded, number of members, membership dues, annual budget, description of objectives, activities, committees, publications, computer and telecommunications services, historical information, convention dates and locations; publications, including title, description, ISSN, circulation, whether advertising is accepted, alternate formats, and former or alternate name(s) of publication. **Arrangement:** By subject keyword within classifications cited above. **Indexes:** Organization name/keyword (including references to organizations listed in International Organizations; also includes addresses and phone numbers after each association's primary reference); separate volume includes geographical and executive indexes (including organization name, address, phone, and name of chief executive in both arrangements).

1445 ■ *National Trade and Professional Associations of the U.S.*
Pub: Columbia Books & Information Services
Contact: Buck Downs
Released: Annual, Latest edition 2011. **Price:** $269, individuals standing order; $299, individuals mailing list; per thousand; minimum order $269. **Covers:** Approximately 7,800 trade associations, professional societies and labor unions. **Entries Include:** Name, year established, name of chief executive and other senior staff, address, phone, toll free, fax, e-mail & internet addresses; number of staff members, budget,

size of membership; date, expected attendance, and location of annual meeting; publications; historical and descriptive data. Title formerly included '. and Canada and Labor Unions'; Canadian coverage was dropped beginning with 1982 edition, but American labor unions are still included. **Arrangement:** Alphabetical. **Indexes:** Geographical, subject, budget, acronym, executive.

1446 ■ *State & Regional Associations of the United States*
Pub: Columbia Books & Information Services
Contact: Buck Downs
Released: Annual, Latest edition 2011. **Price:** $199, individuals. **Covers:** 8,800 state and regional trade associations, professional societies, and labor unions. **Entries Include:** Organization name, address, toll-free phone, fax, e-mail & internet addresses; year established, name of chief executive and select senior staff, number of members, financial data, staff size, requirements for membership, services, publications, annual meetings. **Arrangement:** Geographical, alphabetical within state. **Indexes:** Subject, budget, executive, acronym.

1447 ■ *Who's Who in Association Management*
Pub: American Society of Association Executives
Contact: Karen Sulmonetti
Released: Annual, Latest edition 2007. **Price:** $70, members; $160, nonmembers. **Covers:** Paid executives who are members of the association; suppliers of products and services to associations; supplier listings are paid. **Entries Include:** For members—Name, address, phone, association represented. For suppliers—Company name, address, phone, contact name, description of products and services. **Arrangement:** Members are alphabetical; suppliers are classified by product or service. **Indexes:** Association, geographical, personal name, membership category.

STATISTICAL SOURCES

1448 ■ *Association Meeting Trends*
Pub: American Society of Association Executives (ASAE)
Released: 2004. **Price:** $107.95 (paper) ($86.95 for members). **Description:** Study containing statistics on association conventions, expositions, board and committee meetings, and educational seminars. Includes more than 100 tables.

TRADE PERIODICALS

1449 ■ *ASAE Membership Developments*
Pub: Membership Section
Contact: Meggan Freedman, Section Mgr.
E-mail: mharrison@asaenet.org
Released: Monthly. **Price:** Included in membership. **Description:** Emphasizes direct mail, telemarketing, surveys, and member recruitment and retention. Recurring features include news of the Society.

1450 ■ *Association Meetings*
Pub: Primedia Business Magazines & Media
Contact: Melissa Fromento, Gp. Publisher
E-mail: mfromento@meetingsnet.com
Ed: Sue Pelletier, Editor, spelletier@meetingsnet.com. **Released:** Bimonthly. **Price:** $65 Canada; $98 other countries. **Description:** Magazine for association meeting planners.

1451 ■ *Association News*
Pub: Schneider Publishing Company Inc.
Ed: Ann Shepphird, Editor, ann.shepphird@schneiderpublishing.com. **Released:** Monthly. **Price:** Free. **Description:** Provides timely independent information on association management, meeting planning, and convention business. Seeks to provide a medium for information and news, and offers a communications link among the various nonprofit organizations in the Western U.S. and the commercial entities servicing them. Recurring features include editorials, commentary, news of industry organizations, and articles in the areas of association management and meeting planning.

1452 ■ *Association Trends*
Pub: Martineau Corp.
Contact: Jill M. Cornish, Pres./Publisher
E-mail: jill@assntrends.com
Released: Monthly. **Price:** $165 standard class; $189 1st class; $189 library; $189 Canada standard class. **Description:** Newspaper for staff professionals of volunteer organizations. Covers business, trade associations, and professional societies.

1453 ■ *Communication News*
Pub: American Society of Association Executives
Ed: LaRonda Famodu, Editor, lfamodu@asaenet.org. **Released:** Monthly. **Price:** Included in membership. **Description:** Focuses on public relations, writing and editing, publications management, postal rates and regulations, advertising sales, censorship, and printing and typography. Advises readers on how to improve their publications and alerts them to pertinent legal and legislative action and upcoming conventions and courses.

1454 ■ *Government Relations*
Pub: Government Relations Section
Contact: Tamara Faggen, Assoc.Ed.
Ed: Released: Monthly. **Price:** Included in membership. **Description:** Carries updates on government legislation affecting associations and practical information and suggestions on lobbying techniques. Recurring features include news of Section programs and activities.

1455 ■ *Meetings & Incentive Travel*
Pub: Rogers Media Publishing
Contact: Stephen Dempsey, Editor & Publisher
E-mail: steve.dempsey@mtg.rogers.com
Released: 6/yr. **Price:** $98 two years CAN; $74 Canada; $95 U.S. **Description:** Magazine for corporate meeting planners and incentive travel executives.

TRADE SHOWS AND CONVENTIONS

1456 ■ Holiday Showcase
Association Forum of Chicagoland
10 S. Riverside Plz., Ste. 800
Chicago, IL 60606
Ph:(312)924-7000
Fax:(312)924-7100
URL: http://www.associationforum.org
Released: Annual. **Audience:** Association executives. **Principal Exhibits:** Hotel, airline, and convention center information; printers; insurance and accounting services, banking, technology.

1457 ■ Management and Technology Conferences - ASAE Annual Meeting
American Society of Association Executives ASAE
1575 I St. NW
Washington, DC 20005-1103
Ph:(202)371-0940
Free: 888-950-2723
Fax:(202)371-8315
Co. E-mail: ASAEservice@asaecenter.org
URL: http://www.asaecenter.org
Released: Annual. **Audience:** Association executives and meeting planners. **Principal Exhibits:** Equipment, supplies, and services for associations.

COMPUTERIZED DATABASES

1458 ■ *Associations Canada*
ProQuest LLC
789 E Eisenhower Pky.
PO Box 1346
Ann Arbor, MI 48106
Ph:(734)761-4700
Free: 800-521-0600
Co. E-mail: info@proquest.com
URL: http://www.proquest.com/en-US/products/brands/pl_mm.shtml
Description: Contains information for nearly 20,000 active international, foreign, national, interprovincial, and provincial associations in Canada. Includes association name, founding date, address, telephone number, and facsimile number; executive name and title; annual operating budget; number of paid employees; number of members; affiliations; publications; conference and meeting plans; and mailing lists. Corresponds to *Directory of Associations in Canada*. **Availability:** Online: ProQuest LLC. **Type:** Directory.

LIBRARIES

1459 ■ American Society of Association Executives–The Center for Association Leadership Knowledge Center
Ronald Reagan Bldg. & Intl. Trade Ctr.
1300 Pennsylvania Ave., NW
Washington, DC 20004
Ph:(202)326-9559
Fax:(202)842-1109
Co. E-mail: knowledgecenter@asaecenter.org
URL: http://www.asaenet.org/
Scope: Association management - law, communications, human resources, conventions, education, voluntarism, finance, membership promotion, government relations, International affair chapter relations, marketing. **Services:** Library open to the public by appointment. **Holdings:** 2000 books and research publications; 20 VF drawers containing samples of association management materials. **Subscriptions:** 60 journals and other serials.

START-UP INFORMATION

1460 ▪ *202 Things You Can Buy and Sell for Big Profits*
Pub: Entrepreneur Press
Ed: James Stephenson; Jason R. Rich. **Released:** July 2008. **Price:** $19.95. **Description:** Become an entrepreneur at selling new and used products. This handbook will help individuals cash in on the boom in reselling new and used products online. A new section defines ways to set realistic goals while distinguishing between 'get-rich schemes' and long term, viable businesses. A discussion about targeting and reaching the right customer base is included, along with finding and obtaining the service support needed for starting a new business.

1461 ▪ "Auction Company Grows with Much Smaller Sites" in *Automotive News* (Vol. 86, October 31, 2011, No. 6488, pp. 23)
Pub: Crain Communications Inc.
Ed: Arlena Sawyers. **Description:** Auction Broadcasting Company has launched auction sites and is expanding into new areas. The family-owned business will provide auctions half the size traditionally used. The firm reports that 40 percent of the General Motors factory-owned vehicles sold on consignment were purchased by online buyers, up 30 percent over 2010.

1462 ▪ *Complete Idiot's Guide to Starting an Ebay Business*
Pub: Penguin Books (USA) Incorporated
Ed: Barbara Weltman, Malcolm Katt. **Released:** February 2008. **Price:** $19.95 (US), $29.00 (Canadian). **Description:** Guide for starting an eBay business includes information on products to sell, how to price merchandise, and details for working with services like PayPal, and how to organize fulfillment services.

1463 ▪ *EBay Business Start-up Kit: 100s of Live Links to All the Information and Tools You Need*
Pub: NOLO
Ed: Richard Stim. **Released:** July 2008. **Price:** $24. 99. **Description:** Interactive kit that connects user directly to EBay is presented.

1464 ▪ *eBay Business the Smart Way*
Pub: AMACOM
Ed: Joseph T. Sinclair. **Released:** June 6, 2007. **Price:** $17.95. **Description:** eBay commands ninety percent of all online auction business. Computer and software expert and online entrepreneur shares information to help online sellers get started and move merchandise on eBay. Tips include the best ways to build credibility, find products to sell, manage inventory, create a storefront Website, and more.

1465 ▪ *EBay Income: How ANYONE of Any Age, Location, and/or Background Can Build a Highly Profitable Online Business with eBay (Revised 2nd Edition)*
Pub: Atlantic Publishing Company
Released: December 1, 2010. **Price:** $24.95. **Description:** A complete overview of eBay is given and guides any small company through the entire process of creating the auction and auction strategies, photography, writing copy, text and formatting, multiple sales, programming tricks, PayPal, accounting, creating marketing, merchandising, managing email lists, advertising plans, taxes and sales tax, best time to list items and for how long, sniping programs, international customers, opening a storefront, electronic commerce, buy-it now pricing, keywords, Google marketing and eBay secrets.

1466 ▪ "Power Up" in *Entrepreneur* (Vol. 35, November 2007, No. 11, pp. 140)
Pub: Entrepreneur Media Inc.
Ed: Amanda C. Kooser. **Description:** PowerSeller is a status in the Internet company eBay, wherein sellers average at least $1,000 in sales per month for three consecutive months. There are five tiers in the PowerSeller status, which ranges from Bronze to Titanium. Launching startups at eBay can help entrepreneurs pick up a wide customer base, but getting and maintaining PowerSeller status is a challenge.

1467 ▪ *Start Your Own Business on eBay, 2nd Edition*
Pub: Entrepreneur Press
Ed: Jacquelyn Lynn. **Released:** May 2007. **Price:** $19.95. **Description:** Tips for starring a new online business on eBay are shared.

1468 ▪ *Starting an Ebay Business for Canadians for Dummies*
Pub: John Wiley & Sons, Incorporated
Ed: Marsha Collier; Bill Summers. **Released:** February 2007. **Price:** $35.99. **Description:** Tips for turning a hobby into a successful online eBay company.

ASSOCIATIONS AND OTHER ORGANIZATIONS

1469 ▪ Livestock Marketing Association
10510 NW Ambassador Dr.
Kansas City, MO 64153
Ph:(816)891-0502
Free: 800-821-2048
Fax:(816)891-7926
Co. E-mail: lmainfo@lmaweb.com
URL: http://www.lmaweb.com
Contact: Mark Mackey, CEO
Description: Livestock marketing businesses and livestock dealers. Sponsors annual World Livestock Auctioneer Championships. Offers management and promotional services. .

1470 ▪ National Auctioneers Association
8880 Ballentine St.
Overland Park, KS 66214
Ph:(913)541-8084
Fax:(913)894-5281
Co. E-mail: support@auctioneers.org
URL: http://www.auctioneers.org
Contact: Hannes Combest, CEO
Description: Professional auctioneers. Provides continuing education classes for auctioneers, promotes use of the auction method of marketing in both the private and public sectors. Encourages the highest ethical standards for the profession. .

1471 ▪ National Auto Auction Association
5320 Spectrum Dr., Ste. D
Frederick, MD 21703
Ph:(301)696-0400
Fax:(301)631-1359
Co. E-mail: naaa@naaa.com
URL: http://www.naaa.com
Contact: Jay Cadigan, Pres.
Description: Owners/operators of wholesale automobile and truck auctions; associate members are car and truck manufacturers, insurers of checks and titles, car and truck rental companies, publishers of auto price guide books, and others connected with the industry. Maintains hall of fame. **Publications:** *National Auto Auction Association—Membership Directory* (annual); *On the Block* (quarterly).

REFERENCE WORKS

1472 ▪ "3.4 Million Votes Cast in 2011 eBay Motors People's Pick Poll – Winners Announced at SEMA Show" in *Benzinga.com* (, 2011)
Pub: Benzinga.com
Ed: Benzinga Staff. **Description:** eBay Motors sponsored the 2011 People's Picks survey, an annual poll inviting car enthusiasts to vote on their favorite auto thing, ranging from the best camshaft, favorite ignition, to favorite muscle car. More than 3.4 million votes were counted this year. A complete profile of eBay Motors is also provided.

1473 ▪ "Antwerpen Takes on Chrysler Financial Over Foreclosure Sales" in *Baltimore Business Journal* (Vol. 28, July 30, 2010, No. 12, pp. 1)
Pub: Baltimore Business Journal
Ed: Gary Haber. **Description:** Antwerpen Motorcars Ltd. aims to fight the scheduled foreclosure sale of real estate it leases in Baltimore County, including the showroom for its Hyundai dealership on Baltimore National Pike in Catonsville, Maryland. The company is planning to file papers in court to stop the scheduled August 11, 2010 auction sought by Chrysler Financial Services Americas LLC.

1474 ▪ "Auction-Rate Cash Frees Up" in *The Business Journal-Portland* (Vol. 25, August 15, 2008, No. 23, pp. 1)
Pub: American City Business Journals, Inc.
Ed: Aliza Earnshaw. **Description:** FEI Co. and RadiSys Corp. have received notices that UBS AG will buy back the auction-rate securities that were sold to them in around two years from 2008. FEI had $110.1 million invested in auction-rate securities while RadiSys holds $62.8 million of these securities.

1475 ▪ *Auctioneer—Directory Issue*
Pub: National Auctioneers Association
Contact: Chris Longly, Dir. of Public Affairs & Communications
E-mail: clongly@auctioneers.org
Released: Annual, February. **Publication Includes:** List of about 6,000 auctioneers. **Entries Include:**

Name, address, phone, fax, e-mail, website, specialization. **Arrangement:** Geographical and alphabetical.

1476 ■ "Auctions and Bidding: a Guide for Computer Scientists" in *ACM Computing Surveys* (Vol. 43, Summer 2011, No. 2, pp. 10)
Pub: Association for Computing Machinery
Ed: Simon Parsons, Juan A. Rodriguez-Aguilar, Mark Klein. **Description:** There are various actions: single dimensional, multi-dimensional, single-sided, double-sided, first-price, second-price, English, Dutch, Japanese, sealed-bid, and these have been extensively discussed and analyzed in economics literature. This literature is surveyed from a computer science perspective, primarily from the viewpoint of computer scientists who are interested in learning about auction theory, and to provide pointers into the economics literature for those who want a deeper technical understanding. In addition, since auctions are an increasingly important topic in computer science, the article also looks at work on auctions from the computer science literature. The aim is to identify what both bodies of work tell us about creating electronic auctions.

1477 ■ "B-N Pawn Shop Auctions Off Jimmy Hoffa's Rifle" in *Pantagraph* (September 14, 2010)
Pub: The Pantagraph
Ed: Ryan Denham. **Description:** Midwest Exchange pawn shop located in IAA Drive in Bloomington, Illinois auctioned a rifle once belonging to Jimmy Hoffa.

1478 ■ "Boots Treat Street Rolls Out Trolley Dash App on Androis and iPhone OS" in *Entertainment Close-Up* (October 24, 2011)
Pub: Close-Up Media
Description: Shoppers using Boots Treat Street can now download the Trolley Dash app game, available from the Apple Store and the Android Market, and enjoy the pastel colored street featuring favorite retailers such as eBay, New Look and Play.com collecting prizes while avoiding hazards.

1479 ■ "Brief: US-Business/eBay Earnings Rise 31 Per Cent" in *Denver Post* (July 21, 2011)
Pub: Denver Post
Ed: Andy Goldberg. **Description:** eBay's strong performance in second quarter 2011 is being attributed to Paypal online payments division. eBay's online auction sites reported gross merchandise volume up 34 percent. Statistical data included.

1480 ■ "The Business Case for Mobile Content Acceleration" in *Streaming Media* (November 2011, pp. 78)
Pub: Information Today Inc.
Ed: Dan Rayburn. **Description:** Last holiday season, eBay became a mobile commerce (m-commerce) giant when sales rose by 134 percent, as most online retailers offered customers the ability to purchase items using their mobile devices.

1481 ■ "Cash in Your Attic: Is Your Junk Someone Else's Treasure?" in *Black Enterprise* (Vol. 37, November 2006, No. 4, pp. 156)
Pub: Earl G. Graves Publishing Co. Inc.
Ed: Angela P. Moore-Thorpe. **Description:** Selling items accumulated over the years or purchased at auctions or garage sales can be a lucrative way to make extra cash. Advice and resources on auctions, collecting, and consignment shops included.

1482 ■ "Channelside On the Blocks" in *The Business Journal-Serving Greater Tampa Bay* (Vol. 28, August 29, 2008, No. 36, pp. 1)
Pub: American City Business Journals, Inc.
Ed: Michael Hinman. **Description:** In a bankruptcy auction for The Place, one of the more visible condominium projects at Channelside, the lowest bid is just below $73 a square foot. KeyBank National Association, the Key Developers Group LLC's lender, leads the auction planned for October 15, 2008. The reason behind the low minimum bid required to participate in the said action is discussed.

1483 ■ "Coastal Luxury Management Reports Los Angeles Food and Wine Tickets On Sale" in *Food & Beverage Close-Up* (August 24, 2011)
Pub: Close-Up Media
Description: Wolfgang Puck's Sunday Brunch and Charity Auction will raise money for Saint Vincent Meals on Wheels program.

1484 ■ "Condo Markdown" in *Boston Business Journal* (Vol. 27, November 30, 2007, No. 44, pp. 1)
Pub: American City Business Journals Inc.
Ed: Michelle Hillman. **Description:** Boston real estate market is softening, and condominium developers such as Beacon Communities LLC are sending out various incentives like markdowns and unit upgrades. Developers have also held auctions and even offered brand new cars to lure buyers. Other perks being offered by various Boston developers are discussed.

1485 ■ "The Data Drivers" in *Canadian Business* (Vol. 81, September 15, 2008, No. 14-15, pp. 1)
Pub: Rogers Media Ltd.
Ed: Andrew Wahl. **Description:** Canadian regulators hope that an auction of telecommunications companies will inject more competition into the industry; however, newcomers may not be able to rely on lower prices in order to gain market share from the three major telecommunications companies that already have a stronghold on the market. Analysts feel that providing additional data service is the key to surviving market disruptions.

1486 ■ "Dollar General Selects GSI Commerce to Launch Its eCommerce Business" in *Benzinga.com* (October 29, 2011)
Pub: Benzinga.com
Ed: Benzinga Staff. **Description:** Dollar General Corporation chose GSI Commerce, a leading provider of ecommerce and interactive marketing solutions, to launch its online initiative. GSI Commerce is an eBay Inc. company.

1487 ■ "eBay Business Looking Up" in *Zacks* (July 26, 2011)
Pub: Comtex News Network Inc.
Ed: Sejuti Banerjea. **Description:** eBay reported solid revenue growth for 2011 second quarter, keeping in line with the Zacks Consensus Estimate, and third quarter earnings are expected to be higher. eBay's new strategy is to direct traffic to bigger sellers with improved customer service, making this good for eBay businesses.

1488 ■ "EBay Finally Gaining Traction in China" in *San Jose Mercury News* (October 26, 2011)
Pub: San Jose Mercury News
Ed: John Boudreau. **Description:** eBay has developed a new strategy in China that allows exporters of every type of merchandise to sell directly to eBays 97 million overseas users.

1489 ■ "eBay Inc. Completes Acquisition of Zong" in *Benzinga.com* (October 29, 2011)
Pub: Benzinga.com
Ed: Benzinga Staff. **Description:** eBay Inc. acquired Zong, a provider of payments through mobile carrier billing. Terms of the agreement are outlined.

1490 ■ "eBay Introduces Open Commerce Ecosystem" in *Entertainment Close-Up* (October 24, 2011)
Pub: Close-Up Media
Description: eBay's new X.commerce is an open commerce ecosystem that will arm developers and merchants with the technology tools required to keep pace with the ever-changing industry. X.commerce brings together the technology assets and developer communities of eBay, PayPal, Magento and partners to expand on eBays vision for enabling commerce.

1491 ■ "eBay and Jonathan Adler Team to Launch 'The eBay Inspiration Shop'" in *Entertainment Close-Up* (October 25, 2011)
Pub: Close-Up Media
Description: Designer Jonathan Adler partnered with eBay to create a collection of new must-have merchandise for the fall season. Top trendsetters, including actors, designers, bloggers, stylists, editors, photographers, models and musicians helped curate the items being featured in the windows by sharing their shopping wish lists with users.

1492 ■ *The Ebay Seller's Tax and Legal Answer Book*
Pub: AMACOM
Ed: Cliff Ennico. **Released:** April 30, 2007. **Price:** $19.95. **Description:** Helps sellers using Ebay to file taxes properly, while saving money.

1493 ■ *Ebay the Smart Way: Selling, Burying, and Profiting on the Web's Number One Auction Site*
Pub: AMACOM
Ed: Joseph T. Sinclair. **Released:** May 2007. **Price:** $17.95. **Description:** Resource to help individuals sell, buy and profit using the Internet auction site Ebay.

1494 ■ "Facebook, Adobe, Kenshoo, Outright and Cignex Datamatics Sign On to X.commerce" in *Entertainment Close-Up* (October 24, 2011)
Pub: Close-Up Media
Description: Facebook, Adobe, Kenshoo, Outright and Cignex Datamatics have all partnered with X.commerce's ecosystem, where developers build and merchants can come to shop for new technologies and services.

1495 ■ "Fifty Percent of Global Online Retail Visits Were to Amazon, eBay and Alibaba in June 2011" in *Benzinga.com* (October 29, 2011)
Pub: Benzinga.com
Ed: Benzinga Staff. **Description:** Current statistics and future forecasts through the year 2015 for Amazon, eBay and Alibaba are explored.

1496 ■ "Former Schaefer and Strohminger Dealerships to Hit Auction Block" in *Baltimore Business Journal* (Vol. 28, September 10, 2010)
Pub: Baltimore Business Journal
Ed: Gary Haber. **Description:** Maryland's real estate developers have a chance to vie for almost 11 acres of prime Baltimore County real estate that are on the auction block. The five properties were once home to Schaefer and Strohminger car dealerships and were located in the county's busiest areas. Other potential uses for the properties are also discussed.

1497 ■ "Get Sold On eBay" in *Entrepreneur* (Vol. 36, March 2008, No. 3, pp. 94)
Pub: Entrepreneur Media Inc.
Ed: Marcia Layton Turner. **Description:** Entrepreneurs are increasingly using eBay to sell products. Some tips to start selling products through eBay include: starting with used items, developing a niche to sell specific products, and researching product pricing. Other tips with regard to starting an eBay business are covered.

1498 ■ "Hedge-Fund Titan Cohen Plans Bid for Dodgers" in *Wall Street Journal Eastern Edition* (November 25 , 2011, pp. C3)
Pub: Dow Jones & Company Inc.
Ed: Matthew Futterman, Gregory Zuckerman. **Description:** Steven A. Cohen, the founder and head of hedge-fund SAC Capital Advisors LLC is looking to make an offer at the bankruptcy auction for the financially-troubled Los Angeles Dodgers baseball team.

1499 ■ "HER's: the Future is Free" in *Benzinga.com* (October 29, 2011)
Pub: Benzinga.com
Ed: Benzinga Staff. **Description:** In order to create and maintain electronic health records that connects every physician and hospital it is essential to create a

reliable, easy-to-use, certified Web-based ambulatory ERH using an ad-supported model. eBay seems to be the company showing the most potential for improving services to physicians and consumers, but requires sellers to pay fees based upon sales price.

1500 ■ "High-End Jeweler Loses Street Sparkle" in *Houston Business Journal* (Vol. 40, November 27, 2009, No. 29, pp. 1)
Pub: American City Business Journals
Ed: Allison Wollam. **Description:** High-end jeweler Bailey Banks & Biddle's 7,000 square foot prototype store in Houston, Texas' CityCentre will be ceasing operations despite its parent company's filing for Chapter 11 protection from creditors. According to the bankruptcy filing, parent company Finlay Enterprises Inc. of New York intends to auction off its business and assets. Finlay has 67 Bailey Banks locations throughout the US.

1501 ■ "Luxe Hotels on a Budget" in *Inc.* (Volume 32, December 2010, No. 10, pp. 60)
Pub: Inc. Magazine
Ed: Adam Baer. **Description:** Off & Away Website allows users to vie for discounted hotel rooms at more than 100 luxury properties. To compete, uses buy $1 bids and each time an individual bids the price of the room goes up by 10 cents.

1502 ■ *National Auto Auction Association—Membership Directory*
Pub: National Auto Auction Association
Contact: Frank A. Hackett, Exec. Dir.
E-mail: hackett@naaa.com
Released: Annual, Latest edition 2011. **Price:** $15, members; $35, nonmembers. **Covers:** 25,446 automobile auction firms. **Entries Include:** Company name, address, names and phone numbers of auction personnel; pick up, delivery, and reconditioning services available. **Arrangement:** Geographical.

1503 ■ "Online Reverse Auctions: Common Myths Versus Evolving Reality" in *Business Horizons* (September-October 2007, pp. 373)
Pub: Elsevier Technology Publications
Ed: Tobias Schoenherr, Vincent A. Mabert. **Description:** Common misconceptions about online reverse auctions are examined based on the data obtained from 30 case study companies. Strategies for maintaining a good buyer-supplier relationship and implications for firms and supply managers are presented.

1504 ■ "The Open Mobile Summit Opens in San Francisco Today: John Donahoe CEO eBay to Keynote" in *Benzinga.com* (November 2, 2011)
Pub: Benzinga.com
Ed: Benzinga Staff. **Description:** eBay's CEO, John Donahoe was keynote speaker at the 4th Annual Open Mobile Summit held in San Francisco, California. eBay is one of the 130 companies participating as speakers at the event.

1505 ■ "Points of Light Sells MissionFish to eBay" in *Non-Profit Times* (Vol. 25, May 15, 2011, No. 7, pp. May 15, 2011)
Pub: NPT Publishing Group Inc.
Description: eBay purchased MissionFish, a subsidiary of Points of Light Institute for $4.5 million. MissionFish allows eBay sellers to give proceeds from sales to their favorite nonprofit organization and helps nonprofits raise funds by selling on eBay.

1506 ■ "Pro Livestock Launches Most Comprehensive Virtual Sales Barn for Livestock and Breed Stock" in *Benzinga.com* (October 29, 2011)
Pub: Benzinga.com
Ed: Benzinga Staff. **Description:** Pro Livestock Marketing launched the first online sales portal for livestock and breed stock. The firm has designed a virtual sales barn allowing individuals to purchase and sell cattle, swine, sheep, goats, horses, rodeo stock, show animals, specialty animals, semen and embryos globally. It is like an eBay for livestock and will help ranchers and farmers grow.

1507 ■ "Ritchie Bros. Breaks Record for Internet Sales at Fort Worth Site During Multi-Million Dollar Unreserved Auction" in *Canadian Corporate News*
Pub: Comtex News Network Inc.
Description: Ritchie Bros. Auctioneers, the world's largest auctioneer of trucks and industrial equipment, conducted a large unreserved auction at its permanent auction facility in Fort Worth, Texas, in which the company broke the record for Internet sales with bidders using the company's online bidding service, rbauctionBid-Live. Internet bidders purchased more than 440 lots in the auction.

1508 ■ *The Secret of Exiting Your Business Under Your Terms!*
Pub: Outskirts Press, Incorporated
Ed: Gene H. Irwin. **Released:** August 2005. **Price:** $29.95. **Description:** Topics include how to sell a business for the highest value, tax laws governing the sale of a business, finding the right buyer, mergers and acquisitions, negotiating the sale, and using a limited auction to increase future value of a business.

1509 ■ *Selling Online: Canada's Bestselling Guide to Becoming a Successful E-Commerce Merchant*
Pub: John Wiley and Sons Canada Ltd.
Ed: Jim Carroll; Rick Broadhead. **Released:** September 6, 2002. **Description:** Helps individuals build online retail enterprises; this updated version includes current tools, information and success strategies, how to launch an online storefront, security, marketing strategies, and mistakes to avoid.

1510 ■ "Shoppes of Kenwood Files Chap. 11" in *Business Courier* (Vol. 26, December 18, 2009, No. 34, pp. 1)
Pub: American City Business Journals, Inc.
Ed: Jon Newberry. **Description:** Shoppes of Kenwood filed for Chapter 11 reorganization in US Bankruptcy Court just as the property was scheduled to be offered at a sheriff's auction. Details of the filing are included.

1511 ■ "Tim Tebow Foundation to Hold Pink 'Cleats for a Cure' Auction" in *Travel & Leisure Close-Up* (October 20, 2011)
Pub: Close-Up Media
Description: Tim Tebow Foundation partnered with XV Enterprises to hold the 'Cleats for a Cure' auction on eBay. Tebow is auctioning off a pair of pink cleans he wore during the Denver Broncos vs. Tennessee Titans game October 3, 2010. All funds will go toward finding a cure for breast cancer.

1512 ■ *Titanium EBay: A Tactical Guide to Becoming a Millionaire PowerSeller*
Pub: Penguin Group Incorporated
Ed: Skip McGrath. **Released:** June 2006. **Price:** $24. 95. **Description:** Advice is given to help anyone selling items on eBay to become a Power Seller, an award presented based on monthly gross merchandise sales.

1513 ■ "Treasuries Rally Despite Huge Supply" in *Barron's* (Vol. 89, July 13, 2009, No. 28, pp. M10)
Pub: Dow Jones & Co., Inc.
Ed: Randall W. Forsyth. **Description:** Prices of U.S. Treasuries were sent higher and their yields lower despite four auctions of coupon securities because of the strong appetite for government securities around the world. The reopening of the 10-year note in the week ending July 10, 2009 drew the strongest bidding since 1995.

1514 ■ "Understanding Persuasive Online Sales Messages from eBay Auctions" in *Business Communication Quarterly* (December 2007, pp. 482)
Pub: Sage Publications USA
Ed: Barbara Jo White, Daniel Clapper, Rita Noel, Jenny Fortier, Pierre Grabolosa. **Description:** eBay product listings were studied to determine the requirements of persuasive sales writing. Potential sellers should use the proper keywords and make an authentic description with authentic photographs of the item being auctioned.

1515 ■ "Young Entrepreneur Gets Some Recognition and Some Help for College" in *Philadelphia Inquirer* (August 30, 2010)
Pub: Philadelphia Inquirer
Ed: Susan Snyder. **Description:** Profile of Zachary Gosling, age 18, who launched an online auction Website from his bedroom, using advertising and sponsorship funds rather than charging fees to users.

TRADE PERIODICALS

1516 ■ *The Auctioneer*
Pub: National Auctioneers Association
Contact: Steve Baska, Publications Dir.
E-mail: steve@auctioneers.org
Released: Monthly. **Description:** Trade magazine for auctioneers.

1517 ■ *IAL Auction Newsletter–Auctionier*
Pub: Auction Marketing Institute
Ed: Ann Wood, Editor. **Released:** Quarterly. **Price:** Included in membership. **Description:** Promotes the educational activities of the Institute. Carries miscellaneous items of interest to member auctioneers and for candidates for membership. Recurring features include notices of courses and seminars.

TRADE SHOWS AND CONVENTIONS

1518 ■ National Auctioneers Association National Convention
National Auctioneers Association
8880 Ballentine
Overland Park, KS 66214
Ph:(913)541-8084
Fax:(913)894-5281
URL: http://www.auctioneers.org
Released: Annual. **Principal Exhibits:** Auctioneering equipment, supplies, and services.

FRANCHISES AND BUSINESS OPPORTUNITIES

1519 ■ Certigard (Petro Canada)
2489 N Sheridan Way
Mississauga, ON, Canada L5K 1A8
Free: 888-541-7632
Fax:(905)804-4898
Co. E-mail: hupponen@petro-canada.ca
URL: http://www.petro-canada.ca
No. of Franchise Units: 105. **Founded:** 1987. **Description:** Offers car repair franchise. **Equity Capital Needed:** $75,000 minimum, business development fee 2%, warranty fee 0.2%. **Franchise Fee:** $25,000. **Training:** Yes.

Auto Supply Store

ASSOCIATIONS AND OTHER ORGANIZATIONS

1520 ■ Association of Automotive Aftermarket Distributors/Parts Plus
3085 Fountainside Dr., No. 210
Germantown, TN 38138
Free: 800-727-8112
Fax:(901)682-9098
Co. E-mail: info@networkhq.org
URL: http://www.partsplus.com
Contact: Bob Barstow, Staff Liaison
Description: Represents the independent automotive warehouse distributors. Purchases and markets automotive replacement parts through wholesale/retail auto parts stores. Conducts marketing activities. **Publications:** *Car Care Center*; *Network*; *Parts Plus Magazine* (bimonthly).

1521 ■ Auto International Association
7101 Wisconsin Ave., Ste. 1300
Bethesda, MD 20814
Ph:(301)654-6664
Fax:(301)654-3299
Co. E-mail: aia@aftermarket.org
URL: http://aftermarket.org/Segments/AIA
Contact: Stephen Bearden, Chm.
Description: Manufacturers/importers, distributors/retailers, subcontractors and manufacturers' representatives supporting the import automotive aftermarket products industry. Works to promote and protect the interests of the import auto and accessories industry. Offers Import Parts Specialist certification program for sales personnel. Produces annual AIA World Auto Parts Conference. Compiles statistics. **Publications:** *AIA Facts* (biweekly).

1522 ■ Auto Suppliers Benchmarking Association
4606 FM 1960 W, Ste. 250
Houston, TX 77069-9949
Ph:(281)440-5044
Fax:(281)440-6677
URL: http://www.asbabenchmarking.com
Description: Automotive supplier firms with an interest in benchmarking. Promotes the use of benchmarking, wherein businesses compare their processes with those of their competitors, as a means of improving corporate efficiency and profitability. Facilitates exchange of information among members; conducts target operations, procurement, development, and maintenance studies; identifies model business practices. .

1523 ■ Automotive Aftermarket Industry Association
7101 Wisconsin Ave., Ste. 1300
Bethesda, MD 20814-3415
Ph:(301)654-6664
Fax:(301)654-3299
Co. E-mail: aaia@aftermarket.org
URL: http://www.aftermarket.org
Contact: Kathleen Schmatz, Pres./CEO
Description: Automotive parts and accessories retailers, distributors, manufacturers, and manufacturers' representatives. Conducts research and compiles statistics. Conducts seminars and provides specialized education program. **Publications:** *Aftermarket Insider* (bimonthly); *APAA Who's Who* (annual); *Facts*; *Foreign Buyers Directory* (annual).

1524 ■ Automotive Service Association
PO Box 929
Bedford, TX 76095-0929
Ph:(817)283-6205
Free: 800-272-7467
Fax:(817)685-0225
Co. E-mail: asainfo@asashop.org
URL: http://www.asashop.org
Contact: Ron Pyle, Pres./Chief Staff Exec.
Description: Automotive service businesses including body, paint, and trim shops, engine rebuilders, radiator shops, brake and wheel alignment services, transmission shops, tune-up services, and air conditioning services; associate members are manufacturers and wholesalers of automotive parts, and the trade press. Represents independent business owners and managers before private agencies and national and state legislative bodies. Promotes confidence between consumer and the automotive service industry, safety inspection of motor vehicles, and better highways. **Publications:** *AutoInc* (monthly).

1525 ■ Automotive Warehouse Distributors Association
7101 Wisconsin Ave., Ste. 1300
Bethesda, MD 20814-3415
Ph:(301)654-6664
Fax:(301)654-3299
Co. E-mail: aaia@aftermarket.org
URL: http://www.aftermarket.org/Segments/awda.aspx
Contact: Larry Northup, Exec. Dir.
Description: Warehouse distributors of automotive parts and supplies; manufacturers of automotive parts and suppliers; jobbers, business services, major program groups. **Publications:** *AAIA SmartBrief* (biweekly); *Leadership Directory* (annual); *Life in the Fast Lane: Careers in the Automotive Aftermarket* .

1526 ■ Motor and Equipment Manufacturers Association
PO Box 13966
Research Triangle Park, NC 27709-3966
Ph:(919)549-4800
Fax:(919)549-4824
Co. E-mail: info@mema.org
URL: http://www.mema.org
Contact: Robert E. McKenna, Pres./CEO
Description: Manufacturers of automotive and heavy-duty original equipment and aftermarket components, maintenance equipment, chemicals, accessories, refinishing supplies, tools, and service equipment united for research into all aspects of the automotive and heavy-duty markets. Provides manufacturer-oriented services and programs including marketing consultation for the automotive industry; federal and state legal, safety, and legislative representation and consultation; personnel services; manpower development workshops; international information. **Publications:** *Automotive Industry Status Report* (annual); *Car Maintenance in the U.S. A.*; *Credit and Sales Reference Directory* (3/year); *Market Analysis* (bimonthly); *Sales Force Compensation and Benefits Practice* (annual).

1527 ■ National Truck Equipment Association
37400 Hills Tech Dr.
Farmington Hills, MI 48331-3414
Ph:(248)489-7090
Free: 800-441-NTEA
Fax:(248)489-8590
Co. E-mail: info@ntea.com
URL: http://www.ntea.com
Contact: Jim Carney, Exec. Dir.
Description: Serves as a trade group for commercial truck, truck body, truck equipment, trailer and accessory manufacturers and distributors. Advises members of current federal regulations affecting the manufacturing and installation of truck bodies and equipment; works to enhance the professionalism of management and improve profitability in the truck equipment business. **Publications:** *Excise Tax Bulletin* (periodic); *Membership Roster and Product Directory* (annual); *NTEA News* (monthly); *Truck Equipment Handbook* .

1528 ■ Specialty Equipment Market Association
1575 S Valley Vista Dr.
Diamond Bar, CA 91765
Ph:(909)396-0289
Fax:(909)860-0184
Co. E-mail: member@sema.org
URL: http://www.sema.org
Contact: Christopher J. Kersting CAE, Pres./CEO
Description: Manufacturers, retailers, sales representatives, distributors, motorsports sanctioning groups and other firms related to the automotive high performance and custom vehicle industry. Represents the industry to governmental agencies and consumer groups. Coordinates and conducts research; assists in writing of regulations and codes; collects and disseminates information; compiles statistics. **Publications:** *Fast Facts* (monthly); *SEMA News* (monthly).

REFERENCE WORKS

1529 ■ "3.4 Million Votes Cast in 2011 eBay Motors People's Pick Poll – Winners Announced at SEMA Show" in *Benzinga.com* (, 2011)
Pub: Benzinga.com
Ed: Benzinga Staff. **Description:** eBay Motors sponsored the 2011 People's Picks survey, an annual poll inviting car enthusiasts to vote on their favorite auto thing, ranging from the best camshaft, favorite ignition, to favorite muscle car. More than 3.4 million votes were counted this year. A complete profile of eBay Motors is also provided.

1530 ■ "All Revved Up" in *Barron's* (Vol. 90, September 13, 2010, No. 37, pp. 18)
Pub: Barron's Editorial & Corporate Headquarters
Ed: Christopher C. Williams. **Description:** Shares of Advance Auto Parts has returned 55 percent in a

span of three years and the stock could still reach the mid-60s by 2011 from its price of 46.07 in the second week of September 2010. The shares are trading at just 13 times the 2011 earnings.

1531 ■ "American Axle Sues to Force Steelmaker to Resume Suspended Parts Shipment" in *Crain's Detroit Business* (Vol. 25, June 15, 2009)
Pub: Crain Communications Inc. - Detroit
Ed: Robert Sherefkin. **Description:** American Axle & Manufacturing Holdings Inc. is facing a shutdown if a Michigan court does not force Republic Engineered Products Inc., a specialty steelmaker, to ship parts. If the parts are not shipped, it could cause assembly plants to shutdown.

1532 ■ "Auto Bankruptcies Could Weaken Defense" in *Crain's Detroit Business* (Vol. 25, June 8, 2009, No. 23, pp. 1)
Pub: Crain Communications Inc. - Detroit
Ed: Chad Halcom. **Description:** Bankruptcy and supplier consolidation of General Motors Corporation and Chrysler LLC could interfere with the supply chains of some defense contractors, particularly makers of trucks and smaller vehicles.

1533 ■ *Automotive Warehouse Distributors Association—Membership Directory*
Pub: Automotive Warehouse Distributors Association
Released: Annual, March. **Covers:** Over 200 automotive parts distributors, 300 manufacturers of automotive parts, and marketing associations, manufacturer representatives, and affiliate members. **Entries Include:** Company name, address, phone, names of key personnel, products distributed or manufactured, territories served, number and location of branches. **Arrangement:** Alphabetical. **Indexes:** Geographical.

1534 ■ "Detroit 3's Fall Would Be a Big One in Ohio" in *Business First Columbus* (Vol. 25, November 28, 2008, No. 14, pp. A1)
Pub: American City Business Journals
Ed: Dan Eaton. **Description:** Ohio's economy will suffer huge negative effects in the event of a failure of one or more of the automotive companies, General Motors Corporation, Ford Motor Company, or Chrysler LLC. The state is home to 97,900 jobs in the automotive industry and is a vital link to the industry's supply network.

1535 ■ *Directory of Automotive Aftermarket Suppliers*
Pub: Chain Store Guide
Ed: Arthur Rosenberg, Editor, arosenbe@csgis.com. **Released:** Annual, October. **Price:** $365, individuals. **Covers:** Approximately 1,900 Auto Aftermarket retailers/jobbers; over 1,000 auto parts warehouse distributors; and 100 marine retailers in the United States and Canada, with annual sales of at least $250,000. Included retailers operate approximately 29,500 stores. **Entries Include:** For retailers only—fax number, company e-mail address, sales by customer type, percentage of products installed, total selling square footage, total units, units by trade name, projected openings and remodeling, and average number of checkouts. For distributors only—services provided. For retailers and distributors—company name; physical address; mailing address; company web site address; Internet order processing indicator; listing type; trading areas; distribution center locations; programmed distribution group name and location; year founded; public company indicator; parent company name and location; regional, divisional, and branch office locations; and key personnel with titles. **Arrangement:** Geographical. **Indexes:** Product line, alphabetical.

1536 ■ "Greening the Auto Industry" in *Business Journal-Serving Phoenix & the Valley of the Sun* (Vol. 30, July 23, 2010, No. 46, pp. 1)
Pub: Phoenix Business Journal
Ed: Patrick O'Grady. **Description:** Thermo Fluids Inc. has been recycling used oil products since 1993 and could become Arizona's first home for oil filter recycling after retrofitting its Phoenix facility to include a compaction machine. The new service could help establish Thermo Fluids as a recycling hub for nearby states.

1537 ■ "Japan-Brand Shortages Will Linger Into '12" in *Automotive News* (Vol. 86, October 31, 2011, No. 6488, pp. 1)
Pub: Crain Communications Inc.
Ed: Amy Wilson, Mark Rechtin. **Description:** Floods in Thailand and the tsunami in Japan have caused shortages of Japanese-brand vehicle parts. These shortages are expected to linger into 2012.

1538 ■ "Local Auto Suppliers Upbeat as Detroit 3's Prospects Trend Up" in *Crain's Cleveland Business* (Vol. 30, June 8, 2009, No. 22, pp. 1)
Pub: Crain Communications, Inc.
Ed: Dan Shingler. **Description:** According to the Center for Automotive Research located in Ann Arbor, Michigan, if Detroit automakers can hold their market share, they will end up producing more vehicles as the market recovers.

1539 ■ "Local Dealers Fear Shortages in Car Supply" in *Boston Business Journal* (Vol. 29, May 13, 2011, No. 1, pp. 1)
Pub: American City Business Journals Inc.
Ed: Scott Dance. **Description:** The earthquake and tsunami in Japan are seen to impact the automobile dealers in Baltimore, Maryland. Automobile supply in the area is seen to decrease dramatically during the summer sales season. Shortage of transmission parts and paint colors is also forecasted.

1540 ■ "On a Roll" in *Canadian Business* (Vol. 79, Winter 2006, No. 24, pp. 49)
Pub: Rogers Media
Ed: Thomas Watson. **Description:** The efforts of the Canadian automobile spare parts manufacturer, Magna International Inc., to expand into the the Russian market, are described.

1541 ■ "Reply! Grows at Unprecedented Rate, Rips Beta Off Its Marketplace" in *Marketing Weekly News* (September 19, 2009, pp. 149)
Pub: Investment Weekly News
Description: Profile of Reply.com, a leader in locally-targeted Internet marketing, announced significant growth in terms of revenue, enhanced features and services and new categories since launching its beta Reply! Marketplace platform. Even in the face of an economic downturn, the company has posted over 50 percent revenue growth in the Real Estate and Automotive categories.

1542 ■ "Research Reports: How Analysts Size Up Companies" in *Barron's* (Vol. 88, July 14, 2008, No. 28, pp. M13)
Pub: Dow Jones & Co., Inc.
Ed: Anita Peltonen. **Description:** Shares of Bankrate and AutoZone both get a "Buy" rating from analysts while Zions Bancorporation's shares are downgraded from "Outperform" to "Neutral". The shares of Jet Blue Airline and Deckers Outdoor, a manufacturer of innovative footwear, are also rated and discussed. Statistical data included.

1543 ■ "Shifting Gears" in *Business Journal-Serving Phoenix & the Valley of the Sun* (Vol. 31, November 12, 2010, No. 10, pp. 1)
Pub: Phoenix Business Journal
Ed: Patrick O'Grady. **Description:** Automotive parts recyclers in Arizona are benefiting from the challenging national economic conditions as well as from the green movement. Recyclers revealed that customers prefer recycled parts more because they are cheaper and are more environmentally friendly. Other information about the automotive parts recycling industry is presented.

1544 ■ "Slimmer Interiros Make Small Cars Seem Big" in *Automotive News* (Vol. 86, October 31, 2011, No. 6488, pp. 16)
Pub: Crain Communications Inc.
Ed: David Sedgwick. **Description:** Cost-conscious buyers want luxury car amenities in their smaller vehicles, so automakers are rethinking interiors. Style, efficiency and value could be the next trend in vehicles.

1545 ■ "Steering Toward Profitability" in *Black Enterprise* (Vol. 41, December 2010, No. 5, pp. 72)
Pub: Earl G. Graves Publishing Co. Inc.
Ed: Alan Hughes. **Description:** Systems Electro Coating LLC had to make quick adjustments when auto manufacturers were in a slump. The minority father-daughter team discuss their strategies during the auto industry collapse.

1546 ■ "Suppliers May Follow Fiat" in *Crain's Detroit Business* (Vol. 25, June 15, 2009, No. 24, pp. 1)
Pub: Crain Communications Inc. - Detroit
Ed: Ryan Beene. **Description:** Italian suppliers to Fiat SpA are looking toward Detroit after the formation of Chrysler Group LLC, the Chrysler-Fiat partnership created from Chrysler's bankruptcy. The Italian American Alliance for Business and Technology is aware of two Italy-based powertrain component suppliers that are considering a move to Detroit.

1547 ■ *Tire Review—Performance Tire and Custom Wheel Guide*
Pub: Babcox
Ed: Jim Smith, Editor, jsmith@babcox.com. **Released:** Annual, March. **Publication Includes:** List of about 15 custom wheel and performance tire manufacturers and marketers. **Entries Include:** Manufacturer name, address, phone, names and titles of key personnel, wheel types and sizes, wheel accessories, email and web addresses.

1548 ■ "Wheatfield First Choice for Canadian Manufacturer" in *Business First Buffalo* (November 23, 2007, pp. 1)
Pub: American City Business Journals, Inc.
Ed: James Fink. **Description:** Niagara County Industrial Development Agency is preparing an enticement program that would lure automotive parts manufacturer Pop & Lock Corporation to shift manufacturing operations to Wheatfield, Niagara County, New York. The package includes job-training grants and assistance for acquiring new machinery. Details of the plan are included.

1549 ■ "ZF Revving Up Jobs, Growth" in *Business Courier* (Vol. 26, November 6, 2009, No. 28, pp. 1)
Pub: American City Business Journals, Inc.
Ed: Jon Newberry. **Description:** Proposed $96 million expansion of German-owned automotive supplier ZF Steering systems LLC is anticipated to generate 299 jobs in Boone County, Kentucky. ZF might invest $90 million in equipment, while the rest will go to building and improvements.

SOURCES OF SUPPLY

1550 ■ *Truck Cover and Tarp Association Membership Directory*
Pub: Industrial Fabrics Association International
Released: Annual, October. **Price:** Free. **Publication Includes:** Listings of member companies that manufacture and supply material, equipment or services to the truck cover and tarpaulin industry. **Entries Include:** name, address, phone, fax of company and names and titles of key personnel, along with descriptions of services and products. **Arrangement:** Geographical. **Indexes:** Alphabetical.

1551 ■ *Undercar Digest—Buyer's Guide Issue*
Pub: MD Publications Inc.
Ed: James R. Wilder, Editor, jwilder@mdpublications.com. **Released:** Annual, Latest edition 2011. **Price:** $10, individuals. **Publication Includes:** List of automotive aftermarket manufacturers and suppliers of mufflers, exhaust pipes, brakes, chassis, steering, suspension, driveline, shop equipment and tools, and other products. **Entries Include:** Company name, address, phone, fax, name and title of contact, products. **Arrangement:** Alphabetical. **Indexes:** Product, warehouse distributors, franchise headquarters.

STATISTICAL SOURCES

1552 ■ *The Motor Vehicle Parts Aftermarket*
Pub: Business Trend Analysts, Inc.
Released: 2005-2006. **Price:** $2195.00. **Description:** Profiles the motor vehicle parts aftermarket, covering tires, batteries, engines, brakes, cooling systems, and other replacement parts. Provides information on pricing, factors affecting demand, advertising, foreign trade, and distribution channels. Also contains profiles of leading marketers.

1553 ■ *RMA Annual Statement Studies*
Pub: Robert Morris Associates (RMA)
Released: Annual. **Price:** $175.00 2006-07 edition, $105.00. **Description:** Contains composite balance sheets and income statements for more than 360 industries, including the accounting, auditing, and bookkeeping industries. Also contains five years of comparative historical data for discerning trends. Includes 16 commonly used ratios, computed for most of the size groupings for nearly every industry.

1554 ■ *Standard & Poor's Industry Surveys*
Pub: Standard & Poor's Corp.
Released: Annual. **Price:** $3633.00. **Description:** Two-volume book that examines the prospects for specific industries, including trucking. Also provides analyses of trends and problems, statistical tables and charts, and comparative company analyses.

TRADE PERIODICALS

1555 ■ *Aftermarket Insider*
Pub: Automotive Warehouse Distributors Association
Ed: Jennifer Ortiz, Editor. **Released:** BIM. **Price:** Included in membership. **Description:** Provides Association members with news of developments affecting the warehouse distribution of automotive parts and supplies. Supplies operations tips and articles on marketing and sales techniques. Concentrates on news of members, Association sponsored events and activities, awards, and conferences. Recurring features include news of research, news of educational opportunities, and a calendar of events.

1556 ■ *Automotive Plastics Newsletter*
Pub: Market Search Inc.
Released: Biweekly. **Price:** $498, individuals. **Description:** Reports on news of the automotive and plastics industry. Also includes forecasts.

1557 ■ *Body Language*
Pub: Automotive Body Parts Association
Contact: Stan Rodman, Exec. Dir.
Released: Monthly, 10-12 times/year. **Price:** $90, individuals; $120, elsewhere. **Description:** Reports news impacting the aftermarket body parts industry, industry trends, and Association news. Recurring features include meeting reports and a calendar of events.

1558 ■ *Consumer Electronics Vision*
Pub: Consumer Electronics Association
Ed: Robert MacMillan, Editor, cstevens@ce.org. **Released:** Quarterly, 6/year. **Price:** Free. **Description:** Provides news and information concerning mobile electronics, audio, radar, security, and cellular communications. Examines the manufacture, market trends, and installation of mobile electronics. Covers legislative and regulatory issues at the state and federal levels with particular emphasis on business, manufacturing, and insurance issues. Recurring features include a monthly series of retail management information and news of the Association.

1559 ■ *Counterman*
Pub: Babcox
Ed: Mark Phillips, Editor, mphillips@babcox.com. **Released:** Monthly. **Description:** Magazine devoted to improving the effectiveness of professional automotive parts counter-sales personnel.

1560 ■ *Import Automotive Parts & Accessories*
Pub: Meyers Publishing
Contact: Harriet Kaplan, Asst. Ed.
E-mail: harriet@meyerspublishing.com
Released: Monthly. **Price:** $75 Canada and Mexico; $105 other countries; $55; $10 single issue; $25 import industry sourcebook; $35 import industry sourcebook outside the U.S.; $20 single issue outside the U.S. **Description:** Trade magazine for the automotive aftermarket.

1561 ■ *ImportCar*
Pub: Babcox
Contact: Valli Pantuso, Advertising Svcs.
E-mail: vpantuso@babcox.com
Released: Monthly. **Description:** Magazine focusing on import specialist repair shops that derive more than 50% of revenue from servicing import nameplates.

1562 ■ *SEMA News*
Pub: Specialty Equipment Market Association
Contact: Steve Campbell, Editorial Director
E-mail: stevec@sema.org
Released: Monthly. **Price:** Included in membership. **Description:** Covers the automotive specialty, performance equipment, and accessory sectors. Recurring features include news of government and legislative actions, new products, international markets, and member and Association activities.

1563 ■ *Specialty Automotive Magazine*
Pub: Meyers Publishing
Ed: Steve Relyea, Editor, steve@meyerspublishing.com. **Released:** Bimonthly. **Price:** $40 U.S.; $25 specialty and performance industry sourcebook; $60 Canada and Mexico; $95 other countries; $35 other countries; $10 single issue; $20 single issue outside the U.S. **Description:** Trade magazine for the automotive aftermarket.

TRADE SHOWS AND CONVENTIONS

1564 ■ Florida RV Supershow
Florida RV Trade Association
10510 Gibsonton Dr.
Riverview, FL 33578
Ph:(813)741-0488
Fax:(813)741-0688
Co. E-mail: info@frvta.org
URL: http://www.frvta.org
Released: Annual. **Audience:** First time buyers as well as current owners. **Principal Exhibits:** Recreational vehicle supplies and accessories. **Dates and Locations:** 2011 Jan 11-16, Tampa, FL.

1565 ■ International Big R Show
Automotive Parts Remanufacturers Association
4215 Lafayette Center Dr., Ste. 3
Chantilly, VA 20151-1243
Ph:(703)968-2772
Fax:(703)968-2878
Co. E-mail: mail@apra.com
URL: http://www.apra.org
Released: Annual. **Audience:** Rebuilders of automotive and truck parts and suppliers to rebuilders. **Principal Exhibits:** Cleaning machines for rebuilt parts; test equipment; new and remanufactured products, including alternators, starters, regulators, water pumps, brakes, carburetors, transmissions, cv joints, steering systems, and axles; component parts for rebuilders.

1566 ■ International Midas Dealers Association Annual Conference
International Midas Dealers Association
14 W 3rd St., Ste. 200
Kansas City, MO 64105-1297
Ph:877-543-6203
Fax:(816)472-7765
Released: Annual. **Audience:** Owners of Midas shops. **Principal Exhibits:** Exhibits for Midas muffler and brake shops franchisees.

1567 ■ Minneapolis International Motorcycle Show
Advanstar Communications
641 Lexington Ave., 8th Fl.
New York, NY 10022
Ph:(212)951-6600
Fax:(212)951-6793
Co. E-mail: info@advantstar.com
URL: http://www.advanstar.com
Audience: Public: Motorcycle, watercraft and ATV enthusiasts. **Principal Exhibits:** A marketplace where manufacturers and retailers can display and sell their products such as motorcycles, all-terrain vehicles (ATV), scooters, watercraft, apparel, parts and accessories.

1568 ■ Service Specialists Association Annual Convention
Service Specialists Association
4015 Marks Rd., Ste. 2B
Medina, OH 44256
Ph:(330)725-7160
Free: 800-763-5717
Fax:(330)722-5638
Co. E-mail: trucksvc@aol.com
URL: http://www.truckservice.org
Released: Annual. **Audience:** Trade-Heavy Duty Aftermarket. **Principal Exhibits:** Exhibits related to truck repair operations, rebuilding departments, individuals who have maintained shop equipment such as hydraulic press or heat treating furnace.

1569 ■ Undercar Expo - Showpower-Transmission Expo
MD Publications Inc.
3057 E Cairo
PO Box 2210
Springfield, MO 65802
Ph:(417)866-3917
Free: 800-274-7890
Fax:(417)866-2781
Co. E-mail: showmanager@showpowerexpo.com
URL: http://www.mdpublications.com
Released: Annual. **Audience:** Persons included in the under-the-car and transmission segment of the automotive aftermarket. **Principal Exhibits:** Equipment, supplies, and services for the under-the-car segment of the automotive aftermarket and the transmission aftermarket. **Dates and Locations:** 2011 Mar 17-19, Indianapolis, IN.

CONSULTANTS

1570 ■ ASC Retail Consulting
10 Iverness Center Pky., Ste. 320
Birmingham, AL 35242-4818
Ph:(205)995-5300
Free: 800-633-4767
Fax:(205)995-5360
Co. E-mail: martincic@hoffman.ds.adp.com
URL: http://www.ascconsulting.com
Contact: Sam Yelverton, Principle
E-mail: martincic@hoffman.ds.adp.com
Scope: Offers management consulting for auto dealers, distributors and manufacturers specializing in service, parts and body shop departments. Industries served: Automotive retail, wholesale and manufacturers. **Publications:** "Competitive and Profitable"; "Controlling Service Expense". **Special Services:** Applied Service Management^{TM}; Automated Service Pricing; Customized Solutions.

FRANCHISES AND BUSINESS OPPORTUNITIES

1571 ■ Batteries Plus
925 Walnut Ridge Dr.
Hartland, WI 53029
Free: 800-274-9155
Fax:(262)912-3100
Co. E-mail: franchising@batteriesplus.com
URL: http://www.batteriesplus.com
No. of Franchise Units: 380. **No. of Company-Owned Units:** 25. **Founded:** 1988. **Franchised:** 1992. **Description:** Serves both retail and commercial customers. Program incorporates a unique and recognizable store design, coordinated graphics, color scheme, signage and product brands. **Equity Capital Needed:** $250,000 minimum. **Franchise Fee:** $37,500. **Financial Assistance:** No. **Managerial Assistance:** Ongoing support in retail promotion, customer development, store operations, store opera-

tions and advice **Training:** 3 weeks training at corporate headquarters plus 10 days at franchisees store. Training covers successful company philosophies, store operations and product knowledge.

1572 ■ Top Value Car & Truck Service Centers
International Top Value Automotive, L.L.C.
36887 Schoolcraft Rd.
Livonia, MI 48150
Ph:(734)462-3633
Free: 800-860-8258
Fax:(734)462-1088
No. of Franchise Units: 34. **No. of Company-Owned Units:** 6. **Founded:** 1977. **Franchised:** 1980. **Description:** Offers automobile products and services. **Equity Capital Needed:** $102,500-$158,200, including franchise fee and working capital. **Franchise Fee:** $17,500. **Financial Assistance:** Yes. **Training:** Yes.

COMPUTERIZED DATABASES

1573 ■ *Tire Business*
Crain Communications Inc.
1155 Gratiot Ave.
Detroit, MI 48207
Ph:(313)446-6000
Free: 800-678-2427
Fax:(313)446-1616
Co. E-mail: info@crain.com
URL: http://www.crain.com
Description: Contains news, features, articles, and up-to-date industry information for dealers and businesses in the automotive tire industry. Includes daily news headlines, feature articles on automotive service and management issues, and industry brochures and company material. Includes detailed tire market information, including material on the largest marketing groups, retail chains, commercial dealerships, and more. Includes company market share information, customer loyalty details, tire production data, tire markets, and other market data. Includes classified advertisements, job postings, story archives, and more. **Availability:** Online: Crain Communications Inc. **Type:** Full text; Numeric.

Automobile Detailing/Painting Service

TRADE PERIODICALS

1574 ■ *Automotive Plastics Newsletter*
Pub: Market Search Inc.
Released: Biweekly. **Price:** $498, individuals. **Description:** Reports on news of the automotive and plastics industry. Also includes forecasts.

1575 ■ *ImportCar*
Pub: Babcox
Contact: Valli Pantuso, Advertising Svcs.
E-mail: vpantuso@babcox.com
Released: Monthly. **Description:** Magazine focusing on import specialist repair shops that derive more than 50% of revenue from servicing import nameplates.

1576 ■ *Professional Carwashing & Detailing*
Pub: National Trade Publications Inc.
Contact: Kate Carr, Editor-in-Chief
E-mail: kcarr@carwash.com
Released: Monthly. **Description:** Car care magazine covering carwashing, detailing and oil change facilities.

1577 ■ *Restoration*
Pub: International Society for Vehicle Preservation
Released: Semiannual. **Price:** $20 members; $3 single issue. **Description:** Technical magazine covering the how-to of vehicle restoration.

1578 ■ *Underhood Service*
Pub: Babcox
Released: Monthly. **Description:** Magazine covering service and repair shops doing 50% or more of service underhood.

VIDEOCASSETTES/ AUDIOCASSETTES

1579 ■ *SMART Body Shop Talk: Paint Tips*
Karol Media
Hanover Industrial Estates
375 Stewart Rd.
PO Box 7600
Wilkes Barre, PA 18773-7600
Ph:(570)822-8899
Free: 800-526-4773
Co. E-mail: sales@karolmedia.com
URL: http://www.karolmedia.com
Released: 1991. **Price:** $9.95. **Description:** A guide to the wide variety of paint products available and how to properly use them. **Availability:** VHS.

1580 ■ *Tune Up America: Detailing*
Morris Video
12881 Knott St.
Garden Grove, CA 92841
Ph:(310)533-4800
Fax:(310)320-3171
Released: 1986. **Price:** $19.95. **Description:** The steps you'll need to revitalize and maintain car interiors, exteriors, trim areas, and engine compartments are covered. **Availability:** VHS.

TRADE SHOWS AND CONVENTIONS

1581 ■ AAPEX
William T. Glasgow, Inc.
10729 W. 163rd Pl.
Orland Park, IL 60467
Ph:(708)226-1300
Fax:(708)226-1310
Co. E-mail: brian@wtglasgow.com
URL: http://www.wtglasgow.com
Released: Annual. **Audience:** Retailers, wholesalers, jobbers, manufacturers of the automotive aftermarket. **Principal Exhibits:** Automotive repair parts, tools, equipment, accessories and related services. **Dates and Locations:** 2011 Nov 01-03, Las Vegas, NV; 2012 Oct 30 - Nov 01, Las Vegas, NV; 2013 Nov 05-07, Las Vegas, NV.

1582 ■ Service Specialists Association Annual Convention
Service Specialists Association
4015 Marks Rd., Ste. 2B
Medina, OH 44256
Ph:(330)725-7160
Free: 800-763-5717
Fax:(330)722-5638
Co. E-mail: trucksvc@aol.com
URL: http://www.truckservice.org
Released: Annual. **Audience:** Trade-Heavy Duty Aftermarket. **Principal Exhibits:** Exhibits related to truck repair operations, rebuilding departments, individuals who have maintained shop equipment such as hydraulic press or heat treating furnace.

FRANCHISES AND BUSINESS OPPORTUNITIES

1583 ■ Aero-Colours Inc.
Aero-Colours, Inc.
128 S Tryon St., Ste. 900
Charlotte, NC 28202
Free: 800-275-5200
URL: http://www.aerocolours.com
No. of Franchise Units: 33. **Founded:** 1985. **Franchised:** 1993. **Description:** Mobile paint touch-up process used to repair nicks, chips, scratches and other blemishes in painted surfaces. Service is provided to car dealers, fleet owners, insurance companies and retail customers. Aero-Colours employs a very sophisticated system for paint mixing, matching, application and blending. Each franchisee is granted the right to use the Aero-Colours process in an exclusive territory. **Equity Capital Needed:** $48,350-$62,700. **Franchise Fee:** $25,000. **Royalty Fee:** 7%. **Financial Assistance:** No. **Managerial Assistance:** A toll-free service and technical line is provided. In addition, a staff manager may be reached by a paging system any time Mon — Fri. Annual follow-up visits are made to each franchise at no additional charge. **Training:** Provides 2 weeks classroom/hands-on and 2 weeks onsite training with dealer account development in your exclusive territory.

1584 ■ Altracolor Systems
111 Phlox Ave.
Metairie, LA 70001
Free: 800-727-6567
Fax:(504)456-1714
No. of Franchise Units: 60. **Founded:** 1989. **Franchised:** 1991. **Description:** Mobile auto painting and plastic repair. **Equity Capital Needed:** $37,500-$53,950 total investment; $11,700 cash liquidity. **Franchise Fee:** $8,000-$19,950. **Royalty Fee:** $95/week. **Financial Assistance:** Limited in-house financing available. **Training:** Yes.

1585 ■ CARSTAR Automotive Canada, Inc.
1460 Stonechurch Rd. E
Hamilton, ON, Canada L8W 3V3
Ph:(905)388-4720
Fax:(905)388-1124
Co. E-mail: ldavis@carstar.ca
URL: http://www.carstarcanada.ca
No. of Franchise Units: 150. **Founded:** 1974. **Franchised:** 1994. **Description:** Quality collision service. **Equity Capital Needed:** $30,000-$250,000. **Franchise Fee:** Based on market. **Training:** Full menu of support services.

1586 ■ Colors on Parade
Total Car Franchising Inc.
642 Century Cir.
Conway, SC 29526
Free: 800-726-5677
URL: http://www.colorsfranchise.com
No. of Franchise Units: 215. **No. of Company-Owned Units:** 7. **Founded:** 1989. **Franchised:** 1991. **Description:** Onsite automotive painting and body restoration. **Equity Capital Needed:** $33,800-$441,000. **Franchise Fee:** $5,000-$25,000. **Royalty Fee:** 7-30%. **Financial Assistance:** Limited in-house and third party financing available. **Training:** Provides 2 weeks training at headquarters, 3 months at franchisee's location, and ongoing support.

1587 ■ The Ding King Training Institute
1280 Bison Ave., Ste. B-9
Newport Beach, CA 92660
Ph:(714)775-9450
Free: 800-304-3464
Fax:(714)775-9454
Co. E-mail: todd@dingking.com
URL: http://www.dingking.com
No. of Franchise Units: 1,345. **Founded:** 1991. **Franchised:** 1993. **Description:** Auto reconditioning includes paint less dent removal, paint blemish repair, windshield repair, gold plating, window tinting, odor removal and Patented Chip Magic system. **Equity Capital Needed:** $100,000+. **Franchise Fee:** None. **Financial Assistance:** Yes. **Training:** Includes training at company headquarters and onsite with ongoing support.

1588 ■ Dr. Vinyl & Associates, Ltd.
201 NW Victoria Dr.
Lee's Summit, MO 64086
Ph:(816)525-6060
Free: 800-531-6600
Fax:(816)525-6333
No. of Franchise Units: 253. **No. of Company-Owned Units:** 2. **Founded:** 1972. **Franchised:** 1981. **Description:** Mobile repair, reconditioning and after-market sales and services to auto dealers and other commercial accounts, such as vinyl, leather, velour, fabric, bumper, windshield, plastic and paint less dent repair, application of striping, body moldings, deck racks, graphics, gold plating, etc. **Equity Capital Needed:** $55,000-$85,000. **Franchise Fee:** $38,950. **Financial Assistance:** Yes. **Managerial Assistance:** Ongoing technical assistance via newsletter, conventions and telephone. **Training:** (Missouri for combined classroom and field training and 4-5 days in franchisees territory). Training also available for franchisees employees or sub-contractors.

1589 ■ Fibrenew
Site 16, RR8
Box 33
Calgary, AB, Canada T2J 2T9
Ph:(403)278-7818
Free: 800-345-2951
Fax:(403)278-1434
No. of Franchise Units: 93. **Founded:** 1985. **Franchised:** 1995. **Description:** Mobile interior reconditioning and repair. **Equity Capital Needed:** $75,000. **Franchise Fee:** $59,500. **Financial Assistance:** No. **Training:** Yes.

1590 ■ Line-X Protective Coatings
Line-X Franchise Development Corp.
1862 Sparkman Dr
Huntsville, AL 35816
Free: 877-330-1331
Co. E-mail: sales@line-x.com
URL: http://line-x.com
No. of Franchise Units: 360. **Founded:** 1994. **Franchised:** 1999. **Description:** Spray-on truck bed liners for truck dealers and retail customers. **Equity Capital Needed:** $68,000-$147,000. **Franchise Fee:** $20,000. **Financial Assistance:** No. **Training:** Yes.

1591 ■ Maaco Franchising, Inc.
Maaco Enterprises, Inc.
381 Brooks Rd.
King of Prussia, PA 19406
Ph:(610)265-6606
Free: 800-296-2226
Fax:(610)337-6176
Co. E-mail: Fslprv@maaco.com
URL: http://www.maaco.com
No. of Franchise Units: 500. **Founded:** 1972. **Franchised:** 1972. **Description:** Maaco Auto Painting & Bodyworks Centers are complete production auto paint and body repair centers. No prior automotive experience necessary. **Equity Capital Needed:** $90,000 minimum cash required. **Franchise Fee:** $40,000. **Financial Assistance:** Third party financing available to qualified applicants. **Training:** 4 weeks formal training at corporate headquarters, continuing operational support thereafter. Assistance in financing, site selection and installation of equipment.

1592 ■ Maaco Systems Canada Inc.
Maaco Collision Repair and Auto Painting
8400 Lawson Rd., Ste. 1
Milton, ON, Canada L9T 0A4
Ph:(905)875-1248
Free: 800-387-6780
Fax:(905)875-0105
Co. E-mail: maaco@maaco.com
URL: http://www.maaco.ca
No. of Franchise Units: 34. **Founded:** 1972. **Franchised:** 1974. **Description:** Auto painting and body repair. **Equity Capital Needed:** $299,000-$330,000 investment required; $75,000-$85,000 + SBL. **Franchise Fee:** $30,000. **Training:** Provides 4 weeks in U.S. and 3 man weeks onsite with ongoing support.

1593 ■ The Shine Factory
Shine Factory Systems Inc.
75 Akerley Blvd.
Dartmouth, NS, Canada B3B 1R7
Ph:(902)405-3171
Fax:(902)405-3484
Co. E-mail: info@shinefactory.com
URL: http://www.shinefactory.com
No. of Franchise Units: 16. **Founded:** 1981. **Franchised:** 1981. **Description:** Canada's automotive and polishing franchise. **Equity Capital Needed:** $100,000+. **Franchise Fee:** $25,000+ depending upon market area study. **Financial Assistance:** No. **Training:** Training conducted in Halifax, NS.

1594 ■ Sprayglo Auto Refinishing & Body Repair
Sprayglo USA Inc.
340 Smith Street
Clayton, GA 30525
Ph:877-677-7294
Fax:877-677-7294
Co. E-mail: info@sprayglo.com
URL: http://www.sprayglo.com
No. of Franchise Units: 8. **No. of Company-Owned Units:** 13. **Founded:** 1986. **Franchised:** 1995. **Description:** Automotive painting and body repair. **Equity Capital Needed:** $216,800-$296,000. **Franchise Fee:** $20,000. **Royalty Fee:** 6%. **Financial Assistance:** Equipment leasing can reduce start-up costs along with available financing of initial inventory requirements. **Training:** 30 days at training facilities, and 2 weeks at site location. All paint, materials, and equipment available from franchisor.

1595 ■ Ziebart
Ziebart International Corp.
1290 E. Maple Rd.
Troy, MI 48007-1290
Ph:(248)588-4100
Free: 800-877-1312
Fax:(248)588-0718
No. of Franchise Units: 400. **No. of Company-Owned Units:** 16. **Founded:** 1954. **Franchised:** 1963. **Description:** Automotive application of detailing-accessories and protection services. **Equity Capital Needed:** $145,000-$250,000. **Franchise Fee:** $25,000. **Financial Assistance:** Yes. **Training:** Yes.

COMPUTER SYSTEMS/ SOFTWARE

1596 ■ *Auto Detailing*
Entrepreneur, Inc.
2445 McCabe Way
Irvine, CA 92614
Ph:(949)261-2325
Free: 800-421-2300
Fax:(949)261-7729
URL: http://www.entrepreneur.com
Price: $69.00. **Description:** Software designed to help operate an auto detailing business.

LIBRARIES

1597 ■ Max S. Hayes Vocational School Library
4600 Detroit Ave.
Cleveland, OH 44102
Ph:(216)631-1528
Fax:(216)634-2175
URL: http://www.maxshayes.com/
Contact: Tony Ascota, Libn.
Scope: Automotive trades, metalwork, machine shop work, vocational education, construction, textile fabrication. **Services:** Interlibrary loan; copying; Library open to the public by appointment. **Holdings:** 12,000 volumes; U.S. and foreign car shop manuals, 1965 to present. **Subscriptions:** 85 journals and other serials.

1598 ■ Phoenix Public Library–Burton Barr Central Library–Vehicle and Appliance Repair Collection (1221)
1221 N. Central, 2nd Fl.
Phoenix, AZ 85004
Ph:(602)262-4636
URL: http://www.phoenixpubliclibrary.org/pageView.jsp?id=6029
Scope: Vehicle and motor repair - flat rate, interchange; electronic data and schematics for computers, appliances, transistor and ham radios. **Services:** Interlibrary loan; collection open to the public. **Holdings:** 3500 books; 10,000 schematics and 400 volumes of SAMS photofact publications as well as peripheral publications. **Subscriptions:** 17 journals and other serials.

Automobile/Truck Leasing Service

ASSOCIATIONS AND OTHER ORGANIZATIONS

1599 ■ American Automotive Leasing Association
675 N Washington St., Ste. 410
Alexandria, VA 22314
Ph:(703)548-0777
Fax:(703)548-1925
Co. E-mail: sederholm@aalafleet.com
URL: http://www.aalafleet.com
Contact: Pamela Sederholm, Exec. Dir.

Purpose: Represents the commercial automotive fleet leasing and management industry. .

1600 ■ Automotive Fleet and Leasing Association
1000 Westgate Dr., Ste. 252
St. Paul, MN 55114
Ph:(651)203-7247
Fax:(651)290-2266
Co. E-mail: paulh@aflaonline.com
URL: http://www.aflaonline.org
Contact: Paul Hanscom, Exec. Dir.

Description: New car dealers, fleet administrators, leasing companies, drive-away companies, auto manufacturers, and consultants. Provides a forum for the exchange of information between related segments of the fleet and leasing industry. Seeks to build working relationships with professionals in all phases of the industry, develop new ideas that will help the industry continue to grow, and help the industry find ways to operate more efficiently and profitably. **Publications:** *The Forum* (quarterly).

1601 ■ NAFA Fleet Management Association
125 Village Blvd., Ste. 200
Princeton Forrestal Village
Princeton, NJ 08540
Ph:(609)720-0882
Fax:(609)452-8004
Co. E-mail: info@nafa.org
URL: http://www.nafa.org
Contact: Phillip E. Russo CAE, Exec. Dir.

Description: Persons responsible for the administration of a motor vehicle fleet of 25 or more units for a firm not commercially engaged in the sale, rental, or lease of motor vehicles. Compiles statistics. Maintains placement service and speakers' bureau; conducts research programs. Operates Fleet Information Resource Center. Sponsors professional Certified Automotive Fleet Manager certification. **Publications:** *Fleet Solutions* (bimonthly); *FleetFocus* (biweekly); *NAFA Annual Reference Book*; *NAFA Roster* (annual); *NAFA's Fleet Executive* (monthly).

1602 ■ National Truck Leasing System
1S450 Summit Ave., Ste. 300
Oakbrook Terrace, IL 60181-3990
Ph:(630)925-7710
Free: 800-729-6857
Fax:(630)953-0040
Co. E-mail: passwords@nationalease.com
URL: http://www.ntls.com
Contact: Doug Clark, Pres./CEO
Description: Franchiser of independent companies. Provides full-service truck leasing. Promotes simplification of operating practices. Sponsors seminars. **Publications:** *NationaLease Newsletter* (weekly).

1603 ■ National Vehicle Leasing Association
7250 Pkwy. Dr., Ste. 510
Hanover, MD 21076
Ph:(410)782-2342
Free: 800-225-6852
Fax:(410)712-4038
Co. E-mail: info@nvla.org
URL: http://www.nvla.org
Contact: Ben Carfrae, Pres./Treas.
Description: Companies that lease vehicles. Provides education and information services. Lobbies on behalf of members. Maintains speakers' bureau; offers placement services; compiles statistics. **Publications:** *Lifeline* (bimonthly); *Vehicle Leasing Today* (quarterly).

1604 ■ Recreation Vehicle Rental Association
3930 University Dr.
Fairfax, VA 22030-2515
Ph:(703)591-7130
Fax:(703)359-0152
Co. E-mail: info@rvda.org
URL: http://www.rvra.org
Description: Dealers involved in the rental of recreation vehicles such as folding trailers, travel trailers, and motor homes. Works to improve the professionalism of the RV rental dealer through educational programs and promote the use of rentals by disseminating information. Compiles statistics; conducts seminars. .

1605 ■ Truck Renting and Leasing Association
675 N Washington St., Ste. 410
Alexandria, VA 22314
Ph:(703)299-9120
Fax:(703)299-9115
Co. E-mail: tjames@trala.org
URL: http://www.trala.org
Contact: Thomas James, Pres./CEO
Description: Truck and trailer rental and leasing companies and systems; suppliers to the industry. Seeks to encourage and promote a favorable climate and sound environment conducive to the renting and leasing of trucks, tractors, and trailers, and dedicated contract carriage. **Publications:** *EnRoute* (biweekly); *Inside TRALA* (quarterly); *Truck Renting and Leasing Association—News Digest* (quarterly); *Weekly Wire* (weekly).

REFERENCE WORKS

1606 ■ "Credit Crunch Gives, Takes Away" in *The Business Journal-Serving Metropolitan Kansas City* (Vol. 27, October 17, 2008, No. 5, pp. 1)
Pub: American City Business Journals, Inc.
Ed: Suzanna Stagemeyer. **Description:** Although many Kansas City business enterprises have been adversely affected by the U.S. credit crunch, others have remained relatively unscathed. Examples of how local businesses are being impacted by the crisis are provided including: American Trailer & Storage Inc., which declared bankruptcy after failing to pay a long-term loan; and NetStandard, a technology firm who, on the other hand, is being pursued by prospective lenders.

1607 ■ *Rent-A-Wreck Worldwide Directory*
Pub: Rent-A-Wreck of America Inc.
Contact: Lori Shaffron
Ed: Lori Shaffron, Editor. **Released:** Annual, August. **Price:** Free. **Covers:** Nearly 500 franchise locations worldwide. **Entries Include:** Name, address, phone. **Arrangement:** Geographical.

1608 ■ "Transportation Enterprise" in *Advertising Age* (Vol. 79, June 9, 2008, No. 23, pp. S10)
Pub: Crain Communications, Inc.
Ed: Jean Halliday. **Description:** Overview of Enterprise rent-a-car's plan to become a more environmentally-friendly company. The family-owned business has spent $1 million a year to plant trees since 2006 and has added more fuel-efficient cars, hybrids and flex-fuel models.

STATISTICAL SOURCES

1609 ■ *RMA Annual Statement Studies*
Pub: Robert Morris Associates (RMA)
Released: Annual. **Price:** $175.00 2006-07 edition, $105.00. **Description:** Contains composite balance sheets and income statements for more than 360 industries, including the accounting, auditing, and bookkeeping industries. Also contains five years of comparative historical data for discerning trends. Includes 16 commonly used ratios, computed for most of the size groupings for nearly every industry.

TRADE PERIODICALS

1610 ■ *Automotive Fleet*
Pub: Bobit Business Media
Contact: Cindy Brauer, Managing Editor
E-mail: cindy.brauer@bobit.com
Released: Monthly. **Description:** Automotive magazine covering the car and light truck fleet market.

1611 ■ *Automotive Fleet and Leasing Association—Forum*
Pub: Automotive Fleet and Leasing Association
Contact: Paul Hansman
Ed: Rose Finch, Editor, rose@bobit.com. **Released:** Quarterly. **Price:** Included in membership. **Description:** Seeks to keep automotive fleet dealers and leasing agencies updated on important events, membership news, new legislation, and government programs. Recurring features include editorials and letters to the editor.

1612 ■ *inside TRALA*
Pub: Truck Renting and Leasing Association
Contact: Mary Payne
Ed: Mary S. Payne, Editor, mpayne@trala.org. **Released:** Quarterly. **Price:** Included in membership;

Free. **Description:** Publishes news and activities of TRALA members and suppliers. Addresses federal and state legislation and regulatory issues affecting the industry.

1613 ■ *The Latest Scoop*
Pub: Latest Scoop Publishing
Contact: Tracey Ellis, Publisher
E-mail: scoopautoevents@aol.com
Released: 9/year. **Price:** $15, individuals; $30, Canada. **Description:** Provides current information on car-related events taking place in the Rocky Mountain Region, including auctions, autocross, off-road, parades, races, rallies, rod runs/cruises/tours, swap meets, and shows. Recurring features include a calendar of events and columns titled Club Meetings and The Latest Scoop on. . .

TRADE SHOWS AND CONVENTIONS

1614 ■ Great American Trucking Show
Sellers Expositions
222 Pearl St., Ste. 300
New Albany, IN 47150
Ph:(812)949-9200
Free: 800-558-8767
Fax:(812)949-9600
URL: http://www.sellersexpo.com
Audience: Truck owners and operators, exempt haulers, company drivers and truck drivers for hire, aftermarket parts purchasers, purchasing agents, mechanics, fleet owner. **Principal Exhibits:** Trucks and related equipment, supplies, and services.

1615 ■ Service Specialists Association Annual Convention
Service Specialists Association
4015 Marks Rd., Ste. 2B
Medina, OH 44256
Ph:(330)725-7160
Free: 800-763-5717
Fax:(330)722-5638
Co. E-mail: trucksvc@aol.com
URL: http://www.truckservice.org
Released: Annual. **Audience:** Trade-Heavy Duty Aftermarket. **Principal Exhibits:** Exhibits related to truck repair operations, rebuilding departments, individuals who have maintained shop equipment such as hydraulic press or heat treating furnace.

FRANCHISES AND BUSINESS OPPORTUNITIES

1616 ■ Active Green + Ross
580 Evans Ave.
Toronto, ON, Canada M8W 2W1
Ph:(416)255-5581
Fax:(416)255-4793
Co. E-mail: info@activegreenross.com
URL: http://www.activegreenross.com
No. of Franchise Units: 67. **No. of Company-Owned Units:** 8. **Founded:** 1982. **Description:** This is one of the largest independent groups of tire and automotive service centres in Canada. It is located in Toronto and the surrounding area. **Equity Capital Needed:** $115,000-$200,000. **Franchise Fee:** $25,000. **Financial Assistance:** Yes. **Training:** Training provided for up to 2 months.

1617 ■ Bates International Motor Home Rental Systems, Inc.
Bates Motor Home Rental Network, Inc.
3690 S Eastern Ave., Ste. 220
Las Vegas, NV 89169
Ph:(702)737-9050
Free: 800-732-2283
Fax:(702)737-9149
Co. E-mail: headquarters@batesintl.com
No. of Franchise Units: 16. **Founded:** 1973. **Franchised:** 1995. **Description:** Motor home rentals. **Equity Capital Needed:** $17,000. **Franchise Fee:** $35,000-$50,000. **Financial Assistance:** No. **Training:** Yes.

1618 ■ Budget Brake & Muffler Distributors Ltd
200-185 Golden Dr.
Coquitlam, BC, Canada V3K 6T1
Ph:(604)464-1239
Free: 800-746-9659
Fax:(604)464-1426
Co. E-mail: info@budgetbrake.com
URL: http://www.budgetbrake.com
No. of Franchise Units: 33. **Founded:** 1969. **Franchised:** 1972. **Description:** Provides retail automotive service specializing in brakes, exhaust, shocks and associated service. **Equity Capital Needed:** $185,000-$225,000. **Franchise Fee:** $25,000. **Royalty Fee:** 4% g.s. **Financial Assistance:** No. **Managerial Assistance:** Lease negotiations, site selection, and advisory council provided. **Training:** Offers 2 weeks minimum.

1619 ■ Dollar Rent A Car
Dollar Systems, Inc.
PO Box 33167
Tulsa, OK 74153
Ph:(918)669-3103
Free: 800-951-4268
No. of Franchise Units: 1,300. **No. of Company-Owned Units:** 30. **Founded:** 1967. **Description:** Daily rental car. **Equity Capital Needed:** Dependent on fleet size. **Franchise Fee:** minimum $12,500. **Financial Assistance:** Yes. **Training:** Yes.

1620 ■ Eaglerider Motorcycle Rental
Eaglerider, Inc.
11860 S La Cienga Blvd.
Los Angeles, CA 90250
Ph:(310)536-6777
Free: 800-501-TOUR
Fax:(310)536-6770
No. of Franchise Units: 72. **No. of Company-Owned Units:** 15. **Founded:** 1992. **Franchised:** 1999. **Description:** Motorcycle rental and guide tour company specializing in Harley-Davidson motorcycles. **Equity Capital Needed:** $38,000$160,000. **Franchise Fee:** $20,000-$40,000. **Royalty Fee:** 10%. **Financial Assistance:** Limited in-house and third party financial assistance available. **Training:** Provides 6 days at headquarters, 2 days onsite, and ongoing support. Manuals and procedures of motorcycle rental operations are covered in detail.

1621 ■ Payless Car Rental
Avalon Global Group, Inc.
2350 N 34th St. N
St. Petersburg, FL 33713
Ph:(727)321-6352
Free: 800-729-5255
Fax:(727)322-6540
No. of Franchise Units: 83. **Founded:** 1971. **Franchised:** 1971. **Description:** Automobile rental and sales. **Equity Capital Needed:** Minimum $500,000 net worth. **Franchise Fee:** $20,000-$500,000. **Financial Assistance:** No. **Training:** Yes.

1622 ■ Thrifty Rent-A-Car System, Inc.
Dollar Thrifty Automotive Group
5310 E 31st St.
Tulsa, OK 74135
Ph:(918)669-2219
Free: 800-532-3401
Fax:(918)669-2061
No. of Franchise Units: 545. **No. of Company-Owned Units:** 3. **Founded:** 1962. **Franchised:** 1962. **Description:** Over 90
of retail outlets are owned by independent businesses under the company's trade name. **Equity Capital Needed:** minimum PNW $650,000 unencumbered, + $120,000 minimum working capital. **Franchise Fee:** Varies. **Financial Assistance:** Yes. **Training:** Yes.

1623 ■ Wheelchair Getaways, Inc.
PO Box 1098
Mukilteo, WA 40383
Ph:(425)771-4659
Free: 800-536-5518
Co. E-mail: info@wheelchairgetaways.com
No. of Franchise Units: 47. **No. of Company-Owned Units:** 3. **Founded:** 1988. **Franchised:** 1989. **Description:** Provides rental of speciallyconverted vans on a daily basis to people using wheelchairs. **Equity Capital Needed:** $40,000$112,000. **Franchise Fee:** $25,000. **Financial Assistance:** No. **Training:** Yes.

COMPUTERIZED DATABASES

1624 ■ *Consumer InSite*
Thomson Reuters
610 Opperman Dr.
Eagen, MN 55122
Free: 800-477-4300
Co. E-mail: gale.contentlicensing@cengage.com
URL: http://www.insite2.gale.com
Description: Focuses on consumer behavior, political opinion, contemporary lifestyles, leisure activities, and trends in popular culture. Provides the full text and summaries from more than 350 widely read North American newsstand titles and specialty magazines; derived from Magazine Database. Contains approximately 600,000 articles, including entertainment reviews of books, films, video, theatre, concerts, musical recordings, hotels, and restaurants, consumer buyer's guides, columns, editorials, product evaluations, biographies, speeches, interviews, and obituaries. **Availability:** Online: Thomson Reuters. **Type:** Full text.

1625 ■ *Highway Vehicles Safety Database*
SAE International
400 Commonwealth Dr.
Warrendale, PA 15096-0001
Ph:(724)776-4841
Free: 877-606-7323
Fax:(724)776-0790
Co. E-mail: CustomerService@sae.org
URL: http://www.sae.org
Description: Contains more than 70,000 document summaries (detailed abstracts and bibliographies) of technical papers, journal articles, magazine articles, standards and specifications, Technology books, and research reports relating to highway vehicle safety. Covers topics related to passenger cars, vans, minivans, trucks, buses, and motorcycles, and such safety issues as crashworthiness, stability, vehicle control, human factors, safety equipment, crash impact, occupant protection, collision avoidance, restraint systems, human response, design, testing, modeling, reconstruction, and research. Includes extensive coverage of publications from the United States, Japan, Germany, Italy, the United Kingdom, France, Korea, Brazil, Canada, and other countries. All information is translated from the original language into English. **Availability:** Online: SAE International; CD-ROM: SAE International. **Type:** Bibliographic.

COMPUTER SYSTEMS/ SOFTWARE

1626 ■ Black Book, Inc.
Black Book
PO Box 758
Gainesville, GA 30503
Ph:(770)532-4111
Free: 800-554-1026
Fax:800-357-3444
URL: http://www.blackbookusa.com
Description: Available for IBM computers and MS-DOS compatibles. System provides including cost and retail, options, and finance and lease payments. pricing information on cars and light trucks, including cost and retail, options, and finance and lease payments.

LIBRARIES

1627 ■ Alabama Department of Transportation–Research & Development Bureau–Research Library (1409)
1409 Coliseum Blvd.
Montgomery, AL 36110
Ph:(334)206-2210

Fax:(334)264-2042
Co. E-mail: harrisi@dot.state.al.us
URL: http://www.dot.state.al.us/docs
Contact: Jeffrey W. Brown, Res. & Dev.Engr.
Scope: Transportation. **Services:** Interlibrary loan; Library not open to the public. **Holdings:** 1000 books; 5000 reports. **Subscriptions:** 8 journals and other serials.

1628 ■ California State Department of Motor Vehicles–Licensing Operations Division - Research and Development Branch–Traffic Safety Research Library (2415)
2415 1st Ave., MS F-126
Sacramento, CA 95818
Ph:(916)657-3079
Fax:(916)657-8589
Co. E-mail: dluong@dvm.ca.gov
Contact: Douglas Luong, Staff Svcs.Anl.
Scope: Automobile transportation. **Services:** Copying; Library not open to the public. **Holdings:** 500 books; 10,000 bound periodical volumes; reports; manuscripts. **Subscriptions:** 20 journals and other serials.

1629 ■ Connecticut Department of Transportation–ConnDOT Library and Information Center
2800 Berlin Tpke.
Newington, CT 06111-4116
Ph:(860)594-3035
Fax:(860)594-3039
Co. E-mail: betty.ambler@po.state.ct.us
URL: http://www.ct.gov/dot/site/default.asp
Contact: Betty Ambler, Libn.
Scope: Transportation. **Services:** Interlibrary loan; copying; Library open to the public by appointment. **Holdings:** 10,000 books; 10,000 reports.

1630 ■ Kansas Department of Transportation Library
700 S.W. Harrison St.
Eisenhower State Office Bldg., 4th Fl., W.
Topeka, KS 66603-3745
Ph:(785)291-3854
Fax:(785)291-3717
Co. E-mail: library@ksdot.org
Contact: Marie Manthe, Libn.
Scope: Transportation. **Services:** Interlibrary loan; Library open to the public. **Holdings:** 3000 books; 20,000 reports; 175 CD-ROMs; 100 videos **Subscriptions:** 100 journals and other serials.

1631 ■ Kentucky Transportation Center Library
University of Kentucky
176 Raymond Bldg.
Lexington, KY 40506-0281
Ph:(859)257-2155
Free: 800-432-0719
Fax:(859)257-1815
Co. E-mail: lwhayne@engr.uky.edu
URL: http://www.kyt2.com/
Contact: Laura Whayne, Libn.
Scope: Transportation. **Services:** Interlibrary loan; copying; Library open to the public. **Holdings:** 6000 books; 9000 reports; 800 videotapes. **Subscriptions:** 300 journals and other serials.

1632 ■ Missouri Highway and Transportation Department–Division of Materials Library
PO Box 270
Jefferson City, MO 65102-0270
Ph:(573)751-6735
Fax:(573)526-5636
Co. E-mail: michael.meyerhoff@mail.modot.state.mo.us
URL: http://www.modot.org/
Contact: Mona Scott
Scope: Transportation. **Services:** Library not open to the public. **Holdings:** Figures not available.

1633 ■ Montana Department of Transportation Library
2701 Prospect Ave.
PO Box 201001
Helena, MT 59620-1001
Ph:(406)444-6338
Fax:(406)444-7204
Co. E-mail: ssillick@mt.gov
URL: http://www.mdt.mt.gov/research/unique/services.shtml
Contact: Susan Sillick
Scope: Transportation. **Services:** Interlibrary loan; copying. **Holdings:** 10,000 items; reports; CD-ROMs; video. **Subscriptions:** 10 journals and other serials.

1634 ■ New Jersey Department of Transportation–Research Library
1035 Parkway Ave.
PO Box 600
Trenton, NJ 08625-0600
Ph:(609)530-5289
Fax:(609)530-2052
Co. E-mail: library@dot.state.nj.us
URL: http://www.state.nj.us/transportation/refdata/library/
Contact: Carol Paszamant, Libn.
Scope: Transportation. **Services:** Interlibrary loan; Library open to the public by appointment. **Holdings:** 300 books; 11,000 reports. **Subscriptions:** 50 journals and other serials.

1635 ■ North Carolina Department of Transportation–Research and Development Library
PO Box 25201
Raleigh, NC 27611
Ph:(919)715-2463
Fax:(919)715-0137
Co. E-mail: rhhall@dot.state.nc.us
URL: http://www.ncdot.org/
Contact: Bob Hall
Scope: Transportation. **Services:** Interlibrary loan; copying; Library open to the public for reference use only. **Holdings:** 11,209 books; 20,021 reports; 132 videos. **Subscriptions:** 57 journals and other serials.

1636 ■ North Dakota Department of Transportation–Materials and Research Division Library
300 Airport Rd.
Bismarck, ND 58504-6005
Ph:(701)328-6901
Fax:(701)328-0310
Co. E-mail: gweisger@nd.gov
Contact: Gerri Weisgerber, Adm. Staff Off.
Scope: Transportation. **Services:** Library not open to the public. **Holdings:** 6600 reports. **Subscriptions:** 5 journals and other serials.

1637 ■ South Carolina Department of Transportation Library
955 Park St., Rm. 110
Columbia, SC 29202
Ph:(803)737-9897
Fax:(803)737-0824
Co. E-mail: adcockda@dot.state.sc.us
URL: http://www.dot.state.sc.us
Contact: Ann Adcock, Mgr.
Scope: Transportation, engineering, mass transit. **Services:** Interlibrary loan; transportation related research; Library open to the public. **Holdings:** 5500 books; 90 bound periodical volumes; 1900 reports; 250 videos. **Subscriptions:** 41 journals and other serials; 10 newspapers.

1638 ■ Vermont Agency of Transportation–Policy and Planning Division Library
133 State St.
Montpelier, VT 05633
Ph:(802)828-2544
Fax:(802)828-3983
Contact: Sandy Aja
Scope: Transportation. **Holdings:** Figures not available.

RESEARCH CENTERS

1639 ■ Automotive Market Research Council
10 Laboratory Dr.
PO Box 13966
Research Triangle Park, NC 27709-3966
Ph:(248)650-0603
Fax:(248)650-0606
Co. E-mail: info@amrc.org
URL: http://amrc.org
Contact: Joe Eschenbrenner, Pres.
E-mail: info@amrc.org
Scope: Market research analysis and business planning, focusing on gathering and disseminating market data promptly and accurately and increasing the reliability of demand forecasts in the industry. Also works with government agencies to improve the collection of statistics. **Publications:** The Researcher (quarterly).

REFERENCE WORKS

1640 ■ "Babynut.com to Shut Down" in *Bellingham Business Journal* (Vol. February 2010, pp. 3)
Pub: Sound Publishing Inc.
Description: Saralee Sky and Jerry Kilgore, owners of Babynut.com will close their online store. The site offered a free online and email newsletter to help mothers through pregnancy and the first three years of their child's life. Products being sold at clearance prices include organic and natural maternity and nursing clothing, baby and toddler clothes, books on pregnancy, and more.

1641 ■ "Baby's Room Franchisee Files Bankruptcy" in *Crain's Detroit Business* (Vol. 25, June 22, 2009, No. 25, pp. 15)
Pub: Crain Communications Inc. - Detroit
Ed: Gabe Nelson. **Description:** Emery L, a franchisee of USA Baby Inc. and ran the franchised Baby's Room Nursery Furniture stores in the area has filed for bankruptcy. Details of the bankruptcy are included.

1642 ■ "Consignment Shop Offers Children's Clothes, Products" in *Frederick News-Post* (August 19, 2010)
Pub: Federick News-Post
Ed: Ed Waters Jr. **Description:** Sweet Pea Consignments for Children offers used items for newborns to pre-teens. The shop carries name brand clothing as well as toys, books and baby products.

1643 ■ "Delaware Diaper Maker Wanting To Expand Less Than a Year After Move" in *Business First-Columbus* (December 7, 2007, pp. A6)
Pub: American City Business Journals, Inc.
Ed: Dan Eaton. **Description:** Duluth, Georgia-based Associated Hygienic Products LLC is planning to expand its production operations by 20 percent and hire new workers. The diaper maker was awarded state incentives to facilitate its transfer from Marion to Delaware. Details are included.

1644 ■ "King of the Crib: How Good Samaritan Became Ohio's Baby HQ" in *Business Courier* (Vol. 27, June 18, 2010, No. 7, pp. 1)
Pub: Business Courier
Ed: James Ritchie. **Description:** Cincinnati's Good Samaritan hospital had 6,875 live births in 2009, which is more than any other hospital in Ohio. They specialize in the highest-risk pregnancies and deliveries and other hospitals are trying to grab Good Samaritan's share in this niche.

1645 ■ "Procter & Gamble Boosts Bet on Exclusive Brands" in *Business Courier* (Vol. 27, July 9, 2010, No. 10, pp. 1)
Pub: Business Courier
Ed: Jon Newberry. **Description:** Procter & Gamble is creating more special versions of its brands such as Pringles and Pampers exclusively for retail partners such as Tesco in the U.K. The greater push towards this direction is seen as a way to regain market share.

1646 ■ "Retail Briefs - Dollar Store Opens in Long Leaf Mall" in *Star-News* (November 5, 2010)
Pub: Star-News Media
Ed: Judy Royal. **Description:** Dollar Delight$ opened a new shop in Long Leaf Mall in Wilmington, North Carolina. The store will carry gift bags, balloons, party supplies, greeting cards, school supplies, health and beauty products, hardware, baby items, toys, Christmas goods, crafts, housewares and jewelry in its inventory.

1647 ■ "What's In That Diaper?" in *Inc.* (November 2007, pp. 126)
Pub: Gruner & Jahr USA Publishing
Ed: Nitasha Tiku. **Description:** Profile of Jason and Kimberly Graham-Nye, inventors of the gDiaper, consisting of a washable cotton elastine outer pant and an insert made of fluffed wood pulp and viscose rayon, both harvested from trees certified by the Sustainable Forestry Initiative.

SOURCES OF SUPPLY

1648 ■ *Toys & Games—Buyer's Guide Issue*
Pub: Chelsie Communications Inc.
Contact: Graham Kennedy, Publisher
Released: Annual, Latest edition 2008. **Publication Includes:** List of about 400 Canadian manufacturers and distributors of toys and games for children; trade associations, trade show organizers, and licensors. **Entries Include:** For manufacturers and distributors—Company name, address, phone, key officials, branches, name of firm represented, key to line of business. For associations—Name, address, phone, contact name, property/show represented. **Arrangement:** Alphabetical. **Indexes:** Product, brand name.

VIDEOCASSETTES/ AUDIOCASSETTES

1649 ■ *Baby Massage*
Leslie T. McClure
PO Box 1223
Pebble Beach, CA 93953
Ph:(831)656-0553
Fax:(831)656-0555
Co. E-mail: leslie@411videoinfo.com
URL: http://www.411videoinfo.com
Released: 1998. **Price:** $29.95. **Description:** Instructs how to give a complete massage to your baby. **Availability:** VHS.

TRADE SHOWS AND CONVENTIONS

1650 ■ Denver Apparel and Accessory Market
Denver Merchandise Mart
451 E. 58th Ave., Ste. 4270
Denver, CO 80216-8470
Ph:(303)292-6278
Free: 800-289-6278
Fax:(303)297-8473
Co. E-mail: info@denvermart.com
URL: http://www.denvermart.com
Released: 5/yr. **Audience:** Retailers of women's, children's, and men's apparel and accessories. **Principal Exhibits:** Women's, men's, and children's apparel and accessories. **Dates and Locations:** 2011 Aug 26-29, Denver, CO.

1651 ■ International Juvenile Product Show
Juvenile Products Manufacturers Association
15000 Commerce Pkwy., Ste. C
Mount Laurel, NJ 08054-2267
Ph:(856)638-0420
Fax:(856)439-0525
Co. E-mail: jpma@ahint.com
URL: http://www.jpma.org
Released: Annual. **Audience:** Manufacturers, retailers, reps, wholesalers, importers, and other trade professionals. **Principal Exhibits:** Juvenile products, including furniture, toys, infant accessories, and soft goods.

1652 ■ Just Kidstuff - A Division of the New York International Gift Fair
George Little Management, LLC (New York, New York)
1133 Westchester Ave., Ste. N136
White Plains, NY 10606
Ph:(914)421-3200
Free: 800-272-SHOW
Co. E-mail: cathy_steel@glmshows.com
URL: http://www.glmshows.com
Released: Semiannual. **Audience:** Buyers from specialty and department stores, giftshops, jewelry stores, interior designers, importers and distributors of home products, mail order catalogs. **Principal Exhibits:** Presents a wide variety of upscale products for children of all ages, including bedding, furniture, dolls, toys and games, gifts, clothes, books and educational products and accessories.

1653 ■ Just Kidstuff - A Division of the San Francisco International Gift Fair
George Little Management, LLC (New York, New York)
1133 Westchester Ave., Ste. N136
White Plains, NY 10606
Ph:(914)421-3200
Free: 800-272-SHOW
Co. E-mail: cathy_steel@glmshows.com
URL: http://www.glmshows.com
Released: Semiannual, February and August. **Audience:** Specialty and department stores, gift shops, jewelry stores, interior designers, importers and distributors of home products, mail order catalogs, museums, etc. **Principal Exhibits:** Upscale products for children of all ages, including bedding, furniture, dolls, toys and games, gifts, clothes, books, and educational products and accessories.

1654 ■ Women's and Children's Apparel and Accessories Mart
Dallas Market Center Co.
Attn: SG Marketing Mgr.
2100 Stemmons Fwy.
Dallas, TX 75207

Ph:(214)655-6100
Free: 800-325-6587
Fax:(214)655-6238
Co. E-mail: info@dmcmail.com
Audience: Apparel and accessories and home furnishings retailers. **Principal Exhibits:** Regional Merchandising Mart servicing department and specialty store buyers nationwide.

FRANCHISES AND BUSINESS OPPORTUNITIES

1655 ■ Children's Lighthouse Franchise Co.
101 S Jennings
Fort Worth, TX 76104
Ph:(817)247-0886
Free: 888-338-4466
Fax:(817)887-5772
No. of Franchise Units: 30. **No. of Company-Owned Units:** 8. **Founded:** 1997. **Franchised:** 1999. **Description:** Childcare franchise. **Equity Capital Needed:** $150,000 minimum liquid assets; $500,000 net worth. **Franchise Fee:** $50,000. **Financial Assistance:** No. **Training:** Yes. s.

1656 ■ Stork News
Stork News of America Inc.
1305 Hope Mills Rd., Ste. A
Fayetteville, NC 28304
Ph:(910)426-1357
Free: 800-633-6395
Fax:(910)426-2473
No. of Franchise Units: 140. **No. of Company-Owned Units:** 1. **Founded:** 1983. **Franchised:** 1985. **Description:** Provides announcement services to newborn. **Equity Capital Needed:** $2,000, not including franchise fee. **Franchise Fee:** $10,800+. **Financial Assistance:** No. **Training:** Yes.

LIBRARIES

1657 ■ Art Institute of Philadelphia Library
1610 Chestnut St.
Philadelphia, PA 19103
Ph:(215)405-6402
Co. E-mail: rschachter@aii.edu
URL: http://rs185.aisites.com
Contact: Ruth Schachter, Dir.
Scope: Visual communications, interior design, industrial design, animation, fashion marketing, fashion design, visual merchandising, photography, website design, multimedia. **Services:** Interlibrary loan; Library not open to the public (circulation services provided for students and faculty). **Holdings:** 31,000 volumes; 2000 videocassettes; audiocassettes. **Subscriptions:** 170 print subscriptions and other serials.

1658 ■ Bauder College Library
384 Northyards Blvd. NW, Ste. 190 and 400
Atlanta, GA 30313
Ph:(404)237-7573
Free: 800-986-9710
Fax:(404)237-1619
URL: http://atlanta.bauder.edu
Scope: Fashion design and merchandising, interior design, information technology, business administration, graphic design, criminal justice. **Services:** Library not open to the public. **Holdings:** 7800 books; 500 videotapes; 6500 slide sets; 100 filmstrips. **Subscriptions:** 160 journals and other serials; 6 newspapers.

1659 ■ Fashion Institute of Design & Merchandising–Cyril Magnin Resource and Research Center
55 Stockton St., 5th Fl.
San Francisco, CA 94108-5829
Ph:(415)675-5200, x3361
Free: 800-422-3436
Fax:(415)296-7299
URL: http://fidm.edu
Contact: Jim Glenny, Lib.Dir.
Scope: Fashion design and merchandising, interior design, apparel manufacturing, advertising, merchandising, marketing. **Services:** Center not open to the public. **Holdings:** 4000 books; 800 AV programs; 1000 newspaper clipping files; 4000 videos, DVDs, and slides. **Subscriptions:** 200 journals and other serials.

1660 ■ Fashion Institute of Technology–Gladys Marcus Library
7th Ave. at 27th St.
E-Bldg. E502
New York, NY 10001-5992
Ph:(212)217-4340
Fax:(212)217-4371
Co. E-mail: greta_earnest@fitnyc.edu
URL: http://fitnyc.edu/library
Contact: Prof. N.J. Wolfe, Lib.Dir.
Scope: Costume, fashion, interior design, management engineering technology, fashion buying and merchandising, textiles, toy design, packaging design, advertising. **Services:** Interlibrary loan; copying; Library open to the public for reference use only by appointment. **Holdings:** 130,260 books; 113,265 nonprint units; 20,637 bound periodical volumes; 125,000 fashion slides; 4712 reels of microfilm; 438 CD-ROM serials and digital monographs. **Subscriptions:** 4000 journals and other serials.

START-UP INFORMATION

1661 ■ *How to Bake a Business: Recipes to Turn Your Bright Idea Into a Successful Enterprise*
Pub: Allen & Unwin
Ed: Julia Bickerstaff. **Released:** May 10, 2010. **Price:** $17.95. **Description:** Guide to starting and running a successful baker are offered in a purse-size handbook.

ASSOCIATIONS AND OTHER ORGANIZATIONS

1662 ■ American Bakers Association
1300 I St. NW, Ste. 700 W
Washington, DC 20005
Ph:(202)789-0300
Fax:(202)898-1164
Co. E-mail: rmackie@americanbakers.org
URL: http://www.americanbakers.org
Contact: Robb MacKie, Pres./CEO
Description: Manufacturers and wholesale distributors of bread, rolls, and pastry products; suppliers of goods and services to bakers. Conducts seminars and expositions. .

REFERENCE WORKS

1663 ■ "The Ultimate Vending Machine" in *Benzinga.com* (August 15, 2011)
Pub: Benzinga.com
Ed: Benzinga Staff. **Description:** Louis Hecht, a baker from Hombourg-Haut, France is selling fresh-baked bread in vending machines. Each machine holds 90 pre-cooked loaves which are warmed before being delivered to the customer.

SOURCES OF SUPPLY

1664 ■ *Baking/Snack Directory & Buyer's Guide*
Pub: Sosland Publishing Co.
Contact: Laurie Gorton, Exec. Ed.
E-mail: lgorton@sosland.com
Released: Annual, Latest edition 2010. **Price:** $205, individuals S&H for ea. additional copy is $2 reg., $16 prior.. **Covers:** Wholesale bakers of bread, cake, cookies, crackers, pasta; manufacturers of snack foods, mixes, and frozen dough; licensors of proprietary brands; manufacturers of equipment and products and suppliers of services used in wholesale baking. For bakers—Company name, address, phone, principal headquarters and plant personnel, principal products, sales volume, production method, and number of employees. For manufacturers—Company name, address, phone, name and title of contact. **Entries Include:** Company name, address, phone, executive name. **Arrangement:** Bakers are classified by product type; manufacturers are alphabetical. **Indexes:** Executive name, plant (bakers); product (manufacturers and suppliers).

TRADE PERIODICALS

1665 ■ *Baker's Rack*
Pub: The Retailer's Bakery Association
Ed: Anna Allen, Editor, sesh@rbanet.com. **Released:** Monthly. **Price:** Included in membership. **Description:** Examines trends and issues in the bakery industry. Features items on bakery production, marketing, business management, and other topics of interest. Recurring features include news of research, meeting reports, a calendar of events, and various columns.

1666 ■ *Baking Buyer*
Pub: Sosland Publishing Co.
Released: Monthly. **Price:** Free to qualified subscribers; $80 other countries. **Description:** Magazine for retail, in-store, foodservice, specialty, and wholesale bakers.

1667 ■ *Baking & Snack*
Pub: Sosland Publishing Co.
Contact: Laurie Gorton, Exec. Ed.
E-mail: lgorton@sosland.com
Ed: Steve Berne, Editor, sberne@sosland.com. **Released:** Monthly, (except January). **Price:** $72 other countries print; Free to qualified subscribers; $36. **Description:** Equipment, engineering, production and formulating magazine for commercial manufacturers of baked and snack foods.

1668 ■ *Dairy-Deli-Bake Digest*
Pub: International Dairy-Deli-Bakery Association
Contact: Roberta Rush
Ed: Carol L. Christison, Editor, cchristison@iddba.org. **Released:** Monthly. **Price:** Included in membership. **Description:** Supports the Association, which seeks to increase supermarket dairy-deli-bakery business. Focuses on issues of concern to manufacturers, retailers, brokers, distributors, businesses, and organizations involved with the dairy-deli-bakery industry. Recurring features include research news, reports of meetings, news of educational opportunities and industrial trends, and notices of publications available.

1669 ■ *Milling & Baking News*
Pub: Sosland Publishing Co.
Contact: Jay Sjerven, Sen. Ed.
E-mail: jsjerven@sosland.com
Released: Weekly (Tues.). **Price:** $135 U.S. and Canada; $210 U.S. and Canada 2 years; $290 U.S. and Canada 3 years; $190 out of country; $320 out of country 2 years; $455 out of country 3 years. **Description:** Trade magazine covering the grain-based food industries.

1670 ■ *Modern Baking*
Pub: Penton Media Inc.
Contact: Bill Dooley, Advertising Dir
E-mail: bill.dooley@penton.com
Released: Monthly. **Description:** Magazine on news, products, and trends of the baking industry.

TRADE SHOWS AND CONVENTIONS

1671 ■ Dairy-Deli-Bake Seminar and Expo
International Dairy-Deli-Bakery Association
PO Box 5528
Madison, WI 53705-0528
Ph:(608)310-5000
Fax:(608)238-6330
Co. E-mail: iddba@iddba.org
URL: http://www.iddba.org
Released: Annual. **Audience:** Retailers, wholesalers, distributors, brokers, and manufacturers of the dairy, deli, and bakery industry. **Principal Exhibits:** Dairy, deli, and bakery products, packaging, and equipment. **Dates and Locations:** 2011 Jun 05-07, Anaheim, CA.

FRANCHISES AND BUSINESS OPPORTUNITIES

1672 ■ Bagel Patch
Bagel Patch, Inc.
c/o Marketing Resources Group
83-26 Lefferts Blvd.
Kew Gardens, NY 11415
Ph:(718)261-8882
No. of Franchise Units: 9. **No. of Company-Owned Units:** 1. **Founded:** 1980. **Franchised:** 1994. **Description:** Bagel shop. **Equity Capital Needed:** $120,000-$146,000, including franchise fee. **Franchise Fee:** $15,000. **Financial Assistance:** No. **Training:** Yes.

1673 ■ Between Rounds Bakery Sandwich Cafe
Between Rounds Franchise Corp.
19A John Fitch Blvd.
South Windsor, CT 06074
Ph:(860)291-0323
Fax:(860)289-2732
No. of Company-Owned Units: 3. **Founded:** 1990. **Franchised:** 1994. **Description:** Bagels and other baked goods. **Equity Capital Needed:** $100,000 per unit or $500,000 liquid for area development. **Franchise Fee:** $25,000$175,000. **Financial Assistance:** No. **Training:** Yes.

1674 ■ Big Apple Bagels
BAB, Inc.
500 Lake Cook Rd., Ste. 475
Deerfield, IL 60015
Ph:(847)948-7520
Fax:(847)405-8140
Co. E-mail: tcervini@babcorp.com
URL: http://www.babcorp.com
No. of Franchise Units: 147. **No. of Company-Owned Units:** 1. **Founded:** 1992. **Franchised:** 1993. **Description:** A bakery style cafe featuring our three brands, made from scratch daily Big Apple Bagels and My Favorite Muffin, and freshly roasted Brewster's Coffee. Product offering includes made to order gourmet sandwiches, salads, soups, and espresso beverages. **Equity Capital Needed:**

$174,800-$349,500. **Franchise Fee:** $25,000. **Financial Assistance:** No. **Managerial Assistance:** Ongoing support in operations, marketing, and menu development provided by field reps and in-house staff. **Training:** Extensive training covers all aspects of operations and management, combines hands-on experience at our corporate store training facility with classroom presentations by management and key note vendors.

1675 ■ Big Town Hero

Hero Systems, Inc.
333 SW Taylor St., Ste. 200
Portland, OR 97204
Ph:(503)228-4376
Fax:(503)228-8778

No. of Franchise Units: 45. **Founded:** 1983. **Franchised:** 1989. **Description:** Sandwiches, salads, soups, fresh bread and baked goods from scratch. Fast and friendly. **Equity Capital Needed:** $50,000-$150,000. **Franchise Fee:** $20,000. **Financial Assistance:** No. **Training:** Yes.

1676 ■ Blue Chip Cookies

BDGS, LLC
210 Harrison St.
Loveland, OH 45140
Ph:(513)697-6610
Free: 800-888-9866
Fax:(513)697-2783
Co. E-mail: bluechipcookies@fuse.net
URL: http://www.bluechipcookies.com

No. of Franchise Units: 5. **No. of Company-Owned Units:** 3. **Founded:** 1983. **Franchised:** 1986. **Description:** Cookies, bakery items, ice cream, coffees, depending on model and site. **Equity Capital Needed:** $150,000-$250,000. **Franchise Fee:** $25,000. **Financial Assistance:** Bank SBA assistance. **Training:** Offers 2 weeks of training.

1677 ■ Breadsmith

Breadsmith Franchising, Inc.
409 E Silver Spring Dr.
Whitefish Bay, WI 53217
Ph:(414)962-1965
Fax:(414)431-5789

No. of Franchise Units: 33. **No. of Company-Owned Units:** 1. **Founded:** 1992. **Franchised:** 1993. **Description:** Specialty European artisan bakery. **Equity Capital Needed:** $205,000-$329,500. **Franchise Fee:** $30,000. **Financial Assistance:** No. **Training:** Yes.

1678 ■ Bruegger's

159 Bank St.
Burlington, VT 05401
Free: (886)660-4104
Fax:(802)660-4034
Co. E-mail: franchise@brueggers.com
URL: http://www.brueggers.com

No. of Franchise Units: 99. **No. of Company-Owned Units:** 148. **Founded:** 1983. **Franchised:** 1993. **Description:** Bakery style cafe serving bagels, sandwiches, breads, and fresh salads. **Equity Capital Needed:** $100,000 liquid; $200,000 net worth. **Franchise Fee:** $30,000. **Financial Assistance:** No. **Managerial Assistance:** Franchise Operations Consultants will be assigned to assist with first 2 bakeries opened and provide ongoing site visits, training and operational support. **Training:** Up to 8 weeks of on-the-job training.

1679 ■ Canada Bread Company, Limited

10 Four Seasons Pl.
Etobicoke, ON, Canada M9B 6H7
Ph:(416)641-4521
Fax:(416)626-7506

No. of Franchise Units: 1,000. **Founded:** 1960. **Description:** Bread, rolls, bagels, etc. **Equity Capital Needed:** Initial investment ranges from $60,000-$150,000 Canadian. **Franchise Fee:** $5,000 Canadian. **Financial Assistance:** No. **Training:** Yes. Yes.

1680 ■ Lox of Bagels

11801 Prestwick Rd., Ste. 301
Potomac, MD 20854
Ph:(301)299-8523
Free: 800-879-6927

No. of Franchise Units: 12. **Founded:** 1983. **Franchised:** 1996. **Description:** Bagels and gourmet coffee. **Equity Capital Needed:** $50,000 in equity with typical cost of $150,000-$200,000 per unit. **Franchise Fee:** $9,500. **Financial Assistance:** Yes. **Training:** Yes.

1681 ■ Perfecto's Caffe

Perfecto's Caffe Development LLC
79 N Main St.
Andover, MA 01810
Ph:(978)749-7022
Fax:(978)749-9433

No. of Franchise Units: 2. **No. of Company-Owned Units:** 2. **Founded:** 1993. **Franchised:** 2005. **Description:** Bagels, muffins, coffee, wraps, salads, and cookies. **Equity Capital Needed:** $175,000-$275,000, initial investment. **Franchise Fee:** $20,000. **Financial Assistance:** No. **Training:** Yes.

LIBRARIES

1682 ■ American Society of Baking Information Service and Library

765 Baywood Dr., Ste. 339
Petaluma, CA 94954
Ph:(707)762-8800
Free: (866)920-9885
Fax:(707)762-9500
Co. E-mail: kbrown@asbe.org
URL: http://www.asbe.org
Contact: Kerwin Kerwin, Exec.Dir.

Scope: Baking and allied subjects. **Holdings:** 10,000 references.

REFERENCE WORKS

1683 ■ "Convictions Under the Fisheries Act" in *Canadian Corporate News* (May 16, 2007)
Pub: Comtex News Network Inc.
Description: Fisheries and Oceans Canada is mandated to protect and conserve marine resources and thus released a list of fishers fined for various offences under the Fisheries Act in March and April.

TRADE PERIODICALS

1684 ■ *Fishing Tackle Retailer*
Pub: BASS/ESPN
Contact: Deborah Johnson, Managing Editor
Ed: Dave Ellison, Editor. **Released:** 11/yr. **Description:** Magazine for the fishing tackle industry.

VIDEOCASSETTES/ AUDIOCASSETTES

1685 ■ *Advanced Walleye Systems I*
The In-Fisherman
7819 Highland Scenic Rd.
Baxter, MN 56425-8011
Ph:(218)829-1648
Free: 800-260-6397
Fax:(218)829-2371
Co. E-mail: customerservice@imoutdoors.com
URL: http://www.in-fisherman.com
Description: Covers rigging techniques, hot locations in rivers, beating the postspawn slowdown, and more. **Availability:** VHS.

1686 ■ *Advanced Walleye Systems II*
The In-Fisherman
7819 Highland Scenic Rd.
Baxter, MN 56425-8011
Ph:(218)829-1648
Free: 800-260-6397
Fax:(218)829-2371
Co. E-mail: customerservice@imoutdoors.com
URL: http://www.in-fisherman.com
Description: Provides step-by-step instructions for locating and successfully catching walleye. **Availability:** VHS.

1687 ■ *Advanced Walleye Systems III*
The In-Fisherman
7819 Highland Scenic Rd.
Baxter, MN 56425-8011
Ph:(218)829-1648
Free: 800-260-6397
Fax:(218)829-2371
Co. E-mail: customerservice@imoutdoors.com
URL: http://www.in-fisherman.com
Description: Presents veteran anglers as they combine fishing techniques and boat control maneuvers to catch more fish. **Availability:** VHS.

1688 ■ *Advanced Walleye Trolling Tactics*
The In-Fisherman
7819 Highland Scenic Rd.
Baxter, MN 56425-8011
Ph:(218)829-1648
Free: 800-260-6397
Fax:(218)829-2371
Co. E-mail: customerservice@imoutdoors.com
URL: http://www.in-fisherman.com
Description: Covers boat rigging, bait selection, leadcore line fishing, and more. **Availability:** VHS.

1689 ■ *Bass Tackle: How to Buy & Save*
Bennett Marine Video
2321 Abbot Kinney Blvd., Top Fl.
Venice, CA 90291
Ph:(310)827-8064
Free: 800-733-8862
Fax:(310)827-8074
Co. E-mail: questions@bennettmarine.com
URL: http://www.bennettmarine.com
Released: 1988. **Price:** $29.99. **Description:** This is a guide to fishing tackle, with an emphasis on looking for bargains. **Availability:** VHS.

1690 ■ *The Big Catfish Connection*
The In-Fisherman
7819 Highland Scenic Rd.
Baxter, MN 56425-8011
Ph:(218)829-1648
Free: 800-260-6397
Fax:(218)829-2371
Co. E-mail: customerservice@imoutdoors.com
URL: http://www.in-fisherman.com
Description: Covers pre-spawn staging locations, rigging right, summer hot spots, and how to find wintering holes. **Availability:** VHS.

1691 ■ *The Big Catfish Connection II*
The In-Fisherman
7819 Highland Scenic Rd.
Baxter, MN 56425-8011
Ph:(218)829-1648
Free: 800-260-6397
Fax:(218)829-2371
Co. E-mail: customerservice@imoutdoors.com
URL: http://www.in-fisherman.com
Description: Provides information on night cats, high-water cats, bobber cats, and light-line cats. **Availability:** VHS.

1692 ■ *Big Fish Ontario*
The In-Fisherman
7819 Highland Scenic Rd.
Baxter, MN 56425-8011
Ph:(218)829-1648
Free: 800-260-6397
Fax:(218)829-2371
Co. E-mail: customerservice@imoutdoors.com
URL: http://www.in-fisherman.com
Description: Explains locations and techniques for successful fishing in Ontario. **Availability:** VHS.

1693 ■ *Big Walleye Presentations*
The In-Fisherman
7819 Highland Scenic Rd.
Baxter, MN 56425-8011
Ph:(218)829-1648
Free: 800-260-6397
Fax:(218)829-2371
Co. E-mail: customerservice@imoutdoors.com
URL: http://www.in-fisherman.com
Description: Covers live bait, soft plastics, rod selection, rigging methods, spinners, and drift socks. **Availability:** VHS.

1694 ■ *Big Water Catfish*
The In-Fisherman
7819 Highland Scenic Rd.
Baxter, MN 56425-8011
Ph:(218)829-1648
Free: 800-260-6397
Fax:(218)829-2371
Co. E-mail: customerservice@imoutdoors.com
URL: http://www.in-fisherman.com
Description: Offers tips on anchoring and setting lines and hints on finding the best places to fish. **Availability:** VHS.

1695 ■ *Catfish Fever*
The In-Fisherman
7819 Highland Scenic Rd.
Baxter, MN 56425-8011
Ph:(218)829-1648
Free: 800-260-6397
Fax:(218)829-2371
Co. E-mail: customerservice@imoutdoors.com
URL: http://www.in-fisherman.com
Description: Covers methods and equipment for catching catfish. **Availability:** VHS.

1696 ■ *Crappie Tactics for Lakes and Reservoirs*
The In-Fisherman
7819 Highland Scenic Rd.
Baxter, MN 56425-8011
Ph:(218)829-1648
Free: 800-260-6397
Fax:(218)829-2371
Co. E-mail: customerservice@imoutdoors.com
URL: http://www.in-fisherman.com
Description: Covers methods and equipment for catching crappies. **Availability:** VHS.

1697 ■ *Fly Fishing for Pike*
The In-Fisherman
7819 Highland Scenic Rd.
Baxter, MN 56425-8011
Ph:(218)829-1648
Free: 800-260-6397
Fax:(218)829-2371
Co. E-mail: customerservice@imoutdoors.com
URL: http://www.in-fisherman.com
Description: Covers rigging techniques, and how, when, and where to catch pike with a fly rod. **Availability:** VHS.

1698 ■ *Ice Fishing Secrets I*
The In-Fisherman
7819 Highland Scenic Rd.
Baxter, MN 56425-8011
Ph:(218)829-1648
Free: 800-260-6397
Fax:(218)829-2371
Co. E-mail: customerservice@imoutdoors.com
URL: http://www.in-fisherman.com
Description: Covers jigging methods, tip-ups, and terminal rigs. **Availability:** VHS.

1699 ■ *Northern Pike: The Water World*
The In-Fisherman
7819 Highland Scenic Rd.
Baxter, MN 56425-8011
Ph:(218)829-1648
Free: 800-260-6397
Fax:(218)829-2371
Co. E-mail: customerservice@imoutdoors.com
URL: http://www.in-fisherman.com
Description: Al Lindner explains where to catch pike, what lures to use, trolling patterns, and more. **Availability:** VHS.

1700 ■ *Panfish Patterns*
The In-Fisherman
7819 Highland Scenic Rd.
Baxter, MN 56425-8011
Ph:(218)829-1648
Free: 800-260-6397
Fax:(218)829-2371
Co. E-mail: customerservice@imoutdoors.com
URL: http://www.in-fisherman.com
Description: Covers methods and equipment for catching panfish. **Availability:** VHS.

1701 ■ *Pike in the Dead Zone*
The In-Fisherman
7819 Highland Scenic Rd.
Baxter, MN 56425-8011
Ph:(218)829-1648
Free: 800-260-6397
Fax:(218)829-2371
Co. E-mail: customerservice@imoutdoors.com
URL: http://www.in-fisherman.com
Description: Covers floats, rods, dead bait triggers for early season pike, and more. **Availability:** VHS.

1702 ■ *Prime Time Walleye Locations*
The In-Fisherman
7819 Highland Scenic Rd.
Baxter, MN 56425-8011
Ph:(218)829-1648
Free: 800-260-6397
Fax:(218)829-2371
Co. E-mail: customerservice@imoutdoors.com
URL: http://www.in-fisherman.com
Description: Includes information on shallow water walleyes, night fishing, speed control, lure choice, and equipment selection. **Availability:** VHS.

1703 ■ *River Walleye Location Secrets*
The In-Fisherman
7819 Highland Scenic Rd.
Baxter, MN 56425-8011
Ph:(218)829-1648
Free: 800-260-6397
Fax:(218)829-2371
Co. E-mail: customerservice@imoutdoors.com
URL: http://www.in-fisherman.com
Description: Presents prespawn, summer, and fall techniques. **Availability:** VHS.

1704 ■ *River Walleye Presentation Secrets*
The In-Fisherman
7819 Highland Scenic Rd.
Baxter, MN 56425-8011
Ph:(218)829-1648
Free: 800-260-6397
Fax:(218)829-2371
Co. E-mail: customerservice@imoutdoors.com
URL: http://www.in-fisherman.com
Description: Covers bait options, rod and reel types, depth control , and setting the hook. **Availability:** VHS.

1705 ■ *Secrets of the Walleye Trail*
The In-Fisherman
7819 Highland Scenic Rd.
Baxter, MN 56425-8011
Ph:(218)829-1648
Free: 800-260-6397
Fax:(218)829-2371
Co. E-mail: customerservice@imoutdoors.com
URL: http://www.in-fisherman.com
Description: Covers wind fishing, leadcore trolling, advanced bottom bouncing, jigging spoons, and shallow water fishing techniques. **Availability:** VHS.

1706 ■ *Smallmouth Bass: America's Greatest Sportfish*
The In-Fisherman
7819 Highland Scenic Rd.
Baxter, MN 56425-8011
Ph:(218)829-1648
Free: 800-260-6397
Fax:(218)829-2371
Co. E-mail: customerservice@imoutdoors.com
URL: http://www.in-fisherman.com
Description: Covers location keys and sight fishing, rattle baits, lures, chuggers, and more. **Availability:** VHS.

1707 ■ *Stream Trout Tactics*
The In-Fisherman
7819 Highland Scenic Rd.
Baxter, MN 56425-8011
Ph:(218)829-1648
Free: 800-260-6397
Fax:(218)829-2371
Co. E-mail: customerservice@imoutdoors.com
URL: http://www.in-fisherman.com
Description: Covers methods and equipment for catching stream trout. **Availability:** VHS.

1708 ■ *Trophy Lake Trout Tactics*
The In-Fisherman
7819 Highland Scenic Rd.
Baxter, MN 56425-8011
Ph:(218)829-1648
Free: 800-260-6397
Fax:(218)829-2371
Co. E-mail: customerservice@imoutdoors.com
URL: http://www.in-fisherman.com
Description: Covers methods and equipment for catching lake trout. **Availability:** VHS.

1709 ■ *The World's Greatest Walleye Lure*
The In-Fisherman
7819 Highland Scenic Rd.
Baxter, MN 56425-8011
Ph:(218)829-1648
Free: 800-260-6397
Fax:(218)829-2371
Co. E-mail: customerservice@imoutdoors.com
URL: http://www.in-fisherman.com
Description: Discusses presentation, triggering, snap jigging, and specialty jigs. **Availability:** VHS.

TRADE SHOWS AND CONVENTIONS

1710 ■ Cincinnati Travel, Sports, and Boat Show
Hart Productions, Inc.
2234 Bauer Rd., Ste. B
Batavia, OH 45103
Ph:(513)797-7900
Free: 877-704-8190
Fax:(513)797-1013
URL: http://www.hartproductions.com
Released: Annual. **Audience:** General public. **Principal Exhibits:** Showcasing a world of travel and recreation featuring vacation travel exhibits, boats, sporting goods, fishing and hunting equipment and seminars. **Dates and Locations:** 2011 Jan 14-23, Cincinnati, OH.

1711 ■ Cleveland Sport, Travel & Outdoor Show
Expositions Inc.
PO Box 550, Edgewater Br.
Cleveland, OH 44107-0550
Ph:(216)529-1300
Fax:(216)529-0311
Co. E-mail: expoinc@oinc.com
URL: http://www.expoinc.com
Released: Annual. **Principal Exhibits:** Sport fishing.

1712 ■ Detroit Boat Show
Michigan Boating Industries Association
32398 5 Mile Rd.
Livonia, MI 48154-6109
Ph:(734)261-0123
Free: 800-932-2628
Fax:(734)261-0880
Co. E-mail: boatmichigan@mbia.org
URL: http://www.mbia.org
Released: Annual. **Audience:** Trade professionals and general public. **Principal Exhibits:** Boats, fishing equipment, boat-related accessories, charter rentals, nautical attire, trailer and outboard motors, and personal watercraft.

1713 ■ Eastern Fishing and Outdoor Exposition
Eastern Fishing and Outdoor Exposition Inc.
PO Box 4720
Portsmouth, NH 03801
Ph:(603)431-4315
Fax:(603)431-1971
Co. E-mail: info@sportshows.com
URL: http://www.sportshows.com
Released: Annual. **Audience:** Metro Boston/ Worcester Market. **Principal Exhibits:** Fishing and outdoor sports.

1714 ■ World Fishing and Outdoor Exposition
Eastern Fishing and Outdoor Exposition Inc.
PO Box 4720
Portsmouth, NH 03801
Ph:(603)431-4315
Fax:(603)431-1971
Co. E-mail: info@sportshows.com
URL: http://www.sportshows.com
Released: Annual. **Audience:** Metro New York City Market. **Principal Exhibits:** Fishing and outdoor sports. **Dates and Locations:** 2011 Mar 03-06, Suffern, NY.

FRANCHISES AND BUSINESS OPPORTUNITIES

1715 ■ Cinnzeo
Cinnaroll Bakeries Ltd.
2140 Pegasus Rd., NE
Calgary, AB, Canada T2E 8G8
Ph:(403)255-4556
Free: 877-246-6036
Fax:(403)259-5124
No. of Franchise Units: 20. **No. of Company-Owned Units:** 4. **Founded:** 1987. **Franchised:** 1998. **Description:** Quick service cinnamon roll bakery. **Equity Capital Needed:** $214,000-$621,000. **Franchise Fee:** $15,000. **Royalty Fee:** 7%. **Financial Assistance:** No. **Training:** Offers 3 weeks at headquarters, 2 weeks at franchise's location with ongoing support.

1716 ■ Desert Moon Fresh Mexican Grill
Desert Moon Holdings Corp., Inc.
521 Berlin Cross Keys Rd., PMB 13
Sicklerville, NJ 08081
Ph:(845)267-3300
Free: 877-564-6362
Fax:(845)267-2548
No. of Franchise Units: 15. **No. of Company-Owned Units:** 3. **Founded:** 1992. **Franchised:** 1999. **Description:** Specializes in Mexican food delicacies. **Equity Capital Needed:** $350,000. **Franchise Fee:** $25,000. **Financial Assistance:** Yes. **Training:** Yes.

1717 ■ White Hen Pantry, Inc.
Clark Retail Enterprises Inc.
1722 Routh St., Ste. 1000
Dallas, TX 75201
Ph:(630)366-3100

Fax:(630)366-3447

No. of Franchise Units: 260. **Founded:** 1965. **Franchised:** 1965. **Description:** Convenience food store of approximately 2,500 square feet. Up-front parking for 10-15 cars. Stores are usually open 24 hours (some operate a lesser number of hours) for 365 days a year. Product line includes a service deli, fresh bakery, fresh produce and a wide variety of staples. **Equity Capital Needed:** $40,000-$45,000, not including franchise fee. **Franchise Fee:** $25,000. **Financial Assistance:** Available to qualified candidates. **Managerial Assistance:** Business insurance (group health and plate glass insurance are optional). Store counselor visits regular and frequent. **Training:** 3 weeks of classroom and in-store training precede store opening. Follow-up training provided after taking over store. Detailed operations manuals provided.

LIBRARIES

1718 ■ International Game Fish Association–E.K. Harry Library of Fishes
IGFA Fishing Hall of Fame and Museum, 2nd Fl.
300 Gulf Stream Way
Dania Beach, FL 33004
Ph:(954)927-2628
Fax:(954)924-4299
Co. E-mail: hq@igfa.org
URL: http://www.igfa.org/Museum/IGFA-MUSEUM-LIBRARY.aspx
Contact: Gail M. Morchower, Musm.Mgr.
Scope: Fish, sport fishing. **Services:** Library open to the public for reference use only. **Holdings:** 15,000 books; fishing club yearbooks and newsletters; 2100 fishing videos; stamps; photographs; angling artifacts. **Subscriptions:** 150 journals and other serials.

1719 ■ Virginia Institute of Marine Science–William J. Hargis, Jr. Library
College of William and Mary
School of Marine Science
PO Box 1346
Gloucester Point, VA 23062-1346
Ph:(804)684-7114
Fax:(804)684-7113
Co. E-mail: coughlin@vims.edu
URL: http://web.vims.edu/library/
Contact: Carol Coughlin, Lib.Dir.
Scope: Marine and estuarine biology and ecology, oceanography, aquaculture, Chesapeake Bay. **Services:** Interlibrary loan; copying; Library open to the public. **Holdings:** 29,511 book titles; 30,149 bound periodical volumes; 5007 maps; 51,000 serial volumes. **Subscriptions:** 685 journals and other serials.

Bakery/Doughnut Shop

START-UP INFORMATION

1720 ■ "Hand-Held Heaven: Smallcakes Cupcakery" in *Tulsa World* (February 15, 2011)
Pub: McClatchy Company
Description: Franchisee Carolyn Archer displays her products at Smallcakes Cupcakery, a Jenks shop that's the first to be co-branded with FreshBerry under the Beautiful Brands International banner. The shop's launch is part of a franchise deal between BBI and Jeff and Brandy Martin, co-owners of Smallcakes; twelve concepts have been developed and marketed already by Tulsa-based BBI.

1721 ■ *How to Bake a Business: Recipes to Turn Your Bright Idea Into a Successful Enterprise*
Pub: Allen & Unwin
Ed: Julia Bickerstaff. **Released:** May 10, 2010. **Price:** $17.95. **Description:** Guide to starting and running a successful baker are offered in a purse-size handbook.

1722 ■ *How to Open a Financially Successful Bakery: With a Companion CD-ROM*
Pub: Atlantic Publishing Company
Ed: Sharon Fullen, Douglas R. Brown. **Released:** July 18, 2009. **Price:** $39.95. **Description:** Expert tips, tricks and information is offered to help start and run a bakery.

1723 ■ *My Life From Scratch: A Sweet Journey of Starting Over, One Cake at a Time*
Pub: Broadway Books
Released: June 8, 2010. **Price:** $14.00. **Description:** Lively account of Old World recipes, Bullock-Prado, a former Hollywood film developer and sister to actress Sandra Bullock, recounts the joys and heartbreak of running her own patisserie in Montpelier, Vermont. Having fled Los Angeles with her husband, Ray for the simpler pleasures of a small town near the Green Mountains, she opened her own bake shop, Gesine Confectionary in 2004, mostly on the fame of the macaroons she refashioned from her German mother's favorite almond treat, mandelhoernchen (and the casual mention of her sister in an interview). Her memoir follows one day in a busy baker's life, from waking at 3 a.m. to prepare the batter and bake her croissants, scones, and sticky buns, before opening her shop at 7 a.m., through the hectic lunch, and 3 p.m. tea time.

1724 ■ *The Specialty Shop: How to Create Your Own Unique and Profitable Retail Business*
Pub: AMACOM
Ed: Dorothy Finell. **Released:** February 27, 2007. **Price:** $21.95. **Description:** Advise to start retail businesses, including bakeries, gift shops, toy stores, book shops, tea houses, clothing boutiques, and other unique stores.

1725 ■ "Try a Little Piece of Heaven at this Suffolk Cupcakery" in *Virginia-Pilot* (February 13, 2011)
Pub: McClatchy Company
Ed: Hattie Brown Garrow. **Description:** Profile of Tanya West, owner of the new startup called Divine Creations Cupcakery and Desserts located in Suffolk, Virginia. West is a full-time baker and mother of three children.

ASSOCIATIONS AND OTHER ORGANIZATIONS

1726 ■ AIB International
1213 Bakers Way
PO Box 3999
Manhattan, KS 66505-3999
Ph:(785)537-4750
Free: 800-633-5137
Fax:(785)537-1493
Co. E-mail: aibmarketing@aibonline.org
URL: http://www.aibonline.org
Contact: James Munyon, Pres./CEO
Description: Baking research and educational center. Conducts basic and applied research, educational and hands-on training, and in-plant sanitation and worker safety audits. Maintains museum. Provides bibliographic and reference service. Serves as registrar for ISO-9000 quality certification. **Publications:** *American Institute of Baking—Technical Bulletin* (monthly); *Bakers Way* (quarterly).

1727 ■ American Bakers Association
1300 I St. NW, Ste. 700 W
Washington, DC 20005
Ph:(202)789-0300
Fax:(202)898-1164
Co. E-mail: rmackie@americanbakers.org
URL: http://www.americanbakers.org
Contact: Robb MacKie, Pres./CEO
Description: Manufacturers and wholesale distributors of bread, rolls, and pastry products; suppliers of goods and services to bakers. Conducts seminars and expositions. .

1728 ■ American Society of Baking
PO Box 336
Swedesboro, NJ 08085
Free: 800-713-0462
Fax:888-315-2612
Co. E-mail: info@asbe.org
URL: http://www.asbe.org
Contact: Mr. Kent Van Amburg CAE, Exec. Dir.
Description: Professional organization of persons engaged in bakery production; chemists, production supervisors, engineers, technicians, and others from allied fields. Maintains information service and library references to baking and related subjects. .

1729 ■ Baking Association of Canada–Association Canadienne de la Boulangerie
7895 Tranmere Dr., Ste. 202
Mississauga, ON, Canada L5S 1V9
Ph:(905)405-0288
Free: 888-674-2253
Fax:(905)405-0993
Co. E-mail: info@baking.ca
URL: http://www.bakingassoccanada.com
Contact: Paul Hetherington, Pres./CEO
Description: Bakeries. Promotes growth and development of the domestic baking industries. Represents the interests of bakers (retail, wholesale, in-store, food service) before industrial and labor organizations, government agencies, and the public. **Publications:** *The Bulletin* (10/year).

1730 ■ Independent Bakers Association
PO Box 3731
Washington, DC 20007
Ph:(202)333-8190
Fax:(202)337-3809
Co. E-mail: independentbaker@yahoo.com
URL: http://www.independentbaker.net/independent-bakersassociation
Contact: Nicholas A. Pyle, Pres.
Description: Trade association representing small-medium wholesale bakers and allied trade members. Represents independent wholesale bakers on federal legislative and regulatory issues. Offers annual Smith-Schaus-Smith internships. **Publications:** *The Independent* (annual); *News Release* (biweekly).

1731 ■ Retail Bakers of America
202 Village Cir., Ste. 1
Slidell, LA 70458
Ph:(985)643-6504
Free: 800-638-0924
Fax:(985)643-6929
Co. E-mail: info@rbanet.com
URL: http://www.retailbakersofamerica.org
Contact: Rick Boone, Pres.
Description: Independent and in-store bakeries, food service, specialty bakeries, suppliers of ingredients, tools and equipment; other. Provides information, management, production, merchandising and small business services. **Publications:** *The Business Owner* (bimonthly).

REFERENCE WORKS

1732 ■ "At This Bakery, Interns' Hope Rises Along With the Bread" in *Chicago Tribune* (October 31, 2008)
Pub: McClatchy-Tribune Information Services
Ed: Mary Schmich. **Description:** Profile of Sweet Miss Givings Bakery and its diverse founder, interns and employees; the bakery was founded by Stan Sloan, an Episcopal priest who started the business to help fund his ministry; Sloan saw a need for jobs for those living with HIV and other disabilities and through the bakery the interns learn the skills needed to eventually find work elsewhere.

1733 ■ "Baxter Baker Wins in Hot Finale of 'Cupcake Wars'" in *Fort Mill Times* (September 13, 2011)
Pub: McClatchy Company
Ed: Jenny Overmann. **Description:** Heather McDonnell, owner of Cupcrazed Cakery, and her assistant Debbie McDonnell, vied for a chance to win $10,000

on the cable network show called "Cupcake Wars", and to serve cupcakes at the album release party for country singer Jennette McCurdy. At the end of the show, the sisters-in-law won the top prize.

1734 ■ "Blue Hill Tavern to Host Baltimore's First Cupcake Camp" in *Daily Record* (August 10, 2011)
Pub: Dolan Company

Ed: Rachel Bernstein. **Description:** Cities joining the trend to host cupcake camps are listed. The camps are open to all individuals wishing to share and eat cupcakes in an open environment.

1735 ■ "Breadwinner Tries on Designer Jeans" in *Houston Business Journal* (Vol. 40, December 18, 2009, No. 32, pp. 1)
Pub: American City Business Journals

Ed: Allison Wollam. **Description:** Chuck Cain, the franchisee who introduced Panera Bread to Houston, Texas has partnered with tax accountant Jim Jacobsen to introduce custom-make Tattu Jeans. As more Tattu Jeans outlets are being planned, Cain is using entrepreneurial lessons learned from Panera Bread in the new venture. Both Panera Bread and Tattu Jeans were opened by Cain during economic downturns.

1736 ■ "Canada's Largest Bakery Officially Opened Today" in *Ecology,Environment & Conservation Business* (October 15, 2011, pp. 7)
Pub: HighBeam Research

Description: Maple Leaf Foods opened Canada's largest commercial bakery in Hamilton, Ontario. The firm's 385,000 square foot Trillium bakery benefits from efficient design flow and best-in-class technologies.

1737 ■ "Cold Stone Creamery Offers New Eight-Layer Ice Cream Cakes" in *Ice Cream Reporter* (Vol. 23, October 20, 2010, No. 11, pp. 2)
Pub: Ice Cream Reporter

Description: Cold Stone Creamery is introducing a new line of eight-layer ice cream cakes, which are crafted with three layers of ice cream, three layers of cake and two mid-layers of mix-ins and finished with frosting and a creative design.

1738 ■ "Cupcake Craze" in *Mail Tribune* (March 2, 2011)
Pub: Southern Oregon Media Group

Ed: Sarah Lemon. **Description:** Gourmet cupcake shops are sprouting up in large cities in Oregon. The Cupcake Company, a family business, is profiled.

1739 ■ "Cupcake Eating Contest Draws World-Class Competitors" in *Waterloo Courier* (April 14, 2011)
Pub: Lee Enterprises

Ed: Amie Steffen. **Description:** World Cupcake Eating Championships were held at the Isle Casino Hotel Waterloo, Iowa, April 23, 2011. Major League Eating reports this to be the first time they've held a cupcake eating contest.

1740 ■ "Cupcake Maker Explains Tricks of the Trade" in *Chattanooga Times/Free Press* (September 6, 2011)
Pub: Chattanooga Publishing Company

Ed: Holly Leber. **Description:** Sunny Burden, head baker at Whipped Cupcakes in Chattanooga, Tennessee creates themed cupcakes as well as traditional ones. Burden finds baking therapeutic.

1741 ■ "Cupcake Maker Grabs Outpost" in *Crain's New York Business* (Vol. 27, August 15, 2011, No. 33, pp. 16)
Pub: Crain Communications Inc.

Ed: Jermaine Taylor. **Description:** Family-owned miniature cupcake maker, Baked by Melissa, singed a ten-year lease, expanding their stores to five. The business was started three years ago by advertising executive Melissa Bushell.

1742 ■ "'Cupcake Wars' TV Show Returns to Hampton Roads" in *Virginian-Pilot* (September 11, 2011)
Pub: McClatchy Company

Ed: Carolyn Shapiro. **Description:** Virginia Beach, Virginia sweet shop called Just Cupcakes and Carolina Cupcakery will compete for prizes on cable TV's Food Network Channel. Carla Hesseltine, owner of Just Cupcakes made it to the final rounds.

1743 ■ "Dunkin' Donuts Franchise Looking Possible for 2011" in *Messenger-Inquirer* (January 2, 2010)
Pub: Messenger-Inquirer

Ed: Joy Campbell. **Description:** Dunkin' Donuts has approved expansion of their franchises in the Owensboro, Kentucky region.

1744 ■ "GoodNews.com and the Little Cupcake Shoppe Support Calgary Food Bank With Unique $1.00 Deal" in *Marketwire Canada* (March 9, 2011)
Pub: Marketwire Canada

Description: Socially-conscious group-buying Website, GoodNews.com has partnered with The Little Cupcake Shoppe in Calgary, to raise funds for the Inter-Faith Food Bank. The fundraiser will feature a half dozen, pre-packaged assorted miniature cupcakes for $1.00. The entire amount is donated to the Calgary Food Bank.

1745 ■ "Hostess Reveals Grand Prize Winner of 'CupCake Jackpot' Promotion" in *Entertainment Close-Up* (August 19, 2011)
Pub: Close-Up Media

Description: Tricia Botbyl was the grand prize winner of the Hostess 'CupCake Jackpot' promotion that asked consumers to 'spin' online to win $10,000. Consumers were asked to vote for their favorite Hostess Brand cupcake flavor.

1746 ■ "How Sweet It Is: a Health Hardship Leads to Cupcake Commerce" in *Black Enterprise* (Vol. 41, August 2010, No. 1, pp. 56)
Pub: Earl G. Graves Publishing Co. Inc.

Ed: Tamara E. Holmes. **Description:** Profile of Andra Hall, entrepreneur who started her cupcake business when her one-year-old daughter suffered from sleep apnea and wanted the flexibility to be with her baby. Hall and her husband refinanced their home in order to start the bakery

1747 ■ "It's all Kosher at Downtown Eatery/Bakery" in *AZ Daily Star* (July 10, 2008)
Pub: Arizona Daily Star

Ed: Valerie Vinyard. **Description:** Rabbi James Botwright and partner Wayne Anderson are profiled. Details of how the partners opened their bakery and eatery in Tucson, Arizona. Botwright, who attended culinary school in San Francisco, learned much from his grandfather who was a pastry chef.

1748 ■ "Katie's Cupcakes to Celebrate One-Year Anniversary" in *Bellingham Business Journal* (Vol. March 2010, pp. 3)
Pub: Sound Publishing Inc.

Description: Katie Swanson, owner of Katie's Cupcakes, celebrated her firm's one-year anniversary with a fundraiser for the Whatcom Humane Society by offering free specialty cupcakes and other special events to the public. The specialty cupcakes will feature either a paw or bone and will be available throughout the month of March.

1749 ■ "Lux Coffees, Breads Push Chains to React" in *Advertising Age* (Vol. 77, June 26, 2006, No. 26, pp. S14)
Pub: Crain Communications, Inc.

Ed: Kate MacArthur. **Description:** Fast-food giants such as McDonald's, Burger King, Dunkin' Donuts and Subway have adjusted their menus in order to become more competitive with gourmet coffee shops and bakeries like Panera Bread and Starbucks which have taken a large share in the market. Statistical data included.

1750 ■ "Nation of Islam Businessman Who Became Manager for Muhamnmad Ali Dies" in *Chicago Tribune* (August 28, 2008)
Pub: McClatchy-Tribune Information Services

Ed: Trevor Jensen. **Description:** Profile of Jabir Herbert Muhammad who died on August 25, after heart surgery; Muhammad lived nearly all his life on Chicago's South Side and ran a number of small businesses including a bakery and a dry cleaners before becoming the manager to famed boxer Mohammad Ali.

1751 ■ "New Zealand Natural Co-Branding with Mrs. Fields" in *Ice Cream Reporter* (Vol. 23, November 20, 2010, No. 12, pp. 2)
Pub: Ice Cream Reporter

Description: Mrs. Fields has partnered with a New Zealand firm to co-brand ice cream and cookies in Australian markets.

1752 ■ "Red Velvet Cupcake Bites" in *CandyIndustry* (Vol. 176, September 2011, No. 9, pp. RC4)
Pub: BNP Media

Description: Taste of Nature's Cookie Dough Bites has launched a new candy called, Red Velvet Cupcake Bites. The new product will feature a cupcake center covered in red frosting; ingredients are listed.

1753 ■ "Toughen Up, Cupcake: You Know Who Plays for Keeps These Days? Cupcake Makers" in *Inc* (Vol. 33, May 2011, No. 4, pp. 100)
Pub: Inc. Magazine

Ed: Burt Helm. **Description:** Cupcake shops are sprouting up everywhere across the nation and Washington, DC seems to be the epicenter for the trend. Profile of a new bakery called Sprinkles, that offers cupcake creations, is featured.

1754 ■ "Two Local Bakers Winners of TV's 'Cupcake Wars'" in *Toledo Blade* (July 6, 2011)
Pub: Toledo Times

Description: Winners of cable network Food Channel's Cupcake Wars, Lori Jacobs and Dana Iliev own Cake in a Cup in Toledo, Ohio. The partners shop features creative cupcakes with names such as Monkey Business, Pretty in Pink, and Tropical Getaway.

1755 ■ "The Ultimate Vending Machine" in *Benzinga.com* (August 15, 2011)
Pub: Benzinga.com

Ed: Benzinga Staff. **Description:** Louis Hecht, a baker from Hombourg-Haut, France is selling fresh-baked bread in vending machines. Each machine holds 90 pre-cooked loaves which are warmed before being delivered to the customer.

STATISTICAL SOURCES

1756 ■ *The Market Outlook for Bakery Products*
Pub: Business Trend Analysts, Inc.

Released: 2005-2006. **Price:** $2195.00. **Description:** Profiles markets for bread, rolls, cakes, pies, cookies, crackers, other sweets, and pretzels. Provides information on consumption patterns, distribution trends, pricing, new products, and advertising strategies. Also contains profiles of leading marketers.

1757 ■ *RMA Annual Statement Studies*
Pub: Robert Morris Associates (RMA)

Released: Annual. **Price:** $175.00 2006-07 edition, $105.00. **Description:** Contains composite balance sheets and income statements for more than 360 industries, including the accounting, auditing, and bookkeeping industries. Also contains five years of comparative historical data for discerning trends. Includes 16 commonly used ratios, computed for most of the size groupings for nearly every industry.

1758 ■ *The U.S. Bread Market*
Pub: MarketResearch.com
Released: 1998. **Price:** $2062.50. **Description:** This report from Packaged Facts analyzes the $21 billion U.S. market for packaged, fresh and frozen bread products, focusing on the increasing diversity of the consumer base and the products marketed.

TRADE PERIODICALS

1759 ■ *American Institute of Baking Technical Bulletin*
Pub: American Institute of Baking
Contact: Janette Gelroth, Mgr
Released: Monthly. **Price:** $100 U.S.; $125 other countries; $20 single issue plus shipping; $20 single issue via email and fax. **Description:** Professional journal covering baking.

1760 ■ *Baker's Rack*
Pub: The Retailer's Bakery Association
Ed: Anna Allen, Editor, sesh@rbanet.com. **Released:** Monthly. **Price:** Included in membership. **Description:** Examines trends and issues in the bakery industry. Features items on bakery production, marketing, business management, and other topics of interest. Recurring features include news of research, meeting reports, a calendar of events, and various columns.

1761 ■ *Baking & Snack*
Pub: Sosland Publishing Co.
Contact: Laurie Gorton, Exec. Ed.
E-mail: lgorton@sosland.com
Ed: Steve Berne, Editor, sberne@sosland.com. **Released:** Monthly, (except January). **Price:** $72 other countries print; Free to qualified subscribers; $36. **Description:** Equipment, engineering, production and formulating magazine for commercial manufacturers of baked and snack foods.

1762 ■ *IDDBA Legis-Letter*
Pub: International Dairy-Deli-Bakery Association
Contact: Roberta Rush
Ed: Carol L. Christison, Editor, cchristison@iddba.org. **Price:** Included in membership. **Description:** Reports on legislative activity concerning the supermarket dairy-deli-bakery industry.

1763 ■ *Milling & Baking News*
Pub: Sosland Publishing Co.
Contact: Jay Sjerven, Sen. Ed.
E-mail: jsjerven@sosland.com
Released: Weekly (Tues.). **Price:** $135 U.S. and Canada; $210 U.S. and Canada 2 years; $290 U.S. and Canada 3 years; $190 out of country; $320 out of country 2 years; $455 out of country 3 years. **Description:** Trade magazine covering the grain-based food industries.

1764 ■ *Pastry Art & Design*
Pub: Haymarket Group Ltd.
Contact: Jeff Dryfoos, Publisher
E-mail: jdryfoos@chocolatiermagazine.com
Ed: Tish Boyle, Editor. **Released:** Bimonthly. **Price:** $50; $100 two years; $60 Canada; $120 Canada for two years; $60 other countries; $120 other countries for two years. **Description:** Trade magazine for professional chefs.

1765 ■ *WrapUp*
Pub: International Dairy-Deli-Bakery Association
Ed: Carol L Christison, Editor, cchristison@iddba.org. **Released:** Quarterly. **Price:** Included in membership. **Description:** Reports on news, activities, and topics of interest to the Association.

VIDEOCASSETTES/ AUDIOCASSETTES

1766 ■ *A Baker's Dozen: 13 European Concepts, 144 Great Ideas!*
International Dairy-Deli-Bakery Association (IDDBA)
636 Science Dr.
PO Box 5528
Madison, WI 53705-0528
Ph:(608)310-5000
Fax:(608)238-6330
Co. E-mail: iddba@iddba.org
URL: http://www.iddba.org
Price: $100.00. **Description:** Merchandising and training video. **Availability:** VHS.

1767 ■ *Bakery High Notes from Europe*
International Dairy-Deli-Bakery Association (IDDBA)
636 Science Dr.
PO Box 5528
Madison, WI 53705-0528
Ph:(608)310-5000
Fax:(608)238-6330
Co. E-mail: iddba@iddba.org
URL: http://www.iddba.org
Price: $100.00. **Description:** Merchandising and training video. **Availability:** VHS.

1768 ■ *Bakery Merchandising 101*
International Dairy-Deli-Bakery Association (IDDBA)
636 Science Dr.
PO Box 5528
Madison, WI 53705-0528
Ph:(608)310-5000
Fax:(608)238-6330
Co. E-mail: iddba@iddba.org
URL: http://www.iddba.org
Price: $50.00. **Description:** Discusses ways for successful promotion and product appeal to help increase bakery sales. **Availability:** VHS.

1769 ■ *Bakery Merchandising Certificate Program*
International Dairy-Deli-Bakery Association (IDDBA)
636 Science Dr.
PO Box 5528
Madison, WI 53705-0528
Ph:(608)310-5000
Fax:(608)238-6330
Co. E-mail: iddba@iddba.org
URL: http://www.iddba.org
Price: $160.00. **Description:** Examines the benefits of suggestive selling, sampling, displays, and event merchandising. **Availability:** VHS.

1770 ■ *Cake Decorating for All Occasions*
Cambridge Educational
c/o Films Media Group
132 West 31st Street, 17th Floor
Ste. 124
New York, NY 10001
Free: 800-257-5126
Fax:(609)671-0266
Co. E-mail: custserve@films.com
URL: http://www.cambridgeol.com
Released: 1987. **Price:** $49.95. **Description:** Just about anyone can learn how to make a beautifully decorated cake by watching this program. Available as two half hour tapes or one 60 minute program. **Availability:** VHS.

1771 ■ *More Knowledge, More Sales*
International Dairy-Deli-Bakery Association (IDDBA)
636 Science Dr.
PO Box 5528
Madison, WI 53705-0528
Ph:(608)310-5000
Fax:(608)238-6330
Co. E-mail: iddba@iddba.org
URL: http://www.iddba.org
Price: $160.00. **Description:** Bakery product knowledge training video. **Availability:** VHS.

1772 ■ *Path to Profit*
International Dairy-Deli-Bakery Association (IDDBA)
636 Science Dr.
PO Box 5528
Madison, WI 53705-0528
Ph:(608)310-5000
Fax:(608)238-6330
Co. E-mail: iddba@iddba.org
URL: http://www.iddba.org
Price: $160.00. **Description:** Analyzes strategies for increasing bakery impulse sales and bottom-line profitability. Discusses how to control shrink and effectively schedule labor. **Availability:** VHS.

1773 ■ *Puff Pastry Dough*
Culinary Institute of America
Video Sales
1946 Campus Drive
Hyde Park, NY 12538
Ph:(845)452-9600
Free: 800-888-7850
Co. E-mail: ciaprochef@culinary.edu
URL: http://www.culinary.edu
Released: 1988. **Price:** $100.00. **Description:** Two different ways of making this type of dough are demonstrated. **Availability:** VHS; 3/4U.

1774 ■ *Service That Sells*
International Dairy-Deli-Bakery Association (IDDBA)
636 Science Dr.
PO Box 5528
Madison, WI 53705-0528
Ph:(608)310-5000
Fax:(608)238-6330
Co. E-mail: iddba@iddba.org
URL: http://www.iddba.org
Price: $160.00. **Description:** Bakery customer service training video. **Availability:** VHS.

1775 ■ *Sit-Up Shaped Cakes*
Cine-Video West
112 Annandale Rd.
Pasadena, CA 91105-1406
Ph:(626)792-0842
Released: 1988. **Description:** A video course in creating special party cakes shaped like upright seated figures, such as clowns. **Availability:** VHS.

1776 ■ *Stay Clean, Stay Safe*
International Dairy-Deli-Bakery Association (IDDBA)
636 Science Dr.
PO Box 5528
Madison, WI 53705-0528
Ph:(608)310-5000
Fax:(608)238-6330
Co. E-mail: iddba@iddba.org
URL: http://www.iddba.org
Price: $160.00. **Description:** Bakery food safety training course. **Availability:** VHS.

1777 ■ *Successful Food Demonstration & Sampling*
International Dairy-Deli-Bakery Association (IDDBA)
636 Science Dr.
PO Box 5528
Madison, WI 53705-0528
Ph:(608)310-5000
Fax:(608)238-6330
Co. E-mail: iddba@iddba.org
URL: http://www.iddba.org
Price: $100.00. **Description:** Presents ways supermarket dairy, deli, bakery and food-service employees can sell more through food demonstrations and sampling. **Availability:** VHS.

TRADE SHOWS AND CONVENTIONS

1778 ■ Dairy-Deli-Bake Seminar and Expo
International Dairy-Deli-Bakery Association
PO Box 5528
Madison, WI 53705-0528
Ph:(608)310-5000
Fax:(608)238-6330
Co. E-mail: iddba@iddba.org
URL: http://www.iddba.org
Released: Annual. **Audience:** Retailers, wholesalers, distributors, brokers, and manufacturers of the dairy, deli, and bakery industry. **Principal Exhibits:** Dairy, deli, and bakery products, packaging, and equipment. **Dates and Locations:** 2011 Jun 05-07, Anaheim, CA.

CONSULTANTS

1779 ■ Isaksen Foodservice Consultants Inc.
11228 Georgia Ave.
Silver Spring, MD 20902-2712
Ph:(301)933-2100

Fax:(301)933-2101
Co. E-mail: isaksen@erols.com
Contact: Rosemarie Kellinger, Vice President
Scope: Consultants to architects, developers, and owners regarding layout and design of food service equipment for health care, elder care, country clubs, bakeries, hotels, hospitals, restaurants, nursing homes, schools, prisons and other institutions, as well as government agencies. Also space planning, lighting and acoustic design, laundry layout and design and food service area construction and installation supervision services. **Publications:** "Contemporary Long Term Care," Oct, 1997; "Pantries Take on Non-Institutional Look"; "Hospitality Profiles," Nov, 1994; "Interview: Ron Isak sen of Isak sen Food services Strategies"; "Food service Equipment and Supplies Specialist," Sep, 1991; "Winning Kitchens Show Their Metal"; "Food service Equipment and Supplies Specialist," Jun, 1991; "Isak sen, Others Devote Time to Charity," Restaurants and Institutions, Feb, 1991; "Nothing Fishy About Proper Seafood Refrigeration," Food service Equipment and Supplies Specialist, Oct, 1990; "Seven Great Kitchen Design Ideas". **Seminars:** Recipe for Success: New Concepts in Nutrition for the Aging; Integration of Food Delivery Systems with Decentralized Cluster Concepts.

FRANCHISES AND BUSINESS OPPORTUNITIES

1780 ■ Atlanta Bread Company, Intl.
1200 Wilson Way SE., Ste. A
Smyrna, GA 30082
Ph:(770)432-0933
Fax:(770)444-1991
No. of Franchise Units: 110. **No. of Company-Owned Units:** 4. FND 1993. **Franchised:** 1995. **Description:** Bakery and cafe. **Equity Capital Needed:** $629,700-$831,300. **Franchise Fee:** $40,000. **Financial Assistance:** No. **Training:** Yes.

1781 ■ Blue Chip Cookies
BDGS, LLC
210 Harrison St.
Loveland, OH 45140
Ph:(513)697-6610
Free: 800-888-9866
Fax:(513)697-2783
Co. E-mail: bluechipcookies@fuse.net
URL: http://www.bluechipcookies.com
No. of Franchise Units: 5. **No. of Company-Owned Units:** 3. **Founded:** 1983. **Franchised:** 1986. **Description:** Cookies, bakery items, ice cream, coffees, depending on model and site. **Equity Capital Needed:** $150,000-$250,000. **Franchise Fee:** $25,000. **Financial Assistance:** Bank SBA assistance. **Training:** Offers 2 weeks of training.

1782 ■ Bojangles' Chicken 'n Biscuits
Bojangles' Restaurants, Inc.
9432 Southern Pine Blvd.
Charlotte, NC 28273
Ph:(704)527-2675
Free: 800-366-9921
Fax:(704)523-6803
Co. E-mail: bojbizopp@crs-services.com
URL: http://www.bojangles.com
No. of Franchise Units: 309. **No. of Company-Owned Units:** 194. **Founded:** 1977. **Franchised:** 1979. **Description:** Fast-service chicken and biscuits restaurant. **Equity Capital Needed:** $500,000 liquid assets; $1,000,000 minimum net worth. **Franchise Fee:** $25,000. **Financial Assistance:** Franchise secures own financing. Different sources are available. **Managerial Assistance:** Ongoing training, marketing, and Operations is part of the franchise support. **Training:** Offers an 5 week training program at as well as a one week training program at Bojangles' University.

1783 ■ Breadsmith
Breadsmith Franchising, Inc.
409 E Silver Spring Dr.
Whitefish Bay, WI 53217
Ph:(414)962-1965
Fax:(414)431-5789
No. of Franchise Units: 33. **No. of Company-Owned Units:** 1. **Founded:** 1992. **Franchised:** 1993. **Description:** Specialty European artisan bakery. **Equity Capital Needed:** $205,000-$329,500. **Franchise Fee:** $30,000. **Financial Assistance:** No. **Training:** Yes.

1784 ■ Cinnzeo
Cinnaroll Bakeries Ltd.
2140 Pegasus Rd., NE
Calgary, AB, Canada T2E 8G8
Ph:(403)255-4556
Free: 877-246-6036
Fax:(403)259-5124
No. of Franchise Units: 20. **No. of Company-Owned Units:** 4. **Founded:** 1987. **Franchised:** 1998. **Description:** Quick service cinnamon roll bakery. **Equity Capital Needed:** $214,000-$621,000. **Franchise Fee:** $15,000. **Royalty Fee:** 7%. **Financial Assistance:** No. **Training:** Offers 3 weeks at headquarters, 2 weeks at franchise's location with ongoing support.

1785 ■ Coffee Time Donuts Inc.
77 Progress Ave.
Toronto, ON, Canada M1P 2Y7
Ph:(416)288-8515
Fax:(416)288-8895
Co. E-mail: franchising@coffeetime.ca
URL: http://www.coffeetime.ca
No. of Franchise Units: 184. **No. of Company-Owned Units:** 18. **Founded:** 1982. **Franchised:** 1989. **Description:** The menu includes donuts, muffins, croissants, pastries and gourmet blend coffee, soups, chili, salads, sandwiches and various hot and cold beverages. store, serving customers in a warm and efficient manner and fostering good employee relationships. **Equity Capital Needed:** $100,000-$360,000. **Financial Assistance:** No. **Training:** Yes.

1786 ■ Dunkin' Donuts, Inc.
130 Royall St.
Canton, MA 02021
Free: 800-777-9983
Fax:(781)737-4000
No. of Franchise Units: 4,736. **Founded:** 1950. **Franchised:** 1955. **Description:** Retail coffee, donuts, muffins & bagels. **Equity Capital Needed:** $600,000 liquid assets; $1,200,000 net worth. **Franchise Fee:** $40,000. **Financial Assistance:** Yes. **Training:** Yes.

1787 ■ Einstein Bros. Bagels
Einstein Noah Restaurant Group, Inc.
555 Zang St., Ste. 300
Lakewood, CO 80228
URL: http://www.einsteinbros.com/franchising
No. of Franchise Units: 22. **No. of Company-Owned Units:** 345. **Founded:** 1995. **Franchised:** 2006. **Description:** Quick casual bakery segment that offers cuisine at breakfast, lunch or anytime. **Equity Capital Needed:** $2,500,000 net worth; $1,000,000 liquid. **Franchise Fee:** $35,000. **Financial Assistance:** No. **Training:** Solid corporate infrastructure at headquarters, complete training materials, R&D and local support.

1788 ■ Fuddruckers, Inc.
Magic Restaurants
5700 Mopac Expy. S, Ste. C300
Austin, TX 78749
Ph:(512)275-0421
Fax:(512)275-0670
No. of Franchise Units: 99. **No. of Company-Owned Units:** 113. **Founded:** 1980. **Franchised:** 1983. **Description:** Upscale restaurant that serves fresh ground beef patties from on-premises butcher shop and freshly baked buns from on-premises bakery. Breast of chicken, fish fillet, hot dogs, salads, fries, onion rings, fresh cookies, brownies, pies, milk shakes and beverages with unlimited refills are also available. **Equity Capital Needed:** $740,000-$1,500,000 total investment; $1,500,000 net worth, $550,000 cash liquidity. **Franchise Fee:** $50,000. **Royalty Fee:** 5%. **Financial Assistance:** Third party financing available. **Training:** Provides 6 week training program with ongoing support.

1789 ■ Great American Cookies
Mrs. Fields' Original Cookies, Inc.
1346 Oakbrook Dr., Ste. 170
Norcross, GA 30093
Free: 800-524-6444
No. of Franchise Units: 275. **Founded:** 1977. **Franchised:** 1978. **Description:** Franchises chocolate chip cookie stores, located in shopping centers. **Equity Capital Needed:** $185,150-$288,950. **Franchise Fee:** $25,000. **Royalty Fee:** 6%. **Financial Assistance:** Third party financing available. **Training:** Franchisor offers 5 days training at headquarters with ongoing support.

1790 ■ Great Harvest Franchising, Inc.
Great Harvest Franchising, Inc.
28 S Montana St.
Dillon, MT 59725
Ph:(406)683-6842
Free: 800-442-0424
Fax:(406)683-5537
No. of Franchise Units: 229. **Founded:** 1976. **Franchised:** 1978. **Description:** Retail premium bread bakeries, specializing in whole wheat products. **Equity Capital Needed:** $121,624-$569,248. **Franchise Fee:** $35,000. **Financial Assistance:** No. **Training:** Yes.

1791 ■ House of Bread
299 Marsh St.
San Luis Obispo, CA 93401
Ph:(805)801-4853
Free: 800-545-5146
Fax:(805)542-0257
Co. E-mail: bread@houseofbread.com
URL: http://www.houseofbread.com
No. of Franchise Units: 7. **No. of Company-Owned Units:** 1. **Founded:** 1996. **Franchised:** 2000. **Description:** Specialty bread bakery. **Equity Capital Needed:** $100,000 liquid; $300,000 net worth. **Franchise Fee:** $28,000. **Financial Assistance:** Helps create business plans for obtaining bank financing. **Training:** Offers 3+ weeks of hands-on training and ongoing support.

1792 ■ Insomnia Cookies Franchising LLC
650 5th Ave., 31st Fl.
New York, NY 10019
Ph:(212)286-2403
Fax:(866)422-8402
No. of Company-Owned Units: 14. **Founded:** 2002. **Franchised:** 2006. **Description:** Cookies & baked goods stores/late-night delivery. **Equity Capital Needed:** $65,600-$111,400. **Franchise Fee:** $25,000. **Royalty Fee:** 6%. **Financial Assistance:** No. **Training:** Offer 2-3 weeks training at headquarters, 2-3 weeks onsite and ongoing support.

1793 ■ Jo To Go Coffee
Jo to Go America, Inc.
1263 Main St., Ste. 228
Green Bay, WI 54302
Free: (866)568-6461
Fax:(920)482-5623
No. of Franchise Units: 12. **No. of Company-Owned Units:** 6. **Founded:** 1998. **Franchised:** 2001. **Description:** Drive-thru specialty coffee, smoothies and bakery. **Equity Capital Needed:** $133,000-$409,000. **Franchise Fee:** $25,000. **Royalty Fee:** 7
. **Financial Assistance:** Limited third party financing available. **Training:** Provides 1 week at headquarters, 1 week at franchisee's location, 1 week at a corporate store and ongoing support.

1794 ■ Kolache Factory, Inc.
23240 Westheimer Pkwy.
Katy, TX 77494
Ph:(218)829-6188
Fax:(281)829-6813
No. of Franchise Units: 20. **No. of Company-Owned Units:** 21. **Founded:** 1982. **Franchised:** 2000. **Description:** Bakery/cafe specializing in kolaches. **Equity Capital Needed:** $150,000 liquid; $500,000 net. **Franchise Fee:** $35,000. **Financial Assistance:** No. **Training:** Yes.

1795 ■ Lamar's Donuts
Donut Holdings, Inc.
5601 S 27th St., Ste. 202
Lincoln, NE 68512
Ph:(402)420-0203
Free: 800-533-7489
Fax:(402)420-0209
No. of Franchise Units: 28. **No. of Company-Owned Units:** 4. **Founded:** 1960. **Franchised:** 1993. **Description:** Donuts, specialties and gourmet coffee. **Equity Capital Needed:** $290,000-$390,000. **Franchise Fee:** $28,500. **Financial Assistance:** No. **Training:** Yes.

1796 ■ Michel's Baguette Bakery Cafe
mmmuffins Canada Corp.
7880 Keele St., Ste. 101
Vaughan, ON, Canada L4K 4G7
Ph:(905)482-7300
Free: 877-434-3223
Fax:(905)482-7330
Co. E-mail: franchise@threecaf.com
URL: http://www.mmmuffins.com
No. of Franchise Units: 9. **No. of Company-Owned Units:** 5. **Founded:** 1980. **Franchised:** 1994. **Description:** International experienced bakers, where international breads, pastries, salads, sandwiches and entrees are prepared around the clock, fresh every day. **Equity Capital Needed:** $400,000-$650,000. **Franchise Fee:** $40,000+ applicable taxes. **Training:** Offers 3 week training program.

1797 ■ mmmuffins
Threecaf Brands Canada Inc.
7880 Keele St., Ste. 101
Vaughan, ON, Canada L4K 4G7
Ph:(905)482-7300
Free: 877-434-3223
Fax:(905)482-7330
Co. E-mail: franchise@threecaf.com
URL: http://www.mmmuffins.com
No. of Franchise Units: 25. **No. of Company-Owned Units:** 3. **Founded:** 1979. **Franchised:** 1980. **Description:** mmmuffins products are freshly baked onsite, every day, served with freshly roasted coffee. With our extensive library of recipes, we can customize your menu to suit customer preferences. **Equity Capital Needed:** $300,000-$400,000. **Franchise Fee:** $25,000+ GST. **Training:** Provides 3 weeks training.

1798 ■ Mrs. Field's Original Cookies, Inc.
1141 W 2400 S
Salt Lake City, UT 84119
Free: (866)643-9491
Fax:(801)736-5936
No. of Franchise Units: 378. **No. of Company-Owned Units:** 147. **Founded:** 1977. **Franchised:** 1990. **Description:** Fresh baked cookies and more. **Equity Capital Needed:** $200,000 net worth; $150,000 liquid. **Franchise Fee:** $30,000. **Financial Assistance:** No. **Training:** Yes.

1799 ■ Nestle Toll House Cafe by Chip
Crest Foods, Inc.
101 W Renner Rd., Ste. 240
Richardson, TX 75082
Ph:(214)495-9533
Fax:(214)853-5347
No. of Franchise Units: 93. **No. of Company-Owned Units:** 1. **Founded:** 2000. **Franchised:** 2000. **Description:** The franchise offers fresh baked cookies, baked goods, coffee, ice cream and smoothies. **Equity Capital Needed:** $157,300-$425,000. **Franchise Fee:** $30,000. **Royalty Fee:** 6%. **Financial Assistance:** Third party financing available. **Training:** Offers 12 days at headquarters and ongoing support.

1800 ■ PJ's Coffee of New Orleans
Raving Brands
109 New Camellia Blvd., Ste. 201
Covington, LA 70433
Ph:(404)351-3500
URL: http://www.pjscoffee.com
No. of Franchise Units: 107. **No. of Company-Owned Units:** 1. **Founded:** 1978. **Franchised:** 1989. **Description:** Founded in New Orleans, PJ's has been brewing its distinguished brand of signature roasts for over 25 years. Our beans are hand-selected, hand-roasted and brewed to perfection. PJ's also offers a variety of gourmet pastries and deserts. **Equity Capital Needed:** $400,000 net worth; $100,000 liquid assets. **Franchise Fee:** $25,000. **Financial Assistance:** Relationships with multiple financial institutions with experience in assisting franchisees. **Training:** Raving Brands University classroom and onsite training provided. From register operation to food preparation, from hiring staff to accounting procedures, you'll improve your management skills, setup your back office and develop an airtight sales and marketing plan.

1801 ■ Robin's Donuts
Robin's Foods, Inc.
77 Progress Ave.
Toronto, ON, Canada M1P 2Y7
Ph:(416)646-0987
Fax:(807)637-7745
No. of Franchise Units: 130. **No. of Company-Owned Units:** 10. **Founded:** 1975. **Franchised:** 1977. **Description:** Coffee house, deli, donuts, pastry, and pies. **Equity Capital Needed:** $130,000. **Franchise Fee:** $25,000. **Financial Assistance:** No. **Training:** Yes.

1802 ■ Saint Cinnamon Bake Shoppe
Saint Cinnamon Bakery Ltd.
350 Esna Park Dr.
Markham, ON, Canada L3R 1H5
Ph:(905)470-1517
Free: 877-490-5916
Fax:(905)470-8112
Co. E-mail: markh@saintcinnamon.com
URL: http://www.saintcinnamon.com
No. of Franchise Units: 97. **No. of Company-Owned Units:** 3. **Founded:** 1986. **Franchised:** 1986. **Description:** Freshly-baked cinnamon rolls made in front of the customer and served immediately from the oven. Served with quality coffees in a kiosk or in-line concept. **Equity Capital Needed:** $144,050-$264,700, approximate total investment. **Franchise Fee:** $25,000. **Financial Assistance:** No. **Training:** Franchisee is provided with both local and national assistance in the format of both master franchisee and franchisor.

1803 ■ Southern Maid Donuts
Southern Maid Donut Flour Co.
3615 Cavalier Dr.
Garland, TX 75042
Ph:(972)272-6425
Free: 800-936-6887
Fax:(972)276-3549
No. of Franchise Units: 90. **Founded:** 1937. **Franchised:** 1939. **Description:** Makes and sells donuts, muffins and other delectable items, as well as coffee, juices and soda drinks. **Equity Capital Needed:** Approximately $50,000. **Franchise Fee:** $5,000. **Financial Assistance:** No. **Training:** Yes.

1804 ■ Tim Hortons
T.H.D. Donut,(Delaware), Inc.
4150 Tuller Rd., Ste. 236
Dublin, OH 43017
Ph:(614)791-4200
No. of Franchise Units: 1,763. **No. of Company-Owned Units:** 130. **Founded:** 1964. **Franchised:** 1965. **Description:** Retail coffee, donut and specialty baked goods chain, with over 800 stores across Canada and the US. Franchisee purchases a turnkey operation, the right to use Tim Horton's trademarks and trade names, as well as a comprehensive 7-8 week training program and ongoing operational and marketing support. **Equity Capital Needed:** $300,000-$734,900, includes franchise fee. **Franchise Fee:** $35,000. **Royalty Fee:** 4.5%. **Financial Assistance:** No. **Managerial Assistance:** Assists with initial store opening and provides ongoing support and guidance of head office personnel. **Training:** A 7-8 week training program is conducted at principal offices in Oakville, ON, Canada. Cost incurred while in training (accommodations, meals, etc.) are the responsibility of the franchisee.

LIBRARIES

1805 ■ American Institute of Baking Information Services Department–Ruth Emerson Library
1213 Bakers Way
PO Box 3999
Manhattan, KS 66502-3999
Ph:(785)537-4750
Free: 800-633-5137
Fax:(785)537-1493
Co. E-mail: information@aibonline.org
URL: http://www.aibonline.org
Scope: Baking science and technology, food chemistry, nutrition. **Services:** Interlibrary loan; Library open to the public for reference use only. **Holdings:** 7000 books; 2500 reference and non-circulating volumes; 3500 bound periodical volumes; 80 VF drawers of unbound material on baking and nutrition. **Subscriptions:** 350 journals and other serials.

1806 ■ American Institute of Food Distribution, Inc.–Information and Research Center
1 Broadway Plaza, 2nd Fl.
Elmwood Park, NJ 07407
Ph:(201)791-5570
Fax:(201)791-5222
Co. E-mail: jkastrinsky@foodinstitute.com
URL: http://www.foodinstitute.com/
Contact: Brian Todd, Pres./CEO
Scope: Food industry. **Services:** Center open to the public on fee basis. **Subscriptions:** 400 journals and other serials.

1807 ■ American Society of Baking Information Service and Library
765 Baywood Dr., Ste. 339
Petaluma, CA 94954
Ph:(707)762-8800
Free: (866)920-9885
Fax:(707)762-9500
Co. E-mail: kbrown@asbe.org
URL: http://www.asbe.org
Contact: Kerwin Kerwin, Exec.Dir.
Scope: Baking and allied subjects. **Holdings:** 10,000 references.

1808 ■ Noble and Associates Library
2155 W. Chesterfield Blvd.
Springfield, MO 65807
Ph:(417)875-5000
Co. E-mail: julie.tumy@noble.net
URL: http://www.noble.net
Contact: Julie Tumy, Pres.
Scope: Food, food service, advertising, construction, agriculture. **Services:** Interlibrary loan; copying; SDI; Library not open to the public. **Holdings:** 500 books; 1000 reports. **Subscriptions:** 300 journals and other serials; 5 newspapers.

RESEARCH CENTERS

1809 ■ American Institute of Baking
PO Box 3999
Manhattan, KS 66505-3999
Ph:(785)537-4750
Free: 800—633-5137
Fax:(785)537-1493
Co. E-mail: info@aibonline.org
URL: http://www.aibonline.org
Contact: James Munyon, Pres./CEO
E-mail: info@aibonline.org
Scope: Nutrition, including effects of ingredients, processing, and baked products on physiological responses in humans; and cereal science, particularly applied technology. Contract research projects include performance characteristics of new and improved ingredients for the baking industry and product and process development utilizing laboratory and pilot bakeries. **Services:** Food Safety/Security Audits and Consulting; ISO 9000 registration; Technical assistance group. **Publications:** AIB Update (quarterly); Newsletter (monthly); Technical bulletins (monthly). **Educational Activities:** Correspondence

and CD-Rom courses, in applied baking, food safety, and maintenance engineering; Courses, in baking and maintenance engineering; Training and professional education, for bakers, food safety auditors, and employee safety personnel; Worldwide seminars, in baking, food safety, nutrition, technology transfer.

Bar/Cocktail Lounge

START-UP INFORMATION

1810 ■ "Thirsty Lion on the Prowl" in *Business Journal Portland* (Vol. 27, November 5, 2010, No. 36, pp. 1)
Pub: Portland Business Journal
Ed: Wendy Culverwell. **Description:** Concept Entertainment Inc.'s impending launch of the Thirsty Lion Pub and Grill at the Washington Square in downtown Portland, Oregon is part of its West Coast expansion plan. A discussion of the planning involved in realizing Thirsty Lion is discussed, along with pub offerings that are expected to be enjoyed by customers.

ASSOCIATIONS AND OTHER ORGANIZATIONS

1811 ■ Beverage Network
44 Pleasant St., Ste. 110
Watertown, MA 02472
Ph:(617)715-9670
Fax:(617)812-7740
Co. E-mail: jcraven@bevnet.com
URL: http://www.bevnet.com
Contact: John Craven, Ed.
Description: Beverage distributors dealing primarily in "new wave specialty non-alcoholic" products and some specialty food items. Serves as a forum for the exchange of information among members. Assists members in identifying new products. .

1812 ■ Distilled Spirits Council of the United States
1250 Eye St. NW, Ste. 400
Washington, DC 20005
Ph:(202)628-3544
Fax:(202)682-8888
Co. E-mail: fcoleman@discus.org
URL: http://www.discus.org
Contact: Dr. Peter H. Cressy, Pres./CEO
Description: Serves as national trade association of producers and marketers of distilled spirits sold in the U.S. Provides statistical and legal data for industry and the public and serves as public information source; conducts educational programs. **Publications:** *Summary of State Laws and Regulations Relating to Distilled Spirits* (biennial).

REFERENCE WORKS

1813 ■ "$100 Million Complex To Be Built...On a Bridge" in *Business Courier* (Vol. 27, November 12, 2010, No. 28, pp. 1)
Pub: Business Courier
Ed: Lucy May. **Description:** A development firm closed a deal with the Newport Southbank Bridge Company for a $100M entertainment complex that will be built on tope of the Purple People Bridge. The proposed project will cover 150,000 square feet with attractions such as restaurants, a boutique hotel, and pubs.

1814 ■ "Bars, Restaurants to Offer Prix Fixe Menus, Space to Race Patrons" in *Boston Business Journal* (Vol. 29, July 22, 2011, No. 11, pp. 1)
Pub: American City Business Journals Inc.
Ed: Alexander Jackson. **Description:** Restaurants and bar owners in Baltimore, Maryland have changed the way they do business as the Baltimore Grand Prix approaches. Owners have gone so far as to offering new services or renting out their entire restaurants to companies for the three-day event in September.

1815 ■ "Beer Stocks Rally on Anheuser, InBev Report" in *Globe & Mail* (February 16, 2007, pp. B3)
Pub: CTVglobemedia Publishing Inc.
Ed: Keith McArthur. **Description:** The stock prices of beer manufacturing industries have increased considerably after impressive profit reports from Anheuser Busch Cos Inc. and InBev SA. Complete analysis in this context is presented.

1816 ■ *Beverage Industry—Annual Manual Issue*
Pub: BNP Media
Released: Annual, Latest edition 2010. **Publication Includes:** List of over 1,700 companies supplying equipment and materials to the soft drink, beer, wine, bottled water, and juice industries; industry associations; bottling and supply franchise companies; beer importers distributors; manufacturers' representatives; soft drink distributors. **Entries Include:** For suppliers—Company name, address, phone, code to indicate products. For associations—Name, address, phone, name of president; some association listings also include meeting date and location and names of other executives. For franchise companies—Name, address, phone, names and titles of executives, number of plants, number of franchised plants, products, foreign involvement. For beer importers and distributors—Name, address, phone, names and titles of key executives, brands handled. For manufacturers' representatives—Name, address, phone, names of contacts, market areas, products represented. **Arrangement:** State associations and supplier associations are geographical; other listings are alphabetical. **Indexes:** Trade name, product/service.

1817 ■ *Beverage World—Buyers Guide Issue*
Pub: Beverage World
Contact: Jeff Cioletti, Editor-in-Chief
E-mail: jcioletti@beverageworld.com
Released: Annual, Latest edition June 2008. **Publication Includes:** List of suppliers to the beverage industry. **Entries Include:** Company name, address. **Arrangement:** Classified by product.

1818 ■ "Big Gains Brewing at Anheuser-Busch InBev" in *Barron's* (Vol. 90, August 30, 2010, No. 35, pp. 34)
Pub: Barron's Editorial & Corporate Headquarters
Ed: Christopher C. Williams. **Description:** Anheuser-Busch InBev is realizing cost synergies and it posted better than expected returns two years after the merger that formed the company. One analyst believes its American depositary receipt could be worth as much as 72 in a year.

1819 ■ "Booze Makers Battle Over Turkey Day" in *Advertising Age* (Vol. 78, October 29, 2007, No. 43, pp. 4)
Pub: Crain Communications, Inc.
Ed: Jeremy Mullman. **Description:** Beer and wine marketers are jockeying for position in regards to the Thanksgiving holiday.

1820 ■ "Canada's New Government Introduces Amendments to Deny Work Permits to Foreign Strippers" in *Canadian Corporate News* (May 16, 2007)
Pub: Comtex News Network Inc.
Description: Honourable Diane Finley, Minister of Citizenship and Immigration, introduced amendments to the Immigration and Refugee Protection Act (IRPA) to help prevent the exploitation and abuse of vulnerable foreign workers, such as strippers.

1821 ■ "Closures Pop Cork on Wine Bar Sector Consolidation" in *Houston Business Journal* (Vol. 40, January 22, 2010, No. 37, pp. A2)
Pub: American City Business Journals
Ed: Allison Wollam. **Description:** Wine bar market in Houston, Texas is in the midst of a major shift and heads toward further consolidation due to the closure of pioneering wine bars that opened in the past decade. The Corkscrew owner, Andrew Adams, has blamed the creation of competitive establishments to the closure which helped wear out his concept.

1822 ■ "Counting on Cornhole: Popular Bean Bag Game Brings Crowds to Bars" in *Boston Business Journal* (Vol. 29, July 15, 2011, No. 10, pp. 1)
Pub: American City Business Journals Inc.
Ed: Alexander Jackson. **Description:** Cornhole game is being used by bars to spur business as the games hikes beer and food sales on slow weekdays. The game is played with two cornhole boards facing each other and is played with one or two people on one team who try to place a bag on the board.

1823 ■ "A Crystal Ball" in *Business Journal Portland* (Vol. 27, December 31, 2010, No. 44, pp. 1)
Pub: Portland Business Journal
Ed: Wendy Culverwell. **Description:** McMenamins Pubs and Breweries has resumed construction of its Crystal Hotel project. The company has been working to convert a former bath house into a 51-room hotel. The hotel is expected to open in 2011.

1824 ■ "Deals Still Get Done at Drake's Coq d'Or" in *Crain's Chicago Business* (Vol. 31, November 17, 2008, No. 46, pp. 35)
Pub: Crain Communications, Inc.
Ed: Shia Kapos. **Description:** Chicago's infamous Coq d'Or, a restaurant and lounge located at the Drake Hotel, is still a favorite establishment for noted executives but the eatery is now trying to cater to

younger professionals through marketing and offering new beverages that appeal to that demographic. Many find it the perfect environment in which to close deals, relax or network.

1825 ■ "Discount Beers Take Fizz Out Of Molson" in *Globe & Mail* (February 10, 2006, pp. B3)
Pub: CTVglobemedia Publishing Inc.
Ed: Omar El Akkad. **Description:** The reasons behind the decline in profits by 60 percent for Molson Coors Brewing Co., during fourth quarter 2005, are presented.

1826 ■ "Eat, Drink and Be a Success" in *Entrepreneur* (Vol. 37, August 2009, No. 8, pp. 70)
Pub: Entrepreneur Media, Inc.
Ed: Joel Holland. **Description:** Profile of Fritz Brogan, who is a full time student but also runs a successful bar and restaurant named Gin & Tonic and Kitchen. The bar was built with their target audience in mind which happens to be Brogan's college friends.

1827 ■ "Executive Decision: Damn the Profit Margins, Sleeman Declares War on Buck-a-Beer Foes" in *Globe & Mail* (January 28, 2006, pp. B3)
Pub: CTVglobemedia Publishing Inc.
Ed: Andy Hoffman. **Description:** The cost savings plans of chief executive officer John Sleeman of Sleeman Breweries Ltd. are presented.

1828 ■ "Fair Exchange" in *Food and Drink* (Winter 2010, pp. 84)
Pub: Schofield Media Group
Ed: Don Mardak. **Description:** Bartering can assist firms in the food and beverage industry to attract new customers, maximize resources, and reduce cash expenses.

1829 ■ "Grape Expectations" in *Canadian Business* (Vol. 80, March 12, 2007, No. 6, pp. 55)
Pub: Rogers Media
Ed: Andrea Jezvovit. **Description:** The emergence of Nova Scotia as one of the leading wine-making places in Canada, in view of its favorable climate for growing grapes, is discussed.

1830 ■ "Hike in Md.'s Alcohol Tax May Be Hard For Lawmakers to Swallow" in *Baltimore Business Journal* (Vol. 28, November 19, 2010, No. 28)
Pub: Baltimore Business Journal
Ed: Emily Mullin. **Description:** Maryland's General Assembly has been reluctant to support a dime-per-drink increase in alcohol tax that was drafted in the 2009 bill if the tax revenue goes into a separate fund. The alcohol tax increase is considered unnecessary by some lawmakers and business leaders due to impending federal spending boosts.

1831 ■ "Homes, Not Bars, Stay Well Tended" in *Advertising Age* (Vol. 79, January 28, 2008, No. 4, pp. 8)
Pub: Crain Communications, Inc.
Ed: Jeremy Mullman. **Description:** Due to the downturn in the economy, consumers are drinking less at bars and restaurants; however, according to the Distilled Spirits Council of the United States, they are still purchasing expensive liquor to keep in their homes.

1832 ■ "I Love L.A." in *Canadian Business* (Vol. 81, December 8, 2008, No. 21, pp. S22)
Pub: Rogers Media Ltd.
Ed: Rachel Pulfer. **Description:** Los Angeles-based Standard Downtown, which was built in the 1950s, has a bar that remains popular to Hollywood celebrities. The Standard L.A., which used to house the former headquarters of Superior Oil, offers Devon's Bourbon Sour.

1833 ■ "Imports Frothing Up Beer Market" in *Globe & Mail* (February 16, 2006, pp. B4)
Pub: CTVglobemedia Publishing Inc.
Ed: Andy Hoffman. **Description:** The reasons behind the rise in market share of beer imports, in Canada, are presented.

1834 ■ "Labatt to Swallow Lakeport" in *Globe & Mail* (February 2, 2007, pp. B1)
Pub: CTVglobemedia Publishing Inc.
Ed: Keith McArthur. **Description:** The decision of Labatt Brewing Company Ltd. to acquire Lakeport Brewing Income Fund for $201.4 million is discussed.

1835 ■ "Lawyers Cash In On Alcohol" in *Business Journal Portland* (Vol. 27, November 19, 2010, No. 38, pp. 1)
Pub: Portland Business Journal
Ed: Andy Giegerich. **Description:** Oregon-based law firms have continued to corner big business on the state's growing alcohol industry as demand for their services increased. Lawyers, who represent wine, beer and liquor distillery interests, have seen their workload increased by 20 to 30 percent in 2009.

1836 ■ "Lee's Launches With Focus on Liqueur-based Ice Creams" in *Ice Cream Reporter* (Vol. 23, August 20, 2010, No. 9, pp. 6)
Pub: Ice Cream Reporter
Description: Lee's Cream Liqueur Ice Cream Parlors launched their grand opening in Old Town Scottsdale in July, featuring premium liqueurs to create adult-only ice creams that can be served on their own or blended into exotic drinks.

1837 ■ "Little Cheer in Holiday Forecast for Champagne" in *Advertising Age* (Vol. 88, November 17, 2008, No. 43, pp. 6)
Pub: Crain Communications, Inc.
Ed: Jeremy Mullman. **Description:** Due to a weak economy that has forced consumers to trade down from the most expensive alcoholic beverages as well as a weak U.S. dollar that has driven already lofty Champagne prices higher, makers of the French sparkling wine are anticipating a brutally slow holiday season.

1838 ■ "Moet, Rivals Pour More Ad Bucks Into Bubbly" in *Advertising Age* (Vol. 88, September 3, 2007, No. 35, pp. 4)
Pub: Crain Communications, Inc.
Ed: Jeremy Mullman. **Description:** In an attempt to revive sluggish sales, champagne companies are raising their advertising budgets, transforming themselves from light-spending seasonal players to year-round heavyweights in the advertising world.

1839 ■ *National Conference of State Liquor Administrators—Official Directory*
Pub: National Conference of State Liquor Administrators
Contact: Pamela D. Salario, Exec. Dir.
E-mail: pamsalario@cox.net
Released: Annual. **Covers:** State alcohol beverage control administrators in 36 jurisdictions in the United States, Puerto Rico, District of Columbia, and Guam. **Entries Include:** Name, office address and phone. **Arrangement:** Geographical.

1840 ■ "A New Flavor for Second Street: Lamberts Chef Backs New Restaurant" in *Austin Business JournalInc.* (Vol. 28, January 2, 2009)
Pub: American City Business Journals
Ed: Sandra Zaragoza. **Description:** Chef Larry McGuire has teamed up with the Icon Group to develop the La Condesa restaurant and the Malverde lounge in the Second Street district. The La Condesa restaurant will be a Mexico City-inspired restaurant, while the Malverde lounge atop the La Condesa will host DJs and live music.

1841 ■ "Nighttime Shuttle to Connect Detroit, Ferndale, Royal Oak" in *Crain's Detroit Business* (Vol. 24, October 6, 2008, No. 40, pp. 24)
Pub: Crain Communications, Inc.
Ed: Nancy Kaffer. **Description:** With hopes of bridging the social gap between the cities and suburbs, Chris Ramos has launched The Night Move, a new shuttle service that will ferry passengers between Royal Oak, Ferndale and downtown Detroit. The cost for a round trip ticket is $12.

1842 ■ "Plan B Saloon Opened New Year's Eve" in *Bellingham Business Journal* (Vol. February 2010, pp. 7)
Pub: Sound Publishing Inc.
Description: Plan B Saloon, located in Bellingham, Washington, opened New Year's Eve 2010. The bar/restaurant will feature classic American food consisting of sandwiches and burgers and will host local musicians on Friday and Saturday nights.

1843 ■ "The Price Is Right: What You Can Learn From the Wine Industry" in *Advertising Age* (Vol. 88, February 11, 2008, No. 6, pp. 14)
Pub: Crain Communications, Inc.
Ed: Lenore Skenazy. **Description:** In California a wine study was conducted in which participants' brains were hooked up to an MRI so researchers could watch what was happening in both the taste centers as well as the pleasure centers; the participants were given three different wines but were told that the samples were from a variety of wines that differed radically in price; surprisingly, the differences did not affect the taste centers of the brain, however, when the participants were told that a sample was more expensive, the pleasure centers were greatly affected.

1844 ■ "Startup to Serve Bar Scene" in *Austin Business JournalInc.* (Vol. 29, December 18, 2009, No. 41, pp. 1)
Pub: American City Business Journals
Ed: Christopher Calnan. **Description:** Startup ATX Innovation Inc. of Austin, Texas has developed a test version of TabbedOut, a Web-based tool that would facilitate mobile phone-based restaurant and bar bill payment. TabbedOut has been tested by six businesses in Austin and will be available to restaurant and bar owners for free. Income would be generated by ATX through a 99-cent convenience charge per transaction.

1845 ■ "To Live and Thrive in L.A." in *Canadian Business* (Vol. 81, October 13, 2008, No. 17, pp. 78)
Pub: Rogers Media Ltd.
Ed: Rachel Pulfer. **Description:** Toronto entrepreneur Shereen Arazm thrived in Los Angeles, California as the queen of nightlife. Arazm holds or has held ownership stakes in bars, nightspots and restaurants that include the Geisha House, Concorde, Shag, Parc and Central, and Terroni L.A.

1846 ■ "The Traveling Godfather: Beam Global Spirits & Wine Inc." in *Canadian Business* (Vol. 81, October 13, 2008, No. 17, pp. S10)
Pub: Rogers Media Ltd.
Ed: Andy Holoway. **Description:** Dan Tullio, director of Canadian Club, is seen as a godfather because he gets to be asked a lot of favors. Tullio gets to immerse himself into other cultures because of his employment as global ambassador of Beam Global Spirits & Wine Inc. Tullio's views, as well as information about him are presented.

1847 ■ "Union, Uneven But Imaginative, Works" in *Crain's Chicago Business* (Vol. 34, September 12, 2011, No. 37, pp. 30)
Pub: Crain Communications Inc.
Ed: Alison Neumer Lara. **Description:** Japanese restaurant, Union Sushi & Barbecue Bar opened in Chicago this year. Union is a hip and urban place for business and leisure diners.

1848 ■ "Waite, Cancer Survivor, Readies Sch'dy 'Big House' after Long Delay" in *Business Review, Albany New York* (October 26, 2007)
Pub: American City Business Journals, Inc.
Ed: Michael DeMasi. **Description:** Stephen Waite, owner of Big House Brewing Company, will be opening its new nightclub called Big House Underground. The nightclub is part of a $3.25 million project Waite started in 2005, which was delayed due to his battle with tonsil cancer. Details of turning the building into a restaurant, bar and nightclub are provided.

1849 ■ "What'll You Have Tonight?" in *Barron's* (Vol. 88, July 4, 2008, No. 28, pp. 22)
Pub: Dow Jones & Co., Inc.
Ed: Neil A. Martin. **Description:** Shares of Diageo could rise by 30 percent a year from June 2008 after it slipped due to U.S. sales worries. The company also benefits from the trend toward more premium alcoholic beverage brands worldwide especially in emerging markets.

SOURCES OF SUPPLY

1850 ■ *Beverage Marketing Directory*
Pub: Beverage Marketing Corp.
Contact: Brian Sudano, Mng. Dir.
Released: Annual, Latest edition 33rd; 2011. **Price:** $1,435, individuals softcover or in PDF format; $5,495, individuals database on CD-ROM; $5,495, Canada database on CD-ROM. **Covers:** Over 25,500 beer wholesalers, wine and spirits wholesalers, soft drink bottlers and franchisors, breweries, wineries, distilleries, alcoholic beverage importers, bottled water companies; and trade associations, government agencies, micro breweries, juice, coffee, tea, milk companies, and others concerned with the beverage and bottling industries; coverage includes Canada. **Entries Include:** Beverage and bottling company listings contain company name, address, phone, names of key executives, number of employees, brand names, and other information, including number of franchisees, number of delivery trucks, sales volume. Suppliers and related companies and organizations listings include similar but less detailed information. **Arrangement:** Geographical. **Indexes:** Personnel, supplier's product, company name.

STATISTICAL SOURCES

1851 ■ *RMA Annual Statement Studies*
Pub: Robert Morris Associates (RMA)
Released: Annual. **Price:** $175.00 2006-07 edition, $105.00. **Description:** Contains composite balance sheets and income statements for more than 360 industries, including the accounting, auditing, and bookkeeping industries. Also contains five years of comparative historical data for discerning trends. Includes 16 commonly used ratios, computed for most of the size groupings for nearly every industry.

TRADE PERIODICALS

1852 ■ *Cheers*
Pub: Adams Business Media
Contact: Liza Zimmerman, Editor-in-Chief
E-mail: lzimmerman@m2media360.com
Released: Bimonthly. **Price:** $35 print version only; $50 Canada and Mexico print version only; $130 other countries print version only; $45 print & digital; $60 Canada and Mexico print & digital; $140 other countries print & digital. **Description:** Full service restaurant and bar magazine.

1853 ■ *Cocktails Magazine*
Pub: Destiny Productions for Print, Radio & Cable Promotions
Released: Monthly. **Description:** Trade magazine for the alcohol service industry.

1854 ■ *The Food & Beverage Journal*
Pub: Journal Publications Inc.
Contact: Michael Walsh, Publisher
Ed: Ellen Walsh, Editor, ewalsh@fbworld.com. **Released:** Bimonthly. **Price:** $30; $40 two years. **Description:** Trade magazine for the food and beverage industry in the western U.S.

1855 ■ *Modern Brewery Age*
Pub: Business Journals Inc.
Contact: Mac R. Brighton, Chm., COO
E-mail: macb@busjour.com
Released: Bimonthly. **Price:** $125. **Description:** Magazine for the wholesale and brewing industry.

VIDEOCASSETTES/ AUDIOCASSETTES

1856 ■ *Art of the Cocktail, Part 1*
Tapeworm Video Distributors
25876 The Old Road 141
Stevenson Ranch, CA 91381
Ph:(661)257-4904
Fax:(661)257-4820
Co. E-mail: sales@tapeworm.com
URL: http://www.tapeworm.com
Price: $29.95. **Description:** Offers instruction on cocktail mixing and preparation. **Availability:** VHS.

1857 ■ *Art of the Cocktail, Part 2*
Tapeworm Video Distributors
25876 The Old Road 141
Stevenson Ranch, CA 91381
Ph:(661)257-4904
Fax:(661)257-4820
Co. E-mail: sales@tapeworm.com
URL: http://www.tapeworm.com
Price: $29.95. **Description:** Offers instruction on cocktail mixing and preparation. **Availability:** VHS.

1858 ■ *Mr. Boston's Official Video Bartender's Guide*
MGM/UA
MGM
10250 Constellation Blvd.
Los Angeles, CA 90067
Ph:(310)449-3000
URL: http://www.mgm.com
Released: 1985. **Price:** $14.98. **Description:** In a bar-hopping romp across the U.S.A. the Glenmore Distillery people offer step-by-step instructions for preparing the world's most popular cocktails and punches. **Availability:** VHS.

1859 ■ *100 Fabulous Cocktails*
Tapeworm Video Distributors
25876 The Old Road 141
Stevenson Ranch, CA 91381
Ph:(661)257-4904
Fax:(661)257-4820
Co. E-mail: sales@tapeworm.com
URL: http://www.tapeworm.com
Released: 1997. **Price:** $19.95. **Description:** Professional bartenders instruct how to prepare and order drinks. **Availability:** VHS.

TRADE SHOWS AND CONVENTIONS

1860 ■ Nightclub & Bar/Beverage Retailer/ Food and Beverage Convention & Tradeshow
Oxford Publishing Inc.
307 W Jackson Ave.
Oxford, MS 38655
Ph:(662)236-5510
Free: 800-247-3881
Fax:(662)236-5541
Co. E-mail: oxfordpublishing@oxpub.com
URL: http://www.oxfordpublishinginc.com
Released: Semiannual. **Audience:** Owners and managers of bars, clubs, and restaurants; corporate executives and food/beverage managers of hotels, resorts, state buyers, retailers. **Principal Exhibits:** Equipment, supplies, and services for nightclubs, restaurants, bars, hotels, casinos, and retailers of alcoholic beverages. **Dates and Locations:** 2011 Mar 08-09, Las Vegas, NV.

CONSULTANTS

1861 ■ GEC Consultants Inc.
4604 Birchwood Ave.
Skokie, IL 60076-3835
Ph:(847)674-6310
Fax:(847)674-3946
Co. E-mail: experts@gecconsultants.com
URL: http://www.gecconsultants.com
Contact: Lloyd M. Gordon, CEO
E-mail: legal@gecconsultants.com
Scope: Consulting in all areas of bar and restaurant operations. Restaurant manager development appraises existing locations or sites. Studies the feasibility of projects. Develop new concepts. Assist in expanding, existing food operations, marketing, expert witness (legal) for hospitality/restaurant industry. **Publications:** "How You Can Fight Back to Minimize This Recession!"; "New Thoughts On Leases"; "The Use of Job Analysis to Actually Reduce Payroll Costs"; "Do You Need a Feasibility Study?"; "Combat Negative Hospitality"; "How To Run A Successful Night club"; "Are Capitalists In Your Cabinet?"; "Marketing For The 21st Century"; "Profitability In The Banquet Industry"; "Starting a Restaurant, Bar or Catering Business"; "How To Find And Retain Suitable Employees"; "26 Things To Do To Plan A Restaurant"; "Wall Fabric or Paint: Decor Magic It's Your Call"; "The Art of Cafe Ambiance"; "Why You Need A Consultant". **Seminars:** How to increase restaurant profit, Member MSPC Speakers Bureau; Raising Capital for New Development and Expansion.

FRANCHISES AND BUSINESS OPPORTUNITIES

1862 ■ Bevinco
505 Consumers Rd., Ste. 510
Toronto, ON, Canada M2J 4V8
Ph:(416)490-6266
Free: 888-238-4626
Fax:(416)490-6899
Co. E-mail: info@bevinco.com
URL: http://www.bevinco.com
No. of Franchise Units: 250. **No. of Company-Owned Units:** 1. **Founded:** 1987. **Franchised:** 1991. **Description:** Liquor inventory control system for bars, restaurants, hotels, clubs, etc. **Equity Capital Needed:** $40,000. **Franchise Fee:** $40,000. **Financial Assistance:** Up to $10,000 for qualified candidates. **Training:** 7 days corporate training in Toronto, 5-10 days regional training with state master franchise.

1863 ■ Boston Bartenders School of America
Boston Bartenders School Associates, Inc.
64 Enterprise Rd.
Hyannis, MA 02601
Free: 800-357-3210
Fax:(508)771-1165
No. of Franchise Units: 10. **No. of Company-Owned Units:** 3. **Founded:** 1968. **Franchised:** 1994. **Description:** Program in mixology and alcohol awareness. **Equity Capital Needed:** $50,000. **Franchise Fee:** $10,000. **Financial Assistance:** Yes. **Training:** Yes.

1864 ■ Bridge Business & Property Brokers, Inc.
60 Knickerbocker Ave.
Bohemia, NY 11716
Ph:888-614-6592
Fax:888-605-5727
Co. E-mail: franchising@bridgebrokers.com
URL: http://www.bridgebrokers.com
No. of Franchise Units: 4. **No. of Company-Owned Units:** 19. **Founded:** 2004. **Franchised:** 2005. **Description:** Specialize in bringing together buyers and sellers of businesses to provide a seamless transfer of ownership. Expertise extends into franchise and business consulting, commercial real estate brokerage, helping find commercial insurance and acquiring loans. **Equity Capital Needed:** $38,000-$63,000. **Franchise Fee:** $25,000. **Royalty Fee:** 6%. **Financial Assistance:** No. **Training:** Offers training program designed to expedite the process of making your employees proficient in the art of business brokering.

1865 ■ Cartoon Cuts
5501 NW 21st Ave., Ste. 410
Ft. Lauderdale, FL 33309
Ph:(954)653-CUTS
Free: 800-701-CUTS
Fax:(954)653-9074
No. of Company-Owned Units: 19. **Founded:** 1991. **Franchised:** 2001. **Description:** Hair salons for children. **Equity Capital Needed:** $97,000-$216,000. **Franchise Fee:** $25,000. **Financial Assistance:** Yes. **Training:** Yes.

1866 ■ Dooley's
795 Main St., Ste. 200
Moncton, NB, Canada E1C 8P9
Ph:(506)857-8050
URL: http://franchisedirectory.ca
No. of Franchise Units: 90. **Founded:** 1993. **Description:** Each Dooly's features a comfortable atmosphere with a fireplace, cozy sofas, lounge area

and of course, first-class billiard tables. **Equity Capital Needed:** $350,000-$450,000 total investment; $150,000 minimum cash liquidity. **Managerial Assistance:** Weekly marketing summaries offer many suggestions for increasing your business and optimizing your sales force. Local and national marketing programs are available to customize for your market and our in-house marketing team will work with you to develop your local marketing plan. **Training:** Extensive training, both in operations and marketing are provided. Field representatives will help with hiring and training your manager and staff with ongoing training and support through workshops and annual meetings.

1867 ■ Old Chicago Pizza
Rock Bottom Restaurants, Inc.
248 Centennial Pky.
Louisville, CO 80027
Ph:(303)664-4200
Fax:(303)664-4007

No. of Franchise Units: 22. **No. of Company-Owned Units:** 58. **Founded:** 1976. **Description:** Pizza restaurant with a large high energy bar. **Equity Capital Needed:** $3,000,000 net worth; $750,000 available for investment. **Franchise Fee:** $15,000 area+ $40,000 fee. **Financial Assistance:** No. **Training:** Yes.

LIBRARIES

1868 ■ Anheuser-Busch Companies Corporate Library
1 Busch Pl.
St. Louis, MO 63118
Free: 800-342-5283
URL: http://www.anheuser-busch.com
Contact: Ann Lauenstein, Corp.Libn.

Scope: Brewing chemistry, fermentation technology, food and beverage industries, alcohol and alcoholism, yeast, business and industrial management. **Services:** Interlibrary loan. **Holdings:** 50,000 books; 60,000 bound periodical volumes; 100 pamphlet boxes of Annual reports; 25 VF drawers of U.S. and foreign patents; 70 pamphlet boxes of clippings. **Subscriptions:** 1000 journals and other serials.

1869 ■ Coca-Cola Company–The INFOSOURCE
PO Box 1734
Atlanta, GA 30301
Ph:(404)515-4636
Fax:(404)253-4575
Co. E-mail: koinfo@na.ko.com
URL: http://www.coca-cola.com
Contact: Heather Turnbull, Sr.Res.Anl.

Scope: Business, Legal, Marketing, Technical - including beverages, soft drinks, fruit juices, food technology, nutrition, chemistry, engineering.

1870 ■ Distilled Spirits Council of the U.S. Library
1250 Eye St. NW, Ste. 400
Washington, DC 20005
Ph:(202)628-3544
Fax:(202)682-8888
URL: http://www.discus.org/

Scope: Distilled spirits industry, prohibition, temperance movement, alcoholism, liquor laws, alcohol and health/safety issues, moderate drinking, drinking customs. **Services:** Interlibrary loan; copying; Library open to researchers with prior approval. **Holdings:** 3500 volumes; 72 VF drawers of information on subjects and organizations. **Subscriptions:** 225 journals and other serials.

Beauty Supply Center

ASSOCIATIONS AND OTHER ORGANIZATIONS

1871 ■ American Health and Beauty Aids Institute
PO Box 19510
Chicago, IL 60619-0510
Ph:(708)633-6328
Fax:(708)633-6329
Co. E-mail: ahbai1@sbcglobal.net
URL: http://www.ahbai.org
Contact: Clyde Hammond, Chm.

Description: Minority-owned companies engaged in manufacturing and marketing health and beauty aids for the black consumer. Represents the interests of members and the industry before local, state, and federal governmental agencies. Assists with business development and economic progress within the minority community by providing informational and educational resources. Maintains speakers' bureau. Conducts annual Proud Lady Beauty Show. .

1872 ■ Cosmetic Industry Buyers and Suppliers
Elite Packaging
40-E Cotters Ln.
East Brunswick, NJ 08816
Co. E-mail: cibsmail@cibsonline.com
URL: http://www.cibsonline.com
Contact: Charles Marchese, Pres.

Description: Buyers and suppliers of essential oils, chemicals, packaging, and finished goods relative to the cosmetic industry. Enhances growth, stability, prosperity, and protection of the American cosmetic industry through close personal contact and the exchange of ideas and experiences. .

1873 ■ Fashion Group International
8 W 40th St., 7th Fl.
New York, NY 10018
Ph:(212)302-5511
Fax:(212)302-5533
Co. E-mail: cheryl@fgi.org
URL: http://www.fgi.org
Contact: Cheryl Ingersoll, Regional Dir.

Description: Fashion, apparel, accessories, beauty and home industries. Works to advance professionalism in fashion and its related lifestyle industries with a particular emphasis on the role and development of women. Provides a public forum for examination of important contemporary issues in fashion and the business of fashion. Works to present timely information regarding national and global trends and to attain greater recognition of women's achievements in business and to promote career opportunities in fashion.

1874 ■ International Aloe Science Council
8630 Fenton St., Ste. 918
Silver Spring, MD 20910
Ph:(301)588-2420
Fax:(301)588-1174
Co. E-mail: info@iasc.org
URL: http://www.iasc.org
Contact: Chris Hardy, Chm.
Description: Manufacturers and marketers of foods, drugs and cosmetics containing gel of the aloe vera plant. Aims to provide scientific research for support of product claims. Educates members on the plant and its products and uses. Acts as a liaison for government agency regulations on aloe vera business. .

1875 ■ NAGMR
16A Journey, Ste. 200
Aliso Viejo, CA 92656
Ph:(949)859-4040
Fax:(949)855-2973
Co. E-mail: lball@manaonline.org
URL: http://www.nagmr.com
Contact: Jim Lewis, Membership Committee
Description: Consumer products brokers specializing in selling drug, health, beauty aids, and nonfood products to food chains and the same products and grocery items to the nonfood market. .

1876 ■ Personal Care Product Council
1101 17th St. NW, Ste. 300
Washington, DC 20036-4702
Ph:(202)331-1770
Fax:(202)331-1969
Co. E-mail: membership@ctfa.org
URL: http://www.personalcarecouncil.org
Contact: Pamela G. Bailey, Pres./CEO
Description: Manufacturers and distributors of finished cosmetics, fragrances, and personal care products; suppliers of raw materials and services. Provides scientific, legal, regulatory, and legislative services. Coordinates public service, educational, and public affairs activities. **Publications:** *CTFA News* (biweekly); *International Color Handbook*; *International Resource Manual* .

1877 ■ Professional Beauty Association I National Cosmetology Association
15825 N 71st St., Ste. 100
Scottsdale, AZ 85254
Ph:(480)281-0424
Free: 800-468-2274
Fax:(480)905-0708
Co. E-mail: info@probeauty.org
URL: http://www.probeauty.org
Contact: Max Wexler, Exec. Dir.
Description: Manufacturers and manufacturers' representatives of beauty and barber products, cosmetics, equipment, and supplies used in or resold by beauty salons or barbershops. Promotes the beauty industry; works to ensure product safety; disseminates information. Holds educational seminars; organizes charity events. **Publications:** *PBA Progress* (3/year).

REFERENCE WORKS

1878 ■ "avVaa World Health Care Products Rolls Out Internet Marketing Program" in *Health and Beauty Close-Up* (September 18, 2009)
Pub: Close-Up Media
Description: avVaa World Health Care Products, Inc., a biotechnology company, manufacturer and distributor of nationally branded therapeutic, natural health care and skin products, has signed an agreement with Online Performance Marketing to launch of an Internet marketing campaign in order to broaden its presence online. The impact of advertising on the Internet to generate an increase in sales is explored.

1879 ■ "Cross Atlantic Commodities Launches National Internet Marketing Programs" in *Manufacturing Close-Up* (September 8, 2009)
Pub: Close-Up Media

Description: Profile of the Internet campaign recently launched by Cross Atlantic Commodities, Inc., a manufacturer of specialty beauty and health products.

1880 ■ "Freeman Beauty Labs" in *Retail Merchandiser* (Vol. 51, September-October 2011, No. 5, pp. 74)
Pub: Phoenix Media Corporation

Description: Profile of Freeman Beauty Labs, the family owned beauty product developer supplying retailers and salons with quality products. The firm promotes its bath, foot care, hair care, and skincare brands as a whole, not as individual products.

1881 ■ "In the Raw: Karyn Calabrese Brings Healthy Dining to a New Sophisticated Level" in *Black Enterprise* (Vol. 41, September 2010)
Pub: Earl G. Graves Publishing Co. Inc.

Ed: Sonia Alleyne. **Description:** Profile of Karyn Calabrese whose businesses are based in Chicago, Illinois. Calabrese has launched a complete line of products (vitamins and beauty items), services (spa, chiropractic, and acupuncture treatments), and restaurants to bring health dining and lifestyles to a better level.

1882 ■ *Lessons of a Lipstick Queen: Finding and Developing the Great Idea That Can Change Your Life*
Pub: Simon & Schuster

Ed: Poppy King. **Released:** May 1, 2009. **Price:** $14. 00. **Description:** Poppy King tells how she started her lipstick brand at age eighteen. She reveals how she managed to launch her business using a good idea and finding financing, marketing the product and how she became successful.

1883 ■ *The Perfect Scent: A Year Inside the Perfume Industry in Paris and New York*
Pub: Henry Holt and Company

Ed: Chandler Burr. **Released:** 2009. **Price:** $25.00. **Description:** An insiders glimpse at the development of two new fragrances from Hermes and Coty.

1884 ■ "Retail Briefs - Dollar Store Opens in Long Leaf Mall" in *Star-News* (November 5, 2010)
Pub: Star-News Media

Ed: Judy Royal. **Description:** Dollar Delight$ opened a new shop in Long Leaf Mall in Wilmington, North Carolina. The store will carry gift bags, balloons, party supplies, greeting cards, school supplies, health and beauty products, hardware, baby items, toys, Christmas goods, crafts, housewares and jewelry in its inventory.

1885 ■ "Scream Therapy: A Chain of New York City Beauty Stores Perfect Halloween Pop-Ups" in *Inc.* (Vol. 33, October 2011, No. 8, pp. 99)
Pub: Inc. Magazine
Ed: Amy Barrett. **Description:** Ricky's Halloween stores will open 30 temporary stores for about two months, 28 of which are permanent beauty supply shops the rest of the year.

1886 ■ "White Cat Media Tells You Where to Get a Bargain. Now It's Shopping for $1.5 Million" in *Inc.* (March 2008, pp. 48)
Pub: Gruner & Jahr USA Publishing
Ed: Athena Schindelheim. **Description:** Profile of White Cat Media which runs two shopping Websites: SheFinds.com for fashion and beauty items, and MomFinds.com for mothers. The New York City firm reported revenues for 2007 at $400,000 and is looking for funding capital in the amount of $1.7 million.

1887 ■ "Women Prioritize Luxury Spending" in *Marketing to Women* (Vol. 22, July 2009, No. 7, pp. 8)
Pub: EPM Communications, Inc.
Description: In 2008, women spent 7 percent less on luxury items than in the previous year, according to Unity Marketing. Some luxury items, such as facial care products, are faring better than others. Statistical data included.

STATISTICAL SOURCES

1888 ■ *RMA Annual Statement Studies*
Pub: Robert Morris Associates (RMA)
Released: Annual. **Price:** $175.00 2006-07 edition, $105.00. **Description:** Contains composite balance sheets and income statements for more than 360 industries, including the accounting, auditing, and bookkeeping industries. Also contains five years of comparative historical data for discerning trends. Includes 16 commonly used ratios, computed for most of the size groupings for nearly every industry.

1889 ■ *The Skincare Market*
Pub: Rector Press, Ltd.
Contact: Lewis Sckolnick, Pres
Released: 2009. **Price:** Contact Rector Press. and rankings for both mass-market and limited distribution brands; new product trends, advertising and promotion, and packaging trends; distribution channels (both mass-market and prestige outlets); and consumer usage among adults and teenagers.

1890 ■ *Standard & Poor's Industry Surveys*
Pub: Standard & Poor's Corp.
Released: Annual. **Price:** $3633.00. **Description:** Two-volume book that examines the prospects for specific industries, including trucking. Also provides analyses of trends and problems, statistical tables and charts, and comparative company analyses.

1891 ■ *Suncare - U.S. Report*
Pub: MarketResearch.com
Released: 2008. **Price:** $3995.00. **Description:** This report addresses all the key issues affecting the suncare market, such as the combining of suncare and skincare products, the difficulty attracting teens to suncare products, and how consumer education continues to impact sales.

TRADE PERIODICALS

1892 ■ *Cosmetics & Toiletries*
Pub: Allured Publishing Corp.
Contact: Jane Evison, European Accounts managing editorager
E-mail: jane-evison@btconnect.com
Released: Monthly. **Price:** $98; $137 Canada; $189 other countries; $169 two years; $231 Canada two years; $330 other countries two years. **Description:** Trade magazine on cosmetic and toiletries manufacturing with an emphasis on product research and development issues.

1893 ■ *Skin Inc.*
Pub: Allured Publishing Corp.
Released: Monthly. **Price:** $49; $57 Canada; $98 other countries. **Description:** The complete business guide for face and body care.

TRADE SHOWS AND CONVENTIONS

1894 ■ American Association of Cosmetology Schools Annual Conference - AACS Annual Convention & Expo
American Association of Cosmetology Schools
15825 N. 71st St., Ste. 100
Scottsdale, AZ 85254-1521
Ph:(480)281-0431
Free: 800-831-1086
Fax:(480)905-0993
Co. E-mail: dilsah@beautyschools.org
URL: http://www.beautyschools.org
Released: Annual. **Audience:** School owners. **Principal Exhibits:** Beauty supplies and products, and cosmetology services.

FRANCHISES AND BUSINESS OPPORTUNITIES

1895 ■ Beauty Supply Outlet
210-6465 Millcreek Dr.
Mississauga, ON, Canada L5N 5R6
Ph:(905)363-4105
Free: 800-617-3961
Fax:(952)995-3403
Co. E-mail: franchiseleads@regiscorp.com
URL: http://www.regisfranchise.com
No. of Franchise Units: 37. **Founded:** 1993. **Description:** Retails professional hair care and beauty products, professional hair and beauty tools and trendy and elegant accessories. **Equity Capital Needed:** $100,000 in liquid; $300,000 networth. **Franchise Fee:** $25,000. **Training:** Yes.

1896 ■ Chatters Salon
274-28042 Hwy. 11
Red Deer County, AB, Canada T4S 2L4
Ph:(403)342-5055
Free: 888-944-5055
Fax:(403)347-7759
Co. E-mail: franchise@chatters.ca
URL: http://www.chatters.ca
No. of Franchise Units: 90. **No. of Company-Owned Units:** 8. **Founded:** 1988. **Franchised:** 1991. **Description:** Hair salon and beauty supply full salon services with extensive retail component. **Equity Capital Needed:** $400,000$700,000. **Franchise Fee:** $40,000.

1897 ■ Facelogic
200 W State Hwy. 6, Ste. 225
Woodway, TX 76712
Ph:(254)757-1554
Fax:(254)751-9034
No. of Franchise Units: 43. **No. of Operating Units:** 45. **Founded:** 2005. **Franchised:** 2005. **Description:** Skin care. **Equity Capital Needed:** $212,700-$355,600. **Franchise Fee:** $34,900. **Royalty Fee:** 4%. **Financial Assistance:** Limited third party financial assistance. **Training:** 3 days training provided at headquarters, 5 days onsite and ongoing support.

1898 ■ Glamour Secrets
Glamour Secrets Franchising, Inc.
101 Jevlan Dr.
Woodbridge, ON, Canada L4L 8C2
Free: (866)713-7487
Fax:(905)264-2779
No. of Franchise Units: 31. **No. of Company-Owned Units:** 15. **Founded:** 1990. **Franchised:** 1990. **Description:** Retail stores selling exclusive salon beauty products. **Equity Capital Needed:** $175,000-$400,000. **Franchise Fee:** $25,000. **Financial Assistance:** Yes. **Training:** Yes.

1899 ■ The Woodhouse Day Spa
1 O'Connor Plaza., 12th Fl.
Victoria, TX 77901
Free: 877-570-7772
Fax:(361)578-7116
No. of Franchise Units: 24. **No. of Company-Owned Units:** 1. **Founded:** 2001. **Franchised:** 2003. **Description:** Day spa services, bath and body retail products. **Equity Capital Needed:** $402,750-$530,000. **Franchise Fee:** $45,000. **Royalty Fee:** 6%. **Financial Assistance:** Third party financing available. **Training:** Offers 2-3 weeks training and an additional 1-2 days with ongoing support.

LIBRARIES

1900 ■ Avon Products Research Library
1345 Avenue of the Americas
New York, NY 10020
Ph:(212)282-5000
Co. E-mail: mary.warren@avon.com
URL: http://www.avoncompany.com/
Contact: Mary Warren, Res.Libn.
Scope: Cosmetics, packaging, toxicology, dermatology, pharmacology, chemistry, engineering, microbiology. **Services:** Interlibrary loan; SDI; Library open to the public for reference use only on request. **Holdings:** 6500 books; 5000 bound periodical volumes; 6000 U.S. and foreign patents. **Subscriptions:** 300 journals and other serials.

1901 ■ Johnson and Johnson Consumer and Personal Products Worldwide Library
199 Grandview Rd.
Skillman, NJ 08558
Ph:(908)904-3710
Fax:(908)874-1212
URL: http://www.jnj.com/connect/
Contact: Susan Gleckner, Lib.Hd.
Scope: Infant care, health and beauty aids, toiletries, chemistry, pharmaceuticals, oral care, wound care, skin care, dermatology, women's health. **Holdings:** 2000 books; 1500 bound periodical volumes. **Subscriptions:** 400 journals and other serials.

1902 ■ Mary Kay Inc.–Information Resources
16251 N. Dallas Pkwy.
Addison, TX 75001
Ph:(972)687-5527
Fax:(972)687-1643
Co. E-mail: cecilia.armas@mkcorp.com
Contact: Cecilia Armas-Benavidas, Mgr., Info.Rsrcs.
Scope: Cosmetics, dermatology, toxicology, chemistry, business, marketing. **Services:** Interlibrary loan. **Holdings:** 2000 books; 500 bound periodical volumes. **Subscriptions:** 250 journals and other serials.

1903 ■ Revlon Research Center Library
2121 Rte. 27
Edison, NJ 08818
Ph:(732)287-7650
Fax:(732)248-2230
Contact: Ann Van Dine, Libn.
Scope: Cosmetics, soaps, chemistry, perfumery, dermatology, pharmacology, microbiology, aerosols. **Services:** Interlibrary loan; copying; SDI; Library open to the public by appointment. **Holdings:** 11,000 books; 4000 bound periodical volumes. **Subscriptions:** 100 journals and other serials.

Bed and Breakfast Operation

START-UP INFORMATION

1904 ■ *How to Start and Run a B&B: All You Need to Know to Build a Successful Enterprise*
Pub: How To Books
Ed: David Weston; Louise Weston. **Released:** December 2006. **Price:** $24.75. **Description:** Advice is offered for starting and running a Bed and Breakfast operation. Topics include information on planning, budgeting, pricing, regulation and compliance, accounting and taxation, and defining a market.

REFERENCE WORKS

1905 ■ "B&B to Hit SoCo Next Month" in *Austin Business JournalInc.* (Vol. 28, September 5, 2008, No. 25, pp. 1)
Pub: American City Business Journals
Ed: Sandra Zaragoza. **Description:** The KimberModern bed and breakfast will opening Austin's trendy South Congress neighborhood on October 10, 2008. The establishment will have a secured gate instead of a front desk and will let guests enjoy their breakfasts at their leisure unlike hotels that close their early morning breakfasts to guests at a set time.

1906 ■ "B&B Hopes to Appeal to Fiat Execs" in *Crain's Detroit Business* (Vol. 25, June 15, 2009, No. 24, pp. 21)
Pub: Crain Communications Inc. - Detroit
Ed: Daniel Duggan. **Description:** Cobblestone Manor, a ten-room bed and breakfast in Auburn Hills, Michigan is hoping to provide rooms for Fiat executives. The owners have been working with travel organizations to promote the castle-like bed and breakfast which appeals to European visitors.

1907 ■ *Best Places to Stay in New England*
Pub: Houghton Mifflin Books
Ed: Christina Tree, Editor. **Released:** Biennial. **Price:** $19, individuals trade paperback. **Covers:** Over 350 bed and breakfast homes, inns, hotels, farms, and other accommodations; coverage includes Connecticut, Maine, Massachusetts, New Hampshire, Rhode Island, and Vermont. **Entries Include:** Hotel or inn name, owner, address, rates, credit cards accepted, whether children or pets are allowed, description. **Arrangement:** Classified by type of location (lakeside, beach, farm, etc.), then geographical. **Indexes:** Alphabetical, geographical.

1908 ■ *Buying and Running a Guesthouse or Small Hotel*
Pub: Hot To Books Ltd.
Ed: Dan Marshall. **Released:** December 2007. **Price:** $30.00. **Description:** Teaches how to build and enjoy a lifestyle while running a guesthouse or small hotel.

1909 ■ "'Groundhog Day' B & B Likely Will Be Converted Into One In Real Life" in *Chicago Tribune* (October 21, 2008)
Pub: McClatchy-Tribune Information Services
Ed: Carolyn Starks. **Description:** Everton Martin and Karla Stewart Martin have purchased the Victorian house that was featured as a bed-and-breakfast in the 1993 hit move "Groundhog Day"; the couple was initially unaware of the structure's celebrity status when they purchased it with the hope of fulfilling their dream of owning a bed-and-breakfast.

1910 ■ *How to Open a Financially Successful Bed & Breakfast or Small Hotel*
Pub: Atlantic Publishing Company
Ed: Lora Arduser; Douglas R. Brow. **Released:** May 1, 2004. **Price:** $39.95. **Description:** Handbook with CD ROM demonstrates ways to set up, operate and manage a financially successful bed-and-breakfast or small hotel.

1911 ■ *How to Open and Operate a Bed & Breakfast, 8th Edition*
Pub: Globe Pequot Press
Ed: Jan Stankus. **Released:** January 1, 2007 (paperback). **Price:** $18.95 (paperback). **Description:** Handbook outlines how to set up and run a bed and breakfast, whether using a spare room of a home or a small inn.

1912 ■ *How to Start and Operate Your Own Bed-and-Breakfast: Down-To-Earth Advice from an Award-Winning B&B Owner*
Pub: Owl Books
Ed: Martha W. Murphy. **Released:** May 15, 1994. **Price:** $18.00. **Description:** Bed and breakfast owner shares tip for running a successful business.

1913 ■ *INNside Scoop: Everything You Ever Wanted to Know About Bed & Breakfast Inns*
Pub: The B&B and Country Inn Marketplace
Ed: Maxine Pinson. **Released:** December 2002. **Description:** Guide for running a successful bread and breakfast inn.

1914 ■ "Muirhead Farmhouse B & B Owners Get Hospitality Right" in *Chicago Tribune* (July 31, 2008)
Pub: McClatchy-Tribune Information Services
Ed: Glenn Jeffers. **Description:** Profile of the Muirhead Farmhouse, a bed-and-breakfast owned by Mike Petersdorf and Sarah Muirhead Petersdorf; Frank Lloyd Wright designed the historic farmhouse which blends farm life and history into a unique experience that is enhanced by the couple's hospitality.

1915 ■ "Sleep It Off In a Silo B & B" in *Chicago Tribune* (December 14, 2008)
Pub: McClatchy-Tribune Information Services
Ed: Bill Daley. **Description:** Profile of Oregon's Abbey Road Farm bed-and-breakfast which is located on an 82-acre working farm; guests stay in shiny metal farm silos which have been converted into luxury rooms with views of the farm.

1916 ■ *So, You Want to Be an Innkeeper*
Pub: Chronicle Books LLC
Ed: JoAnn M. Bell; Susan Brown, Mary Davies; Pat Hardy. **Released:** March 2004. **Description:** Provides information for aspiring innkeepers, includes information on cottages, luxury properties, and spa services.

1917 ■ "South Lake Tahoe B & B Blocks Out Neveda's Neon" in *Chicago Tribune* (May 18, 2008)
Pub: McClatchy-Tribune Information Services
Ed: Randall Weissman. **Description:** Profile of the Black Bear Inn, a small bed-and-breakfast in South Lake Tahoe owned by Jerry Birdwell and Kevin Chandler; the welcoming ambience is a delightful departure from ski resort hotel rooms. Pricing and further details of the various rooms are described.

1918 ■ *Start and Run a Profitable Bed and Breakfast*
Pub: Self-Counsel Press Inc.
Ed: Monica Taylor, Richard Taylor. **Released:** October 1999. **Description:** Information for starting and running a successful bed and breakfast is presented.

1919 ■ *Upstart Guide to Owning and Managing a Bed and Breakfast*
Pub: Kaplan Publishing
Ed: Lisa Angowski Rogak. **Released:** November 1, 1994. **Description:** Guide for running a profitable bed and breakfast.

TRADE PERIODICALS

1920 ■ *innkeeping*
Pub: Professional Association of Innkeepers International
Ed: Pat Hardy, Editor, ph@paii.org. **Released:** Monthly. **Price:** $95, individuals. **Description:** Addresses topics of interest to innkeepers who own and operate bed and breakfast operations. Recurring features include letters to the editor, news of research, news of educational opportunities, and notices of publications available.

1921 ■ *The Place*
Pub: Inn Room Visitors Magazine
Contact: Suzanne Wilkinson, Advertising Dir
Released: Monthly. **Description:** Visitor magazine covering restaurants, shopping, entertainment, and television listing placed in hotel-motel rooms for travelers.

1922 ■ *Southern Festivals*
Pub: Southern Festivals
Contact: Jim Taylor
Released: Bimonthly. **Description:** A statewide newspaper covering travel and tourism.

COMPUTERIZED DATABASES

1923 ■ *Food Code - Recommendations of the United States Public Health Service Food and Drug Administration*
U.S. Department of Health and Human Services
10903 New Hampshire Ave.
Silver Spring, MD 20993-0002
Free: 888-INFO-FDA
URL: http://www.fda.gov
Description: Contains information on progress made in monitoring and preventing food borne diseases, including requirements for safeguarding public health.

Provides clarification of the food code based on advances in science and reflective of new technologies. Corresponds in part to the printed version *Food Code*, but the electronic version includes 2 additional manuals. **Availability:** Online: U.S. Department of Health and Human Services; CD-ROM: U.S. Department of Commerce; Diskette: U.S. Department of Commerce. **Type:** Full text.

Beekeeping

ASSOCIATIONS AND OTHER ORGANIZATIONS

1924 ■ American Beekeeping Federation
3525 Piedmont Rd., Bldg. 5, Ste. 300
Atlanta, GA 30305
Ph:(404)760-2875
Co. E-mail: info@abfnet.org
URL: http://www.abfnet.org
Contact: David Mendes, Pres.
Description: Commercial and avocational beekeepers, suppliers, bottlers, packers, and others affiliated with the honey industry. Promotes the industry and serves as an representative before legislative bodies; makes recommendations and helps secure appropriations for research programs. Operates the Honey Defense Fund, which works to insure the purity of honey marketed in the U.S. Sponsors American Honey Queen Program. **Publications:** *Bee Culture* (monthly);Newsletter (bimonthly).

1925 ■ Apiary Inspectors of America
32736 180th St.
Starbuck, MN 56381
Ph:(320)239-4725
Free: 800-967-2474
Co. E-mail: don.hopkins@ncagr.gov
URL: http://www.apiaryinspectors.org
Contact: Don Hopkins, Pres.
Description: State and provincial apiarists; individuals interested in beekeeping and bee research are associate members. Seeks to promote and protect the beekeeping industry of North America. Participates in research meetings at United States Department of Agriculture-Science and Educational Administration laboratories. .

1926 ■ Eastern Apicultural Society of North America
142 Cemetery Rd.
Mocksville, NC 27028
Ph:(336)998-2975
Co. E-mail: secretary@easternapiculture.org
URL: http://www.easternapiculture.org
Contact: Susan Fairiss, Sec.
Description: Hobbyist beekeepers and producers of honey; supporting members are manufacturers of beekeeping equipment and packers of honey. Provides an educational program for hobbyist beekeepers and the public on the science of apiculture (beekeeping). .

1927 ■ National Honey Packers and Dealers Association
3301 Rte. 66, Ste. 205, Bldg. C
Neptune, NJ 07753
Ph:(732)922-3008
Fax:(732)922-3590
Co. E-mail: info@nhpda.org
URL: http://www.mytradeassociation.org/nhpda
Description: Represents cooperative and independent processors, packers, and dealers of honey at either the wholesale or retail level. Offers members information on testing facilities for honey analysis. Consults with Department of Agriculture on research programs in the field of honey marketing. .

REFERENCE WORKS

1928 ■ *Bee Culture—Who's Who in Apiculture Issue*
Pub: The A.I. Root Co.
Ed: Kim Flottum, Editor, kim@beeculture.com. **Released:** Annual, April; Latest edition 2008. **Price:** $23.50, U.S. one year; $38.50, individuals foreign surface; $83.50, individuals foreign airmail. **Publication Includes:** List of United States and Canadian government agencies concerned with apiculture, including university, extension and apiary inspectors, and other groups concerned with apiculture. **Entries Include:** For government agencies—Agency name, address; names, titles, phone numbers, e-mail and webpage of key personnel. For associations and other groups—Name, address, name and title of contact. **Arrangement:** Geographical.

1929 ■ "A Busy Little Parasite" in *Hawaii Business* (Vol. 53, March 2008, No. 9, pp. 1)
Pub: Hawaii Business Publishing
Ed: Jason Ubay. **Description:** Bee mites were first sighted in Hawaii by Michael Kliks on April 6, 2007 and have since been a cause of concern for the beekeeping industry and pollinated-dependent crop industry. Hawaii's agricultural industry estimates that the losses due to bee mites may amount to between $42 million and $62 million. Steps taken to address the issue are discussed.

1930 ■ "Buzz Kill" in *Canadian Business* (Vol. 83, August 17, 2010, No. 13-14, pp. 24)
Pub: Rogers Media Ltd.
Ed: Rachel Mendleson. **Description:** Beekeeping industry has been plagued by a massive wave of honeybee deaths since 2006, which pushed upward the cost of per hive-rental. The death of honeybees has put the food supply at risk since it jeopardized the growth of pumpkins, as well as other crops in large acreage. Insights on the Colony Collapse Disorder are outlined.

TRADE PERIODICALS

1931 ■ *American Bee Journal*
Pub: Dadant & Sons Inc.
Released: Monthly. **Price:** $71.10 other countries airmail; $44 foreign , surface mail; $26 U.S. U.S. standard mail; $56.95 Canada airmail; $49.30 two years; $59.30 Canada two years; $85.30 other countries two years. **Description:** Magazine for hobbyist and professional beekeepers. Covers hive management, honey handling, disease control, honey markets, foreign beekeeping, beekeeping history, bee laws, honey plants, marketing, and government beekeeping research.

1932 ■ *American Beekeeping Federation—News Letter*
Pub: American Beekeeping Federation Inc.
Contact: Troy Fore, Executive Director
Ed: Troy H. Fore, Jr., Editor, troyfore@abfnet.org. **Released:** Bimonthly. **Price:** $35, individuals. **Description:** Discusses Federation activities and national problems of the beekeeping industry. Also covers related legislation, regulations, and marketing and production information. Recurring features include news of research, book reviews, and columns titled President's Page, Washington Update, and Honey Queen Program Activities.

1933 ■ *Hive Lights*
Pub: Canadian Honey Council
Contact: Heather Clay
Ed: Heather Clay, Editor. **Released:** Quarterly. **Price:** Included in membership; $25, nonmembers Canada; $30, nonmembers U.S.; $25, libraries. **Description:** Cover topics related to the beekeeping and honey industry. Recurring features include letters to the editor, news of research, a calendar of events, reports of meetings, news of educational opportunities, and job listings.

1934 ■ *Manitoba Beekeeper*
Pub: Manitoba Beekeepers' Association
Ed: Heather Laird, Editor, hlaird@mb.sympatico.ca. **Released:** Quarterly. **Price:** Included in membership; $20, nonmembers. **Description:** Furnishes information about beekeeping. Recurring features include news of research, a calendar of events, reports of meetings, and honey market news.

1935 ■ *The Speedy Bee*
Pub: The Speedy Bee
Contact: Troy H. Fore Jr., Editor & Publisher
E-mail: troyfore@jesup.net
Released: Quarterly. **Price:** $17.25. **Description:** Monthly trade newspaper for the beekeeping and honey industry.

1936 ■ *The Sting*
Pub: Ontario Beekeepers' Association
Contact: Pat Westlake, Business Administrator
Released: Bimonthly. **Price:** Included in membership. **Description:** Provides news and information for beekeepers in the Ontario area and beyond. Recurring features include letters to the editor, news of research, a calendar of events, reports of meetings, news of educational opportunities, and job listings.

VIDEOCASSETTES/ AUDIOCASSETTES

1937 ■ *Bee Breeding: The Search for the Perfect Honeybee*
Bullfrog Films, Inc.
PO Box 149
Oley, PA 19547
Ph:(610)779-8226
Free: 800-543-3764
Fax:(610)370-1978
Co. E-mail: video@bullfrogfilms.com
URL: http://bullfrogfilms.com
Released: 1988. **Price:** $250.00. **Description:** A look at the work and genetic advances in bee breeding by Brother Adam, a 90-year-old English monk who stands as the world's foremost bee-breeder. **Availability:** VHS; 3/4U.

TRADE SHOWS AND CONVENTIONS

1938 ■ American Beekeeping Federation Convention
American Beekeeping Federation
3525 Piedmont Rd., Bldg. 5, Ste. 300
Atlanta, GA 30305
Ph:(404)760-2875
Fax:(404)240-0998
Co. E-mail: info@abfnet.org
URL: http://www.abfnet.org

Released: Annual. **Audience:** Trade and general public. **Principal Exhibits:** Products to benefit beekeeping/honey industry; gift packs, equipment, packaging, and bee items.

LIBRARIES

1939 ■ Bee Biology and Systematics Laboratory Library
Utah State University
UMC 5310
Logan, UT 84322
Ph:(435)797-2526
Fax:(435)797-0461
Co. E-mail: tgris@biology.usu.edu
Contact: Terry Griswold
Scope: Bees, pollination, crops, systematics, biology, management and control. **Services:** Library not open to the public. **Holdings:** 17,000 volumes.

1940 ■ Florida Department of Agriculture and Consumer Services–Division of Plant Industry Library
PO Box 147100
1911 SW 34th St.
Gainesville, FL 32608-1268
Ph:(352)372-3505
Fax:(352)955-2301
Co. E-mail: popeb@doacs.state.fl.us
URL: http://www.neflin.org/dpi/default.html
Contact: Beverly Pope, Libn.
Scope: Entomology, apiary, plant pathology, plant inspection, nematology. **Services:** Interlibrary loan; copying; Library open to the public for reference use only. **Holdings:** 17,000 volumes; 124 microfiche. **Subscriptions:** 417 journals and other serials.

1941 ■ Michigan State University–Special Collections Library
100 Library
East Lansing, MI 48823
Ph:(517)884-6471
Co. E-mail: berg@msu.edu
URL: http://specialcollections.lib.msu.edu/
Contact: Peter I. Berg, Libn./Hd., Spec.Coll.
Scope: American radicalism; history of French monarchy and revolution; Italian Risorgimento history; English 18th-century studies; comic art; popular fiction; early works in criminology, fencing, agriculture, botany, entomology, toxicology, cookery. **Services:** Interlibrary loan; copying; Library open to the public with required identification. **Holdings:** 450,000 volumes; facsimile editions of illuminated manuscripts. **Subscriptions:** 150 journals and newspapers.

1942 ■ University of California, Davis–University Libraries I Special Collections
100 NW Quad
Shields Library, 1st Fl.
Davis, CA 95616-5292
Ph:(530)752-1621
Fax:(916)754-5758
Co. E-mail: dmorrison@ucdavis.edu
URL: http://www.lib.ucdavis.edu/dept/specol/
Contact: Ms. Daryl Morrison, Dept.Hd.
Scope: Reference. **Services:** Copying; collections open to the public for reference use only. **Holdings:** 129,500 books; 17,200 lin.ft. of archives and manuscripts. **Subscriptions:** 40 journals and other serials; 2 newspapers.

Beeper/Paging Service

ASSOCIATIONS AND OTHER ORGANIZATIONS

1943 ■ Canadian Call Management Association
24 Olive St., Unit 10
Grimsby, ON, Canada L3M 2B6
Ph:(905)309-0224
Free: 800-896-1054
Fax:(905)309-0225
Co. E-mail: info@camx.ca
URL: http://www.camx.ca/call-center/index_ang.cfm
Contact: Linda Osip, Exec. Dir.
Description: Call centers and message exchanges. Promotes excellence in the handling of voice and electronic messages. Represents members' interests; facilitates technical advancement in the field of telecommunications. **Publications:** *Advisor* (bimonthly).

1944 ■ PCIA - The Wireless Infrastructure Association
901 N Washington St., Ste. 600
Alexandria, VA 22314-1535
Ph:(703)836-1608
Free: 800-759-0300
Fax:(703)836-1608
Co. E-mail: nancy.touhill@pcia.com
URL: http://www.pcia.com
Contact: Michael T.N. Fitch, Pres./CEO
Description: Promotes the wireless infrastructure, tower and siting industry through advocacy, education, programs, a trade show and other marketplace initiatives. **Publications:** *PCIA Zoning Field Guide: Information and Resources for Tower Siting* .

RESEARCH CENTERS

1945 ■ Virginia Polytechnic Institute and State University–Center for Wireless Telecommunications
466 Whittemore Hall
Virginia Tech
Blacksburg, VA 24061-0111
Ph:(540)231-5096
Fax:(540)231-3004
Co. E-mail: bostian@vt.edu
URL: http://www.cwt.vt.edu
Contact: Charles W. Bostian, Dir.
E-mail: bostian@vt.edu
Scope: Radio frequency (RF) systems and components; antennas; satellite communications; local multipoint distribution services (LMDS); wireless networks; and business, marketing, financial, and regulatory issues affecting wireless telecommunications. **Services:** Analysis and consulting services; Engineering and business planning development. **Publications:** Newsletter (semiannually). **Educational Activities:** Wireless opportunities workshop. **Awards:** Wireless Entrepreneur of the Year.

ASSOCIATIONS AND OTHER ORGANIZATIONS

1946 ■ Adventure Cycling Association
PO Box 8308
Missoula, MT 59807
Ph:(406)721-1776
Free: 800-755-2453
Fax:(406)721-8754
URL: http://www.adventurecycling.org
Contact: Mr. Jim Sayer, Exec. Dir.

Purpose: Focuses on the research, maintenance, and mapping of over 20,000 miles of bicycle touring and mountain biking routes. Efforts are aimed at promoting bicycle adventure travel and educating the public in bicycle usage and safety. **Publications:** *Adventure Cyclist: The Periodical of Bicycle Adventure* (9/year); *Cyclists' Yellow Pages* (annual).

1947 ■ Bicycle Product Suppliers Association
PO Box 187
Montgomeryville, PA 18936
Ph:(215)393-3144
Fax:(215)893-4872
Co. E-mail: bpsa@bpsa.org
URL: http://bpsa.org
Contact: John Nedeau, Pres.

Description: Wholesalers of bicycles, bicycle parts, and accessories; vendor members are manufacturers and suppliers. Affiliate members supply services and products to bicycle retailers. Offers educational programs; compiles statistics and safety information. **Publications:** *Statistical Report* (annual).

1948 ■ League of American Bicyclists
1612 K St. NW, Ste. 800
Washington, DC 20006-2850
Ph:(202)822-1333
Fax:(202)822-1334
Co. E-mail: bikeleague@bikeleague.org
URL: http://www.bikeleague.org
Contact: Andy D. Clarke, Pres.

Description: Bicyclists and bicycle clubs. Promotes bicycling for fun, fitness, and transportation, and works through advocacy and education for a bicycle-friendly America. Represents members' interests. Seeks to bring better bicycling to all communities. **Publications:** *American Bicyclist* (quarterly); *Bike-League News* (bimonthly).

1949 ■ National Bicycle Dealers Association
3176 Pullman St., No. 117
Costa Mesa, CA 92626
Ph:(949)722-6909
Co. E-mail: info@nbda.com
URL: http://nbda.com
Contact: Fred Clements, Exec. Dir.

Description: Represents independent retail dealers who sell and service bicycles. Sponsors workshops and provides programs. .

1950 ■ National Bicycle League
1000 Creekside Plz., Ste. 300
Gahanna, OH 43230
Ph:(614)416-7680
Free: 800-886-BMX1
Fax:(614)750-1212
Co. E-mail: administration@nbl.org
URL: http://www.nbl.org
Contact: Gary Aragon, CEO

Description: BMX racers. (BMX stands for bicycle motocross, a race of unmotorized bicycles on a tight course of 600 to 1,000 ft. over natural terrain that includes steep hills, sharp turns, and jumps.) Aims to establish rules and regulations for BMX races. Sponsors national competitions; distributes number plates to be earned by the top 40 racers. Maintains file on points earned by members in local races; licenses racers according to age class and proficiency. **Publications:** *BMX Today* (monthly).

1951 ■ National Center for Bicycling and Walking
1612 K St. NW, Ste. 802
Washington, DC 20006
Ph:(202)223-3621
Co. E-mail: mark@bikewalk.org
URL: http://www.bikewalk.org
Contact: Mark Plotz, Program Mgr.

Description: Promotes bicycling for transportation and recreation; encourages increased quality and number of local bicycling programs; facilitates communication within the bicycle community. Disseminates information and provides technical assistance to community bicycle activists and city officials involved in bicycle programs. Designs and manages national bicycle promotion campaigns. Studies liability issues; develops guidelines for community bicycle programs; sponsors training seminars and programs for safety and planning professionals; conducts workshops on bicycle safety. Plans to offer advocacy and promotion services to government, industry, consumers, and organizations. **Publications:** *NCBW Forum* (quarterly); *Pro Bike Directory* (periodic); *Pro Bike News* (monthly); *Pro Bike Proceedings* (biennial).

1952 ■ United States Cycling Federation
210 U.S.A. Cycling Point, Ste. 100
Colorado Springs, CO 80919
Ph:(719)434-4200
Fax:(719)434-4300
Co. E-mail: membership@usacycling.org
URL: http://www.usacycling.org
Contact: Steve Johnson, CEO

Description: National governing body for cycling in the United States. Supervises and controls all elite and amateur bicycle championships, including road, track, mountain bike, BMX, and cyclo-cross; Compiles national bicycle racing records. Conducts development camps, coaching education, mechanics and officials training. **Publications:** *Media Guide*; *National Championship Program* (annual); *NORBA Newsletter* (periodic); *Rule Book* (annual); *Take the Lead*; *U.S.A. Cycling Magazine* (bimonthly).

REFERENCE WORKS

1953 ■ *Achieving Planned Innovation: A Proven System for Creating Successful New Products and Services*
Pub: Simon and Schuster

Ed: Frank R. Bacon. **Released:** August 2007. **Price:** $16.95. **Description:** Planned innovation is a disciplined and practical step-by-step sequence of procedures for reaching the intended destination point: successful products. This easy-to-read book explains the system along with an action-oriented program for continuous success in new-product innovations. Five steps outlined include: a disciplined reasoning process; lasting market orientation; proper selection criteria that reflect both strategic and tactical business objectives and goals along with dynamic matching of resources to present and future opportunities, and positive and negative requirements before making major expenditures; and proper organizational staffing. The author explains what to do and evaluating the potential of any new product or service, ranging from ventures in retail distribution to the manufacture of goods as diverse as bicycles, motorcycles, aerospace communication and navigation equipment, small business computers, food packaging, and medical products.

1954 ■ *Cyclists' Yellow Pages*
Pub: Adventure Cycling Association

Ed: Michael Deme, Editor, mdeme@adventurecycling.org. **Released:** Annual. **Price:** Free. **Covers:** Sources of bicycle maps, books, routes, clubs, tour operators, and organizations in the United States, Canada, and foreign countries. **Entries Include:** For sources—Name of agency or organization, address, phone, e-mail, web sites. For publications—Title, name and address of publisher, description, price. For organizations and shops—Name, address, phone, e-mail, description of activities, interests, or offerings. **Arrangement:** Most sections are geographical; others are classified by topic or line of business.

1955 ■ "Riding High" in *Small Business Opportunities* (November 2008)
Pub: Entrepreneur Media Inc.

Ed: Stan Roberts. **Description:** Profile of David Sanborn who found a way to turn his passion for biking into a moneymaking opportunity by opening his own bicycle shops; Sanborn's goal is to become the largest independent bike retailer in the United States.

STATISTICAL SOURCES

1956 ■ *RMA Annual Statement Studies*
Pub: Robert Morris Associates (RMA)

Released: Annual. **Price:** $175.00 2006-07 edition, $105.00. **Description:** Contains composite balance sheets and income statements for more than 360 industries, including the accounting, auditing, and bookkeeping industries. Also contains five years of comparative historical data for discerning trends. Includes 16 commonly used ratios, computed for most of the size groupings for nearly every industry.

TRADE PERIODICALS

1957 ■ *Adventure Cyclist*
Pub: Adventure Cycling Association
Ed: Daniel D'Ambrosio, Editor. **Released:** 9/year. **Description:** Magazine for members of Adventure Cycling Assn.

1958 ■ *Bicycling*
Pub: Bicycling
Contact: Stephen Madden, Editor-in-Chief
Released: 11/yr. **Price:** $11 plus free delivery; $22 two years plus free delivery. **Description:** World's largest magazine about bicycle riding and equipment.

1959 ■ *Cycling Science*
Pub: Penner Publishing
Released: Quarterly. **Price:** $23.95. **Description:** Science journal for the technical cycling enthusiast.

1960 ■ *Mountain Bike Magazine*
Pub: Mountain Bike Magazine
Released: 11/yr. **Price:** $11 U.S.; $22 two years. **Description:** Riding techniques and product information for the mountain bike enthusiast.

1961 ■ *Outspokin'*
Pub: National Bicycle Dealers Association
Ed: John Francis, Editor. **Released:** 10/year. **Price:** Included in membership. **Description:** Offers bicycle retailing and management tips, and provides consumer survey results. Recurring features include Association and industry news.

VIDEOCASSETTES/ AUDIOCASSETTES

1962 ■ *Cycling: Repair, Correct Riding Position & Safety*
Moonbeam Publications, Inc.
PO Box 5150
Traverse City, MI 49696
Ph:(616)922-0533
Free: 800-445-2391
Fax:800-334-9789
Co. E-mail: custserv@moonbeampublications.com
URL: http://www.moonbeampublications.com
Released: 1991. **Price:** $29.95. **Description:** Master bicycle man Ron Sutphin, owner of the United Bicycle Institute, teaches helpful hints for repair, safety and proper riding techniques. **Availability:** VHS.

TRADE SHOWS AND CONVENTIONS

1963 ■ Interbike
VNU Expo (Laguna Beach, California)
310 Broadway
Laguna Beach, CA 92651
Ph:(946)376-6200
Free: 800-486-2701
Fax:(949)497-5290
Co. E-mail: interbike@wyoming.com
URL: http://www.vnuexpo.com
Released: Annual. **Audience:** Owners and managers of cycling and specialty sports retail store. **Principal Exhibits:** Cycling hard goods, gear and accessories. **Dates and Locations:** 2011 Sep 14-16, Las Vegas, NV.

RESEARCH CENTERS

1964 ■ Cornell University–Cornell BioRobotics and Locomotion Laboratory
206 Kimball Hall
Department of Theoretical & Applied Mechanics
Ithaca, NY 14853-1503
Ph:(607)255-7108
Fax:(607)255-2011
Co. E-mail: ruina@cornell.edu
URL: http://ruina.tam.cornell.edu/research/index.htm
Contact: Prof. Andy L. Ruina
E-mail: ruina@cornell.edu
Scope: Bicycles, rowers, robots, and other human powered or human-like machines. Research on the interaction of human muscles with machines, improving comfort, efficiency, and capacity for the production of mechanical work. Current work focuses on human and robotic locomotion and human power output. Studies also include dynamic issues such as balance and steering, and the non-linear dynamics of frictional systems. **Services:** Recycling services for old bicycles. **Publications:** Journal articles.

START-UP INFORMATION

1965 ■ "Pocket Change?" in *Inc.* (Vol. 30, December 2008, No. 12, pp. 28)
Pub: Mansueto Ventures LLC

Ed: Ryan McCarthy. **Description:** Owner of a chain of nine retail billiard showrooms grew his business by starting to deliver pool tables for Sears. The company, consisting of seven retail locations and two warehouses, is now for sale. Details are included.

ASSOCIATIONS AND OTHER ORGANIZATIONS

1966 ■ Billiard and Bowling Institute of America
PO Box 6573
Arlington, TX 76005
Ph:(817)385-8120
Free: 800-343-1329
Fax:(817)633-2940
Co. E-mail: answer@billiardandbowling.org
URL: http://www.billiardandbowling.org
Contact: Phil Cardinale, Pres.

Description: Represents distributors and manufacturers of billiard and bowling equipment. .

1967 ■ Billiard Congress of America
12303 Airport Way, Ste. 140
Broomfield, CO 80021
Ph:(303)243-5070
Free: (866)852-0999
Fax:(303)243-5075
Co. E-mail: rob@bca-pool.com
URL: http://www.bca-pool.com
Contact: Rob Johnson, CEO

Description: Develops rules for pocket billiards. Serves as national clearinghouse for billiard activities. Compiles statistics. **Publications:** *BCA Break and BCA Open Table* (quarterly); *Official Rules and Records Book* (annual).

TRADE PERIODICALS

1968 ■ *BBIA enews*
Pub: Billiards and Bowling Institute of America

Ed: Sebastian Dicasoli, Editor. **Released:** Monthly, 3/year. **Price:** Free. **Description:** Serves as an update on the Institute's programs for manufacturers, distributors, and retailers of billiard and bowling supplies and equipment. Monitors executive changes, special promotions, new products, and trade show activities. Recurring features include member news.

1969 ■ *Billiards Digest*
Pub: Luby Publishing

Released: Monthly. **Price:** $48; $80 two years; $115 other countries for two years; $115 three years. **Description:** Billiards industry magazine.

VIDEOCASSETTES/ AUDIOCASSETTES

1970 ■ *Billiard Basics*
MNTEX Entertainment, Inc.
500 Kirts Blvd.
Troy, MI 48084-5225
Ph:(248)362-4400
Free: 800-786-8777

Released: 1989. **Description:** A comprehensive guide toward the mastery of billiards. **Availability:** VHS.

1971 ■ *Billiards for All Age Groups*
School-Tech Inc.
745 State Cir.
PO Box 1941
Ann Arbor, MI 48106
Free: 800-521-2832
Fax:800-654-4321
Co. E-mail: service@school-tech.com
URL: http://www.schoolmasters.com

Released: 1990. **Price:** $12.95. **Description:** Pool legend Willie Mosconi demonstrates proper hand position and strategies for making those near-impossible shots. **Availability:** VHS.

1972 ■ *Pool 1: Pool School*
ESPN Home Video
ESPN Plz., 935 Middle St.
Bristol, CT 06010
Ph:(860)766-2000
Fax:(860)585-2213
URL: http://www.espn.go.com

Released: 1988. **Price:** $39.95. **Description:** Champions Jim Rempe and Loree Jon Jones offer techniques for beginner to intermediate pool skills. **Availability:** VHS.

1973 ■ *Pool 2: Power Pool*
ESPN Home Video
ESPN Plz., 935 Middle St.
Bristol, CT 06010
Ph:(860)766-2000
Fax:(860)585-2213
URL: http://www.espn.go.com

Released: 1988. **Price:** $39.95. **Description:** Learn control of the cueball via tip position, jumping the ball and other advanced techniques with Jim Rempe and Loree Jon Jones. **Availability:** VHS.

1974 ■ *Pool 3: Trick Shots*
ESPN Home Video
ESPN Plz., 935 Middle St.
Bristol, CT 06010
Ph:(860)766-2000
Fax:(860)585-2213
URL: http://www.espn.go.com

Released: 1988. **Price:** $39.95. **Description:** Six of the game's greatest show you their signature shots and teach you how to perform them. Hosted by Jim Rempe and Loree Jon Jones. **Availability:** VHS.

TRADE SHOWS AND CONVENTIONS

1975 ■ Billiard Congress of America Trade Expo
William T. Glasgow, Inc.
10729 W. 163rd Pl.
Orland Park, IL 60467
Ph:(708)226-1300
Fax:(708)226-1310
Co. E-mail: brian@wtglasgow.com
URL: http://www.wtglasgow.com
Released: Annual. **Principal Exhibits:** Billiards and pocket billiards equipment, supplies, and services. **Dates and Locations:** 2011 Jul 13-15, Las Vegas, NV.

FRANCHISES AND BUSINESS OPPORTUNITIES

1976 ■ American Poolplayers Association, Inc.
1000 Lake St. Louis Blvd., Ste. 325
Lake St. Louis, MO 63367
Ph:(314)625-8611
Free: 800-3RA-CKEM
Fax:(314)625-2975
No. of Franchise Units: 315. **No. of Company-Owned Units:** 2. **Founded:** 1981. **Franchised:** 1982. **Description:** Governing body of amateur pool; sanctions weekly league play for over 120,000 members through a nationwide franchising network. **Equity Capital Needed:** $17,080-$32,650. **Franchise Fee:** $10,000-$22,500. **Royalty Fee:** $2.50/team/wk. **Financial Assistance:** No. **Training:** Yes.

1977 ■ Dooley's
795 Main St., Ste. 200
Moncton, NB, Canada E1C 8P9
Ph:(506)857-8050
URL: http://franchisedirectory.ca
No. of Franchise Units: 90. **Founded:** 1993. **Description:** Each Dooly's features a comfortable atmosphere with a fireplace, cozy sofas, lounge area and of course, first-class billiard tables. **Equity Capital Needed:** $350,000-$450,000 total investment; $150,000 minimum cash liquidity. **Managerial Assistance:** Weekly marketing summaries offer many suggestions for increasing your business and optimizing your sales force. Local and national marketing programs are available to customize for your market and our in-house marketing team will work with you to develop your local marketing plan. **Training:** Extensive training, both in operations and marketing are provided. Field representatives will help with hiring and training your manager and staff with ongoing training and support through workshops and annual meetings.

1978 ■ West Side Charlie's Bar and Billiards
Churchill Square
PO Box 23071
St. John's, NL, Canada A1B 4J9
Ph:(709)738-4747

Fax:(709)726-4849
Co. E-mail: franchise@westsidecharlies.com
URL: http://www.westsidecharlies.com

No. of Franchise Units: 13. **Founded:** 1996. **Franchised:** 1996. **Description:** Offers customers with an upscale billiard room experience. **Equity Capital Needed:** $150,000-$300,000. **Franchise Fee:** $20,000. **Training:** Offers 1 week and ongoing support.

ASSOCIATIONS AND OTHER ORGANIZATIONS

1979 ■ Asphalt Institute
2696 Research Park Dr.
Lexington, KY 40511-8480
Ph:(859)288-4960
Fax:(859)288-4999
Co. E-mail: info@asphaltinstitute.org
URL: http://www.asphaltinstitute.org
Contact: Mr. Peter T. Grass, Pres.
Description: Composed of petroleum asphalt/bitumen producers, manufacturers and affiliated businesses. Promotes the use, benefits, and quality performance of petroleum asphalt through environmental marketing, research, engineering, and technical development, and through the resolution of issues affecting the industry. **Publications:** *MS-4: The Asphalt Handbook* .

1980 ■ International Slurry Surfacing Association
3 Church Cir.
PMB 250
Annapolis, MD 21401
Ph:(410)267-0023
Fax:(410)267-7546
Co. E-mail: krissoff@slurry.org
URL: http://www.slurry.org
Contact: Michael R. Krissoff, Exec. Dir.
Purpose: Dedicated to the interests, education, and success of slurry surfacing professionals and corporations around the world. Promotes ethics and quality. Provides members with information, technical assistance, and ongoing opportunities for networking and professional development. **Publications:** *Technical Bulletin* (periodic);Membership Directory (annual).

1981 ■ National Asphalt Pavement Association
5100 Forbes Blvd.
Lanham, MD 20706
Ph:(301)731-4748
Free: 877-272-0077
Fax:(301)731-4621
Co. E-mail: napa@hotmix.org
URL: http://www.hotmix.org
Contact: Mike Acott, Pres.
Description: Manufacturers and producers of scientifically proportioned Hot Mix Asphalt for use in all paving, including highways, airfields, and environmental usages. Membership includes hot mix producers, paving contractors, equipment manufacturers, engineering consultants, and others. Supports research and publishes information on: producing, stockpiling, and feeding of the aggregate to the manufacturing facility; drying; methods of screening, storing, and proportioning in the manufacturing facility; production of the hot mix asphalt; transporting mix to paver; lay down procedure and rolling; general workmanship; and related construction practices and materials. Commits to product quality, environmental control, safety and health, and energy conservation. Conducts training programs on a variety of technical and managerial topics for industry personnel. Maintains speakers' bureau and Hot Mix Asphalt Hall of Fame. **Publications:** *National Asphalt Pavement Association—Publications Catalog* (annual);Membership Directory (annual).

REFERENCE WORKS

1982 ■ *Asphalt Emulsion Manufacturers Association—Membership Directory*
Pub: Asphalt Emulsion Manufacturers Association
Contact: Barry Baughman, Pres.
Ed: Michael R. Krissoff, Editor, krissoff@aema.org. **Released:** Biennial, Latest edition 2010-2011. **Covers:** About 100 member manufacturers and their plants and suppliers to the industry; international coverage. **Entries Include:** Company name, address, phone, names and titles of representatives. Plant listings include address and phone. **Arrangement:** Classified by membership type, then alphabetical. Plants are geographical. **Indexes:** Personal name, company name.

1983 ■ *Asphalt Paving Technologists*
Pub: Association of Asphalt Paving Technologists
Ed: Eugene L. Skok, Jr., Editor. **Released:** Annual, Latest edition 2010. **Price:** $25, members; $100, nonmembers. **Covers:** About 850 member engineers and chemists engaged in paving or related fields, such as paving materials and construction equipment; international coverage. **Entries Include:** Name, affiliation, address, phone. **Arrangement:** Alphabetical.

1984 ■ *Asphalt Recycling & Reclaiming Association—Membership Directory*
Pub: Asphalt Recycling & Reclaiming Association
Contact: Michael R. Krissoff, Exec. Dir.
Released: Annual, June. **Covers:** About 200 contractors, manufacturers, consulting engineers, and public works officials involved in asphalt reclaiming and recycling. **Entries Include:** Name of company, address, phone; key personnel; type of organization or company; product line, or contact person. **Arrangement:** By type of membership, then alphabetical. **Indexes:** Personal name, geographical.

1985 ■ "Bridging the Bay" in *Business Journal Serving Greater Tampa Bay* (Vol. 30, November 5, 2010, No. 46, pp. 1)
Pub: Tampa Bay Business Journal
Ed: Mark Holan. **Description:** The Florida Department of Transportation has launched a study to design the proposed addition to the Howard Frankland Bridge. The bridge would be designed to accommodate more than personal vehicles.

1986 ■ "Contracting Firm Sees Timing Right for Expansion" in *Tampa Bay Business Journal* (Vol. 29, November 13, 2009, No. 47, pp. 1)
Pub: American City Business Journals
Ed: Janet Leiser. **Description:** Construction management company Moss & Associates LLC of Fort Lauderdale, Florida has launched its expansion to Tampa Bay. Moss & Associates has started the construction of the Marlins stadium in Miami, Florida's Little Havana section. It also plans to diversify by embarking on other government development, such as health care facilities and airports.

1987 ■ "Contractors Scramble for Jobs" in *Business Journal Portland* (Vol. 26, December 18, 2009, No. 41, pp. 1)
Pub: American City Business Journals Inc.
Ed: Andy Giegerich. **Description:** Contractors in Portland area are expected to bid for capital construction projects that will be funded by municipalities in the said area. Contracts for companies that work on materials handling, road improvement, and public safety structure projects will be issued.

1988 ■ "Downtown Light Rail Plans Up in the Air" in *Business Journal Serving Greater Tampa Bay* (Vol. 30, October 22, 2010, No. 44, pp. 1)
Pub: Tampa Bay Business Journal
Ed: Mark Holan. **Description:** Construction of Tampa's $2 billion light rail transit is suspended pending the result of the November 2, 2010 referendum. The routes, usage, and financing of the light rail project will be decided on the referendum. Whether the light rail will be elevated is also discussed.

1989 ■ "Giant Garages Could Rise Up Downtown" in *Business Courier* (Vol. 27, October 22, 2010, No. 25, pp. 1)
Pub: Business Courier
Ed: Dan Monk. **Description:** More than 2,500 new parking spaces could rise up to the eastern edge of downtown Cincinnati, Ohio as public and private investors collect resources for new garage projects. These projects are expected to accommodate almost 1,500 monthly parkers who will lose access at Broadway Commons due to the construction of Harrah's casino.

1990 ■ "Port Authority Taking Heat in Kenwood Mess" in *Business Courier* (Vol. 26, September 18, 2009, No. 21, pp. 1)
Pub: American City Business Journals, Inc.
Ed: Dan Monk. **Description:** Port of Greater Cincinnati Development Authority is being criticized for not requiring payment and performance bonds to ensure that contractors would be paid. The criticism occurred after the general contractor for the project to build a parking garage at Kenwood Towne Plaza stopped paying its subcontractors.

1991 ■ "A Second Chance at Road Dollars" in *Orlando Business Journal* (Vol. 26, February 5, 2010, No. 36, pp. 1)
Pub: American City Business Journals
Ed: Bill Orben. **Description:** Nearly $10 million worth of construction projects in Central Florida would give construction companies that missed the initial round of federal stimulus-funded local road building projects another opportunity. Cost savings in the initial round of road projects enabled Orange, Osceola, and Seminole Counties to secure additional projects.

SOURCES OF SUPPLY

1992 ■ *Better Roads—Annual Winter Maintenance Equipment & Materials Issue*
Pub: James Informational Media Inc.
Released: Annual, June. **Price:** $95, individuals per year prepaid. **Publication Includes:** List of manufac-

turers of equipment and suppliers of materials and services for winter roads maintenance. Also features information on road agencies, construction/maintenance, and safety. **Entries Include:** Company name, address. **Arrangement:** Alphabetical. **Indexes:** Product/service.

1993 ■ *Parking Products & Services Directory*
Pub: National Parking Association
Contact: Patricia A. Langfeld, Director
E-mail: plangfeld@npapark.org

Released: Annual, Latest edition 2008. **Price:** $25, members; $45, nonmembers. **Covers:** About 300 firms supplying products and services to the parking industry, including about 52 parking consultants. **Entries Include:** Company name, address, phone, fax, product/service descriptions. **Arrangement:** Classified by product/service. **Indexes:** Product/service, trade name.

TRADE PERIODICALS

1994 ■ *The Asphalt Contractor*
Pub: The Asphalt Contractor
Contact: Lisa Cleaver, Managing Editor

Ed: Gregory Udelhofen, Editor. **Released:** Monthly. **Description:** Trade journal for asphalt contractors, asphalt producers, and public work specifiers.

TRADE SHOWS AND CONVENTIONS

1995 ■ National Pavement Maintenance Exposition and Conference
Sellers Expositions
222 Pearl St., Ste. 300
New Albany, IN 47150
Ph:(812)949-9200
Free: 800-558-8767
Fax:(812)949-9600
URL: http://www.sellersexpo.com

Released: Annual. **Audience:** Pavement contractors, distributors, and dealers of pavement maintenance products and equipment, and property owners and managers. **Principal Exhibits:** Pavement maintenance equipment, supplies, and services.

LIBRARIES

1996 ■ Asphalt Institute Research Library
2696 Research Park Dr.
Lexington, KY 40511-8480
Ph:(859)288-4960
Fax:(859)288-4999
Co. E-mail: info@asphatinstitute.org
URL: http://www.asphaltinstitute.org
Contact: Dwight Walker, Assoc.Res.Dir.

Scope: Asphalt - technology, history, industry. **Services:** Library open to serious students by advance application. **Holdings:** 1000 volumes; 288 boxes of fugitive literature. **Subscriptions:** 20 journals and other serials.

1997 ■ Golden Bear Oil Specialties–QC/R & D Library
24152 Park Casino
Calabasas, CA 91302-2538
Ph:(661)393-7110
Fax:(661)392-8584
Contact: Euthene Snell, Libn.

Scope: Petroleum refining, lubricants, asphalt pavements, rubber, emulsions, instrumental analyses. **Services:** Library not open to the public. **Holdings:** 2200 books; 670 bound periodical volumes; 5 catalogs; 5 VF drawers of internal technical reports; preprints; reprints; instrumental scans; 5 VF drawers of patents, technical documents, product development information; 5 VF drawers of government and industry specifications, qualifications, and contracts. **Subscriptions:** 47 journals and other serials.

1998 ■ National Asphalt Pavement Association–Charles R. Foster Technical Library
5100 Forbes Blvd.
Lanham, MD 20706-4413
Ph:(301)731-4748
Free: 888-468-6499
Fax:(301)731-4621
Co. E-mail: napa@hotmix.org
URL: http://www.hotmix.org
Contact: Judy Hornung
Scope: Hot mix asphalt technology and applications, highway engineering. **Services:** Library not open to the public. **Holdings:** Manuals; selected reports (Transportation Research Board, Federal Highway Administration, Federal Aviation Administration, Transport and Road Research Laboratory); selected proceedings; foreign asphalt association publications; 30 VF drawers. **Subscriptions:** 75 journals and other serials.

1999 ■ Saskatchewan Highways and Transportation Library
1855 Victoria Ave., 11th Fl.
Regina, SK, Canada S4P 3V5
Ph:(306)787-4800
Fax:(306)787-8700
Co. E-mail: library@highways.gov.sk.ca
URL: http://www.highways.gov.sk.ca/

Scope: Highway and traffic engineering, transportation, management, traffic safety, rail and air transport; asphalt construction. **Services:** Interlibrary loan; copying; SDI; Library open to the public for reference use only. **Holdings:** 15,000 books. **Subscriptions:** 150 journals and other serials.

2000 ■ U.S. Army–Engineer Research and Development Center–Airfields, Pavements, and Mobility Information Analysis Center (3909)
3909 Halls Ferry Rd.
Vicksburg, MS 39180-6199
Ph:(601)634-2955
Fax:(601)634-3020
Co. E-mail: gsl-info@erdc.usace.army.mil
URL: http://gsl.erdc.usace.army.mil/lgiacs.html
Contact: Gary Anderton, Dir.

Scope: Soil trafficability, mobility, pavements, terrain evaluation. **Services:** Interlibrary loan; copying. **Holdings:** Center is supported by the collection of holdings in the Research Library.

2001 ■ U.S. Army–Engineer Research and Development Center–Research Library (3909)
3909 Halls Ferry Rd.
Bldg. 1000
Vicksburg, MS 39180-6199
Ph:(601)634-2355
Fax:(601)634-2542
Co. E-mail: library-ms@erdc.usace.army.mil
URL: http://itl.erdc.usace.army.mil/library/
Contact: Debbie Carpenter, Libn.

Scope: Hydraulics, soil mechanics, concrete, weapons effects, mobility of vehicles, environmental studies, explosive excavation, pavements, geology, computer science. **Services:** Interlibrary loan; copying; SDI; Center open to the public with restrictions. **Holdings:** 545,100 volumes, including microforms. **Subscriptions:** 1494 journals and other serials.

RESEARCH CENTERS

2002 ■ Auburn University–National Center for Asphalt Technology
277 Technology Pky.
Auburn, AL 36830
Ph:(334)844-6228
Fax:(334)844-6248
Co. E-mail: westran@auburn.edu
URL: http://www.ncat.us
Contact: Randy West PhD, Dir.
E-mail: westran@auburn.edu
Scope: Asphalt technology, including asphalt mixture design and characterization, and asphalt chemistry and material properties. **Educational Activities:** Asphalt Technology (3/year), training course covering asphalt mix design, production and control, construction, pavement design.

2003 ■ Oregon State University–Kiewit Center for Infrastructure and Transportation
220 Owen Hall
Corvallis, OR 97331-3212
Ph:(541)737-4273
Fax:(541)737-3052
Co. E-mail: scott.ashford@oregonstate.edu
URL: http://kiewit.oregonstate.edu
Contact: Prof. Scott A. Ashford PhD, Dir.
E-mail: scott.ashford@oregonstate.edu
Scope: Transportation system economics, regulations, and management; geotechnical engineering and materials testing; transportation system planning, operations, and safety; facility design, construction, and maintenance; transportation for resource development; transportation for persons with disabilities; social impacts of transportation; and environment and energy, including studies on transportation materials and applications of microcomputers. Transportation materials research concerns include alternate surfacings for temporary or intermittent use roads; effect of moisture, aging, and thermal changes on asphalt pavements; modified asphalt; slope stability; and asphalt properties. Microcomputer applications studies include collection and use of data from high-speed traffic monitoring systems, pavement analysis, design, and evaluation with microcomputers, the use of microcomputers to analyze and evaluate traffic operation and safety, the economic feasibility of alternate surfacings, and the performance of Portland cement concrete pavements. **Publications:** Biennial report. **Educational Activities:** Northwest Transportation Conference; Short courses, as part of a continuing education program sponsored by the Oregon Traffic Safety Division; Transportation seminars.

2004 ■ Texas A&M University–Texas Transportation Institute
3135 TAMU
College Station, TX 77843-3135
Ph:(979)845-1713
Fax:(979)845-9356
Co. E-mail: dennis-c@tamu.edu
URL: http://tti.tamu.edu
Contact: Dr. Dennis L. Christiansen, Dir.
E-mail: dennis-c@tamu.edu
Scope: All modes of transportation, including highways, airports, pipelines, waterways, and rail systems. Research areas include all aspects of transportation. **Services:** Contributes to the Texas Transportation Technology Transfer Program. **Publications:** Texas Transportation Researcher (quarterly). **Educational Activities:** Short courses in highway engineering; Traffic engineering schools; Transportation Certificate Program, awarded through Texas A&M University; Undergraduate and graduate instruction in highway, traffic, transportation engineering, and structural mechanics.

2005 ■ University of Texas at Austin–Center for Transportation Research
1616 Guadalupe St., Ste. 4.202, MC D9300
Austin, TX 78701
Ph:(512)232-3100
Fax:(512)232-3153
Co. E-mail: rbm@mail.utexas.edu
URL: http://www.utexas.edu/research/ctr
Contact: Dr. Randy Machemehl, Dir.
E-mail: rbm@mail.utexas.edu
Scope: Coordinates and develops highway, air, rail, pipeline, waterway, intermodal and transportation policy, and mass transportation research activities at the University. Emphasizes improvement of local and state transportation, including studies on optimizing traffic flow, transportation planning and policy, computer methods of structural design, foundation design, alternative fuels, multimodal transportation investment, pavement design, drainage, dynamics of highway loading, safety, and highway structures. Operates a cooperative research program with the Texas Department of Transportation. **Publications:** Annual report. **Educational Activities:** Annual Texas Department of Transportation Symposium, in April, open to the public.

2006 ■ Western Research Institute
365 N 9th St.
Laramie, WY 82072-3380
Ph:(307)721-2011
Free: 888—463-6974
Fax:(307)721-2345
Co. E-mail: don.collins@uwyo.edu
URL: http://www.westernresearch.org
Contact: Donald W. Collins, CEO
E-mail: don.collins@uwyo.edu
Scope: Energy recovery and utilization technology, including engineering research, kinetics and thermodynamics, environmental monitoring, environmental control technology, fossil and alternative fuel technology. Also conducts research on asphalt. **Educational Activities:** Workshops and conferences.

Blind Cleaning/Installation

ASSOCIATIONS AND OTHER ORGANIZATIONS

2007 ■ Home Fashion Products Association
355 Lexington Ave., Ste. 1500
New York, NY 10017-6603
Ph:(212)297-2122
Fax:(212)370-9047
Co. E-mail: contactus@hfpaonline.org
URL: http://www.homefashionproducts.com
Contact: Katie Goshgarian, Exec. Dir.
Description: Manufacturers of curtains, draperies, bedding, rugs and related products. Sponsors annual scholarship for students attending accredited schools in home textiles. .

2008 ■ International Furnishings and Design Association
150 S Warner Rd., Ste. 156
King of Prussia, PA 19406
Ph:(610)535-6422
Fax:(610)535-6423
Co. E-mail: info@ifda.com
URL: http://www.ifda.com
Contact: Janet Stevenson, Pres.
Description: Represents individuals engaged in design, production, distribution, education, promotion and editorial phases of the interior furnishings industry and related fields. Founded IFDA Educational Foundation in 1968. Conducts charitable programs; maintains speakers' bureau. **Publications:** *IFDA Network* (quarterly).

2009 ■ Window Covering Manufacturers Association
355 Lexington Ave., 15th Fl.
New York, NY 10017
Ph:(212)297-2122
URL: http://www.wcmanet.org
Description: Represents corporations engaged in the manufacture or assembly of Venetian blinds, vertical blinds, pleated shades, or their components. Promotes the use, utility, image, and attractiveness of the products and services offered by the window covering industry. .

REFERENCE WORKS

2010 ■ *Draperies & Window Coverings—Directory & Buyer's Guide Issue*
Pub: L.C. Clark Publishing Company Inc.
Ed: Howard Shingle, Editor. **Released:** Annual, fall. **Publication Includes:** List of about 2,000 manufacturers and distributors of window coverings and other products used in the window coverings and interior fashions industry. **Entries Include:** Company name, address, phone, key executives, brand names carried. **Arrangement:** Alphabetical. **Indexes:** Product/service.

FRANCHISES AND BUSINESS OPPORTUNITIES

2011 ■ Blind Man of America
Keller Corp.
606 Fremont Cir.
Colorado Springs, CO 80919
Free: 800-547-9889
Fax:(719)272-4105
No. of Franchise Units: 9. **No. of Company-Owned Units:** 1. **Founded:** 1991. **Franchised:** 1996. **Description:** Mobile window coverings. **Equity Capital Needed:** $45,500-$69,100. **Franchise Fee:** $15,000. **Royalty Fee:** 4.3%. **Financial Assistance:** No. **Training:** Provides 2 weeks at headquarters with ongoing support.

2012 ■ Budget Blinds
Home Franchise Concepts, Inc.
1927 N Glassell St.
Orange, CA 92865
Free: 800-258-7079
No. of Franchise Units: 707. **Founded:** 1992. **Franchised:** 1994. **Description:** Custom window coverings. **Equity Capital Needed:** $82,400-$174,070. **Franchise Fee:** $14,950. **Royalty Fee:** Varies. **Financial Assistance:** Limited in-house financing available. **Training:** Provides 2 weeks at headquarters and ongoing training and support.

2013 ■ Coit Cleaning and Restoration Services
897 Hinckley Rd.
Burlingame, CA 94010
Free: 800-243-8797
Fax:(650)692-8397
Co. E-mail: franchise@coit.com
URL: http://www.coit.com
No. of Franchise Units: 42. **No. of Company-Owned Units:** 8. **Founded:** 1950. **Franchised:** 1962. **Description:** Coit is a multi-service cleaning company, offering drapery cleaning, carpet cleaning, upholstery cleaning, area rug cleaning, air duct cleaning and more. **Equity Capital Needed:** $50,000-$145,000. **Franchise Fee:** $24,000-$40,000. **Financial Assistance:** Limited financing available. **Training:** Includes 10 days in corporate office.

LIBRARIES

2014 ■ Arizona State University–Architectural and Environmental Design Library
College of Architecture
PO Box 871705
Tempe, AZ 85287-1705
Ph:(480)965-6400
Fax:(480)727-6965
Co. E-mail: deborah.koshinsky@asu.edu
URL: http://www.asu.edu
Contact: Deborah Koshinsky, Hd.Archv./Libn.
Scope: Architecture, city planning, landscape architecture, industrial design, interior design, graphic design. **Services:** Interlibrary loan; copying; Library open to the public; special collections open to the public by appointment. **Holdings:** 50,000 volumes; 150 cassette and tape recordings; 563 titles on microfilm; 125 films and videocassettes; archives; microfiche. **Subscriptions:** 140 journals and other serials.

START-UP INFORMATION

2015 ■ "Franchises with an Eye on Chicago" in *Crain's Chicago Business* (Vol. 34, March 14, 2011, No. 11, pp. 20)
Pub: Crain Communications Inc.
Description: Profiles of franchise companies seeking franchisees for the Chicago area include: Extreme Pita, a sandwich shop; Hand and Stone, offering massage, facial and waxing services; Molly Maid, home-cleaning service; Primrose Schools, private accredited schools for children 6 months to 6 hears and after-school programs; Protect Painters, residential and light-commercial painting contractor; and Wingstop, a restaurant offering chicken wings in nine flavors, fries and side dishes.

ASSOCIATIONS AND OTHER ORGANIZATIONS

2016 ■ Cosmetic Industry Buyers and Suppliers
Elite Packaging
40-E Cotters Ln.
East Brunswick, NJ 08816
Co. E-mail: cibsmail@cibsonline.com
URL: http://www.cibsonline.com
Contact: Charles Marchese, Pres.
Description: Buyers and suppliers of essential oils, chemicals, packaging, and finished goods relative to the cosmetic industry. Enhances growth, stability, prosperity, and protection of the American cosmetic industry through close personal contact and the exchange of ideas and experiences. .

2017 ■ International Spa Association
2365 Harrodsburg Rd., Ste. A325
Lexington, KY 40504
Ph:(859)226-4326
Free: 888-651-4772
Fax:(859)226-4445
Co. E-mail: ispa@ispastaff.com
URL: http://www.experienceispa.com
Contact: Ms. Lynne Walker McNees, Pres.
Description: Professional association and voice of the spa industry. Forms and maintains alliances that educate, set standards, provide resources, influence policy and build coalitions for the industry. Raises awareness of the spa industry and educates the public and industry professionals about the benefits of the spa experience. **Publications:** *LiveSpa*; *Pulse* (bimonthly).

2018 ■ Personal Care Product Council
1101 17th St. NW, Ste. 300
Washington, DC 20036-4702
Ph:(202)331-1770
Fax:(202)331-1969
Co. E-mail: membership@ctfa.org
URL: http://www.personalcarecouncil.org
Contact: Pamela G. Bailey, Pres./CEO
Description: Manufacturers and distributors of finished cosmetics, fragrances, and personal care products; suppliers of raw materials and services. Provides scientific, legal, regulatory, and legislative services. Coordinates public service, educational, and public affairs activities. **Publications:** *CTFA News* (biweekly); *International Color Handbook*; *International Resource Manual* .

REFERENCE WORKS

2019 ■ *Avon: Building the World's Premier Company for Women*
Pub: John Wiley & Sons, Incorporated
Ed: Laura Klepacki. **Released:** May 2006. **Price:** $21.99. **Description:** Profile of Avon, the world's largest direct sales company. Avon representatives number four million in over 140 countries.

2020 ■ *Business as Usual*
Pub: HarperBusiness
Ed: Anita Roddick. **Released:** 2005. **Price:** $12.95. **Description:** Founder of The Body Shop shares her story and gives her opinion on everything from cynical cosmetic companies to destructive consultants.

2021 ■ *Cosmetics & Toiletries—Cosmetic Bench Reference*
Pub: Allured Publishing Corp.
Ed: Linda Knott, Editor, lludwig@allured.com. **Released:** Annual. **Price:** $199, individuals. **Publication Includes:** List of cosmetic ingredient suppliers. **Entries Include:** Supplier name, address, phone, fax, chemicals, trade names. Principal content of publication is data on cosmetic ingredients, with label names, trade names, functions, EINECS, INCI names, and CAS numbers. **Arrangement:** Alphabetical by chemical name (includes trade names).

2022 ■ "Every Little Bit Helps" in *Black Enterprise* (Vol. 38, November 2007, No. 4, pp. 102)
Pub: Earl G. Graves Publishing Co. Inc.
Ed: Tennille M. Robinson. **Description:** After a career in the cosmetics industry, Tricialee Riley is marketing and advertising her new venture, the Polish Bar, a salon offering manicures, pedicures, makeup application, and waxing.

2023 ■ "First: Package Deal" in *Entrepreneur* (Vol. 35, October 2007, No. 10, pp. 114)
Pub: Entrepreneur Media Inc.
Ed: Nichole L. Torres. **Description:** Unique packaging of Me! Bath's products proved to be an effective marketing strategy for the company, which has over $3 million dollar sales yearly. Their ice cream-looking bath products have become popular and are much appreciated by vendors. Details of how packaging can affect sales are presented.

2024 ■ *Fragrance and Olfactory Dictionary*
Pub: The Fragrance Foundation Inc.
Released: Irregular. **Price:** $7, nonmembers USA; $5, members USA. **Description:** Principal content of publication definitions of fragrance and olfactory terms. **Arrangement:** Alphabetical.

2025 ■ "Greening the Manscape" in *Canadian Business* (Vol. 81, October 13, 2008, No. 17, pp. S19)
Pub: Rogers Media Ltd.
Ed: David Lackie. **Description:** Buyer's guide of environmentally friendly grooming products for men is provided. Improved formulations have solved the problems of having synthetic ingredients in grooming products. Details about a face scrub, after shave conditioner, and a nourishing cream made of 91 percent organic ingredients are given, including prices.

2026 ■ "How I Did It: It Just Came Naturally" in *Inc.* (November 2007, pp. 110-112)
Pub: Gruner & Jahr USA Publishing
Ed: Athena Schindelheim. **Description:** Profile of Bobbi Brown, CEO and founder of Bobbi Brown Cosmetics, designed to highlight a woman's natural look. Brown opened her first freestanding retail store recently that houses a makeup artistry school in the back.

2027 ■ "How to Keep Your Cool and Your Friends in a Heat Wave" in *Canadian Business* (Vol. 83, August 17, 2010, No. 13-14, pp. 79)
Pub: Rogers Media Ltd.
Ed: Angelina Chapin. **Description:** A buyer's guide of menswear clothing for businessmen is presented. The products include an antiperspirant and deodorant, men's dress shorts, shoes and bamboo fabric undershirt.

2028 ■ "Identify and Conquer" in *Black Enterprise* (Vol. 38, December 2007, No. 5, pp. 76)
Pub: Earl G. Graves Publishing Co. Inc.
Ed: Tennille M. Robinson. **Description:** Twenty-two-year-old entrepreneur wants to expand her wholesale body oil and skincare products business.

2029 ■ "In the Raw: Karyn Calabrese Brings Healthy Dining to a New Sophisticated Level" in *Black Enterprise* (Vol. 41, September 2010)
Pub: Earl G. Graves Publishing Co. Inc.
Ed: Sonia Alleyne. **Description:** Profile of Karyn Calabrese whose businesses are based in Chicago, Illinois. Calabrese has launched a complete line of products (vitamins and beauty items), services (spa, chiropractic, and acupuncture treatments), and restaurants to bring health dining and lifestyles to a better level.

2030 ■ "Ivorydale Looks to Clean Up" in *Business Courier* (Vol. 26, January 15, 2010, No. 39, pp. 1)
Pub: American City Business Journals, Inc.
Ed: Jon Newberry. **Description:** Cincinnati-based St. Bernard Soap Company plans to focus on new services such as product development and logistics and to continue growth and put excess capacity to work. The unit of Ontario, Canada-based Trillium Health Care Products Inc. is the largest contract manufacturer of bar soap in North America.

2031 ■ *Lessons of a Lipstick Queen: Finding and Developing the Great Idea That Can Change Your Life*
Pub: Simon & Schuster
Ed: Poppy King. **Released:** May 1, 2009. **Price:** $14. 00. **Description:** Poppy King tells how she started her lipstick brand at age eighteen. She reveals how she managed to launch her business using a good idea and finding financing, marketing the product and how she became successful.

2032 ■ "Natural Attraction: Bath and Body Products Maker Delivers Wholesome Goodness" in *Black Enterprise* (Vol. 38, November 2007, No. 4)
Pub: Earl G. Graves Publishing Co. Inc.
Ed: Kaylyn Kendall Dines. **Description:** Profile of Dawn Fitch, creator of Pooka Inc., manufacturer of handmade bath and body products that contain no preservatives. Sales are expected to reach $750,000 for 2007.

2033 ■ "New Year's Resolutions: How Three Companies Came Up With Their 2008 Growth Strategies" in *Inc.* (January 2008, pp. 47-49)
Pub: Gruner & Jahr USA Publishing
Ed: Martha C. White. **Description:** Three companies share 2008 growth strategies; companies include a candle company, a voice mail and text messaging marketer, and hotel supplier of soap and shampoo.

2034 ■ "Old Spice Guy (Feb.-July 2010)" in *Canadian Business* (Vol. 83, August 17, 2010, No. 13-14, pp. 23)
Pub: Rogers Media Ltd.
Ed: Andrew Potter. **Description:** Old Spice Guy was played by ex-football player and actor Isaiah Mustafa who made the debut in the ad for Old Spice Red Zone body wash that was broadcast during Super Bowl XLIV in February 2010. Old Spice Guy has become one of social marketing success but was cancelled in July when online viewership started to wane.

2035 ■ "P&G to Mine E-Commerce Potential" in *Business Courier* (Vol. 26, September 18, 2009, No. 21, pp. 1)
Pub: American City Business Journals, Inc.
Ed: Lisa Biank Fasig. **Description:** Procter & Gamble (P&G) is looking to turn the hits to the company's Websites into increased sales. The program will include a shop now option to track all emerging sales.

2036 ■ *The Perfect Scent: A Year Inside the Perfume Industry in Paris and New York*
Pub: Henry Holt and Company
Ed: Chandler Burr. **Released:** 2009. **Price:** $25.00. **Description:** An insiders glimpse at the development of two new fragrances from Hermes and Coty.

2037 ■ "Private Equity Firm Links First Arizona Deal" in *Business Journal-Serving Phoenix and the Valley of the Sun* (November 2, 2007)
Pub: American City Business Journals, Inc.
Ed: Chris Cassacchia. **Description:** Pacific Investment Partners and Your Source Financial launched a $10 million fund and signed their first deal. The two companies acquires a minority stake in Dreambrands Inc. for $3 million. Dreambrands is using the capital to market its personal lubricant product Carrageenana.

2038 ■ "A Team Sport" in *Business Courier* (Vol. 26, October 2, 2009, No. 23, pp. 1)
Pub: American City Business Journals, Inc.
Ed: Lisa Biank Fasig. **Description:** Procter & Gamble (P&G) revised the way it works with marketing, design and public relations firms. Creative discussions will be managed by only two representatives, the franchise leader and the brand agency leader in order for P&G to simplify operations as it grows larger and more global.

2039 ■ "To Catch Up, Colgate May Ratchet Up Its Ad Spending" in *Advertising Age* (Vol. 81, December 6, 2010, No. 43, pp. 1)
Pub: Crain Communications, Inc.
Ed: Jack Neff. **Description:** Colgate-Palmolive Company has been losing market share in the categories of toothpaste, deodorant, body wash, dish soap and pet food.

2040 ■ "Vitabath: Sweet Smell of Success" in *Retail Merchandiser* (Vol. 51, September-October 2011, No. 5, pp. 82)
Pub: Phoenix Media Corporation
Description: After taking over at Vitabath, Rich Brands developed new scents and products and while discovering new channels to distribute these items.

2041 ■ "Want a Facial With That Steak?" in *Charlotte Observer* (February 5, 2007)
Pub: Knight-Ridder/Tribune Business News
Ed: Jen Aronoff. **Description:** Profile of Burke Myotherapy Massage & Spa and Schell's Bistro. Lynn Shell moved her massage therapy business into a 106-year old home that had been used as a restaurant. She opened her own eatery on the first floor and offers massage therapy upstairs.

2042 ■ "Zit Zapper Lands New Funding" in *Houston Business Journal* (Vol. 40, November 27, 2009, No. 29, pp. 1)
Pub: American City Business Journals
Ed: Mary Ann Azevedo. **Description:** Tyrell Inc. of Houston, Texas generated $20 million in funds for making a cheaper version of its acne-removing Zeno device. The upcoming product, Zeno Mini, will be targeted to a mass market with a price tag of about $89. In 2005, the original Zeno acne treatment device could only be bought through medical offices and spas at about $225.

TRADE PERIODICALS

2043 ■ *Cosmetics & Toiletries*
Pub: Allured Publishing Corp.
Contact: Jane Evison, European Accounts managing editorager
E-mail: jane-evison@btconnect.com
Released: Monthly. **Price:** $98; $137 Canada; $189 other countries; $169 two years; $231 Canada two years; $330 other countries two years. **Description:** Trade magazine on cosmetic and toiletries manufacturing with an emphasis on product research and development issues.

2044 ■ *Flavour and Fragrance Journal*
Pub: John Wiley & Sons Inc.
Released: Bimonthly. **Price:** $2,071 institutions print only; $2,278 institutions print & online. **Description:** International journal on essential oils and related products for organic chemists, food scientists, toxicologists, flavor chemists, and technologists.

2045 ■ *The Rose Sheet*
Pub: Elsevier Business Intelligence
Contact: Chirs Morrison, Editor-in-Chief
E-mail: c.morrison@elsevier.com
Released: Weekly (Mon.). **Price:** $1,470 print & online. **Description:** Trade journal for executives in the toiletries, fragrance, cosmetic, and skin care industries.

2046 ■ *Skin Inc.*
Pub: Allured Publishing Corp.
Released: Monthly. **Price:** $49; $57 Canada; $98 other countries. **Description:** The complete business guide for face and body care.

TRADE SHOWS AND CONVENTIONS

2047 ■ Beauty Fair
The Finnish Fair Corp.
Messuaukio 1
PO Box 21
FIN-00521 Helsinki, Finland
Ph:358 9 15091
Fax:358 9 1509218
Co. E-mail: info@finnexpo.fi
Released: Annual. **Audience:** General public. **Principal Exhibits:** Beauty and fashion, cosmetics and services; hair products and services; clothing, showes, bags, accessories, jewelry, education, and publications.

2048 ■ Extracts - A Division of New York International Gift Fair
George Little Management, LLC (New York, New York)
1133 Westchester Ave., Ste. N136
White Plains, NY 10606
Ph:(914)421-3200
Free: 800-272-SHOW
Co. E-mail: cathy_steel@glmshows.com
URL: http://www.glmshows.com
Released: Semiannual. **Audience:** Specialty, chain and department stores, gift and drug stores, mail order catalog houses, cosmetic companies, home furnishings/decorative accessory retailers. **Principal Exhibits:** Personal care products, aromatherapy products, body lotions, bath and shower gels, soaps, fragrances, botanicals, potpourri, candles, home fragrance products, bath accessories, and small appliances.

FRANCHISES AND BUSINESS OPPORTUNITIES

2049 ■ Fruits & Passion
21 Paul-Gaugin
Candiac, QC, Canada J5R 3X8
Ph:(450)638-2212
Fax:(450)638-2430
Co. E-mail: info@fruits-passion.com
URL: http://www.fruits-passion.com
No. of Franchise Units: 36. **No. of Company-Owned Units:** 53. **Founded:** 1992. **Description:** Offers natural body care products, home ambiance and gourmet specialties based on the curative and regenerative properties of fruit with award-winning, high-quality products. **Equity Capital Needed:** $174,000-$400,000. **Franchise Fee:** $25,000. **Training:** Initial and ongoing.

2050 ■ Women's Health Boutique
Women's Health Boutique Franchise System, Inc.
12715 Telge Rd.
Cypress, TX 77429
Free: 888-708-9982
Fax:(281)256-4100
Co. E-mail: w-h-bsales@w-h-b.com
URL: http://www.w-h-b.com
No. of Franchise Units: 13. **Founded:** 1991. **Franchised:** 1994. **Description:** Products and services related to pre and postnatal care, post-mastectomy, compression therapy, hair loss, incontinence, and skin care. **Equity Capital Needed:** $49,000 minimum start-up cash. **Financial Assistance:** Yes. **Training:** Yes.

COMPUTERIZED DATABASES

2051 ■ *Pharmaceutical News Index*
ProQuest LLC
789 E Eisenhower Pky.
PO Box 1346
Ann Arbor, MI 48106-1346
Ph:(734)761-4700
Free: 800-521-0600
Fax:(734)761-6450
Co. E-mail: info@proquest.com
URL: http://www.proquest.com
Description: Contains more than 700,000 citations and indexing for all articles in more than 20 key U.S. and international pharmaceutical, healthcare, biotechnology, and medical device industry newsletters. Also includes citations to company and industry reports in the Investext database (described in a separate entry). Topics covered include drugs and medical devices; sales and earnings reports; mergers and acquisitions; research developments; government regulations and legislation; and new product announcements. **Availability:** Online: Wolters Kluwer Health, Wolters Kluwer Health, ProQuest LLC, ProQuest LLC, STN International, ProQuest LLC. **Type:** Bibliographic.

LIBRARIES

2052 ■ Avon Products Research Library
1345 Avenue of the Americas
New York, NY 10020

Ph:(212)282-5000
Co. E-mail: mary.warren@avon.com
URL: http://www.avoncompany.com/
Contact: Mary Warren, Res.Libn.

Scope: Cosmetics, packaging, toxicology, dermatology, pharmacology, chemistry, engineering, microbiology. **Services:** Interlibrary loan; SDI; Library open to the public for reference use only on request. **Holdings:** 6500 books; 5000 bound periodical volumes; 6000 U.S. and foreign patents. **Subscriptions:** 300 journals and other serials.

2053 ■ Clairol Research Library
1 Blachley Rd.
Stamford, CT 06922
Ph:(203)357-5001
Free: 800-252-4765
Fax:(203)969-2577
URL: http://www.clairol.com
Contact: Linda Massoni, Libn.

Scope: Chemistry and technology of cosmetics, hair dyes and dyeing, personal care. **Services:** Library open to the public with restrictions. **Holdings:** 10,000 books; 6000 bound periodical volumes; 30 titles on microfilm. **Subscriptions:** 350 journals and other serials.

2054 ■ Colgate Palmolive Company Technology Information Center
909 River Rd.
Piscataway, NJ 08854
Ph:(732)878-7574
Fax:(732)878-7128
URL: http://www.colgate.com
Contact: Miranda D. Scott, Tech.Info.Assoc.
Scope: Soaps and detergents, fats and oils, dentifrices, cosmetics, perfumes and essential oils, environmental pollution, foods, chemistry. **Services:** Interlibrary loan; copying; SDI. **Holdings:** 20,000 books; 10,000 bound periodical volumes; 16,000 periodical volumes on 4000 reels of microfilm; 250 VF drawers of internal reports; 10 VF drawers of archival materials. **Subscriptions:** 300 journals and other serials.

2055 ■ Johnson and Johnson Consumer and Personal Products Worldwide Library
199 Grandview Rd.
Skillman, NJ 08558
Ph:(908)904-3710
Fax:(908)874-1212
URL: http://www.jnj.com/connect/
Contact: Susan Gleckner, Lib.Hd.
Scope: Infant care, health and beauty aids, toiletries, chemistry, pharmaceuticals, oral care, wound care, skin care, dermatology, women's health. **Holdings:** 2000 books; 1500 bound periodical volumes. **Subscriptions:** 400 journals and other serials.

2056 ■ Mary Kay Inc.–Information Resources
16251 N. Dallas Pkwy.
Addison, TX 75001
Ph:(972)687-5527
Fax:(972)687-1643
Co. E-mail: cecilia.armas@mkcorp.com
Contact: Cecilia Armas-Benavidas, Mgr., Info.Rsrcs.
Scope: Cosmetics, dermatology, toxicology, chemistry, business, marketing. **Services:** Interlibrary loan. **Holdings:** 2000 books; 500 bound periodical volumes. **Subscriptions:** 250 journals and other serials.

2057 ■ Revlon Research Center Library
2121 Rte. 27
Edison, NJ 08818
Ph:(732)287-7650
Fax:(732)248-2230
Contact: Ann Van Dine, Libn.
Scope: Cosmetics, soaps, chemistry, perfumery, dermatology, pharmacology, microbiology, aerosols. **Services:** Interlibrary loan; copying; SDI; Library open to the public by appointment. **Holdings:** 11,000 books; 4000 bound periodical volumes. **Subscriptions:** 100 journals and other serials.

Book Publishing

START-UP INFORMATION

2058 ■ *How to Start and Run a Small Book Publishing Company: A Small Business Guide to Self-Publishing and Independent Publishing*
Pub: HCM Publishing
Ed: Peter I. Hupalo. **Released:** August 30, 2002. **Price:** $18.95. **Description:** The book teaches all aspects of starting and running a small book publishing company. Topics covered include: inventory accounting in the book trade, just-in-time inventory management, turnkey fulfillment solutions, tax deductible costs, basics of sales and use tax, book pricing, standards in terms of the book industry, working with distributors and wholesalers, cover design and book layout, book promotion and marketing, how to select profitable authors to publish, printing process, printing on demand, the power of a strong backlist, and how to value copyright.

ASSOCIATIONS AND OTHER ORGANIZATIONS

2059 ■ About Books, Inc.
1618 W Colorado Ave.
Colorado Springs, CO 80904
Ph:(719)632-8226
Fax:(719)471-2182
Co. E-mail: deb@about-books.com
URL: http://www.about-books.com
Contact: Debi Flora, Pres./Co-Owner
Description: Information clearinghouse on self-publishing and marketing of books. Provides educational programs; maintains speakers' bureau. Provides audiotape programs and books on the subject.
.

2060 ■ American Book Producers Association
151 W 19th St., 3rd Fl.
New York, NY 10011
Ph:(212)645-2368
Fax:(212)675-1364
Co. E-mail: office@abpaonline.org
URL: http://www.abpaonline.org
Contact: Richard Rothschild, Pres.
Description: Book producing companies that develop the concepts for books and, based on a contractual agreement with a publisher, may produce finished books or production-ready film, camera-ready mechanicals, finished manuscripts, art and layouts. Aims to increase the book industry's awareness of members' capabilities and the state of the book producers' art. Facilitates exchange of information for the purpose of improving business and establishing trade standards. **Publications:** *American Book Producers Association—Newsletter* (monthly).

2061 ■ American Booksellers Association
200 White Plains Rd., Ste. 600
Tarrytown, NY 10591
Free: 800-637-0037
Fax:(914)591-2720
Co. E-mail: info@bookweb.org
URL: http://www.bookweb.org
Contact: Oren Teicher, CEO
Description: Seeks to meet the needs of members, independently owned bookstores with storefront locations, through education, information dissemination, and advocacy. Supports free speech, literacy, and programs that encourage reading. **Publications:** *ABA Electronic Book Buyer's Handbook*; *ABACUS* (annual); *Bookselling this Week* (weekly).

2062 ■ Association of American Publishers
71 5th Ave., 2nd Fl.
New York, NY 10003-3004
Ph:(212)255-0200
Fax:(212)255-7007
Co. E-mail: jplatt@publishers.org
URL: http://www.publishers.org
Contact: Tom Allen, Pres./CEO
Description: Represents the major commercial publishers in the United States as well as smaller and non-profit publishers, university presses and scholarly societies. Helps in the protection of intellectual property rights in all media. Promotes reading and literacy and the freedom to publish at home and abroad. Conducts seminars and workshops on various publishing topics including rights and permission, sales, and educational publishing. Compiles statistics. **Publications:** *AAP Monthly Report* (monthly).

2063 ■ Association of American University Presses
28 W 36th St., Ste. 602
New York, NY 10018
Ph:(212)989-1010
Fax:(212)989-0275
Co. E-mail: info@aaupnet.org
URL: http://www.aaupnet.org
Contact: Peter J. Givler, Exec. Dir.
Description: Helps university presses do their work more economically, creatively, and effectively through its own activities in education-training, fundraising and development, statistical research and analysis, and community and institutional relations. **Publications:** *AAUP Directory* (annual); *Exchange* (quarterly).

2064 ■ Association of Canadian Publishers
174 Spadina Ave., Ste. 306
Toronto, ON, Canada M5T 2C2
Ph:(416)487-6116
Fax:(416)487-8815
Co. E-mail: admin@canbook.org
URL: http://www.publishers.ca
Contact: Carolyn Wood, Exec. Dir.
Description: Canadian-owned book publishers. Supports the development of a vibrant domestic publishing industry. Encourages writing, publishing, distribution, and promotion of Canadian books. Conducts industry research, including salary surveys, book sales analyses, and accounting modifications; facilitates communication among members; makes available promotion, public relations, and marketing services. Serves as a clearinghouse on Canadian writing and publishing; sponsors lobbying activities. **Publications:** *ACP Update* (biweekly).

2065 ■ Association of Catholic Publishers
4725 Dorsey Hall Dr., Ste. A
PMB No. 709
Ellicott City, MD 21042
Ph:(410)988-2926
Fax:(410)571-4946
Co. E-mail: tbrown@cbpa.org
URL: http://www.cbpa.org
Contact: Therese Brown, Exec. Dir.
Description: Facilitates the sharing of professional information, networking, cooperation, and friendship among those involved in Catholic publishing in the United States and abroad. **Publications:** *The Catholic Book Publishers Association Directory* (annual); *CBPA Newsletter*, *The Spirit of Books* (semiannual).

2066 ■ Authors and Publishers Association
25661 Field Store Rd.
Waller, TX 77484-5930
Co. E-mail: info@authorsandpublishers.org
URL: http://www.authorsandpublishers.org
Contact: Ron Kaye, Interim Pres.
Description: Authors, aspiring authors, editors, artists, printers and publishers, marketers, distributors, booksellers, and other corporations and individuals with an interest in the book trade. Seeks to assist writers, authors, and publishers to "keep the literary craft alive". Serves as a clearinghouse on the book publishing industry; provides employment and other information to writers; facilitates networking among members. .

2067 ■ Bay Area Independent Publishers Association
PO Box E
Corte Madera, CA 94976
Ph:(415)456-0247
Co. E-mail: books4women@yahoo.com
URL: http://www.baipa.net
Contact: Paula Hendricks, Pres.
Description: Promotes authors interested in independent publishing as an alternative to the commercial publishing system; printers, artists, typists, and others in allied fields. Aims to become a comprehensive source of self-publishing information and to develop knowledge and expertise to better assist members in promoting, marketing, and publishing their works. Acts as a liaison and clearinghouse of information and provides guidance in all aspects of self-publishing, including copy preparation, book production, and marketing and sales. **Publications:** *SPEX* (monthly).

2068 ■ Book Industry Study Group
370 Lexington Ave., Ste. 900
New York, NY 10017
Ph:(646)336-7141
Fax:(646)336-6214
Co. E-mail: info@bisg.org
URL: http://www.bisg.org
Contact: Scott Lubeck, Exec. Dir.
Description: Represents publishers, manufacturers, suppliers, wholesalers, retailers, librarians, and other

engaged in the business of print and electronic media. **Publications:** *Book Industry TRENDS* (annual).

2069 ■ Book Manufacturers' Institute
Two Armand Beach Dr., Ste. 1B
Palm Coast, FL 32137-2612
Ph:(386)986-4552
Fax:(386)986-4553
Co. E-mail: info@bmibook.com
URL: http://www.bmibook.com
Contact: Daniel N. Bach, Exec. VP/Sec.
Description: Represents the trade association for manufacturers of books. .

2070 ■ Book and Periodical Council
192 Spadina Ave., Ste. 107
Toronto, ON, Canada M5T 2C2
Ph:(416)975-9366
Fax:(416)975-1839
Co. E-mail: info@thebpc.ca
URL: http://www.bookandperiodicalcouncil.ca
Contact: Anne McClelland, Exec. Dir.
Description: Associations representing writers, editors, and publishers of books and periodicals and manufacturers, distributors, and sellers and lenders of printed materials. Promotes improved market conditions for Canadian publications and seeks to insure availability of a representative range of Canadian books and periodicals. Works to strengthen book and periodical distribution systems; supports development of new and existing Canadian-owned publishing companies; serves as a forum for discussion of industry issues.

2071 ■ Canadian Children's Book Centre
40 Orchard View Blvd., Ste. 217
Toronto, ON, Canada M4R 1B9
Ph:(416)975-0010
Fax:(416)975-8970
Co. E-mail: shannon@bookcentre.ca
URL: http://www.bookweek.ca
Contact: Shannon Howe, Program Coor.
Description: Promotes the reading, writing, illustrating and publishing of Canadian books for young readers. Offers programs, publications and resources to help teachers, librarians, booksellers and parents to select the best books for young readers. **Publications:** *Canadian Children's Book News* (quarterly); *Our Choice* (annual).

2072 ■ Canadian Copyright Institute
192 Spadina Ave., Ste. 107
Toronto, ON, Canada M5T 2C2
Ph:(416)975-1756
Fax:(416)975-1839
Co. E-mail: info@thecci.ca
URL: http://www.canadiancopyrightinstitute.ca
Contact: Anne McClelland, Admin.
Description: Creators, producers, and distributors of copyrighted works. Encourages a more complete understanding of copyright laws among members and the public. Consults with government and judicial bodies regarding reform of copyright laws. Conducts and sponsors research on copyright laws worldwide. Works with organizations pursuing similar goals to improve copyright legislation and enforcement. **Publications:** *Copyright Reform Legislation Reporting Service* (periodic).

2073 ■ Canadian Publishers' Council
250 Merton St., Ste. 203
Toronto, ON, Canada M4S 1B1
Ph:(416)322-7011
Fax:(416)322-6999
Co. E-mail: jhushion@pubcouncil.ca
URL: http://www.pubcouncil.ca
Contact: Jacqueline Hushion, Exec. Dir.
Description: English-language publishers. Seeks to advance the domestic book publishing industry; encourages publication of Canadian authors. Facilitates communication and cooperation among members; represents members' interests before trade organizations, government agencies, and the public.

2074 ■ Center for the Book
Library of Congress
101 Independence Ave. SE
Washington, DC 20540-4920
Ph:(202)707-5221
Fax:(202)707-0269
Co. E-mail: glam@loc.gov
URL: http://www.read.gov/cfb
Contact: John Y. Cole, Dir.
Description: Uses resources and prestige of Library of Congress to stimulate public interest in books, reading, literacy, and libraries, and encourage the study of books and the printed word. Sponsors lectures, symposia, reading promotion projects, and publications. Develops partnerships with state center for the book affiliates and national organizations. .

2075 ■ Evangelical Christian Publishers Association
9633 S 48th St., Ste. 140
Phoenix, AZ 85044
Ph:(480)966-3998
Fax:(480)966-1944
Co. E-mail: info@ecpa.org
URL: http://www.ecpa.org
Contact: Mark W. Kuyper, Pres./CEO
Description: Companies that primarily publish Christian religious literature. Conducts annual sales and operation survey, and a series of educational seminars and trade shows. **Publications:** *Monday Rush* (weekly).

2076 ■ Independent Book Publishers Association
627 Aviation Way
Manhattan Beach, CA 90266
Ph:(310)372-2732
Fax:(310)374-3342
Co. E-mail: info@ibpa-online.org
URL: http://www.pma-online.org
Contact: Terry Nathan, Exec. Dir.
Description: Entrepreneurial publishers of trade books and video and audio cassette tapes. Aims to assist independent publishers in the marketing and sale of their titles to bookstores, libraries, and specialty markets. Holds marketing and educational programs. **Publications:** *PMA Resource Directory* (annual).

2077 ■ Let's Face It USA
University of Michigan
School of Dentistry
Dentistry Library
Ann Arbor, MI 48109-1078
Co. E-mail: faceit@umich.edu
URL: http://www.dent.umich.edu/faceit
Contact: Betsy Wilson, Founder/Dir.
Description: Provides information and support for people who have or who care for those with facial disfigurement. Website and annual publication with over 150 resources for professionals and families. Links to all related networks for specific conditions i.e. Genetic Disorders, Burns, Cancer, etc. **Publications:** *Resources for People with Facial Difference* (semiannual).

2078 ■ Literary Press Group of Canada
501-192 Spadina Ave.
Toronto, ON, Canada M5T 2C2
Ph:(416)483-1321
Fax:(416)483-2510
Co. E-mail: jack@lpg.ca
URL: http://www.lpg.ca
Contact: Jack Illingworth, Exec. Dir.
Description: Canadian owned and controlled literary book publishers. Promotes growth and development of members. Makes available cooperative sales and marketing services.

2079 ■ Livres Canada Books
1 Nicholas St., Ste. 504
Ottawa, ON, Canada K1N 7B7
Ph:(613)562-2324
Fax:(613)562-2329
Co. E-mail: info@livrescanadabooks.com
URL: http://www.livrescanadabooks.com
Contact: Francois Charette, Exec. Dir.
Description: Helps Canadian publishers develop foreign markets and promote export sales of books. Provides financial assistance and market intelligence. Organizes collective Canada stands at major international book fairs. **Publications:** *AECB News* (periodic); *Books on Canada* (annual); *Rights Canada* (semiannual).

2080 ■ National Information Standards Organization
1 N Charles St., Ste. 1905
Baltimore, MD 21201
Ph:(301)654-2512
Free: (866)957-1593
Fax:(301)654-1721
Co. E-mail: tcarpenter@niso.org
URL: http://www.niso.org
Contact: Todd Carpenter, Managing Dir.
Description: Identifies, develops, maintains, and publishes technical standards to manage information in the changing environment used by libraries, publishers, and information services. Supports open access to NISO standards. Standards available at website. **Publications:** *Information Standards* (quarterly); *Newsline* (monthly); *Technical Report* (periodic).

2081 ■ Periodical and Book Association of America
481 8th Ave., Ste. 526
New York, NY 10001
Ph:(212)563-6502
Fax:(212)563-4098
Co. E-mail: lscott@pbaa.net
URL: http://www.pbaa.net
Contact: Lisa W. Scott, Exec. Dir.
Description: Magazine and paperback publishers concerned with single copy or newsstand sales. Carries out concerted action in areas of publishing, production, and sales. .

2082 ■ Small Publishers Association of North America
PO Box 9725
Colorado Springs, CO 80932-0725
Ph:(719)924-5534
Fax:(719)213-2602
Co. E-mail: info@spannet.org
URL: http://www.spannet.org
Contact: Scott Flora, Exec. Dir.
Description: For self-publishers, authors and small presses. Works to advance the image and profits of independent publishers through education and marketing. Offers continuing education, co-op buying power and sales and networking opportunities, plus discounts on many products and services. Publishes monthly newsletter. .

2083 ■ Society for Scholarly Publishing
10200 W 44th Ave., Ste. 304
Wheat Ridge, CO 80033
Ph:(303)422-3914
Fax:(303)422-8894
Co. E-mail: info@sspnet.org
URL: http://www.sspnet.org
Contact: Lois Smith, Pres.
Description: Individuals, including librarians, booksellers, publishers, printers, authors, and editors interested in scholarly publication; organizations. Serves as an educational forum. .

2084 ■ Special Libraries Association
331 S Patrick St.
Alexandria, VA 22314-3501
Ph:(703)647-4900
Fax:(703)647-4901
Co. E-mail: janice@sla.org
URL: http://www.sla.org
Contact: Janice R. Lachance, CEO
Description: International association of information professionals who work in specialized information environments such as business, research, government, universities, newspapers, museums, and institutions. Seeks to advance the leadership role of information professionals through learning, networking and advocacy. Offers consulting services to organizations that wish to establish or expand a library or information services. Conducts strategic learning and development courses, public relations, and government relations programs. Provides employment services. Operates knowledge exchange

on topics pertaining to the development and management of special libraries. **Publications:** *Information Outlook* (8/year); *SLA Connections* (monthly).

2085 ■ Women's National Book Association
PO Box 237
New York, NY 10150-0231
Ph:(212)208-4629
Fax:(212)208-4629
Co. E-mail: publicity@bookbuzz.com
URL: http://www.wnba-books.org
Contact: Susannah Greenberg, Public Relations Mgr.

Description: Women and men who work with and value books. Exists to promote reading and to support the role of women in the book community. **Publications:** *The Bookwoman* (3/year).

EDUCATIONAL PROGRAMS

2086 ■ Managing the Publications Department
EEI Communications
66 Canal Center Plz., Ste. 200
Alexandria, VA 22314
Ph:(703)683-7453
Free: 888-253-2762
Fax:(703)683-7310
Co. E-mail: train@eeicom.com
URL: http://www.eeicom.com/training

Price: $745.00. **Description:** Covers the role of the publications manager, techniques for managing multiple projects, standardizing and organizing the publications process, creating productivity standards and quality control procedures, using new technology, and working effectively with peers, subordinates, and superiors. **Locations:** Alexandria, VA.

2087 ■ Production Techniques and Technology
EEI Communications
66 Canal Center Plz., Ste. 200
Alexandria, VA 22314
Ph:(703)683-7453
Free: 888-253-2762
Fax:(703)683-7310
Co. E-mail: train@eeicom.com
URL: http://www.eeicom.com/training

Price: $745.00. **Description:** Seminar for editors, writers, designers, and graphic artists; covers the print production process within the publishing industry, including processes and principles of graphic production, pre-press, and printing; basics of design, typography, and layout; electronic advances on the desktop and in the printing plant; working with vendors; and the basics of scheduling, estimating, and quality control. **Locations:** Alexandria, VA.

2088 ■ Quality Control in Publications
EEI Communications
66 Canal Center Plz., Ste. 200
Alexandria, VA 22314
Ph:(703)683-7453
Free: 888-253-2762
Fax:(703)683-7310
Co. E-mail: train@eeicom.com
URL: http://www.eeicom.com/training

Price: $425.00. **Description:** Covers the process of publication, including planning and quality control systems, error detection processes, effectively using software, and dealing with print vendors. **Locations:** Alexandria, VA.

REFERENCE WORKS

2089 ■ "Africa Rising" in *Harvard Business Review* (Vol. 86, September 2008, No. 9, pp. 36)
Pub: Harvard Business School Press

Ed: John T. Landry. **Description:** Review of the book entitled, "Africa Rising: How 900 Million African Consumers Offer More Than You Think" provides advice for marketing to those on the African continent.

2090 ■ "ALA: Hot Topics for Librarianship" in *Information Today* (Vol. 28, September 2011, No. 8, pp. 17)
Pub: Information Today, Inc.

Ed: Barbara Brynko. **Description:** Highlights from the American Library Association Annual Conference and Exhibition are listed. Thousands of attendees sought out services, displays, demos, new product rollouts, and freebies. Emerging technology for librarians, staff development, gray literature, interlibrary loans, and next-generation interfaces were among the topics discussed.

2091 ■ *Association of American University Presses—Directory*
Pub: Association of American University Presses
Contact: Susan Patton, Membership Mgr.
E-mail: spatton@aaupnet.org

Released: Annual, Latest edition 2011. **Price:** $30, individuals. **Covers:** 124 presses and affiliates worldwide. **Entries Include:** Press name, address, phone, e-mail, URL; titles and names of complete editorial and managerial staffs; editorial program; mailing, warehouse, printing, and/or customer service addresses; other details. **Arrangement:** Classified by press affiliation, alphabetical by press name. **Indexes:** Personal name.

2092 ■ "Back Talk with Chris Gardner" in *Black Enterprise* (Vol. 37, January 2007, No. 6, pp. 112)
Pub: Earl G. Graves Publishing Co. Inc.

Ed: Kenneth Meeks. **Description:** Profile of with Chris Gardner and his Chicago company, Gardner Rich L.L.C., a multimillion-dollar investment firm. During an interview, Gardner discusses his rise from homelessness. His story became a book, The Pursuit of Happyness and was recently released as a film starring Will Smith.

2093 ■ "Because Kids Need To Be Heard: Tina Wells: Buzz Marketing Group: Voorhees, New Jersey" in *Inc.* (Volume 32, December 2010)
Pub: Inc. Magazine

Ed: Tamara Schweitzer. **Description:** Profile of Tina Wells, founder and CEO of Buzz Marketing Group, who writes a tween book series called Mackenzie Blue to reach young girls.

2094 ■ *Book Dealers Dropship Directory*
Pub: North American Bookdealers Exchange
Contact: Al Galasso, Director

Released: Irregular, Latest edition 2005-2006. **Price:** $15, individuals with free shipping in USA and Canada. **Covers:** More than 300 dealers and distributors who ship individual copies of books to customers for publishers and mail order companies. **Entries Include:** Company name, address, titles or types of books handled. **Arrangement:** Alphabetical.

2095 ■ *Book Fairs*
Pub: Para Publishing
Contact: Dan Poynter, Publisher
E-mail: danpoynter@parapublishing.com

Released: Irregular. **Price:** $7.95, individuals plus shipping charges. **Publication Includes:** List of about 30 major book fairs; display equipment suppliers, exhibition services: associations, periodicals, consultants, seminars; international coverage. **Entries Include:** For fairs—Fair name, sponsoring organization name and address. For suppliers—Firm name, address, name of contact, product or service. Principal content is author's advice on taking part in book exhibits and fairs. **Arrangement:** Each list is alphabetical.

2096 ■ "The Book On Indigo" in *Canadian Business* (Vol. 81, July 22, 2008, No. 12-13, pp. 29)
Pub: Rogers Media Ltd.

Ed: Thomas Watson. **Description:** Indigo Books & Music Inc. reported record sales of $922 million resulting in a record net profit of $52.8 million for the 2008 fiscal year ended March 29, 2008. Earnings per share were $2.13, greater than Standard & Poor's expected $1.70 per share. Additional information concerning Indigo Books is presented.

2097 ■ "Book Publishing is Growing" in *Information Today* (Vol. 28, October 2011, No. 9, pp. 10)
Pub: Information Today, Inc.

Ed: Paula J. Hane. **Description:** U.S. book publishing industry is reporting growth in its sector, despite the poor economy. BookStats, a comprehensive statistical survey conducted on the modern publishing industry in the U.S. reported Americans are reading in all print and digital formats. In 2011, 114 million ebooks were sold and now account for 13.6 percent of revenue from adult fiction. In contrast, 603 million trade hardcover books (fiction and nonfiction) were sold in 2011, a 5.8 percent increase over 2008.

2098 ■ *Books in Print*
Pub: R.R. Bowker L.L.C.
Contact: Roy Crego, Mng.Dir.

Released: Annual, Latest edition 2009-2010. **Price:** $995, individuals hardcover; 7 volumes. **Description:** Over 2.8 million entries covering books published and distributed in the U.S. **Entries Include:** For publishers—Company name, address. For books—Authors, title, price, publisher, other bibliographic information as available. The material in "Books in Print" is also available in subject-classified form in "Subject Guide to Books in Print," published as a five-volume set, annually in September. **Arrangement:** Publishers, authors, and titles are alphabetical in separate sections.

2099 ■ "Bridging the Worlds" in *Academy of Management Journal* (Vol. 50, No. 5, October 2007, pp. 1043)
Pub: Academy of Management

Ed: Lise Saari. **Description:** Need to transfer human resource research information published in journals to practitioners and organizations is investigated, along with suggestions on ways of achieving this goal.

2100 ■ "Buying In" in *Harvard Business Review* (Vol. 86, September 2008, No. 9, pp. 36)
Pub: Harvard Business School Press

Ed: Andrew O'Connell. **Description:** Review of the book entitled, "Buying In: The Secret Dialogue between What We Buy and Who We Are" which offers tips that those in the field of marketing will find useful.

2101 ■ *Children's Books in Print*
Pub: R.R. Bowker L.L.C.

Released: Annual, Latest edition 2009. **Price:** $455, individuals 2-vol. set. **Entries Include:** Book entries—Title, subtitle, author(s), editor(s), illustrator(s), publishing date, edition, price, binding, ISBN, LC number, publisher; Publisher entries—Name, address, phone, ISBN prefix. The material in "Children's Books in Print" is also available in subject-classified form in "Subject Guide to Children's Books in Print," also published in December. **Arrangement:** Alphabetical within each index. **Indexes:** Author, title, illustrator, award or prize, publisher.

2102 ■ "Copyright Clearance Center (CCC) Partnered with cSubs" in *Information Today* (Vol. 28, November 2011, No. 10, pp. 14)
Pub: Information Today, Inc.

Description: Copyright Clearance Center (CCC) partnered with cSubs to integrate CCC's point-of-content licensing solution RightsLink Basic directly into cSubs workflow. The partnership will allow cSubs' customers a user-friendly process for obtaining permissions. Csubs is a corporate subscription management service for books, newspapers, and econtent.

2103 ■ *Directory of Small Press—Magazine Editors and Publishers*
Pub: Dustbooks

Ed: Len Fulton, Editor. **Released:** Annual, Latest edition 42nd; 2011-2012. **Price:** $49.95, individuals online; $21, individuals CD-ROM. **Covers:** About 7,500 publishers and editors. **Entries Include:** Individual name, title of press or magazine, address and phone number. **Arrangement:** Alphabetical.

2104 ■ "EBSCO Adds New Features to EBSCOhost Content Viewer" in *Information Today* (Vol. 26, February 2009, No. 2, pp. 31)
Pub: Information Today, Inc.
Description: EBSCOhost Content Viewer historical digital archive collection provides a visual overview of a displayed document, highlighting search keywords on the page as well as providing a document map that shows the number of times a given keyword is mentioned in a periodical, monograph, article, or other document. For periodical content, the viewer lets users browse multiple issues in a volume without leaving the interface; features include zoom and pan technology similar to online maps.

2105 ■ *The Entrepreneurial Author*
Pub: Morgan James Publishing, LLC
Ed: David L. Hancock. **Released:** October 2009. **Price:** $17.95. **Description:** Handbook to help entrepreneurs author and publish a book based on their expertise in their chosen field.

2106 ■ "Etextbook Space Heats Up" in *Information Today* (Vol. 28, November 2011, No. 10, pp. 10)
Pub: Information Today, Inc.
Ed: Paula J. Hane. **Description:** The use of etextbooks is expected to grow with the use of mobile devices and tablets. A new group of activists is asking students, faculty members and others to sign a petition urging higher education leaders to prioritize affordable textbooks or free ebooks over the traditional, expensive new books required for classes.

2107 ■ "Etextbooks: Coming of Age" in *Information Today* (Vol. 28, September 2011, No. 8, pp. 1)
Pub: Information Today, Inc.
Ed: Amanda Mulvihill. **Description:** National average for textbooks costs was estimated at $1,137 annually at a 4-year public college for the 2010-2011 school year. Amazon reported selling 105 etextbooks for every 100 print books, while Barnes and Noble announced that their etextbooks were outselling print 3 to 1.

2108 ■ "Ex Libris Rosetta Hits the Market" in *Information Today* (Vol. 26, February 2009, No. 2, pp. 30)
Pub: Information Today, Inc.
Description: Ex Libris Rosetta, the latest version of the Ex Libris Group's Digital Preservation System supports the acquisition, validation, ingest, storage, management, preservation, and dissemination of digital objects, allowing libraries the infrastructure and technology to preserve and facilitate access to digital collections. The firm's Ex Libris Rosseta Charter Program helps users develop strategic collaboration between Ex Libris and its customers to improve the product.

2109 ■ "Ex-MP? Ex-con? Exactly!" in *Canadian Business* (Vol. 83, October 12, 2010, No. 17, pp. 16)
Pub: Rogers Media Ltd.
Ed: James Cowan. **Description:** British author Jeffrey Archer's novels could be made into movies. Archer sold 250 million books in 63 countries, which include political thrillers, spy novels, and crime capers.

2110 ■ "Facebook Purchased Push Pop Press" in *Information Today* (Vol. 28, October 2011, No. 9, pp. 12)
Pub: Information Today, Inc.
Description: Facebook purchased Push Pop Press, a digital publishing company that developed a multi-touch interface for ebook publishing on the iPad.

2111 ■ *First Editions, a Guide to Identification*
Pub: Spoon River Press
Ed: Edward N. Zempel, Editor. **Released:** Latest edition 4th. **Price:** $60, individuals hardcover, plus $3. 50, postage for U.S. delivery. **Covers:** 4,200 English language publishers and their methods of designating first editions. **Entries Include:** Publisher name, method of designation.

2112 ■ "Five More Great Books on Entrepreneurship" in *Entrepreneur* (Vol. 37, July 2009, No. 7, pp. 19)
Pub: Entrepreneur Media, Inc.
Description: 800-CEO-Read founder, Jack Covert, and president, Todd Stattersten, share five books that would have been included in the book, 'The 100 Business Books of All Time' if space was not an issue. 'You Need to Be a Little Crazy,' 'Oh, the Places You'll Go!,' 'Founders at Work,' 'The Innovator's Dilemma,' and 'Purple Cow' are highly recommended for entrepreneurs.

2113 ■ *From Entrepreneur to Infopreneur: Make Money with Books, E-Books, and Other Information Products*
Pub: John Wiley & Sons, Incorporated
Ed: Stephanie Chandler. **Released:** November 2006. **Price:** $19.95. **Description:** Infopreneurs sell information online in the forms of books, e-books, special reports, audio and video products, seminars, and more.

2114 ■ "A Good Book Is Worth a Thousand Blogs" in *Barron's* (Vol. 88, July 14, 2008, No. 28, pp. 42)
Pub: Dow Jones & Co., Inc.
Ed: Gene Epstein. **Description:** Nine summer book suggestions on economics are presented. The list includes 'The Revolution' by Ron Paul, 'The Forgotten Man' by Amity Shales, 'The Commitments of Traders Bible' by Stephen Briese, and 'Economic Facts and Fallacies' by Thomas Sowell.

2115 ■ "Guide to Carbon Footprinting" in *American Printer* (Vol. 128, June 1, 2011, No. 6)
Pub: Penton Media Inc.
Description: PrintCity Alliance published its new report, 'Carbon Footprint & Energy Reduction for Graphic Industry Value Chain.' The report aims to help improve the environmental performance of printers, converters, publishers, brand owners and their suppliers.

2116 ■ *Guild of Book Workers—Supplies and Services Directory*
Pub: Guild of Book Workers Inc.
Contact: Catherine Burkhard
Ed: Bernadette G. Callery, Editor. **Released:** Irregular, Latest edition November 2008. **Price:** $15, individuals 2001 issue. **Covers:** More than 250 manufacturers and suppliers of products used in bookbinding, calligraphy, and repair and conservation of documents and books; coverage includes Canada. **Entries Include:** Name of firm, address, phone, products or services, minimum order requirements, shipping restrictions, whether catalog or samples are available. **Arrangement:** Geographical, then by product or service. **Indexes:** Alphabetical.

2117 ■ "Harlequin Leads the Way" in *Marketing to Women* (Vol. 22, July 2009, No. 7, pp. 1)
Pub: EPM Communications, Inc.
Description: Although the publishing industry has been slow to embrace new media options, the Internet is now a primary source for reaching women readers. Harlequin has been eager to court their female consumers over the Internet and often uses women bloggers in their campaigns strategies.

2118 ■ "Health Care Leads Sectors Attracting Capital" in *Hispanic Business* (March 2008, pp. 14-16, 18)
Pub: Hispanic Business
Ed: Scott Williams. **Description:** U. S. Hispanic healthcare, media, and food were the key industries in the U.S. gaining investors in 2007.

2119 ■ "Hit the Books" in *Black Enterprise* (Vol. 38, July 2008, No. 12, pp. 42)
Pub: Earl G. Graves Publishing Co. Inc.
Ed: Mellody Hobson. **Description:** Four books that deal with investing are discussed as is the idea that reading even 15 minutes a day from one of these books will give you tools that far exceed what you can learn from magazines and the business section of your daily newspaper.

2120 ■ "Hitting the E-Books" in *Inc.* (Vol. 33, September 2011, No. 7, pp. 36)
Pub: Inc. Magazine
Ed: Shivani Vora. **Description:** Textbooks may be getting cheaper for college students now that they can use electronic textbooks that can be read on a laptop or tablet. The market is growing about 50 percent annually. Statistical data included.

2121 ■ "Ideas at Work: Total Communicator" in *Business Strategy Review* (Vol. 21, Autumn 2010, No. 3, pp. 10)
Pub: Blackwell Publishers Ltd.
Ed: Stuart Crainer. **Description:** Vittorio Colao has been chief executive of Vodafone Group for two years. He brings to the company special experience as CEO of RCS MediaGroup in Milan, which publishes newspapers, magazines and books in Italy, Spain and France. Prior to RCS, he held other positions within Vodaphone. Colao shares his views on business, the global economy and leading Vodafone.

2122 ■ "In It For the Long Run" in *Business Journal-Serving Phoenix & the Valley of the Sun* (Vol. 30, August 20, 2010, No. 50, pp. 1)
Pub: Phoenix Business Journal
Ed: Angela Gonzales. **Description:** Cancer survivor Helene Neville has finished a record-breaking 2,520-mile run in 93 days and then celebrated her 50th birthday despite being diagnosed with Hodgkins' lymphoma in 1991. Neveille, who is also a Phoenix area registered nurse, made stops along the way to promote her book, 'Nurses in Shape'. Neville also discusses how she fought her cancer through running.

2123 ■ *International Directory of Little Magazines and Small Presses*
Pub: Dustbooks
Ed: Len Fulton, Editor. **Released:** Annual, Latest edition 47th; 2011-2012. **Price:** $65, individuals CD-ROM (3 directories); $49.95, individuals online; $30, individuals CD-ROM. **Covers:** Over 4,000 small, independent magazines, presses, and papers. **Entries Include:** Name, address, size, circulation, frequency, price, type of material used, number of issues or books published annually, and other pertinent data. **Arrangement:** Alphabetical. **Indexes:** Subject, regional.

2124 ■ "Lafley Gives Look At His Game Plan" in *Business Courier* (Vol. 24, March 21, 2008, No. 50, pp. 1)
Pub: American City Business Journals, Inc.
Ed: Lisa Biank Fasig. **Description:** Overview of A.G. Lafley's book entitled 'The Game-Changer', is presented. Lafley, Procter & Gamble Co.'s chief executive officer, documented his philosophy and strategy in his book. His work also includes Procter & Gamble's hands-on initiatives such as mock-up grocery stores and personal interviews with homeowners.

2125 ■ *Library and Book Trade Almanac*
Pub: Information Today Inc.
Released: Annual, Latest edition 56th; June 2011. **Price:** $229, individuals hardbound; plus $17 shipping and handling charges; $206.10, individuals first time standing order. **Publication Includes:** Lists of accredited library schools; scholarships for education in library science; library organizations; library statistics; publishing and bookselling organizations. **Entries Include:** Directory listings give name of institution, address, phone, fax, name of officer or contact, publications; scholarship listings include requirements, value of grant, contact name. Principal content is articles and special reports on topics of interest to those in library/information science and publishers; international reports; annual reports from federal agencies and libraries and from national associations; information on legislation, funding, etc. **Arrangement:** Topical. **Indexes:** Organization; subject.

2126 ■ *Literary Market Place*
Pub: Information Today Inc.
Contact: Thomas H. Hogan, Pres. & Publisher
Released: Annual, Latest edition 2012. **Price:** $339, individuals 2-volume set/softbound plus $25 shipping/handling; $305.10, individuals first time standing

order. **Covers:** Over 12,500 firms or organizations offering services related to the publishing industry, including book publishers in the United States and Canada who issued three or more books during the preceding year, plus a small press section of publishers who publish less than three titles per year or those who are self-published. Also included: book printers and binders; book clubs; book trade and literary associations; selected syndicates, newspapers, periodicals, and radio and TV programs that use book reviews or book publishing news; translators and literary agents. **Entries Include:** For publishers—Company name, address, phone, address for orders, principal executives, editorial directors, and managers, date founded, number of titles in previous year, number of backlist titles in print, types of books published, ISBN prefixes, representatives, imprints, and affiliations. For suppliers, etc.—Listings usually show firm name, address, phone, executives, services, etc. **Arrangement:** Classified by line of business. **Indexes:** Principal index is 35,000-item combined index of publishers, publications, and personnel; several sections have geographical and/or subject indexes; translators are indexed by source and target language.

2127 ■ "Negotiating Tips" in *Black Enterprise* (Vol. 37, December 2006, No. 5, pp. 70)
Pub: Earl G. Graves Publishing Co. Inc.

Description: Sekou Kaalund, head of strategy, mergers & acquisitions at Citigroup Securities & Fund Services, states that "Negotiation skills are paramount to success in a business environment because of client, employee, and shareholder relationships". He discusses how the book by George Kohlrieser, Hostage at the Table: How Leaders Can Overcome Conflict, Influence Others, and Raise Performance, has helped him negotiate more powerfully and enhance his skills at conflict-resolution.

2128 ■ "New Approach to Mechanical Binding" in *American Printer* (Vol. 128, July 1, 2011, No. 7)
Pub: Penton Media Inc.

Description: EcoBinder coil binding system from Kugler-Womako eliminates traditional plastic combs or wire spiral with the use of 22-mm wide printable paper rings.

2129 ■ "New Book Takes Alternate View on Ontario's Wind Industry" in *CNW Group* (September 19, 2011)
Pub: CNW Group

Description: Dirty Business: The Reality Behind Ontario's Rush to Wind Power, was written by editor and health care writer Jane Wilson of Ottawa, Ontario, Canada along with contributing editor Parker Gallant. The book contains articles and papers on the wind business, including information on illnesses caused from the environmental noise.

2130 ■ "Online Book Sales Surpass Bookstores" in *Information Today* (Vol. 28, September 2011, No. 8, pp. 11)
Pub: Information Today, Inc.

Ed: Cindy Martine. **Description:** Online book sales outpaced bookstore purchases in the United States, signaling a shift in the US book industry. Statistical data included.

2131 ■ "Online Self-Publishing Services" in *Black Enterprise* (Vol. 37, November 2006, No. 4, pp. 90)
Pub: Earl G. Graves Publishing Co. Inc.

Description: Profiles of five online self-publishing services.

2132 ■ *Publishers' Catalogues*
Pub: Northern Lights Internet Solutions Ltd.
Contact: Peter Scott, Publisher
E-mail: scott@lights.com

Released: Continuous updates. **Price:** Free. **Covers:** Publishing companies worldwide. **Entries Include:** Company name, address, phone, fax, titles. **Arrangement:** Geographical by country, then alphabetical.

2133 ■ *Publishers Directory*
Pub: Gale

Released: Annual, Latest edition 36th; April, 2011. **Price:** $720, individuals. **Covers:** Over 20,000 new and established, commercial and nonprofit, private and alternative, corporate and association, government and institution publishing programs and their distributors; includes producers of books, classroom materials, prints, reports, and databases. **Entries Include:** Firm name, address, phone, fax, company e-mail address, URL, year founded, ISBN prefix, Standard Address Number, whether firm participates in the Cataloging in Publication program of the Library of Congress, names of principal executives, personal e-mail addresses, number of titles in print, description of firm and its main subject interests, discount and returns policies, affiliated and parent companies, mergers and amalgamations, principal markets, imprints and divisions, alternate formats products are offered; distributors also list firms for which they distribute, special services, terms to publishers and regional offices. **Arrangement:** Alphabetical; distributors listed separately. **Indexes:** Subject, geographical, publisher, imprints, and distributor.

2134 ■ *Publishers, Distributors, and Wholesalers of the United States*
Pub: R.R. Bowker L.L.C.

Released: Annual, latest edition 2010. **Price:** $500, individuals in 2 volumes; hard cover. **Covers:** Over 196,066 publishers, distributors, and wholesalers; includes associations, museums, software producers and manufacturers, and others not included in 'Books in Print'. **Entries Include:** Publisher name, editorial and ordering addresses, e-mail, websites, phone, Standard Address Numbers (SANs), International Standard Book Number prefix. **Arrangement:** Alphabetical; distributors and wholesalers are listed separately. **Indexes:** ISBN prefix, abbreviation, type of business, imprint name, geographical, inactive and out of business company name, toll-free phone and fax, wholesaler and distributor.

2135 ■ *The Publishing Game: Publish a Book in 30 Days*
Pub: Peanut Butter and Jelly Press LLC

Ed: Fern Reiss. **Released:** January 31, 2003. **Price:** $19.95. **Description:** Excellent resource for individuals wanting to write a book and become their own publisher.

2136 ■ "Publishing Technology Introduces IngentaConnect Mobile" in *Information Today* (Vol. 26, February 2009, No. 2, pp. 33)
Pub: Information Today, Inc.

Description: College undergraduates will find Publishing Technology's newest publisher product, IngentaConnect Mobile helpful. The product allows users to read articles and abstracts on mobile devices. According to a recent study, 73 percent of young adults with wireless hand-held devices use them to access non-voice data on any given day.

2137 ■ "Reducing the Book's Carbon Footpring" in *American Printer* (Vol. 128, July 1, 2011, No. 7)
Pub: Penton Media Inc.

Description: Green Press Initiative's Book Industry Environmental Council is working to achieve a 20 percent reduction in the book industry's carbon footprint by 2020. The Council is made up of publishers, printers, paper suppliers, and non-governmental organizations.

2138 ■ "SAGE Publications Announced a Partnership with Which Medical Device" in *Information Today* (Vol. 28, November 2011, No. 10, pp. 15)
Pub: Information Today, Inc.

Description: SAGE Publications has partnered with Which Medical Device to offer insights, tutorials, and reviews of medical devices.

2139 ■ "Savvy Solutions" in *Black Enterprise* (Vol. 41, November 2010, No. 4, pp. 42)
Pub: Earl G. Graves Publishing Co. Inc.

Ed: Tennile M. Robinson. **Description:** Society of Children's Book Writers and Illustrators offers members many benefits, including directories of agencies looking for new writers of books.

2140 ■ "Scientific American Builds Novel Blog Network" in *Information Today* (Vol. 28, September 2011, No. 8, pp. 12)
Pub: Information Today, Inc.

Ed: Kurt Schiller. **Description:** Scientific American launched a new blog network that joins a diverse lineup of bloggers cover various scientific topics under one banner. The blog network includes 60 bloggers providing insights into the ever-changing world of science and technology.

2141 ■ "The Seat-Of-The-Pants School of Marketing" in *Brandweek* (Vol. 49, April 21, 2008, No. 16, pp. 24)
Pub: VNU Business Media, Inc.

Ed: David Vinjamuri. **Description:** Excerpt from the book "Accidental Branding: How Ordinary People Build Extraordinary Brands," by David Vinjamuri, discusses six shared principles for creating a brand that is unique and will be successful over the long-term.

2142 ■ *The Self-Publishing Manual: How To Write, Print, and Sell Your Own Book*
Pub: Para Publishing

Ed: Dan Poynter. **Released:** 2007. **Price:** $19.95. **Description:** The book provides a complete course in writing, publishing, marketing, promoting, and distributing books. Poynter offers a step-by-step study of the publishing industry and explains various book-marketing techniques.

2143 ■ "Serials Solutions Launches 360 Resource Manager Consortium Edition" in *Information Today* (Vol. 26, February 2009, No. 2, pp. 32)
Pub: Information Today, Inc.

Description: Serials Solutions new Serials Solutions 360 Resource Manager Consortium Edition helps consortia, groups and member libraries with their e-resource management services. The products allows users to consolidate e-resource metadata and acquisition information into one place, which enables groups to manage holdings, subscriptions, licensing, contacts, and cost information and to streamline delivery of information to members.

2144 ■ *Society for Scholarly Publishing—Membership Directory*
Pub: Society for Scholarly Publishing
Contact: Ann Mehan Crosse CAE, Exec. Dir.
E-mail: amehan@resourcenter.com

Released: Annual. **Database Covers:** More than 1,000 librarians, publishers, printers, authors, and editors interested in scholarly publication; related organizations. **Database Includes:** Name, title, address, phone, organization. **Arrangement:** Alphabetical.

2145 ■ "Spotlight; 'Classroom Focus' at Encyclopaedia Britannica" in *Crain's Chicago Business* (Vol. 34, October 24, 2011, No. 42, pp. 6)
Pub: Crain Communications Inc.

Ed: Paul Merrion. **Description:** Profile of Gregory Healy, product officer for Encyclopaedia Britannica is presented. Healy took the position in May 2010 and is focused on online offerings of their publication and to make them more useful to teachers.

2146 ■ "Swedes Swoop In To Save Time4" in *Advertising Age* (Vol. 78, January 29, 2007, No. 5, pp. 4)
Pub: Crain Communications, Inc.

Ed: Nat Ives. **Description:** Overview of Stockholm's Bonnier Group, a family-owned publisher that is looking to expand its U.S. presence; Bonnier recently acquired a number of Time Inc. magazines.

2147 ■ "The Way I Work: Kim Kleeman" in *Inc.* (October 2007, pp. 110-112, 114)
Pub: Gruner & Jahr USA Publishing

Ed: Leigh Buchanan. **Description:** Profile of Kim Kleemna, founder and president of ShakespeareSquared, a firm that develops educational materials, including lesson plans, teacher guides, activity workbooks, and discussion guides for large publishers. Kleeman talks about the challenges she faces running her nearly all-women company while maintaining a balance with her family.

2148 ■ "Traits that Makes Blogs Attractive to Book Publishers" in *Marketing to Women* (Vol. 22, July 2009, No. 7, pp. 1)
Pub: EPM Communications, Inc.
Description: Book publishers are finding a beneficial relationship between themselves and women bloggers on the Internet. A high visitor count, frequent updates and active readership are criteria for identifying the blogs with the most clout and therefore providing the greatest benefit to publishers.

2149 ■ "University Book Store Inc.: an Act of Independence" in *Retail Merchandiser* (Vol. 51, September-October 2011, No. 5, pp. 68)
Pub: Phoenix Media Corporation
Ed: Lori Sichtermann. **Description:** University Book Store Inc. is a campus bookstore located at the University of Washington, in Seattle. The book store provides more than $1 million in UW customer rebates and discounts annually and donated more than $800,000 in UW student scholarships.

2150 ■ "An Updated Ranking of Academic Journals in Economics" in *Canadian Journal of Economics* (Vol. 44, November 2011, No. 4, pp. 1525)
Pub: Blackwell Publishers Ltd.
Ed: Pantelis Kalaitzidakis, Theofanis P. Mamuneas, Thanasis Stengos. **Description:** An updated list showing the ranking of economic journals (2003) is presented; however this present study differs methodologically from an earlier study by using a rolling window of years between 2003 and 2008, for each year counting the number of citations of articles published in the previous ten years.

2151 ■ "Why Women Blog and What They Read" in *Marketing to Women* (Vol. 22, July 2009, No. 7, pp. 8)
Pub: EPM Communications, Inc.
Description: Listing of topics that are visited the most by female Internet users. Statistical data included.

2152 ■ "Wikinomics: The Sequel" in *Business Strategy Review* (Vol. 21, Summer 2010, No. 2, pp. 64)
Pub: Wiley-Blackwell
Description: Ever-optimistic Don Tapscott and Anthony Williams, coauthors of Wikinomics and individually, of a number of other books that study the Internet and its relation to society, are now working on a new book, one for which they're using the Internet to determine its title.

2153 ■ "Women Prefer Cookbooks Over Word-Of-Mouth for Recipe Suggestions" in *Marketing to Women* (Vol. 23, November 2010, No. 11, pp. 6)
Pub: EPM Communications, Inc.
Description: Sixty-five percent of women surveyed enjoy a sit-down dinner at least five times a week according to Martha Steward Omni-media. Cookbooks, recipe Websites, food-focused magazines, and TV cooking shows are their primary source for new recipes.

STATISTICAL SOURCES

2154 ■ *Book Industry Trends*
Pub: Book Industry Study Group, Inc.
Ed: Compiled by Statistical Service Center staff. **Released:** 2009. **Price:** $875.00 (paper).

2155 ■ *RMA Annual Statement Studies*
Pub: Robert Morris Associates (RMA)
Released: Annual. **Price:** $175.00 2006-07 edition, $105.00. **Description:** Contains composite balance sheets and income statements for more than 360 industries, including the accounting, auditing, and bookkeeping industries. Also contains five years of comparative historical data for discerning trends. Includes 16 commonly used ratios, computed for most of the size groupings for nearly every industry.

2156 ■ *Standard & Poor's Industry Surveys*
Pub: Standard & Poor's Corp.
Released: Annual. **Price:** $3633.00. **Description:** Two-volume book that examines the prospects for specific industries, including trucking. Also provides analyses of trends and problems, statistical tables and charts, and comparative company analyses.

2157 ■ *U.S. Book Publishing Industry*
Pub: Business Trend Analysts, Inc.
Released: 2007. **Price:** $149.00. **Description:** The Book Publishing Industry report features 2008 current and 2009 forecast estimates on the size of the industry (sales, establishments, employment) nationally and for all 50 U.S. States and over 900 metro areas.

TRADE PERIODICALS

2158 ■ *AAP Monthly Report*
Pub: Association of American Publishers Inc.
Ed: Judith Platt, Editor, jplatt@publishers.org. **Released:** Monthly. **Price:** Included in membership. **Description:** Examines subjects of interest to publishers, including copyright issues, First Amendment issues, Washington legislation, and programs and activities of the Association. Recurring features include reports of meetings, and notices of publications available.

2159 ■ *Book Marketing Update*
Pub: Open Horizons
Ed: John Kremer, Editor, johnkremer@bookmarket.com. **Released:** Semimonthly. **Price:** $297, U.S. and Canada; $337, elsewhere. **Description:** Surveys resources for publishers interested in marketing their books to bookstores, libraries, wholesalers, catalogs, book clubs, and other special markets.

2160 ■ *The Bookwoman*
Pub: Women's National Book Association
Ed: Ellen Myrick, Editor, ellenmyrick@ingrambook.com. **Released:** 3/year. **Price:** $10, nonmembers in U.S.; $12, nonmembers elsewhere. **Description:** Covers major topics of interest to publishers, librarians, educators, writers, and agents in the book world. Recurring features include editorials, letters to the editor, book reviews, and news of members, articles, essays, profiles of woman-owned presses, and news of the bookworld and WNBA chapters.

2161 ■ *Fiction Writer's Guideline*
Pub: Fiction Writer's Connection
Contact: Blythe Camenson, Editor & Dir.
E-mail: bcamenson@aol.com
Released: Enewsletter. **Price: Description:** Offers practical advice and support on writing and getting published. Recurring features include interviews, book reviews, and Advice From agents and editors and Writing Tips.

2162 ■ *Guild of Book Workers Newsletter*
Pub: Guild of Book Workers Inc.
Contact: Catherine Burkhard
Ed: Margaret Johnson, Editor. **Released:** Bimonthly, Every 2 months. **Price:** Included in membership. **Description:** Covers issues in book arts, binding, book conservation, calligraphy, and printing. Recurring features include letters to the editor, interviews, news of research, a calendar of events, reports of meetings, news of educational opportunities, job listings, book reviews, and notices of publications available.

2163 ■ *The Horn Book Magazine*
Pub: The Horn Book Inc.
Contact: Andrew Thorne, VP Mktg.
Released: Bimonthly. **Price:** $49; $66 Canada and Mexico; $70 other countries. **Description:** Journal devoted to children's and young adult literature.

2164 ■ *How To Be Your Own Publisher Update*
Pub: Bibliotheca Press
Contact: A. Doyle
Ed: A. Doyle, Editor. **Released:** Annual. **Price:** $12.95, U.S.; $15.95, Canada; $19.95, other countries. **Description:** Acts as a reference for self publishers. Distributed by Prosperity & Profits Unlimited Distribution Services, PO Box 416, Denver, CO, 80201.

2165 ■ *Independent Publisher Online*
Pub: Jenkins Group Inc.
Contact: Jim Barnes, Managing Editor
E-mail: jimb@bookpublishing.com
Released: Monthly. **Description:** Online magazine containing book reviews and articles about independent publishing.

2166 ■ *Journal of Scholarly Publishing*
Pub: University of Toronto Press-Journal Div.
Ed: Tom Radko, Editor, tradko@ala-choice.org. **Released:** Quarterly. **Price:** $40 U.S. and Canada print; $105 institutions print only; $35 members print only. **Description:** Journal covering scholarly publishing from writer to reader.

2167 ■ *Kirkus Reviews*
Pub: Nielsen Business Media
Contact: Anne Larsen, Executive Editor
E-mail: larsenx13@aol.com
Released: Semimonthly. **Price:** $355, institutions libraries according to book budget. **Description:** Publishes book reviews on current titles of both fiction and nonfiction for adults and children. Also provides author, publisher, price, and page count.

2168 ■ *Laughing Bear Newsletter*
Pub: Laughing Bear Press
Ed: Tom Person, Editor, editor@laughingbear.com. **Released:** Monthly. **Price:** $15, U.S.; $17.50, Canada; $25, elsewhere. **Description:** Reviews small press and business publications; provides information and resources on publishing, designs, and planning techniques for self-published books. Contains news and commentary on independent publishing and related services.

2169 ■ *PMA Independent*
Pub: Independent Book Publishers Association
Ed: Jan Nathan, Editor. **Released:** Monthly. **Price:** $12, members; $40, nonmembers others. **Description:** Informs member entrepreneurial book publishers about upcoming marketing programs and other Association activities aimed at helping independent publishers succeed. Also carries articles on topics such as desktop publishing and typesetting systems. Recurring features include member, committee, and research news, notices of educational and cooperative marketing opportunities, a calendar of events, and columns titled News from the "Net" and From the Director's Desk.

2170 ■ *Professional Publishing Report*
Pub: SIMBA Information Inc.
Contact: Jason W. Fuchs, Research Specialist
Released: Monthly. **Price:** $749 USA and Canada. **Description:** Features news on the publishing industry, including company figures, mergers, industry trends, revenue comparisons, and more.

2171 ■ *Publishers Weekly*
Pub: Publishers Weekly
Contact: Sonia Jaffe Robbins, Managing Editor
Released: Weekly. **Price:** $249.99; $299.99 Canada; $399.99 other countries air delivery. **Description:** Magazine for publishers.

2172 ■ *Publishing Executive*
Pub: North American Publishing Co.
Contact: Noelle Skodzinski, Editorial Dir.
E-mail: nskodzinski@napco.com
Released: 10/yr. **Description:** Trade magazine covering current trends in print production of magazines, catalogs, books, direct mail, corporate publishing, and advertising agencies.

2173 ■ *Publishing Poynters*
Pub: Para Publishing
Contact: Dan Poynter
Ed: Dan Poynter, Editor, DanPoynter@ParaPublishing.com. **Released:** Semimonthly, 2/month. **Description:** Contains publishing industry news as well as management and marketing suggestions. Recurring features include news of research, news of educational opportunities, book reviews, and notices of publications available.

2174 ■ *The Russ von Hoelscher Direct Response Profit Report*
Pub: Publishers Media
Contact: Teri Apodaca, office manager
Ed: Russ von Hoelscher, Editor. **Released:** 8/year. **Price:** $36 1 year; $60 2 years. **Description:** Provides marketing advice for independent publishers and small presses, with special emphasis given to the non-bookstore market. Recurring features include letters to the editor, interviews, news of research, and book reviews, plus how to sell by mail and on the internet.

2175 ■ *Sell More Books! Newsletter*
Pub: Florida Publishers Association
Ed: Betsy Wright-Lampe, Editor. **Released:** Bimonthly. **Price:** Included in membership. **Description:** Reports on news, events, and updates of the Florida Publishers Association. Also focuses on publishing companies, book successes, and useful tips.

2176 ■ *SPEX*
Pub: Bay Area Independent Publishers Association (BAIPA)
Contact: Margaret Speaker Yuan, Programs & Editor
E-mail: myuan@slip.net
Released: Monthly. **Description:** Discusses opportunities and changes in the field of publishing. Reviews members' books. Publicizes meetings, seminars, and other information of importance to small publishers. Recurring features include letters to the editor, interviews, news of research, a calendar of events, news of members, and a column titled the President's Message.

VIDEOCASSETTES/ AUDIOCASSETTES

2177 ■ *Inside Business Today*
GPN Educational Media
1550 Executive Drive
Elgin, IL 60123
Ph:(402)472-2007
Free: 800-228-4630
Fax:800-306-2330
Co. E-mail: askgpn@smarterville.com
URL: http://www.shopgpn.com
Released: 1989. **Description:** Leaders in business and industry tell their success stories in this extensive series. **Availability:** VHS; 3/4U.

TRADE SHOWS AND CONVENTIONS

2178 ■ Bologna Children's Book Fair - Fiera Del Libro Per Ragazzi
Bologna Fiere
Via della Fiera 20
40128 Bologna, Italy
Ph:39 51 282111
Fax:39 51 6374004
Co. E-mail: segreteria.generale@bolognafiere.it
URL: http://www.bolognafiere.it
Released: Annual. **Principal Exhibits:** Children's and juvenile books, text books and electronic books.

2179 ■ Special Libraries Association Information Revolution
Special Libraries Association
331 South Patrick St.
Alexandria, VA 22314-3501
Ph:(703)647-4900
Fax:(703)647-4901
Co. E-mail: sla@sla.org
URL: http://www.sla.org
Released: Annual. **Audience:** Information managers and librarians. **Principal Exhibits:** Library equipment, supplies, and services, including computers and software, Database information.

CONSULTANTS

2180 ■ About Books Inc.
1618 W Colorado Ave.
PO Box 1500
Colorado Springs, CO 80904-4029
Ph:(719)632-8226
Free: 800-548-1876
Fax:(719)471-2182
Co. E-mail: infoabi@about-books.com
URL: http://www.about-books.com
Contact: Lisa Gilman, Principle
E-mail: debiflora@atsabout-books.com
Scope: Full service writing and publishing consultants organized to assist corporations, organizations and individuals in the writing, editing, producing and marketing of books. Also develop sponsored and premium books. **Publications:** "Molding Young Athletes," Purington Press.

2181 ■ Donald Wigal
4 Park Ave., Ste. 8M
PO Box 432
New York, NY 10016
Ph:(212)683-3478
Fax:(212)683-8064
Co. E-mail: donwigal@ix.netcom.com
URL: http://www.dwigal.com
E-mail: donwigal@ix.netcom.com
Scope: Offers services and products to businesses and individuals. Newsgroup and web searching consulting services include database searching, ad copy, a-presentations, career guidance and niche marketing. Other services include manuscript preparation, editing, copy editing, abstracting and indexing. **Publications:** "The Cicero Project: A Celebration of Old Age by Common Bonders," 2009; "1000 Beromda Konstverk," 2007; "1000 Genialnich Obrazu," 2007; "Faszination des Opiums in Geschichte und Kunst, Die," Parkstone International, 2004; "Who's Who in the East".

2182 ■ Editorial Code and Data Inc.
814 Wolverine Dr., Ste. 2
Walled Lake, MI 48390
Ph:(248)926-5187
Fax:(248)926-6047
Co. E-mail: monique@marketsize.com
URL: http://www.marketsize.com
Contact: Joyce P. Simkin, Mgr
E-mail: monique@marketsize.com
Scope: Provides data and computer services primarily to the publishing industry, with specialization in statistical data drawn from government sources. Services include data acquisition, analysis, formatting, and typesetting, archiving of computer data on CD-ROM, custom data display, search, and printing software, information brokering services, and related services such as design, writing, and data processing design. Industries served: publishing, in-house printing, non-profit organizations, government agencies, utilities, and manufacturing. **Publications:** "Market Share Reporter"; "Encyclopedia of Products & Industries"; "Economic Indicators Handbook"; "American Salaries and Wages Survey"; "Dun and Bradstreet & Gale: Industrial Handbook"; "Reference American Cost of Living Survey".

2183 ■ Edward F. McCartan Publishing Consultant
220 E 54th St.
New York, NY 10022
Ph:(212)421-2641
Fax:(212)421-4115
Co. E-mail: edmccartan@aol.com
E-mail: edmccartan@aol.com
Scope: Advises potential author or authors with unpublished manuscripts on content, style, and form by written evaluation. Edits manuscripts for spelling, grammar, punctuation, and consistency.

2184 ■ Harian Creative Enterprises
47 Hyde Blvd.
Ballston Spa, NY 12020
Ph:(518)885-6699
Contact: Harry Barba, Publisher
Scope: Literary service for writers and publishers, offering counsel on the writing and completion of literary projects, including titling, book and jacket design and editorial work. Industries served: Education, culture, and art and entertainment. **Seminars:** The Workshop Under the Sky.

2185 ■ Heidelberg Graphics
2 Stansbury Ct.
Chico, CA 95928
Ph:(530)342-6582
Fax:(530)342-6582
Co. E-mail: service@heidelberggraphics.com
URL: http://www.heidelberggraphics.com
Contact: Larry S. Jackson, Owner
Scope: Offers services including scans, disc conversions, layouts, editing and printing for books, catalogs and magazines. Provides the codes on paper, disk, film, embedded in designs, or in variable labeling and personalized printing. Serves private industries as well as government agencies. **Publications:** "Chronicles of the Clandestine Knights: Hyacinth Blue," 2003; "A Book of Thoughts II," 2001; "Historic Shot Glasses: The pre-Prohibition," 1992; "After the War," 1981; "Phantasm," 1980.

2186 ■ J. S. Eliezer Associates Inc.
300 Atlantic St., 7th Fl.
Stamford, CT 06901-3513
Ph:(203)658-1300
Fax:(203)658-1301
Co. E-mail: dmckenna@jseliezer.com
URL: http://www.jseliezer.com
Contact: Mark J. Vallely, Principle
E-mail: jeliezer@atsjseliezer.com
Scope: Management and market research consultants offering design and implementation of manufacturing strategy, feasibility analysis and systems analysis, as well as management information systems and prepress systems; manufacturing proposals analysis, negotiations and contracts; paper purchasing strategy and contract negotiations; catalog distribution effectiveness analysis. Serves the publishing and catalog industries.

2187 ■ James Peter Associates Inc.
PO Box 772
Tenafly, NJ 07670
Ph:(201)568-0760
Fax:(201)568-2959
Co. E-mail: bertholtje@compuserve.com
Contact: Herbert F. Holtje, Principle
E-mail: bholtje@atsattmail.com
Scope: Consults with publishers and industry on such projects for total book production from conception through writing, design and illustration to camera-ready copy, video tapes and programmed instruction. Also works with businesses and non-profit organizations to develop books and periodical publications.

2188 ■ The K.S. Giniger Company Inc.
1045 Park Ave.
New York, NY 10028
Ph:(212)369-6692
Fax:(212)269-6692
Co. E-mail: bernicecullinan@verizon.net
Contact: Kenneth Seeman Giniger, President
Scope: Consultants on book publishing to publishers of books, magazines and newsletters, direct sales organizations, government agencies, educational organizations, financial and investment institutions; public relations and advertising agencies. Clients in the United States, Canada, Mexico, England, Denmark, France, Spain, Switzerland, Germany, Israel, Singapore and Australia.

2189 ■ Leon Gelfond & Associates
17266 Boca Club Blvd., Apt. 1606
Boca Raton, FL 33487-1279
Ph:(561)995-0865
Contact: Renee M. Gelfond, Principle
Scope: Consultants offering services in mail order, fulfillment, data processing, shipping and warehousing, printing, and book packaging. Primarily serving the publishing industry. Also has the capabilities and facilities for providing clients with a complete mail order package, from the creation to the printing and mailing of the promotion. Serves government also.

2190 ■ The Live Oak Press L.L.C.
445 Burgess Dr.
PO Box 60036
Menlo Park, CA 94306-0036
Ph:(650)853-0197

Fax:(815)366-8205
Co. E-mail: mhamilton@liveoakpress.com
URL: http://www.liveoakpress.com
Contact: David M. Hamilton, President
E-mail: mhamilton@liveoakpress.com
Scope: Manages design and implementation of publishing programs. Also offers complete book and magazine preparation and publishing consulting, including web resources, advertising, concept development, manuscript, design, development and production through finished product. Specializes in high-technology clients and electronic publishing. **Publications:** "The Tools of My Trade"; "To the Yukon with Jack London"; "Earthquakes and Young Volcanoes"; "The Lost Cement Mine"; "Inner Voyage"; "Studies in the Development of Consciousness"; "Dialectical Realism: Studies on a Philosophy of Growth"; "Mammoth Lakes Sierra"; "Deepest Valley"; "Mammoth Gold"; "Old Mammoth". **Seminars:** Internet publishing Aeminar.

2191 ■ Martin Cook Associates Ltd.
353 Strawtown Rd.
New City, NY 10956
Ph:(914)639-5316
Fax:(914)639-5318
Co. E-mail: martin@mcabooks.com
URL: http://www.mcabooks.com
Contact: Martin H. Cook, President
E-mail: mcanewcity@aol.com
Scope: Provides book and print production and design management to publishers, foundations, and corporations. Offers allied graphic services, including copy editing, proofreading, design and typography of books, jackets and print materials, typesetting, color separations, printing, binding, warehousing, and distribution. Also conducts budgeting, scheduling, and sourcing of foreign and domestic suppliers based on cost, schedule, and quality requirements.

2192 ■ Moseley Associates Inc.
6 Bart Bull Rd.
Middeltown, NY 10941
Ph:(212)988-2834
Fax:(212)717-2435
Co. E-mail: pwadams@consultmoseley.com
URL: http://www.consultmoseley.com
Contact: Cameron S. Moseley, Chairman of the Board
E-mail: pwadams@consultmoseley.com
Scope: Management consultants to the publishing industry-commercial and nonprofit-in the United States and international markets. Expertise in publishing areas: books, periodicals and non-print media. Consulting in all aspects of the publishing process: management studies, business planning, organization evaluation, research and development, financial analysis, editorial, marketing, market research, sales, production, warehousing and distribution, order fulfillment and related operations. Also has expertise with organization and operating technology for new publishing and information service enterprises, as well as acquisitions, divestitures, and mergers. Extensive experience in appraisals of books, magazines and learning materials; and of entire publishing firms. Has worked with government agencies. **Publications:** "Is This the End of Publishing? As We Know It," Jun, 2007; "US School Publishing," Apr, 2001; "A Century of Progress," Jun, 2006; "Technology in Publishing: A Century of Progress," Against the Grain, May, 2001; "Why I Don't Read Electronic Journals: An Iconoclast Speaks Out," Sep, 1997; "Post-Traumatic Shock Syndrome, Or, Surviving the Merger," Jun, 2009; "Familiar and Unfamiliar Quotations," Apr, 2009.

2193 ■ nSight Inc.
1 Van de Graaff Dr., Ste. 202
Burlington, MA 01803-5171
Ph:(781)273-6300
Fax:(781)273-6301
Co. E-mail: sales@nsightworks.com
URL: http://www.nsightworks.com
Contact: Sharon K. Smith, Mgr
E-mail: ssmith@atsnsightworks.com
Scope: Provides complete communications and publications support and training through its four divisions. Temporary and Permanent Placement Division assigns tested publications professionals to companies. Consulting offers consulting services such as publications evaluation and Internet strategies. Industries served: Computer industry, management and environmental consulting firms, book publishers, banks and government agencies. **Seminars:** Business Writing: Grammar and Usage; XML: An Introduction; XML: DTD Design; Writing and Editing for the Web; Writing for Public Relations; Editing for an International Audience; Creating Effective PowerPoint Presentations; Instructional Design for Blended Learning: A Practical Approach, Apr, 2008; Project Management for Publishing Writers and Editors, Mar, 2008; Online Editing with MS Word and Adobe Acrobat, Mar, 2008; Copyediting for Technical Documentation, Mar, 2008; Advanced Copyediting for Technical Documentation, Mar, 2008; Business Writing: Grammar and Usage, Mar, 2008; Copyediting for BioTech/Medical Documentation, Feb, 2008; Copyediting Fundamentals, Feb, 2008; Editing International Documents, Feb, 2008; Creating Corporate Style Guides, Feb, 2008; Creating a Web Content Style Guide, Feb, 2008; Design for Non-Designers, Feb, 2008; HTML 4.01 Web Authoring Basic, Jan, 2008; Indexing Technical Documentation, Jan, 2008; Polishing Your Writing through Self-Editing, Jan, 2008; Proofreading essentials, Jan, 2008; Substantive and Developmental Editing, Jan, 2008.

2194 ■ Stillman H. Publishers Inc.
21405 Woodchuck Ln.
Boca Raton, FL 33428
Ph:(561)482-6343
Contact: Herbert Stillman, President
Scope: Offers consulting services in the following areas: management, start ups, profit maximization, world wide negotiating, interim management, corporate debt resolution.

FRANCHISES AND BUSINESS OPPORTUNITIES

2195 ■ FinderBinder/SourceBook Directories
5173 Waring Rd., Ste. 8
San Diego, CA 92120
Ph:(619)582-8500
Free: 800-255-2575
No. of Franchise Units: 20. **No. of Company-Owned Units:** 1. **Founded:** 1974. **Franchised:** 1978. **Description:** Current news media directories for specific areas. $20,000-$25,000. **Franchise Fee:** $2,000. **Financial Assistance:** No. **Managerial Assistance:** An operations manual is provided. **Training:** Franchisor provides a field representative to assist franchise for a minimum of 8 hours and for further time as deemed necessary by the franchisor. Supervisory assistance is available at the discretion of the franchisor.

2196 ■ The Little Black Book For Every Busy Woman
LBB LLC
PO Box 21466
Charleston, SC 29413
Free: (866)958-8600
Fax:(843)853-0771
No. of Franchise Units: 7. **No. of Company-Owned Units:** 1. **Founded:** 1999. **Franchised:** 2003. **Description:** Publish a directory for women. **Equity Capital Needed:** $22,000-$47,000, includes franchise fee. **Franchise Fee:** $12,000-$22,000. **Financial Assistance:** No. **Training:** Yes.

COMPUTERIZED DATABASES

2197 ■ *Book Review Index Online*
Cengage Learning Inc.
27500 Drake Rd.
Farmington Hills, MI 48331-3535
Ph:(248)699-4253
Free: 800-877-4253
Fax:(248)699-8069
Co. E-mail: galeord@gale.com
URL: http://gale.cengage.com
Description: Contains access to more than 5.6 million reviews of more than 2.5 million books, periodicals, books-on-tape, and electronic media representing a full range of popular, academic, and professional interests. Includes citations for both newly published and older materials. Publications and newspapers indexed include: *American Journal of Education, Belles Lettres, Books in Canada, Children's Book News, Choice, Essence, German Quarterly, Irish Literary Supplement, Kirkus Reviews, Library Journal, Middle East Policy, Mother Jones, New York Times Book Review, Publishers Weekly, Times Literary Supplement, Village Voice, Women's Review of Books, World Literature Today*, and *Yale Review*. Corresponds to *Book Review Index*. **Availability:** Online: Cengage Learning Inc. **Type:** Bibliographic.

2198 ■ *BooksInPrint.com Professional*
R.R. Bowker LLC
630 Central Ave.
New Providence, NJ 07974
Ph:(908)268-1090
Free: 888-269-5372
Fax:(908)665-3528
Co. E-mail: customerservice@bowker.com
URL: http://www.bowker.com
Description: Contains bibliographic descriptions and ordering information for more than 5 million books currently in print or declared out of print (from July 1979 to date), active and inactive audios and videos, and soon-to-be-published titles from some 200,000 publishers. Also contains more than 700,000 full-text reviews, more than 200,000 book jacket images, author biographies, and 140,000 tables of contents. Coverage includes scholarly, popular, adult, juvenile, reprint, and other books on all subjects published by U.S. publishers or exclusively distributed in the United States and available to the trade or general public for single- or multiple-copy purchases. Such items as government publications, Bibles, free books, and subscription-only titles are excluded. Also provides the complete text of reviews from *Library Journal, Publisher's Weekly*, and *School Library Journal*. Corresponds to *Books in Print, Books Out of Print, Forthcoming Books, Books in Print Supplement, Scientific and Technical Books in Print, Medical and Health Care Books in Print, Children's Books in Print, Paperbound Books in Print*, and *Law Books in Print*. Subject classification scheme utilizes more than 72,000 Library of Congress subject headings as well as Sears headings. **Availability:** Online: R.R. Bowker LLC, Colorado Alliance of Research Libraries, ProQuest LLC; CD-ROM: R.R. Bowker LLC. **Type:** Bibliographic.

2199 ■ *LC MARC: Books All*
U.S. Library of Congress
101 Independence Ave. SE
Washington, DC 20541-4912
Ph:(202)707-6100
Fax:(202)707-1334
Co. E-mail: cdsinfo@loc.gov
URL: http://www.loc.gov/cds
Description: Contains bibliographic and cataloging information on more than 9.1 million monographs published worldwide since 1968. Covers books in English since 1968; in French, since 1973; in German, Portuguese, and Spanish, since 1975; in other Roman alphabet languages, since 1976-77; in South Asian and Cyrillic alphabet languages (in Romanized form), since 1979; in Greek (in Romanized form), since 1980. Also covers Chinese, Japanese, and Korean (in Romanized form) from 1983 to 1989; Hebrew and Yiddish (in Romanized form) from 1983 to 1989; and Arabic and Persian (in Romanized form) from 1983 to 1990. Provides basic bibliographic data from LC Machine Readable Cataloging (MARC) records. Provides information derived from books, pamphlets, manuscripts, maps and atlases, monographic microform publications (both microform reissues and items originally issued in microform), and all monographic national and international government publications. Data provided in each record vary by online service, but may include LC card number, title, author, series, publisher, publication date, place of publication, International Standard Book Number, call number, language, document type, notes, and subject classification. Also includes some Cataloging in Publication data. Includes older PREMARC records called OCLC Replacement Records. Corresponds in part to the *National Union Catalog*. **Availability:** On-

line: ProQuest LLC, ProQuest LLC, British Library, University of Tsukuba, U.S. Library of Congress. **Type:** Bibliographic.

LIBRARIES

2200 ■ American Booksellers Association ABA Information Service Center
200 White Plains Rd. Ste. 600
Tarrytown, NY 10591
Free: 800-637-0037
Fax:(914)591-2720
Co. E-mail: info@bookweb.org
URL: http://www.bookweb.org
Contact: Oren Teicher, CEO
Scope: Book selling and publishing. **Holdings:** 5000 volumes; 1000 bound periodical volumes; 100 newsletters; 11 VF drawers; 2000 publishers catalogs.

2201 ■ Cleveland Public Library–Literature Department
Main Bldg., 2nd Fl.
325 Superior Ave.
Cleveland, OH 44114-1271
Ph:(216)623-2881
Co. E-mail: literature@cpl.org
URL: http://www.cpl.org/TheLibrary/SubjectsCollections/Literature.aspx
Contact: Ron Antonucci, Mgr.
Scope: Fiction, drama and theater, film, radio, television, poetry, essays, humor, oratory and public speaking, craft of writing, literary criticism and biography, classical Greek and Latin, linguistics, journalism, book trade, printing, publishing, Library and information science. **Services:** Department open to the public. **Holdings:** 500,000 volumes; 11,368 bound periodical volumes; 23,000 theater programs and playbills; 16,000 titles of microform editions of plays and miscellanea; 190 vertical files. **Subscriptions:** 825 journals and other serials.

2202 ■ Free Library of Philadelphia–Social Science & History Department
1901 Vine St.
Philadelphia, PA 19103
Ph:(215)686-5396
Fax:(215)563-3628
URL: http://www.freelibrary.org
Contact: Jim DeWalt, Hd.
Scope: History, biography, social sciences, law, travels and geography, archeology, anthropology, sports and games. **Services:** Interlibrary loan. **Holdings:** 228,000 volumes; 53,900 pamphlets; 35 VF drawers of clippings. **Subscriptions:** 610 journals and other serials.

2203 ■ Grolier Club of New York Library
47 E. 60th St.
New York, NY 10022
Ph:(212)838-6690
Fax:(212)838-2445
Co. E-mail: ejh@grolierclub.org
URL: http://www.grolierclub.org
Contact: Eric Holzenberg, Dir.
Scope: Bibliography, history of printing, book-collecting, bookselling, arts of the book. **Services:** Library open to the public with restrictions. **Holdings:** 100,000 volumes; 5000 prints and portraits; bookplates. **Subscriptions:** 100 journals and other serials.

2204 ■ Hanley-Wood, LLC Library
426 S. Westgate St.
Addison, IL 60101-4546
Ph:(630)543-0870
Fax:(630)543-3112
URL: http://www.hanleywood.com
Contact: Kimberly Last, Libn.
Scope: Concrete, cement, masonry, construction, home building. **Services:** Interlibrary loan; copying. **Holdings:** 3000 books; 120 bound periodical volumes. **Subscriptions:** 100 journals and other serials.

2205 ■ Houghton Mifflin Company–School Division Research Center
222 Berkeley St.
Boston, MA 02116
Ph:(617)351-5275
Fax:(617)351-3546
Co. E-mail: april-baglole@hmco.com
URL: http://www.hmco.com
Contact: April Baglole, Des.Libn.
Scope: Publishing, education, textbooks. **Services:** Interlibrary loan; research. **Holdings:** 8000 books. **Subscriptions:** 15 journals and other serials.

2206 ■ John Wiley and Sons Information Center
111 River St.
Hoboken, NJ 07030
Ph:(201)748-6000
Fax:(201)748-6088
Co. E-mail: info@wiley.com
URL: http://as.wiley.com/WileyCDA/Section/index.html
Contact: Nicole Luce Rizzo, Dir.
Scope: Publishing, business and management, higher education. **Services:** Center not open to the public. **Holdings:** 200 books; 9 VF drawers of clippings. **Subscriptions:** 25 journals and other serials.

2207 ■ The McGraw-Hill Companies, Inc.–Business Information Center
1221 Ave. of the Americas, 48th Fl.
New York, NY 10020
Ph:(212)512-4001
Fax:(212)512-4646
Co. E-mail: bic_bic@mcgraw-hill.com
Contact: Susan Gormley, Mgr.
Scope: Finance, education, communications, publishing. **Services:** Library not open to the public. **Holdings:** 800 volumes; archives. **Subscriptions:** 42 journals and other serials.

2208 ■ Omohundro Institute of Early American History and Culture–Kellock Library
College of William and Mary
PO Box 8781
Williamsburg, VA 23187-8781
Ph:(757)221-1126
Fax:(757)221-1047
Co. E-mail: pvhigg@wm.edu
URL: http://oieahc.wm.edu
Contact: Patricia V. Higgs, Libn./Archv.
Scope: Early American history, book publishing. **Services:** Interlibrary loan; Library open to outside users with permission of director. **Holdings:** 8650 books; 942 bound periodical volumes; 2000 reels of microfilm. **Subscriptions:** 54 journals and other serials.

2209 ■ Reed Business Information–Frederic G. Melcher Library
360 Park Ave., S.
New York, NY 11010
Ph:(646)746-6511
Fax:(646)746-6689
Co. E-mail: gink@reedbusiness.com
URL: http://www.reedbusiness.co.uk/rb2_home/rb2_home.htm
Contact: Gary Ink, Libn.
Scope: Book industries and trade, Library science. **Services:** Library not open to the public. **Holdings:** 4000 books; 700 bound periodical volumes; 130 VF drawers. **Subscriptions:** 200 journals and other serials.

2210 ■ Science Associates/International, Inc. Library
6 Hastings Rd.
Marlboro, NJ 07746-1313
Ph:(908)536-7673
Free: 800-721-1080
Fax:(908)536-7673
Contact: Roxy Bauer, Libn.
Scope: Information science, library science, documentation, publishing, computer science. **Services:** Library not open to the public. **Holdings:** 2000 books; 750 library and information science reports; 100 newsletters. **Subscriptions:** 100 journals and other serials.

2211 ■ Silver Burdett & Ginn–Editorial Library
299 Jefferson Rd.
Parsippany, NJ 07054
Ph:(973)739-8000
Fax:(973)898-0114
Scope: General education, publishing, market research. **Services:** Library not open to the public. **Holdings:** 10,000 books. **Subscriptions:** 150 journals and other serials.

2212 ■ Simmons College–Graduate School of Library and Information Science Library
300 The Fenway
Boston, MA 02115
Ph:(617)521-2824
Fax:(617)521-3192
Co. E-mail: gslisadm@simmons.edu
URL: http://www.simmons.edu/gslis
Contact: Linda H. Watkins, Libn.
Scope: Library and information science, publishing, media resources and study, Library management. **Services:** Interlibrary loan; copying; Library open to the public for reference use only by appointment. **Holdings:** 24,258 books; 7537 bound periodical volumes; 4935 microfiche; 911 reels of microfilm; 34 VF drawers; School of Library Science doctoral field studies; information files on 100 library-related subjects; doctoral dissertations on microfilm. **Subscriptions:** 560 journals and other serials.

RESEARCH CENTERS

2213 ■ Simon Fraser University–Canadian Centre for Studies in Publishing
Harbor Ctr.
515 W Hastings St.
Vancouver, BC, Canada V6B 5K3
Ph:(778)782-5242
Fax:(778)782-5239
Co. E-mail: lorimer@sfu.ca
URL: http://tkbr.ccsp.sfu.ca
Contact: Prof. Rowland Lorimer PhD, Dir.
E-mail: lorimer@sfu.ca
Scope: Role of publishing and the dynamics of information in society. **Services:** Consulting, for specialized professional development. **Publications:** Articles (occasionally); Books; Canadian Journal of Communication (quarterly); Reports (occasionally); Scholarly and Research Communication (3/year). **Educational Activities:** Master of Publishing Program (annually), attended by graduate students from Canada and around the world; Seminars and conferences; Summer Publishing Workshops; Writing and Publishing Program (occasionally), for specialized professional development.

ASSOCIATIONS AND OTHER ORGANIZATIONS

2214 ■ Binders' Guild
2925 Powell St.
Eugene, OR 97405
Ph:(541)485-6527
Co. E-mail: editor@bindersguild.org
URL: http://www.bindersguild.org
Description: Amateur and professional hand bookbinders and other interested persons. Facilitates exchange of information among members concerning techniques and sources of supplies. .

2215 ■ Binding Industries Association International
200 Deer Run Rd.
Sewickley, PA 15143
Ph:(412)259-1802
Fax:(412)259-1800
Co. E-mail: jgoldstein@printing.org
URL: http://www.gain.net
Contact: Justin Goldstein, Mgr.
Description: Represents trade binders and loose-leaf manufacturers united to conduct seminars, hold conventions, and formulate and maintain standards. **Publications:** *Binders Bulletin* (monthly).

2216 ■ Book Manufacturers' Institute
Two Armand Beach Dr., Ste. 1B
Palm Coast, FL 32137-2612
Ph:(386)986-4552
Fax:(386)986-4553
Co. E-mail: info@bmibook.com
URL: http://www.bmibook.com
Contact: Daniel N. Bach, Exec. VP/Sec.
Description: Represents the trade association for manufacturers of books. .

2217 ■ Center for Book Arts
28 W 27th St., 3rd Fl.
New York, NY 10001
Ph:(212)481-0295
Fax:(212)481-9853
Co. E-mail: info@centerforbookarts.org
URL: http://www.centerforbookarts.org
Contact: Alexander Campos, Exec. Dir.
Description: Dedicated to the preservation of the traditional crafts of bookmaking, as well as encouraging contemporary interpretations of the book as an art object. Organizes exhibitions related to the art of the book and offers an extensive selection of educational courses, workshops and seminars in traditional and contemporary bookbinding, letterpress printing, fine press publishing, and other associated arts. Other programs include Artist-in-Residence, Broadsides Reading Series, and the Poetry Chapbook Competition. Supported by local businesses, various foundations including the Lenrow Fund, the Milton and Sally Avery Arts Foundation, the NY State Council on the Arts, the National Endowment for the Arts, and its members. .

2218 ■ Guild of Book Workers
521 5th Ave.
New York, NY 10175-0038
Co. E-mail: secretary@guildofbookworkers.org
URL: http://www.guildofbookworkers.org
Contact: Andrew Huot, Pres.
Description: Amateur and professional workers in the handbook crafts such as bookbinding, calligraphy, illuminating, fine presswork, and decorative papermaking. Works to improve standards by the sponsorship of exhibitions, field trips, lectures, workshops, and discussion groups. **Publications:** *Directory of Study Opportunities*; *Guild of Book Workers—Membership Directory* (annual); *Guild of Book Workers—Newsletter* (bimonthly); *Supply Directory* .

2219 ■ Library Binding Institute
4440 PGA Blvd., Ste. 600
Palm Beach Gardens, FL 33410
Ph:(561)745-6821
Fax:(561)472-8401
Co. E-mail: dnolan@lbibinders.org
URL: http://www.lbibinders.org
Contact: Ms. Debra S. Nolan CAE, Exec. Dir.
Description: Firms and certified library binders doing library binding in accordance with LBI Standard for Library Binding, including rebinding of worn volumes, prebinding of new volumes, initial hardcover binding of periodicals, and other binding principally for libraries and schools; associate members are suppliers and manufacturers of library binding materials and equipment. Certifies qualified binding companies after examination of work and investigation of experience, insurance for protection of customers' property, and examination of bank and library references. Conducts research on materials used in library binding. Conducts statistical surveys of unit production, operating statement data, and wage data. .

DIRECTORIES OF EDUCATIONAL PROGRAMS

2220 ■ Directory of Private Accredited Career Schools and Colleges of Technology
Pub: Accrediting Commission of Career Schools and Colleges of Technology
Contact: Michale S. McComis, Exec. Dir.
Released: On web page. **Price:** Free. **Description:** Covers 3900 accredited post-secondary programs that provide training programs in business, trade, and technical fields, including various small business endeavors. Entries offer school name, address, phone, description of courses, job placement assistance, and requirements for admission. Arrangement is alphabetical.

REFERENCE WORKS

2221 ■ Guild of Book Workers—Supplies and Services Directory
Pub: Guild of Book Workers Inc.
Contact: Catherine Burkhard
Ed: Bernadette G. Callery, Editor. **Released:** Irregular, Latest edition November 2008. **Price:** $15, individuals 2001 issue. **Covers:** More than 250 manufacturers and suppliers of products used in bookbinding, calligraphy, and repair and conservation of documents and books; coverage includes Canada. **Entries Include:** Name of firm, address, phone, products or services, minimum order requirements, shipping restrictions, whether catalog or samples are available. **Arrangement:** Geographical, then by product or service. **Indexes:** Alphabetical.

2222 ■ Study Opportunities List
Pub: Guild of Book Workers Inc.
Contact: Catherine Burkhard
Released: Irregular, Latest edition 2011. **Price:** $15, individuals 1995 issue. **Covers:** About 130 teachers, schools, and centers offering hand bookbinding and calligraphic services; international coverage. **Entries Include:** Craftsperson's name, address, special interests, source of expertise, whether apprentices are desired; also includes (for schools and other centers) names and addresses of instructors and courses offered. **Arrangement:** Geographical.

STATISTICAL SOURCES

2223 ■ Book Industry Trends
Pub: Book Industry Study Group, Inc.
Ed: Compiled by Statistical Service Center staff. **Released:** 2009. **Price:** $875.00 (paper).

TRADE PERIODICALS

2224 ■ Guild of Book Workers Newsletter
Pub: Guild of Book Workers Inc.
Contact: Catherine Burkhard
Ed: Margaret Johnson, Editor. **Released:** Bimonthly, Every 2 months. **Price:** Included in membership. **Description:** Covers issues in book arts, binding, book conservation, calligraphy, and printing. Recurring features include letters to the editor, interviews, news of research, a calendar of events, reports of meetings, news of educational opportunities, job listings, book reviews, and notices of publications available.

2225 ■ MCBA Newsletter
Pub: Minnesota Center for Book Arts
Ed: Lori Brink, Editor. **Released:** 3/year (always March, July, and December). **Price:** $40, Included in membership; $15, nonmembers. **Description:** Focuses on the field of book arts, including letterpress printing, bookbinding, and papermaking. Reviews current and future Center exhibitions and announces classes available at the Center. Recurring features include book reviews and news of educational opportunities.

VIDEOCASSETTES/ AUDIOCASSETTES

2226 ■ Papermaking & Bookbinding
Crystal Productions
1812 Johns Dr.
Box 2159
Glenview, IL 60025-6519
Ph:(847)657-8144

Free: 800-255-8629
Fax:(847)657-8149
Co. E-mail: custserv@crystalproductions.com
URL: http://www.crystalproductions.com
Released: 1991. **Price:** $89.50. **Description:** Desktop publishing the old-fashioned way. Learn how to make paper using ordinary household materials. The making of both hard and soft covers is also covered. A teacher's guide is included. **Availability:** VHS.

CONSULTANTS

2227 ■ W. F. Davis Consultants
179 Voelbel Rd.
Hightstown, NJ 08520-2807
Ph:(609)448-0161
Contact: William F. Davis, President
Scope: Offers counsel to corporations on planning, manufacturing, product development, product conception, special purpose machinery development, production methodology, profit enhancement, and manufacturing systems. Specializes in printing and bindery equipment. Clients include paper, printing, publication, graphic arts machinery, disposable products, textile, consumer products, machine tool and instrumentation industries.

LIBRARIES

2228 ■ Book Club of California–Albert Sperisen Library
312 Sutter St., Ste. 510
San Francisco, CA 94108-4320
Ph:(415)781-7532
Free: 800-869-7656
Fax:(415)781-7537
Co. E-mail: bland@bccbooks.org
URL: http://www.bccbooks.org
Contact: Barbara Jane Land, Libn.
Scope: Printing, bookbinding, typography, books, papermaking, private presses, history of printing and printing methods; California and Western history. **Services:** Library open to the public (on written application). **Holdings:** 2500 books; ephemera from private presses. **Subscriptions:** 10 journals and other serials.

2229 ■ Canadian Bookbinders & Book Artists Guild Library
60 Atlantic Ave., Ste. 112
Toronto, ON, Canada M6K 1X9
Ph:(416)581-1071
Co. E-mail: cbbag@cbbag.ca
URL: http://www.cbbag.ca
Contact: Scott Duncan, Pres.
Scope: Bookbinding, fine printing, book arts. **Services:** Library open to the public by appointment. **Holdings:** Figures not available. **Subscriptions:** 500 journals and other serials.

2230 ■ Grolier Club of New York Library
47 E. 60th St.
New York, NY 10022
Ph:(212)838-6690
Fax:(212)838-2445
Co. E-mail: ejh@grolierclub.org
URL: http://www.grolierclub.org
Contact: Eric Holzenberg, Dir.
Scope: Bibliography, history of printing, book-collecting, bookselling, arts of the book. **Services:** Library open to the public with restrictions. **Holdings:** 100,000 volumes; 5000 prints and portraits; bookplates. **Subscriptions:** 100 journals and other serials.

2231 ■ Guild of Book Workers Library
State Historical Society of Iowa
402 Iowa Ave.
Iowa City, IA 52240
Ph:(319)335-3921
Co. E-mail: jane-meggers@uiowa.edu
URL: http://www.lib.uiowa.edu/spec-coll/gbw/gbw1.html
Contact: Jane Meggers, Cons./Guild Libn.
Scope: Bookbinding, history of the book, calligraphy, printing, paper making. **Services:** Library open to members only. **Holdings:** 700 books; videotapes; DVDs.

2232 ■ Mills College–F.W. Olin Library I Special Collections
5000 MacArthur Blvd.
Oakland, CA 94613
Ph:(510)430-2047
Fax:(510)430-2278
Co. E-mail: jbraun@mills.edu
URL: http://www.mills.edu/academics/library/index.php
Contact: Janice Braun, Spec.Coll.Libn.
Scope: English and American literature, printing, dance, Shakespeare, women's history, bookbinding, book arts. **Services:** Copying; collections open to the public for reference use only. **Holdings:** 12,000 books; 10,000 manuscripts. **Subscriptions:** 12 journals and other serials.

2233 ■ Newark Public Library–Special Collections Division
5 Washington St.
PO Box 630
Newark, NJ 07101-0630
Ph:(973)733-7745
Fax:(973)733-5648
Co. E-mail: wgrey@npl.org
URL: http://www.npl.org/Pages/Collections/specialcollections1.html
Contact: William Grey, Dir.
Scope: Graphic arts, commercial art and design, original fine prints, rare books, fine art, artist's book movement, original lithographs, etchings, serigraphs and mixed media, book illustration, and the history of fine printing. **Services:** Division open to the public by appointment. **Holdings:** 10,000 books; about 100 lin. ft. of vertical files on artists in collections, printing history, and art and music topics. **Subscriptions:** 15 journals and other serials.

2234 ■ Rochester Institute of Technology–Melbert B. Cary, Jr. Graphic Arts Collection
Wallace Memorial Library
90 Lomb Memorial Dr.
Rochester, NY 14623-5604
Ph:(585)475-2408
Fax:(585)475-6900
Co. E-mail: dppwml@rit.edu
URL: http://library.rit.edu/cary
Contact: David Pankow, Cur.
Scope: Printing history, type specimens, typography, book arts, press books, calligraphy, papermaking, graphic arts, bookbinding. **Services:** Copying (limited); collection open to the public. **Holdings:** 50,000 books; 20 VF drawers of clippings; ephemera; pamphlets; 50 boxes of posters, broadsides, drawings; 400 boxes of correspondence and manuscript material. **Subscriptions:** 20 journals and other serials.

2235 ■ Yale University–Arts Library I Special Collections
Robert B. Haas Family Arts Library, Lower Level
180 York St.
PO Box 208318
New Haven, CT 06520-8318
Ph:(203)432-4439
Fax:(203)432-0549
Co. E-mail: jae.rossman@yale.edu
URL: http://www.library.yale.edu/arts/specialcollections
Contact: Jae Jennifer Rossman, Asst.Dir., Spec.Coll.
Scope: Typography, book illustration and design, bookbinding, papermaking, bookplates, private presses, artists' books, conceptual books, and fine printing. **Services:** Collection open to the public. **Holdings:** 20,000 books; prints and broadsides; type specimens; archive of student printing, including masters' theses from School of Graphic Design and School of Photography at Yale; 1 million bookplates; Japanese prints; stage and costume designs. **Subscriptions:** 20 journals and other serials.

ASSOCIATIONS AND OTHER ORGANIZATIONS

2236 ■ Canadian Institute of Chartered Accountants–Institut Canadien des Comptables Agrees
277 Wellington St. W
Toronto, ON, Canada M5V 3H2
Ph:(416)977-3222
Fax:(416)977-8585
Co. E-mail: jan.burns@cica.ca
URL: http://www.cica.ca
Contact: Nigel Byars, Exec. VP
Description: Sets national accounting, auditing, and financial reporting standards. Maintains an active professional development program for its members. Represents the profession's viewpoint on federal legislation issues and matters of national concern. Confers with other national organizations to achieve worldwide harmonization of accounting and auditing standards. **Publications:** *Directory of Canadian Chartered Accountants* (periodic).

2237 ■ Canadian Institute of Quantity Surveyors–Institut Canadien des Economistes en Construction
90 Nolan Ct., Unit 19
Markham, ON, Canada L3R 4L9
Ph:(905)477-0008
Free: (866)345-1168
Fax:(905)477-6774
Co. E-mail: info@ciqs.org
URL: http://www.ciqs.org
Contact: Roy Lewis, Pres.
Description: Quantity surveyors and construction estimators. Establishes and maintains standards for certification and provides through advice to members relating to construction costs, management and administration of construction projects. Conducts continuing professional development programs for members. **Publications:** *The Construction Economist* (quarterly). **Telecommunication Services:** electronic mail, president@ciqs.org.

2238 ■ Society of Professional Accountants of Canada–La societe des comptables professionnels du Canada
250 Consumers Rd., Ste. 1007
Toronto, ON, Canada M2J 4V6
Ph:(416)350-8145
Free: 877-515-4447
Fax:(416)350-8146
Co. E-mail: president@professionalaccountant.org
URL: http://www.professionalaccountant.org
Contact: Mr. John Singer RPA, VP
Description: Professional accountants and individuals working to pass qualifying accountancy examinations. Promotes ongoing professional education among accountants; encourages students to enter the accounting field; works to advance the profession of accounting. Gathers and disseminates information on accounting; sponsors educational programs; conducts professional accountancy qualifying examinations. **Publications:** *Professional Accountant* (quarterly).

REFERENCE WORKS

2239 ■ "2011 Tax Information of Interest" in *Business Owner* (Vol. 35, November-December 2011, No. 6, pp. 10)
Pub: DL Perkins Company
Description: Compilation of 2011 tax information to help small business take advantage of all tax incentives.

2240 ■ "Accrual vs. Cash Accounting, Explained" in *Business Owner* (Vol. 35, July-August 2011, No. 4, pp. 13)
Pub: DL Perkins Company
Description: Cash method versus accrual accounting methods are examined, using hypothetical situations.

2241 ■ "Adler Blanchard & Freeman Reports New SmartKeeper Bookkeeping Service" in *Professional Services Close-Up* (March 24, 2011)
Pub: Close-Up Media
Description: Profile of Adler Blanchard & Freeman (AB&F) accountants and business advisors. The firm has expanded its client offerings to include their new SmartKeeper Business and Personal Bookkeeping Service for small to mid-sized companies and individuals.

2242 ■ "Attend To Your Corporate Housekeeping" in *Women Entrepreneur* (December 4, 2008)
Pub: Entrepreneur Media Inc.
Ed: Nina Kaufman. **Description:** Business owners can lose all the benefits and privileges of the corporate form if they do not follow proper corporate formalities such as holding an annual meeting, electing officers and directors and adopting or passing corporate resolutions. Creditors are able to take from one's personal assets if such formalities have not been followed.

2243 ■ "Battling Back from Betrayal" in *Harvard Business Review* (Vol. 88, December 2010, No. 12, pp. 130)
Pub: Harvard Business School Publishing
Ed: Daniel McGinn. **Description:** Stephen Greer's scrap metal firm, Hartwell Pacific, lost several million dollars due to a lack of efficient and appropriate inventory audits, accounting procedures, and new-hire reference checks for his foreign operations. Greer believes that balancing growth with control is a key component of success.

2244 ■ *Beat the Taxman: Easy Ways to Tax Save in Your Small Business*
Pub: John Wiley & Sons, Incorporated
Ed: Stephen Thompson. **Released:** May 2008. **Price:** $26.95. **Description:** Concise tax planner to help entrepreneurs take advantage of current tax laws.

2245 ■ "A Bigger Deal" in *Crain's Cleveland Business* (Vol. 28, November 12, 2007, No. 45, pp. 1)
Pub: Crain Communications, Inc.
Ed: Shawn A. Turner. **Description:** In an attempt to boost its revenue CBiz Inc., a provider of accounting and business services, is looking to balance its acquisitions of smaller companies with larger ones as part of its overall growth strategy.

2246 ■ "Bookkeeping Service Opens First Sacramento Franchise" in *Sacramento Bee* (April 13, 2011)
Pub: Sacramento Bee
Ed: Mark Glover. **Description:** Franchise bookkeeping service called BookKeeping Express opened its new office in Roseville, California; its first shop in the area.

2247 ■ "Cautions On Loans With Your Business" in *Business Owner* (Vol. 35, July-August 2011, No. 4, pp. 5)
Pub: DL Perkins Company
Description: Caution must be used when borrowing from or lending to any small business. Tax guidelines for the borrowing and lending practice are also included.

2248 ■ "Changing the Rules of the Accounting Game" in *Canadian Business* (Vol. 81, December 8, 2008, No. 21, pp. 19)
Pub: Rogers Media Ltd.
Ed: Al Rosen. **Description:** Interference from world politicians in developing accounting standards is believed to have resulted in untested rules that are inferior to current standards. European lawmakers have recently asked to change International Financial Reporting Standards.

2249 ■ "Channeling for Growth" in *The Business Journal-Serving Greater Tampa Bay* (Vol. 28, July 11, 2008, No. 29, pp. 1)
Pub: American City Business Journals, Inc.
Ed: Margie Manning. **Description:** HSN Inc., one of the largest employers in Tampa Bay, Florida, is expected to spend an additional $9.7 million annually as it plans to hire more accounting, internal audit, legal, treasury and tax personnel after its spin-off to a public company. Details on the company's sales growth are provided.

2250 ■ "Convergence Collaboration: Revising Revenue Recognition" in *Management Accounting Quarterly* (Vol. 12, Spring 2011, No. 3, pp. 18)
Pub: Management Accounting Quarterly
Ed: Jack T. Ciesielski, Thomas R. Weirich. **Description:** While revenue recognition is critical, regulations have been developed on an ad hoc basis until now. The joint FASB/IASB proposed accounting standard on revenue recognition is a meaningful convergence of standards that will require a major adjustment for financial statement preparers. The proposal is a radical departure from the way revenue has been recognized by the U.S. GAAP. For industries such as consulting, engineering, construction, and technol-

ogy, it could dramatically change revenue recognition, impacting the top line. The new proposed standard, its potential impact, and the critical role that contracts play is examined thoroughly.

2251 ■ *Deduct It!: Lower Your Small Business Taxes*
Pub: NOLO
Ed: Stephen Fishman. **Released:** November 2009. **Price:** $34.99. **Description:** Ways to make the most of tax deductions for any small business are covered. The book is organized into categories featuring common deductions, start-up expenses, health deductions, entertainment, travel, inventory, equipment and more. Current tax laws and numbers for 2008 are included.

2252 ■ "DHS Finalizes Rules Allowing Electronic I-9s" in *HR Specialist* (Vol. 8, September 2010, No. 9, pp. 5)
Pub: Capitol Information Group Inc.
Description: U.S. Department of Homeland Security issued regulations that give employers more flexibility to electronically sing and store I-9 employee verification forms.

2253 ■ *Directory of Global Professional Accounting and Business Certifications*
Pub: John Wiley & Sons, Incorporated
Ed: Lal Balkaran. **Released:** February 9, 2007. **Price:** $35.00. **Description:** Resource for international accounting, auditing, and business professions.

2254 ■ "Do Fair Value Adjustments Influence Dividend Policy?" in *Accounting and Business Research* (Vol. 41, Spring 2011, No. 2, pp. 51)
Pub: American Institute of CPAs
Ed: Igor Goncharov, Sander van Triest. **Description:** The impact of positive fair value adjustments on corporate distributions is examined using a Russian setting that requires disclosure of unrealized fair value adjustments in income. It was found that there is no rise in dividends due to positive fair value adjustments and that on the contrary, a negative relationship exists between adjustments and dividend changes.

2255 ■ "Economic Crisis and Accounting Evolution" in *Accounting and Business Research* (Vol. 41, Summer 2011, No. 3, pp. 2159)
Pub: American Institute of CPAs
Ed: Gregory Waymire, Sudipta Basu. **Description:** Financial reporting changes at the face of economic crises are studied using a punctuated equilibrium evolution. Findings show that financial reporting has a minor impact but may amplify economic crises. Attempts to enhance accounting amid economic crises may not be as beneficial as planned.

2256 ■ *Electronic Commerce: Technical, Business, and Legal Issues*
Pub: Prentice Hall PTR
Ed: Oktay Dogramaci; Aryya Gangopadhyay; Yelena Yesha; Nabil R. Adam. **Released:** August 1998. **Description:** Provides insight into the goals of using the Internet to grow a business in the areas of networking and telecommunication, security, and storage and retrieval; business areas such as marketing, procurement and purchasing, billing and payment, and supply chain management; and legal aspects such as privacy, intellectual property, taxation, contractual and legal settlements.

2257 ■ "Finally, Justice" in *Canadian Business* (Vol. 82, April 27, 2009, No. 7, pp. 12)
Pub: Rogers Media
Ed: John Gray. **Description:** Former investment adviser Alex Winch feels that he was vindicated with the Canadian Court's ruling that Livent Inc. founders Garth Drabinsky and Myron Gottlieb were guilty of fraud. Drabinsky filed a libel case on Winch over Winch's letter that complained over Livent's accounting procedures. Winch also criticized the inconsistent accounting during Drabinsky's term as chief executive of another firm.

2258 ■ *Finance & Accounting: How to Keep Your Books and Manage Your Finances with an MBA, a CPA, or a Ph.D*
Pub: Adams Media Corporation
Ed: Suzanne Caplan. **Price:** $19.95.

2259 ■ "Furniture Making May Come Back—Literally" in *Business North Carolina* (Vol. 28, March 2008, No. 3, pp. 32)
Pub: Business North Carolina
Description: Due to the weak U.S. dollar and the fact that lumber processors never left the country, foreign furniture manufacturers are becoming interested in moving manufacturing plants to the U.S.

2260 ■ "Give Until It Works" in *Hispanic Business* (Vol. 30, March 2008, No. 3, pp. 26)
Pub: Hispanic Business
Ed: Rick Munarriz. **Description:** Donating to qualified charities and non-profit organizations for maximizing tax advantage to be availed on the income tax bill is examined. The amount that can be deducted from the total taxable amount is usually less then the actual amount donated and must be made during that calendar year.

2261 ■ "Handle With Care" in *Hawaii Business* (Vol. 53, October 2007, No. 5, pp. 66)
Pub: Hawaii Business Publishing
Ed: Kenneth Sheffield. **Description:** Discusses a fiduciary, who may be a board member, business owner, or a trustee, and is someone who supervises and manages the affairs and the resources of a principal. Fiduciary duties, which include accounting, cost review and risk management, must be served with the benefit of the principal as the priority. Ways of breaching fiduciary duties and how to avoid them are discussed.

2262 ■ "The Hidden Tax" in *Canadian Business* (Vol. 81, April 14, 2008, No. 6, pp. 28)
Pub: Rogers Media
Ed: Al Rosen. **Description:** Accounting fraud could take out a sizable sum from one's retirement fund when computed over a long period of time. The much bigger tax on savings is the collective impact of the smaller losses that do not attract the attention they deserve. Ensuring that investors are not unnecessarily taxed 2 percent of their total investments every year outweighs the benefit of a 2 percent reduction in personal tax rates.

2263 ■ *How to Start an Internet Sales Business*
Pub: Lulu.com
Ed: Dan Davis. **Released:** August 2005. **Price:** $19. 95. **Description:** Small business guide for launching an Internet sales company. Topics include business structure, licenses, and taxes.

2264 ■ "How To: Manage Your Cash Better" in *Inc.* (Volume 32, December 2010, No. 10, pp. 69)
Pub: Inc. Magazine
Description: A monthly guide to policies, procedures and practices for managing cash for a small business.

2265 ■ "IFRS Monopoly: the Pied Piper of Financial Reporting" in *Accounting and Business Research* (Vol. 41, Summer 2011, No. 3, pp. 291)
Pub: American Institute of CPAs
Ed: Shyam Sunder. **Description:** The disadvantages of granting monopoly to the international financial reporting standards (IFRS) are examined. Results indicate that an IFRS monopoly removes the chances for comparing alternative practices and learning from them. An IFRS monopoly also eliminates customization of financial reporting to fit local differences in governance, business, economic, and legal conditions.

2266 ■ "IRS Announces New Standards for Tax Preparers" in *Bellingham Business Journal* (Vol. February 2010, pp. 9)
Pub: Sound Publishing Inc.
Ed: Isaac Bonnell. **Description:** A new oversight plan was announced by the Internal Revenue Services (IRS) that will require tax professionals to pass a competency test and register with the government in order to ensure greater accountability in the industry.

2267 ■ "It's Time to Take Full Responsibility" in *Harvard Business Review* (Vol. 88, October 2010, No. 10, pp. 42)
Pub: Harvard Business School Publishing
Ed: Rosabeth Moss Kanter. **Description:** A case for corporate responsibility is cited, focusing on long-term impact and the effects of public accountability.

2268 ■ "Kaboom!" in *Canadian Business* (Vol. 81, November 10, 2008, No. 19, pp. 18)
Pub: Rogers Media Ltd.
Ed: Al Rosen, Mark Rosen. **Description:** International Financial Reporting Standards (IFRS) is a good idea in theory but was implemented in a hurry and had poor quality standards from the beginning.

2269 ■ "Know Your Numbers" in *Inc.* (Volume 32, December 2010, No. 10, pp. 39)
Pub: Inc. Magazine
Ed: Norm Brodsky. **Description:** Ways to maximize profit and minimize tax burden are presented.

2270 ■ "Living in a 'Goldfish Bowl'" in *WorkingUSA* (Vol. 11, June 2008, No. 2, pp. 277)
Pub: Blackwell Publishers Ltd.
Ed: John Lund. **Description:** Recent changes in laws, regulations and even the reporting format of labor organization annual financial reports in both the U.S. and Australia have received surprisingly little attention, yet they have significantly increased the amount of information available both to union members and the public in general, as reports in both countries are available via government Websites. While such financial reporting laws are extremely rare in European countries, with the exception of the UK and Ireland, the U.S. and Australian reporting systems have become among the most detailed in the world. After reviewing these changes in financial reporting and the availability of these reports, as well as comparing and contrasting the specific reporting requirements of each country, this paper then examines the cost-benefit impact of more detailed financial reporting.

2271 ■ "Merger Mania: Regional Snaps Up HVS" in *The Business Journal-Serving Greater Tampa Bay* (Vol. 28, September 26, 2008, No. 40, pp. 1)
Pub: American City Business Journals, Inc.
Ed: Alexis Muellner. **Description:** It was reported that Harper Van Scoik & Co. LLP has finalized a merger with Carr Riggs & Ingram LLC. The agreement, effective October 1, 2008, is a merger of HVS assets into CRI. Bill Carr, a managing partner, revealed that HVS' $5 million in revenue will take CRI from $78 million to $82 million in revenue.

2272 ■ "My Favorite Tool for Managing Expenses" in *Inc.* (Volume 32, December 2010, No. 10, pp. 60)
Pub: Inc. Magazine
Ed: J.J. McCorvey. **Description:** Web-based service called Expensify is outlined. The service allows companies to log expenses while away from the office using the service's iPhone application.

2273 ■ "A Necessary Balancing Act: Bookkeeping" in *Contractor* (Vol. 56, November 2009, No. 11, pp. 22)
Pub: Penton Media, Inc.
Ed: Al Schwartz. **Description:** Pros and cons of getting a bookkeeper or a certified public accountant for the subcontractor are discussed. A bookkeeper can help a subcontractor get new accounting software up and running while an accountant will more than likely keep after the books at regular intervals throughout the year.

2274 ■ "New Century's Fall Has a New Culprit" in *Barron's* (Vol. 88, March 31, 2008, No. 13, pp. 20)
Pub: Dow Jones & Company, Inc.
Ed: Jonathan R. Laing. **Description:** Court examiner Michael Missal reports that New Century Financial's auditor contributed to New Century's demise by its

negligence in permitting improper and imprudent practices related to New Century's accounting processes. New Century's bankruptcy filing is considered the start of the subprime-mortgage crisis.

2275 ■ "New Institutional Accounting and IFRS" in *Accounting and Business Research* (Vol. 41, Summer 2011, No. 3, pp. 309)
Pub: American Institute of CPAs
Ed: Peter Wysocki. **Description:** A new framework for institutional accounting research is presented. It has five fundamental components – efficient versus inefficient results, interdependencies, causation, level of analysis, and institutional structure. The use of the framework for evaluation accounting institutions such as the international financial reporting standards is discussed.

2276 ■ "Paperless Bookkeeping Program" in *Fleet Owner Online* (February 15, 2011)
Pub: Penton Business Media Inc.
Description: TruckTax launched its new paperless bookkeeping system to help manage bookkeeping tasks, accounting and business tax information and filings for truckers.

2277 ■ "Privacy Concern: Are 'Group' Time Sheets Legal?" in *HR Specialist* (Vol. 8, September 2010, No. 9, pp. 4)
Pub: Capitol Information Group Inc.
Description: Under the Fair Labor Standards Act (FLSA) employers are required to maintain and preserve payroll or other records, including the number of hours worked, but it does not prescribe a particular order or form in which these records must be kept.

2278 ■ "Proposed Accounting Changes Could Complicate Tenant's Leases" in *Baltimore Business Journal* (Vol. 28, July 2, 2010, No. 8, pp. 1)
Pub: Baltimore Business Journal
Ed: Daniel J. Sernovitz. **Description:** The Financial Accounting Standards Board has proposed that companies must indicate the value of real estate leases as assets and liabilities on balance sheets instead of expenses. The proposals could cause some companies to document millions of dollars in charges on their books or find difficulty in getting loans.

2279 ■ "Prosecutors Dish Sordid AIPC Story" in *The Business Journal-Serving Metropolitan Kansas City* (Vol. 27, September 19, 2008, No. 1)
Pub: American City Business Journals, Inc.
Ed: Suzanna Stagemeyer. **Description:** Prosecutors in the American Italian Pasta Co.'s accounting fraud case have revealed evidence on the schemes used by then-officers of the company to commit fraud. District attorney John Wood has dubbed the case as the largest corporate fraud lawsuit in the history of the district of Missouri. How AIPC fell from being an industry leader is also discussed.

2280 ■ *QuickBooks All-in-One Desk Reference for Dummies*
Pub: John Wiley & Sons, Incorporated
Ed: Stephen L. Nelson. **Released:** January 2007. **Price:** $29.99 (US), $42.99 (Canadian). **Description:** Compilation of nine self-contained minibooks to get the most from QuickBooks accounting software. Companion Web site with sample business plan workbook and downloadable profit-volume cost analysis workbook included.

2281 ■ *QuickBooks Simple Start for Dummies*
Pub: John Wiley & Sons, Incorporated
Ed: Stephen L. Nelson. **Released:** October 2004. **Price:** $21.99. **Description:** Profile of Intuits new accounting software geared to micro businesses. Advice is offered on daily, monthly, and yearly accounting activities covering records, sales tax, and reports.

2282 ■ *Reading Financial Reports for Dummies*
Pub: John Wiley and Sons, Inc.
Ed: Lita Epstein. **Released:** January 2009. **Price:** $21.99. **Description:** This second edition contains more new and updated information, including new information on the separate accounting and financial reporting standards for private/small businesses versus public/large businesses; updated information reflecting 2007 laws on international financial reporting standards; new content to match SEC and other governmental regulatory changes over the last three years; new information about how the analyst-corporate connection has changed the playing field; the impact of corporate communications and new technologies; new examples that reflect the current trends; and updated Websites and resources.

2283 ■ "Reform or Perish" in *Canadian Business* (Vol. 82, April 27, 2009, No. 7, pp. 20)
Pub: Rogers Media
Ed: Al Rosen. **Description:** It is believed that Canada needs to fix its financial regulatory framework in order to provide more oversight on accounting procedures that is often left up to auditors. While the U.S. has constantly rebuilt its regulatory framework, Canada has not instituted reforms on its regulations. Canada entered the recession with a strong system but needs to build more substance into it.

2284 ■ *Sarbanes-Oxley for Dummies, 2nd Ed.*
Pub: John Wiley and Sons, Inc.
Ed: Jill Gilbert Welytok. **Released:** February 2008. **Price:** $21.99. **Description:** Provides the latest Sarbanes-Oxley (SOX) legislation with procedures to safely and effectively reduce compliance costs. Topics include way to: establish SOX standards for IT professionals, minimize compliances costs for every aspect of a business, survive a Section 404 audit, avoid litigation under SOX, anticipate future rules and trends, create a post-SOX paper trail, increase a company's standing and reputation, work with SOX in a small business, meet new SOX standards, build a board that can't be bought, and to comply with all SOX management mandates.

2285 ■ "SEC Extends Small Business Deadline for SOX Audit Requirement" in *HRMagazine* (Vol. 53, August 2008, No. 8, pp. 20)
Pub: Society for Human Resource Management
Description: Securities and Exchange Commission has approved a one-year extension of the compliance date for smaller public companies to meet the Section 404(b) auditor attestation requirement of the Sarbanes-Oxley Act.

2286 ■ *Self-Employed Tax Solutions: Quick, Simple, Money-Saving, Audit-Proof Tax and Recordkeeping Basics*
Pub: The Globe Pequot Press
Ed: June Walker. **Released:** January 1, 2009. **Price:** $17.95. **Description:** A simple system for maintaining tax records and filing tax forms for any small business is explored.

2287 ■ *The Small Business Bible: Everything You Need to Know to Succeed in Your Small Business*
Pub: John Wiley & Sons, Incorporated
Ed: Steven D. Strauss. **Released:** September 2008. **Price:** $19.95 (US), $28.99 (Canadian). **Description:** Comprehensive guide to starting and running a successful small business. Topics include bookkeeping and financial management, marketing, publicity, and advertising.

2288 ■ "Spotlight on Principles-based Financial Reporting" in *Business Horizons* (September-October 2007, pp. 359)
Pub: Elsevier Technology Publications
Ed: Laureen A. Maines. **Description:** Employment of principles-based standards in order to generate reliable financial reporting and to reduce misrepresentations is discussed. Rules-based standards are distinguished from principles-based standards.

2289 ■ "Staffing Firm Grows by Following Own Advice-Hire a Headhunter" in *Crain's Detroit Business* (Vol. 24, October 6, 2008, No. 40, pp. 1)
Pub: Crain Communications, Inc.
Ed: Sherri Begin. **Description:** Profile of Venator Holdings L.L.C., a staffing firm that provides searches for companies in need of financial-accounting and technical employees; the firm's revenue has increased from $1.1 million in 2003 to a projected $11.5 million this year due to a climate in which more people are exiting the workforce than are coming in with those particular specialized skills and the need for a temporary, flexible workforce for contract placements at companies that do not want to take on the legacy costs associated with permanent employees. The hiring of an external headhunter to find the right out-of-state manager for Venator is also discussed.

2290 ■ "Surviving an IRS Audit: Tips for Small Businesses" in *Agency Sales Magazine* (Vol. 39, July 2009, No. 7, pp. 52)
Pub: MANA
Ed: Joshua D. Mosshart. **Description:** It is a good idea to enlist the services of a tax professional even if an audit is expected to go smoothly since the IRS is likely to scrutinize the unreported income and personal as well as business expenses of a small business during an audit.

2291 ■ "Test Your Structural Integrity" in *Entrepreneur* (Vol. 37, August 2009, No. 8, pp. 60)
Pub: Entrepreneur Media, Inc.
Ed: Jennifer Lawler. **Description:** Tax considerations can be important when choosing a business structure. For example, profits are taxed to the corporation in a C corp while profits are taxed only once at an S corp or a limited liability company. Meeting a tax professional should be done prior to switching to a different structure.

2292 ■ "Throughput Metrics Meet Six Sigma" in *Management Accounting Quarterly* (Vol. 12, Spring 2011, No. 3, pp. 12)
Pub: Management Accounting Quarterly
Ed: Shaun Aghili. **Description:** Throughput accounting (TA) metrics can be combined with six sigma's DMAIC methodology and various time-tested analysis and measurement tools for added effectiveness in resolving resource constraint issues. The goal is to optimize not only the output of a specific department but that of the entire system, by implementing a cost accounting system that is conducive to system optimization while increasing product quality, process integrity, or ideally, both.

2293 ■ "ValienteHernandez Acquired" in *The Business Journal-Serving Greater Tampa Bay* (Vol. 28, September 12, 2008, No. 38, pp. 1)
Pub: American City Business Journals, Inc.
Ed: Alexis Muellner. **Description:** Minnesota accounting firm LarsonAllen LLP has acquired Florida-based ValienteHernandez PA, creating a company with 35 employees to be based in ValienteHernandez's newly built office in Tampa Bay Area. Other details about the merger are provided.

2294 ■ "Welcome Back" in *Canadian Business* (Vol. 82, April 27, 2009, No. 7, pp. 25)
Pub: Rogers Media
Ed: Sarka Halas. **Description:** Some Canadian companies such as Gennum Corporation have taken advantage of corporate sale-leasebacks to raise money at a time when credit is hard to acquire. Corporate sale-leasebacks allow companies to sell their property assets while remaining as tenants of the building. Sale-leasebacks allow firms to increase capital while avoiding the disruptions that may result with moving.

2295 ■ "Where Women Work" in *Marketing to Women* (Vol. 21, April 2008, No. 4, pp. 8)
Pub: EPM Communications, Inc.
Description: According to the U.S. Census Bureau, 60 percent of America's professional tax preparers are women. Also features additional trends concerning women in the workplace. Statistical data included.

2296 ■ *Working Papers, Chapters 1-14 for Needles/Powers/Crosson's Financial and Managerial Accounting*
Pub: Cengage South-Western
Ed: Belverd E. Needles, Marian Powers, Susan V. Crosson. **Released:** May 10, 2010. **Price:** $62.95. **Description:** Appropriate accounting forms for completing all exercises, problems and cases in the text are provided for financial management of a small company.

TRADE SHOWS AND CONVENTIONS

2297 ■ Business & Technology Solutions Show
Illinois Certified Public Accounting Society
550 W. Jackson, Ste. 900
Chicago, IL 60661
Ph:(312)933-0407
Free: 800-993-0407
Fax:(312)993-9954
URL: http://www.icpas.org
Released: Annual. **Audience:** Certified public accountants and their clients, business owners and managers, and others from the financial and business community. **Principal Exhibits:** Computers, office equipment, software publishing and educational supplies, and financial services.

2298 ■ Institute of Management Accountants Conference
Institute of Management Accountants, Inc.
10 Paragon Dr.
Montvale, NJ 07645-1718
Ph:(201)573-9000
Free: 800-638-4427
Fax:(201)573-9000
Co. E-mail: info@imanet.org
URL: http://www.imanet.org
Released: Annual. **Audience:** Management accountants. **Principal Exhibits:** Management accounting equipment, supplies, and services. Review courses, shipping companies, software companies, and risk management consultants.

2299 ■ New Jersey Accounting, Business & Technology Show & Conference
Flagg Management, Inc.
353 Lexington Ave.
New York, NY 10016
Ph:(212)286-0333
Fax:(212)286-0086
Co. E-mail: flaggmgmt@msn.com
URL: http://www.flaggmgmt.com
Released: Annual. **Audience:** CPAs, accounting professionals, business and financial executives of New Jersey, Fortune 1000 corporations, business owners and managers, IT managers. **Principal Exhibits:** Information and technology, financial and business services, computer accounting systems, software, tax preparation, accounting, audit, practice management software - windows, and computer and business systems. Banking, insurance, financial and business software. Internet, online systems and middle market software and investment services. **Dates and Locations:** 2011 May 18-19, Secaucus, NJ.

CONSULTANTS

2300 ■ CFO Service
112 Chester Ave.
Saint Louis, MO 63122
Ph:(314)757-2940
Contact: John D. Skae, President
E-mail: jds217@aol.com
Scope: A group of professional executives that provide upper management services to companies that cannot support a full time COO or CFO. Provides clients in the areas of business planning, company policies, contract negotiations, safety policies, product and service pricing, loans management, taxes, cost analysis, loss control and budgeting.

2301 ■ On-Q Software Inc.
13764 SW 11th St.
Miami, FL 33184
Ph:(305)553-2400
Free: 800-553-2862
Fax:(305)220-2666
Co. E-mail: info@on-qsoftware.com
URL: http://www.on-qsoftware.com
Contact: Terry Cajigas, Principle
E-mail: hcajigas@on-qsoftware.com
Scope: Provides the small business community with simple to use, feature rich software. Provides software solutions including time and fixed fee billing, due date tracking and practice manager.

FRANCHISES AND BUSINESS OPPORTUNITIES

2302 ■ CFO Today Inc.
545 E Tennessee St.
Tallahassee, FL 32308
Ph:(850)681-1941
Free: 888-643-1348
Fax:(850)561-1374
URL: http://www.cfotoday.com
No. of Franchise Units: 103. **No. of Company-Owned Units:** 1. **Founded:** 1989. **Franchised:** 1990. **Description:** Offers regional franchise program through which a regional owner solicits local franchisees. Local franchisees operate an accounting and tax practice, utilizing special marketing techniques, in addition to operational and computer systems, to provide tax, record keeping and other services to clients. **Equity Capital Needed:** $24,400-$40,000. **Franchise Fee:** $24,000. **Royalty Fee:** Varies. **Financial Assistance:** No. **Training:** Provides 5 days training at corporate headquarters and 1 day onsite, with ongoing support.

2303 ■ Ledgers Professional Services
4-17705 Leslie St.
Newmarket, ON, Canada L3Y 3E3
Ph:(905)898-6320
Free: (866)836-6620
Co. E-mail: sales@ledgers.com
URL: http://www.ledgers.com
No. of Franchise Units: 50. **No. of Company-Owned Units:** 1. **Founded:** 1994. **Franchised:** 1996. **Description:** Provides a comprehensive suite of services to small businesses, including bookkeeping, payroll and personal income taxes to corporate financial statement preparation and tax returns. **Equity Capital Needed:** $10,000. **Franchise Fee:** $20,000. **Royalty Fee: Financial Assistance: Training:** Provides 5 days training.

LIBRARIES

2304 ■ Defense Finance & Accounting Service–Denver Center–Learning Center (6760)
6760 E. Irvington Pl.
Denver, CO 80279-5000
Ph:(303)676-7053
Fax:(303)676-7052
URL: http://www.dfas.mil
Contact: Harvey Reynolds, Libn.
Scope: Computers, accounting, finance, management. **Services:** Library not open to the public. **Holdings:** 7000 books. **Subscriptions:** 450 journals and other serials; 20 newspapers.

2305 ■ Deloitte Services LLP Information Center
50 S. 6th St., Ste. 2800
Minneapolis, MN 55402-1538
Ph:(612)397-4342
Co. E-mail: marcollins@deloitte.com
Contact: Marsha Collins, Mgr.
Scope: Accounting, auditing, taxation, healthcare, consulting. **Services:** Library not open to the public. **Holdings:** 3000 books; 178 bound periodical volumes. **Subscriptions:** 300 journals and other serials; 5 newspapers.

2306 ■ Deloitte & Touche Research Center
180 N. Stetson
Chicago, IL 60601
Ph:(312)946-3617
Fax:(312)946-2663
Co. E-mail: badolmon@dttus.com
Contact: Barbara Dolmon, Mgr.
Scope: Accounting, auditing, taxation, business and finance, management, electronic data processing/ information technology. **Services:** Interlibrary loan; copying; Library open to the public by appointment. **Holdings:** 2500 books. **Subscriptions:** 250 journals and other serials; 15 newspapers.

2307 ■ Deloitte & Toucher Library and Information Center
2800 - 1055 Dunsmuir St.
4 Bentall Ctr.
Vancouver, BC, Canada V7X 1P4
Ph:(604)640-3026
Fax:(604)685-0395
URL: http://www.deloitte.com
Contact: Nada Djurovic, Libn.
Scope: Accounting, auditing, taxation, industry. **Services:** Interlibrary loan; Library open to the public with restrictions. **Holdings:** 2000 books; stock, exchange rate, and dividend records. **Subscriptions:** 65 journals and other serials; 6 newspapers.

2308 ■ District of Columbia Public Library–Business, Economics and Vocations Division
Martin Luther King Memorial Library
901 G St. NW, Rm. 107
Washington, DC 20001
Ph:(202)727-1171
Fax:(202)727-1129
Co. E-mail: commentssuggestions.dcpl@dc.gov
URL: http://dclibrary.org
Contact: David Robinson, Div.Mgr.
Scope: Business; statistics, economics, vocations, investment, real estate, import, export, accounting, taxation, business report writing, organizational behavior, commerce, management, marketing, labor, transportation. **Services:** Interlibrary loan; copying; division open to the public. **Holdings:** 55,639 books; 1150 bound periodical volumes; 471 business directories; 6000 pamphlets; 508 telephone directories; 5521 reels of microfilm; 88 microcards; 7268 microfiche. **Subscriptions:** 428 journals and other serials; 35 newspapers and financial services.

2309 ■ Ernst & Young Center for Business Knowledge
1 Victory Pk., Ste. 2000
2323 Victory Ave.
Dallas, TX 75219
Ph:(214)969-8000
Fax:(214)969-8587
URL: http://www.ey.com
Contact: Tommy M. Yardley, Reg.Res.Mgr.
Scope: Consulting, accounting, tax accounting, auditing. **Services:** Center open to the public at librarian's discretion.

2310 ■ Howard University–School of Business–Business Library (2600)
2600 6th St., NW
Washington, DC 20059
Ph:(202)806-1561
Fax:(202)986-4780
Co. E-mail: lsmiley@howard.edu
URL: http://www.howard.edu/businesslibrary
Contact: Lucille B. Smiley, Hd.Libn.
Scope: Business administration, health services administration, management, accounting, real estate, insurance, marketing, finance, computer-based management information systems, hospitality management, International business. **Services:** Interlibrary loan; copying; Library open to the public for reference use only. **Holdings:** 70,000 books; 10,500 bound periodical volumes; 25,000 reels of microfilm; 500,000 10K reports on microfiche. **Subscriptions:** 1372 journals and other serials; 35 newspapers.

2311 ■ KPMG–Research Centre
777 Dunsmuir St.
PO Box 10426
Vancouver, BC, Canada V7Y 1K3
Ph:(604)691-3000
Fax:(604)691-3031
URL: http://www.kpmg.ca
Contact: Julian Richards, Libn.
Scope: Accounting, tax, general business, stocks. **Services:** SDI; Library not open to the public. **Holdings:** 1000 books; 70 bound periodical volumes. **Subscriptions:** 50 journals and other serials; 6 newspapers.

2312 ■ KPMG L.L.P. Library
355 S. Grand Ave., Ste. 2000
Los Angeles, CA 90071-1568
Ph:(213)972-4000
Fax:(213)622-1217
Co. E-mail: baby@kpmg.com
URL: http://www.kpmg.com/us/en/pages/default.aspx
Contact: Brian Aby, Lib.Assoc.
Scope: Accounting, taxation, business management, auditing, economics. **Services:** Interlibrary loan; copying; Library open to the public. **Holdings:** 2500 books; 100 bound periodical volumes. **Subscriptions:** 636 journals and other serials; 2 newspapers.

2313 ■ KPMG L.L.P. Resource Centre
Ste. 2700, Bow Valley Sq. 2
205-5th Ave., SW
Calgary, AB, Canada T2P 4B9
Ph:(403)691-8000
Fax:(403)691-8008
Co. E-mail: rbuhler@kpmg.ca
URL: http://www.kpmg.com
Contact: Roxie Buhler, Info.Mgr.
Scope: Accounting, taxation, oil and gas. **Services:** Interlibrary loan; copying; services open to clients. **Holdings:** 900 books; 900 Annual reports. **Subscriptions:** 50 journals and other serials; 6 newspapers.

2314 ■ Price Waterhouse Library
1300 SW 5th Ave., Ste. 3100
Portland, OR 97201-5638
Ph:(971)544-4000
Fax:(971)544-4100
URL: http://www.pwc.com
Contact: Lynne Trueblood, Libn.
Scope: Tax law, accounting, auditing, management consulting. **Services:** Interlibrary loan; copying; SDI; Library open to the public by appointment. **Holdings:** Figures not available. **Subscriptions:** 80 journals and other serials; 7 newspapers.

2315 ■ PricewaterhouseCoopers–North Toronto Research Centre
1900-5700 Yonge St.
North York, ON, Canada M2M 4K7
Ph:(416)941-8383
Fax:(416)814-3200
Co. E-mail: catherine.southwell@ca.pwc.com
Contact: Catherine Southwell, Info.Spec.
Scope: Taxation, GST/Commodity tax, real estate, estate administration, tax law. **Services:** Interlibrary loan; centre not open to the public. **Holdings:** 1200 books. **Subscriptions:** 100 journals and other serials; 3 newspapers.

RESEARCH CENTERS

2316 ■ Connecticut Society of Certified Public Accountants–Education and Research Foundation
845 Brook St., Bldg. 2
Rocky Hill, CT 06067-3405
Ph:(860)258-4800
Free: 800—232-2232
Fax:(860)258-4859
Co. E-mail: artr@cs-cpa.org
URL: http://www.cs-cpa.org
Contact: Arthur J. Renner, Exec.Dir.
E-mail: artr@cs-cpa.org
Scope: Accounting. **Services:** Consultation. **Publications:** Newsletter (10/year). **Educational Activities:** Colloquium (annually); Seminars, conferences, and technical sessions.

2317 ■ Credit Research Foundation
8840 Columbia 100 Pky.
Columbia, MD 21045
Ph:(410)740-5499
Fax:(410)740-4620
URL: http://www.crfonline.org
Contact: Terry Callahan, Pres.
Scope: Financial management, including management theory, electronic data processing, human resources management, business practices and techniques, economic impact of business credit, credit and receivables management, working capital management, international credit and finance, and related subjects. **Publications:** CRF News (quarterly); Credit Executives Handbook; National Summary of Domestic Trade Receivables (quarterly); Net Bad-Debt Writeoffs and Allowance for Uncollectibles (annually); Quarterly Credit and Financial Management Review; Annual Collection Productivity Report. **Educational Activities:** CRF Credit and Accounts Receivable Forums (3/year), held in various cities around America; CRF Online Classroom, online training for credit personnel.

2318 ■ Financial Executives Research Foundation
West Tower, 7th Fl.
1250 Headquarters Plz.
Morristown, NJ 07960
Ph:(973)765-1000
Fax:(973)765-1023
Co. E-mail: mhollein@financialexecutives.org
URL: http://www.financialexecutives.org/eweb/DynamicPage.aspx?Site=_fei&Webcode=ferf_home
Contact: Marie Hollein, Pres./CEO
E-mail: mhollein@financialexecutives.org
Scope: Business management, with particular emphasis on principles and practices of financial management and their evolving role in the management of business. **Publications:** Executive reports (monthly); Issue alerts (quarterly); Newsletters (quarterly). **Educational Activities:** Professional development presentations (monthly).

2319 ■ New York University–Salomon Center for the Study of Financial Institutions
Stern School of Business
44 W 4th St., Ste. 9-160
New York, NY 10012
Ph:(212)998-0700
Fax:(212)995-4220
Co. E-mail: mrichar0@stern.nyu.edu
URL: http://w4.stern.nyu.edu/salomon
Contact: Prof. Matthew Richardson PhD, Dir.
E-mail: mrichar0@stern.nyu.edu
Scope: Evaluates changing structure of financial instruments and markets and the use of these instruments and markets in financial intermediation and the management of risk by financial institutions and business corporations. Recent projects include modern portfolio management and the prudent man rule, role of financial futures and options in large financial institutions' investment portfolios, information and stock market efficiency, composition of individual investment portfolios, hedging and trading performance of new financial futures and options, new financial instruments, reforming Japan's financial markets, reconfiguration of the insurance industry, and restructuring the U.S. financial and insurance sectors. **Services:** Associates Program, which encourages participation of interested business organizations. **Publications:** Instruments and Markets (5/year); Journal of Derivatives (quarterly); Journal of Financial Institutions; Journal of International Financial Management and Accounting (quarterly); Newsletter (annually); Occasional Papers in Business and Finance (occasionally); Working Paper Series (50-70/year). **Educational Activities:** Short courses (3/year), on advanced topics in finance; Workshops. **Awards:** Doctoral awards.

2320 ■ Shippensburg University of Pennsylvania–Office of Extended Studies
Horton Hall 111
1871 Old Main Dr.
Shippensburg, PA 17257
Ph:(717)477-1348
Fax:(717)477-4050
Co. E-mail: extended@ship.edu
URL: http://www.ship.edu/extended
Contact: Dr. Christina M. Sax
E-mail: extended@ship.edu
Scope: Personnel development programs and problem-solving in organizational function, including accounting, finance, marketing, management, sales, advertising, training, and taxes. **Services:** Provides speakers for professional meetings; Research and data collection services. **Publications:** Working Paper Series. **Educational Activities:** Annual Small Business Management Series, open to small business owners or managers; Tax Institute Small Business Management Seminar.

2321 ■ University of Iowa–RSM McGladrey Institute of Accounting Education and Research
108 John Pappajohn Business Bldg.
Henry B. Tippie College of Business
Iowa City, IA 52242-1994
Ph:(319)335-0958
Fax:(319)335-1956
Co. E-mail: ramji-balakrishnan@uiowa.edu
URL: http://tippie.uiowa.edu/accounting/mcgladrey/index.cfm
Contact: Prof. Ramji Balakrishnan PhD, Dir.
E-mail: ramji-balakrishnan@uiowa.edu
Scope: Accounting, auditing, and financial reporting by public and private organizations. **Publications:** Working papers (occasionally). **Educational Activities:** National Speaker series; PriceWaterhouseCoopers Accounting Research Workshop; Sidney G. Winter lecture series.

2322 ■ University of Rhode Island–Research Center in Business and Economics
College of Business Administration
7 Lippitt Rd.
Kingston, RI 02881
Ph:(401)874-2549
Fax:(401)874-4825
Co. E-mail: rcbe@etal.uri.edu
URL: http://www.cba.uri.edu/offices/research/rcbe/
Contact: Jerri Paquin, Assoc.Dir.
E-mail: rcbe@etal.uri.edu
Scope: Services research activities of faculty members of the College in fields of accounting, business law, economics, finance, insurance, management, marketing, and quantitative analysis. Conducts survey research, economic analyses, and business-related research projects on a contract basis.

Bookstore

START-UP INFORMATION

2323 ■ *How to Open and Operate a Financially Successful Bookstore on Amazon and Other Web Sites: With Companion CD-ROM*
Pub: Atlantic Publishing Company

Released: December 1, 2010. **Price:** $39.95. **Description:** This book was written for every used book aficionado and bookstore owner who currently wants to take advantage of the massive collection of online resources available to start and run your own online bookstore business.

2324 ■ *The Specialty Shop: How to Create Your Own Unique and Profitable Retail Business*
Pub: AMACOM

Ed: Dorothy Finell. **Released:** February 27, 2007. **Price:** $21.95. **Description:** Advise to start retail businesses, including bakeries, gift shops, toy stores, book shops, tea houses, clothing boutiques, and other unique stores.

ASSOCIATIONS AND OTHER ORGANIZATIONS

2325 ■ American Booksellers Association
200 White Plains Rd., Ste. 600
Tarrytown, NY 10591
Free: 800-637-0037
Fax:(914)591-2720
Co. E-mail: info@bookweb.org
URL: http://www.bookweb.org
Contact: Oren Teicher, CEO

Description: Seeks to meet the needs of members, independently owned bookstores with storefront locations, through education, information dissemination, and advocacy. Supports free speech, literacy, and programs that encourage reading. **Publications:** *ABA Electronic Book Buyer's Handbook*; *ABACUS* (annual); *Bookselling this Week* (weekly).

2326 ■ Antiquarian Booksellers Association of America
20 W 44th St., Ste. 507
New York, NY 10036-6604
Ph:(212)944-8291
Fax:(212)944-8293
Co. E-mail: hq@abaa.org
URL: http://www.abaa.org
Contact: Susan Benne, Exec. Dir.

Description: Dealers and appraisers of fine, rare and out-of-print books, manuscripts, and related materials. Sponsors two annual regional international book fairs and four biennial regional international book fairs. Promotes ethical standards in the industry. Sponsors educational programs for members, librarians, archivists, and the public. Administers the Antiquarian Booksellers' Benevolent Fund. .

2327 ■ Antiquarian Booksellers' Association of Canada–Association de la Librairie Ancienne du Canada
783 Bank St.
Ottawa, ON, Canada K1S 3V5
Co. E-mail: info@abac.org
URL: http://www.abac.org
Contact: Liam McGahern, Pres.

Description: Bookselling firms and dealers in rare books and manuscripts. Promotes adherence to high standards of ethics and practice in the trade of antiquarian books. Serves as liaison between members and book collectors and as a clearinghouse on antiquarian books and their trade.

2328 ■ Book Industry Study Group
370 Lexington Ave., Ste. 900
New York, NY 10017
Ph:(646)336-7141
Fax:(646)336-6214
Co. E-mail: info@bisg.org
URL: http://www.bisg.org
Contact: Scott Lubeck, Exec. Dir.

Description: Represents publishers, manufacturers, suppliers, wholesalers, retailers, librarians, and other engaged in the business of print and electronic media. **Publications:** *Book Industry TRENDS* (annual).

2329 ■ Canadian Booksellers Association
1255 Bay St., Ste. 902
Toronto, ON, Canada M5R 2A9
Free: (866)788-0790
Co. E-mail: lefebvr@mcmaster.ca
URL: http://www.cbabook.org
Contact: Mark Lefebvre, Pres.

Description: Represents the interests of Canadian booksellers from coast to coast to government, media, suppliers and other industry stakeholders. Works to improve the status of the book trade. Fosters communication among members. **Publications:** *Canadian Bookseller* (bimonthly).

2330 ■ CBA
PO Box 62000
Colorado Springs, CO 80962-2000
Ph:(719)265-9895
Free: 800-252-1950
Fax:(719)272-3510
Co. E-mail: info@cbaonline.org
URL: http://www.cbaonline.org
Contact: Jim Powell, Pres.

Description: Serves as trade association for retail stores selling Christian books, Bibles, gifts, and Sunday school and church supplies. Compiles statistics; conducts specialized education programs. **Publications:** *Aspiring Retail* .

2331 ■ Great Lakes Independent Booksellers Association
PO Box 901
Grand Haven, MI 49417
Ph:(616)847-2460
Free: 800-745-2460
Fax:(616)842-0051
Co. E-mail: info@gliba.org
URL: http://www.gliba.org
Contact: Deb Leonard, Exec. Dir.

Description: Booksellers. Supports bookstores and promotes excellence in publishing, distribution, promotion and selling of books. Provides a forum for information exchange; fosters a sense of community among booksellers; provides information and services for the advancement of members; promotes literacy; and supports the First Amendment rights of members. **Publications:** *Books for Holiday Giving* (annual); *Great Lakes Bookseller* (bimonthly).

2332 ■ Institute of Communication Agencies
2300 Yonge St., Ste. 3002
Toronto, ON, Canada M4P 1E4
Ph:(416)482-1396
Free: 800-567-7422
Fax:(416)482-1856
Co. E-mail: ica@icacanada.ca
URL: http://www.icacanada.ca
Contact: Jani Yates, Pres.

Description: Aims to represent advertising agencies in a wide variety of beneficial activities.

2333 ■ International League of Antiquarian Booksellers
35 W Maple Ave.
Merchantville, NJ 08109-5141
Ph:(856)665-2284
Fax:(856)665-3639
Co. E-mail: mail@betweenthecovers.com
URL: http://www.ilab.org
Contact: Arnoud Gerits, Pres.

Description: Represents national associations of antiquarian booksellers around the world. Organizes professional training courses for members. Sponsors book fairs. .

2334 ■ National Association of College Stores
500 E Lorain St.
Oberlin, OH 44074
Free: 800-622-7498
Fax:(440)775-4769
Co. E-mail: webteam@nacs.org
URL: http://www.nacs.org
Contact: Brian E. Cartier CAE, CEO

Description: Institutional, private, leased, and cooperative college stores selling books, supplies, and other merchandise to college students, faculty, and staff; associate members include publishers and suppliers. Seeks to effectively serve higher education by providing educational research, advocacy and other to college stores and their suppliers. Maintains NACSCORP, Inc., a wholly owned subsidiary corporation, which distributes trade and mass market books and educational software. Sponsors seminars. Conducts manager certification, specialized education, and research programs. Maintains College Stores Research and Educational Foundation which provides grants for educational programs and conducts research. **Publications:** *Campus Marketplace* (weekly); *The College Store* (bimonthly); *NACS Book*

Buyers Manual (annual); *NACS Directory of Colleges and College Stores* (annual); *NACS Directory of Publishers* (biennial).

2335 ■ Women's National Book Association
PO Box 237
New York, NY 10150-0231
Ph:(212)208-4629
Fax:(212)208-4629
Co. E-mail: publicity@bookbuzz.com
URL: http://www.wnba-books.org
Contact: Susannah Greenberg, Public Relations Mgr.
Description: Women and men who work with and value books. Exists to promote reading and to support the role of women in the book community. **Publications:** *The Bookwoman* (3/year).

REFERENCE WORKS

2336 ■ "Africa Rising" in *Harvard Business Review* (Vol. 86, September 2008, No. 9, pp. 36)
Pub: Harvard Business School Press
Ed: John T. Landry. **Description:** Review of the book entitled, "Africa Rising: How 900 Million African Consumers Offer More Than You Think" provides advice for marketing to those on the African continent.

2337 ■ *Book Dealers Dropship Directory*
Pub: North American Bookdealers Exchange
Contact: Al Galasso, Director
Released: Irregular, Latest edition 2005-2006. **Price:** $15, individuals with free shipping in USA and Canada. **Covers:** More than 300 dealers and distributors who ship individual copies of books to customers for publishers and mail order companies. **Entries Include:** Company name, address, titles or types of books handled. **Arrangement:** Alphabetical.

2338 ■ "The Book On Indigo" in *Canadian Business* (Vol. 81, July 22, 2008, No. 12-13, pp. 29)
Pub: Rogers Media Ltd.
Ed: Thomas Watson. **Description:** Indigo Books & Music Inc. reported record sales of $922 million resulting in a record net profit of $52.8 million for the 2008 fiscal year ended March 29, 2008. Earnings per share were $2.13, greater than Standard & Poor's expected $1.70 per share. Additional information concerning Indigo Books is presented.

2339 ■ "Book Publishing is Growing" in *Information Today* (Vol. 28, October 2011, No. 9, pp. 10)
Pub: Information Today, Inc.
Ed: Paula J. Hane. **Description:** U.S. book publishing industry is reporting growth in its sector, despite the poor economy. BookStats, a comprehensive statistical survey conducted on the modern publishing industry in the U.S. reported Americans are reading in all print and digital formats. In 2011, 114 million ebooks were sold and now account for 13.6 percent of revenue from adult fiction. In contrast, 603 million trade hardcover books (fiction and nonfiction) were sold in 2011, a 5.8 percent increase over 2008.

2340 ■ *Books in Print*
Pub: R.R. Bowker L.L.C.
Contact: Roy Crego, Mng.Dir.
Released: Annual, Latest edition 2009-2010. **Price:** $995, individuals hardcover; 7 volumes. **Description:** Over 2.8 million entries covering books published and distributed in the U.S. **Entries Include:** For publishers—Company name, address. For books—Authors, title, price, publisher, other bibliographic information as available. The material in "Books in Print" is also available in subject-classified form in "Subject Guide to Books in Print," published as a five-volume set, annually in September. **Arrangement:** Publishers, authors, and titles are alphabetical in separate sections.

2341 ■ "Boom and Bust in the Book Biz" in *Canadian Business* (Vol. 83, August 17, 2010, No. 13-14, pp. 16)
Pub: Rogers Media Ltd.
Ed: Jordan Timm. **Description:** Electronic book marketplace is booming with Amazon.com's e-book sales for the Kindle e-reader exceeding the hardcover sales. Kobo Inc. has registered early success with its Kobo e-reader and has partnered with Hong Kong telecom giant on an e-book store.

2342 ■ "Borders Previews New Web Site" in *Crain's Detroit Business* (Vol. 23, October 8, 2007, No. 41, pp. 4)
Pub: Crain Communications Inc. - Detroit
Ed: Sheena Harrison. **Description:** Borders Group Inc. previewed its new Website that allows customers to buy items that include the Magic Shelf, a virtual bookcase that displays available recommended books, movies and music.

2343 ■ "Burdened by Debt, Borders Group Suspends Dividends, May Be Sold" in *Crain's Detroit Business* (Vol. 24, March 24, 2008, No. 12)
Pub: Crain Communications, Inc.
Ed: Nancy Kaffer. **Description:** Ann Arbor-based Borders Group Inc. is exploring its options and may put itself up for sale due to its declining stock price and mounting debt. The company's fiscal year was capped by poor holiday sales and Borders does not have the cash on hand to meet the 2009 goals set in its strategic plan.

2344 ■ "Buying In" in *Harvard Business Review* (Vol. 86, September 2008, No. 9, pp. 36)
Pub: Harvard Business School Press
Ed: Andrew O'Connell. **Description:** Review of the book entitled, "Buying In: The Secret Dialogue between What We Buy and Who We Are" which offers tips that those in the field of marketing will find useful.

2345 ■ *Children's Books in Print*
Pub: R.R. Bowker L.L.C.
Released: Annual, Latest edition 2009. **Price:** $455, individuals 2-vol. set. **Entries Include:** Book entries—Title, subtitle, author(s), editor(s), illustrator(s), publishing date, edition, price, binding, ISBN, LC number, publisher; Publisher entries—Name, address, phone, ISBN prefix. The material in "Children's Books in Print" is also available in subject-classified form in "Subject Guide to Children's Books in Print," also published in December. **Arrangement:** Alphabetical within each index. **Indexes:** Author, title, illustrator, award or prize, publisher.

2346 ■ "Consignment Shop Offers Children's Clothes, Products" in *Frederick News-Post* (August 19, 2010)
Pub: Federick News-Post
Ed: Ed Waters Jr. **Description:** Sweet Pea Consignments for Children offers used items for newborns to pre-teens. The shop carries name brand clothing as well as toys, books and baby products.

2347 ■ "Copyright Clearance Center (CCC) Partnered with cSubs" in *Information Today* (Vol. 28, November 2011, No. 10, pp. 14)
Pub: Information Today, Inc.
Description: Copyright Clearance Center (CCC) partnered with cSubs to integrate CCC's point-of-content licensing solution RightsLink Basic directly into cSubs workflow. The partnership will allow cSubs' customers a user-friendly process for obtaining permissions. Csubs is a corporate subscription management service for books, newspapers, and econtent.

2348 ■ "Gadget Makers Aim for New Chapter in Reading" in *Crain's Cleveland Business* (Vol. 28, October 22, 2007, No. 42, pp. 20)
Pub: Crain Communications, Inc.
Ed: Jennifer McKevitt. **Description:** Although e-books and e-audiobooks are becoming more popular, e-readers, devices that display digital books, still haven't caught on with the public. Experts feel that consumers, many of whom have to look at a computer screen all day for work, still like the feel of a real book in their hands.

2349 ■ "A Good Book Is Worth a Thousand Blogs" in *Barron's* (Vol. 88, July 14, 2008, No. 28, pp. 42)
Pub: Dow Jones & Co., Inc.
Ed: Gene Epstein. **Description:** Nine summer book suggestions on economics are presented. The list includes 'The Revolution' by Ron Paul, 'The Forgotten Man' by Amity Shales, 'The Commitments of Traders Bible' by Stephen Briese, and 'Economic Facts and Fallacies' by Thomas Sowell.

2350 ■ "A Gripping Read: Bargains & Noble" in *Barron's* (Vol. 88, March 17, 2008, No. 11, pp. 20)
Pub: Dow Jones & Company, Inc.
Ed: Jonathan R. Laing. **Description:** Barnes & Noble's earnings forecast for the fiscal year ending in January, 2008 to be $1.70 to $1.90 per share which is way lower than the $2.12 analyst consensus. The company also said that sales at stores one-year old or older dropped 0.5 percent in the fourth quarter. However, the shares are now cheap at 4.9 times enterprise value with some analysts putting a price target of 41 per share.

2351 ■ "Hit the Books" in *Black Enterprise* (Vol. 38, July 2008, No. 12, pp. 42)
Pub: Earl G. Graves Publishing Co. Inc.
Ed: Mellody Hobson. **Description:** Four books that deal with investing are discussed as is the idea that reading even 15 minutes a day from one of these books will give you tools that far exceed what you can learn from magazines and the business section of your daily newspaper.

2352 ■ "Interactive Stores a Big Part of Borders' Turnaround Plan" in *Crain's Detroit Business* (Vol. 24, February 18, 2008, No. 7, pp. 4)
Pub: Crain Communications Inc. - Detroit
Description: Borders Group Inc. is using digital technology and interactive media as a part of the firm's turnaround plan. The digital store will allow shoppers to create CDs, download audio books, publish their own works, print photos and search family genealogy.

2353 ■ "Lafley Gives Look At His Game Plan" in *Business Courier* (Vol. 24, March 21, 2008, No. 50, pp. 1)
Pub: American City Business Journals, Inc.
Ed: Lisa Biank Fasig. **Description:** Overview of A.G. Lafley's book entitled 'The Game-Changer', is presented. Lafley, Procter & Gamble Co.'s chief executive officer, documented his philosophy and strategy in his book. His work also includes Procter & Gamble's hands-on initiatives such as mock-up grocery stores and personal interviews with homeowners.

2354 ■ "Last Founder Standing" in *Conde Nast Portfolio* (Vol. 2, June 2008, No. 6, pp. 124)
Pub: Conde Nast Publications, Inc.
Ed: Kevin Maney. **Description:** Interview with Amazon CEO Jeff Bezos in which he discusses the economy, the company's new distribution center and the hiring of employees for it, e-books, and the overall vision for the future of the firm.

2355 ■ *Library and Book Trade Almanac*
Pub: Information Today Inc.
Released: Annual, Latest edition 56th; June 2011. **Price:** $229, individuals hardbound; plus $17 shipping and handling charges; $206.10, individuals first time standing order. **Publication Includes:** Lists of accredited library schools; scholarships for education in library science; library organizations; library statistics; publishing and bookselling organizations. **Entries Include:** Directory listings give name of institution, address, phone, fax, name of officer or contact, publications; scholarship listings include requirements, value of grant, contact name. Principal content is articles and special reports on topics of interest to those in library/information science and publishers; international reports; annual reports from federal agencies and libraries and from national associations; information on legislation, funding, etc. **Arrangement:** Topical. **Indexes:** Organization; subject.

2356 ■ "Negotiating Tips" in *Black Enterprise* (Vol. 37, December 2006, No. 5, pp. 70)
Pub: Earl G. Graves Publishing Co. Inc.
Description: Sekou Kaalund, head of strategy, mergers & acquisitions at Citigroup Securities & Fund Services, states that "Negotiation skills are paramount to success in a business environment because of cli-

ent, employee, and shareholder relationships". He discusses how the book by George Kohlrieser, Hostage at the Table: How Leaders Can Overcome Conflict, Influence Others, and Raise Performance, has helped him negotiate more powerfully and enhance his skills at conflict-resolution.

2357 ■ "New Book Takes Alternate View on Ontario's Wind Industry" in *CNW Group* (September 19, 2011)
Pub: CNW Group
Description: Dirty Business: The Reality Behind Ontario's Rush to Wind Power, was written by editor and health care writer Jane Wilson of Ottawa, Ontario, Canada along with contributing editor Parker Gallant. The book contains articles and papers on the wind business, including information on illnesses caused from the environmental noise.

2358 ■ "Online Book Sales Surpass Bookstores" in *Information Today* (Vol. 28, September 2011, No. 8, pp. 11)
Pub: Information Today, Inc.
Ed: Cindy Martine. **Description:** Online book sales outpaced bookstore purchases in the United States, signaling a shift in the US book industry. Statistical data included.

2359 ■ *Publishers Directory*
Pub: Gale
Released: Annual, Latest edition 36th; April, 2011. **Price:** $720, individuals. **Covers:** Over 20,000 new and established, commercial and nonprofit, private and alternative, corporate and association, government and institution publishing programs and their distributors; includes producers of books, classroom materials, prints, reports, and databases. **Entries Include:** Firm name, address, phone, fax, company e-mail address, URL, year founded, ISBN prefix, Standard Address Number, whether firm participates in the Cataloging in Publication program of the Library of Congress, names of principal executives, personal e-mail addresses, number of titles in print, description of firm and its main subject interests, discount and returns policies, affiliated and parent companies, mergers and amalgamations, principal markets, imprints and divisions, alternate formats products are offered; distributors also list firms for which they distribute, special services, terms to publishers and regional offices. **Arrangement:** Alphabetical; distributors listed separately. **Indexes:** Subject, geographical, publisher, imprints, and distributor.

2360 ■ "SAGE Publications Announced a Partnership with Which Medical Device" in *Information Today* (Vol. 28, November 2011, No. 10, pp. 15)
Pub: Information Today, Inc.
Description: SAGE Publications has partnered with Which Medical Device to offer insights, tutorials, and reviews of medical devices.

2361 ■ "The Seat-Of-The-Pants School of Marketing" in *Brandweek* (Vol. 49, April 21, 2008, No. 16, pp. 24)
Pub: VNU Business Media, Inc.
Ed: David Vinjamuri. **Description:** Excerpt from the book "Accidental Branding: How Ordinary People Build Extraordinary Brands," by David Vinjamuri, discusses six shared principles for creating a brand that is unique and will be successful over the long-term.

2362 ■ "University Book Store Inc.: an Act of Independence" in *Retail Merchandiser* (Vol. 51, September-October 2011, No. 5, pp. 68)
Pub: Phoenix Media Corporation
Ed: Lori Sichtermann. **Description:** University Book Store Inc. is a campus bookstore located at the University of Washington, in Seattle. The book store provides more than $1 million in UW customer rebates and discounts annually and donated more than $800,000 in UW student scholarships.

2363 ■ "An Updated Ranking of Academic Journals in Economics" in *Canadian Journal of Economics* (Vol. 44, November 2011, No. 4, pp. 1525)
Pub: Blackwell Publishers Ltd.
Ed: Pantelis Kalaitzidakis, Theofanis P. Mamuneas, Thanasis Stengos. **Description:** An updated list showing the ranking of economic journals (2003) is presented; however this present study differs methodologically from an earlier study by using a rolling window of years between 2003 and 2008, for each year counting the number of citations of articles published in the previous ten years.

2364 ■ "What Slump? Davis Likely to Fill Borders Gap Quickly" in *Sacramento Business Journal* (Vol. 28, July 29, 2011, No. 22, pp. 1)
Pub: Sacramento Business Journal
Ed: Kelly Johnson. **Description:** The nationwide shutdown of Borders bookstores worry most cities, but not Davis, California, which is experiencing a relatively low retail vacancy rate of 6.3 percent.

STATISTICAL SOURCES

2365 ■ *Book Industry Trends*
Pub: Book Industry Study Group, Inc.
Ed: Compiled by Statistical Service Center staff. **Released:** 2009. **Price:** $875.00 (paper).

2366 ■ *RMA Annual Statement Studies*
Pub: Robert Morris Associates (RMA)
Released: Annual. **Price:** $175.00 2006-07 edition, $105.00. **Description:** Contains composite balance sheets and income statements for more than 360 industries, including the accounting, auditing, and bookkeeping industries. Also contains five years of comparative historical data for discerning trends. Includes 16 commonly used ratios, computed for most of the size groupings for nearly every industry.

TRADE PERIODICALS

2367 ■ *Book Dealers World*
Pub: North American Bookdealers Exchange
Contact: Russ Von Hoelscher
Released: Quarterly. **Price:** $45; $5 single issue. **Description:** The book marketing magazine for independent publishers and mail order entrepreneurs.

2368 ■ *Bookselling This Week*
Pub: American Booksellers Association
Contact: Robert Keymer, Assoc. Publisher
E-mail: rkeymer@bookweb.org
Ed: Dan Cullen, Editor, dcullen@bookweb.org. **Released:** Weekly. **Price:** $49.99, individuals; $5, single issue. **Description:** Contains information on book selling.

2369 ■ *CBA Marketplace*
Pub: CBA Service Corporation Inc.
Released: Monthly, 12/year. **Price:** $59.95 nonmembers. **Description:** A how-to magazine on the Christian retail industry.

2370 ■ *College Store Executive*
Pub: Executive Business Media Inc.
Released: 8/yr. **Price:** $35; $60 two years; $87 other countries mail. **Description:** Magazine for college store managers and buyers.

2371 ■ *Forecast*
Pub: Baker & Taylor
Contact: Sally Neher, Director
Released: Monthly. **Description:** Prepublication announcement magazine for booksellers and librarians containing bibliographic data and descriptions for new and forthcoming adult hardcover books.

2372 ■ *The New York Review of Books*
Pub: The New York Review of Books
Contact: Rea S. Hederman, Publisher
Released: 20/yr. **Price:** $69; $109 other countries; $89 Canada. **Description:** Literary, cultural, and political magazine.

2373 ■ *The New York Times Book Review*
Pub: The New York Times Co.
Released: Weekly. **Price:** $65 U.S. 52 weeks; $98.80 Canada 52 weeks; $119.60 other countries 52 weeks. **Description:** Magazine containing book reviews.

2374 ■ *Publishers Weekly*
Pub: Publishers Weekly
Contact: Sonia Jaffe Robbins, Managing Editor
Released: Weekly. **Price:** $249.99; $299.99 Canada; $399.99 other countries air delivery. **Description:** Magazine for publishers.

2375 ■ *Sell More Books! Newsletter*
Pub: Florida Publishers Association
Ed: Betsy Wright-Lampe, Editor. **Released:** Bimonthly. **Price:** Included in membership. **Description:** Reports on news, events, and updates of the Florida Publishers Association. Also focuses on publishing companies, book successes, and useful tips.

TRADE SHOWS AND CONVENTIONS

2376 ■ BookExpo America
Reed Exhibitions Contemporary Forums
11900 Silvergate Dr.
Dublin, CA 94568
Ph:(925)828-7100
Fax:800-329-9923
Co. E-mail: info@cforums.com
URL: http://www.contemporaryforums.com
Released: Annual. **Audience:** Book retailers and wholesalers, librarians, literacy agents, and scouts. **Principal Exhibits:** Books and related products. **Dates and Locations:** 2011 May 26-26, New York, NY.

2377 ■ Christian Booksellers Association International Convention
Christian Booksellers Association
9240 Explorer Dr., Ste. 101
Colorado Springs, CO 80920-5001
Ph:(719)265-9895
Free: 800-252-1950
Fax:(719)272-3510
Co. E-mail: info@cbaonline.org
URL: http://www.cbaonline.org
Released: Annual. **Audience:** Christian bookstore trade. **Principal Exhibits:** Christian bookstore merchandise, including literature, music, gifts, cards, jewelry, and curricula.

COMPUTERIZED DATABASES

2378 ■ *Books in Print ON DISC - Canadian Edition*
R.R. Bowker LLC
630 Central Ave.
New Providence, NJ 07974
Ph:(908)268-1090
Free: 888-269-5372
Fax:(908)665-3528
Co. E-mail: customerservice@bowker.com
URL: http://www.bowker.com
Description: Contains bibliographic descriptions of more than 2.8 million books produced and distributed throughout the United States and Canada. Also features Canadian prices and sources for 670,000 bindings including 100,000 records for titles available only from Canada. Enables users to locate and order books from throughout North America, and identify and contact some 200 major Canadian distributors as well as thousands of U.S. dealers. **Availability:** CD-ROM: R.R. Bowker LLC. **Type:** Bibliographic.

2379 ■ *BooksInPrint.com Professional*
R.R. Bowker LLC
630 Central Ave.
New Providence, NJ 07974
Ph:(908)268-1090
Free: 888-269-5372
Fax:(908)665-3528
Co. E-mail: customerservice@bowker.com
URL: http://www.bowker.com
Description: Contains bibliographic descriptions and ordering information for more than 5 million books currently in print or declared out of print (from July 1979 to date), active and inactive audios and videos, and soon-to-be-published titles from some 200,000 publishers. Also contains more than 700,000 full-text reviews, more than 200,000 book jacket images,

author biographies, and 140,000 tables of contents. Coverage includes scholarly, popular, adult, juvenile, reprint, and other books on all subjects published by U.S. publishers or exclusively distributed in the United States and available to the trade or general public for single- or multiple-copy purchases. Such items as government publications, Bibles, free books, and subscription-only titles are excluded. Also provides the complete text of reviews from *Library Journal, Publisher's Weekly,* and *School Library Journal.* Corresponds to *Books in Print, Books Out of Print, Forthcoming Books, Books in Print Supplement, Scientific and Technical Books in Print, Medical and Health Care Books in Print, Children's Books in Print, Paperbound Books in Print,* and *Law Books in Print.* Subject classification scheme utilizes more than 72,000 Library of Congress subject headings as well as Sears headings. **Availability:** Online: R.R. Bowker LLC, Colorado Alliance of Research Libraries, ProQuest LLC; CD-ROM: R.R. Bowker LLC. **Type:** Bibliographic.

2380 ■ *ChildrensBooksInPrint.com*
R.R. Bowker LLC
630 Central Ave.
New Providence, NJ 07974
Ph:(908)268-1090
Free: 888-269-5372
Fax:(908)665-3528
Co. E-mail: customerservice@bowker.com
URL: http://www.bowker.com
Description: Contains comprehensive publication information on reading and educational textbook print and multimedia materials. Includes information on books, textbooks, audio books, DVDs, videos, and e-books. Contains more than 550,000 titles as well as specific series, characters and awards. Offers 167,000 full-text reviews and more than 13,000 annotations. Access to a library's catalog system is also available. **Availability:** Online: R.R. Bowker LLC. **Type:** Bibliographic.

2381 ■ *LC MARC: Books All*
U.S. Library of Congress
101 Independence Ave. SE
Washington, DC 20541-4912
Ph:(202)707-6100
Fax:(202)707-1334
Co. E-mail: cdsinfo@loc.gov
URL: http://www.loc.gov/cds
Description: Contains bibliographic and cataloging information on more than 9.1 million monographs published worldwide since 1968. Covers books in English since 1968; in French, since 1973; in German, Portuguese, and Spanish, since 1975; in other Roman alphabet languages, since 1976-77; in South Asian and Cyrillic alphabet languages (in Romanized form), since 1979; in Greek (in Romanized form), since 1980. Also covers Chinese, Japanese, and Korean (in Romanized form) from 1983 to 1989; Hebrew and Yiddish (in Romanized form) from 1983 to 1989; and Arabic and Persian (in Romanized form) from 1983 to 1990. Provides basic bibliographic data from LC Machine Readable Cataloging (MARC) records. Provides information derived from books, pamphlets, manuscripts, maps and atlases, monographic microform publications (both microform reissues and items originally issued in microform), and all monographic national and international government publications. Data provided in each record vary by online service, but may include LC card number, title, author, series, publisher, publication date, place of publication, International Standard Book Number, call number, language, document type, notes, and subject classification. Also includes some Cataloging in Publication data. Includes older PREMARC records called OCLC Replacement Records. Corresponds in part to the *National Union Catalog.* **Availability:** Online: ProQuest LLC, ProQuest LLC, British Library, University of Tsukuba, U.S. Library of Congress. **Type:** Bibliographic.

2382 ■ *The Title Source III*
Baker & Taylor Inc.
2550 W Tyvola Rd., Ste. 300
Charlotte, NC 28217
Ph:(704)998-3100
Free: 800-775-1800
Co. E-mail: btinfo@btol.com
URL: http://www.btol.com
Description: Contains bibliographic information for more than 3 million titles in 75,000 subject areas available from Baker & Taylor Books. Covers books, spoken-word, music audio, VHS and DVD video titles, and multimedia titles in print, out of print, or being published in the United States. Information on each item includes title, author, publisher, International Standard Book Number (ISBN), Library of Congress (LC) card number, title status (e.g., not yet published), binding (e.g., paper, hardcover), edition, grade level, volume, and list price. Provides the name, address, and phone number for 65,000 U.S. and U.K. publishers. Each monthly update provides up to 133,000 changes. Enables the user to search by paperback or hardcover, grade level, publication status, price, and publication date. Generates and prints bibliographic reports. Allows users to export data to other formats for spreadsheets, databases, and word processors. Also includes B&T Link software that enables the user to create and place custom order requests with Baker & Taylor Books. Also includes availability information for other book wholesalers. **Availability:** Online: Baker & Taylor Inc. **Type:** Bibliographic; Numeric.

LIBRARIES

2383 ■ American Booksellers Association ABA Information Service Center
200 White Plains Rd. Ste. 600
Tarrytown, NY 10591
Free: 800-637-0037
Fax:(914)591-2720
Co. E-mail: info@bookweb.org
URL: http://www.bookweb.org
Contact: Oren Teicher, CEO
Scope: Book selling and publishing. **Holdings:** 5000 volumes; 1000 bound periodical volumes; 100 newsletters; 11 VF drawers; 2000 publishers catalogs.

2384 ■ Grolier Club of New York Library
47 E. 60th St.
New York, NY 10022
Ph:(212)838-6690
Fax:(212)838-2445
Co. E-mail: ejh@grolierclub.org
URL: http://www.grolierclub.org
Contact: Eric Holzenberg, Dir.
Scope: Bibliography, history of printing, book-collecting, bookselling, arts of the book. **Services:** Library open to the public with restrictions. **Holdings:** 100,000 volumes; 5000 prints and portraits; bookplates. **Subscriptions:** 100 journals and other serials.

2385 ■ Hope Foundation Inc.–Margaret L. Tyler Library
132 Hope House Rd.
Windsor, NC 27983
Ph:(252)794-3140
Fax:(252)794-5583
Co. E-mail: hopeplantation@coastalnet.com
URL: http://www.hopeplantation.org
Contact: Gregory Tyler, Cur.
Scope: Rare books 18th and 19th centuries; North Carolina; decorative arts; genealogy; plantation - management, law. **Services:** Copying; Library open to the public by appointment. **Holdings:** 1400 books; 100 reports; 40 cubic ft. archival materials. **Subscriptions:** 4 journals and other serials; 1 newspaper.

2386 ■ Villanova University–Falvey Memorial Library I Special Collections
Villanova, PA 19085
Ph:(610)519-4290
Fax:(610)519-5018
Co. E-mail: bente.polites@villanova.edu
URL: http://www.library.villanova.edu
Contact: Bente Polites, Spec.Coll.Libn.
Scope: Augustiniana, early printed books and general rare books, Irish history, James Joyce. **Services:** Interlibrary loan; copying; Library open to the public. **Holdings:** 15,000 items.

Bottled Water Service

ASSOCIATIONS AND OTHER ORGANIZATIONS

2387 ■ International Bottled Water Association
1700 Diagonal Rd., Ste. 650
Alexandria, VA 22314
Ph:(703)683-5213
Free: 800-WATER-11
Fax:(703)683-4074
Co. E-mail: ibwainfo@bottledwater.org
URL: http://www.bottledwater.org
Contact: Joseph K. Doss, Pres.
Description: Bottled water plants; distributors; manufacturers of bottled water supplies; international bottlers, distributors and suppliers. Conducts seminars and technical research. **Publications:** *IBWA Audit Handbook*; *IBWA Membership Roster* (annual).

REFERENCE WORKS

2388 ■ "CEO Tapped for Perrier, Poland Springs" in *Black Enterprise* (Vol. 38, February 2008, No. 7, pp. 30)
Pub: Earl G. Graves Publishing Co. Inc.
Ed: Brenda Porter. **Description:** John J. Harris, newly appointed CEO, is hoping to increase market share of Nestle's bottled water products.

2389 ■ "Eco-Preneuring" in *Small Business Opportunities* (Jan. 2008)
Pub: Harris Publications Inc.
Description: Iceland Naturally is a joint marketing effort among tourism and business interests hoping to increase demand for Icelandic products including frozen seafood, bottled water, agriculture, and tourism in North America.

2390 ■ "A Precious Resource: Investing In the Fate of Fresh Water" in *Black Enterprise* (Vol. 38, February 2008, No. 7, pp. 44)
Pub: Earl G. Graves Publishing Co. Inc.
Ed: Charles Keenan. **Description:** Despite rising oil prices, water may become the most precious commodity in years to come because the world's supply of drinkable water is dwindling.

2391 ■ "Pulque with Flavor" in *Canadian Business* (Vol. , pp.)
Pub: Rogers Media Ltd.
Ed: Augusta Dwyer. **Description:** Mexico-based Pulque Poliqhui, which has exported 20,000 bottles of Pulque into Canada in March 2008, plans to distribute in Ontario and Quebec. Pulque Poliqhui is introducing Cool Passion, a fruit-flavored version of pulque in Canada.

2392 ■ "Thirsty? Now There's a Water Cooler to Suit Every Taste" in *Inc.* (Vol. 33, October 2011, No. 8, pp. 43)
Pub: Inc. Magazine
Ed: John Brandon. **Description:** Brita's Hydration Station is a wall-mounted unit with a touch-free sensor for dispensing water. This water cooler cuts down on landfill waste and offers special features.

STATISTICAL SOURCES

2393 ■ *The Bottled Water Market*
Pub: Business Trend Analysts, Inc.
Released: 2005-2006 Edition. **Price:** $2195.00. **Description:** An in-depth examination of the size and projected growth (to 2014) of the bottled water market, covering both domestic and imported products.

TRADE PERIODICALS

2394 ■ *Bottled Water Reporter*
Pub: International Bottled Water Association
Released: Bimonthly. **Price:** $50 nonmembers U.S. & Canada; $100 other countries. **Description:** Magazine for bottled water industry.

2395 ■ *Hot Springs, Mineral Waters*
Pub: Bibliotheca Press
Contact: A. Doyle
Ed: A. Doyle, Editor. **Released:** Irregular. **Price:** $7.95, U.S.. **Description:** Lists hot springs and mineral water locations for tourists.

TRADE SHOWS AND CONVENTIONS

2396 ■ International Bottled Water Association Convention and Trade Show
International Bottled Water Association
1700 Diagonal Rd., Ste. 650
Alexandria, VA 22314
Ph:(703)683-5213
Free: 800-WATER-11
Fax:(703)683-4074
URL: http://www.bottledwater.org
Released: Annual. **Audience:** Bottled water company executives and suppliers to the industry. **Principal Exhibits:** Bottled water industry supplies and equipment. **Dates and Locations:** 2011 Sep 26-30, Las Vegas, NV.

CONSULTANTS

2397 ■ Fitzpatrick & Associates Inc.
10133 Cross Green Way
PO Box 19886
Jacksonville, FL 32245
Ph:(904)642-1445
Contact: M. A. Fitzpatrick, Principle
Scope: Firm offers management consulting services to the beverage industry; services include sales and operations management, company purchasing control, production facilities management and loss control programs.

FRANCHISES AND BUSINESS OPPORTUNITIES

2398 ■ Purified Water Store
11566 24 St. SE, Unit 214
Calgary, AB, Canada T2Z 3J3
Ph:(403)261-7873
Free: 800-976-9283
Fax:(403)720-6020
Co. E-mail: info@purifiedwaterstore.com
URL: http://www.purifiedwaterstore.com
No. of Franchise Units: 23. **No. of Company-Owned Units:** 1. **Founded:** 1999. **Franchised:** 2000. **Description:** Offers reverse osmosis bottled water production facilities. Retail show rooms marketing coolers, crocks and purified water accessories are provided. In-home filtration systems and water conditioning equipment is also offered. **Equity Capital Needed:** $154,000. **Franchise Fee:** $20,000. **Training:** 1 week corporate training program, 1 week onsite, and follow up on store opening.

2399 ■ Water Depot
431 Huronia Rd. Unit 8
Barrie, ON, Canada L4N 9B3
Ph:(705)735-6642
Fax:(705)792-5157
Co. E-mail: pstrain@waterdepotinc.com
URL: http://www.waterdepotinc.com
No. of Franchise Units: 20. **No. of Company-Owned Units:** 1. **Founded:** 1989. **Franchised:** 2001. **Description:** Supplies bottled water and water treatment products to consumers. **Franchise Fee:** $25,000. **Training:** Ongoing Water Depot College and University courses, seminars, question and answer Sessions and events.

2400 ■ World of Water International Ltd.
326 Keewatin St.
Winnipeg, MB, Canada R2X 2R9
Ph:(204)774-7770
Free: (866)749-1146
Fax:(204)772-5051
Co. E-mail: info@worldofwater.ca
URL: http://www.worldofwater.ca
No. of Franchise Units: 18. **Founded:** 1976. **Franchised:** 1976. **Description:** Producer and marketer of Dewdrop steam distilled water and franchisor of retail bottled water stores. The retail stores cater to retail as well as home and office delivery customers through our franchise stores. **Equity Capital Needed:** $145,000. **Franchise Fee:** $25,000. **Training:** Yes.

COMPUTERIZED DATABASES

2401 ■ *WATERNET Bibliographic Database*
American Water Works Association
6666 W Quincy Ave.
Denver, CO 80235
Ph:(303)794-7711
Free: 800-926-7337
Fax:(303)347-0804
URL: http://www.awwa.org
Description: Contains more than 50,000 citations, with abstracts, to literature on water quality, water utility management, analytical procedures for water quality testing, energy-related economics, water system materials, water and wastewater treatment and reuse, industrial and potable uses of water, and environmental issues related to water. Typical data elements include author name, article title, journal title, publication date, volume and issue numbers,

page numbers, availability, ISSN, language, document type, and abstract. Items are selected from books, conference proceedings, journals, newsletters, standards, handbooks, water quality standard test methods, and all AWWA and AWWA Research Foundation (AWWARF) publications, e.g., *Annual Conference Proceedings*, *Water Quality Technology Conference Proceedings*, *Distribution System Symposium Proceedings*, and *Conference Seminars.* Also covers selected non-AWWA items. Corresponds to the online WATERNET database. **Availability:** CD-ROM: American Water Works Association. **Type:** Bibliographic.

LIBRARIES

2402 ■ Coca-Cola Company–The INFOSOURCE
PO Box 1734
Atlanta, GA 30301
Ph:(404)515-4636
Fax:(404)253-4575
Co. E-mail: koinfo@na.ko.com
URL: http://www.coca-cola.com
Contact: Heather Turnbull, Sr.Res.Anl.

Scope: Business, Legal, Marketing, Technical - including beverages, soft drinks, fruit juices, food technology, nutrition, chemistry, engineering.

Bowling Alley

ASSOCIATIONS AND OTHER ORGANIZATIONS

2403 ■ Billiard and Bowling Institute of America
PO Box 6573
Arlington, TX 76005
Ph:(817)385-8120
Free: 800-343-1329
Fax:(817)633-2940
Co. E-mail: answer@billiardandbowling.org
URL: http://www.billiardandbowling.org
Contact: Phil Cardinale, Pres.
Description: Represents distributors and manufacturers of billiard and bowling equipment. .

2404 ■ Bowling Proprietors' Association of America
621 Six Flags Dr.
Arlington, TX 76011
Free: 800-343-1329
Fax:(817)633-2940
Co. E-mail: steve@bpaa.com
URL: http://www.bpaa.com
Contact: Steve Johnson, Exec. Dir.
Description: Represents proprietors of bowling establishments. **Publications:** *Bowling Center Management* (monthly); *Talking Human Resources* .

2405 ■ Bowling Proprietors' Association of Canada
250 Shields Ct., Unit 10-A
Markham, ON, Canada L3R 9W7
Ph:(905)479-1560
Fax:(905)479-8613
Co. E-mail: info@bowlcanada.ca
URL: http://www.bowlcanada.ca
Contact: Paul Oliveira, Exec. Dir.
Description: Owners of bowling alleys. Promotes increased participation in recreational and competitive bowling. Represents members' interests before business and labor organizations, government agencies, and the public. Conducts promotional activities.

2406 ■ The National Bowling Association
9944 Reading Rd.
Cincinnati, OH 45241-3106
Ph:(513)769-1985
Fax:(513)769-3596
Co. E-mail: nationaloffice@tnbainc.org
URL: http://www.tnbainc.org
Contact: Dr. Michael L. Boykins, Pres.
Description: Seeks to: foster good sportsmanship, fellowship, and friendship; increase the interests, talents, and skills of adult and youth bowlers; create national awareness and interest in civic and community programs. Participates in and promotes bowling tournaments and other activities. Sponsors fundraising programs for sickle cell anemia and the United Negro College Fund. Bestows bowling awards, annual special bowling and service awards, and annual national and local scholarship awards. Maintains hall of fame; compiles statistics. **Publications:** *Bowler* (quarterly); *NBA History Book*; *Souvenir Yearbook* (annual).

2407 ■ Professional Bowlers Association of America
719 2nd Ave., Ste. 701
Seattle, WA 98104-1747
Ph:(206)332-9688
Fax:(206)332-9722
Co. E-mail: membership@pba.com
URL: http://www.pba.com
Contact: Chris Peters, Chm.
Description: Professional bowlers. Works to promote the status of the qualified bowler to the rank of professional; also promotes bowling as a major sport. Sponsors tournaments; assists the American Bowling Congress in enforcing its rules and regulations; has established code of ethics. Promotes better understanding between professional bowlers and bowling proprietors, bowling manufacturers, and the communications media. Maintains placement service, hall of fame, school, and insurance programs for members. Compiles statistics. **Publications:** *Official Tour Program* (semiannual); *Press-Radio-TV Guide* (annual).

2408 ■ United States Bowling Congress
621 Six Flags Dr.
Arlington, TX 76011
Free: 800-514-2695
Co. E-mail: bowlinfo@bowl.com
URL: http://www.bowl.com
Contact: Susan Merrill, CFO
Description: Aims to be the unified organization of choice focused on the growth of bowling. Ensures the integrity and protects the future of the sport, provides programs and services and enhances the bowling experience. .

EDUCATIONAL PROGRAMS

2409 ■ Vincennes University
1002 N 1st St.
Vincennes, IN 47591
Ph:(812)888-8888
Free: 800-742-9198
Fax:(812)888-5868
URL: http://www.vinu.edu
Description: Two-year college offering a program in business administration; small business management classes; and bowling lane management and technology.

STATISTICAL SOURCES

2410 ■ *RMA Annual Statement Studies*
Pub: Robert Morris Associates (RMA)
Released: Annual. **Price:** $175.00 2006-07 edition, $105.00. **Description:** Contains composite balance sheets and income statements for more than 360 industries, including the accounting, auditing, and bookkeeping industries. Also contains five years of comparative historical data for discerning trends. Includes 16 commonly used ratios, computed for most of the size groupings for nearly every industry.

TRADE PERIODICALS

2411 ■ *BBIA enews*
Pub: Billiards and Bowling Institute of America
Ed: Sebastian Dicasoli, Editor. **Released:** Monthly, 3/year. **Price:** Free. **Description:** Serves as an update on the Institute's programs for manufacturers, distributors, and retailers of billiard and bowling supplies and equipment. Monitors executive changes, special promotions, new products, and trade show activities. Recurring features include member news.

2412 ■ *Bowlers Journal*
Pub: Luby Publishing
Contact: Barbara Peltz
Released: Monthly. **Price:** $32; $44 two years; $54 three years; $57 other countries. **Description:** Sports magazine - bowling's premier magazine.

2413 ■ *Bowling-Golfing News*
Pub: Master Associates
Ed: E.C. Townsend, Editor, edwardctownsend@hotmail.com. **Released:** Weekly. **Description:** Provides news and information on bowling and golf.

TRADE SHOWS AND CONVENTIONS

2414 ■ FUN Expo
Reed Exhibitions North American Headquarters
383 Main Ave.
Norwalk, CT 06851
Ph:(203)840-4800
Fax:(203)840-5805
Co. E-mail: export@reedexpo.com
URL: http://www.reedexpo.com
Released: Annual. **Principal Exhibits:** Amusement and recreation products for family and location based entertainment centers, small amusement parks and family oriented businesses such as bowling centers, skating rinks, sports parks, miniature golf courses, golf driving ranges, family restaurants, resorts and other entertainment/recreation businesses. **Dates and Locations:** 2011 Mar 01-03, Las Vegas, NV.

2415 ■ International Bowl Expo
Bowling Proprietors Association of America
621 Six Flags Dr.
Arlington, TX 76011
Ph:800-343-1329
Fax:(817)633-2940
URL: http://www.bpaa.com
Released: Annual. **Audience:** Bowling center owners/operators billiard center owners, Bowling Pro Shop Owners. **Principal Exhibits:** Equipment, supplies, and services for the bowling industry, , Awards and Promotional Products, Financial and Insurance Services, Redemption Products. **Dates and Locations:** 2011 Jun 26 - Jul 01, Grapevine, TX.

START-UP INFORMATION

2416 ■ *Brewing Up a Business: Adventures in Entrepreneurship from the Founder of Dogfish Head Craft*
Pub: John Wiley & Sons, Incorporated
Ed: Sam Calagione. **Released:** October 2006. **Price:** $16.95. **Description:** Author shares nontraditional success secrets. Calgione began his business with a home brewing kit and grew it into Dogfish Head Craft Beer, the leading craft brewery in the U.S.

ASSOCIATIONS AND OTHER ORGANIZATIONS

2417 ■ American Beverage Institute
1090 Vermont Ave. NW, Ste. 800
Washington, DC 20005
Ph:(202)463-7110
URL: http://www.abionline.org
Contact: Sarah Longwell, Managing Dir.
Description: Provides public information regarding the consumption of adult beverages. Offers research and educational programs. .

2418 ■ American Breweriana Association
PO Box 595767
Fort Gratiot, MI 48059-5767
Ph:(810)385-7101
Fax:(810)385-7121
Co. E-mail: jseelow@americanbreweriana.org
URL: http://www.americanbreweriana.org
Contact: John F. Seelow, Exec. Dir.
Description: Promotes the interest of collectors of brewery advertising and antiques, brewery historians, breweries, beer distributors and retailers, industrial workers, and beer workers. Promotes increased public knowledge of brewing history. Serves collectors and historians. Preserves the memories and artifacts of historic breweries in the U.S. Aims to restore the former brewery at Potosi, WI, into a National Brewery Museum. Provides an exchange service allowing collectors of beer labels, coasters, crown caps, openers, and printed material to exchange duplicates with other members. Assists members with research regarding brewery history and the industry. **Publications:** *American Breweriana Journal* (bimonthly); *Directory of the American Breweriana Association* (annual).

2419 ■ Beer Institute
122 C St. NW, Ste. 350
Washington, DC 20001
Ph:(202)737-2337
Free: 800-379-BREW
Fax:(202)737-7004
Co. E-mail: info@beerinstitute.org
URL: http://www.beerinstitute.org
Contact: Joe McClain, Pres.
Description: Brewers, importers, and suppliers to the industry. Committed to the development of public policy and to the values of civic duty and personal responsibility. **Publications:** *Beer Institute Bulletin* (quarterly); *Membership* .

2420 ■ Brewers Association of Canada–Association des Brasseurs du Canada
100 Queen St., Ste. 650
Ottawa, ON, Canada K1P 1J9
Ph:(613)232-9601
Fax:(613)232-2283
Co. E-mail: info@brewers.ca
URL: http://www.brewers.ca
Contact: Bruce McCubbin, Chm.
Description: Independent breweries operating in Canada. Promotes operation of microbreweries; seeks growth and development of the brewing industry. Represents members' interests; conducts educational programs; makes available promotional services to members. **Publications:** *On Tap* (bimonthly); *Statistical Bulletin* (annual).

2421 ■ Brewing and Malting Barley Research Institute
1510 One Lombard Pl.
Winnipeg, MB, Canada R3B 0X3
Ph:(204)927-1407
Fax:(204)947-5960
Co. E-mail: info@bmbri.ca
URL: http://www.bmbri.ca
Contact: Dr. Michael Brophy, Pres./CEO
Description: Supports the development and evaluation of new malting barley varieties in Canada on behalf of member companies.

2422 ■ Fermenters International Trade Association
PO Box 1373
Valrico, FL 33595
Ph:(813)685-4261
Fax:(813)681-5625
Co. E-mail: droberson1@verizon.net
URL: http://www.fermentersinternational.org
Contact: John Pastor, Pres.
Description: Manufacturers, wholesalers, retailers, authors, and editors having a commercial interest in the home beer-making and winemaking trade. Promotes the development and growth of home brewing, home winemaking, and associated trades. Sponsors wine competition. .

2423 ■ Master Brewers Association of the Americas
3340 Pilot Knob Rd.
St. Paul, MN 55121-2097
Ph:(651)454-7250
Fax:(651)454-0766
Co. E-mail: mbaa@mbaa.com
URL: http://www.mbaa.com
Contact: Steve Nelson, Exec. VP
Description: Provides opportunity for brewing professionals to interact with other fermentation industry professionals and to learn practical solutions, resourceful safeguards, and innovative technologies. **Publications:** *MBAA Technical Quarterly* (quarterly).

REFERENCE WORKS

2424 ■ "Beer Drinkers Wanted More. The Brewer Had No Room to Expand. How Could It Keep the Taps Flowing?" in *Inc.* (October 2007, pp. 65-66)
Pub: Gruner & Jahr USA Publishing
Ed: Alex Salkever. **Description:** Profile of John McDonald, founder of Boulevard, the second-largest beer company located in Kansas City, Missouri. McDonald tells how he was able to expand his turn-of-the-century brick building he had imported from Bavaria by developing a 70,000-square-foot building on four acres adjacent to his existing location rather move to a suburb.

2425 ■ "Beer Sales 'Foament' a Dispute" in *Philadelphia Business Journal* (Vol. 28, October 9, 2009, No. 34, pp. 1)
Pub: American City Business Journals
Ed: Peter van Allen. **Description:** Malt Beverages Distributors Association of Pennsylvania filed a case against the Liquor Control Board (LCB) at the Pennsylvania Supreme Court in order to further restrict store sales. The dispute stems from the supermarket chains circumventing the liquor law with the blessings of LCB.

2426 ■ "Big Gains Brewing at Anheuser-Busch InBev" in *Barron's* (Vol. 90, August 30, 2010, No. 35, pp. 34)
Pub: Barron's Editorial & Corporate Headquarters
Ed: Christopher C. Williams. **Description:** Anheuser-Busch InBev is realizing cost synergies and it posted better than expected returns two years after the merger that formed the company. One analyst believes its American depositary receipt could be worth as much as 72 in a year.

2427 ■ "Black Lotus Brewing Co." in *Crain's Detroit Business* (Vol. 23, October 1, 2007, No. 40, pp. 13)
Pub: Crain Communications Inc. - Detroit
Ed: Leah Boyd. **Description:** Profile of Black Lotus Brewing Company and owner, Mike Allan who converted a drug store location into a brewery while restoring the building's original architecture.

2428 ■ "Coors Execs Listen to Milwaukee Pitch" in *Business Journal-Milwaukee* (Vol. 25, November 2, 2007, No. 5, pp. A1)
Pub: American City Business Journals, Inc.
Ed: Rich Rovito. **Description:** Coors Brewing Company officials met with Wisconsin Governor Jim Doyle and Milwaukee Mayor Tom Barnett about putting the MillerCoors corporate headquarters in Milwaukee. The city is competing with Denver, Colorado for the headquarters of the joint venture.

2429 ■ "A Crystal Ball" in *Business Journal Portland* (Vol. 27, December 31, 2010, No. 44, pp. 1)
Pub: Portland Business Journal
Ed: Wendy Culverwell. **Description:** McMenamins Pubs and Breweries has resumed construction of its Crystal Hotel project. The company has been working to convert a former bath house into a 51-room hotel. The hotel is expected to open in 2011.

2430 ■ "Denver Will Put Up Fight for MillerCoors HQ" in *Business Journal-Milwaukee* (Vol. 25, October 19, 2007, No. 3, pp. A1)
Pub: American City Business Journals, Inc.
Ed: Rich Rovito. **Description:** A contention exists between Milwaukee and Denver over which city will become the new location of the Miller Brewing Company (Milwaukee) and Coors Brewing Company (Colorado) joint venture MillerCoors. Leaders of the breweries since the announcement of the merger, have contended frantically to prepare strategies to back up their own cities. The advantages and disadvantages of both cities are presented.

2431 ■ "Harding Brews Success at Anheuser-Busch" in *Black Enterprise* (Vol. 37, February 2007, No. 7, pp. 1)
Pub: Earl G. Graves Publishing Co. Inc.
Ed: Mashaun D. Simon. **Description:** Profile of Michael S. Harding, president and CEO of Anheuser-Busch packaging Group. Harding oversees five business units, 15 facilities, and over 2,300 workers.

2432 ■ "I Fought the Law: a Brewery Comes Out on Top" in *Inc.* (Vol. 33, November 2011, No. 9, pp. 28)
Pub: Inc. Magazine
Ed: Darren Dahl. **Description:** Profile of Omar Ansari, founder of Surly Brewing is presented. Ansari credits fans on Facebook and Twitter for contacting legislators with phone calls and emails to allow him to sell his beer to customers on site.

2433 ■ *The King of Vodka: The Story of Pyotr Smirnov and the Upheaval of an Empire*
Pub: HarperCollins Publishers
Ed: Linda Himelstein. **Released:** 2009. **Price:** $29. 99. **Description:** Biography of Pyotr Smirnov and how his determination took him from serf to the head of Smirnov Vodka. Smirnov's marketing techniques are defined and show how he expanded the drink worldwide.

2434 ■ "Lawyers Cash In On Alcohol" in *Business Journal Portland* (Vol. 27, November 19, 2010, No. 38, pp. 1)
Pub: Portland Business Journal
Ed: Andy Giegerich. **Description:** Oregon-based law firms have continued to corner big business on the state's growing alcohol industry as demand for their services increased. Lawyers, who represent wine, beer and liquor distillery interests, have seen their workload increased by 20 to 30 percent in 2009.

2435 ■ *North American Brewers Resource Directory*
Pub: Brewers Publications
Contact: Charlie Papazian, President
E-mail: charlie@aob.org
Released: Biennial, latest edition 2009-2010. **Price:** Included in membership; $49, members additional copy; $99, nonmembers. **Covers:** Manufacturers, suppliers, publications, associations, institutions, and breweries concerned with the beer microbrewing industry. **Entries Include:** Organization, company, or institution name, address, phone, contact name, products or services, laws, publications. **Arrangement:** Classified by line of business. **Indexes:** Trade name, product/service (suppliers only), geographical.

2436 ■ "SABMiller Deal Hit by Tax Ruling" in *Wall Street Journal Eastern Edition* (November 21 , 2011, pp. B9)
Pub: Dow Jones & Company Inc.
Ed: David Fickling, Simon Zekaria. **Description:** SABMiller PLC, the giant brewer in the United Kingdom, is acquiring Australian beer icon Foster's Group Ltd. for US$9.9 billion, but will have to come up with another A$582 million following a tax ruling by the Australian Taxation Office in order that shareholders of Foster's don't lose.

2437 ■ "South Park Draws Brewers, Vintners" in *Puget Sound Business Journal* (Vol. 29, August 29, 2008, No. 19, pp. 1)
Pub: American City Business Journals
Ed: Heidi Dietrich. **Description:** Craft breweries and wineries are moving into Seattle, Washington's South Park neighborhood due to the area's low rents, convenience, and ample equipment space. These industries bring a more upscale flavor to the heavily industrial area and the tastings and festivals draw people from throughout the Seattle region.

2438 ■ *Star Spangled Beer*
Pub: Jack Erickson
Price: $13.95, individuals. **Covers:** 100 microbreweries and brewpubs; coverage includes Canada. **Entries Include:** Company name, address, phone, products. **Arrangement:** Geographical. **Indexes:** Company name.

2439 ■ "They're Hopping Mad" in *Canadian Business* (Vol. 80, October 22, 2007, No. 21, pp. 20)
Pub: Rogers Media
Description: Alberta Review Panel is calling for a 20 percent increase in oil and gas development taxes. SABMiller and Molson Coors Brewing Company combined its U.S. and Puerto Rican operations, though the deal is still subject to regulatory approvals. Montreal Exchange Inc. filed for approval of the trade of Montreal Climate Exchange futures contracts.

2440 ■ "The Traveling Godfather: Beam Global Spirits & Wine Inc." in *Canadian Business* (Vol. 81, October 13, 2008, No. 17, pp. S10)
Pub: Rogers Media Ltd.
Ed: Andy Holoway. **Description:** Dan Tullio, director of Canadian Club, is seen as a godfather because he gets to be asked a lot of favors. Tullio gets to immerse himself into other cultures because of his employment as global ambassador of Beam Global Spirits & Wine Inc. Tullio's views, as well as information about him are presented.

2441 ■ "Troy Brewer Opens Own Bottling Operation" in *Business Review, Albany New York* (Vol. 34, November 16, 2007, No. 33, pp. 3)
Pub: American City Business Journals, Inc.
Ed: Michael DeMasi. **Description:** Brown Brewing Company's owner Peter Martin invested in $100,000 worth of bottling equipment and has now doubled his production capacity to 3,000 barrels. Davidson Brothers, another brewery that bottles its own beer, sells 3,000 to 5,000 cases of beer annually. Industry sales of draft breweries are presented.

STATISTICAL SOURCES

2442 ■ *The Microbreweries Market*
Pub: Rector Press, Ltd.
Contact: Lewis Sckolnick, Pres
Released: 2009. **Price:** Contact Rector Press.

2443 ■ *Outlook for the American Beer Market*
Pub: Business Trend Analysts, Inc.
Released: 2004-2005. **Price:** $1895.00. **Description:** Analyzes the U.S. beer market. Covers the influence of new imports and the Canadian beer market through 1991. Profiles companies such as Anheuser-Busch, Coors, Heilemann, Philip Morris, and Stroh. Profiles include financial news, marketing strategies, and brand performance.

2444 ■ *Standard & Poor's Industry Surveys*
Pub: Standard & Poor's Corp.
Released: Annual. **Price:** $3633.00. **Description:** Two-volume book that examines the prospects for specific industries, including trucking. Also provides analyses of trends and problems, statistical tables and charts, and comparative company analyses.

TRADE PERIODICALS

2445 ■ *Ale Street News*
Pub: Tuscarora Inc.
Contact: Jack Babin, Publisher
E-mail: tony@alestreet.news.com
Released: Bimonthly. **Price:** $18.95; $37.90 two years. **Description:** Newspaper for beer enthusiasts, home brewers and the craft brewing industry.

2446 ■ *Cocktails Magazine*
Pub: Destiny Productions for Print, Radio & Cable Promotions
Released: Monthly. **Description:** Trade magazine for the alcohol service industry.

2447 ■ *Modern Brewery Age*
Pub: Business Journals Inc.
Contact: Mac R. Brighton, Chm., COO
E-mail: macb@busjour.com
Released: Bimonthly. **Price:** $125. **Description:** Magazine for the wholesale and brewing industry.

2448 ■ *Modern Brewery Age Tabloid Edition*
Pub: Business Journals Inc.
Contact: Peter Reid, Editor & Publisher
E-mail: pete@breweryage.com
Released: Weekly. **Price:** $95 via email. **Description:** Brewery industry tabloid.

VIDEOCASSETTES/ AUDIOCASSETTES

2449 ■ *How It's Made*
Lucerne Media
37 Ground Pine Rd.
Morris Plains, NJ 07950
Free: 800-341-2293
Fax:(973)538-0855
Co. E-mail: lucernemedia@optonline.net
URL: http://www.lucernemedia.com
Released: 1988. **Price:** $95.00. **Description:** The entire process of the beer industry is distilled into these three programs, plus a look at how bottle caps are made. **Availability:** VHS; 3/4U.

TRADE SHOWS AND CONVENTIONS

2450 ■ National Beer Wholesalers Association Convention and Exposition
Corcoran Expositions, Inc.
100 W. Monroe St., Ste. 1001
Chicago, IL 60603
Ph:(312)541-0567
Fax:(312)541-0573
Co. E-mail: info@corcexpo.com
URL: http://www.corcexpo.com
Released: Biennial. **Audience:** Beer distributors and wholesalers. **Principal Exhibits:** Brewery software and hardware, trucking, beer cleaning equipment, and related equipment, supplies, and services.

2451 ■ Wine and Spirits Wholesalers of America Convention and Exposition
Wine and Spirits Wholesalers of America, Inc.
805 15th St. NW, Ste. 430
Washington, DC 20005
Ph:(202)371-9792
Fax:(202)789-2405
URL: http://www.wswa.org
Released: Annual. **Audience:** Wine and spirits wholesalers; suppliers of any product of service distributed or utilized by wholesalers. **Principal Exhibits:** Producers of spirits, wine, beer, mixes, bottled water; freight routing/forwarding companies; computer hardware/software; point of sale products vendors; warehouse equipment producers; forklifts, security systems, conveyor and packing systems; scanners. **Dates and Locations:** 2011 Apr 10-11, Orlando, FL.

CONSULTANTS

2452 ■ Bio-Technical Resources L.P.
1035 S 7th St.
Manitowoc, WI 54220-5301
Ph:(920)684-5518
Fax:(920)684-5519
Co. E-mail: info@biotechresources.com
URL: http://www.biotechresources.com
Contact: Tom Jerrell, President
E-mail: jerrell@atsbiotechresources.com
Scope: Services include strain improvement, process development and metabolic engineering. Solutions are also offered for the development of biotechnology products and processes through contract services in

research and development, bio process scale-up, pilot scale manufacturing, technology and economic assessments. Target audience: pharmaceutical, biotechnology, chemical and food and feed industries. Client base may be global leaders as well as small companies and startups. **Publications:** "A Novel Fungus for the Production of Efficient Cellulases and Hemi-Cellulases," Jun, 2009; "Linoleic Acid Isomerase from Propionibacterium acnes: Purification, Characterization, Molecular Cloning, and Heterologous Expression," 2007; "Purification and Characterization of a Membrane-Bound Linoleic Acid Isomerase from Clostridium sporogenes," 2007; "Metabolic Engineering of Sesquiterpene Metabolism in Yeast," 2007; "Purification and Characterization of a Membrane-Bound Linoleic AcidIsomerase from Clostridium sporogenes," 2007; "Reduction of Background Interference in the Spectrophotometric Assay of Mevalonate Kinase," 2006; "A Soluble Form of Phosphatase in Saccharomyces cerevisiae Capable of Converting Farnesyl Diphosphate to E, E-Farnesol," 2006; "Ascorbate Biosynthesis: A Diversity of Pathways," BIOS Scientific Publishers, 2004; "The Biotechnology of Ascorbic Acid Manufacture," BIOS Scientific Publishers, 2004; "Detection of Farnesyl Diphosphate Accumulation in YeastERG9 Mutants," 2003; "Reverse Two-Hybrid System: Detecting Critical Interaction Domains and Screening for Inhibitors," Eaton Publishing, 2000. **Seminars:** Metabolic Engineering for Industrial Production of Glucosamine and N-Acetylglucosamine, Aug, 2003; Metabolic Engineering of E. coli for the Industrial Production of Glucosamine, Apr, 2003.

2453 ■ Fitzpatrick & Associates Inc.
10133 Cross Green Way
PO Box 19886
Jacksonville, FL 32245
Ph:(904)642-1445
Contact: M. A. Fitzpatrick, Principle
Scope: Firm offers management consulting services to the beverage industry; services include sales and operations management, company purchasing control, production facilities management and loss control programs.

LIBRARIES

2454 ■ Anheuser-Busch Companies Corporate Library
1 Busch Pl.
St. Louis, MO 63118
Free: 800-342-5283
URL: http://www.anheuser-busch.com
Contact: Ann Lauenstein, Corp.Libn.
Scope: Brewing chemistry, fermentation technology, food and beverage industries, alcohol and alcoholism, yeast, business and industrial management. **Services:** Interlibrary loan. **Holdings:** 50,000 books; 60,000 bound periodical volumes; 100 pamphlet boxes of Annual reports; 25 VF drawers of U.S. and foreign patents; 70 pamphlet boxes of clippings. **Subscriptions:** 1000 journals and other serials.

2455 ■ Brewers Association of Canada Library
650-100 Queen St., Ste. 650
Ottawa, ON, Canada K1P 1J9
Ph:(613)232-9601
Fax:(613)232-2283
Co. E-mail: info@brewers.ca
URL: http://www.brewers.ca
Contact: Edwin P. Gregory, Mgr.
Scope: History and statistical information of the brewing industry, taverns and inns, alcoholic beverage taxation and control policies, beer and brewing. **Services:** Interlibrary loan; Library open to the public by appointment only. **Holdings:** 500 books; 500 papers on use and abuse of alcohol. **Subscriptions:** 60 journals and other serials.

2456 ■ Coors Brewing Company Technical Library
PO Box 4030
Golden, CO 80401
Free: 800-642-6116
URL: http://www.coors.com/
Contact: Stephen Boss, Libn.
Scope: Brewing, microbiology, chemistry, law, engineering. **Services:** Copying; Library open to the public with restrictions. **Holdings:** 7000 books; 40,000 internal reports; patents; clippings; pamphlets. **Subscriptions:** 400 journals and other serials; 15 newspapers.

2457 ■ Miller Brewing Company–Scientific and Technical Information Facility
3939 W. Highland Blvd.
Milwaukee, WI 53208
Ph:(414)931-3640
Fax:(414)931-2818
Co. E-mail: langley.emily@mbco.com
URL: http://www.millerbrewing.com
Contact: Emily A. Langley, Info.Spec.
Scope: Brewing, chemistry, microbiology, chemical engineering, genetics, enzymology. **Services:** Interlibrary loan; facility open to the public with restrictions. **Holdings:** 3000 books; 1500 bound periodical volumes; 10,000 patents; 80 reels of microfilm; 4000 microfiche; 1500 research reports. **Subscriptions:** 200 journals and other serials.

2458 ■ University of California, Davis–University Libraries I Special Collections
100 NW Quad
Shields Library, 1st Fl.
Davis, CA 95616-5292
Ph:(530)752-1621
Fax:(916)754-5758
Co. E-mail: dmorrison@ucdavis.edu
URL: http://www.lib.ucdavis.edu/dept/specol/
Contact: Ms. Daryl Morrison, Dept.Hd.
Scope: Reference. **Services:** Copying; collections open to the public for reference use only. **Holdings:** 129,500 books; 17,200 lin.ft. of archives and manuscripts. **Subscriptions:** 40 journals and other serials; 2 newspapers.

Bridal Shop/Bridal Consultant

START-UP INFORMATION

2459 ■ *How to Open and Operate a Financially Successful Wedding Consultant and Planning Business: With Companion CD-ROM*
Pub: Atlantic Publishing Group, Inc.
Ed: John N. Peragine. **Released:** May 2008. **Price:** $39.95 paperback. **Description:** Consumers are spending a record $46 billion on weddings annually, with the average wedding costing around $32,000. Wedding consultants and planners provide information, ideas and contacts for brides along with guidance on etiquette, invitations, planning and directing the rehearsal and ceremony, and even arranging transportation and accommodations.

2460 ■ *Start Your Own Wedding Consultant Business*
Pub: Entrepreneur Press
Ed: Eileen Figure Sandlin. **Released:** December 2003. **Description:** Advice for starting and running a wedding consulting business.

ASSOCIATIONS AND OTHER ORGANIZATIONS

2461 ■ American Society of Wedding Professionals
26 Roden Way
Closter, NJ 07624
Ph:(201)244-5969
Free: 800-274-3350
Fax:(973)574-7626
Co. E-mail: info@localtrafficbuilder.com
URL: http://www.localtrafficbuilder.com
Contact: Brian D. Lawrence, Exec. Off.
Description: Professionals in the wedding industry. Promotes the wedding professional and educates brides on the experience of working with a consultant. Provides trends, etiquette, marketing, consulting information, directory listing, referrals, networking, and co-op advertising. Offers local forums for information exchange among members. Compiles statistics and conducts educational programs and seminars. **Publications:** *WedPro News* (monthly).

2462 ■ Association of Bridal Consultants
56 Danbury Rd., Ste. 11
New Milford, CT 06776
Ph:(860)355-7000
Fax:(860)354-1404
Co. E-mail: info@bridalassn.com
URL: http://www.bridalassn.com
Contact: David M. Wood III, Pres.
Description: Represents independent bridal and wedding consultants; persons employed by companies in wedding-related businesses and novices looking to get into the business. Strives to improve professionalism and recognition of bridal and wedding consultants. Offers professional development program, startup manual and seminars. Provides advertising, publicity, referrals and information services. Operates speakers' bureau; compiles statistics. **Publications:** *ABCDialogue* (bimonthly); *Ethnic and Specialty by Wedding Guide* (periodic); *Retail Resource Directory* (semiannual); *Weddings As A Business* .

2463 ■ Association for Wedding Professionals International
6700 Freeport Blvd., Ste. 202
Sacramento, CA 95822
Ph:(916)392-5000
Free: 800-242-4461
Fax:(916)392-5222
Co. E-mail: richard@afwpi.com
URL: http://www.afwpi.com
Contact: Richard Markel, Dir.
Description: Professionals working in the wedding industry. Promotes adherence to high standards of ethics and practice by members; seeks to advance members' professional standing. Serves as a network linking members; offers member discounts on business services, insurance, and advertising; sponsors educational programs. **Publications:** *Professional Connection* (quarterly).

2464 ■ Bridal Association of America
531 H St.
Bakersfield, CA 93304
Ph:(661)633-9200
Free: (866)699-3334
Fax:(661)633-9199
Co. E-mail: kyle@bridalassociationofamerica.com
URL: http://www.bridalassociationofamerica.com
Contact: Mr. Kyle Brown, Exec. Dir.
Description: Provides free and accessible information on wedding planning and on how to adjust on living life as a couple. Provides a forum for wedding professionals to express their own approaches and styles when it comes to their own wedding products and services. **Publications:** *The Wedding Book* (annual).

2465 ■ Wedding and Event Videographers Association International
8499 S Tamiami Trail
PMB 208
Sarasota, FL 34238
Ph:(941)923-5334
Fax:(941)921-3836
Co. E-mail: info@weva.com
URL: http://www.weva.com
Contact: Roy Chapman, Founder/Chm.
Description: Professional wedding and event videographers. Serves as a trade organization representing members' commercial interests. Provides educational programs and resources to wedding and event videographers. **Publications:** *The Business of Wedding and Special Event Videography*; *Wedding and Event Videography Resource Guide* .

2466 ■ Wedding and Portrait Photographers International
6059 Bristol Pkwy., Ste. 100
Culver City, CA 90230
Ph:(310)846-4770
Fax:(310)846-5995
URL: http://www.wppionline.com
Contact: Steven Sheanin, Pres./CEO
Description: Represents wedding portrait and digital photographers and photographers employed at general photography studios. Promotes high artistic and technical standards in wedding photography. Serves as a forum for the exchange of technical knowledge and experience; makes available the expertise of top professionals in the field of photographic arts and technology, advertising, sales promotion, marketing, public relations, accounting, business management, tax, and profit planning. Members are offered the opportunity to purchase special products and services. **Publications:** *Marketing and Technical Manual* (quarterly); *Rangefinder*; *Wedding Photographer* (monthly); *WPPI Photography Monthly* (monthly).

REFERENCE WORKS

2467 ■ "2011 Summer Wedding and Party Tips and Must Have's" in *Benzinga.com* (June 17, 2011)
Pub: Benzinga.com
Ed: Benzinga Staff. **Description:** Tips for hosting garden parties and get-togethers, but focusing on wedding receptions are provided.

2468 ■ "Carnival Cruise Lines Hosts First-Ever Wedding at Charleston's Annual 10K Cooper River Bridge Run" in *Benzinga.com* (April 4, 2011)
Pub: Benzinga.com
Ed: Benzinga Staff. **Description:** Carnival Cruise Lines hosted a post-race wedding ceremony after the Cooper River Bridge Run in South Carolina.

2469 ■ "Chesapeake Beach Resort and Spa Announces Dream Waterfront Wedding Giveaway" in *Benzinga.com* (October 29, 2011)
Pub: Benzinga.com
Ed: Benzinga Staff. **Description:** Chesapeake Beach Resort and Spa will give away a Dream Waterfront Wedding to a lucky bride and groom in order to promote their resort as a wedding venue.

2470 ■ "CPI Corporation Acquires Assets of Bella Pictures" in *Benzinga.com* (January 28, 2011)
Pub: Benzinga.com
Ed: Benzinga Staff. **Description:** CPI Corporation acquired assets of Bella Pictures Inc., a leading provider of branded wedding photography services. Details of the acquisition are explained.

2471 ■ "Destination Wedding Giveaway!" in *Benzinga.com* (October 29, 2011)
Pub: Benzinga.com
Ed: Benzinga Staff. **Description:** Eden Condominiums in Perdido Key, Florida will award a beach wedding to a couple in 2012. The event is a marketing tool to draw attention brides as a perfect wedding venue.

2472 ■ "Discover the Wedding Location of Your Dreams" in *Benzinga.com* (December 24, 2011)
Pub: Benzinga.com

Ed: Benzinga Staff. **Description:** Ritz Carlton Hotel Company helps couples choose from their 70 wedding locations worldwide with wedding advisors to assist in planning.

2473 ■ "Esencia Estate to Host 'The Esencia Experience for Upscale Wedding Planners'" in *Benzinga.com* (October 29, 2011)
Pub: Benzinga.com

Ed: Benzinga Staff. **Description:** Esencia Estate located in the Riviera Maya, Mexico is reintroducing the estate as a premier wedding venue. They are hosting an event to help wedding planners envision plans at the estate.

2474 ■ "Fairfax Announces Acquisition of William Ashley" in *Benzinga.com* (August 16, 2011)
Pub: Benzinga.com

Ed: Benzinga Staff. **Description:** Fairfax Financial Holdings Limited acquired the family-owned William Ashley China company, leader within the dinnerware and wedding registry industries and was the first company in North America to introduce a computerized wedding registry system.

2475 ■ "Finally, a Unique Solution to Meet All Wedding Planning Needs" in *Benzinga.com* (September 29, 2011)
Pub: Benzinga.com

Ed: Benzinga Staff. **Description:** WEDdeals.ca, a Canadian-based firm, lists up to 90 percent discounts on wedding vendor services in a particular area to help couples plan their weddings.

2476 ■ "Freelance Writer Creates L.I. Bridal Blog" in *Long Island Business News* (September 10, 2010)
Pub: Dolan Media Newswires

Ed: Gregory Zeller. **Description:** Profile of Claudia Copquin, freelance journalist who created a blog for brides on the Internet.

2477 ■ "Grand Bohemian Hotel in Orlando, Fla. Takes Lead in Wedding Planning" in *Benzinga.com* (August 4, 2011)
Pub: Benzinga.com

Ed: Benzinga Staff. **Description:** MAD-Marketing launched a newly-designed Website for the Grand Bohemian Hotel in Orlando, Florida. The site features the hotel's wedding vanity site to help target prospective couples planning their weddings.

2478 ■ "Host Your Dream Wedding at the Minneapolis Marriott Southwest" in *Benzinga.com* (June 6, 2011)
Pub: Benzinga.com

Ed: Benzinga Staff. **Description:** Minneapolis Marriott Southwest is helping engaged couples plan their wedding destination at their property. Details of wedding reception options are outlined.

2479 ■ "International Monetary Barter Helps Discretionary Industry" in *Benzinga.com* (January 24, 2011)
Pub: Benzinga.com

Ed: Benzinga Staff. **Description:** International Monetary Systems Limited, a business-to-business bartering firm, is helping wedding and event planners close deals with customers with bartering solutions.

2480 ■ "Markel American Insurance Company Announces Wedding and Special Event Insurance for Consumers" in *Benzinga.com* (February 16, 2011)
Pub: Benzinga.com

Ed: Benzinga Staff. **Description:** Markel American Insurance Company, headquartered in Waukesha, Wisconsin has launched its new special event insurance and wedding insurance to protect both liabilities and cancellations associated with these events.

2481 ■ "Memphis Marriott Downtown Offers Wedding Reception Discounts to Soon-To-Be Newlyweds" in *Benzinga.com* (June 23, 2011)
Pub: Benzinga.com

Ed: Benzinga Staff. **Description:** Memphis Marriott Downtown in Memphis, Tennessee is offering wedding reception discounts to couples planning their weddings.

2482 ■ "Military Brides Can Get Free Wedding Gowns" in *Virginian-Pilot* (November 10, 2010)
Pub: The Virginia-Pilot

Ed: Jamesetta Walker. **Description:** Seventy-five designer wedding gowns will be given to military brides on a first-come, first-served basis at Maya Couture through the Brides Across America's wedding gown giveaway program. Gowns are valued between $500 to $3,000 and are donated by designers Maggie Sottero, Pronovias and Essense of Australia.

2483 ■ "Modern Bride Unveiled Exclusively at JCPenney" in *Benzinga.com* (February 3, 2011)
Pub: Benzinga.com

Ed: Benzinga Staff. **Description:** JCPenney created its new Modern Bride concept in its bridal find jewelry departments. The new shopping experience is a collaboration between the retailer and Conde Nast catering to the bridal customer.

2484 ■ "More Brides, Grooms Say 'I Do' to Interracial Marriage" in *Black Enterprise* (Vol. 41, August 2010, No. 1, pp. 36)
Pub: Earl G. Graves Publishing Co. Inc.

Description: According to a recent survey conducted by Pew Research Center, a record 14.6 percent of all new marriages in the U.S. in 2008 were interracial. Statistical data included.

2485 ■ "New York City-Based New Street Realty Advisors has Secured a New Flagship for David's Bridal" in *Chain Store Age* (August 2008)
Pub: Chain Store Age

Description: New York City-based New Street Realty Advisors secured a new flagship store for David's Bridal in the Chelsea district of Manhattan. David's Bridal will occupy 12,800 square feet on two floors in a retail condominium development.

2486 ■ "On Your Marks, American Airlines, Now Vote!" in *Benzinga.com* (, 2011)
Pub: Benzinga.com

Ed: Benzinga Staff. **Description:** Wedding planner, Aviva Samuels, owner of Kiss the Planner boutique wedding and event planning agency in Florida, says that winning this contest would help her increase her knowledge base and provide in-depth, personal experience offering more destination wedding destinations.

2487 ■ "Online Security Crackdown: Scanning Service Oversees Site Security at David's Bridal" in (Vol. 84, July 2008, No. 7, pp. 46)
Pub: Chain Store Age

Ed: Samantha Murphy. **Description:** Online retailers are beefing up security on their Websites. Cyber thieves use retail systems in order to gain entry to consumer data. David's Bridal operates over 275 bridal showrooms in the U.S. and has a one-stop wedding resource for new brides planning weddings.

2488 ■ "Party Animals" in *Business Review, Albany New York* (Vol. 34, November 16, 2007, No. 33, pp. 1)
Pub: American City Business Journals, Inc.

Ed: Donna Abbott Viahos. **Description:** Total Events LLC, an event planning firm founded by Richard Carrier, generated sales from $13,000 to $1.5 million in eight years. Fine Affairs Inc. generates more than a million of revenues a year. Both companies provide party planning, organizing and decorating, wedding, galas, bar mitzvahs and other event planning.

2489 ■ "Peacocks Launches Its First Wedding Dress" in *Benzinga.com* (July 1, 2011)
Pub: Benzinga.com

Ed: Benzinga Staff. **Description:** Peacocks, a leading fashion retailer in the United Kingdom launched its first wedding dress available for sale in August 2011.

2490 ■ "Plan Your Next Event at Newport News Marriott at City Center" in *Benzinga.com* (July 29, 2011)
Pub: Benzinga.com

Ed: Benzinga Staff. **Description:** Newport News Marriott at City Center is promoting itself as the premier venue for business meetings, conventions and weddings.

2491 ■ "Plan Your Wedding with Cleveland Airport Marriott's Certified Event Planners" in *Benzinga.com* (February 2, 2011)
Pub: Benzinga.com

Ed: Benzinga Staff. **Description:** Cleveland's Airport Marriott makes wedding planning easy with its venue spaces and a full team of wedding planners.

2492 ■ "Planning a Wedding Fit for a Royal? Read This First, Urge Legal and General" in *Benzinga.com* (April 21, 2011)
Pub: Benzinga.com

Ed: Benzinga Staff. **Description:** When planning a wedding, the author suggests checking life insurance to be sure you are covered for any situations that may arise.

2493 ■ "The Power of Commitment: Mere Motivation Is Often Not Enough To Achieve Your Goals" in *Black Enterprise* (November 2007)
Pub: Earl G. Graves Publishing Co. Inc.

Ed: Tamara E. Holmes. **Description:** Profile of Michelle Tucker Kirk who opened her bridal shop in 2006. Kirk explains how her commitment and determination were keys to the company's success. Five signs to help any would-be entrepreneur discover if they are truly committed to a business idea are listed.

2494 ■ "Renren Partners With Recruit to Launch Social Wedding Services" in *Benzinga.com* (June 7, 2011)
Pub: Benzinga.com

Ed: Benzinga Staff. **Description:** Renren Inc. and Recruit Company Ltd. partnered to build a wedding social media catering to engaged couples and newlyweds in China. The platform will integrate online wedding related social content and offline media such as magazine and wedding exhibitions.

2495 ■ "Renren Partnership With Recruit to Launch Social Wedding Services" in *Benzinga.com* (June 7, 2011)
Pub: Benzinga.com

Ed: Benzinga Staff. **Description:** Renren Inc., the leading real name social networking Internet platform in China has partnered with Recruit Company Limited, Japan's largest human resource and classified media group to form a joint venture to build a wedding social media catering to the needs of engaged couples and newlyweds in China.

2496 ■ "Research and Markets: Wedding Statistics and Industry Reports" in *Benzinga.com* (June 24, 2011)
Pub: Benzinga.com

Ed: Benzinga Staff. **Description:** The latest trends and statistics regarding weddings and the wedding industry are spotlighted.

2497 ■ "Style Me Pretty on My Wedding Day – Final Chance to Enter" in *Benzinga.com* (October 29, 2011)
Pub: Benzinga.com

Ed: Benzinga Staff. **Description:** Style Me Pretty and Christian Dior have partnered to award one bride the chance to have a personal Dior makeup artist for their wedding day.

2498 ■ "Sylvie Collection Offers a Feminine Perspective and Voice in Male Dominated Bridal Industry" in *Benzinga.com* (October 29, 2011)
Pub: Benzinga.com
Ed: Benzinga Staff. **Description:** Bridal jewelry designer Sylvie Levine has created over 1,000 customizable styles of engagement rings and wedding bands and is reaching out to prospective new brides through a new Website, interactive social media campaign and monthly trunk show appearances.

2499 ■ "TLC's 'Jumping the Broom' Red Carpet Wedding Contest" in *Benzinga.com* (March 30, 2011)
Pub: Benzinga.com
Ed: Benzinga Staff. **Description:** The Learning Channel's 'Jumping the Broom' Red Carpet Wedding Contest provides couples the chance to marry or renew vows at the star-studded Hollywood premier of the new film.

2500 ■ "TripIt Itineraries Show Labor Day is the Most Popular Weekend for Wedding Travel" in *Benzinga.com* (August 26, 2011)
Pub: Benzinga.com
Ed: Benzinga Staff. **Description:** According to TripIt, the leading mobile trip organizer, Labor Day is the most popular weekend to travel for weddings between the months of April and August.

2501 ■ "Trousseaus of Memories Trail Behind Wedding Gowns" in *Oregonian* (September 4, 2010)
Pub: The Oregonian
Ed: Anne Saker. **Description:** Readers are asked to share stories about their wedding gowns and what that garment meant to them at the time and now.

2502 ■ "Wedding Bells on a Budget: Have Your Cake and Eat It Too" in *Benzinga.com* (June 11, 2011)
Pub: Benzinga.com
Ed: Benzinga Staff. **Description:** Typical American weddings cost about $24,000 with most couples spending between $18,000 to $30,000; a checklist and budget are critical. Nine ideas to help couples plan for their big day are outlined.

2503 ■ "Wedding Present Shopping – What to Get the Couple Who Have Everything" in *Benzinga.com* (April 19, 2011)
Pub: Benzinga.com
Ed: Benzinga Staff. **Description:** Tips for purchasing the perfect wedding gift are outlined.

2504 ■ "Wedding: Style Gowns Ready to Go" in *Houston Chronicle* (June 3, 2010)
Pub: Houston Chronicle
Ed: Molly Glentzer. **Description:** Wedding gowns with slender silhouettes travel well for destination weddings. Amsale, Oscar del la Renta and Monique Lhuillier dresses are highlighted.

2505 ■ "WeddingChannel.com Reviews Tops More than 200,000 Wedding Reviews" in *Benzinga.com* (June 23, 2011)
Pub: Benzinga.com
Ed: Benzinga Staff. **Description:** WeddingChannel.com is the leading wedding and gift registry Website for soon-to-be brides with search and review information on over 130,000 of the wedding industry's top vendors and even allows vendors to interact with the prospective brides.

TRADE PERIODICALS

2506 ■ *ABC Dialogue*
Pub: Association of Bridal Consultants
Ed: Gerard J. Monaghan, Editor. **Released:** Bimonthly, 6/year. **Price:** Included in membership. **Description:** Explores the various aspects of wedding consulting, including bridal attire, jewelry, food, photography, and business management and advertising. Recurring features include business tips and profiles of members.

2507 ■ *Cincinnati Wedding*
Pub: Cincinnati Magazine Inc.
Contact: John Lunn, Publisher
E-mail: jlunn@cincinnatimagazine.com
Released: Semiannual. **Description:** Consumer magazine covering weddings for engaged couples in the Cincinnati area.

2508 ■ *Modern Bride*
Pub: Conde Nast Publications Inc.
Released: Monthly. **Price:** $16.95 12 issues; $28 two years 24 issues. **Description:** Magazine for brides.

2509 ■ *New England Bride*
Pub: New England Bride Inc.
Contact: Laura Catizone, Assoc. Publisher
Released: Monthly. **Price:** Free to qualified subscribers; $36. **Description:** Magazine for brides-to-be in six New England states.

2510 ■ *Vows*
Pub: Grimes and Associates
Contact: Kori Grimes, Business & Finance
E-mail: korigrimes@vowsmagazine.com
Released: Bimonthly. **Price:** $30; $52 two years; $55 elsewhere. **Description:** Trade journal for bridal and wedding professionals.

VIDEOCASSETTES/ AUDIOCASSETTES

2511 ■ *Planning a Wedding to Remember*
Cambridge Educational
c/o Films Media Group
132 West 31st Street, 17th Floor
Ste. 124
New York, NY 10001
Free: 800-257-5126
Fax:(609)671-0266
Co. E-mail: custserve@films.com
URL: http://www.cambridgeol.com
Released: 1990. **Price:** $19.95. **Description:** Wedding authority Beverly Clark covers all facets involved in planning a wedding. **Availability:** VHS.

2512 ■ *Planning Your Wedding, Vol. 1: Selecting Your Formal Wear*
Leslie T. McClure
PO Box 1223
Pebble Beach, CA 93953
Ph:(831)656-0553
Fax:(831)656-0555
Co. E-mail: leslie@411videoinfo.com
URL: http://www.411videoinfo.com
Released: 1998. **Price:** $29.95. **Description:** Part of a ten-volume series for brides- and grooms-to-be that follows the steps taken by a typical couple, Jeff and Lisa, in their preparation for the big event. **Availability:** VHS.

2513 ■ *Planning Your Wedding, Vol. 2: A Visit to Your Caterer*
Leslie T. McClure
PO Box 1223
Pebble Beach, CA 93953
Ph:(831)656-0553
Fax:(831)656-0555
Co. E-mail: leslie@411videoinfo.com
URL: http://www.411videoinfo.com
Released: 1998. **Price:** $29.95. **Description:** Part of a ten-volume series for brides- and grooms-to-be that follows the steps taken by a typical couple, Jeff and Lisa, in their preparation for the big event. **Availability:** VHS.

2514 ■ *Planning Your Wedding, Vol. 3: Selecting Your Wedding Cake*
Leslie T. McClure
PO Box 1223
Pebble Beach, CA 93953
Ph:(831)656-0553
Fax:(831)656-0555
Co. E-mail: leslie@411videoinfo.com
URL: http://www.411videoinfo.com
Released: 1998. **Price:** $29.95. **Description:** Part of a ten-volume series for brides- and grooms-to-be that follows the steps taken by a typical couple, Jeff and Lisa, in their preparation for the big event. **Availability:** VHS.

2515 ■ *Planning Your Wedding, Vol. 4: Selecting Your Photographer*
Leslie T. McClure
PO Box 1223
Pebble Beach, CA 93953
Ph:(831)656-0553
Fax:(831)656-0555
Co. E-mail: leslie@411videoinfo.com
URL: http://www.411videoinfo.com
Released: 1998. **Price:** $29.95. **Description:** Part of a ten-volume series for brides- and grooms-to-be that follows the steps taken by a typical couple, Jeff and Lisa, in their preparation for the big event. **Availability:** VHS.

2516 ■ *Planning Your Wedding, Vol. 5: Visiting Your Travel Agent*
Leslie T. McClure
PO Box 1223
Pebble Beach, CA 93953
Ph:(831)656-0553
Fax:(831)656-0555
Co. E-mail: leslie@411videoinfo.com
URL: http://www.411videoinfo.com
Released: 1998. **Price:** $29.95. **Description:** Part of a ten-volume series for brides- and grooms-to-be that follows the steps taken by a typical couple, Jeff and Lisa, in their preparation for the big event. **Availability:** VHS.

2517 ■ *Planning Your Wedding, Vol. 6: Meeting with Your Financial Advisor*
Leslie T. McClure
PO Box 1223
Pebble Beach, CA 93953
Ph:(831)656-0553
Fax:(831)656-0555
Co. E-mail: leslie@411videoinfo.com
URL: http://www.411videoinfo.com
Released: 1998. **Price:** $29.95. **Description:** Part of a ten-volume series for brides- and grooms-to-be that follows the steps taken by a typical couple, Jeff and Lisa, in their preparation for the big event. **Availability:** VHS.

2518 ■ *Planning Your Wedding, Vol. 7: Visiting with Your Jeweler*
Leslie T. McClure
PO Box 1223
Pebble Beach, CA 93953
Ph:(831)656-0553
Fax:(831)656-0555
Co. E-mail: leslie@411videoinfo.com
URL: http://www.411videoinfo.com
Released: 1998. **Price:** $29.95. **Description:** Part of a ten-volume series for brides- and grooms-to-be that follows the steps taken by a typical couple, Jeff and Lisa, in their preparation for the big event. **Availability:** VHS.

2519 ■ *Planning Your Wedding, Vol. 8: Meeting with Your Minister*
Leslie T. McClure
PO Box 1223
Pebble Beach, CA 93953
Ph:(831)656-0553
Fax:(831)656-0555
Co. E-mail: leslie@411videoinfo.com
URL: http://www.411videoinfo.com
Released: 1998. **Price:** $29.95. **Description:** Part of a ten-volume series for brides- and grooms-to-be that follows the steps taken by a typical couple, Jeff and Lisa, in their preparation for the big event. **Availability:** VHS.

2520 ■ *Planning Your Wedding, Vol. 9: Selecting Your Flowers*
Leslie T. McClure
PO Box 1223
Pebble Beach, CA 93953

Ph:(831)656-0553
Fax:(831)656-0555
Co. E-mail: leslie@411videoinfo.com
URL: http://www.411videoinfo.com

Released: 1998. **Price:** $29.95. **Description:** Part of a ten-volume series for brides- and grooms-to-be that follows the steps taken by a typical couple, Jeff and Lisa, in their preparation for the big event. **Availability:** VHS.

2521 ■ *Planning Your Wedding, Vol. 10: Meeting with Your Bridal Consultant*
Leslie T. McClure
PO Box 1223
Pebble Beach, CA 93953
Ph:(831)656-0553
Fax:(831)656-0555
Co. E-mail: leslie@411videoinfo.com
URL: http://www.411videoinfo.com

Released: 1998. **Price:** $29.95. **Description:** Part of a ten-volume series for brides- and grooms-to-be that follows the steps taken by a typical couple, Jeff and Lisa, in their preparation for the big event. **Availability:** VHS.

TRADE SHOWS AND CONVENTIONS

2522 ■ Haus-Garten-Freizeit
Leipziger-Messe GmbH
PO Box 100720
D-04007 Leipzig, Germany
Ph:49 341 67 80
Fax:49 341 678 87 62
Co. E-mail: info@leipziger-messe.de
URL: http://www.leipziger-messe.de

Released: Annual. **Audience:** General public. **Principal Exhibits:** Cooking, eating, housekeeping, home and furnishing, textiles, jewellery, cosmetics, arts and crafts, health, fitness, pets.

2523 ■ National Bridal Market
Merchandise Mart Properties Inc.
222 Merchandise Mart, Ste. 470
Chicago, IL 60654
Free: 800-677-6278
URL: http://www.merchandisemart.com

Released: Annual, and October. **Audience:** Retailers. **Principal Exhibits:** Bridal gowns, special occasion gowns, tuxedos, and related accessories. **Dates and Locations:** 2011 Apr 03-05, Chicago, IL.

2524 ■ Wedding Wishes/Formal Fair
Thunder Bay Chamber of Commerce
200 Syndicate Ave. S., Ste. 102
Thunder Bay, ON, Canada P7E 1C9
Ph:(807)624-2626
Fax:(807)622-7752
Co. E-mail: chamber@tb-chamber.on.ca
URL: http://www.tb-chamber.on.ca
Released: Annual. **Principal Exhibits:** Wedding related supplies and services. **Dates and Locations:** 2011 Nov 06-06, Thunder Bay, ON.

FRANCHISES AND BUSINESS OPPORTUNITIES

2525 ■ Sweet Beginnings
1037 W Broadway, Ste. 105
Vancouver, BC, Canada V6H 1E3
Ph:(604)738-9552
Free: (866)730-5553
Fax:(604)876-6460
No. of Franchise Units: 2. **No. of Company-Owned Units:** 2. **Founded:** 1997. **Franchised:** 2004. **Description:** Wedding & event planning, decorating and chair covers. **Equity Capital Needed:** $29,100-$44,700. **Franchise Fee:** $10,000-$20,000. **Royalty Fee:** $300/month. **Financial Assistance:** Limited third party financing available. **Training:** Provides 5 days training and 3 days onsite.

Building/Home Inspection Service

ASSOCIATIONS AND OTHER ORGANIZATIONS

2526 ■ American Institute of Inspectors
PO Box 248
Lower Lake, CA 95457
Free: 800-877-4770
Fax:(707)277-7852
Co. E-mail: execdir@inspection.org
URL: http://www.inspection.org
Contact: Sylvia Duerksen, Exec. Dir.
Description: Certified home inspectors. Works to set standards for impartial evaluations of residential properties. Certifies members in four areas: residential homes, mobile homes, mechanics, and earthquake hazard reduction. Maintains speakers' bureau.
.

2527 ■ Canadian Association of Home and Property Inspectors–Association Canadienne des Inspecteurs de Biens Immobiliers
PO Box 13715
Ottawa, ON, Canada K2K 1X6
Ph:(613)839-5344
Free: 888-748-2244
Fax:(866)876-9877
Co. E-mail: info@cahpi.ca
URL: http://www.cahpi.ca
Contact: Ms. Sharry Featherston, Admin./Registrar
Description: Home inspectors. Promotes professional advancement of members. Seeks to insure adherence to high standards of ethics and practice among home inspectors. Represents members' collective interests. **Publications:** *The Canadian Home Inspector* (3/year). **Telecommunication Services:** electronic mail, sharry@cahpi.ca.

2528 ■ Canadian Institute of Professional Home Inspectors
999 W Broadway, Ste. 720
Vancouver, BC, Canada
Ph:(604)732-0617
Co. E-mail: info@edwitzke.com
URL: http://www.edwitzke.com
Contact: Ed R.R. Witzke
Description: Home inspectors. Seeks to advance the profession of home inspection; promotes adherence to high standards of ethics and practice among members. Serves as a forum for the exchange of information among members; sponsors educational and training programs. **Publications:** *Complete Canadian Home Inspection Guide* .

2529 ■ Construction Specifications Canada–Devis de Construction Canada
120 Carlton St., Ste. 312
Toronto, ON, Canada M5A 4K2
Ph:(416)777-2198
Free: 800-668-5684
Fax:(416)777-2197
Co. E-mail: info@csc-dcc.ca
URL: http://www.csc-dcc.ca
Contact: Nick Franjic CAE, Exec. Dir.
Description: Construction companies, workers, engineers, and writers of building standards and specifications. Promotes continuing professional development of members; seeks to insure adherence to high standards of practice in the building industries. Conducts educational programs; makes available vocational training courses. Develops industry standards. Represents members' interests before industry organizations and government agencies; advises government agencies responsible for promulgating building codes and construction specifications. Makes available discount insurance and vehicle leasing programs to members. **Publications:** *Chapter Specifiers* (10/year); *Construction Canada* (bimonthly); *News in Brief* (semiannual).

REFERENCE WORKS

2530 ■ *International Conference of Building Officials—Membership Directory*
Pub: International Code Council (Washington, District of Columbia)
Covers: government agencies and officials, primarily in the United States, responsible for preparing and publishing building construction standards and the Uniform Building Code, to be used as a basis for regulations concerning materials and types of construction. **Entries Include:** Name, company name, address, phone. **Arrangement:** Alphabetical.

TRADE PERIODICALS

2531 ■ *The Appraisers Standard*
Pub: New England Appraisers Association
Released: Quarterly. **Price:** $20; $25 Canada; $30 other countries. **Description:** Trade magazine for personal property appraisers.

2532 ■ *The Construction Specifier*
Pub: The Construction Specifications Institute
Released: Monthly. **Price:** $59; $99 two years; $69 Canada; $109 Canada two years; $199 other countries; $16.50 members. **Description:** Magazine.

CONSULTANTS

2533 ■ AEP Associates Inc.
53 Notch Rd.
West Paterson, NJ 07424-1953
Ph:(973)256-7575
Fax:(973)890-7848
Co. E-mail: aep@aepassoc.com
Contact: Stanley John Lacz, President
E-mail: stl@aepassoc.com
Scope: Provides comprehensive professional services in the following areas: Architectural-building, programming, cost analysis, construction documents, construction inspection, and interior design; landscape architecture; engineering-site plans, energy studies, storm drainage, foundations, structures, plumbing, water supply, heating, air conditioning, electrical lighting, and land subdivisions; planning-master plan studies, zoning ordinance, variances, application to government agencies; governmental approvals-stream encroachment, wet lands. Clients include leading corporations; municipal, county, state, and federal governmental agencies; various developers; organizations and individuals for mercantile, educational, and medical projects; and homeowners.

2534 ■ American Forensic Engineers
34 Sammis Ln.
White Plains, NY 10605
Ph:(914)949-5978
Fax:(914)949-0350
Co. E-mail: gusmundel@aol.com
Contact: August B. Mundel, President
E-mail: gusmundel@aol.com
Scope: Provides industrial, safety, and forensic consulting services. Services include relevant engineering studies, sampling, statistical studies, quality and reliability efforts, industrial hygiene, human factors analysis, industrial experimentation, product safety analysis and product liability causes in the electrical, electronic, electro-chemical, chemical, mechanical, and battery industrial areas. Also offers building inspection services. Serves private industries as well as government agencies in the U.S. **Publications:** "Ethics in Quality," Marcell Dekker.

2535 ■ American Roofing Consultants Inc.
785 Briggs Rd.
PO Box 47
Salisbury, NC 28147-9539
Ph:(704)637-0370
Free: 800-455-6207
Fax:(704)630-0774
Contact: F. Lee Russell, President
Scope: Provides investigative roof surveys; on-site roof construction inspection; nuclear, infrared, capacitance moisture surveys; roof maintenance schedules; plan and specification reviews; and specialty roof seminars. Also serves as expert witness.

2536 ■ Applied Fire Protection Engineering Inc.
10501-A Ewing Rd.
Beltsville, MD 20705
Ph:(301)931-3330
Free: 800-331-6373
Fax:(301)931-6412
Co. E-mail: nfse@mindspring.com
URL: http://www.nfse.com
Contact: Dennis A. Sullivan, President
E-mail: dennis@atsnfsa.com
Scope: Provides comprehensive consulting services in the field of fire protection (including building and fire code analysis for new construction and renovations; existing building inspections and analysis; fire alarm system design; and automatic sprinkler system design) as well as annual testing and maintenance of fire alarm systems, fire pumps and sprinkler systems.

2537 ■ Architectural Consultants Ltd.
500 W Central Rd., Ste. 208
Mount Prospect, IL 60056-2381
Ph:(847)577-5777

Fax:(847)577-5784
Contact: Edward S. Busche, President
Scope: Professional activities include forensic services for all types of building and/or construction-related problems; architectural services for the renovation, restoration and expansion of buildings; due diligence studies to determine the condition of buildings and the cost of restoring them to an acceptable condition. Services are provided by a multidisciplinary team of architects, structural, electrical and mechanical engineers with broad experience in building design, construction and restoration.

2538 ■ Architecture, Building Codes & Inspection
0310 Crystal Country Cir.
Carbondale, CO 81623
Ph:(970)963-8209
Fax:(970)963-8209
Co. E-mail: dysart@rof.net
Contact: Jack Dysart, Principle
E-mail: dysart@rof.net
Scope: Architect, building inspector, construction inspector, and contractor who offers forensic support of litigation concerning building design, codes and construction. Recent experience with the Americans with Disabilities Act facilities compliance, architecture, and residential buildings. Industries served building and corporate owners, single family homeowners, realtors, banks lenders, attorneys, insurance companies, architects and contractors, and city building departments. **Publications:** "Ibc International Building Code Research & Critiques"; "Building Code Compliance Checklists"; "Aia "Masterspec" Master Specifications Contributor, American Institute of Architects"; "Cost Estimating Computer Programs for Cmc College Lectures & Private Practice".

2539 ■ Breen & Associates Inc.
PO Box 120424
Arlington, TX 76012
Ph:(817)275-4711
Fax:(817)275-4711
Co. E-mail: jbreen504@aol.com
URL: http://www.breenengineering.com
Contact: James E. Breen, President
E-mail: jbreen504@aol.com
Scope: Building construction consultants offering complete inspection services of residential and commercial structures (includes structural, equipment and systems). Clients include real estate brokers, investors (real estate) and builders/developers.

2540 ■ CAS Financial Advisory Services
38 Chauncy St., Ste. 600
Boston, MA 02111
Ph:(617)338-9484
Fax:(617)338-9422
Co. E-mail: info@casfas.com
URL: http://www.casfas.com
Contact: Todd Trehubenko, President
E-mail: ehandelman@atscasfas.com
Scope: Provides a comprehensive suite of financial, asset management, and physical capital needs services to institutions with a financial position in multifamily residential property. **Publications:** "Physical Needs Due Diligence Related to Recapitalization Transactions". **Seminars:** Capital Needs Assessments and Reserve Analysis.

2541 ■ Foit-Albert Associates
215 W 94th St., Ste. 517
New York, NY 10025
Ph:(716)856-3933
Fax:(716)856-3961
Co. E-mail: info@foit-albert.com
URL: http://www.foit-albert.com
Contact: Warren T. Shaw, Mgr
E-mail: wshaw@foit-albert.com
Scope: Full architectural/engineering surveying consulting firm specializing in historic preservation, educational facilities, full-time construction inspection and engineering coordination. Grant writing services available.

2542 ■ The Hall Partnership Architects L.L.P.
42 E 21st St.
New York, NY 10010-7216
Ph:(212)777-2090
Fax:(212)979-2217
Co. E-mail: info@hallarchitect.com
URL: http://www.hallarchitect.com
Contact: William A. Hall, Partner
E-mail: thall@atshallarchitect.com
Scope: Offers full range of architectural and planning consulting services. Serves private industries as well as government agencies.

2543 ■ Harvey Toub Engineering
6145 Barfield Rd. NE, Ste. 220
Atlanta, GA 30328
Ph:(404)843-1192
Fax:(404)256-9780
Contact: Harvey Toub, President
Scope: Engineering consulting firm which provides HVAC, plumbing and electrical design services for new buildings and for modifications/additions to existing buildings. Also offers boiler testing, energy efficiency studies and design, boiler operator training, building inspection/reports, industrial design for ventilation, electrical installations and preventive maintenance planning. Industries served: Foundry, pharmaceutical, boiler, manufacturing, institutional and government agencies.

2544 ■ InspectAmerica Engineering P.C.
3 School St.
White Plains, NY 10606-1408
Ph:(914)682-9090
Fax:(845)661-5183
Co. E-mail: comments@inspectamerica.com
URL: http://www.inspectamerica.com
Contact: Rick Anderson, Principle
E-mail: raymond.wexler@atskirkland.com
Scope: Provides engineering inspection services for pre-purchase purposes, condominium and cooperative conversions and inspections to analyze and design remedies for problems in homes and buildings. Services encompass both commercial and residential properties. Industries served: real estate, lawyers, bankers, property management, landlords, investors, and government agencies. **Publications:** "Home Inspectors Check for Termites"; "Structural Inspection"; "Healthy Home Inspection". **Special Services:** Home Inspection SuperSite^{TM}; Home Inspection TechTalk^{TM}; InspectAmerica^{R}.

2545 ■ Kohn Engineering
4220 Mountain Rd.
Macungie, PA 18062
Ph:(610)967-4766
Fax:(610)967-6468
Co. E-mail: don@kohnengineering.com
URL: http://www.kohnengineering.com
Contact: Don Kohn, Principle
E-mail: don@kohnengineering.com
Scope: Offers fire protection consulting. Provides a wide range of fire protection consulting services that includes design, code interpretation, expert witness, project management, fire safety program development, and hazard identification. Provides cost effective solutions to fire protection problems. **Seminars:** Fire Protection in Nuclear Power Plants.

2546 ■ Middle Department Inspection Agency Inc.
8673 Commerce Dr., Ste. 2
PO Box 1356
Easton, MD 21601
Ph:(412)931-3028
Free: 800-580-6342
Fax:(724)935-7480
Co. E-mail: radmdia@comcast.net
URL: http://www.mdia.net
E-mail: radmdia@comcast.net
Scope: Offers building, electrical, fire protection and plumbing inspections. Serves private industries as well as government agencies, such as municipalities and counties.

2547 ■ N.R. Goldstein & Associates
1200 US Hwy. 130
Trenton, NJ 08691
Ph:(609)426-1888
Fax:(609)426-1230
Contact: Norman R. Goldstein, President
Scope: Provides forensic safety services regarding slips and falls, machine guarding, construction, and building codes. Primarily serves attorneys and insurance carriers.

2548 ■ Professional Engineering Inspections Inc.
PO Box 271492
Houston, TX 77277
Ph:(713)664-1264
Fax:(713)589-2503
Co. E-mail: mail@profengineering.com
Contact: Sue Lambie, Office Mgr
E-mail: slambie@atsprofengineering.com
Scope: Specializes in residential inspections, commercial inspections and consulting, structural inspection-mechanical and electrical, pools and spas foundation, roof- energy loss, quality of construction-condition of property, and capital reserve studies-special inspections.

2549 ■ Trendzitions Inc.
25691 Atlantic Ocean Dr., Ste. B13
Lake Forest, CA 92630-8842
Ph:(949)727-9100
Free: 800-266-2767
Fax:(949)727-3444
Co. E-mail: ctooker@trendzitions.com
URL: http://www.trendzitions.com
Contact: Christian Tooker, President
E-mail: ctooker@atstrendzitions.com
Scope: Provides services in the areas of communications consulting, project management, construction management, and furniture procurement. Offers information on spatial uses, building codes, ADA compliance and city ordinances. Also offers budget projections.

FRANCHISES AND BUSINESS OPPORTUNITIES

2550 ■ Amerispec Home Inspection Service
ServiceMaster
3839 Forest Hill Irene Rd.
Memphis, TN 38125
Free: 800-338-6833
Fax:(901)820-7580
Co. E-mail: sales@amerispec.net
URL: http://www.amerispecfranchise.com
No. of Franchise Units: 322. **Founded:** 1987. **Franchised:** 1988. **Description:** Home inspection franchise which sells independently-owned and operated businesses to entrepreneurs in exclusive territories. Owners use a proprietary software program to generate a narrative report and/or an onsite report to clients. Large or small area franchises available-priced accordingly. **Equity Capital Needed:** $41,350-$60,900. **Franchise Fee:** $25,900-$35,900. **Royalty Fee:** 7%, or $250 per month ($125 per month for smaller areas). **Financial Assistance:** Financing of up to 80% of initial franchise fee on large areas. Offers loan repayment term option and competitive rates. Also assists in finding outside financing. **Managerial Assistance:** Operations manual, and extensive training during initial 2 week course. Formal 2-3 day follow-up (one-on-one, onsite at owners office), which includes all aspects of business, monthly telephone contact with owners, twice annually regional training and annual national training. All include management review. **Training:** 2 weeks hands-on & classroom training & includes the exclusive AmeriSpec Smart Start 27-week business start-up program.

2551 ■ AmeriSpec Inspection Service
ServiceMaster
5462 Timberlea Blvd.
Mississauga, ON, Canada L4W 2T7
Ph:(905)670-0000
Free: 800-263-5928

Fax:(905)670-0077
Co. E-mail: thould@smclean.com
URL: http://www.amerispec.ca

No. of Franchise Units: 84. **No. of Operating Units:** 384. **Founded:** 1988. **Franchised:** 1988. **Description:** Home inspection franchise in North America. **Equity Capital Needed:** $24,900-$34,900, $30,000-$60,000 total investment, $40,000 start-up capital. **Franchise Fee:** $24,000-$35,900. **Financial Assistance:** Available (OAC). **Training:** Yes.

2552 ■ The BrickKicker
RonLen Enterprises Inc.
849 N Ellsworth St.
Naperville, IL 60563
Free: 888-339-5425
Fax:(630)420-2270
Co. E-mail: linda@brickkicker.com
URL: http://www.brickkicker.com

No. of Franchise Units: 165. **Founded:** 1989. **Franchised:** 1995. **Description:** Building inspection service. **Equity Capital Needed:** $15,000-$40,000. **Franchise Fee:** $7,500-$25,000. **Financial Assistance:** Up to one-third the franchise fee. **Training:** 2 weeks hands-on/in-field work, interactive classroom discussions, lab, telemarketing, report writing, sales calls, roll-play, technical & marketing training manuals, as well as training through yearly national conventions, roundtables, monthly support packages and toll-free support.

2553 ■ Home-Alyze
3740B 11A St. NE, Ste. 201
Calgary, AB, Canada T2E 6M6
Ph:(403)730-9986
Free: 800-831-6272
Fax:(403)274-4821
Co. E-mail: info@homealyze.com
URL: http://www.homealyzefranchise.com

No. of Franchise Units: 9. **Founded:** 1978. **Franchised:** 1999. **Description:** Home-Alyze offers home inspection services. **Equity Capital Needed:** $60,000. **Franchise Fee:** $24,900. **Training:** Initial and ongoing.

2554 ■ The Hometeam Inspection Services, Inc.
575 Chamber Dr.
Milford, OH 45150
Free: 800-598-5297
Co. E-mail: sales@hometeaminspection.com
URL: http://www.hometeaminspection.com

No. of Franchise Units: 220. **Founded:** 1991. **Franchised:** 1992. **Description:** National franchisor of home inspections. **Equity Capital Needed:** $40,000-$80,000. **Franchise Fee:** $9,800. **Financial Assistance:** Finance up to 50% of initial franchise fee. **Managerial Assistance:** Marketing, accounting and management. Ongoing assistance. **Training:** 14 day comprehensive training program at corporate office.

2555 ■ Housemaster, Home Inspections, Done Right
426 Vosseller Ave.
Bound Brook, NJ 08805
Ph:(732)823-4087
Co. E-mail: mkuhn@housemaster.com
URL: http://www.housemaster.com

No. of Franchise Units: 355. **Founded:** 1971. **Franchised:** 1979. **Description:** Home inspections for home buyers and sellers. **Equity Capital Needed:** $43,500-$68,200. **Franchise Fee:** $27,500. **Financial Assistance:** Limited financing available. **Training:** Offers 2-5 weeks of initial training.

2556 ■ Inspect-It 1st LLC
Inspect-It 1st Franchising Corp.
7100 E Pleasant Valley Rd., Ste. 300
Independence, OH 44131
Free: 877-392-6278
Fax:(216)674-0650
Co. E-mail: administrator@inspectit1st.com
URL: http://www.inspectit1st.com
No. of Franchise Units: 39. **Founded:** 1991. **Franchised:** 1998. **Description:** Offers home inspection service. **Equity Capital Needed:** $34,400-$53,400. **Franchise Fee:** $26,900. **Royalty Fee:** $200-$400/month. **Financial Assistance:** Limited in-house and third party financing available. **Training:** Provides 10 days in Phoenix with ongoing support.

2557 ■ Lighthouse Inspections Canada
2400 Dundas St. W, Unit 6
Mississauga, ON, Canada L5K 2R8
Ph:(905)278-7887
Free: 800-217-2450
Fax:(905)278-9582
Co. E-mail: franchise@lighthouseinspections.com
URL: http://www.lighthouseinspections.com
No. of Franchise Units: 19. **No. of Company-Owned Units:** 1. **Founded:** 1999. **Franchised:** 2000. **Description:** Offers lighthouse inspection service. **Franchise Fee:** $20,000. **Training:** Minimum 3 weeks initial training, ongoing support, seminars and re-certification.

2558 ■ National Property Inspections
9375 Burt St., Ste. 201
Omaha, NE 68114
Ph:(402)333-9807
Free: 800-333-9807
Fax:800-933-2508
Co. E-mail: info@npiweb.com
URL: http://www.npiweb.com
No. of Franchise Units: 283. **Founded:** 1987. **Franchised:** 1987. **Description:** NPI offers a home inspection franchise opportunity with exclusive, protected territories and a turn-key start-up package, complete with the training and equipment needed for your business. NPI's support goes beyond training. You'll also receive continual technical assistance & education for both residential & commercial inspections, as well as marketing programs to help you build your business year after year. **Equity Capital Needed:** Working capital of $5,000 or more (not including franchise fee). **Franchise Fee:** $24,900. **Financial Assistance:** Bank or SBA loans. **Managerial Assistance:** State of the art hand held computer/inspection software and support, plus full on-going technology and marketing staff support. **Training:** 2 weeks of training at our home office, plus a third optional week in the field with a veteran NPI inspector in our mentor program.

2559 ■ Pillar to Post Inc.
5805 Whittle Rd., Ste. 211
Mississauga, ON, Canada L4Z 2J1
Ph:(905)568-8608
Fax:(905)568-8137
Co. E-mail: franchise.development@pillartopost.com
URL: http://www.pillartopost.com
No. of Franchise Units: 287. **Founded:** 1994. **Franchised:** 1994. **Description:** Qualified home inspection franchise. **Equity Capital Needed:** $30,700-$42,750. **Franchise Fee:** $14,900. **Royalty Fee:** 7%. **Financial Assistance:** Limited in-house and third party financial assistance available. **Training:** Offers 2 weeks of training.

2560 ■ Prospection
7100 E Pleasant Valley Rd., Ste. 300
Independence, OH 44131
Free: (866)328-7720
Fax:(216)674-0652

No. of Franchise Units: 28. **Founded:** 2003. **Franchised:** 2003. **Description:** Professional home inspection service. **Equity Capital Needed:** $6,000-$12,000. **Financial Assistance:** Yes. **Training:** Yes.

2561 ■ Service One Janitorial
1180 Spring Centre S. Blvd., Ste. 208
Altamonte, FL 32714
Ph:(407)261-1300
Free: 800-522-7111
Fax:800-846-3992

No. of Franchise Units: 420. **Founded:** 1967. **Franchised:** 1985. **Description:** Commercial janitorial business. **Equity Capital Needed:** $10,000. **Franchise Fee:** $9,000. **Royalty Fee:** 8-15%. **Financial Assistance:** In-house finance assistance available.

2562 ■ Sharkey's Cuts For Kids, Franchising Co., LLC
37 Highland Rd.
Westport, CT 06880
Ph:(203)637-8911
Fax:(203)637-0386
Co. E-mail: info@sharkeycutsforkids.com
URL: http://www.sharkeyscutsforkids.com

No. of Franchise Units: 19. **Founded:** 2001. **Franchised:** 2004. **Description:** Kids salon, including Flat Screen/Fun Chairs/PS2, Game cube, X-box/Rides/Pinball/Glamour Parties/Party Favors, and Karaoke Parties for Mom's. **Equity Capital Needed:** $100,000 turnkey. **Franchise Fee:** None. **Financial Assistance:** Limited financing available upon request. **Training:** Provides help with site selection. Once a site is chosen we then come back and create specific modeling prints for your store. Prior to opening, a 3 day training program is given at our headquarters in CT (all expenses covered by Sharkey's).

2563 ■ Snip-Its
The Snip-Its Franchise Co.
6409 City West Pkwy., Ste. 205
Eden Prairie, MN 55344
Ph:(508)651-7052
Free: 800-651-7063
Fax:(508)651-0549
Co. E-mail: mmerrigan@snipits.com
URL: http://www.snipits.com

No. of Franchise Units: 62. **No. of Company-Owned Units:** 1. **Founded:** 1995. **Franchised:** 2003. **Description:** Children's haircuts. **Equity Capital Needed:** $141,189-$273,731 Salon, $127,775-$187,850 Express Salon. **Franchise Fee:** $25,000. **Financial Assistance:** Registered with SBA. **Training:** Yes.

2564 ■ WIN Home Inspection
9238 Madison Blvd., Ste. 750
Madison, AL 35758
Ph:(206)728-8100
Free: 800-967-8127
Fax:800-274-7758
Co. E-mail: joinwin@wini.com
URL: http://www.winfranchise.com

No. of Franchise Units: 227. **Founded:** 1993. **Franchised:** 1994. **Description:** Performs home inspection. **Equity Capital Needed:** $27,800-$49,050. **Franchise Fee:** $16,900-$26,900. **Financial Assistance:** Yes. **Training:** Yes.

START-UP INFORMATION

2565 ■ "Legendary Success" in *Small Business Opportunities* (November 2010)
Pub: Harris Publications Inc.
Description: Von Schrader is famous in the cleaning industry and more than 50,000 individuals have started their own professional cleaning service businesses using the company's air cell technology cleaning systems along with their proven business systems. This is a perfect business for anyone wishing to start and run it from their home.

ASSOCIATIONS AND OTHER ORGANIZATIONS

2566 ■ Building Service Contractors Association International
401 N Michigan Ave., Ste. 2200
Chicago, IL 60611-4267
Ph:(312)321-5167
Free: 800-368-3414
Fax:(312)673-6735
Co. E-mail: info@bscai.org
URL: http://www.bscai.org
Contact: Chris Mundschenk, Exec. VP/CEO
Description: Firms and corporations in 40 countries engaged in contracting building maintenance services including the provision of labor, purchasing materials and janitorial cleaning and maintenance of a building or its surroundings; associate members are manufacturers of cleaning supplies and equipment. Seeks to provide a unified voice for building service contractors and to promote increased recognition by government, property owners and the general business and professional public. Conducts continuing study and action, through committees and special task groups on areas such as public affairs, costs and ratios, uniform accounting, industrial relations and personnel, marketing and sales, contract improvement, research and planning, materials and supplies sources, group insurance, management training, statistics collection, safety and insurance costs. Has developed a certification program for building service executives and a registration program for building service managers. **Publications:** *Who's Who in Building Service Contracting* (annual).

2567 ■ Canadian Association Environmental Management–Association Canadienne de Gestion Environnementale
Aberdeen Hospital
835 E River Rd.
New Glasgow, NS, Canada B2G 3S6
Ph:(902)725-7600
Fax:(902)755-3975
Co. E-mail: rosemary.gillis-bowers@pcha.nshealth.ca
URL: http://www.thecanadiangroup.com/caha/index.htm
Contact: Rosemary Gillis-Bowers CEM, Acting Pres./Sec.-Treas.
Description: Environmental managers. Seeks to advance the environmental (housekeeping) profession; promotes adherence to high standards of ethics and practice by members. Represents members' interests; facilitates communication and cooperation among members. **Publications:** *The Quarterly* (quarterly).

2568 ■ Cleaning Management Institute
19 British American Blvd. W
Latham, NY 12110
Ph:(518)540-9163
Fax:(518)783-1386
Co. E-mail: mgallinger@ntpmedia.com
URL: http://www.cminstitute.net
Contact: Matt Gallinger, Dir.
Description: Represents individuals and organizations active in cleaning maintenance and management, including contract cleaner firms. Develops home study educational courses and publications to promote professional certification, self-improvement, and efficient work methods. .

2569 ■ International Facility Management Association - Toronto Chapter
46 Falcon St.
Toronto, ON, Canada M4S 2P5
Ph:(416)346-4729
Fax:(866)461-6469
Co. E-mail: admin@ifma-toronto.org
URL: http://www.ifma-toronto.org
Contact: Geoff Williams, Pres.
Description: Facilities management professionals. Promotes professionalism in the practice of facilities management; encourages professional advancement of members. Conducts continuing professional development courses; formulates and enforces standards of practice and ethics in facilities management. Conducts research; makes available job referral services; facilitates communication among members. **Publications:** *Facility Management Journal* (bimonthly); *IFMA Membership Services Directory* (periodic); *IFMA News* (monthly); *Toronto News* .

2570 ■ International Sanitary Supply Association
7373 N Lincoln Ave.
Lincolnwood, IL 60712-1799
Ph:(847)982-0800
Free: 800-225-4772
Fax:(847)982-1012
Co. E-mail: info@issa.com
URL: http://www.issa.com
Contact: John Garfinkel, Exec. Dir.
Description: Manufacturers, distributors, wholesalers, manufacturer representatives, publishers, and associate members of cleaning and maintenance supplies, chemicals, and equipment used by janitors, custodians, and maintenance workers in all types of industrial, commercial, and institutional buildings. Represents members in 83 countries. Produces videos and other educational materials. Offers specialized education seminars. **Publications:** *ISSA Today* (bimonthly); *Legislative and Regulatory Update* (monthly).

2571 ■ Sanitary Supply Wholesaling Association
PO Box 98
Swanton, OH 43558
Ph:(419)825-3055
Fax:(419)825-1815
Co. E-mail: info@sswa.com
URL: http://www.sswa.com
Contact: Donna R. Frendt, Exec. Dir.
Description: Wholesalers and manufacturers of janitorial supplies and/or paper products. Seeks to create integrity and recognition of wholesale distribution in the sanitary supply industry. **Publications:** *The Wholesaler* (quarterly);Membership Directory (annual).

EDUCATIONAL PROGRAMS

2572 ■ Air Conditioning and Refrigeration
American Trainco, Inc.
9785 S Maroon Cir., Ste. 300
PO Box 3397
Englewood, CO 80112
Free: 877-978-7246
Fax:(303)531-4565
Co. E-mail: Sales@AmericanTrainco.com
URL: http://www.americantrainco.com
Price: $990.00. **Description:** A two-day course for building, plant, and facility maintenance personnel. Covers understanding principles, components and systems, maintenance, troubleshooting, and operating efficiency. **Locations:** Cities throughout the United States.

2573 ■ Basic Electricity for the Non Electrician (In-House Training)
American Trainco, Inc.
9785 S Maroon Cir., Ste. 300
PO Box 3397
Englewood, CO 80112
Free: 877-978-7246
Fax:(303)531-4565
Co. E-mail: Sales@AmericanTrainco.com
URL: http://www.americantrainco.com
Price: $990.00. **Description:** A two-day hands on training course for building, plant, and facility maintenance personnel. **Locations:** Cities throughout the United States.

2574 ■ Boiler Operation, Maintenance and Safety (In-House Training)
American Trainco, Inc.
9785 S Maroon Cir., Ste. 300
PO Box 3397
Englewood, CO 80112
Free: 877-978-7246
Fax:(303)531-4565
Co. E-mail: Sales@AmericanTrainco.com
URL: http://www.americantrainco.com
Price: $990.00. **Description:** A two-day training course for everyday building, plant, and facility maintenance. **Locations:** Cities throughout the United States.

2575 ■ Electric Motors, Drives and Control Circuits (In-House Training)
American Trainco, Inc.
9785 S Maroon Cir., Ste. 300
PO Box 3397
Englewood, CO 80112
Free: 877-978-7246
Fax:(303)531-4565
Co. E-mail: Sales@AmericanTrainco.com
URL: http://www.americantrainco.com
Price: $990.00. **Description:** A practical course for maintenance personnel working in industrial plants, public facilities, and commercial buildings. **Locations:** Cities throughout the United States.

2576 ■ HVAC Controls and Air Distribution
American Trainco, Inc.
9785 S Maroon Cir., Ste. 300
PO Box 3397
Englewood, CO 80112
Free: 877-978-7246
Fax:(303)531-4565
Co. E-mail: Sales@AmericanTrainco.com
URL: http://www.americantrainco.com
Price: $990.00. **Description:** A two-day course that teaches how to maximize HVAC comfort and efficiency. **Locations:** Cities throughout the United States.

2577 ■ Maintenance Welding
American Trainco, Inc.
9785 S Maroon Cir., Ste. 300
PO Box 3397
Englewood, CO 80112
Free: 877-978-7246
Fax:(303)531-4565
Co. E-mail: Sales@AmericanTrainco.com
URL: http://www.americantrainco.com
Price: $985.00. **Description:** Covers the fundamental, practical applications, and best practices of maintenance welding. **Locations:** Cities throughout the United States.

2578 ■ National College of Appraisal and Property Management
Professional Career Development Institute
430 Technology Pky.
Norcross, GA 30092
Ph:(770)729-8400
Free: 800-224-7234
Fax:(770)729-0961
URL: http://www.pcdi.com
Description: Home study course on property management. I

2579 ■ Pumps and Pump Systems
American Trainco, Inc.
9785 S Maroon Cir., Ste. 300
PO Box 3397
Englewood, CO 80112
Free: 877-978-7246
Fax:(303)531-4565
Co. E-mail: Sales@AmericanTrainco.com
URL: http://www.americantrainco.com
Price: $990.00. **Description:** A comprehensive course designed to benefit mechanics, operators, consulting and design engineers, and multi-craft maintenance technicians. **Locations:** Cities throughout the United States.

2580 ■ Total Productive Maintenance and 5S (In-House Training)
American Trainco, Inc.
9785 S Maroon Cir., Ste. 300
PO Box 3397
Englewood, CO 80112
Free: 877-978-7246
Fax:(303)531-4565
Co. E-mail: Sales@AmericanTrainco.com
URL: http://www.americantrainco.com
Price: $990.00. **Description:** A two-day seminar designed to help reduce breakdowns, stoppages, and lower costs. **Locations:** Cities throughout the United States.

2581 ■ Toubleshooting Mechanical Drive Systems and Rotating Equipment
American Trainco, Inc.
9785 S Maroon Cir., Ste. 300
PO Box 3397
Englewood, CO 80112
Free: 877-978-7246
Fax:(303)531-4565
Co. E-mail: Sales@AmericanTrainco.com
URL: http://www.americantrainco.com
Price: $890.00. **Description:** A practical course designed for building facility and industrial plant maintenance technicians. **Locations:** Cities throughout the United States.

2582 ■ Understanding and Troubleshooting Hydraulics
American Trainco, Inc.
9785 S Maroon Cir., Ste. 300
PO Box 3397
Englewood, CO 80112
Free: 877-978-7246
Fax:(303)531-4565
Co. E-mail: Sales@AmericanTrainco.com
URL: http://www.americantrainco.com
Price: $990.00. **Description:** A two-day training course for everyday building, plant, and facility maintenance, including systems and components and identifying and fixing common problems. **Locations:** Cities throughout the United States.

DIRECTORIES OF EDUCATIONAL PROGRAMS

2583 ■ *Directory of Private Accredited Career Schools and Colleges of Technology*
Pub: Accrediting Commission of Career Schools and Colleges of Technology
Contact: Michale S. McComis, Exec. Dir.
Released: On web page. **Price:** Free. **Description:** Covers 3900 accredited post-secondary programs that provide training programs in business, trade, and technical fields, including various small business endeavors. Entries offer school name, address, phone, description of courses, job placement assistance, and requirements for admission. Arrangement is alphabetical.

REFERENCE WORKS

2584 ■ "ABM Janitorial Services Receives Service Excellence Award from Jones Lang LaSalle" in *Investment Weekly News* (July 16, 2011, pp. 75)
Pub: News RX
Description: ABM Janitorial Services was awarded the 2010 Jones Lang LaSalle Distinction award in the category of Service Excellence. LaSalle is a leading financial and professional services firm that specializes in real estate services and investment management. The program recognizes supplier partners who play a vital role in LaSalle's aim to provide the highest quality of services, value and innovation to clients.

2585 ■ "As Tradesmen Age, New Workers In Short Supply" in *Boston Business Journal* (Vol. 27, November 9, 2007, No. 41, pp. 1)
Pub: American City Business Journals Inc.
Ed: Jackie Noblett. **Description:** It is becoming more difficult to find young people who have the skills for installation and maintenance businesses. Some businesses are unable to complete contracts on time due to lack of staff. Unions are making efforts to address the expected shortfall of laborers in the coming years through apprenticeship programs.

2586 ■ "Brief: Janitorial Company Must Pay Back Wages" in *Buffalo News* (September 24, 2011)
Pub: The Buffalo News
Ed: Jonathan D. Epstein. **Description:** Knights Facilities Management, located in Michigan, provides grounds maintenance and janitorial services at the Ralph Wilson Stadium in Buffalo, New York. The US Department of Labor ordered the firm to pay $22,000 in back wages and damages to 26 employees for overtime and minimum wage compensation. Details of the company's violation of the Fair Labor Standards Act are included.

2587 ■ "Bringing Charities More Bang for Their Buck" in *Crain's Chicago Business* (Vol. 34, May 23, 2011, No. 21, pp. 31)
Pub: Crain Communications Inc.
Ed: Lisa Bertagnoli. **Description:** Marcy-Newberry Association connects charities with manufacturers in order to use excess items such as clothing, janitorial and office supplies.

2588 ■ "Butane Heated Pressure Washer Offers Diverse Cleaning Options" in *Product News Network* (March 8, 2011)
Pub: Product News Network
Description: Profile of the Super Max (TM) 6000B power sprayer the can clean with cold or heated water and wet steam. Daimer Industries, provider of janitorial supplies, announced the availability of the machine that offers a variety of cleaning options for a range of applications.

2589 ■ "Jacksonville-based Interline Expanding in Janitorial-Sanitation Market" in *Florida Times-Union* (May 10, 2011)
Pub: Florida Times-Union
Ed: Mark Basch. **Description:** Interline Brands Inc., located in Jacksonville, Florida, aims to grow its business with two recent acquisitions of firms that distribute janitorial and sanitation products. Interline markets and distributes maintenance, repair and operations products.

2590 ■ "Janitorial Equipment and Supplies US Market" in *PR Newswire* (October 24, 2011)
Pub: PR Newswire
Description: United States demand for janitorial equipment and supplies (excluding chemical products) is predicted to rise 2.4 percent per year to $7.6 billion in 2013. New product development will lead to increased sales of higher-value goods in the industry.

2591 ■ "Knox County Schools Debate Outsourcing Janitorial Services" in (March 29, 2011)
Pub: Knoxville News Sentinel
Ed: Lola Alapo. **Description:** Custodial services of Knox County Schools in Tennessee may be outsourced in move to save money for the school district. Details of the proposed program are included.

2592 ■ "Our Company is Dedicated to the Environment, But We Work With Vendors that Aren't" in *Inc.* (March 2008, pp. 78)
Pub: Gruner & Jahr USA Publishing
Ed: Myra Goodman. **Description:** Insight into working with vendors, such as construction and janitorial contractors, to comploy with your company's environmental policies is given.

2593 ■ "Pride Lands Janitorial Work at New Terminal" in *Sacramento Business Journal* (Vol. 28, June 10, 2011, No. 15, pp. 1)
Pub: Sacramento Business Journal
Ed: Kelly Johnson. **Description:** Pride Industries Inc. won the five-year $9.4 million contract to clean the Sacramento International Airport's new Terminal B, which will open in fall 2011. The nonprofit organization posts a revenue of $191 million for 2011 and currently employs more than 2,400 people with disabilities. The contract is expected to provide savings of over $3 million a year to the airport.

2594 ■ *Sanitary Maintenance—Buyers' Guide Issue*
Pub: Trade Press Media Group
Contact: Dan Weltin, Editor-in-Chief
E-mail: dan.weltin@tradepress.com
Released: Annual, Latest edition 2008. **Publication Includes:** List of manufacturers and suppliers of equipment and products for the sanitary and janitorial supplies and building service contractors industry. **Entries Include:** Companyname, address, phone, fax, trade and brand names, products or services. **Arrangement:** Alphabetical. **Indexes:** Product/service.

2595 ■ "Staples Advantage Receives NJPA National Contract for Janitorial Supplies" in *Professional Services Close-Up* (April 22, 2011)
Pub: Close-Up Media
Description: Staples Advantage, the business-to-business division of Staples Inc. was awarded a contract for janitorial supplies to members of the National Joint Powers Alliance (NJPA). NJPA is a member-owned buying cooperative serving public and private schools, state and local governments, and nonprofit organizations.

2596 ■ "U Overhauling Its Janitorial Program, but Custodians Taking Exception" in *Saint Paul Pioneer Press* (August 20, 2011)
Pub: McClatchy-Tribune Regional News
Ed: Mila Koumpilova. **Description:** University of Minnesota developed a new team cleaning approach for its campus. The new custodian program will save $3.1 million annually while providing a cleaner campus. The union representing the custodians questions both claims.

STATISTICAL SOURCES

2597 ■ *RMA Annual Statement Studies*
Pub: Robert Morris Associates (RMA)
Released: Annual. **Price:** $175.00 2006-07 edition, $105.00. **Description:** Contains composite balance sheets and income statements for more than 360 industries, including the accounting, auditing, and bookkeeping industries. Also contains five years of comparative historical data for discerning trends. Includes 16 commonly used ratios, computed for most of the size groupings for nearly every industry.

TRADE PERIODICALS

2598 ■ *American Window Cleaner Magazine*
Pub: American Window Cleaner Magazine
Contact: Richard Fabry, Consultant
Released: Bimonthly. **Price:** $45 U.S.; $50 Canada; $70 other countries overseas; $80 U.S. two years; $90 Canada two years; $130 other countries overseas. **Description:** Designed to make professional window cleaners work faster, safer and more profitably.

2599 ■ *Contracting Profits*
Pub: Trade Press Media Group
Contact: Dan Weltin, Editor-in-Chief
E-mail: dan.weltin@tradepress.com
Released: 10/yr. **Description:** Trade magazine covering business and operations management issues for commercial and institutional building cleaning service contractors.

2600 ■ *Maintenance Management Newsletter*
Pub: Springfield Resources
Contact: Joel Levitt
Ed: Joel Levitt, Editor, jdl@maintrainer.com. **Released:** Monthly. **Price:** Free. **Description:** Provides information of interest to maintenance professionals and plant engineers. Recurring features include interviews, a calendar of events, book reviews, news of educational opportunities, and notices of publications available. Remarks: Available online only

2601 ■ *Maintenance Supplies*
Pub: Cygnus Business Media Inc.
Contact: Arlette Sambs, Publisher
E-mail: arlette.sambs@maintenancesuppliesmang.com
Ed: Bill Swichtenberg, Editor, bill.swichtenberg@maintenancesuppliesmag.com. **Released:** 7/yr. **Description:** Magazine covering the sanitary supplies industry, geared toward distributors and manufacturers' agents.

2602 ■ *Services*
Pub: Building Service Contractors Association Int'l.
Contact: Trevilynn Blakeslee, Managing Editor
Released: Bimonthly. **Price:** $24 members; $30 nonmembers; $48 other countries members; $54 other countries non-members. **Description:** Trade journal for maintenance and cleaning contractors and facility management companies.

VIDEOCASSETTES/ AUDIOCASSETTES

2603 ■ *School Housekeeping*
AMS Distributors, Inc.
PO Box 658
Lady Lake, FL 32158
Free: 800-424-3464
Fax:(352)750-5635
Co. E-mail: orders@vpats.com
URL: http://www.vpats.com
Released: 1989. **Price:** $1980.00. **Description:** Learn to keep all areas of your school from looking dingy through the techniques illustrated in this series. **Availability:** VHS; 3/4U.

2604 ■ *Supervisory Series*
AMS Distributors, Inc.
PO Box 658
Lady Lake, FL 32158
Free: 800-424-3464
Fax:(352)750-5635
Co. E-mail: orders@vpats.com
URL: http://www.vpats.com
Released: 1986. **Description:** A series training custodial supervisors in staff management. **Availability:** VHS; 3/4U.

TRADE SHOWS AND CONVENTIONS

2605 ■ Cleaning Management Conference and Exposition
Advanstar Communications
641 Lexington Ave., 8th Fl.
New York, NY 10022
Ph:(212)951-6600
Fax:(212)951-6793
Co. E-mail: info@advanstar.com
URL: http://www.advanstar.com
Released: Annual. **Audience:** Housekeeping/environmental services directors, building maintenance and services managers, directors of plant facilities, and related personnel. **Principal Exhibits:** Cleaning equipment, supplies, and services, including brooms, cleaning chemicals, carpet extractors, computer systems, floor machines, floor pads and sealers, mops, paper products, pressure washer pumps, safety equipment, soaps and sponges, steam cleaning equipment and chemicals, stripping machines, vacuum cleaners, and wringers.

CONSULTANTS

2606 ■ Cleaning Consultant Services Inc.
3693 E Marginal Way S
PO Box 1273
Seattle, WA 98134
Ph:(206)682-9748
Fax:(206)622-6876
Co. E-mail: ccs@cleaningconsultants.com
URL: http://www.cleaningconsultants.com
Contact: Wm. R. Griffin, President
E-mail: wgriffin@cleaningconsultants.com
Scope: Management consultants to cleaning and maintenance contractors, property managers, hospitals, schools, hotels, building owners, facility directors, and small business owners in the cleaning industry. Services are designed to increase efficiency and profit through training and the use of time-saving techniques on the job; increase the useful life of building surfaces and equipment; encourage self development of cleaning and maintenance professionals; and make the world a clean and safe place to live. Specific consulting services are related to cleaning contract specifications development and negotiation, claim and dispute resolution, certified carpet and floor covering inspection and corrections, expert court testimony, independent certified cleaning and maintenance inspections, training program and materials development, building startup and long-range maintenance planning, architect and engineering services regarding cleaning, and building maintenance. Serves all industries in need of cleaning and maintenance services. **Publications:** "Raising the Bar with Science, Training and Upward Mobility," Jan, 2010; "Technology Revolutionizes the Cleaning Process "Cleaning for Health" is the New Mantra," Distribution Sales and Management Magazine, May, 2003; "Bill Griffin's Crystal Balls-Cleaning Trends in the Usa 2001," Floor Care is Hot in 2001," Mar, 2001; "In-clean Magazine (Australia), Feb, 2001; "Maintaining Swimming Pools, Spas, Whirlpool Tubs and Saunas," Executive House keeping, Feb, 2001; "Whats New with Floor Care," 2001. **Seminars:** Stone Maintenance Technician (SMT) IICRC Certification Course; Carpet Cleaning Technician; Apprentice/Basic Skills; Organizing Custodial Operations for Maximum Efficiency: How to Sell & Price Contract Cleaning; Starting a House cleaning Business; Rugs & Carpet Cleaning; How to Start and Operate a Successful Cleaning Business; Cleaning Schools in the 2000and Beyond; Bringing About and Working Through Change; Organizing Custodial Operations for Maximum Efficiency; Floor Care Technician (FCT)11 CPC Certified Course; Administering Cleaning Service Contracts.

2607 ■ Erin Services Inc.
111 Travelers Way
PO Box 1048
Saint Simons Island, GA 31522-5632
Ph:(912)638-9916
Free: 800-862-5361
Fax:(912)638-5701
Co. E-mail: dennisd@ns.technonet.com
Contact: Dennis J. Donnelly III, President
E-mail: dennis179@yahoo.com
Scope: Offers assistance in technical proposal production, marketing, and research. Industries served: Food service, janitorial, landscaping, hospitality and lodging, parks, and recreational.

FRANCHISES AND BUSINESS OPPORTUNITIES

2608 ■ 1-800-Got-Junk?
1055 W Hastings St., 14th Fl.
Vancouver, BC, Canada V6E 2E9
Free: 877-408-5865
Fax:(801)751-0634
Co. E-mail: franopps@1800gotjunk.com
URL: http://www.1800gotjunk.com
No. of Franchise Units: 119. **No. of Company-Owned Units:** 1. **Founded:** 1989. **Franchised:** 1999. **Description:** Junk removal service. **Equity Capital Needed:** $60,000-$90,000 minimum, $6,000 for each additional territory. **Franchise Fee:** $16,000+. **Financial Assistance:** SBA registered. **Training:** 1 week at corporate training center, 2 day site visit post launch.

2609 ■ 360Clean
3032 W Montague Ave., Ste. 103
Charleston, SC 29418
Ph:888-241-4865
Free: 888-321-4553
Fax:888-241-4665
Co. E-mail: barry@360clean.com
URL: http://www.360cleanfranchise.com
No. of Franchise Units: 25. **No. of Company-Owned Units:** 1. **Founded:** 2004. **Franchised:** 2007. **Description:** Commercial cleaning. **Equity Capital Needed:** $50,000. **Franchise Fee:** $29,500-$75,000. **Financial Assistance:** Yes. **Training:** Yes.

2610 ■ Aerowest Restroom Deodorizing Service
West Sanitation Services, Inc.
3882 Del Amo Blvd., Ste. 602
Torrance, CA 90503
Ph:(310)793-4242
Fax:(310)793-4250
No. of Franchise Units: 44. **No. of Company-Owned Units:** 36. **Founded:** 1983. **Franchised:** 1983. **Description:** Restroom deodorizing dispenser service. **Equity Capital Needed:** $10,000. **Franchise Fee:** $6,000. **Financial Assistance:** Yes. **Training:** Yes.

2611 ■ Aire-Master of America, Inc.
PO Box 2310
Nixa, MO 65810-2310
Ph:(417)725-2691
Free: 800-525-0957
Fax:(417)725-5737
No. of Franchise Units: 65. **No. of Company-Owned Units:** 5. **Founded:** 1958. **Franchised:** 1976. **Description:** Room deodorizing, restroom deodorizing and disinfecting service. **Equity Capital Needed:** $32,000 start-up cash, $32,000-$85,000 total investment. **Franchise Fee:** $28,000. **Financial Assistance:** Yes. **Training:** Yes.

2612 ■ A All Animal Control
PO Box 330087-8087
Northglenn, CO 80233
Ph:(304)345-1511
No. of Franchise Units: 16. **Founded:** 1995. **Franchised:** 2000. **Description:** wildlife management. **Equity Capital Needed:** $10,000-30,000. **Franchise Fee:** $5,000. **Financial Assistance:** Yes. **Training:** Yes.

2613 ■ American Restoration Services
22 Rutgers Rd.
Pittsburgh, PA 15215
Ph:(412)351-7100
Free: 800-245-1617
No. of Franchise Units: 262. **No. of Company-Owned Units:** 1. **Founded:** 1970. **Franchised:** 1976. **Description:** General restoration of homes and commercial structures, using a unique line of cleaning and sealing products. **Equity Capital Needed:** $22,500, includes franchise fees. **Franchise Fee:** $12,500 (U.S.F.). **Financial Assistance:** Yes. **Training:** Yes.

2614 ■ Anago Franchising, Inc.
Anago Cleaning Systems, Inc.
1100 Park Central Blvd., Ste. 1200
Pompano Beach, FL 33064
Free: 800-213-5857
Fax:(954)752-1200
URL: http://www.anagousa.com
No. of Franchise Units: 1,000. **Founded:** 1989. **Franchised:** 1991. **Description:** Janitorial service. **Equity Capital Needed:** $140,000-$180,000 Master City, $5,000 unit. **Franchise Fee:** $150,000-$800,000 Master. **Financial Assistance:** Yes. **Training:** Onsite training.

2615 ■ Bonus Building Care
Bonus of America
PO Box 300
Indianola, OK 74442
Ph:(918)823-4990
Free: 800-931-1102
Fax:(918)823-4994
Co. E-mail: franchisees@bonusbuildingcare.com
URL: http://www.bonusbuildingcare.com
No. of Franchise Units: 1,778. **No. of Company-Owned Units:** 2. **Founded:** 1996. **Franchised:** 1996. **Description:** Commercial cleaning. **Equity Capital Needed:** $1,000. **Franchise Fee:** $7,500. **Financial Assistance:** Financing guaranteed. A down payment of $1,000 starts your business and guarantees financing of the franchise fee, equipment, supplies and growth. **Training:** Intensive initial training, extended training and special services training all included at no additional cost. Flexible, onsite training coupled with comprehensive written guides gets you up and running.

2616 ■ BuildingStars Inc.
11489 Page Service Dr.
St. Louis, MO 63146
Ph:(314)991-3356
Fax:(314)991-3198
URL: http://www.buildingstars.com
No. of Franchise Units: 310. **Founded:** 1994. **Franchised:** 2000. **Description:** Commercial cleaning services. **Equity Capital Needed:** $2,195-$52,795. **Franchise Fee:** $995-$38,595. **Royalty Fee:** 10%. **Financial Assistance:** In-house financing available. **Training:** 1 week at corporate headquarters with ongoing support.

2617 ■ Certapro Painters
The Franchise Company
150 Green Tree Rd.
Oaks, PA 19456
Free: 800-689-7494
Fax:(610)650-9997
No. of Franchise Units: 325. **Founded:** 1992. **Franchised:** 1992. **Description:** Residential and commercial painting franchise. **Equity Capital Needed:** $129,000-$156,000. **Franchise Fee:** $50,000. **Financial Assistance:** No. **Training:** 2 weeks of training prior to start-up; quarterly training in field. Advance training is also provided.

2618 ■ Chemstation International Inc.
3400 Encrete Ln.
Dayton, OH 45439
Ph:(937)297-8265
Free: 800-554-8265
Fax:(937)534-0426
No. of Franchise Units: 49. **No. of Company-Owned Units:** 2. **Founded:** 1979. **Franchised:** 1981. **Description:** Manufactures and distributes detergents in bulk. **Equity Capital Needed:** $500,000-$600,000. **Franchise Fee:** $45,000. **Financial Assistance:** Yes. **Training:** Yes.

2619 ■ City Wide Maintenance Franchise Co.
8460 Nieman Rd.
Lenexa, KS 66214
Ph:(913)888-5700
Free: (866)887-4029
Fax:(913)888-5151
No. of Franchise Units: 32. **No. of Company-Owned Units:** 1. **Founded:** 1959. **Franchised:** 2001. **Description:** Maintenance services. **Equity Capital Needed:** $102,325-$225,700. **Franchise Fee:** $60,000-$125,000. **Royalty Fee:** 5%. **Financial Assistance:** Assistance with franchise fee. **Training:** Offers 2 weeks at headquarters, 2 weeks at franchisees location, annual training meeting with ongoing support.

2620 ■ Clean & Happy Windows
10019 Des Moines Memorial Dr.
Seattle, WA 98168
Free: (866)762-7617
Fax:(206)762-7637
No. of Franchise Units: 2. **Founded:** 1990. **Franchised:** 1999. **Description:** Franchise offers maintenance and cleaning of windows. **Equity Capital Needed:** $1,000-$3,000. **Franchise Fee:** $4,000. **Financial Assistance:** No. **Training:** Yes.

2621 ■ Clean Living Specialists
2742 Joseph Blvd., Ste. 10
Orleans, ON, Canada K1C 1G5
Ph:(613)860-0436
Free: (866)244-4434
Fax:(613)830-9445
Co. E-mail: admin@cleanliving.net
URL: http://www.cleanliving.net
No. of Franchise Units: 11. **No. of Company-Owned Units:** 14. **Founded:** 1988. **Description:** Clean living specialists offer residential cleaning services. **Equity Capital Needed:** $20,000-$25,000; $150,000 master franchise. **Training:** Provides 2 weeks in Kanata, Ontario, 1 month in new business, followed by ongoing support.

2622 ■ The Cleaning Authority
7230 Lee Deforest Dr.
Columbia, MD 21046
Ph:(410)740-1900
Free: 877-504-6221
URL: http://www.thecleaningauthority.com
No. of Franchise Units: 160. **No. of Company-Owned Units:** 1. **Founded:** 1978. **Franchised:** 1996. **Description:** Cleaning service. **Equity Capital Needed:** $90,000 -$110,000. **Franchise Fee:** $30,000-$50,000. **Financial Assistance:** Third party financing. **Training:** 2 week home office training; onsite visits, quarterly newsletter, ongoing training sessions.

2623 ■ Cleaning Consultant Services Inc.
PO Box 1273
Seattle, WA 98111
Ph:(206)682-9748
No. of Franchise Units: 2. **No. of Company-Owned Units:** 3. **Founded:** 1976. **Franchised:** 1978. **Description:** Support services to those who own, manage and/or supervise cleaning operations. **Equity Capital Needed:** $7,500. **Franchise Fee:** $2,500. **Managerial Assistance:** Manuals and onsite visits provided. **Training:** 2-3 days at out training site in Seattle, WA.

2624 ■ Cleannet USA, Inc.
9861 Broken Land Pky., Ste. 208
Columbia, MD 21046
Ph:(301)621-8838
Free: 800-735-8838
Fax:(410)720-5307
No. of Franchise Units: 3,338. **No. of Company-Owned Units:** 464. **Founded:** 1987. **Franchised:** 1988. **Description:** Commercial facility cleaning services. **Equity Capital Needed:** $1,500-$100,000 for a master franchise. **Franchise Fee:** $3,200-$200,000. **Financial Assistance:** Yes. **Training:** Yes.

2625 ■ Clintar Groundskeeping Services
Truserve Groundcare Inc.
70 Esna Park Dr., Unit 1
Markham, ON, Canada L3R 1E3
Ph:(905)943-9530
Free: 800-361-3542
Fax:(905)943-9529
Co. E-mail: info@clintar.com
URL: http://www.clintar.com
No. of Franchise Units: 21. **Founded:** 1973. **Franchised:** 1984. **Description:** Grounds keeping services including landscape maintenance, snow and ice control, power sweeping, light construction, tree care and irrigation maintenance. **Equity Capital Needed:** $100,000-$125,000; $50,000-$60,000 cash. **Franchise Fee:** $40,000. **Financial Assistance:** No. **Training:** Yes.

2626 ■ Coustic-Glo
CGI International Inc.
7111 Ohms Ln.
Minneapolis, MN 55439
Ph:(952)835-1338
Free: 800-333-8523
Fax:(952)835-1395
Co. E-mail: cgiinc@aol.com
URL: http://www.cousticglo.com
No. of Franchise Units: 100. **No. of Company-Owned Units:** 1. **Founded:** 1978. **Franchised:** 1988. **Description:** Offers a unique opportunity for an individual to pursue financial independence in a virtually untapped industry. The need for ceiling and wall cleaning and restoration is everywhere. Coustic-Glo franchisees are provided with all of the equipment, products, cleaning solutions and the training necessary to prosper in the field. Assistance with field problems, technical questions, etc. Complete test reports on all products are provided, with updating as necessary. A very aggressive national advertising campaign is pursued. Local ad mats and all product identification are provided. **Equity Capital Needed:** $18,000-$32,000. **Franchise Fee:** $15,000-$25,000. **Financial Assistance:** Company offers limited financing. **Training:** Provided with a very intensive 2-3 day training program that takes place in his/her respective exclusive area, under the direct supervision of an experienced franchisee that is brought in form his/her area to assist in the establishment of the new franchisees business. Also available to the new franchisee is the option of a training course provided at the home office under the direct supervision of home office personnel.

2627 ■ Coverall Health-Based Cleaning System
5201 Congress Ave., Ste. 275
Boca Raton, FL 33487
Ph:(516)922-2500
Free: 888-435-9584

Fax:(561)922-2423
Co. E-mail: info@coverall.com
URL: http://www.coverall.com

No. of Franchise Units: 9,468. **Founded:** 1985. **Franchised:** 1985. **Description:** One of the nation's leading commercial cleaning franchise companies with 6,000+ Franchise Owners worldwide. Franchisees are provided with training, equipment, billing & collection services, a quality control program, & a customer base. Ranked as the fastest growing commercial cleaning franchise in the nation by Entrepreneur's 22nd Annual 'Franchise 500'. **Equity Capital Needed:** $10,812-$37,585. **Franchise Fee:** $10,000-$32,200. **Financial Assistance:** flexible credit and leasing options. **Training:** Hands-on training introduces franchisees to innovative cleaning techniques, the latest technology, management, sales and marketing, as well as environmental, safety and security procedures.

2628 ■ Executive Business Maintenance Franchise
5931 Stanley Ave., Ste. S-6
Carmichael, CA 95608
Free: 877-326-8787
Fax:(916)484-3854

Founded: 1996. **Franchised:** 2006. **Description:** Janitorial contract brokerage services. **Equity Capital Needed:** $59,000-$89,000. **Franchise Fee:** $35,000. **Royalty Fee:** 8%. **Financial Assistance:** No. **Training:** Offers 5 business days at headquarters, 5 business days at franchisee's location and ongoing support.

2629 ■ Fibreclean Supplies Ltd.
3750-19th St. NE, Ste. 101
Calgary, AB, Canada T2E 6V2
Ph:(403)291-3991
Free: 800-661-8548
Fax:(403)291-2295
Co. E-mail: kbrown@fibreclean.com
URL: http://www.fibreclean.com

No. of Franchise Units: 1. **No. of Company-Owned Units:** 4. **Founded:** 1977. **Description:** Distributes specialty wholesale supplies to the cleaning industry. One of the soft fibre suppliers in Canada. **Equity Capital Needed:** $70,000-$100,000 minimum investment. **Franchise Fee:** Varies by territory. **Training:** 2 weeks initial and ongoing support.

2630 ■ Fish Window Cleaning
200 Enchanted Pky.
Manchester, MO 63021
Ph:(636)530-7334
Free: 877-707-3474
Fax:(636)530-7856
Co. E-mail: info@fishwindowcleaning.com
URL: http://www.fishwindowcleaning.com

No. of Franchise Units: 220. **No. of Company-Owned Units:** 1. **Founded:** 1978. **Franchised:** 1998. **Description:** Residential and commercial low-rise window cleaning. **Equity Capital Needed:** $59,900-$127,000. **Franchise Fee:** $19,900-$49,900. **Financial Assistance:** Assist with third party or indirect financing. **Managerial Assistance:** Quarterly newsletter, toll-free number, proprietary software, technical support and home page. **Training:** Intensive 10 day training in St. Louis followed by 4 days in franchisee territory. On-going support included.

2631 ■ Goodbye Graffiti Inc.
950 Powell St.
Vancouver, BC, Canada V6A 1H9
Free: 877-684-4747
Fax:(604)684-4547
Co. E-mail: amaddison@goodbyegraffiti.com
URL: http://www.goodbyegraffiti.com

No. of Franchise Units: 11. **Founded:** 1997. **Franchised:** 2000. **Description:** The company is into graffiti removal and abatement franchises. Specializes in environmentally friendly graffiti removal from all surfaces and long-term maintenance. **Equity Capital Needed:** $60-$100,000. **Franchise Fee:** $27,000. **Training:** 2 weeks and ongoing support provided.

2632 ■ International Master Care Janitorial Franchising Inc.
555-6 St., Ste. 327
New Westminster, BC, Canada V3L 5H1
Ph:(604)525-8221
Free: 800-889-2799

No. of Franchise Units: 95. **No. of Company-Owned Units:** 1. **Founded:** 1987. **Franchised:** 1987. **Description:** Commercial cleaning service. **Equity Capital Needed:** $10,000-$150,000. **Franchise Fee:** $6,000-$120,000. **Financial Assistance:** Yes. **Training:** Yes.

2633 ■ Jani-King International, Inc.
16885 Dallas Pky.
Addison, TX 75001
Ph:(972)991-0900
Free: 800-552-5264
Fax:(972)239-7706
Co. E-mail: info@janiking.com
URL: http://www.janiking.com

No. of Franchise Units: 10,500. **No. of Company-Owned Units:** 32. **Founded:** 1969. **Franchised:** 1974. **Description:** Offers entrepreneurs a proven system for operating a business involved in the cleaning of office buildings, retail, medical and other facilities. Franchisees in this growth industry are owner/operators of their own businesses who also have access to regional support centers. **Equity Capital Needed:** $8,200-$33,550 and up. FFE $5,500-$15,750 and up. **Financial Assistance:** Master & associate franchises are also Available. **Training:** Training covers cleaning, personnel, client relations, proposals and sales.

2634 ■ Jantize America
8421 Old Statesville Rd., Ste. 1
Charlotte, NC 28269
Free: 888-540-0001

No. of Franchise Units: 167. **Founded:** 1988. **Franchised:** 1988. **Description:** Commercial cleaning. **Equity Capital Needed:** $29,650-$171,500. **Franchise Fee:** $29,650-$150,500. **Royalty Fee:** 4%. **Financial Assistance:** Limited third party and in-house financing available. **Training:** Includes 3 days training at headquarters, 2 days at franchisee's location and ongoing support.

2635 ■ JDI Cleaning Systems
3380 S Service Rd.
Burlington, ON, Canada L7N 3J5
Ph:(905)634-5228
Free: 800-597-5091
Fax:(905)634-8790
Co. E-mail: jimbrogno@jdicleaning.com
URL: http://www.jdicleaning.com

No. of Franchise Units: 90. **No. of Company-Owned Units:** 1. **Founded:** 1992. **Franchised:** 1992. **Description:** Janitorial franchise. **Equity Capital Needed:** Varies dependent on program chosen. **Franchise Fee:** $10,000 (local); $50,000+ (master). **Training:** 5 days and on the job training provided.

2636 ■ KCS Applications Inc.
4955 Creaser Rd.
Westmoreland, NY 13490
Ph:(315)853-4805
Fax:(315)853-4805
Co. E-mail: kcsapplications@aol.com
URL: http://www.kcs1.com

No. of Franchise Units: 16. **Founded:** 1992. **Franchised:** 1994. **Description:** Asphalt maintenance service. **Equity Capital Needed:** $15,650. **Franchise Fee:** $15,000. **Royalty Fee:** $450/year. **Training:** 2 days at corporate headquarters, 1 day at franchisee's location and ongoing support provided.

2637 ■ Master Care
555 6 St., Ste. 327
New Westminster, BC, Canada V3L 5H1
Ph:(604)525-8221
Free: 800-889-2799
Fax:(604)526-2235
Co. E-mail: info@mastercare.com
URL: http://www.mastercare.com

No. of Franchise Units: 159. **No. of Company-Owned Units:** 1. **Founded:** 1987. **Franchised:** 1995. **Description:** The franchise system is in search of associate master franchisees for metropolitan areas. Provides training in commercial building cleaning. **Equity Capital Needed:** $18,000. **Franchise Fee:** $18,000. **Training:** Provides 3 weeks training and ongoing support.

2638 ■ Octoclean
Octoclean Franchising Systems
5225 Canyon Crest Dr., Ste. 71-339
Riverside, CA 92507
Ph:(951)683-5859
Free: (866)OCT-OCLN
Fax:(951)779-0270
Co. E-mail: chuck@octoclean.com
URL: http://www.octoclean.com

No. of Franchise Units: 196. **Founded:** 1983. **Franchised:** 2000. **Description:** Maintenance and cleaning services are provided. **Financial Assistance:** In-house financing. **Training:** Provides hands on training and ongoing support.

2639 ■ Office Pride Commercial Cleaning Services
Office Pride, Inc.
170 N Jackson St.
Franklin, IN 46131
Free: 888-641-2310
Fax:800-863-8708
URL: http://www.officepride.com

No. of Franchise Units: 93. **Founded:** 1992. **Franchised:** 1996. **Description:** Commercial cleaning service. **Equity Capital Needed:** $14,000-$35,500. **Franchise Fee:** $8,500. **Financial Assistance:** Available from the franchisor for qualified applicants. **Training:** 5 days of classroom training at corporate headquarters, follow-up training, and ongoing support.

2640 ■ Omex Office Maintenance Experts
Omex International, Inc.
205 House Ave.
Camp Hill, PA 17011
Ph:(717)737-7311
Free: 800-827-6639
Fax:(717)737-9271

No. of Franchise Units: 20. **No. of Company-Owned Units:** 1. **Founded:** 1979. **Franchised:** 1994. **Description:** Cleaning services. **Equity Capital Needed:** $40,000-$70,000, including working capital. **Franchise Fee:** $15,000-$25,000. **Financial Assistance:** No. **Training:** Yes.

2641 ■ Openworks
O.P.E.N. America, Inc.
4742 N 24th St., Ste. 300
Phoenix, AZ 85016
Ph:(602)224-0440
Free: 800-777-6736
Fax:(602)468-3788

No. of Franchise Units: 300. **Founded:** 1983. **Franchised:** 1983. **Description:** Offers maintenance and cleaning services. **Equity Capital Needed:** $16,450-$119,950. **Franchise Fee:** $15,200-$67,500. **Royalty Fee:** 10%. **Financial Assistance:** Assistance with franchise fee and equipment. **Training:** Offers training at headquarters and 2 weeks at franchisee's location and ongoing support.

2642 ■ Rainbow International
The Dwyer Group
1020 N University Parks Dr.
Waco, TX 76707
Free: (866)696-1504
Fax:800-209-7621
Co. E-mail: leadgeneration@dwyergroup.com
URL: http://www.rainbowintl.com

No. of Franchise Units: 179. **Founded:** 1981. **Franchised:** 1981. **Description:** Building Maintenance/Cleaning Service/Custodial Service. **Equity Capital Needed:** $103,900-$165,050; includes franchise fee, equipment package, and start-up costs. **Franchise Fee:** $22,000. **Financial Assistance:** Up to 70% of franchise fee and lease packages available, upon qualifying. **Training:** Ongoing support begins with a 2 week program, followed by field mentoring and seminars. Marketing concepts, operations, and the technical A, B, C's are taught. Experienced systems managers monitor the progress and are available for daily contact.

2643 ■ Scrubway
217 Ravenwood Rd.
Exton, PA 19341
Ph:(610)650-8270
Free: 800-355-3000
Fax:(610)650-3268
Co. E-mail: scrubway@comcast.net
No. of Franchise Units: 6. **No. of Company-Owned Units:** 1. **Founded:** 1994. **Franchised:** 1994. **Description:** Commercial restroom hygiene franchise. **Equity Capital Needed:** $50,000-$75,000. **Franchise Fee:** $25,000-$35,000. **Financial Assistance:** Yes. **Training:** Yes.

2644 ■ Service-Tech Corporation
7589 First Pl.
Oakwood Village, OH 44146
Ph:(440)735-1505
Free: 800-992-9302
Fax:(440)735-1433
No. of Franchise Units: 2. **No. of Company-Owned Units:** 2. **Founded:** 1960. **Franchised:** 1990. **Description:** Indoor air quality remediation and industrial cleaning services. Opportunity to join 33 years of experience in solving the growing concerns associated with indoor air pollution. The list of cleaning services offered includes air duct systems, industrial exhaust systems, industrial ovens, overhead structural steel, restaurant hood exhaust systems, laboratory hood exhaust systems, computer room subfloors, laundry and restroom exhaust systems. **Equity Capital Needed:** $13,000-$20,000 working capital, van lease and miscellaneous. **Franchise Fee:** $19,000 + equipment; $30,000. **Financial Assistance:** No. **Managerial Assistance:** Business and accounting forms, reference manuals, advertising and marketing supplies, open line communication with main office, continual updates on industry-related matters and safety. **Training:** 14 days training schedule conducted at the corporate training center, with hands-on field instruction at job sites. Training in marketing, sales, field operations, accounting, personnel and management trainings.

2645 ■ Steamatic, Inc.
BMS Enterprises, Inc.
3333 Quorum Dr., Ste. 280
Ft. Worth, TX 76137
Ph:(817)332-1575
Free: 800-527-1295
Fax:(817)332-5349
No. of Franchise Units: 391. **Founded:** 1948. **Franchised:** 1968. **Description:** Provides water, fire and storm insurance restoration (disaster recovery services); indoor environmental services, air duct and coil cleaning; carpet cleaning; furniture cleaning; drapery cleaning; deodorizing; wood restoration; document restoration; corrosion control; ceiling and wall cleaning. and 24-hour toll-free numbers. **Equity Capital Needed:** $95,000-$165,960. **Franchise Fee:** $7,000-$24,000. **Financial Assistance:** No. **Training:** Initial training is 2 weeks. Advanced training is optional. The first week concentrates on the various cleaning and restoration services. The second week is a mini-business school session. Classes consist of advertising and marketing procedures, selling techniques, accounting methods, financial management, telemarketing skill, commercial pricing, insurance, residential jobs, writing programs, maintenance contracts, brainstorming, role playing and much more.

2646 ■ Swisher Hygiene Franchise Corp.
Swisher International
4725 Piedmont Row Dr., No. 400
Charlotte, NC 28210
Ph:(704)364-7707
Free: 800-444-4138
No. of Franchise Units: 31. **No. of Company-Owned Units:** 42. **Founded:** 1983. **Franchised:** 1990. **Description:** Provides restroom sanitation and other cleaning services. **Equity Capital Needed:** $83,300-$173,900. **Franchise Fee:** $45,000-$75,000. **Royalty Fee:** 6%. **Financial Assistance:** Yes. **Training:** Provides 1 week at headquarters, 1 week at franchisee's location, and ongoing support.

2647 ■ System4
4700 Rockside Rd., No. 610
Independence, OH 44131
Ph:(216)524-6100
No. of Franchise Units: 1,302. **Founded:** 2003. **Franchised:** 2003. **Description:** Commercial cleaning. **Equity Capital Needed:** $6,156-$37,750. **Franchise Fee:** $4,400-$32,000. **Royalty Fee:** 5%. **Financial Assistance:** Limited in-house assistance available. **Training:** Training includes 3 days at franchisees location, 1 day each seminars and ongoing support.

2648 ■ Vacuvent Air Duct Cleaning
Vacuvent Franchising Inc.
13537 US Hwy 1, Ste. 106
Sebastian, FL 32958
Free: 800-690-7292
Fax:800-690-7295
No. of Franchise Units: 5. **No. of Company-Owned Units:** 5. **Founded:** 2003. **Franchised:** 2004. **Description:** Air duct cleaning. **Equity Capital Needed:** $3,500. **Franchise Fee:** $2,500. **Financial Assistance:** No. **Training:** Yes.

2649 ■ Vanguard Cleaning Systems, Inc
655 Mariners Island Blvd., Ste. 303
San Mateo, CA 94404
Ph:(650)287-2414
Free: 800-564-6422
Fax:(650)591-1545
Co. E-mail: wgreen@vanguardcleaning.com
URL: http://www.vanguardcleaning.com
No. of Franchise Units: 2,200. **No. of Company-Owned Units:** 3. **Founded:** 1984. **Franchised:** 1984. **Description:** Cleaning services. **Equity Capital Needed:** $250,000. **Franchise Fee:** $100,000-$400,000. **Financial Assistance:** No. **Training:** Initial training at headquarters followed by onsite training.

2650 ■ Window Brigade
Window Brigade, Inc.
4907 Hollenden Dr., Ste. 208
Raleigh, NC 27616
Ph:(919)834-8215
Free: (866)587-6243
Fax:(919)834-7630
No. of Franchise Units: 7. **No. of Company-Owned Units:** 1. **Founded:** 1989. **Franchised:** 2003. **Description:** Residential & commercial window cleaning. **Equity Capital Needed:** $36,500-$125,000. **Franchise Fee:** $6,000-$55,500. **Financial Assistance:** Yes. **Training:** Yes.

2651 ■ Window Genie
FOR Franchising, LLC
800 E Ross Ave.
Cincinnati, OH 45207
Free: 800-700-0022
URL: http://www.windowgenie.com
No. of Franchise Units: 125. **Founded:** 1994. **Franchised:** 1998. **Description:** Window cleaning service. **Equity Capital Needed:** $60,700-$128,600. **Franchise Fee:** $19,500-$57,000. **Royalty Fee:** 7%. **Financial Assistance:** Third party financing available. **Training:** Offers 5 days at headquarters, 5 days at franchisees location with ongoing support.

2652 ■ Window King
Window King, Inc.
40 West Littleton Blvd. Ste. 210-202
Littleton, CO 80120
Ph:(720)283-8002
Fax:(719)487-9702
No. of Franchise Units: 28. **No. of Company-Owned Units:** 2. **Founded:** 1997. **Franchised:** 1998. **Description:** Window cleaning services. **Equity Capital Needed:** $15,000-$30,000. **Franchise Fee:** $7,000. **Financial Assistance:** No. **Training:** Yes.

2653 ■ Wood Re New
220 S Dysart
Springfield, MO 65802
Ph:(417)865-3665
Fax:(417)833-5479
No. of Franchise Units: 22. **Founded:** 1993. **Franchised:** 2001. **Description:** Wood Re New offers maintenance and cleaning services. **Equity Capital Needed:** $60,000. **Franchise Fee:** $30,000. **Financial Assistance:** No. **Training:** Yes.

REFERENCE WORKS

2654 ■ *Computer Industry Almanac*
Pub: Computer Industry Almanac Inc.
Contact: Karen Petska, Author
Released: Annual. **Price:** $53, individuals paperback; $63, individuals hardcover. **Covers:** Over 3,000 firms involved in the computer industry in the U.S. **Entries Include:** Company Name, address, phone, fax, products, sales, number of employees, names and titles of key personnel, e-mail addresses, websites.

TRADE PERIODICALS

2655 ■ *DCLNews*
Pub: Data Conversion Laboratory
Contact: Mark Gross
Ed: Released: Monthly. **Price:** Included in membership;. **Description:** E-journal providing you insider information on XML and SGML, along with the latest technology and e-publishing news.

2656 ■ *Media Computing*
Pub: Dreamscape Productions
Ed: Sheridan Tatsuno, Editor, statsuno@aol.com. **Released:** Monthly. **Price:** $495, institutions in the U.S. and Canada; $550, institutions elsewhere. **Description:** Supplies analysis of multimedia, internet, intranet, and web computing issues. Recurring features include interviews and reports of meetings.

2657 ■ *Spotlights*
Pub: Internet/Media Strategies Inc.
Released: Weekly. **Description:** Analyzes business opportunities on the Internet and other technologies.

CONSULTANTS

2658 ■ Law Offices of Robert J. Keller, P.C.
Farragut Sta.
PO Box 33428, Farragut Sta.
Washington, DC 20033-3428
Ph:(202)223-2100
Fax:(202)223-2121
Co. E-mail: rjk@telcomlaw.com
URL: http://www.telcomlaw.com
Contact: Robert J. Keller, CEO
E-mail: rjk@telcomlaw.com
Scope: Specializes in telecommunications law, policy, and regulation, with particular emphasis on wireless telecommunications, new and emerging technologies, transactions involving FCC-regulated entities and licensees, and the special legal and regulatory issues relating to toll free telephone numbers. Experience in representing clients before the Federal Communications Commission, federal courts, and state and federal regulatory agencies.

LIBRARIES

2659 ■ Gartner IRC
56 Top Gallant Rd.
Stamford, CT 06904
Ph:(203)964-0096
URL: http://www.gartner.com
Scope: Information technology, computers, system design, telecommunications. **Services:** SDI; Center not open to the public (client research only). **Holdings:** 3000 items. **Subscriptions:** 1200 journals and other serials.

2660 ■ International Data Corp.–IDC Library
2131 Landings Dr.
Mountain View, CA 94043
Ph:(650)962-6481
Fax:(650)691-0531
Co. E-mail: slake@idc.com
URL: http://www.idc.com
Contact: Sara Lake, Mgr.Lib.Svcs.
Scope: Information technology. **Services:** Center not open to the public. **Holdings:** 350 books; 250 subject files. **Subscriptions:** 70 journals and other serials.

RESEARCH CENTERS

2661 ■ University of Minnesota–Charles Babbage Institute for the History of Information Technology
211 Andersen Library
222 21st Ave. S
Minneapolis, MN 55455
Ph:(612)624-5050
Fax:(612)625-8054
Co. E-mail: tmisa@umn.edu
URL: http://www.cbi.umn.edu
Contact: Thomas J. Misa PhD, Dir.
E-mail: tmisa@umn.edu
Scope: History of information science and technology, including development of computer technology, applications of information processing techniques ranging from banking to science research, automation techniques in archival development and historical database generation, history and social impacts of the information processing field, and entrepreneurial activity of the information industry. Identifies and makes accessible important letters, diaries, manuscripts, unpublished reports, industry records, financial information, interviews, and photographs that document and interpret the information revolution. Acts as a clearinghouse on the location of historical material. **Services:** Advises corporations, institutions, and individuals on record management and historical archives development. **Publications:** Charles Babbage Institute Newsletter (semiannually). **Educational Activities:** Conferences and workshops; Lecture series.

Business Broker Service

START-UP INFORMATION

2662 ■ *EBay Business Start-up Kit: 100s of Live Links to All the Information and Tools You Need*
Pub: NOLO
Ed: Richard Stim. **Released:** July 2008. **Price:** $24. 99. **Description:** Interactive kit that connects user directly to EBay is presented.

ASSOCIATIONS AND OTHER ORGANIZATIONS

2663 ■ Broker Management Council
PO Box 150229
Arlington, TX 76015
Ph:(682)518-6008
Fax:(682)518-6476
Co. E-mail: assnhqtrs@aol.com
URL: http://www.bmcsales.com
Contact: Pamela L. Bess, Exec. Dir.
Description: Foodservice sales and marketing companies specializing in institutional and restaurant food and allied products. Aims to: facilitate communication and exchange of management information; increase efficiency and reduce the cost of doing business; promote a favorable image of brokers in order to enhance their acceptance. Compiles statistics; conducts specialized education program. .

2664 ■ NAGMR
16A Journey, Ste. 200
Aliso Viejo, CA 92656
Ph:(949)859-4040
Fax:(949)855-2973
Co. E-mail: lball@manaonline.org
URL: http://www.nagmr.com
Contact: Jim Lewis, Membership Committee
Description: Consumer products brokers specializing in selling drug, health, beauty aids, and nonfood products to food chains and the same products and grocery items to the nonfood market. .

2665 ■ Printing Brokerage/Buyers Association
PO Box 744
Palm Beach, FL 33480
Ph:(215)821-6581
Free: 877-585-7141
Fax:(561)845-7130
URL: http://www.pbba.org
Description: Printing buyers/brokers/distributors, printers, typographers, binders, envelope and book manufacturers, packagers, color separation houses, pre-press service organizations, and related companies in the graphic arts industry. Promotes understanding, cooperation, and interaction among members while obtaining the highest standard of professionalism in the graphic arts industry. Gathers information on current technology in the graphic communications industry. Sponsors seminars for members to learn how to work with buyers, brokers and printers; also conducts technical and management seminars. Maintains referral service; compiles statistics. Conducts charitable programs. **Publications:** *BrokerRatings* (quarterly); *Corporate Print Buyer* (quarterly); *Hot Markets Annual Rankings of Buyers, Print Products and Geographies* (annual); *The Printer's Official Complete Guide to e-Everything-and How to Prevail!*; *Printing Brokerage Directory and Sourcebook* (annual).

REFERENCE WORKS

2666 ■ "Bartering Takes Businesses Back to Basics: Broker's Exchange Helps Members to Reach New Customers" in *Buffalo News* (July 9, 2010)
Pub: The Buffalo News
Ed: Dino Grandoni. **Description:** Bartering clubs can help small businesses reach new customers and to expand their business.

2667 ■ "Cyberwise" in *Black Enterprise* (Vol. 41, September 2010, No. 2, pp. 49)
Pub: Earl G. Graves Publishing Co. Inc.
Ed: Marcia Wade Talbert. **Description:** Advice is given to assist in selling an online store called theupscalegaragesale.com. A listing of business brokers specializing in the sale of Internet businesses is included.

2668 ■ *The Ebay Seller's Tax and Legal Answer Book*
Pub: AMACOM
Ed: Cliff Ennico. **Released:** April 30, 2007. **Price:** $19.95. **Description:** Helps sellers using Ebay to file taxes properly, while saving money.

2669 ■ *Merger and Acquisition Sourcebook*
Pub: NVST Inc.
Ed: Nancy Rothlein, Editor. **Released:** Annual, latest edition 2008. **Price:** $425, single issue discounted price. **Publication Includes:** Profiles of companies most active in mergers and acquisitions in the previous year. **Entries Include:** Company name, address, phone, financial data, history of transactions. Principal content of publication is summary and analysis of merger, acquisition, and divestiture activity in the previous year; company reorganizations; and terminated financial transactions. **Arrangement:** Classified by Standard Industrial Classification (SIC) code.

2670 ■ "The Neighborhood Watch" in *Hawaii Business* (Vol. 53, March 2008, No. 9, pp. 36)
Pub: Hawaii Business Publishing
Ed: David K. Choo. **Description:** OahuRe.com offers information on Hawaii real estate market, with spreadsheets and comparative market analysis page, which shows properties that are active, sold, or in escrow. Other details about OahuRe.com are discussed. A list of other top real estate websites in Hawaii and in the U.S. in general is provided.

2671 ■ "Power Up" in *Entrepreneur* (Vol. 35, November 2007, No. 11, pp. 140)
Pub: Entrepreneur Media Inc.
Ed: Amanda C. Kooser. **Description:** PowerSeller is a status in the Internet company eBay, wherein sellers average at least $1,000 in sales per month for three consecutive months. There are five tiers in the PowerSeller status, which ranges from Bronze to Titanium. Launching startups at eBay can help entrepreneurs pick up a wide customer base, but getting and maintaining PowerSeller status is a challenge.

2672 ■ "Risky Business" in *Canadian Business* (Vol. 79, October 23, 2006, No. 21, pp. 153)
Pub: Rogers Media
Ed: C.J. Burton. **Description:** Tips for Canadian managers on how to handle business risks are presented.

2673 ■ "With New Listings, Business Brokers See Hope" in *Business Courier* (Vol. 27, September 3, 2010, No. 18, pp. 1)
Pub: Business Courier
Ed: Lucy May. **Description:** Business brokers in Cincinnati, Ohio are expecting better prices in view of the strengthening economy.

2674 ■ *World M&A Network*
Pub: NVST.com Inc.
Ed: John W. Bailey, Editor. **Released:** Quarterly, Updated monthly online. **Price:** $395, members annual membership; $39.50, members month-to-month membership. **Covers:** Over 2,000 merger and acquisition leads for companies with annual revenues over $1 million. **Entries Include:** company, size, geographic region and sales. **Arrangement:** Classified by Standard Industrial Classification (SIC) code.

TRADE PERIODICALS

2675 ■ *Barron's*
Pub: Dow Jones & Company Inc.
Contact: Edwin A. Finn Jr., Ed., Pres.
Released: Weekly (Mon.). **Price:** $149 print & online; $99 print only; $79 online only. **Description:** Business and finance magazine.

2676 ■ *Better Investing*
Pub: National Association of Investors Corp.
Ed: Adam Ritt, Editor. **Released:** Monthly. **Price:** $19. **Description:** Magazine focusing on investing in long-term common stock.

2677 ■ *Business Opportunities Journal*
Pub: Business Service Corp.
Ed: Mark Adkins, Editor, news@boj.com. **Released:** Monthly. **Description:** Newspaper covering businesses for sale.

2678 ■ *Computerized Investing*
Pub: American Association of Individual Investors
Released: Bimonthly. **Price:** $20 members; $35 members and other countries, international; $40 nonmembers U.S.; $45 nonmembers and other countries, international. **Description:** Magazine covering the use of computers for investment analysis.

2679 ■ *Dow Theory Forecasts*
Pub: Horizon Publishing Company L.L.C.
Contact: Richard Moroney CFA, Ed./VP
Released: Weekly. **Description:** Financial magazine.

2680 ■ *Futures Magazine*
Pub: Futures Magazine
Contact: Steve Zwick, Ed. at Large
E-mail: steve.zwick@gmail.com
Released: Monthly. **Price:** $78 U.S.; $121 other countries. **Description:** Magazine covering news, analysis and strategies for futures, options and derivatives traders.

2681 ■ *Institutional Investor*
Pub: Institutional Investor
Contact: Gary Mueller, Chm./CEO
Released: Monthly. **Description:** Magazine for the investment or financial industry.

2682 ■ *Investment Advisor Magazine*
Pub: Investment Advisor Group
Contact: Robert Keane, Managing Editor
Released: Monthly. **Price:** $99 Canada; $139 out of country. **Description:** Investment magazine for financial professionals. Includes coverage of mutual funds, insurance products and partnerships combined with feature articles for financial planners.

2683 ■ *The Journal of Futures Markets*
Pub: John Wiley & Sons Inc.
Contact: Ira G. Kawaller, Editorial Board
Ed: Robert I. Webb, Editor, riw4j@virginia.edu. **Released:** Monthly. **Price:** $2,242 institutions print only; $2,362 institutions, Canada print only; $2,464 institutions, other countries print only; $406 print only; $2,467 institutions print with online; $2,587 institutions, Canada print with online; $2,689 institutions, other countries print with online. **Description:** Journal publishing articles of interest to those concerned with futures markets. Topics include financial futures, commodity forecasting techniques, corporate hedging strategies, tax and accounting implications of hedging, analysis of commodity trading systems, legal and regulatory issues and commodity portfolio optimization.

2684 ■ *The Journal of Portfolio Management*
Pub: Institutional Investor
Contact: Peter Bernstein, Founding Editor
Ed: Frank J. Fabozzi, Editor, fabozzi321@aol.com. **Released:** Quarterly. **Price:** $795; $1,351 two years; $1,908 three years. **Description:** Journal focusing on portfolio management and investment strategies.

2685 ■ *Money*
Pub: Time Inc.
Released: Monthly. **Price:** $14.95; $29.90 two years; $44.82 3 years. **Description:** Magazine focusing on personal and family finance.

2686 ■ *Official Summary of Security Transactions and Holdings*
Pub: U.S. Government Printing Office and Superintendent of Documents
Released: Monthly. **Price:** $30 single issue; $42 other countries. **Description:** Journal reporting securities holdings figures and transactions by owner.

VIDEOCASSETTES/ AUDIOCASSETTES

2687 ■ *Anatomy of a Leveraged Buyout*
Chesney Communications
2302 Martin St., Ste. 125
Irvine, CA 92612
Ph:(949)263-5500
Free: 800-223-8878
Fax:(949)263-5506
Co. E-mail: videocc@aol.com
URL: http://www.videocc.com
Released: 1989. **Price:** $49.95. **Description:** Now everyone can pull off a leveraged buyout, because Terry Greve, a man who has been involved with eight of them, tells his secrets in this video. **Availability:** VHS; 3/4U.

2688 ■ *Private Placements and Other Private Financings*
Practicing Law Institute
810 7th Ave., 21st Fl.
New York, NY 10019-5818
Ph:(212)824-5700
Free: 800-260-4PLI
Co. E-mail: info@pli.edu
URL: http://www.pli.edu
Released: 1988. **Price:** $245.00. **Description:** This program focuses on the legal aspects of business finance. **Availability:** VHS.

CONSULTANTS

2689 ■ Allen Business Investments
125 Ryan Industrial Ct., Ste. 100
San Ramon, CA 94583
Ph:(925)838-8150
Fax:(925)838-8173
URL: http://www.abi-bizbrkrs.com
Contact: Ron Johnson, President
E-mail: ron@atsabi-ma.com
Scope: Offers expertise on all phases of business opportunity valuations, and buyers and sellers of any type of business. Provides counsel on business frauds and expert witness services in superior and United States bankruptcy court valuations work for goodwill values; loss revenues; estate planning and dissolution of marriages. **Publications:** "Caution Small Business Owners - Be Wary of Companies That Want to Value and Help You Sell Your Business, for an Up-Front "Valuation" Fee"; "Wanted Considered Dangerous Known for Separating Business Owners From Their Money"; "Allocation of Purchase Price"; "Selling Your Business - a Quick Overview".

2690 ■ Associated Management Systems Inc.
1000 Elwell Ct., Ste. 234
Palo Alto, CA 94303-4306
Ph:(650)852-9041
Fax:(650)967-9992
Co. E-mail: amsn@rcn.com
Contact: M. A. Quraishi, President
Scope: The firm's entrepreneurial and professional expertise includes corporate management, investment banking, finance, strategic planning, risk evaluation, due diligence studies and management audits. Also assists with mergers and acquisitions, and provides management for turnaround situations. Undertakes project packaging, plant relocations, capital restructuring and funding. Industries served: Agriculture, real estate, insurance, computers, communications, retail/wholesale, electronics/instruments, paper/printing, food processing, furniture/home products, travel, transportation, recreation, heavy industry, pharmaceuticals, and government agencies.

2691 ■ Associated Marketers
10 E Hartshorn Dr.
Short Hills, NJ 07078
Ph:(973)376-3835
Contact: Lauren K. Hagaman, President
Scope: Consulting services limited to area of mergers and acquisitions through a network of associates. Active in serving manufacturing, distributing and service businesses seeking new corporate homes, acquiring additional businesses, or divesting divisions or subsidiaries. Fields served include appliances, house wares, advertising, industrial, publishing, building materials, printing and graphic arts, banking, insurance, apparel and textiles, automotive, transportation, home furnishings, food and confectionery products, leisure products, mail order, natural resources, plastics, packaging, and service businesses and retailing.

2692 ■ Boice Dunham Group
30 W 13th St., Ste. 3C
New York, NY 10011-7912
Ph:(212)752-5550
Fax:(212)752-7055
Co. E-mail: bdgbusdevl@msn.com
Contact: Craig K. Boice, President
E-mail: bdgbusdevl@msn.com
Scope: Specialized business development service offering identification, assessment and positioning of new business opportunities; acquisition of new corporate resources and business plan implementation for new ventures based on innovative technologies and growing markets. **Seminars:** Methods of Market Transformation: Breakout from the Niche, Apr, 2007; How will Utilities Grow?, Denver, May, 2006; New Tools and New Strategies to build active Customer Relationships: The State of the Art, Miami, Dec, 2005; Technology management, Decision-making, and business planning; The Role of AMR in Demand Response and Reliability.

2693 ■ Bullitt-Hutchins Inc.
5555 West Loop S, Ste. 255
Bellaire, TX 77401-2112
Ph:(713)464-7705
Fax:(713)668-9710
Contact: Walter C. Bullitt, President
E-mail: kevoc@hal-pc.org
Scope: Provides counseling and appraisal services to commercial, industrial and multi-family real estate in both urban and suburban settings. Specializes in providing negotiations for the acquisition and disposition of properties.

2694 ■ Business Team
1901 S Bascom Ave., Ste. 400
Campbell, CA 95008
Ph:(408)246-1102
Fax:(408)246-2219
Co. E-mail: sanjose@business-team.com
URL: http://www.business-team.com
Contact: William L. Kramer, Vice President
E-mail: mani@atsbusiness-team.com
Scope: Business consulting services offered to companies looking for buyers. Specializes in mergers and acquisitions, business brokerage, and valuations. **Seminars:** Business Valuation Enhancing the Value of Your Company.

2695 ■ Federated Business Agencies
15 Hunter Dr.
Eastchester, NY 10709-5205
Ph:(914)793-2220
Fax:(914)793-2524
Contact: Nathan Papell, President
E-mail: papell@msn.com
Scope: Business brokers and real estate brokers actively involved with acquisitions and mergers; real estate; purchases and sales of various business entities; new business ventures; special situations; business expansion and diversification; management consultation and financing.

FRANCHISES AND BUSINESS OPPORTUNITIES

2696 ■ Business America
Business America Assoc., Inc.
2120 Greentree Rd.
Pittsburgh, PA 15220
Ph:(412)276-7701
No. of Franchise Units: 4. **Founded:** 1984. **Franchised:** 1985. **Description:** Sells businesses and franchise appraisal. **Equity Capital Needed:** $10,000. **Franchise Fee:** $7,995. **Financial Assistance:** No. **Training:** Yes.

2697 ■ Empire Business Brokers
PO Box 129
Buffalo, NY 14225
Ph:(716)240-2544
Fax:(610)535-2544
Co. E-mail: nickgug1@aol.com
URL: http://www.empirebb.com
No. of Franchise Units: 66. **No. of Company-Owned Units:** 1. **Founded:** 1981. **Franchised:** 1989. **Description:** Assist sellers of existing business opportunities in finding buyers. **Equity Capital Needed:** $20,000-$30,000 total investment. **Franchise Fee:** $17,500. **Royalty Fee:** 5%. **Financial Assistance:** At the option of franchiser, directly from franchiser. Office equipment leasing assistance as well. **Training:** 5 days at company Headquarters by the country's foremost business broker, ongoing Seminars and conventions. Manuals, forms and tapes provided.

2698 ■ The Entrepreneur's Source
TES Franchising LLC
900 Main St. S, Bldg. 2
Southbury, CT 06488
Ph:(908)236-2264
Free: 800-289-0086
Fax:(203)264-3516
Co. E-mail: sstilwell@FranchiseSource.com
URL: http://www.franchisesearch.com
No. of Franchise Units: 267. **Founded:** 1984. **Franchised:** 1998. **Description:** Franchising consulting, coaching, placement/selection, and development firm providing services to prospective and existing franchisees and franchisors. **Equity Capital Needed:** $85,000$250,000. **Franchise Fee:** $49,000. **Financial Assistance:** No. **Training:** Initial and ongoing.

2699 ■ Executive Business Maintenance Franchise
5931 Stanley Ave., Ste. S-6
Carmichael, CA 95608
Free: 877-326-8787
Fax:(916)484-3854
Founded: 1996. **Franchised:** 2006. **Description:** Janitorial contract brokerage services. **Equity Capital Needed:** $59,000-$89,000. **Franchise Fee:** $35,000. **Royalty Fee:** 8%. **Financial Assistance:** No. **Training:** Offers 5 business days at headquarters, 5 business days at franchisee's location and ongoing support.

2700 ■ Murphy Business & Financial Corp.
513 N Belcher Rd.
Clearwater, FL 33765
Ph:(727)725-7090
Free: 888-561-3243
Fax:(727)725-8090
No. of Franchise Units: 145. **Founded:** 1994. **Franchised:** 2006. **Description:** Business & franchise brokerage/commercial real estate. **Equity Capital Needed:** $37,000. **Franchise Fee:** $35,000-$49,000. **Royalty Fee:** 10%. **Financial Assistance:** Limited third party financing available.

2701 ■ Realty World
Realty World America, Inc.
1600 Sunflower Ave. Ste. 100
Costa Mesa, CA 92626
Free: 800-685-4984
No. of Franchise Units: 216. **Founded:** 1973. **Franchised:** 1973. **Description:** real estate brokerage. **Equity Capital Needed:** $54,500-$227,000. **Franchise Fee:** $12,500-$50,000. **Royalty Fee:** Varies. **Financial Assistance:** No. **Training:** Provides 1 week training at headquarters, and ongoing support.

2702 ■ Sunbelt Business Brokers
2821 Riverside Dr.
Ottawa, ON, Canada K1V 8N4
Ph:(613)731-9140
Free: 800-905-3557
Fax:(613)526-0997
Co. E-mail: ottawa@sunbeltnetwork.com
URL: http://www.sunbeltnetwork.com
No. of Franchise Units: 29. **Founded:** 2002. **Franchised:** 2002. **Description:** Business brokerage company. **Equity Capital Needed:** $100,000. **Franchise Fee:** $25,000. **Training:** Provides training and ongoing support.

COMPUTERIZED DATABASES

2703 ■ *ABI/INFORM*
ProQuest LLC
789 E Eisenhower Pky.
PO Box 1346
Ann Arbor, MI 48106-1346
Ph:(734)761-4700
Free: 800-521-0600
Fax:(734)761-6450
Co. E-mail: info@proquest.com
URL: http://www.proquest.com
Description: Contains approximately 6 million full text or bibliographic citations to articles from more than 800 business and management publications worldwide. **Availability:** Online: Wolters Kluwer Health, ProQuest LLC, ProQuest LLC, Questel SA, STN International, Colorado Alliance of Research Libraries, Financial Times Ltd., LexisNexis Group, ProQuest LLC. **Type:** Full text; Bibliographic; Image.

2704 ■ *American Banker Financial Publications*
SourceMedia Inc.
1 State St. Plz., 27th Fl.
New York, NY 10004
Ph:(212)803-8200
Free: 800-221-1809
Fax:(212)843-9600
Co. E-mail: custserv@AmericanBanker.com
URL: http://www.americanbanker.com
Description: Provides full text of the daily financial services newspaper and other financial newsletters which follow trends, developments, and news in banking and related financial areas. Includes topics such as capital markets, bank regulation, insurance letters, and public finance letters. **Availability:** Online: ProQuest LLC. **Type:** Full text.

2705 ■ *Best's Statement File - Life/Health - United States*
A.M. Best Company Inc.
Ambest Rd.
Oldwick, NJ 08858
Ph:(908)439-2200
Free: 800-424-2378
Fax:(908)439-3296
Co. E-mail: customer_service@ambest.com
URL: http://www.ambest.com
Description: Contains 11 years of annual and six years of quarterly statutory filing data on some 1300 U.S. life and health insurance companies. For each company, provides complete information from the NAIC annual statement, including assets, liability and surplus, expenses, premiums written by line, exhibit of life insurance, stock and bond summary, and quality and maturity of bonds. Provides industry and segmented total records as well as unique A.M. Best calculated ratios, rankings, and the Best's Ratings. Information may be selected for the total industry or for individual companies. Includes *Best's Review, BestWeek,* and *BestAlert Service.* Also includes a one-year subscription to *Best's Review* magazine. **Availability:** CD-ROM: A.M. Best Company Inc. **Type:** Numeric; Directory.

2706 ■ *Best's Statement File - Property/ Casualty - United States*
A.M. Best Company Inc.
Ambest Rd.
Oldwick, NJ 08858
Ph:(908)439-2200
Free: 800-424-2378
Fax:(908)439-3296
Co. E-mail: customer_service@ambest.com
URL: http://www.ambest.com
Description: Contains 11 years of annual and six years of quarterly statutory filing data on some 4100 U.S. property and casualty insurance companies. For each company, provides complete information from the NAIC annual statement, including assets, liability and surplus, expenses, premiums written by line, exhibit of life insurance, stock and bond summary, and quality and maturity of bonds. Includes *Best's Review, BestWeek,* and *BestAlert Service.* Also includes a one-year subscription to *Best's Review* magazine. **Availability:** CD-ROM: A.M. Best Company Inc. **Type:** Numeric; Directory.

2707 ■ *Dial-Data*
Track Data Corp.
95 Rockwell Pl.
Brooklyn, NY 11217
Ph:(718)522-7373
Free: 800-367-5968
Co. E-mail: info@trackdata.com
URL: http://www.trackdata.com
Description: A database system that contains current and historical data on securities, options, and commodities. Comprises the following three files. Securities—contains data from 1970 to date on more than 12,000 stocks, warrants, rights, bonds, and government issues. Includes both fundamental (e.g., earnings, shares outstanding) and technical data for all issues from the New York Stock Exchange (NYSE), American Stock Exchange (AMEX), NASDAQ Over-The-Counter market, International Stock Exchange (London), Montreal Exchange, Toronto Exchange, and government issues. Data items available include daily price and volume for NYSE and AMEX bonds; daily bid, ask, and yield for government issues; coupon and maturity data for both; and open, high, low, close, and volume interest data for all exchanges. Splits and dividends are reported on the evening of the day they occur. Options—contains data on all options listed on NYSE; Chicago Board Options Exchange (CBOE); AMEX; Philadelphia Exchange; and Pacific Stock Exchange (PSE). Daily price, volume, high, low, open, and close interest data as well as fundamental and technical data are available on all underlying securities from 1973 to date. Commodities—contains daily price, volume, high, low, open, and close interest data by contract on all commodities from the following exchanges: CBOE; Chicago Board of Trade (CBOT); Chicago Mercantile Exchange (CME); Commodity Exchange, Inc.; International Monetary Exchange; Kansas City Board of Trade; Mid America Exchange; Minneapolis Grain Exchange; New York Coffee, Sugar, and Cocoa Exchange; New York Cotton Exchange; New York Futures Exchange; New York Mercantile Exchange; and Winnipeg Grain Exchange. Covers commodities from 1963 to date, with selected cash series data from 1959 to date. Also includes 200 indexes and statistics on the daily or weekly performance of the securities market. Primary sources include NYSE, Dow Jones, Standard & Poor's, Value Line, and daily market summaries compiled from MERLIN data. Indexes and statistics date from 1972, with some data from 1970. **Availability:** Online: Track Data Corp. **Type:** Numeric.

2708 ■ *Dialog Finance and Banking Newsletters*
ProQuest LLC
2250 Perimeter Park Dr., Ste. 300
Morrisville, NC 27560
Ph:(919)804-6400
Free: 800-334-2564
Fax:(919)804-6410
Co. E-mail: contact@dialog.com
URL: http://www.dialog.com
Description: Provides access to more than 30 newsletters and journals published by publishers in the financial services industry. Covers more than 151,000 records. Includes publications from Euromoney Publications, Securities Data Publishing, Investment Dealers Digest, and Phillips Business Information. Includes such publications as: *Asset-Backed Securities Week. Bank Automation News. Bank Investment Marketing. Bank Loan Report. Central European Finance. Credit Risk Management Report. Employee Benefit News. Euromoney. Financial Planning. Financial Services Report. Investment Management Weekly. Mergers & Acquisitions Journal. On Wall Street. Mutual Fund Market News. Private Equity Week. Retail Delivery Systems News. Variable Annuity Market News. Venture Capital Journal.* **Availability:** Online: ProQuest LLC. **Type:** Full text.

2709 ■ *Dividend Record*
Standard & Poor's
55 Water St.
New York, NY 10041
Ph:(212)438-2000
Free: 800-523-4534
Fax:(212)438-7375
Co. E-mail: questions@standardandpoors.com
URL: http://www.standardandpoors.com
Description: Contains dividend disbursement data for more than 22,000 equity securities listed on the New York Stock Exchange (NYSE) and American Stock Exchange (AMEX), the NASDAQ market and the Toronto and Montreal stock exchanges. Also contains data on American Depository Receipts, mutual funds, closed-end investment companies, limited partnerships, and real-estate investment trusts. Comprised of and stock and cash dividend announcements, including initial dividends, dividends resumed, increase or decrease in dividends, omitted or suspended dividends, and additional, extra, special, or optional dividends. Also includes announcements of stock splits, stock redemptions, tender offers, rights offerings, spin-offs, stock ex-

change rulings, and due bill information. Provides, for each dividend, its declaration date, ex-dividend date, stock-of-record date, and payment date, as well as the amount of the dividend. Sources include the stock exchanges, National Association of Securities Dealers (NASD), and company information. Corresponds to Standard & Poor's printed *Dividend Record* services. **Availability:** Online: Standard & Poor's. **Type:** Numeric.

2710 ■ *EIU ViewsWire*
The Economist Group
26 Red Lion Sq.
London WC1R 4HQ, United Kingdom
Ph:44 20 7576 8181
Fax:44 20 7576 8476
Co. E-mail: london@eiu.com
URL: http://www.eiu.com
Description: Provides up to 150 articles daily covering practical business intelligence, including key events, market issues, impending crises, and the business and regulatory environment in emerging and International markets. Covers information from more than 195 countries. Includes: Briefings: critical political, economic, and business changes around the world organized by the topics of company, economy, finance, politics, regulations, and industry. Forecasts: Country updates-continuously updated overviews of GDP, inflation, demand, investment, fiscal policy, interest rates, currency, external accounts, and the political scene in more than 190 countries. Consensus forecasts-monthly currency, interest rate, and equity market short-term outlooks provided by multinational companies and investment banks. Country risk summary-political and credit risk ratings and analysis for 100 countries. Five-year forecasts—quarterly growth, inflation, and trade indicators for 60 countries. Forecast summaries—quarterly key economic indicators and business watchlist. Background: facts and figures on current conditions in more than 190 countries. Key economic indicators—quarterly statistics on growth, trade, reserves, and currencies. Basic data and country fact sheet-population data, per capita GDP, political structure, taxes, foreign trade and policy issues. Trade, tax and forex regulations-Connecticut updated full regulatory profiles on 60 countries. **Availability:** Online: The Economist Group, Thomson Reuters, Financial Times Ltd., LexisNexis Group. **Type:** Full text; Numeric.

2711 ■ *Mergers Unleashed*
Investcorp International Inc.
1 State St. Plaza, 27th Fl.
New York, NY 10004
Ph:(212)803-8200
Free: 800-221-1809
Co. E-mail: custserv@sourcemedia.com
URL: http://www.sourcemedia.com
Description: Contains the complete text of *Mergers & Acquisitions Report* and *Mergers & Acquisitions Journal*. Covers pending and ongoing deals as well as insights into industry trends, strategies, and the firms and individuals involved. **Availability:** Online: LexisNexis Group, Investcorp International Inc. **Type:** Full text.

2712 ■ *Quarterly Financial Report*
Haver Analytics
60 E 42nd St.
New York, NY 10165
Ph:(212)986-9300
Fax:(212)986-5857
Co. E-mail: data@haver.com
URL: http://www.haver.com
Description: Contains statistics on the financial position of U.S. corporations aggregated by Industry from the *Quarterly Financial Report* and financial ratios for Manufacturing corporations. Includes quarterly data of income statements and balance sheet items for all Manufacturing, large mining, and trade corporations. Covers 8700 surveyed corporations, classified by Industry and asset size. **Availability:** Online: Haver Analytics. **Type:** Time series.

2713 ■ *SNL Financial Banks & Thrifts Module*
SNL Financial LC
One SNL Plaza
PO Box 2124
Charlottesville, VA 22902
Ph:(434)977-1600
Fax:(434)977-4466
Co. E-mail: support@snl.com
URL: http://www.snl.com
Description: Provides Information on more than 120,000 branches of banks and thrifts. Includes major exchange, OTC and pinksheet traded commercial banks and thrifts; GAAP balance sheet; detailed asset quality, loan and deposit composition, capital adequacy, and banking-specific performance and profitability ratios; mutual-to-stock thrift conversion data; historical financial data from the FDIC (Call Report), OTS (TFR), Federal Reserve (Y-9) and credit union regulatory agency filings; financial soundness ratings and regulatory enforcement actions; CRA ratings; Links to Uniform Bank Performance Reports (UBPR); and banking transactions. **Availability:** Online: SNL Financial LC. **Type:** Full text; Directory; Numeric; Statistical.

2714 ■ *SNL Financial North American Real Estate Module*
SNL Financial LC
One SNL Plaza
PO Box 2124
Charlottesville, VA 22902
Ph:(434)977-1600
Fax:(434)977-4466
Co. E-mail: support@snl.com
URL: http://www.snl.com
Description: Provides information on more than 40,000 publicly traded and private REITs (Real Estate Investment Trusts) and selected REOCs (Real Estate Operating Companies) in North America. Includes GAAP balance sheet, income statement, cash flow statement and debt composition; key financial ratios; NAV, NAV per share and price/NAV ratios; analyst consensus estimates for EPS, FFO, and AFFO. Includes property name, location and ownership percentage, size of property and demographic information. Offers Information on capital issues giving detailed description for each company's individual capital issues including preferred operating partnership units. Includes access to searchable database of SEC documents. **Availability:** Online: SNL Financial LC. **Type:** Directory; Numeric; Statistical.

2715 ■ *Value Line Electronic Convertibles*
Value Line Inc.
220 E 42nd St., 6th Fl.
New York, NY 10017
Ph:(212)907-1500
Free: 800-531-1425
Fax:(212)907-1992
Co. E-mail: vlcr@valueline.com
URL: http://www.valueline.com
Description: Contains evaluation data for approximately 600 convertible securities. Includes price, yield, premium, issue size, liquidity, and maturity. Enables the user to perform calculations to evaluate the effects of changes in prices, common dividends, quality ratings, and interest rates. **Availability:** Online: Value Line Inc. **Type:** Numeric.

Business Consulting Service

START-UP INFORMATION

2716 ■ *How to Start a Home-Based Consulting Business: Define Your Specialty Build a Client Base Make Yourself Indispensable*
Pub: The Globe Pequot Press
Ed: Bert Holtje. **Released:** January 10, 2010. **Price:** $18.95. **Description:** Everything needed for starting and running a successful consulting business from home.

2717 ■ *Starting and Running a Coaching Business*
Pub: How To Books
Ed: Aryanne Oade. **Released:** August 9, 2010. **Price:** $26.00. **Description:** Guide for the comprehensive, practical and personalized process of starting and running a coaching business is presented.

2718 ■ *Starting Up On Your Own: How to Succeed as an Independent Consultant or Freelance*
Pub: FT Press
Ed: Mike Johnson. **Released:** February 1, 2010. **Price:** $24.99. **Description:** Concise guide for anyone wanting to start their own consulting firm is provided.

ASSOCIATIONS AND OTHER ORGANIZATIONS

2719 ■ Association of Consulting Engineering Companies - Canada–Association des Ingenieurs-Conseils du Canada
130 Albert St., Ste. 616
Ottawa, ON, Canada K1P 5G4
Ph:(613)236-0569
Free: 800-565-0569
Fax:(613)236-6193
Co. E-mail: info@acec.ca
URL: http://www.acec.ca
Contact: John D. Gamble CET, Pres.
Description: Promotes the interests of independent consulting engineers; represents electrical, civil, environmental, geotechnical, metallurgical, cultural, and other engineering fields. Standardizes forms of agreement, contracts, and guidelines for consulting engineers; acts as clearinghouse. **Publications:** *Canadian Consulting Engineer* (bimonthly); *Communique* (monthly).

2720 ■ Association for Corporate Growth - Toronto Chapter
1 Concorde Gate, Ste. 802
Toronto, ON, Canada M3C 3N6
Ph:(416)868-1881
Fax:(416)391-3633
Co. E-mail: acgtoronto@acg.org
URL: http://www.acg.org/toronto/default.aspx
Contact: Stephen B. Smith, Pres.
Description: Professionals with a leadership role in strategic corporate growth. Seeks to facilitate the professional advancement of members, and the practice of corporate growth management. Fosters communication and cooperation among members; conducts continuing professional education programs. **Publications:** *Mergers & Acquisitions - The Dealmaker's Journal* (monthly).

2721 ■ Association of Independent Consultants
15 Wilson St.
Markham, ON, Canada L3P 1M9
Ph:(416)410-8163
Fax:(905)669-5233
Co. E-mail: info1@aiconsult.ca
URL: http://www.aiconsult.ca/en
Contact: Lawrence Fox, Pres.
Description: Independent consultants. Promotes professional advancement of members. Facilitates communication and cooperation among members; makes available volume discounts to members. Conducts business education courses; maintains speakers' bureau. **Publications:** *Thrive-on-Line* . **Telecommunication Services:** electronic mail, president1@aiconsult.ca.

2722 ■ Canadian Association of International Development Consultants–Regroupement des consultants canadiens en developpement internationale
260 St. Patrick St., Ste. 101
Ottawa, ON, Canada K1N 5K5
Ph:(613)244-1050
Fax:(613)244-8315
Co. E-mail: caidc_rccdi@yahoo.ca
URL: http://www.caidc-rccdi.ca
Contact: Amitav Rath, Treas.
Description: Aims to provide services for, and to represent the interests of, Canadian international development consultants.

2723 ■ International Association for Time Use Research
University of Oxford
Dept. of Sociology
Manor Road Bldg.
Oxford OX1 3UQ, United Kingdom
Co. E-mail: kimberly.fisher@sociology.ox.ac.uk
URL: http://iatur.timeuse.org
Contact: Prof. Michael Bittman, Pres.
Description: The International Association for Time Use Research (IATUR) facilitates exchange of ideas, methodology, and data collection techniques among researchers and compilers of official statistics on the patterns of daily activities and changes in people's behaviours over time. **Publications:** *Electronic International Journal for Time Use Research* (annual); *Fifteenth Reunion of the International Association for Time Use Research Amsterdam* (periodic); *Time Use Methodology: Towards Consensus* .

REFERENCE WORKS

2724 ■ "Achieving Greatness" in *Black Enterprise* (Vol. 38, January 2008, No. 6, pp. 50)
Pub: Earl G. Graves Publishing Co. Inc.
Description: Randall Pinkett, winner of a reality show on television and chairman of BCT Partners, insists that a business cannot survive by doing just enough or more of the same. Pinkett's New Jersey company provides management, technology and consulting to other firms.

2725 ■ "Altegrity Acquires John D. Cohen, Inc." in (November 19, 2009, pp. 14)
Pub: Investment Weekly News
Description: John D. Cohen, Inc., a contract provider of national security policy guidance and counsel to the federal government, was acquired by Altegrity, Inc., a global screening and security solutions provider; the company will become part of US Investigations Services, LLC and operate under the auspices of Altegrity's new business, Altegrity Security Consulting.

2726 ■ "The Art of War for Women" in *Hawaii Business* (Vol. 54, July 2008, No. 1, pp. 23)
Pub: Hawaii Business Publishing
Description: Business consultant Chi-Ning Chu talks about her new book 'The Art of War for Women: Sun Tzu's Ancient Strategies and Wisdom for Winning at Work', which discusses how women can more effectively win in business. She also shares her thoughts about the advantages that women have, which they can use in businesses decisions.

2727 ■ "BDC Launches New Online Business Advice Centre" in *Internet Wire* (July 13, 2010)
Pub: Comtex
Description: The Business Development Bank of Canada (BDC) offers entrepreneurs the chance to use their new online BDC Advice Centre in order to seek advice regarding the challenges of entrepreneurship. Free online business tools and information to help both startups and established firms are also provided.

2728 ■ "Best Foot Forward" in *Canadian Business* (Vol. 80, October 22, 2007, No. 21, pp. 115)
Pub: Rogers Media
Ed: Jeremy Shinewald. **Description:** Jeremy Shinewald's mbaMission admissions consulting business helps prospective MBA students with essay writing, mock interview preparation and school selection. The consulting fee for application to one school is $2,250. Details of the business schools' MBA programs and tuition fees are explored.

2729 ■ "Brite-Strike Tactical Launches New Internet Marketing Initiatives" in *Internet Wire* (September 15, 2009)
Pub: Comtex News Network, Inc.
Description: Brite-Strike Tactical Illumination Products, Inc. has enlisted the expertise of Internet marketing guru Thomas J. McCarthy to help revamp the company's Internet campaign. An outline of the Internet marketing strategy is provided.

2730 ■ "Designing Events Updates Online Suite" in *Wireless News* (October 25, 2009)
Pub: Close-Up Media
Description: Designing Events, an outsourcing and consulting firm for conferences and meetings, announced the release of an update to its Designing

Events Online suite of web-based management and marketing tools; features include enhanced versions of online registration and collaboration, content management, session development, social media and conference websites.

2731 ■ "The End of Clock-Punching" in *Canadian Business* (Vol. 83, September 14, 2010, No. 15, pp. 96)
Pub: Rogers Media Ltd.
Ed: Lyndsie Bourgon. **Description:** Workplace consultant Peter Hadwen is pushing for the transformation of Canada's government departments into results-only work environments (ROWE). ROWE does not require employees to show up to work at a certain time as long as they are meeting goals and achieving results in their jobs. Details of studies regarding ROWE in US companies are examined.

2732 ■ "Federal Fund Valuable Tool For Small-Biz Innovators" in *Crain's Detroit Business* (Vol. 24, September 29, 2008, No. 39, pp. 42)
Pub: Crain Communications, Inc.
Ed: Nancy Kaffer. **Description:** Grants from the Small Business Innovation Research Program, or SBIR grants, are federal funds that are set aside for 11 federal agencies to allocate to tech-oriented small-business owners. Firms such as Biotechnology Business Consultants help these companies apply for SBIR grants.

2733 ■ "Five Low-Cost Home Based Startups" in *Women Entrepreneur* (December 16, 2008)
Pub: Entrepreneur Media Inc.
Ed: Lesley Spencer Pyle. **Description:** During tough economic times, small businesses have an advantage over large companies because they can adjust to economic conditions more easily and without having to go through corporate red tape that can slow the implementation process. A budding entrepreneur may find success by taking inventory of his or her skills, experience, expertise and passions and utilizing those qualities to start a business. Five low-cost home-based startups are profiled. These include starting an online store, a virtual assistant service, web designer, sales representative and a home staging counselor.

2734 ■ *Franchise: Freedom or Fantasy*
Pub: iUniverse
Ed: Mitchell York. **Released:** June 22, 2009. **Price:** $13.95. **Description:** Successful franchisee and professional certified coach guides individuals through the many steps involved in deciding whether or not to buy a franchise and how to do it correctly.

2735 ■ "Hire Power" in *Entrepreneur* (Vol. 35, November 2007, No. 11, pp. 105)
Pub: Entrepreneur Media Inc.
Ed: Mark Henricks. **Description:** Companies with big resources may hire human resource (HR) consultants to help with writing manuals, drafting policies and designing benefits for employees. HR consultants may also be hired to assist with specific functions or other strategic aspects.

2736 ■ "Interbrand's Creative Recruiting" in *Business Courier* (Vol. 27, November 12, 2010, No. 28, pp. 1)
Pub: Business Courier
Ed: Dan Monk. **Description:** Global brand consulting firm Interbrand uses a creative recruitment agency to attract new employees into the company. Interbrand uses themed parties to attract prospective employees. The 'Alice In Wonderland' tea party for example, allowed the company to hire five new employees.

2737 ■ "International Growth" in *Black Enterprise* (Vol. 38, July 2008, No. 12, pp. 64)
Pub: Earl G. Graves Publishing Co. Inc.
Ed: Marcia A. Reed-Woodard. **Description:** Becoming an increasingly smaller portion of the global business environment is the U.S. economy. Christopher Catlin, an associate with Booz Allen Hamilton, a technology management and strategy-consulting firm, shares what he has learned about the global market.

2738 ■ "Into the Groove: Fine-Tune Your Biz By Getting Into the Good Habit Groove" in *Small Business Opportunities* (Spring 2008)
Pub: Harris Publications Inc.
Description: Profile of Ty Freyvogel and his consulting firm Freyvogel Communications. Freyvogel serves the telecommunications need of Fortune 500 and mid-sized businesses.

2739 ■ "Leadership: The Couch in the Corner Office: Surveying the Landscape of the CEO Psyche" in *Inc.* (January 2008, pp. 33-34)
Pub: Gruner & Jahr USA Publishing
Description: Profile of Leslie G. Mayer, founder of the Leadership Group, a firm that provides assistance to CEOs of firms by offering a deep understanding of the relationships, insecurities, and blind spots that can weaken strong leadership.

2740 ■ "Managing the Facebookers; Business" in *The Economist* (Vol. 390, January 3, 2009, No. 8612, pp. 10)
Pub: Economist Newspaper Ltd.
Description: According to a report from PricewaterhouseCoopers, a business consultancy, workers from Generation Y, also known as the Net Generation, are more difficult to recruit and integrate into companies that practice traditional business acumen. 61 percent of chief executive managers say that they have trouble with younger employees who tend to be more narcissistic and more interested in personal fulfillment with a need for frequent feedback and an over-precise set of objectives on the path to promotion which can be hard for managers who are used to a different relationship with their subordinates. Older bosses should prepare to make some concessions to their younger talent since some of the issues that make them happy include cheaper online ways to communicate and additional coaching, both of which are good for business.

2741 ■ "Meet Rebecca. She's Here to Fire You" in *Inc.* (November 2007, pp. 25-26)
Pub: Gruner & Jahr USA Publishing
Ed: Max Chafkin. **Description:** Amid liability concerns as well as CEO guilt, more and more firms are using consulting companies to fire workers. These outsourced firms help small companies structure severance and document information in order to limit legal liability when firing an employee.

2742 ■ *The Mirror Test: How to Breathe New Life Into Your Business*
Pub: Grand Central Publishing
Ed: Jeffrey W. Hayzlett. **Released:** May 10, 2010. **Price:** $24.99. **Description:** Consultant and author, Jeffrey Hayzlett, explains why a business is not doing well and asks the questions that most business managers are afraid to ask.

2743 ■ "Montgomery & Barnes: a Service-Disabled, Veteran-Owned Small Business" in *Underground Construction* (Vol. 65, October 2010, No. 10)
Pub: Oildom Publishing Company of Texas Inc.
Description: Gary Montgomery, chairman of Montgomery and Barnes announced that President Wendell (Buddy) Barnes is now majority owner, thus making the Houston-based civil engineering and consulting services firm, eligible to quality as a Service-Disabled Veteran-Owned Small Business (SDVOSB).

2744 ■ "More Sales Leads, Please: Or, What Happened When Frontline Selling Started Practicing What It Preaches" in *Inc.* (November 2007)
Pub: Gruner & Jahr USA Publishing
Description: Frontline Selling located in Oakland, New Jersey helps train sales teams to generate and convert sales leads. The consulting firm doubled their marketing budget to increase their own sales.

2745 ■ "Nampa Police Department: Electronic Systems Just One Tool in Business Security Toolbox" in *Idaho Business Review* (October 29, 2010)
Pub: Dolan Media Newswires
Ed: Brad Carlson. **Description:** Police departments and private security firms can help small businesses with hard security and business consultants can assist with internal audit security and fraud prevention.

2746 ■ "New Database Brings Doctors Out of the Dark" in *Business Courier* (Vol. 26, October 23, 2009, No. 26, pp. 1)
Pub: American City Business Journals, Inc.
Ed: James Ritchie. **Description:** A database created by managed care consulting firm Praesentia allows doctors in Cincinnati to compare average reimbursements from health insurance companies to doctors in different areas. Specialist doctors in the city are paid an average of $172.25 for every office consultation.

2747 ■ "Nothing But Net: Fran Harris Offers Advice On Winning the Game of Business" in *Black Enterprise* (Vol. 38, March 2008, No. 8, pp. 50)
Pub: Earl G. Graves Publishing Co. Inc.
Ed: Chana Garcia. **Description:** Fran Harris, certified life coach, business consultant, and CEO of her business, a multimedia development company, reveals five tips to ensure entrepreneurial success.

2748 ■ "On Hire Ground" in *Entrepreneur* (Vol. 36, February 2008, No. 2, pp. 19)
Pub: Entrepreneur Media Inc.
Description: ADP Small Business Services, an economic consulting firm, showed that small businesses had increased employment rates in 2007 and added 77,000 jobs in November 2007. Entrepreneurial employment and data showing the contribution of small businesses to job growth are presented.

2749 ■ "Outplacement Services" in *Black Enterprise* (Vol. 38, March 2008, No. 8, pp. 60)
Pub: Earl G. Graves Publishing Co. Inc.
Ed: Marcia Reed Woodard. **Description:** Tips to use while in career-transition are offered. Many times outplacement services are provided as part of a severance package to employees.

2750 ■ "Plan Your Next Event at Newport News Marriott at City Center" in *Benzinga.com* (July 29, 2011)
Pub: Benzinga.com
Ed: Benzinga Staff. **Description:** Newport News Marriott at City Center is promoting itself as the premier venue for business meetings, conventions and weddings.

2751 ■ *PPC's Guide to Small Business Consulting Engagements*
Pub: Practitioners Publishing Company
Released: March 2004. **Price:** $226.00. **Description:** Technical guide for conducting consulting engagements for small business.

2752 ■ *PPC's Guide to Small Business Consulting Engagements, Vol. 2*
Pub: Practitioners Publishing Company
Released: March 2004. **Description:** Second volume of the technical guide for conducting consulting engagements for small business.

2753 ■ *PPC's Guide to Small Business Consulting Engagements, Vol. 3*
Pub: Practitioners Publishing Company
Released: March 2004. **Description:** Third volume of the technical guide for conducting consulting engagements for small business.

2754 ■ "Reduce the Risk of Failed Financial Judgments" in *Harvard Business Review* (Vol. 86, July-August 2008, No. 8, pp. 24)
Pub: Harvard Business School Press
Ed: Robert G. Eccles; Edward J. Fiedl. **Description:** Utilization of business consultants, evaluators, appraisers, and actuaries to decrease financial management risks is discussed.

2755 ■ "Restoring Grandeur" in *Business Courier* (Vol. 26, December 4, 2009, No. 32, pp. 1)
Pub: American City Business Journals, Inc.
Ed: Dan Monk. **Description:** Eagle Realty Group intends to spend more than $10 to restore the historic 12-story Phelps apartment building in Lytle Park in Cincinnati. Its president, Mario San Marco, expressed

the need to invest in the building in order to maintain operations. The building could be restored into a hotel catering to executives and consultants.

2756 ■ "Risky Business" in *Canadian Business* (Vol. 79, October 23, 2006, No. 21, pp. 153)
Pub: Rogers Media
Ed: C.J. Burton. **Description:** Tips for Canadian managers on how to handle business risks are presented.

2757 ■ "The Secret Life of a Serial CEO" in *Inc.* (January 2008, pp. 80-88)
Pub: Gruner & Jahr USA Publishing
Ed: David H. Freedman. **Description:** Profile of Bob Cramer, who has lead six successful companies and is now searching for a new business venture and thinks he's found it. Cramer shares his journey from wooing venture capital, handling founders and his hunt for his newest venture.

2758 ■ "Seven Ways to Fail Big" in *Harvard Business Review* (Vol. 86, September 2008, No. 9, pp. 82)
Pub: Harvard Business School Press
Ed: Paul B. Carroll; Chunka Mui. **Description:** Seven factors involved in business failures are identified, and ways to avoid them are described. These factors include flawed financial engineering, hurrying into consolidation, and investing in technology that is not a good fit.

2759 ■ *The Sticking Point Solution: 9 Ways to Move Your Business from Stagnation to Stunning Growth in Tough Economic Times*
Pub: Vanguard Press
Ed: Jay Abraham. **Released:** May 10, 2010. **Price:** $25.95. **Description:** Renowned business consultant, Jay Abraham, reveals the nine ways even successful businesses get stuck, hit plateaus, and fail to achieve their dreams and he explains how to get unstuck and create exponential growth.

2760 ■ "Think Disruptive! How to Manage In a New Era of Innovation" in *Strategy & Leadership* (Vol. 38, July-August 2010, No. 4, pp. 5-10)
Pub: Emerald Inc.
Ed: Brian Leavy, John Sterling. **Description:** The views expressed by Scott Anthony, president of an innovation consultancy Innosight, on the need for corporate leaders to apply disruptive innovation in a recessionary environment are presented. His suggestion that disruptive innovation is the only way to survive during the economic crisis is discussed.

2761 ■ "Trend: Tutors to Help You Pump Up the Staff" in *Business Week* (September 22, 2008, No. 4100, pp. 45)
Pub: McGraw-Hill Companies, Inc.
Ed: Reena Janaj. **Description:** High-level managers are turning to innovation coaches in an attempt to obtain advice on how to better sell new concepts within their companies. Individuals as well as consulting firms are now offering this service.

2762 ■ "Your Booming Business: How You Can Align Sales and Marketing for Dynamic Growth" in *Small Business Opportunities* (Spring 2008)
Pub: Harris Publications Inc.
Ed: Voss W. Graham. **Description:** Voss Graham, founder and CEO of Inneractive Consulting Group Inc., works with companies to develop and hire successful sales teams. A checklist from the American Bankers Association to help write a business plan is included.

TRADE PERIODICALS

2763 ■ *The GreenMoney Journal & Online Guide*
Pub: The Greenmoney Journal
Contact: Cliff Feigenbaum, Editor & Publisher
E-mail: cliff@greenmoney.com
Released: Bimonthly. **Price:** $50, individuals; $50, Canada plus $10 postage; $50, elsewhere plus $20 postage. **Description:** Encourages and promotes the awareness of socially and environmentally responsible business, investing and consumer resources in publications and online. Our goal is to educate and empower individuals and businesses to make informed financial decisions through aligning their personal, corporate and financial principles. Recurring features include a calendar

2764 ■ *Make It A Winning Life*
Pub: Wolf Rinke Associates,Inc.
Ed: Wolf J. Rinke, Ph.D., Editor, wolfrinke@aol.com. **Released:** Bimonthly. **Price:** Free. **Description:** Features ideas and strategies to help individuals succeed faster and improve the quality of their life. Remarks: America Online, Inc.

VIDEOCASSETTES/ AUDIOCASSETTES

2765 ■ *Building a Profitable Consulting Practice Series*
Instructional Video
2219 C St.
Lincoln, NE 68502
Ph:(402)475-6570
Free: 800-228-0164
Fax:(402)475-6500
Co. E-mail: feedback@insvideo.com
URL: http://www.insvideo.com
Description: Two-part business educational series by Howard Shenson offers tips on how to build a profitable consulting practice. Covers consulting opportunities, market strategies, proposal writing, contracting strategies, fee setting, disclosure, and collection techniques. **Availability:** VHS.

2766 ■ *Exceeding Customer Expectations*
Service Quality Institute
9201 E. Bloomington Fwy.
Minneapolis, MN 55420-3437
Ph:(952)884-3311
Free: 800-548-0538
Fax:(952)884-8901
URL: http://www.customer-service.com
Price: $149.95. **Description:** Teaches good customer interaction and how to treat co-workers as internal customers. **Availability:** VHS.

2767 ■ *Managing the Emerging Company*
Leslie T. McClure
PO Box 1223
Pebble Beach, CA 93953
Ph:(831)656-0553
Fax:(831)656-0555
Co. E-mail: leslie@411videoinfo.com
URL: http://www.411videoinfo.com
Released: 1997. **Price:** $990.00. **Description:** Ten-volume set deals with the functions of developing and running a business. **Availability:** VHS.

CONSULTANTS

2768 ■ Allen Business Investments
125 Ryan Industrial Ct., Ste. 100
San Ramon, CA 94583
Ph:(925)838-8150
Fax:(925)838-8173
URL: http://www.abi-bizbrkrs.com
Contact: Ron Johnson, President
E-mail: ron@atsabi-ma.com
Scope: Offers expertise on all phases of business opportunity valuations, and buyers and sellers of any type of business. Provides counsel on business frauds and expert witness services in superior and United States bankruptcy court valuations work for goodwill values; loss revenues; estate planning and dissolution of marriages. **Publications:** "Caution Small Business Owners - Be Wary of Companies That Want to Value and Help You Sell Your Business, for an Up-Front "Valuation" Fee"; "Wanted Considered Dangerous Known for Separating Business Owners From Their Money"; "Allocation of Purchase Price"; "Selling Your Business - a Quick Overview".

2769 ■ The Alliance Management Group Inc.
38 Old Chester Rd., Ste. 300
Gladstone, NJ 07934
Ph:(908)234-2344
Fax:(908)234-0638
Co. E-mail: kathy@strategicalliance.com
URL: http://www.strategicalliance.com
Contact: Dan G. Watson, Senior Partner
E-mail: gene@atsstrategicalliance.com
Scope: The firm enables leading companies to maximize the value of their strategic alliances, mergers and acquisitions. Offers services in partner evaluation process, a planning and negotiating program, mergers and acquisition integration, management issues, the turnaround or termination of poorly performing alliances, and a competitive strategic analysis program. **Publications:** "Effective Practices For Sourcing Innovation," Jan-Feb, 2009; "Intellectual Property Issues in Collaborative Research Agreements," Nov-Dec, 2008; "Building University Relationships in China," Sep-Oct, 2008; "Reinventing Corporate Growth: Implementing the Transformational Growth Model"; "The Strongest Link"; "Allocating Patent Rights in Collaborative Research Agreements"; "Protecting Know-how and Trade Secrets in Collaborative Research Agreements," Aug, 2006; "Sourcing External Technology for Innovation," Jun, 2006. **Special Services:** "Want, Find, Get, Manage" Model[R]; "Want, Find, Get, Manage" Framework[R]; WFGM Framework[R]; The Alliance Implementation Program[R]; WFGM Paradigm[R]; WFGM Model[R]; "Want, Find, Get, Manage" Paradigm[R], Transformational Growth[R]; T-growth[R].

2770 ■ Alliance Management International Ltd.
PO Box 470691
Cleveland, OH 44147-0691
Ph:(440)838-1922
Fax:(440)740-1434
Co. E-mail: bob@bgruss.com
Contact: Ken Gruss, Mgr
E-mail: bgruss@cox.net
Scope: A consulting company that helps to form national and international strategic alliances. Handles alliances between companies forming joint ventures. Staff specialized in small company-large company alliance, alliance assessment and analysis, and alliance strategic planning. **Seminars:** Joint Business Planning; Developing a Shared Vision; Current and New/Prospective Partner Assessment; Customer Service; Sales Training; Leader and Management Skills.

2771 ■ Allin Corp.
2841 W Cypress Creek Rd.
Fort Lauderdale, FL 33309
Ph:(412)928-8800
Fax:(412)928-0887
Co. E-mail: webpitt@allin.com
URL: http://www.allin.com
Contact: William C. Kavan, Director
Scope: A information technology consulting company that teams with businesses to help them transform the promise of the Internet into practical business realities through five interrelated solution areas: Information Technology Infrastructure, Business Operations, Knowledge Management, Electronic Business and Interactive Media. **Seminars:** Automate Business Processes using XML, Microsoft's new InfoPath 2003 andK2.net 2003.

2772 ■ Alternative Services Inc.
32625 7 Mile Rd., Ste. 10
Livonia, MI 48152-4269
Ph:(248)471-4880
Fax:(248)471-5230
URL: http://www.asi-mi.org
Contact: Arthur Mack, President
E-mail: bmcluckie@asi-mi.org
Scope: Provides social services management support to group homes for the mentally disabled. Also offers marketing, training, and financial services to businesses and nonprofit organizations.

2773 ■ Ambler Growth Strategy Consultants Inc.
3432 Reading Ave.
Hammonton, NJ 08037-8008
Ph:(609)567-9669
Free: 888-253-6662
Fax:(609)567-3810
Co. E-mail: thegrowthstrategist@ambler.com
URL: http://www.thegrowthstrategist.com
Contact: Melissa Norcross, Chief Marketing Officer
E-mail: melissa@atsambler.com
Scope: Growth strategies, strategic assessments, CEO coaching. **Publications:** "A joint venture can deliver more than growth"; "Achieving competitive advantage"; "Achieving resilience for your business during difficult times"; "Achieving resilient growth during challenging times"; "Acquisitions: A growth strategy to consider"; "Attracting and retaining long-term corporate sponsors"; "Celebrate Selling: The Consultative Relationship Way"; "A Joint Venture Can Deliver More Than Growth"; "Achieving Competitive Advantage"; "Achieving Resilience for Your Business During Difficult Times"; "Balancing Revenue Growth with Growth of a Business"; "Capture Your Competitive Advantage"; "Ease Succession Planning"; "Games Employees Play"; "How to Spark Innovation in an Existing Company"; "Managers demands must change with growth"; "Motivating Generation employees"; "Knowing when to hire ratios provide answers"; "Better customer service can bring black ink". **Seminars:** Strategic Leadership; Managing Innovation; Breaking Through Classic Barriers to Growth; Energize Your Enterprise; Capture Your Competitive Advantage; Four Entrepreneurial Styles; Perservance and Resilience; Real-Time Strategic Planning/RO1. **Special Services:** The Growth Strategist™.

2774 ■ American English Academy
111 N Atlantic Blvd., Ste. 112
Monterey Park, CA 91754
Ph:(626)457-2800
Fax:(626)457-2808
Co. E-mail: admission@aea-usa.com
URL: http://www.aea-usa.com
Contact: Charles Policky, President
Scope: Specializes in providing on-site English language and communication development for corporations and individuals. Also develops and delivers training in speaking, writing, pronunciation, grammar, and idioms with an emphasis on business communication. Offers individual, small group, intensive, and long-distance learning. Programs tailor-made for each client.

2775 ■ Association of Home-Based Women Entrepreneurs
PO Box 31561
Saint Louis, MO 63131-1561
Ph:(314)805-9519
Fax:(314)909-8179
Co. E-mail: aschaefer@advbizsol.com
URL: http://www.hbwe.org
Contact: Sue Lunnemann, Treasurer
E-mail: sue@atssl-solutions.biz
Scope: Organization dedicated to women working from home-based offices. Focuses on the needs and interests of women doing their own business. It also focuses on business-related programs and issues, networking, leads and mentoring for professional growth in a dynamic and friendly atmosphere. **Publications:** "Taking Your Business International"; "Dressing For Success"; "Web 2.0 The Future of the Internet"; "Assertiveness Skills for Women in Business". **Seminars:** Making Connections, Jul, 2008; One Inch Wide, One Mile Deep, Jun, 2008; Accelerating Your Business, May, 2008; Change is Good, Apr, 2008; Pyro Marketing, Jan, 2007; Twenty Five Key Steps To Maintaining A Successful Home-Based Business, Nov, 2006.

2776 ■ Aurora Management Partners Inc.
4485 Tench Rd., Ste. 340
Suwanee, GA 30024
Ph:(770)904-5209
Co. E-mail: rturcotte@auroramp.com
URL: http://www.auroramp.com
Contact: William A. Barbee, Director
E-mail: abarbee@atsauroramp.com
Scope: Firm specializes in turnaround management and reorganization consulting. Firm develop strategic initiatives, organize and analyze solutions, deal with creditor issues, review organizational structure and develop time frames for decision making. Turnaround services offered include Recovery plans and their implementation, Viability analysis, Crisis management, Financial restructuring, Corporate and organizational restructuring, Facilities rationalization, Liquidation management, Loan workout, Litigation support and Expert testimony, Contract renegotiation, Sourcing loan refinancing and Sourcing equity investment. **Publications:** "TMA Turnaround of the Year Award, Small Company, Honorable Mention," Nov, 2005; "Back From The Brink - Bland Farms," Progressive Farmer, Oct, 2004; "New Breed of Turnaround Managers," Catalyst Magazine, Aug, 2004; "Key Performance Drivers - Bland Farms," The Produce News, Apr, 2004; "Corporate Governance: Averting Crisis's Before They Happen," ABJ journal, Feb, 2004.

2777 ■ Automated Accounting
23325 Gerbera St.
Moreno Valley, CA 92553
Ph:(951)653-5053
Co. E-mail: autoacc@earthlink.net
Contact: Gary Capolino, Owner
Scope: A business management consulting firm that caters to small businesses. Offers software installation services, tax preparation services and business plan advisory services. **Publications:** "Inflated Real Estate Prices. . .How Did This Happen," Moreno Valley Magazine, Aug, 2005.

2778 ■ Beacon Management Group Inc.
1000 W McNab Rd., Ste. 150
Pompano Beach, FL 33069-4719
Ph:(954)782-1119
Free: 800-771-8721
Fax:(954)969-2566
Co. E-mail: md@beaconmgmt.com
URL: http://www.beaconmgmt.com
Contact: Chris Roy, Treasurer
E-mail: md@beaconmgmt.com
Scope: Specializes in change management, organized workplaces, multicultural negotiations and dispute resolutions and internet based decision making.

2779 ■ Beeline Learning Solutions
14911 Quorum Dr., Ste. 120
Dallas, TX 75254
Ph:(972)813-0465
Fax:(972)386-8667
Co. E-mail: info@consultingpartners.com
URL: http://www.beeline.com
Contact: Debra Gann, Managering Director
E-mail: gann@atsconsultingpartners.com
Scope: Consulting firm offering technology, content, and services addressing recruitment and sourcing, talent management, and learning and performance optimization. Solutions offered include contingent workforce solutions, vendor management software, talent management solutions, recruitment process outsourcing, performance management, applicant tracking, learning management and eLearning. **Special Services:** Beeline®.

2780 ■ Benchmark Consulting Group Inc.
283 Franklin St., Ste. 400
PO Box 126
Boston, MA 02110-3100
Ph:(617)482-7661
Fax:(617)423-2158
Co. E-mail: werobb35@aol.com
Contact: Walter E. Robb III, President
E-mail: werobb35@aol.com
Scope: Provides financial and management services to companies. Helps companies grow through debt, equity sourcing and restructuring, business valuation, acquisition and divestiture, computer information systems and improved operation profitability.

2781 ■ Bio-Technical Resources L.P.
1035 S 7th St.
Manitowoc, WI 54220-5301
Ph:(920)684-5518
Fax:(920)684-5519
Co. E-mail: info@biotechresources.com
URL: http://www.biotechresources.com
Contact: Tom Jerrell, President
E-mail: jerrell@atsbiotechresources.com
Scope: Services include strain improvement, process development and metabolic engineering. Solutions are also offered for the development of biotechnology products and processes through contract services in research and development, bio process scale-up, pilot scale manufacturing, technology and economic assessments. Target audience: pharmaceutical, biotechnology, chemical and food and feed industries. Client base may be global leaders as well as small companies and startups. **Publications:** "A Novel Fungus for the Production of Efficient Cellulases and Hemi-Cellulases," Jun, 2009; "Linoleic Acid Isomerase from Propionibacterium acnes: Purification, Characterization, Molecular Cloning, and Heterologous Expression," 2007; "Purification and Characterization of a Membrane-Bound Linoleic Acid Isomerase from Clostridium sporogenes," 2007; "Metabolic Engineering of Sesquiterpene Metabolism in Yeast," 2007; "Purification and Characterization of a Membrane-Bound Linoleic AcidIsomerase from Clostridium sporogenes," 2007; "Reduction of Background Interference in the Spectrophotometric Assay of Mevalonate Kinase," 2006; "A Soluble Form of Phosphatase in Saccharomyces cerevisiae Capable of Converting Farnesyl Diphosphate to E, E-Farnesol," 2006; "Ascorbate Biosynthesis: A Diversity of Pathways," BIOS Scientific Publishers, 2004; "The Biotechnology of Ascorbic Acid Manufacture," BIOS Scientific Publishers, 2004; "Detection of Farnesyl Diphosphate Accumulation in YeastERG9 Mutants," 2003; "Reverse Two-Hybrid System: Detecting Critical Interaction Domains and Screening for Inhibitors," Eaton Publishing, 2000. **Seminars:** Metabolic Engineering for Industrial Production of Glucosamine and N-Acetylglucosamine, Aug, 2003; Metabolic Engineering of E. coli for the Industrial Production of Glucosamine, Apr, 2003.

2782 ■ BioChem Technology Inc.
3620 Horizon Dr., Ste. 200
King of Prussia, PA 19406-2110
Ph:(610)768-9360
Fax:(610)768-9363
Co. E-mail: sales@biochemtech.com
URL: http://www.biochemtech.com
Contact: Allan Myers, Principle
E-mail: charlesxu@atsbiochemtech.com
Scope: A process consultation firm specializing in the monitoring, optimization and control of wastewater treatment processes. The technological optimization services include assessment of treatment capacities, facility re-rating, optimization services, debottlenecking services, flow dynamics/mixing pattern analysis. **Publications:** "A Novel Approach for Monitoring and Control of Denitrification in a Biological Nutrient Removal Facility," Oct, 1999; "A Unique Approach for Assessing the Capacity of a Biological Nutrient Removal Facility," Oct, 1999; "Enhancing Competitiveness of an Operations Staff: Five Years Experience with a BNR Wastewater Treatment Facility," Oct, 1998; "Optimization of Nitrification Process By On-Line Monitoring of Nitrification Time," Jun, 1997; "Monitoring and Control of the Nitrification Process Marine Park Water Reclamation Facility, City of Vancouver, WA," Oct, 1997; "Operational Improvements in a Biological Nutrient Removal Facility Using an Innovative Biological Activity Meter," May, 1996; "Operator Education and an Innovative Monitoring Technology Improve Performance of a Biological Nutrient Removal Facility," Oct, 1996; "Performance Enhancement of a BNR Wastewater Treatment Facility Utilizing a Microcosm Reactor Equipped With a Biological Activity Meter," Oct, 1996; "Optimization of Biological Denitrification Through Biological Activity Monitoring: System Development," Jun, 1995. **Seminars:** A Five Year Case Study of a Feed Forward Nitrogen Reduction Process Control System, Jun, 2009; Alternate DO Control Based on On-line Ammonia Measurement, Jun, 2009.

2783 ■ BioSciCon Inc.
14905 Forest Landing Cir.
Rockville, MD 20850-3924
Ph:(301)610-9130

Fax:(301)610-7662
Co. E-mail: info@bioscicon.com
URL: http://www.bioscicon.com
Contact: Olivera Markovic, Director
E-mail: info@bioscicon.com
Scope: Sponsoring development of the technology of the Pap test accuracy via introduction of a new bio-marker that enhances visibility of abnormal cells on Pap smears or mono-layers of cervical cells obtained in solution. Conducts clinical trials for assessment of the test efficacy and safety, manufactures research tools for conduct of trials, and markets IP to license manufacturing, marketing, sales and distribution rights of the new technology line of products. **Publications:** "Cervical Acid Phosphates: A Biomarker of Cervical Dysplasia and Potential Surrogate Endpoint for Colposcopy," 2004; "Enhancing Pap test with a new biological marker of cervical dysplasia," 2004; "A cytoplasmic biomarker for liquid-based Pap," The FACEB Journal Experimental Biology, 2004; "Pap test and new biomarker-based technology for enhancing visibility of abnormal cells," 2004. **Special Services:** MarkPap[R]; PreservCyt[R].

2784 ■ Birchfield Jacobs Foodsystems Inc.
519 N Charles St., Ste. 350A
Baltimore, MD 21201-5022
Ph:(410)528-8700
Fax:(410)528-6060
URL: http://www.birchfieldjacobs.com
Contact: Robert Jacobs, Principle
E-mail: rjacobs@atsbirchfieldjacobs.com
Scope: Food facilities design consultants for colleges; universities; schools; healthcare facilities; government; military; correctional; country clubs and restaurants. Services include facilities design; feasibility studies; operations analysis and master planning.

2785 ■ BPT Consulting Associates Ltd.
12 Parmenter Rd., Ste. B-6
Londonderry, NH 03053
Ph:(603)437-8484
Free: 888-278-0030
Fax:(603)434-5388
Co. E-mail: bptcons@tiac.net
Contact: John Kuczynski, President
E-mail: bptcons@tiac.net
Scope: Provides management consulting expertise and resources to cross-industry clients with services for: Business Management consulting, People/Human Resources Transition and Training programs, and a full cadre of multi-disciplined Technology Computer experts. Virtual consultants with expertise in e-commerce, supply chain management, organizational development, and business application development consulting.

2786 ■ Bran Management Services Inc.
2106 High Ridge Rd.
Louisville, KY 40207-1128
Ph:(502)896-1632
Contact: Robert C. Braverman, CEO
Scope: Offers management consulting services to companies in manufacturing, distribution and services to help them cope with growth and change. Helps small businesses create and identify product strategies. Services include developing international business opportunities; turnaround management; sales and marketing development; business planning; acquisitions and mergers.

2787 ■ Business Consulting Services
207 Dickinson Ave.
PO Box 431
Swarthmore, PA 19081-1630
Ph:(610)328-9806
Contact: Thomas K. Casey, President
Scope: Management consulting organization dedicated to providing high quality, professional services to the business, government and non-profit communities. Specializes in the two key areas of business performance improvement and information technology consulting. Specifically for small business owners. **Publications:** "If You Fail To Plan"; "The True Cost Of Technology"; "Why Projects Fail"; "Planning For A Business Disruption". **Seminars:** How To Select, Manage and Contract Consultants, and Other Resources; How To Market Professional Services; Introduction To Management Consulting.

2788 ■ Business Improvement Architects
33 Riderwood Dr.
Toronto, ON, Canada M2L 2X4
Ph:(416)444-8225
Free: (866)346-3242
Fax:(416)444-6743
Co. E-mail: info@bia.ca
URL: http://www.bia.ca
Contact: Susan Lee, Principle
E-mail: slee@atsbia.ca
Scope: Provides the following services: strategic planning, leadership development, innovation and project and quality management. Specialize in strategic planning, change management, leadership assessment, and development of skills. **Publications:** "Avoiding Pit falls to Innovation"; "Create a New Dimension of Performance with Innovation"; "The Power of Appreciation in Leadership"; "Why It Makes Sense To Have a Strategic Enterprise Office"; "Burning Rubber at the Start of Your Project"; "Accounting for Quality"; "How Pareto Charts Can Help You Improve the Quality of Business Processes"; "Managing Resistance to Change". **Seminars:** The Innovation Process. . .From Vision to Reality, San Diego, Oct, 2007; Critical Thinking, Kuala Lump or, Sep, 2007; Critical Thinking, Brunei, Sep, 2007; Delivering Project Assurance, Auckland, Jun, 2007; From Crisis to Control: A New Era in Strategic Project Management, Prague, May, 2007; What Project Leaders Need to Know to Help Them Sleep Better At Night, London, May, 2007; Innovation Process. . .From Vision To Reality, Orlando, Apr, 2007. **Special Services:** Project Planning Tool[TM].

2789 ■ ByrneMRG
22 Isle of Pines Dr.
Hilton Head Island, SC 29928
Ph:(215)630-7411
Free: 888-816-8080
Co. E-mail: info@byrnemrg.com
URL: http://www.byrnemrg.com
Contact: Patrick J. Boyle, CEO
E-mail: pjboyle@byrnemrg.com
Scope: Firm specializes in management consulting, including department management, equipment evaluation and selection, project management, research and development planning; and database design and management. **Publications:** "Implementing Solutions to Everyday Issues".

2790 ■ C. Clint Bolte & Associates
809 Philadelphia Ave.
Chambersburg, PA 17201-1268
Ph:(717)263-5768
Fax:(717)263-8954
Co. E-mail: clint@clintbolte.com
URL: http://www.clintbolte.com
Contact: C. Clint Bolte, Principle
E-mail: cbolte3@comcast.net
Scope: Provides management consulting services to firms involved with the printing industry. Services include outsourcing studies, graphics supply chain management studies, company and equipment valuations, plant layout services, litigation support, fulfillment warehouse consulting and product development services. **Publications:** "UV Cost Savings Environmental Advantage"; "Possible Quebecor World Fall Out"; "80-20 Rule for Managing"; "Options Available in Starting Up a Mailing Operation"; "High Volume Print Buyers at Print 2009"; "Diversifying With Mailing & Fulfillment Services"; "New Business Model Needed for Magazine News stand Distribution"; "Purchasing Incentives Can Be Costly..".; "In-Plant New Product Opportunity for 2009: Tran promo Printing"; "Possible Quebecor World Fall Out"; "Offshore Print Evolution"; "Benefits of Third Party Lease Review"; "Unique Information Fulfillment Opportunities for In-Plant Printers"; "Tough Competition Forces New Strategic Realities for In-Plants"; "Direct Mail Industry Group Files Interpretive Ruling Requests with the Ssta"; "Interesting Opportunities Amid the Gray Clouds of 2007 Postal Rate Increases"; "Time to Break Through the Glass Ceiling," the Seybold Report, May, 2006; "Challenges and Opportunities Presented By Postal Rate Increases," the Seybold Report, May, 2006; "Packaging Roll Sheeting Comes of Age," the Seybold Report, May, 2006; "Diversifying with Mailing and Fulfillment Services," the Seybold Report, Jan, 2006. **Seminars:** How to compete with the majors.

2791 ■ Canadian Business Resource Centre
145 Front St. E, Ste. 101
Toronto, ON, Canada M5A 1E3
Ph:(416)415-2370
Fax:(416)415-2371
Co. E-mail: info@cbrc.com
Contact: Gabriella Zoltan-Johan, Principle
E-mail: info@cbrc.com
Scope: Management consulting and training services to the small and medium enterprise sector, to design and deliver entrepreneurship and small business training and provide consulting advice and information to individuals, organizations and municipalities interested in developing businesses and/or community economic development projects.

2792 ■ Capell & Associates
601 Central Ave.
PO Box 742
Barnegat Light, NJ 08006
Ph:(202)572-8774
Fax:(609)494-7369
Co. E-mail: contact@capellandassociates.com
URL: http://www.capellandassociates.com
Contact: E. Daniel Capell, President
E-mail: dan_capell@att.net
Scope: Specialized consulting firm focused on direct marketing, magazine publishing and circulation. Consulting services include due diligence, circulation audits, benchmarking and list rental analysis. **Seminars:** Circulation for the Non-Circulator.

2793 ■ Casino, Hotel & Resort Consultants L.L.C.
8100 Via Del Cerro Ct.
Las Vegas, NV 89117
Ph:(702)646-7200
Fax:(702)646-6680
Co. E-mail: info@hraba.com
URL: http://www.hraba.com
Contact: John S. Hraba, President
E-mail: jshraba@aol.com
Scope: Casino and hospitality industry consultants. Firm specializes in developing and implementing customized forecast and labor management control systems that deliver immediate, positive impact to the company's bottom line. Involved in production planning, employ surveys and communication, inventory management, business process reviews, audits, development and implementation of key management reports. **Seminars:** Payroll Cost Control; Effective Staff Scheduling.

2794 ■ Center for Lifestyle Enhancement - Columbia Medical Center of Plano
3901 W 15th St.
Plano, TX 75075
Ph:(972)596-6800
Fax:(972)519-1299
Co. E-mail: mcp.cle@hcahealthcare.com
URL: http://www.medicalcenterofplano.com
Contact: Doug Browning, Vice President
E-mail: boesdorfer@hcahealthcare.com
Scope: Provides professional health counseling in the areas of general nutrition for weight management, eating disorders, diabetic education, cholesterol reduction and adolescent weight management. Offers work site health promotion and preventive services. Also coordinates speaker's bureau, cooking classes and physician referrals. Industries served: education, insurance, healthcare, retail or wholesale, data processing and manufacturing throughout Texas. **Seminars:** Rx Diet and Exercise; Smoking Cessation; Stress Management; Health Fairs; Fitness Screenings; Body Composition; Nutrition Analysis; Exercise Classes; Prenatal Nutrition; SHAPEDOWN; Successfully Managing Diabetes; Gourmet Foods for Your Heart; The Aging Heart; Heart Smart Saturday featuring Day of Dance; Weight-Loss Management Seminars; The Right Stroke for Men; Peripheral Artery Disease Screening; Menstruation: The Cycle Begins; Boot Camp for New Dads; Grand parenting 101: Caring for Kids Today; Teddy Bear Camp; New Baby Day Camp; Safe Sitter Baby-Sitting Class.

2795 ■ The Center for Organizational Excellence Inc.
15204 Omega Dr., Ste. 300
Rockville, MD 20850
Ph:(301)948-1922
Free: 877-674-3923
Fax:(301)948-2158
Co. E-mail: results@center4oe.com
URL: http://www.center4oe.com
Contact: Kirstin Austin, Mgr
E-mail: kaustin@atscenter4oe.com
Scope: An organizational effectiveness consulting firm specializing in helping organizations achieve results through people, process, and performance. Service areas include organizational performance systems, leadership systems, customer systems, and learning systems.

2796 ■ Center for Personal Empowerment
102 N Main St., Ste. 1
Columbia, IL 62236-1702
Ph:(618)281-3565
Free: 888-657-1530
Fax:(618)476-7083
Co. E-mail: personalempowerment@wholenet.net
Contact: Cherri Hendrix, Vice President
Scope: Private consultations and trainings to educate on how to determine which emotions, events, beliefs from the past prevent you from achieving success. Methods used include time line therapy, news linguistic programming and hypnosis. Behavior modification through NLP trainings. **Seminars:** NLP Practitioner Training; Hypnosis Certification Training; Lifemap Seminars.

2797 ■ Century Business Services Inc.
6050 Oak Tree Blvd. S, Ste. 500
Cleveland, OH 44131-6951
Ph:(216)525-1947
Fax:(216)447-9007
Co. E-mail: info@cbiz.com
URL: http://www.cbiz.com
Contact: Steven L. Gerard, CEO
E-mail: gdufour@cbiz.com
Scope: A business consulting and tax services firm providing financial, consulting, tax and business services through seven groups: Financial management, tax advisory, construction and real estate, health-care, litigation support, capital resource and CEO outsource. **Publications:** "FAS 154: Changes in the Way We Report Changes," 2006; "Equity-Based Compensation: How Much Does it Really Cost Your Business," 2006; "Preventing Fraud - Tips for Nonprofit Organizations"; "Today's Workforce and Nonprofit Organizations: Meeting a Critical Need"; "IRS Highlights Top Seven Form 990 Errors". **Seminars:** Health Care - What the Future Holds; Consumer Driven Health Plans; Executive Plans; Health Savings Accounts; Healthy Wealthy and Wise; Legislative Update; Medicare Part D; Retirement Plans.

2798 ■ CEO Advisors
848 Brickell Ave., Ste. 603
Miami, FL 33131
Ph:(305)371-8560
Fax:(305)371-8563
Co. E-mail: ciaizpurua@ceoadvisors.us
URL: http://www.ceoadvisors.us
Contact: Mario Castro, Vice President
E-mail: mcastro@atsceoadvisors.us
Scope: Business consulting firm offering clients services in strategy, mergers and acquisitions, corporate finance, corporate advisory, supply chain management, government relations and public affairs. Specializes in strategic planning, profit enhancement, start-up businesses, venture capital, appraisals and valuations.

2799 ■ Chamberlain & Cansler Inc.
2251 Perimeter Park Dr.
Atlanta, GA 30341
Ph:(770)457-5699
Contact: Charles L. Cansler, Owner
Scope: Firm specializes in strategic planning; profit enhancement; small business management; interim management; crisis management; turnarounds.

2800 ■ Charismedia
610 W End Ave., Ste. B1
New York, NY 10001
Ph:(212)362-6808
Fax:(212)362-6809
Co. E-mail: charismedia@earthlink.net
URL: http://www.charismedia.net
Contact: Ying Jo Wong, Principle
E-mail: charismedia@earthlink.net
Scope: Offers speech and image training as well as speech writing services for effective presentation skills. Conducts workshops like anti-stage fright breathing, psychophysical exercises, transformational success imagery, face reading and body language, EMDR (Eye Movement Desensitization Re-Processing) for Permanent Trauma and Fear Removal, Bach Flower remedies, thought field therapy, cross-cultural communication, speech, voice and diction; regional and foreign accent elimination and acquisition, Positive Perception Management (P.P.M.), Ad-libbing, humor and spontaneity training, fast creative speech preparation, Neuro-Linguistic Programming and Hypnosis. **Publications:** "Flaunt It"; "Improve Your Sex Life"; "Phone Power"; "Train Your Voice"; "Turning Tinny, Tiny Tones To Gold"; "The New Secrets of Charisma: How to Discover and Unleash your Hidden Powers," McGraw-Hill, Jul, 1999. **Seminars:** Services for Comfortable Effective Speaking.

2801 ■ Chartered Management Co.
125 S Wacker Dr.
Chicago, IL 60606
Ph:(312)214-2575
Contact: William B. Avellone, President
Scope: Operations improvement consultants. Specializes in strategic planning; feasibility studies; management audits and reports; profit enhancement; start-up businesses; mergers and acquisitions; joint ventures; divestitures; interim management; crisis management; turnarounds; business process re-engineering; venture capital; and due diligence.

2802 ■ The Children's Psychological Trauma Center
2105 Divisadero St.
San Francisco, CA 94115
Ph:(415)292-7119
Fax:(415)749-2802
Co. E-mail: gil.kliman@cphc-sf.org
URL: http://www.cphc-sf.org
Contact: Charlotte E. Burchard, Managing Director
E-mail: charlotte.burchard@atscphn-sf.org
Scope: Treats those with psychological trauma claimed from stressors including institutional negligence, vehicular and aviation accidents, wrongful death in the family, rape, molestation, fire, explosion, flood, earthquake, loss of parents, terrorism, kidnapping, disfiguring events, emotional damage from social work, medical malpractice or defective products. Provides evaluation and reports to referring professionals. Experienced in forensic consultation and testimony. **Publications:** "My Personal Story About Tropical Storm Stan," Feb, 2006; "My Personal Story About Hurricanes Katrina and Rita: A guided activity workbook to help coping, learning and Healthy expression," Sep, 2005; "Helping Patients and their Families Cope in a National Disaster," Jan, 2002; "The practice of behavioral treatment in the acute rehabilitation setting".

2803 ■ Claremont Consulting Group
4525 Castle Ln.
La Canada, CA 91011-1436
Ph:(818)249-0584
Fax:(818)249-5811
Contact: Donald S. Remer, Partner
E-mail: amruskin@compuserve.com
Scope: Consulting, coaching, training, and litigation support in project management, engineering management, system engineering and cost estimating. **Publications:** "What Every Engineer Should Know About Project Management"; "100%product-oriented work breakdown structures and their importance to system engineering". **Seminars:** Project Management, System Engineering and Cost Estimating.

2804 ■ Clayton/Curtis/Cottrell
1722 Madison Ct.
Louisville, CO 80027-1121
Ph:(303)665-2005
Contact: Robert Cottrell, President
Scope: Market research firm specializes in providing consultations for packaged goods, telecommunications, direct marketing and printing, and packaging industries. Services include strategic planning; profit enhancement; startup businesses; mergers and acquisitions; joint ventures; divestitures; interim management; crisis management; turnarounds; market size, segmentation and rates of growth; competitor intelligence; image and reputation, and competitive analysis. **Publications:** "Turn an attitude into a purchase," Jul, 1995; "Mixed results for private label; price assaults by the national brands are getting heavy, but there's still a place for private label," Jun, 1995; "In-store promotion goes high-tech: is the conventional coupon destined for obsolescence?," Jun, 1995.

2805 ■ Colmen Menard Company Inc.
The Woods, 994 Old Eagle School Rd., Ste. 1000
Wayne, PA 19087
Ph:(484)367-0300
Fax:(484)367-0305
Co. E-mail: cmci@colmenmenard.com
URL: http://www.colmenmenard.com
Contact: David W. Menard, Managering Director
E-mail: dmenard@atscolmenmenard.com
Scope: Merger and acquisition corporate finance and business advisory services for public and private companies located in North America. **Publications:** "Success in Selling a Troubled Company," Nov, 2002; "Savvy Dealmakers," May, 2001; "Truisms," M&A Today, Nov, 2000.

2806 ■ Columbia Consultants
8950 Old Annapolis Rd., Rte. 108, Ste. 226
Columbia, MD 21045
Ph:(410)992-4700
Free: 800-783-7574
Fax:(410)992-4518
Contact: Anela Brooks, Principle
E-mail: abrooks@columbiaconsultants.net
Scope: A complete personnel service offering placement of both permanent and temporary employees. Provides professional services and integrated solutions.

2807 ■ Comer & Associates L.L.C.
5255 Holmes Pl.
Boulder, CO 80303
Ph:(303)786-7986
Free: 888-950-3190
Fax:(303)895-2347
URL: http://www.comerassociates.com
Contact: Jerry C. Comer, President
E-mail: jcomer@comer-associates.com
Scope: Specialize in developing markets and businesses. Marketing support includes: Developing and writing strategic and tactical business plans; developing and writing focused, effective market plans; researching market potential and competition; implementing targeted marketing tactics to achieve company objectives; conducting customer surveys to determine satisfaction and attitudes toward client. Organization development support includes: Executive/management training programs; executive coaching; team building; developing effective organization structures; and management of change in dynamic and competitive environments; individual coaching for management and leadership effectiveness. **Seminars:** Developing a Strategic Market Plan; Market Research: Defining Your Opportunity; Management and Leadership Effectiveness; Team Building; Developing a Business Plan; How to Close; Using Questions to Sell; Sales System Elements and Checklist; Working With Independent Reps; Features vs. Benefits; Overcoming Objections; Sales Force Automation.

2808 ■ Consultants National Resource Center
27-A Big Spring Rd.
PO Box 430
Clear Spring, MD 21722
Ph:(301)791-9332

Free: 800-290-3196
Fax:(301)582-3639
Co. E-mail: cnrc@erols.com
Contact: Lewis Williams, Director
E-mail: steve@mynabc.com
Scope: Provides marketing and strategic planning services for consultants. Also serves as membership center for the professional management institute. Industries served: all consulting disciplines. **Publications:** "Consulting Opportunities Journal"; "How to Master Continuous Learning". **Seminars:** How to Series on Starting and Building a Consulting Practice; Introduction to the Professional Management Institute; Consulting Boot camp; Planagement[R].

2809 ■ Consulting & Conciliation Service
2830 I St., Ste. 301
Sacramento, CA 95816
Ph:(916)396-0480
Free: 888-898-9780
Fax:(916)441-2828
Co. E-mail: service@azurewings.net
Contact: Jane A. McCluskey, Principle
E-mail: service@azurewings.net
Scope: Offers consulting and conciliation services. Provides pre-mediation counseling, training and research on preparing for a peaceful society, mediation and facilitation, and preparation for shifts in structure, policy and personnel. Offers sliding scale business rates and free individual consultation. **Publications:** "Native America and Tracking Shifts in US Policy"; "Biogenesis: A Discussion of Basic Social Needs and the Significance of Hope". **Seminars:** Positive Approaches to Violence Prevention: Peace building in Schools and Communities.

2810 ■ The Consulting Exchange
1770 Mass Ave., Ste. 288
PO Box 391050
Cambridge, MA 02140
Ph:(617)576-2100
Free: 800-824-4828
Co. E-mail: gday@consultingexchange.com
URL: http://www.cx.com
Contact: Geoffrey Day, President
E-mail: gday@consultingexchange.com
Scope: A consultant referral service for management and technical consultants. Serves a local, regional and international client base. **Publications:** "Looking for a Consultant? Success Points for Finding the Right One," Boston Business Journal, Jun, 2001; "Getting Full Value From Consulting is in Your Hands," Mass High Tech, May, 1998; "Developing Knowledge-Based Client Relationships, The Future of Professional Services"; "The Consultant's Legal Guide"; "The Business of Consulting: The Basics and Beyond".

2811 ■ The Corlund Group L.L.C.
101 Federal St., Ste. 310
Boston, MA 02110
Ph:(617)423-9364
Fax:(617)423-9371
Co. E-mail: info@corlundgroup.com
URL: http://www.corlundgroup.com
Contact: Deborah J. Cornwall, Managing Director
E-mail: dcornwall@atscorlundgroup.com
Scope: Boutique firm offering services in the areas of leadership, governance, and change with a particular focus on CEO and senior executive succession planning, including assessment, development, and orchestrating succession processes with management and Boards of Directors. Also Board governance effectiveness. **Publications:** "Are You Rolling the Dice on CEO Succession?" Center for Healthcare Governance, 2006; "Leadership Due Diligence: The Neglected Governance Frontier," Directorship, Sep, 2001; "Leadership Due Diligence: Managing the Risks," The Corporate Board, Aug, 2001; "Succession: The need for detailed insight," Directors and Boards, 2001; "CEO Succession: Who's Doing Due Diligence?," 2001.

2812 ■ Corporate Consulting Inc.
3333 Belcaro Dr.
Denver, CO 80209-4912
Ph:(303)698-9292
Fax:(303)698-9292
Co. E-mail: corpcons@compuserve.com
Contact: Devereux C. Josephs, President
E-mail: corpcons@compuserve.com
Scope: Specializes in feasibility studies, organizational development, small business management, mergers and acquisitions, joint ventures, divestitures, interim management, crisis management, turnarounds, financing, appraisals valuations and due diligence studies.

2813 ■ Coyne Associates
4010 E Lake St.
Minneapolis, MN 55406-2201
Ph:(612)724-1188
Fax:(612)722-1379
Contact: Sandra Blanton, Principle
Scope: A marketing and public relations consulting firm that specializes in assisting architectural, engineering, and contractor/developer firms. Services include: marketing plains and audits, strategic planning, corporate identity, turnarounds, and sales training.

2814 ■ Creative Computer Resources Inc.
5001 Horizons Dr., Ste. 200
Columbus, OH 43220-5291
Ph:(614)384-7557
Free: (866)720-0209
Fax:(614)573-6331
Co. E-mail: team@planet-ccr.com
URL: http://www.planet-ccr.com
Contact: M. Erik Mueller, President
E-mail: merikm@atsplanet-ccr.com
Scope: Firm offers information systems support, custom software development, website design, development and implementation. Provides information technology support and management services to small and mid-size businesses.

2815 ■ Crystal Clear Communications Inc.
1633 W Winslow Dr., Ste. 210
Mequon, WI 53092
Ph:(262)240-0072
Fax:(262)240-0073
Co. E-mail: contact@crystalclear1.com
URL: http://www.crystalclear1.com
Contact: Chez Fogel, Principle
E-mail: chfogel@atscrystalclear.com
Scope: Specialize in helping executives identify impediments to success, and then develop strategies to surmount them. Serves to identify core problems, suggest appropriate business changes, work with the organization to support these changes, and help executives articulate the behavior that will uphold these changes. Specializes in strategic planning; organizational development; small business management; executive coaching. **Publications:** "Weakest Link"; "Aware Leadership"; "Integrity"; "When Your Plate is Full"; "Problem Solving"; "Strategic Thinking".

2816 ■ CUFFE & Associates Inc.
27435 Everett St.
PO Box 7123
Southfield, MI 48076-5130
Ph:(248)557-8541
Fax:(248)557-5144
Co. E-mail: caimmts@aol.com
Contact: Stafford S. Cuffe, President
E-mail: caimmts@aol.com
Scope: Specializes in the following areas: E-commerce, analysis, assessment, mapping and research and planning, risk mitigation and crisis management, glass technology, business process re-engineering, productivity improvements, quality tools. Performed assessments in manufacturing, management, financial, operations, and IT.

2817 ■ De Bellas & Co.
2700 Post Oak Blvd., Ste. 1400
Houston, TX 77056
Ph:(949)859-3332
Fax:(949)859-9333
Co. E-mail: info@debellas.com
URL: http://www.debellas.com
Contact: Royal J. Brown, Vice President
E-mail: rbrown@debellas.com
Scope: Provides merger, acquisition and financial advisory services to staffing and information technology services businesses and professional employer service organizations. **Publications:** "Tools to Take Advantage of the Current IT Staffing M and A Market," 2005; "Healthcare Staffing: Buy, Sell or Build," 2005.

2818 ■ The Devine Group Inc.
7755 Montgomery Rd., Ste. 180
Cincinnati, OH 45236
Ph:(513)792-7500
Free: (866)792-7500
Fax:(513)793-8535
Co. E-mail: sales@devinegroup.com
URL: http://www.devinegroup.com
Contact: Dr. Syed Saad, VP of Research
E-mail: rwalker@atsdevinegroup.com
Scope: A human resource consulting company devoted to providing reliable and responsive information focusing on performance issues and answers. Dedicated to analyzing and enhancing job performance. Custom design and implement programs and workshops that will result in demonstrable behavior change on the job. Assist clients enhance their productivity via behavior analysis. **Publications:** "Leveraging Assessments for Enterprise Improvement," Oct, 2006; "Evaluation of Assessment Tools: The Five Criteria," Oct, 2006; "People Improvement Using Behavior Assessment," Aug, 2005; "Measuring Personality: The Good, the Bad and the Ugly," Jul, 25. **Special Services:** The Devine Inventory[TM].

2819 ■ Diamond Management & Technology Consultants Inc.
1101 Pennsylvania Ave. NW, Ste. 600
Washington, DC 20004
Ph:(312)255-5000
Fax:(312)255-6000
Co. E-mail: info@diamondcluster.com
URL: http://www.diamondconsultants.com
Contact: Melvyn E. Bergstein, Chairman of the Board
Scope: Provides business consulting services to help companies develop business strategies; information advantage services to help clients make better decisions about opportunities and risks by extracting the untapped value of data and by increasing the value of information management investments. Customer impact services help companies design and implement superior experiences across all interactions, which lead to passionate, profitable customer relationships; and execution services turn high-level strategies into measurable results. **Publications:** "Answer To a New Set of Shareholders," Jan, 2009; "Subprime Fallout: Investing in Data Management," Jun, 2008; "Billion-Dollar Lessons: What You Can Learn From the Most Inexcusable Business Failures of the Last 25 Years," Portfolio, 2008; "Unleashing the Killer App: Digital Strategies for Market Dominance," Harvard Business School Press, 1998; "The Compliance Conundrum: Guarding the Firm, Controlling Costs". **Seminars:** Banking for the Rural and the Underprivileged, Mumbai, Oct, 2007.

2820 ■ Dimond Hospitality Consulting Group Inc.
5710 Stoneway Trl.
Nashville, TN 37209
Ph:(615)353-0033
Fax:(615)352-5290
Co. E-mail: drew@dimondhotelconsulting.com
URL: http://www.dimondhotelconsulting.com
Contact: Drew W. Dimond, President
E-mail: drew@dimondhotelconsulting.com
Scope: Specializes in strategic planning; start-up businesses; business process re-engineering; team building; competitive analysis; venture capital; competitive intelligence; and due diligence. Offers litigation support. Comprehensive hospitality consulting firm that serves as an adviser to leading hotel companies, independent hotels, lending institutions, trustees, law firms, investment companies and municipalities in the areas of: Asset management,

Acquisition due diligence, Arbitration, Disposition advisory services, Exit strategies, Financial review and analysis, Impact studies, Mediation. **Publications:** "The distressed debt conundrum," Jul, 2009; "How to buy distressed assets," Apr, 2009; "Cmbs Loans: A History and the Future," Apr, 2009; "Opportunity Knocks," Apr, 2009; "Another Reality Check," Mar, 2009; "An Inkling of Hope," Mar, 2009; "Strong World Tourism Growth in 2007," 2007; "Les U.S. Construction Pipeline Sets Another Record at 5011 Hotels with 654503 Rooms"; "Hotel Capitalization Rates Hold for Now"; "Winning Cornell Hotel and Restaurant Administration Quarterly Article Provides Hotel Brand Analysis"; "Breaking News for Lifestyle Hotels. Ian Schrager and Bill Marriott Announce Their Marriage Will the Schrager-Marriott Marriage Lead to Eternal Bliss Or End in Divorce What Will the M Hotels Children Be Named"; "Brands Vs Independents"; "Nyu Conf Takes Industry Temp"; "Economy Hotel Performance Indication of Travel Trends"; "Hotel Sales Continue at Brisk Pace"; "Fundamentals Strong, Weakening Undercurrent"; "Hotel Investments: Where Do We Go From Here"; "On the Road: Aahoa Panel Commits to Change"; "Cuba Not Ready, But Expecting U.S. Tourists".

2821 ■ Diversified Health Resources Inc.
875 N Michigan Ave., Ste. 3250
Chicago, IL 60611-1901
Ph:(312)266-0466
Fax:(312)266-0715
Contact: Andrea R. Rozran, President
E-mail: yablon@ix.netcom.com
Scope: Offers health care consulting for hospitals, nursing homes including homes for the aged, and other health related facilities and companies. Specializes in planning and marketing. Also conducts executive searches for top level health care administrative positions. Serves private industries as well as government agencies. **Publications:** "City Finance".

2822 ■ Dropkin & Co.
390 George St.
New Brunswick, NJ 08901
Ph:(732)828-3211
Fax:(732)828-4118
Co. E-mail: murray@dropkin.com
URL: http://www.dropkin.com
Contact: Mel Nusbaum, Principle
E-mail: mel@atsdropkin.com
Scope: Firm specializes in feasibility studies; business management; business process re-engineering; and team building, health care and housing. **Publications:** "Bookkeeping for Nonprofits," Jossey Bass, 2005; "Guide to Audits of Nonprofit Organizations," PPC; "The Nonprofit Report," Warren, Gorham & Lamont; "The Budget Building Book for Nonprofits," Jossey-Bass; "The Cash Flow Management Book for Nonprofits," Jossey-Bass.

2823 ■ Dubuc Lucke & Company Inc.
120 W 5th St.
Cincinnati, OH 45202-2713
Ph:(513)579-8330
Fax:(513)241-6669
Contact: Kenneth E. Dubuc, President
Scope: Provides consulting services in the areas of profit enhancement; small business management; mergers and acquisitions; joint ventures; divestitures; interim management; crisis management; turnarounds; appraisals; valuations; due diligence; and international trade.

2824 ■ The DuMond Group
5282 Princeton Ave.
Westminster, CA 92683-2753
Ph:(714)373-0610
Contact: David L. Dumond, Principle
Scope: Human resources and executive search consulting firm that specializes in organizational development; small business management; employee surveys and communication; performance appraisals; and team building.

2825 ■ Dunelm International
437 Colebrook Ln.
Bryn Mawr, PA 19010-3216
Ph:(610)989-0144
Fax:(610)964-9524
Co. E-mail: jecdunelm@worldnet.att.net
Contact: John E. Crowther, President
E-mail: jecdunelm@dunelm.org.uk
Scope: Firm specializes in feasibility studies; start-up businesses; interim management; crisis management; turnarounds; business process re-engineering; sales forecasting; supply chain solution and project management.

2826 ■ Eastern Point Consulting Group Inc.
36 Glen Ave.
Newton, MA 02464
Ph:(617)965-4141
Fax:(617)965-4172
Co. E-mail: info@eastpt.com
URL: http://www.eastpt.com
Contact: Mary MacMahon, Principal
E-mail: kherzog@eastpt.com
Scope: Specializes in bringing practical solutions to complex challenges. Provides consulting and training in managing diversity; comprehensive sexual-harassment policies and programs; organizational development; benchmarks 360 skills assessment; executive coaching; strategic human resource planning; team building; leadership development for women; mentoring programs; and gender issues in the workplace. **Seminars:** Leadership Development for Women.

2827 ■ Education Development Center Inc.
55 Chapel St.
Newton, MA 02458-1060
Ph:(617)969-7100
Free: 800-225-4276
Fax:(617)969-5979
Co. E-mail: comment@edc.org
URL: http://www.edc.org
Contact: Luther Luedtke, President
E-mail: rrotner@atsedc.org
Scope: Services include research, training, educational materials and strategy, with activities ranging from seed projects to large-scale national and international initiatives. Specialize in program and fiscal management. Serves to design, deliver and evaluate innovative programs to address some of the world's most urgent challenges in education, health, and economic opportunity. Renders services to U.S. and foreign government agencies, private foundations, healthcare sectors, educational institutions, nonprofit organizations, universities, and corporations. **Publications:** "A Call to Action: HIV/AIDS, Health, Safety, and the Youth Employment Summit"; "A Case Against "Binge" as the Term of Choice: How to Get College Students to Personalize Messages about Dangerous Drinking"; "A Description of Foundation Skills Interventions for Struggling Middle-Grade Readers in Four Urban Northeast and Islands Region School Districts"; "A Guide to Facilitating Cases in Education"; "A Look at Social, Emotional, and Behavioral Screening Tools for Head Start and Early Head Start"; "A Multifaceted Social Norms Approach to Reduce High-Risk Drinking: Lessons from Hobart and William Smith Colleges"; "The New Media Literacy Handbook"; "Helping Children Outgrow War"; "Worms, Shadows, and Whirlpools: Science in the Early Childhood Classroom"; "Teacher Leadership in Mathematics and Science Casebook and Facilitator's Guide"; "Teachers' Professional Development and the Elementary Mathematics Classroom: Bringing Understandings to Light". **Seminars:** Designed to Introduce the Materials; To Guide Schools Through the Issues.

2828 ■ Edward M. Hepner & Associates
4667 Macarthur Blvd., Ste. 405
Newport Beach, CA 92660
Ph:(714)250-0818
Fax:(714)553-8437
Contact: Edward M. Hepner, President
Scope: An immigration consultant and labor certification specialist. Assists in obtaining visa for work, immigration and business development within the United States and Canada.

2829 ■ Effective Compensation Inc.
3609 S Wadsworth Blvd., Ste. 260
Lakewood, CO 80235
Ph:(303)854-1000
Free: 877-746-4324
Fax:(303)854-1030
Co. E-mail: eci@effectivecompensation.com
URL: http://www.effectivecompensation.com
Contact: Mike Sanchez, Principle
E-mail: tisselhardt@atseffectivecompensation.com
Scope: Independent compensation consulting firm specializing in working with clients on a collaborative basis to improve their organization's efficiency through competitive, focused total compensation processes. Helps organizations determine how to competitively pay their employees. Provides quality, culture sensitive, compensation consulting assistance to all types of employers. Specializes in surveys like drilling industry compensation surveys, environmental industry compensation surveys, liquid pipeline round table compensation surveys; and oil and gas E and P industry compensation surveys. **Publications:** "Alternative Job Evaluation Approaches"; "Broad Banding: A Management Overview"; "Job Evaluation: Understanding the Issues"; "Industry Compensation Surveys"; "Skill Based Pay"; "Four Levels of Team Membership"; "Factors in Designing an Incentive Plan"; "Key Stock Allocation Issues"; "Stock Plans Primer". **Seminars:** Alternative Job Evaluation Approaches; Broad Banding: A Management Overview; Skill Based Pay; Job Evaluation: Understanding the Issues; Designing Compensation Programs that Motivate Employees; Master the Compensation Maze; Base Salary Administration Manual.

2830 ■ Effectiveness Resource Group Inc.
2529 170th Pl. SE
PO Box 7149
Bellevue, WA 98008-5520
Ph:(206)949-4171
Fax:(425)957-9186
Co. E-mail: don@consultdon.com
URL: http://www.consultdon.com
Contact: Donald H. Swartz, President
E-mail: dhsergsri@aol.com
Scope: Provides problem solving help to client organizations in public and private sectors so they can release and mobilize the full potential of their personnel to achieve productive and satisfying results. Emphasis is on technical or human productivity improvement projects and systems, total human resource systems design and implementation, and a whole systems approach to organizational change design and implementation. Serves private industries as well as government agencies. Consults with both internal and external consultants via e-mail and phone. Also offers executive coaching. **Seminars:** Life/Work Goals Exploration; Influencing Change Thru Consultation; Designing and Leading Participative Meetings; Designing, Leading and Managing Change; Project Management and Leadership; Performance Management; Productive Management of Differences; Performance Correction.

2831 ■ Environmental Business International Inc.
4452 Park Blvd. Ste. 306
PO Box 371769
San Diego, CA 92116-4049
Ph:(619)295-7685
Fax:(619)295-5743
Co. E-mail: moe@ebiusa.com
URL: http://www.ebiusa.com
Contact: Grant Ferrier, President
E-mail: gf@atsebiusa.com
Scope: Offers a variety of research and professional services to deliver the market information and business intelligence required for growth and profit in today's rapidly changing business climate. **Publications:** "Water view Report: Water & Wastewater Markets," Dec, 2006; "Report 2020 the U.S. Environmental Industry & Global Markets"; "Mergers & Acquisitions in the Environmental Industry".

2832 ■ Environmental Health Science Inc.
418 Wall St.
Princeton, NJ 08540
Ph:(609)924-7616
Free: 800-841-8923

Fax:(609)924-0793
Co. E-mail: healthscience@comcast.net
URL: http://www.speechgeneratingdevices.com
Contact: Wilma Solomon, Principle
E-mail: davidg@atspatmedia.net
Scope: Specialists in rehabilitation technology for speech disorder and physically disabled persons. Offers demonstrations, evaluations and sales of the following types of equipment: augmentative speech communication systems, adaptive switches and specialty controls, and computer access devices. Industries served: hospitals and rehabilitation centers, schools, and special service organizations such as United Cerebral Palsy Association, Department of Human Services, etc. **Publications:** "Play & Learn"; "Bookworm Literacy Tool"; "Meville to Weville". **Seminars:** Augmentative Communication and Assistive Devices. **Special Services:** Boardmaker[R]; Dynamically Pro[R].

2833 ■ Everest Marketing
957 Ashland Ave.
Saint Paul, MN 55104-7019
Ph:(612)581-1333
Fax:(651)221-1978
Co. E-mail: aistrup@aistrup.com
Contact: Becky Aistrup, Principle
E-mail: mike@aistrup.com
Scope: Provides business-to-business marketing services including marketing plan development, marketing communications, market research and business intelligence. **Publications:** "Finding and Using Local Market Research To Improve Your Sales"; "Marketing to the Right People at the Right Time"; "Marketing in a Sales-Driven Environment"; "Money Well Spent! (Eight Steps to a successful consulting project)"; "Does this sound like you?"; "Marketing Quickies". **Seminars:** Market Research Basics for Managers; Profiting from Your Customer Database; Developing Your Strategic Marketing Plan from the Ground Up; A Team Process for Developing Your Marketing Plan; Developing a Commercialization Plan for Your SBIR (Small Business Innovation Research)Proposal; Using Marketing Strategies to Jump-Start Your Sales; Marketing in a Sales-Driven Environment and Marketing in a Technology-Driven Environment.

2834 ■ Everett & Co.
3126 S Franklin St.
Englewood, CO 80113
Ph:(303)761-7999
Fax:(303)781-8296
Contact: Wayne Everett, Principle
Scope: Provides strategic real estate solutions and project management.

2835 ■ Facility Directions Inc.
PO Box 761
Manchester, MO 63011
Ph:(636)256-4400
Free: 800-536-0044
Fax:(636)227-2868
Co. E-mail: walty@facilitydirections.com
URL: http://www.facilitydirections.com
Contact: Walter E. Yesberg, President
E-mail: walty@facilitydirections.com
Scope: Firm specializes in service to financial institutions; strategic planning; feasibility studies; facility and space planning; attitude surveys; site selection.

2836 ■ Family Business Institute Inc.
904 Steffi Ct.
Lawrenceville, GA 30044-6933
Ph:(770)952-4085
Fax:(770)432-6660
Co. E-mail: asktheexpert@family-business-experts.com
URL: http://www.family-business-experts.com
Contact: Wayne Rivers, President
E-mail: don@family-business-experts.com
Scope: Assists families in business to achieve personal, family, and organizational goals by meeting challenges that are unique to family-owned businesses. Provides coordinated and integrated assessments and solutions for family issues and needs; for company finance and for human resource and operational requirements. **Publications:** "Professional Intervention in the Family Owned Business"; "Building Consensus in a Family Business"; "Professionalizing Family Business Management"; "Recognizing generations - know them by their weekends"; "Succession planning tactics"; "Succession Planning Obstacles in Family Business"; "Succession: three ways to ease the transition"; "Pruning the family business tree"; "Responsibility diffusion - the most critical impediment to successfully growing any kind of business"; "Breaking Up is Hard to Do: Divorce in the Family Business".

2837 ■ Family Resource Center on Disabilities
20 E Jackson Blvd., Ste. 300
Chicago, IL 60604-2265
Ph:(312)939-3513
Free: 800-952-4199
Fax:(312)939-7297
Co. E-mail: contact@frcd.org
URL: http://www.frcd.org
Contact: Charlotte des Jardins, Director
E-mail: contact@frcd.org
Scope: Provides consulting services to advocacy groups and individuals seeking support for children with disabilities. **Publications:** "How to Get Services By Being Assertive"; "How to Organize an Effective Parent/Advocacy Group and Move Bureaucracies"; "Main roads Travel to Tomorrow - a Road Map for the Future"; "Does Your Child Have Special Education Needs"; "How to Prepare for a Successful Due Process Hearing"; "How to Participate Effectively in Your Child's IEP Meeting"; "Tax Guide for Parents". **Seminars:** How to Support Parents as Effective Advocates; How to Get Services by Being Assertive; How to Develop an Awareness Program for Nondisabled Children; How to Organize a Parent Support Group; How to Move Bureaucratic Mountains; How to Raise Money Painlessly through Publishing; How to Use Humor in Public Presentations.

2838 ■ FCP Consulting
500 Sutter St., Ste. 507
San Francisco, CA 94102-1114
Ph:(415)956-5558
Fax:(415)956-5722
Contact: Cox Ferrall, President
Scope: Management consulting in Business-To-Business sales.

2839 ■ Flett Research Ltd.
440 DeSalaberry Ave.
Winnipeg, MB, Canada R2L 0Y7
Ph:(204)667-2505
Fax:(204)667-2505
Co. E-mail: flett@flettresearch.ca
URL: http://www.flettresearch.ca
Contact: Dawn Gilbert, Principle
E-mail: flett@flettresearch.ca
Scope: Provides environmental audits and assessments. Offers contract research and consultation on environmental topics, specializing in limnology, with emphasis in microbiology, bio-geochemistry and radio-chemistry. Performs dating of sediments via Pb-210 and CS-137 methods, to determine sediment accumulation rates in lakes. One of a handful of labs in the world able to carry out total mercury and methyl mercury analyses at the sub-nanogram and L concentration in water.

2840 ■ Fowler, Anthony & Co.
20 Walnut St.
Wellesley, MA 02481
Ph:(781)237-4201
Fax:(781)237-7718
Co. E-mail: jquagliaroli@comcast.net
Contact: John A. Quagliaroli, President
E-mail: jquagliaroli@mediaone.net
Scope: Offers consulting services and direct investment into small businesses in mergers and acquisitions, capital financing and venture capital. Active with the following industries: Communications, computer related, consumer, distribution, electronic components and instrumentation, multimedia, on-line database/publishing, industrial products and equipment, food processing, multimedia, health care services, medical/health related and publishing.

2841 ■ The Franchise Consulting Group
1801 Century Pk. E, Ste. 2400
Los Angeles, CA 90067-2302
Ph:(310)552-2901
Fax:(310)440-2604
Co. E-mail: info@franchiseconsulting.com
URL: http://www.franchiseconsulting.com
Contact: Edward Kushell, President
E-mail: ekushell@franchiseconsulting.com
Scope: Offers consulting services specializing in new business start up and company expansion programs. Performs analysis, research, planning and development of product service distribution systems, national and international. Serves as consultants to new and established franchisers and as expert witness in franchise litigation.

2842 ■ Freese & Associates Inc.
PO Box 814
Chagrin Falls, OH 44022-0814
Ph:(440)564-9183
Fax:(440)564-7339
Co. E-mail: tfreese@freeseinc.com
URL: http://www.freeseinc.com
Contact: James H. Muir, Principle
E-mail: tfreese@freeseinc.com
Scope: A management consulting firm offering advice in all forms of business logistics. Consulting services are in the areas of strategic planning; network analysis, site selection, facility layout and design, outsourcing, warehousing, transportation and customer service. Typical projects include 3PL marketing surveys; third party outsourcing selection; operational audits; competitive analysis; inventory management; due diligence; and implementation project management. **Publications:** "Building Relationships is Key to Motivation," Distribution Center Management, Apr, 2006; "Getting Maximum Results from Performance Reviews," WERC Sheet, Oct, 2003; "SCM: Making the Vision a Reality," Supply Chain Management Review, Oct, 2003; "Contents Under Pressure," DC Velocity, Aug, 2003; "When Considering Outsourcing, It's Really a Financial Decision," Inventory Management Report, Mar, 2003. **Seminars:** WERC/CAWS Warehousing in China Conference, Sep, 2008; CSCMP Annual Conference, Denver, Oct, 2008; Keys to Retaining and Motivating Your Associates, Dallas, Mar, 2006; The Value and Challenges of Supply Chain Management, Dubai, Feb, 2006; Best Practices in Logistics in China, Jun, 2005; Keys to Motivating Associates, Dallas, May, 2005; The Goal and the Way of International Cooperation in Logistics, Jenobuk, Apr, 2005.

2843 ■ Full Voice
3217 Broadway Ave., Ste. 300
Kansas City, MO 64111
Ph:(816)941-0011
Free: 800-684-8764
Fax:(816)931-8887
Co. E-mail: info@infullvoice.com
URL: http://www.fullvoice.us
Contact: Michienne Dixon, Principle
E-mail: garrett@infullvoice.com
Scope: Vocal performance training firm offering consulting services and personal training sessions in the implementation of effective vocal communication techniques for the development of business relationships and career enhancement. Formalizes a program of proven techniques into a practical method of helping individuals improve their ability to better present themselves when speaking in a professional situation. Industries served: All. **Publications:** "You Can Sound Like You Know What You're Saying". **Seminars:** You Can Sound Like You Know What You're Saying; The Psychology of Vocal Performance; Security. . .the Ability to Accept Change; Knowing. . .the Key to Relaxed Public Communication; The Effective Voice for Customer Service Enhancement; You Can Speak With Conviction; How To Make Yours a Championship Team; Functional English For Foreign Trade. **Special Services:** FULL VOICE[TM].

2844 ■ GEC Consultants Inc.
4604 Birchwood Ave.
Skokie, IL 60076-3835
Ph:(847)674-6310

Fax:(847)674-3946
Co. E-mail: experts@gecconsultants.com
URL: http://www.gecconsultants.com
Contact: Lloyd M. Gordon, CEO
E-mail: legal@gecconsultants.com
Scope: Consulting in all areas of bar and restaurant operations. Restaurant manager development appraises existing locations or sites. Studies the feasibility of projects. Develop new concepts. Assist in expanding, existing food operations, marketing, expert witness (legal) for hospitality/restaurant industry. **Publications:** "How You Can Fight Back to Minimize This Recession!"; "New Thoughts On Leases"; "The Use of Job Analysis to Actually Reduce Payroll Costs"; "Do You Need a Feasibility Study?"; "Combat Negative Hospitality"; "How To Run A Successful Night club"; "Are Capitalists In Your Cabinet?"; "Marketing For The 21st Century"; "Profitability In The Banquet Industry"; "Starting a Restaurant, Bar or Catering Business"; "How To Find And Retain Suitable Employees"; "26 Things To Do To Plan A Restaurant"; "Wall Fabric or Paint: Decor Magic It's Your Call"; "The Art of Cafe Ambiance"; "Why You Need A Consultant". **Seminars:** How to increase restaurant profit, Member MSPC Speakers Bureau; Raising Capital for New Development and Expansion.

2845 ■ Gerson Goodson Inc.
2451 McMullen Booth Rd., Ste. 201
Clearwater, FL 33759
Ph:(727)726-7619
Free: 888-237-7424
Fax:(727)726-2406
Co. E-mail: getrich@richgerson.com
URL: http://www.richgerson.com
Contact: Richard F. Gerson, Principal
E-mail: richard.gerson@atsrichgerson.com
Scope: Independent consulting firm provides performance management solutions to improve performance and maximize productivity in organizations. Provides assistance to organizations in talent and performance management, leadership development, selection and hiring practices, employee and customer retention, and customer service. Conducts a systematic needs analysis of the entire marketing, sales and customer service operations of the company. Identifies hidden, neglected and underutilized marketing, sales and customer service assets. **Publications:** "Winning The Inner Game Of Selling," 1999; "Marketing Strategies for Small Businesses," 1994; "Measuring Customer Satisfaction," 1993; "Beyond Customer Service," 1992; "Achieving High Performance"; "Guaranteeing Performance Improvement"; "The Executive Athlete"; "Positive Performance Improvement". **Seminars:** Marketing Real Estate Services Management Development, Oct, 2007; Presentation Skills, Oct, 2007; From Member Service to Sales, Sep, 2007; Leadership Development, Sep, 2007; The Marketing Difference That Makes The Difference: How To Position Your Company For Rapid Growth Regardless Of The Economy Or The Competition; Growing Your Business With What You Already Have: How To Identify And Profit From The Hidden Marketing Assets That Are Currently Costing You Money; The R Factor In Customer Service: 5Ways To Grow Your Business For Little Or No Cost.

2846 ■ Global Business Consultants
200 Lake Hills Rd.
PO Box 776
Pinehurst, NC 28374-0776
Ph:(910)295-5991
Fax:(910)295-5991
Co. E-mail: gbc@pinehurst.net
Contact: Gerd Hofielen, Partner
E-mail: mcoin@atsyourculturecoach.com
Scope: Firm specializes in human resources management; project management; software development; and international trade. Offers litigation support. **Publications:** "Culture to Culture: Mission Trip Do's and Don'ts," Jul, 2005; "Rules of the Game: Global Business Protocol". **Seminars:** Cross-Cultural Training.

2847 ■ Global Technology Transfer L.L.C.
1500 Dixie Hwy.
Park Hills, KY 41011-2819
Ph:(859)431-1262
Fax:(859)431-5148
Co. E-mail: arzembrodt@worldnet.att.net
Contact: Michelle Hartley, CFO
Scope: Firm specializes in product development; quality assurance; new product development; and total quality management focusing on household chemical specialties, especially air fresheners. Utilizes latest technology from global resources. Specializes in enhancement products for home and automobile.

2848 ■ Goldore Consulting Inc.
120-5 St. NW, Ste. 1
PO Box 590
Linden, AB, Canada T0M 1J0
Ph:(403)546-4208
Fax:(403)546-4208
Co. E-mail: goldore@leadershipessentials.com
Contact: Robert A. Orr, President
E-mail: orr@leadershipessentials.com
Scope: Provides consulting service in leadership and management skills. Industries served: primarily charities, non-profits; some businesses. **Seminars:** The Challenge Of Leadership.

2849 ■ Great Lakes Consulting Group Inc.
54722 Little Flower Trl.
Mishawaka, IN 46545
Ph:(574)287-4500
Fax:(574)233-2688
Contact: James E. Schrager, President
Scope: Provides consulting services in the areas of strategic planning; feasibility studies; start-up businesses; small business management; mergers and acquisitions; joint ventures; divestitures; interim management; crisis management; turnarounds; business process re-engineering; venture capital; and international trade.

2850 ■ The Greystone Group Inc.
440 N Wells, Ste. 570
Chicago, IL 60610
Ph:(616)451-8880
Fax:(616)451-9180
Co. E-mail: consult@greystonegp.com
E-mail: consult@greystonegp.com
Scope: Firm specializes in strategic planning and communications; organizational development; start-up businesses; business management; mergers and acquisitions; joint ventures; divestitures; business process re-engineering.

2851 ■ Grief Counseling & Support Services
8600 W Chester Pke., Ste. 304
Upper Darby, PA 19082
Ph:(610)789-7707
Fax:(610)469-9499
Contact: Jeffrey Kauffman, President
E-mail: jkharry@voicenet.com
Scope: Specializing in consulting and training services for organizations dealing with loss, trauma and grief issues. These services may include management consultations, crisis intervention, educational programming, policy development, program design, group process work, individual counseling or other support services. Training and support services also provided for loss issues for mental retardation service providers. Serves private industries as well as government agencies.

2852 ■ Grimmick Consulting Services
455 Donner Way
San Ramon, CA 94582
Ph:(925)735-1036
Fax:(925)735-1100
Co. E-mail: hank@grimmickconsulting.com
URL: http://www.grimmickconsulting.com
Contact: Henry Grimmick, President
E-mail: hank@grimmickconsulting.com
Scope: Provides consulting services in the areas of strategic planning; organizational assessment; organizational development; leadership and management development Baldridge criteria, process improvement and balanced scorecards and team dynamics.

2853 ■ Hardy Stevenson and Associates Ltd.
364 Davenport Rd.
Toronto, ON, Canada M5R 1K6
Ph:(416)944-8444
Free: 877-267-7794
Fax:(416)944-0900
Co. E-mail: hsa@hardystevenson.com
URL: http://www.hardystevenson.com
Contact: Glynn Gomes, Principle
E-mail: davehardy@atshardystevenson.com
Scope: Firm specialize in land use and environmental planning social economic impact assessment facilitation, conflict resolution community relations, public consultation strategic planning policy and project management consulting.

2854 ■ Harris Advertising
G4162 Fenton Rd.
Flint, MI 48507-3637
Ph:(810)232-4120
Contact: Susan Kay Harris, President
Scope: Marketing and advertising firm provides advertisement services to private industries as well as government agencies.

2855 ■ Harvey A. Meier Co.
410 W Nevada St., Billings Ranch, Ste. 245
Ashland, OR 97520-1043
Ph:(509)458-3210
Fax:(541)488-7905
Co. E-mail: harvey@harveymeier.com
URL: http://www.harveymeier.com
Contact: Harvey A. Meier, President
E-mail: harvey@harveymeier.com
Scope: Firm provides service to chief executive officers and board of directors. Specializes in interim management, strategic planning, financial planning and organization governance. **Publications:** "The D'Artagnan Way".

2856 ■ Health Strategy Group Inc.
46 River Rd.
Chatham, NY 12037
Ph:(518)392-6770
Contact: John Fiorillo, Principle
Scope: Provides consulting services in the areas of strategic planning, feasibility studies, start-up businesses, organizational development, market research, customer service audits, new product development, marketing, public relations. **Publications:** "Online Consumer Surveys as a Methodology for Assessing the Quality of the United States Health Care System," 2004.

2857 ■ Hewitt Development Enterprises
18 Lindley Ave.
North Kingstown, RI 02852
Ph:(305)372-0941
Free: 800-631-3098
Fax:(305)372-0941
Co. E-mail: info@hewittdevelopment.com
URL: http://www.hewittdevelopment.com
Contact: Robert G. Hewitt, Principal
E-mail: bob@hewittdevelopment.com
Scope: Specializes in strategic planning; profit enhancement; start-up businesses; interim management; crisis management; turnarounds; production planning; just-in-time inventory management; and project management. Serves senior management (CEOs, CFOs, division presidents, etc.) and acquirers of distressed businesses.

2858 ■ Hickey & Hill Inc.
1009 Oak Hill Rd., Ste. 201
Lafayette, CA 94549-3812
Ph:(925)906-5331
Contact: Edwin L. Hill, CEO
Scope: Firm provides management consulting services to companies in financial distress. Expertise area: Corporate restructuring and turnaround.

2859 ■ hightechbiz.com
4209 Santa Monica Blvd., Ste. 201
PO Box 189
Los Angeles, CA 90029-3027
Ph:(323)913-3355
Free: 877-648-4753

Fax:(323)913-3355
Contact: Jack Potter, Principal
Scope: A full service marketing agency specializing in integrated marketing solutions. Services include: marketing surveys; positioning surveys; strategic and tactical plans; implementation plans; management consulting; product brochures; product catalogs; product packaging; product data sheets; direct mail programs; media research; competitive research; complete creative; production and film; media placement; corporate identity; in-house creative; public relations.

2860 ■ Hills Consulting Group Inc.
6 Partridge Ct.
Novato, CA 94945-1315
Ph:(415)898-3944
Contact: Michael R. Hills, President
Scope: Specializes in strategic planning; marketing surveys; market research; customer service audits; new product development; competitive analysis; and sales forecasting.

2861 ■ Holt Capital
1916 Pike Pl., Ste. 12-344
Seattle, WA 98101
Ph:(206)484-0403
Fax:(206)789-8034
Co. E-mail: info@holtcapital.com
URL: http://www.holtcapital.com
Contact: David Brazeau, Principle
E-mail: mjholt@holtcapital.com
Scope: Registered investment advisory firm. Services include: Debt planning, private equity, mergers, divestitures and acquisitions, transaction support services. Connects companies with capital. **Publications:** "Early Sales Key to Early-Stage Funding"; "Financial Transactions: Who Should Be At Your Table"; "Get the Deal Done: The Four Keys to Successful Mergers and Acquisitions"; "Is Your First Paragraph a Turn-off"; "Bubble Rubble: Bridging the Price Gap for an Early-Stage Business"; "Are You Ready For The new Economy"; "Could I Get Money or Jail Time With That The Sarbanes-Oxley Act Of 2002 gives early-stage companies More Risks". **Seminars:** Attracting Private Investors; Five Proven Ways to Finance Your Company; How to Get VC Financing; Venture Packaging; How to Finance Company Expansion.

2862 ■ Hornberger & Associates
1966 Lombard St.
San Francisco, CA 94123
Ph:(415)346-2106
Fax:(415)346-9993
Co. E-mail: info@hornbergerassociates.com
URL: http://www.hornbergerassociates.com
Contact: Deborah Hornberger, Principle
E-mail: deborah@hornbergerassociates.com
Scope: Specialized services include wealth management, retirement programs, small business banking, personal trust, investment management, brokerage services, mutual funds, relationship management, private banking and employee banking. Help clients by offering strategic marketing plans, market segmentation/niche marketing, website strategies and development; product development and introduction; client communications; product, sales and referral training; client retention programs and project management. **Publications:** "Establishing a Mini-trust Product," Bank Marketing, Oct, 1997. **Seminars:** Building a Marketing Plan Directed at Emerging Wealth Baby Boomers, Strategy Institute conference, Jun, 1999.

2863 ■ I.H.R. Solutions
3333 E Bayaud Ave., Ste. 219
Denver, CO 80209
Ph:(303)588-4243
Fax:(303)978-0473
Co. E-mail: dhollands@ihrsolutions.com
Contact: Deborah Hollands, President
E-mail: dhollands@ihrsolutions.com
Scope: Provides joint-venture and start-up human resource consulting services as well as advice on organization development for international human capital. Industries served: high-tech and telecommunications.

2864 ■ IMC Consulting & Training
901 McHenry Ave., Ste. A
Modesto, CA 95350
Ph:(209)572-2271
Fax:(209)572-2862
Co. E-mail: info@imc-1.net
URL: http://www.imc-1.net
Contact: Ed Stout, Principle
E-mail: michael@imc-1.net
Scope: Firm helps businesses and professionals identify, develop and market their selling proposition to increase profits. Services include B-to-B surveys, direct marketing, media relations, planning and strategy, sales management, training and leadership coaching. **Publications:** "Consultant Earns Advanced Certificate," Hccsc Business Review, Dec, 2004; "Adapting to Change - the New Competitive Advantage," Business Journal, Jul, 2004; "Loyalty Marketing Can Divide New Business," Jun, 2004; "Eleven Major Marketing Mistakes," Jul, 2003; "Planning to Win or Racing to Fail," Jun, 2003. **Seminars:** Negotiating High Profit Sales; How to Write Winning Proposals, Modesto Chamber of Commerce, Oct, 2007; Winning the 2nd Half: A 6-month Plan to Score New Customers and Profits.

2865 ■ In Plain English
14501 Antigone Dr.
PO Box 3300
Gaithersburg, MD 20885-3300
Ph:(301)340-2821
Free: 800-274-9645
Fax:(301)279-0115
Co. E-mail: rwohl@inplainenglish.com
URL: http://www.inplainenglish.com
Contact: Ronald H. Wohl, CEO
E-mail: rwohl@inplainenglish.com
Scope: Management consultants helping government and businesses research, design, write and produce user oriented management information for human resources, employee benefits, business process, corporate and marketing needs. Services include: GSA mob is schedule for consulting to the government; employee benefit communications, plain English business writing workshops for print and electronic media; communicating strategy and tactics; marketing research, business planning and communications; readability testing; usability testing and monitoring strategy. **Publications:** "The Benefits Communication"; "The Employee Benefits Communication ToolKit," Commerce Clearinghouse; "Benefits Communication," Business and Legal Reports. **Seminars:** Plain English Writing Training; Summary Plan Description Compliance workshops; Re-Humanizing the Corporation, Human Resources and Employee Benefits Communication Workshop; 21 Writing Tips for the 21st Century; Make the Write Impression; Writing to Inform and Instruct; The Dreaded Nuts and Bolts; Writing to Persuade; Writing Policy and Procedure Manuals In Plain English; Writing for Accountants and Auditors In Plain English. **Special Services:** In Plain English[R].

2866 ■ Innovative Scientific Analysis & Computing
6168 Flagstaff Rd.
PO Box 1636
Boulder, CO 80302
Ph:(303)440-7673
Fax:(303)545-6674
Co. E-mail: ros5e@isaac.com
URL: http://www.ros5e.com
Contact: Herrn C. Rose, Principle
E-mail: ros5e@isaac.com
Scope: Engineering services includes mathematical analysis specializing in optimal estimation, scientific programming, and database design and development, data encryption and security.

2867 ■ The Institute for Management Excellence
PO Box 5459
Lacey, WA 98509-5459
Ph:(360)412-0404
Co. E-mail: pwoc@itstime.com
URL: http://www.itstime.com
Contact: Michael Anthony, Director
E-mail: btaylor@itstime.com
Scope: Management consulting and training focuses on improving productivity, using practices and creative techniques. Practices based on the company's theme: It's time for new ways of doing business. Industries served: public sector, law enforcement, finance or banking, non profit, computers or high technology, education, human resources, utilities. **Publications:** "Income Without a Job," 2008; "The Other Side of Midnight, 2000: An Executive Guide to the Year 2000 Problem"; "Concordance to the Michael Teachings"; "Handbook of Small Business Advertising"; "The Personality Game"; "How to Market Yourself for Success". **Seminars:** The Personality Game; Power Path Seminars; Productivity Plus; Sexual Harassment and Discrimination Prevention; Worker's Comp Cost Reduction; Americans with Disabilities Act; In Search of Identify: Clarifying Corporate Culture.

2868 ■ Institute of Public Administration
411 Lafayette St., Ste. 303
New York, NY 10003
Ph:(212)992-9898
Free: 800-258-1102
Fax:(212)995-4876
Co. E-mail: p553@nyu.edu
URL: http://www.theipa.org
Contact: Yoshihiro Asano, Principle
Scope: A private nonprofit consulting, research and education organization experienced in management of governments and public enterprises. Firm's activities are directed toward the solution of emerging problems of government, organization, financial management and policies, and public enterprises in the United States and abroad. Programs are financed chiefly by contracts with local, state and federal governments, international aid agencies and foreign governments, public enterprises, and by foundation grants. Areas of concentration include personnel administration, structures and resources of local legislative bodies, training, structure and financing of public enterprises, public finance and fiscal reform, financial management and anti-corruption systems, sustainable urban development, urban and regional planning, organization and management, city/county charter revision, urban transportation, public sector ethics and citizenship, and management of government procurement systems. **Publications:** "Local Governance Approach to Social Reintegration and Economic Recovery in Post Conflict Countries: The Political Context for Programs of UNDP/UNCDF Assistance"; "Local Governance Approach to Social Reintegration and Economic Recovery in Post Conflict Countries: Programming Options for UNDP/UNCDF Assistance"; "Local Governance Approach to Social Reintegration and Economic Recovery in Post Conflict Countries: The View from Mozambique"; "Local Governance Approach to Social Reintegration and Economic Recovery in Post Conflict Countries: Towards a Definition and a Rationale"; "Local Governance Approach to Post Conflict Recovery: Perspective from Cambodia"; "The Sustainable Human Development Strategy: A Proposal for Post Conflict Recovery Societies"; "Local Governance Approach to Post Conflict Recovery: Proceedings Report on the Workshop Organized by the Institute of Public Administration". **Seminars:** A Local Governance Approach to Post Conflict Recovery.

2869 ■ Interminds & Federer Resources Inc.
106 E 6th St., Ste. 310
Austin, TX 78701-3659
Ph:(512)476-8800
Fax:(512)476-8811
URL: http://www.interminds.com
Contact: Salvador Apud, Partner
E-mail: sapud@atsintegra100.com
Scope: Firm specializes in feasibility studies; startup businesses; small business management; mergers and acquisitions; joint ventures; divestitures; interim management; crisis management; turnarounds; production planning; team building; appraisals and valuations.

2870 ■ Interpersonal Coaching & Consulting
1516 W Lake St., Ste. 2000S
Minneapolis, MN 55408
Ph:(612)381-2494

Fax:(612)381-2494
Co. E-mail: mail@interpersonal-coaching.com
URL: http://www.interpersonal-coaching.com
Contact: Mary Belfry, Partner
E-mail: mail@interpersonal-coaching.com
Scope: Provides coaching and consulting to businesses and organizations. Assesses the interpersonal workplace through interviews, assessment instruments and individual group settings. Experienced as a therapist for over a decade. **Seminars:** Sexual harassment and discrimination issues.

2871 ■ Jest for the Health of It Services
PO Box 8484
Santa Cruz, CA 95061-8484
Ph:(831)425-8436
Fax:(831)425-8437
Co. E-mail: pwooten@jesthealth.com
URL: http://www.jesthealth.com
Contact: Shirley Trout, Mgr
E-mail: strout@atsnurseswhostay.com
Scope: Develops and presents seminars, keynotes and skill shops about the power of humor. Provides consulting services for development of humor rooms and comedy carts in hospitals. Conducts training for clowns to make visits in hospitals and nursing homes. Industries served: health professionals and businesses wishing to educate staff about healthy lifestyle choices. **Publications:** "Heart Humor and Healing"; "Compassionate Laughter: Jest for Your Health"; "The Hospital Clown: A Closer Look"; "Humor: An Antidote for Stress"; "Humor, Laughter and Play: Maintaining Balance in a Serious World"; "You've Got to Be Kidding: Humor Skills for Surviving Managed Care"; "Laughter as Therapy for Patient and Caregiver"; "Patty Wooten: Nurse Healer"; "Humor: An antidote for stress".

2872 ■ Jim Castello Marketing Communications Consultants
711 Red Wing Dr.
Lake Mary, FL 32746
Ph:(407)321-6322
Contact: James E. Castello Jr., President
Scope: Consultant develops creative ideas and marketing strategies, including collateral programs, public relations, advertising, and brochures. Industries served: All golf related industry/business, golf manufacturers, golf resorts, golf residential developments, golf professionals, golf clothing, golf accessories, golf associations, and golf travel. **Seminars:** How To Seminar for Family Fun Center Entrepreneurs; How To Seminar for Creativity in Golf Marketing; The Golf Business on the Internet.

2873 ■ Joel Greenstein & Associates
6212 Nethercombe Ct.
McLean, VA 22101
Ph:(703)893-1888
Co. E-mail: jgreenstein@contractmasters.com
Contact: Joel Greenstein, Principle
E-mail: jgreenstein@contractmasters.com
Scope: Provides services to minority and women-owned businesses and government agencies. Specializes in interpreting federal, agency-specific acquisition regulations and contract terms and conditions. Offers assistance with preparing technical, cost proposals and sealed bids.

2874 ■ Johnston Co.
1646 Massachusetts Ave., Ste. 22
Lexington, MA 02420
Ph:(781)862-7595
Fax:(781)862-9066
Co. E-mail: info@johnstoncompany.com
URL: http://www.johnstoncompany.com
Contact: Terry Sugrue, Mgr
E-mail: tzsugrue@atshotmail.com
Scope: Firm specializes in management audits and reports; start-up businesses; small business management; mergers and acquisitions; joint ventures; divestitures; interim management; crisis management; turnarounds; cost controls; financing; venture capital; controller services; financial management, strategic and advisory services. **Publications:** "Why are board meetings such a waste of time," Boston Business Journal, Apr, 2004.

2875 ■ Kaufman Global L.L.C.
5975 Castle Creek Pky., Ste. 440
Indianapolis, IN 46250
Ph:(317)818-2430
Fax:(317)818-2434
Co. E-mail: info@kaufmanglobal.com
URL: http://www.kaufmanglobal.com
Contact: Jerry Timpson, President
E-mail: iscott@atskaufmanglobal.com
Scope: Consulting firm addresses cultural, emotional and political elements of change throughout the workplace. **Publications:** "ArvinMeritor: A Lean Culture"; "The Struggle to Get Lean"; "The Missing Link of Lean Success"; "Using a Full-Court Press to Transform a Business"; "Managing Growth - BD Finds Success Integrating Lean and Six Sigma". **Special Services:** Lean Leadership[R]; SLIM-IT[R]; Lean Daily Management System LDMS[R]; 20 Keys[R]; WIn-Lean[R]; Lean Six Sigma.

2876 ■ Keiei Senryaku Corp.
19191 S Vermont Ave., Ste. 530
Torrance, CA 90502-1049
Ph:(310)366-3331
Free: 800-951-8780
Fax:(310)366-3330
Co. E-mail: takenakaes@earthlink.net
Contact: Kurt Miyamoto, President
Scope: Offers consulting services in the areas of strategic planning; feasibility studies; profit enhancement; organizational development; start-up businesses; mergers and acquisitions; joint ventures; divestitures; executive searches; sales management; and competitive analysis.

2877 ■ Koch Group Inc.
240 E Lake St., Ste. 300
Addison, IL 60101-2874
Ph:(630)941-1100
Free: 800-470-7845
Fax:(630)941-3865
Co. E-mail: info@kochgroup.com
URL: http://www.kochgroup.com
Contact: Charissa Pachucki, Treasurer
E-mail: rgg@atskochgroup.com
Scope: Provides industrial marketing consulting services to small to mid-sized manufacturers. Primary assistance includes industrial market research and analysis, identification of potential markets, strategic planning and plan implementation, market planning, sales analysis, competitor analysis. Specializes in assisting manufacturers identify, recruit, and manage agents and reps and developing website for business promotion. **Seminars:** Niche Marketing; Regional Industrial Association Recruiting; Strategic Marketing for Manufacturers; Strategic Marketing; How To Identify, Screen, Interview and Select High Quality Agents; Basics of Industrial Market Research; Elements of Industrial Marketing; Trade Adjustment Assistance For Firms; Developing New Business; Selecting An Industrial Web Site Developer; Strategic Selling; Pick Your Customer; Strategic and Tactical Marketing.

2878 ■ Kostka & Company Inc.
9 Wild Rose Ct.
Cromwell, CT 06416
Ph:(860)257-1045
Co. E-mail: mail@mmgnet.com
URL: http://www.mmgnet.com
Contact: Tom Steiner, Managing Partner
E-mail: peterpk@gmail.com
Scope: Areas of expertise: management consulting, global technology sourcing, complex project management, SKU management and new product introduction, application development, medical point-of-sale, multi-touch user interface, made-to-order management systems and Smartphone ERP connectivity. Clients include global fortune 500 companies as well as small and medium-sized businesses and startups.

2879 ■ Kroll Zolfo Cooper L.L.C.
777 S Figueroa St., 24th Fl.
Los Angeles, CA 90017
Ph:(212)561-4000
Fax:(212)948-4226
Co. E-mail: mwyse@krollzolfocooper.com
URL: http://www.krollzolfocooper.com
Contact: Stephen F. Cooper, Principal
E-mail: scooper@kroll.com
Scope: Firm provides accounting consulting services to businesses. Specializes in restructuring and turnaround consulting; interim and crisis management; performance improvement; creditor advisory; cross-border restructuring and corporate finance.

2880 ■ Kubba Consultants Inc.
1255 Montgomery Dr.
Deerfield, IL 60015
Ph:(847)729-0051
Fax:(847)729-8765
Co. E-mail: edkubba@aol.com
URL: http://www.kubbainc.com
Contact: Sam Sampat, Mgr
E-mail: edkubba@aol.com
Scope: Industrial and business-to-business marketing research and consulting. Services include new product research, new market evaluation, competitor analysis and customer value analysis.

2881 ■ L G Anthony Associates
40 Wellington Blvd.
Reading, PA 19610
Ph:(610)670-0477
Contact: Louis G. Anthony, Owner
Scope: Provides food service facility planning, layout and design, including equipment selection and specification. Also offers management systems and operations analysis, such as the development of operating policies and procedures. Firm can design menu planning and recipe development, food selection and specification, work simplification, service, and quality control around current concepts in the field. Industries served: hospital, nursing home, restaurant, group homes; commercial and institutional food service industries. **Seminars:** Food Service Sanitation; Menu Planning; Work Simplification; Quality Control in Food Service.

2882 ■ Liberty Business Strategies Ltd.
The Times Bldg., Ste. 400, Suburban Sq.
Ardmore, PA 19003
Ph:(610)649-3800
Fax:(610)649-0408
Co. E-mail: info@libertystrategies.com
URL: http://www.libertystrategies.com
Contact: Dr. Emmy S. Miller, President
E-mail: emmym@atslibertystrategies.com
Scope: Management consulting firm working with clients to gain speed and agility in driving their business strategy. The consulting model builds the alignment of strategy, organization commitment, and technology. Provides senior leader coaching and team development coaching. **Seminars:** Winning with Talent, Morison Annual Conference, Jul, 2009.

2883 ■ Linda Lipsky Restaurant Consultants Inc.
216 Foxcroft Rd.
PO Box 489
Broomall, PA 19008
Ph:(610)325-3663
Free: 877-425-3663
Fax:(610)325-3329
Co. E-mail: lipsky@restaurantconsult.com
URL: http://www.restaurantconsult.com
Contact: Linda J. Lipsky, President
E-mail: lipsky@restaurantconsult.com
Scope: Helps food and beverage operations achieve their highest level of profits, product consistency and service quality. Concentrates on implementing cost cutting measures, developing training programs for both front and heart of the house employees, engineering menus, performing Spotter's reports and creating organizational manuals and procedures for restaurant, bar, hotel, banquet facility, country clubs, or caterer. Key areas of specialization include on site operations evaluations to identify in effective cost controls, flaws in the organizational structure and inadequacies of management systems, policies and procedures; profit enhancement as a result of implementing cost-cutting measures in all prime cost areas; server training, sales incentive training, and management training and evaluation programs;

recipe documentation, cost analysis, menu pricing and menu copy writing; competitive market surveys and market positioning analysis, and bridge management. **Seminars:** Designing Menus for Maximum Sales and Profits; How to Maximize Your Check Average; Going Beyond Your Customer's Expectations; Seeing Your Restaurant Through a Customer's Eyes; Making the Best First and Last Impression; Basic Training in Kitchen Management Techniques; Basic Training in Bar Management Techniques; Make Every Labor Dollar Count; Back to Basics/More Than Shift Management; Conducting Your Own In-House Inspection; Basics of Sanitation Training for Kitchen Employees; Basics of Sanitation Training for Dining Room Employees.

2884 ■ Lupfer & Associates
92 Glen St.
Natick, MA 01760-5646
Ph:(508)655-3950
Fax:(508)655-7826
Co. E-mail: donlupfer@aol.com
Contact: Donald Lupfer, President
E-mail: don.lupfer@lupferassociates.com
Scope: Assists off shore hi-tech companies in entering United States markets and specializes in channel development for all sorts of products. Perform MARCOM support for hi-tech United States clients. **Publications:** "What's Next For Distribution-Feast or Famine"; "The Changing Global Marketplace"; "Making Global Distribution Work". **Seminars:** How to do Business in the United States.

2885 ■ Management Network Group Inc.
7300 College Blvd., Ste. 302
Overland Park, KS 66210-1879
Ph:(913)345-9315
Free: 888-480-8664
Fax:(913)451-1845
Co. E-mail: info@tmng.com
URL: http://www.tmng.com
Contact: Donald Klumb, CFO
E-mail: ronald.angner@atstmng.com
Scope: A provider of strategy, management, marketing, operational and technology consulting services to the global telecommunications industry. **Special Services:** Lexicon™; QBC™; QSA™.

2886 ■ Management Resource Partners
181 2nd Ave., Ste. 542
San Mateo, CA 94401
Ph:(650)401-5850
Fax:(650)401-5850
Contact: John C. Roberts, Principle
Scope: Firm specializes in strategic planning; small business management; mergers and acquisitions; joint ventures; divestitures; interim management; crisis management; turn around; venture capital; appraisals and valuations.

2887 ■ Management Strategies
1000 S Old Woodward, Ste. 105
Birmingham, MI 48009
Ph:(248)258-2756
Fax:(248)258-3407
Co. E-mail: bob@hois.com
Contact: Robert E. Hoisington, President
E-mail: bob@hois.com
Scope: Firm specializes in strategic planning; feasibility studies; profit enhancement; organizational studies; start up businesses; turnarounds; business process re engineering; industrial engineering; marketing; ecommerce.

2888 ■ Mankind Research Foundation Inc.
1315 Apple Ave.
Silver Spring, MD 20910-3614
Ph:(301)587-8686
Fax:(301)585-8959
Contact: Carl Schleicher, CEO
Scope: Firm provide an organization for scientific development and application of technology that could have positive impact on the health, education, and welfare of mankind. Provide solution to seek and apply futuristic solutions to current problems. Provides services in the areas of advanced sciences, biotechnical, bionic, biocybernetic, biomedical, holistic health, bioimmunology, solar energy, accelerated learning, and sensory aids for handicapped. Current specific activities involve research in AIDS, drug abuse, affordable housing, food for the hungry, and literacy and remedial education.

2889 ■ Marketing Leverage Inc.
2022 Laurel Oak
Palm City, FL 34990
Free: 800-633-1422
Fax:(772)659-8664
Co. E-mail: lkelly@marketingleverage.com
URL: http://www.marketingleverage.com
Contact: Genina Gravlin, Principle
E-mail: davery@atsmarketingleverage.com
Scope: Consulting and research firm focusing on the targeting, retention and satisfaction of customers. Consulting is offered for due diligence; marketing and customer retention strategy; program design and implementation. Research services offered help clients determine service improvements that increase customer loyalty; boosting sales through better understanding buyer motivations; increasing the odds of product acceptance through new product concept testing; and improving the effectiveness of advertising, collateral, publications through audience evaluation. Clients include top financial services, insurance, health care, technology and management services organizations. **Publications:** "Creating Strategic Leverage"; "Exploring Corporate Strategy"; "Competitive Advantage"; "Breakpoint and Beyond "; "Competitive Strategy ". **Seminars:** Best Practices in Brainstorming; Getting Results in the Real World; Finding the Leverage in Your Customer Strategy; The Role of Communications in Building Customer Loyalty; Building a Customer Centered Relationship and Making it Pay. **Special Services:** The Marketing Leverage Win/Loss Tracking System™.

2890 ■ May Toy Lukens
3226 NE 26th Ct.
Renton, WA 98056
Ph:(425)891-3226
Contact: May T. Lukens, Principle
Scope: Provides training to teach people to think of ways to improve their operations continuously by changing the way they think. Industries served: All, particularly financial. Operational analysis and training. **Seminars:** Seminars and workshops in maximizing resource utilization and staff potential.

2891 ■ McCreight & Company Inc.
36 Grove St., Ste. 4
New Canaan, CT 06840-5329
Ph:(203)801-5000
Fax:(866)646-8339
Co. E-mail: roc@implementstrategy.com
URL: http://www.implementstrategy.com
Contact: Laraine Mehr-Turlis, CFO
E-mail: jas@atsimplementstrategy.com
Scope: The firm assist the global clients with strategy implementation involving large scale change, including mergers, divestitures, alliances, and new business launches. Along with the alliance partners, focus on issues that energize or constrain strategic change including: plans and goals; transition design; management competence; organization structure, effectiveness, and staffing; roles and responsibilities; management processes; information management and technology; and change management effectiveness. **Publications:** "The Board's Role in Strengthening M&A Success," Boardroom Briefing, 2008; "Creating the Future," Ask Magazine, 2007; "Strategy Implementation Insights," Mccreight and Company Inc., Oct, 2007; "Sustaining Growth," Deloitte and Ct Technology Council, Jul, 2006; "A Four Phase Approach to Succession Planning," Southern Connecticut Newspapers Inc., 2005; E perspective; Board Effectiveness Insights; and Information Technology Insights. **Seminars:** Successful Mergers and Acquisitions - An Implementation Guide; Global 100One-Face-to-the-Customer; Implementation of Strategic Change.

2892 ■ McDonald Consulting Group Inc.
1900 W Park Dr., Ste. 280
Westborough, MA 01581
Ph:(952)841-6357
Fax:(507)664-9389
Co. E-mail: rmcdonald@mcdonaldconsultinggroup.com
URL: http://www.mcdonaldconsultinggroup.com
Contact: Ron A. McDonald, President
E-mail: rmcdonald@mcdonaldconsultinggroup.com
Scope: A management consulting firm specializing in assisting insurance companies improve operations. Provides services in the areas of strategic planning; profit enhancement; organizational development; interim management; crisis management; turnarounds; business process re-engineering; benefits and compensation planning and total quality management. **Publications:** "Improving Customer Focus through Organizational Structure," AASCIF News; "Changing Strategies in Hard Markets," The National Underwriter; "Moving Beyond Management 101: Postgraduate Time Management for Executives," The National Underwriter; "A New Attitude: 3 Clients Improved Results Through Our Fundamental Change Process," Bests Review; "How to Organize Your Company Around Your Customers," Bests Review. **Seminars:** How to establish "expense allowable"; How to design an incentive compensation plan around a units core success measures.

2893 ■ McMann & Ransford
1 Sugar Creek Center Blvd., Ste. 300
Sugar Land, TX 77478
Free: (866)267-0299
URL: http://www.mcmannransford.com
Contact: Dean E. McMann, CEO
E-mail: dmcmann@mcmannransford.com
Scope: Provides of management consulting, training, executive recruiting and market research services specializing in the professional services industry.

2894 ■ McShane Group Inc.
2345 York Rd., Ste. 102
Timonium, MD 21093
Ph:(410)560-0077
Fax:(410)560-2718
Co. E-mail: tmcshane@mcshanegroup.com
URL: http://www.mcshanegroup.com
Contact: Richard D. Montgomery, Principle
E-mail: rdm@atsmcshanegroup.com
Scope: Turnaround consulting and crisis management firm. Specializes in due diligence services, interim management, strategic business realignments, business sale and asset depositions and debt restructuring. Industries served: technology, financial, retail, distribution, medical, educational, manufacturing, contracting, environmental and health care.

2895 ■ MeasureNet
137 Pioneer Dr.
West Hartford, CT 06117
Ph:(860)913-3767
Co. E-mail: greilly@business.uconn.edu
URL: http://www.measure.net
Contact: Greg Reilly, President
E-mail: greilly@sbcglobal.net
Scope: Firm seeks to improve corporate performance measurement systems through measurement audit and improvement services. **Publications:** "Value-linked Measurement at Dell," Journal of Cost Management, Jul, 2002; "Performance Measurement for Improved Working Capital Management," Journal of Cost Management, May, 2002; "Improving the Quality of Performance Information," Journal of Cost Management, Mar, 2002; "Developing Managers Through Performance Measurement," Journal of Cost Management, Nov, 2001; "Improving Corporate Performance Measurement," Journal of Cost Management, Jul, 2001; "Value Measurement: Using a Measure Network to Understand and Deliver Value," Journal of Cost Management, Nov, 2000. **Special Services:** Measure Network™.

2896 ■ Medical Imaging Consultants Inc.
1037 US Highway 46, Ste. G-2
Clifton, NJ 07013-2445
Ph:(973)574-8000
Free: 800-589-5685

Fax:(973)574-8001
Co. E-mail: info@micinfo.com
URL: http://www.micinfo.com
Contact: Dr. Philip A. Femano, President
E-mail: phil@micinfo.com
Scope: Provides professional support services for radiology management and comprehensive continuing education programs for radiologic technologists. Management services include resource-critical database logistics; customer registration in educational programs; educational program development and Category A accreditation; national agency notification (e.g., ASRT, SNM-TS) of CE credits earned; meeting planning; manpower assessment; market research; expert witness; think-tank probes and executive summaries of industry issues. **Seminars:** Sectional Anatomy and Imaging Strategies; CT Cross-Trainer; CT Registry Review Program; MR Cross Trainer; MRI Registry Review Program; Digital Mammography Essentials for Technologists; Radiology Trends for Technologists.

2897 ■ Medical Outcomes Management Inc.
132 Central St., Ste. 215
Foxborough, MA 02035-2422
Ph:(508)543-0050
Fax:(508)543-1919
Co. E-mail: info@mom-inc.com
Contact: Vinit P. Nair, Mgr
E-mail: vinit@atsmom-inc.com
Scope: Management and technology consulting firm providing a specially focused group of services such as disease management programs and pharmacoeconomic studies. Services include clinical and educational projects, medical writing and editing, marketing and sales projects, disease registries, educational seminars, strategic planning projects, managed care organizations; and pharmaceutical and biotechnology companies. **Publications:** "Treatment of acute exacerbation's of chronic bronchitis in patients with chronic obstructive pulmonary disease: A retrospective cohort analysis logarithmically extended release vs. Azithromycin," 2003; "A retrospective analysis of cyclooxygenase-II inhibitor response patterns," 2002; "DUE criteria for use of regional urokinase infusion for deep vein thrombosis,"2002; "The formulary management system and decision-making process at Horizon Blue Cross Blue Shield of New Jersey," Pharmaco therapy, 2001. **Seminars:** Economic Modeling as a Disease Management Tool, Academy of Managed Care Pharmacy, Apr, 2005; Integrating Disease State Management and Economics, Academy of Managed Care Pharmacy, Oct, 2004; Clinical and economic outcomes in the treatment of peripheral occlusive diseases, Mar, 2003.

2898 ■ Mefford, Knutson & Associates Inc.
6437 Lyndale Ave. S, Ste. 103
Richfield, MN 55423-1465
Ph:(612)869-8011
Free: 800-831-0228
Fax:(612)869-8004
Co. E-mail: info@mkaonline.net
URL: http://www.mkaonline.net
Contact: Jennifer Thompson, Director
E-mail: jthompson@atsmkaonline.com
Scope: A consulting and licensed business brokerage firm specializing in start-up businesses; strategic planning; mergers and acquisitions; joint ventures; divestitures; business process re-engineering; personnel policies and procedures; market research; new product development and cost controls.

2899 ■ Melvin E. Barnette & Associates Inc.
805 Hopkins Ave.
Pendleton, SC 29670
Ph:(864)646-7622
Co. E-mail: melvin@mbarnette.com
URL: http://www.mbarnette.com
Contact: Melvin E. Barnette, President
Scope: Management consulting firm specializing in higher education and public sector consulting services. Offers services including higher education administrative, business and financial operations studies; structuring of upper-level management organizations; state government operations; legislative liaison; personnel evaluation; crisis resolution and management; and management training.

2900 ■ Midwest Computer Group L.L.C.
6060 Franks Rd.
House Springs, MO 63051-1101
Ph:(636)677-0287
Fax:(636)677-0287
Co. E-mail: sales@mcgcomputer.com
URL: http://www.mcgcomputer.com
Contact: Jeffrey A. Sanford, Mgr
E-mail: jeffrey@atsmcgcomputer.com
Scope: Firm specializes in helping businesses create accounting, marketing and business information systems; software development; and database design and management.

2901 ■ Midwest Research Institute
425 Volker Blvd.
Kansas City, MO 64110-2241
Ph:(816)753-7600
Fax:(816)753-8420
Co. E-mail: info@mriresearch.org
URL: http://www.mriresearch.org
Contact: Dr. William Hall, Chairman of the Board
E-mail: jshular@atsmriresearch.org
Scope: Independent not-for-profit research institute offering scientific services in the areas of national defense, health sciences, agriculture and food safety, engineering, energy, and infrastructure. Services include biomedical electronics, remote sensing, automation and control electromagnetic radiation, environmental sampling and analysis programs for industry and government, program management, engineering studies, exposure and risk assessment, waste management strategies, contaminant identification, pollution prevention, and waste minimization. Expertise in highway safety/accident analysis, chemometrics/pattern recognition/neural networks, statistical support, process and product engineering.

2902 ■ Miller, Hellwig Associates
150 W End Ave.
New York, NY 10023-5713
Ph:(212)799-0471
Fax:(212)877-0186
Co. E-mail: millerhelwig@earthlink.net
Contact: Ernest C. Miller, President
Scope: Consulting services in the areas of start-up businesses; small business management; employee surveys and communication; performance appraisals; executive searches; team building; personnel policies and procedures; market research. Also involved in improving cross-cultural and multi-cultural relationships, particularly with Japanese clients. **Seminars:** Objectives and standards/recruiting for boards of directors.

2903 ■ National Center for Public Policy Research
501 Capitol Ct. NE
Washington, DC 20002
Ph:(202)543-4110
Fax:(202)543-5975
Co. E-mail: info@nationalcenter.org
URL: http://www.nationalcenter.org
Contact: Amy Moritz Ridenour, Principal
E-mail: aridenour@atsnationalcenter.org
Scope: A communications and research nonprofit organization offering advice and information on international affairs and United States domestic affairs. Sponsors Project 21. Gives special emphasis an environmental and regulatory issues and civil rights issues. **Publications:** "National Policy Analysis"; "Legal Briefs"; "White Paper: National Policy Analysis 523"; "Shattered Dreams: One Hundred Stories of Government Abuse"; "Shattered Lives: 100 Victims of Government Health Care".

2904 ■ National Insurance Professionals Corp.
1040 NE Hostmark St., Ste. 200
Poulsbo, WA 98370-7454
Ph:(360)697-3611
Free: 800-275-6472
Fax:(360)697-3688
Co. E-mail: kathy_schufreider@rpsvcs.com
URL: http://www.nipc.com
Contact: Jamie Augustine, Mgr
E-mail: jamie_augustine@atsrpsins.com
Scope: Program administrators for alternative specialty markets. Includes social service agencies and bicycle tour operators. Provides retail and wholesale insurance brokers access to specialty insurance carriers.

2905 ■ Navarro, Kim & Associates
529 N Charles St., Ste. 202
Baltimore, MD 21201
Ph:(410)837-6317
Fax:(410)837-6294
Co. E-mail: bnavarro@sprynet.com
Contact: Beltran Navarro, Director
E-mail: bnavarro@sprynet.com
Scope: Specializes in bridging the gap between firms and non-traditional ethnic communities, especially in community development and institutional building.

2906 ■ New Commons
545 Pawtucket Ave., Studio 106A
PO Box 116
Pawtucket, RI 02860
Ph:(401)351-7110
Fax:(401)351-7158
Co. E-mail: info@newcommons.com
URL: http://www.newcommons.com
Contact: Robert Leaver, Principal
E-mail: rleaver@atsnewcommons.com
Scope: Builder of agile human networks to champion innovation and mobilize change; to pursue business opportunities; to custom design agile organizations and communities, to foster civic engagement. Clients include organizations on-profits, corporations, government agencies, educational institutions; networks-Trade/professional groups, IT services collaborations, service-sharing collectives; and communities- municipalities, states and statewide agencies, regional collaborations. **Publications:** "Plexus Imperative," Sep, 2005; "Creating 21st Century Capable Innovation Systems," Aug, 2004; "Call to Action: Building Providences Creative and Innovative Economy"; "Getting Results from Meetings"; "The Entrepreneur as Artist," Commonwealth Publications; "Leader and Agent of Change," Commonwealth Publications; "Achieving our Providence: Lessons of City-Building," Commonwealth Publications. **Seminars:** Introduction to Social Computing (Web 2.0), Jan, 2009; Every Company Counts, Jun, 2009; Facilitating for Results; Story-Making and Story-Telling.

2907 ■ The New Marketing Network Inc.
300 Park Ave., 17th Fl.
New York, NY 10022
Ph:(212)572-6392
Co. E-mail: info@newmarketingnetwork.com
URL: http://www.newmarketingnetwork.com
Contact: Sherri Coffelt, Vice President
E-mail: pwallace@newmarketingnetwork.com
Scope: Full service firm assisting companies in marketing, creative, research, branding and communications specialties. The firm assists companies achieve their growth initiatives, increase profits and establish a sustainable competitive advantage through successful new products, accurate trend identification; application; business and brand franchise expansion. Additional services include strategic planning and positioning; qualitative and quantitative research.

2908 ■ Nightingale Associates
7445 Setting Sun Way
Columbia, MD 21046-1261
Ph:(410)381-4280
Fax:(410)381-4280
Co. E-mail: fredericknightingale@nightingaleassociates.net
URL: http://www.nightingaleassociates.net
Contact: Frederick C. Nightingale, Managing Director
E-mail: fredericknightingale@nightingaleassociates.net
Scope: Management training and consulting firm offering the following skills: productivity and accomplishment; leadership skills for the experienced manager; management skills for the new manager; leadership and teambuilding; supervisory development; creative problem solving; real strategic planning; providing superior customer service; international purchasing and supply chain management; negotiation skills development and fundamentals of purchasing. **Seminars:** Productivity and Accomplishment Management Skills for the New Manager;

Leadership and Team building; Advanced Management; Business Process Re engineering; Strategic Thinking; Creative Problem Solving; Customer Service; International Purchasing and Materials Management; Fundamentals of Purchasing; Negotiation Skills Development; Providing superior customer service; Leadership skills for the experienced manager.

2909 ■ Norman E Joe and Associates
700 - 6th Ave. SW, Ste. 100
Calgary, AB, Canada T2P 0T8
Ph:(952)595-8000
Fax:(952)595-0679
Co. E-mail: info@focustools.com
URL: http://www.focustools.com
E-mail: info@focustools.com
Scope: Consultants specializing in the development and implementation of problem-solving, decision-making and team processes for managers/supervisors and key people in a variety of organizations. Industries served: manufacturing, industrial, insurance/banking, healthcare and government. **Publications:** "What is the Decision Leader Review"; "Decision Focus Executive Learning". **Seminars:** How To Create Innovative Solutions On Demand, Jul, 2006; Essential tools to solve problems, make decisions and execute plans, faster and more effectively, Jul, 2006; Decision Focus; Creative Focus; The Focus; Team Focus. **Special Services:** Decision Focus 7.0[R].

2910 ■ North Carolina Fair Share
3824 Barrett Dr., Ste. 312
PO Box 12543
Raleigh, NC 27609
Ph:(919)786-7474
Fax:(919)786-7475
Co. E-mail: ncfslrw@aol.com
URL: http://www.ncfairshare.org
Contact: Lynice Williams, Principle
Scope: Social services firm consults on community organizing and lobbying for health issues.

2911 ■ Occupational & Environmental Health Consulting Services Inc.
635 Harding Rd.
Hinsdale, IL 60521-4814
Ph:(630)325-2083
Fax:(630)325-2098
Co. E-mail: bobb@safety-epa.com
URL: http://www.oehcs.com
Contact: Gail Brandys, Principle
E-mail: metromom@atssafety-epa.com
Scope: Provides consulting to industry on safety program development and implementation, industrial hygiene monitoring programs, occupational health nursing, wellness programs, medical monitoring, accident trending and statistics, emergency response planning, multilingual training, right-to-know compliance and training, hazardous waste management, random monitoring and mitigation, asbestos school inspection, and project management. Also offers indoor air quality, expert witnessing service. **Publications:** "Worldwide Exposure Standards for Mold and Bacteria"; "Global Occupational Exposure Limits for Over 5000 Specific Chemicals"; "Post-Remediation Verification and Clearance Testing for Mold and Bacteria Risk Based Levels of Cleanliness". **Seminars:** Right-To-Know Compliance; Setting Internal Exposure Standards; Hospital Right-to-Know and Contingency Response; Ethylene Oxide Control; Industrial Hygiene Training; Asbestos Worker Training; Biosafety; Asbestos Operations and Maintenance. **Special Services:** Safety Software Program, Audiogram Analysis, First Report of Injury Form, Human Resources Database; Material Safety Data Sheet (MSDS); NPDES Monthly Reports; Lockout/ Tagout (LOTO) Procedure Software; VOC Usage Tracking and Reporting Software, Medical Department Patient Records Database, Pictorial Labels for Chemical Containers, TIER II Hazardous Material Inventory Form & Database.

2912 ■ Optial Corp.
13 Curtain Rd.
London EC2A 3LT, United Kingdom
Ph:(770)753-0128
Fax:(770)216-1841
Co. E-mail: info@optial.com
URL: http://www.optial.com
Contact: Judith Graham, COO
Scope: Consultants in the following areas to develop integrated compliance and risk management solutions: Financial operational risk management, healthcare administration, business and property insurance, occupational safety and health, environmental. **Special Services:** Optial[TM].

2913 ■ Organization Counselors Inc.
44 W Broadway, Ste. 1102
PO Box 987
Salt Lake City, UT 84101
Ph:(801)363-2900
Fax:(801)363-0861
Co. E-mail: jpanos@xmission.com
Contact: John E. Panos, President
E-mail: jpanos@xmission.com
Scope: Organizational development; employee surveys and communication; outplacement; team building; total quality management and continuous improvement. **Seminars:** Correcting Performance Problems; Total Quality Management; Employee Selection; Performance Management.

2914 ■ Organizational Improvement Associates L.L.C.
40 Gilbert St.
Ridgefield, CT 06877
Ph:(203)417-4957
Fax:(203)244-5737
Co. E-mail: daveknibbe@oiaus.com
URL: http://www.oiaus.com
Contact: Valentina Espinosa-Shimizu, Principle
E-mail: daveknibbe@oiaus.com
Scope: Specializes in high-performance team development, executive coaching, employee development programs, performance management and reward systems and dispute mediation. Industries served: Consumer products, telecommunications, finance, health-care, amusement/leisure, hospitality/lodging, retail and pharmaceuticals.

2915 ■ P2C2 Group Inc.
4101 Denfeld Ave.
Kensington, MD 20895-1514
Ph:(301)942-7985
Fax:(301)942-7986
Co. E-mail: info@p2c2group.com
URL: http://www.p2c2group.com
Contact: Jim Kendrick, President
E-mail: kendrick@p2c2group.com
Scope: Works with clients on the business side of federal program and project management. Services include program/project planning and optimization; acquisition strategy and work statements; IT Capital Planning and Investment Control (CPIC); business cases - new, revisions, critiques; budget analysis - cost benefits- alternatives; CPIC, SELC, and security documentation; research, metrics, analysis, and case studies. Consulting support helping to: Define or redefine programs; strengthen portfolio management; identify alternatives for lean budgets; improve capital planning and investment; develop better plans and documentation, and evaluate performance of existing program investments. **Publications:** "OMB 300s Go Online," Federal Sector Report, Mar, 2007; "Using Risk-Adjusted Costs for Projects," Federal Sector Report, Feb, 2007; "Make Better Decisions Using Case Studies," Federal Sector Report, Jan, 2007; "PMO Performance Measurement & Metrics"; "Executive Sponsors for Projects"; "ABCs of the Presidential Transition"; "Financial Systems and Enterprise Portfolio Management"; "The Future of CPIC"; "Critical Factors for Program and Project Success"; "Using Risk-Adjusted Costs for Projects"; "Tactics for a Successful Year of CPIC"; "Operational Analysis Reviews"; "Successful IT Strategic Planning"; "Information Technology Investment Management". **Seminars:** How to Hire a Management Consultant and Get the Results You Expect.

2916 ■ Papa and Associates Inc.
200 Consumers Rd., Ste. 305
Toronto, ON, Canada M2J 4R4
Ph:(416)512-7272
Fax:(416)512-2016
Co. E-mail: ppapa@papa-associates.com
URL: http://www.papa-associates.com
Contact: Roxanne Wilson, Mgr
E-mail: ppapa@atspapa-associates.com
Scope: Firm provides broad based management consulting services in the areas of quality assurance, environmental, health and safety and integrated management systems.

2917 ■ Parker Consultants Inc.
230 Mason St.
Greenwich, CT 06830-6633
Ph:(203)869-9400
Contact: William P. Hartl, Chairman of the Board
Scope: Firm specializes in strategic planning; organizational development; small business management; performance appraisals; executive searches; team building; and customer service audits.

2918 ■ Partners for Market Leadership Inc.
400 Galleria Pky., Ste. 1500
Atlanta, GA 30339
Ph:(770)850-1409
Free: 800-984-1110
Co. E-mail: dcarpenter@market-leadership.com
URL: http://www.market-leadership.com
Contact: Nancy Surdyka, Mgr
E-mail: nsurdyka@atsmarket-leadership.com
Scope: Boutique consulting firm focused on assisting clients to develop sustainable market leadership in geographic, practice area and/or industry markets. Provides consulting on market leadership, revenue enhancement, strategic development and change facilitation. Additional services are offered to legal, accounting, valuation and financial firms.

2919 ■ Pathways To Wellness
617 Everhart Rd.
Corpus Christi, TX 78411
Ph:(361)985-9642
Fax:(361)949-4627
Co. E-mail: path2wellness@earthlink.net
URL: http://www.path2wellness.com
Contact: Evy Coppola, Owner
Scope: Offer natural holistic health counseling, yoga and hatha yoga classes, teachers training and cookery classes for individuals and companies. Health counseling includes nutritional guidance, kinesiology, iridology, reflexology, energy healing, massage therapy, herbal and vitamin therapy, creative visualization and meditation. Provides supplements which bring about the same effects as that of natural sunshine. **Seminars:** Is It You Holding You Back?; The Balancing Act. . .Career. . . Family. . .and Self; Learning the Art of Friendly Persuasion; Stop Accepting What You Are Getting and Start Asking for What You Want!; Introduction to Natural Health and Healthy Living; Learn Why One Size Approaches to the Answers on Health Do Not Work; Introduction to Yoga. What is it? Who can do it? What can it do for you.

2920 ■ Performance Consulting Associates Inc.
3700 Crestwood Pky., Ste. 100
Duluth, GA 30096
Ph:(770)717-2737
Fax:(770)717-7014
Co. E-mail: info@pcaconsulting.com
URL: http://www.pcaconsulting.com
Contact: Robert Wilson, Mgr
E-mail: wilson@atspcaconsulting.com
Scope: Maintenance consulting and engineering firm specializing in production planning, project management, team building, and re-engineering maintenance. **Publications:** "Does Planning Pay," Plant Services, Nov, 2000; "Asset Reliability Coordinator," Maintenance Technology, Oct, 2000; "Know What it is You Have to Maintain," Maintenance Technology; May, 2000; "Does Maintenance Planning Pay," Maintenance Technology, Nov, 2000.; "What is Asset Management?"; "Implementing Best Business Practices".

2921 ■ Performance Consulting Group Inc.
8031 SW 35th Terr.
Miami, FL 33155-3443
Ph:(305)264-5577

Fax:(305)264-9079
Contact: Patrick J. O'Brien, President
Scope: Firm provides consulting services in the areas of strategic planning; profit enhancement; product development; and production planning.

2922 ■ Performance Dynamics Group L.L.C.
One Ridge Rd.
Green Brook, NJ 08812
Ph:(732)537-0381
Free: 888-720-7337
Co. E-mail: info@performance-dynamics.net
URL: http://www.performance-dynamics.net
Contact: Mark E. Green, President
E-mail: mark.green@atsperformance-dynamics.net
Scope: An organizational consulting group whose approach to learning and employee empowerment is designed to be both effective and efficient in achieving the specific knowledge and skill goals of a given program, in developing changes in thinking and behavior and also to foster and develop initiative, self confidence, creative problem-solving ability and interpersonal effectiveness of all participants. Brings improvement in areas of revenue growth, profitability, sales, marketing effectiveness, and employee and customer loyalty. **Seminars:** Accelerated Approach to Change; Commitment to Quality; Managing Cultural Diversity; The Corporate Energizer; The Power Pole Experience; Team Assessment; Self-Directed Work Teams.

2923 ■ Practice Development Counsel
60 Sutton Pl. S
New York, NY 10022
Ph:(212)593-1549
Fax:(212)980-7940
Co. E-mail: pwhaserot@pdcounsel.com
URL: http://www.pdcounsel.com
Contact: Steven A. Lauer, Mgr
E-mail: stevelauer@atssprintmail.com
Scope: Specializes in business development, service quality, retention, organizational development work/ life excellence, and conflict resolution for professional firms. Provides coaching, client relationship management and quality service programs; strategic marketing planning/implementation; ancillary businesses/ diversification; market research, trend watching, bench marking; facilitation and planning for retreats and creative decision making; new business proposals and presentations; marketing communications and public relations; and business development training, coaching, and materials. Also offers speaker's services - engagements, publicity, etc. Industries served: law, accounting, and financial services, executive search, design, architecture, real estate, and management consultants worldwide. **Publications:** "The Rainmaking Machine: Marketing Planning, Strategy and Management For Law Firms"; "The Marketer's Handbook of Tips & Checklists"; "Venturesome Questions: The Law Firms Guide to Developing a New Business Venture"; "Navigating the Whitewater of Internal Politics"; "Changing Attitudes on Firm Flexibility"; "Transition Planning: A Looming Challenge"; "Don't You Think the Solution Is to Bring In a Good Rainmaker?"; "Aligning Firm Culture with the Needs of the Times"; "What New Partners Need to Know"; "Dangers of Lack of Diversity"; "Learn to Respect Emotion in Business"; "What New Partners Need to Know"; "Taking Responsibility: Implementing Personal Marketing Plans"; "How to Change Unwritten Rules"; "Mentoring and Networking Converge"; "Integrating a New Practice into the Firm"; "Using Conflict Resolution Skills for Marketing Success"; "Sports Team Models for Law Firm Management". **Seminars:** Managing Work Expectations; Effective Coaching Skills; Service Quality; End-Running the Resistance Professionals Have to Getting Client Input; Ancillary Business Activities; Marketing for Professional Firms; Marketing Ethics; Business Development Training; Trends in Professional Services Marketing; Client Relationship Management; Collaborative Culture; Reaching Consensus; Conflict Resolution; Work life Balance; Generaltional Issues; Preparing New Partners; Becoming the Employer of Choice; A Marketing Approach to Recruiting; Implementing Workplace Flexibility; The Business Case for Flexible Work Arrangements.

2924 ■ Praxis Media Inc.
48 Harbourview Ave.
South Norwalk, CT 06854
Ph:(203)866-6666
Fax:(203)853-8299
Co. E-mail: aldo@praxismediainc.com
Contact: Deborah Winegrad, Vice President
Scope: Media needs analysis and project planning specialists provide services in product introductions, communications planning, technology application, promotion and marketing communications. Also assists with focus groups, research, concept development, creative development, scripting and executive speech coaching/training. Industries served: Financial services, high-tech, travel and leisure, health and pharmaceutical and telecommunications.

2925 ■ Professional Counseling Centers Inc.
543 Coventry Way
Noblesville, IN 46062-9024
Ph:(317)877-3111
Contact: Margie Hanrahan, Owner
Scope: Business counselors offering services in the following areas: employee assistance, managed care, alcohol and drug treatment, labor and union consultation, and industrial mental health.

2926 ■ Public Administration Service
7927 Jones Branch Dr., Ste. 100 S
McLean, VA 22102-3322
Ph:(703)734-8970
Fax:(703)734-4965
Contact: Ramesh Khatiwada, Treasurer
Scope: Performs a variety of consulting and research work in serving the special needs of governments and other public service institutions. Services range from technical studies of central management problems to analyses of public policy issues, and in development administration water sewerage management and systems, rural development, and small farmer organization privatization, and management. Devoted exclusively to improving the conduct of public activities. Consulting services in the United States include organization and management, data processing and automation plans, position classification and compensation plans, police and fire service studies, public works and utilities studies, and parks management studies.

2927 ■ Public Policy Communications
4163 Dingman Dr.
Sanibel, FL 33957
Ph:(941)395-6773
Fax:(941)395-6779
Contact: Robert Schaeffer, President
E-mail: bobschaeffer@earthlink.net
Scope: Provides strategic communications for progressive causes, candidates and socially-responsible businesses. These include public relations strategies, political campaign planning, organizational development and training. Substantial work in report writing, editing and design as well as production of a full range of media materials. Industries served: nonprofit, social change organizations, foundations, political campaigns, environmentally and consumer-oriented businesses, government agencies. **Publications:** "Winning Local and State Elections," Free Press MacMillan; "Giving the Media Your Message, and The News Media and the Big Lie". **Seminars:** Giving the Media Your Message; Effective Public Relations Practices; Winning Your Election; Understanding the Government Budget Process; How to Be an Effective Advocate; Strategic Planning for Non-Profits; How to Run a News Conference: Ten Key Steps, 1998.

2928 ■ Public Sector Consultants Inc.
600 W St. Joseph St., Ste. 10
Lansing, MI 48933-2267
Ph:(517)484-4954
Fax:(517)484-6549
Co. E-mail: psc@pscinc.com
URL: http://www.pscinc.com
Contact: Julie Metty Bennett, Vice President
E-mail: jmettybennett@atspscinc.com
Scope: Offers policy research expertise, specializing in opinion polling, public relations, conference planning, and legislative and economic analysis. Industries served: Associations, education, environment, health-care, and public finance. **Publications:** "Ingham Community Voices Final Evaluation Report," Nov, 2008; "First Class Schools Analysis," Aug, 2008; "Opportunities for Achieving Efficiency in the Aging, Community Mental Health, Local Public Health, and Substance Abuse Coordinating Agency Networks," Aug, 2008; "Saginaw River Bay Area of Concern," Jun, 2008; "Portage Lake Water shed Forever Plan," May, 2008; "Smoke Free Workplaces," Apr, 2008; "Protecting and Restoring the Upper Looking Glass River," Feb, 2008; "Market Structures and the 21st Century Energy Plan," Sep, 2007; "The Growing Crisis of Aging Dams," Apr, 2007; "Financing Community Health Workers Why and How," Jan, 2007; "Hastings Area: Inter local Approaches to Growth Management," Jan, 2007; "Michigan's Part 201 Environmental Remediation Program Review," Jan, 2007.

2929 ■ The Purchasing Department
34 Claremont Ave.
Maplewood, NJ 07040-2118
Fax:(973)275-0749
Co. E-mail: eostpd@aol.com
Contact: James Thomas Milway, Principle
E-mail: jtmtpd@aol.com
Scope: Provides state of the art procurement arrangements, process re-engineering and outsourcing assistance to any business wishing to achieve purchasing savings and efficiencies to improve bottom line results. Available to provide contract services to businesses requiring specialized supplemental assistance to back up own personnel on special projects. **Seminars:** Green Purchasing: Buying Recycled Products; Ethics; Measuring Purchasing Performance; Supplier Teaming and Quality; Preparing for ISO 9000 in the Purchasing Department.

2930 ■ Queens Business Consulting
Queens School of Business, Goodes Hall, 143 Union St.
Kingston, ON, Canada K7L 3N6
Ph:(613)533-2309
Fax:(613)533-2370
Co. E-mail: qbc@business.queensu.ca
URL: http://www.qsbc.com
Contact: Amber Wallace, Principle
E-mail: awallace@atsbusiness.queensu.ca
Scope: Provides business plans, feasibility studies, financial planning, competitor analysis, market research, marketing strategies, production planning and systems implementation.

2931 ■ R.E. Moulton Inc.
50 Doaks Ln.
Marblehead, MA 01945
Ph:(781)631-1325
Fax:(781)631-2165
Co. E-mail: mike_lee@remoultoninc.com
URL: http://www.oneamerica.com/wps/wcm/connect/REMoulton
Contact: Reynolds E. Moulton Jr., Chairman of the Board
E-mail: dick@atsremoultoninc.com
Scope: Offers underwriting services, marketing solutions, claims administration and adjudication; policy and commission administration; and risk management solutions to clients. Supplementary service s include risk management and employee assistance. Clients include individuals, business men, employers and finance professionals.

2932 ■ Reed Royalty Public Affairs Inc.
30205 Hillside Terr.
San Juan Capistrano, CA 92675-1542
Ph:(949)240-2022
Fax:(949)240-0304
Co. E-mail: reed.royauy@home.com
Contact: Reed L. Royalty, President
E-mail: rroyalty@ocers.org
Scope: A governmental relations consultant who provides lobbying for changes in laws and government regulations, helps in obtaining licenses and permits, provides corporate training in governmental relations and assistance in winning government contracts. Services include crisis management, business association management and issue-specific community and media relations.

2933 ■ Rental Relocation Inc.
281 S Atlanta St.
Roswell, GA 30075
Ph:(770)641-8393
Free: 800-641-7368
Fax:(770)641-8607
Co. E-mail: ahlsinfo@rentalrelocation.com
URL: http://www.rentalrelocation.com
Contact: Christopher Bliss, President
E-mail: cbliss@atsrentalrelocation.com
Scope: Relocation firm offering services in corporate housing, rentals, free metro Atlanta apartment locating service, property management, house and condo rental relocation tours.

2934 ■ Rose & Crangle Ltd.
117 N 4th St.
PO Box 285
Lincoln, KS 67455
Ph:(785)524-5050
Fax:(785)524-3130
Co. E-mail: rcltd@nckcn.com
URL: http://www.roseandcrangle.com
Contact: Jeanne Crangle, Principle
E-mail: rcltd@nckcn.com
Scope: Firm provides evaluation, planning and policy analyzes for universities, associations, foundations, governmental agencies and private companies engaged in scientific, technological or educational activities. Special expertise in the development of new institutions. Special skills in providing planning and related group facilitation workshops. **Publications:** "Preface to Bulgarian Integration Into Europe and NATO: Issues of Science Policy And research Evaluation Practice," Ios Press, 2006; "Allocating Limited National Resources for Fundamental Research," 2005.

2935 ■ Rothschild Strategies Unlimited L.L.C.
19 Thistle Rd.
PO Box 7568
Norwalk, CT 06851-1909
Ph:(203)846-6898
Fax:(203)847-1426
Co. E-mail: bill@strategyleader.com
URL: http://www.strategyleader.com
Contact: William Rothchild, CEO
E-mail: billrothschild@atsoptonline.net
Scope: Consults with senior management and business level strategy teams to develop overall strategic direction, set priorities and creates sustainable competitive advantages and differentiators. Enables organizations to enhance their own strategic thinking and leadership skills so that they can continue to develop and implement profitable growth strategies. **Publications:** "Putting It All Together-a guide to strategic thinking"; "Competitive Advantage"; "Ristaker, Caretaker, Surgeon & Undertaker four faces of strategic leadership"; "The Secret to GE's Success"; "Having the Right Strategic Leader and Team". **Seminars:** Who is going the WRONG way?; Learning from your Successes and Failures. **Special Services:** StrategyLeader[R].

2936 ■ Sanford Consulting
52 Perry Corners Rd., RR 1
PO Box 314A
Amenia, NY 12501
Ph:(845)373-8960
Fax:(845)373-8961
Co. E-mail: sanford@mohawk.com
Contact: Anne Sanford, President
E-mail: sanford@mohawk.com
Scope: Helps businesses find, sell, to, and keep customers. Provides management and marketing services, including problem analysis and solution design for new business development, market analysis and segmentation, departmental organization and administrative policies and procedures. Industries served: small business, telecommunications, professional services, health care and nonprofits in the continental United States. **Seminars:** Trade show success; Finding customers; Business attitudes at not for profit and others.

2937 ■ S.B. Smith Consulting Group Inc.
837 Millwood Rd.
Toronto, ON, Canada M4G 1W5
Ph:(416)467-0011
Fax:(416)467-0071
Co. E-mail: susan@sbsconsulting.ca
URL: http://www.sbsconsulting.ca
Contact: Susan Smith, President
E-mail: susan@sbsconsulting.ca
Scope: Seeks to help overworked and overstressed entrepreneurs regain effective control and release ineffective control. **Publications:** "What You Can Measure, You Can Manage"; "Leadership By Design". **Seminars:** Advisory Boards - Accelerating Success; Alternative Growth Strategies Beyond Succession; Leadership - Understanding Styles and Developing new Leaders; Facing Change Head On - Avoiding Frustrations and Mistrust; Hiring Right and Retaining the Best; Keeping Your Balance - Walking the Cash Flow Tightrope; Strategic Planning - Begin with the End in Mind; What You Can Measure You Can Measure - Developing Polices and Procedures; Understanding your Financial Statements; Financial Management - Beyond the Basics.

2938 ■ SBR International
3 - 14 College St.
The Graeme Bldg.
Toronto, ON, Canada M5G 1K2
Ph:(416)962-7500
Fax:(416)962-7505
Co. E-mail: bizdev@sbr-global.com
URL: http://www.sbr-global.com
Contact: Chris Anstead, Managering Director
Scope: Specializes in the leasing of multi-disciplinary, high-performance work teams at customer in-house cost, under a mixed military/general contracting model. Engagements include BPR, IE, SA, market and competitor intelligence, logistics, strategy, audit, workouts/turnarounds, M and A support/targeting, statistics and micro-economic modeling, PMO support. **Seminars:** Electronic counter measures; Strategic planning; Project management.

2939 ■ Schneider Consulting Group Inc.
50 S Steele St., Ste. 390
Denver, CO 80209
Ph:(303)320-4413
Fax:(303)320-5795
Contact: Kim Schneider Malek, Vice President
E-mail: kim@atsscgfambus.com
Scope: Assists family-owned and privately-held business transition to the next generation and/or to a more professionally managed company, turn around consulting for small and medium size companies.

2940 ■ Scott Ashby Teleselling Inc.
1102 Ben Franklin Dr., Ste. 309
Sarasota, FL 34236
Ph:(941)388-4283
Fax:(941)388-5240
Co. E-mail: rscottashby@netscape.net
URL: http://www.scottashbyteleselling.com
Contact: R. Scott Ashby, Owner
E-mail: rscottashby@netscape.net
Scope: Provides consulting services and customized training programs that emphasize consultative telephone selling techniques. **Publications:** "How Will the Internet Affect Teleselling Programs?"; "When is Telemarketing Really Not Telemarketing?"; "The Future of Account Management Telesales". **Seminars:** Start-Up Educational, Planning and Strategy Development; Existing Program Audit, Evaluation, State-of-the-Art Best Practices Comparison, Tracking and Measurement Review, Systems and Procedures Analysis, and Optional Selling Skills; Develop New or Revised Consultative Telephone Selling; Helping Clients Build Relationship and Grow Their Business by Phone.

2941 ■ Sklar and Associates Inc.
242 Laurel Bay Dr.
Murrells Inlet, SC 29576
Ph:(202)257-5061
Fax:(843)651-3090
Co. E-mail: sklarincdc@aol.com
URL: http://www.sklarinc.com
Contact: Tim Sklar, President
Scope: Provides consulting services for business acquisitions, business development and project finance. Provides audit oversight services to listed corporations on Sarbanes-Oxley compliance. Services include: Due diligence analyses and corporate governance. Industries served: transportation sectors, energy sector and commercial real estate industries. **Seminars:** Financial Analysis in MBA; Emerging Company Finance; Due Diligence in Business Acquisition; Business Valuation.

2942 ■ Straightline Services Inc.
11 Centre St., Ste. 10
Salem, CT 06420-3845
Ph:(860)889-7929
Fax:(860)885-1894
Co. E-mail: straitln@aol.com
Contact: Wayne J. S. France CPCM, President
Scope: Design and implementation of organizational infrastructure, business plans and troubleshooting. Emphasizes on operations with a central and field or satellite offices. Industries served: Construction, resorts, Indian tribes, academies, small-medium sized business, mostly privately held.

2943 ■ Strategic MindShare Consulting
1401 Brickell Ave., Ste. 640
Miami, FL 33131
Ph:(305)377-2220
Fax:(305)377-2280
Co. E-mail: dee@strategicmindshare.com
URL: http://www.strategicmindshare.com
Contact: Cynthia R. Cohen, President
E-mail: cohen@strategicmindshare.com
Scope: Firm specializes in strategic planning; feasibility studies; profit enhancement; organizational development; start-up businesses; mergers and acquisitions; joint ventures; divestitures; interim management; crisis management; turnarounds; new product development and competitive analysis. **Publications:** "Top Ten CEO Burning Issues for 2005"; "Top Ten Consumer Behavioral Trends for 2005"; "The Influence Factors"; "New Profit Opportunities for Retailers and Consumer Product Companies".

2944 ■ TC International Marketing Inc.
11 Iliffe House, Iliffe Ave.
Leicester LE2 5LS, United Kingdom
Ph:(845)258-7482
Fax:(845)986-2130
Co. E-mail: tcintl@warwick.net
Contact: Graeme Wright, Partner
Scope: Business expansion consulting including feasibility studies, mergers and acquisitions, divestment, market research and strategizing.

2945 ■ Technology Management Group Co.
PO Box 3260
New Haven, CT 06515-0360
Ph:(203)387-1430
Fax:(203)387-1470
Co. E-mail: info@commtechsoftware.com
URL: http://www.ratafia.net
Contact: Manny Ratafia, President
E-mail: manny@commtechsoftware.com
Scope: Consulting services include analysis of market opportunities; product introductions; new ventures; acquisitions analysis; licensing, joint ventures, and OEM arrangements. Emphasis on polymers, medical devices, biotechnology, pharmaceuticals, and chemicals. **Special Services:** CommTechPowerSearch[R].

2946 ■ TQM Consulting
1821 Lodgepole Dr.
Kamloops, BC, Canada V1S 1X7
Ph:(250)828-0420
Fax:(250)828-6859
Co. E-mail: info@tqmconsulting.ca
URL: http://www.tqmconsulting.ca
Contact: Don Anderson, President
Scope: Provides individuals and organizations with a competitive edge through our training and consulting services. **Seminars:** Pre-Entrepreneurial Program for Human Resources Development.

2947 ■ Trendzitions Inc.
25691 Atlantic Ocean Dr., Ste. B13
Lake Forest, CA 92630-8842
Ph:(949)727-9100
Free: 800-266-2767

Fax:(949)727-3444
Co. E-mail: ctooker@trendzitions.com
URL: http://www.trendzitions.com
Contact: Christian Tooker, President
E-mail: ctooker@atstrendzitions.com
Scope: Provides services in the areas of communications consulting, project management, construction management, and furniture procurement. Offers information on spatial uses, building codes, ADA compliance and city ordinances. Also offers budget projections.

2948 ■ Turnaround Inc.
3415 A St. NW
Gig Harbor, WA 98335
Ph:(253)857-6730
Fax:(253)857-6344
Co. E-mail: info@turnround-inc.com
URL: http://www.turnaround-inc.com
Contact: Miles Stover, President
E-mail: mstover@turnaround-inc.com
Scope: Firm provides interim executive management assistance and management advisory to small, medium and family-owned businesses that are not meeting their goals. Services include acting as an interim executive or on-site manager. Extensive practices in arena of bankruptcy management. **Publications:** "How to Identify Problem and Promising Management"; "How to Tell if Your Company is a Bankruptcy Candidate"; "Signs that Your Company is in Trouble"; "The Turnaround Specialist: How to File a Petition Under 11 USC 11". **Seminars:** Competitive Intelligence Gathering.

2949 ■ ValueNomics Value Specialists
50 W San Fernando St., Ste. 600
San Jose, CA 95113
Ph:(408)200-6400
Fax:(408)200-6401
Co. E-mail: info@amllp.com
Contact: Jeff A. Stegner, Partner
Scope: Consulting is offered in the areas of financial management, process re-engineering, growth business services; governance, risk/compliance, SOX readiness and compliance, SAS 70, enterprise risk management, system security, operational and internal audit; business advisory services; valuation services; CORE assessment; contract assurance; transaction advisory services, IT solutions and litigation support services. **Publications:** "Dueling Appraisers: How Differences in Input and Assumptions May Control the Value," Apr, 2005; "The Business of Business Valuation and the CPA as an expert witness"; "The Business of Business Valuation," McGraw-Hill Professional Publishers Inc.

2950 ■ Via Nova Consulting
1228 Winburn Dr.
Atlanta, GA 30344
Ph:(404)761-7484
Fax:(404)762-7123
Scope: Consulting services in the areas of strategic planning; privatization; executive searches; market research; customer service audits; new product development; competitive intelligence; and Total Quality Management (TQM).

2951 ■ Vision Management
149 Meadows Rd.
Lafayette, NJ 07848-3120
Ph:(973)702-1116
Fax:(973)702-8311
Contact: Norman L. Naidish, President
Scope: Firm specializes in profit enhancement; strategic planning; business process reengineering; industrial engineering; facilities planning; team building; inventory management; and total quality management (TQM). **Publications:** "To increase profits, improve quality," Manufacturing Engineering, May, 2000.

2952 ■ The Visioneering Institute
2780 rue de Lanoraie St.
Quebec, QC, Canada G1W 1M4
Ph:(418)948-1553
Free: 888-788-8844
Co. E-mail: info@visioneering-institute.com
URL: http://www.visioneering-institute.com
Contact: Davender Gupta, President
E-mail: davender@davender.com
Scope: Supports entrepreneurs to create high-performance organizations that unlock the potential of every member of the team, through coaching, consulting, training and leadership. Areas include leadership training, corporate retreat facilitation, mission and vision statement building and corporate culture assessment. **Seminars:** High Performance Success Coaching.

2953 ■ The Walk The Talk Co.
1100 Parker Sq., Ste. 250
Flower Mound, TX 75028-7458
Ph:(972)899-8300
Free: 800-888-2811
Fax:(972)899-9291
Co. E-mail: info@walkthetalk.com
URL: http://www.walkthetalk.com
Contact: Doug Westmoreland, VP of Operations
E-mail: ericharvey@walkthetalk.com
Scope: Assists a wide variety of organizations in implementing proprietary performance management system developed by the firm which concentrates on individual responsibility and decision making instead of disciplinary penalties. Helps organizations develop and implement peer review, a proven system that helps solve employee problems in a remarkable way-through employees and an evaluation process software is used whereby feedback is compiled from a full-range of sources, including a self-evaluation, leadership development workshops and keynote presentations and publications. **Publications:** "Positive Discipline"; "Leadership Secrets of Santa Claus"; "Start Right-Stay Right"; "Walk Awhile in My Shoes"; "Listen Up, Leader!"; "Five Star Teamwork"; "Ethics4Everyone"; "Leadership Courage"; "The Manager's Communication Handbook"; "180 Ways to Walk the Recognition Talk"; "The Manager's Coaching Handbook"; "The Best Leadership Advice I Ever Got"; "Power Exchange". **Seminars:** Walk the Talk; Coaching for Continuous Improvement; Managing Employee Performance; Customized Management Development Forums; Keynote presentations; Leadership Development Workshops; Consulting Services and Publications; Customer service training; Ethics and Values training.

2954 ■ Weich & Bilotti Inc.
600 Worcester Rd., 4th Fl.
Framingham, MA 01702
Ph:(508)663-1600
Fax:(508)663-1682
Co. E-mail: info@weich-bilotti.com
URL: http://www.weich-bilotti.com
Contact: Mervyn D. Weich, President
E-mail: mweich@weich-bilotti.com
Scope: Specializes in business plans, venture capital, computer information systems, turnaround/ interim management, retail consulting, start-up process, college recruiting and IS and IT personnel.

2955 ■ Western Business Services Ltd.
1269 Lindsay St.
Regina, SK, Canada S4N 3B4
Ph:(306)522-1493
Fax:(306)522-9076
Co. E-mail: wbs@accesscomm.ca
URL: http://www.wbs.bz
Contact: Lenore M. Zuck, Principle
Scope: Provides marketing, financial and accounting services to individuals, on-profit organizations and commercial companies.

2956 ■ Wheeler and Young Inc.
33 Peter St.
Markham, ON, Canada L3P 2A5
Ph:(905)471-5709
Fax:(905)471-9989
Co. E-mail: wheeler@ericwheeler.ca
URL: http://www.ericwheeler.ca
Contact: Eric S. Wheeler, Managing Partner
E-mail: ewheeler@yorku.ca
Scope: Provides consulting services to high-tech companies on the implementation of software development processes; quality management systems (including ISO 9000 compliance) and business management systems. Offers business management and knowledge-management services to organizations. Industries served: Knowledge-based industries, including software and hardware development, medical and legal professionals, information service providers.

2957 ■ William E. Kuhn & Associates
234 Cook St.
Denver, CO 80206-5305
Ph:(303)322-8233
Fax:(303)331-9032
Co. E-mail: billkuhn1@cs.com
Contact: William E. Kuhn, Owner
E-mail: billkuhn1@cs.com
Scope: Firm specializes in strategic planning; profit enhancement; small business management; mergers and acquisitions; joint ventures; divestitures; human resources management; performance appraisals; team building; sales management; appraisals and valuations. **Publications:** "Creating a High-Performance Dealership," Office SOLUTIONS & Office DEALER, Jul-Aug, 2006.

2958 ■ ZS Engineering P.C.
99 Tulip Ave.
Floral Park, NY 11001
Ph:(516)328-3200
Fax:(516)328-6195
Co. E-mail: office@zsengineering.com
URL: http://www.zsengineering.com
Contact: Donna Conte, Mgr
E-mail: staszewski@atszsengineering.com
Scope: Offers engineering consulting services to building owners, building managers and contractors. Specializes in design and inspections of fire alarm systems, sprinkler systems, smoke control systems, building evaluations for fire code compliance, violations removal. **Seminars:** Fire protection courses for contractors and building management.

FRANCHISES AND BUSINESS OPPORTUNITIES

2959 ■ ABX-Associates Business Xchange
7604 Oak St.
Frisco, TX 75034
Ph:(214)850-6131
Fax:(866)462-7229
Founded: 1971. **Description:** Nationwide franchise brokers network.

2960 ■ ActionCoach
5781 S Fort Apache
Las Vegas, NV 89118
Ph:(702)795-3188
Fax:(702)795-3183
No. of Franchise Units: 292. **No. of Operating Units:** 1,022. **Founded:** 1993. **Franchised:** 1997. **Description:** Business consulting and coaching service. **Equity Capital Needed:** $82,500-$490,030. **Franchise Fee:** $50,000-$275.000. **Royalty Fee:** $1,500-$1,800/month. **Financial Assistance:** Third party financing available. **Training:** Offers 10 days at headquarters, 10 days at various locations with ongoing support.

2961 ■ Alliance Cost Containment LLC
222 S First St., Ste. 301
Louisville, KY 40202
Ph:(502)635-3208
Fax:(502)238-1830
No. of Franchise Units: 28. **No. of Company-Owned Units:** 1. **Founded:** 1992. **Franchised:** 2004. **Description:** Expense-reduction consulting services. **Equity Capital Needed:** $47,600-$64,600. **Franchise Fee:** $34,500. **Royalty Fee:** 9%. **Financial Assistance:** No. **Training:** Training includes 3-4 days at headquarters, 3 days at annual conference and ongoing support.

2962 ■ Alpha Legal Forms & More, Inc.
Alpha Publications of America, Inc.
PO Box 12488
Tucson, AZ 85732
Ph:(520)795-7100

Free: 800-770-4329
Founded: 1976. **Description:** Legal forms.

2963 ■ The Alternative Board
Tab Boards International, Inc.
11031 Sheridan Blvd.
Westminster, CO 80020
Ph:(303)839-4744
Free: 800-727-0126
Fax:(303)839-0012
No. of Franchise Units: 128. **No. of Company-Owned Units:** 9. **Founded:** 1990. **Franchised:** 1996. **Description:** Coordination of advisory business groups. **Equity Capital Needed:** $56,821-$112,981 total investment. **Franchise Fee:** $17,500-$52,500. **Royalty Fee:** Varies. **Financial Assistance:** Third party financing available. **Training:** Training available at headquarters for 6 days and 4 weeks on-site with monthly/quarterly conference calls.

2964 ■ American Association of Franchisees and Dealers
PO Box 10158
Palm Desert, CA 92255
Ph:(619)209-3775
Free: 800-733-9858
Fax:(619)209-3777
Founded: 1992. **Description:** Franchisees and business services.

2965 ■ American Franchise Consultants
520 W Gleneagles Dr.
Phoenix, AZ 85023
Free: 800-424-0749
Founded: 1995. **Description:** Business consultants.

2966 ■ Crestcom International, Ltd.
6900 E Belleview Ave., 3rd Fl.
Greenwood Village, CO 80111
Ph:(303)267-8200
Free: 888-CRE-STCO
Fax:(303)267-8207
Co. E-mail: franchiseinfo@crestcom.com
URL: http://www.crestcom.com
No. of Franchise Units: 200. **Founded:** 1987. **Franchised:** 1992. **Description:** Business centers around marketing and conducting video-based management and sales training. Training is a combination of video instruction, featuring renowned business and management personalities, and hands-on monthly seminars. Training is currently used by many leading organizations throughout the world. **Equity Capital Needed:** $12,500-$62,500. **Franchise Fee:** $12,500-$62,500. **Financial Assistance:** Some. **Managerial Assistance:** Training for franchisees'employees, newsletters, awards and incentive programs, and regional and international conferences. **Training:** Initial classroom and field training, ongoing training, a lead assistance program.

2967 ■ Criterium Engineers
22 Monument Sq., Ste. 600
Portland, ME 04101
Ph:(207)828-1969
Free: 800-242-1969
Fax:(207)775-4405
No. of Franchise Units: 71. **Founded:** 1957. **Franchised:** 1958. **Description:** Nationwide network of registered professional engineers, specializing in buildings and related consulting services. Services include residential and commercial inspections, insurance investigations, environmental assessments, capital reserve studies, design and related services. Clients include buyers, building owners and managers, lenders, attorneys, insurance companies and government agencies. Customized software and unlimited toll-free support. **Equity Capital Needed:** $41,000-$64,000. **Franchise Fee:** $26,500. **Financial Assistance:** Yes. **Training:** Yes.

2968 ■ Days Inns-Canada
Realstar Hotel Services Corp.
77 Bloor St. W, Ste. 2000
Toronto, ON, Canada M5S 1M2
Ph:(416)966-8387
Free: 800-840-8162
Fax:(416)923-5424
Co. E-mail: irwin.prince@daysinn.ca
URL: http://www.daysinn.ca
No. of Franchise Units: 94. **Founded:** 1992. **Franchised:** 1992. **Description:** Has established franchised properties in all major cities across the country in the moderate-priced segment of the market. **Equity Capital Needed:** $5,000,000. **Franchise Fee:** $350/room, minimum $35,000 and $10,000. **Royalty Fee:** Marketing fee included in Royalty Fee 6.5%, reservation fee 2.3% of gross room revenue (GRR). **Financial Assistance:** No. **Training:** Training provided at opening and ongoing. Site selection and advisory council are provided.

2969 ■ DirectBuild
DirectBuild Franchising, LLC
19201 E Mainstreet, Ste. 103
PO Box 2019
Parker, CO 80134
Ph:(303)805-9294
Fax:(720)851-7160
No. of Franchise Units: 1. **No. of Company-Owned Units:** 2. **Founded:** 1995. **Franchised:** 2006. **Description:** Home building & remodeling consulting. **Equity Capital Needed:** $176,000. **Franchise Fee:** $29,900. **Royalty Fee:** 7%. **Financial Assistance:** No. **Training:** Yes.

2970 ■ ESAPP Financial, LLC
6520 E 82nd St., Ste.200
Indianapolis, IN 46250
Ph:(317)577-4995
Fax:(317)577-4996
Founded: 1996. **Description:** Financial services company.

2971 ■ Expense Reduction Analysts
5050 Avenida Encinas, Ste. 200
Carlsbad, CA 92008
Ph:(760)712-3600
Free: 877-972-3721
Fax:(760)712-3700
No. of Franchise Units: 246. **No. of Company-Owned Units:** 5. **Founded:** 1992. **Franchised:** 2003. **Description:** Cost management consultancy. **Equity Capital Needed:** $65,000-$300,000. **Franchise Fee:** $59,900-$250,000. **Financial Assistance:** No. **Training:** Yes.

2972 ■ FD & MG Franchise Company Inc.
949 E Pioneer Rd., Ste. B-2
Draper, UT 84020
Ph:(801)352-1400
Fax:(801)619-4038
No. of Franchise Units: 2. **No. of Company-Owned Units:** 1. **Founded:** 2003. **Franchised:** 2007. **Description:** Franchise consulting. **Equity Capital Needed:** $120,500-$152,100. **Franchise Fee:** $75,000. **Royalty Fee:** 6%. **Financial Assistance:** Third party financing available and in-house assistance with franchise fee. **Training:** Includes 2 weeks training at headquarters and ongoing support.

2973 ■ Focal Point Business Coaching
5740 S Eastern Ave., Ste. 100
Las Vegas, NV
Ph:(702)932-3870
Free: 877-433-6225
Fax:(702)932-3871
No. of Franchise Units: 60. **Founded:** 1999. **Franchised:** 2005. **Description:** Business coaching and consulting. **Equity Capital Needed:** $75,550-$121,950. **Franchise Fee:** $40,000. **Royalty Fee:** $1,800/month. **Financial Assistance:** Assistance with franchise fee. **Training:** Provides 1 week at headquarters, 2 months at franchisees location, virtual training and ongoing support.

2974 ■ Franchise Compliance, Inc.
PO Box 982662
Park City, UT 84098
Ph:(435)757-5071
Fax:(435)563-0163
Description: Provides franchise services and mystery shopping.

2975 ■ Franchise Consultants, Inc.
558 S Osprey Ave.
Sarasota, FL 34236
Ph:(941)954-6484
Free: (866)372-6484
Fax:(941)954-8462
Founded: 1986. **Description:** UFOC preparation, registration and franchise sales.

2976 ■ Franchise Development International, LLC
370 SE 15 Ave.
Pompano Beach, FL 33060
Ph:(954)942-9424
Fax:(954)783-5177
Founded: 1991. **Description:** Franchise development and marketing.

2977 ■ Franchise Development & Marketing Group
Franchise Development & Marketing Group, Inc.
949 E Pioneer Rd., Ste. 2B
Draper, UT 84020
Ph:(801)352-1400
Fax:(801)619-4038
Founded: 2003. **Description:** Assist businesses in all franchise phase.

2978 ■ Franchise Developments, Inc.
The Design Center, Ste. 660
5001 Baum Blvd.
Pittsburgh, PA 15213
Ph:(412)687-8484
Fax:(412)687-0541
Founded: 1970. **Description:** Develop, implement and launch franchise programs.

2979 ■ Franchise Foundations
4157 23rd St.
San Francisco, CA 94114
Free: 800-942-4402
Founded: 1980. **Description:** Franchise consulting.

2980 ■ Franchise Recruiters Ltd.
Saddlebrooke Country Club
63284 E Flower Ridge Dr.
Tucson, AZ 85739
Ph:(520)825-9588
Free: 800-334-6257
Founded: 1977. **Description:** Placement of franchise management professionals.

2981 ■ Franchise Sales
1315 S Villa Ave.
Villa Park, IL 60181
Ph:(630)819-2418
Fax:(630)827-0174
Founded: 1991. **Description:** Self franchisees in business now.

2982 ■ Franchise Search, Inc.
Kushell Associates Inc.
48 Burd St., Ste. 101
Nyack, NY 10960
Ph:(845)727-4103
Founded: 1982. **Description:** International executive search firm for franchisors.

2983 ■ Franchise Selection Specialists Inc.
14408 E Carroll Blvd.
Cleveland, OH 44118
Ph:(216)831-2610
Fax:(216)765-7118
Founded: 1990. **Description:** Franchise related advice and consulting.

2984 ■ Franchise Specialists, Inc.
1234 Maple St. Ext.
Moon Twp, PA 15108
Free: 800-261-5055
Founded: 1978. **Description:** Professional franchise development and sales.

2985 ■ Franchise Strategies Group, Inc.
6008 Avenue Of The Palms
Weeki Wachee, FL 34607
Ph:(352)556-2430
Free: 800-795-9116
Founded: 1984. **Description:** Franchise consultants.

2986 ■ FranchiseInc!
2148 Pelham Pky., Bldg. 300
Pelham, AL 35124
Free: 800-961-0420
Fax:(205)682-2939
No. of Franchise Units: 24. **No. of Company-Owned Units:** 1. **Founded:** 1995. **Franchised:** 2006. **Description:** Franchise consulting service. **Equity Capital Needed:** $36,600-$48,500. **Franchise Fee:** $29,500. **Financial Assistance:** No. **Training:** Includes 5 days training at headquarters, 52 weeks mentoring via teleconference and ongoing support.

2987 ■ Franchiseknowhow, LLC
PO Box 714
Stony Brook, NY 11790
Ph:(631)246-5782
Fax:(631)689-6905
Description: Franchise consulting service.

2988 ■ FranchiseMart / Biz1Brokers
2121 Vista Pky.
West Palm Beach, FL 33411
Ph:(561)868-1390
Free: 877-757-6550
Fax:(561)478-4340
Co. E-mail: franchise@franchisemart.com
URL: http://www.franchisemart.com
No. of Franchise Units: 5. **Founded:** 2006. **Franchised:** 2007. **Description:** Franchise consulting services. **Equity Capital Needed:** $30,000-$35,000 initial, total investment $110,000-$115,000. **Franchise Fee:** $29,500. **Financial Assistance:** Limited third party financing available. **Training:** Yes.

2989 ■ Franchises Unlimited Network LLC
36601 Samoa Dr.
Sterling Heights, MI 48312
Free: (866)583-5311
Description: Franchise consulting service.

2990 ■ Francorp, Inc.
20200 Governors Dr.
Olympia Fields, IL 60461
Ph:(708)481-2900
Free: 800-372-6244
Co. E-mail: info@francorp.com
URL: http://www.francorp.com
Founded: 1976. **Description:** Offers consultancy on franchising business. Consultants have provided full development programs, including feasibility studies, business plans, legal documents, operations manuals, and marketing materials for clients since 1976. **Training:** Provides post-development services for establishing franchisors, including lead generation programs, brochures, videotapes, international brokerage, PR, and expert witness service.

2991 ■ Frandocs, Experts in Franchising
Franchise 123, Inc.
PO Box 149
Islamorada, FL 33036
Free: 800-655-0343
Co. E-mail: frandocs@aol.com
URL: http://www.frandocs.com
Founded: 1980. **Description:** Frandocs has developed franchise software and the Franchisor fills in the blanks to complete the documents. **Managerial Assistance:** Provides toll free 800 consulting throughout the franchise development and includes consulting on franchise sales.

2992 ■ Global Recruiters Network - GRN
2001 Butterfield Rd., Ste. 102
Downers Grove, IL 60515
Free: (866)476-8200
No. of Franchise Units: 150. **Founded:** 2003. **Franchised:** 2003. **Description:** Employee search and placement services. **Franchise Fee:** $89,000. **Financial Assistance:** Yes. **Training:** Yes.

2993 ■ The Growth Coach, Inc.
10700 Montgomery Rd., Ste. 300
Cincinnati, OH 45242
Free: (866)708-9188
Fax:(513)563-2691
Co. E-mail: inquiry@TheGrowthCoach.com
URL: http://www.TheGrowthCoach.com
No. of Franchise Units: 144. **Founded:** 2002. **Franchised:** 2002. **Description:** Small business and self-employed coaching. Since you will be taught how to facilitate a proven-strategic process, you only need minimal business experience. You'll be able to leverage your time and enjoy a huge income potential while serving groups of small business owners and managers on a regular and ongoing basis. **Equity Capital Needed:** $47,200-$76,400 total investment. **Franchise Fee:** $39,900. **Financial Assistance:** Yes. **Training:** 5 day training program to provide the systems, tools and confidence to be successful as an entrepreneur and a coach. The training covers all aspects of successful business ownership: marketing, operations, coaching, and financial management. Ongoing support provided.

2994 ■ iFranchise Group
905 W 175th St., 2nd Fl.
Homewood, IL 60430
Ph:(708)957-2300
Fax:(708)957-2395
Co. E-mail: info@ifranchise.net
URL: http://www.ifranchise.com
Description: Offers services on strategic planning, franchise law, operations documentation, marketing and sales, and executive recruiting for franchisors.

2995 ■ IMTEC (International Management Tech. Co., LLC)
78 Fox Hill Rd.
Stamford, CT 06903
Ph:(203)322-6175
Fax:(203)322-6274
Founded: 1982. **Description:** Full services to achieve international expansion.

2996 ■ Inner Circle
Inner Circle International, LTD
3208 W Lake St., Unit 3
Minneapolis, MN 55416
Ph:(952)933-6629
Fax:(952)935-5269
No. of Franchise Units: 5. **No. of Company-Owned Units:** 1. **Founded:** 1989. **Franchised:** 1996. **Description:** Peer groups for business owners. **Equity Capital Needed:** $67,000-$84,000. **Franchise Fee:** $56,000. **Financial Assistance:** No. **Training:** Yes.

2997 ■ International Business Opportunities
Worldwide Canadian Management Consultants, Inc.
PO Box 639
Pickering, ON, Canada L1V 3T3
Ph:(905)686-0469
Fax:(905)686-0469
No. of Franchise Units: 37. **No. of Company-Owned Units:** 2. **Founded:** 1976. **Franchised:** 1981. **Description:** Worldwide virtual and home office. **Equity Capital Needed:** Canadian and U.S. $6,599; other countries $15,000 U.S.; home offices $15,000 U.S. **Franchise Fee:** $6,599 U.S. **Financial Assistance:** Yes. **Training:** Yes.

2998 ■ International Mergers and Acquisitions
International Mergers and Acquisitions, Inc.
4300 N Miller Rd., Ste. 230
Scottsdale, AZ 85251
Ph:(480)990-3899
Fax:(480)990-7480
No. of Franchise Units: 30. **Founded:** 1969. **Franchised:** 1979. **Description:** Members are engaged in the profession of serving merger and acquisition-minded companies in the areas of consulting, financing, divestitures, mergers and acquisitions. Creative work sessions throughout the year. **Equity Capital Needed:** Suggested $40,000-$50,000. **Franchise Fee:** $15,000. **Financial Assistance:** No. **Training:** Yes.

2999 ■ The Lease Coach
Terrace Plaza
4445 Calgary Trl., Unit 820
Edmonton, AB, Canada T6H 5R7
Free: 800-738-9202
Fax:(780)448-2670
No. of Franchise Units: 2. **No. of Company-Owned Units:** 1. **Founded:** 1999. **Franchised:** 2001. **Description:** Commercial lease consulting services. **Equity Capital Needed:** $25,000-$45,000. **Franchise Fee:** $11,800. **Royalty Fee:** $2,200-$3,200/month. **Financial Assistance:** No. **Training:** Includes 1 week training at headquarters and ongoing training via teleconference/webconference.

3000 ■ Leon Gottlieb USA/Int'l Franchise/ Restaurant Consultants
Leon Gottlieb & Associates
4601 Sendero Pl.
Tarzana, CA 91356-4821
Ph:(818)757-1131
Fax:(818)757-1816
Founded: 1960. **Description:** Consultant, expert witness, arbitrator.

3001 ■ Manufacturing Management Associates
700 Commerce Dr., Ste. 500
Oak Brook, IL 60523
Ph:(630)575-8700
No. of Franchise Units: 8. **No. of Company-Owned Units:** 1. **Founded:** 1982. **Franchised:** 1993. **Description:** Has built its reputation providing small to mid-sized manufacturing and distribution companies with the technical and advisory services they need to achieve their individual business goals. Areas of expertise include manufacturing systems and network technology, process flow (JIT), quality (TQC), cost management, human resource change management, ISO 9000 certification preparation and work cell design/factory layout. days of training in Chicago, IL. Will also assist the franchisee in sales and marketing efforts to promote the success of the franchise. Other notable benefits include potential client leads, alliances with industry experts, project management methodologies, proprietary computer software systems, reference proposals and R & D. **Equity Capital Needed:** $14,900-$49,450. **Franchise Fee:** $10,000. **Financial Assistance:** No. **Training:** An intensive 8 day seminar in Chicago, IL, where the franchisee will be exposed to a working office and receive extensive training in the policies of running a successful franchise. The franchisee will receive a thorough explanation of proven methodologies, as well as training in proprietary software and business systems.

3002 ■ Marketing Resources Group
83-26 Lefferts Blvd.
Kew Gardens, NY 11415
Ph:(718)261-8882
Description: Franchise development, marketing, and sales.

3003 ■ McGrow Consulting
30 North St.
Hingham, MA 02043
Ph:(781)740-2211
Free: 800-358-8011
Founded: 1980. **Description:** Franchise consulting firm.

3004 ■ MFV Expositions
210 E Rte 4, Ste. 403
Paramus, NJ 07652
Ph:(201)226-1130
Fax:(201)226-1131
Description: Producer of franchise expos.

3005 ■ Moresales.ca
231 Shearson Crescent, Ste. 207B
Cambridge, ON, Canada N1T 1J5
Ph:(519)620-8127
Co. E-mail: mike@moresales.ca
URL: http://www.moresales.ca
No. of Franchise Units: 3. **No. of Company-Owned Units:** 1. **Founded:** 2005. **Franchised:** 2007. **Description:** MoreSALES.ca is a unique franchise opportunity. If you are a Sales or Marketing Professional looking to own your own business, we offer low start-up costs, a fixed franchise fee, a proven training program & a short ramp-up time. We make owning your own business a reality! Structured as a network of business growth professionals, MoreSALES.ca franchisees offer cost effective sales & marketing

expertise to help companies reach more customers, communicate more effectively & close more sales. **Equity Capital Needed:** $50,000. **Franchise Fee:** $25,000. **Training:** 5-part training program included in franchise fee.

3006 ■ National Franchise Associates Inc.
240 Lake View Ct.
Lavonia, GA 30553
Ph:(770)945-0660
Fax:(770)338-1603
Co. E-mail: nfa@nationalfranchise.com
URL: http://www.nationalfranchise.com
Founded: 1981. **Description:** Full service consulting and developmental firm with expertise in feasibility studies, Franchise agreements and UFOC's, advertising and public relations campaigns, operations and training manuals, franchise sales programs, and ongoing franchise consulting.

3007 ■ Nationwide Franchise Marketing Services
18715 Gibbons Dr.
Dallas, TX 75287-4045
Ph:(972)248-9667
Free: (866)740-5815
Fax:(972)248-9667
Founded: 1971. **Description:** Full service franchise development evaluations.

3008 ■ OneCoach Int'l. LLC
5963 La Place Ct., Ste. 105
Carlsbad, CA 92008
Ph:(760)904-5287
Fax:(858)792-1270
No. of Franchise Units: 17. **No. of Company-Owned Units:** 1. **Founded:** 2005. **Franchised:** 2007. **Description:** Small business coaching services. **Equity Capital Needed:** $40,100-$318,800. **Franchise Fee:** $23,500-$265,000. **Royalty Fee:** $750/month. **Financial Assistance:** Limited financial assistant available. **Training:** Provides 8-10 days training at headquarters, 6-9 days virtual training and ongoing training and boot camps.

3009 ■ Osler, Hoskin & Harcourt LLP
1 First Canadian Pl.
PO Box 50
Toronto, ON, Canada M5X 1B8
Ph:(416)362-2111
Fax:(416)862-6666
Founded: 1862. **Description:** Canadian and international franchise law.

3010 ■ "Partner" On-Call Network
"Partner" On-Call Network LLC
730 Sandy Point Ln.
N Palm Beach, FL 33410
Ph:(561)776-2515
Fax:(561)868-6892
Co. E-mail: partneroncall@comcast.net
URL: http://www.PartnerOnCall.com
No. of Franchise Units: 23. **Founded:** 2005. **Franchised:** 2006. **Description:** Consulting business. **Equity Capital Needed:** $56,000-$76,000. **Franchise Fee:** $25,000. **Financial Assistance:** Yes. **Managerial Assistance:** CDs, DVDs and numerous how-to manuals and books. **Training:** 10 day home study, plus 5 days at headquarters and 3 days on-call via telephone and fax, conferences and proactive training & mentoring from a consultant seasoned in our business.

3011 ■ Performance Group, Ltd.
PO Box 437
Barrington, IL 60011
Ph:(847)526-9298
Founded: 1979. **Description:** Franchise program development and enhancement.

3012 ■ PRO, President's Resource Organization
100 E Bellevue, Ste. 4E
Chicago, IL 60611
Ph:(312)337-3658
Free: 800-276-2233
Fax:(312)944-6815
No. of Franchise Units: 3. **No. of Company-Owned Units:** 2. **Founded:** 1993. **Franchised:** 1999. **Description:** Facilitate peer advisory boards. **Equity Capital Needed:** $12,000-$40,000. **Franchise Fee:** $8,500-$36,000. **Financial Assistance:** Yes. **Training:** Yes.

3013 ■ Red Wheel Fundraising
RWFR, Inc.
16 S 15th St.
Council Bluffs, IA 51501
Ph:(816)221-2699
Free: 800-269-0667
Co. E-mail: redwheel@mitec.net
URL: http://www.redwheelfundraising.com
No. of Franchise Units: 18. **Founded:** 1984. **Franchised:** 1988. **Description:** The franchise offers general business. **Equity Capital Needed:** $10,000-$12,000. **Franchise Fee:** $10,000. **Financial Assistance:** Yes. **Training:** Yes.

3014 ■ Renaissance Executive Forums, Inc.
7855 Ivanhoe Ave., Ste. 300
La Jolla, CA 92037
Ph:(858)551-6600
Fax:(858)551-8777
No. of Franchise Units: 45. **Founded:** 1994. **Franchised:** 1994. **Description:** Interactive peer review forums for business professionals. **Equity Capital Needed:** $76,000 liquid capital; $500,000 net worth. **Franchise Fee:** $24,500. **Financial Assistance:** No. **Training:** Yes.

3015 ■ Seller Direct, Inc.
1954 First St., Ste. 161
Highland Park, IL 60035
Ph:(847)266-0082
Founded: 1995. **Description:** Brokerage support of franchise resales.

3016 ■ Sunbelt Business Brokers
Sunbelt Business Advisors Network
3212 Rice St.
St. Paul, MN 55126
Ph:(651)484-2677
Fax:(651)484-9658
Co. E-mail: hschilling@sunbeltnetwork.com
URL: http://www.sunbeltnetwork.com
Founded: 1979. **Description:** Offer franchise consulting & re-sales programs for prospective franchisors and franchisees. Provides consumers a no-cost personal consultation to determine the best available business to meet your personal and financial needs.

3017 ■ Turbo Leadership Systems Ltd.
36280 NE Wilsonville Rd.
Newberg, OR 97132
Ph:(503)625-1867
Fax:(503)625-2699
No. of Company-Owned Units: 1. **Founded:** 1985. **Franchised:** 1995. **Description:** Management training and team building training. **Equity Capital Needed:** $49,000. **Franchise Fee:** $39,000. **Financial Assistance:** No. **Training:** Yes.

3018 ■ Upside Group Franchise Consulting Corp.
11445 E Via Linda, Ste. 2-495
Scottsdale, AZ 85259
Free: 888-445-2882
Fax:(480)664-1627
Founded: 2000. **Description:** Full franchise consulting/sales development. **Training:** Yes.

3019 ■ Venture Marketing Associates
800 Palisade Ave., Ste. 907
Fort Lee, NJ 07024
Ph:(201)924-7435
Founded: 1976. **Description:** Business development/franchise consultants.

3020 ■ West Coast Commercial Credit
PO Box 19241
San Diego, CA 92159
Ph:(619)280-2484
Free: 800-804-7901
Fax:(619)280-2575
Founded: 1987. **Description:** Nationwide commercial financing.

COMPUTERIZED DATABASES

3021 ■ *ABI/INFORM*
ProQuest LLC
789 E Eisenhower Pky.
PO Box 1346
Ann Arbor, MI 48106-1346
Ph:(734)761-4700
Free: 800-521-0600
Fax:(734)761-6450
Co. E-mail: info@proquest.com
URL: http://www.proquest.com
Description: Contains approximately 6 million full text or bibliographic citations to articles from more than 800 business and management publications worldwide. **Availability:** Online: Wolters Kluwer Health, ProQuest LLC, ProQuest LLC, Questel SA, STN International, Colorado Alliance of Research Libraries, Financial Times Ltd., LexisNexis Group, ProQuest LLC. **Type:** Full text; Bibliographic; Image.

3022 ■ *NewsEdge*
ProQuest LLC
2250 Perimeter Park Dr., Ste. 300
Morrisville, NC 27560
Ph:(919)804-6400
Free: 800-334-2564
Fax:(919)804-6410
Co. E-mail: contact@dialog.com
URL: http://www.dialog.com
Description: Provides relevant news on specific industries, along with an archive of stories from more than 12,000 global and business information sources. Includes such business information as company and brand developments, earning forecasts, economic indicators, geopolitical shifts, industry events, product launches, and regulatory announcements. The My Live News feature provides streaming headlines from some 2300 sources. **Availability:** Online: ProQuest LLC. **Type:** Full text; Numeric; Statistical.

3023 ■ *PROMT - Predicast's Overview of Markets and Technology*
Cengage Learning Inc.
27500 Drake Rd.
Farmington Hills, MI 48331-3535
Ph:(248)699-4253
Free: 800-877-4253
Fax:(248)699-8069
Co. E-mail: galeord@gale.com
URL: http://gale.cengage.com
Description: Contains more than 16 million citations, with abstracts and/or full text, to the worldwide business literature on companies, markets, products, and technologies for major international, national, and regional manufacturing and service industries. Covers new products and technologies, mergers and acquisitions, capital expenditures, market data, product sales, marketing strategies, foreign trade, and regulations. Sources include more than 1600 business, financial, and trade magazines, newspapers, newsletters, reports, and news releases. Includes summaries from Investext investment and brokerage firm reports. **Availability:** Online: Cengage Learning Inc., ProQuest LLC, ProQuest LLC. **Type:** Bibliographic; Full text.

LIBRARIES

3024 ■ Alameda County Library Business Library
2400 Stevenson Blvd.
Fremont, CA 94538
Ph:(510)505-7001
URL: http://www.aclibrary.org
Contact: Sallie Pine, Lib.Br.Mgr.
Scope: Starting and managing a business, small business, investments, real estate, International business, management and personnel, career planning, San Francisco Bay area business. **Services:** Interlibrary loan; copying; Library open to the public. **Hold-**

ings: 18,000 books; 300 audiocassettes; 100 videocassettes. **Subscriptions:** 400 journals and other serials; 20 newspapers.

3025 ■ American Society for Training and Development ASTD Information Center
1640 King St.
PO Box 1443
Alexandria, VA 22313-2043
Ph:(703)683-8100
Free: 800-628-2783
Fax:(703)683-1523
Co. E-mail: customercare@astd.org
URL: http://www.astd.org
Contact: Greg Bindner, Mgr.

Scope: Human resource development - general, management, training, career development, Organization development, consulting skills. **Services:** Library open to national members of the Society. **Holdings:** 3000 bound volumes. **Subscriptions:** 60 journals and other serials.

3026 ■ Franchise Consultants International Association Library
5147 S. Angela Rd.
Memphis, TN 38117
Ph:(901)368-3361
Fax:(901)368-1144
Co. E-mail: franmark@msn.com
URL: http://www.FranchiseStores.com
Contact: R. Richey
Scope: Franchise law, demographics, statistics, logistics, suppliers, technology, advertising, management, legal consulting. **Services:** Members only participants for reference use. **Holdings:** 2800 books, periodicals, clippings, audio/visuals, and audio recordings; reports; manuscripts; archives; patents. **Subscriptions:** 143 magazines.

RESEARCH CENTERS

3027 ■ Auburn University at Montgomery–Center for Business
600 S Court St.
Montgomery, AL 36104
Ph:(334)244-3700
Free: 888—94CENTER
Fax:(334)244-3718
Co. E-mail: cforehand@cbed.aum.edu
URL: http://cbed.aum.edu
Contact: Cynthia W. Forehand, Sr.Dir.
E-mail: cforehand@cbed.aum.edu

Scope: Economic impact studies, revenue forecasting, market research, equipment use and need analysis, management, and personnel research. **Services:** Human resources consulting. **Publications:** Research reports (periodically).

Business Services Operation

START-UP INFORMATION

3028 ■ "Visual Appeal" in *Small Business Opportunities* (Fall 2007)
Pub: Harris Publications Inc.

Ed: Michael L. Corne. **Description:** Profile of Jim Huffman, who launched his new Video Business Card Distributorship. The business cards allow companies and individuals to put personal video messages on their cards explaining the benefits of doing business with them. The cards take prospective customers to Websites and even provide a printable document for brochures or special offers.

ASSOCIATIONS AND OTHER ORGANIZATIONS

3029 ■ National Association for Business Organizations
5432 Price Ave.
Baltimore, MD 21215
Ph:(410)367-5309
Co. E-mail: nahbb@msn.com
URL: http://www.ameribizs.com/global
Contact: Rudolph Lewis, Pres.

Description: Business organizations that develop and support small businesses that have the capability to provide their products or services on a national level. Promotes small business in a free market system; represents the interests of small businesses to government and community organizations on small business affairs; monitors and reviews laws that affect small businesses; promotes a business code of ethics. Supplies members with marketing and management assistance; encourages joint marketing services between members. Operates a Home Based Business Television Network that provides an affordable audio/visual media for small and home based businesses. .

REFERENCE WORKS

3030 ■ "Windstream Expands Business Service Into Monroe" in *Marketing Weekly News* (January 23, 2010, pp. 77)
Pub: Investment Weekly News

Description: Windstream Corp. announces the expansion of its data and voice services into Monroe, N.C., which will give local businesses a new choice for advanced communication services and network security.

TRADE PERIODICALS

3031 ■ *Worldgram Newsletter*
Pub: Worldprofit Inc.

Ed: Dr. Jeffrey Lant, Editor, drjlant@worldprofit.com. **Released:** Bimonthly. **Price:** Free. **Description:** Internet newsletter with a marketing focus for businesses. Also offers tips on how to profit from the World Wide Web.

CONSULTANTS

3032 ■ Automated Accounting
23325 Gerbera St.
Moreno Valley, CA 92553
Ph:(951)653-5053
Co. E-mail: autoacc@earthlink.net
Contact: Gary Capolino, Owner

Scope: A business management consulting firm that caters to small businesses. Offers software installation services, tax preparation services and business plan advisory services. **Publications:** "Inflated Real Estate Prices. . .How Did This Happen," Moreno Valley Magazine, Aug, 2005.

3033 ■ BioSciCon Inc.
14905 Forest Landing Cir.
Rockville, MD 20850-3924
Ph:(301)610-9130
Fax:(301)610-7662
Co. E-mail: info@bioscicon.com
URL: http://www.bioscicon.com
Contact: Olivera Markovic, Director
E-mail: info@bioscicon.com

Scope: Sponsoring development of the technology of the Pap test accuracy via introduction of a new bio-marker that enhances visibility of abnormal cells on Pap smears or mono-layers of cervical cells obtained in solution. Conducts clinical trials for assessment of the test efficacy and safety, manufactures research tools for conduct of trials, and markets IP to license manufacturing, marketing, sales and distribution rights of the new technology line of products. **Publications:** "Cervical Acid Phosphates: A Biomarker of Cervical Dysplasia and Potential Surrogate Endpoint for Colposcopy," 2004; "Enhancing Pap test with a new biological marker of cervical dysplasia," 2004; "A cytoplasmic biomarker for liquid-based Pap," The FACEB Journal Experimental Biology, 2004; "Pap test and new biomarker-based technology for enhancing visibility of abnormal cells," 2004. **Special Services:** MarkPap[R]; PreservCyt[R].

3034 ■ BPT Consulting Associates Ltd.
12 Parmenter Rd., Ste. B-6
Londonderry, NH 03053
Ph:(603)437-8484
Free: 888-278-0030
Fax:(603)434-5388
Co. E-mail: bptcons@tiac.net
Contact: John Kuczynski, President
E-mail: bptcons@tiac.net

Scope: Provides management consulting expertise and resources to cross-industry clients with services for: Business Management consulting, People/Human Resources Transition and Training programs, and a full cadre of multi-disciplined Technology Computer experts. Virtual consultants with expertise in e-commerce, supply chain management, organizational development, and business application development consulting.

3035 ■ Carelli & Associates
17 Reid Pl.
Delmar, NY 12054
Ph:(518)439-0233
Fax:(518)439-3006
Co. E-mail: anneobriencarelli@yahoo.com
URL: http://www.carelli.com
Contact: Dr. Anne Obrien Carelli, Owner
E-mail: anneobriencarelli@yahoo.com

Scope: Provides writing and editing services to industry and businesses, health care and educational institutions, and government agencies. Also provides program management in creating and disseminating publications and in implementing related training. Assists organizations in designing and implementing team-based management. Offers supervisory skills training and problem-solving work sessions for managers. Individual Consultation are provided for managers, CEOs, potential supervisors including 360 degree assessments. **Publications:** "The Truth About Supervision: Coaching, Teamwork, Interviewing, Appraisals, 360 degree Assessments, and Recognition". **Seminars:** Supervisory Skills Training Series; Problem-Solving Work Sessions for Managers; Effective Leadership.

3036 ■ CFO Service
112 Chester Ave.
Saint Louis, MO 63122
Ph:(314)757-2940
Contact: John D. Skae, President
E-mail: jds217@aol.com

Scope: A group of professional executives that provide upper management services to companies that cannot support a full time COO or CFO. Provides clients in the areas of business planning, company policies, contract negotiations, safety policies, product and service pricing, loans management, taxes, cost analysis, loss control and budgeting.

3037 ■ Charismedia
610 W End Ave., Ste. B1
New York, NY 10001
Ph:(212)362-6808
Fax:(212)362-6809
Co. E-mail: charismedia@earthlink.net
URL: http://www.charismedia.net
Contact: Ying Jo Wong, Principle
E-mail: charismedia@earthlink.net

Scope: Offers speech and image training as well as speech writing services for effective presentation skills. Conducts workshops like anti-stage fright breathing, psychophysical exercises, transformational success imagery, face reading and body language, EMDR (Eye Movement Desensitization Re-Processing) for Permanent Trauma and Fear Removal, Bach Flower remedies, thought field therapy, cross-cultural communication, speech, voice and diction; regional and foreign accent elimination and acquisition, Positive Perception Management (P.P.M.), Ad-libbing, humor and spontaneity training, fast creative speech preparation, Neuro-Linguistic Programming and Hypnosis. **Publications:** "Flaunt It"; "Improve Your Sex Life"; "Phone Power"; "Train Your Voice"; "Turning Tinny, Tiny Tones To Gold"; "The New Secrets of Charisma: How to Discover and Unleash your Hidden Powers," McGraw-Hill, Jul, 1999. **Seminars:** Services for Comfortable Effective Speaking.

3038 ■ The Consulting Exchange
1770 Mass Ave., Ste. 288
PO Box 391050
Cambridge, MA 02140
Ph:(617)576-2100
Free: 800-824-4828
Co. E-mail: gday@consultingexchange.com
URL: http://www.cx.com
Contact: Geoffrey Day, President
E-mail: gday@consultingexchange.com
Scope: A consultant referral service for management and technical consultants. Serves a local, regional and international client base. **Publications:** "Looking for a Consultant? Success Points for Finding the Right One," Boston Business Journal, Jun, 2001; "Getting Full Value From Consulting is in Your Hands," Mass High Tech, May, 1998; "Developing Knowledge-Based Client Relationships, The Future of Professional Services"; "The Consultant's Legal Guide"; "The Business of Consulting: The Basics and Beyond".

3039 ■ Custom Consulting Inc.
6315 Bayside Dr.
New Port Richey, FL 34652-2040
Ph:(727)844-5065
Fax:(727)844-5064
Co. E-mail: diwago@customconsulting.com
URL: http://www.customconsulting.com
Contact: David Wong, Mgr
E-mail: dwong@atscustomconsulting.com
Scope: Provides systems development personnel on a temporary basis. Specializes in mainframe, mini and Client/server development environments.

3040 ■ David G. Schantz
29 Wood Run Cir.
Rochester, NY 14612-2271
Ph:(716)723-0760
Fax:(716)723-8724
Co. E-mail: daveschantz@yahoo.com
URL: http://www.daveschantz.freeservers.com
E-mail: daveschantz@yahoo.com
Scope: Provides industrial engineering services for photofinishing labs, including amateur-wholesale, professional, commercial, school, and package.

3041 ■ Development Resource Consultants
PO Box 118
Rancho Cucamonga, CA 91729
Ph:(909)902-7655
Fax:(909)476-6942
Co. E-mail: drc@gotodrc.com
URL: http://www.gotodrc.com
Contact: Jerry R. Frey, Partner
E-mail: jfrey@atsgotodrc.com
Scope: Specializes in office re-organization, employee training in office organization, communication skills, sales training and career counseling. **Publications:** "Institute of Management Consultants Southern California Chapter," Jan, 2006.

3042 ■ DRI Consulting
2 Otter Ln.
North Oaks, MN 55127-6436
Ph:(651)415-1400
Free: (866)276-4600
Fax:(651)415-9968
Co. E-mail: dric@dric.com
URL: http://www.dric.com
Contact: Dr. Heather Mortensen, Principle
E-mail: heathermortensen@atsdric.com
Scope: Licensed psychologists providing organization and management consulting. Developing leaders, managers and individuals through coaching, business strategy, career development, crisis management, policy consultation and technology optimization.

3043 ■ Edward M. Hepner & Associates
4667 Macarthur Blvd., Ste. 405
Newport Beach, CA 92660
Ph:(714)250-0818
Fax:(714)553-8437
Contact: Edward M. Hepner, President
Scope: An immigration consultant and labor certification specialist. Assists in obtaining visa for work, immigration and business development within the United States and Canada.

3044 ■ Family Business Institute Inc.
904 Steffi Ct.
Lawrenceville, GA 30044-6933
Ph:(770)952-4085
Fax:(770)432-6660
Co. E-mail: asktheexpert@family-business-experts.com
URL: http://www.family-business-experts.com
Contact: Wayne Rivers, President
E-mail: don@family-business-experts.com
Scope: Assists families in business to achieve personal, family, and organizational goals by meeting challenges that are unique to family-owned businesses. Provides coordinated and integrated assessments and solutions for family issues and needs; for company finance and for human resource and operational requirements. **Publications:** "Professional Intervention in the Family Owned Business"; "Building Consensus in a Family Business"; "Professionalizing Family Business Management"; "Recognizing generations - know them by their weekends"; "Succession planning tactics"; "Succession Planning Obstacles in Family Business"; "Succession: three ways to ease the transition"; "Pruning the family business tree"; "Responsibility diffusion - the most critical impediment to successfully growing any kind of business"; "Breaking Up is Hard to Do: Divorce in the Family Business".

3045 ■ First Strike Management Consulting Inc.
401 Loblolly Ave.
PO Box 1188
Little River, SC 29566-1188
Ph:(843)385-6338
Fax:(843)390-1004
Co. E-mail: fsmc.hq@fsmc.com
URL: http://www.fsmc.com
Contact: J.D. Lewis, President
E-mail: jd.lewis@fsmc.com
Scope: Offers proposal management and program management services. Specializes in enterprise systems, management systems, and staff augmentation. Serves the following industries: Nuclear/Fossil Power, Petro-Chemical, Aerospace and Defense, Telecommunications, Engineering and Construction, Information Technology, Golf Course Construction/ Management, Utility Engineering/Construction, Civil Works, and Housing Development. **Publications:** "Project Management for Executives"; "Project Risk Management"; "Project Communications Management"; "Winning Proposals, Four Computer Based Training (CBT) courses"; "Principles of Program Management". **Seminars:** Preparing Winning Proposals in Response to Government RFPs.

3046 ■ Full Voice
3217 Broadway Ave., Ste. 300
Kansas City, MO 64111
Ph:(816)941-0011
Free: 800-684-8764
Fax:(816)931-8887
Co. E-mail: info@infullvoice.com
URL: http://www.fullvoice.us
Contact: Michienne Dixon, Principle
E-mail: garrett@infullvoice.com
Scope: Vocal performance training firm offering consulting services and personal training sessions in the implementation of effective vocal communication techniques for the development of business relationships and career enhancement. Formalizes a program of proven techniques into a practical method of helping individuals improve their ability to better present themselves when speaking in a professional situation. Industries served: All. **Publications:** "You Can Sound Like You Know What You're Saying". **Seminars:** You Can Sound Like You Know What You're Saying; The Psychology of Vocal Performance; Security. . .the Ability to Accept Change; Knowing. . .the Key to Relaxed Public Communication; The Effective Voice for Customer Service Enhancement; You Can Speak With Conviction; How To Make Yours a Championship Team; Functional English For Foreign Trade. **Special Services:** FULL VOICE™.

3047 ■ Great Western Association Management Inc.
7995 E Prentice Ave., Ste. 100
Greenwood Village, CO 80111
Ph:(303)770-2220
Fax:(303)770-1614
Co. E-mail: info83@gwami.com
URL: http://www.gwami.com
Contact: Sheryl Pitts, Principle
E-mail: kwojdyla@atsgwami.com
Scope: Provides clients with products and services to effectively manage existing and startup, for- and not-for-profit organizations. Clients select from a menu of services including association development and public relations, conferences and seminars, financial management, membership communications, and governance. Expertise also includes association strategic planning, compliance, lobbying, meeting planning, fundraising, marketing and communications. Serves national, regional and state organizations. **Seminars:** Site selection; Creative program development; Contract negotiations; On-site conference management; Trade show management; Travel and logistics.

3048 ■ I.H.R. Solutions
3333 E Bayaud Ave., Ste. 219
Denver, CO 80209
Ph:(303)588-4243
Fax:(303)978-0473
Co. E-mail: dhollands@ihrsolutions.com
Contact: Deborah Hollands, President
E-mail: dhollands@ihrsolutions.com
Scope: Provides joint-venture and start-up human resource consulting services as well as advice on organization development for international human capital. Industries served: high-tech and telecommunications.

3049 ■ IMC Consulting & Training
901 McHenry Ave., Ste. A
Modesto, CA 95350
Ph:(209)572-2271
Fax:(209)572-2862
Co. E-mail: info@imc-1.net
URL: http://www.imc-1.net
Contact: Ed Stout, Principle
E-mail: michael@imc-1.net
Scope: Firm helps businesses and professionals identify, develop and market their selling proposition to increase profits. Services include B-to-B surveys, direct marketing, media relations, planning and strategy, sales management, training and leadership coaching. **Publications:** "Consultant Earns Advanced Certificate," Hccsc Business Review, Dec, 2004; "Adapting to Change - the New Competitive Advantage," Business Journal, Jul, 2004; "Loyalty Marketing Can Divide New Business," Jun, 2004; "Eleven Major Marketing Mistakes," Jul, 2003; "Planning to Win or Racing to Fail," Jun, 2003. **Seminars:** Negotiating High Profit Sales; How to Write Winning Proposals, Modesto Chamber of Commerce, Oct, 2007; Winning the 2nd Half: A 6-month Plan to Score New Customers and Profits.

3050 ■ The Institute for Management Excellence
PO Box 5459
Lacey, WA 98509-5459
Ph:(360)412-0404
Co. E-mail: pwoc@itstime.com
URL: http://www.itstime.com
Contact: Michael Anthony, Director
E-mail: btaylor@itstime.com
Scope: Management consulting and training focuses on improving productivity, using practices and creative techniques. Practices based on the company's theme: It's time for new ways of doing business. Industries served: public sector, law enforcement, finance or banking, non profit, computers or high technology, education, human resources, utilities. **Publications:** "Income Without a Job," 2008; "The Other Side of Midnight, 2000: An Executive Guide to the Year 2000 Problem"; "Concordance to the Michael Teachings"; "Handbook of Small Business Advertis-

ing"; "The Personality Game"; "How to Market Yourself for Success". **Seminars:** The Personality Game; Power Path Seminars; Productivity Plus; Sexual Harassment and Discrimination Prevention; Worker's Comp Cost Reduction; Americans with Disabilities Act; In Search of Identify: Clarifying Corporate Culture.

3051 ■ Interpersonal Coaching & Consulting
1516 W Lake St., Ste. 2000S
Minneapolis, MN 55408
Ph:(612)381-2494
Fax:(612)381-2494
Co. E-mail: mail@interpersonal-coaching.com
URL: http://www.interpersonal-coaching.com
Contact: Mary Belfry, Partner
E-mail: mail@interpersonal-coaching.com
Scope: Provides coaching and consulting to businesses and organizations. Assesses the interpersonal workplace through interviews, assessment instruments and individual group settings. Experienced as a therapist for over a decade. **Seminars:** Sexual harassment and discrimination issues.

3052 ■ Invent Resources Inc.
PO Box 548
Lexington, MA 02420-0005
Ph:(781)862-0200
Fax:(781)721-2300
Co. E-mail: pavelle@comcast.net
URL: http://www.weinvent.com
Contact: Sol Aisenberg, Principle
E-mail: pavelle@comcast.net
Scope: Provides consultancy services to provide support in developing and prototyping new, proprietary products. Offer inventory services on demand. Assist clients who need innovations in product lines, have hit technical bottlenecks, or need improvements in manufacturing processes. Provide assistance to individuals and clients in obtaining, reviewing, and strengthening patents.

3053 ■ Joel Greenstein & Associates
6212 Nethercombe Ct.
McLean, VA 22101
Ph:(703)893-1888
Co. E-mail: jgreenstein@contractmasters.com
Contact: Joel Greenstein, Principle
E-mail: jgreenstein@contractmasters.com
Scope: Provides services to minority and women-owned businesses and government agencies. Specializes in interpreting federal, agency-specific acquisition regulations and contract terms and conditions. Offers assistance with preparing technical, cost proposals and sealed bids.

3054 ■ Kroll Zolfo Cooper L.L.C.
777 S Figueroa St., 24th Fl.
Los Angeles, CA 90017
Ph:(212)561-4000
Fax:(212)948-4226
Co. E-mail: mwyse@krollzolfocooper.com
URL: http://www.krollzolfocooper.com
Contact: Stephen F. Cooper, Principal
E-mail: scooper@kroll.com
Scope: Firm provides accounting consulting services to businesses. Specializes in restructuring and turnaround consulting; interim and crisis management; performance improvement; creditor advisory; cross-border restructuring and corporate finance.

3055 ■ May Toy Lukens
3226 NE 26th Ct.
Renton, WA 98056
Ph:(425)891-3226
Contact: May T. Lukens, Principle
Scope: Provides training to teach people to think of ways to improve their operations continuously by changing the way they think. Industries served: All, particularly financial. Operational analysis and training. **Seminars:** Seminars and workshops in maximizing resource utilization and staff potential.

3056 ■ Navarro, Kim & Associates
529 N Charles St., Ste. 202
Baltimore, MD 21201
Ph:(410)837-6317
Fax:(410)837-6294
Co. E-mail: bnavarro@sprynet.com
Contact: Beltran Navarro, Director
E-mail: bnavarro@sprynet.com
Scope: Specializes in bridging the gap between firms and non-traditional ethnic communities, especially in community development and institutional building.

3057 ■ On-Q Software Inc.
13764 SW 11th St.
Miami, FL 33184
Ph:(305)553-2400
Free: 800-553-2862
Fax:(305)220-2666
Co. E-mail: info@on-qsoftware.com
URL: http://www.on-qsoftware.com
Contact: Terry Cajigas, Principle
E-mail: hcajigas@on-qsoftware.com
Scope: Provides the small business community with simple to use, feature rich software. Provides software solutions including time and fixed fee billing, due date tracking and practice manager.

3058 ■ Pathways To Wellness
617 Everhart Rd.
Corpus Christi, TX 78411
Ph:(361)985-9642
Fax:(361)949-4627
Co. E-mail: path2wellness@earthlink.net
URL: http://www.path2wellness.com
Contact: Evy Coppola, Owner
Scope: Offer natural holistic health counseling, yoga and hatha yoga classes, teachers training and cookery classes for individuals and companies. Health counseling includes nutritional guidance, kinesiology, iridology, reflexology, energy healing, massage therapy, herbal and vitamin therapy, creative visualization and meditation. Provides supplements which bring about the same effects as that of natural sunshine. **Seminars:** Is It You Holding You Back?; The Balancing Act. . .Career. . . Family. . .and Self; Learning the Art of Friendly Persuasion; Stop Accepting What You Are Getting and Start Asking for What You Want!; Introduction to Natural Health and Healthy Living; Learn Why One Size Approaches to the Answers on Health Do Not Work; Introduction to Yoga. What is it? Who can do it? What can it do for you.

3059 ■ ProActive English
4355 SE 29th Ave.
Portland, OR 97202
Ph:(503)231-2906
Co. E-mail: infopae@proactive-english.com
URL: http://www.proactive-english.com
Contact: David Kertzner, Managing Director
E-mail: dkertzner@atsproactive-english.com
Scope: Offers on-site individual and small group language and communication training. Sets up learning plans tailored to the needs and schedules of managers and executives who are non-native English speakers. Serves all industries. **Seminars:** Communicating in Business Situations; Presentations and Pronunciation; Tailored Curriculum; One-on-One Programs.

3060 ■ Rose & Crangle Ltd.
117 N 4th St.
PO Box 285
Lincoln, KS 67455
Ph:(785)524-5050
Fax:(785)524-3130
Co. E-mail: rcltd@nckcn.com
URL: http://www.roseandcrangle.com
Contact: Jeanne Crangle, Principle
E-mail: rcltd@nckcn.com
Scope: Firm provides evaluation, planning and policy analyzes for universities, associations, foundations, governmental agencies and private companies engaged in scientific, technological or educational activities. Special expertise in the development of new institutions. Special skills in providing planning and related group facilitation workshops. **Publications:** "Preface to Bulgarian Integration Into Europe and NATO: Issues of Science Policy And research Evaluation Practice," Ios Press, 2006; "Allocating Limited National Resources for Fundamental Research," 2005.

3061 ■ Rothschild Strategies Unlimited L.L.C.
19 Thistle Rd.
PO Box 7568
Norwalk, CT 06851-1909
Ph:(203)846-6898
Fax:(203)847-1426
Co. E-mail: bill@strategyleader.com
URL: http://www.strategyleader.com
Contact: William Rothchild, CEO
E-mail: billrothschild@atsoptonline.net
Scope: Consults with senior management and business level strategy teams to develop overall strategic direction, set priorities and creates sustainable competitive advantages and differentiators. Enables organizations to enhance their own strategic thinking and leadership skills so that they can continue to develop and implement profitable growth strategies. **Publications:** "Putting It All Together-a guide to strategic thinking"; "Competitive Advantage"; "Ristaker, Caretaker, Surgeon & Undertaker four faces of strategic leadership"; "The Secret to GE's Success"; "Having the Right Strategic Leader and Team". **Seminars:** Who is going the WRONG way?; Learning from your Successes and Failures. **Special Services:** StrategyLeader[R].

3062 ■ Schneider Consulting Group Inc.
50 S Steele St., Ste. 390
Denver, CO 80209
Ph:(303)320-4413
Fax:(303)320-5795
Contact: Kim Schneider Malek, Vice President
E-mail: kim@atsscgfambus.com
Scope: Assists family-owned and privately-held business transition to the next generation and/or to a more professionally managed company, turn around consulting for small and medium size companies.

3063 ■ Sklar and Associates Inc.
242 Laurel Bay Dr.
Murrells Inlet, SC 29576
Ph:(202)257-5061
Fax:(843)651-3090
Co. E-mail: sklarincdc@aol.com
URL: http://www.sklarinc.com
Contact: Tim Sklar, President
Scope: Provides consulting services for business acquisitions, business development and project finance. Provides audit oversight services to listed corporations on Sarbanes-Oxley compliance. Services include: Due diligence analyses and corporate governance. Industries served: transportation sectors, energy sector and commercial real estate industries. **Seminars:** Financial Analysis in MBA; Emerging Company Finance; Due Diligence in Business Acquisition; Business Valuation.

3064 ■ TC International Marketing Inc.
11 Iliffe House, Iliffe Ave.
Leicester LE2 5LS, United Kingdom
Ph:(845)258-7482
Fax:(845)986-2130
Co. E-mail: tcintl@warwick.net
Contact: Graeme Wright, Partner
Scope: Business expansion consulting including feasibility studies, mergers and acquisitions, divestment, market research and strategizing.

3065 ■ Trendzitions Inc.
25691 Atlantic Ocean Dr., Ste. B13
Lake Forest, CA 92630-8842
Ph:(949)727-9100
Free: 800-266-2767
Fax:(949)727-3444
Co. E-mail: ctooker@trendzitions.com
URL: http://www.trendzitions.com
Contact: Christian Tooker, President
E-mail: ctooker@atstrendzitions.com
Scope: Provides services in the areas of communications consulting, project management, construction management, and furniture procurement. Offers information on spatial uses, building codes, ADA compliance and city ordinances. Also offers budget projections.

3066 ■ Turnaround Inc.
3415 A St. NW
Gig Harbor, WA 98335
Ph:(253)857-6730

Fax:(253)857-6344
Co. E-mail: info@turnround-inc.com
URL: http://www.turnaround-inc.com
Contact: Miles Stover, President
E-mail: mstover@turnaround-inc.com
Scope: Firm provides interim executive management assistance and management advisory to small, medium and family-owned businesses that are not meeting their goals. Services include acting as an interim executive or on-site manager. Extensive practices in arena of bankruptcy management. **Publications:** "How to Identify Problem and Promising Management"; "How to Tell if Your Company is a Bankruptcy Candidate"; "Signs that Your Company is in Trouble"; "The Turnaround Specialist: How to File a Petition Under 11 USC 11". **Seminars:** Competitive Intelligence Gathering.

3067 ■ Weich & Bilotti Inc.
600 Worcester Rd., 4th Fl.
Framingham, MA 01702
Ph:(508)663-1600
Fax:(508)663-1682
Co. E-mail: info@weich-bilotti.com
URL: http://www.weich-bilotti.com
Contact: Mervyn D. Weich, President
E-mail: mweich@weich-bilotti.com
Scope: Specializes in business plans, venture capital, computer information systems, turnaround/ interim management, retail consulting, start-up process, college recruiting and IS and IT personnel.

3068 ■ William J. Yang & Associates
847 N Hollywood Way, Ste. 100
Burbank, CA 91505-2848
Ph:(818)841-8888
Fax:(818)841-7900
Contact: William J. Yang, President
Scope: A mechanical engineering firm that serves commercial businesses.

3069 ■ Zogby International
150 SE 2nd Ave., Ste. 600
Miami, FL 33131
Ph:(315)624-0200
Free: 877-462-7655
Fax:(315)624-0210
Co. E-mail: marketing@zogby.com
URL: http://www.zogby.com
Contact: Stephanie Vogel, COO
Scope: Specializes in providing market research and analysis services. **Publications:** "Just who are you calling anyway"; "All of this leads to a very basic question". **Seminars:** The Research Authority, Oct, 2006; Christian Science Monitor Break fast, Oct, 2006.

FRANCHISES AND BUSINESS OPPORTUNITIES

3070 ■ Alpha Legal Forms & More, Inc.
Alpha Publications of America, Inc.
PO Box 12488
Tucson, AZ 85732
Ph:(520)795-7100
Free: 800-770-4329
Founded: 1976. **Description:** Legal forms.

3071 ■ American Association of Franchisees and Dealers
PO Box 10158
Palm Desert, CA 92255
Ph:(619)209-3775
Free: 800-733-9858
Fax:(619)209-3777
Founded: 1992. **Description:** Franchisees and business services.

3072 ■ AmSpirit Business Connections
AmSpirit Franchise Corp.
158 W Johnstown Rd.
PO Box 30724
Columbus, OH 43230-0724
Ph:(614)476-5540
Free: 888-267-7474
Fax:(614)476-6699
No. of Franchise Units: 2. **No. of Company-Owned Units:** 7. **Founded:** 1997. **Description:** Establish and support networking groups. **Equity Capital Needed:** $10,000. **Franchise Fee:** $10,000. **Financial Assistance:** No. **Training:** Yes.

3073 ■ Business Cards Tomorrow
Business Cards Tomorrow, Inc.
3000 NE 30th Pl., 5th Fl.
Ft. Lauderdale, FL 33306
Ph:(954)563-1224
Free: 800-627-9998
Fax:(954)565-0742
No. of Franchise Units: 64. **No. of Company-Owned Units:** 5. **Founded:** 1975. **Franchised:** 1977. **Description:** Professional, niche wholesale service business. **Equity Capital Needed:** $991,700-$1,100,000. **Franchise Fee:** $35,000. **Financial Assistance:** Third party financing available. **Training:** Provides 2 weeks at headquarters, 4 weeks onsite and ongoing support.

3074 ■ The Canadian Badge Maker Ltd.
2806 W King Edward Ave.
Vancouver, BC, Canada V6L 1T9
Ph:(604)733-4323
Fax:(604)736-8419
Co. E-mail: wunday@shae.ca
URL: http://www.recognitionexpress.ca
No. of Franchise Units: 8. **Founded:** 1978. **Franchised:** 1978. **Description:** Focus on corporate employee identification through name tags with full corporate logos, colours, etc. **Franchise Fee:** $39,500. **Training:** Offers 1 week training.

3075 ■ Cybertary
1217 Pleasant Grove Blvd., Ste. 100
Roseville, CA 95678
Ph:(916)781-7799
Free: 888-CYB-TARY
Fax:877-CYB-TARY
Co. E-mail: Franchise@Cybertary.com
URL: http://www.CybertaryFranchise.com
No. of Franchise Units: 23. **Founded:** 2005. **Franchised:** 2006. **Description:** Virtual assistant (VA) industry providing on-demand administrative support to businesses, entrepreneurs, and busy people through a nationwide team network to meet the needs of any business. This home-based B2B service offers low overhead and a flexible schedule. **Equity Capital Needed:** $39,500-$78,500. **Franchise Fee:** $37,500-$56,250. **Royalty Fee:** 5%+. **Financial Assistance:** 50% down, balance financed over 1 year and applies to franchise fee and startup costs. **Training:** Receive 4 days of intensive training before you launch your business & 90 days of weekly one-on-one coaching sessions to build your business once you are up and running.

3076 ■ A Day to Cherish Wedding Videos
10174 S Memorial Dr.
South Jordan, UT 84095
Ph:(801)253-2450
No. of Franchise Units: 2. **No. of Company-Owned Units:** 1. **Founded:** 2004. **Franchised:** 2004. **Description:** Wedding and special occasion videos. **Equity Capital Needed:** $33,400-$39,400 total investment. **Franchise Fee:** $17,500. **Royalty Fee:** 6%. **Financial Assistance:** No. **Training:** Provides 6 days at headquarters and 2 days at franchisee's location with ongoing support.

3077 ■ Decorating Elves
Decorative Lighting, Inc.
10460 Roosevelt Blvd., Ste. 292
St. Petersburg, FL 33716
Ph:(813)935-5087
Free: 800-695-4837
Fax:(813)425-5799
No. of Franchise Units: 2. **No. of Company-Owned Units:** 2. **Founded:** 2006. **Franchised:** 2007. **Description:** Holiday lighting. **Equity Capital Needed:** $15,500$62,500. **Franchise Fee:** $8,500+. **Financial Assistance:** Yes. **Training:** Yes.

3078 ■ Discount Imaging Franchise Corporation
206 Texas Ave.
Monroe, LA 71201
Ph:(318)324-8977
Co. E-mail: tim@discountimaging.com
URL: http://www.difcorp.com
No. of Franchise Units: 11. **No. of Company-Owned Units:** 1. **Founded:** 1995. **Franchised:** 1998. **Description:** Business to business model providing solutions for the full range of printer, fax and copier supplies and service. **Equity Capital Needed:** $75,000. **Franchise Fee:** $25,000. **Financial Assistance:** SBA approved and offers special financing to experienced salespersons who qualify. **Managerial Assistance:** 4 weeks of local market development in your hometown with ongoing sales and technical support. **Training:** Provides 2 week training at home office.

3079 ■ ESAPP Financial, LLC
6520 E 82nd St., Ste.200
Indianapolis, IN 46250
Ph:(317)577-4995
Fax:(317)577-4996
Founded: 1996. **Description:** Financial services company.

3080 ■ Franchise Recruiters Ltd.
Saddlebrooke Country Club
63284 E Flower Ridge Dr.
Tucson, AZ 85739
Ph:(520)825-9588
Free: 800-334-6257
Founded: 1977. **Description:** Placement of franchise management professionals.

3081 ■ Franchise Sales
1315 S Villa Ave.
Villa Park, IL 60181
Ph:(630)819-2418
Fax:(630)827-0174
Founded: 1991. **Description:** Self franchisees in business now.

3082 ■ Franchise Search, Inc.
Kushell Associates Inc.
48 Burd St., Ste. 101
Nyack, NY 10960
Ph:(845)727-4103
Founded: 1982. **Description:** International executive search firm for franchisors.

3083 ■ Goin' Postal
4941 4th St.
Zephyrhills, FL 33542
Ph:(813)782-1500
Fax:(813)782-1599
No. of Franchise Units: 275. **No. of Company-Owned Units:** 1. **Founded:** 2002. **Franchised:** 2004. **Description:** Retail shipping & business services. **Equity Capital Needed:** $46,865-$133,115. **Franchise Fee:** $15,000. **Royalty Fee:** $345/month. **Financial Assistance:** Third party financing available. **Training:** 1 week training at headquarters, 1 week at franchisee's location, refresher training at corporate location throughout term of the franchise and ongoing support.

3084 ■ Handyman-Network Franchise Systems LLC
Handyman Franchise Systems, Inc.
2760 E Spring St., Ste. 212
Long Beach, CA 90806
Ph:(562)216-9292
Free: 877-942-6396
Fax:(562)216-9296
Co. E-mail: franchise@handyman-network.com
URL: http://www.handyman-network.com
No. of Franchise Units: 5. **Founded:** 2000. **Franchised:** 2002. **Description:** Provides homeowners with service, people, systems, and technology. **Equity Capital Needed:** $67,388-$107,044 total start-up, including franchise fee. **Franchise Fee:** $30,000. **Royalty Fee:** 6%. **Financial Assistance:** Assistance with franchise fee. **Training:** Start-up program is an extensive 3 module training program. Includes 2 weeks of on the

job training at headquarters, and 4 days of onsite training. Each module is supported with manuals with ongoing support.

3085 ■ Ink Solution & Postal
9524 Hebron Commerce Dr.
Charlotte, NC 28273
Free: (866)482-4657
Fax:(704)523-8720
No. of Franchise Units: 19. **Founded:** 2001. **Franchised:** 2007. **Description:** Inkjet & toner cartridge recycling/postal services. **Equity Capital Needed:** $118,000. **Franchise Fee:** $29,000. **Royalty Fee:** 4%. **Financial Assistance:** No. **Training:** Provides 1 week training at headquarters, 1 week at franchisee's location, 1 week at corporate store and ongoing support.

3086 ■ InkTone
26722 Plaza Dr.
Mission Viejo, CA 92691
Free: 888-465-9481
Fax:888-465-9452
Founded: 2006. **Franchised:** 2006. **Description:** Inkjet & toner replacements. **Equity Capital Needed:** $130,000-$170,000. **Franchise Fee:** $25,000. **Royalty Fee:** 6%. **Financial Assistance:** No. **Training:** Offers 2 weeks training at headquarters, 1 week at franchisee's location and ongoing support.

3087 ■ Liberty Tax Service
800 Denison St., Unit 18
Markham, ON, Canada L3R 5M9
Ph:(905)943-2640
Free: 800-790-3863
Fax:(866)902-1245
Co. E-mail: kstrongoli@libtax.com
URL: http://www.libertytaxcanada.ca
No. of Franchise Units: 233. **No. of Company-Owned Units:** 19. **Founded:** 1972. **Franchised:** 1982. **Description:** Tax preparation service. **Equity Capital Needed:** $33,350-$54,900. **Franchise Fee:** $25,000. **Training:** Provides 5 days training.

3088 ■ Lord & Partners
9-741 Muskoka Rd., Ste. 3 N
Huntsville, ON, Canada P1H 2L3
Ph:(705)788-1966
Free: 877-490-6660
Fax:(705)788-1969
Co. E-mail: busadmin@lordandpartners.com
URL: http://www.lordandpartners.com
No. of Franchise Units: 4. **No. of Company-Owned Units:** 2. **Founded:** 1990. **Franchised:** 2005. **Description:** Unique business to business franchise network serving a growing $30 billion market in representing Canadian manufactured environmentally responsible solutions that replace hazardous traditional chemicals in the workplace and reduce environmental aspects and impacts on the community. **Equity Capital Needed:** $200,000. **Franchise Fee:** $50,000. **Training:** Provides 29 days training on the proven proprietary business, marketing systems, a demo "showroom on wheels," with ongoing support for a protected territory.

3089 ■ Luxury Bath Systems
1958 Brandon Ct.
Glendale Heights, IL 60139
Ph:(630)295-9084
Free: 800-354-2284
Fax:(630)295-9418
URL: http://www.luxurybath.com
No. of Franchise Units: 100. **Founded:** 1994. **Description:** Acrylic and solid surface bathroom remodeling using the latest technology. **Equity Capital Needed:** $20,000-$40,000. **Franchise Fee:** $16,000. **Financial Assistance:** Limited in-house assistance available. **Training:** 5 days covering marketing, installation and support and 3 days at franchisee's location with ongoing support.

3090 ■ Mail Boxes Etc.–MBEC Communications, Inc.
MBEC Communications, Inc.
1115 North Service Rd. W, Unit 1
Oakville, ON, Canada L6M 2V9
Ph:(905)338-9754
Free: 800-661-6232
Fax:(905)338-7491
Co. E-mail: customerservice@theupsstore.ca
URL: http://www.mbe.ca
No. of Franchise Units: 351. **Founded:** 1990. **Franchised:** 1991. **Description:** With over 4,000 locations worldwide and over 260 centers operating in Canada, MBE is one of the largest and fastest growing business and communications service franchise. Services include expert packing services, shipping, worldwide courier services, black and white and color photocopies, electronic document services, digital color printing, fax sending and receiving, computer rental, word processing, Internet/email access and mail receiving services. **Equity Capital Needed:** $146,150-$179,550 plus working capital. **Franchise Fee:** $35,900. **Royalty Fee:** 6% of gross. **Training:** Complete pre-opening support provided, including site selection, lease negotiation, design and construction, training, marketing, as well as ongoing operational and marketing field support.

3091 ■ Padgett Business Services
400 Blue Hill Dr., Ste. 201
Westwood, MA 02090
Free: 877-729-8725
Co. E-mail: padgett@smallbizpros.com
URL: http://www.smallbizpros.com
No. of Franchise Units: 400. **Founded:** 1966. **Franchised:** 1975. **Description:** Padgett provides an array of services to small businesses, such as consulting, financial reporting, government compliance, payroll and tax preparation services. Padgett also offers credit card processing, pension and 125 plan administration, equipment financing and workers' compensation payment service. **Equity Capital Needed:** Total investment and net worth &105,955; liquid or cash $78,750. **Franchise Fee:** $56,000. **Financial Assistance:** Third party financing up to $75,000. Also enrolled in the SBA registry. **Training:** Initial training 12 days + field visits, covering marketing, operations, and software. Ongoing training and support is provided through regular seminars in marketing, operations, tax, etc. Support is delivered through toll-free telephone and a wide range of information and material is provided via the company's web site.

3092 ■ Padgett Business Services (Canada)
775 Pacific Rd, Ste. 38
Oakville, ON, Canada L6L 6M4
Free: 888-723-4388
Fax:800-428-5297
Co. E-mail: hcanaan@smallbizpros.ca
URL: http://www.smallbizpros.ca
No. of Franchise Units: 120. **Founded:** 1966. **Franchised:** 1975. **Description:** Supplier of small business services including accounting, tax preparation and consultation, payroll services and business advice. **Equity Capital Needed:** $45,000. **Franchise Fee:** $25,000. **Financial Assistance:** No. **Training:** Yes.

3093 ■ Profit-Tell International, Inc.
201 Ogden Ave.
Hinsdale, IL 60521
Ph:(630)655-3700
Fax:(630)655-4100
URL: http://www.Profit-Tell.com
No. of Franchise Units: 31. **No. of Company-Owned Units:** 1. **Founded:** 1993. **Franchised:** 2002. **Description:** Cutting edge marketing systems. **Equity Capital Needed:** $42,000-$60,000. **Franchise Fee:** $42,000 turnkey. **Financial Assistance:** Yes. **Training:** Yes.

3094 ■ ProFleet Care Franchising
51 Sundial Dr.
Dundas, ON, Canada L9M 7R6
Ph:(905)667-8595
Free: (866)787-8645
Co. E-mail: info@profleetcare.com
URL: http://www.profleetcare.com
No. of Franchise Units: 15. **No. of Company-Owned Units:** 1. **Founded:** 1981. **Franchised:** 2007. **Description:** Pro Fleet Care is a unique and comparatively low start-up cost franchise in the highly profitable rust protection industry. Being the only mobile concept in the industry, Pro Fleet Care prides itself in offering its customers the ability to save money, protect and extend the life of expensive equipment. We are providers of Exceptional Rust Control Service, On site, On time and as Promised. The franchise package includes everything you need to get started in this highly profitable industry. **Equity Capital Needed:** $33,000-$70,000, varies if purchase truck outright. **Franchise Fee:** $20,000. **Training:** Provides 2 weeks training, including technical and operational and ongoing.

3095 ■ Resource Associates Corp.
One Meridian Blvd., Ste. 1C02
Wyomissing, PA 19601
Ph:(610)775-5222
Free: 800-799-6277
Fax:(610)775-9686
URL: http://www.rac-tqi.com
No. of Franchise Units: 600. **Founded:** 1978. **Description:** Network of consultants focusing on people development, strategy, and processes. **Equity Capital Needed:** $29,000. **Franchise Fee:** None. **Financial Assistance:** Yes. **Training:** Yes.

3096 ■ Services Select Franchise Company, LLC
1206 Pointe Centre Dr., Ste. 120
Chattanooga, TN 37421
Ph:(423)413-6258
Fax:(423)892-1803
No. of Franchise Units: 4. **Founded:** 2004. **Franchised:** 2007. **Description:** Award system for businesses. **Equity Capital Needed:** $51,850-$57,350. **Franchise Fee:** $50,000. **Financial Assistance:** No. **Training:** Yes.

3097 ■ We the People USA Inc.
Dollar Financial Group
1436 Lancaster Ave., Ste. 340
Berwyn, PA 19312
Free: (866)429-2785
Fax:(866)480-6970
Co. E-mail: info@wethepeopleusa.com
URL: http://www.wethepeopleusa.com
No. of Franchise Units: 151. **No. of Company-Owned Units:** 26. **Founded:** 1985. **Franchised:** 1996. **Description:** Legal document preparation. **Equity Capital Needed:** $123,200-$169,500. **Franchise Fee:** $89,500. **Financial Assistance:** Limited in-house and third party financing available. **Training:** Offers 1 week at headquarters, 1 week at franchisee's location and ongoing support.

COMPUTERIZED DATABASES

3098 ■ *Business & Management Practices*
Cengage Learning Inc.
27500 Drake Rd.
Farmington Hills, MI 48331-3535
Ph:(248)699-4253
Free: 800-877-4253
Fax:(248)699-8069
Co. E-mail: galeord@gale.com
URL: http://gale.cengage.com
Description: Provides access to more than 831,000 records from more than 1200 management sources, and selected records from more than 300 Business and Industry sources. Includes information on how companies and managers make decisions, implement new technology, plan for the future, and expand. Includes definitions of key terms in business methodology and management issues. Contains book reviews, how-to articles, interviews, speeches, and surveys. Includes case studies, practical applications and guidelines. Defines more than 400 searchable management concept terms. Indexes include company and industry names, product codes and names and geographic codes. Available as part of the RDS Business Suite. **Availability:** Online: Cengage Learning Inc., Alacra Inc., LexisNexis Group, Nerac Inc., Thomson Reuters, Wolters Kluwer Health, ProQuest LLC, GENIOS - German Business Information/Deutsche Wirtschaftsdatenbank GmbH. **Type:** Full text; Bibliographic.

3099 ■ *Florida Trend*
Trend Magazines Inc.
490 First Ave. S, 8th Fl.
St. Petersburg, FL 33701
Ph:(727)821-5800
Fax:(727)822-5083
Co. E-mail: custrelations@floridatrend.com
URL: http://www.floridatrend.com
Description: Provides the complete text of Florida Trend, a monthly publication covering Florida business, economics, finance, and real estate. Includes profiles of Florida corporations and executives, analysis of economic trends, and columns covering state and federal government, public policy, fine dining, and real estate. **Availability:** Online: Trend Magazines Inc. **Type:** Full text.

LIBRARIES

3100 ■ Alabama A & M University–J.F. Drake Memorial Learning Resources Center
4900 Meridian St.
Normal, AL 35762
Ph:(256)372-4747
Fax:(256)372-5764
URL: http://www.aamu.edu/library/
Contact: Veronica Acklin, Adm.Sec.
Scope: Education, business and economics, agriculture, the sciences, computer science, literature. **Services:** Interlibrary loan; copying; media services; Center open to the public (courtesy card must be purchased for check out of materials by persons not enrolled at the university or at one of the cooperating institutions). **Holdings:** 236,147 books; 25,517 bound periodical volumes; 5044 AV programs; 20,869 periodicals on microfilm; 1053 college catalogs; various telephone directories; 16,166 ERIC microfiche; 141,376 government documents; *Wall Street Journal* on microfiche (11,643). **Subscriptions:** 1657 journals and other serials; 93 newspapers; 359 microfilm subscriptions.

3101 ■ Alameda County Library Business Library
2400 Stevenson Blvd.
Fremont, CA 94538
Ph:(510)505-7001
URL: http://www.aclibrary.org
Contact: Sallie Pine, Lib.Br.Mgr.
Scope: Starting and managing a business, small business, investments, real estate, International business, management and personnel, career planning, San Francisco Bay area business. **Services:** Interlibrary loan; copying; Library open to the public. **Holdings:** 18,000 books; 300 audiocassettes; 100 videocassettes. **Subscriptions:** 400 journals and other serials; 20 newspapers.

3102 ■ A.T. Kearney, Inc.–Information Research Center
222 W. Adams St.
Chicago, IL 60606
Ph:(312)648-0111
Fax:(312)223-7242
URL: http://www.atkearney.com
Scope: Management consulting, automotive industries, benchmarking, business processes, consumer industries, economics, information technology, knowledge management, manufacturing, retail, strategic innovation, strategic sourcing, supply chain integration, transportation. **Services:** Interlibrary loan; Center not open to the public. **Holdings:** 4300 books; 3 CD-ROMs. **Subscriptions:** 150 journals and other serials.

3103 ■ Balch & Bingham LLP Library
1901 6th Ave. N., Ste. 1500
Birmingham, AL 35203
Ph:(205)251-8100
Fax:(205)226-8799
Co. E-mail: ctabereaux@balch.com
URL: http://www.balch.com
Contact: Christina Tabereaux, Dir. of Lib.Svcs.
Scope: Law, business. **Services:** Interlibrary loan; Library not open to the public. **Holdings:** 35,000 volumes; legislative and government documents. **Subscriptions:** 266 journals and other serials.

3104 ■ The Boston Consulting Group–Chicago Information and Research Group
300 N. La Salle
Chicago, IL 60654
Ph:(312)993-3300
Fax:(312)876-0771
Co. E-mail: bcgchicago@bcg.com
URL: http://www.bcg.com
Contact: Vera Ward
Scope: Statistics, finance, industry. **Services:** Interlibrary loan; Library not open to the public. **Holdings:** 4500 books; 3000 Annual reports; 21 lin.ft. of microfiche; 84 reels of microfilm. **Subscriptions:** 100 journals and other serials; 5 newspapers.

3105 ■ Business Trend Analysts Library
2171 Jericho Tpke., Ste. 200
Commack, NY 11725
Ph:(631)462-5454
Free: 800-866-4648
Fax:(631)462-1842
Co. E-mail: sales@bta-ler.com
URL: http://www.businesstrendanalysts.com
Contact: J. Marquardt, Libn.
Scope: Marketing, business, economics. **Services:** Library not open to the public. **Holdings:** 200 reports. **Subscriptions:** 400 journals and other serials; 8 newspapers.

3106 ■ California Polytechnic State University–Robert F. Kennedy Library - Government Documents and Map Department–Diablo Canyon Power Plant Depository Library (Bldg.)
Bldg. 35
University Dr. cor. N. Perimeter Rd.
San Luis Obispo, CA 93407
Ph:(805)756-2345
Fax:(805)756-2346
URL: http://lib.calpoly.edu
Contact: Michael D. Miller, Dean of Lib. Svcs.
Scope: Nuclear power plants. **Services:** Library open to the public. **Holdings:** Figures not available.

3107 ■ Canada Public Works & Government Services–Consulting and Audit Canada Information Centre
112 Kent St., Tower B
Ottawa, ON, Canada K1A 0S5
Ph:(613)943-8387
Fax:(613)947-2436
Co. E-mail: svcinfo-ascinfo@tpsgc-pwgsc.gc.ca
URL: http://www.tpsgc-pwgsc.gc.ca/comm/index-eng.html
Contact: Henne Kahwa, Mgr., Lib.Svcs.
Scope: Business, finance, public administration, management consulting. **Services:** Library not open to the public. **Holdings:** Figures not available.

3108 ■ Golden Gate University–University Library
536 Mission St.
San Francisco, CA 94105-2968
Ph:(415)442-7244
Free: 877-448-8543
Fax:(415)543-6779
Co. E-mail: jcarter@ggu.edu
URL: http://www.ggu.edu/university_library
Contact: Janice Carter, Lib.Dir.
Scope: Business, public administration, information systems, telecommunications. **Services:** Interlibrary loan; libraries open to the public on Annual fee basis. **Holdings:** 90,000 volumes; 264 microfiche; 435 microfilms. **Subscriptions:** 3000 journals and other serials.

3109 ■ McKinsey & Company, Inc.–Resource Library
110 Charles St., W.
Toronto, ON, Canada M5S 1K9
Ph:(416)313-3700
Fax:(416)313-2999
URL: http://www.mckinsey.com
Contact: Marie Gadula, Mgr., Res. & Info.Svc.
Scope: Strategic planning, Organization and operations effectiveness, management consulting. **Services:** Interlibrary loan; SDI; Center open to clients. **Holdings:** 3000 books; full depository collection of Statistics Canada documentation. **Subscriptions:** 350 journals and other serials; 12 newspapers.

3110 ■ Towers Watson Information Center
1800 McGill College Ave., 22nd Fl.
Montreal, QC, Canada H3A 3J6
Fax:(514)982-9269
URL: http://www.towerswatson.com/
Scope: Employee benefits, compensation, actuarial science, taxation, labor, social security, employee communications, insurance, human resource management. **Services:** Center not open to the public. **Holdings:** 2000 books; 100 internal reports; 40 VF drawers of pamphlets and clippings; 1000 microfiche; AV materials. **Subscriptions:** 100 journals and other serials; 6 newspapers.

Butcher Shop

ASSOCIATIONS AND OTHER ORGANIZATIONS

3111 ■ American Association of Meat Processors
PO Box 269
Elizabethtown, PA 17022
Ph:(717)367-1168
Free: 877-877-0168
Fax:(717)367-9096
Co. E-mail: aamp@aamp.com
URL: http://www.aamp.com
Contact: Jay Wenther PhD, Exec. Dir.
Description: Represents small and mid-sized packers, processors, wholesalers, home food service businesses, meat retailers, deli, mail order businesses and catering operators and their suppliers. Represents its members at the federal level of government. Provides education, insurance options and business management assistance to the independent segment of the meat industry. **Publications:** *AAMPlifier* (semimonthly); *Capitol Line-Up* (semimonthly); *The Membership Directory and Buyers' Guide of the American Association of Meat Processors* (biennial).

3112 ■ American Meat Institute
1150 Connecticut Ave. NW, 12th Fl.
Washington, DC 20036
Ph:(202)587-4200
Fax:(202)587-4300
Co. E-mail: memberservices@meatami.com
URL: http://www.meatami.com
Contact: J. Patrick Boyle, Pres./CEO
Description: Represents the interests of packers and processors of beef, pork, lamb, veal, and turkey products and their suppliers throughout North America. Provides legislative, regulatory, and public relations services. Conducts scientific research. Offers marketing and technical assistance. Sponsors educational programs. .

3113 ■ Canadian Meat Council–Conseil des Viandes du Canada
955 Green Valley Crescent, Ste. 305
Ottawa, ON, Canada K2C 3V4
Ph:(613)729-3911
Fax:(613)729-4997
Co. E-mail: info@cmc-cvc.com
URL: http://www.cmc-cvc.com
Contact: James M. Laws, Exec. Dir.
Description: Meat packers and distributors. Promotes growth and development of the meat industries. Represents members' interests; sponsors promotional campaigns. **Publications:** *Food Service Meat Manual* .

3114 ■ National Cattlemen's Beef Association
9110 E Nichols Ave., Ste. 300
Centennial, CO 80112
Ph:(303)694-0305
Free: (866)233-3872
Fax:(303)694-2851
Co. E-mail: membership@beef.org
URL: http://www.beefusa.org
Contact: J.D. Alexander, Pres.-Elect
Description: Represents 149 organizations of livestock marketers, growers, meat packers, food retailers, and food service firms. Conducts extensive program of promotion, education and information about beef, veal, and associated meat products. Conducts projects such as recipe testing and development, food demonstrations, food photography, educational service to colleges, experimental meat cutting methods, merchandising programs, and preparation of materials for newspapers, magazines, radio, and television. .

REFERENCE WORKS

3115 ■ "Dick Haskayne" in *Canadian Business* (Vol. 81, March 31, 2008, No. 5, pp. 72)
Pub: Rogers Media
Ed: Andy Holloway. **Description:** Dick Haskayne says that he learned a lot about business from his dad who ran a butcher shop where they had to make a decision on buying cattle and getting credit. Haskayne says that family, friends, finances, career, health, and infrastructure are benchmarks that have to be balanced.

3116 ■ *Urner Barry's Meat and Poultry Directory*
Pub: Urner Barry Publications Inc.
Ed: Joseph Soja, Editor. **Released:** Biennial, latest edition 2010-2011. **Price:** $199, individuals. **Covers:** More than 10,000 slaughterers, wholesalers, importers and exporters, brokers, and other processors and handlers of meat and poultry. **Entries Include:** Company name, address, phone, fax, names and titles of key personnel, branch offices, brand names, type or nature of business, products handled, and other information, e-mail address. **Arrangement:** Geographical. **Indexes:** Type of business, product, brand name, key personnel, fax.

STATISTICAL SOURCES

3117 ■ *Poultry - U.S.*
Pub: MarketResearch.com
Released: 2008. **Price:** $3995.00.

TRADE PERIODICALS

3118 ■ *AAMPlifier*
Pub: American Association of Meat Processors
Ed: Steve Krut, Editor, steve@aamp.com. **Released:** Bimonthly, 2/month. **Description:** Covers association meetings, news of members, industry trends and guidelines, the activities of related organizations.

3119 ■ *Capitol Line-Up*
Pub: American Association of Meat Processors
Contact: Bernard F. Shire
Ed: Bernard F. Shire, Editor, bernie@aamp.com. **Released:** Bimonthly, 26/year. **Price:** $50, nonmembers. **Description:** Features news and information on meat products, issues brought up by the United States Department of Agriculture (USDA) and its Food Safety and Inspection Service (FSIS), other government agencies, and current market conditions. Recurring features include news of research, a calendar of events, reports of meetings, and legislative and regulatory news.

3120 ■ *Iowa Grocer*
Pub: Iowa Grocery Industry Association
Contact: Jerry Fleagle, President
Released: Bimonthly. **Description:** Magazine for grocery industry - retail and supply.

3121 ■ *Lean Trimmings*
Pub: National Meat Association
Contact: Kiran Kernellu
Ed: Kiran Kernellu, Editor, kiran@nmaonline.org. **Released:** Weekly. **Price:** Included in membership. **Description:** Deals with the latest regulatory and business news on the meat industry. Recurring features include news of research, a calendar of events, reports of meetings, job listings, and sections on members, labor relations, and marketing trends. Remarks: Also available via e-mail.

3122 ■ *Meat & Poultry*
Pub: Sosland Publishing Co.
Contact: Dave Crost, Publisher
E-mail: dcrost@sosland.com
Released: Monthly. **Price:** Free to qualified subscribers; $85 other countries print; $165 other countries print, airmail delivery. **Description:** Magazine serving the meat and poultry processing, distributing, and wholesaling industries in the U.S. and Canada.

VIDEOCASSETTES/ AUDIOCASSETTES

3123 ■ *Practice Beef Quality Grading II*
CEV Multimedia
1020 SE Loop 289
Lubbock, TX 79404
Ph:(806)745-8820
Free: 877-610-5017
Fax:800-243-6398
Co. E-mail: cev@cevmultimedia.com
URL: http://www.cevmultimedia.com
Price: $49.95. **Description:** Centers on the practice of beef quality grading by presenting a wide variety of 50 carcasses for practice grading. **Availability:** VHS.

3124 ■ *Practice Retail Cut Identification II*
CEV Multimedia
1020 SE Loop 289
Lubbock, TX 79404
Ph:(806)745-8820
Free: 877-610-5017
Fax:800-243-6398
Co. E-mail: cev@cevmultimedia.com
URL: http://www.cevmultimedia.com
Price: $49.95. **Description:** Furnishes 25 second views of 75 retail cuts from five different meat classes allowing the viewer a chance to practice their retail

cut identification skills. Also provides a scoring key. Cuts were selected from the National FFA Meats Evaluation and Management ontest list of 126 approved cuts. **Availability:** VHS.

3125 ■ *Practice Retail Cut Identification III*
CEV Multimedia
1020 SE Loop 289
Lubbock, TX 79404
Ph:(806)745-8820
Free: 877-610-5017
Fax:800-243-6398
Co. E-mail: cev@cevmultimedia.com
URL: http://www.cevmultimedia.com

Price: $59.95. **Description:** Practice retail cut identification program which offers 25-second views of 75 different cuts of meat from five different classes. Provides a scoring key. The cuts were selected from the National FFA Meat Evaluation and Management Contest approved list of more than 100 cuts. **Availability:** VHS.

3126 ■ *Practice Retail Cut Identification IV*
CEV Multimedia
1020 SE Loop 289
Lubbock, TX 79404
Ph:(806)745-8820
Free: 877-610-5017
Fax:800-243-6398
Co. E-mail: cev@cevmultimedia.com
URL: http://www.cevmultimedia.com

Price: $59.95. **Description:** Presents 25-second views of 75 retail cuts from five different classes allowing the viewer to practice their retail cut identification skills. Provides a scoring key. Cuts were selected from the National FFA Meat Evaluation and Management Contest approved list of 126 cuts. **Availability:** VHS.

TRADE SHOWS AND CONVENTIONS

3127 ■ American Convention of Meat Processors
American Association of Meat Processors
One Meating Pl.
PO Box 269
Elizabethtown, PA 17022
Ph:(717)367-1168
Free: 877-877-0168
Fax:(717)367-9096
Co. E-mail: info@aamp.com
URL: http://www.aamp.com

Released: Annual. **Audience:** Slaughtering; packing; meat, poultry and seafood processors; wholesalers, retailers, and supermarkets; catalog businesses; catering and deli operators/owners. **Principal Exhibits:** Processing equipment; packaging supplies and equipment; technical and computer services; deli, mail order, and catering supplies; marketing aids; transportation; chilling and building information; laboratory services and testing equipment; consultants in various food processing areas. **Dates and Locations:** 2011 Jun 16-18, Reno, NV.

FRANCHISES AND BUSINESS OPPORTUNITIES

3128 ■ Logan Farms Honey Glazed Hams
10560 Westheimer Rd.
Houston, TX 77042
Ph:(713)781-4335
Free: 800-833-HAMS

No. of Franchise Units: 12. **No. of Company-Owned Units:** 1. **Founded:** 1984. **Description:** Gourmet meat stores, specializing in the sale of honey-glazed, spiral-sliced hams. Also sells gourmet rib eye roast, pork loins, chicken breast, smoked turkeys, spiral-sliced boneless hams, spiral-sliced honey-glazed turkey breast, smoked sausage, bacon, cheesecakes and a variety of honey mustard and preserves. Stores also have a deli department making a variety of sub sandwiches and poor-boys. conduct of the franchisees business. **Equity Capital Needed:** $100,000 cash. **Franchise Fee:** $30,000. **Financial Assistance:** No. **Training:** 2 weeks on procedures and techniques in manufacturing and marketing the products, manuals for advertising and market programs, record-keeping and inventory control.

3129 ■ M & M Meat Shops, Ltd.
640 Trillium Dr.
PO Box 2488
Kitchener, ON, Canada N2H 6M3
Ph:(519)895-1075
Fax:(519)895-0762

No. of Company-Owned Units: 4. **Founded:** 1980. **Franchised:** 1981. **Description:** Sells specialty flash-frozen foods, including beef, pork, poultry, seafood, party foods, vegetables, desserts, etc. Primarily heat-and-serve convenience foods. Most portions are controlled. **Equity Capital Needed:** $320,000. **Franchise Fee:** $30,000. **Royalty Fee:** 3%. **Financial Assistance:** No. **Training:** Provides 2 weeks at headquarters, 2 days at franchisees location with ongoing support.

LIBRARIES

3130 ■ National Cattlemen's Beef Association Library
444 N. Michigan Ave., Ste. 1800
Chicago, IL 60611
Ph:(312)467-5520
Fax:(312)670-9414
Co. E-mail: nationalcattlemen@beef.org
URL: http://www.beefusa.org/
Contact: Charles P. Schroeder, CEO

Scope: Meat, nutrition, food economics, cookery. **Services:** Interlibrary loan; copying; Center open to industry members by appointment. **Holdings:** 5000 books; 600 reports; 28 VF drawers of reprints, clippings, government documents. **Subscriptions:** 400 journals and other serials; 8 newspapers.

ASSOCIATIONS AND OTHER ORGANIZATIONS

3131 ■ CTAM - Cable and Telecommunications Association for Marketing
201 N Union St., Ste. 440
Alexandria, VA 22314
Ph:(703)549-4200
Fax:(703)684-1167
Co. E-mail: info@ctam.com
URL: http://www.ctam.com
Contact: Char Beales, Pres./CEO
Description: Network of cable and telecommunications professionals dedicated to the pursuit of marketing excellence. Provides its members with competitive marketing resources including education, research, networking and leadership opportunities. **Publications:** *CTAM Quarterly Journal* (quarterly).

3132 ■ Jones/NCTI
9697 E Mineral Ave.
Centennial, CO 80112
Ph:(303)797-9393
Free: (866)575-7206
Fax:(303)797-9394
Co. E-mail: info@jonesncti.com
URL: http://www.jonesncti.com
Contact: Glenn R. Jones, Chm./CEO
Description: Provides comprehensive broadband training for the cable television industry. Offers career training resources and courses in areas ranging from customer service procedures to optical fiber system design, installation, and maintenance. **Publications:** *Spanish/English CATV Dictionary* .

3133 ■ National Cable and Telecommunications Association
25 Massachusetts Ave. NW, Ste. 100
Washington, DC 20001-1413
Ph:(202)222-2300
Fax:(202)222-2514
Co. E-mail: webmaster@ncta.com
URL: http://www.ncta.com
Contact: Michael Powell, Pres./CEO
Description: Franchised cable operators, programmers, and cable networks; associate members are cable hardware suppliers and distributors; affiliate members are brokerage and law firms and financial institutions; state and regional cable television associations cooperate, but are not affiliated, with the organization. Serves as national medium for exchange of experiences and opinions through research, study, discussion, and publications. Represents the cable industry before Congress, the Federal Communications Commission and various courts on issues of primary importance. Conducts research program in conjunction with National Academy of Cable Programming. Sponsors, in conjunction with Motion Picture Association of America, the Coalition Opposing Signal Theft, an organization designed to deter cable signal theft and to develop anti-piracy materials. Provides promotional aids and information on legal, legislative and regulatory matters. Compiles statistics. **Publications:** *Cable Industry Overview* (semiannual).

3134 ■ Society of Cable Telecommunications Engineers
140 Philips Rd.
Exton, PA 19341-1318
Ph:(610)363-6888
Free: 800-542-5040
Fax:(610)363-5898
Co. E-mail: scte@scte.org
URL: http://www.scte.org
Contact: Mark Dzuban, Pres./CEO
Description: Persons engaged in engineering, construction, installation, technical direction, management, or administration of cable telecommunications and broadband communications technologies. Also eligible are students in communications, educators, government and regulatory agency employees, and affiliated trade associations. Dedicated to the technical training and further education of members. Provides technical training and certification and is an American National Standards Institute (ANSI) approved Standards Development Organization for the cable communications industry. **Publications:** *Communications Technology* (monthly); *Interval* (monthly).

3135 ■ Women in Cable Telecommunications
14555 Avion Pkwy., Ste. 250
Chantilly, VA 20151
Ph:(703)234-9810
Fax:(703)817-1595
Co. E-mail: mbrennan@wict.org
URL: http://www.wict.org
Contact: Maria Brennan, Pres./CEO
Description: Empowers and educates women to achieve their professional goals by providing opportunities for leadership, networking and advocacy. **Publications:** *The Catalyst*; *Insights* (quarterly); *WICT Wire*;Membership Directory (annual).

REFERENCE WORKS

3136 ■ "10 Trends That Are Shaping Global Media Consumption" in *Advertising Age* (Vol. 81, December 6, 2010, No. 43, pp. 3)
Pub: Crain Communications, Inc.
Ed: Ann Marie Kerwin. **Description:** Ad Age offers the statistics from the TV penetration rate in Kenya to the number of World Cup watchers and more.

3137 ■ "Advertising May Take a Big Hit in Southwest/AirTran Merger" in *Baltimore Business Journal* (Vol. 28, October 1, 2010, No. 21, pp. 1)
Pub: Baltimore Business Journal
Ed: Gary Haber. **Description:** Advertising on television stations and the publishing industry in Baltimore could drop as a result of the merger between rival discount airlines Southwest Airlines and AirTran Airways. Southwest is among the top advertisers in the U.S., spending $126 million in 2009. No local jobs are expected to be affected because neither airline uses a local advertising firm.

3138 ■ "At 5-Year Mark, News 9 Makes Presence Felt in Competition for Ad Dollars" in *Business Review, Albany New York* (October 5, 2007)
Pub: American City Business Journals, Inc.
Ed: Barbara Pinckney. **Description:** The 24-hour news channel Capital News 9 can be watched live by viewers on their cell phones beginning late 2007 or early 2008 as part of a deal between Time Warner Cable and Sprint Nextel Corporation to bring Sprint's Pivot technology. News 9 marked its fifth year and plans to continue expanding coverage and provide better services to viewers.

3139 ■ "Baxter Baker Wins in Hot Finale of 'Cupcake Wars'" in *Fort Mill Times* (September 13, 2011)
Pub: McClatchy Company
Ed: Jenny Overmann. **Description:** Heather McDonnell, owner of Cupcrazed Cakery, and her assistant Debbie McDonnell, vied for a chance to win $10,000 on the cable network show called "Cupcake Wars", and to serve cupcakes at the album release party for country singer Jennette McCurdy. At the end of the show, the sisters-in-law won the top prize.

3140 ■ "Black Network Shifts Gears: Struggling Channel To Focus On Broadband TV" in *Black Enterprise* (Vol. 38, November 2007, No. 4, pp. 34)
Pub: Earl G. Graves Publishing Co. Inc.
Ed: Wendy Isom. **Description:** Rick Newberger, president and CEO of Black Family Channel's television platform discusses its plans to switch to broadband format programming offering various channels simultaneously with fewer costs.

3141 ■ *Bowdens International Directory*
Pub: Cision Canada
Released: 3 times a year. **Price:** $275, individuals per year (book). **Covers:** Daily and community newspapers, periodicals, radio and television broadcasting stations, and cable television systems; network television personnel, wire service offices, and other media in Canada. **Entries Include:** For newspapers and periodicals—Name, address, phone, fax, telex, circulation, ownership, news service, publisher and editors. For radio and television stations—Call letters, address, phone, fax, telex, type of programming, names and titles of key personnel, watts, air personalities, local programs aired including times and names of contacts. For cable television systems—Firm name, address, fax, names and titles of key personnel, ownership, programming hours. **Arrangement:** Geographical.

3142 ■ *Burrelle's New Jersey Media Directory*
Pub: BurrellesLuce
Released: Annual. **Price:** $60 plus $4.00 shipping. **Covers:** Over 1,200 New Jersey periodicals, newspapers, college publications, radio and television stations, and cable television systems. Also includes New York City and Philadelphia daily newspapers. **Entries Include:** For publications—Title, publisher name, address, phone, names and titles of key

personnel, frequency, circulation, geographical area covered, advertising and editorial deadlines. For others—Call letters and/or company name and address, names and titles of key personnel, markets covered. **Arrangement:** Classified by type of media, then town. **Indexes:** Alphabetical, geographical (county).

3143 ■ *Cable TV Facts*
Pub: Cabletelevision Advertising Bureau
Contact: Sean Cunningham, Pres./CEO
Released: Annual, Latest edition 2011. **Price:** $10. 99, members 1-49 each; $24, nonmembers; $10.25, members 50-99 each; $9.25, members 100-249 each. **Publication Includes:** List of ad-supported cable networks. Principal content of publication is discussion of the growth of the cable television industry, changes in viewership, marketing, and research trends. Covers demographic information, audience ratings, cable penetration, regional sports and news networks, major market inter-connects.

3144 ■ *Call Me Ted*
Pub: Grand Central Publishing
Ed: Ted Turner. **Released:** 2008. **Price:** $30.00. **Description:** Media mogul, Ted Turner's biography is full of personal and business details from his careers in advertising and broadcasting.

3145 ■ "Comcast Launches New Home Security Service, Developed in Portland" in *The Oregonian* (June 7, 2011)
Pub: McClatchy-Tribune Regional News
Ed: Mike Rogoway. **Description:** Comcast introduced its new high-end home security system that provides 24-hour monitoring and control of homes and utilities, along with Web and mobile access.

3146 ■ "Commercials Make Us Like TV More" in *Harvard Business Review* (Vol. 88, October 2010, No. 10, pp. 36)
Pub: Harvard Business School Publishing
Ed: Leif Nelson. **Description:** Research indicates that people prefer commercial interruption over uninterrupted shows due to the break creating a reactivation of the initial pleasure when beginning a desirable activity.

3147 ■ "'Cupcake Wars' TV Show Returns to Hampton Roads" in *Virginian-Pilot* (September 11, 2011)
Pub: McClatchy Company
Ed: Carolyn Shapiro. **Description:** Virginia Beach, Virginia sweet shop called Just Cupcakes and Carolina Cupcakery will compete for prizes on cable TV's Food Network Channel. Carla Hesseltine, owner of Just Cupcakes made it to the final rounds.

3148 ■ "Detroit Pawn Shop to be Reality TV Venue" in *UPI NewsTrack* (July 10, 2010)
Pub: United Press International-USA
Description: TruTV will present a new series called 'Hardcore Pawn' to compete with the History Channel's successful show 'Pawn Stars'. The show will feature American Jewelry and Loan in Detroit, Michigan and its owner Les Gold, who runs the store with his wife and children.

3149 ■ "Don't' Hate the Cable Guy" in *Saint Louis Business Journal* (Vol. 31, August 5, 2011, No. 50, pp. 1)
Pub: Saint Louis Business Journal
Ed: Angela Mueller. **Description:** Charter Communications named John Birrer as senior vice president of customer experience. The company experienced problems with its customer services.

3150 ■ "Exiting Stage Left" in *Baltimore Business Journal* (Vol. 28, June 18, 2010, No. 6, pp. 1)
Pub: Baltimore Business Journal
Ed: Scott Dance. **Description:** Film professionals including crew members and actors have been leaving Maryland to find work in other states such as Michigan, Louisiana, and Georgia where bigger budgets and film production incentives are given. Other consequences of this trend in local TV and film production are discussed.

3151 ■ "For Apple, It's Showtime Again" in *Barron's* (Vol. 90, August 30, 2010, No. 35, pp. 29)
Pub: Barron's Editorial & Corporate Headquarters
Ed: Eric J. Savitz. **Description:** Speculations on what Apple Inc. will unveil at its product launch event are presented. These products include a possible new iPhone Nano, a new update to its Apple TV, and possibly a deal with the Beatles to distribute their songs over iTunes.

3152 ■ *Freelancing for Journalists*
Pub: Routledge
Ed: Diana Harris. **Released:** January 1, 2010. **Price:** $110.00. **Description:** Comprehensive guide showing the specific skills required for those wishing to freelance in newspapers, magazines, radio, television, and as online journalists.

3153 ■ "iControl Networks Powers Comcast's XFINITY (Reg) Home Security Service" in *Benzinga.com* (June 9, 2011)
Pub: Benzinga.com
Ed: Benzinga Staff. **Description:** Comcast's XFINITY Home Security Service is powered by iControl Networks' OpenHome (TM) software platform. The service provides intrusion and fire protection along with interactive features such as home monitoring, home management, and energy management services with Web and mobile access.

3154 ■ *International Television and Video Almanac*
Pub: Quigley Publishing Company Inc.
Ed: Eileen Quigley, Editor. **Released:** Annual, January; latest edition 2011. **Price:** $235, individuals. **Covers:** "Who's Who in Motion Pictures and Television and Home Video," television networks, major program producers, major group station owners, cable television companies, distributors, firms serving the television and home video industry, equipment manufacturers, casting agencies, literary agencies, advertising and publicity representatives, television stations, associations, list of feature films produced for television; statistics, industry's year in review, award winners, satellite and wireless cable provider, primetime programming, video producers, distributors, wholesalers. **Entries Include:** Generally, company name, address, phone; manufacturer and service listings may include description of products and services and name of contact; producing, distributing, and station listings include additional detail, and contacts for cable and broadcast networks. **Arrangement:** Classified by service or activity. **Indexes:** Full.

3155 ■ "Johnson Publishing Expands: Moving Into Television and Internet To Extend Brand" in *Black Enterprise* (October 2007)
Pub: Earl G. Graves Publishing Co. Inc.
Ed: Tamara E. Holmes. **Description:** Johnson Publishing Company has followed the lives of black families in both Ebony and Jet magazines. The media firm has expanded its coverage by developing entertainment content for television, the Internet and other digital arenas.

3156 ■ "KXAN Seeks Larger Studio, Office Space" in *Austin Business Journal* (Vol. 31, May 27, 2011, No. 12, pp. A1)
Pub: American City Business Journals Inc.
Ed: Cody Lyon. **Description:** Austin NBC affiliate KXAN Television is opting to sell its property north of downtown and relocate to another site. The station is now inspecting possible sites to house its broadcasting facility and employees totaling as many as 200 people. Estimated cost of the construction of the studios and offices is $13 million plus another million in moving the equipment.

3157 ■ "Local TV Hits Media Radar Screen" in *Business Courier* (Vol. 27, July 2, 2010, No. 9, pp. 1)
Pub: Business Courier
Ed: Dan Monk. **Description:** Fort Wright, Kentucky-based broadcasting company Local TV LLC has acquired 18 television stations since its founding in 2007, potentially boosting its chances of becoming a media empire. In the last twelve months that ended in March 2010, Local TV LLC has posted total revenues of $415 million. How Local TV LLC has entered into cost-sharing deals with other stations is also discussed.

3158 ■ *Matthews CATV Directory*
Pub: Marketwire
Released: Annual, Published in May and November. **Price:** $280, single issue blue and green; $415, individuals blue and green (one year); $740, two years blue and green; $350, single issue red plus green or blue. **Covers:** Cable television systems and pay television specialty channels, microwave, and satellite services in Canada.

3159 ■ *Media, Organizations and Identity*
Pub: Palgrave Macmillan
Ed: Lilie Chouliaraki, Mette Morsing. **Released:** January 19, 2010. **Price:** $90.00. **Description:** The mass media, press and television are a essential in the formation of corporate identity and the promotion of business image and reputation. This book offers a new perspective into the interrelationships between media and organizations over three dimensions: media as business, media in business and business in the media.

3160 ■ "Political Ads Big Boost to Local Media" in *Baltimore Business Journal* (Vol. 28, October 22, 2010, No. 24, pp. 1)
Pub: Baltimore Business Journal
Ed: Scott Dance. **Description:** Information about the intense demand for advertising time from political campaigns in Baltimore, Maryland is provided. The surge in political advertisement spending would mean big money for local broadcasters, because they see a surging demand for local advertising time for virtually any time of day.

3161 ■ "Prime-Time Exposure" in *Inc.* (March 2008, pp. 66, 68)
Pub: Gruner & Jahr USA Publishing
Ed: Adam Bluestein. **Description:** Product placement in television shows has increase sales for many companies. Tips for placing products or services into TV shows are explained: consider hiring an agency, target efforts, dream up a plot point, be ready to go on short notice, and work the niches.

3162 ■ "Ready, Aim, (Cool) Fire" in *Saint Louis Business Journal* (Vol. 32, September 2, 2011, No. 1, pp. 1)
Pub: Saint Louis Business Journal
Ed: E.B. Solomont. **Description:** Coolfire Originals' CEO Jeff Keane is co-producing 'Welcome Sweetie Pie's' with Los Angeles, California-based Pilgrims Films and Television Films for the Oprah Winfrey Network. The reality show focuses on restaurant owner Robbie Montgomery of Sweetie Pie's in St. Louis, Missouri.

3163 ■ "Recovery on Tap for 2010?" in *Orlando Business Journal* (Vol. 26, January 1, 2010, No. 31, pp. 1)
Pub: American City Business Journals
Ed: Melanie Stawicki Azam, Richard Bilbao, Christopher Boyd, Anjali Fluker. **Description:** Economic forecasts for Central Florida's leading business sectors in 2010 are presented. These sectors include housing, film and TV, sports business, law, restaurants, aviation, tourism and hospitality, banking and finance, commercial real estate, retail, health care, insurance, higher education, and manufacturing. According to some local executives, Central Florida's economy will slowly recover in 2010.

3164 ■ "Reds Hit Ratings Homer" in *Business Courier* (Vol. 27, July 30, 2010, No. 13, pp. 1)
Pub: Business Courier
Ed: Steve Watkins, James Ourand. **Description:** Cincinnati Reds fans have tuned in to their TVs and radios as their team made a hottest start to a season. The Reds TV ratings have increased 49 percent during the first six months of 2010 and continued to rise while the Reds' games broadcast on WLW-AM reported the highest average audience share per game of any Major League Baseball team.

3165 ■ "Storytelling Star of Show for Scripps" in *Business Courier* (Vol. 26, November 13, 2009, No. 29, pp. 1)
Pub: American City Business Journals, Inc.
Ed: Dan Monk. **Description:** Rich Boehne, CEO Of the EW Scripps Company in Cincinnati has authorized a new training program in storytelling for employees at Scripps' 10 television stations. He believes that the training will improve the quality of broadcasting content. His plans to improve quality of newspaper content are also discussed.

3166 ■ "Summit, Lions Gate are in Talks to Merge Studios" in *Wall Street Journal Eastern Edition* (November 29, 2011, pp. B2)
Pub: Dow Jones & Company Inc.
Ed: Erica Orden, Michelle Kung. **Description:** Movie studio Summit Entertainment LLC is in talks with television producer Lions Gate Entertainment Corporation about a possible merger. Previous talks have taken place, but no deal was ever reached. Such a deal would create a large, independent studio able to compete in the market with the big Hollywood giants.

3167 ■ "Television Broadcasting" in *MarketingMagazine* (Vol. 115, September 27, 2010, No. 13, pp. 16)
Pub: Rogers Publishing Ltd.
Description: Market statistics covering the Canadian television broadcasting industry are covered.

3168 ■ "Two Local Bakers Winners of TV's 'Cupcake Wars'" in *Toledo Blade* (July 6, 2011)
Pub: Toledo Times
Description: Winners of cable network Food Channel's Cupcake Wars, Lori Jacobs and Dana Iliev own Cake in a Cup in Toledo, Ohio. The partners shop features creative cupcakes with names such as Monkey Business, Pretty in Pink, and Tropical Getaway.

3169 ■ "Waco Pawn Shop Owners Say Reality Isn't Much Like 'Pawn Stars' TV Show" in *Waco Tribune-Herald* (August 15, 2010)
Pub: Waco Tribune-Herald
Ed: Mike Copeland. **Description:** Area pawn shop owners report that the television show on cable TV does not represent the true life operations of a pawn shop. The Las Vegas shop represented on TV boasts 30 employees and 21 on-call experts, which is not the case in reality.

3170 ■ *The Weather Channel*
Pub: Harvard Business School Press
Ed: Frank Batten with Jeffrey L. Cruikshank. **Released:** 2002. **Price:** $29.95. **Description:** Frank Batten illustrates the power of a resourceful growth strategy along with details the journey he successfully took his small, private newspaper into the cable industry.

3171 ■ "A Whiff of TV Reality" in *Houston Business Journal* (Vol. 40, January 22, 2010, No. 37, pp. A1)
Pub: American City Business Journals
Ed: Christine Hall. **Description:** Houston, Texas-based Waste Management Inc.'s president and chief operation officer, Larry O'Donnell shares some of his experience as CBS Television Network reality show 'Undercover Boss' participant. O'Donnell believes the show was a great way to show the customers how tough their jobs are and reveals that the most difficult job was being a sorter at the recycling center.

SOURCES OF SUPPLY

3172 ■ *FINDERBINDER—Arizona*
Pub: Rita Sanders Advertising Public Relations
Released: Annual. **Description:** "FINDERBINDER" directories are loose-leaf directories of broadcast and print media covering states or smaller areas published by companies, licensed to use the name and format by Finderbinder (see entry for "FINDERBINDER—San Diego"). Types of media covered include daily and weekly local and outstate newspapers; religious, ethnic, and labor papers; business, trade, sports, recreation, and general interest publications; college papers; and radio and television stations in Arizona. **Entries Include:** Publication or station name, names of management, editorial, and advertising personnel, deadlines, frequency or circulation as appropriate, and other data; cable TV listings. **Arrangement:** Classified by type of medium. **Indexes:** Publication or station name.

3173 ■ *FINDERBINDER—Greater Detroit*
Pub: C & E Communications Inc.
Contact: Sharon Castle, Publisher
Released: Annual, September; bimonthly updates. **Price:** $250, individuals set including outside Michigan. **Description:** "FINDERBINDER" directories are loose-leaf directories of broadcast and print media covering states or smaller areas published by companies, usually advertising and public relations firms, licensed to use the name and format by Finderbinder. Detroit's FINDERBINDER covers more than 440 media, including daily and weekly newspapers; religious, ethnic, and labor papers; business, trade, sports, recreation, and general interest publications; college papers; and radio and television stations in the seven-county Detroit metro area. **Entries Include:** Publication or station name, names of management, editorial, and advertising personnel, deadlines, frequency or circulation as appropriate, and other data; radio, TV, and cable TV listings give name of public service announcement (PSA) director, interview format programs. **Arrangement:** Classified by type of medium. **Indexes:** Publication or station name, geographical, cable by community.

3174 ■ *FINDERBINDER—Oklahoma*
Pub: FINDERBINDER of Oklahoma
Contact: Iris Park, Publisher
Released: Annual. **Description:** 'FINDERBINDER' directories are loose-leaf directories of broadcast and print media covering states or smaller areas published by companies, usually advertising and public relations firms, licensed to use the name and format by Finderbinder (see entry for 'FINDERBINDER—San Diego'). Types of media covered include daily and weekly local and outstate newspapers; religious, ethnic, and labor papers; business, trade, sports, recreation, and general interest publications; college papers; and radio and television stations in Oklahoma. **Entries Include:** Publication or station name, names of management, editorial, and advertising personnel, deadlines, frequency or circulation as appropriate, and other data; cable TV listings show homes served. **Arrangement:** Classified by type of medium. **Indexes:** Publication or station name.

TRADE PERIODICALS

3175 ■ *Cable Yellow Pages*
Pub: Teton Media Inc.
Contact: Glenn Schrader, Assoc. Pub.
Released: Annual. **Price:** $32.95. **Description:** Cable TV industry directory.

3176 ■ *Financial Manager for the Media Professional*
Pub: Broadcast Cable Financial Management Association
Ed: Janet Stilson, Editor, jstilson@bcfm.com. **Released:** Bimonthly. **Price:** $69. **Description:** Trade magazine for professionals in the broadcast and cable industry.

3177 ■ *Movie Entertainment*
Pub: Feature Publishing Ltd.
Contact: Nik Reitz
E-mail: nikr@movieentertainment.ca
Released: Monthly. **Price:** $17. **Description:** Consumer magazine used as a viewing guide for readers to find out what's on The Movie Network, A&E, Playboy and Viewer's Choice. Includes movies, music, and games. Content also covers a range of pop culture interests—celebrities, technology, happenings, trends, events and style, and what's hot and what's not.

3178 ■ *Russian Telecom Newsletter*
Pub: Information Gatekeepers Inc.
Contact: Jeremy Awori, Publisher
Ed: Prof. Sergei L. Galkin, Editor. **Released:** Monthly. **Price:** $695, U.S. and Canada; $745, elsewhere; $695 PDF email version. **Description:** Covers the telecommunications industry in Russia, including competition, government regulations, international business and ventures, cellular, satellites, and market intelligence. Also features new products and conference reports.

3179 ■ *TelevisionWeek*
Pub: Crain Communications Inc. (Detroit, Michigan)
Contact: Rance Crain, Pres/Ed.-in-Ch.
Released: Weekly. **Price:** $119; $171 Canada incl. GST; $309 other countries airmail. **Description:** Newspaper covering management, programming, cable and trends in the television and the media industry.

3180 ■ *TV Blueprint*
Pub: Wilen Media Corp.
Released: Monthly. **Description:** Magazine serving cable television subscribers and companies.

3181 ■ *TV Guide*
Pub: TV Guide Magazine
Contact: Gary Kleinman, VP, Assoc. Publisher
E-mail: gary.kleinman@tvguide.com
Released: Weekly. **Price:** $15.96 28 issues. **Description:** Special interest publication serving cable television customers and cable television system companies.

3182 ■ *TV International Daily*
Pub: Informa Publishing Group
Contact: Mr.
Released: Daily. **Price:** $1,995, U.S. via fax; $1,995, U.S. via e-mail; $2,495, U.S. via fax and e-mail. **Description:** Provides news on international television, cable, satellite, digital, and pay and pay-per-view. Remarks: Available via fax or e-mail.

3183 ■ *Utilities Telecommunications News*
Pub: Information Gatekeepers Inc.
Contact: Paul Polishuk, Managing Editor
Released: Monthly. **Price:** $695, U.S. and Canada; $745, elsewhere; $695 PDF email version. **Description:** Focuses on the role of utilities in telecommunications. Topics include government and regulations, business, and the Internet. Also features new products and conferences.

VIDEOCASSETTES/ AUDIOCASSETTES

3184 ■ *Cable TV, Video, and Imaging*
Filmakers Library, Inc.
124 E. 40th St.
New York, NY 10016
Ph:(212)808-4980
Free: 800-555-9815
Fax:(212)808-4983
URL: http://www.filmakers.com
Price: $5,000.00. **Description:** In 28 separate volumes, University of Colorado Adj. Prof. Gary Bardsley talks about trends in the cable industry including technology, policy, economics, roles, and responsibilities. **Availability:** VHS.

TRADE SHOWS AND CONVENTIONS

3185 ■ Broadcast Cable Financial Management Association Conference
Broadcast Cable Financial Management Association
550 Frontage Rd., Ste. 3600
Northfield, IL 60093
Ph:(847)716-7000
Fax:(847)716-7004
Co. E-mail: info@bcfm.com
URL: http://www.bcfm.com
Released: Annual. **Audience:** Business managers, CFOs. **Principal Exhibits:** Exhibits relating to the financial management of radio, television, and cable television operations, including issues such as industry - specific software, collection agencies, insurance, investments, banking, accounting firms and music licensing. **Dates and Locations:** 2011 May 15-17, Atlanta,, GA.

3186 ■ Cabletelevision Advertising Bureau - Cable Advertising Conference
Cabletelevision Advertising Bureau
830 3rd Ave., 2nd Fl.
New York, NY 10022
Ph:(212)508-1200
Fax:(212)832-3268
URL: http://www.thecab.tv/
Released: Annual. **Audience:** Cable television and advertising trade. **Principal Exhibits:** Cable television and advertising equipment, supplies, and services.

FRANCHISES AND BUSINESS OPPORTUNITIES

3187 ■ The Utility Company Ltd.
One Hines Rd., Ste. 101
Kanata, ON, Canada K2K 3C7
Ph:(613)591-9800
Fax:(613)591-3966
Co. E-mail: abradley@theutilitycompany.com
URL: http://www.theutilitycompany.com
No. of Franchise Units: 57. **No. of Company-Owned Units:** 1. **Founded:** 2006. **Franchised:** 2006. **Description:** Supplier of information technology delivered as a utility service to small and medium businesses, providing the required hardware, software and service for a monthly fee per user. Our Connected Office service suite empowers people to operate, communicate and manage their business more effectively. **Equity Capital Needed:** $45,119-$70,357. **Franchise Fee:** $39,000. **Royalty Fee:** 7%. **Training:** Yes.

LIBRARIES

3188 ■ Alliance for Community Media Library
666 11th St. NW, Ste. 740
Washington, DC 20001
Ph:(202)393-2650
Fax:(202)393-2653
Co. E-mail: sylvia@alliancecm.org
URL: http://www.alliancecm.org
Contact: Sylvia Strobel, Exec.Dir.
Scope: Cable television - community access, local origination, legislation, industry, franchising; public television; educational television; governmental access television. **Services:** Library not open to the public. **Holdings:** 6 books; 1 bound periodical volume. **Subscriptions:** 1 journal.

3189 ■ American Film Institute–Louis B. Mayer Library
2021 N. Western Ave.
Box 27999
Los Angeles, CA 90027-1657
Ph:(323)856-7654
Fax:(323)467-4578
URL: http://www.afi.com/about/library.aspx
Contact: Caroline Sisneros, Libn.
Scope: Moving pictures, television, video, cable, satellite. **Services:** Copying; Library open to the public. Indexing Service (microfiche); Film Production Index, 1930-1969 (card). **Holdings:** 14,000 books; 900 bound periodical volumes; 6000 motion picture and television scripts; 44 oral history transcripts; 535 seminar transcripts; 600 seminar audiotapes; 75 reels of microfilm. **Subscriptions:** 100 journals and other serials (approximately); 5 newspapers.

3190 ■ CBS Television Law Library
51 W. 52nd St., 36th Fl.
New York, NY 10019
Ph:(212)975-4260
Fax:(212)975-7292
URL: http://www.cbs.com
Contact: Marilee N. Martel, Mgr., Info.Svc.
Scope: Communications, copyright, cable television, entertainment law, broadcasting, intellectual property. **Services:** Copying; Library open to the public by appointment (LLAGNY and SLA members only). **Holdings:** 4800 books. **Subscriptions:** 30 journals and other serials; 5 newspapers.

3191 ■ Communications Institute–Phillip D. Greenleaf Communications Library
Marina Sta.
PO Box 472139
San Francisco, CA 94147-2139
Ph:(415)346-4466
Co. E-mail: comlibrary@aol.com
URL: http://www.nvo.com/cinst
Contact: Theodore S. Connelly, Dir.
Scope: Communications - education, cable television, history, languages of, media; children's art. **Services:** Library open only by appointment to professionals and students. **Holdings:** 13,000 cable TV vertical file items; 100 reports; 500 archival items; manuscripts. **Subscriptions:** 100 journals and other serials; 8 newspapers.

3192 ■ National Cable Television Institute Resource Center
9697 E. Mineral Ave.
Centennial, CO 80112
Ph:(303)797-9393
Free: (866)575-7206
URL: http://www.jonesncti.com
Contact: Glen R. Jones, CEO
Scope: Technical careers in broadband communications. **Services:** Library not open to the public. **Holdings:** 20,000 training manuals.

3193 ■ Quebec Province Communications et Societe–Centre de Documentation
1340 Boulevard St. Joseph, E.
Montreal, QC, Canada H2J 1M3
Ph:(514)524-8223
Fax:(514)524-8522
Co. E-mail: ocs@officecom.qc.ca
URL: http://www.officecom.qc.ca
Contact: Bertrand Ouellet, Dir.Gen.
Scope: Cinema, radio, television, cablevision, videotext, the press. **Services:** Copying; Library open to the media, with restrictions. **Holdings:** 6000 books; 400 bound periodical volumes; microfilm; unbound documents. **Subscriptions:** 60 journals and other serials; 10 newspapers.

Calligraphy Service

ASSOCIATIONS AND OTHER ORGANIZATIONS

3194 ■ Association for the Calligraphic Arts
26 Main St.
East Greenwich, RI 02818
Co. E-mail: aca@calligraphicarts.org
URL: http://www.calligraphicarts.org
Contact: Joan Merrell, Pres.
Purpose: Promotes the art of calligraphy. **Publications:** *The Newsletter* (quarterly).

3195 ■ Society of Scribes
PO Box 933
New York, NY 10150
Ph:(212)452-0139
Co. E-mail: info@societyofscribes.org
URL: http://www.societyofscribes.org
Contact: Cara Di Edwardo, Pres.
Description: Calligraphers, bookbinders, lettering artists, and individuals with an interest in book arts. Promotes calligraphy and related lettering arts. Collects and disseminates information. Conducts exhibitions, workshops, lecturers, programs, and publications. **Publications:** *Classes and Workshops* (semiannual); *Letters from New York* (semiannual); *NewSOS* (semiannual).

3196 ■ Washington Calligraphers Guild
PO Box 3688
Merrifield, VA 22116-3688
Co. E-mail: swerdloff@gmail.com
URL: http://www.calligraphersguild.org
Contact: Pamela Klinedinst, Pres.
Description: Calligraphers and individuals interested in calligraphy. Promotes the appreciation of calligraphy and its applications and history. Seeks to foster a greater understanding of calligraphy as an art. Conducts studies on calligraphy; sponsors charitable and educational programs. **Publications:** *Scripsit* (semiannual);Newsletter (monthly);Membership Directory (annual).

REFERENCE WORKS

3197 ■ Guild of Book Workers—Supplies and Services Directory
Pub: Guild of Book Workers Inc.
Contact: Catherine Burkhard
Ed: Bernadette G. Callery, Editor. **Released:** Irregular, Latest edition November 2008. **Price:** $15, individuals 2001 issue. **Covers:** More than 250 manufacturers and suppliers of products used in bookbinding, calligraphy, and repair and conservation of documents and books; coverage includes Canada. **Entries Include:** Name of firm, address, phone, products or services, minimum order requirements, shipping restrictions, whether catalog or samples are available. **Arrangement:** Geographical, then by product or service. **Indexes:** Alphabetical.

3198 ■ Society for Calligraphy—Membership Directory
Pub: Society for Calligraphy
Contact: DeAnn Singh
E-mail: describe25@aol.com
Released: Annual, September. **Covers:** About 1,200 members and societies interested in calligraphy, including calligraphers, illustrators, graphic artists, and curators; international coverage. **Entries Include:** For individual members—Name, address, phone, title. For societies—Contact name, address, phone; committee members. **Arrangement:** Alphabetical. **Indexes:** Personal name.

TRADE PERIODICALS

3199 ■ Amphora
Pub: Alcuin Society
Contact: Howard Greaves, Chairperson
E-mail: hgreaves@axion.net
Released: Quarterly. **Price:** Included in membership. **Description:** Carries articles about all aspects of the book and reading, including the book arts, private presses, book selling, book collecting, and notable library collections.

3200 ■ Colorado Calligraphers' Guild Newsletter
Pub: Colorado Calligraphers' Guild
Ed: Margaret Stookesberry, Editor. **Released:** Quarterly. **Price:** Included in membership. **Description:** Reports the business of the Guild. Supplies tips on techniques and materials used by calligraphers, and news of other calligraphic organizations. Recurring features include book reviews, workshop reprints, and listings of educational opportunities.

3201 ■ Guild of Book Workers Newsletter
Pub: Guild of Book Workers Inc.
Contact: Catherine Burkhard
Ed: Margaret Johnson, Editor. **Released:** Bimonthly, Every 2 months. **Price:** Included in membership. **Description:** Covers issues in book arts, binding, book conservation, calligraphy, and printing. Recurring features include letters to the editor, interviews, news of research, a calendar of events, reports of meetings, news of educational opportunities, job listings, book reviews, and notices of publications available.

3202 ■ Ink, Inc.
Pub: New Orleans Lettering Arts Association Inc.
Ed: Theresa P. Williams, Editor. **Released:** 3/year. **Price:** Included in membership. **Description:** Dedicated to promoting calligraphy and the fine art of lettering. Contains articles on such topics as copperplate calligraphy, paper for calligraphers, and Chinese ink lettering. Alerts calligraphers to new supplies and where to obtain them. Recurring features include profiles of successful calligraphers and typographers, news of the Association and its activities, announcements of calligraphy classes and exhibitions, and book reviews.

3203 ■ Valley Calligraphy Guild Newsletter
Pub: Valley Calligraphy Guild
Contact: Barbara Snow, Membership Officer
Released: 3/year. **Price:** Included in membership. **Description:** Dedicated to preserving the art of calligraphy. Contains tips and techniques on lettering, italic handwriting, design, color use, and such crafts as papermaking, bookmaking, and bookbinding. Offers articles on workshop reviews, supplies, projects, artists, and activities of the Guild. Recurring features include schedules of classes, meetings, workshops, shows, and news of the activities of other societies of interest. Remarks: Newsletter text is primarily handwritten in calligraphy.

VIDEOCASSETTES/ AUDIOCASSETTES

3204 ■ Learn & Earn with Calligraphy
Instructional Video
2219 C St.
Lincoln, NE 68502
Ph:(402)475-6570
Free: 800-228-0164
Fax:(402)475-6500
Co. E-mail: feedback@insvideo.com
URL: http://www.insvideo.com
Price: $39.95. **Description:** Demonstrates eight different techniques that can be used to learn and develop calligraphy skills to produce items such as invitations, certificates, awards, advertising, T-shirts, wine labels, and framed quotations. **Availability:** VHS.

LIBRARIES

3205 ■ Long Beach Public Library–Performing Arts Department
101 Pacific Ave.
Long Beach, CA 90822
Ph:(562)570-7500
Fax:(562)570-7408
Co. E-mail: rstewart@lbpl.org
URL: http://www.lbpl.org
Contact: Ruth Stewart, Dept.Libn.
Scope: Art history and techniques, music history and scores, dance, flower arranging, antiques, theater, moving pictures, sports. **Services:** Interlibrary loan; department open to the public with restrictions. **Holdings:** 34,103 books; 8624 bound scores; 7099 pieces of sheet music; 91,043 mounted pictures; 9000 videocassettes; 10,000 phonograph records; 5000 cassettes; 5500 CDs.

3206 ■ Rochester Institute of Technology–Melbert B. Cary, Jr. Graphic Arts Collection
Wallace Memorial Library
90 Lomb Memorial Dr.
Rochester, NY 14623-5604
Ph:(585)475-2408
Fax:(585)475-6900
Co. E-mail: dppwml@rit.edu
URL: http://library.rit.edu/cary
Contact: David Pankow, Cur.
Scope: Printing history, type specimens, typography, book arts, press books, calligraphy, papermaking, graphic arts, bookbinding. **Services:** Copying (limited); collection open to the public. **Holdings:** 50,000 books; 20 VF drawers of clippings; ephemera; pamphlets; 50 boxes of posters, broadsides, drawings; 400 boxes of correspondence and manuscript material. **Subscriptions:** 20 journals and other serials.

3207 ■ Society for Calligraphy Library
PO Box 64174
Los Angeles, CA 90064
Fax:(310)398-3506
Co. E-mail: resources@societyforcalligraphy.org
URL: http://www.societyforcalligraphy.com
Contact: Kathleen Dunning-Torbett, Libn.

Scope: Calligraphy, lettering, bookbinding, paper arts, and related fields. **Services:** Library not open to the public. **Holdings:** 450 volumes; slides; movies; videos.

3208 ■ Yale University–Arts Library I Special Collections
Robert B. Haas Family Arts Library, Lower Level
180 York St.
PO Box 208318
New Haven, CT 06520-8318
Ph:(203)432-4439
Fax:(203)432-0549
Co. E-mail: jae.rossman@yale.edu
URL: http://www.library.yale.edu/arts/specialcollections
Contact: Jae Jennifer Rossman, Asst.Dir., Spec.Coll.
Scope: Typography, book illustration and design, bookbinding, papermaking, bookplates, private presses, artists' books, conceptual books, and fine printing. **Services:** Collection open to the public. **Holdings:** 20,000 books; prints and broadsides; type specimens; archive of student printing, including masters' theses from School of Graphic Design and School of Photography at Yale; 1 million bookplates; Japanese prints; stage and costume designs. **Subscriptions:** 20 journals and other serials.

Camera Shop

ASSOCIATIONS AND OTHER ORGANIZATIONS

3209 ■ Photoimaging Manufacturers and Distributors Association
7600 Jericho Tpke., Ste. 301
Woodbury, NY 11797
Ph:(516)802-0895
Fax:(516)364-0140
Co. E-mail: jerry@pmda.com
URL: http://www.pmda.com
Contact: Jerry Grossman, Exec. Dir.

Description: Represents manufacturers, wholesalers, distributors, and importers of photographic equipment. Holds lecture meetings presenting programs on topics facing the photographic industry. Helps to further the consumer's interest in photography through its website and a traveling information booth.
.

3210 ■ PMA - The Worldwide Community of Imaging Associations
3000 Picture Pl.
Jackson, MI 49201-8853
Ph:(517)788-8100
Free: 800-762-9287
Fax:(517)788-8371
Co. E-mail: pma_membership@pmai.org
URL: http://www.pmai.org
Contact: Brian Wood, Pres.

Description: Retailers of photo and video equipment, film, and supplies; firms developing and printing film. Maintains hall of fame. Compiles statistics; conducts research and educational programs. **Publications:** *NAPET News* (bimonthly); *Photo Marketing Association International—Newsline* (semimonthly); *Photo Marketing Magazine* (monthly); *Sales Counter* (monthly); *Specialty Lab Update* (monthly); *Who's Who in Photographic Management* (annual).

REFERENCE WORKS

3211 ■ "Five Things...For Photo Fun" in *Hawaii Business* (Vol. 53, October 2007, No. 4, pp. 20)
Pub: Hawaii Business Publishing

Ed: Cathy S. Cruz-George. **Description:** Featured is a buyers guide of products used for capturing or displaying digital photos; products featured include the Digital Photo Wallet and Light Affection.

3212 ■ "Get the Picture: Here's How to Choose the Best Digital Camera For Your Needs" in *Black Enterprise* (November 2007)
Pub: Earl G. Graves Publishing Co. Inc.

Ed: Laura Turley. **Description:** Information for finding the best digital camera for your needs is provided. A professional photographer and digital media/photography teacher at the International Center of Photography recommends several cameras from each category.

3213 ■ "Olympus is Urged to Revise Board" in *Wall Street Journal Eastern Edition* (November 28, 2011, pp. B3)
Pub: Dow Jones & Company Inc.

Ed: Phred Dvorak. **Description:** Koji Miyata, once a director on the board of troubled Japanese photographic equipment company, is urging the company to reorganize its board, saying the present group should resign their board seats but keep their management positions. The company has come under scrutiny for its accounting practices and costly acquisitions.

3214 ■ "Our Gadget of the Week: Easy as a Snap" in *Barron's* (Vol. 90, September 13, 2010, No. 37, pp. 35)
Pub: Barron's Editorial & Corporate Headquarters

Ed: Jay Palmer. **Description:** SanMyPhotos.com offers a service whereby people can receive an empty box they can fill with photos then send back to the company to be stored digitally. The photos are returned to the customer with a disc containing the digital photographs. The service costs $150 for one box and $300 for three boxes.

3215 ■ "Play By Play: These Video Products Can Add New Life to a Stagnant Website" in *Black Enterprise* (Vol. 41, December 2010, No. 5)
Pub: Earl G. Graves Publishing Co. Inc.

Ed: Marcia Wade Talbert. **Description:** Web Visible, provider of online marketing products and services, cites video capability as the fastest-growing Website feature for small business advertisers. Profiles of various devices for adding video to a Website are included.

3216 ■ "Red One and The Rain Chronicles" in *Michigan Vue* (Vol. 13, July-August 2008, No. 4, pp. 30)
Pub: Entrepreneur Media Inc.

Ed: Evan Cornish. **Description:** Troy-based film school the Motion Picture Institute (MPI) implemented the latest technology by shooting the second of their trilogy, "The Rain Chronicles", on the Red One camera. This is the first feature film in Michigan to utilize this exciting new camera, which includes proprietary software for rendering and color correction. Brian K. Johnson heads up the visual effects team as visual effects supervisor and lead CG artist. His company, Dream Conduit Studios, had to tackle the task of employing the new work flow through a post-production pipeline that would allow him to attack complex visual effects shots, many of which were shot with a moving camera, a technique rarely seen in films at this budgetary level where the camera is traditionally locked off.

STATISTICAL SOURCES

3217 ■ *RMA Annual Statement Studies*
Pub: Robert Morris Associates (RMA)

Released: Annual. **Price:** $175.00 2006-07 edition, $105.00. **Description:** Contains composite balance sheets and income statements for more than 360 industries, including the accounting, auditing, and bookkeeping industries. Also contains five years of comparative historical data for discerning trends. Includes 16 commonly used ratios, computed for most of the size groupings for nearly every industry.

TRADE PERIODICALS

3218 ■ *Light and Shade*
Pub: Pictorial Photographers of America

Ed: Sylvia Mavis, Editor. **Released:** Monthly. **Price:** Included in membership. **Description:** Designed to help amateur and professional photographers perfect their photographic techniques. Carries how-to articles and information on photography equipment. Recurring features include organizational news, announcements of educational opportunities, and book reviews.

3219 ■ *Professional Photographer*
Pub: Professional Photographers of America Inc.
Contact: Karisa Gilmer, managing editorager of Sales
E-mail: kgilmer@ppa.com

Released: Monthly. **Price:** $19.95 print (U.S.); $35.95 print (Canada). **Description:** Magazine for photographers.

VIDEOCASSETTES/ AUDIOCASSETTES

3220 ■ *Home Video Hits: Great Ideas for Creating Better Home Videos*
Leslie T. McClure
PO Box 1223
Pebble Beach, CA 93953
Ph:(831)656-0553
Fax:(831)656-0555
Co. E-mail: leslie@411videoinfo.com
URL: http://www.411videoinfo.com

Released: 1997. **Price:** $19.95. **Description:** Demonstrates a variety of camera angles, focus options, camera movements and in-camera editing techniques. **Availability:** VHS.

TRADE SHOWS AND CONVENTIONS

3221 ■ Photo Marketing Association International Annual Convention and Trade Show
Photo Marketing Association International
3000 Picture Pl.
Jackson, MI 49201
Ph:(517)788-8100
Fax:(517)788-8371
Co. E-mail: PMA_Trade_Exhibits@pmai.org
URL: http://www.pmai.org

Released: Annual. **Audience:** Trade professionals from the following groups: photo/video/optics/imaging products retailers; photo processing equipment and related service groups. **Principal Exhibits:** Profile of exhibitors: film, cameras and photo accessory manufacturers and distributors; photo processing equipment and materials suppliers; digital imaging hardware and software marketers; studio imaging equipment distributors; and original equipment manufacturers (OEMs).

Campground Management

ASSOCIATIONS AND OTHER ORGANIZATIONS

3222 ■ American Camp Association
5000 State Rd., 67 N
Martinsville, IN 46151-7902
Ph:(765)342-8456
Free: 800-428-CAMP
Fax:(765)342-2065
Co. E-mail: 2020@acacamps.org
URL: http://www.acacamps.org
Contact: Peter Surgenor CCD, Pres.
Description: Camp owners, directors, program directors, businesses, and students interested in resident and day camp programming for youth and adults. Conducts camp standards. Offers educational programs in areas of administration, staffing, child development, promotion, and programming. **Publications:** *Guide to Accredited Camps* (annual).

3223 ■ Best Holiday Trav-L-Park Association
4809 E Marshall Dr.
Vestal, NY 13850
Ph:(607)241-7531
Co. E-mail: info@bestholiday.org
URL: http://www.bestholiday.org
Description: Independently owned campgrounds. Seeks to increase business of members through networking and the establishment of a common logo.
.

3224 ■ Canadian Camping Association–Association des Camps du Canada
4545 Pierre de Coubertin
CP 1000 Succursale M
Montreal, QC, Canada H1V 3R2
Ph:(514)252-3113
Free: 800-361-3586
Fax:(514)252-1650
Co. E-mail: info@camps.qc.ca
URL: http://www.ccamping.org
Contact: Jeff Bradshaw, Pres.
Description: Commercial camps and nonprofit organizations and individuals with an interest in camping. Promotes the "growth and development of organized camping for all populations in Canada." Furthers the interests and welfare of children, youth and adults through camping. Functions as a coordinating body for organized camping nationwide. Develops and enforces standards of practice and facilities among commercial camps; provides guidance, advocacy, and resources for camping leaders. Offers services to members including discount insurance, credit card, and online programs. Compiles industry statistics; operates bookstore.

3225 ■ Canadian Family Camping Federation
PO Box 397
Rexdale, ON, Canada M9W 5L4
Co. E-mail: cfcf@canada.com
URL: http://www.cfcf.cjb.net
Description: Families with an interest in camping. Promotes camping as a recreational pastime. Serves as a clearinghouse on family camping opportunities; conducts social and educational programs.

3226 ■ Christian Camp and Conference Association
PO Box 62189
Colorado Springs, CO 80962-2189
Ph:(719)260-9400
Fax:(719)260-6398
Co. E-mail: info@ccca.org
URL: http://www.ccca.org
Contact: Greg Anderson, Chm.
Description: Exists to proclaim the power of the Christian camp and conference experience and to interpret its benefits to the Church and the public at large; and to provide leaders at member organizations with ongoing encouragement, professional training, and timely resources. **Publications:** *Executive Briefing* (monthly).

3227 ■ Family Campers and RVers
4804 Transit Rd., Bldg. 2
Depew, NY 14043
Ph:(716)668-6242
Free: 800-245-9755
Co. E-mail: fcrvnat@verizon.net
URL: http://www.fcrv.org
Contact: Jack Smye, Pres.
Description: Family campers and hikers; others interested in outdoor activities. Promotes and enhances the experience of "family" style camping/RVing. **Publications:** *Camping Today* (monthly).

3228 ■ KampGround Owners Association
3416 Primm Ln.
Birmingham, AL 35216
Ph:(205)824-0022
Free: 800-678-9976
Co. E-mail: info@koaowners.org
URL: http://www.koaowners.org
Contact: William Ranieri, Exec. Dir.
Description: Represents KOA franchisees. Offers seminars and workshops. Compiles statistics; maintains speakers' bureau, charitable program, and several committees. .

3229 ■ National Association of RV Parks and Campgrounds
9085 E Mineral Cir., Ste. 200
Centennial, CO 80112
Ph:(303)681-0401
Free: 800-395-2267
Fax:(303)681-0426
Co. E-mail: lprofaizer@arvc.org
URL: http://www.arvc.org
Contact: Paul Bambei, Pres./CEO
Description: Regular members are commercial campground owners and operators; associate members are manufacturers and suppliers of campground products and services. Promotes and protects the interests of the commercial campground industry, with government officials and agencies, campers, the press and the general public. Represents the campground industry in contact with RV manufacturers, RV dealers and other branches of the camping business. Offers specialized education. Works to develop better, more efficient, more profitable campground management and business methods. Compiles statistics. Operates National RV Park and Campground Industry Education Foundation and a Certified Park Operators program. **Publications:** *ARVC Report* (monthly); *Direct Line* (monthly); *Membership Directory and Buyer's Guide* (annual).

3230 ■ National Forest Recreation Association
PO Box 488
Woodlake, CA 93286
Ph:(559)564-2365
Fax:(559)564-2048
Co. E-mail: info@nfra.org
URL: http://www.nfra.org
Contact: Marily Reese, Exec. Dir.
Description: Owners and operators of resorts, winter sports areas, marinas, campgrounds, stores, river trip outfitters, packer-outfitters, restaurants, and motels located on or adjacent to federal land. Participates in trade and public relations matters that is of interest to members, including legislation and relationships with U.S. agencies; state and local officials in matters of taxation, insurance, finance, health, and building requirements; and employment. .

3231 ■ North American Family Campers Association
PO Box 318
Lunenburg, MA 01462
Ph:(401)828-0579
Co. E-mail: ka1rcy1@msn.com
URL: http://www.nafca.org
Contact: Ron Barratt, Pres.
Description: Families interested in camping; sustaining members are manufacturers and dealers of camping equipment, campgrounds, and other services related to family campers. Works to improve camping conditions, inform members about camping areas, equipment, and techniques, promote good camping manners, and foster fellowship among family campers. Encourages and guides development of campgrounds; cooperates with conservation and legislative agencies for the good of camping. Conducts conservation and antilitter programs. **Publications:** *Campfire Chatter* (monthly).

REFERENCE WORKS

3232 ■ *Camping Magazine—Buyer's Guide Issue*
Pub: American Camp Association
Released: Annual, September/October Issue; Latest edition 2011. **Price:** $7.25, individuals. **Publication Includes:** List of over 200 firms providing sporting equipment, food, infirmary supplies, etc. For children's and other organized camps. **Entries Include:** Company name, address, product or service provided. **Arrangement:** Alphabetical. **Indexes:** Product.

3233 ■ *Frontier West/Great Plains & Mountain Region Campground Guide*
Pub: Woodall Publications Corp.
Released: Annual, latest edition 2010. **Price:** $4.95, individuals 2010 edition. **Covers:** Campground site listings for Colorado, Montana, Nebraska, North

Dakota, South Dakota, Utah, and Wyoming. **Entries Include:** Site name, address, phone, facility description, driving directions, camping fees, attractions and seasonal events. It also includes, new for 2004, "Discover Outdoor RV Adventures" and Woodall's Guide to Seasonal Sites.

3234 ■ *Guide to ACA-Accredited Camps*
Pub: American Camp Association

Released: Annual, January; Latest edition 2004. **Covers:** Over 2,400 summer camps. **Entries Include:** Name of camp, address, phone, fax, email addresses, age and sex of children accepted, rates, season, capacity, facilities, programs, activities offered and camp philosophy. **Arrangement:** Geographical, then by day or resident camp. **Indexes:** Activity, special clientele, camp name, specific disabilities.

3235 ■ *Guide to Summer Camps and Summer Schools*
Pub: Porter Sargent Publishers Inc.
Contact: J. Yonce, President

Released: Biennial, Latest edition 32nd, 2010-2011. **Price:** $45, individuals cloth, plus shipping; $27, individuals paper, plus shipping. **Covers:** 1,700 residential summer camping, recreational, pioneering, and academic programs in the United States and Canada, as well as travel programs worldwide. Includes special programs for the handicapped, maladjusted, and those with learning disabilities. **Entries Include:** Program name, address, phone, fax, enrollment, director's name, title and winter address, fees, length of camping period, type of housing, whether camp has counselor-in-training program, year established, description of programs, sex and age range, amenities, URL, e-mail, term length, descriptive paragraph. **Arrangement:** Classified by type of camp, or school then geographical, cross indexed by enrollment, age ranges, sexes accepted. **Indexes:** Alphabetical by school name, features, religion, military programs.

3236 ■ *New York/New England & Eastern Canada Campground Guide*
Pub: Woodall Publications Corp.

Released: Annual, Latest edition 2010. **Price:** $9.95 retail price; $4.95 discounted price. **Covers:** Campground site listings for New England states, including Maine, Connecticut, Massachusetts, New Hampshire, New York, Rhode Island, Vermont, and Ontario. **Entries Include:** Site name, address, phone, facility description, driving directions, camping fees, attractions and seasonal events.

3237 ■ *Who's Who in Grounds Management*
Pub: Professional Grounds Management Society
Contact: Thomas C. Shaner, Exec. Dir.

Released: Annual, October. **Covers:** About 1400 managers of large institutional grounds, grounds maintenance firms, parks, recreation areas, golf courses, cemeteries, botanical gardens, arboretums, and other private and public grounds; educators; certified grounds managers; researchers and horticulturists; and government and university officials engaged in extension services; coverage includes Canada. **Entries Include:** Name, home address, office address, title or affiliation. **Arrangement:** Alphabetical. **Indexes:** Geographical.

3238 ■ *Woodall's Campground Directory*
Pub: Woodall Publications Corp.

Released: Annual, Latest edition 2011. **Price:** $14. 95, individuals North American edition; $25.95, individuals retail price. **Covers:** Private and public campgrounds in the United States, Canada, and Mexico. Separate listing of over 15,000 service locations for recreational vehicles. Three major editions: North America; eastern United States and Canada; and western United States, Canada, and Mexico. Also editions for New York, New England, Mid-Atlantic, Great Lakes, Great Plains and Mountain States, Far West, Frontier West, South, Canada. These eight regional editions cover all of the United States and Canada. **Entries Include:** Name of campground, location, directions from major highways, camping rates per night, ratings of facilities and of recreation. **Arrangement:** Geographical.

3239 ■ *Woodall's Canada Campground Guide*
Pub: Woodall Publications Corp.

Released: Latest edition 2010. **Price:** $8.96, individuals discounted; $9.95, individuals retail price. **Covers:** Campground site listings for all Canadian provinces. **Entries Include:** Site name, address, phone, facility description, driving directions, camping fees, attractions and seasonal events.

3240 ■ *Woodall's Far West Campground Guide*
Pub: Woodall Publications Corp.

Released: Annual, Latest edition 2010. **Price:** $4.95, individuals; $9.95 retail price. **Covers:** Campground site listings for the Far West U.S., including Alaska, Arizona, California, Idaho, Nevada, Oregon, Washington, and British Columbia, Mexico, and the Yukon. **Entries Include:** Site name, address, phone, facility description, driving directions, camping fees, attractions and seasonal events.

3241 ■ *Woodall's Frontier West/Great Plains & Mountain Region Campground Guide*
Pub: Woodall Publications Corp.

Released: Latest edition 2010. **Price:** $4.95, individuals; $9.95, individuals retail price. **Covers:** Campground site listings for Arkansas, Kansas, Missouri, New Mexico, Oklahoma, Texas, and Mexico. **Entries Include:** Site name, address, phone, facility description, driving directions, camping fees, attractions and seasonal events.

3242 ■ *Woodall's Great Lakes Regional Campground Guide*
Pub: Woodall Publications Corp.

Released: Annual, Latest edition 2010. **Price:** $4.95, individuals; $9.95, individuals retail price. **Covers:** Campground site listings for Great Lakes states, including Illinois, Indiana, Iowa, Michigan, Minnesota, Ohio, and Wisconsin. **Entries Include:** Site name, address, phone, facility description, driving directions, camping fees, attractions and seasonal events.

3243 ■ *Woodall's Mid-Atlantic Regional Campground Guide*
Pub: Woodall Publications Corp.

Released: Annual, latest edition 2010. **Price:** $4.95, individuals; $9.95 retail price. **Covers:** Campground site listings for Mid-Atlantic states, including Delaware, District of Columbia, Maryland, New Jersey, Pennsylvania, Virginia, and West Virginia. **Entries Include:** Site name, address, phone, facility description, driving directions, camping fees, attractions and seasonal events.

3244 ■ *Woodall's South Campground Guide*
Pub: Woodall Publications Corp.

Released: Annual, Latest edition 2010. **Price:** $9.95, individuals Retail price; $4.95, individuals Discounted. **Covers:** Campground site listings for the 9 Southern U.S. states, including Alabama, Florida, Georgia, Kentucky, Louisiana, Mississippi, North Carolina, South Carolina, and Tennessee. **Entries Include:** Site name, address, phone, facility description, driving directions, camping fees, attractions and seasonal events.

3245 ■ *YMCA Resident Camp Directory*
Pub: Camping Programs

Ed: Robert Telleen, Editor, telleen@ymcausa.org. **Released:** updated weekly. **Entries Include:** Association name, camp name, address and phone of winter office, camp location and summer address and phone, name of director, seasons of operation, capacity; whether coed or restricted to boys or girls, or available for family and adult camping; special programs offered. **Database Covers:** Over 235 resident camps and conference and retreat centers operated by local YMCA associations in the United States. **Arrangement:** Classified by type of camp (resident, family, conference centers).

TRADE PERIODICALS

3246 ■ *Campgroundata*
Pub: Campground Data Resource

Ed: Dale S. Bourdette, Editor, dale_bourdette@worldnet.att.net. **Released:** Bimonthly. **Description:** Provides information for campground buyers and sellers to help them make informed buy or sell decisions.

3247 ■ *Camping Magazine*
Pub: American Camp Association

Released: Bimonthly. **Price:** $29.95 U.S. mainland; $56 two years U.S. mainland; $48 Alaska, Hawaii, Puerto Rico; Canada & Mexico; $92 two years Alaska, Hawaii, Puerto Rico; Canada & Mexico; $54 other countries; $104 other countries 2 years. **Description:** Magazine on organized camp management.

3248 ■ *InSite*
Pub: Christian Camp and Conference Association

Ed: Martha Krienke, Editor, editor@ccca.org. **Released:** Bimonthly. **Price:** $29.95 nonmembers; $39.95 out of country non-members; $4.95 single issue. **Description:** Religious magazine covering Christian camps and conferences.

3249 ■ *Trailer Life*
Pub: TL Enterprises Inc.
Contact: Terry Thompson, VP, Sales

Released: Monthly. **Price:** $15.97; $27.97 two years. **Description:** Magazine for recreational vehicle (RV) enthusiasts.

3250 ■ *Woodall's Northeast Outdoors*
Pub: Woodall Publications Corp.

Released: Bimonthly. **Price:** $20. **Description:** Magazine serving campers and RVers in the Northeast.

TRADE SHOWS AND CONVENTIONS

3251 ■ American Camping Association Conference & Exhibits
American Camping Association
5000 State Rd., 67 N.
Martinsville, IN 46151-7902
Ph:(765)342-8456
Free: 800-428-2267
Fax:(765)342-2065
Co. E-mail: exhibitors@ACAcamps.org
URL: http://www.acacamps.org

Released: Annual. **Audience:** Camp directors, counselors, and exhibitors. **Principal Exhibits:** Arts and crafts, computer software, sporting goods, waterfront equipment, insurance imprinted wear, bedding, and food.

3252 ■ California Travel Parks Association Convention and Trade Show
California Travel Parks Association
PO Box 5648
Auburn, CA 95604
Ph:(530)885-1624
Free: 888-782-9287
Fax:(530)823-6331
Co. E-mail: info@rvandcampoutwest.com
URL: http://www.camp-california.com

Released: Annual. **Audience:** Campgrounds and recreational vehicle parks in the western United States, including CA, NV, OR, WA, MT, ID, UT, and WY. **Principal Exhibits:** Equipment, supplies, and services for the recreational vehicle industry.

FRANCHISES AND BUSINESS OPPORTUNITIES

3253 ■ Kampgrounds of America, Inc
550 N 31st St.
PO Box 30558
Billings, MT 59114
Ph:(406)248-7444
Free: 800-548-7239
Fax:(406)254-7440

No. of Franchise Units: 482. **No. of Company-Owned Units:** 27. **Founded:** 1961. **Franchised:** 1962. **Description:** Franchisor of campgrounds. **Equity Capital Needed:** $200,000+. **Franchise Fee:** $7,750-$22,500. **Financial Assistance:** No. **Training:** Yes.

3254 ■ Yogi Bear's Jellystone Park Camp-Resorts
Leisure Systems, Inc.
50 W TechneCenter Dr., Ste. G
Milford, OH 45150
Ph:(513)831-2100
Free: 800-626-3720
Fax:(513)576-8670
URL: http://www.jellystonefranchise.com

No. of Franchise Units: 71. **Founded:** 1969. **Franchised:** 1970. **Description:** Leisure Systems, Inc. holds an exclusive license to franchise Yogi Bear's Jellystone Park Camp/Resorts in the US and Canada. Presently, there are 70 units in the U.S. and 3 in Canada. **Equity Capital Needed:** $25,000+. **Franchise Fee:** $20,000. **Financial Assistance:** Yes. **Training:** Franchisees are required to attend a 5 day training program held at the home office in Cincinnati, OH. Additional onsite training is also conducted for a period of 2-3 days.

LIBRARIES

3255 ■ American Camp Association Library
5000 State Rd., 67 N.
Martinsville, IN 46151-7902
Ph:(765)349-3313
Fax:(765)342-2065
Co. E-mail: psmith@acacamps.org
URL: http://www.acacamps.org
Contact: Peg Smith, CEO

Scope: Camping, ecosystems. **Holdings:** Figures not available.

ASSOCIATIONS AND OTHER ORGANIZATIONS

3256 ■ American Association of Candy Technologists
PO Box 266
Princeton, WI 54968
Ph:(920)295-6969
Fax:(920)295-6843
Co. E-mail: aactinfo@gomc.com
URL: http://www.aactcandy.org
Contact: Allen R. Allured, Treas.

Description: Candy technologists who seek to further the education of the technical community of the confectionery industry. .

3257 ■ American Wholesale Marketers Association
2750 Prosperity Ave., Ste. 530
Fairfax, VA 22031
Ph:(703)208-3358
Free: 800-482-2962
Fax:(703)573-5738
Co. E-mail: info@awmanet.org
URL: http://www.awmanet.org
Contact: Bill Marshall, Pres.

Description: Represents the interests of distributors of convenience-related products. Its members include wholesalers, retailers, manufacturers, brokers and allied organizations from across the U.S. and abroad. Programs include strong legislative representation in Washington and a broad spectrum of targeted education, business and information services. Sponsors the country's largest show for candy and convenience related products in conjunction with its semi-annual convention. **Publications:** *Buying Guide and Membership Directory* (annual).

3258 ■ National Confectioners Association of the U.S.
1101 30th St. NW, Ste. 200
Washington, DC 20007
Ph:(202)534-1440
Fax:(202)337-0637
Co. E-mail: info@candyusa.org
URL: http://www.candyusa.org
Contact: Lawrence T. Graham, Pres.

Description: Represents manufacturers of confectionery products; suppliers to the industry. Conducts research and technical and governmental services; provides information to the public; conducts annual confectionery technology course at the University of Wisconsin, Madison; gathers statistics on the industry. **Publications:** *A Year of Confectionery* (annual).

3259 ■ National Confectionery Sales Association
10225 Berea Rd., Ste. B
Cleveland, OH 44102
Ph:(216)631-8200
Fax:(216)631-8210
Co. E-mail: info@candyhalloffame.org
URL: http://www.candyhalloffame.org
Contact: Michael F. Gilmore, Dir./Chm.

Description: Salespersons, brokers, sales managers, wholesalers, and manufacturers in the candy industry. Maintains Candy Hall of Fame. **Publications:** *National Confectionery Sales Association of America-Journal* (annual).

3260 ■ PMCA: An International Association of Confectioners
2980 Linden St., Ste. E3
Bethlehem, PA 18017
Ph:(610)625-4655
Fax:(610)625-4657
Co. E-mail: info@pmca.com
URL: http://www.pmca.com
Contact: W. David Hess, Chm.

Description: Manufacturers and suppliers of confectionery and chocolate products. Conducts research and educational programs. **Publications:** *Annual Production Conference Proceedings* (annual); *PMCA News Update* (quarterly).

3261 ■ Retail Confectioners International
2053 S Waverly, Ste. C
Springfield, MO 65804
Ph:(417)883-2775
Free: 800-545-5381
Fax:(417)883-1108
Co. E-mail: info@retailconfectioners.org
URL: http://www.retailconfectioners.org
Contact: Kelly Brinkmann, Exec. Dir.

Description: Manufacturing retail confectioners who make and sell their own candies through directly-owned retail candy shops; associates are suppliers to the industry. Provides education, promotion and legislative and information service. Monitors legislative activities that affect the industry at state and national levels. Holds comprehensive two-week course and one-week specialized course on retail candy making biennially. .

REFERENCE WORKS

3262 ■ *Candy Buyers' Directory*
Pub: Manufacturing Confectioner Publishing Corp.

Released: Annual, latest edition 2011. **Price:** $80, individuals. **Covers:** Wholesale confectionery manufacturers and candy importers. **Entries Include:** Company name, address, phone, name of sales manager (for manufacturers and importers), and products and brand names manufactured or distributed. Broker and importer listings also show territory covered and countries from which imported. **Arrangement:** Alphabetical; brokers are listed geographically. **Indexes:** Brand, product, brokers, manufacturer.

3263 ■ *Candy Industry Buyer's Guide*
Pub: BNP Media
Contact: Bernard Pacyniak, Editor-in-Chief
E-mail: bpacyniak@stagnito.com

Released: Annual, Latest edition 2010. **Publication Includes:** List of approximately 682 suppliers of ingredients, equipment, and services to the candy industry. **Entries Include:** Company name, address, phone. **Arrangement:** Alphabetical. **Indexes:** Product.

3264 ■ "Cold Stone in Licensing Agreement with Turin Chocolates" in *Ice Cream Reporter* (Vol. 22, December 20, 2008, No. 1, pp. 2)
Pub: Ice Cream Reporter

Description: Cold Stone Creamery and Turin Chocolatier are teaming up to offer a new line of chocolate truffles under the Cold Stone label. The treats will feature four the most popular Cold Stone flavors: Coffee Lovers Only, Chocolate Devotion, Our Strawberry Blonde, and Peanut Butter Cup Perfection.

3265 ■ *Distribution Channels Buying Guide & AWMA Membership Directory*
Pub: American Wholesale Marketers Association
Contact: Joan R. Fay, Assoc. Publisher and Bus. Mgr.
E-mail: joanf@awmanet.org

Released: Monthly, except January/February and August/September,10/yr. **Price:** $36, individuals domestic (within the U.S. and territories); $66, individuals Canada/international. **Publication Includes:** List of 3,000 manufacturers, suppliers, brokers, and wholesalers of confectionery, tobacco, and snack products; state associations of the candy and tobacco industry; industry events calendar. **Entries Include:** Firm name, address, phone, fax, product line carried, description of products. **Arrangement:** Separate alphabetical sections for members, associations, and suppliers. **Indexes:** Distribution Channels magazine 2001 editorial index.

3266 ■ "Hyde Park Hungry for Expansion at Cap" in *Business First-Columbus* (October 12, 2007, pp. A1)
Pub: American City Business Journals, Inc.

Ed: Dan Eaton. **Description:** The Cap, an area developed for the retail and restaurant industry, is experiencing major changes such as Hyde Park Restaurant System's planned expansion, and the expected departure of other tenants. The expansion of Hyde Park will lead to the relocation of Schakolad Chocolate Factory.

3267 ■ "Juicy Feud; Deal Caps Years of Rancor in Wrigley Gum Dynasty" in *Crain's Chicago Business* (Vol. 31, May 5, 2008, No. 18, pp. 1)
Pub: Crain Communications, Inc.

Ed: David Sterrett. **Description:** Discusses the sale of Wm. Wrigley Jr. Co. to Mars Inc. and Warren Buffett for $23 billion as well as the intra-family feuding which has existed for nearly a decade since William Wrigley Jr. took over as CEO of the company following his father's death.

3268 ■ "Kaminsky Back in the Business of Selling Her Chocolate Treats" in *Business First Buffalo* (October 5, 2007, pp. 4)
Pub: American City Business Journals, Inc.

Ed: Tracey Drury. **Description:** Loretta Kaminsky, the original owner of Lou-Retta's Custom Chocolates brand, has decided to bring her products back into the market after winning a breach of contract lawsuit against Art Coco. Kaminsky sold her business to Art Coco in 2003, agreeing to the deal that Kaminsky will promote the products for two years in exchange for royalties and Art Coco's maintaining of product quality. Details of the distribution agreement with Wegmans, which will reintroduce Kaminsky's products are presented.

3269 ■ *Manufacturing Confectioner—Directory of Ingredients, Equipment and Packaging*
Pub: Manufacturing Confectioner Publishing Corp.
Ed: Kate Allured, Editor. **Released:** Annual, July. **Price:** $50, individuals. **Publication Includes:** Suppliers of machinery, equipment, raw materials, and supplies to the confectionery industry; laboratory instrumentation and services. **Entries Include:** Company name, address, phone, telex, fax. **Arrangement:** Separate alphabetical sections for raw materials, equipment, agents, packaging, laboratory instrumentation, and services. **Indexes:** Product, trade name.

3270 ■ "The Oracle's Endgame; Wrigley Investment Isn't What Many Call a Classic Buffett Play" in *Crain's Chicago Business* (May 5, 2008)
Pub: Crain Communications, Inc.
Ed: Ann Saphir. **Description:** Discusses Warren Buffett's deal with Mars Inc. to buy Wm. Wrigley Jr. Co., a move which would make Mr. Buffett a minority shareholder in a privately held company, a departure from his typical investment strategy. Mr. Buffett's Berkshire Hathaway Inc. agreed to provide $4.4 billion to help finance the $23 billion deal to pay another $2.1 billion for an equity stake in the company once it became a subsidiary of Mars.

3271 ■ *Progressive Grocer's Marketing Guidebook*
Pub: Trade Dimensions
Released: Annual, Latest edition 2011. **Covers:** Over 1,000 U.S. and Canadian supermarket chains, large independents and wholesalers; also includes 350 specialty distributors include smaller food wholesalers, food brokers, non-food distributors, and candy/tobacco/media distributors and over 15,000 key executives and buyers. **Entries Include:** For retailers and wholesalers—Company name, address, phone, email and websites, number of stores operated or served, areas of operation, major grocery supplier, three-year financial summary, buying policies, private label information, lists of executives, buyers, and merchandisers. For specialty distributors—Name, address, phone, list of key personnel including buyers' categories, list of items handled, URL. **Arrangement:** Alphabetical by hierarchy, geographical by eight regions and 50 market areas. **Indexes:** Grocery related organizations, chain and wholesalers, state index, store operating name/parent company reference.

3272 ■ "Shari's Berries Founder Shuts Last of Her Stores" in *Sacramento Business Journal* (Vol. 28, September 2, 2011, No. 27, pp. 1)
Pub: Sacramento Business Journal
Ed: Kelly Johnson. **Description:** Sacramento, California-based Shari's Berries owner Shari Fitzpatrick closed the company's last three stores called The Berry Factory. Fitzpatrick also filed for business bankruptcy protection. The weak economy is blamed for the company's failure.

3273 ■ "The Sky's the Limit" in *Retail Merchandiser* (Vol. 51, July-August 2011, No. 4, pp. 64)
Pub: Phoenix Media Corporation
Ed: John Capizzi. **Description:** Mars Retail Group (MRG) is the licensing division handling M&M's Brand Candies. Since taking over the brand they have expanded from 12 licensees to 50 licensees with new offerings.

3274 ■ "Wrigley's a Rich Meal for Mars" in *Crain's Chicago Business* (Vol. 31, May 5, 2008, No. 18, pp. 2)
Pub: Crain Communications, Inc.
Ed: Steven R. Strahler. **Description:** Mars Inc. will have to manage wisely in order to make their acquisition of Wm. Wrigley Jr. Co. profitable due to the high selling price of Wrigley which far exceeds the industry norm. Statistical data included.

TRADE PERIODICALS

3275 ■ *Candy Industry*
Pub: BNP Media
Released: Monthly. **Description:** Magazine serving candy industry management.

3276 ■ *Convenience Distribution*
Pub: American Wholesale Marketers Association
Contact: Traci Carneal, Editor-in-Chief
E-mail: tracic@awmanet.org
Released: 10/yr. **Price:** $36 domestic; $66 other countries. **Description:** For service based distributors marketing to the retail trade.

3277 ■ *Fancy Food & Culinary Products*
Pub: Talcott Communication Corp.
Contact: Erika Flynn, Contributing Ed.
Released: Monthly. **Price:** $26; $37 two years; $47 Canada 3 years; $32 Canada; $60 other countries. **Description:** Trade magazine for specialty food retailers.

3278 ■ *Quick Topics Newsletter*
Pub: American Wholesale Marketers Association
Ed: Barbara Valakos, Editor, barbarav@awmanet.org. **Released:** 12/year. **Price:** Included in membership. **Description:** Provides wholesalers of candy and tobacco products, brokers, salespersons, and manufacturers with industry news. Recurring features include news of members and notices of Association activities, events, awards, and research and educational programs.

TRADE SHOWS AND CONVENTIONS

3279 ■ International Fancy Food and Confection Show/Winter
National Association for the Specialty Food Trade, Inc.
120 Wall St., 27th Fl.
New York, NY 10005
Ph:(212)482-6440
Fax:(212)482-6459
URL: http://www.fancyfoodshows.com
Released: Annual. **Audience:** Retailers, brokers, importers, buyers, chefs, caterers and related personnel. **Principal Exhibits:** Pates, cheeses, specialty meats and seafood, condiments, sauces, mustards, vinegars, chocolates, fine candies, biscuits, cookies, cakes, jams, jellies, preserves, coffees, teas, fruits, nuts, special beverages, beer, wine, ice creams, desserts, and cooking accessories.

FRANCHISES AND BUSINESS OPPORTUNITIES

3280 ■ AmeriCandy Retail Interactive Kiosk
AmeriCandy Co., Inc.
3618 St. Germaine Ct.
Louisville, KY 40207
Ph:(502)583-1776
Fax:(502)583-1776
No. of Company-Owned Units: 1. **Founded:** 2006. **Franchised:** 2009. **Description:** Markets confections and chocolates representing 50 states in red and gold AmeriCandy presentation boxes. Distributes its products through retail stores, specialty shops and catalogs. **Equity Capital Needed:** $51,000. **Franchise Fee:** $15,000. **Financial Assistance:** Yes. **Training:** Yes.

3281 ■ Candy Bouquet International
423 E 3rd St.
Little Rock, AR 72201
Ph:(501)375-9990
Free: 877-226-3901
Fax:(501)375-9998
URL: http://www.candybouquet.com
No. of Franchise Units: 550. **Founded:** 1989. **Franchised:** 1993. **Description:** Hand-crafted candy bouquet gift arrangements. **Equity Capital Needed:** $8,500. **Franchise Fee:** $5,000-$33,500. **Financial Assistance:** No. **Training:** Hands-on training program.

3282 ■ Kilwin's Chocolates and Ice Cream
355 N Division Rd.
Petoskey, MI 49770
Ph:(231)439-0972
Fax:(231)439-6829
No. of Franchise Units: 75. **Founded:** 1947. **Franchised:** 1981. **Description:** Full-line confectionery shops, featuring Kilwin's handmade chocolates, fudge and original-recipe ice cream. **Equity Capital Needed:** $336,000-$550,000 all inclusive; $100,000-$120,000 cash. **Franchise Fee:** $40,000. **Financial Assistance:** No. **Training:** Yes.

3283 ■ Powell's Sweet Shoppe
Powell's Sweet Shoppe USA, LLC
PO Box 1079
Windsor, CA 95492
Ph:(707)838-4898
Fax:(707)838-8318
Co. E-mail: Michael.powell@powellsss.com
URL: http://www.powellsss.com
No. of Franchise Units: 8. **No. of Company-Owned Units:** 1. **Founded:** 2003. **Franchised:** 2005. **Description:** Candy, gelato, and nostalgic toys. **Equity Capital Needed:** $370,000-$440,000. **Franchise Fee:** $30,000. **Royalty Fee:** 6%. **Financial Assistance:** Third party financing available.

3284 ■ Ricky's Candy, Cones And Chaos
Ricky's Franchise Group, LLC
2865 S Eagle Rd.
Newtown, PA 18940
Ph:(267)987-2287
Fax:(215)579-2748
No. of Franchise Units: 43. **No. of Company-Owned Units:** 1. **Founded:** 2004. **Franchised:** 2004. **Description:** Nostalgic and bulky candy, ice cream. **Equity Capital Needed:** $100,000 initial investment. **Franchise Fee:** $30,000. **Financial Assistance:** Yes. **Training:** Yes.

3285 ■ Rocky Mountain Chocolate Factory, Inc.
265 Turner Dr.
Durango, CO 81301
Ph:(970)259-0554
Free: 800-438-7623
Fax:(970)259-5895
Co. E-mail: franchise@rmcf.net
URL: http://www.sweetfranchise.com
No. of Franchise Units: 355. **No. of Company-Owned Units:** 12. **Founded:** 1981. **Franchised:** 1982. **Description:** Retail and wholesale of packaged and bulk chocolates, brittles, truffles, sauces, cocoas, coffees and related chocolate and non-chocolate items. In-store preparation of fudges, caramel apples and dipped fruits via interactive cooking demonstrations. Complete line of gift and holiday items. Supplemental retail sale of soft drinks, ice cream, cookies and brewed coffee. **Equity Capital Needed:** $50,000 cash; ability to finance an additional $199,771-$599,336. **Franchise Fee:** $24,500. **Financial Assistance:** No. **Training:** Training provided in customer service, record keeping, merchandising, inventory control and marketing during 10 day program at corporate headquarters, in addition to several days onsite for store opening.

3286 ■ Schakolad Chocolate Factory
5966 Lakehurst Dr.
Orlando, FL 32819
Ph:(407)248-6400
Fax:(407)248-1466
No. of Franchise Units: 26. **Founded:** 1995. **Franchised:** 1999. **Description:** Handmade fine chocolate. **Equity Capital Needed:** $111,600-$144,000.

Franchise Fee: $30,000. **Royalty Fee:** $600/month. **Financial Assistance:** Limited third party financing available. **Training:** Offers 1-2 weeks at headquarters and onsite.

3287 ■ South Bend Chocolate Co.
3300 W Sample St.
South Bend, IN 46619
Ph:(574)233-2577
Free: 800-301-4961
Fax:(574)233-3150

No. of Franchise Units: 13. **No. of Company-Owned Units:** 10. **Founded:** 1991. **Franchised:** 1997. **Description:** Gourmet chocolate and confectionery manufacturer. **Equity Capital Needed:** $74,950-$295,500. **Franchise Fee:** $35,000. **Royalty Fee:** 4%. **Financial Assistance:** No. **Training:** Offers 10 days at headquarters, 80 hours at franchisees location with ongoing support.

LIBRARIES

3288 ■ M&M/Mars Research Library
800 High St.
Hackettstown, NJ 07840-1500
Ph:(908)852-1000
Fax:(908)850-2624
URL: http://www.mars.com
Contact: B.J. Restrepo

Scope: Confectionery, business. **Services:** Interlibrary loan (responds to fax requests); Library not open to the public. **Holdings:** 500 books; 75 reels of microfilm; 160 videocassettes; 8 journals. **Subscriptions:** 50 journals and other serials; 3 newspapers.

3289 ■ PMCA - an International Association of Confectioners–Bibliography of Technical Papers Collection
2980 Linden St., Ste. E3
Bethlehem, PA 18017
Ph:(610)625-4655
Fax:(610)625-4657
Co. E-mail: yvette.thomas@pmca.com
URL: http://www.pmca.com
Contact: Yvette Thomas, Adm.Dir.
Scope: Chocolate technology; confectionery products production. **Services:** Copying (fee); Library not open to the public. **Holdings:** Annual Production Proceedings (1947 to present).

Car Alarm and Stereo Store

ASSOCIATIONS AND OTHER ORGANIZATIONS

3290 ■ International Auto Sound Challenge Association
2200 S Ridgewood Ave.
South Daytona, FL 32119
Ph:(386)322-1551
Fax:(386)761-2120
Co. E-mail: paul@iasca.com
URL: http://www.iasca.com
Contact: Paul Papadeas, Pres.

Description: Manufacturers, retailers, and representatives/distributors of auto stereos; other interested individuals. Promotes the automotive stereo industry; holds sound quality and security contests; conducts consumer education. .

REFERENCE WORKS

3291 ■ *Surviving in the Security Alarm Business*
Pub: Butterworth-Heinemann

Ed: Lou Sepulveda. **Released:** 1998. **Price:** $19.95.

TRADE PERIODICALS

3292 ■ *Consumer Electronics Vision*
Pub: Consumer Electronics Association
Ed: Robert MacMillan, Editor, cstevens@ce.org. **Released:** Quarterly, 6/year. **Price:** Free. **Description:** Provides news and information concerning mobile electronics, audio, radar, security, and cellular communications. Examines the manufacture, market trends, and installation of mobile electronics. Covers legislative and regulatory issues at the state and federal levels with particular emphasis on business, manufacturing, and insurance issues. Recurring features include a monthly series of retail management information and news of the Association.

3293 ■ *Security Sales & Integration*
Pub: Bobit Business Media
Released: Monthly. **Description:** Magazine covering the security industry.

FRANCHISES AND BUSINESS OPPORTUNITIES

3294 ■ Alta Mere Toys for Your Car
Alta Mere Industries
4444 W 147th St.
Midlothian, IL 60445
Ph:(708)389-5922
Free: 800-581-8468

No. of Franchise Units: 14. **Founded:** 1986. **Franchised:** 1993. **Description:** Auto tinting and alarm installation facilities. **Equity Capital Needed:** $134,100-$166,880. **Franchise Fee:** $30,000. **Royalty Fee:** 7%. **Financial Assistance:** Limited third party financing available. **Training:** Provides 1 week training at headquarters, 3 weeks at franchisee's location with ongoing support.

3295 ■ Ziebart
Ziebart International Corp.
1290 E. Maple Rd.
Troy, MI 48007-1290
Ph:(248)588-4100
Free: 800-877-1312
Fax:(248)588-0718

No. of Franchise Units: 400. **No. of Company-Owned Units:** 16. **Founded:** 1954. **Franchised:** 1963. **Description:** Automotive application of detailing-accessories and protection services. **Equity Capital Needed:** $145,000-$250,000. **Franchise Fee:** $25,000. **Financial Assistance:** Yes. **Training:** Yes.

REFERENCE WORKS

3296 ▪ "How Not to Build a Website" in *Women Entrepreneur* (December 24, 2008)
Pub: Entrepreneur Media Inc.

Ed: Erica Ruback; Joanie Reisen. **Description:** Tips for producing a unique and functional Website are given as well as a number of lessons a pair of entrepreneurs learned while trying to launch their networking website, MomSpace.com.

VIDEOCASSETTES/ AUDIOCASSETTES

3297 ▪ *Automotive Quick Test*
Practicing Law Institute
810 7th Ave., 21st Fl.
New York, NY 10019-5818
Ph:(212)824-5700
Free: 800-260-4PLI
Co. E-mail: info@pli.edu
URL: http://www.pli.edu
Released: 1988. **Description:** Mechanics are taught how to quickly and efficiently check out a car. **Availability:** VHS; 3/4U.

CONSULTANTS

3298 ▪ Dynamotive Engineering Inc.
101 Foxfell Dr.
Kennett Square, PA 19348
Ph:(610)444-3636
Fax:(610)444-3636
Co. E-mail: dynamotive@kennett.net
Contact: William G. Mears, President
Scope: Specialist in the design, application and use of chassis roll dynamometers for testing automobiles and trucks. This includes facilities, such as environmental chambers, in which chassis roll dynamometers are operated and accessory equipment such as vehicle restraints and automatic drivers used in conjunction with chassis roll operation. Industries served: Automotive, petroleum, automotive accessories, dynamometer fabrication and control, automotive emissions testing, automotive diagnostic systems and inspection-maintenance programs. **Seminars:** Available for seminars on chassis roll dynamometer simulation accuracy and estimation of vehicle road load settings on chassis roll dynameters.

FRANCHISES AND BUSINESS OPPORTUNITIES

3299 ▪ Snap-On Tools Of Canada Ltd.
6500 Millcreek Dr.
Mississauga, ON, Canada L5N 2W6
Free: 800-665-8665
Fax:877-234-0180
Co. E-mail: bill.preston@snapon.com
URL: http://www.snaponfranchise.com
No. of Franchise Units: 350. **No. of Company-Owned Units:** 110. **Founded:** 1931. **Franchised:** 1994. **Description:** Distributes quality automotive and industrial tools and diagnostic equipments. **Equity Capital Needed:** $198,243-$292,433. **Franchise Fee:** $7,500-$15,000. **Financial Assistance:** No. **Training:** Initial training and ongoing.

Car Towing Service

ASSOCIATIONS AND OTHER ORGANIZATIONS

3300 ■ Towing and Recovery Association of America

2121 Eisenhower Ave., Ste. 200
Alexandria, VA 22314
Ph:(703)684-7713
Free: 800-728-0136
Fax:(703)684-6720
Co. E-mail: towserver@aol.com
URL: http://www.towserver.net
Contact: Harriet Cooley, Exec. Dir.

Description: Tow truck owners or operators; associate members are wrecker and accessory manufacturers and vendors. Aims to upgrade and promote the industry. Promotes uniform legislation; offers specialized education and National Driver Certification Program. **Publications:** *TRAA Membership Directory* (annual).

REFERENCE WORKS

3301 ■ *Tow Times' Annual Sourcebook*
Pub: T.T. Publications Inc.
Contact: Eleanor Joyce, VP
Released: Annual, Latest edition 2011-2012. **Publication Includes:** Lists of approximately 100 suppliers in the U.S. serving towing and recovery operators. **Entries Include:** Company name, address, phone, fax, name and title of contact, cross reference code to products and services. Principal content of publication is articles of interest to towing and recovery professionals. **Arrangement:** Classified by line of business. **Indexes:** Product/service.

SOURCES OF SUPPLY

3302 ■ *Truck Frame & Axle Repair Association—Membership Directory*
Pub: Truck Frame and Axle Repair Association
Contact: Bob Razenberg, President
E-mail: razenberg@sbcglobal.net
Released: Biennial, August of odd years. **Price:** Free. **Covers:** About 150 regular and associate members that repair heavy-duty truck equipment or supply the industry. **Entries Include:** Firm name, address, phone, key personnel, coding to indicate specialties. **Arrangement:** Geographical.

TRADE PERIODICALS

3303 ■ *National Towing News*
Pub: Towing & Recovery Association of America
Ed: Released: Monthly. **Price:** Included in membership. **Description:** Gives news of the Association. Recurring features include a column titled From the State Line.

3304 ■ *Towing and Recovery Footnotes*
Pub: Dominion Enterprises
Contact: Bill Candler, Sen. Ed.
E-mail: bcandler@traderonline.com
Released: Monthly. **Price:** $30; $55 two years. **Description:** Trade magazine covering business management for the towing industry.

START-UP INFORMATION

3305 ■ "Cleaning Up" in *Small Business Opportunities* (Get Rich At Home 2010)
Pub: Harris Publications Inc.
Ed: Description: Break into the $23 billion pro car wash business with no experience needed. Profile of Team Blue, founded by father and son team, Jeff and Jason Haas along with franchise opportunities is included.

ASSOCIATIONS AND OTHER ORGANIZATIONS

3306 ■ Canadian Carwash Association
4195 Dundas St. W, Ste. 346
Toronto, ON, Canada M8X 1Y4
Ph:(416)239-0339
Fax:(416)239-1076
Co. E-mail: office@canadiancarwash.ca
URL: http://www.canadiancarwash.ca
Contact: Scott Murray, Pres.
Description: Owners of car wash facilities. Promotes growth and development of the industry. Facilitates exchange of information among members; monitors legislation of interest to members and conducts lobbying activities; makes available continuing professional education programs; conducts public relations campaigns. Provides benefits to members including discount insurance programs and customer handouts. **Publications:** *Wash-Word* (quarterly).

3307 ■ International Carwash Association
401 N Michigan Ave., Ste. 2200
Chicago, IL 60611
Free: 888-422-8422
Co. E-mail: info@carwash.org
URL: http://www.carwash.org
Contact: Eric Wulf CAE, Exec. Dir./CEO
Description: Membership consists of car wash and detail operators, manufacturers, and supplier's distributors. Promotes the car wash industry by providing educational opportunities to members and gathering information on the industry and its customer. **Publications:** *ICA Directory and Buyer's Guide* (annual); *ICA News* (monthly).

REFERENCE WORKS

3308 ■ "Casey's Buys Second Marion Convenience Store" in *Gazette* (December 14, 2010)
Pub: Gazette
Ed: Dave DeWitte. **Description:** Casey's General Stores Inc. has acquired a Short Stop convenience store on Marion's west side in Iowa. The new store includes a car and truck wash.

3309 ■ "Dry Idea" in *Entrepreneur* (Vol. 36, April 2008, No. 4, pp. 20)
Pub: Entrepreneur Media, Inc.
Ed: Tiffany Meyers. **Description:** Lucky Earth LLC is an Inglewood, California-based company that markets "Waterless" Carwash, an organic product that is sprayed on to the car and wiped down without using water. Businesses related to water conservation are being created, as water shortage is anticipated in 36 states in the U.S. by 2013.

STATISTICAL SOURCES

3310 ■ *RMA Annual Statement Studies*
Pub: Robert Morris Associates (RMA)
Released: Annual. **Price:** $175.00 2006-07 edition, $105.00. **Description:** Contains composite balance sheets and income statements for more than 360 industries, including the accounting, auditing, and bookkeeping industries. Also contains five years of comparative historical data for discerning trends. Includes 16 commonly used ratios, computed for most of the size groupings for nearly every industry.

TRADE PERIODICALS

3311 ■ *Auto Laundry News*
Pub: E.W. Williams Publications Co.
Released: Monthly. **Price:** $72; $83 Canada; $125 elsewhere airmail; $108 two years; $106 Canada 2 years; $200 elsewhere 2 years, airmail; $125 3 years; $15 annual directory; $20 Canada annual directory; $7 single issue. **Description:** Trade magazine covering the car wash and quick lube industry.

3312 ■ *Professional Carwashing & Detailing*
Pub: National Trade Publications Inc.
Contact: Kate Carr, Editor-in-Chief
E-mail: kcarr@carwash.com
Released: Monthly. **Description:** Car care magazine covering carwashing, detailing and oil change facilities.

TRADE SHOWS AND CONVENTIONS

3313 ■ International Carwash Association Annual Convention and Exhibition
International Carwash Association
401 N. Michigan Ave., Ste. 2200
Chicago, IL 60611
Ph:(312)321-5199
Free: 888-422-8422
Fax:(312)527-6774
Co. E-mail: ica@sba.com
Released: Annual. **Audience:** Carwash and detail shop operators. **Principal Exhibits:** Carwash and detailing equipment, supplies and services.

FRANCHISES AND BUSINESS OPPORTUNITIES

3314 ■ Cactus Car Wash
2980-A Piedmont Rd.
Atlanta, GA 30080
Ph:(770)436-0985
Fax:(770)818-5885
No. of Company-Owned Units: 4. **Founded:** 1996. **Franchised:** 2005. **Description:** Full-service car wash. **Equity Capital Needed:** $1,200,000-$1,600,000. **Franchise Fee:** $30,000. **Royalty Fee:** 5.5%. **Financial Assistance:** No. **Training:** Offers 2 weeks at headquarters, 2 weeks onsite and ongoing support.

3315 ■ Fine Details Inc.
481 N Service Rd., W Unit A13
Oakville, ON, Canada L6M 2V6
Ph:(905)825-4200
Free: 888-843-9274
Fax:(905)825-4035
Co. E-mail: michelle@finedetails.ca
URL: http://www.finedetails.ca
No. of Franchise Units: 22. **No. of Company-Owned Units:** 1. **Founded:** 1995. **Franchised:** 1998. **Description:** Offers interior/exterior hand car cleaning. There are 13 different types of services to satisfy the needs of the vehicle as well as the client's budget. **Equity Capital Needed:** $120,000. **Franchise Fee:** $30,000. **Training:** 2 weeks training with ongoing operational and marketing support.

3316 ■ The Shine Factory
Shine Factory Systems Inc.
75 Akerley Blvd.
Dartmouth, NS, Canada B3B 1R7
Ph:(902)405-3171
Fax:(902)405-3484
Co. E-mail: info@shinefactory.com
URL: http://www.shinefactory.com
No. of Franchise Units: 16. **Founded:** 1981. **Franchised:** 1981. **Description:** Canada's automotive and polishing franchise. **Equity Capital Needed:** $100,000+. **Franchise Fee:** $25,000+ depending upon market area study. **Financial Assistance:** No. **Training:** Training conducted in Halifax, NS.

3317 ■ Super Wash
707 W Lincolnway
Morrison, IL 61270
Ph:(815)772-2111
Fax:(815)772-7160
URL: http://www.superwash.com
No. of Franchise Units: 288. **No. of Company-Owned Units:** 65. **Founded:** 1982. **Franchised:** 2001. **Description:** Franchisor of car washes. **Equity Capital Needed:** $468,000-$1,100,100. **Franchise Fee:** $9,000. **Royalty Fee:** Varies. **Financial Assistance:** Third party financing available. **Training:** Training available at headquarters, onsite and ongoing support provided.

Career Counseling

ASSOCIATIONS AND OTHER ORGANIZATIONS

3318 ■ American Counseling Association
5999 Stevenson Ave.
Alexandria, VA 22304
Free: 800-347-6647
Fax:(703)823-0252
Co. E-mail: ryep@counseling.org
URL: http://www.counseling.org
Contact: Richard Yep, Exec. Dir.
Description: Counseling professionals in elementary and secondary schools, higher education, community agencies and organizations, rehabilitation programs, government, industry, business, private practice, career counseling, and mental health counseling. Conducts professional development institutes and provides liability insurance. Maintains Counseling and Human Development Foundation to fund counseling projects. **Publications:** *Career Development Quarterly* (quarterly); *Counseling and Values* (3/year); *Journal of Addictions and Offender Counseling* (semiannual); *Journal of College Counseling* (semiannual); *Journal of Counseling and Development* (quarterly); *The Journal of Humanistic Counseling, Education and Development* (quarterly); *Journal of Multicultural Counseling and Development* (quarterly).

3319 ■ Association of Canadian Search, Employment and Staffing Services–Association Nationale des Enterprises en Recrutement et Placement de Personnel
2233 Argentina Rd., Ste. 100
Mississauga, ON, Canada L5N 2X7
Ph:(905)826-6869
Free: 888-232-4962
Fax:(905)826-4873
Co. E-mail: acsess@acsess.org
URL: http://www.acsess.org
Contact: Amanda Curtis, Exec. Dir.
Description: Promotes employment, recruitment, and staffing services industry in Canada, including direct-hire and executive search services, temporary and contract staffing services. Promotes advancement and growth, advocates for professional ethics and standards in the industry; coordinates government relations, educational and promotional and communications initiatives; provides support services on relevant legislative, regulatory and procurement issues. Promotes best industry practices and adherence to employment legislation and regulations. Monitors industry standards. Provides professional certification and training, including Certified Personnel Consultant Designation Program. Coordinates educational programs and conferences. Promotes public awareness of the industry and keeps members informed of issues affecting the industry. Collects and provides industry statistics. **Publications:** *Dialogue* (3/year).

3320 ■ Career Planning and Adult Development Network
543 Vista Mar Ave.
Pacifica, CA 94044
Ph:(650)773-0982
Co. E-mail: admin@careernetwork.org
URL: http://www.careernetwork.org
Contact: Howard Figler PhD
Description: Counselors, trainers, consultants, therapists, educators, personnel specialists, and graduate students who work in business, educational, religious, and governmental organizations, and focus on career planning and adult development issues. Seeks to: establish a link between professionals working with adults in a variety of settings; identify and exchange effective adult development methods and techniques; develop a clearer understanding of the directions and objectives of the career planning and the adult development movement. Keeps members informed of developments in career decision-making, career values clarification, preretirement counseling, dual-career families, job search techniques, and mid-life transitions. Cosponsors professional seminars; maintains biographical archives. **Publications:** Journal (quarterly);Newsletter (bimonthly).

3321 ■ International Association of Counseling Services
101 S Whiting St., Ste. 211
Alexandria, VA 22304
Ph:(703)823-9840
Fax:(703)823-9843
Co. E-mail: iacsinc@earthlink.net
URL: http://www.iacsinc.org
Contact: Nancy E. Roncketti, Exec. Dir.
Description: Represents accredited university and four-year college counseling services in the U.S., Canada, and Australia. Fosters communications and cooperation among counseling services. **Publications:** *National Survey of Counseling Center Directors* (annual).

3322 ■ National Board for Certified Counselors and Affiliates
3 Terrace Way
Greensboro, NC 27403-3660
Ph:(336)547-0607
Fax:(336)547-0017
Co. E-mail: nbcc@nbcc.org
URL: http://www.nbcc.org
Contact: Dr. Thomas W. Clawson, Pres./CEO
Purpose: Establishes and monitors professional credentialing standards for counselors. Identifies individuals who have obtained voluntary certification as a National Certified Counselor, one who assists persons with aging, vocational development, adolescence, family, and marital concerns, or a National Certified School Counselor, one who specializes in counseling within the school setting, or a Certified Clinical Mental Health Counselor, one who specializes in working in clinical settings, or a Master Addictions Counselor, one who specializes in addictions counseling. Maintains a database of nearly 37,000 certified counselors. **Publications:** *The National Certified Counselor* (3/year); *Preparation Guide for the National Clinical Mental Health Counseling Examination*; *Preparation Guide for the National Counselor Examination for Licensure and Certification* .

3323 ■ National Career Development Association
305 N Beech Cir.
Broken Arrow, OK 74012
Ph:(918)663-7060
Free: (866)367-6232
Fax:(918)663-7058
Co. E-mail: dpennington@ncda.org
URL: http://associationdatabase.com/aws/NCDA/pt/sp/Home_Page
Contact: Deneen Pennington, Exec. Dir.
Description: Represents professionals and others interested in career development or counseling in various work environments. Supports counselors, education and training personnel, and allied professionals working in schools, colleges, business/industry, community and government agencies, and in private practice. Provides publications, support for state and local activities, human equity programs, and continuing education and training for these professionals. Provides networking opportunities for career professionals in business, education, and government. .

3324 ■ National Employment Counseling Association
6836 Bee Cave Rd., Ste. 260
Austin, TX 78746
Free: 800-347-6647
Co. E-mail: kimberly@encompasswf.com
URL: http://www.employmentcounseling.org
Contact: Kimberly Key, Pres.
Description: Serves as a division of the American Counseling Association. Represents individuals who are engaged in employment counseling, counselor education, research, administration or supervision in business and industry, colleges and universities, and federal and state governments; students. Offers professional leadership and development services; provides opportunities for professional growth through workshops and special projects. **Publications:** *Journal of Employment Counseling* (quarterly).

DIRECTORIES OF EDUCATIONAL PROGRAMS

3325 ■ *The Directory of Canadian Recruiters*
Pub: Continental Records Company Ltd.
Contact: Neil Patte, Publisher
Released: Annual, Latest edition 2011-12. **Price:** $79.95, individuals GST plus shipping cost; $99.95, individuals Professional CD ed. plus shipping cost plus tax. **Covers:** 2,655 recruiting firms and more than 5,600 executive recruiting firms in Canada. **Entries Include:** Firm name, address, phone, fax, e-mail, URL, industries, positions, salary levels, name and title of contact.

3326 ■ *Who's Hiring*
Pub: Mediacorp Canada Inc.
Ed: Anthony W. Meehan, Editor. **Released:** Annual, 2005. **Price:** $42.95, individuals book and CD-ROM. **Covers:** Ranks Canada's 5,000 fastest-growing employers in 61 major occupational categories. **Entries Include:** Company name, address, phone, fax,

e-mail, and URL addresses, human resources contacts, positions recently advertised, description of employer's business.

REFERENCE WORKS

3327 ■ "Design program in Athletic Footwear" in *Occupational Outlook Quarterly* (Vol. 55, Fall 2011, No. 3, pp. 21)
Pub: U.S. Bureau of Labor Statistics
Description: The Fashion Institute of Technology offers the only certificate program in performance athletic footwear design in the U.S. The program focuses on conceptualizing and sketching shoe designs and covers ergonomic, anatomical, and material considerations for athletic footwear design.

3328 ■ "Encouraging Study in Critical Languages" in *Occupational Outlook Quarterly* (Vol. 55, Summer 2011, No. 2, pp. 23)
Pub: U.S. Bureau of Labor Statistics
Description: Proficiency in particular foreign languages is vital to the defense, diplomacy, and security of the United States. Several federal programs provide scholarships and other funding to encourage high school and college students to learn languages of the Middle East, China, and Russia.

3329 ■ "Finishing High School Leads to Better Employment Prospects" in *Occupational Outlook Quarterly* (Vol. 55, Summer 2011, No. 2, pp. 36)
Pub: U.S. Bureau of Labor Statistics
Description: Students who drop out of high school are more likely to face unemployment than those who finish. Statistical data included.

3330 ■ "Genetic Counselor" in *Occupational Outlook Quarterly* (Vol. 55, Summer 2011, No. 2, pp. 34)
Pub: U.S. Bureau of Labor Statistics
Ed: John Mullins. **Description:** Genetic counseling involves the practice of informing clients about genetic disorders and to help them understand and manage a disorder. There are approximately 2,400 certified genetic counselors in the U.S. and earn a median annual salary of about $63,000, according to the American Board of Genetic Counseling. The US Bureau of Labor Statistics does not have data on employment or wages for genetic counselors.

3331 ■ "Online Tools for Jobseekers" in *Occupational Outlook Quarterly* (Vol. 55, Fall 2011, No. 3, pp. 20)
Pub: U.S. Bureau of Labor Statistics
Description: U.S. Department of Labor's CareerOneStop provides a collection of Web-based tools serving students, jobseekers, employers, and the workforce. The top six categories for job listings nationwide include general job boards, niche job boards, career planning tools, career explorations sites, social media job search sites, and other tools which include interview preparation tools and training grants.

3332 ■ "Paid to Persuade: Careers in Sales" in *Occupational Outlook Quarterly* (Vol. 55, Summer 2011, No. 2, pp. 24)
Pub: U.S. Bureau of Labor Statistics
Ed: Ilka Maria Torpey. **Description:** Sales workers are paid to persuade others to buy goods and services. There were over 13 million wage and salary sales workers in the US in 2010. Wages in sales careers can vary and some become lucrative, lifelong career positions. Seven sales occupations with annual wages higher than $33,000 are profiled.

3333 ■ "Physics for Females" in *Occupational Outlook Quarterly* (Vol. 55, Summer 2011, No. 2, pp. 22)
Pub: U.S. Bureau of Labor Statistics
Description: Free resources to help females investigate careers in medical physics and health physics are available from the American Physical Society. The booklet is designed for girls in middle and high school and describes the work of 15 women who use physics to solve medical mysteries, discover planets, research new materials, and more.

3334 ■ "Plan Your Future with My Next Move" in *Occupational Outlook Quarterly* (Vol. 55, Summer 2011, No. 2, pp. 22)
Pub: U.S. Bureau of Labor Statistics
Description: My Next Move, an online tool offering a variety of user-friendly ways to browse more than 900 occupations was created by the National Center for O NET Development for the US Department of Labor's Employment and Training Administration. Clicking on an occupation presents a one-page profile summarizing key information for specific careers.

3335 ■ "Work for Play: Careers in Video Game Development" in *Occupational Outlook Quarterly* (Vol. 55, Fall 2011, No. 3, pp. 2)
Pub: U.S. Bureau of Labor Statistics
Ed: Drew Liming, Dennis Vilorio. **Description:** Game developers make a living creating the games the public enjoys playing. The video gaming industry reported sales over $10 billion in 2009 and employed 32,000 people in 34 states. Career options in video game development are featured.

TRADE PERIODICALS

3336 ■ *AACE Bonus Briefs*
Pub: American Association for Career Education
Ed: Pat Nellor Wickwire, Editor. **Released:** Quarterly. **Price:** Included in membership. **Description:** Contains brief papers by American Association for Career Education members on current issues in careers, education, and employment.

3337 ■ *AACE Distinguished Member Series*
Pub: American Association for Career Education
Ed: Pat Nellor Wickwire, Editor. **Released:** Periodic. **Price:** Included in membership. **Description:** Publication of the American Association for Career Education. Provides information on careers, education, and employment.

3338 ■ *Career Development Quarterly*
Pub: National Career Development Association
Ed: Dr. Jerry Trusty, Editor. **Released:** Quarterly. **Price:** $65; $100 institutions. **Description:** Journal for career counseling and career education professionals in schools, colleges, private practice, government agencies, personnel departments in business and industry, and employment counseling centers.

3339 ■ *Career Planning & Adult Development Network Newsletter*
Pub: Career Planning & Adult Development Network
Ed: **Released:** BIM. **Price:** $59, Free payment must accompany order; $74, other countries payment must accompany order; $11, single issue; $12.50, single issue other countries. **Description:** Contains features and news items on career development and human resources: theory, methodology, research, practices, and techniques. Deals with manpower, organizational planning, counseling, training, equal opportunity, career transition, marketing skills, and adult learning. Recurring features include notices of resources, materials, publications of interest, conferences, workshops, seminars, employment opportunities, book reviews, network news, and a column on publishers of career development books.

3340 ■ *Career World*
Pub: Weekly Reader Corp.
Released: Bimonthly, during academic year. **Price:** $10.25. **Description:** Magazine serving as a guide to jobs and careers for students in grades 7-12.

3341 ■ *Careers & Colleges*
Pub: 360 Youth L.L.C.
Contact: Tim Clancy, Publisher
E-mail: tclancy@alloyeducation.com
Released: Bimonthly, (during the school year). **Description:** Magazine providing career and college information to high school students throughout the United States.

3342 ■ *Changing Course*
Pub: Making Waves, Publishers
Contact: Valerie Young
Ed: Valerie Young, Editor, vyoung@changingcourse.com. **Released:** Bimonthly. **Price:** $29, U.S.; $49, two years USA; $35, Canada; $57, two years Canada. **Description:** Contains inspiration and information on creating more satisfying work lives outside the 9-to-5 job world. Recurring features include letters to the editor, interviews, book reviews, and columns titled Opportunities Knock: Creative Alternatives to Working 9-5, Resources for a Change, and Dollar/Sense.

3343 ■ *Counseling Today*
Pub: American Counseling Association
Ed: Jonathan Rollins, Editor. **Released:** Monthly. **Description:** Association newspaper (tabloid) on counseling and human services.

3344 ■ *Enrich!*
Pub: National Chamber of Commerce for Women
Contact: Jay Orson, Ad.Mgr.
Ed: R. Wright, Editor. **Released:** Bimonthly. **Price:** $96. **Description:** Strives to assist readers on business-plan, career-path, and pay-comparison goals.

3345 ■ *Journal of Employment Counseling*
Pub: American Association for Counseling and Development
Ed: Dr. Roberta A. Neault, Editor, roberta@lifestrategies.ca. **Released:** Quarterly. **Price:** $44; $55 institutions. **Description:** Journal covering state employee, vocational, college placement, education, business, and industry counseling.

VIDEOCASSETTES/ AUDIOCASSETTES

3346 ■ *The American Professionals Series*
RMI Media
1365 N. Winchester St.
Olathe, KS 66061-5880
Ph:(913)768-1696
Free: 800-745-5480
Fax:800-755-6910
Co. E-mail: actmedia@act.org
URL: http://www.actmedia.com
Released: 1984. **Description:** In this series of 21 half hour programs, various occupations are examined in depth, including a day in the life of each worker. **Availability:** VHS; 3/4U.

3347 ■ *Career Assessment Video*
Cambridge Educational
c/o Films Media Group
132 West 31st Street, 17th Floor
Ste. 124
New York, NY 10001
Free: 800-257-5126
Fax:(609)671-0266
Co. E-mail: custserve@films.com
URL: http://www.cambridgeol.com
Released: 1991. **Price:** $395.00. **Description:** Contains information on the requirements and typical settings of different careers, including interests, abilities, work areas, work activities, school subjects, aptitudes, work situations, math and language, work load, physical skills, indoor-outdoor, work environment, and education level. Includes guidebook, test booklet, worksheet, and two diskettes. **Availability:** VHS; Special order formats.

3348 ■ *The Career Encounters Series*
Cambridge Educational
c/o Films Media Group
132 West 31st Street, 17th Floor
Ste. 124
New York, NY 10001
Free: 800-257-5126
Fax:(609)671-0266
Co. E-mail: custserve@films.com
URL: http://www.cambridgeol.com
Released: 199?. **Price:** $599.00. **Description:** Nine-part career information series that provides information on matching individual characteristics to appropriate careers. Covers academic routes to take to prepare for a certain career, opportunities and challenges in each career field, and other career-related information. **Availability:** VHS.

3349 ■ *Career Moves: A Winning Strategy*
University of Wisconsin-Madison Center on Education & Work
1025 W. Johnson St., Rm. 964
Madison, WI 53706-1796
Ph:(608)265-6700
Free: 800-862-1071
Co. E-mail: cewmail@education.wisc.edu
URL: http://www.cew.wisc.edu
Price: $48.00. **Description:** Discusses various career issues, including the state of job opportunities, employment and training options, and balancing family and work. **Availability:** VHS.

3350 ■ *Career Planning Steps*
Cambridge Educational
c/o Films Media Group
132 West 31st Street, 17th Floor
Ste. 124
New York, NY 10001
Free: 800-257-5126
Fax:(609)671-0266
Co. E-mail: custserve@films.com
URL: http://www.cambridgeol.com
Price: $98.00. **Description:** Uses real-life examples and realistic scenarios to outline the career development process, including self-examination, career exploration methods, interviewing for information, training and educational options available, and job searching. Includes study manual. **Availability:** VHS.

3351 ■ *Career Strategies*
Educational Video Network
1401 19th St.
Huntsville, TX 77340
Ph:(936)295-5767
Free: 800-762-0060
Fax:(936)294-0233
URL: http://www.evndirect.com
Price: $59.95. **Description:** Offers methods for career planners to use to succeed in their quest. **Availability:** VHS.

3352 ■ *Choosing Careers*
Cambridge Educational
c/o Films Media Group
132 West 31st Street, 17th Floor
Ste. 124
New York, NY 10001
Free: 800-257-5126
Fax:(609)671-0266
Co. E-mail: custserve@films.com
URL: http://www.cambridgeol.com
Released: 1986. **Description:** A series of tapes, available separately, aimed toward the high school student choosing his or her life's path. **Availability:** VHS.

3353 ■ *Choosing a Job*
Encyclopedia Britannica
331 N. LaSalle St.
Chicago, IL 60654
Ph:(312)347-7159
Free: 800-323-1229
Fax:(312)294-2104
URL: http://www.britannica.com
Released: 1971. **Description:** How career education programs may save young students from frustrating job-hopping after finishing school. From the "Careers in the Office" series. **Availability:** VHS; 3/4U.

3354 ■ *Effective Resumes & Job Applications*
Cambridge Educational
c/o Films Media Group
132 West 31st Street, 17th Floor
Ste. 124
New York, NY 10001
Free: 800-257-5126
Fax:(609)671-0266
Co. E-mail: custserve@films.com
URL: http://www.cambridgeol.com
Released: 1992. **Price:** $99.00. **Description:** Provides tips on writing effective job resumes and cover letters and filling out applications. Includes user guide. **Availability:** VHS.

3355 ■ *How to Get a Job*
Home Vision Cinema
c/o Image Entertainment
20525 Nordhoff St., Ste. 200
Chatsworth, CA 91311
Co. E-mail: inquiries@image-entertainment.com
URL: http://www.homevision.com
Released: 1979. **Description:** The Self-Directed Placement Corporation helps unemployed people recognize their self-worth, providing direction and hope in their search for jobs. **Availability:** VHS; 3/4U.

3356 ■ *In the Prime: Changing Careers with Carole Hyatt*
Leslie T. McClure
PO Box 1223
Pebble Beach, CA 93953
Ph:(831)656-0553
Fax:(831)656-0555
Co. E-mail: leslie@411videoinfo.com
URL: http://www.411videoinfo.com
Released: 1997. **Price:** $19.95. **Description:** Presents simple exercises to discover what your next career move should be. **Availability:** VHS.

3357 ■ *Lifelines: A Career Profile Study*
The Cinema Guild
115 West 30th St., Ste. 800
New York, NY 10001
Ph:(212)685-6242
Free: 800-723-5522
Fax:(212)685-4717
Co. E-mail: info@cinemaguild.com
URL: http://www.cinemaguild.com
Released: 1977. **Description:** Dr. Edgar Schein of the Sloan School of Management at the Massachusetts Institute of Technology discusses some the results of his research studies in career formation. Dr. Schein explains that each of us has a "career lifeline"-a path that directs our choice of work. With illustrations from three actual cases, Dr. Schein's concept of "career anchors"-patterns by which people discover what they are good at and what they would like to do for the rest of their lives is examined. **Availability:** 3/4U; Special order formats.

3358 ■ *People in Management*
Phoenix Learning Group
2349 Chaffee Dr.
St. Louis, MO 63146-3306
Ph:(314)569-0211
Free: 800-221-1274
Fax:(314)569-2834
URL: http://www.phoenixlearninggroup.com
Released: 1976. **Description:** This documentary film follows the daily activities of several men and women at all stages of management, from trainee to company president of a large corporation. **Availability:** VHS; 3/4U.

3359 ■ *People Who Help: Health Careers*
Phoenix Learning Group
2349 Chaffee Dr.
St. Louis, MO 63146-3306
Ph:(314)569-0211
Free: 800-221-1274
Fax:(314)569-2834
URL: http://www.phoenixlearninggroup.com
Released: 1975. **Description:** Few of us realize how many different professions and jobs it takes to run a modern hospital. This film creates, through documentary footage, the atmosphere of such a hospital. **Availability:** VHS; 3/4U.

3360 ■ *People Who Sell Things*
Phoenix Learning Group
2349 Chaffee Dr.
St. Louis, MO 63146-3306
Ph:(314)569-0211
Free: 800-221-1274
Fax:(314)569-2834
URL: http://www.phoenixlearninggroup.com
Released: 1975. **Description:** What kind of people are best suited to work in sales? This documentary film follows the lively daily activities of four successful salespersons. **Availability:** VHS; 3/4U.

3361 ■ *People Who Work in Manufacturing*
Phoenix Learning Group
2349 Chaffee Dr.
St. Louis, MO 63146-3306
Ph:(314)569-0211
Free: 800-221-1274
Fax:(314)569-2834
URL: http://www.phoenixlearninggroup.com
Released: 1975. **Description:** Creates, through exciting documentary footage, the atmosphere of a sophisticated electronics factory. **Availability:** VHS; 3/4U.

3362 ■ *People Who Work with People*
Phoenix Learning Group
2349 Chaffee Dr.
St. Louis, MO 63146-3306
Ph:(314)569-0211
Free: 800-221-1274
Fax:(314)569-2834
URL: http://www.phoenixlearninggroup.com
Released: 1976. **Description:** Service workers discuss why they chose service work, what they get out of their jobs, and what they offer in return. **Availability:** VHS; 3/4U.

3363 ■ *Power Interviewing: A Headhunter's Guide to Getting Hired in the '90s*
Waterford Executive Group Ltd.
1 N. 141 County Farm Rd.
Winfield, IL 60190-2023
Ph:(630)690-0055
Fax:(630)690-5533
Co. E-mail: info@waterfordgroup.com
URL: http://waterfordgroup.com
Released: 1991. **Price:** $59.95. **Description:** A detailed examination of how to interview successfully, including proper wardrobe, resumes, acquiring interviews and more. **Availability:** VHS.

3364 ■ *Resume Preparation*
University of Arizona
University Teaching Center
1600 E. 1st St.
PO Box 210102
Tucson, AZ 85721-0129
Ph:(520)621-7788
Fax:(520)626-7314
URL: http://www.utc.arizona.edu
Released: 197?. **Description:** This program is designed to aid the prospective job-hunter or job-changer in presenting the necessary information to an employer through a resume. **Availability:** VHS; EJ; 3/4U.

3365 ■ *Strategic Job Search*
American Media, Inc.
4621 121st St.
Urbandale, IA 50323-2311
Ph:(515)224-0919
Free: 888-776-8268
Fax:(515)327-2555
Co. E-mail: custsvc@ammedia.com
URL: http://www.ammedia.com
Released: 1989. **Price:** $425.00. **Description:** A course is plotted for people who are looking for a new job. **Availability:** VHS; 3/4U.

3366 ■ *The Video Career Library*
RMI Media
1365 N. Winchester St.
Olathe, KS 66061-5880
Ph:(913)768-1696
Free: 800-745-5480
Fax:800-755-6910
Co. E-mail: actmedia@act.org
URL: http://www.actmedia.com
Released: 1987. **Description:** Information on 165 occupations is provided, including job duties, working conditions, wages and salaries, job outlook, and required education and training. Also describes current labor market status and offers a list of addresses where one can write for more information about each job. **Availability:** VHS; 3/4U.

3367 ■ *Vocational Visions Career Series*
Cambridge Educational
c/o Films Media Group
132 West 31st Street, 17th Floor
Ste. 124
New York, NY 10001
Free: 800-257-5126
Fax:(609)671-0266
Co. E-mail: custserve@films.com
URL: http://www.cambridgeol.com
Released: 1989. **Price:** $39.95. **Description:** A series of tapes providing insight into various careers through interviews with people working in those jobs. The ten tapes can be purchased individually or as a set. **Availability:** VHS.

TRADE SHOWS AND CONVENTIONS

3368 ■ International Career Development Conference
Career Planning and Adult Development Network
543 Vista Mar Ave.
Pacifica, CA 94044
Ph:(650)359-6911
Fax:(650)359-3089
Co. E-mail: admin@careernetwork.org
URL: http://www.careernetwork.org
Released: Annual. **Audience:** Career counselors from schools, universities, business, and other industries. **Principal Exhibits:** Career education and guidance information, including books, tests, and computer software.

CONSULTANTS

3369 ■ Career Dimensions Inc.
6330 LBJ Fwy., Ste. 136
Dallas, TX 75240-6412
Ph:(972)239-1399
Fax:(972)239-1439
Co. E-mail: tauneeb@careerdimensions-dfw.com
URL: http://www.careerdimensions-dfw.com
Contact: Jane Warren, Principle
E-mail: tauneeb@atscareerdimensions-dfw.com
Scope: Provides seminars and consulting in the following areas: career planning, spouse employment relocation, outplacement, employee career development, and small business strategies; life planning time and stress management, pre retirement planning, balancing personal and professional responsibilities; and professional development team building, goal setting and action planning, effective communication, negotiating, networking within the organization and community, employee recruiting and selection, management development, and women and their careers, recruiting strategies for women and minorities. **Publications:** "What Do I Say When I Don't Know What Career to Pursue?"; "How Do I Choose a College Major?"; "The National Business Employment Weekly's Premier Guide to Resumes"; "The National Business Employment Weekly's Premier Guide to Cover Letters"; "Ten Common Interview Mistakes and How to Avoid Them"; "Eating Your Way Through an Interview"; "How to Respond to 'Tell Me About Yourself'"; "Interview to Stand Out From the Crowd". **Seminars:** What Do I Do When I am Bored With My Job?.

3370 ■ Career Evaluation Systems Inc.
1022 N Oakley Blvd.
Chicago, IL 60622
Ph:(312)645-1363
Co. E-mail: dougfaller@aol.com
Contact: Doug Faller, Vice President
E-mail: dougfaller@aol.com
Scope: Provides vocational testing instruments to evaluation and counseling facilities, and serves those facilities with computerized test scoring and counseling advice. Facilities may be career counselors, businesses, schools, psychologists, hospitals, rehabilitation centers, and prisons. Used for assessing occupational potential, pre-training screening, worker's compensation and SSD depositions.

3371 ■ Centennial Rehabilitation Associates
2401 S Downing St.
Denver, CO 80210
Ph:(303)368-4500
Fax:(303)368-1333
Co. E-mail: centen@centen.net
URL: http://www.centen.net
Contact: Dr. William Boyd, Principal
E-mail: wboyd@centen.net
Scope: Offers vocational rehabilitation and medical case management services in Colorado and Nebraska.

3372 ■ Constructive Leisure
511 N La Cienega Blvd.
Los Angeles, CA 90048
Ph:(310)652-7389
Fax:(213)874-0663
Co. E-mail: nvab@aol.com
Contact: Patsy B. Edwards, President
Scope: A life planning, career, and leisure consulting firm serving adults and youth. Develops and markets original books, surveys, audio tapes, software, and materials for career or leisure counseling and assessment. Materials are designed mainly to assist adults and youth with career or leisure guidance in terms of life planning, self-knowledge, career changing, educational selection, pre retirement or retirement, and preventive health services through life satisfaction. **Publications:** "Adapting to Change: The NVAB Program" Jul, 2000. **Special Services:** Leisure PREF and The NVAB Program.

3373 ■ Jobs In Horticulture Inc.
57 Rosedown Blvd.
PO Box 521731
Debary, FL 32713-4115
Ph:(386)753-0996
Free: 800-428-2474
Fax:(386)753-0997
Co. E-mail: info@hortjobs.com
URL: http://www.hortjobs.com
Contact: Joan Ferrell, Principal
E-mail: joan@hortjobs.com
Scope: Career consulting and career services with emphasis on horticulture.

3374 ■ Lou Antonelli
175 Cooper St.
Sonoma, CA 95476-6709
Ph:(707)996-0629
Fax:(707)996-2316
Co. E-mail: lantonel@sonic.net
E-mail: lantonel@sonic.net
Scope: Rehabilitation consultant who provides vocational consulting services to industrial insurance carriers and injured workers. Services include dissolution evaluations and career workshops. Recent experience with compliance of new Americans with Disabilities Act. Provides forensic expert witness services also.

FRANCHISES AND BUSINESS OPPORTUNITIES

3375 ■ AAA Franchise Legal Help Hotline
Franchise Foundations
4157 23rd St.
San Francisco, CA 94114
Free: 800-942-4402
Founded: 1980. **Description:** Advice on franchise legal issues.

3376 ■ Carter & Tani
402 E Roosevelt Rd., Ste. 206
Wheaton, IL 60187
Ph:(630)668-2135
Founded: 1977. **Description:** Assist start-up franchisees and franchisors.

COMPUTERIZED DATABASES

3377 ■ *Annual Employment by Industry*
Haver Analytics
60 E 42nd St.
New York, NY 10165
Ph:(212)986-9300
Fax:(212)986-5857
Co. E-mail: data@haver.com
URL: http://www.haver.com
Description: Contains annual time series on wages and employment by place of work. Data are available by 3-digit Standard Industrial Classification (SIC) codes for all 50 states and the 8 Bureau of Economic Analysis (BEA) regions, and by 2-digit SIC codes for Metropolitan Statistical Areas (MSAs). Source is the U.S. Bureau of Economic Analysis (BEA). **Availability:** Online: Haver Analytics. **Type:** Time series.

3378 ■ *Oregon Career Information System*
Oregon Career Information System
1244 University of Oregon
Eugene, OR 97403-1244
Ph:(541)346-3872
Free: 800-495-1266
Fax:(541)346-3823
Co. E-mail: rlee@orcis.uoregon.edu
URL: http://oregoncis.uoregon.edu
Description: Provides career information, including occupational profiles; local, state, and national labor market trends; job search techniques; self-employment options; programs of study; postsecondary educational institutions; and financial aid. For each occupation, covers job duties, required abilities, working conditions, earnings, employment outlooks, relevant school subjects, ways to prepare, self-employment options, and entry routes. For programs of study and training, covers typical course work, teaching methods, related occupations, admission requirements, lists of schools offering the programs, and transfer programs. For profiles of postsecondary schools and the kinds of programs they offer, covers admission requirements, costs, housing, and the types of financial aid and student services available. **Availability:** Online: Oregon Career Information System. **Type:** Directory.

LIBRARIES

3379 ■ Chicago Public Library Central Library–Business/Science/Technology Division
Harold Washington Library Center
400 S. State St., 4th Fl.
Chicago, IL 60605
Ph:(312)747-4450
Fax:(312)747-4975
URL: http://www.chipublib.org/branch/details/library/harold-washington/p/Bst
Contact: Marcia Dellenbach, BST Div.Chf.
Scope: Small business, marketing, technology, corporate reports, investments, management, personnel, patents, physical and biological sciences, medicine, health, computer science, careers, environmental information, gardening, cookbooks. **Services:** Interlibrary loan; copying; division open to the public. **Holdings:** 415,000 books; 52,100 bound periodical volumes; 33,000 reels of microfilm; Securities and Exchange Commission (SEC) reports; federal specifications and standards; American National Standards Institute standards; corporate Annual reports. **Subscriptions:** 4000 journals and other serials; 8 newspapers.

3380 ■ Eureka, The California Career Information System Library
PO Box 647
Richmond, CA 94808-0647
Ph:(510)669-0996
Free: 888-463-2247
Fax:(510)669-0992
Co. E-mail: msb@eurekanet.org
URL: http://www.eurekanet.org
Contact: M. Sumyyah Bilal, Dir.
Scope: Career exploration, California and National occupational and school information, International occupational information, job search and financial aid, programs of study and training, skills assessment. **Services:** Copying. **Holdings:** Figures not available.

3381 ■ Florida State University–Career Center Library
PO Box 3064162
100 S. Woodward Ave.
Tallahassee, FL 32306-4162

Ph:(850)644-6431
Fax:(850)644-3273
URL: http://www.career.fsu.edu/library
Contact: Brianna Frank, Libn.
Scope: Career planning, occupational information, education and training, work experience, job hunting, employer information. **Services:** Library open to the public. **Holdings:** 1000 books; 600 occupational files; 44 VF drawers; 100 videotapes; 66 CD-ROMs. **Subscriptions:** 35 journals and other serials.

3382 ■ Howard High School of Technology–Media Center
401 E. 12th St.
Wilmington, DE 19801
Ph:(302)571-5437
Fax:(302)571-5849
Co. E-mail: jlaugin@nccvt.k12.de.us
URL: http://www.howard.nccvt.k12.de.us/
Contact: Jane M. Lauginiger, Libn.
Scope: Vocational and technical careers. **Services:** Interlibrary loan; Library not open to the public. **Holdings:** 6000 books. **Subscriptions:** 50 journals and other serials; 3 newspapers.

3383 ■ Indian River Area Library
PO Box 160
Indian River, MI 49749
Ph:(231)238-8581
Fax:(231)238-9494
Co. E-mail: indrivl@northland.lib.mi.us
URL: http://www.libnet.org/iriver/
Contact: Cindy Lou Poquette, Dir.
Scope: Small business, careers, fine arts, music, dance. **Services:** Interlibrary loan; copying; Library open to the public (fee for non-residents to check out materials). **Holdings:** 52,000 books; 2500 videocassettes; 2000 microfiche; videocassettes; sound cassettes; DVDs; CDs; periodicals; large print books. **Subscriptions:** 78 journals and other serials; 3 newspapers.

3384 ■ Kershaw County Applied Technology Education Campus–Vocational-Technical Library
874 Vocational Ln.
Camden, SC 29020
Ph:(803)425-8980
Fax:(803)425-8988
URL: http://atec.kcsdschools.com/home.asp
Contact: Cynthia Addison, Libn.
Scope: Vocational education. **Services:** Library open to the public. **Holdings:** 5000 books. **Subscriptions:** 80 journals and other serials; 2 newspapers.

3385 ■ Lee Hecht Harrison–Business Information Center
50 Tice Blvd.
Woodcliff Lake, NJ 07677
Ph:(201)930-9333
Free: 800-611-4LHH
Fax:(201)307-0778
Co. E-mail: info@lhh.com
URL: http://www.lhh.com
Contact: Kim Glinsky, Dir., Bus.Info.Svcs.
Scope: Business, career transition and development. **Services:** Library not open to the public. **Holdings:** 200 books. **Subscriptions:** 30 journals and other serials; 5 newspapers.

3386 ■ National Association of Colleges & Employers Information Center
62 Highland Ave.
Bethlehem, PA 18017
Ph:(610)868-1421
Free: 800-544-5272
Fax:(610)868-0208
Co. E-mail: infocenter@naceweb.org
URL: http://www.naceweb.org/
Scope: Career planning and development, employer relations and recruitment, education statistics. **Services:** Center available to NACE members only. **Holdings:** Figures not available.

3387 ■ Ohio State University–Career Connection
Younkin Success Ctr., 2nd Fl.
1640 Neil Ave.
Columbus, OH 43201
Ph:(614)688-3898
Fax:(614)688-3440
Co. E-mail: careerconnection@studentlife.osu.edu
URL: http://careerconnection.osu.edu
Contact: Christina A. Rideout, PhD, Dir.
Scope: Personal and career self-assessment, career exploration, training opportunities, job search resources. **Services:** Copying; Center open to the public for reference use only. **Holdings:** 400 books. **Subscriptions:** 15 journals and other serials.

3388 ■ Social Development Canada and Human Resources and Skills Development Canada–Departmental Library–Career Library (235 L)
235 Lansdowne St.
Kamloops, BC, Canada V2C 1X8
Ph:(819)953-9134
Fax:(250)372-0761
Co. E-mail: matt.treger@hrdc-drhc.gc.ca
URL: http://www.hrdc-drhc.gc.ca/redirect_hr.html
Contact: Helen Apouchtine, Departmental Lib.
Scope: Human resources. **Services:** Library open to the public for reference use only. **Holdings:** 50 reports.

3389 ■ University of Oregon–Career Center Library
1408 University St.
220 Hendricks Hall
PO Box 3257
Eugene, OR 97403-0257
Ph:(541)346-6006
Fax:(541)346-6038
Co. E-mail: thaynes@uoregon.edu
URL: http://career.uoregon.edu
Contact: Tina Haynes, Career Libn.
Scope: Career direction, career information, job search, employment preparation tools, employer directories, International resources, majors and careers resources, internships, graduate school resources, computer lab. **Services:** Career Library services provided to current students and UO alumni; Career Library is open to the public with limited services. **Holdings:** 800-850 books and binders. **Subscriptions:** 5 journals and other periodicals; 4 newspapers.

3390 ■ University of South Carolina–Career Center Library
H. William Close Bldg., 6th Fl.
Columbia, SC 29208
Ph:(803)777-7280
Fax:(803)777-7556
Contact: Anne Orange, Prog.Mgr.
Scope: Career development, self-assessment, career planning, job searching. **Holdings:** Figures not available.

3391 ■ West Virginia Junior College Library
1000 Virginia St. E.
Charleston, WV 25301
Ph:(304)345-2820
Fax:(304)345-1425
Co. E-mail: wvjc_chas@hotmail.com
URL: http://www.wvjc.edu
Contact: Belinda L. Yerkey-Hammack
Scope: Business, medical assisting, legal office assisting, computer technology. **Services:** Copying; Library not open to the public. **Holdings:** 6000 books; 50 CD-ROMs. **Subscriptions:** 25 journals and other serials; 2 newspapers.

3392 ■ York University, Glendon Campus Counselling & Career Centre
Glendon Hall, E103
2275 Bayview Ave.
Toronto, ON, Canada M4N 3M6
Ph:(416)487-6709
Fax:(416)440-9237
Co. E-mail: starshis@glendon.yorku.ca
URL: http://www.glendon.yorku.ca/counselling/career.html
Contact: Sharon Tarshis, Couns.
Scope: Careers for liberal arts graduates. **Services:** Library not open to the public. **Holdings:** Figures not available.

3393 ■ YWCA–Resource Center Library
2222 14th St.
Boulder, CO 80302
Ph:(303)443-0419, x101
Fax:(303)443-5098
Co. E-mail: frontdesk@ywcaboulder.org
URL: http://www.ywcaboulder.org
Contact: Janet L. Beardsley, Exec.Dir.
Scope: Careers, job searching, educational resources, parenting, divorce, women's literature. **Services:** Copying; Library open to the public. **Holdings:** 550 books. **Subscriptions:** 6 journals and other serials; 2 newspapers.

ASSOCIATIONS AND OTHER ORGANIZATIONS

3394 ■ Architectural Woodwork Institute
46179 Westlake Dr., Ste. 120
Potomac Falls, VA 20165
Ph:(571)323-3636
Fax:(571)323-3630
Co. E-mail: info@awinet.org
URL: http://www.awinet.org
Contact: Philip Duvic, Exec. VP

Description: Manufacturers of architectural woodwork products (casework, fixtures, and paneling) and associated suppliers of equipment and materials. Works to: raise industry standards; research new and improved materials and methods; publish technical data helpful in the design and use of architectural woodwork. Conducts seminars and training course. **Publications:** *Newsbriefs* (monthly); *Quality Standards Illustrated* (periodic);Membership Directory (annual).

3395 ■ Association of Millwork Distributors
10047 Robert Trent Jones Pkwy.
New Port Richey, FL 34655-4649
Ph:(727)372-3665
Free: 800-786-7274
Fax:(727)372-2879
Co. E-mail: mail@amdweb.com
URL: http://www.amdweb.com
Contact: Rosalie Leone, CEO

Description: Wholesale distributors of windows, door, millwork and related products. Conducts research and statistical studies. Offers millwork home study course and audiovisual program dealing with product knowledge; furnishes group insurance. Compiles statistics. **Publications:** *AMD News* (monthly); *Membership Directory and Products' Guide* (annual).

3396 ■ Moulding and Millwork Producers Association
507 1st St.
Woodland, CA 95695
Ph:(530)661-9591
Free: 800-550-7889
Fax:(530)661-9586
Co. E-mail: info@wmmpa.com
URL: http://wmmpa.com
Contact: Kellie A. Schroeder, Exec. VP/CEO

Description: Represents manufacturers of wood mouldings and millwork. Provides promotion, standardization and marketing information services. **Publications:** *Case 'n Base News* (monthly); *Wood Moulding and Millwork Producers Association—Products and Services Membership Directory* (annual).

3397 ■ Window and Door Manufacturers Association
401 N Michigan Ave., Ste. 2200
Chicago, IL 60611
Ph:(312)321-6802
Fax:(312)673-6922
Co. E-mail: wdma@wdma.com
URL: http://www.wdma.com
Contact: Michael O'Brien, Pres./CEO

Description: Manufacturers of doors, windows, frames, and related products. Fosters, promotes, and protects members' interests; encourages product use. Establishes quality and performance standards; conducts research in all areas of door and window manufacture. Issues seals of approval for wood preservative treatment, hardwood doors, and window unit manufacture. **Publications:** *Millwork Sources of Supply* (annual); *WDMA Newsletter* (monthly).

DIRECTORIES OF EDUCATIONAL PROGRAMS

3398 ■ *Directory of Private Accredited Career Schools and Colleges of Technology*
Pub: Accrediting Commission of Career Schools and Colleges of Technology
Contact: Michale S. McComis, Exec. Dir.

Released: On web page. **Price:** Free. **Description:** Covers 3900 accredited post-secondary programs that provide training programs in business, trade, and technical fields, including various small business endeavors. Entries offer school name, address, phone, description of courses, job placement assistance, and requirements for admission. Arrangement is alphabetical.

REFERENCE WORKS

3399 ■ "Hard Rock on Pike" in *Puget Sound Business Journal* (Vol. 29, September 5, 2008, No. 20, pp. 1)
Pub: American City Business Journals

Ed: Jeanne Lang Jones. **Description:** A branch of the Hard Rock Cafe is opening in 2009 in the Liberty Building on Pike Street in downtown Seattle, Washington. The location is being renovated as a green building; the restaurant and concert venue will seat 300 patrons and has a rooftop deck and memorabilia shop.

3400 ■ "Ronald Taketa" in *Hawaii Business* (Vol. 54, September 2008, No. 3, pp. 28)
Pub: Hawaii Business Publishing

Ed: Shara Enay. **Description:** Interview with Ronald Taketa of the Hawaii Carpenters Union who states that the economic downturn has affected the construction industry as 20 percent of the union's 7,800 members are unemployed. He shares his thoughts about the industry's economic situation, the union's advertisements, and his role as a leader of the union.

3401 ■ "Troubled Project In Court" in *The Business Journal-Portland* (Vol. 25, July 25, 2008, No. 20, pp. 1)
Pub: American City Business Journals, Inc.

Ed: Wendy Culverwell. **Description:** Views and information on Salpare Bay's Hayden Island project, as well as on financing problems and cases associated with the project, are presented. Construction of luxurious waterside condominiums stopped last fall, after the discovery of financing problems and subcontractors and other parties started filing claims and counterclaims.

STATISTICAL SOURCES

3402 ■ *RMA Annual Statement Studies*
Pub: Robert Morris Associates (RMA)

Released: Annual. **Price:** $175.00 2006-07 edition, $105.00. **Description:** Contains composite balance sheets and income statements for more than 360 industries, including the accounting, auditing, and bookkeeping industries. Also contains five years of comparative historical data for discerning trends. Includes 16 commonly used ratios, computed for most of the size groupings for nearly every industry.

TRADE PERIODICALS

3403 ■ *AMD Newsletter*
Pub: Association of Millwork Distributors

Released: Monthly. **Price:** $40. **Description:** Provides information on the activities of the National Sash and Door Jobbers Association. Promotes wholesale distribution of windows, door, millwork, and related products.

3404 ■ *Architectural Designs*
Pub: Architectural Designs Inc.

Released: Quarterly. **Description:** Consumer magazine offering over 200 house plans.

3405 ■ *The Carpenter*
Pub: United Brotherhood of Carpenters and Joiners of America, AFL-CIO
Contact: Dave Ransom, Managing Editor

Released: Bimonthly. **Price:** $10; $2 single issue. **Description:** Official magazine of the Carpenters' Union.

3406 ■ *CWB Custom Woodworking Business*
Pub: Vance Publishing Corp.

Released: Monthly. **Price:** Free to qualified subscribers; $55 U.S., Canada, and Mexico; $125 other countries. **Description:** Magazine for professional custom woodworkers.

3407 ■ *Fine Woodworking*
Pub: Taunton Press Inc.
Contact: Jon Miller, Publisher

Ed: Timothy D. Schreiner, Editor. **Released:** 7/yr. **Price:** $34.95 U.S. and Canada; $59.95 U.S. and Canada two years; $83.95 U.S. and Canada three years. **Description:** Technical magazine for the amateur and professional woodworker.

3408 ■ *Modern Woodworking*
Pub: BNP Media
Contact: Brooke Wisdom, Exec. Ed.
E-mail: bwisdom@rrpub.com

Description: Magazine for management in the primary and secondary wood products industry.

3409 ■ *Wood Digest*
Pub: Cygnus Business Media
Contact: Kim Kaiser, Editor-in-Chief
Released: Monthly. **Description:** Manufactures of wood products trade magazine.

3410 ■ *Wood & Wood Products*
Pub: Vance Publishing Corp.
Contact: Rich Christianson, Assoc. Publisher/Ed.-at-Large
E-mail: rchristianson@vancepublishing.com
Released: Monthly. **Description:** Magazine for furniture, cabinet, and woodworking industry.

3411 ■ *Woodshop News*
Pub: Dominion Enterprises
Contact: Jennifer Hicks, Staff Writer
E-mail: j.hicks@woodshopnews.com
Ed: Tod Riggio, Editor, t.riggio@woodshopnews.com. **Released:** Monthly. **Price:** $21.95; $33.95 Canada; $35.95 other countries; $35.95 two years. **Description:** Newspaper (tabloid) focusing on people and businesses involved in woodworking.

3412 ■ *Woodwork*
Pub: Ross Periodicals
Ed: John Lavine, Editor. **Released:** Bimonthly. **Price:** $22 Canada; $25 other countries. **Description:** Covers all aspects of woodworking.

3413 ■ *Words From Woody*
Pub: David W. Wood
Ed: David W. Wood, Editor. **Released:** Quarterly. **Price:** $24.95; $39.95, two years. **Description:** Contains information of interest to construction-related firms. Also includes business and marketing tips.

VIDEOCASSETTES/ AUDIOCASSETTES

3414 ■ *Building Dreams*
CA Working Group/We Do the Work
1611 Telegraph Ave Suite 1550
Oakland, CA 94612
Ph:(510)268-9675
Fax:(510)268-3606
Co. E-mail: info@theworkinggroup.org
URL: http://www.pbs.org/livelyhood
Price: $59.00. **Description:** Examination of Los Angeles carpenters at work on various projects. Offers insight from the carpenters on passing on their skills and knowledge to the young men and women of South Central L.A. **Availability:** VHS.

3415 ■ *Small Shop Tips and Techniques*
Taunton Press
63 S. Main St.
PO Box 5506
Newtown, CT 06470-5506
Ph:(203)426-8171
Free: 800-888-8286
Fax:(203)426-3434
URL: http://www.taunton.com
Released: 1989. **Price:** $29.95. **Description:** The former editor of "Fine Woodworking" magazine shows off a few carpentry tips. **Availability:** VHS.

3416 ■ *Woodworking*
RMI Media
1365 N. Winchester St.
Olathe, KS 66061-5880
Ph:(913)768-1696
Free: 800-745-5480
Fax:800-755-6910
Co. E-mail: actmedia@act.org
URL: http://www.actmedia.com
Released: 1987. **Price:** $39.95. **Description:** Offers step-by-step instructions for special woodworking projects. **Availability:** VHS; 3/4U.

FRANCHISES AND BUSINESS OPPORTUNITIES

3417 ■ Archadeck
U.S. Structures Inc.
2924 Emerywood Pky., Ste. 101
Richmond, VA 23294
Ph:(804)353-6999
Free: 800-789-3325
Fax:(804)358-1878
Co. E-mail: Franchising@ussi.net
URL: http://www.archadeck.com
No. of Franchise Units: 73. **No. of Company-Owned Units:** 1. **Founded:** 1980. **Franchised:** 1984. **Description:** Custom design deck franchise. When a deck design is chosen, franchisees send preliminary sketches to the company's drafting division which will supply full construction plans with complete material layouts and specifications. Subcontracted Archadecktrained carpenters will usually build the deck in 2-3 days. **Equity Capital Needed:** $91,700-$142,900. **Franchise Fee:** $39,500-$49,500. **Royalty Fee:** 3.5%-5.5%+. **Financial Assistance:** Limited assistance. **Managerial Assistance:** Marketing director assists with a marketing plan before opening. Provides guidance in opening the business and preparing a business plan. Consultants help in the first 3 months of operation, with ongoing assistance with sales and construction. Toll-free numbers to all personnel at headquarters. Construction and drafting departments assist franchisees anytime. Regional and national workshops and seminars all year round. **Training:** Trains franchisee in construction, design, product knowledge, computer software, marketing plan, sales and business operations in a 3 week training. Also will train any employees that are hired later on. Before training, franchisees will receive start-up materials, manuals, Videotapes, and audio tapes that will help prepare them for the training.

3418 ■ Dollar Castle Inc.
7031 Orchard Lake Rd., Ste. 201
West Bloomfield, MI 48322
Ph:(248)539-3100
Free: 888-682-7379
Fax:(248)539-1778
No. of Franchise Units: 25. **No. of Company-Owned Units:** 7. **Founded:** 1992. **Franchised:** 1992. **Description:** Retail dollar store. **Equity Capital Needed:** $200,000. **Franchise Fee:** $30,000. **Financial Assistance:** No. **Training:** Yes.

3419 ■ DreamMaker Bath and Kitchen
1020 N University Parks Dr.
Waco, TX 76707
Ph:(254)745-2481
Free: 800-253-9153
Fax:800-396-6154
Co. E-mail: franchising@dwyergroup.com
URL: http://www.dreammaker-remodel.com
No. of Franchise Units: 46. **Founded:** 1970. **Franchised:** 1971. **Description:** Specializes in bath and kitchen remodeling options. **Equity Capital Needed:** $88,150-$315,000 cash; $112,750-$237,000 total investment. **Franchise Fee:** $37,000. **Financial Assistance:** Yes. **Training:** Extensive business, marketing and management training provided including team training conferences, an annual convention (Reunion) offers networking opportunities with other DreamMaker Bath & Kitchen franchisees, and continuous training.

3420 ■ DRY-B-LO International, Inc.
5287 Camp Wahsega Rd.
Dahlonega, GA 30533
Ph:(706)864-0049
Co. E-mail: corporate@dry-b-lo.com
URL: http://www.dry-b-lo.com
No. of Franchise Units: 39. **Founded:** 1993. **Franchised:** 1997. **Description:** Professionally installed deck drain system company in the United States. Multi-patented system that provides homeowners with a new approach to outdoor entertainment areas. **Equity Capital Needed:** $44,700-$150,300. **Franchise Fee:** $25,000. **Royalty Fee:** 7.5%. **Financial Assistance:** Third party equipment financing available. **Training:** Offers 1 week at headquarters, 3 days at franchisee's location, 1 week in Denver, CO and ongoing support.

3421 ■ Exovations
1550-A Oak Industrial Ln.
Cumming, GA 30041
Ph:(770)205-2995
Fax:(678)947-1800
No. of Franchise Units: 1. **No. of Company-Owned Units:** 2. **Founded:** 1996. **Franchised:** 2006. **Description:** Exterior home remodeling. **Equity Capital Needed:** $86,050-$198,750. **Franchise Fee:** $28,000-$75,000. **Royalty Fee:** 5%. **Financial Assistance:** Assistance with Payroll. **Training:** Offers 2 weeks at headquarters, 2 weeks at franchisees location and ongoing support.

3422 ■ Garagetek
5 Aerial Way, Ste. 200
Syosset, NY 11791
Ph:(516)621-4300
Free: (866)664-2724
Fax:(516)992-8600
Co. E-mail: SBarrett@GarageTek.com
URL: http://www.GarageTek.com
No. of Franchise Units: 55. **No. of Company-Owned Units:** 2. **Founded:** 2000. **Franchised:** 2001. **Description:** Franchise of construction, remodeling, bath and closet services. **Equity Capital Needed:** $250,000. **Franchise Fee:** $50,000. **Financial Assistance:** No. **Training:** Provides 2 weeks at corporate and ongoing field support.

3423 ■ Granite Transformations
RockSolid Granit USA Inc.
10360 USA Today Way
Miramar, FL 33025
Ph:(954)435-5538
Free: (866)685-5300
Fax:(954)435-5579
Co. E-mail: info@granittransformations.com
URL: http://www.granitetransformations.com
No. of Franchise Units: 79. **No. of Company-Owned Units:** 1. **Founded:** 2001. **Franchised:** 2001. **Description:** Construction, remodeling, and bath and closets services. **Equity Capital Needed:** $127,000-$350,000. **Franchise Fee:** $25,000-$75,000. **Financial Assistance:** No. **Training:** Training program consists of operations, installations, and sales training. Each training module is supported with training material. Training facility is an actual working location allowing trainees to evaluate, test, and see results. Grand opening supported by sales manager onsite and ongoing support.

3424 ■ House Doctors Handyman Service
575 Chamber Dr.
Milford, OH 45150
Free: 800-319-3359
Co. E-mail: info@housedoctors.com
URL: http://www.housedoctors.com
No. of Franchise Units: 90. **Founded:** 1994. **Description:** Minor home repairs. **Equity Capital Needed:** $70,000-$120,000. **Franchise Fee:** $9,800. **Financial Assistance:** Offers financing up to 50% of franchise fee. **Training:** 5 days of training includes marketing, technical knowledge, and business procedures.

3425 ■ Interior Door Replacement Co.
IDRC Franchising Corp.
300 Pioneer Way, Ste. B
Mountain View, CA 94041
Ph:(650)965-IDRC
Free: (866)315-IDRC
Fax:(650)938-6879
No. of Company-Owned Units: 1. **Founded:** 1997. **Franchised:** 2001. **Description:** Franchise of construction, remodeling and carpentry services. **Equity Capital Needed:** $126,500-$178,000. **Franchise Fee:** $10,000. **Financial Assistance:** No. **Training:** Yes.

3426 ■ Kitchen Solvers
301 4th St. S
La Crosse, WI 54601
Free: 800-845-6779
Fax:(608)784-2917
No. of Franchise Units: 78. **Founded:** 1982. **Franchised:** 1984. **Description:** Kitchen cabinet refacing, replacing doors and drawer fronts with new solid wood doors and covering framework with 1/8 wood panel. **Equity Capital Needed:** $38,400-$96,650. **Franchise Fee:** $15,000. **Financial Assistance:** Yes. **Training:** Yes.

3427 ■ Kitchen Tune-Up & Kitchen Tune-Up Express
KTU Worldwide Inc.
813 Circle Dr.
Aberdeen, SD 57401
Ph:(605)225-4049
Free: 800-333-6385
Fax:(605)225-1371
Co. E-mail: ktu@kitchentuneup.com
URL: http://www.kitchentuneup.com

No. of Franchise Units: 204. **Founded:** 1975. **Franchised:** 1989. **Description:** Provides inexpensive wood care services to both the residential homeowner and the commercial property owner. Also offers door replacement materials. This is a home-based, no-inventory, high-profit margin business. Offers potential franchise owners the unique opportunity to attend training and evaluate the franchise before signing the franchise agreement. **Equity Capital Needed:** $58,000- $66,000 or $22,000-$25,000 for Express. **Franchise Fee:** $25,000 or $10,000 for Kitchen Tune-Up Express. **Financial Assistance:** In-house and third party. **Training:** Initial training and ongoing support.

3428 ■ Millicare Commercial Carpet Care
201 Lukken Industrial Dr., W
LaGrange, GA 30240
Free: 877-812-8803
Fax:(706)880-3279
No. of Franchise Units: 79. **Founded:** 1979. **Franchised:** 1996. **Description:** Offers maintenance and cleaning services. **Equity Capital Needed:** $50,000 liquid; $150,000 net worth. **Franchise Fee:** $20,000. **Financial Assistance:** No. **Training:** Yes.

3429 ■ Ready Decks Franchise Systems Inc.
1250 New Natchitoches Rd.
West Monroe, LA 71295
Ph:(318)362-9990
Fax:(713)621-8200
No. of Franchise Units: 2. **No. of Company-Owned Units:** 2. **Founded:** 2001. **Franchised:** 2005. **Description:** Decking services. **Equity Capital Needed:** $84,000-$168,000. **Franchise Fee:** $29,000. **Royalty Fee:** 5%. **Financial Assistance:** Third party financing available. **Training:** Offers 2 weeks at headquarters, 1 week onsite and ongoing support.

3430 ■ RENOCanada-Bathroom & Kitchen Makeover Specialists
1534 Midland Ave.
Scarborough, ON, Canada M1P 3C2
Ph:(416)285-6798
Fax:(416)285-1825
Co. E-mail: info@renosystems.com
URL: http://www.renosystems.com
No. of Franchise Units: 3. **No. of Company-Owned Units:** 3. **Founded:** 2006. **Description:** New concept in home renovation where home improvement is not about the house, it's about self-improvement (lifestyle) and that bathrooms and kitchens are personal. **Franchise Fee:** $25,000.

3431 ■ United States Seamless
United States Seamless, Inc.
474 45th St. S
PO Box 2426
Fargo, ND 58108
Ph:(701)241-8888
Fax:(701)241-9999

No. of Franchise Units: 54. **Founded:** 1992. **Franchised:** 1992. **Description:** Seamless steel siding. **Equity Capital Needed:** $58,300-$108,700. **Franchise Fee:** $8,500. **Royalty Fee:** Varies. **Financial Assistance:** Third party financing available. **Training:** YES.

Catering Service

START-UP INFORMATION

3432 ■ *55 Surefire Food-Related Businesses: You Can Start for Under $5000*
Pub: Entrepreneur Press
Ed: Cheryl Kimball. **Released:** March 1, 2009. **Price:** $17.95. **Description:** Advice is given to start 55 various food-related companies and goes beyond restaurant or catering services. Home-based, retail and mail order ventures are covered, as well as food safety and standards.

3433 ■ *Culinary Careers: How to Get Your Dream Job in Food with Advice from Top Culinary Professionals*
Pub: Crown Business Books
Ed: Rick Smilow, Anne E. McBride. **Released:** May 4, 2010. **Price:** $16.99. **Description:** Top culinary experts offer advice for working in or owning a food service firm.

3434 ■ *How to Start a Home-Based Catering Business*
Pub: Globe Pequot Press, The
Ed: Denise Vivaldo. **Released:** 2002, 4th edition. **Price:** $17.95.

3435 ■ *How to Start a Home-Based Personal Chef Business*
Pub: Globe Pequot Press
Ed: Denise Vivaldo. **Released:** December 2006. **Price:** $18.95. **Description:** Everything needed to know to start a personal chef business is featured.

3436 ■ "It Sure Beats Pizza: San Francisco Company Delivers Gourmet Lunches to Businesses" in *Inc.* (Vol. 33, November 2011, No. 9, pp. 30)
Pub: Inc. Magazine
Ed: Bobbie Gossage. **Description:** Gastronaut caters daily meals to local companies. The firm was started by two former chefs at Google and employs 24 people to deliver buffet-style meals to eight businesses, with lunches costing $16 to $18 per serving.

3437 ■ *The Professional Chef: The Business of Doing Business As a Personal Chef*
Pub: John Wiley and Sons Inc.
Ed: Candy Wallace; Greg Forte. **Released:** February 2007. **Price:** $50.00. **Description:** Resources for starting a personal chef business are covered; CD-ROM included.

3438 ■ *Start and Run a Home-Based Food Business*
Pub: Self-Counsel Press, Inc.
Ed: Mimi Shotland Fix. **Released:** January 10, 2010. **Price:** $21.95. **Description:** Information is shared to help start and run a home-based food business, selling your own homemade foods.

ASSOCIATIONS AND OTHER ORGANIZATIONS

3439 ■ Canadian Restaurant and Foodservices Association–Association Canadienne des Restaurateurs et des Services Alimentaires
316 Bloor St. W
Toronto, ON, Canada M5S 1W5
Ph:(416)923-8416
Free: 800-387-5649
Fax:(416)923-1450
Co. E-mail: info@crfa.ca
URL: http://www.crfa.ca
Contact: Garth Whyte, Pres./CEO
Description: Restaurant and food service corporations, hotels, caterers, and food service suppliers and educators. Seeks to create a favorable business environment for members. Represents members' interests before government; conducts trade research. Makes available group buying programs and other services to members; owns and operates three industry trade shows. **Publications:** *Canadian Foodservice Industry Operations Report* (biennial); *Foodservice Facts* (annual); *Legislation Guide* (quarterly).

3440 ■ Convenience Caterers and Food Manufacturers Association
1205 Spartan Dr.
Madison Heights, MI 48071
Ph:(248)982-5379
Co. E-mail: ccfma@ymail.com
URL: http://www.mobilecaterers.com
Description: Firms and corporations engaged in the mobile catering business and in any other business catering to industrial feeding by mobile equipment; associate members are suppliers and manufacturers. Deals with common intra-industry problems through exchange of ideas, advice on legal problems, and safety standards and licensing regulations. **Publications:** *alaCARTE* (monthly).

3441 ■ National Association of Catering Executives
9891 Broken Land Pkwy., Ste. 301
Columbia, MD 21046
Ph:(410)290-5410
Fax:(410)290-5460
Co. E-mail: bfedchock@nacenet.org
URL: http://www.nace.net
Contact: Bonnie Fedchock, Exec. Dir.
Description: Professional caterers, affiliate members, the local and national suppliers and vendors in the many disciplines that impact and influence the catering business. Addresses banquet facilities, off-premise, country club, military and resort catering. Provides continuing education, certification, networking and career support. **Publications:** *NACE News Network* (monthly); *Professional Caterer* (quarterly).

3442 ■ National Barbecue Association
455 S Fourth St., Ste. 650
Louisville, KY 40202
Free: 888-909-2121
Fax:(502)589-3602
Co. E-mail: nbbqa@hqtrs.com
URL: http://www.nbbqa.org
Contact: Kell Phelps, Pres.
Description: Industry professionals and barbecue enthusiasts including restaurants, caterers, specialty equipment retailers, grill manufacturers and distributors, smoker manufacturers and distributors, food product suppliers and distributors, sauces and spice distributors, backyard hobbyists. **Publications:** *National Barbecue News* (monthly); *NBBQA Barbecue Buyers' Guide* (annual).

DIRECTORIES OF EDUCATIONAL PROGRAMS

3443 ■ *Major Food & Drink Companies of the World*
Pub: Graham & Whiteside
Ed: Heather Brewin, Editor. **Released:** Annual, Latest edition 16th; Published May, 2012. **Price:** $1,460, individuals. **Covers:** Over 9,200 worldwide companies involved in the food and drink industry. **Entries Include:** Company name, address, phone and names and titles of key personnel.

REFERENCE WORKS

3444 ■ "The Caterer and Hotelkeeper Interview Patrick Harbour and Nathan Jones" in *Caterer & Hotelkeeper* (October 28, 2011, No. 288)
Pub: Reed Reference Publishing
Description: Profiles of Patrick Harbour and Nathan Jones who quit their jobs to start their own catering business. The partners discuss their business strategy when launching their boutique catering firm and ways they are adapting to the slow economy in order to remain successful.

3445 ■ *Directory of Foodservice Distributors*
Pub: Chain Store Guide
Released: Annual, Latest edition 2011. **Price:** $425, individuals Directory; $495, individuals online lite; $1,175, individuals online pro. **Covers:** About 4,700 companies in the United States and Canada with at least $500,000 in sales to foodservice companies. Included companies must distribute more than one product line and obtain no more than 95% of its total sales volume from self-manufactured merchandise. **Entries Include:** Company name, address, phone and fax numbers, e-mail and web addresses; Internet order processing indicator and sales percentage; total sales; foodservice and wholesale sales; product lines; total units served; foodservice accounts served; trading areas; distribution center locations; markets served; buying/marketing group name and location; subsidiaries names and locations; divisional, regional and branch office locations; year founded; public company indicator; key personnel with titles; 20,500 foodservice distribution contacts; 9,642 Name, address, phone, fax. **Arrangement:** Geographical. **Indexes:** Product lines, alphabetical, exclusions.

3446 ■ "Edible Endeavors" in *Black Enterprise* (March 2008)
Pub: Earl G. Graves Publishing Co. Inc.
Ed: Carolyn M. Brown. **Description:** Profile of Jacqueline Frazer, woman entrepreneur who turned her love for cooking into a catering business. She is chef

and owner of Command Performance in New York City. The firm works with more than 50 clients annually and generates annual revenues of about $350,000.

3447 ■ *Foodservice Consultants Society International—Membership Directory*
Pub: Foodservice Consultants Society International
Contact: Mr. Scott D. Legge, Exec. Dir.
E-mail: scott@fcsi.org

Released: Annual, 2002-2003. **Price:** $450. **Covers:** About 1,400 members who design and advise on management and other aspects of food service operations. **Entries Include:** Name, company name, address, business phone, home phone (if available), fax, e-mail, areas of specialty. **Arrangement:** Classified by membership type. **Indexes:** Geographical, company name.

3448 ■ "Prepping for the Unpredictable" in *Crain's Cleveland Business* (Vol. 30, June 15, 2009, No. 23, pp. 16)
Pub: Crain Communications, Inc.

Ed: Joel Hammond. **Description:** Michael Ferrara, event planner and designer for Executive Caterers discusses the many events he has planned.

3449 ■ "Professional Help: Cross That Off Your To-Do List" in *Inc.* (November 2007, pp. 89-90, 92)
Pub: Gruner & Jahr USA Publishing

Ed: Alison Stein Wellner. **Description:** Small business owners are finding that it pays to hire someone to takeover the personal tasks of daily living, including hiring a personal assistant, chauffeur, chef, stylist, pet caregiver, or concierge service.

3450 ■ "Revelations Derek Johnstone, Head Chef, Greywalls Hotel and Chez Roux" in *Caterer & Hotelkeeper* (October 28, 2011, No. 288)
Pub: Reed Reference Publishing

Description: Profile of Derek Johnstone, head chef at Greywalls Hotel and Chez Roux and his love for catering.

3451 ■ "Savvy Solutions" in *Black Enterprise* (Vol. 41, October 2010, No. 3, pp. 52)
Pub: Earl G. Graves Publishing Co. Inc.

Ed: Tennille M. Robinson. **Description:** Husband and wife team seek advice for expanding their catering business. They are also seeking funding resources.

TRADE PERIODICALS

3452 ■ *Cooking for Profit*
Pub: CP Publishing, Inc.

Released: Monthly. **Price:** $30; $55 two years; $52 Canada; $98 Canada 2 years; $85 other countries; $160 other countries 2 years. **Description:** Food service trade publication for owners/operators of food service businesses. Profiles successful operations, offers management tips, recipes with photos and step-by-step instructions, new and improved uses and maintenance of gas equipment.

3453 ■ *The National Culinary Review*
Pub: American Culinary Federation Inc.

Ed: Kay Orde, Editor, korde@acfchefs.net. **Released:** Monthly. **Price:** $60; $200 other countries. **Description:** Trade magazine covering food and cooking.

VIDEOCASSETTES/ AUDIOCASSETTES

3454 ■ *Food Services*
RMI Media
1365 N. Winchester St.
Olathe, KS 66061-5880
Ph:(913)768-1696
Free: 800-745-5480
Fax:800-755-6910
Co. E-mail: actmedia@act.org
URL: http://www.actmedia.com

Released: 1987. **Description:** Methods of food preparation and equipment maintenance used in the food industry are discussed. **Availability:** VHS; 3/4U.

3455 ■ *Le Cordon Bleu II*
PBS Home Video
Catalog Fulfillment Center
PO Box 751089
Charlotte, NC 28275-1089
Ph:800-531-4727
Free: 800-645-4PBS
Co. E-mail: info@pbs.org
URL: http://www.pbs.org

Released: 1998. **Price:** $99.95. **Description:** The Master Chefs of Le Cordon Bleu, one of the finest schools of French cuisine in the world, show the viewer how to prepare Tournedos Montagnarde (filet mignon with goat cheese and pine nuts in a red wine sauce), Coq au Vin and show how to prepare a menu for a dinner party or holiday gathering. Four hours on four videocassettes. **Availability:** VHS.

TRADE SHOWS AND CONVENTIONS

3456 ■ ApEx
Canadian Restaurant and Food Services Association
316 Bloor St. W.
Toronto, ON, Canada M5S 1W5
Ph:(416)923-8416
Free: 800-387-5649
Fax:(416)923-1450
Co. E-mail: info@crfa.ca
URL: http://www.crfa.ca

Audience: Trade. **Principal Exhibits:** Products and services for the restaurant and hospitality industry, as well as institutions, convenience stores, delis and bakeries. **Dates and Locations:** 2011 Apr 03-04, Moncton, NB.

3457 ■ HSMAI - Affordable Meetings West
George Little Management, LLC (New York, New York)
1133 Westchester Ave., Ste. N136
White Plains, NY 10606
Ph:(914)421-3200
Free: 800-272-SHOW
Co. E-mail: cathy_steel@glmshows.com
URL: http://www.glmshows.com

Released: Annual. **Audience:** Trade professionals. **Principal Exhibits:** Equipment, supplies, and services for the hospitality and marketing industry. **Dates and Locations:** 2011 Jun 15-16, Long Beach, CA.

3458 ■ International Restaurant & Foodservice Show of New York
Reed Exhibitions North American Headquarters
383 Main Ave.
Norwalk, CT 06851
Ph:(203)840-4800
Fax:(203)840-5805
Co. E-mail: export@reedexpo.com
URL: http://www.reedexpo.com

Released: Annual. **Principal Exhibits:** Equipment, supplies, and services for the food products, foodservice, restaurant, and institutional food service industries.

3459 ■ Ottawa Wine and Food Show
Player Expositions International
255 Clemow Ave.
Ottawa, ON, Canada K1S 2B5
Ph:(613)567-6408
Fax:(613)567-2718
URL: http://www.playerexpo.com

Released: Annual. **Audience:** Restaurant, hotels, clubs, catering-fine food stores, specialty food stores, wine clubs, and the general public. **Principal Exhibits:** Fine wines and foods, and beer from around the world.

CONSULTANTS

3460 ■ Cini-Little International Inc.
20251 Century Blvd., Ste. 375
Germantown, MD 20874-1114
Ph:(301)528-9700
Fax:(301)528-9711
Co. E-mail: info@cinilittle.com
URL: http://www.cinilittle.com
Contact: William V. Eaton, Principle
E-mail: weaton@atscinilittle.com

Scope: Offers a full range of independent management and design consulting services in all aspects of food service to industries such as hospitality, business, and health care. Services include feasibility studies and or operations analyses, food service programs and concepts, operational training programs and manuals, food service contractor selection, contract documents, review of contractor submittal and site inspections. Offers consulting in materials management, materials handling, vertical horizontal transport elevator escalator moving sidewalks to all segments of the construction, hospitality, health-care and related industries.

FRANCHISES AND BUSINESS OPPORTUNITIES

3461 ■ City Kitchen
950 S Flower St., Ste. 105
Los Angeles, CA 90015
Free: 800-704-2070
Fax:(213)236-0951

No. of Company-Owned Units: 1. **Founded:** 2001. **Franchised:** 2004. **Description:** Fine food catering. **Equity Capital Needed:** $150,000-$500,000. **Franchise Fee:** $30,000. **Royalty Fee:** 6%. **Financial Assistance:** Third party financing available.

3462 ■ Corporate Caterers Franchise LLC
4155 SW 130th Ave., Ste. 208
Miami, FL 33175
Ph:(305)223-1230
Free: 877-523-1230
Fax:(305)223-2165

No. of Franchise Units: 7. **No. of Company-Owned Units:** 2. **Founded:** 1997. **Franchised:** 2007. **Description:** Catering for professional offices & business events. **Equity Capital Needed:** $86,000-$188,000. **Franchise Fee:** $30,000. **Royalty Fee:** 4%. **Financial Assistance:** No. **Training:** Offers 4 weeks at headquarters, 10 days at franchisees location and ongoing support.

3463 ■ Steak-Out Charbroiled Delivery
Steak-Out Franchising, Inc.
3091 Governors Lake Dr., Ste. 500
Norcross, GA 30071
Ph:(678)533-6000
Free: 877-878-3257
Fax:(678)291-0222
Co. E-mail: jmccord@steakout.com
URL: http://www.steakout.com

No. of Franchise Units: 42. **No. of Company-Owned Units:** 2. **Founded:** 1986. **Franchised:** 1987. **Description:** Full meal delivery chain featuring charbroiled steaks, chicken, seafood, burgers, chef salads & deserts. Steak-Out serves the busy office worker that doesn't have time to go for lunch & the on-the-go family that needs a wholesome meal when there is no time to cook. Steak-Out features delivery, carry-out & catering. **Equity Capital Needed:** $100,000 liquid; $400,000 net worth. **Franchise Fee:** $30,000. **Financial Assistance:** Third party and SBA approved. **Training:** Training is 4 weeks in the store and at headquarters for 3 to 4 management employees. Complete support in site finding, store opening, marketing and ongoing.

LIBRARIES

3464 ■ American Institute of Food Distribution, Inc.–Information and Research Center
1 Broadway Plaza, 2nd Fl.
Elmwood Park, NJ 07407
Ph:(201)791-5570

Fax:(201)791-5222
Co. E-mail: jkastrinsky@foodinstitute.com
URL: http://www.foodinstitute.com/
Contact: Brian Todd, Pres./CEO
Scope: Food industry. **Services:** Center open to the public on fee basis. **Subscriptions:** 400 journals and other serials.

3465 ■ City College of San Francisco Culinary Arts and Hospitality Studies Department–Alice Statler Library
50 Phelan Ave.
Statler Wing, Rm. 10
San Francisco, CA 94112
Ph:(415)239-3460
Fax:(415)239-3026
Co. E-mail: aniosi@ccsf.edu
URL: http://www.ccsf.edu/library/alice/statler.html
Contact: Andrea Niosi, Libn.
Scope: Public hospitality industries - hotels, motels, restaurants, catering services, cookery and nutrition; tourism; beverages. **Services:** Copying; Library open to the public for reference use only. **Holdings:** 10,000 books; 3500 pamphlets; 900 menus; videotapes; archives. **Subscriptions:** 80 journals and other serials.

3466 ■ Culinary Institute of America–Conrad N. Hilton Library
1946 Campus Dr.
Hyde Park, NY 12538-1499
Ph:(845)451-1322
Co. E-mail: c_crawfo@culinary.edu
URL: http://library.culinary.edu/
Contact: Christine Crawford-Oppenheimer, Info.Svcs. Libn.
Scope: Cookery, food service, restaurant management, hospitality. **Services:** Interlibrary loan; copying; Library open to the public by appointment. **Holdings:** 84,000 volumes; 30,000 menus; 3800 DVDs and videos. **Subscriptions:** 280 journals and other serials.

3467 ■ Johnson & Wales University–Harborside Culinary Library
321 Harborside Blvd.
Providence, RI 02905
Ph:(401)598-1282
Fax:(401)598-1834
Co. E-mail: barbara.janson@jwu.edu
URL: http://www.jwu.edu
Contact: Barbara Janson, Hd.Libn.
Scope: Cookbooks, food service, menu planning, nutrition, professional management, catering and banquets, household manuals, canning, preserving and freezing, hotel and motel management. **Services:** Copying; Library open to the public. **Holdings:** 10,000 books; 700 menus. **Subscriptions:** 100 journals and other serials.

3468 ■ Johnson and Wales University Charleston Campus–Barry L. Gleim Library
701 E. Bay St.
Charleston, SC 29403
Ph:(843)727-3045
Fax:(843)727-3078
Co. E-mail: Joanne.Letendre@jwu.edu
Contact: Joanne N. Letendre
Scope: Culinary arts, food service, hospitality management, travel and tourism. **Services:** Library open to the public with restrictions. **Holdings:** 10,681 books; 1230 videos; 6 CD-ROMs. **Subscriptions:** 174 journals and other serials; 5 newspapers.

3469 ■ Noble and Associates Library
2155 W. Chesterfield Blvd.
Springfield, MO 65807
Ph:(417)875-5000
Co. E-mail: julie.tumy@noble.net
URL: http://www.noble.net
Contact: Julie Tumy, Pres.
Scope: Food, food service, advertising, construction, agriculture. **Services:** Interlibrary loan; copying; SDI; Library not open to the public. **Holdings:** 500 books; 1000 reports. **Subscriptions:** 300 journals and other serials; 5 newspapers.

START-UP INFORMATION

3470 ■ *The 100 Best Businesses to Start When You Don't Want To Work Hard Anymore*
Pub: Career Press Inc.
Ed: Lisa Rogak. **Price:** $16.99. **Description:** Author helps burned-out workers envision a new future as a small business owner. Systems analysis, adventure travel outfitting, bookkeeping, food delivery, furniture making, and software development are among the industries examined.

3471 ■ "Local Startup Hits Big Leagues" in *Austin Business JournalInc.* (Vol. 28, December 19, 2008, No. 40, pp. 1)
Pub: American City Business Journals
Ed: Christopher Calnan. **Description:** Qcue LLC, an Austin, Texas-based company founded in 2007 is developing a software system that can be used by Major League Baseball teams to change the prices of their single-game tickets based on variables affecting demand. The company recently completed a trial with the San Francisco Giants in 2008.

3472 ■ "OtherInbox Ready for Revenue: Software Startup Expects Profits in '09" in *Austin Business JournalInc.* (Vol. 28, January 2, 2009)
Pub: American City Business Journals
Ed: Christopher Calnan. **Description:** Founder of Austin, Texas-based OtherBox Inc. expects the company to generate revenue through subscriptions and advertising and also reach profitability in 2009. The company's email management tool sends secondary mail to an alternate location thereby freeing up the work inbox for more urgent messages.

REFERENCE WORKS

3473 ■ "A Dog-Day Pooch" in *Canadian Business* (Vol. 79, September 11, 2006, No. 18, pp. 19)
Pub: Rogers Media
Ed: Andrew Wahl. **Description:** Acquisition deal of Hummingbird Ltd by Canadian software maker Open Text Corp., is discussed.

3474 ■ "Abacast, Citadel Strike Radio Ad Deal" in *Business Journal Portland* (Vol. 27, December 31, 2010, No. 44, pp. 3)
Pub: Portland Business Journal
Ed: Erik Siemers. **Description:** Software firm Abacast Inc. has partnered with Citadel Media to aid the latter's advertising sales. Citadel provides radio networks and syndicated programs to 4,200 affiliate stations.

3475 ■ "ACC Game Development Program Opens" in *Austin Business JournalInc.* (Vol. 28, October 31, 2008, No. 33, pp. 1)
Pub: American City Business Journals
Ed: Sandra Zaragoza. **Description:** Austin, Texas-based Austin Community College has launched its Game Development Institute. The institute was created to meet the gaming industry's demand for skilled workers. One hundred students have enrolled with the institute.

3476 ■ "All Those Applications, and Phone Users Just Want to Talk" in *Advertising Age* (Vol. 79, August 11, 2008, No. 31, pp. 18)
Pub: Crain Communications, Inc.
Ed: Mike Vorhaus. **Description:** Although consumers are slowly coming to text messaging and other data applications, a majority of those Americans surveyed stated that they simply want to use their cell phones to talk and do not care about other activities. Statistical data included.

3477 ■ "AMT's Partner Program Enables New Security Business Models" in *Internet Wire* (August 12, 2010)
Pub: Comtex
Description: AMT, technical provider of physical access control Software as a Service (Saas) solutions, has developed a new Partner Program that allows partners to outsource any technical abilities lacking to AMT with no upfront fees.

3478 ■ "Angel Investments Tripled in 2009" in *Austin Business JournalInc.* (Vol. 29, January 8, 2010, No. 44, pp. 1)
Pub: American City Business Journals
Ed: Christopher Calnan. **Description:** Central Texas Angel Network (CTAN) has invested $3.5 million in 12 ventures, which include 10 in Austin, Texas in 2009 to triple the amount it invested during 2008. The largest recipient of CTAN's investments is life sciences, which attracted 20 percent of the capital, while software investments fell to 18 percent. The new screening process that helps startups secure CTAN capital is explored.

3479 ■ "Apps For Anybody With an Idea" in *Advertising Age* (Vol. 79, October 20, 2008, No. 39, pp. 29)
Pub: Crain Communications, Inc.
Ed: Beth Snyder Bulik. **Description:** Apple's new online App Store is open to anyone with an idea and the ability to write code and many of these developers are not only finding a sense of community through this venue but are also making money since the sales are split with Apple, 30/70 in the developer's favor.

3480 ■ "Arctic IT Honored" in *Alaska Business Monthly* (Vol. 27, October 2011, No. 10, pp. 10)
Pub: Alaska Business Publishing Company
Ed: Nancy Pounds. **Description:** Arctic Information Technology Inc. was named to Everything Channel's 2011 Computer Reseller News (CRN) Next-Generation 250 list. The firm provides business software and network infrastructure solutions.

3481 ■ "Arizona Firms In Chicago Go For Gold With '08 Games" in *The Business Journal - Serving Phoenix and the Valley of the Sun* (Vol. 28, August 8, 2008, No. 49, pp. 1)
Pub: American City Business Journals, Inc.
Ed: Patrick O'Grady. **Description:** More than 20 U.S. athletes will wear Arizona-based eSoles LLC's custom-made insoles to increase their performance at the 2008 Beijing Olympics making eSoles one of the beneficiaries of the commercialization of the games. Translation software maker Auralog Inc saw a 60 percent jump in sales from its Mandarin Chinese language applications.

3482 ■ "Attivio Brings Order to Data" in *Information Today* (Vol. 26, February 2009, No. 2, pp. 14)
Pub: Information Today, Inc.
Ed: Marji McClure. **Description:** Profile of Attivio, the high tech firm offering next-generation software that helps businesses to consolidate data and eliminate enterprise silos.

3483 ■ "AVG Introduces Security Software Suite for SMBs 551179" in *eWeek* (October 12, 2010)
Pub: Ziff Davis Enterprise
Description: AVG Technologies is offering its AVG Internet Security 2011 Business Edition and AVG Anti-Virus Business Edition designed to give Internet-active SMB owners protection. The system protects online transactions and email communications as well as sensitive customer data and AVG Anti-Virus 2011 Business edition offers real-time protection against the latest online threats.

3484 ■ "BancVue to Expand" in *Austin Business JournalInc.* (Vol. 29, November 27, 2009, No. 38, pp. 1)
Pub: American City Business Journals
Ed: Kate Harrington. **Description:** Significant growth of BancVue in the past six years has prompted the company to look for a site that could increase its office space from 25,000 square feet to 65,000 square feet. BancVue offers bank and credit union software solutions and is planning to lease or buy a property in Austin, Texas.

3485 ■ "Bar Hopping: Your Numbers At a Glance" in *Inc.* (January 2008, pp. 44-45)
Pub: Gruner & Jahr USA Publishing
Ed: Michael Fitzgerald. **Description:** Software that helps any company analyze data include Crystal Xcelsius, a program that takes data from Excel documents and turns them into animated gauges, charts and graphs; CashView, a Web-based application that tracks receivables and payables; iDashboards, a Web-based programs that produces animated gauges, maps, pie charts and graphs; Corda Human Capital Management, that transforms stats like head count, productivity, and attrition into graphs and dials; NetSuite, a Web-based application that tracks key indicators; and Cognos Now, that gauges, dials, and graphs data.

3486 ■ "BayTSP, NTT Data Corp. Enter Into Reseller Pact to Market Online IP Monitoring" in *Professional Services Close-Up* (Sept. 11, 2009)
Pub: Close-Up Media
Description: Due to incredible interest from distributors and content owners across Asia, NTT Data Corp. will resell BayTSP's online intellectual property monitoring, enforcement, business intelligence and monetization services in Japan.

3487 ■ "Behind the Scenes: Companies At the Heart of Everyday Life" in *Inc.* (February 2008, pp. 26-27)
Pub: Gruner & Jahr USA Publishing

Ed: Athena Schindelheim. **Description:** Profiles of companies providing services to airports, making the environment safer and more efficient, as well as more comfortable for passengers and workers. Centerpoint Manufacturing provides garbage bins that can safely contain explosions producing thousands of pounds of pressure; Infax, whose software displays arrival and departure information on 19-foot-wide screens; Lavi Industries, whose products include security barricades, hostess stands, and salad-bar sneeze guards; and SATech maker of rubber flooring that helps ease discomfort for workers having to stand for long periods of time.

3488 ■ "Being all a-Twitter" in *Canadian Business* (Vol. 81, December 8, 2008, No. 21, pp. 22)
Pub: Rogers Media Ltd.

Ed: Andrew Wahl. **Description:** Marketing experts suggest that advertising strategies have to change along with new online social media. Companies are advised to find ways to incorporate social software because workers and customers are expected to continue its use.

3489 ■ "Best Managed Companies (Canada)" in *Canadian Business* (Vol. 82, Summer 2009, No. 8, pp. 38)
Pub: Rogers Media

Ed: Calvin Leung. **Description:** Agrium Inc. and Barrick Gold Corporation are among those that are found to be the best managed companies in Canada. Best managed companies also include software firm Open Text Corporation, which has grown annual sales by 75 percent and annual profits by 160 percent since 1995. Open Text markets software that allow firms to manage word-based data, and has 46,000 customers in 114 countries.

3490 ■ "Beyond Microsoft and Yahoo!: Some M&A Prospects" in *Barron's* (Vol. 88, March 17, 2008, No. 11, pp. 39)
Pub: Dow Jones & Company, Inc.

Ed: Eric J. Savitz. **Description:** Weak quarterly earnings report for Yahoo! could pressure the company's board to cut a deal with Microsoft. Electronic Arts is expected to win its $26-a-share bid for Take-Two Interactive Software. Potential targets and buyers for mergers and acquisitions are mentioned.

3491 ■ "Beyond YouTube: New Uses for Video, Online and Off" in *Inc.* (October 2007, pp. 53-54)
Pub: Gruner & Jahr USA Publishing

Ed: Leah Hoffmann. **Description:** Small companies are using video technology for embedding messages into email, broadcasting live interactive sales and training seminars, as well as marketing campaigns. Experts offer insight into producing and broadcasting business videos.

3492 ■ *The Big Switch*
Pub: W. W. Norton & Company, Inc.

Ed: Nicholas Carr. **Released:** January 19, 2009. **Price:** $16.95 paperback. **Description:** Today companies are dismantling private computer systems and tapping into services provided via the Internet. This shift is remaking the computer industry, bringing competitors such as Google to the forefront ant threatening traditional companies like Microsoft and Dell. The book weaves together history, economics, and technology to explain why computing is changing and what it means for the future.

3493 ■ "Blog Buzz Heralds Arrival of IPhone 2.0" in *Advertising Age* (Vol. 79, June 9, 2008, No. 40, pp. 8)
Pub: Crain Communications, Inc.

Ed: Abbey Klaassen. **Description:** Predictions concerning the next version of the iPhone include a global-positioning-system technology as well as a configuration to run on a faster, 3G network.

3494 ■ *Business Feasibility Analysis Pro*
Pub: Prentice Hall PTR

Ed: Palo Alto Software. **Released:** August 2006. **Price:** $28.40. **Description:** Profile of software developed to support small business management and/or entrepreneurship text. Step-by-step instructions are provided.

3495 ■ "BusinessOnLine Launches a New Web-Based Search Engine Optimization Tool" in *Internet Wire* (October 19, 2009)
Pub: Comtex News Network, Inc.

Description: First Link Checker, a complimentary new search engine optimization tool that helps site owners optimize their on-page links by understanding which of those links are actually being counted in Google's relevancy algorithm, was developed by BusinessOnLine, a rapidly growing Internet marketing agency. This tool will make it easy for the average web master to ensure that their internal link structure is optimized.

3496 ■ "A Case Study: Real-Life Business Planning" in *Entrepreneur* (February 3, 2009)
Pub: Entrepreneur Media Inc.

Ed: Tim Berry. **Description:** Provides a case study of a two-day planning meeting for Palo Alto Software in which the executives of the company met for their annual planning cycle and discussed ways in which the company needed to change in order to stay viable in today's tough economic climate.

3497 ■ "Cerner Works the Business Circuit" in *Business Journal-Serving Metropolitan Kansas City* (Vol. 26, October 5, 2007, No. 4, pp. 1)
Pub: American City Business Journals, Inc.

Ed: Rob Roberts. **Description:** Cerner Corporation is embracing the coming of the electronic medical record exchange by creating a regional health information organization (RHIO) called the CareEntrust. The RHIO convinced health insurers to share claims data with patients and clinicians. At the Center Health Conference, held October 7 to 10, Cerner will demonstrate the software it developed for CareEntrust to the 40,000 healthcare and information technology professionals.

3498 ■ "ChemSW Software Development Services Available for Outsourcing" in *Information Today* (Vol. 26, February 2009, No. 2, pp. 30)
Pub: Information Today, Inc.

Description: ChemSW software development services include requirements analysis, specification development, design, development, testing, and system documentation as an IT outsourcing solution. The company can also develop software tracking systems for satellite stockrooms, provide asset management integration solutions and more.

3499 ■ "ClickFuel Launches New Products to Help Small and Mid-Sized Businesses Bolster Their Brand Online" in *Internet Wire* (Dec. 3,2009)
Pub: Comtex News Network, Inc.

Description: Boostability, a provider of Enterprise Search Engine Optimization (SEO) software technology, has partnered with ClickFuel, a firm that designs, tracks and manages Internet marketing campaigns in order to leverage Boostability's technology in order to deliver comprehensive SEO solutions to small and mid-size businesses; three new products will also become available for these business clients to help them manage all facets of their online presence.

3500 ■ "ClickFuel Unveils Internet Marketing Tools for Small Businesses" in *Internet Wire* (October 19, 2009)
Pub: Comtex News Network, Inc.

Description: ClickFuel, a firm that manages, designs and tracks marketing campaigns has unveiled a full software suite of affordable services and technology solutions designed to empower small business owners and help them promote and grow their businesses through targeted Internet marketing campaigns.

3501 ■ "Clouds in the Forecast" in *Information Today* (Vol. 28, September 2011, No. 8, pp. 10)
Pub: Information Today, Inc.

Ed: Paula J. Hane. **Description:** Cloud computing is software, applications, and data stored remotely and accessed via the Internet with output displayed on a client device. Recent developments in cloud computing are explored.

3502 ■ *Computer Accounting Essentials with Microsoft Office Accounting 2010*
Pub: McGraw-Hill Higher Education

Ed: Carol Yacht, Susan Crosson. **Released:** March 10, 2010. **Description:** Step-by-step guide to using Microsoft's Office Professional 2007 Accounting program.

3503 ■ "Cut Energy Waste" in *Inc.* (Vol. 31, January-February 2009, No. 1, pp. 42)
Pub: Mansueto Ventures LLC

Description: Carbon Control, Edison, and Saver software programs help companies cut carbon emissions by reducing the amount of energy consumed by computers while they are idle.

3504 ■ "Dear Customer: Managing E-Mail Campaigns" in *Inc.* (March 2008, pp. 58-59)
Pub: Gruner & Jahr USA Publishing

Ed: Ryan Underwood. **Description:** Internet services that help firms manage their online business including email marketing, to manage subscriber lists, comply with spam regulations, monitor bouncebacks, and track potential customers are profiled. Constant Contact, MobileStorm Stun, Campaign Monitor, Pop Commerce, Emma, and StrongMail E-mail Server are among software and services highlighted.

3505 ■ "Design Programs for HVAC Sizing Solutions" in *Contractor* (Vol. 57, January 2010, No. 1, pp. 44)
Pub: Penton Media, Inc.

Ed: William Feldman; Patti Feldman. **Description:** Rhvac 8 is an HVAC design program that lets users calculate peak heating and cooling load requirements for rooms, zones, systems, and entire buildings. The HVAC Pipe Sizer software for the iPhone enables quick sizing of a simple piping system.

3506 ■ "Don't Touch My Laptop, If You Please Mr. Customs Man" in *Canadian Electronics* (Vol. 23, June-July 2008, No. 4, pp. 6)
Pub: Action Communication Inc.

Ed: Mark Borkowski. **Description:** Canadian businessmen bringing electronic devices to the US can protect the contents of their laptops by hiding their data from US border agents. They can also choose to clean up the contents of their laptop using file erasure programs.

3507 ■ "DST Turns to Banks for Credit" in *The Business Journal-Serving Metropolitan Kansas City* (Vol. 27, October 3, 2008, No. 3, pp. 1)
Pub: American City Business Journals, Inc.

Ed: Rob Roberts. **Description:** Kansas City, Missouri-based DST Systems Inc., a company that provides sophisticated information processing, computer software services and business solutions, has secured a new five-year, $120 million credit facility from Enterprise Bank and Bank of the West. The deal is seen to reflect that the region and community-banking model remain stable. Comments from executives are also provided.

3508 ■ "Eagles Measure Suite Success" in *Philadelphia Business Journal* (Vol. 30, September 9, 2011, No. 30, pp. 1)
Pub: American City Business Journals Inc.

Ed: John George. **Description:** Philadelphia Eagles have a new software program that helps suite holders keep track of how their suite is being used and whether they are getting a return on their investment. The software allows suite holders to better utilize and distribute their tickets.

3509 ■ "EBSCO Adds New Features to EBSCOhost Content Viewer" in *Information Today* (Vol. 26, February 2009, No. 2, pp. 31)
Pub: Information Today, Inc.
Description: EBSCOhost Content Viewer historical digital archive collection provides a visual overview of a displayed document, highlighting search keywords on the page as well as providing a document map that shows the number of times a given keyword is mentioned in a periodical, monograph, article, or other document. For periodical content, the viewer lets users browse multiple issues in a volume without leaving the interface; features include zoom and pan technology similar to online maps.

3510 ■ "Elastic Path Software Joins Canada in G20 Young Entrepreneur Summit" in *Internet Wire* (June 14, 2010)
Pub: Comtex
Description: The Canadian Youth Business Foundation hosted the G20 Young Entrepreneur Summit and announced that Harry Chemko of British Columbia's Elastic Path Software will be a member of the Canadian delegation at the G20 Young Entrepreneur Summit. Details are included.

3511 ■ "The Emergence of Governance In an Open Source Community" in *Academy of Management Journal* (Vol. 50, No. 5, October 2007, pp. 1079)
Pub: Academy of Management
Ed: Siiobhan O'Mahony, Fabrizio Ferraro. **Description:** Study examined the method of self-governance among small communities producing collective goods, focusing on an open source software community. Results revealed that a combination of bureaucratic and democratic practices helped its governance system.

3512 ■ "Empire of Pixels" in *Entrepreneur* (Vol. 37, September 2009, No. 9, pp. 50)
Pub: Entrepreneur Media, Inc.
Ed: Jason Daley. **Description:** Entrepreneur Jack Levin has successfully grown Imageshack, an image-hosting Web service. The Website currently gets 50 million unique visitors a month. Levin has launched Y-Frog, an application that uses Imageshack to allow Twitter users to add images to their posts.

3513 ■ *The Entrepreneurial Culture Network Advantage Within Chinese and Irish Software Firms*
Pub: Edward Elgar Publishing, Incorporated
Ed: Tsang. **Released:** October 2006. **Price:** $95.00. **Description:** Ways national cultural heritage influences entrepreneurial ventures are discussed.

3514 ■ "Ex Libris Rosetta Hits the Market" in *Information Today* (Vol. 26, February 2009, No. 2, pp. 30)
Pub: Information Today, Inc.
Description: Ex Libris Rosetta, the latest version of the Ex Libris Group's Digital Preservation System supports the acquisition, validation, ingest, storage, management, preservation, and dissemination of digital objects, allowing libraries the infrastructure and technology to preserve and facilitate access to digital collections. The firm's Ex Libris Rosseta Charter Program helps users develop strategic collaboration between Ex Libris and its customers to improve the product.

3515 ■ "Fly Phishing" in *Canadian Business* (Vol. 80, October 22, 2007, No. 21, pp. 42)
Pub: Rogers Media
Ed: Andy Holloway. **Description:** Symantec Corporation's report shows consumers and companies have effectively installed network defenses that prevent unwanted access. Phishing packages are readily available and are widely used. Other details of the Internet Security Threat Report are presented.

3516 ■ "The Folly of Google's Latest Gambit" in *Barron's* (Vol. 89, July 13, 2009, No. 28, pp. 23)
Pub: Dow Jones & Co., Inc.
Ed: Eric J. Savitz. **Description:** Google will enter the operating systems business with the introduction of the Google Chrome OS but its success is dubious because the project is still a year or so away while Microsoft will release an updated version of Windows by then; another problem is that Google already has another OS called Android which will overlap with the Chrome OS's market.

3517 ■ "Game On! African Americans Get a Shot at $17.9 Billion Video Game Industry" in *Black Enterprise* (Vol. 38, July 2008, No. 12, pp. 56)
Pub: Earl G. Graves Publishing Co. Inc.
Ed: Carolyn M. Brown. **Description:** Despite the economic crisis, consumers are still purchasing the hottest video games and hardware. Tips for African American developers who want to become a part of this industry that lacks content targeting this demographic are offered.

3518 ■ "Game Plan" in *Canadian Business* (Vol. 79, September 11, 2006, No. 18, pp. 50)
Pub: Rogers Media
Ed: Joe Castaldo. **Description:** Strategies adopted by gaming companies to revitalize their business and give a stimulus to their falling resources are presented.

3519 ■ "German Win Through Sharing" in *Canadian Business* (Vol. 83, September 14, 2010, No. 15, pp. 16)
Pub: Rogers Media Ltd.
Ed: Jordan Timm. **Description:** German economic historian Eckhard Hoffner has a two-volume work showing how German's relaxed attitude toward copyright and intellectual property helped it catch up to industrialized United Kingdom. Hoffner's research was in response to his interest in the usefulness of software patents. Information on the debate regarding Canada's copyright laws is given.

3520 ■ "Getting Rid of Global Glitches: Choosing Software For Trade Compliance" in *Black Enterprise* (Vol. 41, September 2010, No. 2, pp. 48)
Pub: Earl G. Graves Publishing Co. Inc.
Ed: Marcia Wade Talbert. **Description:** Compliance software for trading with foreign companies must be compatible with the U.S. Census Bureau's Automated Export System (www.aesdirect.gov). It has to be current with regulatory requirements for any country in the world. Whether owners handle their own compliance or hire a logistics company, they need to be familiar with this software in order to access reports and improve transparency and efficiency of theft supply chain.

3521 ■ "Global: Put It on Autopilot" in *Entrepreneur* (Vol. 35, October 2007, No. 10, pp. 110)
Pub: Entrepreneur Media Inc.
Ed: Laurel Delaney. **Description:** A business that aims to enter the global market must first streamline its global supply chain (GSC). A streamlined GSC can be achieved by laying out the company's processes and by automating it with supply chain management software. Advantages of GSC automation such as credibility are provided.

3522 ■ "Google Places a Call to Bargain Hunters" in *Advertising Age* (Vol. 79, September 29, 2008, No. 36, pp. 13)
Pub: Crain Communications, Inc.
Ed: Abbey Klaassen. **Description:** Google highlighted application developers who have created tools for its Android mobile phone in the device's unveiling; applications such as ShopSavvy and CompareEverywhere help shoppers to find bargains by allowing them to compare prices in their local areas and across the web.

3523 ■ "A Hacker in India Hijacked His Website Design and Was Making Good Money Selling It" in *Inc.* (December 2007, pp. 77-78, 80)
Pub: Gruner & Jahr USA Publishing
Ed: Darren Dahl. **Description:** John Anton, owner of an online custom T-shirt business and how a company in India was selling software Website templates identical to his firm's Website.

3524 ■ "His Banking Industry Software Never Caught On, so Bill Randle is Now Targeting the Health Care Market" in *Inc.* (March 2008)
Pub: Gruner & Jahr USA Publishing
Ed: Alex Salkever. **Description:** Profile of Bill Randle, bank executive turned entrepreneur; Randle tells how he changed his focus for his company from banking software to healthcare software. The firm employs ten people who secure online billing and recordkeeping systems for hospitals and insurers. Randle discusses critical decisions that will impact his firm in the coming year. Three experts offer advice.

3525 ■ "Holiday Sales Look Uncertain for Microsoft and PC Sellers" in *Puget Sound Business Journal* (Vol. 29, November 28, 2008, No. 32)
Pub: American City Business Journals
Ed: Todd Bishop. **Description:** Personal computer makers face uncertain holiday sales for 2008 as a result of the weak U.S. economy and a shift toward low-cost computers. Personal computer shipments for the fourth quarter 2008 are forecast to drop 1 percent compared to the same quarter 2007.

3526 ■ "How Hard Could It Be? Adventures In Software Demol'ling" in *Inc.* (December 2007, pp. 99-100)
Pub: Gruner & Jahr USA Publishing
Ed: Joel Spolsky. **Description:** Founder and CEO of Fog Creek Software, a New York City software developer shares insight into his software demo tour used to promote his firm's products.

3527 ■ "HR Tech on the Go" in *Workforce Management* (Vol. 88, November 16, 2009, No. 12, pp. 1)
Pub: Crain Communications, Inc.
Ed: Ed Frauenheim. **Description:** Examination of the necessity of mobile access of human resources software applications that allow managers to recruit, schedule and train employees via their mobile devices; some industry leaders believe that mobile HR applications are vital while others see this new technology as hype.

3528 ■ "iControl Networks Powers Comcast's XFINITY (Reg) Home Security Service" in *Benzinga.com* (June 9, 2011)
Pub: Benzinga.com
Ed: Benzinga Staff. **Description:** Comcast's XFINITY Home Security Service is powered by iControl Networks' OpenHome (TM) software platform. The service provides intrusion and fire protection along with interactive features such as home monitoring, home management, and energy management services with Web and mobile access.

3529 ■ "Image Conscious" in *Canadian Business* (Vol. 81, March 17, 2008, No. 4, pp. 36)
Pub: Rogers Media
Ed: Andrew Wahl. **Description:** Idee Inc. is testing an Internet search engine for images that does not rely on tags but compares its visual data to a database of other images. The company was founded and managed by Leila Boujnane as an off-shoot of their risk-management software firm. Their software has already been used by image companies to track copyrighted images and to find images within their own archives.

3530 ■ "Inside Intel's Effectiveness System for Web Marketing" in *Advertising Age* (Vol. 81, January 25, 2010, No. 4, pp. 4)
Pub: Crain's Communications
Ed: Beth Snyder Bulik. **Description:** Overview of Intel's internally developed program called Value Point System in which the company is using in order to evaluate and measure online marketing effectiveness.

3531 ■ "Intel to Buy McAfee Security Business for 768B" in *eWeek* (August 19, 2010)
Pub: Ziff Davis Enterprise
Description: Intel will acquire security giant McAfee for approximately $7.68 billion, whereby McAfee would become a wholly owned subsidiary of Intel and would report to Intel's Software and Services Group.

3532 ■ "iPhone Apps Big Business" in *Austin Business JournalInc.* (Vol. 28, November 14, 2008, No. 35, pp. 1)
Pub: American City Business Journals
Ed: Christopher Calnan. **Description:** Members of the computer software industry in Austin, Texas have benefited from developing applications for Apple Inc.'s iPhone. Pangea Software Inc.'s revenues have grown by developing iPhone applications. Lexcycle LLC, on the other hand, has created an application that enables users to read books on the iPhone.

3533 ■ "iPhone Apps In a Flash" in *Entrepreneur* (Vol. 37, October 2009, No. 10, pp. 38)
Pub: Entrepreneur Media, Inc.
Description: Ansca is developing Corona, a software development kit for the Apple iPhone. The kit reduces development time and allows individuals with knowledge of software to develop iPhone applications.

3534 ■ "Is It Time to Ban Swearing at Work?" in *HR Specialist* (Vol. 8, September 2010, No. 9, pp. 2)
Pub: Capitol Information Group Inc.
Description: Screening software has been developed to identify profanity used in business correspondence.

3535 ■ "iSymmetry's Technological Makeover Or, How a Tech Company Finally Grew Up and Discovered the World Wide Web" in *Inc.* (October 2007)
Pub: Gruner & Jahr USA Publishing
Description: Profile of iSymmetry, an Atlanta, Georgia-based IT recruiting firm, covering the issues the company faces keeping its technology equipment up-to-date. The firm has devised a program that will replace its old server-based software systems with on-demand software delivered via the Internet, known as software-as-a-service. Statistical information included.

3536 ■ "Johnny Royal of Luthier Society Unveils Archimedes 1.0 Trailer" in *Internet Wire* (October 22, 2009)
Pub: Comtex News Network, Inc.
Description: Luthier Society, a social media and viral branding agency, has released the first viral video for the company's ROI weighted-value software platform named Archimedes 1.0; users of the software will be able to determine the depth of their outreach efforts, saturation rate, value of their Internet presence and the geo-spatial location of their audience; this will give a true, monetized value for ROI (Return on Investment) in social media marketing.

3537 ■ "Keeping Up With the Joneses: Outfitting Your Company With Up-To-Date Technology is Vital" in *Black Enterprise* (November 2007)
Pub: Earl G. Graves Publishing Co. Inc.
Ed: Sonya A. Donaldson. **Description:** Small businesses, whether home-based or not, need to keep up with new technological developments including hardware, software, and the Internet.

3538 ■ "Lights, Camera, Action: Tools for Creating Video Blogs" in *Inc.* (Volume 32, December 2010, No. 10, pp. 57)
Pub: Inc. Magazine
Ed: John Brandon. **Description:** A video blog is a good way to spread company news, talk about products, and stand out among traditional company blogs. New editing software can create two- to four-minute blogs using a webcam and either Windows Live Essentials, Apple iLife 2011, Powerdirector 9 Ultra, or Adobe Visual Communicator 3.

3539 ■ "Make Relationships Count: CRM Software That Works" in *Black Enterprise* (Vol. 38, February 2008, No. 7, pp. 60)
Pub: Earl G. Graves Publishing Co. Inc.
Ed: Fiona Haley. **Description:** Customer relationship management (CRM) software can help any small business keep track of clients. Descriptions of the latest CRM software offered are profiled, including Salesforce.com, Microsoft Dynamics, and Saga Software.

3540 ■ "Media Software and Data Services" in *MarketingMagazine* (Vol. 115, September 27, 2010, No. 13, pp. 78)
Pub: Rogers Publishing Ltd.
Description: Media software and data services information in Canada is presented.

3541 ■ "Meetings Go Virtual" in *HRMagazine* (Vol. 54, January 2009, No. 1, pp. 74)
Pub: Society for Human Resource Management
Ed: Elizabeth Agnvall. **Description:** Microsoft Office Live Meeting conferencing software allows companies to schedule meetings from various company locations, thus saving travel costs.

3542 ■ "Microsoft Clicks Into High Speed" in *Hispanic Business* (Vol. 30, July-August 2008, No. 7-8, pp. 54)
Pub: Hispanic Business, Inc.
Ed: Derek Reveron. **Description:** Microsoft's diversity hiring and vendor diversity program to capture more Hispanic consumer and business-to-business market is described. One of the main goals of these programs is to hire more Hispanic executives and managers who will help the company develop and market products and services that will appeal and benefit Hispanic consumers.

3543 ■ "Microsoft Goes Macrosoft" in *Barron's* (Vol. 89, July 27, 2009, No. 30, pp. 25)
Pub: Dow Jones & Co., Inc.
Ed: Mark Veverka. **Description:** Microsoft reported a weak quarter on the heels of a tech rally which suggests the economy has not turned around. Marc Andreesen describes his new venture-capital fund as focused on "classic tech" and that historical reference places him in the annals of the last millennium.

3544 ■ "Microsoft Releases Office Security Updates" in *Mac World* (Vol. 27, November 2010, No. 11, pp. 66)
Pub: Mac Publishing
Ed: David Dahlquist. **Description:** Office for Mac and Mac Business Unit are Microsoft's pair of security- and stability-enhancing updates for Office 2008 and Office 2004. The software will improve the stability and compatibility and fixes vulnerabilities that would allow attackers to overwrite Mac's memory with malicious code.

3545 ■ "Mimosa Systems Gains 150,000 New NearPoint Users" in *Information Today* (Vol. 26, February 2009, No. 2, pp. 31)
Pub: Information Today, Inc.
Description: Mimosa System's NearPoint archive solution features email and file archiving, e-discovery, archive virtualization, and disaster recovery capabilities.

3546 ■ "More Leading Retailers Using Omniture Conversion Solutions to Boost Sales and Ecommerce Performance" in *Internet Wire* (Sept. 22,2009)
Pub: Comtex News Network, Inc.
Description: Many retailers are utilizing Omniture conversion solutions to improve the performance of their ecommerce businesses; recent enhancements to Omniture Merchandising and Omniture Recommendations help clients drive increased conversion to their Internet ventures.

3547 ■ "My Favorite Tool for Organizing Data" in *Inc.* (Vol. 33, November 2011, No. 9, pp. 46)
Pub: Inc. Magazine
Ed: Abram Brown. **Description:** Intelligence software firm uses Roambi, a Web-based service that turns spreadsheet data into interactive files for iPhones and iPads.

3548 ■ "New Database Brings Doctors Out of the Dark" in *Business Courier* (Vol. 26, October 23, 2009, No. 26, pp. 1)
Pub: American City Business Journals, Inc.
Ed: James Ritchie. **Description:** A database created by managed care consulting firm Praesentia allows doctors in Cincinnati to compare average reimbursements from health insurance companies to doctors in different areas. Specialist doctors in the city are paid an average of $172.25 for every office consultation.

3549 ■ "New IPhone Also Brings New Way of Mobile Marketing" in *Advertising Age* (Vol. 79, June 16, 2008, No. 24, pp. 23)
Pub: Crain Communications, Inc.
Ed: Abbey Klaasen. **Description:** Currently there are two kinds of applications for the iPhone and other mobile devices: native applications that allow for richer experiences and take advantage of features that are built into a phone and web applications, those that allow access to the web through specific platforms. Marketers are interested in creating useful experiences for customers and opening up the platforms which will allow them to do this.

3550 ■ "New Sprint Phone Whets Appetite for Applications" in *The Business Journal-Serving Metropolitan Kansas City* (Vol. 26, July 25, 2008)
Pub: American City Business Journals, Inc.
Ed: Suzanna Stagemeyer. **Description:** Firms supporting the applications of the new Samsung Instinct, which was introduced by Sprint Nextel Corp. in June 2008, have reported usage rates increase for their products. Handmark, whose mobile services Pocket Express comes loaded with Instinct, has redirected employees to meet the rising demand for the services. Other views and information on Instinct, are presented.

3551 ■ "New Wave of Business Security Products Ushers in the Kaspersky Anti-Malware Protection System" in *Internet Wire* (October 26, 2010)
Pub: Comtex
Description: Kaspersky Anti-Malware System provides anti-malware protection that requires minimal in-house resources for small businesses. The system offers a full range of tightly integrated end-to-end protection solutions, ensuring unified protection across an entire network, from endpoint and mobile device protection to file server, mail server, network storage and gateway protection. It provides flexible centralized management, immediate threat visibility and a level of responsiveness not seen in other anti-malware approaches.

3552 ■ "Nonprofit NAIC Acquires Software Developer as For-Profit Arm" in *Crain's Detroit Business* (Vol. 25, June 22, 2009, No. 25, pp. 10)
Pub: Crain Communications Inc. - Detroit
Ed: Sherri Begin Welch. **Description:** Details of National Association of Investors Corporation's acquisition of a Massachusetts investment software developer in order to offer more products to investment clubs and individual investors nationwide.

3553 ■ "Not Your Father's Whiteboard" in *Inc.* (Vol. 33, November 2011, No. 9, pp. 50)
Pub: Inc. Magazine
Ed: Adam Baer. **Description:** Sharp's new interactive whiteboard is really a 70-inch touch screen monitor with software for importing presentations from any Windows 7 computer.

3554 ■ "Nothing Like a Weak Team Or An Unrealistic Schedule To Start a Project Off Right" in *Inc.* (November 2007, pp. 85-87)
Pub: Gruner & Jahr USA Publishing
Ed: Joel Spolsky. **Description:** Five easy ways to fail meeting a project deadline are discussed by the owner of a software development company: start with second-rate team of developers, set weekly milestones, negotiate a deadline, divide tasks equitably, and work until midnight.

3555 ■ "OCE Boosts JetStream Productivity" in *American Printer* (Vol. 128, August 1, 2011, No. 8)
Pub: Penton Media Inc.
Description: New Oce JetStream 1400 and 3000 digital full-color inkjet presses are profiled. The new models promise higher speed to grow print volume.

3556 ■ "Oce Business Services: Discovery Made Easy" in *Information Today* (Vol. 26, February 2009, No. 2, pp. 31)
Pub: Information Today, Inc.
Ed: Barbara Brynko. **Description:** Oce Business Services provides document process management and electronic discovery through its CaseData repertoire of legal management solutions.

3557 ■ "Omniture's Next Version of SearchCenter Delivers Landing Page Optimization" in *Internet Wire* (September 24, 2009)
Pub: Comtex News Network, Inc.
Description: Omniture, Inc., a leading provider of online business optimization software, has announced a new release of Omniture SearchCenter; this latest version will allow search engine marketers to test landing pages across campaigns and ad groups.

3558 ■ "On Beyond Powerpoint: Presentations Get a Wake-Up Call" in *Inc.* (November 2007, pp. 58-59)
Pub: Gruner & Jahr USA Publishing
Ed: Michael Fitzgerald. **Description:** New software that allows business presentations to be shared online are profiled, including ProfCast, audio podcasts for sales, marketing, and training; SmartDraw2008, software that creates professional graphics; Dimdim, an open-Web conferencing tool; Empressr, a hosted Web service for creating, managing, and sharing multimedia presentations; Zentation, a free tool that allows users to watch slides and a videos of presenter; Spresent, a Web-based presentation tool for remote offices or conference calls.

3559 ■ *Open Source Solutions for Small Business Problems*
Pub: Charles River Media
Ed: John Locke. **Released:** May 2004. **Price:** $35. 95. **Description:** Open source software provides solutions to many small business problems such as tracking electronic documents, scheduling, accounting functions, managing contact lists, and reducing spam.

3560 ■ "Oracle and Tauri Group Honored by Homeland Security and Defense Business Council" in *Wireless News* (December 15, 2009)
Pub: Close-Up Media
Description: Selected as members of the year by the Homeland Security and Defense Business Council were Oracle, a software company that has provided thought leadership and strategic insights as well as The Tauri Group, an analytical consultancy, that has demonstrated a unique understanding of the role of small business and its vital contribution to the success of the country's security.

3561 ■ "Our Gadget of the Week" in *Barron's* (Vol. 88, March 24, 2008, No. 12, pp. 47)
Pub: Dow Jones & Company, Inc.
Ed: Tiernan Ray. **Description:** Review of the $299 Apple Time Capsule, which is a 500-megabyte hard disk drive and a Wi-Fi router, rolled into one device. The device allows users to create backup files without the need for sophisticated file management software.

3562 ■ "Owner of IT Firm MK2 Tying Future to Software" in *Crain's Cleveland Business* (Vol. 30, June 15, 2009, No. 23, pp. 3)
Pub: Crain Communications, Inc.
Ed: Chuck Soder. **Description:** Donald Kasper, owner of MK2 Technologies LLC of Cleveland, Ohio discusses his recent acquisition of a portion of ProSource Solution. The move will help expand the two companies' custom software development plans.

3563 ■ "Paging Dr. Phil" in *Canadian Business* (Vol. 79, September 25, 2006, No. 19, pp. 21)
Pub: Rogers Media
Ed: John Gray. **Description:** Increasing corporate crimes in software industry is discussed by focusing on recent case of Hewlett and Packard.

3564 ■ "Panda Security for Business 4.05" in *SC Magazine* (Vol. 21, July 2010, No. 7, pp. 50)
Pub: Haymarket Media Inc.
Description: Profile of Panda Security for Business, software offering endpoint security protection for computer desktops and servers is presented.

3565 ■ "The Paper Shredder" in *Business Courier* (Vol. 26, September 11, 2009, No. 20, pp. 1)
Pub: American City Business Journals, Inc.
Ed: Dan Monk. **Description:** DotLoop Company, owned by entrepreneur Austin Allison, is developing the DotLoop software, which eliminates paperwork in the processing of real estate contracts. The software allows realtors to take control of the negotiation process and is adaptable to the rules of different US states.

3566 ■ "Paperless Bookkeeping Program" in *Fleet Owner Online* (February 15, 2011)
Pub: Penton Business Media Inc.
Description: TruckTax launched its new paperless bookkeeping system to help manage bookkeeping tasks, accounting and business tax information and filings for truckers.

3567 ■ "PC Connection Acquires Cloud Software Provider" in *New Hampshire Business Review* (Vol. 33, March 25, 2011, No. 6, pp. 8)
Pub: Business Publications Inc.
Description: Merrimack-based PC Connection Inc. acquired ValCom Technology, a provider of cloud-based IT service management software. Details of the deal are included.

3568 ■ "PC Running Slowly? How to Rev Up Your Machine" in *Inc.* (Vol. 33, November 2011, No. 9, pp. 46)
Pub: Inc. Magazine
Ed: John Brandon. **Description:** Software that keeps PCs tuned up and running smoothing are profiled: AUSLO6ICS BOOSTSPEED 5, $50; Tuneup Utilities 2011, $40; Slimware Slimcleaner 1.9, free; and IOBIT Advanced Systemcare Pro 4, $20 a year.

3569 ■ "PopCap Games Achieves Significant Increase in Return on Ad Spend With Omniture SearchCenter" in *Internet Wire* (September 15, 2009)
Pub: Comtex News Network, Inc.
Description: PopCap Games, a leading computer games provider, is using Omniture SearchCenter together with Omniture SiteCatalyst to increase revenue from its search engine marketing campaign. Omniture, Inc. is a leading provider of Internet business optimization software.

3570 ■ "The Power of Negative Thinking" in *Inc.* (Volume 32, December 2010, No. 10, pp. 43)
Pub: Inc. Magazine
Ed: Jason Fried. **Description:** A Website is software and most businesses have and need a good Website to generate business. Understanding for building a powerful Website is presented.

3571 ■ "Power Ranger" in *Inc.* (November 2007, pp. 131)
Pub: Gruner & Jahr USA Publishing
Ed: Nitasha Tiku. **Description:** Surveyor software is designed to power down computers when not in use, in order to save energy.

3572 ■ *Practical Tech for Your Business*
Pub: Kiplinger Books and Tapes
Ed: Michael J. Martinez. **Released:** 2002. **Description:** Advice is offered to help small business owners choose the right technology for their company. The guide tells how to get started, network via the Internet, create an office network, use database software, and conduct business using mobile technology.

3573 ■ "Precision Crop Control with Valley Irrigation/CropMetrics Partnership" in *Farm Industry News* (January 6, 2011)
Pub: Penton Business Media Inc.
Description: Irrigation systems have become a precision farming tool since partnering with agronomic software systems to apply products across the field by prescription. Valley Irrigation and CropMetrics have partnered in order to variably control water, fertilizer and other crop management products through a center pivot irrigation system.

3574 ■ "Press Release: Trimble Introduces CFX-750 Display" in *Farm Industry News* (January 4, 2011)
Pub: Penton Business Media Inc.
Description: Trimble is offering a touch screen display called the CFX-750. The new 8-inch full-color display allows farmers to choose the specific guidance, steering and precision agriculture capabilities that best fit their farm's particular needs. The display can be upgraded as business needs change, including the addition of GLONASS capabilities, or the addition of section and rate control for crop inputs such as seed, chemicals and fertilizer.

3575 ■ "Programs Provide Education and Training" in *Contractor* (Vol. 56, September 2009, No. 9, pp. 56)
Pub: Penton Media, Inc.
Ed: William Feldman; Patti Feldman. **Description:** Opportunity Interactive's Showroom v2 software provides uses computer graphics to provide education and training on HVAC equipment and systems. It can draw heat pump balance points for a specific home. Meanwhile, Simutech's HVAC Training Simulators provide trainees with 'hands-on' HVACR training.

3576 ■ "Protection One Introduces Home and Business Security iPhone App" in *Wireless News* (November 13, 2009)
Pub: Close-Up Media
Description: Protection One, Inc., a provider of security systems to business and residential customers, has developed an application that allows users to access their security panels and receive real-time updates from their iPhone or iPod touch devices.

3577 ■ "Providers Ride First Wave of eHealth Dollars" in *Boston Business Journal* (Vol. 31, June 10, 2011, No. 20, pp. 1)
Pub: Boston Business Journal
Ed: Julie M. Donnelly. **Description:** Health care providers in Massachusetts implementing electronic medical records technology started receiving federal stimulus funds. Beth Israel Deaconess Medical Center was the first hospital to qualify for the funds.

3578 ■ "Publishing Technology Introduces IngentaConnect Mobile" in *Information Today* (Vol. 26, February 2009, No. 2, pp. 33)
Pub: Information Today, Inc.
Description: College undergraduates will find Publishing Technology's newest publisher product, IngentaConnect Mobile helpful. The product allows users to read articles and abstracts on mobile devices. According to a recent study, 73 percent of young adults with wireless hand-held devices use them to access non-voice data on any given day.

3579 ■ "Putting the App in Apple" in *Inc.* (Vol. 30, November 2008, No. 11, pp.)
Pub: Mansueto Ventures LLC
Ed: Nitasha Tiku. **Description:** Aftermarket companies are scrambling to develop games and widgets for Apple's iPhone. Apple launched a kit for developers interested in creating iPhone-specific software along with the App Store, and an iTunes spinoff. Profiles of various software programs that may be used on the iPhone are given.

3580 ■ *QuickBooks All-in-One Desk Reference for Dummies*
Pub: John Wiley & Sons, Incorporated
Ed: Stephen L. Nelson. **Released:** January 2007. **Price:** $29.99 (US), $42.99 (Canadian). **Description:** Compilation of nine self-contained minibooks to get the most from QuickBooks accounting software. Companion Web site with sample business plan workbook and downloadable profit-volume cost analysis workbook included.

3581 ■ *QuickBooks Simple Start for Dummies*
Pub: John Wiley & Sons, Incorporated
Ed: Stephen L. Nelson. **Released:** October 2004. **Price:** $21.99. **Description:** Profile of Intuits new ac-

counting software geared to micro businesses. Advice is offered on daily, monthly, and yearly accounting activities covering records, sales tax, and reports.

3582 ■ *QuickBooks X on Demand*
Pub: Que
Ed: Gail Perry. **Released:** December 2006. **Price:** $34.99. **Description:** Step-by-step training for using various small business financial software programs; includes illustrated, full color explanations.

3583 ■ *QuickBooks X for Dummies*
Pub: John Wiley & Sons, Incorporated
Ed: Stephen L. Nelson. **Released:** November 2006. **Price:** $21.99. **Description:** Key features of QuickBooks software for small business are introduced. Invoicing and credit memos, recoding sales receipts, accounting, budgeting, taxes, payroll, financial reports, job estimating, billing, tracking, data backup, are among the features.

3584 ■ "Quickoffice's MobileFiles Pro App Enables Excel Editing On-the-Go" in *Information Today* (Vol. 26, February 2009, No. 2, pp. 31)
Pub: Information Today, Inc.
Description: Quickoffice Inc. introduced MobileFiles Pro, which features editable Microsoft Office functionality for the iPone and iPod touch. The application allows users to edit and save Microsoft Excel files in .xls format, transfer files to and from PC and Mac desktops via Wi-Fi, and access and synchronize with Apple MobileMe accounts.

3585 ■ "Remote Control: Working From Wherever" in *Inc.* (February 2008, pp. 46-47)
Pub: Gruner & Jahr USA Publishing
Ed: Ryan Underwood. **Description:** New technology allows workers to perform tasks from anywhere via the Internet. Profiles of products to help connect to your office from afar include, LogMein Pro, a Web-based service that allowsaccess to a computer from anywhere; Xdrive, an online service that allows users to store and swap files; Basecamp, a Web-based tools that works like a secure version of MySpace; MojoPac Freedom, is software that allows users to copy their computer's desktop to a removable hard drive and plug into any PC; WatchGuard Firebox X Core e-Series UTM Bundle, hardware that blocks hackers and viruses while allowing employees to work remotely; TightVNC, a free open-source software that lets you control another computer via the Internet.

3586 ■ "RES Stakes Its Claim in Area" in *Philadelphia Business Journal* (Vol. 28, January 29, 2010, No. 50, pp. 1)
Pub: American City Business Journals
Ed: Peter Key. **Description:** RES Software Company Inc. of Amsterdam, Netherlands appointed Jim Kirby as president for the Americas and Klaus Besier as chairman in an effort to boost the firm's presence in the US. Brief career profiles of Kirby and Besier are included. RES develops software that allows management of information flow between an organization and its employees regardless of location.

3587 ■ "Route Optimization Impacts the Bottom Line" in *Contractor* (Vol. 56, November 2009, No. 11, pp. 48)
Pub: Penton Media, Inc.
Ed: Dave Beaudry. **Description:** Plumbing and HVAC businesses can save a significant amount of money from route optimization. The process begins with gathering information on a fleet and a routing software tool can determine the effectiveness of current route configurations and identify preferable route plans.

3588 ■ *Salesforce.com Secrets of Success: Best Practices for Growth and Profitability*
Pub: Prentice Hall Business Publishing
Ed: David Taber. **Released:** May 15, 2009. **Price:** $34.99. **Description:** Guide for using Salesforce.com; it provides insight into navigating through user groups, management, sales, marketing and IT departments in order to achieve the best results.

3589 ■ "Save the Date" in *Barron's* (Vol. 90, September 13, 2010, No. 37, pp. 35)
Pub: Barron's Editorial & Corporate Headquarters
Ed: Mark Veverka. **Description:** Mark Hurd is the new Co-President of Oracle after being forced out at Hewlett-Packard where he faced a harassment complaint. HP fired Hurd due to expense account malfeasance. Hurd is also set to speak at an Oracle trade show in San Francisco on September 20, 2010.

3590 ■ "Scitable Puts Nature Education on the Map" in *Information Today* (Vol. 26, February 2009, No. 2, pp. 29)
Pub: Information Today, Inc.
Description: Nature Education, a division of the Nature Publishing Group, released its first product, Scitable, a free online resource for undergraduate biology students and educators. The service includes over 180 overviews of key genetics concepts as well as social networking features, including groups and functionality, that lets students work with classmates and others. Teachers can use the service to set up public or private groups for students.

3591 ■ "Second Cup?" in *Canadian Business* (Vol. 81, July 21, 2008, No. 11, pp. 50)
Pub: Rogers Media Ltd.
Ed: Calvin Leung. **Description:** Profile of James Gosling who is credited as the inventor of the Java programming language; however, the 53-year-old software developer feels ambivalent for being credited as inventor since many people contributed to the language. Netscape and Sun Microsystems incorporation of the programming language into Java is presented.

3592 ■ "Sense of Discovery" in *Business Journal Portland* (Vol. 27, November 19, 2010, No. 38, pp. 1)
Pub: Portland Business Journal
Ed: Erik Siemers. **Description:** Tigard, Oregon-based Exterro Inc. CEO Bobby Balachandran announced plans to go public without the help of an institutional investor. Balachandran believes Exterro could grow to a $100 million legal compliance software company in the span of three years. Insights on Exterro's growth as market leader in the $1 billion legal governance software market are also given.

3593 ■ "Serials Solutions Launches 360 Resource Manager Consortium Edition" in *Information Today* (Vol. 26, February 2009, No. 2, pp. 32)
Pub: Information Today, Inc.
Description: Serials Solutions new Serials Solutions 360 Resource Manager Consortium Edition helps consortia, groups and member libraries with their e-resource management services. The products allows users to consolidate e-resource metadata and acquisition information into one place, which enables groups to manage holdings, subscriptions, licensing, contacts, and cost information and to streamline delivery of information to members.

3594 ■ "A Side Project Threatens To Get Totally Out of Control and I Think, 'How Fun'" in *Inc.* (October 2007, pp. 81-82)
Pub: Gruner & Jahr USA Publishing
Ed: Joel Spolsky. **Description:** Profile of Fog Creek Software, makers of project-management software for other software developers. Fog Creek's owner discusses his idea to create a new product for his firm.

3595 ■ "Skype on Steroids" in *Inc.* (Vol. 31, January-February 2009, No. 1, pp. 46)
Pub: Mansueto Ventures LLC
Ed: Nitasha Tiku. **Description:** Free software called VoxOx allows users to make calls over the Internet and connects all email and IM accounts.

3596 ■ "Small is Bountiful for Intuit" in *Barron's* (Vol. 90, September 13, 2010, No. 37, pp. 22)
Pub: Barron's Editorial & Corporate Headquarters
Ed: Mark Veverka. **Description:** Finance software maker Intuit wants to tap the underserved small business market. One analyst sees Intuit's shares rising 25 percent to 55 percent in the next 12 months from September 2010.

3597 ■ "A Software Company's Whimsical Widgets Were an Instant Hit. But Its Core Product Was Getting Overshadowed" in *Inc.* (Jan. 2008)
Pub: Gruner & Jahr USA Publishing
Ed: Alex Salkever. **Description:** A widget designed as a marketing tool tuned into a hit on Facebook. Should ChipIn shift its focus?

3598 ■ "Software Solutions Increase Productivity" in *Contractor* (Vol. 57, February 2010, No. 2, pp. 26)
Pub: Penton Media, Inc.
Ed: William Feldman; Patti Feldman. **Description:** Singletouch is a real-time data capture solution for mechanical and other contractors that work in jobs that require materials and workload tracking. Contractors get information on extreme weather and sudden changes in the cost of materials. The OptimumHVAC optimization software by Optimum Energy is designed to optimize energy savings in commercial buildings.

3599 ■ "Software Solutions from Trane and Carrier" in *Contractor* (Vol. 56, July 2009, No. 7, pp. 38)
Pub: Penton Media, Inc.
Ed: William Feldman; Patti Feldman. **Description:** Trane Trace 700 software helps HVAC contractors optimize the design of a building's HVAC system and aids in the evaluation of various key energy-saving concepts, including daylighting, high-performance glazing, and other optimization strategies. Carrier's E20-II family of software programs lets contractors increase the accuracy of an HVAC system estimate.

3600 ■ "Software's Last Hurrah" in *Canadian Business* (Vol. 81, December 24, 2007, No. 1, pp. 27)
Pub: Rogers Media
Ed: Andrew Wahl. **Description:** Canada's software industry could be facing a challenge with IBM's acquisition of Cognos, which was the country's last major independent business intelligence company and was also IBM's largest acquisition ever. Next in line to Cognos in terms of prominence is Open Text Corporation, which could also be a possible candidate for acquisition, as analysts predict.

3601 ■ "Startup on Cusp of Trend" in *Austin Business JournalInc.* (Vol. 29, January 8, 2010, No. 44, pp. 1)
Pub: American City Business Journals
Ed: Christopher Calnan. **Description:** Austin-based Socialware Inc. introduced a new business called social middleware, which is a software that is layered between the company network and social networking Website used by workers. The software was designed to give employers a measure of control over content while allowing workers to continue using online social networks.

3602 ■ "The State of the Art in End-User Software Engineering" in *ACM Computing Surveys* (Vol. 43, Fall 2011, No. 3, pp. 21)
Pub: Association for Computing Machinery
Description: Most programs today are not written by professional software developers but by people with expertise in other domains working towards goals for which they need computational support. A discussion of empirical research about end-user software engineering activities and the technologies designed to support them is presented. Several crosscutting issues in the design of EUSE tools, including the roles of risk, reward, and domain complexity, and self-efficacy in the design of EUSE tools and the potential of educating users about software engineering principles are also examined.

3603 ■ "The Story Of Diane Greene" in *Barron's* (Vol. 88, July 14, 2008, No. 28, pp. 31)
Pub: Dow Jones & Co., Inc.
Ed: Mark Veverka. **Description:** Discusses the ousting of Diane Greene as a chief executive of VMWare, a developer of virtualization software, after the firm went public; in this case Greene, a brilliant engineer, should not be negatively impacted by the decision

because it is common for companies to bring in new executive leadership that is more operations oriented after the company goes public.

3604 ■ "A Survey of Combinatorial Testing" in *ACM Computing Surveys* (Vol. 43, Summer 2011, No. 2, pp. 11)
Pub: Association for Computing Machinery
Ed: Changhai Nie, Hareton Leung. **Description:** Combinatorial Testing (CT) can detect failures triggered by interactions of parameters in the Software Under Test (SUT) with a covering array test suite generated by some sampling mechanisms. Basic concepts and notations of CT are covered.

3605 ■ "A Survey of Comparison-Based System-Level Diagnosis" in *ACM Computing Surveys* (Vol. 43, Fall 2011, No. 3, pp. 22)
Pub: Association for Computing Machinery
Ed: Elias P. Duarte Jr., Roverli P. Ziwich, Luiz C.P. Albini. **Description:** The growing complexity and dependability requirements of hardware, software, and networks demand efficient techniques for discovering disruptive behavior in those systems. Comparison-based diagnosis is a realistic approach to detect faulty units based on the outputs of tasks executed by system units. This survey integrates the vast amount of research efforts that have been produced in this field.

3606 ■ "Taking the Steps Into the Clouds" in *New Hampshire Business Review* (Vol. 33, March 25, 2011, No. 6, pp. 19)
Pub: Business Publications Inc.
Ed: Tim Wessels. **Description:** Cloud services include Internet and Web security, spam filtering, message archiving, work group collaboration, IT asset management, help desk and disaster recovery backup.

3607 ■ "Tech Deal Couples Homegrown Firms" in *The Business Journal-Serving Greater Tampa Bay* (Vol. 28, July 4, 2008, No. 28, pp. 1)
Pub: American City Business Journals, Inc.
Ed: Michael Hinman. **Description:** Tampa Bay, Florida-based Administrative Partners Inc. was acquired by Tribridge Inc. resulting in the strengthening of the delivery of Microsoft products to clients. Other details of the merger of the management consulting services companies are presented.

3608 ■ "Technology to the Rescue" in *Contractor* (Vol. 56, July 2009, No. 7, pp. 22)
Pub: Penton Media, Inc.
Ed: Candace Ruolo. **Description:** Features of several products that will make the job of a mechanical contractor easier are discussed. These include Ridgid's line of drain and sewer inspection cameras and monitors, Motion Computing's Motion F5 tablet rugged tablet PC, the JobClock from Exaktime, and the TeleNav Track tool for mobile workforce management.

3609 ■ "Technology: What Seems To Be the Problem? Self Service Gets a Tune-Up" in *Inc.* (February 2008, pp. 43-44)
Pub: Gruner & Jahr USA Publishing
Ed: Darren Dahl. **Description:** Self-service software can save companies money when responding to customer service phone calls, text or email messages. More companies are relying on alternatives such as automated Web-based self-service systems.

3610 ■ "Ted Stahl: Executive Chairman" in *Inside Business* (Vol. 13, September-October 2011, No. 5, pp. NC6)
Pub: Great Lakes Publishing Company
Ed: Miranda S. Miller. **Description:** Profile of Ted Stahl, who started working in his family's business when he was ten years old is presented. The firm makes dies for numbers and letters used on team uniforms. Another of the family firms manufactures stock and custom heat-printing products, equipment and supplies. It also educates customers on ways to decorate garments with heat printing products and offers graphics and software for customers to create their own artwork.

3611 ■ "Thinking Strategically About Technology" in *Franchising World* (Vol. 42, August 2010, No. 8, pp. 9)
Pub: International Franchise Association
Ed: Bruce Franson. **Description:** Nearly 25 percent of companies waste money from their technology budget. Most of the budget is spent on non-strategic software. Ways to spend money on technology for any franchise are examined.

3612 ■ "A Timely Boon for Small Investors" in *Barron's* (Vol. 88, March 24, 2008, No. 12, pp. 48)
Pub: Dow Jones & Company, Inc.
Ed: Theresa W. Carey. **Description:** Nasdaq Data Store's new program called Market Replay allows investors to accurately track stock price movements. The replay can be as long as a day of market time and allows investors to determine whether they executed stock trades at the best possible price.

3613 ■ "Touching the Future" in *Canadian Business* (Vol. 81, July 21, 2008, No. 11, pp. 41)
Pub: Rogers Media Ltd.
Ed: Matt McClearn. **Description:** Microsoft Corp. has launched a multi-touch product which is both a software and hardware technology called Microsoft Surface. The innovative product allows people to use it at the same time, however touch-based computers are reported to be around $100,000. Other features and benefits of the product are presented.

3614 ■ "Trust But Verify: FMLA Software Isn't Foolproof, So Apply a Human Touch" in *HR Specialist* (Vol. 8, September 2010, No. 9, pp. 3)
Pub: Capitol Information Group Inc.
Description: Employers are using software to track FMLA information, however, it is important for employers to review reasons for eligibility requirements, particularly when an employee is reportedly overstepping the bounds within leave regulations due to software error.

3615 ■ "Two Field Service Management Solutions" in *Contractor* (Vol. 56, November 2009, No. 11, pp. 37)
Pub: Penton Media, Inc.
Ed: William Feldman; Patti Feldman. **Description:** Bella Solutions Field Service Software v. 4.2 is a web based solution for HVAC service contractors that enables scheduling of emergency, one-time, multi-visit or periodically recurring jobs with drag and drop appointments. VaZing is another web based solution that costs $99 per month for contractors. It can handle line-item discounting and invoices aside from scheduling.

3616 ■ "Two Ways to Find New Customers" in *Inc.* (Vol. 31, January-February 2009, No. 1, pp. 41)
Pub: Mansueto Ventures LLC
Description: Latest software programs that help sales staff connect to new leads are profiled. Salesconx provides online leads while Demandbase reports users on a particular Website.

3617 ■ "Unbound ID Raises $2 Million" in *Austin Business JournalInc.* (Vol. 28, December 12, 2008, No. 39, pp. 1)
Pub: American City Business Journals
Ed: Christopher Calnan. **Description:** Austin, Texas-based Unbound ID Corporation has secured $2 million in funding from venture capital firm Silverton Partners. The company has developed identity management software for network directories. The market for identity management technology is expected to grow to more than $12.3 billion by 2014.

3618 ■ "uTest Discusses the Evolution of Crowdsourcing Models at CrowdConf 2010" in *Internet Wire* (October 1, 2010)
Pub: Comtex
Description: World's largest software testing marketplace, uTest, announces its first conference dedicated to the emerging field of crowdsourcing along with the future of distributed work. A panel of experts will discuss common misconceptions about crowdsourcing using real-world examples.

3619 ■ "Video Surveillance Enters Digital Era, Makes Giant Strides" in *Arkansas Business* (Vol. 26, September 28, 2009, No. 39, pp. 1)
Pub: Journal Publishing Inc.
Ed: Jamie Walden. **Description:** Arkansas business owners are finding that the newest technology in video surveillance is leading to swift apprehension of thieves due to the high-quality digital imagery now being captured on surveillance equipment. Motion detection software for these systems is enhancing the capabilities of these systems and providing opportunities for businesses that would normally have problems integrating these systems.

3620 ■ "A Virtual Jog Mode for CAM" in *Modern Machine Shop* (Vol. 84, November 2011, No. 6, pp. 22)
Pub: Gardner Publications
Ed: Edwin Gasparraj. **Description:** In many cases, CAM programming required a specific, user-defined path. Siemens PLMs Generic Motion Controller is an alternative that defines the tool path within CAM. The program is a virtual 'teach' mode that enables the user to capture cutter locations by jogging machines axes within CAM.

3621 ■ "What Has Sergey Wrought?" in *Barron's* (Vol. 89, July 13, 2009, No. 28, pp. 8)
Pub: Dow Jones & Co., Inc.
Ed: Alan Abelson. **Description:** Sergey Aleynikov is a computer expert that once worked for Goldman Sachs but he was arrested after he left the company and charged with theft for bringing with him the code for the company's proprietary software for high-frequency trading. The stock market has been down for four straight weeks as of July 13, 2009 which reflects the reality of how the economy is still struggling.

3622 ■ "Will the Force Be With Salesforce?" in *Barron's* (Vol. 88, March 24, 2008, No. 12, pp. 20)
Pub: Dow Jones & Company, Inc.
Ed: Mark Veverka. **Description:** Shares of Salesforce.com are likely to drop from the $44.83-a-share level in the face of a deteriorating economy and financial sector and thus lower demand for business software. The company is unlikely to deliver on its ambitious earnings forecasts for 2008 especially with strengthening competition from Oracle.

3623 ■ "Women Losing IT Ground" in *Marketing to Women* (Vol. 21, February 2008, No. 2, pp. 6)
Pub: EPM Communications, Inc.
Description: According to a study conducted by The National Center for Women & Information Technology, women in technology are losing ground. Statistical data included.

3624 ■ "Yammer Gets Serious" in *Inc.* (Volume 32, December 2010, No. 10, pp. 58)
Pub: Inc. Magazine
Ed: Eric Markowitz. **Description:** Yammer, an internal social network for companies, allows coworkers to share ideas and documents in real-time. Details of this service are included.

3625 ■ "Yes, No, and Somewhat Likely: Survey the World with Web Polls" in *Inc.* (October 2007, pp. 58-59)
Pub: Gruner & Jahr USA Publishing
Ed: Don Steinberg. **Description:** Online tools for surveying customers, employees and the general public include Zoomergan zPro and Zoomerang Sample, software designed to send surveys and allows viewing results; SurveyMonkey software creates, administers and allows viewing online surveys and results; Vizu software places a one-question poll on a particular Website; and Vovici EFM Feedback, a subscription service providing ongoing surveys to customers or employees.

3626 ■ "Zeon Solutions Teams with Endeca for SaaS Version of Endeca InFront" in *Entertainment Close-Up* (October 25, 2011)
Pub: Close-Up Media
Description: Zeon Solutions, an enterprise e-commerce and Website development firm announced a special licensing partnership with Endecca Technologies. Endeca is an information management software company that provides small and mid-size retailers with high-performance Customer Experience Management technology.

TRADE PERIODICALS

3627 ■ *CD Computing News*
Pub: Worldwide Videotex
Contact: Mark Wright
Ed: Mark Wright, Editor, markedit@juno.com. **Released:** Monthly. **Price:** $165, U.S. and Canada; $180, elsewhere. **Description:** Provides coverage of the projects, products, and developments of the commercial applications of CD-ROM, CD-I, and all the other optical storage devices used in computing. Concentrates on information relating to successful marketing strategies.

3628 ■ *DCLNews*
Pub: Data Conversion Laboratory
Contact: Mark Gross
Ed: Released: Monthly. **Price:** Included in membership;. **Description:** E-journal providing you insider information on XML and SGML, along with the latest technology and e-publishing news.

3629 ■ *Electric Pages*
Pub: International Informatics Institute
Ed: Released: Enewsletter. **Price:** Free. **Description:** Covers new publishing and media technologies from a publisher's perspective. Discusses such topics as digital printing, fax publishing, CD-ROM audiotex, videotex, electronic advertising, telecommunications, multimedia, and other interactive publishing tools. Recurring features include letters to the editor, interviews, news of research, book reviews, notices of publications available, and technology reviews. Publishes solely on the Internet.

3630 ■ *EMediaLive*
Pub: Online, A Division of Information Today Inc.
Contact: Dan Huggins, Publisher
E-mail: dhuggins@infotoday.com
Released: Monthly. **Description:** Professional trade journal for CD publishers and developers using or considering CD-ROM, CD-Recordable, DVD, and other optical media. Contains product reviews and comparisons, surveys, newspages, columns, and interviews.

3631 ■ *Media Computing*
Pub: Dreamscape Productions
Ed: Sheridan Tatsuno, Editor, statsuno@aol.com. **Released:** Monthly. **Price:** $495, institutions in the U.S. and Canada; $550, institutions elsewhere. **Description:** Supplies analysis of multimedia, internet, intranet, and web computing issues. Recurring features include interviews and reports of meetings.

TRADE SHOWS AND CONVENTIONS

3632 ■ ARMA International Annual Conference and Expo
ARMA International
11880 College Blvd., Ste. 450
Lenexa, KS 66215
Ph:(913)341-3808
Free: 800-422-2762
Fax:(913)341-3742
Co. E-mail: hq@arma.org
URL: http://www.arma.org
Released: Annual. **Audience:** Record managers. **Principal Exhibits:** Optical disk, CD-ROM, and optical storage technology; automated document storage and retrieval, micrographics, and reprographics; information management software; WORM; copying/duplicating equipment; image management systems; and record management systems.

CONSULTANTS

3633 ■ Century Small Business Solutions
152 N El Camino Real
Encinitas, CA 92024-2849
Ph:(760)633-4725
Contact: John R. Todd, Principle
Scope: Focuses on improving the profitability of growth-oriented small businesses through business planning, controlling expenses, marketing to find new customers and tax planning to minimize taxes. **Seminars:** QuickBooks training and Budgeting for your Small Business.

3634 ■ CheckMark Software Inc.
724 Whalers Way, Bldg. H, Ste. 101
Fort Collins, CO 80525-7578
Ph:(970)225-0522
Free: 800-444-9922
Fax:(970)225-0611
Co. E-mail: info@checkmark.com
URL: http://www.checkmark.com
Contact: Terry Stone, Dir of Sales
E-mail: rgilmore@checkmark.com
Scope: Developer of accounting software tools for small businesses and provides fast, easy to use, affordable accounting and payroll solutions to small and medium sized businesses. Provides payroll software and multiledger integrated accounting software. **Special Services:** MultiLedger™; Payroll.

3635 ■ Cognetics Corp.
52 Mill Rd.
PO Box 386
Princeton Junction, NJ 08550-1706
Ph:(609)799-5005
Free: 800-229-8437
Fax:(609)799-8555
Co. E-mail: info@cognetics.com
URL: http://www.cognetics.com
Contact: Anne Pauker-Kreitzberg, Principle
E-mail: scottg@atscognetics.com
Scope: Offers services including technical, programming, human factors, content, graphics, and writing. Designs interactive products such as website, web applications and web communities. **Publications:** "10 Steps to Creating the Perfect Web Site"; "The Beginning of the End or the End of the Beginning"; "Is Your Project at Risk"; "Selling Usability: Scope and Schedule Estimates," Society for Technical Communication, Dec, 2003. **Special Services:** LUCID™.

3636 ■ DacEasy Inc.
1715 N Brown Rd.
Lawrenceville, GA 30043
Ph:(770)492-6414
Free: 800-322-3279
Fax:(770)724-2874
Co. E-mail: sales@daceasy.com
URL: http://www.daceasy.com
Contact: Marchell Gillis
E-mail: marchell.gillis@sage.com
Scope: Develops an accounting system for small businesses that integrates accounting, invoicing, payroll, communications, and management software into a single package. **Seminars:** DacEasy Training. **Special Services:** DacEasy.

3637 ■ Data Conversion Laboratory Inc.
61-18 190th St., 2nd Fl.
Fresh Meadows, NY 11365-2721
Ph:(718)357-8700
Fax:(718)357-8776
Co. E-mail: convert@dclab.com
URL: http://www.dclab.com
Contact: David Skurich, Chief Technical Officer
E-mail: mikegross@atsdclab.com
Scope: Specializes in information transfer, and data and text conversion services with particular emphasis on SGML or XML conversion and CD ROM publishing. Serves publishing, pharmaceuticals, financial, manufacturers. Specializes in document conversion strategy; identifies document redundancy; extracts meta data and transform legacy. **Seminars:** Data Conversion Panel, May, 2010.

3638 ■ Earth View Inc.
6523 California Ave. SW, Ste. 322
PO Box 172
Seattle, WA 98136
Ph:(206)527-3168
Fax:(206)524-6803
Co. E-mail: bryanb@earthview.com
URL: http://www.earthview.com
Contact: Bryan Brewer, President
E-mail: bryanb@earthview.com
Scope: Offers market analysis, application design, and development of CD-ROM and Internet publishing for business and consumer markets. Also works with government agencies. Provides Internet consulting services. **Publications:** "Eclipse," 1978; "The Compact Disc Book".

3639 ■ Future Communications Corp.
104 W 40th St.
New York, NY 10018
Ph:(212)400-6000
Fax:(212)937-3892
Co. E-mail: info@futurecomusa.com
URL: http://www.futurecomusa.com
Contact: Michael Bischoff, Director
E-mail: mbischoff@atsipvideoconferencing.com
Scope: Provides video conferencing solutions including custom room solution for conference rooms, board rooms, distance education and command centers; room rental and equipment rental solutions; video consulting solutions such as managing video conferencing room and equipment, implementing video in an IP and ISDN environment; virtual private network design solutions and PC/Network solutions.

3640 ■ Missile Defense Systems Group
103 Quality Cir., Ste. 200
Huntsville, AL 35806
Ph:(703)998-3900
Fax:(703)824-5699
URL: http://www.asd-inc.com
Contact: Todd Mauzy, Chief Technical Officer
Scope: Provides management and technical support to private industries and government in the development and implementation of user-oriented computer systems. Offers expert LAN operation, administration, and user support. Specialists in optical disk technology, including CD-ROM and other image-based optical information systems.

3641 ■ SiteShapers
4070 Goldfinch St., Ste. D
San Diego, CA 92103
Ph:(619)231-6907
Fax:(619)231-7061
Co. E-mail: inquiry@siteshapers.com
URL: http://www.siteshapers.com
Contact: Irene Jernigan, Principal
E-mail: jaime@atssiteshapers.com
Scope: Conducts needs assessment and marketing productivity workshops for high-technology manufacturers and service firms. Specializes in web site strategies and design, marketing strategies, planning, research and promotion. Serves electronics and software, instruments and health care industries.

3642 ■ S.V. Writing Services
4471 Park Bristol Pl.
San Jose, CA 95136-2510
Ph:(408)972-2476
Fax:(408)224-8496
Co. E-mail: nahal@ix.netcom.com
Contact: Tarlochan S. Nahal, President
Scope: Firm specializes in computer hardware and software documentation; online documentation; wafer processing equipment manuals; desktop publishing and illustration. Uses in-house Macintosh Quadra and Pentium-based computers running Inter leaf, Frame Maker, Word Perfect, Microsoft Word, and Ventura. Serves the semiconductor, electronics, and computer hardware or software industries.

3643 ■ Users First Inc.
2162 Pine Knoll Ave.
PO Box 26385
Columbus, OH 43229
Ph:(614)523-2177

Fax:(614)899-7886
Co. E-mail: mjlmail@aol.com
Contact: Dr. Martha Lindeman, President
E-mail: lindemam@franklin.edu

Scope: Design and/or test user interfaces for any type of computer or telephony systems or for the computer-telephony integration. Participates in any phase of the design and development process. Provide off-site prototyping and usability evaluation services. Customize training materials for combined training/consulting workshops for specific projects. Serves all industries. **Publications:** "A New Design Framework for Computer-Telephony Integration"; "Human Factors and Voice Interactive Systems"; "Automatic Speech Recognition".

3644 ■ Write Job Inc.
538 W Sunnyoaks Ave.
Campbell, CA 95008-5335
Ph:(408)370-2855
Co. E-mail: writejob@dnai.com
Contact: Richard J. Collins, President

Scope: Offers editorial services specializing in technical manual writing, editing, illustration, and document preparation.

LIBRARIES

3645 ■ Automated Sciences Group Library
1100 N. Glebe Rd.
Arlington, VA 22201-4798
Ph:(703)587-8750
Fax:(703)565-9412
Contact: Marvin L. Doxie, Sr.
Scope: Telecommunications, systems and software engineering, system integration, hardware, software, peripherals. **Services:** Library not open to the public. **Holdings:** 400 books; 200 reports; hardware and software specifications; government directories; ADP forecast/industry profiles. **Subscriptions:** 75 journals and other serials.

3646 ■ University of Guam–Robert F. Kennedy Memorial Library–Instructional Media Division (Tan S)
Tan Siu Lin Bldg.
UOG Station
Mangilao, GU 96923
Ph:(671)735-2326
Fax:(671)734-6882
Co. E-mail: millhoff@uog9.uog.edu
URL: http://www.uog.edu
Contact: Brian L. Millhoff, Inst. Media
Scope: Multimedia; graphics. **Services:** Interlibrary loan. **Holdings:** 2388 videotapes; 110 CD-ROMs; 28 laser discs; 139 audio programs tape/CD; 200 pieces of media equipment.

RESEARCH CENTERS

3647 ■ Santa Clara University–Institute for Information Storage Technology
IIST Engineering Bldg.
Santa Clara, CA 95053
Ph:(408)554-4032
Fax:(408)554-7841
Co. E-mail: ahoagland@scu.edu
URL: http://www.iist.scu.edu/iist/hoagland/about.html
Contact: Dr. Albert S. Hoagland, Dir.
E-mail: ahoagland@scu.edu

Scope: Conducts studies of recording systems, particularly components, materials, design, and manufacturability. Activities focus on read/write transducers and include studies of data storage devices, head-medium interface, the magnetic recording channel, magnetic head design, and optical recording systems. Produces textbooks and videotapes. **Services:** Cooperative research projects with corporate sponsors, and technical support. **Educational Activities:** Undergraduate and graduate courses and short courses to the professional community; Workshops.

Cellular Phone/Telephone Business

START-UP INFORMATION

3648 ■ "Head West, Young Startup?" in *Boston Business Journal* (Vol. 30, October 22, 2010, No. 39, pp. 1)
Pub: Boston Business Journal
Ed: Galen Moore. **Description:** Startup companies Lark Technologies, Baydin and E la Cart Inc. are planning to leave Boston, Massachusetts for Silicon Valley. Lark has developed a vibrating wrist strap that syncs with a mobile phone's alarm clock.

3649 ■ *Starting an iPhone Application Business for Dummies*
Pub: Wiley Publishing
Ed: Aaron Nicholson, Joel Elad, Damien Stolarz. **Released:** October 26, 2009. **Price:** $24.99. **Description:** Ways to create a profitable, sustainable business developing and marketing iPhone applications are profiled.

ASSOCIATIONS AND OTHER ORGANIZATIONS

3650 ■ Canadian Wireless Telecommunications Association–Association Canadienne des Telecommunications Sans Fil
130 Albert St., Ste. 1110
Ottawa, ON, Canada K1P 5G4
Ph:(613)233-4888
Fax:(613)233-2032
Co. E-mail: info@cwta.ca
URL: http://www.cwta.ca
Contact: Bernard Lord, Pres./CEO
Description: Promotes the wireless communications industry in Canada in order to create and maintain a positive economic environment; encourages further investment by the industry to improve the delivery of existing services and create further innovation. **Publications:** *CWTA Membership - Products and Services Directory*; *Wireless Telecom* (3/year).

3651 ■ Communications Marketing Association
PO Box 36275
Denver, CO 80236
Ph:(303)988-3515
Fax:(303)988-3517
Co. E-mail: mercycontreras@comcast.net
URL: http://www.cma-cmc.org
Contact: Mercy Contreras, Exec. Dir.
Description: Manufacturers, independent manufacturers' representatives, and distributors who deal in two-way radio and wireless communication equipment and associated products. Promotes effective marketing and ensures professional industry standards. **Publications:** *CMA Newsletter* (quarterly).

3652 ■ CTIA - The Wireless Association
1400 16th St. NW, Ste. 600
Washington, DC 20036
Ph:(202)736-3200
Fax:(202)785-0721
Co. E-mail: memberservices@ctia.org
URL: http://www.ctia.org
Contact: Steve Largent, Pres./CEO
Description: Individuals and organizations actively engaged in cellular radiotelephone communications, including: telephone companies and corporations providing radio communications; lay firms; engineering firms; consultants and manufacturers. (A cellular radiotelephone is a mobile communications device. An area is geographically divided into low frequency cells monitored by a computer that switches callers from one frequency to another as they move from cell to cell.) Objectives are to: promote, educate, and facilitate the professional interests, needs, and concerns of members with respect to the development and commercial applications of cellular technology; provide an opportunity for exchanging experience and concerns; broaden the understanding and importance of cellular communication technology. Conducts discussions, studies, and courses. **Publications:** *Cellular Technology Report* (monthly); *Industry Data Survey* (semiannual).

3653 ■ Organization for the Promotion and Advancement of Small Telecommunications Companies
2020 K St. NW, 7th Fl.
Washington, DC 20006
Ph:(202)659-5990
Fax:(202)659-4619
Co. E-mail: mks@opastco.org
URL: http://www.opastco.org
Contact: Martha Silver, Dir. of Public Relations
Description: Small, independent telephone companies and cooperatives serving rural areas; associate members are telephone equipment and service suppliers. Seeks to promote and advance small, independent telephone companies and provide a forum for the exchange of ideas and discussion of mutual problems. Represents rural companies' interests before Congress and regulatory bodies. Provides clearinghouse for the compilation, publication, and distribution of information of interest to members. Offers guidance to members on matters of industry-wide importance. Encourages recognition of the contribution made to the telephone industry by members. **Publications:** *OPASTCO 411* (biweekly); *OPASTCO Online Membership Directory* (annual); *OPASTCO Roundtable: The Magazine of Ideas for Small Telephone Companies* (quarterly).

3654 ■ PCIA - The Wireless Infrastructure Association
901 N Washington St., Ste. 600
Alexandria, VA 22314-1535
Ph:(703)836-1608
Free: 800-759-0300
Fax:(703)836-1608
Co. E-mail: nancy.touhill@pcia.com
URL: http://www.pcia.com
Contact: Michael T.N. Fitch, Pres./CEO
Description: Promotes the wireless infrastructure, tower and siting industry through advocacy, education, programs, a trade show and other marketplace initiatives. **Publications:** *PCIA Zoning Field Guide: Information and Resources for Tower Siting* .

3655 ■ Telecommunications Industry Association
2500 Wilson Blvd., Ste. 300
Arlington, VA 22201-3834
Ph:(703)907-7700
Fax:(703)907-7727
Co. E-mail: gseiffert@tiaonline.org
URL: http://www.tiaonline.org
Contact: Grant Seiffert, Pres.
Description: Serves the communications and IT industry, with proven strengths in standards development, domestic and international public policy, and trade shows. Facilitates business development and opportunities and a competitive market environment; provides a forum for member companies, the manufacturers and suppliers of products and services used in global communications. Represents the communications sector of the Electronic Industries Alliance. **Publications:** *Channel Intelligence Report*; *Industry Beat* (weekly); *PulseOnline* (monthly); *TIA Network* (weekly).

REFERENCE WORKS

3656 ■ "Actiontec and Verizon Team Up for a Smarter Home" in *Ecology,Environment & Conservation Business* (November 5, 2011, pp. 3)
Pub: HighBeam Research
Description: Verizon is implementing Actiontec Electronics' SG200 Service Gateway as a basic component of its Home Monitoring and Control service. This new smart home service allows customers to remotely check their homes, control locks and appliances, view home-energy use and more using a smartphone, PC, or FiOS TV.

3657 ■ "After Price Cuts, Competition GPS Makers Lose Direction" in *Brandweek* (Vol. 49, April 21, 2008, No. 16, pp. 16)
Pub: VNU Business Media, Inc.
Ed: Steve Miller. **Description:** Garmin and TomTom, two of the leaders in portable navigation devices, have seen lowering revenues due to dramatic price cuts and unexpected competition from the broadening availability of personal navigation on mobile phones. TomTom has trimmed its sales outlook for its first quarter while Garmin's stock dropped 40 percent since February.

3658 ■ "Agricharts Launches New Mobile App for Ag Market" in *Farm Industry News* (December 1, 2011)
Pub: Penton Business Media Inc.
Description: AgriCharts provides market data, agribusiness Website hosting and technology solutions for the agricultural industry. AgriCharts is a division of Barchart.com Inc. and announced the release of a new mobile applications that offers real-time or delayed platform for viewing quotes, charts and analysis of grains, livestock and other commodity markets.

3659 ■ "Aiming at a Moving Web Target" in *Entrepreneur* (Vol. 37, August 2009, No. 8, pp. 30)
Pub: Entrepreneur Media, Inc.
Ed: Dan O'Shea. **Description:** Rapidly increasing numbers of businesspeople are web surfing on mobile phones. To make a website that is accessible to people on the move, the main page should be light on images and graphics and the most important information should be put near the top. A more intensive route is to create a separate mobile-specific website.

3660 ■ "All Those Applications, and Phone Users Just Want to Talk" in *Advertising Age* (Vol. 79, August 11, 2008, No. 31, pp. 18)
Pub: Crain Communications, Inc.
Ed: Mike Vorhaus. **Description:** Although consumers are slowly coming to text messaging and other data applications, a majority of those Americans surveyed stated that they simply want to use their cell phones to talk and do not care about other activities. Statistical data included.

3661 ■ "App Time: Smartphone Applications Aren't Just for Fun and Games Anymore" in *Inc.* (Volume 32, December 2010, No. 10, pp. 116)
Pub: Inc. Magazine
Ed: Jason Del Rey. **Description:** Smart phone technology can help any small business market their products and services.

3662 ■ "Apps For Anybody With an Idea" in *Advertising Age* (Vol. 79, October 20, 2008, No. 39, pp. 29)
Pub: Crain Communications, Inc.
Ed: Beth Snyder Bulik. **Description:** Apple's new online App Store is open to anyone with an idea and the ability to write code and many of these developers are not only finding a sense of community through this venue but are also making money since the sales are split with Apple, 30/70 in the developer's favor.

3663 ■ "Aptitudes for Apps" in *Boston Business Journal* (Vol. 31, July 1, 2011, No. 23, pp. 3)
Pub: Boston Business Journal
Ed: Kyle Alspach. **Description:** Startups Apperian Inc. and Kinvey Inc. are aiming to accelerate the development and deployment of mobile applications and have received fund pledges from Boston-area venture capital firms.

3664 ■ "At 5-Year Mark, News 9 Makes Presence Felt in Competition for Ad Dollars" in *Business Review, Albany New York* (October 5, 2007)
Pub: American City Business Journals, Inc.
Ed: Barbara Pinckney. **Description:** The 24-hour news channel Capital News 9 can be watched live by viewers on their cell phones beginning late 2007 or early 2008 as part of a deal between Time Warner Cable and Sprint Nextel Corporation to bring Sprint's Pivot technology. News 9 marked its fifth year and plans to continue expanding coverage and provide better services to viewers.

3665 ■ "AT&T To Acquire Black Telecom Firm" in *Black Enterprise* (Vol. 38, January 2008, No. 6, pp. 24)
Pub: Earl G. Graves Publishing Co. Inc.
Ed: Alan Hughes. **Description:** Details of AT&T's acquisition of ChaseCom LP, a telecommunications company based in Houston, Texas, are covered.

3666 ■ "Awaiting a Call from Deutsche Telekom" in *Barron's* (Vol. 90, September 6, 2010, No. 36, pp. M5)
Pub: Barron's Editorial & Corporate Headquarters
Ed: Vito J. Racanelli. **Description:** Deutsche Telekom's (DT) T-Mobile USA Unit has settled in the number four position in the market and the parent company will need to decide if it will hold onto the company in the next 12-18 months from September 2010. T-Mobile's rivals will make critical improvements during this time and DT has the option to upgrade T-Mobile at the cost of improvements to its other units.

3667 ■ "BCE Wireless Growth Flags in Fourth Quarter" in *Globe & Mail* (February 8, 2007, pp. B5)
Pub: CTVglobemedia Publishing Inc.
Ed: Catherine McLean. **Description:** BCE Inc., the largest telecommunications provider in Canada, reported $699 million profit in the final quarter of 2006. The company signed up 169,000 wireless customers in the important holiday season.

3668 ■ "Bet on China" in *Canadian Business* (Vol. 80, November 5, 2007, No. 22, pp. 30)
Pub: Rogers Media
Ed: Thomas Watson. **Description:** Former U.S. Federal Reserve Board head, Alan Greenspan, warns that contraction will happen in the Chinese market. However, the economic success of China does not seem to be at the point of ending, as the country remains the largest market for mobile telecommunications. Forecasts for Chinese trading and investments are provided.

3669 ■ "Beyond the RAZR's Edge" in *Canadian Business* (Vol. 79, November 6, 2006, No. 22, pp. 15)
Pub: Rogers Media
Ed: Andrew Wahl. **Description:** Features of Motorola RAZR, such as low weight and camera accessibility, are presented.

3670 ■ "Big Trouble at Sony Ericsson" in *Barron's* (Vol. 88, March 24, 2008, No. 12, pp. M9)
Pub: Dow Jones & Company, Inc.
Ed: Angelo Franchini. **Description:** Sony Ericsson is facing trouble as it warned that its sales and net income before taxes will fall by nearly half for the first quarter of 2008. The joint venture of Sony and Ericsson has a global mobile phone market share of nine percent as of 2007, fourth largest in the world.

3671 ■ "Blog Buzz Heralds Arrival of IPhone 2.0" in *Advertising Age* (Vol. 79, June 9, 2008, No. 40, pp. 8)
Pub: Crain Communications, Inc.
Ed: Abbey Klaasen. **Description:** Predictions concerning the next version of the iPhone include a global-positioning-system technology as well as a configuration to run on a faster, 3G network.

3672 ■ "Bon Voyager" in *Entrepreneur* (Vol. 36, April 2008, No. 4, pp. 58)
Pub: Entrepreneur Media, Inc.
Ed: Heather Clancy. **Description:** LG Voyager, especially made for Verizon Wireless, is a smart phone that is being compared to Apple iPhone. The Voyager has a 2.8-inch external touchscreen and has a clamshell design, which features an internal keyboard. It does not have Wi-Fi support like iPhone, but it has 3G support. Other differences between the two phones are discussed.

3673 ■ "Boosting Your Merchant Management Services With Wireless Technology" in *Franchising World* (Vol. 42, August 2010, No. 8, pp. 27)
Pub: International Franchise Association
Ed: Michael S. Slominski. **Description:** Franchises should have the capability to accept credit cards away from their businesses. This technology will increase sales.

3674 ■ "Boots Treat Street Rolls Out Trolley Dash App on Androis and iPhone OS" in *Entertainment Close-Up* (October 24, 2011)
Pub: Close-Up Media
Description: Shoppers using Boots Treat Street can now download the Trolley Dash app game, available from the Apple Store and the Android Market, and enjoy the pastel colored street featuring favorite retailers such as eBay, New Look and Play.com collecting prizes while avoiding hazards.

3675 ■ "Break Up the Gang?" in *Canadian Business* (Vol. 81, November 10, 2008, No. 19, pp. 24)
Pub: Rogers Media Ltd.
Ed: Andrew Wahl. **Description:** Nortel Networks Corporation announced they will their Metro Ethernet Network division, suggesting desperation on the part of the company. Some analysts suggest the division is promising, if still unprofitable.

3676 ■ "Broadband Reaches Access Limits in Europe" in *Information Today* (Vol. 26, February 2009, No. 2, pp. 22)
Pub: Information Today, Inc.
Ed: Jim Ashling. **Description:** Eurostat (the Statistical Office of the European communities) reports results from is survey regarding Internet use by businesses throughout its 27-member states. Iceland, Finland and the Netherlands provide the most access at broadband speeds, followed by Belgium, Spain and France.

3677 ■ "The Business Case for Mobile Content Acceleration" in *Streaming Media* (November 2011, pp. 78)
Pub: Information Today Inc.
Ed: Dan Rayburn. **Description:** Last holiday season, eBay became a mobile commerce (m-commerce) giant when sales rose by 134 percent, as most online retailers offered customers the ability to purchase items using their mobile devices.

3678 ■ *Buyology: Truth and Lies About Why We Buy*
Pub: Doubleday, a Division of Random House
Ed: Martin Lindstrom. **Released:** 2009. **Price:** $24. 95. **Description:** Marketers study brain scans to determine how consumers rate Nokia, Coke, and Ford products.

3679 ■ "Call of Prepaid Heard by More" in *Chicago Tribune* (November 26, 2008)
Pub: McClatchy-Tribune Information Services
Ed: Wailin Wong. **Description:** Due to the economic downturn, more consumers are switching to no-contract, prepaid cell phone service. Customers find that the cost savings, flexibility and lack of contract are appealing in such uncertain times.

3680 ■ "Call Them Gorgeous" in *Entrepreneur* (Vol. 35, October 2007, No. 10, pp. 54)
Pub: Entrepreneur Media Inc.
Ed: Amanda C. Kooser. **Description:** Smart phones are known for their high technology features, unique names and extraordinary design. Features of the Apple iPhone, Helio Ocean, Blackberry Curve, T-Mobile Wing and Motorola Razr2 V9 are described.

3681 ■ "Can You Hear Them Now?" in *Hawaii Business* (Vol. 54, August 2008, No. 2, pp. 48)
Pub: Hawaii Business Publishing
Ed: Jason Ubay. **Description:** Coral Wireless LLC (dba Mobi PCS) is ranked 237 in Hawaii Business' list of the state's top 250 companies for 2008. The company is a local wireless phone provider, which has expanded its market to Oahu, Maui and the Big Island since opening in 2006, offering 13 phones and unlimited texts and calls. Details on the company's sales are provided.

3682 ■ "Cell Phone the Ticket on American Airlines" in *Chicago Tribune* (November 14, 2008)
Pub: McClatchy-Tribune Information Services
Ed: Julie Johnsson. **Description:** American Airlines is testing a new mobile boarding pass at O'Hare International Airport. Travelers on American can board flights and get through security checkpoints by flashing a bar code on their phones. Passengers must have an Internet-enabled mobile device and an active e-mail address in order to utilize this service.

3683 ■ *Cisco Network Design Solutions for Small-Medium Businesses*
Pub: Cisco Press
Ed: Peter Rybaczyk. **Released:** August 2004. **Price:** $55.00. **Description:** Solutions for computer networking professionals using computer networks within a small to medium-sized business. Topics cover not only core networking issues and solutions, but security, IP telephony, unified communications, customer relations management, wireless LANs, and more.

3684 ■ "Citizens Unveils Mobile App for Business Customers" in *New Hampshire Business Review* (Vol. 33, March 25, 2011, No. 6, pp. 27)
Pub: Business Publications Inc.
Description: Citizens Financial Group offers a new mobile banking application that allows business

customers to manage cash and payments from a mobile device.

3685 ■ "Comcast Launches New Home Security Service, Developed in Portland" in *The Oregonian* (June 7, 2011)
Pub: McClatchy-Tribune Regional News
Ed: Mike Rogoway. **Description:** Comcast introduced its new high-end home security system that provides 24-hour monitoring and control of homes and utilities, along with Web and mobile access.

3686 ■ "Connections: United We Gab" in *Entrepreneur* (Vol. 35, October 2007, No. 10, pp. 60)
Pub: Entrepreneur Media Inc.
Ed: Mike Hogan. **Description:** T-Mobile and AT&T introduced dual-mode service to consumers, helping them to switch between cellular and Wi-Fi networks easily. These services, such as Hotspot@Home, reduces the cost of long distance calls by routing them over the Internet with the use of WiFi. Benefits of dual mode service, such as lower hardware price and better call coverage are given.

3687 ■ "Consumer Electronics: Brick and Mortar Vs. Online" in *Retail Merchandiser* (Vol. 51, September-October 2011, No. 5, pp. 15)
Pub: Phoenix Media Corporation
Description: Brick and mortar retailers with Websites are discovering that the Internet is used more for research than purchasing when it comes to electronics products. According to a recent study conducted by The NPD Group shows that 56 percent of consumers research televisions online before purchasing, but only 19 percent actually buy them online.

3688 ■ "Corporate Elite Face Steep Challenges" in *Hispanic Business* (January-February 2008, pp. 20, 22, 24, 26, 28, 30, 32)
Pub: Hispanic Business
Ed: Jonathan Higuera. **Description:** Hispanic men and women are moving up corporate ranks at leading companies in the U.S., including Ralph de la Vega, president and CEO of AT&T Mobility. Profiles of Vega and other Hispanic business leaders are included.

3689 ■ "Cox Opens Norfolk Mall Kiosk; Wireless Service Not Ready" in *Virginian-Pilot* (September 20, 2010)
Pub: Virginian-Pilot
Ed: Carolyn Shapiro. **Description:** Cox Communications opened a kiosk at MacArthur Center that will sell wireless telephone devices and plans.

3690 ■ "Cyberwise" in *Black Enterprise* (Vol. 41, December 2010, No. 5, pp. 50)
Pub: Earl G. Graves Publishing Co. Inc.
Ed: Marica Wade Talbert. **Description:** Information is given regarding single platforms that can be used to develop applications for iPhone, Android, Blackberry, and Nokia.

3691 ■ "The Data Drivers" in *Canadian Business* (Vol. 81, September 15, 2008, No. 14-15, pp. 1)
Pub: Rogers Media Ltd.
Ed: Andrew Wahl. **Description:** Canadian regulators hope that an auction of telecommunications companies will inject more competition into the industry; however, newcomers may not be able to rely on lower prices in order to gain market share from the three major telecommunications companies that already have a stronghold on the market. Analysts feel that providing additional data service is the key to surviving market disruptions.

3692 ■ "Death of the PC" in *Canadian Business* (Vol. 83, October 12, 2010, No. 17, pp. 44)
Pub: Rogers Media Ltd.
Ed: Joe Castaldo. **Description:** The future of the personal computer (PC) is looking bleak as consumers are relying more on new mobile devices instead of their PC. A 'Wall Street Journal' article published in September 2010 reported that the iPad had cannibalized sales of laptops by as much as 50 percent. The emergence of tablet computers running alternative operating systems is also explained.

3693 ■ "The Digital Revolution is Over. Long Live the Digital Revolution!" in *Business Strategy Review* (Vol. 21, Spring 2010, No. 1, pp. 74)
Pub: Wiley-Blackwell
Ed: Gianvito Lanzolla, Jamie Anderson. **Description:** Many businesses are now involved in the digital marketplace. The authors argue that the new reality of numerous companies offering overlapping products means that it is critical for managers to understand digital convergence and to observe the imperatives for remaining competitive.

3694 ■ "A Direct Approach" in *Business Journal-Portland* (Vol. 24, November 9, 2007, No. 36, pp. 1)
Pub: American City Business Journals, Inc.
Ed: Matthew Kish. **Description:** Respond 2 LLC's annual revenue has increased from $14.2 million in 2004 to almost $50 million in 2007. The growth is attributed to a $100 million contract with Vonage. The role of the popularity of infomercials on the success of the Portland-based marketing company is evaluated.

3695 ■ "Diversity Elite Scorecard" in *Hispanic Business* (September 2007, pp. 72-74, 76, 78, 80, 82, 84)
Pub: Hispanic Business
Description: Special report on companies committed to diversity in 2007 is presented along with a brief profile of each company. Southern California Edison and AT&T Inc. topped the list.

3696 ■ "Don't' Hang Up On FairPoint" in *Barron's* (Vol. 88, July 7, 2008, No. 27, pp. M5)
Pub: Dow Jones & Co., Inc.
Ed: Fleming Meeks. **Description:** Shares of FairPoint Communications, priced at $6.63 each, are undervalued and should be worth over $12 each. The company increased its size by more than five times by acquiring Verizon's local telephone operations in Vermont, New Hampshire, and Maine, but must switch customers in those areas into their system by the end of September 2007.

3697 ■ "Don't' Hate the Cable Guy" in *Saint Louis Business Journal* (Vol. 31, August 5, 2011, No. 50, pp. 1)
Pub: Saint Louis Business Journal
Ed: Angela Mueller. **Description:** Charter Communications named John Birrer as senior vice president of customer experience. The company experienced problems with its customer services.

3698 ■ "Double Duty" in *Black Enterprise* (Vol. 38, February 2008, No. 7, pp. 56)
Pub: Earl G. Graves Publishing Co. Inc.
Description: Pantech Wireless is offering its new Duo cellular phone that combines multiple features of a phone with the high speed data functions of a Blackberry-style smartphone.

3699 ■ "Dow Jones Gives Apple-Loving Sales Professionals a Boost" in *Information Today* (Vol. 26, February 2009, No. 2, pp. 30)
Pub: Information Today, Inc.
Description: Dow Jones Sales Triggers for iPhone and iPod program helps sales professionals stay current to prospects and customers in their fields by providing real-time news on business changes, including management moves, mergers, and new investments. The application presents events that trigger best opportunities and allows users to look up companies and executives to retrieve information.

3700 ■ "Dropped Calls" in *Canadian Business* (Vol. 80, November 5, 2007, No. 22, pp. 34)
Pub: Rogers Media
Ed: Andrew Wahl. **Description:** Control over Canada's telecommunications market by Telus, Rogers and Bell Canada has resulted in a small number of innovations. The pricing regimes of these carriers have also stifled innovations in the telecommunications industry. The status of Canada's telecommunications industry is further analyzed.

3701 ■ "eBay Inc. Completes Acquisition of Zong" in *Benzinga.com* (October 29, 2011)
Pub: Benzinga.com
Ed: Benzinga Staff. **Description:** eBay Inc. acquired Zong, a provider of payments through mobile carrier billing. Terms of the agreement are outlined.

3702 ■ *Electronic Commerce*
Pub: Course Technology
Ed: Gary Schneider, Bryant Chrzan, Charles McCormick. **Released:** May 1, 2010. **Price:** $117.95. **Description:** E-commerce can open the door to more opportunities than ever before for small business. Packed with real-world examples and cases, the book delivers comprehensive coverage of emerging online technologies and trends and their influence on the electronic marketplace. It details how the landscape of online commerce is evolving, reflecting changes in the economy and how business and society are responding to those changes. Balancing technological issues with the strategic business aspects of successful e-commerce, the new edition includes expanded coverage of international issues, social networking, mobile commerce, Web 2.0 technologies, and updates on spam, phishing, and identity theft.

3703 ■ "Etextbook Space Heats Up" in *Information Today* (Vol. 28, November 2011, No. 10, pp. 10)
Pub: Information Today, Inc.
Ed: Paula J. Hane. **Description:** The use of etextbooks is expected to grow with the use of mobile devices and tablets. A new group of activists is asking students, faculty members and others to sign a petition urging higher education leaders to prioritize affordable textbooks or free ebooks over the traditional, expensive new books required for classes.

3704 ■ "Executive Decision: To Make Inroads Against RIM, Palm Steals Its Strategy" in *Globe & Mail* (March 25, 2006, pp. B3)
Pub: CTVglobemedia Publishing Inc.
Ed: Simon Avery. **Description:** The Palm Inc., global leader in portable device manufacturing, is looking forward to improve its sales of Palm Treos, a wireless portable device that connects to internet and email. Palm is also planning to build partnerships, under the efficient management of Michael Moskowitz, general manager and vice-president of Palm Inc., with the other companies to increase the sales of its wireless devices.

3705 ■ *Extraordinary Circumstances: The Journey of a Corporate Whistleblower*
Pub: John Wiley & Sons, Inc.
Ed: Cynthia Cooper. **Released:** 2009. **Price:** $27.95. **Description:** Cynthia Cooper offers details of the events that led to the implosion of telecom giant WorldCom.

3706 ■ "Faster and Shorter" in *Canadian Business* (Vol. 81, October 13, 2008, No. 17, pp. 25)
Pub: Rogers Media Ltd.
Ed: Terri Goveia. **Description:** Study revealed that instant messaging (IM) technologies are slowly becoming legitimate in the corporate world. IM is traditionally considered as a distraction, but it was found to let workers make targeted inquiries that gives them what they need in an instant. Other views and information about IMs is included.

3707 ■ "Firm Restricts Cellphone Use While Driving" in *Globe & Mail* (January 30, 2006, pp. B3)
Pub: CTVglobemedia Publishing Inc.
Ed: Catherine McLean. **Description:** The details on AMEC Plc, which adopted cellphone-free driving policy, are presented.

3708 ■ "For Apple, It's Showtime Again" in *Barron's* (Vol. 90, August 30, 2010, No. 35, pp. 29)
Pub: Barron's Editorial & Corporate Headquarters
Ed: Eric J. Savitz. **Description:** Speculations on what Apple Inc. will unveil at its product launch event are

presented. These products include a possible new iPhone Nano, a new update to its Apple TV, and possibly a deal with the Beatles to distribute their songs over iTunes.

3709 ■ "gdgt: The New Online Home for Gadget Fans" in *Hispanic Business* (July-August 2009, pp. 15)
Pub: Hispanic Business
Ed: Jeremy Nisen. **Description:** Profile of the new online Website for gadget lovers. The site combines a leek interface, gadget database, and social networking-type features which highlights devices for the consumer.

3710 ■ "Generation Y Chooses the Mobile Web" in *PR Newswire* (November 24, 2010)
Pub: PR Newswire Association LLC
Description: Generation Y individuals between the ages of 18 - 27 use their mobile phones to browse the Internet more often than a desktop or laptop computer, according to a survey conducted by Opera, a Web browser company.

3711 ■ "Get Paid and Get Moving" in *Entrepreneur* (Vol. 37, October 2009, No. 10, pp. 38)
Pub: Entrepreneur Media, Inc.
Description: GoPayments application from Intuit allows mobile telephones to process payments like credit card terminals. The application costs $19.95 a month and can be used on the Internet browsers of mobile telephones.

3712 ■ "Google Places a Call to Bargain Hunters" in *Advertising Age* (Vol. 79, September 29, 2008, No. 36, pp. 13)
Pub: Crain Communications, Inc.
Ed: Abbey Klaassen. **Description:** Google highlighted application developers who have created tools for its Android mobile phone in the device's unveiling; applications such as ShopSavvy and CompareEverywhere help shoppers to find bargains by allowing them to compare prices in their local areas and across the web.

3713 ■ "Growing at the Margins" in *Business Journal Serving Greater Tampa Bay* (Vol. 30, November 5, 2010, No. 46, pp. 1)
Pub: Tampa Bay Business Journal
Ed: Margie Manning. **Description:** Jabil Circuit Inc. has reported an increase in revenues from its smart phones and medical devices. The company has been focusing on its core services such as making smart phone parts and medical devices.

3714 ■ "Hewlett-Packard Mini: Ultra-Portable, and Affordable" in *Hispanic Business* (July-August 2009, pp. 36)
Pub: Hispanic Business
Ed: Jeremy Nisen. **Description:** Hewlett-Packard's 1151 NR computers works a lot like a smartphone online, it can dial up fast speeds on Verizon's 3G network almost anywhere.

3715 ■ "Hold the IPhone" in *Canadian Business* (Vol. 80, January 15, 2007, No. 2, pp. 22)
Pub: Rogers Media
Ed: Andrew Wahl. **Description:** The rise in the price of shares of Apple Inc. after the introduction of its new product, the iPhone, is discussed.

3716 ■ "Hoover's Mobile, MobileSP Now Available" in *Information Today* (Vol. 26, February 2009, No. 2, pp. 29)
Pub: Information Today, Inc.
Description: Hoover's Inc. introduced its Hoover's Mobile for iPhone, BlackBerry and Windows Mobile smartphones along with Hoover's MobileSP for BlackBerry and Windows Mobile. Both products allow users to access customer, prospect, and partner information; analyze competitors; prepare for meetings; and find new opportunities. In addition, MobileSP adds one-click calling to executives, GPS-enabled location searches, advanced search and list building, and a custom call queue and a 'save to contacts' capabilities.

3717 ■ "How Dell Will Dial for Dollars" in *Austin Business JournalInc.* (Vol. 29, December 4, 2009, No. 39, pp. 1)
Pub: American City Business Journals
Ed: Christopher Calnan. **Description:** Dell Inc. revealed plans to launch a Mini3i smartphone in China which could enable revenue sharing by bundling with wireless service subscription. Dell's smartphone plan is similar to the netbook business, which Dell sold with service provided by AT&T Inc.

3718 ■ "How to Play the Tech Mergers" in *Barron's* (Vol. 90, August 30, 2010, No. 35, pp. 18)
Pub: Barron's Editorial & Corporate Headquarters
Ed: Tiernan Ray. **Description:** The intense bidding by Hewlett-Packard and Dell for 3Par was foreseen in a previous Barron's cover story and 3Par's stock has nearly tripled since reported. Other possible acquisition targets in the tech industry include Brocade Communication Systems, NetApp, Xyratex, and Isilon Systems.

3719 ■ "HR Tech on the Go" in *Workforce Management* (Vol. 88, November 16, 2009, No. 12, pp. 1)
Pub: Crain Communications, Inc.
Ed: Ed Frauenheim. **Description:** Examination of the necessity of mobile access of human resources software applications that allow managers to recruit, schedule and train employees via their mobile devices; some industry leaders believe that mobile HR applications are vital while others see this new technology as hype.

3720 ■ "iControl Networks Powers Comcast's XFINITY (Reg) Home Security Service" in *Benzinga.com* (June 9, 2011)
Pub: Benzinga.com
Ed: Benzinga Staff. **Description:** Comcast's XFINITY Home Security Service is powered by iControl Networks' OpenHome (TM) software platform. The service provides intrusion and fire protection along with interactive features such as home monitoring, home management, and energy management services with Web and mobile access.

3721 ■ "Ideas at Work: Total Communicator" in *Business Strategy Review* (Vol. 21, Autumn 2010, No. 3, pp. 10)
Pub: Wiley-Blackwell
Ed: Stuart Crainer. **Description:** Vittorio Colao has been chief executive of Vodafone Group for two years. He brings to the company some special experience: from 2004-2006 he was CEO of RCS MediaGroup in Milan, which publishes newspapers, magazines and books in Italy, Spain and France. Colao shares his views on business, the global economy and leading Vodafone.

3722 ■ "Impressive Numbers: Companies Experience Substantial Increases in Dollars, Employment" in *Hispanic Business* (July-August 2007)
Pub: Hispanic Business
Ed: Derek Reveron. **Description:** Profiles of five fastest growing Hispanic companies reporting increases in revenue and employment include Brightstar, distributor of wireless products; Greenway Ford Inc., a car dealership; Fred Loya Insurance, auto insurance carrier; and Group O, packaging company; and Diverse Staffing, Inc., an employment and staffing firm.

3723 ■ "Internet and Mobile Media" in *MarketingMagazine* (Vol. 115, September 27, 2010, No. 13, pp. 60)
Pub: Rogers Publishing Ltd.
Description: Market data covering the Internet and mobile media in Canada is given.

3724 ■ "Into the Groove: Fine-Tune Your Biz By Getting Into the Good Habit Groove" in *Small Business Opportunities* (Spring 2008)
Pub: Harris Publications Inc.
Description: Profile of Ty Freyvogel and his consulting firm Freyvogel Communications. Freyvogel serves the telecommunications need of Fortune 500 and mid-sized businesses.

3725 ■ "IPhone 3G" in *Advertising Age* (Vol. 79, November 17, 2008, No. 43, pp. 15)
Pub: Crain Communications, Inc.
Ed: Beth Snyder Bulik. **Description:** Review of Apple's new iPhone 3G which includes the addition of smart-phone applications as well as a price drop; the new functionalities as well as the lower price seems to be paying off for Apple who reported sales of 6.9 million iPhones in its most recent quarter, in which the 3G hit store shelves.

3726 ■ "iPhone Apps Big Business" in *Austin Business JournalInc.* (Vol. 28, November 14, 2008, No. 35, pp. 1)
Pub: American City Business Journals
Ed: Christopher Calnan. **Description:** Members of the computer software industry in Austin, Texas have benefited from developing applications for Apple Inc.'s iPhone. Pangea Software Inc.'s revenues have grown by developing iPhone applications. Lexcycle LLC, on the other hand, has created an application that enables users to read books on the iPhone.

3727 ■ "The iPhone Gets Some Competition" in *Inc.* (Vol. 31, January-February 2009, No. 1, pp. 42)
Pub: Mansueto Ventures LLC
Ed: Mark Spoonauer. **Description:** RIM's BlackBerry Storm and T-Mobile's G1 are competing with the iPhone 3G technology; the three systems are profiled.

3728 ■ "Israeli Spam Law May Have Global Impact" in *Information Today* (Vol. 26, February 2009, No. 2, pp. 28)
Pub: Information Today, Inc.
Ed: David Mirchin. **Description:** Israels new law, called Amendment 40 of the Communications Law, will regulate commercial solicitations including those sent without permission via email, fax, automatic phone dialing systems, or short messaging technologies.

3729 ■ "It Was a Very Good Year...To Be Ted Rogers" in *Canadian Business* (Vol. 80, Winter 2007, No. 24, pp. 121)
Pub: Rogers Media
Ed: Andrew Wahl. **Description:** Ted Rogers had a banner year in 2007 as Rogers Communications Inc. (RCI) took in huge profits from its phone and wireless business and his personal wealth grew sixty-seven percent to $7.6 billion. Rogers has record of betting on technologies that get the best returns relative to the investment in the marketplace such as its use of the GSM network and its cable hybrid fiber coaxial network.

3730 ■ "It's Not About the G1; Google Just Wants You to Use the Mobile Web" in *Advertising Age* (Vol. 79, September 29, 2008, No. 36, pp. 32)
Pub: Crain Communications, Inc.
Ed: Abbey Klaassen. **Description:** Google's Android is the first serious competitor to Apple's iPhone; the company says that its goal is to simplify the mobile market and get wireless subscribers to use the mobile Internet and purchase smartphones.

3731 ■ "Jump Ship On Your Wireless Contract" in *Black Enterprise* (Vol. 38, January 2008, No. 6, pp. 87)
Pub: Earl G. Graves Publishing Co. Inc.
Ed: Nicole Norfleet. **Description:** Better Business Bureau reported it received more than 28,000 complaints in 2007. Four situations that allow consumers to be released from a long-term service contract with a carrier without paying penalty fees are addressed.

3732 ■ "Kenyans Embrace Moving Money By Text Message" in *Chicago Tribune* (October 7, 2008)
Pub: McClatchy-Tribune Information Services
Ed: Laurie Goering. **Description:** Cell phone banking services are becoming more common, especially for foreign residents; customers are able to establish a virtual cell phone bank account through companies such as M-Pesa which allows their customers to pay bills, withdraw cash, pay merchants or text money to relatives.

3733 ■ "Like All Great Visionaries, Steve Jobs has a Dark Side" in *Canadian Business* (Vol. 83, July 20, 2010, No. 11-12, pp. 11)
Pub: Rogers Media Ltd.
Ed: Steve Maich. **Description:** All the adoration piled onto Apple can go to a man's head, especially its CEO Steve Jobs. Jobs is a true visionary but his leadership comes with an autocratic side that is worth watching out for; this is shown by his condescending response to the reported reception problems of the iPhone 4.

3734 ■ "Look, No Hands!" in *Inc.* (Vol. 33, September 2011, No. 7, pp. 52)
Pub: Inc. Magazine
Ed: John Brandon. **Description:** The Jabra Freeway, a small Bluetooth speakerphone clips to a car visor and allows the user to place, answer and ignore calls by speaking commands.

3735 ■ "Looking Out for the Little Guys" in *Black Enterprise* (Vol. 38, October 2007, No. 3, pp. 58)
Pub: Earl G. Graves Publishing Co. Inc.
Ed: Kaylyn Kendall Dines. **Description:** Biz TechConnect is a Web portal that offers free online and social networking, along with four modules that help small businesses with marketing and advertising, communications and mobility, financial management, and customer relationship management.

3736 ■ "Making Visitors Out Of Listeners" in *Hawaii Business* (Vol. 54, July 2008, No. 1, pp. 18)
Pub: Hawaii Business Publishing
Ed: Casey Chin. **Description:** Japanese workers are subscribing to the Official Hawaii Podcast in iTunes, which offers a free 20-minute, Japanese-language audio content on different topics, such as dining reviews and music from local artists. The concept is a way to attract Japanese travelers to come to Hawaii.

3737 ■ "Marketers Push for Mobile Tuesday as the New Black Friday" in *Advertising Age* (Vol. 79, December 1, 2008, No. 44, pp. 21)
Pub: Crain Communications, Inc.
Ed: Natalie Zmuda. **Description:** Marketers are using an innovative approach in an attempt to stimulate business on the Tuesday following Thanksgiving by utilizing consumer's cell phones to alert them of sales or present them with coupons for this typically slow retail business day; with this campaign both advertisers and retailers are hoping to start Mobile Tuesday, another profitable shopping day in line with Black Friday and Cyber Monday.

3738 ■ "Mobile: Juanes Fans Sing for Sprint" in *Advertising Age* (Vol. 79, November 3, 2008, No. 41, pp. 22)
Pub: Crain Communications, Inc.
Ed: Laurel Wentz. **Description:** Marketers are appealing to the Hispanic market since they are more prone to use their cell phones to respond to contests, download videos, ringtones, or other data activity. Sprint recently sponsored a contest inviting people to sing like Colombian megastar Juanes; the participants filmed and sent their videos using their cell phones rather than laptops or camcorders illustrating the Hispanic overindex on mobile-phone technology. The contest generated hundreds of thousands of dollars in additional fee revenue, as monthly downloads increased 63 percent.

3739 ■ "Mobile Marketing Grows With Size of Cell Phone Screens" in *Crain's Detroit Business* (Vol. 24, January 14, 2008, No. 2, pp. 13)
Pub: Crain Communications Inc. - Detroit
Ed: Bill Shea. **Description:** Experts are predicting increased marketing for cell phones with the inception of larger screens and improved technology.

3740 ■ *Mobile Office: The Essential Small Business Guide to Office Technology*
Pub: Double Storey Books
Ed: Arthur Goldstruck, Steven Ambrose. **Released:** September 1, 2009. **Price:** $6.95. **Description:** Essential pocket guide for startup businesses and entrepreneurs which provides information to create a mobile office in order to maximize business potential while using current technologies.

3741 ■ "Mobile Presence, in a Flash: DIY Tools for Creating Smartphone-Friendly Websites" in *Inc.* (Vol. 33, November 2011, No. 9, pp. 50)
Pub: Inc. Magazine
Ed: John Brandon. **Description:** DudaMobile and FiddleFly convert regular Websites into mobile sites that work on most smartphones. Profiles of both apps services are included.

3742 ■ "Mobile Security for Business V5" in *SC Magazine* (Vol. 20, August 2009, No. 8, pp. 55)
Pub: Haymarket Media, Inc.
Description: Review of F-Secure's Mobile Security for Business v5 which offers protection for business smartphones that can be centralized for protection monitoring by IT administrators.

3743 ■ "Mobility: So Happy Together" in *Entrepreneur* (Vol. 35, October 2007, No. 10, pp. 64)
Pub: Entrepreneur Media Inc.
Ed: Heather Clancy. **Description:** Joshua Burnett, CEO and founder of 9ci, uses index cards to keep track of what he needs to do despite the fact that he has a notebook computer, cell phone and PDA. Kim Hahn, a media entrepreneur, prefers jotting her ideas down in a spiral notebook, has a team that would organize her records for her, and a personal assistant that would keep track of changes to her schedule. Reasons why these entrepreneurs use old-fashioned methods along with new technology are given.

3744 ■ "Moosylvania Releases Latest XL Marketing Trends Report" in *Wireless News* (October 6, 2009)
Pub: Close-Up Media
Description: Moosylvania, a digital promotion and branding agency that also has an on-site research facility, has released its 2nd XL Marketing Trends Report which focuses on digital video; the study defines the top digital video trends marketers must focus on now and well into the future and notes that in 2010, Mobile Web Devices, such as smart phones will outnumber computers in this country. Statistical data included.

3745 ■ "More Callers Are Cutting Their Landlines" in *Chicago Tribune* (December 30, 2008)
Pub: McClatchy-Tribune Information Services
Ed: Eric Benderoff. **Description:** Despite sporadic outages for cell phone users, the trend for consumers to cut out the expense of a landline does not appear to be slowing; experts believe that the recession will further increase the number of consumers who decide to go completely wireless.

3746 ■ "A Motorola Spinoff Is No Panacea" in *Barron's* (Vol. 88, March 31, 2008, No. 13, pp. 19)
Pub: Dow Jones & Company, Inc.
Ed: Mark Veverka. **Description:** Motorola's plan to try and spinoff their handset division is bereft of details as to how or specifically when in 2009 the spinoff would occur. There's no reason to buy the shares since there's a lot of execution risk to the plan. Motorola needs to hire a proven cellphone executive and develop a compelling new cellphone platform.

3747 ■ "Motorola's New Cell Phone Lineup Includes Green Effort" in *Chicago Tribune* (January 14, 2009)
Pub: McClatchy-Tribune Information Services
Ed: Eric Benderoff. **Description:** Motorola Inc. introduced a new line of mobile phones at the Consumer Electronics Show in Las Vegas; the phones are made using recycled water bottles for the plastic housing.

3748 ■ "My Favorite Tool for Managing Expenses" in *Inc.* (Volume 32, December 2010, No. 10, pp. 60)
Pub: Inc. Magazine
Ed: J.J. McCorvey. **Description:** Web-based service called Expensify is outlined. The service allows companies to log expenses while away from the office using the service's iPhone application.

3749 ■ "My Favorite Tool for Organizing Data" in *Inc.* (Vol. 33, November 2011, No. 9, pp. 46)
Pub: Inc. Magazine
Ed: Abram Brown. **Description:** Intelligence software firm uses Roambi, a Web-based service that turns spreadsheet data into interactive files for iPhones and iPads.

3750 ■ "Naked Ambitions Put Telus on the Spot" in *Globe & Mail* (February 6, 2007, pp. B3)
Pub: CTVglobemedia Publishing Inc.
Ed: Catherine McLean. **Description:** The offering of pornographic content on mobile phones by the telecommunications company Telus Corp., is discussed.

3751 ■ "The New Basics of Marketing" in *Inc.* (February 2008, pp. 75-81)
Pub: Gruner & Jahr USA Publishing
Ed: Leigh Buchanan. **Description:** New tools for marketing a business or service include updating or upgrading a Website, using email or texting, or advertising on a social Internet network.

3752 ■ "The New Guard" in *Entrepreneur* (Vol. 36, February 2008, No. 2, pp. 46)
Pub: Entrepreneur Media Inc.
Ed: Amanda C. Kooser. **Description:** A natural language search engine is being developed by Powerset for better online searching. Zannel Inc. offers Instant Media Messaging platform, which allows for social networking using phones. Ning is an online platform that allows users to customize and control their social networks.

3753 ■ "New IPhone Also Brings New Way of Mobile Marketing" in *Advertising Age* (Vol. 79, June 16, 2008, No. 24, pp. 23)
Pub: Crain Communications, Inc.
Ed: Abbey Klaasen. **Description:** Currently there are two kinds of applications for the iPhone and other mobile devices: native applications that allow for richer experiences and take advantage of features that are built into a phone and web applications, those that allow access to the web through specific platforms. Marketers are interested in creating useful experiences for customers and opening up the platforms which will allow them to do this.

3754 ■ "New Sprint Phone Whets Appetite for Applications" in *The Business Journal-Serving Metropolitan Kansas City* (Vol. 26, July 25, 2008)
Pub: American City Business Journals, Inc.
Ed: Suzanna Stagemeyer. **Description:** Firms supporting the applications of the new Samsung Instinct, which was introduced by Sprint Nextel Corp. in June 2008, have reported usage rates increase for their products. Handmark, whose mobile services Pocket Express comes loaded with Instinct, has redirected employees to meet the rising demand for the services. Other views and information on Instinct, are presented.

3755 ■ "New Ways To Think About Data Loss: Data Loss Is Costly and Painful" in *Franchising World* (Vol. 42, August 2010, No. 8, pp. 21)
Pub: International Franchise Association
Ed: Ken Colburn. **Description:** Information for maintaining data securely for franchised organizations, including smart phones, tablets, copiers, computers and more is given.

3756 ■ "New Year's Resolutions: How Three Companies Came Up With Their 2008 Growth Strategies" in *Inc.* (January 2008, pp. 47-49)
Pub: Gruner & Jahr USA Publishing
Ed: Martha C. White. **Description:** Three companies share 2008 growth strategies; companies include a candle company, a voice mail and text messaging marketer, and hotel supplier of soap and shampoo.

3757 ■ "The Next Generation of Bluetooth Headsets" in *Inc.* (Vol. 31, January-February 2009, No. 1, pp. 41)
Pub: Mansueto Ventures LLC
Ed: Mark Spoonauer. **Description:** Information on the latest Bluetooth headsets that allow users to talk hands-free and the new technology that blocks ambient sounds is given. Aliph Jawbone, Plantronics Voyager Jabra BT530, and Motorola Motopure H15 are profiled.

3758 ■ "Nine Sectors to Watch: Telecom" in *Canadian Business* (Vol. 81, December 24, 2007, No. 1, pp. 44)
Pub: Rogers Media
Ed: Andrew Wahl. **Description:** Forecasts on the Canadian telecommunications industry for 2008 are presented. Details on consumer spending growth, the popularity of broadband, and activities in the wireless sector are also discussed.

3759 ■ *The Nokia Revolution: The Story of an Extraordinary Company That Transformed an Industry*
Pub: AMACOM
Ed: Dan Steinbock. **Released:** May 31, 2001. **Description:** Profile of Nokia, the world's largest wireless communications company. Nokia started in 1865 in rural Finland and merged its rubber company and a cabling firm to form the corporation around 1965. The firm's corporate strategy in the mobile communications industry is highlighted.

3760 ■ "Note-Taking App, Supercharged" in *Inc.* (Vol. 33, October 2011, No. 8, pp. 48)
Pub: Inc. Magazine
Ed: Adam Baer. **Description:** Note Taker HD is an iPad app that lets the user text by typing with finger or stylus with various colors, fonts and sizes; Extensive Notes creates notes, records audio memos, and takes photos and videos; Evernote allows users to create notes, take snapshots, and record voice memos.

3761 ■ "One Charger, Many Devices: the Skinny on Wireless Power Pads" in *Inc.* (Volume 32, December 2010, No. 10, pp. 58)
Pub: Inc. Magazine
Ed: John Brandon. **Description:** Wireless charging pads eliminate the need for multiple cords and wall outlets. Powermat 2X, Energizer Q1, Pure Energy Solutions Wildcharge Pad, and Curacell mygrid are profiled.

3762 ■ "Online Translation Service Aids Battlefield Troops" in *Product News Network* (August 30, 2011)
Pub: Thomas Publishing Company
Description: Linquist online service, LinGo Link provides real-time interpreter support to military troops overseas. Interpreters skilled in multiple languages and dialects are used in various areas and in multiple instances without requiring physical presence. The service is available through commercial cellular or WiFi services or tactical communications network. The system accommodates exchange of audio, video, photos, and text during conversations via smartphones and mobile peripheral devices.

3763 ■ "Our Gadget of the Week: Mostly, I Liked It" in *Barron's* (Vol. 88, July 14, 2008, No. 28, pp. 31)
Pub: Dow Jones & Co., Inc.
Ed: Jay Palmer. **Description:** Review of the Apple iPhone 3G, which costs $199, has better audio and is slightly thicker than its predecessor; using the 3G wireless connection makes going online faster but drains the battery faster too.

3764 ■ "Our Hoarder Mentality: Blame the Hard Disk" in *PC Magazine* (Vol. 30, November 2011, No. 11, pp. 46)
Pub: Ziff Davis Inc.
Ed: John C. Dvorak. **Description:** Computer programmers, once referred to as computer users, are slowly being replaced by passive consumers of products and content of tablets and handheld mobile phones and devices of the future. Understanding is garnered as this article examines this industry trend.

3765 ■ "Play By Play: These Video Products Can Add New Life to a Stagnant Website" in *Black Enterprise* (Vol. 41, December 2010, No. 5)
Pub: Earl G. Graves Publishing Co. Inc.
Ed: Marcia Wade Talbert. **Description:** Web Visible, provider of online marketing products and services, cites video capability as the fastest-growing Website feature for small business advertisers. Profiles of various devices for adding video to a Website are included.

3766 ■ *Power Up Your Small-Medium Business: A Guide to Enabling Network Technologies*
Pub: Cisco Press
Ed: Robyn Aber. **Released:** March 2004. **Price:** $39.95 (US), $57.95 (Canadian). **Description:** Network technologies geared to small and medium-size business, focusing on access, IP telephony, wireless technologies, security, and computer network management.

3767 ■ *Practical Tech for Your Business*
Pub: Kiplinger Books and Tapes
Ed: Michael J. Martinez. **Released:** 2002. **Description:** Advice is offered to help small business owners choose the right technology for their company. The guide tells how to get started, network via the Internet, create an office network, use database software, and conduct business using mobile technology.

3768 ■ "Prepaid Phones Surge in Bad Economy" in *Advertising Age* (Vol. 79, November 17, 2008, No. 43, pp. 6)
Pub: Crain Communications, Inc.
Ed: Rita Chang. **Description:** Prepay cell phone offerings are becoming increasingly competitive amid a greater choice of plans and handsets. In an economic environment in which many consumers are unable to pass the credit checks required for traditional cell phone plans, the prepay market is surging.

3769 ■ "Presidential Address: Innovation in Retrospect and Prospect" in *Canadian Journal of Electronics* (Vol. 43, November 2010, No. 4)
Pub: Journal of the Canadian Economics Association
Ed: James A. Brander. **Description:** Has innovation slowed in recent decades? While there has been progress in information and communications technology, the recent record of innovation in agriculture, energy, transportation and healthcare sectors is cause for concern.

3770 ■ "Providing Expertise Required to Develop Microsystems" in *Canadian Electronics* (Vol. 23, February 2008, No. 1, pp. 6)
Pub: CLB Media Inc.
Ed: Ian McWalter. **Description:** CMC Microsystems, formerly Canadian Microelectronics Corporation, is focused on empowering microelectronics and Microsystems research in Canada. Microsystems offers the basis for innovations in the fields of science, environment, technology, automotives, energy, aerospace and communications technology. CMC's strategy in developing Microsystems in Canada is described.

3771 ■ "Publishing Technology Introduces IngentaConnect Mobile" in *Information Today* (Vol. 26, February 2009, No. 2, pp. 33)
Pub: Information Today, Inc.
Description: College undergraduates will find Publishing Technology's newest publisher product, IngentaConnect Mobile helpful. The product allows users to read articles and abstracts on mobile devices. According to a recent study, 73 percent of young adults with wireless hand-held devices use them to access non-voice data on any given day.

3772 ■ "Put a Projector in Your Pocket" in *Inc.* (Vol. 31, January-February 2009, No. 1, pp. 42)
Pub: Mansueto Ventures LLC
Description: PowerPoint presentations can be given using the Optoma Pico Pocket Projector. The device can be connected to laptops, cell phones, digital cameras, and iPods.

3773 ■ "Putting the App in Apple" in *Inc.* (Vol. 30, November 2008, No. 11, pp.)
Pub: Mansueto Ventures LLC
Ed: Nitasha Tiku. **Description:** Aftermarket companies are scrambling to develop games and widgets for Apple's iPhone. Apple launched a kit for developers interested in creating iPhone-specific software along with the App Store, and an iTunes spinoff. Profiles of various software programs that may be used on the iPhone are given.

3774 ■ "Q&A Patrick Pichette" in *Canadian Business* (Vol. 81, October 13, 2008, No. 17, pp. 6)
Pub: Rogers Media Ltd.
Ed: Andrew Wahl. **Description:** Patrick Pichette finds challenge in taking over the finances of an Internet company that has a market cap of about $140 billion. He feels, however, that serving as Google's chief financial officer is nothing compared to running Bell Canada Enterprises (BCE). Pichette's other views on Google and BCE are presented.

3775 ■ "Qualcomm Could Win Big as the IPhone 3G Calls" in *Barron's* (Vol. 88, July 4, 2008, No. 28, pp. 30)
Pub: Dow Jones & Co., Inc.
Ed: Eric J. Savitz. **Description:** Apple iPhone 3G's introduction could widen the smartphone market thereby benefiting handset chipmaker Qualcomm in the process. Qualcomm Senior V.P., Bill Davidson sees huge potential for his company's future beyond phones with their Snapdragon processor. The prospects of Sun Microsystems' shares are also discussed.

3776 ■ "Quickoffice's MobileFiles Pro App Enables Excel Editing On-the-Go" in *Information Today* (Vol. 26, February 2009, No. 2, pp. 31)
Pub: Information Today, Inc.
Description: Quickoffice Inc. introduced MobileFiles Pro, which features editable Microsoft Office functionality for the iPone and iPod touch. The application allows users to edit and save Microsoft Excel files in .xls format, transfer files to and from PC and Mac desktops via Wi-Fi, and access and synchronize with Apple MobileMe accounts.

3777 ■ "Remote Control: Working From Wherever" in *Inc.* (February 2008, pp. 46-47)
Pub: Gruner & Jahr USA Publishing
Ed: Ryan Underwood. **Description:** New technology allows workers to perform tasks from anywhere via the Internet. Profiles of products to help connect to your office from afar include, LogMein Pro, a Web-based service that allowsaccess to a computer from anywhere; Xdrive, an online service that allows users to store and swap files; Basecamp, a Web-based tools that works like a secure version of MySpace; MojoPac Freedom, is software that allows users to copy their computer's desktop to a removable hard drive and plug into any PC; WatchGuard Firebox X Core e-Series UTM Bundle, hardware that blocks hackers and viruses while allowing employees to work remotely; TightVNC, a free open-source software that lets you control another computer via the Internet.

3778 ■ "Research and Markets Adds Report: The U.S. Mobile Web Market" in *Entertainment Close-Up* (December 10, 2009)
Pub: Close-Up Media
Description: Highlights of the new Research and Markets report "The U.S. Mobile Web Market: Taking Advantage of the iPhone Phenomenon" include: mobile Internet marketing strategies; the growth of mobile web usage; the growth of revenue in the mobile web market; and a look at Internet business communications, social media and networking.

3779 ■ "RIM Opts to Be Little Less Open" in *Canadian Business* (Vol. 83, October 12, 2010, No. 17, pp. 13)
Pub: Rogers Media Ltd.
Ed: Joe Castaldo. **Description:** RIM is planning to stop releasing quarterly subscriber updates. However, some analysts are skeptical about the change due to the previous drop in company subscribers. The company also decided to stop reporting the average selling price of the BlackBerry, which analysts have also scrutinized.

3780 ■ "Rough and Ready: Putting Rugged Phones to the Test" in *Inc.* (Vol. 33, November 2011, No. 9, pp. 45)
Pub: Inc. Magazine
Ed: John Brandon. **Description:** Smartphones were roughed up in order to discover their durability. Tests involved the Casio G'Zone Commando, the Sonim XP3300 Force, Motorola Titaniu, and the Samsung Convoy 2.

3781 ■ "Sales Communications in a Mobile World" in *Business Communication Quarterly* (December 2007, pp. 492)
Pub: Sage Publications USA
Ed: Daniel T. Norris. **Description:** Salespeople can take advantage of the latest mobile technologies while maintaining a personal touch with clients and customers through innovation, formality in interactions, client interactions, and protection and security of mobile data.

3782 ■ "Samsung's Metamorphosis" in *Austin Business Journal* (Vol. 31, May 20, 2011, No. 11, pp. 1)
Pub: American City Business Journals Inc.
Ed: Christopher Calnan. **Description:** Samsung Austin Semiconductor LP, a developer of semiconductors for smartphones and tablet computers, plans to diversify its offerings to include niche products: flash memory devices and microprocessing devices. In light of this strategy, Samsung Austin will be hiring 300 engineers as part of a $3.6 billion expansion of its plant.

3783 ■ "Show and Tell" in *Entrepreneur* (Vol. 36, May 2008, No. 5, pp. 54)
Pub: Entrepreneur Media, Inc.
Ed: Heather Clancy. **Description:** FreshStart Telephone uses recorded video testimonials of customers, by using Pure Digital Flip Video that downloads content directly to the computer, and uploads it in the company's website to promote their wireless phone service.

3784 ■ "Skype Ltd. Acquired GroupMe" in *Information Today* (Vol. 28, October 2011, No. 9, pp. 12)
Pub: Information Today, Inc.
Description: Skype Ltd. acquired GroupMe, a group messaging company that allows users to form impromptu groups where they can text message, share data, and make conference calls for free and is supported on Android, iPhone, BlackBerry, and Windows phones.

3785 ■ "Skype on Steroids" in *Inc.* (Vol. 31, January-February 2009, No. 1, pp. 46)
Pub: Mansueto Ventures LLC
Ed: Nitasha Tiku. **Description:** Free software called VoxOx allows users to make calls over the Internet and connects all email and IM accounts.

3786 ■ "A Socko Payout Menu: Rural Phone Carrier Plots to Supercharge Its Shares" in *Barron's* (Vol. 88, June 30, 2008, No. 26, pp. M5)
Pub: Dow Jones & Co., Inc.
Ed: Shirley A. Lazo. **Description:** CenturyTel boosted its quarterly common payout to 70 cents from 6.75 cents per share die to its strong cash flows and solid balance sheet. Eastman Kodak's plan for a buyback will be partially funded by its $581 million tax refund. CME Group will buyback stocks through 2009 worth $1.1 billion.

3787 ■ "Sprint Tries to Wring Out Positives" in *The Business Journal-Serving Metropolitan Kansas City* (Vol. 26, August 8, 2008, No. 48)
Pub: American City Business Journals, Inc.
Ed: Suzanna Stagemeyer. **Description:** Sprint Nextel Corp. reported that 901,000 subscribers left the company in the quarter ending June 30, 2008; fewer than the nearly 1.1 million it lost in the previous quarter. Customer turnover also dropped to just less than 2 percent, compared to 2.45 percent in the first quarter of 2008.

3788 ■ "Startup to Serve Bar Scene" in *Austin Business JournalInc.* (Vol. 29, December 18, 2009, No. 41, pp. 1)
Pub: American City Business Journals
Ed: Christopher Calnan. **Description:** Startup ATX Innovation Inc. of Austin, Texas has developed a test version of TabbedOut, a Web-based tool that would facilitate mobile phone-based restaurant and bar bill payment. TabbedOut has been tested by six businesses in Austin and will be available to restaurant and bar owners for free. Income would be generated by ATX through a 99-cent convenience charge per transaction.

3789 ■ "State Efforts to Boost Contract Efficiency Hurt Smaller Firms" in *Boston Business Journal* (Vol. 27, November 9, 2007, No. 41, pp. 1)
Pub: American City Business Journals Inc.
Ed: Lisa van der Pool. **Description:** Massachusetts Operational Services Division, which provides statewide telecommunications and data infrastructure contracts, announced that it is cutting the list of companies on the new contract from twelve to six. The cost-cutting efforts began in 2005, after a review by an independent consultant advised the state to adopt strategies that would save millions of dollars.

3790 ■ "Stay in Touch, Wherever You Roam: Smartphones for Overseas Travel" in *Inc.* (Volume 32, December 2010, No. 10, pp. 60)
Pub: Inc. Magazine
Description: International cell phones services are profiled, including HTC Aria, Nokia E73 Mode, Samsung Captivate, and Blackberry Bold 9650.

3791 ■ "Strictly Business" in *Black Enterprise* (Vol. 38, October 2007, No. 3, pp. 62)
Pub: Earl G. Graves Publishing Co. Inc.
Description: Profile of the HP iPAQ hw6925 smartphone suited to small business use. The phone offers mobile word processing and messaging features great for the tech-savvy business traveler.

3792 ■ "Study: Instant Messaging Can Benefit Workplaces" in *HRMagazine* (Vol. 53, August 2008, No. 8, pp. 20)
Pub: Society for Human Resource Management
Description: Using text messaging at work is less, not more disruptive, even as it promotes more frequent communication, according to a study published in the Journal of Compute-Mediated Communication.

3793 ■ "Tale of the Tape: IPhone Vs. G1" in *Advertising Age* (Vol. 79, October 27, 2008, No. 40, pp. 6)
Pub: Crain Communications, Inc.
Ed: Rita Chang. **Description:** T-Mobile's G1 has been positioned as the first serious competitor to Apple's iPhone. G1 is the first mobile phone to run on the Google-backed, open-source platform Android.

3794 ■ "Tap the iPad and Mobile Internet Device Market" in *Franchising World* (Vol. 42, September 2010, No. 9, pp. 43)
Pub: International Franchise Association
Ed: John Thomson. **Description:** The iPad and other mobile Internet devices will help franchise owners interact with customers. It will be a good marketing tool for these businesses.

3795 ■ "Technology Drivers to Boost Your Bottom Line" in *Franchising World* (Vol. 42, August 2010, No. 8, pp. 15)
Pub: International Franchise Association
Ed: Dan Dugal. **Description:** Technological capabilities are expanding quickly and smart franchises should stay updated on all the new developments, including smart phones, global positioning systems, and social media networks.

3796 ■ *Telecommunications Directory*
Pub: Gale
Released: Annual, Latest edition 23rd; April, 2012. **Price:** $993, individuals. **Covers:** Two volumes-North America and International, Cover approximately 6,000 national and international voice and data communications networks, electronic mail services, teleconferencing facilities and services, facsimile services, Internet access providers, videotex and teletext operations, transactional services, local area networks, audiotex services, microwave systems/networkers, satellite facilities, and others involved in telecommunications, including related consultants, advertisers/marketers; associations, regulatory bodies, and publishers. **Entries Include:** Company or organization name, address, phone, fax, year established, name and title of contact, executive officers and board of directors, function or type of service; geographical area served; NAICS and SIC codes; number of employees; general description, including telecommunications-related activities; product/service; specific applications; means of access and equipment required; publications; intended market and availability; pricing; stock exchanges traded and ticker symbols; financial figures. **Arrangement:** Alphabetical by company name; within geographic region. **Indexes:** Name of firm/acronym, personal name, geographical (with name, address, phone, and director), and function/type of service (with name, address, phone). Indexes are cumulative.

3797 ■ "TELUS Drawing More Power From Its Wireless Operations" in *Globe & Mail* (February 17, 2007, pp. B3)
Pub: CTVglobemedia Publishing Inc.
Ed: Catherine McLean. **Description:** TELUS Corp., the fast-growing wireless business company, posted tripled profits in the fourth quarter of 2006. The revenues of the company increased 8 percent in the same period.

3798 ■ "Titan to Become New York's Largest Provider of Phone Kiosk Advertising" in *Marketing Weekly News* (September 11, 2010, pp. 150)
Pub: VerticalNews
Description: Titan will acquire from Verizon 1,900 payphones at 1,300 phone kiosk locations in New York City, New York. This transaction will triple the firm's inventory of New York Phone Kiosk media to over 5,000 advertising faces. Details are included.

3799 ■ "Top IPhone Apps" in *Advertising Age* (Vol. 79, December 15, 2008, No. 46, pp. 17)
Pub: Crain Communications, Inc.
Ed: Marissa Miley. **Description:** Free and low cost applications for the iPhone are described including Evernote, an application that allows users to outsource their memory to keep track of events, notes, ides and more; Handshake, a way for users to exchange business cards and pictures across Wi-Fi and 3G; CityTransit, an interactive map of the New York subway system that uses GPS technology to find nearby stations and also tells the user if a train is out of commission that day; and Stage Hand which allows users to deliver a presentation, control timing and slide order on the spot.

3800 ■ "A Torch in the Darkness" in *Canadian Business* (Vol. 83, August 17, 2010, No. 13-14, pp. 66)
Pub: Rogers Media Ltd.
Ed: Joe Castaldo. **Description:** Research In Motion (RIM) unveiled the BlackBerry Touch, featuring a touch screen as well as a physical keyboard, in an attempt to repel competitors and expand share in the consumer smart phone market. RIM shares have fallen 43 percent from its peak in 2009.

3801 ■ "Touch and Go" in *Black Enterprise* (Vol. 38, January 2008, No. 6, pp. 46)
Pub: Earl G. Graves Publishing Co. Inc.
Ed: Anthony Calypso. **Description:** Profile of HTC Touch Smartphone, which operates on the Windows Mobile 6 Pro platform. The phone is about the size of a credit card and weighs less than four ounces and can connect to Bluetooth, GSM/GPRS/EDGE/Wi-Fi.

3802 ■ "Turnaround Plays: The Return of Wi-LAN" in *Canadian Business* (Vol. 80, January 29, 2007, No. 3, pp. 68)
Pub: Rogers Media
Ed: Joe Castaldo. **Description:** The recovery of the wireless equipment manufacturing firm Wi-LAN from near-bankruptcy, under the leadership of Jim Skippen, is described.

3803 ■ "U.S. Enters BlackBerry Dispute Compromise Sought Over Security Issues" in *Houston Chronicle* (August 6, 2010)
Pub: Houston Chronicle
Ed: Matthew Lee. **Description:** U.S. State Department is working for a compromise with Research in Motion, manufacturer of the BlackBerry, over security issues. The Canadian company makes the smartphones and foreign governments believe they pose a security risk.

3804 ■ "Uniting Spring in OP Could Reduce Static" in *Business Journal-Serving Metropolitan Kansas City* (October 19, 2007)
Pub: American City Business Journals, Inc.
Ed: Jim Davis, Steve Vockrodt. **Description:** Sprint Nextel, the result of Sprint Corporation and Nextel Communications Inc. has been using Nextel's Reston office as corporate headquarters. The consolidation of Sprint Nextel's headquarters is expected to result in saving on cost of living and leases. The benefits of choosing Kansas City as the headquarters are evaluated.

3805 ■ "VeriFone Announces Global Security Solutions Business" in *Marketing Weekly News* (October 3, 2009)
Pub: Investment Weekly News
Description: Focused on delivering innovative security solutions, VeriFone Holdings, Inc. announced the formation of its Global Security Solutions Business Unit, including VeriShield Protect, an end-to-end encryption to protect cardholder data throughout the merchant and processor systems. The business will focus on consulting, sales and implementation of these new products in order to help retailers and processors protect customer data.

3806 ■ "Verizon Comes Calling With 500 Jobs" in *Business First Columbus* (Vol. 25, September 15, 2008, No. 4, pp. 1)
Pub: American City Business Journals
Ed: Brian R. Ball. **Description:** Hilliard, Ohio offered Verizon Wireless a 15-year incentive package worth $3.4 million for the company to move 300 customer financial services jobs to the city in addition to the 200 jobs from their facility in Dublin, Ohio. The incentives include a return of 15 percent of the income tax generated by the jobs.

3807 ■ "Verizon Small Business Awards Give Companies a Technology Edge" in *Hispanic Business* (July-August 2009, pp. 32)
Pub: Hispanic Business
Ed: Patricia Marroquin. **Description:** Verizon Wireless awards grants to twenty-four companies in California. The winning businesses ranged from barbershop to coffee shop, tattoo parlor to florist.

3808 ■ "Verizon, Union Dispute is a Vestige of the Past" in *Philadelphia Business Journal* (Vol. 30, August 26, 2011, No. 28, pp. 1)
Pub: American City Business Journals Inc.
Ed: Peter Key. **Description:** Verizon is arguing that some of the provisions of its unionized workers' contracts date back to the days before AT&T were forced to spin off its local phone-service providers in 1984. The evolution of Verizon through the years and its relations with its unions are discussed.

3809 ■ "Vonage V-Phone: Use Your Laptop to Make Calls Via the Internet" in *Black Enterprise* (Vol. 37, January 2007, No. 6, pp. 52)
Pub: Earl G. Graves Publishing Co. Inc.
Ed: James C. Johnson. **Description:** Overview of the Vonage V-Phone, which is small flash drive device that lets you make phone calls through a high-speed Internet connection and plugs into any computer's USB port. Business travels may find this product to be a wonderful solution as it includes 250MB of memory and can store files, digital photos, MP3s, and more.

3810 ■ "Wattles Plugs Back Into State" in *Business Journal Portland* (Vol. 27, November 19, 2010, No. 38, pp. 1)
Pub: Portland Business Journal
Ed: Wendy Culverwell. **Description:** Denver, Colorado-based Ultimate Electronics Inc.'s first store in Oregon was opened in Portland and the 46th store in the chain of electronic superstores is expected to employ 70-80 workers. The venture is the latest for Mark Wattles, one of Oregon's most successful entrepreneurs, who acquired Ultimate from bankruptcy.

3811 ■ "Weathering the BlackBerry Storm" in *Hispanic Business* (January-February 2009, pp. 52)
Pub: Hispanic Business
Ed: Jeremy Nisen. **Description:** Profile of BlackBerry Storm, the smartphone from Research in Motion.

3812 ■ "Why-Max?" in *Canadian Business* (Vol. 81, July 22, 2008, No. 12-13, pp. 19)
Pub: Rogers Media Ltd.
Ed: Andrew Wahl. **Description:** Nascent technology known as LTE (Long Term Evolution) is expected to challenge Intel's WiMax wireless technology as the wireless broadband standard. LTE , which is believed to be at least two years behind WiMax in development, is likely to be supported by wireless and mobile-phone carriers. Views and information on WiMax and LTE are presented.

3813 ■ "Will mCommerce Make Black Friday Green?" in *Retail Merchandiser* (Vol. 51, September-October 2011, No. 5, pp. 8)
Pub: Phoenix Media Corporation
Ed: Scott Miller. **Description:** Retailers speculate the possibilities of mobile commerce and are implementing strategies at their stores. Consumers using mobile devices accounted for only 0.1 percent of visits to retail Websites on Black Friday 2009 and rose to 5.6 percent in 2010; numbers are expected to rise for 2011.

3814 ■ "Wireless: Full Service" in *Entrepreneur* (Vol. 35, October 2007, No. 10, pp. 60)
Pub: Entrepreneur Media Inc.
Ed: Amanda C. Kooser. **Description:** Palm Foleo, the $599 smart phone enables users to access and compose email, browse the Internet, view documents and play Powerpoint files. It weighs 2.5 pounds and has a 10-inch screen. Other features, such as built-in WiFi are described.

3815 ■ "A Wireless Makes 8 Store-In-Store Kiosk Acquisitions" in *Wireless News* (October 16, 2010)
Pub: Close-Up Media Inc.
Description: A Wireless, a retailer for Verizon Wireless has acquired eight of Verizon's retail kiosks that are positioned in home appliance and electronics stores.

3816 ■ "Wireless Provider's Star Grows $283 Million Brighter" in *Hispanic Business* (July-August 2007, pp. 60)
Pub: Hispanic Business
Description: Profile of Brightstar Corporation, the world's largest wireless phone distribution and supply chain reported record growth in 2007.

3817 ■ "Words at Work" in *Information Today* (Vol. 26, February 2009, No. 2, pp. 25)
Pub: Information Today, Inc.
Description: Current new buzzwords include the following: digital amnesia, or overload by availability, speed and volume of digital information; maternal profiling, a form a discrimination against women; recipe malpractice, a reminder that just because you can turn on a stove it doesn't make you a chef; ringxiety, the act when everyone reaches for their cell phone when one rings; verbing, the practice of turning good nouns into verbs.

STATISTICAL SOURCES

3818 ■ *RMA Annual Statement Studies*
Pub: Robert Morris Associates (RMA)
Released: Annual. **Price:** $175.00 2006-07 edition, $105.00. **Description:** Contains composite balance sheets and income statements for more than 360 industries, including the accounting, auditing, and bookkeeping industries. Also contains five years of comparative historical data for discerning trends. Includes 16 commonly used ratios, computed for most of the size groupings for nearly every industry.

3819 ■ *Standard & Poor's Industry Surveys*
Pub: Standard & Poor's Corp.
Released: Annual. **Price:** $3633.00. **Description:** Two-volume book that examines the prospects for specific industries, including trucking. Also provides analyses of trends and problems, statistical tables and charts, and comparative company analyses.

3820 ■ *Wireless Communications*
Pub: Business Communications Co., Inc.
Released: 1993. **Price:** $2250.00. **Description:** Report analyzing and forecasting the market for wireless frequencies transmitting voice and data to 1997. Covers wireless LANS, cellular data/voice, wireless WANS/MANS, pagers, and wireless PBX/Centrex.

TRADE PERIODICALS

3821 ■ *1394 Newsletter*
Pub: Information Gatekeepers Inc.
Ed: Paul Polishuk, Editor. **Released:** Monthly. **Price:** $695, U.S. and Canada; $745, elsewhere. **Description:** Covers developments in the computer and consumer electronic markets, including new technology and related fields.

3822 ■ *Communications Daily*
Pub: Warren Communications News
Contact: Mike Feazel, Managing Editor
Released: Daily, 5/wk. **Price:** $3,695. **Description:** Covers telephone and data communications, broadcasting, cable TV, teleconferencing, satellite communications, electronic publishing, and emerging technologies. Recurring features include personnel updates, obituaries, statistics, trade show news, and news of research.

3823 ■ *Industry Pulse*
Pub: Telecommunications Industry Association
Ed: Ian Martinez, Editor. **Released:** 4/year. **Price:** Included in membership. **Description:** Publishes news of the Association, its members, and its activities.

3824 ■ *Internet Telephone–Green Data Centers*
Pub: Information Gatekeepers Inc.
Ed: Tony Carmona, Editor. **Released:** Monthly. **Price:** $695, U.S. and Canada; $745, elsewhere. **Description:** Provides marketing and technology information on new developments in the internet telephone industry on a worldwide basis.

3825 ■ *Russian Telecom Newsletter*
Pub: Information Gatekeepers Inc.
Contact: Jeremy Awori, Publisher
Ed: Prof. Sergei L. Galkin, Editor. **Released:** Monthly. **Price:** $695, U.S. and Canada; $745, elsewhere; $695 PDF email version. **Description:** Covers the telecommunications industry in Russia, including competition, government regulations, international business and ventures, cellular, satellites, and market intelligence. Also features new products and conference reports.

3826 ■ *Sound & Communications Magazine*
Pub: Testa Communications
Contact: Gary Kayye
E-mail: gkayye@testa.com
Released: Monthly. **Price:** Free to qualified subscribers. **Description:** Magazine focusing on sound and communications systems equipment, installations, and technology.

3827 ■ *TelephonyOnline*
Pub: Penton Media Inc.
Contact: Wayne Madden, Gp. Publisher
E-mail: wayne.madden@penton.com
Released: Monthly. **Description:** Magazine providing analytical reporting on all aspects of broadband economy. Features perspectives on network technology innovations, content development, and business drivers that affect broadband communications service providers.

3828 ■ *Urgent Communications*
Pub: Penton Media Inc.
Contact: Dennis Hegg, Assoc. Publisher
E-mail: dennis.hegg@penton.com
Released: Monthly. **Description:** Technical magazine for the mobile communications industry.

3829 ■ *Utilities Telecommunications News*
Pub: Information Gatekeepers Inc.
Contact: Paul Polishuk, Managing Editor
Released: Monthly. **Price:** $695, U.S. and Canada; $745, elsewhere; $695 PDF email version. **Description:** Focuses on the role of utilities in telecommunications. Topics include government and regulations, business, and the Internet. Also features new products and conferences.

3830 ■ *Wireless Business & Technology*
Pub: SYS-CON Media
Contact: Jeremy Geelan, Pres./COO
E-mail: jeremy@sys-con.com
Released: Bimonthly. **Price:** $4 single issue; $129 two years digital edition; $99 digital edition. **Description:** Professional journal covering the wireless industry.

3831 ■ *Wireless Cellular–WMAX*
Pub: Information Gatekeepers Inc.
Ed: Paul Polishuk, Editor. **Released:** Monthly. **Price:** $695, U.S. and Canada; $745, elsewhere. **Description:** Covers international developments in the wireless cellular industry, including new products, market opportunities and forecasts, regulations and standards, procurements, mergers and acquisitions, and applications.

3832 ■ *Wireless Review*
Pub: Penton Media Inc.
Contact: Michael Hanley, Managing Editor
E-mail: mhanley@primediabusiness.com
Released: Monthly. **Description:** Magazine serving the cellular and PCS communications industry.

TRADE SHOWS AND CONVENTIONS

3833 ■ Wireless
Cellular Telecommunications Industry Association
1400 16th St. NW, Ste. 600
Washington, DC 20036
Ph:(202)785-0081
Fax:(202)785-0721
Co. E-mail: research@ctia.org
URL: http://www.ctia.org
Released: Annual. **Audience:** Managerial level members of the cellular and wireless communications industry. **Principal Exhibits:** Cellular and wireless equipment and support services. **Dates and Locations:** 2011 Mar 22-24, Orlando, FL.

CONSULTANTS

3834 ■ CTA Communications Inc.
20715 Timberlake Rd., Ste. 106
PO Box 4579
Lynchburg, VA 24502
Ph:(434)239-9200
Fax:(434)239-9221
Co. E-mail: home@ctacommunications.com
Contact: Cheryl Giggetts, President
E-mail: forrestpe@ctacommunications.com
Scope: An engineering and consulting firm, providing service in the area of specification, design, installation and implementation of communication systems including mobile, cellular, fiber optics, data and telecommunications systems. Work involves system planning, system design, system implementation, requirement analysis, specification development, site management, traffic studies, proposal development, training, analog design, digital design, path loss analysis, and data communication design. Industries served: public safety, local government, utilities, and general industry. **Publications:** "Alternative Centers: Where's My Backup," Sep, 2006; "Are you ready for Narrowband," May, 2006; "Rebanding the 800 MHz Frequencies: Just retuning? Think again," Aug, 2005; "Wireless 9-1-1: Help, or Needs Help," Feb, 2004. **Seminars:** Wide Area Trunking Considerations-Applications in Systems Large and Small; Coverage Proof of Performance-Hocus Pocus or Real World; Digital Radio Concepts for Public Safety Applications; The Digital Journey; Daddy Aren't We There Yet?.

3835 ■ Trott Communications Group Inc.
4320 N Beltline Rd., Ste. A100
Irving, TX 75038
Ph:(972)518-1811
Fax:(972)518-1969
Co. E-mail: info@trottgroup.com
URL: http://www.trottgroup.com
Contact: Walter J. Stewart, President
E-mail: tom.murphy@atstrottgroup.com
Scope: Provides engineering consulting services to the land mobile and telecommunications industries. Services include: RF system design, microwave path engineering, propagation analyzes, interference studies, site management services, specification preparation, and equipments election and RF radiation studies.

3836 ■ W & J Partnership
18876 Edwin Markham Dr.
PO Box 2499
Castro Valley, CA 94546-0499
Ph:(510)583-7751
Fax:(510)583-7645
Co. E-mail: jemorgan@wjpartnership.com
URL: http://www.wjpartnership.com
Contact: Judith E. Morgan, Partner
E-mail: jemorgan@atswjpartnership.com
Scope: Management and technical consulting in complex network design, operations, administration, maintenance and products for large enterprises, carriers and service providers (wire-line and wireless) and governments, especially VoIP, security; R and D for vendors. Review product plans and investment opportunities. Software and hardware: Architectures, design, development and testing for manufacturers. No work for vendors and business at the same time. **Seminars:** Fiber Optics Communications; Networks & Networks Management; Structured Cabling; Public Safety Radio; Computer and Communications Security Systems; Hands-On Fiber Optic Communications; Cabling & Wiring for Local Communications. **Special Services:** Systems Software; Networking Software; Communications Embedded Systems; SAP; Siebel; Software and Firmware Quality Assurance.

FRANCHISES AND BUSINESS OPPORTUNITIES

3837 ■ Worldwide Wireless
Worldwide Wireless Franchise Services LLC
1000 Eagle Ridge Dr.
Schererville, IN 46375
Ph:(219)864-9991
Free: 877-FIN-DWWW
Fax:(219)864-9992
URL: http://www.worldwidewirelessinc.com
Founded: 1999. **Franchised:** 2006. **Description:** Exclusive Sprint dealership. **Equity Capital Needed:** $75,000-$150,000. **Franchise Fee:** $30,000. **Financial Assistance:** Yes. **Training:** Yes.

3838 ■ Yakety Yak Wireless
3400 Irvine Ave., Ste. 118
Newport Beach, CA 92660
Ph:(949)851-1900
Free: 888-925-4887
Fax:(949)486-6001
No. of Franchise Units: 30. **Founded:** 1999. **Franchised:** 2005. **Description:** Wireless services & related products. **Equity Capital Needed:** $79,000-$301,500. **Franchise Fee:** $29,000. **Royalty Fee:** $300-$1,000/month. **Financial Assistance:** Third party financing available. **Training:** Offers 2 weeks at headquarters, daily conference calls and ongoing support.

COMPUTERIZED DATABASES

3839 ■ *The Telecom Manager's Voice Report*
United Communications Group
2 Washingtonian Ctr., Ste. 100
9737 Washingtonian Blvd.
Gaithersburg, MD 20878
Ph:(301)287-2700
Free: 888-275-2264
Fax:(301)287-2170
Co. E-mail: support@ccmi.com
URL: http://www.ccmi.com
Description: Contains the complete text of *The Telecom Manager's Voice Report*, providing information for corporate telecommunications managers. Covers selection of local and long-distance services, design and installation of private networks, emerging technology, system maintenance and expansion, and telephone bill auditing. Also covers telecommunications industry developments, including changes in tariffs and regulations. **Availability:** Online: ProQuest LLC, United Communications Group. **Type:** Full text.

LIBRARIES

3840 ■ GTE Telephone Operations Headquarters Library
600 Hidden Ridge
MCF04P01
Irving, TX 75038
Ph:(972)718-5549
Fax:(214)718-2399
Contact: Charlotte Wixx Clark, Lib.Hd.
Scope: Market research, telecommunications, technology, business telecommunication-related products. **Services:** Interlibrary loan; Library not open to the public. **Holdings:** 450 books; 8 CD-ROM; 10,000 studies; reports; manuscripts. **Subscriptions:** 152 journals and other serials.

3841 ■ Manitoba Telecom Services Corporate Library
333 Main St.
PO Box 6666
Winnipeg, MB, Canada R3C 3V6
Ph:(204)941-6344
Fax:(204)944-0830
URL: http://www.mts.ca
Contact: Tanya L. Evancio, Libn.
Scope: Telecommunications industry. **Services:** Library not open to the public. **Holdings:** 2000 books. **Subscriptions:** 100 journals and other serials.

3842 ■ Museum of Independent Telephony–Archives Collection
412 S. Campbell
Abilene, KS 67410
Ph:(785)263-2681
Fax:(785)263-0380
Co. E-mail: heritagecenterdk@sbcglobal.net
URL: http://www.heritagecenterdk.com/museum_of_independent_telephony.html
Contact: Jeff Sheets
Scope: Telephone history and technology. **Services:** Copying; collection open to the public. **Holdings:** 1000 books; 1000 bound periodical volumes; 1000 other cataloged items; 500 manuscripts; 120 boxes of loose periodicals; 150 tapes. **Subscriptions:** 10 journals and other serials.

3843 ■ Ohio Bell–Corporate Information Resource Center
45 Erieview Plaza, Rm. 820
Cleveland, OH 44114-1813
Ph:(216)822-2740
Contact: John Jakovcic, Asst.Mgr.
Scope: Business, management, telecommunications, personnel, computers, marketing, Ohio Bell and Bell System history. **Services:** Interlibrary loan; copying; Library open to the public at librarian's discretion. **Holdings:** 5000 books. **Subscriptions:** 150 journals and other serials; 10 newspapers.

3844 ■ U.S. Federal Communications Commission Library
445 12th St. SW, Rm. TW-8505
Washington, DC 20554
Ph:(202)418-0450
Free: 888-225-5322
Fax:(202)418-2805
Co. E-mail: ecclibrary@fcc.gov
URL: http://www.fcc.gov
Contact: Gloria Thomas, Mgr., Lib. Group
Scope: Telecommunications, electrical engineering, law, economics, public utility regulation, public administration, management, statistics. **Services:** SDI; Library not open to the public. **Holdings:** 45,000 books; 123 bound periodical volumes; 6200 VF materials; 3000 reels of microfilm. **Subscriptions:** 305 journals and other serials.

Charter Boat Service

ASSOCIATIONS AND OTHER ORGANIZATIONS

3845 ■ Boat Owners Association of the United States
880 S Pickett St.
Alexandria, VA 22304
Ph:(703)823-9550
Free: 800-395-2628
Fax:(703)461-2847
Co. E-mail: mail@boatus.com
URL: http://www.boatus.com
Contact: Richard Schwartz, Chm./Founder
Description: Represents owners or prospective owners of recreational boats. Independent, consumer service organization offering representation, benefits, and programs for boat owners. Services include: legislative and regulatory representation on issues affecting boaters' interests; marine insurance; magazines; trailering club; marina discounts; long-term boat financing; boating regulations and forms service; charter and group travel services; sale and chartering exchange; marine surveyor and admiralty lawyer reference service; assistance with individual boating problems and towing reimbursement; association flag. Maintains Consumer Protection Bureau, which utilizes comprehensive consumer experience files to pursue individual complaints. **Publications:** *BOAT U.S. Magazine* (bimonthly); *Boat U.S. Trailering Magazine* (bimonthly); *Equipment Catalog* (annual); *Seaworthy* (quarterly).

3846 ■ National Women's Sailing Association
1 Esquire Dr.
Peabody, MA 01960
Ph:(401)682-2064
Co. E-mail: wsf@womensailing.org
URL: http://www.womensailing.org
Contact: Joan Thayer, Pres.
Description: Works to enhance the lives of women and girls through education and access to the sport of sailing. **Publications:** *Women's Sailing Resource* (biennial).

3847 ■ Passenger Vessel Association
103 Oronoco St., Ste. 200
Alexandria, VA 22314
Ph:(703)518-5005
Free: 800-807-8360
Fax:(703)518-5151
Co. E-mail: pvainfo@passengervessel.com
URL: http://www.passengervessel.com
Contact: Jay Spence, Pres.
Description: Owners, operators and suppliers of U.S. and Canadian flagged passenger vessels, including dinner vessels, private charter, tour and excursion boats, casino gambling boats, overnight cruise vessels and whale watching and eco-tourism operators. Monitors and disseminates information on current and proposed federal regulation and legislation affecting passenger ship owners; represents the industry's views to legislative and regulatory bodies. **Publications:** *Foghorn* (monthly).

3848 ■ States Organization for Boating Access
231 S LaSalle St., Ste. 2050
Chicago, IL 60604
Ph:(312)946-6283
Fax:(312)946-0388
Co. E-mail: info@sobaus.org
URL: http://www.sobaus.org
Contact: James Adams, Pres.
Description: Individuals interested in recreational boating facilities. Provides information regarding the construction, maintenance, financing and administration of recreational boating facilities to state program administrators charged with their management. **Publications:** *Design Handbook and Operations and Maintenance Guidelines* .

REFERENCE WORKS

3849 ■ *Atlantic Boating Almanac*
Pub: Atlantic Boating Almanac
Released: Annual, Latest edition 2006. **Price:** $26. 95, individuals. **Covers:** Listings on coast piloting, electronics, GPS by Gordon West, first aid, weather, facilities and fuel docks. There are four separate regional editions: Florida & Bahamas; North & South Carolina and Georgia; Massachusetts, Rhode Island, Connecticut and Long Island; and Maine, New Hampshire & Massachusetts. **Arrangement:** Geographical.

TRADE PERIODICALS

3850 ■ *Current*
Pub: National Marine Manufacturers Association (NMMA)
Ed: Released: Semiannual. **Price:** Included in membership. **Description:** Reviews boat shows. Reports industry trends. Offers trade and consumer show advice. Recurring features include interviews, a calendar of events, and reports of meetings.

3851 ■ *Marine Business Journal*
Pub: Marine Business Journal Inc.
Contact: Skip Allen, Publisher/Editorial Dir.
E-mail: skip@southernboating.com
Ed: Marilyn Mower, Editor, marilyn@southernboating.com. **Released:** Bimonthly. **Price:** $30 other countries. **Description:** Trade magazine.

3852 ■ *Seaworthy*
Pub: Boat Owners Association of The United States
Ed: Robert Adriance, Jr., Editor, badriance@boatus.com. **Released:** Quarterly. **Price:** $10 for noninsured; Free. **Description:** Seeks to help boaters avoid accidents or problems by listing actual insurance claims. Includes case stuides that provide insight in to how to avoid accidents, breakdowns, injuries, and other "unexpected" circumstances that can jeopardize the safety of their boat, themselves, and guests.

TRADE SHOWS AND CONVENTIONS

3853 ■ Cleveland Sport, Travel & Outdoor Show
Expositions Inc.
PO Box 550, Edgewater Br.
Cleveland, OH 44107-0550
Ph:(216)529-1300
Fax:(216)529-0311
Co. E-mail: expoinc@oinc.com
URL: http://www.expoinc.com
Released: Annual. **Principal Exhibits:** Sport fishing.

3854 ■ Eastern Fishing and Outdoor Exposition
Eastern Fishing and Outdoor Exposition Inc.
PO Box 4720
Portsmouth, NH 03801
Ph:(603)431-4315
Fax:(603)431-1971
Co. E-mail: info@sportshows.com
URL: http://www.sportshows.com
Released: Annual. **Audience:** Metro Boston/ Worcester Market. **Principal Exhibits:** Fishing and outdoor sports.

3855 ■ Louisville Boat, RV & Sportshow
Douglas Expositions Inc.
10000 Shelbyville Rd., No. 111
Anchorage, KY 40223-2950
Ph:(502)244-5660
Fax:(502)244-5160
Released: Annual. **Principal Exhibits:** Sports, boating and vacations, hunting and fishing, recreational vehicles.

3856 ■ Quad City Boat and Vacation Show
Iowa Show Productions Inc.
PO Box 2460
Waterloo, IA 50704-2460
Ph:(319)232-0218
Fax:(319)235-8932
Co. E-mail: info@iowashows.com
URL: http://www.iowashows.com/
Released: Annual. **Principal Exhibits:** Boats, fishing tackle, resorts, tourism associations, motorhomes.

FRANCHISES AND BUSINESS OPPORTUNITIES

3857 ■ The Cruising Club Fractional Boat Ownership
20 Calabria Ave., Ste. 505
Coral Gables, FL 33134
Ph:(972)212-5079
No. of Franchise Units: 6. **No. of Company-Owned Units:** 5. **Founded:** 1998. **Franchised:** 2004. **Description:** Fractional boat ownership. **Equity Capital Needed:** Varies, $35,000-$500,000+. **Franchise Fee:** $25,000-$100,000+. **Financial Assistance:** Yes. **Training:** Yes.

REFERENCE WORKS

3858 ■ "Kenyans Embrace Moving Money By Text Message" in *Chicago Tribune* (October 7, 2008)
Pub: McClatchy-Tribune Information Services
Ed: Laurie Goering. **Description:** Cell phone banking services are becoming more common, especially for foreign residents; customers are able to establish a virtual cell phone bank account through companies such as M-Pesa which allows their customers to pay bills, withdraw cash, pay merchants or text money to relatives.

FRANCHISES AND BUSINESS OPPORTUNITIES

3859 ■ ACE America's Cash Express
ACE Cash Express Inc.
1231 Greenway Dr., Ste. 600
Irving, TX 75038
Ph:(972)550-5000
Free: 800-713-3338
Fax:(972)582-1409
Co. E-mail: franchisedevelopment@acecashexpress.com
URL: http://www.acecashexpress.com
No. of Franchise Units: 220. **No. of Company-Owned Units:** 1,353. **Founded:** 1968. **Franchised:** 1996. **Description:** Check cashing, loans, money orders, wire transfers, bill payments, cash advances, prepaid telecommunication products. **Equity Capital Needed:** $141,632-$227,950/$240,132-$282,950. **Franchise Fee:** $15,000-$30,000. **Financial Assistance:** Third party nationwide lenders lenders/SBA. **Managerial Assistance:** Proprietary computer system with network connectivity to national database. **Training:** Site selection, store design, complete classroom and onsite training, manuals, advertising, annual conference and ongoing operation evaluations.

3860 ■ Advantage Cash Advance
Advantage Cash Corp.
4744 Keithdale Ln.
Bloomfield Hills, MI 48302
Ph:(810)423-1375
Fax:(248)399-4771
No. of Franchise Units: 7. **Founded:** 2005. **Franchised:** 2005. **Description:** Payday advance business. **Equity Capital Needed:** $90,000-$135,000. **Financial Assistance:** No. **Training:** Yes.

3861 ■ Cash Plus
Cash Plus, Inc.
3002 Dow Ave., Ste, 120
Tustin, CA 92780
Ph:(714)731-2274
Free: 888-707-2274
Fax:(714)731-2099
No. of Franchise Units: 91. **No. of Company-Owned Units:** 2. **Founded:** 1984. **Franchised:** 1988. **Description:** Check cashing service and related services, including money orders, wire transfers, cash advances, mailboxes, notary, UPS, fax, snacks, tax filing and other items. **Equity Capital Needed:** $190,200-$269,700. **Franchise Fee:** $35,000. **Financial Assistance:** Provides guidance on credit applications and business plans used by franchisees seeking third party financing. **Training:** Provides training including easy-to-run computerized operating system, promotions and check verification and payday advance process.

3862 ■ Commission Express
Commission Express National
8306 Professional Hill Dr.
Fairfax, VA 22031
Ph:(703)560-5500
Fax:(703)560-5502
Co. E-mail: manager@commissionexpress.com
URL: http://www.commissionexpress.com
No. of Franchise Units: 74. **No. of Company-Owned Units:** 1. **Founded:** 1992. **Franchised:** 1996. **Description:** Buy real estate agent commissions. **Equity Capital Needed:** $94,300-$213,500. **Franchise Fee:** $20,000-$80,000. **Financial Assistance:** No. **Training:** Provides 1 week at Fairfax, VA and annual conference.

3863 ■ Family Financial Centers
202 Farm Ln.
Doylestown, PA 18901
Ph:(215)230-5508
Fax:(215)230-5535
No. of Franchise Units: 25. **Founded:** 2004. **Franchised:** 2004. **Description:** Check cashing & other financial services. **Equity Capital Needed:** $146,000-$229,300. **Franchise Fee:** $33,500. **Royalty Fee:** 0.2%. **Financial Assistance:** Financial assistance with equipment. **Training:** Offers 1 week training at headquarters, 1 week field training and ongoing support.

3864 ■ FastBucks
FastBucks Franchise Corp.
7920 Beltline Rd., Ste. 600
Dallas, TX 75254
Ph:(972)490-3330
Fax:(972)490-8297
No. of Franchise Units: 6. **No. of Company-Owned Units:** 52. **Founded:** 1998. **Franchised:** 2003. **Description:** Payday loans. **Equity Capital Needed:** $125,000-$150,000. **Franchise Fee:** $27,500. **Royalty Fee:** 7%. **Financial Assistance:** In-house financing available. **Training:** Offers 2 weeks at headquarters, 1 week at franchisee's location with ongoing support.

3865 ■ United Check Cashing
United Financial Services Group, Inc.
325 Chestnut St., Ste. 3000
Philadelphia, PA 19106
Ph:(215)238-0300
Free: 800-626-0787
Fax:(215)238-9056
Co. E-mail: info@unitedfsg.com
URL: http://www.unitedfsg.com
No. of Franchise Units: 132. **Founded:** 1977. **Franchised:** 1992. **Description:** Check cashing, money orders, wire transfers, authorized bill payments, fax, copies, notary, consumer loans, ATM's, lottery, credit card advances, tax service, photo ID systems and beeper sales. **Equity Capital Needed:** $103,500 (kiosk)-$297,000 which allows for $50,000 (kiosk)-$120,000 in operating cash. **Franchise Fee:** $30,000. **Financial Assistance:** Yes. **Managerial Assistance:** Training provided on procedures and legal processes. **Training:** Receive training in customer servicing, sales, human resources, loss prevention and risk management.

Children's Apparel Shop

START-UP INFORMATION

3866 ■ *In Fashion: From Runway to Retail, Everything You Need to Know to Break Into the Fashion Industry*
Pub: Crown Business Books
Ed: Annemarie Iverson. **Released:** August 10, 2010. **Price:** $16.99. **Description:** Whether your dream is to photograph models, outfit celebrities, design fashions, this book provides details into every aspect for working in the fashion industry.

3867 ■ "Mount Laurel Woman Launches Venture Into Children's Used Clothing" in *Philadelphia Inquirer* (September 17, 2010)
Pub: Philadelphia Media Network
Ed: Maria Panaritis. **Description:** Profile of Jennifer Frisch, stay-at-home mom turned entrepreneur. Frisch started a used-clothing store Once Upon a Child after opening her franchised Plato's Closet, selling unwanted and used baby clothing and accessories at her new shop, while offering used merchandise to teens at Plato's Closet.

ASSOCIATIONS AND OTHER ORGANIZATIONS

3868 ■ American Apparel and Footwear Association
1601 N Kent St., Ste. 1200
Arlington, VA 22209
Ph:(703)797-9037
Free: 800-520-2262
Fax:(703)522-6741
Co. E-mail: pcarty@apparelandfootwear.org
URL: http://www.apparelandfootwear.org
Contact: Kevin M. Burke, Pres./CEO
Description: Manufacturers of infants', children's, boys', girls', juniors', men's, and women's wearing apparel; associate members are suppliers of fabrics, equipment, accessories, and services to the apparel industry. Operates the Apparel Foundation; offers placement service through newsletter. Compiles statistics. **Publications:** *AAFA Directory of Members and Associate Members* (annual); *Technical Advisory Committee Bulletin* (periodic).

REFERENCE WORKS

3869 ■ "Consignment Shop Offers Children's Clothes, Products" in *Frederick News-Post* (August 19, 2010)
Pub: Federick News-Post
Ed: Ed Waters Jr. **Description:** Sweet Pea Consignments for Children offers used items for newborns to pre-teens. The shop carries name brand clothing as well as toys, books and baby products.

3870 ■ *Directory of Apparel Specialty Stores*
Pub: Chain Store Guide
Released: Annual, Latest edition 2011. **Price:** $395, individuals Directory; $445, individuals online lite; $1,075, individuals online pro. **Covers:** 5,040 apparel and sporting goods specialty retailers in the United States and Canada, operating more than 70,700 stores. Apparel retailers must have annual retail sales of at least $500,000; sporting goods specialty retailers must also have $500,000 in annual sales, with the condition that at least 20% of product sales are from sporting goods equipment. **Entries Include:** Company name, phone, and fax numbers; physical and mailing addresses; company e-mail and web addresses; Internet order processing indicator; percentage of Internet sales; type of business; listing type; product lines; total, industry, and product group sales; total selling square footage; store prototype sizes; total stores; trading areas; projected openings and remodeling; units by trade name; distribution center locations; resident buyer's name and location; mail order indicator; percentage of mail order sales; catalog names; private label indicator; private label credit card indicator; apparel price lines; average number of checkouts; year founded; public company indicator; parent company name and location; and key personnel with titles; 7,200 personnel email addresses . **Arrangement:** Geographical. **Indexes:** Alphabetical, product lines, exclusions.

3871 ■ "Green It Like You Mean It" in *Special Events Magazine* (Vol. 28, February 1, 2009, No. 2)
Pub: Special Events Magazine
Ed: Christine Landry. **Description:** Eco-friendly party planners offer advice for planning and hosting green parties or events. Tips include information for using recycled paper products, organic food and drinks. The Eco Nouveau Fashion Show held by Serene Star Productions reused old garments to create new fashions as well as art pieces from discarded doors and window frames for the show; eco-friendly treats and gift bags were highlighted at the event.

3872 ■ "Intrepid Souls: Meet a Few Who've Made the Big Leap" in *Crain's Chicago Business* (Vol. 31, November 10, 2008, No. 45, pp. 26)
Pub: Crain Communications, Inc.
Ed: Meredith Landry. **Description:** Advice is given from entrepreneurs who have launched businesses in the last year despite the economic crisis. Among the types of businesses featured are a cooking school, a child day-care center, a children's clothing store and an Internet-based company.

3873 ■ "Let It Shine: Organization Helps Disadvantaged Girls See Their Worth" in *Black Enterprise* (Vol. 38, February 2008, No. 7, pp. 142)
Pub: Earl G. Graves Publishing Co. Inc.
Ed: George Alexander. **Description:** Wilson Mourning, founder of the clothing label Honey Child, attributes her success to her mother and other positive women who helped her through her adolescence. Mourning created a mentoring organization that helps young girls in the Miami, Florida area to develop life skills.

3874 ■ *Men's & Boys' Wear Buyers*
Pub: Briefings Media Group
Contact: Alan M. Douglas, President
Released: Annual, latest edition 2011-2012. **Price:** $329, individuals directory price; $659, individuals directory/CD combo price. **Covers:** 9,000 buyers and 5,100 stores in the men's and boys' retail industry. **Entries Include:** Store name, address, phone, fax; names and titles of key personnel; e-mail; URL; financial data; branch/subsidiary name and address; products/services provided; price points and sales volume; parent company; type and number of stores for companies; corporate buying office. **Arrangement:** Geographical. **Indexes:** Store name, new listings, mail order, buying office, online retailer.

3875 ■ "Research and Market Adds: 2010 US Women's and Children's Clothing Wholesale Report" in *Wireless News* (November 8, 2009)
Pub: Close-Up Media
Description: Highlights of the annual Research and Markets "2010 U.S. Women's and Children's Clothing Wholesale Report" include industry statistics, demographics and forecasts.

3876 ■ "Research and Markets Adds: 2011 U.S. Women's & Children's Clothing Wholesale Report" in *Health & Beauty Close-Up* (October 16, 2010)
Pub: Close-Up Media Inc.
Description: The Women's & Children's Clothing Wholesale Report is an annual report containing timely and accurate industry statistics, forecasts and demographics.

3877 ■ "Retail News: Children's Boutique Relocates to Conway" in *Sun News* (June 4, 2010)
Pub: The Sun News
Description: Little Angel's Children's Boutique and Big Oak Frame Shop have moved to downtown locations in Conway, South Carolina. Little Angel's will sell children's clothing and accessories, shoes and gifts, while the frame shop will offer custom framing along with the sale of stationary, invitations and local prints.

3878 ■ "Weaving a Stronger Fabric: Organizing a Global Sweat-Free Apparel Production Agreement" in *WorkingUSA* (Vol. 11, June 2008, No. 2)
Pub: Blackwell Publishers Ltd.
Ed: Eric Dirnbach. **Description:** Tens of millions of workers working under terrible sweatshop conditions in the global apparel industry. Workers are employed at apparel contractors and have been largely unsuccessful in organizing and improving their working conditions. The major apparel manufacturers and retailers have the most power in this industry, and they have adopted corporate social responsibility programs as a false solution to the sweatshop problem. The major North American apparel unions dealt with similar sweatshop conditions a century ago by organizing the contractors and brands into joint association contracts that significantly raised standards. Taking inspiration from their example, workers and their anti-sweatshop allies need to work together to coordinate a global organizing effort that builds worker power and establishes a global production

agreement that negotiates with both contractors and the brands for improved wages, benefits, and working conditions.

3879 ■ *Women's & Children's Wear Buyers*
Pub: Briefings Media Group
Contact: Alan M. Douglas, President
Released: Annual, latest edition 2011-2012. **Price:** $329 directory price; $659 directory/CD combo price. **Covers:** Over 9,000 retailers and 17,000 buyers in women's and children's wear industry. **Entries Include:** Company name, address, phone, fax; e-mail; URL; names and titles of key personnel; financial data; branch or subsidiary name and address; products and/or services provided; names and titles of buyers; price points and sales volume; type and number of stores for companies; parent companies, and corporate buying offices. **Arrangement:** Geographical. **Indexes:** Store name, new listings, mail order, buying office, online retailer.

3880 ■ "Zakkamono Taps Growing Market for Collectibles" in *Hawaii Business* (Vol. 54, September 2008, No. 3, pp. 68)
Pub: Hawaii Business Publishing
Ed: Casey Chin. **Description:** Profile of Zakkamono, a business that designs and sells designer toys, shirts and other collectibles; the first toys being Mousubi and Miao figurines. Owners Zakka and Rae Huo say that one of the business' challenges is finding manufacturing resources. Other details about Zakkamono are discussed.

SOURCES OF SUPPLY

3881 ■ *Denver Merchandise Mart Directory*
Pub: Denver Merchandise Mart
Released: Annual, December/January. **Covers:** About 4,000 manufacturers, importers, and wholesale distributors of men's, women's, and children's clothing, western apparel, shoes, gifts, gourmet items, bath accessories, jewelry, resort merchandise, and home furnishings who are represented in the Denver Merchandise Mart. **Entries Include:** Firm name, mart address; alphabetical listings include phone. **Arrangement:** Alphabetical by product classification.

TRADE PERIODICALS

3882 ■ *Apparel News South*
Pub: Apparel News Group
Contact: Martin Wernicke, Publisher/CEO
Released: 5/yr. **Price:** $89. **Description:** Clothing industry magazine containing textile information on garments for women and children.

3883 ■ *California Apparel News*
Pub: Apparel News Group
Contact: Deborah Belgum, Sen. Ed.
E-mail: deborah@apparelnews.net
Released: Weekly (Fri.). **Price:** $89 print; $99 online. **Description:** Weekly newspaper covering the apparel industry and providing information about textiles, trimmings, fashion trends, retailing and business.

3884 ■ *Chicago Apparel News*
Pub: Apparel News Group
Contact: Martin Wernicke, Publisher/CEO
Released: Weekly. **Price:** $83; $140 two years. **Description:** Magazine covering the apparel industry; providing information about retail, fashion, textiles and accessories for women and children.

3885 ■ *Dallas Apparel News*
Pub: Apparel News Group
Contact: N. Jayne Seward, Fashion Ed.
E-mail: jayne@apparelnews.net
Released: 5/yr. **Description:** Women's and children's garment industry magazine providing textile, retail, fashion and accessory information.

3886 ■ *DNR*
Pub: Fairchild Publications Inc.
Contact: Edward Nardoza, Editor-in-Chief
E-mail: edward_nardoza@condenast.com
Released: Daily (morn.). **Price:** $129; $99 online; $169 online print; $895 online archive. **Description:** Daily newspaper reporting on men's and boys' clothing, retailing, and textiles.

3887 ■ *Kids Creations*
Pub: Children's Apparel Manufacturers' Association
Contact: Myron MacKlovitch, International Sales Dir.
E-mail: myronmak@attcanada.ca
Released: Quarterly. **Price:** $37 Canada; $50 U.S.; $110 other countries; $64 two years Canada; $90 two years U.S.; $210 two years and other countries. **Description:** Children's wear trade magazine (English and French).

3888 ■ *New York Apparel News*
Pub: Apparel News Group
Contact: Alison A. Neider, Exec. Ed.
E-mail: alison@apparelnews.net
Released: 5/yr. **Price:** $20; $4 single issue. **Description:** Apparel magazine covering textiles and accessories for women and children.

TRADE SHOWS AND CONVENTIONS

3889 ■ Dallas Men's and Boys' Apparel Market
Dallas Market Center Co.
Attn: SG Marketing Mgr.
2100 Stemmons Fwy.
Dallas, TX 75207
Ph:(214)655-6100
Free: 800-325-6587
Fax:(214)655-6238
Co. E-mail: info@dmcmail.com
Released: Quarterly. **Principal Exhibits:** Men's clothing and accessories.

3890 ■ Denver Apparel and Accessory Market
Denver Merchandise Mart
451 E. 58th Ave., Ste. 4270
Denver, CO 80216-8470
Ph:(303)292-6278
Free: 800-289-6278
Fax:(303)297-8473
Co. E-mail: info@denvermart.com
URL: http://www.denvermart.com
Released: 5/yr. **Audience:** Retailers of women's, children's, and men's apparel and accessories. **Principal Exhibits:** Women's, men's, and children's apparel and accessories. **Dates and Locations:** 2011 Aug 26-29, Denver, CO.

3891 ■ Florida Fashion Focus Show
Southern Apparel Exhibitors, Inc.
1856 Sheridan St.
Evanston, IL 60201
Ph:(847)475-1856
Free: 888-249-1377
Co. E-mail: info@saemiami.com.
URL: http://www.saemiami.com
Released: 5/yr. **Audience:** Trade buyers. **Principal Exhibits:** Ladies ready-to-wear clothing; handbags, jewelry, and accessories. Order-writing for future delivery.

3892 ■ Just Kidstuff - A Division of the New York International Gift Fair
George Little Management, LLC (New York, New York)
1133 Westchester Ave., Ste. N136
White Plains, NY 10606
Ph:(914)421-3200
Free: 800-272-SHOW
Co. E-mail: cathy_steel@glmshows.com
URL: http://www.glmshows.com
Released: Semiannual. **Audience:** Buyers from specialty and department stores, giftshops, jewelry stores, interior designers, importers and distributors of home products, mail order catalogs. **Principal Exhibits:** Presents a wide variety of upscale products for children of all ages, including bedding, furniture, dolls, toys and games, gifts, clothes, books and educational products and accessories.

3893 ■ Just Kidstuff - A Division of the San Francisco International Gift Fair
George Little Management, LLC (New York, New York)
1133 Westchester Ave., Ste. N136
White Plains, NY 10606
Ph:(914)421-3200
Free: 800-272-SHOW
Co. E-mail: cathy_steel@glmshows.com
URL: http://www.glmshows.com
Released: Semiannual, February and August. **Audience:** Specialty and department stores, gift shops, jewelry stores, interior designers, importers and distributors of home products, mail order catalogs, museums, etc. **Principal Exhibits:** Upscale products for children of all ages, including bedding, furniture, dolls, toys and games, gifts, clothes, books, and educational products and accessories.

3894 ■ Women's and Children's Apparel and Accessories Mart
Dallas Market Center Co.
Attn: SG Marketing Mgr.
2100 Stemmons Fwy.
Dallas, TX 75207
Ph:(214)655-6100
Free: 800-325-6587
Fax:(214)655-6238
Co. E-mail: info@dmcmail.com
Audience: Apparel and accessories and home furnishings retailers. **Principal Exhibits:** Regional Merchandising Mart servicing department and specialty store buyers nationwide.

FRANCHISES AND BUSINESS OPPORTUNITIES

3895 ■ Baby News Children's Stores
6909 Las Positas Rd., Ste. A
Livermore, CA 94551
Ph:(925)245-1370
No. of Franchise Units: 50. **No. of Company-Owned Units:** 1. **Founded:** 1949. **Description:** Children's store. **Equity Capital Needed:** $200,000. **Franchise Fee:** $15,000. **Financial Assistance:** No. **Training:** Yes.

3896 ■ Children's Orchard
Children's Orchard, Inc.
900 Victors Way, Ste. 200
Ann Arbor, MI 48108
Ph:(734)994-9199
Free: 800-999-5437
Fax:(734)994-9323
No. of Franchise Units: 93. **No. of Company-Owned Units:** 1. **Founded:** 1980. **Franchised:** 1985. **Description:** Children's upscale/resale retail store. **Equity Capital Needed:** $115,600-$197,000. **Franchise Fee:** $25,000. **Royalty Fee:** 5%. **Financial Assistance:** No. **Training:** Provides 12 days training at headquarters, 3 days onsite and ongoing support.

3897 ■ Educational Outfitters
8002 East Brainerd Rd.
Chattanooga, TN 37421
Ph:(423)894-1222
Free: 877-814-1222
Fax:(423)894-9222
Co. E-mail: info@eschoolclothes.com
URL: http://www.eschoolclothes.com
No. of Franchise Units: 22. **No. of Company-Owned Units:** 1. **Founded:** 1999. **Franchised:** 2001. **Description:** Franchise of school uniforms and dress-code apparel for schools. **Equity Capital Needed:** $80,000-$198,000. **Franchise Fee:** $29,500. **Financial Assistance:** No. **Training:** initial training at store, additional training at the franchisees location along with on-going support.

RESEARCH CENTERS

3898 ■ Texas A&M University–Center for Retailing Studies
Wehner Bldg., Ste. 201
Mays Business School
4112 TAMU
College Station, TX 77843-4112
Ph:(979)845-0325
Fax:(979)845-5230
Co. E-mail: c-bridges@mays.tamu.edu
URL: http://www.crstamu.org
Contact: Cheryl Holland Bridges, Dir.
E-mail: c-bridges@mays.tamu.edu

Scope: Retailing. **Publications:** Faculty retailing research Papers; Retailing Issues Letter (quarterly). **Educational Activities:** Retailing Summit, held in September for retailing executives and academics; Thought Leadership Conference (annually), brings together academic scholars and industry professionals from around the globe to develop position papers on retailing research issues. **Awards:** M.B. Zale Visionary Merchant Award and Lecture (annually), held in spring to honor outstanding performance by a leading retailer.

START-UP INFORMATION

3899 ■ "Franchises with an Eye on Chicago" in *Crain's Chicago Business* (Vol. 34, March 14, 2011, No. 11, pp. 20)
Pub: Crain Communications Inc.
Description: Profiles of franchise companies seeking franchisees for the Chicago area include: Extreme Pita, a sandwich shop; Hand and Stone, offering massage, facial and waxing services; Molly Maid, home-cleaning service; Primrose Schools, private accredited schools for children 6 months to 6 hears and after-school programs; Protect Painters, residential and light-commercial painting contractor; and Wingstop, a restaurant offering chicken wings in nine flavors, fries and side dishes.

3900 ■ "Fun And Easy Gold Mines" in *Small Business Opportunities* (Fall 2008)
Pub: Entrepreneur Media Inc.
Description: Twenty-five businesses that cater to the booming children's market are profiled; day care services, party planning, special events video-making, tutoring, personalized children's toys and products and other services geared toward the kids market are included.

3901 ■ "Making Money? Child's Play!" in *Small Business Opportunities* (March 2008)
Pub: Harris Publications Inc.
Description: Proven system helps launch a successful child care business.

ASSOCIATIONS AND OTHER ORGANIZATIONS

3902 ■ American Montessori Society
281 Park Ave. S
New York, NY 10010-6102
Ph:(212)358-1250
Fax:(212)358-1256
Co. E-mail: ams@amshq.org
URL: http://www.amshq.org
Contact: Richard A. Ungerer, Exec. Dir.
Description: School affiliates and teacher training affiliates; heads of schools, teachers, parents, non-Montessori educators, and other interested individuals dedicated to stimulating the use of the Montessori teaching approach and promoting better education for all children. Seeks to meet demands of growing interest in the Montessori approach to early learning. Assists in establishing schools; supplies information and limited services to member schools in other countries. Maintains school consultation and accreditation service; provides information service; assists research and gathers statistical data; offers placement service. Maintains Montessori and related materials exhibit. **Publications:** *Montessori Life* (quarterly); *Salary & Tuition Surveys* (biennial); *School Directory* (annual).

3903 ■ Association for Childhood Education International
17904 Georgia Ave., Ste. 215
Olney, MD 20832
Ph:(301)570-2111
Free: 800-423-3563
Fax:(301)570-2212
Co. E-mail: headquarters@acei.org
URL: http://acei.org
Contact: Diane Whitehead, Exec. Dir.
Description: Promotes and supports in the global community, optimal education and development of children, from birth through early adolescence. Influences the professional growth of educators and the efforts of others who are committed to the needs of children in a changing society. Strives to dedicate to a flexible, child-centered approach to education. Conducts advocacy through a variety of public forums and major coalitions for children and education. **Publications:** *Childhood Education* (bimonthly); *Focus on Elementary* (quarterly); *Journal of Research in Childhood Education* (quarterly).

3904 ■ Child Welfare League of America
1726 M St. NW, Ste. 500
Washington, DC 20036-4522
Ph:(202)688-4200
Fax:(202)833-1689
Co. E-mail: register@cwla.org
URL: http://www.cwla.org
Contact: Christine James-Brown, Pres./CEO
Description: Works to improve care and services for abused, dependent, or neglected children, youth, and their families. Provides training and consultation; conducts research; maintains information service and develops standards for child welfare practice. .

3905 ■ Children's Defense Fund
25 E St. NW
Washington, DC 20001
Ph:(202)628-8787
Free: 800-233-1200
Co. E-mail: cdfinfo@childrensdefense.org
URL: http://www.childrensdefense.org
Contact: Marian Wright Edelman, Founder/Pres.
Purpose: Provides systematic, long-range advocacy on behalf of the nation's children and teenagers. Engages in research, public education, monitoring of federal agencies, litigation, legislative drafting and testimony, assistance to state and local groups, and community organizing in areas of child welfare, child health, adolescent pregnancy prevention, child care and development, family income, family services, prevention of violence against and by children and child mental health. Works with individuals and groups to change policies and practices resulting in neglect or maltreatment of millions of children. Advocates: access to existing programs and services; creation of new programs and services where necessary; consistent emphasis on prevention; enforcement of civil rights laws; program accountability; strong parent and community role in decision-making; adequate funding for essential programs for children. Compiles statistics. **Publications:** *America's Cradle to Prison Pipeline* .

3906 ■ National Association of Child Care Professionals
PO Box 90723
Austin, TX 78709
Ph:(512)301-5557
Free: 800-537-1118
Fax:(512)301-5080
Co. E-mail: admin@naccp.org
URL: http://www.naccp.org
Contact: Bobette Thompson, Pres.
Description: Child care supervisors and individuals involved in decision-making at a child care facility. Offers networking opportunities and support services to child care professionals. Dedicated to the professional development of child care directors. Conducts educational programs. **Publications:** *Caring for Your Children* (quarterly); *Immunizing Children Against Disease: A Guide For Child Care Providers*; *Professional Connections* (quarterly); *Team Work* (quarterly).

3907 ■ National Association for the Education of Young Children
PO Box 97156
Washington, DC 20090-7156
Ph:(202)232-8777
Free: 800-424-2460
Fax:(202)328-1846
Co. E-mail: naeyc@naeyc.org
URL: http://www.naeyc.org
Contact: Stephanie Fanjul, Pres.
Description: Teachers and directors of preschool and primary schools, kindergartens, child care centers, and early other learning programs for young childhood; early childhood education and child development educators, trainers, and researchers and other professionals dedicated to young children's healthy development. **Publications:** *Young Children* (bimonthly).

3908 ■ National Black Child Development Institute
1313 L St. NW, Ste. 110
Washington, DC 20005-4110
Ph:(202)833-2220
Free: 800-556-2234
Fax:(202)833-8222
Co. E-mail: moreinfo@nbcdi.org
URL: http://nbcdi.org
Contact: Carol Brunson Day, Pres./CEO
Description: Aims to improving the quality of life for African American children and youth. Conducts direct services and advocacy campaigns aimed at both national and local public policies focusing on issues of health, child welfare, education, and child care. Organizes and trains network of members in a volunteer grassroots affiliate system to voice concerns regarding policies that affect black children and their families. Stimulates communication between black community groups, through conferences and seminars, to discuss and make recommendations that will be advantageous to the development of black children. Analyzes selected policy decisions and legislative and administrative regulations to determine their impact on black children and youth. Informs national policymakers of issues critical to black children. **Publications:** *Child Health Talk* (quarterly); *School Readiness and Social Emotional Development: Perspectives on Cultural Diversity* .

3909 ■ National Coalition for Campus Children's Centers
950 Glenn Dr., Ste. 150
Folsom, CA 95630
Free: 877-736-6222
Fax:(916)932-2209
Co. E-mail: info@campuschildren.org
URL: http://www.campuschildren.org
Contact: Betty Pearsall, Pres.

Description: Promotes child care centers on college campuses and provides information on organizing and operating these centers. Believes that campus child care programs should be an integral part of higher education systems and should provide safe and healthy environments for children, developmentally sound educational programs, and services to both parents and campus programs. .

3910 ■ National Head Start Association
1651 Prince St.
Alexandria, VA 22314
Ph:(703)739-0875
Fax:(703)739-0878
Co. E-mail: nhsamembership@nhsa.org
URL: http://www.nhsa.org
Contact: Ron Herndon, Chm.

Description: Members of National Head Start Parent Association, National Head Start Directors Association, National Head Start Staff Association, National Head Start Friends Association, and others interested in the Head Start Program. Upgrades the quality and quantity of Head Start Program services. Integrates the activities of the 4 divisions to present cohesive policies, positions, and statements. Conducts seminars and training sessions in early childhood education. Maintains speakers' bureau. **Publications:** *Children and Families* (quarterly); *NHSA Newsletter* (quarterly).

3911 ■ National Resource Center for Health and Safety in Child Care and Early Education
Campus Mail Stop F541
13120 E 19th Ave.
Aurora, CO 80045-0508
Ph:(303)724-0654
Free: 800-598-KIDS
Fax:(303)724-0960
Co. E-mail: info@nrckids.org
URL: http://nrckids.org
Contact: Marilyn J. Krajicek EdD, Dir.

Description: Seeks to enhance the quality of child care and early education by supporting state and local health departments, child care regulatory agencies, child care providers/teachers, and parents/guardians in their effort to promote health and safety in child care and early education. Provides information services and technical assistance. .

3912 ■ Southern Early Childhood Association
PO Box 55930
Little Rock, AR 72215-5930
Ph:(501)221-1648
Free: 800-305-7322
Fax:(501)227-5297
Co. E-mail: info@southernearlychildhood.org
URL: http://www.southernearlychildhood.org
Contact: Janie Humphries, Pres.

Description: Early childhood educators, day care providers, program administrators, researchers, teacher trainers, and parents from the U.S. and abroad who share a common concern for the well-being of young children. Provides a unified voice on vital local, state, and federal issues affecting young children. Exchanges information and ideas through conferences and workshops. Explores contemporary issues in child development and early education through publications. **Publications:** *Dimensions of Early Childhood* (3/year).

3913 ■ U.S.A. Toy Library Association
2719 Broadway Ave.
Evanston, IL 60201
Ph:(847)612-6966
Fax:(847)864-8473
Co. E-mail: jqi@comcast.net
URL: http://usatla.org/Welcome.html
Contact: Judith Q. Iacuzzi, Exec. Dir.

Description: Child care professionals, parents, and others interested in the role of toys and play in child development. Promotes the importance of play and the development of toy libraries in public and school libraries, hospitals, day care centers, and mobile collections. Seeks to broaden understanding of how toys can educate, increase parent-child interaction, and aid in development and therapy of disabled children. .

3914 ■ World Organization for Early Childhood Education–Organisation Mondiale pour l'Education Prescolaire
PO Box 37
Montreal-Nord, QC, Canada H1H 5L1
Ph:(514)987-3000
Co. E-mail: omep-canada@sympatico.ca
URL: http://www.omep-canada.org
Contact: Ginette Beausejour, Pres.

Description: Organizations and individuals in 72 countries concerned with the health, education, and welfare of children. Promotes greater understanding of children from birth to age 8. Facilitates international exchange of research experience and knowledge on topics including child psychology, toys and play materials, living conditions of families with young children, preschool education and care, and other issues in education. Members promote research on early childhood education, conduct surveys of nursery schools and teacher training, and encourage parent education. Maintains speakers' bureau; conducts seminars and forums.

DIRECTORIES OF EDUCATIONAL PROGRAMS

3915 ■ *Directory of Private Accredited Career Schools and Colleges of Technology*
Pub: Accrediting Commission of Career Schools and Colleges of Technology
Contact: Michale S. McComis, Exec. Dir.

Released: On web page. **Price:** Free. **Description:** Covers 3900 accredited post-secondary programs that provide training programs in business, trade, and technical fields, including various small business endeavors. Entries offer school name, address, phone, description of courses, job placement assistance, and requirements for admission. Arrangement is alphabetical.

REFERENCE WORKS

3916 ■ "The Best Advice I Ever Got" in *Harvard Business Review* (Vol. 86, September 2008, No. 9, pp. 29)
Pub: Harvard Business School Press

Ed: Daisy Wademan Dowling. **Description:** Bright Horizons Family Solutions founder and chair Linda Mason illustrates how letting one's life passion direct entrepreneurship and business success. She describes how her humanitarian interests and efforts gave her the drive to launch a childcare service.

3917 ■ "Child-Care Policy and the Labor Supply of Mothers with Young Children" in *University of Chicago Press* (Vol. 26, July 2008, No. 3)
Pub: University of Chicago Press

Ed: Pierre Lefebvre, Philip Merrigan. **Description:** In 1997, the provincial government of Quebec, the second most populous province in Canada, initiated a new childcare policy. Licensed childcare service providers began offering day care spaces at the reduced fee of $5 per day per child for children aged four. By 2000, the policy applied to all children not in kindergarten. Using annual data (1993-2002) drawn from Statistics Canada's Survey of Labour and Income Dynamics, the results show that the policy had a large and statistically significant impact on the labor supply of mothers with preschool children.

3918 ■ "Day Care for Affluent Drawing a Crowd" in *Business First Columbus* (Vol. 24, August 15, 2008, No. 52, pp. 1)
Pub: American City Business Journals

Ed: Carrie Ghose. **Description:** Day care centers for affluent families have grown in popularity in Columbus, Ohio. Primrose Schools Franchising Company has opened three such schools in the area. Statistical data included.

3919 ■ "Day-Care Center Owner to Argue Against Liquor Store Opening Nearby" in *Chicago Tribune* (March 13, 2008)
Pub: McClatchy-Tribune Information Services

Ed: Matthew Walberg. **Description:** NDLC's owner feels that Greenwood Liquors should not be granted its liquor license due to the claim that the NDLC is not only a day-care center but also a school that employs state-certified teachers.

3920 ■ "Daycare Dollars" in *Small Business Opportunities* (Winter 2009)
Pub: Entrepreneur Media Inc.

Description: Profile of Maui Playcare, a franchise that provides parents drop-in daycare for their children without having to purchase a membership, make reservations or pay costly dues; the company is expanding beyond its Hawaiian roots onto the mainland and is expected to have between 40 and 50 locations signed by the end of 2010.

3921 ■ "Intrepid Souls: Meet a Few Who've Made the Big Leap" in *Crain's Chicago Business* (Vol. 31, November 10, 2008, No. 45, pp. 26)
Pub: Crain Communications, Inc.

Ed: Meredith Landry. **Description:** Advice is given from entrepreneurs who have launched businesses in the last year despite the economic crisis. Among the types of businesses featured are a cooking school, a child day-care center, a children's clothing store and an Internet-based company.

3922 ■ "Manulife Posts Billion-Dollar Profit" in *Globe & Mail* (February 14, 2007, pp. B7)
Pub: CTVglobemedia Publishing Inc.

Ed: Andrew Willis. **Description:** Manulife Financial Corp., Canada's largest insurer, reported $1.1 billion profit in the fourth quarter of 2006. The financial results of Manulife reflected a 39 percent rise in quarterly profit at the nation's wealth management division.

3923 ■ "Susan Leger Ferraro Built a $7.2 Million Day Care Business. Now She Wants To Expand-And Cash Out" in *Inc.* (January 2008, pp. 50-53)
Pub: Gruner & Jahr USA Publishing

Ed: Dalia Fahmy. **Description:** Profile of Susan Leger Ferraro who wants to expand her chain of day care centers into Florida and California and sell part of her 87 percent stake to reduce financial risk.

STATISTICAL SOURCES

3924 ■ *RMA Annual Statement Studies*
Pub: Robert Morris Associates (RMA)

Released: Annual. **Price:** $175.00 2006-07 edition, $105.00. **Description:** Contains composite balance sheets and income statements for more than 360 industries, including the accounting, auditing, and bookkeeping industries. Also contains five years of comparative historical data for discerning trends. Includes 16 commonly used ratios, computed for most of the size groupings for nearly every industry.

3925 ■ *U.S. Child Day Care Services: An Industry Analysis 6th Edition*
Pub: MarketResearch.com

Released: 2005. **Price:** $2695.00. **Description:** A major source of public information about any industry or market analyzed by Marketdata is the U.S. Government—the most prolific producer of business information in the world.

TRADE PERIODICALS

3926 ■ *ACEI Exchange*
Pub: Association for Childhood Education International
Contact: Deborah Jordan Kravitz
Ed: Deborah Jordan Kravitz, Editor, aceied@aol.com. **Released:** 5/year. **Price:** Included in membership. **Description:** Concerned with the Association's goal of promoting good educational programs and practices for children from infancy through early adolescence. Provides information on resources, publications, and Association activities. Recurring features include calls for papers and presenters, letters to the editor, and a calendar of events.

3927 ■ *Change*
Pub: Heldref Publications
Released: Bimonthly. **Price:** $52 print only; $39 institutions print only; $64 print and online; $207 institutions print and online. **Description:** Magazine dealing with contemporary issues in higher learning.

3928 ■ *Child Care Bridges*
Pub: Manitoba Child Care Association
Contact: Pat Wedge, Exec. Dir.
E-mail: clairefunk@mccahouse.org
Ed: Released: Price: Description: advocates for a quality system of child care, to advance early childhood education as a profession , and to provide services to our members.

3929 ■ *Child Care Plus*
Pub: University of Montana
Ed: Sandra L. Morris, Editor, slmorris@selway.umt.edu. **Released:** Quarterly. **Price:** $8; $15, two years; $20 three years. **Description:** Aims to support the efforts of care providers who care for children with physical, developmental, or medical disabilities in the child-care setting. Provides practical hints, notes from parents, community collaboration, answers to common questions, and spotlighted programs and resources.Includes columns titled Spotlight, What Do I Do When, From the Source, Notes from Home, Making it Work, and Resource Review.

3930 ■ *Child Welfare*
Pub: Child Welfare League of America Inc.
Released: Bimonthly. **Price:** $140 Canada and Mexico; $195 institutions; $210 other countries; $265 institutions, other countries; $255 2 years; $395 other countries 2 years; $340 institutions 2 years; $480 institutions, other countries 2 years. **Description:** Child welfare services journal.

3931 ■ *School Age Notes*
Pub: Richard T. Scofield
Ed: Richard T. Scofield, Editor. **Released:** Monthly. **Price:** $31.95, U.S.; $31.95, Canada; $33.95, elsewhere. **Description:** Carries ideas for activities and games that are developmentally oriented for school-age children. Offers curricula, advice, news, and think-pieces for improving school-age child care. Recurring features include book reviews, a list of resources, notices of events, and columns titled Director's Corner, Developmental Notes, Activities, Curriculum Corner, and Administrative Notes.

3932 ■ *Young Children*
Pub: National Association for the Education of Young Children
Released: Bimonthly. **Price:** $60 non U.S.; $95 institutions non U.S.; $80 other countries; $115 institutions, other countries. **Description:** Peer-reviewed professional journal focusing on issues in the field of early childhood education.

VIDEOCASSETTES/ AUDIOCASSETTES

3933 ■ *The Adventures of Elmer and Friends: Freedom Rocks*
Leslie T. McClure
PO Box 1223
Pebble Beach, CA 93953
Ph:(831)656-0553
Fax:(831)656-0555
Co. E-mail: leslie@411videoinfo.com
URL: http://www.411videoinfo.com
Released: 1998. **Price:** $14.95. **Description:** Live action musical program for children stars Elmer the tree and a variety of friends. Stresses the importance of nature and equality. **Availability:** VHS.

3934 ■ *The Adventures of Elmer and Friends: Pirate Island*
Leslie T. McClure
PO Box 1223
Pebble Beach, CA 93953
Ph:(831)656-0553
Fax:(831)656-0555
Co. E-mail: leslie@411videoinfo.com
URL: http://www.411videoinfo.com
Released: 1998. **Price:** $14.95. **Description:** Live action musical program for children stars Elmer the tree and a variety of friends. Stresses the importance of friendship. **Availability:** VHS.

3935 ■ *The Adventures of Elmer and Friends: The Magic Map*
Leslie T. McClure
PO Box 1223
Pebble Beach, CA 93953
Ph:(831)656-0553
Fax:(831)656-0555
Co. E-mail: leslie@411videoinfo.com
URL: http://www.411videoinfo.com
Released: 1998. **Price:** $14.95. **Description:** Live action musical program for children stars Elmer the tree and a variety of friends. Stresses the importance of reading. **Availability:** VHS.

3936 ■ *The Adventures of Elmer and Friends: Treasure Beyond Measure*
Leslie T. McClure
PO Box 1223
Pebble Beach, CA 93953
Ph:(831)656-0553
Fax:(831)656-0555
Co. E-mail: leslie@411videoinfo.com
URL: http://www.411videoinfo.com
Released: 1998. **Price:** $14.95. **Description:** Live action musical program for children stars Elmer the tree and a variety of friends. Stresses the importance of self-esteem. **Availability:** VHS.

3937 ■ *Ages of Infancy: Caring for Young, Mobile, and Older Infants*
California State Department of Education
CDE Press
1430 N St.
Sacramento, CA 95814-5901
Ph:(916)445-1260
Free: 800-995-4099
Fax:(916)323-0823
URL: http://www.cde.ca.gov/
Released: 1990. **Price:** $65.00. **Description:** Identifies the three stages of infant development, as well as each stage's accompanying development issue. Provides guidelines and suggestions for caregiving in each stage. A 10-page video magazine is included. **Availability:** VHS.

3938 ■ *The Alphabet Jungle Game*
Sony Wonder
550 Madison Ave.
New York, NY 10022-3211
Ph:(212)833-8100
Co. E-mail: Lisa_Davis@sonyusa.com
URL: http://www.sonywondertechlab.com
Released: 1998. **Price:** $12.98. **Description:** Sesame Street characters Elmo, Zoe, and Telly explore the alphabet in this collection of segments from the popular children's show. **Availability:** VHS.

3939 ■ *Art Surprises*
Tapeworm Video Distributors
25876 The Old Road 141
Stevenson Ranch, CA 91381
Ph:(661)257-4904
Fax:(661)257-4820
Co. E-mail: sales@tapeworm.com
URL: http://www.tapeworm.com
Released: 1998. **Price:** $29.95. **Description:** Donna Erickson presents creative projects for children of all ages, including Fish Prints and Potato Jewelry. **Availability:** VHS.

3940 ■ *Baby See, Baby Do*
Leslie T. McClure
PO Box 1223
Pebble Beach, CA 93953
Ph:(831)656-0553
Fax:(831)656-0555
Co. E-mail: leslie@411videoinfo.com
URL: http://www.411videoinfo.com
Released: 1998. **Price:** $14.95. **Description:** Contains images and sounds intended to delight infants and their caregivers. **Availability:** VHS.

3941 ■ *Backyard Safari*
GPN Educational Media
1550 Executive Drive
Elgin, IL 60123
Ph:(402)472-2007
Free: 800-228-4630
Fax:800-306-2330
Co. E-mail: askgpn@smarterville.com
URL: http://www.shopgpn.com
Released: 1998. **Price:** $467.35. **Description:** Series of 13 30-minute videos designed to teach preschool children through grade six basic science and natural history. **Availability:** VHS.

3942 ■ *The Big Comfy Couch: Are You Ready for School?*
Tapeworm Video Distributors
25876 The Old Road 141
Stevenson Ranch, CA 91381
Ph:(661)257-4904
Fax:(661)257-4820
Co. E-mail: sales@tapeworm.com
URL: http://www.tapeworm.com
Released: 1998. **Price:** $12.99. **Description:** Loonette and Molly entertain children and stress important themes, including sharing and cooperation. **Availability:** VHS.

3943 ■ *The Big Comfy Couch: Be Nice, Snicklefritz!*
Tapeworm Video Distributors
25876 The Old Road 141
Stevenson Ranch, CA 91381
Ph:(661)257-4904
Fax:(661)257-4820
Co. E-mail: sales@tapeworm.com
URL: http://www.tapeworm.com
Released: 1998. **Price:** $12.99. **Description:** Loonette and Molly entertain children and stress important themes, including sharing and cooperation. **Availability:** VHS.

3944 ■ *The Big Comfy Couch: Dustbunny Dreams*
Tapeworm Video Distributors
25876 The Old Road 141
Stevenson Ranch, CA 91381
Ph:(661)257-4904
Fax:(661)257-4820
Co. E-mail: sales@tapeworm.com
URL: http://www.tapeworm.com
Released: 1998. **Price:** $12.99. **Description:** Loonette and Molly entertain children and stress important themes, including sharing and cooperation. **Availability:** VHS.

3945 ■ *Blue's Clues: Arts and Crafts*
Paramount Home Video
5555 Melrose Ave.
Los Angeles, CA 90038
Ph:(323)956-5000
URL: http://www.paramount.com
Released: 1998. **Price:** $9.95. **Description:** Animated puppy "Blue" and live action host Steve invite youngsters to learn through solving clues in "Adventures in Art" and "What Does Blue Want to Make?". **Availability:** VHS.

3946 ■ *Blue's Clues: Story Time*
Paramount Home Video
5555 Melrose Ave.
Los Angeles, CA 90038
Ph:(323)956-5000
URL: http://www.paramount.com
Released: 1998. **Price:** $9.95. **Description:** Animated puppy "Blue" and live action host Steve invite youngsters to learn through solving clues in "What's Blue's Favorite Story?" and "What Story Does Blue Want to Play?". **Availability:** VHS.

3947 ■ *Child Safety*
Janson Media
88 Semmens Rd.
Harrington Park, NJ 07640
Ph:(201)784-8488
Fax:(201)784-3993
URL: http://www.janson.com
Released: 1998. **Price:** $19.95. **Description:** Guides parents and caregivers in keeping children safe from accidental harm. **Availability:** VHS.

3948 ■ *Child's Play: The World of Learning*
Educational Productions Inc.
7101 Wisconsin Ave., Ste. 700
Bethesda, MD 20814
Free: (1-8)00-637-3652
Fax:(301)634-0826
Co. E-mail: customerrelations@teachingstrategies.com
URL: http://www.edpro.com
Released: 1990. **Price:** $295.00. **Description:** This video for teachers, administrators, parents, students and aides takes a look at the implications of children's play, including how they build thinking, language, motor, social and emotional skills, prepare for academic learning, set foundations for reading and writing and much more. **Availability:** VHS; 3/4U.

3949 ■ *Colors and Shapes Circus*
Leslie T. McClure
PO Box 1223
Pebble Beach, CA 93953
Ph:(831)656-0553
Fax:(831)656-0555
Co. E-mail: leslie@411videoinfo.com
URL: http://www.411videoinfo.com
Released: 1998. **Price:** $19.95. **Description:** Teaches young children primary and secondary colors and basic shapes. **Availability:** VHS.

3950 ■ *Connecting—Grades K-8*
Crystal Productions
1812 Johns Dr.
Box 2159
Glenview, IL 60025-6519
Ph:(847)657-8144
Free: 800-255-8629
Fax:(847)657-8149
Co. E-mail: custserv@crystalproductions.com
URL: http://www.crystalproductions.com
Price: $239.00. **Description:** Still-frame teaching aid for art appreciation presents art work in themes so that relationships, comparisons, and connections are more easily seen. **Availability:** VHS.

3951 ■ *Day Care Grows Up*
Films for the Humanities & Sciences
132 West 31st Street
New York, NY 10001
Ph:(609)671-1000
Free: 800-257-5126
Fax:(609)671-0266
Co. E-mail: custserv@films.com
URL: http://www.films.com
Released: 1991. **Price:** $159.00. **Description:** Discusses the new attitudes and measures being taken to increase the quality of childcare in the U.S. **Availability:** VHS.

3952 ■ *Fingerplays and Footplays*
Educational Activities, Inc.
PO Box 87
Baldwin, NY 11510
Free: 800-797-3223
Fax:(516)623-9282
URL: http://www.edact.com
Released: 1997. **Price:** $19.95. **Description:** Presents activities that encourage dramatic play and help focus children's attention. **Availability:** VHS.

3953 ■ *First Moves: Welcoming a Child to a New Caregiving Setting*
California State Department of Education
CDE Press
1430 N St.
Sacramento, CA 95814-5901
Ph:(916)445-1260
Free: 800-995-4099
Fax:(916)323-0823
URL: http://www.cde.ca.gov/
Released: 1988. **Price:** $65.00. **Description:** Child-care professionals are taught how to make their kids comfortable right from the start. **Availability:** VHS.

3954 ■ *Friends and Strangers*
Tapeworm Video Distributors
25876 The Old Road 141
Stevenson Ranch, CA 91381
Ph:(661)257-4904
Fax:(661)257-4820
Co. E-mail: sales@tapeworm.com
URL: http://www.tapeworm.com
Price: $14.95. **Description:** Provides children with tips to distinguish the differences between friends and strangers. **Availability:** VHS.

3955 ■ *Good Choices . . . Bad Choices*
Tapeworm Video Distributors
25876 The Old Road 141
Stevenson Ranch, CA 91381
Ph:(661)257-4904
Fax:(661)257-4820
Co. E-mail: sales@tapeworm.com
URL: http://www.tapeworm.com
Price: $14.95. **Description:** Provides children with tips to distinguish the differences between good choices and bad choices. **Availability:** VHS.

3956 ■ *Good Discipline, Good Kids*
Sunburst Technology
1550 Executive Dr.
Elgin, IL 60123
Free: 888-492-8817
Fax:888-800-3028
Co. E-mail: service@sunburst.com
URL: http://www.sunburst.com
Released: 1998. **Price:** $99.95. **Description:** Parenting experts Adele Faber and Elaine Mazlish provide tips and techniques to develop a consistent approach to disciplining children. **Availability:** VHS.

3957 ■ *The Great Numbers Game*
Sony Wonder
550 Madison Ave.
New York, NY 10022-3211
Ph:(212)833-8100
Co. E-mail: Lisa_Davis@sonyusa.com
URL: http://www.sonywondertechlab.com
Released: 1998. **Price:** $12.98. **Description:** Sesame Street characters Elmo, Gabi, and Telly learn about numbers in this collection of segments from the popular children's show. **Availability:** VHS.

3958 ■ *Help Your Child Succeed in School*
Sunburst Technology
1550 Executive Dr.
Elgin, IL 60123
Free: 888-492-8817
Fax:888-800-3028
Co. E-mail: service@sunburst.com
URL: http://www.sunburst.com
Released: 1998. **Price:** $99.95. **Description:** Parenting experts Adele Faber and Elaine Mazlish provide tips and techniques to develop the self-discipline and self-confidence needed for a child's success in school. **Availability:** VHS.

3959 ■ *Hola Amigos: Spanish for Kids*
PBS Home Video
Catalog Fulfillment Center
PO Box 751089
Charlotte, NC 28275-1089
Ph:800-531-4727
Free: 800-645-4PBS
Co. E-mail: info@pbs.org
URL: http://www.pbs.org
Released: 1998. **Price:** $54.95. **Description:** Roung viewers will learn the basics of Spanish, including the words for colors, letters, numbers, pets and animals, musical instuments and sports. Uses the adventures of cartoon dog Paco to ease youngsters into the Spanish language. Two hours and 30 minutes on three videocassettes. **Availability:** VHS.

3960 ■ *Imagineria*
Crystal Productions
1812 Johns Dr.
Box 2159
Glenview, IL 60025-6519
Ph:(847)657-8144
Free: 800-255-8629
Fax:(847)657-8149
Co. E-mail: custserv@crystalproductions.com
URL: http://www.crystalproductions.com
Price: $9.98. **Description:** Computer animated teaching aid for art education designed for children. **Availability:** VHS.

3961 ■ *Imaginit*
Crystal Productions
1812 Johns Dr.
Box 2159
Glenview, IL 60025-6519
Ph:(847)657-8144
Free: 800-255-8629
Fax:(847)657-8149
Co. E-mail: custserv@crystalproductions.com
URL: http://www.crystalproductions.com
Price: $12.98. **Description:** Computer animated teaching aid for art education that encourages children to imagine. **Availability:** VHS.

3962 ■ *Inside Business Today*
GPN Educational Media
1550 Executive Drive
Elgin, IL 60123
Ph:(402)472-2007
Free: 800-228-4630
Fax:800-306-2330
Co. E-mail: askgpn@smarterville.com
URL: http://www.shopgpn.com
Released: 1989. **Description:** Leaders in business and industry tell their success stories in this extensive series. **Availability:** VHS; 3/4U.

3963 ■ *The Just So Stories, Vol. 1*
Interama, Inc.
301 W. 53rd St., Ste. 19E
New York, NY 10019
Ph:(212)977-4830
Fax:(212)581-6582
Released: 1998. **Price:** $14.95. **Description:** Animated rendering of Rudyard Kipling's tales of the natural world. Includes "How the Elephant Got His Trunk," "How the Rhinoceros Got His Skin," and "The Beginning of Armadillos." **Availability:** VHS.

3964 ■ *The Just So Stories, Vol. 2*
Interama, Inc.
301 W. 53rd St., Ste. 19E
New York, NY 10019
Ph:(212)977-4830
Fax:(212)581-6582
Released: 1998. **Price:** $14.95. **Description:** Animated rendering of Rudyard Kipling's tales of the natural world. Includes "How the Whale Got His Throat," "How the Leopard Got His Spots," and "How the Camel Got His Hump." **Availability:** VHS.

3965 ■ *The Just So Stories, Vol. 3*
Interama, Inc.
301 W. 53rd St., Ste. 19E
New York, NY 10019
Ph:(212)977-4830
Fax:(212)581-6582
Released: 1998. **Price:** $14.95. **Description:** Animated rendering of Rudyard Kipling's tales of the natural world. Includes "Why the Cat Is Walking By Himself" and "How the Crab Played with the Sea." **Availability:** VHS.

3966 ■ *Kitchen Capers*
Tapeworm Video Distributors
25876 The Old Road 141
Stevenson Ranch, CA 91381
Ph:(661)257-4904
Fax:(661)257-4820
Co. E-mail: sales@tapeworm.com
URL: http://www.tapeworm.com
Released: 1998. **Price:** $9.99. **Description:** Donna Erickson presents creative projects for children of all ages, including Wacky Bubble Brew, Handmade Ice Cream, and Gooey Goop. **Availability:** VHS.

3967 ■ *Learning about Honesty*
Sunburst Technology
1550 Executive Dr.
Elgin, IL 60123
Free: 888-492-8817
Fax:888-800-3028
Co. E-mail: service@sunburst.com
URL: http://www.sunburst.com
Released: 1998. **Price:** $59.95. **Description:** Provides children grades K-2 with a basis for understanding honesty through vignettes and an entertaining host, "The Truth Fairy." **Availability:** VHS.

3968 ■ *Let's Create for Halloween*
Crystal Productions
1812 Johns Dr.
Box 2159
Glenview, IL 60025-6519
Ph:(847)657-8144
Free: 800-255-8629
Fax:(847)657-8149
Co. E-mail: custserv@crystalproductions.com
URL: http://www.crystalproductions.com
Price: $24.95. **Description:** Guides children through a number of art activities appropriate for Halloween. **Availability:** VHS.

3969 ■ *Let's Create for Thanksgiving*
Crystal Productions
1812 Johns Dr.
Box 2159
Glenview, IL 60025-6519
Ph:(847)657-8144
Free: 800-255-8629
Fax:(847)657-8149
Co. E-mail: custserv@crystalproductions.com
URL: http://www.crystalproductions.com
Price: $24.95. **Description:** Guides children through a number of art activities appropriate for Thanksgiving. **Availability:** VHS.

3970 ■ *Moving Freely: A Creative Dance Class*
Tapeworm Video Distributors
25876 The Old Road 141
Stevenson Ranch, CA 91381
Ph:(661)257-4904
Fax:(661)257-4820
Co. E-mail: sales@tapeworm.com
URL: http://www.tapeworm.com
Price: $14.95. **Description:** Presents a movement class for children 3-10 incorporating elements of technique, rhythm, locomotion, composition and sharing. **Availability:** VHS.

3971 ■ *The Number Express*
Leslie T. McClure
PO Box 1223
Pebble Beach, CA 93953
Ph:(831)656-0553
Fax:(831)656-0555
Co. E-mail: leslie@411videoinfo.com
URL: http://www.411videoinfo.com
Released: 1998. **Price:** $19.95. **Description:** The engineer of a steam engine teaches young children numbers, number relationships, and counting skills. **Availability:** VHS.

3972 ■ *101 Dalmatians: Pongo and Perdita Sing Along Songs*
Buena Vista Home Entertainment
500 S. Buena Vista St.
Burbank, CA 91521-1120
Free: 800-723-4763
URL: http://www.bvhe.com
Released: 1997. **Price:** $12.99. **Description:** Encourages children to sing, dance and play along with a collection of "dog-themed" tunes. **Availability:** VHS.

3973 ■ *Potty Training One, Two, Three*
Tapeworm Video Distributors
25876 The Old Road 141
Stevenson Ranch, CA 91381
Ph:(661)257-4904
Fax:(661)257-4820
Co. E-mail: sales@tapeworm.com
URL: http://www.tapeworm.com
Released: 1997. **Price:** $19.95. **Description:** Genie Z. Laborde, Ph.D., provides guidelines for quick and easy potty training. **Availability:** VHS.

3974 ■ *Respectfully Yours: Magda Gerber's Approach to Professional Infant/Toddler Care*
California State Department of Education
CDE Press
1430 N St.
Sacramento, CA 95814-5901
Ph:(916)445-1260
Free: 800-995-4099
Fax:(916)323-0823
URL: http://www.cde.ca.gov/
Released: 1988. **Price:** $65.00. **Description:** This is an introductory guide for people who want to learn how to care for young children. **Availability:** VHS.

3975 ■ *Schedules and Routines: Why Bother?*
AAVIM (American Association for Vocational Instructional Materials)
220 Smithonia Rd.
Winterville, GA 30683-9257
Ph:(706)742-5355
Free: 800-228-4689
Fax:(706)742-7005
Co. E-mail: sales@aavim.com
URL: http://www.aavim.com
Price: $89.95. **Description:** Part of the Child Care Worker Series. Offers advice on planning schedules according to objectives of the child care facility, including times children arrive and leave, amount of time at the facility, number and ages of children and adults, balance of active and quiet activities, and the time of the year and weather. Includes study guide. **Availability:** VHS.

3976 ■ *See How They Grow: Farm Animals*
Environmental Media
PO Box 99
Beaufort, SC 29901
Ph:(843)474-0147
Free: 800-368-3382
Fax:(843)986-9093
Co. E-mail: bpendergraft@envmedia.com
URL: http://www.envmedia.com
Price: $12.95. **Description:** Part of a ten-volume teaching aid for environmental education that presents the birth and growth of different animal groups in a manner appropriate for young children. Covers chickens, pigs, calves, and lambs. **Availability:** VHS.

3977 ■ *See How They Grow: Forest Animals*
Environmental Media
PO Box 99
Beaufort, SC 29901
Ph:(843)474-0147
Free: 800-368-3382
Fax:(843)986-9093
Co. E-mail: bpendergraft@envmedia.com
URL: http://www.envmedia.com
Price: $12.95. **Description:** Part of a ten-volume teaching aid for environmental education that presents the birth and growth of different animal groups in a manner appropriate for young children. Covers owls, mice, ants, and chipmunks. **Availability:** VHS.

3978 ■ *See How They Grow: Insects and Spiders*
Environmental Media
PO Box 99
Beaufort, SC 29901
Ph:(843)474-0147
Free: 800-368-3382
Fax:(843)986-9093
Co. E-mail: bpendergraft@envmedia.com
URL: http://www.envmedia.com
Price: $12.95. **Description:** Part of a ten-volume teaching aid for environmental education that presents the birth and growth of different animal groups in a manner appropriate for young children. Covers ladybugs, spiders, butterflies, and grasshoppers. **Availability:** VHS.

3979 ■ *See How They Grow: Pets*
Environmental Media
PO Box 99
Beaufort, SC 29901
Ph:(843)474-0147
Free: 800-368-3382
Fax:(843)986-9093
Co. E-mail: bpendergraft@envmedia.com
URL: http://www.envmedia.com
Price: $12.95. **Description:** Part of a ten-volume teaching aid for environmental education that presents the birth and growth of different animal groups in a manner appropriate for young children. Covers puppies, kittens, parakeets, and goldfish. **Availability:** VHS.

3980 ■ *See How They Grow: Pond Animals*
Environmental Media
PO Box 99
Beaufort, SC 29901
Ph:(843)474-0147
Free: 800-368-3382
Fax:(843)986-9093
Co. E-mail: bpendergraft@envmedia.com
URL: http://www.envmedia.com
Price: $12.95. **Description:** Part of a ten-volume teaching aid for environmental education that presents the birth and growth of different animal groups in a manner appropriate for young children. Covers dragonflies, frogs, ducks, and salamanders. **Availability:** VHS.

3981 ■ *See How They Grow: Wild Animals*
Environmental Media
PO Box 99
Beaufort, SC 29901
Ph:(843)474-0147
Free: 800-368-3382
Fax:(843)986-9093
Co. E-mail: bpendergraft@envmedia.com
URL: http://www.envmedia.com
Price: $12.95. **Description:** Part of a ten-volume teaching aid for environmental education that presents the birth and growth of different animal groups in a manner appropriate for young children. Covers rabbits, foxes, pheasants, and snakes. **Availability:** VHS.

3982 ■ *So Smart*
Tapeworm Video Distributors
25876 The Old Road 141
Stevenson Ranch, CA 91381
Ph:(661)257-4904
Fax:(661)257-4820
Co. E-mail: sales@tapeworm.com
URL: http://www.tapeworm.com
Released: 1997. **Price:** $14.95. **Description:** Infant stimulation video designed to enhance intellectual development. **Availability:** VHS.

3983 ■ *S.O.S. Kids: Infant/Child Emergency Life Saving Video*
Tapeworm Video Distributors
25876 The Old Road 141
Stevenson Ranch, CA 91381
Ph:(661)257-4904
Fax:(661)257-4820
Co. E-mail: sales@tapeworm.com
URL: http://www.tapeworm.com
Released: 1997. **Price:** $19.95. **Description:** EMT Paramedic Richard Hardman describes and demonstrates what to do in various medical emergencies. **Availability:** VHS.

3984 ■ *Table Time for Tots*
Tapeworm Video Distributors
25876 The Old Road 141
Stevenson Ranch, CA 91381

Ph:(661)257-4904
Fax:(661)257-4820
Co. E-mail: sales@tapeworm.com
URL: http://www.tapeworm.com

Released: 1997. **Price:** $14.95. **Description:** Introduces children to the basic food groups using poem and song. **Availability:** VHS.

3985 ■ *Wilbur Sings the Classics*
Tapeworm Video Distributors
25876 The Old Road 141
Stevenson Ranch, CA 91381
Ph:(661)257-4904
Fax:(661)257-4820
Co. E-mail: sales@tapeworm.com
URL: http://www.tapeworm.com

Released: 1997. **Price:** $14.95. **Description:** Wilbur the Cow leads children in singing nursery rhyme favorites. **Availability:** VHS.

3986 ■ *Wilton Appreciation Series 100—Grades K-4*
Crystal Productions
1812 Johns Dr.
Box 2159
Glenview, IL 60025-6519
Ph:(847)657-8144
Free: 800-255-8629
Fax:(847)657-8149
Co. E-mail: custserv@crystalproductions.com
URL: http://www.crystalproductions.com

Price: $199.00. **Description:** Still-frame teaching aid for art appreciation introduces children to the elements of design. **Availability:** VHS.

TRADE SHOWS AND CONVENTIONS

3987 ■ Association for Childhood Education International Annual International Conference & Exhibition
Association for Childhood Education International
17904 Georgia Ave., Ste. 215
Olney, MD 20832
Ph:(301)570-2111
Free: 800-423-3563
Fax:(301)570-2212
Co. E-mail: headquarters@acei.org
URL: http://www.acei.org

Released: Annual. **Audience:** Teachers, teacher educators, day-care personnel, and related professionals. **Principal Exhibits:** Commercial and educational exhibits of interest to teachers, teacher educators, college students, daycare personnel and other care givers.

3988 ■ National Association for the Education of Young Children Annual Conference
National Association for the Education of Young Children
1313 L St. NW, Ste. 500
Washington, DC 20005
Ph:(202)232-8777
Free: 800-424-2460
Fax:(202)328-1846
Co. E-mail: naeyc@naeyc.org
URL: http://www.naeyc.org

Released: Annual. **Audience:** Professionals in early childhood education. **Principal Exhibits:** Educational materials and equipment designed for children ages birth through eight years old. **Dates and Locations:** 2011 Nov 02-05, Orlando, FL.

FRANCHISES AND BUSINESS OPPORTUNITIES

3989 ■ Baby Power / Forever Kids
Searles Corp.
PO Box 526
Annandale, NJ 08801
Ph:(908)713-6547
Free: 800-365-4847
Fax:(908)713-6547

No. of Franchise Units: 5. **Founded:** 1975. **Franchised:** 1998. **Description:** Developmentally appropriate gymnastic & musical parent/child play and enrichment programs. Carefully designed to build confidence and promote child development, parent communication and bonding. The purpose of the Baby Power program is to stimulate during the most formative growth period 6 months to 3 years. The Forever Kids programs at Baby Power are designed to develop the second phase in a child's development, 3-5 years. **Equity Capital Needed:** $85,000-$105,000, total investment. **Franchise Fee:** $25,000. **Financial Assistance:** No. **Training:** Yes.

3990 ■ Children's Lighthouse Franchise Co.
101 S Jennings
Fort Worth, TX 76104
Ph:(817)247-0886
Free: 888-338-4466
Fax:(817)887-5772

No. of Franchise Units: 30. **No. of Company-Owned Units:** 8. **Founded:** 1997. **Franchised:** 1999. **Description:** Childcare franchise. **Equity Capital Needed:** $150,000 minimum liquid assets; $500,000 net worth. **Franchise Fee:** $50,000. **Financial Assistance:** No. **Training:** Yes. s.

3991 ■ CHIP - The Child ID Program
30961 Agoura Rd., No. 101
Westlake Village, CA 91361
Ph:(805)557-0577
Fax:(805)557-0587

No. of Franchise Units: 152. **No. of Company-Owned Units:** 1. **Founded:** 2001. **Franchised:** 2002. **Description:** Child ID and school safety program. **Equity Capital Needed:** $10,990-$14,990. **Franchise Fee:** $10,990-$14,990. **Financial Assistance:** Limited in-house financial assistance available. **Training:** Yes.

3992 ■ CLIX (TM)
COMON Group, Inc.
2496 W Ridge Rd.
Rochester, NY 14626
Ph:(585)262-2549
Free: 888-2GO-CLIX
Fax:(203)413-6311
Co. E-mail: franchise@getyourclix.com
URL: http://www.clixfranchise.com

No. of Franchise Units: 8. **Founded:** 1999. **Franchised:** 2005. **Description:** Dedicated to creating a digital portrait experience like no other. With the latest in technology, a proprietary proven system, and focus on service and our customer's experience. Offering a unique multifaceted business opportunity. **Equity Capital Needed:** $50,184-$398,000. **Franchise Fee:** $21,000 or $29,500. **Financial Assistance:** No. **Training:** Training includes pre-opening, store set-up and onsite training.

3993 ■ College Nannies & Tutors
Franchise Development Group
1415 Wayzata Blvd., E
Wayzata, MN 55391
Ph:(952)476-0262
Free: 888-92N-anny
Fax:(952)476-0264

No. of Franchise Units: 42. **Founded:** 2001. **Franchised:** 2005. **Description:** Childcare and academic support. **Equity Capital Needed:** $50,000-$125,000. **Franchise Fee:** $25,000-$35,000. **Financial Assistance:** No. **Training:** Yes.

3994 ■ Creative World School Franchising Co., Inc.
Creative World School, Inc.
25110 Bernwood Dr., St. 104
Bonita Springs, FL 34135
Ph:(561)755-3635
Free: 800-362-5940
Fax:(239)437-0507
URL: http://www.creativeworldschool.com

No. of Franchise Units: 9. **No. of Company-Owned Units:** 11. **Founded:** 1970. **Franchised:** 2000. **Description:** Childcare centers. **Equity Capital Needed:** $200,000+. **Franchise Fee:** $50,000. **Financial Assistance:** No. **Training:** Extensive training at our facility and onsite staff training at your location with ongoing support.

3995 ■ DigiKids
DIGIKIDS, INC.
9463 Hwy. 377 S, Ste. 111
Fort Worth, TX 76126
Free: 888-DIGI-KIDS
Fax:(817)886-3655

No. of Franchise Units: 11. **Founded:** 2003. **Franchised:** 2004. **Description:** Onsite child safety ID program. **Equity Capital Needed:** $30,000 single territory; $50,000 master franchise. **Franchise Fee:** $26,500. **Financial Assistance:** No. **Training:** Yes.

3996 ■ Goddard School
Goddard Systems
1016 9th Ave.
King of Prussia, PA 19406
Free: 800-272-4901
Fax:(610)265-6931

No. of Franchise Units: 290. **Founded:** 1988. **Franchised:** 1988. **Description:** High-quality pre-school, offering day care hours. All Goddard teachers hold 4-year degrees in early childhood or elementary education. **Equity Capital Needed:** $120,000 liquid; $477,260-$524,600 total investment. **Franchise Fee:** $135,000. **Financial Assistance:** Help with document preparation. **Training:** Yes.

3997 ■ Guard-A-Kid
Guard-A-Kid Franchising Corp.
3785 NW 82nd Ave., Ste. 106
Miami, FL 33166
Ph:(305)477-3301
Free: 800-679-4256
Fax:(305)489-0311

No. of Franchise Units: 155. **Founded:** 2004. **Franchised:** 2005. **Description:** Digital child identification and safety program. **Equity Capital Needed:** $15,000-$27,900. **Franchise Fee:** $14,900-$24,900. **Financial Assistance:** Limited third party financing available. **Training:** Provides 2 days training at headquarters, including monthly conference calls, bi-weekly workshops, and ongoing support.

3998 ■ Gymboree Play and Music
Gymboree Corp.
500 Howard St.
San Francisco, CA 94105
Ph:(415)278-7925
Fax:(415)278-7452
Co. E-mail: play_franchise@gymboree.com
URL: http://www.gymboree.com

No. of Franchise Units: 658. **No. of Company-Owned Units:** 8. **Founded:** 1976. **Franchised:** 1978. **Description:** Parent and child participation play & music program. Specialized equipment, songs and games. Classes offered for children - newborn through 5 years of age. **Equity Capital Needed:** $77,000-$270,950. **Franchise Fee:** $45,000/$25,000 metro model. **Financial Assistance:** No. **Training:** Offers initial training and also regional training. Franchises receive continued support in programming, operations, and marketing.

3999 ■ The Honors Learning Center
PO Box 24055
Chattanooga, TN 37422-4055
Ph:(423)892-1803
Fax:(423)892-1803

No. of Franchise Units: 1. **Founded:** 1987. **Franchised:** 1992. **Description:** Supplemental education and academic testing. **Equity Capital Needed:** $64,500-$68,700. **Franchise Fee:** $25,000. **Financial Assistance:** No. **Training:** Yes.

4000 ■ JumpBunch, Inc.
302 Annapolis St.
Annapolis, MD 21401
Ph:(410)703-2300
Free: (866)826-5645

Fax:(410)268-0465
Co. E-mail: tbunchman@jumpbunch.com
URL: http://www.jumpbunch.com

No. of Franchise Units: 28. **Founded:** 1997. **Franchised:** 2002. **Description:** Teaching sports and fitness to children. **Equity Capital Needed:** $75,000. **Franchise Fee:** $25,000-$30,000. **Financial Assistance:** No. **Training:** Yes.

4001 ■ J.W. Tumbles
312 S Cedros, Ste. 329
Solana Beach, CA 92075
Ph:(858)794-0484
Fax:(858)794-0398

No. of Franchise Units: 33. **No. of Company-Owned Units:** 1. **Founded:** 1994. **Franchised:** 2004. **Description:** Children's gym for fitness & fun. **Equity Capital Needed:** $138,600-$215,600. **Franchise Fee:** $42,850. **Financial Assistance:** No. **Training:** Yes.

4002 ■ Kid to Kid
BaseCamp Franchising, LLC
170 S 1000 E
Salt Lake City, UT 84102
Ph:(801)359-0071
Free: 888-543-2543
Fax:(801)359-3207
Co. E-mail: sterling@kidtokid.com
URL: http://www.kidtokid.com

No. of Franchise Units: 72. **No. of Company-Owned Units:** 1. **Founded:** 1992. **Franchised:** 1994. **Description:** Resale store for children's clothing and toys. **Equity Capital Needed:** $196,028-$272,718. **Franchise Fee:** $25,000. **Royalty Fee:** 5%. **Financial Assistance:** Third party financing available. **Training:** Offers 10 days at headquarters, 3 days at franchisee's location, 5 days at existing location, and ongoing support.

4003 ■ Kiddie Academy Child Care Learning Centers
3415 Box Hill Corporate Ctr. Dr.
Abingdon, MD 21009
Ph:(410)515-0788
Free: 800-554-3343
Fax:(410)569-1448
Co. E-mail: sales@kiddieacademy.com
URL: http://www.kiddieacademy.com

No. of Franchise Units: 100. **No. of Company-Owned Units:** 2. **Founded:** 1981. **Franchised:** 1992. **Description:** Offers an advanced, tested, state-of-the-art curriculum incorporating traditional development milestones, with emphasis on reading skills, language development and social skills. Classes in computers and foreign languages. Infant through age 12. **Equity Capital Needed:** $180,000 liquid; $342,600-$643,500 investment required. **Franchise Fee:** $50,000. **Royalty Fee:** 7%. **Financial Assistance:** Identified third party lenders to provide financing to franchisees and will assist in developing a business plan and loan packaging. **Managerial Assistance:** Assists with demographic and competitive surveys, site selection, lease negotiation, staff recruitment, training, licensing, grand-opening, accounting, marketing, advertising and curriculum. Turn-key program provides full support. **Training:** Yes.

4004 ■ Kidokinetics
304 Indian Trace, Ste. 121
Weston, FL 33326
Ph:(954)385-8511
Free: 888-kid-okin
Fax:(954)217-5928

No. of Franchise Units: 3. **No. of Company-Owned Units:** 1. **Founded:** 2000. **Franchised:** 2006. **Description:** Children's mobile sports/fitness. **Equity Capital Needed:** $42,900-$57,000. **Franchise Fee:** $30,000. **Financial Assistance:** No. **Training:** Yes.

4005 ■ Kidspark, Inc.
2858 Stevens Creek Blvd., Ste. 100
San Jose, CA 95128
Ph:(408)213-0973
Fax:(408)260-7366

No. of Franchise Units: 14. **No. of Company-Owned Units:** 2. **Founded:** 1988. **Franchised:** 2004. **Description:** Hourly childcare. **Equity Capital Needed:** $172,500-$300,000. **Franchise Fee:** $19,500. **Financial Assistance:** No. **Training:** Yes.

4006 ■ Kinderdance International, Inc.
1333 Gateway Dr., Ste. 1003
Melbourne, FL 32901
Ph:(321)984-4448
Free: 800-554-2334
Fax:(321)984-4490
Co. E-mail: leads@kinderdance.com
URL: http://www.kinderdance.com

No. of Franchise Units: 131. **No. of Company-Owned Units:** 2. **Founded:** 1979. **Franchised:** 1985. **Description:** If you enjoy children and have high energy, you can qualify to join in the quality preschool education through dance, gymnastics and creative movement. No studio required. The program has been taught to thousands of children in hundreds of child-care centers since 1979. Enjoy flexible hours, fulfilling work and adorable customers. Rated one of the top 15 franchises for women by Working Woman Magazine. 24-hours a day, an operations manual, newsletters and active franchisee advisory counsel. **Equity Capital Needed:** $14,950-$46,100, including franchise fee. **Franchise Fee:** $12,000-$40,000. **Financial Assistance:** Third party financing available. **Training:** 1 week training class, field support, ongoing support and an annual training conference provides continuing education.

4007 ■ Little City Kids LLC
10127 Northwestern Ave.
Franksville, WI 53126
Ph:(262)884-4226
Fax:(262)884-4230
Co. E-mail: littlecitykids@tds.net
URL: http://www.littlecitykids.com

No. of Company-Owned Units: 1. **Founded:** 1998. **Franchised:** 2004. **Description:** Educational playcare for your child. The environment is set into action in an interactive world filled with imagination stations, innovative online curriculum and team teaching methods. We offer two models, the Little City Kids model is for children ages 2-13 years and the Itty Bitty Kids model adds infant and toddler care. **Equity Capital Needed:** $118,000-$189,000. **Franchise Fee:** $35,000. **Royalty Fee:** 7%. **Financial Assistance:** No. **Training:** Thorough training includes administrative and facility management, operating procedures, development procedures, staff hiring, curriculum and team teaching methods.

4008 ■ The Little Gym
7001 N Scottsdale Rd., Ste. 1050
Scottsdale, AZ 85253
Ph:(480)948-2878
Free: 888-228-2878
Fax:(480)948-2765
Co. E-mail: sales@thelittlegym.com
URL: http://www.thelittlegym.com

No. of Franchise Units: 219. **No. of Company-Owned Units:** 2. **Founded:** 1976. **Franchised:** 1992. **Description:** Children's fitness centers. **Equity Capital Needed:** $147,500-$294,000. **Franchise Fee:** $39,500-$69,500. **Royalty Fee:** 8%. **Financial Assistance:** Third party financing available. **Training:** Yes.

4009 ■ Little Scientists
25 Higgins Dr.
Milford, CT 06460
Ph:(203)783-1114
Free: 800-FAC-TFUN
Fax:(203)397-2165

No. of Franchise Units: 20. **No. of Company-Owned Units:** 2. **Founded:** 1995. **Franchised:** 1996. **Description:** Hands-on science education for children. **Equity Capital Needed:** $25,000-$50,000. **Franchise Fee:** $25,000. **Financial Assistance:** No. **Training:** Yes.

4010 ■ Oxford Learning Centers
747 Hyde Park Rd., Ste. 230
London, ON, Canada N6H 3S3
Ph:(519)473-1207
Free: 888-559-2212
Fax:(519)473-6086
Co. E-mail: franchise@oxfordlearning.com
URL: http://www.oxfordlearning.com

No. of Franchise Units: 104. **No. of Company-Owned Units:** 5. **Founded:** 1984. **Franchised:** 1991. **Description:** Oxford is an educational franchise in Canada, which provides extensive training in all fields. **Equity Capital Needed:** $140,000-$210,000 + applicable taxes. **Franchise Fee:** $40,000 + applicable taxes. **Training:** Provides 2 weeks training and ongoing support.

4011 ■ Pee Wee Workout
Cardiac Carr Co.
34976 Aspenwood Ln.
Willoughby, OH 44094
Ph:(440)946-7888
Fax:(440)946-7888

No. of Franchise Units: 25. **No. of Company-Owned Units:** 1. **Founded:** 1986. **Franchised:** 1987. **Description:** Fitness programs for children. **Equity Capital Needed:** $2,700. **Franchise Fee:** $2,000. **Financial Assistance:** No. **Training:** Yes.

4012 ■ Primrose School Franchising Co.
3660 Cedarcrest Rd.
Acworth, GA 30101
Ph:(770)529-4100
Free: 800-PRI-MROS
Fax:(770)529-1551
Co. E-mail: kmusso@primroseschools.com
URL: http://www.primroseschools.com

No. of Franchise Units: 200+. **No. of Company-Owned Units:** 1. **Founded:** 1982. **Franchised:** 1989. **Description:** Quality educational childcare, with proven, traditional curriculum for infants through 4/5 kindergarten, after-school explorers club ages 5-12 years, Spanish, computer intergenerational program and strong parental communication. Programs develop positive self-esteem and a joy of learning. ongoing after opening. **Equity Capital Needed:** $350,000 minimum liquid assets; $500,000 net worth; $2,800,000-$4,200,000 (includes land/building). **Franchise Fee:** $70,000. **Financial Assistance:** No. **Managerial Assistance:** Day-to-day business management and online Intranet, manuals, support materials and other communication tools. **Training:** Initial training and ongoing support.

4013 ■ Pump It Up - The Inflatable Party Zone
PIU Management, LLC
1860 W University Dr., Ste. 108
Tempe, AZ 85281
Free: (866)635-0029
Fax:(480)371-1201
Co. E-mail: info@pumpitupparty.com
URL: http://www.pumpitupparty.com

No. of Franchise Units: 160. **Franchised:** 2002. **Description:** Offers a unique way to celebrate children's milestones. With interactive inflateables in a clean, private party facility. We take care of organization, child supervision, party setup & clean up. Offers entrepreneurs a unique, differentiated brand backed by an experienced, dedicated franchise development team. **Equity Capital Needed:** $304,550-$703,900, includes franchise fee. **Franchise Fee:** $40,000. **Financial Assistance:** No. **Training:** Training both onsite and at our main offices. Training includes logistics, sales, marketing and more. Ongoing phone support is provided.

4014 ■ Reading Friends Franchise Co.
Reading Friends Holdings Co. L.L.C.
5228 Pershing
Fort Worth, TX 76107
Ph:(817)738-9430
Fax:(817)732-2079

No. of Franchise Units: 4. **No. of Company-Owned Units:** 1. **Founded:** 1980. **Franchised:** 2002. **Description:** Preschool for children. **Equity Capital Needed:** $119,000-$325,000. **Franchise Fee:** $35,000. **Training:** Yes.

4015 ■ Sunbrook Academy
Sunbrook Franchising Inc.
2933 Cherokee St., Ste. 100
Kennesaw, GA 30144
Ph:(770)426-0619
Fax:(770)426-0724
Co. E-mail: info@sunbrookacademy.com
URL: http://www.sunbrookacademy.com
No. of Franchise Units: 8. **No. of Company-Owned Units:** 3. **Founded:** 1984. **Franchised:** 1999. **Description:** Provider of childcare programs. **Equity Capital Needed:** $250,000-$450,000. **Franchise Fee:** $55,000. **Financial Assistance:** Several interested third party lenders and have received SBA approval. Also provide assistance with business plan, and loan package. **Managerial Assistance:** Provides operations manuals, pre-opening manuals, marketing manuals, all forms, documents, and handbooks. **Training:** 21 day training program prior to opening, and 30 days onsite training with ongoing assistance after opening.

LIBRARIES

4016 ■ BOCES–Putnam/Northern Westchester–BOCES Professional Library (200 B)
200 BOCES Dr.
Yorktown Heights, NY 10598-4399
Ph:(914)245-2700
Fax:(914)248-4519
Co. E-mail: mfeldman@pnwboces.org
URL: http://www.pnwboces.org
Contact: Anita Feldman, Pres.
Scope: Education, child psychology. **Services:** Interlibrary loan; copying; Library open to the public with restrictions (reference use only for those not residing or working in the 18 school districts). **Holdings:** 8000 books; 16,000 bound periodical volumes; 300,000 nonbook items. **Subscriptions:** 119 journals and other serials.

4017 ■ Georgetown University–Maternal and Child Health Library
PO Box 571272
2115 Wisconsin Ave. NW, Ste. 601
Washington, DC 20057-1272
Ph:(202)784-9770
Free: 877-624-1935
Fax:(202)784-9777
Co. E-mail: mchgroup@georgetown.edu
URL: http://www.mchlibrary.info
Contact: Olivia K. Pickett, Dir., Lib.Svcs.
Scope: Maternal and child health - genetics, prenatal care, adolescent health, chronic illness/disability, developmental disabilities, infant mortality, nutrition, violence and injury prevention, child health, women's health, public health. **Services:** Library open to health professionals; responds to requests from the public. **Holdings:** 20,000 books; ephemeral literature; reports from state MCH agencies and discretionary grants of the U.S. Maternal and Child Health Bureau; manuscripts; microfiche; microfilm; archives. **Subscriptions:** 100 journals and other serials.

4018 ■ Illinois Early Childhood Intervention Clearinghouse Library
Early Childhood and Parenting Collaborative
University of Illinois at Urbana-Champaign
Children's Research Ctr., Rm. 20
51 Gerty Dr.
Champaign, IL 61820-7469
Ph:(217)333-1386
Free: 877-275-3227
Fax:(217)244-7732
Co. E-mail: illinois-eic@illlnois.edu
URL: http://www.eiclearinghouse.org/library.html
Contact: Logan Moore, Libn.
Scope: Early childhood, at-risk children, developmental disabilities. **Services:** Interlibrary loan; copying; clearinghouse open to Illinois residents. **Holdings:** 9850 books; 1785 audiovisuals. **Subscriptions:** 20 journals and other serials.

RESEARCH CENTERS

4019 ■ Arizona State University–Child Development Laboratory
PO Box 873701
Tempe, AZ 85287-3701
Ph:(480)965-7257
Fax:(480)965-6779
Co. E-mail: mary.zuzich@asu.edu
URL: http://sites.google.com/a/asu.edu/asu-child-development-lab
Contact: Mary Zuzich, Asst.Dir.
E-mail: mary.zuzich@asu.edu
Scope: Children and their families, including emotional development, sex-role development, parent-child interaction, and children and television. Provides surrounding communities with an extended day program for children 3 through 6 years and acts as a research and training center for professionals who work with the children and their families. **Educational Activities:** Parent Education Seminars.

4020 ■ Arizona State University–Child Study Laboratory
Department of Psychology
950 S McAllister
PO Box 871104
Tempe, AZ 85287-1104
Ph:(480)965-5320
Fax:(480)965-8544
URL: http://psychology.clas.asu.edu/csl
Contact: Beth Wiley, Dir.
Scope: Children and, in some studies, their parents. Conducts a preschool program for children from Tempe and surrounding communities who are 15 months through five years of age.

4021 ■ Jewish Board of Family and Children's Services, Inc.–Child Development Center
120 W 57th St., 11 Fl.
New York, NY 10019
Ph:(212)632-4733
Free: 888—523-2769
Fax:(212)632-4534
Co. E-mail: admin@jbfcs.org
URL: http://www.jbfcs.com
Contact: Marian Davidson-Amodeo, Dir.
E-mail: admin@jbfcs.org
Scope: Therapeutic and educational techniques for emotionally disturbed, language-impaired, and central nervous system-impaired children; development of criteria for assessment and monitoring; and onsite group treatment of preschool children in daycare centers. **Educational Activities:** Early Childhood Workshops, for early childhood educators and related service providers; Institute for Infants, Toddlers, and Parents, a two-year, post-graduate training program.

4022 ■ University of California at Berkeley–Institute of Human Development–Harold E. Jones Child Study Center
2425 Atherton St., No. 6070
Berkeley, CA 94720-6070
Ph:(510)642-7031
Fax:(510)643-7350
Co. E-mail: lisabranum@berkeley.edu
URL: http://ihd.berkeley.edu/child.htm
Contact: Lisa Branum
E-mail: lisabranum@berkeley.edu
Scope: Developmental psychology, physical growth, and sociology of preschoolers. **Educational Activities:** Conducts two preschool classrooms.; Research in child development (annually).

4023 ■ University of Georgia–Institute for Behavioral Research–Center for Family Research
1095 College Station Rd.
Athens, GA 30602
Ph:(706)425-2992
Free: 888—542-3068
Fax:(706)425-2985
Co. E-mail: gbrody@uga.edu
URL: http://www.cfr.uga.edu
Contact: Gene H. Brody PhD, Dir.
E-mail: gbrody@uga.edu
Scope: Family study, including topics such as divorce rates, women entering the work force, isolation of the family, child abuse and incest, governmental family welfare programs, daycare, and family care for elderly parents. **Educational Activities:** Colloquium (annually); Seminar Series (monthly).

ASSOCIATIONS AND OTHER ORGANIZATIONS

4024 ■ National Chimney Sweep Guild
2155 Commercial Dr.
Plainfield, IN 46168
Ph:(317)837-1500
Fax:(317)837-5365
Co. E-mail: mmcsweeney@ncsg.org
URL: http://www.ncsg.org
Contact: Mark T. McSweeney CAE, Exec. Dir.
Description: Individuals in the chimney service profession. Provides an opportunity for chimney service professionals to learn about technical aspects of trade and new equipment, and to share ideas for building strong businesses and promoting chimney safety. Conducts training and certification seminars. **Publications:** *Newslink* (monthly); *Sweeping* (monthly).

Christmas Decoration Store

STATISTICAL SOURCES

4025 ■ *RMA Annual Statement Studies*
Pub: Robert Morris Associates (RMA)
Released: Annual. **Price:** $175.00 2006-07 edition, $105.00. **Description:** Contains composite balance sheets and income statements for more than 360 industries, including the accounting, auditing, and bookkeeping industries. Also contains five years of comparative historical data for discerning trends. Includes 16 commonly used ratios, computed for most of the size groupings for nearly every industry.

TRADE SHOWS AND CONVENTIONS

4026 ■ Annual Dickens Christmas Show and Festivals Week
Leisure Time Unlimited, Inc.
708 Main St.
PO Box 332
Myrtle Beach, SC 29577
Ph:(843)448-9483
Free: 800-261-5591
Fax:(843)626-1513
Co. E-mail: dickensshow@sc.rr.com
Released: Annual. **Audience:** General public. **Principal Exhibits:** Crafts, art, paintings, gifts, and Christmas related items. **Dates and Locations:** 2011 Nov 10-13, Myrtle Beach, SC.

4027 ■ Christmas Gift and Hobby Show
HSI Show Productions
PO Box 502797
Indianapolis, IN 46250
Ph:(317)576-9933
Free: 800-215-1700
Fax:(317)576-9955
Co. E-mail: info@hsishows.com
URL: http://www.hsishows.com
Released: Annual. **Audience:** General public. **Principal Exhibits:** Art, crafts, and giftware.

4028 ■ Holiday Fair
Textile Hall Corp.
PO Box 5823
Greenville, SC 29606
Ph:(864)331-2277
Fax:(864)331-2282
Co. E-mail: atmei@textilehall.com
Released: Annual. **Audience:** General public. **Principal Exhibits:** Arts and crafts.

4029 ■ Southern Christmas Show
Southern Shows, Inc.
PO Box 36859
Charlotte, NC 28236
Ph:(704)376-6594
Free: 800-849-0248
Fax:(704)376-6345
Co. E-mail: sabernethy@southernshows.com
URL: http://www.southernshows.com
Released: Annual. **Audience:** General public. **Principal Exhibits:** Christmas gifts, crafts, arts, foods, and educational materials, Christmas tree lane, and decorating competitions, and Santa Claus. **Dates and Locations:** 2011 Nov 10-20, Charlotte, NC.

FRANCHISES AND BUSINESS OPPORTUNITIES

4030 ■ Christmas Decor Inc.
The Decor Group
PO Box 5946
Lubbock, TX 79408-5946
Ph:(806)722-1225
Free: 800-687-9551
Fax:(806)722-9627
Co. E-mail: info@thedecorgroup.com
URL: http://www.christmasdecor.com
No. of Franchise Units: 240. **Founded:** 1984. **Franchised:** 1996. **Description:** Holiday and event decorations. **Equity Capital Needed:** $13,150-$35,350. **Franchise Fee:** $5,000. **Royalty Fee:** 5%. **Financial Assistance:** No. **Training:** 4 day quick start training at headquarters, 4 days at regional locations and ongoing support.

ASSOCIATIONS AND OTHER ORGANIZATIONS

4031 ■ National Christmas Tree Association
16020 Swingley Ridge Rd., Ste. 300
Chesterfield, MO 63017
Ph:(636)449-5070
Fax:(636)449-5051
Co. E-mail: info@realchristmastrees.org
URL: http://www.realchristmastrees.org
Contact: Rick Dungey
Description: Exists to promote the use of real Christmas trees and support the industry that provides them. Includes grower-wholesalers, grower-retailers, and all other retailers that sell real Christmas trees and related green products. Sponsors National Christmas Tree Contest. Maintains information and referral service and provides the option of liability insurance for retailers, and choose and cut growers. **Publications:** *American Christmas Tree Journal* (quarterly).

REFERENCE WORKS

4032 ■ *Pacific Northwest Christmas Tree Association Buy-Sell Directory*
Pub: Pacific Northwest Christmas Tree Association
Released: Annual, April. **Price:** Free. **Covers:** Christmas tree sellers and buyers in Washington, Oregon, California, Idaho, and southwestern Canada. **Entries Include:** For sellers—Farm or company name, address, phone, name and title of contact, number of acres, year established, number of trees for sale by species. For buyers—Company or individual name, address, phone, name and title of contact, number of trees to be purchased by species. **Arrangement:** Separate alphabetical seller and buyer sections.

TRADE PERIODICALS

4033 ■ *American Christmas Tree Journal*
Pub: National Christmas Tree Association
Released: Quarterly. **Price:** $57 U.S., Canada, and Mexico; $92 other countries; $37 members. **Description:** Christmas tree industry trade magazine covering growing, harvesting, and retailing.

4034 ■ *Christmas Trees*
Pub: Tree Publishers Inc.
Released: Quarterly. **Price:** $25; $48 two years; $6.25 U.S., Canada, and Mexico single; $25 Canada and Mexico; $48 Canada and Mexico 2 years; $45 other countries; $75 other countries two years; $9.25 single issue and other countries. **Description:** Magazine covering the Christmas tree industry.

4035 ■ *NAA Reporter*
Pub: Tree Care Industry Association
Ed: Peter Gerstenberger, Editor. **Released:** Monthly. **Price:** Included in membership. **Description:** Concerned with the profession of arboriculture. Provides information on "recognized methods of tree care, new products and services, effective business management, and kindred activities of the association."

4036 ■ *The Treeworker*
Pub: Tree Care Industry Association
Contact: B. Rouse
Ed: Robert Rouse, Editor, rouse@natlarb.com. **Released:** Monthly. **Price:** $24.95, Included in membership. **Description:** Provides practical information on worker safety, tree care techniques, skills development, general knowledge of trees, and occupational safety and health in tree care operations.

CONSULTANTS

4037 ■ Hutchison Forestry Inc.
1627 Shackett Rd.
Leicester, VT 05733
Ph:(802)247-3117
Free: 800-439-3117
Co. E-mail: info@mountpleasantmaple.com
URL: http://www.mountpleasantmaple.com
Contact: Hutchison Forestry, Principle
Scope: Consulting forester offering counsel on timber and woodland management and Christmas tree management. Serves private industries as well as government agencies.

4038 ■ Joseph Grahame
PO Box 503
Elkins, WV 26241-3833
Ph:(304)636-6672
Fax:(304)636-9337
Co. E-mail: jgrahame@foreconinc.com
E-mail: jgrahame@foreconinc.com
Scope: Provides services including timber cruises and appraisals, fire damage appraisals, trespass appraisals, timber sales, forest and game management, forest litigation, wild land surveying, logging road design, court house research and mapping of large surface and mineral ownerships. Serves private industries as well as government agencies.

4039 ■ Timmerlinn Inc.
18 Saint-Henri E
Sainte-Agathe-des-Monts, QC, Canada J8H 1S9
Ph:(819)326-3559
Fax:(819)326-3602
Contact: Garage M. Boyer, Principle
Scope: Offers counsel, planning and management of renewable resources to private land owners, municipalities, governments and companies in forestry, recreation and wildlife. Main activities include forest resource inventories and plans, timber brokerage, silviculture, reforestation, re-vegetation, land reclamation, maple syrup production, Christmas tree production, soil studies, planning of parks, ski areas, and other recreation facilities. The firm has considerable experience in erosion control and forestry work. **Seminars:** Marketing Forestry Services to Private Land Owners.

FRANCHISES AND BUSINESS OPPORTUNITIES

4040 ■ Christmas Decor Inc.
The Decor Group
PO Box 5946
Lubbock, TX 79408-5946
Ph:(806)722-1225
Free: 800-687-9551
Fax:(806)722-9627
Co. E-mail: info@thedecorgroup.com
URL: http://www.christmasdecor.com
No. of Franchise Units: 240. **Founded:** 1984. **Franchised:** 1996. **Description:** Holiday and event decorations. **Equity Capital Needed:** $13,150-$35,350. **Franchise Fee:** $5,000. **Royalty Fee:** 5%. **Financial Assistance:** No. **Training:** 4 day quick start training at headquarters, 4 days at regional locations and ongoing support.

RESEARCH CENTERS

4041 ■ Purdue University–Southeast-Purdue Agricultural Center
4425 E County Rd. 350 N
PO Box 216
Butlerville, IN 47223-0216
Ph:(812)458-6977
Fax:(812)458-6979
Co. E-mail: biehled@purdue.edu
URL: http://www.agriculture.purdue.edu/pac/sepac/index.html
Contact: Donald J. Biehle, Supt.
E-mail: biehled@purdue.edu
Scope: Soils and crops, including soil drainage, water quality, tillage, fertility, varieties, insects, diseases, and weeds. Forestry research includes studies on Christmas trees, walnuts, and oaks. **Educational Activities:** Field and Research Report Days (annually).

4042 ■ Texas A&M University–Texas Forest Service
John B. Connally Bldg., Ste. 364
301 Tarrow, Ste. 364
College Station, TX 77840-7896
Ph:(979)458-6606
Fax:(979)458-6610
Co. E-mail: tboggus@tfs.tamu.edu
URL: http://txforestservice.tamu.edu/main/default.aspx
Contact: Thomas G. Boggus, Dir.
E-mail: tboggus@tfs.tamu.edu
Scope: Tree production.

4043 ■ University of Wisconsin—Madison–Hancock Agricultural Research Station
N3909 County Rd. V
Hancock, WI 54943
Ph:(715)249-5961

Fax:(715)249-5850
Co. E-mail: lemere@wisc.edu
URL: http://www.ars.wisc.edu/hancock
Contact: Mary LeMere, Interim Supt.
E-mail: lemere@wisc.edu
Scope: Potato, vegetable, and fruit production under irrigation. Integrated efforts are directed at refining cultural practices to control wind erosion and eliminate groundwater contamination.

START-UP INFORMATION

4044 ■ "Online Fortunes" in *Small Business Opportunities* (Fall 2008)
Pub: Entrepreneur Media Inc.
Description: Fifty hot, e-commerce enterprises for the aspiring entrepreneur to consider are featured; virtual assistants, marketing services, party planning, travel services, researching, web design and development, importing as well as creating an online store are among the businesses featured.

4045 ■ "Startup Aims to Cut Out Coupon Clipping" in *The Business Journal-Serving Metropolitan Kansas City* (Vol. 26, August 15, 2008, No. 49)
Pub: American City Business Journals, Inc.
Ed: Suzanna Stagemeyer. **Description:** TDP Inc., who started operations 18 months ago, aims to transform stale coupon promotions using technology by digitizing the entire coupon process. The process is expected to enable consumers to hunt coupons online where they will be automatically linked to loyalty cards. Other views and information on TDP and its services are presented.

REFERENCE WORKS

4046 ■ *Gale Directory of Publications and Broadcast Media*
Pub: Gale
Released: Annual, Latest edition April 2011. **Price:** $1,297, individuals. **Covers:** Approximately 57,000 publications and broadcasting stations, including newspapers, magazines, journals, radio stations, television stations, radio/television/cable networks, syndicates and cable systems in the U.S. and Canada. Newsletters and directories are excluded. **Entries Include:** For publications—Title, publishing and editorial addresses, phone, fax, description, names of editor, publisher, and advertising manager, base advertising rate, page specifications, subscription rate, circulation, frequency, ISSN, former names, additional contacts. For broadcast media—Call letters or cable system name, address, phone, fax, format, networks, owner, date founded, former call letters, operating hours, names and titles of key personnel, local programming, wattage, ad rates, additional contacts. **Arrangement:** Geographical. **Indexes:** Title; radio station format; publisher; geographic market; lists of agricultural, college, foreign language, Jewish, fraternal, black, women's, Hispanic, religious, general circulation, and trade and technical publications (by subject and/or geographical as needed); daily newspaper; daily periodical; free circulation newspaper; and shopping guides (each geographical); list of feature editors at daily newspapers with 50,000 or more circulation.

4047 ■ *Gebbie Press All-in-One Media Directory*
Pub: Gebbie Press Inc.
Ed: Mark Gebbie, Editor. **Released:** Annual, Latest edition 40th edition, 2011. **Price:** $175, individuals 2006 all-in-one media directory: print version; $175, individuals daily and weekly newspaper CD-ROM; $175, individuals radio and television CD-ROM; $175, individuals trade and consumer magazines CD-ROM. **Covers:** 1,453 daily newspapers, 6,202 weekly newspapers, 10,789 radio stations, 1,445 television stations, 268 general-consumer magazines, 430 professional business publications, 3,100 trade magazines, 320 farm publications, list of the Black press and radio, Hispanic press and radio, and a list of news syndicates. **Entries Include:** For periodicals—Name, address, phone, fax, frequency, editor, circulation, readership. For newspapers—Name, address, phone, fax, circulation. For radio and television stations—Call letters, address, phone, format. **Arrangement:** Classified by type of media.

4048 ■ *National Directory of Magazines*
Pub: Oxbridge Communications Inc.
Released: latest edition 2011. **Price:** $995, individuals print version; $1,195, individuals CD-ROM single user; $1,995, individuals print and CD-ROM. **Covers:** Over 20,000 magazines; coverage includes Canada. **Entries Include:** Title, publisher name, address, phone, fax number, names and titles of contact and key personnel, financial data, editorial and advertising information, circulation. **Arrangement:** Classified by subject. **Indexes:** Title, geographical, publisher.

4049 ■ *Oxbridge Directory of Newsletters*
Pub: Oxbridge Communications Inc.
Released: Annual, Latest edition 2011. **Price:** $995, individuals print version; $1,195, individuals CD-ROM single user; $1,995, individuals print and CD-ROM. **Covers:** Approximately 15,000 newsletters in the U.S. and Canada. **Entries Include:** Publication name, publisher name, address, phone; names of editor and other key personnel; description of contents and types of material used, year founded, frequency, advertising and subscription rates, print method, page size, number of pages. **Arrangement:** Classified by subject. **Indexes:** Title, geographical, publisher.

4050 ■ *SRDS International Media Guides*
Pub: SRDS
Released: Annual. **Price:** $455, individuals annual unlimited single-user access. **Covers:** approximately 19,000 newspapers and color newspaper magazines/supplements from 200 countries, including the United States. **Entries Include:** Publication name; publisher name, address, phone, fax, e-mail, URL, names of editor, advertising manager, and representatives in the United States and worldwide; advertising rates in U.S. dollars and/or local currency, circulation, mechanical data, ad closing, readership description, etc. **Arrangement:** Geographical.

4051 ■ *Standard Periodical Directory*
Pub: Oxbridge Communications Inc.
Ed: Deborah Striplin, Editor, dstriplin@oxbridge.com. **Released:** Annual, Latest edition January 2011. **Price:** $1,995, individuals print version; $1,995, single issue CD-ROM single user; $2,995, individuals print and CD-ROM. **Covers:** 63,000 magazines, journals, newsletters, directories, house organs, association publications, etc. , in the United States and Canada. **Entries Include:** Publication current and former title; publisher name, address, phone; names and titles of key personnel; circulation and advertising rates; description of contents; ISSN, year founded, frequency; subscription rates, print method, page size, number of pages. **Arrangement:** Classified by subject. **Indexes:** Subject, title.

4052 ■ *Ulrich's Periodicals Directory*
Pub: R.R. Bowker L.L.C.
Released: Annual, Latest edition 2010. **Price:** $1,260, individuals Hardcover, 4 volumes. **Covers:** Nearly 200,000 current periodicals and newspapers published worldwide. **Entries Include:** In main list—Publication title; Dewey Decimal Classification number, Library of Congress Classification Number (where applicable), CODEN designation (for sci-tech serials), British Library Document Supply Centre shelfmark number, country code, ISSN; subtitle, language(s) of text, year first published, frequency, subscription prices, sponsoring organization, publishing company name, address, phone, fax, e-mail and website addresses, editor and publisher names; regular features (reviews, advertising, abstracts, bibliographies, trade literature, etc.), indexes, circulation, format, brief description of content; availability of microforms and reprints; whether refereed; CD-ROM availability with vendor name; online availability with service name; services that index or abstract the periodical, with years covered; advertising rates and contact; right and permissions contact name and phone; availability through document deliver **Arrangement:** Main listing is classified by subject; U.S. general daily and weekly newspapers are listed in a separate volume; lists of cessations, online services, and CD-ROM vendors are alphabetical. **Indexes:** Cessations, subjects, title (including variant, former, and ceased titles), ISSN, periodicals available on CD-ROM, online periodical title, refereed serial, and international organization publication title.

TRADE PERIODICALS

4053 ■ *Business Periodicals Index*
Pub: The H.W. Wilson Co.
Released: Monthly. **Price:** $600. **Description:** Index of business periodicals.

COMPUTERIZED DATABASES

4054 ■ *Business Periodicals Index*
EBSCO Publishing
10 Estes St.
Ipswich, MA 01938
Ph:(978)356-6500
Free: 800-653-2726
Fax:(978)356-6565
Co. E-mail: information@ebscohost.com
URL: http://www.ebscohost.com/wilson
Description: Contains citations to articles and book reviews in more than 650 general business periodicals and trade journals, covering 25 business specialties. Includes feature articles, interviews, biographical sketches of business leaders, book reviews, research developments, new product reviews, and reports of

associations, societies, and conferences. Features indexing of publications from 1982 to date. Covers such general topics as accounting, advertising, economics, finance, management, marketing, and occupational health and safety, as well as such specific industries as banking, computers, and real estate. Corresponds to *Business Periodicals Index*. **Availability:** Online: EBSCO Publishing, Wolters Kluwer Health, Wolters Kluwer Health. **Type:** Bibliographic.

4055 ■ *Newspaper Abstracts*
ProQuest LLC
789 E Eisenhower Pky.
PO Box 1346
Ann Arbor, MI 48106-1346
Ph:(734)761-4700
Free: 800-521-0600
Fax:(734)761-6450
Co. E-mail: info@proquest.com
URL: http://www.proquest.com

Description: Contains more than 2.6 million citations, with abstracts, to articles from 9 major newspapers, including: *Atlanta Constitution/Journal*, *Boston Globe*, *Chicago Tribune*, *Christian Science Monitor*, *Los Angeles Times*, *New York Times*, *USA Today*, *The Wall Street Journal*, and *Washington Post*. Covers international, national, regional, and local news, business and finance, editorials, commentaries, letters to the editor from prominent people, arts and leisure, special series and supplements, sports, and obituaries of eminent persons. Articles include complete bibliographic information, as well as either an abstract or annotated headline. On ProQuest, available as one of three versions of the ProQuest Newspaper Abstracts Database. **Availability:** Online: ProQuest LLC, ProQuest LLC. **Type:** Bibliographic.

START-UP INFORMATION

4056 ■ *Design and Launch Your Online Boutique in a Week*
Pub: Entrepreneur Press
Ed: Melissa Campanelli. **Released:** June 2008. **Price:** $17.95. **Description:** Guide to start an online boutique includes information on business planning, Website design and funding.

4057 ■ *In Fashion: From Runway to Retail, Everything You Need to Know to Break Into the Fashion Industry*
Pub: Crown Business Books
Ed: Annemarie Iverson. **Released:** August 10, 2010. **Price:** $16.99. **Description:** Whether your dream is to photograph models, outfit celebrities, design fashions, this book provides details into every aspect for working in the fashion industry.

4058 ■ "Money Matters: Using Sound Resources, You Can Find Capital For Your Business" in *Black Enterprise* (Vol. 38, November 2007, No. 4)
Pub: Earl G. Graves Publishing Co. Inc.
Ed: Carolyn M. Brown. **Description:** Profile of fashion designer Kara Saun who inspired an angel investor from Connecticut to help launch her Fall 2006 clothing line.

4059 ■ *Start Your Own Fashion Accessories Business*
Pub: Entrepreneur Press
Released: March 1, 2009. **Price:** $17.95. **Description:** Entrepreneurs wishing to start a fashion accessories business will find important information for setting up a home workshop and office, exploring the market, managing finances, publicizing and advertising the business and more.

ASSOCIATIONS AND OTHER ORGANIZATIONS

4060 ■ Association of Knitwear Designers
4532 17th St.
San Francisco, CA 94114
Ph:(415)552-8414
Co. E-mail: info@knitwear-designers.org
URL: http://www.knitwear-designers.org
Contact: Jill Wolcott, Pres.
Purpose: Promotes the art and business of knitting. Provides networking, professional accreditation and helps freelance knitwear designers worldwide. **Publications:** *Teachers Directory* (annual).

4061 ■ Association of Sewing and Design Professionals
PO Box 897
Higley, AZ 85236
Free: 877-755-0303
Co. E-mail: admin@sewingprofessionals.org
URL: http://www.paccprofessionals.org
Contact: Ms. Rae Cumbie, Pres.
Description: Encourages the interchange of ideas among individuals involved in the sewing and design fields. Promotes professions in the industry; represents members' interests. Conducts educational and training programs. .

4062 ■ Council of Fashion Designers of America
1412 Broadway, Ste. 2006
New York, NY 10018
Co. E-mail: info@cfda.com
URL: http://www.cfda.com
Contact: Steven Kolb, Exec. Dir.
Description: Persons of "recognized ability, standing, and integrity, who are actively engaged in creative fashion design in the United States, in the fields of wearing apparel, fabrics, accessories, jewelry, or related products." (Membership is individual and does not extend to the firm or associates.) Seeks "to further the position of fashion design as a recognized branch of American art and culture, to advance its artistic and professional standards, to establish and maintain a code of ethics and practices of mutual benefit in professional, public, and trade relations, and to promote and improve public understanding and appreciation of the fashion arts through leadership in quality and taste". .

4063 ■ Custom Tailors and Designers Association of America
42732 Ridgeway Dr.
Broadlands, VA 20148
Free: 888-248-2832
Fax:(866)661-1240
Co. E-mail: info@ctda.com
URL: http://www.ctda.com
Contact: David Eisele, Pres.
Description: Designers and makers of men's custom tailored outerwear and clothing. .

4064 ■ Fashion Group International
8 W 40th St., 7th Fl.
New York, NY 10018
Ph:(212)302-5511
Fax:(212)302-5533
Co. E-mail: cheryl@fgi.org
URL: http://www.fgi.org
Contact: Cheryl Ingersoll, Regional Dir.
Description: Fashion, apparel, accessories, beauty and home industries. Works to advance professionalism in fashion and its related lifestyle industries with a particular emphasis on the role and development of women. Provides a public forum for examination of important contemporary issues in fashion and the business of fashion. Works to present timely information regarding national and global trends and to attain greater recognition of women's achievements in business and to promote career opportunities in fashion.

4065 ■ Men's Clothing Manufacturers Association–Association des manufacturiers de vetements pour hommes
555, Chabanel Ouest, Ste. 801
Montreal, QC, Canada H2N 2H8
Ph:(514)382-3846
Fax:(514)383-1689
Co. E-mail: amiq@macten.net
URL: http://www.asp-habillement.org/fr/partners/patronales.html
Contact: Alain Plourde, Exec. Dir.
Description: Manufacturers of men's clothing and accessories. Promotes international competitiveness among members. Serves as a clearinghouse on the apparel industry; conducts research and educational programs. **Publications:** *On The Button* (quarterly).

4066 ■ Organization of Black Designers
300 M St. SW, Ste. N110
Washington, DC 20024
Ph:(202)659-3918
Co. E-mail: info@obd.org
URL: http://www.core77.com/OBD/welcome.html
Contact: David H. Rice, Founder/Chm.
Description: African American designers holding college degrees who are practicing graphic advertising, industrial, fashion, textile, and interior design. Provides forum for discussion and educational programs, business, career and economic development. Sponsors competitions and speakers' bureau. **Publications:** *DesigNation* (biennial); *OBData* .

REFERENCE WORKS

4067 ■ "Apparel" in *Retail Merchandiser* (Vol. 51, July-August 2011, No. 4, pp. 14)
Pub: Phoenix Media Corporation
Description: NPD Group Inc. released current sales statistics for the women's apparel market along with men's apparel. It also reported annual shoes sales for 2010. Statistical data included.

4068 ■ "As Seen On TV" in *Canadian Business* (Vol. 80, November 5, 2007, No. 22, pp. 93)
Pub: Rogers Media
Ed: Zena Olijnyk. **Description:** StarBrand Media Inc. is one of the companies providing fans with information on how and where to purchase the items that television characters are using. StarBrand created the style section found on different television shows' Websites, such as that of the Gossip Girl and Smallville. The benefits of using sites like StarBrand are evaluated.

4069 ■ "The Bottom Line" in *Retail Merchandiser* (Vol. 51, July-August 2011, No. 4, pp. 60)
Pub: Phoenix Media Corporation
Description: Hanky Panky believes that comfort and style don't have to be mutually exclusive when designing their line of intimate apparel for women. The lingerie retailer was launched in 1977.

4070 ■ "Breadwinner Tries on Designer Jeans" in *Houston Business Journal* (Vol. 40, December 18, 2009, No. 32, pp. 1)
Pub: American City Business Journals
Ed: Allison Wollam. **Description:** Chuck Cain, the franchisee who introduced Panera Bread to Houston, Texas has partnered with tax accountant Jim Jacob-

sen to introduce custom-make Tattu Jeans. As more Tattu Jeans outlets are being planned, Cain is using entrepreneurial lessons learned from Panera Bread in the new venture. Both Panera Bread and Tattu Jeans were opened by Cain during economic downturns.

4071 ■ "Bringing Charities More Bang for Their Buck" in *Crain's Chicago Business* (Vol. 34, May 23, 2011, No. 21, pp. 31)
Pub: Crain Communications Inc.
Ed: Lisa Bertagnoli. **Description:** Marcy-Newberry Association connects charities with manufacturers in order to use excess items such as clothing, janitorial and office supplies.

4072 ■ "Buying Chanel (All Of It)" in *Conde Nast Portfolio* (Vol. 2, June 2008, No. 6, pp. 34)
Pub: Conde Nast Publications, Inc.
Ed: Willow Duttge. **Description:** Overview of the luxury company Chanel and an estimated guess as to what the company is worth.

4073 ■ "A Change Would Do You Good" in *Canadian Business* (Vol. 80, November 19, 2007, No. 23, pp. 15)
Pub: Rogers Media
Ed: Geoff Kirbyson. **Description:** Western Glove Works will be manufacturing clothing offshore, including Sheryl Crow's jeans collection, in countries such as China and the Philippines. The company decided to operate offshore after 86 years of existence due to the high price of manufacturing jeans in Canada. Western Glove's focus on producing celebrity-endorsed goods is discussed.

4074 ■ *Chief Culture Officer: How to Create a Living, Breathing Corporation*
Pub: Basic Books
Ed: Grant McCracken. **Price:** $26.95. **Description:** Business consultant argues that corporations need to focus on 'reading' what's happening in the culture around them. Otherwise, companies will suffer the consequences, as Levi Strauss did when it missed out on the rise of hip-hop (and the baggy pants that are part of that lifestyle).

4075 ■ "Common Thread" in *Entrepreneur* (Vol. 36, March 2008, No. 3, pp. 144)
Pub: Entrepreneur Media Inc.
Ed: Sara Wilson. **Description:** Profile of Stacey Benet and her business, Alice and Olivia, and how she jumpstarted her career in the clothing industry after she wore a self-designed pair of pants that caught the attention of a Barney's New York representative is presented.

4076 ■ "Consignment Shop Closes Without Warning to Customers, Landlord" in *Sun Journal* (June 30, 2010)
Pub: Freedom Communications Inc.
Ed: Laura Oleniacz. **Description:** Off The Racks consignment shop located on Glenburnie Road in New Bern, North Carolina closed without warning to customers or its landlord. The consignors who donated clothing to the store were left unpaid.

4077 ■ "Consignment Shop Offers Children's Clothes, Products" in *Frederick News-Post* (August 19, 2010)
Pub: Federick News-Post
Ed: Ed Waters Jr. **Description:** Sweet Pea Consignments for Children offers used items for newborns to pre-teens. The shop carries name brand clothing as well as toys, books and baby products.

4078 ■ "Design program in Athletic Footwear" in *Occupational Outlook Quarterly* (Vol. 55, Fall 2011, No. 3, pp. 21)
Pub: U.S. Bureau of Labor Statistics
Description: The Fashion Institute of Technology offers the only certificate program in performance athletic footwear design in the U.S. The program focuses on conceptualizing and sketching shoe designs and covers ergonomic, anatomical, and material considerations for athletic footwear design.

4079 ■ "Designer is Walking Ad for TIBI Line" in *Charlotte Observer* (February 5, 2007)
Pub: Knight-Ridder/Tribune Business News
Ed: Crystal Dempsey. **Description:** Profile of Amy Smilovic, mother of two children, and clothing designer. Smilovic wears what she designs, making her a great marketing tool for her clothing line TIBI.

4080 ■ *The Designer's Guide to Marketing and Pricing: How to Win Clients and What to Charge Them*
Pub: F and W Publications, Inc.
Ed: Ilise Benun. **Released:** March 2008. **Price:** $19.99. **Description:** Guide to running a creative services business teaches designers how to be more effective, attract new clients, wages, and how to accurately estimate a project.

4081 ■ "Designers' Hats Foretell a Big Comeback Next Fall" in *Charlotte Observer* (February 8, 2007)
Pub: Knight-Ridder/Tribune Business News
Ed: Crystal Dempsey. **Description:** According to designer experts, hats are making a comeback and will make a big fashion statement, fall 2007.

4082 ■ "Doing Good: Fair Fashion" in *Entrepreneur* (Vol. 35, October 2007, No. 10, pp. 36)
Pub: Entrepreneur Media Inc.
Ed: J.J. Ramberg. **Description:** Indigenous Designs was launched in 1993, when organic clothing was not yet popular. However, the company has become successful in the industry, with $4 million dollars in revenue, owing to the growing environment awareness of consumers. A history of how the company was formed and an overview of their production process are provided.

4083 ■ "eBay and Jonathan Adler Team to Launch 'The eBay Inspiration Shop'" in *Entertainment Close-Up* (October 25, 2011)
Pub: Close-Up Media
Description: Designer Jonathan Adler partnered with eBay to create a collection of new must-have merchandise for the fall season. Top trendsetters, including actors, designers, bloggers, stylists, editors, photographers, models and musicians helped curate the items being featured in the windows by sharing their shopping wish lists with users.

4084 ■ "Fall Fever" in *Canadian Business* (Vol. 81, October 13, 2008, No. 17, pp. S12)
Pub: Rogers Media Ltd.
Description: Buyer's guide of men's suits and jackets for fall are presented, including a suit by Boss Hugo Boss recommended for fun in the city after finishing work. Designers Ermenegildo, Michael Kors, and Arnold Brant are also highlighted.

4085 ■ *Fashion Calendar*
Pub: Ruth Finley
Contact: Ruth Finley, Founder/Publisher
Released: Semimonthly, Latest edition 2010. **Covers:** Events of interest to the fashion industry, including private and public fashion openings, and important events in other fields which are scheduled for principal fashion cities; coverage is heavily New York City, but major cities worldwide are also covered. **Entries Include:** For openings—Event name, date, address, phone. For other events—Event name, date, time, location, phone. **Arrangement:** Openings are alphabetical; events are chronological.

4086 ■ *The Fashion Designer Survival Guide*
Pub: Kaplan Publishing
Ed: Mary Gehlhar; Zac Posen. **Released:** September 1, 2005. **Description:** Professional advice from an insider to help start and run a fashion business.

4087 ■ "Fashionistas Weigh in on the Super-Thin" in *Charlotte Observer* (February 7, 2007)
Pub: Knight-Ridder/Tribune Business News
Ed: Crystal Dempsey. **Description:** Council of Fashion Designers of America held a panel discussion regarding the weight and ages of models used to highlight clothing.

4088 ■ "Fight Ensues Over Irreplaceable Gowns" in *Tampa Bay Business Journal* (Vol. 30, January 15, 2010, No. 4, pp. 1)
Pub: American City Business Journals
Ed: Janet Leiser. **Description:** People's Princess Charitable Foundation Inc. founder Maureen Rorech Dunkel has sought Chapter 11 bankruptcy protection before a state court decides on the fate of the five of 13 Princess Diana Gowns. Dunkel and the nonprofit were sued by Patricia Sullivan of HRH Venture LLC who claimed they defaulted on $1.5 million in loans.

4089 ■ "Fledgling Brands May Take the Fall With Steve & Barry's" in *Advertising Age* (Vol. 79, July 7, 2008, No. 26, pp. 6)
Pub: Crain Communications, Inc.
Ed: Natalie Zmuda. **Description:** Steve & Barry's, a retailer that holds licensing deals with a number of designers and celebrities, may have to declare bankruptcy; this leaves the fate of the retailer's hundreds of licensing deals and exclusive celebrity lines in question.

4090 ■ *Fugitive Denim: A Moving Story of People and Pants in the Borderless World of Global Trade*
Pub: W.W. Norton & Company
Ed: Rachel Snyder. **Released:** April 2009. **Price:** $16.95. **Description:** In-depth study of the global production and processes of how jeans are designed, sewn, and transported as well as how the cotton for denim is grown, regulated, purchased and processed.

4091 ■ "Going Western with a Touch of Style" in *Women In Business* (Vol. 63, Summer 2011, No. 2, pp. 8)
Pub: American Business Women's Association
Ed: Maureen Sullivan. **Description:** Tips on ways women should dress up in Western style are presented. The wearing of Western-style denims is recommended. Use of accessories such as belt buckles, boots and hats is also encouraged.

4092 ■ "H&M Offers a Dress for Less" in *Canadian Business* (Vol. 83, September 14, 2010, No. 15, pp. 20)
Pub: Rogers Media Ltd.
Ed: Laura Cameron. **Description:** Swedish clothing company H&M has implemented loss leader strategy by pricing some dresses at extremely low prices. The economy has forced retailers to keep prices down despite the increasing cost of manufacturing, partly due to Chinese labor becoming more expensive. How the trend will affect apparel companies is discussed.

4093 ■ "Haute Flyers" in *Canadian Business* (Vol. 80, November 19, 2007, No. 23, pp. 68)
Pub: Rogers Media
Ed: Rachel Pulfer. **Description:** Duckie Brown has been nominated by the Council of Fashion Designers of America as best menswear designer in the U.S. for 2007, along with leaders Calvin Klein and Ralph Lauren. The New York-based company was formed the day after September 11, 2001, but the timing did not hamper its growth. The works and plans of owners Steven Cox and Daniel Silver are described.

4094 ■ "How to Keep Your Cool and Your Friends in a Heat Wave" in *Canadian Business* (Vol. 83, August 17, 2010, No. 13-14, pp. 79)
Pub: Rogers Media Ltd.
Ed: Angelina Chapin. **Description:** A buyer's guide of menswear clothing for businessmen is presented. The products include an antiperspirant and deodorant, men's dress shorts, shoes and bamboo fabric undershirt.

4095 ■ "How This First Lady Moves Markets" in *Harvard Business Review* (Vol. 88, November 2010, No. 11, pp. 38)
Pub: Harvard Business School Publishing
Description: A chart is presented demonstrating how First Lady Michelle Obama's choice of fashion designer has impacted the clothing industry.

4096 ■ *Hug Your Customers*
Pub: Hyperion Books
Ed: Jack Mitchell. **Price:** $19.95. **Description:** The CEO of Mitchells/Roberts, two very successful clothing stores, professes his belief in showering customers with attention. His secrets for long-term business success include advice about attracting a good staff, lowering marketing costs, and maintaining higher gross margins and revenues.

4097 ■ *If You Have to Cry, Go Outside: And Other Things Your Mother Never Told You*
Pub: HarperOne
Ed: Kelly Cutrone. **Released:** February 2, 2010. **Price:** $22.99. **Description:** Women's mentor advices on how to make it in one of the most competitive industries in the world, fashion. She has kicked people out of fashion shows, forced some of reality television's shiny start to fire their friends, and built her own company which is one of the most powerful public relations firms in the fashion business.

4098 ■ "Insider" in *Canadian Business* (Vol. 80, Winter 2007, No. 24, pp.)
Pub: Rogers Media
Ed: Zena Olijnyk. **Description:** Luluemon Athletica started in 1998 after Dennis Wilson takes a yoga class and notices a demand from women for breathable clothes. The company opened their first outlet in Vancouver in November 2000 then opened their first U.S. store in 2003 until finally going public July 27, 2007 where its stocks doubled in value within days of trading.

4099 ■ "Integral USA Magazine Sponsors Eco-Fashion in the Park" in *Entertainment Close-Up* (September 2, 2011)
Pub: Close-Up Media
Description: Integral Magazine sponsored Eco-Fashion in the Park, a fashion show for the fashion conscious. Eleven independent designers will show their eco-friendly fashions at the event.

4100 ■ *International Textile & Apparel Association—Membership Directory*
Pub: International Textile & Apparel Association
Contact: Sandra S. Hutton, Member
Released: Irregular, Latest edition 2007-2008. **Covers:** About 1,000 college professors of clothing and textile studies. **Entries Include:** Name, address, phone, academic credentials. **Arrangement:** Alphabetical; geographical by zip code.

4101 ■ "Island Co.: Isle Style" in *Entrepreneur* (Vol. 35, October 2007, No. 10, pp. 172)
Pub: Entrepreneur Media Inc.
Ed: Sara Wilson. **Description:** Island Co., producer of travel clothing and swimsuits was formed by Spencer Antle in 2002. Its office projects the Caribbean atmosphere, a strategy Antle used to promote the company's theme to its clients. Future plans for the company are also indicated.

4102 ■ "It's So You! Consignment Chop Owner Thrilled to See Vision Come to Fruition" in *News-Herald* (August 27, 2010)
Pub: News-Herald
Ed: Brandon C. Baker. **Description:** Profile of Laurel Howes and her It's So You! Boutique. The consignment shop is located in Willoughby's Pine Ride Plaza in Ohio. The shop targets all women, but particularly those who are not that comfortable with shopping consignment.

4103 ■ "Let It Shine: Organization Helps Disadvantaged Girls See Their Worth" in *Black Enterprise* (Vol. 38, February 2008, No. 7, pp. 142)
Pub: Earl G. Graves Publishing Co. Inc.
Ed: George Alexander. **Description:** Wilson Mourning, founder of the clothing label Honey Child, attributes her success to her mother and other positive women who helped her through her adolescence. Mourning created a mentoring organization that helps young girls in the Miami, Florida area to develop life skills.

4104 ■ "Life's Work: Manolo Blahnik" in *Harvard Business Review* (Vol. 88, December 2010, No. 12, pp. 144)
Pub: Harvard Business School Publishing
Ed: Alison Beard. **Description:** Shoe designer Manolo Blahnik recounts his beginnings in the shoe industry and the influence art has had on his work, as well as balancing art and commerce. He also discusses the importance of quality materials and craftsmanship and the benefits of managing an independent, family-owned business.

4105 ■ "Making It Work" in *Retail Merchandiser* (Vol. 51, July-August 2011, No. 4, pp. 43)
Pub: Phoenix Media Corporation
Ed: Anthony DiPaolo. **Description:** Profile of Anthony DiPaolo and his purchase of the Work 'N Gear retail store in 2002. The brick and mortar shop sells work wear and healthcare apparel and DiPaolo believes customer respect is essential to his success.

4106 ■ "Meet Joe Fresh" in *Canadian Business* (Vol. 79, November 6, 2006, No. 22, pp. 49)
Pub: Rogers Media
Ed: Calvin Leung. **Description:** The efforts of Joseph Mimran, a fashion designer, in improving the business of Joe Fresh style products are analyzed.

4107 ■ "Military Brides Can Get Free Wedding Gowns" in *Virginian-Pilot* (November 10, 2010)
Pub: The Virginia-Pilot
Ed: Jamesetta Walker. **Description:** Seventy-five designer wedding gowns will be given to military brides on a first-come, first-served basis at Maya Couture through the Brides Across America's wedding gown giveaway program. Gowns are valued between $500 to $3,000 and are donated by designers Maggie Sottero, Pronovias and Essense of Australia.

4108 ■ "Not All Contracts a Good Fit for Fashion Reps" in *Agency Sales Magazine* (Vol. 39, September-October 2009, No. 9, pp. 10)
Pub: MANA
Ed: Jack Foster. **Description:** Difficult situations regarding the relationship between sales representatives and their principals in the fashion industry are presented and suggestions on how to create contracts that seek to prevent potential problems are provided. Sales reps should make sure that manufacturer has a viable business that is well thought-out and adequately financed.

4109 ■ "On a Mission: Ginch Gonch Wants You to Get Rid of Your Tighty Whities" in *Canadian Business* (Vol. 81, September 29, 2008, No. 16)
Pub: Rogers Media Ltd.
Ed: Michelle Magnan. **Description:** New Equity Capital acquired underwear maker Ginch Gonch in July 2008; founder Jason Sutherland kept his position as creative director of the company and will retain his title as 'director of stitches and inches'. The company is known for its products, which are reminiscent of the days when people wore underwear covered in cowboys and stars as kids. The company also claims that Nelly, Justin Timberlake, and Hilary Duff have worn their products.

4110 ■ "Options Abound in Winter Wares" in *Pet Product News* (Vol. 64, November 2010, No. 11, pp. 1)
Pub: BowTie Inc.
Ed: Maggie M. Shein. **Description:** Pet supply manufacturers emphasize creating top-notch construction and functional design in creating winter clothing for pets. Meanwhile, retailers and pet owners seek human-inspired style, quality, and versatility for pets' winter clothing. How retailers generate successful sales of pets' winter clothing outside of traditional brand marketing is also examined.

4111 ■ "Peacocks Launches Its First Wedding Dress" in *Benzinga.com* (July 1, 2011)
Pub: Benzinga.com
Ed: Benzinga Staff. **Description:** Peacocks, a leading fashion retailer in the United Kingdom launched its first wedding dress available for sale in August 2011.

4112 ■ "Portland Wooing Under Armour to West Coast Facility" in *Baltimore Business Journal* (Vol. 27, January 29, 2010, No. 39, pp. 1)
Pub: American City Business Journals
Ed: Andy Giegerich. **Description:** Baltimore, Maryland sports apparel maker, Under Armour, is planning a west coast expansion with Portland, Oregon among the sites considered to house its apparel and footwear design center. Portland officials counting on the concentration of nearly 10,000 activewear workers in the city will help lure the company to the city.

4113 ■ "Research and Markets Adds: 2011 U.S. Women's & Children's Clothing Wholesale Report" in *Health & Beauty Close-Up* (October 16, 2010)
Pub: Close-Up Media Inc.
Description: The Women's & Children's Clothing Wholesale Report is an annual report containing timely and accurate industry statistics, forecasts and demographics.

4114 ■ "Retail News: Children's Boutique Relocates to Conway" in *Sun News* (June 4, 2010)
Pub: The Sun News
Description: Little Angel's Children's Boutique and Big Oak Frame Shop have moved to downtown locations in Conway, South Carolina. Little Angel's will sell children's clothing and accessories, shoes and gifts, while the frame shop will offer custom framing along with the sale of stationary, invitations and local prints.

4115 ■ "Rule of the Masses: Reinventing Fashion Via Crowdsourcing" in *WWD* (Vol. 200, July 26, 2010, No. 17, pp. 1)
Pub: Conde Nast Publications Inc.
Ed: Cate T. Corcoran. **Description:** Large apparel brands and retailers are crowdsourcing as a way to increase customer loyalty and to build their businesses.

4116 ■ "Skinny Jeans Sticking Around for Fall" in *Charlotte Observer* (February 5, 2007)
Pub: Knight-Ridder/Tribune Business News
Ed: Crystal Dempsey. **Description:** Clothing designers were showing skinny jeans in the fall/winter fashion shows for 2007.

4117 ■ "Stylish Successes" in *Women In Business* (Vol. 61, October-November 2009, No. 5, pp. 12)
Pub: American Business Women's Association
Ed: Leigh Elmore; Megan L. Reese. **Description:** Amanda Horan Kennedy, Angela Samuels, Barbara Nast Saletan, and Patty Nast Canton are career women who ventured into entrepreneurship. They are deemed to possess networking and teamwork skills that ensured their success in the garment industry.

4118 ■ *They Made America*
Pub: Little Brown Company/Time Warner Book Group
Ed: Harold Evans, Gail Buckland, David Lefer. **Released:** 2006. **Price:** $18.95. **Description:** Coffee table book highlighting entrepreneurship; this book is filled with interesting illustrated portraits of entrepreneurs and innovators like Thomas Edison, George Doriot (a venture capital pioneer), and Ida Rosenthal (inventor of the Maidenform bra).

4119 ■ "Trousseaus of Memories Trail Behind Wedding Gowns" in *Oregonian* (September 4, 2010)
Pub: The Oregonian
Ed: Anne Saker. **Description:** Readers are asked to share stories about their wedding gowns and what that garment meant to them at the time and now.

4120 ■ "The Ultimate Home Shopping Network" in *Austin Business JournalInc.* (Vol. 28, October 17, 2008, No. 31, pp. A1)
Pub: American City Business Journals
Ed: Sandra Zaragoza. **Description:** New York-based Etcetera sells their clothing through more than 850 fashion consultants in the U.S. Central Texas is one

of the company's top markets and the company is looking to increase its fashion consultants in the area from five to about 20 since they believe there is plenty of room to expand their customer base in the area.

4121 ■ "Web Sight: Do You See What I See?" in *Entrepreneur* (Vol. 35, October 2007, No. 10, pp. 58)
Pub: Entrepreneur Media Inc.
Ed: Heather Clancy. **Description:** Owners of Trunkt, a boutique in New York that showcases independent designs, have created a new style of Website called Trunkt.org. The Website allows buyers to select the products they want to see and designers can choose anytime which of their items will be displayed on the site. An explanation of the strategy that helped bring Trunkt closer to its clients is presented.

4122 ■ "Wedding: Style Gowns Ready to Go" in *Houston Chronicle* (June 3, 2010)
Pub: Houston Chronicle
Ed: Molly Glentzer. **Description:** Wedding gowns with slender silhouettes travel well for destination weddings. Amsale, Oscar del la Renta and Monique Lhuillier dresses are highlighted.

4123 ■ "Well-Heeled Startup" in *Business Journal Portland* (Vol. 27, November 12, 2010, No. 37, pp. 1)
Pub: Portland Business Journal
Ed: Erik Siemers. **Description:** Oh! Shoes LLC expects to receive about $1.5 million in funding from angel investors, while marketing a new line of high heel shoes that are comfortable, healthy, and attractive. The new line of shoes will use the technology of athletic footwear while having the look of an Italian designer. Oh! Shoes hopes to generate $35 million in sales by 2014.

4124 ■ "What's Next, Pup Tents in Bryant Park?" in *Advertising Age* (Vol. 78, January 29, 2007, No. 5, pp. 4)
Pub: Crain Communications, Inc.
Ed: Stephanie Thompson. **Description:** Designers such as Ralph Lauren, Juicy Couture, Burberry and Kiehl's have been expanding their businesses with new clothing lines for pets. Packaged Facts, a division of MarketResearch.com, predicts that pet expenditures will continue to grow in the years to come.

4125 ■ "When Dov Cries" in *Canadian Business* (Vol. 83, June 15, 2010, No. 10, pp. 71)
Pub: Rogers Media Ltd.
Ed: Joe Castaldo. **Description:** American Apparel disclosed that they will have problems meeting one of its debt covenants which could trigger a chain reaction that could lead to bankruptcy. The prospects look bleak, but eccentric company founder Dov Charney, has always defied expectations.

4126 ■ "Work that Skirt!" in *Entrepreneur* (Vol. 37, October 2009, No. 10, pp. 17)
Pub: Entrepreneur Media, Inc.
Ed: Donnell Alexander. **Description:** Steven Villegas, also called Krash, has captured a segment of the men's clothing market with his skirts called Utilikilts. Villegas has sold 100,000 kilts since starting his business in 2000.

SOURCES OF SUPPLY

4127 ■ *American Apparel Producers' Network—Directory for Sourcing Apparel*
Pub: American Apparel Producers' Network
Contact: Sue C. Strickland, Exec. Dir.
Released: Annual, First quarter. **Covers:** Over 300 member contractors, manufacturers, and suppliers in the apparel industry. **Entries Include:** Firm name, address, phone, names and titles of key personnel, apparel and services provided. **Arrangement:** Alphabetical. **Indexes:** Company name, type of apparel.

TRADE PERIODICALS

4128 ■ *Clothing Manufacturers Association—News Bulletin*
Pub: Clothing Manufacturers Association of the U.S.A.
Ed: Robert A. Kaplan, Editor. **Released:** Semimonthly. **Price:** Included in membership; $297 Associate (supplier) members. **Description:** Disseminates information for the Association relating to developments in or affecting the manufacturing of men's and boy's tailored clothing in the U.S. Contains statistics on sales, production, size, and industry earnings. Recurring features include notices of publications available, labor advisories, import and export statistics and advisories, and news of business opportunities.

4129 ■ *Dallas Apparel News*
Pub: Apparel News Group
Contact: N. Jayne Seward, Fashion Ed.
E-mail: jayne@apparelnews.net
Released: 5/yr. **Description:** Women's and children's garment industry magazine providing textile, retail, fashion and accessory information.

4130 ■ *DNR*
Pub: Fairchild Publications Inc.
Contact: Edward Nardoza, Editor-in-Chief
E-mail: edward_nardoza@condenast.com
Released: Daily (morn.). **Price:** $129; $99 online; $169 online print; $895 online archive. **Description:** Daily newspaper reporting on men's and boys' clothing, retailing, and textiles.

4131 ■ *New York Apparel News*
Pub: Apparel News Group
Contact: Alison A. Neider, Exec. Ed.
E-mail: alison@apparelnews.net
Released: 5/yr. **Price:** $20; $4 single issue. **Description:** Apparel magazine covering textiles and accessories for women and children.

4132 ■ *Sew News*
Pub: Primedia Consumer Media and Magazine Group
Contact: Beth Bradley, Assoc. Ed.
Released: 6/yr. **Price:** $21.98; $38.98 two years; $27.98 Canada; $33.98 other countries; $50.98 two years; $62.98 institutions 2 years. **Description:** Magazine on fashion sewing home decor, products, and patterns. Includes interviews with designers.

4133 ■ *Threads*
Pub: Taunton Press Inc.
Contact: Carol Spier, Editor-in-Chief
Released: Bimonthly. **Price:** $32.95 U.S. and Canada; $54.95 U.S. and Canada two years; $78.95 U.S. and Canada 3/yr. **Description:** Magazine for sewers, and quilters. Focus is on garment design, materials, and techniques.

4134 ■ *Visionaire*
Pub: Visionaire Publishing
Released: 3/yr. **Price:** $675. **Description:** Limited edition multi-format journal of art and fashion.

VIDEOCASSETTES/ AUDIOCASSETTES

4135 ■ *Cloth by the Yard*
New Jersey Network
25 S. Stockton St.
P.O. Box 777
Trenton, NJ 08625-0777
Ph:(609)777-5000
Free: 800-792-8645
Fax:(973)643-4004
Co. E-mail: njnvideo@njn.org
URL: http://www.njn.net
Released: 1983. **Description:** This documentary visits the Klopman Mills cloth factory to show how designs are woven into fabric. **Availability:** VHS; 3/4U.

4136 ■ *Clothes That Fit*
American Educational Products, LLC
401 Hickory St.
PO Box 2121
Fort Collins, CO 80522
Ph:(970)484-7445
Free: 800-289-9299
Fax:(970)484-1198
Co. E-mail: custserv@amep.com
URL: http://www.amep.com
Released: 1981. **Description:** This program in the "Good Life" series emphasizes the importance of proper fit and appropriate length of clothes, for developmentally disabled adolescents and adults. **Availability:** VHS; EJ; 3/4U.

4137 ■ *Clothing Around the World*
Phoenix Learning Group
2349 Chaffee Dr.
St. Louis, MO 63146-3306
Ph:(314)569-0211
Free: 800-221-1274
Fax:(314)569-2834
URL: http://www.phoenixlearninggroup.com
Released: 1981. **Description:** This film demonstrates many styles of clothing around the world. **Availability:** VHS; 3/4U.

4138 ■ *Clothing and Fashion: A History*
Benchmark Media
72 N. State Rd., Ste. 415
Briarcliff Manor, NY 10510-1542
Ph:(914)762-3838
Free: 800-438-5564
Fax:(914)762-3895
Co. E-mail: benchmedia@aol.com
Released: 1972. **Description:** From ancient to modern times, the evolution of fashions in clothing are explored. **Availability:** VHS; 3/4U.

4139 ■ *Clothing Sewing Techniques Series*
Time-Life Video and Television
1450 Palmyra Ave.
Richmond, VA 23227-4420
Ph:(804)266-6330
Free: 800-950-7887
Fax:(757)427-7905
URL: http://www.timelife.com
Released: 1972. **Description:** This series introduces the parts of the sewing machine, how to follow pattern instructions, and how to apply various types of zippers. **Availability:** VHS; 3/4U; Special order formats.

4140 ■ *Cotton Production*
CEV Multimedia
1020 SE Loop 289
Lubbock, TX 79404
Ph:(806)745-8820
Free: 877-610-5017
Fax:800-243-6398
Co. E-mail: cev@cevmultimedia.com
URL: http://www.cevmultimedia.com
Price: $59.95. **Description:** Outlines all areas of the cotton industry from planting to clothing production. **Availability:** VHS.

4141 ■ *Not by Jeans Alone*
Phoenix Learning Group
2349 Chaffee Dr.
St. Louis, MO 63146-3306
Ph:(314)569-0211
Free: 800-221-1274
Fax:(314)569-2834
URL: http://www.phoenixlearninggroup.com
Released: 1981. **Description:** A look at how Levi Strauss Company plans to branch out into the clothing industry. Part of the "Enterprise" series. **Availability:** VHS; 3/4U.

4142 ■ *Sins*
Anchor Bay Entertainment
1699 Stutz Dr.
Troy, MI 48084
Ph:(248)816-0909
Free: 800-786-8777
Fax:(248)816-3335
URL: http://www.anchorbayentertainment.com
Released: 1985. **Price:** $29.95. **Description:** On her way up the ladder of success in the fashion industry, Helene has stepped on a few toes. Those rivals and her ever-increasing acquisition of power and money make this film an exciting drama. **Availability:** VHS; VHS.

TRADE SHOWS AND CONVENTIONS

4143 ■ Beauty Fair
The Finnish Fair Corp.
Messuaukio 1
PO Box 21
FIN-00521 Helsinki, Finland
Ph:358 9 15091
Fax:358 9 1509218
Co. E-mail: info@finnexpo.fi
Released: Annual. **Audience:** General public. **Principal Exhibits:** Beauty and fashion, cosmetics and services; hair products and services; clothing, showes; bags, accessories, jewelry, education, and publications.

4144 ■ Mitteldeutsche Handwerksmesse: Central German Handicrafts Fair
Leipziger-Messe GmbH
PO Box 100720
D-04007 Leipzig, Germany
Ph:49 341 67 80
Fax:49 341 678 87 62
Co. E-mail: info@leipziger-messe.de
URL: http://www.leipziger-messe.de
Released: Annual. **Audience:** General public. **Principal Exhibits:** Building and conversion, home, arts and crafts, health, lifestyle, food crafts, vehicles, rare handicrafts.

4145 ■ National Costumers Association Annual Convention
National Costumers Association
6914 E. Upper Trail Cir.
Mesa, AZ 85207-0943
Ph:(480)654-6220
Free: 800-622-1321
Fax:(480)654-6223
Released: Annual. **Principal Exhibits:** Exhibits for designers, producers and renters of costumes for all occasions including parties and dance.

LIBRARIES

4146 ■ Academy of Art University Library
180 New Montgomery St., 6th Fl.
San Francisco, CA 94105
Ph:(415)618-3842
Co. E-mail: library@academyart.edu
URL: http://library.academyart.edu
Contact: Debra Sampson, Lib.Dir.
Scope: Commercial arts, photography, fine arts, art history, interior architecture design, fashion, industrial design, film, advertising art, graphic design, computer graphics. **Services:** Copying; scanning; Internet access; Library open to the public for reference use only. **Holdings:** 50,000 books; 112,000 slides; VF drawers of art-related ephemera; picture file; 253 CD-ROMs; 1400 videocassettes. **Subscriptions:** 300 journals and other serials.

4147 ■ American Intercontinental University Library
12655 W. Jefferson Blvd.
Los Angeles, CA 90066
Ph:(310)302-2111
Co. E-mail: nkleban@la.aiuniv.edu
URL: http://la.aiuniv.edu/about_aiu/library.aspx
Contact: Eric Zakem, Libn.
Scope: Fashion, busines, commercial art, costume history, interior design, information technology, criminal justice, media production. **Services:** Copying; Library not open to the public. **Holdings:** 25,000 books; 225 bound periodical volumes; 25,000 microfiche; fashion clipping file. **Subscriptions:** 200 journals and other serials; 15 newspapers.

4148 ■ Art Institute of Philadelphia Library
1610 Chestnut St.
Philadelphia, PA 19103
Ph:(215)405-6402
Co. E-mail: rschachter@aii.edu
URL: http://rs185.aisites.com
Contact: Ruth Schachter, Dir.
Scope: Visual communications, interior design, industrial design, animation, fashion marketing, fashion design, visual merchandising, photography, website design, multimedia. **Services:** Interlibrary loan; Library not open to the public (circulation services provided for students and faculty). **Holdings:** 31,000 volumes; 2000 videocassettes; audiocassettes. **Subscriptions:** 170 print subscriptions and other serials.

4149 ■ Art Institute of Portland Library
1122 NW Davis St.
Portland, OR 97209-2911
Ph:(503)382-4759
Free: (88)
Fax:(503)228-4227
Co. E-mail: nthurston@aii.edu
URL: http://www.artinstitute.edu/portland/
Contact: Nancy Thurston, LRC Dir.
Scope: Fashion and costume history, interior decoration, furniture history, world history, textiles, clothing and fashion industry, graphic design, multimedia, digital media production, media arts and animation, game art, advertising. **Services:** Copying; color copying; A/V viewing; Library open to professionals in the field. **Holdings:** 21,933 books; 900 videocassettes. **Subscriptions:** 204 journals and other serials; 3 newspapers.

4150 ■ Bauder College Library
384 Northyards Blvd. NW, Ste. 190 and 400
Atlanta, GA 30313
Ph:(404)237-7573
Free: 800-986-9710
Fax:(404)237-1619
URL: http://atlanta.bauder.edu
Scope: Fashion design and merchandising, interior design, information technology, business administration, graphic design, criminal justice. **Services:** Library not open to the public. **Holdings:** 7800 books; 500 videotapes; 6500 slide sets; 100 filmstrips. **Subscriptions:** 160 journals and other serials; 6 newspapers.

4151 ■ Brooklyn Museum Library
200 Eastern Pkwy.
Brooklyn, NY 11238
Ph:(718)501-6307
Fax:(718)501-6136
Co. E-mail: library@brooklynmuseum.org
URL: http://www.brooklynmuseum.org
Contact: Deirdre E. Lawrence, Prin.Libn.
Scope: American and European painting and sculpture; decorative arts; art African, Oceanic, Native American; prints and drawings; Asian art; costumes and textiles. **Services:** Interlibrary loan; copying; Library open to the public by appointment. **Holdings:** 300,000 volumes; 25,000 bound periodical volumes; 200 VF drawers of ephemeral materials; 1900 lin.ft. museum archival materials. **Subscriptions:** 400 journals and other serials.

4152 ■ Centennial College of Applied Arts & Technology–Warden Woods Campus Learning & Resource Centre
PO Box 631, Sta. A
Scarborough, ON, Canada M1K 5E9
Ph:(416)289-5000
Co. E-mail: illocen@centennialcollege.ca
URL: http://library.centennialcollege.ca
Contact: Gladys Watson, Dir.
Scope: Nursing, travel, early childhood education, social services. **Services:** Interlibrary loan; Center open to the public. **Holdings:** 26,995 volumes. **Subscriptions:** 189 periodicals.

4153 ■ Conde Nast Publications Library and Information Services
4 Times Sq., 17th Fl.
New York, NY 10036
Ph:(212)286-2860
URL: http://www.condenastdigital.com
Contact: Sarah Chubb, Pres.
Scope: Fashion, houses, gardens, home furnishings, interior design, health, personalities, photographs. **Holdings:** 7000 volumes. **Subscriptions:** 200 journals and other serials; 4 newspapers.

4154 ■ Fashion Institute of Design & Merchandising–Cyril Magnin Resource and Research Center
55 Stockton St., 5th Fl.
San Francisco, CA 94108-5829
Ph:(415)675-5200, x3361
Free: 800-422-3436
Fax:(415)296-7299
URL: http://fidm.edu
Contact: Jim Glenny, Lib.Dir.
Scope: Fashion design and merchandising, interior design, apparel manufacturing, advertising, merchandising, marketing. **Services:** Center not open to the public. **Holdings:** 4000 books; 800 AV programs; 1000 newspaper clipping files; 4000 videos, DVDs, and slides. **Subscriptions:** 200 journals and other serials.

4155 ■ Fashion Institute of Design & Merchandising–Orange County Library
17590 Gillette Ave.
Irvine, CA 92614-5610
Ph:(949)851-6200
Fax:(949)851-6808
Co. E-mail: rmarkman@fidm.com
URL: http://www.fidm.com
Contact: Rebecca Markman, Campus Libn.
Scope: Apparel manufacturing management, cosmetics and fragrance merchandising, fashion design, interior design, merchandise marketing, textile design, visual presentation and space design. **Services:** Library open to the public by appointment. **Holdings:** 3000 books; 130 bound periodical volumes; 40 pamphlet headings; 475 videotapes; 135 slide sets; 300 retail catalogs; 100 Annual reports; 50 CD-ROMs. **Subscriptions:** 80 journals and other serials; 8 newspapers.

4156 ■ Fashion Institute of Technology–Gladys Marcus Library
7th Ave. at 27th St.
E-Bldg. E502
New York, NY 10001-5992
Ph:(212)217-4340
Fax:(212)217-4371
Co. E-mail: greta_earnest@fitnyc.edu
URL: http://fitnyc.edu/library
Contact: Prof. N.J. Wolfe, Lib.Dir.
Scope: Costume, fashion, interior design, management engineering technology, fashion buying and merchandising, textiles, toy design, packaging design, advertising. **Services:** Interlibrary loan; copying; Library open to the public for reference use only by appointment. **Holdings:** 130,260 books; 113,265 nonprint units; 20,637 bound periodical volumes; 125,000 fashion slides; 4712 reels of microfilm; 438 CD-ROM serials and digital monographs. **Subscriptions:** 4000 journals and other serials.

4157 ■ George Brown College of Applied Arts & Technology Archives
500 Macpherson Ave., Rm. F-103
PO Box 1015, Sta. B
Toronto, ON, Canada M5T 2T9
Ph:(416)415-5000, x4771
Fax:(416)415-4772
Co. E-mail: rmacaula@georgebrown.ca
URL: http://llc.georgebrown.ca/llc/er_dept/archives/gb_er_archives.aspx
Contact: Robert Macaulay, Coll.Archv.
Scope: College history, labor relations, fashion industry, post-secondary education, nursing schools, collegiate sports. **Services:** Copying; archives open to the public with restrictions and by appointment only. **Holdings:** 190 cubic meters of records and manuscripts; 2700 linear meters publications, clippings, photographs, filsm, audio and video recordings.

4158 ■ Illinois Institute of Art/ Schaumburg–Learning Resource Center
1000 N. Plaza Dr., Ste. 100
Schaumburg, IL 60173-4913
Ph:(847)619-3450

Free: 800-314-3450
URL: http://www.artinstitutes.edu/schaumburg/
Scope: Graphic design, interior design, applied art and design, furniture history. **Services:** Interlibrary loan. **Holdings:** Books; slides; periodicals; videotapes; DVDs; CD-ROMs. **Subscriptions:** 175 journals and other serials.

4159 ■ Metropolitan Museum of Art–Irene Lewisohn Costume Reference Library
1000 Fifth Ave.
New York, NY 10028-0198
Ph:(212)650-2723
Fax:(212)570-3970
Co. E-mail: julie.le@metmuseum.org
URL: http://www.metmuseum.org/education/er_lib.asp#ire
Scope: History of costume, fashion, fashion designers, social history. **Services:** Copying; Library open to professional designers and research scholars by appointment. **Holdings:** 40,000 cataloged books and journals; 100,000 pieces of ephemera, including swatch books, fashion sketches, fashion plates, postcards, and vertical files; 50 fashion periodical subscriptions. **Subscriptions:** 70 journals and other serials.

4160 ■ Otis College of Art and Design–Millard Sheets Library
Ahmanson Bldg., 3rd Fl.
9045 Lincoln Blvd.
Goldsmith Campus
Los Angeles, CA 90045
Ph:(310)665-6930
Co. E-mail: maberry@otis.edu
URL: http://www.otis.edu/life_otis/library/index.html
Contact: Sue Maberry, Lib.Dir.
Scope: Fine arts, communication design, architecture, fashion, ceramics, photography. **Services:** Interlibrary loan; copying; Library open to the public by appointment only. **Holdings:** 45,000 books; 2900 bound periodical volumes; 100,000 slides; 54 VF drawers of artists' ephemera files; 8 VF drawers of clipping files; 267 audiocassettes; 123 films; 150 videocassettes and cassettes; 5000 videos/DVDs; 20,000 images. **Subscriptions:** 150 journals and other serials.

4161 ■ Parsons School of Design–Adam & Sophie Gimbel Design Library
2 W. 13th St.
New York, NY 10011
Ph:(212)229-8914, x4121
Fax:(212)229-2806
Co. E-mail: luedkej@newschool.edu
URL: http://library.newschool.edu/gimbel/
Contact: Jill Luedke, Ref. and Instr.Libn.
Scope: Fine arts, architecture, costume, crafts, design, environmental design, fashion, graphic arts, photography, typography. **Services:** Interlibrary loan. **Holdings:** 61,000 books; 55,000 mounted picture plates; 85,000 slides; archives. **Subscriptions:** 200 journals and other serials.

4162 ■ Philadelphia University–Paul J. Gutman Library
School House Ln. and Henry Ave.
Philadelphia, PA 19144
Ph:(215)951-2840
Fax:(215)951-2574
Co. E-mail: reference@philau.edu
URL: http://www.philau.edu/library
Contact: Stanley Gorski, Interim Dir.
Scope: Textiles, textile manufacturing, apparel, fashion, architecture, design, business. **Services:** Interlibrary loan; copying; Library open to the public for research only. **Holdings:** 113,600 books; 12,000 bound periodical volumes; 4900 microforms; 2000 AV; 8000 archival items. **Subscriptions:** 929 journals and other serials; 20 newspapers.

4163 ■ Southern New Hampshire University–Shapiro Library
2500 N. River Rd.
Manchester, NH 03106-1394
Ph:(603)645-9605
Fax:(603)645-9685
Co. E-mail: reference@snhu.edu
URL: http://www.snhu.edu/library.asp
Contact: Kathy Growney, Dean of Univ.Lib.
Scope: Economics, accounting, computer sciences, business management, finance, taxes, marketing and retailing, hotel/resort/tourism, community economic development, mathematics, fashion merchandising. **Services:** Interlibrary loan; copying; Library open to the public. **Holdings:** 81,010 books; 514 bound periodical volumes; 6949 reels of microfilm; 10 VF drawers of archival materials; 345,612 microfiche. **Subscriptions:** 654 journals and other serials; 11 newspapers.

4164 ■ Tavy Stone Fashion Library
Detroit Historical Museum
5401 Woodward Ave.
Detroit, MI 48202
Ph:(313)833-1805
Fax:(313)833-5342
Co. E-mail: webmaster@detroithistorical.org
URL: http://www.detroithistorical.org
Contact: Jill M. Koepke, Libn.
Scope: Fashion (antiquity to present) - American and European fashion designers, careers, advertising, merchandising, management, textiles and fabrics, cosmetics and fragrances, historic costume, fashion retailers; the business, sociological, and psychological aspects of fashion. **Services:** Copying; Library open to the public with restrictions. **Holdings:** 800 books; 40 VF drawers; 500 slides; 10 color swatches; 21 AV programs. **Subscriptions:** 6 journals and other serials.

4165 ■ University of British Columbia–Art, Architecture, and Planning Division
Irving K. Barber Learning Centre
1961 East Mall
Vancouver, BC, Canada V6T 1Z1
Ph:(604)822-3943
Fax:(604)822-3779
Co. E-mail: lcontact@interchange.ubc.ca
URL: http://www.library.ubc.ca/aarp/
Contact: D. Vanessa Kam, Hd.Libn.
Scope: Fine arts, architecture, community and regional planning, history of costume and dance, artistic photography, fashion design. **Services:** Library open to the public with restrictions. **Holdings:** 220,000 books and bound periodical volumes. **Subscriptions:** 400 journals and other serials.

4166 ■ University of Cincinnati–Design, Architecture, Art & Planning Library
5480 Aronoff Center for Design and Art
PO Box 210016
Cincinnati, OH 45221-0016
Ph:(513)556-1335
Fax:(513)556-3006
Co. E-mail: jennifer.pollock@uc.edu
URL: http://www.libraries.uc.edu/libraries/daap/index.html
Contact: Jennifer Pollock, Dept.Hd.
Scope: Architecture, art history, art education, planning, interior design, industrial design, fine arts, fashion design, urban studies, health planning, graphic design. **Services:** Interlibrary loan; copying; Library open to the public. **Holdings:** 70,000 books; 11,000 serial volumes; 5000 microforms; 100 planning reports; 200,000 35mm slides; digital images. **Subscriptions:** 400 journals and other serials.

4167 ■ Woodbury University Library
7500 Glenoaks Blvd.
Burbank, CA 91504-1052
Ph:(818)252-5201
Fax:(818)767-4534
Co. E-mail: jennifer.rosenfeld@woodbury.edu
URL: http://library.woodbury.edu
Contact: Nedra Peterson, Dir.
Scope: Business and management, International business, art, architecture, interior design, fashion marketing and design, psychology, animation. **Services:** Interlibrary loan; copying; Library open to the public for reference use only. **Holdings:** 65,000 books; 3070 bound periodical volumes; 17,401 slides; 2000 DVD/VHS. **Subscriptions:** 300 journals and other serials; 5 newspapers.

START-UP INFORMATION

4168 ■ *Design and Launch Your Online Boutique in a Week*
Pub: Entrepreneur Press
Ed: Melissa Campanelli. **Released:** June 2008. **Price:** $17.95. **Description:** Guide to start an online boutique includes information on business planning, Website design and funding.

4169 ■ *In Fashion: From Runway to Retail, Everything You Need to Know to Break Into the Fashion Industry*
Pub: Crown Business Books
Ed: Annemarie Iverson. **Released:** August 10, 2010. **Price:** $16.99. **Description:** Whether your dream is to photograph models, outfit celebrities, design fashions, this book provides details into every aspect for working in the fashion industry.

4170 ■ "Money Matters: Using Sound Resources, You Can Find Capital For Your Business" in *Black Enterprise* (Vol. 38, November 2007, No. 4)
Pub: Earl G. Graves Publishing Co. Inc.
Ed: Carolyn M. Brown. **Description:** Profile of fashion designer Kara Saun who inspired an angel investor from Connecticut to help launch her Fall 2006 clothing line.

4171 ■ "Mount Laurel Woman Launches Venture Into Children's Used Clothing" in *Philadelphia Inquirer* (September 17, 2010)
Pub: Philadelphia Media Network
Ed: Maria Panaritis. **Description:** Profile of Jennifer Frisch, stay-at-home mom turned entrepreneur. Frisch started a used-clothing store Once Upon a Child after opening her franchised Plato's Closet, selling unwanted and used baby clothing and accessories at her new shop, while offering used merchandise to teens at Plato's Closet.

4172 ■ *The Specialty Shop: How to Create Your Own Unique and Profitable Retail Business*
Pub: AMACOM
Ed: Dorothy Finell. **Released:** February 27, 2007. **Price:** $21.95. **Description:** Advise to start retail businesses, including bakeries, gift shops, toy stores, book shops, tea houses, clothing boutiques, and other unique stores.

4173 ■ *Start Your Own Fashion Accessories Business*
Pub: Entrepreneur Press
Released: March 1, 2009. **Price:** $17.95. **Description:** Entrepreneurs wishing to start a fashion accessories business will find important information for setting up a home workshop and office, exploring the market, managing finances, publicizing and advertising the business and more.

ASSOCIATIONS AND OTHER ORGANIZATIONS

4174 ■ International Formalwear Association
244 E Main St.
Galesburg, IL 61401
Ph:(309)721-5450
Fax:(309)342-5921
Co. E-mail: admin@formalwear.org
URL: http://www.formalwear.org
Contact: Rod Benbrook, Pres.
Description: Specialists working to promote the formal wear industry. Conducts educational programs through seminars and exhibitions. **Publications:** *IFA Membership Directory* (annual).

4175 ■ National Retail Federation
325 7th St. NW, Ste. 1100
Washington, DC 20004
Ph:(202)783-7971
Free: 800-673-4692
Fax:(202)737-2849
Co. E-mail: shaym@nrf.com
URL: http://www.nrf.com
Contact: Matt Shay, Pres./CEO
Description: Represents state retail associations, several dozen national retail associations, as well as large and small corporate members representing the breadth and diversity of the retail industry's establishment and employees. Conducts informational and educational conferences related to all phases of retailing including financial planning and cash management, taxation, economic forecasting, expense planning, shortage control, credit, electronic data processing, telecommunications, merchandise management, buying, traffic, security, supply, materials handling, store planning and construction, personnel administration, recruitment and training, and advertising and display. **Publications:** *NRF Foundation Focus* (quarterly); *NRF Update*; *STORES Magazine* (monthly); *Washington Retail Report* (weekly).

REFERENCE WORKS

4176 ■ "Always Striving" in *Women In Business* (Vol. 61, December 2009, No. 6, pp. 28)
Pub: American Business Women's Association
Ed: Kathleen Leighton. **Description:** Jennifer Mull discusses her responsibilities and how she attained success as CEO of Backwoods, a gear and clothing store founded by her father in 1973. She places importance on being true to one's words and beliefs, while emphasizing the capacity to tolerate risks in business. Mull defines success as an evolving concept and believes there must always be something to strive for.

4177 ■ "Apparel Apparatchic at Kmart" in *Barron's* (Vol. 88, March 17, 2008, No. 11, pp. 16)
Pub: Dow Jones & Company, Inc.
Description: Kmart began a nationwide search for women to represent the company in a national advertising campaign. Contestants need to upload their photos to Kmart's website and winners will be chosen by a panel of celebrity judges. The contest aims to reverse preconceived negative notions about the store's quality and service.

4178 ■ "Apparel" in *Retail Merchandiser* (Vol. 51, July-August 2011, No. 4, pp. 14)
Pub: Phoenix Media Corporation
Description: NPD Group Inc. released current sales statistics for the women's apparel market along with men's apparel. It also reported annual shoes sales for 2010. Statistical data included.

4179 ■ "Are You Looking for an Environmentally Friendly Dry Cleaner?" in *Inc.* (Vol. 30, December 2008, No. 12, pp. 34)
Pub: Mansueto Ventures LLC
Ed: Shivani Vora. **Description:** Greenopia rates the greenness of 52 various kinds of businesses, including restaurants, nail salons, dry cleaners, and clothing stores. The guidebooks are sold through various retailers including Barnes & Noble and Amazon.com.

4180 ■ "As Seen On TV" in *Canadian Business* (Vol. 80, November 5, 2007, No. 22, pp. 93)
Pub: Rogers Media
Ed: Zena Olijnyk. **Description:** StarBrand Media Inc. is one of the companies providing fans with information on how and where to purchase the items that television characters are using. StarBrand created the style section found on different television shows' Websites, such as that of the Gossip Girl and Smallville. The benefits of using sites like StarBrand are evaluated.

4181 ■ "Babynut.com to Shut Down" in *Bellingham Business Journal* (Vol. February 2010, pp. 3)
Pub: Sound Publishing Inc.
Description: Saralee Sky and Jerry Kilgore, owners of Babynut.com will close their online store. The site offered a free online and email newsletter to help mothers through pregnancy and the first three years of their child's life. Products being sold at clearance prices include organic and natural maternity and nursing clothing, baby and toddler clothes, books on pregnancy, and more.

4182 ■ "Better Than New" in *Bellingham Business Journal* (Vol. February 2010, pp. 16)
Pub: Sound Publishing Inc.
Ed: Ashley Mitchell. **Description:** Profile of family owned Better Than New clothing store that sells overstock items from department stores and clothing manufacturers. The stores location makes it easy to miss and its only advertising is a large sign posted outside. This is the sixth store owned by the couple, Keijeo and Sirba Halmekanqas.

4183 ■ "Breadwinner Tries on Designer Jeans" in *Houston Business Journal* (Vol. 40, December 18, 2009, No. 32, pp. 1)
Pub: American City Business Journals
Ed: Allison Wollam. **Description:** Chuck Cain, the franchisee who introduced Panera Bread to Houston, Texas has partnered with tax accountant Jim Jacobsen to introduce custom-make Tattu Jeans. As more Tattu Jeans outlets are being planned, Cain is using

entrepreneurial lessons learned from Panera Bread in the new venture. Both Panera Bread and Tattu Jeans were opened by Cain during economic downturns.

4184 ■ "Bringing Charities More Bang for Their Buck" in *Crain's Chicago Business* (Vol. 34, May 23, 2011, No. 21, pp. 31)
Pub: Crain Communications Inc.
Ed: Lisa Bertagnoli. **Description:** Marcy-Newberry Association connects charities with manufacturers in order to use excess items such as clothing, janitorial and office supplies.

4185 ■ "Buy the Pants, Save the Planet?" in *Globe & Mail* (February 5, 2007, pp. B1)
Pub: CTVglobemedia Publishing Inc.
Ed: Keith McArthur. **Description:** The marketing campaign of the clothing company Diesel S.p.A. is discussed. The company has based its latest collection of T-shirt designs on the problem of global warming.

4186 ■ "Buying Chanel (All Of It)" in *Conde Nast Portfolio* (Vol. 2, June 2008, No. 6, pp. 34)
Pub: Conde Nast Publications, Inc.
Ed: Willow Duttge. **Description:** Overview of the luxury company Chanel and an estimated guess as to what the company is worth.

4187 ■ "Can Avenue be Fashionable Again? Livernois Merchants, City Want Revival" in *Crain's Detroit Business* (March 10, 2008)
Pub: Crain Communications, Inc.
Ed: Nancy Kaffer. **Description:** Once a busy retail district, the Avenue of Fashion, a Livernois Avenue strip between Six Mile and Eight Mile roads, is facing a community business effort being backed by city support whose aim is to restore the area to its former glory.

4188 ■ *Canadian Apparel Directory*
Pub: Canadian Apparel Federation
Contact: Bob Kirke, Exec. Dir.
E-mail: bkirke@apparel.ca
Released: Biennial, May/June. **Price:** $132, members; $350, nonmembers. **Publication Includes:** Lists of Canadian industry suppliers, and manufacturers of apparel. **Entries Include:** Company name, address, phone, fax, names and titles of key personnel, name and title of contact, product/service, description of company business activities. **Arrangement:** Alphabetical. **Indexes:** Trade name, product/service, geographical.

4189 ■ "A Change Would Do You Good" in *Canadian Business* (Vol. 80, November 19, 2007, No. 23, pp. 15)
Pub: Rogers Media
Ed: Geoff Kirbyson. **Description:** Western Glove Works will be manufacturing clothing offshore, including Sheryl Crow's jeans collection, in countries such as China and the Philippines. The company decided to operate offshore after 86 years of existence due to the high price of manufacturing jeans in Canada. Western Glove's focus on producing celebrity-endorsed goods is discussed.

4190 ■ *Chief Culture Officer: How to Create a Living, Breathing Corporation*
Pub: Basic Books
Ed: Grant McCracken. **Price:** $26.95. **Description:** Business consultant argues that corporations need to focus on 'reading' what's happening in the culture around them. Otherwise, companies will suffer the consequences, as Levi Strauss did when it missed out on the rise of hip-hop (and the baggy pants that are part of that lifestyle).

4191 ■ "Clothier Delays Opening" in *The Business Journal-Serving Metropolitan Kansas City* (Vol. 27, November 14, 2008, No. 10, pp. 1)
Pub: American City Business Journals, Inc.
Ed: Suzanna Stagemeyer. **Description:** Jos A. Bank Clothiers Inc. has delayed the opening of its store at the Kansas City Power and Light District in Missouri for the first quarter of 2009. The company is still waiting for other tenants to open shop in the district. Comments from officials concerning the retail sector are also presented.

4192 ■ "Common Thread" in *Entrepreneur* (Vol. 36, March 2008, No. 3, pp. 144)
Pub: Entrepreneur Media Inc.
Ed: Sara Wilson. **Description:** Profile of Stacey Benet and her business, Alice and Olivia, and how she jumpstarted her career in the clothing industry after she wore a self-designed pair of pants that caught the attention of a Barney's New York representative is presented.

4193 ■ "Consignment Shop Closes Without Warning to Customers, Landlord" in *Sun Journal* (June 30, 2010)
Pub: Freedom Communications Inc.
Ed: Laura Oleniacz. **Description:** Off The Racks consignment shop located on Glenburnie Road in New Bern, North Carolina closed without warning to customers or its landlord. The consignors who donated clothing to the store were left unpaid.

4194 ■ "Consignment Shop Offers Children's Clothes, Products" in *Frederick News-Post* (August 19, 2010)
Pub: Federick News-Post
Ed: Ed Waters Jr. **Description:** Sweet Pea Consignments for Children offers used items for newborns to pre-teens. The shop carries name brand clothing as well as toys, books and baby products.

4195 ■ "Crowdsourcing their Way into One Big Mess" in *Brandweek* (Vol. 51, October 25, 2010, No. 38, pp. 26)
Pub: Nielsen Business Media, Inc.
Ed: Gregg S. Lipman. **Description:** The Gap, was counting on crowdsourcing to provide feedback for its new logo, but it did not prove positive for the retailer. However, a massive outcry of negative opinion, via crowdsourcing, may not always equal valid, constructive criticism.

4196 ■ "Designer is Walking Ad for TIBI Line" in *Charlotte Observer* (February 5, 2007)
Pub: Knight-Ridder/Tribune Business News
Ed: Crystal Dempsey. **Description:** Profile of Amy Smilovic, mother of two children, and clothing designer. Smilovic wears what she designs, making her a great marketing tool for her clothing line TIBI.

4197 ■ *Directory of Apparel Specialty Stores*
Pub: Chain Store Guide
Released: Annual, Latest edition 2011. **Price:** $395, individuals Directory; $445, individuals online lite; $1,075, individuals online pro. **Covers:** 5,040 apparel and sporting goods specialty retailers in the United States and Canada, operating more than 70,700 stores. Apparel retailers must have annual retail sales of at least $500,000; sporting goods specialty retailers must also have $500,000 in annual sales, with the condition that at least 20% of product sales are from sporting goods equipment. **Entries Include:** Company name, phone, and fax numbers; physical and mailing addresses; company e-mail and web addresses; Internet order processing indicator; percentage of Internet sales; type of business; listing type; product lines; total, industry, and product group sales; total selling square footage; store prototype sizes; total stores; trading areas; projected openings and remodeling; units by trade name; distribution center locations; resident buyer's name and location; mail order indicator; percentage of mail order sales; catalog names; private label indicator; private label credit card indicator; apparel price lines; average number of checkouts; year founded; public company indicator; parent company name and location; and key personnel with titles; 7,200 personnel email addresses . **Arrangement:** Geographical. **Indexes:** Alphabetical, product lines, exclusions.

4198 ■ "Doing Good: Fair Fashion" in *Entrepreneur* (Vol. 35, October 2007, No. 10, pp. 36)
Pub: Entrepreneur Media Inc.
Ed: J.J. Ramberg. **Description:** Indigenous Designs was launched in 1993, when organic clothing was not yet popular. However, the company has become successful in the industry, with $4 million dollars in revenue, owing to the growing environment awareness of consumers. A history of how the company was formed and an overview of their production process are provided.

4199 ■ "Don't Tweak Your Supply Chain - Rethink It End to End" in *Harvard Business Review* (Vol. 88, October 2010, No. 10, pp. 62)
Pub: Harvard Business School Publishing
Ed: Hau L. Lee. **Description:** Hong Kong apparel firm Esquel Apparel Ltd. is used to illustrate supply chain reorganization to improve a firm's sustainability. Discussion focuses on taking a broad approach rather than addressing individual steps or processes.

4200 ■ "Dots Sings To New Tune With Its Radio Station" in *Crain's Cleveland Business* (Vol. 30, June 15, 2009, No. 23, pp. 7)
Pub: Crain Communications, Inc.
Description: Dots LLC, a women's clothing retailer, has launched an online radio station on its Website. The station plays the in-store music to customers while they are shopping online.

4201 ■ "Dress Professionally Cool for Summer" in *Women In Business* (Vol. 62, June 2010, No. 2, pp. 38)
Pub: American Business Women's Association
Ed: Maureen Sullivan. **Description:** Summer clothing for business and career women is discussed with regard to traditional and relaxed work places. Fabric considerations, tips on choosing blazers and a list of clothes and other items that are not appropriate for the workplace are presented.

4202 ■ "Echo Vintage Clothing Fundraiser Set July 24" in *Tri-City Herald* (July 22, 2010)
Pub: McClathcy-Tribune
Description: Bicentennial Echo Vintage Clothing Show and Tea was held July 24, 2010 at the Echo City Hall Ballroom in Echo, Oregon. The event is held every two years to fund project in Echo and to maintain the vintage clothing collection.

4203 ■ "The Endless Flow of Russell Simmons" in *Entrepreneur* (Vol. 37, September 2009, No. 9, pp. 24)
Pub: Entrepreneur Media, Inc.
Ed: Josh Dean. **Description:** Entrepreneur Russell Simmons has successfully grown his businesses by focusing on underserved markets. Simons has never given up on any business strategy. He has also entered the music, clothing and television industries.

4204 ■ "Fall Fever" in *Canadian Business* (Vol. 81, October 13, 2008, No. 17, pp. S12)
Pub: Rogers Media Ltd.
Description: Buyer's guide of men's suits and jackets for fall are presented, including a suit by Boss Hugo Boss recommended for fun in the city after finishing work. Designers Ermenegildo, Michael Kors, and Arnold Brant are also highlighted.

4205 ■ "Fall Wardrobe on a Budget" in *Women In Business* (Vol. 62, September 2010, No. 3, pp. 38)
Pub: American Business Women's Association
Ed: Kathleen Leighton. **Description:** Things women should keep in mind when putting together a fall wardrobe are discussed. Women should aim for at least two jackets, five tops, four pants or skirts, two twin sets, five pairs of pantyhose, and two pair of shoes. They should also be ruthless when it comes to quality and practicality.

4206 ■ *The Fashion Designer Survival Guide*
Pub: Kaplan Publishing
Ed: Mary Gehlhar; Zac Posen. **Released:** September 1, 2005. **Description:** Professional advice from an insider to help start and run a fashion business.

4207 ■ "Fashion Forward - Frugally" in *Entrepreneur* (Vol. 37, July 2009, No. 7, pp. 18)
Pub: Entrepreneur Media, Inc.
Ed: Jason Daley. **Description:** Staci Deal, a Fayetteville-based franchisee of fashion brand Plato's Closet, shares her experiences on the company's growth. Deal believes that the economy, and the fact

that Fayetteville is a college town, played a vital role in boosting the used clothing store's popularity. Her thoughts on being a young business owner, and the advantages of running a franchise are also given.

4208 ■ "Fashionistas Weigh in on the Super-Thin" in *Charlotte Observer* (February 7, 2007)
Pub: Knight-Ridder/Tribune Business News
Ed: Crystal Dempsey. **Description:** Council of Fashion Designers of America held a panel discussion regarding the weight and ages of models used to highlight clothing.

4209 ■ "Finishing Touches: the Fashion Statement is in the Detail" in *Black Enterprise* (Vol. 37, January 2007, No. 6, pp. 106)
Pub: Earl G. Graves Publishing Co. Inc.
Ed: Sonia Alleyne. **Description:** Men are discovering the importance of dressing for success. Paying attention to the details such as shoes, socks, cuffs, and collars are just as important as finding the right suit.

4210 ■ "Five Reasons Why the Gap Fell Out of Fashion" in *Globe & Mail* (January 27, 2007, pp. B4)
Pub: CTVglobemedia Publishing Inc.
Ed: Keith McArthur. **Description:** The five major market trends that have caused the decline of fashion clothing retailer Gap Inc.'s sales are discussed. The shift in brand, workplace fashion culture, competition, demographics, and consumer preferences have lead to the Gap's brand identity.

4211 ■ "Fledgling Brands May Take the Fall With Steve & Barry's" in *Advertising Age* (Vol. 79, July 7, 2008, No. 26, pp. 6)
Pub: Crain Communications, Inc.
Ed: Natalie Zmuda. **Description:** Steve & Barry's, a retailer that holds licensing deals with a number of designers and celebrities, may have to declare bankruptcy; this leaves the fate of the retailer's hundreds of licensing deals and exclusive celebrity lines in question.

4212 ■ "Forget Your Pants, Calvin Klein Wants Into Your Bedroom" in *Globe & Mail* (March 31, 2007, pp. B4)
Pub: CTVglobemedia Publishing Inc.
Ed: Barrie McKenna. **Description:** The plans of Phillips-Van Heusen Corp. to open more Calvin Klein stores for selling the new ranges of clothing, personal care products, luggage and mattresses are discussed.

4213 ■ *Fugitive Denim: A Moving Story of People and Pants in the Borderless World of Global Trade*
Pub: W.W. Norton & Company
Ed: Rachel Snyder. **Released:** April 2009. **Price:** $16.95. **Description:** In-depth study of the global production and processes of how jeans are designed, sewn, and transported as well as how the cotton for denim is grown, regulated, purchased and processed.

4214 ■ "Green It Like You Mean It" in *Special Events Magazine* (Vol. 28, February 1, 2009, No. 2)
Pub: Special Events Magazine
Ed: Christine Landry. **Description:** Eco-friendly party planners offer advice for planning and hosting green parties or events. Tips include information for using recycled paper products, organic food and drinks. The Eco Nouveau Fashion Show held by Serene Star Productions reused old garments to create new fashions as well as art pieces from discarded doors and window frames for the show; eco-friendly treats and gift bags were highlighted at the event.

4215 ■ "H&M Offers a Dress for Less" in *Canadian Business* (Vol. 83, September 14, 2010, No. 15, pp. 20)
Pub: Rogers Media Ltd.
Ed: Laura Cameron. **Description:** Swedish clothing company H&M has implemented loss leader strategy by pricing some dresses at extremely low prices. The economy has forced retailers to keep prices down despite the increasing cost of manufacturing, partly due to Chinese labor becoming more expensive. How the trend will affect apparel companies is discussed.

4216 ■ "Haute Flyers" in *Canadian Business* (Vol. 80, November 19, 2007, No. 23, pp. 68)
Pub: Rogers Media
Ed: Rachel Pulfer. **Description:** Duckie Brown has been nominated by the Council of Fashion Designers of America as best menswear designer in the U.S. for 2007, along with leaders Calvin Klein and Ralph Lauren. The New York-based company was formed the day after September 11, 2001, but the timing did not hamper its growth. The works and plans of owners Steven Cox and Daniel Silver are described.

4217 ■ "Home Shows Signs of Life at Target" in *Home Textiles Today* (Vol. 31, May 24, 2011, No. 13, pp. 1)
Pub: Reed Business Information
Description: Retailer, Target, is experience a boost in sales for apparel and products for the home.

4218 ■ "Hot Kicks, Cool Price" in *Black Enterprise* (Vol. 37, December 2006, No. 5, pp. 34)
Pub: Earl G. Graves Publishing Co. Inc.
Ed: Topher Sanders. **Description:** Stephon Marbury of the New York Nicks introduced a new basketball shoe, the Starbury One, costing $14.98. The shoes are an addition to the Starbury clothing line and although the privately owned company would not disclose figures; stores sold out of a month's worth of inventory in merely three days.

4219 ■ "How to Keep Your Cool and Your Friends in a Heat Wave" in *Canadian Business* (Vol. 83, August 17, 2010, No. 13-14, pp. 79)
Pub: Rogers Media Ltd.
Ed: Angelina Chapin. **Description:** A buyer's guide of menswear clothing for businessmen is presented. The products include an antiperspirant and deodorant, men's dress shorts, shoes and bamboo fabric undershirt.

4220 ■ "How This First Lady Moves Markets" in *Harvard Business Review* (Vol. 88, November 2010, No. 11, pp. 38)
Pub: Harvard Business School Publishing
Description: A chart is presented demonstrating how First Lady Michelle Obama's choice of fashion designer has impacted the clothing industry.

4221 ■ *Hug Your Customers*
Pub: Hyperion Books
Ed: Jack Mitchell. **Price:** $19.95. **Description:** The CEO of Mitchells/Roberts, two very successful clothing stores, professes his belief in showering customers with attention. His secrets for long-term business success include advice about attracting a good staff, lowering marketing costs, and maintaining higher gross margins and revenues.

4222 ■ "Insider" in *Canadian Business* (Vol. 80, Winter 2007, No. 24, pp.)
Pub: Rogers Media
Ed: Zena Olijnyk. **Description:** Luluemon Athletica started in 1998 after Dennis Wilson takes a yoga class and notices a demand from women for breathable clothes. The company opened their first outlet in Vancouver in November 2000 then opened their first U.S. store in 2003 until finally going public July 27, 2007 where its stocks doubled in value within days of trading.

4223 ■ "Island Co.: Isle Style" in *Entrepreneur* (Vol. 35, October 2007, No. 10, pp. 172)
Pub: Entrepreneur Media Inc.
Ed: Sara Wilson. **Description:** Island Co., producer of travel clothing and swimsuits was formed by Spencer Antle in 2002. Its office projects the Caribbean atmosphere, a strategy Antle used to promote the company's theme to its clients. Future plans for the company are also indicated.

4224 ■ "It's All in the Details" in *Canadian Business* (Vol. 80, December 25, 2006, No. 1, pp. 11)
Pub: Rogers Media
Description: The failure of several Canadian clothing retailers to disclose their labor practices is discussed.

4225 ■ "It's So You! Consignment Chop Owner Thrilled to See Vision Come to Fruition" in *News-Herald* (August 27, 2010)
Pub: News-Herald
Ed: Brandon C. Baker. **Description:** Profile of Laurel Howes and her It's So You! Boutique. The consignment shop is located in Willoughby's Pine Ride Plaza in Ohio. The shop targets all women, but particularly those who are not that comfortable with shopping consignment.

4226 ■ "Izod, Loft Outlets Coming To Tanger" in *New Hampshire Business Review* (Vol. 33, March 25, 2011, No. 6, pp. 30)
Pub: Business Publications Inc.
Description: Izod and Lots stores will open at the Tanger Outlet Center in Tilton, New Hampshire. Both stores will feature fashions and accessories.

4227 ■ "Jeans Draw a Global Following" in *Marketing to Women* (Vol. 21, April 2008, No. 4, pp. 6)
Pub: EPM Communications, Inc.
Description: According to a global study by Synovate of jeans and the women who wear them uncovered trends such as brand loyalty and if given a choice 45 percent of all respondents say that if given a choice, they would wear jeans every day.

4228 ■ "Let It Shine: Organization Helps Disadvantaged Girls See Their Worth" in *Black Enterprise* (Vol. 38, February 2008, No. 7, pp. 142)
Pub: Earl G. Graves Publishing Co. Inc.
Ed: George Alexander. **Description:** Wilson Mourning, founder of the clothing label Honey Child, attributes her success to her mother and other positive women who helped her through her adolescence. Mourning created a mentoring organization that helps young girls in the Miami, Florida area to develop life skills.

4229 ■ "Longtime Peoria Heights Second-Hand Clothing Shop Closing" in *Journal Star* (December 18, 2010)
Pub: Journal Star
Ed: Scott Hilyard. **Description:** The Happy Hangar, a consignment clothing store located in Peoria Heights, Illinois is closing after 31 years of selling second-hand clothing.

4230 ■ "Luxe Men Are In Style" in *Brandweek* (Vol. 49, April 21, 2008, No. 16, pp. 12)
Pub: VNU Business Media, Inc.
Description: According to a recent survey by Unity Marketing, among 1,300 luxury shoppers found that men spent an average of $2,401 on fashion items over a three-month period which is nearly $1,000 more than women. Men also spring for more luxury items such as vehicles and memberships to exclusive clubs.

4231 ■ "Luxury Still Sells Well" in *Puget Sound Business Journal* (Vol. 29, September 5, 2008, No. 20, pp. 1)
Pub: American City Business Journals
Ed: Jeanne Lang Jones. **Description:** High fashion retailers are planning to open stores in the Puget Sound area despite the economic slowdown, citing high incomes in the area despite the weak U.S. dollar.

4232 ■ "Making It Work" in *Retail Merchandiser* (Vol. 51, July-August 2011, No. 4, pp. 43)
Pub: Phoenix Media Corporation
Ed: Anthony DiPaolo. **Description:** Profile of Anthony DiPaolo and his purchase of the Work 'N Gear retail store in 2002. The brick and mortar shop sells work wear and healthcare apparel and DiPaolo believes customer respect is essential to his success.

4233 ■ "Maternity Wear Goes Green" in *Marketing to Women* (Vol. 21, March 2008, No. 3, pp. 3)
Pub: EPM Communications, Inc.
Description: Mother's Work Inc. has launched a series of environmentally-friendly products made from such sustainable fibers as organic cotton and bamboo.

4234 ■ "Meet Joe Fresh" in *Canadian Business* (Vol. 79, November 6, 2006, No. 22, pp. 49)
Pub: Rogers Media
Ed: Calvin Leung. **Description:** The efforts of Joseph Mimran, a fashion designer, in improving the business of Joe Fresh style products are analyzed.

4235 ■ *Men's & Boys' Wear Buyers*
Pub: Briefings Media Group
Contact: Alan M. Douglas, President
Released: Annual, latest edition 2011-2012. **Price:** $329, individuals directory price; $659, individuals directory/CD combo price. **Covers:** 9,000 buyers and 5,100 stores in the men's and boys' retail industry. **Entries Include:** Store name, address, phone, fax; names and titles of key personnel; e-mail; URL; financial data; branch/subsidiary name and address; products/services provided; price points and sales volume; parent company; type and number of stores for companies; corporate buying office. **Arrangement:** Geographical. **Indexes:** Store name, new listings, mail order, buying office, online retailer.

4236 ■ "Military Brides Can Get Free Wedding Gowns" in *Virginian-Pilot* (November 10, 2010)
Pub: The Virginia-Pilot
Ed: Jamesetta Walker. **Description:** Seventy-five designer wedding gowns will be given to military brides on a first-come, first-served basis at Maya Couture through the Brides Across America's wedding gown giveaway program. Gowns are valued between $500 to $3,000 and are donated by designers Maggie Sottero, Pronovias and Essense of Australia.

4237 ■ "Not All Contracts a Good Fit for Fashion Reps" in *Agency Sales Magazine* (Vol. 39, September-October 2009, No. 9, pp. 10)
Pub: MANA
Ed: Jack Foster. **Description:** Difficult situations regarding the relationship between sales representatives and their principals in the fashion industry are presented and suggestions on how to create contracts that seek to prevent potential problems are provided. Sales reps should make sure that manufacturer has a viable business that is well thought-out and adequately financed.

4238 ■ "Office Party Attire" in *Women In Business* (Vol. 61, October-November 2009, No. 5, pp. 27)
Pub: American Business Women's Association
Ed: Leigh Elmore. **Description:** Office holiday party attire should conform to factors such as time, location, scheduled events, and other company-furnished details. Observing this guideline can help in upholding the business nature of the party. Party attendees are also encouraged to network with other attendees, while tips on how to behave during the party are also presented.

4239 ■ "On a Mission: Ginch Gonch Wants You to Get Rid of Your Tighty Whities" in *Canadian Business* (Vol. 81, September 29, 2008, No. 16)
Pub: Rogers Media Ltd.
Ed: Michelle Magnan. **Description:** New Equity Capital acquired underwear maker Ginch Gonch in July 2008; founder Jason Sutherland kept his position as creative director of the company and will retain his title as 'director of stitches and inches'. The company is known for its products, which are reminiscent of the days when people wore underwear covered in cowboys and stars as kids. The company also claims that Nelly, Justin Timberlake, and Hilary Duff have worn their products.

4240 ■ "One Paddle, Two Paddle" in *Hawaii Business* (Vol. 53, October 2007, No. 4, pp. 65)
Pub: Hawaii Business Publishing
Ed: Kyle Galdeira. **Description:** Oiwi Ocean Gear's strategy may not give instant profits, but it works well for the company's goal of providing high-quality apparel for paddlers. The apparel company produces and markets swimwear, paddling jerseys and active wear. The company's strategy is compared with the selling of mass-produced clothes lower prices.

4241 ■ "Pink Label: Victoria's Sales Secret" in *Advertising Age* (Vol. 79, July 7, 2008, No. 26, pp. 4)
Pub: Crain Communications, Inc.
Ed: Natalie Zmuda. **Description:** Victoria Secret's Pink label accounted for roughly 17 percent of the retailer's total sales last year. The company is launching a Collegiate Collection which will be promoted by a campus tour program.

4242 ■ "Portland Wooing Under Armour to West Coast Facility" in *Baltimore Business Journal* (Vol. 27, January 29, 2010, No. 39, pp. 1)
Pub: American City Business Journals
Ed: Andy Giegerich. **Description:** Baltimore, Maryland sports apparel maker, Under Armour, is planning a west coast expansion with Portland, Oregon among the sites considered to house its apparel and footwear design center. Portland officials counting on the concentration of nearly 10,000 activewear workers in the city will help lure the company to the city.

4243 ■ "Prime Time for Vintage" in *Daily Variety* (Vol. 308, August 23, 2010, No. 35, pp. 12)
Pub: Reed Business Information Inc.
Ed: Cynthia Littleton. **Description:** The week of August 23 starts the busy season for owners of Los Angeles' vintage couture shops due to Emmy-related events.

4244 ■ "Pssst! Buzz About Target" in *Barron's* (Vol. 89, July 27, 2009, No. 30, pp. 15)
Pub: Dow Jones & Co., Inc.
Ed: Katherine Cheng. **Description:** Target rebutted the rumor that they will disassociate themselves from a line of clothing inspired by the television show 'Gossip Girl'. Target's spokesman says that the retailer intends to remain closely identified with the show. Target's sales should benefit from the hotly anticipated clothing line.

4245 ■ "Q&A: Joseph Ribkoff" in *Canadian Business* (Vol. 81, March 31, 2008, No. 5, pp. 4)
Pub: Rogers Media
Ed: Zena Olijnyk. **Description:** Joseph Ribkoff started his career in the garment trade by sweeping floors and running deliveries for a dress manufacturer called Town & Country and earned $16 a week. Ribkoff says that the key to controlling costs in Canada is to invest in the latest equipment and technology to stay competitive.

4246 ■ "Research and Market Adds: 2010 US Women's and Children's Clothing Wholesale Report" in *Wireless News* (November 8, 2009)
Pub: Close-Up Media
Description: Highlights of the annual Research and Markets "2010 U.S. Women's and Children's Clothing Wholesale Report" include industry statistics, demographics and forecasts.

4247 ■ "Research and Markets Adds: 2011 U.S. Women's & Children's Clothing Wholesale Report" in *Health & Beauty Close-Up* (October 16, 2010)
Pub: Close-Up Media Inc.
Description: The Women's & Children's Clothing Wholesale Report is an annual report containing timely and accurate industry statistics, forecasts and demographics.

4248 ■ "Retail News: Children's Boutique Relocates to Conway" in *Sun News* (June 4, 2010)
Pub: The Sun News
Description: Little Angel's Children's Boutique and Big Oak Frame Shop have moved to downtown locations in Conway, South Carolina. Little Angel's will sell children's clothing and accessories, shoes and gifts, while the frame shop will offer custom framing along with the sale of stationary, invitations and local prints.

4249 ■ "Rule of the Masses: Reinventing Fashion Via Crowdsourcing" in *WWD* (Vol. 200, July 26, 2010, No. 17, pp. 1)
Pub: Conde Nast Publications Inc.
Ed: Cate T. Corcoran. **Description:** Large apparel brands and retailers are crowdsourcing as a way to increase customer loyalty and to build their businesses.

4250 ■ "Shop Around" in *Houston Chronicle* (December 7, 2010, pp. 3)
Pub: Houston Chronicle
Ed: Tara Dooley. **Description:** Profile of Diana Candida and Maria Martinez who partnered to open Beatniks, a shop carrying vintage clothing, art from various artists, dance shoes, and jewelry.

4251 ■ "Size Obsession" in *Marketing to Women* (Vol. 22, August 2009, No. 8, pp. 2)
Pub: EPM Communications, Inc.
Description: Clothing size is becoming a marketing tool for retailers who wish to seize more of the female market share. Women are more likely to purchase an item in a smaller size.

4252 ■ "Skinny Jeans Sticking Around for Fall" in *Charlotte Observer* (February 5, 2007)
Pub: Knight-Ridder/Tribune Business News
Ed: Crystal Dempsey. **Description:** Clothing designers were showing skinny jeans in the fall/winter fashion shows for 2007.

4253 ■ "S.M. Whitney Co. (1868-2010)" in *Canadian Business* (Vol. 83, October 12, 2010, No. 17, pp. 27)
Pub: Rogers Media Ltd.
Ed: Angelina Chapin. **Description:** A history of S.M. Whitney Company is presented. The cotton company was opened in 1868. The cotton is sold to textile manufacturers after crops have been picked, ginned and baled. The company closed down in 2010 after chief executive officer Barry Whitney decided to sell his last bale of cotton.

4254 ■ "The Smell of Fear: Is a Bottom Near?" in *Barron's* (Vol. 88, March 17, 2008, No. 11, pp. M3)
Pub: Dow Jones & Company, Inc.
Ed: Kopin Tan. **Description:** Liquidity problems at Bear Stearns frightened investors in markets around the world due to the fear of the prospects of a big bank's failure. Shares of health maintenance organizations got battered led by WellPoint, and Humana but longer-term investors who could weather short-term volatility may find value here. The value of J. Crew shares is also discussed.

4255 ■ "Spell It Out" in *Entrepreneur* (Vol. 36, April 2008, No. 4, pp. 123)
Pub: Entrepreneur Media, Inc.
Ed: Emily Weisberg. **Description:** IM:It is an apparel and accessories company that markets products with instant messaging (IM) acronyms and emoticons. Examples of these are "LOL" and "GTG". Other details on IM:It products are discussed.

4256 ■ "Stylish Successes" in *Women In Business* (Vol. 61, October-November 2009, No. 5, pp. 12)
Pub: American Business Women's Association
Ed: Leigh Elmore; Megan L. Reese. **Description:** Amanda Horan Kennedy, Angela Samuels, Barbara Nast Saletan, and Patty Nast Canton are career women who ventured into entrepreneurship. They are deemed to possess networking and teamwork skills that ensured their success in the garment industry.

4257 ■ "Suited for Success" in *Retail Merchandiser* (Vol. 51, July-August 2011, No. 4, pp. 6)
Pub: Phoenix Media Corporation
Description: MyBestFit is a size-matching body scanner that helps consumers find the perfect size clothing for themselves, giving brick and mortar retailers an edge on ecommerce competitors.

4258 ■ "Suiting Up; Yes, You're Smart, But Can You Look the Part" in *Crain's Chicago Business* (Vol. 30, February 2007, No. 6, pp. 39)
Pub: Crain Communications, Inc.
Ed: Kate Ryan. **Description:** For investment bankers, fashion is a must. Advice for men and women included.

4259 ■ "Timberland's CEO On Standing Up to 65,000 Angry Activists" in *Harvard Business Review* (Vol. 88, September 2010, No. 9, pp. 39)
Pub: Harvard Business School Publishing
Ed: Jeff Swartz. **Description:** Timberland Company avoided a potential boycott by taking a two-way approach. It addressed a supplier issue that posed a threat to the environment, and launched an email campaign to keep Greenpeace activists informed of the development of a new supplier agreement.

4260 ■ *Too Good to be Threw: The Complete Operations Manual for Resale and Consignment Shops*
Pub: Katydid Press
Price: $69.95. **Description:** Revised edition covers all the information needfed to start and run a buy-outright or consignment shop, covering anything from clothing to furniture resale.

4261 ■ "The Transparent Supply Chain" in *Harvard Business Review* (Vol. 88, October 2010, No. 10, pp. 76)
Pub: Harvard Business School Publishing
Ed: Steve New. **Description:** Examination of the use of new technologies to create a transparent supply chain, such as next-generation 2D bar codes in clothing labels that can provide data on a garment's provenance.

4262 ■ "Trousseaus of Memories Trail Behind Wedding Gowns" in *Oregonian* (September 4, 2010)
Pub: The Oregonian
Ed: Anne Saker. **Description:** Readers are asked to share stories about their wedding gowns and what that garment meant to them at the time and now.

4263 ■ "The Ultimate Home Shopping Network" in *Austin Business JournalInc.* (Vol. 28, October 17, 2008, No. 31, pp. A1)
Pub: American City Business Journals
Ed: Sandra Zaragoza. **Description:** New York-based Etcetera sells their clothing through more than 850 fashion consultants in the U.S. Central Texas is one of the company's top markets and the company is looking to increase its fashion consultants in the area from five to about 20 since they believe there is plenty of room to expand their customer base in the area.

4264 ■ "Under Armour Wants to Equip Athletes, Too" in *Boston Business Journal* (Vol. 29, July 8, 2011, No. 9, pp. 1)
Pub: American City Business Journals Inc.
Ed: Ryan Sharrow. **Description:** Baltimore sportswear maker Under Armour advances plans to enter into the equipment field, aiming to strengthen its hold on football, basketball and lacrosse markets where it already has a strong market share. The company is now cooking up licensing deals to bolster the firm's presence among athletes.

4265 ■ "Uptick in Clicks: Nordstrom's Online Sales Surging" in *Puget Sound Business Journal* (Vol. 29, August 22, 2008, No. 18, pp. 1)
Pub: American City Business Journals
Ed: Gregg Lamm. **Description:** Nordstrom Inc.'s online division grew its sales by 15 percent in the second quarter of 2008, compared to 2007's 4.3 percent in overall decline. The company expects their online net sales to reach $700 million in 2008 capturing eight percent of overall sales.

4266 ■ "Weaving a Stronger Fabric: Organizing a Global Sweat-Free Apparel Production Agreement" in *WorkingUSA* (Vol. 11, June 2008, No. 2)
Pub: Blackwell Publishers Ltd.
Ed: Eric Dirnbach. **Description:** Tens of millions of workers working under terrible sweatshop conditions in the global apparel industry. Workers are employed at apparel contractors and have been largely unsuccessful in organizing and improving their working conditions. The major apparel manufacturers and retailers have the most power in this industry, and they have adopted corporate social responsibility programs as a false solution to the sweatshop problem. The major North American apparel unions dealt with similar sweatshop conditions a century ago by organizing the contractors and brands into joint association contracts that significantly raised standards. Taking inspiration from their example, workers and their anti-sweatshop allies need to work together to coordinate a global organizing effort that builds worker power and establishes a global production agreement that negotiates with both contractors and the brands for improved wages, benefits, and working conditions.

4267 ■ "Web Sight: Do You See What I See?" in *Entrepreneur* (Vol. 35, October 2007, No. 10, pp. 58)
Pub: Entrepreneur Media Inc.
Ed: Heather Clancy. **Description:** Owners of Trunkt, a boutique in New York that showcases independent designs, have created a new style of Website called Trunkt.org. The Website allows buyers to select the products they want to see and designers can choose anytime which of their items will be displayed on the site. An explanation of the strategy that helped bring Trunkt closer to its clients is presented.

4268 ■ "Wedding: Style Gowns Ready to Go" in *Houston Chronicle* (June 3, 2010)
Pub: Houston Chronicle
Ed: Molly Glentzer. **Description:** Wedding gowns with slender silhouettes travel well for destination weddings. Amsale, Oscar del la Renta and Monique Lhuillier dresses are highlighted.

4269 ■ "When Dov Cries" in *Canadian Business* (Vol. 83, June 15, 2010, No. 10, pp. 71)
Pub: Rogers Media Ltd.
Ed: Joe Castaldo. **Description:** American Apparel disclosed that they will have problems meeting one of its debt covenants which could trigger a chain reaction that could lead to bankruptcy. The prospects look bleak, but eccentric company founder Dov Charney, has always defied expectations.

4270 ■ "White Cat Media Tells You Where to Get a Bargain. Now It's Shopping for $1.5 Million" in *Inc.* (March 2008, pp. 48)
Pub: Gruner & Jahr USA Publishing
Ed: Athena Schindelheim. **Description:** Profile of White Cat Media which runs two shopping Websites: SheFinds.com for fashion and beauty items, and MomFinds.com for mothers. The New York City firm reported revenues for 2007 at $400,000 and is looking for funding capital in the amount of $1.7 million.

4271 ■ *Women's & Children's Wear Buyers*
Pub: Briefings Media Group
Contact: Alan M. Douglas, President
Released: Annual, latest edition 2011-2012. **Price:** $329 directory price; $659 directory/CD combo price. **Covers:** Over 9,000 retailers and 17,000 buyers in women's and children's wear industry. **Entries Include:** Company name, address, phone, fax; e-mail; URL; names and titles of key personnel; financial data; branch or subsidiary name and address; products and/or services provided; names and titles of buyers; price points and sales volume; type and number of stores for companies; parent companies, and corporate buying offices. **Arrangement:** Geographical. **Indexes:** Store name, new listings, mail order, buying office, online retailer.

4272 ■ "Work that Skirt!" in *Entrepreneur* (Vol. 37, October 2009, No. 10, pp. 17)
Pub: Entrepreneur Media, Inc.
Ed: Donnell Alexander. **Description:** Steven Villegas, also called Krash, has captured a segment of the men's clothing market with his skirts called Utilikilts. Villegas has sold 100,000 kilts since starting his business in 2000.

STATISTICAL SOURCES

4273 ■ *RMA Annual Statement Studies*
Pub: Robert Morris Associates (RMA)
Released: Annual. **Price:** $175.00 2006-07 edition, $105.00. **Description:** Contains composite balance sheets and income statements for more than 360 industries, including the accounting, auditing, and bookkeeping industries. Also contains five years of comparative historical data for discerning trends. Includes 16 commonly used ratios, computed for most of the size groupings for nearly every industry.

4274 ■ *Standard & Poor's Industry Surveys*
Pub: Standard & Poor's Corp.
Released: Annual. **Price:** $3633.00. **Description:** Two-volume book that examines the prospects for specific industries, including trucking. Also provides analyses of trends and problems, statistical tables and charts, and comparative company analyses.

TRADE PERIODICALS

4275 ■ *Apparel News South*
Pub: Apparel News Group
Contact: Martin Wernicke, Publisher/CEO
Released: 5/yr. **Price:** $89. **Description:** Clothing industry magazine containing textile information on garments for women and children.

4276 ■ *DNR*
Pub: Fairchild Publications Inc.
Contact: Edward Nardoza, Editor-in-Chief
E-mail: edward_nardoza@condenast.com
Released: Daily (morn.). **Price:** $129; $99 online; $169 online print; $895 online archive. **Description:** Daily newspaper reporting on men's and boys' clothing, retailing, and textiles.

4277 ■ *Formaltimes*
Pub: International Formalwear Association
Ed: Released: Bimonthly. **Description:** Concerned with the promotion of the formalwear industry, providing specialized information on profit strategies, marketing, merchandising, advertising, sales, and other areas of interest. Includes Association news and columns titled President's Message, and Member Profile. Recurring features include reports of meetings and a calendar of events.

4278 ■ *Made to Measure*
Pub: Halper Publishing Co.
Released: Semiannual. **Price:** $5 single issue; $20 single issue international. **Description:** Trade magazine for the uniform, career apparel, and allied trades.

4279 ■ *Stores*
Pub: NRF Enterprises Inc.
Contact: Susan Reda, Exec. Dir.
Released: Monthly. **Price:** $120 nonmembers. **Description:** Magazine for retail traders.

TRADE SHOWS AND CONVENTIONS

4280 ■ Big and Tall Men's Apparel Needs Show
Specialty Trade Show, Inc.
3939 Hardie Rd.
Coconut Grove, FL 33133-6437
Ph:(305)663-6635
Fax:(305)661-8118
Co. E-mail: info@spectrade.com
URL: http://www.spectrade.com
Released: Semiannual. **Audience:** Retailers. **Principal Exhibits:** Menswear.

4281 ■ Denver Apparel and Accessory Market
Denver Merchandise Mart
451 E. 58th Ave., Ste. 4270
Denver, CO 80216-8470
Ph:(303)292-6278
Free: 800-289-6278
Fax:(303)297-8473
Co. E-mail: info@denvermart.com
URL: http://www.denvermart.com
Released: 5/yr. **Audience:** Retailers of women's, children's, and men's apparel and accessories. **Principal Exhibits:** Women's, men's, and children's apparel and accessories. **Dates and Locations:** 2011 Aug 26-29, Denver, CO.

4282 ■ Florida Fashion Focus Show
Southern Apparel Exhibitors, Inc.
1856 Sheridan St.
Evanston, IL 60201
Ph:(847)475-1856
Free: 888-249-1377
Co. E-mail: info@saemiami.com.
URL: http://www.saemiami.com
Released: 5/yr. **Audience:** Trade buyers. **Principal Exhibits:** Ladies ready-to-wear clothing; handbags, jewelry, and accessories. Order-writing for future delivery.

4283 ■ Mitteldeutsche Handwerksmesse: Central German Handicrafts Fair
Leipziger-Messe GmbH
PO Box 100720
D-04007 Leipzig, Germany
Ph:49 341 67 80
Fax:49 341 678 87 62
Co. E-mail: info@leipziger-messe.de
URL: http://www.leipziger-messe.de
Released: Annual. **Audience:** General public. **Principal Exhibits:** Building and conversion, home, arts and crafts, health, lifestyle, food crafts, vehicles, rare handicrafts.

4284 ■ New England Apparel Club
New England Apparel Club, Inc.
75 McNeal Way, Ste. 207
Dedham, MA 02026
Ph:(781)326-9223
Fax:(781)326-6892
Co. E-mail: neacrlg@aol.com
Released: 5/yr. **Principal Exhibits:** Clothing and related equipment, supplies, and services. **Dates and Locations:** 2011 Jun 12-15, Marlboro, MA.

4285 ■ Women's and Children's Apparel and Accessories Mart
Dallas Market Center Co.
Attn: SG Marketing Mgr.
2100 Stemmons Fwy.
Dallas, TX 75207
Ph:(214)655-6100
Free: 800-325-6587
Fax:(214)655-6238
Co. E-mail: info@dmcmail.com
Audience: Apparel and accessories and home furnishings retailers. **Principal Exhibits:** Regional Merchandising Mart servicing department and specialty store buyers nationwide.

FRANCHISES AND BUSINESS OPPORTUNITIES

4286 ■ Children's Orchard
Children's Orchard, Inc.
900 Victors Way, Ste. 200
Ann Arbor, MI 48108
Ph:(734)994-9199
Free: 800-999-5437
Fax:(734)994-9323
No. of Franchise Units: 93. **No. of Company-Owned Units:** 1. **Founded:** 1980. **Franchised:** 1985. **Description:** Children's upscale/resale retail store. **Equity Capital Needed:** $115,600-$197,000. **Franchise Fee:** $25,000. **Royalty Fee:** 5%. **Financial Assistance:** No. **Training:** Provides 12 days training at headquarters, 3 days onsite and ongoing support.

4287 ■ Compuchild
Compuchild Services of America
1800 Halifax St.
Camel, IN 46032
Ph:(317)817-9817
Free: 800-619-5437
Fax:(317)818-8184
No. of Franchise Units: 69. **No. of Company-Owned Units:** 1. **Founded:** 1994. **Franchised:** 1995. **Description:** Computer education to children. **Equity Capital Needed:** $15,000. **Franchise Fee:** $12,500 or $17,500. **Financial Assistance:** No. **Training:** Yes.

4288 ■ Embroidme
2121 Vista Pky.
West Palm Beach, FL 33411
Ph:(561)640-7367
Free: 800-727-6720
Fax:(561)478-4340
Co. E-mail: franchise@embroidme.com
URL: http://www.embroidme.com
No. of Franchise Units: 450. **Founded:** 2000. **Franchised:** 2000. **Description:** Custom apparel and merchandise specializing in embroidered pieces. **Equity Capital Needed:** $184,000-$187,000 total investment. **Franchise Fee:** $42,500. **Financial Assistance:** Secured financing for entire equipment package and up to 70% of the total package. **Training:** 4 weeks of training, marketing, merchandising and support (2 weeks in FL, 2 weeks onsite) and ongoing support.

4289 ■ Pickles & Ice Cream Franchising, Inc.
5001 Spring Valley Rd., Ste. 385-W
Dallas, TX 75244
Ph:(214)742-5537
Fax:(972)980-9861
No. of Franchise Units: 4. **No. of Company-Owned Units:** 2. **Founded:** 1997. **Franchised:** 1999. **Description:** Maternity clothing franchise. **Equity Capital Needed:** $167,200-$366,000. **Franchise Fee:** $30,000. **Royalty Fee:** 6%. **Financial Assistance:** No. **Training:** Offers 10 days at headquarters, 2 days at franchisees location with ongoing support.

COMPUTERIZED DATABASES

4290 ■ *Consumer Buying Power*
The Nielsen Co.
770 Broadway
New York, NY 10003-9595
URL: http://www.claritas.com/sitereports/default.jsp
Description: Contains current-year estimates and 5-year projections of total household expenditures for more than 350 product categories, including goods and services, and 73 summary categories. Provides estimated potential consumer expenditures by store types for 41 retail store types, such as eating places; furniture; grocery; shoes; and sporting goods; as well as a breakdown of average household expenditures, such as apparel; education; electronic devices; food at home; furniture; major appliances; medical expenses; and personal care. Also includes average household expenditures for 53 Yellow Page headings. **Availability:** Online: The Nielsen Co. **Type:** Statistical.

LIBRARIES

4291 ■ Conde Nast Publications Library and Information Services
4 Times Sq., 17th Fl.
New York, NY 10036
Ph:(212)286-2860
URL: http://www.condenastdigital.com
Contact: Sarah Chubb, Pres.
Scope: Fashion, houses, gardens, home furnishings, interior design, health, personalities, photographs. **Holdings:** 7000 volumes. **Subscriptions:** 200 journals and other serials; 4 newspapers.

4292 ■ Fashion Institute of Design & Merchandising–Cyril Magnin Resource and Research Center
55 Stockton St., 5th Fl.
San Francisco, CA 94108-5829
Ph:(415)675-5200, x3361
Free: 800-422-3436
Fax:(415)296-7299
URL: http://fidm.edu
Contact: Jim Glenny, Lib.Dir.
Scope: Fashion design and merchandising, interior design, apparel manufacturing, advertising, merchandising, marketing. **Services:** Center not open to the public. **Holdings:** 4000 books; 800 AV programs; 1000 newspaper clipping files; 4000 videos, DVDs, and slides. **Subscriptions:** 200 journals and other serials.

4293 ■ Fashion Institute of Technology–Gladys Marcus Library
7th Ave. at 27th St.
E-Bldg. E502
New York, NY 10001-5992
Ph:(212)217-4340
Fax:(212)217-4371
Co. E-mail: greta_earnest@fitnyc.edu
URL: http://fitnyc.edu/library
Contact: Prof. N.J. Wolfe, Lib.Dir.
Scope: Costume, fashion, interior design, management engineering technology, fashion buying and merchandising, textiles, toy design, packaging design, advertising. **Services:** Interlibrary loan; copying; Library open to the public for reference use only by appointment. **Holdings:** 130,260 books; 113,265 nonprint units; 20,637 bound periodical volumes; 125,000 fashion slides; 4712 reels of microfilm; 438 CD-ROM serials and digital monographs. **Subscriptions:** 4000 journals and other serials.

4294 ■ Illinois Institute of Art/ Schaumburg–Learning Resource Center
1000 N. Plaza Dr., Ste. 100
Schaumburg, IL 60173-4913
Ph:(847)619-3450
Free: 800-314-3450
URL: http://www.artinstitutes.edu/schaumburg/
Scope: Graphic design, interior design, applied art and design, furniture history. **Services:** Interlibrary loan. **Holdings:** Books; slides; periodicals; videotapes; DVDs; CD-ROMs. **Subscriptions:** 175 journals and other serials.

4295 ■ Tavy Stone Fashion Library
Detroit Historical Museum
5401 Woodward Ave.
Detroit, MI 48202
Ph:(313)833-1805
Fax:(313)833-5342
Co. E-mail: webmaster@detroithistorical.org
URL: http://www.detroithistorical.org
Contact: Jill M. Koepke, Libn.
Scope: Fashion (antiquity to present) - American and European fashion designers, careers, advertising, merchandising, management, textiles and fabrics, cosmetics and fragrances, historic costume, fashion retailers; the business, sociological, and psychological aspects of fashion. **Services:** Copying; Library open to the public with restrictions. **Holdings:** 800 books; 40 VF drawers; 500 slides; 10 color swatches; 21 AV programs. **Subscriptions:** 6 journals and other serials.

ASSOCIATIONS AND OTHER ORGANIZATIONS

4296 ■ National Coffee Association of U.S.A.
45 Broadway, Ste. 1140
New York, NY 10006
Ph:(212)766-4007
Fax:(212)766-5815
Co. E-mail: info@ncausa.org
URL: http://www.ncausa.org
Contact: Robert F. Nelson, Pres./CEO

Description: Green coffee importers, jobbers, brokers, and agents; instant coffee and liquid extract processors; roasters and allied coffee industries; exporters; retailers. Promotes sound business relations and mutual understanding among members of the trade, and to increase coffee consumption. Collects and publishes consumer, market and technical information on the coffee industry. **Publications:** *CoffeeTrax* (quarterly); *National Coffee Drinking Trends* (annual); *US Coffee Industry Review 2005* .

4297 ■ Specialty Coffee Association of America
330 Golden Shore, Ste. 50
Long Beach, CA 90802
Ph:(562)624-4100
Fax:(562)624-4101
Co. E-mail: info@scaa.org
URL: http://www.scaa.org
Contact: Tim O'Connor, Pres.

Description: Coffee roasters, green coffee brokers, retailers, distributors, and others involved in the gourmet coffee industry. Provides business, professional, promotional, and educational assistance in the areas of cultivation, processing, preparation, and marketing of specialty coffee; increase consumer awareness, understanding, and consumption of specialty coffee. Provides a forum for discussion of the purpose and unified character of the industry and represents members in national and regional coffee concerns. Distributes posters, surveys, articles, and other promotional information; develops coffee education curricula for culinary school programs. Maintains reference materials. Sponsors tastings of specialty coffees. **Publications:** Membership Directory (annual).

SOURCES OF SUPPLY

4298 ■ *Automatic Merchandiser—Blue Book Buyer's Guide Issue*
Pub: Cygnus Business Media
Contact: Michael Martin, President

Released: Annual. **Publication Includes:** Suppliers of products, services, and equipment to the merchandise vending, contract foodservice, and office coffee service industries. **Entries Include:** Company name, address, phone, names of executives, trade and brand names, and products or services offered. **Arrangement:** Classified by type of business. **Indexes:** Alphabetical, product.

4299 ■ *Vending Times—Buyers Guide and Directory Issue*
Pub: Vending Times Inc.
Contact: Alicia Lavay-Kertes, Pres./Publisher
E-mail: alicia@vendingtimes.net

Released: Annual, Latest edition 2009. **Price:** $40, individuals includes shipping and handling. **Publication Includes:** Lists of manufacturers and suppliers of equipment and products used by vending machine industry operators, including product venders, juke boxes, pinball and other games; industry trade associations. **Entries Include:** Company name, address, phone, names of key personnel, description of products. **Arrangement:** Classified by product or service.

STATISTICAL SOURCES

4300 ■ *Standard & Poor's Industry Surveys*
Pub: Standard & Poor's Corp.

Released: Annual. **Price:** $3633.00. **Description:** Two-volume book that examines the prospects for specific industries, including trucking. Also provides analyses of trends and problems, statistical tables and charts, and comparative company analyses.

TRADE PERIODICALS

4301 ■ *Automatic Merchandiser*
Pub: Cygnus Business Media
Contact: Emily Refermat, Managing Editor
E-mail: emily.refermat@vendingmarketwatch.com

Released: Monthly. **Description:** Vending and office coffee service industry trade magazine.

4302 ■ *Tea and Coffee Trade Journal*
Pub: Lockwood Trade Publications Inc.

Released: Monthly. **Price:** $49; $83 two years; $152 other countries airmail; $68 other countries surface mail; $258 two years airmail; $116 two years surface mail. **Description:** Magazine on coffee and tea roasters and packers.

TRADE SHOWS AND CONVENTIONS

4303 ■ Atlantic Coast Exposition - Showcasing the Vending and Food Service Industry
IMI Association Executives Inc.
2501 Aerial Center Pkwy.
Suite 103
Morrisville, NC 27560
Ph:(919)459-2070
Free: 800-729-2776
Fax:(919)459-2075
Co. E-mail: info@imiae.com
URL: http://www.imiae.com

Released: Annual. **Audience:** Vending, food service, and OCS personnel. **Principal Exhibits:** Vending machines, office coffee service equipment, food stuffs, and related goods and services.

FRANCHISES AND BUSINESS OPPORTUNITIES

4304 ■ Blenz Coffee
535 Thurlow St., Ste. 300
Vancouver, BC, Canada V6E 3L2
Ph:(604)682-2995
Fax:(604)684-2542

No. of Franchise Units: 25. **No. of Company-Owned Units:** 2. **Founded:** 1990. **Franchised:** 1992. **Description:** Coffee beverages and coffee beans. **Equity Capital Needed:** $30,000-$70,000+ equity. **Financial Assistance:** No. **Training:** Yes.

4305 ■ Cafe Ala Carte
Cafe Ala Carte Corp.
19512 S Coquina Way
Weston, FL 33332
Ph:(949)349-1030
Fax:(954)349-3100

No. of Franchise Units: 2. **No. of Company-Owned Units:** 13. **Founded:** 1996. **Franchised:** 2000. **Description:** Carts serving coffee and espresso drinks. **Equity Capital Needed:** $56,200-$80,800 total investment. **Franchise Fee:** $25,000. **Royalty Fee:** 8-5%. **Financial Assistance:** Third party financing available. **Training:** Provides 1 week at headquarters, 1 week in Fort Lauderdale, FL with ongoing support.

4306 ■ Coffee Beanery
Coffee Beanery, Ltd.
3429 Pierson Pl.
Flushing, MI 48433
Ph:(810)733-1020
Free: 888-385-2326
Fax:(810)733-1536
Co. E-mail: stacyp@beanerysupport.com
URL: http://www.coffeebeanery.com

No. of Franchise Units: 93. **No. of Company-Owned Units:** 2. **Founded:** 1976. **Franchised:** 1985. **Description:** The Coffee Beanery retails whole bean coffees and beverages, espresso and cappuccino in a variety of styles in carts, kiosks, in-line mall stores and street front cafes. **Equity Capital Needed:** $74,250-$545,000. **Franchise Fee:** $27,500. **Financial Assistance:** No. **Training:** 4 weeks training at corporate headquarters plus 1 week orientation including customer service, merchandising, marketing & daily operations. Additional onsite training, site selection assistance, lease negotiation, layout & construction supervision, and on-going support via 800 line, Internet, fax, enewsletter, & field support.

4307 ■ Java Hut Drive Thru
148 Bamboo Ln.
Fallbrook, CA 92028
Ph:(760)630-4245

No. of Franchise Units: 2. **No. of Company-Owned Units:** 2. **Founded:** 1993. **Description:** Drive-thru coffee, tea & smoothie shop. **Equity Capital Needed:** $12,000-$50,000. **Franchise Fee:** $10,000. **Financial Assistance:** No. **Training:** Yes.

4308 ■ Jo To Go Coffee
Jo to Go America, Inc.
1263 Main St., Ste. 228
Green Bay, WI 54302
Free: (866)568-6461
Fax:(920)482-5623
No. of Franchise Units: 12. **No. of Company-Owned Units:** 6. **Founded:** 1998. **Franchised:** 2001. **Description:** Drive-thru specialty coffee, smoothies and bakery. **Equity Capital Needed:** $133,000-$409,000. **Franchise Fee:** $25,000. **Royalty Fee:** 7%. **Financial Assistance:** Limited third party financing available. **Training:** Provides 1 week at headquarters, 1 week at franchisee's location, 1 week at a corporate store and ongoing support.

4309 ■ Williams Fresh Cafe Inc.
202 Grand River Ave.
Brantford, ON, Canada N3T 4X9
Ph:(519)752-4850
Fax:(519)752-2671
Co. E-mail: franchiseinfo@williamsfreshcafe.com
URL: http://www.williamsfreshcafe.com
No. of Franchise Units: 39. **Founded:** 1993. **Franchised:** 1994. **Description:** Serves best cafe, coffee bar and restaurant and caters to its customers with convenient hours of operation, a comprehensive easy-to-prepare menu, quick, modified table service and popular pricing. **Equity Capital Needed:** $300,000-$675,000. **Franchise Fee:** $35,000. **Training:** Offers 8-12 weeks of training.

LIBRARIES

4310 ■ Noble and Associates Library
2155 W. Chesterfield Blvd.
Springfield, MO 65807
Ph:(417)875-5000
Co. E-mail: julie.tumy@noble.net
URL: http://www.noble.net
Contact: Julie Tumy, Pres.
Scope: Food, food service, advertising, construction, agriculture. **Services:** Interlibrary loan; copying; SDI; Library not open to the public. **Holdings:** 500 books; 1000 reports. **Subscriptions:** 300 journals and other serials; 5 newspapers.

ASSOCIATIONS AND OTHER ORGANIZATIONS

4311 ■ American Hatpin Society
2505 Indian Creek Rd.
Diamond Bar, CA 91765-3307
Co. E-mail: info@americanhatpinsociety.com
URL: http://www.americanhatpinsociety.com
Contact: Jodi Lenocker, Pres.
Description: Collectors of hatpins. Promotes collection, preservation, and restoration of hatpins and related fashion accessories. Serves as a clearinghouse on hatpins and their history; facilitates exchange of information among members; conducts educational programs. .

4312 ■ American Numismatic Association
818 N Cascade Ave.
Colorado Springs, CO 80903-3279
Ph:(719)632-2646
Free: 800-367-9723
Fax:(719)634-4085
Co. E-mail: ana@money.org
URL: http://www.money.org
Contact: Larry Shepherd, Exec. Dir.
Description: Collectors of coins, medals, tokens, and paper money. Promotes the study, research, and publication of articles on coins, coinage, and history of money. Sponsors correspondence courses; conducts research. Maintains museum, archive, authentication service for coins, and hall of fame. Sponsors National Coin Week; operates speakers' bureau. **Publications:** *The ABC's of Money - A Numismatic Primer*; *ANA Grading Guide*; *ANA Numismatic Correspondence Course*; *Consumer Alert - Investing in Rare Coins*; *First Strike Supplement: Emerging Collectors* (quarterly); *The Numismatist: For Collectors of Coins, Medals, Tokens and Paper Money* (monthly).

4313 ■ American Numismatic Society
75 Varick St., 11th Fl.
New York, NY 10038
Ph:(212)571-4470
Fax:(212)571-4479
Co. E-mail: meadows@numismatics.org
URL: http://www.numismatics.org
Contact: Ute W. Kagan, Exec. Dir.
Description: Collectors and others interested in coins, medals, and related materials. Advances numismatic knowledge as it relates to history, art, archaeology, and economics by collecting coins, medals, tokens, decorations, and paper money. Maintains only museum devoted entirely to numismatics. Presents annual Graduate Fellowship in Numismatics. Sponsors Graduate Seminar in Numismatics, a nine-week individual study program for ten students. **Publications:** *American Coins in North American Collections*; *American Journal of Numismatics* (annual); *American Numismatic Society—Numismatic Studies* (periodic); *Ancient Coins in North American Collections* (periodic); *ANS Magazine* (3/year); *Biennial Indexes to Numismatic Literature, 1947-65*; *Coinage of the Americas Conference*; *The Colonial Newsletter* (3/year); *Index to American Journal of Numismatics*; *Numismatic Literature* (semiannual); *Numismatic Notes and Monographs*; *Numismatic Studies*; *Sylloge Nummorum Graecorum: The Collection of the American Numismatic Society* (periodic).

4314 ■ American Philatelic Congress
400 Clayton St.
San Francisco, CA 94117-1912
Co. E-mail: rosstowle@yahoo.com
URL: http://www.americanphilateliccongress.org/index.html
Contact: Dr. Mark E. Banchik, Pres.
Description: Promotes philatelic writing and research. **Publications:** *American Philatelic Congress Book* (annual); *Congress Comments* (3/year).

4315 ■ American Philatelic Society
100 Match Factory Pl.
Bellefonte, PA 16823
Ph:(814)933-3803
Fax:(814)933-6128
Co. E-mail: wade@pencom.com
URL: http://www.stamps.org
Contact: Wade E. Saadi, Pres.
Description: Collectors of postage and revenue stamps, first day covers, postal history, and related philatelic items. Helps members buy and sell stamps; operates expertise service; offers stamp insurance program; circulates slide programs. Maintains hall of fame; offers correspondence courses; accredits judges for philatelic competitions. Conducts philatelic seminars. **Publications:** *The American Philatelist* (monthly).

4316 ■ American Stamp Dealers Association
217-14 Northern Blvd., Ste. 205
Bayside, NY 11361
Ph:(718)224-2500
Fax:(718)224-2501
Co. E-mail: asda@asdaonline.com
URL: http://www.asdaonline.com
Contact: Mr. Joseph B. Savarese, Exec. Dir.
Description: Dealers and wholesalers of stamps, albums and other philatelic materials. Sponsors National Stamp Collecting Week in November. **Publications:** *The American Stamp Dealer and Collector* (10/year); *Members Only Newsletter* (monthly).

4317 ■ Bicycle Stamps Club
21304 2nd Ave. SE
Bothell, WA 98021-7550
Co. E-mail: tonimaur@bigpond.com
URL: http://bicyclestamps.tripod.com
Contact: Bill Eubanks
Description: Philatelists interested in collecting stamps depicting bicycles and cycling themes. **Publications:** *Bicycle Stamps* (quarterly).

4318 ■ Canadian Aerophilatelic Society
203A Woodfield Dr.
Nepean, ON, Canada K2G 4P2
Co. E-mail: bjnepean@trytel.com
URL: http://www.aerophilately.ca
Contact: Chris Hargreaves, Pres.
Description: Individuals interested in the history of Canadian and Newfoundland air mail service and aerophilately. Promotes study of Canadian postal history and collection of aerophilatelic materials. Conducts research and educational programs; sponsors competitions. **Publications:** *Canadian Aerophilatelist* (quarterly).

4319 ■ Canadian Association of Numismatic Dealers–L'Association Canadienne Marchands Numismatiques
PO Box 10272
Winona Postal Outlet
Stoney Creek, ON, Canada L8E 5R1
Ph:(905)643-4988
Fax:(905)643-6329
Co. E-mail: email@cand.org
URL: http://www.cand.org
Contact: Jo-Anne M. Simpson, Exec. Sec.
Description: Dealers in numismatic materials. Seeks to advance the numismatic collectibles industry. Facilitates communication and cooperation among members; represents members' interests.

4320 ■ Canadian Numismatic Research Society
PO Box 1351
Victoria, BC, Canada V8W 2W7
Fax:(250)598-5539
Co. E-mail: ragreene@telus.net
URL: http://www.nunetcan.net/cnrs.htm
Contact: Ronald Greene, Sec.
Description: Numismatists and other individuals with an interest in coins, tokens, paper money, and medals; membership by invitation only. Seeks to advance numismatic study. Sponsors research and educational programs. **Publications:** *Numismatica Canada* (annual).

4321 ■ Cracker Jack Collectors Association
4908 N Holborn Dr.
Muncie, IN 47304
Co. E-mail: lindajfarris@comcast.net
URL: http://www.crackerjackcollectors.com
Contact: Nancy Schultz, Pres.
Description: Collectors of Cracker Jack prizes and related items. Promotes collection and preservation of Cracker Jack memorabilia. Gathers and disseminates information on Cracker Jack collectibles and their availability; facilitates exchange of information and promotes good fellowship among members.
.

4322 ■ Craft and Hobby Association
319 E 54th St.
Elmwood Park, NJ 07407
Ph:(201)835-1200
Free: 800-822-0494
Fax:(201)797-0657
Co. E-mail: info@craftandhobby.org
URL: http://www.craftandhobby.org
Contact: Tony Lee, Acting Pres./CEO
Description: Manufacturers, wholesalers, retailers, publishers, and allied firms in the craft and hobby industry. Promotes the interest of all companies engaged in the buying, selling, or manufacturing of craft and hobby merchandise; conceives, develops, and implements programs for members to achieve greater individual growth. Conducts seminars and

educational workshops; sponsors national trade show. Compiles statistics. **Publications:** Membership Directory (annual).

4323 ■ Fostoria Glass Collectors
PO Box 826
Moundsville, WV 26041
Ph:(304)845-9188
URL: http://www.fostoriacollectors.org
Contact: Jim Davis, Pres.
Description: Collectors and admirers of handmade American glassware. Promotes appreciation of handmade American glass products. Serves as a clearinghouse on handmade American glassware and its collection; sponsors research and educational programs; participates in charitable activities; maintains museum. **Publications:** *The Glass Works* (bimonthly).

4324 ■ Industry Council for Tangible Assets
PO Box 1365
Severna Park, MD 21146-8365
Ph:(410)626-7005
Fax:(410)626-7007
Co. E-mail: eloise.ullman@ictaonline.org
URL: http://ictaonline.org
Contact: Gary Adkins, Chm.
Description: Individuals and firms engaged in the fabrication, manufacture, importation, wholesale distribution, or retail sale of any tangible asset (precious or other metals, coins, antiques, stamps, or art objects). Cooperates in maintaining an appropriate and favorable regulatory climate in the U.S.; serves as liaison with governmental and other agencies. **Publications:** *ICTA Washington Wire* (quarterly).

4325 ■ International Harvester Collectors
310 Busse Hwy.
PMB 250
Park Ridge, IL 60068-3251
Ph:(847)823-8612
Fax:(847)823-7069
Co. E-mail: ihcclub@aol.com
URL: http://www.nationalihcollectors.com
Contact: Ben Trapani, Pres.
Description: Owners and admirers of farm machinery produced by International Harvester. Promotes preservation and restoration of International Harvester equipment. Facilitates communication among members; serves as a clearinghouse on International Harvester tractors and other farm equipment. **Publications:** *Red Power Round-Up* (annual).

4326 ■ International Paperweight Society
761 Chestnut St.
Santa Cruz, CA 95060
Ph:(408)427-1177
Free: 800-538-0766
Co. E-mail: lselman@got.net
URL: http://www.paperweight.com
Contact: Wibarine Favre, Pres.
Description: Promotes paperweight collecting. Conducts educational programs. Runs a speakers' bureau. .

4327 ■ National Shaving Mug Collectors Association
366 Lake Shore Dr.
Hewitt, NJ 07421
URL: http://www.nsmca.net
Contact: Don Allain, Treas.
Description: Collectors of shaving mugs and other shaving equipment. Promotes collection of shaving paraphernalia as a hobby. Facilitates communication and trading among members; gathers and disseminates information on shaving mugs and related equipment. .

4328 ■ Numismatics International
PO Box 570842
Dallas, TX 75357-0842
Co. E-mail: johnvan@tx.rr.com
URL: http://www.numis.org
Contact: Mr. John E. Vandigriff, Chm.
Description: Numismatists, coin dealers, students, and numismatic authors in 35 countries. Works to: encourage and promote the science of numismatics; cultivate fraternal relations among collectors and numismatic students; encourage new collectors and foster the interest of youth in numismatics; stimulate and advance affiliations among collectors and kindred organizations; acquire, share, and disseminate numismatic knowledge including cultural and historical information on coins. Sponsors periodic lectures. Maintains coin collection. **Publications:** *NI Bulletin* (periodic).

4329 ■ Postal History Society of Canada
255 Shakespeare St.
Ottawa, ON, Canada K1L 5M7
Co. E-mail: secretary@postalhistorycanada.net
URL: http://postalhistorycanada.net
Contact: Stephane Cloutier, Sec.-Treas.
Description: Postal historians and philatelists. Disseminates information on Canadian postal history. Conducts postal history mail auction. Maintains specialized study groups. **Publications:** *Index to the PHSC Journal* (annual).

4330 ■ Professional Currency Dealers Association
PO Box 7157
Westchester, IL 60154
Co. E-mail: nge3@comcast.net
URL: http://www.pcdaonline.com
Contact: Sergio Sanches Jr., Pres.
Description: Dealers of rare paper money and other printed media of exchange including stocks, bonds, fiscal documents, and related ephemera. Promotes the study of and interest in collectible paper media of exchange; maintains standards in commercial aspects of syngraphics. Sponsors research project to identify U.S. national banks whose large size note issues are undiscovered. .

4331 ■ Professional Numismatists Guild
28441 Rancho California Rd., Ste. 106
Temecula, CA 92590
Ph:(951)587-8300
Free: 800-375-4653
Fax:(951)587-8301
Co. E-mail: info@pngdealers.com
URL: http://www.pngdealers.com
Contact: Robert Brueggeman, Exec. Dir.
Description: Represents coin dealers who have been involved full-time in the profession for at least five years. Establishes, promotes, and defends ethics in the hobby of numismatics. **Publications:** *The Pleasure of Coin Collecting*; *What You Should Know Before You Invest in Coins* .

4332 ■ Royal Canadian Numismatic Association
5694 Hwy. No. 7 E, Ste. 432
Markham, ON, Canada L3P 1B4
Ph:(647)401-4014
Fax:(905)472-9645
Co. E-mail: info@rcna.ca
URL: http://www.canadian-numismatic.org
Contact: William Waychison, Pres.
Description: Individuals interested in coins and other Canada numismatic artifacts. Promotes collection of numismatic materials. Serves as a clearinghouse on numismatic materials and their collection and preservation; provides assistance to members. **Publications:** *The CN Journal* .

4333 ■ Royal Philatelic Society of Canada–La Societe Royale de Philatelie du Canada
PO Box 929
Sta. Q
Toronto, ON, Canada M4T 2P1
Ph:(416)921-2077
Free: 888-285-4143
Fax:(416)921-1282
Co. E-mail: info@rpsc.org
URL: http://www.rpsc.org
Contact: George Pepall, Pres.
Description: Individuals with an interest in philately. Promotes interest in stamps and postal history. Conducts educational and social programs; facilitates exchange of information among members. Sponsors competitions. **Publications:** *The Canadian Philatelist* (bimonthly). **Telecommunication Services:** electronic mail, president@rpsc.org.

4334 ■ Strawberry Shortcake Chat Group
138 E Main Cross St.
Greenville, KY 42345
Ph:(270)338-4318
Fax:(270)338-6856
Co. E-mail: jenniferbowles@bellsouth.net
URL: http://www.strawberrybonkers.com
Contact: Jennifer Bowles, Ed.
Description: Owners and admirers of Strawberry Shortcake dolls. Promotes collection and preservation of Strawberry Shortcake dolls. Facilitates communication among members; serves as a clearinghouse on Strawberry Shortcake dolls. .

TRADE PERIODICALS

4335 ■ *American Philatelic Society CAC Newsletter*
Pub: American Philatelic Society
Ed: Jane King Fohn, Editor, jkfohn1442@aol.com. **Released:** Quarterly. **Description:** Provides service to stamp clubs affiliated with the Society.

4336 ■ *Americana Philatelic News*
Pub: Americana Unit
Ed: Melvin Morris, Editor. **Released:** Quarterly. **Description:** Contains information about stamps and other philatelic materials relating to the U.S., emphasizing stamps issued by countries other than the U.S. Includes news of the Americana Unit and its members. Publishes checklists of new and old stamps on a specific subject within the Americana topic. Recurring features include a schedule of activities and a list of newly-issued Americana stamps.

4337 ■ *Artistamp News*
Pub: Ed Varney
Ed: Ed Varney, Editor, evarney@mars.ark.com. **Released:** Semiannual. **Price:** $10 2 issues. **Description:** Contains articles on the production of stamp art editions. Provides reviews of shows and editions, profiles of artists, and mail art show and project information. Recurring features include notices of publications available.

4338 ■ *Canadian Coin News*
Pub: Trajan Publishing Corp.
Contact: Bret Evans, Mng. Ed./Assoc. Publisher
E-mail: bret@trajan.ca
Released: Biweekly. **Price:** $43.95; $76.95 two years; $43 Canada; $172 other countries. **Description:** Newspaper consumer magazine for coin collectors.

4339 ■ *The Canadian Stamp News*
Pub: Trajan Publishing Corp.
Contact: Mary-Anne Luzba, Display Advertising
E-mail: advertising@trajan.ca
Released: Biweekly. **Price:** $43 in Canada; $75.34 Canada in Canada, 2 years; $172 other countries; $43.95; $76.95 two years. **Description:** Hobby newspaper presenting philatelic news.

4340 ■ *Certified Coin Dealer Newsletter*
Pub: Shane Downing
Contact: Shane Downing, Publisher
Released: Weekly. **Price:** $117, U.S., Canada, and Mexico; $193, U.S., Canada, and Mexico two years; $190, other countries; $340, two years other countries. **Description:** Provides current prices and market commentary on certified coins (Mint State Grades of MS61-MS67 and PR61-PR67) of Professional Coin Grading Service (PCGS), Numismatic Guaranty Corporation of America (NGC) Weekly, ANACS, NCI, PCI, and INS.

4341 ■ *The Coin Dealer Newsletter*
Pub: Shane Downing
Ed: Keith M. Zaner, Editor. **Released:** Weekly, Plus a monthly and quarterly for a total of 75 newsletters. **Price:** $98, individuals. **Description:** Provides information on U.S. coinage, 1793 to present. Gives current prices and market commentary and analysis. Issues The Monthly Supplement and Complete Series Pricing Guide as an adjunct to the newsletter. Recurring features include columns titled The Market in Depth and This Week's Market.

4342 ■ *Coin Prices*
Pub: FW Media Inc.
Contact: Debbie Bradley, Editorial Dir.
Released: Bimonthly. **Price:** $18.98. **Description:** Price guide for United States coins.

4343 ■ *Coin World*
Pub: Amos Press Inc.
Contact: Brenda Wyen
E-mail: bwyen@coinworld.com
Released: Weekly. **Price:** $19.99; $34.99 Canada; $127.97 Canada 52 issues; $49.97 52 issues. **Description:** Newspaper for coin collectors.

4344 ■ *The COINfidential Report*
Pub: Bale Publications
Ed: Don Bale, Jr., Editor. **Released:** Bimonthly, except July and August. **Price:** $19.95, individuals; $99 lifetime subscription. **Description:** Features coin, stock and bullion market forecasts and analyses, plus inside information and best coin and stock bets. Recurring features include interviews, book reviews, and notices of publications available.

4345 ■ *Coins Magazine*
Pub: FW Media Inc.
Contact: Dean Listle, Publisher
Ed: Robert R. Van Ryzin, Editor. **Released:** Monthly. **Price:** $22.98. **Description:** Magazine on coin collecting.

4346 ■ *The Collectors Club Philatelist*
Pub: Collectors Club Inc.
Ed: Robert P. Odenweller, Editor. **Released:** Bimonthly. **Price:** $45 members; $7 single issue; $7.50 institutions; $7.50 nonmembers. **Description:** Magazine devoted to philatelic study and research.

4347 ■ *The Colonial Newsletter*
Pub: American Numismatic Society
Ed: Gary Trudgen, Editor, gtrudgen@aol.com. **Released:** 3/year. **Price:** $35; $35, members; $45, nonmembers. **Description:** Contains original research papers on the scientific and humanistic aspects of early American numismatics, especially die varieties of the American coinages produced prior to the establishment of the U.S. Mint in 1793. Also covers paper money and early tokens.

4348 ■ *The Currency Dealer Newsletter*
Pub: Shane Downing
Ed: Keith M. Zaner, Editor. **Released:** Monthly. **Price:** $44, individuals $44/year; $78, two years; $5, single issue. **Description:** Concerned with U.S. currency, 1861 to present. Recurring features include current wholesale price lists (from dealer-to-dealer transactions), and an analysis of a particular issue of currency with a Bid/Ask Pricing Chart.

4349 ■ *David Hall's Inside View*
Pub: David Hall Rare Coins
Ed: David Hall, Editor. **Released:** Monthly, 10-12/year. **Description:** Provides advisory information on collecting and investing in rare coins.

4350 ■ *Lambda Philatelic Journal*
Pub: Gay-Lesbian History Stamp Club
Released: Quarterly. **Price:** $15, U.S., Canada, and Mexico; $15, elsewhere. **Description:** Journal of the Gay-Lesbian History Stamp Club. Provides information and articles on stamp collecting.

4351 ■ *Linn's Stamp News*
Pub: Linn's Stamp News
Contact: Michael Laurence, Editorial Dir.
E-mail: mlaurence@linns.com
Released: Weekly. **Price:** $45.95; $90.95 Canada; $120.95 other countries; $9.99 digital. **Description:** Magazine (tabloid) for stamp collectors.

4352 ■ *Numismatic News*
Pub: Krause Publications Inc.
Contact: Scott Tappa, Publisher
Ed: David C. Harper, Editor. **Released:** 52/yr. **Price:** $29.99; $96.99 Canada; $146.99 other countries. **Description:** U.S. coin collecting magazine.

4353 ■ *The Numismatist*
Pub: American Numismatic Association
Contact: David Truesdell, Sales Mgr
E-mail: truesdell@money.org
Released: Monthly. **Price:** $28 online delivery; $46 mail delivery. **Description:** Magazine for collectors of coins, medals, tokens, and paper money.

4354 ■ *Philatelic Literature Review*
Pub: American Philatelic Society
Contact: Bonny Farmer, Assoc. Ed.
Released: Quarterly. **Description:** Journal featuring bibliographies, indexes, and commentary on philatelic literature.

4355 ■ *The Posthorn*
Pub: Scandinavian Collectors Club
Contact: Paul Albright, Ed./Interim Business managing editorager
Released: Quarterly. **Price:** $20. **Description:** Journal covering philately, specifically Scandinavian stamps and postal history.

4356 ■ *Proof Collectors Corner*
Pub: World Proof Numismatic Association
Ed: Edward J. Moschetti, Editor. **Released:** Bimonthly. **Price:** Included in membership. **Description:** Provides information on coin collecting. Recurring features include news of research and reports of meetings, news releases on new world-wide coin issues including photos. A free coin selling and swapping section for members.

4357 ■ *Rosen Numismatic Advisory*
Pub: Numismatic Counseling Inc.
Ed: Maurice Rosen, Editor, mauricerosen@aol.com. **Released:** 6-8/year. **Description:** In-depth analysis for rare coin investors. Comprehensive coverage of all active areas, key interviews and no-holes-barred examination of controversal subjects.

4358 ■ *Scott Stamp Monthly*
Pub: Scott Publishing Co.
Contact: Renee Davis, Advertising
E-mail: rdavis@cottonline.com
Ed: Michael Baadke, Editor, mbaadke@scottonline.com. **Released:** Monthly. **Price:** $29.90 print; $55 two years; $45.90 other countries; $87 other countries two years. **Description:** Focuses on entertaining aspects of stamp collecting. Includes monthly update of all new stamps issued.

4359 ■ *Stamps*
Pub: American Publishing Co.
Released: Weekly (Sat.). **Description:** Stamp collecting magazine.

4360 ■ *World Coin News*
Pub: FW Media Inc.
Contact: Dennis Piotrowski, Advertising Dir
E-mail: dennis.piotrowski@fwpubs.com
Ed: Maggie Pahl, Editor. **Released:** Monthly. **Price:** $25.99; $41.99 Canada; $53.99 other countries. **Description:** World coin collectors' magazine.

TRADE SHOWS AND CONVENTIONS

4361 ■ Canadian Numismatic Association Convention
Canadian Numismatic Association
5694 Highway 7 East, Ste. 432
Markham, ON, Canada L3P 1B4
Ph:(647)401-4014
Fax:(905)472-9645
Co. E-mail: cnainfo@rogers.com
URL: http://www.canadian-numismatic.org
Released: Annual. **Audience:** Coin collectors. **Principal Exhibits:** Coins, currency, medals, and tokens.

4362 ■ National Topical Stamp Show
American Topical Association
PO Box 8
Carterville, IL 62918-0008
Ph:(618)985-5100
Fax:(618)985-5100
Co. E-mail: americantopical@msn.com
URL: http://www.americantopicalassn.org
Released: Annual. **Audience:** Stamp collectors. **Principal Exhibits:** Topical stamp and 200 frames of stamp exhibits. **Dates and Locations:** 2011 Jun 24-26, Milwaukee, WI.

4363 ■ Spring '11 Postage Stamp Mega Event
American Stamp Dealers Association
217-14 Northern Blvd., Ste. 205
Glen Cove, NY 11361
Ph:(718)224-2500
Fax:(718)224-2501
Co. E-mail: asda@asdaonline .com
URL: http://www.asdaonline.com
Released: Annual. **Audience:** Stamp collectors and the general public. **Principal Exhibits:** Stamps, philatelic supplies, and related displays. **Dates and Locations:** 2011 Apr 07-10, New York, NY.

LIBRARIES

4364 ■ American Numismatic Society Library
75 Varick St., Fl. 11
New York, NY 10013
Ph:(212)571-4470, x-4
Fax:(212)571 4479
Co. E-mail: library@numismatics.org
URL: http://www.numismatics.org/Library/Library
Contact: Elizabeth Hahn, Hd.Libn.
Scope: Numismatics. **Services:** Copying (limited); Library open to the public with restrictions. **Holdings:** 100,000 books; 10,000 bound periodical volumes; 10,000 other cataloged items; 350 reels of microfilm. **Subscriptions:** 260 journals and other serials.

4365 ■ American Philatelic Research Library
100 Match Factory Pl.
Bellefonte, PA 16823
Ph:(814)933-3803, x-241
Fax:(814)237-6128
Co. E-mail: aprl@stamps.org
URL: http://stamplibrary.org/thelibrary/lib_abouttheaprl.htm
Contact: Tara Murray, Dir., Info.Svcs./Libn.
Scope: Stamp collecting, postal history, U.S. postal records, stamp production. **Services:** Interlibrary loan; copying; Library open to the public for reference use only. **Holdings:** 20,000 book titles; 5500 periodical titles; 5000 stamp auction firms' catalogs; dealer price lists; new issue releases; clipping files. **Subscriptions:** 400 journals and other serials; 5 newspapers.

4366 ■ Bick International Library
Box 854
Van Nuys, CA 91408
Ph:(818)997-6496
Fax:(818)988-4337
Co. E-mail: iibick@sbcglobal.net
URL: http://www.bick.net
Contact: Israel Bick, Pres.
Scope: Philately. **Services:** Library open to the public by appointment. **Holdings:** 200 books; 50 bound periodical volumes; other cataloged items. **Subscriptions:** 75 journals and other serials; 50 newspapers.

4367 ■ Canadian Numismatic Association Library
c/o Daniel Gosling
49 Sierra Grande Estates
52131 Range Rd. 210
Sherwood Park, AB, Canada T8G 1A2
Ph:(780)922-5743
Co. E-mail: dan@gosling.ca
URL: http://www.canadian-numismatic.org
Contact: Daniel Gosling, Libn.
Scope: Numismatics. **Services:** Library open to the public with restrictions. **Holdings:** 3500 books. **Subscriptions:** 15 journals and other serials; 1 newspaper.

4368 ■ Collectors Club of Chicago Library
1029 N. Dearborn St.
Chicago, IL 60610
Co. E-mail: info@askphil.org
URL: http://www.askphil.org
Contact: Edward Waterous, Chm., Lib.Comm.
Scope: Philately. **Services:** Interlibrary loan; Library open to the public by appointment. **Holdings:** 4000 books; 2000 bound periodical volumes. **Subscriptions:** 100 journals and other serials.

4369 ■ Collectors Club Library
22 E. 35th St.
New York, NY 10016
Ph:(212)683-0559
Fax:(212)481-1269
Co. E-mail: collectorsclub@verizon.net
URL: http://www.collectorsclub.org
Contact: Mark E. Banchik, Jr., Chm., Lib.Comm.
Scope: Philately, postal history. **Services:** Interlibrary loan (fee); copying; Library open to the public for reference use only by appointment (members may borrow books). **Holdings:** 150,000 volumes. **Subscriptions:** 200 journals and other serials.

4370 ■ Franklin Mint Information Research Center
US Rte. 1
Chester Heights, PA 19017
Ph:(610)459-6868
Fax:(610)459-7526
Contact: Cheryl Towne, Dir.
Scope: Antiques, American history, art, die-cast, decorative arts, travel, numismatics, natural history, philatelics, direct mail, collectibles, home decor, dolls. **Services:** Center not open to the public. **Holdings:** 45,000 volumes; 100 VF drawers of pictures and slides. **Subscriptions:** 500 journals and other serials; 6 newspapers.

4371 ■ Friends of the Western Philatelic Library
PO Box 2219
Sunnyvale, CA 94087-2219
Ph:(408)733-0336
Co. E-mail: stulev@ix.netcom.com
URL: http://www.fwpl.org
Contact: Stuart Leven, Pres.
Scope: Stamp collecting. **Services:** Interlibrary loan; copying; Library open to the public. **Holdings:** 5000 books; 7000 bound periodical volumes; 12 cabinets of pamphlets and files; microfilm. **Subscriptions:** 150 journals and other serials.

4372 ■ Numismatics International Library
PO Box 570842
Dallas, TX 75357-0842
Co. E-mail: davidfg248@grandecom.net
URL: http://www.numis.org/index-5.html
Contact: David Gracey, Libn.
Scope: Coins, currency. **Services:** Interlibrary loan (fee); Library open to members and other numismatic organizations. **Holdings:** 3000 books; slide sets.

4373 ■ Philatelic Foundation–Archives and Library
70 W. 40th St., 15th Fl.
New York, NY 10018
Ph:(212)221-6555
Fax:(212)221-6208
Co. E-mail: philatelicfoundation@verizon.net
URL: http://www.philatelicfoundation.org
Contact: Robert Waterman, Archv.
Scope: Philately. **Services:** Copying; Library open to contributors by appointment. **Holdings:** 1500 books; 600 bound periodical volumes; 5000 documents and archival materials. **Subscriptions:** 25 journals and other serials; 10 newspapers.

4374 ■ Smithsonian Institution Libraries–National Postal Museum Library
2 Massachusetts Ave., NE
Washington, DC 20560-0570
Ph:(202)633-5544
Fax:(202)633-9371
Co. E-mail: libmail@si.edu
URL: http://www.sil.si.edu/libraries/npm
Contact: Paul McCutcheon, Libn.
Scope: Philately, stamp and postal history (domestic and foreign). **Services:** Library open to the public by appointment. **Holdings:** 40,000 books, journals, catalogues, and archival documents. **Subscriptions:** 250 journals and other serials.

4375 ■ Stack's Rare Coin Company of New York–Technical Information Center
123 W. 57th St.
New York, NY 10019
Ph:(212)582-2580
Fax:(212)245-5018
Scope: Rare coins - U.S., ancient, foreign; medals and decorations. **Services:** Center open to the public by appointment. **Holdings:** 10,000 books; 5000 bound periodical volumes.

4376 ■ Women on Stamps Study Unit Library
c/o D. Kristy
515 Ocean Ave., No. 608S
Santa Monica, CA 90402
Ph:(310)394-5587
Fax:(310)899-3927
Co. E-mail: dkristy@sprintmail.com
Scope: Postage stamps; philately. **Services:** Library not open to the public but information is available on request. **Holdings:** Archival materials. **Subscriptions:** 70 journals and other serials.

RESEARCH CENTERS

4377 ■ American Numismatic Society
75 Varick St., 11th Fl.
New York, NY 10013
Ph:(212)571-4470
Fax:(212)571-4479
Co. E-mail: uwk@numismatics.org
URL: http://www.numismatics.org
Contact: Dr. Ute Wartenberg Kagan, Exec.Dir.
E-mail: uwk@numismatics.org
Scope: Numismatics. Supports study and research through grants-in-aid and fellowships including the Frances M. Schwartz Fellowship. **Services:** Technical advice on specialized photography of numismatic material. **Publications:** American Journal of Numismatics (annually); Annual Report; Numismatic Literature (semiannually); American Numismatic Society Magazine (quarterly). **Educational Activities:** Coinage of the Americas Conference (annually); Educational slide programs which provide visual aids to assist in the instruction of history and art history (annually); Graduate Seminar in Numismatics (annually). **Awards:** Donald Groves Fund Grants for research and publications in early American numismatics.

REFERENCE WORKS

4378 ■ "Ask Inc." in *Inc.* (October 2007, pp. 74)
Pub: Gruner & Jahr USA Publishing
Description: Promoting a new comedy club using television, radio and print advertising and tracking results is discussed.

4379 ■ "Waite, Cancer Survivor, Readies Sch'dy 'Big House' after Long Delay" in *Business Review, Albany New York* (October 26, 2007)
Pub: American City Business Journals, Inc.
Ed: Michael DeMasi. **Description:** Stephen Waite, owner of Big House Brewing Company, will be opening its new nightclub called Big House Underground. The nightclub is part of a $3.25 million project Waite started in 2005, which was delayed due to his battle with tonsil cancer. Details of turning the building into a restaurant, bar and nightclub are provided.

Comic Book/Collectibles Store

ASSOCIATIONS AND OTHER ORGANIZATIONS

4380 ■ Canadian Association of Token Collectors
Box 21018 Meadowvale RPO
Mississauga, ON, Canada L5N 6A2
Co. E-mail: len.kuenzig@sympatico.ca
URL: http://www.nunet.ca/catc.htm
Contact: Scott E. Douglas, VP
Description: Collectors of Canadian tokens. Promotes collection of tokens and other memorabilia as a recreational pastime. Facilitates exchange of information among members; serves as a clearinghouse on the preservation, availability, and value of tokens. **Publications:** *Canada Numismatica* (quarterly).

4381 ■ Cartoonists Northwest
PO Box 31122
Seattle, WA 98103
Co. E-mail: cartoonistsnw@gmail.com
URL: http://sites.google.com/site/cartoonistnw/home
Contact: Keith Curtis
Description: Cartoonists, writers, publishers, illustrators, agents, and others interested in cartooning. Members are accepted nationwide and internationally. Provides information on all aspects of the cartooning profession to amateur, aspiring, and practicing cartoonists. Promotes cartooning as an art form. Provides networking opportunities and referral services. Conducts educational programs. .

4382 ■ Haviland Collectors International Foundation
PO Box 271383
Fort Collins, CO 80527
Co. E-mail: art@aeroinc.net
URL: http://www.havilandcollectors.com
Description: Owners and admirers of Haviland China objects. Promotes "the study of porcelain and pottery produced by the Haviland family in France and America". Facilitates communication and cooperation among members; serves as a clearinghouse on Haviland China; promotes China exhibits. **Publications:** *Charles Field Haviland: China Identification Guide*; *Dining with Flowers: Haviland Porcelain from 1860 to 1910*; *Haviland Quarterly* (quarterly); *Porcelain Theodore Haviland* .

REFERENCE WORKS

4383 ■ *Bookman's Price Index*
Pub: Gale
Ed: Anne F. McGrath, Editor. **Released:** 3 to 4 volumes per year. **Price:** $595, individuals. **Covers:** Rare and collectible books offered for sale by 150 bookdealers in the United States, Canada, and the United Kingdom. **Entries Include:** Book title, author's name, date and place of publication, description of book's condition, name of dealer, catalog and item number, year of catalog in which listing appeared, price; dealer's address is given in a separate list. **Arrangement:** Alphabetical by author name; separate sections for association copies, books with special bindings, and books with fore-edge paintings.

4384 ■ *Collectibles Market Guide & Price Index*
Pub: Collectors' Information Bureau
Released: Annual, latest edition 19th; February, 2005. **Price:** $24.95, individuals suggested retail; $19.96, individuals sales price. **Publication Includes:** List of manufacturers of limited edition collectible plates, figurines, bells, graphics, ornaments, dolls, and steins; related associations and museums; price guide to secondary market values of limited edition collectibles. **Entries Include:** Company name and address, history, current projects, values of retired editions. **Arrangement:** Membership organization. Editorial restricted to member companies. **Indexes:** Price index of collectibles. Biographies of collectibles artists; collectibles price index; feature articles; glossary; directory of secondary market dealers.

4385 ■ *Fandom Directory*
Pub: Fandata Publications
Contact: Harry A. Hopkins, Publisher
E-mail: harry@fandata.com
Released: Biennial, Latest edition 2011. **Price:** $19.95 plus $4.50 shipping. **Covers:** over 20,000 fans, fan clubs, fan magazine publishers, and fan events in the field of science fiction, fantasy, television and movies, old radio programs, computer games, comic books; location of large or rare manuscript collections; over 9,000 stores that serve fans and collectors. **Entries Include:** Club, individual, or firm name, address, phone, special interest(s). **Arrangement:** Geographical. **Indexes:** Alphabetical, interest, geographical.

4386 ■ *Old-Stuff—Directory of Shops Section*
Pub: VBM Printers Inc.
Contact: Donna Miller, Editor & Publisher
E-mail: donna@oldstuffnews.com
Released: 6 times a year. **Price:** $20, individuals yearly subscription; $5.50, single issue; $35, two years; $35, Canada. **Publication Includes:** List of approximately 900 antiques shops in the northwestern United States. **Entries Include:** Shop name, address, phone. **Arrangement:** Geographical. **Indexes:** Shops, alphabetical by city.

TRADE PERIODICALS

4387 ■ *Antique Bottle and Glass Collector*
Pub: Antique Bottle and Glass Collector
Released: Monthly. **Price:** $32 2nd class; $47 Canada; $57 other countries by airmail; $95 other countries by airmail; $54 1st class. **Description:** Trade magazine for antique bottle and glass collectors.

4388 ■ *Antiques & Collecting Magazine*
Pub: Lightner Publishing Corp.
Contact: Gregory K. Graham, Gen Mgr
Released: Monthly. **Price:** $38; $66 two years. **Description:** Magazine for antique and hobby collectors.

4389 ■ *Beer Cans and Brewery Collectibles*
Pub: Brewery Collectibles Club of America
Contact: Laurie Zell
Ed: Marcia Butterbaugh, Editor. **Released:** Bimonthly. **Price:** $38. **Description:** Contains information on collecting beer cans and brewery paraphernalia.

4390 ■ *Collectors News*
Pub: Pioneer Communications Inc.
Ed: Linda Kruger, Editor, lkruger@pioneermagazines.com. **Released:** Monthly. **Price:** $26.95. **Description:** Magazine covering antiques and collecting for pleasure and profit.

4391 ■ *Comics Buyer's Guide*
Pub: Krause Publications Inc.
Contact: Norma Jean Fochs, Advertising Mgr
E-mail: normajean.fochs@fwpubs.com
Released: Monthly. **Price:** $24.95; $74.95 other countries; $59.95 Canada; $5.99 single issue. **Description:** Weekly newspaper for comic book collectors, professionals and the industry.

4392 ■ *Comics & Games Retailer*
Pub: Krause Publications Inc.
Contact: Lori Hauser, Ad Sales Asst.
Ed: Brent Frankenhoff, Editor. **Released:** Monthly. **Price:** $151.13; $119.95 other countries. **Description:** Provides industry news and general business information to comics and gaming retailers, Publishers, and distributors.

4393 ■ *The Comics Journal*
Pub: Fantagraphics Books Inc.
Contact: Michael Dean, Managing Editor
E-mail: dean@tcj.com
Released: Monthly. **Price:** $72; $193 other countries; $128 Canada; $36 5 issues; $64 Canada 5 issues; $96 other countries 5 issues. **Description:** News, reviews and interviews with and about comics.

4394 ■ *Postcard History Society*
Pub: Postcard History Society
Contact: Jim Ward, Director
Released: Quarterly. **Price:** $9. **Description:** Supplies information on the hobby of collecting postcards.

VIDEOCASSETTES/ AUDIOCASSETTES

4395 ■ *Baseball Card Collector*
Karol Media
Hanover Industrial Estates
375 Stewart Rd.
PO Box 7600
Wilkes Barre, PA 18773-7600
Ph:(570)822-8899
Free: 800-526-4773
Co. E-mail: sales@karolmedia.com
URL: http://www.karolmedia.com
Released: 1989. **Price:** $19.99. **Description:** Mel Allen narrates this guide to the buying and selling of baseball cards. Also available as a "deluxe edition," half an hour longer for $29.99. **Availability:** VHS.

4396 ■ *Big Kids Baseball Cards*
ESPN Home Video
ESPN Plz., 935 Middle St.
Bristol, CT 06010
Ph:(860)766-2000
Fax:(860)585-2213
URL: http://www.espn.go.com
Released: 1988. **Price:** $19.95. **Description:** Strategies on buying and collecting baseball cards. Includes hints on speculating on tomorrow's stars, and tips from card shark Alan "Mr. Mint" Rosen. **Availability:** VHS.

4397 ■ *Comic Book Collector*
Anchor Bay Entertainment
1699 Stutz Dr.
Troy, MI 48084
Ph:(248)816-0909
Free: 800-786-8777
Fax:(248)816-3335
URL: http://www.anchorbayentertainment.com
Released: 1990. **Price:** $19.99. **Description:** Comprehensive guide to collecting, including what's valuable and what's not, how to find find rare comics, and proper care and storage for maximum protection. **Availability:** VHS.

TRADE SHOWS AND CONVENTIONS

4398 ■ VEGASPEX - Las Vegas International Stamp, Coin, Antique Watch, Jewelry & Collectibles Expo
Bick International
PO Box 854
Van Nuys, CA 91408
Ph:(818)997-6496
Fax:(818)988-4337
Co. E-mail: iibick@sbcglobal.net
URL: http://www.bick.net
Released: Biennial. **Audience:** General public. **Principal Exhibits:** Coin, stamp, currency, collectible and antique watch collecting show.

4399 ■ Washington Gift Show
George Little Management, LLC (New York, New York)
1133 Westchester Ave., Ste. N136
White Plains, NY 10606
Ph:(914)421-3200
Free: 800-272-SHOW
Co. E-mail: cathy_steel@glmshows.com
URL: http://www.glmshows.com
Released: Semiannual. **Audience:** Specialty and department store retailers, importers, and distributors. **Principal Exhibits:** Gifts, stationery, gourmet products, floral industry products and services, decorative accessories, souvenirs, crafts, jewelry, personal accessories, china, glass, fine and fashion jewelry, collectibles, and related tabletop items.

FRANCHISES AND BUSINESS OPPORTUNITIES

4400 ■ All Nations Flag Co., Inc.
Patriot Enterprises LLC
118 W 5th St.
Kansas City, MO 64105
Ph:(816)842-8798
Free: 800-533-3524
No. of Company-Owned Units: 1. **Founded:** 1924. **Franchised:** 1996. **Description:** Custom flags and banners. **Equity Capital Needed:** $125,000 minimum. **Franchise Fee:** $15,000. **Financial Assistance:** No. **Training:** Yes.

LIBRARIES

4401 ■ American Matchcover Collecting Club Library
PO Box 18481
Asheville, NC 28814
Ph:(828)254-4487
Fax:(828)254-1066
Co. E-mail: bill@matchcovers.com
URL: http://www.matchcovers.net
Contact: Bill Retskin, Pres.
Scope: Matchcovers. **Services:** Library not open to the public. **Holdings:** 150,000 archival items. **Subscriptions:** 600 journals and other serials.

4402 ■ Comics Magazine Association of America Library
355 Lexington Ave.
New York, NY 10017-6603
Ph:(212)661-4261
Fax:(212)370-9047
Scope: Comics magazines. **Services:** Library not open to the public. **Holdings:** 100 books; 2000 periodicals; 2 VF drawers.

4403 ■ Interlac Library
97 Woodmere Rd.
Stamford, CT 06905
Ph:(203)975-1554
URL: http://members.aol.com/interlac/
Contact: Tom Burkert
Scope: Comic books, popular culture. **Services:** Library not open to the public. **Holdings:** 20,000 volumes. **Subscriptions:** 20 journals and other serials.

4404 ■ Michigan State University–Special Collections Division–Russel B. Nye Popular Culture Collection (100 L)
100 Library
East Lansing, MI 48824
Ph:(517)432-6123, x-100
Fax:(517)353-5069
Co. E-mail: comics@msu.edu
URL: http://specialcollections.lib.msu.edu/index.jsp
Contact: Randall W. Scott, Libn./Asst.Hd.
Scope: Comic books; fiction - juvenile, detective, science fiction, western, gay and lesbian pulp fiction, romance; popular arts and entertainment; popular information. **Services:** Copying; Interlibrary loan; collections open to the public for reference use only with required identification. **Holdings:** 450,000 volumes. **Subscriptions:** 30 journals and other serials; 5 newspapers.

4405 ■ Museum of Western Colorado–Loyd Files Research Library
PO Box 20000
Grand Junction, CO 81502-5020
Ph:(970)242-0971
Free: 888-488-DINO
Fax:(970)242-3960
Co. E-mail: mmenard@westcomuseum.org
URL: http://www.museumofwesternco.com
Contact: Michael Menard, Libn./Archv.
Scope: Western Colorado, Mesa County, and Grand Junction history; genealogy; paleontology; geology; anthropology. **Services:** Copying; photographic reproduction (including scanning); Center open to the public. **Holdings:** 3500 books and monographs; 18,000 historical and aerial photographs; 2200 audiocassettes; maps and vertical files; institutional archives; reels of microfilm; National Park Service publications on historic preservation; site inventories. **Subscriptions:** 15 journals and other serials; 7 newspapers.

4406 ■ Ohio State University–Cartoon Library and Museum
Wexner Ctr., Rm. 023L
27 W. 17th Ave. Mall
Columbus, OH 43210-1393
Ph:(614)292-0538
Fax:(614)292-9101
Co. E-mail: cartoons@osu.edu
URL: http://cartoons.osu.edu
Contact: Lucy Shelton Caswell, Cur. & Prof.
Scope: Comic strips, editorial cartoons, magazine cartoons, comic books, graphic novels, illustrations, movie posters and stills, photographs. **Services:** Copying; digital reproduction services; Library open to the public upon registration. **Holdings:** 36,000 books on cartoon art; more than 450,000 original cartoons; representative holdings of original art from editorial cartoonists, comic book artists, and comic strip artists; comic strip clippings; Association of American Editorial Cartoonists and National Cartoonists Society Archives; Newspaper Features Council Archives; Collections of San Francisco Academy of Comic Art. **Subscriptions:** 51,000 journals and other serials.

4407 ■ University of California, Los Angeles–Department of Special Collections
A1713 Young Research Library
Box 951575
Los Angeles, CA 90095-1575
Ph:(310)825-4988
Fax:(310)206-1864
Co. E-mail: speccoll-paging@library.ucla.edu
URL: http://www.library.ucla.edu/specialcollections/researchlibrary/index.cfm
Contact: Annie A. Watanabe-Rocco, Off.Coord.
Scope: California and the West; children's books; literature; motion pictures; radio; television; dance; African Americans; Japanese Americans; Latinos; visual arts; photography; popular culture; printing history (especially Aldines and early Italian printing); fine press printing, fine bindings, and artists' books; fashion; Brazil; Southern California architecture; Leonardo da Vinci. **Services:** Copying (mediated); department open to the public for reference use only. **Holdings:** 333,000 volumes; 30 million manuscripts; 632 volumes of newspapers; 5 million photographs and negatives, ephemera, maps, works of art, architectural drawings and models, and other graphic arts material; 13,806 reels of microfilm; 4828 sound recordings; 15,285 slides; 9743 videotapes. **Subscriptions:** 212 journals and other serials.

4408 ■ University of Minnesota–Children's Literature Research Collections
113 Elmer L. Andersen Library
222 - 21st Ave., S.
Minneapolis, MN 55455
Ph:(612)624-4576
Fax:(612)626-0377
Co. E-mail: k-hoyl@umn.edu
URL: http://special.lib.umn.edu/clrc
Contact: Karen Nelson Hoyle, Cur.
Scope: Children's books - first editions, manuscripts, illustrations; children's literary history and criticism; children's periodicals; American and British dime novels, periodicals, story papers, pulps; Big Little Books; comic books. **Services:** Copying (limited); Collection open for research only. **Holdings:** 60,000 monographs; 2600 feet of manuscripts; 1913.41 lin.ft. of illustrations; 771 reels of microfilm or 83 dime novel titles; 1732 posters; 65 audio/visual titles. **Subscriptions:** 37 journals and other serials.

START-UP INFORMATION

4409 ■ "Savvy Solutions" in *Black Enterprise* (Vol. 41, December 2010, No. 5, pp. 42)
Pub: Earl G. Graves Publishing Co. Inc.
Ed: Tennille M. Robinson. **Description:** Individual asks for advice in launching a graphic design business, particularly grants available in a slow economy.

ASSOCIATIONS AND OTHER ORGANIZATIONS

4410 ■ Advertising Production Club of New York
Euro RSCG Life, 7th Fl.
200 Madison Ave.
New York, NY 10016
Ph:(212)251-7295
Fax:(212)726-5057
Co. E-mail: admin@apc-ny.org
URL: http://www.apc-ny.org
Contact: Dan Marselle, Pres.
Description: Production and traffic department personnel from advertising agencies, corporate or retail advertising departments, and publishing companies; college level graphic arts educators. Meetings include educational programs on graphic arts procedures and plant tours. Maintains employment service for members. .

4411 ■ American Institute of Graphic Arts
164 5th Ave.
New York, NY 10010-5901
Ph:(212)807-1990
Fax:(212)807-1799
Co. E-mail: grefe@aiga.org
URL: http://www.aiga.org
Contact: Richard Grefe, Exec. Dir.
Description: Graphic designers, art directors, illustrators and packaging designers. Sponsors exhibits and projects in the public interest. Sponsors traveling exhibitions. Operates gallery. Maintains library of design books and periodicals; offers slide archives. **Publications:** *365: AIGA Year in Design 24* (annual).

4412 ■ Associated Designers of Canada–Association des Designers Canadiens
201-192 Spadina Ave.
Toronto, ON, Canada M5T 2C2
Ph:(416)410-4209
Free: 800-361-2721
Fax:(416)703-6601
Co. E-mail: adc@designers.ca
URL: http://www.designers.ca
Contact: Phillip Silver, Pres.
Description: Theatre designers, including set, costume, lighting, and sound. Promotes the professional advancement of members. Facilitates communication and cooperation among members. Conducts continuing professional development programs.

4413 ■ California Society of Printmakers
PO Box 194202
San Francisco, CA 94119
Co. E-mail: info@caprintmakers.org
URL: http://www.caprintmakers.org
Contact: Mark Welschmeyer, Pres.
Description: Fosters the appreciation of prints and printmaking; sponsors education programs, including exhibitions. **Publications:** *California Printmaker* (annual).

4414 ■ Canadian Association of Photographers and Illustrators in Communications–Association Canadienne de Photographes et Illustrateurs de Publicite
720 Spadina Ave., Ste. 202
Toronto, ON, Canada M5S 2T9
Ph:(416)462-3677
Free: 888-252-2742
Fax:(416)929-5256
Co. E-mail: administrator@capic.org
URL: http://www.capic.org
Contact: Andre Cornellier, Chm.
Description: Photographers and illustrators employed in communications. Promotes professional and artistic advancement of members. Represents members' interests before industrial organizations; formulates standards of ethics and practice for members.

4415 ■ Digital Printing and Imaging Association
10015 Main St.
Fairfax, VA 22031-3489
Ph:(703)385-1335
Free: 888-385-3588
Fax:(703)273-0456
Co. E-mail: sgia@sgia.org
URL: http://www.sgia.org
Contact: Michael E. Robertson, Pres.
Description: Electronic printing, pre-press companies, commercial printers, service bureaus, photo labs, reprographic companies, and printer suppliers, and educational institutions. Works to advance the electronic imaging field by promoting the use of digital printing devices, responding to industry needs and concerns, and improving the industry's ability to serve its market and customers. Conducts educational programs. **Publications:** *RIP* (quarterly).

4416 ■ National Association of Quick Printers
2250 E Devon Ave., Ste. 245
Des Plaines, IL 60018
Ph:(847)298-8680
Free: 800-234-0040
Fax:(847)298-8705
Co. E-mail: info@naqp.com
URL: http://www.naqp.com
Contact: Steven D. Johnson, Pres./CEO
Description: Independent printers and printing franchise businesses; industry suppliers. Seeks to bring recognition, improved quality, and increased profits to the entire quick printing field. Provides services to members; works to advance the collective interests of the printing industries at the national and international levels. **Publications:** *NAQP Network* (monthly).

4417 ■ National Oil and Acrylic Painters' Society
PO Box 676
Osage Beach, MO 65065-0676
Ph:(573)348-1764
Co. E-mail: noaps1991_usa@noaps.org
URL: http://www.noaps.org
Contact: Joe Ray Kelly, Pres.
Description: Represents artists and others interested in exhibition and sales of original oil and acrylic paintings. **Publications:** *NOAPS Newsletter* (semiannual).

4418 ■ Organization of Black Designers
300 M St. SW, Ste. N110
Washington, DC 20024
Ph:(202)659-3918
Co. E-mail: info@obd.org
URL: http://www.core77.com/OBD/welcome.html
Contact: David H. Rice, Founder/Chm.
Description: African American designers holding college degrees who are practicing graphic advertising, industrial, fashion, textile, and interior design. Provides forum for discussion and educational programs, business, career and economic development. Sponsors competitions and speakers' bureau. **Publications:** *DesigNation* (biennial); *OBData* .

4419 ■ Rank and File–Au Bas de l'Echelle
6839A rue Drolet, Bur. 305
Montreal, QC, Canada H2S 2T1
Ph:(514)270-7878
Fax:(514)270-7726
Co. E-mail: abe@aubasdelechelle.ca
URL: http://www.aubasdelechelle.ca
Contact: Pierre-Antoine Harvey, Pres.
Description: Promotes increased recognition of the working rights of nonsyndicated workers. Represents members' interests; gathers and disseminates information to increase public awareness of conditions faced by nonsyndicated workers. **Publications:** *Aub bas de l'echelle...pas pour toujours* (3/year).

4420 ■ Screen Printing Technical Foundation
10015 Main St.
Fairfax, VA 22031
Ph:(703)385-1335
Free: 888-385-3588
Fax:(703)273-0456
Co. E-mail: sptf@sgia.org
URL: http://www.sgia.org/sptf
Contact: Dawn Hohl, Technical Training Mgr.
Description: Participants include corporations, institutions, and individuals interested in screen-printing. Advances the screen-printing industry. Conducts technical research and hands-on training programs to address production problems and processes. Sponsors educational programs and prepares educational materials. **Publications:** *SPTF Update* (quarterly).

4421 ■ Society for Environmental Graphic Design
1000 Vermont Ave. NW, Ste. 400
Washington, DC 20005
Ph:(202)638-5555
Fax:(202)638-0891
Co. E-mail: segd@segd.org
URL: http://www.segd.org
Contact: Wayne McCutcheon, Pres.

Description: Designers and manufacturers of sign systems and environmental graphics. Establishes educational guidelines for professional development as well as governmental guidelines for environmental graphics programs; provides a forum for interaction and communication among members who are from a variety of design disciplines and with manufacturers; compiles and disseminates technical data. Offers members the opportunity to participate in government hearings, code reviews, and related proceedings regarding environmental graphic design. Conducts educational programs and develops resource materials. Maintains slide collection, library and educational materials. **Publications:** *SEGD Compensation and Billing Survey*; *SEGD Green Paper: Best Practices, Strategies, and Scenarios for Sustainability in Environmental Graphic Design*; *SEGdesign* (quarterly); *What is Exhibition Design?*; *You are Here, Graphics that Direct, Explain and Entertain* (bimonthly).

4422 ■ Society of Graphic Designers of Canada–Societe des designers graphiques du Canada
Arts Ct.
2 Daly Ave.
Ottawa, ON, Canada K1N 6E2
Ph:(613)567-5400
Free: 877-496-4453
Fax:(613)564-4428
Co. E-mail: info@gdc.net
URL: http://www.gdc.net
Contact: Roderick C.J. Roodenburg, Pres.

Description: Graphic designers, administrators, educators, students, and organizations promoting graphic design in Canada. Provides for professional development and information exchange within the field; promotes high standards in the industry. Represents the interests of members; maintains communication with federal and provincial bodies. Sponsors shows and competitions for professional designers and students. Conducts educational programs and seminars. **Publications:** *Graphic Design* (periodic); *The National* (quarterly); *Regional Newsletter* (periodic).

DIRECTORIES OF EDUCATIONAL PROGRAMS

4423 ■ *Directory of Private Accredited Career Schools and Colleges of Technology*
Pub: Accrediting Commission of Career Schools and Colleges of Technology
Contact: Michale S. McComis, Exec. Dir.

Released: On web page. **Price:** Free. **Description:** Covers 3900 accredited post-secondary programs that provide training programs in business, trade, and technical fields, including various small business endeavors. Entries offer school name, address, phone, description of courses, job placement assistance, and requirements for admission. Arrangement is alphabetical.

REFERENCE WORKS

4424 ■ "Agfa: M-Press Leopard Debuts" in *American Printer* (Vol. 128, June 1, 2011, No. 6)
Pub: Penton Media Inc.

Description: M-Press Leopard is a new version of the machine that offers advanced ink jet technology at a lower price point. Agfa Graphics introduced the new version that allows for new applications that require more manual handling.

4425 ■ "Art Attack 2007 Comes to Minneapolis" in *Art Business News* (Vol. 34, November 2007, No. 11, pp. 11)
Pub: Pfingsten Publishing, LLC

Description: Overview of Art Attack 2007, an open studio and gallery crawl in the Northeast Minneapolis Arts District which featured artists working in glass, ceramics, jewelry, mosaics, mixed media, photography, painting, pottery, sculpture, textiles and wood.

4426 ■ "Art Miami Comes to Miami's Wynwood Art District" in *Art Business News* (Vol. 34, November 2007, No. 11, pp. 18)
Pub: Pfingsten Publishing, LLC

Description: In December, The Art Group will hold its Art Miami fair in the Wynwood Art District; the exhibitors range from painting, sculpture, video and works on paper.

4427 ■ "Artexpo Celebrates 30th Anniversary" in *Art Business News* (Vol. 34, November 2007, No. 11, pp. 18)
Pub: Pfingsten Publishing, LLC

Description: In honor of its 30th anniversary Artexpo New York 2008 will be an unforgettable show offering a collection of fine-art education courses for both trade and consumer attendees and featuring a variety of artists working in all mediums.

4428 ■ "Avanti Hosts Users Conference" in *American Printer* (Vol. 128, July 1, 2011, No. 7)
Pub: Penton Media Inc.

Description: Avanti Computer Systems Ltd. hosted its 19th annual users conference in Washington DC. In-plant and commercial printers were in attendance.

4429 ■ "Avoid a Tablet Generation Gap" in *American Printer* (Vol. 128, July 1, 2011, No. 7)
Pub: Penton Media Inc.

Description: Individuals between the ages of 18-34 are the only generation that is more likely to own a laptop computer or netbook insead of a desktop computer. Statistical data included.

4430 ■ *Black Book Photography*
Pub: Black Book Marketing Group
Contact: Magi Lipson, Vice President
E-mail: mlipson@blackbook.com

Released: Annual, Latest edition 2008. **Price:** $60, individuals Deluxe Edition - Hardcover. **Publication Includes:** Over 19,000 art directors, creative directors, photographers and photographic services, design firms, advertising agencies, and other firms whose products or services are used in advertising. **Entries Include:** Company name, address, phone. Principal content of publication is 4-color samples from the leading commercial photographers. **Arrangement:** Classified by product/service.

4431 ■ "Boston Printer Celebrates 60th Anniversary" in *American Printer* (Vol. 128, August 1, 2011, No. 8)
Pub: Penton Media Inc.

Description: Shawmut printing is celebrating its 60th anniversary. The family business plans to increase efficiency through automation, monitoring job progress online from start to finish.

4432 ■ "Business is Unbelievable" in *American Printer* (Vol. 128, August 1, 2011, No. 8)
Pub: Penton Media Inc.

Ed: Katherine O'Brien. **Description:** Most commercial printers have seen an increase in business over the last year.

4433 ■ "Calendar" in *Crain's Detroit Business* (Vol. 26, January 11, 2010, No. 2, pp. 16)
Pub: Crain Communications, Inc.

Description: Listing of events includes seminars sponsored by the Detroit Economic Club as well as conferences dealing with globalization and graphic design.

4434 ■ "Catching Creatives; Detroit Group Gets Grant to Attract 1,000 Design Pros" in *Crain's Detroit Business* (March 24, 2008)
Pub: Crain Communications, Inc.

Ed: Sherri Begin. **Description:** Design Detroit was given a $200,000 planning grant by the Knight Foundation, an organization that strives to back initiatives that leverage talent and resources in each of the 26 U.S. cities it funds, to inspire strategies to attract up to 1,000 creative professionals to live in Detroit.

4435 ■ "Challenges Await Quad in Going Public" in *Milwaukee Business Journal* (Vol. 27, January 29, 2010, No. 18, pp. A1)
Pub: American City Business Journals

Ed: Rich Rovito. **Description:** Sussex, Wisconsin-based Quad/Graphics Inc.'s impending acquisition of rival Canadian World Color Press Inc. will transform it into a publicly held entity for the first time. Quad has operated as a private company for nearly 40 years and will need to adjust to changes, such as the way management shares information with Quad/Graphics' employees. Details of the merger are included.

4436 ■ "City Slickers" in *Canadian Business* (Vol. 81, March 31, 2008, No. 5, pp. 36)
Pub: Rogers Media

Ed: Joe Castaldo. **Description:** Richard Florida believes that the creative class drives the economy and the prosperity of countries depends on attracting and retaining these people. Florida has brought attention to developing livable and economically vibrant cities thanks in part to his promotional skills. However, he has also drawn critics who see his data on his theories as flimsy and inadequate.

4437 ■ "ContiTech Celebrates 100 Years" in *American Printer* (Vol. 128, July 1, 2011, No. 7)
Pub: Penton Media Inc.

Description: ContiTech celebrated 100 years in business. The firm started in 1911 after developing the first elastic printing blanket. Other milestones for the firm include its manufacturing process for compressible printing blankets, the Conti-Air brand and climate-neutral printing blankets.

4438 ■ *The Creative Business Guide to Running a Graphic Design Business*
Pub: W.W. Norton & Company, Incorporated

Ed: Cameron S. Foote. **Released:** April 2004. **Price:** $23.10. **Description:** Advice for running a graphic design firm, focusing on organizations, marketing, personnel and operations.

4439 ■ "Crouser Offers UV Coating Price Report" in *American Printer* (Vol. 128, June 1, 2011, No. 6)
Pub: Penton Media Inc.

Description: Crouser and Associates will offer the 'Pricing Off-Line UV Coating' report that provides background information on all three types of protective printing coatings and price guidance. The report will also offer comparisons of four popular types of offline equipment.

4440 ■ "Customer OKs on Press" in *American Printer* (Vol. 128, August 1, 2011, No. 8)
Pub: Penton Media Inc.

Description: Printers discuss the value of having customers meet at the plant in order to okay print colors for projects.

4441 ■ "Design Center Shows Quality of Digital Paper" in *American Printer* (Vol. 128, June 1, 2011, No. 6)
Pub: Penton Media Inc.

Description: Digital Design Centers allows printers to customize marketing tools in order to promote their own digital printing capabilities.

4442 ■ "Digital Printing Walks the Plank" in *American Printer* (Vol. 128, August 1, 2011, No. 8)
Pub: Penton Media Inc.

Description: Digital print manufacturing is discussed.

4443 ■ "F1 Makes Room(s) for Aspiring Entrepreneur" in *Austin Business Journal* (Vol. 31, July 1, 2011, No. 17, pp. 1)
Pub: American City Business Journals Inc.
Ed: Vicky Garza. **Description:** Formula One fan and graphic designer Danielle Crespo cashes in on the June 17, 2012 racing event in Austin, Texas via hosting a Website that allows users to book hotel rooms. She invested less than $100 and long hours on this enterprise which now has 74,000-plus visitors.

4444 ■ *Fashion & Print Directory*
Pub: Peter Glenn Publications
Ed: Gregory James, Editor. **Released:** Annual, November; latest edition 47th. **Price:** $39.95, individuals. **Covers:** Advertising agencies, PR firms, marketing companies, 1,000 client brand companies and related services in the U.S. and Canada. Includes photographers, marketing agency, suppliers, sources of props and rentals, fashion houses, beauty services, locations. **Entries Include:** Company name, address, phone; paid listings numbering 5,000 include description of products or services, key personnel. **Arrangement:** Classified by line of business.

4445 ■ "Feeding the Elephants While Searching for Greener Pastures" in *American Printer* (Vol. 128, July 1, 2011, No. 7)
Pub: Penton Media Inc.
Ed: Bob Rosen. **Description:** Three steps to help printers to build a new business while facing the challenges to the existing business are outlined.

4446 ■ "First U.S. :M-Press Tiger with Inline Screen Printing" in *American Printer* (Vol. 128, June 1, 2011, No. 6)
Pub: Penton Media Inc.
Description: Graphic Tech located in California bought :M-Press Tiger, the first in North America with an inline screen printing unit.

4447 ■ "Flint Group Raises Prices" in *American Printer* (Vol. 128, August 1, 2011, No. 8)
Pub: Penton Media Inc.
Description: Due to the rising cost for raw materials, Flint Group is raising their prices for inks and coatings in North American.

4448 ■ "Four Exhibition Considerations" in *American Printer* (Vol. 128, August 1, 2011, No. 8)
Pub: Penton Media Inc.
Description: Four questions to ask at the Graph Expo will help printers improve their own business.

4449 ■ "Fujifilm Invites Printers to Take the 'Onset Challenge'" in *American Printer* (Vol. 128, August 1, 2011, No. 8)
Pub: Penton Media Inc.
Description: Fujifilm North American Corporation's Graphic Systems Division offers a new five-step product selection and return-on-investment calculator for the Onset family of wide-format printers.

4450 ■ "Gallery Street Launches ArtCandy" in *Art Business News* (Vol. 34, November 2007, No. 11, pp. 8)
Pub: Pfingsten Publishing, LLC
Description: Fine-art reproduction house Gallery Street recently launched its new division, ArtCandy Editions; the division was created in order to help a network of artists expand the distribution of their work.

4451 ■ "Giovanni Sanfilippo" in *Art Business News* (Vol. 34, November 2007, No. 11, pp. 14)
Pub: Pfingsten Publishing, LLC
Description: GSG Publishing is marketing a new release of Maestro Sanfilippo's "Timida", in a limited edition.

4452 ■ *Graphic Monthly—Estimators' & Buyers' Guide Issue*
Pub: Masthead Publishing Ltd.
Ed: Filomena Tamburri, Editor. **Released:** Annual, Latest edition 2009-2010. **Price:** $25, individuals. **Publication Includes:** List of about 800 suppliers of graphic arts products and services, such as trade printers, art studios, film houses, binding equipment manufacturers, and printing equipment manufacturers. **Entries Include:** Company name, address, phone, product or service. **Arrangement:** Classified by product/service. **Indexes:** Product/service.

4453 ■ "Guide to Carbon Footprinting" in *American Printer* (Vol. 128, June 1, 2011, No. 6)
Pub: Penton Media Inc.
Description: PrintCity Alliance published its new report, 'Carbon Footprint & Energy Reduction for Graphic Industry Value Chain.' The report aims to help improve the environmental performance of printers, converters, publishers, brand owners and their suppliers.

4454 ■ "A Home's Identity in Black and White" in *Crain's Chicago Business* (Vol. 31, April 21, 2008, No. 16, pp. 35)
Pub: Crain Communications, Inc.
Ed: Lisa Bertagnoli. **Description:** Real estate agents are finding that showing customers a written floor plan is a trend that is growing since many buyers feel that Online virtual tours distort a room. Although floor plans cost up to $500 to have drawn up, they clearly show potential buyers the exact dimensions of rooms and how they connect.

4455 ■ "How to Save Money on Ink" in *American Printer* (Vol. 128, July 1, 2011, No. 7)
Pub: Penton Media Inc.
Description: Tips are shared to help graphic arts and printing companies save money on raw materials. Factors to consider once the type of ink is decided are also outlined.

4456 ■ "Improving the USPS" in *American Printer* (Vol. 128, July 1, 2011, No. 7)
Pub: Penton Media Inc.
Description: National Postal Forum held in San Diego, California May 1-4, 2011 hosted 4,000 attendees. Highlights of the event are provided.

4457 ■ "Industry/Events 2011" in *American Printer* (Vol. 128, July 1, 2011, No. 7)
Pub: Penton Media Inc.
Description: PMA, the Worldwide Community of Imaging Association launched its new CliQ with how-to tips, product reviews and monthly photo contests. PMA formed a partnership with the Consumer Electronics Association to make changes to this year's annual convention.

4458 ■ "Inside an Online Bazaar" in *Entrepreneur* (Vol. 37, September 2009, No. 9, pp. 38)
Pub: Entrepreneur Media, Inc.
Ed: Kara Ohngren. **Description:** Etsy.com is a website that provides a marketplace for handmade products. The site has attracted more than 250,000 sellers since its launch in 2005. Site features and services are also supplied.

4459 ■ "Interchangeable or Irreplaceable?" in *American Printer* (Vol. 128, August 1, 2011, No. 8)
Pub: Penton Media Inc.
Description: Creating and maintaining customers is important for all graphic design and printing companies. Tips are shared to help maintain good customer satisfaction and repeat business.

4460 ■ "IPEX Moves to London Venue" in *American Printer* (Vol. 128, July 1, 2011, No. 7)
Pub: Penton Media Inc.
Description: IPES 2014 is being relocated to London's ExCeL International Exhibition and Conference Centre from March 26 to April 2, 2014.

4461 ■ "JDF Integration: 3 Key Tips" in *American Printer* (Vol. 128, August 1, 2011, No. 8)
Pub: Penton Media Inc.
Description: Three tips for implementing cross-vendor integrations are outlined.

4462 ■ "KBA, Graphic Art System Partner on Cold Foil" in *American Printer* (Vol. 128, June 1, 2011, No. 6)
Pub: Penton Media Inc.
Description: KBA North America has partnered with Graphic Art System to retrofit and equip presses with cold foil machines.

4463 ■ "Kodak Offers Cloud-Based Operating Option" in *American Printer* (Vol. 128, June 1, 2011, No. 6)
Pub: Penton Media Inc.
Description: Kodak partnered with VMware to offer its first Virtual Operating Environment option for Kodak Unified Workflow Solutions. The new feature enables cost savings, increased efficiency and failover protection.

4464 ■ "Metallics Education" in *American Printer* (Vol. 128, June 1, 2011, No. 6)
Pub: Penton Media Inc.
Description: Guide 'Curious About Print: Your Guide to the World of Curious Metallics' provides hints and tips to help printers maximize selection and reproduction, advice on working with metallic and UV inks, and recommendations for gaining quantity without sacrificing quality.

4465 ■ "MFSA Officially Endorses Five-Day USPS Delivery" in *American Printer* (Vol. 128, August 1, 2011, No. 8)
Pub: Penton Media Inc.
Description: Board of Directors of the Mailing and Fulfillment Service Association (MFSA) voted to support the US Postal Service's move to five-day delivery service.

4466 ■ "New Approach to Mechanical Binding" in *American Printer* (Vol. 128, July 1, 2011, No. 7)
Pub: Penton Media Inc.
Description: EcoBinder coil binding system from Kugler-Womako eliminates traditional plastic combs or wire spiral with the use of 22-mm wide printable paper rings.

4467 ■ "No Straight Lines: How Video Visionary Julien 'Little X' Lutz Creates His Images" in *Black Enterprise* (Vol. 38, January 2008)
Pub: Earl G. Graves Publishing Co. Inc.
Ed: Sonia Alleyne. **Description:** Profile of Julien Lutz, who turned his passion for drawing into a successful career.

4468 ■ "OCE Boosts JetStream Productivity" in *American Printer* (Vol. 128, August 1, 2011, No. 8)
Pub: Penton Media Inc.
Description: New Oce JetStream 1400 and 3000 digital full-color inkjet presses are profiled. The new models promise higher speed to grow print volume.

4469 ■ "One World" in *American Printer* (Vol. 128, August 1, 2011, No. 8)
Pub: Penton Media Inc.
Description: Graph Expo will highlight entrepreneurs focused on the connection between content, technology and business models.

4470 ■ "Paper a la Carte" in *American Printer* (Vol. 128, June 1, 2011, No. 6)
Pub: Penton Media Inc.
Description: Blurb, the online publishing platform, launched ProLine which features Mohawk Superfine and Mohawk proPhoto papers. ProLine papers offer two finishes: Pearl Photo and Uncoated.

4471 ■ "Paper Choices Made Simple" in *American Printer* (Vol. 128, June 1, 2011, No. 6)
Pub: Penton Media Inc.
Description: Choices, a new initiative by Boise, provides professional guidance to help customers and consumers make informed, effective choices for using paper.

4472 ■ "Paper Replaces PVC for Gift Cards" in *American Printer* (Vol. 128, June 1, 2011, No. 6)
Pub: Penton Media Inc.
Description: Monadnock Envi Card Stock replaces paper for gift cards, loyalty cards, membership cards, hotel keys and durable signage. This renewable wood fiber alternative to PVC card materials comes from Monadock Paper Mills.

4473 ■ "Partnering for Success" in *Art Business News* (Vol. 36, October 2009, No. 10, pp. 4)
Pub: Summit Business Media
Ed: Jennifer Dulin Wiley. **Description:** In such a volatile economy many savvy artists and gallery owners are turning to out-of-the-box partnerships for continued success; these partnerships are also pervading the Internet, especially with such social media networks as Facebook and Twitter where artists and businesses can develop a loyal following.

4474 ■ *The Pixar Touch: The Making of a Company*
Pub: Pantheon Books
Ed: David A. Price. **Released:** 2009. **Price:** $27.95. **Description:** Profile of how Pixar's founders turned their computer-animated films into a successful movie studio.

4475 ■ "Prices Continue to Rise" in *American Printer* (Vol. 128, June 1, 2011, No. 6)
Pub: Penton Media Inc.
Description: Prices were increased by both Flint Group and Ashland Performance Materials by 7-10 percent and 5-15 percent respectively.

4476 ■ "Printers to the Trade" in *American Printer* (Vol. 128, July 1, 2011, No. 7)
Pub: Penton Media Inc.
Description: Wholesale printing is discussed. Two wholesale printers share insight into their success, from business philosophies in general to practices that build strong relationships.

4477 ■ "QR Codes: OK, I Get It Now" in *American Printer* (Vol. 128, July 1, 2011, No. 7)
Pub: Penton Media Inc.
Description: QR Code technology is discussed. It is up to the user to enter the proper QR Code.

4478 ■ "The Rage Offstage at Marvel" in *Barron's* (Vol. 88, June 30, 2008, No. 26, pp. 19)
Pub: Dow Jones & Co., Inc.
Ed: Bill Alpert. **Description:** Lawsuits against Marvel Entertainment and Stan Lee are pushing the claims from Peter F. Paul that Stan Lee Media was undone by the actions of the accused. Paul's associates argue that Stan Lee Media owns rights to Marvel characters and that they want half the profits that Marvel is making.

4479 ■ "Red One and The Rain Chronicles" in *Michigan Vue* (Vol. 13, July-August 2008, No. 4, pp. 30)
Pub: Entrepreneur Media Inc.
Ed: Evan Cornish. **Description:** Troy-based film school the Motion Picture Institute (MPI) implemented the latest technology by shooting the second of their trilogy, "The Rain Chronicles", on the Red One camera. This is the first feature film in Michigan to utilize this exciting new camera, which includes proprietary software for rendering and color correction. Brian K. Johnson heads up the visual effects team as visual effects supervisor and lead CG artist. His company, Dream Conduit Studios, had to tackle the task of employing the new work flow through a post-production pipeline that would allow him to attack complex visual effects shots, many of which were shot with a moving camera, a technique rarely seen in films at this budgetary level where the camera is traditionally locked off.

4480 ■ "Reducing the Book's Carbon Footpring" in *American Printer* (Vol. 128, July 1, 2011, No. 7)
Pub: Penton Media Inc.
Description: Green Press Initiative's Book Industry Environmental Council is working to achieve a 20 percent reduction in the book industry's carbon footprint by 2020. The Council is made up of publishers, printers, paper suppliers, and non-governmental organizations.

4481 ■ "Root, Root, Root for the P.A. Hutchison Co." in *American Printer* (Vol. 128, August 1, 2011, No. 8)
Pub: Penton Media Inc.
Description: The P.A. Hutchison Company celebrate 100 years in the printing business. President and CEO Chris Hutchison presented awards to employees, however employees also presented awards to Chris and his father as Employer of the Century.

4482 ■ *RSVP*
Pub: RSVP: The Directory of Illustration and Design
Contact: Richard Lebenson
Released: Annual, January/February latest edition 2005. **Price:** $20, individuals. **Covers:** about 250 illustrators and designers in the graphic arts industry. All listings are paid. **Entries Include:** Name, address, phone, sample of work. **Arrangement:** Separate sections for illustrators and designers; each subdivided into color and black and white. **Indexes:** Specialty (with phone), geographical, alphabetical.

4483 ■ "Sappi Awards Gold NA Printers of the Year Winners" in *American Printer* (Vol. 128, July 1, 2011, No. 7)
Pub: Penton Media Inc.
Description: Sappi Fine Paper North America honored ten gold winners of its 14th North American Printers of the Year awards. Each gold winning printer will receive $20,000 to support marketing and brand initiatives.

4484 ■ "Seeing the Light" in *American Printer* (Vol. 128, July 1, 2011, No. 7)
Pub: Penton Media Inc.
Description: Four printing demos on sheetfed, digital, label and pad printing equipment were highlighted at the Fifth UV Days held in Stuttgart, Germany in May 2011.

4485 ■ *Seven Days in the Art World*
Pub: W.W. Norton & Company
Ed: Sarah Thornton. **Released:** 2009. **Price:** $24.95. **Description:** A sociologist renders the interplay among buyers, critics, curators and makers of contemporary art.

4486 ■ "Seven Tips for Continuous Improvement" in *American Printer* (Vol. 128, July 1, 2011, No. 7)
Pub: Penton Media Inc.
Description: Seven tips are given to help any graphic arts or printing company improve by integrating lean manufacturing into operations.

4487 ■ "Show Dates" in *Art Business News* (Vol. 34, November 2007, No. 11, pp. 18)
Pub: Pfingsten Publishing, LLC
Description: Listing of conferences, trade shows and gallery openings for artists and those in the art industry.

4488 ■ "Something Old and Something New" in *American Printer* (Vol. 128, August 1, 2011, No. 8)
Pub: Penton Media Inc.
Description: Trade journalists and industry analysts were invited to Fujifilm North America Corporation's Hanover Park, Illinois facility to view it's sheetfed inkjet press. The JPress 720 is the first and only of its kind in the world.

4489 ■ "Successful First Year for Twin Rivers" in *American Printer* (Vol. 128, June 1, 2011, No. 6)
Pub: Penton Media Inc.
Description: Profile of Twin Rivers located in Maine. The firm manufactured 380,000 tons of free sheet and hybrid-groundwood papers in its first year.

4490 ■ "Ted Stahl: Executive Chairman" in *Inside Business* (Vol. 13, September-October 2011, No. 5, pp. NC6)
Pub: Great Lakes Publishing Company
Ed: Miranda S. Miller. **Description:** Profile of Ted Stahl, who started working in his family's business when he was ten years old is presented. The firm makes dies for numbers and letters used on team uniforms. Another of the family firms manufactures stock and custom heat-printing products, equipment and supplies. It also educates customers on ways to decorate garments with heat printing products and offers graphics and software for customers to create their own artwork.

4491 ■ "Tic-Tac-Show" in *American Printer* (Vol. 128, August 1, 2011, No. 8)
Pub: Penton Media Inc.
Description: Graph Expo has become the US print industry's main event. There will be as many as 500 exhibitors at this year's event and the Graphic Arts Show Company lists over 30 co-located events as well as 53 new sessions in the seminar program's 28 education categories.

4492 ■ "Transcontinental to Exchange Assets with Quad/Graphics" in *American Printer* (Vol. 128, August 1, 2011, No. 8)
Pub: Penton Media Inc.
Description: Transcontinental Inc. and Quad/Graphics Inc. entered into an agreement where Transcontinental will indirectly acquire all shares of Quad Graphics Canada Inc.

4493 ■ "Try a Little Social Media" in *American Printer* (Vol. 128, June 1, 2011, No. 6)
Pub: Penton Media Inc.
Description: Social media helps keep Ussery Printing on customers radar. Jim David, VP of marketing for the firm, states that 350 people following them on Facebook are from the local area.

4494 ■ "Use Ink Presets to Minimize Makeready" in *American Printer* (Vol. 128, July 1, 2011, No. 7)
Pub: Penton Media Inc.
Description: Automatic registration systems enable most printers to be in register very quickly after press startup. If the paper, ink and press time wasted during makeready can be reduced, these savings will flow directly to the bottom line. Ink presetting as an economical solution to set color quickly is a trend that continues to gain momentum.

4495 ■ "UV Suppliers Form Strategic Alliance" in *American Printer* (Vol. 128, June 1, 2011, No. 6)
Pub: Penton Media Inc.
Description: British ultra-violent curing systems developer Integration Technology Ltd. formed a strategic alliance with UV technology provider IST Metz GmbH of Germany in order to offer a complete line of UV solutions for the printing industry.

4496 ■ "A Vegas Sensation Inaugural Artexpo Las Vegas" in *Art Business News* (Vol. 34, November 2007, No. 11, pp. 1)
Pub: Pfingsten Publishing, LLC
Ed: Jennifer Dulin. **Description:** Overview of the first Artexpo Las Vegas which featured exhibitors, artists and buyers and was a wonderful place for networking.

4497 ■ "Web to Print" in *American Printer* (Vol. 128, August 1, 2011, No. 8)
Pub: Penton Media Inc.
Description: Jerry Kennelly, CEO and founder of Tweak.com believes that Web-to-Design is middleware with no content. His firm offers an easy to use interface that flows right into the printer's workflow with no additional costs.

STATISTICAL SOURCES

4498 ■ *RMA Annual Statement Studies*
Pub: Robert Morris Associates (RMA)
Released: Annual. **Price:** $175.00 2006-07 edition, $105.00. **Description:** Contains composite balance sheets and income statements for more than 360

industries, including the accounting, auditing, and bookkeeping industries. Also contains five years of comparative historical data for discerning trends. Includes 16 commonly used ratios, computed for most of the size groupings for nearly every industry.

TRADE PERIODICALS

4499 ■ *Applied Arts Magazine*
Pub: Applied Arts Inc.
Contact: Georges Haroutiun, Art Dir./Founder
E-mail: art@appliedartsmag.com
Ed: Peter Giffen, Editor, editor@appliedartsmag.com. **Released:** 6/yr. **Price:** $60; $100 two years; $75 U.S. and other countries; $150 two years U.S. & and other countries. **Description:** Visual communication arts magazine for designers, art directors, photographers, illustrators, and other professionals in related fields.

4500 ■ *Before & After*
Pub: JMS Publishing L.L.C.
Contact: John McWade, Creative Dir./Founder
E-mail: mailbox@bamagazine.com
Released: Bimonthly. **Price:** $48. **Description:** Trade magazine covering graphic design.

4501 ■ *Country Home*
Pub: Meredith Corp.
Released: Monthly, 10/yr. **Price:** $4.95 newstand; $21.97 two years. **Description:** Magazine furnishing information on American interior design, architecture, antiques and collectibles, gardening, art, and culinary endeavor.

4502 ■ *Economic Edge*
Pub: National Association for Printing Leadership
Released: Quarterly. **Price:** Included in membership. **Description:** Provides current economic data for the printing industry. Also covers sales growth projections, capital spending, and employment.

4503 ■ *Gain*
Pub: American Institute of Graphic Arts
Contact: Richard Grefe, Publisher
E-mail: grefe@aiga.org
Released: Semiannual. **Description:** Journal covering graphic art and design.

4504 ■ *Graphic Communicator*
Pub: Graphic Communication Conference of the International Brotherhood of Teamsters
Contact: George Tedeschi, President
Released: 5/yr. **Price:** $12 U.S. and Canada; $15 other countries. **Description:** Trade newspaper of the Graphic Communications International Union.

4505 ■ *The Graphic Monthly*
Pub: North Island Publishing
Released: Bimonthly. **Price:** $28 Free to qualified subscribers; $40. **Description:** Printing and graphic design magazine.

4506 ■ *Trace*
Pub: American Institute of Graphic Arts
Contact: Connie Birdsall, Director
E-mail: connie.birdsall@lm.mmc.com
Released: Triennial. **Price:** $13 quantity available: 1. **Description:** Journal of design and visual culture.

VIDEOCASSETTES/ AUDIOCASSETTES

4507 ■ *The Application of Good Design*
Instructional Video
2219 C St.
Lincoln, NE 68502
Ph:(402)475-6570
Free: 800-228-0164
Fax:(402)475-6500
Co. E-mail: feedback@insvideo.com
URL: http://www.insvideo.com
Price: $39.95. **Description:** Outlines techniques in creating graphic designs that sell. Provides demonstrations by professional designers working on rough layouts, comprehensives, and dummies. Also discusses computer aids. **Availability:** VHS.

4508 ■ *Harvard Graphics 2.3*
Moonbeam Publications, Inc.
PO Box 5150
Traverse City, MI 49696
Ph:(616)922-0533
Free: 800-445-2391
Fax:800-334-9789
Co. E-mail: custserv@moonbeampublications.com
URL: http://www.moonbeampublications.com
Released: 1991. **Price:** $24.95. **Description:** Get the most from your Harvard Graphics package with this video. **Availability:** VHS.

4509 ■ *Lithography: How to Paint and Sell Lithographs*
Instructional Video
2219 C St.
Lincoln, NE 68502
Ph:(402)475-6570
Free: 800-228-0164
Fax:(402)475-6500
Co. E-mail: feedback@insvideo.com
URL: http://www.insvideo.com
Price: $19.95. **Description:** Provides information on how professional print makers plan and print original lithographs to sell. Also contains demonstrations of tools, techniques, materials, and marketing. **Availability:** VHS.

TRADE SHOWS AND CONVENTIONS

4510 ■ Graph Expo and Converting Expo
Graphic Arts Show Co. GASC
1899 Preston White Dr.
Reston, VA 20191-5468
Ph:(703)264-7200
Fax:(703)620-9187
Co. E-mail: info@gasc.org
URL: http://www.gasc.org
Released: Annual. **Audience:** Commercial printers, designers, publishers, typographers, converters. **Principal Exhibits:** Graphic art equipment, supplies, and services. Printing, publishing, and converting equipment. **Dates and Locations:** 2011 Sep 11-14, Chicago, IL; 2012 Sep 30 - Oct 03, Chicago, IL; 2013 Sep 06-11, Chicago, IL.

4511 ■ Graphics of the Americas
Printing Association of Florida, Inc.
6275 Hazeltine National Dr.
Orlando, FL 32822
Ph:(407)240-8009
Free: 800-749-4855
Fax:(407)240-8333
Co. E-mail: agaither@pafgraf.org
URL: http://www.pafgraf.org
Released: Annual. **Audience:** Graphics arts trade. **Principal Exhibits:** Graphic arts and specialty printing equipment, supplies, and services.

4512 ■ Graphics Canada
dmg world media
180 Duncan Mill Rd., Ste. 400
4th Fl.
Toronto, ON, Canada M3B 1Z6
Ph:(416)385-1880
Free: 888-823-7469
Fax:(416)385-1855
Co. E-mail: corpinfo@ca.dmgworldmedia.com
URL: http://www.dmgworldmedia.com
Released: Annual. **Audience:** People who are interested in the graphic arts and printing industry. **Principal Exhibits:** Printing and graphic art industries equipment, supplies, and services, including computer graphics, desktop publishing, and art supplies. **Dates and Locations:** 2011 Nov 10-12, Toronto, ON.

CONSULTANTS

4513 ■ AT Associates
63 Old Rutherford Ave.
Charlestown, MA 02129-3750
Ph:(617)242-6004
Contact: Dan Kovacevic, Partner
Scope: Provides consulting services in industrial design, model making and graphic design.

4514 ■ CATTAN Services Group Inc.
1006 Haywood Dr.
College Station, TX 77845-5688
Ph:(979)260-7200
Fax:(979)260-7100
Co. E-mail: cattan@cattan.com
URL: http://www.cattan.com
Contact: Thomas L. Tanel, CEO
E-mail: tanel@cattan.com
Scope: Consultants offering supply chain and logistics advisory; counseling and training services. Specialists in purchasing and procurement; distribution and warehousing; inventory control; traffic management and supply chain strategy. Works with client organizations to assist in personnel; organizational; procedural; policy or strategic issues. Conducts functional operational audits; interfunctional problem-solving; productivity improvement programs; facility layouts; coaching; seminars and strategic planning. Industries served: business services, distribution, oil and gas, processors and manufacturing; financial services; building owners; local; state and federal government; nonprofit organizations and utilities. **Seminars:** Advanced Cargo Traffic Management; Bar Coding, RFID and Automatic Identification; Effective Purchasing Negotiations; Improving Supplier Performance; Strategic Planning from a Purchasing and Supply Management Perspective; Advanced Purchasing & Supply Management Techniques; Fundamentals of International Purchasing; Fundamentals of Traffic; Improving Supplier Performance; Legal Aspects of Purchasing; Maximizing Purchasing Power; Outsourcing to Success; Warehouse Operations & Inventory Management; Strategic Sourcing; Strategic Planning from a Purchasing & Supply Management Perspective; Purchasing Techniques for Effective Buying; Logistics & Supply Chain Management; Purchasing Negotiation Process & Communication Skills.

4515 ■ Concord Associates Co.
16 Chambers Cir.
West Lebanon, NH 03784
Ph:(603)643-6768
Fax:(603)643-6768
Contact: Elliott D. Novak, President
Scope: Offers business counsel and market and marketing consulting assistance in key areas of both the consumer and professional digital imaging fields. Primary emphasis is in digital cameras; ink jet and dye sublimation printers; digital mini labs; and related or ancillary products such as flash memory cards for digital cameras.

4516 ■ Gate Group USA Inc.
137 Varick St., Ste. 400
New York, NY 10013-1105
Ph:(212)989-9797
Free: 800-966-9889
Fax:(212)989-9363
Co. E-mail: gategroupusa@graphicartstech.com
URL: http://www.graphicartstech.com
Contact: Isaac M. Savitt, President
E-mail: ike@graphicartstech.com
Scope: Provides foreign trade and international marketing consulting services. S specializes in the graphic arts and printing-related industries.

4517 ■ Jack J. Bulloff Consulting and Expert Witness Services
8140 Township Line Rd., Ste. 5220
Indianapolis, IN 46260-5866
Ph:(317)824-0014
Fax:(317)824-0589
Contact: Dr. Jack J. Bulloff, Owner
Scope: Chemical and environmental consultant and expert witness specializing in the following areas: occupational and environmental safety and health, hazardous chemicals and waste management/disposal, research and development and innovation information development, environmental impact/technology assessment, technological forecasting and planning.

4518 ■ Ki Systems Inc.
432 Knollwood Dr.
Newbury Park, CA 91320-4840
Ph:(805)499-4912
Free: 800-946-2854

Fax:(805)499-8048
Co. E-mail: ki@kibizsystems.com
URL: http://www.kibizsystems.com
Contact: Allen Imbarrato, Product Development Manager
Scope: Training company specializing in learning technologies. Develops customized program to develop a high performance organization. Do esextensive needs analysis on current level of organizational functioning. Assesses leadership skills, and develops individualized leadership development programs to improve leadership skills. Facilitates a VISIONING process to develop clear corporate mission, goals, and strategy. Does personal computer consulting to achieve optimum use of computers and network. Industries served: retail, video production, real estate development, graphic arts, advertising, telephone, communications, computer, aerospace, defense, government agencies, and health. **Seminars:** Winning at Work and at Life; Developing a High Performance Organization; Maximizing Productivity with Fundamental Macintosh Tools; Creating Presentations with a Computer; Break through Technology. **Special Services:** KiBizSystem 4.5; KiShop; KiPoint; KiBizSystem 5.0.; KiBiz Accounting; KiBiz Production Management; Ki Sales Automation via EDI or XML.

4519 ■ LandaJob Advertising Staffing Specialists
222 W Gregory Blvd., Ste. 304
Kansas City, MO 64114
Ph:(816)523-1881
Free: 800-931-8806
Fax:(816)523-1876
Co. E-mail: adstaff@landajobnow.com
URL: http://www.landajobnow.com
Contact: Elisa Haake, Principle
E-mail: ehaake@atslandajobnow.com
Scope: Personnel consultants and recruiters for advertising, marketing, and communications positions. Industries served: advertising, communications, marketing, graphic arts, printing and publishing.

4520 ■ Landor Associates
1001 Front St.
San Francisco, CA 94111-1424
Ph:(415)365-1700
Free: 888-252-6367
Fax:(415)365-3190
Co. E-mail: more_info@landor.com
URL: http://www.landor.com
Contact: Rob Horjus, Managering Director
E-mail: joseph_pantigoso@atslandor.com
Scope: A global brand consulting and strategic design firm. **Publications:** "Brand simple" Palgrave Macmillan, 2006.

4521 ■ Miles F. Southworth, Consultant to the Graphic Arts
3100 Bronson Hill Rd.
Livonia, NY 14487-9716
Ph:(716)346-2776
Fax:(716)346-2276
Co. E-mail: mfsouth@aol.com
E-mail: mfsouth@aol.com
Scope: Graphic arts consultant active in the areas of color reproduction, quality control, and total quality management, productivity audit and training. **Publications:** "Quality and Productivity in the Graphic Arts and How to Implement Total Quality Management," Southworth and Southworth; "Pocket Guide to Color Reproduction," 1995; "Color Separation on the Desktop," 1994. **Seminars:** As need relating to topics listed under consulting activities; 10 Steps to good color reproduction; GRACOL. Productivity and Color Quality Improvement Newspaper.

4522 ■ Naramore, Bain, Brady and Johanson
130 Sutter St., 2nd Fl.
San Francisco, CA 94104
Ph:(206)223-5555
Fax:(206)621-2300
Co. E-mail: info@nbbj.com
URL: http://www.nbbj.com
Contact: Steve McConnell, Managing Partner
E-mail: smcconnell@nbbj.com
Scope: Offers services in architecture, branding and design, interiors, landscape design, lighting design, planning and urban design. Additional services include land use planning, economic and financial feasibility studies, facilities management, graphic design and signage. Industries served: airport and transportation, civic, commercial mixed-use, corporate, healthcare, higher education, hospitality, resort and recreation, retail, sports and entertainment. **Special Services:** MicroStation/TriForma.

4523 ■ Sales Directors Inc.
1034 Lake St.
Oak Park, IL 60301
Ph:(708)383-4038
Fax:(708)383-4081
Co. E-mail: info@salesdirectors.com
URL: http://www.salesdirectors.com
Contact: Linda Stanley, Director
E-mail: linda@atssalesdirectors.com
Scope: Sales and marketing consultants for the printing and graphic arts industries. Specializes in sales training for personnel of graphic arts firms, and search/placement of sales people. **Publications:** "Bull's Eye Selling. A Guide to Target Account Sales"; "Twelve Steps to Success in Selling"; "Sales basics for newer sales people"; "Selling Graphic Arts in the Electronic Age"; "How To Manage a Sales Force That Sells". **Seminars:** Twelve Steps to Success in Selling; How to Manage a Sales Force That Sells; Selling Graphic Arts in this Electronic Age; Great Training Great Price, Personal Support Real Development.

4524 ■ Smith, Bridges & Associates
555 S Old Woodward Ave., Ste. 603
Birmingham, MI 48009-6658
Ph:(248)540-2448
Free: 800-728-0168
Fax:(248)540-2801
Contact: Michael Smith, Partner
E-mail: mike@atssmithbridges.com
Scope: Offers contingency executive search for national and regional companies and nonprofit organizations. Recruiting activity includes sourcing candidates for executive level positions with a minimum of five years industry experience and income in the 80, 000 to 160, 000 dollar range.

4525 ■ Strack Vaughan L.L.C.
4833 Rugby Ave., Ste. 201
Bethesda, MD 20814-3035
Ph:(301)654-7778
Fax:(301)951-0063
Contact: Janice Hartmann, Partner
Scope: Business and financial planning consultants providing services in mergers and acquisitions, strategic planning, and tax planning. Serves insurance agencies and the graphic arts industry.

4526 ■ Teague
2727 Western Ave., Ste. 200
Seattle, WA 98121
Ph:(206)838-4200
Fax:(206)838-4299
Co. E-mail: newbiz@teague.com
URL: http://www.teague.com
Contact: William Scott, Chairman of the Board
E-mail: jbarratt@teague.com
Scope: Offers counsel in industrial design, graphics design, environmental and interior design, packaging design, transportation design, quality assurance and reliability and maintainability engineering.

4527 ■ VMS Inc.
805 Airway Dr.
Allegan, MI 49010-8516
Ph:(269)673-2200
Free: 800-343-6430
Fax:(269)673-9509
Co. E-mail: sales@vms-online.com
URL: http://www.vms-online.com
Contact: Lydia E. Walsh, Vice President
E-mail: mike@vms-online.com
Scope: Provides marketing services to clients producing training materials for vocational schools, colleges, and industry. Assists in identifying and preparing training materials, training staff to prepare training materials, packaging, and developing marketing plans. Works with traditional publishers and clients wishing to convert internal training materials for external sale. Industries served: Automotive, building and machine trades, software, graphic arts and government in the U.S. and Canada. **Seminars:** Product Marketing; Direct Mail; Trade Show Boothmanship; Product Evaluation. **Special Services:** Corel WordPerfect X4: Academic Version; WordPerfect Office X3 Essential Training; CorelDRAW Graphics Suite X4: Academic Version; AutoCAD LT 2010 for Windows; AutoCAD LT 2010 Student Version: 61 month License; TurboCAD Pro 16 Platinum Ed: Academic; TurboCAD PRO 16 Architectural: Academic; TurboCAD Mac PRO: Academic; TurboCAD Mac Deluxe 2D/3D: Academic; TurboFLOORPLAN 3D Home and Landscape PRO.

4528 ■ W. F. Davis Consultants
179 Voelbel Rd.
Hightstown, NJ 08520-2807
Ph:(609)448-0161
Contact: William F. Davis, President
Scope: Offers counsel to corporations on planning, manufacturing, product development, product conception, special purpose machinery development, production methodology, profit enhancement, and manufacturing systems. Specializes in printing and bindery equipment. Clients include paper, printing, publication, graphic arts machinery, disposable products, textile, consumer products, machine tool and instrumentation industries.

FRANCHISES AND BUSINESS OPPORTUNITIES

4529 ■ Greenbaum Marketing Communications
12 Sunset Way, Ste. A-104
Henderson, NV 89014
Ph:(702)898-8818
Fax:(702)898-8870
Founded: 2004. **Description:** Marketing/graphic design firm.

4530 ■ Kwik Kopy Business Centers
Kwik Kopy Business Centers, Inc.
12715 Telge Rd.
Cypress, TX 77429
Free: 888-638-8722
Fax:(281)256-4178
Co. E-mail: franchisedevelopment@iced.net
URL: http://www.iced.net
No. of Franchise Units: 16. **No. of Company-Owned Units:** 1. **Founded:** 2001. **Franchised:** 2001. **Description:** Offers business advertisement aids and printing and copying services. **Equity Capital Needed:** $65,000 liquid capital; $250,000 net worth. **Franchise Fee:** $35,000. **Financial Assistance:** Conventional bank and SBA loans, and through in-house financing with sufficient collateral. **Managerial Assistance:** Provide business support, advertising, and marketing materials. **Training:** Owners attend classroom and field training, as well as ongoing training through workshops and conferences.

4531 ■ Sign Biz, Inc.
24681 La Plaza, Ste. 270
Dana Point, CA 92629
Ph:(949)234-0408
Free: 800-633-5580
Fax:(949)234-0426
URL: http://www.signbiz.com
No. of Franchise Units: 185. **Founded:** 1989. **Franchised:** 1990. **Description:** Visual communication stores developing digital sign making. **Equity Capital Needed:** $45,000-$50,000 liquid. **Franchise Fee:** None. **Financial Assistance:** SBA registered. **Training:** 2 weeks initial training at corporate office and 1-2 week home study program.

COMPUTERIZED DATABASES

4532 ■ *Art Index*
EBSCO Publishing
10 Estes St.
Ipswich, MA 01938
Ph:(978)356-6500
Free: 800-653-2726

Fax:(978)356-6565
Co. E-mail: information@ebscohost.com
URL: http://www.ebscohost.com/wilson
Description: Contains more than 870,000 citations to articles, reproductions, and book reviews in 400 periodicals, yearbooks, and museum bulletins published worldwide. Covers archaeology, architecture, art history, city planning, crafts, landscape architecture, film, fine arts, folk art, graphic arts, industrial design, interior design, and photography. Corresponds to *Art Index*. **Availability:** Online: EBSCO Publishing, Wolters Kluwer Health, Wolters Kluwer Health. **Type:** Bibliographic.

4533 ■ *Art on Screen Database*
Program for Art on Film Inc.
200 Willoughby Ave.
Brooklyn, NY 11205-3817
Ph:(718)399-4506
Fax:(718)399-4507
Co. E-mail: info@artfilm.org
URL: http://www.artfilm.org
Description: Contains bibliographic information on more than 25,000 videos, films, multimedia, and CD-ROM productions about the visual arts. For each product, provides title, credits, length, year, country, language, synopsis, production date, distributors, formats, awards, reviews, and in many cases evaluations. Includes entries for more than 5000 distribution sources, providing name, address, telephone, and fax numbers for each entry. Users may perform searches by artist name, style or period, materials, techniques, genre or by associated concepts. **Availability:** Online: Program for Art on Film Inc. **Type:** Directory.

4534 ■ *Graphic Arts Blue Book*
Reed Business Information Ltd.
Quadrant House
The Quadrant
Surrey
Sutton SM2 5AS, United Kingdom
Ph:44 20 8652 3500
Fax:44 20 8652 8932
Co. E-mail: rbi.subscriptions@qss-uk.com
URL: http://www.rbi.co.uk
Description: Contains directory information on more than 40,000 specialty printers and graphic arts suppliers. Contains listings of more than 1200 products and services. Includes listings of graphics arts equipment, supplies, and services. Provides menu-based and full-text search capability. Available in several regional editions. **Availability:** Online: Reed Business Information Ltd. **Type:** Full text; Directory.

4535 ■ *Impressionism and Its Sources*
Technology Dynamics Corp.
1601 N Sepulveda Blvd., Ste. 374
PO Box 219
Manhattan Beach, CA 90267
Ph:(310)406-1803
Fax:(310)406-0833
Co. E-mail: contact@tdcinteractive.com
URL: http://www.tdcinteractive.net
Description: Presents over 1000 paintings and drawings in the impressionist style along with instruction in understanding and appreciating impressionism. Contains examples of works by major artists along with biographical essays. Includes an interactive essay explaining impressionism's importance to art history. **Availability:** CD-ROM: Technology Dynamics Corp. **Type:** Full text.

LIBRARIES

4536 ■ Art Center College of Design–James Lemont Fogg Memorial Library
1700 Lida St.
Pasadena, CA 91103
Ph:(626)396-2233
Co. E-mail: betsy.galloway@artcenter.edu
URL: http://hera.artcenter.edu
Contact: Betsy Galloway, Lib.Dir.
Scope: Fine arts, communications design, graphics/packaging, advertising design, industrial design, illustration, photography and film. **Services:** Copying; Library open to the public by appointment. **Holdings:** 86,000 volumes of books and periodicals; 4200 bound periodical volumes; 2086 exhibition catalogs; 32 VF drawers; 1900 Annual reports; 110,000 slides; 133 films; 8000 videotapes and DVDs; 90,000 photographs. **Subscriptions:** 400 journals and other serials; 10 newspapers.

4537 ■ Art Institute of Boston at Lesley University Library
700 Beacon St.
Boston, MA 02215
Ph:(617)585-6671
Co. E-mail: dverhoff@lesley.edu
URL: http://www.lesley.edu/aib/studentlife/services.html
Contact: Deb Verhoff, Hd.Libn.
Scope: Art history, photography, graphics, design, humanities, graphic design, illustration, animation, humanities. **Services:** Copying; scanning; Library open to the public for reference use only. **Holdings:** 11,000 books; 45,000 slides; 7 VF drawers of picture reference files; 4 VF drawers of exhibition catalogs; 6 VF drawer of pamphlets; 450 videos; 10,000 photographs. **Subscriptions:** 95 journals and other serials.

4538 ■ Art Institute of Philadelphia Library
1610 Chestnut St.
Philadelphia, PA 19103
Ph:(215)405-6402
Co. E-mail: rschachter@aii.edu
URL: http://rs185.aisites.com
Contact: Ruth Schachter, Dir.
Scope: Visual communications, interior design, industrial design, animation, fashion marketing, fashion design, visual merchandising, photography, website design, multimedia. **Services:** Interlibrary loan; Library not open to the public (circulation services provided for students and faculty). **Holdings:** 31,000 volumes; 2000 videocassettes; audiocassettes. **Subscriptions:** 170 print subscriptions and other serials.

4539 ■ The Baltimore Museum of Art–E. Kirkbride Miller Art Research Library
10 Art Museum Dr.
Baltimore, MD 21218-3898
Ph:(443)573-1778
Fax:(443)573-1582
Co. E-mail: bmalibrary@artbma.org
URL: http://www.artbma.org/about/library.html
Contact: Doreen Bolger, Dir.
Scope: History of art with special strengths in: modern and contemporary art; 19th-century French art; American and British decorative arts; prints, drawings, and photography; arts of Africa, Asia, Oceania, and the Americas. **Services:** Library open to the public. **Holdings:** 47,530 books; 3056 bound periodical volumes; 14,600 auction catalogs; 168 drawers of vertical files (artists, museums, and dealers); manuscripts; archives; microfilm. **Subscriptions:** 100 journals and other serials; 1 newspaper.

4540 ■ California College of the Arts Libraries–Meyer Library
5212 Broadway
Oakland, CA 94618
Ph:(510)594-3658
Co. E-mail: meyerlib@cca.edu
URL: http://library.cca.edu
Contact: Janice Woo, Dir. of Libs.
Scope: Art, architecture, design, humanities. **Services:** Library limited to the CCA community (specialized research by appointment). **Holdings:** 62,000 volumes; 150,000 slides and pictures; 100 lin.ft. of archival material. **Subscriptions:** 275 journals and other serials.

4541 ■ Cleveland Institute of Art–Jessica R. Gund Memorial Library
11141 East Blvd.
Cleveland, OH 44106
Ph:(216)421-7440
Fax:(216)421-7439
Co. E-mail: referencehelp@cia.edu
URL: http://www.cia.edu/academicResources/library.php
Contact: Cristine C. Rom, Lib.Dir.
Scope: Fine arts, crafts, industrial design, general design, graphic arts, new media, glass, ceramics, medical illustration, textiles, metals. **Services:** Interlibrary loan; copying; Library open to the public. **Holdings:** 45,000 books; 10,000 bound periodical volumes; 125,000 slides; 9000 pictures; 37 volumes and boxes of archival materials; 4000 reels of microfilm; 15,000 microfiche; 500 videocassettes and DVDs; 3000 sound recordings; 600 videotapes. **Subscriptions:** 220 journals and other serials; 2 newspapers.

4542 ■ Des Moines Art Center Library
4700 Grand Ave.
Des Moines, IA 50312-2099
Ph:(515)277-4405
Fax:(515)271-0357
Co. E-mail: informationdesk@desmoinesartcenter.org
URL: http://www.desmoinesartcenter.org
Contact: Mary Morman-Graham, Libn.
Scope: 19th- and 20th-century painting, graphics, sculpture, architecture, drawing, photography. **Services:** Library open to the public by appointment for reference use only. **Holdings:** 16,750 books; 850 bound periodical volumes; 36 VF drawers of publications on individual artists; 36 VF drawers of museum catalogs, art collection catalogs, and allied materials; archives; slides. **Subscriptions:** 70 journals and other serials.

4543 ■ Free Library of Philadelphia–Art Department
1901 Vine St.
Philadelphia, PA 19103-1189
Ph:(215)686-5403
Fax:(215)563-3628
URL: http://www.freelibrary.org
Contact: Deborah Litwack, Hd.
Scope: Art history, African and African-American art, architecture, painting, sculpture, costume history, drawing, decorative arts, ceramics, cartoons, crafts, design, commercial art, photography, graphic arts, numismatics. **Services:** Interlibrary loan; copying. **Holdings:** 60,000 volumes; 35,000 pamphlets and clippings; 735 periodical titles; card index of 15,700 artists; 1500 original graphics (1491 to present); 800,000 photographs and art reproductions in loan collection; postcards; greeting cards; posters. **Subscriptions:** 220 journals and other serials.

4544 ■ Graphic Communications World Library
PO Box 1126
Port Orchard, WA 98366
Ph:(360)769-5417
Fax:(360)769-5622
URL: http://www.quoinpublishing.com
Contact: William Esler, Pres.
Scope: Printing and graphic communications technology. **Services:** Library open to subscribers. **Holdings:** Figures not available. **Subscriptions:** 150 journals and other serials.

4545 ■ Hallmark Cards, Inc.–Creative Research Library
2501 McGee, No. 146
Kansas City, MO 64108
Ph:(816)274-5525
Fax:(816)274-7245
Co. E-mail: hallmarkplus@hallmark.com
URL: http://www.hallmark.com
Contact: Mark Spencer, Mgr., Creative Rsrc.Ctr.
Scope: Fine art, lettering, advertising, graphic art, design, illustration, photography. **Services:** Library open to Hallmark employees only. **Holdings:** 18,000 books; 60 bound periodical volumes. **Subscriptions:** 150 journals and other serials; 3 newspapers.

4546 ■ Library of Congress–Prints & Photographs Division
101 Independence Ave., SE
James Madison Bldg., Rm. LM 337
Washington, DC 20540-4730
Ph:(202)707-6394
Fax:(202)707-6647
URL: http://www.loc.gov/rr/print/
Contact: Jeremy Adamson, Div.Chf.
Scope: Architecture, design, engineering, popular and applied graphic art, documentary photographs, fine prints, master photographs, posters. **Services:** Photoduplication service. **Holdings:** 190,000 prints

and drawings; 80,000 posters; 14 million photographic prints and negatives, daguerreotypes, slides; 1.8 million prints, posters, architectural drawings, and related materials; 200,000 images (electronic).

4547 ■ Milwaukee Area Technical College–Rasche Memorial Library
Downtown Milwaukee Campus
700 W. State St.
Milwaukee, WI 53233-1443
Ph:(414)297-7030
Co. E-mail: jackson@qwise1.matc.edu
URL: http://www.matc.edu/library/matclibrary.html
Contact: Jeff Jackson, MATC Dist.Lib.Dir.
Scope: Applied science and technology, graphic arts, liberal arts, health sciences. **Services:** Interlibrary loan; copying; Library open to the public. **Holdings:** 70,000 volumes. **Subscriptions:** 856 journals and other serials; 15 newspapers.

4548 ■ Milwaukee Art Museum–George Peckham Miller Art Research Library
700 N. Art Museum Dr.
Milwaukee, WI 53202
Ph:(414)224-3270
Co. E-mail: library@mam.org
URL: http://www.mam.org/collection/library.php
Contact: Heather Winter, Libn./Archv.
Scope: Visual arts in all forms, including painting, graphic arts, sculpture, drawing, design, and photography. **Services:** Library open to Art Museum patrons. **Subscriptions:** 66 journals and other serials.

4549 ■ Milwaukee Institute of Art & Design Library
273 E. Erie St.
Milwaukee, WI 53202
Ph:(414)847-3342
Fax:(414)291-8077
URL: http://www.miad.edu
Contact: Cynthia Lynch, Dir. of Lib.Svcs.
Scope: Artists, graphic design, art history, aesthetics, industrial design, decorative arts, photography, sculpture, painting, illustration, interior design, history, social sciences, literature, natural sciences. **Services:** Copying; Library open to the public with restrictions. **Holdings:** 22,920 books; 47,500 slides. **Subscriptions:** 125 journals and other serials.

4550 ■ Minneapolis College of Art and Design Library
2501 Stevens Ave., S.
Minneapolis, MN 55404
Ph:(612)874-3791
Fax:(612)874-3704
Co. E-mail: library@mcad.edu
URL: http://intranet.mcad.edu/modules/library
Contact: Suzanne Degler, Lib.Dir.
Scope: Painting, sculpture, graphic arts, design, films and film making, photography, video, performance art. **Services:** Interlibrary loan (limited); copying; Library open to the public for reference use only. **Holdings:** 60,000 volumes; 350 artists' books; 140,000 slides; college archives; compact discs; video cassettes, CD-ROMs. **Subscriptions:** 200 journals and other serials.

4551 ■ Modern Art Museum of Fort Worth Library
3200 Darnell St.
Fort Worth, TX 76107-2872
Ph:(817)738-9215
Free: (866)824-5566
Fax:(817)735-1161
Co. E-mail: info@themodern.org
URL: http://www.themodern.org
Scope: 20th-century art in all countries, focusing on media consisting of painting, sculpture, and graphics. **Services:** Library not open to the public. **Holdings:** 10,000 books.

4552 ■ Paier College of Art, Inc. Library
20 Gorham Ave.
Hamden, CT 06514-3902
Ph:(203)287-3023
Fax:(203)287-3021
URL: http://www.paiercollegeofart.edu/generalinfo/misc.htm
Contact: Beth R. Harris, Libn.
Scope: Fine arts, graphic design, interior design, photography, illustration, general academics. **Services:** Library open to the public for research only. **Holdings:** 13,000 books; 71 periodical titles; 30,000 pictures; 16,000 slides. **Subscriptions:** 71 journals and other serials.

4553 ■ Parsons School of Design–Adam & Sophie Gimbel Design Library
2 W. 13th St.
New York, NY 10011
Ph:(212)229-8914, x4121
Fax:(212)229-2806
Co. E-mail: luedkej@newschool.edu
URL: http://library.newschool.edu/gimbel/
Contact: Jill Luedke, Ref. and Instr.Libn.
Scope: Fine arts, architecture, costume, crafts, design, environmental design, fashion, graphic arts, photography, typography. **Services:** Interlibrary loan. **Holdings:** 61,000 books; 55,000 mounted picture plates; 85,000 slides; archives. **Subscriptions:** 200 journals and other serials.

4554 ■ Printing Brokerage/Buyers Association Library
PO Box 744
Palm Beach, FL 33480
Ph:877-585-7141
Fax:(561)845-7130
Co. E-mail: info@pbbai.net
URL: http://www.pbba.org/
Scope: Management techniques in the graphic arts industries. **Services:** Library open to the public for reference use only. **Holdings:** 500 books. **Subscriptions:** 25 journals and other serials.

4555 ■ Printing Industries of America/ Graphic Arts Technical Foundation–Edward H. Wadewitz Memorial Library
200 Deer Run Rd.
Sewickley, PA 15143-2324
Ph:(412)741-6860
Free: (866)PIA-GATF
Fax:(412)741-2311
Co. E-mail: library@piagatf.org
URL: http://www.printing.org/page/4506
Contact: Hallie Barcalow, Adm.
Scope: Printing processes, lithography, paper, ink, graphic design, desktop publishing, packaging, chemistry, physics, environmental control, safety and health, photography. **Services:** Document delivery; Library open to the public by appointment. **Holdings:** 15,000 volumes. **Subscriptions:** 180 journals and other serials.

4556 ■ Ringling College of Art and Design–Verman Kimbrough Memorial Library
2700 N. Tamiami Trail
Sarasota, FL 34234
Ph:(941)359-7587
Fax:(941)359-7632
Co. E-mail: library@ringling.edu
URL: http://www.ringling.edu
Contact: Kathleen List, Dir., Lib.Svcs.
Scope: Art history, interior design, graphic design, computer animation, photography, architecture, fine arts, decorative arts, illustration. **Services:** Interlibrary loan; copying; Library open to artists and researchers. **Holdings:** 49,000 books; 110,000 art slides; 34 16mm films; 3000 videocassettes and DVDs. **Subscriptions:** 320 journals and other serials.

4557 ■ Rochester Institute of Technology–Melbert B. Cary, Jr. Graphic Arts Collection
Wallace Memorial Library
90 Lomb Memorial Dr.
Rochester, NY 14623-5604
Ph:(585)475-2408
Fax:(585)475-6900
Co. E-mail: dppwml@rit.edu
URL: http://library.rit.edu/cary
Contact: David Pankow, Cur.
Scope: Printing history, type specimens, typography, book arts, press books, calligraphy, papermaking, graphic arts, bookbinding. **Services:** Copying (limited); collection open to the public. **Holdings:** 50,000 books; 20 VF drawers of clippings; ephemera; pamphlets; 50 boxes of posters, broadsides, drawings; 400 boxes of correspondence and manuscript material. **Subscriptions:** 20 journals and other serials.

4558 ■ School of Visual Arts–Visual Arts Library
380 2nd Ave., 22nd St., 2nd Fl.
New York, NY 10010-3994
Ph:(212)592-2660
Fax:(212)592-2655
Co. E-mail: rlobe@sva.edu
URL: http://www.schoolofvisualarts.edu/sr/index.jsp?sid0=258&sid1=290
Contact: Robert Lobe, Lib.Dir.
Scope: Fine arts, graphic design, advertising, photography, film, computer graphics, humanities. **Services:** Copying; Library open to students, faculty, staff, and alumni (METRO passes honored). **Holdings:** 70,000 books and bound periodical volumes; 2000 pamphlets; 270,000 pictures; 152,000 slides. **Subscriptions:** 300 journals and other serials.

4559 ■ Smithsonian Institution–Smithsonian American Art Museum–National Portrait Gallery Library (750 9)
750 9th St. NW, Ste. 2100
PO Box 37012
Washington, DC 20013-7012
Ph:(202)633-8230
Fax:(202)275-1929
Co. E-mail: chinc@si.edu
URL: http://www.sil.si.edu/libraries/aapg
Contact: Cecilia H. Chin, Chf.Libn.
Scope: American painting, sculpture, graphic arts, biography, history, photography; portraiture; contemporary art. **Services:** Interlibrary loan; copying; Library open to the public for reference use only. **Holdings:** 180,000 books; exhibitions catalogs; catalogues raisonnes; serials; dissertations; artists' books; ephemeral materials; auction catalogs; scrapbooks; microforms; CD-ROMs.

4560 ■ Smithsonian Institution–Smithsonian American Art Museum–Photograph Archives (PO Box)
PO Box 37012
MRC 970
Washington, DC 20013-7012
Ph:(202)633-8390
Fax:(202)633-8373
Co. E-mail: sapa@si.edu
URL: http://sirismm.si.edu/siris/saam.htm
Contact: Christine Hennessey, Chf., Res. & Scholars
Scope: American art, painting, sculpture, graphics. **Services:** Study prints open to the public with restrictions.

4561 ■ Springfield Art Museum–Art Reference Library
1111 E. Brookside Dr.
Springfield, MO 65807
Ph:(417)837-5700
Fax:(417)837-5704
Co. E-mail: artmuseum@springfieldmo.gov
URL: http://www.springfieldmogov.org/egov/art
Contact: Susan Potter, Libn.
Scope: Art history, painting, sculpture, graphics, decorative arts, photography. **Services:** Library open to the public. **Holdings:** 8000 volumes; periodicals; catalogs; AV materials. **Subscriptions:** 65 journals and other serials.

4562 ■ University of Guam–Robert F. Kennedy Memorial Library–Instructional Media Division (Tan S)
Tan Siu Lin Bldg.
UOG Station
Mangilao, GU 96923

Ph:(671)735-2326
Fax:(671)734-6882
Co. E-mail: millhoff@uog9.uog.edu
URL: http://www.uog.edu
Contact: Brian L. Millhoff, Inst. Media

Scope: Multimedia; graphics. **Services:** Interlibrary loan. **Holdings:** 2388 videotapes; 110 CD-ROMs; 28 laser discs; 139 audio programs tape/CD; 200 pieces of media equipment.

4563 ■ University of Minnesota–Eric Sevareid Journalism Library
20 Murphy Hall
206 Church St., SE
Minneapolis, MN 55455
Ph:(612)625-7892
Fax:(612)626-8251
Co. E-mail: j-nybe@umn.edu
URL: http://www.lib.umn.edu/journalism/
Contact: Kathleen A. Hansen, Prof./Libn.

Scope: Mass communications, new media arts studies, newspaper journalism, broadcasting, magazine journalism, graphic arts, advertising, International communication, public relations, behavioral research, media management, visual communication. **Services:** Interlibrary loan; copying; Library open to the public. **Holdings:** 12,000 books; 2800 bound periodical volumes; 200 theses; 14 DVDs; CD-ROMs; 22 videotapes. **Subscriptions:** 250 journals and other serials; newspapers.

4564 ■ University of Puerto Rico–Library System–Arts Collection (PO Box)
PO Box 23302
San Juan, PR 00931-3302
Ph:(787)764-0000, x3492
Fax:(787)772-1479
Co. E-mail: artes@uprrp.edu
URL: http://biblioteca.uprrp.edu/index.html
Contact: Iris D. Rodriguez Falcon?, Chf.Libn.

Scope: Fine arts, dance. **Services:** Copying; Library open to the public with restrictions. **Holdings:** 27,900 books; 205 slides; manuscripts; photographs; artist books; rare books.

4565 ■ Walker Art Center–Staff Reference Library
1750 Hennepin Ave.
Vineland Pl.
Minneapolis, MN 55403
Ph:(612)375-7680
Co. E-mail: rosemary.furtak@walkerart.org
URL: http://www.walkerart.org
Contact: Rosemary Furtak, Libn.

Scope: Contemporary art, art history, architecture, design, film, artists' books, graphics, photography, painting, sculpture. **Services:** Copying; Internet searches; Library open to the public by appointment. **Holdings:** 35,000 books; 550 bound periodical volumes; vertical files. **Subscriptions:** 140 journals.

4566 ■ Williams College–Chapin Library
PO Box 426
96 School St., Apartment 3
Williamstown, MA 01267
Ph:(413)597-2462
Fax:(413)597-2929
Co. E-mail: chapin.library@williams.edu
URL: http://chapin.williams.edu
Contact: Wayne Hammond, Asst.Libn.

Scope: Education, reference. **Services:** Copying; answers correspondence requests for bibliographical information; Library open to the public with restrictions. **Holdings:** 50,000 volumes; 40,000 manuscripts. **Subscriptions:** 25 journals and other serials.

RESEARCH CENTERS

4567 ■ Graphic Arts Education and Research Foundation
1899 Preston White Dr.
Reston, VA 20191-4367
Ph:(703)264-7200
Free: (866)-381-9839
Fax:(703)620-3165
Co. E-mail: gaerf@npes.org
URL: http://www.gaerf.org
Contact: Stephen L. Johnson, Chm.
E-mail: gaerf@npes.org

Scope: Educational and research projects designed to enhance the future of the graphic arts industry. **Services:** Career Focus, a graphic communications awareness campaign. **Publications:** Guidelines Booklet; Resource (annually); Vanguard Annual Report. **Educational Activities:** Grants.

4568 ■ University of California, Los Angeles–Grunwald Center for the Graphic Arts
Hammer Museum of Art & Cultural Ctr.
10899 Wilshire Blvd.
Los Angeles, CA 90024
Ph:(310)443-7000
Fax:(310)443-7099
Co. E-mail: cburlingham@hammer.ucla.edu
URL: http://www.hammer.ucla.edu/collections/3/
Contact: Ann Philbin, Dir.
E-mail: cburlingham@hammer.ucla.edu

Scope: Graphic arts, including 15th through 21st century prints and drawings, contemporary American photography, and artist illustrated books. **Services:** Friends of the Graphic Arts Support Group. **Publications:** Exhibition catalogues (occasionally).

ASSOCIATIONS AND OTHER ORGANIZATIONS

4569 ■ Association of Alternate Postal Systems
1725 Oaks Way
Oklahoma City, OK 73131
Ph:(405)478-0006
Co. E-mail: aaps@cox.net
URL: http://www.aapsinc.org
Contact: John White, Exec. Dir.
Description: Companies in the business of delivering private postal advertising material to residences. Seeks to improve industry credibility and increase the public's awareness of the private postal industry. **Publications:** *Association of Alternate Postal Systems—Member Directory* (annual); *Association of Alternate Postal Systems—Update* (quarterly).

4570 ■ Women in Packaging
4290 Bells Ferry Rd., Ste. 106-17
Kennesaw, GA 30144-1300
Ph:(678)594-6872
Co. E-mail: joann@womeninpackaging.org
URL: http://womeninpackaging.org
Contact: JoAnn R. Hines, Founder
Description: Works to promote and encourage women in the packaging industry. Educates the packaging industry about the contributions of women to the industry; helps to eliminate stereotypes and discrimination in the profession; offers networking opportunities; conducts career enhancement programs; compiles statistics; maintains speakers' bureau. **Publications:** *Packaging Horizons* .

REFERENCE WORKS

4571 ■ "Contest Produce Ad Designs on a Dime" in *San Diego Business Journal* (Vol. 31, August 23, 2010, No. 31, pp. 1)
Pub: San Diego Business Journal
Ed: Mike Allen. **Description:** San Diego-based Prova.fm runs design contests for clients such as the U.S. Postal Service. The client then chooses the best entry from the contest. Prova.fm relies on the Internet to deliver a range of possible graphic solutions and allowing the customer to make the right selection for its business through a process called crowdsourcing.

4572 ■ *Directory of Major Mailers*
Pub: North American Publishing Co.
Ed: Cheryl Cagle, Editor, ccagle@napco.com. **Released:** Annual, latest edition 2011. **Price:** $299, individuals Print; plus shipping and handling; $599, individuals online; $799, individuals print and CD-ROM; plus shipping and handling; $14.95, individuals print. **Covers:** About 7,000 mailers and 19,000 mailing efforts. **Entries Include:** Company name, address, phone, fax; names and titles of key personnel, marketing and production, product/service, and mailing campaigns from the previous year. **Arrangement:** Alphabetical. **Indexes:** Geographical, product/service, mailing formats.

4573 ■ "The Question: Who Do You Think Is the Most Genuine?" in *Advertising Age* (Vol. 79, July 7, 2008, No. 26, pp. 4)
Pub: Crain Communications, Inc.
Ed: Ken Wheaton. **Description:** According to a survey conducted by Harris Interactive Reputation Quotient, Johnson & Johnson was deemed the most genuine brand. Google came in second followed by UPS.

TRADE PERIODICALS

4574 ■ *Distribution Sales and Management*
Pub: NPTA Alliance
Contact: Debra Ray, Editor & Publisher
E-mail: debra@gonpta.com
Released: Monthly. **Description:** Trade magazine covering the paper, packaging and allied products distribution industry.

4575 ■ *Fastline—Bluegrass Truck Edition*
Pub: Fastline
Released: 13/yr. **Price:** $18; $30 two years; $45 Canada and Mexico; $95 other countries. **Description:** Illustrated buying guide for the trucking industry.

4576 ■ *Fastline—Florida Truck Edition*
Pub: Fastline
Released: 13/yr. **Price:** $18; $30 two years; $45 Canada and Mexico; $95 other countries. **Description:** Illustrated buying guide for the trucking industry.

4577 ■ *Fastline—Georgia Truck Edition*
Pub: Fastline
Released: 13/yr. **Price:** $18; $30 two years; $45 Canada and Mexico; $95 other countries. **Description:** Illustrated buying guide for the trucking industry.

4578 ■ *Fastline—Tennessee Truck Edition*
Pub: Fastline
Released: Monthly. **Price:** $18; $30 two years; $45 Canada and Mexico; $95 other countries; $35 3 years. **Description:** Illustrated buying guide for the trucking industry.

4579 ■ *Fastline—Tri-State Truck Edition*
Pub: Fastline
Released: 13/yr. **Price:** $18; $30 two years; $45 Canada and Mexico; $95 other countries. **Description:** Illustrated buying guide for the trucking industry.

4580 ■ *Food & Beverage Packaging*
Pub: BNP Media
Contact: Mike Barr, Publisher
E-mail: barrm@bnpmedia.com
Ed: Pan Demetrakakes, Editor, pand@bnpmedia.com. **Released:** Monthly. **Description:** Trade magazine for packaging professionals in food and pharmaceutical industries.

4581 ■ *Mailing Systems Technology MAST*
Pub: RB Publishing Co.
Contact: John E. Thompson, Managing Editor
E-mail: john.t@rbpub.com
Ed: Dan O'Rourke, Editor, dan.o@rbpub.com. **Description:** Trade magazine covering mailing and office practices.

4582 ■ *Postal Bulletin*
Pub: U.S. Government Printing Office and Superintendent of Documents
Released: 26/yr. **Price:** $163; $228 other countries. **Description:** Bulletin reporting U.S. Postal Service news.

TRADE SHOWS AND CONVENTIONS

4583 ■ National Association of Postmasters of the United States Convention
National Association of Postmasters of the United States
8 Herbert St.
Alexandria, VA 22305-2600
Ph:(703)683-9027
Fax:(703)683-6820
Co. E-mail: napusinfo@napus.org
URL: http://www.napus.org
Released: Annual. **Audience:** Postmasters. **Principal Exhibits:** Office supplies and materials for the postal service.

FRANCHISES AND BUSINESS OPPORTUNITIES

4584 ■ Navis Pack & Ship Centers
Navis Logistics Network
5675 DTC Blvd., Ste. 280
Greenwood Village, CO 80111
Ph:(303)741-6626
Free: (866)738-6820
Fax:(303)531-6530
URL: http://www.gonavis.com
Founded: 1984. **Franchised:** 2001. **Description:** Packaging and shipping industry. **Equity Capital Needed:** $100,000 liquid capital; $350,000 net worth. **Franchise Fee:** $46,950/$93,900. **Financial Assistance:** No. **Training:** Offers 3 weeks training and certification course.

4585 ■ Packaging and Shipping Specialists
5211 85th St., Ste. 104
Lubbock, TX 79424
Ph:(806)794-0202
Free: 800-877-8884
Fax:(806)794-9997
Co. E-mail: mike@packship.com
URL: http://www.packship.com
No. of Franchise Units: 904. **No. of Company-Owned Units:** 1. **Founded:** 1981. **Franchised:** 1987. **Description:** Business center, including copying and shipping services. **Equity Capital Needed:** $50,000. **Franchise Fee:** $28,900. **Financial Assistance:** Develop business plan for loan package; up to $30,000 in equipment leasing. **Training:** In classroom and on-the-job training.

4586 ■ Pak Mail
7173 S Havan St., Ste. 600
Centennial, CO 80112
Free: 800-833-2821

Fax:800-336-7363
Co. E-mail: sales@pakmail.org
URL: http://www.pakmail.com
No. of Franchise Units: 500. **Founded:** 1983. **Franchised:** 1984. **Description:** One-stop shop offers the customer a convenient location to send packages, make copies, send or receive a fax or rent a private mailbox. **Equity Capital Needed:** $130,000-$164,300. **Franchise Fee:** $29,950. **Financial Assistance:** Third party finance packages. **Managerial Assistance:** Offers assistance with site selection, lease negotiation, build-out & merchandising, operations processes, & marketing programs and ongoing networking. **Training:** Provides training, education & ongoing support to build your business.

4587 ■ Pak Mail Centres (Canada) Ltd.
501 Passmore Ave., Ste, 30
Toronto, ON, Canada M1V 5G4
Ph:(416)335-6245
Free: 800-387-8335
Fax:(416)335-9080
Co. E-mail: georgek@pakmailcanada.com
URL: http://www.pakmailcanada.com
No. of Franchise Units: 10. **No. of Company-Owned Units:** 1. **Founded:** 1983. **Franchised:** 1996. **Description:** Offers mailing services like customer packaging, domestic and international shipping by means of courier, truck, planes, train and ocean freight. **Equity Capital Needed:** $114,000-$140,000. **Franchise Fee:** $25,000. **Training:** Offers 4 weeks initial and ongoing support.

4588 ■ Postal Connections of America
Templar Franchise Company
275 E. Douglas Ave., Ste. 115
El Cajon, CA 92020
Ph:(619)294-7550
Free: 800-767-8257
Fax:(619)294-4550
Co. E-mail: info@postalconnections.com
URL: http://www.postalconnections.com.
No. of Franchise Units: 99. **Founded:** 1985. **Franchised:** 1996. **Description:** Postal Connections stores offer packaging, shipping, mail receiving & forwarding, copies, printing, scanning & storage of digital documents, eBay auction support, office & packing supplies, crate & freight shipping and more. **Equity Capital Needed:** $119,000-$153,900, average initial investment. **Franchise Fee:** $23,900. **Financial Assistance:** Third party financing sources available. **Managerial Assistance:** Online 24/7 "business coaching" on private website. **Training:** Extensive training prior to & after opening. Franchisees receive 5 days live action training in a regional training store, Unique Act video training program & 4 days onsite.

4589 ■ Postalannex+
Annex Brands, Inc.
7580 Metropolitan Dr., Ste. 200
San Diego, CA 92108-4417
Ph:(619)563-4800
Free: 800-456-1525
Fax:(619)563-9850
Co. E-mail: ryan@postalannex.com
URL: http://www.postalannex.com
No. of Franchise Units: 321. **Founded:** 1985. **Franchised:** 1986. **Description:** Provides postal, communication, and business services in the convenience of a store setting. Services rendered include mailbox rental, mail check, express money services, passport photos, metered mail, word processing, secretarial services, packaging and packaging supplies, laminating, copy services, office supplies, printing, business cards and stationery, binding, and notary. Also provides a fax network and telephone message center. **Equity Capital Needed:** $200,000 net worth; $50,000 liquid assets; actual cost $138,800-$200,050. **Franchise Fee:** $29,950. **Financial Assistance:** Third party lenders offering SBA and conventional loans. **Training:** 2 week training at home office, plus 1 week at location. Ongoing training and support provided.

4590 ■ PostNet
PostNet Intl. Franchise Corp.
1819 Wazee St.
Denver, CO 80202
Ph:(303)771-7100
Free: 800-338-7401
Fax:(303)771-7133
Co. E-mail: info@postnet.net
URL: http://www.postnet.net
No. of Franchise Units: 900+. **Founded:** 1985. **Franchised:** 1993. **Description:** PostNet International, 'a different kind of franchise,' offers site location assistance based on proven criteria, high tech design layout, development services, stateof-the-art equipment, startup inventory, full color promotional materials, plus 800 line, fax, Internet and regional support. Centers offer shipping, packaging, private mailboxes, fax, office/packaging supplies, printing, voice mail and the latest information and communication services available. **Equity Capital Needed:** $175,875-$197,600, total investment includes working capital. **Franchise Fee:** $29,900. **Financial Assistance:** Assistance with the preparation of loan packages is provided to franchisees. Several 3rd party sources available. **Managerial Assistance:** Each network member has access to an 800 line, member workshops, and seminars. A quarterly newsletter & an online member network/bulletin board updates information. **Training:** In-depth 3-step training process includes classroom, onsite and follow-up. Continuous ongoing support provided.

4591 ■ Sunshine Pack & Ship
7580 Metropolitan Dr., Ste. 200
San Diego, CA 92108-4417
Ph:(619)563-4800
Free: 800-456-1525
Fax:(619)563-9850
No. of Franchise Units: 27. **No. of Company-Owned Units:** 2. **Founded:** 1993. **Franchised:** 2000. **Description:** Packing, shipping & eBay drop-off stores. **Equity Capital Needed:** $69,000-$123,000. **Franchise Fee:** $19,900. **Royalty Fee:** 5%. **Financial Assistance:** Third party financing available. **Training:** Offers 40 hours at headquarters, 40 hours at franchisees location and additional training as needed.

4592 ■ The UPS Store
1115 North Service Rd., Unit 1
Oakville, ON, Canada L6M 2V9
Ph:(905)338-9754
Free: 800-661-6232
Fax:(905)338-7491
Co. E-mail: development@theupsstore.ca
URL: http://www.theupsstore.ca
Founded: 1990. **Description:** Offering one-stop convenience for small business: digital print & photocopies (colour & B/W), document finishing, worldwide courier services, packaging services & supplies, fax services, computer rental, WIFI and mail receiving services. **Equity Capital Needed:** $146,150-$179,550. **Franchise Fee:** $35,000.

4593 ■ The UPS Store / Mail Boxes Etc.
6060 Cornerstone Ct., W
San Diego, CA 92121
Ph:(858)455-8962
Free: 877-623-7253
Fax:(858)546-7493
Co. E-mail: usafranchise@mbe.com
URL: http://www.theupsstore.com
No. of Franchise Units: 4,357. **Founded:** 1980. **Franchised:** 1980. **Description:** Retail shipping, postal and business services. **Equity Capital Needed:** $150,196-$371,022. **Franchise Fee:** $29,950. **Royalty Fee:** 5%. **Financial Assistance:** In-house and third party financing available. **Training:** Offers 2 weeks at headquarters, 2 weeks at franchisees location and ongoing support.

4594 ■ Worldwide Express
CGI Franchise Systems, Inc.
2828 Raith St., Ste. 400
Dallas, TX 75201
Ph:(214)720-2400
Free: 800-758-SHIP
Fax:(214)720-2446
URL: http://www.wwex.com
No. of Franchise Units: 192. **No. of Company-Owned Units:** 33. **Founded:** 1991. **Franchised:** 1994. **Description:** Discounted air express services. **Equity Capital Needed:** $46,500-$364,850. **Franchise Fee:** $33,120-$327,500. **Royalty Fee:** 6%. **Financial Assistance:** No. **Training:** Training available at headquarters and onsite.

RESEARCH CENTERS

4595 ■ University of Colorado at Boulder–Center for Advanced Manufacturing and Packaging of Microwave, Optical and Digital Electronics
University of Colorado
Boulder, CO 80309-0427
Ph:(303)492-7750
Fax:(303)492-3498
Co. E-mail: mahajan@spot.colorado.edu
URL: http://www.nsf.gov/eng/iip/iucrc/directory/camp.jsp
Contact: Prof. Roop L. Mahajan, Dir.
E-mail: mahajan@spot.colorado.edu
Scope: Development of computer-aided designs, packaging and manufacturing technologies for high-quality, low-cost production of electronic systems.

ASSOCIATIONS AND OTHER ORGANIZATIONS

4596 ■ National Association of Recording Merchandisers
9 Eves Dr., Ste. 120
Marlton, NJ 08053
Ph:(856)596-2221
Fax:(856)596-3268
Co. E-mail: donio@narm.com
URL: http://www.narm.com
Contact: Jim Donio, Pres.

Description: Serves the music and other prerecorded entertainment software industry as a forum for insight and dialogue; members include retailers, wholesalers, distributors, entertainment software suppliers, and suppliers of related products and services. **Publications:** *NARM Convention Official Guide* (annual); *NARM Membership Directory and Buyer's Guide* (annual); *NARM News Bits* (monthly); *NARM Research Briefs* (monthly).

REFERENCE WORKS

4597 ■ *The Rhythm of Success: How an Immigrant Produced His Own American Dream*
Pub: Penguin Group (USA) Inc.

Ed: Emilio Estefan. **Released:** January 10, 2010. **Price:** $24.95. **Description:** Emilio Estafan, husband to singer Gloria Estefan and founder of the Latin pop legend Miami Sound Machine, is the classic example of the American dream. He shares his guiding principles that entrepreneurs need to start and grow a business.

4598 ■ "Scoring Music" in *Canadian Business* (Vol. 81, December 8, 2008, No. 21, pp. S3)
Pub: Rogers Media Ltd.
Ed: Jay Somerset. **Description:** Boyd Devereaux, who plays with the Toronto Maple Leafs, collaborates with musicians through his record label Elevation Records. Devereaux won a Stanley Cup with the Detroit Red Wings in 2002 and has released five limited edition discs through Elevation records.

4599 ■ "Sound Fundamentals" in *Hispanic Business* (September 2007, pp. 12, 14, 16)
Pub: Hispanic Business
Ed: Michael T. Mena. **Description:** Profile of Ozomatli, a Los Angeles-based multicultural, multi-ethnic musical group that has topped Billboard's Latin Pop chart without relying on record sales. Members explain how they run the group like a small business.

TRADE PERIODICALS

4600 ■ *Music Inc.*
Pub: Maher Publications Inc.
Contact: Kevin Maher, Publisher
Released: 11/yr. **Price:** $17. **Description:** Magazine serving retailers of music and sound products.

4601 ■ *Turok's Choice*
Pub: Paul Turok
Ed: Paul Turok, Editor. **Released:** 11/year. **Price:** $14.95, individuals; $19, Canada and Mexico; $23, elsewhere. **Description:** Publishes reviews of classical compact discs.

FRANCHISES AND BUSINESS OPPORTUNITIES

4602 ■ CD Tradepost
826 S Kansas Ave.
Topeka, KS 66612
Ph:(785)233-0675
Fax:(785)232-4444
No. of Franchise Units: 5. **No. of Company-Owned Units:** 14. **Founded:** 1998. **Franchised:** 2002. **Description:** Used CDs, videos & video games. **Equity Capital Needed:** $98,000-$159,000. **Franchise Fee:** $30,000. **Royalty Fee:** 5-6%. **Financial Assistance:** No. **Training:** Provides 2 weeks at headquarters with ongoing support including grand opening support.

LIBRARIES

4603 ■ Chicago Public Library–Visual & Performing Arts Division–Music Information Center (Harol)
Harold Washington Library Center
400 S. State St., 8th Fl.
Chicago, IL 60605
Ph:(312)747-4850
URL: http://www.chipublib.org/branch/details/library/harold-washington/p/Vpa
Contact: Richard Schwegel
Scope: History and theory of music, biographies of musicians and composers, music education, opera, musical comedy, sacred music, popular music, discography, music business, musical instruments, vocal and instrumental pedagogy, music therapy, folk music, composition and orchestration, arranging. **Services:** Interlibrary loan; copying; listening/viewing Center; practice rooms; music chamber; Center open to the public. **Holdings:** 49,800 books; 8025 bound periodical volumes; 67,000 bound volumes of music; 30,000 pieces of music; 15 VF drawers of pamphlets and clippings; 6102 microfiche of music; 2220 reels of microfilm of periodicals; 169,000 phonograph records, compact discs, audiocassettes; 3900 music videos; 334 laserdiscs; 4250 photographs; 51,957 uncatalogued scores. **Subscriptions:** 561 journals and other serials.

Computer Consulting

ASSOCIATIONS AND OTHER ORGANIZATIONS

4604 ■ Association of Professional Computer Consultants
2323 Yonge St., Ste. 400
Toronto, ON, Canada M4P 2C9
Ph:(416)545-5275
Free: 888-487-2722
Co. E-mail: information@apcconline.com
URL: http://www.apcconline.com

Description: Promotes the interests of Independent Computer Consultants. **Publications:** *Gateway* (periodic).

4605 ■ British Columbia Technology Industries Association
1188 W Georgia St., Ste. 900
Vancouver, BC, Canada V6E 4A2
Ph:(604)683-6159
Fax:(604)683-3879
Co. E-mail: info@bctia.org
URL: http://www.bctia.org
Contact: Bill Tam, Pres./CEO

Description: Fosters the growth and development of the Province's technology industries and member companies. Provides programs, services and activities designed to meet the needs and interests of members in the areas of networking, education, public awareness, and government relations. Offers a forum for members to review industry issues, acquire new business knowledge from leading industry professionals, to supply input on existing and proposed legislation and generally work together to advance the industry's interests. **Publications:** *Impact* (annual).

4606 ■ Canadian Image Processing and Pattern Recognition Society–Association Canadienne de Traitement d'Images et de Reconnaissance des Formes
University of Western Ontario
Middlesex College 379
Dept. of Computer Science
London, ON, Canada N6A 5B7
Ph:(519)661-2111
Fax:(519)661-3515
Co. E-mail: cipprs@csd.uwo.ca
URL: http://www.gel.ulaval.ca
Contact: Prof. John Barron, Treas.

Description: Strives to advance the theory and practice of signal and image processing for pattern analysis and classification, scene or speech understanding and recognition, computer vision, on-line and off-line document analysis and recognition, robotic perception, intelligent autonomous systems, biomedical imaging, neural networks and modeling, remote sensing, specialized architecture and industrial applications. **Publications:** *Vision Interface* .

4607 ■ International Association for Computer Information Systems
Quinnipiac University
School of Business
275 Mt. Carmel Ave.
Hamden, CT 06518
Co. E-mail: richard.mccarthy@quinnipiac.edu
URL: http://www.iacis.org
Contact: Lori Willoughby, Pres.

Description: Educators and computer professionals. Seeks to promote the knowledge, use, and teaching of computers, and technology; dedicated to the improvement of information systems and computer professionals. **Publications:** *IACIS Newsletter* (semiannual); *Journal of Computer Information Systems* (quarterly).

4608 ■ TechServe Alliance
1420 King St., Ste. 610
Alexandria, VA 22314
Ph:(703)838-2050
Fax:(703)838-3610
Co. E-mail: staff@techservealliance.org
URL: http://www.techservealliance.org
Contact: Mark Roberts, CEO

Description: Businesses that provide the services of highly technical professionals, such as computer programmers, systems analysts, engineers, to clients in need of temporary technical support. Promotes legal and economic environment favorable to the technical services industry, including protection of a firm's freedom to choose either employees or independent contractors when supplying services to clients. Encourages professional standards in the industry; serves as a support mechanism for members. Provides industry-specific educational information and insurance discounts. **Publications:** *Directory of Members Firms* (periodic); *NACCB Monitor* (quarterly); *NACCB Newsletter* (quarterly).

REFERENCE WORKS

4609 ■ "Arctic IT Honored" in *Alaska Business Monthly* (Vol. 27, October 2011, No. 10, pp. 10)
Pub: Alaska Business Publishing Company

Ed: Nancy Pounds. **Description:** Arctic Information Technology Inc. was named to Everything Channel's 2011 Computer Reseller News (CRN) Next-Generation 250 list. The firm provides business software and network infrastructure solutions.

4610 ■ "Auctions and Bidding: a Guide for Computer Scientists" in *ACM Computing Surveys* (Vol. 43, Summer 2011, No. 2, pp. 10)
Pub: Association for Computing Machinery

Ed: Simon Parsons, Juan A. Rodriguez-Aguilar, Mark Klein. **Description:** There are various actions: single dimensional, multi-dimensional, single-sided, double-sided, first-price, second-price, English, Dutch, Japanese, sealed-bid, and these have been extensively discussed and analyzed in economics literature. This literature is surveyed from a computer science perspective, primarily from the viewpoint of computer scientists who are interested in learning about auction theory, and to provide pointers into the economics literature for those who want a deeper technical understanding. In addition, since auctions are an increasingly important topic in computer science, the article also looks at work on auctions from the computer science literature. The aim is to identify what both bodies of work tell us about creating electronic auctions.

4611 ■ "Burton Group Answers Industry Need for Practical Data Center Advice" in *Canadian Corporate News* (May 14, 2007)
Pub: Comtex News Network Inc.

Description: Burton Group, an IT research firm focused on in-depth technical analysis of enterprise IT infrastructures, launched a new service providing practical advice for IT professionals facing critical data center decisions which due to technological advances can be more efficient while reducing costs.

4612 ■ "Consumer Trust in E-Commerce Web Sites: a Meta-Study" in *ACM Computing Surveys* (Vol. 43, Fall 2011, No. 3, pp. 14)
Pub: Association for Computing Machinery

Ed: Patricia Beatty, Ian Reay, Scott Dick, James Miller. **Description:** Trust is at once an elusive, imprecise concept, and a critical attribute that must be engineered into e-commerce systems. Engineering trust is examined.

4613 ■ "Discrete Wavelet Transform-Based Time Series Analysis and Mining" in *ACM Computing Surveys* (Vol. 43, Summer 2011, No. 2, pp. 6)
Pub: Association for Computing Machinery

Ed: Pimwadee Chaovalit, Aryya Gangopadhyay, George Karabatis, Zhiyuan Chen. **Description:** Time series are recorded values of an interesting phenomenon such as stock prices, household items, or patient heart rates over a period of time. Time series data mining focuses on discovering interesting patterns in such data. An introduction to a wavelet-based times series data analysis is provided with a systematic survey of various analysis techniques that use discrete wavelet transformation (DWT) in time series data mining, and outlines the benefits of this approach demonstrated by previous studies performed on diverse application domains, including image classification, multimedia retrieval, and computer network anomaly detection.

4614 ■ "The Failure Detector Abstraction" in *ACM Computing Surveys* (Vol. 43, Summer 2011, No. 2, pp. 9)
Pub: Association for Computing Machinery

Ed: Felix C. Freiling, Rachid Guerraoui, Petr Kuznetsov. **Description:** A failure detector is a fundamental abstraction in distributed computing. This article surveys this abstraction through two dimensions. First it studies failure detectors as building blocks to simplify the design of reliable distributed algorithms, particularly how failure detectors can factor out timing assumptions to detect failures in distributed agreement algorithms. Second, failure detectors as computability benchmarks are studied. Some limitations of the failure detector abstraction along each of the dimensions is also highlighted.

4615 ■ "Free Speech Vs. Privacy in Data Mining" in *Information Today* (Vol. 28, September 2011, No. 8, pp. 22)
Pub: Information Today, Inc.
Ed: George H. Pike. **Description:** The U.S. Constitution does not explicitly guarantee the right of privacy. Organizations and businesses that require obtaining and disseminating information can be caught in the middle of privacy rights. The long-term impact on data mining, Internet marketing, and Internet privacy issues are examined.

4616 ■ "Human Activity Analysis: a Review" in *ACM Computing Surveys* (Vol. 43, Fall 2011, No. 3, pp. 16)
Pub: Association for Computing Machinery
Ed: J.K. Aggarwal, M.S. Ryoo. **Description:** Human activity recognition is an important area of computer vision research and is studied in this report.

4617 ■ "Implementing Statically Typed Object-Oriented Programming Languages" in *ACM Computing Surveys* (Vol. 43, Fall 2011, No. 3, pp. 18)
Pub: Association for Computing Machinery
Ed: Roland Ducournau. **Description:** Object-oriented programming represents an original implementation issue due to its philosophy of making the program behavior depend on the dynamic type of objects. A review of the various implementation techniques available in static typing and in the three cases of single inheritance, multiple inheritance, and multiple subtyping are reviewed.

4618 ■ "Lighter Than Air" in *Game Developer* (Vol. 18, November 1, 2011, No. 10, pp. 38)
Pub: Think Services
Ed: Andy Firth. **Description:** Floating point performance tips and tricks are outlined. Floating point allows freedom of representation when implementing algorithms and is both intuitive to set up and simple to work with; hardware is also improved so that it is faster to use floating point math as opposed to integer in many environments.

4619 ■ "Machine Transliteration Survey" in *ACM Computing Surveys* (Vol. 43, Fall 2011, No. 3, pp. 17)
Pub: Association for Computing Machinery
Ed: Sarvnaz Karimi, Falk Scholer, Andrew Turpin. **Description:** Machine transliteration is the process of automatically transforming the script of a word from a source language to a target language, while preserving pronunciation. The development of algorithms specifically for machine transliteration began over a decade ago based on the phonetics of source and target languages, followed by approaches using statistical and language-specific methods. In this survey, the key methodologies introduced in transliteration literature are reviewed. The approaches are categorized based on the resources and algorithms used, and the effectiveness is compared.

4620 ■ "Nampa Police Department: Electronic Systems Just One Tool in Business Security Toolbox" in *Idaho Business Review* (October 29, 2010)
Pub: Dolan Media Newswires
Ed: Brad Carlson. **Description:** Police departments and private security firms can help small businesses with hard security and business consultants can assist with internal audit security and fraud prevention.

4621 ■ "Our Hoarder Mentality: Blame the Hard Disk" in *PC Magazine* (Vol. 30, November 2011, No. 11, pp. 46)
Pub: Ziff Davis Inc.
Ed: John C. Dvorak. **Description:** Computer programmers, once referred to as computer users, are slowly being replaced by passive consumers of products and content of tablets and handheld mobile phones and devices of the future. Understanding is garnered as this article examines this industry trend.

4622 ■ *Pro Windows Small Business Server 2003*
Pub: Apress L.P.
Ed: Tony Campbell. **Released:** July 2006. **Price:** $39.99. **Description:** Profile of Microsoft's Windows Small Business Server, designed for companies with 50 or fewer employees.

4623 ■ "The State of the Art in End-User Software Engineering" in *ACM Computing Surveys* (Vol. 43, Fall 2011, No. 3, pp. 21)
Pub: Association for Computing Machinery
Description: Most programs today are not written by professional software developers but by people with expertise in other domains working towards goals for which they need computational support. A discussion of empirical research about end-user software engineering activities and the technologies designed to support them is presented. Several crosscutting issues in the design of EUSE tools, including the roles of risk, reward, and domain complexity, and self-efficacy in the design of EUSE tools and the potential of educating users about software engineering principles are also examined.

4624 ■ "Strict Intersection Types for the Lambda Calculus" in *ACM Computing Surveys* (Vol. 43, Fall 2011, No. 3, pp. 20)
Pub: Association for Computing Machinery
Ed: Steffen Van Bakel. **Description:** The usefulness and elegance of strict intersection types for the Lambda Calculus, that are strict in the sense that they are the representatives of equivalence classes of types in the BCD-system is shown. Focus in directed on the essential intersection type assignment; this system is almost syntax directed, and the article will show that all major properties hold that are known to hold for other intersection systems, like the approximation theorem, the characterization of (head/strong) normalization, completeness of type assignment using filter semantics, strong normalization for cut-elimination and the principal pair property. In part, the proofs for these properties are new. A brief comparison of the essential system with other existing systems is given.

4625 ■ "A Survey of Combinatorial Testing" in *ACM Computing Surveys* (Vol. 43, Summer 2011, No. 2, pp. 11)
Pub: Association for Computing Machinery
Ed: Changhai Nie, Hareton Leung. **Description:** Combinatorial Testing (CT) can detect failures triggered by interactions of parameters in the Software Under Test (SUT) with a covering array test suite generated by some sampling mechanisms. Basic concepts and notations of CT are covered.

4626 ■ "A Survey of Comparison-Based System-Level Diagnosis" in *ACM Computing Surveys* (Vol. 43, Fall 2011, No. 3, pp. 22)
Pub: Association for Computing Machinery
Ed: Elias P. Duarte Jr., Roverli P. Ziwich, Luiz C.P. Albini. **Description:** The growing complexity and dependability requirements of hardware, software, and networks demand efficient techniques for discovering disruptive behavior in those systems. Comparison-based diagnosis is a realistic approach to detect faulty units based on the outputs of tasks executed by system units. This survey integrates the vast amount of research efforts that have been produced in this field.

4627 ■ "A Survey of DHT Security Techniques" in *ACM Computing Surveys* (Vol. 43, Summer 2011, No. 2, pp. 8)
Pub: Association for Computing Machinery
Ed: Guido Urdaneta, Guillaume Pierre, Maarten Van Steen. **Description:** Peer-to-peer networks based on distributed hash tables (DHTs) have received considerable attention since their introduction in 2001. Unfortunately, DHT-based systems have been shown to be difficult to protect against security attacks. An overview of techniques reported in literature for making DHT-based systems resistant to the three most important attacks that can be launched by malicious nodes participating in the DHT is given: the Sybil attack, the Eclipse attack, and routing and storage attacks.

4628 ■ "What is the Future of Disk Drives, Death or Rebirth?" in *ACM Computing Surveys* (Vol. 43, Fall 2011, No. 3, pp. 23)
Pub: Association for Computing Machinery
Ed: Yuhui Deng. **Description:** Disk drives have experienced dramatic development to meet performance requirements since the IBM 1301 disk drive was announced in 1961. However, the performance gap between memory and disk drives has widened to 6 orders of magnitude and continues to widen by about 50 percent per year. Challenges and opportunities facing these storage devices are explored.

TRADE PERIODICALS

4629 ■ *Association for Computing Machinery*
Pub: Special Interest Group on Data Communication
Ed: Martha Steenstrup, Editor. **Released:** Quarterly. **Price:** $50. **Description:** Serves as a forum for computing professionals in the data communications field. Focuses on network architecture, including the Internet, network protocols, and distributed systems.

4630 ■ *Computer Link Magazine*
Pub: Millennium Publishing Inc.
Released: Monthly. **Price:** $20. **Description:** Magazine covering computer news.

4631 ■ *Consultants News*
Pub: Kennedy Information
Contact: Wayne Cooper, CEO
E-mail: editor@kennedyinfo.com
Released: Monthly. **Price:** $349, U.S. and Canada; $399, elsewhere. **Description:** The authoritative voice of the consulting industry, covering news, analysis, practice advice, proprietary data and opinion.

4632 ■ *DCLNews*
Pub: Data Conversion Laboratory
Contact: Mark Gross
Ed: Released: Monthly. **Price:** Included in membership;. **Description:** E-journal providing you insider information on XML and SGML, along with the latest technology and e-publishing news.

4633 ■ *Information Technology Adviser*
Pub: Progressive Business Publications
Ed: Robin Nelson, Editor. **Released:** Semimonthly. **Price:** $299, individuals. **Description:** Presents information to keep IT/IS managers up to date on how technology cuts costs, boosts productivity, and makes companies more successful. Recurring features include interviews, news of research, a calendar of events, news of educational opportunities, and a column titled Sharpen Your Judgment.

4634 ■ *Maximum PC*
Pub: Future Network USA
Contact: Michael Brown, Review Ed.
E-mail: michael@maximumpc.com
Released: Monthly. **Price:** $14.95; $24.95 12 CDs; $29.95 other countries; $49.95 other countries two years; $1.95 single issue. **Description:** Consumer magazine covering computing, hardware and software reviews, games and work programs for personal computer users.

4635 ■ *Media Computing*
Pub: Dreamscape Productions
Ed: Sheridan Tatsuno, Editor, statsuno@aol.com. **Released:** Monthly. **Price:** $495, institutions in the U.S. and Canada; $550, institutions elsewhere. **Description:** Supplies analysis of multimedia, internet, intranet, and web computing issues. Recurring features include interviews and reports of meetings.

4636 ■ *Microprocessor Report*
Pub: MicroDesign Resources
Contact: Max Baron
E-mail: mbaron@mdr.cahners.com
Released: 17x/yr. **Price:** $695, U.S. and Canada for print version; $495, U.S. and Canada pounds; $995, U.S. and Canada for print and online version; $995, elsewhere for print version. **Description:** The leading technical publication for the microprocessor industry. Dedicated to providing unbiased, in-depth, critical

analysis of new high-performance microprocessor developments. This newsletter is exclusively subscriber-supported.

4637 ■ *Online*
Pub: Online, A Division of Information Today Inc.
Ed: Marydee Ojala, Editor, marydee@infotoday.com. **Released:** Bimonthly. **Price:** $129.50; $243 two years; $145 Canada and Mexico; $172 other countries. **Description:** Professional magazine covering online and CD-ROM databases with practical how-to articles covering the entire online industry.

4638 ■ *PATCA Journal*
Pub: Professional and Technical Consultants Association
Ed: Stan Turnbull, Editor, stant@ix.netcom.com. **Released:** Quarterly. **Price:** Included in membership. **Description:** Acts as a forum for the exchange of information on consulting and consulting practices. Provides professional support for member independent consultants active in business, industry, and government. Recurring features include book reviews, seminar announcements, interviews, letters to the editor, news of educational opportunities, and member profiles.

4639 ■ *Productivity Software*
Pub: Worldwide Videotex
Released: Monthly. **Price:** $150. **Description:** Provides information on computer software.

TRADE SHOWS AND CONVENTIONS

4640 ■ Computer Fest
ShowFest Productions, Inc.
75 Dufflaw Rd., Ste. 202
Toronto, ON, Canada M6A 2W4
Ph:(416)782-0063
Fax:(416)782-3178
Released: Semiannual. **Audience:** General public and industry professionals. **Principal Exhibits:** Computer equipment, supplies, and services.

4641 ■ ON DEMAND Digital Printing & Publishing Strategy Conference and Exposition
Advanstar Communications
641 Lexington Ave., 8th Fl.
New York, NY 10022
Ph:(212)951-6600
Fax:(212)951-6793
Co. E-mail: info@advantstar.com
URL: http://www.advanstar.com
Released: Annual. **Audience:** Corporate executives, print providers, government users. **Principal Exhibits:** Addresses the digitalization of workflow in the printing and publishing marketplace.

CONSULTANTS

4642 ■ COTC Technologies Inc.
172 E Industrial Blvd.
PO Box 7615
Pueblo, CO 81007-4406
Ph:(719)547-0938
Free: 888-547-0938
Fax:(719)547-1105
Contact: Karen Renz, CFO
E-mail: karen@atscotc-consulting.com
Scope: Provides software consulting services to organizations that require assistance with their HP3000 computer system. Provides systems analysis, programming, operations support, and system management. Also provides PC software and hardware support and consulting. Additionally provides various training for the HP3000 computer system. Industries served: healthcare, aerospace procurement, aerospace proposal activities, and HP3000 computer systems.

4643 ■ Custom Consulting Inc.
6315 Bayside Dr.
New Port Richey, FL 34652-2040
Ph:(727)844-5065
Fax:(727)844-5064
Co. E-mail: diwago@customconsulting.com
URL: http://www.customconsulting.com
Contact: David Wong, Mgr
E-mail: dwong@atscustomconsulting.com
Scope: Provides systems development personnel on a temporary basis. Specializes in mainframe, mini and Client/server development environments.

4644 ■ Executive Analytics & Design Inc.
10 Malcolm X Blvd.
PO Box 191623
Roxbury, MA 02119-1775
Ph:(617)445-5200
Fax:(617)445-5224
Co. E-mail: info@eadfinancialit.com
URL: http://www.eadfinancialit.com
Contact: Gilbert Cole, Mgr
E-mail: gil@atseadfinancialit.com
Scope: A technology consulting firm, specializing in custom financial solutions, that provides systems, software and website development solutions. Provides services including o-the-shelf accounting software selection, custom software development, financial management consulting, project management and financial and technology outsourcing. **Seminars:** Technology and Networking for Better Business Performance.

4645 ■ Globalport.com Inc.
2414 Bayou Dr.
League City, TX 77573
Ph:(281)332-0361
Fax:(281)332-3054
Contact: Janis Robin Scott, Mgr
Scope: Specializes in corporate web site development, database interfaces and business applications.

4646 ■ Hardy Stevenson and Associates Ltd.
364 Davenport Rd.
Toronto, ON, Canada M5R 1K6
Ph:(416)944-8444
Free: 877-267-7794
Fax:(416)944-0900
Co. E-mail: hsa@hardystevenson.com
URL: http://www.hardystevenson.com
Contact: Glynn Gomes, Principle
E-mail: davehardy@atshardystevenson.com
Scope: Firm specialize in land use and environmental planning social economic impact assessment facilitation, conflict resolution community relations, public consultation strategic planning policy and project management consulting.

4647 ■ Richard I. Anderson
101 Spear St., Ste. 203
San Francisco, CA 94105
Ph:(415)383-5689
Co. E-mail: riander@well.com
URL: http://www.well.com/user/riander
E-mail: riander@well.com
Scope: Provides guidance to organizations seeking to increase the influence of user-centered design, ethnographic research, multidisciplinary collaboration, on business strategy, organizational process, product conceptualization and design. **Seminars:** User-Centered Design/Usability Engineering, May, 2000; Addressing Organizational Obstacles to and Achieving Greater Business Benefits; User-Centered Design; Ethnographic Research; Multidisciplinary Collaboration; Managing User Experience Groups; Meeting the Needs of a Multidisciplinary Profession; User Experience Managers and Executives Speak; Changing the Role User Experience Plays in Your Business.

4648 ■ Strategic Systems & Products Corp.
320 Decker Dr., Ste. 100
Irving, TX 75062
Ph:(972)719-2543
Fax:(972)719-2540
Co. E-mail: sales@sspcorp.com
URL: http://www.sspcorp.com
Contact: Lyndy Nierman, Principle
E-mail: lnierman@atssspcorp.com
Scope: Specializes in the implementation and support of application development, project management and e-business consulting services to the exploration and production business unit of petroleum companies.

4649 ■ Weich & Bilotti Inc.
600 Worcester Rd., 4th Fl.
Framingham, MA 01702
Ph:(508)663-1600
Fax:(508)663-1682
Co. E-mail: info@weich-bilotti.com
URL: http://www.weich-bilotti.com
Contact: Mervyn D. Weich, President
E-mail: mweich@weich-bilotti.com
Scope: Specializes in business plans, venture capital, computer information systems, turnaround/interim management, retail consulting, start-up process, college recruiting and IS and IT personnel.

FRANCHISES AND BUSINESS OPPORTUNITIES

4650 ■ Rescuecom
2560 Burnet Ave.
Syracuse, NY 13206
Free: 800-RES-CUE7
Fax:(315)433-5228
URL: http://www.rescuecom.com
No. of Franchise Units: 40. **Founded:** 1985. **Franchised:** 1997. **Description:** Computer consulting and repair services. **Franchise Fee:** $1,495-$18,800. **Financial Assistance:** Yes. **Training:** Yes.

4651 ■ Silution Franchise Corp.
1472 E Walnut St.
Pasadena, CA 91106
Free: 877-745-8846
Fax:(626)535-0566
Founded: 1998. **Franchised:** 2006. **Description:** Computer services & support. **Equity Capital Needed:** $39,950-$71,800. **Franchise Fee:** $22,000. **Royalty Fee:** 10%. **Financial Assistance:** Third party financing available. **Training:** Provides 5 days at headquarters, 1 day at franchisees location with ongoing support.

LIBRARIES

4652 ■ AT & T Middletown Technical Library
200 Laurel Ave., S.
Middletown, NJ 07748
Ph:(732)420-5092
Fax:(732)420-5208
URL: http://www.research.att.com/
Contact: John T. Shaw, Mgr.
Scope: Computer science, data communications, telecommunications. **Services:** Interlibrary loan; Library not open to the public. **Holdings:** 20,000 books; 5000 bound periodical volumes; 200 U.S. and foreign standards. **Subscriptions:** 500 journals and other serials.

4653 ■ Colorado Technical University Library
4435 N. Chestnut St.
Colorado Springs, CO 80907-3896
Ph:(719)590-6708
Fax:(719)590-6818
Co. E-mail: aphillips@coloradotech.edu
URL: http://library.colorado-tech.com/cos.htm
Contact: Amy Phillips, Libn.
Scope: Computer science, logistics, electronics, electrical engineering, business management, quality, computer engineering. **Services:** Interlibrary loan; copying; Library open to the public with restrictions. **Holdings:** 32,000 books; 60 microfiche titles; 400 videocassettes. **Subscriptions:** 2400 journals and other serials (print and Internet); 4 newspapers.

4654 ■ DeVry University Library
2149 W. Dunlap Ave.
Phoenix, AZ 85021
Ph:(602)870-9222
Fax:(602)734-1999
Co. E-mail: maltschuler@devry.edu
URL: http://www.devry.edu
Contact: Margot Altschuler, Dir., Lib.Svcs.
Scope: Electronics, bio/med technology, game programming, computer languages, business operations, computers, accounting, electronic engineering, telecommunications, Internet. **Services:** Copying; virtual reference service; Library open to the public for reference use only. **Holdings:** 25,000 books; 25

CD audio books; 3 cabinets of microfiche; 800 videotapes; 250 DVDs; 500 CD-ROMs; 250 computer disks. **Subscriptions:** 100 journals and other serials; 10 newspapers.

4655 ■ District of Columbia Public Library–Technology and Science Division
Martin Luther King Memorial Library
901 G St., NW, Rm. 107
Washington, DC 20001
Ph:(202)727-1175
Fax:(202)727-1129
Co. E-mail: commentssuggestions.dcpl@dc.gov
URL: http://dclibrary.org
Contact: Lessie O. Mtewa, Asst.Libn.

Scope: Automobile and appliance repair, botany, cookery, general science, geology, genetics, manufacturing, nutrition, paleontology, pet care, printing, zoology, mathematics, computer science, biology, domestic arts, earth science, chemistry and chemical technology, physics, engineering, agriculture, gardening, medicine, psychiatry, astronomy, consumer information, health, veterinary science, physical anthropology. **Services:** Interlibrary loan; copying; Library open to the public. **Holdings:** 92,127 books; 2500 bound periodical volumes; 5755 microforms; 65 VF drawers. **Subscriptions:** 300 journals and other serials.

4656 ■ Goldey Beacom College–J. Wilbur Hirons Library
4701 Limestone Rd.
Joseph West Jones College Center
Wilmington, DE 19808
Ph:(302)225-6247
Fax:(302)998-6189
Co. E-mail: stewarp@gbc.edu
URL: http://www.gbc.edu/library/
Contact: Pamela Stewart, Lib.Dir.

Scope: Business, management, accounting, business administration, marketing, computer science. **Services:** Interlibrary loan; copying; Library open to the public for reference use only. **Holdings:** 60,000 books; 19,500 bound periodical volumes; transparencies; maps; 786 AV programs; 1234 reels of microfilm; 44,637 microfiche; 700 corporation Annual reports. **Subscriptions:** 250 journals and other serials; 6 newspapers.

4657 ■ Intel Corporation Library
1900 Prairie City Rd.
FM5-50
Folsom, CA 95630
Ph:(916)356-8080
URL: http://www.intel.com/
Contact: Cary O'Keeffe, Info.Spec.

Scope: Semiconductor industry, business, microcomputer components and systems, telecommunications. **Services:** Library not open to the public. **Holdings:** 1000 books. **Subscriptions:** 100 journals and other serials.

4658 ■ Walt Disney World–Global Business Technology Strategy Library
Team Disney 336-N
1375 Buena Vista Dr.
PO Box 10000
Lake Buena Vista, FL 32830-1000
Ph:(407)828-4250
Co. E-mail: david.w.hartman@disney.com
URL: http://disneyworld.disney.go.com/wdw
Contact: David Hartman, Libn.

Scope: Computer science, human resources, general business. **Services:** Center not open to the public. **Holdings:** 4000 books, videos, DVDs, and CDs; 100 AV equipment. **Subscriptions:** 200 journals and other serials; 3 newspapers.

Computer Data Storage Company

ASSOCIATIONS AND OTHER ORGANIZATIONS

4659 ■ Automated Storage/Retrieval Systems
8720 Red Oak Blvd., Ste. 201
Charlotte, NC 28217
Ph:(704)676-1190
Fax:(704)676-1199
Co. E-mail: gforger@mhia.org
URL: http://www.mhia.org/industrygroups/as-rs
Contact: Brian Cohen, Chm.
Description: Companies manufacturing automated storage/retrieval systems. Develops and promotes standard nomenclature, codes for equipment operations, fire prevention, and personnel safety; assists and coordinates efforts of related trade associations pertaining to total systems. Develops and promotes a code of ethics; prepares and distributes publicity and educational materials. Cooperates with private and governmental groups that establish standards or safety codes. Sponsors educational programs and maintains speaker's bureau. **Publications:** *Roster of Members* (periodic).

4660 ■ Information Storage Industry Consortium
12396 World Trade Dr., Ste. 201
San Diego, CA 92128
Ph:(858)279-7230
Fax:(858)279-8591
Co. E-mail: insic@insic.org
URL: http://www.insic.org
Contact: Dr. Paul D. Frank, Exec. Dir.
Description: Brings together companies and universities involved in computer data storage research, united to accomplish mutual goals. Creates and manages joint precompetitive research programs among its members. Performs studies to develop long-term roadmaps for various data storage technologies. .

4661 ■ Order Fulfillment Council I Material Handling Industry of America
8720 Red Oak Blvd., Ste. 201
Charlotte, NC 28217-3992
Ph:(704)676-1190
Free: 800-345-1815
Fax:(704)676-1199
Co. E-mail: jnofsinger@mhia.org
URL: http://www.mhia.org/industrygroups/ofc
Contact: John Nofsinger, CEO
Description: Trade associations comprising storage industries. Compiles statistics; sponsors research and educational programs. **Publications:** *Storage and Handling Idea Book* .

4662 ■ PRISM International
1418 Aversboro Rd., Ste. 201
Garner, NC 27529
Ph:(919)771-0657
Fax:(919)771-0457
Co. E-mail: jim@prismintl.org
URL: http://www.prismintl.org
Contact: Jim Booth, Exec. Dir.
Description: Represents owners and operators of commercial information management facilities, which include: commercial record centers, media vaults, imaging service bureaus, confidential destruction vendors, digital archiving operations, vendors to the industry, self-vended records and data repositories, government records repositories and educators. Seeks to provide operating guidelines, education, and research in the industry. Promotes professional quality of services offered by commercial and non-commercial information management organizations; facilitates exchange of technical and management information; provides conferences and educational events in the United States, Europe and Asia; works to advocate for and improve public image of commercial information management industry. .

REFERENCE WORKS

4663 ■ "3Par: Storing Up Value" in *Barron's* (Vol. 90, August 30, 2010, No. 35, pp. 30)
Pub: Barron's Editorial & Corporate Headquarters
Ed: Mark Veverka. **Description:** Dell and Hewlett Packard are both bidding for data storage company 3Par. The acquisition would help Dell and Hewlett Packard provide customers with a one-stop shop as customers move to a private cloud in the Internet.

4664 ■ "Also Check Out..." in *Black Enterprise* (Vol. 38, October 2007, No. 3, pp. 64)
Pub: Earl G. Graves Publishing Co. Inc.
Description: Profile of Lenovo's Think Vantage Rescue and Recovery system that performs backup files for CD/DVDs.

4665 ■ "Attivio Brings Order to Data" in *Information Today* (Vol. 26, February 2009, No. 2, pp. 14)
Pub: Information Today, Inc.
Ed: Marji McClure. **Description:** Profile of Attivio, the high tech firm offering next-generation software that helps businesses to consolidate data and eliminate enterprise silos.

4666 ■ "Beam My Data Up" in *Canadian Business* (Vol. 80, February 12, 2007, No. 4, pp. 42)
Pub: Rogers Media
Ed: Marlene Rego. **Description:** Innovations in the field of teleportation since its invention by Gilles Brassard in 1992 is discussed.

4667 ■ "Best Managed Companies (Canada)" in *Canadian Business* (Vol. 82, Summer 2009, No. 8, pp. 38)
Pub: Rogers Media
Ed: Calvin Leung. **Description:** Agrium Inc. and Barrick Gold Corporation are among those that are found to be the best managed companies in Canada. Best managed companies also include software firm Open Text Corporation, which has grown annual sales by 75 percent and annual profits by 160 percent since 1995. Open Text markets software that allow firms to manage word-based data, and has 46,000 customers in 114 countries.

4668 ■ *The Big Switch: Rewiring the World, From Edison to Google*
Pub: W.W. Norton & Company
Ed: Nicholas Carr. **Released:** 2009. **Price:** $25.95. **Description:** Companies such as Google, Microsoft, and Amazon.com are building huge centers in order to create massive data centers. Together these centers form a giant computing grid that will deliver the digital universe to scientific labs, companies and homes in the future. This trend could bring about a new, darker phase for the Internet, one where these networks could operate as a fearsome entity that will dominate the lives of individuals worldwide.

4669 ■ "Burton Group Answers Industry Need for Practical Data Center Advice" in *Canadian Corporate News* (May 14, 2007)
Pub: Comtex News Network Inc.
Description: Burton Group, an IT research firm focused on in-depth technical analysis of enterprise IT infrastructures, launched a new service providing practical advice for IT professionals facing critical data center decisions which due to technological advances can be more efficient while reducing costs.

4670 ■ "Cerner Works the Business Circuit" in *Business Journal-Serving Metropolitan Kansas City* (Vol. 26, October 5, 2007, No. 4, pp. 1)
Pub: American City Business Journals, Inc.
Ed: Rob Roberts. **Description:** Cerner Corporation is embracing the coming of the electronic medical record exchange by creating a regional health information organization (RHIO) called the CareEntrust. The RHIO convinced health insurers to share claims data with patients and clinicians. At the Center Health Conference, held October 7 to 10, Cerner will demonstrate the software it developed for CareEntrust to the 40,000 healthcare and information technology professionals.

4671 ■ "Clouds in the Forecast" in *Information Today* (Vol. 28, September 2011, No. 8, pp. 10)
Pub: Information Today, Inc.
Ed: Paula J. Hane. **Description:** Cloud computing is software, applications, and data stored remotely and accessed via the Internet with output displayed on a client device. Recent developments in cloud computing are explored.

4672 ■ "Cloudy Future for VMware?" in *Barron's* (Vol. 90, September 13, 2010, No. 37, pp. 21)
Pub: Barron's Editorial & Corporate Headquarters
Ed: Jonathan R. Laing. **Description:** VMWare dominated the virtualization market for years, but it may be ending as it faces more competition from rivals that offer cloud computing services. The company's stocks are also expensive and are vulnerable to the smallest mishap.

4673 ■ "CMS Products and Avecto Team for Business Security Product Solutions" in *Wireless News* (November 11, 2009)
Pub: Close-Up Media
Description: CMS Products, a provider of data security, backup, content management and disaster

recovery, has agreed on a strategic partnership with Avect, a provider in least privilege management. The partnership will allow the companies to bundle their products.

4674 ■ *Contingency Planning and Disaster Recovery: A Small Business Guide*
Pub: John Wiley & Sons, Incorporated
Ed: Donna R. Childs, Stefan Dietrich. **Released:** October 2002. **Description:** Four keys issues to help a business plan for disasters include: preparation, response, recovery, and sample IT solutions in order to secure property and confidential data files and covers the six types of disasters: human errors, equipment failures, third-party failures, environmental hazards, fires and other structural catastrophes, and terrorism and sabotage.

4675 ■ "County Tract Pitched for Data Center" in *Baltimore Business Journal* (Vol. 28, July 23, 2010, No. 11, pp. 1)
Pub: Baltimore Business Journal
Ed: Scott Dance. **Description:** One hundred acres of land in Woodlawn, Maryland is set to be sold for use in the construction of a data center for the U.S. Social Security Administration. Baltimore County has submitted a bid for the $750M construction project.

4676 ■ "Data Center Plan Bearing Fruit From Apple, Spec Center" in *Charlotte Business Journal* (Vol. 25, October 15, 2010, No. 30, pp. 1)
Pub: Charlotte Business Journal
Ed: Ken Elkins. **Description:** Apple Inc. is planning to expand its server farm at the North Carolina Data Center Corridor in Catawba County. T5 Partners, on the other hand, will build a shell building to house a server on the site. Infocrossing Inc. will also build an open data center in the area.

4677 ■ "Data Firm Growth 'Opportunistic'" in *Tampa Bay Business Journal* (Vol. 30, January 29, 2010, No. 6, pp. 1)
Pub: American City Business Journals
Ed: Michael Hinman. **Description:** E Solutions Corporation is experiencing growth amid the economic downturn, with its Park Tower data center occupancy in Tampa Florida expanding from 14,000 square feet to 20,000 square feet. Details on the increased operations fueled by demand for information storage and management services offered by the company are discussed.

4678 ■ "Data Security is No. 1 Compliance Concern" in *HRMagazine* (Vol. 53, October 2008, No. 10, pp. 32)
Pub: Society for Human Resource Management
Ed: Aliah D. Wright. **Description:** Electronic data protection and data privacy are the leading ethics and compliance issues faced by companies today.

4679 ■ "Discrete Wavelet Transform-Based Time Series Analysis and Mining" in *ACM Computing Surveys* (Vol. 43, Summer 2011, No. 2, pp. 6)
Pub: Association for Computing Machinery
Ed: Pimwadee Chaovalit, Aryya Gangopadhyay, George Karabatis, Zhiyuan Chen. **Description:** Time series are recorded values of an interesting phenomenon such as stock prices, household items, or patient heart rates over a period of time. Time series data mining focuses on discovering interesting patterns in such data. An introduction to a wavelet-based times series data analysis is provided with a systematic survey of various analysis techniques that use discrete wavelet transformation (DWT) in time series data mining, and outlines the benefits of this approach demonstrated by previous studies performed on diverse application domains, including image classification, multimedia retrieval, and computer network anomaly detection.

4680 ■ "E-Medical Records Save Money, Time in Ann Arbor" in *Crain's Detroit Business* (Vol. 24, January 21, 2008, No. 3, pp. 6)
Pub: Crain Communications Inc. - Detroit
Ed: Jay Greene. **Description:** Ann Arbor Area Health Information Exchange is improving patient outcomes by sharing clinical and administrative data in electronic medical record systems.

4681 ■ "EBSCO Adds New Features to EBSCOhost Content Viewer" in *Information Today* (Vol. 26, February 2009, No. 2, pp. 31)
Pub: Information Today, Inc.
Description: EBSCOhost Content Viewer historical digital archive collection provides a visual overview of a displayed document, highlighting search keywords on the page as well as providing a document map that shows the number of times a given keyword is mentioned in a periodical, monograph, article, or other document. For periodical content, the viewer lets users browse multiple issues in a volume without leaving the interface; features include zoom and pan technology similar to online maps.

4682 ■ "Ex Libris Rosetta Hits the Market" in *Information Today* (Vol. 26, February 2009, No. 2, pp. 30)
Pub: Information Today, Inc.
Description: Ex Libris Rosetta, the latest version of the Ex Libris Group's Digital Preservation System supports the acquisition, validation, ingest, storage, management, preservation, and dissemination of digital objects, allowing libraries the infrastructure and technology to preserve and facilitate access to digital collections. The firm's Ex Libris Rosseta Charter Program helps users develop strategic collaboration between Ex Libris and its customers to improve the product.

4683 ■ "The Failure Detector Abstraction" in *ACM Computing Surveys* (Vol. 43, Summer 2011, No. 2, pp. 9)
Pub: Association for Computing Machinery
Ed: Felix C. Freiling, Rachid Guerraoui, Petr Kuznetsov. **Description:** A failure detector is a fundamental abstraction in distributed computing. This article surveys this abstraction through two dimensions. First it studies failure detectors as building blocks to simplify the design of reliable distributed algorithms, particularly how failure detectors can factor out timing assumptions to detect failures in distributed agreement algorithms. Second, failure detectors as computability benchmarks are studied. Some limitations of the failure detector abstraction along each of the dimensions is also highlighted.

4684 ■ "The Fort" in *Hawaii Business* (Vol. 53, November 2007, No. 5, pp. 19)
Pub: Hawaii Business Publishing
Ed: Jason Ubay. **Description:** DRFortress' flagship data center The Fort located at Honolulu's Airport Industrial Park provides companies a place to store their servers in an ultra-secure environment. Anything stored in here that requires power has a back up and in case of an outage generators can supply power up to 80 hrs. The Fort caters to major carriers and Internet service providers.

4685 ■ "Free Speech Vs. Privacy in Data Mining" in *Information Today* (Vol. 28, September 2011, No. 8, pp. 22)
Pub: Information Today, Inc.
Ed: George H. Pike. **Description:** The U.S. Constitution does not explicitly guarantee the right of privacy. Organizations and businesses that require obtaining and disseminating information can be caught in the middle of privacy rights. The long-term impact on data mining, Internet marketing, and Internet privacy issues are examined.

4686 ■ "Health IT Regulations Generate Static Among Providers" in *Philadelphia Business Journal* (Vol. 28, January 29, 2010, No. 50, pp. 1)
Pub: American City Business Journals
Ed: John George. **Description:** US Centers for Medicaid and Medicare Services and the Office of the National Coordinator for Health Information Technology have proposed rules regarding the meaningful use of electronic health records. The rules must be complied with by hospitals and physicians to qualify for federal stimulus funds.

4687 ■ "Help Wanted: 100 Hospitals IT Workers" in *Business Courier* (Vol. 27, October 8, 2010, No. 23, pp. 1)
Pub: Business Courier
Ed: James Ritchie. **Description:** Hospitals in the Greater Cincinnati area are expected to hire more than 100 information technology (IT) workers to help digitize medical records. Financial incentives from the health care reform bill encouraged investments in electronic medical record systems, increasing the demand for IT workers that would help make information exchange across the healthcare system easier.

4688 ■ "How to Play the Tech Mergers" in *Barron's* (Vol. 90, August 30, 2010, No. 35, pp. 18)
Pub: Barron's Editorial & Corporate Headquarters
Ed: Tiernan Ray. **Description:** The intense bidding by Hewlett-Packard and Dell for 3Par was foreseen in a previous Barron's cover story and 3Par's stock has nearly tripled since reported. Other possible acquisition targets in the tech industry include Brocade Communication Systems, NetApp, Xyratex, and Isilon Systems.

4689 ■ "Image Conscious" in *Canadian Business* (Vol. 81, March 17, 2008, No. 4, pp. 36)
Pub: Rogers Media
Ed: Andrew Wahl. **Description:** Idee Inc. is testing an Internet search engine for images that does not rely on tags but compares its visual data to a database of other images. The company was founded and managed by Leila Boujnane as an off-shoot of their risk-management software firm. Their software has already been used by image companies to track copyrighted images and to find images within their own archives.

4690 ■ *Information Industry Directory*
Pub: Gale
Released: Annual, Latest edition 36th; April, 2011. **Price:** $1105, individuals. **Covers:** Approximately 12,000 organizations, systems, and services involved in the production and distribution of information in electronic form: database producers and their products online host services, transactional services, library and information networks, bibliographic utilities, library management systems, information retrieval software, mailing list services, fee-based information on demand services, document delivery sources, data collection and analysis centers and firms, and related consultants, service companies, professional and trade associations, publishers, and research activities. **Entries Include:** Name of parent organization, name of system of service, address, phone, toll-free phone, fax, telex, email address, year founded name of unit head, size of staff, names of any affiliated organizations, financial information. Internet access information, general description of electronic product, system, or service, subjects covered or areas of service offered, sources of data for the system, type and quantity of stored information in all forms, publications and microform products and services, computer-based products and services, other services, clientele served, availability and restrictions, name of contact. **Arrangement:** Alphabetical. **Indexes:** Master, database name, software name, publication/microform title, function/service, personal name, subject, geographical.

4691 ■ *Information Sources*
Pub: Software & Information Industry Association
Contact: Ken Wasch, President
Released: Continuous. **Covers:** More than 800 companies involved in the creation, distribution, and use of information products, services, and technology. Entries are prepared by companies described. **Entries Include:** Company name, address, phone, names of executives, international partners, regional offices, trade and brand names, and description of products and services. **Arrangement:** Alphabetical. **Indexes:** Product, personal name, trade name, geographical, corporate parents, international and niche markets.

4692 ■ *Information Technology for the Small Business: How to Make IT Work For Your Company*
Pub: TAB Computer Systems, Incorporated
Ed: T.J. Benoit. **Released:** June 2006. **Price:** $17. 95. **Description:** Basics of information technology to help small companies maximize benefits are covered. Topics include pitfalls to avoid, email and Internet use, data backup, recovery and overall IT organization.

4693 ■ "Media Software and Data Services" in *MarketingMagazine* (Vol. 115, September 27, 2010, No. 13, pp. 78)
Pub: Rogers Publishing Ltd.
Description: Media software and data services information in Canada is presented.

4694 ■ "Mimosa Systems Gains 150,000 New NearPoint Users" in *Information Today* (Vol. 26, February 2009, No. 2, pp. 31)
Pub: Information Today, Inc.
Description: Mimosa System's NearPoint archive solution features email and file archiving, e-discovery, archive virtualization, and disaster recovery capabilities.

4695 ■ "New Database Brings Doctors Out of the Dark" in *Business Courier* (Vol. 26, October 23, 2009, No. 26, pp. 1)
Pub: American City Business Journals, Inc.
Ed: James Ritchie. **Description:** A database created by managed care consulting firm Praesentia allows doctors in Cincinnati to compare average reimbursements from health insurance companies to doctors in different areas. Specialist doctors in the city are paid an average of $172.25 for every office consultation.

4696 ■ "New Wave of Business Security Products Ushers in the Kaspersky Anti-Malware Protection System" in *Internet Wire* (October 26, 2010)
Pub: Comtex
Description: Kaspersky Anti-Malware System provides anti-malware protection that requires minimal in-house resources for small businesses. The system offers a full range of tightly integrated end-to-end protection solutions, ensuring unified protection across an entire network, from endpoint and mobile device protection to file server, mail server, network storage and gateway protection. It provides flexible centralized management, immediate threat visibility and a level of responsiveness not seen in other anti-malware approaches.

4697 ■ "New Ways To Think About Data Loss: Data Loss Is Costly and Painful" in *Franchising World* (Vol. 42, August 2010, No. 8, pp. 21)
Pub: International Franchise Association
Ed: Ken Colburn. **Description:** Information for maintaining data securely for franchised organizations, including smart phones, tablets, copiers, computers and more is given.

4698 ■ *Pro Windows Small Business Server 2003*
Pub: Apress L.P.
Ed: Tony Campbell. **Released:** July 2006. **Price:** $39.99. **Description:** Profile of Microsoft's Windows Small Business Server, designed for companies with 50 or fewer employees.

4699 ■ "Put Your Data to Work in the Marketplace" in *Harvard Business Review* (Vol. 86, September 2008, No. 9, pp. 34)
Pub: Harvard Business School Press
Ed: Thomas C. Redman. **Description:** Nine strategies are presented for data asset marketing including exploiting asymmetries, unbundling, repackaging, and offering new content.

4700 ■ "Scanning Dell's Shopping List" in *Barron's* (Vol. 89, July 13, 2009, No. 28, pp. 24)
Pub: Dow Jones & Co., Inc.
Ed: Mark Veverka. **Description:** It is believed that Dell will be looking for companies to acquire since they poached an experienced mergers-and-acquisitions executive. In addition Dell's CEO is reportedly telling people he plans to go shopping. Dell executives have also stated an interest in data storage.

4701 ■ "Serials Solutions Launches 360 Resource Manager Consortium Edition" in *Information Today* (Vol. 26, February 2009, No. 2, pp. 32)
Pub: Information Today, Inc.
Description: Serials Solutions new Serials Solutions 360 Resource Manager Consortium Edition helps consortia, groups and member libraries with their e-resource management services. The products allows users to consolidate e-resource metadata and acquisition information into one place, which enables groups to manage holdings, subscriptions, licensing, contacts, and cost information and to streamline delivery of information to members.

4702 ■ *Strategies for Growth in SMEs: The Role of Information and Information Systems*
Pub: Elsevier Science & Technology Books
Ed: Margi Levy, Philip Powell. **Released:** December 2004. **Price:** $62.95. **Description:** Role of information and information systems in the growth of small and medium-sized enterprises in the U.S.

4703 ■ "A Survey of DHT Security Techniques" in *ACM Computing Surveys* (Vol. 43, Summer 2011, No. 2, pp. 8)
Pub: Association for Computing Machinery
Ed: Guido Urdaneta, Guillaume Pierre, Maarten Van Steen. **Description:** Peer-to-peer networks based on distributed hash tables (DHTs) have received considerable attention since their introduction in 2001. Unfortunately, DHT-based systems have been shown to be difficult to protect against security attacks. An overview of techniques reported in literature for making DHT-based systems resistant to the three most important attacks that can be launched by malicious nodes participating in the DHT is given: the Sybil attack, the Eclipse attack, and routing and storage attacks.

4704 ■ "Tech Data Launches Unified Communications and Network Security Specialized Business Units" in *Wireless News* (October 22,2009)
Pub: Close-Up Media
Description: Responding to the growing demand for unified communications and network security, Tech Data announced the formation of two new Specialized Business Units.

4705 ■ "The Total Cost of Ignorance: Avoiding Top Tech Mistakes" in *Black Enterprise* (Vol. 38, October 2007, No. 3, pp. 64)
Pub: Earl G. Graves Publishing Co. Inc.
Ed: Alwin A.D. Jones. **Description:** Cost of data loss for any small business can be devastating; lack of security is another mistake companies make when it comes to technology.

4706 ■ "Wegmans Uses Database for Recall" in *Supermarket News* (Vol. 56, September 22, 2008, No. 38)
Pub: Penton Business Media, Inc.
Ed: Carol Angrisani. **Description:** Wegmans used data obtained through its loyalty card that, in turn, sent automated telephone calls to every customer who had purchased tainted pet food when Mars Petcare recalled dog food products.

4707 ■ "What is the Future of Disk Drives, Death or Rebirth?" in *ACM Computing Surveys* (Vol. 43, Fall 2011, No. 3, pp. 23)
Pub: Association for Computing Machinery
Ed: Yuhui Deng. **Description:** Disk drives have experienced dramatic development to meet performance requirements since the IBM 1301 disk drive was announced in 1961. However, the performance gap between memory and disk drives has widened to 6 orders of magnitude and continues to widen by about 50 percent per year. Challenges and opportunities facing these storage devices are explored.

4708 ■ "Z-Tech Lands Contract with CMS" in *Black Enterprise* (Vol. 37, October 2006, No. 3, pp. 36)
Pub: Earl G. Graves Publishing Co. Inc.
Ed: Glenn Townes. **Description:** Z-Tech Corp., a Maryland-based company providing database design and warehousing, was awarded a five-year government contract with the Centers for Medicare and Medicaid Services' Chronic Care Improvement Program worth $20 million.

TRADE PERIODICALS

4709 ■ *DSSCourse*
Pub: Data Storage Systems Center
Ed: Meg A. Papa, Editor. **Released:** 2/year. **Price:** Free. **Description:** Reports on research conducted at the Center as well as the activities of faculty and students. Recurring features include notices of publications available and news of seminars and workshops.

4710 ■ *Journal of Database Management*
Pub: IGI Global
Contact: Dinesh Batra, Assoc. Ed.
Released: Quarterly. **Price:** $205 print only; $835 institutions print and free online; $575 institutions online only; $575 institutions print only. **Description:** Journal covering the research of database administrators and managers.

4711 ■ *Online*
Pub: Online, A Division of Information Today Inc.
Ed: Marydee Ojala, Editor, marydee@infotoday.com. **Released:** Bimonthly. **Price:** $129.50; $243 two years; $145 Canada and Mexico; $172 other countries. **Description:** Professional magazine covering online and CD-ROM databases with practical how-to articles covering the entire online industry.

4712 ■ *SIGIR Forum*
Pub: Special Interest Group on Programming Languages
Ed: Peter Anick, Editor. **Released:** 2/year. **Price:** $30, Included in membership; $30, nonmembers; $15, students. **Description:** Concerned with how machines may be used in the storage, retrieval, and dissemination of information, including news and information relating to retrieval theory, programming, file preparation, searching strategy, output schemes, systems evaluation, and development of equipment best suited for these tasks. Also contains proceedings of annual international SIGIR conferences.

VIDEOCASSETTES/ AUDIOCASSETTES

4713 ■ *Communications: The Wired World*
The Cinema Guild
115 West 30th St., Ste. 800
New York, NY 10001
Ph:(212)685-6242
Free: 800-723-5522
Fax:(212)685-4717
Co. E-mail: info@cinemaguild.com
URL: http://www.cinemaguild.com
Released: 198?. **Description:** The methods we will use to store and disseminate information in the future are examined. Developments considered for the future include instant transmission of diagnostic data to any hospital, robot manufacturing plants, and homemakers shopping electronically. **Availability:** 3/4U; Special order formats.

TRADE SHOWS AND CONVENTIONS

4714 ■ COMDEX
Ziff-Davis, Inc.
28 E. 28th St.
New York, NY 10016-7930
Ph:(212)503-3500
Co. E-mail: info@ziffdavis.com
URL: http://www.ziffdavis.com
Released: Annual. **Audience:** Volume resellers and value-adders of small computers and related items; only a virtual trade show since 2003. **Principal Exhibits:** Small computer systems, related peripherals, software, accessories, services, and supplies.

CONSULTANTS

4715 ■ Thomas Wilds Associates Inc.
PO Box 3534, Church St. Sta.
New York, NY 10008-3534
Ph:(508)657-1356
Fax:(508)478-2235
Co. E-mail: thomwilds@aol.com
Contact: Thomas Wilds, President
E-mail: thomwilds@aol.com
Scope: Provider of management consulting services in the design and implementation of records retention programs for large organizations and not-for-profits.

Industries served: Finance, industry and government. **Seminars:** Records Retention, Hilton New York, Sep, 2006.

COMPUTERIZED DATABASES

4716 ■ *Business Wire*

Berkshire Hathaway Inc.
44 Montgomery St., 39th Fl.
San Francisco, CA 94104
Ph:(415)986-4422
Free: 800-227-0845
Fax:(415)788-5335
Co. E-mail: SF_sales_group@bizwire.com
URL: http://www.businesswire.com

Description: Contains more than 1.4 million records that make up the complete text of press releases from public and private companies and other organizations, such as hospitals and universities. Covers new products, stock offerings, mergers, legal actions, financial information, personnel changes, and company announcements of general interest. Includes headline recaps hourly plus recaps of high tech headlines in some systems. Records include company name, headline, publication date, ticker symbol, byline; dateline, time, word count (usually less than 500), and text, including contact information. Covers industries such as banking, computers, telecommunications, entertainment, aviation, biotechnology, and mining; general news and features; some international events; and sports. **Availability:** Online: Thomson Reuters, Mzinga Inc., ProQuest LLC, Dow Jones & Company Inc., LexisNexis Group, Bloomberg LP. **Type:** Full text.

4717 ■ *Computer Database*

Cengage Learning Inc.
27500 Drake Rd.
Farmington Hills, MI 48331-3535
Ph:(248)699-4253
Free: 800-877-4253
Fax:(248)699-8069
Co. E-mail: galeord@gale.com
URL: http://gale.cengage.com

Description: Contains more than 1 million citations, abstracts, and full text to literature from some 800 trade journals, industry newsletters, and platform-specific publications covering the computer, telecommunications, and electronics industries. Topics covered include business and industry applications; computer graphics; consumer information; database management systems; hardware and software design, development, and reviews; peripherals; home computers; new products; performance evaluations; programming languages; operating systems; phototypesetting; and word processing. Includes descriptive and financial information for companies covered in the industry literature. **Availability:** Online: ProQuest LLC, ProQuest LLC, Cengage Learning Inc. **Type:** Bibliographic; Full text.

4718 ■ *Computer and Information Systems Abstracts*

ProQuest LLC
789 E Eisenhower Pky.
Ann Arbor, MI 48103
Ph:(734)761-4700
Fax:(734)997-4222
Co. E-mail: info@proquest.com
URL: http://www.csa.com

Description: Contains more than 740,000 citations, with abstracts, to the worldwide literature on theoretical and applied computer science. Sources include books, journals, conference proceedings, and government reports. Corresponds to *Computer and Information Systems Abstracts Journal.* **Availability:** Online: STN International, STN International. **Type:** Bibliographic.

4719 ■ *Computerworld*

International Data Group Inc.
One Exeter Plz., 15th Fl.
Boston, MA 02116
Ph:(617)534-1200
Co. E-mail: idgcorpcom@idg.com
URL: http://www.idg.com

Description: Contains the complete text of *Computerworld,* a newspaper on the computer industry. Covers personal computers, workstations, systems and software, systems management, and business news, including the computer market and industry trends. **Availability:** Online: LexisNexis Group, International Data Group Inc. **Type:** Full text.

4720 ■ *Gartner Online*

Gartner Inc.
56 Top Gallant Rd.
Stamford, CT 06904-7700
Ph:(203)964-0096
Fax:(203)316-6488
Co. E-mail: inquiry@gartner.com
URL: http://www.gartner.com

Description: Contains research and survey data on the information processing industry, covering data processing revenue, revenue by class, earnings, capital spending, research spending, and related data. **Availability:** Online: Gartner Inc. **Type:** Numeric.

4721 ■ *TecTrends*

Information Sources Inc.
PO Box 8120
Berkeley, CA 94707
Ph:(510)525-6220
Co. E-mail: tectrendsinfo@tectrends.com
URL: http://www.tectrends.com

Description: Contains information on the information technology industry, with detailed descriptions on more than 12,000 information technology products. Includes company information, including personnel names, addresses, telephone numbers, URLs, e-mails, and a description of the company. Product information includes system requirements, availability, vendor support, and a product description. These product and company descriptions are linked to independent third-party reviews abstracted from more than 200 trade journals and industry magazines. **Availability:** Online: Information Sources Inc., ProQuest LLC, ProQuest LLC. **Type:** Bibliographic; Directory.

LIBRARIES

4722 ■ University of Minnesota–Charles Babbage Institute–Center for the History of Information Technology (211 A)

211 Andersen Library
222 21st Ave., S.
Minneapolis, MN 55455
Ph:(612)624-5050
Fax:(612)625-8054
Co. E-mail: cbi@umn.edu
URL: http://www.cbi.umn.edu
Contact: Thomas J. Misa, PhD, Dir.

Scope: History - information and technology, information storage and retrieval systems, computers, programming languages, computing; software industry; computer industry; Burroughs Corporation; Control Data Corporation. **Services:** Copying; collection open to researchers. **Holdings:** 600 volumes; 5500 lin.ft. of documents, oral interview transcripts, records; 300,000 photographs and other AV material; 1062 microforms. **Subscriptions:** 3 journals and other serials.

4723 ■ University of Minnesota Business Library

Wilson Library, Basement Level
309 19th Ave., S.
Minneapolis, MN 55455
Ph:(612)624-5073
Fax:(612)626-9353
Co. E-mail: busref@umn.edu
URL: http://busref.lib.umn.edu
Contact: Caroline Lilyard, Bus.Libn.

Scope: Business, finance and investments, marketing, accounting, management information systems, human resources & industrial relations, advertising, medical industry leadership, computer hardware and software, insurance, management science, transportation. **Services:** Interlibrary loan; copying; reference collection open to the public for reference use only. **Holdings:** 6511 volumes; 108,420 microforms. **Subscriptions:** 8530 journals and other serials.

RESEARCH CENTERS

4724 ■ Boston University–Multimedia Communications Laboratory

Department of Electrical & Computer Engineering
8 St. Mary's St.
Boston, MA 02215
Ph:(617)353-9877
Fax:(617)353-6440
Co. E-mail: tdcl@bu.edu
URL: http://hulk.bu.edu
Contact: Prof. Thomas D.C. Little, Dir.
E-mail: tdcl@bu.edu

Scope: Time-dependent data and their support by storage and communication as typified by on demand interactive multimedia applications. Topics include physical data organizations for audio and video storage, protocols for scalable video services, scheduling in real-time communications, data distribution and management in distributed multimedia systems, temporal data modeling, and content-based retrieval of multimedia. **Publications:** Technical reports. **Educational Activities:** Research seminars.

4725 ■ University of Florida–Database Systems Research Center

CSE Bldg., Rm. E452, Box 116125
Gainesville, FL 32611-6125
Ph:(352)392-1200
Fax:(352)392-1220
Co. E-mail: jhammer@cise.ufl.edu
URL: http://www.cise.ufl.edu/dbcenter/index.shtml
Contact: Dr. Joachim Hammer, Dir.
E-mail: jhammer@cise.ufl.edu

Scope: The Center focuses on solving complex problems requiring the use and integration of technologies such as database management, distributed objects, information retrieval, artificial intelligence, knowledge management, data transformations and warehousing, database triggering and alerting systems, mobile computing, web services, and distributed and parallel computing. Current research projects include algorithms for collecting and analyzing data for decision support; transnational digital government, advanced technologies for automating e-commerce and e-business with a special focus on internet-based negotiation, dynamic workflow, web services, and supply chain management; data cube query processing; an architecture and technologies for simplifying the access to and querying of heterogeneous information sources; and an intelligent middleware architecture for ubiquitous access to heterogeneous data. **Services:** Editorial services, to technical journals. **Publications:** Conference proceedings (10/year); Journal (5/year). **Educational Activities:** Research workshops, offered to industrial companies, government organizations, and academic institutions; Technical seminars.

ASSOCIATIONS AND OTHER ORGANIZATIONS

4726 ■ AFCOM
742 E Chapman Ave.
Orange, CA 92866
Ph:(714)997-7966
Fax:(714)997-9743
Co. E-mail: afcom@afcom.com
URL: http://www.afcom.com
Contact: Jill Yaoz, CEO
Description: Data center, networking and enterprise systems management professionals from medium and large scale mainframe, midrange and client/server data centers worldwide. Works to meet the professional needs of the enterprise system management community. Provides information and support through educational events, research and assistance hotlines, and surveys. **Publications:** *AFCOM's Fall Program Proceedings* (annual); *Annual Survey of Data Processing Operations Salaries* (annual); *The Communique* (monthly); *DCM Magazine* (bimonthly); *Digest of Conference Sessions* (annual); *Enterprise Management Issues* (bimonthly).

4727 ■ ASTD
Box 1443
Alexandria, VA 22313-1443
Ph:(703)683-8100
Free: 800-628-2783
Fax:(703)683-8103
Co. E-mail: customercare@astd.org
URL: http://www.astd.org
Contact: Tony Bingham, Pres./CEO
Description: Represents workplace learning and performance professionals. **Publications:** *ASTD Buyer's Guide* (annual); *Info-Line: Tips, Tools, and Intelligence for Trainers* (monthly); *Learning Circuits* (monthly).

4728 ■ Capital PC User Group
19209 Mt. Airey Rd.
Brookeville, MD 20833
Ph:(301)560-6442
Fax:(301)760-3303
Co. E-mail: admin@cpcug.org
URL: http://www.cpcug.org
Contact: Dennis Courtney, Pres.
Description: An educational and support group for users of IBM personal computers and compatible computers. Objectives are to: provide a forum for members of the IBM PC and compatible equipment; increase understanding and utilization of the personal computer; encourage experimentation and research on current and potential uses of personal computers; exchange information and experience for the benefit of all concerned; provide an opportunity for both formal and informal education in computer applications and hardware and software technologies. Provides speakers, instructors, materials, and experienced consultants to local educational institutions and nonprofit groups. Conducts charitable program. Sponsors special interest groups. Although it operates primarily in the Washington, DC, area, membership is international. .

4729 ■ Computer Assisted Language Instruction Consortium
Texas State University
214 Centennial Hall
601 University Dr.
San Marcos, TX 78666
Ph:(512)245-1417
Fax:(512)245-9089
Co. E-mail: info@calico.org
URL: http://calico.org
Contact: Ms. Esther Horn, Mgr.
Description: Individuals, corporations, and institutions from the academic, business, research, manufacturing, and government sectors. Seeks to apply primarily computer-related technology to the teaching, learning, and processing of first and second languages. Acts as clearinghouse; facilitates and coordinates information sharing. Conducts software fairs, workshops, and annual conferences on the application of computer-assisted language instruction. **Publications:** *CALICO Monograph Series*; *CALICO Resource Guide* .

4730 ■ International Association for Computer Information Systems
Quinnipiac University
School of Business
275 Mt. Carmel Ave.
Hamden, CT 06518
Co. E-mail: richard.mccarthy@quinnipiac.edu
URL: http://www.iacis.org
Contact: Lori Willoughby, Pres.
Description: Educators and computer professionals. Seeks to promote the knowledge, use, and teaching of computers, and technology; dedicated to the improvement of information systems and computer professionals. **Publications:** *IACIS Newsletter* (semiannual); *Journal of Computer Information Systems* (quarterly).

4731 ■ Jobs for the Future
88 Broad St.
Boston, MA 02110
Ph:(617)728-4446
Fax:(617)728-4857
Co. E-mail: info@jff.org
URL: http://www.jff.org
Contact: Norma DeGraffenreid, Receptionist
Description: Seeks to integrate quality education and work opportunities. Offers technical assistance and training to educators, executives, and policy makers. Conducts research and disseminates results on trends in learning among students and employees. **Publications:** *Newswire* (bimonthly).

4732 ■ Learning Resources Network
PO Box 9
River Falls, WI 54022
Ph:(715)426-9777
Free: 800-678-5376
Co. E-mail: info@lern.org
URL: http://www.lern.org
Contact: William A. Draves CAE, Pres.
Description: Represents college and university affiliated groups, community education organizations, associations, recreation departments, and learning networks; continuing professional educators and individuals interested in lifelong learning. Objectives are: to help people and communities start adult learning programs; to provide technical assistance to existing adult learning organizations; to promote alternative education and social change at the national level. Serves as a national technical assistance network in adult learning and noncredit programming. Provides speakers and technical assistance to members and nonmembers. Sponsors seminars; compiles statistics.
.

4733 ■ Society for Applied Learning Technology
50 Culpeper St.
Warrenton, VA 20186
Ph:(540)347-0055
Fax:(540)349-3169
URL: http://www.salt.org
Contact: Raymond G. Fox, Pres.
Description: Senior executives from military, academic, and industrial organizations which design, manufacture, or use training technology, including computer assisted instruction, simulators, trainers, audio-visual instruction delivery devices, and job performance aids. Objectives are to contribute to the development of the highest standards and practices in the application of technology to training; to assist individuals, agencies, and institutions in applying training technology to the definition and solution of social problems; to facilitate the exchange of information and experience; to promote understanding and knowledge in actual and potential uses of technology in the field of training; to provide an effective educational channel among scientists, managers, and users of training technology in the private and public sectors in order to assure adequate skills, understanding, and effective management of training technology. Maintains special interest groups. **Publications:** *Conference Proceedings* (annual); *Journal of Educational Technology Systems* (quarterly); *Journal of Instruction Delivery Systems* (quarterly); *Journal of Interactive Instruction Development* (quarterly).

REFERENCE WORKS

4734 ■ "MindLeaders' Online Training Courses Come to ePath Learning" in *Information Today* (Vol. 26, February 2009, No. 2, pp. 4)
Pub: Information Today, Inc.
Description: MindLeaders has partnered with ePath Learning to provide clients with over 2,200 new online courses. ePath's integrated Learning Management Service (iLMS) allows organizations to create online training programs for employees.

TRADE PERIODICALS

4735 ■ *Alpha Forum*
Pub: Alpha Forum Inc.
Ed: Tom Marcellus, Editor. **Released:** Monthly. **Price:** $59, individuals in the U.S.; $69, individuals elsewhere. **Description:** Contains tips, techniques, and application articles for Alpha Software's Alpha Four.

4736 ■ *Computer Science Education*
Pub: Routledge Journals
Released: Quarterly. **Price:** $194 print only; $631 online only; $665 print and online. **Description:** Computer journal.

4737 ■ *Computer Science Index*
Pub: EBSCO Publishing Inc.
Contact: Hansi Kess
E-mail: hkess@epnet.com
Description: A bibliography of computer-related publications.

4738 ■ *DCLNews*
Pub: Data Conversion Laboratory
Contact: Mark Gross
Ed: Released: Monthly. **Price:** Included in membership;. **Description:** E-journal providing you insider information on XML and SGML, along with the latest technology and e-publishing news.

4739 ■ *Educational Technology Magazine*
Pub: Educational Technology Publications
Ed: Lawrence Lipsitz, Editor. **Released:** 6/yr. **Price:** $199; $229 other countries; $529 three years; $599 other countries three years. **Description:** Magazine featuring computers, video, telecommunications, the internet and education, all aspects of technology in the schools.

4740 ■ *Learning and Leading with Technology*
Pub: International Society for Technology in Education
Contact: Anita McAnear, Acquisitions Ed.
E-mail: amcanear@iste.org
Ed: Kate Conley, Editor, kconley@iste.org. **Released:** 8/year. **Description:** Journal promoting technology and computer-aided teaching at the precollege level.

4741 ■ *Media Computing*
Pub: Dreamscape Productions
Ed: Sheridan Tatsuno, Editor, statsuno@aol.com. **Released:** Monthly. **Price:** $495, institutions in the U.S. and Canada; $550, institutions elsewhere. **Description:** Supplies analysis of multimedia, internet, intranet, and web computing issues. Recurring features include interviews and reports of meetings.

4742 ■ *Online*
Pub: Online, A Division of Information Today Inc.
Ed: Marydee Ojala, Editor, marydee@infotoday.com. **Released:** Bimonthly. **Price:** $129.50; $243 two years; $145 Canada and Mexico; $172 other countries. **Description:** Professional magazine covering online and CD-ROM databases with practical how-to articles covering the entire online industry.

4743 ■ *Smart Access*
Pub: Pinnacle Publishing Inc.
Contact: Paul Litwin
Ed: Farlon Grove, Editor. **Released:** Monthly. **Price:** $149, individuals in the U.S.;; $169, individuals elsewhere. **Description:** Contains tips, techniques, and application articles for Microsoft Corporation's Microsoft Access. Also includes an accompanying source code disk.

4744 ■ *TechTrends*
Pub: Association for Educational Communications and Technology
Contact: Abie Brown, Editor-in-Chief
Released: Bimonthly. **Price:** $44 nonmembers; $44 other countries. **Description:** Professional magazine for educators and trainers.

VIDEOCASSETTES/ AUDIOCASSETTES

4745 ■ *Adult Learning? You've Got to Be Kidding!*
American Society for Training and Development (ASTD)
1640 King St.
Box 1443
Alexandria, VA 22313-2043
Ph:(703)683-8100
Free: 800-628-2783
Fax:(703)683-8103
URL: http://www.astd.org
Released: 1989. **Description:** A look at the seven steps to becoming an all-star trainer in business and industry. Describes how to use the principles of learning theory to improve training sessions. Focuses on the issues of the adult learner, including fear of failure, new technology vs. past experience, and bureaucractic systems. **Availability:** VHS; 3/4U.

4746 ■ *Computer Applications: Lifestyle*
Encyclopedia Britannica
331 N. LaSalle St.
Chicago, IL 60654
Ph:(312)347-7159
Free: 800-323-1229
Fax:(312)294-2104
URL: http://www.britannica.com
Released: 1982. **Description:** A look at how computers are affecting the job, life at home and the marketplace. **Availability:** VHS; 3/4U.

4747 ■ *Computer Literacy Series*
RMI Media
1365 N. Winchester St.
Olathe, KS 66061-5880
Ph:(913)768-1696
Free: 800-745-5480
Fax:800-755-6910
Co. E-mail: actmedia@act.org
URL: http://www.actmedia.com
Released: 1981. **Description:** A series intended for computer buffs, offering them a better understanding of various computer terminologies and functions. Programs are available individually. **Availability:** VHS; 3/4U.

4748 ■ *The Computer Literacy Training Series*
American Media, Inc.
4621 121st St.
Urbandale, IA 50323-2311
Ph:(515)224-0919
Free: 888-776-8268
Fax:(515)327-2555
Co. E-mail: custsvc@ammedia.com
URL: http://www.ammedia.com
Released: 1990. **Price:** $495.00. **Description:** This video series explains most computer terminology and uses in a non-technical manner. **Availability:** VHS; 3/4U.

4749 ■ *The Computer Training Library*
School-Tech Inc.
745 State Cir.
PO Box 1941
Ann Arbor, MI 48106
Free: 800-521-2832
Fax:800-654-4321
Co. E-mail: service@school-tech.com
URL: http://www.schoolmasters.com
Released: 1991. **Price:** $24.95. **Description:** A series of video programs designed to orient the viewer to computer operations and provide tutoring in most popular applications software. Some are oriented to children, and all include a training manual. **Availability:** VHS.

4750 ■ *Computers: From Pebbles to Programs*
Center for Humanities, Inc./Guidance Associates
31 Pine View Rd.
Mount Kisco, NY 10549
Ph:(914)666-4100
Free: 800-431-1242
Fax:(914)666-5319
Co. E-mail: willg1961@gmail.com
URL: http://www.guidanceassociates.com
Released: 1975. **Description:** A look at computers-what they really are, how they were developed, and what they can do. **Availability:** VHS; 3/4U.

4751 ■ *A Crash Course on the Internet*
Tapeworm Video Distributors
25876 The Old Road 141
Stevenson Ranch, CA 91381
Ph:(661)257-4904
Fax:(661)257-4820
Co. E-mail: sales@tapeworm.com
URL: http://www.tapeworm.com
Price: $69.95. **Description:** Presents a thorough explanation of many facets of the Internet, including definitions, file transfers, and plug-in installations. **Availability:** VHS.

4752 ■ *How Computers Work: A Journey into the Walk-Through Computer*
Karol Media
Hanover Industrial Estates
375 Stewart Rd.
PO Box 7600
Wilkes Barre, PA 18773-7600
Ph:(570)822-8899
Free: 800-526-4773
Co. E-mail: sales@karolmedia.com
URL: http://www.karolmedia.com
Released: 1987. **Price:** $19.95. **Description:** A walking tour of the innards of a desktop computer 50 times normal size, to show how the various components work. **Availability:** VHS.

4753 ■ *Industrial Computer Control*
Williams Learning Network
15400 Calhoun Dr.
Rockville, MD 20855-2762
Fax:(301)315-6880
Co. E-mail: mait@willearn.com
URL: http://www.willearn.com
Description: Four-module, 42-section comprehensive industrial training program aimed at training industrial technicians to maintain state-of-the-art computer-based instrumentation and control equipment, including digital instrumentation, programmable controllers, distributed control systems, and other types of computer-controlled equipment. Comes with five student guides, five textbooks, and an instructor guide. **Availability:** VHS.

4754 ■ *The Information Machine*
Encyclopedia Britannica
331 N. LaSalle St.
Chicago, IL 60654
Ph:(312)347-7159
Free: 800-323-1229
Fax:(312)294-2104
URL: http://www.britannica.com
Released: 1973. **Description:** Using animation, ways in which man uses the computer to help define and solve problems are explored. From the Eames Film Collection. **Availability:** VHS; 3/4U.

4755 ■ *Instrument Technician Training Program (ITTP)*
Instrument Society of America
67 Alexander Dr.
Research Triangle Park, NC 27709
Ph:(919)549-8411
Fax:(919)549-8288
Co. E-mail: info@isa.org
URL: http://www.isa.org
Released: 1982. **Description:** Twenty-two modules provide basic information on the maintenance and repair of pneumatic instruments, electronic instruments, and microprocessors and digital systems. **Availability:** 3/4U; Special order formats.

4756 ■ *The New Literacy: An Introduction to Computers*
Annenberg Media
1301 Pennsylvania NW, 302
Washington, DC 20004
Ph:(202)783-0500
Free: 800-LEA-RNER
Fax:(202)783-0333
Co. E-mail: order@leanrer.org
URL: http://www.learner.org
Released: 1988. **Price:** $350.00. **Description:** Provides a comprehensive look at computers, data processing, terminology, computer applications, and computer environments. **Availability:** VHS; 3/4U.

4757 ■ *Personal Computer Training Series*
Learning Communications
5520 Trabuco Rd.
Irvine, CA 92620

Free: 800-622-3610
URL: http://www.learncom.com
Released: 1984. **Description:** This is a series consisting of video demonstrations and training for the personal computer and the most popular software programs. **Availability:** VHS; 3/4U.

4758 ■ *Shake Hands with Your Computer*
Educational Video Network
1401 19th St.
Huntsville, TX 77340
Ph:(936)295-5767
Free: 800-762-0060
Fax:(936)294-0233
URL: http://www.evndirect.com
Price: $59.95. **Description:** Teaches basic computer skills in layman's terms. **Availability:** VHS.

4759 ■ *Teaching Computer Literacy and Programming*
Alameda County Office of Education
Learning Resource Services
313 W. Winton Ave.
Hayward, CA 94544-1136
Ph:(510)887-0152
Fax:(510)670-4146
Co. E-mail: askacoe@acoe.org
URL: http://www.acoe.k12.ca.us/acoe/
Released: 1984. **Description:** This program develops a rationale for teaching computer literacy at any grade level, and suggests possible content and approaches. Part of the "Classroom Uses of Microcomputers" series. **Availability:** VHS; 3/4U.

4760 ■ *What Is a Computer?*
Encyclopedia Britannica
331 N. LaSalle St.
Chicago, IL 60654
Ph:(312)347-7159
Free: 800-323-1229
Fax:(312)294-2104
URL: http://www.britannica.com
Released: 1970. **Description:** Through the use of animation, this film dispels some of the mysteries about how a computer operates. **Availability:** VHS; 3/4U.

TRADE SHOWS AND CONVENTIONS

4761 ■ COMDEX
Ziff-Davis, Inc.
28 E. 28th St.
New York, NY 10016-7930
Ph:(212)503-3500
Co. E-mail: info@ziffdavis.com
URL: http://www.ziffdavis.com
Released: Annual. **Audience:** Volume resellers and value-adders of small computers and related items; only a virtual trade show since 2003. **Principal Exhibits:** Small computer systems, related peripherals, software, accessories, services, and supplies.

4762 ■ Michigan Association for Computer Users in Learning Conference
Michigan Association for Computer Users in Learning
3410 Belle Chase Way, Ste. 100
Holt, MI 48842-0518
Ph:(517)694-9756
Fax:(517)694-9773
Co. E-mail: macul@macul.org
URL: http://www.macul.org
Released: Annual. **Audience:** Educational technology professionals. **Principal Exhibits:** Computer and educational equipment, supplies, and services.

FRANCHISES AND BUSINESS OPPORTUNITIES

4763 ■ CMIT Solutions
500 N Capital of TX Highway, Bldg. 6, Ste. 200
Austin, TX 78744
Ph:(512)477-6667
Free: 800-710-2648
Fax:(512)692-3711
Co. E-mail: sara@cmit.biz
URL: http://www.cmitsolutions.com
No. of Franchise Units: 125. **Founded:** 1994. **Franchised:** 1998. **Description:** Offers IT service and computer support to small businesses. Franchise can be home-based, as we service the client at their place of business. **Equity Capital Needed:** $100,000-$125,000 total investment. **Franchise Fee:** $39,500. **Royalty Fee:** 6%. **Financial Assistance:** No. **Training:** Offers 1 week training.

4764 ■ Compuchild
Compuchild Services of America
1800 Halifax St.
Camel, IN 46032
Ph:(317)817-9817
Free: 800-619-5437
Fax:(317)818-8184
No. of Franchise Units: 69. **No. of Company-Owned Units:** 1. **Founded:** 1994. **Franchised:** 1995. **Description:** Computer education to children. **Equity Capital Needed:** $15,000. **Franchise Fee:** $12,500 or $17,500. **Financial Assistance:** No. **Training:** Yes.

4765 ■ Computer Explorers
ICED
PO Box 1511
Cypress, TX 77410
Free: 888-638-8722
Fax:(281)256-4178
Co. E-mail: ctsales@iced.net
URL: http://www.computerexplorers.com
No. of Franchise Units: 65. **Founded:** 1983. **Franchised:** 1988. **Description:** Turnkey educational technology franchise. Home office based business providing educational technology solutions for childcare centers, preschools, public and private schools, recreation and community centers. Provides trained technology resource teachers who plan and guide the lessons for students ages 3 to adult. Also offers training for professional development. No retail site is established. **Equity Capital Needed:** $30,000, minimum start-up cash required. **Franchise Fee:** $35,000. **Financial Assistance:** Yes. **Training:** Provides 2 week instruction at training facility in Texas and ongoing training and support.

4766 ■ Executrain Corporation
2500 Northwinds Pky., Ste. 460
Alpharetta, GA 30009
Ph:(770)667-7700
Free: 800-908-7246
Fax:(770)521-6084
No. of Franchise Units: 166. **Founded:** 1984. **Franchised:** 1986. **Description:** Specializes in the education of business professionals, teaching clients how to use popular business related software through hands-on classroom training. **Equity Capital Needed:** $500,000. **Franchise Fee:** Varies by territory. **Financial Assistance:** Yes. **Training:** Yes.

4767 ■ New Horizons Computer Learning Centers, Inc.
New Horizons Worldwide, Inc.
1900 S State College Blvd., Ste. 120
Anaheim, CA 92806
Ph:(714)940-8000
Fax:(714)938-6008
Co. E-mail: na.franchising@newhorizons.com
URL: http://www.newhorizons.com
No. of Franchise Units: 115. **No. of Company-Owned Units:** 25. **Founded:** 1982. **Franchised:** 1992. **Description:** Complete PC, Macintosh, Novell and Unix training company. Provides 1 and 2 day classes to businesses and individuals at the center or at the client's location. **Equity Capital Needed:** $370,000-$560,000. **Franchise Fee:** $25,00-$75,000. **Royalty Fee:** 6%. **Financial Assistance:** Third party financing available. **Training:** Training provided at corporate headquarters with ongoing support.

4768 ■ PC Kidz
PO Box 133002
Tyler, TX 75713
Free: 888-311-5259
Fax:(903)726-7014
No. of Franchise Units: 12. **No. of Company-Owned Units:** 3. **Founded:** 2001. **Franchised:** 2005. **Description:** Children's computer education. **Equity Capital Needed:** $19,800-$91,300. **Franchise Fee:** $15,000-$45,000. **Royalty Fee:** 7%. **Financial Assistance:** No. **Training:** Offers 4 days at headquarters, 3 days onsite, onsite at child care facilities (part of 4 days at HQ) with ongoing support.

COMPUTERIZED DATABASES

4769 ■ *Business Wire*
Berkshire Hathaway Inc.
44 Montgomery St., 39th Fl.
San Francisco, CA 94104
Ph:(415)986-4422
Free: 800-227-0845
Fax:(415)788-5335
Co. E-mail: SF_sales_group@bizwire.com
URL: http://www.businesswire.com
Description: Contains more than 1.4 million records that make up the complete text of press releases from public and private companies and other organizations, such as hospitals and universities. Covers new products, stock offerings, mergers, legal actions, financial information, personnel changes, and company announcements of general interest. Includes headline recaps hourly plus recaps of high tech headlines in some systems. Records include company name, headline, publication date, ticker symbol, byline; dateline, time, word count (usually less than 500), and text, including contact information. Covers industries such as banking, computers, telecommunications, entertainment, aviation, biotechnology, and mining; general news and features; some international events; and sports. **Availability:** Online: Thomson Reuters, Mzinga Inc., ProQuest LLC, Dow Jones & Company Inc., LexisNexis Group, Bloomberg LP. **Type:** Full text.

4770 ■ *Computer Database*
Cengage Learning Inc.
27500 Drake Rd.
Farmington Hills, MI 48331-3535
Ph:(248)699-4253
Free: 800-877-4253
Fax:(248)699-8069
Co. E-mail: galeord@gale.com
URL: http://gale.cengage.com
Description: Contains more than 1 million citations, abstracts, and full text to literature from some 800 trade journals, industry newsletters, and platform-specific publications covering the computer, telecommunications, and electronics industries. Topics covered include business and industry applications; computer graphics; consumer information; database management systems; hardware and software design, development, and reviews; peripherals; home computers; new products; performance evaluations; programming languages; operating systems; phototypesetting; and word processing. Includes descriptive and financial information for companies covered in the industry literature. **Availability:** Online: ProQuest LLC, ProQuest LLC, Cengage Learning Inc. **Type:** Bibliographic; Full text.

4771 ■ *Computer and Information Systems Abstracts*
ProQuest LLC
789 E Eisenhower Pky.
Ann Arbor, MI 48103
Ph:(734)761-4700
Fax:(734)997-4222
Co. E-mail: info@proquest.com
URL: http://www.csa.com
Description: Contains more than 740,000 citations, with abstracts, to the worldwide literature on theoretical and applied computer science. Sources include books, journals, conference proceedings, and government reports. Corresponds to *Computer and Information Systems Abstracts Journal*. **Availability:** Online: STN International, STN International. **Type:** Bibliographic.

4772 ■ *Computerworld*
International Data Group Inc.
One Exeter Plz., 15th Fl.
Boston, MA 02116
Ph:(617)534-1200
Co. E-mail: idgcorpcom@idg.com
URL: http://www.idg.com
Description: Contains the complete text of *Computerworld*, a newspaper on the computer industry. Covers personal computers, workstations, systems and software, systems management, and business news, including the computer market and industry trends. **Availability:** Online: LexisNexis Group, International Data Group Inc. **Type:** Full text.

4773 ■ *TecTrends*
Information Sources Inc.
PO Box 8120
Berkeley, CA 94707
Ph:(510)525-6220
Co. E-mail: tectrendsinfo@tectrends.com
URL: http://www.tectrends.com
Description: Contains information on the information technology industry, with detailed descriptions on more than 12,000 information technology products. Includes company information, including personnel names, addresses, telephone numbers, URLs, e-mails, and a description of the company. Product information includes system requirements, availability, vendor support, and a product description. These product and company descriptions are linked to independent third-party reviews abstracted from more than 200 trade journals and industry magazines. **Availability:** Online: Information Sources Inc., ProQuest LLC, ProQuest LLC. **Type:** Bibliographic; Directory.

RESEARCH CENTERS

4774 ■ Los Alamos National Laboratory–Advanced Computing Laboratory
TA-3, Bldg. SM-2011, Rm. 202
Los Alamos, NM 87545
Ph:(505)665-2000
Fax:(505)665-4939
URL: http://www.ccs.lanl.gov/ccs1/
Contact: Richard Graham, Actg.Gp.Ldr.
Scope: Computational science and technology, computer science, systems simulation, and mathematical analysis, focusing on parallel computers with teraflop computational rates, local and national networks operating at gigabit speeds, high-performance graphics workstations capable of 3-D color imaging, high-performance computing, distributed computing, and visualization. **Services:** Technology transfer agreements with universities, industry, vendors, and funding agencies. **Publications:** Journal of the Advanced Computer Laboratory. **Educational Activities:** Classes, workshops, and seminars, on high performance computing; Cyber security student program, in summer; Seminar series.

4775 ■ Massachusetts Institute of Technology–Center for Collective Intelligence
5 Cambridge Ctr., NE25-753
Sloan School of Management
Cambridge, MA 02142
Ph:(617)253-6843
Fax:(617)253-2242
Co. E-mail: rjl@mit.edu
URL: http://cci.mit.edu
Contact: Robert Laubacher
E-mail: rjl@mit.edu
Scope: How new communications technologies, especially the Internet, allow large numbers of people all over the world to work together in new ways. **Publications:** Working papers (occasionally). **Educational Activities:** Seminars and conferences.

4776 ■ Michigan State University–Software Engineering and Network Systems Laboratory
3115 Engineering Bldg.
East Lansing, MI 48224
Ph:(517)355-8344
Fax:(517)432-1061
Co. E-mail: chengb@cse.msu.edu
URL: http://www.cse.msu.edu/sens
Contact: Dr. Betty H.C. Cheng, Dir.
E-mail: chengb@cse.msu.edu
Scope: Methods for software systems development. **Educational Activities:** IEEE International Conference on Requirements Engineering; IEEE International Conference on Software Engineering; International Software Engineering Week; Workshop on Industrial Strength Formal Specification Techniques.

4777 ■ Rice University–Computer and Information Technology Institute
MS-39
PO Box 1892
Houston, TX 77251-1892
Ph:(713)348-5823
Fax:(866)596-1062
Co. E-mail: vardi@rice.edu
URL: http://www.k2i.rice.edu
Contact: Prof. Moshe Y. Vardi PhD, Dir.
E-mail: vardi@rice.edu
Scope: Parallel computation, performance of parallel and distributed architectures, advanced programming systems, distributed software systems, supercomputer compiler systems, computational mathematics, computational science, robotics, machine vision and image processing, motion planning and control, digital signal processing and communications, and cognitive science. Develops methods for the generation, transmission, storage, and processing of information. Activities emphasize parallel computation, including parallel computational architectures, software support for parallel programs, and parallel algorithms. Also studies the use of technologies for teaching and learning. **Services:** Electronic Software Distribution System, for access to public domain and licensable software. **Publications:** Technical reports. **Educational Activities:** Artificial Intelligence Symposium; Compaq/Rice High Performance Software Symposium; Graduate and undergraduate student training; Short courses and research symposia; U.S. Army Conference on Applied Statistics, on Applied Statistics.

4778 ■ University of Michigan–Collaboratory for Research on Electronic Work
School of Information North, Rm. 2226
1075 Beal Ave.
Ann Arbor, MI 48109-2112
Ph:(734)764-6131
Fax:(734)647-8045
Co. E-mail: finholt@umich.edu
URL: http://crew.umich.edu/
Contact: Thomas A. Finholt PhD, Dir.
E-mail: finholt@umich.edu
Scope: Focuses on the design of new organizations and the technology of voice, data and video communication that makes them possible. Research draws on computer, information, cognitive, and social science. **Publications:** Technical Report Series. **Educational Activities:** Seminars, colloquia, conferences, and workshops.

Computer Maintenance and Repair Service

ASSOCIATIONS AND OTHER ORGANIZATIONS

4779 ■ International Society of Certified Electronics Technicians
3608 Pershing Ave.
Fort Worth, TX 76107-4527
Ph:(817)921-9101
Free: 800-946-0201
Fax:(817)921-3741
Co. E-mail: info@iscet.org
URL: http://www.iscet.org
Contact: Mack Blakely, Exec. Dir.

Description: Technicians in 50 countries who have been certified by the society. Seeks to provide a fraternal bond among certified electronics technicians, raise their public image and improve the effectiveness of industry education programs for technicians. Offers training programs in new electronics information. Maintains library of service literature for consumer electronic equipment, including manuals and schematics for out-of-date equipment. Offers all FCC licenses. Sponsors testing program for certification of electronics technicians in the fields of audio, communications, computer, consumer, industrial, medical electronics, radar, radio-television and video. **Publications:** *ISCET Update* (quarterly).

4780 ■ National Electronics Service Dealers Association
3608 Pershing Ave.
Fort Worth, TX 76107-4527
Ph:(817)921-9061
Free: 800-797-9197
Fax:(817)921-3741
Co. E-mail: info@nesda.com
URL: http://www.nesda.com
Contact: Mack Blakely, Exec. Dir.

Description: Local and state electronic service associations and companies. Supplies technical service information on business management training to electronic service dealers. Offers certification and training programs through International Society of Certified Electronics Technicians. Conducts technical service and business management seminars. **Publications:** *ProService Directory and Yearbook* (annual).

EDUCATIONAL PROGRAMS

4781 ■ Penn Foster Career School
925 Oak St.
Scranton, PA 18515
Ph:(570)342-7701
Free: 800-233-4191
Fax:(570)343-0560
Co. E-mail: info@pennfoster.com
URL: http://www.educationdirect.com

Description: Home-study school offering a small business management program.

DIRECTORIES OF EDUCATIONAL PROGRAMS

4782 ■ *Directory of Private Accredited Career Schools and Colleges of Technology*
Pub: Accrediting Commission of Career Schools and Colleges of Technology
Contact: Michale S. McComis, Exec. Dir.

Released: On web page. **Price:** Free. **Description:** Covers 3900 accredited post-secondary programs that provide training programs in business, trade, and technical fields, including various small business endeavors. Entries offer school name, address, phone, description of courses, job placement assistance, and requirements for admission. Arrangement is alphabetical.

REFERENCE WORKS

4783 ■ *Cisco Network Design Solutions for Small-Medium Businesses*
Pub: Cisco Press

Ed: Peter Rybaczyk. **Released:** August 2004. **Price:** $55.00. **Description:** Solutions for computer networking professionals using computer networks within a small to medium-sized business. Topics cover not only core networking issues and solutions, but security, IP telephony, unified communications, customer relations management, wireless LANs, and more.

4784 ■ "CMS Products and Avecto Team for Business Security Product Solutions" in *Wireless News* (November 11, 2009)
Pub: Close-Up Media

Description: CMS Products, a provider of data security, backup, content management and disaster recovery, has agreed on a strategic partnership with Avect, a provider in least privilege management. The partnership will allow the companies to bundle their products.

4785 ■ "iMozi Integrates Esprida LiveControl for Advanced DVD Kiosk Hardware" in *Wireless News* (December 20, 2010)
Pub: Close-Up Media Inc.

Description: Provider of self-service entertainment technology, iMozi Canada has partnered with Esprida to make its automated DVD Kiosk solutions Esprida-enabled. Esprida develops remote device management solutions and will offer enhanced capabilities and to improve customer experience for users.

4786 ■ "PCI Express Powers Machine Vision" in *Canadian Electronics* (Vol. 23, February 2008, No. 1, pp. 8)
Pub: CLB Media Inc.

Ed: Inder Kohli. **Description:** PCI Express is an innovative peripheral bus that can be used in industrial computing. The peripheral bus delivers a high-bandwidth, scaleable, point-to-point path from peripheral cards to the computing core. Features and functions of PCI Express are described in detail.

4787 ■ *Power Up Your Small-Medium Business: A Guide to Enabling Network Technologies*
Pub: Cisco Press

Ed: Robyn Aber. **Released:** March 2004. **Price:** $39.95 (US), $57.95 (Canadian). **Description:** Network technologies geared to small and medium-size business, focusing on access, IP telephony, wireless technologies, security, and computer network management.

TRADE PERIODICALS

4788 ■ *Association for Computing Machinery*
Pub: Special Interest Group on Data Communication

Ed: Martha Steenstrup, Editor. **Released:** Quarterly. **Price:** $50. **Description:** Serves as a forum for computing professionals in the data communications field. Focuses on network architecture, including the Internet, network protocols, and distributed systems.

4789 ■ *Electronic Products*
Pub: Hearst Business Communications/Electronics Group
Contact: Bryan DeLuca, Managing Editor
E-mail: bdeluca@hearst.com

Ed: Christina Nickolas, Editor, cnickolas@hearst.com. **Released:** Monthly. **Price:** $12. **Description:** Magazine for electronic design engineers and management.

4790 ■ *The High-Tech News*
Pub: ETA International

Ed: Bryan Allen, Editor, bryan@eta-i.org. **Released:** Monthly. **Price:** Included in membership. **Description:** Serves member technicians with news of the Association and the electronics industry, including items on service, education, employment, management, and events. Contains information on membership, management, telecommunications, and business and technical training programs. Recurring features include editorials, news of research, letters to the editor, book reviews, and a calendar of events.

4791 ■ *Microprocessor Report*
Pub: MicroDesign Resources
Contact: Max Baron
E-mail: mbaron@mdr.cahners.com

Released: 17x/yr. **Price:** $695, U.S. and Canada for print version; $495, U.S. and Canada pounds; $995, U.S. and Canada for print and online version; $995, elsewhere for print version. **Description:** The leading technical publication for the microprocessor industry. Dedicated to providing unbiased, in-depth, critical analysis of new high-performance microprocessor developments. This newsletter is exclusively subscriber-supported.

VIDEOCASSETTES/ AUDIOCASSETTES

4792 ■ *Apple II Repair, Maintenance and Expansion*
Bergwall Productions, Inc.
1 DIckinson Drive, Brandywine BUilding 5, Ste. 105
PO Box 1481
Chadds Ford, PA 19317

Ph:(610)361-0334
Free: 800-934-8696
Fax:(610)361-0092
URL: http://www.bergwall.com
Released: 1987. **Price:** $249.00. **Description:** Many different repair techniques and applications for the Apple II are explored. **Availability:** VHS.

4793 ■ *Troubleshooting the IBM PC*
Bergwall Productions, Inc.
1 DIckinson Drive, Brandywine BUilding 5, Ste. 105
PO Box 1481
Chadds Ford, PA 19317
Ph:(610)361-0334
Free: 800-934-8696
Fax:(610)361-0092
URL: http://www.bergwall.com
Released: 1987. **Price:** $269.00. **Description:** Complete guide to isolating and repairing the problems of an IBM PC. **Availability:** VHS.

4794 ■ *Troubleshooting the IBM PC II*
Bergwall Productions, Inc.
1 DIckinson Drive, Brandywine BUilding 5, Ste. 105
PO Box 1481
Chadds Ford, PA 19317
Ph:(610)361-0334
Free: 800-934-8696
Fax:(610)361-0092
URL: http://www.bergwall.com
Released: 1987. **Price:** $359.00. **Description:** More information on IBM PC problems and solutions is given. **Availability:** VHS.

TRADE SHOWS AND CONVENTIONS

4795 ■ COMDEX
Ziff-Davis, Inc.
28 E. 28th St.
New York, NY 10016-7930
Ph:(212)503-3500
Co. E-mail: info@ziffdavis.com
URL: http://www.ziffdavis.com
Released: Annual. **Audience:** Volume resellers and value-adders of small computers and related items; only a virtual trade show since 2003. **Principal Exhibits:** Small computer systems, related peripherals, software, accessories, services, and supplies.

FRANCHISES AND BUSINESS OPPORTUNITIES

4796 ■ Cm It Solutions (TM)
500 N Capital of TX Hwy., Bldg. 6, Ste. 200
Austin, TX 78746
Ph:(512)477-6667
Free: 800-710-2648
Fax:(512)692-3711
Co. E-mail: franchise@computermoms.com
URL: http://www.computermoms.com
No. of Franchise Units: 125. **Founded:** 1994. **Franchised:** 1998. **Description:** Computer support services: system maintenance, problem resolution, upgrades, network design, and training needs to business to business owners and professionals. **Equity Capital Needed:** $100,000-$125,000. **Franchise Fee:** $44,950 + terr. fee. **Financial Assistance:** No. **Managerial Assistance:** Offers sales, marketing, business management and team building. **Training:** Training includes 2 weeks at corporate office, business coaching, support website and telephone line, email exchange, newsgroups, meetings and conferences.

4797 ■ Computer Medics of America, Inc.
2260 N Green Forest Dr.
Palmer, AK 99645
Ph:(907)694-0371
Fax:800-665-8568
Co. E-mail: marketing@computermedicsofamerica.com
URL: http://www.computermedicsofamerica.com
No. of Franchise Units: 58. **No. of Company-Owned Units:** 3. **Founded:** 2000. **Franchised:** 2003. **Description:** Mobile repair computer services. **Equity Capital Needed:** $10,300-$60,000. **Franchise Fee:** $5,000-$20,000. **Financial Assistance:** Limited in-house financing available. **Training:** Includes 1 week training at headquarters and ongoing support.

4798 ■ Computer Troubleshooters
Computer Troubleshooters USA, Inc.
2296 Henderson Mill Rd. NE, Ste. 405
Atlanta, GA 30345
Free: 877-704-1702
Fax:(770)234-6162
Co. E-mail: info@comptroub.com
URL: http://www.comptroub.com
No. of Franchise Units: 460. **No. of Company-Owned Units:** 1. **Founded:** 1997. **Franchised:** 1997. **Description:** Onsite computer service franchise, with over 340 locations in 18 countries. Provide IT services to small businesses and residential users in their area. **Equity Capital Needed:** $29,000 estimated start-up costs. **Franchise Fee:** $14,500. **Financial Assistance:** Provide documentation to assist with SBA and other external financing. **Training:** 3 day training course on business operations and marketing, followed with ongoing support through newsletters, manuals, our intranet, annual conferences, regional meetings, and a 24/7 technical support hotline.

4799 ■ Concerto Networks
9808 Waples St.
San Diego, CA 92121
Ph:(858)875-5189
Free: (866)551-4007
No. of Franchise Units: 38. **Founded:** 2002. **Franchised:** 2003. **Description:** Onsite Simple Office Solutions. **Equity Capital Needed:** $12,500. **Franchise Fee:** $1,250-$12,500. **Royalty Fee:** $199/month. **Financial Assistance:** No. **Training:** Yes.

4800 ■ Data Doctors
2090 E University, Ste. 101
Tempe, AZ 85281
Ph:(480)921-2444
Fax:(480)921-2975
No. of Franchise Units: 69. **No. of Company-Owned Units:** 4. **Founded:** 1988. **Franchised:** 2002. **Description:** Computer sales & services, including web services. **Equity Capital Needed:** $83,400-$114,700. **Franchise Fee:** $35,000. **Royalty Fee:** 5%. **Financial Assistance:** Third party financing available. **Training:** Training at headquarters and onsite varies with video & Internet training ongoing.

4801 ■ Debugit Computer Services
922 Rte. 70, W
Marlton, NJ 08053
Ph:(856)489-9704
No. of Company-Owned Units: 1. **Founded:** 2000. **Franchised:** 2005. **Description:** Computer maintenance services. **Equity Capital Needed:** $127,000-$163,500. **Franchise Fee:** $30,000. **Royalty Fee:** 7%. **Financial Assistance:** Third party financing available. **Training:** 5 days at headquarters, 3 days at franchisee's location and ongoing.

4802 ■ Expetec Technology Services
Expetec Corp.
12 2nd Ave., SW
Aberdeen, SD 57401
Free: 888-209-2292
Fax:(605)225-5176
Co. E-mail: sales@cdfs.com
URL: http://www.expetec.biz
No. of Franchise Units: 40. **No. of Company-Owned Units:** 1. **Founded:** 1992. **Franchised:** 1996. **Description:** Provides computer repair and technology services. **Equity Capital Needed:** $82,000-$121,000. **Franchise Fee:** $45,000. **Financial Assistance:** Yes. **Training:** Provides training on franchise management, customer service, marketing & advertising.

4803 ■ Fast-teks Onsite Computer Serviced
15310 Amberly Dr., Ste. 185
Tampa, FL 33647
Free: 800-262-1671
Fax:(813)932-2485
No. of Franchise Units: 266. **Founded:** 2003. **Franchised:** 2004. **Description:** Onsite computer repair services. **Equity Capital Needed:** $34,650-$60,600. **Franchise Fee:** $19,750-$42,250. **Royalty Fee:** 7%. **Financial Assistance:** Yes. **Training:** Offers 2 days training at headquarters and 2 days onsite with ongoing support provided.

4804 ■ Friendly Computers
Big L's, Inc.
3616 North Rancho
Las Vegas, NV 89130
Ph:(702)458-2780
Free: 800-656-3115
Fax:(702)869-2780
URL: http://www.friendlycomputers.com/franchise
No. of Franchise Units: 70. **Founded:** 1992. **Franchised:** 2000. **Description:** Onsite service and sales of computers to homes and businesses within a given territory. **Equity Capital Needed:** Home based $46,750-$75,250; Retail $128,010-$179,000. **Franchise Fee:** $15,000-$25,000. **Financial Assistance:** Yes. **Training:** 1 Week training at Corporate Store and an additional week of training at franchisees location. .

4805 ■ Geeks On The Way
1223 Macleod Tr., SE
Calgary, AB, Canada L6T 4Z2
Ph:(403)283-3316
Fax:(403)206-7270
Co. E-mail: franchise@geeksontheway.com
URL: http://www.geeksontheway.com
No. of Company-Owned Units: 4. **Founded:** 2001. **Franchised:** 2006. **Description:** Provides quality computer support from removing viruses and spy ware to diagnosing and replacing defective hardware to maintaining corporate networks. **Equity Capital Needed:** $43,400. **Franchise Fee:** $15,000. **Training:** Provides 2 weeks then weekly consultations for one year.

4806 ■ Nerd Force
97 New Drop Plz.
Staten Island, NY 10306
Free: 800-979-6373
Fax:(718)370-6731
No. of Franchise Units: 24. **No. of Company-Owned Units:** 3. **Founded:** 2003. **Franchised:** 2007. **Description:** Onsite tech support services. **Equity Capital Needed:** $34,100-$59,000. **Franchise Fee:** $14,000. **Royalty Fee:** $100/week. **Financial Assistance:** Assistance with franchise fee. **Training:** Provides 1 week at headquarters, 1 week at franchisee's location and ongoing support.

4807 ■ Teamlogic IT
Franchise Services, Inc.
26722 Plaza Dr.
Mission Viejo, CA 92691
Ph:(949)582-6300
Free: (866)TEA-MLOG
Fax:(949)582-6301
Co. E-mail: franchise.sales@teamlogicIT.com
URL: http://www.teamlogicIT.com
No. of Franchise Units: 46. **Founded:** 2004. **Franchised:** 2005. **Description:** Offers computer consultation, maintenance & repair service to small & mid-sized businesses. **Equity Capital Needed:** $120,000 total investment. **Franchise Fee:** $35,000. **Financial Assistance:** Third party financial available. **Training:** Provides a 5 day business building training program.

LIBRARIES

4808 ■ DeVry University–James E. Lovan Library
11224 Holmes Rd.
Kansas City, MO 64131
Ph:(816)941-0430, x5220
Fax:(816)941-0896
Co. E-mail: bcaldarello@devry.edu
URL: http://www.kc.devry.edu/Library.html
Contact: Beth Caldarello, Dir. of Lib.Svcs.
Scope: Electronics, computer information systems, business, accounting, telecommunications. **Services:** Center open to the public for reference use only. **Holdings:** 15,500 books; 450 videos; 750 CD-ROMs. **Subscriptions:** 1500 journals and other serials.

4809 ■ DeVry University, Chicago Campus Library
3300 N. Campbell Ave.
Chicago, IL 60618
Ph:(773)929-8500
Fax:(773)697-2714
Co. E-mail: ccarter@devry.edu
URL: http://www.chi.devry.edu/Library.html
Contact: Catherine J. Carter, PhD, Lib.Dir.
Scope: Business, electronics, computer science, telecommunications. **Services:** Interlibrary loan; Center open to the public for reference use only. **Holdings:** 20,000 volumes. **Subscriptions:** 70 journals and other serials.

4810 ■ DeVry University, Columbus Campus Library
1350 Alum Creek Dr.
Columbus, OH 43209-2705
Ph:(614)253-7291
Free: 800-426-2206
Fax:(614)252-4108
Co. E-mail: bweaver@devry.edu
URL: http://www.cols.devry.edu/library.html
Contact: Bruce Weaver, Dir.
Scope: Electronics technology, computer science, business operations, accounting. **Holdings:** 23,000 volumes. **Subscriptions:** 50 journals and other serials.

4811 ■ DeVry University Library Services
4800 Regent Blvd.
Irving, TX 75063-2440
Ph:(972)929-9347
Fax:(972)929-6778
Co. E-mail: gferdman@devry.edu
URL: http://www.dal.devry.edu/Library.html
Contact: Glenn Ferdman, Univ.Libn.
Scope: Electronics, computer science, electronic engineering, business information, telecommunications, accounting, information technology, electrical engineering. **Services:** Copying; information services for handicapped; Center open to the public for reference use only. **Holdings:** 15,300 books; 875 videotapes; computer software. **Subscriptions:** 57 journals and other serials.

4812 ■ IBM Corporation–Burlington Technical Library
967-B, 1000 River St.
Essex Junction, VT 05452-4299
Ph:(802)769-6519
Fax:(802)769-6501
Co. E-mail: karenlyn@us.ibm.com
URL: http://www.ibm.com/us/en/
Contact: Karen Kromer Lynch, Tech.Lib.Mgr.
Scope: Semiconductor manufacturing, chemistry, computing, solid-state electronics, physics, business and professional, project management, programming, management science, mathematics. **Services:** Interlibrary loan; Center not open to the public. **Holdings:** 10,000 books; 100 reels of microfilm. **Subscriptions:** 160 journals and other serials.

4813 ■ Walt Disney World–Global Business Technology Strategy Library
Team Disney 336-N
1375 Buena Vista Dr.
PO Box 10000
Lake Buena Vista, FL 32830-1000
Ph:(407)828-4250
Co. E-mail: david.w.hartman@disney.com
URL: http://disneyworld.disney.go.com/wdw
Contact: David Hartman, Libn.
Scope: Computer science, human resources, general business. **Services:** Center not open to the public. **Holdings:** 4000 books, videos, DVDs, and CDs; 100 AV equipment. **Subscriptions:** 200 journals and other serials; 3 newspapers.

START-UP INFORMATION

4814 ■ "Probability Processing Chip: Lyric Semiconductor" in *Inc.* (Volume 32, December 2010, No. 10, pp. 52)
Pub: Inc. Magazine
Ed: Christine Lagorio. **Description:** Lyric Semiconductor, a start up located in Cambridge, Massachusetts, has developed a computer chip that also uses values that fall between zero and one, resulting in a chip that can process information using probabilities, considering many possible answers that find the best fit.

ASSOCIATIONS AND OTHER ORGANIZATIONS

4815 ■ Association for Women in Computing
PO Box 2768
Oakland, CA 94602
Co. E-mail: info@awc-hq.org
URL: http://www.awc-hq.org
Contact: Jill Sweeney, Pres.
Description: Individuals interested in promoting the education, professional development, and advancement of women in computing. **Publications:** Membership Directory (annual).

4816 ■ Black Data Processing Associates
9500 Arena Dr., Ste. 350
Largo, MD 20774
Ph:(301)584-3135
Free: 800-727-BDPA
Fax:(301)560-8300
Co. E-mail: office@bdpa.org
URL: http://www.bdpa.org
Contact: Yvette Graham, Natl. Pres.
Description: Represents persons employed in the information processing industry, including electronic data processing, electronic word processing and data communications; others interested in information processing. Seeks to accumulate and share information processing knowledge and business expertise to increase the career and business potential of minorities in the information processing field. Conducts professional seminars, workshops, tutoring services and community introductions to data processing. Makes annual donation to the United Negro College Fund. .

4817 ■ Blissymbolics Communication International
1630 Lawrence Ave. W, Ste. 104
Toronto, ON, Canada M6L 1C5
Ph:(416)644-8291
Fax:(416)244-6543
Co. E-mail: bci@blissymbolics.org
URL: http://www.blissymbolics.org
Contact: Mats Lundalv, Pres.
Description: Promotes appropriate use of Blissymbol applications in software, publications, and educational materials. Conducts research and educational programs.

4818 ■ British Columbia Technology Industries Association
1188 W Georgia St., Ste. 900
Vancouver, BC, Canada V6E 4A2
Ph:(604)683-6159
Fax:(604)683-3879
Co. E-mail: info@bctia.org
URL: http://www.bctia.org
Contact: Bill Tam, Pres./CEO
Description: Fosters the growth and development of the Province's technology industries and member companies. Provides programs, services and activities designed to meet the needs and interests of members in the areas of networking, education, public awareness, and government relations. Offers a forum for members to review industry issues, acquire new business knowledge from leading industry professionals, to supply input on existing and proposed legislation and generally work together to advance the industry's interests. **Publications:** *Impact* (annual).

4819 ■ Canadian Image Processing and Pattern Recognition Society–Association Canadienne de Traitement d'Images et de Reconnaissance des Formes
University of Western Ontario
Middlesex College 379
Dept. of Computer Science
London, ON, Canada N6A 5B7
Ph:(519)661-2111
Fax:(519)661-3515
Co. E-mail: cipprs@csd.uwo.ca
URL: http://www.gel.ulaval.ca
Contact: Prof. John Barron, Treas.
Description: Strives to advance the theory and practice of signal and image processing for pattern analysis and classification, scene or speech understanding and recognition, computer vision, on-line and off-line document analysis and recognition, robotic perception, intelligent autonomous systems, biomedical imaging, neural networks and modeling, remote sensing, specialized architecture and industrial applications. **Publications:** *Vision Interface* .

4820 ■ Institute for Certification of Computing Professionals
2400 E Devon Ave., Ste. 281
Des Plaines, IL 60018-4610
Ph:(847)299-4227
Free: 800-843-8227
Fax:(847)299-4280
Co. E-mail: office2@iccp.org
URL: http://www.iccp.org
Contact: John Whitehouse, Dir. of Certification
Description: Professional societies. Promotes the development of computer examinations which are of high quality, directed toward information technology professionals, and designed to encourage competence and professionalism. Individuals passing the exams automatically become members of the Institute for Certification of Computing Professionals and become certified as CCP or ACP. Has developed code of ethics and good practice to which those taking the exams promise to adhere. Maintains speakers' bureau; compiles statistics. **Publications:** *Certified Business Intelligence Professional*; *ICCP Complete Guide to Professional Computing*; *ICCP Examinations Review Manual for Conference Exam-Cram Sessions*; *Official Exam Review Outline* .

4821 ■ I.T. Financial Management Association
PO Box 30188
Santa Barbara, CA 93130
Ph:(805)687-7390
Fax:(805)687-7382
Co. E-mail: info@itfma.com
URL: http://www.itfma.com
Contact: Terence Quinlan, Dir.
Description: Individuals and corporations interested in the financial management of information technology (IT) organizations. Works for the education and improvement of members and the industry. Offers certification in IT financial management. Conducts peer studies, in-house seminars, and chargeback system reviews. Operates educational programs. .

4822 ■ TechServe Alliance
1420 King St., Ste. 610
Alexandria, VA 22314
Ph:(703)838-2050
Fax:(703)838-3610
Co. E-mail: staff@techservealliance.org
URL: http://www.techservealliance.org
Contact: Mark Roberts, CEO
Description: Businesses that provide the services of highly technical professionals, such as computer programmers, systems analysts, engineers, to clients in need of temporary technical support. Promotes legal and economic environment favorable to the technical services industry, including protection of a firm's freedom to choose either employees or independent contractors when supplying services to clients. Encourages professional standards in the industry; serves as a support mechanism for members. Provides industry-specific educational information and insurance discounts. **Publications:** *Directory of Members Firms* (periodic); *NACCB Monitor* (quarterly); *NACCB Newsletter* (quarterly).

DIRECTORIES OF EDUCATIONAL PROGRAMS

4823 ■ *Directory of Private Accredited Career Schools and Colleges of Technology*
Pub: Accrediting Commission of Career Schools and Colleges of Technology
Contact: Michale S. McComis, Exec. Dir.
Released: On web page. **Price:** Free. **Description:** Covers 3900 accredited post-secondary programs that provide training programs in business, trade, and technical fields, including various small business endeavors. Entries offer school name, address, phone, description of courses, job placement assistance, and requirements for admission. Arrangement is alphabetical.

REFERENCE WORKS

4824 ■ "AMT's Partner Program Enables New Security Business Models" in *Internet Wire* (August 12, 2010)
Pub: Comtex
Description: AMT, technical provider of physical access control Software as a Service (Saas) solutions, has developed a new Partner Program that allows partners to outsource any technical abilities lacking to AMT with no upfront fees.

4825 ■ "Auctions and Bidding: a Guide for Computer Scientists" in *ACM Computing Surveys* (Vol. 43, Summer 2011, No. 2, pp. 10)
Pub: Association for Computing Machinery
Ed: Simon Parsons, Juan A. Rodriguez-Aguilar, Mark Klein. **Description:** There are various actions: single dimensional, multi-dimensional, single-sided, double-sided, first-price, second-price, English, Dutch, Japanese, sealed-bid, and these have been extensively discussed and analyzed in economics literature. This literature is surveyed from a computer science perspective, primarily from the viewpoint of computer scientists who are interested in learning about auction theory, and to provide pointers into the economics literature for those who want a deeper technical understanding. In addition, since auctions are an increasingly important topic in computer science, the article also looks at work on auctions from the computer science literature. The aim is to identify what both bodies of work tell us about creating electronic auctions.

4826 ■ "Beam My Data Up" in *Canadian Business* (Vol. 80, February 12, 2007, No. 4, pp. 42)
Pub: Rogers Media
Ed: Marlene Rego. **Description:** Innovations in the field of teleportation since its invention by Gilles Brassard in 1992 is discussed.

4827 ■ "Burton Group Answers Industry Need for Practical Data Center Advice" in *Canadian Corporate News* (May 14, 2007)
Pub: Comtex News Network Inc.
Description: Burton Group, an IT research firm focused on in-depth technical analysis of enterprise IT infrastructures, launched a new service providing practical advice for IT professionals facing critical data center decisions which due to technological advances can be more efficient while reducing costs.

4828 ■ "ChemSW Software Development Services Available for Outsourcing" in *Information Today* (Vol. 26, February 2009, No. 2, pp. 30)
Pub: Information Today, Inc.
Description: ChemSW software development services include requirements analysis, specification development, design, development, testing, and system documentation as an IT outsourcing solution. The company can also develop software tracking systems for satellite stockrooms, provide asset management integration solutions and more.

4829 ■ *Cisco Network Design Solutions for Small-Medium Businesses*
Pub: Cisco Press
Ed: Peter Rybaczyk. **Released:** August 2004. **Price:** $55.00. **Description:** Solutions for computer networking professionals using computer networks within a small to medium-sized business. Topics cover not only core networking issues and solutions, but security, IP telephony, unified communications, customer relations management, wireless LANs, and more.

4830 ■ "Cloudy Future for VMware?" in *Barron's* (Vol. 90, September 13, 2010, No. 37, pp. 21)
Pub: Barron's Editorial & Corporate Headquarters
Ed: Jonathan R. Laing. **Description:** VMWare dominated the virtualization market for years, but it may be ending as it faces more competition from rivals that offer cloud computing services. The company's stocks are also expensive and are vulnerable to the smallest mishap.

4831 ■ "Consumer Trust in E-Commerce Web Sites: a Meta-Study" in *ACM Computing Surveys* (Vol. 43, Fall 2011, No. 3, pp. 14)
Pub: Association for Computing Machinery
Ed: Patricia Beatty, Ian Reay, Scott Dick, James Miller. **Description:** Trust is at once an elusive, imprecise concept, and a critical attribute that must be engineered into e-commerce systems. Engineering trust is examined.

4832 ■ "Data Center Plan Bearing Fruit From Apple, Spec Center" in *Charlotte Business Journal* (Vol. 25, October 15, 2010, No. 30, pp. 1)
Pub: Charlotte Business Journal
Ed: Ken Elkins. **Description:** Apple Inc. is planning to expand its server farm at the North Carolina Data Center Corridor in Catawba County. T5 Partners, on the other hand, will build a shell building to house a server on the site. Infocrossing Inc. will also build an open data center in the area.

4833 ■ "Data Firm Growth 'Opportunistic'" in *Tampa Bay Business Journal* (Vol. 30, January 29, 2010, No. 6, pp. 1)
Pub: American City Business Journals
Ed: Michael Hinman. **Description:** E Solutions Corporation is experiencing growth amid the economic downturn, with its Park Tower data center occupancy in Tampa Florida expanding from 14,000 square feet to 20,000 square feet. Details on the increased operations fueled by demand for information storage and management services offered by the company are discussed.

4834 ■ "Discrete Wavelet Transform-Based Time Series Analysis and Mining" in *ACM Computing Surveys* (Vol. 43, Summer 2011, No. 2, pp. 6)
Pub: Association for Computing Machinery
Ed: Pimwadee Chaovalit, Aryya Gangopadhyay, George Karabatis, Zhiyuan Chen. **Description:** Time series are recorded values of an interesting phenomenon such as stock prices, household items, or patient heart rates over a period of time. Time series data mining focuses on discovering interesting patterns in such data. An introduction to a wavelet-based times series data analysis is provided with a systematic survey of various analysis techniques that use discrete wavelet transformation (DWT) in time series data mining, and outlines the benefits of this approach demonstrated by previous studies performed on diverse application domains, including image classification, multimedia retrieval, and computer network anomaly detection.

4835 ■ "Experts Take the Temp of Obama Plan" in *The Business Journal-Serving Metropolitan Kansas City* (Vol. 27, November 14, 2008, No. 10)
Pub: American City Business Journals, Inc.
Ed: Rob Roberts. **Description:** Kansas City, Missouri-based employee benefits experts say president-elect Barack Obama's health care reform plan is on track. Insurance for children and capitalization for health information technology are seen as priority areas. The plan is aimed at reducing the number of uninsured people in the United States.

4836 ■ "The Failure Detector Abstraction" in *ACM Computing Surveys* (Vol. 43, Summer 2011, No. 2, pp. 9)
Pub: Association for Computing Machinery
Ed: Felix C. Freiling, Rachid Guerraoui, Petr Kuznetsov. **Description:** A failure detector is a fundamental abstraction in distributed computing. This article surveys this abstraction through two dimensions. First it studies failure detectors as building blocks to simplify the design of reliable distributed algorithms, particularly how failure detectors can factor out timing assumptions to detect failures in distributed agreement algorithms. Second, failure detectors as computability benchmarks are studied. Some limitations of the failure detector abstraction along each of the dimensions is also highlighted.

4837 ■ *Faulkner Information Services*
Pub: Faulkner Information Services
Released: Monthly, Updates; base volumes available with subscription. **Description:** The "Faulkner FACCTs" series includes separate reference services for many areas of data processing, communications, and related fields (the full information service is available as well). Titles include: "Enterprise Computing"; "Enterprise Communications"; "Local Area Networks"; "Telecommunications"; "Converging Communications Technologies"; "Large and Midrange Systems and Software"; "Micro Systems and Software"; "The Internet"; "Wireless Communications" **Entries Include:** All reports contain company name, address, phone, fax, URL if available, and product list or description. Some reports also contain sales reports, financial data, products carried or distributed, and/or distribution statistics. Some comprise technology overviews or "how-to" guides.

4838 ■ *Graduate Assistantship Directory in Computing*
Pub: Association for Computing Machinery
Contact: Mark Mandelbaum
Entries Include: Institution name, address, name and title of contact, degrees offered, area of expertise, financial aid offered, stipend amount, department facilities (hardware and software), school enrollment, required exams, admission deadlines. **Database Covers:** Fellowships and assistantships in the computer sciences offered at U.S. and Canadian educational institutions. **Arrangement:** Geographical.

4839 ■ "Health IT Regulations Generate Static Among Providers" in *Philadelphia Business Journal* (Vol. 28, January 29, 2010, No. 50, pp. 1)
Pub: American City Business Journals
Ed: John George. **Description:** US Centers for Medicaid and Medicare Services and the Office of the National Coordinator for Health Information Technology have proposed rules regarding the meaningful use of electronic health records. The rules must be complied with by hospitals and physicians to qualify for federal stimulus funds.

4840 ■ "Help Wanted: 100 Hospitals IT Workers" in *Business Courier* (Vol. 27, October 8, 2010, No. 23, pp. 1)
Pub: Business Courier
Ed: James Ritchie. **Description:** Hospitals in the Greater Cincinnati area are expected to hire more than 100 information technology (IT) workers to help digitize medical records. Financial incentives from the health care reform bill encouraged investments in electronic medical record systems, increasing the demand for IT workers that would help make information exchange across the healthcare system easier.

4841 ■ "Human Activity Analysis: a Review" in *ACM Computing Surveys* (Vol. 43, Fall 2011, No. 3, pp. 16)
Pub: Association for Computing Machinery
Ed: J.K. Aggarwal, M.S. Ryoo. **Description:** Human activity recognition is an important area of computer vision research and is studied in this report.

4842 ■ "Identity Crisis: The Battle For Your Data" in *Canadian Business* (Vol. 81, March 17, 2008, No. 4, pp. 12)
Pub: Rogers Media
Description: Nigel Brown explains that businesses must protect their data through encryption and tightening up access to data. Brown also points out that banks and merchants bear most of the costs for identity fraud and leaves individuals with a lot of pain and heartache in clearing their name.

4843 ■ "Image Conscious" in *Canadian Business* (Vol. 81, March 17, 2008, No. 4, pp. 36)
Pub: Rogers Media
Ed: Andrew Wahl. **Description:** Idee Inc. is testing an Internet search engine for images that does not rely on tags but compares its visual data to a database of other images. The company was founded and managed by Leila Boujnane as an off-shoot of their risk-management software firm. Their software has already been used by image companies to track copyrighted images and to find images within their own archives.

4844 ■ "iMozi Integrates Esprida LiveControl for Advanced DVD Kiosk Hardware" in *Wireless News* (December 20, 2010)
Pub: Close-Up Media Inc.
Description: Provider of self-service entertainment technology, iMozi Canada has partnered with Esprida to make its automated DVD Kiosk solutions Esprida-enabled. Esprida develops remote device management solutions and will offer enhanced capabilities and to improve customer experience for users.

4845 ■ "Implementing Statically Typed Object-Oriented Programming Languages" in *ACM Computing Surveys* (Vol. 43, Fall 2011, No. 3, pp. 18)
Pub: Association for Computing Machinery
Ed: Roland Ducournau. **Description:** Object-oriented programming represents an original implementation issue due to its philosophy of making the program behavior depend on the dynamic type of objects. A review of the various implementation techniques available in static typing and in the three cases of single inheritance, multiple inheritance, and multiple subtyping are reviewed.

4846 ■ "In the Mobikey of Life" in *Canadian Business* (Vol. 81, July 21, 2008, No. 11, pp. 42)
Pub: Rogers Media Ltd.
Ed: John Gray. **Description:** Toronto-based Route1 has created a data security software system that allows employees to access files and programs stored in the head office without permanently transferring data to the actual computer being used. Mobikey technology is useful in protecting laptops of chief executive officers, which contain confidential financial and customer data.

4847 ■ "Lighter Than Air" in *Game Developer* (Vol. 18, November 1, 2011, No. 10, pp. 38)
Pub: Think Services
Ed: Andy Firth. **Description:** Floating point performance tips and tricks are outlined. Floating point allows freedom of representation when implementing algorithms and is both intuitive to set up and simple to work with; hardware is also improved so that it is faster to use floating point math as opposed to integer in many environments.

4848 ■ "Machine Transliteration Survey" in *ACM Computing Surveys* (Vol. 43, Fall 2011, No. 3, pp. 17)
Pub: Association for Computing Machinery
Ed: Sarvnaz Karimi, Falk Scholer, Andrew Turpin. **Description:** Machine transliteration is the process of automatically transforming the script of a word from a source language to a target language, while preserving pronunciation. The development of algorithms specifically for machine transliteration began over a decade ago based on the phonetics of source and target languages, followed by approaches using statistical and language-specific methods. In this survey, the key methodologies introduced in transliteration literature are reviewed. The approaches are categorized based on the resources and algorithms used, and the effectiveness is compared.

4849 ■ "Make It Easy" in *Entrepreneur* (Vol. 36, May 2008, No. 5, pp. 49)
Pub: Entrepreneur Media, Inc.
Ed: Mike Hogan. **Description:** Zoho has a Planner that keep contacts, notes and reminders and a DB & Reports feature for reports, data analysis and pricing comparisons. WebEx WebOffice Workgroup supports document management and templates for contacts lists, time sheets and sales tracking. Other online data manages are presented.

4850 ■ "Media Software and Data Services" in *MarketingMagazine* (Vol. 115, September 27, 2010, No. 13, pp. 78)
Pub: Rogers Publishing Ltd.
Description: Media software and data services information in Canada is presented.

4851 ■ "New Database Brings Doctors Out of the Dark" in *Business Courier* (Vol. 26, October 23, 2009, No. 26, pp. 1)
Pub: American City Business Journals, Inc.
Ed: James Ritchie. **Description:** A database created by managed care consulting firm Praesentia allows doctors in Cincinnati to compare average reimbursements from health insurance companies to doctors in different areas. Specialist doctors in the city are paid an average of $172.25 for every office consultation.

4852 ■ "New Ways To Think About Data Loss: Data Loss Is Costly and Painful" in *Franchising World* (Vol. 42, August 2010, No. 8, pp. 21)
Pub: International Franchise Association
Ed: Ken Colburn. **Description:** Information for maintaining data securely for franchised organizations, including smart phones, tablets, copiers, computers and more is given.

4853 ■ "Our Hoarder Mentality: Blame the Hard Disk" in *PC Magazine* (Vol. 30, November 2011, No. 11, pp. 46)
Pub: Ziff Davis Inc.
Ed: John C. Dvorak. **Description:** Computer programmers, once referred to as computer users, are slowly being replaced by passive consumers of products and content of tablets and handheld mobile phones and devices of the future. Understanding is garnered as this article examines this industry trend.

4854 ■ "Panda Security for Business 4.05" in *SC Magazine* (Vol. 21, July 2010, No. 7, pp. 50)
Pub: Haymarket Media Inc.
Description: Profile of Panda Security for Business, software offering endpoint security protection for computer desktops and servers is presented.

4855 ■ *Power Up Your Small-Medium Business: A Guide to Enabling Network Technologies*
Pub: Cisco Press
Ed: Robyn Aber. **Released:** March 2004. **Price:** $39.95 (US), $57.95 (Canadian). **Description:** Network technologies geared to small and medium-size business, focusing on access, IP telephony, wireless technologies, security, and computer network management.

4856 ■ "Save the Date" in *Barron's* (Vol. 90, September 13, 2010, No. 37, pp. 35)
Pub: Barron's Editorial & Corporate Headquarters
Ed: Mark Veverka. **Description:** Mark Hurd is the new Co-President of Oracle after being forced out at Hewlett-Packard where he faced a harassment complaint. HP fired Hurd due to expense account malfeasance. Hurd is also set to speak at an Oracle trade show in San Francisco on September 20, 2010.

4857 ■ "The State of the Art in End-User Software Engineering" in *ACM Computing Surveys* (Vol. 43, Fall 2011, No. 3, pp. 21)
Pub: Association for Computing Machinery
Description: Most programs today are not written by professional software developers but by people with expertise in other domains working towards goals for which they need computational support. A discussion of empirical research about end-user software engineering activities and the technologies designed to support them is presented. Several crosscutting issues in the design of EUSE tools, including the roles of risk, reward, and domain complexity, and self-efficacy in the design of EUSE tools and the potential of educating users about software engineering principles are also examined.

4858 ■ "Strict Intersection Types for the Lambda Calculus" in *ACM Computing Surveys* (Vol. 43, Fall 2011, No. 3, pp. 20)
Pub: Association for Computing Machinery
Ed: Steffen Van Bakel. **Description:** The usefulness and elegance of strict intersection types for the Lambda Calculus, that are strict in the sense that they are the representatives of equivalence classes of types in the BCD-system is shown. Focus in directed on the essential intersection type assignment; this system is almost syntax directed, and the article will show that all major properties hold that are known to hold for other intersection systems, like the approximation theorem, the characterization of (head/strong) normalization, completeness of type assignment using filter semantics, strong normalization for cut-elimination and the principal pair property. In part, the proofs for these properties are new. A brief comparison of the essential system with other existing systems is given.

4859 ■ "A Survey of Combinatorial Testing" in *ACM Computing Surveys* (Vol. 43, Summer 2011, No. 2, pp. 11)
Pub: Association for Computing Machinery
Ed: Changhai Nie, Hareton Leung. **Description:** Combinatorial Testing (CT) can detect failures triggered by interactions of parameters in the Software Under Test (SUT) with a covering array test suite generated by some sampling mechanisms. Basic concepts and notations of CT are covered.

4860 ■ "A Survey of Comparison-Based System-Level Diagnosis" in *ACM Computing Surveys* (Vol. 43, Fall 2011, No. 3, pp. 22)
Pub: Association for Computing Machinery
Ed: Elias P. Duarte Jr., Roverli P. Ziwich, Luiz C.P. Albini. **Description:** The growing complexity and dependability requirements of hardware, software, and networks demand efficient techniques for discovering disruptive behavior in those systems. Comparison-based diagnosis is a realistic approach to detect faulty units based on the outputs of tasks executed by system units. This survey integrates the vast amount of research efforts that have been produced in this field.

4861 ■ "A Survey of DHT Security Techniques" in *ACM Computing Surveys* (Vol. 43, Summer 2011, No. 2, pp. 8)
Pub: Association for Computing Machinery
Ed: Guido Urdaneta, Guillaume Pierre, Maarten Van Steen. **Description:** Peer-to-peer networks based on distributed hash tables (DHTs) have received considerable attention since their introduction in 2001. Unfortunately, DHT-based systems have been shown to be difficult to protect against security attacks. An overview of techniques reported in literature for making DHT-based systems resistant to the three most important attacks that can be launched by malicious nodes participating in the DHT is given: the Sybil attack, the Eclipse attack, and routing and storage attacks.

4862 ■ "Tektronix Buys Arbor Networks for Security Business" in *eWeek* (August 9, 2010)
Pub: Ziff Davis Enterprise
Description: Tektronix Communications, provider of communications test and network intelligence solutions will acquire Arbor Networks. The deal will help Tektronix build a brand in security. Details of the transaction are included.

4863 ■ "What is the Future of Disk Drives, Death or Rebirth?" in *ACM Computing Surveys* (Vol. 43, Fall 2011, No. 3, pp. 23)
Pub: Association for Computing Machinery
Ed: Yuhui Deng. **Description:** Disk drives have experienced dramatic development to meet performance requirements since the IBM 1301 disk drive was announced in 1961. However, the performance gap between memory and disk drives has widened to 6 orders of magnitude and continues to widen by about 50 percent per year. Challenges and opportunities facing these storage devices are explored.

4864 ■ "Xtium Has Its Head in the Clouds" in *Philadelphia Business Journal* (Vol. 30, September 23, 2011, No. 32, pp. 1)
Pub: American City Business Journals Inc.
Ed: Peter Key. **Description:** Philadelphia-based cloud computing firm Xtium LLC received an $11.5 million first-round investment from Boston-Massachusetts-based OpenView Venture Partners. Catering to midsize businesses and unit of bigger firms, Xtium offers disaster-recovery, hosting, and managed-information-technology-infrastructure services.

4865 ■ "Z-Tech Lands Contract with CMS" in *Black Enterprise* (Vol. 37, October 2006, No. 3, pp. 36)
Pub: Earl G. Graves Publishing Co. Inc.
Ed: Glenn Townes. **Description:** Z-Tech Corp., a Maryland-based company providing database design and warehousing, was awarded a five-year govern-

ment contract with the Centers for Medicare and Medicaid Services' Chronic Care Improvement Program worth $20 million.

STATISTICAL SOURCES

4866 ■ *RMA Annual Statement Studies*
Pub: Robert Morris Associates (RMA)
Released: Annual. **Price:** $175.00 2006-07 edition, $105.00. **Description:** Contains composite balance sheets and income statements for more than 360 industries, including the accounting, auditing, and bookkeeping industries. Also contains five years of comparative historical data for discerning trends. Includes 16 commonly used ratios, computed for most of the size groupings for nearly every industry.

4867 ■ *Standard & Poor's Industry Surveys*
Pub: Standard & Poor's Corp.
Released: Annual. **Price:** $3633.00. **Description:** Two-volume book that examines the prospects for specific industries, including trucking. Also provides analyses of trends and problems, statistical tables and charts, and comparative company analyses.

TRADE PERIODICALS

4868 ■ *Computerworld*
Pub: 101 Communications
Contact: Sharon Machlis, Managing Editor
E-mail: smachlis@computerworld.com
Released: Weekly. **Price:** $129; $129 Canada; $295 other countries; $250 Mexico/Central/South America; $29 digital edition. **Description:** Newspaper for information systems executives.

4869 ■ *Computing Reviews*
Pub: Association for Computing Machinery
Contact: Eric A. Weiss, Assoc. Ed.-in-Ch.
Released: Monthly. **Price:** $3,085 institutions PhD or equivalent; $2,015 institutions MS or equivalent; $1,345 institutions BA or equivalent; $3,015 institutions other non-profit; $7,180 institutions large corporate; $5,360 institutions medium corporate; $4,180 institutions small corporate. **Description:** Journal presenting reviews of literature on computer science and computer applications.

4870 ■ *Datamation*
Pub: Reed Business Information
Contact: Renee Munshi, Sen. Ed.
Released: Semimonthly. **Description:** Magazine on computers and information processing.

4871 ■ *Dr. Dobb's Journal*
Pub: United Business Media
Released: Monthly. **Price:** $25; $99.95 CD-ROM library. **Description:** Magazine covering computer programming.

4872 ■ *Embedded Systems Design*
Pub: United Business Media
Contact: Richard Nass, Editor-in-Chief
E-mail: mass@techinsights.com
Released: Monthly, including an additional issue in July. **Description:** Magazine covering microprocessors and microcontrollers, high-level languages and real-time operating systems for design engineers, engineering managers, software developers, and programmers.

4873 ■ *The Independent*
Pub: Independent Computer Consultants Association
Released: Bimonthly. **Price:** Included in membership. **Description:** Supports the Association by seeking to promote professionalism among member computer consultants, to increase awareness of products and services available, and to disseminate news and information about Association activities and benefits. Reports legislative and regulatory developments as well as information on marketing and business materials available. Recurring features include reports of meetings, news of educational opportunities, book reviews, and a calendar of events.

4874 ■ *InfoWorld*
Pub: InfoWorld Media Group
Contact: Eric Knorr, Editor-in-Chief
E-mail: eric_knorr@infoworld.com
Released: Weekly. **Price:** Free to qualified subscribers; $180. **Description:** Weekly publication.

4875 ■ *International Journal of Computers and Applications*
Pub: ACTA Press
Contact: Dr. Leone C. Monticone, Editor-in-Chief
E-mail: lmontico@mitre.org
Released: 4/yr. **Price:** $635 online; $635 hardcopy. **Description:** Professional journal covering computers and their applications.

4876 ■ *International Journal of Intelligent Systems*
Pub: John Wiley & Sons Inc.
Contact: John R. Anderson, Editorial Board
Ed: Ronald R. Yager, Editor. **Released:** Monthly. **Price:** $220 U.S., Canada, and Mexico print only; $304 other countries print only; $3,083 institutions print only; $3,251 institutions, Canada and Mexico print only; $3,335 institutions, other countries print only. **Description:** Journal featuring peer-reviewed work on the systematic development of theory used in the construction of intelligent systems. Covers areas such as man-computer interactions and the use of language, neural networks, and machine learning; includes book reviews.

4877 ■ *IT Forecaster*
Pub: International Data Corp.
Ed: Released: Weekly. **Description:** Provides news of original research and explains important trends in the worldwide information technology industry. Analyzes, segments, and sizes worldwide computer markets. Remarks: available online only.

4878 ■ *Java Report*
Pub: SIGS Publications & Conferences
Contact: Henry Allain, President
E-mail: hallain@1105media.com
Released: Monthly. **Price:** $4.95 local; annual; $39 annual; $4.95 single copy. **Description:** Technical magazine covering computer programming.

4879 ■ *Journal of Database Management*
Pub: IGI Global
Contact: Dinesh Batra, Assoc. Ed.
Released: Quarterly. **Price:** $205 print only; $835 institutions print and free online; $575 institutions online only; $575 institutions print only. **Description:** Journal covering the research of database administrators and managers.

4880 ■ *MIS Quarterly*
Pub: MIS Research Center
Contact: Alok Gupta, Publisher
E-mail: alok@csom.umn.edu
Released: Quarterly, (March, June, September, and December). **Price:** $100; $115 other countries; $175 institutions library; $200 institutions, other countries; $90 students; $105 students, other countries; $90 members. **Description:** Refereed research journal for academics and practitioners in the management information systems field.

4881 ■ *Online*
Pub: Online, A Division of Information Today Inc.
Ed: Marydee Ojala, Editor, marydee@infotoday.com. **Released:** Bimonthly. **Price:** $129.50; $243 two years; $145 Canada and Mexico; $172 other countries. **Description:** Professional magazine covering online and CD-ROM databases with practical how-to articles covering the entire online industry.

4882 ■ *PC AI Online*
Pub: Knowledge Technology Inc.
Contact: Robin Okun, Managing Editor
E-mail: robin@pcai.com
Released: Bimonthly. **Description:** Geared toward practical application of intelligent technology, covers developments in robotics, expert systems, neural networks, fuzzy logic, object-oriented development, languages and all other areas of artificial intelligence.

4883 ■ *SIGACT News*
Pub: Association for Computing Machinery
Ed: Mumey Brendan, Editor. **Released:** Quarterly. **Price:** Included in membership. **Description:** Provides information on the practical and theoretical aspects of design, analysis, and application of algorithms, data structures, systems and languages for algebraic and symbolic mathematical computation.

4884 ■ *SIGPLAN Notices*
Pub: Special Interest Group on Programming Languages
Ed: Michael Berman, Editor. **Released:** Monthly. **Price:** $35, Included in membership; $57, nonmembers; $10, students. **Description:** Examines all aspects of programming languages and programming languages processors. Utilizes practical and theoretical approaches to such areas as programming methodology; language definition and design; principles and techniques of computer implementation; general purpose and application-oriented languages; and teaching of programming languages. Recurring features include standards information and proceedings of SIGPLAN symposia.

4885 ■ *SIGSOFT Software Engineering Notes*
Pub: Association for Computing Machinery
Contact: Julie Goetz
Ed: Will Tracz, Editor, will.tracz@lmco.com. **Released:** Quarterly. **Price:** Included in membership. **Description:** Tracks developments in programming and software maintenance processes, as well as the use of computers to provide and maintain timely, higher quality, cost-effective, and durable software. Contains proceedings of software engineering workshops and symposia.

VIDEOCASSETTES/ AUDIOCASSETTES

4886 ■ *Career Possibilities: Computer Programming*
Silver Mine Video Inc.
31316 Via Colinas, Ste. 104
Westlake Village, CA 91362-3905
Ph:(818)707-0300
URL: http://www.quicksilverrecords.zoomshare.com
Released: 1984. **Price:** $29.95. **Description:** Examines all the aspects of computer programming: the fields where programmers are needed, a programmer's responsibilities and a look into the future of computer programming. **Availability:** VHS.

4887 ■ *The Computer Literacy Training Series*
American Media, Inc.
4621 121st St.
Urbandale, IA 50323-2311
Ph:(515)224-0919
Free: 888-776-8268
Fax:(515)327-2555
Co. E-mail: custsvc@ammedia.com
URL: http://www.ammedia.com
Released: 1990. **Price:** $495.00. **Description:** This video series explains most computer terminology and uses in a non-technical manner. **Availability:** VHS; 3/4U.

4888 ■ *Introduction to Computer Law*
Practicing Law Institute
810 7th Ave., 21st Fl.
New York, NY 10019-5818
Ph:(212)824-5700
Free: 800-260-4PLI
Co. E-mail: info@pli.edu
URL: http://www.pli.edu
Released: 1985. **Description:** A look at the laws governing computer use and purchase. **Availability:** VHS; 3/4U.

4889 ■ *The New Literacy: An Introduction to Computers*
Annenberg Media
1301 Pennsylvania NW, 302
Washington, DC 20004
Ph:(202)783-0500
Free: 800-LEA-RNER

Fax:(202)783-0333
Co. E-mail: order@leanrer.org
URL: http://www.learner.org
Released: 1988. **Price:** $350.00. **Description:** Provides a comprehensive look at computers, data processing, terminology, computer applications, and computer environments. **Availability:** VHS; 3/4U.

4890 ■ *1-2-3: Advanced Features*
Bergwall Productions, Inc.
1 DIckinson Drive, Brandywine BUilding 5, Ste. 105
PO Box 1481
Chadds Ford, PA 19317
Ph:(610)361-0334
Free: 800-934-8696
Fax:(610)361-0092
URL: http://www.bergwall.com
Released: 1985. **Description:** A study of computer language for the experienced programmer. **Availability:** VHS; 3/4U.

TRADE SHOWS AND CONVENTIONS

4891 ■ COMDEX
Ziff-Davis, Inc.
28 E. 28th St.
New York, NY 10016-7930
Ph:(212)503-3500
Co. E-mail: info@ziffdavis.com
URL: http://www.ziffdavis.com
Released: Annual. **Audience:** Volume resellers and value-adders of small computers and related items; only a virtual trade show since 2003. **Principal Exhibits:** Small computer systems, related peripherals, software, accessories, services, and supplies.

4892 ■ FOSE
Co. Post Newsweek Tech Media
10 G St. NE, Ste. 500
Washington, DC 20002-4228
Ph:(202)772-2500
Free: (866)447-6864
Fax:(202)772-2500
URL: http://www.postnewsweektech.com
Released: Annual. **Audience:** Government professionals, suppliers to government and systems integrators. **Principal Exhibits:** Computer systems and services, image management equipment, networks, communications and office systems and services. **Dates and Locations:** 2011 Jul 19-21, Washington, DC.

CONSULTANTS

4893 ■ Beeline Learning Solutions
14911 Quorum Dr., Ste. 120
Dallas, TX 75254
Ph:(972)813-0465
Fax:(972)386-8667
Co. E-mail: info@consultingpartners.com
URL: http://www.beeline.com
Contact: Debra Gann, Managering Director
E-mail: gann@atsconsultingpartners.com
Scope: Consulting firm offering technology, content, and services addressing recruitment and sourcing, talent management, and learning and performance optimization. Solutions offered include contingent workforce solutions, vendor management software, talent management solutions, recruitment process outsourcing, performance management, applicant tracking, learning management and eLearning. **Special Services:** Beeline[R].

4894 ■ Broadsword Solutions Corp.
3795 Dorothy Ln.
Waterford, MI 48329
Ph:(248)341-3367
Fax:(248)341-3672
Co. E-mail: info@broadswordsolutions.com
URL: http://www.broadswordsolutions.com
Contact: Jeff Dalton, Product Development Manager
E-mail: jeff@atsbroadswordsolutions.com
Scope: Firm helps small and medium-sized organizations build software with solutions such as Agile CMMI and Traditional CMMI Consulting. **Seminars:** CMMI Accelerator Boxed Set v2.1. **Special Services:** AgileCMMI.

4895 ■ Meg Consulting Group L.L.C.
35452 Edgeton Ct., Ste. 204
Farmington Hills, MI 48335
Ph:(248)477-1186
Fax:(248)579-0226
Co. E-mail: support@megcg.com
URL: http://www.megcg.com
Contact: Mohit Sethi, Owner
Scope: Offers business consulting services in custom and boxed software solutions and network design. Also offers financial, real estate and travel services.

4896 ■ Sterling-Hoffman
425 University Ave., Ste. 800
Toronto, ON, Canada M5G 1T6
Ph:(416)979-6701
Free: 888-758-0942
Fax:(416)979-3030
Co. E-mail: customerservice@sterlinghoffman.com
URL: http://www.sterlinghoffman.com
Contact: Angel Mehta, CEO
E-mail: amehta@atssterlinghoffman.com
Scope: A retained search firm for emerging software companies needing high-performance sales, marketing and business development executives. **Publications:** "Missed the Number? Send Your CEO a Japanese Death Poem"; "Want to Win? Forget YOU Exist"; "Secrets from the Farm: On Fear, Honor, and Building Companies"; "Bruce Lee says your new VP Sales will Fail"; "'Tragic Flaws: Why Software Companies Really Fail". **Seminars:** What CEOs want HR to know, Toronto.

4897 ■ Wheeler and Young Inc.
33 Peter St.
Markham, ON, Canada L3P 2A5
Ph:(905)471-5709
Fax:(905)471-9989
Co. E-mail: wheeler@ericwheeler.ca
URL: http://www.ericwheeler.ca
Contact: Eric S. Wheeler, Managing Partner
E-mail: ewheeler@yorku.ca
Scope: Provides consulting services to high-tech companies on the implementation of software development processes; quality management systems (including ISO 9000 compliance) and business management systems. Offers business management and knowledge-management services to organizations. Industries served: Knowledge-based industries, including software and hardware development, medical and legal professionals, information service providers.

COMPUTERIZED DATABASES

4898 ■ *Computer Database*
Cengage Learning Inc.
27500 Drake Rd.
Farmington Hills, MI 48331-3535
Ph:(248)699-4253
Free: 800-877-4253
Fax:(248)699-8069
Co. E-mail: galeord@gale.com
URL: http://gale.cengage.com
Description: Contains more than 1 million citations, abstracts, and full text to literature from some 800 trade journals, industry newsletters, and platform-specific publications covering the computer, telecommunications, and electronics industries. Topics covered include business and industry applications; computer graphics; consumer information; database management systems; hardware and software design, development, and reviews; peripherals; home computers; new products; performance evaluations; programming languages; operating systems; phototypesetting; and word processing. Includes descriptive and financial information for companies covered in the industry literature. **Availability:** Online: ProQuest LLC, ProQuest LLC, Cengage Learning Inc. **Type:** Bibliographic; Full text.

LIBRARIES

4899 ■ Boston University–Corporate Education Center Library
1 Exec. Dr., Ste. 301
Chelmsford, MA 01824-2558
Ph:(978)649-8200
Free: 800-288-7246
Fax:(978)649-2145
URL: http://butrain.bu.edu
Scope: Software engineering, business administration and management, computer programming languages, program methodology, project management, computer science, social work. **Services:** Interlibrary loan; copying; SDI; Library open to the public by appointment. **Holdings:** 5000 books. **Subscriptions:** 150 journals and other serials; 10 newspapers.

4900 ■ Computer Sciences Corporation Corporate Library
3170 Fairview Park Dr.
Falls Church, VA 90245
Ph:(703)876-1000
Co. E-mail: alawrence@csc.com
URL: http://www.csc.com
Contact: Anita Lawrence, Libn.
Scope: Data processing, communications, information retrieval, programming, systems analysis, business, management, operations research, systems integration, outsourcing, company background information. **Services:** Interlibrary loan; copying; Library not open to the public. **Holdings:** 150 books. **Subscriptions:** 70 journals and other serials.

4901 ■ Ernst & Young LLP–Center for Business Knowledge Library
8484 Westpark Dr.
McLean, VA 22102
Ph:(703)747-1000
Fax:(703)747-0100
URL: http://www.ey.com
Contact: Katherine Vogt, Res.Coord.
Scope: Data communication, computers and data processing. **Services:** Interlibrary loan; Library not open to the public. **Holdings:** 300 volumes. **Subscriptions:** 200 journals and other serials.

4902 ■ IBM Corporation–Burlington Technical Library
967-B, 1000 River St.
Essex Junction, VT 05452-4299
Ph:(802)769-6519
Fax:(802)769-6501
Co. E-mail: karenlyn@us.ibm.com
URL: http://www.ibm.com/us/en/
Contact: Karen Kromer Lynch, Tech.Lib.Mgr.
Scope: Semiconductor manufacturing, chemistry, computing, solid-state electronics, physics, business and professional, project management, programming, management science, mathematics. **Services:** Interlibrary loan; Center not open to the public. **Holdings:** 10,000 books; 100 reels of microfilm. **Subscriptions:** 160 journals and other serials.

4903 ■ IBM Corporation–Library/Information Resource Center
Dept. LVUS, B/908 Z/9819
11400 Burnet Rd.
Austin, TX 78758
Ph:(512)823-0404
Co. E-mail: gillen@us.ibm.com
URL: http://www.ibm.com/us/en/
Contact: Bev Gerzcvske, Mgr.
Scope: Computer architecture, RISC, personal computing, telecommunications, management, human factors, communications. **Services:** Interlibrary loan; Library not open to the public. **Holdings:** 11,000 books; 500 bound periodical volumes; 400 videotapes; 200 audiocassettes; 2000 reels of microfilm. **Subscriptions:** 300 journals, newsletters, and other serials; 15 newspapers.

4904 ■ International Data Corp. Library
5 Speen St.
Framingham, MA 01701
Ph:(508)872-8200
Co. E-mail: leads@idc.com
URL: http://www.idc.com
Contact: Kirk Campbell, Pres./CEO
Scope: Computer technology, management. **Services:** Interlibrary loan; Center not open to the public. **Holdings:** 2200 books; 50 Annual reports; 235 subject files; 12 CD-ROMs. **Subscriptions:** 200 journals and other serials.

4905 ■ Kansas State University, Salina–Libraries
2310 Centennial Rd.
Technology Center Bldg.
Salina, KS 67401-8058
Ph:(785)826-2637
Fax:(785)826-2937
Co. E-mail: astarkey@k-state.edu
URL: http://www.sal.ksu.edu/library/index.html
Contact: Alysia Starkey, Dir. of Libs.
Scope: Computers, electronics, environmental, aeronautics, civil and mechanical engineering. **Services:** Interlibrary loan; copying; Library open to the public. **Holdings:** 26,000 books; videotapes collection; 300 electronic databases. **Subscriptions:** 300 journals and other serials; 9 newspapers.

4906 ■ Lockheed Martin–Manassas Library
105/029
9500 Godwin Dr.
Manassas, VA 20110
Ph:(703)367-6508
Fax:(703)367-4698
Co. E-mail: manassas.library@lmco.com
URL: http://www.lockheedmartin.com
Contact: Jennifer Hatfield, Mgr.
Scope: Computer systems and technology; signal processing; electronics; sonar. **Services:** Interlibrary loan. **Holdings:** 10,000 books; 2000 bound periodical volumes; 100 reports. **Subscriptions:** 200 journals and other serials; 10 newspapers.

4907 ■ MAGNET–Information Resource Center
4600 Prospect Ave.
Cleveland, OH 44103-4314
Ph:(216)432-5369
Fax:(216)432-5205
Co. E-mail: joel.anyim@camp.org
URL: http://www.camp.org
Contact: Linda Barita, Mgr., Tech.Info.
Scope: Manufacturing technology; ECOMM, EDI, CAD/CAM, Business Systems. **Services:** SDI; Library open to members. **Holdings:** 2000 books; 200 periodical titles; 1000 archival reports; CD-ROMs. **Subscriptions:** 200 journals and other serials.

4908 ■ Mayo Biomedical Imaging Resource Library
Mayo Clinic
200 First St., SW
Rochester, MN 55905
Ph:(507)284-2511
Fax:(507)284-0161
Co. E-mail: robb.richard@mayo.edu
URL: http://mayoresearch.mayo.edu/mayo/research/robb_lab/
Contact: Richard A. Robb, Ph.D., Dir.
Scope: Biomedical imaging, visualization science, software systems, workstations, networks, computer graphics, virtual reality. **Services:** Interlibrary loan; Library open to the public. **Holdings:** 100 books; 200 bound periodical volumes; 100 reports; 35 patents. **Subscriptions:** 20 journals and other serials; 5 newspapers.

4909 ■ Sargent & Lundy Engineers–Computer Software Library
55 E. Monroe St.
Chicago, IL 60603
Ph:(312)269-2000
Fax:(312)269-3680
Co. E-mail: thinkingpower@sargentlundy.com
URL: http://www.slchicago.com
Contact: John Wittenauer, IT Dir.
Scope: Computer applications. **Services:** Copying; Library open to the public by appointment. **Holdings:** 250 books; 723 computer program manuals; 70 VF drawers of computer program documentation; microfiche. **Subscriptions:** 27 journals and other serials.

4910 ■ UNISYS Corporation–Technical Information Center
41100 Plymouth Rd.
Plymouth, MI 48170
Ph:(313)451-4512
Contact: Mark Stuart Berna, Libn.
Scope: Computer technology, banking, imaging, business. **Services:** Library not open to the public. **Holdings:** 1800 books. **Subscriptions:** 72 journals and other serials; 5 newspapers.

4911 ■ UNISYS Corporation–West Coast Information Center
25725 Jeronimo Rd., MS-260
Mission Viejo, CA 92691
Ph:(714)380-5061
Fax:(714)380-5138
Contact: M. Patricia Feeney, Mgr., Tech.Info.Ctr.
Scope: Computer architecture, computer programming, software design, hardware engineering design, data communications, management. **Services:** Interlibrary loan; center open to the public at librarian's discretion. **Holdings:** 5000 books; 3500 technical reports; 3000 other cataloged items. **Subscriptions:** 225 journals and other serials.

4912 ■ UNISYS Corporation Corporate Library
One Unisys Way
PO Box 500
Blue Bell, PA 19424
Ph:(215)986-2324
Fax:(215)986-6733
Contact: Susan H. Hahn, Mgr.
Scope: Business, computer science, computer industry, computer services, computer security. **Services:** Library not open to the public. **Holdings:** 9000 books; 200 audiobooks, 350 videocassettes. **Subscriptions:** 100 journals and other serials; 6 newspapers.

4913 ■ Walt Disney World–Global Business Technology Strategy Library
Team Disney 336-N
1375 Buena Vista Dr.
PO Box 10000
Lake Buena Vista, FL 32830-1000
Ph:(407)828-4250
Co. E-mail: david.w.hartman@disney.com
URL: http://disneyworld.disney.go.com/wdw
Contact: David Hartman, Libn.
Scope: Computer science, human resources, general business. **Services:** Center not open to the public. **Holdings:** 4000 books, videos, DVDs, and CDs; 100 AV equipment. **Subscriptions:** 200 journals and other serials; 3 newspapers.

4914 ■ Xerox Corporation–Wilsonville Library
Box 1000, M/S 63-531
Wilsonville, OR 97070
Ph:(503)685-3986
Fax:(503)685-2296
Co. E-mail: linda.appel@opbu.xerox.com
Contact: Linda K. Appel, Libn.
Scope: Color computer printers, programming, electronics, business and management. **Services:** Interlibrary loan; SDI. **Holdings:** 4000 books. **Subscriptions:** 100 journals and other serials; 9 newspapers.

RESEARCH CENTERS

4915 ■ Massachusetts Institute of Technology–Laboratory for Computer Science–Programming Methodology Group
32 Vasaar St., 32-G942
Cambridge, MA 02139
Ph:(617)253-5886
Fax:(617)253-8460
Co. E-mail: liskov@csail.mit.edu
URL: http://www.pmg.lcs.mit.edu/
Contact: Prof. Barbara Liskov, Gp.Ldr.
E-mail: liskov@csail.mit.edu
Scope: Distributed systems, object oriented databases, programming languages, and software design. Ongoing projects include techniques that allow systems to continue to provide service in spite of malicious attacks and software errors, software infrastructure to enable writing of applications that run on distributed collections of embedded computers, and support for automatic software upgrades in distributed systems and object-oriented databases.

4916 ■ Ohio State University–Advanced Computing Center for the Arts and Design
1224 Kinnear Rd.
Columbus, OH 43212-1154
Ph:(614)292-3416
Fax:(614)292-7776
Co. E-mail: mpalazzi@accad.ohio-state.edu
URL: http://accad.osu.edu
Contact: Prof. Maria Palazzi, Dir.
E-mail: mpalazzi@accad.ohio-state.edu
Scope: Computer arts and design, and scientific visualization. Research and development, outreach and collaboration are essential components of ACCAD's mission. Partnerships within academia, industry, public and social services enable our students and faculty to have impact beyond our Center. As a result of our multidisciplinary community, we possess a wealth of cultural and intellectual resources as well as technological knowledge. ACCAD has supported the development of hundreds of industry and research experts from both the sciences and the arts in the field of computer graphics and animation for over 30 years. **Publications:** Newsletter On-line. **Educational Activities:** Digital Animation: A Technology Mentoring Program for Young Women (annually), free summer program for 8th and 9th grade young women to learn computer animation; Open House (annually), held in the beginning of May.

4917 ■ University at Albany, State University of New York–Institute for Informatics, Logics, and Security Studies
SUNY, Social Science Bldg., Rm. 262
Albany, NY 12222
Ph:(518)442-2605
Fax:(518)442-2606
Co. E-mail: nvm@cs.albany.edu
URL: http://www.ils.albany.edu
Contact: Prof. Neil V. Murray PhD, Co-Dir.
E-mail: nvm@cs.albany.edu
Scope: Formal methods and associated logic for hardware and software systems, as well as in algebraic and geometric reasoning methods in solid modeling and computer vision. **Publications:** Technical reports. **Educational Activities:** Conferences.

4918 ■ University of California, Irvine–Distributed Real-time Ever Available Microcomputing Laboratory
4111 Engineering Hall
Irvine, CA 92697
Ph:(949)824-5542
Fax:(949)824-4148
Co. E-mail: khkim@uci.edu
URL: http://dream.eng.uci.edu/
Contact: Prof. Kane Kim, Dir.
E-mail: khkim@uci.edu
Scope: Designs computer systems with guaranteed response times by combining real-time, object oriented, fault tolerant, and distributed and parallel computing. Research has applications in space exploration, transportation automation, automated manufacturing, automated hospital equipment, and other safety-critical areas.

4919 ■ University of Georgia–Center for Remote Sensing and Mapping Science
Geography-Geology Bldg., Rm. 209a
Department of Geography
Athens, GA 30602-2503
Ph:(706)542-2379
Fax:(706)542-2388
Co. E-mail: mmadden@uga.edu
URL: http://www.crms.uga.edu
Contact: Prof. Marguerite Madden PhD, Dir.
E-mail: mmadden@uga.edu
Scope: Image and geographic information system data processing technologies for applications in the physical, biological, and mapping sciences.

4920 ■ University of Southern California–Information Sciences Institute
4676 Admiralty Way, Ste. 1001
Marina del Rey, CA 90292
Ph:(310)822-1511

Fax:(310)823-6714
Co. E-mail: schorr@isi.edu
URL: http://www3.isi.edu/home
Contact: Prof. Herbert Schorr PhD, Exec.Dir.
E-mail: schorr@isi.edu
Scope: Computer science research.

Computer Store

START-UP INFORMATION

4921 ■ *The Mousedriver Chronicles*
Pub: Perseus Books Group
Ed: John Lusk; Kyle Harrison. **Released:** 2003. **Price:** $16.95. **Description:** Entrepreneurial voyage through the startup business of two ivy-league business school graduates and the lessons they learned while developing their idea of a computer mouse that looks like a golf driver into the marketplace. The book is an inspiration for those looking to turn an idea into a company.

ASSOCIATIONS AND OTHER ORGANIZATIONS

4922 ■ Information Technology Industry Council
1101 K St. NW, Ste. 610
Washington, DC 20005
Ph:(202)737-8888
Fax:(202)638-4922
Co. E-mail: kkriner@itic.org
URL: http://www.itic.org
Contact: Dean Garfield, Pres./CEO
Description: Represents manufacturers of information technology products. Serves as secretariat and technology for ANSI-accredited standards committee x3 information technology group. Conducts public policy programs; compiles industry statistics. **Publications:** *Washington Letter* (biweekly).

4923 ■ Transaction Processing Performance Council
PO Box 29920
San Francisco, CA 94129-0920
Ph:(415)561-6272
Fax:(415)561-6120
Co. E-mail: info@tpc.org
URL: http://www.tpc.org
Contact: Omri Serlin, Co-Founder
Description: Represents computer hardware and software companies, computer users and vendors, and industry organizations. Defines transaction processing and database benchmarks. Disseminates objective, verifiable TPC performance data to the industry. Conducts activities such as Benchmark development and maintenance, publication and dissemination of TPC results. **Publications:** *Benchmark Status Report* (bimonthly); *Complete Listing of TPC Results*; *TPC Background*; *TPC Benchmark Specifications* .

DIRECTORIES OF EDUCATIONAL PROGRAMS

4924 ■ *Directory of Private Accredited Career Schools and Colleges of Technology*
Pub: Accrediting Commission of Career Schools and Colleges of Technology
Contact: Michale S. McComis, Exec. Dir.
Released: On web page. **Price:** Free. **Description:** Covers 3900 accredited post-secondary programs that provide training programs in business, trade, and technical fields, including various small business endeavors. Entries offer school name, address, phone, description of courses, job placement assistance, and requirements for admission. Arrangement is alphabetical.

REFERENCE WORKS

4925 ■ "3Par: Storing Up Value" in *Barron's* (Vol. 90, August 30, 2010, No. 35, pp. 30)
Pub: Barron's Editorial & Corporate Headquarters
Ed: Mark Veverka. **Description:** Dell and Hewlett Packard are both bidding for data storage company 3Par. The acquisition would help Dell and Hewlett Packard provide customers with a one-stop shop as customers move to a private cloud in the Internet.

4926 ■ *Achieving Planned Innovation: A Proven System for Creating Successful New Products and Services*
Pub: Simon and Schuster
Ed: Frank R. Bacon. **Released:** August 2007. **Price:** $16.95. **Description:** Planned innovation is a disciplined and practical step-by-step sequence of procedures for reaching the intended destination point: successful products. This easy-to-read book explains the system along with an action-oriented program for continuous success in new-product innovations. Five steps outlined include: a disciplined reasoning process; lasting market orientation; proper selection criteria that reflect both strategic and tactical business objectives and goals along with dynamic matching of resources to present and future opportunities, and positive and negative requirements before making major expenditures; and proper organizational staffing. The author explains what to do and evaluating the potential of any new product or service, ranging from ventures in retail distribution to the manufacture of goods as diverse as bicycles, motorcycles, aerospace communication and navigation equipment, small business computers, food packaging, and medical products.

4927 ■ "Agricharts Launches New Mobile App for Ag Market" in *Farm Industry News* (December 1, 2011)
Pub: Penton Business Media Inc.
Description: AgriCharts provides market data, agribusiness Website hosting and technology solutions for the agricultural industry. AgriCharts is a division of Barchart.com Inc. and announced the release of a new mobile applications that offers real-time or delayed platform for viewing quotes, charts and analysis of grains, livestock and other commodity markets.

4928 ■ "Also Check Out..." in *Black Enterprise* (Vol. 38, October 2007, No. 3, pp. 64)
Pub: Earl G. Graves Publishing Co. Inc.
Description: Profile of Lenovo's Think Vantage Rescue and Recovery system that performs backup files for CD/DVDs.

4929 ■ "Aptitudes for Apps" in *Boston Business Journal* (Vol. 31, July 1, 2011, No. 23, pp. 3)
Pub: Boston Business Journal
Ed: Kyle Alspach. **Description:** Startups Apperian Inc. and Kinvey Inc. are aiming to accelerate the development and deployment of mobile applications and have received fund pledges from Boston-area venture capital firms.

4930 ■ "Avanti Hosts Users Conference" in *American Printer* (Vol. 128, July 1, 2011, No. 7)
Pub: Penton Media Inc.
Description: Avanti Computer Systems Ltd. hosted its 19th annual users conference in Washington DC. In-plant and commercial printers were in attendance.

4931 ■ *The Big Switch*
Pub: W. W. Norton & Company, Inc.
Ed: Nicholas Carr. **Released:** January 19, 2009. **Price:** $16.95 paperback. **Description:** Today companies are dismantling private computer systems and tapping into services provided via the Internet. This shift is remaking the computer industry, bringing competitors such as Google to the forefront ant threatening traditional companies like Microsoft and Dell. The book weaves together history, economics, and technology to explain why computing is changing and what it means for the future.

4932 ■ "Buyer's Guide: Room for Improvement" in *Entrepreneur* (Vol. 35, October 2007, No. 10, pp. 62)
Pub: Entrepreneur Media Inc.
Ed: Amanda C. Kooser. **Description:** Buyers guide for wireless routers is presented. Price, features and availability of the Belkin N1 Vision, Buffalo Wireless-N Nfinit Router, D-Link Xtreme Gigabit Router DIR 655, Linksys Wireless-N Gigabit Security Router, Netgear RangeMax Next Wireless-N Router and Zyxel NBG-460N are provided.

4933 ■ *Cisco Network Design Solutions for Small-Medium Businesses*
Pub: Cisco Press
Ed: Peter Rybaczyk. **Released:** August 2004. **Price:** $55.00. **Description:** Solutions for computer networking professionals using computer networks within a small to medium-sized business. Topics cover not only core networking issues and solutions, but security, IP telephony, unified communications, customer relations management, wireless LANs, and more.

4934 ■ "Clouds in the Forecast" in *Information Today* (Vol. 28, September 2011, No. 8, pp. 10)
Pub: Information Today, Inc.
Ed: Paula J. Hane. **Description:** Cloud computing is software, applications, and data stored remotely and accessed via the Internet with output displayed on a client device. Recent developments in cloud computing are explored.

4935 ■ *Computing Technology Industry Association—Membership Directory*
Pub: Computing Technology Industry Association
Contact: Bob O'Malley, Chm.
Released: Annual, winter. **Covers:** 7,500 member computer hardware and software manufacturers, distributors, associate members, and resellers. **Entries Include:** For manufacturers and distributors—

Company name, address, phone, fax, name and title of contact, products. For resellers—Personal name, company name, address, phone, fax, vertical markets served and CPU brands sold. **Arrangement:** Alphabetical. **Indexes:** Company name, geographical, vertical market, CPU, contact name.

4936 ■ "Cyberwise" in *Black Enterprise* (Vol. 41, December 2010, No. 5, pp. 50)
Pub: Earl G. Graves Publishing Co. Inc.
Ed: Marica Wade Talbert. **Description:** Information is given regarding single platforms that can be used to develop applications for iPhone, Android, Blackberry, and Nokia.

4937 ■ "Death of the PC" in *Canadian Business* (Vol. 83, October 12, 2010, No. 17, pp. 44)
Pub: Rogers Media Ltd.
Ed: Joe Castaldo. **Description:** The future of the personal computer (PC) is looking bleak as consumers are relying more on new mobile devices instead of their PC. A 'Wall Street Journal' article published in September 2010 reported that the iPad had cannibalized sales of laptops by as much as 50 percent. The emergence of tablet computers running alternative operating systems is also explained.

4938 ■ "The Digital Revolution is Over. Long Live the Digital Revolution!" in *Business Strategy Review* (Vol. 21, Spring 2010, No. 1, pp. 74)
Pub: Wiley-Blackwell
Ed: Gianvito Lanzolla, Jamie Anderson. **Description:** Many businesses are now involved in the digital marketplace. The authors argue that the new reality of numerous companies offering overlapping products means that it is critical for managers to understand digital convergence and to observe the imperatives for remaining competitive.

4939 ■ "Facebook Purchased Push Pop Press" in *Information Today* (Vol. 28, October 2011, No. 9, pp. 12)
Pub: Information Today, Inc.
Description: Facebook purchased Push Pop Press, a digital publishing company that developed a multi-touch interface for ebook publishing on the iPad.

4940 ■ *Faulkner Information Services*
Pub: Faulkner Information Services
Released: Monthly, Updates; base volumes available with subscription. **Description:** The "Faulkner FACCTs" series includes separate reference services for many areas of data processing, communications, and related fields (the full information service is available as well). Titles include: "Enterprise Computing"; "Enterprise Communications"; "Local Area Networks"; "Telecommunications"; "Converging Communications Technologies"; "Large and Midrange Systems and Software"; "Micro Systems and Software"; "The Internet"; "Wireless Communications" **Entries Include:** All reports contain company name, address, phone, fax, URL if available, and product list or description. Some reports also contain sales reports, financial data, products carried or distributed, and/or distribution statistics. Some comprise technology overviews or "how-to" guides.

4941 ■ "Featherweight Contenders: Thin and Light, But Heavy On Features" in *Inc.* (Vol. 33, October 2011, No. 8, pp. 44)
Pub: Inc. Magazine
Ed: John Brandon. **Description:** Profiles of ultraportable notebooks include Sony Z Series VPCZ212GX/B, Samsung Series 9 NP900X1B, ASUS U36SJC, and Macbook Air.

4942 ■ "For Apple, It's Showtime Again" in *Barron's* (Vol. 90, August 30, 2010, No. 35, pp. 29)
Pub: Barron's Editorial & Corporate Headquarters
Ed: Eric J. Savitz. **Description:** Speculations on what Apple Inc. will unveil at its product launch event are presented. These products include a possible new iPhone Nano, a new update to its Apple TV, and possibly a deal with the Beatles to distribute their songs over iTunes.

4943 ■ "Funny Business" in *Canadian Business* (Vol. 82, April 27, 2009, No. 7, pp. 27)
Pub: Rogers Media
Ed: Rachel Pulfer. **Description:** Companies are advised to use humor in marketing to drive more revenue. IBM Canada, for example, commissioned Second City Communications for a marketing campaign that involved humor. While IBM Canada declined to give sales or traffic figures, firm executives rank the marketing campaign as an overall success.

4944 ■ "gdgt: The New Online Home for Gadget Fans" in *Hispanic Business* (July-August 2009, pp. 15)
Pub: Hispanic Business
Ed: Jeremy Nisen. **Description:** Profile of the new online Website for gadget lovers. The site combines a leek interface, gadget database, and social networking-type features which highlights devices for the consumer.

4945 ■ "Googly Eyed" in *Entrepreneur* (Vol. 36, February 2008, No. 2, pp. 48)
Pub: Entrepreneur Media Inc.
Ed: Mike Hogan. **Description:** Linux has developed desktops that boot into the Google toolbar and applications. These desktops include: Zonbu, Everex gPCTC2502, and Asus Eee PC 4G mini laptop. Details on the applications of these desktops are discussed.

4946 ■ "Hewlett-Packard Mini: Ultra-Portable, and Affordable" in *Hispanic Business* (July-August 2009, pp. 36)
Pub: Hispanic Business
Ed: Jeremy Nisen. **Description:** Hewlett-Packard's 1151 NR computers works a lot like a smartphone online, it can dial up fast speeds on Verizon's 3G network almost anywhere.

4947 ■ "Holiday Sales Look Uncertain for Microsoft and PC Sellers" in *Puget Sound Business Journal* (Vol. 29, November 28, 2008, No. 32)
Pub: American City Business Journals
Ed: Todd Bishop. **Description:** Personal computer makers face uncertain holiday sales for 2008 as a result of the weak U.S. economy and a shift toward low-cost computers. Personal computer shipments for the fourth quarter 2008 are forecast to drop 1 percent compared to the same quarter 2007.

4948 ■ "Homing In On the Future" in *Black Enterprise* (Vol. 38, October 2007, No. 3, pp. 61)
Pub: Earl G. Graves Publishing Co. Inc.
Ed: Sean Drakes. **Description:** More and more people are wanting new homes wired automated systems that integrate multiple home devices such as computers, audio/visual entertainment, security, communications, utilities, and lighting and environmental controls.

4949 ■ "How Dell Will Dial for Dollars" in *Austin Business JournalInc.* (Vol. 29, December 4, 2009, No. 39, pp. 1)
Pub: American City Business Journals
Ed: Christopher Calnan. **Description:** Dell Inc. revealed plans to launch a Mini3i smartphone in China which could enable revenue sharing by bundling with wireless service subscription. Dell's smartphone plan is similar to the netbook business, which Dell sold with service provided by AT&T Inc.

4950 ■ *How to Get Rich*
Pub: Ebury Press
Ed: Felix Dennis. **Released:** 2008. **Price:** $25.95. **Description:** Publisher of Maxim, The Week, and Stuff magazines, discusses the mistakes he made running his companies. He didn't understand that people who buy computer gaming magazines wanted a free game with each copy, as one of his rivals was offering. And he laments not diversifying into television and exploiting the Internet.

4951 ■ "How to Play the Tech Mergers" in *Barron's* (Vol. 90, August 30, 2010, No. 35, pp. 18)
Pub: Barron's Editorial & Corporate Headquarters
Ed: Tiernan Ray. **Description:** The intense bidding by Hewlett-Packard and Dell for 3Par was foreseen in a previous Barron's cover story and 3Par's stock has nearly tripled since reported. Other possible acquisition targets in the tech industry include Brocade Communication Systems, NetApp, Xyratex, and Isilon Systems.

4952 ■ *IBM on Demand Technology for the Growing Business: How to Optimize Your Computing Environment for Today and Tomorrow*
Pub: Maximum Press
Ed: Jim Hoskins. **Released:** June 2005. **Price:** $29. 95. **Description:** IBM is offering computer solutions to small companies entering the On Demand trend in business.

4953 ■ *Information Technology for the Small Business: How to Make IT Work For Your Company*
Pub: TAB Computer Systems, Incorporated
Ed: T.J. Benoit. **Released:** June 2006. **Price:** $17. 95. **Description:** Basics of information technology to help small companies maximize benefits are covered. Topics include pitfalls to avoid, email and Internet use, data backup, recovery and overall IT organization.

4954 ■ "Intel: Tax Breaks Key" in *Business Journal Portland* (Vol. 27, October 22, 2010, No. 34, pp. 1)
Pub: Portland Business Journal
Ed: Erik Siemers. **Description:** Intel Corporation believes that state tax incentives will be critical, especially in the purchase of manufacturing equipment, as they build a new chip factory in Hillsboro, Oregon. The tax breaks would help Intel avoid paying 10 times more in property taxes compared to average Washington County firms. Critics argue that Intel has about $15 billion in cash assets, and can afford the factory without the tax breaks.

4955 ■ "It Was a Very Good Year...To Be Ted Rogers" in *Canadian Business* (Vol. 80, Winter 2007, No. 24, pp. 121)
Pub: Rogers Media
Ed: Andrew Wahl. **Description:** Ted Rogers had a banner year in 2007 as Rogers Communications Inc. (RCI) took in huge profits from its phone and wireless business and his personal wealth grew sixty-seven percent to $7.6 billion. Rogers has record of betting on technologies that get the best returns relative to the investment in the marketplace such as its use of the GSM network and its cable hybrid fiber coaxial network.

4956 ■ "Keeping Up With the Joneses: Outfitting Your Company With Up-To-Date Technology is Vital" in *Black Enterprise* (November 2007)
Pub: Earl G. Graves Publishing Co. Inc.
Ed: Sonya A. Donaldson. **Description:** Small businesses, whether home-based or not, need to keep up with new technological developments including hardware, software, and the Internet.

4957 ■ "Kids, Computers and the Social Networking Evolution" in *Canadian Business* (Vol. 81, October 27, 2008, No. 18, pp. 93)
Pub: Rogers Media Ltd.
Ed: Penny Milton. **Description:** Social networking was found to help educate students in countries like the U.S., Canada and Mexico. Schools that embrace social networking teach students how to use computers safely and responsibility in order to counter threats to children on the Internet.

4958 ■ "Microsoft Releases Office Security Updates" in *Mac World* (Vol. 27, November 2010, No. 11, pp. 66)
Pub: Mac Publishing
Ed: David Dahlquist. **Description:** Office for Mac and Mac Business Unit are Microsoft's pair of security- and stability-enhancing updates for Office

2008 and Office 2004. The software will improve the stability and compatibility and fixes vulnerabilities that would allow attackers to overwrite Mac's memory with malicious code.

4959 ■ *Mobile Office: The Essential Small Business Guide to Office Technology*
Pub: Double Storey Books
Ed: Arthur Goldstruck, Steven Ambrose. **Released:** September 1, 2009. **Price:** $6.95. **Description:** Essential pocket guide for startup businesses and entrepreneurs which provides information to create a mobile office in order to maximize business potential while using current technologies.

4960 ■ "Mobility: So Happy Together" in *Entrepreneur* (Vol. 35, October 2007, No. 10, pp. 64)
Pub: Entrepreneur Media Inc.
Ed: Heather Clancy. **Description:** Joshua Burnett, CEO and founder of 9ci, uses index cards to keep track of what he needs to do despite the fact that he has a notebook computer, cell phone and PDA. Kim Hahn, a media entrepreneur, prefers jotting her ideas down in a spiral notebook, has a team that would organize her records for her, and a personal assistant that would keep track of changes to her schedule. Reasons why these entrepreneurs use old-fashioned methods along with new technology are given.

4961 ■ "Motors and Motion Control" in *Canadian Electronics* (Vol. 23, February 2008, No. 1, pp. 23)
Pub: CLB Media Inc.
Description: A new version of MicroMo Electronics Inc.'s Smoovy Series 0303...B has been added to MicroMo's DC motor product line. United Electronic Industries, on the other hand, has introduced the new UEIPAC series of programmable automation controllers that can offer solutions to various applications such as unmanned vehicle controllers. Features and functions of other new motors and motion control devices are given.

4962 ■ "My Favorite Tool for Organizing Data" in *Inc.* (Vol. 33, November 2011, No. 9, pp. 46)
Pub: Inc. Magazine
Ed: Abram Brown. **Description:** Intelligence software firm uses Roambi, a Web-based service that turns spreadsheet data into interactive files for iPhones and iPads.

4963 ■ "Nat'l Instruments Connects with Lego" in *Austin Business JournalInc.* (Vol. 28, August 22, 2008, No. 23, pp. 1)
Pub: American City Business Journals
Ed: Laura Hipp. **Description:** Austin-based National Instruments Corporation has teamed with Lego Group from Denmark to create a robot that can be built by children and can be used to perform tasks. Lego WeDo, their latest product, uses computer connection to power its movements. The educational benefits of the new product are discussed.

4964 ■ "The New Breed of Wi-Fi Only Tablets: No Data Plan Required" in *Inc.* (Vol. 33, September 2011, No. 7, pp. 52)
Pub: Inc. Magazine
Ed: John Brandon. **Description:** New Wi-Fi only tablets are available from Samsung, Hewlett Packard, Asus and Acer. A description of offerings from these companies is included.

4965 ■ "New Ways To Think About Data Loss: Data Loss Is Costly and Painful" in *Franchising World* (Vol. 42, August 2010, No. 8, pp. 21)
Pub: International Franchise Association
Ed: Ken Colburn. **Description:** Information for maintaining data securely for franchised organizations, including smart phones, tablets, copiers, computers and more is given.

4966 ■ "Not Your Father's Whiteboard" in *Inc.* (Vol. 33, November 2011, No. 9, pp. 50)
Pub: Inc. Magazine
Ed: Adam Baer. **Description:** Sharp's new interactive whiteboard is really a 70-inch touch screen monitor with software for importing presentations from any Windows 7 computer.

4967 ■ "Note-Taking App, Supercharged" in *Inc.* (Vol. 33, October 2011, No. 8, pp. 48)
Pub: Inc. Magazine
Ed: Adam Baer. **Description:** Note Taker HD is an iPad app that lets the user text by typing with finger or stylus with various colors, fonts and sizes; Extensive Notes creates notes, records audio memos, and takes photos and videos; Evernote allows users to create notes, take snapshots, and record voice memos.

4968 ■ "One Laptop Per Child Weighs Going For-Profit" in *Boston Business Journal* (Vol. 31, May 20, 2011, No. 17, pp. 1)
Pub: Boston Business Journal
Ed: Mary Moore. **Description:** Nonprofit organization One Laptop Per Child is thinking of shifting into a for-profit structure in order to raise as much as $10 million in capital to achieve its goal of distributing more XO laptops to poor children worldwide. The organization has distributed 2 million computers since 2008 with Uruguay, Peru and Rwanda as its biggest markets.

4969 ■ "Our Hoarder Mentality: Blame the Hard Disk" in *PC Magazine* (Vol. 30, November 2011, No. 11, pp. 46)
Pub: Ziff Davis Inc.
Ed: John C. Dvorak. **Description:** Computer programmers, once referred to as computer users, are slowly being replaced by passive consumers of products and content of tablets and handheld mobile phones and devices of the future. Understanding is garnered as this article examines this industry trend.

4970 ■ "Panda Security for Business 4.05" in *SC Magazine* (Vol. 21, July 2010, No. 7, pp. 50)
Pub: Haymarket Media Inc.
Description: Profile of Panda Security for Business, software offering endpoint security protection for computer desktops and servers is presented.

4971 ■ "PC Connection Acquires Cloud Software Provider" in *New Hampshire Business Review* (Vol. 33, March 25, 2011, No. 6, pp. 8)
Pub: Business Publications Inc.
Description: Merrimack-based PC Connection Inc. acquired ValCom Technology, a provider of cloud-based IT service management software. Details of the deal are included.

4972 ■ "PC Running Slowly? How to Rev Up Your Machine" in *Inc.* (Vol. 33, November 2011, No. 9, pp. 46)
Pub: Inc. Magazine
Ed: John Brandon. **Description:** Software that keeps PCs tuned up and running smoothing are profiled: AUSLO6ICS BOOSTSPEED 5, $50; Tuneup Utilities 2011, $40; Slimware Slimcleaner 1.9, free; and IOBIT Advanced Systemcare Pro 4, $20 a year.

4973 ■ "PCI Express Powers Machine Vision" in *Canadian Electronics* (Vol. 23, February 2008, No. 1, pp. 8)
Pub: CLB Media Inc.
Ed: Inder Kohli. **Description:** PCI Express is an innovative peripheral bus that can be used in industrial computing. The peripheral bus delivers a high-bandwidth, scaleable, point-to-point path from peripheral cards to the computing core. Features and functions of PCI Express are described in detail.

4974 ■ "Port of Call" in *Entrepreneur* (Vol. 35, November 2007, No. 11, pp. 66)
Pub: Entrepreneur Media Inc.
Ed: Amanda C. Kooser. **Description:** List of the latest USB (universal serial bus) devices for upgrading technology for a small business is presented.

4975 ■ *Power Up Your Small-Medium Business: A Guide to Enabling Network Technologies*
Pub: Cisco Press
Ed: Robyn Aber. **Released:** March 2004. **Price:** $39.95 (US), $57.95 (Canadian). **Description:** Network technologies geared to small and medium-size business, focusing on access, IP telephony, wireless technologies, security, and computer network management.

4976 ■ *Practical Tech for Your Business*
Pub: Kiplinger Books and Tapes
Ed: Michael J. Martinez. **Released:** 2002. **Description:** Advice is offered to help small business owners choose the right technology for their company. The guide tells how to get started, network via the Internet, create an office network, use database software, and conduct business using mobile technology.

4977 ■ "Press Release: Trimble Introduces CFX-750 Display" in *Farm Industry News* (January 4, 2011)
Pub: Penton Business Media Inc.
Description: Trimble is offering a touch screen display called the CFX-750. The new 8-inch full-color display allows farmers to choose the specific guidance, steering and precision agriculture capabilities that best fit their farm's particular needs. The display can be upgraded as business needs change, including the addition of GLONASS capabilities, or the addition of section and rate control for crop inputs such as seed, chemicals and fertilizer.

4978 ■ *Pro Windows Small Business Server 2003*
Pub: Apress L.P.
Ed: Tony Campbell. **Released:** July 2006. **Price:** $39.99. **Description:** Profile of Microsoft's Windows Small Business Server, designed for companies with 50 or fewer employees.

4979 ■ "Quickoffice's MobileFiles Pro App Enables Excel Editing On-the-Go" in *Information Today* (Vol. 26, February 2009, No. 2, pp. 31)
Pub: Information Today, Inc.
Description: Quickoffice Inc. introduced MobileFiles Pro, which features editable Microsoft Office functionality for the iPone and iPod touch. The application allows users to edit and save Microsoft Excel files in .xls format, transfer files to and from PC and Mac desktops via Wi-Fi, and access and synchronize with Apple MobileMe accounts.

4980 ■ "Remote Control: Working From Wherever" in *Inc.* (February 2008, pp. 46-47)
Pub: Gruner & Jahr USA Publishing
Ed: Ryan Underwood. **Description:** New technology allows workers to perform tasks from anywhere via the Internet. Profiles of products to help connect to your office from afar include, LogMein Pro, a Web-based service that allowsaccess to a computer from anywhere; Xdrive, an online service that allows users to store and swap files; Basecamp, a Web-based tools that works like a secure version of MySpace; MojoPac Freedom, is software that allows users to copy their computer's desktop to a removable hard drive and plug into any PC; WatchGuard Firebox X Core e-Series UTM Bundle, hardware that blocks hackers and viruses while allowing employees to work remotely; TightVNC, a free open-source software that lets you control another computer via the Internet.

4981 ■ *Resource Directory*
Pub: Closing the Gap Inc.
Contact: Connie Kneip, Vice President
Released: Annual, February/March. **Price:** $16.95, individuals plus $4 shipping; $36 one-year subscription; $50 online subscription; $40, students online subscription. **Covers:** About 300 suppliers of computer hardware and software designed for use by persons with disabilities. **Entries Include:** Company or organization name, address, phone, description of products. **Arrangement:** Alphabetical. **Indexes:** Product/service, subject, supplier name.

4982 ■ *Running Your Small Business on a Mac*
Pub: Pearson Technology Group Canada
Ed: Doug Hanley. **Released:** November 2006. **Price:** $39.99. **Description:** Tips for using a Mac computer for small business is presented. The book offers shortcuts to iWork and email.

4983 ■ "Samsung's Metamorphosis" in *Austin Business Journal* (Vol. 31, May 20, 2011, No. 11, pp. 1)
Pub: American City Business Journals Inc.
Ed: Christopher Calnan. **Description:** Samsung Austin Semiconductor LP, a developer of semiconductors for smartphones and tablet computers, plans to diversify its offerings to include niche products: flash memory devices and microprocessing devices. In light of this strategy, Samsung Austin will be hiring 300 engineers as part of a $3.6 billion expansion of its plant.

4984 ■ "Save the Date" in *Barron's* (Vol. 90, September 13, 2010, No. 37, pp. 35)
Pub: Barron's Editorial & Corporate Headquarters
Ed: Mark Veverka. **Description:** Mark Hurd is the new Co-President of Oracle after being forced out at Hewlett-Packard where he faced a harassment complaint. HP fired Hurd due to expense account malfeasance. Hurd is also set to speak at an Oracle trade show in San Francisco on September 20, 2010.

4985 ■ *The Small Business Owner's Manual: Everything You Need to Know to Start Up and Run Your Business*
Pub: Career Press, Incorporated
Ed: Joe Kennedy. **Released:** June 2005. **Price:** $19.99 (US), $26.95 (Canadian). **Description:** Comprehensive guide for starting a small business, focusing on twelve ways to obtain financing, business plans, selling and advertising products and services, hiring and firing employees, setting up a Web site, business law, accounting issues, insurance, equipment, computers, banks, financing, customer credit and collection, leasing, and more.

4986 ■ "A Souped-Up Digital Pen" in *Inc.* (Vol. 33, November 2011, No. 9, pp. 50)
Pub: Inc. Magazine
Ed: Adam Baer. **Description:** Wacom's Inkling is a digital pen designed to record drawings and can save layers of sketches and add or remove them at a later date. Animation of these drawings can also be played. Files can be saved on the receiver which has a 2GB memory and they can then be transferred to a computer.

4987 ■ "Taiwan Technology Initiatives Foster Growth" in *Canadian Electronics* (Vol. 23, February 2008, No. 1, pp. 28)
Pub: CLB Media Inc.
Description: A study conducted by the Market Intelligence Center shows that currently, Taiwan is the world's larges producer of information technology products such as motherboards, servers, and LCD monitors. In 2006, Taiwan's LED industry reached a production value of NTD 21 billion. This push into the LED sector shows the Ministry of Economic Affairs' plan to target industries that are environmentally friendly.

4988 ■ "Taking the Steps Into the Clouds" in *New Hampshire Business Review* (Vol. 33, March 25, 2011, No. 6, pp. 19)
Pub: Business Publications Inc.
Ed: Tim Wessels. **Description:** Cloud services include Internet and Web security, spam filtering, message archiving, work group collaboration, IT asset management, help desk and disaster recovery backup.

4989 ■ "Tap the iPad and Mobile Internet Device Market" in *Franchising World* (Vol. 42, September 2010, No. 9, pp. 43)
Pub: International Franchise Association
Ed: John Thomson. **Description:** The iPad and other mobile Internet devices will help franchise owners interact with customers. It will be a good marketing tool for these businesses.

4990 ■ "Tech Tax Heroes Go from Political Neophytes to Savvy Fundraisers" in *Baltimore Business Journal* (Vol. 27, November 20, 2009, No. 28)
Pub: American City Business Journals
Ed: Scott Dance. **Description:** A group of computer services and information technology executives in Maryland have arranged a private dinner that will function as a fundraiser for Governor Martin O'Malley and Lieutenant Governor Anthony Brown. The event is seen as an effort to ensure the industry's involvement in the state after fighting for the repeal of the tech tax in 2007.

4991 ■ "TomTom GO910: On the Road Again" in *Black Enterprise* (Vol. 37, January 2007, No. 6, pp. 52)
Pub: Earl G. Graves Publishing Co. Inc.
Ed: Stephanie Young. **Description:** TomTom GO 910 is a GPS navigator that offers detailed maps of the U.S., Canada, and Europe. Consumers view their routes by a customizable LCD screen showing everything from the quickest to the shortest routes available or how to avoid toll roads. Business travelers may find this product invaluable as it also functions as a cell phone and connects to a variety of other multi-media devices.

4992 ■ "Two Local Firms Make Inc. List: Minority Business" in *Indianapolis Business Journal* (Vol. 31, August 30, 2010, No. 26, pp. 13A)
Pub: Indianapolis Business Journal Corporation
Description: Smart IT staffing agency and Entap Inc., an IT outsourcing firm were among the top ten fastest growing black-owned businesses in the U.S. by Inc. magazine.

4993 ■ "U.S. Trade Body Clears Apple in Patent Case" in *Wall Street Journal Eastern Edition* (November 23 , 2011, pp. C1)
Pub: Dow Jones & Company Inc.
Ed: Matt Jarzemsky, Paul Mozur. **Description:** HTC Corporation alleged in its patent-infringement case against Apple Inc. that Apple violated patents of S3 Graphics Inc., a company which was acquired by HTC Corporation. Now the International Trade Commission has issued a ruling saying that Apple did not violate the patents.

4994 ■ "What is the Future of Disk Drives, Death or Rebirth?" in *ACM Computing Surveys* (Vol. 43, Fall 2011, No. 3, pp. 23)
Pub: Association for Computing Machinery
Ed: Yuhui Deng. **Description:** Disk drives have experienced dramatic development to meet performance requirements since the IBM 1301 disk drive was announced in 1961. However, the performance gap between memory and disk drives has widened to 6 orders of magnitude and continues to widen by about 50 percent per year. Challenges and opportunities facing these storage devices are explored.

4995 ■ "Will mCommerce Make Black Friday Green?" in *Retail Merchandiser* (Vol. 51, September-October 2011, No. 5, pp. 8)
Pub: Phoenix Media Corporation
Ed: Scott Miller. **Description:** Retailers speculate the possibilities of mobile commerce and are implementing strategies at their stores. Consumers using mobile devices accounted for only 0.1 percent of visits to retail Websites on Black Friday 2009 and rose to 5.6 percent in 2010; numbers are expected to rise for 2011.

4996 ■ "Work for Play: Careers in Video Game Development" in *Occupational Outlook Quarterly* (Vol. 55, Fall 2011, No. 3, pp. 2)
Pub: U.S. Bureau of Labor Statistics
Ed: Drew Liming, Dennis Vilorio. **Description:** Game developers make a living creating the games the public enjoys playing. The video gaming industry reported sales over $10 billion in 2009 and employed 32,000 people in 34 states. Career options in video game development are featured.

4997 ■ "Xbox 360 Excels as a Media Hub" in *Hispanic Business* (October 2009, pp. 40)
Pub: Hispanic Business
Ed: Jeremy Nisen. **Description:** Xbox 360 video game console from Microsoft offers games, amazing graphics and state-of-the-art accessories. The trend towards purchase of the Xbox includes more than teenagers.

4998 ■ "Xtium Has Its Head in the Clouds" in *Philadelphia Business Journal* (Vol. 30, September 23, 2011, No. 32, pp. 1)
Pub: American City Business Journals Inc.
Ed: Peter Key. **Description:** Philadelphia-based cloud computing firm Xtium LLC received an $11.5 million first-round investment from Boston-Massachusetts-based OpenView Venture Partners. Catering to midsize businesses and unit of bigger firms, Xtium offers disaster-recovery, hosting, and managed-information-technology-infrastructure services.

STATISTICAL SOURCES

4999 ■ *RMA Annual Statement Studies*
Pub: Robert Morris Associates (RMA)
Released: Annual. **Price:** $175.00 2006-07 edition, $105.00. **Description:** Contains composite balance sheets and income statements for more than 360 industries, including the accounting, auditing, and bookkeeping industries. Also contains five years of comparative historical data for discerning trends. Includes 16 commonly used ratios, computed for most of the size groupings for nearly every industry.

5000 ■ *Standard & Poor's Industry Surveys*
Pub: Standard & Poor's Corp.
Released: Annual. **Price:** $3633.00. **Description:** Two-volume book that examines the prospects for specific industries, including trucking. Also provides analyses of trends and problems, statistical tables and charts, and comparative company analyses.

TRADE PERIODICALS

5001 ■ *Computer Link Magazine*
Pub: Millennium Publishing Inc.
Released: Monthly. **Price:** $20. **Description:** Magazine covering computer news.

5002 ■ *DCLNews*
Pub: Data Conversion Laboratory
Contact: Mark Gross
Ed: Released: Monthly. **Price:** Included in membership;. **Description:** E-journal providing you insider information on XML and SGML, along with the latest technology and e-publishing news.

5003 ■ *Maximum PC*
Pub: Future Network USA
Contact: Michael Brown, Review Ed.
E-mail: michael@maximumpc.com
Released: Monthly. **Price:** $14.95; $24.95 12 CDs; $29.95 other countries; $49.95 other countries two years; $1.95 single issue. **Description:** Consumer magazine covering computing, hardware and software reviews, games and work programs for personal computer users.

5004 ■ *Media Computing*
Pub: Dreamscape Productions
Ed: Sheridan Tatsuno, Editor, statsuno@aol.com. **Released:** Monthly. **Price:** $495, institutions in the U.S. and Canada; $550, institutions elsewhere. **Description:** Supplies analysis of multimedia, internet, intranet, and web computing issues. Recurring features include interviews and reports of meetings.

5005 ■ *Microprocessor Report*
Pub: MicroDesign Resources
Contact: Max Baron
E-mail: mbaron@mdr.cahners.com
Released: 17x/yr. **Price:** $695, U.S. and Canada for print version; $495, U.S. and Canada pounds; $995, U.S. and Canada for print and online version; $995, elsewhere for print version. **Description:** The leading technical publication for the microprocessor industry. Dedicated to providing unbiased, in-depth, critical analysis of new high-performance microprocessor developments. This newsletter is exclusively subscriber-supported.

5006 ■ *Multimedia Internet@Schools*
Pub: Information Today Inc.
Released: Bimonthly. **Price:** $45.95 U.S.; $60 Canada and Mexico; $69 other countries; $86 U.S. 2 years; $132 U.S. 3 years. **Description:** Consumer

guide to high-tech school products. Includes purchasing recommendations, cost-saving tips, and technical advice. Written for and by K-12 school professionals.

5007 ■ *Online*
Pub: Online, A Division of Information Today Inc.
Ed: Marydee Ojala, Editor, marydee@infotoday.com. **Released:** Bimonthly. **Price:** $129.50; $243 two years; $145 Canada and Mexico; $172 other countries. **Description:** Professional magazine covering online and CD-ROM databases with practical how-to articles covering the entire online industry.

VIDEOCASSETTES/ AUDIOCASSETTES

5008 ■ *Introduction to Computer Law*
Practicing Law Institute
810 7th Ave., 21st Fl.
New York, NY 10019-5818
Ph:(212)824-5700
Free: 800-260-4PLI
Co. E-mail: info@pli.edu
URL: http://www.pli.edu
Released: 1985. **Description:** A look at the laws governing computer use and purchase. **Availability:** VHS; 3/4U.

TRADE SHOWS AND CONVENTIONS

5009 ■ COMDEX
Ziff-Davis, Inc.
28 E. 28th St.
New York, NY 10016-7930
Ph:(212)503-3500
Co. E-mail: info@ziffdavis.com
URL: http://www.ziffdavis.com
Released: Annual. **Audience:** Volume resellers and value-adders of small computers and related items; only a virtual trade show since 2003. **Principal Exhibits:** Small computer systems, related peripherals, software, accessories, services, and supplies.

5010 ■ Computer Game Developers' Conference
CMP Media LLC (San Mateo, California)
2800 Campus Dr.
San Mateo, CA 94403
Ph:(650)513-4300
Co. E-mail: cmp@cmp.com
URL: http://www.cmp.com
Released: Annual. **Principal Exhibits:** Equipment, supplies, and services for developers and producers of computer games.

5011 ■ Expo Comm Wireless Korea
E.J. Krause & Associates, Inc.
6550 Rock Spring Dr., Ste. 500
Bethesda, MD 20817
Ph:(301)493-5500
Fax:(301)493-5705
Co. E-mail: ejkinfo@ejkrause.com
URL: http://www.ejkrause.com
Released: Annual. **Principal Exhibits:** Equipment, supplies, and services for computers.

FRANCHISES AND BUSINESS OPPORTUNITIES

5012 ■ Computer Renaissance
3440 W Cheyenne Ave., No. 100
Las Vegas, NV 89032
Ph:(702)458-2780
Free: 800-656-3115
Fax:(702)869-2780
URL: http://www.computerrenaissance.com
No. of Franchise Units: 37. **Founded:** 1988. **Franchised:** 1993. **Description:** Computer stores that buy, sell, and trade new and used computer equipment. **Equity Capital Needed:** Liquid capital of $193,000-$283,000. **Franchise Fee:** $25,000. **Financial Assistance:** Yes. **Training:** Includes 2 weeks training at headquarters, 1 week at franchisee's location and ongoing support.

5013 ■ Data Doctors
2090 E University, Ste. 101
Tempe, AZ 85281
Ph:(480)921-2444
Fax:(480)921-2975
No. of Franchise Units: 69. **No. of Company-Owned Units:** 4. **Founded:** 1988. **Franchised:** 2002. **Description:** Computer sales & services, including web services. **Equity Capital Needed:** $83,400-$114,700. **Franchise Fee:** $35,000. **Royalty Fee:** 5%. **Financial Assistance:** Third party financing available. **Training:** Training at headquarters and onsite varies with video & Internet training ongoing.

5014 ■ Palm Tree Computer Systems
Palm Tree Franchise Corp.
119 N Central Ave.
Oviedo, FL 32765
Ph:(407)796-5001
No. of Franchise Units: 3. **No. of Company-Owned Units:** 1. **Founded:** 1996. **Franchised:** 2006. **Description:** Retail computer store. **Equity Capital Needed:** $116,300-$285,500. **Financial Assistance:** Yes. **Training:** Yes.

COMPUTERIZED DATABASES

5015 ■ *Computer Database*
Cengage Learning Inc.
27500 Drake Rd.
Farmington Hills, MI 48331-3535
Ph:(248)699-4253
Free: 800-877-4253
Fax:(248)699-8069
Co. E-mail: galeord@gale.com
URL: http://gale.cengage.com
Description: Contains more than 1 million citations, abstracts, and full text to literature from some 800 trade journals, industry newsletters, and platform-specific publications covering the computer, telecommunications, and electronics industries. Topics covered include business and industry applications; computer graphics; consumer information; database management systems; hardware and software design, development, and reviews; peripherals; home computers; new products; performance evaluations; programming languages; operating systems; phototypesetting; and word processing. Includes descriptive and financial information for companies covered in the industry literature. **Availability:** Online: ProQuest LLC, ProQuest LLC, Cengage Learning Inc. **Type:** Bibliographic; Full text.

5016 ■ *CRN Direct*
United Business Media Ltd.
600 Community Dr.
Manhasset, NY 11030
Ph:(516)562-5000
Fax:(516)562-7830
Co. E-mail: inquiries@ubm-us.com
URL: http://www.ubmtechnology.com
Description: Contains the complete text of *CRN: The Newsweekly for Builders of Technology Solutions*, a weekly newspaper for dealers and distributors of microcomputer hardware, software, and peripherals. Covers new products, industry statistics and trends, and marketing strategies. **Availability:** Online: United Business Media Ltd. **Type:** Full text.

5017 ■ *INSPEC Ondisc - Technology*
Institution of Engineering and Technology
Michael Faraday House
Stevenage SG1 2AY, United Kingdom
Ph:44 1438 313 311
Fax:44 1438 765 526
Co. E-mail: postmaster@theiet.org
URL: http://www.theiet.org
Description: Contains abstracts and citations to the worldwide literature on electrical engineering and electronics, computers, and information technology. Covers: electronic components, devices, and circuits, Telecommunication, power engineering, and instrumentation; computer theory, hardware, software, applications of computing, control theory, and technology; and the gathering, processing, storage, distribution, and uses of information in Business, Industry, Education, and recreation. Sources include more than 4000 scientific and technical journals, more than 2000 conference proceedings, as well as books, dissertations, and technical reports. A subset of, and corresponds in part to, the INSPEC database (described in a separate entry). **Availability:** CD-ROM: Institution of Engineering and Technology. **Type:** Bibliographic.

LIBRARIES

5018 ■ Fujitsu Microelectronics, Inc.–FMI Library
1250 E. Arques Ave., No. 333
Sunnyvale, CA 94085-5401
Ph:(408)746-6000
Free: 800-831-3183; (800)866
Fax:(408)992-2674
Co. E-mail: fsa_inquiry@us.fujitsu.com
URL: http://www.fujitsu.com/us
Contact: Jasmine Kuen, Mktg.Anl.
Scope: Semiconductor industry and products, computer industry and products, telecommunications, electronics industry. **Services:** Interlibrary loan; SDI; Library not open to the public. **Holdings:** 500 books and conference proceedings; 250 market research reports and newsletters; CD-ROMs. **Subscriptions:** 70 journals and other serials; 2 newspapers.

5019 ■ Walt Disney World–Global Business Technology Strategy Library
Team Disney 336-N
1375 Buena Vista Dr.
PO Box 10000
Lake Buena Vista, FL 32830-1000
Ph:(407)828-4250
Co. E-mail: david.w.hartman@disney.com
URL: http://disneyworld.disney.go.com/wdw
Contact: David Hartman, Libn.
Scope: Computer science, human resources, general business. **Services:** Center not open to the public. **Holdings:** 4000 books, videos, DVDs, and CDs; 100 AV equipment. **Subscriptions:** 200 journals and other serials; 3 newspapers.

START-UP INFORMATION

5020 ■ "Probability Processing Chip: Lyric Semiconductor" in *Inc.* (Volume 32, December 2010, No. 10, pp. 52)
Pub: Inc. Magazine

Ed: Christine Lagorio. **Description:** Lyric Semiconductor, a start up located in Cambridge, Massachusetts, has developed a computer chip that also uses values that fall between zero and one, resulting in a chip that can process information using probabilities, considering many possible answers that find the best fit.

ASSOCIATIONS AND OTHER ORGANIZATIONS

5021 ■ British Columbia Technology Industries Association
1188 W Georgia St., Ste. 900
Vancouver, BC, Canada V6E 4A2
Ph:(604)683-6159
Fax:(604)683-3879
Co. E-mail: info@bctia.org
URL: http://www.bctia.org
Contact: Bill Tam, Pres./CEO

Description: Fosters the growth and development of the Province's technology industries and member companies. Provides programs, services and activities designed to meet the needs and interests of members in the areas of networking, education, public awareness, and government relations. Offers a forum for members to review industry issues, acquire new business knowledge from leading industry professionals, to supply input on existing and proposed legislation and generally work together to advance the industry's interests. **Publications:** *Impact* (annual).

REFERENCE WORKS

5022 ■ "ChemSW Software Development Services Available for Outsourcing" in *Information Today* (Vol. 26, February 2009, No. 2, pp. 30)
Pub: Information Today, Inc.

Description: ChemSW software development services include requirements analysis, specification development, design, development, testing, and system documentation as an IT outsourcing solution. The company can also develop software tracking systems for satellite stockrooms, provide asset management integration solutions and more.

5023 ■ *Cisco Network Design Solutions for Small-Medium Businesses*
Pub: Cisco Press

Ed: Peter Rybaczyk. **Released:** August 2004. **Price:** $55.00. **Description:** Solutions for computer networking professionals using computer networks within a small to medium-sized business. Topics cover not only core networking issues and solutions, but security, IP telephony, unified communications, customer relations management, wireless LANs, and more.

5024 ■ *Information Industry Directory*
Pub: Gale

Released: Annual, Latest edition 36th; April, 2011. **Price:** $1105, individuals. **Covers:** Approximately 12,000 organizations, systems, and services involved in the production and distribution of information in electronic form: database producers and their products online host services, transactional services, library and information networks, bibliographic utilities, library management systems, information retrieval software, mailing list services, fee-based information on demand services, document delivery sources, data collection and analysis centers and firms, and related consultants, service companies, professional and trade associations, publishers, and research activities. **Entries Include:** Name of parent organization, name of system of service, address, phone, toll-free phone, fax, telex, email address, year founded name of unit head, size of staff, names of any affiliated organizations, financial information. Internet access information, general description of electronic product, system, or service, subjects covered or areas of service offered, sources of data for the system, type and quantity of stored information in all forms, publications and microform products and services, computer-based products and services, other services, clientele served, availability and restrictions, name of contact. **Arrangement:** Alphabetical. **Indexes:** Master, database name, software name, publication/microform title, function/service, personal name, subject, geographical.

5025 ■ *Information Sources*
Pub: Software & Information Industry Association
Contact: Ken Wasch, President

Released: Continuous. **Covers:** More than 800 companies involved in the creation, distribution, and use of information products, services, and technology. Entries are prepared by companies described. **Entries Include:** Company name, address, phone, names of executives, international partners, regional offices, trade and brand names, and description of products and services. **Arrangement:** Alphabetical. **Indexes:** Product, personal name, trade name, geographical, corporate parents, international and niche markets.

5026 ■ "PCI Express Powers Machine Vision" in *Canadian Electronics* (Vol. 23, February 2008, No. 1, pp. 8)
Pub: CLB Media Inc.

Ed: Inder Kohli. **Description:** PCI Express is an innovative peripheral bus that can be used in industrial computing. The peripheral bus delivers a high-bandwidth, scaleable, point-to-point path from peripheral cards to the computing core. Features and functions of PCI Express are described in detail.

5027 ■ *Power Up Your Small-Medium Business: A Guide to Enabling Network Technologies*
Pub: Cisco Press

Ed: Robyn Aber. **Released:** March 2004. **Price:** $39.95 (US), $57.95 (Canadian). **Description:** Network technologies geared to small and medium-size business, focusing on access, IP telephony, wireless technologies, security, and computer network management.

5028 ■ *Pro Windows Small Business Server 2003*
Pub: Apress L.P.

Ed: Tony Campbell. **Released:** July 2006. **Price:** $39.99. **Description:** Profile of Microsoft's Windows Small Business Server, designed for companies with 50 or fewer employees.

5029 ■ "Tech Data Launches Unified Communications and Network Security Specialized Business Units" in *Wireless News* (October 22,2009)
Pub: Close-Up Media

Description: Responding to the growing demand for unified communications and network security, Tech Data announced the formation of two new Specialized Business Units.

5030 ■ "The Web Gets Real" in *Canadian Business* (Vol. 79, July 17, 2006, No. 14-15, pp. 19)
Pub: Rogers Media

Ed: Andrew Wahl. **Description:** Ron Lake's efforts of bringing the virtual and physical worlds more closely together by using Geographic Markup Language (GML) are presented.

5031 ■ "Xtium Has Its Head in the Clouds" in *Philadelphia Business Journal* (Vol. 30, September 23, 2011, No. 32, pp. 1)
Pub: American City Business Journals Inc.

Ed: Peter Key. **Description:** Philadelphia-based cloud computing firm Xtium LLC received an $11.5 million first-round investment from Boston-Massachusetts-based OpenView Venture Partners. Catering to midsize businesses and unit of bigger firms, Xtium offers disaster-recovery, hosting, and managed-information-technology-infrastructure services.

TRADE PERIODICALS

5032 ■ *ClieNT Server News*
Pub: G2 Computer Intelligence Inc.

Ed: Maureen O'Gara, Editor, ogara@g2news.com. **Released:** Weekly. **Price:** $595. **Description:** Provides news on Windows 2000, XPad NT, and NT and Microsoft. Covers software and hardware roll-outs, developments of marketing strategies and client server moves competitive to Windows XP 2000 and NT. Recurring features include letters to the editor, news of research, and interviews. Remarks: Available in Acrobat, HTML, and ASCII.

5033 ■ *Engineering Design and Automation*
Pub: John Wiley & Sons Inc.

Released: Quarterly. **Description:** Journal of new research on the design and analysis of production systems, artificial intelligence, and neural networks.

5034 ■ *ePostal News*
Pub: G2 Computer Intelligence Inc.
Ed: Maureen O'Gara, Editor, ogara@g2news.com. **Released:** Weekly. **Price:** $595. **Description:** Reports news on digital media and e-commerce, e-business, Internet security, and Internet Post and e-mail matters.

5035 ■ *International Journal of Intelligent Systems*
Pub: John Wiley & Sons Inc.
Contact: John R. Anderson, Editorial Board
Ed: Ronald R. Yager, Editor. **Released:** Monthly. **Price:** $220 U.S., Canada, and Mexico print only; $304 other countries print only; $3,083 institutions print only; $3,251 institutions, Canada and Mexico print only; $3,335 institutions, other countries print only. **Description:** Journal featuring peer-reviewed work on the systematic development of theory used in the construction of intelligent systems. Covers areas such as man-computer interactions and the use of language, neural networks, and machine learning; includes book reviews.

5036 ■ *Microprocessor Report*
Pub: MicroDesign Resources
Contact: Max Baron
E-mail: mbaron@mdr.cahners.com
Released: 17x/yr. **Price:** $695, U.S. and Canada for print version; $495, U.S. and Canada pounds; $995, U.S. and Canada for print and online version; $995, elsewhere for print version. **Description:** The leading technical publication for the microprocessor industry. Dedicated to providing unbiased, in-depth, critical analysis of new high-performance microprocessor developments. This newsletter is exclusively subscriber-supported.

5037 ■ *Online*
Pub: Online, A Division of Information Today Inc.
Ed: Marydee Ojala, Editor, marydee@infotoday.com. **Released:** Bimonthly. **Price:** $129.50; $243 two years; $145 Canada and Mexico; $172 other countries. **Description:** Professional magazine covering online and CD-ROM databases with practical how-to articles covering the entire online industry.

VIDEOCASSETTES/ AUDIOCASSETTES

5038 ■ *Computer Network Software Functions (82-1XX)*
Skillsoft
107 Northeastern Blvd.
Nashua, NH 03062
Free: 877-545-5763
Co. E-mail: info@netg.com
URL: http://www.skillsoft.com/
Released: 1981. **Description:** Part of an integrated course which focuses on computer networks and the functions of software that must be used in building them. **Availability:** 3/4U.

5039 ■ *Data Base and Organizational Structure*
Skillsoft
107 Northeastern Blvd.
Nashua, NH 03062
Free: 877-545-5763
Co. E-mail: info@netg.com
URL: http://www.skillsoft.com/
Released: 1984. **Description:** This program explains the concepts and importance of data base systems in business. **Availability:** 3/4U.

5040 ■ *Distributed Processor Communication Architecture*
Skillsoft
107 Northeastern Blvd.
Nashua, NH 03062
Free: 877-545-5763
Co. E-mail: info@netg.com
URL: http://www.skillsoft.com/
Released: 1980. **Description:** A course which provides an overview of the entire field of computer interconnection strategies. **Availability:** VHS; 3/4U.

5041 ■ *The Strategic Impact of Information Technology*
Skillsoft
107 Northeastern Blvd.
Nashua, NH 03062
Free: 877-545-5763
Co. E-mail: info@netg.com
URL: http://www.skillsoft.com/
Released: 1984. **Description:** This series of programs examines the impact of information technology on business and how it can be managed. **Availability:** 3/4U.

5042 ■ *The Systems Development Series (27-0XX)*
Skillsoft
107 Northeastern Blvd.
Nashua, NH 03062
Free: 877-545-5763
Co. E-mail: info@netg.com
URL: http://www.skillsoft.com/
Released: 1981. **Description:** Part of an integrated course which teaches an approach for designing and developing computer-based information systems. **Availability:** 3/4U.

5043 ■ *The Systems Series*
Skillsoft
107 Northeastern Blvd.
Nashua, NH 03062
Free: 877-545-5763
Co. E-mail: info@netg.com
URL: http://www.skillsoft.com/
Released: 197?. **Description:** This series explains how to analyze, design, and manage the implementation of new application systems. As part of an integrated study course, the video series is suitable for use in any computer hardware or software environment. **Availability:** 3/4U.

5044 ■ *Using Information Technology*
Educational Activities, Inc.
PO Box 87
Baldwin, NY 11510
Free: 800-797-3223
Fax:(516)623-9282
URL: http://www.edact.com
Price: $99.00. **Description:** Part of the Management Speaks Series. Outlines the effect of information technology on business. Covers the difference between computers and information technology, integrating technology, the necessary education that managers and technologists need, where and how information technology works, and how to replace management information systems with worker information systems. **Availability:** VHS.

TRADE SHOWS AND CONVENTIONS

5045 ■ COMDEX
Ziff-Davis, Inc.
28 E. 28th St.
New York, NY 10016-7930
Ph:(212)503-3500
Co. E-mail: info@ziffdavis.com
URL: http://www.ziffdavis.com
Released: Annual. **Audience:** Volume resellers and value-adders of small computers and related items; only a virtual trade show since 2003. **Principal Exhibits:** Small computer systems, related peripherals, software, accessories, services, and supplies.

CONSULTANTS

5046 ■ Advanced Computer Consulting Inc.
17-24 Parsons Blvd.
Whitestone, NY 11357
Ph:(718)746-0900
Fax:(718)746-2099
Co. E-mail: accidrg@aol.com
Contact: Dr. Gus A. Galatianos, President
E-mail: accidrg@aol.com
Scope: Services include management consulting, technology assessment, strategic systems planning, feasibility studies, computer and communications hardware and software evaluations, systems analysis through implementation, project management, systems integration, and computer training. Industries served include banking, defense, distribution, healthcare, insurance and manufacturing. **Publications:** "Distributed DDBMS: Problems and Prospects," Scientific Computing &Automation Magazine, Nov, 1992; "Expert Systems Give PCs a Piece of Mind," Office Technology Management Magazine, Dec, 1991. **Seminars:** Principles of Software Engineering; Principles of Database Systems; Principles of Artificial Intelligence and Expert Systems; Principles of Object-oriented Programming and C Plus Plus.

5047 ■ The Centech Group Inc.
6402 Arlington Blvd. 10th Fl.
Falls Church, VA 22042
Ph:(703)525-4444
Free: 800-938-1026
Fax:(703)525-2349
Co. E-mail: clientinterest@centechgroup.com
URL: http://www.centechgroup.com
Contact: Kelly Davidson, Principal
E-mail: whittingtonp@atscentechgroup.com
Scope: Firm provides a variety of computer and information systems services. Work involves program management support, computer systems analysis and integration, software engineering and development, network services, imaging, document conversion, manufacturing and engineering, LAN/WAN; work-flow, and document management and data warehousing, including analysis, design, and implementation, information systems modernization and integration, is a lot to be said for the company you keep, whether it is your customers, your partners or your team members (employees) and information engineering.

5048 ■ Computer Integrations Inc.
1670 Bayview Ave.
Toronto, ON, Canada M4S 1H7
Ph:(416)485-4712
Fax:(416)481-4220
Contact: Ivo Zivkov, President
E-mail: izivkov@onramp.ca
Scope: Specializes in the integration of hardware software products from different vendors as well as custom software development. Provides the following services feasibility study cost benefit analysis participating in RFP preparation and evaluation project design, development, and management installation planning application integration user needs analysis vendor selection, hardware and software; software hardware integration and configuration technical support, maintenance installation assistance training program for trainer and end users phone support for trainer information resource management and documentation preparation. Industries served computer and retail companies.

5049 ■ COTC Technologies Inc.
172 E Industrial Blvd.
PO Box 7615
Pueblo, CO 81007-4406
Ph:(719)547-0938
Free: 888-547-0938
Fax:(719)547-1105
Contact: Karen Renz, CFO
E-mail: karen@atscotc-consulting.com
Scope: Provides software consulting services to organizations that require assistance with their HP3000 computer system. Provides systems analysis, programming, operations support, and system management. Also provides PC software and hardware support and consulting. Additionally provides various training for the HP3000 computer system. Industries served: healthcare, aerospace procurement, aerospace proposal activities, and HP3000 computer systems.

5050 ■ Pathways Unlimited Inc.
1331 S Knoxville Ave.
Tulsa, OK 74112-5805
Ph:(918)744-7482
Fax:(918)744-8909
Co. E-mail: sales@pathways-unlimited.com
URL: http://www.pathways-unlimited.com
Contact: Sandy Ollah, Director
E-mail: sales@pathways-unlimited.com
Scope: Specializes in database publishing. Serving as a Microsoft fox pro development partner, data

publishing systems have been developed to input and process directory information seamlessly from databases and lotus into publishing systems. Serves the publishing industry.

5051 ■ Saffire Systems & Development Inc.
2919 Lucky John Dr.
PO Box 680119
Park City, UT 84060
Ph:(435)649-4146
Fax:(435)647-5708
Co. E-mail: info@saffiresystems.com
URL: http://www.saffiresystems.com
Contact: Kim Page, Principle
E-mail: gdd@atssaffiresystems.com
Scope: Diverse consulting firm that provides system integration, including software and utility development, training and technical writing. Serves private industries as well as government agencies. Woman owned firm. **Publications:** "Interleaf Tips & Tricks," Onward Press, Santa Fe, NM; "The Interleaf Exercise Book," Onward Press, Santa Fe, NM. **Seminars:** Desktop publishing. **Special Services:** HAGNET.

5052 ■ STN Inc.
2126 Espey Ct., Ste. C
Crofton, MD 21114
Ph:(410)721-4004
Free: 800-321-1969
Fax:(410)721-9011
Co. E-mail: ask@stn.com
URL: http://www.stn.com
Contact: Michael Bacastow, Mgr
E-mail: meb@stn.com
Scope: Computer systems consultants specializing in custom software for multi-user computers. All work based on the UNIX environment, with C language and database management system expertise on staff. Provides a full range of solutions, from computer hardware, software and services, to LAN and WAN technology and Internet assistance. Serves private industry and government agencies worldwide. **Publications:** "File Pro Developers Reference Manual". **Seminars:** Browser-Based filePro On Your Local Area Network, 2009; Advanced filePro Input and Output Techniques, Sep, 2008; filePro for Database Managers and Programmers New To filePro, Jul, 2008. **Special Services:** filePro^R; WorkLine^{TM}; MoveTrac^{TM}; LeadTrac^{TM}; MoveBill^{TM}.

5053 ■ Sygenex Inc.
4770 Eastgate Mall
San Diego, CA 92121-1970
Ph:(858)455-5530
Fax:(858)453-9274
Co. E-mail: sygenex@orincon.com
Contact: Linda Gooden, Exec VP of Info Systems
Scope: Supplier of advanced technology products and services in key niches essential to the United States intelligence community and its partners. Engaged in the research, design, development, manufacture and integration of advanced technology systems, products and services.

FRANCHISES AND BUSINESS OPPORTUNITIES

5054 ■ Silution Franchise Corp.
1472 E Walnut St.
Pasadena, CA 91106
Free: 877-745-8846
Fax:(626)535-0566
Founded: 1998. **Franchised:** 2006. **Description:** Computer services & support. **Equity Capital Needed:** $39,950-$71,800. **Franchise Fee:** $22,000. **Royalty Fee:** 10%. **Financial Assistance:** Third party financing available. **Training:** Provides 5 days at headquarters, 1 day at franchisees location with ongoing support.

5055 ■ Vehicle Tracking Solutions
10 E 5th St.
Deer Park, NY 11729
Ph:(631)586-7400
Fax:(866)873-0066
Co. E-mail: jmcjr@VTSN.com
URL: http://www.VTSN.com
No. of Franchise Units: 9. **No. of Company-Owned Units:** 3. **Founded:** 2001. **Franchised:** 2007. **Description:** Companies that have fleets of vehicles use VTS Systems and software to gauge the productivity of their vehicles. **Equity Capital Needed:** $58,150-$64,600. **Franchise Fee:** $24,900. **Financial Assistance:** Limited in-house financing available. **Training:** 1 week training program provided at headquarters followed by 2 days onsite.

COMPUTERIZED DATABASES

5056 ■ *Business Wire*
Berkshire Hathaway Inc.
44 Montgomery St., 39th Fl.
San Francisco, CA 94104
Ph:(415)986-4422
Free: 800-227-0845
Fax:(415)788-5335
Co. E-mail: SF_sales_group@bizwire.com
URL: http://www.businesswire.com
Description: Contains more than 1.4 million records that make up the complete text of press releases from public and private companies and other organizations, such as hospitals and universities. Covers new products, stock offerings, mergers, legal actions, financial information, personnel changes, and company announcements of general interest. Includes headline recaps hourly plus recaps of high tech headlines in some systems. Records include company name, headline, publication date, ticker symbol, byline; dateline, time, word count (usually less than 500), and text, including contact information. Covers industries such as banking, computers, telecommunications, entertainment, aviation, biotechnology, and mining; general news and features; some international events; and sports. **Availability:** Online: Thomson Reuters, Mzinga Inc., ProQuest LLC, Dow Jones & Company Inc., LexisNexis Group, Bloomberg LP. **Type:** Full text.

5057 ■ *Computer Database*
Cengage Learning Inc.
27500 Drake Rd.
Farmington Hills, MI 48331-3535
Ph:(248)699-4253
Free: 800-877-4253
Fax:(248)699-8069
Co. E-mail: galeord@gale.com
URL: http://gale.cengage.com
Description: Contains more than 1 million citations, abstracts, and full text to literature from some 800 trade journals, industry newsletters, and platform-specific publications covering the computer, telecommunications, and electronics industries. Topics covered include business and industry applications; computer graphics; consumer information; database management systems; hardware and software design, development, and reviews; peripherals; home computers; new products; performance evaluations; programming languages; operating systems; phototypesetting; and word processing. Includes descriptive and financial information for companies covered in the industry literature. **Availability:** Online: ProQuest LLC, ProQuest LLC, Cengage Learning Inc. **Type:** Bibliographic; Full text.

5058 ■ *Computer and Information Systems Abstracts*
ProQuest LLC
789 E Eisenhower Pky.
Ann Arbor, MI 48103
Ph:(734)761-4700
Fax:(734)997-4222
Co. E-mail: info@proquest.com
URL: http://www.csa.com
Description: Contains more than 740,000 citations, with abstracts, to the worldwide literature on theoretical and applied computer science. Sources include books, journals, conference proceedings, and government reports. Corresponds to *Computer and Information Systems Abstracts Journal.* **Availability:** Online: STN International, STN International. **Type:** Bibliographic.

5059 ■ *Computerworld*
International Data Group Inc.
One Exeter Plz., 15th Fl.
Boston, MA 02116
Ph:(617)534-1200
Co. E-mail: idgcorpcom@idg.com
URL: http://www.idg.com
Description: Contains the complete text of *Computerworld*, a newspaper on the computer industry. Covers personal computers, workstations, systems and software, systems management, and business news, including the computer market and industry trends. **Availability:** Online: LexisNexis Group, International Data Group Inc. **Type:** Full text.

5060 ■ *TecTrends*
Information Sources Inc.
PO Box 8120
Berkeley, CA 94707
Ph:(510)525-6220
Co. E-mail: tectrendsinfo@tectrends.com
URL: http://www.tectrends.com
Description: Contains information on the information technology industry, with detailed descriptions on more than 12,000 information technology products. Includes company information, including personnel names, addresses, telephone numbers, URLs, e-mails, and a description of the company. Product information includes system requirements, availability, vendor support, and a product description. These product and company descriptions are linked to independent third-party reviews abstracted from more than 200 trade journals and industry magazines. **Availability:** Online: Information Sources Inc., ProQuest LLC, ProQuest LLC. **Type:** Bibliographic; Directory.

LIBRARIES

5061 ■ Agilent Technologies–Santa Clara Site Library
5301 Stevens Creek Blvd.
MS 55/27
Santa Clara, CA 95051
Ph:(408)345-8886
Free: 877-424-4536
Fax:(408)345-8474
Co. E-mail: contact_us@agilent.com
URL: http://www.home.agilent.com
Contact: Diana Robba, Res.Info.Spec. & Mgr.
Scope: Electronics, business, computer science, biological sciences. **Services:** Interlibrary loan; copying; Library not open to the public. **Holdings:** 4000 books. **Subscriptions:** 160 journals and other serials; 2 newspapers.

5062 ■ AMS–Knowledge Center Library
4050 Legato Rd.
Fairfax, VA 22033
Ph:(703)267-5669
Fax:(703)276-5094
Co. E-mail: AMS_know@mail.amsinc.com
Contact: Nancy Gregory, Libn.
Scope: Business, economics, computers, data processing, software engineering, computer programming, telecommunications. **Services:** Interlibrary loan; Library open to the public by appointment. **Holdings:** 3500 volumes; CD-ROMs. **Subscriptions:** 200 journals and other serials.

5063 ■ CitiBank Technical Library
820 Stillwater Rd., 2nd Fl.
West Sacramento, CA 95605-1629
Ph:(916)374-7486
Free: 800-374-9700
Co. E-mail: mjones3@calfed.com
URL: http://www.citibank.com/domain/calfed_converts.htm
Contact: Michael Jones, Tech.Libn.
Scope: Computer systems, telecommunications. **Services:** Library not open to the public. **Holdings:** 500 books; 4000 mainframe computer documents. **Subscriptions:** 10 journals and other serials.

5064 ■ Computer Sciences Corporation Corporate Library
3170 Fairview Park Dr.
Falls Church, VA 90245
Ph:(703)876-1000
Co. E-mail: alawrence@csc.com
URL: http://www.csc.com
Contact: Anita Lawrence, Libn.
Scope: Data processing, communications, information retrieval, programming, systems analysis, business, management, operations research, systems integration, outsourcing, company background information. **Services:** Interlibrary loan; copying; Library not open to the public. **Holdings:** 150 books. **Subscriptions:** 70 journals and other serials.

5065 ■ Hewlett-Packard Company–Roseville Research Library
8000 Foothills Blvd.
MS 5621
Roseville, CA 95747
Ph:(916)785-5548
Fax:(916)785-3266
Contact: Rick Shallenberger, Info.Res.Anl.
Scope: Computer science, electrical engineering, computer networking, business. **Services:** Interlibrary loan; copying; SDI; Library not open to the public. **Holdings:** 2000 books. **Subscriptions:** 125 journals and other serials.

5066 ■ Northrop Grumman Mission Systems–Technology Library
12011 Sunset Hills Rd.
Reston, VA 20190
Ph:(703)345-7738
Fax:(703)345-7735
Co. E-mail: norma.j.draper@ngc.com
Contact: Norma Draper, Sr.Tech.Libn.
Scope: Systems engineering, information technology, computer science, systems integration. **Services:** Interlibrary loan; Library not open to the public. **Holdings:** 500 books and technical reports. **Subscriptions:** 35 journals and other serials.

RESEARCH CENTERS

5067 ■ HEC Montreal–Information Systems Research Group–Groupe de recherche en systèmes d'information
3000 Chemin de la Cote-Sainte-Catherine
Montreal, QC, Canada H3T 2A7
Ph:(514)340-6852
Fax:(514)340-6132
Co. E-mail: guy.pare@hec.ca
URL: http://gresi.hec.ca
Contact: Prof. Guy Pare, Co-Dir.
E-mail: guy.pare@hec.ca
Scope: Information technology management, group decision support systems, organizational impact of information technology, and information systems development. **Publications:** Cahiers du GReSI.

5068 ■ National Research Council Canada–Institute for Information Technology
46 Dinnen Dr.
Fredericton, NB, Canada E3B 9W4
Ph:(506)451-2500
Fax:(506)452-4031
Co. E-mail: christian.couturier@nrc-cnrc.gc.ca
URL: http://www.nrc-cnrc.gc.ca/eng/ibp/iit.html
Contact: Christian Couturier, Dir.Gen.
E-mail: christian.couturier@nrc-cnrc.gc.ca
Scope: Software and systems technology for various industry sectors in Canada in order to help the nation prosper in the knowledge economy. Research is focused on knowledge from data, people-oriented systems, and e-business. **Services:** Business mentoring; Licensing opportunities; Research and development support; Strategic partnerships. **Publications:** NRC Annual Report. **Educational Activities:** Colloquium series (monthly).

5069 ■ Stanford University–Information Systems Laboratory
350 Serra Mall
Department of Electrical Engineering
Stanford, CA 94305-9510
Ph:(650)723-3473
Fax:(650)723-8473
Co. E-mail: abbas@ee.stanford.edu
URL: http://isl.stanford.edu
Contact: Prof. Abbas El Gamal PhD, Dir.
E-mail: abbas@ee.stanford.edu
Scope: Signal processing, information and communication theory, error control coding, array processing and adaptive filtering, broadcast and multiple access communication systems, analog to digital conversion, data compression, speech coding and recognition, multivariable systems, identification and digital control, and algorithms and architecture for very-large-scale integrated circuits. Adaptive signal processing, pattern recognition, machine learning, diagnostic medical imaging systems, fourier and statistical optics, optical data processing and computing.

5070 ■ University of Illinois at Urbana-Champaign–Center for Reliable and High Performance Computing
Coordinated Science Laboratory
1308 W Main St.
Urbana, IL 61801
Ph:(217)333-6201
Fax:(217)244-5685
Co. E-mail: patel@crhc.uiuc.edu
URL: http://www.crhc.illinois.edu
Contact: Prof. Janak H. Patel, Co-Dir.
E-mail: patel@crhc.uiuc.edu
Scope: Reliable and fault-tolerant computing, testing and design for testability, high performance very-large-scale integrated (VLSI) architectures, high performance knowledge and data engineering, and computer-aided design tools for VLSI. Performs experimental studies of computer systems.

5071 ■ University of Maryland at College Park–Institute for Advanced Computer Studies
3143 A.V. Williams Bldg.
College Park, MD 20740
Ph:(301)405-6722
Fax:(301)314-9658
Co. E-mail: varshney@cs.umd.edu
URL: http://www.umiacs.umd.edu/
Contact: Prof. Amitabh Varshney, Dir.
E-mail: varshney@cs.umd.edu
Scope: High performance computing, computer vision, artificial intelligence, software engineering, internet computing, databases, multimedia, natural language processing, computational science, and theory of computing. **Publications:** Technical report series.

5072 ■ University of Maryland at College Park–Institute for Systems Research
2173 A.V. Williams Bldg.
College Park, MD 20742
Ph:(301)405-6615
Fax:(301)314-9920
Co. E-mail: rebeccac@isr.umd.edu
URL: http://www.isr.umd.edu
Contact: Rebecca Copeland, Dir., PR and Info. Management
E-mail: rebeccac@isr.umd.edu
Scope: Complex, heterogeneous, and dynamic problems of engineering technology and systems. Research includes: global communication systems, next generation manufacturing operations research, societal infrastructures, systems engineering education, and sensor and actuator networks. **Services:** Research Review Day, annual free showcase event of research held in the spring. **Publications:** Institute for Systems Research Technical Reports; Newsletter (quarterly). **Educational Activities:** Colloquia; Seminars; Workshops.

5073 ■ Washington University in St. Louis–Computer and Communications Research Center
CB 1045
Department of Computer Science & Engineering
St. Louis, MO 63130-4899
Ph:(314)935-6107
Fax:(314)935-7302
Co. E-mail: jbf@wustl.edu
URL: http://www.ccrc.wustl.edu
Contact: Prof. Mark A. Franklin, Dir.
E-mail: jbf@wustl.edu
Scope: High performance computer systems design, wideband large area packet-based communications networks, and VLSI (very-large-scale integration) design techniques. Studies areas of parallel processor design, telecommunications systems design, interconnection network design, and systems simulation and performance analysis.

REFERENCE WORKS

5074 ■ "Cerner Works the Business Circuit" in *Business Journal-Serving Metropolitan Kansas City* (Vol. 26, October 5, 2007, No. 4, pp. 1)
Pub: American City Business Journals, Inc.
Ed: Rob Roberts. **Description:** Cerner Corporation is embracing the coming of the electronic medical record exchange by creating a regional health information organization (RHIO) called the CareEntrust. The RHIO convinced health insurers to share claims data with patients and clinicians. At the Center Health Conference, held October 7 to 10, Cerner will demonstrate the software it developed for CareEntrust to the 40,000 healthcare and information technology professionals.

5075 ■ "The Keeper of Records" in *Black Enterprise* (Vol. 41, December 2010, No. 5, pp. 54)
Pub: Earl G. Graves Publishing Co. Inc.
Ed: Denise Campbell. **Description:** Medical billing and coding, submission of claims to health insurance companies and Medicare or Medicaid for payment is one of the fastest growing disciplines in healthcare.

TRADE PERIODICALS

5076 ■ *Office Technology*
Pub: Business Technology Association
Released: Monthly. **Price:** $45; $50 Canada; $60 other countries. **Description:** Magazine reporting industry news and trends for dealers of copiers, word processors, computers, software, cash registers, facsimile equipment, and other business equipment and machines, including mailing equipment.

5077 ■ *Print Solutions*
Pub: Print Services & Distribution Association
Ed: John Delavan, Editor. **Released:** Monthly. **Price:** $29 nonmembers. **Description:** Trade magazine on business forms and other printed products, document management, electronic data interchange, and electronic forms.

TRADE SHOWS AND CONVENTIONS

5078 ■ Business & Technology Solutions Show
Illinois Certified Public Accounting Society
550 W. Jackson, Ste. 900
Chicago, IL 60661
Ph:(312)933-0407
Free: 800-993-0407
Fax:(312)993-9954
URL: http://www.icpas.org
Released: Annual. **Audience:** Certified public accountants and their clients, business owners and managers, and others from the financial and business community. **Principal Exhibits:** Computers, office equipment, software publishing and educational supplies, and financial services.

5079 ■ COMDEX
Ziff-Davis, Inc.
28 E. 28th St.
New York, NY 10016-7930
Ph:(212)503-3500
Co. E-mail: info@ziffdavis.com
URL: http://www.ziffdavis.com
Released: Annual. **Audience:** Volume resellers and value-adders of small computers and related items; only a virtual trade show since 2003. **Principal Exhibits:** Small computer systems, related peripherals, software, accessories, services, and supplies.

CONSULTANTS

5080 ■ Bass & Co.
9800 Thunderhill Ct.
Great Falls, VA 22066
Ph:(703)759-4720
Fax:(703)759-0465
Co. E-mail: info@bassandco.com
Contact: Shirley A. Bass, Chief Information Officer
E-mail: shirley@atsbassandco.com
Scope: Offers business consulting on selection and implementation of microcomputer-based accounting systems. Also offers consulting on Federal Acquisition Regulation (FAR) compliance for accounting, purchasing, and estimating systems. Practice includes litigation support, policy and procedure development, DCAA audit assistance, incurred cost submissions and proposal pricing. Industries served: Government contractors, nonprofits, and general service businesses. **Publications:** "The Sba Loan Programs". **Seminars:** Accounting for Government Contracts; Doing Business With the Federal Government; Cost Proposals for Federal Government Contracts; Selecting and Implementing an Accounting System; Financing Alternatives for Small Businesses.

5081 ■ Health Management Systems Inc.
401 Park Ave. S
New York, NY 10016-8008
Ph:(212)857-5000
Free: 877-467-0184
Co. E-mail: info@hmsy.com
URL: http://www.hmsy.com
Contact: Bill Lucia, President
E-mail: blucia@atshmsy.com
Scope: Specializes in cost containment, program integrity and coordination of benefits solutions for government-funded and commercial healthcare entities. Helps clients ensure that healthcare claims are paid correctly and by the responsible party and that those enrolled to receive program benefits meet qualifying criteria. Focuses exclusively on the healthcare industry. **Publications:** "Credit Balance Recovery"; "Preparing for a Historic 2009"; "Introducing the New HMS"; "HMS Acquires Prudent Rx".

5082 ■ Kluger & Associates Inc.
70 Mitchell Blvd., Ste. 106
San Rafael, CA 94903-2019
Ph:(415)479-7900
Free: 800-776-5060
Fax:(415)472-3534
Contact: Andrew M. Kluger, President
E-mail: akluger@pacbell.net
Scope: Provides professional practice management specialization in accounting and billing services. Industries served health care.

5083 ■ McLeod Associates Inc.
3 Mayfair Ln.
PO Box 2164
Westport, CT 06880
Ph:(203)227-3767
Fax:(203)227-9554
Co. E-mail: bernicestine@mcleodassociatesinc.com
URL: http://www.mcleodassociatesinc.com
Contact: Bernicestine E. McLeod Jr., President
E-mail: bemcleo@attglobal.net
Scope: Management information systems consulting firm specializes in providing computer-related project management, education, database design and development, systems analysis and design, systems and application programming services in the mainframe, workstation, and client/server environments. Offers expertise in implementing user oriented computer solutions to facilitate business objectives in all environments. Application areas include accounts receivable, order entry, billing, leasing, credit, and inventory management/control. Firm also specializes in workgroup applications, for example, Lotus Notes as well as personal computer software products (word processors, database managers, spreadsheets). Industries served: manufacturing, distribution, retail, hospital, financial services.

LIBRARIES

5084 ■ International Data Corp.–IDC Library
2131 Landings Dr.
Mountain View, CA 94043
Ph:(650)962-6481
Fax:(650)691-0531
Co. E-mail: slake@idc.com
URL: http://www.idc.com
Contact: Sara Lake, Mgr.Lib.Svcs.
Scope: Information technology. **Services:** Center not open to the public. **Holdings:** 350 books; 250 subject files. **Subscriptions:** 70 journals and other serials.

5085 ■ International Data Corp. Library
5 Speen St.
Framingham, MA 01701
Ph:(508)872-8200
Co. E-mail: leads@idc.com
URL: http://www.idc.com
Contact: Kirk Campbell, Pres./CEO
Scope: Computer technology, management. **Services:** Interlibrary loan; Center not open to the public. **Holdings:** 2200 books; 50 Annual reports; 235 subject files; 12 CD-ROMs. **Subscriptions:** 200 journals and other serials.

RESEARCH CENTERS

5086 ■ University of Tennessee at Chattanooga–Center of Excellence in Applied Computational Science and Engineering
615 Mccallie Ave., Dept. 7200
Chattanooga, TN 37403

Ph:(423)425-5493
Fax:(423)425-5517
Co. E-mail: henry-mcdonald@utc.edu
URL: http://www.utc.edu/Research/CEACSE
Contact: Dr. H. McDonald, Dir.
E-mail: henry-mcdonald@utc.edu
Scope: New computer applications, especially in the fields of industry and education. Activities include studies of artificial intelligence, knowledge engineering, expert systems, productivity enhancement, office/factory automation systems, the development of voice-activated hardware for physically disabled persons, multimedia and hypermedia systems, and visualization technology.

5087 ■ University of Texas at Arlington–Center for Information Technologies Management
Department of Information Systems & Operations Management, B
Arlington, TX 76019-0437
Ph:(817)272-3546
Fax:(817)272-5801
Co. E-mail: pobeck@uta.edu
URL: http://www2.uta.edu/infosys/citm/
Contact: Phil Beck PhD, Dir.
E-mail: pobeck@uta.edu
Scope: Information resource management, business systems planning, disaster recovery planning, business process reengineering, software development, decision support systems, executive information systems, artificial intelligence applications, expert systems, computer system modeling, multivariate statistical methods, database analysis and design, regression analysis, and distributed data processing. Provides research and development facilities to outside organizations. **Services:** Consulting for industry in information systems, management science, production and operations management, and statistics; Coordinates research activities to complement the needs of local industry. **Educational Activities:** Disaster Recovery Institute seminars (3/year).

REFERENCE WORKS

5088 ■ "55-Alive! Wants To Be MySpace for the Baby Boomer Set. Can It Raise $250,000?" in *Inc.* (October 2007, pp. 50)
Pub: Gruner & Jahr USA Publishing
Description: Profile of 55-Alive! The online community created especially for individuals over the age of 50. The Website offers blogs, a dating section, listings for recreational vehicles for sale, movie reviews, advertising and articles of interest to users.

5089 ■ "And the Money Comes Rolling In" in *Inc.* (Vol. 31, January-February 2009, No. 1, pp. 62)
Pub: Mansueto Ventures LLC
Ed: Max Chafkin. **Description:** Profile of Markus Frind, founder of the online dating service in British Columbia called Plenty of Fish. Frind works one hour a day and earns $10 million a year by keeping things simple.

5090 ■ "Ask Inc." in *Inc.* (October 2007, pp. 73-74)
Pub: Gruner & Jahr USA Publishing
Description: An online marketing research firm investigates the use of online communities such as MySpace and Second life in order to recruit individuals to answer surveys.

5091 ■ "On Target" in *Canadian Business* (Vol. 81, July 22, 2008, No. 12-13, pp. 45)
Pub: Rogers Media Ltd.
Ed: Calvin Leung. **Description:** Companies such as LavalifePRIME, a dating website devoted to singles 45 and older, discuss the value of marketing and services aimed at Canada's older consumers. One-third of Canada's 33 million people are 50-plus, controlling 77 percent of the countries wealth.

TRADE SHOWS AND CONVENTIONS

5092 ■ COMDEX
Ziff-Davis, Inc.
28 E. 28th St.
New York, NY 10016-7930
Ph:(212)503-3500
Co. E-mail: info@ziffdavis.com
URL: http://www.ziffdavis.com
Released: Annual. **Audience:** Volume resellers and value-adders of small computers and related items; only a virtual trade show since 2003. **Principal Exhibits:** Small computer systems, related peripherals, software, accessories, services, and supplies.

FRANCHISES AND BUSINESS OPPORTUNITIES

5093 ■ The Right One
200 Cordwainer Dr., Ste. 102
Norwell, MA 02061
Ph:(781)982-4522
Fax:(781)982-0455
URL: http://www.therightone.com
No. of Franchise Units: 15. **No. of Company-Owned Units:** 12. **Founded:** 1990. **Franchised:** 1999. **Description:** Dating service. **Equity Capital Needed:** $98,400-$254,000. **Franchise Fee:** $50,000-$150,000. **Royalty Fee:** 6%. **Training:** 1 week at headquarters, 1 week at franchisees location, 2 weeks at existing locations and ongoing support.

Concession Stand Business

ASSOCIATIONS AND OTHER ORGANIZATIONS

5094 ■ Canadian Restaurant and Foodservices Association–Association Canadienne des Restaurateurs et des Services Alimentaires
316 Bloor St. W
Toronto, ON, Canada M5S 1W5
Ph:(416)923-8416
Free: 800-387-5649
Fax:(416)923-1450
Co. E-mail: info@crfa.ca
URL: http://www.crfa.ca
Contact: Garth Whyte, Pres./CEO
Description: Restaurant and food service corporations, hotels, caterers, and food service suppliers and educators. Seeks to create a favorable business environment for members. Represents members' interests before government; conducts trade research. Makes available group buying programs and other services to members; owns and operates three industry trade shows. **Publications:** *Canadian Foodservice Industry Operations Report* (biennial); *Foodservice Facts* (annual); *Legislation Guide* (quarterly).

5095 ■ National Association of Concessionaires
35 E Wacker Dr., Ste. 1816
Chicago, IL 60601
Ph:(312)236-3858
Fax:(312)236-7809
Co. E-mail: info@naconline.org
URL: http://www.naconline.org
Contact: Charles A. Winans, Exec. Dir.
Description: Represents popcorn processors, manufacturers, and merchandisers; operators of food and beverage concessions in theaters, amusement parks, sports arenas, and other recreational facilities; equipment manufacturers and suppliers. Works to professionalize the concession industry. Provides information services and audiovisual training programs for concession managers and employees. Maintains certification program for concession industry. **Publications:** *Concession Profession* (semiannual); *Concessionworks* (semiannual).

5096 ■ National Restaurant Association
1200 17th St. NW
Washington, DC 20036
Ph:(202)331-5900
Free: 800-424-5156
Fax:(202)331-2429
URL: http://www.restaurant.org
Contact: Sally Smith, Chair
Description: Represents restaurants, cafeterias, clubs, contract foodservice management, drive-ins, caterers, institutional food services and other members of the foodservice industry; also represents establishments belonging to non-affiliated state and local restaurant associations in governmental affairs. Supports foodservice education and research in several educational institutions. Is affiliated with the Educational Foundation of the National Restaurant Association to provide training and education for operators, food and equipment manufacturers, distributors and educators. Has 300,000 member locations. **Publications:** *National Restaurant Association—Washington Report* (semimonthly).

5097 ■ Outdoor Amusement Business Association
1035 S Semoran Blvd., Ste. 1045A
Winter Park, FL 32792
Ph:(407)681-9444
Free: 800-517-OABA
Fax:(407)681-9445
Co. E-mail: oaba@oaba.org
URL: http://www.oaba.org
Contact: Robert W. Johnson, Pres.
Description: Represents executives and employees of carnivals and fairs; ride owners; independent food and games concessionaires; manufacturers and suppliers of equipment. Promotes and lobbies on behalf of the interests of the outdoor amusement industry; provides a center for dissemination of information. **Publications:** *Midway Marquee* (annual).

5098 ■ Western Fairs Association
1776 Tribute Rd., Ste. 210
Sacramento, CA 95815-4495
Ph:(916)927-3100
Fax:(916)927-6397
Co. E-mail: wfa@fairsnet.org
URL: http://www.fairsnet.org
Contact: Stephen J. Chambers, Exec. Dir.
Description: State and county fairs, carnival operators, food concessionaires, entertainment agents, and commercial exhibitors. Seeks to improve conditions in the fair industry by maintaining good relations with governmental agencies. Maintains hall of fame. Compiles statistics. **Publications:** *Western Fairs Association—Date List and Membership Directory* (annual); *WFA Newsletter* (quarterly).

REFERENCE WORKS

5099 ■ *Concession Profession*
Pub: National Association of Concessionaires
Contact: Susan M. Cross, Director
E-mail: scross@naconline.org
Ed: Charles A. Winans, Editor, cwinans@naconline.org. **Released:** Biennial, Latest edition 2010-2011. **Covers:** About 900 member equipment manufacturers, suppliers, jobber/distributors, popcorn processors, theaters, amusement parks, stadiums, rinks, and other concession operators in the United States and Canada. **Entries Include:** For operators—Company name, address, phone, name of contact. For manufacturers and suppliers—Company name, address, phone, names and titles of up to four executives, brief description of service or products. **Arrangement:** Classified by type of concession or business activity. **Indexes:** Name, geographical.

5100 ■ "Working the Streets" in *Baltimore Business Journal* (Vol. 28, July 30, 2010, No. 12, pp. 1)
Pub: Baltimore Business Journal
Ed: Amanda Pino. **Description:** Reports show that street vendors are popping up on new corners in Baltimore, Maryland, with city-inspected stainless steel food carts in tow. Applications for street vending licenses shot up at the end of 2009 and into this summer. It is believed that pinning down the exact number of vendors operating at any one point is difficult.

TRADE PERIODICALS

5101 ■ *Tourist Attractions & Parks Magazine*
Pub: Kane Communications Inc.
Contact: Larry White, Assoc. Publisher
Released: 7/yr. **Price:** $49; $55 two years; $55 other countries; $61 other countries 2 years. **Description:** Magazine on the management of amusement parks, carnivals, arcades, museums, zoos, campgrounds, fun centers, arenas, miniature golf, and water sports.

TRADE SHOWS AND CONVENTIONS

5102 ■ International Association of Fairs and Expositions Trade Show
International Association of Fairs and Expositions
3043 E. Cairo
Springfield, MO 65802
Ph:(417)862-5771
Free: 800-516-0313
Fax:(417)862-0156
Co. E-mail: iafe@fairsandexpos.com
URL: http://www.fairsandexpos.com
Released: Annual. **Audience:** Fair managers, staffs, and board members; carnival owners and staffs; concessionaires; talent and other agencies related to the fair industry. **Principal Exhibits:** Talent agencies, concessionaires, novelties, amusement devices, insurance, ribbons, plaques, attractions, and equipment. Products and services for the fair industry.

FRANCHISES AND BUSINESS OPPORTUNITIES

5103 ■ Camille's Sidewalk Cafe
Camille's Franchise System, LLC
8801 S Yale Ave., Ste. 400
Tulsa, OK 74137-3575
Ph:(918)488-9727
Free: 800-230-7004
Fax:(918)497-1916
No. of Franchise Units: 21. **No. of Company-Owned Units:** 1. **Founded:** 1996. **Franchised:** 1999. **Description:** Sidewalk cafe serving wraps and sandwiches. **Equity Capital Needed:** $214,000-$280,000. **Franchise Fee:** $25,000. **Financial Assistance:** Yes. **Training:** Yes.

5104 ■ Carvel Ice Cream
Focus Brands, Inc.
200 Glenridge Point Pky., Ste. 200
Atlanta, GA 30342
Ph:(404)255-3250

Fax:(404)255-4978
URL: http://www.carvel.com
No. of Franchise Units: 449. **Founded:** 1934. **Franchised:** 1947. **Description:** Custom ice cream desserts and novelties. **Equity Capital Needed:** $100,000 liquid cash; $300,000 net worth. **Franchise Fee:** $30,000. **Financial Assistance:** Does not provide financing, but you will have access to the Carvel Development Network, which includes lenders. **Training:** 2 week ice cream training school; access to the Carvel Development Network (real estate brokers, architects, lenders, contractors, etc.); Design & construction support & assistance; Grand opening support and toll-free hotline available.

5105 ■ The Different Twist Pretzel Co.
6052 Rte. 8
PO Box 334
Bakerstown, PA 15007
Ph:(724)443-8010
Fax:(724)443-7287
No. of Franchise Units: 15. **Founded:** 1992. **Franchised:** 1992. **Description:** Soft pretzels in ten flavors. **Equity Capital Needed:** $40,000-$80,000. **Franchise Fee:** $5,000. **Training:** Yes.

5106 ■ Pretzelmaker, Inc.
Global Franchise Group
1346 Oakbrook Dr., Ste. 170
Norcross, GA 30093
Ph:(770)514-4500
Free: 800-524-6444
Fax:(770)514-4903
No. of Franchise Units: 350. **Founded:** 1991. **Franchised:** 1992. **Description:** Franchises concession stands featuring pretzels. **Equity Capital Needed:** $250,000 net worth; $85,000 liquid. **Franchise Fee:** $25,000. **Financial Assistance:** No. **Training:** Yes.

5107 ■ Willy Dog
120 Clarence St., Ste. 1141
Kingston, ON, Canada K7L 4Y5
Ph:(613)389-6118
Free: 800-915-4683
Fax:(613)389-6138
Co. E-mail: sales@willydogs.com
URL: http://www.willydogs.com
No. of Franchise Units: 115. **No. of Company-Owned Units:** 5. **Founded:** 1989. **Franchised:** 1993. **Description:** Hot dog cart resembling giant hot dog. **Equity Capital Needed:** $6,500. **Franchise Fee:** $6,500. **Financial Assistance:** No. **Training:** Yes.

LIBRARIES

5108 ■ American Beverage Association Information Center
1101 16th St., NW
Washington, DC 20036
Ph:(202)463-6732
Fax:(202)659-5349
Co. E-mail: info@ameribev.org
URL: http://www.ameribev.org/
Contact: Susan K. Neely, Pres./CEO
Scope: Beverage industry. **Services:** Library open to the public for reference use only. **Holdings:** 500 books, articles, papers, and historical materials. **Subscriptions:** 115 journals and other serials.

5109 ■ American Institute of Food Distribution, Inc.–Information and Research Center
1 Broadway Plaza, 2nd Fl.
Elmwood Park, NJ 07407
Ph:(201)791-5570
Fax:(201)791-5222
Co. E-mail: jkastrinsky@foodinstitute.com
URL: http://www.foodinstitute.com/
Contact: Brian Todd, Pres./CEO
Scope: Food industry. **Services:** Center open to the public on fee basis. **Subscriptions:** 400 journals and other serials.

5110 ■ Noble and Associates Library
2155 W. Chesterfield Blvd.
Springfield, MO 65807
Ph:(417)875-5000
Co. E-mail: julie.tumy@noble.net
URL: http://www.noble.net
Contact: Julie Tumy, Pres.
Scope: Food, food service, advertising, construction, agriculture. **Services:** Interlibrary loan; copying; SDI; Library not open to the public. **Holdings:** 500 books; 1000 reports. **Subscriptions:** 300 journals and other serials; 5 newspapers.

RESEARCH CENTERS

5111 ■ National Food Laboratory
365 N Canyons Pky., Ste. 201
Livermore, CA 94551
Ph:(925)828-1440
Fax:(925)243-0117
Co. E-mail: buckk@thenfl.com
URL: http://www.thenfl.com
Contact: Kevin Buck, Pres./CEO
E-mail: buckk@thenfl.com
Scope: Food and thermal processing and engineering, analytical chemistry, microbiology, product development, federal and state regulations, sensory evaluation, and sanitation.

Concierge/Virtual Assistant Service

START-UP INFORMATION

5112 ■ "Five Low-Cost Home Based Startups" in *Women Entrepreneur* (December 16, 2008)
Pub: Entrepreneur Media Inc.
Ed: Lesley Spencer Pyle. **Description:** During tough economic times, small businesses have an advantage over large companies because they can adjust to economic conditions more easily and without having to go through corporate red tape that can slow the implementation process. A budding entrepreneur may find success by taking inventory of his or her skills, experience, expertise and passions and utilizing those qualities to start a business. Five low-cost home-based startups are profiled. These include starting an online store, a virtual assistant service, web designer, sales representative and a home staging counselor.

5113 ■ "Online Fortunes" in *Small Business Opportunities* (Fall 2008)
Pub: Entrepreneur Media Inc.
Description: Fifty hot, e-commerce enterprises for the aspiring entrepreneur to consider are featured; virtual assistants, marketing services, party planning, travel services, researching, web design and development, importing as well as creating an online store are among the businesses featured.

ASSOCIATIONS AND OTHER ORGANIZATIONS

5114 ■ National Concierge Association
2920 Idaho Ave. N
Minneapolis, MN 55427
Ph:(612)317-2932
Fax:(612)317-2910
Co. E-mail: info@nationalconciergeassociation.com
URL: http://www.nationalconciergeassociation.com
Contact: Sara-ann G. Kasner, Pres.
Description: Represents concierges of all types and affiliated hospitality related businesses whose exceptional products and services are of benefit to concierge clientele. **Publications:** *NCA Keynotes* (biennial).

REFERENCE WORKS

5115 ■ "Anybody Out There?" in *Canadian Business* (Vol. 81, July 21 2008, No. 11, pp. 31)
Pub: Rogers Media Ltd.
Ed: Andrew Wahl. **Description:** Virtual offices or shared office services provide solutions to companies that can no longer accommodate additional workspaces. The alternative working arrangement allows the company to have a kind of distributed work system. The disadvantages of employing virtual offices are presented.

5116 ■ "At Your Service: Corporate Concierges Come in Three Varieties" in *Incentive* (August 25, 2008)
Pub: Nielson Business Media
Ed: Nathan Adkisson. **Description:** Companies are offering corporate concierge services to handle tasks for new employees as a sign-on benefit. Concierge of Boston has six employees that focus on fulfilling the needs of individuals.

5117 ■ "Attending to the Needs of the Too Busy" in *New York Times* (Vol. 158, October 1, 2008, No. 54450, pp. 7)
Pub: New York Times Co./Globe Newspaper Co.
Ed: Ken Belson. **Description:** Profiles of individuals working as concierges to meet the needs of their clients are presented.

5118 ■ *The Concierge Manual: A Step-by-Step Guide to Starting Your Own Concierge Service or Lifestyle Management Company*
Pub: New Road Publishing
Ed: Katharine C. Giovanni. **Released:** September 9, 2010. **Price:** $23.00. **Description:** Answering some of the biggest questions about the logistics of running a concierge business, this guide provides all the tools necessary to create a successful concierge, lifestyle management, errand service, or personal assistant company.

5119 ■ "Concierges Get New Marching Orders" in *New York Times* (Vol. 158, January 11, 2009, No. 54552, pp. 1)
Pub: New York Times Co./Globe Newspaper Co.
Ed: Vivian S. Toy. **Description:** Effects of the slowing economy are felt by individuals working as concierges.

5120 ■ "Fitness Made Fun" in *Playthings* (Vol. 106, September 1, 2008, No. 8, pp. 12)
Pub: Reed Business Information
Ed: Karyn M. Peterson. **Description:** Nintendo Wii has developed the Wii Fit game that allows gamers to engage in over forty physical activities through its Balance Board accessory, an engineered platform that senses weight and shifts in movement and balance. It also offers virtual trainers to talk participants through the activities and keeps track of the progress of multiple users.

5121 ■ "Mobility: So Happy Together" in *Entrepreneur* (Vol. 35, October 2007, No. 10, pp. 64)
Pub: Entrepreneur Media Inc.
Ed: Heather Clancy. **Description:** Joshua Burnett, CEO and founder of 9ci, uses index cards to keep track of what he needs to do despite the fact that he has a notebook computer, cell phone and PDA. Kim Hahn, a media entrepreneur, prefers jotting her ideas down in a spiral notebook, has a team that would organize her records for her, and a personal assistant that would keep track of changes to her schedule. Reasons why these entrepreneurs use old-fashioned methods along with new technology are given.

5122 ■ "Opportunity Knocks" in *Small Business Opportunities* (September 2008)
Pub: Entrepreneur Media Inc.
Description: Profile of YourOffice USA, a franchise that provides home-based and small businesses cost-effective and efficient support through "virtual" offices that are available as much or as little as the client needs it; they also supply necessary tools such as a professional business address, private mailbox service, personalized telephone answering and more that supports clients who want to look, act and operate with an advanced business image.

5123 ■ "The Personal Touch: Entrepreneur Turns Good Taste, Love of Luxury Into Lucrative Venture" in *Black Enterprise* (October 2007)
Pub: Earl G. Graves Publishing Co. Inc.
Ed: Tamara E. Holmes. **Description:** Profile of Chaka Fattah Jr. who turned his taste for luxurious things into a successful luxury travel and concierge service catering to business owners, corporate executives, athletes, and entertainers.

5124 ■ "Professional Help: Cross That Off Your To-Do List" in *Inc.* (November 2007, pp. 89-90, 92)
Pub: Gruner & Jahr USA Publishing
Ed: Alison Stein Wellner. **Description:** Small business owners are finding that it pays to hire someone to takeover the personal tasks of daily living, including hiring a personal assistant, chauffeur, chef, stylist, pet caregiver, or concierge service.

5125 ■ "The Way I Work" in *Inc.* (March 2008, pp. 102-104, 106)
Pub: Gruner & Jahr USA Publishing
Ed: Hannah Clark Steiman. **Description:** Profile of Howard Lefkowitz, CEO of Vegas.com, a Website that allows visitors to book flights, reserve hotel rooms, buy show tickets, make spa appointments, and coordinate any and all aspects of a trip to Las Vegas. The firm also runs brick-and-mortar box offices and concierge desks at various cities.

START-UP INFORMATION

5126 ■ *202 Things You Can Buy and Sell for Big Profits*
Pub: Entrepreneur Press
Ed: James Stephenson; Jason R. Rich. **Released:** July 2008. **Price:** $19.95. **Description:** Become an entrepreneur at selling new and used products. This handbook will help individuals cash in on the boom in reselling new and used products online. A new section defines ways to set realistic goals while distinguishing between 'get-rich schemes' and long term, viable businesses. A discussion about targeting and reaching the right customer base is included, along with finding and obtaining the service support needed for starting a new business.

5127 ■ *The Complete Idiot's Guide to Starting and Running a Thrift Store*
Pub: Alpha Publishing House
Ed: Ravel Buckley, Carol Costa. **Released:** January 5, 2010. **Price:** $18.95. **Description:** Thrift stores saw a 35 percent increase in sales during the falling economy in 2008. Despite the low startup costs, launching and running a thrift store is complicated. Two experts cover the entire process, including setting up a store on a nonprofit basis, choosing a location, funding, donations for saleable items, recruiting and managing staff, sorting items, pricing, and recycling donations.

5128 ■ *EBay Business Start-up Kit: 100s of Live Links to All the Information and Tools You Need*
Pub: NOLO
Ed: Richard Stim. **Released:** July 2008. **Price:** $24. 99. **Description:** Interactive kit that connects user directly to EBay is presented.

5129 ■ *eBay Business the Smart Way*
Pub: AMACOM
Ed: Joseph T. Sinclair. **Released:** June 6, 2007. **Price:** $17.95. **Description:** eBay commands ninety percent of all online auction business. Computer and software expert and online entrepreneur shares information to help online sellers get started and move merchandise on eBay. Tips include the best ways to build credibility, find products to sell, manage inventory, create a storefront Website, and more.

5130 ■ "Mount Laurel Woman Launches Venture Into Children's Used Clothing" in *Philadelphia Inquirer* (September 17, 2010)
Pub: Philadelphia Media Network
Ed: Maria Panaritis. **Description:** Profile of Jennifer Frisch, stay-at-home mom turned entrepreneur. Frisch started a used-clothing store Once Upon a Child after opening her franchised Plato's Closet, selling unwanted and used baby clothing and accessories at her new shop, while offering used merchandise to teens at Plato's Closet.

ASSOCIATIONS AND OTHER ORGANIZATIONS

5131 ■ NARTS - The Association of Resale Professionals
PO Box 80707
St. Clair Shores, MI 48080-5707
Ph:(586)294-6700
Free: 800-544-0751
Fax:(586)294-6776
Co. E-mail: info@narts.org
URL: http://www.narts.org
Contact: Adele Meyer, Exec. Dir.

Description: Owners, managers, professionals, and other individuals involved in the resale and thrift shop industry. Works for the exchange of ideas and information among members, develops public recognition and knowledge of the field, and promotes professionalism in the industry. Helps members to become more professional and to increase profits. Offers educational materials. **Publications:** *The Budget Guide to Retail Store Planning and Design*; *Operating Survey*; *Retail in Detail*; *Your NARTS Network* (monthly).

REFERENCE WORKS

5132 ■ "Auction Company Grows with Much Smaller Sites" in *Automotive News* (Vol. 86, October 31, 2011, No. 6488, pp. 23)
Pub: Crain Communications Inc.

Ed: Arlena Sawyers. **Description:** Auction Broadcasting Company has launched auction sites and is expanding into new areas. The family-owned business will provide auctions half the size traditionally used. The firm reports that 40 percent of the General Motors factory-owned vehicles sold on consignment were purchased by online buyers, up 30 percent over 2010.

5133 ■ "Cash in Your Attic: Is Your Junk Someone Else's Treasure?" in *Black Enterprise* (Vol. 37, November 2006, No. 4, pp. 156)
Pub: Earl G. Graves Publishing Co. Inc.

Ed: Angela P. Moore-Thorpe. **Description:** Selling items accumulated over the years or purchased at auctions or garage sales can be a lucrative way to make extra cash. Advice and resources on auctions, collecting, and consignment shops included.

5134 ■ "Consignment Shop Closes Without Warning to Customers, Landlord" in *Sun Journal* (June 30, 2010)
Pub: Freedom Communications Inc.

Ed: Laura Oleniacz. **Description:** Off The Racks consignment shop located on Glenburnie Road in New Bern, North Carolina closed without warning to customers or its landlord. The consignors who donated clothing to the store were left unpaid.

5135 ■ "Consignment Shop Offers Children's Clothes, Products" in *Frederick News-Post* (August 19, 2010)
Pub: Federick News-Post

Ed: Ed Waters Jr. **Description:** Sweet Pea Consignments for Children offers used items for newborns to pre-teens. The shop carries name brand clothing as well as toys, books and baby products.

5136 ■ *The Ebay Seller's Tax and Legal Answer Book*
Pub: AMACOM
Ed: Cliff Ennico. **Released:** April 30, 2007. **Price:** $19.95. **Description:** Helps sellers using Ebay to file taxes properly, while saving money.

5137 ■ *Ebay the Smart Way: Selling, Burying, and Profiting on the Web's Number One Auction Site*
Pub: AMACOM
Ed: Joseph T. Sinclair. **Released:** May 2007. **Price:** $17.95. **Description:** Resource to help individuals sell, buy and profit using the Internet auction site Ebay.

5138 ■ "Get Sold On eBay" in *Entrepreneur* (Vol. 36, March 2008, No. 3, pp. 94)
Pub: Entrepreneur Media Inc.
Ed: Marcia Layton Turner. **Description:** Entrepreneurs are increasingly using eBay to sell products. Some tips to start selling products through eBay include: starting with used items, developing a niche to sell specific products, and researching product pricing. Other tips with regard to starting an eBay business are covered.

5139 ■ *How to Market and Sell Your Art, Music, Photographs, and Handmade Crafts Online*
Pub: Atlantic Publishing Group, Inc.
Ed: Lee Rowley. **Released:** May 2008. **Price:** $24. 95. **Description:** The book provides all the basics for starting and running an online store selling arts, crafts, photography or music. There are more than 300 Websites listed to help anyone market and promote their arts and/or crafts online.

5140 ■ "It's So You! Consignment Chop Owner Thrilled to See Vision Come to Fruition" in *News-Herald* (August 27, 2010)
Pub: News-Herald
Ed: Brandon C. Baker. **Description:** Profile of Laurel Howes and her It's So You! Boutique. The consignment shop is located in Willoughby's Pine Ride Plaza in Ohio. The shop targets all women, but particularly those who are not that comfortable with shopping consignment.

5141 ■ "Longtime Peoria Heights Second-Hand Clothing Shop Closing" in *Journal Star* (December 18, 2010)
Pub: Journal Star
Ed: Scott Hilyard. **Description:** The Happy Hangar, a consignment clothing store located in Peoria Heights, Illinois is closing after 31 years of selling second-hand clothing.

5142 ■ "Power Up" in *Entrepreneur* (Vol. 35, November 2007, No. 11, pp. 140)
Pub: Entrepreneur Media Inc.
Ed: Amanda C. Kooser. **Description:** PowerSeller is a status in the Internet company eBay, wherein sellers average at least $1,000 in sales per month for three consecutive months. There are five tiers in the PowerSeller status, which ranges from Bronze to

Titanium. Launching startups at eBay can help entrepreneurs pick up a wide customer base, but getting and maintaining PowerSeller status is a challenge.

5143 ■ "Shore Total Office Liquidates Massive Supply of Bank Furniture and Used Furniture" in *Internet Wire* (June 21, 2010)
Pub: Comtex
Description: Shore Total Office, located in San Diego, California, is liquidating quality bank furniture and used furniture to customers hoping to outfit their facilities with stylish new furnishings. Shore Total Office is a leading supplier of high quality office furniture and designs.

5144 ■ *Too Good to be Threw: The Complete Operations Manual for Resale and Consignment Shops*
Pub: Katydid Press
Price: $69.95. **Description:** Revised edition covers all the information needfed to start and run a buy-outright or consignment shop, covering anything from clothing to furniture resale.

5145 ■ "Understanding Persuasive Online Sales Messages from eBay Auctions" in *Business Communication Quarterly* (December 2007, pp. 482)
Pub: Sage Publications USA
Ed: Barbara Jo White, Daniel Clapper, Rita Noel, Jenny Fortier, Pierre Grabolosa. **Description:** eBay product listings were studied to determine the requirements of persuasive sales writing. Potential sellers should use the proper keywords and make an authentic description with authentic photographs of the item being auctioned.

TRADE PERIODICALS

5146 ■ *Swap Meet Magazine*
Pub: Forum Publishing Co.
Released: Monthly. **Price:** $29.97; $59.94 two years. **Description:** Trade magazine covering merchandise suppliers for flea market and swap meet vendors.

FRANCHISES AND BUSINESS OPPORTUNITIES

5147 ■ Once Upon a Child
Winmark Corp.
605 Highway 169 N., Ste. 400
Minneapolis, MN 55441
Ph:(763)520-8490
Free: 800-592-8049
Fax:(763)520-8501
URL: http://www.onceuponachild.com
No. of Franchise Units: 241. **Founded:** 1985. **Franchised:** 1993. **Description:** Franchises consignment shops featuring children's products including toys, books, furniture, and apparel. **Equity Capital Needed:** $204,200-$309,500; approximately 30%cash requirement. **Franchise Fee:** $25,000. **Financial Assistance:** No financing available from corporation; Support given in developing 3 year business plan and cash flow analysis to use in securing financing. **Training:** Program includes product acquisition, inventory management, retail store operations, advertising and marketing, proprietary point-of-sale computer system. Training conferences held annually. Owner only website provides tools, resources and a network of fellow franchisees.

5148 ■ Plato's Closet
Winmark Corp.
605 Highway 169 N, Ste. 400
Minneapolis, MN 55441
Ph:(763)520-8500
Free: 800-592-8049
Fax:(763)520-8501
Co. E-mail: pc-franchise-development@platoscloset.com
URL: http://www.platoscloset.com
No. of Franchise Units: 328. **Founded:** 1998. **Franchised:** 1999. **Description:** Teen and young adult apparel and accessories consignment. **Equity Capital Needed:** $196,100-$313,100; $58,830-$93,930 start-up capital required. **Franchise Fee:** $25,000. **Financial Assistance:** In-house financing not available. Assistance given in developing 3 year business plan and cash flow analysis to use in securing loans. **Training:** Training program includes product acquisition, fashion trends, inventory management, and proprietary point-of-sale computer system. Annual franchise conferences, owner only website, and on-site business consultations.

5149 ■ Play it Again Sports
Winmark Corp.
605 Highway 169 N, Ste. 400
Minneapolis, MN 55441
Free: 800-592-8049
URL: http://www.playitagainsports.com
NFU 328. **Founded:** 1983. **Franchised:** 1988. **Description:** Sells new and used sports equipment and clothing. Franchisees purchase discount inventory through closeouts and overruns and accept used equipment in trade from customers, reducing retail prices by 40-60%. **Equity Capital Needed:** $236,400-$374,500; Approximately 30%cash requirement. **Franchise Fee:** $25,000. **Financial Assistance:** No in-house financing available. Support given in developing 3 year business plan and cash flow analysis to use in securing loans. **Managerial Assistance:** Owner only website provides resources and operational support tools to franchisee. **Training:** Training includes product acquisition, inventory management, staff hiring and training, customer service, advertising and marketing, and merchandising. Ongoing regional meetings and national training conferences held annually.

5150 ■ Terri's New & Consigned Furnishings
Consign & Design Franchise Corp.
1375 W Drivers Way
Tempe, AZ 85284
Ph:(480)969-1121
Free: 800-455-0400
Fax:(480)969-5052
No. of Franchise Units: 8. **No. of Company-Owned Units:** 8. **Founded:** 1979. **Franchised:** 1993. **Description:** Upscale home furnishings on consignment. **Equity Capital Needed:** $100,000+. **Franchise Fee:** $10,000-$40,000. **Financial Assistance:** No. **Training:** Yes.

START-UP INFORMATION

5151 ■ "Builder Comes Back Home" in *Houston Business Journal* (Vol. 40, September 18, 2009, No. 19, pp. 1A)
Pub: American City Business Journals
Ed: Allison Wollam. **Description:** Jason Hammonds, who has been previously involved in the local home building market in Texas, has launched a new home building company called J. Kyle Homes. The new company has chosen Cinco Ranch, a neo-traditional styled neighborhood in Katy, Texas to build its first housing community.

5152 ■ "Building a Business: Directbuild Helps Clients Build Their Own Home" in *Small Business Opportunities* (Winter 2007)
Pub: Harris Publications Inc.
Description: Mike New, founder of Directbuild, a franchise company that helps individuals with no construction knowledge build their own home.

5153 ■ "Driving Home Success: Stamped Asphalt for Driveways and Paths is Hottest New Trend" in *Small Business Opportunities* (Winter 2007)
Pub: Harris Publications Inc.
Description: Profile of technology that turns asphalt into three-dimensional replicas of hand-laid brick, slate, cobblestone and other design effects. Profiles of franchise opportunities in this industry are included.

5154 ■ *How to Open and Operate a Financially Successful Construction Company*
Pub: Atlantic Publishing Group, Inc.
Ed: Tanya R. Davis. **Released:** April 2008. **Price:** $39.95 paperback. **Description:** Construction businesses are predicted to be one of the fastest growing industries in the U.S. economy, according to the U.S. Bureau of Labor Statistics. A comprehensive guide is offered detailing the practical side of starting and growing a construction firm. The step-by-step guide provides sample business forms, leases, contracts, worksheets and checklists for planning and running the day-to-day operations.

ASSOCIATIONS AND OTHER ORGANIZATIONS

5155 ■ American Council for Construction Education
1717 N Loop 1604 E, Ste. 320
San Antonio, TX 78232-1570
Ph:(210)495-6161
Fax:(210)495-6168
Co. E-mail: acce@acce-hq.org
URL: http://www.acce-hq.org
Contact: Mr. Steve Nellis, Pres.
Description: Represents construction-oriented associations, corporations, and individuals. Promotes and improves construction education at the postsecondary level. Engages in accrediting construction education programs offered by colleges and universities nationwide. Maintains procedures consistent with the accrediting policies of the Council for Higher Education Accreditation and reports the results of its activities and list the colleges and universities with accredited programs of study in construction. Reviews at regular intervals the criteria, standards, and procedures that the council has adopted to evaluate programs in construction education. Provides visiting teams for campus program evaluations; compiles statistics. .

5156 ■ American Institute of Constructors
700 N Fairfax St., Ste. 510
Alexandria, VA 22314
Ph:(703)683-4999
Fax:(571)527-3105
URL: http://www.professionalconstructor.org
Contact: Andi Wasiniak AIC, Pres.
Description: Professionals engaged in construction practice, education, and research. Serves as the certifying body for the professional constructor. Promotes the study and advances the practice of construction. Facilitates the exchange of information and ideas relating to construction. Conducts educational programs. **Publications:** *Constructor Certification Exam Study Guide Level II*; *Roster of Members* (annual).

5157 ■ American Society of Professional Estimators
2525 Perimeter Place Dr., Ste. 103
Nashville, TN 37214
Ph:(615)316-9200
Free: 888-EST-MATE
Fax:(615)316-9800
Co. E-mail: psmith@aspenational.org
URL: http://www.aspenational.org
Contact: Patsy Smith, Dir. of Admin.
Description: Construction cost estimators. Develops professional and ethical standards in construction estimating. Offers continuing education to established professionals; provides certification for estimators. **Publications:** *Standard Estimating Practice Manual* .

5158 ■ American Sports Builders Association
8480 Baltimore National Pike, No. 307
Ellicott City, MD 21043
Ph:(410)730-9595
Free: (866)501-2722
Fax:(410)730-8833
Co. E-mail: info@sportsbuilders.org
URL: http://sportsbuilders.org
Contact: Sam Fisher, Chm.
Description: Contractors who install running tracks, synthetic turf fields, tennis courts and indoor sports surfaces; manufacturers who supply basic materials for construction; accessory suppliers, designers, architects, and consultants of facilities. Provides guidelines for tennis court construction, running track construction, fencing, synthetic turf field construction and lighting. Offers certification and awards programs. **Publications:** *Buyers Guide for Tennis Court Construction* (periodic); *Running Tracks: A Construction and Maintenance Manual* (semiannual); *Tennis and Track Construction Guidelines* (periodic);Membership Directory (annual).

5159 ■ Architectural Glass and Metal Contractors Association
619 Liverpool Rd.
Pickering, ON, Canada L1W 1R1
Ph:(905)420-7272
Fax:(905)420-7288
Co. E-mail: info@agmca.ca
URL: http://www.agmca.ca
Contact: Mr. Dennis Haatvedt
Description: Architectural glass and metal contractors. Promotes advancement of the building industries; seeks to insure adherence to high standards of ethics and practice among members. Represents members' interests before industrial organizations, government agencies, and the public. Facilitates communication and cooperation among members; serves as a clearinghouse on the architectural glass and metal industries.

5160 ■ Associated Builders and Contractors
4250 N Fairfax Dr., 9th Fl.
Arlington, VA 22203-1607
Ph:(703)812-2000
Fax:(703)812-8201
Co. E-mail: gotquestions@abc.org
URL: http://www.abc.org
Contact: Michael D. Bellaman, Pres./CEO
Description: Construction contractors, subcontractors, suppliers and associates. Aims to foster and perpetuate the principles of rewarding construction workers and management on the basis of merit. Sponsors management education programs and craft training; also sponsors apprenticeship and skill training programs. Disseminates technological and labor relations information. .

5161 ■ Associated Builders and Contractors I National Mechanical Contractors Council
4250 N Fairfax Dr., 9th Fl.
Arlington, VA 22203-1607
Ph:(703)812-2000
Co. E-mail: mechanical@abc.org
URL: http://www.abc.org
Description: A council of Associated Builders and Contractors. Seeks to meet the needs of workers in sheet metal, plumbing, heating, ventilation, and air conditioning. **Publications:** *Construction Executive* .

5162 ■ Associated General Contractors of America
2300 Wilson Blvd., Ste. 400
Arlington, VA 22201
Ph:(703)548-3118
Free: 800-242-1767
Fax:(703)548-3119
Co. E-mail: info@agc.org
URL: http://www.agc.org
Contact: Stephen E. Sandherr, CEO
Description: General construction contractors; subcontractors; industry suppliers; service firms. Provides market services through its divisions. Conducts special conferences and seminars designed specifically for construction firms. Compiles statistics on job accidents reported by member firms. Maintains 65 committees, including joint cooperative

committees with other associations and liaison committees with federal agencies. **Publications:** *AGC Membership Directory and Buyers' Guide* (annual); *Associated General Contractors of America—News and Views* (biweekly).

5163 ■ Associated Schools of Construction
PO Box 1312
Fort Collins, CO 80522
Ph:(970)222-4459
Fax:(970)223-3859
Co. E-mail: sue.asc@gmail.com
URL: http://www.ascweb.org
Contact: Dr. Charles W. Berryman, Pres.

Description: Represents colleges and universities offering a program leading to an undergraduate or advanced degree with major emphasis on construction. Aims to establish objectives for the development of construction education and to assist institutions of higher education in establishing construction education and management programs. Compiles statistics. **Publications:** *International Journal of Construction Education and Research* (triennial); *Proceedings of the Annual Meeting* (annual).

5164 ■ Associated Specialty Contractors
3 Bethesda Metro Ctr., Ste. 1100
Bethesda, MD 20814
Co. E-mail: dgw@necanet.org
URL: http://www.assoc-spec-con.org
Contact: Daniel G. Walter, Pres./COO

Description: Works to promote efficient management and productivity. Coordinates the work of specialized branches of the industry in management information, research, public information, government relations and construction relations. Serves as a liaison among specialty trade associations in the areas of public relations, government relations, and with other organizations. Seeks to avoid unnecessary duplication of effort and expense or conflicting programs among affiliates. Identifies areas of interest and problems shared by members, and develops positions and approaches on such problems. **Publications:** *Contract Documents* .

5165 ■ Canadian Construction Association–Association Canadienne de la Construction
275 Slater St., 19th Fl.
Ottawa, ON, Canada K1P 5H9
Ph:(613)236-9455
Fax:(613)236-9526
Co. E-mail: cca@cca-acc.com
URL: http://www.cca-acc.com
Contact: Dianna Fournier, Exec. Dir.

Description: Construction companies and building contractors. Promotes growth and development of the building industries. Serves as a forum for the discussion of construction industry issues; establishes voluntary standards of ethics, materials, and practice for use by members. Facilitates communication and cooperation among members; represents the commercial, labor, and regulatory interests of the construction industry; sponsors promotional programs.

5166 ■ Canadian Home Builders' Association
150 Laurier Ave. W, Ste. 500
Ottawa, ON, Canada K1P 5J4
Ph:(613)230-3060
Fax:(613)232-8214
Co. E-mail: chba@chba.ca
URL: http://www.chba.ca
Contact: John Kenward, Chief Operating Off.

Description: Home builders and contractors. Promotes growth and development of the residential building industries. Represents members' interests. **Publications:** *The National* (quarterly).

5167 ■ Canadian Institute of Steel Construction–Institut canadien de la construction en acier
3760 14th Ave., Ste. 200
Markham, ON, Canada L3R 3T7
Ph:(905)946-0864
Fax:(905)946-8574
Co. E-mail: info@cisc-icca.ca
URL: http://www.cisc-icca.ca
Contact: Stephen Benson, Chm.

Description: Represents the structural steel, open-web steel joist and steel platework fabricating industries; operates as a technical, marketing and government relations organization. **Publications:** *Advantage Steel* (quarterly); *Design and Construction of Composite Floor Systems*; *Handbook of Steel Construction* .

5168 ■ Ceilings and Interior Systems Construction Association
405 Illinois Ave., Unit 2B
St. Charles, IL 60174
Ph:(630)584-1919
Fax:(866)560-8537
Co. E-mail: cisca@cisca.org
URL: http://www.cisca.org
Contact: Bill Shannon, Pres.

Description: International trade association for the advancement of the interior commercial construction industry. Provides quality education, resources and a forum for communication among its members. **Publications:** *Ceiling Systems* .

5169 ■ Construction Financial Management Association
100 Village Blvd., Ste. 200
Princeton, NJ 08540
Ph:(609)452-8000
Fax:(609)452-0474
Co. E-mail: jburkett@cafcoconstruction.com
URL: http://www.cfma.org
Contact: Joseph Burkett, Chm.

Description: Contractors, subcontractors, architects, real estate developers and engineers; associate members are equipment and material suppliers, accountants, lawyers, bankers and others involved with the financial management of the construction industry. Provides a forum for the exchange of ideas; coordinates educational programs dedicated to improving the professional standards of financial management in the construction industry. Offers expanded national programs, technical assistance and industry representation. Conducts research programs; maintains speakers' bureau and placement service; compiles statistics. **Publications:** *CFMA Building Profits* (bimonthly); *CFMA's Information Technology Survey for the Construction Industry* (biennial); *The Source* (annual).

5170 ■ Construction Management Association of America
7926 Jones Branch Dr., Ste. 800
McLean, VA 22102
Ph:(703)356-2622
Fax:(703)356-6388
Co. E-mail: info@cmaanet.org
URL: http://www.cmaanet.org
Contact: Bruce D'Agostino, Pres./CEO

Description: Promotes the growth and development of construction management as a professional service; encourages high professional standards. Conducts conferences and forums on construction management topics. Sponsors a professional certification program. **Publications:** *CMAA Documents: Standard CM Services and Practice* (annual).

5171 ■ Construction Owners Association of America
Overlook III, Ste. 445
2859 Paces Ferry Rd. SE
Atlanta, GA 30339
Ph:(770)433-0820
Free: 800-994-2622
Fax:(404)577-3551
Co. E-mail: coaa@coaa.org
URL: http://www.coaa.org
Contact: Lisa DeGolyer, Chief Exec.

Description: Represents public and private owners and developers of construction projects all across America. Aims to make a significant and lasting impact on the construction industry by educating its membership and by providing a collective voice for owners and developers of construction projects. **Publications:** *The Owner's Perspective* (semiannual)-;Membership Directory (annual).

5172 ■ Construction Specifications Canada–Devis de Construction Canada
120 Carlton St., Ste. 312
Toronto, ON, Canada M5A 4K2
Ph:(416)777-2198
Free: 800-668-5684
Fax:(416)777-2197
Co. E-mail: info@csc-dcc.ca
URL: http://www.csc-dcc.ca
Contact: Nick Franjic CAE, Exec. Dir.

Description: Construction companies, workers, engineers, and writers of building standards and specifications. Promotes continuing professional development of members; seeks to insure adherence to high standards of practice in the building industries. Conducts educational programs; makes available vocational training courses. Develops industry standards. Represents members' interests before industry organizations and government agencies; advises government agencies responsible for promulgating building codes and construction specifications. Makes available discount insurance and vehicle leasing programs to members. **Publications:** *Chapter Specifiers* (10/year); *Construction Canada* (bimonthly); *News in Brief* (semiannual).

5173 ■ Construction Specifications Institute
110 S Union St., Ste. 100
Alexandria, VA 22314-3351
Free: 800-689-2900
Fax:(703)236-4600
Co. E-mail: csi@csinet.org
URL: http://www.csinet.org
Contact: Dennis J. Hall FCSI, Pres.

Description: Individuals concerned with the specifications and documents used for construction projects. Membership includes architects, professional engineers, specifiers, contractors, product manufacturers, teachers and research workers in architectural and engineering fields, and building maintenance engineers. Advances construction technology through communication, service, education, and research. Certifies construction specifiers and others involved in construction and allied industries. Maintains 20 committees including Certification, Credentials, Specifications Competition, and Technical Documents. Sponsors competitions; maintains speakers' bureau; offers seminars. **Publications:** *The Construction Specifier* (monthly); *NewsBrief* (weekly).

5174 ■ Energy and Environmental Building Association
6520 Edenvale Blvd., Ste. 112
Eden Prairie, MN 55346
Ph:(952)881-1098
Fax:(952)881-3048
Co. E-mail: inquiry@eeba.org
URL: http://www.eeba.org
Contact: Kathleen Guidera, Exec. Dir.

Description: Professional association of builders, architects, consultants, designers, researchers, educators, government agencies, suppliers, and manufactures. Promotes the awareness, education, and development of energy-efficient and environmentally responsible buildings and communities. **Publications:** *EEBA News* (quarterly).

5175 ■ Engineering Contractors Association
8310 Florence Ave.
Downey, CA 90240
Ph:(562)861-0929
Free: 800-293-2240
Fax:(562)923-6179
Co. E-mail: info.eca@verizon.net
URL: http://www.ecaonline.net
Contact: Michael Prlich, Pres.

Description: Engineering construction contractors and suppliers. Represents members in labor and legislation matters and negotiates disputes within the industry. **Publications:** *ECA Magazine* (monthly).

5176 ■ International Masonry Institute
The James Brice House
42 East St.
Annapolis, MD 21401

Ph:(410)280-1305
Free: 800-803-0295
Fax:(301)261-2855
Co. E-mail: masonryquestions@imiweb.org
URL: http://www.imiweb.org
Contact: Joan Baggett Calambokidis, Pres.
Description: Joint labor/management trust fund of the International Union of Bricklayers and Allied Craftworkers and union masonry contractors. Aims for the advancement of quality masonry construction through national and regional training, promotion, advertising and labor management relations programs in the U.S. and Canada. Provides support and materials for local/regional masonry promotion groups in the U.S. and Canada, and cooperates with national groups and organizations promoting the industry. Sponsors craft training and research programs. Offers educational programs. Maintains museum. **Publications:** *IMI Today* (bimonthly).

5177 ■ Mechanical Contractors Association of Canada
No. 601-280 Albert St.
Ottawa, ON, Canada K1P 5G8
Ph:(613)232-0492
Fax:(613)235-2793
Co. E-mail: mcac@mcac.ca
URL: http://mcac.ca
Contact: Richard McKeagan, Pres.
Description: Mechanical contractors and providers of related services. Promotes growth and development of members' businesses; works to ensure high standards of ethics and practice in the mechanical contracting industry. Formulates standards of practice in mechanical contracting; facilitates exchange of information among members; represents members' interests before government agencies, industrial associations, and the public. **Publications:** *Just the Fax* (weekly); *National Bulletin* (periodic). **Telecommunication Services:** electronic mail, rick@mcac.ca.

5178 ■ National Association of Home Builders
1201 15th St. NW
Washington, DC 20005
Ph:(202)266-8200
Free: 800-368-5242
Fax:(202)266-8400
Co. E-mail: jhoward@nahb.com
URL: http://www.nahb.org
Contact: Gerald M. Howard, Pres./CEO
Description: Single and multifamily home builders, commercial builders, and others associated with the building industry. Lobbies on behalf of the housing industry and conducts public affairs activities to increase public understanding of housing and the economy. Collects and disseminates data on current developments in home building and home builders' plans through its Economics Department and nationwide Metropolitan Housing Forecast. Maintains NAHB Research Center, which functions as the research arm of the home building industry. Sponsors seminars and workshops on construction, mortgage credit, labor relations, cost reduction, land use, remodeling, and business management. Compiles statistics; offers charitable program, spokesman training, and placement service; maintains speakers' bureau, and Hall of Fame. Subsidiaries include the National Council of the Housing Industry. Maintains over 50 committees in many areas of construction; operates National Commercial Builders Council, National Council of the Multifamily Housing Industry, National Remodelers Council, and National Sales and Marketing Council. **Publications:** *Builder Magazine* (monthly); *Land Development Magazine* (quarterly); *Nation's Building News* (semimonthly).

5179 ■ National Association of Home Builders I Leading Suppliers Council
1201 15th St. NW
Washington, DC 20005-2800
Ph:(202)266-8200
Free: 800-368-5242
Fax:(202)266-8400
Co. E-mail: cday@nahb.org
URL: http://www.nahb.org/page.aspx/category/sectionID=469
Contact: Cindy Day
Description: Manufacturers of goods and services for the American housing industry. Provides support for the effort of the industry to fill the housing needs of American families. .

5180 ■ National Association of Women in Construction
327 S Adams St.
Fort Worth, TX 76104
Ph:(817)877-5551
Free: 800-552-3506
Fax:(817)877-0324
Co. E-mail: nawic@nawic.org
URL: http://www.nawic.org
Contact: Debra M. Gregoire, Pres.
Description: Seeks to enhance the success of women in the construction industry. .

5181 ■ National Demolition Association
16 N Franklin St., Ste. 203
Doylestown, PA 18901-3536
Ph:(215)348-4949
Free: 800-541-2412
Fax:(215)348-8422
Co. E-mail: drachel@rachelcontracting.com
URL: http://www.demolitionassociation.com
Contact: Don Rachel, Pres.
Description: Demolition contractors and equipment manufacturers. Seeks to foster goodwill and to encourage the exchange of ideas among the public and members. **Publications:** *Demolition Safety Manual* (annual).

5182 ■ National Frame Builders Association
4700 W Lake Ave.
Glenview, IL 60025
Free: 800-557-6957
Fax:(847)375-6495
Co. E-mail: nfba@nfba.org
URL: http://www.nfba.org
Contact: Anne Cordes, Interim Exec. Dir.
Description: Construction contractors specializing in post frame structures for agricultural, residential, industrial and commercial uses. Seeks to enhance the image of the industry and improve management and construction techniques. Conducts educational programs on safety and other vital matters. **Publications:** *Frame Building News* (5/year).

5183 ■ National Housing Endowment
1201 15th St. NW
Washington, DC 20005
Free: 800-368-5242
Fax:(202)266-8177
Co. E-mail: nhe@nahb.com
URL: http://www.nationalhousingendowment.com
Contact: Bruce S. Silver, Pres./CEO
Description: Works to 'build a foundation' to help make the American dream of homeownership a reality for present and future generations. Provides a permanent source of funds to address long-term industry concerns at the national level. Helps the industry to develop more effective approaches to home building. Enhances the ways to educate and train future generations of leaders in residential construction and increase the body of knowledge on housing issues. Supports innovative and effective programs that further Education, Training, and Research. **Publications:** *Blueprint* .

5184 ■ National Insulation Association
12100 Sunset Hills Rd., Ste. 330
Reston, VA 20190
Ph:(703)464-6422
Fax:(703)464-5896
Co. E-mail: mjones@insulation.org
URL: http://www.insulation.org
Contact: Michele M. Jones, Exec. VP/CEO
Description: Insulation contractors, distributors, and manufacturers. **Publications:** *Insulation Outlook* (monthly); *National Industries and Commercial Standards Manual*; *NIA News* (monthly); *Safety Handbook* .

5185 ■ North American Building Material Distribution Association
401 N Michigan Ave.
Chicago, IL 60611
Ph:(312)321-6845
Free: 888-747-7862
Fax:(312)644-0310
Co. E-mail: info@nbmda.org
URL: http://www.nbmda.org
Contact: Brian Schell, Pres.
Description: Building material distributors and manufacturers operating in more than 1500 locations. Represents the industry when appropriate. Distributes member and industry information; provides networking opportunities to distributors and manufacturers in the building material industry. Maintains education foundation; provides charitable programs. **Publications:** *NBMDA Membership and Product Directory* (annual); *The Sales Trainer: A Bi-Monthly Digest of Marketing Techniques for Aggressive Salespeople* (bimonthly).

5186 ■ Professional Construction Estimators Association of America
PO Box 680336
Charlotte, NC 28216
Ph:(704)489-1494
Free: 877-521-7232
Fax:(704)489-1495
Co. E-mail: pcea@pcea.org
URL: http://www.pcea.org
Contact: Randall Williams, Pres.
Description: Professional construction estimators. Objectives are to further recognition of construction estimating as a professional field of endeavor; to collect and disseminate information; to research and solve problems related to the construction industry; to establish educational programs for youth and promote construction estimating as a career; to maintain ethical standards. **Publications:** *National PCEA Directory* (annual).

5187 ■ Professional Women in Construction
315 E 56th St.
New York, NY 10022-3730
Ph:(212)486-4712
Fax:(212)486-0228
Co. E-mail: pwc@pwcusa.org
URL: http://www.pwcusa.org
Contact: Lenore Janis, Pres./Co-Founder
Description: Management-level women and men in construction and allied industries; owners, suppliers, architects, engineers, field personnel, office personnel and bonding/surety personnel. Provides a forum for exchange of ideas and promotion of political and legislative action, education and job opportunities for women in construction and related fields; forms liaisons with other trade and professional groups; develops research programs. Strives to reform abuses and to assure justice and equity within the construction industry. Sponsors mini-workshops. Maintains Action Line, which provides members with current information on pertinent legislation and on the association's activities and job referrals. **Publications:** *e-PWC* (quarterly).

5188 ■ Women Construction Owners and Executives U.S.A.
1004 Duke St.
Alexandria, VA 22314
Free: 800-788-3548
Fax:(202)330-5151
Co. E-mail: info@wcoeusa.org
URL: http://www.wcoeusa.org
Contact: Rosana Privitera Biondo, Pres.
Description: Promotes the interests of women construction owners and executives. Provides legislation, business, educational, and networking opportunities. .

EDUCATIONAL PROGRAMS

5189 ■ Construction Contracting
Seminar Information Service, Inc.
20 Executive Park, Ste. 120
Irvine, CA 92614
Ph:(949)261-9104
Free: 877-SEM-INFO
Fax:(949)261-1963
Co. E-mail: info@seminarinformation.com
URL: http://www.seminarinformation.com
Price: $1,845.00. **Description:** Gain an understanding of the entire contracting process to deal effectively with all parties involved. **Locations:** Atlanta, GA; Chicago, IL; Washington, DC; and San Diego, CA.

DIRECTORIES OF EDUCATIONAL PROGRAMS

5190 ■ *Directory of Private Accredited Career Schools and Colleges of Technology*
Pub: Accrediting Commission of Career Schools and Colleges of Technology
Contact: Michale S. McComis, Exec. Dir.
Released: On web page. **Price:** Free. **Description:** Covers 3900 accredited post-secondary programs that provide training programs in business, trade, and technical fields, including various small business endeavors. Entries offer school name, address, phone, description of courses, job placement assistance, and requirements for admission. Arrangement is alphabetical.

REFERENCE WORKS

5191 ■ "3CDC's Biggest Year" in *Business Courier* (Vol. 26, December 18, 2009, No. 34, pp. 1)
Pub: American City Business Journals, Inc.
Ed: Lucy May. **Description:** Cincinnati Center City Development Corporation (3CDC) will make 2010 its biggest year with nearly $164 million projects in the works. Historic tax credits and continued help from the city have allowed the private nonprofit organization to finance mega projects such as the $43 million renovation and expansion of Washington Park. Other projects that 3CDC will start or complete in 2010 are presented.

5192 ■ "21st Century Filling Station" in *Austin Business JournalInc.* (Vol. 29, December 11, 2009, No. 40, pp. 1)
Pub: American City Business Journals
Ed: Jacob Dirr. **Description:** Clean Energy Fuels Corporation announced plans for the construction of a $1 million, 17,000 square foot compressed natural gas fueling station at or near the Austin-Bergstrom International Airport (ABIA). Clean Energy Fuels hopes to encourage cab and shuttle companies in the ABIA to switch from gasoline to natural gas.

5193 ■ "$100 Million Complex To Be Built...On a Bridge" in *Business Courier* (Vol. 27, November 12, 2010, No. 28, pp. 1)
Pub: Business Courier
Ed: Lucy May. **Description:** A development firm closed a deal with the Newport Southbank Bridge Company for a $100M entertainment complex that will be built on tope of the Purple People Bridge. The proposed project will cover 150,000 square feet with attractions such as restaurants, a boutique hotel, and pubs.

5194 ■ "$100 Million Plan for Jefferson Arms" in *Saint Louis Business Journal* (Vol. 32, October 14, 2011, No. 7, pp. 1)
Pub: Saint Louis Business Journal
Ed: Evan Binns. **Description:** Teach for America is planning a $100 million renovation project of the former Jefferson Arms hotel in St. Louis, Missouri. The organization has signed a letter of intent to occupy the space. Financing of the project will be mainly through tax credits.

5195 ■ "$100 Million in Projects Jeopardized" in *Business Courier* (Vol. 24, March 28, 2008, No. 51, pp. 1)
Pub: American City Business Journals, Inc.
Ed: Dan Monk. **Description:** Ohio's historic preservation tax credit program may be reinstated after some companies planned to sue over its stoppage. The Ohio Department of Development said the program was halted because it exceeded the allocated budget for the credit. $34 million in credits are at stake for more than two dozen local projects if the program is reinstated.

5196 ■ "217 Homes Planned for Former Crystal Cream Site" in *Sacramento Business Journal* (Vol. 25, August 8, 2008, No. 23, pp. 1)
Pub: American City Business Journals, Inc.
Ed: Michael Shaw. **Description:** MetroNova Development LLC plans to develop housing at the former Crystal Cream & Butter Co. site near downtown Sacramento. The developer expects to sell the new loft houses for about $300,000 without public subsidies. Views and other information on the planned development project, is presented.

5197 ■ "$161.9M 'Pit Stop' Fix-Up Will Create About 1,600 Jobs" in *Orlando Business Journal* (Vol. 26, January 22, 2010, No. 34, pp. 1)
Pub: American City Business Journals
Ed: Anjali Fluker. **Description:** State of Florida will be providing $161.9 million to renovate eight service plazas starting November 2010. The project is expected to create 1,600 jobs across the state and is expected to be completed by 2012. Details on bid advertisements and facilities slated for improvement are discussed.

5198 ■ "2010: Important Year Ahead for Waterfront" in *Bellingham Business Journal* (Vol. March 2010, pp. 2)
Pub: Sound Publishing Inc.
Ed: Isaac Bonnell. **Description:** A tentative timeline has been established for the environmental impact statement (EIS) slated for completion in May 2010. The plan for the Waterfront District includes detailed economic and architectural analysis of the feasibility of reusing remaining structures and retaining some industrial icons.

5199 ■ *ABC Today—Associated Builders and Contractors National Membership Directory Issue*
Pub: Associated Builders and Contractors Inc.
Contact: Doug Curtis, Dir. of Chapter Devel.
E-mail: curtis@abc.org
Released: Annual, December. **Price:** $150 plus $7.00 shipping. **Publication Includes:** List of approximately 19,000 member construction contractors and suppliers. **Entries Include:** Company name, address, phone, name of principal executive, code to volume of business, business specialty. **Arrangement:** Classified by chapter, then by work specialty.

5200 ■ "Adventures at Hydronicahh" in *Contractor* (Vol. 56, September 2009, No. 9, pp. 52)
Pub: Penton Media, Inc.
Ed: Mark Eatherton. **Description:** Installation of the heating system of a lakeview room are described. The room's radiant windows are powered by electricity from a solar PV array and a propane-powered hydrogen fuel cell. The system will be programmed to use the most energy available.

5201 ■ "Advertisers Hooked on Horns, their Playground" in *Austin Business JournalInc.* (Vol. 28, July 25, 2008, No. 19, pp. A1)
Pub: American City Business Journals
Ed: Sandra Zaragoza. **Description:** Renovation of the D.K. Royal-Texas Memorial Stadium has increased its advertising revenue from $570,000 in 1993 to $10 in 2008. Sponsorship has grown in the past years due to the revenue-sharing agreement, a ten-year contract through 2015 between the University of Texas and IMG College Sports.

5202 ■ "Affordable Housing on the Rise" in *Philadelphia Business Journal* (Vol. 28, October 23, 2009, No. 36, pp. 1)
Pub: American City Business Journals
Ed: Natalie Kostelni. **Description:** Philadelphia, Pennsylvania led an affordable housing boom with more than 800 new affordable housing units in the works in spite of the recession. The converging of developers and federal stimulus money has driven the sudden increase with the launching of several projects across the city.

5203 ■ "Agricultural Community Implements Green Technologies, Building Team" in *Contractor* (Vol. 56, September 2009, No. 9, pp. 5)
Pub: Penton Media, Inc.
Ed: Candace Ruolo. **Description:** John DeWald and Associates has initiated a residential development project which uses green technologies in Illinois. The community features a community center, organic farm and recreational trails. Comments from executives are also provided.

5204 ■ "Aircraft Maker May Land Here" in *Austin Business Journal* (Vol. 31, April 15, 2011, No. 6, pp. 1)
Pub: American City Business Journals Inc.
Ed: Jacob Dirr. **Description:** Icon Aircraft Inc. is planning to build a manufacturing facility in Austin, Texas. The company needs 100,000 square feet of space in a new or renovated plant. Executive comments are included.

5205 ■ "All About The Benjamins" in *Canadian Business* (Vol. 81, September 29, 2008, No. 16, pp. 92)
Pub: Rogers Media Ltd.
Ed: David Baines. **Description:** Discusses real estate developer Royal Indian Raj International Corp., a company that planned to build a $3 billion "smart city" near the Bangalore airport; to this day nothing has ever been built. The company was incorporated in 1999 by Manoj C. Benjamin one investor, Bill Zack, has been sued by the developer for libel due to his website that calls the company a scam. Benjamin has had a previous case of fraud issued against him as well as a string of liabilities and lawsuits.

5206 ■ *American Society of Professional Estimators—Membership Directory and Buyers' Guide*
Pub: American Society of Professional Estimators
Contact: Beverly Perrell
Released: Annual, Latest edition 2010-2011. **Covers:** 3,000 members allied to the building industry as construction estimators. **Entries Include:** Name, address, phone, business address and phone, category of membership. **Arrangement:** Classified by numbered chapter. **Indexes:** Alphabetical.

5207 ■ "Amid Recession, Companies Still Value Supplier Diversity Programs" in *Hispanic Business* (July-August 2009, pp. 34)
Pub: Hispanic Business
Ed: Joshua Molina. **Description:** The decline of traditionally strong industries, from automotive manufacturing to construction, has shaken today's economy and has forced small businesses, especially suppliers and minority-owned firms, turn to diversity programs in order to make changes.

5208 ■ "Analysts: Intel Site May Be Last Major U.S.-Built Fab" in *Business Journal-Serving Phoenix and the Valley of the Sun* (Oct. 19, 2007)
Pub: American City Business Journals, Inc.
Ed: Ty Young. **Description:** Intel's million-square-foot manufacturing facility, called Fab 32, is expected to open in 2007. The plant will mass-produce the 45-nanometer microchip. Industry analysts believe Fab 32 may be the last of its kind to be built in the U.S., as construction costs are higher in America than in other countries. Intel's future in Chandler is examined.

5209 ■ "Analysts Not Fazed By Constellation's Halt to New Nuclear Plants" in *Baltimore Business Journal* (Vol. 28, October 22, 2010, No. 24)
Pub: Baltimore Business Journal
Ed: Scott Dance. **Description:** Wall Street analysts believe that Constellation Energy Group Inc.'s decision to pull out of the nuclear construction business would not change their outlook on the company. New nuclear power had been one of Constellation's long-term goals, but the company pulled the plug on the project. It is believed that most investors were not expecting any payoff from the venture.

5210 ■ "Are We There Yet?" in *Business Courier* (Vol. 24, April 4, 2008, No. 52, pp. 1)
Pub: American City Business Journals, Inc.
Ed: Lucy May; Dan Monk. **Description:** Groundbreaking for The Banks project happened in April 2, 2008, however, the future of the development remains uncertain due to some unresolved issues such as financing. Developers Harold A. Dawson Co. and

Carter still have to pass final financing documents to Hamilton County and Cincinnati. The issue of financial commitment for the central riverfront project is examined.

5211 ■ "Areva Diversifies Further Into Wind" in *Wall Street Journal Eastern Edition* (November 29, 2011, pp. B7)
Pub: Dow Jones & Company Inc.
Ed: Max Colchester, Noemie Bisserbe. **Description:** French engineering company Areva SA is diversifying and moving away from nuclear energy projects. One sign of that is its recent discussion to construct 120 wind turbines to be located at two German wind farms. Such a deal, if signed, would be worth about US$1.59 billion.

5212 ■ "As Tradesmen Age, New Workers In Short Supply" in *Boston Business Journal* (Vol. 27, November 9, 2007, No. 41, pp. 1)
Pub: American City Business Journals Inc.
Ed: Jackie Noblett. **Description:** It is becoming more difficult to find young people who have the skills for installation and maintenance businesses. Some businesses are unable to complete contracts on time due to lack of staff. Unions are making efforts to address the expected shortfall of laborers in the coming years through apprenticeship programs.

5213 ■ "Athletes' Performance Building $10 Million Facility In ASU Park" in *The Business Journal - Serving Phoenix and the Valley of the Sun* (Vol. 28, August 8, 2008, No. 49, pp. 1)
Pub: American City Business Journals, Inc.
Ed: Jan Buchholz. **Description:** Athletes' Performance's planned facility at Arizona State University is scheduled to begin in November 2008 and expected to be completed by September 2009. The new building will almost double the company's training space as it will expand from around 19,000 square feet to 35,000 square feet.

5214 ■ "Austin Homes are Overpriced, Study Says" in *Austin Business JournalInc.* (Vol. 29, January 1, 2010, No. 43, pp. 1)
Pub: American City Business Journals
Ed: Kate Harrington. **Description:** Study by Forbes. com shows that Austin-Round Rock metropolitan statistical area ranked 10th on the list of cities with the most over-priced homes. For instance, the average price for a single-family home pegged at $188,000.

5215 ■ "Austin Ponders Annexing FI Racetrack" in *Austin Business Journal* (Vol. 31, July 8, 2011, No. 18, pp. 1)
Pub: American City Business Journals Inc.
Ed: Vicky Garza. **Description:** City planners in Austin, Texas are studying the feasibility of annexing the land under and around the Circuit of the Americas Formula One Racetrack being constructed east of the city. The annexation could generate at least $13 million in financial gain over 25 years from property taxes alone.

5216 ■ "BABs in Bond Land" in *Barron's* (Vol. 89, July 6, 2009, No. 27, pp. 14)
Pub: Dow Jones & Co., Inc.
Ed: Jim McTague. **Description:** American Recovery and Reinvestment Act has created taxable Build America Bonds (BAB) to finance new construction projects. The issuance of the two varieties of taxable BABs is expected to benefit the municipal bond market.

5217 ■ "Bad News for Canada: U.S. New-Home Starts Sink" in *Globe & Mail* (February 17, 2007, pp. B7)
Pub: CTVglobemedia Publishing Inc.
Ed: Tavia Grant. **Description:** The new-home construction in the United States dropped by 14.3 percent in January 2007. The sinking construction activity shows significant impact on the Canadian factories and lumber companies.

5218 ■ "Bankruptcies" in *Crain's Detroit Business* (Vol. 24, March 24, 2008, No. 12, pp. 6)
Pub: Crain Communications, Inc.
Description: Current list of business that filed for Chapter 7 or 11 protection in U.S. Bankruptcy Court in Detroit include a construction company, a medical care company, a physical therapy firm and a communications firm.

5219 ■ "Banks Could Greet Tenants in One Year" in *Business Courier* (Vol. 26, October 16, 2009, No. 25, pp. 1)
Pub: American City Business Journals, Inc.
Ed: Lucy May. **Description:** The Banks project's initial phase is expected to start in 60 days, which may mean that the project's first tenant could move in by the end of 2010 or beginning of 2011. Carter, an Atlanta-based firm has partnered with Dawson Company in this riverfront development. The first phase will include 80,000 square feet of retail and 300 apartments.

5220 ■ "Be Proactive - Closely Review Contracts" in *Contractor* (Vol. 56, July 2009, No. 7, pp. 19)
Pub: Penton Media, Inc.
Ed: Al Schwartz. **Description:** Contract disputes can make subcontractors suffer big financial losses or even cause a new subcontractor to fail. Subcontractors should scour the plans and specifications for any references to work that might remotely come under their scope and to cross out any line in the contract that does not accurately reflect the work that they agreed to.

5221 ■ "Be Wary of Dual-Flush Conversion Kits" in *Contractor* (Vol. 56, September 2009, No. 9, pp. 66)
Pub: Penton Media, Inc.
Ed: John Koeller; Bill Gauley. **Description:** Recommendation of untested dual-flush conversion devices for tank-type toilets in the United States have been questioned. The products are being advertised as having the ability to convert single-flush to a dual-flush toilet. No evidence of water conservation from using such devices has been recorded.

5222 ■ "Behind the Scenes: Companies at the Heart of Everyday Life" in *Inc.* (March 2008, pp. 34-35)
Pub: Gruner & Jahr USA Publishing
Ed: Athena Schindelheim. **Description:** Profiles of companies used to improve road conditions at the Bedford, New Hampshire Toll Plaza are presented. General Traffic Equipment provides LED traffic lights; TRMI, provided 8-foot strips treadles that count the number of axles that drive over them; E-Z Pass system is an antenna from Mark IV Industries that uses radio-frequency identification (RFID) technology to scan a small device attached to a car's windshield; and Transport Data Systems installed cameras that snap photos of passengers and license plates in order to catch individuals who try to dodge fees.

5223 ■ "Belmont Annexation Approved" in *Charlotte Observer* (February 7, 2007)
Pub: Knight-Ridder/Tribune Business News
Ed: Jefferson George. **Description:** Belmont, North Carolina City Council approved annexation of nearly 64 acres. The land will be used to develop a residential community.

5224 ■ "Bigger TIF Makes Development Inroads" in *The Business Journal-Serving Metropolitan Kansas City* (Vol. 26, July 11, 2008, No. 44)
Pub: American City Business Journals, Inc.
Ed: Rob Roberts. **Description:** On July 9, 2008 the Tax Increment Financing Commission voted to expand a TIF district to Tiffany Springs Road. The plan for the TIF district close to Kansas City International Airport is to include a-half mile of the road. The impacts of the expansion on construction projects and on the road network are analyzed.

5225 ■ "BIM and LPS Improve Project Management" in *Contractor* (Vol. 57, January 2010, No. 1, pp. 56)
Pub: Penton Media, Inc.
Ed: Dennis Sowards. **Description:** Building Information Modeling helps reduce workspace conflicts and construction problems that are not seen in typical design efforts for mechanical contractors. The Last Planner System in Lean Construction also helps improve productivity in project management.

5226 ■ "BIM and You: Know Its Benefits and Risks" in *Contractor* (Vol. 57, January 2010, No. 1, pp. 46)
Pub: Penton Media, Inc.
Ed: Susan Linden McGreevy. **Description:** Building Information Modeling is intended to be "collaborative" and this could raise legal issues if a contractor sends an electronic bid and it is filtered out. Other legal issues that mechanical contractors need to consider before using this technology are discussed.

5227 ■ "Block Plans Office Park Along K-10 Corridor" in *The Business Journal-Serving Metropolitan Kansas City* (Vol. 27, October 3, 2008)
Pub: American City Business Journals, Inc.
Ed: Rob Roberts. **Description:** Kansas City, Missouri-based Block and Co. is planning to build four office buildings at the corner of College Boulevard and Ridgeview Road in Olathe. Features of the planned development are provided. Comments from executives are also presented.

5228 ■ "Block Pulls Plug On Riverside Deal" in *The Business Journal-Serving Metropolitan Kansas City* (Vol. 27, October 10, 2008, No. 4)
Pub: American City Business Journals, Inc.
Ed: Rob Roberts. **Description:** Real estate developer Ken Block has backed out from a $300 million Riverside industrial project. Block says he has already invested $1 million of his own money into the deal. Details regarding the project are given.

5229 ■ "Bond Hill Cinema Site To See New Life" in *Business Courier* (Vol. 27, October 29, 2010, No. 26, pp. 1)
Pub: Business Courier
Ed: Dan Monk. **Description:** Avondale, Ohio's Corinthian Baptist Church will redevelop the 30-acre former Showcase Cinema property to a mixed-use site that could feature a college, senior home, and retail. Corinthian Baptist, which is one of the largest African-American churches in the region, is also planning to relocate the church.

5230 ■ "Bond OK Could Bring Back the Housing Battle?" in *Charlotte Business Journal* (Vol. 25, November 5, 2010, No. 33, pp. 1)
Pub: Charlotte Business Journal
Ed: Susan Stabley. **Description:** The approval of the $15 million housing bond in Charlotte, North Carolina could bring back the debates on housing in the region. Protesters have opposed affordable housing developments that were proposed in the area since 2008. Other information on the recently approved housing bond and on other real estate issues in North Carolina is presented.

5231 ■ "Bridging the Bay" in *Business Journal Serving Greater Tampa Bay* (Vol. 30, November 5, 2010, No. 46, pp. 1)
Pub: Tampa Bay Business Journal
Ed: Mark Holan. **Description:** The Florida Department of Transportation has launched a study to design the proposed addition to the Howard Frankland Bridge. The bridge would be designed to accommodate more than personal vehicles.

5232 ■ "Brookfield Eyes 'New World'" in *Globe & Mail* (February 6, 2007, pp. B1)
Pub: CTVglobemedia Publishing Inc.
Ed: Sinclair Stewart; Elizabeth Church. **Description:** The efforts of Brookfield Asset Management Inc. to acquire American paper company, Longview Fibre Co., and Australian construction company Multiplex Ltd. are discussed.

5233 ■ "Builder's Bankruptcy Fans Fears" in *Crain's Cleveland Business* (Vol. 28, October 22, 2007, No. 42, pp. 1)
Pub: Crain Communications, Inc.
Ed: Stan Bullard. **Description:** Whitlatch & Co., Northeast Ohio's largest builder by unit volume in the early 1990s, has filed for Chapter 11 bankruptcy. This

is causing builders and others in the real estate industry to wonder how long and severe the housing slump will be and which companies will survive.

5234 ■ "Builder's Comeback Highlights Uptick in Demand for New Homes" in *Boston Business Journal* (Vol. 29, June 3, 2011, No. 4, pp. 1)
Pub: American City Business Journals Inc.
Ed: Gary Haber. **Description:** The return of builder Michael Canock after a series of credit crisis and the funding for his new projects are discussed in light of the recent upsurge in the home-building industry in the Baltimore area. New single-family homes numbered 318 in first quarter 2011 which is a 20 percent increase from first quarter 2010.

5235 ■ "Builders Land Rutenberg Deal" in *Charlotte Observer* (February 2, 2007)
Pub: Knight-Ridder/Tribune Business News
Ed: Bob Fliss. **Description:** Jim and Larry Sanders purchased a franchise from builder, Arthur Rutenberg Homes. The brothers will build custom homes in the area.

5236 ■ "Builders, Unions Aim to Cut Costs; Pushing Changes to Regain Share of Residential Market; Seek Council's Help" in *Crain's New York Business*
Pub: Crain Communications, Inc.
Ed: Erik Engquist. **Description:** Union contractors and workers are worried about a decline in their market share for housing so they intend to ask the City Council to impose new safety and benefit standards on all contractors to avoid being undercut by nonunion competitors.

5237 ■ "Building Targeted for Marriott in Violation" in *Business Journal-Milwaukee* (Vol. 28, December 24, 2010, No. 12, pp. A1)
Pub: Milwaukee Business Journal
Ed: Sean Ryan. **Description:** Milwaukee, Wisconsin's Department of Neighborhood Services has ordered structural improvements and safeguards for the Pioneer Building after three violations from structural failures were found. Pioneer was among the five buildings wanted by Jackson Street Management LLC to demolish for the new Marriott Hotel.

5238 ■ "A Burning Issue: Lives Are at Stake Every Day" in *Contractor* (Vol. 56, October 2009, No. 10, pp. 29)
Pub: Penton Media, Inc.
Ed: Julius A. Ballanco; Stanley Wolfson. **Description:** American Society of Plumbing Engineers has been accused of being biased for supporting rules that require residential fire sprinklers although the society's members will not receive any benefit from their installation. The organization trains and certifies plumbing engineers who design life-saving fire protection systems.

5239 ■ "Buy Now?" in *Hawaii Business* (Vol. 53, March 2008, No. 9, pp. 32)
Pub: Hawaii Business Publishing
Ed: David K. Choo. **Description:** Discusses the Honolulu Board of REALTORS which said that the last two months of 2007 saw double-digit housing sales drop, with December figures showing 30.6 percent and 22.9 percent decline in sales of single-family homes and condominiums, respectively. Forecasts on Hawaii's real estate market for 2008 are discussed.

5240 ■ "Cadillac Tower Largest to Start in a Decade" in *Globe & Mail* (March 28, 2006, pp. B5)
Pub: CTVglobemedia Publishing Inc.
Ed: Elizabeth Church. **Description:** The plans of Cadillac Fairview Corporation Ltd. to build office towers, in downtown Canada, are presented.

5241 ■ "Cal-ISO Plans $125 Million Facility" in *Sacramento Business Journal* (Vol. 25, August 1, 2008, No. 22, pp. 1)
Pub: American City Business Journals, Inc.
Ed: Celia Lamb; Michael Shaw. **Description:** Sacramento, California-based nonprofit organization California Independent System Operator (ISO) is planning to build a new headquarters in Folsom. The new building would double its current leased space to 227,000 square feet. The ISO will seek tax-exempt bond financing for the project.

5242 ■ "Can HOAs Stop You From Going Green?" in *Contractor* (Vol. 56, July 2009, No. 7, pp. 39)
Pub: Penton Media, Inc.
Ed: Susan Linden McGreevy. **Description:** There have been cases concerning homeowners' associations objections to the installation of wind turbines and solar panels. Precedence with the courts show that they will look at several factors when deciding to uphold restrictions on property use including whether the item encroaches on the rights of others, is likely to adversely affect property values, and also the state of enforcement.

5243 ■ "Canada's Largest Bakery Officially Opened Today" in *Ecology,Environment & Conservation Business* (October 15, 2011, pp. 7)
Pub: HighBeam Research
Description: Maple Leaf Foods opened Canada's largest commercial bakery in Hamilton, Ontario. The firm's 385,000 square foot Trillium bakery benefits from efficient design flow and best-in-class technologies.

5244 ■ "Capital Metro May Soon Seek Contractor to Replace Star Tran" in *Austin Business Journal* (Vol. 31, June 10, 2011, No. 14, pp. 1)
Pub: American City Business Journals Inc.
Ed: Vicky Garza. **Description:** Capital Metropolitan Transportation Authority may be forced to contract out its bus services provided by StarTran Inc. as early as September 2012 following legislation approved by the Texas legislature. The bill originates in a report by the Sunset Advisory Commission. Details are included.

5245 ■ "Casino Minority Spend: $80 Million" in *Business Courier* (Vol. 27, August 20, 2010, No. 16, pp. 1)
Pub: Business Courier
Ed: Lucy May. **Description:** Real estate developers are planning to invest $80 million to build the Harrah's casino project in Cincinnati, Ohio. Rock Ventures LLC is seeking a 20 percent inclusion rate in the project.

5246 ■ "Chicago Public School District Builds Green" in *Contractor* (Vol. 56, October 2009, No. 10, pp. 5)
Pub: Penton Media, Inc.
Ed: Candace Roulo. **Description:** Chicago Public Schools district has already built six U.S. Green Building Council LEED certified schools and one addition in five years and will continue to build new green buildings. The district has an Environmental Action Plan that strives to reduce energy usage, improve indoor air quality, and reduce contribution to climate change.

5247 ■ "Children's Hospital to Build in New Berlin" in *The Business Journal-Milwaukee* (Vol. 25, August 1, 2008, No. 45, pp. A1)
Pub: American City Business Journals, Inc.
Ed: Corrinne Hess. **Description:** Children's Hospital of Wisconsin plans a clinic in the 35-acre medical office park in New Berlin, Wisconsin, owned by Froedtert Memorial Lutheran Hospital and Medical College of Wisconsin Real Estate Ventures LLC. The hospital will be the first major tenant in the park, to be built by Irgens Development Partners LLC.

5248 ■ "Children's Hospital to Grow" in *Austin Business Journal* (Vol. 31, July 22, 2011, No. 20, pp. A1)
Pub: American City Business Journals Inc.
Ed: Sandra Zaragoza. **Description:** Austin, Texas-based Dell Children's Medical Center is set to embark on a tower expansion. The plan will accommodate more patients and make room for the hospital's growing specialty program.

5249 ■ "Chinese Solar Panel Manufacturer Scopes Out Austin" in *Austin Business JournalInc.* (Vol. 29, October 30, 2009, No. 34, pp. 1)
Pub: American City Business Journals
Ed: Jacob Dirr. **Description:** China's Yingli Green Energy Holding Company Ltd. is looking for a site in order to construct a $20 million photovoltaic panel plant. Both Austin and San Antonio are vying to house the manufacturing hub. The project could create about 300 jobs and give Austin a chance to become a player in the solar energy market. Other solar companies are also considering Central Texas as an option to set up shop.

5250 ■ "Christ Hospital to Expand" in *Business Courier* (Vol. 27, June 25, 2010, No. 8, pp. 3)
Pub: Business Courier
Ed: Dan Monk, James Ritchie. **Description:** Christ Hospital intends to invest more than $300 million and generate 200 jobs in an expansion of its Mount Auburn campus in Cincinnati, Ohio. About $22 million in retail activity can be created by the hospital expansion, which will also include a replacement garage and new surgery facilities.

5251 ■ "Cincinnati's Senior Moment" in *Business Courier* (Vol. 27, June 11, 2010, No. 6, pp. 1)
Pub: Business Courier
Ed: James Ritchie. **Description:** It is believed that the high demand in housing that will accompany the aging population has yet to arrive, and is not due for years to come. The next few years could lead to leaner times for long-standing independent-living properties and a slow climb for newer centers looking to build occupancy.

5252 ■ "City Eyeing Tax Breaks for Arena" in *Boston Business Journal* (Vol. 29, June 3, 2011, No. 4, pp. 1)
Pub: American City Business Journals Inc.
Ed: Daniel J. Sernovitz. **Description:** Baltimore City is opting to give millions of dollars in tax breaks and construction loans to a group of private investors led by William Hackerman who is proposing to build a new arena and hotel at the Baltimore Convention Center. The project will cost $500 million with the state putting up another $400 million for the center's expansion.

5253 ■ "City Seeks More Minorities" in *Austin Business JournalInc.* (Vol. 28, November 7, 2008, No. 34, pp. A1)
Pub: American City Business Journals
Ed: Jean Kwon. **Description:** Austin, Texas is planning to increase the participation of minority- and women-owned businesses in government contracts. Contractors are required to show 'good faith' to comply with the specified goals. The city is planning to effect the changes in the construction and professional services sector.

5254 ■ "City Sets Yamhill Makeover" in *The Business Journal-Portland* (Vol. 25, July 4, 2008, No. 17, pp. 1)
Pub: American City Business Journals, Inc.
Ed: Andy Giegerich. **Description:** City government is scheduled to redevelop Peterson's property on Yamhill Street in Portland. The redevelopment is seen as a way to better developing commercial properties in the area. Problems associated with the project, which include cost and developer selection, are also discussed.

5255 ■ "City Struggles to Iron Out Tangled Transportation" in *Crain's New York Business* (Vol. 24, January 14, 2008, No. 2, pp. 33)
Pub: Crain Communications, Inc.
Ed: Judith Messina. **Description:** Discusses the possible solutions to improve lower Manhattan's transportation infrastructure including the construction of three new transit centers, an expansion in ferry service and the plan to get parked buses off the street.

5256 ■ "CityLink Project On Hold" in *Business Courier* (Vol. 24, November 9, 2008, No. 30, pp. 3)
Pub: American City Business Journals, Inc.
Ed: Dan Monk. **Description:** Developers of the CityLink project have indicated that it will be at least a year before they start the planned social services mall at 800 Bank West End. According to Tim Senff, Citylink CEO, the company wants to build bridges before constructing the buildings. The project's critics are still considering whether to appeal a court ruling regarding the facility's compliance with the city's zoning code.

5257 ■ "Civil Council Almost On Board With Light Rail Plan" in *The Business Journal-Serving Metropolitan Kansas City* (September 5, 2008)
Pub: American City Business Journals, Inc.
Ed: Steve Vockrodt. **Description:** Civic Council of Greater Kansas City has taken back its demand for the city to show a 10-year financial plan to win its endorsement of a light rail plan. The council said it will accept a five-year financial plan for the project. Details of the light rail plan are also presented.

5258 ■ "Clean Wind Energy Tower Transitions from R&D Stage Company" in *Professional Services Close-Up* (September 30, 2011)
Pub: Close-Up Media
Description: Clean Wind Energy designed and is developing large downdraft towers that use benevolent, non-toxic natural elements to generate electricity and clean water. The firm is closing its internally staffed engineering office in Warrenton, Virginia and transitioning a development team to oversee and coordinate industry consultants and advisors to construct their first dual renewable energy tower.

5259 ■ "Clock Ticking for Hotel Berry" in *Sacramento Business Journal* (Vol. 25, July 25, 2008, No. 21, pp. 1)
Pub: American City Business Journals, Inc.
Ed: Michael Shaw. **Description:** Federal tax credits worth $13.6 million have been awarded to boost the renovation project for the aging Hotel Berry in downtown Sacramento, California. The owners of the hotel have five months before the expiration of the tax credits to raise the remaining funding for the $20 million renovation.

5260 ■ "Collateral Damage" in *Business Courier* (Vol. 26, October 16, 2009, No. 25, pp. 1)
Pub: American City Business Journals, Inc.
Ed: Jon Newberry. **Description:** Non-union construction firms representing Ohio Valley Associated Builders and Contractors Inc. have filed cases against unionized shops claiming violations of wage law in Ohio. Defendants say the violations are minor, however, they believe they are caught in the middle of the group's campaign to change the state's wage law.

5261 ■ "Columbia Sale Narrowed To Two Developers" in *The Business Journal-Milwaukee* (Vol. 25, July 18, 2008, No. 43, pp. A1)
Pub: American City Business Journals, Inc.
Ed: Corrinne Hess. **Description:** Officials of Columbia St. Mary's Inc plan to pick one of two real-estate developers who will buy the 8-acre property of the Columbia Hospital which the company will move away from when their new hospital has been constructed. The hospital on Newport Ave. has been on the market since 2001.

5262 ■ "Combo Dorm-Field House Built to Attain LEED Gold" in *Contractor* (Vol. 56, September 2009, No. 9, pp. 1)
Pub: Penton Media, Inc.
Ed: Candace Roulo; Robert P. Mader. **Description:** North Central College in Illinois has built a new dormitory that is expected to attain Leadership in Energy and Environmental Design Gold certification from the United States Green Building Council. The structure features a geo-exchange heat pump system and radiant floor heat. A description of the facility is also provided.

5263 ■ "Commercial Builders Take It on the Chin" in *Crain's Chicago Business* (Vol. 31, April 28, 2008, No. 17, pp. 16)
Pub: Crain Communications, Inc.
Ed: Alby Gallun. **Description:** Although the health care development sector has seen growth, the rest of Chicago's local commercial building industry has seen steep declines in the first quarter of this year. According to McGraw-Hill Construction, Chicago-area non-residential construction starts totaled $731 million in the quarter, a 60 percent drop from the year-earlier period. Volume in the retail, office and hotel markets fell by nearly 70 percent.

5264 ■ "Condo Markdown" in *Boston Business Journal* (Vol. 27, November 30, 2007, No. 44, pp. 1)
Pub: American City Business Journals Inc.
Ed: Michelle Hillman. **Description:** Boston real estate market is softening, and condominium developers such as Beacon Communities LLC are sending out various incentives like markdowns and unit upgrades. Developers have also held auctions and even offered brand new cars to lure buyers. Other perks being offered by various Boston developers are discussed.

5265 ■ "Condominium Sales Fall to a Seven-Year Low" in *Crain's Chicago Business* (Vol. 31, November 10, 2008, No. 45, pp. 2)
Pub: Crain Communications, Inc.
Ed: Alby Gallun. **Description:** Downtown Chicago condominium market is experiencing the lowest number of sales in years due to the tightening of the mortgage lending market, the Wall Street crisis and the downturn in the economy. The supply of new condos is soaring, the result of the building boom of 2005 and 2006; many developers are finding it difficult to pay off construction loans and fear foreclosure on their properties. Additional information and statistical data related to the downtown condominium market is provided.

5266 ■ "Construction Companies Think Smaller, Find Niches as Projects Become Fewer" in *Crain's Detroit Business* (March 10, 2008)
Pub: Crain Communications, Inc.
Ed: Daniel Duggan. **Description:** Due to the decline in development projects, construction firms are facing stronger competition for bids and are relying on their good track records or developing expertise in specific niches to get the job.

5267 ■ "Contracting Firm Sees Timing Right for Expansion" in *Tampa Bay Business Journal* (Vol. 29, November 13, 2009, No. 47, pp. 1)
Pub: American City Business Journals
Ed: Janet Leiser. **Description:** Construction management company Moss & Associates LLC of Fort Lauderdale, Florida has launched its expansion to Tampa Bay. Moss & Associates has started the construction of the Marlins stadium in Miami, Florida's Little Havana section. It also plans to diversify by embarking on other government development, such as health care facilities and airports.

5268 ■ "Contractors Debate Maximizing Green Opportunities, Education" in *Contractor* (Vol. 56, November 2009, No. 11, pp. 3)
Pub: Penton Media, Inc.
Ed: Robert P. Mader. **Description:** Attendees at the Mechanical Service Co ntractors Association convention were urged to get involved with their local U.S. Green Building Council chapter by one presenter. Another presenter says that one green opportunity for contractors is the commissioning of new buildings.

5269 ■ "Contractors Must be Lead Certified by April 2010" in *Contractor* (Vol. 57, February 2010, No. 2, pp. 3)
Pub: Penton Media, Inc.
Description: Contractors should be trained and certified to comply with the U.S. Environmental Protection Agency's Lead Renovation, Repair, and Painting regulation if they work on housing built before 1978 by April 2010. Contractors with previous lead abatement training must be trained and certified under this new program.

5270 ■ "Contractors Scramble for Jobs" in *Business Journal Portland* (Vol. 26, December 18, 2009, No. 41, pp. 1)
Pub: American City Business Journals Inc.
Ed: Andy Giegerich. **Description:** Contractors in Portland area are expected to bid for capital construction projects that will be funded by municipalities in the said area. Contracts for companies that work on materials handling, road improvement, and public safety structure projects will be issued.

5271 ■ "Contractors: Slots MBE Goal a Test" in *Baltimore Business Journal* (Vol. 27, November 20, 2009, No. 28, pp. 1)
Pub: American City Business Journals
Ed: Scott Dance. **Description:** Slot machine manufacturers in Maryland have been searching minority business enterprises (MBEs) that will provide maintenance and delivery services to the machines. MBEs will also build the stands where the machines will be mounted.

5272 ■ "Convenience Store Expanding" in *Clovis News Journal* (November 9, 2010)
Pub: Freedom Communications Inc.
Description: Allsup's convenience store on North Prince Street in Clovis, New Mexico will expand its facilities. The current building is being demolished to make way for the new construction.

5273 ■ "Corporate Park Retrofits for Water Savings" in *Contractor* (Vol. 56, October 2009, No. 10, pp. 5)
Pub: Penton Media, Inc.
Description: Merrit Corporate Park in Norwalk, Connecticut has been interested in improving building efficiency and one of their buildings has been retrofitted with water-efficient plumbing systems which will allow them to save as much as two million gallons of water. ADP Service Corp. helped the park upgrade their plumbing system.

5274 ■ "Corporex Checks Into Hotel Niche" in *Business Courier* (Vol. 24, October 12, 2008, No. 26, pp. 1)
Pub: American City Business Journals, Inc.
Ed: Laura Baverman. **Description:** Corporex Companies Inc. is investing $900 million on select-service hotels ranging from $12 million to $20 million each, with eight hotels under construction and nine sites under contract.

5275 ■ "Corus Eases Off Ailing Condo Market; Office Developers Get Majority of 1Q Loans" in *Crain's Chicago Business* (April 28, 2008)
Pub: Crain Communications, Inc.
Ed: H. Lee Murphy. **Description:** Corus Bankshares Inc., a specialist in lending for the condominium high-rise construction market, is diversifying its portfolio by making loans to office developers and expects to be investing in hotels through the rest of the year. Corus' $7.57 billion loan portfolio is also discussed in detail as well as the company's earnings and share price. Statistical data included.

5276 ■ "Could This Be Your Next Office Building?" in *Austin Business Journal* (Vol. 31, May 13, 2011, No. 10, pp. A1)
Pub: American City Business Journals Inc.
Ed: Cody Lyon. **Description:** Falcon Containers moved to a 51-acre site in Far East Austin, Texas and started construction of a 2,500-square-foot headquarters made from eight 40-foot shipping containers. Falcon's CEO Stephen Shang plans to

use his headquarters building as a showroom to attract upscale, urban hipsters. Insights on the construction's environmental and social impact are shared.

5277 ■ "Councilman May Revive Labor Bill" in *Baltimore Business Journal* (Vol. 28, August 13, 2010, No. 14, pp. 1)
Pub: Baltimore Business Journal
Ed: Daniel J. Sernovitz. **Description:** Baltimore, Maryland Councilman Bill Henry has started reviving controversial legislation that would force developers and contractors to give preference to union labor. The legislation requires contractors to give preference to city workers in order to lower Baltimore's unemployment rate.

5278 ■ "County Tract Pitched for Data Center" in *Baltimore Business Journal* (Vol. 28, July 23, 2010, No. 11, pp. 1)
Pub: Baltimore Business Journal
Ed: Scott Dance. **Description:** One hundred acres of land in Woodlawn, Maryland is set to be sold for use in the construction of a data center for the U.S. Social Security Administration. Baltimore County has submitted a bid for the $750M construction project.

5279 ■ "Covington's Business Owners Get Bridge Relief" in *Business Courier* (Vol. 27, October 29, 2010, No. 26, pp. 1)
Pub: Business Courier
Ed: Dan Monk. **Description:** Engineers of Brent Spence Bridge have developed a new 'second chance' exit that preserves highway access to Covington, Kentucky's main business districts. It is believed that the planned ramp off Interstate 75 represents a compromise between highway planners, who wish to maintain continuous traffic for interstate users.

5280 ■ "Creativity is Essential in Sagging Relocation Market" in *Crain's Cleveland Business* (Vol. 28, November 5, 2007, No. 44, pp. 19)
Pub: Crain Communications, Inc.
Ed: Christine Gordillo. **Description:** Since Northeast Ohio was headquarters to a number of Fortune 500 companies, residential real estate builders and brokers could count on corporate relocation clients for a steady stream of business. Today, corporations have become more cautious when relocating talent due to the costs involved which has forced industry experts to be more patient and more creative in the ways they attract out-of-town buyers who are likely to be a sure sell.

5281 ■ "A Crystal Ball" in *Business Journal Portland* (Vol. 27, December 31, 2010, No. 44, pp. 1)
Pub: Portland Business Journal
Ed: Wendy Culverwell. **Description:** McMenamins Pubs and Breweries has resumed construction of its Crystal Hotel project. The company has been working to convert a former bath house into a 51-room hotel. The hotel is expected to open in 2011.

5282 ■ "Customer Service Center Will Rise in Indian Land" in *Charlotte Observer* (February 4, 2007)
Pub: Knight-Ridder/Tribune Business News
Ed: Taylor Bright. **Description:** Kennametal is building a new customer service center in Lancaster County, North Carolina. Kennametal makes metal tools and parts, specializing in metals highly resistant to heat.

5283 ■ "D.A.G. Sues to Stay on Job" in *Business Courier* (Vol. 24, November 9, 2008, No. 30, pp. 4)
Pub: American City Business Journals, Inc.
Ed: Jon Newberry. **Description:** D.A.G. Construction Co. filed a breach of contract lawsuit against the Cincinnati Metropolitan Housing Authority. The company asked the Hamilton County Pleas Court to stop the housing authority from taking over a $10 million senior housing project. According to the company, the agency displaced D.A.G. and its subcontractors without warning.

5284 ■ "Data Center Plan Bearing Fruit From Apple, Spec Center" in *Charlotte Business Journal* (Vol. 25, October 15, 2010, No. 30, pp. 1)
Pub: Charlotte Business Journal
Ed: Ken Elkins. **Description:** Apple Inc. is planning to expand its server farm at the North Carolina Data Center Corridor in Catawba County. T5 Partners, on the other hand, will build a shell building to house a server on the site. Infocrossing Inc. will also build an open data center in the area.

5285 ■ "Decorated Marine Sues Contractor" in *Wall Street Journal Eastern Edition* (November 29, 2011, pp. A4)
Pub: Dow Jones & Company Inc.
Ed: Julian E. Barnes. **Description:** Marine Devon Maylie, who was awarded the Congressional Medal of Honor for bravery, has filed a lawsuit against defense contractor BAE Systems PLC claiming that the company prevented his hiring by another firm by saying he has a mental condition and a drinking problem. Maylie says that this was in retaliation for his objections to the company's plan to sell the Pakistani military high-tech sniper scopes.

5286 ■ "Deltona to Get First Movie Theater, Shopping Center" in *Orlando Business Journal* (Vol. 26, December 4, 2009, No. 26, pp. 1)
Pub: American City Business Journals
Ed: Anjali Fluker. **Description:** Epic Theaters Inc. revealed plans to build a new 900,000 square foot retail center anchored by a 12-screen movie theater in the city of Deltona in Volusia County, Florida by 2010. The project, dubbed Deltona Village, would provide the city with its first movie theater and shopping center.

5287 ■ "Design Programs for HVAC Sizing Solutions" in *Contractor* (Vol. 57, January 2010, No. 1, pp. 44)
Pub: Penton Media, Inc.
Ed: William Feldman; Patti Feldman. **Description:** Rhvac 8 is an HVAC design program that lets users calculate peak heating and cooling load requirements for rooms, zones, systems, and entire buildings. The HVAC Pipe Sizer software for the iPhone enables quick sizing of a simple piping system.

5288 ■ "Detroit Residential Market Slows; Bright Spots Emerge" in *Crain's Detroit Business* (Vol. 24, October 6, 2008, No. 40, pp. 11)
Pub: Crain Communications, Inc.
Ed: Daniel Duggan. **Description:** Discusses the state of the residential real estate market in Detroit; although condominium projects receive the most attention, deals for single-family homes are taking place in greater numbers due to financing issues. Buyers can purchase a single family home with a 3.5 percent down payment compared to 20 percent for some condo deals because of the number of first-time homebuyer programs under the Federal Housing Administration.

5289 ■ "Developer Banks On East Submarket, Slowdown Not a Hinderance" in *The Business Journal-Serving Greater Tampa Bay* (August 1, 2008)
Pub: American City Business Journals, Inc.
Ed: Janet Leiser. **Description:** CLW Industrial Group and Cobalt Industrial REIT II have teamed up to develop a 14-acre area in northeast Hillsborough County, Florida. The $15 million industrial park project includes the 175,000-square-foot New Tampa Commerce Center, scheduled for completion in the first quarter of 2009.

5290 ■ "Developer Tries to Bring Homes to Buda" in *Austin Business JournalInc.* (Vol. 28, December 26, 2008, No. 41, pp. 1)
Pub: American City Business Journals
Ed: Kate Harrington. **Description:** Real estate developer Jeremiah Venture LP is planning a residential, single-family development on about 600 acres near Buda, Texas. The company also plans to construct a membrane waste treatment plant, and has applied to do land application. However, several groups have come forward to ask for more information on the application due to concerns about soil density.

5291 ■ "Developers Await Hotel" in *The Business Journal-Portland* (Vol. 25, July 11, 2008, No. 18, pp. 1)
Pub: American City Business Journals, Inc.
Ed: Wendy Culverwell. **Description:** Developers are eager to start the construction of a new hotel at the Oregon Convention Center in Portland, Oregon as hey say that the project will help boost the convention center neighborhood. The project, called The Westin Portland at the Convention Center, is partly handled by Ashforth Pacific Inc.

5292 ■ "Developers Compete for APG Project" in *Baltimore Business Journal* (Vol. 27, October 16, 2009, No. 23, pp. 1)
Pub: American City Business Journals
Ed: Daniel J. Sernovitz. **Description:** Corporate Office Properties Trust has lost the case in Delaware bankruptcy court to prevent rival St. John Properties Inc. from going ahead with its plans to develop the 400 acres at Aberdeen Proving Ground (APG) in Maryland. Both developers have competed for the right to develop the two million square foot business park in APG.

5293 ■ "Developers Give Big to Mayor's Bid" in *Boston Business Journal* (Vol. 29, August 26, 2011, No. 16, pp. 1)
Pub: American City Business Journals Inc.
Ed: Scott Dance. **Description:** Mayor Stephanie Rawlings-Blake received thousands of dollars in her political campaign from companies of real estate developers who are vying to build key development projects in Baltimore, Maryland. Rawlings-Blake created a major fundraising advantage over other mayoral candidates with the help of those contributions.

5294 ■ "Developers Give City Dwellings a Modern Spin" in *Crain's Cleveland Business* (Vol. 28, November 5, 2007, No. 44, pp. 18)
Pub: Crain Communications, Inc.
Description: Cleveland is increasingly becoming a canvas for fresh, cutting-edge design due to several recent projects, some at prominent sites.

5295 ■ "Developers Poised to Pull Trigers" in *Boston Business Journal* (Vol. 30, November 12, 2010, No. 42, pp. 1)
Pub: Boston Business Journal
Ed: Craig M. Douglas. **Description:** Large residential projects are expected to break ground in Boston, Massachusetts in 2011, as real estate developers expect growth for the industry. Real estate experts expect more than 2,000 rental units to be available by 2011. Information on key real estate projects in Boston is presented.

5296 ■ "Developers Vie for UWM Dorm" in *The Business Journal-Milwaukee* (Vol. 25, July 11, 2008, No. 42, pp. A1)
Pub: American City Business Journals, Inc.
Ed: Rich Kirchen. **Description:** Eight developers are competing to build a 500- to 700-student residence hall for the University of Wisconsin-Milwaukee. The residence hall will probably be developed within two miles of the main campus. It was revealed that the university's real estate foundation will select the successful bidder on July 25, 2008, and construction will begin by January 2009.

5297 ■ "Docs Might Hold Cure for Real Estate, Banks" in *Baltimore Business Journal* (Vol. 28, November 5, 2010, No. 26, pp. 1)
Pub: Baltimore Business Journal
Ed: Gary Haber. **Description:** Health care providers, including physicians are purchasing their office space instead of renting it as banks lower interest rates to 6 percent on mortgages for medical offices. The rise in demand offers relief to the commercial real estate market. It has also resulted in a boom in building new medical offices.

5298 ■ "Donated Sprinkler System Honors Fallen Firefighter" in *Contractor* (Vol. 56, July 2009, No. 7, pp. 3)
Pub: Penton Media, Inc.
Ed: Steve Spaulding. **Description:** Capital City District Habitat for Humanity has constructed a home with a residential fire sprinkler system in honor of Ted Abriel, a firefighter who died on the job. Albany Fire Protection donated the labor for the installation of the fire sprinkler system.

5299 ■ "Downtown Light Rail Plans Up in the Air" in *Business Journal Serving Greater Tampa Bay* (Vol. 30, October 22, 2010, No. 44, pp. 1)
Pub: Tampa Bay Business Journal
Ed: Mark Holan. **Description:** Construction of Tampa's $2 billion light rail transit is suspended pending the result of the November 2, 2010 referendum. The routes, usage, and financing of the light rail project will be decided on the referendum. Whether the light rail will be elevated is also discussed.

5300 ■ "Drawn to York County: Less-Expensive Homes, Good Schools Attract Charlotteans" in *Charlotte Observer* (February 4, 2007)
Pub: Knight-Ridder/Tribune Business News
Ed: Taylor Bright. **Description:** York County, North Carolina offers low-priced homes and good schools, making it attractive to workers and small business.

5301 ■ "East Coast Solar" in *Contractor* (Vol. 57, February 2010, No. 2, pp. 17)
Pub: Penton Media, Inc.
Ed: Dave Yates. **Description:** U.S. Department of Energy's Solar Decathlon lets 20 college student-led teams from around the world compete to design and build a solar-powered home. A mechanical contractor discusses his work as an advisor during the competition.

5302 ■ "Eclipse to Hire 50 for Airp;ort Hangar" in *Business Review, Albany New York* (Vol. 34, November 9, 2007, No. 32, pp. 3)
Pub: American City Business Journals, Inc.
Ed: Robin K. Cooper. **Description:** Eclipse Aviation, a jet manufacturer will hire fifty workers who will operate its new maintenance hangar at Albany International Airport. The company was expected to hire around twenty-five employees after it announced its plan to open one of the seven U.S. Factory Service Centers in 2005. Denise Zieske, the airport Economic Development Manager, expects the hangar construction to be completed by December 2007.

5303 ■ "Eco Smart Home Will Showcase Green Technology" in *Contractor* (Vol. 56, September 2009, No. 9, pp. 3)
Pub: Penton Media, Inc.
Ed: Steve Spaulding. **Description:** Eco Smart World Wide is building the Eco Smart Demonstration House to promote the latest in sustainable, renewable and high-efficiency practices and products. The company will use insulated concrete forms in the construction of the building. Features and dimensions of the structure are also presented.

5304 ■ "Economy Hammers Local Builders" in *Business Courier* (Vol. 24, February 8, 2008, No. 44, pp. 1)
Pub: American City Business Journals, Inc.
Ed: Laura Baverman. **Description:** Home builders in Cincinnati, Ohio, have lower revenue and smaller workforces as a result of the housing crisis and economic slowdown. Only four out of the top 25 home builders registered revenue gains, average revenue for 2007 is down 21 percent from 2006 levels, and employment declined by 37 percent from 2006.

5305 ■ "El Paso Firm Rides Boom to the Top" in *Hispanic Business* (Vol. 30, July-August 2008, No. 7-8, pp. 28)
Pub: Hispanic Business, Inc.
Ed: Jeremy Nisen. **Description:** VEMAC, a commercial construction management and general contracting firm that is experiencing success despite the plummeting construction market is discussed. VEMAC's success is attributed to the Pentagons' $5 billion investment in construction for the benefit of new personnel and their families to be transferred to Fort Bliss, a U.S. army base adjacent to El Paso.

5306 ■ "Energy Sparks Job Growth" in *The Business Journal-Serving Greater Tampa Bay* (Vol. 28, August 8, 2008, No. 33, pp. 1)
Pub: American City Business Journals, Inc.
Ed: Margie Manning. **Description:** Energy infrastructure projects in Tampa Bay, Florida, are increasing the demand for labor in the area. Energy projects requiring an increase in labor include TECO Energy Inc.'s plan for a natural gas pipeline in the area and the installation of energy management system in Bank of America's branches in the area.

5307 ■ "Entrepreneurship: As Cool As It Gets" in *Canadian Business* (Vol. 80, January 29, 2007, No. 3, pp. 10)
Pub: Rogers Media
Ed: Norman de Bono. **Description:** The proposed construction of a restaurant with ice in Dubai by the Canadian firm Iceculture Inc. for the Sharaf Group is discussed. The growth of the clientele of Iceculture Inc. is described.

5308 ■ "EPA 'Finalizes' WaterSense for Homes" in *Contractor* (Vol. 57, January 2010, No. 1, pp. 70)
Pub: Penton Media, Inc.
Ed: Bob Mader. **Description:** U.S. Environmental Protection Agency released its "final" version of the WaterSense for Homes standard. The standard's provisions that affect plumbing contractors includes the specification that everything has to be leak tested and final service pressure cannot exceed 60 psi.

5309 ■ "EPA to Tighten Energy Star Standards for 2011" in *Contractor* (Vol. 56, September 2009, No. 9, pp. 6)
Pub: Penton Media, Inc.
Description: United States Environmental Protection Agency will tighten standards for its Energy Star for Homes program in 2011. The green trend in the construction industry has been cited as reason for the plan. The agency is adding requirements for energy-efficient equipment and building techniques.

5310 ■ *Equipment World's Top Bid*
Pub: Randall-Reilly Publishing Co.
Contact: Michael Reilly, Pres./CEO
E-mail: mreilly@randallpub.com
Released: Annual, Latest edition 2008. **Price:** $395, individuals annual; $269, individuals semi-annual; $395, individuals CD-ROM; $189, individuals serial number book. **Publication Includes:** List of suppliers of new, used, and surplus construction equipment and services. **Entries Include:** Company name, address, phone, description of products or services offered. **Arrangement:** Classified by product or service. **Indexes:** Product or service, geographical.

5311 ■ "Everett Dowling" in *Hawaii Business* (Vol. 54, August 2008, No. 2, pp. 32)
Pub: Hawaii Business Publishing
Ed: Jason Ubay. **Description:** Real estate developer Everett Dowling, president of Dowling Company Inc., talks about the company's sustainable management and services. The company's office has been retrofitted to earn a Leadership in Energy and Environmental Design (LEED) certification. Dowling believes that real estate development can be part of the sustainable solution.

5312 ■ "Everett Hospice Planned" in *Puget Sound Business Journal* (Vol. 29, September 26, 2008, No. 23, pp. 1)
Pub: American City Business Journals
Ed: Peter Neurath. **Description:** Providence Senior and Community Services is pursuing a purchase-and-sales agreement for land in Everett to build a $9.7 million 20-bed hospice facility. The organization plans to break ground on the new facility in 2009.

5313 ■ "Federal Buildings to Achieve Zero-Net Energy by 2030" in *Contractor* (Vol. 56, December 2009, No. 12, pp. 5)
Pub: Penton Media, Inc.
Ed: Candace Roulo. **Description:** United States president Barack Obama has issued sustainable goals for federal buildings. Federal agencies are also required to increase energy efficiency, conserve water and support sustainable communities. Obama has also announced a $3.4 billion investment in a smart energy creed.

5314 ■ "Feldman Pushing Past 'Pain' of Cost Overruns, Delays at Colonie Center" in *Business Review, Albany New York* (November 9, 2007)
Pub: American City Business Journals, Inc.
Ed: Michael DeMasi. **Description:** Details of major improvements at Colonie Center are presented. The total cost for these projects increased by $15 million, and the construction of the nearly ten-story theater in the mall is experiencing delays. According to Larry Feldman, chairman of Feldman Mall Properties, which owns a minority stake in the mall, the cost overruns have pushed the company's renovation costs to around $85 million.

5315 ■ "Fewer People Dying At Work" in *Sacramento Business Journal* (Vol. 25, August 29, 2008, No. 26, pp. 1)
Pub: American City Business Journals, Inc.
Ed: Kathy Robertson. **Description:** Statistics show that workplace deaths in California dropped by 24 percent in 2007 compared with the previous year. Much of the decline was observed in the construction industry, where a slowing economy affected employment and dangerous work. The number of workplace deaths in the state also declined in all major categories except fires and explosions.

5316 ■ "Financing for NNSA Plant Is a Work in Progress" in *The Business Journal-Serving Metropolitan Kansas City* (October 24, 2008)
Pub: American City Business Journals, Inc.
Ed: Rob Roberts. **Description:** The Kansas City Council approved a development plan for a $500 million nuclear weapons parts plant in south Kansas City. The US Congress approved a $59 million annual lease payment to the plant's developer. Financing for the construction of the plant remains in question as the plant's developers have to shoulder construction costs.

5317 ■ "Firm Takes 'Local' Worldwide" in *Hispanic Business* (July-August 2007, pp. 48)
Pub: Hispanic Business
Ed: Keith Rosenblum. **Description:** Willy A. Bermello tells how he has expanded his architectural, engineering and construction firm globally.

5318 ■ "Firms Sue Doracon to Recoup More Than $1M in Unpaid Bills" in *Baltimore Business Journal* (Vol. 28, July 9, 2010, No. 9, pp. 1)
Pub: Baltimore Business Journal
Ed: Scott Dance. **Description:** Concrete supplier Paul J. Rach Inc., Selective Insurance Company, and equipment leasing firm Colonial Pacific Leasing Corporation intend to sue Baltimore, Maryland-based Doracon Contracting Inc. for $1 million in unpaid bills. Doracon owed Colonial Pacific $794,000 and the equipment is still in Doracon's possession. Selective Insurance and Paul J. Rach respectively seek $132,000 and $88,000.

5319 ■ "First-Time Homebuyer Credit May Add Some Momentum to Market" in *Crain's Cleveland Business* (Vol. 30, May 18, 2009, No. 20)
Pub: Crain Communications, Inc.
Ed: Stan Bullard. **Description:** Federal tax credits for first-time homebuyers have increased the number of homes being sold. Details of the tax credit are defined.

5320 ■ "Fogg Planning Twinsburg Warehouse Project" in *Crain's Cleveland Business* (Vol. 28, November 26, 2007, No. 47, pp. 6)
Pub: Crain Communications, Inc.
Ed: Stan Bullard. **Description:** Discusses such projects as the proposed 205,000-square-foot distribution center in the works by Ray Fogg Corporate

Properties LLC as well as other industrial real estate developments that are looking to target tenants that need larger spaces.

5321 ■ "Food Bank to Move, Double in Size" in *Austin Business Journal* (Vol. 31, July 8, 2011, No. 18, pp. 1)
Pub: American City Business Journals Inc.
Ed: Sandra Zaragoza. **Description:** The Capital Area Food Bank (CAFB) of Texas intends to construct a 125,000-square-foot hub on the land it purchased in East Texas. The hub will accommodate administrative offices, warehouse and refrigeration space, and a production kitchen.

5322 ■ "For Kenwood, Cavalry Could Be Close" in *Business Courier* (Vol. 26, October 2, 2009, No. 23, pp. 1)
Pub: American City Business Journals, Inc.
Ed: Dan Monk. **Description:** New York-based BlackRock Inc. is believed to be participating in the settlement liens at Kenwood Towne Place, a mixed-use development site in Cincinnati, Ohio. BlackRock may play a key role as an advisor or investor representative to an unnamed investors.

5323 ■ "Fred Weber CEO Tom Dunne: Sales Talks Confidential" in *Saint Louis Business Journal* (Vol. 32, September 23, 2011, No. 4, pp. 1)
Pub: Saint Louis Business Journal
Ed: Evan Binns. **Description:** Fred Weber Inc. CEO Tom Dunne Sr. signed a letter of confidentiality as part of an inquiry made by interested party to the construction company. However, Dunne denied the company is in a fire sale and has been continuing to bid for work and has not stopped securing projects.

5324 ■ "From Malls to Steel Plants" in *Crain's Chicago Business* (Vol. 31, April 28, 2008, No. 17, pp. 30)
Pub: Crain Communications, Inc.
Ed: Samantha Stainburn. **Description:** Profile of the company Graycor Inc. which started out as a sandblasting and concrete-breaking firm but has grown into four businesses due to innovation and acquisitions. Graycor's businesses include: Graycor Industrial Constructors Inc., which builds and renovates power plants and steel mills; Graycor Construction Co., which erects stores, medical centers and office buildings; Graycor Blasting Co., which uses explosives and blasts tunnels for industrial cleaning, and Graycor International Inc., which provides construction services in Mexico.

5325 ■ "Funding Drought Stalls Biotech Incubators" in *Saint Louis Business Journal* (Vol. 31, July 29, 2011, No. 49, pp. 1)
Pub: Saint Louis Business Journal
Ed: Angela Mueller. **Description:** Economic slowdown took its toll on cash-strapped startups that fill incubators such as the Bio-Research and Development Growth (BRDG) Park in Creve Coeur, Missouri and the Center for Emerging Technologies in Midtown St. Louis. BRDG put a hold on construction of of its two buildings.

5326 ■ "Funkhouser Wants Region to Get On Board Light Rail" in *Business Journal-Serving Metropolitan Kansas City* (November 30, 2007)
Pub: American City Business Journals, Inc.
Ed: Suzanna Stagemeyer. **Description:** Mark Funhouser, Mayor of Kansas City, is planning to construct a regional multimodal public transit system. A previous light rail plan was rescinded due to logistical, financial and legal problems. Details of the light transit plans are discussed.

5327 ■ "Gables Unveils Plan for Downtown Tower" in *Austin Business JournalInc.* (Vol. 28, August 8, 2008, No. 21, pp. A1)
Pub: American City Business Journals
Ed: Jean Kwon. **Description:** Gables Residential plans to develop a residential tower with 220 units and 15,000 square feet of retail and commercial spaces in the Warehouse District in Ohio. The development is expected to start in late 2009 and be completed in 18 to 24 months.

5328 ■ "Gateway Delays Start" in *The Business Journal-Serving Metropolitan Kansas City* (Vol. 27, October 31, 2008, No. 8, pp. 1)
Pub: American City Business Journals, Inc.
Ed: Rob Roberts. **Description:** Economic problems caused, in part, by the Wall Street crisis has resulted in the setback of a proposed mixed-use redevelopment project, The Gateway. The $307 million project, which includes the Kansas Aquarium, will be delayed due to financing problems. Details of the project are given.

5329 ■ "Generation Y Driving Portland Multifamily Market" in *Daily Journal of Commerce, Portland* (October 29, 2010)
Pub: Dolan Media Newswires
Ed: Nick Bjork. **Description:** Generation Y, young adults between the ages of 18-30, are interested in multifamily residents in the Portland, Oregon area. Developers in the area, particularly North Portland, have recognized this trend and are looking into multifamily investments.

5330 ■ "Germans Win Solar Decathlon - Again" in *Contractor* (Vol. 56, November 2009, No. 11, pp. 1)
Pub: Penton Media, Inc.
Ed: Robert P. Mader. **Description:** Students from Technische Universtat Darmstadt won the U.S. Department of Energy's Solar Decathlon by designing and building the most attractive and efficient solar-powered home. The winner's design produced a surplus of power even during three days of rain and photovoltaic panels covered nearly every exterior surface.

5331 ■ "Get Online Quick in the Office Or in the Field" in *Contractor* (Vol. 56, October 2009, No. 10, pp. 47)
Pub: Penton Media, Inc.
Ed: William Feldman; Patti Feldman. **Description:** Contractors can set up a web site in minutes using the www.1and1.com website. Verizon's Novatel MIFI 2372 HSPA personal hotspot device lets contractors go online in the field. The StarTech scalable business management system helps contractors manage daily operations.

5332 ■ "Getting in the Game" in *Baltimore Business Journal* (Vol. 27, October 16, 2009, No. 23, pp. 1)
Pub: American City Business Journals
Ed: Ryan Sharrow. **Description:** Crystal Palace FC USA is finalizing a deal with a North Carolina development team to build a 7,000 seat stadium by early 2012 in spite of efforts by Baltimore Mayor Sheila Dixon to bring in professional soccer's DC United. The planned stadium is in the Carroll Camden Industrial area near M&T Bank Stadium. Plans for the new stadium are included.

5333 ■ "Ghazi Insists Downtown Project Still On" in *The Business Journal-Milwaukee* (Vol. 25, August 1, 2008, No. 45, pp. A1)
Pub: American City Business Journals, Inc.
Ed: Rich Kirchen. **Description:** Afshin Ghazi remains confident that his $200 million Catalyst project in downtown Milwaukee, Wisconsin, will push through despite financial disputes delaying his EpiCentre project in Charlotte, North Carolina. He added that the Catalyst is on schedule for groundbreaking in the spring of 2009.

5334 ■ "Giant Garages Could Rise Up Downtown" in *Business Courier* (Vol. 27, October 22, 2010, No. 25, pp. 1)
Pub: Business Courier
Ed: Dan Monk. **Description:** More than 2,500 new parking spaces could rise up to the eastern edge of downtown Cincinnati, Ohio as public and private investors collect resources for new garage projects. These projects are expected to accommodate almost 1,500 monthly parkers who will lose access at Broadway Commons due to the construction of Harrah's casino.

5335 ■ "GL Homes Buys 1,000 Acres in Former Agricultural Reserve" in *Miami Daily Business Review* (March 26, 2008)
Pub: ALM Media Inc.
Ed: Polyana da Costa. **Description:** One of the nation's largest home builders, GL Homes, purchased over 1,000 acres of agricultural land in Southern Palm Beach County, Florida. Plans for 554 residential units are detailed.

5336 ■ "Glendale Pumping $29 Million Into Redevelopment" in *The Business Journal - Serving Phoenix and the Valley of the Sun* (Vol. 28, August 1, 2008, No. 48, pp. 1)
Pub: American City Business Journals, Inc.
Ed: Mike Sunnucks. **Description:** Glendale City is planning to invest $29 million to improve city infrastructure like roadways and water and sewer lines over the next five years. Glendale's city council is also planning to hold a workshop on the redevelopment projects in September 2008. Other views and information on the redevelopment project, are presented.

5337 ■ "GM's Decision to Boot Dealer Prompts Sale" in *Baltimore Business Journal* (Vol. 27, November 6, 2009, No. 26, pp. 1)
Pub: American City Business Journals
Ed: Daniel J. Sernovitz. **Description:** General Motors Corporation's (GM) decision to strip Baltimore's Anderson Automotive Group Inc. of its GM franchise has prompted the owner, Bruce Mortimer, to close the automotive dealership and sell the land to a developer. The new project could make way for new homes, a shopping center and supermarket.

5338 ■ "Good Track Record Helps Developer Secure Construction Loan for Offices" in *Miami Daily Business Review* (March 26, 2008)
Pub: ALM Media Inc.
Description: Luis Lamar, developer, has secured a $64.75 million construction loan to construct a Class A office building in Kendall, Florida. Details of the loan and proposed construction are presented.

5339 ■ "Got to be Smarter than the Average Bear" in *Contractor* (Vol. 56, September 2009, No. 9, pp. 82)
Pub: Penton Media, Inc.
Ed: Bob Mader. **Description:** International Association of Plumbing and Mechanical Officials Green Technical Committee has debated the need for contractors to have certifications in installing green plumbing. Some have argued that qualifications would discourage homeowners from improving their properties. Comments from executives are also included.

5340 ■ "Grainger Show Highlights Building Green, Economy" in *Contractor* (Vol. 57, February 2010, No. 2, pp. 3)
Pub: Penton Media, Inc.
Ed: Candace Roulo. **Description:** chief U.S. economist told attendees of the Grainger's 2010 Total MRO Solutions National Customer Show that the economic recovery would be subdued. Mechanical contractors who attended the event also learned about building sustainable, green products, and technologies, and economic and business challenges.

5341 ■ "Green Energy Exec Hits State Policy" in *Boston Business Journal* (Vol. 30, December 3, 2010, No. 45, pp. 1)
Pub: Boston Business Journal
Ed: Kyle Alspach. **Description:** American Superconductor Corporation President Dan McGahn believes that the state government of Massachusetts is not proactive enough to develop the state into a manufacturing hub for wind power technology. McGahn believes that while Governor Deval Patrick campaigned for wind turbines in the state, his administration does not have the focus required to build the turbines in the state.

5342 ■ "Groundbreaking 2.0" in *Philadelphia Business Journal* (Vol. 30, September 23, 2011, No. 32, pp. 1)
Pub: American City Business Journals Inc.
Ed: Natalie Kostelni. **Description:** University Place Associates, the developer of 2.0 University Place in

West Philadelphia, Pennsylvania, will break ground on a five-story, 97,000-square-foot office building in December 2011. The decision follows the Citizenship and Immigration Services signing of a 15-year lease as anchor tenant.

5343 ■ "'Groundhog Day' B & B Likely Will Be Converted Into One In Real Life" in *Chicago Tribune* (October 21, 2008)
Pub: McClatchy-Tribune Information Services
Ed: Carolyn Starks. **Description:** Everton Martin and Karla Stewart Martin have purchased the Victorian house that was featured as a bed-and-breakfast in the 1993 hit move "Groundhog Day"; the couple was initially unaware of the structure's celebrity status when they purchased it with the hope of fulfilling their dream of owning a bed-and-breakfast.

5344 ■ "Growing Pains" in *Crain's Cleveland Business* (Vol. 30, June 22, 2009, No. 24, pp. 3)
Pub: Crain Communications, Inc.
Ed: Shannon Mortland. **Description:** Judson's latest retirement community, called South Franklin Circle, is near completion despite a faltering economy and delays. Details of the project are explored.

5345 ■ "Habitat, Home Depot Expand Building Programs" in *Contractor* (Vol. 56, September 2009, No. 9, pp. 16)
Pub: Penton Media, Inc.
Description: Habitat for Humanity International and The Home Depot Foundation are planning to expand their Partners in Sustainable Building program. The program will provide funds to help Habitat affiliates build 5,000 homes. Comments from executives are also included.

5346 ■ "Hard Rock on Pike" in *Puget Sound Business Journal* (Vol. 29, September 5, 2008, No. 20, pp. 1)
Pub: American City Business Journals
Ed: Jeanne Lang Jones. **Description:** A branch of the Hard Rock Cafe is opening in 2009 in the Liberty Building on Pike Street in downtown Seattle, Washington. The location is being renovated as a green building; the restaurant and concert venue will seat 300 patrons and has a rooftop deck and memorabilia shop.

5347 ■ "Hard Times for Hard Money" in *Sacramento Business Journal* (Vol. 25, July 18, 2008, No. 20, pp. 1)
Pub: American City Business Journals, Inc.
Ed: Michael Shaw. **Description:** Three private lenders who supplied $1 million sued VLD Realty, its associated companies and owners Volodymyr and Leonid Dubinsky accusing them of default after a plan to build two subdivisions fell through. Investigators are finding that borrowers and lenders ignored most rules on private investments on real estate.

5348 ■ "He Has a Sky-High Outlook on His Business" in *Charlotte Observer* (February 4, 2007)
Pub: Knight-Ridder/Tribune Business News
Ed: Stella M. Hopkins. **Description:** Profile of Chuck Boyle, former Army pilot; Boyle patrols over construction sites in the Charlotte, North Carolina area. The firm's team of engineers and geologists specialize in services such as: rock blasting, roads, testing concrete and other construction materials, and more.

5349 ■ "Health-Care Highway" in *Saint Louis Business Journal* (Vol. 32, October 14, 2011, No. 7, pp. 1)
Pub: Saint Louis Business Journal
Ed: Angela Mueller. **Description:** Around $2.6 billion will be invested in health care facilities along the Highway 64/40 corridor in St. Louis, Missouri. Mercy Hospital is planning to invest $19 million in a virtual care center. St. Elizabeth's Hospital on the other hand, will purchase 105 acres in the corridor.

5350 ■ "Health Centers Plan Expansion" in *Crain's Detroit Business* (Vol. 25, June 15, 2009, No. 24, pp. 3)
Pub: Crain Communications Inc. - Detroit
Ed: Jay Greene. **Description:** Detroit has five federally qualified health centers that plan to receive over $3 million in federal stimulus money that will be used to expand projects that will care for uninsured patients.

5351 ■ "Heavy Industry" in *Business North Carolina* (Vol. 28, February 2008, No. 2, pp. 54)
Pub: Business North Carolina
Ed: Arthur O. Murray. **Description:** Volvo Construction Equipment factory in Asheville, North Carolina expanded its factory that builds road-construction machinery.

5352 ■ "Henry Ford Health Leases Lab Space at TechTown" in *Crain's Detroit Business* (Vol. 24, March 31, 2008, No. 13, pp. 5)
Pub: Crain Communications, Inc.
Ed: Tom Henderson. **Description:** Henry Ford Health System has signed a seven-year lease at TechTown, the high-tech incubator and research park affiliated with Wayne State University, to take over 14,000 square feet of space for four research groups and laboratories. Construction has already begun and Henry Ford officials hope to take occupancy as early as June 1.

5353 ■ "High Hopes: Ralph Mitchell's Picks Have Growth Potential" in *Black Enterprise* (Vol. 37, February 2007, No. 7, pp. 42)
Pub: Earl G. Graves Publishing Co. Inc.
Ed: Carolyn M. Brown. **Description:** Ralph Mitchell, president and senior financial advisor of Braintree-Carthage Financial Group, offers three recommendations: Toll Brothers, Home Depot, and Lowe's.

5354 ■ "Higher Thread Count for Metropole" in *Business Courier* (Vol. 26, September 25, 2009, No. 22, pp. 1)
Pub: American City Business Journals, Inc.
Ed: Lisa Biank Fasig, Lucy May. **Description:** Cincinnati Center City Development Corporation is under contract to buy the 225-unit apartment building called Metropole Apartments and 21c Museum Hotel is the lead candidate for the space. Advocates of some residents of the low-income rental complex complain that this move could leave them homeless.

5355 ■ "Historic Tax Credit Plan Gains Support" in *Baltimore Business Journal* (Vol. 27, January 8, 2010, No. 36, pp. 1)
Pub: American City Business Journals
Ed: Heather Harlan Warnack. **Description:** Maryland Governor Martin O'Malley plans to push legislation in the General Assembly to extend for three more years the tax credit program for rehabilitation of obsolete buildings. The Maryland Heritage Structure Rehabilitation Tax Credit Program has declined from almost $75 million in expenses in 2001 to roughly $5 million in 2010 fiscal year. Details on the projects that benefited from the program are explored.

5356 ■ "HOK Sport May Build Own Practice" in *The Business Journal-Serving Metropolitan Kansas City* (Vol. 26, August 29, 2008, No. 51, pp. 1)
Pub: American City Business Journals, Inc.
Ed: Rob Roberts. **Description:** HOK Sport Venue Event is considering a spin-off from its parent company, HOK Group Inc. HOK Sport spokeswoman Gina Leo confirms that the firm is exploring structures, including a management buyout. Some of HOK Sport Venue Event's Minnesota projects are discussed.

5357 ■ "Hollander 95 Project Getting Bigger" in *Boston Business Journal* (Vol. 29, September 23, 2011, No. 20, pp. 1)
Pub: American City Business Journals Inc.
Ed: Gary Haber. **Description:** Hollander 95 Business Park is in for a huge change as its new owners plan a $50 million expansion which calls for building as many as eight more buildings or a total of more than 500,000 square feed. FRP Development bought the site for $4.35 million at a foreclosure sale in July 2010 and is now seeking city approval for an Industrial Planned Unit Development designation.

5358 ■ "Home Builder, Four Others, Face Sentencing" in *Business Courier* (Vol. 27, November 26, 2010, No. 30, pp. 1)
Pub: Business Courier
Ed: Jon Newberry. **Description:** Home builder Bernie Kurlemann was convicted on November 10, 2010 on six felony counts and faces up to 65 years in prison due to his part in a 2006 Warren County mortgage fraud scheme. Four other business people have pleaded guilty to related charges, and all are awaiting sentencing in early 2011.

5359 ■ "A Home of Her Own" in *Hawaii Business* (Vol. 53, October 2007, No. 4, pp. 51)
Pub: Hawaii Business Publishing
Ed: Maria Torres-Kitamura. **Description:** It was observed that the number of single women in Hawaii purchasing their own home has increased, as that in the whole United States where the percentage has increased from 14 percent in 1995 to 22 percent in 2006. However, First Hawaiian Bank's Wendy Lum thinks that the trend will not continue in Hawaii due to lending restrictions. The factors that women consider in buying a home of their own are presented.

5360 ■ "Home Prices Sag" in *Crain's Chicago Business* (Vol. 31, April 28, 2008, No. 17, pp. 3)
Pub: Crain Communications, Inc.
Ed: Alby Gallun. **Description:** Since the slump in the housing market is continuing with no sign of recovery, Chicago-area home prices are poised for an even steeper drop this year. In 2007, the region's home prices fell nearly 5 percent and according to a forecast by Fiserv Inc., they will decline 8.1 percent this year and another 2.2 percent in 2009. Statistical data included.

5361 ■ "Home Sprinklers Blocked in Texas, Long Beach, California" in *Contractor* (Vol. 56, July 2009, No. 7, pp. 1)
Pub: Penton Media, Inc.
Ed: Robert P. Mader. **Description:** Long Beach, California has exempted older residential high rises and large apartment complexes from a rule to install fire sprinkler systems. Texas has also prohibited municipalities from enacting residential sprinkler ordinances.

5362 ■ "Homebuilders Continue to be Our Nemesis" in *Contractor* (Vol. 56, July 2009, No. 7, pp. 50)
Pub: Penton Media, Inc.
Ed: Bob Mader. **Description:** Homebuilders rank high on the greed scale along with Wall Street brokers. There is this one instance when a builder gave copies of another contractor's quotes that have just been blackened out and another instance when one builder let other bidders visit a site while the current mechanical contractor is working.

5363 ■ "Homing In On the Future" in *Black Enterprise* (Vol. 38, October 2007, No. 3, pp. 61)
Pub: Earl G. Graves Publishing Co. Inc.
Ed: Sean Drakes. **Description:** More and more people are wanting new homes wired automated systems that integrate multiple home devices such as computers, audio/visual entertainment, security, communications, utilities, and lighting and environmental controls.

5364 ■ "Honcoop Honored as BIAWC's Builder of the Year" in *Bellingham Business Journal* (Vol. February 2010, pp. 17)
Pub: Sound Publishing Inc.
Description: Gary Honcoop, co-owner and president of Roosendaal-Honcoop Construction Inc. was honored by the Building Industry Association of Whatcom County as Builder of the Year. The construction company was founded in 1979.

5365 ■ "Hospital to Get $72M Makeover" in *Austin Business JournalInc.* (Vol. 29, January 15, 2010, No. 45, pp. 1)
Pub: American City Business Journals
Ed: Sandra Zaragoza. **Description:** St. David's South Austin Medical Center, formerly St. David's South Austin Hospital, is undertaking an expansion

and renovation project worth $72 million. Meanwhile, CEO Erol Akdamar has resigned to serve as CEO of Medical City Hospital in Dallas, Texas. A new CEO and a general contractor for the project are yet to be chosen by the hospital.

5366 ■ "Hospital Jobs" in *Baltimore Business Journal* (Vol. 28, June 25, 2010, No. 7, pp. 1)
Pub: Baltimore Business Journal
Ed: Scott Graham. **Description:** Greater Baltimore, Maryland has four hospitals that are in the middle of transforming their campuses with new facilities for treating various patients. Construction at Mercy Medical Center, Johns Hopkins Hospital, Franklin Square Hospital and Anne Rundle Hospital has helped bring the construction industry back to life. Insights into the hiring plans of these hospitals are also included.

5367 ■ "Hospital Pegged for Lakeway" in *Austin Business JournalInc.* (Vol. 28, August 8, 2008, No. 21, pp. A1)
Pub: American City Business Journals
Ed: Kate Harrington. **Description:** Views and information on the development of the Lakeway Regional Medical Center in Texas, are presented. The hospital, which is expected to cost more than $250 million, will include 244,000 square feet of medical space. Shops, offices, hike-and-bike trails are also planned around hospital.

5368 ■ "Hotel Woes Reflect Area Struggle" in *Business Journal Serving Greater Tampa Bay* (Vol. 30, December 3, 2010, No. 50, pp. 1)
Pub: Tampa Bay Business Journal
Ed: Mark Holan. **Description:** Quality Inn and Suites in East Tampa, Florida has struggled against the sluggish economy but remained open to guests despite facing a foreclosure. The hotel project is the center of East Tampa's redevelopment plans and public officials defend the $650,000 investment in public amenities near the building.

5369 ■ "Housing Slide Picks Up Speed" in *Crain's Chicago Business* (Vol. 31, April 21, 2008, No. 16, pp. 2)
Pub: Crain Communications, Inc.
Ed: Eddie Baeb. **Description:** According to Tracy Cross & Associates Inc., a real estate consultancy, sales of new homes in the Chicago area dropped 61 percent from the year-earlier period which is more bad news for homebuilders, contractors and real estate agents who are eager for an indication that market conditions are improving.

5370 ■ "How I Did It: Mel Zuckerman" in *Inc.* (December 2007, pp. 140-142)
Pub: Gruner & Jahr USA Publishing
Ed: Daniel McGinn. **Description:** Profile of Mel Zuckerman, who tells how transformed his life as a middle-aged, overweight homebuilder to a healthy addition to the fitness and spa industry with his posh Canyon Ranch retreats.

5371 ■ "Hydronicahh - Everything in Modulation" in *Contractor* (Vol. 56, December 2009, No. 12, pp. 24)
Pub: Penton Media, Inc.
Ed: Mark Eatherton. **Description:** Management and the environmental impact of a home hydronic system are discussed. Radiant windows have the potential to reduce energy consumption. A variable speed delta T pump is required for the construction of a hydronic wood pit.

5372 ■ "IAPMO GTC Votes to Limit Showers to 2.0-GPM" in *Contractor* (Vol. 56, September 2009, No. 9, pp. 1)
Pub: Penton Media, Inc.
Ed: Robert P. Mader. **Description:** Green Technical Committee of the International Association of Plumbing and Mechanical Officials has voted to limit showers to 2.0 GPM. It is also developing a Green Plumbing and Mechanical Supplement. Comments from executives are also supplied.

5373 ■ "ICC Works on Prescriptive Green Construction Code" in *Contractor* (Vol. 56, October 2009, No. 10, pp. 1)
Pub: Penton Media, Inc.
Ed: Robert P. Mader. **Description:** International Code Council launched an initiative to create a green construction code that focuses on existing commercial buildings. The initiative's timeline will include public meetings leading up to a final draft that will be available in 2010.

5374 ■ "Illinois Residential Building Legislation Includes New HVAC Requirements" in *Contractor* (Vol. 56, July 2009, No. 7, pp. 3)
Pub: Penton Media, Inc.
Ed: Candace Roulo. **Description:** Illinois' Energy Efficient Building Act will require all new buildings and houses to conform to the International Energy Conservation Code. The code includes a duct leakage requirement followed by a post-construction test to verify leakage rates and requires programmable thermostats on all houses.

5375 ■ "IMRA's Ultrafast Lasers Bring Precision, profits; Ann Arbor Company Eyes Expansion" in *Crain's Detroit Business* (March 10, 2008)
Pub: Crain Communications, Inc.
Ed: Tom Henderson. **Description:** IMRA America Inc. plans to expand its headquarters and has applied for permits to build a fourth building that will house research and development facilities and allow the company more room for manufacturing; the company plans to add about 20 more employees that would include research scientists, manufacturing and assembly workers, engineers and salespeople. The growth is due mainly to a new technology of ultrafast fiber lasers that reduce side effects for those getting eye surgeries and help manufacturers of computer chips to reduce their size and cost.

5376 ■ "Incentives Debate Rages On Unabated" in *The Business Journal-Serving Metropolitan Kansas City* (Vol. 26, September 5, 2008, No. 52)
Pub: American City Business Journals, Inc.
Ed: Rob Roberts. **Description:** Debate on the new economic development and incentives policy adopted by the Kansas City Council is still on. The city's Planned Industrial Expansion Authority has rejected a standard property tax abatement proposal. The real estate development community has opposed the rejection of proposed the tax incentives policy.

5377 ■ "Increased Competition Prompts Detroit Hotels to Make Upgrades" in *Crain's Detroit Business* (Vol. 24, March 31, 2008, No. 13, pp. 1)
Pub: Crain Communications, Inc.
Ed: Daniel Duggan. **Description:** Five Detroit hotels have recently undergone upgrades or are preparing for major construction projects due to a more competitive hospitality market in the city.

5378 ■ "Increasing Building Work at Ryan Cos." in *Crain's Chicago Business* (Vol. 34, May 23, 2011, No. 21, pp. 6)
Pub: Crain Communications Inc.
Ed: Eddie Baeb. **Description:** Profile of Tim Hennelly, who is working to make Ryan Company known as a pure builder rather than a developer-builder.

5379 ■ "Independence Station Utilizes Sustainable Technologies" in *Contractor* (Vol. 56, September 2009, No. 9, pp. 3)
Pub: Penton Media, Inc.
Ed: Candace Ruolo. **Description:** Independence Station building in Oregon is seen to receive the most LEED points ever awarded by the United States Green Building Council. The building will use an ice-based cooling storage system, biofuel cogeneration system and phovoltaic system. Other building features and dimensions are also supplied.

5380 ■ "Independence's Day Keeps on Getting Brighter" in *Business Courier* (Vol. 27, June 11, 2010, No. 6, pp. 1)
Pub: Business Courier
Ed: Lucy May. **Description:** Reports show that residential and commercial development continues in Independence, Kentucky despite the recession, with a 144-unit apartment complex under construction. The city recorded 152 new-home closings in 2009, or 25 percent of all new homes closed in Boone, Campbell, and Kenton counties.

5381 ■ *Innovation in Small Construction Firms*
Pub: Taylor & Francis Group
Ed: Peter Barrett. **Released:** March 2008. **Price:** $120.00. **Description:** Examination into the ways construction firms can introduce innovation into working practices in order to meet the demands of this rapidly changing industry.

5382 ■ "Intel: Tax Breaks Key" in *Business Journal Portland* (Vol. 27, October 22, 2010, No. 34, pp. 1)
Pub: Portland Business Journal
Ed: Erik Siemers. **Description:** Intel Corporation believes that state tax incentives will be critical, especially in the purchase of manufacturing equipment, as they build a new chip factory in Hillsboro, Oregon. The tax breaks would help Intel avoid paying 10 times more in property taxes compared to average Washington County firms. Critics argue that Intel has about $15 billion in cash assets, and can afford the factory without the tax breaks.

5383 ■ "Iogen in Talks to Build Ethanol Plant in Canada" in *Globe & Mail* (March 21, 2007, pp. B7)
Pub: CTVglobemedia Publishing Inc.
Ed: Shawn McCarthy. **Description:** Ottawa based Iogen Corp. is planning to construct a cellulosic ethanol plant in Saskatchewan region. The company will be investing an estimated $500 million for this purpose.

5384 ■ "It's Not Easy Being Small" in *Baltimore Business Journal* (Vol. 27, October 9, 2009, No. 22, pp. 1)
Pub: American City Business Journals
Ed: Scott Dance. **Description:** A look at how small businesses were left out of the stimulus-funded federal contracts in Maryland. Small contractors were not listed in the federal contracts database USAspending.gov and none were hired for work in the state.

5385 ■ "It's What You Know. It's Who You Know. It's China" in *Inc.* (Vol. 33, October 2011, No. 8, pp. 80)
Pub: Inc. Magazine
Ed: David H. Freedman. **Description:** Michael Lee will be the first American entrepreneur to build big in China. The company is piloting two large commercial real estate developments, one in New York City the other in Nanjing, China.

5386 ■ "J.C. Evans Seeks Bankruptcy Protection" in *Austin Business Journal* (Vol. 31, August 12, 2011, No. 23, pp. A1)
Pub: American City Business Journals Inc.
Ed: Vicky Garza. **Description:** J.C. Evans Construction Holdings Inc., as well as its affiliated companies, has filed for Chapter 11 bankruptcy following its continued financial breakdown which it blames on the tough economy. Details are included.

5387 ■ "Jennifer Hernandez Helps Developers Transform Contaminated Properties" in *Hispanic Business* (Vol. 30, April 2008, No. 4, pp. 32)
Pub: Hispanic Business
Ed: Hildy Medina. **Description:** Jennifer Hernandez is a partner and head of the law firm of Holland & Knight's environmental practice which specializes in the restoration of polluted land where former industrial and commercial buildings once stood, known as brownfields. Brownfield redevelopment can be lucrative but costly due to the cleaning up of contaminated land and challenging because of federal and state environmental laws.

5388 ■ "Joint Venture Plans Bronzeville Project" in *Business Journal-Milwaukee* (Vol. 25, October 5, 2007, No. 1, pp. A1)
Pub: American City Business Journals, Inc.
Ed: Rich Kirchen. **Description:** Proposal for construction of an apartment building and possible expansion of Northtown Mall in Milwaukee, Wisconsin

is being planned by developers in the city's Bronzeville area. The project for rehabilitating the existing mall and building of a 50-unit apartment would amount to about $12.5 million.

5389 ■ "Kenosha 'Lifestyle Center' Delayed" in *The Business Journal-Milwaukee* (Vol. 25, August 8, 2008, No. 46, pp. A1)
Pub: American City Business Journals, Inc.
Ed: Rich Kirchen. **Description:** Quality Centers of Orlando, Florida has postponed construction plans for the Kenosha Town Center in Kenosha County, Wisconsin to 2009 due to the economic downturn and lending concerns. The $200-million, 750,000-square-foot retail and residential center will be located near the corner of Wisconsin Highway 50 and I-94.

5390 ■ "Kimball Hill Files for Chapter 11" in *Crain's Chicago Business* (Vol. 31, April 28, 2008, No. 17, pp. 12)
Pub: Crain Communications, Inc.
Description: Homebuilder Kimball Hill filed for Chapter 11 bankruptcy protection after months of negotiations with lenders. The firm plans to continue operations as it restructures its debt.

5391 ■ "Kroger Forges Ahead with Fuel Centers" in *Business Courier* (Vol. 26, December 25, 2009, No. 35, pp. 1)
Pub: American City Business Journals, Inc.
Ed: Jon Newberry. **Description:** Cincinnati-based grocery chain Kroger Company plans to construct more fuel centers near supermarkets and food stores despite declining profit margins in gasoline sales. Statistical data included.

5392 ■ "KXAN Seeks Larger Studio, Office Space" in *Austin Business Journal* (Vol. 31, May 27, 2011, No. 12, pp. A1)
Pub: American City Business Journals Inc.
Ed: Cody Lyon. **Description:** Austin NBC affiliate KXAN Television is opting to sell its property north of downtown and relocate to another site. The station is now inspecting possible sites to house its broadcasting facility and employees totaling as many as 200 people. Estimated cost of the construction of the studios and offices is $13 million plus another million in moving the equipment.

5393 ■ "LA Passes HET Ordinance, California Greens Code" in *Contractor* (Vol. 56, September 2009, No. 9, pp. 1)
Pub: Penton Media, Inc.
Ed: Candace Ruolo. **Description:** Los Angeles City Council has passed a Water Efficiency Requirements ordinance. The law mandates lower low-flow plumbing requirements for plumbing fixtures installed in new buildings and retrofits. Under the ordinance, a toilet's maximum flush volume may not exceed 1.28-gpf.

5394 ■ "Land Swap Key to Ending Royal Oak Project Impasse" in *Crain's Detroit Business* (Vol. 25, June 8, 2009, No. 23, pp. 20)
Pub: Crain Communications Inc. - Detroit
Ed: Chad Halcom. **Description:** Details of the new construction of the LA Fitness health club near Woodward and Washington Avenues in Royal Oak, Michigan are discussed.

5395 ■ "Large Homes can be Energy Efficient Too" in *Contractor* (Vol. 56, October 2009, No. 10, pp. 5)
Pub: Penton Media, Inc.
Ed: Candace Roulo. **Description:** Eco Estate at Briggs Chaney subdivision in Silver Spring, Maryland has model houses that use sustainable technologies and products and the homes that will be built on the subdivision will feature some of the technologies featured on the model home. The energy efficient HVAC system of the model homes are discussed.

5396 ■ "The Latest on E-Verify" in *Contractor* (Vol. 56, September 2009, No. 9, pp. 58)
Pub: Penton Media, Inc.
Ed: Susan McGreevy. **Description:** United States government has required federal contractors to use its E-Verify program to verify the eligibility of incoming and existent employees. The use of the program is seen to eliminate Social Security mismatches.

5397 ■ "Latest Falls, Ontario Hotel Will Be 25-Story Westin" in *Business First Buffalo* (October 19, 2007, pp. 1)
Pub: American City Business Journals, Inc.
Ed: James Fink. **Description:** Niagara Falls, Ontario-based Canadian Niagara Hotels has announced the construction of a Westin Hotel on Robinson Street that is 25-stories high and has 518 suites starting in 2008. The scope of the $120 million construction project is expected to be completed in 2010.

5398 ■ "Latest Volley Tries to Press Port Group" in *Business Courier* (Vol. 26, November 20, 2009, No. 30, pp. 1)
Pub: American City Business Journals, Inc.
Ed: Dan Monk. **Description:** Subcontractors filed a new legal argument to force the Port of Greater Cincinnati Development Authority to pursue default claim against Bank of America. The bank issued letters of credit to guarantee bond payments in addition to holding the mortgage of the Kenwood Towne Place. Details of the claim are discussed.

5399 ■ "Laugh or Cry?" in *Barron's* (Vol. 88, March 24, 2008, No. 12, pp. 7)
Pub: Dow Jones & Company, Inc.
Ed: Alan Abelson. **Description:** Discusses the American economy which is just starting to feel the effect of the credit and housing crises. JPMorgan Chase purchased Bear Stearns for $2 a share, much lower than its share price of $60, while quasi-government entities Fannie Mae and Freddie Mac are starting to run into trouble.

5400 ■ "Legislature Passes Increased Tax Credit for Urban Brownfield Projects" in *Crain's Detroit Business* (Vol. 24, March 31, 2008, No. 13)
Pub: Crain Communications, Inc.
Ed: Amy Lane. **Description:** Discusses the bill passed by the Legislature that creates a tax credit of up to 20 percent for projects in urban development areas.

5401 ■ "Legoland Florida Theme Park Construction to Start in May" in *Orlando Business Journal* (Vol. 26, January 29, 2010, No. 35, pp. 1)
Pub: American City Business Journals
Ed: Richard Bilbao. **Description:** Merlin Entertainments Group purchased the closed Cypress Garden theme park in Winter Haven, Florida for $22.3 million and plans to spend a reported $100 million or more to begin transforming it into the world's largest Legoland. Winter Haven businesses are expecting a windfall from the theme park's constructions workers.

5402 ■ "Lenders" in *The Business Journal - Serving Phoenix and the Valley of the Sun* (Vol. 28, July 25, 2008, No. 47, pp. 1)
Pub: American City Business Journals, Inc.
Ed: Jan Buchholz. **Description:** Private equity lender Investor Mortgage Holdings Inc. has continued growing despite the crisis surrounding the real estate and financial industries and has accumulated a $700 million loan portfolio. Private lending has become increasingly important in financing real estate deals as commercial credit has dried up.

5403 ■ "Lending Door Slams" in *Puget Sound Business Journal* (Vol. 29, October 24, 2008, No. 27, pp. 1)
Pub: American City Business Journals
Ed: Jeanne Lang Jones, Kirsten Grind. **Description:** KeyBank's closure of its Puget Sound unit that services single-family homebuilders is part of a nationwide shutdown that includes similar closures in other cities. Bank of America is adopting more conservative terms for homebuilding loans while Union Bank of California is still offering credit for market rate housing.

5404 ■ "Long Live Rock" in *Inc.* (November 2007, pp. 130)
Pub: Gruner & Jahr USA Publishing
Ed: Nitasha Tiku. **Description:** Profile of a family business using chemistry to recycle concrete products.

5405 ■ "Loop 360 Offices Planned" in *Austin Business JournalInc.* (Vol. 28, December 5, 2008, No. 38, pp. A1)
Pub: American City Business Journals
Ed: Kate Harrington. **Description:** Nearly 356,000 square feet of office space is planned in the South Capital of Texas Highway Corridor, also known as Loop 360 in Austin. Riverside Developers plans to wait until the economy improves before starting construction.

5406 ■ "Major Advances in Heat Pump Technology" in *Contractor* (Vol. 57, January 2010, No. 1, pp. 42)
Pub: Penton Media, Inc.
Ed: Mark Eatherton. **Description:** Tax credits make ground-source heat pump technology more economically feasible. Suggestions on how to choose the right ground-source heat pump technology to install in a house are discussed.

5407 ■ "Major Renovation Planned for Southridge" in *Business Journal-Milwaukee* (Vol. 28, November 12, 2010, No. 6, pp. A1)
Pub: Milwaukee Business Journal
Ed: Stacy Vogel Davis. **Description:** Simon Property Group plans to invest more than $20 million in upgrading and renovating Southridge Mall in Milwaukee County, Wisconsin. The project, which is partially financed by a $10 million grant from the Village of Greendale, could boost the property's value by $52.5 million.

5408 ■ "Mann to Lead Builders" in *Charlotte Observer* (January 31, 2007)
Pub: Knight-Ridder/Tribune Business News
Ed: Allen Norwood. **Description:** Elliot Mann of Standard Pacific Homes was sworn in as president of Home Builders Association of Charlotte, North Carolina.

5409 ■ "Marine Act Amendments Gain Parliamentary Approval" in *Canadian Sailings* (July 7, 2008)
Pub: Commonwealth Business Media
Ed: Alex Binkley. **Description:** Changes to the Canada Marine Act provides better borrowing deals as well as an ability to tap into federal infrastructure funding for environmental protection measures, security improvements and other site enhancements.

5410 ■ "Martin Marietta Expands Rock Solid Port Manatee Presence" in *Tampa Bay Business Journal* (Vol. 30, January 8, 2010, No. 3, pp. 1)
Pub: American City Business Journals
Ed: Jane Meinhardt. **Description:** Raleigh, North Carolina-based Martin Marietta Materials Inc. has been granted by Florida's Manatee County Port Authority with a 30-year, $42 million contract. Through the contract, an aggregate terminal will be built by Martin Marietta at the port. Construction work is anticipated to start in earl 2010 with terminal operations commencing by late summer 2010.

5411 ■ "McDonald's Founders Fund $80 Million Project" in *The Business Journal - Serving Phoenix and the Valley of the Sun* (Vol. 28, September 12, 2008, No. 53, pp. 1)
Pub: American City Business Journals, Inc.
Ed: Jan Buchholz. **Description:** Construction will begin in early 2009 on an $80 million Ray and Joan Kroc Community Center in Phoenix, Arizona. It will be located adjacent to the Salvation Army, which received a $1.9 billion contribution from Joan Kroc after her death in 2003. This fund will be divided to construct 30 community centers across the country.

5412 ■ "Medical Office Developers To Merge November 1" in *The Business Journal - Serving Phoenix and the Valley of the Sun* (Vol. 29, September 26, 2008, No. 4, pp. 1)
Pub: American City Business Journals, Inc.
Ed: Angela Gonzales. **Description:** Ensemble Real Estate Services LLC and DevMan Co. will merge effective November 1, 2008 and will call the firm Ensemble DevMan of Arizona after the merger. The two companies will combine their resources and

expertise on planned projects that include the Phoenix Children's Hospital's Specialty Clinic and Banner Ironwood Medical Office Building.

5413 ■ "Mequon Plan On Tracks, Bucks Housing Trend" in *The Business Journal-Milwaukee* (Vol. 25, September 26, 2008, No. 53, pp. A1)
Pub: American City Business Journals, Inc.
Ed: Pete Millard. **Description:** Insight Development Group plans to build condominium units and single-family homes despite the residential market downturn. The Orchard Glen project, a planned development in Mequon, is a $22 million project which will include 38 condos and 12 single-family homes. Details of the project are provided.

5414 ■ "Merchants Association Working on Deal for Large Wholesale Warehouse" in *Austin Business JournalInc.* (September 19, 2008)
Pub: American City Business Journals
Ed: Jean Kwon. **Description:** Greater Austin Merchants Association planning to buy a former Dell Outlet Factory in Austin, Texas and convert it into a warehouse for convenience stores and gas stations.

5415 ■ *Metal Construction News—Metal Architecture Building Systems Product File and Directory Issue*
Pub: Modern Trade Communications Inc.
Ed: Shawn Zuver, Editor, shawnzuver@moderntrade.com. **Released:** Annual, January. **Price:** $60, Canada and Mexico; $140, other countries. **Publication Includes:** List of more than 990 manufacturers and suppliers of building components and accessories, insulation, doors and frames, mechanical products, cranes, manufacturing and construction equipment; nearly 90 steel erectors; and about 35 industry associations. **Entries Include:** Company or association name, address, phone, contacts. Listings for associations also include trade show and convention dates; erector listings include geographic areas served; other listings include product information. **Arrangement:** Separate alphabetical sections for manufacturers/suppliers, erectors, and associations. **Indexes:** Product (manufacturers and suppliers).

5416 ■ "Midtown Tampa Bay Taking Shape" in *The Business Journal-Serving Greater Tampa Bay* (Vol. 28, September 12, 2008, No. 38, pp. 1)
Pub: American City Business Journals, Inc.
Ed: Janet Leiser. **Description:** Midtown Tampa Bay's 610,000 square foot shopping and entertainment center is being planned in Florida and is to replace the Tampa Bay One project proposed years earlier. The retail center is to be developed by Bromley Cos. and Opus South Corp. and is expected to have five buildings. Other details about the plan are discussed.

5417 ■ "Military Center a Go" in *Austin Business JournalInc.* (Vol. 29, December 11, 2009, No. 40, pp. 1)
Pub: American City Business Journals
Ed: Kate Harrington. **Description:** The $40 million Armed Forces Guard and Reserve Center project at Austin-Bergstrom International Airport has resumed work after a delay of several years. The project is in both the House and Senate versions of the fiscal 2010 Military Construction and Veterans Appropriations Bill that would earmark $16.5 million for the center and $5.7 million for the maintenance facility. Details of construction plans are covered.

5418 ■ "Minnesota ABC Event Looks at Government Contracting" in *Finance and Commerce Daily Newspaper* (November 23, 2010)
Pub: Dolan Media Newswires
Ed: Brian Johnson. **Description:** Minnesota Associated Builders and Contractors hosted an event focusing on doing business with government agencies. Topics included bidding work, awarding jobs, paperwork, guidelines, certifications and upcoming projects.

5419 ■ "Minor-League Baseball's Sliders Plan Stock Offering" in *Crain's Detroit Business* (Vol. 25, June 15, 2009, No. 24, pp. 3)
Pub: Crain Communications Inc. - Detroit
Ed: Bill Shea. **Description:** New minor-league baseball team is raising funds to build a new stadium in Waterford Township, Michigan because banks are unwilling to provide loans for the project. Owners of the Midwest Sliders in Ypsilanti, Michigan are waiting for the federal Securities and Exchange Commission to approve a Regulation A public offering.

5420 ■ "A Model Development" in *Crain's Cleveland Business* (Vol. 28, October 1, 2007, No. 39, pp. 12)
Pub: Crain Communications, Inc.
Description: Profile a Forest City Enterprises Inc., a firm that is developing a project in New Mexico called Mesa del Sol. The Albuquerque development is being seen as the vanguard of master-planned communities with its high-tech economic development center which is expected to become the site of 60,000 jobs, 38,000 homes and a town center.

5421 ■ "Modular Home Center Opens in Arcadia" in *Charlotte Observer* (February 1, 2007)
Pub: Knight-Ridder/Tribune Business News
Ed: John Lawhorne. **Description:** Arcadia Home Center features modular homes constructed on a steel frame; regulations regarding the manufacture and moving of these homes are included.

5422 ■ "The Money Train: How Public Projects Shape Our Economic Future" in *Hawaii Business* (Vol. 54, September 2008, No. 3, pp. 31)
Pub: Hawaii Business Publishing
Ed: Jason Ubay. **Description:** Public projects impact the construction industry as such projects create jobs and new infrastructure that can lead to private developments. Details on the government contracts and construction projects in Hawaii and their rising costs and impact on the state's economy are discussed.

5423 ■ "More Contractors Unpaid" in *Puget Sound Business Journal* (Vol. 29, October 3, 2008, No. 24, pp. 1)
Pub: American City Business Journals
Ed: Brad Berton. **Description:** An 80 percent rise in the filing of mechanics' liens was reported in Seattle, Washington. It is believed that financial problems are spreading to construction companies and contractors as home sales slide and builders default on construction loans. Delinquencies of single-family construction homes has increased.

5424 ■ "More Details Emerge on Maersk Plan" in *Charlotte Business Journal* (Vol. 25, August 13, 2010, No. 21, pp. 1)
Pub: Charlotte Business Journal
Ed: Will Boye. **Description:** Children Klen Properties has announced the details of its redevelopment plan for a property in Charlotte, North Carolina. The plan includes office and retail space and residential units. The construction of a hotel has also been proposed.

5425 ■ "More Gains in the Pipeline" in *Barron's* (Vol. 89, August 3, 2009, No. 31, pp. M5)
Pub: Dow Jones & Co., Inc.
Ed: Fleming Meeks. **Description:** Shares of El Paso Corp. could recover as the company concludes a deal with a private-equity group to fund pipeline construction. The company's shares are trading at $10.06 and could move up to $12 as bad news has already been priced into the stock.

5426 ■ "Museum Center to Exhibit New Look" in *Business Courier* (Vol. 24, February 22, 2008, No. 46, pp. 1)
Pub: American City Business Journals, Inc.
Ed: Dan Monk. **Description:** Discusses a $120 million renovation is being planned for the Cincinnati Museum Center complex at Union Terminal. The project aims to build a 14-acre park and office spaces in the area. Details of the Museum Center's renovation plans are given.

5427 ■ "A Necessary Balancing Act: Bookkeeping" in *Contractor* (Vol. 56, November 2009, No. 11, pp. 22)
Pub: Penton Media, Inc.
Ed: Al Schwartz. **Description:** Pros and cons of getting a bookkeeper or a certified public accountant for the subcontractor are discussed. A bookkeeper can help a subcontractor get new accounting software up and running while an accountant will more than likely keep after the books at regular intervals throughout the year.

5428 ■ "New-Home Sales Grab a Foothold With Q2 Boost" in *Sacramento Business Journal* (Vol. 25, July 11, 2008, No. 19, pp. 1)
Pub: American City Business Journals, Inc.
Ed: Michael Shaw. **Description:** Statistics show that homebuilders in Sacramento, California experienced an increase in new-home sales during the second quarter of 2008. It was also reported that builders moved more homes without slashing prices significantly. Barry Grant, president of KB Home's Sacramento division, believes that the improvement is caused by the stability in the supply of resale homes.

5429 ■ "New Hydronic Heating Technologies Work" in *Contractor* (Vol. 57, January 2010, No. 1, pp. 58)
Pub: Penton Media, Inc.
Ed: Carol Fey. **Description:** Technology behind hydronic heating systems is reviewed. These technologies include radiant and geothermal hydronic heating. System requirements for installing these greener forms of heating are discussed.

5430 ■ "New ICA, Ex-Builder Tangle Over Construction" in *Boston Business Journal* (Vol. 27, October 12, 2007, No. 37, pp. 1)
Pub: American City Business Journals Inc.
Ed: Michelle Hillman. **Description:** Now-defunct George B.H. Macomber Company is suing the Institute of Contemporary Art (ICA) in Boston, Massachusetts as it believes that it has done extra work worth more than $6.6 million that was not included in the original contract with the construction of the museum. A series of setbacks and minor repairs has caused delays in the opening of the ICA, which was further complicated when Macomber began having financial difficulties.

5431 ■ "New State Rules Require Cranes and Operators to be Certified" in *Bellingham Business Journal* (Vol. February 2010, pp. 11)
Pub: Sound Publishing Inc.
Ed: Isaac Bonnell. **Description:** All construction cranes in Washington state must be inspected annually to be certified for use. The move is part of a larger L&I crane safety program that also requires crane operators to pass a written exam and a skill test.

5432 ■ "New Stores, New Headquarters in Schenectady for Golub Corporation" in *Business Review, Albany New York* (November 23, 2007)
Pub: American City Business Journals, Inc.
Ed: Michael DeMasi. **Description:** Details of Golub Corporation's expansion plan are presented. The supermarket chain, which has 116 stores in six northeastern states, plans to open thirty more stores within the next three or four years. The company will also build 524,000 square feet of warehouse space which will help in supplying new stores. Its corporate headquarters will also move to a vacant lot in Schenectady, New York.

5433 ■ "Newcomers Join Roster of Indoor Sports Venues" in *Business Review, Albany New York* (Vol. 34, October 12, 2007, No. 28, pp. 1)
Pub: American City Business Journals, Inc.
Ed: Adam Sichko. **Description:** Indoor sports scene in Albany, New York is growing, with several indoor training facilities with a special attention to baseball and softball being built. These facilities include the $2.2 million Extra Innings facility in Ballston Corporate Technology Park and the Warning Track facility on Route 9 in Malta. The market for indoor sports, which is seen as saturated, is analyzed.

5434 ■ "The Next Chapter" in *Business Courier* (Vol. 26, November 20, 2009, No. 30, pp. 1)
Pub: American City Business Journals, Inc.
Ed: Lucy May. **Description:** Eric Browne and Mel Gravely purchased controlling interest in TriVersity Construction Group from CM-GC CEO Schulyler Mur-

doch and MBJ Consultants President Monroe Barnes. One third of the company was still owned by Cincinnati-based Messer and TriVersity and will continue to be a certified minority business enterprise.

5435 ■ "The Next Government Bailout?" in *Barron's* (Vol. 88, March 10, 2008, No. 10, pp. 21)
Pub: Dow Jones & Company, Inc.
Ed: Jonathan Laing. **Description:** Fannie Mae may need a government bailout as it faces huge hits brought about by the effects of the housing crisis. The shares of the government-sponsored enterprise have dropped 65 percent since the housing crisis began.

5436 ■ "Next Stage of Green Building will be Water Efficiency" in *Contractor* (Vol. 56, July 2009, No. 7, pp. 41)
Pub: Penton Media, Inc.
Description: One market report says that water efficiency and conservation will become critical factors in green design, construction, and product selection in the next five years from 2009. The report outlines how critical it will be for the construction industry to address responsible water practices in the future.

5437 ■ "N.H. Near the LEED in Green Space" in *New Hampshire Business Review* (Vol. 33, March 25, 2011, No. 6, pp. 30)
Pub: Business Publications Inc.
Description: New Hamphire's architects, contractors and suppliers are among the leaders with LEED-certified space per capita.

5438 ■ "Nine Sectors to Watch: Construction" in *Canadian Business* (Vol. 81, December 24, 2007, No. 1, pp. 48)
Pub: Rogers Media
Ed: Jeff Sanford. **Description:** Infrastructure deficit of C$123 billion, and still growing, was recently reported by the Federation of Canadian Municipalities. Details on plans for infrastructure projects and forecasts on the construction sector for 2008 are discussed.

5439 ■ "No Rooms for the Inn In This High-Rise" in *Chicago Tribune* (October 4, 2008)
Pub: McClatchy-Tribune Information Services
Ed: Ameet Sachdev; Jim Kirk. **Description:** Construction has stalled for several hotel expansion projects due to the economy which has caused a decline in occupancy and little growth in average daily room rates in downtown Chicago because consumers and businesses are becoming more cautious in the amount of money they spend on travel.

5440 ■ "Noah's Park: $150M Project Eyed in Ky." in *Business Courier* (Vol. 27, November 19, 2010, No. 29, pp. 1)
Pub: Business Courier
Ed: Lucy May. **Description:** Grant County, Kentucky has been abuzz with speculation about a $150M Noah's Ark-themed project being planned for Williamstown, Kentucky. The theme park's planned location is halfway between Cincinnati, Ohio and Louisville, Kentucky and about 40 minutes south of the Answers in Genesis Creation Museum in Petersburg.

5441 ■ "Nonprofit to Grow" in *Austin Business JournalInc.* (Vol. 29, January 22, 2010, No. 46, pp. 1)
Pub: American City Business Journals
Ed: Sandra Zaragoza. **Description:** Southwest Key Programs Inc. received a $2.1 million grant from the U.S. Economic Development Administration to help finance the building of a $3.6 million 'Social Enterprise Complex'. The complex is expected to create at least 100 jobs in East Austin, Texas. Details of the plan for the complex are presented.

5442 ■ "Northwest Washington Fair Building Larger Horse Arena" in *Bellingham Business Journal* (Vol. March 2010, pp. 6)
Pub: Sound Publishing Inc.
Description: Northwest Washington Fair is building a new equestrian arena that will provide larger show space for the horse community. The existing arena will function as a warm-up arena when hosting large shows.

5443 ■ "Not Enough Room" in *Austin Business JournalInc.* (Vol. 29, November 13, 2009, No. 36, pp. A1)
Pub: American City Business Journals
Ed: Jacob Dirr. **Description:** Hotel and convention business in downtown Austin, Texas lost nearly $5.3 million when Dell Inc. relocated its annual convention to Las Vegas. However, lack of capital caused the postponement of various hotel projects which need to be finished in order to attract well-attended conventions. Makeover projects on Austin's Waller Creek and Sixth Street are discussed.

5444 ■ "Novi Eyed for $11 Million, 100-Bed Medilodge" in *Crain's Detroit Business* (Vol. 25, June 1, 2009, No. 22, pp. M032)
Pub: Crain Communications Inc. - Detroit
Description: Novi, Michigan is one of the cities being considered for construction of a new 110-bed skilled nursing facility. Details of the project are included.

5445 ■ "O'Reilly Will Soup Up KC Warehouse" in *The Business Journal-Serving Metropolitan Kansas City* (Vol. 26, August 15, 2008, No. 49)
Pub: American City Business Journals, Inc.
Ed: Rob Roberts. **Description:** O'Reilly Automotive Inc. plans to construct a 215,000-square foot warehouse in Kansas City. The move is expected to triple the size of the company's distribution center. Other views and information on the planned warehouse construction, are presented.

5446 ■ "Orlando Health to Build $24M Proton Therapy Facility" in *Orlando Business Journal* (Vol. 26, January 22, 2010, No. 34, pp. 1)
Pub: American City Business Journals
Ed: Melanie Stawicki Azam. **Description:** Orlando Health is planning to construct a $24 million proton therapy facility at its MD Anderson Cancer Center Orlando in Florida. The facility, which aims for a 2011 opening, will be using radiation for more accurate targeting of tumors and avoiding the damage to surrounding tissues and organs.

5447 ■ "Our Company is Dedicated to the Environment, But We Work With Vendors that Aren't" in *Inc.* (March 2008, pp. 78)
Pub: Gruner & Jahr USA Publishing
Ed: Myra Goodman. **Description:** Insight into working with vendors, such as construction and janitorial contractors, to comploy with your company's environmental policies is given.

5448 ■ "Overseas Marketing Key to Success of Chicago Spire" in *Commercial Property News* (March 17, 2008)
Pub: Nielsen Company
Description: New construction of the Chicago Spire, a condominium project located on Lake Michigan's shore, is being marketed to would-be clients in Asia where Chicago is viewed as an emerging world city.

5449 ■ "Pain Ahead as Profit Pressure Increases" in *Crain's Chicago Business* (Vol. 31, May 5, 2008, No. 18, pp. 4)
Pub: Crain Communications, Inc.
Ed: Daniel Rome Levine. **Description:** Interview with David Klaskin, the chairman and chief investment officer at Oak Ridge Investments LLC, who discusses the outlook for the economy and corporate earnings, particularly in the housing and auto industries, the impact of economic stimulus checks, the weakness of the dollar and recommendations of stocks that individual investors may find helpful.

5450 ■ "P&L Building Owner Nears Start of $157M Condo Plan" in *Business Journal-Serving Metropolitan Kansas City* (November 23, 2007)
Pub: American City Business Journals, Inc.
Ed: Jim Davis. **Description:** The owner of Power and Light Building is ready to begin a $157 million plan to refurbish the Kansas City landmark and redevelop a property right next to it after receiving tax increment refinancing for the project.

5451 ■ "Pavilions Poised for Image Overhaul" in *The Business Journal - Serving Phoenix and the Valley of the Sun* (Vol. 28, August 22, 2008)
Pub: American City Business Journals, Inc.
Ed: Jan Buchholz. **Description:** DeRitto Partners Inc. is expected to push through with plans for a major renovation of the 1.1 million-square foot Scottsdale Pavilions in Scottsdale, Arizona. An aggressive marketing campaign is planned to be included in the renovation, which aims to address high vacancy rates and competition. Views and information on the planned renovation are presented.

5452 ■ "Peter Gilgan" in *Canadian Business* (Vol. 82, April 27, 2009, No. 7, pp. 58)
Pub: Rogers Media
Ed: Calvin Leung. **Description:** Mattamy Homes Ltd. president and chief executive officer Peter Gilgan believes that their business model of building communities in an organized way brings advantages to the firm and for their customers. He also believes in adopting their product prices to new market realities. Gilgan considers the approvals regime in Ontario his biggest challenge in the last 20 years.

5453 ■ "Pierre's Ice Cream" in *Ice Cream Reporter* (Vol. 23, October 20, 2010, No. 11, pp. 8)
Pub: Ice Cream Reporter
Description: Pierre's Ice Cream has started work on its new $8 million manufacturing facility in Cleveland, Ohio.

5454 ■ "Pinellas Leaders Want First Leg of Light Rail" in *The Business Journal-Serving Greater Tampa Bay* (Vol. 28, August 8, 2008, No. 33)
Pub: American City Business Journals, Inc.
Ed: Larry Halstead. **Description:** Proposed routes for the first leg of the planned light railway system in the Tampa Bay, Florida area are being presented as the Tampa Bay Area Regional Transportation Authority is about to make its master plan for the project. A sales tax for transit is being proposed to fund the project, as well as an expansion of the accompanying bus system.

5455 ■ "Pipeline Dreams" in *Canadian Business* (Vol. 80, October 22, 2007, No. 21, pp. 19)
Pub: Rogers Media
Ed: Rachel Pulfer. **Description:** Northwest Mackenzie Valley Pipeline has been under review by the National Energy Board since 2004. Hearings on the construction of the gas pipeline will wrap up in 2008. Pius Rolheiser, the spokesman of Imperial Oil Company Inc. believes the change of government in the area will not affect the negotiations on the pipeline construction.

5456 ■ "Placer Land Sells for $12 Million" in *Sacramento Business Journal* (Vol. 25, July 25, 2008, No. 21, pp. 1)
Pub: American City Business Journals, Inc.
Ed: Michael Shaw; Celia Lamb. **Description:** Reynen & Bardis Communities Inc., a Sacramento, California-based homebuilder, has purchased the Antonio Mountain Ranch in Placer County, California shortly before the property's scheduled foreclosure on June 27, 2008. Placer County Recorder's data show that the purchase price of the 808-acre wetland-rich property is $12 million.

5457 ■ "Plans for $160M Condo Resort in Wisconsin Dells Moves Forward" in *Commercial Property News* (March 18, 2008)
Pub: Nielsen Company
Description: Plans for the Grand Cambrian Resort in the Wisconsin Dells is discussed. The luxury condominium resort will include condos, townhomes, and condo-hotel style residences, two water parts, meeting space and indoor entertainment space, as well as a spa, four restaurants and retail offerings.

5458 ■ "Playing Defense" in *Crain's Chicago Business* (Vol. 31, November 10, 2008, No. 45, pp. 4)
Pub: Crain Communications, Inc.
Ed: Monee Fields-White. **Description:** Chicago's money managers are increasingly investing in local companies such as Caterpillar Inc., a maker of

construction and mining equipment, Kraft Foods Inc. and Baxter International Inc., a manufacturer of medical products, in an attempt to bolster their portfolios. These companies have a history of surviving tough economic times.

5459 ■ "Port Authority Taking Heat in Kenwood Mess" in *Business Courier* (Vol. 26, September 18, 2009, No. 21, pp. 1)
Pub: American City Business Journals, Inc.
Ed: Dan Monk. **Description:** Port of Greater Cincinnati Development Authority is being criticized for not requiring payment and performance bonds to ensure that contractors would be paid. The criticism occurred after the general contractor for the project to build a parking garage at Kenwood Towne Plaza stopped paying its subcontractors.

5460 ■ "Possible Green Light On Transit" in *The Business Journal-Milwaukee* (Vol. 25, July 25, 2008, No. 44, pp. A1)
Pub: American City Business Journals, Inc.
Ed: David Doege. **Description:** $50 million in federal funding is being sought by Wisconsin's Milwaukee County Executive Scott Walker for the creation of two bus rapid transit lines, and is to be added to the unspent Milwaukee area federal funds worth $91.5 million. The new transit line will have new higher-speed buses and fewer stops than the traditional line.

5461 ■ "Power Partnerships" in *Business Courier* (Vol. 27, October 22, 2010, No. 25, pp. 1)
Pub: Business Courier
Ed: Lucy May. **Description:** The $400 million Harrah's casino and the $47 million redevelopment and expansion of Washington Park are project aimed at boosting the economy in downtown Cincinnati, Ohio. These projects will be done in cooperation with the National Association for the Advancement of Colored People. Insights into the role of minority-owned businesses in regional economic development are explored.

5462 ■ "'Pre-Sale' for Planned Could Mich Tower" in *Crain's Chicago Business* (Vol. 31, March 24, 2008, No. 12, pp. 14)
Pub: Crain Communications, Inc.
Ed: Eddie Baeb. **Description:** Condominium developer William Warman is planning to build a mixed-use tower at 300 North Michigan Avenue which would include a hotel, retail space, apartments and a parking garage. Mr. Warman is looking for investors to buy part or all of the space in order to make it easier to land financing.

5463 ■ "Prince of the City" in *Canadian Business* (Vol. 80, November 19, 2007, No. 23, pp. 62)
Pub: Rogers Media
Ed: Rachel Pulfer. **Description:** Robert Fung and the Salilent Group aim to revive the poverty-stricken communities in Vancouver by transforming the city's old buildings into designer condominiums using city incentives. Fung and his partners have increased property values in the most unlikely neighborhoods by creating luxury real estate. Fung's recommendations on Vancouver's real estate development are given.

5464 ■ "Project Could Forge Path to Jobs, Growth" in *Business Courier* (Vol. 26, September 11, 2009, No. 20, pp. 1)
Pub: American City Business Journals, Inc.
Ed: Lucy May. **Description:** The planned 13.5 mile Mill Creek Greenway Trail extension could create 445 jobs and bring $52 million to the economy of Cincinnati, Ohio. The trail extension would cost $24 million and would be used for recreational purposes.

5465 ■ "Prominent Hispanic Businessman Signs with Choice Hotels" in *Hispanic Business* (March 2008, pp. 36)
Pub: Hispanic Business
Ed: Melinda Burns. **Description:** Profile of John C. Lopez, who has signed an agreement with Choice Hotels International to build five new Cambria Suites in the U.S.; cost of the project will total $14 million.

5466 ■ "Prominent Hispanic Businessman Signs With Choice Hotels" in *Hispanic Business* (Vol. 30, March 2008, No. 3, pp. 36)
Pub: Hispanic Business
Ed: Melinda Burns. **Description:** Chairman of the board of Lopez Food Inc., John C. Lopez signs the agreement with Choice Hotels International to build five new Cambria suites in the USA. This is his first hotel venture and also the first Hispanic franchisee to enter into business with Choice Hotels.

5467 ■ "Proposal Ruffles Builders" in *Austin Business JournalInc.* (Vol. 29, November 20, 2009, No. 37, pp. 1)
Pub: American City Business Journals
Ed: Jacob Dirr. **Description:** A proposal that requires heating, ventilation and cooling equipment checking for a new commercial building having an area of at least 10,000 square feet might cost 25 cents to 50 cents per square foot for the owners. This may lead to higher housing costs. Both the Building and Fire Code Board of Appeals and the Mechanical Plumbing and Solar Board have recommended the plan.

5468 ■ "PSU Launches $90 Million Project" in *The Business Journal-Portland* (Vol. 25, July 18, 2008, No. 19, pp. 1)
Pub: American City Business Journals, Inc.
Ed: Aliza Earnshaw. **Description:** Portland State University (PSU) has launched a $90-million project for a new business school building, which is to be located at Southwest Market and Southwest Park. The business school is expected to move in to its new 130,000-suqare-foot building by 2013. PSU business school needs to raise $30 million for the project.

5469 ■ "Public Bathroom Pressure Woes Resolved" in *Contractor* (Vol. 56, September 2009, No. 9, pp. 44)
Pub: Penton Media, Inc.
Ed: Dave Yates. **Description:** Design and construction of a public bathroom's plumbing system in the United States are discussed. Installed plumbing fixtures with flush valves would not function properly. The installation of Grundfos SQE variable-speed pumps has resolved problems with the bathroom's water pressure.

5470 ■ "Pulp Friction: Spin Off Mills to Boost Wood Products" in *Globe & Mail* (February 18, 2006, pp. B3)
Pub: CTVglobemedia Publishing Inc.
Ed: Peter Kennedy. **Description:** The reasons behind the decision of chief executive officer Jim Shepherd of Canfor Corp. to sell pulp mills are presented.

5471 ■ "Pulte May Be Bouncing Back From Stock-Price Doldrums" in *Crain's Detroit Business* (Vol. 23, October 8, 2007, No. 41, pp. 4)
Pub: Crain Communications Inc. - Detroit
Ed: Daniel Duggan. **Description:** Pulte Homes saw a jump in its stocks due to Citigroup's analysts rating Pulte and other builders higher due to strong balance sheets.

5472 ■ "Real Estate Ambitions" in *Black Enterprise* (Vol. 37, January 2007, No. 6, pp. 101)
Pub: Earl G. Graves Publishing Co. Inc.
Ed: Description: National Real Estate Investors Association is a nonprofit trade association for both advanced as well as novice real estate investors that offers information on builders to contractors to banks. When looking to become a real estate investor utilize this organization, talk to various investors like the president of your local chapter, let people know your aspirations, and see if you can find a partner who has experience in the field. Resources included.

5473 ■ "Realities May Blur Vision" in *The Business Journal-Serving Metropolitan Kansas City* (Vol. 27, September 19, 2008, No. 1, pp. 1)
Pub: American City Business Journals, Inc.
Ed: Rob Roberts. **Description:** Vision Metcalf is a study by Kansas City that depicts how Metcalf Avenue could look like if redeveloped. Redevelopment plans for the Metcalf corridor include a 20-story mixed-use building on a vacant car dealership. The challenges that the redevelopment plans will face are also analyzed.

5474 ■ "Recovery on Tap for 2010?" in *Orlando Business Journal* (Vol. 26, January 1, 2010, No. 31, pp. 1)
Pub: American City Business Journals
Ed: Melanie Stawicki Azam, Richard Bilbao, Christopher Boyd, Anjali Fluker. **Description:** Economic forecasts for Central Florida's leading business sectors in 2010 are presented. These sectors include housing, film and TV, sports business, law, restaurants, aviation, tourism and hospitality, banking and finance, commercial real estate, retail, health care, insurance, higher education, and manufacturing. According to some local executives, Central Florida's economy will slowly recover in 2010.

5475 ■ "Redcorp Ventures Ltd.: Tulsequah Camp Construction Begins" in *Canadian Corporate News* (May 16, 2007)
Pub: Comtex News Network Inc.
Description: Redfern Reources Ltd., a subsidiary of Redcorp Ventures Ltd., announced that Modular Transportable Solutions LLC was selected to design and manufacture its prefabricated, modular construction camp, cookhouse, administration buildings, and mine dry at the Tulsequah Mine location in northwest British Columbia due to the virtually indestructible design of the units that withstand extreme weather conditions.

5476 ■ "A Renewal in Rentals" in *Barron's* (Vol. 88, March 17, 2008, No. 11, pp. 17)
Pub: Dow Jones & Company, Inc.
Ed: Description: Discusses the projected entry of the estimated 82 million echo-boomers into the rentals market and the influx of immigrants and displaced homeowners which could turn apartments into lucrative investments again. While apartment-building completions rose slowly since 2003, demand is expected to increase steeply until 2015.

5477 ■ "Restoring Grandeur" in *Business Courier* (Vol. 26, December 4, 2009, No. 32, pp. 1)
Pub: American City Business Journals, Inc.
Ed: Dan Monk. **Description:** Eagle Realty Group intends to spend more than $10 to restore the historic 12-story Phelps apartment building in Lytle Park in Cincinnati. Its president, Mario San Marco, expressed the need to invest in the building in order to maintain operations. The building could be restored into a hotel catering to executives and consultants.

5478 ■ "Retail Center Pitched" in *Business Courier* (Vol. 27, June 18, 2010, No. 7, pp. 1)
Pub: Business Courier
Ed: Dan Monk. **Description:** Jeffrey R. Anderson Real Estate Inc.'s plan for a retail center in Butler County, Ohio could have three department stores in the 1.1 million-square-foot property. An outdoor sports retailer is also part of the plans.

5479 ■ "Retail Center Planned for Canton Site" in *Boston Business Journal* (Vol. 29, May 20, 2011, No. 2, pp. 1)
Pub: American City Business Journals Inc.
Ed: Daniel J. Sernovitz. **Description:** A real estate development team is planning to build a shopping center at Canton Crossing in Baltimore, Maryland and is near closing the deal with ExxonMobil Corporation who owns the waterfront site.

5480 ■ "ReVenture Plan Appears Close to Landing Key Legislative Deal" in *Charlotte Business Journal* (Vol. 25, July 9, 2010, No. 16, pp. 1)
Pub: Charlotte Business Journal
Ed: John Downey. **Description:** North Carolina lawmakers acted on special legislation that would boost development of Forsite Development 667-acre ReVenture Energy Park. The legislation could also improve chances that Duke Energy Carolinas will contract to purchase the power from the planned 50-megawatt biomass power plant located at the park. How utilities would benefit from the legislation is also discussed.

5481 ■ "Rise in Occupancy Rate Fuels Area Hotel Building Boom" in *Crain's Detroit Business* (Vol. 24, March 10, 2008, No. 10, pp. 14)
Pub: Crain Communications, Inc.
Ed: Jonathan Eppley. **Description:** Due to a rise in the region's yearly occupancy rate, a number of new hotel construction and renovation projects are slated for the Detroit area.

5482 ■ "A Rise in Rental Units" in *Philadelphia Business Journal* (Vol. 30, October 7, 2011, No. 34, pp. 1)
Pub: American City Business Journals Inc.
Ed: Natalie Kostelni. **Description:** Housing developers have been stepping up the construction of new apartment complexes throughout the suburbs of Pennsylvania in order to capture growing demand for rental properties. BPG Properties Ltd. has nearly 1,000 new apartments under construction.

5483 ■ "Ritz Kapalua Sells 93 Suites for $176M to Fund Renovation" in *Commercial Property News* (March 17, 2008)
Pub: Nielsen Company
Description: Ritz-Carlton, Kapalua in Lahaina, Hawaii sold ninety-three of its units in order to fund renovations of 463 rooms and suites along with construction of a new spa and fitness center, new and expanded restaurants and pools and an environmental education center for children.

5484 ■ "Rivals Blow In" in *Crain's Cleveland Business* (Vol. 30, June 1, 2009, No. 21, pp. 1)
Pub: Crain Communications, Inc.
Ed: Chuck Soder. **Description:** U.S. and Canadian competitors are hoping to start construction of offshore wind farm project proposed by Cuyahoga County's Great Lakes Energy Development Task Force. Details of the project are included.

5485 ■ "River Plan in Disarray" in *Business Journal Portland* (Vol. 26, December 4, 2009, No. 39, pp. 1)
Pub: American City Business Journals Inc.
Ed: Andy Giegerich. **Description:** Portland's proposed rules on a waterfront development plan for the Willamette River calls for fees intended for river bank preservation, a move that could drive industrial manufacturers away. The manufacturers, under the Working Waterfront Coalition, claim that the proposals could increase riverfront building costs by 15 percent.

5486 ■ "Roger Hickel Contracting: Smoothing the Road for Owners" in *Alaska Business Monthly* (Vol. 27, October 2011, No. 10, pp. 114)
Pub: Alaska Business Publishing Company
Ed: Gail West. **Description:** Profile of Roger Hickel and his contracting company that reports nearly $60 million annually in gross revenue. The firm focuses on customer service.

5487 ■ "Ronald Taketa" in *Hawaii Business* (Vol. 54, September 2008, No. 3, pp. 28)
Pub: Hawaii Business Publishing
Ed: Shara Enay. **Description:** Interview with Ronald Taketa of the Hawaii Carpenters Union who states that the economic downturn has affected the construction industry as 20 percent of the union's 7,800 members are unemployed. He shares his thoughts about the industry's economic situation, the union's advertisements, and his role as a leader of the union.

5488 ■ "RT Seeking Ways to Finance Expansion" in *Sacramento Business Journal* (Vol. 28, July 29, 2011, No. 22, pp. 1)
Pub: Sacramento Business Journal
Ed: Melanie Turner. **Description:** Sacramento Regional Transit District is considering ways to finance all its capital projects outlined in a 30-year transit master plan which would cost more than $7 billion to complete. Current funding sources include developer fees and state and federal assistance and fares. Part of the master plan is a light-rail line to Sacramento International Airport.

5489 ■ "Saratoga Eagle Project Quenches Thirst To Grow" in *Business Review, Albany New York* (Vol. 34, November 30, 2007, No. 35, pp. 3)
Pub: American City Business Journals, Inc.
Ed: Robin K. Cooper. **Description:** Saratoga Eagle Sales and Service will be searching for contractors for the construction of its new beverage distribution center at the WJ Grande Industrial Park in Saratoga Springs, New York. The $8 million, 107,000 square foot facility is part of Saratoga Eagle's expansion plan. The company's growth in the Capital Region market and $1.3 million tax break are discussed.

5490 ■ "Schlitterbahn Broadens" in *Austin Business JournalInc.* (Vol. 28, September 19, 2008, No. 27, pp. A1)
Pub: American City Business Journals
Ed: Kate Harrington. **Description:** Schlitterbahn is planning to introduce a Christmas-themed event this winter 2008 in its water amusement park that will keep it open from November to January. The company is also constructing its first out-of-Texas park, which is a $170 million, 376-acre project in Kansas City, Missouri. Other details about Schlitterbahn's expansion are discussed.

5491 ■ "A Second Chance at Road Dollars" in *Orlando Business Journal* (Vol. 26, February 5, 2010, No. 36, pp. 1)
Pub: American City Business Journals
Ed: Bill Orben. **Description:** Nearly $10 million worth of construction projects in Central Florida would give construction companies that missed the initial round of federal stimulus-funded local road building projects another opportunity. Cost savings in the initial round of road projects enabled Orange, Osceola, and Seminole Counties to secure additional projects.

5492 ■ "Seeing Green in Going Green" in *The Business Journal-Serving Greater Tampa Bay* (Vol. 28, July 4, 2008, No. 28, pp. 1)
Pub: American City Business Journals, Inc.
Ed: Janet Leiser. **Description:** Atlanta, Georgia-based developer IDI Corp. is pushing for Leadership in Energy and Environmental Design certification for the warehouse that is currently under construction at Madison Business Center along Port Sutton and U.S. 41. The industrial building is the first in Tampa Bay to seek certification for LEED as set by the U.S. Green Building Council.

5493 ■ "Self-Employment in the United States" in *Montly Labor Review* (Vol. 133, September 2010, No. 9, pp. 17)
Pub: Bureau of Labor Statistics
Description: Self employment in 2009 in the U.S. continued to be more common among men, Whites, Asians, and older workers and in the agriculture, construction, and services industries.

5494 ■ "Sellers Face Excess Land Dilemma" in *Crain's Cleveland Business* (Vol. 28, November 12, 2007, No. 45, pp. 1)
Pub: Crain Communications, Inc.
Ed: Stan Bullard. **Description:** Overview on the way in which the housing slump is effecting builders, land developers and lot prices. Statistical data included.

5495 ■ *Shedworking: The Alternative Workplace Revolution*
Pub: Frances Lincoln Limited
Ed: Alex Johnson. **Released:** June 10, 2010. **Price:** $29.95. **Description:** Shedworking is an alternative office space for those working at home. The book features shedworkers and shedbuilders from around the world who are leading this alternative workplace revolution and why this trend is working.

5496 ■ "Sixty-Acre Vision for North Suburbs" in *Business Courier* (Vol. 24, April 4, 2008, No. 52, pp. 1)
Pub: American City Business Journals, Inc.
Ed: Laura Baverman. **Description:** Al Neyer Inc. plans for a mixed-use development at the 60-acre site it has recently purchased. The mixed-use project could cost up to $100 million, and will include medical offices, residential buildings, and corporate offices. Details of Al Neyer's plans for the site are given.

5497 ■ "Sneak Preview: Alamo Revamp" in *Austin Business JournalInc.* (Vol. 28, December 12, 2008, No. 39, pp. 1)
Pub: American City Business Journals
Ed: Sandra Zaragoza. **Description:** Austin, Texas-based Alamo Drafthouse Cinemas is planning to build a new Circle C Ranch. The new theater will showcase digital projectors and the latest sound systems to show 3-D movies. The company is in lease negotiations with developer Stratus Properties Inc.

5498 ■ "Son of Sandman: Can Tom Gaglardi Really Outdo His Old Man?" in *Canadian Business* (Vol. 80, Winter 2007, No. 24, pp. 106)
Pub: Rogers Media
Ed: Calvin Leung. **Description:** Bob Gagliardi of Northland Properties started to learn about his family's business by working at a construction site at one of the high-rise buildings in downtown Vancouver. Gagliardi wants to expand their Moxie's restaurant chain and increase the market share of their Sandman hotel by 2018.

5499 ■ "South Lake Hospital Starting $47M Patient Tower" in *Orlando Business Journal* (Vol. 26, December 4, 2009, No. 26, pp. 1)
Pub: American City Business Journals
Ed: Melanie Stawicki Azam. **Description:** Clermont, Florida's South Lake Hospital has divulged intentions to issue $50.9 million in bonds in order to fund construction of the $47 million patient tower. The three-story, 124,000 square foot tower would add eighteen inpatient rooms, a new lobby and expanded pharmacy, diagnostic and lab services, and treatment areas.

5500 ■ "South Loop Site Lands a Buyer" in *Crain's Chicago Business* (Vol. 31, March 24, 2008, No. 12, pp. 1)
Pub: Crain Communications, Inc.
Ed: Alby Gallun. **Description:** Russland Capital Group, a little-known condominium developer from Skokie, recently purchased a 6.5-acre riverside property in the site known as Franklin Point for $40 million.

5501 ■ "State Center Lease Deal High for Md." in *Baltimore Business Journal* (Vol. 28, August 6, 2010, No. 13, pp. 1)
Pub: Baltimore Business Journal
Ed: Daniel J. Sernovitz. **Description:** The proposed $1.5 billion State Center development project in Midtown Baltimore might cause the State of Maryland to pay the most expensive rental rates in the city. The state will have to pay an effective rental rate of $34 per square foot, including expenses, on the leasing. Other details of the redevelopment project are discussed.

5502 ■ "State Printing Plant on the Move" in *Sacramento Business Journal* (Vol. 25, August 29, 2008, No. 26, pp. 1)
Pub: American City Business Journals, Inc.
Ed: Michael Shaw; Celia Lamb. **Description:** California is planning to replace its printing plant on Richards Boulevard and 7th Street with a newly built or leased facility in the Sacramento area. It was revealed that the project will meet the state's standards for new buildings. It is believed that the new site will require 15 acres or more depending on requirements.

5503 ■ "State Weighs Tearing Down Hoan" in *The Business Journal-Milwaukee* (Vol. 25, August 22, 2008, No. 48, pp. A1)
Pub: American City Business Journals, Inc.
Ed: Pete Millard. **Description:** Department of Transportation of Wisconsin is studying the feasibility of tearing the Daniel Hoan Memorial Bridge down because rehabilitating the bridge is costly. Rebuilding the Interstate 794 at street level could be less expensive. The potential plans for the bridge are discussed further.

5504 ■ "Still No Arena Financing Plan" in *Sacramento Business Journal* (Vol. 28, May 27, 2011, No. 13, pp. 1)
Pub: Sacramento Business Journal
Ed: Kelly Johnson. **Description:** The government of Sacramento, California has yet to devise a plan to

finance the construction of a proposed stadium. The arena is estimated to cost $387 million. A brief description of the facility is also included.

5505 ■ "Stimulus 'Loser' Won't Build Plant in Mass." in *Boston Business Journal* (Vol. 30, November 5, 2010, No. 41, pp. 1)
Pub: Boston Business Journal
Ed: Kyle Alspach. **Description:** Boston-Power Inc. no longer plans to build an electric vehicle battery plant in Massachusetts after it failed to obtain stimulus funds from the federal government. The company is instead looking to build a lithium-ion battery plant in China and possibly Europe.

5506 ■ "Stone Company Slated to Expand Here" in *Austin Business Journallnc.* (Vol. 28, September 12, 2008, No. 26, pp. 1)
Pub: American City Business Journals
Ed: Jean Kwon. **Description:** Architectural Granite & Marble Inc. has a $6 million investment that moved the company from 2,500 square feet of space to a 10,000 square foot office in Southwest Austin, Texas. The investment will also provide for the company's expansion in Nashville, Tennessee and San Antonio, Texas.

5507 ■ "Stung by Recession, Hemmer Regroups with New Strategy" in *Business Courier* (Vol. 27, June 4, 2010, No. 5, pp. 1)
Pub: Business Courier
Ed: Lucy May. **Description:** Paul Hemmer Companies reduced its work force and outsourced operations such as marketing and architecture, in order for the commercial and construction firm to survive the recession. Hammer's total core revenue in 2009 dropped to less than $30 million forcing the closure of its Chicago office.

5508 ■ "Sundt, DPR Score $470 Million Biotech Project" in *The Business Journal - Serving Phoenix and the Valley of the Sun* (Vol. 29, September 19, 2008, No. 3, pp. 1)
Pub: American City Business Journals, Inc.
Ed: Jan Buchholz. **Description:** Sundt Inc. and DPR Construction Inc. were awarded the winning joint-venture contract to develop the second phase of the Arizona Biomedical Collaborative on the Phoenix Biomedical Campus. Both firms declined to comment, but an employee of the Arizona Board of Regents confirmed that the firms won the bidding. Views and information on the development project are presented.

5509 ■ "Sunriver Venture Hits Snag" in *The Business Journal-Portland* (Vol. 25, August 1, 2008, No. 21, pp. 1)
Pub: American City Business Journals, Inc.
Ed: Robin J. Moody. **Description:** Portland, Oregon based-Sunwest Management Inc. has divided its Sunriver resort community to make way for a redevelopment plan. Sunwest owner Jon Harder and three partners formed SilverStar Destinations LLC to broker the purchase and redevelopment of the property. Details and description of the redevelopment project are also presented.

5510 ■ "Surplus Store Rebuilding Again" in *Spokesman-Review* (November 17, 2010)
Pub: Spokesman Review
Ed: Chelsea Bannach. **Description:** Retail business owner, David Arnold Sr., is rebuilding his Army Surplus store in Spokane, Washington after a truck crashed into the building.

5511 ■ "Survey: Don't Expect Big Results From Stimulus" in *Crain's Detroit Business* (Vol. 25, June 1, 2009, No. 22)
Pub: Crain Communications Inc. - Detroit
Ed: Nancy Kaffer, Chad Halcom. **Description:** In a recent survey, Michigan business owners, operators or managers showed that 48 percent of respondents oppose the President's stimulus package and believe it will have little or no effect on the economy.

5512 ■ "Sustainability Is Top Priority for GreenTown Chicago" in *Contractor* (Vol. 56, November 2009, No. 11, pp. 1)
Pub: Penton Media, Inc.
Ed: Candace Roulo. **Description:** GreenTown Chicago 2009 conference tackled energy-efficient practices and technologies, green design and building, and sustainable policies. Water conservation was also a topic at the conference and one mayor who made a presentation said that reducing the water loss in the system is a priority in the city's endeavor.

5513 ■ "Swope: Breakup Won't Delay Job" in *The Business Journal-Serving Metropolitan Kansas City* (Vol. 26, August 22, 2008, No. 50, pp. 1)
Pub: American City Business Journals, Inc.
Ed: Rob Roberts. **Description:** Swope Community Builders said that the Kansas City Redevelopment Project will not be delayed by the breakup of their partnership with Sherman Associates Inc. Swopes will be the sole master developer of the project.

5514 ■ "Tax Abatement Changes Seen as Home Run for Cleveland Condo Market" in *Crain's Cleveland Business* (Vol. 30, June 15, 2009, No. 23)
Pub: Crain Communications, Inc.
Ed: Jay Miller. **Description:** Condominium ownership became a bit more affordable for Cleveland residents since changes in both state and local tax abatement policy changes. The tax credits are examined.

5515 ■ "Tax Credit Crunch" in *Miami Daily Business Review* (March 26, 2008)
Pub: ALM Media Inc.
Ed: Paula Iuspa-Abbott. **Description:** Uncertainty is growing over the future of the low-income housing project in South Florida and the tax credit program that helps fuel the projects.

5516 ■ "Tax Deal Yields Polaris Offices" in *Business First-Columbus* (October 26, 2007, pp. A1)
Pub: American City Business Journals, Inc.
Ed: Brian R. Ball. **Description:** Speculation on a possible office building construction is increasing with the expansion of tax incentives to build at the Polaris Centers of Commerce. Details of community reinvestment in the Columbus, Ohio area along with possible 15-year 100 percent tax abatements for Polaris office buildings are discussed.

5517 ■ "Taylor Tests Land Grant Program" in *Austin Business Journal* (Vol. 31, June 3, 2011, No. 13, pp. 1)
Pub: American City Business Journals Inc.
Ed: Vicky Garza. **Description:** Taylor Economic Development Corporation implemented a land grant program called Build On Our Lot to lure businesses to Taylor City, Austin, Texas. They are targeting small businesses, especially those in the renewable energy, advanced manufacturing, technical services and food products. Program details are included.

5518 ■ "Testing Firm to Add Jobs" in *Business Courier* (Vol. 26, December 11, 2009, No. 33, pp. 1)
Pub: American City Business Journals, Inc.
Ed: Dan Monk. **Description:** Cincinnati-based Q Laboratories announced plans to add dozens of jobs with the $1.6 million stimulus assisted expansion. The company hired Michael Lichtenberg & Sons Construction Co. to build a new 9,000 square foot laboratory building.

5519 ■ "Texas State Poised for Boom" in *Austin Business Journallnc.* (Vol. 29, January 29, 2010, No. 47, pp. 1)
Pub: American City Business Journals
Ed: Sandra Zaragoza. **Description:** Texas State University, San Marcos has seen its student population grow to 30,800 and the university is set for $633 million in construction projects to address demand for student housing and building expansions and renovations. Details on the buildings and student housing plans for the projects are provided.

5520 ■ "That Empty Feeling" in *Crain's Cleveland Business* (Vol. 28, October 15, 2007, No. 41, pp. 1)
Pub: Crain Communications, Inc.
Ed: Stan Bullard. **Description:** Townhouses, cluster homes and condominiums lured both buyers and builders for most of this decade but now that market is suffering to an even greater degree than the single-family home market. Statistical data included.

5521 ■ "Things Fall Apart" in *Canadian Business* (Vol. 80, October 8, 2007, No. 20, pp. 187)
Pub: Rogers Media
Ed: Jeff Sanford. **Description:** Infrastructure crisis in Canada and in other countries in North America is examined. Incidents that demonstrate this crisis, such as the collapse of a bridge in Minneapolis and the collapse of an overpass in Quebec, Canada are presented. It is estimated that the reconstruction in the country will cost between C$44 billion and C$200 billion.

5522 ■ "This Just In" in *Crain's Detroit Business* (Vol. 25, June 22, 2009, No. 25, pp. 1)
Pub: Crain Communications Inc. - Detroit
Description: Yamasaki Associates, an architectural firm has been sued for non payment of wages to four employees. Yamasaki spokesperson stated the economy has affected the company and it is focusing marketing efforts on areas encouraged by recovery funding.

5523 ■ "Threat of New Office Space Records Rent Hikes" in *Globe & Mail* (March 21, 2007, pp. B4)
Pub: CTVglobemedia Publishing Inc.
Ed: Elizabeth Church. **Description:** The increasing commercial rent prices in the Toronto region amid the high office building construction market are discussed.

5524 ■ "Times are Tough, I Figure I'm Tougher" in *Inc.* (Vol. 33, September 2011, No. 7, pp. 92)
Pub: Inc. Magazine
Ed: April Joyner. **Description:** Profile of Frank Campanaro and his company, Trillacorpe Construction located in Bingham Farms, Michigan. Campanaro has partnered with other companies that have bonding in reserve and lets them take the lion's share.

5525 ■ "Top 100 Consolidate Gains" in *Hispanic Business* (Vol. 30, July-August 2008, No. 7-8, pp. 30)
Pub: Hispanic Business, Inc.
Ed: Richard Kaplan. **Description:** Data developed by HispanTelligence on the increase in revenue posted by the top 100 fastest-growing U.S. Hispanic firms over the last five years is reported. Despite the economic downturn, the service sector, IT and health suppliers showed an increase in revenue whereas construction companies showed a marginal slump in revenue growth.

5526 ■ "Traffic Slows at O'Hare; As Airlines Cut Flights, City Tries to Push Expansion Forward" in *Crain's Chicago Business* (April 28, 2008)
Pub: Crain Communications, Inc.
Ed: Paul Merrion; John Pletz. **Description:** O'Hare International Airport is seeing a decline in passenger traffic just as the city of Chicago presses cash-strapped airlines to fund the second phase of the airport's expansion which would include the extension of one runway, the relocation of two others and the construction of a new western terminal.

5527 ■ "Trisun Healthcare Eager to Add Centers" in *Austin Business Journallnc.* (Vol. 28, August 22, 2008, No. 23, pp. 1)
Pub: American City Business Journals
Ed: Kate Harrington. **Description:** Austin-based nursing and rehabilitation centers operator Trisun Healthcare plans to build more facilities as part of a growth strategy that can expand beyond Texas. Trisun has 16 facilities along the corridor from San Antonio to Temple, and projects to have three more in Texas in 2008.

5528 ■ "Troubled Project In Court" in *The Business Journal-Portland* (Vol. 25, July 25, 2008, No. 20, pp. 1)
Pub: American City Business Journals, Inc.
Ed: Wendy Culverwell. **Description:** Views and information on Salpare Bay's Hayden Island project, as well as on financing problems and cases associated with the project, are presented. Construction of

luxurious waterside condominiums stopped last fall, after the discovery of financing problems and subcontractors and other parties started filing claims and counterclaims.

5529 ■ "The Turkey Has Landed" in *Canadian Business* (Vol. 79, November 20, 2006, No. 23, pp. 38)
Pub: Rogers Media
Ed: Erik Heinrich. **Description:** The design and construction of Toronto Pearson International Airport to handle domestic, international and transborder flights in one facility is discussed.

5530 ■ "UA Turns Ann Arbor Green" in *Contractor* (Vol. 56, September 2009, No. 9, pp. 5)
Pub: Penton Media, Inc.
Ed: Robert P. Mader. **Description:** Instructors at the United Association of Plumbers and Steamfitters have studied the latest in green and sustainable construction and service at the Washtenaw Community College in Michigan. Classes included building information modeling, hydronic heating and cooling and advanced HVACR troubleshooting. The UA is currently focusing on green training.

5531 ■ "The Ultimate Comfort System" in *Contractor* (Vol. 56, July 2009, No. 7, pp. 30)
Pub: Penton Media, Inc.
Ed: Mark Eatherton. **Description:** Retrofitting of a hydronic heating system to an existing home is presented. The project approaches near net-zero energy production.

5532 ■ "UMKC, Hospital Drill Down on Deal" in *The Business Journal-Serving Metropolitan Kansas City* (Vol. 26, July 18, 2008, No. 45, pp. 1)
Pub: American City Business Journals, Inc.
Ed: Rob Roberts. **Description:** University of Missouri Kansas City and Children's Mercy Hospital are negotiating the hospital's potential acquisition of the university's School of Dentistry building. The deal would transfer the 240,000-square foot dental school building to Children's Mercy. Plans for a new dental school building for the UMKC are also presented.

5533 ■ "USF Plans $30M Sports Complex" in *Tampa Bay Business Journal* (Vol. 29, October 23, 2009, No. 44, pp. 1)
Pub: American City Business Journals
Ed: Jane Meinhardt. **Description:** University of South Florida (USF) is going to build a new sports complex with the aid of a $30 million loan from BB&T. The project, which is also comprised of new and renovated athletic facilities on USF's Tampa campus, is projected to create more than $37 million in revenue in its first year. Revenues from the said facilities are expected to achieve an annual growth of at least four percent.

5534 ■ "VA Seeking Bidders for Ft. Howard" in *Baltimore Business Journal* (Vol. 28, June 25, 2010, No. 7, pp. 1)
Pub: Baltimore Business Journal
Ed: Daniel J. Sernovitz. **Description:** The Veterans Affairs Maryland Health Care Systems has requested proposals from developers to build a retirement community at Fort Howard in Baltimore County. The historic site, which has about 36 mostly vacant buildings, could become the home to hundreds of war veterans. Details of the proposed development are discussed.

5535 ■ "Vernon Revamp" in *Business Courier* (Vol. 26, October 9, 2009, No. 24, pp. 1)
Pub: American City Business Journals, Inc.
Ed: Dan Monk. **Description:** Al Neyer Inc. will redevelop the Vernon Manor Hotel as an office building for the Cincinnati Children's Hospital Medical Center. The project will cost $35 million and would generate a new investment vehicle for black investors who plan to raise $2.7 million in private offerings to claim majority ownership of the property after its renovations.

5536 ■ "Vision for Camden in Better Focus" in *Philadelphia Business Journal* (Vol. 30, September 30, 2011, No. 33, pp. 1)
Pub: American City Business Journals Inc.
Ed: Natalie Kostelni. **Description:** More than $500 million worth of projects aimed at redeveloping the downtown and waterfront areas of Camden, New Jersey are being planned. These include the construction of residential, commercial, and education buildings.

5537 ■ "Wal-Mart Proposed for Timmerman Plaza" in *Business Journal-Milwaukee* (Vol. 28, December 31, 2010, No. 14, pp. A1)
Pub: Milwaukee Business Journal
Ed: Sean Ryan. **Description:** Dickson, Tennessee-based Gatlin Development Company Inc. owner Franklin C. Gatlin III revealed plans for a new Wal-Mart store in Timmerman Plaza in Milwaukee, Wisconsin. Wal-Mart plans to open up approximately 18 new stores in southeast Wisconsin in 2012 and the Timmerman project is the first of four that Gatlin will submit for city approval.

5538 ■ "Was Mandating Solar Power Water Heaters For New Homes Good Policy?" in *Hawaii Business* (Vol. 54, August 2008, No. 2, pp. 28)
Pub: Hawaii Business Publishing
Description: Senator Gary L. Kooser of District 7 Kauai-Niihau believes that the mandating of energy-efficient water heaters for new single-family homes starting in 2010 will help cut Hawaii's oil consumption. Ron Richmond of the Hawaii Solar Energy Association says that the content of SB 644 has negative consequences as it allows for choice of energy and not just solar, and it also eliminates tax credits for new homebuyers.

5539 ■ "Water Conservation Helps GC's Building Attain LEED Gold Status" in *Contractor* (Vol. 56, September 2009, No. 9, pp. 5)
Pub: Penton Media, Inc.
Description: Green contractor Marshall Erdman has built a new office building using green design. The facility is seen to become a prime Leadership in Energy and Environmental Design (LEED) building model. Details of the building's design and features are also provided.

5540 ■ "Water Park, Convention Center Plan Matures" in *Austin Business JournalInc.* (Vol. 28, July 18, 2008, No. 18, pp. 1)
Pub: American City Business Journals
Ed: Kate Harrington. **Description:** Plans for the proposed water park in Cedar Park in Austin, Texas is moving forward as it grows in size from 40 to 90 acres, with first phase of construction to begin in early 2009.

5541 ■ "Watershed Solution" in *Business Courier* (Vol. 24, December 14, 2008, No. 35, pp. 1)
Pub: American City Business Journals, Inc.
Ed: Dan Monk. **Description:** Discusses the Metropolitan Sewer District of Greater Cincinnati which is planning to spend around $128 million for its 20-year green-infrastructure improvement projects. Part of the project involves construction of green roofs, rain gardens and restored wetlands to manage water overflows.

5542 ■ "Wayne, Oakland Counties Create Own 'Medical Corridor'" in *Crain's Detroit Business* (Vol. 24, October 6, 2008, No. 40, pp. 8)
Pub: Crain Communications, Inc.
Ed: Jay Greene. **Description:** Woodward Medical Corridor that runs along Woodward Avenue and currently encompasses twelve hospitals and is rapidly growing with additional physician offices, advanced oncology centers and new hospitals. Beaumont Hospital is building a $160 million proton-beam therapy cancer center on its Royal Oak campus in a joint venture with Procure Treatment Centers of Bloomington Ind. That is expected to open in 2010 and will employ approximately 145 new workers.

5543 ■ "What Happens in Vegas Could Happen in Baltimore, Too" in *Boston Business Journal* (Vol. 29, June 17, 2011, No. 6, pp. 1)
Pub: American City Business Journals Inc.
Ed: Daniel J. Sernovitz. **Description:** At least 36 companies expressed their interest in developing a casino in South Baltimore following the state commission's announcement for bids. Developers have until July 28, 2011 to submit their proposals. Baltimore's strong economy is the major factor for the interest, yet the fact that blackjack and poker are outlawed in Maryland could be a drawback.

5544 ■ "What Homes Do Retirees Want?" in *Canadian Business* (Vol. 79, July 17, 2006, No. 14-15, pp.)
Pub: Rogers Media
Ed: Joe Cataldo. **Description:** The obstacles and challenges faced by homebuilders in Canada as well as the approach adopted by them to appeal to the mature homebuilders segment, is discussed.

5545 ■ "What Players in the Midmarket Are Talking About" in *Mergers & Acquisitions: The Dealmaker's Journal* (March 1, 2008)
Pub: SourceMedia, Inc.
Description: Sports Properties Acquisition Corp. went public at the end of January; according to the company's prospectus, it is not limiting its focus to just teams, it is also considering deals for stadium construction companies, sports leagues, facilities, sports-related advertising and licensing of products, in addition to other related segments.

5546 ■ "What's Good Faith Got to Do With Contracts?" in *Contractor* (Vol. 56, November 2009, No. 11, pp. 41)
Pub: Penton Media, Inc.
Ed: Susan Linden McGreevy. **Description:** Uniform Commercial Code makes the obligation to act in good faith a term of every commercial transaction. The code generally applies to the sale of goods and not to construction contracts but parties to a construction contract have the right to expect people to act in good faith and forego actions not related to the contract itself.

5547 ■ "Where Are the Vultures?" in *Mergers & Acquisitions: The Dealmaker's Journal* (March 1, 2008)
Pub: SourceMedia, Inc.
Ed: Ken MacFadyen. **Description:** Although the real estate market is distressed, not many acquisitions are being made by distress private equity investors; this is due, in part, to the difficulty in assessing real estate industry firms since it is a sector which is so localized.

5548 ■ "Will Home Buyers Pay for Green Features?" in *Contractor* (Vol. 56, October 2009, No. 10, pp. 70)
Pub: Penton Media, Inc.
Ed: Bob Mader. **Description:** National Association of Home Builders commissioned a survey which shows that homeowners are interested in green as long as they do no have to pay much for it. The association did not allow a board member to read the survey which raises questions about how the questions were phrased and how the sample was selected.

5549 ■ "Will Workers Be Left To Build It Here?" in *Boston Business Journal* (Vol. 31, June 3, 2011, No. 19, pp. 1)
Pub: Boston Business Journal
Ed: Kyle Alspach. **Description:** Lack of skilled workers has resulted in delayed expansion of local manufacturing operations in Massachusetts. Acme Packet Inc. expects to add only 10 jobs by the end of 2011.

5550 ■ "With Building Plans in Flux, County Could Sell Key Site" in *Crain's Cleveland Business* (Vol. 28, October 8, 2007, No. 40, pp. 1)
Pub: Crain Communications, Inc.
Ed: Jay Miller. **Description:** Due to such issues as financial and administrative problems, Cuyahoga County commissioners have pushed back the con-

struction timeline for a planned county administration center and are saying that they are considering selling the site in downtown Cleveland to developers who would erect a new office building that another large tenant could occupy.

5551 ■ "Yates Helps Turn Log Home Green" in *Contractor* (Vol. 56, November 2009, No. 11, pp. 1)
Pub: Penton Media, Inc.
Description: Dave Yates of F.W. Behler Inc. helped homeowners from James Creek, Pennsylvania achieve energy efficiency on the heating system of their log cabin. The mechanical system installed on the cabin had high-temp "THW" water-to-water geothermal system by ClimateMaster, two twin-coil indirect water heaters, and several pre-assembled, pre-engineered Hydronex panels by Watts Radiant.

5552 ■ "Your Place: Housing Developers Try to Read Generation Y" in *Philadelphia Inquirer* (December 2, 2010)
Pub: Philadelphia Media Network Inc.
Ed: Al Heavens. **Description:** Results of a survey conducted with Generation Y individuals are examined, focusing on housing developments and whether this particular generation prefers suburban or rural lifestyles. Generation Y encompasses people ages 18 to 32 years old. Statistical data included.

5553 ■ "Yudelson Challenges San Antonio Groups" in *Contractor* (Vol. 56, October 2009, No. 10, pp. 6)
Pub: Penton Media, Inc.
Description: Green building consultant and author Jerry Yudelson made a presentation for the Central Texas Green Building Council and Leadership San Antonio where he discussed the European approach to sustainability and how it can be used for designing green buildings. Yudelson also discussed how to use sustainable practices for planning 25 years into the future.

5554 ■ "ZF Revving Up Jobs, Growth" in *Business Courier* (Vol. 26, November 6, 2009, No. 28, pp. 1)
Pub: American City Business Journals, Inc.
Ed: Jon Newberry. **Description:** Proposed $96 million expansion of German-owned automotive supplier ZF Steering systems LLC is anticipated to generate 299 jobs in Boone County, Kentucky. ZF might invest $90 million in equipment, while the rest will go to building and improvements.

STATISTICAL SOURCES

5555 ■ *Means Labor Rates for the Construction Industry*
Pub: R. S. Means Co., Inc.
Released: Annual. **Price:** $379.95 (paper).

5556 ■ *RMA Annual Statement Studies*
Pub: Robert Morris Associates (RMA)
Released: Annual. **Price:** $175.00 2006-07 edition, $105.00. **Description:** Contains composite balance sheets and income statements for more than 360 industries, including the accounting, auditing, and bookkeeping industries. Also contains five years of comparative historical data for discerning trends. Includes 16 commonly used ratios, computed for most of the size groupings for nearly every industry.

5557 ■ *Standard & Poor's Industry Surveys*
Pub: Standard & Poor's Corp.
Released: Annual. **Price:** $3633.00. **Description:** Two-volume book that examines the prospects for specific industries, including trucking. Also provides analyses of trends and problems, statistical tables and charts, and comparative company analyses.

TRADE PERIODICALS

5558 ■ *AMD Newsletter*
Pub: Association of Millwork Distributors
Ed: Released: Monthly. **Price:** Included in membership; $40, nonmembers. **Description:** Reports on Association activities, government rulings, home building statistics, activities of members, and various other subjects of interest to sash and door jobbers.

5559 ■ *AppendX*
Pub: Appendx
Released: Annual. **Description:** Professional journal covering architecture criticism.

5560 ■ *Architects' Guide to Glass, Metal & Glazing*
Pub: Key Communications Inc.
Released: 6/yr. **Price:** $19 one day; $39 one month; $259; Free to qualified subscribers. **Description:** Trade annual covering glass for architects.

5561 ■ *Architectural Designs*
Pub: Architectural Designs Inc.
Released: Quarterly. **Description:** Consumer magazine offering over 200 house plans.

5562 ■ *Builder*
Pub: Hanley-Wood L.L.C.
Contact: Deborah Leopold, Managing Editor
E-mail: dleopold@hanleywood.com
Released: 13/yr. **Price:** $29.95 U.S. and Canada; $54.95 U.S. and Canada 2 years; $192 other countries. **Description:** Magazine covering housing and construction industry.

5563 ■ *Builder Insider*
Pub: Divibest Inc.
Contact: Michael J. Anderson, Editor & Publisher
Released: Monthly. **Description:** Magazine (tabloid) for builders, architects, and remodelers of the Greater Texas Region.

5564 ■ *Building Standards*
Pub: International Code Council
Contact: Peggy Nila
Ed: Greg Layne, Editor, glayne@icbo.org. **Released:** 6/year. **Price:** $25; $40 2 years; $55 3 years. **Description:** Provides articles of interest to building officials, architects, engineers, and others in the construction industry. The newsletter is part of Building Standards magazine subscription.

5565 ■ *California Builder & Engineer*
Pub: California Builder & Engineer Inc.
Released: Biweekly. **Price:** $30; $2 single issue. **Description:** Magazine on California, Hawaii, Western Nevada, and Western Arizona building and engineering.

5566 ■ *CE News*
Pub: Mercor Media
Contact: Shanon M. Fauerbach, Editorial Inquiries
Released: Monthly. **Description:** Trade magazine serving civil engineers and land surveyors engaged in land development, highways, bridges, structural, environmental, geotechnical, water resources, and industrial engineering projects including surveying.

5567 ■ *C.F.M.A. Building Profits*
Pub: Construction Financial Management Association
Contact: Ron Kress, Sales & Advertising managing editorager
E-mail: rkress@cfma.org
Released: Bimonthly. **Price:** $320 contractor; $420 industry service provider. **Description:** Trade magazine covering construction financial management.

5568 ■ *CM Advisor*
Pub: Construction Management Association of America Inc.
Contact: Dannelle Prezioso
Ed: Dannelle Prezioso, Editor, dprezioso@cmaanet.org. **Released:** Bimonthly. **Price:** Included in membership. **Description:** Provides information on construction management and its technical, legal, and legislative issues. Recurring features include letters to the editor, news of research, a calendar of events, reports of meetings, news of educational opportunities, book reviews, notices of publications available, and columns titled Government Affairs and For Your Information

5569 ■ *Construction Briefings*
Pub: Thomson West
Ed: Lisa C. Weltsch, Editor, lisa.weltsch@westgroup.com. **Released:** Monthly. **Price:** $1464.00. **Description:** Covers issues in construction contracting.

5570 ■ *Construction Contracts Law Report*
Pub: Thomson West
Ed: Richard L. Shea, Editor, richard.shea@westgroup.com. **Released:** Biweekly. **Price:** $1679.04 year. **Description:** Contains news, insight, and analysis of construction industry developments and cases.

5571 ■ *Construction Division Newsletter*
Pub: NSC Press
Ed: Laura Coyne, Editor. **Released:** Bimonthly. **Price:** $15, members; $19, nonmembers. **Description:** Focuses on industrial and occupational safety in the construction industry. Carries items on such topics as safe work practices and products; accident prevention; and successful industrial safety programs and policies. Remarks: Available online only

5572 ■ *Construction Exec.*
Pub: Associated Builders and Contractors Inc.
Contact: Lisa A. Nardone, Editor-in-Chief
E-mail: nardone@abc.org
Released: Monthly. **Price:** Free to qualified subscribers. **Description:** Magazine for contractors and subcontractors. Includes articles on national and regional construction news, construction management, project case histories, new products, building design, and legislative and regulatory updates.

5573 ■ *Construction Litigation Reporter*
Pub: Thomson West
Contact: Susan M Anderson
Ed: Marc Schneier, Editor. **Released:** 11/year. **Price:** $1322.96, individuals. **Description:** Consists of articles, case digests, and commentary covering recent litigation in the construction field. Recurring features include lists of expert witnesses.

5574 ■ *Construction Reports*
Pub: U.S. Government Printing Office and Superintendent of Documents
Released: Monthly. **Price:** $16; $22.40 other countries; $4.25 single issue; $5.95 other countries single issue. **Description:** Provides monthly statistics for the United States and regions on new privately owned housing units started, authorized in permit-issuing places; and authorized, but not started at end of period.

5575 ■ *Construction Specifications Institute—Newsdigest*
Pub: The Construction Specifications Institute
Ed: Dan Merriman, Editor, dmerriman@csinet.org. **Released:** Monthly. **Price:** Included in membership; $48, nonmembers. **Description:** Covers the technical and certification programs offered by the Institute, which is "dedicated to the advancement of construction technology through service, education, and research." Also reports on regional and chapter activities and carries items on educational programs related to the construction industry. Recurring features include news of members, a calendar of events, listings of new publications available through the Institute, and columns titled Board Flash, Convention Briefs, and T.I.E. (Technical Information and Education Activities).

5576 ■ *The Construction Specifier*
Pub: The Construction Specifications Institute
Released: Monthly. **Price:** $59; $99 two years; $69 Canada; $109 Canada two years; $199 other countries; $16.50 members. **Description:** Magazine.

5577 ■ *Constructor*
Pub: Associated General Contractors of America
Contact: Monica Cardenas, Assoc. Dir.
E-mail: cardenasm@agc.org
Released: Bimonthly. **Price:** $95. **Description:** Management magazine for the Construction Industry.

5578 ■ *Construire*
Pub: Association de la construction du Quebec
Released: Bimonthly. **Description:** French language trade magazine for the commercial industrial, institutional, and residential construction companies within the province of Quebec.

5579 ■ *Contractors Hot Line Monthly*
Pub: Heartland Communications Group Inc.
Released: Monthly. **Price:** $15.95 single issue. **Description:** Buy, sell, trade publication for the heavy construction industry.

5580 ■ *Current Housing Reports*
Pub: U.S. Government Printing Office and Superintendent of Documents
Released: Quarterly. **Price:** $18; $25.20 other countries. **Description:** Provides statistics on apartments completed in the United States and regions, based on preliminary figures from the survey of market absorptions. covers only privately financed, nonsubsidized apartments in buildings with five units or more.

5581 ■ *Design Cost Data*
Pub: DC & D Technologies Inc.
Contact: Barbara Castelli, Pres./Publisher
E-mail: barb@dcd.com
Released: Bimonthly. **Price:** $94 silver; $99 two years silver; $149 gold; $149.01 two years gold. **Description:** Publication providing real cost data case studies of various types completed around the country for design and building professionals.

5582 ■ *ECA Magazine*
Pub: Engineering Contractors Association
Contact: Michael Prlich, President
Released: Monthly. **Description:** Magazine for the construction engineering field.

5583 ■ *Environmental Building News*
Pub: Building Green Inc.
Ed: Alexander T. Wilson, Editor, alex@buildinggreen.com. **Released:** Monthly. **Price:** $99, individuals U.S.; $199 for organization; $169, two years for individuals; $359, two years for organization. **Description:** Covers the building trade with an environmental slant. Covers nontoxic materials, better landscaping and water use, and resources for energy conservation in a technical manner.

5584 ■ *Fine Homebuilding*
Pub: Taunton Press Inc.
Ed: Kevin Ireton, Editor, kireton@taunton.com. **Released:** 8/yr. **Price:** $37.95 U.S. and Canada; $65.95 U.S. and Canada two years; $93.95 U.S. and Canada three years. **Description:** Magazine for builders, architects, designers, and owner-builders.

5585 ■ *Heavy Equipment Guide*
Pub: Baum Publications Ltd.
Contact: Robin McCabe
E-mail: circulation@baumpub.com
Released: 10/yr. **Description:** Trade publication for the construction, mining, truck, and municipal industries.

5586 ■ *Housing Economics*
Pub: Economics Dept.
Released: Monthly. **Description:** Presents statistical data on the housing industry and includes news of governmental agency actions, business and economic trends, and housing trends. Analyzes the interrelationship between housing and the economy as well as between the industry and government policy. Recurring features include building permit activity, employment rates, and housing opportunity index.

5587 ■ *Interior Construction*
Pub: Ceilings and Interior Systems Construction Association
Released: Bimonthly. **Price:** $35 nonmembers; $35 members. **Description:** Magazine covering interior system construction.

5588 ■ *Intermountain Contractor*
Pub: McGraw-Hill Inc.
Contact: Mark Shaw, Editor-in-Chief
E-mail: mark_shaw@mcgraw-hill.com
Ed: Melissa Leslie, Editor, melissa_leslie@mcgraw-hill.com. **Released:** Weekly. **Price:** $40. **Description:** Building and construction industry magazine covering upcoming engineering and building projects in the mountain regions of the western U.S., and construction business news.

5589 ■ *Journal of Construction Accounting and Taxation*
Pub: RIA
Contact: Rosanne Dobbin, Managing Editor
Released: Bimonthly. **Price:** $285 print; $310 online. **Description:** Trade journal covering construction business management.

5590 ■ *Metal Architecture*
Pub: Modern Trade Communications Inc.
Contact: Kate Gawlik, Editorial Dir.
E-mail: kgawlik@moderntrade.com
Released: Monthly. **Price:** $75 Canada and Mexico; $150 other countries; $45. **Description:** Trade journal serving architectural, engineering, and construction firms.

5591 ■ *Midwest Contractor*
Pub: Reed Construction Data
Contact: Greg Sitek, Editorial Dir.
E-mail: gsitek@reedbusiness.com
Released: Semimonthly. **Description:** Construction news magazine covering project bids and awards, new construction planning, industry trend articles, legislation, regulations, meeting coverage, interviews, and new products. News source for contractors, public officials, and equipment and material suppliers, in Iowa, Kansas, Nebraska, and western and northeastern Missouri.

5592 ■ *The NAWIC Image*
Pub: National Association of Women in Construction (NAWIC)
Contact: Tamie Taylor, President
E-mail: karar@nawic.org
Ed: Leona P. Dalavai, Editor, leonad@nawic.org. **Released:** 6/year. **Price:** $50, nonmembers. **Description:** Fosters career advancement for women in construction. Features women business owners, training for construction trades and educational programs. Recurring features include columns titled Issues and Trends, Road to Success, Chapter Highlights, Members on the Move, and Q&A.

5593 ■ *Panel World*
Pub: Hatton-Brown Publishers Inc.
Contact: Jennifer McCary, Sen. Assoc. Ed.
E-mail: jmccary@hattonbrowwn.com
Ed: Rich Donnell, Editor, rich@hattonbrown.com. **Released:** Bimonthly. **Price:** $50; $60 Canada; $24.95 full online; $9.95 limited online; $95 other countries. **Description:** Business magazine serving the worldwide veneer, plywood, and panel board industry.

5594 ■ *Pavement*
Pub: Cygnus Business Media
Contact: Barb Levin, Sales Rep.
E-mail: barb.levin@cygnuspub.com
Released: 8/yr. **Description:** Trade magazine serving contractors who work in the paving, sealcoating, pavement marking and sweeping industry.

5595 ■ *Practice Periodical on Structural Design and Construction*
Pub: American Society of Civil Engineers
Contact: Anatol Longinow PhD, Exec. Council Ed.
Released: Quarterly. **Price:** $389 institutions print & online; $409 institutions, other countries print & online; $342 institutions print; $362 institutions, other countries print; $311 U.S. and other countries online; $97 members print & online; $117 members international; print & online; $86 members print; $106 members international; print; $78 U.S. and other countries online only. **Description:** Peer-reviewed journal tracking topics and future developments in structural design and construction.

5596 ■ *Professional Builder*
Pub: SGC Horizon LLC
Contact: Patrick O'Toole, Editorial Dir./Publisher
E-mail: potoole@sgcmail.com
Ed: David Barista, Editor, dbarista@sgcmail.com. **Released:** Monthly. **Description:** The integrated engineering magazine of the building construction industry.

5597 ■ *Remodeling*
Pub: Hanley-Wood L.L.C.
Released: 13/yr. **Price:** $25; $40 Canadian residents; $192 international residents. **Description:** Trade magazine for the professional remodeling industry.

5598 ■ *Roofing Contractor*
Pub: BNP Media
Contact: Jill Bloom, Gp. Publisher
E-mail: blooj@bnpmedia.com
Released: Monthly. **Price:** $25 Free to qualified subscribers; $5; $5 single issue. **Description:** Trade magazine on roofing and insulation.

5599 ■ *Rural Builder*
Pub: FW Media Inc.
Contact: Kyler Pope, Advertising Rep.
E-mail: kyler.pope@fwmedia.com
Released: 7/yr. **Description:** Trade magazine serving the rural construction market and covering building/remodeling of grain, commercial, light industrial, recreational, residential, farm and turn-key equipment projects.

5600 ■ *Solar Today*
Pub: American Solar Energy Society
Contact: Brooke Simmons, managing editorager of Online Publishing
E-mail: bsimmons@solartoday.org
Released: 6/yr. **Description:** Journal covering the business, policy and technology of renewable energy, from wind systems and energy-efficient devices to green building.

5601 ■ *System-Built Advantage*
Pub: National Association of Home Builders
Ed: Barbara Martin, Editor. **Released:** Monthly. **Price:** Included in membership. **Description:** Carries industry and Council news for manufacturers of systems-built housing and suppliers. Recurring features include legislative updates, a calendar of events, news of research, announcements of educational opportunities, and meeting reports.

5602 ■ *Timber Framing*
Pub: Timber Framers Guild
Ed: Ken Rower, Editor. **Released:** Quarterly. **Price:** $25 Free with membership; $25 nonmembers. **Description:** Trade magazine covering timber frame design home construction, history, restoration, and preservation.

5603 ■ *Traditional Building*
Pub: Historical Trends Corp.
Contact: Judith Lief, Managing Editor
Released: Bimonthly. **Price:** $21.95; $65 Canada; $35.95 two years. **Description:** Magazine for architects, contractors, and interior designers.

5604 ■ *Western Builder*
Pub: Reed Construction Data
Released: Weekly (Thurs.). **Price:** $125. **Description:** Magazine for construction industry.

5605 ■ *Wood Design & Building*
Pub: Canadian Wood Council
Ed: Bernadette Johnson, Editor, bjohnson@dvtail.com. **Released:** Quarterly. **Price:** $24; $40 two years; $55 two years and other countries; $35 other countries; $50 Canada 3 years; $70 other countries 3 years. **Description:** Trade magazine for construction professionals in the U.S.

5606 ■ *Words From Woody*
Pub: David W. Wood
Ed: David W. Wood, Editor. **Released:** Quarterly. **Price:** $24.95; $39.95, two years. **Description:** Contains information of interest to construction-related firms. Also includes business and marketing tips.

VIDEOCASSETTES/ AUDIOCASSETTES

5607 ■ *Construction Systems Technology*
Bergwall Productions, Inc.
1 DIckinson Drive, Brandywine BUilding 5, Ste. 105
PO Box 1481
Chadds Ford, PA 19317

Ph:(610)361-0334
Free: 800-934-8696
Fax:(610)361-0092
URL: http://www.bergwall.com
Released: 1989. **Price:** $369.00. **Description:** Modern construction technologies and methodologies are examined. **Availability:** VHS.

5608 ■ *Safety Orientation for Construction Contractors*
DuPont Safety Resources
PO Box 80013
Wilmington, DE 19880-0013
Free: 800-532-7233
Fax:888-644-7233
URL: http://www2.dupont.com/Sustainable_Solutions/en_US/practice_areas/safety_consultants/index.html
Released: 1993. **Price:** $475.00. **Description:** Designed to raise and promote safety consciousness among construction contractors and their employees. Includes an administrator's guide and personal handbooks outlining site safety rules and work practices. **Availability:** VHS.

5609 ■ *The 3-Point Contact*
Film Library/National Safety Council California Chapter
4553 Glencoe Ave., Ste. 150
Marina Del Rey, CA 90292
Ph:(310)827-9781
Free: 800-421-9585
Fax:(310)827-9861
Co. E-mail: California@nsc.org
URL: http://www.nsc.org/nsc_near_you/FindYourLocalChapter/Pages/California.aspx
Released: 198?. **Description:** This program demonstrates the safest ways to mount and dismount heavy construction equipment. **Availability:** VHS; 3/4U; Special order formats.

TRADE SHOWS AND CONVENTIONS

5610 ■ AEC-ST
Ecobuild Federal, LCC
1645 Falmouth Rd., Ste. 1A
Centerville, MA 02632
Ph:(508)790-4751
Free: 800-996-2863
Fax:(508)790-4750
Co. E-mail: support@ecobuildamerica.com
URL: http://www.aececobuild.com/
Released: Annual. **Audience:** Design and construction professionals, engineers, government officials, facility managers. **Principal Exhibits:** Sustainable and environmental design, energy efficiency, green building, best practices and expert strategies, building information modeling, future of IT trends.

5611 ■ The Builders' Show
National Association of Home Builders of the United States
1201 15th St. NW
Washington, DC 20005
Ph:(202)266-8200
Free: 800-368-5242
Fax:(202)266-8223
Co. E-mail: exposales@nahb.com
URL: http://www.nahb.org
Released: Annual. **Audience:** Trade. **Principal Exhibits:** Building products, equipment, and services. **Dates and Locations:** 2011 Jan 14 - Feb 17, Orlando, FL; 2012 Jan 13-16, Orlando, FL.

5612 ■ CAM Expo
Construction Association of Michigan
43636 Woodward Ave.
PO Box 3204
Bloomfield Hills, MI 48302
Ph:(248)972-1000
Fax:(248)972-1001
Co. E-mail: marketing@cam-online.com
URL: http://www.cam-online.com
Released: Annual. **Audience:** Trade professionals. **Principal Exhibits:** Construction industry equipment, supplies, and services.

5613 ■ CONEXPO-CON/AGG
Association of Equipment Manufacturers AEM
6737 W. Washington St., Ste. 2400
Milwaukee, WI 53214-5647
Ph:(414)272-0943
Fax:(414)272-1170
Co. E-mail: aem@aem.org
URL: http://www.aem.org
Released: Annual. **Audience:** Construction and related equipment contractors, manufacturers, distributors, engineers, and government officials. **Principal Exhibits:** Construction and construction materials industry equipment, supplies, and services. **Dates and Locations:** 2011 Mar 22-26, Las Vegas, NV.

5614 ■ Indiana's Midwest Builders Convention
Indiana Builders Association
101 W. Ohio St., Ste. 1111
Indianapolis, IN 46204
Ph:(317)917-1100
Free: 800-377-6334
Fax:(317)917-0335
Co. E-mail: info@buildindiana.org
URL: http://www.buildindiana.org
Released: Annual. **Audience:** Builders, remodelers, and subcontractors. **Principal Exhibits:** Building supplies, including windows, doors, and insulation; title insurance information.

5615 ■ Power Show Ohio
Ohio-Michigan Equipment Dealers Association
6124 Avery Rd.
PO Box 68
Dublin, OH 43017
Ph:(614)889-1309
Fax:(614)889-0463
Co. E-mail: ostaff@omeda.org
URL: http://www.omeda.org
Released: Annual. **Audience:** Trade professionals and general public. **Principal Exhibits:** Construction equipment, agricultural equipment, and outdoor power equipment.

CONSULTANTS

5616 ■ A/R/C Associates Inc.
601 N Fern Creek Ave., Ste. 100
Orlando, FL 32803-4899
Ph:(407)896-7875
Fax:(407)898-6043
Co. E-mail: info@arc-arc.com
URL: http://www.arc-arc.com
Contact: Donald G. Dorner, President
E-mail: jjw@atsarc-arc.com
Scope: Architectural firm with specialized capacities in roof consulting and construction technology. Services include: Facility evaluation reports, construction document preparation, bidding and negotiation, construction contract observation and contract administration; roof consulting-roof investigation and analysis, roof inspection and maintenance scheduling, roof litigation and expert testimony, and historical roof preservation and restoration.

5617 ■ Breen & Associates Inc.
PO Box 120424
Arlington, TX 76012
Ph:(817)275-4711
Fax:(817)275-4711
Co. E-mail: jbreen504@aol.com
URL: http://www.breenengineering.com
Contact: James E. Breen, President
E-mail: jbreen504@aol.com
Scope: Building construction consultants offering complete inspection services of residential and commercial structures (includes structural, equipment and systems). Clients include real estate brokers, investors (real estate) and builders/developers.

5618 ■ C. E. Jackson, Jr.
1103 Virginia Ave.
PO Box 1226
McComb, MS 39649-1226
Ph:(601)684-1107
Fax:(601)684-4232
Co. E-mail: cejjrpe@telepak.net
URL: http://www.telapex.com/lAtcejjrpe/resour01.htm
Contact: C.E. Jackson Jr., President
E-mail: cejjrpe@telepak.net
Scope: Construction consulting services in construction safety, civil engineering, construction management, electrical safety, construction engineering, OSHA regulations, arbitration/mediation, public safety, demolition, steel erection, trenching/excavation, highway work-zone safety, and construction equipment safety.

5619 ■ Capital Project Management Inc.
9 Law Dr., 2nd Fl.
Fairfield, NJ 07004-3233
Ph:(267)464-0500
Free: 888-260-2626
Fax:(267)464-0400
Co. E-mail: cpmi@cpmiteam.com
URL: http://www.cpmiteam.com
Contact: William M. Wolf Jr., Principal
E-mail: wwolf@cpmiteam.com
Scope: Engineering consulting firm specializing in contract dispute analysis and resolution; project management oversight; project controls; and surety evaluations. Specializes in analyzing and resolving construction and manufacturing contract disputes. Evaluates technical, schedule and cost issues; develops dispute resolution strategies; assists in settlement negotiations and provides expert witness testimony. **Publications:** "Dealing with Mid-Course Adjustments in Project Planning and Scheduling, and Resultant Claims"; "The ABCs of DRBs"; "Identifying Concurrent Delay"; "When the Best-Laid Plans Go Astray"; "Techniques and Methods for Assessing Delays". **Seminars:** Demystifying Scheduling, New York, Mar, 2007; Handling Construction Risks2006, Allocate Now or Litigate Later, New York, Apr, 2006; 2005 CPM Case Law - Year in Review and One Slice In Time: Two Competing Perspectives for Analyzing Project Delay, Orlando, Apr, 2006.

5620 ■ Commercial Cost Control Inc.
7399 E Wingspan Way
Scottsdale, AZ 85255
Ph:(770)971-2557
Fax:(817)656-3310
Co. E-mail: info@commercialcostcontrol.com
URL: http://www.commercialcostcontrol.com
Contact: Suzanne Mulcay, Partner
E-mail: smulcay@aol.com
Scope: A construction audit firm dedicated to providing value to clients by reducing or recovering capital and expense cost items while maintaining sensitivity to the partnership between clients and their vendors. Services include construction audit services, lease audit services, subtenant portfolio audits, utility audit and consultation, bill verification, rate audits, deregulation opportunity assessments and accounts payable audit services.

5621 ■ Construction Experts Inc.
2419 Sacada Cir.
PO Box 231832
Encinitas, CA 92023-1832
Ph:(760)634-2474
Co. E-mail: info@constructionguy.com
URL: http://www.constructionguy.com
Contact: David Hahn, Mgr
E-mail: bob@constructionclasses.com
Scope: Provides consultation, assistance and guidance to construction companies in the process of developing in-house construction training programs for both craft and supervisory workers. Provides self-paced and paced online courses for educational institutions and non-profit industry organizations. **Publications:** "Scheduling for Estimators"; "The Cost of Training Construction People"; "Eichleay Formula Calculations". **Seminars:** Training Programs for Construction; Introduction to Construction Estimating; Construction Blueprint Reading; Eichleay Formula Calculations; How to Estimate the Cost of Training.

5622 ■ Construction Interface Services Inc.
2 N Front St., 5th Fl.
PO Box 2582
Wilmington, NC 28401
Ph:(910)762-4165

Free: 888-899-6312
Fax:(910)762-4703
Co. E-mail: info@constructor.com
URL: http://www.constructor.com
Contact: John Bahr, President
E-mail: jlb@constructor.com
Scope: Provides project management consulting services and seminars to contractors, attorneys, sureties, lending institutions, owners and design professionals. **Seminars:** Training and seminars on scheduling, productivity, cost control, documentation, negotiation, change order preparation and claims management.

5623 ■ Construction Testing Inc.
925 N Jerome St.
Allentown, PA 18109
Ph:(610)433-6871
Fax:(610)433-7594
Contact: Dolores J. Demyan, President
Scope: Specializing in testing and inspection of concrete, soil structural steel, aggregates, concrete masonry units and mortar, structural clay brick, bituminous concrete, and high strength non-shrink grout.

5624 ■ Corporate Facility Services Inc.
9 Daffodil Ln.
San Carlos, CA 94070-1552
Ph:(650)610-9111
Fax:(650)610-9119
Co. E-mail: info@corpfacserv.com
URL: http://www.corpfacserv.com
Contact: Jeff Watney, Principle
E-mail: jeff.watney@atscorpfacserv.com
Scope: Provides project management services for construction, furniture and relocation projects in Silicon Valley and the San Francisco Bay Area. Services provided include: planning and budgeting; assessing current and future facility requirements; exploring and analyzing logical approaches; articulating objectives on behalf of management; directing the conceptual design process and developing budget estimates documenting plans for evaluation by management.

5625 ■ Draper & Associates
300 Cahaba Park S, Ste. 202
Birmingham, AL 35243
Ph:(404)256-3601
Free: 800-257-0691
Fax:(404)256-3922
Co. E-mail: crivers@draperandassociates.com
URL: http://www.draperandassociates.com
Contact: Thomas T. Covington, Principal
Scope: Provides construction project management services. Has managed projects ranging from single facility renovations to billion-dollar multi-project environments. **Publications:** "Our Economy Stinks. Your Projects Don't Have To," Sep, 2009; "The Demolition of Bowen Homes," Jul, 2009; "The Art of Listening," Jul, 2009; "Another Meeting," May, 2009; "Giving Hope to All Atlantans," May, 2009; "Do You Need an Upgrade," May, 2009. **Seminars:** Champagne Services of a Beer Budget, Sep, 2009.

5626 ■ Empire Building Diagnostics Inc.
2 Main St.
PO Box 412
Depew, NY 14043
Ph:(716)685-4588
Fax:(716)685-6055
Co. E-mail: empire@ebdinc.com
URL: http://www.ebdinc.com
Contact: Mark Young, President
E-mail: michaely@atsebdinc.com
Scope: Consulting firm that provides a full range of pre-renovation contracting services. Specializes in asbestos abatement, asbestos inspections/consulting, asbestos emergency response, lead testing and abatement, third party representation, project management/specification, concrete/CMU saw cutting/removal, radon testing/consulting, site and structure demolition, industrial services and contracting, commercial cleaning, indoor air quality and tank removal and soil remediation.

5627 ■ Engineering and Technical Consultants Inc.
8930 Old Annapolis Rd., Ste. A
Columbia, MD 21045
Ph:(703)450-6220
Fax:(703)444-2285
Co. E-mail: info@etc-web.com
URL: http://www.etc-web.com
Contact: Thomas Dugger, Mgr
Scope: Provides evaluations, intrusive evaluation, design and specifications, solicitation and review of bids, construction monitoring, administration, forensic investigation, testing, document review, research and negotiations services.

5628 ■ Environmental & Engineering Services Inc.
687 NW 5th St.
Corvallis, OR 97330
Ph:(541)754-1062
Fax:(541)753-3948
Co. E-mail: kelly.guenther@eesinet.com
URL: http://www.eesinet.com
Contact: Ron Anderson, Principle
E-mail: fred.shaub@atseesinet.com
Scope: Provides mechanical, electrical engineering and commissioning services, with a special emphasis in renovation and energy upgrades. Offers a wide range of HVAC, electrical and controls engineering services including feasibility assessments, master planning, budgeting, cost analysis, design, computer aided drafting, energy use modeling, facility management and construction management.

5629 ■ Fanning, Fanning & Associates Inc.
2555 74th St.
Lubbock, TX 79423-1405
Ph:(806)745-2533
Fax:(806)745-3596
Co. E-mail: nfanning@fanningfanning.com
URL: http://www.fanningfanning.com
Contact: William White, Principle
E-mail: bwhite@atsfanningfanning.com
Scope: Firm specializes in engineering services including mechanical, electrical, plumbing design and plant layout, HVAC, energy conservation and management, utilities, fire protection and alarms, central heating and cooling plants and communications for institutional, commercial and industrial buildings. Offers design services for drawings, specifications and bid documents, master planning, engineering reports, estimates, analysis, feasibility studies and construction phase services.

5630 ■ Fard Engineers Inc.
3570 Camino Del Rio N, Ste. 100
San Diego, CA 92108
Ph:(925)932-5505
Fax:(925)932-0555
Co. E-mail: mailbox@fard.com
URL: http://www.fard.com
Contact: Steve Jang, Techical Mgr.
Scope: Designs mechanical and electrical systems for all types of buildings. Serves the construction industry in California, Oregon, Arizona, Washington and Nevada. Specialized in apartment buildings, senior housing complexes and school renovation. **Special Services:** Autocad and Paradox.

5631 ■ Franz Wolf Design & Construction Consultants
96 MacGregor Dr.
Mahopac, NY 10541-2779
Ph:(845)628-5159
Fax:(206)781-1911
Contact: Franz Wolf, Owner
Scope: Architectural consultant offers a wide range of particular and specialized areas of design and construction consulting. Particular expertise available in planning and master planning (sites, buildings, interior space planning, design and review); architectural (interior and exterior from concept to finish); building and zoning codes; and handicapped, local, state and federal laws. Industries served: owners, businesses, corporations, builders, contractors, entrepreneurs, law firms, architects, interior designers, and engineers. **Seminars:** NYC code sessions by NY state code division; NY state energy sessions.

5632 ■ GHT Ltd.
1010 N Glebe Rd., Ste. 200
Arlington, VA 22201-4749
Ph:(703)243-1200
Fax:(703)276-1376
Co. E-mail: ght@ghtltd.com
URL: http://www.ghtltd.com
Contact: Robert M. Menuet Jr., Principle
E-mail: rmenuet@ghtltd.com
Scope: Provides design services in mechanical engineering. Offers telecommunications and security engineering services. Provides life safety engineering services and utilities planning services. Provides estimates of life expectancy and replacement or upgrade costs for mechanical and electrical equipment and systems. **Publications:** "Critical spaces keep the pace of business humming," May, 2004; "To avoid staticlater, hire right telecom consultant," Oct, 2007. **Special Services:** LEED[R].

5633 ■ Greacen Consulting Engineers Inc.
919 Old Hwy. 8 NW, Ste. 200
Saint Paul, MN 55112
Ph:(651)633-1318
Fax:(651)633-1885
Contact: Ed Greacen, Principle
Scope: Specializes in plumbing, heating, ventilating, air conditioning and project management. Designs domestic water and water treatment systems, fire protection, fuel and gas piping, humidification and de-humidification systems, variable air volume (VAV), fan-powered VAV, and retrofit systems for Indoor Air Quality (IAQ).

5634 ■ Hatch Associates
Sheridan Science and Technology Pk., 2800 Speakman Dr.
Mississauga, ON, Canada L5K 2R7
Ph:(905)855-7600
Fax:(905)855-8270
Co. E-mail: tomreid@hatch.ca
URL: http://www.hatch.ca
Contact: Tony Hylton, Director
E-mail: rfrancki@atshatch.ca
Scope: Firm supplies process and business consulting, information technology, engineering and project and construction management to the mining, metallurgical, manufacturing, energy and infrastructure industries.

5635 ■ H.H. Holmes Testing Laboratories Inc.
1301 E Arapaho Rd., Ste. 102
Richardson, TX 75081
Ph:(847)541-4040
Fax:(847)537-9098
Co. E-mail: scott@hhholmestesting.com
URL: http://www.hhholmestesting.com
Contact: Todd R. Nelson, Senior VP
Scope: Offers soil, packaging and construction materials testing on-site and in laboratory. Provides reports and engineering recommendations. Laboratory services include: Full range of construction materials testing and research in soils, concrete, aggregate, asphalt, masonry, steel, paper, corrugated, wood, metals and plastics testing for retail, industrial and medical applications.

5636 ■ Historic Exterior Paint Colors Consulting
3661 Waldenwood Dr.
Ann Arbor, MI 48105
Ph:(734)668-0298
Co. E-mail: robs@umich.edu
URL: http://www.historichousecolors.com
Contact: Robert Schweitzer, Owner
E-mail: robs@umich.edu
Scope: Provides exterior paint color consulting services. Provides services for historic, contemporary, new, commercial and residential services; museums. **Publications:** "Proof that Paint Color Lends Detail," Arts and Crafts Homes, 2006; "Bungalow Colors-Exteriors," Gibbs-Smith Publishers, 2002; "Color Scheming," Design NJ, 2002; "Colonial Revival Homes," Victorian Homes, Feb, 2003; "America's Favorite Homes"; "Color a New World," 60s Ranch

Color Makeover, Romantic Homes, Aug, 2001; "How Shall I Paint my House," American Bungalow, 1999; "Color Concepts and Bungalow Basics," Cottages & Bungalows.

5637 ■ Home Builders Network Inc.
205 E Ridgeville Blvd., Ste. C
Mount Airy, MD 21771
Ph:(301)829-6549
Free: 800-823-4344
Fax:(301)829-8907
Co. E-mail: info@hbnnet.com
URL: http://www.hbnnet.com
Contact: William Watkins, Partner
E-mail: altrellis@hbnnet.com
Scope: Assists builders increase their competitiveness through information, education and consulting. Works directly with builders in the areas of marketing, product design, land acquisition, and management. Assists architects to facilitate the creation of housing product lines for builders. Services include: management, marketing, residential design, and land planning. **Publications:** "Documents, Contracts and Worksheets for Home Builders". **Seminars:** Negotiation for Profit, Creating the Customer; Beating the Competition, Marketing Success; Creating the Brand Image; Lots of Opportunity - Land and Spec Houses; The Rd. to Success; The Sequence of Success; Its About Time; Making a Difference in the Marketplace.

5638 ■ The Home Star Group
4646 N Hermitage Ave.
Chicago, IL 60640-4506
Ph:(773)878-7078
Fax:(773)878-7255
Co. E-mail: homestar1@aol.com
Contact: John Krenger, Principle
Scope: A full service construction consulting firm specializing in analyzing and reorganizing construction projects that not progressing as planned. Provides project analysis, financial analysis, project recovery services and litigation support.

5639 ■ Irvine Team
4900 Woodway Dr., Ste. 1100
Houston, TX 77056
Ph:(713)840-1880
Fax:(713)840-1891
Co. E-mail: rmonsour@irvineteam.com
URL: http://www.irvineteam.com
Contact: Angie Chen, Vice President
E-mail: achen@atsirvineteam.com
Scope: A design and construction strategy company that directs from concept to completion, incorporating project management and quality assurance services. Projects have included theaters, museums, civic facilities, health care and institutional entities, and large churches. Offers a range of strategic services to support design and construction, including project leadership, cost strategy development and management, procurement and sourcing, scheduling, project control/construction management, and project accounting.

5640 ■ IRZ Consulting L.L.C.
505 E Main St.
Hermiston, OR 97838
Ph:(541)567-0252
Free: 800-823-7352
Fax:(541)567-4239
Co. E-mail: irz@irz.com
URL: http://www.irz.com
Contact: Rosa Ortiz, Principle
E-mail: rosa@atsirz.com
Scope: A full-service irrigation engineering and consulting firm that specializes in large scale irrigation development, design and construction management. **Seminars:** Umatilla Sub-Basin Replacement Water (SB 1069) Workshop, Oct, 2008.

5641 ■ JDE Construction Management Ltd.
14321-112 Ave.
Edmonton, AB, Canada T5M 2W3
Ph:(780)429-4849
Free: 800-667-4849
Fax:(780)429-4843
Co. E-mail: jde@jdecm.com
Contact: John Dawson-Edwards, President
E-mail: john@atsjdecm.com
Scope: Construction consultants. Specializes in providing solutions that encourage the prevention, mitigation, and equitable settlement of construction disputes.

5642 ■ Joe Turner
3525 Sandybrook Ln., 2nd Fl.
Napa, CA 94558
Ph:(707)224-6344
Free: 888-754-6900
Fax:(707)224-6392
Co. E-mail: jmturner@joeturner.com
URL: http://www.joeturner.com
E-mail: jmturner@joeturner.com
Scope: Provides customer service consulting, materials, software and training for the new home industry. Specializes in construction defect litigation. Specific problem solving, including recruiting, validating employment information, meeting with homeowners and strategic assessment are available. Produces homeowner manuals for builders and developers. **Seminars:** TeamTraks.

5643 ■ Kalin Associates Inc.
1121 Washington St.
Newton, MA 02465
Ph:(617)964-5477
Free: 800-565-2546
Fax:(617)964-5788
Co. E-mail: mark@kalinassociates.com
URL: http://www.kalinassociates.com
Contact: Lisa Goodwin Robbins, Mgr
E-mail: lisa@atskalinassociates.com
Scope: Independent specifications firm specializing in preparation of technical specifications and bidding documents for construction projects, and preparation of guide specifications for building product manufacturers. Related service include development of master specifications for agencies and design firms; computer automation of technical documents; specification coordination for large projects. **Publications:** "Specifying Green Building Products," Rs Means, 2002. **Seminars:** Integrating BIM and Specifications at Ecobuild, Washington, DC.

5644 ■ Kohn Engineering
4220 Mountain Rd.
Macungie, PA 18062
Ph:(610)967-4766
Fax:(610)967-6468
Co. E-mail: don@kohnengineering.com
URL: http://www.kohnengineering.com
Contact: Don Kohn, Principle
E-mail: don@kohnengineering.com
Scope: Offers fire protection consulting. Provides a wide range of fire protection consulting services that includes design, code interpretation, expert witness, project management, fire safety program development, and hazard identification. Provides cost effective solutions to fire protection problems. **Seminars:** Fire Protection in Nuclear Power Plants.

5645 ■ Kora Management Ltd.
200-2005 Sheppard Ave. E
Toronto, ON, Canada M2J 5B4
Ph:(705)675-2251
Free: (866)705-4447
Fax:(705)675-6302
Co. E-mail: mrspeigel@koramgt.com
URL: http://www.koramgt.com
Contact: Mitchell R. Speigel, President
E-mail: mrspeigel@atskoramgt.com
Scope: Specializes in construction, real estate development, management advice and dispute resolution services. Specializes in property management, administration and on-site construction. Offers services in five languages throughout North and South America. Provides personal and commercial loans; recruiting and financial consulting globally.

5646 ■ Lawrence Siegel-Consultant
5292 Eliots Oak Rd.
PO Box 869
Columbia, MD 21044
Ph:(410)997-9210
Fax:(410)997-0927
Co. E-mail: consult@lscourt.com
URL: http://www.lscourt.com
Contact: Lawrence Siegel, President
E-mail: lscourt@cs.com
Scope: Serves government agencies and architects with needs assessment, security analysis and design, facility planning, master planning, feasibility and predesign, facility programming. **Publications:** "The Image Of Justice"; "Space Management and the Courts"; "Some Issues inCourt Security," The Court Manager, 1997.

5647 ■ Lee and Baldauf Consulting Engineers Inc.
12980 Pandora Dr., Ste. 201
Dallas, TX 75238
Ph:(214)342-0399
Fax:(214)342-2600
Co. E-mail: hlee@lbce.com
Contact: Steven H. Baldauf, Director
E-mail: sbaldauf@atslbce.com
Scope: Provides structural engineering services to architects and owners in the commercial, institutional and industrial building markets.

5648 ■ Lundquist, Killeen, Potvin and Bender Inc.
1935 W County Rd. B2, Ste. 300
Saint Paul, MN 55113-2722
Ph:(651)633-1223
Fax:(651)633-1355
Co. E-mail: nbart@lkpb.com
URL: http://www.lkpb.com
Contact: Stephen J. Gentilini, Principle
E-mail: sgent@atslkpb.com
Scope: Provides services in heating, ventilation, plumbing, piping, refrigeration, air conditioning, fire protection, lighting design and fixture selection, communications, electrical power distribution, security, life safety system design, energy conservation analysis, design and implementation.

5649 ■ Maharishi Global Construction L.L.C.
500 N 3rd St., Ste. 110
Fairfield, IA 52556
Ph:(641)472-7570
Free: 888-532-7686
Fax:(515)472-9083
Co. E-mail: vedicarchitecture@maharishi.net
URL: http://www.vedicarchitecture.org
Contact: Eloise Raymond, Director
E-mail: eraymond@globalcountry.net
Scope: Consulting services to designers and builders of homes and institutional and commercial buildings, pre-designed homes and office buildings providing drawings and specifications. **Publications:** "Austin House and Home," Jul, 2000.

5650 ■ Materials Advisory Group Inc.
PO Box 7553
PO Box 632270
San Diego, CA 92167
Ph:(303)757-6284
Fax:(303)757-3363
Co. E-mail: matladvgrp@aol.com
Contact: Robert Cox, Mgr
Scope: Mining, mineral and construction materials consultants whose services include business sales, acquisitions, divestitures, valuations, succession planning, management consulting, marketing and market research.

5651 ■ McKay/Moore Consultants L.L.C.
7323 11th Ave. NW
Seattle, WA 98117-4142
Ph:(206)781-0676
Fax:888-680-4987
Co. E-mail: mckaymoore@strabo.com
URL: http://www.mckaymoore.com
Contact: Patricia Moore, Owner
E-mail: mckaymoore@strabo.com
Scope: Provides cost estimating/consulting services for all disciplines of a construction project - architectural, structural, mechanical, electrical, and civil. Services include: value engineering cost support, expert witness, and cost estimate review/quality;

control and administrative support services. **Publications:** "Estimating Mechanical Systems". **Seminars:** Plywood Manufacturing.

5652 ■ MDA Engineering Inc.
1415 Holland Rd.
Maumee, OH 43537
Ph:(419)893-3141
Fax:(419)893-0687
Co. E-mail: info@mdaengr.com
URL: http://www.mdaengr.com
Contact: Kevin Lafferty, President
E-mail: klafferty@atsmdaengr.com
Scope: Provides mechanical, electrical and telecommunications engineering services. Engineers systems for new building construction, building renovations and industrial process support. Services include: Commercial, municipal, educational, industrial, research and development and healthcare facilities. Offers a spectrum of mechanical engineering and consulting services.

5653 ■ Meridian Consulting Group Inc.
771 E Southlake Blvd.
Southlake, TX 76092
Ph:(817)310-6420
Fax:(817)310-6435
Co. E-mail: dallas@meridian-consulting.com
URL: http://www.meridian-consulting.com
Contact: David Alvarez, Mgr
E-mail: davetx2004@atsyahoo.com
Scope: Construction consulting firm that specializes in construction management, construction consulting services and technical support of construction related litigation to the Surety Industry. Services include: project evaluation, cost estimating, contract negotiation and a full range of project management services; writing construction specifications, develop and conduct construction related continuing education and training seminars, evaluate and manage troubled construction projects, evaluate contract compliance, monitor environmental projects. Provides expert testimony and litigation support. Assists in the preparation of affirmative and defensive construction claims.

5654 ■ Mueser Rutledge Consulting Engineers
14 Penn Plz., 225 W 34th St., 2nd Fl.
New York, NY 10122-0002
Ph:(917)339-9300
Fax:(917)339-9400
Co. E-mail: mhuguet@mrce.com
URL: http://www.mrce.com
Contact: Francis J. Arland, Partner
E-mail: farland@atsmrce.com
Scope: Geotechnical and structural foundation engineering services provided for: Foundation design: Building foundations; transportation structures; special structures and excavation support; temporary structures; claim support; underpinning. Geotechnical services: investigations, analysis and recommendations; field observation and testing; groundwater control and waste containment; ground improvement. Instrumentation: marine and water-related structures; waterfront development studies; piers, wharves and bulkheads; outfalls and intakes; cellular cofferdams; dams and dikes; waste water treatment plants. **Publications:** "Construction Dewatering and Groundwater Control"; "90 Years of Foundation Engineering: The Last 15 Years"; "A Tale of Two Towers," Civil Engineering Magazine, Jun, 2004; "Cantilever Frozen Ground Structure to Support 18M Deep Excavation"; "North American Tunneling," Apr, 2004.

5655 ■ The Panigas Group of Companies
946 Edgeley Blvd.
Concord, ON, Canada L4K 4V4
Ph:(416)798-7199
Free: (866)726-4427
Fax:(905)669-4385
Contact: Michael Mittleman, Principle
E-mail: lou_panigas@atspanigas.com
Scope: Firm provides services in design, signage and construction to the retail industry. Experience in feasibility studies, conceptual development of building and marketing parameters, site planning and civic coordination, base building design signage, communication and fixture design, full coordination of construction, construction documents and contract administration and post construction services.

5656 ■ PJ Materials Consultants Ltd.
11 Wagoners Trl.
Guelph, ON, Canada N1G 3M9
Ph:(519)767-0702
Fax:(519)821-2870
Co. E-mail: pjeffs@pjmc.net
Contact: Paul Jeffs, President
E-mail: pjeffs@pjmc.net
Scope: Provides a wide range of specialist concrete and masonry consultant services for concrete and masonry structures. Services include: provision of materials technology expertise and technical training. Provides technical consulting services for the design, specification, construction, restoration and protection of concrete and masonry structures. **Seminars:** Restoration and Conservation of Masonry Structures; Concrete in the Arabian Peninsular Today; Concrete Slabs on Grade; Modern Concrete Materials and Practices; Modern Concrete Materials and Practices.

5657 ■ R. L. Townsend & Associates Inc.
3941 Legacy Dr., Ste. 204-218A
Plano, TX 75023
Ph:(972)208-1222
Free: 800-559-4471
Fax:(214)853-5287
Co. E-mail: info@rltownsend.com
URL: http://www.rltownsend.com
Contact: Nick Milburn, Mgr
E-mail: nick.milburn@atsrltownsend.com
Scope: Firm provides construction contract cost control advisory and audit services to owner organizations. Clients include organizations contracting with design firms, construction management firms and construction contractors to build new facilities and/or renovate existing facilities. Construction projects include manufacturing plants, petrochemical plants, office buildings, retail developments, hotel/resort buildings, gas and oil pipelines, local government buildings, banks, airport terminals, airport infrastructure, college and university buildings, hospitals and medical centers. Construction cost control and audit services: Construction contract compliance audit services; construction contract control advisory services; construction cost monitoring services; comprehensive advisory/audit services; construction cost control and audit training. **Publications:** "Contracting for Construction Projects," Rich Townsend, Jun, 1993. **Seminars:** Auditing Construction Activity, Austin, 2009; Controlling Construction Costs, Madison, 2009; Controlling Construction Costs, Madison, 2007; Managing Construction Projects, Madison, 2007; Effective Auditing of Construction Activity, Orlando, 2007.

5658 ■ Reed Construction Data Co.
30 Technology Pky. S, Ste. 100
Norcross, GA 30092-2925
Ph:(770)417-4000
Free: 800-424-3996
Fax:(770)417-4344
Co. E-mail: marketing@reedbusiness.com
URL: http://www.reedconstructiondata.com
Contact: Rich Remington, Vice President, Production
Scope: Provides products and services including national, regional and local construction data, building product information, construction cost data, market analytics and advertising channels to construction industry professionals in the US and Canada. Offers information on commercial construction, architects and specifiers and CAD and technical information for manufacturer's building products.

5659 ■ Revay and Associates Ltd.
4333 St. Catherine St. W, Ste. 500
Montreal, QC, Canada H3Z 1P9
Ph:(514)932-2188
Fax:(514)939-0776
Co. E-mail: montreal@revay.com
URL: http://www.revay.com
Contact: Zey Emir, Vice President
E-mail: zemir@atsrevay.com
Scope: Services include construction claims preparation; project management services; cost estimating; planning and scheduling; risk analysis; dispute resolution services; in-depth surveys and studies for the government and the construction industry.

5660 ■ Richmond Sterling Inc.
2870 Pharr Ct. S, Ste. 2007
Atlanta, GA 30305
Ph:(404)525-9606
Fax:(404)525-4416
Co. E-mail: contact@richmondsterling.com
URL: http://www.richmondsterling.com
Contact: Paul N. Marston, President
E-mail: pnm@richmondsterling.com
Scope: An independent construction consulting firm that provides project management, owner's representative services and independent cost management to users of the construction industry. Provides a complete management and control system; supervises the overall budget and schedule; solicits and evaluates bids, recommends a contractor, and awards the contract; directs the contractor in the performance of the contract; operates as the in-house manager of design and construction processes; ensures the owner's directives are accurately given to the design; professionals and contractor, then correctly executed; enables the owner to properly manage the project's development within schedule and budget constraints; monitors and controls the project budgets independently of design and construction teams; monitors contractor pricing and valuations of the work in progress; controls and mitigate extra costs; monitors the cash flow through all phases of construction.

5661 ■ Robert G. Thomas Jr.
1417 Sadler Rd., Ste. 269
Fernandina Beach, FL 32034
Ph:(904)343-2365
Co. E-mail: rgt@rgthomas.com
URL: http://www.eifs.com
E-mail: rgt@rgthomas.com
Scope: Provides insulation, weatherproofing and a finished surface in a single integrated product. **Publications:** "EIFS Design Handbook"; "EIFS New Construction Inspection Guide"; "EIFS Existing Construction Inspection Maintenance and Repair Guide"; "EIFS Homeowners Guide".

5662 ■ Saunders Construction Inc.
6950 S Jordan Rd.
PO Box 3908
Centennial, CO 80112
Ph:(303)699-9000
Fax:(303)269-8340
Co. E-mail: businessdevelopment@saundersci.com
URL: http://www.saundersci.com
Contact: Richard C. Saunders, Chairman of the Board
E-mail: dick@atssaundersci.com
Scope: Specializes in serving healthcare providers and organizations with practice mergers/acquisition/divestiture, practice valuation, strategic planning, compensation, and development of business plans. **Seminars:** Pilot Leadership Training, Jan, 2008.

5663 ■ Seventh Generation Strategies Inc.
650 Mullis St., Ste. 201
Friday Harbor, WA 98250-7951
Ph:(360)378-8588
Fax:(360)378-6477
Co. E-mail: tom.harman@sevengensys.com
Contact: James G. Sackett, President
E-mail: sackett@buildingsnet.com
Scope: A multi-disciplinary firm offering performance and economic solutions to building owners, designers and developers. Provides whole system design and technologies to meet power, heating, cooling, sewage, water and other project requirements on an integrated basis. **Publications:** "Low-Impact Commercial Complex in a Small Town".

5664 ■ Shoreline General Contractors Inc.
3828 Herman Ave.
San Diego, CA 92104-3714
Ph:(619)283-2024
Contact: Paula Harmer, Operations Mgr
Scope: General building contractors involved from the initial concept, through design, contracting and completion of a project.

5665 ■ Smith-Emery Co.
791 E Washington Blvd.
Los Angeles, CA 90021-3043
Ph:(213)749-3411
Fax:(213)741-8620
Co. E-mail: mktla@smithemery.com
URL: http://www.smithemery.com
Contact: James Partridge, President
E-mail: jpartridge@atssmithemery.com
Scope: Provides construction testing and inspection services. Acts as a single source of testing and inspection for all construction related services in the commercial building market, from the soil to the roof. Offers inspection, testing and failure analysis services including post tensioning, curtain wall testing, masonry inspection and tests, flatness testing, flat jack testing, batch plant inspection, seismic evaluation, on destructive examinations, laboratory mock ups, concrete placement, construction materials testing, concrete compression tests, roofing inspections and tests, wood structure inspection, reinforcing steel placement, gypsum inspection, and metallurgical lab testing.

5666 ■ Space Management Programs Inc.
55 W Wacker Dr., Ste. 600
Chicago, IL 60601-1609
Ph:(312)263-0700
Fax:(312)263-1228
Contact: Michael J. Cohen, President
E-mail: mcohen@ghk.net
Scope: A facilities and technology consulting firm experienced in all aspects of design and corporate relocation. Available for site evaluation, strategic planning through the writing of briefs, or architectural programs through space planning, design and construction documents.

5667 ■ Steinmann Facility Development Consultants
9702 N Lake Blvd.
PO Box 909
Kings Beach, CA 96143
Ph:(530)546-4428
Fax:(530)546-0422
Co. E-mail: sfdc@jimsteinmann.com
URL: http://www.jimsteinmann.com
Contact: James H. Steinmann, Exec VP
E-mail: sfdc@jimsteinmann.com
Scope: Provides facility programming and planning consulting services to government and private sector space users. Specializes in needs assessment, facility programming, pre architectural planning, strategic planning, justice system planning, industrial engineering, design/build development and project management.

5668 ■ Stueven Engineering Consultants
140 W 3rd Ave.
Escondido, CA 92025
Ph:(760)735-8577
Fax:(760)735-8578
Co. E-mail: sb@stueven-engineering.com
URL: http://www.stueven-engineering.com
Contact: Steve Balderrama, Principle
E-mail: sb@atsstueven-engineering.com
Scope: Provides services in professional engineering, planning, design, and construction support services for mechanical and plumbing systems.

5669 ■ Swanson Associates
6705 Hwy. 290 W, Ste. 502-126
PO Box 126
Austin, TX 78735
Ph:(512)288-9097
Fax:(512)288-9096
Co. E-mail: gps@flash.net
URL: http://www.geoswan.com
Contact: George Paul Swanson, President
E-mail: gps@flash.net
Scope: Environmentally-conscience construction firm services include non-toxic, breathing construction consulting; natural low impact energy and site utility development consulting; CADD custom and stock natural building design plans; site supervision, construction management and general contracting. **Publications:** "Dome Scrapbook," 1981. **Seminars:** Sustainable Development and Concrete Technology; Traditional Straw/Clay Slip form Construction; Natural design and construction; Benefits of natural building design.

5670 ■ TechniScan Inc.
155 S Madison St., Ste. 228
Denver, CO 80209-3013
Ph:(303)329-0535
Free: 800-266-8565
Fax:(303)377-2740
Co. E-mail: inquiries@techniscan.com
URL: http://www.techniscan.com
Contact: David Michaels, Principle
E-mail: david.g.davis@atstechniscan.com
Scope: An architecturally based consulting practice that performs diagnostic scanning, remedial repair and design, project management, and expert witness services for roofing and curtain wall systems. **Seminars:** Roofing asset portfolio. **Special Services:** TechniScan[R].

5671 ■ Tempest Co.
13326 A St.
Omaha, NE 68144-3641
Ph:(402)334-3332
Free: 888-334-3332
Fax:(402)334-9033
Co. E-mail: inquire@tempestcompany.com
URL: http://www.tempestcompany.com
Contact: Justin E. Short, Principle
E-mail: justins@atstempestcompany.com
Scope: A construction consulting firm specializing in management consulting, marketing and proposal preparation, strategic bidding and estimating and bidding practices. Services include: Estimating, scheduling, project controls, construction consulting and expert services such as arbitration. **Publications:** "Some Estimates Are Wishful Thinking"; "The Nine Secrets of Estimating"; "Fallacy of the Contract Schedule of Values"; "CPM Scheduling Will Work For Your Project"; "Controlling Capital Costs Prior to Construction".

5672 ■ US Aquatics Inc.
124 Bridge Ave.
PO Box 86
Delano, MN 55328
Ph:(763)972-5897
Fax:(763)972-5864
Co. E-mail: info@usaquaticsinc.com
URL: http://www.usaquaticsinc.com
Contact: Aaron Hunter, Mgr
E-mail: ahunter@atsusaquaticsinc.com
Scope: Engineering/design firm specializes in consultation, aquatic design and project construction management for renovations, expansion or new construction of multiuse swimming pools, aquatic facilities and aquatic parks.

FRANCHISES AND BUSINESS OPPORTUNITIES

5673 ■ A-1 Concrete Leveling Inc.
388 S Main St., Ste. 402
Akron, OH 44311
Free: 888-675-3835
Fax:(330)253-1261
No. of Franchise Units: 47. **Founded:** 1992. **Franchised:** 1993. **Description:** Concrete leveling service. **Equity Capital Needed:** $115,500-$145,900 total investment. **Franchise Fee:** $85,000. **Royalty Fee:** 6%. **Financial Assistance:** Limited third-party financing available. **Training:** Provides 1 week at headquarters, 2 weeks of onsite and ongoing support including newsletter, meetings toll-free phone line, Internet, security/safety procedures, and field operations/evaluations.

5674 ■ ABC Seamless Siding
ABC, Inc.
3001 Fiechtner Dr.
Fargo, ND 58103
Ph:(701)293-5952
Free: 800-732-6577
Fax:(701)293-3107
No. of Franchise Units: 109. **No. of Company-Owned Units:** 9. **Founded:** 1973. **Franchised:** 1978. **Description:** Sales and installation of seamless steel and steel gutters. **Equity Capital Needed:** $81,000-$207,500. **Franchise Fee:** $12,000+. **Financial Assistance:** Yes. **Training:** Yes.

5675 ■ Andy Oncall
Franchise Dept.
921 E Main St.
Chattanooga, TN 37408
Free: 877-263-9662
Fax:(423)622-0580
Co. E-mail: info@andyoncall.com
URL: http://www.andyoncall.com
No. of Franchise Units: 54. **Founded:** 1993. **Franchised:** 1999. **Description:** Manage independent contractors to fulfill homeowners' small job needs; management and organizational skills, no construction experience needed, strong and growing demand for service in marketplace. **Equity Capital Needed:** $48,150-$62,050. **Franchise Fee:** $25,000 or $30,000 based on pop. **Financial Assistance:** Will finance up to 30% of franchise fee. **Training:** Training at corporate office, onsite, and ongoing support in all areas of business.

5676 ■ The BrickKicker
RonLen Enterprises Inc.
849 N Ellsworth St.
Naperville, IL 60563
Free: 888-339-5425
Fax:(630)420-2270
Co. E-mail: linda@brickkicker.com
URL: http://www.brickkicker.com
No. of Franchise Units: 165. **Founded:** 1989. **Franchised:** 1995. **Description:** Building inspection service. **Equity Capital Needed:** $15,000-$40,000. **Franchise Fee:** $7,500-$25,000. **Financial Assistance:** Up to one-third the franchise fee. **Training:** 2 weeks hands-on/in-field work, interactive classroom discussions, lab, telemarketing, report writing, sales calls, roll-play, technical & marketing training manuals, as well as training through yearly national conventions, roundtables, monthly support packages and toll-free support.

5677 ■ Case Handyman & Remodeling Services LLC
Case Design/Remodeling Inc.
North Plz., Ste. 40
4701 Sangamore Rd.
Bethesda, MD 20816
Ph:(301)229-4600
Free: 800-426-9434
Fax:(301)229-2089
Co. E-mail: info@casehandyman.com
URL: http://www.casehandyman.com
No. of Franchise Units: 45. **No. of Company-Owned Units:** 5. **Founded:** 1992. **Franchised:** 1997. **Description:** Handyman services. **Equity Capital Needed:** $105,000-$150,000. **Franchise Fee:** $25,000. **Royalty Fee:** 4-6%. **Financial Assistance:** No. **Training:** Includes 3 weeks training at headquarters, 2 days at franchisee's location and ongoing support.

5678 ■ Epcon Communities
500 Stonehenge Pky.
Columbus, OH 43017
Ph:(614)761-1010
Fax:(614)761-2672
URL: http://www.epmarkinc.com
No. of Franchise Units: 200+. **Founded:** 1986. **Franchised:** 1995. **Description:** Franchiser of condo communities. **Equity Capital Needed:** $1,000,000. **Franchise Fee:** $50,000. **Royalty Fee:** $2,500 per unit. **Training:** Available at headquarters, onsite and with ongoing support. Provides additional training at sales conference (2 days) and construction conference (2 days).

5679 ■ Handyman Connection
Mamar, Inc.
10250 Alliance Rd., Ste.100
Cincinnati, OH 45242
Ph:(513)771-3003

Free: 800-466-5530
Fax:(513)771-6439
Co. E-mail: soaks@handymanconnection.com
URL: http://www.handymanconnection.com
No. of Franchise Units: 160. **No. of Company-Owned Units:** 1. **Founded:** 1990. **Franchised:** 1993. **Description:** Small to medium home repairs and remodeling. **Equity Capital Needed:** $90,000-$125,000. **Franchise Fee:** $25,000-$40,000. **Financial Assistance:** No. **Training:** 2 weeks at corporate training center, and 1 week grand opening onsite.

5680 ■ Handyman Matters Franchise Corp.
Handyman Matters, Inc.
12567 W Cedar Dr., Ste. 150
Lakewood, CO 80228
Ph:(866)808-8401
Free: 888-448-3451
Fax:(303)942-5993
Co. E-mail: info@HandymanMatters.com
URL: http://www.HandymanMatters.com
No. of Franchise Units: 121. **Founded:** 1997. **Franchised:** 2001. **Description:** Repairs, maintains, and improves properties including carpentry, plumbing, electrical, drywall, painting, roofing & flooring. **Equity Capital Needed:** $48,930-$89,425. **Franchise Fee:** $30,000. **Financial Assistance:** No. **Training:** Offers 1-2 weeks training at corporate office and 1 week onsite.

5681 ■ Hickory Dickory Decks
115 Dundas St., W
Hamilton, ON, Canada L9H 7L6
Ph:(905)689-4774
Free: 800-263-4774
Fax:(905)689-9753
Co. E-mail: tomjacques@bellnet.ca
URL: http://www.hickorydickorydecks.com
No. of Franchise Units: 30. **No. of Company-Owned Units:** 12. **Founded:** 1987. **Franchised:** 1999. **Description:** Custom builders of decks and gazebo's. **Equity Capital Needed:** $50,000-$100,000. **Franchise Fee:** $25,000. **Training:** Provides 3 weeks training.

5682 ■ Janbury
Synergy Franchising LLC
Sawyer Oaks Professional Park
5674 Marquesas Ctr.
Sarasota, FL 34233
Ph:(941)927-9400
Fax:(941)927-9401
No. of Franchise Units: 2. **No. of Company-Owned Units:** 1. **Founded:** 2001. **Franchised:** 2006. **Description:** Construction support/cleaning service. **Equity Capital Needed:** $156,900-$271,000. **Franchise Fee:** $45,000. **Royalty Fee:** 7%. **Financial Assistance:** No. **Training:** Includes 1 week training at headquarters, 1 week at franchisee's location and ongoing support.

5683 ■ Maintenance Made Simple
4919 Albemarle Rd. Suite 203
Charlotte, NC 28205
Ph:(704)584-9999
Free: (866)778-6283
No. of Franchise Units: 32. **Founded:** 2003. **Franchised:** 2003. **Description:** Handyman and home improvement services. **Equity Capital Needed:** $69,900-$114,900. **Franchise Fee:** $30,000. **Royalty Fee:** 7%. **Financial Assistance:** Third party financing available. **Training:** Yes.

5684 ■ National Franchise Resources, Inc.
Hoey Construction Co.
3310 Southwest Blvd.
Tulsa, OK 74107
Ph:(918)270-4886
Fax:(918)270-4889
Founded: 1979. **Description:** Franchise design build general contractor. **Financial Assistance:** No. **Training:** No.

5685 ■ Perma-Jack Co.
9066 Watson Rd.
St. Louis, MO 63126-2234
Ph:(314)843-1957
Free: 800-843-1888
No. of Franchise Units: 38. **Founded:** 1974. **Description:** Franchises a fast, patented building foundation stabilizing system. **Equity Capital Needed:** $25,000-$200,000. **Franchise Fee:** None. **Financial Assistance:** No. **Training:** Yes.

5686 ■ Sealmaster
InFrasys Inc.
2520 S Campbell St.
Sandusky, OH 44870
Ph:(419)626-4375
Free: 800-395-7325
Fax:(419)626-5477
Co. E-mail: info@sealmaster.net
URL: http://www.sealmaster.net
No. of Franchise Units: 28. **No. of Company-Owned Units:** 1. **Founded:** 1969. **Franchised:** 1993. **Description:** Manufacture pavement sealers and supply a complete line of pavement maintenance products and equipment including crack fillers, traffic paints, sport surfaces and tools. **Equity Capital Needed:** $500,000-$700,000 total investment required, possible start-up equipment. **Franchise Fee:** $35,000. **Financial Assistance:** Possible financing on start-up operations. **Training:** Technical and administrative training, operations manual. Scheduled consulting visits by operations experts.

5687 ■ Tile Outlet Always in Stock
3329 Fitzgerald Rd., Ste. 1
Rancho Cordova, CA 95742
Ph:(916)861-0855
Free: 888-328-4374
Fax:(916)861-0859
Co. E-mail: info@tileoutlet.net
URL: http://www.tileoutlet.net
No. of Franchise Units: 44. **No. of Company-Owned Units:** 6. **Founded:** 2001. **Franchised:** 2002. **Description:** Discount retail tile store selling granite counters, tile, slate, travertine, marble and related products. Our customers include the general public, contractors and builders. The corporate office directly imports products and sells to our franchisees to allow them to focus on selling. Great overhead, high profit margin business with no previous experience required. **Equity Capital Needed:** $59,850-$104,600, franchise fee for additional units $15,000. **Franchise Fee:** $20,000 for 1st. **Financial Assistance:** 60 day terms on initial inventory purchase. **Training:** Provides 3 days of complete training at our corporate facility, 5 days of onsite training at your location and unlimited ongoing support through phone, fax, email, web page and in person visits.

5688 ■ UBuildIt
UBuildit Corp.
PO Box 588
Woodinville, WA 98072
Ph:(425)821-6200
Free: 800-992-4357
Fax:(425)821-6876
Co. E-mail: franchiseinfo@ubuildit.com
URL: http://www.ubuildit.com
No. of Franchise Units: 101. **Founded:** 1988. **Franchised:** 1998. **Description:** Building or remodeling general contractors. **Equity Capital Needed:** $100,000-$225,000. **Franchise Fee:** $25,000. **Financial Assistance:** No. **Training:** Pretraining business start-up assistance, 2 week training and ongoing support.

COMPUTERIZED DATABASES

5689 ■ *Construction Labor Report*
The Bureau of National Affairs Inc.
1801 S Bell St.
Arlington, VA 22202
Free: 800-372-1033
Co. E-mail: customercare@bna.com
URL: http://www.bna.com
Description: Contains labor and employment issues for all segments of the construction industry, including union, non-union, dual shop, and government officials tracking the industry. Topics include apprentices, arbitration decisions, collective bargaining, contractor associations, court and administrative decisions, EEO, employee benefits, federal and state legislation, government regulations, health and safety, independent contractors, jobsite accidents, jurisdictional disputes, labor laws, union organizing, worker shortages, workers' compensation insurance, workforce demographics, regulatory, legislative, and industry developments impacting the construction industry; legal news, state news, economic statistics, lists of relevant meetings, seminars, and conferences; and full text of court decisions, legislation approved by Congress, minority business enterprises, mixed crews, NLRB decisions, pension and benefits matters, prevailing wage laws, productivity, project labor agreements, substance abuse and control, training, transportation, and union job targeting programs. Includes summaries of all reports covered in each issue. **Availability:** Online: The Bureau of National Affairs Inc., Thomson Reuters. **Type:** Full text.

5690 ■ *Residential Building Permits*
Haver Analytics
60 E 42nd St.
New York, NY 10165
Ph:(212)986-9300
Fax:(212)986-5857
Co. E-mail: data@haver.com
URL: http://www.haver.com
Description: Contains monthly, year-to-date, and annual time series on residential building permits expressed in number of units, number of buildings, and thousands of dollars. Also provides data on addition and demolition permits. Data are available for Metropolitan Areas (MAs), U.S. states, census regions, counties, and permit-issuing places. Monthly and annual data are compiled from a sample of permit-issuing places. Source of data is the United States Department of Commerce, Construction Statistics Division. **Availability:** Online: Haver Analytics. **Type:** Time series.

COMPUTER SYSTEMS/ SOFTWARE

5691 ■ Activant
Enterprise Computer Systems, Inc.
5 Independence Pointe
Greenville, SC 29602-2383
Ph:(864)234-7676
Free: 800-569-6309
Fax:(864)987-6400
Co. E-mail: ecs-inc@activant.com
URL: http://www.activant.com
Description: Available for IBM computers. System provides a construction management system with accounting capabilities.

LIBRARIES

5692 ■ Associated General Contractors of America–James L. Allhands Memorial Library
333 John Carlyle St., Ste. 200
Alexandria, VA 22314
Ph:(703)837-5308
Fax:(703)548-3119
Co. E-mail: dayd@agc.org
URL: http://www.agc.org/
Contact: Dennis Day, Sr.Dir., Pub.Aff.
Scope: History of construction industry. **Services:** Interlibrary loan; Library open to the public by appointment. **Holdings:** 400 books. **Subscriptions:** 4 newspapers.

5693 ■ Boston Architectural Center–Alfred Shaw and Edward Durell Stone Library
320 Newbury St., 6th Fl.
Boston, MA 02115
Ph:(617)585-0155
Free: (87)
Fax:(617)585-0151
Co. E-mail: library@the-bac.edu
URL: http://www.the-bac.edu/x459.xml
Contact: Susan Lewis, Lib.Dir.
Scope: Architectural design and history, building technology, urban planning, urban design, landscape architecture, photography, interior design, energy conservation, solar energy. **Services:** Copying; Library open to the public for reference only. **Holdings:** 25,000 books; 800 bound periodical volumes;

800 student theses; 40,000 slides; 500 other cataloged items; archives. **Subscriptions:** 120 journals and other serials.

5694 ■ California Real Estate Services Division Library
707 3rd St., Ste. 6-100
West Sacramento, CA 95605
Ph:(916)376-1900
Fax:(916)376-1895
Co. E-mail: dbrakowi@dgs.ca.gov
URL: http://www.resd.dgs.ca.gov/default.htm
Scope: Construction industry standards, architecture, electrical and mechanical engineering, building products, interior design. **Services:** Interlibrary loan; copying; Library open to other state agencies. **Holdings:** 400 books; 30 bound periodical volumes; 1500 catalogs; titles 1-26 of the California Code of Regulations. **Subscriptions:** 30 journals and other serials.

5695 ■ Canada–National Research Council–CISTI - Institute for Research in Construction Branch (1200)
1200 Montreal Rd., Bldg. M-55
Ottawa, ON, Canada K1A 0R6
Ph:(613)993-2013
Free: 800-668-1222 (US and C
Fax:(613)993-7619
Co. E-mail: info.cisti@nrc-cnrc.gc.ca
URL: http://cisti-icist.nrc-cnrc.gc.ca/eng/locations/cisti/ottawa.html
Contact: Mike Culhane, Mgr.
Scope: Construction, acoustics, building services, fire research, building codes, building structures, materials, infrastructure, indoor environment. **Services:** Interlibrary loan; copying; branch open to the public. **Holdings:** 100,000 books; 200,000 reports. **Subscriptions:** 700 journals and other serials.

5696 ■ Foundation of the Wall & Ceiling Industry–John H. Hampshire Memorial Library
513 W Broad St., Ste. 210
Falls Church, VA 22046
Ph:(703)538-1600
Fax:(703)534-8307
Co. E-mail: smith@awci.org
URL: http://www.awci.org/thefoundation.shtml
Contact: Don Smith, Dir., Tech.Svcs.
Scope: Construction - specifications and standards, management, and law; asbestos removal; fire standards; insulation. **Services:** Copying; Library open to the public. **Holdings:** 10,000 volumes; 3000 books; 500 unbound reports; manufacturers' catalogs. **Subscriptions:** 100 journals and other serials.

5697 ■ Hanley-Wood, LLC Library
426 S. Westgate St.
Addison, IL 60101-4546
Ph:(630)543-0870
Fax:(630)543-3112
URL: http://www.hanleywood.com
Contact: Kimberly Last, Libn.
Scope: Concrete, cement, masonry, construction, home building. **Services:** Interlibrary loan; copying. **Holdings:** 3000 books; 120 bound periodical volumes. **Subscriptions:** 100 journals and other serials.

5698 ■ Harrington College of Design–Design Library
200 W. Madison St., 2nd Fl.
Chicago, IL 60606-3433
Ph:(312)939-4975
Free: (866)590-4423
Co. E-mail: elaine@interiordesign.edu
URL: http://www.interiordesign.edu
Contact: Elaine Lowenthal, Lib.Dir.
Scope: Architecture, design, building materials, furniture, decorative arts, modern design. **Services:** Interlibrary loan; copying; Library open to the public by appointment for reference use only with referral from another Library. **Holdings:** 22,000 books; 900 bound periodical volumes; 23,000 slides; 450 videotapes; 35,000 digital images. **Subscriptions:** 125 journals and other serials.

5699 ■ H.B. Zachry Company–Central Records and Library
PO Box 240130
San Antonio, TX 78224-0130
Ph:(210)922-1213
Fax:(210)927-8060
Contact: Leroy Rome, Dir.
Scope: Construction specifications, industrial relations, tax laws, electronic data processing, accounting procedures, building codes. **Services:** Interlibrary loan; copying; Library open to the public by permission. **Holdings:** 1500 books; 60 bound periodical volumes; film; maps. **Subscriptions:** 135 journals and other serials.

5700 ■ Hill International, Inc. Library
303 Lippincott Ctr.
Marlton, NJ 08053
Ph:(856)810-6200
Fax:(856)810-1309
URL: http://www.hillintl.com/
Contact: Irvin E. Richter, Chm./CEO
Scope: Construction claims avoidance and resolution. **Services:** Interlibrary loan; Library not open to the public. **Holdings:** Comprehensive case histories of claims.

5701 ■ Intertek Testing Services–Warnock Hersey Library
1500 Brigantine Dr.
Coquitlam, BC, Canada V3K 7C1
Ph:(604)520-3321
Fax:(604)524-9186
Co. E-mail: lawrence.gibson@intertek.com
URL: http://www.intertek.com/
Scope: Building codes, electrical codes, plumbing codes, standards. **Services:** Library open to potential clients at librarian's discretion. **Holdings:** Standards; codes; handbooks; manuals; directories. **Subscriptions:** 20 journals and other serials.

5702 ■ Missouri Historical Society Archives–Architecture Collection
PO Box 11940
St. Louis, MO 63112-0040
Ph:(314)746-4599
Fax:(314)454-3162
Co. E-mail: archives@mohistory.org
URL: http://www.mohistory.org
Contact: Christopher Gordon, Archv.
Scope: Construction. **Services:** Copying; collection open to the public by appointment. **Holdings:** Drawings of 2500 different projects; research file specifications; job files; models.

5703 ■ Murphy/Jahn Library
35 E. Wacker Dr., 3rd Fl.
Chicago, IL 60601
Ph:(312)427-7300
Fax:(312)332-0274
Co. E-mail: info@murphyjahn.com
URL: http://www.murphyjahn.com/
Contact: Joseph A. Stypka, Dir. Specifications
Scope: Architecture, codes, construction products. **Services:** Library open to the public by appointment. **Holdings:** 7000 books and articles; 4 bound periodical volumes; 7000 product catalogs; 1900 construction consultant. **Subscriptions:** 200 journals and other serials; 2 newspapers.

5704 ■ Noble and Associates Library
2155 W. Chesterfield Blvd.
Springfield, MO 65807
Ph:(417)875-5000
Co. E-mail: julie.tumy@noble.net
URL: http://www.noble.net
Contact: Julie Tumy, Pres.
Scope: Food, food service, advertising, construction, agriculture. **Services:** Interlibrary loan; copying; SDI; Library not open to the public. **Holdings:** 500 books; 1000 reports. **Subscriptions:** 300 journals and other serials; 5 newspapers.

5705 ■ North Carolina State University–Libraries–D.H. Hill Library Special Collections Research Center (2 Bro)
2 Broughton Dr.
Ground Fl., Rm. G-142
Raleigh, NC 27695-7111
Ph:(919)515-2273
Fax:(919)515-1787
Co. E-mail: lisa_carter@ncsu.edu
URL: http://www.lib.ncsu.edu/specialcollections/
Contact: Lisa Carter, Hd.
Scope: Architecture and design, engineering and technology, history of science, natural resources, textiles, history of NCSU, plant and forestry genetics and genomics, history of computing and simulation, veterinary medicine, entomology, animal welfare. **Services:** Copying; digitization; Library open to the public. **Holdings:** 32,000 books; 7665 lin.ft. of manuscripts; 6778 lin.ft. of University archives.

5706 ■ Pacific Gas and Electric Company–Energy Resource Center
851 Howard St.
San Francisco, CA 94103
Ph:(415)973-7206
Fax:(415)896-1290
Co. E-mail: mxv6@pge.com
URL: http://www.pge.com/mybusiness/edusafety/training/pec/inforesource/
Contact: Marlene Vogelsang, Rsrc.Spec.
Scope: Energy conservation, architecture, design, lighting. **Services:** Copying; Library open to the public. **Holdings:** 1500 books; reports. **Subscriptions:** 120 journals and other serials.

5707 ■ Portland Cement Association Library
5420 Old Orchard Rd.
Skokie, IL 60077
Ph:(847)966-6200
Fax:(847)966-8389
Co. E-mail: library@cement.org
URL: http://www.cement.org/library
Contact: Connie Field, Dir.
Scope: Concrete technology, cement chemistry, structural engineering, civil engineering, construction. **Services:** Interlibrary loan; document delivery; research services available to nonmembers on fee basis. **Holdings:** 10,000 books; 13,500 bound periodical volumes; 40,000 technical reports; 100,000 abstracts; 300 CD publications; 70,000 images. **Subscriptions:** 200 journals and other serials.

5708 ■ Saskatchewan Home Builders' Association Library
11-3012 Louise St.
Saskatoon, SK, Canada S7J 3L8
Ph:(306)955-5188
Free: 888-955-5188
Fax:(306)373-3735
Co. E-mail: info@chbasaskatchewan.com
URL: http://www.shba.ca
Contact: Alan H.J. Thomarat, CEO
Scope: Home construction. **Services:** Library open to the public. **Holdings:** 100 books; 20 reports; slides; videocassettes.

5709 ■ Societe d'Habitation du Quebec–Centre de Documentation
500, boul. Rene-Levesque Quest, 5e etage
Montreal, QC, Canada H2Z 1W7
Ph:(514)873-8775
Free: 800-463-4315
Fax:(514)873-8340
Co. E-mail: centredoc@shq.gouv.qc.ca
URL: http://www.habitation.gouv.qc.ca/en/index.html
Contact: Barbara Maass, Libn.
Scope: Housing, residential construction, architecture, urban planning. **Services:** Interlibrary loan; copying; Library open to the public by appointment. **Holdings:** 15,000 books and reports; 150 audio/visual materials. **Subscriptions:** 360 journals and other serials.

5710 ■ U.S. Dept. of Housing and Urban Development Library
451 7th St. SW, Rm. 8141
Washington, DC 20410
Ph:(202)708-2370
URL: http://www.hud.gov/library/index.cfm
Contact: Donna McCurley, Proj.Mgr.
Scope: Housing, community development, urban planning, sociology, law, mortgage and construction finance, architecture, land use, environmental con-

cerns. **Services:** Interlibrary loan; copying (limited); Library open to the public. **Holdings:** 680,000 items. **Subscriptions:** 2200 journals and other serials.

5711 ■ U.S. National Park Service–Blue Ridge Parkway–Archives (199 H)
199 Hemphill Knob Rd.
Asheville, NC 28803-8686
Ph:(828)271-4779
Fax:(828)271-4313
Co. E-mail: jackie_holt@nps.gov
URL: http://www.nps.gov/blri
Contact: Jackie Holt, Cur.
Scope: Blue Ridge Parkway - history, development, design, construction, landscape, resource management. **Services:** Archives open to researchers by appointment only. **Holdings:** 350,000 archives.

5712 ■ University of Nevada, Las Vegas–Architecture Studies Library
Box 454049
4505 Maryland Pkwy.
Las Vegas, NV 89154-4049
Ph:(702)895-1959
Fax:(702)895-1975
Co. E-mail: jeanne.brown@unlv.edu
URL: http://www.library.unlv.edu/arch/index.html
Contact: Jeanne M. Brown, Hd., Arch.Stud.
Scope: Architecture - history, design, theory, and criticism; landscape architecture; interior design; construction; urban planning. **Services:** Interlibrary loan; copying; scanners; Library open to the public. **Holdings:** 25,000 volumes; 600 videos/DVDs; archives; microfiche and microfilm. **Subscriptions:** 150 journals and other serials.

5713 ■ USG Corporation–USG Research and Technology Center Library
700 N. Hwy. 45
Libertyville, IL 60048
Ph:(847)970-5036
Fax:(847)214-1466
Co. E-mail: jsteffen@usg.com
Contact: Joy Steffen, Lib.Info.Spec.
Scope: Building materials, gypsum products, acoustical products. **Services:** Interlibrary loan; copying; SDI. **Holdings:** 6862 books; 1150 bound periodical volumes; 1846 pamphlets; 32,240 laboratory reports; 987 reels of microfilm; 970 microfiche; 10,000 patents. **Subscriptions:** 125 journals and other serials.

5714 ■ Virginia Tech University–Art & Architecture Library
100 Cowgill Hall
Blacksburg, VA 24061
Ph:(540)231-9271
Fax:(540)231-9263
Co. E-mail: tomlin@vt.edu
URL: http://www.lib.vt.edu/artarch/index.html
Contact: Patrick Tomlin, Art & Arch.Libn.
Scope: Architecture, art, art history, building construction, landscape architecture. **Services:** Interlibrary loan; copying; Library open to the public. **Holdings:** 78,000 volumes; 400 architectural drawing sets; 900 multimedia items, including DVDs, videotapes, and slides. **Subscriptions:** 200 journals and other serials.

RESEARCH CENTERS

5715 ■ Concordia University–Centre for Building Studies–Centre d'études sur le bâtimentbâtiment
Department of Building, Civil & Environmental Engineering, R
1455 de Maisonneuve Blvd. W
Montreal, QC, Canada H3G 1M8
Ph:(514)848-2424
Fax:(514)848-7965
Co. E-mail: zmeur@bcee.concordia.ca
URL: http://www.bcee.concordia.ca/index.php/Centre_for_Building_Studies
Contact: Prof. Radu Zmeureanu PhD, Dir.
E-mail: zmeur@bcee.concordia.ca
Scope: Building environment, building science, building structures, and construction management, including energy efficiency, air quality, air infiltration and rain penetration of enclosure systems, building envelope performance, durability of building materials, polymers in construction, acoustical performance of building elements, wind effects on buildings and building aerodynamics, performance of HVAC components, thermal environment, productivity measurement for the construction industry, decision analysis, and computer-aided design. **Services:** Research development and information transfer services. **Publications:** Annual Report; Research papers. **Educational Activities:** Master's and doctoral degrees, in building engineering through the U.S. Department of of Building, Civil and Environment Engineering.

5716 ■ National Institute of Building Sciences
1090 Vermont Ave. NW, Ste. 700
Washington, DC 20005-4905
Ph:(202)289-7800
Fax:(202)289-1092
Co. E-mail: nibs@nibs.org
URL: http://www.nibs.org
Contact: Henry L. Green, Pres.
E-mail: nibs@nibs.org
Scope: Improvement of the building and the construction regulation process in the U.S. and to encourage the use of safe, innovative building technology. Specific areas of interest include environmental hazard abatement in buildings (focusing on lead, asbestos, indoor air quality, and radon), reduced housing costs through rehabilitation, seismic, wind and flood hazards mitigation, building environment and thermal envelope research needs, building code studies, model manuals for operating and maintaining facilities, conversion to metric measurement, and the development of research projects. Serves to bring together the nation's building community in order to identify and resolve common building process problems. **Publications:** Building Sciences Newsletter (bimonthly); CCB Bulletin (quarterly). **Educational Activities:** BETEC Symposia, in spring and fall; Workshops and seminars on seismic design, moisture control, and building envelope energy issues. **Awards:** BSSC Exceptional Service Award (annually); BSSC Honor Award (annually); Institute Honor Award (annually); Institute Member Award (annually); President's Award (annually).

5717 ■ University of Hartford–Construction Institute
260 Girard Ave., 2nd Fl.
Hartford, CT 06105
Ph:(860)768-5659
Fax:(860)768-5662
Co. E-mail: wcianci@construction.org
URL: http://www.construction.org
Contact: William H. Cianci PhD, Exec.Dir.
E-mail: wcianci@construction.org
Scope: Construction industry and concerns, especially in Connecticut, including the infrastructure system in Connecticut, labor relations, affordable insurance, and the size, scope, and impact of the Connecticut construction industry. Serves as a neutral forum in which construction industry professionals from all disciplines examine issues and resolve major problems. **Services:** Provides information, to industry and public officials. **Publications:** Newsletter. **Educational Activities:** Forums (8/year); Seminars and conferences, on critical industry issues September to June; Training, to help industry professionals improve management skills, add to their technical knowledge, develop personnel, and increase productivity.

5718 ■ University of Illinois at Urbana-Champaign–Building Research Council
School of Architecture
1 Saint Mary's Rd.
Champaign, IL 61820
Ph:(217)333-4698
Fax:(217)244-2204
Co. E-mail: dfournie@illinois.edu
URL: http://brc.arch.uiuc.edu
Contact: Donald Fournier, Ch.
E-mail: dfournie@illinois.edu
Scope: Methods and materials for building construction, particularly light frame construction including thermographic analysis, environmental effects on building materials, mitigation of natural disasters, and roofing and waterproofing materials. Investigates and develops planning standards for space design in housing construction. **Publications:** SEDAC Newsletter (monthly). **Educational Activities:** Weatherization training and building energy assessments; High performance building analyses.

5719 ■ University of Texas at Arlington–Construction Research Center
PO Box 19347
Arlington, TX 76019-0347
Ph:(817)272-3701
Fax:(817)272-7575
Co. E-mail: matthys@uta.edu
URL: http://www.uta.edu/ce/crc
Contact: John H. Matthys PhD, Dir.
E-mail: matthys@uta.edu
Scope: Addresses the needs of the construction industry through construction research and educational programs. **Educational Activities:** Seminars (10/year), open to builders, architects, engineers, contractors, and other personnel of the construction industry.

Consumer Electronics Store

ASSOCIATIONS AND OTHER ORGANIZATIONS

5720 ■ Electronics Representatives Association
111 N Canal St., Ste. 885
Chicago, IL 60606
Ph:(312)559-3050
Free: 800-776-7377
Fax:(312)559-4566
Co. E-mail: info@era.org
URL: http://www.era.org
Contact: Robert Walsh, Chm.
Description: Professional field sales organizations selling components and materials; computer, instrumentation and data communications products; audiovisual, security, land/mobile communications and commercial sound components and consumer products to the electronics industry. Sponsors insurance programs and educational conference for members. **Publications:** *Lines Available* (weekly); *Representor* (quarterly).

5721 ■ National Electronics Service Dealers Association
3608 Pershing Ave.
Fort Worth, TX 76107-4527
Ph:(817)921-9061
Free: 800-797-9197
Fax:(817)921-3741
Co. E-mail: info@nesda.com
URL: http://www.nesda.com
Contact: Mack Blakely, Exec. Dir.
Description: Local and state electronic service associations and companies. Supplies technical service information on business management training to electronic service dealers. Offers certification and training programs through International Society of Certified Electronics Technicians. Conducts technical service and business management seminars. **Publications:** *ProService Directory and Yearbook* (annual).

REFERENCE WORKS

5722 ■ "After Price Cuts, Competition GPS Makers Lose Direction" in *Brandweek* (Vol. 49, April 21, 2008, No. 16, pp. 16)
Pub: VNU Business Media, Inc.
Ed: Steve Miller. **Description:** Garmin and TomTom, two of the leaders in portable navigation devices, have seen lowering revenues due to dramatic price cuts and unexpected competition from the broadening availability of personal navigation on mobile phones. TomTom has trimmed its sales outlook for its first quarter while Garmin's stock dropped 40 percent since February.

5723 ■ *Appliance—Appliance Industry Purchasing Section Issue*
Pub: Dana Chase Publications Inc.
Ed: David Chase, Editor, david@appliance.com. **Released:** Annual, January. **Publication Includes:** Suppliers to manufacturers of consumer, commercial, and business appliances. Membership directories for the following associations: Air-Conditioning and Refrigeration Institute, Association of Home Appliance Manufacturers, Commercial Refrigerator Manufacturers Association, Computer and Business Equipment Manufacturers Association, Consumer Electronics Group/Electronic Industries Association, Gas Appliance Manufacturers Association, Cookware Manufacturers Association, National Association of Food Equipment Manufacturers, National Housewares Manufacturers Association, Power Tool Institute, and Vacuum Cleaner Manufacturers Association. **Entries Include:** Company name, address, phone, fax, and products. **Arrangement:** Classified by product. **Indexes:** Manufacturer, product heading.

5724 ■ "Bag It" in *Entrepreneur* (Vol. 36, May 2008, No. 5, pp. 48)
Pub: Entrepreneur Media, Inc.
Ed: Amanda C. Kooser. **Description:** Buyer's guide featuring bags and carrying cases for laptops is presented. Prices and attributes of the bags are provided.

5725 ■ "Best Buy's CEO On Learning to Love Social Media" in *Harvard Business Review* (Vol. 88, December 2010, No. 12, pp. 43)
Pub: Harvard Business School Publishing
Ed: Brian J. Dunn. **Description:** Effective utilization of online social networks to enhance brand identity, connect with consumers, and address bad publicity scenarios is examined.

5726 ■ "The Big Picture" in *Canadian Business* (Vol. 79, Winter 2006, No. 24, pp. 142)
Pub: Rogers Media
Ed: Andy Holloway. **Description:** The features of the new range of high-definition television sets released by Matushita Electric Corporation of America are described. The pricing of the television sets is discussed.

5727 ■ "Bon Voyager" in *Entrepreneur* (Vol. 36, April 2008, No. 4, pp. 58)
Pub: Entrepreneur Media, Inc.
Ed: Heather Clancy. **Description:** LG Voyager, especially made for Verizon Wireless, is a smart phone that is being compared to Apple iPhone. The Voyager has a 2.8-inch external touchscreen and has a clamshell design, which features an internal keyboard. It does not have Wi-Fi support like iPhone, but it has 3G support. Other differences between the two phones are discussed.

5728 ■ "Canon Focuses on New Moms" in *Marketing to Women* (Vol. 21, January 2008, No. 1, pp. 3)
Pub: EPM Communications, Inc.
Description: Canon launches a photo contest aimed at spotlighting baby's first pictures in an attempt to connect with new mothers.

5729 ■ "Clusters Last Stand?" in *Canadian Electronics* (Vol. 23, February 2008, No. 1, pp. 6)
Pub: CLB Media Inc.
Description: Survival of technology clusters was the focus of Strategic Microelectronics Council's conference entitled, "The Power of Community: Building Technology Clusters in Canada". Clusters can help foster growth in the microelectronics sector, and it was recognized that government intervention is needed to maintain these clusters.

5730 ■ "Consumer Electronics: Brick and Mortar Vs. Online" in *Retail Merchandiser* (Vol. 51, September-October 2011, No. 5, pp. 15)
Pub: Phoenix Media Corporation
Description: Brick and mortar retailers with Websites are discovering that the Internet is used more for research than purchasing when it comes to electronics products. According to a recent study conducted by The NPD Group shows that 56 percent of consumers research televisions online before purchasing, but only 19 percent actually buy them online.

5731 ■ "Craig Muhlhauser" in *Canadian Business* (Vol. 81, September 15, 2008, No. 14-15, pp. 6)
Pub: Rogers Media Ltd.
Ed: Andrew Wahl. **Description:** Interview with Craig Muhlhauser who is the CEO of Celestica, a manufacturing company that provides services for the electronics sector; Muhlhauser discusses the company's restructuring program, which he feels was the secret to their surprising first-quarter results. Muhlhauser states that the company is operating with more forward visibility and that understanding the opportunities during the current economic situation presents the biggest challenge.

5732 ■ "Customers Turned Off? Not at Best Buy" in *Barron's* (Vol. 88, March 24, 2008, No. 12, pp. 29)
Pub: Dow Jones & Company, Inc.
Ed: Sandra Ward. **Description:** Shares of Best Buy, trading at $42.41 each, are expected to rise to an average of $52 a share due to the company's solid fundamentals. The company's shares have fallen 20 percent from their 52-week high and are attractive given the company's bright prospects in the video game sector and high-definition video.

5733 ■ "Dear Diary, Arbitron is Dumping You" in *Business Courier* (Vol. 26, September 25, 2009, No. 22, pp. 1)
Pub: American City Business Journals, Inc.
Ed: Dan Monk. **Description:** Arbitron Inc. is replacing hand-written ratings diaries with Portable People Meters or electronic sensors that measure local radio audiences. The technology counts all exposure to radio and stations; those that penetrate the workplace will see success, while the more 'niche' oriented formats will have a more difficult time.

5734 ■ "Digital Edge: Stay Tuned" in *Entrepreneur* (Vol. 35, October 2007, No. 10, pp. 56)
Pub: Entrepreneur Media Inc.
Ed: Mike Hogan. **Description:** Future of set-top boxes, particularly the digital video recorders is promising. TiVo HD, for example, already receives

content from Websites, while companies such as Diego and Microsoft are soon to release similar devices. The potential applications of television and computer convergence are provided.

5735 ■ "Digital Power Management and the PMBus" in *Canadian Electronics* (Vol. 23, June-July 2008, No. 4, pp. 8)
Pub: Action Communication Inc.
Ed: Torbjorn Hohnberg. **Description:** PMBus is an interface that can be applied to a variety of devices including power management devices. Information on digital power management products using this interface are also provided.

5736 ■ "The Easy Route" in *Entrepreneur* (Vol. 36, April 2008, No. 4, pp. 60)
Pub: Entrepreneur Media, Inc.
Ed: Amanda C. Kooser. **Description:** Buyer's guide of wireless office routers is presented. All products included in the list use the latest draft-n technology. Price and availability of the products are provided.

5737 ■ "EDCO Doling Out Capital Along Border" in *Austin Business JournalInc.* (Vol. 28, August 1, 2008, No. 20, pp. 1)
Pub: American City Business Journals
Ed: Sandra Zaragoza. **Description:** Non-profit business incubator Economic Development Catalyst Organization Ventures is searching for promising startup companies. The company is targeting startups in green energy, technology and consumer markets. EDCO has partnered with consumer electronics repair company CherryFusion and technology firm MiniDonations.

5738 ■ "Electronic Design and a Greener Environment" in *Canadian Electronics* (Vol. 23, June-July 2008, No. 4, pp. 6)
Pub: Action Communication Inc.
Ed: Nicholas Deeble. **Description:** Companies seeking to minimize their environmental impact are using Design methodologies of Cadence Design Systems Ltd. The company's Low Power Format and Low Power Design Flow help reduce carbon dioxide emissions.

5739 ■ "Electronics Recycler Poised to Grow" in *Austin Business Journal* (Vol. 31, July 22, 2011, No. 20, pp. A1)
Pub: American City Business Journals Inc.
Ed: Cody Lyon. **Description:** Electronic Recycling and Trading Inc. has leased 138,000 square feet of space in North Austin, Texas. The company requires more space for bigger equipment.

5740 ■ "Five Things...For Photo Fun" in *Hawaii Business* (Vol. 53, October 2007, No. 4, pp. 20)
Pub: Hawaii Business Publishing
Ed: Cathy S. Cruz-George. **Description:** Featured is a buyers guide of products used for capturing or displaying digital photos; products featured include the Digital Photo Wallet and Light Affection.

5741 ■ "Game On! African Americans Get a Shot at $17.9 Billion Video Game Industry" in *Black Enterprise* (Vol. 38, July 2008, No. 12, pp. 56)
Pub: Earl G. Graves Publishing Co. Inc.
Ed: Carolyn M. Brown. **Description:** Despite the economic crisis, consumers are still purchasing the hottest video games and hardware. Tips for African American developers who want to become a part of this industry that lacks content targeting this demographic are offered.

5742 ■ "HR Tech on the Go" in *Workforce Management* (Vol. 88, November 16, 2009, No. 12, pp. 1)
Pub: Crain Communications, Inc.
Ed: Ed Frauenheim. **Description:** Examination of the necessity of mobile access of human resources software applications that allow managers to recruit, schedule and train employees via their mobile devices; some industry leaders believe that mobile HR applications are vital while others see this new technology as hype.

5743 ■ "Industry/Events 2011" in *American Printer* (Vol. 128, July 1, 2011, No. 7)
Pub: Penton Media Inc.
Description: PMA, the Worldwide Community of Imaging Association launched its new CliQ with how-to tips, product reviews and monthly photo contests. PMA formed a partnership with the Consumer Electronics Association to make changes to this year's annual convention.

5744 ■ "IPod Killers?" in *Canadian Business* (Vol. 79, November 20, 2006, No. 23, pp. 68)
Pub: Rogers Media
Ed: Gerry Blackwell. **Description:** The features of Apple iPod that distinguishes it from other MP3 players available in the market are discussed.

5745 ■ "Kodiak Bucks Bear Market" in *Austin Business JournalInc.* (Vol. 29, December 18, 2009, No. 41, pp. 1)
Pub: American City Business Journals
Ed: Kate Harrington. **Description:** Austin, Texas-based Kodiak Assembly Solutions LLC, a company that installs components into printed circuit boards for product or evaluation tool kit prototyping purposes, will expand despite the recession. It will relocate from a 28,000 square foot space to a 42,000 square foot space in North Austin. The firm will also increase its workforce by 20 employees.

5746 ■ "LED Screen Technology Takes Centre Stage" in *Canadian Electronics* (Vol. 23, June-July 2008, No. 4, pp. 17)
Pub: Action Communication Inc.
Ed: Ed Whitaker. **Description:** Display technologies based on light emitting diodes are becoming more popular due to their flexibility, versatility and reproducibility of displays. These are being increasingly used in different applications, such as advertising and concerts.

5747 ■ "Manufacturing Behind the Great Wall: What Works, What Doesn't" in *Canadian Electronics* (Vol. 23, February 2008, No. 1, pp. 6)
Pub: CLB Media Inc.
Ed: Michel Jullian. **Description:** Electronic component producers are increasingly transitioning their manufacturing operations to China in order to take advantage of the growing Chinese manufacturing industry. It is believed that manufacturers have to carefully consider whether their run sizes are appropriate for Chinese manufacturing before moving their operations.

5748 ■ "Meet the Jetsons" in *Entrepreneur* (Vol. 35, November 2007, No. 11, pp. 21)
Pub: Entrepreneur Media Inc.
Ed: Amanda C. Kooser. **Description:** An overview of modern home devices is presented, including an organic light-emitting diode (OLED) wall display with changeable artwork, networked appliances like refrigerators, biometric door locks, and a television that can serve as a computer monitor.

5749 ■ "Miller's Crossroad" in *Canadian Business* (Vol. 83, September 14, 2010, No. 15, pp. 58)
Pub: Rogers Media Ltd.
Ed: Joe Castaldo. **Description:** Future Electronics founder and billionaire Robert Miller shares the secret of Future's unique operating model, which is based on inventory and market research. Miller attributes much of the company's success to its privately held status that enables quick movement against competitors.

5750 ■ "Mosaid Grants First Wireless Parent License To Matsushita" in *Canadian Electronics* (Vol. 23, June-July 2008, No. 5, pp. 1)
Pub: Action Communication Inc.
Description: Matsushita Electric Industrial Co. Ltd. has been granted a six-and-a-half-year license by Mosaid Technologies Inc. to manufacture the latter's products. The patent portfolio license agreement covers Mosaid's Wi-Fi, Wi-Max, CDMA-enabled notebook computers and other products.

5751 ■ "Motors and Motion Control" in *Canadian Electronics* (Vol. 23, February 2008, No. 1, pp. 23)
Pub: CLB Media Inc.
Description: A new version of MicroMo Electronics Inc.'s Smoovy Series 0303...B has been added to MicroMo's DC motor product line. United Electronic Industries, on the other hand, has introduced the new UEIPAC series of programmable automation controllers that can offer solutions to various applications such as unmanned vehicle controllers. Features and functions of other new motors and motion control devices are given.

5752 ■ *National Electronic Distributors Association—Membership Directory*
Pub: National Electronic Distributors Association
Contact: Janet Wood
Released: Annual, summer; latest edition 2003-2004. **Covers:** Approximately 150 member distributors and 150 member manufacturers of electronics products, plus 1,100 branch offices. **Entries Include:** Company name, address, branch locations, phones, names of principal executives, size of firm, products handled, territory served, product cross-reference of distributors, geographical listing, e-mail and web site addresses. **Arrangement:** Alphabetical. **Indexes:** Geographical (includes about 1,100 branches), product category (includes distributors).

5753 ■ "Network TV" in *Canadian Business* (Vol. 79, September 11, 2006, No. 18, pp. 136)
Pub: Rogers Media
Ed: Gerry Blackwell. **Description:** The functions and features of the new Mediasmart LCD TV offered by Hewlett-Packard are discussed.

5754 ■ "Now See This" in *Entrepreneur* (Vol. 36, April 2008, No. 4, pp. 53)
Pub: Entrepreneur Media, Inc.
Ed: Mike Hogan. **Description:** New high definition (HD) products are to be introduced in 2008 at the Consumer Electronics Show and the Macworld Conference & Expo. HD lineup from companies such as Dell Inc. and Hewlett-Packard Co. are discussed.

5755 ■ "Nvidia Shares Clobbered After Gloomy Warning" in *Barron's* (Vol. 88, July 7, 2008, No. 27, pp. 25)
Pub: Dow Jones & Co., Inc.
Ed: Eric J. Savitz. **Description:** Shares of graphics chip manufacturer Nvidia suffered a 30 percent drop in its share price after the company warned that revenue and gross margin forecasts for the quarter ending July 27, 2008 will be below expectations. Stan Glasgow, chief operating officer of Sony Electronics, believes the US economic slowdown will not affect demand for the company's products. Statistical data included.

5756 ■ "Pressed for Time" in *Marketing to Women* (Vol. 21, March 2008, No. 3, pp. 1)
Pub: EPM Communications, Inc.
Description: Statistical data concerning the tools women use for time management which include gadgets as well as traditional media such as calendars.

5757 ■ "Products and Services" in *Canadian Electronics* (Vol. 23, August 2008, No. 5, pp. 46)
Pub: Action Communication Inc.
Description: Directory of companies under the alphabetical listing of electronic equipment and allied components that they offer is presented.

5758 ■ "Providing Expertise Required to Develop Microsystems" in *Canadian Electronics* (Vol. 23, February 2008, No. 1, pp. 6)
Pub: CLB Media Inc.
Ed: Ian McWalter. **Description:** CMC Microsystems, formerly Canadian Microelectronics Corporation, is focused on empowering microelectronics and Microsystems research in Canada. Microsystems offers the basis for innovations in the fields of science,

environment, technology, automotives, energy, aerospace and communications technology. CMC's strategy in developing Microsystems in Canada is described.

5759 ■ "Provinces Tackle E-Waste Problem" in *Canadian Electronics* (Vol. 23, June-July 2008, No. 4, pp. 1)
Pub: Action Communication Inc.
Ed: Ken Manchen. **Description:** Canadian provinces are implementing measures concerning the safe and environmentally friendly disposal of electronic waste. Alberta, British Columbia, Nova Scotia, and Saskatchewan impose an e-waste recycling fee on electronic equipment purchases.

5760 ■ "RIM Gets Smart" in *Canadian Business* (Vol. 79, October 23, 2006, No. 21, pp. 157)
Pub: Rogers Media
Ed: Gerry Blackwell. **Description:** Details of the features of Blackberry Pearl, the new personal digital assistant from Research in Motion Inc., are presented.

5761 ■ "Samsung 'Holding Breath'" in *Austin Business JournalInc.* (Vol. 29, January 29, 2010, No. 47, pp. 1)
Pub: American City Business Journals
Ed: Jacob Dirr. **Description:** Samsung Austin Semiconductor LLC entered into an incentives agreement with the State of Texas in 2005, which involved $230 million in tax breaks and public financing. Terms of the agreement have been met, but some are questioning whether the company will be able to meet its goals for the Austin operations in 2010.

5762 ■ "Sources" in *Canadian Electronics* (Vol. 23, August 2008, No. 5, pp. 12)
Pub: Action Communication Inc.
Description: Directory of electronic manufacturers, distributors and representatives in Canada is provided. The list presents distributors and representatives under each manufacturer.

5763 ■ "STMicroelectronics" in *Canadian Electronics* (Vol. 23, February 2008, No. 1, pp. 1)
Pub: CLB Media Inc.
Description: STMicroelectronics, a semiconductor maker, revealed that it plans to acquire Genesis Microchip Inc. Genesis develops image and video processing systems. It was reported that the acquisition has been approved by Genesis' Board of Directors. It is expected that Genesis will enhance STMicroelectronics' technological capabilities.

5764 ■ "Taiwan Technology Initiatives Foster Growth" in *Canadian Electronics* (Vol. 23, February 2008, No. 1, pp. 28)
Pub: CLB Media Inc.
Description: A study conducted by the Market Intelligence Center shows that currently, Taiwan is the world's larges producer of information technology products such as motherboards, servers, and LCD monitors. In 2006, Taiwan's LED industry reached a production value of NTD 21 billion. This push into the LED sector shows the Ministry of Economic Affairs' plan to target industries that are environmentally friendly.

5765 ■ "Thumbing Around" in *Canadian Business* (Vol. 79, October 9, 2006, No. 20, pp. 143)
Pub: Rogers Media
Ed: Gerry Blackwell. **Description:** The features, functions of Cruzer Titanium, a serial bus standard to interface device developed by SanDisk Corporation are discussed.

5766 ■ "TomTom GO910: On the Road Again" in *Black Enterprise* (Vol. 37, January 2007, No. 6, pp. 52)
Pub: Earl G. Graves Publishing Co. Inc.
Ed: Stephanie Young. **Description:** TomTom GO 910 is a GPS navigator that offers detailed maps of the U.S., Canada, and Europe. Consumers view their routes by a customizable LCD screen showing everything from the quickest to the shortest routes available or how to avoid toll roads. Business travelers may find this product invaluable as it also functions as a cell phone and connects to a variety of other multi-media devices.

5767 ■ "Tony Hawk Carves a New Niche" in *Entrepreneur* (Vol. 37, October 2009, No. 10, pp. 26)
Pub: Entrepreneur Media, Inc.
Ed: Gary Cohn. **Description:** Professional skateboarder Tony Hawk discusses the growth of Birdhouse, the skateboard company he founded. He is excited about the release of Tony Hawk Ride, a videogame with a skateboard controller.

5768 ■ "VTech Targets Tots With a Wee Wii" in *Advertising Age* (Vol. 79, September 8, 2008, No. 33, pp. 14)
Pub: Crain Communications, Inc.
Ed: Beth Snyder Bulik. **Description:** V-Motion is a video-game console targeting 3-to-7-year-olds and is manufactured by educational toy company VTech. The company is marketing the product as a kind of Wii for preschoolers and hopes to build a formidable brand presence in the kids' electronics market.

5769 ■ "Wattles Plugs Back Into State" in *Business Journal Portland* (Vol. 27, November 19, 2010, No. 38, pp. 1)
Pub: Portland Business Journal
Ed: Wendy Culverwell. **Description:** Denver, Colorado-based Ultimate Electronics Inc.'s first store in Oregon was opened in Portland and the 46th store in the chain of electronic superstores is expected to employ 70-80 workers. The venture is the latest for Mark Wattles, one of Oregon's most successful entrepreneurs, who acquired Ultimate from bankruptcy.

5770 ■ "Winning With Women" in *Marketing to Women* (Vol. 22, August 2009, No. 8, pp. 6)
Pub: EPM Communications, Inc.
Description: Women shoppers are buying more utilitarian categories despite the overall fall in consumer electronics sales. Among the top five purchases women will defer in the next three months are personal consumer electronics, such as MP3 players and digital cameras, as well as home entertainment items.

5771 ■ "A Wireless Makes 8 Store-In-Store Kiosk Acquisitions" in *Wireless News* (October 16, 2010)
Pub: Close-Up Media Inc.
Description: A Wireless, a retailer for Verizon Wireless has acquired eight of Verizon's retail kiosks that are positioned in home appliance and electronics stores.

STATISTICAL SOURCES

5772 ■ *RMA Annual Statement Studies*
Pub: Robert Morris Associates (RMA)
Released: Annual. **Price:** $175.00 2006-07 edition, $105.00. **Description:** Contains composite balance sheets and income statements for more than 360 industries, including the accounting, auditing, and bookkeeping industries. Also contains five years of comparative historical data for discerning trends. Includes 16 commonly used ratios, computed for most of the size groupings for nearly every industry.

TRADE PERIODICALS

5773 ■ *NARDA Independent Retailer*
Pub: North American Retail Dealers Association
Released: Monthly. **Price:** $78. **Description:** Magazine for appliance, consumer electronics, furniture, and computer dealers.

5774 ■ *Wireless Week*
Pub: Wireless Week
Contact: Holly Hoffer, Publisher
E-mail: holly.hoffer@advantagemedia.com
Released: Weekly. **Description:** Trade tabloid covering the wireless industry including cellular, paging, satellite, and microwave.

TRADE SHOWS AND CONVENTIONS

5775 ■ National Professional Service Convention and Trade Show
National Electronics Service Dealers Association
3608 Pershing Ave.
Fort Worth, TX 76107-4527
Ph:(817)921-9061
Free: 800-797-9197
Fax:(817)921-3741
Co. E-mail: info@nesda.com
URL: http://www.nesda.com
Released: Annual. **Audience:** Electronic product servicers, dealers. **Principal Exhibits:** Electronics, receivers, recorders, and supplies; software; telecommunications equipment; computers; videocassette recorders; parts and accessories, business forms, warranty companies, and magazines/associations.

FRANCHISES AND BUSINESS OPPORTUNITIES

5776 ■ Handypro Handyman Service
HandyPro Franchise, Inc.
995 S Main St.
Plymouth, MI 48170
Ph:(734)254-9160
Fax:(734)254-9171
No. of Franchise Units: 5. **No. of Company-Owned Units:** 1. **Founded:** 1993. **Franchised:** 2001. **Description:** Professional handyman services. **Equity Capital Needed:** $38,350-$61,900. **Franchise Fee:** $25,000. **Financial Assistance:** No. **Training:** Yes.

5777 ■ K & N Mobile Distribution Systems
K & N Electric Franchising, Inc.
4909 Rondo Dr.
Ft. Worth, TX 76106
Free: 800-433-2170
Fax:(817)624-3721
No. of Franchise Units: 12. **No. of Company-Owned Units:** 13. **Founded:** 1972. **Description:** Distribution and sale of electrical products and fasteners from a "mobile warehouse." Six-month, money-back guarantee in applicable states. **Equity Capital Needed:** $87,000. **Franchise Fee:** $10,000. **Royalty Fee:** 13%. **Financial Assistance:** No. **Managerial Assistance:** Manages franchisees accounts receivables; manages inventory by automatically restocking parts sold during the previous week; also provides computer-generated reports each month that help the franchisee manage the business. **Training:** Initial 10-day training course is conducted at corporate headquarters. Trainer accompanies franchisee during the first 3-10 days in the field. During the first year, a trainer rides with the franchisee at least 2 days per quarter. After the franchisee has been in business for 1 year, a corporate representative will spend 4 or more days with the franchisee each year.

5778 ■ RadioShack
RadioShack Dealer Franchise
RadioShack Riverfrt Campus
300 RadioShack Cr
Ft. Worth, TX 76102
Ph:(817)415-9138
No. of Franchise Units: 1,172. **No. of Company-Owned Units:** 4,473. **Founded:** 1921. **Franchised:** 1968. **Description:** Retail electronics. **Equity Capital Needed:** $149,875-$542,351. **Franchise Fee:** $39,900. **Royalty Fee:** 7%. **Financial Assistance:** Yes. **Training:** Offers 1 week training at franchisee's location, local workshops, annual convention and ongoing support.

5779 ■ Rapid Refill Ink
Rapid Refill Ink Intl., Corp.
18732 Lake Dr. E
Chanhassen, MN 55317
Ph:(952)238-1000
Free: 877-880-4465

Fax:(952)238-1009
No. of Franchise Units: 92. **No. of Company-Owned Units:** 1. **Founded:** 2002. **Franchised:** 2004. **Description:** Remanufacturing of inkjet & laser toner cartridges. **Equity Capital Needed:** $84,350-$135,300. **Franchise Fee:** $30,000. **Royalty Fee:** 6%. **Financial Assistance:** Third party financing available. **Training:** Provides 2 weeks training at headquarters, including 3 days business training.

COMPUTERIZED DATABASES

5780 ■ *INSPEC Ondisc - Technology*
Institution of Engineering and Technology
Michael Faraday House
Stevenage SG1 2AY, United Kingdom
Ph:44 1438 313 311
Fax:44 1438 765 526
Co. E-mail: postmaster@theiet.org
URL: http://www.theiet.org
Description: Contains abstracts and citations to the worldwide literature on electrical engineering and electronics, computers, and information technology. Covers: electronic components, devices, and circuits, Telecommunication, power engineering, and instrumentation; computer theory, hardware, software, applications of computing, control theory, and technology; and the gathering, processing, storage, distribution, and uses of information in Business, Industry, Education, and recreation. Sources include more than 4000 scientific and technical journals, more than 2000 conference proceedings, as well as books, dissertations, and technical reports. A subset of, and corresponds in part to, the INSPEC database (described in a separate entry). **Availability:** CD-ROM: Institution of Engineering and Technology. **Type:** Bibliographic.

LIBRARIES

5781 ■ Agilent Technologies–Santa Clara Site Library
5301 Stevens Creek Blvd.
MS 55/27
Santa Clara, CA 95051
Ph:(408)345-8886
Free: 877-424-4536
Fax:(408)345-8474
Co. E-mail: contact_us@agilent.com
URL: http://www.home.agilent.com
Contact: Diana Robba, Res.Info.Spec. & Mgr.
Scope: Electronics, business, computer science, biological sciences. **Services:** Interlibrary loan; copying; Library not open to the public. **Holdings:** 4000 books. **Subscriptions:** 160 journals and other serials; 2 newspapers.

5782 ■ Fujitsu Microelectronics, Inc.–FMI Library
1250 E. Arques Ave., No. 333
Sunnyvale, CA 94085-5401
Ph:(408)746-6000
Free: 800-831-3183; (800)866
Fax:(408)992-2674
Co. E-mail: fsa_inquiry@us.fujitsu.com
URL: http://www.fujitsu.com/us
Contact: Jasmine Kuen, Mktg.Anl.
Scope: Semiconductor industry and products, computer industry and products, telecommunications, electronics industry. **Services:** Interlibrary loan; SDI; Library not open to the public. **Holdings:** 500 books and conference proceedings; 250 market research reports and newsletters; CD-ROMs. **Subscriptions:** 70 journals and other serials; 2 newspapers.

Convenience Store

ASSOCIATIONS AND OTHER ORGANIZATIONS

5783 ■ Food Marketing Institute
2345 Crystal Dr., Ste. 800
Arlington, VA 22202-4801
Ph:(202)452-8444
Fax:(202)429-4519
Co. E-mail: fmi@fmi.org
URL: http://www.fmi.org
Contact: Leslie G. Sarasin, Pres./CEO
Description: Grocery retailers and wholesalers. Maintains liaison with government and consumers. Conducts 30 educational conferences and seminars per year. Conducts research programs; compiles statistics. **Publications:** *Facts About Supermarket Development* (annual); *Food Marketing Industry Speaks* (annual).

5784 ■ National Association of Convenience Stores
1600 Duke St.
Alexandria, VA 22314
Ph:(703)684-3600
Free: 800-966-6227
Fax:(703)836-4564
Co. E-mail: information@nacsonline.com
URL: http://www.nacsonline.com
Contact: Henry Armour, Pres./CEO

5785 ■ National Grocers Association
1005 N Glebe Rd., Ste. 250
Arlington, VA 22201-5758
Ph:(703)516-0700
Fax:(703)812-1821
Co. E-mail: feedback@nationalgrocers.org
URL: http://www.nationalgrocers.org
Contact: Peter J. Larkin, Pres./CEO
Description: Independent food retailers; wholesale food distributors servicing 29,000 food stores. Promotes industry interests and works to advance understanding, trade and cooperation among all sectors of the food industry. Represents members' interests before the government. Aids in the development of programs designed to improve the productivity and efficiency of the food distribution industry. Offers services in areas such as store planning and engineering, personnel selection and training, operations and advertising. Sponsors seminars and in-house training. Maintains liaison with Women Grocers of America, which serves as an advisory arm. **Publications:** *Congressional or Regulatory Update* (periodic).

REFERENCE WORKS

5786 ■ "7-Eleven Considers Private Label Ice Cream" in *Ice Cream Reporter* (Vol. 22, December 20, 2008, No. 1, pp. 1)
Pub: Ice Cream Reporter
Description: 7-Eleven is considering the introduction of a private label of snack foods, including ice cream desserts.

5787 ■ "Amcon Distributing Co." in *Arkansas Business* (Vol. 26, November 9, 2009, No. 45, pp. 13)
Pub: Journal Publishing Inc.
Description: Amcon Distributing Co., a consumer products company, has bought the convenience store distribution assets of Discount Distributors from its parent, Harps Food Stores Inc., significantly increasing its wholesale distribution presence in the northwest Arkansas market. The acquisition will be funded through Amcon's existing credit facilities.

5788 ■ "Ampm Focus Has BP Working Overtime; New Convenience-Store Brand Comes to Chicago" in *Crain's Chicago Business* (April 28, 2008)
Pub: Crain Communications, Inc.
Ed: John T. Slania. **Description:** Britian's oil giant BP PLC is opening its ampm convenience stores in the Chicago market and has already begun converting most of its 78 Chicago-area gas stations to ampms. The company has also started to franchise the stores to independent operators. BP is promoting the brand with both traditional and unconventional marketing techniques such s real or simulated 3D snacks embedded in bus shelter ads and an in-store Guitar Hero contest featuring finalists from a recent contest at the House of Blues.

5789 ■ "Casey's Buys Second Marion Convenience Store" in *Gazette* (December 14, 2010)
Pub: Gazette
Ed: Dave DeWitte. **Description:** Casey's General Stores Inc. has acquired a Short Stop convenience store on Marion's west side in Iowa. The new store includes a car and truck wash.

5790 ■ "Clean Bathrooms Are Big Key to Convenience Store's Success" in *Marketing to Women* (Vol. 23, January 2010, No. 1, pp. 3)
Pub: EPM Communications, Inc.
Description: Buc-ee's, a Texas-based convenience store chain, is attributing its large female consumer base to the cleanliness of its bathrooms. The chain actually markets itself specifically to female consumers.

5791 ■ "Convenience Store Deal for Cardtronics" in *American Banker* (Vol. 174, July 28, 2009, No. 143, pp. 12)
Pub: SourceMedia, Inc.
Description: Royal Buying Group, Inc., a convenience store marketing company, has agreed to recommend automated teller machine services from Cardtronics Inc., to its clients.

5792 ■ "Convenience Store Expanding" in *Clovis News Journal* (November 9, 2010)
Pub: Freedom Communications Inc.
Description: Allsup's convenience store on North Prince Street in Clovis, New Mexico will expand its facilities. The current building is being demolished to make way for the new construction.

5793 ■ "Convenience Store Owners Will Request New Zoning Once More" in *Daily Republic* (November 1, 2010)
Pub: McClatchy Tribune Information Services
Ed: Tom Lawrence. **Description:** Zoning change has been requested for a proposed convenience store in Mitchell, South Dakota. Details are included.

5794 ■ "December 19 Is a Great Day to be Terrible" in *Internet Wire* (December 15, 2009)
Pub: Comtex News Network, Inc.
Description: Overview of the plans to market the grand opening of the newest Terrible Herbst location in Las Vegas, Nevada. Terrible Herbst is a complete convenience destination offering a gas station, convenience store, car wash and lube center.

5795 ■ *Directory of Supermarket, Grocery & Convenience Store Chains*
Pub: Chain Store Guide
Released: Annual, Latest edition 2011. **Price:** $425, individuals Directory; $495, individuals Online lite; $1,175, individuals Online pro. **Covers:** Over 3,269 supermarket, grocery, and convenience store chains operating 71,000 stores in the United States and Canada. **Entries Include:** For supermarkets/groceries—company name, address, phone, fax, e-mail and web address; total annual sales; grocery sales; Internet order processing indicator; total units; number of units by type; number of units by trade name; number of units franchised to and from; total selling square feet; prototype sizes; average number of checkouts; projected number of units by specialty department; primary wholesaler type, name and location; parent company name and location; subsidiary name and location; divisional and branch office locations; warehouse locations; year founded; public company indicator; key personnel with titles. For convenience stores—company name, address, phone and fax numbers, web and e-mail addresses; total annual sales; convenience store sales; gasoline sales percentage; Internet order processing indicator; total units; number of units by trade name; number of units franchised to and from; total selling square footage; prototype sizes; average number of checkouts; projected number of openings and remodeling; packaged liquor indicators; trading areas; distribution center locations; number of units by specialty department; primary wholesaler type, name and location; parent company, subsidiary, warehouse, divisional and branch office names and locations; year founded; public company indicator; key personnel with titles. **Arrangement:** Geographical with sections for supermarkets and convenience stores. **Indexes:** Top 200 chains, trading area, alphabetical, exclusions.

5796 ■ "Green and Clean" in *Retail Merchandiser* (Vol. 51, July-August 2011, No. 4, pp. 56)
Pub: Phoenix Media Corporation
Description: Green Valley Grocery partnered with Paragon Solutions consulting firm to make their stores environmentally green.

5797 ■ "Hy-Vee Plans Expansion, Convenience Store in Cedar Rapids" in *Gazette* (November 26, 2010)
Pub: Gazette
Ed: George Ford. **Description:** Hy-Vee Inc. is awaiting approval to expand its supermarket in Cedar

Rapids, Iowa. Hy-Vee is a food and drug store chain will construct a convenience store and gas station on the site.

5798 ■ "In the Fast Lane" in *Chain Store Age* (Vol. 85, November 2009, No. 11, pp. 44)
Pub: Chain Store Age

Ed: Samantha Murphy. **Description:** Quick Chek, which operates some 120 convenience stores in New Jersey and southern New York, is testing a new self-checkout system in order to examine how speed affects its in-store experience.

5799 ■ "Javo Beverage to Feature On-Demand Coffee System" in *GlobeNewswire* (October 20, 2009)
Pub: Comtex News Network, Inc.

Description: During the National Association of Convenience Store Show (NACS) at the Las Vegas Convention Center, Javo Beverage Company, Inc., a leading provider of premium dispensable coffee and tea-based beverages to the foodservice industry, will introduce its on-demand hot coffee system as well as a new line of products for the convenience store industry.

5800 ■ "Killings Remind Convenience Store Workers of Job's Potential Risks" in *Waterloo Courier* (November 19, 2010)
Pub: Gazette

Ed: Tina Hinz. **Description:** Potential risks for convenience store workers is stressed citing shootings in area shops; safety plans are important for these stores.

5801 ■ "McD's Picks a Soda Fight; Takes on 7-Eleven With $1 Pop as Economy Softens" in *Crain's Chicago Business* (April 14, 2008)
Pub: Crain Communications, Inc.

Ed: David Sterrett. **Description:** McDonald's Corp. is urging franchise owners to slash prices on large soft drinks to one dollar this summer to win customers from convenience store chains like 7-Eleven.

5802 ■ "Merchants Association Working on Deal for Large Wholesale Warehouse" in *Austin Business JournalInc.* (September 19, 2008)
Pub: American City Business Journals

Ed: Jean Kwon. **Description:** Greater Austin Merchants Association planning to buy a former Dell Outlet Factory in Austin, Texas and convert it into a warehouse for convenience stores and gas stations.

5803 ■ "MillerCoors Needs the Quickie Mart" in *Crain's Chicago Business* (Vol. 32, November 16, 2009, No. 46, pp. 2)
Pub: Crain Communications, Inc.

Ed: David Sterrett. **Description:** Power Marts convenience store owner Sam Odeh says that Chicago-based MillerCoors LLC has done a poor job at promoting its brand, keeping its signs up to date and stocking the shelves at his stores. He complains that the company's service has been awful and the marketing pathetic. Convenience stores accounted for more than $14 billion in beer sales in the past year.

5804 ■ *Progressive Grocer's Marketing Guidebook*
Pub: Trade Dimensions

Released: Annual, Latest edition 2011. **Covers:** Over 1,000 U.S. and Canadian supermarket chains, large independents and wholesalers; also includes 350 specialty distributors include smaller food wholesalers, food brokers, non-food distributors, and candy/tobacco/media distributors and over 15,000 key executives and buyers. **Entries Include:** For retailers and wholesalers—Company name, address, phone, email and websites, number of stores operated or served, areas of operation, major grocery supplier, three-year financial summary, buying policies, private label information, lists of executives, buyers, and merchandisers. For specialty distributors—Name, address, phone, list of key personnel including buyers' categories, list of items handled, URL. **Arrangement:** Alphabetical by hierarchy, geographical by eight regions and 50 market areas. **Indexes:** Grocery related organizations, chain and wholesalers, state index, store operating name/parent company reference.

5805 ■ "QuikTrip Makes Fortune 'Best' List" in *Tulsa World* (January 22, 2010)
Pub: Tulsa World

Ed: Kyle Arnold. **Description:** According to a list released by Fortune Magazine, QuikTrip Corp. is once again ranked among the best companies in the country to work for due to the core values and culture held by the company's management.

5806 ■ "Shout and Devour" in *Tulsa World* (November 7, 2009)
Pub: Tulsa World

Ed: Kyle Arnold. **Description:** Profile of convenience store Shout and Sack whose owners have distanced themselves from the corporate fray of the chain stores by offering homemade lunches served at a counter; the store recently gained national exposure that highlighted the popularity despite a market share heavily dominated by franchises and chains.

5807 ■ "Some Atlantic Beach Leaders Leery About Convenience Store Safety Measure" in *Florida Times-Union* (November 3, 2010)
Pub: Florida Times-Union

Ed: Drew Dixon. **Description:** Jacksonville, Florida authorities are proposing a new ordinance that would require convenience stores to upgrade safety measures to protect store workers and customers from robbery and other crimes.

5808 ■ "TMC Development Closes $1.1 Million Real Estate Purchase" in *Internet Wire* (September 17, 2009)
Pub: Comtex News Network, Inc.

Description: TMC Development announced the closing of a $1.1 million real estate purchase for Mansa, LLC dba Kwikee Mart, a Napa-based convenience store; TMC helped the company secure a Small Business Administration 504 loan in order to purchase the acquisition of a 3,464 square foot building. SBA created the 504 loan program to provide financing for growing small and medium-sized businesses.

5809 ■ *Trade Dimensions—Directory of Convenience Stores*
Pub: Trade Dimensions
Contact: Carley Staron, Directories Mktg. Mgr.

Released: Annual, Latest edition 2009. **Price:** $290, individuals print; $645, individuals CD. **Covers:** Over 1,600 U.S. and Canadian convenience store companies, each having four or more convenience stores. **Entries Include:** Company name, address, phone, fax, email, website; URL; operating names; financial data; key personnel; number of stores operated; number of stores selling gasoline; number of stores franchised; number of stores selling fast food, number of stores with ATMs; names of grocery wholesalers, gasoline suppliers; candy, tobacco, and other distributors. **Arrangement:** Geographical (in 50 market areas). **Indexes:** Organization name, store operating name, major grocery supplier.

5810 ■ "Walmart, Target Moving to Convenience Store Near You" in *Hardware Retailing* (Vol. 199, November 2010, No. 5, pp. 60)
Pub: North American Retail Hardware Association

Description: Walmart has plans to move into small convenience stores in Chicago, Detroit, San Francisco, and Los Angeles.

STATISTICAL SOURCES

5811 ■ *RMA Annual Statement Studies*
Pub: Robert Morris Associates (RMA)

Released: Annual. **Price:** $175.00 2006-07 edition, $105.00. **Description:** Contains composite balance sheets and income statements for more than 360 industries, including the accounting, auditing, and bookkeeping industries. Also contains five years of comparative historical data for discerning trends. Includes 16 commonly used ratios, computed for most of the size groupings for nearly every industry.

5812 ■ *Standard & Poor's Industry Surveys*
Pub: Standard & Poor's Corp.

Released: Annual. **Price:** $3633.00. **Description:** Two-volume book that examines the prospects for specific industries, including trucking. Also provides analyses of trends and problems, statistical tables and charts, and comparative company analyses.

TRADE PERIODICALS

5813 ■ *Grocery Headquarters*
Pub: Macfadden Communications Group L.L.C.
Contact: Seth Mendelson, Publisher/Editorial Dir./VP
E-mail: smendelson@groceryheadquarters.com

Released: Monthly. **Price:** Free to qualified subscribers. **Description:** Magazine (tabloid) serving the supermarket industry.

5814 ■ *NACS*
Pub: National Association of Convenience Stores (NACS)

Ed: Pressley Erin, Editor, ssmall@cstorecentral.com. **Released:** Monthly. **Price:** Included in membership. **Description:** Reports on key industry trends and innovative practices of convenience store companies. Recurring features include news of research, a calendar of events, reports of meetings, news of educational opportunities, and notices of publications available.

5815 ■ *VFDA Update*
Pub: Virginia Food Dealers Association Inc.

Ed: Nadine Kadlubowski, Editor. **Released:** Monthly. **Price:** Included in membership. **Description:** Carries news and items of interest to those in retail food industries.

FRANCHISES AND BUSINESS OPPORTUNITIES

5816 ■ 7-Eleven Inc.
One Arts Plz., Ste. 1000
1722 Routh St.
Dallas, TX 75201
Free: 800-255-0711

No. of Franchise Units: 6,515. **No. of Company-Owned Units:** 457. **Founded:** 1927. **Franchised:** 1964. **Description:** Convenience store. **Equity Capital Needed:** $30,800-$604,500. **Franchise Fee:** $10,000-$440,400. **Royalty Fee:** Varies. **Financial Assistance:** Third party financing available. **Training:** Provides 6 weeks training and ongoing support.

5817 ■ Circle K
1130 W Warner Rd.
Tempe, AZ 85284
Ph:(602)728-8000
Fax:(602)728-5248

No. of Franchise Units: 491. **No. of Company-Owned Units:** 2,901. **Founded:** 1991. **Franchised:** 1995. **Description:** Convenience store. **Equity Capital Needed:** $171,000-$1,882,150. **Franchise Fee:** $25,000. **Royalty Fee:** 3.7-4.5%. **Financial Assistance:** Financial ssistance with equipment. **Training:** 2 weeks training at headquarters, 2 weeks at franchisee's location and ongoing support.

5818 ■ Express Mart Franchising Corp.
Petr-All Petroleum Corp.
6567 Kinne Rd.
DeWitt, NY 13214
Ph:(315)446-0125

No. of Franchise Units: 21. **No. of Company-Owned Units:** 44. **Founded:** 1975. **Franchised:** 1987. **Description:** Convenience stores the franchise is a license to utilize the franchisor's service name "Express Mart," related service mark and logotype, as well as the franchisor's system for identification, layout and operation of convenience stores. Features pre-packaged and prepared foods, beverages, sundries, motor fuels and convenience store goods at a single approved location. **Equity Capital Needed:** $86,000-$450,000. **Franchise Fee:** $15,000. **Financial Assistance:** No. **Managerial Assistance:** Coordination and counsel from highly-skilled professional managers with considerable experience in convenience store and petroleum marketing. Provides tested programs, a comprehensive procedures manual and a strong field support network. **Training:** Provides comprehensive training: 1 week of classroom training in Phase I, and 1 week of in-store training in Phase II. Phase I deals with gasoline merchandising, convenience-store merchandising, alcohol management, inventory and loss control, recruiting, hiring, interviewing and customer relations. Phase II is onsite training on all applications.

5819 ■ Just-A-Buck
Just-A-Buck Licensing, Inc
563 Temple Hill Rd.
New Windsor, NY 12553
Ph:(845)561-7411
Fax:(845)561-7433
Co. E-mail: rs@spryal.net
URL: http://www.just-a-buck.com

No. of Franchise Units: 21. **No. of Company-Owned Units:** 6. **Founded:** 1988. **Franchised:** 1992. **Description:** Dollar store. **Equity Capital Needed:** Minimum initial liquid capital required $50,000. **Franchise Fee:** $25,000. **Financial Assistance:** Third party financing. **Training:** Provides corporate and onsite training.

5820 ■ Street Corner
McColla Enterprises Ltd.
2945 SW Wanamaker Dr.
Topeka, KS 66614
Ph:(782)272-8529
Fax:(785)272-2384
URL: http://www.streetcornernews.com

No. of Franchise Units: 50. **Founded:** 1988. **Franchised:** 1995. **Description:** A convenience store and newsstand. **Equity Capital Needed:** $30,000 liquid. **Franchise Fee:** $19,900. **Financial Assistance:** No. **Training:** Training available at headquarters upon request, 1 week at franchisee's location and ongoing support.

5821 ■ White Hen Pantry, Inc.
Clark Retail Enterprises Inc.
1722 Routh St., Ste. 1000
Dallas, TX 75201
Ph:(630)366-3100
Fax:(630)366-3447

No. of Franchise Units: 260. **Founded:** 1965. **Franchised:** 1965. **Description:** Convenience food store of approximately 2,500 square feet. Up-front parking for 10-15 cars. Stores are usually open 24 hours (some operate a lesser number of hours) for 365 days a year. Product line includes a service deli, fresh bakery, fresh produce and a wide variety of staples. **Equity Capital Needed:** $40,000-$45,000, not including franchise fee. **Franchise Fee:** $25,000. **Financial Assistance:** Available to qualified candidates. **Managerial Assistance:** Business insurance (group health and plate glass insurance are optional). Store counselor visits regular and frequent. **Training:** 3 weeks of classroom and in-store training precede store opening. Follow-up training provided after taking over store. Detailed operations manuals provided.

LIBRARIES

5822 ■ National Association of Convenience Stores–NACS Information Center
1600 Duke St.
Alexandria, VA 22314-3436
Ph:(703)684-3600
Free: 800-966-6227
Fax:(703)836-4564
Co. E-mail: nacs@nacsonline.com
URL: http://www.nacsonline.com
Contact: Henry Armour, Pres./CEO

Scope: Convenience stores, retail trade, petroleum marketing, food service. **Services:** Center open to the public by appointment only. **Holdings:** 600 books; 200 video cassettes; archives. **Subscriptions:** 100 journals and other serials.

ASSOCIATIONS AND OTHER ORGANIZATIONS

5823 ■ American Culinary Federation
180 Center Place Way
St. Augustine, FL 32095
Ph:(904)824-4468
Free: 800-624-9458
Fax:(904)825-4758
Co. E-mail: acf@acfchefs.net
URL: http://www.acfchefs.org
Contact: Heidi Cramb, Exec. Dir.
Description: Aims to promote the culinary profession and provide on-going educational training and networking for members. Provides opportunities for competition, professional recognition, and access to educational forums with other culinary experts at local, regional, national, and international events. Operates the National Apprenticeship Program for Cooks and pastry cooks. Offers programs that address certification of the individual chef's skills, accreditation of culinary programs, apprenticeship of cooks and pastry cooks, professional development, and the fight against childhood hunger. **Publications:** *The Culinary Insider* (biweekly); *Culinary Olympic Cookbook*; *National Culinary Review* (monthly); *Sizzle* (quarterly).

5824 ■ International Association of Culinary Professionals
1100 Johnson Ferry Rd., Ste. 300
Atlanta, GA 30342
Ph:(404)252-3663
Free: 800-928-4227
Fax:(404)252-0774
Co. E-mail: info@iacp.com
URL: http://www.iacp.com
Contact: Cynthia Glover, Pres.
Description: Represents cooking school owners, food writers, chefs, caterers, culinary specialists, directors, teachers, cookbook authors, food stylists, food photographers, student/apprentices, and individuals in related industries in 20 countries. Promotes the interests of cooking schools, teachers, and culinary professionals. Encourages the exchange of information and education. Promotes professional standards and accreditation procedures. Maintains a Foundation to award culinary scholarships and grants. **Publications:** *International Association of Culinary Professionals Food Forum Quarterly* (quarterly).

5825 ■ International Council on Hotel, Restaurant, and Institutional Education
2810 N Parham Rd., Ste. 230
Richmond, VA 23294
Ph:(804)346-4800
Fax:(804)346-5009
Co. E-mail: kmccarty@chrie.org
URL: http://www.chrie.org
Contact: Kathy McCarty, CEO
Description: Schools and colleges offering specialized education and training in hospitals, recreation, tourism and hotel, restaurant, and institutional administration; individuals, executives, and students. Provides networking opportunities and professional development. **Publications:** *Guide to Hospitality Education* (semiannual); *Hosteur Magazine* (biennial); *The Journal of Hospitality and Tourism Education* (quarterly); *The Journal of Hospitality and Tourism Research* (3/year); *Membership Directory and Research Guide* (annual).

5826 ■ National Restaurant Association Educational Foundation
175 W Jackson Blvd., Ste. 1500
Chicago, IL 60604-2702
Ph:(312)715-1010
Free: 800-765-2122
Co. E-mail: info@restaurant.org
URL: http://www.nraef.org
Contact: Linda Bacin, Interim Exec. Dir.
Description: Serves as an educational foundation supported by the National Restaurant Association and all segments of the foodservice industry including restaurateurs, foodservice companies, food and equipment manufacturers, distributors and trade associations. Advances the professional standards of the industry through education and research. Offers video training programs, management courses and careers information. Conducts research and maintains hall of fame. .

REFERENCE WORKS

5827 ■ "Beyond Grits: The Many Varieties of Southern Cuisine" in *Women In Business* (Vol. 62, June 2010, No. 2, pp. 14)
Pub: American Business Women's Association
Ed: Debbie Gold. **Description:** Southern cuisine is believed to be associated with grits, but the cuisine is not always with grits and offers varieties from Europe, Native American and African cooking. Southern cuisine varieties include soul food, Creole food, Cajun food and Low Country food. Examples are provided.

5828 ■ "A Failed Promise: A Dream Job Gone...or Just Delayed?" in *Restaurant Business* (Vol. 107, September 2008, No. 9, pp. 34)
Pub: Ideal Media
Ed: Patricia Cobe, Joan M. Lang, Dana Tanyeri. **Description:** Profile of Jeremy Lycanwas, executive chef who taught at the California Culinary Academy. Lycanwas tells of accepting a position as executive chef from his mentor, and later started his own restaurant.

5829 ■ "Holy Wasabi! Sushi Not Just For Parents Anymore" in *Chicago Tribune* (March 13, 2008)
Pub: McClatchy-Tribune Information Services
Ed: Christopher Borrelli. **Description:** Wicker Park cooking school, The Kid's Table, specializes in cooking classes for pre-teens; Elena Marre who owns the school was surprised when she was asked to plan a children's party in which she would teach a course in sushi making. More and more adolescents and small children are eating sushi.

5830 ■ "Intrepid Souls: Meet a Few Who've Made the Big Leap" in *Crain's Chicago Business* (Vol. 31, November 10, 2008, No. 45, pp. 26)
Pub: Crain Communications, Inc.
Ed: Meredith Landry. **Description:** Advice is given from entrepreneurs who have launched businesses in the last year despite the economic crisis. Among the types of businesses featured are a cooking school, a child day-care center, a children's clothing store and an Internet-based company.

5831 ■ "It's all Kosher at Downtown Eatery/ Bakery" in *AZ Daily Star* (July 10, 2008)
Pub: Arizona Daily Star
Ed: Valerie Vinyard. **Description:** Rabbi James Botwright and partner Wayne Anderson are profiled. Details of how the partners opened their bakery and eatery in Tucson, Arizona. Botwright, who attended culinary school in San Francisco, learned much from his grandfather who was a pastry chef.

5832 ■ *Martha, Inc.*
Pub: John Wiley and Sons, Inc.
Ed: Christopher Byron. **Released:** 2002. **Price:** $28. 00. **Description:** Profile of Martha Stewart's rise from working class to a billionaire businesswoman is presented. The book covers Stewart's power struggles and personal conflicts as well as her triumphs.

5833 ■ "Nurturing Talent for Tomorrow" in *Restaurants and Institutions* (Vol. 118, September 15, 2008, No. 14, pp. 90)
Pub: Reed Business Information
Description: Hormel Foods Corporation and The Culinary Institute of America (CIA) have teamed to develop The Culinary Enrichment and Innovation Program that supports future culinary leaders by providing creative and competitive staff development. Sixteen students attend four three-day sessions at the CIA's campus in Hyde Park, New York; sessions include classroom teaching, one-on-one interaction with leading culinarians, and hands-on kitchen time.

5834 ■ *The Pampered Chef*
Pub: Doubleday Broadway Publishing Group
Ed: Doris Christopher. **Price:** $24.95.

TRADE PERIODICALS

5835 ■ *Bon Appetit*
Pub: Conde Nast Publications Inc.
Contact: Jamie Pallot, Editorial Dir.
Released: Monthly. **Price:** $12 plus 3 shipping & handling; $24 plus 6 shipping & handling. **Description:** Lifestyle magazine covering food, travel, and entertaining.

5836 ■ *Cooking for Profit*
Pub: CP Publishing, Inc.
Released: Monthly. **Price:** $30; $55 two years; $52 Canada; $98 Canada 2 years; $85 other countries; $160 other countries 2 years. **Description:** Food service trade publication for owners/operators of food service businesses. Profiles successful operations,

offers management tips, recipes with photos and step-by-step instructions, new and improved uses and maintenance of gas equipment.

5837 ■ *ESSENCE*
Pub: Canadian Federation of Chefs & Cooks
Ed: Julius Pokomandy, Editor. **Released:** Quarterly. **Price:** Included in membership; $15, nonmembers. **Description:** Promotes national culinary events, information from chefs, skills upgrading, and product information. Recurring features include letters to the editor, interviews, news of research, a calendar of events, reports of meetings, and news of educational opportunities.

5838 ■ *No Salt Week-The Newsletter*
Pub: Prosperity & Profits Unlimited, Distribution Services
Contact: A. Doyle
Ed: A. Doyle, Editor. **Released:** Annual. **Price:** $2, U.S.; $3, Canada; $4, elsewhere. **Description:** Presents possibilities for herb and spice blends that contain no added salt. Also contains ideas for cooking and much more.

VIDEOCASSETTES/ AUDIOCASSETTES

5839 ■ *Jacques Pepin's Cooking Techniques*
PBS Home Video
Catalog Fulfillment Center
PO Box 751089
Charlotte, NC 28275-1089
Ph:800-531-4727
Free: 800-645-4PBS
Co. E-mail: info@pbs.org
URL: http://www.pbs.org
Released: 1998. **Price:** $69.95. **Description:** Master chef Jacques Pepin, host of public TV series "Today's Gourmet," teaches the fundamentals that turn good recipes into great meals. He reveals secrets of cooking from sharpening knives to making the perfect omelette. Five hours and 30 minutes on five videocassettes. **Availability:** VHS.

5840 ■ *Le Cordon Bleu II*
PBS Home Video
Catalog Fulfillment Center
PO Box 751089
Charlotte, NC 28275-1089
Ph:800-531-4727
Free: 800-645-4PBS
Co. E-mail: info@pbs.org
URL: http://www.pbs.org
Released: 1998. **Price:** $99.95. **Description:** The Master Chefs of Le Cordon Bleu, one of the finest schools of French cuisine in the world, show the viewer how to prepare Tournedos Montagnarde (filet mignon with goat cheese and pine nuts in a red wine sauce), Coq au Vin and show how to prepare a menu for a dinner party or holiday gathering. Four hours on four videocassettes. **Availability:** VHS.

FRANCHISES AND BUSINESS OPPORTUNITIES

5841 ■ Batter Up Kids Culinary Center
4403 Canyonside Trail
Austin, TX 78731
Ph:(512)342-8682
Free: (866)345-8682
Fax:(512)343-8810
No. of Company-Owned Units: 1. **Founded:** 1991. **Franchised:** 2006. **Description:** Children's culinary program. **Equity Capital Needed:** $178,100-$256,000 total investment; $70,000 net worth. **Franchise Fee:** $25,000. **Royalty Fee:** 4%. **Financial Assistance:** No. **Training:** Provides 4-5 days at headquarters, 4-5 days at franchisee's location with ongoing support.

LIBRARIES

5842 ■ Atlantic Cape Community College–William Spangler Library
Mays Landing Campus
5100 Black Horse Pike
Mays Landing, NJ 08330-2699
Ph:(609)343-4951
Co. E-mail: wilinski@atlantic.edu
URL: http://www.atlantic.edu/library/index.htm
Contact: Grant Wilinski, Dir.
Scope: Business, criminal justice, culinary arts, dance, education, English, general studies, geography, history, hospitality, Library vocabulary, nursing, psychology, sociology. **Services:** Interlibrary loan; copying; Library open to the public. **Holdings:** 71,000 books; audio and video materials. **Subscriptions:** 320 journals and other serials; 8 newspapers.

5843 ■ California Culinary Academy Library
625 Polk St.
San Francisco, CA 94102
Ph:800-229-2433
Free: 888-897-3222
Co. E-mail: bgk@baychef.com
URL: http://www.baychef.com
Contact: Beth Klein, Dean, Lib.Svcs.
Scope: Culinary arts, nutrition, restaurant and hospitality industry. **Services:** Library open to the public by special appointment only. **Holdings:** 3500 books. **Subscriptions:** 90 journals and other serials.

5844 ■ Canadian Restaurant & Foodservices Association Resource Centre
316 Bloor St., W.
Toronto, ON, Canada M5S 1W5
Ph:(416)923-8416
Free: 800-387-5649
Fax:(416)923-1450
Co. E-mail: info@crfa.ca
URL: http://www.crfa.ca/research/
Contact: Mimy Taylor, Info.Coord.
Scope: Food service, quantity cooking, legislation, administration, management, statistics, training, customer attitude surveys. **Services:** Copying; Center open to the public on fee basis. **Holdings:** 1000 books. **Subscriptions:** 100 journals and other serials.

5845 ■ City College of San Francisco Culinary Arts and Hospitality Studies Department–Alice Statler Library
50 Phelan Ave.
Statler Wing, Rm. 10
San Francisco, CA 94112
Ph:(415)239-3460
Fax:(415)239-3026
Co. E-mail: aniosi@ccsf.edu
URL: http://www.ccsf.edu/library/alice/statler.html
Contact: Andrea Niosi, Libn.
Scope: Public hospitality industries - hotels, motels, restaurants, catering services, cookery and nutrition; tourism; beverages. **Services:** Copying; Library open to the public for reference use only. **Holdings:** 10,000 books; 3500 pamphlets; 900 menus; videotapes; archives. **Subscriptions:** 80 journals and other serials.

5846 ■ Culinary Institute of America–Conrad N. Hilton Library
1946 Campus Dr.
Hyde Park, NY 12538-1499
Ph:(845)451-1322
Co. E-mail: c_crawfo@culinary.edu
URL: http://library.culinary.edu/
Contact: Christine Crawford-Oppenheimer, Info.Svcs. Libn.
Scope: Cookery, food service, restaurant management, hospitality. **Services:** Interlibrary loan; copying; Library open to the public by appointment. **Holdings:** 84,000 volumes; 30,000 menus; 3800 DVDs and videos. **Subscriptions:** 280 journals and other serials.

5847 ■ Indianapolis-Marion County Public Library–Business, Science and Technology Service Section
40 E. St. Clair St.
Indianapolis, IN 46204
Ph:(317)275-4100
Fax:(317)269-1768
Co. E-mail: ofields@imcpl.org
URL: http://www.imcpl.org/
Contact: Mark Leggett, Mgr.
Scope: Science, engineering, space science, agriculture, electronics, computer science, building, health, cookery, television, accounting, advertising, economics, business, insurance, investment, management. **Services:** Interlibrary loan; copying. **Holdings:** 65,000 titles; 10 VF drawers. **Subscriptions:** 950 journals and other serials.

5848 ■ Johnson & Wales University–Harborside Culinary Library
321 Harborside Blvd.
Providence, RI 02905
Ph:(401)598-1282
Fax:(401)598-1834
Co. E-mail: barbara.janson@jwu.edu
URL: http://www.jwu.edu
Contact: Barbara Janson, Hd.Libn.
Scope: Cookbooks, food service, menu planning, nutrition, professional management, catering and banquets, household manuals, canning, preserving and freezing, hotel and motel management. **Services:** Copying; Library open to the public. **Holdings:** 10,000 books; 700 menus. **Subscriptions:** 100 journals and other serials.

5849 ■ Lamar University–Mary and John Gray Library–Justice Cookery Collection (Lamar)
Lamar University
PO Box 10021
Beaumont, TX 77710-0021
Ph:(409)880-8118
Fax:(409)880-2318
Co. E-mail: david.carroll@lamar.edu
URL: http://library.lamar.edu
Contact: David Carroll, Dean of Lib.Svcs.
Scope: Southeast Texas - settlement, politics, trails, environment and conservation, mining and petroleum industries, shipping, air and rail transportation, performing arts. **Services:** Photoduplication; imaging; Library open to the public. **Holdings:** 3000 volumes. **Subscriptions:** 2700 journals and other serials; 11 newspapers.

5850 ■ Paul Smith's College of Arts and Sciences–Joan Weill Adirondack Library
Rte. 86 and 30
PO Box 265
Paul Smiths, NY 12970-0265
Ph:(518)327-6227
Free: 800-421-2605
Fax:(518)327-6016
Co. E-mail: nsurprenant@paulsmiths.edu
URL: http://www.paulsmiths.edu/library
Contact: Neil Surprenant, Dir., Lib.Svcs.
Scope: Hotel and restaurant management, chef training, culinary arts, forestry, urban tree management, environmental science, forest recreation, surveying, ecotourism, natural resources management, fisheries management, business management. **Services:** Interlibrary loan; copying; Library open to the public with restrictions. **Holdings:** 54,000 books; pamphlets. **Subscriptions:** 504 journals and other serials; 7 newspapers.

5851 ■ Prince Edward Island Food Technology Centre–Information Services
PO Box 2000
Charlottetown, PE, Canada C1A 7N8
Ph:(902)368-5548
Fax:(902)368-5549
Co. E-mail: peiftc@gov.pe.ca
URL: http://www.gov.pe.ca/ftc/
Contact: Kathy MacEwen, Lib.Techn.
Scope: Agriculture, food, technology, food research. **Services:** Interlibrary loan; Library open to the public by permission only. **Holdings:** 200 books; 9 bound periodical volumes. **Subscriptions:** 38 journals and other serials.

5852 ■ Societe Culinaire–Philanthropique
305 E. 47th St., Ste. 11B
New York, NY 10017
Ph:(212)308-0628

Fax:(212)308-0588
Co. E-mail: salon@societeculinaire.com
URL: http://www.societeculinaire.com
Contact: Jean-Pierre Stoehr, Pres.
Scope: Professional cooking. **Services:** Library open to members only. **Holdings:** Cookbooks.

5853 ■ Unilever Foods R&D Information Center
800 Sylvan Ave.
Englewood Cliffs, NJ 07632-3201
Ph:(732)894-7569
Fax:(732)627-8506
Co. E-mail: john.troisi@unilever.com
Contact: Karla Cicciari, Info.Spec.
Scope: Nutrition, food technology, cookery, food microbiology, food analysis. **Services:** Interlibrary loan. **Holdings:** 10,000 books; company reports and patents on microfiche; archives; microfilm. **Subscriptions:** 300 journals and other serials.

5854 ■ University of Denver–Penrose Library–Special Collections & Archives (2150)
2150 E. Evans Ave., Lower Level
Denver, CO 80208-0287
Ph:(303)871-3428
Fax:(303)871-2290
Co. E-mail: archives@du.edu
Contact: Steven Fisher, Cur.
Scope: University of Denver archives, cookery, Judaica, dance, Civil War. **Services:** Interlibrary loan; copying; collections open to the public. **Holdings:** 30,000 books. 15,000 lin. ft. of archives.

5855 ■ University of Nebraska—Kearney–Nebraska Career and Technical Education Resource Center
West Center, E212
Kearney, NE 68849
Ph:(308)865-8462
Fax:(308)865-8669
Co. E-mail: klesathmj@unk.edu
URL: http://www.unk.edu
Contact: Mary Jo Klesath
Scope: Vocational education, family and consumer science, tech prep, applied academics, gender equity, industrial technology, career education, business education, agriculture, marketing, health occupations. **Services:** Interlibrary loan; Library open to the public. **Holdings:** 7000 books; 500 audio/visual materials; curriculum guides; games; kits.

Copy Shop

ASSOCIATIONS AND OTHER ORGANIZATIONS

5856 ■ Copyright Clearance Center
222 Rosewood Dr.
Danvers, MA 01923
Ph:(978)750-8400
Fax:(978)646-8600
Co. E-mail: info@copyright.com
URL: http://www.copyright.com
Contact: Tracey L. Armstrong, Pres./CEO
Description: Facilitates compliance with U.S. copyright law. Provides licensing systems for the reproduction and distribution of copyrighted materials in print and electronic formats throughout the world. Manages rights relating to over 1.75 million works and represents more than 9600 publishers and hundreds of thousands of authors and other creators, directly or through their representatives. .

5857 ■ International Reprographic Association
401 N Michigan Ave.
Chicago, IL 60611
Ph:(312)673-4805
Free: 800-833-4742
Fax:(312)321-5150
Co. E-mail: sbova@irga.com
URL: http://www.irga.com
Contact: Steve Bova CAE, Exec. Dir.
Description: Commercial blue print and photocopy firms, engineering supply stores, and materials and equipment suppliers. Conducts annual photo-tech, marketing, management, and business planning seminars. **Publications:** *IRgA News Digest* (monthly); *Repro Report* (bimonthly).

REFERENCE WORKS

5858 ■ "Funny Business" in *Canadian Business* (Vol. 82, April 27, 2009, No. 7, pp. 27)
Pub: Rogers Media
Ed: Rachel Pulfer. **Description:** Companies are advised to use humor in marketing to drive more revenue. IBM Canada, for example, commissioned Second City Communications for a marketing campaign that involved humor. While IBM Canada declined to give sales or traffic figures, firm executives rank the marketing campaign as an overall success.

5859 ■ "Xerox Diverts Waste from Landfills" in *Canadian Electronics* (Vol. 23, February 2008, No. 1, pp. 1)
Pub: CLB Media Inc.
Description: Xerox Corporation revealed that it was able to divert more than two billion pounds of electronic waste from landfills through waste-free initiatives. The company's program, which was launched in 1991, covers waste avoidance in imaging supplies and parts reuse. Environmental priorities are also integrated into manufacturing operations.

STATISTICAL SOURCES

5860 ■ *RMA Annual Statement Studies*
Pub: Robert Morris Associates (RMA)
Released: Annual. **Price:** $175.00 2006-07 edition, $105.00. **Description:** Contains composite balance sheets and income statements for more than 360 industries, including the accounting, auditing, and bookkeeping industries. Also contains five years of comparative historical data for discerning trends. Includes 16 commonly used ratios, computed for most of the size groupings for nearly every industry.

TRADE PERIODICALS

5861 ■ *NAQP News*
Pub: PrintImage International
Contact: C. Bennett
Released: Monthly. **Price:** Included in membership. **Description:** Features information on the newest technologies in electronic publishing, color copying, mailing services, and computer hardware and software. Includes association news, advice on management and marketing methods, government issues affecting the industry, and an ideas exchange forum.

5862 ■ *Quick Printing*
Pub: Cygnus Business Media Inc.
Contact: JeanneMarie Graziano, Production Mgr
E-mail: jeannemarie.graziano@cygnusb2b.com
Released: Monthly. **Description:** For Quick and Small Commercial Printers.

TRADE SHOWS AND CONVENTIONS

5863 ■ International Reprographic Association Annual Convention and Trade Show
International Reprographic Association
401 N. Michigan Ave.
Chicago, IL 60611
Ph:(312)245-1026
Fax:(312)527-6705
URL: http://www.irga.com
Released: Annual. **Audience:** Reprographic professionals. **Principal Exhibits:** Reprographic equipment, supplies, and services for color graphics, reprographic and digital imaging service supplies. **Dates and Locations:** 2011 Apr 27-28, Las Vegas, NV.

5864 ■ Print Ontario
North Island Trade Shows, Ltd.
1606 Sedlescomb Dr. Unit 8 & 9
Mississauga, ON, Canada L4X 1M6
Ph:(905)625-7070
Free: 800-331-7408
Fax:(905)625-4856
URL: http://www.printontario.com
Released: Biennial. **Audience:** Small and mid-size commercial printers, instant printers, implant shops, brokers and forms distributors. **Principal Exhibits:** Press manufactures, bindery equipment, high speed photocopiers, color copiers, paper manufactures, ink manufactures, trade business, manufactures, trade labels. **Dates and Locations:** 2012 Nov 17-19, Toronto, ON.

CONSULTANTS

5865 ■ Concord Associates Co.
16 Chambers Cir.
West Lebanon, NH 03784
Ph:(603)643-6768
Fax:(603)643-6768
Contact: Elliott D. Novak, President
Scope: Offers business counsel and market and marketing consulting assistance in key areas of both the consumer and professional digital imaging fields. Primary emphasis is in digital cameras; ink jet and dye sublimation printers; digital mini labs; and related or ancillary products such as flash memory cards for digital cameras.

FRANCHISES AND BUSINESS OPPORTUNITIES

5866 ■ Kwik Kopy Business Centers
Kwik Kopy Business Centers, Inc.
12715 Telge Rd.
Cypress, TX 77429
Free: 888-638-8722
Fax:(281)256-4178
Co. E-mail: franchisedevelopment@iced.net
URL: http://www.iced.net
No. of Franchise Units: 16. **No. of Company-Owned Units:** 1. **Founded:** 2001. **Franchised:** 2001. **Description:** Offers business advertisement aids and printing and copying services. **Equity Capital Needed:** $65,000 liquid capital; $250,000 net worth. **Franchise Fee:** $35,000. **Financial Assistance:** Conventional bank and SBA loans, and through in-house financing with sufficient collateral. **Managerial Assistance:** Provide business support, advertising, and marketing materials. **Training:** Owners attend classroom and field training, as well as ongoing training through workshops and conferences.

5867 ■ Pip Printing and Document Services
26722 Plz. Dr., Ste. 200
Mission Viejo, CA 92691
Free: 800-894-7498
Fax:800-747-0679
Co. E-mail: karen.brock@pip.com
URL: http://www.pip.com
No. of Franchise Units: 285. **Founded:** 1965. **Franchised:** 1968. **Description:** Offers complete range of business including multi-color printing, high-volume copying, desktop publishing, layout, design and finishing on newsletters, brochures, bound presentations, business stationery and forms. **Equity Capital Needed:** Minimum cash investment $83,000 + living expenses; Total investment $232,850-$465,840. **Franchise Fee:** $20,000. **Royalty Fee:** 1%- 7%(-sliding scale). **Financial Assistance:** 3rd party financing and SBA loan programs are available with equipment and leasehold packages for qualified

individuals. **Managerial Assistance:** After initial 2 weeks training, owners may request a visit from business consultants trained in sales, marketing, operations and finance. Also, workshops, regional meetings and biennial conclaves held nationwide, covering topics from customer services to the future of the printing industry. Training, operations and safety manuals. **Training:** 2 1/2 weeks of training at PIP University and field visit within the first six months of operation.

5868 ■ Postal Connections of America
Templar Franchise Company
275 E. Douglas Ave., Ste. 115
El Cajon, CA 92020
Ph:(619)294-7550
Free: 800-767-8257
Fax:(619)294-4550
Co. E-mail: info@postalconnections.com
URL: http://www.postalconnections.com.

No. of Franchise Units: 99. **Founded:** 1985. **Franchised:** 1996. **Description:** Postal Connections stores offer packaging, shipping, mail receiving & forwarding, copies, printing, scanning & storage of digital documents, eBay auction support, office & packing supplies, crate & freight shipping and more. **Equity Capital Needed:** $119,000-$153,900, average initial investment. **Franchise Fee:** $23,900. **Financial Assistance:** Third party financing sources available. **Managerial Assistance:** Online 24/7 "business coaching" on private website. **Training:** Extensive training prior to & after opening. Franchisees receive 5 days live action training in a regional training store, Unique Act video training program & 4 days onsite.

5869 ■ Sir Speedy, Inc.
26722 Plz. Dr.
Mission Viejo, CA 92691
Free: 888-465-9481
Fax:(949)348-5010
URL: http://www.sirspeedy.com

No. of Franchise Units: 400. **Founded:** 1968. **Franchised:** 1968. **Description:** Franchisor of printing, copying, graphic design and digital networking centers. **Equity Capital Needed:** $261,000-$268,413; net worth $300,000+. **Franchise Fee:** $25,000. **Financial Assistance:** No. **Training:** Sir Speedy University, Regional training.

5870 ■ Sure Print & Copy Centers
12465 82nd Ave., Ste. 101
Surrey, BC, Canada V3W 3E8
Ph:(604)594-8334
Free: 800-914-7873
Fax:(604)594-8320
Co. E-mail: sadru@surecopy.com

No. of Franchise Units: 90. **No. of Company-Owned Units:** 3. **Founded:** 1984. **Franchised:** 1990. **Description:** A print and copy service provider. **Equity Capital Needed:** $50,000 cash + minimum $15,000 working capital. **Franchise Fee:** $20,000. **Financial Assistance:** Yes. **Training:** Yes.

LIBRARIES

5871 ■ Xerox Corporation–Technical Information Center
800 Philips Rd.
Mail Stop 0105-66C
Webster, NY 14580
Ph:(716)422-3505
Fax:(716)265-5722
Contact: Laura R. Tucker, Mgr.

Scope: Xerography, electrophotography, reprography, electronics, chemistry, physics, photography, materials and processes, computer science. **Services:** Interlibrary loan; SDI; center open to the public by appointment. **Holdings:** 17,318 books; 10,728 microfilm reels/rolls; 126,531 internal reports; 16,937 external reports; 55 VF drawers; 5500 reels of microfilm; 455,426 microfiche; 3,793,423 patents. **Subscriptions:** 90 journals and other serials.

Cosmetics Business

ASSOCIATIONS AND OTHER ORGANIZATIONS

5872 ■ Canadian Cosmetic, Toiletry and Fragrance Association–Association Canadienne des Cosmetiques, Produits de Toilette et Parfums
420 Britannia Rd. E, Ste. 102
Mississauga, ON, Canada L4Z 3L5
Ph:(905)890-5161
Fax:(905)890-2607
Co. E-mail: cctfa@cctfa.ca
URL: http://www.cctfa.ca/site/cctfa
Contact: Ms. Michele Davis
Description: Manufacturers of personal care products, cosmetics, and perfumes. Seeks to advance the cosmetics and toiletries industries. Represents members before labor and industrial organizations, government agencies, and the public. Sponsors cosmetic safety research. **Publications:** *CCTFA News and Events Newsletter* (monthly).

5873 ■ Cosmetic Executive Women
286 Madison Ave., 19th Fl.
New York, NY 10017
Ph:(212)685-5955
Fax:(212)685-3334
Co. E-mail: cjacobson@cew.org
URL: http://cew.org
Contact: Carlotta Jacobson, Pres.
Description: Women in the cosmetic and allied industries. Unites women executives in the cosmetic field for industry awareness and business advancement. Promotes products, people, professional development and philanthropy. **Publications:** *Membership Roster* (periodic).

5874 ■ Cosmetic Industry Buyers and Suppliers
Elite Packaging
40-E Cotters Ln.
East Brunswick, NJ 08816
Co. E-mail: cibsmail@cibsonline.com
URL: http://www.cibsonline.com
Contact: Charles Marchese, Pres.
Description: Buyers and suppliers of essential oils, chemicals, packaging, and finished goods relative to the cosmetic industry. Enhances growth, stability, prosperity, and protection of the American cosmetic industry through close personal contact and the exchange of ideas and experiences. .

5875 ■ Cosmetic Ingredient Review
1101 17th St. NW, Ste. 412
Washington, DC 20036-4702
Ph:(202)331-0651
Fax:(202)331-0088
Co. E-mail: cirinfo@cir-safety.org
URL: http://www.cir-safety.org
Contact: Wilma F. Bergfeld MD, Chair
Description: A cosmetic industry self-regulatory organization sponsored by the Cosmetic, Toiletry, and Fragrance Association. Seeks to assure the safety of ingredients used in cosmetics. Reviews scientific data on the safety of ingredients used in cosmetics; documents validity of tests used to study ingredients. **Publications:** *CIR Annual Report* (annual); *Final Reports on Cosmetic Ingredient Safety Assessments* (quarterly); *Ingredient Report* .

5876 ■ International Spa Association
2365 Harrodsburg Rd., Ste. A325
Lexington, KY 40504
Ph:(859)226-4326
Free: 888-651-4772
Fax:(859)226-4445
Co. E-mail: ispa@ispastaff.com
URL: http://www.experienceispa.com
Contact: Ms. Lynne Walker McNees, Pres.
Description: Professional association and voice of the spa industry. Forms and maintains alliances that educate, set standards, provide resources, influence policy and build coalitions for the industry. Raises awareness of the spa industry and educates the public and industry professionals about the benefits of the spa experience. **Publications:** *LiveSpa*; *Pulse* (bimonthly).

5877 ■ National Beauty Culturists' League
25 Logan Cir. NW
Washington, DC 20005-3725
Ph:(202)332-2695
Fax:(202)332-0940
Co. E-mail: nbcl@bellsouth.net
URL: http://www.nbcl.org
Contact: Dr. Katie B. Catalon, Pres.
Description: Beauticians, cosmetologists, and beauty products manufacturers. Encourages standardized, scientific, and approved methods of hair, scalp, and skin treatments. Offers scholarships and plans to establish a research center. Sponsors: National Institute of Cosmetology, a training course in operating and designing and business techniques. Maintains hall of fame; conducts research program. .

5878 ■ National - Interstate Council of State Boards of Cosmetology
7622 Briarwood Cir.
Little Rock, AR 72205
Ph:(501)227-8262
Fax:(501)227-8212
Co. E-mail: dnorton@nictesting.org
URL: http://www.nictesting.org
Contact: Kay Kendrick, Pres.
Description: Persons commissioned by 50 state governments as administrators of cosmetology laws and examiners of applicants for licenses to practice cosmetology. .

5879 ■ Personal Care Product Council
1101 17th St. NW, Ste. 300
Washington, DC 20036-4702
Ph:(202)331-1770
Fax:(202)331-1969
Co. E-mail: membership@ctfa.org
URL: http://www.personalcarecouncil.org
Contact: Pamela G. Bailey, Pres./CEO
Description: Manufacturers and distributors of finished cosmetics, fragrances, and personal care products; suppliers of raw materials and services. Provides scientific, legal, regulatory, and legislative services. Coordinates public service, educational, and public affairs activities. **Publications:** *CTFA News* (biweekly); *International Color Handbook*; *International Resource Manual* .

REFERENCE WORKS

5880 ■ *Avon: Building the World's Premier Company for Women*
Pub: John Wiley & Sons, Incorporated
Ed: Laura Klepacki. **Released:** May 2006. **Price:** $16.95. **Description:** Profile of Avon and how it grew from a small business selling door-to-door to one of the largest cosmetics companies in the world.

5881 ■ *Business as Usual*
Pub: HarperBusiness
Ed: Anita Roddick. **Released:** 2005. **Price:** $12.95. **Description:** Founder of The Body Shop shares her story and gives her opinion on everything from cynical cosmetic companies to destructive consultants.

5882 ■ "Eco-Preneuring" in *Small Business Opportunities* (Jan. 2008)
Pub: Harris Publications Inc.
Description: Iceland Naturally is a joint marketing effort among tourism and business interests hoping to increase demand for Icelandic products including frozen seafood, bottled water, agriculture, and tourism in North America.

5883 ■ "Every Little Bit Helps" in *Black Enterprise* (Vol. 38, November 2007, No. 4, pp. 102)
Pub: Earl G. Graves Publishing Co. Inc.
Ed: Tennille M. Robinson. **Description:** After a career in the cosmetics industry, Tricialee Riley is marketing and advertising her new venture, the Polish Bar, a salon offering manicures, pedicures, makeup application, and waxing.

5884 ■ "Greening the Manscape" in *Canadian Business* (Vol. 81, October 13, 2008, No. 17, pp. S19)
Pub: Rogers Media Ltd.
Ed: David Lackie. **Description:** Buyer's guide of environmentally friendly grooming products for men is provided. Improved formulations have solved the problems of having synthetic ingredients in grooming products. Details about a face scrub, after shave conditioner, and a nourishing cream made of 91 percent organic ingredients are given, including prices.

5885 ■ "How I Did It: It Just Came Naturally" in *Inc.* (November 2007, pp. 110-112)
Pub: Gruner & Jahr USA Publishing
Ed: Athena Schindelheim. **Description:** Profile of Bobbi Brown, CEO and founder of Bobbi Brown Cosmetics, designed to highlight a woman's natural look. Brown opened her first freestanding retail store recently that houses a makeup artistry school in the back.

5886 ■ "Identify and Conquer" in *Black Enterprise* (Vol. 38, December 2007, No. 5, pp. 76)
Pub: Earl G. Graves Publishing Co. Inc.
Ed: Tennille M. Robinson. **Description:** Twenty-two-year-old entrepreneur wants to expand her wholesale body oil and skincare products business.

5887 ■ *Lessons of a Lipstick Queen: Finding and Developing the Great Idea That Can Change Your Life*
Pub: Simon & Schuster
Ed: Poppy King. **Released:** May 1, 2009. **Price:** $14.00. **Description:** Poppy King tells how she started her lipstick brand at age eighteen. She reveals how she managed to launch her business using a good idea and finding financing, marketing the product and how she became successful.

5888 ■ "Master of His Domain" in *Canadian Business* (Vol. 81, December 8, 2008, No. 21, pp. S17)
Pub: Rogers Media Ltd.
Ed: Andy Holloway. **Description:** L'Oreal Canada chief executive Javier San Juan believes in being close to consumers and travels to one of his company's fifteen locations in Canada about once a month. San Juan's job is to build the L'Oreal brand in Canada.

5889 ■ *More Than a Pink Cadillac*
Pub: McGraw-Hill
Ed: Jim Underwood. **Released:** 2002. **Price:** $23.95. **Description:** Profile of Mary Kay Ash who turned her $5,000 investment into a billion-dollar corporation. Ash's nine principles that form the foundation of her company's global success are outlined. Stories from her sales force leaders share ideas for motivating employees, impressing customers and building a successful company. The book emphasizes the leadership skills required to drive performance in any successful enterprise.

5890 ■ "Natural Attraction: Bath and Body Products Maker Delivers Wholesome Goodness" in *Black Enterprise* (Vol. 38, November 2007, No. 4)
Pub: Earl G. Graves Publishing Co. Inc.
Ed: Kaylyn Kendall Dines. **Description:** Profile of Dawn Fitch, creator of Pooka Inc., manufacturer of handmade bath and body products that contain no preservatives. Sales are expected to reach $750,000 for 2007.

5891 ■ *The Perfect Scent: A Year Inside the Perfume Industry in Paris and New York*
Pub: Henry Holt and Company
Ed: Chandler Burr. **Released:** 2009. **Price:** $25.00. **Description:** An insiders glimpse at the development of two new fragrances from Hermes and Coty.

5892 ■ "Style Me Pretty on My Wedding Day – Final Chance to Enter" in *Benzinga.com* (October 29, 2011)
Pub: Benzinga.com
Ed: Benzinga Staff. **Description:** Style Me Pretty and Christian Dior have partnered to award one bride the chance to have a personal Dior makeup artist for their wedding day.

5893 ■ "Want a Facial With That Steak?" in *Charlotte Observer* (February 5, 2007)
Pub: Knight-Ridder/Tribune Business News
Ed: Jen Aronoff. **Description:** Profile of Burke Myotherapy Massage & Spa and Schell's Bistro. Lynn Shell moved her massage therapy business into a 106-year old home that had been used as a restaurant. She opened her own eatery on the first floor and offers massage therapy upstairs.

5894 ■ *Who's Who—Personal Care Products Council Membership Directory*
Pub: Personal Care Products Council
Released: Annual, Latest edition 2012. **Covers:** More than 1,000 member companies. **Entries Include:** Company name, address, phone, telex/TWX number, Internet site, names and titles of key personnel, parent company name, affiliates and subsidiaries, products and services, designation as manufacturer, distributor, supplier, or private-label manufacturer. **Arrangement:** Alphabetical within membership categories. **Indexes:** Company name.

TRADE PERIODICALS

5895 ■ *Cosmetics & Toiletries*
Pub: Allured Publishing Corp.
Contact: Jane Evison, European Accounts managing editorager
E-mail: jane-evison@btconnect.com
Released: Monthly. **Price:** $98; $137 Canada; $189 other countries; $169 two years; $231 Canada two years; $330 other countries two years. **Description:** Trade magazine on cosmetic and toiletries manufacturing with an emphasis on product research and development issues.

5896 ■ *The Food & Drug Letter*
Pub: Washington Business Information Inc.
Ed: Released: Biweekly. **Price:** $1,245, individuals. **Description:** Seeks to provide a detailed analysis of federal regulatory activity relating to food, drugs, and cosmetics. Interprets policy and regulatory changes, focusing on the impact of specific actions on industry in both the long and short term. .

5897 ■ *For Formulation Chemists Only*
Pub: CITA International
Contact: E.M. Mosby, Founder & Ed.-in-Ch.
E-mail: f2co@knowledge21.org
Released: Quarterly. **Price:** $100 online. **Description:** Online journal covering chemical industrial technology for technicians in the chemical specialty and consumer product industries.

5898 ■ *The Rose Sheet*
Pub: Elsevier Business Intelligence
Contact: Chirs Morrison, Editor-in-Chief
E-mail: c.morrison@elsevier.com
Released: Weekly (Mon.). **Price:** $1,470 print & online. **Description:** Trade journal for executives in the toiletries, fragrance, cosmetic, and skin care industries.

5899 ■ *Skin Inc.*
Pub: Allured Publishing Corp.
Released: Monthly. **Price:** $49; $57 Canada; $98 other countries. **Description:** The complete business guide for face and body care.

VIDEOCASSETTES/ AUDIOCASSETTES

5900 ■ *Cosmetic and Personal Services*
Morris Video
12881 Knott St.
Garden Grove, CA 92841
Ph:(310)533-4800
Fax:(310)320-3171
Released: 1985. **Price:** $24.95. **Description:** Occupations involving cosmetology, hair styling and manicures are covered. **Availability:** VHS.

5901 ■ *Puttin' on Your Lips*
Tapeworm Video Distributors
25876 The Old Road 141
Stevenson Ranch, CA 91381
Ph:(661)257-4904
Fax:(661)257-4820
Co. E-mail: sales@tapeworm.com
URL: http://www.tapeworm.com
Released: 1997. **Price:** $14.95. **Description:** Demonstrates proper make-up application techniques. **Availability:** VHS.

TRADE SHOWS AND CONVENTIONS

5902 ■ American Association of Cosmetology Schools Annual Conference - AACS Annual Convention & Expo
American Association of Cosmetology Schools
15825 N. 71st St., Ste. 100
Scottsdale, AZ 85254-1521
Ph:(480)281-0431
Free: 800-831-1086
Fax:(480)905-0993
Co. E-mail: dilsah@beautyschools.org
URL: http://www.beautyschools.org
Released: Annual. **Audience:** School owners. **Principal Exhibits:** Beauty supplies and products, and cosmetology services.

5903 ■ Beauty Fair
The Finnish Fair Corp.
Messuaukio 1
PO Box 21
FIN-00521 Helsinki, Finland
Ph:358 9 15091
Fax:358 9 1509218
Co. E-mail: info@finnexpo.fi
Released: Annual. **Audience:** General public. **Principal Exhibits:** Beauty and fashion, cosmetics and services; hair products and services; clothing, showes, bags, accessories, jewelry, education, and publications.

5904 ■ Beauty Prague
Expona spol. s.r.o.
Masovicka 263/22
CZ-142 00 Praha, Czech Republic
Ph:42 271 961305
Fax:42 274 869807
Co. E-mail: expona@expona.cz
Audience: professionals mostly. **Principal Exhibits:** National Championships in make-up and nail-design.

5905 ■ Extracts - A Division of New York International Gift Fair
George Little Management, LLC (New York, New York)
1133 Westchester Ave., Ste. N136
White Plains, NY 10606
Ph:(914)421-3200
Free: 800-272-SHOW
Co. E-mail: cathy_steel@glmshows.com
URL: http://www.glmshows.com
Released: Semiannual. **Audience:** Specialty, chain and department stores, gift and drug stores, mail order catalog houses, cosmetic companies, home furnishings/decorative accessory retailers. **Principal Exhibits:** Personal care products, aromatherapy products, body lotions, bath and shower gels, soaps, fragrances, botanicals, potpourri, candles, home fragrance products, bath accessories, and small appliances.

5906 ■ National Beauty Show - HAIRWORLD
National Cosmetology Association
401 N Michigan Ave., 22nd Floor
Chicago, IL 60611-4255
Ph:(312)527-6765
Free: 800-527-1683
Fax:(312)464-6118
Co. E-mail: nca1@ncacares.org
URL: http://www.behindthechairexchange.com/nca
Released: Annual. **Audience:** Salon owners and cosmetologists. **Principal Exhibits:** Hair products, cosmetics, and jewelry.

FRANCHISES AND BUSINESS OPPORTUNITIES

5907 ■ Caryl Baker Visage
31 Wingold Ave.
Toronto, ON, Canada M6B 1P8
Ph:(416)789-7191
Fax:(416)789-2594
Co. E-mail: info@carylbakervisage.com
URL: http://www.carylbakervisage.com
No. of Franchise Units: 30. **Founded:** 1969. **Franchised:** 1974. **Description:** A professional salon selling a comprehensive line of cosmetics and skin care products with a selection of services designed to pamper a wide range of clientele. Locations available in major shopping centers across Canada. **Equity Capital Needed:** $220,000-$270,000. **Franchise Fee:** $20,000. **Training:** 9-12 weeks and ongoing training and support.

5908 ■ FACES
Faces, Inc.
30 Machintosh Blvd., Unit 6
Vaughan, ON, Canada L4K 4P1
Ph:(905)760-0110
Fax:(905)760-0901
URL: http://www.faces-cosmetics.com
No. of Franchise Units: 57. **No. of Company-Owned Units:** 12. **Founded:** 1974. **Franchised:** 1976. **Description:** Retail cosmetics business featuring in-mall, stand-alone boutiques and in-line stores selling FACES own extensive, affordable and distinct brand of prestige color cosmetics and bath and body care. **Equity Capital Needed:** Approximate total cost of turn-key business is from $180,000-$380,000 U.S. **Franchise Fee:** $25,000. **Financial Assistance:** Third party financing is available. **Training:** FACES Academy is a 2 week, comprehensive training program at FACES head office in Toronto. Courses in beauty health theory, cosmetic product knowledge, business & counter sales management, cosmetic application and retail sales strategies will earn franchisees Retail Cosmetic Management certification.

5909 ■ Faces Cosmetics
3010 LBJ Fwy., Ste. 1200
Dallas, TX 75234
Free: 877-773-2237
Co. E-mail: Jennifer@faces-cosmetics.com
URL: http://www.faces-cosmentics.com
No. of Franchise Units: 45. **No. of Company-Owned Units:** 11. **Founded:** 1976. **Franchised:** 1976. **Description:** Retailer of cosmetics, skincare and anti-aging products and services for make-up, aesthetics and mini-spa treatments. Provides a turn-key package including a fully-equipped boutique with complete inventory. **Equity Capital Needed:** $219,500-$372,500. **Franchise Fee:** $27,500. **Royalty Fee:** 6%. **Financial Assistance:** No. **Managerial Assistance:** Marketing and advertising programs included. **Training:** Initial 2 week training and ongoing Head-Office support.

5910 ■ Ideal Image
4830 W Kennedy Blvd., Ste. 440
Tampa, FL 33609
Ph:(813)286-8100
Fax:(866)866-4390
No. of Franchise Units: 60. **No. of Company-Owned Units:** 7. **Founded:** 2001. **Franchised:** 2004. **Description:** Laser hair removal. **Equity Capital Needed:** $551,300-$903,400. **Franchise Fee:** $25,000-$35,000. **Royalty Fee:** 9%. **Financial Assistance:** Limited third party financing available. **Training:** Offers 2-4 weeks at headquarters, onsite as needed, and i-Learn online training ongoing.

5911 ■ Merle Norman Cosmetics Studio
Merle Norman Cosmetics
9130 Bellanca Ave.
Los Angeles, CA 90045
Ph:(310)641-3000
Free: 800-421-6648
Fax:(310)337-2370
URL: http://www.merlenorman.com
No. of Franchise Units: 2,000. **No. of Company-Owned Units:** 6. **Founded:** 1931. **Franchised:** 1989. **Description:** Offers a complete line of Merle Norman cosmetics along with professional cosmetic advice from trained consultants. Locations feature unique interior designs and are situated in major shopping centers and strip malls. **Equity Capital Needed:** Varies. **Franchise Fee:** None. **Financial Assistance:** Yes. **Training:** Offers 2 week home office training and ongoing field support.

5912 ■ Top of the Line Fragrances
515 Bath Ave.
Long Branch, NJ 07740
Ph:(732)229-0014
Free: 800-929-3083
Fax:(732)222-1762
Co. E-mail: info@tolfranchise.com
URL: http://www.tolfranchise.com
No. of Franchise Units: 11. **Founded:** 1983. **Franchised:** 1987. **Description:** Cosmetics and fragrances. **Equity Capital Needed:** $164,800-$237-800. **Franchise Fee:** $20,000. **Royalty Fee:** 5%. **Financial Assistance:** Third party financing available. **Training:** Offered at franchisees location for 7-10 days with ongoing support.

5913 ■ Women's Health Boutique
Women's Health Boutique Franchise System, Inc.
12715 Telge Rd.
Cypress, TX 77429
Free: 888-708-9982
Fax:(281)256-4100
Co. E-mail: w-h-bsales@w-h-b.com
URL: http://www.w-h-b.com
No. of Franchise Units: 13. **Founded:** 1991. **Franchised:** 1994. **Description:** Products and services related to pre and postnatal care, post-mastectomy, compression therapy, hair loss, incontinence, and skin care. **Equity Capital Needed:** $49,000 minimum start-up cash. **Financial Assistance:** Yes. **Training:** Yes.

LIBRARIES

5914 ■ Avon Products Research Library
1345 Avenue of the Americas
New York, NY 10020
Ph:(212)282-5000
Co. E-mail: mary.warren@avon.com
URL: http://www.avoncompany.com/
Contact: Mary Warren, Res.Libn.
Scope: Cosmetics, packaging, toxicology, dermatology, pharmacology, chemistry, engineering, microbiology. **Services:** Interlibrary loan; SDI; Library open to the public for reference use only on request. **Holdings:** 6500 books; 5000 bound periodical volumes; 6000 U.S. and foreign patents. **Subscriptions:** 300 journals and other serials.

5915 ■ Clairol Research Library
1 Blachley Rd.
Stamford, CT 06922
Ph:(203)357-5001
Free: 800-252-4765
Fax:(203)969-2577
URL: http://www.clairol.com
Contact: Linda Massoni, Libn.
Scope: Chemistry and technology of cosmetics, hair dyes and dyeing, personal care. **Services:** Library open to the public with restrictions. **Holdings:** 10,000 books; 6000 bound periodical volumes; 30 titles on microfilm. **Subscriptions:** 350 journals and other serials.

5916 ■ Colgate Palmolive Company Technology Information Center
909 River Rd.
Piscataway, NJ 08854
Ph:(732)878-7574
Fax:(732)878-7128
URL: http://www.colgate.com
Contact: Miranda D. Scott, Tech.Info.Assoc.
Scope: Soaps and detergents, fats and oils, dentifrices, cosmetics, perfumes and essential oils, environmental pollution, foods, chemistry. **Services:** Interlibrary loan; copying; SDI. **Holdings:** 20,000 books; 10,000 bound periodical volumes; 16,000 periodical volumes on 4000 reels of microfilm; 250 VF drawers of internal reports; 10 VF drawers of archival materials. **Subscriptions:** 300 journals and other serials.

5917 ■ Gillette Company Technical Information Center
37 A St.
Needham, MA 02492-9120
Ph:(781)292-8406
Fax:(781)292-8455
Co. E-mail: susan_fox@gillette.com
URL: http://www.gillette.com
Contact: Susan R. Fox, Sr.Info.Spec.
Scope: Chemistry, hair, skin, cosmetics, materials, polymers, plastics, electrochemistry. **Services:** Interlibrary loan; Center not open to the public. **Holdings:** 12,000 books; 8000 reports; 350 patents. **Subscriptions:** 150 journals and other serials.

5918 ■ Mary Kay Inc.–Information Resources
16251 N. Dallas Pkwy.
Addison, TX 75001
Ph:(972)687-5527
Fax:(972)687-1643
Co. E-mail: cecilia.armas@mkcorp.com
Contact: Cecilia Armas-Benavidas, Mgr., Info.Rsrcs.
Scope: Cosmetics, dermatology, toxicology, chemistry, business, marketing. **Services:** Interlibrary loan. **Holdings:** 2000 books; 500 bound periodical volumes. **Subscriptions:** 250 journals and other serials.

5919 ■ Revlon Research Center Library
2121 Rte. 27
Edison, NJ 08818
Ph:(732)287-7650
Fax:(732)248-2230
Contact: Ann Van Dine, Libn.
Scope: Cosmetics, soaps, chemistry, perfumery, dermatology, pharmacology, microbiology, aerosols. **Services:** Interlibrary loan; copying; SDI; Library open to the public by appointment. **Holdings:** 11,000 books; 4000 bound periodical volumes. **Subscriptions:** 100 journals and other serials.

5920 ■ Tavy Stone Fashion Library
Detroit Historical Museum
5401 Woodward Ave.
Detroit, MI 48202
Ph:(313)833-1805
Fax:(313)833-5342
Co. E-mail: webmaster@detroithistorical.org
URL: http://www.detroithistorical.org
Contact: Jill M. Koepke, Libn.
Scope: Fashion (antiquity to present) - American and European fashion designers, careers, advertising, merchandising, management, textiles and fabrics, cosmetics and fragrances, historic costume, fashion retailers; the business, sociological, and psychological aspects of fashion. **Services:** Copying; Library open to the public with restrictions. **Holdings:** 800 books; 40 VF drawers; 500 slides; 10 color swatches; 21 AV programs. **Subscriptions:** 6 journals and other serials.

5921 ■ Unilever HPC NA Research Library
40 Merritt Blvd.
Trumbull, CT 06611
Ph:(203)377-8300
Fax:(203)381-4355
Co. E-mail: mary.m.davis@unilever.com
URL: http://www.unileverna.com
Contact: Mary Davis, Res.Libn.
Scope: Cosmetic science, dermatology. **Holdings:** 5000 books; 2000 bound periodical volumes. **Subscriptions:** 250 journals and other serials.

5922 ■ U.S. Food & Drug Administration–Biosciences Library–CFSAN Branch Library (5100)
5100 Paint Branch Pkwy.
HFS-678
College Park, MD 20740
Ph:(301)436-2163
Fax:(301)436-2653
Co. E-mail: cfsanlib@fda.hhs.gov
Contact: Lee S. Bernstein, Br.Mgr.
Scope: Chemistry, analytical chemistry, toxicology, food technology, nutrition, medicine, biology, cosmetics. **Services:** Interlibrary loan; Library open to the public. **Holdings:** 1000 books; 500 reports, documents, pamphlets; 16,000 cartridges of microfilm. **Subscriptions:** 100 journals and other serials.

ASSOCIATIONS AND OTHER ORGANIZATIONS

5923 ■ Costume Society of America
390 Amwell Rd., Ste. 402
Hillsborough, NJ 08844
Ph:(908)359-1471
Free: 800-272-9447
Fax:(908)450-1118
Co. E-mail: national.office@costumesocietyamerica.com
URL: http://www.costumesocietyamerica.com
Contact: Robin Campbell, Pres.-Elect

Description: Represents museum and historical society personnel; college/university faculty of costume history, retailing, material culture, apparel design, social-psychological aspects, economics; theatre/film fashion designers; conservators; costume and textile collectors/dealers; and re-enactors. Focuses on the scholarly study of all aspects of dress and appearance. Promotes the study of dress through education, research, preservation, and design. Supports scholarship and its dissemination through research papers and publications; collects and disseminates information on the preservation, interpretation, and exhibition of costumes; provides referrals for the identification and conservation of costumes, sponsors international study tours. **Publications:** *CSA E-News* (monthly); *CSA News* (3/year); *DRESS* (annual).

5924 ■ National Costumers Association
121 N Bosart Ave.
Indianapolis, IN 46201
Ph:(317)351-1940
Free: 800-NCA-1321
Fax:(317)351-1941
Co. E-mail: office@costumers.org
URL: http://www.costumers.org
Contact: Jennifer Skarstedt, Admin. Sec.

Description: Designers, producers, and renters of costumes for all occasions. Works to establish and maintain professional and ethical standards of business in the costume industry. Encourages and promotes a greater and more diversified use of costumes in all fields of human activity. Offers Play Plot, Book services; conducts educational programs during conventions; buyer's group discounts, website listing, book service, and debt recovery source. **Publications:** *National Costumers Magazine* (8/year); *Operations Guide Book* (periodic).

REFERENCE WORKS

5925 ■ "Ghouls, Goblins, and Harry Potter: Cashing In On Halloween" in *Inc.* (Vol. 33, October 2011, No. 8, pp. 24)
Pub: Inc. Magazine

Ed: Darren Dahl. **Description:** Costume Craze, an online costume retailer reports $13.2 million in sales last year. Originally the family business started out as a software company called StaticAdvantage, but switched gears.

5926 ■ "Scream Therapy: A Chain of New York City Beauty Stores Perfect Halloween Pop-Ups" in *Inc.* (Vol. 33, October 2011, No. 8, pp. 99)
Pub: Inc. Magazine

Ed: Amy Barrett. **Description:** Ricky's Halloween stores will open 30 temporary stores for about two months, 28 of which are permanent beauty supply shops the rest of the year.

TRADE SHOWS AND CONVENTIONS

5927 ■ National Costumers Association Annual Convention
National Costumers Association
6914 E. Upper Trail Cir.
Mesa, AZ 85207-0943
Ph:(480)654-6220
Free: 800-622-1321
Fax:(480)654-6223

Released: Annual. **Principal Exhibits:** Exhibits for designers, producers and renters of costumes for all occasions including parties and dance.

FRANCHISES AND BUSINESS OPPORTUNITIES

5928 ■ Halloween Express
100 Progress Way
Owenton, KY 40359
Ph:(513)300-0000
Fax:(513)677-8641

No. of Franchise Units: 135. **No. of Company-Owned Units:** 7. **Founded:** 1992. **Description:** Costumes, masks, and make-up. **Equity Capital Needed:** $75,000+. **Franchise Fee:** $10,000. **Financial Assistance:** No. **Training:** Train and assist you in setting up your business, including site selection and guidance throughout the lease process.

LIBRARIES

5929 ■ BMV Archives: Butterick, McCall's, Vogue–Patterns Archives
11 Penn Plaza, 18th Fl.
New York, NY 10001-2000
Ph:(212)620-2790
Fax:(212)465-6962
Co. E-mail: sherryh@mccallpattern.com
Contact: Lillian Esposito, Promotion Mgr.

Scope: Vogue/Butterick costume and marketing history. **Services:** Archives open to students and researchers by appointment, for reference use only. **Holdings:** 200 books; 1500 bound periodical volumes; 1300 cubic feet of archival materials; 100 cubic feet of pictures, clippings, posters. **Subscriptions:** 10 journals and other serials.

5930 ■ Carnegie Library of Pittsburgh–Music Department
4400 Forbes Ave.
Pittsburgh, PA 15213
Ph:(412)622-3105
Fax:(412)687-8982
Co. E-mail: musicdept@carnegielibrary.org
URL: http://www.clpgh.org/locations/music
Contact: Kathryn Logan, Dept.Hd.

Scope: Music, art, architecture, interior design, collectibles, dance. **Services:** Reference and reader's assistance; department open to the public. **Holdings:** 110,000 music books and scores; 63,000 art books; 1500 dance books; 30,000 sound recordings; 1200 videocassettes; 280,000 mounted pictures; 54,000 slides; 69 VF drawers; 1700 videos and DVDs. **Subscriptions:** 320 journals and other serials.

5931 ■ Eugene O'Neill Theater Center–Leibling-Wood Library–Monte Cristo Cottage Collection (325 P)
325 Pequot Ave.
New London, CT 06320
Ph:(860)443-5378
Fax:(860)443-9653
Co. E-mail: montecristo@theoneill.org
URL: http://www.theoneill.com/prog/monte/montprog.htm
Contact: Preston Whiteway, Exec.Dir.

Scope: Drama, dramatic literature, costume design, theater memorabilia. **Services:** Copying; collection open to the public. **Holdings:** 5000 books; playbills; theater scrapbooks; photographic stills; manuscripts; letters; set and costume designs; television manuscripts; clipping files; periodicals.

5932 ■ Fashion Institute of Design & Merchandising–Orange County Library
17590 Gillette Ave.
Irvine, CA 92614-5610
Ph:(949)851-6200
Fax:(949)851-6808
Co. E-mail: rmarkman@fidm.com
URL: http://www.fidm.com
Contact: Rebecca Markman, Campus Libn.

Scope: Apparel manufacturing management, cosmetics and fragrance merchandising, fashion design, interior design, merchandise marketing, textile design, visual presentation and space design. **Services:** Library open to the public by appointment. **Holdings:** 3000 books; 130 bound periodical volumes; 40 pamphlet headings; 475 videotapes; 135 slide sets; 300 retail catalogs; 100 Annual reports; 50 CD-ROMs. **Subscriptions:** 80 journals and other serials; 8 newspapers.

5933 ■ Fashion Institute of Technology–Gladys Marcus Library
7th Ave. at 27th St.
E-Bldg. E502
New York, NY 10001-5992
Ph:(212)217-4340
Fax:(212)217-4371
Co. E-mail: greta_earnest@fitnyc.edu
URL: http://fitnyc.edu/library
Contact: Prof. N.J. Wolfe, Lib.Dir.

Scope: Costume, fashion, interior design, management engineering technology, fashion buying and merchandising, textiles, toy design, packaging design, advertising. **Services:** Interlibrary loan; copying; Library open to the public for reference use only by appointment. **Holdings:** 130,260 books; 113,265 nonprint units; 20,637 bound periodical volumes; 125,000 fashion slides; 4712 reels of microfilm; 438 CD-ROM serials and digital monographs. **Subscriptions:** 4000 journals and other serials.

5934 ■ Guthrie Theater Foundation–Staff Reference Library
818 S. 2nd St.
Minneapolis, MN 55415
Ph:(612)225-6000
Fax:(612)225-6004
Co. E-mail: joh@guthrietheater.org
URL: http://www.guthrietheater.org
Contact: Jo Holcomb, Libn.
Scope: Costume design and history, decorative arts, architecture, history of theater, actors and acting, stage lighting and design, technical production, dramatic literature and critical works, poetry, music, general history and geography. **Services:** Library not open to the public. **Holdings:** 4500 books; 3900 plays; 8 VF drawers of slides; 12 VF drawers of photographs of past productions; 10 VF drawers of scripts from past productions. **Subscriptions:** 6 journals and other serials.

5935 ■ Kansas State University–Richard L.D. and Marjorie J. Morse Department of Special Collections
506 Hale Library
Manhattan, KS 66506
Ph:(785)532-7456
Fax:(785)532-7415
Co. E-mail: rarebooks@k-state.edu
URL: http://www.lib.k-state.edu/depts/spec/index.html
Contact: Roger C. Adams, Assoc.Prof./Libn.
Scope: Cookery, Kanzana, literature, agriculture, military history, milling and grain science, botany, prairie ecology, Oz, science fiction/fantasy, historic costumes and textiles. **Services:** Collections open to the public. **Holdings:** 100,000 volumes.

5936 ■ Los Angeles County Museum of Art–Balch Art Research Library
5905 Wilshire Blvd.
Los Angeles, CA 90036
Ph:(323)857-6118
Co. E-mail: library@lacma.org
URL: http://www.lacma.org
Contact: Alexis Curry, Hd.Libn.
Scope: Art, photography, costumes and textiles, prints and drawings, conservation, European art, American art, Asian art, South and Southeast Asian art, ancient and Islamic art, Latin American art, Craft and Folk Art. **Services:** Interlibrary loan; copying; Library open to the public by appointment only. **Holdings:** 175,000 books; 450 current periodical; 24,107 microfiche; 74 reels of microfilm; current auction catalogs; 150 VF drawers of artist ephemera.

5937 ■ Metropolitan Museum of Art–Irene Lewisohn Costume Reference Library
1000 Fifth Ave.
New York, NY 10028-0198
Ph:(212)650-2723
Fax:(212)570-3970
Co. E-mail: julie.le@metmuseum.org
URL: http://www.metmuseum.org/education/er_lib.asp#ire
Scope: History of costume, fashion, fashion designers, social history. **Services:** Copying; Library open to professional designers and research scholars by appointment. **Holdings:** 40,000 cataloged books and journals; 100,000 pieces of ephemera, including swatch books, fashion sketches, fashion plates, postcards, and vertical files; 50 fashion periodical subscriptions. **Subscriptions:** 70 journals and other serials.

5938 ■ Minneapolis College of Art and Design Library
2501 Stevens Ave., S.
Minneapolis, MN 55404
Ph:(612)874-3791
Fax:(612)874-3704
Co. E-mail: library@mcad.edu
URL: http://intranet.mcad.edu/modules/library
Contact: Suzanne Degler, Lib.Dir.
Scope: Painting, sculpture, graphic arts, design, films and film making, photography, video, performance art. **Services:** Interlibrary loan (limited); copying; Library open to the public for reference use only. **Holdings:** 60,000 volumes; 350 artists' books; 140,000 slides; college archives; compact discs; video cassettes, CD-ROMs. **Subscriptions:** 200 journals and other serials.

5939 ■ Museum of the City of New York–Department of Collections Access
1220 5th Ave.
New York, NY 10029
Ph:(212)534-1672
Fax:(917)492-3960
Co. E-mail: research@mcny.org
URL: http://www.mcny.org
Contact: Peter Simmons, Mgr., Coll. Access
Scope: New York City history; history of theater in New York City; costumes; scene and costume designs. **Services:** Copying; collection open to qualified scholars and researchers only by appointment. **Holdings:** 1000 books; 1000 manuscripts; clippings; documents; prints; photographs; paintings; sheet music.

5940 ■ Newark Public Library–Reference Center
5 Washington St.
PO Box 630
Newark, NJ 07101-0630
Ph:(973)733-7779
Fax:(973)733-7840
Co. E-mail: reference@npl.org
URL: http://www.npl.org
Contact: Wilma J. Grey, Lib.Dir.
Scope: Art and art history, theory, and practice; architecture; biography; bibliography; business; costume; decorative arts; historical stock prices; history; literature and literary criticism; music and music history; religion; social science. **Services:** Interlibrary loan; copying; public fax; Center open to the public. **Holdings:** 300,000 books; 1500 periodical titles (including 19th-century journals); 6.7 million patents; 15,500 scores and song books; 7500 compact discs. **Subscriptions:** 170 journals and other serials.

5941 ■ University of Wisconsin—Madison–Ruth Ketterer Harris Library–Helen Louise Allen Textile Collection (1300)
1300 Linden Dr., Rm. 378
School of Human Ecology
Madison, WI 53706-1524
Ph:(608)262-1162
Fax:(608)265-5099
Co. E-mail: hlatc@mail.sohe.wisc.edu
URL: http://sohe.wisc.edu/depts/hlatc/library.html
Contact: Terry Boyd, Dir.
Scope: Textiles (history), folk art, costume, design. **Services:** Copying; Library open to the public with restrictions (non-circulating). **Holdings:** 4000 books, pamphlets, and journals; 1000 periodical volumes; folios. **Subscriptions:** 30 journals and other serials.

5942 ■ Wayne Finkelman Research Library at Western Costume Company
11041 Vanowen St.
North Hollywood, CA 91605
Ph:(818)760-0900
Fax:(818)508-2190
Co. E-mail: wccmail@westerncostume.com
URL: http://westerncostume.com
Contact: Bobi Garland, Dir., Res.
Scope: Clothing, military and civilian uniforms, insignia, medals and decorations, police uniforms, occupational clothing, sports clothing, ecclesiastical clothing, costume, fashion, folk dress. **Services:** Copying; Library open to the public on a fee basis. **Holdings:** 15,000 volumes; 130 VF drawers; bound periodical volumes. **Subscriptions:** 60 journals and other serials.

5943 ■ Yale University–Drama Collection (Arts Library)
180 York St.
Box 208318
New Haven, CT 06520-8318
Ph:(203)432-2645
Fax:(203)432-0549
Co. E-mail: allen.townsend@yale.edu
URL: http://www.library.yale.edu/arts/arts_collections.html#drama
Contact: Allen Townsend, Dir.
Scope: Plays by American, British, and foreign playwrights; history of the theater; theater architecture; drama criticism; costume and set design; stage lighting; acting; direction; production; theater administration. **Services:** Interlibrary loan; copying; audio and video cassette players; Library open to the public for reference use only (circulation limited to Yale University card holders). **Holdings:** 20,000 volumes; 150 production books; 300 masters' theses; 130 dissertations; 120 scrapbooks of clippings. All unpublished material is under the responsibility of Special collections/Arts Library. **Subscriptions:** 44 journals and other serials; 3 newspapers.

START-UP INFORMATION

5944 ■ *Craft Inc: Turn Your Creative Hobby into a Business*
Pub: Chronicle Books LLC

Ed: Meg Mateo Ilasco. **Released:** September 2007. **Price:** $16.95. **Description:** Guide to help any crafter turn their hobby into a successful business. The book covers all aspects including pricing, sales and marketing, trade shows, as well as interviews with successful craft artisans Jonathan Adler, Lotta Jansdotter, Denyse Schmidt and Jill Bliss.

5945 ■ *How to Start a Faux Painting or Mural Business, Second Edition*
Pub: Allworth Press

Ed: Rebecca Pittman. **Released:** October 1, 2010. **Price:** $24.95. **Description:** Updated and expanded to cover better ways to advertise, innovative supplies (such as Venetian plasters and stained cements), unique bidding and studio setups required for new plasters and varnishes.

5946 ■ *How to Start a Home-Based Craft Business, 5th Ed.*
Pub: Globe Pequot Press

Ed: Kenn Oberrecht. **Released:** July 2007. **Price:** $18.95. **Description:** Step-by-step guide for starting and growing a home-based craft business.

5947 ■ *How to Start a Home-Based Craft Business, 5th Edition*
Pub: Globe Pequot Press

Ed: Kenn Oberrecht. **Released:** July 2007. **Price:** $18.95. **Description:** Advice for starting a home-based craft business is given, including sources for finding supplies on the Internet, writing a business plan, publicity, zoning ordinances, and more.

5948 ■ *Scrapbooking for Profit: Cashing in on Retail, Home-Based and Internet Opportunities*
Pub: Allworth Press

Ed: Rebecca Pittman. **Released:** June 2005. **Price:** $19.95 (US), $22.95 (Canadian). **Description:** Eleven strategies for starting a scrapbooking business, including brick-and-mortar stores, home-based businesses, and online retail and wholesale outlets.

5949 ■ *Setting Up Your Ceramic Studio: Ideas and Plans from Working Artists*
Pub: Lark Books

Ed: Virginia Scotchie. **Released:** March 2005. **Price:** $45.00. **Description:** Floor plans and advice for setting up a creative ceramics studio are provided, focusing on equipment, workflow, and safety issues.

5950 ■ *Will Work for Fun: 3 Simple Steps for Turning Any Hobby or Interest into Cash*
Pub: John Wiley and Sons, Inc.

Ed: Allan R. Bechtold. **Released:** May 2008. **Price:** $24.95. **Description:** Tips for turning any hobby or interest into a lucrative business are shared.

ASSOCIATIONS AND OTHER ORGANIZATIONS

5951 ■ Aid to Artisans
1030 New Britain Ave., Ste. 102
West Hartford, CT 06110
Ph:(860)756-5550
Fax:(860)756-7558
Co. E-mail: info@aidtoartisans.org
URL: http://www.aidtoartisans.org
Contact: Alfredo Espinosa, Pres.
Description: Offers practical assistance worldwide to artisans. Fosters artistic traditions and cultural vitality to improve livelihood and keep communities healthy, strong and growing. Works with its artisan partners to develop products with the appeal to compete successfully in new markets around the world and to improve their business skills so that the changes achieved are enduring. **Publications:** *Artisans of Haiti* .

5952 ■ American Craft Council
72 Spring St., 6th Fl.
New York, NY 10012-4019
Ph:(212)274-0630
Free: 800-836-3470
Fax:(212)274-0650
Co. E-mail: council@craftcouncil.org
URL: http://www.craftcouncil.org
Contact: Chris Amundsen, Exec. Dir.
Description: Promotes understanding and appreciation of contemporary American craft. **Publications:** *American Craft* (bimonthly).

5953 ■ American Society of Artists
PO Box 1326
Palatine, IL 60078
Ph:(312)751-2500
Co. E-mail: asoa@webtv.net
URL: http://community-2.webtv.net/ASOA/ASA
Description: Professional artists and craftspeople. Maintains art referral service and information exchange service. Sponsors art and craft festivals and a Lecture and Demonstration Service; the Special Arts Services Division aids disabled individuals to either practice or enjoy the visual arts. Presents demonstrations in visual arts to better acquaint the public with various processes in different media. **Publications:** *Art Lovers Art and Craft Fair Bulletin* (quarterly).

5954 ■ Guild of American Papercutters
PO Box 384
Somerset, PA 15501
URL: http://www.papercutters.org
Contact: Marie-Helene Grabman, Pres.
Purpose: Unites fellow papercutters to share ideas, display artwork, and increase public appreciation and awareness of this art form. Offers demonstrations and exhibits. .

5955 ■ Handweavers Guild of America
1255 Buford Hwy., Ste. 211
Suwanee, GA 30024
Ph:(678)730-0010
Fax:(678)730-0836
Co. E-mail: hga@weavespindye.org
URL: http://www.weavespindye.org
Contact: Sandra Bowles, Exec. Dir./Ed.-in-Chief
Description: Individuals, weaving arts guilds, educational institutions, teachers, suppliers, and libraries. Seeks to promote participation and interest in hand-crafted textiles; encourage the development of places to work, sell, exhibit, and teach; bring about cooperation among agencies and individuals interested in the textile arts, fiber arts and related fields. **Publications:** *Shuttle Spindle and Dyepot* (quarterly).

5956 ■ Indian Arts and Crafts Association
4010 Carlisle Blvd. NE, Ste. C
Albuquerque, NM 87107
Ph:(505)265-9149
Fax:(505)265-8251
Co. E-mail: info@iaca.com
URL: http://www.iaca.com
Contact: Joseph P. Zeller, Pres.
Description: Indian craftspeople and artists, museums, dealers, collectors, and others. Works to promote, preserve, protect, and enhance the understanding of authentic American Indian arts and crafts. Sets code of ethics for members and standards for the industry. Conducts consumer education seminars, meetings, and display programs; works with related government groups. Operates speakers' bureau. **Publications:** *Indian Arts and Crafts Association—Directory* (annual); *Membership Directory/Buyer's Guide* (annual).

5957 ■ International Wildfowl Carvers Association
194 Summerside Dr.
Centralia, WA 98531
Ph:(360)736-1082
Co. E-mail: jobyrn@comcast.net
URL: http://iwfca.com
Contact: Bob L. Sutton, Chm.
Description: Wildlife carvers. Sets the rules and helps the IWCA member shows.

5958 ■ Knifemakers' Guild
2914 Winters Ln.
La Grange, KY 40031
Ph:(502)222-1397
Fax:(502)222-2676
Co. E-mail: gil@hibbenknives.com
URL: http://www.knifemakersguild.com
Contact: Gil Hibben, Pres.
Description: Knifemakers and interested others. Promotes knives and knifemakers; provides technical assistance to knifemakers; encourages ethical and professional business conduct. .

5959 ■ The Knitting Guild Association
1100-H Brandywine Blvd.
Zanesville, OH 43701-7303
Ph:(740)452-4541

Fax:(740)452-2552
Co. E-mail: tkga@tkga.com
URL: http://www.tkga.com
Contact: Ms. Penny Sitler, Exec. Dir.
Description: Represents shop owners and individuals interested in knitting. Provides education and a means of communication to those wishing to improve the quality of workmanship and creativity of their knitting projects. **Publications:** *Convention Brochure* (annual); *Seminar Brochure* (quarterly).

5960 ■ Smocking Arts Guild of America
PO Box 2846
Grapevine, TX 76099
Free: 800-520-3101
Fax:(817)886-0393
Co. E-mail: president@smocking.org
URL: http://www.smocking.org
Contact: Bobbi Smith, Pres.
Description: Needleart enthusiasts, designers, instructors, business owners, and others interested in smocking, embroidery, fine hand sewing, and/or fine machine sewing. Works to preserve and foster the art of smocking and related needlework through education communication and quality workmanship. Conducts artisan program in four areas of study including smocking, embroidery and heirloom stitching. Offers correspondence courses. .

REFERENCE WORKS

5961 ■ *202 Things You Can Make and Sell for Big Profits*
Pub: Entrepreneur Press
Ed: James Stephenson. **Released:** September 2005. **Price:** $19.95. **Description:** Instructions for 202 products that can be made and sold over the Internet.

5962 ■ *American Craft—News Section*
Pub: American Craft Council
Contact: Lori Key, Asst. Ed.
Ed: Lois Moran, Editor. **Released:** Bimonthly. **Price:** $5 per issue; $40 per year. **Publication Includes:** List of exhibitions, sales, workshops, seminars, conferences, and competitions for contemporary American craftspersons. **Entries Include:** Event name, dates, location; name of gallery, museum, or sponsoring organization. For shows and sales—Whether juried, deadline for applications, fees, contact name and address, media accepted. For workshops, courses, conferences, etc.—Contact name and address, guest artist presiding, dates of events. **Arrangement:** Classified by type of event, then geographical.

5963 ■ "Arario Gallery Opens First American Space" in *Art Business News* (Vol. 34, November 2007, No. 11, pp. 14)
Pub: Pfingsten Publishing, LLC
Description: Opening a new space in New York's Chelsea gallery district is Arario Gallery, a leader in the field of Asian contemporary art; the gallery will feature new works by Chinese artists at its opening.

5964 ■ "Art Attack 2007 Comes to Minneapolis" in *Art Business News* (Vol. 34, November 2007, No. 11, pp. 11)
Pub: Pfingsten Publishing, LLC
Description: Overview of Art Attack 2007, an open studio and gallery crawl in the Northeast Minneapolis Arts District which featured artists working in glass, ceramics, jewelry, mosaics, mixed media, photography, painting, pottery, sculpture, textiles and wood.

5965 ■ "Art Miami Comes to Miami's Wynwood Art District" in *Art Business News* (Vol. 34, November 2007, No. 11, pp. 18)
Pub: Pfingsten Publishing, LLC
Description: In December, The Art Group will hold its Art Miami fair in the Wynwood Art District; the exhibitors range from painting, sculpture, video and works on paper.

5966 ■ "Artexpo Celebrates 30th Anniversary" in *Art Business News* (Vol. 34, November 2007, No. 11, pp. 18)
Pub: Pfingsten Publishing, LLC
Description: In honor of its 30th anniversary Artexpo New York 2008 will be an unforgettable show offering a collection of fine-art education courses for both trade and consumer attendees and featuring a variety of artists working in all mediums.

5967 ■ *ASA Artisan*
Pub: American Society of Artists
Released: Quarterly. **Publication Includes:** Lists of shows and competitions accepting fine art, art and craft work and other information for and about members. **Entries Include:** Show or competition name, location, sponsor, name and address of contact, dates, requirements, supple exhibit info, etc. Principal content of publication is information for and about ASA members. **Arrangement:** Chronological.

5968 ■ "Ask Inc." in *Inc.* (January 2008, pp. 61)
Pub: Gruner & Jahr USA Publishing
Description: Information to help crafter of custom quilts made from old T-shirts, baby clothes, jeans, and neckties to market her items on a small budget.

5969 ■ "Carving Passion, Talent Help Couple Craft Business on Wood-Rich Land" in *Crain's Cleveland Business* (October 8, 2007)
Pub: Crain Communications, Inc.
Ed: Sharon Schnall. **Description:** Profile of Wood-carved Art Gallery & Studio, a family-owned business which includes several ventures of the husband-and-wife team, Jim Stadtlander and Diane Harto.

5970 ■ "Catching Creatives; Detroit Group Gets Grant to Attract 1,000 Design Pros" in *Crain's Detroit Business* (March 24, 2008)
Pub: Crain Communications, Inc.
Ed: Sherri Begin. **Description:** Design Detroit was given a $200,000 planning grant by the Knight Foundation, an organization that strives to back initiatives that leverage talent and resources in each of the 26 U.S. cities it funds, to inspire strategies to attract up to 1,000 creative professionals to live in Detroit.

5971 ■ "City Slickers" in *Canadian Business* (Vol. 81, March 31, 2008, No. 5, pp. 36)
Pub: Rogers Media
Ed: Joe Castaldo. **Description:** Richard Florida believes that the creative class drives the economy and the prosperity of countries depends on attracting and retaining these people. Florida has brought attention to developing livable and economically vibrant cities thanks in part to his promotional skills. However, he has also drawn critics who see his data on his theories as flimsy and inadequate.

5972 ■ *The Craft Business Answer Book: Starting, Managing, and Marketing a Home-Based Art, Crafts, Design Business*
Pub: M. Evans and Company, Incorporated
Ed: Barbara Brabec. **Released:** August 2006. **Price:** $16.95. **Description:** Expert advice for starting a home-based art or crafts business is offered.

5973 ■ *Craft, Inc.*
Pub: Chronicle Books LLC
Ed: Meg Mateo Ilasco. **Released:** August 2007. **Price:** $16.95. **Description:** Business primer for entrepreneurial crafters wishing to turn their hobbies into a small business, including tips for developing products, naming the company, writing a business plan, applying for licenses, and paying taxes.

5974 ■ *The Crafts Report—Shows & Fairs Column*
Pub: The Crafts Report
Ed: Bernadette Finnerty, Editor. **Released:** Monthly. **Publication Includes:** List of forthcoming arts and crafts shows, articles for craft industry. **Entries Include:** Show name, name and address of contact, sizes, fees, attendance. **Arrangement:** Chronological.

5975 ■ "A Decent Proposal" in *Hawaii Business* (Vol. 53, March 2008, No. 9, pp. 52)
Pub: Hawaii Business Publishing
Ed: Jacy L. Youn. **Description:** Bonnie Cooper and Brian Joy own Big Rock Manufacturing Inc., a stone manufacturing company, which sells carved rocks and bowls, lava benches, waterfalls, and Buddhas. Details about the company's growth are discussed.

5976 ■ "Doing Good: Cause and Effect" in *Entrepreneur* (Vol. 36, February 2008, No. 2, pp. 23)
Pub: Entrepreneur Media Inc.
Description: Lisa Knoppe established Art for a Cause LLC that employs people with mental and physical disabilities. The company makes hand-painted tools and furniture to be sold at gift retailers and hardware stores.

5977 ■ "A Doll That Looks Like You: Will Custom Toys Take Off?" in *Inc.* (Volume 32, December 2010, No. 10, pp. 144)
Pub: Inc. Magazine
Ed: Shivani Vora. **Description:** Profiles of various companies that provide custom items that look like people.

5978 ■ *Earn Cash Crafting at Home: An MBA At-Home Mom Explains Step-by-Step Her Fun, Proven, Money-Making, Own-Your-Own Business Formula*
Pub: Dark Horse, Incorporated
Ed: Maria Colman. **Released:** March 2006. **Price:** $10.00. **Description:** Manual offering advice to start and run an at-home craft business.

5979 ■ *Enterprising Women in Urban Zimbabwe: Gender, Microbusiness, and Globalization*
Pub: Indiana University Press
Ed: Mary Johnson Osirim. **Released:** April 1, 2009. **Price:** $39.95. **Description:** An investigation into the business and personal experiences of women entrepreneurs in the microenterprise sector in Zimbabwe. Many of these women work as market traders, crocheters, seamstresses, and hairdressers.

5980 ■ "From Craft Biz To Wholesale Giant" in *Women Entrepreneur* (January 19, 2009)
Pub: Entrepreneur Media Inc.
Ed: Maria Falconer. **Description:** Advice is given on how to turn a small craft business into a full-time venture; tips to help one transition from a part-time designer to a full-time wholesaler and brand are also included.

5981 ■ "Gallery Street Launches ArtCandy" in *Art Business News* (Vol. 34, November 2007, No. 11, pp. 8)
Pub: Pfingsten Publishing, LLC
Description: Fine-art reproduction house Gallery Street recently launched its new division, ArtCandy Editions; the division was created in order to help a network of artists expand the distribution of their work.

5982 ■ "Getting It Sold" in *Black Enterprise* (Vol. 38, November 2007, No. 4, pp. 54)
Pub: Earl G. Graves Publishing Co. Inc.
Ed: Tennille M. Robinson. **Description:** Artist is given advice for marketing and selling paintings, as well as getting artwork published.

5983 ■ "Greg Lueck: Glass Blowing" in *Inc.* (Volume 32, December 2010, No. 10, pp. 36)
Pub: Inc. Magazine
Ed: April Joyner. **Description:** Profile of Greg Lueck, partner and COO of Centerstance, a tech consulting firm in Portland, Oregon. Lueck opened Firehouse Glass, a studio that provides workspace and equipment for glass blowers. He says glass blowing serves as a welcome counterbalance to the cerebral work he does at the office.

5984 ■ *How to Market and Sell Your Art, Music, Photographs, and Handmade Crafts Online*
Pub: Atlantic Publishing Group, Inc.
Ed: Lee Rowley. **Released:** May 2008. **Price:** $24. 95. **Description:** The book provides all the basics for starting and running an online store selling arts, crafts, photography or music. There are more than 300 Websites listed to help anyone market and promote their arts and/or crafts online.

5985 ■ "Innovation Can Be Imperative for Those in Hands-On Trades" in *Crain's Cleveland Business* (Vol. 28, November 12, 2007, No. 45)
Pub: Crain Communications, Inc.
Ed: Harriet Tramer. **Description:** Discusses the importance of networking and innovative marketing concerning those in art and restoration trades.

5986 ■ "Inside an Online Bazaar" in *Entrepreneur* (Vol. 37, September 2009, No. 9, pp. 38)
Pub: Entrepreneur Media, Inc.
Ed: Kara Ohngren. **Description:** Etsy.com is a website that provides a marketplace for handmade products. The site has attracted more than 250,000 sellers since its launch in 2005. Site features and services are also supplied.

5987 ■ "Jo-Ann Fabric and Craft Stores Joins ArtFire.com to Offer Free Online Craft Marketplace" in *Internet Wire* (January 26, 2010)
Pub: Comtex News Network, Inc.
Description: Jo-Ann Fabric and Craft Stores has entered into a partnership with ArtFire.com which will provide sewers and crafters all the tools they need in order to make and sell their products from an online venue.

5988 ■ "Let the Light Shine" in *Retail Merchandiser* (Vol. 51, July-August 2011, No. 4, pp. 74)
Pub: Phoenix Media Corporation
Description: For over 25 years, The Thomas Kinkade Company has been producing art that is collected by both old and young, and is the only company that publishes Thomas Kinkade art.

5989 ■ *Martha, Inc.*
Pub: John Wiley and Sons, Inc.
Ed: Christopher Byron. **Released:** 2002. **Price:** $28. 00. **Description:** Profile of Martha Stewart's rise from working class to a billionaire businesswoman is presented. The book covers Stewart's power struggles and personal conflicts as well as her triumphs.

5990 ■ "Midas Touch" in *Entrepreneur* (Vol. 36, April 2008, No. 4, pp. 160)
Pub: Entrepreneur Media, Inc.
Ed: Sara Wilson. **Description:** Lana Fertelmeister is a model-turned-jewelry designer. Her company, Lana Jewelry, designs fine jewelry for women. Her jewelry line is available in more than 100 stores worldwide and has been worn by celebrities like Cameron Diaz and Sandra Bullock.

5991 ■ "Off the Wall: Keith Collins' Larger-Than-Life Designs" in *Black Enterprise* (Vol. 37, February 2007, No. 7, pp. 138)
Pub: Earl G. Graves Publishing Co. Inc.
Description: Profile of Keith Collins, an entrepreneur who makes carpets for the likes of Jay Leno, Nicolas Cage, Arnold Schwartzenegger, Janet Jackson, and Will Smith. Collins is passionate about this ancient art form and saw a future in it despite the negative feedback from those around him.

5992 ■ "Partnering for Success" in *Art Business News* (Vol. 36, October 2009, No. 10, pp. 4)
Pub: Summit Business Media
Ed: Jennifer Dulin Wiley. **Description:** In such a volatile economy many savvy artists and gallery owners are turning to out-of-the-box partnerships for continued success; these partnerships are also pervading the Internet, especially with such social media networks as Facebook and Twitter where artists and businesses can develop a loyal following.

5993 ■ "Pick A Name, Not Just Any Name" in *Women Entrepreneur* (December 17, 2008)
Pub: Entrepreneur Media Inc.
Ed: Maria Falconer. **Description:** Craft business owners must choose a name that sounds personal since customers who buy hand-made products want to feel that they are buying from an individual rather than an institution. Tips for choosing a name are provided.

5994 ■ *Seven Days in the Art World*
Pub: W.W. Norton & Company
Ed: Sarah Thornton. **Released:** 2009. **Price:** $24.95. **Description:** A sociologist renders the interplay among buyers, critics, curators and makers of contemporary art.

5995 ■ "Show Dates" in *Art Business News* (Vol. 34, November 2007, No. 11, pp. 18)
Pub: Pfingsten Publishing, LLC
Description: Listing of conferences, trade shows and gallery openings for artists and those in the art industry.

5996 ■ "Ted Stahl: Executive Chairman" in *Inside Business* (Vol. 13, September-October 2011, No. 5, pp. NC6)
Pub: Great Lakes Publishing Company
Ed: Miranda S. Miller. **Description:** Profile of Ted Stahl, who started working in his family's business when he was ten years old is presented. The firm makes dies for numbers and letters used on team uniforms. Another of the family firms manufactures stock and custom heat-printing products, equipment and supplies. It also educates customers on ways to decorate garments with heat printing products and offers graphics and software for customers to create their own artwork.

5997 ■ "A Vegas Sensation Inaugural Artexpo Las Vegas" in *Art Business News* (Vol. 34, November 2007, No. 11, pp. 1)
Pub: Pfingsten Publishing, LLC
Ed: Jennifer Dulin. **Description:** Overview of the first Artexpo Las Vegas which featured exhibitors, artists and buyers and was a wonderful place for networking.

TRADE PERIODICALS

5998 ■ *American Ceramic Society Bulletin*
Pub: The American Ceramic Society
Ed: Peter Wray, Editor, pwray@ceramics.org. **Released:** Monthly. **Price:** $75 U.S. and Canada non-members; $131 other countries non-members. **Description:** Contains items of interest to the ceramics community, and provides current information on R&D, technology, manufacturing, engineered ceramics, fuel cells, nanotechnology, glass, refractories, environmental concerns, whitewares, etc. Bulletin publishes "the Glass Researcher" as a quarterly feature section. The December issue of Bulletin includes ceramic Source, an annual buyer's guide.

5999 ■ *Ceramics Monthly*
Pub: The American Ceramic Society
Contact: Cynthia Griffith, Production Ed.
Released: 10/yr. **Price:** $34.95; $40 Canada; $60 other countries; $59.95 two years; $75 Canada two years; $99 other countries two years. **Description:** Consumer magazine containing ceramic art and craft. Features articles on ceramic artists, exhibitions, production processes, critical commentary, book and video reviews, clay and glaze recipes, and kiln designs.

6000 ■ *The China Painter*
Pub: World Organization of China Painters
Contact: Mary Early, Asst. Ed.
Ed: Pat Dickerson, Editor. **Released:** Bimonthly. **Price:** $34; $39 other countries. **Description:** Magazine about china painting for students, teachers, and artists.

6001 ■ *Chip Chats*
Pub: National Wood Carvers Association
Released: Bimonthly. **Price:** $16; $22 other countries. **Description:** Journal for amateur and professional wood carvers.

6002 ■ *CityArt Magazine*
Pub: Fleisher Fine Arts Inc.
Contact: Pat Fleisher, Publisher
E-mail: info@artfocus.com
Released: 3/yr. **Price:** $15 Canada 7%GST. **Description:** Magazine on the contemporary arts scene, including overview articles and reviews of exhibits, artbooks, and an annual summer art school directory.

6003 ■ *Country Home*
Pub: Meredith Corp.
Released: Monthly, 10/yr. **Price:** $4.95 newstand; $21.97 two years. **Description:** Magazine furnishing information on American interior design, architecture, antiques and collectibles, gardening, art, and culinary endeavor.

6004 ■ *The Crafts Fair Guide*
Pub: Crafts Fair Guide
Released: Quarterly. **Price:** $45; $80 two years. **Description:** Magazine reviewing West Coast craft fairs, providing information about a show's environment, weather, attendance, fees, promoters' names and addresses, and old and new dates.

6005 ■ *Crafts 'n things*
Pub: Amos Press Inc.
Ed: Abby Foster, Editor, afoster@amoscraft.com. **Released:** 6/yr. **Price:** $21.97 print and online; $19.97 online only; $29.47 Canada print and online; $36.97 other countries print and online. **Description:** Craft magazine.

6006 ■ *Crafts News*
Pub: The Crafts Center
Contact: Sarah Bernhardt
Released: Quarterly. **Price:** $50. **Description:** Features practical and timely news on market and trade information, sources of microcredit, successful artisan products, artisan advocacy issues, and crafts-related publications and events worldwide.

6007 ■ *Crafts—Newsletter*
Pub: Craft Council of Newfoundland and Labrador
Ed: Sandy Newton, Editor, sandy@nfld.com. **Released:** Bimonthly. **Price:** Included in membership. Contains news and information of the Association and of interest to members. Covers members' achievements, meetings, arts and craft shows, workshops, art supply resources, and gallery openings. Recurring features include a member profile, a product profile, the executive director's report, a calendar of events and news of educational and professional opportunities.

6008 ■ *CWB Custom Woodworking Business*
Pub: Vance Publishing Corp.
Released: Monthly. **Price:** Free to qualified subscribers; $55 U.S., Canada, and Mexico; $125 other countries. **Description:** Magazine for professional custom woodworkers.

6009 ■ *Doll Crafter*
Pub: Jones Publishing Inc.
Contact: Joe Jones, Owner
Released: Monthly. **Price:** $39.95; $74.95 two years; $89.95 3 years. **Description:** Dollcrafting magazine focusing on porcelain dollmaking with emphasis on reproductions.

6010 ■ *Doll World*
Pub: House of White Birches
Contact: Scott Moss, Mktg. Dir.
Ed: Vicki Steensma, Editor. **Released:** Bimonthly. **Description:** Magazine on doll-making, history, costuming, restoration, and information on doll-identification services.

6011 ■ *European Clinical Laboratory*
Pub: International Scientific Communications Inc.
Contact: Brian Howard, Publisher, Ed. in Ch.
Released: Bimonthly, 6 times. **Description:** Magazine for clinical laboratory scientists.

6012 ■ *Fine Woodworking*
Pub: Taunton Press Inc.
Contact: Jon Miller, Publisher
Ed: Timothy D. Schreiner, Editor. **Released:** 7/yr. **Price:** $34.95 U.S. and Canada; $59.95 U.S. and Canada two years; $83.95 U.S. and Canada three years. **Description:** Technical magazine for the amateur and professional woodworker.

6013 ■ *Fired Arts & Crafts*
Pub: Jones Publishing Inc.
Contact: Bill Bright, Publisher
Released: Monthly. **Price:** $39.95; $74.95 two years; $89.95 3 years. **Description:** Magazine for the hobby ceramic industry; includes color photos and step-by-step instructions to complete projects.

6014 ■ *The Home Shop Machinist*
Pub: The Home Shop Machinist
Released: Bimonthly. **Price:** $29.95. **Description:** Magazine for the amateur small shop machinist.

6015 ■ *Loomsong*
Pub: Atlantic Spinners & Handweavers
Ed: Fran Nowakowski, Editor, fcn@dal.ca. **Released:** Monthly, 10/year. **Price:** Included in membership. **Description:** Discusses weaving and spinning. Recurring features include a calendar of events, reports of meetings, news of educational opportunities, book reviews.

6016 ■ *Machinist's Workshop*
Pub: Village Press Publications
Contact: Gretchen Christensen, Advertising Mgr
E-mail: gretchenchris@villagepress.com
Ed: George Buliss, Editor, gbulliss@villagepress.com. **Released:** Bimonthly. **Price:** $26.95. **Description:** Magazine describing metal working techniques and projects for hobby machinists.

6017 ■ *Modern Woodworking*
Pub: BNP Media
Contact: Brooke Wisdom, Exec. Ed.
E-mail: bwisdom@rrpub.com
Description: Magazine for management in the primary and secondary wood products industry.

6018 ■ *National Guild of Decoupeurs—Dialogue*
Pub: National Guild of Decoupeurs
Ed: Marion D. Peer, Editor, mdpeer@aol.com. **Released:** 4/year. **Price:** $40, Included in membership. **Description:** Publishes "how to" articles on decoupage. Recurring features include news of the activities of the Guild.

6019 ■ *Painting*
Pub: Amos Press Inc.
Ed: Irene Mueller, Editor, imueller@amoscraft.com. **Released:** Bimonthly. **Price:** $24.95 online only; $26.95 print and online; $34.45 Canada print and online; $41.95 other countries print and online. **Description:** Magazine for tole and decorative painters, featuring columns, and how-to and educational articles.

6020 ■ *PaintWorks*
Pub: All American Crafts Inc.
Contact: Jerry Cohen, Publisher
Ed: Linda R. Heller, Editor, editors@paintworksmag.com. **Released:** 7/yr. **Price:** $24.97; $38.97 Canada; $45.97 out of country; $39.97 two years; $67.97 Canada two years; $81.97 out of country two years. **Description:** Magazine featuring multimedia arts and crafts projects for all skill levels.

6021 ■ *Paper Crafts Magazine*
Pub: Primedia Special Interest Publications
Contact: Cath Edvalson, Creative Ed.
Released: 8/yr. **Price:** $17.95; $31.93 two years; $23.95 Canada; $29.95 other countries. **Description:** Crafts is a how-to magazine which offers attractive projects in a variety in crafting techniques, such as painting, cross stitch, papercrafts, plastic canvas, polymer clay, fabric crafts, florals, dollmaking, crochet and others. Crafts provides full-size patterns, complete instructions and clear photos that show the projects' details.

6022 ■ *Scentouri News*
Pub: Scentouri
Ed: A. Doyle, Editor. **Description:** Contains recipes and suggestions for making potpourri. Distributed by Prosperity & Profits Unlimited.

6023 ■ *Selling Christmas Decorations*
Pub: Edgell Communications Inc.
Contact: Dorene VanHouten, Gp. Publisher
E-mail: dvanhouten@edgellmail.com
Ed: Mary Ford, Editor, mford@hvc.rr.com. **Released:** Quarterly. **Description:** Trade magazine for the Christmas industry.

6024 ■ *Soft Dolls & Animals*
Pub: Scott Publications
Contact: Cathy Schnoes
Released: Bimonthly. **Price:** $29.95; $53.90 two years; $41.95 out of country non-US; $77.90 two years non-US. **Description:** Magazine covering fabric dolls, teddy bears, and other fabric figures for hobbyists and crafters.

6025 ■ *This Time*
Pub: Homeworkers Organized for More Employment
Ed: Released: Quarterly. **Price:** $5. **Description:** Provides information about H.O.M.E. Furthers the purpose of the organization, which is to provide supplemental income for low-income families through sale of their crafts through the organization. Reports on the education, social service, job training, home building, shelters for the homeless, and a food bank the organization promotes.

6026 ■ *Threads*
Pub: Taunton Press Inc.
Contact: Carol Spier, Editor-in-Chief
Released: Bimonthly. **Price:** $32.95 U.S. and Canada; $54.95 U.S. and Canada two years; $78.95 U.S. and Canada 3/yr. **Description:** Magazine for sewers, and quilters. Focus is on garment design, materials, and techniques.

6027 ■ *Tole World*
Pub: EGW.com Inc.
Contact: Rickie Wilson, Advertising Mgr
E-mail: rwilson@egw.com
Ed: Sandra Yarmolich, Editor, syarmolich@egw.com. **Released:** Bimonthly. **Price:** $17. **Description:** Magazine for tole and decorative painting hobbyists.

6028 ■ *WoodenBoat*
Pub: WoodenBoat Publications Inc.
Contact: Carl Cramer, Publisher
E-mail: carl@woodenboat.com
Ed: Matthew Murphy, Editor, matt@woodenboat.com. **Released:** Bimonthly. **Price:** $32; $59 two years; $85 three years; $37 Canada; $64 Canada two years; $45 other countries. **Description:** Magazine covering the design, building, care, preservation, and use of wooden boats, including commercial and pleasure, old and new, sail and power.

6029 ■ *Woodshop News*
Pub: Dominion Enterprises
Contact: Jennifer Hicks, Staff Writer
E-mail: j.hicks@woodshopnews.com
Ed: Tod Riggio, Editor, t.riggio@woodshopnews.com. **Released:** Monthly. **Price:** $21.95; $33.95 Canada; $35.95 other countries; $35.95 two years. **Description:** Newspaper (tabloid) focusing on people and businesses involved in woodworking.

6030 ■ *Woodsmith*
Pub: August Home Publishing
Contact: Donald Peschke, Publisher
Released: Bimonthly. **Price:** $33 two years; $37 Canada includes additional postage & GST; $36 other countries includes additional postage; $22. **Description:** Magazine for woodworking hobbyists.

6031 ■ *Woodwork*
Pub: Ross Periodicals
Ed: John Lavine, Editor. **Released:** Bimonthly. **Price:** $22 Canada; $25 other countries. **Description:** Covers all aspects of woodworking.

6032 ■ *Wool Gathering*
Pub: Schoolhouse Press
Ed: Meg Swansen, Editor. **Released:** Semiannual. **Price:** $25, other countries airmail; $30, elsewhere. **Description:** Provides hand-knitters with original designs by Elizabeth Zimmermann and Meg Swansen. Includes reviews of knitting trends, information on wools, book reviews, and video news.

VIDEOCASSETTES/ AUDIOCASSETTES

6033 ■ *Craftsmen*
Phoenix Learning Group
2349 Chaffee Dr.
St. Louis, MO 63146-3306
Ph:(314)569-0211
Free: 800-221-1274
Fax:(314)569-2834
URL: http://www.phoenixlearninggroup.com
Released: 1972. **Description:** Six master craftsmen discuss their work and their personal concept of craftsmanship. **Availability:** VHS; 3/4U.

6034 ■ *Lithography: How to Paint and Sell Lithographs*
Instructional Video
2219 C St.
Lincoln, NE 68502
Ph:(402)475-6570
Free: 800-228-0164
Fax:(402)475-6500
Co. E-mail: feedback@insvideo.com
URL: http://www.insvideo.com
Price: $19.95. **Description:** Provides information on how professional print makers plan and print original lithographs to sell. Also contains demonstrations of tools, techniques, materials, and marketing. **Availability:** VHS.

6035 ■ *Maskmaking with Clay*
Crystal Productions
1812 Johns Dr.
Box 2159
Glenview, IL 60025-6519
Ph:(847)657-8144
Free: 800-255-8629
Fax:(847)657-8149
Co. E-mail: custserv@crystalproductions.com
URL: http://www.crystalproductions.com
Released: 1997. **Price:** $24.95. **Description:** Demonstrates complete techniques and materials for creating masks from clay. **Availability:** VHS.

6036 ■ *With These Hands*
Time-Life Video and Television
1450 Palmyra Ave.
Richmond, VA 23227-4420
Ph:(804)266-6330
Free: 800-950-7887
Fax:(757)427-7905
URL: http://www.timelife.com
Released: 1979. **Description:** This program contains footage of craftspeople at work. Potters Toshiko Takaezu and Paul Soldner, sculptors Peter Voulkos, Harry Nohr, Clayton Bailey, and J.B. Blunk, fiber artist Dorian Zachai, and glass blower James Tanner tell why they do what they do. **Availability:** VHS; 3/4U; Special order formats.

TRADE SHOWS AND CONVENTIONS

6037 ■ Annual Dickens Christmas Show and Festivals Week
Leisure Time Unlimited, Inc.
708 Main St.
PO Box 332
Myrtle Beach, SC 29577
Ph:(843)448-9483
Free: 800-261-5591
Fax:(843)626-1513
Co. E-mail: dickensshow@sc.rr.com
Released: Annual. **Audience:** General public. **Principal Exhibits:** Crafts, art, paintings, gifts, and Christmas related items. **Dates and Locations:** 2011 Nov 10-13, Myrtle Beach, SC.

6038 ■ Atlanta International Gift and Home Furnishing Market
AMC Inc.
240 Peachtree St. NW, Ste. 2200
Atlanta, GA 30303-1327
Ph:(404)220-3000
Free: 800-285-6278
Fax:(404)220-3030
Released: Semiannual. **Audience:** Buyers. **Principal Exhibits:** Gifts, stationery, souvenirs, home accents, furniture, Americana, home textiles, designer gifts, homemade gifts, holiday merchandise, florals, and jewelry. **Dates and Locations:** 2011 Jan 12-19, Atlanta, GA.

6039 ■ Atlantic Craft Trade Show
Nova Scotia Department of Economic Development
PO Box 2311
1660 Hollis St., Suite 600
Halifax, NS, Canada B3J 3C8
Ph:(902)424-0377
Fax:(902)424-7008
Released: Annual. **Audience:** Craft, giftware, and apparel trade professionals. **Principal Exhibits:** Crafts and giftware, including porcelain, silver and pewter ware, jewelry, hand knits, hooked rugs, hand blown glass, toys; apparel, wood, and food products. **Dates and Locations:** 2011 Feb 05-07, Halifax, NS; 2012 Feb 04-06, Halifax, NS; 2013 Mar 06 - Feb 05, Halifax, NS.

6040 ■ Border Security Expo
E.J. Krause & Associates, Inc.
6550 Rock Spring Dr., Ste. 500
Bethesda, MD 20817
Ph:(301)493-5500
Fax:(301)493-5705
Co. E-mail: ejkinfo@ejkrause.com
URL: http://www.ejkrause.com
Released: Annual. **Audience:** Law enforcement personnel, government officials. **Principal Exhibits:** GPS systems, wireless communications, law enforcement training, fingerprinting technology, voice recognition systems, documentation checking, guards and bomb sniffing dogs, motion detectors, intelligence sharing, unmanned ground vehicles, armored vehicles, surveillance cameras, sensors, radar systems, scanning systems, control monitors, barriers, biohazard detection systems.

6041 ■ CHA Winter Convention and Trade Show
Hobby Industry Association HIA
319 E. 54th St.
Elmwood Park, NJ 07407
Ph:(201)835-1200
Fax:(201)797-0657
Co. E-mail: info@craftandhobby.org
URL: http://www.hobby.org
Released: Annual. **Audience:** Owners, corporate officers and buyers from craft, hobby, DIY stores, general merchandise stores, wholesalers, and professional crafters. **Principal Exhibits:** Crafts, ceramics, floral accessories, dollhouse miniatures, aromatics, art materials and frames, jewelry findings, fabrics, needlework and quilting supplies, home decor, rubber stamps, stencils and scrapbooking supplies.

6042 ■ Charlotte Gift and Jewelry Show
Charlotte Gift and Jewelry Show
3710 Latrobe Dr., Ste. 110
Charlotte, NC 28211
Ph:(704)365-4150
Fax:(704)365-4154
Co. E-mail: michael@charlottegiftshow.com
URL: http://www.charlottegiftshow.com
Released: Quarterly. **Audience:** Trade buyers. **Principal Exhibits:** Gifts, housewares, jewelry, crafts, silk plants and flowers, tabletop, glassware, collectibles, accessories, home decorating accessories, basketry, and other related products.

6043 ■ Christmas Gift and Hobby Show
HSI Show Productions
PO Box 502797
Indianapolis, IN 46250
Ph:(317)576-9933
Free: 800-215-1700
Fax:(317)576-9955
Co. E-mail: info@hsishows.com
URL: http://www.hsishows.com
Released: Annual. **Audience:** General public. **Principal Exhibits:** Art, crafts, and giftware.

6044 ■ Connecticut Craft Show
Sugarloaf Mountain Works, Inc.
19807 Executive Park Circle
Germantown, MD 20874
Ph:(301)990-1400
Free: 800-210-9900
Fax:(301)253-9620
Co. E-mail: sugarloafinfo@sugarloaffest.com
URL: http://www.sugarloafcrafts.com
Released: Annual. **Audience:** General public. **Principal Exhibits:** Arts and crafts. **Dates and Locations:** 2011 Nov 11-13, Hartford, CT.

6045 ■ The Craftmen's Christmas Classic Arts & Crafts Festival
Gilmore Enterprises
3514-A Drawbridge Pkwy.
Greensboro, NC 27410-8584
Ph:(336)282-5550
Co. E-mail: contact@gilmoreshows.com
URL: http://www.gilmoreshows.com
Released: Annual. **Audience:** Trade and general public. **Principal Exhibits:** Original arts and crafts.

6046 ■ Craftsmen's Classic Arts & Crafts Festival-Columbia
Gilmore Enterprises
3514-A Drawbridge Pkwy.
Greensboro, NC 27410-8584
Ph:(336)282-5550
Co. E-mail: contact@gilmoreshows.com
URL: http://www.gilmoreshows.com
Released: Annual. **Audience:** Trade and general public. **Principal Exhibits:** Original arts and crafts, hand made and presented by their creator. **Dates and Locations:** 2011 Mar 04-06, Columbia, SC.

6047 ■ The Craftsmen's Classic Arts & Crafts Festival—Greensboro
Gilmore Enterprises
3514-A Drawbridge Pkwy.
Greensboro, NC 27410-8584
Ph:(336)282-5550
Co. E-mail: contact@gilmoreshows.com
URL: http://www.gilmoreshows.com
Released: Annual. **Audience:** General public. **Principal Exhibits:** Originals arts and crafts. **Dates and Locations:** 2011 Apr 08-10, Greensboro, NC.

6048 ■ The Craftsmen's Classic Arts & Crafts Festival—Myrtle Beach
Gilmore Enterprises
3514-A Drawbridge Pkwy.
Greensboro, NC 27410-8584
Ph:(336)282-5550
Co. E-mail: contact@gilmoreshows.com
URL: http://www.gilmoreshows.com
Released: Annual. **Audience:** Trade and general public. **Principal Exhibits:** Original arts and crafts. **Dates and Locations:** 2011 Aug 05-07, Myrtle Beach, SC.

6049 ■ Handmade - A Division of the New York International Gift Fair
George Little Management, LLC (New York, New York)
1133 Westchester Ave., Ste. N136
White Plains, NY 10606
Ph:(914)421-3200
Free: 800-272-SHOW
Co. E-mail: cathy_steel@glmshows.com
URL: http://www.glmshows.com
Released: Semiannual. **Audience:** Buyers of specialty, department, jewelry, and stationery stores; gift shops, interior designers, importers/distributors of home products, mail order catalogs. **Principal Exhibits:** Handmade merchandise, including functional and decorative home furnishings, fashion accessories, jewelry plus an array of other unique craft objects. All merchandise is selected by a panel of craft professionals for uniqueness, originality and marketability.

6050 ■ Handmade - A Division of the San Francisco International Gift Fair
George Little Management, LLC (New York, New York)
1133 Westchester Ave., Ste. N136
White Plains, NY 10606
Ph:(914)421-3200
Free: 800-272-SHOW
Co. E-mail: cathy_steel@glmshows.com
URL: http://www.glmshows.com
Released: Semiannual. **Audience:** Specialty, department, stationery, juvenile, and jewelry stores, interior designers, gift shops, mail order catalogs, importers/distributors of home products. **Principal Exhibits:** Handmade merchandise, including functional and decorative home furnishings, fashion accessories, jewelry plus an array of other unique craft objects. All merchandise is selected by a panel of craft professionals for uniqueness, originality and marketability.

6051 ■ Holiday Fair
Textile Hall Corp.
PO Box 5823
Greenville, SC 29606
Ph:(864)331-2277
Fax:(864)331-2282
Co. E-mail: atmei@textilehall.com
Released: Annual. **Audience:** General public. **Principal Exhibits:** Arts and crafts.

6052 ■ Home Entertainment Show
Trigger Agency
3539 Clipper Mill Rd.
Baltimore, MD 21211
Free: 800-830-3976
Fax:(410)878-9911
Co. E-mail: info@triggeragency.com
URL: http://www.triggeragency.com/
Released: Biennial. **Audience:** Consumers, trade and press. **Principal Exhibits:** Home theater and high-fidelity audio equipment, supplies, and services.

6053 ■ Memories Expo
Offinger Management Co.
1100-H Brandywine Blvd.
PO Box 3388
Zanesville, OH 43702-3388
Ph:(740)452-4541
Free: 888-878-6334
Fax:(740)452-2552
Co. E-mail: OMC.Info@Offinger.com
URL: http://www.offinger.com
Released: 5/year. **Audience:** Trade and public. **Principal Exhibits:** Scrapbook supplies. **Dates and Locations:** 2011 Mar 25-26, Columbus, OH.

6054 ■ Mid-South Jewelry & Accessories Fair Fall
Helen Brett Enterprises, Inc.
5111 Academy Dr.
Lisle, IL 60532-2171
Ph:(630)241-9865
Free: 800-541-8171
Fax:(630)241-9870
URL: http://www.gift2jewelry.com
Released: Semiannual. **Audience:** Wholesaler buyers. **Principal Exhibits:** Fine/costume jewelry, apparel, leathers, silks, beaded items, home decor, novelties.

6055 ■ Society of Craft Designers Educational Seminar
Offinger Management Co.
1100-H Brandywine Blvd.
PO Box 3388
Zanesville, OH 43702-3388
Ph:(740)452-4541
Free: 888-878-6334
Fax:(740)452-2552
Co. E-mail: OMC.Info@Offinger.com
URL: http://www.offinger.com
Released: Annual. **Audience:** Designers, manufacturers, editors, and publishers. **Principal Exhibits:** Craft designer showcases and education.

6056 ■ Southern Christmas Show
Southern Shows, Inc.
PO Box 36859
Charlotte, NC 28236
Ph:(704)376-6594
Free: 800-849-0248
Fax:(704)376-6345
Co. E-mail: sabernethy@southernshows.com
URL: http://www.southernshows.com
Released: Annual. **Audience:** General public. **Principal Exhibits:** Christmas gifts, crafts, arts, foods, and educational materials, Christmas tree lane, and decorating competitions, and Santa Claus. **Dates and Locations:** 2011 Nov 10-20, Charlotte, NC.

6057 ■ Sugarloaf Art Fair Novi, Spring
Sugarloaf Mountain Works, Inc.
19807 Executive Park Circle
Germantown, MD 20874
Ph:(301)990-1400
Free: 800-210-9900
Fax:(301)253-9620
Co. E-mail: sugarloafinfo@sugarloaffest.com
URL: http://www.sugarloafcrafts.com
Released: Annual. **Audience:** Women ages 25 through 54. **Principal Exhibits:** Arts and crafts.

6058 ■ Sugarloaf Crafts Festival Gaithersburg, Fall
Sugarloaf Mountain Works, Inc.
19807 Executive Park Circle
Germantown, MD 20874
Ph:(301)990-1400
Free: 800-210-9900
Fax:(301)253-9620
Co. E-mail: sugarloafinfo@sugarloaffest.com
URL: http://www.sugarloafcrafts.com
Released: Annual. **Audience:** Women ages 25 through 54. **Principal Exhibits:** Arts and crafts. **Dates and Locations:** 2011 Nov 18-20, Gaithersburg, MD.

6059 ■ Sugarloaf Crafts Festival Gaithersburg, Spring
Sugarloaf Mountain Works, Inc.
19807 Executive Park Circle
Germantown, MD 20874
Ph:(301)990-1400
Free: 800-210-9900
Fax:(301)253-9620
Co. E-mail: sugarloafinfo@sugarloaffest.com
URL: http://www.sugarloafcrafts.com
Released: Annual. **Audience:** Women ages 25 through 54. **Principal Exhibits:** Arts and crafts. **Dates and Locations:** 2011 Apr 08-10, Gaithersburg, MD.

6060 ■ Sugarloaf Crafts Festival Manassas, Fall
Sugarloaf Mountain Works, Inc.
19807 Executive Park Circle
Germantown, MD 20874
Ph:(301)990-1400
Free: 800-210-9900
Fax:(301)253-9620
Co. E-mail: sugarloafinfo@sugarloaffest.com
URL: http://www.sugarloafcrafts.com
Released: Annual. **Audience:** Women ages 25 through 54. **Principal Exhibits:** Arts and crafts.

6061 ■ Sugarloaf Crafts Festival Philadelphia
Sugarloaf Mountain Works, Inc.
19807 Executive Park Circle
Germantown, MD 20874
Ph:(301)990-1400
Free: 800-210-9900
Fax:(301)253-9620
Co. E-mail: sugarloafinfo@sugarloaffest.com
URL: http://www.sugarloafcrafts.com
Released: Semiannual. **Audience:** Women ages 25 through 54. **Principal Exhibits:** Arts and crafts.

6062 ■ Sugarloaf Crafts Festival Somerset, Fall
Sugarloaf Mountain Works, Inc.
19807 Executive Park Circle
Germantown, MD 20874
Ph:(301)990-1400
Free: 800-210-9900
Fax:(301)253-9620
Co. E-mail: sugarloafinfo@sugarloaffest.com
URL: http://www.sugarloafcrafts.com
Released: Annual. **Audience:** Women ages 25 through 54. **Principal Exhibits:** Arts and crafts. **Dates and Locations:** 2011 Oct 28-30, Somerset, NJ.

6063 ■ Sugarloaf Crafts Festival Somerset, Spring
Sugarloaf Mountain Works, Inc.
19807 Executive Park Circle
Germantown, MD 20874
Ph:(301)990-1400
Free: 800-210-9900
Fax:(301)253-9620
Co. E-mail: sugarloafinfo@sugarloaffest.com
URL: http://www.sugarloafcrafts.com
Released: Semiannual. **Audience:** Women ages 25 through 54. **Principal Exhibits:** Arts and crafts. **Dates and Locations:** 2011 Mar 11-13, Somerset, NJ.

6064 ■ Sugarloaf Crafts Festival Timonium, Fall
Sugarloaf Mountain Works, Inc.
19807 Executive Park Circle
Germantown, MD 20874
Ph:(301)990-1400
Free: 800-210-9900
Fax:(301)253-9620
Co. E-mail: sugarloafinfo@sugarloaffest.com
URL: http://www.sugarloafcrafts.com
Released: Annual. **Audience:** Women ages 25 through 54. **Principal Exhibits:** Arts and crafts. **Dates and Locations:** 2011 Sep 30 - Oct 02, Timonium, MD.

6065 ■ Sugarloaf Crafts Festival Timonium, Spring
Sugarloaf Mountain Works, Inc.
19807 Executive Park Circle
Germantown, MD 20874
Ph:(301)990-1400
Free: 800-210-9900
Fax:(301)253-9620
Co. E-mail: sugarloafinfo@sugarloaffest.com
URL: http://www.sugarloafcrafts.com
Released: Annual. **Audience:** Women ages 25 through 54. **Principal Exhibits:** Arts and crafts. **Dates and Locations:** 2011 Apr 29 - May 01, Timonium, MD.

6066 ■ TNNA Winter Trade Show
Offinger Management Co.
1100-H Brandywine Blvd.
PO Box 3388
Zanesville, OH 43702-3388
Ph:(740)452-4541
Free: 888-878-6334
Fax:(740)452-2552
Co. E-mail: OMC.Info@Offinger.com
URL: http://www.offinger.com
Released: Semiannual. **Audience:** Trade-retail buyers of needle art products. **Principal Exhibits:** Upscale needle art products such as needlepoint, knitting, counted thread, embroidery, and crochet supplies as well as related products such as buttons, beads, trims, frames, fibers, books, etc.

FRANCHISES AND BUSINESS OPPORTUNITIES

6067 ■ Crock A Doodle Inc.
101 Osler Dr., Unit 101
Dundas, ON, Canada L9H 4H4
Ph:(519)757-5522
Co. E-mail: franchise@crockadoodle.com
URL: http://www.crockadoodle.com
No. of Franchise Units: 10. **No. of Company-Owned Units:** 2. **Founded:** 2002. **Franchised:** 2004. **Description:** Provides a variety of pottery painting events and activities for groups of all kinds. For women, we offer a calendar full of pottery-painting workshops and classes, as well as creative activities for girls' nights, bridal showers and special occasions. For children, we offer birthday parties, seasonal events and pottery-painting classes, as well as creative programming for camps, schools, teams and groups. The opportunity extends throughout the community to corporate team builders, fundraisers and community events of all kinds. **Equity Capital Needed:** Total investment from $75,000. **Franchise Fee:** $20,000. **Training:** Provides 2 weeks plus ongoing support.

6068 ■ The Painted Penguin, LLC
6115 Monroe Ct.
Morton Grove, IL 60053
Ph:(847)681-0005
Free: (847)681-0005
Fax:(847)432-3437
Co. E-mail: franchise@thepaintedpenguin.com
URL: http://www.thepaintedpenguin.com
No. of Franchise Units: 1. **No. of Company-Owned Units:** 2. **Founded:** 2000. **Franchised:** 2003. **Description:** Offers the opportunity to get in on the ground floor of the booming craft industry with a well respected, growth oriented franchise that combines business ownership with a fun environment. **Equity Capital Needed:** $115,000-$199,000. **Franchise Fee:** $35,000. **Financial Assistance:** None. **Training:** Comprehensive training, marketing guidance, site selection assistance and other on-going support.

COMPUTERIZED DATABASES

6069 ■ *Art on Screen Database*
Program for Art on Film Inc.
200 Willoughby Ave.
Brooklyn, NY 11205-3817
Ph:(718)399-4506
Fax:(718)399-4507
Co. E-mail: info@artfilm.org
URL: http://www.artfilm.org
Description: Contains bibliographic information on more than 25,000 videos, films, multimedia, and CD-ROM productions about the visual arts. For each product, provides title, credits, length, year, country, language, synopsis, production date, distributors, formats, awards, reviews, and in many cases evaluations. Includes entries for more than 5000 distribution sources, providing name, address, telephone, and fax numbers for each entry. Users may perform searches by artist name, style or period, materials, techniques, genre or by associated concepts. **Availability:** Online: Program for Art on Film Inc. **Type:** Directory.

6070 ■ *Consumer InSite*
Thomson Reuters
610 Opperman Dr.
Eagen, MN 55122
Free: 800-477-4300
Co. E-mail: gale.contentlicensing@cengage.com
URL: http://www.insite2.gale.com
Description: Focuses on consumer behavior, political opinion, contemporary lifestyles, leisure activities, and trends in popular culture. Provides the full text and summaries from more than 350 widely read North American newsstand titles and specialty magazines; derived from Magazine Database. Contains approximately 600,000 articles, including entertainment reviews of books, films, video, theatre, concerts, musical recordings, hotels, and restaurants, consumer buyer's guides, columns, editorials, product evaluations, biographies, speeches, interviews, and obituaries. **Availability:** Online: Thomson Reuters. **Type:** Full text.

6071 ■ *Humanities Full Text*
EBSCO Publishing
10 Estes St.
Ipswich, MA 01938
Ph:(978)356-6500
Free: 800-653-2726
Fax:(978)356-6565
Co. E-mail: information@ebscohost.com
URL: http://www.ebscohost.com/wilson
Description: Contains more than 640,000 full-text articles from approximately 600 humanities periodicals from 1995 to date in the subject areas of humanities, including literature and language, history, philosophy, archaeology, classical studies, folklore, gender studies, performing arts, history, religion and theology. Includes indexing of some 600 periodicals from 1984 and abstracts of 50 to 150 words. **Availability:** Online: Wolters Kluwer Health, ProQuest LLC, Wolters Kluwer Health, EBSCO Publishing. **Type:** Full text; Bibliographic.

LIBRARIES

6072 ■ American Craft Council Library
72 Spring St., 6th Fl.
New York, NY 10012-4019
Ph:(212)274-0630
Free: 800-836-3470

Fax:(212)274-0650
Co. E-mail: library@craftcouncil.org
URL: http://www.craftcouncil.org/html/resources/library.shtml
Contact: David Shuford, Libn.
Scope: 20th-century contemporary fine crafts - fiber, clay, metal, wood, glass, enamel, plastics, mixed media; decorative arts; design. **Services:** Library open to the public by appointment (Mondays, Wednesdays, and Fridays). **Holdings:** 6400 books; 700 bound periodical volumes; 7000 exhibition catalogs; 200 videocassettes. **Subscriptions:** 100 journals and other serials.

6073 ■ American Society of Artists Resource Center
Box 1326
Palatine, IL 60078
Ph:(312)751-2500
Co. E-mail: asoa@webtv.net
URL: http://www.americansocietyofartists.org
Contact: Donald Metcoff, Libn.
Scope: Art, crafts, supplies. **Services:** Lectures; demonstrations; seminars; workshops. **Holdings:** 50 volumes; 43 VF drawers. **Subscriptions:** 11 journals and other serials.

6074 ■ California College of the Arts Libraries–Meyer Library
5212 Broadway
Oakland, CA 94618
Ph:(510)594-3658
Co. E-mail: meyerlib@cca.edu
URL: http://library.cca.edu
Contact: Janice Woo, Dir. of Libs.
Scope: Art, architecture, design, humanities. **Services:** Library limited to the CCA community (specialized research by appointment). **Holdings:** 62,000 volumes; 150,000 slides and pictures; 100 lin.ft. of archival material. **Subscriptions:** 275 journals and other serials.

6075 ■ Cleveland Institute of Art–Jessica R. Gund Memorial Library
11141 East Blvd.
Cleveland, OH 44106
Ph:(216)421-7440
Fax:(216)421-7439
Co. E-mail: referencehelp@cia.edu
URL: http://www.cia.edu/academicResources/library.php
Contact: Cristine C. Rom, Lib.Dir.
Scope: Fine arts, crafts, industrial design, general design, graphic arts, new media, glass, ceramics, medical illustration, textiles, metals. **Services:** Interlibrary loan; copying; Library open to the public. **Holdings:** 45,000 books; 10,000 bound periodical volumes; 125,000 slides; 9000 pictures; 37 volumes and boxes of archival materials; 4000 reels of microfilm; 15,000 microfiche; 500 videocassettes and DVDs; 3000 sound recordings; 600 videotapes. **Subscriptions:** 220 journals and other serials; 2 newspapers.

6076 ■ Haystack Mountain School of Crafts Library
PO Box 518
Deer Isle, ME 04627-0518
Ph:(207)348-2306
Fax:(207)348-2307
Co. E-mail: haystack@haystack-mtn.org
URL: http://www.haystack-mtn.org/
Scope: Fine arts, ceramics, weaving, glassblowing, flat glass, jewelry, surface and textile design, wood, blacksmithing, printmaking, papermaking, weaving. **Services:** Library open to the public on a limited basis. **Holdings:** 1000 books. **Subscriptions:** 20 journals and other serials.

6077 ■ Manitoba Crafts Museum & Library–Gladys Chown Memorial Library
1B-183 Kennedy St.
Winnipeg, MB, Canada R3C 1S6
Ph:(204)487-6117
Fax:(204)487-6117
Co. E-mail: mcml1@mts.net
URL: http://www.mts.net/lAtmcml
Contact: Andrea Reichert, Cur.
Scope: Crafts - weaving, pottery, embroidery, knitting, crochet, quilting, paper, wood, Inuit and Aboriginal, polymer clay, lace; craft design; color theory; history of craft. **Services:** Library open to the public. **Holdings:** 3500 volumes; 2000 slides; 9000 artifacts. **Subscriptions:** 4 journals and other serials.

6078 ■ Museum of Contemporary Craft Library
724 NW Davis St.
Portland, OR 97209
Ph:(503)223-2654
Fax:(503)223-0190
Co. E-mail: info@museumofcontemporarycraft.org
URL: http://www.museumofcontemporarycraft.org/
Contact: Linda Brower, Treas.
Scope: Ceramics and pottery, weaving and textiles, Pacific Northwest craftsmen, contemporary designers, metalwork and jewelry, contemporary glass, sculpture, woodworking, architecture. **Services:** Library open during Museum hours. **Holdings:** 420 books; 74 bound and 125 unbound periodical volumes.

6079 ■ Parsons School of Design–Adam & Sophie Gimbel Design Library
2 W. 13th St.
New York, NY 10011
Ph:(212)229-8914, x4121
Fax:(212)229-2806
Co. E-mail: luedkej@newschool.edu
URL: http://library.newschool.edu/gimbel/
Contact: Jill Luedke, Ref. and Instr.Libn.
Scope: Fine arts, architecture, costume, crafts, design, environmental design, fashion, graphic arts, photography, typography. **Services:** Interlibrary loan. **Holdings:** 61,000 books; 55,000 mounted picture plates; 85,000 slides; archives. **Subscriptions:** 200 journals and other serials.

6080 ■ University of Hartford–William H. Mortensen Library–Anne Bunce Cheney Art Collection (200 B)
200 Bloomfield Ave.
West Hartford, CT 06117
Ph:(860)768-4397
Fax:(860)768-5298
Co. E-mail: bigazzi@hartford.edu
URL: http://library-new.hartford.edu
Contact: Anna B. Bigazzi, Art Ref.Libn.
Scope: Art history, architecture, art education, applied art, decorative arts, crafts, photography, typography. **Services:** Interlibrary loan; copying; Library open to the public. **Holdings:** 24,000 books; 3200 bound periodical volumes; 19,000 mounted reproductions; 2500 pamphlets; CD-ROMs; videos. **Subscriptions:** 70 journals and other serials.

Craft/Hobby Business

START-UP INFORMATION

6081 ■ *Careers for Self-Starters and Other Entrepreneurial Types*
Pub: McGraw-Hill Companies

Ed: Blythe Camenson. **Released:** September 2004. **Price:** $9.99 (US). **Description:** Advice to entrepreneurs wishing to start their own small company. Tips for turning hobbies into job skills are included.

6082 ■ *The Craft Business Answer Book: Starting, Managing, and Marketing a Home-Based Art, Crafts, Design Business*
Pub: M. Evans and Company, Incorporated

Ed: Barbara Brabec. **Released:** August 2006. **Price:** $16.95. **Description:** Expert advice for starting a home-based art or crafts business is offered.

6083 ■ *Craft Inc: Turn Your Creative Hobby into a Business*
Pub: Chronicle Books LLC

Ed: Meg Mateo Ilasco. **Released:** September 2007. **Price:** $16.95. **Description:** Guide to help any crafter turn their hobby into a successful business. The book covers all aspects including pricing, sales and marketing, trade shows, as well as interviews with successful craft artisans Jonathan Adler, Lotta Jansdotter, Denyse Schmidt and Jill Bliss.

6084 ■ *Earn Cash Crafting at Home: An MBA At-Home Mom Explains Step-by-Step Her Fun, Proven, Money-Making, Own-Your-Own Business Formula*
Pub: Dark Horse, Incorporated

Ed: Maria Colman. **Released:** March 2006. **Price:** $10.00. **Description:** Manual offering advice to start and run an at-home craft business.

6085 ■ *How to Start a Home-Based Craft Business, 5th Ed.*
Pub: Globe Pequot Press

Ed: Kenn Oberrecht. **Released:** July 2007. **Price:** $18.95. **Description:** Step-by-step guide for starting and growing a home-based craft business.

6086 ■ *How to Start a Home-Based Craft Business, 5th Edition*
Pub: Globe Pequot Press

Ed: Kenn Oberrecht. **Released:** July 2007. **Price:** $18.95. **Description:** Advice for starting a home-based craft business is given, including sources for finding supplies on the Internet, writing a business plan, publicity, zoning ordinances, and more.

6087 ■ *Scrapbooking for Profit: Cashing in on Retail, Home-Based and Internet Opportunities*
Pub: Allworth Press

Ed: Rebecca Pittman. **Released:** June 2005. **Price:** $19.95 (US), $22.95 (Canadian). **Description:** Eleven strategies for starting a scrapbooking business, including brick-and-mortar stores, home-based businesses, and online retail and wholesale outlets.

6088 ■ *Setting Up Your Ceramic Studio: Ideas and Plans from Working Artists*
Pub: Lark Books

Ed: Virginia Scotchie. **Released:** March 2005. **Price:** $45.00. **Description:** Floor plans and advice for setting up a creative ceramics studio are provided, focusing on equipment, workflow, and safety issues.

6089 ■ *Soul Proprietor: 101 Lessons from a Lifestyle Entrepreneur*
Pub: Crossing Press, Incorporated

Ed: Jane Pollak. **Released:** September 2004. **Description:** More than 100 tips and stores to inspire and guide any would-be entrepreneur to earn a living from a favorite hobby or passion.

6090 ■ *Will Work for Fun: 3 Simple Steps for Turning Any Hobby or Interest into Cash*
Pub: John Wiley and Sons, Inc.

Ed: Allan R. Bechtold. **Released:** May 2008. **Price:** $24.95. **Description:** Tips for turning any hobby or interest into a lucrative business are shared.

ASSOCIATIONS AND OTHER ORGANIZATIONS

6091 ■ American Craft Council
72 Spring St., 6th Fl.
New York, NY 10012-4019
Ph:(212)274-0630
Free: 800-836-3470
Fax:(212)274-0650
Co. E-mail: council@craftcouncil.org
URL: http://www.craftcouncil.org
Contact: Chris Amundsen, Exec. Dir.

Description: Promotes understanding and appreciation of contemporary American craft. **Publications:** *American Craft* (bimonthly).

6092 ■ American Sewing Guild
9660 Hillcroft, Ste. 510
Houston, TX 77096
Ph:(713)729-3000
Fax:(713)721-9230
Co. E-mail: ddias@asg.org
URL: http://www.asg.org
Contact: Denise Dias, Chair

Description: Home sewers and people interested in sewing. Provides current sewing information and advice through lectures, demonstrations, classes, seminars, and fashion shows. Seeks to improve communication between home sewers and sewing industry. Encourages the development of neighborhood workshop groups. .

6093 ■ Canadian Craft and Hobby Association
PO Box 101
Orangeville, ON, Canada L9W 2Z5
Ph:(519)940-5969
Free: (866)386-8853
Fax:(519)941-0492
Co. E-mail: paul.laplante@asi-tapedots.com
URL: http://www.cdncraft.org
Contact: Paul Laplante, Pres.
Description: Hobbyists and craftspeople. Promotes recreational and commercial participation in the production of craft objects. Facilitates communication and cooperation among members; provides support and services to craftspeople; conducts promotional activities. **Publications:** *Canadian Craft Trade* (semiannual); Membership Directory (annual).

6094 ■ Craft and Hobby Association
319 E 54th St.
Elmwood Park, NJ 07407
Ph:(201)835-1200
Free: 800-822-0494
Fax:(201)797-0657
Co. E-mail: info@craftandhobby.org
URL: http://www.craftandhobby.org
Contact: Tony Lee, Acting Pres./CEO
Description: Manufacturers, wholesalers, retailers, publishers, and allied firms in the craft and hobby industry. Promotes the interest of all companies engaged in the buying, selling, or manufacturing of craft and hobby merchandise; conceives, develops, and implements programs for members to achieve greater individual growth. Conducts seminars and educational workshops; sponsors national trade show. Compiles statistics. **Publications:** Membership Directory (annual).

6095 ■ Embroiderers' Guild of America
1355 Bardstown Rd., Ste. 157
Louisville, KY 40202
Ph:(502)589-6956
Fax:(502)584-7900
Co. E-mail: egahq@egausa.org
URL: http://www.egausa.org
Contact: Lorie Welker, Pres.
Description: People interested in the art of needlework. Aims to set and maintain high standards of design, color, and workmanship in all kinds of embroidery. Sponsors exhibitions; offers examinations for teaching certification; serves as an information source for needlework in the U.S. Conducts classes and correspondence on all types of needlework. Presents certificate for successful completion of Master Craftsman Programs. **Publications:** *Inside EGA* (quarterly); *Needle Arts* (quarterly).

6096 ■ Indian Arts and Crafts Association
4010 Carlisle Blvd. NE, Ste. C
Albuquerque, NM 87107
Ph:(505)265-9149
Fax:(505)265-8251
Co. E-mail: info@iaca.com
URL: http://www.iaca.com
Contact: Joseph P. Zeller, Pres.
Description: Indian craftspeople and artists, museums, dealers, collectors, and others. Works to promote, preserve, protect, and enhance the understanding of authentic American Indian arts and crafts. Sets code of ethics for members and standards for the industry. Conducts consumer education seminars, meetings, and display programs; works with related

government groups. Operates speakers' bureau. **Publications:** *Indian Arts and Crafts Association—Directory* (annual); *Membership Directory/Buyer's Guide* (annual).

6097 ■ The National Needle Arts Association
1100-H Brandywine Blvd.
Zanesville, OH 43701-7303
Ph:(740)455-6773
Free: 800-889-8662
Fax:(740)452-2552
Co. E-mail: tnna.info@offinger.com
URL: http://www.tnna.org
Contact: Matt Bryant, Pres.
Description: Manufacturers, retailers and distributors of upscale needle art products (needlepoint, embroidery, cross stitch, crochet, knitting, books and accessories). Advances its community of professional businesses by encouraging the passion for needle arts though education, industry knowledge exchange and a strong marketplace. **Publications:** *Directory of Exhibitors* (semiannual).

REFERENCE WORKS

6098 ■ *202 Things You Can Make and Sell for Big Profits*
Pub: Entrepreneur Press
Ed: James Stephenson. **Released:** September 2005. **Price:** $19.95. **Description:** Instructions for 202 products that can be made and sold over the Internet.

6099 ■ "Ask Inc." in *Inc.* (January 2008, pp. 61)
Pub: Gruner & Jahr USA Publishing
Description: Information to help crafter of custom quilts made from old T-shirts, baby clothes, jeans, and neckties to market her items on a small budget.

6100 ■ *Craft, Inc.*
Pub: Chronicle Books LLC
Ed: Meg Mateo Ilasco. **Released:** August 2007. **Price:** $16.95. **Description:** Business primer for entrepreneurial crafters wishing to turn their hobbies into a small business, including tips for developing products, naming the company, writing a business plan, applying for licenses, and paying taxes.

6101 ■ *The Crafts Report—Shows & Fairs Column*
Pub: The Crafts Report
Ed: Bernadette Finnerty, Editor. **Released:** Monthly. **Publication Includes:** List of forthcoming arts and crafts shows, articles for craft industry. **Entries Include:** Show name, name and address of contact, sizes, fees, attendance. **Arrangement:** Chronological.

6102 ■ "A Curious Appeal (Market for Scientific Toys)" in *Playthings* (Vol. 106, October 1, 2008, No. 9, pp. 26)
Pub: Reed Business Information
Ed: Pamela Brill. **Description:** Science and nature toys are still popular with children. Kits allow kids to make candy, soap, grow miniature gardens, catch bugs and more. These hands-on kits have manufacturers watching trends to create more toys in this category.

6103 ■ "Fabric, Craft Store Opens in North Bibb" in *Macon Telegraph* (July 17, 2010)
Pub: Macon Telegraph
Ed: Linda S. Morris. **Description:** Ohio-based Jo-Ann Fabrics and Craft Stores opened a new shop in Macon, Georgia. The store will feature items for crafters, hobbyists, needle artists and seamstresses.

6104 ■ "Greg Lueck: Glass Blowing" in *Inc.* (Volume 32, December 2010, No. 10, pp. 36)
Pub: Inc. Magazine
Ed: April Joyner. **Description:** Profile of Greg Lueck, partner and COO of Centerstance, a tech consulting firm in Portland, Oregon. Lueck opened Firehouse Glass, a studio that provides workspace and equipment for glass blowers. He says glass blowing serves as a welcome counterbalance to the cerebral work he does at the office.

6105 ■ "Hobbies Hold Fast" in *Playthings* (Vol. 106, November 1, 2008, No. 1, pp. 6)
Pub: Reed Business Information
Ed: Karyn M. Peterson. **Description:** Profile of the 24th Annual iHobby Expo is presented. The event is a combined trade and consumer show offering a look at the latest releases in die-cast collectibles, model railroads and aircraft, slot cars, remote control vehicles, rocketry, robotics, military toys, wood/plastic model kits, games, etc.

6106 ■ *Hobby Merchandiser Annual Trade Directory*
Pub: Hobby Publications Inc.
Contact: Dennis McFarlane, Editor-in-Chief
E-mail: editor@hobbymerchandiser.com
Released: Annual, December. **Covers:** Manufacturers, wholesalers, industry suppliers, and publishers of books and periodicals in the hobby trade industry. **Entries Include:** For manufacturers—Company name, address, phone, name and title of contact. For wholesalers—Company name, address, phone, specialty, geographical area covered. For publishers—Company name, address, phone, name and title of contact; types of books, periodicals, or other media published or produced. For industry suppliers—Company name, address, phone, name and title of contact, product. **Arrangement:** Manufacturers, publishers, and suppliers are alphabetical; wholesalers are geographical. **Indexes:** Product.

6107 ■ *How to Market and Sell Your Art, Music, Photographs, and Handmade Crafts Online*
Pub: Atlantic Publishing Group, Inc.
Ed: Lee Rowley. **Released:** May 2008. **Price:** $24. 95. **Description:** The book provides all the basics for starting and running an online store selling arts, crafts, photography or music. There are more than 300 Websites listed to help anyone market and promote their arts and/or crafts online.

6108 ■ "Jo-Ann Fabric and Craft Stores Joins ArtFire.com to Offer Free Online Craft Marketplace" in *Internet Wire* (January 26, 2010)
Pub: Comtex News Network, Inc.
Description: Jo-Ann Fabric and Craft Stores has entered into a partnership with ArtFire.com which will provide sewers and crafters all the tools they need in order to make and sell their products from an online venue.

6109 ■ "Jo-Ann Launches Quilt Your Colors Contest to Celebrate National Sewing Month" in *Internet Wire* (September 10, 2010)
Pub: Comtex
Description: Jo-Ann Fabric and Craft Stores featured a contest to create a quilt in order to promote National Sewing Month.

6110 ■ *Martha, Inc.*
Pub: John Wiley and Sons, Inc.
Ed: Christopher Byron. **Released:** 2002. **Price:** $28. 00. **Description:** Profile of Martha Stewart's rise from working class to a billionaire businesswoman is presented. The book covers Stewart's power struggles and personal conflicts as well as her triumphs.

6111 ■ "Paper Cache" in *Playthings* (Vol. 106, October 1, 2008, No. 9, pp. 9)
Pub: Reed Business Information
Ed: Karyn M. Peterson. **Description:** New toys in the paper play category are capturing children's imaginations with pirate ships and fairy houses and more they can build or design themselves. Hands-on paper and cardboard-based kits offer options for all ages.

6112 ■ "Remodeled Stores Help Fabric Retailer Stitch Up Profit Growth" in *Investor's Business Daily* (January 7, 2010, pp. A06)
Pub: Investor's Business Daily
Ed: Marilyn Much. **Description:** Overview of the successful plan implemented by Darrell Webb for Jo-Ann Fabric and Craft stores to stimulate growth and generate revenue; changes include better inventory controls and remodeling; statistical data included.

6113 ■ "Retail Briefs - Dollar Store Opens in Long Leaf Mall" in *Star-News* (November 5, 2010)
Pub: Star-News Media
Ed: Judy Royal. **Description:** Dollar Delight$ opened a new shop in Long Leaf Mall in Wilmington, North Carolina. The store will carry gift bags, balloons, party supplies, greeting cards, school supplies, health and beauty products, hardware, baby items, toys, Christmas goods, crafts, housewares and jewelry in its inventory.

6114 ■ "Sewing Is a Life Skill; Teaching To Sew Is An Art" in *Virginia-Pilot* (August 31, 2010)
Pub: Virginian-Pilot
Ed: Jamesetta Walker. **Description:** In conjunction with National Sewing Month, the American Sewing Guild is sponsoring a two-day workshop featuring Stephanie Kimura.

6115 ■ "Sewing Shoppe Is All His" in *News & Observer* (October 8, 2010)
Pub: News & Observer
Ed: Sue Stock. **Description:** Profile of My Sewing Shoppe, authorized sales and service dealers for Pfaff and Singer sewing machines, and also sells items for sewing, embroider and quilting. The store is located in Raleigh, North Carolina area.

6116 ■ "Up, Up and Away" in *Small Business Opportunities* (November 2007)
Pub: Harris Publications Inc.
Ed: Stan Roberts. **Description:** Profile of Miniature Aircraft USA, a mail order business providing kits to build flying machines priced from $500 to $2,500.

STATISTICAL SOURCES

6117 ■ *RMA Annual Statement Studies*
Pub: Robert Morris Associates (RMA)
Released: Annual. **Price:** $175.00 2006-07 edition, $105.00. **Description:** Contains composite balance sheets and income statements for more than 360 industries, including the accounting, auditing, and bookkeeping industries. Also contains five years of comparative historical data for discerning trends. Includes 16 commonly used ratios, computed for most of the size groupings for nearly every industry.

6118 ■ *Size of Craft/Hobby Industry*
Pub: MarketResearch.com
Released: 1992. **Price:** $500.00. **Description:** Report from the Hobby Industries of America (HIA) evaluating 1990 and 1991 sales volumes by six main craft categories, including art materials, florals and naturals, frames, hard crafts, needlecrafts, and sewing and notions. Also contains copies of all research materials, including questionnaires and regional data for manufacturers, retailers, and consumers.

TRADE PERIODICALS

6119 ■ *American Craft*
Pub: American Craft Council
Contact: John Gourlay, Publisher
E-mail: jgourlay@craftcouncil.org
Released: Bimonthly. **Price:** $40; $55 other countries. **Description:** Journal covering contemporary crafts.

6120 ■ *Annie's Plastic Canvas Magazine*
Pub: The Needlecraft Shop L.L.C.
Released: Bimonthly. **Price:** $20 plus postage and processing; $25 Canada plus postage and processing. **Description:** Craft magazine offering patterns (plastic canvas).

6121 ■ *Antique Bottle and Glass Collector*
Pub: Antique Bottle and Glass Collector
Released: Monthly. **Price:** $32 2nd class; $47 Canada; $57 other countries by airmail; $95 other countries by airmail; $54 1st class. **Description:** Trade magazine for antique bottle and glass collectors.

6122 ■ *Bead and Button*
Pub: Kalmbach Publishing Co.
Ed: Ann Dee Allen, Editor. **Released:** Bimonthly. **Price:** $28.95; $42.95 other countries; $55.95 12 issues; $83.95 other countries 12 issues; $79.95 18 issues; $121.95 other countries 18 issues. **Description:** Magazine highlighting beading techniques and uses of buttons in jewelry and designing. Includes historical articles.

6123 ■ *Ceramics Monthly*
Pub: The American Ceramic Society
Contact: Cynthia Griffith, Production Ed.
Released: 10/yr. **Price:** $34.95; $40 Canada; $60 other countries; $59.95 two years; $75 Canada two years; $99 other countries two years. **Description:** Consumer magazine containing ceramic art and craft. Features articles on ceramic artists, exhibitions, production processes, critical commentary, book and video reviews, clay and glaze recipes, and kiln designs.

6124 ■ *Country Home*
Pub: Meredith Corp.
Released: Monthly, 10/yr. **Price:** $4.95 newstand; $21.97 two years. **Description:** Magazine furnishing information on American interior design, architecture, antiques and collectibles, gardening, art, and culinary endeavor.

6125 ■ *Craft Train News*
Pub: Wm. K. Walthers Inc.
Description: Contains information such as prices and detailed descriptions on new model railroad products.

6126 ■ *Crafts 'n things*
Pub: Amos Press Inc.
Ed: Abby Foster, Editor, afoster@amoscraft.com. **Released:** 6/yr. **Price:** $21.97 print and online; $19.97 online only; $29.47 Canada print and online; $36.97 other countries print and online. **Description:** Craft magazine.

6127 ■ *Discover Mid-America*
Pub: Discovery Publications Inc.
Contact: Bruce Rodgers, Exec. Ed./Publisher
E-mail: publisher@discoverypub.com
Released: Monthly. **Description:** Trade magazine covering antiques, arts, crafts, regional history, and events.

6128 ■ *Doll Costuming*
Pub: Jones Publishing Inc.
Released: 6/yr. **Price:** $20; $74.95 two years; $89.95 3 years. **Description:** Consumer magazine covering dolls and doll costuming.

6129 ■ *Doll Crafter*
Pub: Jones Publishing Inc.
Contact: Joe Jones, Owner
Released: Monthly. **Price:** $39.95; $74.95 two years; $89.95 3 years. **Description:** Dollcrafting magazine focusing on porcelain dollmaking with emphasis on reproductions.

6130 ■ *Dragon Magazine*
Pub: Wizards of the Coast Inc.
Released: Monthly. **Description:** Magazine featuring Dungeons & Dragons and other role-playing games.

6131 ■ *Fine Woodworking*
Pub: Taunton Press Inc.
Contact: Jon Miller, Publisher
Ed: Timothy D. Schreiner, Editor. **Released:** 7/yr. **Price:** $34.95 U.S. and Canada; $59.95 U.S. and Canada two years; $83.95 U.S. and Canada three years. **Description:** Technical magazine for the amateur and professional woodworker.

6132 ■ *Fired Arts & Crafts*
Pub: Jones Publishing Inc.
Contact: Bill Bright, Publisher
Released: Monthly. **Price:** $39.95; $74.95 two years; $89.95 3 years. **Description:** Magazine for the hobby ceramic industry; includes color photos and step-by-step instructions to complete projects.

6133 ■ *Garden Railways*
Pub: Kalmbach Publishing Co.
Contact: Terry Thompson, Publisher
Released: Bimonthly. **Price:** $29.95; $39.95 other countries; $56 12 issues; $76 other countries 12 issues; $80 18 issues; $110 other countries 18 issues. **Description:** Magazine highlighting outdoor railroading, including layouts, projects with instructions, product reviews, and planting tips.

6134 ■ *Glass Craftsman*
Pub: Arts & Media Inc.
Contact: Joe Porcelli, Publisher
Released: Bimonthly. **Price:** $19.95; $39.95 two years; $15.95 other countries digital only; $29.90 other countries digital, 2 years; $27.95 other countries; $54.95 other countries 2 years. **Description:** Consumer magazine covering the craft of art glass for collectors, hobbyists, and professionals.

6135 ■ *Glass Patterns Quarterly*
Pub: Glass Patterns Quarterly Inc.
Contact: Maureen James, Editor-in-Chief
Released: Quarterly. **Price:** $24; $29 other countries; $59 other countries via air; $43 two years; $53 other countries 2 years; $118 other countries 2 years, via air; $61 3 years; $76 other countries 3 years; $170 other countries 3 years, via air. **Description:** Consumer magazine covering instructional stained glass making for a general and professional audience. Leading international glass magazine featuring patterns and instruction on glass etching, fusing, leading, copper foil, beveling, tiffany-style lamp construction, slumping, painting, beadmaking. Over 100 how-to photographs, steb-by-step instructions.

6136 ■ *Hobby Merchandiser*
Pub: Hobby Publications Inc.
Contact: Robert Gherman, Publisher
E-mail: publisher@hobbymerchandiser.com
Ed: Dennis McFarlane, Editor, dmcfarlane@hobbypub.com. **Released:** 15/yr. **Price:** $20; $35 other countries surface mail; $120 other countries airmail; $20 renewal. **Description:** Trade magazine for the model and hobby industry.

6137 ■ *Model Airplane News*
Pub: Air Age Publishing Inc.
Contact: Debra Cleghorn, Exec. Ed.
E-mail: debrac@airage.com
Released: Monthly. **Price:** $24.95; $44 two years; $30.95 Canada; $39.95 other countries; $50 Canada 2 years; $59 other countries 2 years. **Description:** Magazine on radio-controlled model airplanes and helicopters.

6138 ■ *Model Railroader*
Pub: Kalmbach Publishing Co.
Contact: Terry Thompson, Publisher
E-mail: tthompson@modelrailroader.com
Released: Monthly. **Price:** $42.95; $77.95 two years; $107.95 3 years; $52.95 Canada; $97.95 Canada 2 years; $137.95 Canada 3 years. **Description:** Model railroad hobby magazine.

6139 ■ *Model Retailer*
Pub: Kalmbach Publishing Co.
Contact: Rick Albers, Gp. Advertising Sales
E-mail: ralbers@modelretailer.com
Ed: Hal Miller, Editor, hmiller@modelretailer.com. **Released:** Monthly. **Price:** $85; $85 other countries surface mail. **Description:** Trade magazine for the hobby industry.

6140 ■ *Needlework Retailer*
Pub: Yarn Tree Design Inc.
Released: Bimonthly. **Description:** Trade magazine for the needlework industry, especially small, independent needlework retailers.

6141 ■ *Out Your Backdoor*
Pub: Out Your Backdoor
Contact: Jeff Potter, Editor & Publisher
E-mail: jeff@outyourbackdoor.com
Released: Monthly. **Description:** Magazine focusing on bicycling, adventure, culture, the outdoors, hobbies, and sports.

6142 ■ *Railroad Model Craftsman*
Pub: Carstens Publications Inc.
Contact: Christopher D'Amato, Assoc. Ed.
E-mail: chrisd@rrmodelcraftsman.com
Released: Monthly. **Price:** $37.95; $50 out of country including Canada; $69.95 two years; $94 two years foreign. **Description:** Model railroading (building, operating, and collecting) magazine.

6143 ■ *Scrap & Stamp Arts*
Pub: Scott Publications
Released: 8/yr. **Price:** $29.90; $55 two years; $45.90 out of country; $87 two years and other countries. **Description:** Consumer magazine covering rubber stamping for hobbyists.

6144 ■ *Soft Dolls & Animals*
Pub: Scott Publications
Contact: Cathy Schnoes
Released: Bimonthly. **Price:** $29.95; $53.90 two years; $41.95 out of country non-US; $77.90 two years non-US. **Description:** Magazine covering fabric dolls, teddy bears, and other fabric figures for hobbyists and crafters.

6145 ■ *Uncoverings*
Pub: American Quilt Study Group
Contact: Judy Brott Buss PhD, Exec. Dir.
Ed: Lauren Horton, Editor. **Released:** Annual. **Price:** $20 single issue. **Description:** Scholarly journal covering quilts, textiles and quilt makers.

VIDEOCASSETTES/ AUDIOCASSETTES

6146 ■ *Angel Crafts Video Vol. 1*
Tapeworm Video Distributors
25876 The Old Road 141
Stevenson Ranch, CA 91381
Ph:(661)257-4904
Fax:(661)257-4820
Co. E-mail: sales@tapeworm.com
URL: http://www.tapeworm.com
Released: 1996. **Price:** $19.95. **Description:** Kathy Peterson provides instruction for creating six heirloom angels. **Availability:** VHS.

6147 ■ *Christmas Entertaining*
Cambridge Educational
c/o Films Media Group
132 West 31st Street, 17th Floor
Ste. 124
New York, NY 10001
Free: 800-257-5126
Fax:(609)671-0266
Co. E-mail: custserve@films.com
URL: http://www.cambridgeol.com
Description: Instructs on how to create foods, crafts, and gifts for the holidays. **Availability:** VHS.

6148 ■ *Crafts in Less Than 10 Minutes Video Vol. 1*
Tapeworm Video Distributors
25876 The Old Road 141
Stevenson Ranch, CA 91381
Ph:(661)257-4904
Fax:(661)257-4820
Co. E-mail: sales@tapeworm.com
URL: http://www.tapeworm.com
Released: 1996. **Price:** $19.95. **Description:** Kathy Peterson provides instruction for creating nine fast and easy craft projects. **Availability:** VHS.

6149 ■ *Holiday Centerpieces*
Videomaker
PO Box 4591
Chico, CA 95927
Ph:(530)891-8410
Free: 800-284-3226
Fax:(530)891-8443
Co. E-mail: customerservice@videomaker.com
URL: http://www.videomaker.com
Price: $14.95. **Description:** Provides instruction for creating flower arrangements for Fall and Christmas. **Availability:** VHS.

6150 ■ *Kids Make Puppets: Easy Scarf Marionettes*
Tapeworm Video Distributors
25876 The Old Road 141
Stevenson Ranch, CA 91381
Ph:(661)257-4904
Fax:(661)257-4820
Co. E-mail: sales@tapeworm.com
URL: http://www.tapeworm.com
Price: $14.95. **Description:** Provides instruction for making marionettes from materials found at home. **Availability:** VHS.

6151 ■ *Pets Crafts Video Vol. 1*
Tapeworm Video Distributors
25876 The Old Road 141
Stevenson Ranch, CA 91381
Ph:(661)257-4904
Fax:(661)257-4820
Co. E-mail: sales@tapeworm.com
URL: http://www.tapeworm.com
Released: 1996. **Price:** $19.95. **Description:** Kathy Peterson provides instruction for creating seven pet projects. **Availability:** VHS.

6152 ■ *Santa Crafts Video Vol. 1*
Tapeworm Video Distributors
25876 The Old Road 141
Stevenson Ranch, CA 91381
Ph:(661)257-4904
Fax:(661)257-4820
Co. E-mail: sales@tapeworm.com
URL: http://www.tapeworm.com
Released: 1996. **Price:** $19.95. **Description:** Kathy Peterson provides instruction for creating five heirloom Santas. **Availability:** VHS.

6153 ■ *The Secrets of Magic and Illusion*
MPI Home Video
16101 S. 108th Ave.
Orland Park, IL 60467
Ph:(708)460-0555
Free: 800-323-0442
Fax:(708)873-3177
URL: http://www.mpihomevideo.com
Released: 1997. **Price:** $19.98. **Description:** Reveals the secrets of famous illusions including the Sword Suspension, Cards and Coins, and the Chinese Linking Rings. **Availability:** VHS.

6154 ■ *Silk Arrangements*
Videomaker
PO Box 4591
Chico, CA 95927
Ph:(530)891-8410
Free: 800-284-3226
Fax:(530)891-8443
Co. E-mail: customerservice@videomaker.com
URL: http://www.videomaker.com
Price: $14.95. **Description:** Provides instruction for creating four attractive flower arrangements for all seasons. **Availability:** VHS.

6155 ■ *Table Centerpieces*
Videomaker
PO Box 4591
Chico, CA 95927
Ph:(530)891-8410
Free: 800-284-3226
Fax:(530)891-8443
Co. E-mail: customerservice@videomaker.com
URL: http://www.videomaker.com
Price: $14.95. **Description:** Provides instruction for creating two fresh Spring flower arrangements and how to make a florists bow. **Availability:** VHS.

6156 ■ *Victorian Crafts Video Vol. 1*
Tapeworm Video Distributors
25876 The Old Road 141
Stevenson Ranch, CA 91381
Ph:(661)257-4904
Fax:(661)257-4820
Co. E-mail: sales@tapeworm.com
URL: http://www.tapeworm.com
Released: 1996. **Price:** $19.95. **Description:** Kathy Peterson provides instruction for creating seven Victorian heirlooms. **Availability:** VHS.

TRADE SHOWS AND CONVENTIONS

6157 ■ Annual Dickens Christmas Show and Festivals Week
Leisure Time Unlimited, Inc.
708 Main St.
PO Box 332
Myrtle Beach, SC 29577
Ph:(843)448-9483
Free: 800-261-5591
Fax:(843)626-1513
Co. E-mail: dickensshow@sc.rr.com
Released: Annual. **Audience:** General public. **Principal Exhibits:** Crafts, art, paintings, gifts, and Christmas related items. **Dates and Locations:** 2011 Nov 10-13, Myrtle Beach, SC.

6158 ■ Atlantic Craft Trade Show
Nova Scotia Department of Economic Development
PO Box 2311
1660 Hollis St., Suite 600
Halifax, NS, Canada B3J 3C8
Ph:(902)424-0377
Fax:(902)424-7008
Released: Annual. **Audience:** Craft, giftware, and apparel trade professionals. **Principal Exhibits:** Crafts and giftware, including porcelain, silver and pewter ware, jewelry, hand knits, hooked rugs, hand blown glass, toys; apparel, wood, and food products. **Dates and Locations:** 2011 Feb 05-07, Halifax, NS; 2012 Feb 04-06, Halifax, NS; 2013 Mar 06 - Feb 05, Halifax, NS.

6159 ■ CHA Winter Convention and Trade Show
Hobby Industry Association HIA
319 E. 54th St.
Elmwood Park, NJ 07407
Ph:(201)835-1200
Fax:(201)797-0657
Co. E-mail: info@craftandhobby.org
URL: http://www.hobby.org
Released: Annual. **Audience:** Owners, corporate officers and buyers from craft, hobby, DIY stores, general merchandise stores, wholesalers, and professional crafters. **Principal Exhibits:** Crafts, ceramics, floral accessories, dollhouse miniatures, aromatics, art materials and frames, jewelry findings, fabrics, needlework and quilting supplies, home decor, rubber stamps, stencils and scrapbooking supplies.

6160 ■ Christmas Gift and Hobby Show
HSI Show Productions
PO Box 502797
Indianapolis, IN 46250
Ph:(317)576-9933
Free: 800-215-1700
Fax:(317)576-9955
Co. E-mail: info@hsishows.com
URL: http://www.hsishows.com
Released: Annual. **Audience:** General public. **Principal Exhibits:** Art, crafts, and giftware.

6161 ■ Holiday Fair
Textile Hall Corp.
PO Box 5823
Greenville, SC 29606
Ph:(864)331-2277
Fax:(864)331-2282
Co. E-mail: atmei@textilehall.com
Released: Annual. **Audience:** General public. **Principal Exhibits:** Arts and crafts.

6162 ■ Home Entertainment Show
Trigger Agency
3539 Clipper Mill Rd.
Baltimore, MD 21211
Free: 800-830-3976
Fax:(410)878-9911
Co. E-mail: info@triggeragency.com
URL: http://www.triggeragency.com/
Released: Biennial. **Audience:** Consumers, trade and press. **Principal Exhibits:** Home theater and high-fidelity audio equipment, supplies, and services.

6163 ■ International Model and Hobby Expo
Radio Control Hobby Trade Association
PO Box 315
Butler, NJ 07405-0315
Ph:(973)283-9088
Fax:(973)838-7124
Co. E-mail: pkoziol@rchta.org
URL: http://www.rchta.org
Released: Annual. **Audience:** Hobby retailers, distributors. **Principal Exhibits:** Model kits and hobby equipment, supplies, and services, radio control products and accessories, model railroad products and accessories, aerodynamics, games, rockets, die cast, adhesives, plastic models, minatures, tools, slot cars, astronomy, paints, publications, apparel, collectables, kites, science/educational, videos, and speciality items.

6164 ■ Memories Expo
Offinger Management Co.
1100-H Brandywine Blvd.
PO Box 3388
Zanesville, OH 43702-3388
Ph:(740)452-4541
Free: 888-878-6334
Fax:(740)452-2552
Co. E-mail: OMC.Info@Offinger.com
URL: http://www.offinger.com
Released: 5/year. **Audience:** Trade and public. **Principal Exhibits:** Scrapbook supplies. **Dates and Locations:** 2011 Mar 25-26, Columbus, OH.

6165 ■ Society of Craft Designers Educational Seminar
Offinger Management Co.
1100-H Brandywine Blvd.
PO Box 3388
Zanesville, OH 43702-3388
Ph:(740)452-4541
Free: 888-878-6334
Fax:(740)452-2552
Co. E-mail: OMC.Info@Offinger.com
URL: http://www.offinger.com
Released: Annual. **Audience:** Designers, manufacturers, editors, and publishers. **Principal Exhibits:** Craft designer showcases and education.

FRANCHISES AND BUSINESS OPPORTUNITIES

6166 ■ Hobbytown USA
Hobby Town Unlimited Inc.
1233 Libra Dr.
Lincoln, NE 68512
Ph:(402)434-5064
Free: 800-858-7370
Fax:(402)434-5055
Co. E-mail: nichole@hobbytown.com
URL: http://www.hobbytown.com
No. of Franchise Units: 175. **Founded:** 1980. **Franchised:** 1986. **Description:** full-line hobby stores featuring model railroading, models, radio controlled vehicles, games, collectible cards, die cast, toys, gifts, accessories and more. provides store owners with a comprehensive package of systems and services to be competitive in the hobby and entertainment industries. **Equity Capital Needed:** $75,000-$200,000 cash investment; total investment $250,000-$350,000. **Franchise Fee:** $19,500 ($15,000 veterans). **Financial Assistance:** Third party. **Training:** 3 week comprehensive training program, including home office and onsite field training.

6167 ■ Pinch A Penny, Inc.
14480 62nd St. N
Clearwater, FL 33760
Ph:(727)531-8913
Fax:(727)536-8066
URL: http://www.pinchapenny.com/franchise
No. of Franchise Units: 200+. **No. of Company-Owned Units:** 2. **Founded:** 1974. **Franchised:** 1976. **Description:** Swimming pool supplies & spa supplies. **Equity Capital Needed:** $180,000-$350,000. **Franchise Fee:** $30,000. **Financial Assistance:** No. **Training:** Offers 4 weeks training in Clearwater, FL.

6168 ■ Remote Control Hobbies
5435 Boatworks Dr., Ste. 1
Littleton, CO 80126
Ph:(303)804-0470
Fax:(303)531-5273

No. of Franchise Units: 12. **Founded:** 2003. **Franchised:** 2004. **Description:** Remote control hobby vehicles, parts & accessories. **Equity Capital Needed:** $111,900-$315,900. **Franchise Fee:** $18,000-$22,000. **Royalty Fee:** 2.5%. **Financial Assistance:** Limited in-house assistance. **Training:** Provides 7 weeks training at headquarters, 6 weeks onsite with ongoing support.

LIBRARIES

6169 ■ American Craft Council Library
72 Spring St., 6th Fl.
New York, NY 10012-4019
Ph:(212)274-0630
Free: 800-836-3470
Fax:(212)274-0650
Co. E-mail: library@craftcouncil.org
URL: http://www.craftcouncil.org/html/resources/library.shtml
Contact: David Shuford, Libn.

Scope: 20th-century contemporary fine crafts - fiber, clay, metal, wood, glass, enamel, plastics, mixed media; decorative arts; design. **Services:** Library open to the public by appointment (Mondays, Wednesdays, and Fridays). **Holdings:** 6400 books; 700 bound periodical volumes; 7000 exhibition catalogs; 200 videocassettes. **Subscriptions:** 100 journals and other serials.

6170 ■ American Museum of Magic–Lund Memorial Library
107 E. Michigan Ave.
PO Box 5
Marshall, MI 49068
Ph:(269)781-7570
Co. E-mail: info@americanmuseumofmagic.org
URL: http://www.americanmuseumofmagic.org

Scope: Conjuring, confidence games, superstition. **Services:** Library open to the public with restrictions. **Holdings:** 15,000 books; 30,000 magazines; 150,000 letters; 3000 posters; newspaper clippings; programs; photographs; films; manuscripts. **Subscriptions:** 25 journals and other serials.

6171 ■ American Society of Artists Resource Center
Box 1326
Palatine, IL 60078
Ph:(312)751-2500
Co. E-mail: asoa@webtv.net
URL: http://www.americansocietyofartists.org
Contact: Donald Metcoff, Libn.

Scope: Art, crafts, supplies. **Services:** Lectures; demonstrations; seminars; workshops. **Holdings:** 50 volumes; 43 VF drawers. **Subscriptions:** 11 journals and other serials.

6172 ■ California College of the Arts Libraries–Meyer Library
5212 Broadway
Oakland, CA 94618
Ph:(510)594-3658
Co. E-mail: meyerlib@cca.edu
URL: http://library.cca.edu
Contact: Janice Woo, Dir. of Libs.

Scope: Art, architecture, design, humanities. **Services:** Library limited to the CCA community (specialized research by appointment). **Holdings:** 62,000 volumes; 150,000 slides and pictures; 100 lin.ft. of archival material. **Subscriptions:** 275 journals and other serials.

6173 ■ Craft Council of Newfoundland and Labrador Library
Devon House Craft Ctr.
59 Duckworth St.
St. John's, NL, Canada A1C 1E6
Ph:(709)753-2749
Fax:(709)753-2766
Co. E-mail: info@craftcouncil.nl.ca
URL: http://www.craftcouncil.nl.ca

Scope: Craft promotion and development. **Services:** Library open to the public. **Holdings:** 400 books; 20 serials; 50 reports. **Subscriptions:** 10 journals and other serials.

6174 ■ Ferrum College–Blue Ridge Heritage Archive
20 Museum Dr.
PO Box 1000
Ferrum College
Ferrum, VA 24088-9001
Ph:(540)365-4412
Fax:(540)365-4419
Co. E-mail: bri@ferrum.edu
URL: http://www.blueridgeinstitute.org
Contact: Vaughan Webb, Asst.Dir.

Scope: Folk culture, legends, crafts, music, and customs of Virginia, especially the Blue Ridge Mountain area, 1780 to present. **Services:** Copying; archive open to the public by appointment. **Holdings:** Videotapes; audio tapes; CDs; DVDs; phonograph records; manuscripts; photographs; films; books; correspondence; transcripts.

6175 ■ Haystack Mountain School of Crafts Library
PO Box 518
Deer Isle, ME 04627-0518
Ph:(207)348-2306
Fax:(207)348-2307
Co. E-mail: haystack@haystack-mtn.org
URL: http://www.haystack-mtn.org/

Scope: Fine arts, ceramics, weaving, glassblowing, flat glass, jewelry, surface and textile design, wood, blacksmithing, printmaking, papermaking, weaving. **Services:** Library open to the public on a limited basis. **Holdings:** 1000 books. **Subscriptions:** 20 journals and other serials.

6176 ■ John Michael Kohler Arts Center Resource Center
608 New York Ave.
Box 489
Sheboygan, WI 53081
Ph:(920)458-6144, x-147
Fax:(920)458-4473
Co. E-mail: jmcfarlane@jmkac.org
URL: http://www.jmkac.org
Contact: Jamie McFarlane, Libn./Archv.

Scope: Art environments; self-taught vernacular art; contemporary art, contemporary crafts, non-traditional photography. **Services:** Onsite assistance available by appointment; reference and research services, including image reproduction services, available by phone or email. **Holdings:** 5000 monographs; 150 serials; 90,000 images of Arts Center programming including permanent collection objects and works in exhibitions. **Subscriptions:** 50 serials.

6177 ■ Manitoba Crafts Museum & Library–Gladys Chown Memorial Library
1B-183 Kennedy St.
Winnipeg, MB, Canada R3C 1S6
Ph:(204)487-6117
Fax:(204)487-6117
Co. E-mail: mcml1@mts.net
URL: http://www.mts.net/lAtmcml
Contact: Andrea Reichert, Cur.

Scope: Crafts - weaving, pottery, embroidery, knitting, crochet, quilting, paper, wood, Inuit and Aboriginal, polymer clay, lace; craft design; color theory; history of craft. **Services:** Library open to the public. **Holdings:** 3500 volumes; 2000 slides; 9000 artifacts. **Subscriptions:** 4 journals and other serials.

6178 ■ Museum of Contemporary Craft Library
724 NW Davis St.
Portland, OR 97209
Ph:(503)223-2654
Fax:(503)223-0190
Co. E-mail: info@museumofcontemporarycraft.org
URL: http://www.museumofcontemporarycraft.org/
Contact: Linda Brower, Treas.

Scope: Ceramics and pottery, weaving and textiles, Pacific Northwest craftsmen, contemporary designers, metalwork and jewelry, contemporary glass, sculpture, woodworking, architecture. **Services:** Library open during Museum hours. **Holdings:** 420 books; 74 bound and 125 unbound periodical volumes.

6179 ■ Oregon College of Art and Craft Library
8245 SW Barnes Rd.
Portland, OR 97225
Ph:(503)297-5544
Free: 800-390-0632
Fax:(503)297-9651
Co. E-mail: ljohnson@ocac.edu
URL: http://www.ocac.edu
Contact: Lori Johnson, Vis.Rsrcs.Libn.

Scope: Textiles, ceramics, woodworking, drawing and design, metals, book arts, photography, calligraphy, painting, sculpture, art history, art criticism. **Services:** Interlibrary loan; Library open to the public. **Holdings:** 9000 books; 27,000 slides. **Subscriptions:** 90 journals and other serials.

6180 ■ San Francisco Public Library–Bernard Osher Foundation–Art, Music & Recreation Center (100 L)
100 Larkin St.
San Francisco, CA 94102
Ph:(415)557-4525
Fax:(415)557-4524
Co. E-mail: info@sfpl.org
URL: http://www.sfpl.org/librarylocations/main/art/art.htm
Contact: Mark Hall, Fl.Mgr.

Scope: Arts - visual, graphic; sports and recreation; photography; architecture; arts and crafts; performing arts; music - orchestral, chamber, opera, popular, folk, jazz. **Services:** Center open to the public. **Holdings:** Books; serials; scores.

6181 ■ University of Hartford–William H. Mortensen Library–Anne Bunce Cheney Art Collection (200 B)
200 Bloomfield Ave.
West Hartford, CT 06117
Ph:(860)768-4397
Fax:(860)768-5298
Co. E-mail: bigazzi@hartford.edu
URL: http://library-new.hartford.edu
Contact: Anna B. Bigazzi, Art Ref.Libn.

Scope: Art history, architecture, art education, applied art, decorative arts, crafts, photography, typography. **Services:** Interlibrary loan; copying; Library open to the public. **Holdings:** 24,000 books; 3200 bound periodical volumes; 19,000 mounted reproductions; 2500 pamphlets; CD-ROMs; videos. **Subscriptions:** 70 journals and other serials.

RESEARCH CENTERS

6182 ■ Canadian Crafts Federation–Fédération canadienne des métiers d'art
PO Box 1231
Fredericton, NB, Canada E3B 5C8
Ph:(506)464-9560
Fax:(506)457-6010
Co. E-mail: info@canadiancraftsfederation.ca
URL: http://canadiancraftsfederation.typepad.com/canadian-crafts-federatn
Contact: Simon Wroot, Pres.
E-mail: info@canadiancraftsfederation.ca

Scope: Market development strategies for Canadian crafts in Canada and internationally.

6183 ■ Museum of International Folk Art–El Museo de Arte Popular Internacional
PO Box 2087
Santa Fe, NM 87504-2087
Ph:(505)476-1200

Fax:(505)476-1300
Co. E-mail: marsha.bol@state.nm.us
URL: http://www.internationalfolkart.org
Contact: Marsha C. Bol PhD, Dir.
E-mail: marsha.bol@state.nm.us

Scope: International folk arts and crafts, anthropology, and folklore. Research is conducted by staff and independent and associate researchers and relates to the Museum's ongoing exhibition and curatorial programs. **Publications:** Exhibition Catalogs; Reports Curriculum for K-12. **Educational Activities:** Docent-led tours (daily), for the public, artist demonstrations; Exhibitions (weekly), of traditional arts; Gallery talks (periodically); Lecture/film series, in relation to exhibits, family and school programs; Public school outreach programs; Staff development programs; Teacher Training Institute for Elementary Teachers; Workshops, demonstrations.

"Create-Your-Own..." Store

START-UP INFORMATION

6184 ■ *Setting Up Your Ceramic Studio: Ideas and Plans from Working Artists*
Pub: Lark Books
Ed: Virginia Scotchie. **Released:** March 2005. **Price:** $45.00. **Description:** Floor plans and advice for setting up a creative ceramics studio are provided, focusing on equipment, workflow, and safety issues.

TRADE PERIODICALS

6185 ■ *Small Business Opportunities*
Pub: Harris Publications Inc.
Contact: Melissa Zinker
E-mail: melissa@harris-pub.com
Ed: Susan Rakowski, Editor, sr@harris-pub.com. **Released:** Bimonthly, (plus 4 special editions). **Price:** $14.97 U.S. and Canada; $29.94 other countries. **Description:** How-to magazine for small business owners.

TRADE SHOWS AND CONVENTIONS

6186 ■ American Quilt Study Group Seminar
American Quilt Study Group
1610 L St.
Lincoln, NE 68508-2509
Ph:(402)477-1181
Fax:(402)477-1181
Co. E-mail: aqsg2@americanquiltstudygroup.org
URL: http://www.americanquiltstudygroup.org
Released: Annual. **Principal Exhibits:** Quilt-related articles.

6187 ■ Handmade - A Division of the San Francisco International Gift Fair
George Little Management, LLC (New York, New York)
1133 Westchester Ave., Ste. N136
White Plains, NY 10606
Ph:(914)421-3200
Free: 800-272-SHOW
Co. E-mail: cathy_steel@glmshows.com
URL: http://www.glmshows.com
Released: Semiannual. **Audience:** Specialty, department, stationery, juvenile, and jewelry stores, interior designers, gift shops, mail order catalogs, importers/distributors of home products. **Principal Exhibits:** Handmade merchandise, including functional and decorative home furnishings, fashion accessories, jewelry plus an array of other unique craft objects. All merchandise is selected by a panel of craft professionals for uniqueness, originality and marketability.

FRANCHISES AND BUSINESS OPPORTUNITIES

6188 ■ Color Me Mine Franchising, Inc.
Versent Inc.
3722 San Fernando Rd.
Glendale, CA 91204
Ph:(818)291-5900
Free: 888-265-6764
Fax:(818)240-9712
No. of Franchise Units: 120. **Founded:** 1992. **Franchised:** 1996. **Description:** Paint-your-own ceramics studio. **Franchise Fee:** $25,000. **Financial Assistance:** No. **Training:** Yes.

6189 ■ Dream Dinners Inc.
PO Box 889
Snohomish, WA 98291
Ph:(425)397-3511
Fax:(425)397-7211
No. of Franchise Units: 234. **No. of Company-Owned Units:** 2. **Founded:** 2002. **Franchised:** 2003. **Description:** Do-it-yourself home meal preparation. **Equity Capital Needed:** $245,000-$367,000. **Franchise Fee:** $35,000. **Royalty Fee:** 6%. **Financial Assistance:** No. **Training:** Provides 1 week at headquarters, 2 days at franchisees location with ongoing support.

6190 ■ GourMade Franchise
7060 Koll Center Pky., Ste. 320
Pleasanton, CA 94566
Ph:(925)846-4774
Fax:(925)484-3324
No. of Company-Owned Units: 1. **Founded:** 2004. **Franchised:** 2006. **Description:** Meal assembly and meals-to-go. **Equity Capital Needed:** $141,000-$256,000. **Franchise Fee:** $20,000. **Royalty Fee:** 5%. **Financial Assistance:** No.

6191 ■ Mr. Food No-Fuss Meals
NFM Franchise, LLC
1770 NW 64th St., Ste. 500
Ft. Lauderdale, FL 33309
Ph:(954)938-0400
Fax:(954)938-2005
No. of Franchise Units: 6. **No. of Company-Owned Units:** 1. **Founded:** 2004. **Franchised:** 2006. **Description:** Make-and-take meal assembly. **Equity Capital Needed:** $350,000 net worth, including $75,000 in liquid assets. **Franchise Fee:** $35,000. **Financial Assistance:** No. **Training:** Yes.

6192 ■ Super Suppers
6100 Camp Bowie Blvd.
Fort Worth, TX 76132
Ph:(817)732-6100
Fax:(817)732-6106
No. of Franchise Units: 206. **No. of Company-Owned Units:** 1. **Founded:** 1986. **Franchised:** 2004. **Description:** Do-it-yourself home meal preparation. **Equity Capital Needed:** $175,400-$263,200. **Franchise Fee:** $35,000. **Royalty Fee:** 5%. **Financial Assistance:** No. **Training:** Offers 1 week at headquarters, 3 days at franchisees location, regional seminars and ongoing support.

6193 ■ Wacky Bear Factory Express
5953 W Park Ave., Ste. L13
Houma, LA 70360
Ph:(985)872-1212
Fax:(985)872-1357
No. of Company-Owned Units: 3. **Founded:** 2000. **Franchised:** 2004. **Description:** Custom stuffed toy animals & related accessories. **Equity Capital Needed:** $150,500-$187,500. **Franchise Fee:** $30,000. **Royalty Fee:** 4%. **Financial Assistance:** No. **Training:** Training includes 2 weeks at headquarters and ongoing support.

DIRECTORIES OF EDUCATIONAL PROGRAMS

6194 ■ *International Association of Credit Card Investigators—Membership Directory*
Pub: International Association of Financial Crimes Investigators
Released: Annual. **Covers:** Approximately 3,500 firms and individuals involved in investigating fraudulent credit card use who are members of the International Association of Credit Card Investigators. **Entries Include:** Contact information. **Arrangement:** Alphabetical by name. **Indexes:** Geographical; alphabetical by firm name.

REFERENCE WORKS

6195 ■ *All About Credit*
Pub: Kaplan Publishing
Ed: Deborah McNaughton **Released:** April 1999. **Price:** $15.95. **Description:** Debt solution to specific credit problems for individuals denied credit, trying to mortgage a home, problems with creditors, and bankruptcy.

6196 ■ "At Wine Kiosk, Show ID, Face Camera, Swipe Card and Blow" in *Pittsburgh Post-Gazette* (November 28, 2010)
Pub: Pittsburgh-Post Gazette
Ed: Dennis B. Roddy. **Description:** New technology installed on wine kiosks enables sellers to abide by the law. This technology tests blood alcohol levels and warns people if they have recently used a mouthwash before testing.

6197 ■ *BIN Number Directory of All Visa/ Mastercard Issuing Banks*
Pub: Fraud & Theft Information Bureau
Contact: Larry Schwartz
Ed: Pearl Sax, Editor. **Released:** Annual, January. **Price:** $1,175, individuals postpaid print edition; $5,075, individuals on CD-ROM, postpaid. **Covers:** About 30,000 banks worldwide issuing Visa and Mastercard credit cards. **Entries Include:** Name of issuing bank, bank identification number, address, phone. BIN numbers, the digits on credit cards that identify a credit card holder's issuing bank are also called prefix numbers and ISO numbers. Directory is used by merchants to prevent fraud by verifying that customer is actually the cardholder. **Arrangement:** Numerical.

6198 ■ *Chain of Blame: How Wall Street Caused the Mortgage and Credit Crisis*
Pub: John Wiley & Sons, Inc.
Ed: Paul Muolo, Mathew Padilla. **Released:** 2009. **Price:** $27.95. **Description:** The book describes how risky loans given irresponsibly put big investment banks at the center of the subprime crisis.

6199 ■ "Collection Industry Fights Stigma, Lagging Payments" in *Crain's Cleveland Business* (Vol. 30, June 8, 2009, No. 22, pp. 15)
Pub: Crain Communications, Inc.
Ed: Joel Hammond. **Description:** John Murray, co-owner and president of JP Recovery Services Inc. in Rocky River, Ohio discusses the burden of the collection industry during a financial crisis like a recession. Statistical data included.

6200 ■ "Cost of Business Banking May Soon Go Up" in *Baltimore Business Journal* (Vol. 28, October 29, 2010, No. 25, pp. 1)
Pub: Baltimore Business Journal
Ed: Gary Haber. **Description:** Experts in the financial industry expect banks to charge credit card transactions, especially to small business owners and consumers to recover about $11 million in lost revenue annually. Banks are expected to charge old fees and new ones, including $5 to $10 a month for a checking account.

6201 ■ "Credit Card Crackdown" in *Business Journal-Portland* (Vol. 24, November 23, 2007, No. 38, pp. 1)
Pub: American City Business Journals, Inc.
Ed: Andy Giegerich. **Description:** Oregon's U.S. Senator Ron Wyden is sponsoring Credit Card Safety Act of 2007, a bill that requires credit card companies to reduce the jargon of credit card agreements and require the Federal Reserve Board to launch a public education campaign among credit card users. The legislation will also impose a rating system for credit card contracts with five being the safest for consumers to use.

6202 ■ "Curbing the Debt Collector" in *Business Journal-Portland* (Vol. 24, October 5, 2007, No. 32, pp. 1)
Pub: American City Business Journals, Inc.
Ed: Andy Giegerich. **Description:** Republican representative Sal Esquivel, who had a bad personal experience with a Houston collector, is developing legislation that would give the state attorney general's office enforcement powers over debt collecting agencies. The existing Oregon legislation concerning the debt collection industry is also discussed.

6203 ■ "Economic Trends for Small Business" in *Small Business Economic Trends* (April 2008, pp. 1)
Pub: National Federation of Independent Business
Ed: William C. Dunkelberg, Holly Wade. **Description:** Summary of economic trends for small businesses in the U.S. is presented. Economic indicators such as capital spending, inventories and sales, inflation, and profits are given. Analysis of credit markets is also provided.

6204 ■ "End of the Beginning" in *Canadian Business* (Vol. 81, November 10, 2008, No. 19, pp. 17)
Pub: Rogers Media Ltd.
Ed: David Wolf. **Description:** The freeze in the money markets and historic decline in equity markets around the world finally forced governments into aggressive coordinated action. The asset price inflation brought on by cheap credit will now work in reverse and the tightening of credit will be difficult economically. Canada is exposed to the fallout everywhere, given that the U.S, the U.K. and Japan buy 30 percent of Canada's output.

6205 ■ "Fees Fueling Frustration for Region's Gas Retailers" in *Business First Buffalo* (December 7, 2007, pp. 1)
Pub: American City Business Journals, Inc.
Ed: David Bertola. **Description:** Credit card fees are a major cause of concern to gas retailers along with higher gasoline prices. Statistical details included.

6206 ■ *The Girl's Guide to Building a Million-Dollar Business*
Pub: AMACOM
Ed: Susan Wilson Solovic. **Released:** 2008. **Price:** $21.95. **Description:** Success plan for women business owners; the book includes tips for determination, managing changing relationships, keeping employees and customers happy, getting and maintaining credit, overcoming gender bias, and creating a good business plan and solid brand.

6207 ■ "A New FICO Scoring Model: Get Ready For Changes That Could Affect Your Score" in *Black Enterprise* (Vol. 38, March 2008, No. 8)
Pub: Earl G. Graves Publishing Co. Inc.
Ed: Sheiresa McRae. **Description:** Fair Isaac Corporation, creator of the FICO credit score has developed a new scoring model that provides a more accurate way for lenders to determine a borrower's creditworthiness.

6208 ■ "New Money" in *Entrepreneur* (Vol. 36, February 2008, No. 2, pp. 62)
Pub: Entrepreneur Media Inc.
Ed: C.J. Prince. **Description:** Tips on how to handle business finance, with regard to the tightened credit standards imposed by leading institutions, are provided. These include: selling receivables, margining blue chips, and selling purchase orders.

6209 ■ "New Rule Rankles In Jersey" in *Philadelphia Business Journal* (Vol. 30, September 16, 2011, No. 31, pp. 1)
Pub: American City Business Journals Inc.
Ed: Jeff Blumenthal. **Description:** A new rule in New Jersey which taxes out-of-state companies that conduct business in the state earned the ire of several banks, mortgage lenders and credit card companies and prompted opponents to threaten to file lawsuits. The new rule is an amendment to New Jersey Division of Taxation's corporate business tax regulation and is retroactive to 2002. Details are given.

6210 ■ "Prepaid Cards and State Unclaimed Property Laws" in *Franchise Law Journal* (Vol. 27, Summer 2007, No. 1, pp. 23)
Pub: American Bar Association
Ed: Phillip W. Bohl, Kathryn J. Bergstrom, Kevin J. Moran. **Description:** Unredeemed value of electronic prepaid stored-value credit cards for retail purchases is known as breakage. Laws governing unclaimed property as it relates to these gift cards is covered.

6211 ■ "Small Business Credit Conditions" in *Small Business Economic Trends* (April 2008, pp. 12)
Pub: National Federation of Independent Business
Ed: William C. Dunkelberg, Holly Wade. **Description:** Graphs and tables that present the credit condi-

tions of small businesses in the U.S. are provided. The tables include figures on availability of loans, interest rates, and expected credit conditions.

6212 ■ "State Targets Credit Fixers" in *Business Journal-Portland* (Vol. 24, October 12, 2007, No. 33, pp. 1)
Pub: American City Business Journals, Inc.
Ed: Andy Giegerich, Justin Matlick. **Description:** Number of companies that offer quick fix to consumers is growing; the State of Oregon is considering rules to target them. A group working on a study in the state's mortgage lending regulations could craft bills to be examined for legislative session in February 2008.

6213 ■ "Summary. Economic Trends for Small Business" in *Small Business Economic Trends* (February 2008, pp. 1)
Pub: National Federation of Independent Business
Ed: William C. Dunkelberg, Holly Wade. **Description:** Summary of economic trends for small businesses in the U.S. is provided. Economic indicators such as capital spending, inventories and sales, inflation, and profits are given. Analysis of credit markets is also provided.

6214 ■ "Survival Guide: There Can Be an Upside to Managing a Downturn" in *Canadian Business* (Vol. 81, November 10, 2008, No. 19, pp. 54)
Pub: Rogers Media Ltd.
Ed: Sharda Prashad. **Description:** Canada-based Foxy is already limiting its exposure to retailers who could be a credit problem in case of recession. Retirement Life Communities is entering into fixed-rate and fixed-term loans for them to have sufficient financing to grow. Business owners need to realize that customers want more for less.

6215 ■ "Travel Rewards Take Off" in *Inc.* (Vol. 33, October 2011, No. 8, pp. 46)
Pub: Inc. Magazine
Ed: Matthew DeLuca. **Description:** Credit card companies are offering travel reward cards with special perks, including sign-up bonuses; three such cards are described.

6216 ■ *The Trillion Dollar Meltdown: Easy Money, High Rollers, and the Great Credit Crash*
Pub: Public Affairs
Ed: Charles R. Morris. **Released:** 2009. **Price:** $22.95. **Description:** Former banker believes that Wall Street and the financial community have too much power in America. He estimates that writedowns and defaults of residential mortgages, commercial mortgages, junk bonds, leveraged loans, credit cards, and complex securitized bonds could reach $1 trillion.

6217 ■ *The Visa Approval Backlog and Its Impact on American Small Business: Congressional Hearing*
Pub: DIANE Publishing Company
Ed: Donald A. Manzullo. **Released:** July 2006. **Price:** $30.00. **Description:** Information regarding the Congressional hearing involving the Visa approval backlog is discussed.

TRADE PERIODICALS

6218 ■ *Bankcard Barometer*
Pub: RAM Research Group
Ed: Robert B. McKinley, Editor. **Released:** Monthly. **Price:** $1295, individuals. **Description:** Provides proprietary statistical data on specific U.S. credit card issuers, including gross receivables, gross accounts, delinquincy rate (30/60 day), attrition rate (voluntary/ involuntary), charge-offs, recoveries, acquisitions, average balance for standard and gold accounts, number of standard and gold cards, average cash advance for gold and standard accounts, active accounts, interest income, number of business cards, non-interest income, card/merchant processor, bankruptcy losses, fraud losses, average portfolio A.P.R.

6219 ■ *Bankcard Update*
Pub: RAM Research Group
Ed: Robert B. McKinley, Editor. **Released:** Monthly. **Price:** $1295, individuals. **Description:** Focuses on the pricing and marketing of bank credit cards. Covers standard, gold, secured, and business bank credit cards from more than 1,000 issuers (500 monitored on a monthly basis) and provides national and regional breakouts. Recurring features include news of research and departments titled Top 10 Issuer Scorecard, National Top 25 Low-Card Survey, Weighted and Unweighted A.P.R./Fee Averages for Standard and Gold Cards, Average Delinquency Rates, Average Charge-Off Rates, Average Balance Per Account, Average Volume Per Account, Average Bankruptcy Losses, Late Payment Fees,.

6220 ■ *Cardfax*
Pub: SourceMedia Inc.
Ed: Andrea McKenna Findlay, Editor. **Released:** Daily. **Description:** Contains news of the credit and debit card industry. Emphasizes company plans, ventures, programs, performance, competition, and legal and regulatory issues.

VIDEOCASSETTES/ AUDIOCASSETTES

6221 ■ *Credit Card Basics: Play Now Pay Forever*
Cambridge Educational
c/o Films Media Group
132 West 31st Street, 17th Floor
Ste. 124
New York, NY 10001
Free: 800-257-5126
Fax:(609)671-0266
Co. E-mail: custserve@films.com
URL: http://www.cambridgeol.com
Released: 1992. **Price:** $79.00. **Description:** Defines terms and explains procedures associated with credit. Emphasizes the need to keep accounts current in order to maintain a good credit rating. **Availability:** VHS.

6222 ■ *Credit Cards: Living with Plastic*
The Learning Seed
641 W. Lake St., Ste. 301
Chicago, IL 60661
Free: 800-634-4941
Fax:800-998-0854
Co. E-mail: info@learningseed.com
URL: http://www.learningseed.com
Released: 199?. **Price:** $89.00. **Description:** How to evaluate and "shop" for the credit card that best fits your needs. Discusses how to match a credit card to your spending patterns, grace periods, computing interest, annual percentage rates, yearly fees, and cardholders' legal rights. **Availability:** VHS.

6223 ■ *Credit Connection*
Commonwealth Films, Inc.
223 Commonwealth Ave.
Boston, MA 02116
Ph:(617)262-5634
Fax:(617)262-6948
Co. E-mail: info@commonwealthfilms.com
URL: http://www.commonwealthfilms.com
Released: 1986. **Price:** $295.00. **Description:** Increase your knowledge of the use of credit in the business world. **Availability:** VHS; 3/4U.

LIBRARIES

6224 ■ Loan Brokers Association–Information Services
917 S. Park St.
Owosso, MI 48867-4422
Contact: Ben Campbell, Dir.
Scope: Loan brokers, loan consulting, credit repair, lending, credit cards, venture capital. **Services:** Copying; SDI; Library to members or by permission.

START-UP INFORMATION

6225 ■ *How to Start a Bankruptcy Forms Processing Service*
Pub: Graphico Publishing Company
Ed: Victoria Ring. **Released:** September 2004. **Price:** $39.00. **Description:** Due to the increase in bankruptcy filings, attorneys are outsourcing related jobs in order to reduce overhead.

ASSOCIATIONS AND OTHER ORGANIZATIONS

6226 ■ American Financial Services Association
919 18th St. NW, Ste. 300
Washington, DC 20006-5526
Ph:(202)296-5544
Fax:(202)223-0321
Co. E-mail: susie@afsamail.org
URL: http://www.afsaonline.org
Contact: Susie Irvine, Pres./CEO
Description: Represents companies whose business is primarily direct credit lending to consumers and/or the purchase of sales finance paper on consumer goods. Has members that have insurance and retail subsidiaries; some are themselves subsidiaries of highly diversified parent corporations. Encourages the business of financing individuals and families for necessary and useful purposes at reasonable charges, including interest; promotes consumer understanding of basic money management principles as well as constructive uses of consumer credit. Includes educational services such as films, textbooks and study units for the classroom and budgeting guides for individuals and families. Compiles statistical reports; offers seminars. **Publications:** *Credit* (bimonthly); *Spotlight* (monthly).

6227 ■ Credit Professionals International
10726 Manchester Rd., Ste. 210
St. Louis, MO 63122
Ph:(314)821-9393
Fax:(314)821-7171
Co. E-mail: creditpro@creditprofessionals.org
URL: http://www.creditprofessionals.org
Contact: Billie Plasker PCS, Pres.
Description: Represents individuals employed in credit or collection departments of business firms or professional offices. Conducts educational program in credit work. Sponsors Career Club composed of members who have been involved in credit work for at least 25 years. **Publications:** *The Credit Professional* (annual).

6228 ■ Credit Research Foundation
8840 Columbia 100 Pkwy.
Columbia, MD 21045
Ph:(410)740-5499
Fax:(410)740-4620
URL: http://www.crfonline.org
Contact: Karren Salter, Chm.
Description: Represents credit, financial, and working capital executives of manufacturing and banking concerns. Aims to create a better understanding of the impact of credit on the economy. Plans, supervises, and administers research and educational programs. Conducts surveys on economic conditions, trends, policies, practices, theory, systems, and methodology. Sponsors formal educational programs in credit and financial management. Maintains library on credit, collections, and management. **Publications:** *Credit Professional's Handbook*; *CRF News* (quarterly); *National Summary of Domestic Trade Receivables* (quarterly).

6229 ■ National Association of Credit Management
8840 Columbia 100 Pkwy.
Columbia, MD 21045-2158
Ph:(410)740-5560
Free: 800-955-8815
Fax:(410)740-5574
URL: http://www.nacm.org
Contact: Robin D. Schauseil CAE, Pres./COO
Description: Credit and financial executives representing manufacturers, wholesalers, financial institutions, insurance companies, utilities, and other businesses interested in business credit. Promotes sound credit practices and legislation. Conducts Graduate School of Credit and Financial Management at Dartmouth College, Hanover, NH. **Publications:** *Business Credit* (9/year); *Credit Executives Handbook*; *Manual of Credit and Commercial Laws* (annual).

6230 ■ National Foundation for Credit Counseling
2000 M St. NW, Ste. 505
Washington, DC 20036
Free: 800-388-2227
URL: http://www.nfcc.org
Contact: Susan C. Keating, Pres./CEO
Description: Umbrella group for 200 member services operating over 1,500 offices throughout the United States and Canada. Promotes the wise use of credit through education, counseling and debt repayment programs. Member agencies provide teaching units and other money management educational materials to high schools, universities, employee assistance programs and community groups. Sponsors confidential credit and budget and homeownership counseling. .

REFERENCE WORKS

6231 ■ *All About Credit*
Pub: Kaplan Publishing
Ed: Deborah McNaughton **Released:** April 1999. **Price:** $15.95. **Description:** Debt solution to specific credit problems for individuals denied credit, trying to mortgage a home, problems with creditors, and bankruptcy.

6232 ■ "The Best Option for All" in *American Executive* (Vol. 7, September 2009, No. 5, pp. 170)
Pub: RedCoat Publishing, Inc.
Ed: Ashley McGown. **Description:** Plaza Associates, a collections agency that conducts business primarily in the accounts receivable management sector, is the first in the industry to purchase 100 percent of the company from the founders through the formation of a leveraged Employee Stock Ownership Plan (ESOP).

6233 ■ *Chain of Blame: How Wall Street Caused the Mortgage and Credit Crisis*
Pub: John Wiley & Sons, Inc.
Ed: Paul Muolo, Mathew Padilla. **Released:** 2009. **Price:** $27.95. **Description:** The book describes how risky loans given irresponsibly put big investment banks at the center of the subprime crisis.

6234 ■ "Collection Agencies Industry Rankings" in *Collections and Credit Risk* (Vol. 14, September 1, 2009, No. 8, pp. 18)
Pub: SourceMedia, Inc.
Description: Ranking of the top collection agencies in the United States in terms of the revenue generated in 2007 and 2088; statistical data included.

6235 ■ "Collection Agency Issues Whitepaper on Legal and Ethical Methods of Collecting on Overdue Accounts" in *Internet Wire* (July 20, 2009)
Pub: Comtex News Network, Inc.
Description: American Profit Recovery, a collection agency based in Massachusetts and Michigan, has updated and reissued a whitepaper on what businesses can and cannot do regarding conversing with their customers in an attempt to collect on overdue accounts and payments. A detailed summary on the federal laws associated with collecting on overdue accounts is outlined in such a way that any business owner, manager, or responsible party can easily understand.

6236 ■ "Collection Industry Fights Stigma, Lagging Payments" in *Crain's Cleveland Business* (Vol. 30, June 8, 2009, No. 22, pp. 15)
Pub: Crain Communications, Inc.
Ed: Joel Hammond. **Description:** John Murray, co-owner and president of JP Recovery Services Inc. in Rocky River, Ohio discusses the burden of the collection industry during a financial crisis like a recession. Statistical data included.

6237 ■ "Credit Card Crackdown" in *Business Journal-Portland* (Vol. 24, November 23, 2007, No. 38, pp. 1)
Pub: American City Business Journals, Inc.
Ed: Andy Giegerich. **Description:** Oregon's U.S. Senator Ron Wyden is sponsoring Credit Card Safety Act of 2007, a bill that requires credit card companies to reduce the jargon of credit card agreements and require the Federal Reserve Board to launch a public education campaign among credit card users. The legislation will also impose a rating system for credit card contracts with five being the safest for consumers to use.

6238 ■ "Curbing the Debt Collector" in *Business Journal-Portland* (Vol. 24, October 5, 2007, No. 32, pp. 1)
Pub: American City Business Journals, Inc.
Ed: Andy Giegerich. **Description:** Republican representative Sal Esquivel, who had a bad personal

experience with a Houston collector, is developing legislation that would give the state attorney general's office enforcement powers over debt collecting agencies. The existing Oregon legislation concerning the debt collection industry is also discussed.

6239 ■ "Debt Buyers Industry Rankings" in *Collections and Credit Risk* (Vol. 14, September 1, 2009, No. 8, pp. 19)
Pub: SourceMedia, Inc.
Description: Ranking of the top debt buyers in the United States in terms of the revenue generated in 2007 and 2088; statistical data included.

6240 ■ "Economic Trends for Small Business" in *Small Business Economic Trends* (April 2008, pp. 1)
Pub: National Federation of Independent Business
Ed: William C. Dunkelberg, Holly Wade. **Description:** Summary of economic trends for small businesses in the U.S. is presented. Economic indicators such as capital spending, inventories and sales, inflation, and profits are given. Analysis of credit markets is also provided.

6241 ■ "End of the Beginning" in *Canadian Business* (Vol. 81, November 10, 2008, No. 19, pp. 17)
Pub: Rogers Media Ltd.
Ed: David Wolf. **Description:** The freeze in the money markets and historic decline in equity markets around the world finally forced governments into aggressive coordinated action. The asset price inflation brought on by cheap credit will now work in reverse and the tightening of credit will be difficult economically. Canada is exposed to the fallout everywhere, given that the U.S, the U.K. and Japan buy 30 percent of Canada's output.

6242 ■ *Get Your Credit Straight: A Sister's Guide to Ditching Your Debt, Mending Your Credit, and Building a Strong Financial Future*
Pub: Broadway Books
Ed: Glinda Bridgforth. **Price:** $19.95. **Description:** Third book in the series is aimed primarily at African American women and offers helpful and understandable information for a larger audience. The sidebars on how women in particular tend to get into credit trouble and ways they can increase their financial knowledge and reign in their spending habits are especially notable.

6243 ■ *Grow Your Money: 101 Easy Tips to Plan, Save and Invest*
Pub: HarperBusiness
Ed: Jonathan D. Pond. **Released:** December 2007. **Price:** $26.95. **Description:** In what should be required reading for anyone entering the work world, the author offers helpful investment and financial definitions, debt-management strategies, retirement and home ownerships considerations and more.

6244 ■ "The Letter of the Law" in *Collections and Credit Risk* (Vol. 14, November 1, 2009, No. 9, pp. 40)
Pub: SourceMedia, Inc.
Ed: Michelle Dunn. **Description:** Analyzes the regulatory landscape regarding debt collection and the ways in which those in the field are dealing with a tough economy, unclear laws and the newest regulations.

6245 ■ "A New FICO Scoring Model: Get Ready For Changes That Could Affect Your Score" in *Black Enterprise* (Vol. 38, March 2008, No. 8)
Pub: Earl G. Graves Publishing Co. Inc.
Ed: Sheiresa McRae. **Description:** Fair Isaac Corporation, creator of the FICO credit score has developed a new scoring model that provides a more accurate way for lenders to determine a borrower's creditworthiness.

6246 ■ "New Money" in *Entrepreneur* (Vol. 36, February 2008, No. 2, pp. 62)
Pub: Entrepreneur Media Inc.
Ed: C.J. Prince. **Description:** Tips on how to handle business finance, with regard to the tightened credit standards imposed by leading institutions, are provided. These include: selling receivables, margining blue chips, and selling purchase orders.

6247 ■ "Portfolio Recovery Associates Expands Its Hampton Call Center" in *Internet Wire* (January 20, 2010)
Pub: Comtex News Network, Inc.
Description: Entering into a lease amendment in order to expand its Hampton, Virginia call center and extend its lease agreement, Portfolio Recovery Associates, Inc., a company that collects, purchases and manages defaulted consumer debt, plans to upgrade the existing space enabling them to draw on local talent.

6248 ■ "Research and Markets Adds Report: Credit and Collection Practices 2009" in *Wireless News* (August 12, 2009)
Pub: Close-Up Media
Description: Research and Markets announced the addition of the "Credit and Collection Practices 2009" report which will highlight credit and collection industry practices and technologies. The report also includes an overview of the best practices in the field.

6249 ■ "'Rocket Docket' Leaves Memphis Debtors Behind" in *Commercial Appeal* (November 28, 2009)
Pub: Commercial Appeal
Ed: Bartholomew Sullivan. **Description:** According to an investigation by the Scripps Howard News Service, Memphians lodged 807 formal complaints about debt-collection practices to the Federal Trade Commission in a 2 1/2 -year period ending in July; Nearly 1/3 of the complaints involved some type of error with the debt in question. The majority of the complaints were leveled at NCO Group, which also generated the most complaints around the country.

6250 ■ "Small Business Credit Conditions" in *Small Business Economic Trends* (April 2008, pp. 12)
Pub: National Federation of Independent Business
Ed: William C. Dunkelberg, Holly Wade. **Description:** Graphs and tables that present the credit conditions of small businesses in the U.S. are provided. The tables include figures on availability of loans, interest rates, and expected credit conditions.

6251 ■ "State Targets Credit Fixers" in *Business Journal-Portland* (Vol. 24, October 12, 2007, No. 33, pp. 1)
Pub: American City Business Journals, Inc.
Ed: Andy Giegerich, Justin Matlick. **Description:** Number of companies that offer quick fix to consumers is growing; the State of Oregon is considering rules to target them. A group working on a study in the state's mortgage lending regulations could craft bills to be examined for legislative session in February 2008.

6252 ■ "Summary. Economic Trends for Small Business" in *Small Business Economic Trends* (February 2008, pp. 1)
Pub: National Federation of Independent Business
Ed: William C. Dunkelberg, Holly Wade. **Description:** Summary of economic trends for small businesses in the U.S. is provided. Economic indicators such as capital spending, inventories and sales, inflation, and profits are given. Analysis of credit markets is also provided.

6253 ■ "The Survey Says" in *Collections and Credit Risk* (Vol. 14, September 1, 2009, No. 8, pp. 16)
Pub: SourceMedia, Inc.
Ed: Bill Grabarek; Darren Waggoner. **Description:** Revenue for the top accounts receivable management firms rose nearly 20 percent in 2008 despite lower liquidation rates, a poor economy and riskier, albeit cheaper debt portfolios; the trend may continue this year as collection agencies expect revenue, on average, to increase 5.8 percent. Debt buyers, however, found that their revenue fell nearly 7 percent in 2008 and expect it to fall another 12 percent this year.

6254 ■ "Survival Guide: There Can Be an Upside to Managing a Downturn" in *Canadian Business* (Vol. 81, November 10, 2008, No. 19, pp. 54)
Pub: Rogers Media Ltd.
Ed: Sharda Prashad. **Description:** Canada-based Foxy is already limiting its exposure to retailers who could be a credit problem in case of recession. Retirement Life Communities is entering into fixed-rate and fixed-term loans for them to have sufficient financing to grow. Business owners need to realize that customers want more for less.

6255 ■ "Taking Collections" in *Investment Dealers' Digest* (Vol. 75, October 9, 2009, No. 38, pp. 19)
Pub: SourceMedia, Inc.
Ed: Aleksandrs Rozens. **Description:** Although the nation's debt-collection industry has grown with increased reliance by consumers on credit, valuations of these firms have lessened due to the economy which has hurt some of the success of these firms in obtaining the debt back from consumers who are experiencing trying economic times.

6256 ■ *The Trillion Dollar Meltdown: Easy Money, High Rollers, and the Great Credit Crash*
Pub: Public Affairs
Ed: Charles R. Morris. **Released:** 2009. **Price:** $22.95. **Description:** Former banker believes that Wall Street and the financial community have too much power in America. He estimates that writedowns and defaults of residential mortgages, commercial mortgages, junk bonds, leveraged loans, credit cards, and complex securitized bonds could reach $1 trillion.

TRADE PERIODICALS

6257 ■ *Notables*
Pub: National Foundation for Credit Counseling
Contact: Lydia Sermons-Ward, Executive Editor
E-mail: lsward@nfcc.org
Released: Monthly. **Description:** Covers issues concerning consumer credit counseling, family finances, and debt counseling. Recurring features include news of research, reports of meetings, and notices of publications available.

LIBRARIES

6258 ■ Loan Brokers Association–Information Services
917 S. Park St.
Owosso, MI 48867-4422
Contact: Ben Campbell, Dir.
Scope: Loan brokers, loan consulting, credit repair, lending, credit cards, venture capital. **Services:** Copying; SDI; Library to members or by permission.

6259 ■ National Foundation for Credit Counseling Library
801 Roeder Rd., Ste. 900
Silver Spring, MD 20910
Ph:(301)589-5600
Fax:(301)495-5623
URL: http://www.nfcc.org/
Contact: Paul Weiss, Chf.Fin.Off/Chf. of Staff
Scope: Consumer credit, credit counseling, credit research and education. **Services:** Library not open to the public. **Holdings:** Brochures and pamphlets.

START-UP INFORMATION

6260 ■ *How to Start a Bankruptcy Forms Processing Service*
Pub: Graphico Publishing Company
Ed: Victoria Ring. **Released:** September 2004. **Price:** $39.00. **Description:** Due to the increase in bankruptcy filings, attorneys are outsourcing related jobs in order to reduce overhead.

ASSOCIATIONS AND OTHER ORGANIZATIONS

6261 ■ ACA International
PO Box 390106
Minneapolis, MN 55439-0106
Ph:(952)926-6547
Fax:(952)926-1624
Co. E-mail: aca@acainternational.org
URL: http://www.acainternational.org
Contact: Patrick J. Morris, CEO
Description: Collection services handling overdue accounts for retail, professional, and commercial credit grantors. Maintains specialized programs in the areas of healthcare, checks, and government which provide services for members who work with credit grantors in these areas. Conducts research. Offers specialized education; compiles statistics. **Publications:** *Collector* (monthly); *Consumer Trends* (monthly); *Cred-Alert* (monthly); *Management Trends* (bimonthly).

6262 ■ Consumer Data Industry Association
1090 Vermont Ave. NW, Ste. 200
Washington, DC 20005-4964
Ph:(202)371-0910
Fax:(202)371-0134
Co. E-mail: cdia@cdiaonline.org
URL: http://www.cdiaonline.org
Contact: Betty Byrnes
Description: Serves as international association of credit reporting and collection service offices. Maintains hall of fame and biographical archives; conducts specialized educational programs. Offers computerized services and compiles statistics. .

6263 ■ Credit Professionals International
10726 Manchester Rd., Ste. 210
St. Louis, MO 63122
Ph:(314)821-9393
Fax:(314)821-7171
Co. E-mail: creditpro@creditprofessionals.org
URL: http://www.creditprofessionals.org
Contact: Billie Plasker PCS, Pres.
Description: Represents individuals employed in credit or collection departments of business firms or professional offices. Conducts educational program in credit work. Sponsors Career Club composed of members who have been involved in credit work for at least 25 years. **Publications:** *The Credit Professional* (annual).

6264 ■ International Association of Commercial Collectors
4040 W 70th St.
Minneapolis, MN 55435
Ph:(952)925-0760
Fax:(952)926-1624
Co. E-mail: iacc@commercialcollector.com
URL: http://www.commercialcollector.com
Contact: Tammy Schoenberg, Exec. Dir.
Description: Debt collection professionals who are specialists in the recovery of commercial accounts receivable. **Publications:** *Commercial Collection Guidelines for Credit Grantors*; *Scope* (monthly).

6265 ■ International Association of Financial Crimes Investigators
1020 Suncast Ln., Ste. 102
El Dorado Hills, CA 95762
Ph:(916)939-5000
Fax:(916)939-0395
Co. E-mail: admin@iafci.org
URL: http://www.iafci.org
Contact: Jan Moffett
Description: Special agents, investigators, and investigation supervisors who investigate criminal violations of credit card laws and prosecute offenders; law enforcement officers, prosecutors, or related officials who investigate, apprehend, and prosecute credit card offenders; employees of card issuing institutions who are responsible for credit card security and investigations; management personnel of companies performing services for the credit card industry. Aids in the establishment of effective credit card security programs; suppresses fraudulent use of credit cards; and detects and proceeds with the apprehension of credit card thieves. Emphasizes a professional approach to the investigative function, a free exchange of criminal intelligence, and a vigorous prosecution policy. Encourages members to use existing federal and local criminal statutes and to seek more effective legislation in areas where it is lacking. Provides workshops and training conferences to acquaint law enforcement bodies and the membership with technological advances in the industry. **Publications:** *IAFCI News* (quarterly).

6266 ■ National Association of Credit Management
8840 Columbia 100 Pkwy.
Columbia, MD 21045-2158
Ph:(410)740-5560
Free: 800-955-8815
Fax:(410)740-5574
URL: http://www.nacm.org
Contact: Robin D. Schauseil CAE, Pres./COO
Description: Credit and financial executives representing manufacturers, wholesalers, financial institutions, insurance companies, utilities, and other businesses interested in business credit. Promotes sound credit practices and legislation. Conducts Graduate School of Credit and Financial Management at Dartmouth College, Hanover, NH. **Publications:** *Business Credit* (9/year); *Credit Executives Handbook*; *Manual of Credit and Commercial Laws* (annual).

DIRECTORIES OF EDUCATIONAL PROGRAMS

6267 ■ *International Association of Credit Card Investigators—Membership Directory*
Pub: International Association of Financial Crimes Investigators
Released: Annual. **Covers:** Approximately 3,500 firms and individuals involved in investigating fraudulent credit card use who are members of the International Association of Credit Card Investigators. **Entries Include:** Contact information. **Arrangement:** Alphabetical by name. **Indexes:** Geographical; alphabetical by firm name.

REFERENCE WORKS

6268 ■ "11th Circuit: Don't Break the Law to Comply with It" in *Miami Daily Business Review* (October 21, 2009)
Pub: Incisive Media Ltd.
Ed: Janet L. Conley. **Description:** Niagara Credit Solutions argued with a three-judge panel that the company broke the rule saying debt collectors must identify themselves so that they could comply with a rule barring debt collectors from communicating about a debt with third parties.

6269 ■ *ACA International—Membership Roster*
Pub: ACA International
Ed: Tim Dressen, Editor. **Released:** Annual, Latest edition 2008. **Publication Includes:** List of about 3,600 debt collection agencies, 1,000 credit grantors and 700 collection attorneys, and services in 55 countries. **Entries Include:** Firm name, address, phone, fax, URL, e-mail, names and names and titles of key personnel. **Arrangement:** Geographical.

6270 ■ "All-Star Advice 2010" in *Black Enterprise* (Vol. 41, October 2010, No. 3, pp. 97)
Pub: Earl G. Graves Publishing Co. Inc.
Ed: Renita Burns, Sheiresa Ngo, Marcia Wade Talbert. **Description:** Financial experts share tips on real estate, investing, taxes, insurance and debt management.

6271 ■ "B2B Commercial Collection Agency Accounts Fall" in *Managing Credit, Receivables & Collections* (November 2010, No. 10-11, pp. 9)
Pub: Institute of Management & Administration
Description: A fall in the number of Business-To-Business collection accounts reflects the pace of the global economic recovery.

6272 ■ "Banks, Retailers Squabble Over Fees" in *Baltimore Business Journal* (Vol. 28, June 18, 2010, No. 6, pp. 1)
Pub: Baltimore Business Journal
Ed: Gary Haber. **Description:** How an amendment to the financial regulatory reform bill would affect the bankers' and retailers' conflict over interchange fees

is discussed. Interchange fees are paid for by retailers every time consumers make purchases through debit cards. Industry estimates indicate that approximately $50 million in such fees are paid by retailers.

6273 ■ "Barred Collection Agency Sued by Colorado AG" in *Collections & Credit Risk* (Vol. 15, August 1, 2010, No. 7, pp. 7)
Pub: SourceMedia Inc.
Description: Collection agency run by Chad Lee received notice that it is barred from collecting in the State of Colorado by Attorney General John Suther's office. A ruling cited that the firm engages in harassment or abuse and/or threats of violence, made false representations as to its legal status of debts, made false and misleading representations of nonpayment of debts that would result in arrest, and that Lee failed to disclose his previous felony conviction.

6274 ■ "The Best Option for All" in *American Executive* (Vol. 7, September 2009, No. 5, pp. 170)
Pub: RedCoat Publishing, Inc.
Ed: Ashley McGown. **Description:** Plaza Associates, a collections agency that conducts business primarily in the accounts receivable management sector, is the first in the industry to purchase 100 percent of the company from the founders through the formation of a leveraged Employee Stock Ownership Plan (ESOP).

6275 ■ "Boosting Your Merchant Management Services With Wireless Technology" in *Franchising World* (Vol. 42, August 2010, No. 8, pp. 27)
Pub: International Franchise Association
Ed: Michael S. Slominski. **Description:** Franchises should have the capability to accept credit cards away from their businesses. This technology will increase sales.

6276 ■ "Boring Bonds Gain Pizzazz as Investors Flock to Debt Issues" in *Baltimore Business Journal* (Vol. 28, June 11, 2010, No. 5, pp. 1)
Pub: Baltimore Business Journal
Ed: Gary Haber. **Description:** Companies and nonprofit organizations have increased the pace of bond offerings in order to take advantage of the bonds' appeal among willing investors. Companies mostly issued corporate bonds to replace existing debt at lower interest rates and save them money from interest payments.

6277 ■ *Chain of Blame: How Wall Street Caused the Mortgage and Credit Crisis*
Pub: John Wiley & Sons, Inc.
Ed: Paul Muolo, Mathew Padilla. **Released:** 2009. **Price:** $27.95. **Description:** The book describes how risky loans given irresponsibly put big investment banks at the center of the subprime crisis.

6278 ■ "China's Dagong Show" in *Canadian Business* (Vol. 83, August 17, 2010, No. 13-14, pp. 15)
Pub: Rogers Media Ltd.
Ed: Matthew McClearn. **Description:** Beijing, China-based Dagong Global Credit Rating has downgraded US credit ratings, as well as other developed countries such as Canada, while granting higher ratings to China, Russia and Brazil. However, there is a perceived disconnection between Dagong's ratings and its official pronouncements.

6279 ■ "Clock Ticks On Columbia Sussex Debt" in *Business Courier* (Vol. 27, July 30, 2010, No. 13, pp. 1)
Pub: Business Courier
Ed: Dan Monk. **Description:** Cincinnati, Ohio-based Columbia Sussex Corporation has made plans to restructure a $1 billion loan bundle that was scheduled to mature in October 2010. The privately held hotel has strived in a weak hotel market to keep pace with its $3 billion debt load.

6280 ■ "Collection Agencies Industry Rankings" in *Collections and Credit Risk* (Vol. 14, September 1, 2009, No. 8, pp. 18)
Pub: SourceMedia, Inc.
Description: Ranking of the top collection agencies in the United States in terms of the revenue generated in 2007 and 2088; statistical data included.

6281 ■ "Collection Agency Issues Whitepaper on Legal and Ethical Methods of Collecting on Overdue Accounts" in *Internet Wire* (July 20, 2009)
Pub: Comtex News Network, Inc.
Description: American Profit Recovery, a collection agency based in Massachusetts and Michigan, has updated and reissued a whitepaper on what businesses can and cannot do regarding conversing with their customers in an attempt to collect on overdue accounts and payments. A detailed summary on the federal laws associated with collecting on overdue accounts is outlined in such a way that any business owner, manager, or responsible party can easily understand.

6282 ■ "Collection Industry Fights Stigma, Lagging Payments" in *Crain's Cleveland Business* (Vol. 30, June 8, 2009, No. 22, pp. 15)
Pub: Crain Communications, Inc.
Ed: Joel Hammond. **Description:** John Murray, co-owner and president of JP Recovery Services Inc. in Rocky River, Ohio discusses the burden of the collection industry during a financial crisis like a recession. Statistical data included.

6283 ■ "Companies Warned About California Collection Agency" in *Cardline* (Vol. 10, June 4, 2010, No. 23, pp. 3)
Pub: SourceMedia Inc.
Description: Maxwell, Turner & Associates has received an F-rating from the Better Business Bureau of Central California, citing 32 unanswered complaints in less than a year.

6284 ■ *Complete Idiot's Guide to Starting an Ebay Business*
Pub: Penguin Books (USA) Incorporated
Ed: Barbara Weltman, Malcolm Katt. **Released:** February 2008. **Price:** $19.95 (US), $29.00 (Canadian). **Description:** Guide for starting an eBay business includes information on products to sell, how to price merchandise, and details for working with services like PayPal, and how to organize fulfillment services.

6285 ■ "Cost of Business Banking May Soon Go Up" in *Baltimore Business Journal* (Vol. 28, October 29, 2010, No. 25, pp. 1)
Pub: Baltimore Business Journal
Ed: Gary Haber. **Description:** Experts in the financial industry expect banks to charge credit card transactions, especially to small business owners and consumers to recover about $11 million in lost revenue annually. Banks are expected to charge old fees and new ones, including $5 to $10 a month for a checking account.

6286 ■ "Credit Card Crackdown" in *Business Journal-Portland* (Vol. 24, November 23, 2007, No. 38, pp. 1)
Pub: American City Business Journals, Inc.
Ed: Andy Giegerich. **Description:** Oregon's U.S. Senator Ron Wyden is sponsoring Credit Card Safety Act of 2007, a bill that requires credit card companies to reduce the jargon of credit card agreements and require the Federal Reserve Board to launch a public education campaign among credit card users. The legislation will also impose a rating system for credit card contracts with five being the safest for consumers to use.

6287 ■ "Credit Reporting Myths and Reality" in *Black Enterprise* (Vol. 41, December 2010, No. 5, pp. 34)
Pub: Earl G. Graves Publishing Co. Inc.
Ed: Denise Campbell. **Description:** It is critical to understand all the factors affecting credit scores before making any major purchase.

6288 ■ "Curbing the Debt Collector" in *Business Journal-Portland* (Vol. 24, October 5, 2007, No. 32, pp. 1)
Pub: American City Business Journals, Inc.
Ed: Andy Giegerich. **Description:** Republican representative Sal Esquivel, who had a bad personal experience with a Houston collector, is developing legislation that would give the state attorney general's office enforcement powers over debt collecting agencies. The existing Oregon legislation concerning the debt collection industry is also discussed.

6289 ■ "Death Spiral" in *Business Journal Serving Greater Tampa Bay* (Vol. 30, October 29, 2010, No. 45, pp. 1)
Pub: Tampa Bay Business Journal
Ed: Margie Manning. **Description:** Bay Cities Bank has started working on the loan portfolio of its acquisition, Progress Bank of Florida. Regulators closed Progress Bank in October 2010 after capital collapsed due to charge-offs and increases in the provision for future loan losses.

6290 ■ "Debt Buyers Industry Rankings" in *Collections and Credit Risk* (Vol. 14, September 1, 2009, No. 8, pp. 19)
Pub: SourceMedia, Inc.
Description: Ranking of the top debt buyers in the United States in terms of the revenue generated in 2007 and 2088; statistical data included.

6291 ■ "Debt-Collection Agency to Lay Off 368 in Hampton Center" in *Virginian-Pilot* (December 4, 2010)
Pub: Virginian-Pilot
Ed: Tom Shean. **Description:** NCO Financial Systems Inc., provider of debt-collection and outsourcing services will permanently lay off 368 workers at its Hampton call center in 2011.

6292 ■ "Delinquent Properties on the Rise" in *Business Courier* (Vol. 27, June 11, 2010, No. 6, pp. 1)
Pub: Business Courier
Ed: Dan Monk. **Description:** Reports show that Cincinnati now ranks in the U.S. Top 20 for its delinquency rate on securitized commercial real estate loans. In December 2009, the region ranked 28th out of 50 cities studied by Trepp LLC. As of May 30, 2010, more than $378 million in commercial mortgage-backed security loans were more than 60 days past due.

6293 ■ "Developer Wins Bout with Bank in Roundabout Way" in *Tampa Bay Business Journal* (Vol. 30, January 29, 2010, No. 6, pp. 1)
Pub: American City Business Journals
Ed: Janet Leiser. **Description:** Developer Donald E. Phillips of Phillips Development and Realty LLC won against the foreclosure filed by First Horizon National Corporation, which is demanding the company to fully pay its $2.9 million loan. Phillips requested that his company pay monthly mortgage and extend the loan's maturity date.

6294 ■ "Direct Recovery Associates Debt Collection Agency Beats Industry Record" in *Internet Wire* (June 24, 2010)
Pub: Comtex
Description: Direct Recovery Associates Inc. was named as one of the highest collection records in the industry, which has consistently improved over 18 years. The firm is an international attorney-based debt collection agency.

6295 ■ "Direct Recovery Associates, Inc. Debt Collection Agency Founder Featured in China Daily" in *Internet Wire* (November 9, 2010)
Pub: Comtex
Description: Richard Hart, founder of Direct Recovery Associates, was featured in an article published in the China Daily. The article discussed the increased credit and debt collection demands involving the U.S. and China.

6296 ■ "Doctors, Health Insurers Squabble Over Who Sends Patients the Bill" in *Baltimore Business Journal* (Vol. 27, February 6, 2010)
Pub: American City Business Journals
Ed: Scott Graham. **Description:** Issue of allowing patients to send reimbursement checks to physicians who are not part of their health insurer's provider

network is being debated in Maryland. Details on the proposed Maryland bill and the arguments presented by doctors and insurers are outlined.

6297 ■ *EBay Income: How ANYONE of Any Age, Location, and/or Background Can Build a Highly Profitable Online Business with eBay (Revised 2nd Edition)*
Pub: Atlantic Publishing Company
Released: December 1, 2010. **Price:** $24.95. **Description:** A complete overview of eBay is given and guides any small company through the entire process of creating the auction and auction strategies, photography, writing copy, text and formatting, multiple sales, programming tricks, PayPal, accounting, creating marketing, merchandising, managing email lists, advertising plans, taxes and sales tax, best time to list items and for how long, sniping programs, international customers, opening a storefront, electronic commerce, buy-it now pricing, keywords, Google marketing and eBay secrets.

6298 ■ "Economic Trends for Small Business" in *Small Business Economic Trends* (April 2008, pp. 1)
Pub: National Federation of Independent Business
Ed: William C. Dunkelberg, Holly Wade. **Description:** Summary of economic trends for small businesses in the U.S. is presented. Economic indicators such as capital spending, inventories and sales, inflation, and profits are given. Analysis of credit markets is also provided.

6299 ■ "End of the Beginning" in *Canadian Business* (Vol. 81, November 10, 2008, No. 19, pp. 17)
Pub: Rogers Media Ltd.
Ed: David Wolf. **Description:** The freeze in the money markets and historic decline in equity markets around the world finally forced governments into aggressive coordinated action. The asset price inflation brought on by cheap credit will now work in reverse and the tightening of credit will be difficult economically. Canada is exposed to the fallout everywhere, given that the U.S, the U.K. and Japan buy 30 percent of Canada's output.

6300 ■ "Ethics Commission May Hire Collection Agency" in *Tulsa World* (August 21, 2010)
Pub: World Publishing
Ed: Barbara Hoberock. **Description:** Oklahoma Ethics Commission is considering a more to hire a collection agency or law firm in order to collect fees from candidates owing money for filing late financial reports.

6301 ■ "Fight Ensues Over Irreplaceable Gowns" in *Tampa Bay Business Journal* (Vol. 30, January 15, 2010, No. 4, pp. 1)
Pub: American City Business Journals
Ed: Janet Leiser. **Description:** People's Princess Charitable Foundation Inc. founder Maureen Rorech Dunkel has sought Chapter 11 bankruptcy protection before a state court decides on the fate of the five of 13 Princess Diana Gowns. Dunkel and the nonprofit were sued by Patricia Sullivan of HRH Venture LLC who claimed they defaulted on $1.5 million in loans.

6302 ■ "Firms Sue Doracon to Recoup More Than $1M in Unpaid Bills" in *Baltimore Business Journal* (Vol. 28, July 9, 2010, No. 9, pp. 1)
Pub: Baltimore Business Journal
Ed: Scott Dance. **Description:** Concrete supplier Paul J. Rach Inc., Selective Insurance Company, and equipment leasing firm Colonial Pacific Leasing Corporation intend to sue Baltimore, Maryland-based Doracon Contracting Inc. for $1 million in unpaid bills. Doracon owed Colonial Pacific $794,000 and the equipment is still in Doracon's possession. Selective Insurance and Paul J. Rach respectively seek $132,000 and $88,000.

6303 ■ *Get Your Credit Straight: A Sister's Guide to Ditching Your Debt, Mending Your Credit, and Building a Strong Financial Future*
Pub: Broadway Books
Ed: Glinda Bridgforth. **Price:** $19.95. **Description:** Third book in the series is aimed primarily at African American women and offers helpful and understandable information for a larger audience. The sidebars on how women in particular tend to get into credit trouble and ways they can increase their financial knowledge and reign in their spending habits are especially notable.

6304 ■ "The Great Deleveraging" in *Canadian Business* (Vol. 81, October 13, 2008, No. 17, pp. 45)
Pub: Rogers Media Ltd.
Ed: Jeff Sanford. **Description:** 'Hell Week' of financial crisis on Wall Street is believed to have started with the downgrade of AIG Inc.'s credit rating. AIG is a major player in the credit derivatives market, and its bankruptcy would have affected firms on Wall Street.

6305 ■ "High-End Jeweler Loses Street Sparkle" in *Houston Business Journal* (Vol. 40, November 27, 2009, No. 29, pp. 1)
Pub: American City Business Journals
Ed: Allison Wollam. **Description:** High-end jeweler Bailey Banks & Biddle's 7,000 square foot prototype store in Houston, Texas' CityCentre will be ceasing operations despite its parent company's filing for Chapter 11 protection from creditors. According to the bankruptcy filing, parent company Finlay Enterprises Inc. of New York intends to auction off its business and assets. Finlay has 67 Bailey Banks locations throughout the US.

6306 ■ "Hospitals Feel Pain from Slow Economy" in *Business Courier* (Vol. 27, September 3, 2010, No. 18, pp. 1)
Pub: Business Courier
Ed: James Ritchie. **Description:** Hospitals in Cincinnati, Ohio have suffered from decreased revenues owing to the economic crises. Declining patient volumes and bad debt have also adversely impacted hospitals.

6307 ■ "Illinois Regulators Revoke Collection Agency's License" in *Collections & Credit Risk* (Vol. 15, August 1, 2010, No. 7, pp. 13)
Pub: SourceMedia Inc.
Description: Creditors Service Bureau of Springfield, Illinois had its license revoked by a state regulatory agency and was fined $55,000 because the owner and president, Craig W. Lewis, did not turn over portions of collected funds to clients.

6308 ■ "The Letter of the Law" in *Collections and Credit Risk* (Vol. 14, November 1, 2009, No. 9, pp. 40)
Pub: SourceMedia, Inc.
Ed: Michelle Dunn. **Description:** Analyzes the regulatory landscape regarding debt collection and the ways in which those in the field are dealing with a tough economy, unclear laws and the newest regulations.

6309 ■ "Making Automated Royalty Payments Work for Your Franchise" in *Franchising World* (Vol. 42, October 2010, No. 10, pp. 30)
Pub: International Franchise Association
Ed: J.P. O'Brien. **Description:** In the past, royalty payments were sent by franchisees through regular postal mail and accompanied by a single slip of paper with handwritten notes indicating the month's revenue numbers and royalty amounts.

6310 ■ "Media Industry Collection Agency Completes Acquisition" in *Collections & Credit Risk* (Vol. 15, December 1, 2010, No. 11, pp. 22)
Pub: SourceMedia Inc.
Description: Media Receivable Management Inc. (MRM) will take over the collection operations at Borden, Jones & Mitchell, in Miami, Florida. MRM clients are basically magazine and electronic media publishers.

6311 ■ "More Ad Shops Link Payment to Results" in *Boston Business Journal* (Vol. 30, November 12, 2010, No. 42, pp. 1)
Pub: Boston Business Journal
Ed: Lisa van der Pool. **Description:** A growing number of advertising firms are proposing a 'value-based' payment scheme where they are paid a base fee plus a bonus if certain sales goals or other targets are met. The proposed shift in payment scheme is seen as reminiscent of the dot-com boom about ten years ago. Advertising firms are traditionally paid by the hour.

6312 ■ "A New FICO Scoring Model: Get Ready For Changes That Could Affect Your Score" in *Black Enterprise* (Vol. 38, March 2008, No. 8)
Pub: Earl G. Graves Publishing Co. Inc.
Ed: Sheiresa McRae. **Description:** Fair Isaac Corporation, creator of the FICO credit score has developed a new scoring model that provides a more accurate way for lenders to determine a borrower's creditworthiness.

6313 ■ "New Money" in *Entrepreneur* (Vol. 36, February 2008, No. 2, pp. 62)
Pub: Entrepreneur Media Inc.
Ed: C.J. Prince. **Description:** Tips on how to handle business finance, with regard to the tightened credit standards imposed by leading institutions, are provided. These include: selling receivables, margining blue chips, and selling purchase orders.

6314 ■ "New York Collection Agency's Bribery Case Resolved" in *Collections & Credit Risk* (Vol. 15, August 1, 2010, No. 7, pp. 19)
Pub: SourceMedia Inc.
Description: Criminal conviction and civil settlement in a bribery case and Medicaid scam involving H.I.S. Holdings Inc. and owner Deborah Kantor is examined.

6315 ■ "Ohio Collection Agency Settles Second Lawsuit" in *Collections & Credit Risk* (Vol. 15, July 1, 2010, No. 6, pp. 9)
Pub: SourceMedia Inc.
Description: National Enterprise Systems, will pay $75,000 for illegal and abusive collection charged in a lawsuit filed by West Virginia's Attorney General's office. Money will be used to reimburse students and consumers who paid the illegal fees to the company.

6316 ■ "Pay Me! How to Get the Money You're Owed When No One Seems to Have Any" in *Entrepreneur* (Vol. 37, July 2009, No. 7, pp. 49)
Pub: Entrepreneur Media, Inc.
Ed: Randy B. Hecht. **Description:** How certain collections scenarios with clients, who have already fallen behind on their payments, should be handled is discussed. During a down economy, business owners should properly manage collection and billing because this can actually strengthen client relationships. Insights on hiring a collections agency are also presented.

6317 ■ "Portfolio Recovery Associates Expands Its Hampton Call Center" in *Internet Wire* (January 20, 2010)
Pub: Comtex News Network, Inc.
Description: Entering into a lease amendment in order to expand its Hampton, Virginia call center and extend its lease agreement, Portfolio Recovery Associates, Inc., a company that collects, purchases and manages defaulted consumer debt, plans to upgrade the existing space enabling them to draw on local talent.

6318 ■ *Practical Debt Collecting for Small Companies and Traders*
Pub: Meadow Books
Ed: Robin Evelegh. **Released:** December 2006. **Price:** $12.99. **Description:** Credit and collection guide for small companies.

6319 ■ "Regulators Revoke Mann Bracken's Collection Agency Licenses" in *Collections & Credit Risk* (Vol. 15, September 1, 2010, No. 8, pp. 19)
Pub: SourceMedia Inc.
Description: Maryland regulators have revoked the collections licenses of defunct law firm Mann Bracken LLP.

6320 ■ "Research and Markets Adds Report: Credit and Collection Practices 2009" in *Wireless News* (August 12, 2009)
Pub: Close-Up Media
Description: Research and Markets announced the addition of the "Credit and Collection Practices 2009" report which will highlight credit and collection industry practices and technologies. The report also includes an overview of the best practices in the field.

6321 ■ "'Rocket Docket' Leaves Memphis Debtors Behind" in *Commercial Appeal* (November 28, 2009)
Pub: Commercial Appeal
Ed: Bartholomew Sullivan. **Description:** According to an investigation by the Scripps Howard News Service, Memphians lodged 807 formal complaints about debt-collection practices to the Federal Trade Commission in a 2 1/2 -year period ending in July; Nearly 1/3 of the complaints involved some type of error with the debt in question. The majority of the complaints were leveled at NCO Group, which also generated the most complaints around the country.

6322 ■ "Small Business Credit Conditions" in *Small Business Economic Trends* (April 2008, pp. 12)
Pub: National Federation of Independent Business
Ed: William C. Dunkelberg, Holly Wade. **Description:** Graphs and tables that present the credit conditions of small businesses in the U.S. are provided. The tables include figures on availability of loans, interest rates, and expected credit conditions.

6323 ■ "State Targets Credit Fixers" in *Business Journal-Portland* (Vol. 24, October 12, 2007, No. 33, pp. 1)
Pub: American City Business Journals, Inc.
Ed: Andy Giegerich, Justin Matlick. **Description:** Number of companies that offer quick fix to consumers is growing; the State of Oregon is considering rules to target them. A group working on a study in the state's mortgage lending regulations could craft bills to be examined for legislative session in February 2008.

6324 ■ "Summary. Economic Trends for Small Business" in *Small Business Economic Trends* (February 2008, pp. 1)
Pub: National Federation of Independent Business
Ed: William C. Dunkelberg, Holly Wade. **Description:** Summary of economic trends for small businesses in the U.S. is provided. Economic indicators such as capital spending, inventories and sales, inflation, and profits are given. Analysis of credit markets is also provided.

6325 ■ "The Survey Says" in *Collections and Credit Risk* (Vol. 14, September 1, 2009, No. 8, pp. 16)
Pub: SourceMedia, Inc.
Ed: Bill Grabarek; Darren Waggoner. **Description:** Revenue for the top accounts receivable management firms rose nearly 20 percent in 2008 despite lower liquidation rates, a poor economy and riskier, albeit cheaper debt portfolios; the trend may continue this year as collection agencies expect revenue, on average, to increase 5.8 percent. Debt buyers, however, found that their revenue fell nearly 7 percent in 2008 and expect it to fall another 12 percent this year.

6326 ■ "Survival Guide: There Can Be an Upside to Managing a Downturn" in *Canadian Business* (Vol. 81, November 10, 2008, No. 19, pp. 54)
Pub: Rogers Media Ltd.
Ed: Sharda Prashad. **Description:** Canada-based Foxy is already limiting its exposure to retailers who could be a credit problem in case of recession. Retirement Life Communities is entering into fixed-rate and fixed-term loans for them to have sufficient financing to grow. Business owners need to realize that customers want more for less.

6327 ■ "Taking Collections" in *Investment Dealers' Digest* (Vol. 75, October 9, 2009, No. 38, pp. 19)
Pub: SourceMedia, Inc.
Ed: Aleksandrs Rozens. **Description:** Although the nation's debt-collection industry has grown with increased reliance by consumers on credit, valuations of these firms have lessened due to the economy which has hurt some of the success of these firms in obtaining the debt back from consumers who are experiencing trying economic times.

6328 ■ "Tampa Bay's CMBS Exposure Looms Large" in *Tampa Bay Business Journal* (Vol. 30, December 4, 2009, No. 50, pp. 1)
Pub: American City Business Journals
Ed: Margie Manning. **Description:** Tampa, Florida's metropolitan statistical area have listed 50 to 601 commercial mortgage-backed securities loans as delinquent with a total delinquent loan balance of $439 million. The total was 9.7 percent of the $4.5 billion loans outstanding and was higher than the delinquency rate in New York and Los Angeles.

6329 ■ "Travel Rewards Take Off" in *Inc.* (Vol. 33, October 2011, No. 8, pp. 46)
Pub: Inc. Magazine
Ed: Matthew DeLuca. **Description:** Credit card companies are offering travel reward cards with special perks, including sign-up bonuses; three such cards are described.

6330 ■ *The Trillion Dollar Meltdown: Easy Money, High Rollers, and the Great Credit Crash*
Pub: Public Affairs
Ed: Charles R. Morris. **Released:** 2009. **Price:** $22.95. **Description:** Former banker believes that Wall Street and the financial community have too much power in America. He estimates that writedowns and defaults of residential mortgages, commercial mortgages, junk bonds, leveraged loans, credit cards, and complex securitized bonds could reach $1 trillion.

6331 ■ *Ultimate Credit and Collection Handbook*
Pub: Entrepreneur Press
Ed: Michelle Dunn. **Released:** August 2006. **Price:** $36.95. **Description:** Entrepreneurial experts offer advice for successful credit and collection procedures.

6332 ■ "Unfair Distraction of Employees" in *Business Owner* (Vol. 35, March-April 2011, No. 2, pp. 8)
Pub: DL Perkins Company
Description: Fair Credit Collection Practices Act makes it illegal for collectors to contact a debtor at his or her place of employment if the collector is made aware that it is against personnel policy of the employer for the worker to take such a call.

6333 ■ "Unlicensed Utah Collection Agency Settles with Idaho Department of Finance" in *Idaho Business Review, Boise* (July 15, 2010)
Pub: Idaho Business Review
Description: Federal Recovery Acceptance Inc., doing business as Paramount Acceptance in Utah, agreed to pay penalties and expenses after the firm was investigated by the state for improprieties. The firm was charged with conducting unlicensed collection activity.

6334 ■ *The Visa Approval Backlog and Its Impact on American Small Business: Congressional Hearing*
Pub: DIANE Publishing Company
Ed: Donald A. Manzullo. **Released:** July 2006. **Price:** $30.00. **Description:** Information regarding the Congressional hearing involving the Visa approval backlog is discussed.

6335 ■ "Welcome Back" in *Canadian Business* (Vol. 82, April 27, 2009, No. 7, pp. 25)
Pub: Rogers Media
Ed: Sarka Halas. **Description:** Some Canadian companies such as Gennum Corporation have taken advantage of corporate sale-leasebacks to raise money at a time when credit is hard to acquire. Corporate sale-leasebacks allow companies to sell their property assets while remaining as tenants of the building. Sale-leasebacks allow firms to increase capital while avoiding the disruptions that may result with moving.

6336 ■ "What the Future Holds for Consumers" in *Black Enterprise* (Vol. 41, August 2010, No. 1, pp. 47)
Pub: Earl G. Graves Publishing Co. Inc.
Ed: Sheiresa Ngo. **Description:** The way people purchase goods and service has changed with technology. With an increased focus on security (as well as privacy and fairness) the U.S. Congress began regulating the credit card industry with the Fair Credit Reporting Act of 1970 and the Credit Card Accountability, Responsibility, and Disclosure (CARD) Act of 2009.

6337 ■ "When Dov Cries" in *Canadian Business* (Vol. 83, June 15, 2010, No. 10, pp. 71)
Pub: Rogers Media Ltd.
Ed: Joe Castaldo. **Description:** American Apparel disclosed that they will have problems meeting one of its debt covenants which could trigger a chain reaction that could lead to bankruptcy. The prospects look bleak, but eccentric company founder Dov Charney, has always defied expectations.

STATISTICAL SOURCES

6338 ■ *U.S. Credit Bureau and Collections Agencies: An Industry Analysis*
Pub: MarketResearch.com
Released: 2003. **Price:** $1595.00. **Description:** This newly updated bestseller by Marketdata examines the growth businesses of credit reporting services and debt collection agencies.

TRADE PERIODICALS

6339 ■ *Collections & Credit Risk*
Pub: SourceMedia Inc.
Contact: Darren Waggoner, Editor-in-Chief
Released: Monthly. **Price:** $119; $148; $213 two years; $376 two years in Canada. **Description:** Business publication tracking trends in the credit and collections industry.

6340 ■ *Collector*
Pub: ACA International
Contact: Gary D. Rippentrop, CEO
Released: Monthly. **Price:** $35 members; $70 nonmembers; $45 Canada members; $90 Canada nonmembers; $60 other countries members; $120 other countries non-members. **Description:** Magazine on consumer credit and debt collection services.

VIDEOCASSETTES/ AUDIOCASSETTES

6341 ■ *The Secrets of Locating Past-Due Debtors*
Cambridge Educational
c/o Films Media Group
132 West 31st Street, 17th Floor
Ste. 124
New York, NY 10001
Free: 800-257-5126
Fax:(609)671-0266
Co. E-mail: custserve@films.com
URL: http://www.cambridgeol.com
Released: 1986. **Description:** For training debt collectors, how to track down welchers. **Availability:** VHS; 3/4U.

FRANCHISES AND BUSINESS OPPORTUNITIES

6342 ■ National Tenant Network
PO Box 1664
Lake Grove, OR 97035
Ph:(503)635-1238
Free: 800-228-0989
No. of Franchise Units: 25. **No. of Company-Owned Units:** 2. **Founded:** 1980. **Franchised:** 1987. **Description:** Residential and commercial tenant performance reporting. **Equity Capital Needed:** $75,000-$120,000. **Franchise Fee:** $30,000 + $40,000. **Financial Assistance:** Yes. **Training:** Yes.

COMPUTER SYSTEMS/ SOFTWARE

6343 ■ Collection-Master
Commercial Legal Software, Inc.
170 Changebridge Rd., Ste. A4-2
Montville, NJ 07045
Ph:(973)575-5646
Free: 800-435-7257
Fax:(781)207-0219
Co. E-mail: cmaster@collectionsoftware.com
URL: http://www.collectionsoftware.com
Description: Available for IBM computers and compatibles. System provides collection agencies with data management and word processing.

6344 ■ Collection Resource System
CR Software, Inc.
4035 Ridge Top Rd., Ste. 600
Fairfax, VA 22030
Ph:(703)934-9060
Free: 800-222-1722
Fax:(703)293-7510
URL: http://www.crsoftwareinc.com
Description: Contact CR Software.

6345 ■ Comtronic Debtmaster: Software for Debt Collection
Comtronic Systems, Inc.
205 N Harris Ave.
Cle Elum, WA 98922
Ph:(509)573-4300
Fax:(509)674-2383
Co. E-mail: sales@comtronic.com
URL: http://www.comtronic.com
Price: Description: Debt collector software with varied capabilities such as collector work schedules, account assignments, and general ledger accounting.

LIBRARIES

6346 ■ Loan Brokers Association–Information Services
917 S. Park St.
Owosso, MI 48867-4422
Contact: Ben Campbell, Dir.
Scope: Loan brokers, loan consulting, credit repair, lending, credit cards, venture capital. **Services:** Copying; SDI; Library to members or by permission.

6347 ■ RMA Risk Management Association Information Center
1 Liberty Pl.
1801 Market St., Ste. 300
Philadelphia, PA 19103-1628
Ph:(215)446-4000
Free: 800-677-7621
Fax:(215)446-4101
Co. E-mail: rmainfo@rmahq.org
URL: http://www.rmahq.org/RMA/
Contact: Heng You, Info.Spec.
Scope: Banking and finance, lending/credit, industry/analysis. **Services:** Library not open to the public. **Holdings:** 1500 books. **Subscriptions:** 150 journals and other serials.

Damage Restoration Service

ASSOCIATIONS AND OTHER ORGANIZATIONS

6348 ■ National Association of Flood and Storm Water Management Agencies
1333 H St. NW, West Tower, 10th Fl.
Washington, DC 20005
Ph:(202)289-8625
Fax:(202)530-3389
Co. E-mail: info@nafsma.org
URL: http://www.nafsma.org
Contact: Susan Gilson, Exec. Dir.
Description: State, county, and local governments; special districts concerned with management of water resources. Objectives are to reduce or eliminate flooding and provide for improved storm water management and conservation of watersheds. **Publications:** *NAFSMA Bulletin* (periodic); *NAFSMA Newsletter* (monthly); *Survey of Local Storm Water Utilities* .

6349 ■ Natural Hazards Research and Applications Information Center
University of Colorado
483 UCB
Boulder, CO 80309-0482
Ph:(303)492-6818
Fax:(303)492-2151
Co. E-mail: hazctr@colorado.edu
URL: http://www.colorado.edu/hazards
Contact: Kathleen Tierney, Dir.
Description: Advances and communicates knowledge on hazards mitigation and disaster preparedness, response, and recovery. Fosters information sharing and integration of activities among researchers, practitioners, and policy makers from around the world; supports and conducts research; and provides educational opportunities for the next generation of hazards scholars and professionals. **Publications:** *Disaster Research* (biweekly); *Environment and Behavior Monograph Series* (periodic); *Natural Hazards Observer* (bimonthly); *Natural Hazards Working Papers Series* (periodic); *Quick Response Research Reports Series* (periodic); *Special Publications Series* (periodic); *Topical Bibliographies Series* (periodic).

TRADE PERIODICALS

6350 ■ *Cleaning & Restoration*
Pub: Restoration Industry Association
Contact: Tony Greenfield, Sales Mgr
E-mail: ria@rcn.com
Released: Monthly. **Price:** $69 nonmembers; $79 nonmembers Canada; $99 nonmembers international; $49 members; $59 members Canada; $79 members international. **Description:** Journal covering drapery, rug, upholstery, and carpet cleaning; fire and water damage; and disaster restoration and mechanical systems cleaning and inspection.

6351 ■ *Natural Hazards Observer*
Pub: Natural Hazards Research and Applications Information Center
Ed: Christa Rabenold, Editor. **Released:** Bimonthly. **Description:** Discusses methods of mitigating the effects of all natural hazards on humans, especially earthquakes, floods, hurricanes, and some technological hazards. Emphasizes research into land use planning, disaster contingency planning, and reconstruction. Recurring features include reports of relevant legislative and government actions, announcements of research grants awarded, lists of new publications, hazard maps and videos, and schedules of workshops, conferences, and significant programs.

TRADE SHOWS AND CONVENTIONS

6352 ■ Can Clean
Canadian Sanitation Supply Association CSSA
910 Dundas St. West
PO Box 10009
Whitby, ON, Canada L1P 1P7
Ph:(905)430-7267
Free: 800-561-1359
Fax:(905)430-6418
Co. E-mail: cssa@cssa.com
URL: http://www.cssa.com
Released: Annual. **Audience:** Distributors and end-users of sanitary maintenance products. **Principal Exhibits:** Sanitary maintenance products. **Dates and Locations:** 2011 Apr 19-20, Mississauga, ON.

6353 ■ Restoration Industry Association Annual Convention and Exhibition
Restoration Industry Association
9810 Patuxent Woods Dr., Ste. K
Columbia, MD 21046-1595
Ph:(443)878-1000
Free: 800-272-7012
Fax:(443)878-1010
URL: http://www.restorationindustry.org
Released: Annual. **Audience:** Owners and managers of cleaning and restoration firms. **Principal Exhibits:** Carpet, upholstery, and draperies cleaning and restoration equipment, duct cleaning supplies and services.

FRANCHISES AND BUSINESS OPPORTUNITIES

6354 ■ Deck Renewal Systems USA
2369 Promenade Way
Miamisburg, OH 45342
Ph:(937)434-3256
Free: 800-430-4711
Fax:(937)434-2931
No. of Franchise Units: 3. **Founded:** 1993. **Franchised:** 2006. **Description:** Wood restoration. **Equity Capital Needed:** $29,000. **Franchise Fee:** $29,000. **Royalty Fee:** 5%. **Financial Assistance:** No. **Training:** 1 week training at headquarters, 1 week at franchisee's location and ongoing support.

6355 ■ Disaster Kleenup Int'l.
1555 Mittel Blvd., No. 5
Wood Dale, IL 60191
Ph:(630)350-3000
Fax:(630)350-9354
No. of Franchise Units: 185. **Founded:** 1974. **Franchised:** 1994. **Description:** Insurance restoration services. **Equity Capital Needed:** $17,895-$118,250. **Franchise Fee:** $15,750-$40,000. **Royalty Fee:** $575-$1,980/month. **Financial Assistance:** No. **Training:** Offers 1 day and ongoing training, including 2-5 days national & regional conferences & meetings.

6356 ■ Servpro
Servpro Industries, Inc.
801 Industrial Blvd.
Gallatin, TN 37066
Ph:(615)451-0600
Free: 800-826-9586
Fax:(615)451-1602
Co. E-mail: franchise@servpronet.com
URL: http://www.servpro.com
No. of Franchise Units: 1,500+. **Founded:** 1967. **Franchised:** 1969. **Description:** A completely diversified cleaning & restoration business, with multiple income opportunities. The insurance restoration market (fire, smoke and water damage) is their main focus. Specialize in commercial & residential cleaning. **Equity Capital Needed:** $132,050-$180,450. **Franchise Fee:** $41,000. **Financial Assistance:** May offer partial financing in addition to assisting with2third party lenders. **Training:** Intensive home study curriculum, manuals and videos. Provides 2 weeks training in state of the art national training facility, 1 week set up/opening assistance, and trainer assistance. Ongoing support, convention, regional and area meetings, formal business reviews, newsletters, bulletins, and more.

ASSOCIATIONS AND OTHER ORGANIZATIONS

6357 ■ American Ballet Competition
4701 Bath St., No. 46
Philadelphia, PA 19137-2229
Ph:(215)636-9000
Fax:(215)672-2912
Co. E-mail: info@danceaffiliates.org
URL: http://www.dancecelebration.org
Contact: F. Randolph Swartz, Artistic Dir.
Description: Selects and prepares the U.S. team for participation in the annual International Ballet Competition (the "Olympics of Dance"). Works to establish the U.S. as a major force in ballet; to stimulate interest in international competitions and festivals; to encourage young American dancers to strive for world-class excellence; and to build an ongoing program to finance and support further international competitions. Raises funds from private and corporate sources; secures federal grants and sells promotional items. Sponsors trips to observe performing arts in other countries. .

6358 ■ American Dance Guild
240 W 14th St.
New York, NY 10011
Ph:(212)627-9407
Co. E-mail: info@americandanceguild.org
URL: http://www.americandanceguild.org
Contact: Gloria McLean, Pres.
Description: Serves the dance professional by providing: a networking system between dance artists and dance educators; an informed voice on behalf of the dance field to governmental, educational and corporate institutions and the general public; international dance festivals, conferences and dance film festivals; educational publications and videos; the ADG Fannie Weiss Scholarship; the ADG Harkness Resource for Dance Study. **Publications:** *ADG Newsletter* (semiannual); *Souvenir Journal* (annual).

6359 ■ American Dance Therapy Association
10632 Little Patuxent Pkwy., Ste. 108
Columbia, MD 21044
Ph:(410)997-4040
Fax:(410)997-4048
URL: http://www.adta.org
Contact: Sharon Goodill PhD, Pres.
Description: Individuals professionally practicing dance therapy, students interested in becoming dance therapists, university departments with dance therapy programs, and individuals in related therapeutic fields. Establishes and maintains high standards of professional education and competence in dance therapy. Acts as information center; develops guidelines for educational programs and for approval of programs; maintains registry of qualified dance therapists. Maintains Marian Chace Memorial Fund to be used for educational, literary, or scientific projects related to dance in the field of mental health. **Publications:** *Capturing the Essence of Chase: A Teacher's Journey Schmais*; *Conference Proceedings*; *Dance Therapy Bibliography*; *Dance Therapy Notebook*; *Metamorphosis in Movement: Mart Stark Whitehouse - a Video Retrospective*;Membership Directory (annual);Newsletter (quarterly).

6360 ■ American Society for the Alexander Technique
PO Box 2307
Dayton, OH 45401-2307
Ph:(937)586-3732
Free: 800-473-0620
Fax:(937)586-3699
Co. E-mail: info@amsatonline.org
URL: http://www.amsatonline.org
Contact: Nanette Walsh, Chair
Description: Individuals who have completed a three-year training course and have been certified by the society; students currently enrolled in an approved AmSAT teacher training course. Promotes and trains teachers of the Alexander Technique. Created by Australian actor F. M. Alexander (1863-1955), the technique employs reeducation of habitual movement patterns so the body is used efficiently with the least amount of "wear and tear". Seeks to: promote proficiency, knowledge, and skill in the field of psycho-physical reeducation; encourage education and study in the Alexander Technique; approve the establishment and continuation of teacher training courses. Promotes communication and the interchange of skills and information between the society and other organizations of teachers in the Alexander Technique; works to achieve reciprocal memberships between such organizations. Promotes and conducts research. Compiles information regarding teacher members and members of affiliated societies and disseminates this information to the public. Maintains speakers' bureau. **Publications:** *AMSAT News* (quarterly); *List of Certified Training Courses* (annual); *Teaching Members List* (annual).

6361 ■ Cecchetti Council of America
23393 Meadows Ave.
Flat Rock, MI 48134
Ph:(734)379-6710
Fax:(734)379-3886
Co. E-mail: info@cecchetti.org
URL: http://www.cecchetti.org
Contact: Jean Gloria Newell, Pres.
Description: Teachers of ballet and ballet dancers. Aims to raise the quality of ballet teaching and to promote the Cecchetti method of ballet training. (Named for Cavalier Enrico Cecchetti, 1850-1928, Italian ballet dancer and teacher.) Uses the teachings and writings of Cecchetti in a sequence of grades measured to the degree of difficulty and physical development; provides a system of accredited examinations to test the student's proficiency within those grades. Holds exams regularly for teachers and students; conducts refresher courses. Maintains close liaison with Cecchetti Society Branch of the Imperial Society of Teachers of Dancing . **Publications:** *National CCA Newsletter* (semiannual).

6362 ■ Country Dance and Song Society
PO Box 338
Haydenville, MA 01039-0338
Ph:(413)268-7426
Fax:(413)268-7471
Co. E-mail: office@cdss.org
URL: http://www.cdss.org
Contact: Bradley R. Foster, Exec. and Artistic Dir.
Description: Amateur and professional musicians; dance historians and recreational dancers. Promotes modern use of English and Anglo-American folk dances, songs, and music. Holds 11 week-long adult camps per year and 3 week-long family camps. **Publications:** *A Choice Selection of American Country Dances of the Revolutionary Era*; *Country Dance and Song Society—Group Directory* (annual); *Country Dance and Song Society—Newsletter* (bimonthly); *Legacy: 50 Years of Dance and Song*; *The Playford Ball: 103 Early English Country Dances*; *Twenty-four Early American Country Dances: Cotillions and Reels*
.

6363 ■ Cross-Cultural Dance Resources
518 S Agassiz St.
Flagstaff, AZ 86001-5711
Ph:(928)774-8108
Fax:(928)774-8108
Co. E-mail: ccdr-researchcenter@ccdr.org
URL: http://www.ccdr.org
Contact: Pegge Vissicaro, Managing Dir.
Description: Promotes dance performances; preserves and researches dance materials; fosters a dynamic environment for dance events; provides rehearsal space. Offers consultation in areas such as dance theory and methods, ethnomusicology, cultural dynamics, and ethics. Awards internships. Sponsors concerts, visiting artists, and lecture demonstrations. Maintains museum of musical instruments and costumes. Archive includes material of Gertrude Prokosch Kurath, Eleanor King. **Publications:** *Half a Century of Dance Research: Essays by Gertrude Prokosch Kurath*; *Tibet Week in Flagstaff* .

6364 ■ Dance Educators of America
PO Box 8607
Pelham, NY 10803-0607
Ph:(914)636-3200
Free: 800-229-3868
Fax:(914)636-5895
Co. E-mail: dea@deadance.com
URL: http://www.deadance.com
Description: Qualified dance teachers who pass an examination and subscribe to a code of ethics and advertising rules and regulations. Works to further and promote the education of teachers in the performing arts and stage arts and of dance in all its forms. Conducts training schools at New York and Las Vegas. **Publications:** *To Teach Is To Learn Twice* .

6365 ■ Dance Notation Bureau
111 John St., Ste. 704
New York, NY 10038
Ph:(212)571-7011
Fax:(212)571-7012
Co. E-mail: dnbinfo@dancenotation.org
URL: http://www.dancenotation.org
Contact: Lynne Weber, Exec. Dir.
Description: Documents and preserves dance works through the use of graphic notation. Conducts research into movement-related analysis techniques

and programs. Maintains extension at Ohio State University, Columbus. Maintains placement service; assists choreographers in copyrighting, licensing, and restaging of their dance works. Offers service for dance reconstructors and circulating library materials to members. Maintains archive of original Labanotated dance scores in the world. .

6366 ■ International Association for Creative Dance
103 Princeton Ave.
Providence, RI 02907
Ph:(401)521-0546
Co. E-mail: doug.dance@juno.com
URL: http://www.dancecreative.org
Contact: Douglas R. Victor, Co-Founder
Description: Represents individuals with an interest in Mettler-based creative dance. Works to advance the field of creative dance and sponsors opportunities for the study and teaching of creative dance. .

6367 ■ International Council of Kinetography Laban
2801 Northwest Blvd.
Columbus, OH 43221
Co. E-mail: treasurer@ickl.org
URL: http://www.ickl.org
Contact: Richard Allan Ploch, Sec.
Description: Professional dancers, teachers, and others in 20 countries using the Labanotation system for recording dance movements. Supports Kinetography Laban/Labanotation by: guiding the unified development of the system; encouraging consistent standards of practice; acting as the authoritative body with regard to orthography; promoting research into notation matters likely to increase the efficiency and usage of the system. Maintains archive of papers and conference reports. .

6368 ■ International Tap Association
PO Box 150574
Austin, TX 78715
Ph:(303)443-7989
Co. E-mail: info@tapdance.org
URL: http://www.tapdance.org
Contact: Acia Gray, Pres.
Description: Represents the interests of tap dancers, performers, studios, choreographers, teachers, scholars, historians, students, and other tap enthusiasts. Promotes understanding, preservation, and development of tap dance as an art form. Encourages the creation of new tap performance venues and touring circuits. Preserves the history of tap through archival documentation and research. Establishes support mechanisms and communication networks for tap. **Publications:** *On Tap* (5/year).

6369 ■ National Association of Schools of Dance
11250 Roger Bacon Dr., Ste. 21
Reston, VA 20190-5248
Ph:(703)437-0700
Fax:(703)437-6312
Co. E-mail: info@arts-accredit.org
URL: http://nasd.arts-accredit.org
Contact: Samuel Hope, Exec. Dir.
Description: Serves as accrediting agency for educational programs in dance. Provides prospective students with current, accurate information about schools offering instruction in dance. Seeks to establish standards in the field regarding budget, class time requirements, faculty qualifications, faculty-student ratios, and library and physical facilities. Fosters public understanding and acceptance of the educational disciplines inherent in the creative arts in the nation's system of higher education. Encourages high-quality teaching, as well as varied and experimental methods and theories of dance instruction. Provides national representation in matters pertaining to dance and affecting member institutions and their goals. Encourages the collaboration of individuals and professional dance groups in formulating curricula and standards. Offers members general assistance and counseling in program development and encourages self-evaluation and continuing efforts toward improvement. Evaluates dance schools and dance instruction programs through voluntary accreditation processes; assures students and parents that accredited programs offer competent instructors and adequate curricula and facilities. **Publications:** *NASD Handbook* (biennial).

6370 ■ National Ballroom and Entertainment Association
2799 Locust Rd.
Decorah, IA 52101-7600
Ph:(563)382-3871
Co. E-mail: nbea@q.com
URL: http://www.nbea.com
Contact: John Matter, Exec. Dir.
Description: Represents owners and operators of ballrooms; entertainment members are band leaders and others in positions related to live music dancing. .

6371 ■ National Dance Association
1900 Association Dr.
Reston, VA 20191
Ph:(703)476-3400
Free: 800-213-7193
Fax:(703)476-9527
Co. E-mail: nda@aahperd.org
URL: http://www.aahperd.org/nda
Contact: Freddie Thompson-Esters, Pres.-Elect
Description: Dance educators, choreographers, schools and dance/arts administrators, researchers, performers, dance medicine/science specialists, technologists, therapists and others associated with dance/arts education. Works with 160 federal and state agencies, arts and education associations, foundations, and businesses and corporations to ensure that: (1) quality dance/arts education is available to all Americans regardless of age, sex, ability, interest, or culture; and (2) quality dance/arts education becomes a part of U.S. education for all children. **Publications:** *Dance Movement Therapy: A Healing Book*; *The National Standards for Dance Education*; *Seeing While Being Seen: Dance Photography & the Creative Process* .

6372 ■ Royal Academy of Dance
1712 19th St., No. 215 B
Bakersfield, CA 93301-4313
Ph:(661)336-0160
Fax:(661)336-0162
Co. E-mail: info@radusa.org
URL: http://www.radusa.org
Contact: Mrs. Patti Ashby
Description: International examining body working to maintain a high standard of classical ballet training. Provides teachers with an examination syllabus. Conducts teachers' courses and summer schools for children and teachers. .

REFERENCE WORKS

6373 ■ *Dance Magazine College Guide*
Pub: Dance Magazine Inc.
Contact: Karen Hildebrand, VP/Ed.
E-mail: khildebrand@dancemedia.com
Released: Annual, Latest edition 2011. **Price:** $29. 95, individuals plus shipping and handling. **Covers:** Approximately 600 college-level dance programs. **Entries Include:** College name, address, phone, and name of contact for dance department; degrees offered; degree requirements; facilities; special programs; admission requirements; tuition and fees; financial aid available. Also includes articles on issues in dance education. **Arrangement:** Alphabetical, geographical. **Indexes:** College or University name.

6374 ■ *National Guild of Community Schools of the Arts—Membership Directory*
Pub: National Guild of Community Schools of the Arts
Released: Annual, August. **Covers:** Over 320 member schools, including community schools, social service centers, and collegiate divisions with programs in music, dance, drama, visual arts, and creative writing; about 150 individual members, business affiliate members, trustees, and board members; coverage includes Canada. **Entries Include:** For schools—School name, address, phone, fax, e-mail addresses, website addresses, name and title of director, year established, year and status of NGCSA membership, number of branches (affiliate programs), areas of instruction, organizational affiliations, profile of school guild membership, special programs and classes, number of students. For individuals—Name, title, affiliation, address. For business affilates—Name, address, phone, fax, e-mail, website, name and title of main contacts, description of products and services. **Arrangement:** Institutions are geographical; individuals and business affiliates are alphabetical. **Indexes:** Regional chapter; school director; geographical.

6375 ■ "Shop Around" in *Houston Chronicle* (December 7, 2010, pp. 3)
Pub: Houston Chronicle
Ed: Tara Dooley. **Description:** Profile of Diana Candida and Maria Martinez who partnered to open Beatniks, a shop carrying vintage clothing, art from various artists, dance shoes, and jewelry.

6376 ■ "Toes for Business" in *Hispanic Business* (October 2007, pp. 10, 12)
Pub: Hispanic Business
Ed: Gabriel Rodriguez. **Description:** Prima ballerinas, Lorena and Lorna Feijoo, have increased box office sales by at least 30 to 40 percent. A discussion with Pedro Pablo Pena, artistic director of the Miami Hispanic Ballet Corps and founder of the first Choreographic Workshop of Havana is included.

TRADE PERIODICALS

6377 ■ *AAHPERD Update*
Pub: American Alliance for Health, Physical Education, Recreation & Dance
Ed: Getchen O'Brien, Editor. **Released:** 6/year. **Price:** $45, individuals; $48.15, Canada; $53, other countries. **Description:** Provides news and information on the Alliance. Discusses current issues and research in the areas of health, physical education, recreation, dance, fitness, and adapted physical education. Recurring features include a calendar of events, reports of meetings, news of educational opportunities, job listings, notices of publications available, and columns titled President's Message, Membership Corner, and From the EVP's Desk.

6378 ■ *Ballet Review*
Pub: Dance Research Foundation Inc.
Contact: Roberta Hellman, Circulation Mgr
E-mail: info@balletreview.com
Ed: Francis Mason, Editor. **Released:** Quarterly. **Price:** $23; $5.95 single issue; $9 back issues; $42. **Description:** Journal covering all aspects of dance and related arts.

6379 ■ *Country Dance and Song Society Newsletter*
Pub: Country Dance and Song Society
Contact: Caroline Batson, Editor-in-Chief
Released: 6/year. **Price:** Included in membership. **Description:** Promotes the study and enjoyment of traditional Anglo-American and English folk dances, songs, and music. Carries Society news, reports from dance centers across the country, book reviews, and recordings.

6380 ■ *Dance International*
Pub: Vancouver Ballet Society
Contact: Maureen Riches, Managing Editor
E-mail: danceint@direct.ca
Released: Quarterly. **Price:** $41 U.S.; $69 two years within USA; $26 Canada; $66 U.S. library/institution; $46 Canada library/institution; $48 other countries beyond North America; $86 other countries library/institution, beyond North America. **Description:** Magazine covering dance in Canada and worldwide.

6381 ■ *Dance Magazine*
Pub: Dance Magazine Inc.
Released: Monthly. **Price:** $34.95; $64.90 two years; $46.95 Canada; $88.90 Canada 2 years; $66.95 other countries; $128.90 other countries 2 years. **Description:** Performing arts magazine featuring all forms of dance with profiles, news, photos, reviews of performances, and information on books, videos, films, schools, health, and technique.

6382 ■ *Spotlight on Dance*
Pub: National Dance Association
Released: 3/year. **Price:** Included in membership. **Description:** Promotes the development of sound philosophies and policies in all forms of dance and dance education. Reports on dance research, current information on dance education, professional preparation, and certification.

VIDEOCASSETTES/ AUDIOCASSETTES

6383 ■ *Advanced Progressions for Across the Floor*
Stagestep
4701 Bath St., 46B
Philadelphia, PA 19137
Ph:(215)636-9000
Free: 800-523-0960
Fax:(267)672-2912
Co. E-mail: stagestep@stagestep.com
URL: http://stagestep.com
Price: $39.95. **Description:** Cathy Roe demonstrates a number of dance progressions, including time steps, jumps, and kicks. **Availability:** VHS.

6384 ■ *Ballet 101*
Tapeworm Video Distributors
25876 The Old Road 141
Stevenson Ranch, CA 91381
Ph:(661)257-4904
Fax:(661)257-4820
Co. E-mail: sales@tapeworm.com
URL: http://www.tapeworm.com
Released: 1997. **Price:** $19.95. **Description:** Introduces basic ballet warm-up exercises and technique. Based on a University of California major program. **Availability:** VHS.

6385 ■ *Bellydance! Fast Moves*
Tapeworm Video Distributors
25876 The Old Road 141
Stevenson Ranch, CA 91381
Ph:(661)257-4904
Fax:(661)257-4820
Co. E-mail: sales@tapeworm.com
URL: http://www.tapeworm.com
Released: 1996. **Description:** Presents beginner through intermediate movements and combinations designed to increase vitality. **Availability:** VHS.

6386 ■ *Bellydance! Slow Moves*
Tapeworm Video Distributors
25876 The Old Road 141
Stevenson Ranch, CA 91381
Ph:(661)257-4904
Fax:(661)257-4820
Co. E-mail: sales@tapeworm.com
URL: http://www.tapeworm.com
Released: 1996. **Description:** Presents beginner through intermediate movements and combinations designed to tone and reduce stress. **Availability:** VHS.

6387 ■ *Beyond Routine*
Stagestep
4701 Bath St., 46B
Philadelphia, PA 19137
Ph:(215)636-9000
Free: 800-523-0960
Fax:(267)672-2912
Co. E-mail: stagestep@stagestep.com
URL: http://stagestep.com
Price: $49.95. **Description:** Joffrey Ballet dancers deconstruct a theatre dance production number to demonstrate the elements involved. "Happy Feet" from the ballet "A Shoestring Revue" is used as the example. **Availability:** VHS.

6388 ■ *Bob Rizzo's Dance New York: Jazz*
Stagestep
4701 Bath St., 46B
Philadelphia, PA 19137
Ph:(215)636-9000
Free: 800-523-0960
Fax:(267)672-2912
Co. E-mail: stagestep@stagestep.com
URL: http://stagestep.com
Price: $39.95. **Description:** Bob Rizzo teaches three jazz routines for beginner through advanced dancers. **Availability:** VHS.

6389 ■ *Bob Rizzo's Dance New York: Lyrical*
Stagestep
4701 Bath St., 46B
Philadelphia, PA 19137
Ph:(215)636-9000
Free: 800-523-0960
Fax:(267)672-2912
Co. E-mail: stagestep@stagestep.com
URL: http://stagestep.com
Price: $39.95. **Description:** Ray Leeper teaches three lyrical routines for beginner through advanced dancers. **Availability:** VHS.

6390 ■ *Bob Rizzo's Dance New York: Tap*
Stagestep
4701 Bath St., 46B
Philadelphia, PA 19137
Ph:(215)636-9000
Free: 800-523-0960
Fax:(267)672-2912
Co. E-mail: stagestep@stagestep.com
URL: http://stagestep.com
Price: $39.95. **Description:** Alan Onickel teaches three tap routines for beginner through advanced dancers. **Availability:** VHS.

6391 ■ *Creating the Dancer's Body*
Stagestep
4701 Bath St., 46B
Philadelphia, PA 19137
Ph:(215)636-9000
Free: 800-523-0960
Fax:(267)672-2912
Co. E-mail: stagestep@stagestep.com
URL: http://stagestep.com
Price: $39.95. **Description:** Cathy Roe demonstrates exercises for dancers intended to improve muscular strength and endurance. **Availability:** VHS.

6392 ■ *Dances for Drill and Dance Teams*
Stagestep
4701 Bath St., 46B
Philadelphia, PA 19137
Ph:(215)636-9000
Free: 800-523-0960
Fax:(267)672-2912
Co. E-mail: stagestep@stagestep.com
URL: http://stagestep.com
Price: $39.95. **Description:** Presents three routines for drill teams and other large dancing groups. Jazz-funk, precision, and lyrical styles are used. **Availability:** VHS.

6393 ■ *Dancing in Hollywood: A Guide for the Professional Dancer*
Stagestep
4701 Bath St., 46B
Philadelphia, PA 19137
Ph:(215)636-9000
Free: 800-523-0960
Fax:(267)672-2912
Co. E-mail: stagestep@stagestep.com
URL: http://stagestep.com
Price: $34.95. **Description:** Provides tips and techniques for becoming a professional dancer in Hollywood, including how to prepare a resume and get a dance agent. **Availability:** VHS.

6394 ■ *Dynamic Dance: Principles of Choreography*
Stagestep
4701 Bath St., 46B
Philadelphia, PA 19137
Ph:(215)636-9000
Free: 800-523-0960
Fax:(267)672-2912
Co. E-mail: stagestep@stagestep.com
URL: http://stagestep.com
Price: $34.95. **Description:** Provides instruction on how to use the basic principles of choreography to create powerful modern and jazz dance routines. **Availability:** VHS.

6395 ■ *Eight Great Steps to Choreography*
Stagestep
4701 Bath St., 46B
Philadelphia, PA 19137
Ph:(215)636-9000
Free: 800-523-0960
Fax:(267)672-2912
Co. E-mail: stagestep@stagestep.com
URL: http://stagestep.com
Price: $49.95. **Description:** Students from the Joffrey Ballet School demonstrate eight choreographic concepts, including the use of patterns, pace, and orchestration. **Availability:** VHS.

6396 ■ *Flatfooting Workshop*
Stagestep
4701 Bath St., 46B
Philadelphia, PA 19137
Ph:(215)636-9000
Free: 800-523-0960
Fax:(267)672-2912
Co. E-mail: stagestep@stagestep.com
URL: http://stagestep.com
Price: $50.00. **Description:** Presents 27 flatfooting steps, beginning with the basics and moving through to an advanced level. Features Ira Bernstein in three dancing samples. **Availability:** VHS.

6397 ■ *Funk, Funk & More Funk*
Stagestep
4701 Bath St., 46B
Philadelphia, PA 19137
Ph:(215)636-9000
Free: 800-523-0960
Fax:(267)672-2912
Co. E-mail: stagestep@stagestep.com
URL: http://stagestep.com
Price: $39.95. **Description:** Cathy Roe and Lyn Cramer present three high energy dances for beginners, intermediate, and advanced dancers. **Availability:** VHS.

6398 ■ *Irish Dance*
Leslie T. McClure
PO Box 1223
Pebble Beach, CA 93953
Ph:(831)656-0553
Fax:(831)656-0555
Co. E-mail: leslie@411videoinfo.com
URL: http://www.411videoinfo.com
Released: 1997. **Price:** $12.99. **Description:** Two-volume set celebrates authentic Irish dance, culture, and tradition. **Availability:** VHS.

6399 ■ *Jazzin' across the Floor*
Stagestep
4701 Bath St., 46B
Philadelphia, PA 19137
Ph:(215)636-9000
Free: 800-523-0960
Fax:(267)672-2912
Co. E-mail: stagestep@stagestep.com
URL: http://stagestep.com
Price: $39.95. **Description:** Instructor Bob Rizzo provides step-by-step instruction for jazz and lyrical dance. **Availability:** VHS.

6400 ■ *Learn to Dance Overnight*
Cambridge Educational
c/o Films Media Group
132 West 31st Street, 17th Floor
Ste. 124
New York, NY 10001
Free: 800-257-5126
Fax:(609)671-0266
Co. E-mail: custserve@films.com
URL: http://www.cambridgeol.com
Description: Provides instruction for learning the Two-Step, Key Step, the Stroll, and more. **Availability:** VHS.

6401 ■ *Learn to Dance Overnight Vol. 2*
Cambridge Educational
c/o Films Media Group
132 West 31st Street, 17th Floor
Ste. 124
New York, NY 10001
Free: 800-257-5126

Fax:(609)671-0266
Co. E-mail: custserve@films.com
URL: http://www.cambridgeol.com
Description: Provides instruction for learning the Box Step, 3-Step Box, the Break-Away Technique, and more. **Availability:** VHS.

6402 ■ *Leonard Reed's Shim Sham Shimmy*
Stagestep
4701 Bath St., 46B
Philadelphia, PA 19137
Ph:(215)636-9000
Free: 800-523-0960
Fax:(267)672-2912
Co. E-mail: stagestep@stagestep.com
URL: http://stagestep.com
Price: $48.00. **Description:** Tap instructor Rusty Frank teaches the Shim Sham Shimmy, the Freeze Chorus, and the Shim Sham II. **Availability:** VHS.

6403 ■ *Lifts for Your Choreography: From Beginner to Spectacular, Vol. 1*
Stagestep
4701 Bath St., 46B
Philadelphia, PA 19137
Ph:(215)636-9000
Free: 800-523-0960
Fax:(267)672-2912
Co. E-mail: stagestep@stagestep.com
URL: http://stagestep.com
Price: $34.95. **Description:** Presents a variety of easy dance lifts and explains how they are incorporated into routines. **Availability:** VHS.

6404 ■ *Rommett Floor-Barre Technique: A Method to Develop and Refine Ballet Technique*
Stagestep
4701 Bath St., 46B
Philadelphia, PA 19137
Ph:(215)636-9000
Free: 800-523-0960
Fax:(267)672-2912
Co. E-mail: stagestep@stagestep.com
URL: http://stagestep.com
Price: $53.00. **Description:** Zena Rommett combines ballet and anatomical principles to develop a teaching method that helps dancers increase vitality, prevent injury, and more. **Availability:** VHS.

6405 ■ *Suhaila Unveiled*
Tapeworm Video Distributors
25876 The Old Road 141
Stevenson Ranch, CA 91381
Ph:(661)257-4904
Fax:(661)257-4820
Co. E-mail: sales@tapeworm.com
URL: http://www.tapeworm.com
Released: 1996. **Description:** Suhaila Salimpour performs exotic dances. **Availability:** VHS.

6406 ■ *Tap Dancin'*
Stagestep
4701 Bath St., 46B
Philadelphia, PA 19137
Ph:(215)636-9000
Free: 800-523-0960
Fax:(267)672-2912
Co. E-mail: stagestep@stagestep.com
URL: http://stagestep.com
Price: $26.95. **Description:** Judy Ann Bassing demonstrates two tap routines, with each step presented independently. **Availability:** VHS.

6407 ■ *Tappin' across the Floor*
Stagestep
4701 Bath St., 46B
Philadelphia, PA 19137
Ph:(215)636-9000
Free: 800-523-0960
Fax:(267)672-2912
Co. E-mail: stagestep@stagestep.com
URL: http://stagestep.com
Price: $39.95. **Description:** Instructor Jimmy Kichler presents more than 30 tap progressions, suitable for the beginner or the professional. **Availability:** VHS.

6408 ■ *Tappin' Rhythm*
Stagestep
4701 Bath St., 46B
Philadelphia, PA 19137
Ph:(215)636-9000
Free: 800-523-0960
Fax:(267)672-2912
Co. E-mail: stagestep@stagestep.com
URL: http://stagestep.com
Price: $39.95. **Description:** Charles Kelley demonstrates more than 50 tap steps, including the Waltz Clog, Cramproll, and Heel Grind. **Availability:** VHS.

FRANCHISES AND BUSINESS OPPORTUNITIES

6409 ■ Fred Astaire Dance Studios, Inc.
Fred Astaire Dance of N.A. Inc.
10 Bliss Rd.
Longmeadow, MA 01106
Ph:(413)567-3200
Fax:(413)565-2298
No. of Franchise Units: 117. **Founded:** 1947. **Franchised:** 1952. **Description:** Adult ballroom dance instruction. **Equity Capital Needed:** $125,000. **Franchise Fee:** $15,000 and up. **Financial Assistance:** No. **Training:** Yes.

6410 ■ Webby Dance Company
H & R Dance, Inc.
190 Pomona Ave.
Long Beach, CA 90803
Ph:(513)438-4466
Free: 888-243-2623
Fax:(513)438-3466
No. of Franchise Units: 4. **No. of Company-Owned Units:** 2. **Founded:** 1975. **Franchised:** 1999. **Description:** Mobile dance business. **Equity Capital Needed:** $22,700-$31,000. **Franchise Fee:** $15,000. **Financial Assistance:** No. **Training:** Yes.

LIBRARIES

6411 ■ Beverly Hills Public Library Fine Arts Division
444 N. Rexford Dr.
Beverly Hills, CA 90210
Ph:(310)288-2233
Co. E-mail: library@beverlyhills.org
URL: http://www.beverlyhills.org/services/library/
Scope: Art, film, theater, dance, music, photography. **Services:** Interlibrary loan; copying; collection open to the public for reference use only. **Holdings:** 22,000 books/exhibition catalogs; 19,000 slides. **Subscriptions:** 120 journals and other serials.

6412 ■ Dance Films Association, Inc.
48 W. 21st St., No. 907
New York, NY 10010
Ph:(212)727-0764
Fax:(212)727-0764
Co. E-mail: info@dancefilms.org
URL: http://www.dancefilmsassn.org
Contact: Beni Matias, Exec.Dir.
Scope: Dance on film and videotape. **Services:** Public and members may view DVDs and VHS in the Library. **Holdings:** Films/video on dance; articles; journals; programs; videos.

6413 ■ Los Angeles Public Library–Arts, Music and Recreation Department
630 W. 5th St.
Los Angeles, CA 90071
Ph:(213)228-7225
Fax:(213)228-7239
Co. E-mail: art@lapl.org
URL: http://www.lapl.org/central/art.html
Contact: Youngsil Lee, Actg.Dept.Mgr.
Scope: Art, architecture, music, opera, sports and recreation, film, photography, dance, costume, urban planning, gardening, circus. **Services:** Interlibrary loan; copying; department open to the public. **Holdings:** 166,000 volumes; 155,000 clippings; 34,000 scores; 220,000 mounted pictures; 3000 music CDs. **Subscriptions:** 600 journals and other serials.

6414 ■ New York Public Library–The Research Libraries–Jerome Robbins Dance Division (40 Li)
40 Lincoln Center Plaza
New York, NY 10023-7498
Ph:(212)870-1657
Fax:(212)870-1869
Co. E-mail: dance@nypl.org
URL: http://www.nypl.org/locations/lpa/jerome-robbins-dance-division
Contact: Jan Schmidt, Cur.
Scope: All forms of dance. **Services:** Copying; collection open to the public. **Holdings:** 42,000 books; 2200 original drawings and stage designs; manuscripts (1 million items); 1700 reels of microfilm; 38,500 reels of videotape and film; 3270 hours of oral history tapes; 2200 scrapbooks; 25,800 files of clippings and reviews; 325,800 photographs and negatives; 4500 posters; 6000 prints; 100,800 programs. **Subscriptions:** 247 journals and other serials.

6415 ■ St. Norbert Arts Centre Archives
PO Box 175
Winnipeg, MB, Canada R3V 1L6
Ph:(204)269-0564
Fax:(204)261-1927
Co. E-mail: snac@snac.mb.ca
URL: http://www.snac.mb.ca
Contact: Gerry Atwell, Dir.
Scope: Art - visual art, music, theater, and dance. **Services:** Archives open to the public. **Holdings:** Graphic materials; textual records.

6416 ■ Toronto Reference Library–Performing Arts Centre
789 Yonge St., 5th Fl.
Toronto, ON, Canada M4W 2G8
Ph:(416)393-7131
Fax:(416)393-7147
Co. E-mail: mmilne@torontopubliclibrary.ca
URL: http://www.torontopubliclibrary.ca/books-video-music/specialized-collection s/
Contact: Mary Shantz, Mgr.
Scope: Music, dance, film, theatre. **Services:** Library open to the public. **Holdings:** 17,000 LPs; 12,000 CDs; 47,000 music scores; 11,000 photographs; 4000 original stage drawings; prints; engravings; Canadian theatre and concert programs; clippings; archival materials; Canadian sheet music; microfiche; microfilm. **Subscriptions:** 150 journals and other serials.

6417 ■ University of Cincinnati–College Conservatory of Music–Gorno Memorial Music Library (Carl)
Carl Blegen Library
PO Box 210152
Cincinnati, OH 45221-0152
Ph:(513)556-1970
Fax:(513)556-3777
Co. E-mail: mark.palkovic@uc.edu
URL: http://www.libraries.uc.edu/libraries/ccm/index.html
Contact: Mark Palkovic, Hd., CCM Lib.
Scope: Music performance, history, and theory; musicology; dance; theater arts; music education. **Services:** Interlibrary loan; copying; Library open to the public for reference use only. **Holdings:** 38,000 bound volumes; 72,000 scores; 55,000 sound recordings; 6000 microforms. **Subscriptions:** 550 journals and other serials.

6418 ■ University of North Carolina at Greensboro–Special Collections & Rare Books, Jackson Library–Dance Collection (PO Box)
PO Box 26170
Greensboro, NC 27402-6170
Ph:(336)334-5246
Fax:(336)334-5399
Co. E-mail: carolyn_shankle@uncg.edu
URL: http://library.uncg.edu/info/depts/scua
Contact: William K. Finley, Hd., Spec.Coll.
Scope: History of the dance, modern dance, dance notation. **Services:** Collection open to the public for research.

6419 ■ University of North Carolina School of the Arts–Semans Library
UNC School of the Arts
1533 S. Main St.
Winston-Salem, NC 27127
Ph:(336)770-3270
Fax:(336)770-3271
Co. E-mail: rebeccab@uncsa.edu
URL: http://www.uncsa.edu/library
Contact: Rebecca Brown, Hd. of Access Svcs.
Scope: Music, art and design, theater, film, dance, humanities. **Services:** Interlibrary loan; Library open to the public. **Holdings:** 111,000 books; 9000 bound periodical volumes; 50,000 music scores; 45,000 sound recordings; 5200 DVDs and videos. **Subscriptions:** 470 journals and other serials; 25 newspapers.

RESEARCH CENTERS

6420 ■ Congress on Research in Dance
3416 Primm Ln.
Birmingham, AL 35216
Ph:(205)823-5517
Fax:(205)823-2760
Co. E-mail: cord@primemanagement.net
URL: http://www.cordance.org
Contact: Marta Savigliano PhD, Pres.
E-mail: cord@primemanagement.net
Scope: All aspects of dance. **Publications:** Annual conference proceeding; CORD Newsletter (semiannually); Dance Research Journal (semiannually); Membership Directory. **Educational Activities:** National and regional conferences (annually); Workshops.

6421 ■ Laban/Bartenieff Institute of Movement Studies
520 8th Ave., Ste. 304
New York, NY 10018
Ph:(212)643-8888
Fax:(212)643-8388
Co. E-mail: info@limsonline.org
URL: http://www.limsonline.org
Contact: Virginia Reed, Pres.
E-mail: info@limsonline.org
Scope: Perception, description, and analysis of human movement for applications in dance and theater, physical therapy, psychotherapy, nonverbal communication, management consulting, anthropology, and fitness and sports training. The Institute's mission is to further the studies of the principles of movement formulated by Rudolf Laban (1879-1958), an Austro-Hungarian dancer, choreographer, and philosopher, and Irmgard Bartenieff (1900-1981), who applied her Laban training to physical therapy, dance therapy, anthropology, and dance. **Publications:** Journal of Laban Movement Studies; Movement News. **Educational Activities:** Bartenieff Program, experiential approach to somatic movement; Certification Program in Laban Movement Studies.

Delicatessen/Sandwich Shop

START-UP INFORMATION

6422 ■ *Culinary Careers: How to Get Your Dream Job in Food with Advice from Top Culinary Professionals*
Pub: Crown Business Books
Ed: Rick Smilow, Anne E. McBride. **Released:** May 4, 2010. **Price:** $16.99. **Description:** Top culinary experts offer advice for working in or owning a food service firm.

6423 ■ "Franchises with an Eye on Chicago" in *Crain's Chicago Business* (Vol. 34, March 14, 2011, No. 11, pp. 20)
Pub: Crain Communications Inc.
Description: Profiles of franchise companies seeking franchisees for the Chicago area include: Extreme Pita, a sandwich shop; Hand and Stone, offering massage, facial and waxing services; Molly Maid, home-cleaning service; Primrose Schools, private accredited schools for children 6 months to 6 hears and after-school programs; Protect Painters, residential and light-commercial painting contractor; and Wingstop, a restaurant offering chicken wings in nine flavors, fries and side dishes.

6424 ■ *Start and Run a Delicatessen: Small Business Starters Series*
Pub: How To Books
Ed: Deborah Penrith. **Released:** November 9, 2010. **Price:** $30.00. **Description:** Information for starting and running a successful delicatessen is provided. Insight is offered into selecting a location, researching the market, writing a business plan and more.

6425 ■ *Start Small, Finish Big*
Pub: Business Plus/Warner Business Books
Ed: Fred DeLuca with John P. Hayes. **Released:** April 2009. **Price:** $16.95. **Description:** Fred DeLuca is profiled; after founding the multi-billion dollar chain of Subway sandwich restaurants, DeLuca is committed to helping microentrepreneurs, people who start successful small businesses with less than $1,000.

ASSOCIATIONS AND OTHER ORGANIZATIONS

6426 ■ Canadian Restaurant and Foodservices Association–Association Canadienne des Restaurateurs et des Services Alimentaires
316 Bloor St. W
Toronto, ON, Canada M5S 1W5
Ph:(416)923-8416
Free: 800-387-5649
Fax:(416)923-1450
Co. E-mail: info@crfa.ca
URL: http://www.crfa.ca
Contact: Garth Whyte, Pres./CEO
Description: Restaurant and food service corporations, hotels, caterers, and food service suppliers and educators. Seeks to create a favorable business environment for members. Represents members' interests before government; conducts trade research. Makes available group buying programs and other services to members; owns and operates three industry trade shows. **Publications:** *Canadian Foodservice Industry Operations Report* (biennial); *Foodservice Facts* (annual); *Legislation Guide* (quarterly).

6427 ■ International Dairy-Deli-Bakery Association
PO Box 5528
Madison, WI 53705-0528
Ph:(608)310-5000
Fax:(608)238-6330
Co. E-mail: iddba@iddba.org
URL: http://www.iddba.org
Contact: Carol Christison, Exec. Dir.
Description: Companies and organizations engaged in the production, processing, packaging, marketing, promotion, and/or selling of cheese and cheese products, bakery, or delicatessen and delicatessen-related items. Aims to further the relationship between manufacturing, production, marketing and distribution channels utilized in the delivery of deli, dairy, and bakery foods to the marketplace. Develops and disseminates information concerning deli, dairy, and bakery foods. **Publications:** *Dairy-Deli-Bake Digest* (monthly); *IDDBA and You* (monthly); *Trainer's Tool Kit*; *Who's Who in Dairy-Deli-Bakery* (periodic).

6428 ■ National Restaurant Association
1200 17th St. NW
Washington, DC 20036
Ph:(202)331-5900
Free: 800-424-5156
Fax:(202)331-2429
URL: http://www.restaurant.org
Contact: Sally Smith, Chair
Description: Represents restaurants, cafeterias, clubs, contract foodservice management, drive-ins, caterers, institutional food services and other members of the foodservice industry; also represents establishments belonging to non-affiliated state and local restaurant associations in governmental affairs. Supports foodservice education and research in several educational institutions. Is affiliated with the Educational Foundation of the National Restaurant Association to provide training and education for operators, food and equipment manufacturers, distributors and educators. Has 300,000 member locations. **Publications:** *National Restaurant Association—Washington Report* (semimonthly).

REFERENCE WORKS

6429 ■ "Burger Market Sizzling with Newcomers" in *Boston Business Journal* (Vol. 29, June 10, 2011, No. 5, pp. 1)
Pub: American City Business Journals Inc.
Ed: Ryan Sharrow. **Description:** The burger trend in Maryland is on the rise with burger joints either opening up or expanding into several branches. Startup costs for this kind of business range between $250,000 to $400,000. With a growth rate of roughly 17 percent in 2009, this so-called better burger segment of the burger categories is expected to dominate the market for quite some time.

6430 ■ *Eastern Perishable Products Association—Membership Directory*
Pub: Eastern Perishable Products Association Inc.
Contact: Mike Ryan, Exec. Dir.
E-mail: mike@eppainc.org
Released: Continuous. **Price:** Free. **Covers:** About 400 member manufacturers, retailers, brokers, and distributors of perishable products located primarily in the New York metropolitan area (including New Jersey, Pennsylvania and Connecticut). **Entries Include:** Company name, address, phone, name of contact, product or service provided. **Arrangement:** Alphabetical Company name, company type, contact Alpa last name.

TRADE PERIODICALS

6431 ■ *ConcepTrac*
Pub: Technomic Information Services
Ed: Eric Giandelone, Editor, egiandelone@technomic.com. **Released:** Monthly. **Price:** $395, individuals. **Description:** Provides news on chain restaurant development. Includes information on decor, atmosphere, service styles, cooking preparation methods, and unit economics.

VIDEOCASSETTES/ AUDIOCASSETTES

6432 ■ *Be Safe, Not Sorry*
International Dairy-Deli-Bakery Association (IDDBA)
636 Science Dr.
PO Box 5528
Madison, WI 53705-0528
Ph:(608)310-5000
Fax:(608)238-6330
Co. E-mail: iddba@iddba.org
URL: http://www.iddba.org
Price: $160.00. **Description:** Deli food safety training course. **Availability:** VHS.

6433 ■ *Center on Profit*
International Dairy-Deli-Bakery Association (IDDBA)
636 Science Dr.
PO Box 5528
Madison, WI 53705-0528
Ph:(608)310-5000
Fax:(608)238-6330
Co. E-mail: iddba@iddba.org
URL: http://www.iddba.org
Price: $160.00. **Description:** Teaches managers how to reduce unknown shrink, write effective orders and schedules, plus calculate deli items' profit and gross margin contribution to margin. **Availability:** VHS.

6434 ■ *A Classic Guide to Custom Deli Trays*
International Dairy-Deli-Bakery Association (IDDBA)
636 Science Dr.
PO Box 5528
Madison, WI 53705-0528
Ph:(608)310-5000

Fax:(608)238-6330
Co. E-mail: iddba@iddba.org
URL: http://www.iddba.org
Price: $100.00. **Description:** Merchandising and training video. **Availability:** VHS.

6435 ■ *Clean, Fresh & Friendly*
International Dairy-Deli-Bakery Association (IDDBA)
636 Science Dr.
PO Box 5528
Madison, WI 53705-0528
Ph:(608)310-5000
Fax:(608)238-6330
Co. E-mail: iddba@iddba.org
URL: http://www.iddba.org
Price: $160.00. **Description:** Deli customer service training video. **Availability:** VHS.

6436 ■ *Deli Meats 101*
International Dairy-Deli-Bakery Association (IDDBA)
636 Science Dr.
PO Box 5528
Madison, WI 53705-0528
Ph:(608)310-5000
Fax:(608)238-6330
Co. E-mail: iddba@iddba.org
URL: http://www.iddba.org
Price: $50.00. **Description:** Discusses why deli sliced meats are a high turn product; different kinds of deli ham, turkey and beef products; and information to speak knowledgeably about them. **Availability:** VHS.

6437 ■ *Deli Meats & Poultry: Classic Tastes for Today's Consumer*
International Dairy-Deli-Bakery Association (IDDBA)
636 Science Dr.
PO Box 5528
Madison, WI 53705-0528
Ph:(608)310-5000
Fax:(608)238-6330
Co. E-mail: iddba@iddba.org
URL: http://www.iddba.org
Price: $100.00. **Description:** Merchandising and training video. **Availability:** VHS.

6438 ■ *Know What You're Selling*
International Dairy-Deli-Bakery Association (IDDBA)
636 Science Dr.
PO Box 5528
Madison, WI 53705-0528
Ph:(608)310-5000
Fax:(608)238-6330
Co. E-mail: iddba@iddba.org
URL: http://www.iddba.org
Price: $160.00. **Description:** Deli product knowledge training video. **Availability:** VHS.

6439 ■ *Successful Food Demonstration & Sampling*
International Dairy-Deli-Bakery Association (IDDBA)
636 Science Dr.
PO Box 5528
Madison, WI 53705-0528
Ph:(608)310-5000
Fax:(608)238-6330
Co. E-mail: iddba@iddba.org
URL: http://www.iddba.org
Price: $100.00. **Description:** Presents ways supermarket dairy, deli, bakery and food-service employees can sell more through food demonstrations and sampling. **Availability:** VHS.

TRADE SHOWS AND CONVENTIONS

6440 ■ Dairy-Deli-Bake Seminar and Expo
International Dairy-Deli-Bakery Association
PO Box 5528
Madison, WI 53705-0528
Ph:(608)310-5000
Fax:(608)238-6330
Co. E-mail: iddba@iddba.org
URL: http://www.iddba.org
Released: Annual. **Audience:** Retailers, wholesalers, distributors, brokers, and manufacturers of the dairy, deli, and bakery industry. **Principal Exhibits:** Dairy, deli, and bakery products, packaging, and equipment. **Dates and Locations:** 2011 Jun 05-07, Anaheim, CA.

6441 ■ International Restaurant & Foodservice Show of New York
Reed Exhibitions North American Headquarters
383 Main Ave.
Norwalk, CT 06851
Ph:(203)840-4800
Fax:(203)840-5805
Co. E-mail: export@reedexpo.com
URL: http://www.reedexpo.com
Released: Annual. **Principal Exhibits:** Equipment, supplies, and services for the food products, foodservice, restaurant, and institutional food service industries.

CONSULTANTS

6442 ■ Erin Services Inc.
111 Travelers Way
PO Box 1048
Saint Simons Island, GA 31522-5632
Ph:(912)638-9916
Free: 800-862-5361
Fax:(912)638-5701
Co. E-mail: dennisd@ns.technonet.com
Contact: Dennis J. Donnelly III, President
E-mail: dennis179@yahoo.com
Scope: Offers assistance in technical proposal production, marketing, and research. Industries served: Food service, janitorial, landscaping, hospitality and lodging, parks, and recreational.

6443 ■ Market Discoveries Inc.
82-50 217th St.
Queens Village, NY 11427
Ph:(718)464-0690
Fax:(718)468-6089
Contact: Arlene Spiegel, President
Scope: Provides operational, management and marketing services for all aspects of food service and food retail business facilities. Also offers expertise in strategic planning, business and development. Industries served: restaurants, hotels, specialty food, supermarkets, franchise, fast food, entertainment and contract management companies. **Seminars:** How to Develop a Healthy Deli; Supermarkets - The New Competition; How to Upscale in a Downscale Market; How to Identify Profit Opportunities in90s; How to Develop an Effective Sales Force; How to Get Free Publicity; What Makes You So Special; Taste of Tuscany Food Program; Full Service Nutrition Analysis.

6444 ■ Riedel Marketing Group
5327 E Pinchot Ave.
Phoenix, AZ 85018-2963
Ph:(602)840-4948
Fax:(602)840-4928
Co. E-mail: ajr@4rmg.com
URL: http://www.4rmg.com
Contact: A. J. Riedel, Senior Partner
E-mail: ajr@4rmg.com
Scope: The house wares and food service industry strategic marketing planning experts. Help manufacturers of house wares and food products solve marketing problems and identify and exploit marketing opportunities. Provides a full-range of strategic marketing planning services including development of marketing strategy, development of fact-based sales presentations, category management, definition of market opportunities and new product development exclusively to the house wares and food service industries. **Publications:** "Your Key Consumer: Her Take on the International Home & Housewares Show," Mar, 2008; "What's Hot, What's Not: The Consumer Speaks," Mar, 2006; "HIPsters SPEAK: What We Love to Buy and Why," Apr, 2005; "Influentials: Who They Are and Why You Should Care," Jun, 2004; "The Seven Secrets to Selling More Housewares," Jan, 2003. **Seminars:** Consumers Speak: What We Love to Buy and Why, What Do Those Consumers Think; The Seven Secrets to Selling More House wares. **Special Services:** Home Trend Influentials Panel.

FRANCHISES AND BUSINESS OPPORTUNITIES

6445 ■ Atlantic City Sub Shops Inc.
124 Warf Rd.
Egg Harbor Twp., NJ 08234
Ph:(609)926-4560
Fax:(609)641-2121
No. of Franchise Units: 1. **No. of Company-Owned Units:** 2. **Founded:** 1968. **Franchised:** 1990. **Description:** Sandwich shop. **Equity Capital Needed:** $100,000-$275,000. **Franchise Fee:** $15,000. **Royalty Fee:** 5%. **Financial Assistance:** No. **Training:** Yes.

6446 ■ Baker Bros. American Deli
BB Franchising, Inc.
5500 Greenville Ave., Ste. 1102
Dallas, TX 75206
Ph:(214)696-8780
Fax:(214)696-8809
No. of Franchise Units: 8. **No. of Company-Owned Units:** 8. **Founded:** 1998. **Franchised:** 2000. **Description:** Sandwich shop. **Equity Capital Needed:** $1,500,000 net worth; $750,000 liquid assets. **Franchise Fee:** $25,000. **Financial Assistance:** No. **Training:** Yes.

6447 ■ Big Town Hero
Hero Systems, Inc.
333 SW Taylor St., Ste. 200
Portland, OR 97204
Ph:(503)228-4376
Fax:(503)228-8778
No. of Franchise Units: 45. **Founded:** 1983. **Franchised:** 1989. **Description:** Sandwiches, salads, soups, fresh bread and baked goods from scratch. Fast and friendly. **Equity Capital Needed:** $50,000-$150,000. **Franchise Fee:** $20,000. **Financial Assistance:** No. **Training:** Yes.

6448 ■ Blendz Franchise System, Inc.
267 E Campbell Ave., Ste., 200
Campbell, CA 95008
Free: (866)4BL-ENDZ
Fax:(408)273-6766
No. of Franchise Units: 11. **Founded:** 2002. **Franchised:** 2005. **Description:** Tossed-to-order salads, panini, smoothies and soups. **Equity Capital Needed:** $277,100-$350,400. **Franchise Fee:** $25,000. **Financial Assistance:** Limited third party financing available. **Training:** Yes.

6449 ■ Camille's Sidewalk Cafe
Camille's Franchise System, LLC
8801 S Yale Ave., Ste. 400
Tulsa, OK 74137-3575
Ph:(918)488-9727
Free: 800-230-7004
Fax:(918)497-1916
No. of Franchise Units: 21. **No. of Company-Owned Units:** 1. **Founded:** 1996. **Franchised:** 1999. **Description:** Sidewalk cafe serving wraps and sandwiches. **Equity Capital Needed:** $214,000-$280,000. **Franchise Fee:** $25,000. **Financial Assistance:** Yes. **Training:** Yes.

6450 ■ Capt. Sub
Grinner Food Systems
105 Walker St.
Truro, NS, Canada B2N 5G9
Ph:(902)820-3108
Fax:(902)820-3109
Co. E-mail: d.crane@grinners.ca
URL: http://www.captsub.ca
No. of Franchise Units: 30. **No. of Company-Owned Units:** 2. **Founded:** 1972. **Franchised:** 1972. **Description:** The franchise specializes in delicious oven roasted submarine sandwiches. **Equity Capital Needed:** $120,000-$160,000. **Franchise Fee:** $20,000. **Training:** Offers management and staff on start-up.

6451 ■ Cheba Hut Roasted Subs
600 S Sherwood St.
Fort Collins, CO 80521
Ph:(970)420-7082
No. of Franchise Units: 14. **Founded:** 1998. **Franchised:** 2002. **Description:** Toasted sandwiches & salads. **Equity Capital Needed:** $149,500-$299,500. **Franchise Fee:** $25,000. **Royalty Fee:** 4%. **Financial Assistance:** Limited third party financing available. **Training:** provides 14 days at headquarters, 7 days onsite and ongoing support.

6452 ■ Chedd's Gourmet Grilled Cheese
1906 Pearl St.
Denver, CO 80203
Ph:(303)948-1520
Fax:(303)948-8801
No. of Company-Owned Units: 2. **Founded:** 2003. **Franchised:** 2007. **Description:** Gourmet grilled cheese sandwiches. **Equity Capital Needed:** $126,500-$323,500. **Franchise Fee:** $35,000. **Royalty Fee:** 6%. **Financial Assistance:** No. **Training:** Provides 2-3 weeks training at headquarters, 1 week at franchisee's location and ongoing support.

6453 ■ Coffee Time Donuts Inc.
77 Progress Ave.
Toronto, ON, Canada M1P 2Y7
Ph:(416)288-8515
Fax:(416)288-8895
Co. E-mail: franchising@coffeetime.ca
URL: http://www.coffeetime.ca
No. of Franchise Units: 184. **No. of Company-Owned Units:** 18. **Founded:** 1982. **Franchised:** 1989. **Description:** The menu includes donuts, muffins, croissants, pastries and gourmet blend coffee, soups, chili, salads, sandwiches and various hot and cold beverages. store, serving customers in a warm and efficient manner and fostering good employee relationships. **Equity Capital Needed:** $100,000-$360,000. **Financial Assistance:** No. **Training:** Yes.

6454 ■ Coney Beach
8801 S Yale, Ste. 400
Tulsa, OK 74137
Ph:(918)488-9727
Fax:(918)497-1916
No. of Franchise Units: 4. **No. of Company-Owned Units:** 1. **Founded:** 2006. **Franchised:** 2007. **Description:** Hot dogs, hamburgers & fries. **Equity Capital Needed:** $240,500-$493,000. **Franchise Fee:** $25,000. **Royalty Fee:** 6%. **Financial Assistance:** Limited third party financing available.

6455 ■ Cousins Subs
Cousins Subs Systems, Inc.
N83 W13400 Leon Rd.
Menomonee Falls, WI 53051
Ph:(262)253-7700
Free: 800-238-9736
Fax:(262)253-7710
Co. E-mail: betterfranchise@counsinssubs.com
URL: http://www.cousinssubs.com
No. of Franchise Units: 145. **No. of Company-Owned Units:** 16. **Founded:** 1972. **Franchised:** 1985. **Description:** Submarine sandwich operation, with over 20 years of expertise. Volume-oriented, fast-service concept in an upscale, in-line, strip or free-standing location, some with drive-up windows. Franchising opportunities available for single, multi-unit and area developer franchisees, seminars and training classes. A corporate area representative meets with each franchise location management 3 times per month to maintain communications and assist in problem solving. **Equity Capital Needed:** $80,000 cash, $106,700-$288,300 total investment. **Franchise Fee:** $17,500 ltd. time. **Financial Assistance:** No. **Training:** Includes a store building seminar for site selection, lease negotiation and construction 30 days of hands-on training, plus 10 days of opening assistance and training. National and local store marketing support.

6456 ■ Doc Green's Gourmet Salads
782 Ponce de Leon Ave.
Atlanta, GA 30306
Ph:(404)844-3225
Fax:(404)446-1755
No. of Franchise Units: 12. **No. of Company-Owned Units:** 1. **Founded:** 2003. **Franchised:** 2004. **Description:** Salads, flatbread sandwiches & bistro fare. **Equity Capital Needed:** $367,000-$655,000. **Franchise Fee:** $25,000. **Royalty Fee:** 5%. **Financial Assistance:** Third party financing available. **Training:** Offers 2 1/2 weeks training at headquarters, 1 week at franchisee's location and ongoing support.

6457 ■ Earl of Sandwich (USA) LLC
6052 Turkey Lake Rd.
Orlando, FL 32819
Ph:(407)992-2989
Fax:(407)992-2987
No. of Franchise Units: 6. **No. of Company-Owned Units:** 2. **Founded:** 2003. **Franchised:** 2005. **Description:** Sandwiches, wraps, salads, and desserts. **Equity Capital Needed:** $375,000-$400,000. **Franchise Fee:** $25,000. **Royalty Fee:** 6%. **Financial Assistance:** Third party financing available.

6458 ■ East Coast Subs
RCLC Enterprises, Inc.
949 E Pioneer Rd., St. 2B
Draper, UT 84020
Ph:(801)352-1400
Fax:(801)619-4038
No. of Franchise Units: 2. **No. of Company-Owned Units:** 2. **Founded:** 1991. **Franchised:** 2005. **Description:** Sandwiches and Philly subs. **Equity Capital Needed:** $90,500-$113,500. **Franchise Fee:** $12,500. **Financial Assistance:** No. **Training:** Yes.

6459 ■ Erbert & Gerbert's Subs & Clubs
Erbert & Gerbert's & Friends
205 E Grand Ave.
Eau Claire, WI 54701
Ph:(715)833-1375
Free: 800-283-5241
Fax:(715)833-8523
No. of Franchise Units: 47. **No. of Company-Owned Units:** 1. **Founded:** 1988. **Franchised:** 1992. **Description:** Offers top-quality, gourmet submarine and club sandwiches on bread baked fresh onsite. A delivery service complements eat-in and carry-out services. **Equity Capital Needed:** Net worth of $250,000, $50,000 liquid. **Franchise Fee:** $25,000. **Financial Assistance:** No. **Training:** 3 week training with control and quality standards covered in the first weekly section. The second week involves administrative and management training required for cost control, payroll, financial management, etc. This is followed by 1 week of training at the time of start-up in the franchisees store.

6460 ■ Frankitude
21 NW Miami Ct.
Miami, FL 33128
Ph:(305)371-9875
Free: 877-275-8778
No. of Franchise Units: 1. **No. of Company-Owned Units:** 1. **Founded:** 2006. **Franchised:** 2006. **Description:** Hot dogs, salads, panini, and wraps. **Equity Capital Needed:** $170,200-$325,000 (Express/kiosk option available). **Franchise Fee:** $25,000. **Royalty Fee:** 6%. **Financial Assistance:** No. **Training:** Offers 2+ weeks training at headquarters, 1+ weeks onsite and ongoing support.

6461 ■ Frullati Cafe & Bakery
Kahala Corp.
9311 E Via De Ventura
Scottsdale, AZ 85258
Ph:(480)362-4800
Free: 800-438-2590
No. of Franchise Units: 32. **Founded:** 1994. **Franchised:** 1994. **Description:** Deli sandwiches, smoothies, salads, soups, etc. **Equity Capital Needed:** $150,900-$511,300. **Franchise Fee:** $30,000. **Royalty Fee:** 6%. **Financial Assistance:** Limited third party financing available. **Training:** Provides 1 week at headquarters, 2 weeks at franchise's location and ongoing support.

6462 ■ Groucho's Deli
611 Harden St.
Columbia, SC 29205
Ph:(803)799-9867
Fax:(803)799-2297
No. of Franchise Units: 23. **No. of Company-Owned Units:** 1. **Founded:** 1941. **Franchised:** 2001. **Description:** Subs & salads. **Equity Capital Needed:** $72,700-$310,030. **Franchise Fee:** $10,000-$20,000. **Royalty Fee:** 5.25%. **Financial Assistance:** Third party financing available. **Training:** Available at headquarters: 134-166 hours. Available at franchisee's location and ongoing support.

6463 ■ Jersey Mike's Subs
Jersey Mike's Franchise Systems, Inc.
2251 Landmark Pl.
Manasquan, NJ 08736
Ph:(732)223-4044
Free: 800-321-7676
Fax:(732)292-8256
Co. E-mail: sales@jerseymikes.com
URL: http://www.jerseymikes.com
No. of Franchise Units: 500. **No. of Company-Owned Units:** 22. **Founded:** 1956. **Franchised:** 1987. **Description:** Restaurants that serve sandwiches and related items. **Equity Capital Needed:** $100,000 start-up cost; $150,082$519,970 total investment. **Franchise Fee:** $18,500. **Financial Assistance:** No. **Training:** Offers 9 week training program with ongoing support.

6464 ■ Jimmy John's Gourmet Sandwiches
2212 Fox Dr.
Champaign, IL 61820
Free: 800-546-6904
Fax:(217)359-2956
URL: http://www.jimmyjohns.com
No. of Franchise Units: 1,208. **No. of Company-Owned Units:** 26. **Founded:** 1983. **Franchised:** 1993. **Description:** Gourmet sandwich shops, which make, sell and deliver an up-scale signature line of French bread subs and wheat club sandwiches. Stores require small investment and can be located in strip centers, downtown store frontages and food courts in malls. management. **Equity Capital Needed:** $300,000 net worth; $80,000 liquid assets. **Franchise Fee:** $35,000. **Financial Assistance:** No. **Training:** Provides 3 week training course in Champaign, IL.

6465 ■ Larry's Giant Subs
4479 Deerwood Lake Pky., Ste. 1
Jacksonville, FL 32216
Ph:(904)739-9069
Free: 800-358—687
Fax:(904)739-1218
Co. E-mail: Bigone@larryssubs.com
URL: http://www.larryssubs.com
No. of Franchise Units: 70. **No. of Company-Owned Units:** 6. **Founded:** 1982. **Franchised:** 1986. **Description:** An up-scale, New York-style submarine sandwich shop, featuring 50 varieties of subs and numerous salads. Features easy operation, no experience necessary, non-cooking environment and low royalty. Full training in corporate shop. Additional training at your franchise location. **Equity Capital Needed:** $159,000-$225,000. **Franchise Fee:** $20,000. **Royalty Fee:** 6%. **Financial Assistance:** Third party financing available. **Training:** Provides 3 weeks at corporate headquarters, 1-2 weeks onsite with ongoing support.

6466 ■ Lenny's Sub Shop
Lenny's Franchisor, LLC
8295 Tournament Dr., Ste. 200
Memphis, TN 38125
Ph:(901)753-4002
Fax:(901)753-4395
No. of Franchise Units: 175. **No. of Company-Owned Units:** 2. **Founded:** 1998. **Franchised:** 2001. **Description:** Subs & philly cheesesteak sandwiches. **Equity Capital Needed:** $210,000-$348,500. **Franchise Fee:** $15,000-$25,000. **Financial Assistance:** Yes. **Training:** Yes.

6467 ■ Little King
Little King, Inc.
11811 "I" St.
Omaha, NE 68137
Ph:(402)330-8019
Free: 800-788-9978
Fax:(402)330-3221
No. of Franchise Units: 15. **Founded:** 1968. **Franchised:** 1978. **Description:** Subs and deli-style sandwiches. **Equity Capital Needed:** $145,000-$200,000 start-up & minimum net worth of $250,000. **Franchise Fee:** $19,000. **Financial Assistance:** Yes. **Training:** Offers 15 days in Omaha and 7-10 days when opening.

6468 ■ Maid-Rite Sandwich Shoppes
Maid-Rite Corp.
2951 86th St.
Des Moines, IA 50322
Ph:(515)276-5448
Fax:(515)276-5449
No. of Franchise Units: 77. **No. of Company-Owned Units:** 3. **Founded:** 1926. **Franchised:** 1926. **Description:** Fast casual dining franchise. **Equity Capital Needed:** $100,000 liquid; $500,000 net worth. **Franchise Fee:** $35,000. **Financial Assistance:** No. **Training:** Yes. Yes. .

6469 ■ McAlister's Deli
McAlister's Corp.
731 S Pear Orchard, Ste. 51
Ridgeland, MS 39157
Ph:(601)519-8985
Free: 888-855-3354
Fax:(601)957-0964
No. of Franchise Units: 253. **No. of Company-Owned Units:** 34. **Founded:** 1989. **Franchised:** 1994. **Description:** Southern style deli. **Equity Capital Needed:** $600,000-$700,000. **Franchise Fee:** $35,000. **Financial Assistance:** No. **Training:** Yes.

6470 ■ Miami Subs Grill
Miami Subs Capital Partners 1
6300 NW 31st Ave.
Ft. Lauderdale, FL 33309
Ph:(954)973-0000
Fax:(954)973-7616
No. of Franchise Units: 40. **Founded:** 1983. **Franchised:** 1986. **Description:** Quick service, made to order menu. **Equity Capital Needed:** $75,000-$550,000. **Franchise Fee:** $20,000-$30,000. **Financial Assistance:** No. **Training:** Yes.

6471 ■ Mikes Restaurants Inc.
8250 Decarie Blvd., Ste. 310
Montreal, QC, Canada H4P 2P5
Ph:(514)341-5544
Free: (866)341-9782
Fax:(514)341-5635
Co. E-mail: iroy@mikesrestaurants.com
URL: http://www.mikes.com
No. of Franchise Units: 87. **Founded:** 1967. **Franchised:** 1968. **Description:** Restaurant serving delicious Italian pizza, sandwiches and pasta. **Equity Capital Needed:** $300,000-$700,000. **Franchise Fee:** $45,000, includes training. **Training:** Provides 10 weeks training.

6472 ■ Mr. Goodcents Franchise Systems Inc.
8997 Commerce Dr.
De Soto, KS 66018
Ph:(913)583-8400
Free: 800-648-2368
Fax:(913)583-3500
No. of Franchise Units: 92. **No. of Company-Owned Units:** 3. **Founded:** 1988. **Franchised:** 1990. **Description:** Quick service submarine sandwiches and pasta. **Equity Capital Needed:** $161,650-$274,300. **Franchise Fee:** $10,000-$20,000. **Royalty Fee:** 5%. **Financial Assistance:** Third party financing available. **Training:** Offers 5 days training at headquarters, 20 days at franchisee's location and ongoing support.

6473 ■ Mr. Goodcents Subs & Pastas
Mr. Goodcents Franchise Systems, Inc.
8997 Commerce Dr.
DeSoto, KS 66018
Ph:(913)583-8400
Free: 800-648-2368
Fax:(913)583-3500
Co. E-mail: frandev@mrgoodcents.com
URL: http://www.mrgoodcents.com
No. of Franchise Units: 100. **No. of Company-Owned Units:** 1. **Founded:** 1989. **Franchised:** 1990. **Description:** Quick service restaurant serving lunch and dinner featuring submarine sandwiches with fresh meat and cheese on bread. **Equity Capital Needed:** $75,000. **Franchise Fee:** $20,000. **Financial Assistance:** No. **Training:** 30 days of comprehensive in-house training.

6474 ■ Mr. Pickle's Sandwich Shop
670 Auburn-Folsom Rd., Ste. 106-571
Auburn, CA 95603
Ph:(916)746-7727
Fax:(916)746-7787
No. of Franchise Units: 24. **Founded:** 1996. **Franchised:** 2006. **Description:** Sandwiches, soups, and salads. **Equity Capital Needed:** $249,000 (Express/kiosk option available). **Franchise Fee:** $25,000. **Royalty Fee:** None. **Financial Assistance:** No. **Training:** 2 weeks training included at franchisee's location and ongoing support.

6475 ■ Mr. Pita
Papa Romano's Enterprises, Inc.
24901 Northwestern Hwy., Ste. 444
Southfield, MI 48075
Ph:(248)888-7242
Free: (866)738-7482
Fax:(248)888-0011
No. of Franchise Units: 29. **Founded:** 1993. **Franchised:** 1994. **Description:** Deli serving pita sandwiches, soups, and salads. **Equity Capital Needed:** $80,000 liquid; $250,000. **Franchise Fee:** $25,000. **Financial Assistance:** Yes. **Training:** Yes.

6476 ■ Must Be Heaven Franchise Corp.
107 W Alamo
Brenham, TX 77833
Ph:(979)830-8536
Fax:(979)836-9913
Co. E-mail: franchise@mustbeheaven.com
URL: http://www.mustbeheaven.com
No. of Franchise Units: 10. **Founded:** 1987. **Franchised:** 1999. **Description:** Soup, sandwiches, salads, pies and ice cream. **Equity Capital Needed:** $75,000-$100,000. **Franchise Fee:** $30,000. **Financial Assistance:** No. **Training:** Yes.

6477 ■ Mustard Cafe
41 Auto Center Drive, Ste. 103
Foothill Ranch, CA 92610
Ph:(949)716-1000
No. of Franchise Units: 5. **No. of Company-Owned Units:** 1. **Founded:** 2002. **Franchised:** 2004. **Description:** Sandwiches, soups, and salads. **Equity Capital Needed:** $338,000-$536,500. **Franchise Fee:** $25,000. **Royalty Fee:** 5%. **Financial Assistance:** Limited third party financing available. **Training:** Offers 2 weeks training at headquarters, 4 weeks at franchisee's location and ongoing support.

6478 ■ The Original SoupMan
1110 South Ave., Ste. 300
Staten Island, NY 10314
Free: 877-768-7626
No. of Franchise Units: 16. **No. of Company-Owned Units:** 2. **Founded:** 1984. **Franchised:** 2005. **Description:** Soups. **Equity Capital Needed:** $79,500-$198,500. **Franchise Fee:** $30,000. **Royalty Fee:** 5%. **Financial Assistance:** No.

6479 ■ Penn Station East Coast Subs
Penn Station, Inc.
1226 US Hwy. 50
Milford, OH 45150
Ph:(513)474-5957
Fax:(513)474-7116
No. of Franchise Units: 183. **No. of Company-Owned Units:** 2. **Founded:** 1985. **Franchised:** 1987. **Description:** Retail sale of various cheesecake and submarine sandwiches, fresh-cut fries and fresh-squeezed lemonade. **Equity Capital Needed:** $100,000 liquidity. **Franchise Fee:** $25,000. **Financial Assistance:** No. **Training:** Yes.

6480 ■ Perfecto's Caffe
Perfecto's Caffe Development LLC
79 N Main St.
Andover, MA 01810
Ph:(978)749-7022
Fax:(978)749-9433
No. of Franchise Units: 2. **No. of Company-Owned Units:** 2. **Founded:** 1993. **Franchised:** 2005. **Description:** Bagels, muffins, coffee, wraps, salads, and cookies. **Equity Capital Needed:** $175,000-$275,000, initial investment. **Franchise Fee:** $20,000. **Financial Assistance:** No. **Training:** Yes.

6481 ■ Port of Subs
Port of Subs, Inc.
5365 Mae Anne Ave., No. A-29
Reno, NV 89523
Ph:(775)747-0555
Free: 800-245-0245
Fax:(775)747-1510
No. of Franchise Units: 115. **No. of Company-Owned Units:** 25. **Founded:** 1972. **Franchised:** 1985. **Description:** Submarine sandwich franchise, featuring unique front-line method of preparing specialty sandwiches, soups, salads and party platters. Bread is baked fresh daily on premises. **Equity Capital Needed:** $80,000 liquid assets, $250,000 net worth. **Franchise Fee:** $20,000. **Financial Assistance:** No. **Managerial Assistance:** operations assistance. **Training:** Offers 2+ weeks of training, plus 2 weeks in the franchisees unit during initial opening.

6482 ■ Quizno's Subs
The Quizno's Corp.
1001 17th St., Ste. 175
Denver, CO 80202-2212
Ph:(720)359-3300
Free: 800-335-4782
No. of Franchise Units: 2,772. **No. of Company-Owned Units:** 62. **Founded:** 1981. **Franchised:** 1983. **Description:** Italian deli theme, specializing in subs, soups, salads and pasta. **Equity Capital Needed:** $157,547-$217,527, estimated initial investment for new store. **Franchise Fee:** $5,000-$12,500. **Financial Assistance:** Assistance with third party financing. **Training:** Twenty two day training program includes classroom and in-store training. Grand opening and initial onsite assistance.

6483 ■ Schlotzsky's
Focus Brands Inc.
Franchise Licensing Dept.
200 Glenridge Point Pky., Ste. 200
Atlanta, GA 30342
Ph:(404)255-3250
Free: 800-846-2867
Fax:800-335-4329
No. of Franchise Units: 353. **No. of Company-Owned Units:** 38. **Founded:** 1971. **Franchised:** 1976. **Description:** Fast, casual restaurant. **Equity Capital Needed:** $600,000 liquidity; $1,500,000 net worth (3 store minimum required). **Franchise Fee:** $30,000. **Financial Assistance:** No. **Training:** Yes.

6484 ■ Smash Hit Subs
Orion Food Systems
2930 W Maple
Sioux Falls, SD 57101
Ph:(605)336-6961
Free: 800-648-6227
Fax:(605)336-0141
No. of Franchise Units: 1,300. **No. of Company-Owned Units:** 12. **Founded:** 1984. **Franchised:** 1986. **Description:** Sub sandwiches. **Equity Capital Needed:** $25,000. **Franchise Fee:** $4,950. **Financial Assistance:** Yes. **Training:** Yes.

6485 ■ Subway
Franchise Sales Dept.
325 Bic Dr.
Milford, CT 06460
Ph:(203)877-4281
Free: 800-888-4848
Fax:(203)783-7325
Co. E-mail: franchise@subway.com
URL: http://www.subway.com
No. of Franchise Units: 33,000. **No. of Company-Owned Units:** 1. **Founded:** 1974. **Franchised:** 1974. **Description:** Submarine sandwich category with fresh, great tasting, made-for-you sandwiches and salads, many of which have 6 grams of fat or less. Offering a healthful alternative to fatty fast food has made Subway a popular destination for health-conscious consumers. **Equity Capital Needed:** $114,800-$258,300 total investment. **Franchise Fee:** $15,000. **Financial Assistance:** Third party financing, and equipment leasing is available for qualified franchisees. **Training:** Provides training and assistance to franchisees in all areas of business operation.

6486 ■ Sweet Peppers Deli
Sweet peppers Franchise Systems, LLC
PO Box 1368
Columbus, OH 39703
Ph:(662)327-6982
Free: 888-222-9550
Fax:(662)327-1672
No. of Franchise Units: 14. **No. of Company-Owned Units:** 5. **Founded:** 1984. **Franchised:** 2002. **Description:** Fast casual, deli-style restaurant. **Equity Capital Needed:** $200,000. **Franchise Fee:** $25,000. **Financial Assistance:** No. **Training:** Yes.

6487 ■ Togo's Eatery
Togo's Franchisor, LLC
18 N San Pedro St
San Jose, CA 95110
Ph:(408)280-6569
Free: 877-718-6467
Fax:(866)394-4902
Co. E-mail: franchisesales@togos.com
URL: http://www.togos.com
No. of Franchise Units: 245. **No. of Company-Owned Units:** 1. **Founded:** 1971. **Franchised:** 1977. **Description:** Fast-food sandwiches. Only Resales are available in the United States. **Equity Capital Needed:** $300,000 net worth; $150,000 liquid; $256,650-$417,300 total investment. **Franchise Fee:** $25,000 10 year term; $40,000 20 year term. **Financial Assistance:** No. **Managerial Assistance:** Provides purchasing, cost control, sanitation, product development, promotion and general assistance for the life of the franchise. **Training:** Offers 2 weeks of onsite training, with periodic follow-up.

6488 ■ Tubby's Sub Shops, Inc.
18357 E 14 Mile Rd.
Fraser, MI 48026
Ph:(586)293-5099
Free: 800-752-0644
Fax:(586)293-5088
No. of Franchise Units: 70. **No. of Company-Owned Units:** 2. **Founded:** 1968. **Franchised:** 1978. **Description:** Specialty submarine sandwich shop, featuring grilled sandwiches, soups, salads and ice cream. **Equity Capital Needed:** $500,000 net worth; $75,000 cash/assets convertible to cash. **Franchise Fee:** $5,000-$13,000 (varies by type of store). **Financial Assistance:** No. **Training:** Classroom sessions where very facet of your business is covered. Additional onsite assistance is given just prior to opening and during your first few weeks of operation.

6489 ■ Uno Chicago Grill
Pizzeria Uno Corp.
100 Charles Park Rd.
Boston, MA 02132
Ph:(617)218-5272
Free: 877-855-8667
Fax:(617)218-5376
No. of Franchise Units: 86. **No. of Company-Owned Units:** 124. **Founded:** 1943. **Franchised:** 1979. **Description:** Full service casual theme restaurant. **Equity Capital Needed:** $1,000,000 net worth per location; $700,000 liquidity. **Franchise Fee:** $40,000. **Financial Assistance:** No. **Training:** Yes.

6490 ■ W.G. Grinders
Grinders Inc.
9002 Cotter St.
Lewis Center, OH 43035
Ph:(614)578-6701
Free: 877-477-DELI
Fax:(614)766-4030
No. of Franchise Units: 13. **No. of Company-Owned Units:** 8. **Founded:** 1989. **Franchised:** 1995. **Description:** Upscale quick service gourmet deli. **Equity Capital Needed:** $239,000-$314,000 estimated initial investment required. **Franchise Fee:** $15,000 thru 2011. **Financial Assistance:** No. **Training:** Yes.

6491 ■ Which Wich Superior Sandwiches
Which Wich Franchise, Inc.
1310 Elm St., Ste. 180LL
Dallas, TX 75202
Ph:(214)747-WICH
Fax:(214)242-4329
No. of Franchise Units: 136. **No. of Company-Owned Units:** 1. **Founded:** 2003. **Franchised:** 2005. **Description:** Modern sandwich concept. **Equity Capital Needed:** $195,000-$488,750. **Franchise Fee:** $30,000 **Financial Assistance:** Third party financing available. **Training:** Provides 3 weeks training at headquarters, 1-2 weeks at franchisee's location and ongoing support.

6492 ■ Zero's Subs
2859 Virginia Beach Blvd., Ste. 105
Virginia Beach, VA 23452
Ph:(757)486-8338
Free: 800-588-0782
Fax:(818)545-9132
Co. E-mail: zeros@zeros.com
URL: http://www.zeros.com
No. of Franchise Units: 70. **Founded:** 1967. **Franchised:** 1996. **Description:** A Fast-food, sit-down and to-go restaurant, serving Italian submarine sandwiches and pizzas. **Equity Capital Needed:** $137,880-$242,300. **Franchise Fee:** $20,000. **Financial Assistance:** Yes. **Training:** Yes.

LIBRARIES

6493 ■ American Institute of Food Distribution, Inc.–Information and Research Center
1 Broadway Plaza, 2nd Fl.
Elmwood Park, NJ 07407
Ph:(201)791-5570
Fax:(201)791-5222
Co. E-mail: jkastrinsky@foodinstitute.com
URL: http://www.foodinstitute.com/
Contact: Brian Todd, Pres./CEO
Scope: Food industry. **Services:** Center open to the public on fee basis. **Subscriptions:** 400 journals and other serials.

6494 ■ Noble and Associates Library
2155 W. Chesterfield Blvd.
Springfield, MO 65807
Ph:(417)875-5000
Co. E-mail: julie.tumy@noble.net
URL: http://www.noble.net
Contact: Julie Tumy, Pres.
Scope: Food, food service, advertising, construction, agriculture. **Services:** Interlibrary loan; copying; SDI; Library not open to the public. **Holdings:** 500 books; 1000 reports. **Subscriptions:** 300 journals and other serials; 5 newspapers.

START-UP INFORMATION

6495 ■ *How to Start and Run a Small Book Publishing Company: A Small Business Guide to Self-Publishing and Independent Publishing*
Pub: HCM Publishing

Ed: Peter I. Hupalo. **Released:** August 30, 2002. **Price:** $18.95. **Description:** The book teaches all aspects of starting and running a small book publishing company. Topics covered include: inventory accounting in the book trade, just-in-time inventory management, turnkey fulfillment solutions, tax deductible costs, basics of sales and use tax, book pricing, standards in terms of the book industry, working with distributors and wholesalers, cover design and book layout, book promotion and marketing, how to select profitable authors to publish, printing process, printing on demand, the power of a strong backlist, and how to value copyright.

ASSOCIATIONS AND OTHER ORGANIZATIONS

6496 ■ Association of Proposal Management Professionals
PO Box 668
Dana Point, CA 92629-0668
Co. E-mail: memberservices@apmp.org
URL: http://www.apmp.org
Contact: Rick Harris, Exec. Dir.

Description: Proposal managers, proposal planners, proposal writers, consultants, desktop publishers and marketing managers. Encourages unity and cooperation among industry professionals. Seeks to broaden member knowledge and skills through developmental, educational and social activities. Maintains speakers' bureau. Provides current information and developments in the field. .

6497 ■ Macrocosm USA
PO Box 185
Cambria, CA 93428
Ph:(805)927-2515
Co. E-mail: brockway@macronet.org
URL: http://www.macronet.org
Contact: Sandi Brockway, Pres./Founder

Description: Publishes reader/directories for educators, journalists, students, and activists. Compiles and edits materials into utilitarian formats such as handbooks, databases, a databank, and newsletters. Networks people, projects, and organizations. Self-serve, searchable directory, calendar, and forums on-line. **Publications:** *Macrocosm USA: Possibilities For A New Progressive Era* .

6498 ■ Small Publishers Association of North America
PO Box 9725
Colorado Springs, CO 80932-0725
Ph:(719)924-5534
Fax:(719)213-2602
Co. E-mail: info@spannet.org
URL: http://www.spannet.org
Contact: Scott Flora, Exec. Dir.

Description: For self-publishers, authors and small presses. Works to advance the image and profits of independent publishers through education and marketing. Offers continuing education, co-op buying power and sales and networking opportunities, plus discounts on many products and services. Publishes monthly newsletter. .

EDUCATIONAL PROGRAMS

6499 ■ Becoming a Publications Manager
EEI Communications
66 Canal Center Plz., Ste. 200
Alexandria, VA 22314
Ph:(703)683-7453
Free: 888-253-2762
Fax:(703)683-7310
Co. E-mail: train@eeicom.com
URL: http://www.eeicom.com/training
Price: $425.00. **Description:** For new managers, this seminar covers defining responsibilities, managing workflow, organizational and recruitment skills, providing feedback, and utilizing technology. **Locations:** Alexandria, VA.

6500 ■ Design for Print
EEI Communications
66 Canal Center Plz., Ste. 200
Alexandria, VA 22314
Ph:(703)683-7453
Free: 888-253-2762
Fax:(703)683-7310
Co. E-mail: train@eeicom.com
URL: http://www.eeicom.com/training
Price: $745.00. **Description:** Covers basic design principles, utilizing color and typography, composition, and preparing files for the printing process. **Locations:** Silver Spring, MD; Alexandria, VA; Hunt Valley, MD; and Columbia, MD.

6501 ■ Visual Thinking II: Color Theory
EEI Communications
66 Canal Center Plz., Ste. 200
Alexandria, VA 22314
Ph:(703)683-7453
Free: 888-253-2762
Fax:(703)683-7310
Co. E-mail: train@eeicom.com
URL: http://www.eeicom.com/training
Price: $1,395.00. **Description:** Covers the design elements of color, including the color wheel, the seven color contrasts, and the psychological aspects of color. **Locations:** Silver Spring, MD; Alexandria, VA; Hunt Valley, MD; and Columbia, MD.

REFERENCE WORKS

6502 ■ "Career Transition" in *Crain's Detroit Business* (Vol. 26, January 4, 2010, No. 1, pp. 14)
Pub: Crain Communications, Inc.
Description: Profile of Nicole Longhini-McElroy who has opted to radically change her career path from working in the manufacturing sector to becoming a self-published author of "Charmed Adventures", a book series created to engage children in creative thought.

6503 ■ "Freelance Writer Creates L.I. Bridal Blog" in *Long Island Business News* (September 10, 2010)
Pub: Dolan Media Newswires
Ed: Gregory Zeller. **Description:** Profile of Claudia Copquin, freelance journalist who created a blog for brides on the Internet.

6504 ■ *Freelancing for Journalists*
Pub: Routledge
Ed: Diana Harris. **Released:** January 1, 2010. **Price:** $110.00. **Description:** Comprehensive guide showing the specific skills required for those wishing to freelance in newspapers, magazines, radio, television, and as online journalists.

6505 ■ *From Entrepreneur to Infopreneur: Make Money with Books, E-Books, and Other Information Products*
Pub: John Wiley & Sons, Incorporated
Ed: Stephanie Chandler. **Released:** November 2006. **Price:** $19.95. **Description:** Infopreneurs sell information online in the forms of books, e-books, special reports, audio and video products, seminars, and more.

6506 ■ "Getting It Sold" in *Black Enterprise* (Vol. 38, November 2007, No. 4, pp. 54)
Pub: Earl G. Graves Publishing Co. Inc.
Ed: Tennille M. Robinson. **Description:** Artist is given advice for marketing and selling paintings, as well as getting artwork published.

6507 ■ *How to Start a Home-Based Writing Business, 5th Edition*
Pub: Globe Pequot Press
Ed: Lucy Parker. **Released:** December 2007. **Price:** $18.95. **Description:** Guide for starting and running a home-based writing business.

6508 ■ "Interactive Stores a Big Part of Borders' Turnaround Plan" in *Crain's Detroit Business* (Vol. 24, February 18, 2008, No. 7, pp. 4)
Pub: Crain Communications Inc. - Detroit
Description: Borders Group Inc. is using digital technology and interactive media as a part of the firm's turnaround plan. The digital store will allow shoppers to create CDs, download audio books, publish their own works, print photos and search family genealogy.

6509 ■ *Literary Market Place*
Pub: Information Today Inc.
Contact: Thomas H. Hogan, Pres. & Publisher
Released: Annual, Latest edition 2012. **Price:** $339, individuals 2-volume set/softbound plus $25 shipping/handling; $305.10, individuals first time standing order. **Covers:** Over 12,500 firms or organizations offering services related to the publishing industry, including book publishers in the United States and Canada who issued three or more books during the

preceding year, plus a small press section of publishers who publish less than three titles per year or those who are self-published. Also included: book printers and binders; book clubs; book trade and literary associations; selected syndicates, newspapers, periodicals, and radio and TV programs that use book reviews or book publishing news; translators and literary agents. **Entries Include:** For publishers—Company name, address, phone, address for orders, principal executives, editorial directors, and managers, date founded, number of titles in previous year, number of backlist titles in print, types of books published, ISBN prefixes, representatives, imprints, and affiliations. For suppliers, etc.—Listings usually show firm name, address, phone, executives, services, etc. **Arrangement:** Classified by line of business. **Indexes:** Principal index is 35,000-item combined index of publishers, publications, and personnel; several sections have geographical and/or subject indexes; translators are indexed by source and target language.

6510 ■ "Online Self-Publishing Services" in *Black Enterprise* (Vol. 37, November 2006, No. 4, pp. 90)
Pub: Earl G. Graves Publishing Co. Inc.
Description: Profiles of five online self-publishing services.

6511 ■ "Paper a la Carte" in *American Printer* (Vol. 128, June 1, 2011, No. 6)
Pub: Penton Media Inc.
Description: Blurb, the online publishing platform, launched ProLine which features Mohawk Superfine and Mohawk proPhoto papers. ProLine papers offer two finishes: Pearl Photo and Uncoated.

6512 ■ "Pretentious and Loving It" in *Entrepreneur* (Vol. 37, August 2009, No. 8, pp. 34)
Pub: Entrepreneur Media, Inc.
Ed: Eric Mahoney. **Description:** Pitchfork.com features reviews of albums from independent artists. Their most innovative section is Pitchfork.tv, featuring videos of bands, and Forkcast along with their Features section that contains articles about bands and their histories.

6513 ■ *The Publishing Game: Publish a Book in 30 Days*
Pub: Peanut Butter and Jelly Press LLC
Ed: Fern Reiss. **Released:** January 31, 2003. **Price:** $19.95. **Description:** Excellent resource for individuals wanting to write a book and become their own publisher.

6514 ■ "Savvy Solutions" in *Black Enterprise* (Vol. 41, November 2010, No. 4, pp. 42)
Pub: Earl G. Graves Publishing Co. Inc.
Ed: Tennile M. Robinson. **Description:** Society of Children's Book Writers and Illustrators offers members many benefits, including directories of agencies looking for new writers of books.

6515 ■ *The Self-Publishing Manual: How To Write, Print, and Sell Your Own Book*
Pub: Para Publishing
Ed: Dan Poynter. **Released:** 2007. **Price:** $19.95. **Description:** The book provides a complete course in writing, publishing, marketing, promoting, and distributing books. Poynter offers a step-by-step study of the publishing industry and explains various book-marketing techniques.

6516 ■ "The Way I Work: Kim Kleeman" in *Inc.* (October 2007, pp. 110-112, 114)
Pub: Gruner & Jahr USA Publishing
Ed: Leigh Buchanan. **Description:** Profile of Kim Kleemna, founder and president of ShakespeareSquared, a firm that develops educational materials, including lesson plans, teacher guides, activity workbooks, and discussion guides for large publishers. Kleeman talks about the challenges she faces running her nearly all-women company while maintaining a balance with her family.

TRADE PERIODICALS

6517 ■ *Economic Edge*
Pub: National Association for Printing Leadership
Released: Quarterly. **Price:** Included in membership. **Description:** Provides current economic data for the printing industry. Also covers sales growth projections, capital spending, and employment.

6518 ■ *How To Be Your Own Publisher Update*
Pub: Bibliotheca Press
Contact: A. Doyle
Ed: A. Doyle, Editor. **Released:** Annual. **Price:** $12.95, U.S.; $15.95, Canada; $19.95, other countries. **Description:** Acts as a reference for self publishers. Distributed by Prosperity & Profits Unlimited Distribution Services, PO Box 416, Denver, CO, 80201.

6519 ■ *Independent Publisher Online*
Pub: Jenkins Group Inc.
Contact: Jim Barnes, Managing Editor
E-mail: jimb@bookpublishing.com
Released: Monthly. **Description:** Online magazine containing book reviews and articles about independent publishing.

6520 ■ *The Kleper Report on Digital Publishing*
Pub: Graphic Dimensions
Contact: Michael Kleper
E-mail: scott@printerport.com
Ed: Michael Kleper, Editor, mkleper@printerport.com. **Released:** 6/year. **Price:** $24.95, individuals $150/year, U.S. and Canada; $225 elsewhere;. **Description:** Reviews software program packages for desktop, electronic, and digital publishing, imaging, multimedia, and Web publishing.

6521 ■ *KMWorld*
Pub: Information Today Inc.
Contact: Hugh McKellar, Editor-in-Chief
E-mail: hugh_mckellar@kmworld.com
Released: Monthly. **Price:** Free to qualified subscribers. **Description:** Journal focusing on the applications of knowledge management solutions as they apply to business and corporations.

6522 ■ *Min's b2b*
Pub: Phillips Business Information Inc.
Contact: Angela Duff, Publisher
Ed: Jeremy Greenfield, Editor. **Released:** Biweekly. **Price: Description:** Provides news on business relations and strategies and tactics to increase online publishing and new media business.

6523 ■ *Oregon Publisher*
Pub: Oregon Newspaper Publishers Association
Contact: LeRoy Yorgason, Publisher
E-mail: leroy@orenews.com
Ed: David Merrill, Editor, dmerrill@orenews.com. **Released:** Every other month. **Price:** Included in membership. **Description:** Covers journalism and publishing topics.

VIDEOCASSETTES/ AUDIOCASSETTES

6524 ■ *Desktop Design 1: Basic Electronic Graphic Techniques*
Cambridge Educational
c/o Films Media Group
132 West 31st Street, 17th Floor
Ste. 124
New York, NY 10001
Free: 800-257-5126
Fax:(609)671-0266
Co. E-mail: custserve@films.com
URL: http://www.cambridgeol.com
Price: $39.95. **Description:** Presents basic electronic design techniques and principles through a series of step-by-step projects. **Availability:** VHS.

6525 ■ *Desktop Design 2: Creative Design with PostScript Drawing Software*
Cambridge Educational
c/o Films Media Group
132 West 31st Street, 17th Floor
Ste. 124
New York, NY 10001
Free: 800-257-5126
Fax:(609)671-0266
Co. E-mail: custserve@films.com
URL: http://www.cambridgeol.com
Price: $39.95. **Description:** Step-by-step project introduces major applications of Adobe Illustrator 88 and Aldus FreeHand. Covers charts and graphs, logo design, advertising, illustration, font creation, and a magazine cover. **Availability:** VHS.

6526 ■ *Desktop Design 3: Creative Design with Page-Layout Software*
Cambridge Educational
c/o Films Media Group
132 West 31st Street, 17th Floor
Ste. 124
New York, NY 10001
Free: 800-257-5126
Fax:(609)671-0266
Co. E-mail: custserve@films.com
URL: http://www.cambridgeol.com
Price: $39.95. **Description:** Illustrates the use of Aldus Pagemaker; Ready, Set, Go!; and Quark XPress for newsletters, brochures, and full-page ad layout. Includes tips and tricks. **Availability:** VHS.

6527 ■ *Introduction to Desktop Publishing*
RMI Media
1365 N. Winchester St.
Olathe, KS 66061-5880
Ph:(913)768-1696
Free: 800-745-5480
Fax:800-755-6910
Co. E-mail: actmedia@act.org
URL: http://www.actmedia.com
Released: 1987. **Price:** $89.95. **Description:** Computer expert and consultant Julie Gomoll explains what desktop publishing is, how it can be used, and who should use it. **Availability:** VHS; 3/4U.

6528 ■ *Introduction to PageMaker*
RMI Media
1365 N. Winchester St.
Olathe, KS 66061-5880
Ph:(913)768-1696
Free: 800-745-5480
Fax:800-755-6910
Co. E-mail: actmedia@act.org
URL: http://www.actmedia.com
Released: 1987. **Price:** $89.95. **Description:** Introduces viewers to Aldus PageMaker 3.0 software capability and operation. Assuming no prior knowledge of publishing or printing, shows how to create a sample four-page newsletter. **Availability:** VHS; 3/4U.

6529 ■ *Microsoft Word, Desktop Publishing*
Learn.com
14001 NW 4th St
Sunrise, FL 33325
Ph:(954)233-4000
Free: 800-842-3294
Fax:(954)233-4001
Co. E-mail: info@learn.com
URL: http://www2.stlu.com/fd/viagrafix.asp
Released: 1991. **Price:** $69.95. **Description:** Learn to create newsletters, letterheads, brochures and other documents in this easy-to-follow video. Also covers printers and graphics handling. Includes learning diskette. **Availability:** VHS.

6530 ■ *Understanding Desktop Publishing*
Chesney Communications
2302 Martin St., Ste. 125
Irvine, CA 92612
Ph:(949)263-5500
Free: 800-223-8878
Fax:(949)263-5506
Co. E-mail: videocc@aol.com
URL: http://www.videocc.com
Released: 1987. **Description:** Instruction for the lone businessman in using a MacIntosh computer to produce his own published materials instead of giving it to outside houses. **Availability:** VHS; 3/4U.

6531 ■ *Word Processing/Desktop Publishing/ Graphics Library*
Moonbeam Publications, Inc.
PO Box 5150
Traverse City, MI 49696

Ph:(616)922-0533
Free: 800-445-2391
Fax:800-334-9789
Co. E-mail: custserv@moonbeampublications.com
URL: http://www.moonbeampublications.com
Released: 1991. **Description:** Pick your favorite type of computer work and learn all there is to know about it in this 13-volume set. **Availability:** VHS.

6532 ■ *WordPerfect for Desktop Publishing*
Learn.com
14001 NW 4th St
Sunrise, FL 33325
Ph:(954)233-4000
Free: 800-842-3294
Fax:(954)233-4001
Co. E-mail: info@learn.com
URL: http://www2.stlu.com/fd/viagrafix.asp
Released: 1991. **Price:** $69.95. **Description:** How to use graphics, fonts, and other design tools in creating newsletters, brochures, and other useful publications. **Availability:** VHS.

TRADE SHOWS AND CONVENTIONS

6533 ■ ON DEMAND Digital Printing & Publishing Strategy Conference and Exposition
Advanstar Communications
641 Lexington Ave., 8th Fl.
New York, NY 10022
Ph:(212)951-6600
Fax:(212)951-6793
Co. E-mail: info@advantstar.com
URL: http://www.advanstar.com
Released: Annual. **Audience:** Corporate executives, print providers, government users. **Principal Exhibits:** Addresses the digitalization of workflow in the printing and publishing marketplace.

6534 ■ Seybold San Francisco Conference and Exposition
Keith Reed Media Events
303 Vintage Park Dr.
Foster City, CA 94404
Ph:(650)578-6897
Free: 800-488-2883
Fax:(650)525-0193
Co. E-mail: mtrask@zdcf.com
Released: Annual. **Audience:** Computer publishing trade. **Principal Exhibits:** Equipment, supplies, and services for computer publishing.

CONSULTANTS

6535 ■ Barb Gordon Graphic Design
14107 Wilden Dr.
Urbandale, IA 50323
Ph:(515)278-9738
Co. E-mail: bgordon@myarbonne.com
URL: http://www.barbgordon.com
Contact: Barbara J. Gordon, Principle
E-mail: gordon@dwx.com
Scope: Consultant offers training in desktop publishing and in popular graphics software. Training is generally presented in-house and is available on a one-to-one basis. Industries served: graphic artists.

6536 ■ Editorial Code and Data Inc.
814 Wolverine Dr., Ste. 2
Walled Lake, MI 48390
Ph:(248)926-5187
Fax:(248)926-6047
Co. E-mail: monique@marketsize.com
URL: http://www.marketsize.com
Contact: Joyce P. Simkin, Mgr
E-mail: monique@marketsize.com
Scope: Provides data and computer services primarily to the publishing industry, with specialization in statistical data drawn from government sources. Services include data acquisition, analysis, formatting, and typesetting, archiving of computer data on CD-ROM, custom data display, search, and printing software, information brokering services, and related services such as design, writing, and data processing design. Industries served: publishing, in-house printing, non-profit organizations, government agencies, utilities, and manufacturing. **Publications:** "Market Share Reporter"; "Encyclopedia of Products & Industries"; "Economic Indicators Handbook"; "American Salaries and Wages Survey"; "Dun and Bradstreet & Gale: Industrial Handbook"; "Reference American Cost of Living Survey".

6537 ■ Intercollegiate Broadcasting System Inc.
367 Windsor Hwy.
New Windsor, NY 12553-7900
Ph:(845)565-0003
Fax:(845)565-7446
Co. E-mail: ibs@ibsradio.org
URL: http://www.ibsradio.org
Contact: Jeff Tellis, Vice President, Public Relations
Scope: Communications media specialists with focus on Macintosh computing, desktop publishing, graphic production layout, database, spreadsheet, and training. Possesses particular expertise on AV systems and setups. Serves private industries as well as government agencies.

6538 ■ The Live Oak Press L.L.C.
445 Burgess Dr.
PO Box 60036
Menlo Park, CA 94306-0036
Ph:(650)853-0197
Fax:(815)366-8205
Co. E-mail: mhamilton@liveoakpress.com
URL: http://www.liveoakpress.com
Contact: David M. Hamilton, President
E-mail: mhamilton@liveoakpress.com
Scope: Manages design and implementation of publishing programs. Also offers complete book and magazine preparation and publishing consulting, including web resources, advertising, concept development, manuscript, design, development and production through finished product. Specializes in high-technology clients and electronic publishing. **Publications:** "The Tools of My Trade"; "To the Yukon with Jack London"; "Earthquakes and Young Volcanoes"; "The Lost Cement Mine"; "Inner Voyage"; "Studies in the Development of Consciousness"; "Dialectical Realism: Studies on a Philosophy of Growth"; "Mammoth Lakes Sierra"; "Deepest Valley"; "Mammoth Gold"; "Old Mammoth". **Seminars:** Internet publishing Aeminar.

6539 ■ Lovelady Consulting
1100 Martin Ridge Rd.
Roswell, GA 30076-2852
Ph:(770)992-1545
Fax:(770)992-7238
Co. E-mail: carol@loveladyconsulting.com
URL: http://www.loveladyconsulting.com
Contact: Carol Lovelady, Owner
E-mail: clovelady@venturalady.com
Scope: Specialist on electronic publishing and office automation applications, offers consultation, design and training. Specializes in Ventura, Page Maker, Corel Draw, quark press, graphics and related applications. Develops customized corporate training programs. Serves private industries as well as government agencies. **Publications:** "Adobe Acrobat 9 Quick start Guide"; "Adobe Acrobat 9 How-To's "; "How to Do Everything with Acrobat 9"; "Corel Ventura 10"; "CorelDraw X4 Upgrade"; "CorelDraw X4 Full Version"; "Adobe Acrobat 9 Professional Upgrade"; "Adobe Acrobat 9 Standard Upgrade"; "CorelDraw Graphics Suite X3"; "Adobe Acrobat 8 Quick Start Guide"; "How To Do Everything with Acrobat 7"; "Acrobat 8 Upgrade from Standard to Professional". **Seminars:** Corel Ventura 10 Introduction, 2007; Adobe Acrobat Advanced; Corel Ventura 10 Transition; CorelDRAW X3 Introduction, 2007; CorelDRAW X3 Advanced; Adobe Acrobat Advanced; Corel Database Publisher 8/10; Ventura Tips and Tricks, 2005; Adobe In Design Introduction, 2005; Corel Database Publisher 8/10; CorelDRAW 11/12 Introduction; Ventura Tips & Tricks; Corel PhotoPAINT Introduction. **Special Services:** CorelDraw X4 or X3; Adobe Acrobat 8 or 9; Corel Ventura 10; CorelDRAW 11/12; Corel Ventura 10.

6540 ■ LPD Enterprises
925 Salamanca St. NW
Los Ranchos de Albuquerque, NM 87107-5647
Ph:(505)344-9382
Fax:(505)345-5129
Co. E-mail: info@nmsantos.com
URL: http://www.nmsantos.com
Contact: Paul F. Rhetts, Director
Scope: Offers services in public relations, publications, desktop and electronic publishing, management, and organizational development. Specializes in serving small- to medium-sized businesses, nonprofit organizations and educational institutions. **Publications:** "Shoes for Santo Nino"; "Genizaro & the Artist"; "Old West Trivia"; "Tale of Pronghorned Cantaloupe"; "Saints of the Pueblos"; "A Century of Masters"; "Visions Underground"; "Avenging Victorio". **Seminars:** Balloon Safety.

6541 ■ Nicholas J. Naclerio and Associates Inc.
7463 Cross Gate Ln.
PO Box 278
Alexandria, VA 22315-4620
Ph:(703)451-7557
Fax:(703)922-0173
Co. E-mail: njnaclerio@cs.com
Contact: Nicholas J. Naclerio, Owner
E-mail: njnaclerio@cs.com
Scope: Provides administrative and personnel, and information management consulting to business and government in such areas as document creation and office automation, desktop publishing, database design, career development programs, and organizational development. Also, offers hands-on microcomputer training on all popular software for both IBM and Macintosh computers including Lotus Suite, Microsoft Office, Word Perfect and the Internet.

6542 ■ Nostradamus Advertising
884 W End Ave., Ste. 2
New York, NY 10025
Ph:(212)581-1362
Fax:(212)662-8625
Co. E-mail: nos@nostradamus.net
URL: http://www.nostradamus.net
Contact: Barry Nostradamus Sher, President
Scope: Provides graphic design, advertising and marketing services to small companies and organizations. Other services include consulting; designing direct mail for politicians; creating and updating Websites, book design and communication services. Serves government agencies.

6543 ■ PubCom/i-Imagery Design
7417 Holly Ave.
PO Box 11007
Takoma Park, MD 20912-4219
Ph:(301)585-8805
Fax:(301)585-7289
Co. E-mail: info@pubcom.com
URL: http://www.pubcom.com
Contact: Bevi Chagnon, President
E-mail: bevi@atspubcom.com
Scope: Specializes in cross media publishing for print, multimedia, and the Internet. Provides training in desktop publishing and website design. Also offers system analyses, installation, and software for publishing multimedia and website development. Industries served graphic arts, publishing, typesetting, nonprofits, government, corporations, and federal contractors in the mid Atlantic states. **Seminars:** Advertising 101 for Small Businesses, 2006; Marketing on a Small Budget, 2006; Strategies for Promoting your Exhibit Booth, 2006; Beginner and advanced hands-on training in desktop publishing; Cross-Media Publishing with Adobe In Design: Publishing for Press and Web; 508 Compliance with Adobe In Design; Management of Multi-Tiered Enterprise Websites and Intranets; New Directions in Publishing Technology.

6544 ■ SketchPad Graphic Design
812 Mountain View St.
Fillmore, CA 93015
Ph:(805)524-2740

Fax:(805)524-2795
Co. E-mail: info@sketch.com
URL: http://www.sketch.com
Contact: Norma Holt, Director
E-mail: holt@atssketch.com
Scope: Provides desktop publishing, including text capture, graphic capture, typesetting, layout, design, photographs and printing, color separation, file management, software and hardware usage. Also designs and hosts web pages. Industries served: public and private sector in Ventura County and rest of U.S. via mail and facsimile. **Seminars:** Desktop publishing; Ventura Publisher and PageMaker.

6545 ■ Stillman H. Publishers Inc.
21405 Woodchuck Ln.
Boca Raton, FL 33428
Ph:(561)482-6343
Contact: Herbert Stillman, President
Scope: Offers consulting services in the following areas: management, start ups, profit maximization, world wide negotiating, interim management, corporate debt resolution.

6546 ■ Systems Service Enterprises Inc.
77 W Port Plz., Ste. 500
Saint Louis, MO 63146-3126
Ph:(314)439-4700
Fax:(314)439-4799
Co. E-mail: info@sseinc.com
URL: http://www.sseinc.com
Contact: Brenda Enders, Principle
E-mail: eeniedringhaus@sseinc.com
Scope: Develops information technology solutions and services such as application development, business intelligence, e learning, network design, IT outsourcing, and technical staff augmentation services. **Publications:** "IT Budget Got your Stomach in Knots"; "We Have a Guy Who Does That"; "Considering Telecommute Questions to Answer"; "Is Your IT MOOSE Spending Too Loose"; "Exponential Growth of Spyware in Q4"; "Knowing the Tricks of the Trade"; "93 percent of Firms with Major Data Losses File for Bankruptcy"; "70 percent of Security Threats Originate Inside Your Office"; "99 percent of Computers Worldwide are Vulnerable to Online Attacks". **Special Services:** Pretecht™; SSEwinEngine™; SSElearn Portal™; SSEanalytics™.

LIBRARIES

6547 ■ Printing Industries of America/ Graphic Arts Technical Foundation–Edward H. Wadewitz Memorial Library
200 Deer Run Rd.
Sewickley, PA 15143-2324
Ph:(412)741-6860
Free: (866)PIA-GATF
Fax:(412)741-2311
Co. E-mail: library@piagatf.org
URL: http://www.printing.org/page/4506
Contact: Hallie Barcalow, Adm.
Scope: Printing processes, lithography, paper, ink, graphic design, desktop publishing, packaging, chemistry, physics, environmental control, safety and health, photography. **Services:** Document delivery; Library open to the public by appointment. **Holdings:** 15,000 volumes. **Subscriptions:** 180 journals and other serials.

TRADE PERIODICALS

6548 ■ *Audiotex News*
Pub: Audiotex News
Contact: Carol Morse, Editor & Publisher
E-mail: carol@audiotex.news.com
Released: Monthly. **Description:** Covers news, trends, regulations, and information on the 900/800 pay-per-call business. Recurring features include interviews, news of research, calendar of events, reports of meetings, book reviews, and notices of publications available.

6549 ■ *Telephone IP News*
Pub: Worldwide Videotex
Contact: Mark Wright
Released: Monthly. **Price:** $165, U.S. and Canada; $180, elsewhere outside North America; $25, single issue U.S. and Canada; $30, single issue outside North America. **Description:** Provides information provider (IP) industry news for various telephone services, such as 900, 970, and 976 numbers. Covers new products, public service commission rulings, and marketing strategies.

LIBRARIES

6550 ■ Manitoba Telecom Services Corporate Library
333 Main St.
PO Box 6666
Winnipeg, MB, Canada R3C 3V6
Ph:(204)941-6344
Fax:(204)944-0830
URL: http://www.mts.ca
Contact: Tanya L. Evancio, Libn.
Scope: Telecommunications industry. **Services:** Library not open to the public. **Holdings:** 2000 books. **Subscriptions:** 100 journals and other serials.

6551 ■ U.S. Federal Communications Commission Library
445 12th St. SW, Rm. TW-8505
Washington, DC 20554
Ph:(202)418-0450
Free: 888-225-5322
Fax:(202)418-2805
Co. E-mail: ecclibrary@fcc.gov
URL: http://www.fcc.gov
Contact: Gloria Thomas, Mgr., Lib. Group
Scope: Telecommunications, electrical engineering, law, economics, public utility regulation, public administration, management, statistics. **Services:** SDI; Library not open to the public. **Holdings:** 45,000 books; 123 bound periodical volumes; 6200 VF materials; 3000 reels of microfilm. **Subscriptions:** 305 journals and other serials.

Disc Jockey Service

ASSOCIATIONS AND OTHER ORGANIZATIONS

6552 ■ American Disc Jockey Association
20118 N 67th Ave., Ste. 300-605
Glendale, AZ 85308
Free: 888-723-5776
Co. E-mail: office@adja.org
URL: http://www.adja.org

Description: Mobile and night club disc jockeys. Seeks to promote the disc jockey as a professional form of entertainment; improves the industry by establishing standards, procedures, and benefits. Assists and trains members; provides forums for professional disc jockeys; conducts educational, charitable, and research programs. **Publications:** *Mobile Beat* (annual).

6553 ■ Canadian Disc Jockey Association
1008 Manchester Rd.
London, ON, Canada N6H 5J1
Ph:(519)287-3600
Free: 877-472-0653
Fax:(519)472-0242
Co. E-mail: pres@cdja.ca
URL: http://www.cdja.ca
Contact: Doug Scott, Pres.

Description: Disc jockeys and others promote excellence in service through education, information, networking, and support. Promotes professional development among members. Facilitates exchange of information among members; represents members' interests. **Publications:** *CUED-UP Street* (annual); *DJ Pulse* (quarterly).

TRADE PERIODICALS

6554 ■ *DJ Times*
Pub: Testa Communications
Contact: Vincent Testa, Pres./Publisher
Ed: Jim Tremayne, Editor, jtremayne@testa.com. **Released:** Monthly. **Price:** $19.40; $36.99 two years; $39.99 Canada; $75.99 two years Canada; $59.99 other countries; $99.99 two years foreign. **Description:** DJ Times offers the most comprehensive coverage of what the professional DJ wants and needs.

START-UP INFORMATION

6555 ■ "Franchises with an Eye on Chicago" in *Crain's Chicago Business* (Vol. 34, March 14, 2011, No. 11, pp. 20)
Pub: Crain Communications Inc.

Description: Profiles of franchise companies seeking franchisees for the Chicago area include: Extreme Pita, a sandwich shop; Hand and Stone, offering massage, facial and waxing services; Molly Maid, home-cleaning service; Primrose Schools, private accredited schools for children 6 months to 6 hears and after-school programs; Protect Painters, residential and light-commercial painting contractor; and Wingstop, a restaurant offering chicken wings in nine flavors, fries and side dishes.

6556 ■ "Green Clean Machine" in *Small Business Opportunities* (Winter 2010)
Pub: Harris Publications Inc.

Description: Eco-friendly maid franchise plans to grow its $62 million sales base. Profile of Maid Brigade, a green-cleaning franchise is planning to expand across the country.

6557 ■ *Housecleaning Business: Organize Your Business - Get Clients and Referrals - Set Rates and Services*
Pub: The Globe Pequot Press

Ed: Laura Jorstad, Melinda Morse. **Released:** June 1, 2009. **Price:** $18.95. **Description:** This book shares insight into starting a housecleaning businesses. It shows how to develop a service manual, screen clients, serve customers, select cleaning products, competition, how to up a home office, using the Internet to grow the business and offering green cleaning options to clients.

ASSOCIATIONS AND OTHER ORGANIZATIONS

6558 ■ Canadian Association Environmental Management–Association Canadienne de Gestion Environnementale
Aberdeen Hospital
835 E River Rd.
New Glasgow, NS, Canada B2G 3S6
Ph:(902)725-7600
Fax:(902)755-3975
Co. E-mail: rosemary.gillis-bowers@pcha.nshealth.ca
URL: http://www.thecanadiangroup.com/caha/index.htm
Contact: Rosemary Gillis-Bowers CEM, Acting Pres./Sec.-Treas.

Description: Environmental managers. Seeks to advance the environmental (housekeeping) profession; promotes adherence to high standards of ethics and practice by members. Represents members' interests; facilitates communication and cooperation among members. **Publications:** *The Quarterly* (quarterly).

REFERENCE WORKS

6559 ■ "Domestic Workers Organize!" in *WorkingUSA* (Vol. 11, December 2008, No. 4, pp. 413)
Pub: Blackwell Publishers Ltd.

Ed: Eileen Boris, Premilla Nadasen. **Description:** History of domestic workers in the U.S. is examined. The article challenges the long-standing assumption that these, primarily women of color cleaners, nannies, and elder care providers are unable to organize and assesses the possibilities and limitations of recent organizing efforts. The nature of the occupation, its location in the home, the isolated character of the work, informal arrangements with employers, and exclusions from labor law protection, has fostered community-based, social movement organizing to build coalitions, reform legislation and draw public attention to the plight of domestic workers.

6560 ■ *International Sanitary Supply Association—Membership Directory*
Pub: ISSA
Contact: Lisa Veeck, Web and Communications Dir.
E-mail: lisav@issa.com

Ed: Michael McQueen, Editor, mike@issa.com. **Released:** Annual, spring. **Covers:** About 5,500 member associates, manufacturers, manufacturers' representatives, distributors, publishers, and wholesalers of industrial and institutional cleaning and maintenance chemicals, equipment, and supplies; international coverage. **Entries Include:** Company name, address, phone, names of key personnel, line of business; manufacturer listings include product information, email and website. **Arrangement:** Geographical. **Indexes:** Alphabetical, product.

6561 ■ "What Moms Want" in *Marketing to Women* (Vol. 21, February 2008, No. 2, pp. 6)
Pub: EPM Communications, Inc.

Description: According to a survey conducted by Eureka's Spa, moms would rather have an experience gift than flowers or chocolate. The top five dream gifts include a spa day, a weekend getaway, maid service, a bathroom makeover or a getaway weekend with girlfriends.

TRADE PERIODICALS

6562 ■ *Services*
Pub: Building Service Contractors Association Int'l.
Contact: Trevilynn Blakeslee, Managing Editor

Released: Bimonthly. **Price:** $24 members; $30 nonmembers; $48 other countries members; $54 other countries non-members. **Description:** Trade journal for maintenance and cleaning contractors and facility management companies.

CONSULTANTS

6563 ■ Cleaning Consultant Services Inc.
3693 E Marginal Way S
PO Box 1273
Seattle, WA 98134
Ph:(206)682-9748
Fax:(206)622-6876
Co. E-mail: ccs@cleaningconsultants.com
URL: http://www.cleaningconsultants.com
Contact: Wm. R. Griffin, President
E-mail: wgriffin@cleaningconsultants.com
Scope: Management consultants to cleaning and maintenance contractors, property managers, hospitals, schools, hotels, building owners, facility directors, and small business owners in the cleaning industry. Services are designed to increase efficiency and profit through training and the use of time-saving techniques on the job; increase the useful life of building surfaces and equipment; encourage self development of cleaning and maintenance professionals; and make the world a clean and safe place to live. Specific consulting services are related to cleaning contract specifications development and negotiation, claim and dispute resolution, certified carpet and floor covering inspection and corrections, expert court testimony, independent certified cleaning and maintenance inspections, training program and materials development, building startup and long-range maintenance planning, architect and engineering services regarding cleaning, and building maintenance. Serves all industries in need of cleaning and maintenance services. **Publications:** "Raising the Bar with Science, Training and Upward Mobility," Jan, 2010; "Technology Revolutionizes the Cleaning Process "Cleaning for Health" is the New Mantra," Distribution Sales and Management Magazine, May, 2003; "Bill Griffin's Crystal Balls-Cleaning Trends in the Usa 2001," Floor Care is Hot in 2001," Mar, 2001; "Inclean Magazine (Australia), Feb, 2001; "Maintaining Swimming Pools, Spas, Whirlpool Tubs and Saunas," Executive House keeping, Feb, 2001; "Whats New with Floor Care," 2001. **Seminars:** Stone Maintenance Technician (SMT) IICRC Certification Course; Carpet Cleaning Technician; Apprentice/Basic Skills; Organizing Custodial Operations for Maximum Efficiency: How to Sell & Price Contract Cleaning; Starting a House cleaning Business; Rugs & Carpet Cleaning; How to Start and Operate a Successful Cleaning Business; Cleaning Schools in the 2000and Beyond; Bringing About and Working Through Change; Organizing Custodial Operations for Maximum Efficiency; Floor Care Technician (FCT)11 CPC Certified Course; Administering Cleaning Service Contracts.

FRANCHISES AND BUSINESS OPPORTUNITIES

6564 ■ BearCom Building Services
BearCom Building Services, Inc.
7022 S 400 West
Midvale, UT 84047
Ph:(801)569-9500
Free: 888-569-9533
Fax:(801)569-8400
No. of Franchise Units: 58. **Founded:** 1979. **Franchised:** 1990. **Description:** Commercial cleaning. **Equity Capital Needed:** $12,787-$39,287. **Franchise Fee:** $9,995-$14,995. **Royalty Fee:** 8%. **Financial Assistance:** Yes. **Training:** Offers 24 hours training with ongoing support.

6565 ■ The Cleaning Authority
7230 Lee Deforest Dr.
Columbia, MD 21046
Ph:(410)740-1900
Free: 877-504-6221
URL: http://www.thecleaningauthority.com

No. of Franchise Units: 160. **No. of Company-Owned Units:** 1. **Founded:** 1978. **Franchised:** 1996. **Description:** Cleaning service. **Equity Capital Needed:** $90,000 -$110,000. **Franchise Fee:** $30,000-$50,000. **Financial Assistance:** Third party financing. **Training:** 2 week home office training; onsite visits, quarterly newsletter, ongoing training sessions.

6566 ■ Cleaning Consultant Services Inc.
PO Box 1273
Seattle, WA 98111
Ph:(206)682-9748

No. of Franchise Units: 2. **No. of Company-Owned Units:** 3. **Founded:** 1976. **Franchised:** 1978. **Description:** Support services to those who own, manage and/or supervise cleaning operations. **Equity Capital Needed:** $7,500. **Franchise Fee:** $2,500. **Managerial Assistance:** Manuals and onsite visits provided. **Training:** 2-3 days at out training site in Seattle, WA.

6567 ■ Cottage Care Canada
816 Willow Park Dr. SE, Ste. 105
Calgary, AB, Canada T2J 5S1
Ph:(403)225-3441
Free: 800-718-8200
Fax:(403)225-3502
Co. E-mail: housecleaning@cottagecare.ca
URL: http://www.cottagecare.com

No. of Franchise Units: 6. **Founded:** 1996. **Franchised:** 1996. **Description:** Cottage Care Canada are into general housecleaning services. **Equity Capital Needed:** $75,000-$100,000. **Franchise Fee:** $19,500. **Training:** Provides 2 weeks training prior to start-up and ongoing support.

6568 ■ CottageCare, Inc.
6323 W 110th St.
Overland Park, KS 66211
Ph:(913)469-8778
Free: 800-469-6303
Fax:(913)469-0822
URL: http://www.cottagecare.com

No. of Franchise Units: 32. **No. of Company-Owned Units:** 8. **Founded:** 1988. **Franchised:** 1989. **Description:** Big business approach to housecleaning. Franchisor markets and signs-up new customers. Franchisee operates business and has a staff that cleans. Jumbo territories with availability of multiple offices in each territory. **Equity Capital Needed:** $69,500 total investment. **Franchise Fee:** $17,500-$19,500. **Royalty Fee:** 5.5%. **Financial Assistance:** Yes. **Managerial Assistance:** Continual support includes all marketing, analysis of weekly operational and financial reports, teleconferences and weekly news letter. Routine business reviews and onsite visits. **Training:** Provides training at headquarters for 10 days and ongoing support.

6569 ■ Home Cleaning Centers of America
4851 W 134th St., Unit D
Leawood, KS 66209
Ph:(913)327-5227
Free: 800-767-1118
Fax:(913)327-5272
Co. E-mail: Mcalhoon@homecleaningcenters.com
URL: http://www.homecleaningcenters.com

No. of Franchise Units: 34. **Founded:** 1981. **Franchised:** 1984. **Description:** Home and office cleaning service. **Equity Capital Needed:** $35,000-$45,000. **Franchise Fee:** $12,500. **Financial Assistance:** No. **Training:** Begins with a 1 week training in Denver. Then franchisee will be monitored and supported by a "District Manager" who also has owned and managed a franchise. All decisions are made by "Policy Committee" comprised of franchise owners. That is followed up with an Annual Franchise Meeting.

6570 ■ Jani-King Canada
23 Cornwallis St.
Kentville, NS, Canada B4N 2E2
Ph:(902)678-3200
Free: 800-565-1873
Fax:(902)678-3500
Co. E-mail: info@janiking.ca
URL: http://www.janiking.ca

No. of Franchise Units: 593. **No. of Company-Owned Units:** 21. **Founded:** 1969. **Franchised:** 1976. **Description:** Commercial cleaning franchise. **Franchise Fee:** $10,900-$24,000. **Training:** Initial and ongoing support provided.

6571 ■ Maid Brigade
Maid Brigade, Inc.
4 Concourse Pky., Ste. 200
Atlanta, GA 30328
Ph:(770)551-9630
Free: 800-722-MAID
Fax:(770)391-9092
Co. E-mail: franrec@maidbrigade.com
URL: http://www.maidbrigade.com

No. of Franchise Units: 413. **Founded:** 1979. **Franchised:** 1981. **Description:** Cleaning service serving from 20,000 to 150,000 qualified households. We provide unparalleled support, business development, and the latest technology in the industry. If lifestyle, safe investment, quick-start, building equity & generating income are important to you contact us. **Equity Capital Needed:** From $87,000-$132,500. **Franchise Fee:** From $29,500-$58,500. **Financial Assistance:** Yes. **Training:** Pre-opening throughout the life of your business, support never stops. New training DVDs, manuals, on-line training, home office training, onsite training, bulletin board, e-mail, councils, conferences, technical support, etc. Our support staff is comprised of former successful Maid Brigade franchisees.

6572 ■ Maid to Perfection
Maid to Perfection Global, Inc.
3111 Innovation Dr.
St. Cloud, FL 34769
Ph:(407)870-2474
Free: 800-648-6243
Fax:(407)932-0587
Co. E-mail: MAIDSVC@aol.com
URL: http://www.maidtoperfectioncorp.com

No. of Franchise Units: 305. **Founded:** 1980. **Franchised:** 1990. **Description:** Maid to Perfection provides customized cleaning designed for today's sophisticated customer, making service easy to sell. A residential and commercial business. Proven record of offering choices & diversification to franchisees, which leads to higher profits. Unmatched operational format ensures continuous growth. Your business plan adjusts to your market to meet your goals. Success Magazine ranked Maid To Perfection 1 for franchise support & satisfaction 1999. **Equity Capital Needed:** $54,937-$62,635. **Franchise Fee:** $15,000. **Financial Assistance:** Entire investment if qualified, and all expansion territories. **Training:** 6-8 week business start-up planning, 5 day HQ training, includes live in-home estimating, 5 day office setup & field training, training manuals & CD, 11 instructional videos, advertising materials and assistance, computer program available, 800 help line, national convention, monthly newsletters, ongoing support.

6573 ■ Maid to Sparkle Inc.
2151 Carbon Hill Drive
Midlothian, VA 23113
Ph:(804)382-7749
Fax:(804)272-0723

No. of Franchise Units: 2. **No. of Company-Owned Units:** 2. **Founded:** 1998. **Franchised:** 2003. **Description:** Maid services. **Equity Capital Needed:** $15,000. **Franchise Fee:** $20,000. **Royalty Fee:** 7%. **Financial Assistance:** Yes. **Training:** Provides 1 week training at headquarters, 1 week onsite and ongoing support.

6574 ■ Maidpro
180 Canal St.
Boston, MA 02114
Ph:(617)742-8787
Free: 888-MAI-DPRO
Fax:(617)720-0700
Co. E-mail: chuck@maidpro.com
URL: http://www.maidpro.com

No. of Franchise Units: 109. **No. of Company-Owned Units:** 1. **Founded:** 1991. **Franchised:** 1997. **Description:** Maid services. **Equity Capital Needed:** $80,709-$103,959. **Franchise Fee:** $7,900. **Financial Assistance:** Third party financing available. **Training:** Includes 6-8 weeks in training and ongoing support.

6575 ■ MAIDS ETC.
4907 Hollenden Dr., Ste. 208
Raleigh, NC 27616
Ph:(919)834-8215
Free: 877-624-3738
Fax:(919)834-7630
Co. E-mail: franchise@maidsetc.com
URL: http://www.maidsetc.com

No. of Franchise Units: 15. **No. of Company-Owned Units:** 3. **Founded:** 1989. **Franchised:** 2003. **Description:** It's time to clean up with MAIDS ETC. and create your own future in residential and commercial cleaning, which is experiencing explosive growth. We are the 'full service people' offering full-service residential and commercial bull's-eye cleaning systems. We provide our owner-operators with training, consultation, operational support and access to the latest technological advances. **Equity Capital Needed:** $36,500-$56,500. **Franchise Fee:** $9,995. **Financial Assistance:** Available up to 100% of the franchise fee for qualified candidates. **Training:** 6 week business start-up training, 5 day headquarter training and 5 day onsite office setup and field training, start-up equipment and supplies, 800 assist line, computer software, and advertisement materials.

6576 ■ The Maids Home Service
The Maids International, Inc.
4820 Dodge St.
Omaha, NE 68132
Free: 800-843-6243
Fax:(402)558-4112
Co. E-mail: franchising@themaids.net
URL: http://www.maids.com

No. of Franchise Units: 1,058. **No. of Company-Owned Units:** 26. **Founded:** 1979. **Franchised:** 1981. **Description:** Residential maid service franchise. **Equity Capital Needed:** $92,545-$120,295. **Franchise Fee:** $10,000. **Royalty Fee:** 3.9%-6.9%. **Financial Assistance:** Third party financing available. **Training:** Includes 10 days training at corporate headquarters, 5 days at franchisee's location and 7-10 weeks phone consultation (before & after corporate training) and ongoing support.

6577 ■ Maid2Clean
3054 Dundas St., W
Toronto, ON, Canada M6P 1Z7
Ph:(905)877-0777
Free: 877-265-6243
Fax:(905)702-8801
Co. E-mail: mike.walsh@maid2clean.ca
URL: http://www.maid2clean.ca

No. of Franchise Units: 60. **Founded:** 1993. **Franchised:** 1999. **Description:** Domestic housekeeping, cleaning and ironing services provided to private residential homes. **Equity Capital Needed:** $29,500. **Franchise Fee:** $19,500. **Training:** Provides 2 days training and ongoing support.

6578 ■ Merry Maids
3839 Forest Hill-Irene Rd.
Memphis, TN 38125
Ph:800-263-5928
Free: 800-798-8000
Fax:(901)597-7580
Co. E-mail: franchisesales@mmhomeoffice.com
URL: http://www.merrymaids.com

No. of Franchise Units: 689. **No. of Company-Owned Units:** 257. **Founded:** 1979. **Franchised:** 1980. **Description:** Residential cleaning service. Entrepreneur Magazine has ranked Merry Maids 1 in the industry for 9 consecutive yrs. Black Enterprise magazine ranked Merry Maids one of the Fabulous 15 low cost franchises! The company's commitment to training and support is unmatched. Merry Maids provides comprehensive software and equipment and supply package. Products and supplies available online. Member of the ServiceMaster Quality Service Network. **Equity Capital Needed:** $55,350-$73,850 Total capital requirement. **Franchise Fee:** $33,500-$43,500. **Financial Assistance:** Up to 80% available toward franchise fee. **Training:** 8 day HQ training; all start-up equipment and supplies for 2 teams Buddy Program, educational programs, 800 number for assistance, national TV ads, free website for each franchise, weekly intranet bulletin board, newsletters, regional meetings, national convention, proprietary intranet website, 17 field regional coordinators.

6579 ■ Merry Maids of Canada
ServiceMaster
5462 Timberlea Blvd.
Mississauga, ON, Canada L4W 2T7
Ph:(905)670-0000
Free: 800-263-5928
Fax:(905)670-0077
Co. E-mail: thould@smclean.com
URL: http://www.merrymaids.com

No. of Franchise Units: 72. **No. of Company-Owned Units:** 100. **Founded:** 1979. **Franchised:** 1980. **Description:** Residential cleaning service with a majority of workers being women. **Equity Capital Needed:** $35,000-$60,000. **Franchise Fee:** $28,000-$35,000. **Financial Assistance:** Yes. **Training:** Training includes 10 days at Merry Maids University and ongoing support from Canadian home office included.

6580 ■ Mini Maid
3020 Canton Rd., Ste. 13
Marietta, GA 30066-3800
Ph:(770)794-9938
Free: 800-627-6464
Fax:(770)794-1877

No. of Franchise Units: 85. **No. of Company-Owned Units:** 10. **Founded:** 1973. **Description:** Maid services. **Equity Capital Needed:** $28,000. **Franchise Fee:** $15,500. **Financial Assistance:** No. **Training:** Yes.

6581 ■ Mint Condition Franchising, Inc.
Mint Condition, Inc.
1057 521 Corporate Center Dr., Ste. 165
Fort Mill, SC 29707
Ph:(803)548-6121
Fax:(803)548-4578
Co. E-mail: info@mintconditioninc.com
URL: http://www.mintconditioninc.com

No. of Franchise Units: 60. **No. of Company-Owned Units:** 1. **Franchised:** 1996. **Description:** A Mint Condition Franchise gives you immediate access to a proven and successful model. Our Franchisees are provided with an initial customer base, training, equipment packages, billing and collections from customers, and field support. I invite you to ask about our unique contract guarantees. **Equity Capital Needed:** $1,000-$20,900 start-up cash; $4,384-$45,100 total initial investment. **Franchise Fee:** $3,000-$22,000. **Financial Assistance:** Available for the initial business plan, equipment packages, and for securing additional business. **Training:** Training includes both classroom and field support. Our extensive training includes cleaning techniques and standards, customer service, sales and marketing, personnel, floor care maintenance.

6582 ■ Molly Maid, Inc.
Service Brands Intl.
3948 Ranchero Dr.
Ann Arbor, MI 48108
Ph:(734)822-6800
Free: 800-886-6559
Fax:(734)822-6666
Co. E-mail: info@mollymaid.com
URL: http://www.mollymaid.com

No. of Franchise Units: 614. **Founded:** 1979. **Franchised:** 1984. **Description:** Maid service industry. Since 1979, they have cleaned more than 10 million homes in 5 countries. MOLLY MAID has received awards for franchise excellence, and has a stellar reputation nationwide. Learn more about MOLLY MAID by browsing through their web site or feel free to give them a call at 800-665-5962. **Equity Capital Needed:** Total investment $150,000-$175,000, including working capital. **Franchise Fee:** $14,900. **Royalty Fee:** 3-6.5% declining. **Financial Assistance:** No. **Training:** 6-8 pre-train program, followed by a week at the home office and week at a Regional Training Center. Industry-leading software, a dedicated support staff, publications and national meetings are available.

6583 ■ Mr. Handyman
Service Brands Intl.
3948 Ranchero Dr.
Ann Arbor, MI 48108
Ph:(734)822-6535
Free: 800-289-4600
Fax:(734)822-6666
Co. E-mail: info@mrhandyman.com
URL: http://www.mrhandyman.com

No. of Franchise Units: 248. **Founded:** 1996. **Franchised:** 2000. **Description:** Mr. Handyman caters to U.S. homeowners and commercial customers needing property repairs. Mr. Handyman is the solution for millions of time-starved, two-income families needing assistance in maintaining their households. There are hundreds of to-do lists on refrigerator doors waiting for Mr. Handyman. Learn more about Mr. Handyman by browsing their web site or give them a call at 800-289-4600. **Equity Capital Needed:** $120,000-$130,000. **Franchise Fee:** $19,900 **Financial Assistance:** Yes. **Training:** Intensive 4-8 pre-training program, followed by a week at the home office and a personal onsite visit. Industry-leading software, a dedicated support staff, publications and national meetings are available.

6584 ■ MTOclean Inc.
Maids to Order of Ohio, Inc.
7100 E Pleasant Valley Rd., Ste. 300
Independence, OH 44131
Free: 877-392-6278
Fax:(216)674-0650
Co. E-mail: kgolubski@mtoclean.com
URL: http://www.mtoclean.com

No. of Franchise Units: 35. **Founded:** 1988. **Franchised:** 1992. **Description:** Maid service. **Equity Capital Needed:** $17,300-$86,600 working capital. **Franchise Fee:** $5,000-$9,900. **Royalty Fee:** 3-6%. **Financial Assistance:** In-house financing available. **Training:** Training provided at corporate headquarters for 1 week, 1-2 days at franchisee's location and ongoing support.

6585 ■ Nature Stone
O.C.R. Products Inc.
15 N Park St.
Bedford, OH 44146
Ph:(440)786-9100
Free: 800-358-0583
Fax:(440)786-1927
Co. E-mail: jteresi@naturestonefloors.com
URL: http://www.naturestonefloors.com

No. of Franchise Units: 41. **No. of Company-Owned Units:** 3. **Founded:** 1989. **Franchised:** 2005. **Description:** Franchisee will receive a franchise to own and operate a Nature Stone business, involving the sale and installation of a line of flooring and concrete resurfacing products used as a floor surface for garages, patios, driveways, basements, pool decks, and related surfaces, for an initial term of 5 years with the right, upon payment of a renewal fee and compliance with other conditions, to renew for up to three additional 5 year renewal terms. **Equity Capital Needed:** $141,500-$398,630, includes franchise fee. **Franchise Fee:** $24,950-$34,950. **Financial Assistance:** No. **Training:** Yes.

6586 ■ Royal Maid Enterprises
Enterprise House
1574 Pointe Tarpon Blvd.
Tarpon Springs, FL 34689
Ph:(727)943-9521
Co. E-mail: rmaids@knology.net
URL: http://www.royalmaidservice.com

No. of Franchise Units: 36. **Founded:** 1992. **Description: Equity Capital Needed:** $39,000-$60,000. **Franchise Fee:** From $25,000. **Financial Assistance:** No. **Managerial Assistance:** Manual and training DVD, computer program, advertising materials and assistance. **Training:** Offers 6-8 week business start up planning, 5 day office set up and on site training including in home estimating and field training and ongoing support.

6587 ■ ServiceMaster Residential and Commercial Services, L.P.
ServiceMaster Clean
3839 Forest Hill-Irene Rd.
Memphis, TN 38125
Ph:(901)597-7500
Free: 800-786-9687
Fax:(901)597-7580
Co. E-mail: smfranchiseinfo@smclean.com
URL: http://www.ownafranchise.com

No. of Franchise Units: 4,500. **Founded:** 1947. **Franchised:** 1952. **Description:** Provides heavy cleaning services for homes, including carpet, upholstery, draperies, windows and disaster restoration. Janitorial services are also provided for the commercial market. Provides all the research, equipment, supplies, initial and continuous training franchisees need. **Equity Capital Needed:** $47,860-$161,125. **Franchise Fee:** $24,900-$79,200. **Financial Assistance:** Offers financing on up to 80% of the franchise fee and equipment. **Training:** 2 weeks training at corporate headquarters; monthly newsletters; local and national conferences. Regional operations managers assist the franchisees in the growth and development of their business. All of the departments within ServiceMaster have at least one person who handles franchise relations. Each distributor has owned and operated his/her own ServiceMaster for at least 5 years, as have the regional operations managers.

6588 ■ Servpro
Servpro Industries, Inc.
801 Industrial Blvd.
Gallatin, TN 37066
Ph:(615)451-0600
Free: 800-826-9586
Fax:(615)451-1602
Co. E-mail: franchise@servpronet.com
URL: http://www.servpro.com

No. of Franchise Units: 1,500+. **Founded:** 1967. **Franchised:** 1969. **Description:** A completely diversified cleaning & restoration business, with multiple income opportunities. The insurance restoration market (fire, smoke and water damage) is their main focus. Specialize in commercial & residential cleaning. **Equity Capital Needed:** $132,050-$180,450. **Franchise Fee:** $41,000. **Financial Assistance:** May offer partial financing in addition to assisting with2third party lenders. **Training:** Intensive home study curriculum, manuals and videos. Provides 2 weeks training in state of the art national training facility, 1 week set up/opening assistance, and trainer assistance. Ongoing support, convention, regional and area meetings, formal business reviews, newsletters, bulletins, and more.

Driving School

ASSOCIATIONS AND OTHER ORGANIZATIONS

6589 ■ American Driver and Traffic Safety Education Association
Highway Safety Services, LLC
1434 Trim Tree Rd.
Indiana, PA 15701
Ph:(724)801-8246
Free: 877-485-7172
Fax:(724)349-5042
Co. E-mail: office@adtsea.org
URL: http://www.adtsea.org/adtsea
Contact: Fred Nagao, Pres.

Description: Professional organization of teachers and supervisors interested in improving driver and traffic safety education in colleges and secondary and elementary schools. Awards honorary memberships to retired persons distinguished in the field. Provides assistance to state departments of education, colleges and universities, state associations, and local school districts. **Publications:** *Journal of Traffic Safety Education* (quarterly); *Washington Wire* (periodic).

6590 ■ Governors Highway Safety Association
444 N Capitol St. NW, Ste. 722
Washington, DC 20001
Ph:(202)789-0942
Fax:(202)789-0946
Co. E-mail: headquarters@ghsa.org
URL: http://www.ghsa.org
Contact: Barbara L. Harsha, Exec. Dir.

Description: Represents the interests of state and territorial officials who administer the Highway Safety Act of 1966. (The Highway Safety Act requires that states receiving highway safety grants under 23 U.S. Code 402 may not receive program approval unless the governor of each state or territory is responsible for administration of the program.) Works to reduce highway fatalities and automobile accidents; enforces the 55 mph speed limit; develops and maintains driver education and pedestrian and bicycle safety programs; manages alcohol safety and occupant protection programs. Conducts research through grant programs. Provides highway safety training in such areas as judicial training, engineering, traffic engineering, and traffic safety engineering. **Publications:** *Directions in Highway Safety* (quarterly).

TRADE PERIODICALS

6591 ■ *Dual News*
Pub: Driving School Association of Americas

Ed: George R. Hensel, Editor, grhensel@aol.com. **Released:** Quarterly. **Price:** Free. **Description:** Focuses on traffic safety, automobile care (repair and maintenance), teaching methods, and driving, in general. Recurring features include news of research and columns titled Legislation Pertaining to Driving, Teaching Methods, and President's Corner.

6592 ■ *Highway Safety Directions*
Pub: Highway Safety Research Center
Contact: Shannon Walters

Ed: Katy Jones **Released:** Biennial. **Price:** Free. **Description:** Reports on research being done by the University of North Carolina Highway Safety Research Center, including alcohol and highway safety, motor vehicle inspection, accident investigation and analysis, driver behavior, and education and licensing. Carries news on adult and child passenger safety, including seat belts and child seats, passenger protection laws, and statewide passenger safety efforts.

6593 ■ *In Motion*
Pub: General Learning Communications

Released: Annual. **Description:** Driver education magazine.

VIDEOCASSETTES/ AUDIOCASSETTES

6594 ■ *At the Wheel*
National Film Board of Canada
1123 Broadway, Ste. 307
New York, NY 10010
Ph:(212)629-8890
Free: 800-542-2164
Fax:(212)629-8502
URL: http://www.nfb.ca

Released: 1989. **Price:** $400.00. **Description:** This video series documents the consequences and aftereffects of a serious automobile crash. **Availability:** VHS; 3/4U.

6595 ■ *Defensive Driving Techniques*
Gun Video
4585 Murphy Canyon Rd.
San Diego, CA 92123
Ph:(858)569-4000
Free: 800-942-8273
Fax:(858)569-0505
Co. E-mail: info2@gunvideo.com
URL: http://www.gunvideo.com

Price: $49.95. **Description:** Advice on high-speed driving from expert instructors. **Availability:** VHS.

6596 ■ *General Driving Safety*
Gulf Publishing Co.
PO Box 2608
Houston, TX 77252
Ph:(713)529-4301
Free: 800-231-6275
Fax:(713)520-4433
Co. E-mail: customerservices@gulfpub.com
URL: http://www.gulfpub.com

Description: Eleven-part series that provides instruction on driving safety, including information on road conditions and speed, drunk driving, accidents, sleepiness and driving, mountain driving, skidding, convoys, safety devices, seat belts, fire-resistant clothing, and backing up. **Availability:** VHS; 3/4U.

TRADE SHOWS AND CONVENTIONS

6597 ■ Driving School Association of America Annual Conference
Driving School Association of America
12676 Bass Lake Rd.
Maple Grove, MN 55369
Free: 800-270-3722
Fax:(763)398-0778
Co. E-mail: info@thedssa.org
URL: http://www.thedsaa.org

Released: Annual. **Audience:** social functions only. **Principal Exhibits:** Automobile safety products related to driver training and traffic safety. **Dates and Locations:** 2011 Nov 09-12, San Francisco, CA.

FRANCHISES AND BUSINESS OPPORTUNITIES

6598 ■ All Star Franchising, LLC
All Star Driver Education, Inc.
1011 S Main St.
Ann Arbor, MI 48104
Ph:(734)665-7374
Free: 800-967-7719
Fax:(734)665-7680

No. of Company-Owned Units: 30. **Founded:** 1997. **Franchised:** 2007. **Description:** Driver education. **Equity Capital Needed:** $83,700-$199,900. **Franchise Fee:** $30,000. **Financial Assistance:** Yes. **Training:** Yes.

LIBRARIES

6599 ■ Alabama Department of Transportation–Research & Development Bureau–Research Library (1409)
1409 Coliseum Blvd.
Montgomery, AL 36110
Ph:(334)206-2210
Fax:(334)264-2042
Co. E-mail: harrisi@dot.state.al.us
URL: http://www.dot.state.al.us/docs
Contact: Jeffrey W. Brown, Res. & Dev.Engr.

Scope: Transportation. **Services:** Interlibrary loan; Library not open to the public. **Holdings:** 1000 books; 5000 reports. **Subscriptions:** 8 journals and other serials.

6600 ■ American Automobile Association Research Library
1000 AAA Dr.
Heathrow, FL 32746-5060
Ph:(407)444-7965
Fax:(407)444-7759
Co. E-mail: rinesta@aaasouth.com
URL: http://www.aaasouth.com
Contact: Renaldo Inesta, Div.Mgr.

Scope: Travel guide books; market studies; highway and traffic safety; driver education; automobiles - history, statistics, insurance. **Services:** Interlibrary loan;

Library open to researchers with permission. **Holdings:** 10,000 books; 20 VF drawers of pamphlets; reports. **Subscriptions:** 100 journals and other serials.

6601 ■ California State Department of Motor Vehicles–Licensing Operations Division - Research and Development Branch–Traffic Safety Research Library (2415)
2415 1st Ave., MS F-126
Sacramento, CA 95818
Ph:(916)657-3079
Fax:(916)657-8589
Co. E-mail: dluong@dvm.ca.gov
Contact: Douglas Luong, Staff Svcs.Anl.
Scope: Automobile transportation. **Services:** Copying; Library not open to the public. **Holdings:** 500 books; 10,000 bound periodical volumes; reports; manuscripts. **Subscriptions:** 20 journals and other serials.

6602 ■ Connecticut Department of Transportation–ConnDOT Library and Information Center
2800 Berlin Tpke.
Newington, CT 06111-4116
Ph:(860)594-3035
Fax:(860)594-3039
Co. E-mail: betty.ambler@po.state.ct.us
URL: http://www.ct.gov/dot/site/default.asp
Contact: Betty Ambler, Libn.
Scope: Transportation. **Services:** Interlibrary loan; copying; Library open to the public by appointment. **Holdings:** 10,000 books; 10,000 reports.

6603 ■ Kansas Department of Transportation Library
700 S.W. Harrison St.
Eisenhower State Office Bldg., 4th Fl., W.
Topeka, KS 66603-3745
Ph:(785)291-3854
Fax:(785)291-3717
Co. E-mail: library@ksdot.org
Contact: Marie Manthe, Libn.
Scope: Transportation. **Services:** Interlibrary loan; Library open to the public. **Holdings:** 3000 books; 20,000 reports; 175 CD-ROMs; 100 videos **Subscriptions:** 100 journals and other serials.

6604 ■ Kentucky Transportation Center Library
University of Kentucky
176 Raymond Bldg.
Lexington, KY 40506-0281
Ph:(859)257-2155
Free: 800-432-0719
Fax:(859)257-1815
Co. E-mail: lwhayne@engr.uky.edu
URL: http://www.kyt2.com/
Contact: Laura Whayne, Libn.
Scope: Transportation. **Services:** Interlibrary loan; copying; Library open to the public. **Holdings:** 6000 books; 9000 reports; 800 videotapes. **Subscriptions:** 300 journals and other serials.

6605 ■ Missouri Highway and Transportation Department–Division of Materials Library
PO Box 270
Jefferson City, MO 65102-0270
Ph:(573)751-6735
Fax:(573)526-5636
Co. E-mail: michael.meyerhoff@mail.modot.state.mo.us
URL: http://www.modot.org/
Contact: Mona Scott
Scope: Transportation. **Services:** Library not open to the public. **Holdings:** Figures not available.

6606 ■ Montana Department of Transportation Library
2701 Prospect Ave.
PO Box 201001
Helena, MT 59620-1001
Ph:(406)444-6338
Fax:(406)444-7204
Co. E-mail: ssillick@mt.gov
URL: http://www.mdt.mt.gov/research/unique/services.shtml
Contact: Susan Sillick
Scope: Transportation. **Services:** Interlibrary loan; copying. **Holdings:** 10,000 items; reports; CD-ROMs; video. **Subscriptions:** 10 journals and other serials.

6607 ■ New Jersey Department of Transportation–Research Library
1035 Parkway Ave.
PO Box 600
Trenton, NJ 08625-0600
Ph:(609)530-5289
Fax:(609)530-2052
Co. E-mail: library@dot.state.nj.us
URL: http://www.state.nj.us/transportation/refdata/library/
Contact: Carol Paszamant, Libn.
Scope: Transportation. **Services:** Interlibrary loan; Library open to the public by appointment. **Holdings:** 300 books; 11,000 reports. **Subscriptions:** 50 journals and other serials.

6608 ■ North Carolina Department of Transportation–Research and Development Library
PO Box 25201
Raleigh, NC 27611
Ph:(919)715-2463
Fax:(919)715-0137
Co. E-mail: rhhall@dot.state.nc.us
URL: http://www.ncdot.org/
Contact: Bob Hall
Scope: Transportation. **Services:** Interlibrary loan; copying; Library open to the public for reference use only. **Holdings:** 11,209 books; 20,021 reports; 132 videos. **Subscriptions:** 57 journals and other serials.

6609 ■ North Dakota Department of Transportation–Materials and Research Division Library
300 Airport Rd.
Bismarck, ND 58504-6005
Ph:(701)328-6901
Fax:(701)328-0310
Co. E-mail: gweisger@nd.gov
Contact: Gerri Weisgerber, Adm. Staff Off.
Scope: Transportation. **Services:** Library not open to the public. **Holdings:** 6600 reports. **Subscriptions:** 5 journals and other serials.

6610 ■ South Carolina Department of Transportation Library
955 Park St., Rm. 110
Columbia, SC 29202
Ph:(803)737-9897
Fax:(803)737-0824
Co. E-mail: adcockda@dot.state.sc.us
URL: http://www.dot.state.sc.us
Contact: Ann Adcock, Mgr.
Scope: Transportation, engineering, mass transit. **Services:** Interlibrary loan; transportation related research; Library open to the public. **Holdings:** 5500 books; 90 bound periodical volumes; 1900 reports; 250 videos. **Subscriptions:** 41 journals and other serials; 10 newspapers.

6611 ■ U.S. National Highway Traffic Safety Administration–Technical Information Services
1200 New Jersey Ave., SE
Washington, DC 20590
Ph:888-327-4236
Fax:(202)493-2833
Co. E-mail: tis@nhtsa.dot.gov
URL: http://www.nhtsa.dot.gov/cars/problems/trd/?name=
Contact: Kevin M. Ball
Scope: Motor vehicle safety, highway traffic safety, alcohol countermeasures for driving safety, vehicle occupant protection, emergency medical services. **Services:** Copying; TIS open to the public. **Holdings:** 200 books; 52,000 agency and related publications and reports; 920,000 microfiche. **Subscriptions:** 40 journals and other serials.

6612 ■ Vermont Agency of Transportation–Policy and Planning Division Library
133 State St.
Montpelier, VT 05633
Ph:(802)828-2544
Fax:(802)828-3983
Contact: Sandy Aja
Scope: Transportation. **Holdings:** Figures not available.

RESEARCH CENTERS

6613 ■ Indiana University Bloomington–Center for Health and Safety Studies
1025 E 7th, HPER Rm. 116
Bloomington, IN 47405
Ph:(812)855-2429
Fax:(812)855-3936
Co. E-mail: torabi@indiana.edu
URL: http://www.research.iu.edu/centers/chss.html
Contact: Dr. Mohammad R. Torabi, Ch.
E-mail: torabi@indiana.edu
Scope: Health behavior, quantitative and qualitative evaluation of instructional materials, and human behavior and attitudes relating to safety and driver education, including studies on industrial safety, health and safety practices in industry and recreational settings, childhood accident prevention and injury control, nutrition, family life, and human development. **Services:** Health and safety consulting to industry and government. **Educational Activities:** Conferences on health and safety issues (occasionally).

6614 ■ University of North Carolina at Chapel Hill–Highway Safety Research Center
730 Martin Luther King Jr. Blvd., CB 3430
Chapel Hill, NC 27599-3430
Ph:(919)962-2202
Free: 800—672-4527
Fax:(919)962-8710
Co. E-mail: david_harkey@unc.edu
URL: http://www.hsrc.unc.edu/index.cfm
Contact: David L. Harkey, Dir.
E-mail: david_harkey@unc.edu
Scope: Highway traffic safety, including evaluation of state's operational highway safety program, analysis of mass traffic accident data; roadway hazards; seat belt and restraint system incentives; law, policy and usage studies; evaluation of highway safety countermeasure programs; alcohol and highway safety; driver education and licensing; commercial motor vehicle safety; bicycle and pedestrian safety; older and younger driver studies; and driver distraction studies. **Publications:** Highway Safety Directions (e-format only 2002 forward) (occasionally). **Educational Activities:** Annual series of traffic records workshops; Occupant protection workshops (occasionally), for health and safety professionals, law enforcement officials, and researchers; Safe Routes to School Course (occasionally), for planners.

Drug Store/Pharmacy

ASSOCIATIONS AND OTHER ORGANIZATIONS

6615 ■ American Association of Colleges of Pharmacy
1727 King St.
Alexandria, VA 22314
Ph:(703)739-2330
Fax:(703)836-8982
Co. E-mail: mail@aacp.org
URL: http://www.aacp.org
Contact: Lucinda L. Maine, Exec. VP/CEO
Description: College of pharmacy programs accredited by American Council on Pharmaceutical Education; corporations and individuals. Compiles statistics. **Publications:** *American Association of Colleges of Pharmacy—Graduate Programs in the Pharmaceutical Sciences* (annual); *American Journal of Pharmaceutical Education* (quarterly); *Pharmacy School Admission Requirements* (annual); *Prescription for a Rewarding Career* (periodic); *Roster of Faculty and Professional Staff* (annual); *Roster of Teaching Personnel in Colleges of Pharmacy* (annual).

6616 ■ American Association of Pharmacy Technicians
PO Box 1447
Greensboro, NC 27402
Ph:(336)333-9356
Free: 877-368-4771
Fax:(336)333-9068
Co. E-mail: aapt@pharmacytechnician.com
URL: http://www.pharmacytechnician.com
Contact: Ms. Ann Oberg CPhT, Pres.
Description: Pharmacy technicians. Promotes professional advancement of members. Represents members before health care and public organizations; conducts continuing professional development courses; publicizes the role of the pharmacy technician as an "integral part of the patient care team". **Publications:** Newsletters (quarterly).

6617 ■ American College of Apothecaries
2830 Summer Oaks Dr.
Bartlett, TN 38134
Ph:(901)383-8119
Free: 800-828-5933
Fax:(901)383-8882
Co. E-mail: aca@acainfo.org
URL: http://www.americancollegeofapothecaries.com
Contact: Edward J. Hesterlee, Exec. VP
Description: Professional society of pharmacists owning and operating ethical prescription pharmacies, including hospital pharmacists, pharmacy students, and faculty of colleges of pharmacy. Translates, transforms, and disseminates knowledge, research data, and recent developments in the pharmaceutical industry and public health. Offers continuing education courses and certificate program. Conducts research programs; sponsors charitable program; compiles statistics; operates speakers' bureau. **Publications:** *American College of Apothecaries Newsletter* (monthly); *American College of Apothecaries—Patron's Newsletter* (monthly); *American College of Apothecaries—Physician's Newsletter* (monthly); *Voice of the Pharmacist* (quarterly).

6618 ■ American Foundation for Pharmaceutical Education
1 Church St., Ste. 400
Rockville, MD 20850-4184
Ph:(301)738-2160
Fax:(301)738-2161
Co. E-mail: info@afpenet.org
URL: http://www.afpenet.org
Contact: Robert M. Bachman CAE, Pres.
Description: Established by pharmaceutical and drug trade associations to improve pharmaceutical education, colleges of pharmacy, and pharmacy student performance. Accepts and administers gifts, legacies, bequests, and funds and makes disbursements for fellowships and the promotion of pharmaceutical education. .

6619 ■ American Institute of the History of Pharmacy
777 Highland Ave.
Madison, WI 53705-2222
Ph:(608)262-6234
Fax:(608)262-3943
Co. E-mail: bdfisher@aihp.org
URL: http://pharmacy.wisc.edu/aihp
Contact: Dr. Gregory J. Higby PhD, Exec. Dir.
Description: Pharmacists, firms, and organizations interested in historical and social aspects of the pharmaceutical field. Maintains pharmaceutical Americana collection; conducts research programs. **Publications:** *AIHP Notes* (quarterly); *Pharmacy in History* (quarterly).

6620 ■ American Society of Consultant Pharmacists
1321 Duke St.
Alexandria, VA 22314-3563
Ph:(703)739-1300
Free: 800-355-2727
Fax:(703)739-1321
Co. E-mail: info@ascp.com
URL: http://www.ascp.com
Contact: John Feather, Exec. Dir./CEO
Description: Provides leadership, education, advocacy and resources enabling consultant and senior care pharmacists to enhance quality of care and quality of life for older individuals through the provision of pharmaceutical care and the promotion of healthy aging. Excels in the areas of: knowledge and skills in geriatric pharmacotherapy; expertise in long-term care settings for the frail at-risk elderly and other residents; and patient-centered advocate for seniors at-risk for medication related problems. Improves drug therapy and quality of life of geriatric patients and other individuals residing in a variety of environments, including nursing facilities, subacute care and assisted living facilities, psychiatric hospitals, hospice programs, and in home and community settings. **Publications:** *The Consultant Pharmacist* (monthly); *UPDATE* (monthly).

6621 ■ American Society of Health System Pharmacists
7272 Wisconsin Ave.
Bethesda, MD 20814
Ph:(301)657-3000
Free: (866)279-0681
Fax:(301)664-8867
Co. E-mail: custserv@ashp.org
URL: http://www.ashp.org
Contact: Henri R. Manasse Jr., Exec. VP/CEO
Description: Professional society of pharmacists employed by hospitals, HMOs, clinics, and other health systems. Provides personnel placement service for members; sponsors professional and personal liability program. Conducts educational and exhibit programs. Maintains 30 practice interest areas, special sections for home care practitioners and clinical specialists, and research and education foundation. **Publications:** *American Journal of Health System Pharmacy* (semimonthly); *ASHP Newsletter* (monthly); *Handbook on Injectable Drugs* (biennial); *Intersections* (quarterly).

6622 ■ American Society for Pharmacy Law
3085 Stevenson Dr., Ste. 200
Springfield, IL 62703-4270
Ph:(217)529-6948
Fax:(217)529-9120
Co. E-mail: nchatara@associationcentral.org
URL: http://www.aspl.org
Contact: Nathela Chatara, Exec. Dir.
Description: Pharmacists, lawyers, and students. Aims are to: further legal knowledge; communicate accurate legal information to pharmacists; foster knowledge and education pertaining to the rights and duties of pharmacists; distribute information of interest to members; provide a forum for exchange of information pertaining to pharmacy law. **Publications:** *Pharma-Law eNews* (monthly); *Rx Ipsa Loquitur* (bimonthly).

6623 ■ Canadian Pharmacists Association–Association des Pharmaciens du Canada
1785 Alta Vista Dr.
Ottawa, ON, Canada K1G 3Y6
Ph:(613)523-7877
Free: 800-917-9489
Fax:(613)523-0445
Co. E-mail: info@pharmacists.ca
URL: http://www.pharmacists.ca
Contact: Jeff Poston, Exec. Dir.
Description: Pharmacists in Canada. Works to provide leadership for the pharmacy profession. Monitors government health care policies and legislation; lobbies for the interests of pharmacists. Maintains liaison with government departments, pharmaceutical manufacturers, and health care organizations. Conducts education and research programs. **Publications:** *Canadian Pharmaceutical Journal* (10/year); *Compendium of Pharmaceuticals and Specialties* (annual); *Sterile Preparations* .

6624 ■ Chain Drug Marketing Association
PO Box 995
43157 W Nine Mile Rd.
Novi, MI 48376-0995
Ph:(248)449-9300
Free: 800-935-2362
Fax:(248)449-9396
Co. E-mail: customerservice@qualitychoice.com
URL: http://www.chaindrug.com
Contact: James R. Devine, Pres.
Description: Drug store chains located throughout the world. Represents members in the market for merchandise; keeps them abreast of trends in relevant fields. .

6625 ■ Foreign Pharmacy Graduate Examination Committee
Natl. Assn. of Boards of Pharmacy
1600 Feehanville Dr.
Mount Prospect, IL 60056
Ph:(847)391-4406
Fax:(847)391-4502
Co. E-mail: custserv@nabp.net
URL: http://www.nabp.net
Contact: William T. Winsley MS, Chm.
Purpose: Provides information to foreign pharmacy graduates regarding entry into the U.S. pharmacy profession and health care systems. Evaluates qualifications of foreign pharmacy graduates. Gathers and disseminates data on foreign graduates; maintains information on foreign pharmacy schools in order to produce an examination that measures academic competence with regard to U.S. pharmacy school standards. **Publications:** *National Pharmacy Compliance News* (quarterly); *State Newsletter Program* (quarterly).

6626 ■ Generic Pharmaceutical Association
777 6th St. NW, Ste. 510
Washington, DC 20001
Ph:(202)249-7100
Co. E-mail: info@gphaonline.org
URL: http://www.gphaonline.org
Contact: Kathleen Jaeger, Pres./CEO
Description: Promotes the common interests of the members and the general welfare of the pharmaceutical industry; prepares and disseminates among members and others, accurate and reliable information concerning the industry, products, needs and requirements; participates in international, federal, state and municipal legislative, regulatory and administrative proceedings with respect to law, rules and orders affecting the pharmaceutical industry; participates in scientific research and product development with intent to increase consumer access to generic products; and raises awareness and visibility of the significant benefits and value of generic drugs to the consumers. .

6627 ■ Healthcare Distribution Management Association
901 N Glebe Rd., Ste. 1000
Arlington, VA 22203
Ph:(703)787-0000
Fax:(703)812-5282
Co. E-mail: lkanfer@hdmanet.org
URL: http://www.healthcaredistribution.org
Contact: David Moody, Chm.
Description: Wholesalers and manufacturers of drug and health care products and industry service providers. Seeks to secure safe and effective distribution of healthcare products, create and exchange industry knowledge affecting the future of distribution management, and influence standards and business processes that produce efficient health care commerce. Compiles statistics; sponsors research and specialized education programs. .

6628 ■ International Academy of Compounding Pharmacists
4638 Riverstone Blvd.
Missouri City, TX 77459
Ph:(281)933-8400
Free: 800-927-4227
Fax:(281)495-0602
Co. E-mail: iacpinfo@iacprx.org
URL: http://www.iacprx.org
Contact: L.D. King, Exec. Dir.
Description: Pharmacists who compound custom medications to meet unique patient needs. Seeks to "enhance credibility and respect of the compounding pharmacy practice to the health care community and its patients"; promotes empowerment of compounding pharmacists. Develops and enforces codes of ethics and practice for members; facilitates cooperation and exchange of information among members; sponsors research and educational programs. **Publications:** *The eLink* (weekly); *The Pharmacists' Link* (quarterly).

6629 ■ International Federation of Pharmaceutical Wholesalers
10569 Crestwood Dr.
Manassas, VA 20109
Ph:(703)331-3714
Fax:(703)331-3715
Co. E-mail: info@ifpw.com
URL: http://www.ifpw.com
Contact: Eric V. Zwisler, Vice Chm.
Description: Wholesalers and distributors of pharmaceutical products. Promotes efficient delivery of pharmaceuticals to hospitals, physicians, and pharmacists; seeks to increase public awareness of the role played by members in the health care system. Facilitates cooperation and exchange of information among members; represents members' commercial and regulatory interests; sponsors educational and promotional programs. .

6630 ■ National Association of Chain Drug Stores
413 N Lee St.
Alexandria, VA 22314
Ph:(703)549-3001
Fax:(703)683-1451
URL: http://www.nacds.org
Contact: Steven C. Anderson, Pres./CEO
Description: Represents the concerns of community pharmacies in Washington, in state capitals, and across the country. Members are more than 210 chain community pharmacy companies. Collectively, community pharmacy comprises the largest component of pharmacy practice with over 107,000 FTE pharmacists. .

6631 ■ National Community Pharmacists Association
100 Daingerfield Rd.
Alexandria, VA 22314
Ph:(703)683-8200
Free: 800-544-7447
Fax:(703)683-3619
Co. E-mail: info@ncpanet.org
URL: http://www.ncpanet.org
Contact: Robert Greenwood, Pres.
Description: Owners and managers of independent drugstores and pharmacists employed in community pharmacies offering pharmacy service. Provides support for undergraduate pharmacy education through National Community Pharmacists Association Foundation. **Publications:** *America's Pharmacist* (monthly); *NCPA Newsletter* (semimonthly).

6632 ■ Pharmaceutical Care Management Association
601 Pennsylvania Ave. NW, Ste. 740 S
Washington, DC 20004
Ph:(202)207-3610
Co. E-mail: kpumphrey@pcmanet.org
URL: http://www.pcmanet.org
Contact: Mark Merritt, Pres./CEO
Description: Represents managed care pharmacy, Pharmaceutical Benefits Management companies (PBMs) and their healthcare partners in pharmaceutical care. Promotes education, legislation, practice standards, and research to foster quality, affordable pharmaceutical care. .

6633 ■ Pharmaceutical Research and Manufacturers of America
950 F St. NW, Ste. 300
Washington, DC 20004
Ph:(202)835-3400
Fax:(202)835-3414
URL: http://www.phrma.org
Contact: John J. Castellani, Pres./CEO
Description: Research based manufacturers of ethical pharmaceutical and biological products that are distributed under their own labels. Encourages high standards for quality control and good manufacturing practices; researches toward the development of new and better medical products; enactment of uniform and reasonable drug legislation for the protection of public health. Disseminates information on governmental regulations and policies, but does not maintain or supply information on specific products, prices, distribution, promotion, or sales policies of its individual members. Has established the Pharmaceutical Manufacturers Association Foundation to promote public health through scientific and medical research. .

REFERENCE WORKS

6634 ■ "Analysts Not Too Sad Over Gemunder" in *Business Courier* (Vol. 27, August 6, 2010, No. 14, pp. 1)
Pub: Business Courier
Ed: James Ritchie. **Description:** Analysts and investors do not understand why Omnicare chief executive officer (CEO) Joel Gemunder suddenly retired after nearly thirty years with the Covington, Kentucky company. They believe that new leadership might invigorate the firm, which provides pharmacy and related services to the long-term care industry.

6635 ■ "Angiotech to Buy Top Medical Devices Company" in *Globe & Mail* (February 1, 2006, pp. B1)
Pub: CTVglobemedia Publishing Inc.
Ed: Leonard Zehr. **Description:** The details on Angiotech Pharmaceuticals Inc.'s acquisition of American Medical Instruments Holdings Inc. are presented.

6636 ■ "ART Announces New Distribution Arrangement with GE Healthcare for eXplore Optix" in *Canadian Corporate News* (May 14, 2007)
Pub: Comtex News Network Inc.
Description: ART Advanced Research Technologies Inc., a medical device company and a leader in optical molecular imaging products for the pharmaceutical and healthcare industries, announced that it signed an agreement with GE Healthcare regarding worldwide distribution of its eXplore Optix preclinical optical molecular imaging system.

6637 ■ "At the Drugstore, the Nurse Will See You Now" in *Globe & Mail* (April 13, 2007, pp. B1)
Pub: CTVglobemedia Publishing Inc.
Ed: Marina Strauss. **Description:** The appointment of several health professionals including nurse, podiatrists, etc. by Rexall Co. at its drugstores to face competition from rivals, is discussed.

6638 ■ "Auxilium Drug's New Use: Putting Squeeze On Cellulite" in *Philadelphia Business Journal* (Vol. 30, September 16, 2011, No. 31, pp. 1)
Pub: American City Business Journals Inc.
Ed: John George. **Description:** Auxilium Pharmaceuticals and BioSpecifics Technologies are getting on with their plans of finding new uses for their drug Xiaflex, a possible treatment for cellulite. The two firms have dismissed their pending litigations and mapped out an amended licensing agreement for their search for the potential uses of the drug.

6639 ■ "Best Growth Stocks" in *Canadian Business* (Vol. 82, Summer 2009, No. 8, pp. 28)
Pub: Rogers Media
Ed: Calvin Leung. **Description:** Canadian stocks that are considered as the best growth stocks, and whose price-earnings ratio is less than their earnings growth rate, are suggested. Suggestions include pharmaceutical firm Paladin Labs, which was found to have 13 consecutive years of revenue growth. Paladin Labs acquires or licenses niche drugs and markets them in Canada.

6640 ■ "Changing Prescriptions" in *Business North Carolina* (Vol. 28, March 2008, No. 3, pp. 52)
Pub: Business North Carolina
Description: Profile of Moose Drug Company, founded by Archibald Walter Moose in 1882. Family owners share how they focus on pharmacoeconomics (cost-benefit analyses of drugs or drug therapy) and customer service.

6641 ■ *ComputerTalk for the Pharmacist—Buyers Guide Issue*
Pub: ComputerTalk Associates Inc.
Released: Annual, Latest edition 2011. **Publication Includes:** List of more than 50 retail pharmacy data processing system suppliers. All listings are paid. **Entries Include:** Company, name, address, phone; number of installations, entry-level system configuration and price, software available, expandability, additional costs, length and cost of training period, largest system installed, map showing states where systems are marketed, supplier's statement. **Arrangement:** Alphabetical. **Indexes:** Geographical (code indicates whether location of installation, sales or service office, or distributor), alphabetical (including addresses and phone numbers of headquarters and sales offices or distributors).

6642 ■ "Despite Hot Toys, Holiday Sales Predicted To Be Ho-Ho-Hum" in *Drug Store News* (Vol. 29, November 12, 2007, No. 14, pp. 78)
Pub: Drug Store News
Ed: Doug Desjardins. **Description:** Summer toy recalls have retailers worried about holiday sales in 2007. Mattel was heavily impacted from the recall of millions of toys manufactured in China.

6643 ■ "A Different Kind of Waiting List" in *Canadian Business* (Vol. 80, April 9, 2007, No. 8, pp. 17)
Pub: Rogers Media
Ed: Erin Pooley. **Description:** The adverse impact on drug companies' profitability due to regulatory delays in approving drugs is discussed.

6644 ■ *Directory of Drug Store & HBC Chains*
Pub: Chain Store Guide
Released: Annual, Latest edition 2010. **Price:** $395, individuals print; $445, individuals online lite. **Covers:** More than 1,200 drug store chains operation two or more units, including mass merchants and grocers with pharmacies; 215 wholesale drug companies in the United States and Canada. **Entries Include:** For retailers—company name; phone and fax numbers; physical and mailing addresses; company e-mail and web addresses; listing type; number of stores; product lines; percentage of sales by product line; total sales; prescription drug sales; percentage of prescriptions filled with generic drugs; number of prescriptions filled daily; percentage of prescriptions filled with private third party, cash, and Medicaid; number of stores by type; mail order pharmacy indicator; managed care division indicator; projected openings and remodeling; store prototype sizes; total selling square footage; trading area; franchise group headquarters' name and location; distribution center and primary wholesaler names and locations; number of specialty departments; packaged liquor indicators; private label indicators; computerized pharmacy indicator; average number of checkouts; year founded; public company indicator; parent company name and location; regional and divisional office locations; headquarters personnel with titles. For wholesalers—company name, address, phone, and fax; e-mail and web addresses; listing type; product lines; percentage of sales by product line; total sales; percentage of sales by customer type; total stores served; number of member and non-member stores served; trading area; group store trading names; wholesaler type; distribution center locations; private label indicator; year founded; public company indicator; headquarters personnel with titles. **Arrangement:** Separate geographical sections for retailers and wholesalers. **Indexes:** Alphabetical, exclusions.

6645 ■ "Eckerd Sales Spell Relief for Coutu" in *Globe & Mail* (January 18, 2006, pp. B4)
Pub: CTVglobemedia Publishing Inc.
Ed: Bertrand Marotte. **Description:** The details on Eckerd Corp., which posted rise in sales by 2.7 percent in December 2005, are presented. Eckerd Corp. is a unit of Jean Coutu Group (PJC) Inc.

6646 ■ "Elder Care, Rx Drugs Reforms Top Zoeller's Agenda" in *Times* (December 21, 2010)
Pub: The Times
Ed: Sarah Tompkins. **Description:** Indiana Attorney General Greg Zoeller is hoping to develop a program in the state that will help regulate care for the elderly; freeze medical licenses for doctors involved in criminal investigations; address illegal drug use; and to establish a program to help individuals dispose of old prescription medications easily at pharmacies.

6647 ■ "Engine of Growth: U.S. Industry Funk hasn't Hurt Cummins or Its Investors" in *Barron's* (Vol. 88, July 14, 2008, No. 28, pp. 43)
Pub: Dow Jones & Co., Inc.
Ed: Shirley A. Lazo. **Description:** Engine maker Cummins increased its quarterly common dividend by 40 percent to 17.5 cents per share from 12.5 cents. CVS Caremark's dividend saw a hike of 18.4 percent from 9.5 cents to 11.25 cents per share while its competitor Walgreen is continuing its 75th straight year of dividend distribution and its 33rd straight year of dividend hikes.

6648 ■ "Executive Decision: Just What the Doctor Ordered" in *Globe & Mail* (February 11, 2006, pp. B3)
Pub: CTVglobemedia Publishing Inc.
Ed: Leonard Zehr. **Description:** The leadership ability of chief executive William Hunter of Angiotech Pharmaceuticals Inc., who acquired American Medical Instruments Holdings Inc. for $785 million, is discussed.

6649 ■ "The Grass is Greener" in *Canadian Business* (Vol. 79, August 14, 2006, No. 16-17, pp. 43)
Pub: Rogers Media
Ed: Thomas Watson. **Description:** Owner of New Image Plans LLC, Joe White, shares his views on the Canadian market for the marijuana drug.

6650 ■ "Healthy Dose of Vitality" in *Business Courier* (Vol. 24, February 29, 2008, No. 47, pp. 1)
Pub: American City Business Journals, Inc.
Ed: Dan Monk. **Description:** Healthy Advice plans to become a leading consumer brand and expand to pharmacies and hospitals. The growth opportunities for healthy Advice are discussed.

6651 ■ "Key FDA Approval Yanked for Avastin" in *Wall Street Journal Eastern Edition* (November 19 , 2011, pp. B1)
Pub: Dow Jones & Company Inc.
Ed: Thomas M. Burton, Jennifer Corbett Dooren. **Description:** Avastin, a drug manufactured by Genetech Inc. and used in the treatment of metastatic breast cancer in women, has had its approval by the US Food and Drug Administration withdrawn by the agency, which says there is no evidence the widely-used drug is successful in increasing the longevity of breast cancer patients.

6652 ■ "Luster Lost" in *Saint Louis Business Journal* (Vol. 32, September 16, 2011, No. 3, pp. 1)
Pub: Saint Louis Business Journal
Ed: E.B. Solomont. **Description:** Express Cripts shares have plunged 22.71 percent since late July amid regulatory concerns, as the luster of the second-largest deal announced for 2011 wore off. Express Scripts has become the largest pharmacy benefit manager in the country after the $29 billion deal to take rival Medco Health Solutions.

6653 ■ *Medical and Health Information Directory*
Pub: Gale
Released: Annual, Latest edition April 2011. **Price:** $1190, individuals set; $501, individuals per volume. **Covers:** In volume 1, more than 33,000 medical and health oriented associations, organizations, institutions, and government agencies, including health maintenance organizations (HMOs), preferred provider organizations (PPOs), insurance companies, pharmaceutical companies, research centers, and medical and allied health schools. In Volume 2, over 20,000 medical book publishers; medical periodicals, directories, audiovisual producers and services, medical libraries and information centers, electronic resources, and health-related internet search engines. In Volume 3, more than 40,500 clinics, treatment centers, care programs, and counseling/diagnostic services for 34 subject areas. **Entries Include:** Institution, service, or firm name, address, phone, fax, email and URL; many include names of key personnel and, when pertinent, descriptive annotation. Volume 3 was formerly listed separately as Health Services Directory. **Arrangement:** Classified by organization activity, service, etc. **Indexes:** Each volume has a complete alphabetical name and keyword index.

6654 ■ "MPI Expansion Goes Back to Family Roots" in *Crain's Detroit Business* (Vol. 25, June 1, 2009, No. 22, pp. M007)
Pub: Crain Communications Inc. - Detroit
Ed: Sherri Begin Welch. **Description:** William Parfet, grandson of Upjohn Company founder, is expanding MPI Research's clinical and early clinical research operations into two buildings in Kalamazoo, land which was once part of his grandfather's farm.

6655 ■ *National Drug Code Directory*
Pub: U.S. Food and Drug Administration
Released: Irregular, Latest edition 2011. **Publication Includes:** List of manufacturers of commercially marketed human prescription drugs. **Entries Include:** Drug company name, address, labeler code, product name, description of product, National Drug Code (NDC) number. Principal content of publication is a listing of about 32,000 drug products. **Arrangement:** Alphabetical. **Indexes:** NDC number, drug class, drug name.

6656 ■ "Retail in Austin Strong, Will Continue to Be" in *Austin Business JournalInc.* (Vol. 29, January 22, 2010, No. 46, pp. 1)
Pub: American City Business Journals
Ed: Jacob Dirr. **Description:** Retail sector in Austin, Texas has outpaced the national average in value, mid-tier, high-end and drugs retail sectors, according to a report by Pitney Bowes. The national consulting firm's report has projected growth in every sector until the end of fiscal 2012. Data regarding other sectors is also included.

6657 ■ "Shire Seeking New Digs for Headquarters" in *Philadelphia Business Journal* (Vol. 30, September 2, 2011, No. 29, pp. 1)
Pub: American City Business Journals Inc.
Ed: Natalie Kostelni. **Description:** Dublin, Ireland-based Shire PLC announced plans to relocate its North American headquarters from Chesterbrook Corporate Center in Wayne, Pennsylvania and currently evaluating their options. The specialty biopharmaceutical firm is also considering a move to New Jersey or Delaware.

6658 ■ "Sinai Doctor Seeks FDA OK for Drug" in *Baltimore Business Journal* (Vol. 28, July 16, 2010, No. 10, pp. 1)
Pub: Baltimore Business Journal
Ed: Emily Mullin. **Description:** Paul Gurbel, Sinai Hospital Center for Thrombosis Research director, is seeking an FDA approval of Brilinta, a drug which he helped create and test. Gurbel says that the approval could bring the drug to market as early as December 2010. The drug is expected to rival Bristol-Myers' Plavix, which generated almost $6.2 billion in 2009.

6659 ■ "Turning Trust Into Success" in *Retail Merchandiser* (Vol. 51, July-August 2011, No. 4, pp. 52)
Pub: Phoenix Media Corporation
Ed: Karen Kondilis. **Description:** Shopko Stores employs tenured and trustworthy pharmacists and believes it is the core to their success.

6660 ■ "Walgreen Takes Up Doctoring" in *Crain's Chicago Business* (Vol. 31, March 31, 2008, No. 13, pp. 18)
Pub: Crain Communications, Inc.
Ed: Mark Bruno. **Description:** Walgreen Co. has agreed to acquire two firms that provide on-site medical and pharmaceutical services to large companies. Walgreen feels that these facilities mark the future of health care for a number of large corporations.

6661 ■ "'We Are Not a Marketing Company'" in *Boston Business Journal* (Vol. 31, June 10, 2011, No. 20, pp. 1)
Pub: Boston Business Journal
Ed: Julie M. Donnelly. **Description:** Vertex Pharmaceuticals Inc. is marketing its new Hepatitis C treatment, Incivek. The company hired people to connect patients to the drug. Vertex is also set to move to a new facility in Boston, Massachusetts.

6662 ■ "Wielding a Big Ax" in *Barron's* (Vol. 89, July 13, 2009, No. 28, pp. 26)
Pub: Dow Jones & Co., Inc.
Ed: Shirley A. Lazo. **Description:** Weyerhaeuser cut their quarterly common payout by 80 percent from 25 cents to a nickel a share which they say will help them preserve their long-term value and improve their performance. Paccar also cut their quarterly dividend by half to nine cents a share. Walgreen however, boosted their quarterly dividend by 22.2 percent to 13.75 cents a share.

SOURCES OF SUPPLY

6663 ■ *Scott's Canadian Pharmacists Directory*
Pub: Business Information Group
Released: Biennial, Latest edition 2009. **Price:** $239, individuals Plus S/H + Applicable Taxes; $289, individuals CD-pinpointer; $599, individuals CD-profiler; $1,399, individuals CD-prospector. **Covers:** Approximately 18,000 pharmacists, university pharmacy faculty members, pharmacy suppliers, and drug and poison information centers in Canada, chain drug stores, independent. **Entries Include:** Name, address, phone, names and titles of key personnel, biographical data (for pharmacists), geographical area served. **Arrangement:** For pharmacists—Same information available in geographical and alphabetical sections. For others—Classified by line of business, then alphabetical.

STATISTICAL SOURCES

6664 ■ *RMA Annual Statement Studies*
Pub: Robert Morris Associates (RMA)
Released: Annual. **Price:** $175.00 2006-07 edition, $105.00. **Description:** Contains composite balance sheets and income statements for more than 360 industries, including the accounting, auditing, and bookkeeping industries. Also contains five years of comparative historical data for discerning trends. Includes 16 commonly used ratios, computed for most of the size groupings for nearly every industry.

6665 ■ *Standard & Poor's Industry Surveys*
Pub: Standard & Poor's Corp.
Released: Annual. **Price:** $3633.00. **Description:** Two-volume book that examines the prospects for specific industries, including trucking. Also provides analyses of trends and problems, statistical tables and charts, and comparative company analyses.

TRADE PERIODICALS

6666 ■ *America's Pharmacist*
Pub: National Community Pharmacists Association
Contact: Chris Linville, Managing Editor
Released: Monthly. **Description:** Professional magazine.

6667 ■ *Community Pharmacist*
Pub: ELF Publications Inc.
Contact: Judy Lane, Editor & Publisher
E-mail: judy.lane@elfpublications.com
Released: Bimonthly. **Description:** National magazine addressing the professional and business needs, concerns and continuing education of retail pharmacists practicing in independent, chain and supermarket pharmacies.

6668 ■ *Compendium of Pharmaceuticals and Specialties*
Pub: Canadian Pharmacists Association
Contact: Leesa D. Bruce, Publisher
Released: Annual. **Price:** $245. **Description:** Medical periodical covering all Canadian prescription drugs.

6669 ■ *The Consultant Pharmacist*
Pub: American Society of Consultant Pharmacists
Released: Monthly. **Price:** $105; $150 elsewhere; $130 institutions; $190 institutions elsewhere. **Description:** Journal containing peer-reviewed articles, news, and information relevant to pharmacy practice in long-term care facilities, hospices, adult day care centers, home health care, and other extended-care settings.

6670 ■ *Drug Discovery/Technology News*
Pub: Business Communications Company Inc.
Ed: Steve Edwards, Editor, salaned@aol.com. **Released:** Monthly. **Price:** $450; $821, two years; $1,160 3/years. **Description:** Covers developments in the drug industry. Recurring features include a column titled Industry News.

6671 ■ *Drug Topics*
Pub: Advanstar Communications Inc.
Released: Bimonthly. **Price:** $61; $30.50 students; $109 out of country; $10 single issue; $10 Canada and Mexico for single issue; $15 other countries for single issue. **Description:** Newsmagazine for pharmacists.

6672 ■ *FDA Week*
Pub: Inside Washington Publishers
Ed: Donna Haseley, Editor. **Released:** Weekly (Fri.). **Price:** $595, U.S. and Canada; $645, elsewhere. **Description:** Reports on Food and Drug Administration policy, regulation, and enforcement.

6673 ■ *HealthCare Distributor*
Pub: ELF Publications Inc.
Contact: Judy D. Lane, Editor & Publisher
Released: Bimonthly. **Price:** $29.95; $80 elsewhere. **Description:** Magazine covering the issues and opportunities facing companies that distribute pharmaceuticals, medical/surgical products, and other healthcare goods and services.

6674 ■ *Impact*
Pub: Canadian Pharmacists Association
Ed: Louie Chatelain, Editor, lchatelain@pharmacists.ca. **Released:** 4/year. **Price:** Included in membership; $27.50. **Description:** Tracks activities of the Association; provides information on national and provincial programs, projects and regulatory changes. Recurring features include letters to the editor, news of research, a calendar of events, reports of meetings, and news of educational opportunities.

6675 ■ *Journal of the American Pharmacists Association*
Pub: American Pharmacists Association
Contact: Alex Egervary, Sen. Asst. Ed.
Ed: L. Michael Posey, Editor, mposey@aphanet.org. **Released:** Bimonthly. **Price:** $495 institutions print and online; $395 institutions online only. **Description:** Peer-reviewed journal for pharmacy professionals.

6676 ■ *Journal of Pharmaceutical Sciences*
Pub: American Pharmacists Association
Contact: Bradley D. Anderson, Assoc. Ed.
Ed: Dr. Ronald T. Borchardt, Editor. **Released:** Monthly. **Price:** $325 print; $382 other countries print; $1,399 institutions print only; $1,456 institutions, other countries print only; $1,539 institutions print and online; $1,596 institutions, other countries print and online. **Description:** Professional journal publishing research articles in the pharmaceutical sciences.

6677 ■ *NCPA Newsletter*
Pub: National Community Pharmacists Association
Ed: Released: Semimonthly. **Price:** Included in membership; $50, nonmembers. **Description:** Reports on topics affecting independents, including developments within the pharmaceutical industry, regulatory and legislative activity, and pricing and import information. Recurring features include reports of meetings, news of educational opportunities, notices of publications available, and news of NARD activities and events.

6678 ■ *Pharmaceutical Approvals Monthly*
Pub: F-D-C Reports Inc.
Contact: Lee Szilagyi, Assistant editor
Ed: Jon Dobson, Editor. **Released:** Monthly. **Price:** $975. **Description:** Reports on current and future drug/pharmaceutical approvals. Also provides lists of drugs pending FDA approval.

6679 ■ *Pharmacy Times*
Pub: Ascend Integrated Media
Contact: Bill Schu, Gp. Editorial Dir.
E-mail: bschu@mdng.com
Released: Monthly, 1 OTC supplement. **Description:** Journal providing information on health items (including prescription and over-the-counter drugs and surgical supplies) to independent, chain, and hospital pharmacists.

6680 ■ *Pharmacy Today*
Pub: American Pharmacists Association
Contact: Carli Richard, Managing Editor
Released: Monthly. **Price:** Included in membership; $200, nonmembers U.S.; $250, nonmembers other countries. **Description:** Reports news and opinions of interest to pharmacists. Includes comprehensive coverage of pharmacotherapeutic, legislative, and socioeconomic news of every segment of the pharmacy profession.

6681 ■ *Pharmacy Week*
Pub: Pharmacy Week
Contact: Paul Barnes, Publisher
Released: Weekly. **Price:** Free. **Description:** Employment newsletter for pharmacists.

6682 ■ *The Pink Sheet*
Pub: F-D-C Reports Inc.
Contact: Danielle Foullon, Exec. Editor
Ed: M. Nielsen Hobbs, Editor. **Released:** Weekly, 50x/yr. **Price:** $2,145 print and web. **Description:** Provides in-depth news and analysis about developments affecting prescription medicines, including FDA, FTC, and HCFA policies and actions, as well as federal and state legislation affecting the drug industry. Coverage includes FDA recalls and seizures, mergers and acquisitions, biotechnology startups, new product activity, and company research and development.

6683 ■ *Provincial Drug Benefit Programs*
Pub: Canadian Pharmacists Association
Released: Semiannual. **Price:** $275. **Description:** Professional periodical covering provincial government drug benefit programs.

6684 ■ *Validation Times*
Pub: Washington Information Source
Contact: Kenneth Reid, Editor & Publisher
Released: Monthly, plus weekly email updates. **Price:** $1,021, U.S. and Canada. **Description:** Covers pre-approval and post-approval regulatory news on pharmaceutical products and biologics. Recurring features include letters to the editor, interviews, news of research, and a calendar of events.

6685 ■ *Voice of the Pharmacist Newsletter*
Pub: American College of Apothecaries
Ed: Dr. D.C. Huffman, Jr., Editor. **Released:** Quarterly. **Price:** Included in membership; $40, nonmembers. **Description:** Examines current issues and opportunities affecting the retail, hospital, and consultant practices of pharmacy. Discusses controversial issues, often with commentary by pharmacists. Recurring features include editorials, news of research, and letters to the editor.

TRADE SHOWS AND CONVENTIONS

6686 ■ American Society of Consultant Pharmacists Annual Meeting and Exhibition
American Society of Consultant Pharmacists
1321 Duke St.
Alexandria, VA 22314-3563
Ph:(703)739-1300

Free: 800-355-2727
Fax:(703)739-1321
Co. E-mail: info@ascp.com
URL: http://www.ascp.com
Released: Annual. **Audience:** Pharmacists in the long-term care field, allied professionals, and general public. **Principal Exhibits:** Pharmaceuticals, drug distribution systems, packaging equipment, computers, durable medical equipment, and medical supplies. **Dates and Locations:** 2011 Nov 16-19, Phoenix, AZ; 2012 Nov 07-10, National Harbor, MD.

6687 ■ Florida Pharmacy Association Annual Meeting and Convention
Florida Pharmacy Association
610 N. Adams St.
Tallahassee, FL 32301
Ph:(850)222-2400
Fax:(850)561-6758
Co. E-mail: fpa@pharmview.com
URL: http://www.pharmview.com
Released: Annual. **Audience:** Trade professionals and general public. **Principal Exhibits:** Pharmaceuticals and other product lines and services provided for and by pharmacists. **Dates and Locations:** 2011 Jun 22-26, Miami, FL.

6688 ■ NCPA 113th Annual Convention and Trade Exposition
National Community Pharmacists Association
100 Daingerfield Rd.
Alexandria, VA 22314
Ph:(703)683-8200
Fax:(703)683-3619
Co. E-mail: info@ncpanet.org
URL: http://www.ncpanet.org
Released: Annual. **Audience:** Pharmacy owners and managers. **Principal Exhibits:** Pharmaceutical and related equipment, supplies, and services. **Dates and Locations:** 2011 Oct 08-12, Nashville, TN.

6689 ■ PDA Annual Meeting
Parenteral Drug Association, Inc.
3 Bethesda Metro Center, No. 1500
Bethesda, MD 20814
Ph:(301)656-5900
Fax:(301)986-1093
Co. E-mail: info@pda.org
URL: http://www.pda.org
Released: Annual. **Audience:** Pharmaceutical manufacturers. **Principal Exhibits:** Supplies and services related to pharmaceuticals manufacturing the science and technology. **Dates and Locations:** 2011 Apr 11-15, San Antonio, TX.

6690 ■ Texas Pharmacy Association Annual Meeting and Exhibit
Texas Pharmacy Association
12007 Research Blvd., Ste. 201
Austin, TX 78759
Ph:(512)836-8350
Free: 800-505-5463
Fax:(512)836-0308
URL: http://www.txpharmacy.com
Released: Annual. **Audience:** Pharmacists, students. **Principal Exhibits:** Pharmaceuticals and various services provided to pharmacists.

CONSULTANTS

6691 ■ Thole Associates
1400 Shadwell Cir.
Lake Mary, FL 32746-4344
Ph:(407)333-2174
Fax:(407)333-2174
Contact: Jerome L. Thole, President
Scope: Consulting organization specializing in food and drug store merchandising and operations. In addition to serving retailers, the firm provides consulting service to wholesalers and manufacturers as well. Areas of expertise include store operations, store conditions, operating cost control, customer service training, research, and budget control and scheduling. Industries served: retail food supermarket and drug companies. **Seminars:** How to Improve Customer Service-Without Sacrificing Productivity; Customer Satisfaction-Develop a Strategy for Success; How to Control Expense in Tough Economic Times.

FRANCHISES AND BUSINESS OPPORTUNITIES

6692 ■ Medicap Pharmacy
Medicap Pharmacies, Inc.
1 Rider Trail Plaza Dr.
Earth City, MO 63045
Ph:(515)224-8400
Free: 800-445-2244
No. of Franchise Units: 201. **Founded:** 1971. **Franchised:** 1974. **Description:** Professional pharmacy that typically operates in an 800-1,000 square foot location. Ninety percent of the business is prescription and the remaining 10% consists of over-the-counter medications. New store start-ups and conversion of full-line drug stores and independent pharmacies to the Medicap concept. continued support. **Equity Capital Needed:** Equity capital $10,000-$55,000; total investment $22,100-$414,700. **Franchise Fee:** $15,000 new/$8,500 converted. **Financial Assistance:** Yes. **Training:** 3 days of orientation at corporate office and 3 days of onsite training, plus continued support.

6693 ■ Medicine Shoppe Canada
1600-10104 103 Avenue NW
Edmonton, AB, Canada T5J 0H8
Free: 800-267-8877
Fax:(780)425-3980
Co. E-mail: info@medicineshoppe.ca
URL: http://www.futureofpharmacy.com
No. of Franchise Units: 162. **Founded:** 1992. **Franchised:** 1992. **Description:** Franchise of retail pharmacies. Focuses on patient care, health screenings and risk assessments. **Equity Capital Needed:** $175,000-$200,000. **Franchise Fee:** $9,000-$25,000. **Training:** Yes.

6694 ■ Medicine Shoppe International
Cardinal Health
7000 Cardinal Place
Dublin, OH 43107
Ph:(314)993-6000
Free: 800-325-1397
URL: http://www.medicineshoppe.com
No. of Franchise Units: 927. **Founded:** 1970. **Franchised:** 1970. **Description:** Retail professional pharmacy and health care. **Equity Capital Needed:** $74,300-$253,400. **Franchise Fee:** $10,000-$18,000. **Royalty Fee:** 2-5.5%. **Financial Assistance:** In-house financial assistance available. **Training:** Provides 6 days training at headquarters, at franchisee's location twice a year, regional meetings and seminars and ongoing support.

6695 ■ Shoppers Drug Mart
Pharamaprix
243 Consumers Rd.
North York, ON, Canada M2J 4W8
Ph:(416)490-2690
Fax:(416)490-2700
Co. E-mail: wlack@shoppersdrugmart.ca
URL: http://www.shoppersdrugmart.ca
No. of Franchise Units: 1,090. **Founded:** 1962. **Description:** Licensing of retail drug stores with licenses available only to qualified registered pharmacists. **Franchise Fee:** Provided by franchiser (minimum of $25,000 in Quebec). **Training:** Yes.

COMPUTERIZED DATABASES

6696 ■ *Clinical Pharmacology*
Elsevier
302 Knights Run Ave., Ste. 800
Tampa, FL 33602
Ph:(813)258-4747
Free: 800-375-0943
Fax:(813)259-1585
Co. E-mail: info@goldstandard.com
URL: http://www.goldstandard.com
Description: Provides comprehensive information and clinical monographs on drugs and pharmaceuticals available in the United States. Offers data intended for health care professionals and students. Provides detailed drug data, including indications, interactions, adverse reactions, contraindications, IV admixtures, and chemical structures. Provides information on new and investigational drugs. Covers nutritional and herbal products. Supports electronic prescription writing, recording, and printing with allergy and contraindication warnings. Features a Product Identification utility which enables the user to search for drugs based on physical appearance and verify them with color photographs. Also includes a patient database for creating patient-specific profiles and printing therapy information reports. Enables the user to print prescriptions and drug information for patients. **Availability:** Online: Elsevier; CD-ROM: United Business Media LLC, Elsevier, American Society of Health-System Pharmacists; Handheld: Elsevier. **Type:** Full text; Image.

6697 ■ *Compendium of Pharmaceuticals and Specialties*
Canadian Pharmacists Association
1785 Alta Vista Dr.
Ottawa, ON, Canada K1G 3Y6
Ph:(613)523-7877
Free: 800-917-9489
Fax:(613)523-0445
Co. E-mail: info@pharmacists.ca
URL: http://www.pharmacists.ca
Description: Provides health care professionals with web access to the most current Canadian drug information available. Containing thousands of Health Canada-approved drug monographs, links to Health Canada advisories, printable information for patients, searchable product images and more, this product is an advanced yet user-friendly resource that is updated regularly. **Availability:** Online: Canadian Pharmacists Association. **Type:** Full text; Image.

6698 ■ *International Pharmaceutical Abstracts*
Thomson Reuters
3501 Market St.
Philadelphia, PA 19104
Ph:(215)386-0100
Free: 800-336-4474
Fax:(215)386-2911
Co. E-mail: general.info@thomsonreuters.com
URL: http://science.thomsonreuters.com
Description: Contains more than 381,000 citations, with abstracts, to the world's literature dealing with the development and use of drugs or the clinical, practical, theoretical, scientific, economic, and ethical aspects of professional pharmaceutical practice. Covers adverse drug reactions and toxicity; drug evaluations, analyses, and interactions; pharmaceutical chemistry; and information processing for the pharmaceutical industry; legislation, laws, and regulations. Sources include more than 850 pharmaceutical, medical, and health-related journals. **Availability:** Online: Wolters Kluwer Health, ProQuest LLC, ProQuest LLC, STN International, DIMDI, the German Institute of Medical Documentation and Information, EBSCO Publishing, American Society of Health-System Pharmacists; CD-ROM: Wolters Kluwer Health. **Type:** Bibliographic.

6699 ■ *KINETIDEX System*
Thomson Reuters
6200 S Syracuse Way, Ste. 300
Greenwood Village, CO 80111-4740
Ph:(303)486-6444
Free: 800-525-9083
Fax:(303)486-6460
Co. E-mail: mdx.info@thomson.com
URL: http://www.micromedex.com
Description: Contains information on therapeutic drugs and drug dosages. For each drug, provides such information as recommended therapeutic levels, physical IV incompatibilities, clinically significant drug interactions, adverse effects, and guidelines for clinical monitoring. Designed for use by clinicians, enables the user to establish an optimal drug therapy

regimen for any patient at any point in time based on age, various disease and physiologic states, multiple drug therapy, social habits, and drug absorption. Software facilitates calculation of drug dose, interval, peak, trough, and other critical pharmacokinetic parameters. Features tables for drug use in patients with renal dysfunction or liver disease as well as the ability to maintain a database of patient records for use in subsequent drug monitoring and drug utilization review. **Availability:** Online: Thomson Reuters; CD-ROM: Thomson Reuters. **Type:** Full text; Numeric.

6700 ■ *State Health Care Regulatory Developments*
The Bureau of National Affairs Inc.
1801 S Bell St.
Arlington, VA 22202
Free: 800-372-1033
Co. E-mail: customercare@bna.com
URL: http://www.bna.com
Description: Contains information on health care regulatory news and developments in the United States. Subjects include community-based care, home care, emergency care, infectious diseases, managed care, insurance, laboratories, Medicaid, mental health, medical waste, nursing homes, pharmaceuticals, physician services, professional licensing, provider relationships, worker protection and compensation. Entries are organized by state, topic, and register citation. **Availability:** Online: The Bureau of National Affairs Inc., Thomson Reuters. **Type:** Full text.

LIBRARIES

6701 ■ American Pharmacists Association Foundation Library
2215 Constitution Ave., NW
Washington, DC 20037
Ph:(202)429-7524
Fax:(202)783-2351
Co. E-mail: gnorheim@aphanet.org
URL: http://www.pharmacist.com
Contact: Gwen Norheim
Scope: Pharmacy, pharmacology, medicine, pharmaceutical care. **Services:** Library open to the public by appointment. **Holdings:** 2000 books; 7000 bound periodical volumes. **Subscriptions:** 225 journals and other serials.

6702 ■ Amgen, Inc.–Amgen Libraries
One Amgen Center Dr., 14-1-A
Thousand Oaks, CA 91320-1789
Ph:(805)447-1000
Fax:(805)447-1010
Co. E-mail: larrym@amgen.com
URL: http://www.amgen.com
Contact: Larry Markworth
Scope: Biotechnology, molecular biology, pharmaceutical industry. **Services:** Interlibrary loan; SDI; group open to the public by appointment. **Holdings:** 7000 books; 50 reports; patents on microfilm and CDs. **Subscriptions:** 400 journals and other serials; 10 newspapers.

6703 ■ Anderson Area Medical Center Library
800 N. Fant St.
Anderson, SC 29621
Ph:(864)261-1253
Fax:(864)261-1552
Contact: Beth Addis
Scope: Medicine, nursing. **Services:** Interlibrary loan, literature searches. **Holdings:** 750 books. **Subscriptions:** 125 journals and other serials; 2 newspapers.

6704 ■ AstraZeneca Pharmaceuticals LP Library and Information Services
PO Box 15437
Wilmington, DE 19850-5437
Ph:(302)886-3000
Free: 800-236-9933
URL: http://www.astrazeneca-us.com/
Scope: Pharmacology, pharmacy, chemistry, bioscience, medicine, pharmaceutical industry. **Services:** Interlibrary loan. **Holdings:** 3500 books; 4750 bound periodical volumes. **Subscriptions:** 360 journals and other serials.

6705 ■ Block Drug Company–Research and Development Library
257 Cornelison Ave.
Jersey City, NJ 07302
Ph:(201)434-3000
Fax:(201)434-0842
Co. E-mail: karen_berryman@BlockDrug.com
Contact: Karen Berryman, Tech.Libn.
Scope: Dentistry, medicine, pharmacology, dermatology. **Services:** SDI; Library not open to the public. **Holdings:** 2000 books. **Subscriptions:** 350 journals and other serials; 2 newspapers.

6706 ■ Emmanuel College–Cardinal Cushing Library
400 The Fenway
Boston, MA 02115
Ph:(617)735-9927
Co. E-mail: tholl@emmanuel.edu
URL: http://www1.emmanuel.edu/library/
Contact: Dr. Susan von Daum Tholl, Dir.
Scope: Theology, pastoral ministry, religious history, women's studies, arts, humanities, education. **Services:** Interlibrary loan; Library open to the public. **Holdings:** 130,000 volumes. **Subscriptions:** 1000 journals and other serials.

6707 ■ Fisons Corporation Limited–Information Resources Centre
2235 Sheppard Ave. E.
Atria 11, 18th Fl.
Pickering, ON, Canada M2J 5B5
Ph:(416)497-8444
Fax:(416)498-2869
Contact: David Thompson, Mgr.Med.Info.
Scope: Pharmaceuticals. **Services:** Copying; online searching. **Holdings:** Figures not available.

6708 ■ GlaxoSmithKline–U.S. Medical Information Library (FP1045)
1 Franklin Plaza
Philadelphia, PA 19102-1225
Free: 888-825-5249
Co. E-mail: betty.j.kelley@gsk.com
URL: http://www.gsk.com/
Contact: Betty-Jane Kelley, Hd.Libn.
Scope: Medicine, pharmaceutical science, chemistry, biology, business, regulatory affairs. **Services:** Library not open to the public. **Holdings:** 3500 books; 9000 bound periodical volumes. **Subscriptions:** 400 journals and other serials.

6709 ■ GlaxoSmithKline Information and Library Services
5 Moore Dr.
PO Box 13398
Research Triangle Park, NC 27709
Ph:(919)483-5395
Free: 888-825-5249
Fax:(919)483-3015
URL: http://us.gsk.com
Contact: Alberta McKay, Mgr., Info.Svcs.
Scope: Organic chemistry, medicine, biochemistry, pharmacology, microbiology, toxicology, business. **Services:** Document delivery; copying; SDI. **Holdings:** 14,331 books; 34,039 bound periodical volumes. **Subscriptions:** 1300 journals and other serials; 5 newspapers.

6710 ■ Johnson & Johnson Pharmaceutical Research & Development–Hartman Library
920 Rte. 202
Mailstop E1756
Raritan, NJ 08869
Co. E-mail: glblpharmardcom@prdus.jnj.com
URL: http://www.jnjpharmarnd.com
Contact: Donna Wahl
Scope: Medicine, pharmacy, endocrinology, biological sciences, chemistry. **Holdings:** 5000 books; 20,000 bound periodical volumes; 300 reels of microfilm. **Subscriptions:** 600 journals and other serials.

6711 ■ Keller and Heckman LLP–Law Firm Library
1001 G St. NW, Ste. 500 W.
Washington, DC 20001
Ph:(202)434-4100
Fax:(202)434-4646
Co. E-mail: khlibrary@khlaw.com
URL: http://www.khlaw.com
Contact: Abigail Ross, Lib.Mgr.
Scope: Food and drug, the environment, telecommunications, transportation, intellectual property, International trade. **Services:** Interlibrary loan; Library not open to the public. **Holdings:** 8000 books. **Subscriptions:** 140 journals and other serials; 8 newspapers.

6712 ■ Lexington Medical Center–LMC Health Library
2720 Sunset Blvd.
West Columbia, SC 29169
Ph:(803)791-2000
URL: http://www.lexmed.com/
Scope: Medicine, nursing, and allied health sciences. **Holdings:** Figures not available.

6713 ■ Maryland Pharmacists Association Library
1800 Washington Blvd.
Baltimore, MD 21230
Ph:(410)727-0746
Fax:(410)727-2253
Co. E-mail: schiff@marylandpharmacist.org
URL: http://marylandpharmacist.org
Contact: Howard Schiff, Exec.Dir.
Scope: Pharmacy, allied health sciences. **Services:** Library not open to the public. **Holdings:** 1000 volumes. **Subscriptions:** 1 journal.

6714 ■ McKenna Long & Aldridge LLP Law Library
1900 K St. NW, Lower Level
Washington, DC 20006-1108
Ph:(202)496-7752
Fax:(202)496-7756
Co. E-mail: kmartin@mckennalong.com
URL: http://www.mckennalong.com
Contact: Kate Martin, Dir. of Lib.Svcs.
Scope: Law - government contracts, environmental, litigation, food and drug, International, health care, labor, insurance, energy. **Services:** Interlibrary loan; Library not open to the public. **Holdings:** 15,000 books; 5000 bound periodical volumes. **Subscriptions:** 400 journals and other serials.

6715 ■ McNeil Consumer and Specialty Pharmaceuticals–Pharmaceutical Research Center
7050 Camp Hill Rd.
Fort Washington, PA 19034-2799
Ph:(215)273-7603
Fax:(215)273-4082
Co. E-mail: hhohman@mccus.jnj.com
Contact: Helen J. Hohman, Mgr., Pharm.Info. & Comm.
Scope: Pharmaceutics, medicine, chemistry, marketing, finance, nutritionals. **Services:** Interlibrary loan; center not open to the public. **Holdings:** 600 books. **Subscriptions:** 300 journals and other serials; 5 newspapers.

6716 ■ Merck Frosst Canada Ltd.–Research Library and Information Centre
16711 Trans Canada Hwy.
Kirkland, QC, Canada H9H 3L1
Ph:(514)428-2666
Fax:(514)428-8535
Co. E-mail: josee_schepper@merck.com
URL: http://www.merckfrosstlab.ca
Contact: Josee Schepper, Mgr.
Scope: Biochemistry, chemistry, molecular biology, pharmacology, pharmacy, biology. **Services:** Interlibrary loan; Library open to professionals based on need to access. **Holdings:** 3000 books; 10,000 bound periodical volumes. **Subscriptions:** 300 journals and other serials; 1300 e-journals; 4 newspapers.

6717 ■ National Association of Boards of Pharmacy Library
1600 Feehanville Dr.
Mount Prospect, IL 60056
Ph:(847)391-4406
Fax:(847)391-4502
Co. E-mail: exec-office@nabp.net
URL: http://www.nabp.net
Contact: Carmen A. Catizone, Exec.Dir./Sec.
Scope: Pharmacy - law and regulation, education, licensure. **Holdings:** Figures not available.

6718 ■ National Association of Chain Drug Stores Resource Center
413 N. Lee St.
PO Box 1417-D49
Alexandria, VA 22314-1417
Ph:(703)549-3001
URL: http://www.nacds.org
Contact: Larry J. Merlo, Ch.
Scope: Industry-related topics; community pharmacy. **Services:** Interlibrary loan; Library open to the public at director's discretion. **Holdings:** 10,000 volumes; 1000 videocassettes; 500 audiocassettes. **Subscriptions:** 150 journals and other serials.

6719 ■ Oak Ridge National Laboratory–Toxicology Information Response Center
1060 Commerce Park, MS-6480
Oak Ridge, TN 37830
Ph:(865)576-1746
Fax:(865)574-9888
Co. E-mail: slusherkg@ornl.gov
URL: http://www.ornl.gov/TechResources/tirc/hmepg.html
Contact: Kim Slusher
Scope: Toxicology, pharmacology, veterinary toxicology, heavy metals, pesticides, chemistry, biology, medicine, industrial hygiene. **Services:** SDI; Center open to the public. **Holdings:** 10,000 search files; 250 microfiche of published bibliographies. **Subscriptions:** 300 journals and other serials.

6720 ■ Sanofi-Synthelabo–Research Division–Research Information Services (9 Gre)
9 Great Valley Pkwy.
Malvern, PA 19355
Ph:(610)889-8652
Fax:(610)889-8988
Contact: Don Miles, Dir.
Scope: Biomedicine, biochemistry, clinical medicine, chemistry, pharmacology, toxicology. **Services:** Interlibrary loan; copying; SDI. **Holdings:** 4000 books; 1000 bound periodical volumes; 6000 reels of microfilm; 2000 nonbook items. **Subscriptions:** 300 journals and other serials.

6721 ■ Sanofi-Synthelabo Inc.–Virtual Information Center
90 Park Ave.
New York, NY 10016
Ph:(212)551-4105
Fax:(212)551-4908
Contact: Donna A. Brown
Scope: Pharmaceuticals, clinical medicine. **Services:** Library open to the public by appointment. **Holdings:** 300 books and bound periodical volumes. **Subscriptions:** 120 journals and other serials.

6722 ■ Schering-Plough Healthcare, Inc.–R & D Library
3030 Jackson Ave.
PO Box 377
Memphis, TN 38151-0001
Ph:(901)320-2702
Fax:(901)320-3017
Co. E-mail: martha.hurst@spcorp.com
Contact: Martha Hurst, Libn.
Scope: Pharmacology, toxicology, medicine, chemistry, pharmaceutical technology. **Services:** Interlibrary loan; Library open to the public by permission only. **Holdings:** 1600 books; 1800 bound periodical volumes; 3000 reprints. **Subscriptions:** 150 journals and other serials.

6723 ■ Sentron Medical Inc.–Senmed Medical Ventures Library
4445 Lake Forest Dr., No. 600
Cincinnati, OH 45242-3798
Ph:(513)563-3240
Fax:(513)563-3261
URL: http://www.senmed.com/organization.htm
Contact: Rosanne Wohlwender
Scope: Biotechnology, medical devices and diagnostics, technology transfer, pharmaceuticals, venture capital, licensing. **Services:** Library not open to the public. **Holdings:** 800 books; 50 reports. **Subscriptions:** 100 journals and other serials; 2 newspapers.

6724 ■ Southwest Health Center Medical Library
1400 East Side Rd.
Platteville, WI 53818
Ph:(608)348-2331
Fax:(608)342-5011
Co. E-mail: library@southwesthealth.org
URL: http://www.southwesthealth.org/index.php
Scope: Medicine, nursing, and allied health sciences. **Services:** Interlibrary loan; copying; Library open to the public. **Holdings:** 500 books. **Subscriptions:** 80 journals and other serials.

6725 ■ Thomson Physicians World–Knowledge Management & Medical Library
150 Meadowlands Pkwy.
Secaucus, NJ 07094
Ph:(201)271-6105
Free: 800-223-8978
Fax:(201)865-9247
Co. E-mail: pw.contact@pwnj.thomson.com
URL: http://www.physiciansworld.com
Contact: Maria V. Kwonn, Dir.
Scope: Medicine, pharmaceuticals, medical education, clinicals. **Services:** Interlibrary loan; Library not open to the public. **Holdings:** 1200 books; 1400 bound periodical volumes. **Subscriptions:** 110 journals and other serials.

6726 ■ Tri-Meridian, Inc.–MEDSEARCH Division Library
PO Box 7664
Wilmington, NC 28406
Ph:(910)793-6456
Fax:(910)793-8280
Co. E-mail: michaels2@worldnet.att.net
Contact: Debbra D. Michaels, Dir.
Scope: Medicine, pharmaceuticals, consumer health, nursing, allied health. **Services:** Interlibrary loan; Library not open to the public. **Holdings:** 150 books. **Subscriptions:** 10 journals and other serials.

RESEARCH CENTERS

6727 ■ University of Maryland at Baltimore–Center on Drugs and Public Policy
School of Pharmacy
220 Arch St.
Baltimore, MD 21201
Ph:(410)706-0133
Fax:(410)706-5394
Co. E-mail: fpalumbo@rx.umaryland.edu
URL: http://www.pharmacy.umaryland.edu/cdpp
Contact: Francis B. Palumbo JD, Exec.Dir.
E-mail: fpalumbo@rx.umaryland.edu
Scope: Dug policy, legal and regulatory; drug utilization review; outpatient drug benefits under the OBRA 90; cost effective drug therapies; pharmaceutical care services; health outcomes related to drug therapy; pharmacoepidemiology, pharmacy manpower; the pharmaceutical industry; impact of changes in the organization and financing of health care services; and patient compliance with prescribed drug regimen. **Educational Activities:** Conferences.

6728 ■ University of Tennessee–Drug Information Center
875 Monroe Ave., Ste. 116
Memphis, TN 38163
Ph:(901)448-5555
Fax:(901)448-5419
Co. E-mail: ksuda@utmem.edu
URL: http://www.uthsc.edu/pharmacy/dcp/dic
Contact: Dr. Katie Suda, Dir.
E-mail: ksuda@utmem.edu
Scope: Outcomes and epidemiology of therapeutic and pharmaceutical drugs. Provides therapeutic and pharmaceutic drug information to health care professionals. **Educational Activities:** Drug Information Clerkship, offered to doctoral candidates; Drug Information Course, for doctoral students.

START-UP INFORMATION

6729 ■ *Coin Laundries - Road to Financial Independence: A Complete Guide to Starting and Operating Profitable Self-Service Laundries*
Pub: Mountain Publishing Company
Ed: Emerson G. Higdon. **Released:** June 2001. **Description:** Guide to starting and operating a self-service laundry.

ASSOCIATIONS AND OTHER ORGANIZATIONS

6730 ■ Coin Laundry Association
1 S 660 Midwest Rd., Ste. 205
Oakbrook Terrace, IL 60181
Ph:(630)953-7920
Free: 800-570-5629
Fax:(630)953-7925
Co. E-mail: info@coinlaundry.org
URL: http://coinlaundry.org
Contact: Brian Wallace, Pres./CEO
Description: Manufacturers of equipment or supplies used in self-service (coin-operated) laundry or dry cleaning establishments; distributors of equipment services and supplies; owners and operators of self-service laundry and/or dry cleaning stores. Compiles statistics. **Publications:** *CLA Management Guidelines* (quarterly); *The Journal of the Coin Laundry Industry* (monthly).

6731 ■ Drycleaning and Laundry Institute International
14700 Sweitzer Ln.
Laurel, MD 20707
Ph:(301)622-1900
Free: 800-638-2627
Fax:(240)295-0685
Co. E-mail: techline@ifi.org
URL: http://www.ifi.org
Contact: David Silliman, Chm.
Description: Retail and industrial drycleaners, hospital laundries, linen supply and drapery services, distributors and manufacturers of supplies and machinery, dry-cleaning and laundry associations, and individual launders in 43 countries. Provides washability and dry-cleanability testing for manufacturers of fabrics and related products; offers quality testing and consulting services; conducts research for members. Organizes courses in dry-cleaning, laundering, management, and maintenance. Maintains consulting service, speakers' bureau, research facilities, and library. **Publications:** *International Fabricare Institute—Bulletins* (periodic); *International Fabricare Institute—Industry FOCUS* .

6732 ■ Multi-Housing Laundry Association
1500 Sunday Dr., Ste. 102
Raleigh, NC 27607
Ph:(919)861-5579
Fax:(919)787-4916
Co. E-mail: nshore@mla-online.com
URL: http://www.mla-online.com
Contact: David J. Feild, Exec. Dir.
Description: Operating and supplier companies. Strives to provide tenants with professionally operated laundry facilities. Sponsors annual convention and trade show. **Publications:** *MLA News* (bimonthly).

6733 ■ Textile Care Allied Trades Association
271 Rte. 46 W, No. D203
Fairfield, NJ 07004
Ph:(973)244-1790
Fax:(973)244-4455
Co. E-mail: info@tcata.org
URL: http://www.tcata.org
Contact: David H. Cotter, CEO
Description: Represents Manufacturers and distributors of laundry and dry-cleaning machinery, and supplies. **Publications:** *Roster and Buyers Guide* (annual).

REFERENCE WORKS

6734 ■ "Are You Looking for an Environmentally Friendly Dry Cleaner?" in *Inc.* (Vol. 30, December 2008, No. 12, pp. 34)
Pub: Mansueto Ventures LLC
Ed: Shivani Vora. **Description:** Greenopia rates the greenness of 52 various kinds of businesses, including restaurants, nail salons, dry cleaners, and clothing stores. The guidebooks are sold through various retailers including Barnes & Noble and Amazon.com.

6735 ■ *Coin Laundry Association Supplier Directory*
Pub: Coin Laundry Association
Contact: Brian Wallace, President, CEO
E-mail: brian@coinlaundry.org
Ed: Michael Sokolowski, Editor, michael@coinlaundry.org. **Released:** Annual, August. **Covers:** about 500 manufacturers and suppliers of products and services to the coin laundry and dry cleaning industries. **Entries Include:** Name of firm, address, phone, e-mail, URL, products or services; distributors show area served. **Arrangement:** Manufacturers are alphabetical; distributors are geographical.

6736 ■ "'Green' Cleaner Buys Local Firm" in *Puget Sound Business Journal* (Vol. 29, December 19, 2008, No. 35, pp. 3)
Pub: American City Business Journals
Ed: Greg Lamm. **Description:** Washington-based Blue Sky Cleaners has purchased Four Seasons Cleaners. The green company also purchased Queen Anne store and Four Seasons' routes fro Snohomish County through Seattle.

6737 ■ "Nation of Islam Businessman Who Became Manager for Muhamnmad Ali Dies" in *Chicago Tribune* (August 28, 2008)
Pub: McClatchy-Tribune Information Services
Ed: Trevor Jensen. **Description:** Profile of Jabir Herbert Muhammad who died on August 25, after heart surgery; Muhammad lived nearly all his life on Chicago's South Side and ran a number of small businesses including a bakery and a dry cleaners before becoming the manager to famed boxer Mohammad Ali.

STATISTICAL SOURCES

6738 ■ *RMA Annual Statement Studies*
Pub: Robert Morris Associates (RMA)
Released: Annual. **Price:** $175.00 2006-07 edition, $105.00. **Description:** Contains composite balance sheets and income statements for more than 360 industries, including the accounting, auditing, and bookkeeping industries. Also contains five years of comparative historical data for discerning trends. Includes 16 commonly used ratios, computed for most of the size groupings for nearly every industry.

TRADE PERIODICALS

6739 ■ *American Coin-Op*
Pub: American Trade Magazines
Ed: Paul Partyka, Editor, ppartyka@crain.com. **Released:** Monthly. **Price:** Free to qualified subscribers. **Description:** Trade magazine on coin-operated laundries and dry-cleaners.

6740 ■ *American Drycleaner*
Pub: American Trade Magazines
Released: Monthly. **Price:** Free to qualified subscribers. **Description:** Magazine on drycleaning.

6741 ■ *CLA Member Journal*
Pub: Coin Laundry Association
Contact: Bob Nieman, Dir. Of Media Sales
E-mail: sara@coinlaundry.org
Released: Quarterly. **Price:** Included in membership. **Description:** Provides management and technical information for members of the self-service (coin-operated) laundry and drycleaning industry.

6742 ■ *Cycles*
Pub: Service Directions Inc.
Released: Semiannual. **Price:** Free. **Description:** Describes new laundry equipment, advances in laundryroom management, and analyzes problems in residential laundryrooms. Recurring features include interviews.

6743 ■ *Drycleaners News*
Pub: Zackin Publications Inc.
Contact: Cheryl Samide, Accounting/Office managing editorager
Released: Monthly. **Price:** $36. **Description:** Trade magazine (tabloid) for the dry-cleaning industry in the Northeastern U.S.

6744 ■ *Fabricare*
Pub: Drycleaning & Laundry Institute
Contact: Jillian Handman, Contributing Editor
Released: Monthly. **Price:** Included in membership. **Description:** Informs drycleaners and launderers of industry developments and Institute activities. Carries legislative updates, technical data, management ideas, and tips on problem fabrics and garments.

6745 ■ *Fabricare Canada*
Pub: Fabricare Canada
Contact: Marcia Todd, Publisher
E-mail: marcia@fabricarecanada.com
Released: Bimonthly. **Price:** Free to qualified subscribers; $25 other countries. **Description:** Magazine covering the laundry, dry-cleaning industry.

6746 ■ *The National Clothesline*
Pub: BPS Communications
Ed: Hal Horning, Editor. **Released:** Monthly. **Description:** Newspaper (tabloid) for laundry and dry cleaning industry.

TRADE SHOWS AND CONVENTIONS

6747 ■ Clean Show - World Educational Congress for Laundering and Drycleaning
Riddle & Associates, Show Management
3091 Maple Dr., Ste. 305
Atlanta, GA 30305
Ph:(404)876-1988
Fax:(404)876-5121
Co. E-mail: info@jriddle.com
URL: http://www.jriddle.com
Released: Biennial. **Audience:** Laundering and dry cleaning personnel, equipment manufacturers, suppliers and industry professionals. **Principal Exhibits:** Laundry and dry cleaning equipment, supplies, and services. **Dates and Locations:** 2011 Jun 06-09, Las Vegas, NV.

6748 ■ FABRICARE - Great Western Exhibit
California Cleaners Association
530 Bercut Dr., Ste. G
Sacramento, CA 95814
Ph:(916)443-0986
Free: 800-390-8409
Fax:(916)325-9990
Co. E-mail: cca@camgmt.com
URL: http://www.calcleaners.com
Released: Biennial. **Audience:** Dry cleaning and laundry plant owners, managers, employees, and investors. **Principal Exhibits:** Laundry and dry cleaning equipment, supplies, and services.

CONSULTANTS

6749 ■ Colburn & Guyette Consulting Partners Inc.
201 Oak St., Ste. 12
Pembroke, MA 02359
Ph:(781)826-5522
Free: 800-343-3310
Fax:(781)826-5523
Co. E-mail: info@colburnguyette.com
URL: http://www.colburnguyette.com
Contact: R. Todd Guyette, Principle
E-mail: rtg@colburnguyette.com
Scope: Offers a variety of consulting services to the foodservice Industry. Serves private industries as well as government agencies.

FRANCHISES AND BUSINESS OPPORTUNITIES

6750 ■ Comet Cleaners
Comet Cleaners Franchise Group
406 W Division St.
Arlington, TX 76011
Ph:(817)461-3555
Fax:(817)861-4779
Co. E-mail: info@cometcleaners.com
URL: http://www.cometcleaners.com
No. of Franchise Units: 250. **Founded:** 1941. **Franchised:** 1967. **Description:** Dry cleaning and laundry packages. 1-to-2 weeks. **Equity Capital Needed:** Estimated capital investment: $90,000$513,000. **Franchise Fee:** $15,000-$30,000. **Financial Assistance:** Various options available. **Training:** Yes.

6751 ■ Door-To-Door Dry Cleaning
8400 E Prentice Ave., Ste. 1500
Greenwood Village, CO 80111
Free: 877-769-3667
Fax:(866)731-5471
No. of Franchise Units: 28. **Founded:** 2004. **Franchised:** 2006. **Description:** Dry cleaning delivery. **Equity Capital Needed:** $40,950-$57,700. **Franchise Fee:** $25,000. **Royalty Fee:** 5-7%. **Financial Assistance:** No. **Training:** Provides 1 week training at headquarters, 1 week onsite and ongoing support.

6752 ■ Dove Cleaners & Cadet Cleaners
1560 Yonge St.
Toronto, ON, Canada M4T 289
Ph:(416)413-7900
Fax:(416)413-0619
Co. E-mail: sam@dovecorp.com
URL: http://www.dovecleaners.com
No. of Franchise Units: 98. **No. of Company-Owned Units:** 1. **Founded:** 1994. **Franchised:** 2000. **Description:** Named "Best Dry Cleaner" by Flare, Toronto Life and 680 News, Dove Cleaners is Toronto's leading dry cleaner. Franchises operate as depot locations with all cleaning performed off-site at Dove's central processing plant using state-of-the-art equipment and only hypo-allergenic detergents. Dove is an ISO registered company offering free pick-up and delivery to customers via call-in and online ordering service. **Equity Capital Needed:** $30,000. **Franchise Fee:** $30,000.

6753 ■ Dry Cleaning To-Your-Door
1121 NW Bayshore Dr.
Waldport, OR 97394
Free: 800-318-1800
Fax:(541)563-6938
No. of Franchise Units: 85. **Founded:** 1994. **Franchised:** 1996. **Description:** Dry cleaning business. **Equity Capital Needed:** $10,000-$16,000. **Franchise Fee:** $29,450. **Financial Assistance:** No. **Training:** Yes.

6754 ■ ImageFirst Healthcare Laundry Specialists
5 Radnor Corporate Center, Ste. 503
100 Matsonford Rd.
Radnor, PA 19087
Ph:(484)253-7200
Free: 800-932-7472
Fax:(484)253-7210
Co. E-mail: dburnette@myimagefirst.com
URL: http://www.imagefirstmedical.com
No. of Franchise Units: 21. **No. of Company-Owned Units:** 10. **Founded:** 1967. **Franchised:** 1997. **Description:** ImageFIRST provides laundry services on a rental basis for dentists, physicians and medical clinics. The main services offered are delivering, washing, picking up, monitoring usage and managing inventories. **Equity Capital Needed:** $50,00-$150,000. **Franchise Fee:** $30,000. **Financial Assistance:** No. **Training:** 4 weeks onsite marketing and sales assistance.

6755 ■ Lapels Dry Cleaning
Next Step Franchising
962 Washington St.
Hanover, MA 02339
Ph:(781)829-9935
Free: (866)695-2735
Fax:(781)829-9546
URL: http://www.lapelsdrycleaning.com
No. of Franchise Units: 47. **Founded:** 2000. **Franchised:** 2001. **Description:** Dry cleaning retail stores. **Equity Capital Needed:** $20,000-$100,000. **Franchise Fee:** $20,000-$30,000. **Financial Assistance:** Yes. **Training:** Full training with ongoing support.

6756 ■ Martinizing Dry Cleaning
Martin Franchises Inc.
422 Wards Corner Rd., Ste. F
Loveland, OH 45140
Ph:(513)699-4242
Free: 800-827-0345
Fax:(513)731-0818
Co. E-mail: cleanup@martinizing.com
URL: http://www.martinizing.com
No. of Franchise Units: 466. **Founded:** 1949. **Franchised:** 1949. **Description:** Dry cleaning stores. **Equity Capital Needed:** $400,000 minimum net worth; $385,000 typical investment. **Franchise Fee:** $40,000 initial fee. **Financial Assistance:** No. **Training:** Comprehensive managerial and technical training in classroom as well as franchisees store; equipment shakedown and ongoing service hotline; grand opening marketing package and ongoing local store and market wide promotional programs; field and operations assistance; ongoing support staff only a toll-free call away.

6757 ■ Nu-Look 1-Hour Cleaners
NLF, Inc.
5970 SW 18th St., Ste. 331
Boca Raton, FL 33433-7197
Ph:(561)362-4190
Free: (866)533-0146
Fax:(561)362-4229
No. of Franchise Units: 46. **Founded:** 1967. **Franchised:** 1969. **Description:** Retail dry cleaner. **Equity Capital Needed:** $195,000. **Franchise Fee:** $20,000. **Financial Assistance:** Third party financing available. **Training:** Offers 2 weeks at headquarters, 2 weeks at franchisee's location and ongoing support.

6758 ■ Oxxo Care Cleaners
1874 N Young Cir.
Hollywood, FL 33020
Ph:(954)927-7410
Free: (866)G02-0XX0
Fax:(954)927-7357
Co. E-mail: info@oxxousa.com
URL: http://www.oxxousa.com
No. of Franchise Units: 30. **No. of Company-Owned Units:** 2. **Founded:** 2001. **Franchised:** 2002. **Description:** State of the art dry cleaners. This is not your traditional drycleaners. We have eliminated the antiquated equipment and hazardous chemicals. Oxxo brings a successful venture directly from Europe that sets us apart from all other cleaners. Our unique boutique style air conditioning garment care centers use the most technologically advanced equipment, environmentally safe cleaning solutions, hand ironing, and offer a 24 hours a day and 7 days a week pick up and drop off through a 24-hour ATM garment retrieval system. **Equity Capital Needed:** $225,000 net worth; $150,000 liquid. **Franchise Fee:** $30,000. **Financial Assistance:** Associated with SBA lenders, offering third party financing. **Training:** Training is provided in all areas. Technical training in classroom, Training center, as well as franchisees store. Training in customer service, marketing, quality control, maintenance and ongoing support.

6759 ■ Pressed 4 Time
8 Clock Tower Pl., Ste. 110
Maynard, MA 01754
Ph:(978)823-8300
Free: 800-423-8711
Fax:(978)823-8301
Co. E-mail: franchiseinfo@pressed4time.com
URL: http://www.pressed4time.com
No. of Franchise Units: 165. **Founded:** 1987. **Franchised:** 1990. **Description:** Dry cleaning and shoe repair pick-up and delivery service, serving executives and staff at local businesses. A high repeat business, a low stress operation (5-day workweek, and local cleaning plants do the actual cleaning). **Equity Capital Needed:** $35,910-$44,810. **Franchise Fee:** $29,900. **Financial Assistance:** No. **Training:** Includes 2 days at the corporate offices, including 1 day of hands-on operations, the corporate vehicle and 1 day of intensive classroom training, covering start-up, record keeping, administration, dry cleaning, operations and sales. Also, 2 days of training in the franchisees territory, consisting of marketing training in the field to establish initial accounts.

6760 ■ Zips Dry Cleaners
Zips Franchising LLC
7500 Greenway Center Dr., Ste. 400
Greenbelt, MD 20770
Ph:(301)313-0389
Fax:(301)345-2895
No. of Franchise Units: 28. **Founded:** 1996. **Franchised:** 2006. **Description:** One price, same day

service dry cleaning. **Equity Capital Needed:** $616,150-$778,500. **Franchise Fee:** $50,000. **Royalty Fee:** 6%. **Financial Assistance:** Third party financing available. **Training:** Yes.

LIBRARIES

6761 ■ Drycleaning and Laundry Institute International Library
14700 Sweitzer Ln.
Silver Spring, MD 20707
Ph:(301)622-1900
Free: 800-638-2627
Fax:(240)295-0685
Co. E-mail: techline@ifi.org
URL: http://www.ifi.org/index.html
Scope: Chemistry, textiles, dry cleaning, laundering. **Services:** Library open to the public by appointment only. **Holdings:** Reference materials; CD-ROMs.

RESEARCH CENTERS

6762 ■ Drycleaning and Laundry Institute International
14700 Sweitzer Ln.
Laurel, MD 20707
Ph:(301)622-1900
Free: 800—638-2627
Fax:(240)295-0685
Co. E-mail: techline@ifi.org
URL: http://www.ifi.org
Contact: David Silliman, Chm.
E-mail: techline@ifi.org
Scope: Drycleaning, laundering, and related problems of textiles and detergency, including studies of mechanism of soil removal and redeposition, role of chemical and engineering factors that affect cleaning of textiles, alternative cleaning methods, alternative dry cleaning solvents, and dry cleaning-related environmental issues. **Services:** Counseling for members on sales, advertising, engineering methods, washroom formulas, drycleaning technology, and textiles maintenance. **Publications:** Fabric Bulletins (bimonthly); Fabricare (monthly); Fabricare Resources (bimonthly); Industry Focus (bimonthly); Shirt Laundry Procedures (bimonthly); Technical Bulletins (bimonthly). **Educational Activities:** Educational facilities for members; Laundering and drycleaning clinics.

START-UP INFORMATION

6763 ■ *How to Start a Home-Based Writing Business, 5th Edition*
Pub: Globe Pequot Press

Ed: Lucy Parker. **Released:** December 2007. **Price:** $18.95. **Description:** Guide for starting and running a home-based writing business.

ASSOCIATIONS AND OTHER ORGANIZATIONS

6764 ■ American Book Producers Association
151 W 19th St., 3rd Fl.
New York, NY 10011
Ph:(212)645-2368
Fax:(212)675-1364
Co. E-mail: office@abpaonline.org
URL: http://www.abpaonline.org
Contact: Richard Rothschild, Pres.

Description: Book producing companies that develop the concepts for books and, based on a contractual agreement with a publisher, may produce finished books or production-ready film, camera-ready mechanicals, finished manuscripts, art and layouts. Aims to increase the book industry's awareness of members' capabilities and the state of the book producers' art. Facilitates exchange of information for the purpose of improving business and establishing trade standards. **Publications:** *American Book Producers Association—Newsletter* (monthly).

6765 ■ American Society of Journalists and Authors
1501 Broadway, Ste. 302
New York, NY 10036
Ph:(212)997-0947
Fax:(212)937-2315
Co. E-mail: director@asja.org
URL: http://www.asja.org
Contact: Alexandra Owens, Exec. Dir.

Description: Represents freelance writers of nonfiction magazine articles and books. Seeks to elevate the professional and economic position of nonfiction writers, provide a forum for discussion of common problems among writers and editors, and promote a code of ethics for writers and editors. Operates writer referral service for individuals, institutions, or companies seeking writers for special projects; sponsors Llewellyn Miller Fund to aid professional writers who no longer able to work due to age, disability, or extraordinary professional crisis. **Publications:** *American Society of Journalists and Authors—Directory of Writers* (annual); *The ASJA Guide to Freelance Writing*; *ASJA Monthly* (monthly).

6766 ■ Asian American Writers' Workshop
110-112 W 27th St., 6th Fl.
New York, NY 10001
Ph:(212)494-0061
Fax:(212)494-0062
Co. E-mail: desk@aaww.org
URL: http://www.aaww.org
Contact: Ken Chen, Exec. Dir.
Description: Dedicated to the creation, development, publication, and dissemination of Asian American literature. **Publications:** *Asian Pacific American Journal* (semiannual).

6767 ■ Association of Teachers of Technical Writing
Texas Tech University
PO Box 43091
Lubbock, TX 79409
Co. E-mail: amy.koerber@ttu.edu
URL: http://www.attw.org
Contact: Kelli Cargile Cook, Pres.
Description: Teachers and students of technical communication at all levels and all types of educational institutions; technical communicators from government and industry. Serves as a forum of communication among technical writing teachers and acts as a liaison with other professional organizations. Provides current bibliographies of teaching/learning materials and reports of current research in the teaching of technical writing. Sponsors meetings and workshops at the annual conventions of the Modern Language Association of America and the Conference on College Composition and Communication. **Publications:** *Technical Communication Quarterly* (quarterly).

6768 ■ Association of Writers and Writing Programs
George Mason University
Mail Stop 1E3
Fairfax, VA 22030-4444
Ph:(703)993-4301
Fax:(703)993-4302
Co. E-mail: awp@awpwriter.org
URL: http://www.awpwriter.org
Contact: David W. Fenza, Exec. Dir.
Description: Writers; students and teachers in creative writing programs in university departments of English; editors, publishers, and freelance creative and professional writers. Fosters literary talent and achievement; advocates the craft of writing as primary to a liberal and humane education; provides publications and services to the makers and readers of contemporary literature. Operates career services and job listings; sponsors literary competitions. **Publications:** *AWP Official Guide to Writing Programs* (biennial); *The Writer's Chronicle* (periodic).

6769 ■ Bay Area Independent Publishers Association
PO Box E
Corte Madera, CA 94976
Ph:(415)456-0247
Co. E-mail: books4women@yahoo.com
URL: http://www.baipa.net
Contact: Paula Hendricks, Pres.
Description: Promotes authors interested in independent publishing as an alternative to the commercial publishing system; printers, artists, typists, and others in allied fields. Aims to become a comprehensive source of self-publishing information and to develop knowledge and expertise to better assist members in promoting, marketing, and publishing their works. Acts as a liaison and clearinghouse of information and provides guidance in all aspects of self-publishing, including copy preparation, book production, and marketing and sales. **Publications:** *SPEX* (monthly).

6770 ■ Boating Writers International
108 9th St.
Wilmette, IL 60091
Ph:(847)736-4142
Co. E-mail: info@bwi.org
URL: http://www.bwi.org
Contact: Zuzana Prochazka, Pres.
Description: Individuals in numerous countries including newspaper, magazine, radio, and television writers and photographers covering boating, fishing, and outdoor recreation and public relations. Seeks to: cover boating as a competitive as well as recreational sport; promote boating safety; encourage enjoyment of other outdoor water sports. **Publications:** *BWI Journal* (11/year);Directory (annual).

6771 ■ Bowling Writers Association of America
621 Six Flags Dr.
Arlington, TX 76011
Free: 800-343-1329
Co. E-mail: bwaa@bowlingwriters.com
URL: http://www.bowlingwriters.com
Contact: Jim Goodwin, Pres.
Description: Reporters of bowling news. **Publications:** *BWAA Newsletter* (semiannual).

6772 ■ Broad Universe
51 Watkins Ln.
Walnut Creek, CA 94596
Co. E-mail: info@broaduniverse.org
URL: http://www.broaduniverse.org
Contact: Karen Meng, Treas.
Description: Promotes science fiction, fantasy, and horror written by women. **Publications:** *The Broadsheet* .

6773 ■ Canadian Association of Journalists–L'Association Canadienne des Journalistes
Algonquin College
1106 Wellington St.
Ottawa, ON, Canada K1Y 4V3
Ph:(613)526-8061
Co. E-mail: canadianjour@magma.ca
URL: http://www.caj.ca
Contact: John Dickins, Exec. Dir.
Description: Professional organization representing the interests of journalists in Canada. Promotes high professional standards. Disseminates information. **Publications:** *Media* (3/year).

6774 ■ Canadian Copyright Institute
192 Spadina Ave., Ste. 107
Toronto, ON, Canada M5T 2C2
Ph:(416)975-1756

Fax:(416)975-1839
Co. E-mail: info@thecci.ca
URL: http://www.canadiancopyrightinstitute.ca
Contact: Anne McClelland, Admin.

Description: Creators, producers, and distributors of copyrighted works. Encourages a more complete understanding of copyright laws among members and the public. Consults with government and judicial bodies regarding reform of copyright laws. Conducts and sponsors research on copyright laws worldwide. Works with organizations pursuing similar goals to improve copyright legislation and enforcement. **Publications:** *Copyright Reform Legislation Reporting Service* (periodic).

6775 ■ Canadian Writers Foundation–La Fondation des ecrivains canadiens
PO Box 13281
Kanata Sta.
Ottawa, ON, Canada K2K 1X4
Ph:(613)256-6937
Fax:(613)256-5457
Co. E-mail: info@canadianwritersfoundation.org
URL: http://www.canadianwritersfoundation.org
Contact: Suzanne Williams, Exec. Sec.

Description: Provides ongoing assistance to notable senior Canadian writers who have made a significant contribution to Canadian writing and are experiencing extreme financial distress.

6776 ■ Communications Workers of America/ Canada–Syndicat des Communications d'Amerique
7B-1050 Baxter Rd.
Ottawa, ON, Canada K2C 3P1
Ph:(613)820-9777
Free: 877-486-4292
Fax:(613)820-8188
Co. E-mail: info@cwa-scacanada.ca
URL: http://www.cwa-scacanada.ca
Contact: Arnold Amber, Chm.

Description: Primarily union of journalists and media workers in Canada, as well as social workers and employees in the manufacturing industry. **Publications:** *TNG Canada Today* (monthly).

6777 ■ Crime Writers of Canada
2160 Colonel William Pkwy.
Oakville, ON, Canada L6M 0B8
Co. E-mail: info@crimewriterscanada.com
URL: http://www.crimewriterscanada.com
Contact: Garry Ryan, Pres.

Description: Canadian crime writers, associated professionals, and others with serious interest in Canadian crime writing. Promotes Canadian crime writing and increases awareness of Canadian crime writers from coast to coast. **Publications:** *Dishes to Die For*, *Fingerprints* (quarterly); *In Cold Blood* (semiannual).

6778 ■ Editorial Freelancers Association
71 W 23rd St., 4th Fl.
New York, NY 10010
Ph:(212)929-5400
Free: (866)929-5439
Fax:(212)929-5439
Co. E-mail: office@the-efa.org
URL: http://www.the-efa.org
Contact: J.P. Partland, Co-Exec.

Description: Represents persons who work full or part-time as freelance writers or editorial freelancers. Promotes professionalism and facilitates the exchange of information and support. Conducts professional training seminars; and offers job listings. **Publications:** *The Freelancer* (bimonthly).

6779 ■ Editors' Association of Canada–Association canadienne des reviseurs
502-27 Carlton St.
Toronto, ON, Canada M5B 1L2
Ph:(416)975-1379
Free: (866)226-3348
Fax:(416)975-1637
Co. E-mail: info@editors.ca
URL: http://www.editors.ca
Contact: Michelle Boulton, Pres.

Description: Editors, proofreaders, copy editors, and researchers working on both English and French language printed materials. Promotes advancement of the profession of editing, and of members' capabilities. Conducts professional development courses for members; makes available to members job hotline services and discount long-term disability, extended health, and dental and life insurance. Sets and enforces editorial standards of practice; establishes payment levels and conditions of employment for editorial work. Cooperates with other organizations pursuing similar goals. **Publications:** *Active Voice* (bimonthly).

6780 ■ Federation of BC Writers
PO Box 3887
Station Terminal
Vancouver, BC, Canada V6B 2Z3
Ph:(604)683-2057
Co. E-mail: fedbcwriters@gmail.com
URL: http://www.bcwriters.com
Contact: Sylvia Taylor, Exec. Dir.

Description: Contributes to a supportive environment for writing in the community.

6781 ■ Horror Writers Association
244 5th Ave., Ste. 2767
New York, NY 10001-7604
Co. E-mail: hwa@horror.org
URL: http://www.horror.org
Contact: Rocky Wood, Pres.

Description: Horror writers, including creators of comic strips, screenplays, and role-playing games, who have sold at least one work at professional rates are active members; horror writers who have sold something but not at professional rates are affiliate members. Non-writing professionals are associate members. Seeks to assist aspiring and accomplished horror writers in advancing their art and careers. Facilitates networking among members; gathers and disseminates information on horror fiction markets; serves as liaison between members and writers' agents and publishers. **Publications:** *Handbook/ Directory* (annual).

6782 ■ International Black Writers
PO Box 43576
Los Angeles, CA 90043
Ph:(213)964-3721
Co. E-mail: ibwa_la@yahoo.com
URL: http://ibwa.tripod.com/home.htm

Description: Seeks to discover and support new black writers. Conducts research and monthly seminars in poetry, fiction, nonfiction, music, and jazz. Provides writing services and children's services. Maintains speakers' bureau. Offers referral service. Plans to establish hall of fame, biographical archives, and museum. **Publications:** *The Black Writer* (quarterly); *Directory of Afro-American Writers* (periodic); *Griots Benaate, the Baobab: Tales From Los Angeles*; *In Touch Newsletter* (monthly); *Poetry Contest* (annual); *River Crossings: Voices of the Diaspora*; *Urban Voices Poetry* (annual);Bulletin (periodic).

6783 ■ International Food, Wine and Travel Writers Association
1142 S Diamond Bar Blvd., No. 177
Diamond Bar, CA 91765-2203
Ph:(909)860-6914
Free: 877-439-8929
Fax:(909)396-0014
Co. E-mail: admin@ifwtwa.org
URL: http://www.ifwtwa.org
Contact: Ms. Patricia A. Anis, Exec. Dir.

Description: Professional food, wine, and travel journalists, photographers, broadcasters and industry professionals in 28 countries; associate members are organizations in the hospitality industries. Seeks to bring recognition to those in the food, wine, and travel industry who have met the association's criteria. Offers scholarships in culinary arts and sciences journalism (food-wine-travel). **Publications:** *Global Writes* (weekly); *International Food, Wine and Travel Writers Association—Membership Roster* (annual); *Membership Benefits* (annual); *New Asian Cuisine: Fabulous Recipes from Celebrity Chefs*; *Press Pass* (monthly).

6784 ■ International Foodservice Editorial Council
PO Box 491
Hyde Park, NY 12538-0491
Ph:(845)229-6973
Fax:(845)229-6973
Co. E-mail: ifec@ifeconline.com
URL: http://ifeconline.com
Contact: Carol Lally, Exec. Dir.

Description: Key communicators within the U.S. foodservice industry, including top editors and marketing and public relations personnel for leading food companies and foodservice educational institutions. Organized to sound the marketing directions of the industry on all levels; seeks to improve communications. .

6785 ■ Investigative Reporters and Editors
Missouri School of Journalism
141 Neff Annex
Columbia, MO 65211
Ph:(573)882-2042
Fax:(573)882-5431
Co. E-mail: info@ire.org
URL: http://www.ire.org
Contact: Mark Horvit, Exec. Dir.

Description: Persons who report or edit in-depth journalism; journalism educators and students. Provides educational services, including computer-assisted reporting through its National Institute for Computer-Assisted Reporting. **Publications:** *Beat Book Series* (quarterly); *IRE Journal* (bimonthly); *IRE Members Directory* (annual); *Uplink* (bimonthly).

6786 ■ Let's Face It USA
University of Michigan
School of Dentistry
Dentistry Library
Ann Arbor, MI 48109-1078
Co. E-mail: faceit@umich.edu
URL: http://www.dent.umich.edu/faceit
Contact: Betsy Wilson, Founder/Dir.

Description: Provides information and support for people who have or who care for those with facial disfigurement. Website and annual publication with over 150 resources for professionals and families. Links to all related networks for specific conditions i.e. Genetic Disorders, Burns, Cancer, etc. **Publications:** *Resources for People with Facial Difference* (semiannual).

6787 ■ National Writers Association
10940 S Parker Rd., No. 508
Parker, CO 80134
Ph:(303)841-0246
Fax:(303)841-2607
Co. E-mail: natlwritersassn@hotmail.com
URL: http://www.nationalwriters.com

Description: Professional full- or part-time freelance writers who specialize in business writing. Aims to serve as a marketplace whereby business editors can easily locate competent writing talent. Establishes communication among editors and writers. .

6788 ■ North American Snowsports Journalists Association
460 Sarsons Rd.
Kelowna, BC, Canada V1W 1C2
Ph:(250)764-2143
Fax:(250)764-2145
Co. E-mail: nasja@shaw.ca
URL: http://www.nasja.org
Contact: Phil Johnson, Pres.

Description: Newspaper, magazine, book, television, radio writers and broadcasters, and photographers who report on skiing and other snow sports. Covers skiing and other snow sports. **Publications:** *The Inside Edge* (quinquennial); *NASJA Directory* (annual).

6789 ■ Novelists, Inc.
PO Box 2037
Manhattan, KS 66505
Fax:(785)837-1877
Co. E-mail: ninc@varney.com
URL: http://www.ninc.com
Contact: Kay Hooper, Pres.

Description: Works to serve the needs of multi-published writers of popular fiction. .

6790 ■ Outdoor Writers Association of America
615 Oak St., Ste. 201
Missoula, MT 59801
Ph:(406)728-7434
Fax:(406)728-7445
Co. E-mail: info@owaa.org
URL: http://www.owaa.org
Contact: Robin Giner, Exec. Dir.

Description: Professional organization of newspaper, magazine, radio, television and motion picture writers and photographers (both staff and free-lance) concerned with outdoor recreation and conservation. Conducts surveys for educational and industrial organizations; compiles market data for writer members and offers liaison aid in writer assignments.
.

6791 ■ Quebec Writers' Federation
1200 Atwater Ave.
Westmount, QC, Canada H3Z 1X4
Ph:(514)933-0878
Co. E-mail: admin@qwf.org
URL: http://www.qwf.org
Contact: Lori Schubert, Exec. Dir.

Description: Works toward ensuring a lasting place for English literature and practitioners on the Quebec cultural scene.

6792 ■ Sisters in Crime
PO Box 442124
Lawrence, KS 66044
Ph:(785)842-1325
Co. E-mail: sinc@sistersincrime.org
URL: http://www.sistersincrime.org
Contact: Cathy Pickens, Pres.

Description: Represents writers, librarians, editors, booksellers, agents and publishers. Promotes the professional development and advancement of women crime writers. .

6793 ■ Society for Technical Communication
9401 Lee Hwy., Ste. 300
Fairfax, VA 22031
Ph:(703)522-4114
Fax:(703)522-2075
Co. E-mail: stc@stc.org
URL: http://www.stc.org
Contact: Dr. Hillary Hart, Pres.

Description: Writers, editors, educators, scientists, engineers, artists, publishers, and others professionally engaged in or interested in the field of technical communication; companies, corporations, organizations and agencies interested in the aims of the society. Seeks to advance the theory and practice of technical communication in all media. Sponsors high school writing contests. **Publications:** *Technical Communication* (quarterly).

6794 ■ United States Harness Writers' Association
PO Box 1314
Mechanicsburg, PA 17055
Ph:(717)651-5889
Co. E-mail: ushwa@paonline.com
URL: http://www.ushwa.org
Contact: Jason Settlemoir, Pres.

Description: Writers, reporters, editors, broadcasters, columnists, and cartoonists who cover harness racing for the press. Seeks to further the interests of light harness racing. Maintains hall of fame and charitable program. Votes on national awards. .

6795 ■ Women Writing the West
8547 E Arapahoe Rd., No. J-541
Greenwood Village, CO 80112-1436
Co. E-mail: info@womenwritingthewest.org
URL: http://www.womenwritingthewest.org
Contact: Pam Tartaglio, Pres.-Elect

Description: Serves as a forum for writers and other professionals writing and promoting the Women's West founded by Sybil Downing and Jerrie Hurd. Promotes the legacy of earlier women writers who depicted the life during the hard and dangerous times of the Western American era. .

EDUCATIONAL PROGRAMS

6796 ■ Copywriting I
EEI Communications
66 Canal Center Plz., Ste. 200
Alexandria, VA 22314
Ph:(703)683-7453
Free: 888-253-2762
Fax:(703)683-7310
Co. E-mail: train@eeicom.com
URL: http://www.eeicom.com/training

Price: $745.00. **Description:** Topics include understanding your audience, defining your purpose, communication methods, and effective writing structures. **Locations:** Alexandria, VA.

6797 ■ Copywriting II
EEI Communications
66 Canal Center Plz., Ste. 200
Alexandria, VA 22314
Ph:(703)683-7453
Free: 888-253-2762
Fax:(703)683-7310
Co. E-mail: train@eeicom.com
URL: http://www.eeicom.com/training

Price: $425.00. **Description:** Geared towards the experienced writer, this seminar covers forming ideas and brainstorming, impact writing, and improving the creative process. **Locations:** Alexandria, VA.

6798 ■ The Designing Editor
EEI Communications
66 Canal Center Plz., Ste. 200
Alexandria, VA 22314
Ph:(703)683-7453
Free: 888-253-2762
Fax:(703)683-7310
Co. E-mail: train@eeicom.com
URL: http://www.eeicom.com/training

Price: $745.00. **Description:** Seminar for editors who must also perform design tasks; covers the basics of effective design, including the design process, page layout, design evaluation techniques, and related issues. **Locations:** Alexandria, VA.

6799 ■ Intensive Review of Grammar
EEI Communications
66 Canal Center Plz., Ste. 200
Alexandria, VA 22314
Ph:(703)683-7453
Free: 888-253-2762
Fax:(703)683-7310
Co. E-mail: train@eeicom.com
URL: http://www.eeicom.com/training

Price: $745.00. **Description:** Seminar for writers and editors; covers the advanced elements of grammar and usage, including adverbs and adjectives, restrictive and nonrestrictive clauses, dependent and independent clauses, tricky punctuation rules, pronoun/antecedent agreement, and subject/verb agreement. **Locations:** Silver Spring, MD; and Alexandria, VA.

6800 ■ Scientific Editing
EEI Communications
66 Canal Center Plz., Ste. 200
Alexandria, VA 22314
Ph:(703)683-7453
Free: 888-253-2762
Fax:(703)683-7310
Co. E-mail: train@eeicom.com
URL: http://www.eeicom.com/training

Price: $745.00. **Description:** Covers techniques for editing scientific and technical prose, including convincing writers to revise their manuscript; reducing author reliance on jargon and wordiness; locating and using scientific editing resources; meeting title, abstract, and keyword requirements; editing math and scientific data in graphs, diagrams, and illustrations; handling units, measurements, and numbers; and using scientific and engineering symbols. **Locations:** Alexandria, VA.

DIRECTORIES OF EDUCATIONAL PROGRAMS

6801 ■ *Contemporary Women Poets*
Pub: St. James Press

Ed: Pamela L. Shelton, Editor. **Released:** Latest edition October 2007. **Covers:** 250 prominent women poets writing and publishing in the English language and including some foreign-language authors. **Entries Include:** Biographical data, list of publications, author's comments when available, signed essay about the author. **Arrangement:** Alphabetical. **Indexes:** Nationality, title.

6802 ■ *FACSNET*
Pub: Foundation for American Communications
FACS

Entries Include: For experts—Name, address, phone, E-mail address. For others—Contact information. **Database Covers:** Internet resources for journalists, including traditional news beats, seminars, institutes, conferences, and experts in the field.

6803 ■ *Who's Who in the Media and Communications*
Pub: Marquis Who's Who L.L.C.

Covers: More than 18,500 professionals in print journalism, broadcasting, publishing, television, public relations, advertising, radio, telecommunications, interactive multimedia, and education. **Entries Include:** Biographical data.

REFERENCE WORKS

6804 ■ *American Society of Journalists and Authors—Directory*
Pub: American Society of Journalists & Authors

Released: Annual, January. **Price:** $98, individuals. **Covers:** 1,000 member freelance nonfiction writers. **Entries Include:** Writer's name, home and office addresses and phone numbers, specialties, areas of expertise; name, address and phone of agent; memberships; books; periodicals to which contributed; awards. **Arrangement:** Alphabetical. **Indexes:** Subject specialty, type of material written, geographical.

6805 ■ *The AWP Official Guide to Writing Programs*
Pub: Association of Writers & Writing Programs
Contact: Katherine Perry
E-mail: awpchron@mason.gmu.edu

Released: Annual, February of even years; Latest edition 11th. **Price:** $28.45, individuals including shipping and handling. **Covers:** About 300 graduate and 400 undergraduate programs in creative writing; approximately 250 writers' conferences, festivals, and centers; coverage includes Canada and the United Kingdom. **Entries Include:** Institution name, department name, contact name and address; web site, description of program, including degree or other credit offered; description of faculty, including titles of their publications; tuition fees and dates. **Arrangement:** Alphabetical. **Indexes:** Geographical, degree.

6806 ■ *Be a Brilliant Business Writer: Write Well, Write Fast, and Whip the Competition*
Pub: Crown Business Books

Ed: Jane Curry, Diana Young. **Released:** October 5, 2010. **Price:** $13.99. **Description:** Tools for mastering the art of persuasive writing in every document created, from email and client letters to reports and presentations, this book will help any writer convey their message with clarity and power, increase productivity by reducing rewrites, and provide the correct tone for navigating office politics.

6807 ■ *Editorial Freelancers Association—Membership Directory*
Pub: Editorial Freelancers Association Inc.
Contact: Sheila Buff
Released: Annual, spring. **Covers:** 1,100 member editorial freelancers. **Entries Include:** Personal name, address, phone, services provided, specialties. **Arrangement:** Alphabetical. **Indexes:** Product/service, special interest, geographical, computer skills.

6808 ■ "Freelance Writer Creates L.I. Bridal Blog" in *Long Island Business News* (September 10, 2010)
Pub: Dolan Media Newswires
Ed: Gregory Zeller. **Description:** Profile of Claudia Copquin, freelance journalist who created a blog for brides on the Internet.

6809 ■ *Freelancing for Journalists*
Pub: Routledge
Ed: Diana Harris. **Released:** January 1, 2010. **Price:** $110.00. **Description:** Comprehensive guide showing the specific skills required for those wishing to freelance in newspapers, magazines, radio, television, and as online journalists.

6810 ■ *International Literary Market Place*
Pub: Information Today Inc.
Contact: Thomas H. Hogan, Publisher/Pres.
Released: Annual, Latest edition 2012. **Price:** $289, individuals softbound; $260.10, individuals first time standing order. **Covers:** Over 10,500 publishers in over 180 countries outside the United States and Canada, and about 1,499 trade and professional organizations related to publishing abroad; includes major printers, binders, typesetters, book manufacturers, book dealers, libraries, literary agencies, translators, book clubs, reference books and journals, periodicals, prizes, and international reference section. **Entries Include:** For publishers—Name, address, phone, fax, telex, names and titles of key personnel, branches, type of publications, subjects, ISBN prefix. Listings for others include similar information but less detail. **Arrangement:** Classified by business activities, then geographical. **Indexes:** Company name, subject, type of publication.

6811 ■ *Midwest Travel Writers Association—Membership Directory*
Pub: Midwest Travel Writers Association
Contact: Glenda Hinz, Admin. Asst.
Released: Annual, February. **Price:** $50; $65 book & CD. **Covers:** Over 100 travel writers, editors, and representatives of the travel and tourism industry, located in 13 Midwestern states. **Entries Include:** Name, spouse's name, address, phone; title, year membership began, publications, professional affiliations, writing specialties. **Arrangement:** Alphabetical. **Indexes:** Geographical.

6812 ■ *My So-Called Freelance Life: How to Survive and Thrive as a Creative Professional for Hire*
Pub: Seal Press
Ed: Michelle Goodman. **Released:** October 1, 2008. **Price:** $15.95. **Description:** Guidebook for women wishing to start a freelancing business; tips, advice, how-to's and all the information needed to survive working from home are included.

6813 ■ "A Network of One: Local Writer Adds Web Interviews to Creative Output" in *La Crosse Tribune* (September 14, 2009)
Pub: La Crosse Tribune
Ed: Geri Parlin. **Description:** Profile of Andrew Revels, a freelance and aspiring writer, who has created a website in order to help gain attention for his own writing as well as for other local artists, musicians and comedians. His latest endeavor includes interviewing local talent and broadcasting the interviews on his site each week.

6814 ■ "Pretentious and Loving It" in *Entrepreneur* (Vol. 37, August 2009, No. 8, pp. 34)
Pub: Entrepreneur Media, Inc.
Ed: Eric Mahoney. **Description:** Pitchfork.com features reviews of albums from independent artists. Their most innovative section is Pitchfork.tv, featuring videos of bands, and Forkcast along with their Features section that contains articles about bands and their histories.

6815 ■ *Professional Freelance Writers Directory*
Pub: The National Writers Association
Contact: Anita Whelchel
E-mail: anitaedits@aol.com
Released: Annual. **Price:** Free. **Entries Include:** Name, address, phone (home and business numbers), special fields of writing competence, titles of books published by royalty firms, mention of contributions to specific magazines, journals, newspapers or anthologies, recent awards received, relevant activities and skills (photography, etc.). **Database Covers:** About 200 professional members selected from the club's membership on the basis of significant articles or books, or production of plays or movies. **Arrangement:** Alphabetical. **Indexes:** By author alphabetical, by state, by subject.

6816 ■ *Publishers Directory*
Pub: Gale
Released: Annual, Latest edition 36th; April, 2011. **Price:** $720, individuals. **Covers:** Over 20,000 new and established, commercial and nonprofit, private and alternative, corporate and association, government and institution publishing programs and their distributors; includes producers of books, classroom materials, prints, reports, and databases. **Entries Include:** Firm name, address, phone, fax, company e-mail address, URL, year founded, ISBN prefix, Standard Address Number, whether firm participates in the Cataloging in Publication program of the Library of Congress, names of principal executives, personal e-mail addresses, number of titles in print, description of firm and its main subject interests, discount and returns policies, affiliated and parent companies, mergers and amalgamations, principal markets, imprints and divisions, alternate formats products are offered; distributors also list firms for which they distribute, special services, terms to publishers and regional offices. **Arrangement:** Alphabetical; distributors listed separately. **Indexes:** Subject, geographical, publisher, imprints, and distributor.

6817 ■ "Savvy Solutions" in *Black Enterprise* (Vol. 41, November 2010, No. 4, pp. 42)
Pub: Earl G. Graves Publishing Co. Inc.
Ed: Tennile M. Robinson. **Description:** Society of Children's Book Writers and Illustrators offers members many benefits, including directories of agencies looking for new writers of books.

6818 ■ *Short Story Writers*
Pub: Magill's Choice
Ed: Frank N. Magill, Editor. **Released:** Published October 2007. **Price:** $217, individuals 3 volumes. **Covers:** 102 short story writers of the 19th and 20th centuries. **Entries Include:** Writer name, principal works of short fiction, other literary forms produced, notable career and technical achievements related to the short story form, brief biography, glossary. **Arrangement:** Alphabetical. **Indexes:** Author surname, title.

6819 ■ "Welcome to a New Kind of Cubicle Culture" in *Boston Business Journal* (Vol. 29, August 19, 2011, No. 15, pp. 1)
Pub: American City Business Journals Inc.
Ed: Alexander Jackson. **Description:** Beehive Baltimore offers a co-working space where independent freelancers and entrepreneurs can work. There are two other companies that provide the same service and the value of these services to these professional is that it provides them with an office that is both convenient and affordable aside from letting them network with peers.

TRADE PERIODICALS

6820 ■ *American Society of Journalists and Authors Newsletter*
Pub: American Society of Journalists & Authors
Ed: Barbara DeMarco Barrett, Editor, newsletter@asja.org. **Released:** Monthly, July and August issues clubbed. **Description:** Reports on the business meetings of the Society and provides market news as well as news of members, publishers, editors, and association chapters. Recurring features include professional market reports and discussions of magazines, books, and other media.

6821 ■ *Authorship*
Pub: The National Writers Association
Contact: Sandy Whelchel
Ed: Sandy Whelchel, Editor. **Released:** Quarterly. **Price:** $18, nonmembers. **Description:** Contains information about the freelance writing and publishing fields. Carries market news, lists of editors and publishers against whom many have registered complaints, and updates on publications that have gone out of business or are no longer considering freelance submissions. Recurring features include news of members, editorials, letters to the editor, book reviews, and columns titled Director's Corner and Business Writing News.

6822 ■ *AWP Job List*
Pub: Association of Writers & Writing Programs
Ed: David Sherwin, Editor, awpchron@mason.gmu.edu. **Released:** Monthly, 7/year. **Price:** Included in membership. **Description:** Lists job opportunities for writers, both in academia and in the business sector.

6823 ■ *Children's Book Insider*
Pub: Children's Book Insider
Contact: Laura Backes, Publisher
E-mail: laura@write4kids.com
Released: Monthly. **Price:** $29.95, individuals; $26.95 online. **Description:** Discusses writing and selling books and stories for children. Recurring features include interviews, news of educational opportunities, job listings, and columns titled Writing Workshop, Market News, and Trends.

6824 ■ *Fiction Writer's Guideline*
Pub: Fiction Writer's Connection
Contact: Blythe Camenson, Editor & Dir.
E-mail: bcamenson@aol.com
Released: Enewsletter. **Price: Description:** Offers practical advice and support on writing and getting published. Recurring features include interviews, book reviews, and Advice From agents and editors and Writing Tips.

6825 ■ *Freelance Writer's Report*
Pub: CNW Publishing, Editing, & Promotion Inc.
Contact: Dana K. Cassell
Ed: Dana K. Cassell, Editor, danakcnw@ncia.net. **Released:** Monthly. **Price:** Included in membership. **Description:** Offers up-to-date news and information concerning effective marketing/production techniques, writing tips, self-promotion, and other topics of interest "to freelance writers who intend to earn a good income from their work and improve the quality of their work." Recurring features include interviews, book reviews, news of writing seminars, conferences, and market news. Remarks: Members of the Florida Freelance Writers Association receive an extra association section (4 pages).

6826 ■ *The Freelancer*
Pub: Editorial Freelancers Association Inc.
Ed: Mary Ratcliffe, Editor, gamut@mratcliffe.com. **Released:** Bimonthly. **Price:** Included in membership; $20, nonmembers. **Description:** Publishes news of the concerns and activities of EFA, whose members "provide freelance editorial services to the publishing and communications industries." Recurring features include letters to the editor, news of members, book reviews, a calendar of events, columns on usage and business, reports on on general meetings, news of member, and columns titled Grammatical Gleanings and Tax Tips.

6827 ■ *How To Be Your Own Publisher Update*
Pub: Bibliotheca Press
Contact: A. Doyle
Ed: A. Doyle, Editor. **Released:** Annual. **Price:** $12.95, U.S.; $15.95, Canada; $19.95, other countries. **Description:** Acts as a reference for self publishers. Distributed by Prosperity & Profits Unlimited Distribution Services, PO Box 416, Denver, CO, 80201.

6828 ■ *International Women's Writing Guild—Network*
Pub: International Women's Writing Guild
Contact: Tatiana Stoumen
Ed: Tatiana Stoumen, Editor. **Released:** Bimonthly. **Price:** Included in membership. **Description:** Carries a variety of items for women who write both for personal growth and professionally. Announces opportunities for retreat, publication, and awards. Recurring features include Guild and member news; writing conferences, and workshops; letters; and contests, environmental news, market and publication information.

6829 ■ *Journal of Technical Writing and Communication*
Pub: Baywood Publishing Company Inc.
Contact: Elizabeth Tebeaux, Book Review Ed.
Ed: Charles H. Sides, Editor. **Released:** Quarterly. **Price:** $402 institutions; $381 institutions online. **Description:** Peer-reviewed journal addressed to technical writers, editors, communication specialists, and everyone engaged in the exchange of technical and scientific information.

6830 ■ *NABJ Update*
Pub: National Association of Black Journalists
Ed: Ernie Suggs, Editor. **Released:** 6/year. **Description:** Reports on activities of the National Association of Black Journalists.

6831 ■ *NAHWW Newsletter*
Pub: National Association of Home and Workshop Writers (NAHWW)
Ed: Richard Day, Editor. **Released:** Quarterly. **Price:** Included in membership. **Description:** Promotes communication among member writers by sharing information on publishers, marketing conditions, and mutual problems. Offers how-to tips, do-it-yourself field growth projections, and news of association activities. Recurring features include letters from members, book reviews, jokes, and columns titled Market Report and Resources.

6832 ■ *New Writer's Magazine*
Pub: New Writer's Magazine
Ed: George S. Haborak, Editor, newriters@aol.com. **Released:** Bimonthly. **Price:** $25. **Description:** Magazine covering the craft of writing.

6833 ■ *Poetalk*
Pub: Bay Area Poets Coalition Inc.
Contact: John B. Rowe, President
Released: Quarterly. **Price:** $15, Included in membership; $6, nonmembers; $12, institutions. **Description:** Publishes quality work by beginner and experienced poets.

6834 ■ *PWAContact*
Pub: Professional Writers Association of Canada
Contact: Lauren Stewart
Ed: Phil Moscovitch, Editor. **Released:** Quarterly. **Description:** Provides news and information to help further the careers of professional freelance writers in Canada. Examines copyright changes and implications and discusses available markets, industry news, computer programs and technology, and various aspects of the writing profession. Recurring features include letters to the editor, reports of meetings, a calendar of events, and columns titled New Tech, Professional Practice, and Copyright. Remarks: PWAC members receive a special section titled PWAC Inside, which provides an insider's view and tips about working for specific magazines, information on new publications, awards, chapter updates, and a column titled Red Flag.

6835 ■ *Travel Publicity Leads*
Pub: Scott American Corp.
Contact: Frank Scott, Editor & Publisher
Released: Weekly. **Price:** $400, individuals by mail or fax. **Description:** Summarizes the information, trip invitations, data, and interviews travel writers and broadcasters desire. Provides global editorial placement opportunities for PR specialists at travel service providers, worldwide, and their PR firms. Includes an annual compilation of editorial calendars of worldwide travel media, with key-worded and time-sequenced topics.

6836 ■ *Travel Writer*
Pub: Society of American Travel Writers
Contact: Al Sandner
Released: 10/year. **Description:** Advises and provides information for travel writers.

6837 ■ *Washington Writer*
Pub: Washington Independent Writers
Contact: Claude Berube, President
E-mail: editor@washwriter.org
Released: Monthly, July/August issue combined. **Price:** Included in membership; $45, nonmembers. **Description:** Carries information for freelance writers about current issues of interest, including developments in the book and magazine publishing businesses, new markets, and alerts concerning unfair editorial practices. Recurring features include a calendar of events, news of members, announcements of workshops, conference reports, and columns titled Bylines, Resources, Small Groups, and Classified Ads. Remarks: Subscribers must live outside the Washington metropolitan area. Members of the organization receive the newsletter as part of their membership.

6838 ■ *The Writer Magazine*
Pub: Kalmbach Publishing Co.
Contact: Jeff Felbab, Advertising Mgr
E-mail: jfelbab@writermag.com
Released: Monthly. **Price:** $32.95; $42.95 Canada; $61 two years; $44.95 other countries. **Description:** Magazine for free-lance writers. Publishing practical information and advice on how to write publishable material and where to sell it.

6839 ■ *Writer's Digest*
Pub: FW Media Inc.
Contact: Nancy Miller, Advertising Sales Rep.
E-mail: nancymiller@fwmedia.com
Released: 8/yr. **Price:** $19.96; $29.96 Canada including GST/HST; $29.96 other countries surface delivery. **Description:** Professional magazine for writers.

6840 ■ *Writers' Union of Canada Newsletter*
Pub: Writers' Union of Canada
Contact: Deborah Windsor, Dir.
Released: Quarterly, 6/year. **Price:** Included in membership. **Description:** Informs members of the activities of the Union.

VIDEOCASSETTES/ AUDIOCASSETTES

6841 ■ *Get Published*
Instructional Video
2219 C St.
Lincoln, NE 68502
Ph:(402)475-6570
Free: 800-228-0164
Fax:(402)475-6500
Co. E-mail: feedback@insvideo.com
URL: http://www.insvideo.com
Price: $149.95. **Description:** New York literary and film agent Peter Miller furnishes information on what it takes to get published, includes advise on selling fiction, defending author's rights, and developing nonfiction book proposals. He also discusses industry practices, procedures, and the television and motion picture markets. **Availability:** VHS.

6842 ■ *Jane Rule...Writing*
The Cinema Guild
115 West 30th St., Ste. 800
New York, NY 10001
Ph:(212)685-6242
Free: 800-723-5522
Fax:(212)685-4717
Co. E-mail: info@cinemaguild.com
URL: http://www.cinemaguild.com
Released: 1996. **Price:** $250. **Description:** Documentary features novelist Jane Rule discussing her philosophy of creative writing. **Availability:** VHS.

CONSULTANTS

6843 ■ Career Pro
7825 Midlothian Tpke., Ste. 220
Richmond, VA 23235-5247
Ph:(804)323-0120
Free: 800-513-1666
Fax:(804)560-4098
Contact: John Myers, Principle
Scope: Firm provides professional resume and cover letter writing deliverable in Word or HTML format.

6844 ■ Carelli & Associates
17 Reid Pl.
Delmar, NY 12054
Ph:(518)439-0233
Fax:(518)439-3006
Co. E-mail: anneobriencarelli@yahoo.com
URL: http://www.carelli.com
Contact: Dr. Anne Obrien Carelli, Owner
E-mail: anneobriencarelli@yahoo.com
Scope: Provides writing and editing services to industry and businesses, health care and educational institutions, and government agencies. Also provides program management in creating and disseminating publications and in implementing related training. Assists organizations in designing and implementing team-based management. Offers supervisory skills training and problem-solving work sessions for managers. Individual Consultation are provided for managers, CEOs, potential supervisors including 360 degree assessments. **Publications:** "The Truth About Supervision: Coaching, Teamwork, Interviewing, Appraisals, 360 degree Assessments, and Recognition". **Seminars:** Supervisory Skills Training Series; Problem-Solving Work Sessions for Managers; Effective Leadership.

6845 ■ The Center for Technical Communication
590 Delcina Dr.
River Vale, NJ 07675
Ph:(201)505-9451
Fax:(201)385-1138
Co. E-mail: rwbly@bly.com
URL: http://www.bly.com
Contact: Bob Bly, President
E-mail: rwbly@bly.com
Scope: An independent consultant and copywriter specializing in business-to-business, industrial, hi-tech, and direct response advertising, marketing, publicity, and promotion. Writes marketing plans, ad campaigns, sales brochures, publicity materials, direct response ads, sales letters, and direct mail packages for clients nationwide. Industries served: publishing, business-to-business products or services, software or computers, electronics, financial, healthcare, medical equipment, industrial equipment, chemicals, consulting, and professional services. **Publications:** "The Bulletproof Book Proposal "; "Finding A Good Idea For Your Book"; "A Fine Position to Be In"; "What to Do When Your Book Goes Out of Print"; "How To Write a Good Advertisement"; "31 -derfully Simple Ways To Make Your Ads Generate More Inquiries"; "On Target Advertising"; "How to Write More Effective Product Brochures "; "Classy Outfit...Classy Brochure?"; "Improving Your Listening Skills"; "Improving Your Interpersonal Skills"; "10 Ways To Get More Done in Less Time"; "How to Give a Successful Presentation". **Seminars:** Active Listening; Become an Instant Guru; Get More Done In Less Time: How To Double Your Personal Productivity; How To Write A Nonfiction Book And Get It Published; How To Succeed as a Freelance Writer; The 1-Hour E-Zine Writing Formula; World's Best-Kept Copywriting Secrets; What's Working in Direct Mail Today; What's Working in E-Mail Marketing Today; Copywriting for Non-Copywriters; Effective Business Writing; Effective Technical Writing; How To Write Copy That Sells; Selling Your Services.

6846 ■ Great Western Association Management Inc.
7995 E Prentice Ave., Ste. 100
Greenwood Village, CO 80111
Ph:(303)770-2220

Fax:(303)770-1614
Co. E-mail: info83@gwami.com
URL: http://www.gwami.com
Contact: Sheryl Pitts, Principle
E-mail: kwojdyla@atsgwami.com
Scope: Provides clients with products and services to effectively manage existing and startup, for- and not-for-profit organizations. Clients select from a menu of services including association development and public relations, conferences and seminars, financial management, membership communications, and governance. Expertise also includes association strategic planning, compliance, lobbying, meeting planning, fundraising, marketing and communications. Serves national, regional and state organizations. **Seminars:** Site selection; Creative program development; Contract negotiations; On-site conference management; Trade show management; Travel and logistics.

6847 ■ Harian Creative Enterprises
47 Hyde Blvd.
Ballston Spa, NY 12020
Ph:(518)885-6699
Contact: Harry Barba, Publisher
Scope: Literary service for writers and publishers, offering counsel on the writing and completion of literary projects, including titling, book and jacket design and editorial work. Industries served: Education, culture, and art and entertainment. **Seminars:** The Workshop Under the Sky.

LIBRARIES

6848 ■ Cleveland Public Library–Literature Department
Main Bldg., 2nd Fl.
325 Superior Ave.
Cleveland, OH 44114-1271
Ph:(216)623-2881
Co. E-mail: literature@cpl.org
URL: http://www.cpl.org/TheLibrary/SubjectsCollections/Literature.aspx
Contact: Ron Antonucci, Mgr.
Scope: Fiction, drama and theater, film, radio, television, poetry, essays, humor, oratory and public speaking, craft of writing, literary criticism and biography, classical Greek and Latin, linguistics, journalism, book trade, printing, publishing, Library and information science. **Services:** Department open to the public. **Holdings:** 500,000 volumes; 11,368 bound periodical volumes; 23,000 theater programs and playbills; 16,000 titles of microform editions of plays and miscellanea; 190 vertical files. **Subscriptions:** 825 journals and other serials.

6849 ■ National Press Club–Eric Friedheim Library & News Information Center
529 14th St. NW, 13th Fl.
Washington, DC 20045
Ph:(202)662-7523
Fax:(202)879-6725
Co. E-mail: info@press.org
URL: http://press.org/library
Contact: Julie Schoo, Dir./Libn.
Scope: Current events; journalism - craft, history; print and broadcast media. **Services:** Copying; audio cassette copying (fee); Library open to members. **Holdings:** 2500 books; NPC luncheon audiocassettes & videotapes; newsletters; microfilm; CDs. **Subscriptions:** 250 newspapers, magazines, journals, and newsletters.

Electrical Contractor

ASSOCIATIONS AND OTHER ORGANIZATIONS

6850 ■ Independent Electrical Contractors
4401 Ford Ave., Ste. 1100
Alexandria, VA 22302-1432
Ph:(703)549-7351
Free: 800-456-4324
Fax:(703)549-7448
Co. E-mail: info@ieci.org
URL: http://www.ieci.org
Contact: Larry Mullins, Exec. VP/CEO
Description: Independent electrical contractors, small and large, primarily oPEN shop. Promotes the interests of members; works to eliminate "unwise and unfair business practices" and to protect its members against "unfair or unjust taxes and legislative enactments." Sponsors electrical apprenticeship programs; conducts educational programs on cost control and personnel motivation. Represents independent electrical contractors to the National Electrical Code panel. Conducts surveys on volume of sales and purchases and on type of products used. Has formulated National Pattern Standards for Apprentice Training for Electricians. **Publications:** *IEC Insights* (8/year);Membership Directory (annual).

6851 ■ National Association of Electrical Distributors
1181 Corporate Lake Dr.
St. Louis, MO 63132
Ph:(314)991-9000
Free: 888-791-2512
Fax:(314)991-3060
Co. E-mail: customerservice@naed.org
URL: http://www.naed.org
Contact: Tom Naber, Pres./CEO
Description: Serves as wholesale distributors of electrical supplies and apparatus. Aims to serve and protect the electrical distribution channel; maintains several committees. **Publications:** *The Electrical Distributor* (monthly); *NAED Newsline* (weekly); *Performance Analysis Report* .

6852 ■ National Electrical Contractors Association
3 Bethesda Metro Ctr., Ste. 1100
Bethesda, MD 20814
Ph:(301)657-3110
Fax:(301)215-4500
URL: http://www.necanet.org
Contact: John M. Grau, CEO
Description: Contractors erecting, installing, repairing, servicing, and maintaining electric wiring, equipment, and appliances. Provides management services and labor relations programs for electrical contractors; conducts seminars for contractor sales and training. Conducts research and educational programs; compiles statistics. Sponsors honorary society, the Academy of Electrical Contracting. **Publications:** *A Comparison of Operational Cost of Union vs. Non-Union Contractors*; *Electrical Contractor Magazine* (monthly); *Electrical Maintenance Pays Dividends*; *NECA Manual of Labor Units*; *This is NECA* .

6853 ■ National Electrical Manufacturers Association
1300 N 17th St., Ste. 1752
Rosslyn, VA 22209
Ph:(703)841-3200
Fax:(703)841-5900
Co. E-mail: communications@nema.org
URL: http://www.nema.org
Contact: Evan R. Gaddis, Pres./CEO
Description: Aims to maintain and improve quality and reliability of products; insure safety standards in manufacture and use of products; organize and act upon members' interests in productivity, competition from overseas suppliers, energy conservation and efficiency, marketing opportunities, economic matters, and product liability. Develops product standards covering such matters as nomenclature, ratings, performance, testing, and dimensions; actively participates in regional and international standards process for electrical products; participates in developing National Electrical Code and National Electrical Safety Codes, and advocates their acceptance by state and local authorities; conducts regulatory and legislative analyses on issues of concern to electrical manufacturers; compiles and issues market data of all kinds, and statistical data on such factors as sales, new orders, unfilled orders, cancellations, production, and inventories. **Publications:** *Electroindustry*; *National Electrical Manufacturers Association—Publications and Materials Catalog* (semiannual).

6854 ■ National Electrical Manufacturers Representatives Association
28 Deer St., Ste. 302
Portsmouth, NH 03801
Ph:(914)524-8650
Free: 800-446-3672
Fax:(914)524-8655
Co. E-mail: nemra@nemra.org
URL: http://www.nemra.org
Contact: Michael Gorin CPMR, Chm.-Elect
Purpose: North American trade association dedicated to promoting continuing education, professionalism, and the use of independent manufacturers representatives in the electrical industry. Offers professional development programs in business management and sales training, and offers a proprietary computer system for independent electrical representatives. Sponsors educational programs; compiles statistics; and holds an annual networking conference for its representative members and their manufacturers. **Publications:** *NEMRA Locator* (annual).

EDUCATIONAL PROGRAMS

6855 ■ Arc Flash Protection & Electrical Safety 70E (In-House Training)
American Trainco, Inc.
9785 S Maroon Cir., Ste. 300
PO Box 3397
Englewood, CO 80112
Free: 877-978-7246
Fax:(303)531-4565
Co. E-mail: Sales@AmericanTrainco.com
URL: http://wwww.americantrainco.com
Price: $990.00. **Description:** A two-day training course designed to save lives, eliminate injuries, and prevent damage to plants, buildings, and equipment. **Locations:** Cities throughout the United States.

6856 ■ Electrical Ladder Drawings, Schematics and Diagrams
American Trainco, Inc.
9785 S Maroon Cir., Ste. 300
PO Box 3397
Englewood, CO 80112
Free: 877-978-7246
Fax:(303)531-4565
Co. E-mail: Sales@AmericanTrainco.com
URL: http://wwww.americantrainco.com
Price: $990.00. **Description:** A two-day course for everyone in industrial plants, public facilities, and commercial buildings. **Locations:** Cities throughout the United States.

6857 ■ Electrical Troubleshooting and Preventive Maintenance
American Trainco, Inc.
9785 S Maroon Cir., Ste. 300
PO Box 3397
Englewood, CO 80112
Free: 877-978-7246
Fax:(303)531-4565
Co. E-mail: Sales@AmericanTrainco.com
URL: http://wwww.americantrainco.com
Price: $990.00. **Description:** A two-day course for everyday building, plant, and facility maintenance. **Locations:** Cities throughout the United States.

6858 ■ Generators and Emergency Power
American Trainco, Inc.
9785 S Maroon Cir., Ste. 300
PO Box 3397
Englewood, CO 80112
Free: 877-978-7246
Fax:(303)531-4565
Co. E-mail: Sales@AmericanTrainco.com
URL: http://wwww.americantrainco.com
Price: $990.00. **Description:** A two-day seminar specifically designed to help understand the types, applications, operation, maintenance, and testing of onsite power generation systems. **Locations:** Cities throughout the United States.

6859 ■ Hands-On PLCs: Operation, Installation, Maintenance and Troubleshooting
American Trainco, Inc.
9785 S Maroon Cir., Ste. 300
PO Box 3397
Englewood, CO 80112
Free: 877-978-7246

Fax:(303)531-4565
Co. E-mail: Sales@AmericanTrainco.com
URL: http://wwww.americantrainco.com
Price: $980.00. **Description:** An intensive, two-day course for those needing "hands-on" work experience with programmable logic controllers. **Locations:** Cities throughout the United States.

6860 ■ Uninterruptable Power Supply Systems for First Responders (In-House Training)
American Trainco, Inc.
9785 S Maroon Cir., Ste. 300
PO Box 3397
Englewood, CO 80112
Free: 877-978-7246
Fax:(303)531-4565
Co. E-mail: Sales@AmericanTrainco.com
URL: http://wwww.americantrainco.com
Price: $990.00. **Description:** Understanding the application, installation, operation, and troubleshooting of UPS systems and storage batteries. **Locations:** Oakland, CA; Orange County, CA; Baton Rouge, LA; Boston, MA; Long Island, NY; Columbus, OH; Oklahoma City, OK.

6861 ■ Variable Frequency Drives
American Trainco, Inc.
9785 S Maroon Cir., Ste. 300
PO Box 3397
Englewood, CO 80112
Free: 877-978-7246
Fax:(303)531-4565
Co. E-mail: Sales@AmericanTrainco.com
URL: http://wwww.americantrainco.com
Price: $990.00. **Description:** A practical two-day seminar for maintenance technicians. **Locations:** Cities throughout the United States.

DIRECTORIES OF EDUCATIONAL PROGRAMS

6862 ■ *Directory of Private Accredited Career Schools and Colleges of Technology*
Pub: Accrediting Commission of Career Schools and Colleges of Technology
Contact: Michale S. McComis, Exec. Dir.
Released: On web page. **Price:** Free. **Description:** Covers 3900 accredited post-secondary programs that provide training programs in business, trade, and technical fields, including various small business endeavors. Entries offer school name, address, phone, description of courses, job placement assistance, and requirements for admission. Arrangement is alphabetical.

REFERENCE WORKS

6863 ■ "Acing the Test" in *Contractor* (Vol. 57, January 2010, No. 1, pp. 32)
Pub: Penton Media, Inc.
Ed: Robert P. Mader. **Description:** A ward winning mechanical system retrofitting of a middle school in Ohio is discussed. The school now operates at 37,800 Btu/sq. ft and reduced a significant amount of pollutants from being emitted into the environment.

6864 ■ "Advances in Pump Technology - Part Two" in *Contractor* (Vol. 57, February 2010, No. 2, pp. 22)
Pub: Penton Media, Inc.
Ed: Mark Eatherton. **Description:** Chinese and Japanese companies have come up with refrigerant based heat pump products that are air based which will significantly lower the installed cost of heat pump based systems. Some of these newer models have variable speed, soft start compressors and have the ability to perform high-efficiency heat pump operation on a modulating basis.

6865 ■ "Be Proactive - Closely Review Contracts" in *Contractor* (Vol. 56, July 2009, No. 7, pp. 19)
Pub: Penton Media, Inc.
Ed: Al Schwartz. **Description:** Contract disputes can make subcontractors suffer big financial losses or even cause a new subcontractor to fail. Subcontractors should scour the plans and specifications for any references to work that might remotely come under their scope and to cross out any line in the contract that does not accurately reflect the work that they agreed to.

6866 ■ "BIM and You: Know Its Benefits and Risks" in *Contractor* (Vol. 57, January 2010, No. 1, pp. 46)
Pub: Penton Media, Inc.
Ed: Susan Linden McGreevy. **Description:** Building Information Modeling is intended to be "collaborative" and this could raise legal issues if a contractor sends an electronic bid and it is filtered out. Other legal issues that mechanical contractors need to consider before using this technology are discussed.

6867 ■ *Buyer's Guide & Membership Directory*
Pub: Independent Electrical Contractors Inc.
Contact: Thayer Long, Exec. VP/CEO
E-mail: tlong@ieci.org
Released: Annual. **Covers:** Member electrical contracting firms, electrical manufacturers, and distributors. **Entries Include:** Name of company, address, names of principals. **Arrangement:** Geographical.

6868 ■ "Chicago Public School District Builds Green" in *Contractor* (Vol. 56, October 2009, No. 10, pp. 5)
Pub: Penton Media, Inc.
Ed: Candace Roulo. **Description:** Chicago Public Schools district has already built six U.S. Green Building Council LEED certified schools and one addition in five years and will continue to build new green buildings. The district has an Environmental Action Plan that strives to reduce energy usage, improve indoor air quality, and reduce contribution to climate change.

6869 ■ "Contractors Fret Over Credit, People, Government" in *Contractor* (Vol. 57, February 2010, No. 2, pp. 7)
Pub: Penton Media, Inc.
Ed: Robert P. Mader. **Description:** Telephone interviews with 22 plumbing and HVAC contractors reveal that only two had sales increases for 2009 and that overall, contractors were down anywhere from seven to 25 percent. In the repair/service market, the residential sector was holding its own but the commercial portion was lagging behind.

6870 ■ "The Customer Is Right Even If He's Wrong" in *Contractor* (Vol. 57, February 2010, No. 2, pp. 12)
Pub: Penton Media, Inc.
Ed: Al Schwarz. **Description:** Mechanical contractors should note that customers will make a judgment based upon the impression that they form on their first meeting. Contractors can maintain a professional image by washing their trucks and having the personnel dress uniformly. Contractors have every right to demand that employees clean up and make a better impression on customers.

6871 ■ "East Coast Solar" in *Contractor* (Vol. 57, February 2010, No. 2, pp. 17)
Pub: Penton Media, Inc.
Ed: Dave Yates. **Description:** U.S. Department of Energy's Solar Decathlon lets 20 college student-led teams from around the world compete to design and build a solar-powered home. A mechanical contractor discusses his work as an advisor during the competition.

6872 ■ *Electrical Construction Equipment Directory*
Pub: Underwriters Laboratories Inc.
Contact: Susan Druktenis, Asst. Mgr.
Released: Annual, Latest edition 2011. **Covers:** Companies that have qualified to use the UL listing mark or classification marking on or in connection with products that have been found to be in compliance with UL's requirements. Coverage includes foreign companies that manufacture for distribution in the United States. **Entries Include:** Company name, city, ZIP code, UL file number, and type of product. **Arrangement:** Classified by type of product. **Indexes:** Company name.

6873 ■ "EPA to Tighten Energy Star Standards for 2011" in *Contractor* (Vol. 56, September 2009, No. 9, pp. 6)
Pub: Penton Media, Inc.
Description: United States Environmental Protection Agency will tighten standards for its Energy Star for Homes program in 2011. The green trend in the construction industry has been cited as reason for the plan. The agency is adding requirements for energy-efficient equipment and building techniques.

6874 ■ "Federal Buildings to Achieve Zero-Net Energy by 2030" in *Contractor* (Vol. 56, December 2009, No. 12, pp. 5)
Pub: Penton Media, Inc.
Ed: Candace Roulo. **Description:** United States president Barack Obama has issued sustainable goals for federal buildings. Federal agencies are also required to increase energy efficiency, conserve water and support sustainable communities. Obama has also announced a $3.4 billion investment in a smart energy creed.

6875 ■ "FSU's OGZEB Is Test Bed for Sustainable Technology" in *Contractor* (Vol. 56, October 2009, No. 10, pp. 1)
Pub: Penton Media, Inc.
Ed: Candace Roulo. **Description:** Florida State University has one of 14 off-grid zero emissions buildings (OGZEB) in the U.S. ; it was built to research sustainable and alternative energy systems. The building produces electricity from 30 photovoltaic panels and it also has three AET water heating solar panels on the roof.

6876 ■ "Get Online Quick in the Office Or in the Field" in *Contractor* (Vol. 56, October 2009, No. 10, pp. 47)
Pub: Penton Media, Inc.
Ed: William Feldman; Patti Feldman. **Description:** Contractors can set up a web site in minutes using the www.1and1.com website. Verizon's Novatel MIFI 2372 HSPA personal hotspot device lets contractors go online in the field. The StarTech scalable business management system helps contractors manage daily operations.

6877 ■ "Grainger Show Highlights Building Green, Economy" in *Contractor* (Vol. 57, February 2010, No. 2, pp. 3)
Pub: Penton Media, Inc.
Ed: Candace Roulo. **Description:** chief U.S. economist told attendees of the Grainger's 2010 Total MRO Solutions National Customer Show that the economic recovery would be subdued. Mechanical contractors who attended the event also learned about building sustainable, green products, and technologies, and economic and business challenges.

6878 ■ "Hansen Mechanical Performs Boiler Upgrade at Brookfield Zoo" in *Contractor* (Vol. 57, February 2010, No. 2, pp. 7)
Pub: Penton Media, Inc.
Description: Hansen Mechanical installed a donated boiler in the Brookfield Zoo from Weil-McLain. The boilers were installed in the zoo's 'The Swamp' and 'The Living Coast' exhibits.

6879 ■ "Housing Slide Picks Up Speed" in *Crain's Chicago Business* (Vol. 31, April 21, 2008, No. 16, pp. 2)
Pub: Crain Communications, Inc.
Ed: Eddie Baeb. **Description:** According to Tracy Cross & Associates Inc., a real estate consultancy, sales of new homes in the Chicago area dropped 61 percent from the year-earlier period which is more bad news for homebuilders, contractors and real estate agents who are eager for an indication that market conditions are improving.

6880 ■ "The Latest on E-Verify" in *Contractor* (Vol. 56, September 2009, No. 9, pp. 58)
Pub: Penton Media, Inc.
Ed: Susan McGreevy. **Description:** United States government has required federal contractors to use its E-Verify program to verify the eligibility of incoming and existent employees. The use of the program is seen to eliminate Social Security mismatches.

6881 ■ "Major Advances in Heat Pump Technology" in *Contractor* (Vol. 57, January 2010, No. 1, pp. 42)
Pub: Penton Media, Inc.
Ed: Mark Eatherton. **Description:** Tax credits make ground-source heat pump technology more economically feasible. Suggestions on how to choose the right ground-source heat pump technology to install in a house are discussed.

6882 ■ "Minnesota State Park Building Exemplifies Sustainability" in *Contractor* (Vol. 56, November 2009, No. 11, pp. 5)
Pub: Penton Media, Inc.
Ed: Candace Roulo. **Description:** Camden State Park's newly remodeled information/office building in Lynd, Minnesota features a 10 kw wind turbine which is capable of offsetting most of the facility's electricity and a geothermal heat pump system. The heat pump is a 4-ton vertical closed-loop ground source heat pump by ClimateMaster.

6883 ■ "Most Popular Tools? The Survey Says" in *Contractor* (Vol. 57, February 2010, No. 2, pp. 1)
Pub: Penton Media, Inc.
Ed: Robert P. Mader. **Description:** According to a survey of individuals in the field, mechanical contractors are purchasing more of their tools at home centers and they are also increasingly working in the service, repair, and retrofit markets. The survey also found that the reciprocating saw is the most used corded power tool. Additional purchasing habits of mechanical contractors are listed.

6884 ■ *National Electrical Manufacturers Representatives Association—Locator*
Pub: National Electrical Manufacturers Representatives Association
Contact: Kenneth W. Hooper, President
E-mail: khooper@nemra.org
Released: Annual, September. **Price:** Free. **Covers:** Approximately 1,000 electrical manufacturers representatives companies. **Entries Include:** Company name, address, phone, telex, fax, number of employees, geographical area served, subsidiary and branch names and locations, products. **Arrangement:** Geographical. **Indexes:** Company name.

6885 ■ "A Necessary Balancing Act: Bookkeeping" in *Contractor* (Vol. 56, November 2009, No. 11, pp. 22)
Pub: Penton Media, Inc.
Ed: Al Schwartz. **Description:** Pros and cons of getting a bookkeeper or a certified public accountant for the subcontractor are discussed. A bookkeeper can help a subcontractor get new accounting software up and running while an accountant will more than likely keep after the books at regular intervals throughout the year.

6886 ■ "New Hydronic Heating Technologies Work" in *Contractor* (Vol. 57, January 2010, No. 1, pp. 58)
Pub: Penton Media, Inc.
Ed: Carol Fey. **Description:** Technology behind hydronic heating systems is reviewed. These technologies include radiant and geothermal hydronic heating. System requirements for installing these greener forms of heating are discussed.

6887 ■ "San Diego Museum Receives LEED Certification" in *Contractor* (Vol. 57, January 2010, No. 1, pp. 14)
Pub: Penton Media, Inc.
Description: San Diego Natural History Museum received an LEED certification for existing buildings. The certification process began when they committed to displaying the Dead Sea Scrolls in 2007 and they had to upgrade their buildings' air quality and to control for air moisture, temperature, and volume. They reduced their energy consumption by upwards of 20 percent.

6888 ■ "Selling a Job When There's Buyer's Remorse" in *Contractor* (Vol. 56, December 2009, No. 12, pp. 37)
Pub: Penton Media, Inc.
Ed: H. Kent Craig. **Description:** Advice on how contractors should manage low-profit jobs in the United States are presented. Efforts should be made to try and find at least one quality field foreman or superintendent. Contractors should also try to respectfully renegotiate the terms of the job.

6889 ■ "Software Solutions Increase Productivity" in *Contractor* (Vol. 57, February 2010, No. 2, pp. 26)
Pub: Penton Media, Inc.
Ed: William Feldman; Patti Feldman. **Description:** Singletouch is a real-time data capture solution for mechanical and other contractors that work in jobs that require materials and workload tracking. Contractors get information on extreme weather and sudden changes in the cost of materials. The OptimumHVAC optimization software by Optimum Energy is designed to optimize energy savings in commercial buildings.

6890 ■ "Sustainability Is Top Priority for GreenTown Chicago" in *Contractor* (Vol. 56, November 2009, No. 11, pp. 1)
Pub: Penton Media, Inc.
Ed: Candace Roulo. **Description:** GreenTown Chicago 2009 conference tackled energy-efficient practices and technologies, green design and building, and sustainable policies. Water conservation was also a topic at the conference and one mayor who made a presentation said that reducing the water loss in the system is a priority in the city's endeavor.

6891 ■ "Synthetic Drywall Rots Mechanical Parts" in *Contractor* (Vol. 56, December 2009, No. 12, pp. 50)
Pub: Penton Media, Inc.
Ed: Bob Mader. **Description:** Chinese-made synthetic drywalls have been found to corrode mechanical and electrical products in homes. Drywalls always contain a certain amount of sulfur. The hydrogen sulfide gas component of synthetic drywalls causes copper and silver sulfide corrosion.

6892 ■ "Tracking Your Fleet Can Increase Bottom Line" in *Contractor* (Vol. 56, November 2009, No. 11, pp. 26)
Pub: Penton Media, Inc.
Ed: Candace Roulo. **Description:** GPS fleet management system can help boost a contractor's profits, employee productivity, and efficiency. These are available as a handheld device or a cell phone that employees carry around or as a piece of hardware installed in a vehicle. These lets managers track assets and communicate with employees about jobs.

6893 ■ "Trade Craft: Take Pride in Your Trade, Demand Excellence" in *Contractor* (Vol. 56, October 2009, No. 10, pp. 24)
Pub: Penton Media, Inc.
Ed: Al Schwartz. **Description:** There is a need for teaching, developing, and encouraging trade craft. An apprentice plumber is not only versed in the mechanical aspects of the trade but he also has a working knowledge of algebra, trigonometry, chemistry, and thermal dynamics. Contractors should be demanding on their personnel regarding their trade craft and should only keep and train the very best people they can hire.

6894 ■ "Yudelson Challenges San Antonio Groups" in *Contractor* (Vol. 56, October 2009, No. 10, pp. 6)
Pub: Penton Media, Inc.
Description: Green building consultant and author Jerry Yudelson made a presentation for the Central Texas Green Building Council and Leadership San Antonio where he discussed the European approach to sustainability and how it can be used for designing green buildings. Yudelson also discussed how to use sustainable practices for planning 25 years into the future.

STATISTICAL SOURCES

6895 ■ *RMA Annual Statement Studies*
Pub: Robert Morris Associates (RMA)
Released: Annual. **Price:** $175.00 2006-07 edition, $105.00. **Description:** Contains composite balance sheets and income statements for more than 360 industries, including the accounting, auditing, and bookkeeping industries. Also contains five years of comparative historical data for discerning trends. Includes 16 commonly used ratios, computed for most of the size groupings for nearly every industry.

TRADE PERIODICALS

6896 ■ *EE Product News*
Pub: Penton Media Inc.
Released: Monthly. **Description:** Trade magazine covering new products for electronic design engineers.

6897 ■ *Electrical Contractor*
Pub: National Electrical Contractors Association
Contact: Astra Hudson, Circulation Mgr
E-mail: ajh@necanet.org
Released: Monthly. **Price:** $5 single issue. **Description:** Electrical engineering.

6898 ■ *Electrical Wholesaling*
Pub: Penton Media Inc.
Contact: Doug Chandler, Exec. Ed.
E-mail: doug.chandler@penton.com
Released: Monthly. **Description:** Magazine focusing on electrical wholesaling for distributors of electrical supplies.

6899 ■ *IAEI News*
Pub: International Association of Electrical Inspectors (IAEI)
Contact: Kathryn P. Ingley, Managing Editor
E-mail: kpingley@compuserv.com
Ed: P.H. Cox, Editor. **Released:** Bimonthly. **Price:** Included in membership; $50, nonmembers. **Description:** Concerned with electrical safety and inspection. Supplies explanations of the more complicated sections of the National Electrical Code and information on electrical devices, materials, and methods. Provides news of the Association and of related organizations. Recurring features include editorials, news of research, articles on sections of the National Electrical Code (NEC), code editors responses to questions on NEC, letters to the editor, listings of new publications and products, and a calendar of events.

6900 ■ *TED The Electrical Distributor Magazine*
Pub: National Association of Electrical Distributors Inc.
Contact: Michael Martin, Publisher
E-mail: mmartin@naed.org
Ed: Misty Byers, Editor, mbyers@naed.org. **Released:** Monthly. **Price:** $32; $45 other countries. **Description:** Magazine for electrical distributors.

VIDEOCASSETTES/ AUDIOCASSETTES

6901 ■ *Low Voltage Safety*
Film Library/National Safety Council California Chapter
4553 Glencoe Ave., Ste. 150
Marina Del Rey, CA 90292
Ph:(310)827-9781
Free: 800-421-9585
Fax:(310)827-9861
Co. E-mail: California@nsc.org
URL: http://www.nsc.org/nsc_near_you/FindYourLocalChapter/Pages/California.aspx
Released: 198?. **Description:** This tape describes the safety precautions electricians should take when working with 660 volts or less. **Availability:** VHS; 3/4U.

TRADE SHOWS AND CONVENTIONS

6902 ■ North Carolina RV and Camping Show
Affinity Events/Affinity, Inc.
6420 Sycamore Ln., Ste. 100
Maple Grove, MN 55369
Free: 800-848-6247

Fax:(763)383-4499
URL: http://www.agievents.com
Released: Annual. **Audience:** RV and camping enthusiasts. **Principal Exhibits:** Motor home, mini-homes, travel trailers, folding campers, and fifth wheels.

6903 ■ Upper Midwest Electrical Expo
North Central Electrical League
2901 Metro Dr. Ste. 203
Bloomington, MN 55425-1556
Ph:(952)854-4405
Free: 800-925-4985
Fax:(952)854-7076
Co. E-mail: dale@ncel.org
URL: http://www.ncel.org
Released: Biennial. **Audience:** Electrical contractors, distributors, utilities, industrial plant engineers, consulting engineers, and purchasing agents. **Principal Exhibits:** Electrical equipment, supplies, and services.

CONSULTANTS

6904 ■ Environmental & Engineering Services Inc.
687 NW 5th St.
Corvallis, OR 97330
Ph:(541)754-1062
Fax:(541)753-3948
Co. E-mail: kelly.guenther@eesinet.com
URL: http://www.eesinet.com
Contact: Ron Anderson, Principle
E-mail: fred.shaub@atseesinet.com
Scope: Provides mechanical, electrical engineering and commissioning services, with a special emphasis in renovation and energy upgrades. Offers a wide range of HVAC, electrical and controls engineering services including feasibility assessments, master planning, budgeting, cost analysis, design, computer aided drafting, energy use modeling, facility management and construction management.

6905 ■ GHT Ltd.
1010 N Glebe Rd., Ste. 200
Arlington, VA 22201-4749
Ph:(703)243-1200
Fax:(703)276-1376
Co. E-mail: ght@ghtltd.com
URL: http://www.ghtltd.com
Contact: Robert M. Menuet Jr., Principle
E-mail: rmenuet@ghtltd.com
Scope: Provides design services in mechanical engineering. Offers telecommunications and security engineering services. Provides life safety engineering services and utilities planning services. Provides estimates of life expectancy and replacement or upgrade costs for mechanical and electrical equipment and systems. **Publications:** "Critical spaces keep the pace of business humming," May, 2004; "To avoid staticlater, hire right telecom consultant," Oct, 2007. **Special Services:** LEED[R].

6906 ■ Lundquist, Killeen, Potvin and Bender Inc.
1935 W County Rd. B2, Ste. 300
Saint Paul, MN 55113-2722
Ph:(651)633-1223
Fax:(651)633-1355
Co. E-mail: nbart@lkpb.com
URL: http://www.lkpb.com
Contact: Stephen J. Gentilini, Principle
E-mail: sgent@atslkpb.com
Scope: Provides services in heating, ventilation, plumbing, piping, refrigeration, air conditioning, fire protection, lighting design and fixture selection, communications, electrical power distribution, security, life safety system design, energy conservation analysis, design and implementation.

FRANCHISES AND BUSINESS OPPORTUNITIES

6907 ■ Handyman Connection
Mamar, Inc.
10250 Alliance Rd., Ste.100
Cincinnati, OH 45242
Ph:(513)771-3003
Free: 800-466-5530
Fax:(513)771-6439
Co. E-mail: soaks@handymanconnection.com
URL: http://www.handymanconnection.com
No. of Franchise Units: 160. **No. of Company-Owned Units:** 1. **Founded:** 1990. **Franchised:** 1993. **Description:** Small to medium home repairs and remodeling. **Equity Capital Needed:** $90,000-$125,000. **Franchise Fee:** $25,000-$40,000. **Financial Assistance:** No. **Training:** 2 weeks at corporate training center, and 1 week grand opening onsite.

6908 ■ Mr. Electric
1010 N. University Dr.
Waco, TX 76707
Free: 800-805-0575
Fax:800-483-5809
Co. E-mail: ronnie.musick@dwyergroup.com
URL: http://www.mrelectric.com
No. of Franchise Units: 27. **Founded:** 1994. **Franchised:** 1994. **Description:** Residential and commercial electrical repair, installation, and maintenance and services. **Equity Capital Needed:** $35,000 investment required; $35,000 start-up capital required. **Franchise Fee:** $26,000, per $100,000 population. **Training:** Initial, onsite, intranet and ongoing support.

LIBRARIES

6909 ■ IEEE Information Center
445 Hoes Ln.
PO Box 1331
Piscataway, NJ 08855-1331
Co. E-mail: library@ieee.org
URL: http://www.ieee.org
Contact: Mary Jane Miller, Libn.
Scope: Electrical and electronic engineering, computer science. **Services:** Library open to IEEE members and staff. **Holdings:** 1000 books; periodicals, conference proceedings and standards in hard copy, electronic, and microform formats. **Subscriptions:** 25 journals and other serials.

6910 ■ Intertek Testing Services–Warnock Hersey Library
1500 Brigantine Dr.
Coquitlam, BC, Canada V3K 7C1
Ph:(604)520-3321
Fax:(604)524-9186
Co. E-mail: lawrence.gibson@intertek.com
URL: http://www.intertek.com/
Scope: Building codes, electrical codes, plumbing codes, standards. **Services:** Library open to potential clients at librarian's discretion. **Holdings:** Standards; codes; handbooks; manuals; directories. **Subscriptions:** 20 journals and other serials.

6911 ■ James Madison University–Carrier Library I Special Collections
MSC 1704, rm. 207
880 Madison Dr.
Harrisonburg, VA 22807
Ph:(540)568-3612
Fax:(540)568-3405
Co. E-mail: library-special@jmu.edu
URL: http://www.lib.jmu.edu/special
Contact: Tracy Harter, Spec.Coll.Libn.
Scope: Central Shenandoah Valley region. **Services:** Limited copying; scanning; faxing; manuscript finding aids; Library open to the public. **Holdings:** 4482 books; 100 manuscript collections; 2000 photographs. **Subscriptions:** 89 journals and other serials; 20 newspapers.

RESEARCH CENTERS

6912 ■ Tennessee Technological University–Center for Energy Systems Research
1020 Stadium Dr., Box 5032
Cookeville, TN 38505
Ph:(931)372-3615
Fax:(931)372-6369
Co. E-mail: deivy@tntech.edu
URL: http://www.tntech.edu/cesr/home
Contact: Prof. Subramaniam Deivanayagam, Interim Dir.
E-mail: deivy@tntech.edu
Scope: Electric power, including electric power industry problems, generation, power systems performance improvement, fossil fuel utilization, advanced technologies, integrated software systems for simulating and analyzing power systems, online techniques for measuring coal and coal ash composition, electromagnetic transients capabilities, environmental issues and energy conservation. **Services:** Third party review of technical issues. **Publications:** Annual report.

Electrical Lighting Supply Store

ASSOCIATIONS AND OTHER ORGANIZATIONS

6913 ■ American Lighting Association
PO Box 420288
Dallas, TX 75342-0288
Ph:(214)698-9898
Free: 800-274-4484
Fax:(214)698-9899
Co. E-mail: dupton@americanlightingassoc.com
URL: http://www.americanlightingassoc.com
Contact: Richard D. Upton, Pres./CEO

Description: Manufacturers, manufacturers' representatives, distributors, and retailers of residential lighting fixtures, portable lamps, component parts, accessories, and bulbs. Trains and certifies lighting consultants; conducts showroom sales seminars; disseminates marketing and merchandising information. Compiles statistics. **Publications:** *Light Up Your Kitchen and Bath*; *Lighting Your Life*; *Lightrays* (bimonthly).

6914 ■ International Association of Lighting Designers
Merchandise Mart, Ste. 9-104
Chicago, IL 60654
Ph:(312)527-3677
Fax:(312)527-3680
Co. E-mail: iald@iald.org
URL: http://www.iald.org
Contact: Marsha L. Turner CAE, Exec. VP

Description: Represents professionals, educators, students, and others working in the field of lighting design worldwide. Promotes the benefits of quality lighting design and emphasizes the potential impact of lighting on architectural design and environmental quality. Furthers professional standards of lighting designers and seeks to increase their function in the interior design industry. Sponsors national awards program, summer intern program for qualified college students interested in lighting design as a profession, and career development lectures and seminars. **Publications:** *e-Reflections* (monthly); *International Association of Lighting Designers—Membership Directory* (annual); *Why Hire an IALD Lighting Designer?* .

6915 ■ National Association of Independent Lighting Distributors
2207 Elmwood Ave.
Buffalo, NY 14216-1009
Ph:(716)875-3670
Fax:(716)875-0734
Co. E-mail: info@naild.org
URL: http://www.naild.org
Contact: Linda Daniel, Admin.

Description: Distributors of specialized lighting products; vendor members are manufacturers and suppliers of lighting goods. Increases effectiveness and profitability through educational programs. Makes available information on the distribution of lighting products develop marketing techniques through an exchange of ideas. Develops methods of exchanging slow-moving inventory among members. Shares solutions to supply and distribution problems. Sponsors educational programs in the areas of accounting, finance, inventory control, general management, personnel training, and product cost analysis. .

6916 ■ National Lighting Bureau
8811 Colesville Rd., Ste. G106
Silver Spring, MD 20910
Ph:(301)587-9572
Fax:(301)589-2017
Co. E-mail: info@nlb.org
URL: http://www.nlb.org
Contact: John P. Bachner, Exec. Dir.

Description: Information source sponsored by trade associations, professional societies, manufacturers, utilities, and agencies of the federal government. Focuses on High-Benefit lighting (tm). Does not promote any specific form of lighting or brand name component. .

REFERENCE WORKS

6917 ■ *American Lighting Association—Membership Directory*
Pub: American Lighting Association
Contact: Eric Jacobson, VP Membership
E-mail: ejacobson@americanlightingassoc.com

Released: Annual, January/February. **Covers:** about 110 member manufacturers of lighting fixtures, portable lamps, accessories, components, and bulbs; 720 retail lighting showrooms, 220 manufacturing representative firms, 50 component manufacturing firms. **Entries Include:** Company name, address, phone, name and title of chief executive or contact. **Arrangement:** Classified. **Indexes:** Classified by manufacturer; regional manufacturing representatives.

6918 ■ *Home Lighting & Accessories—Suppliers Directory Issue*
Pub: Doctorow Communications Inc.
Contact: Linda Longo, Editor-in-Chief
E-mail: linda@homelighting.com

Released: Semiannual. **Price:** $15, U.S., Canada, and Mexico 1 year; $20, elsewhere 1 year; $100, elsewhere 1 year (air mail); $22.50, U.S., Canada, and Mexico 2 years. **Publication Includes:** List of almost 1,000 suppliers of lighting fixtures, lamp and lighting parts, and other products primarily for the retail lighting industry. **Entries Include:** Company name, address, phone and fax. **Arrangement:** Alphabetical. **Indexes:** Product.

6919 ■ "Homing In On the Future" in *Black Enterprise* (Vol. 38, October 2007, No. 3, pp. 61)
Pub: Earl G. Graves Publishing Co. Inc.

Ed: Sean Drakes. **Description:** More and more people are wanting new homes wired automated systems that integrate multiple home devices such as computers, audio/visual entertainment, security, communications, utilities, and lighting and environmental controls.

6920 ■ *LDA—Lighting Equipment Accessories Directory Issue*
Pub: Illuminating Engineering Society of North America
Contact: Leslie Prestia, Advertising Coord.
E-mail: lprestia@iesna.org

Ed: Paul Tarricone, Editor, ptarricone@iesna.org. **Released:** Annual, June. **Publication Includes:** List of over 800 manufacturers and suppliers of custom designed and manufactured lighting products, fixtures, accessories and equipment, parts, housings, and instruments; coverage includes Canada. **Entries Include:** Name of firm, address, phone, description of products. **Arrangement:** Alphabetical. **Indexes:** Product, geographical.

STATISTICAL SOURCES

6921 ■ *The U.S. Lighting Fixtures Industry*
Pub: Business Trend Analysts, Inc.

Released: 2001-2002. **Price:** $1450.00. **Description:** This in-depth report analyzes the size, growth, and projected growth of the markets for all types of residential, industrial, commercial, institutional, and vehicular lighting fixtures, on a product-by-product basis.

TRADE PERIODICALS

6922 ■ *Architectural Lighting*
Pub: Hanley Wood L.L.C.

Released: 7/yr. **Price:** $48; $60 Canada; $96 other countries. **Description:** Magazine for professionals involved in the design, specification, and application of lighting.

6923 ■ *Home Lighting & Accessories*
Pub: Doctorow Communications Inc.
Contact: Abbie Liehr, Art Dir.
E-mail: abbie@homelighting.com

Released: Monthly. **Price:** $15 U.S., Canada, and Mexico; $20 other countries; $100 other countries airmail; $22.50 U.S., Canada, and Mexico two years; $30 other countries two years. **Description:** Business magazine about the residential lighting business for retailers, electrical distributors, manufacturers, and lighting professionals.

6924 ■ *LDA*
Pub: Illuminating Engineering Society of North America
Contact: William Hanley, Publisher
E-mail: whanley@iesna.org

Released: Monthly. **Price:** $44 nonmembers; $85 two years; $59 other countries; $115 two years international; $32 members; $110 three years; $155 other countries three years. **Description:** Magazine presenting current lighting and energy news and applications.

FRANCHISES AND BUSINESS OPPORTUNITIES

6925 ■ Living Lighting
Franchise Bancorp Inc.
294 Walker Dr., Unit 2
Brampton, ON, Canada L6T 4Z2

Ph:(905)790-9023
Free: (866)463-4124
Fax:(905)790-7059
Co. E-mail: franchises@franchisebancorp.com
URL: http://www.livinglighting.com
No. of Franchise Units: 27. **Founded:** 1968. **Franchised:** 1968. **Description:** Retail and residential lighting. **Equity Capital Needed:** $270,000-$470,000. **Franchise Fee:** $30,000. **Financial Assistance:** No. **Training:** Yes.

6926 ■ Nite Time Decor Inc.
The Decor Group
PO Box 5183
Lubbock, TX 79408-5183
Free: (866)321-4077
Fax:(806)722-9627
No. of Franchise Units: 37. **Founded:** 1986. **Franchised:** 1999. **Description:** Landscape lighting products and services. **Equity Capital Needed:** $37,500-$74,350. **Franchise Fee:** $16,900. **Royalty Fee:** 5%. **Financial Assistance:** Assistance with franchise fee. **Training:** Includes 4 days training at headquarters and ongoing support.

6927 ■ Outdoor Lighting Perspectives Franchise, Inc.
2924 Emerywood Parkway, Ste. 101
Richmond, VA 23294
Ph:(704)841-2666
Free: 800-722-4668
Fax:(704)341-8182
Co. E-mail: tiffany@outdoorlights.com
URL: http://www.olpfranchise.com
No. of Franchise Units: 70. **No. of Company-Owned Units:** 1. **Founded:** 1995. **Franchised:** 1998. **Description:** Design and installation of landscape lighting. **Equity Capital Needed:** $69,000-$102,000. **Franchise Fee:** $49,000. **Financial Assistance:** No. **Managerial Assistance:** Access to corporate personnel at all times. **Training:** 5 days of training at corporate location and 3 days within ninety days of start-up in that city. Product & technical training at manufacturing plant shortly after start-up.

LIBRARIES

6928 ■ TLA Lighting Consultants, Inc. Library
7 Pond St.
Salem, MA 01970
Ph:(978)745-6870
Fax:(978)741-4420
Scope: Illumination, optics, lighting systems, architectural lighting design. **Services:** Library not open to the public. **Holdings:** 150 books; 5000 bound periodical volumes; 250 reports; 75 manuscripts; 150 patents.

Electronic/Online Publishing

ASSOCIATIONS AND OTHER ORGANIZATIONS

6929 ■ Electronic Literature Organization
University of Maryland
Maryland Institute for Technology in the Humanities
B0131 McKeldin Library
College Park, MD 20742
Ph:(301)314-6545
Co. E-mail: hdevinney@gmail.com
URL: http://www.eliterature.org
Contact: Helen DeVinney, Managing Dir.
Description: Strives to facilitate and promote the writing, publishing, and reading of literature in electronic media. **Publications:** *Acid-Free Bits: Recommendations for Long-Lasting Electronic Literature*; *Born-Again Bits: A Framework for Migrating Electronic Literature*; *Electronic Literature Directory*; *State of the Arts* .

REFERENCE WORKS

6930 ■ "Boom and Bust in the Book Biz" in *Canadian Business* (Vol. 83, August 17, 2010, No. 13-14, pp. 16)
Pub: Rogers Media Ltd.
Ed: Jordan Timm. **Description:** Electronic book marketplace is booming with Amazon.com's e-book sales for the Kindle e-reader exceeding the hardcover sales. Kobo Inc. has registered early success with its Kobo e-reader and has partnered with Hong Kong telecom giant on an e-book store.

6931 ■ "Media Wars" in *Canadian Business* (Vol. 83, August 17, 2010, No. 13-14, pp. 32)
Pub: Rogers Media Ltd.
Ed: Thomas Watson. **Description:** Canada's newspaper industry has changed considerably with The Glove, under Philip Crawley, positioned as corporate Canada's newspaper of record. However, the National Post under Paul Godfrey is making a comeback by re-launching it as the flagship of a national chain of so-called digital first news organizations.

TRADE SHOWS AND CONVENTIONS

6932 ■ Bologna Children's Book Fair - Fiera Del Libro Per Ragazzi
Bologna Fiere
Via della Fiera 20
40128 Bologna, Italy
Ph:39 51 282111
Fax:39 51 6374004
Co. E-mail: segreteria.generale@bolognafiere.it
URL: http://www.bolognafiere.it
Released: Annual. **Principal Exhibits:** Children's and juvenile books, text books and electronic books.

FRANCHISES AND BUSINESS OPPORTUNITIES

6933 ■ Wireless Toyz
Wireless Toyz Franchise LLC
29155 Northwestern Hwy
Southfield, MI 48034
Ph:(248)426-8200
Free: (866)2FR-ANCH
Fax:(248)671-0346
Co. E-mail: franchise@wirelesstoyz.com
URL: http://www.wirelesstoyz.com
No. of Franchise Units: 160. **No. of Company-Owned Units:** 3. **Founded:** 1995. **Franchised:** 2001. **Description:** Telecommunication products and services are offered. **Equity Capital Needed:** $75,000 cash minimum. **Franchise Fee:** $30,000. **Financial Assistance:** Referrals to SBA lenders. **Training:** 4 weeks in Michigan and 5 days onsite.

TRADE PERIODICALS

6934 ■ *Staffing Industry Analysts*
Pub: Staffing Industry Analysts Inc.
Contact: Craig Johnson, Analyst and Assoc. Ed.
E-mail: basin@staffingindustry.com
Released: Bimonthly, 22/year. **Description:** Focuses on the temporary help and employment services industry. Provides information on economic forecasts, employment indicators, finance, labor and market trends, stocks, and statistics.

VIDEOCASSETTES/ AUDIOCASSETTES

6935 ■ *From Law School to Law Practice: What Every Associate Needs to Know—The Set*
American Law Institute
American Bar Association Committee on Continuing Education
4025 Chestnut St.
Philadelphia, PA 19104
Ph:(215)243-1600
Free: 800-CLE-NEWS
Fax:(215)243-1636
Co. E-mail: custserv@ali-aba.org
URL: http://www.ali.org
Released: 1989. **Price:** $190. **Description:** Uses brief dramatizations to outline various skills and strategies for law firm success. Complete with study guide. **Availability:** VHS.

Employment Agency

ASSOCIATIONS AND OTHER ORGANIZATIONS

6936 ■ American Staffing Association
277 S Washington St., Ste. 200
Alexandria, VA 22314-3675
Ph:(703)253-2020
Fax:(703)253-2053
Co. E-mail: asa@americanstaffing.net
URL: http://www.americanstaffing.net
Contact: Mr. Richard Wahlquist, Pres./CEO
Description: Promotes and represents the staffing industry through legal and legislative advocacy, public relations, education, and the establishment of high standards of ethical conduct. **Publications:** *ASA Managers Guide to Employment Law*; *Co-Employment Guide*; *Membership and Resource Directory*; *Staffing Success* (bimonthly).

6937 ■ Association of Career Firms North America
8509 Crown Crescent C., Ste. ACF
Charlotte, NC 28227
Ph:(704)849-2500
Fax:(704)845-2420
Co. E-mail: bcrigger@oipartners.net
URL: http://www.acf-northamerica.com
Contact: Annette Summers, Exec. Dir.
Description: Represents firms providing displaced employees, who are sponsored by their organization, with counsel and assistance in job searching and the techniques and practices of choosing a career. Develops, improves and encourages the art and science of outplacement consulting and the professional standards of competence, objectivity, and integrity in the service of clients. Cooperates with other industrial, technical, educational, professional, and governmental bodies in areas of mutual interest and concern. .

6938 ■ Association of Executive Search Consultants
12 E 41st St., 17th Fl.
New York, NY 10017
Ph:(212)398-9556
Fax:(212)398-9560
Co. E-mail: aesc@aesc.org
URL: http://www.aesc.org
Contact: Peter M. Felix, Pres.
Description: Represents executive search consulting firms worldwide, establishes professional and ethical standards for its members, and serves to broaden public understanding of the executive search process. Specialized form of management consulting, conducted through an exclusive engagement with a client organization. **Publications:** *eSearch Connection* (monthly).

6939 ■ Career Planning and Adult Development Network
543 Vista Mar Ave.
Pacifica, CA 94044
Ph:(650)773-0982
Co. E-mail: admin@careernetwork.org
URL: http://www.careernetwork.org
Contact: Howard Figler PhD
Description: Counselors, trainers, consultants, therapists, educators, personnel specialists, and graduate students who work in business, educational, religious, and governmental organizations, and focus on career planning and adult development issues. Seeks to: establish a link between professionals working with adults in a variety of settings; identify and exchange effective adult development methods and techniques; develop a clearer understanding of the directions and objectives of the career planning and the adult development movement. Keeps members informed of developments in career decision-making, career values clarification, preretirement counseling, dual-career families, job search techniques, and mid-life transitions. Cosponsors professional seminars; maintains biographical archives. **Publications:** Journal (quarterly);Newsletter (bimonthly).

6940 ■ International Association of Workforce Professionals
1801 Louisville Rd.
Frankfort, KY 40601
Ph:(502)223-4459
Free: 888-898-9960
Fax:(502)223-4127
Co. E-mail: iawp@iawponline.org
URL: http://www.iawponline.org
Contact: Rich Vincent, Pres.
Description: Officials and others engaged in job placement, unemployment compensation, and labor market information administration through municipal, state, provincial, and federal government employment agencies and unemployment compensation agencies. Conducts workshops and research. Offers professional development program of study guides and tests. .

6941 ■ National Association of Colleges and Employers
62 Highland Ave.
Bethlehem, PA 18017-9481
Ph:(610)868-1421
Free: 800-544-5272
Fax:(610)868-0208
Co. E-mail: mmackes@naceweb.org
URL: http://www.naceweb.org
Contact: Marilyn Mackes, Exec. Dir.
Description: Connects more than 5,200 college career services professionals at nearly 2,000 college and universities nationwide, and more than 3,000 HR/staffing professionals focused on college relations and recruiting. Forecasts trends in the job market; tracks legal issues in employment, the job search, and hiring practices; and provides college and employer professionals with benchmarks for their work. Provides research and information to its professional members through website, quarterly surveys of starting salary offers to new college graduates, and surveys of employer and college members. Provides members with primary tools for reaching and educating college students through Job Choices publications. **Publications:** *Job Choices in Business and Liberal Arts Students* (annual); *NACE Journal* (quarterly); *NACE—Salary Survey* (quarterly).

6942 ■ National Association of Personnel Services
131 Prominence Ct., Ste. 130
Dawsonville, GA 30534
Ph:(706)531-0060
Fax:(866)739-4750
Co. E-mail: conrad.taylor@recruitinglife.com
URL: http://www.recruitinglife.com
Contact: Conrad Taylor, Pres.
Description: Private employment and temporary service firms. Compiles statistics on professional agency growth and development; conducts certification program and educational programs. Association is distinct from former name of National Association of Personnel Consultants. **Publications:** Membership Directory (annual).

6943 ■ National Business and Disability Council
201 I.U. Willets Rd.
Albertson, NY 11507
Ph:(516)465-1516
Co. E-mail: jtowles@abilitiesonline.org
URL: http://www.business-disability.com
Contact: John Kemp, Pres./CEO
Description: Acts as a resource for employers seeking to integrate people with disabilities into the workplace and companies seeking to reach them in the consumer market. **Publications:** *Giving Us the Tools: A Human Resources Training Package on Employing Individuals with Disabilities*; *Interviewing Individuals with Disabilities*; *NBDC News* (quarterly).

DIRECTORIES OF EDUCATIONAL PROGRAMS

6944 ■ *Adams Jobs Almanac*
Pub: Adams Media Corp.
Released: Annual, Latest edition 9th. **Price:** $10, individuals list price. **Covers:** Job listings nationwide. **Entries Include:** Firm or organization name, address, phone, name and title of contact; description of organization, headquarters location, typical titles for entry- and middle-level positions, educational backgrounds desired, fringe benefits offered, stock exchange listing, training programs, internships, parent company, number of employees, revenues, e-mail and web address, projected number of hires.

REFERENCE WORKS

6945 ■ "Albany Molecular on Hiring Spree as Big Pharma Slashes Work Force" in *Business Review, Albany New York* (December 28, 2007)
Pub: American City Business Journals, Inc.
Ed: Barbara Pinckney. **Description:** Albany Molecular Research Inc. (AMRI) is an outsourcing company that provides work forces for pharmaceutical companies due to large numbers of downsizings in the year 2007. In 2008, AMRI plans to hire several workers.

6946 ■ "AT&T To Acquire Black Telecom Firm" in *Black Enterprise* (Vol. 38, January 2008, No. 6, pp. 24)
Pub: Earl G. Graves Publishing Co. Inc.
Ed: Alan Hughes. **Description:** Details of AT&T's acquisition of ChaseCom LP, a telecommunications company based in Houston, Texas, are covered.

6947 ■ "Beyond Auto; Staffing Firm Malace Grabs Revenue Jump" in *Crain's Detroit Business* (Vol. 26, January 18, 2010, No. 3, pp. 3)
Pub: Crain Communications, Inc.
Ed: Sherri Welch. **Description:** Malace & Associates Inc., the Troy-based human resources management company, expects its diversification into nonautomotive industries to help double its revenues this year. Due to the automotive downturn, between October 2008 and March 2009 the company lost approximately 48 percent of its business.

6948 ■ "Calling All Recruiters: Agent HR Puts Staffing Agents In Charge" in *Black Enterprise* (Vol. 38, December 2007, No. 5, pp. 72)
Pub: Earl G. Graves Publishing Co. Inc.
Ed: Chana Garcia. **Description:** Recruiting and staffing agencies are seeing a drop in services due to slow economic growth. AgentHR partners with full-service recruiters who have three to five year's experience-specialists soliciting their own clients, provide staffing services, and manage their own accounts, thus combining the roles of recruiter and salesperson.

6949 ■ *The Career Guide—Dun's Employment Opportunities Directory*
Pub: Dun & Bradstreet Corp.
Released: Annual. **Covers:** More than 10,000 companies on leading employers throughout the U.S. that provide career opportunities in sales, marketing, management, engineering, life and physical sciences, computer science, mathematics, statistics planning, accounting and finance, liberal arts fields, and other technical and professional areas; based on data supplied on questionnaires and through personal interviews. Also covers personnel consultants; includes some public sector employers (governments, schools, etc.) usually not found in similar lists. **Entries Include:** Company name, location of headquarters and other offices or plants; entries may also include name, title, address, and phone of employment contact; disciplines or occupational groups hired; brief overview of company, discussion of types of positions that may be available, training and career development programs, benefits offered, internship and work-study programs. **Arrangement:** Employers are alphabetical; geographically by industry, employer branch offices geographically, disciplines hired geographically, employees offering work-study or internship programs and personnel consultants. **Indexes:** Geographical, SIC code.

6950 ■ *The Directory of Toronto Recruiters*
Pub: Continental Records Company Ltd.
Contact: Neil Patte
Released: Annual, latest edition 2008. **Price:** $49. 95, individuals plus express post shipping cost and GST. **Covers:** More than 1,200 recruiting firms in the Toronto, Canada area. **Entries Include:** Firm name, address, phone, fax, e-mail, URL, name and title of contact, and industry and professional specialties.

6951 ■ "Growing Strong" in *Entrepreneur* (Vol. 35, November 2007, No. 11, pp. 36)
Pub: Entrepreneur Media Inc.
Ed: Nichole L. Torres. **Description:** Amy Langer founded Salo LL with partner John Folkestad. The company is growing fast since its 2002 launch, with over $40 million in projections for 2007. The finance and accounting staffing company tops the list of the fastest-growing women-led companies in North America.

6952 ■ "Impressive Numbers: Companies Experience Substantial Increases in Dollars, Employment" in *Hispanic Business* (July-August 2007)
Pub: Hispanic Business
Ed: Derek Reveron. **Description:** Profiles of five fastest growing Hispanic companies reporting increases in revenue and employment include Brightstar, distributor of wireless products; Greenway Ford Inc., a car dealership; Fred Loya Insurance, auto insurance carrier; and Group O, packaging company; and Diverse Staffing, Inc., an employment and staffing firm.

6953 ■ "Interbrand's Creative Recruiting" in *Business Courier* (Vol. 27, November 12, 2010, No. 28, pp. 1)
Pub: Business Courier
Ed: Dan Monk. **Description:** Global brand consulting firm Interbrand uses a creative recruitment agency to attract new employees into the company. Interbrand uses themed parties to attract prospective employees. The 'Alice In Wonderland' tea party for example, allowed the company to hire five new employees.

6954 ■ "iSymmetry's Technological Makeover Or, How a Tech Company Finally Grew Up and Discovered the World Wide Web" in *Inc.* (October 2007)
Pub: Gruner & Jahr USA Publishing
Description: Profile of iSymmetry, an Atlanta, Georgia-based IT recruiting firm, covering the issues the company faces keeping its technology equipment up-to-date. The firm has devised a program that will replace its old server-based software systems with on-demand software delivered via the Internet, known as software-as-a-service. Statistical information included.

6955 ■ "The Jobs Man" in *Business Courier* (Vol. 26, December 25, 2009, No. 35, pp. 1)
Pub: American City Business Journals, Inc.
Ed: Lucy May. **Description:** Entrepreneur Bob Messer, a volunteer for Jobs Plus Employment Network in Cincinnati's Over-the-Rhine neighborhood, regularly conducts a seminar that aims to help attendees prepare for employment. Jobs Plus founder Burr Robinson asked Messer to create the seminar in order to help unemployed jobseekers. So far, the program has helped 144 individuals with full time jobs in 2009.

6956 ■ "Matchmakers Anticipating Tech Valley Boom" in *Business Review, Albany New York* (Vol. 34, November 2, 2007, No. 31, pp. 1)
Pub: American City Business Journals, Inc.
Ed: Adam Sichko. **Description:** Qualified candidates are coming to permanent placement companies after being downsized elsewhere. The top five projected fastest-growing and top five projected fasted-decreasing jobs in the Capital Region are presented.

6957 ■ *Occupational Outlook Handbook*
Pub: U.S. Bureau of Labor Statistics
Contact: Chet Levine
Released: Biennial, Latest edition 2010-2011. **Price:** $22, individuals. **Publication Includes:** Various occupational organizations that provide career information on hundreds of occupations. **Entries Include:** For organizations—Organization name, address. Principal content of publication is profiles of various occupations, which include description of occupation, educational requirements, job outlook, and expected earnings. **Arrangement:** Organizations are classified by occupation.

6958 ■ "On the Clock" in *Canadian Business* (Vol. 82, April 27, 2009, No. 7, pp. 28)
Pub: Rogers Media
Ed: Sarka Halas. **Description:** Survey of 100 Canadian executives found that senior managers can be out of a job for about nine months before their careers are adversely affected. The nine month mark can be avoided if job seekers build networks even before they lose their jobs. Job seekers should also take volunteer work and training opportunities to increase their changes of landing a job.

6959 ■ "Overseas Overtures" in *Business Journal-Portland* (Vol. 24, October 26, 2007, No. 35, pp. 1)
Pub: American City Business Journals, Inc.
Ed: Robin J. Moody. **Description:** Oregon has a workforce shortage, specifically for the health care industry. Recruiting agencies, such as the International Recruiting Network Inc., answers the high demand for workforce by recruiting foreign employees. The difficulties recruiting companies experience with regards to foreign labor laws are investigated.

6960 ■ "Priority: Business For Sale" in *Inc.* (January 2008, pp. 28)
Pub: Gruner & Jahr USA Publishing
Ed: Elaine Appleton Grant. **Description:** Profile of an employment agency providing registered nurses to hospitals and nursing homes. The company began as an temporary placement agency for IT professionals and is now for sale at the asking price of $4.2 million.

6961 ■ "Q&A With Devin Ringling: Franchise's Services Go Beyond Elder Care" in *Gazette* (October 2, 2010)
Pub: The Gazette
Ed: Bill Radford. **Description:** Profile of franchise, Interim HealthCare, in Colorado Springs, Colorado; the company offers home care services that include wound care and specialized feedings to shopping and light housekeeping. It also runs a medical staffing company that provides nurses, therapists and other health care workers to hospitals, prisons, schools and other facilities.

6962 ■ "Regional Talent Network Unveils Jobs Web Site" in *Crain's Cleveland Business* (Vol. 30, June 1, 2009, No. 21, pp. 11)
Pub: Crain Communications, Inc.
Description: Regional Talent Network launched WhereToFindHelp.org, a Website designed to act as a directory of all Northeast Ohio resources that can help employers recruit and job seekers look for positions. The site also lists organizations offering employment and training services.

6963 ■ "Sign of the Times: Temp-To-Perm Attorneys" in *HRMagazine* (Vol. 54, January 2009, No. 1, pp. 24)
Pub: Society for Human Resource Management
Ed: Bill Leonard. **Description:** A growing number of law firms are hiring professional staff on a temp-to-perm basis according to the president of Professional Placement Services in Florida. Firms can save money while testing potential employees on a temporary basis.

6964 ■ "Staffing Firms are Picking Up the Pieces, Seeing Signs of Life" in *Milwaukee Business Journal* (Vol. 27, February 5, 2010, No. 19)
Pub: American City Business Journals
Ed: Rich Rovito. **Description:** Milwaukee, Wisconsin-based staffing firms are seeing signs of economic rebound as many businesses turned to temporary employees to fill the demands for goods and services. Economic observers believe the growth in temporary staffing is one of the early indicators of economic recovery.

6965 ■ "Temporary Measures" in *Occupational Outlook Quarterly* (Vol. 54, Fall 2010, No. 3, pp. 36)
Pub: U.S. Bureau of Labor Statistics
Description: Data on temporary help services employment from the U.S. Bureau of Labor Statistics suggests good news for all nonfarm workers. The data had been rising steadily for most of 2009.

6966 ■ "What You Look Like Online" in *Black Enterprise* (Vol. 37, January 2007, No. 6, pp. 56)
Pub: Earl G. Graves Publishing Co. Inc.
Ed: Marcia A. Reed-Woodard. **Description:** Of 100 executive recruiters 77 percent stated that they use search engines to check the backgrounds of potential job candidates, according to a survey conducted by ExecuNet. Of those surveyed 35 percent stated that they eliminate potential candidates based on information they find online so it is important to create a positive Web presence which highlights professional image qualities.

6967 ■ "Winner: Private Company, $100M-$1B" in *Crain's Detroit Business* (Vol. 25, June 22, 2009, No. 25, pp. E004)
Pub: Crain Communications Inc. - Detroit
Ed: Sherri Begin Welch. **Description:** Profile of Strategic Staffing Solutions Inc. is presented.

6968 ■ "Work To Do" in *Canadian Business* (Vol. 81, July 22, 2008, No. 12-13, pp. 22)
Pub: Rogers Media Ltd.

Ed: Jane Bao. **Description:** Recruiting firm Manpower revealed that 36 percent of Canadian employers had trouble filling positions in 2007, highlighting the labor shortage and the need to bring in more workers. Underemployment of immigrants costs up to $6 billion to Canada's economy every year. Other views regarding Canada's labor shortage and on its economic impact are presented.

STATISTICAL SOURCES

6969 ■ *RMA Annual Statement Studies*
Pub: Robert Morris Associates (RMA)

Released: Annual. **Price:** $175.00 2006-07 edition, $105.00. **Description:** Contains composite balance sheets and income statements for more than 360 industries, including the accounting, auditing, and bookkeeping industries. Also contains five years of comparative historical data for discerning trends. Includes 16 commonly used ratios, computed for most of the size groupings for nearly every industry.

TRADE PERIODICALS

6970 ■ *AACE Bonus Briefs*
Pub: American Association for Career Education

Ed: Pat Nellor Wickwire, Editor. **Released:** Quarterly. **Price:** Included in membership. **Description:** Contains brief papers by American Association for Career Education members on current issues in careers, education, and employment.

6971 ■ *AACE Distinguished Member Series*
Pub: American Association for Career Education

Ed: Pat Nellor Wickwire, Editor. **Released:** Periodic. **Price:** Included in membership. **Description:** Publication of the American Association for Career Education. Provides information on careers, education, and employment.

6972 ■ *Journal of Employment Counseling*
Pub: American Association for Counseling and Development

Ed: Dr. Roberta A. Neault, Editor, roberta@lifestrategies.ca. **Released:** Quarterly. **Price:** $44; $55 institutions. **Description:** Journal covering state employee, vocational, college placement, education, business, and industry counseling.

6973 ■ *National Association of Colleges and Employers—Spotlight*
Pub: National Association of Colleges and Employers

Ed: Mimi Collins, Editor. **Released:** 21/year. **Description:** Devoted to career planning and employment of college graduates. Recurring features include news of regulations and legislation, technological developments statistics, research, trends, publications, and events related to career development and employment. Remarks: Subscription includes the Journal of Career Planning & Employment.

6974 ■ *Occupational Outlook Quarterly*
Pub: U.S. Government Printing Office and Superintendent of Documents
Contact: John Mullins, Managing Editor

Ed: Kathleen Green, Editor. **Released:** Quarterly. **Price:** $30 two years; $15; $42 other countries 2 years; $6 single issue; $8.40 other countries single copy. **Description:** Magazine providing occupational and employment information.

6975 ■ *Recruiting Trends*
Pub: Kennedy Information Inc.
Contact: R.E. Harling

Ed: Joseph Daniel McCool, Editor, rt-editor@kennedyinfo.com. **Released:** Bimonthly. **Price:** $249, Included in membership; $249, U.S., Canada, and Mexico; $289, elsewhere. **Description:** Provides strategies and tactics for creating and maintaining a competitive work force.

VIDEOCASSETTES/ AUDIOCASSETTES

6976 ■ *Career Moves: A Winning Strategy*
University of Wisconsin-Madison Center on Education & Work
1025 W. Johnson St., Rm. 964
Madison, WI 53706-1796
Ph:(608)265-6700
Free: 800-862-1071
Co. E-mail: cewmail@education.wisc.edu
URL: http://www.cew.wisc.edu

Price: $48.00. **Description:** Discusses various career issues, including the state of job opportunities, employment and training options, and balancing family and work. **Availability:** VHS.

6977 ■ *Day in the Career Series*
The Bureau for At-Risk Youth
PO Box 1246
Wilkes-Barre, PA 18703-1246
Free: 800-99-YOUTH
Fax:800-2620-1886
Co. E-mail: Email is a form at the site
URL: http://www.at-risk.com

Released: 1994. **Price:** $1575.00. **Description:** Twenty-tape vocational series that allows one to explore the various career opportunities within the top 100 vocations of the '90s. **Availability:** VHS.

6978 ■ *Employability Skills Video Series*
University of Wisconsin-Madison Center on Education & Work
1025 W. Johnson St., Rm. 964
Madison, WI 53706-1796
Ph:(608)265-6700
Free: 800-862-1071
Co. E-mail: cewmail@education.wisc.edu
URL: http://www.cew.wisc.edu

Released: 199?. **Price:** $295.00. **Description:** Eight-part job hunting series focusing on the skills needed for career and job success. Includes "Going to Work" workbook. **Availability:** VHS.

6979 ■ *Empowerment: It's Your Career*
International Training Consultants, Inc.
1838 Park Oaks
Kemah, TX 77565
Free: 800-998-8764
Co. E-mail: itc@trainingitc.com
URL: http://www.trainingitc.com

Price: $495.00. **Description:** Part of the "Empowerment: The Employee Development Series." Examines career development as an organizational system and teaches the employee's role in this system. Provides tools and information which will help employees determine and plan their career goals and interests. Emphasis is placed on individual responsibility for career development. **Availability:** VHS.

6980 ■ *From Law School to Law Practice: What Every Associate Needs to Know—The Set*
American Law Institute
American Bar Association Committee on Continuing Education
4025 Chestnut St.
Philadelphia, PA 19104
Ph:(215)243-1600
Free: 800-CLE-NEWS
Fax:(215)243-1636
Co. E-mail: custserv@ali-aba.org
URL: http://www.ali.org

Released: 1989. **Price:** $190. **Description:** Uses brief dramatizations to outline various skills and strategies for law firm success. Complete with study guide. **Availability:** VHS.

6981 ■ *Inside Business Today*
GPN Educational Media
1550 Executive Drive
Elgin, IL 60123
Ph:(402)472-2007
Free: 800-228-4630
Fax:800-306-2330
Co. E-mail: askgpn@smarterville.com
URL: http://www.shopgpn.com

Released: 1989. **Description:** Leaders in business and industry tell their success stories in this extensive series. **Availability:** VHS; 3/4U.

6982 ■ *Shhh! I'm Finding a Job: The Library and Your Self-Directed Job Search*
Cambridge Educational
c/o Films Media Group
132 West 31st Street, 17th Floor
Ste. 124
New York, NY 10001
Free: 800-257-5126
Fax:(609)671-0266
Co. E-mail: custserve@films.com
URL: http://www.cambridgeol.com

Released: 1993. **Price:** $79.95. **Description:** The library can be a powerful resource in locating and landing the job that's right for you. Learn how to utilize this tool to maximize your strengths and minimize your weaknesses. **Availability:** VHS.

CONSULTANTS

6983 ■ Custom Consulting Inc.
6315 Bayside Dr.
New Port Richey, FL 34652-2040
Ph:(727)844-5065
Fax:(727)844-5064
Co. E-mail: diwago@customconsulting.com
URL: http://www.customconsulting.com
Contact: David Wong, Mgr
E-mail: dwong@atscustomconsulting.com

Scope: Provides systems development personnel on a temporary basis. Specializes in mainframe, mini and Client/server development environments.

FRANCHISES AND BUSINESS OPPORTUNITIES

6984 ■ 10 Til 2- Part-Time Placement Service
10 Til 2 Franchising, LLC
3151 S Vaughn Way., Ste. 500
Aurora, CO 80014
Ph:(303)909-3868
Free: 877-999-1022
Fax:(303)617-1371

No. of Franchise Units: 19. **No. of Company-Owned Units:** 2. **Founded:** 2003. **Franchised:** 2006. **Description:** Part-time employment placement services. **Equity Capital Needed:** TBD. **Franchise Fee:** $35,000. **Financial Assistance:** No. **Training:** Yes.

6985 ■ AAA Employment
5533 Central Ave.
St. Petersburg, FL 33710
Ph:(727)343-3044
Free: 800-801-5627
Fax:(727)343-2953
Co. E-mail: aaaemployment@ij.net
URL: http://www.aaaemployment.net

No. of Franchise Units: 11. **Founded:** 1957. **Franchised:** 1967. **Description:** Employment agency. **Equity Capital Needed:** $25,000. **Franchise Fee:** $25,000. **Royalty Fee:** 10%. **Financial Assistance:** Direct financial assistance available. **Training:** Provides 2 weeks-30 days training.

6986 ■ AHEAD Human Resources, Inc.
AHEAD Human Resources, Inc.
2209 Heather Ln.
Louisville, KY 40218
Free: 877-485-5858
Fax:(502)485-0801

No. of Franchise Units: 7. **Founded:** 1995. **Franchised:** 2000. **Description:** Temporary staffing. **Equity Capital Needed:** Need working capital. **Franchise Fee:** $17,700-$23,700. **Financial Assistance:** No. **Training:** Yes.

6987 ■ Careers USA
6501 Congress Ave., Ste. 200
Boca Raton, FL 33487
Ph:(561)995-7000
Free: 888-227-3375
Fax:(561)995-7001

No. of Franchise Units: 7. **No. of Company-Owned Units:** 18. **Founded:** 1981. **Franchised:** 1988. **Description:** Staffing service. **Equity Capital Needed:** $129,700-$170,600. **Franchise Fee:** $14,500. **Royalty Fee:** Varies. **Financial Assistance:** Limited third party financing available. **Training:** Provides 2 weeks at headquarters, 1 week at franchisees location and ongoing sales support.

6988 ■ CareersUSA Franchise
Careers Franchising Inc.
6501 Congress Ave., Ste. 200
Boca Raton, FL 33487
Ph:(561)995-7000
Free: 888-CAR-EERS
Fax:(561)995-7001
Co. E-mail: tfeldman@careerusa.com
URL: http://www.careerusa.com

No. of Franchise Units: 9. **No. of Company-Owned Units:** 17. **Founded:** 1981. **Franchised:** 1987. **Description:** A temporary, temp-to-hire and direct hire placement staffing service specializing in clerical, administrative, accounting and light service personnel in varied industries and organizations. **Equity Capital Needed:** $110,000-$154,500. **Franchise Fee:** $14,500. **Financial Assistance:** 100% payroll funding. **Managerial Assistance:** Proprietary computerized software provided. **Training:** Comprehensive business and sales training including site selection advice, advertising support and staff status.

6989 ■ Express Employment Professionals
8516 NW Expy.
Oklahoma City, OK 73162
Free: 877-652-6400
Co. E-mail: franchising@expresspersonnel.com
URL: http://www.franchising.expresspersonnel.com

No. of Franchise Units: 550. **Founded:** 1983. **Franchised:** 1985. **Description:** Is an international fullservice staffing corporation with three distinct divisions available in one franchise agreement. The franchised offices provide clients with temporary help, full-time placements, and executive recruitment. **Equity Capital Needed:** $153,750-$242,500 depending on the market. Can be a combo of cash and equity. **Franchise Fee:** $35,000. **Financial Assistance:** Express finances temporary associate payroll. **Managerial Assistance:** Continuous follow-up training in the field and in regular seminars and workshops. **Training:** 2 week initial training at headquarters, 1 week in certified training office and ongoing field training and support. Followed by additional time in new office with assigned field representative.

6990 ■ Interim HomeStyle Services
1601 Sawgrass Corporate Pky.
Sunrise, FL 33323
Ph:(954)858-2699
Free: 800-338-7786
Fax:(954)858-2720
Co. E-mail: johnmarquez@interimhealthcare.com
URL: http://www.interimhealthcare.com

No. of Franchise Units: 293. **No. of Company-Owned Units:** 22. **Founded:** 1956. **Franchised:** 1966. **Description:** Interim HomeStyle Services is the brand for non-medical services provided by Interim Healthcare, the country's oldest health care franchise organization. **Equity Capital Needed:** $35,000-$70,000 total investment. **Franchise Fee:** $10,000. **Royalty Fee:** 5%. **Financial Assistance:** Direct financial assistance available. **Training:** Offers 1 week training.

6991 ■ Labor Finders International, Inc.
11426 N Jog Rd.
Palm Beach Gardens, FL 33418
Ph:(561)273-8222
Free: 800-864-7749
Fax:(561)273-8163
Co. E-mail: lfi@laborfinders.com
URL: http://www.laborfinders.com

No. of Franchise Units: 256. **No. of Company-Owned Units:** 29. **Founded:** 1975. **Franchised:** 1975. **Description:** Personnel services. **Equity Capital Needed:** $96,150-$157,320. **Franchise Fee:** $20,000. **Financial Assistance:** No. **Training:** Sales, operation, and owners training program software, and helpdesk.

6992 ■ Management Recruiters International Inc.
CDI Corp.
75 Erieview Plc., Ste. 100
Cleveland, OH 44114
Ph:(216)416-8467
Free: 800-875-4000
Fax:(216)696-6612

No. of Franchise Units: 1,128. **No. of Company-Owned Units:** 32. **Founded:** 1957. **Franchised:** 1965. **Description:** Management level and general personnel placement, search and recruiting service on an employer-paid, contingency fee basis. **Equity Capital Needed:** $112,855-$154,345. **Franchise Fee:** $100,000. **Financial Assistance:** Yes. **Training:** Initial training program of approximately 3 weeks at headquarters, plus an additional on-the-job training program of approximately 3 weeks in licensee's first office. Training thereafter as needed. Also assists in securing suitable office space, lease negotiations, design and layout, office furniture, equipment, telephone systems, etc.

6993 ■ Pridestaff
7535 N Palm Ave., Ste. 101
Fresno, CA 93711-1393
Ph:(559)449-5804

No. of Franchise Units: 35. **No. of Company-Owned Units:** 3. **Founded:** 1978. **Franchised:** 1995. **Description:** Recruiting Agency. **Equity Capital Needed:** $162,000-$237,000. **Franchise Fee:** $32,000. **Financial Assistance:** No. **Training:** Yes.

6994 ■ Sanford Rose Associates
SRA International, Inc.
1305 Mall of Georgia Blvd., Ste. 160
Buford, GA 30519
Ph:(678)833-9305
Free: 800-731-7724
Fax:(770)904-0359

No. of Franchise Units: 64. **Founded:** 1959. **Franchised:** 1970. **Description:** Employee search service that uses a database of candidates and custom computer software to allow each office to match employees with client openings. **Equity Capital Needed:** $91,350-$129,680. **Franchise Fee:** $65,000. **Financial Assistance:** Yes. **Managerial Assistance:** The first 6-9 months, franchisee works with staff in strategic planning. **Training:** Provides a minimum of 10 days of training at corporate headquarters and an additional 5 days of training in franchisees office.

6995 ■ Snelling Staffing, LLC
Snelling Staffing, LLC
4055 Valley View Ln., Ste. 700
Dallas, TX 75244
Free: 800-756-7500
Fax:(972)383-3839

No. of Franchise Units: 126. **No. of Company-Owned Units:** 54. **Founded:** 1951. **Franchised:** 1955. **Description:** Full-service temporary and permanent personnel service franchise. Computerized national matching network. Services inclusive of sales and marketing, accounting and finance, data processing, engineering, health care and office support. **Equity Capital Needed:** $104,700-$183,500. **Franchise Fee:** $25,000. **Royalty Fee:** 4.5/7%. **Financial Assistance:** Limited third party financing available. **Training:** Provides 8 days training at headquarters, at franchisee's location as needed, and at field location as needed.

6996 ■ TRC Staffing Services, Inc.
115 Perimeter Center Pl. NE, Ste. 850
Atlanta, GA 30346
Ph:(770)392-1411
Free: 800-488-8008

No. of Franchise Units: 30. **No. of Company-Owned Units:** 23. **Founded:** 1980. **Description:** Provides office support, clerical, word processing, data processing, marketing and light industrial personnel to businesses. **Equity Capital Needed:** $15,000. **Franchise Fee:** $75,000 minimum liquid. **Financial Assistance:** No. **Training:** Yes.

6997 ■ White Glove Placement, Inc.
We Know How, Inc.
155 Lorimer St.
Brooklyn, NY 11206
Ph:(718)387-8181
Free: (866)862-8994

No. of Company-Owned Units: 1. **Founded:** 1995. **Franchised:** 2004. **Description:** Staff hospitals, etc. w/nursing personnel. **Equity Capital Needed:** $89,000-$242,900. **Franchise Fee:** $25,000. **Training:** Yes.

COMPUTERIZED DATABASES

6998 ■ *The Ohio JobBank*
Adams Media Corp.
57 Littlefield St.
Avon, MA 02322-1944
Ph:(508)427-7100
Fax:(508)427-6790
Co. E-mail: rights@adamsmedia.com
URL: http://www.adamsmedia.com

Released: Biennial, Latest edition 12th. **Price:** $17. 95, individuals Paperback. **Covers:** 4,800 Employers and employment services in Ohio. **Entries Include:** Firm or organization name, address, phone, name and title of contact; description of organization, headquarters location, typical titles for entry- and middle-level positions, educational backgrounds desired, fringe benefits offered, stock exchange listing, training programs, internships, parent company, number of employees, revenues, e-mail and web address, projected number of hires. **Arrangement:** Alphabetical.

6999 ■ *Oregon Career Information System*
Oregon Career Information System
1244 University of Oregon
Eugene, OR 97403-1244
Ph:(541)346-3872
Free: 800-495-1266
Fax:(541)346-3823
Co. E-mail: rlee@orcis.uoregon.edu
URL: http://oregoncis.uoregon.edu

Description: Provides career information, including occupational profiles; local, state, and national labor market trends; job search techniques; self-employment options; programs of study; postsecondary educational institutions; and financial aid. For each occupation, covers job duties, required abilities, working conditions, earnings, employment outlooks, relevant school subjects, ways to prepare, self-employment options, and entry routes. For programs of study and training, covers typical course work, teaching methods, related occupations, admission requirements, lists of schools offering the programs, and transfer programs. For profiles of postsecondary schools and the kinds of programs they offer, covers admission requirements, costs, housing, and the types of financial aid and student services available. **Availability:** Online: Oregon Career Information System. **Type:** Directory.

7000 ■ *SkillSearch*
SkillSearch Ltd.
22-23 Kensington St.
East Sussex
Brighton BN1 4AJ, United Kingdom
Ph:44 1273 64 7280
Fax:44 1273 64 7290
Co. E-mail: mail@skillsearch.com
URL: http://www.skillsearch.com

Description: Provides information on new employment opportunities for individuals in the United Kingdom and Europe. Searchable by product area, location, and position. **Availability:** Online: SkillSearch Ltd. **Type:** Directory.

LIBRARIES

7001 ■ Employment Support Center Library
1556 Wisconsin Ave., NW
Washington, DC 20007
Ph:(202)628-2919
Fax:(703)790-1469
Co. E-mail: escjobclubs@yahoo.com
URL: http://jobclubs.angelfire.com/
Contact: Ellie Wegener, Exec.Dir.
Scope: Employment networking, self-esteem, starting your own business, setting up job clubs, training facilitators, maintaining a large job bank, providing job-searching skills. **Services:** Library open to the public. **Holdings:** 150 articles; books; periodicals; videos on job search; interviews; reports; manuscripts. **Subscriptions:** 4 journals and other serials; 2 newspapers.

7002 ■ Muskegon Community College–Hendrik Meijer Library I Special Collections
221 S. Quarterline Rd.
Muskegon, MI 49442
Ph:(231)777-0260
Fax:(231)777-0279
Co. E-mail: library@muskegoncc.edu
URL: http://muskegoncc.edu/pages/309.asp
Contact: Carol Briggs-Erickson, Lib.Coord.
Scope: Reference. **Services:** Interlibrary loan; copying; Library open to the public. **Holdings:** 54,000 books; 600 bound periodical volumes; 2000 archives; 20,000 microfiche; 2000 microfilms. **Subscriptions:** 320 journals and other serials; 10 newspapers.

RESEARCH CENTERS

7003 ■ W.E. Upjohn Institute for Employment Research
300 S Westnedge Ave.
Kalamazoo, MI 49007-4686
Ph:(269)343-5541
Fax:(269)343-3308
Co. E-mail: eberts@upjohninstitute.org
URL: http://www.upjohninstitute.org
Contact: Dr. Randall W. Eberts, Pres.
E-mail: eberts@upjohninstitute.org
Scope: Causes and effects of unemployment, including studies on social insurance and income maintenance programs, earnings and benefits, economic development and local labor issues, work arrangements, education and training issues for the workplace, and other methods of alleviating problems related to unemployment. **Publications:** Business Outlook for West Michigan; Employment Research Newsletter. **Educational Activities:** Conference (annually). **Awards:** Upjohn Institute Dissertation Award.

DIRECTORIES OF EDUCATIONAL PROGRAMS

7004 ▪ *Directory of Private Accredited Career Schools and Colleges of Technology*
Pub: Accrediting Commission of Career Schools and Colleges of Technology
Contact: Michale S. McComis, Exec. Dir.
Released: On web page. **Price:** Free. **Description:** Covers 3900 accredited post-secondary programs that provide training programs in business, trade, and technical fields, including various small business endeavors. Entries offer school name, address, phone, description of courses, job placement assistance, and requirements for admission. Arrangement is alphabetical.

TRADE PERIODICALS

7005 ▪ *Recognition Review*
Pub: Awards and Recognition Association
Ed: Joseph Agnew, Editor. **Released:** Monthly. **Price:** Included in membership; $42, nonmembers. **Description:** Covers news and general information on the awards and engraving industry. Focuses on the association's trade shows, product developments and additions, Association business, and industry success stories.

VIDEOCASSETTES/ AUDIOCASSETTES

7006 ▪ *Machine Embroidery*
Nancy's Notions Ltd.
333 Beichl Ave.
P.O. Box 683
Beaver Dam, WI 53916-0683
Ph:(920)887-7321
Free: 800-725-0361
Fax:800-255-8119
Co. E-mail: customerservice@nancysnotions.com
URL: http://www.nancysnotions.com
Released: 1987. **Description:** Complete instruction is given in how to use your sewing machine to embroider like a pro. **Availability:** VHS.

7007 ▪ *Machine Monogramming*
Nancy's Notions Ltd.
333 Beichl Ave.
P.O. Box 683
Beaver Dam, WI 53916-0683
Ph:(920)887-7321
Free: 800-725-0361
Fax:800-255-8119
Co. E-mail: customerservice@nancysnotions.com
URL: http://www.nancysnotions.com
Released: 1987. **Description:** How to effectively monogram through the use of a zigzag sewing machine. **Availability:** VHS.

7008 ▪ *Machine Monogramming & Embroidery Combo*
Nancy's Notions Ltd.
333 Beichl Ave.
P.O. Box 683
Beaver Dam, WI 53916-0683
Ph:(920)887-7321
Free: 800-725-0361
Fax:800-255-8119
Co. E-mail: customerservice@nancysnotions.com
URL: http://www.nancysnotions.com
Released: 1987. **Description:** Two instructional programs on monogramming and embroidery using the sewing machine. **Availability:** VHS.

FRANCHISES AND BUSINESS OPPORTUNITIES

7009 ▪ Crown Trophy, Inc.
9 Skyline Dr.
Hawthorne, NY 10532
Ph:(914)347-7700
Free: 800-583-8228
Fax:(914)347-0211
No. of Franchise Units: 142. **Founded:** 1978. **Franchised:** 1987. **Description:** Offers a complete line of trophies and awards. **Equity Capital Needed:** $50,000-$60,000. **Franchise Fee:** $35,000. **Financial Assistance:** Yes. **Training:** Yes.

7010 ▪ Recognition Express
Recognition Express Intl.
6290 Harrison Dr., Ste. 7
Las Vegas, NV 89120
Ph:(702)795-4550
Free: (866)838-5888
Fax:(702)795-4551
No. of Franchise Units: 10. **Founded:** 1972. **Franchised:** 1974. **Description:** Name badges, awards, and specialty products. **Equity Capital Needed:** $82,100-$118,500 total investment. **Franchise Fee:** $29,500. **Royalty Fee:** 4-6%. **Financial Assistance:** No. **Training:** Provides 5 days training at headquarters, 2 days at franchisee's location and ongoing support.

Environmental Consultant

START-UP INFORMATION

7011 ■ "EDCO Doling Out Capital Along Border" in *Austin Business JournalInc.* (Vol. 28, August 1, 2008, No. 20, pp. 1)
Pub: American City Business Journals
Ed: Sandra Zaragoza. **Description:** Non-profit business incubator Economic Development Catalyst Organization Ventures is searching for promising startup companies. The company is targeting startups in green energy, technology and consumer markets. EDCO has partnered with consumer electronics repair company CherryFusion and technology firm MiniDonations.

7012 ■ *How to Start a Home-Based Consulting Business: Define Your Specialty Build a Client Base Make Yourself Indispensable*
Pub: The Globe Pequot Press
Ed: Bert Holtje. **Released:** January 10, 2010. **Price:** $18.95. **Description:** Everything needed for starting and running a successful consulting business from home.

7013 ■ *Starting Green: An Ecopreneur's Guide to Starting a Green Business from Business Plans to Profits*
Pub: Entrepreneur Press
Ed: Glenn E. Croston. **Released:** September 9, 2010. **Price:** $21.95. **Description:** Entrepreneur and scientist outlines green business essentials and helps uncover eco-friendly business opportunities, build a sustainable business plan, and gain the competitive advantage.

ASSOCIATIONS AND OTHER ORGANIZATIONS

7014 ■ Canadian Environmental Law Association
130 Spadina Ave., Ste. 301
Toronto, ON, Canada M5V 2L4
Ph:(416)960-2284
Fax:(416)960-9392
Co. E-mail: theresa@cela.ca
URL: http://www.cela.ca
Contact: Theresa McClenaghan, Exec. Dir./Counsel
Description: Protects and enhances public health and environmental quality throughout Canada. Advocates for comprehensive laws, standards and policies. Seeks to increase public participation in environmental decision-making. **Publications:** *Intervenor* (quarterly).

7015 ■ Canadian Environmental Network–Reseau canadien de l'environment
39 McArthur Ave., Level 1-1
Ottawa, ON, Canada K1L 8L7
Ph:(613)728-9810
Fax:(613)728-2963
Co. E-mail: info@cen-rce.org
URL: http://www.cen-rce.org
Contact: Ms. Olivier Kolmel, Chm.
Description: Environmental organizations. Seeks to advance the projects and activities of members. Promotes ecologically sustainable development. Serves as a clearinghouse on environmental issues; provides support and assistance to members. **Publications:** *Canadian Environmental Network News* (annual).

7016 ■ Canadian Institute for Environmental Law and Policy–L'institut canadien du droit et de la politique en l'environnement
729 St. Clair Ave. W, Rm. 13
Toronto, ON, Canada M6C 1B2
Ph:(416)923-3529
Fax:(416)923-5949
Co. E-mail: cielap@cielap.org
URL: http://www.cielap.org
Contact: Thomas Esakin, Exec. Dir.
Description: Works to improve legal and economic policies affecting the environment. Conducts research and disseminates information on current environmental policies. Promotes dialogue among governments, the private sector, and nongovernmental groups. Provides educational programs. **Publications:** *The Citizen's Guide to Biotechnology*; *Electricity Competition and Clean Air*; *Environment on Trial*; *Environment Technology Support Program in Canada*; *Sustainable Agriculture: An Overview and Assessment of Critical Needs in Canada* . **Telecommunication Services:** electronic mail, thomas@cielap.org.

7017 ■ Canadian Institute of Resources Law–Institut canadien du droit des ressources
University of Calgary
Murray Fraser Hall, Rm. 3353
2500 University Dr. NW
Calgary, AB, Canada T2N 1N4
Ph:(403)220-3200
Fax:(403)282-6182
Co. E-mail: cirl@ucalgary.ca
URL: http://www.cirl.ca
Contact: J. Owen Saunders, Exec. Dir.
Description: Promotes research, education, and publication on law relating to Canada's renewable and nonrenewable natural resources. Conducts research and educational programs on topics including the relationship between legal systems, laws, and natural resources, and the development of public policies governing environmental protection and natural resources extraction. Provides advice and assistance to legal and policy-making bodies; gathers and disseminates information on environmental law. **Publications:** *Resources* (quarterly). **Telecommunication Services:** electronic mail, josaunde@ucalgary.ca.

7018 ■ Canadian Network of Toxicology Centres
University of Guelph
Edmund Bovey Bldg., No. 80, 2nd Fl.
Gordon St.
Guelph, ON, Canada N1G 2W1
Ph:(519)824-4120
Fax:(519)837-3861
Co. E-mail: dwarner@uoguelph.ca
URL: http://www.uoguelph.ca/cntc
Contact: Dr. Len Ritter, Exec. Dir.
Description: University based toxicology research centers. Seeks to improve human and environmental health through increased understanding of toxic substances and their impact on the environment. Coordinates research efforts of research team members; advises government agencies and industrial organizations concerned with the release of toxic substances into the environment. Supports educational programs in toxicology at all levels. Serves as a clearinghouse on toxicology and environmental health issues. **Publications:** *Toxicology Educators Resource Guide for Secondary School Audiences* .

7019 ■ Canadian Parks and Wilderness Society–Societe pour la nature et les parcs du Canada
250 City Centre Ave., Ste. 506
Ottawa, ON, Canada K1R 6K7
Ph:(613)569-7226
Free: 800-333-9453
Fax:(613)569-7098
Co. E-mail: info@cpaws.org
URL: http://www.cpaws.org
Contact: Eric Hebert-Daly, Natl. Exec. Dir.
Description: Individuals and organizations with an interest in the preservation of wilderness areas. Promotes establishment of new protected areas; seeks to improve management of existing parks and wildernesses. Develops proposals for reform of public policies governing wilderness preservation and parks management. Conducts advocacy and educational programs to raise public awareness of wilderness preservation issues. Facilitates formation of partnerships linking environmental groups, aboriginal people's governments and organizations, industries, and government agencies. **Publications:** *Canadian Wilderness* (semiannual).

7020 ■ Canadian Society of Environmental Biologists–Societe Canadienne des Biologistes l'Environnement
PO Box 962
Sta. F
Toronto, ON, Canada M4Y 2N9
Ph:(780)427-7765
Fax:(780)427-5120
Co. E-mail: bfree@cseb-scbe.org
URL: http://www.cseb-scbe.org
Contact: Brian Free, Pres.
Description: Environmental biologists. Promotes conservation and wise use of Canada's natural resources. Facilitates communication and cooperation among members. Promulgates and enforces professional standards for environmental biology practice, education, and research. Conducts professional training programs; sponsors public education projects to raise awareness of environmental issues. Evaluates conservation and environmental protection programs maintained by government agencies and industries; makes recommendations regarding improvement of conservation practices. **Publications:** *CSEB Newsletter* (quarterly).

7021 ■ Earth Day Canada
111 Peter St., Ste. 503
Toronto, ON, Canada M5V 2H1
Ph:(416)599-1991
Free: 888-283-2784

Fax:(416)599-3100
Co. E-mail: info@earthday.ca
URL: http://www.earthday.ca
Contact: Keith Treffry, Dir. of Communications
Description: Individuals and organizations. Promotes respect for the environment. Seeks to raise public awareness of environmental protection and conservation issues. Conducts educational and charitable programs; makes available children's services. **Publications:** *Earth Tones* (quarterly).

7022 ■ Earth Energy Society of Canada–Societe de l'Energie solaire du Canada
7885 Jock Trail
Ottawa, ON, Canada K0A 2Z0
Ph:(613)222-6920
Fax:(613)822-4987
Co. E-mail: info@earthenergy.ca
URL: http://www.earthenergy.ca
Contact: Mr. Bill Eggertson, Coor.
Description: Promotes the feasible application of geothermal (earth energy) heat pumps for low-grade thermal energy, both as a standalone technology and as an integral part of the Green Heat Global partnership.

7023 ■ EarthSave Canada
SPEC Bldg.
2150 Maple St.
Vancouver, BC, Canada V6J 3T3
Ph:(604)731-5885
Fax:(604)731-5805
URL: http://www.earthsave.ca
Contact: Dave Steele, Pres.
Description: Seeks to increase the awareness of the health, ethical, and environmental impacts of food choices. Promotes transition to a plant-based diet for optimum health, environmental sustainability, and compassion. **Publications:** *Canada EarthSaver* (bimonthly).

7024 ■ Ecojustice Canada
131 Water St., Ste. 214
Vancouver, BC, Canada V6B 4M3
Ph:(604)685-5618
Free: 800-926-7744
Fax:(604)685-7813
Co. E-mail: info@ecojustice.ca
URL: http://www.ecojustice.ca
Contact: Devon Page, Exec. Dir.
Description: Represents attorneys and others with an interest in conservation and environmental law. Provides free legal advice and representation to organizations and individuals seeking judgments in cases involving environmental protection.

7025 ■ Ecology Action Centre
2705 Fern Ln.
Halifax, NS, Canada B3K 4L7
Ph:(902)429-2202
Fax:(902)405-3716
Co. E-mail: info@ecologyaction.ca
URL: http://www.ecologyaction.ca
Contact: Karen Hollett, Co-Chair
Description: Works to develop solutions to ecological problems. Fosters communication between members. **Publications:** *Between the Issues* (quarterly); Brochures (periodic).

7026 ■ Energy Probe Research Foundation
225 Brunswick Ave.
Toronto, ON, Canada M5S 2M6
Ph:(416)964-9223
Fax:(416)964-8239
Co. E-mail: webadmin@eprf.ca
URL: http://www.eprf.ca/eprf/index.html
Contact: Patricia Adams, Pres.
Description: Seeks to inform public opinion on matters of environmental protection, energy resources and consumption, international development, and consumer policies. Promotes social change through participation in democratic political institutions. Functions as a watchdog organization, monitoring public and corporate policies related to energy production and consumption and environmental protection. Provides advice and information to government agencies and corporations in matters of energy and environmental protection. Conducts research and educational programs; makes available teaching aids and other informative materials.

7027 ■ Environmental Business Council of New England
375 Harvard St., Ste. 2
Brookline, MA 02446
Ph:(617)505-1818
Co. E-mail: ebc@ebcne.org
URL: http://www.ebcne.org
Contact: Daniel K. Moon, Pres./Exec. Dir.
Description: Firms that manufacture environmental and/or energy products and provide environmental and/or energy services. Fosters the development of an effective and competitive envirotech industry for the purpose of enhancing and maintaining a clean and productive environment. Provides a forum for environmental and energy company executives to network with each other and to meet leading members of the academic, nonprofit, and government communities to discuss issues of concern to the environmental industry. Provides business development and educational services. **Publications:** Newsletter (monthly).

7028 ■ Environmental Defence
116 Spadina Ave. W, Ste. 300
Toronto, ON, Canada M5V 2K6
Ph:(416)323-9521
Free: 877-399-2333
Fax:(416)323-9301
Co. E-mail: info@environmentaldefence.ca
URL: http://environmentaldefence.ca
Contact: Dr. Rick Smith, Exec. Dir.
Description: Provides Canadians with the tools and knowledge needed to protect and improve the environment and health; committed to engaging the public, finding solutions, and protecting the environmental rights of future generations. **Publications:** *Eco News* .

7029 ■ Environnement Jeunesse
454 Ave. Laurier E
Montreal, QC, Canada H2J 1E7
Ph:(514)252-3016
Free: (866)377-3016
Fax:(514)254-5873
Co. E-mail: infoenjeu@enjeu.qc.ca
URL: http://enjeu.qc.ca
Contact: Amelie Trottier-Picard, Pres.
Description: Youth and adult leaders. Promotes development in youth of a worldview conducive to sustainable use of natural resources. Conducts educational and social programs to raise awareness among youth of environmental consequences of lifestyle choices. **Publications:** *L'Enjeu* (quarterly).

7030 ■ Harmony Foundation–Harmony
PO Box 50022
Victoria, BC, Canada V8S 1G1
Ph:(250)380-3001
Fax:(250)380-0887
Co. E-mail: harmony@islandnet.com
URL: http://www.harmonyfdn.ca
Contact: Mr. Michael Bloomfield, Founder/Exec. Dir.
Description: Environmental educators, community and youth leaders, government officials, and other interested individuals. Seeks to ensure the availability of environmental education resources and skills in schools, workplaces, and the community. Works with educators and community leaders to improve environmental programs; develops and conducts leadership training courses for educators and community leaders.

7031 ■ Municipal Waste Association
127 Wyndham St. N, Ste. 100
Guelph, ON, Canada N1H 4E9
Ph:(519)823-1990
Fax:(519)823-0084
Co. E-mail: mwa@municipalwaste.ca
URL: http://www.municipalwaste.ca
Contact: Vivian De Giovanni, Exec. Dir.
Description: Municipal waste management professionals. Promotes more effective and environmentally sustainable removal of solid wastes. Facilitates sharing of municipal waste management, reduction, recycling, and reuse information and facilities. Conducts continuing professional education courses for members; operates job hotline; represents members' interests before government agencies and the public. Sponsors research; compiles statistics. **Publications:** *For R Information* (quarterly).

7032 ■ Natural Products Marketing Council
PO Box 550
Truro, NS, Canada B2N 5E3
Ph:(902)893-6511
Co. E-mail: crouseea@gov.ns.ca
URL: http://www.gov.ns.ca/agri/npmc
Contact: Dave Davies, Chm.
Description: Producers and processors of natural food products and wool. Promotes growth and development of the natural products industries. Supervises natural product marketing boards.

7033 ■ Ontario Nature
366 Adelaide St. W, Ste. 201
Toronto, ON, Canada M5V 1R9
Ph:(416)444-8419
Free: 800-440-2366
Fax:(416)444-9866
Co. E-mail: info@ontarionature.org
URL: http://www.ontarionature.org
Contact: Caroline Schultz, Exec. Dir.
Description: Works to protect Ontario's nature through research, education and conservation action. Champions woodlands, wetlands and wildlife, and preserves essential habitat through a system of nature reserves. **Publications:** *On Nature* (quarterly).

7034 ■ Pembina Institute for Appropriate Development
Box 7558
Drayton Valley, AB, Canada T7A 1S7
Ph:(403)269-3344
Fax:(780)542-6464
Co. E-mail: info@pembina.org
URL: http://www.pembina.org
Contact: Marlo Raynolds, Exec. Dir.
Description: Organizations and individuals with an interest in environmental protection and global development. Promotes increased public awareness of environmental and development issues. Conducts environmental research and educational programs; provides corporate environmental strategic management services, sponsors charitable activities. **Telecommunication Services:** electronic mail, marlor@pembina.org.

7035 ■ Pitch-In Canada
Box 45011, Ocean Park PO
White Rock, BC, Canada V4A 9L1
Free: 877-474-8244
Fax:(604)535-4653
Co. E-mail: pitch-in@pitch-in.ca
URL: http://www.pitch-in.ca
Contact: Misha Cook, Exec. Dir.
Description: Individuals and organizations with an interest in community beautification and pollution control. Promotes reduction of packaging and other refuse discarded in public and wild places. Conducts educational and public relations programs to discourage littering and stimulate community-based clean-up campaigns, including annual Pitch-In Week. Makes available resources and other support and assistance to local antilittering and clean-up projects. Sponsors research; compiles statistics.

7036 ■ Pollution Probe
150 Ferrand Dr., Ste. 208
Toronto, ON, Canada M3C 3E5
Ph:(416)926-1907
Fax:(416)926-1601
Co. E-mail: pprobe@pollutionprobe.org
URL: http://www.pollutionprobe.org
Contact: Bob Oliver, CEO
Description: Works to define environmental problems through research; seeks to raise public awareness of environmental issues through education; lobbies for environmental protection and remediation before government agencies and industrial associations. Focuses on smog and climate change, reduction and elimination of mercury in water, child health and the environment, indoor air quality, and water quality. **Publications:** *ProbeAbilities* (quarterly).

7037 ■ Recycling Council of Alberta
PO Box 23
Bluffton, AB, Canada T0C 0M0
Ph:(403)843-6563
Fax:(403)843-4156
Co. E-mail: info@recycle.ab.ca
URL: http://www.recycle.ab.ca
Contact: Jason London, Pres.
Description: Promotes and facilitates waste reduction, recycling and resource conservation in the province of Alberta. **Publications:** *Connector* (quarterly); *Enviro Business Guide* .

7038 ■ Saskatchewan Environmental Society
Box 1372
Saskatoon, SK, Canada S7K 3N9
Ph:(306)665-1915
Fax:(306)665-2128
Co. E-mail: info@environmentalsociety.ca
URL: http://www.environmentalsociety.ca
Contact: Allyson Brady, Exec. Dir.
Description: Seeks to support and encourage the creation of a global community in which all needs are met in sustainable ways. **Publications:** *SES Newsletter* (bimonthly).

7039 ■ Sierra Club of Canada
412-1 Nicholas St.
Ottawa, ON, Canada K1N 7B7
Ph:(613)241-4611
Free: 888-810-4204
Fax:(613)241-2292
Co. E-mail: info@sierraclub.ca
URL: http://www.sierraclub.ca
Contact: John Bennett, Exec. Dir.
Description: Individuals and organizations concerned about conservation and environmental protection. Promotes development of public policies mandating environmental responsibility. Seeks to raise public awareness of environmental protection issues. Conducts national campaigns on matters including: increased energy efficiency; clear-cutting of forests; health risks associated with pesticide use; protection of biodiversity. **Telecommunication Services:** electronic mail, membership@sierraclub.ca.

7040 ■ Society Promoting Environmental Conservation
2060-B Pine St.
Vancouver, BC, Canada V6J 4P8
Ph:(604)736-7732
Fax:(604)736-7115
Co. E-mail: admin@spec.bc.ca
URL: http://www.spec.bc.ca
Contact: Joanna Robinson, Pres.
Description: Promotes environmental research, advocacy, and education. **Publications:** *SPECTRUM* (quarterly).

7041 ■ Trout Unlimited Canada
6712 Fisher St. SE, Ste. 160
Calgary, AB, Canada T2H 2A7
Ph:(403)221-8360
Free: 800-909-6040
Fax:(403)221-8368
Co. E-mail: tuc@tucanada.org
URL: http://www.tucanada.org
Contact: Jeff Surtees, CEO
Description: Individuals with interest in trout fishing and conservation of riparian habitats and freshwater ecosystems. Promotes the protection, conservation and restoration of Canada's freshwater ecosystems and their coldwater resources for current and future generations. Conducts educational programs and restoration projects in areas including responsible disposal of household chemicals and other wastes; sustainable fishing practices such as catch and release; sustainable development; purchase and preservation of unique coldwater habitats. Sponsors research and educational programs; maintains speakers' bureau. **Publications:** *Currents* (quarterly).

7042 ■ Western Canada Wilderness Committee
PO Box 2205
Station Terminal
Vancouver, BC, Canada V6B 3W2
Ph:(604)683-8220
Free: 800-661-9453
Fax:(604)683-8229
Co. E-mail: info@wildernesscommittee.org
URL: http://www.wildernesscommittee.org
Contact: Joe Foy, Exec. Dir.
Description: Individuals interested in preserving wilderness areas, with emphasis on old-growth forests, and their inhabitants. Promotes social justice as a prerequisite of environmental protection in developing regions. Conducts educational campaigns to raise public awareness of environmental protection issues and the dangers posed to the environment by economic development. Works with local environmental groups and indigenous people associations to insure appropriate and sustainable economic growth in developing regions. Maintains trails in unprotected temperate rainforests on the coast of British Columbia. Acts as hub for a global network of environmental groups. **Publications:** Newspaper (monthly).

7043 ■ Women's Healthy Environments Network
215 Spadina Ave., Ste. 400
Toronto, ON, Canada M5T 2C7
Ph:(416)928-0880
Fax:(416)644-0116
Co. E-mail: office@womenshealthyenvironments.ca
URL: http://www.womenshealthyenvironments.ca
Contact: Marie Lorenzo, Co-Chair
Description: Women experts in environmental studies and issues. Works to implement community development projects to improve the environment. Provides a forum for discussion, information exchange, and the conducting of research related to women in the fields of planning, health, workplace, design, economy, urban and rural sociology, and community development. Initiates and organizes community projects. Advocates environmental protection, anti-discriminatory zoning practices, and the development of affordable housing. **Publications:** *Whitewash*; *Women and Environments* (quarterly).

7044 ■ Young Naturalists' Circle–Cercles des Jeunes Naturalistes
Jardin botanique de Montreal
4101 Rue Sherbrooke Est, Bureau 262
Montreal, QC, Canada H1X 2B2
Ph:(514)252-3023
Fax:(514)254-8744
Co. E-mail: info@jeunesnaturalistes.org
URL: http://www.jeunesnaturalistes.org
Contact: Mr. Jean Sebastien Labrecque, CEO
Description: Youth with an interest in nature; nature clubs. Promotes interest in nature and the natural and environmental sciences among youth. Encourages environmental protection. Conducts educational programs; maintains speakers' bureau and museum. **Publications:** *Les Naturalistes* (quarterly).

7045 ■ Yukon Conservation Society
302 Hawkins St.
Whitehorse, YT, Canada Y1A 1X6
Ph:(867)668-5678
Fax:(867)668-6637
Co. E-mail: ycs@ycs.yk.ca
URL: http://www.yukonconservation.org
Contact: Karen Baltgailis, Exec. Dir.
Description: Seeks to protect Canada's natural environment; particularly that of the Yukon region. Encourages the conservation of Yukon wilderness, wildlife and natural resources. **Publications:** *Walk Softly* (quarterly).

DIRECTORIES OF EDUCATIONAL PROGRAMS

7046 ■ *The Guide to Graduate Environmental Programs*
Pub: Island Press
Price: $29.96, individuals hardcover; $20, individuals paperback. **Covers:** Graduate study facilities and 160 programs in the environmental sciences in the U.S. **Entries Include:** Facility name, address, phone, program name, profile, Number of students and faculty in the program, requirements for master's and doctoral degrees, faculty/advisee ratio, e-mail contact and Web site address, special program features, auxiliary services.

7047 ■ *Recycling in America*
Pub: ABC-CLIO
Contact: Debra Kimball Strong, Author
Released: Latest edition 2nd, November 1997. **Publication Includes:** Lists of private, state, and federal agencies and organizations, and online sources. Principal content of publication is a history of recycling; brief biographical section; facts on recycled materials; and laws and regulations.

REFERENCE WORKS

7048 ■ "Burner Handles Everything From 2 to B100" in *Indoor Comfort Marketing* (Vol. 70, May 2011, No. 5, pp. 24)
Pub: Industry Publications Inc.
Description: A new oil burner being offered by AMERIgreen Energy is profiled.

7049 ■ "21st Century Filling Station" in *Austin Business JournalInc.* (Vol. 29, December 11, 2009, No. 40, pp. 1)
Pub: American City Business Journals
Ed: Jacob Dirr. **Description:** Clean Energy Fuels Corporation announced plans for the construction of a $1 million, 17,000 square foot compressed natural gas fueling station at or near the Austin-Bergstrom International Airport (ABIA). Clean Energy Fuels hopes to encourage cab and shuttle companies in the ABIA to switch from gasoline to natural gas.

7050 ■ "$40M Fund Created for Big Energy Project" in *Austin Business JournalInc.* (Vol. 29, November 27, 2009, No. 38, pp. 1)
Pub: American City Business Journals
Ed: Christopher Calnan. **Description:** A group of Texas businessmen, called Republic Power Partners LP, is planning to raise $40 million in order to launch an alternative energy project. The 6,000-megawatt initiative would generate solar, biomass and wind power in West Texas and could cost as much as $10 billion.

7051 ■ "2010: Important Year Ahead for Waterfront" in *Bellingham Business Journal* (Vol. March 2010, pp. 2)
Pub: Sound Publishing Inc.
Ed: Isaac Bonnell. **Description:** A tentative timeline has been established for the environmental impact statement (EIS) slated for completion in May 2010. The plan for the Waterfront District includes detailed economic and architectural analysis of the feasibility of reusing remaining structures and retaining some industrial icons.

7052 ■ "2011 FinOvation Awards" in *Farm Industry News* (January 19, 2011)
Pub: Penton Business Media Inc.
Ed: Jodie Wehrspann. **Description:** The 2011 FinOvation Award winners are announced, covering new products that growers need for corn and soybean crops. Winners range from small turbines and a fuel-efficient pickup to a Class 10 combine and drought-tolerant hybrids.

7053 ■ "2011 a Record Year for New Wind Energy Installations in Canada" in *CNW Group* (September 26, 2011)
Pub: CNW Group
Description: Canada reports a record for new wind energy projects in 2011 with about 1,338 MW of newly installed wind energy capacity expected to come on line, compared to 690 MW installed in 2010. Statistical data included.

7054 ■ "2011 U.S. Smart Grid – Saving Energy/Saving Money" in *Ecology,Environment & Conservation Business* (October 8, 2011, pp. 3)
Pub: HighBeam Research
Description: Highlights of the '2011 U.S. Smart Grid –Saving Energy/Saving Money Customers' Prospective Demand-Response assesses residential energy consumers' willingness to decrease their power consumption in order to mitigate power issues. Statistical details included.

7055 ■ "The ABCs of a Good Show" in *Playthings* (Vol. 106, October 1, 2008, No. 9, pp. 18)
Pub: Reed Business Information
Ed: Karyn M. Peterson. **Description:** ABC Kids Expo 2008 made a strong showing with products for babies, kids and new/expecting parents. The new Naturally Kids section promoting eco-friendly products was the highlight of the show.

7056 ■ "Acing the Test" in *Contractor* (Vol. 57, January 2010, No. 1, pp. 32)
Pub: Penton Media, Inc.
Ed: Robert P. Mader. **Description:** A ward winning mechanical system retrofitting of a middle school in Ohio is discussed. The school now operates at 37,800 Btu/sq. ft and reduced a significant amount of pollutants from being emitted into the environment.

7057 ■ "Actiontec and Verizon Team Up for a Smarter Home" in *Ecology,Environment & Conservation Business* (November 5, 2011, pp. 3)
Pub: HighBeam Research
Description: Verizon is implementing Actiontec Electronics' SG200 Service Gateway as a basic component of its Home Monitoring and Control service. This new smart home service allows customers to remotely check their homes, control locks and appliances, view home-energy use and more using a smartphone, PC, or FiOS TV.

7058 ■ "Adventures at Hydronicahh" in *Contractor* (Vol. 56, October 2009, No. 10, pp. 42)
Pub: Penton Media, Inc.
Ed: Mark Eatherton. **Description:** Design and installation of a solar thermal system for a hydronic heating project is described. This portion has two 32-square feet of flat plate glazed solar collectors that are tied to a 120-gallon reverse indirect DHW heater.

7059 ■ "AF Expands in New Green Building in Gothenburg" in *Ecology,Environment & Conservation Business* (September 24, 2011, pp. 2)
Pub: HighBeam Research
Description: AF signed a ten-year tenancy contract with Skanska for the premises of its new green building in Gothenburg, Sweden. AF offers qualified services and solutions for industrial processes, infrastructure projects and the development of products and IT systems.

7060 ■ "Agricultural Community Implements Green Technologies, Building Team" in *Contractor* (Vol. 56, September 2009, No. 9, pp. 5)
Pub: Penton Media, Inc.
Ed: Candace Ruolo. **Description:** John DeWald and Associates has initiated a residential development project which uses green technologies in Illinois. The community features a community center, organic farm and recreational trails. Comments from executives are also provided.

7061 ■ "Ahead of the Pack" in *Small Business Opportunities* (Fall 2010)
Pub: Harris Publications Inc.
Description: Profile of an organic fast-food business that is carving out a niche that is gaining favor. Elevation Burger is a unique concept offering healthier burgers in sustainable buildings.

7062 ■ "Allowing Ethanol Tax Incentive to Expire Would Risk Jobs, RFAas Dinneen Says" in *Farm Industry News* (November 3, 2010)
Pub: Penton Business Media Inc.
Description: Jobs would be at risk if the ethanol tax incentive expires.

7063 ■ "Alstom Launches te ECO 122 – 2.7MW Wind Turbine for Low Wind Sites" in *CNW Group* (September 28, 2011)
Pub: CNW Group
Description: Alstom is launching its new ECO 122, a 2.7MW onshore wind turbine that combines high power and high capacity factor (1) to boost energy yield in low wind regions around the world. The ECO 122 will produce about 25 percent increased wind farm yield that current turbines and fewer turbines would be installed in areas.

7064 ■ "Alternative Energy Calls for Alternative Marketing" in *Indoor Comfort Marketing* (Vol. 70, June 2011, No. 6, pp. 8)
Pub: Industry Publications Inc.
Ed: Richard Rutigliano. **Description:** Advice for marketing solar energy products and services is given.

7065 ■ "Alternative Energy is a Major Topic at Agritechnica 2011" in *Farm Industry News* (November 16, 2011)
Pub: Penton Business Media Inc.
Ed: Mark Moore. **Description:** Sustainable agricultural systems were a hot topic at this year's Agritechnia 2011, held in Germany. Germany is a leader in the development of on-farm biogas systems.

7066 ■ "American Chemistry Council Launches Flagship Blog" in *Ecology,Environment & Conservation Business* (October 29, 2011, pp. 5)
Pub: HighBeam Research
Description: American Chemistry Council (ACC) launched its blog, American Chemistry Matters, where interactive space allows bloggers to respond to news coverage and to discuss policy issues and their impact on innovation, competitiveness, job creation and safety.

7067 ■ "ANATURALCONCEPT" in *Crain's Cleveland Business* (Vol. 30, June 22, 2009, No. 24, pp. 1)
Pub: Crain Communications, Inc.
Ed: Dan Shingler. **Description:** Cleveland-based Biomimicry Institute, led by Cleveland's Entrepreneurs for Sustainability and the Cuyahoga County Planning Commission, are using biomimicry to incorporate eco-friendliness with industry. Biomimicry studies nature's best ideas then imitates these designs and processes to solve human problems.

7068 ■ "Answers About Commercial Wind Farms Could Come from Downstate" in *Erie Times-News* (September 27, 2011)
Pub: Erie Times-News
Ed: Valerie Myers. **Description:** Texas-based Pioneer Green Energy is measuring wind and leasing land in North East Township, Pennsylvania. The firm plans to build a 7,000-acre wind farm along wine-country ridges. About 70 turbines would harness wind in order to generate electricity that would be sold into the eastern power grid.

7069 ■ "Aquarium's Solar Demonstration Project Exceeds Expectations" in *Contractor* (Vol. 57, February 2010, No. 2, pp. 1)
Pub: Penton Media, Inc.
Ed: Candace Roulo. **Description:** Seattle Aquarium cafe installed flat-plate solar collectors to preheat water and data has shown that the system has allowed them to off-set almost double their expected consumption of natural gas. It is estimated that rthe solar panels will shrink the aquarium's carbon footprint by 2.5 tons of carbon dioxide each year.

7070 ■ "Are You Looking for an Environmentally Friendly Dry Cleaner?" in *Inc.* (Vol. 30, December 2008, No. 12, pp. 34)
Pub: Mansueto Ventures LLC
Ed: Shivani Vora. **Description:** Greenopia rates the greenness of 52 various kinds of businesses, including restaurants, nail salons, dry cleaners, and clothing stores. The guidebooks are sold through various retailers including Barnes & Noble and Amazon.com.

7071 ■ "Areva Diversifies Further Into Wind" in *Wall Street Journal Eastern Edition* (November 29, 2011, pp. B7)
Pub: Dow Jones & Company Inc.
Ed: Max Colchester, Noemie Bisserbe. **Description:** French engineering company Areva SA is diversifying and moving away from nuclear energy projects. One sign of that is its recent discussion to construct 120 wind turbines to be located at two German wind farms. Such a deal, if signed, would be worth about US$1.59 billion.

7072 ■ "Art Institute of Chicago Goes Green" in *Contractor* (Vol. 56, July 2009, No. 7, pp. 1)
Pub: Penton Media, Inc.
Ed: Candace Roulo. **Description:** Art Institute of Chicago's Modern Wing museum addition will receive a certification that makes them one of the most environmentally sound museum expansions in the U.S. A modified variable-air-volume system is being used to meet temperature and humidity requirements in the building and it also has a double curtain wall to capture summer heat.

7073 ■ "Attorney Covers Climate in Copenhagen" in *Houston Business Journal* (Vol. 40, December 25, 2009, No. 33, pp. 1)
Pub: American City Business Journals
Ed: Ford Gunter. **Description:** Houston environmental attorney Richard Faulk talks to the United Nations Climate Change Conference in Copenhagen, Denmark. Faulk believes the conference failed due to political differences between countries like US and China. Faulk believed the discussion of developed and developing countries on verification and limits on carbon emissions is something good that came from the conference.

7074 ■ "Austin to Buy $1.1B of Wind Power from Two" in *Austin Business Journal* (Vol. 31, August 19, 2011, No. 24, pp. A1)
Pub: American City Business Journals Inc.
Ed: Vicky Garza. **Description:** Austin City Council is set to approve contracts to purchase wind energy from Duke Energy Corporation and MAP Royalty Inc. The city will get 200MW from Duke and 91MW from MAP and the total contract is estimated to be worth $1.1 million.

7075 ■ "Austin Energy May Build $2.3B Biomass Plant" in *Austin Business JournalInc.* (Vol. 28, July 25, 2008, No. 19, pp. A1)
Pub: American City Business Journals
Ed: Kate Harrington. **Description:** An approval from the Austin City Council is being sought by Austin Energy for a 20-year supply contract with Nacogdoches Power LLC to build a $2.3 billion biomass plant in East Texas. The 100-megawatt biomass plant, which is to run on waste wood, will have Austin Energy as its sole buyer.

7076 ■ "Award Win Highlights Slingsby's Green Credentials" in *Ecology,Environment & Conservation Business* (August 20, 2011, pp. 3)
Pub: HighBeam Research
Description: Slingsby, an industrial and commercial equipment supplier, was joint winner with Hallmark Cards of the Baildon Business in the Community's Yorkshire and Humber Long Term Environmental Improvement Award. The firm cites its commitment to reducing environmental impact.

7077 ■ "Babynut.com to Shut Down" in *Bellingham Business Journal* (Vol. February 2010, pp. 3)
Pub: Sound Publishing Inc.
Description: Saralee Sky and Jerry Kilgore, owners of Babynut.com will close their online store. The site offered a free online and email newsletter to help mothers through pregnancy and the first three years of their child's life. Products being sold at clearance prices include organic and natural maternity and nursing clothing, baby and toddler clothes, books on pregnancy, and more.

7078 ■ "Be Wary of Dual-Flush Conversion Kits" in *Contractor* (Vol. 56, September 2009, No. 9, pp. 66)
Pub: Penton Media, Inc.
Ed: John Koeller; Bill Gauley. **Description:** Recommendation of untested dual-flush conversion devices for tank-type toilets in the United States have been questioned. The products are being advertised as

having the ability to convert single-flush to a dual-flush toilet. No evidence of water conservation from using such devices has been recorded.

7079 ■ "BETC Backers Plot Future" in *Business Journal Portland* (Vol. 27, December 10, 2010, No. 41, pp. 1)
Pub: Portland Business Journal
Ed: Erik Siemers. **Description:** A coalition of clean energy groups and industrial manufacturers have spearheaded a campaign aimed at persuading Oregon legislators that the state's Business Energy Tax Credit (BETC) is vital in job creation. Oregon's BETC grants tax credits for 50 percent of an eligible renewable or clean energy project's cost. However, some legislators propose BETC's abolition.

7080 ■ "Beware of E15" in *Rental Product News* (Vol. 33, October 2011)
Pub: Cygnus Business Media
Ed: Curt Bennink. **Description:** Environmental Protection Agency (EPA) set a new regulation that grants partial waivers to allow gasoline containing up to 15 percent ethanol (E15) to be introduced into commerce for use in model year 2001 and newer light-duty motor vehicles, subject to certain conditions.

7081 ■ "Big Energy Deals Power OptiSolar's Local Growth" in *Sacramento Business Journal* (Vol. 25, August 22, 2008, No. 25, pp. 1)
Pub: American City Business Journals, Inc.
Ed: Celia Lamb. **Description:** Solar energy projects are driving Sacramento, California-based OptiSolar's growth. The company is set to begin construction of its first photovoltaic project in Ontario. It also plans to build the world largest photovoltaic project in San Luis Obispo County.

7082 ■ "Big Energy Ideas for Our Times" in *Canadian Business* (Vol. 83, August 17, 2010, No. 13-14, pp. 49)
Pub: Rogers Media Ltd.
Description: Five ideas Canada must consider in the production of energy are explored. These ideas are run-off-river hydroelectric projects, the tapping of natural gas inside shale formation, the water's role in creating energy, the development of a smart grid, and the reduction of energy consumption.

7083 ■ "Bigger is Definitely Not Better When It Comes to Cooling" in *Indoor Comfort Marketing* (Vol. 70, May 2011, No. 5, pp. 49)
Pub: Industry Publications Inc.
Ed: Eugene Silberstein. **Description:** Efficiency is more important when installing air conditioning equipment over size of the unit. Details are provided.

7084 ■ "Biodiesel Poised to Regain Growth" in *Farm Industry News* (January 21, 2011)
Pub: Penton Business Media Inc.
Description: According to Gary Haer, vice president of sales and marketing for Renewable Energy Group, the biodiesel industry is positioned to regain growth in 2011 with the reinstatement of the biodiesel blendersa tax credt of $1 per gallon.

7085 ■ "Bioheat – Alternative for Fueling Equipment" in *Indoor Comfort Marketing* (Vol. 70, May 2011, No. 5, pp. 14)
Pub: Industry Publications Inc.
Ed: Gary Hess. **Description:** Profile of Worley and Obetz, supplier of biofuels used as an alternative for fueling industry equipment.

7086 ■ "Blackwater is LEED Golden for Port of Portland Building" in *Contractor* (Vol. 56, October 2009, No. 10, pp. 3)
Pub: Penton Media, Inc.
Ed: Robert P. Mader. **Description:** Worrel Water Technologies' Tidal Wetlands Living Machine recycles blackwater from the toilets and sends it right back to flush the toilets. The Technology is being installed in the new headquarters of the Port of Portland which aims to get awarded a gold certificate from the Leadership in Energy and Environmental Design.

7087 ■ "Brown At Center of Local CleanTech Lobbying Efforts" in *Boston Business Journal* (Vol. 30, October 15, 2010, No. 36, pp. 1)
Pub: Boston Business Journal
Ed: Kyle Alspach. **Description:** U.S. Senator Scott Brown has been active in lobbying for energy reform in Massachusetts. Brown has been meeting with business groups seeking the reforms.

7088 ■ "Burning Issues: Four of Today's Hottest Energy Topics" in *Canadian Business* (Vol. 83, August 17, 2010, No. 13-14, pp. 45)
Pub: Rogers Media Ltd.
Description: A look at four issues dominating Canada's energy industry is presented. These issues are lack of transmission capacity and difficulty in transferring power across provincial boundaries, the management of intermittency of renewable generation, techniques that would clean up the Alberta's oil sands, and the impending massive use of electric cars in North America.

7089 ■ "The Business of Activism" in *Entrepreneur* (Vol. 37, September 2009, No. 9, pp. 43)
Pub: Entrepreneur Media, Inc.
Ed: Mary Catherine O'Connor. **Description:** San Francisco, California-based business incubator Virgance has been promoting sustainable projects by partnering with businesses. The company has launched campaigns which include organizing homeowners in negotiating with solar installers. The company is also planning to expand its workforce.

7090 ■ "Caber Engineering Helps to Reduce Canada's Carbon Footprint" in *Ecology,Environment & Conservation Business* (July 16, 2011, pp. 7)
Pub: HighBeam Research
Description: Calgary-based Caber Engineering Inc. will assist in the engineering design of the Alberta Carbon Trunk Line (ACTL). The ACTL is Alberta's first sizable commercial carbon capture and storage project focusing on the reduction of environmental impacts while being economically beneficial.

7091 ■ "Campaign Not Stirred by Wind Issue in Roanoke County" in *Roanoke Times* (September 18, 2011)
Pub: Roanoke Times
Ed: Katelyn Polantz. **Description:** Wind energy has brought citizens of the Roanoke area into activism this year. Comments from citizen on both sides of the issue are provided.

7092 ■ "Canada's Clean Energy Advantages Offer a Bright Future" in *Canadian Business* (Vol. 83, August 17, 2010, No. 13-14, pp. 38)
Pub: Rogers Media Ltd.
Ed: Don McKinnon. **Description:** Canada has clean energy advantages in the greenhouse gas emission-free CANada Deuterium Uranium reactor technology and carbon neutral biomass fuels that were continuously ignored by policy makers. Both are proven to significantly reduce emissions while providing reliable, affordable and secure electricity.

7093 ■ "Canada's Largest Bakery Officially Opened Today" in *Ecology,Environment & Conservation Business* (October 15, 2011, pp. 7)
Pub: HighBeam Research
Description: Maple Leaf Foods opened Canada's largest commercial bakery in Hamilton, Ontario. The firm's 385,000 square foot Trillium bakery benefits from efficient design flow and best-in-class technologies.

7094 ■ "Canadian Hydronics Businesses Promote 'Beautiful Heat'" in *Indoor Comfort Marketing* (Vol. 70, September 2011, No. 9, pp. 20)
Pub: Industry Publications Inc.
Description: Canadian hydronics companies are promoting their systems as beautiful heat. Hydronics is the use of water as the heat-transfer medium in heating and cooling system.

7095 ■ "Canadian Wind Farm Sued Due to Negative Health Effects" in *PC Magazine Online* (September 22, 2011)
Pub: PC Magazine
Description: Suncor Energy is being sued by a family in Ontario, Canada. The family claims that Suncor's wind turbines have created health problems for them, ranging from vertigo and sleep disturbance to depression and suicidal thoughts. The family's home is over 1,000 meters from the eight wind turbines, and according to Ontario officials, wind turbines must be a minimum of 550 meters from existing homes.

7096 ■ "Candidates Differ On State's Green Streak" in *Business Journal Portland* (Vol. 27, October 22, 2010, No. 34, pp. 1)
Pub: Portland Business Journal
Ed: Andy Giegerich. **Description:** The views of Oregon gubernatorial candidates Chris Dudley and John Kitzhaber on the state's economy and on environmental policies are presented. Both Dudley, who is a Republican, and his Democratic challenger believe that biomass could help drive the state's economy. Both candidates also pledged changes in Oregon's business energy tax credit (BETC) program.

7097 ■ "CanWEA Unveils WindVision for BC: 5,250 MW of Wind Energy by 2025" in *CNW Group* (October 4, 2011)
Pub: CNW Group
Description: Wind industry leaders are asking British Columbia, Canada policy makers to created conditions to further develop and integrate wind energy in accordance with greenhouse gas emission targets and projected economic growth. Statistical data included.

7098 ■ "The Carbon Equation" in *Canadian Business* (Vol. 81, October 27, 2008, No. 18, pp. 109)
Pub: Rogers Media Ltd.
Ed: Jack M. Mintz. **Description:** Economic and environmental impacts of the likely rejection of a carbon tax for the cap-and-trade system in Canada are discussed. The Conservative Party is expected tow in the 2008 elections and would likely pursue the cap-and-trade system.

7099 ■ "Carbon Trading: Current Schemes and Future Developments" in *Energy Policy* (Vol. 39, October 2011, No. 10, pp. 6040-6054)
Pub: Reed Elsevier Reference Publishing
Ed: Slobodan Perdan, Adisa Azapagic. **Description:** Current and future developments regarding carbon trading is highlighted.

7100 ■ "Case IH Announces Strategy to Meet 2014 Clean Air Standards" in *Farm Industry News* (September 15, 2011)
Pub: Penton Business Media Inc.
Ed: Jodie Wehrspann. **Description:** Case IH will meet EPA's stringent engine emissions limits imposed in 2014, called Tier 4. The limits call for a 90 percent reduction in particulate matter and nitrogen oxides (NOx) over the Tier 3 requirements from a few years ago.

7101 ■ "Cash for Appliances Targets HVAC Products, Water Heaters" in *Contractor* (Vol. 56, October 2009, No. 10, pp. 1)
Pub: Penton Media, Inc.
Ed: Candace Roulo. **Description:** States and territories would need to submit a full application that specifies their implementation plans if they are interested in joining the Cash for Appliances program funded by the American Recovery and Reinvestment Act. The Department of Energy urges states to focus on heating and cooling equipment, appliances and water heaters since these offer the greatest energy savings potential.

7102 ■ "Catch the Wind Announces Filing of Injunction Against Air Data Systems LLC and Philip Rogers" in *CNW Group* (September 30, 2011)
Pub: CNW Group
Description: Catch the Wind, providers of laser-based wind sensor products and technology, filed an injunction against Optical Air Data Systems (OADS)

LLC and its former President and CEO Philip L. Rogers. The complaint seeks to have OADS and Rogers return tangible and intangible property owned by Catch the Wind, which the firm believes to be critical to the operations of their business.

7103 ■ "Catch the Wind to Hold Investor Update Conference Call on October 18, 2011" in *CNW Group* (October 4, 2011)
Pub: CNW Group
Description: Catch the Wind Ltd., providers of laser-based wind sensor products and technology, held a conference call for analysts and institutional investors. The high-growth technology firm is headquartered in Manassas, Virginia.

7104 ■ "CE2 Carbon Capital and Dogwood Carbon Solutions Partner With Missouri Landowners" in *Nanotechnolgy Business Journal* (Jan. 25, 2010)
Pub: Investment Weekly News
Description: Dogwood Carbon Solutions, a developer of agriculture and forestry based conservation projects, has partnered with CE2 Carbon Capital, one of the largest investors and owners of U.S. carbon commodities and carbon emissions reduction projects, to develop high-quality carbon offsets from over 30,000 acres of privately-owned non-industrial forest in the Ozark mountain region of Arkansas and Missouri.

7105 ■ "CEO Forecast" in *Hispanic Business* (January-February 2009, pp. 34, 36)
Pub: Hispanic Business
Ed: Jessica Haro, Richard Kaplan. **Description:** As economic uncertainty fogs the future, executives turn to government contracts in order to boost business. Revenue sources, health care challenges, environmental consulting and remediation services, as well as technological strides are discussed.

7106 ■ "Changing Fuel Compositions: What It Means To You and Your Business" in *Indoor Comfort Marketing* (Vol. 70, June 2011, No. 6, pp. 30)
Pub: Industry Publications Inc.
Ed: Paul Nazzaro. **Description:** Biofuels are outlined and the way it is changing the HVAC/R industry are discussed.

7107 ■ "Charged Up for Sales" in *Charlotte Business Journal* (Vol. 25, October 15, 2010, No. 30, pp. 1)
Pub: Charlotte Business Journal
Ed: Susan Stabley. **Description:** Li-Ion Motors Corporation is set to expand its production lines of electric cars in Sacramento, California. The plan is seen to create up to 600 jobs. The company's total investment is seen to reach $500 million.

7108 ■ "China Wind Power Generates Stronger First Quarter Results" in *Marketwire Canada* (September 28, 2011)
Pub: MarketWire Canada
Description: China Wind Power International Corporation, an independent wind power producer in China reported strong growth for the first quarter 2011. Details of the company and its future developments are highlighted.

7109 ■ "China's Transition to Green Energy Systems" in *Energy Policy* (Vol. 39, October 2011, No. 10, pp. 5909-5919)
Pub: Reed Elsevier Reference Publishing
Ed: Wei Li, Guojun Song, Melanie Beresford, Ben Ma. **Description:** The economics of home solar water heaters and their growing popularity in Dezhous City, China is discussed.

7110 ■ "Chinese Solar Panel Manufacturer Scopes Out Austin" in *Austin Business JournalInc.* (Vol. 29, October 30, 2009, No. 34, pp. 1)
Pub: American City Business Journals
Ed: Jacob Dirr. **Description:** China's Yingli Green Energy Holding Company Ltd. is looking for a site in order to construct a $20 million photovoltaic panel plant. Both Austin and San Antonio are vying to house the manufacturing hub. The project could create about 300 jobs and give Austin a chance to become a player in the solar energy market. Other solar companies are also considering Central Texas as an option to set up shop.

7111 ■ "City's New Energy Audits to Spawn 'Fantastic' Market" in *Austin Business JournalInc.* (Vol. 28, November 14, 2008, No. 35, pp. 1)
Pub: American City Business Journals
Ed: Jean Kwon. **Description:** A new law requiring older homes to undergo energy use audits is seen to provide new business for some companies in the Austin, Texas area. The new law is seen to create a new industry of performance testers. Details of the new ordinance are also given.

7112 ■ "Clean-Tech Focus Sparks Growth" in *Philadelphia Business Journal* (Vol. 28, January 15, 2010, No. 48, pp. 1)
Pub: American City Business Journals
Ed: Peter Key. **Description:** Keystone Redevelopment Group and economic development organization Ben Franklin Technology Partners of Southeastern Pennsylvania have partnered in supporting the growth of new alternative energy and clean technology companies. Keystone has also been developing the Bridge Business Center.

7113 ■ "Clean Wind Energy Tower Transitions from R&D Stage Company" in *Professional Services Close-Up* (September 30, 2011)
Pub: Close-Up Media
Description: Clean Wind Energy designed and is developing large downdraft towers that use benevolent, non-toxic natural elements to generate electricity and clean water. The firm is closing its internally staffed engineering office in Warrenton, Virginia and transitioning a development team to oversee and coordinate industry consultants and advisors to construct their first dual renewable energy tower.

7114 ■ "Climate Law Could Dig into our Coal-Dusted Pockets" in *Business Courier* (Vol. 26, November 20, 2009, No. 30, pp. 1)
Pub: American City Business Journals, Inc.
Ed: Lucy May. **Description:** Passage of federal climate legislation into law is set to increase household cost for Greater Cincinnati, according to the calculation by the Brookings Institute. The increase for residents of the area will amount to $244 in 2020 and the city was ranked the sixth-highest rate in the nation, behind Indianapolis.

7115 ■ "Cloudy Skies" in *Canadian Business* (Vol. 81, October 27, 2008, No. 18, pp. 101)
Pub: Rogers Media Ltd.
Ed: Andrew Wahl. **Description:** Canada's federal government is expected to implement its regulations on greenhouse-gas emissions by January 1, 2010, but companies are worried because the plan took so long and some details are yet to be revealed. Corporate Canada wants a firm, long-range plan similar to the European Union Emissions Trading Scheme in dealing with greenhouse-gas emissions.

7116 ■ "CO2 Emissions Embodied in China-US Trade" in *Energy Policy* (Vol. 39, October 2011, No. 10, pp. 5980-5987)
Pub: Reed Elsevier Reference Publishing
Ed: Huibin Du, Guozhu Mao, Alexander M. Smith, Xuxu Wang, Yuan Wang, Jianghong Guo. **Description:** Input and output analysis based on the energy per dollar ratio for carbon dioxide emissions involved in China-United States trade is outlined.

7117 ■ "Combo Dorm-Field House Built to Attain LEED Gold" in *Contractor* (Vol. 56, September 2009, No. 9, pp. 1)
Pub: Penton Media, Inc.
Ed: Candace Roulo; Robert P. Mader. **Description:** North Central College in Illinois has built a new dormitory that is expected to attain Leadership in Energy and Environmental Design Gold certification from the United States Green Building Council. The structure features a geo-exchange heat pump system and radiant floor heat. A description of the facility is also provided.

7118 ■ "Coming Soon: Electric Tractors" in *Farm Industry News* (November 21, 2011)
Pub: Penton Business Media Inc.
Ed: Jodie Wehrspann. **Description:** The agricultural industry is taking another look at electric farm vehicles. John Deere Product Engineering Center said that farmers can expect to see more diesel-electric systems in farm tractors, sprayers, and implements.

7119 ■ "Community Food Co-op Creates Revolving Loan Program for Local Farmers" in *Bellingham Business Journal* (Vol. February 2010, pp. 3)
Pub: Sound Publishing Inc.
Description: Community Food Co-op's Farm Fund received a $12,000 matching grant from the Sustainable Whatcom Fund of the Whatcom Community Foundation. The Farm Fund will create a new revolving loan program for local farmers committed to using sustainable practices.

7120 ■ *Consultants and Consulting Organizations Directory*
Pub: Gale
Released: Annual, New edition expected 37th; February, 2012. **Price:** $1,392, individuals. **Covers:** Over 26,000 firms, individuals, and organizations active in consulting. **Entries Include:** Individual or organization name, address, phone, fax, e-mail, URL, specialties, founding date, branch offices, names and titles of key personnel, number of employees, financial data, publications, seminars and workshops. **Arrangement:** By broad subject categories. **Indexes:** Subject, geographical, organization name.

7121 ■ "Consumers Like Green, But Not Mandates" in *Business Journal-Milwaukee* (Vol. 28, December 10, 2010, No. 10, pp. A1)
Pub: Milwaukee Business Journal
Ed: Sean Ryan. **Description:** Milwaukee, Wisconsin consumers are willing to spend more on green energy, a survey has revealed. Respondents also said they will pay more for efficient cars and appliances. Support for public incentives for homeowners and businesses that reduce energy use has also increased.

7122 ■ "Convert New Customers to Long Term Accounts" in *Indoor Comfort Marketing* (Vol. 70, February 2011, No. 2, pp. 22)
Pub: Industry Publications Inc.
Description: Marketing to new customers and suggestions for retaining them is covered.

7123 ■ "Corporate Responsibility" in *Professional Services Close-Up* (July 2, 2010)
Pub: Close-Up Media
Description: List of firms awarded the inaugural Best Corporate Citizens in Government Contracting by the Corporate Responsibility Magazine is presented. The list is based on the methodology of the Magazine's Best Corporate Citizen's List, with 324 data points of publicly-available information in seven categories which include: environment, climate change, human rights, philanthropy, employee relations, financial performance, and governance.

7124 ■ "The Cost of Energy" in *Canadian Business* (Vol. 83, August 17, 2010, No. 13-14, pp. 39)
Pub: Rogers Media Ltd.
Description: Canada's cheap energy has bred complacency among Canadian companies and most have not strived to conserve or develop other forms of energy. However, even costs of traditional energy such as oil are set to rise, fueled by recent events in Saudi Arabia and the Gulf of Mexico.

7125 ■ "Could This Be Your Next Office Building?" in *Austin Business Journal* (Vol. 31, May 13, 2011, No. 10, pp. A1)
Pub: American City Business Journals Inc.
Ed: Cody Lyon. **Description:** Falcon Containers moved to a 51-acre site in Far East Austin, Texas and started construction of a 2,500-square-foot headquarters made from eight 40-foot shipping containers. Falcon's CEO Stephen Shang plans to

use his headquarters building as a showroom to attract upscale, urban hipsters. Insights on the construction's environmental and social impact are shared.

7126 ■ "Council Power Shift Could Benefit Business" in *Business Courier* (Vol. 26, November 6, 2009, No. 28, pp. 1)
Pub: American City Business Journals, Inc.
Ed: Lucy May. **Description:** A majority in the Cincinnati City Council, which is comprised of reelected members, might be created by Charlie Winburn's impending return to the council. It would be empowered to decide on public safety, stock options taxes, and environmental justice. How the presumed majority would affect the city's economic progress is discussed.

7127 ■ "Crude Awakening" in *Canadian Business* (Vol. 81, October 27, 2008, No. 18, pp. 14)
Pub: Rogers Media Ltd.
Ed: Jeff Sanford. **Description:** Jim Grays believes that a global liquid fuels crisis is coming and hopes the expected transition from oil dependence will be smooth. Charles Maxwell, on the other hand, predicts that a new world economy will arrive in three waves. Views of both experts are examined.

7128 ■ "Customized Before Custom Was Cool" in *Green Industry Pro* (July 2011)
Pub: Cygnus Business Media
Ed: Gregg Wartgow. **Description:** Profile of Turf Care Enterprises and owner Kevin Vogeler, who discusses his desire to use more natural programs using little or no chemicals in 1986. At that time, that sector represented 20 percent of his business, today it shares 80 percent.

7129 ■ "Cut Energy Waste" in *Inc.* (Vol. 31, January-February 2009, No. 1, pp. 42)
Pub: Mansueto Ventures LLC
Description: Carbon Control, Edison, and Saver software programs help companies cut carbon emissions by reducing the amount of energy consumed by computers while they are idle.

7130 ■ "David Robinson Column" in *Buffalo News* (October 2, 2011)
Pub: Buffalo News
Ed: David Robinson. **Description:** New York Power Authority ceased development of an offshore wind farm project. Wind farming in the waters of Lake Erie or Lake Ontario would be too costly. Details of the project are discussed.

7131 ■ "A Day Late and a Dollar Short" in *Indoor Comfort Marketing* (Vol. 70, March 2011, No. 3, pp. 30)
Pub: Industry Publications Inc.
Ed: Philip J. Baratz. **Description:** A discussion involving futures options and fuel oil prices is presented.

7132 ■ "Despite Economic Upheaval Generation Y is Still Feeling Green: RSA Canada Survey" in *CNW Group* (October 28, 2010)
Pub: CNW Group
Description: Canadian Generation Y individuals believe it is important for their company to be environmentally-friendly and one-third of those surveyed would quit their job if they found their employer was environmentally irresponsible, despite the economy.

7133 ■ "Detroit Hosts Conferences on Green Building, IT, Finance" in *Crain's Detroit Business* (Vol. 25, June 1, 2009, No. 22, pp. 9)
Pub: Crain Communications Inc. - Detroit
Ed: Tom Henderson. **Description:** Detroit will host three conferences in June 2009, one features green technology, one information technology and the third will gather black bankers and financial experts from across the nation.

7134 ■ "DeWind Delivering Turbines to Texas Wind Farm" in *Professional Services Close-Up* (September 25, 2011)
Pub: Close-Up Media
Description: DeWind Company has begun shipment of turbines to the 20 MW Frisco Wind Farm located in Hansford County, Texas. DeWind is a subsidiary of Daewoo Shipbuilding and Marine Engineering Company. Details of the project are discussed.

7135 ■ "DOE Proposes New Water Heater Efficiency Standards" in *Contractor* (Vol. 57, January 2010, No. 1, pp. 3)
Pub: Penton Media, Inc.
Ed: Robert P. Mader. **Description:** U.S. Department of Energy is proposing higher efficiency standards for gas and electric water heaters which will not take effect until 2015. The proposal calls for gas-fired storage water heaters less than 60 gallons to have an Energy Factor of 0.675 and those larger than 60 gallons to have an Energy Factor of 0.717.

7136 ■ "Dow Champions Innovative Energy Solutions for Auto Industry at NAIAS" in *Business of Global Warming* (January 25, 2010, pp. 7)
Pub: Investment Weekly News
Description: This year's North American International Auto Show in Detroit will host the "Electric Avenue" exhibit sponsored by the Dow Chemical Company. The display will showcase the latest in innovative energy solutions from Dow as well as electric vehicles and the technology supporting them. This marks the first time a non-automotive manufacturer is part of the main floor of the show.

7137 ■ "Earth Angels" in *Playthings* (Vol. 106, September 1, 2008, No. 8, pp. 10)
Pub: Reed Business Information
Ed: Karyn M. Peterson. **Description:** ImagiPlay toy company has partnered with Whole Foods Market to distribute the company's wooden playthings across the country. The company's Earth-friendly business model is outlined.

7138 ■ "East Coast Solar" in *Contractor* (Vol. 57, February 2010, No. 2, pp. 17)
Pub: Penton Media, Inc.
Ed: Dave Yates. **Description:** U.S. Department of Energy's Solar Decathlon lets 20 college student-led teams from around the world compete to design and build a solar-powered home. A mechanical contractor discusses his work as an advisor during the competition.

7139 ■ *Eco Barons: The New Heroes of Environmental Activism*
Pub: Ecco/HarperCollins
Ed: Edward Humes. **Released:** January 19, 2010. **Price:** $14.99. **Description:** Profiles of business leaders who have dedicated their lives to saving the planet from ecological devastation.

7140 ■ "Eco-Preneuring" in *Small Business Opportunities* (July 2008)
Pub: Entrepreneur Media Inc.
Ed: Mary C. Pearl. **Description:** Profile of Wildlife Trust, a rapidly growing global organization dedicated to innovative conservation science linking health and ecology. With partners in nearly twenty countries, Wildlife Trust draws on global strengths in order to respond to well-defined local needs. In the Dominican Republic, they are working with the community and local biologists in order to restore fishing and create jobs in the field of ecotourism.

7141 ■ "Eco Smart Home Will Showcase Green Technology" in *Contractor* (Vol. 56, September 2009, No. 9, pp. 3)
Pub: Penton Media, Inc.
Ed: Steve Spaulding. **Description:** Eco Smart World Wide is building the Eco Smart Demonstration House to promote the latest in sustainable, renewable and high-efficiency practices and products. The company will use insulated concrete forms in the construction of the building. Features and dimensions of the structure are also presented.

7142 ■ "EMC Greens Its Machines" in *Boston Business Journal* (Vol. 31, July 15, 2011, No. 25, pp. 3)
Pub: Boston Business Journal
Ed: Kyle Alspach. **Description:** Hopkinton, Massachusetts-based EMC Corporation has been pursuing a sustainability strategy even though it would not directly pay back money to the company or customers who use the products. EMC has been increasingly requiring sustainable practices from its suppliers and evaluating the full lifecycle impacts of its products.

7143 ■ "Energy Consulting Company to Expand" in *Austin Business JournalInc.* (Vol. 28, November 7, 2008, No. 34, pp. A1)
Pub: American City Business Journals
Ed: Kate Harrington. **Description:** CLEAResult Consulting Inc. is planning to increase its workforce and move its headquarters to a larger office. The company has posted 1,000 percent increase in revenues. The company's adoption of best practices and setting of benchmark goals are seen as the reason for its growth.

7144 ■ "Energy Efficiency Ordinance Softened" in *Austin Business JournalInc.* (Vol. 28, October 3, 2008, No. 29)
Pub: American City Business Journals
Ed: Jean Kwon. **Description:** City of Austin has eliminated mandatory energy efficiency upgrades to single-family housing as a condition for selling or renting homes or buildings. The new law proposes that an energy performance audit be conducted on single-family homes before being sold and the results of the audit disclosed to perspectives buyers.

7145 ■ "Energy Is Put to Good Use in Antarctica" in *Contractor* (Vol. 56, July 2009, No. 7, pp. 32)
Pub: Penton Media, Inc.
Ed: Carol Fey. **Description:** Recapturing waste heat is an important part of the heating system at the McMurdo Station in Antarctica. The radiators of generators are the heat source and this is supplemented by modular boilers when seasonal demands for heat increase. Waste heat is also used to make 55,000 gallons of fresh water a day.

7146 ■ *Environmental Guide to the Internet*
Pub: Government Institutes
Ed: Carol Briggs-Erickson, Editor. **Price:** $83, individuals. **Covers:** 1,200 resources covering the environment on the Internet, including organizations, products, and resources, including discussion groups, electronic journals, newsgroups, and discussion groups. **Entries Include:** Name, online address, description, e-mail address. **Arrangement:** Categories.

7147 ■ "EPA 'Finalizes' WaterSense for Homes" in *Contractor* (Vol. 57, January 2010, No. 1, pp. 70)
Pub: Penton Media, Inc.
Ed: Bob Mader. **Description:** U.S. Environmental Protection Agency released its "final" version of the WaterSense for Homes standard. The standard's provisions that affect plumbing contractors includes the specification that everything has to be leak tested and final service pressure cannot exceed 60 psi.

7148 ■ "EPA Grants E15 Waiver for 2001-2006 Vehicles" in *Farm Industry News* (January 21, 2011)
Pub: Penton Business Media Inc.
Description: U.S. Environmental Protection Agency waived a limitation on selling gasoline that contains more than 10 percent ethanol for model year 2001-2006 cars and light trucks, allowing fuel to contain up to 15 percent ethanol (E15) for these vehicles.

7149 ■ "ESolar Partners With Penglai on Landmark Solar Thermal Agreement for China" in *Business of Global Warming* (January 25, 2010, pp. 8)
Pub: Investment Weekly News
Description: Penglai Electric, a privately-owned Chinese electrical power equipment manufacturer, and eSolar, a global provider of cost-effective and

reliable solar power plants, announced a master licensing agreement in which eSolar will build at least 2 gigawatts of solar thermal power plants in China over the next 10 years.

7150 ■ "Everett Dowling" in *Hawaii Business* (Vol. 54, August 2008, No. 2, pp. 32)
Pub: Hawaii Business Publishing
Ed: Jason Ubay. **Description:** Real estate developer Everett Dowling, president of Dowling Company Inc., talks about the company's sustainable management and services. The company's office has been retrofitted to earn a Leadership in Energy and Environmental Design (LEED) certification. Dowling believes that real estate development can be part of the sustainable solution.

7151 ■ "Family Takes Wind Turbine Companies to Court Over Gag Clauses on Health Effects of Turbines" in *CNW Group* (September 12, 2011)
Pub: CNW Group
Description: Shawn and Trisha Drennan are concerned about the negative experiences other have had with wind turbines close to their homes, including adverse health effects. The couple's home will be approximately 650 meters from the Kingsbridge II wind farm project in Ontario, Canada.

7152 ■ "Federal Buildings to Achieve Zero-Net Energy by 2030" in *Contractor* (Vol. 56, December 2009, No. 12, pp. 5)
Pub: Penton Media, Inc.
Ed: Candace Roulo. **Description:** United States president Barack Obama has issued sustainable goals for federal buildings. Federal agencies are also required to increase energy efficiency, conserve water and support sustainable communities. Obama has also announced a $3.4 billion investment in a smart energy creed.

7153 ■ "Find Private Money for FutureGen Plant" in *Crain's Chicago Business* (Vol. 34, September 12, 2011, No. 37, pp. 18)
Pub: Crain Communications Inc.
Description: FutureGen is a clean-coal power plant being developed in Southern Illinois. The need for further funding is discussed.

7154 ■ "First Suzlon S97 Turbines Arrive in North America for Installation" in *PR Newswire* (September 28, 2011)
Pub: United Business Media
Description: Suzlon Energy Ltd., the world's fifth largest manufacturer of wind turbines, will install its first S97 turbine at the Amherst Wind Farm Project. These turbines will be installed on 90-meter hub height towers and at full capacity, will generate enough electricity to power over 10,000 Canadian homes.

7155 ■ *The Flaw of Averages: Why We Underestimate Risk in the Face of Uncertainty*
Pub: John Wiley & Sons, Inc.
Ed: Sam L. Savage. **Released:** June 3, 2009. **Price:** $22.95. **Description:** Personal and business plans are based on uncertainties on a daily basis. The common avoidable mistake individuals make in assessing risk in the face of uncertainty is defined. The explains why plans based on average assumptions are wrong, on average, in areas as diverse as finance, healthcare, accounting, the war on terror, and climate change.

7156 ■ "Florida's Bright Upside" in *Tampa Bay Business Journal* (Vol. 29, November 6, 2009, No. 46, pp. 1)
Pub: American City Business Journals
Ed: Michael Hinman. **Description:** Florida's Public Service Commission (PSC) decision on a power purchase agreement that could add 25 megawatts of solar energy on Tampa Electric Company's offerings is presented. The decision could support the growing market for suppliers and marketers of renewable energy such as Jabil Circuit Inc., which manufactures photovoltaic modules. Details of the agreement are discussed.

7157 ■ "Floyd County Considers Wind Farms" in *Roanoke Times* (September 19, 2011)
Pub: Roanoke Times
Ed: Jeff Sturgeon. **Description:** German firm, Nordex USA Inc. is proposing a $100 million, 30-50 megawatt wind farm atop Wills Ridge, Virginia within the next four years. This project is one of several large wind project considered in the Roanoke and New River valleys of Virginia.

7158 ■ "Flue Vaccines are Going Green" in *Canadian Business* (Vol. 83, September 14, 2010, No. 15, pp. 24)
Pub: Rogers Media Ltd.
Ed: Angelia Chapman. **Description:** Quebec-based Medicago has found a solution to the bottleneck in the production of influenza vaccines by using plant-based processes instead of egg-based systems. Medicago's US Department of Defense funded research has produced the technology that speeds up the production time for vaccines by almost two-thirds. Insights into Medicago's patented process are also given.

7159 ■ "For Giving Us a Way To Say Yes To Solar: Lynn Jurich and Edward Fenster" in *Inc.* (Volume 32, December 2010, No. 10, pp. 110)
Pub: Inc. Magazine
Description: Profile of entrepreneurs Lynn Jurich and Edward Fenster, cofounders of SunRun. The firm installs solar panels at little or no cost and homeowners sign 20-year contracts to buy power at a fixed price.

7160 ■ "For Putting Down Roots in Business: Amy Norquist: Greensulate, New York City" in *Inc.* (Volume 32, December 2010, No. 10, pp. 106)
Pub: Inc. Magazine
Ed: Christine Lagorio. **Description:** Profile of Amy Norquist who left her position at an environmental nonprofit organization to found Greensulate. Her firm insulates rooftops with lavender, native grasses and succulents called sedum in order to eliminate carbon from the atmosphere.

7161 ■ "Forum at UNCW to Explore Offshore Wind Farming" in *Star-News* (October 4, 2011)
Pub: Star-News
Ed: Kate Elizabeth Queram. **Description:** North Carolina is poised to profit from offshore wind farming, according to regional environmental experts. The Sierra Club, in conjunction with the University of North Carolina Wilmington and Oceana are hosting an offshore wind forum featuring five panelists, focusing on potential impacts on birds and sea life, tourism and cost, as well as other pertinent issues.

7162 ■ "Fossil Fuel, Renewable Fuel Shares Expected to Flip Flop" in *Farm Industry News* (April 29, 2011)
Pub: Penton Business Media Inc.
Description: Total energy use of fossil fuels is predicted to fall 5 percent by the year 2035, with renewable fuel picking it up.

7163 ■ "FSU's OGZEB Is Test Bed for Sustainable Technology" in *Contractor* (Vol. 56, October 2009, No. 10, pp. 1)
Pub: Penton Media, Inc.
Ed: Candace Roulo. **Description:** Florida State University has one of 14 off-grid zero emissions buildings (OGZEB) in the U.S. ; it was built to research sustainable and alternative energy systems. The building produces electricity from 30 photovoltaic panels and it also has three AET water heating solar panels on the roof.

7164 ■ "Fuel King: The Most Fuel-Efficient Tractor of the Decade is the John Deere 8295R" in *Farm Industry News* (November 10, 2011)
Pub: Penton Business Media Inc.
Description: Farm Industry News compiled a list of the most fuel-efficient tractors with help from the Nebraska Tractor Test Lab, with the John Deere 8295R PTO winner of the most fuel-efficient tractor of the decade.

7165 ■ "Fuel for Thought; Canadian Business Leaders on Energy Policy" in *Canadian Business* (Vol. 81, September 15, 2008, No. 14-15, pp. 12)
Pub: Rogers Media Ltd.
Ed: Joe Castaldo. **Description:** Most Canadian business leaders worry about the unreliability of the oil supply but feel that Canada is in a better position to benefit from the energy supply crisis than other countries. Many respondents also highlighted the need to invest in renewable energy sources.

7166 ■ "GE Milestone: 1,000th Wind Turbine Installed in Canada" in *CNW Group* (October 4, 2011)
Pub: CNW Group
Description: GE installed its 1,000th wind turbine in Canada at Cartier Wind Energy's Gros Morne project in the Gaspesie Region of Quebec, Canada. As Canada continues to expand its use of wind energy, GE plans to have over 1,100 wind turbines installed in the nation by the end of 2011.

7167 ■ "Germans Win Solar Decathlon - Again" in *Contractor* (Vol. 56, November 2009, No. 11, pp. 1)
Pub: Penton Media, Inc.
Ed: Robert P. Mader. **Description:** Students from Technische Universtat Darmstadt won the U.S. Department of Energy's Solar Decathlon by designing and building the most attractive and efficient solar-powered home. The winner's design produced a surplus of power even during three days of rain and photovoltaic panels covered nearly every exterior surface.

7168 ■ "Getting the Bioheat Word Out" in *Indoor Comfort Marketing* (Vol. 70, September 2011, No. 9, pp. 32)
Pub: Industry Publications Inc.
Description: Ways to market advanced liquid fuels to the public are outlined.

7169 ■ "Getting Going on Going Green" in *HRMagazine* (Vol. 53, August 2008, No. 8, pp. 8)
Pub: Society for Human Resource Management
Ed: Rita Zeidner. **Description:** Being eco-friendly can help recruit and retain workers. Resources to help firms create green initiatives are presented.

7170 ■ "Getting NORA reauthorized is high priority" in *Indoor Comfort Marketing* (Vol. 70, February 2011, No. 2, pp. 14)
Pub: Industry Publications Inc.
Description: The importance of reauthorizing the National Oilheat Research Alliance is stressed.

7171 ■ "The GHG Quandary: Whose Problem Is It Anyway?" in *Canadian Business* (Vol. 81, September 15, 2008, No. 14-15, pp. 72)
Pub: Rogers Media Ltd.
Ed: Matthew McClearn. **Description:** Nongovernmental organizations were able to revoke the permit for Imperial Oil Ltd's Kearl oilsands project on the grounds of its expected greenhouse gas emission but the court's ruling was rendered irrelevant by bureaucratic paper-shuffling shortly after. The idea of an environmental impact assessment as a guide to identify the consequences of a project is also discussed.

7172 ■ "The Global Environment Movement is Bjorn Again" in *Canadian Business* (Vol. 83, September 14, 2010, No. 15, pp. 11)
Pub: Rogers Media Ltd.
Ed: Steve Maich. **Description:** Danish academic Bjorn Lomborg is in favor of decisive action to combat climate change in his new book and was given front page treatment by a London newspaper. Environmentalist groups see this as a victory since Lomborg had not previously considered climate change an immediate issue.

7173 ■ "GM's Volt Woes Cast Shadow on E-Cars" in *Wall Street Journal Eastern Edition* (November 28, 2011, pp. B1)
Pub: Dow Jones & Company Inc.
Ed: Sharon Terlep. **Description:** The future of electric cars is darkened with the government investigation by the National Highway Traffic Safety Administration

into General Motor Company's Chevy Volt after two instances of the car's battery packs catching fire during crash tests conducted by the Agency.

7174 ■ "Go Green Or Go Home" in *Black Enterprise* (Vol. 41, August 2010, No. 1, pp. 53)
Pub: Earl G. Graves Publishing Co. Inc.
Ed: Tennille M. Robinson. **Description:** The green economy has become an essential part of every business, however, small business owners need to learn how to participate, including minority owned entrepreneurs.

7175 ■ "Going Green, Going Slowly" in *Playthings* (Vol. 106, September 1, 2008, No. 8, pp. 17)
Pub: Reed Business Information
Ed: Nancy Zwiers. **Description:** Sustainability and greener materials for both product and packaging in the toy industry has become important for protecting our environment. However, in a recent survey nearly 60 percent of responders stated environmental issues did not play a part in purchasing a toy or game for their children.

7176 ■ "Golden Valley, Fling Hills Plan LNG Plant" in *Alaska Business Monthly* (Vol. 27, October 2011, No. 10, pp. 9)
Pub: Alaska Business Publishing Company
Ed: Nancy Pounds. **Description:** Golden Valley Electric Association and Flint Hills Resources have partnered on a natural gas liquefaction facility on the North Slope. The deal will deliver gas at cost to GVEA and Flint Hills and Flint Hills will become more competitive and efficient by burning LNG instead of refined crude oil at the refinery.

7177 ■ *Good Green Guide for Small Businesses: How to Change the Way Your Business Works for the Better*
Pub: A & C Black
Ed: Impetus Consulting Ltd. Staff. **Released:** September 1, 2009. **Price:** $19.95. **Description:** Guide for small businesses to take an environmental audit of their company and shows how to minimize the impact of office essentials such as utilities, insulation, recycling and waste, electrical equipment, water systems, lighting options, food and drink, and office cleaning arrangements and products.

7178 ■ "Gov. Kasich to Put DOD On Short Leash" in *Business Courier* (Vol. 27, November 26, 2010, No. 30, pp. 1)
Pub: Business Courier
Ed: Dan Monk. **Description:** Ohio Governor-elect John Kasich proposed the privatization of the Ohio Department of Development in favor of a nonprofit corporation called JobsOhio. Kasich believes that the department has lost its focus by adding to its mission issues such as energy efficiency and tourism.

7179 ■ "Grainger Show Highlights Building Green, Economy" in *Contractor* (Vol. 57, February 2010, No. 2, pp. 3)
Pub: Penton Media, Inc.
Ed: Candace Roulo. **Description:** chief U.S. economist told attendees of the Grainger's 2010 Total MRO Solutions National Customer Show that the economic recovery would be subdued. Mechanical contractors who attended the event also learned about building sustainable, green products, and technologies, and economic and business challenges.

7180 ■ "Green Acre$ Tope 10 Green Biz To Start Right Now" in *Small Business Opportunities* (September 2010)
Pub: Harris Publications Inc.
Description: A list of the top ten green businesses to start in 2010 is provided.

7181 ■ "Green Acres" in *Hawaii Business* (Vol. 54, September 2008, No. 3, pp. 48)
Pub: Hawaii Business Publishing
Ed: Jan Tenbruggencate. **Description:** Bill Cowern's Hawaiian Mahogany is a forestry business that processes low-value trees to be sold as wood chips, which can be burned to create biodiesel. Cowern is planning to obtain certification to market carbon credits and is also working with Green Energy Hawaii for the permit of a biomass-fueled power plant. Other details about Cowern's business are discussed.

7182 ■ "Green and Clean" in *Retail Merchandiser* (Vol. 51, July-August 2011, No. 4, pp. 56)
Pub: Phoenix Media Corporation
Description: Green Valley Grocery partnered with Paragon Solutions consulting firm to make their stores environmentally green.

7183 ■ "'Green' Cleaner Buys Local Firm" in *Puget Sound Business Journal* (Vol. 29, December 19, 2008, No. 35, pp. 3)
Pub: American City Business Journals
Ed: Greg Lamm. **Description:** Washington-based Blue Sky Cleaners has purchased Four Seasons Cleaners. The green company also purchased Queen Anne store and Four Seasons' routes fro Snohomish County through Seattle.

7184 ■ *The Green Collar Economy: How One Solution Can Fix Our Two Biggest Problems*
Pub: HarperCollins Publishers
Ed: Van Jones. **Released:** November 1, 2009. **Price:** $14.99. **Description:** This book offers insight into rebuilding the nation's infrastructure and creating alternative energy sources that could boost the economy through increased employment and higher wages while decreasing our dependence on fossil fuels.

7185 ■ "Green Counting" in *Canadian Business* (Vol. 81, October 13, 2008, No. 17, pp. 27)
Pub: Rogers Media Ltd.
Ed: Joe Castaldo. **Description:** Procter and Gamble research revealed that only 10 percent of North American consumers are willing to accept trade-offs for a greener product. Three out of four North American consumers will not accept a higher price or a decrease in a product's performance for an environmental benefit. Details on green marketing are also discussed.

7186 ■ "Green Energy Exec Hits State Policy" in *Boston Business Journal* (Vol. 30, December 3, 2010, No. 45, pp. 1)
Pub: Boston Business Journal
Ed: Kyle Alspach. **Description:** American Superconductor Corporation President Dan McGahn believes that the state government of Massachusetts is not proactive enough to develop the state into a manufacturing hub for wind power technology. McGahn believes that while Governor Deval Patrick campaigned for wind turbines in the state, his administration does not have the focus required to build the turbines in the state.

7187 ■ "Green Firm Scouts Sites in Tri-State" in *Business Courier* (Vol. 27, July 23, 2010, No. 12, pp. 1)
Pub: Business Courier
Ed: Dan Monk. **Description:** CresaPartners is searching for a manufacturing facility in Cincinnati, Ohio. The company is set to tour about ten sites in the area.

7188 ■ *The Green Guide for Business: The Ultimate Environment for Businesses of All Sizes*
Pub: Profile Books Limited
Ed: Roger East, Hannah Bullock, Chris Goodall. **Released:** May 10, 2010. **Description:** Everyone wants to go green these days, but for small businesses that's easier said than done. How do you measure a company's carbon footprint? Are dryers or hand towels more eco-friendly? Recycled paper or FSC-certified? All these questions and more are explored.

7189 ■ "Green It Like You Mean It" in *Special Events Magazine* (Vol. 28, February 1, 2009, No. 2)
Pub: Special Events Magazine
Ed: Christine Landry. **Description:** Eco-friendly party planners offer advice for planning and hosting green parties or events. Tips include information for using recycled paper products, organic food and drinks. The Eco Nouveau Fashion Show held by Serene Star Productions reused old garments to create new fashions as well as art pieces from discarded doors and window frames for the show; eco-friendly treats and gift bags were highlighted at the event.

7190 ■ "Green Light" in *The Business Journal-Portland* (Vol. 25, July 11, 2008, No. 18, pp. 1)
Pub: American City Business Journals, Inc.
Ed: Erik Siemers. **Description:** Ecos Consulting, a sustainability consulting company based in Portland, Oregon, is seeing a boost in revenue as more businesses turn to sustainable practices. The company's revenue rose by 50 percent in 2007 and employees increased from 57 to 150. Other details about Ecos' growth are discussed.

7191 ■ "Green Shift Sees Red" in *Canadian Business* (Vol. 81, September 29, 2008, No. 16)
Pub: Rogers Media Ltd.
Ed: Jeff Sanford. **Description:** Green Shift Inc. is suing the Liberal Party of Canada in an $8.5 million lawsuit for using the phrase "green shift" when they rolled out their carbon tax and climate change policy. The company has come to be recognized as a consultant and provider of green products such as non-toxic, biodegradable cups, plates, and utensils for events.

7192 ■ "Greenhouse Announces Merger With Custom Q, Inc." in *Investment Weekly* (January 30, 2010, pp. 338)
Pub: Investment Weekly News
Description: In accordance with an Agreement and Plan of Share Exchange, GreenHouse Holdings, Inc., an innovative green solutions provider, has gone public via a reverse merger with Custom Q, Inc.

7193 ■ "Greening the Auto Industry" in *Business Journal-Serving Phoenix & the Valley of the Sun* (Vol. 30, July 23, 2010, No. 46, pp. 1)
Pub: Phoenix Business Journal
Ed: Patrick O'Grady. **Description:** Thermo Fluids Inc. has been recycling used oil products since 1993 and could become Arizona's first home for oil filter recycling after retrofitting its Phoenix facility to include a compaction machine. The new service could help establish Thermo Fluids as a recycling hub for nearby states.

7194 ■ "Greening the Manscape" in *Canadian Business* (Vol. 81, October 13, 2008, No. 17, pp. S19)
Pub: Rogers Media Ltd.
Ed: David Lackie. **Description:** Buyer's guide of environmentally friendly grooming products for men is provided. Improved formulations have solved the problems of having synthetic ingredients in grooming products. Details about a face scrub, after shave conditioner, and a nourishing cream made of 91 percent organic ingredients are given, including prices.

7195 ■ *Greening Your Small Business: How to Improve Your Bottom Line, Grow Your Brand, Satisfy Your Customers and Save the Planet*
Pub: Prentice Hall Press
Ed: Jennifer Kaplan. **Released:** November 3, 2009. **Price:** $19.95. **Description:** A definitive resource for anyone who wants their small business to be cutting-edge, competitive, profitable, and eco-conscious. Stories from small business owners address every aspect of going green, from basics such as recycling waste, energy efficiency, and reducing information technology footprint, to more in-depth concerns such as green marketing and communications, green business travel, and green employee benefits.

7196 ■ *Guerrilla Marketing Goes Green: Winning Strategies to Improve Your Profits and Your Planet*
Pub: John Wiley & Sons, Inc.
Ed: Jay Conrad Levinson, Shel Horowitz. **Released:** January 10, 2010. **Price:** $21.95. **Description:** The latest tips on green marketing and sustainable business strategies are shared.

7197 ■ "Guide to Carbon Footprinting" in *American Printer* (Vol. 128, June 1, 2011, No. 6)
Pub: Penton Media Inc.
Description: PrintCity Alliance published its new report, 'Carbon Footprint & Energy Reduction for Graphic Industry Value Chain.' The report aims to help improve the environmental performance of printers, converters, publishers, brand owners and their suppliers.

7198 ■ "Habitat, Home Depot Expand Building Programs" in *Contractor* (Vol. 56, September 2009, No. 9, pp. 16)
Pub: Penton Media, Inc.
Description: Habitat for Humanity International and The Home Depot Foundation are planning to expand their Partners in Sustainable Building program. The program will provide funds to help Habitat affiliates build 5,000 homes. Comments from executives are also included.

7199 ■ *Habitats and Ecosystems*
Pub: ABC-CLIO
Contact: Mark Crawford, Author
Released: Published December 1999. **Price:** $75, individuals print; $51.95, individuals. **Covers:** A listing of more than 1,400 of the most hazardous pollution sites since 1980. **Entries Include:** Location. **Arrangement:** Geographical by state.

7200 ■ "Hard Rock on Pike" in *Puget Sound Business Journal* (Vol. 29, September 5, 2008, No. 20, pp. 1)
Pub: American City Business Journals
Ed: Jeanne Lang Jones. **Description:** A branch of the Hard Rock Cafe is opening in 2009 in the Liberty Building on Pike Street in downtown Seattle, Washington. The location is being renovated as a green building; the restaurant and concert venue will seat 300 patrons and has a rooftop deck and memorabilia shop.

7201 ■ "Hey, You Can't Do That" in *Green Industry Pro* (Vol. 23, September 2011)
Pub: Cygnus Business Media
Ed: Rod Dickens. **Description:** Manufacturers of landscape equipment are making better use of energy resources, such as the use of fuel-injection systems instead of carburetors, lightweight materials, better lubricants, advanced battery technology, and innovative engine designs.

7202 ■ "Hot Air" in *Canadian Business* (Vol. 81, July 22, 2008, No. 12-13, pp. 16)
Pub: Rogers Media Ltd.
Ed: Joe Castaldo. **Description:** Over half of 101 business leaders who were recently surveyed oppose Liberal leader Stephane Dion's carbon-tax proposal, saying that manufacturers in Canada are likely to suffer from the plan. Additional key results of the survey are presented.

7203 ■ "Hot Air: On Global Warming and Carbon Tax" in *Canadian Business* (Vol. 81, October 13, 2008, No. 17, pp. 12)
Pub: Rogers Media Ltd.
Ed: Joe Castaldo. **Description:** Survey of Canadian business leaders revealed that the environment is a key issue in Canada's federal elections. Respondents believe that Prime Minister Stephen Harper's views on global warming and climate change are closer to their own views. Other key information on the survey is presented.

7204 ■ *Hot, Flat and Crowded: Why We Need a Green Revolution - and How It Can Renew America*
Pub: Farrar, Straus and Giroux
Ed: Thomas L. Friedman. **Released:** September 8, 2008. **Price:** $27.95. **Description:** Author explains how global warming, rapidly growing populations, and the expansion of the world's middle class through globalization have impacted the environment.

7205 ■ *Housecleaning Business: Organize Your Business - Get Clients and Referrals - Set Rates and Services*
Pub: The Globe Pequot Press
Ed: Laura Jorstad, Melinda Morse. **Released:** June 1, 2009. **Price:** $18.95. **Description:** This book shares insight into starting a housecleaning businesses. It shows how to develop a service manual, screen clients, serve customers, select cleaning products, competition, how to up a home office, using the Internet to grow the business and offering green cleaning options to clients.

7206 ■ "How Bad Is It?" in *Hawaii Business* (Vol. 54, July 2008, No. 1, pp. 35)
Pub: Hawaii Business Publishing
Ed: Jolyn Okimoto Rosa. **Description:** Donald G. Horner, chief executive officer of First Hawaiian Bank, says that the current Hawaiian economic situation is a cyclical slowdown. Maurice Kaya, an energy consultant, says the slowdown is due to overdependence on imported fuels. Other local leaders, such as Constance H. Lau, also discuss their view on the current economic situation in Hawaii.

7207 ■ "How Green Is The Valley?" in *Barron's* (Vol. 88, July 4, 2008, No. 28, pp. 13)
Pub: Dow Jones & Co., Inc.
Description: San Jose, California has made a good start towards becoming a leader in alternative energy technology through the establishment of United Laboratories' own lab in the city. The certification process for photovoltaic cells will be dramatically shortened with this endeavor.

7208 ■ "IAPMO GTC Debates Supplement" in *Contractor* (Vol. 56, September 2009, No. 9, pp. 3)
Pub: Penton Media, Inc.
Ed: Robert P. Mader. **Description:** Green Technical Committee of the International Association of Plumbing and Mechanical Officials is developing a Green Plumbing and Mechanical Supplement. The supplement provides for installation of systems by licensed contractors and installers. Comments from officials are also presented.

7209 ■ "IAPMO GTC Finalizes Green Supplement" in *Contractor* (Vol. 57, January 2010, No. 1, pp. 1)
Pub: Penton Media, Inc.
Description: International Association of Plumbing and Mechanical Officials' Green Technical Committee finalized the Green Plumbing & Mechanical Code Supplement. The supplement was created to provide a set of provisions that encourage sustainable practices and work towards the design and construction of plumbing and mechanical systems.

7210 ■ "IAPMO GTC Votes to Limit Showers to 2.0-GPM" in *Contractor* (Vol. 56, September 2009, No. 9, pp. 1)
Pub: Penton Media, Inc.
Ed: Robert P. Mader. **Description:** Green Technical Committee of the International Association of Plumbing and Mechanical Officials has voted to limit showers to 2.0 GPM. It is also developing a Green Plumbing and Mechanical Supplement. Comments from executives are also supplied.

7211 ■ "Independence Station Utilizes Sustainable Technologies" in *Contractor* (Vol. 56, September 2009, No. 9, pp. 3)
Pub: Penton Media, Inc.
Ed: Candace Ruolo. **Description:** Independence Station building in Oregon is seen to receive the most LEED points ever awarded by the United States Green Building Council. The building will use an ice-based cooling storage system, biofuel cogeneration system and phovoltaic system. Other building features and dimensions are also supplied.

7212 ■ "Indoor Air Quality – a Tribute to Efficiency" in *Indoor Comfort Marketing* (Vol. 70, August 2011, No. 8, pp. 8)
Pub: Industry Publications Inc.
Ed: Matthew Maleske. **Description:** Efficiency of new HVAC/R equipment has helped improve indoor air quality.

7213 ■ "Industry Escalates Lobbying Efforts For Loan Program" in *Crain's Detroit Business* (Vol. 24, September 22, 2008, No. 38, pp. 22)
Pub: Crain Communications, Inc.
Ed: Jay Greene; Ryan Beene; Harry Stoffer. **Description:** Auto suppliers such as Lear Corp., which is best known for vehicle seating, also supplies high-voltage wiring for Ford hybrids and is developing other hybrid components. These suppliers are joining automakers in lobbying for the loan program which would promote the accelerated development of fuel-efficient vehicles.

7214 ■ "Info Junkie" in *Crain's Chicago Business* (Vol. 34, October 24, 2011, No. 42, pp. 35)
Pub: Crain Communications Inc.
Ed: Christina Le Beau. **Description:** Greg Colando, president of Flor Inc., an eco-friendly carpet company located I Chicago discusses his marketing program to increase sales.

7215 ■ "Interested in 12 Billion Dollars?" in *Indoor Comfort Marketing* (Vol. 70, March 2011, No. 3, pp. 18)
Pub: Industry Publications Inc.
Ed: Matthew Maleske. **Description:** Trends in the indoor quality industry are cited, with insight into expanding an existing indoor heating and cooling business.

7216 ■ "It's Always 55 Degrees F" in *Contractor* (Vol. 56, September 2009, No. 9, pp. 38)
Pub: Penton Media, Inc.
Ed: Carol Fey. **Description:** Geothermal-exchange heating and cooling systems can save businesses up to 60 percent on energy costs for heating and cooling. Geothermal systems get heat from the earth during winter. Design, features and installation of geothermal systems are also discussed.

7217 ■ "It's Not Easy Investing Green" in *Entrepreneur* (Vol. 37, August 2009, No. 8, pp. 64)
Pub: Entrepreneur Media, Inc.
Ed: Rosalind Resnick. **Description:** Some venture capitalists remain bullish on green investing despite signs of stagnation. One way for an investor to cash in on green investing is to invest in large public companies that are investing big in green initiatives. Being an angel investor to a local clean-tech company is another avenue.

7218 ■ "Know the Facts About Natural Gas!" in *Indoor Comfort Marketing* (Vol. 70, August 2011, No. 8, pp. 26)
Pub: Industry Publications Inc.
Description: AEC Activity Update is presented on the American Energy Coalition's Website.

7219 ■ "Kohler Building Earns LEED Silver Certification" in *Contractor* (Vol. 56, September 2009, No. 9, pp. 12)
Pub: Penton Media, Inc.
Description: United States Green Building Council has awarded Kohler Co. with the Silver Leadership in Energy and Environmental Design Status. The award has highlighted the company's work to transform its building into a more environmentally efficient structure. A description of the facility is also provided.

7220 ■ "Large Homes can be Energy Efficient Too" in *Contractor* (Vol. 56, October 2009, No. 10, pp. 5)
Pub: Penton Media, Inc.
Ed: Candace Roulo. **Description:** Eco Estate at Briggs Chaney subdivision in Silver Spring, Maryland has model houses that use sustainable technologies and products and the homes that will be built on the subdivision will feature some of the technologies featured on the model home. The energy efficient HVAC system of the model homes are discussed.

7221 ■ "Legislation Introduced" in *Indoor Comfort Marketing* (Vol. 70, July 2011, No. 7, pp. 6)
Pub: Industry Publications Inc.
Description: New industry legislation is examined by the National Oilheat Research Alliance.

7222 ■ "Letting the Sunshine In" in *Barron's* (Vol. 89, July 6, 2009, No. 27, pp. 11)
Pub: Dow Jones & Co., Inc.
Ed: Katherine Cheng. **Description:** Solar energy industry leaders believe the industry needs aid from the US government regarding the funding of its

research efforts and lowering solar energy costs. The climate change bill passed by the US House of Representatives signifies the US government's desire to significantly reduce carbon dioxide emissions.

7223 ■ "Lincoln Electric Installs Large Wind Tower" in *Modern Machine Shop* (Vol. 84, October 2011, No. 5, pp. 42)
Pub: Gardner Publications
Description: Lincoln Electric, a welding product manufacturer, constructed a 443-foot-tall wind tower at its plant in Euclid, Ohio. The tower is expected to generate as much as 10 percent of the facility's energy and save as much as $500,000 annually in energy costs.

7224 ■ "The Lithium Deficit" in *Canadian Business* (Vol. 82, April 27, 2009, No. 7, pp. 17)
Pub: Rogers Media
Ed: Joe Castaldo. **Description:** Experts are concerned that there may not be enough lithium available to support the expected rise in demand for the natural resource. Lithium is used in lithium ion batteries, the standard power source for electric and hybrid vehicles. Experts believe that the demand for lithium can only be measured once the technology is out in the market.

7225 ■ "Loan Dollars Sit Idle for Energy Plan" in *Baltimore Business Journal* (Vol. 28, September 10, 2010, No. 18, pp. 1)
Pub: Baltimore Business Journal
Ed: Scott Dance. **Description:** The Maryland Energy Administration has millions of dollars in Federal stimulus and state energy efficiency cash sitting idle and might be lost once the window for stimulus spending is gone. However, businesses have no interest in betting on renewable energy because some cannot afford to take out more loans. Other challenges faced by these businesses are presented.

7226 ■ "The Long View: Roberta Bondar on Science and the Need for Education" in *Canadian Business* (Vol. 81, October 27, 2008, No. 18)
Pub: Rogers Media Ltd.
Ed: Alex Mlynek. **Description:** Roberta Bondar believes that energy and renewable energy is a critical environmental issue faced by Canada today. Bondar is the first Canadian woman and neurologist in space.

7227 ■ "A Look At Three Gas-Less Cars" in *Hispanic Business* (Vol. 30, September 2008, No. 9, pp. 90)
Pub: Hispanic Business, Inc.
Ed: Daniel Soussa. **Description:** Three major car manufacturers, Chevrolet, BMW, and Honda, are giving market leader Toyota competition for the next generation of eco-friendly car. The latest and most advanced of the gasoline-less cars designed by the three firms, namely, the Chevrolet Volt, BMW's Hydrogen 7, and the Honda FCX Clarity, are reviewed.

7228 ■ "Lunch Box Maker Gives Back" in *Marketing to Women* (Vol. 23, November 2010, No. 11, pp. 5)
Pub: EPM Communications, Inc.
Description: Female entrepreneurs launched a new program called, "Share Your Lunch Project" that encourages mothers to give back and replace their child's lunchbox with their eco-friendly lunch boxes, which are available at select retailers. All proceeds from the project will benefit the World Food Program USA, which feeds children in developing countries.

7229 ■ "Magpower May Build Solar Panels Here" in *Austin Business Journal* (Vol. 31, May 13, 2011, No. 10, pp. A1)
Pub: American City Business Journals Inc.
Ed: Christopher Calnan. **Description:** RRE Austin Solar LLC CEO Doven Mehta has revealed plans to partner with Portugal-based Magpower SA, only if Austin energy buys electricity from planned solar energy farm in Pflugerville. Austin Energy has received 100 bids from 35 companies to supply 200 megawatts of solar- and wind-generated electricity.

7230 ■ "Making Waves" in *Business Journal Portland* (Vol. 27, November 26, 2010, No. 39, pp. 1)
Pub: Portland Business Journal
Ed: Erik Siemers. **Description:** Corvallis, Oregon-based Columbia Power Technologies LLC is about to close a $2 million Series A round of investment initiated by $750,000 from Oregon Angel Fund. The wave energy startup company was formed to commercialize the wave buoy technology developed by Oregon State University researchers.

7231 ■ "Missouri Public Service Commission Chooses APX" in *Wireless News* (January 22, 2010)
Pub: Investment Weekly News
Description: Missouri Public Service Commission, with the help of APX Inc., an infrastructure provider for environmental and energy markets, has selected the North American Registry as the renewable energy certificate management system for Missouri Renewable Energy Standard compliance. APX will continue to support the state's renewable energy programs and manage their environmental assets.

7232 ■ "Mixing Business and Pleasure On the Green" in *Black Enterprise* (Vol. 41, October 2010, No. 3, pp. 65)
Pub: Earl G. Graves Publishing Co. Inc.
Ed: Annya M. Lott. **Description:** Glow Golf, sponsored by Glow Sports, will offer instruction to 150 female corporate executives and entrepreneurs to learn the fundamentals of the game of golf.

7233 ■ "Molycorp Funds Wind Energy Technology Company" in *Manufacturing Close-Up* (September 19, 2011)
Pub: Close-Up Media
Description: Molycorp Inc., producer of rare earth oxides (REO) and a REO producer outside of China, announced it will invest in Boulder Wind Power, which has designed a rare earth magnet powered wind turbine generator. This new generator can produce electricity as low as $0.04 per Kilowatt Hour. Boulder Wind Power's patented wind turbine technology allows for use of rare earth permanent magnets that do not require dysprosium, which is relatively scarce.

7234 ■ "Mr. Clean" in *Canadian Business* (Vol. 81, October 27, 2008, No. 18, pp. 74)
Pub: Rogers Media Ltd.
Ed: Rachel Pulfer. **Description:** Profile of Nicholas Parker, co-founder of Cleantech Group LLC, a pioneer in clean technology investing. Cleantech, now a global industry, accounts for 10 percent of all venture capital investments made by U.S. companies in 2007.

7235 ■ *The Necessary Revolution: Working Together to Create a Sustainable World*
Pub: Broadway Books
Ed: Peter M. Senge, Bryan Smith, Nina Kruschwitz, Joe Laur, Sara Schley. **Released:** April 6, 2010. **Price:** $18.00. **Description:** The book outlines various examples for companies to implement sustainable change and go green in the process.

7236 ■ "N.E.'s Largest Solar Site Set for Scituate Landfill" in *Boston Business Journal* (Vol. 30, December 17, 2010, No. 47, pp. 1)
Pub: Boston Business Journal
Ed: Kyle Alspach. **Description:** A closed 12-acre landfill in Scituate, Massachusetts is the proposed site for a 2.4-megawatt solar power plant. The town government will buy the power at a discounted rate, saving it $200,000 annually.

7237 ■ "The New Alchemists" in *Canadian Business* (Vol. 81, October 27, 2008, No. 18, pp. 22)
Pub: Rogers Media Ltd.
Ed: Joe Castaldo. **Description:** Ethanol industry expects second-generation ethanol or cellulosic biofuels to provide ecologically friendly technologies than the ethanol made from food crops. Government and industries are investing on producing cellulosic biofuels.

7238 ■ "A New Alliance For Global Change" in *Harvard Business Review* (Vol. 88, September 2010, No. 9, pp. 56)
Pub: Harvard Business School Publishing
Ed: Bill Drayton, Valeria Budinich. **Description:** Collaboration between social organizations and for-profit firms through the development of hybrid value chains to target complex global issues is promoted. While social organizations offer links to communities and consumers, firms provide financing and scale expertise.

7239 ■ "New Book Takes Alternate View on Ontario's Wind Industry" in *CNW Group* (September 19, 2011)
Pub: CNW Group
Description: Dirty Business: The Reality Behind Ontario's Rush to Wind Power, was written by editor and health care writer Jane Wilson of Ottawa, Ontario, Canada along with contributing editor Parker Gallant. The book contains articles and papers on the wind business, including information on illnesses caused from the environmental noise.

7240 ■ "A New Day is Dawning" in *Indoor Comfort Marketing* (Vol. 70, August 2011, No. 8, pp. 18)
Pub: Industry Publications Inc.
Ed: Paul Nazzaro. **Description:** New trends in the HVAC/R industry regarding biofuels and bioheat are explored.

7241 ■ "Next Stage of Green Building will be Water Efficiency" in *Contractor* (Vol. 56, July 2009, No. 7, pp. 41)
Pub: Penton Media, Inc.
Description: One market report says that water efficiency and conservation will become critical factors in green design, construction, and product selection in the next five years from 2009. The report outlines how critical it will be for the construction industry to address responsible water practices in the future.

7242 ■ "N.H. Near the LEED in Green Space" in *New Hampshire Business Review* (Vol. 33, March 25, 2011, No. 6, pp. 30)
Pub: Business Publications Inc.
Description: New Hamphire's architects, contractors and suppliers are among the leaders with LEED-certified space per capita.

7243 ■ "NStar Feels the Heat" in *Cape Cod Times* (September 30, 2011)
Pub: Cape Cod Media Group
Ed: Patrick Cassidy. **Description:** Massachusetts energy officials wish to delay a merger between NStar and Northeast Utilities until it is clear how the partnership would meet the state's green energy goals. Governor Deval Patrick supports the proposed Nantucket Sound wind farm.

7244 ■ "Nuclear Renaissance" in *Canadian Business* (Vol. 83, August 17, 2010, No. 13-14, pp. 46)
Pub: Rogers Media Ltd.
Description: Nuclear energy has come back into the public's favor in Canada because it has virtually no emissions and is always available anytime of the day. Canada's nuclear industry has also achieved an incomparable record of safe, economic and reliable power generation in three provinces for 48 years.

7245 ■ "On Growth Path of Rising Star" in *Boston Business Journal* (Vol. 31, June 24, 2011, No. 22, pp. 3)
Pub: Boston Business Journal
Ed: Kyle Alspach. **Description:** 1366 Technologies Inc. of Lexington, Massachusetts is considered a rising solar power technology company. The firm secured $150 million loan guarantee from the US Department of Energy that could go to the construction of a 1,000 megawatt solar power plant.

7246 ■ "One on One With SEIA's President, CEO" in *Contractor* (Vol. 57, January 2010, No. 1, pp. 40)
Pub: Penton Media, Inc.
Ed: Dave Yates. **Description:** Solar Energy Industries Association President and CEO Rhone Resch says that the deployment of solar systems in the U.S.

has exploded since 2005 and that there is a need to make inroads for shaping the U.S. energy policy. Resch says one of the hurdles they face is that there are no universal standards.

7247 ■ "OPEC Exposed" in *Hawaii Business* (Vol. 54, September 2008, No. 3, pp. 2)
Pub: Hawaii Business Publishing
Ed: Serena Lim. **Description:** Organization of the Petroleum Exporting Countries (OPEC) has said that their effort in developing an alternative energy source has driven prices up. The biofuel sector is criticizing the statement, saying that a research study found that biofuels push petroleum prices down by 15 percent. Details on the effect of rising petroleum prices are discussed.

7248 ■ "Out of Juice?" in *Canadian Business* (Vol. 81, October 27, 2008, No. 18, pp. 32)
Pub: Rogers Media Ltd.
Ed: Joe Castaldo. **Description:** Alternative energy experts suggest Canada should be more aggressive and should make major policy changes on energy alternatives despite an Ernst & Young research that rated the country high on renewable energy.

7249 ■ "Overheating Taking Place? Pay Attention to Details..." in *Indoor Comfort Marketing* (Vol. 70, March 2011, No. 3, pp.)
Pub: Industry Publications Inc.
Ed: George R. Carey. **Description:** Boiler facts are outlined to help the small HVAC company when servicing customers.

7250 ■ "An Overview of Energy Consumption of the Globalized World Economy" in *Energy Policy* (Vol. 39, October 2011, No. 10, pp. 5920-2928)
Pub: Reed Elsevier Reference Publishing
Ed: Z.M. Chen, G.Q. Chen. **Description:** Energy consumption and its impact on the global world economy is examined.

7251 ■ "Phoenix Conference Reveals Opportunities are Coming" in *Indoor Comfort Marketing* (Vol. 70, March 2011, No. 3, pp. 24)
Pub: Industry Publications Inc.
Ed: Paul J. Nazzaro. **Description:** Advanced liquid fuels were spotlighted at the Phoenix conference revealing the opportunities for using liquid fuels.

7252 ■ "Positive Transformational Change" in *Indoor Comfort Marketing* (Vol. 70, April 2011, No. 4, pp. 30)
Pub: Industry Publications Inc.
Ed: Blaine Fox. **Description:** Management changes taking place at Shark Bites HVAC firm are discussed.

7253 ■ "PPC's Major Commitment to Biofuel Infrastructure" in *Indoor Comfort Marketing* (Vol. 70, April 2011, No. 4, pp. 6)
Pub: Industry Publications Inc.
Description: Petroleum Products Corporation's commitment to the biofuel infrastructure is outlined.

7254 ■ "Pre-Certified LEED Hotel Prototype Reduces Energy Use, Conserves Water" in *Contractor* (Vol. 57, January 2010, No. 1, pp. 3)
Pub: Penton Media, Inc.
Ed: Candace Roulo. **Description:** Marriott International Inc.'s LEED pre-certified prototype hotel will reduce a hotel's energy and water consumption by 25 percent and save owners approximately $100,000. Their Courtyard Settler's Ridge in Pittsburgh will be the first hotel built based on the prototype.

7255 ■ "Programs Provide Education and Training" in *Contractor* (Vol. 56, September 2009, No. 9, pp. 56)
Pub: Penton Media, Inc.
Ed: William Feldman; Patti Feldman. **Description:** Opportunity Interactive's Showroom v2 software provides uses computer graphics to provide education and training on HVAC equipment and systems. It can draw heat pump balance points for a specific home. Meanwhile, Simutech's HVAC Training Simulators provide trainees with 'hands-on' HVACR training.

7256 ■ "PSC Approves $130M TECO Solar Project" in *Tampa Bay Business Journal* (Vol. 30, December 18, 2009, No. 52, pp. 1)
Pub: American City Business Journals
Ed: Michael Hinman. **Description:** Florida's Public Service Commission has endorsed Tampa Electric Company's plan to add 25 megawatts of solar energy to its portfolio. TECO's plan needed the approval by PSC to defray additional costs for the project through ratepayers.

7257 ■ "Radiant – the Hottest Topic in ... Cooling" in *Indoor Comfort Marketing* (Vol. 70, February 2011, No. 2, pp. 8)
Pub: Industry Publications Inc.
Description: Examination of radiant cooling systems, a new trend in cooling homes and buildings.

7258 ■ "Recycling 202: How to Take Your Recycling Practices to the Next Level" in *Black Enterprise* (Vol. 41, September 2010, No. 2, pp. 38)
Pub: Earl G. Graves Publishing Co. Inc.
Ed: Tamara E. Holmes. **Description:** Consumer Electronics Association and other organizations, manufacturers and retailers list ways to recycle all household items.

7259 ■ "Reducing the Book's Carbon Footpring" in *American Printer* (Vol. 128, July 1, 2011, No. 7)
Pub: Penton Media Inc.
Description: Green Press Initiative's Book Industry Environmental Council is working to achieve a 20 percent reduction in the book industry's carbon footprint by 2020. The Council is made up of publishers, printers, paper suppliers, and non-governmental organizations.

7260 ■ "Reinventing Marketing to Manage the Environmental Imperative" in *Journal of Marketing* (Vol. 75, July 2011, No. 4, pp. 132)
Pub: American Marketing Association
Ed: Philip Kotler. **Description:** Marketers must now examine their theory and practices due to the growing recognition of finite resources and high environmental costs. Companies also need to balance more carefully their growth goals with the need to purse sustainability. Insights on the rise of demarketing and social marketing are also given.

7261 ■ "Renewable Energy Adoption in an Aging Population" in *Energy Policy* (Vol. 39, October 2011, No. 10, pp. 6021-6029)
Pub: Reed Elsevier Reference Publishing
Ed: Ken Willis, Riccardo Scarpa, Rose Gilroy, Neveen Hamza. **Description:** Attitudes and impacts of renewable energy adoption on an aging population is examined.

7262 ■ "Renewable Energy Market Opportunities: Wind Testing" in *PR Newswire* (September 22, 2011)
Pub: United Business Media
Description: Global wind energy test systems markets are discussed. Research conducted covers both non-destructive test equipment and condition monitoring equipment product segments.

7263 ■ "ReVenture Plan Appears Close to Landing Key Legislative Deal" in *Charlotte Business Journal* (Vol. 25, July 9, 2010, No. 16, pp. 1)
Pub: Charlotte Business Journal
Ed: John Downey. **Description:** North Carolina lawmakers acted on special legislation that would boost development of Forsite Development 667-acre ReVenture Energy Park. The legislation could also improve chances that Duke Energy Carolinas will contract to purchase the power from the planned 50-megawatt biomass power plant located at the park. How utilities would benefit from the legislation is also discussed.

7264 ■ "Rivals Blow In" in *Crain's Cleveland Business* (Vol. 30, June 1, 2009, No. 21, pp. 1)
Pub: Crain Communications, Inc.
Ed: Chuck Soder. **Description:** U.S. and Canadian competitors are hoping to start construction of offshore wind farm project proposed by Cuyahoga County's Great Lakes Energy Development Task Force. Details of the project are included.

7265 ■ "Rosewood Site Faces Big Cleanup" in *Baltimore Business Journal* (Vol. 27, February 6, 2010, No. 40, pp. 1)
Pub: American City Business Journals
Ed: Daniel J. Sernovitz. **Description:** Environmental assessment report states that Maryland's Rosewood Center for the Developmentally Disabled has significant amounts of toxic chemicals, which could impact Stevenson University's decision to purchase the property. Senator Robert A. Zirkin believes that the state should pay for the cleanup, which is expected to cost millions.

7266 ■ "Rough Headwinds" in *Boston Business Journal* (Vol. 30, November 12, 2010, No. 42, pp. 1)
Pub: Boston Business Journal
Ed: Kyle Alspach. **Description:** Views of residents, as well as key information on First Wind's plan to install wind power turbines in Brimfield, Massachusetts are presented. Residents believe that First Wind's project will devalue properties, compromise quality of life, and ruin the rural quality of Brimfield. First Wind expects to produce 2,000 megawatts of power from wind by 2020.

7267 ■ "San Diego Museum Receives LEED Certification" in *Contractor* (Vol. 57, January 2010, No. 1, pp. 14)
Pub: Penton Media, Inc.
Description: San Diego Natural History Museum received an LEED certification for existing buildings. The certification process began when they committed to displaying the Dead Sea Scrolls in 2007 and they had to upgrade their buildings' air quality and to control for air moisture, temperature, and volume. They reduced their energy consumption by upwards of 20 percent.

7268 ■ "Sandvik Expands Energy-Saving Program" in *Modern Machine Shop* (Vol. 84, September 2011, No. 4, pp. 48)
Pub: Gardner Publications
Description: Sandvik Coromant, based in Fair Lawn, New Jersey, expanded its Sustainable Manufacturing Program that originally was developed to help Japanese-based firms reduce electricity consumption by 15 percent after the recent earthquake that cause loss of electrical power. The program now provides energy reduction through the Sandvick cutting tool technology, application techniques and productivity increases.

7269 ■ "The Second Most Fuel-Efficient Tractor of the Decade: John Deere 8320R" in *Farm Industry News* (November 10, 2011)
Pub: Penton Business Media Inc.
Description: John Deere's 8320R Tractor was ranked second in the Farm Industry News listing of the top 40 most fuel-efficient tractors of the decade, following the winner, John Deere's 8295R PTO tractor.

7270 ■ "Shaw Joins Green Institute Launch" in *Home Textiles Today* (Vol. 31, May 24, 2011, No. 13, pp. 4)
Pub: Reed Business Information
Description: Shaw Industries Group joined the Green Products Innovation Institute, the first nonprofit institute of its kind in America. The institute promotes the concepts of reverse engineering, elimination of waste, safe chemistries, and closed loop technical nutrients.

7271 ■ "Shifting Gears" in *Business Journal-Serving Phoenix & the Valley of the Sun* (Vol. 31, November 12, 2010, No. 10, pp. 1)
Pub: Phoenix Business Journal
Ed: Patrick O'Grady. **Description:** Automotive parts recyclers in Arizona are benefiting from the challenging national economic conditions as well as from the green movement. Recyclers revealed that customers prefer recycled parts more because they are cheaper and are more environmentally friendly. Other information about the automotive parts recycling industry is presented.

7272 ■ "Slick Science" in *Canadian Business* (Vol. 81, September 15, 2008, No. 14-15, pp. 55)
Pub: Rogers Media Ltd.
Ed: Andrew Nikiforuk. **Description:** N-Solv Corp's John Nenniger has discovered a better alternative to steam-assisted gravity drainage methods for extracting bitumen. Nenniger's technique also relies on gravity but replaces steam with propane, which leaves behind impurities like asphaltenes and heavy metals that are too dirty to burn.

7273 ■ "Small Wind Power Market to Double by 2015 at $634 Million" in *Western Farm Press* (September 30, 2011)
Pub: Penton Media Inc.
Description: Small wind power provides cost-effective electricity on a highly localized level, in both remote settings as well as in conjunction with power from the utility grid. Government incentives are spurring new growth in the industry.

7274 ■ "Smart Car Sales Take Big Hit in Recession" in *Business Journal-Milwaukee* (Vol. 28, December 10, 2010, No. 10, pp. A1)
Pub: Milwaukee Business Journal
Ed: Stacey Vogel Davis. **Description:** Sales of smart cars in Milwaukee declined in 2010. Smart Center Milwaukee sold only 52 new cars through October 2010. Increased competition is seen as a reason for the decline in sales.

7275 ■ "Snow Melt Systems Offer Practical Solutions" in *Contractor* (Vol. 56, October 2009, No. 10, pp. S6)
Pub: Penton Media, Inc.
Ed: Lisa Murton Beets. **Description:** Cases are discussed in which the installation of a snow melt system becomes a necessity. One example describes how limited space means there would be no place to put plowed snow; snow melt systems can also resolve problems that arise due to an excess of melting snow.

7276 ■ "Solar Choices" in *Contractor* (Vol. 56, October 2009, No. 10, pp. 32)
Pub: Penton Media, Inc.
Ed: Tom Scheel. **Description:** Price, performance, and ease of installation of a flat plate versus an evacuated tube collector for a plumbing and heating job are compared. The better choice with regards to weight, aesthetics, efficiency in warm or cool climates, year round load, and space heating is discussed.

7277 ■ "Solar Credit Lapse Spur Late Demand" in *The Business Journal - Serving Phoenix and the Valley of the Sun* (Vol. 28, July 18, 2008)
Pub: American City Business Journals, Inc.
Ed: Patrick O'Grady. **Description:** Businesses looking to engage in the solar energy industry are facing the problems of taxation and limited solar panel supply. Solar panels manufacturers are focusing more on the European market. Political issues surrounding the federal tax credit policy on solar energy users are also discussed.

7278 ■ "Something Different in the Air? The Collapse of the Schwarzenegger Health Plan in Calfornia" in *WorkingUSA* (June 2008)
Pub: Blackwell Publishers Ltd.
Ed: Daniel J.B. Mitchell. **Description:** In January 2007, California Governor Arnold Schwarzenegger proposed a state universal health care plan modeled after the Massachusetts individual mandate program. A year later, the plan was dead. Although some key interest groups eventually backed the plan, it was overwhelmed by a looming state budget crisis and a lack of gubernatorial focus. Although much acclaimed for his stance on greenhouse gases, stem cells, hydrogen highways, and other Big Ideas, diffused gubernatorial priorities and a failure to resolve California's chronic fiscal difficulties let the clock run out on universal health care.

7279 ■ "Start Connecting Today" in *Indoor Comfort Marketing* (Vol. 70, May 2011, No. 5, pp. 34)
Pub: Industry Publications Inc.
Ed: Paul Nazzaro. **Description:** An in-depth discussion regarding the use of biofuels on bioheat use and dealership.

7280 ■ "Start Moving Toward Advanced Fuels" in *Indoor Comfort Marketing* (Vol. 70, March 2011, No. 3, pp. 4)
Pub: Industry Publications Inc.
Ed: Michael L. SanGiovanni. **Description:** Commentary on advanced fuels is presented.

7281 ■ "Start Thinking About Carbon Assets - Now" in *Harvard Business Review* (Vol. 86, September 2008, No. 9, pp. 28)
Pub: Harvard Business School Press
Ed: Alex Rau; Robert Toker. **Description:** Economic and strategic benefits of adopting a corporate carbon assets policy are discussed. Topics include renewable energy and capturing waste energy.

7282 ■ "State Investment Goes Sour" in *Business Journal Portland* (Vol. 26, December 4, 2009, No. 39, pp. 1)
Pub: American City Business Journals Inc.
Ed: Erik Siemers. **Description:** Oregon might recoup only $500,000 of a $20 million loan to Vancouver-based Cascade Grain Products LLC. Cascade Grain's ethanol plant in Clatskanie, OR will be put into auction under the supervision of a bankruptcy court.

7283 ■ *State Wildlife Laws Handbook*
Pub: Government Institutes
Contact: Ruth S. Musgrave, Author
Price: $127, individuals cloth. **Publication Includes:** Listing of state fish and wildlife agencies. **Entries Include:** Name, address, phone. Principal content of publication is an analysis of wildlife management and protection laws for all fifty states.

7284 ■ "Stimulus 'Loser' Won't Build Plant in Mass." in *Boston Business Journal* (Vol. 30, November 5, 2010, No. 41, pp. 1)
Pub: Boston Business Journal
Ed: Kyle Alspach. **Description:** Boston-Power Inc. no longer plans to build an electric vehicle battery plant in Massachusetts after it failed to obtain stimulus funds from the federal government. The company is instead looking to build a lithium-ion battery plant in China and possibly Europe.

7285 ■ "The Superpower Dilemma" in *Canadian Business* (Vol. 83, August 17, 2010, No. 13-14, pp. 42)
Pub: Rogers Media Ltd.
Description: Canada has been an energy superpower partly because it controls the energy source and the production means, particularly of fossil fuels. However, Canada's status as superpower could diminish if it replaces petroleum exports with renewable technology for using sources of energy available globally.

7286 ■ "Sustainability Is Top Priority for GreenTown Chicago" in *Contractor* (Vol. 56, November 2009, No. 11, pp. 1)
Pub: Penton Media, Inc.
Ed: Candace Roulo. **Description:** GreenTown Chicago 2009 conference tackled energy-efficient practices and technologies, green design and building, and sustainable policies. Water conservation was also a topic at the conference and one mayor who made a presentation said that reducing the water loss in the system is a priority in the city's endeavor.

7287 ■ "Suzlon S88-Powered Wind Farm in Minnesota Secures Long-Term Financing" in *PR Newswire* (September 21, 2011)
Pub: United Business Media
Description: Suzlon Energy Limited is the world's fifth largest manufacturer of wind turbines. Owners of the Grant County Wind Farm in Minnesota have secured a long-term financing deal for the ten Suzlon S88 2.1 MW wind turbines that generate enough electricity to power 7,000 homes.

7288 ■ "Taxis Are Set to Go Hybrid" in *Philadelphia Business Journal* (Vol. 30, September 16, 2011, No. 31, pp. 1)
Pub: American City Business Journals Inc.
Ed: Natalie Kostelni. **Description:** Taxis are going hybrid in several major states such as New York, California and Maryland where it is mandated, but it is yet to happen in Philadelphia, Pennsylvania with the exception of one taxi company. Freedom Taxi is awaiting Philadelphia Parking Authority's sign off.

7289 ■ "Think the Oilsands Are an Environmental Disaster?" in *Canadian Business* (Vol. 83, October 12, 2010, No. 17, pp. 52)
Pub: Rogers Media Ltd.
Ed: Michael McCullough. **Description:** Studies which were commissioned by the Alberta Energy Research Institute in 2008 found that the life-cycle carbon emissions of oil derived from oilsands was 10 percent greater than the average from all sources. Synthetic crude from the oilsands is 38 percent less carbon-intensive than it was 20 years ago due to productivity improvements.

7290 ■ "Thirsty? Now There's a Water Cooler to Suit Every Taste" in *Inc.* (Vol. 33, October 2011, No. 8, pp. 43)
Pub: Inc. Magazine
Ed: John Brandon. **Description:** Brita's Hydration Station is a wall-mounted unit with a touch-free sensor for dispensing water. This water cooler cuts down on landfill waste and offers special features.

7291 ■ *The Three Secrets of Green Business: Unlocking Competitive Advantage in a Low Carbon Economy*
Pub: Earthscan
Ed: Gareth Kane. **Released:** February 10, 2010. **Price:** $96.00. **Description:** Small business is coming under increasing pressure from government, customers and campaigning groups to improve environmental performance. Soaring utility and compliance costs are critical financial burdens on small companies.

7292 ■ "Timberland's CEO On Standing Up to 65,000 Angry Activists" in *Harvard Business Review* (Vol. 88, September 2010, No. 9, pp. 39)
Pub: Harvard Business School Publishing
Ed: Jeff Swartz. **Description:** Timberland Company avoided a potential boycott by taking a two-way approach. It addressed a supplier issue that posed a threat to the environment, and launched an email campaign to keep Greenpeace activists informed of the development of a new supplier agreement.

7293 ■ "Time to Green Your Business" in *Gallup Management Journal* (April 22, 2011)
Pub: Gallup
Ed: Bryant Ott. **Description:** It's Earth Day, so expect to hear companies touting their commitment to the environment. However, according to Gallup, more companies are finding it more interested to talk about being green than actually taking the steps to become a green business.

7294 ■ "Toolmakers' New Tack" in *Crain's Detroit Business* (Vol. 25, June 8, 2009,)
Pub: Crain Communications Inc. - Detroit
Ed: Ryan Beene, Amy Lane. **Description:** MAG Industrial Automation Systems LLC and Dowding Machining Inc. have partnered to advance wind-turbine technology. The goal is to cut costs of wind energy to the same level as carbon-based fuel.

7295 ■ "Toward a Better Future" in *Canadian Business* (Vol. 83, August 17, 2010, No. 13-14, pp. 51)
Pub: Rogers Media Ltd.
Description: A look at certain realities in order to build a better future for Canada's energy industry is presented. Canada must focus on making the oil cleaner, instead of replacing it with another source since dependency on oil will remain in this lifetime. Canada must also develop solutions toward clean technology power sources.

7296 ■ "Traer Turning to Wind Power to Meet Long-Term Energy Needs" in *Waterloo Courier* (September 20, 2011)
Pub: Lee Enterprises
Ed: Josh Nelson. **Description:** Traer Municipal Utilities is working with Clark Thompson, a Story City wind turbine developer, to erect a wind turbine to supply electrical energy to the city. Details are included.

7297 ■ "Tucson Tech Column" in *AZ Daily Star* (September 27, 2011)
Pub: Arizona Daily Star
Ed: David Wichner. **Description:** Western Wind Energy, based in Vancouver, British Columbia, Canada is able to harness energy from the sun when the wind is not blowing at the Kingman I Project wind farm. Details of this technology are outlined.

7298 ■ "UA Turns Ann Arbor Green" in *Contractor* (Vol. 56, September 2009, No. 9, pp. 5)
Pub: Penton Media, Inc.
Ed: Robert P. Mader. **Description:** Instructors at the United Association of Plumbers and Steamfitters have studied the latest in green and sustainable construction and service at the Washtenaw Community College in Michigan. Classes included building information modeling, hydronic heating and cooling and advanced HVACR troubleshooting. The UA is currently focusing on green training.

7299 ■ "Ultra Green Energy Services Opens NJ Biodiesel Transload Facility" in *Indoor Comfort Marketing* (Vol. 70, June 2011, No. 6, pp. 35)
Pub: Industry Publications Inc.
Description: Profile of Ultra Green Energy Services and the opening of their new biodiesel facility in New Jersey is discussed.

7300 ■ "Ultra Low Sulfur Diesel: The Promise and the Reality" in *Indoor Comfort Marketing* (Vol. 70, July 2011, No. 7, pp. 22)
Pub: Industry Publications Inc.
Ed: Ed Kitchen. **Description:** Impacts of ultra low sulfur diesel are examined.

7301 ■ "Unilever to Sustainably Source All Paper and Board Packaging" in *Ice Cream Reporter* (Vol. 23, July 20, 2010, No. 8, pp. 1)
Pub: Ice Cream Reporter
Description: Unilever, a leader in the frozen dessert market, has developed a new sustainable paper and board packaging sourcing policy that will reduce environmental impact by working with suppliers to source 75 percent of paper and board packaging from sustainably managed forests or from recycled material. Unilever is parent company to Breyers, Haagen-Dazs, Klondike, Popsicle and other ice cream brands.

7302 ■ "University Data Center Goes Off-Grid, Is Test Bed" in *Contractor* (Vol. 57, February 2010, No. 2, pp. 1)
Pub: Penton Media, Inc.
Ed: Candace Roulo. **Description:** Syracuse University's Green Data Center has gone off-grid through the use of natural gas fired turbines. It is expected to use 50 percent less energy than a typical computer center. The center's heating and cooling system setup is also discussed.

7303 ■ "Valener Announces that Gaz Metro has Achieved a Key Step in Acquiring CVPS" in *CNW Group* (September 30, 2011)
Pub: CNW Group
Description: Valener Inc., which owns about 29 percent of Gaz Metro Ltd. Partnership, announced that Gaz Metro welcomes the sale of Central Vermont Public Service Corporation (CVPS). Valener owns an indirect interest of 24.5 percent in the wind power projects jointly developed by Beaupre Eole General Partnership and Boralex Inc. on private lands in Quebec. Details of the deal are included.

7304 ■ "VeriFone Announces Global Security Solutions Business" in *Marketing Weekly News* (October 3, 2009)
Pub: Investment Weekly News
Description: Focused on delivering innovative security solutions, VeriFone Holdings, Inc. announced the formation of its Global Security Solutions Business Unit, including VeriShield Protect, an end-to-end encryption to protect cardholder data throughout the merchant and processor systems. The business will focus on consulting, sales and implementation of these new products in order to help retailers and processors protect customer data.

7305 ■ "Voices: Climategate Leads Nowhere" in *Business Strategy Review* (Vol. 21, Summer 2010, No. 2, pp. 76)
Pub: Wiley-Blackwell
Ed: Mick Blowfield. **Description:** Examination of the recent Climategate scandal and an exploration of the damage it can cause managers who are too easily mystified or misled.

7306 ■ "Volunteers Needed" in *Canadian Business* (Vol. 81, October 27, 2008, No. 18, pp. 60)
Pub: Rogers Media Ltd.
Ed: Megan Harman. **Description:** Emissions-targeting regulations focus on the biggest polluters, missing out on other companies that leave carbon footprints in things such as shipping and travel. Some companies in Canada have initiated programs to offset their carbon emissions. Critics claim that offsetting does not reduce emissions and the programs merely justify pollution.

7307 ■ "Warm Floors Make Warm Homes" in *Contractor* (Vol. 56, October 2009, No. 10, pp. S18)
Pub: Penton Media, Inc.
Ed: Lisa Murton Beets. **Description:** Three award winning radiant floor-heating installations are presented. The design and the equipment used for these systems are discussed.

7308 ■ "Was Mandating Solar Power Water Heaters For New Homes Good Policy?" in *Hawaii Business* (Vol. 54, August 2008, No. 2, pp. 28)
Pub: Hawaii Business Publishing
Description: Senator Gary L. Kooser of District 7 Kauai-Niihau believes that the mandating of energy-efficient water heaters for new single-family homes starting in 2010 will help cut Hawaii's oil consumption. Ron Richmond of the Hawaii Solar Energy Association says that the content of SB 644 has negative consequences as it allows for choice of energy and not just solar, and it also eliminates tax credits for new homebuyers.

7309 ■ "Water Conservation Helps GC's Building Attain LEED Gold Status" in *Contractor* (Vol. 56, September 2009, No. 9, pp. 5)
Pub: Penton Media, Inc.
Description: Green contractor Marshall Erdman has built a new office building using green design. The facility is seen to become a prime Leadership in Energy and Environmental Design (LEED) building model. Details of the building's design and features are also provided.

7310 ■ "Water Distiller" in *Canadian Business* (Vol. 81, September 29, 2008, No. 16, pp. 52)
Pub: Rogers Media Ltd.
Ed: Matthew McClearn. **Description:** Les Fairn's invention of a water distiller called a Solarsphere was recognized in the Great Canadian Invention Competition. Fairn's invention resembles a buoy that uses the sun's energy to vaporize dirty water then leaves the impurities behind in a sump. The invention has an application for producing potable water in impoverished countries.

7311 ■ "Western Wind Energy Corporation" in *CNW Group* (October 4, 2011)
Pub: CNW Group
Description: Profile of Western Wind Energy Corporation will complete the installation of 60 wind turbines by the end of 2011. The first 106MW are ready for pre-commissioning with the ability to sell power in November when the site is interconnected.

7312 ■ "What Are Canada's Industrial Polluters Doing to Reduce Emissions?" in *Canadian Business* (Vol. , pp.)
Pub: Rogers Media Ltd.
Ed: Matthew McClearn. **Description:** Efforts by Canada's industrial polluters to reduce emissions are examined. Syncrude Canada plans to reduce sulphur emissions by 60 percent in 2011, while TransAlta invests in emission reduction programs. Environmental groups, however, claim that companies are not doing enough to protect the environment.

7313 ■ "What Is a Geothermal Heat Pump" in *Indoor Comfort Marketing* (Vol. 70, August 2011, No. 8, pp. 14)
Pub: Industry Publications Inc.
Ed: George Carey. **Description:** Examination of geothermal heat pumps is provided, citing new trends in the industry.

7314 ■ "Where the Future is Made" in *Indoor Comfort Marketing* (Vol. 70, May 2011, No. 5, pp. 48)
Pub: Industry Publications Inc.
Description: Research being performed at Brookhaven National Laboratory, located in Upton, New York, is discussed, focusing on new energy sources for our nation.

7315 ■ "A Whiff of TV Reality" in *Houston Business Journal* (Vol. 40, January 22, 2010, No. 37, pp. A1)
Pub: American City Business Journals
Ed: Christine Hall. **Description:** Houston, Texas-based Waste Management Inc.'s president and chief operation officer, Larry O'Donnell shares some of his experience as CBS Television Network reality show 'Undercover Boss' participant. O'Donnell believes the show was a great way to show the customers how tough their jobs are and reveals that the most difficult job was being a sorter at the recycling center.

7316 ■ "Will Home Buyers Pay for Green Features?" in *Contractor* (Vol. 56, October 2009, No. 10, pp. 70)
Pub: Penton Media, Inc.
Ed: Bob Mader. **Description:** National Association of Home Builders commissioned a survey which shows that homeowners are interested in green as long as they do no have to pay much for it. The association did not allow a board member to read the survey which raises questions about how the questions were phrased and how the sample was selected.

7317 ■ "Wind Gets Knocked Out of Energy Farm Plan" in *Buffalo News* (September 28, 2011)
Pub: Buffalo News
Ed: David Robinson. **Description:** New York Power Authority formally killed the proposal for a wind energy farm off the shores of Lake Erie and Lake Ontario. The Authority cited high subsidy costs would be required to make the wind farm economically feasible. Details of the proposal are outlined.

7318 ■ "Yates Helps Turn Log Home Green" in *Contractor* (Vol. 56, December 2009, No. 12, pp. 40)
Pub: Penton Media, Inc.
Description: Upgrading and greening of a log home's HVAC system in Pennsylvania is discussed. F. W. Behler Inc. president Dave Yates was chosen to manage the project. A large coil of R-flex was used to connect the buffer tank to the garage's radiant heat system.

7319 ■ "Yates Turns Log Home Green - Part Three" in *Contractor* (Vol. 57, January 2010, No. 1, pp. 5)
Pub: Penton Media, Inc.
Description: Dave Yates of F.W. Behler Inc. discusses remodeling a log home's HVAC system with geo-to-radiant heat and thermal-solar systems. The solar heater's installation is discussed.

7320 ■ "You're a What? Wind Turbine Service Technician" in *Occupational Outlook Quarterly* (Vol. 54, Fall 2010, No. 3, pp. 34)
Pub: U.S. Bureau of Labor Statistics
Ed: Drew Liming. **Description:** Profile of Brandon Johnson, former member of the Air Force, found a career as a wind turbine service technician.

7321 ■ "Yudelson Challenges San Antonio Groups" in *Contractor* (Vol. 56, October 2009, No. 10, pp. 6)
Pub: Penton Media, Inc.
Description: Green building consultant and author Jerry Yudelson made a presentation for the Central Texas Green Building Council and Leadership San

Antonio where he discussed the European approach to sustainability and how it can be used for designing green buildings. Yudelson also discussed how to use sustainable practices for planning 25 years into the future.

SOURCES OF SUPPLY

7322 ■ *Environmental Management Information Systems Report*
Pub: Donley Technology
Contact: Elizabeth Donley
Released: Latest edition 6th, Published May, 2007. **Price:** $389, individuals single; $699, individuals multiple; $999, individuals company-wide license. **Covers:** 26 software systems that manage environmental data, including inventory and waste tracking, air pollution tracking, report and label generation, mapping, and help with emergency response. **Entries Include:** Company name, address, phone, hardware and software requirements, description of system, cost.

TRADE PERIODICALS

7323 ■ *Composting News*
Pub: McEntee Media Corp.
Ed: Ken McEntee, Editor, ken@recycle.cc. **Released:** Monthly. **Price:** $83, individuals; $93, Canada and Mexico; $105, other countries. **Description:** Covers news and trends in the composting industry. Also reports on compost product prices. Recurring features include letters to the editor, interviews, news of research, a calendar of events, reports of meetings, and notices of publications available.

7324 ■ *E*
Pub: Earth Action Network
Contact: Doug Moss, Founder, Publisher & Exec. Dir.
E-mail: doug@emagazine.com
Ed: Brita Belli, Editor, bbelli@emagazine.com. **Released:** Bimonthly. **Price:** $24.95; $34.95 two years; $34.95 Canada; $64.95 other countries. **Description:** Clearinghouse of news, information and commentary on environmental issues.

7325 ■ *Earth Island Journal*
Pub: Earth Island Institute
Contact: John A. Knox, Exec. Dir.
E-mail: johnknox@earthisland.org
Ed: Jason Mark, Editor, jmark@earthisland.org. **Released:** Quarterly. **Price:** $9.95. **Description:** Magazine publishing environmental alerts and success stories from around the world.

7326 ■ *Environmental Compliance Alert*
Pub: Progressive Business Publications
Ed: Tom Guay, Editor. **Released:** Semimonthly. **Price:** $299. **Description:** Explains the latest air, water and waste regulatory changes affect business in plain English. Recurring features include interviews, news of research, a calendar of events, news of educational opportunities, and a column titled Sharpen Your Judgment.

7327 ■ *Environmental News Network*
Pub: Environmental News Network
Contact: Jeff London, Mktg. Dir.
E-mail: jlondon@enn.com
Released: Daily. **Price:** $12.95 world-wide. **Description:** Online magazine covering environmental and science topics.

7328 ■ *Everyone's Backyard*
Pub: Center for Health, Environment and Justice
Contact: Patty Lovera
Ed: Stephen U. Lester, Editor. **Released:** Quarterly. **Price:** $35, individuals; $5, single issue. **Description:** Includes information on the grassroots environmental movement. Presents community victories and how the groups organized and succeeded. Supports community activists around the United States.

7329 ■ *The Green Business Letter*
Pub: Tilden Press Inc.
Ed: Joel Makower, Editor. **Released:** Monthly. **Price:** $95 electronic edition; $45 for students and academics. **Description:** Helps companies integrate environmental considerations into their operations in a way that creates business value and environmental improvement. Recurring features include interviews, news of research, reports of meetings, book reviews, and notices of publications available.

7330 ■ *The GreenMoney Journal & Online Guide*
Pub: The Greenmoney Journal
Contact: Cliff Feigenbaum, Editor & Publisher
E-mail: cliff@greenmoney.com
Released: Bimonthly. **Price:** $50, individuals; $50, Canada plus $10 postage; $50, elsewhere plus $20 postage. **Description:** Encourages and promotes the awareness of socially and environmentally responsible business, investing and consumer resources in publications and online. Our goal is to educate and empower individuals and businesses to make informed financial decisions through aligning their personal, corporate and financial principles. Recurring features include a calendar

7331 ■ *Inside Cal/EPA*
Pub: Inside Washington Publishers
Contact: Rick Weber, Publisher
Released: Weekly (Fri.). **Price:** $585, U.S. and Canada; $635, elsewhere. **Description:** Reports on environmental legislation, regulation, and litigation.

7332 ■ *Navigator*
Pub: Hudson River Sloop Clearwater Inc.
Ed: Linda Richards, Editor. **Released:** Bimonthly. **Description:** Contains information on environmental issues, globally, nationally, and locally. Recurring features include letters to the editor, interviews, news of research, a calendar of events, and reports of meetings.

7333 ■ *Water Policy Report*
Pub: Inside Washington Publishers
Contact: Charlie Mitchell, Chief Editor
Released: Biweekly, every other Monday. **Price:** $650, U.S. and Canada; $700, elsewhere. **Description:** Reports on federal water quality programs and policies. Covers topics such as drinking water, toxics, enforcement, monitoring, and state/EPA relations.

7334 ■ *Wind Energy Weekly*
Pub: American Wind Energy Association
Ed: Thomas O. Gray, Editor, tom_gray@igc.org. **Released:** Weekly. **Price:** Included in membership; $595, nonmembers. **Description:** Provides wind energy trade news, plus covers energy and environmental policy. Recurring features include news of research, reports of meetings, job listings, and notices of publications available. Remarks: Available only via E-mail account.

7335 ■ *Windstar Wildlife Garden Weekly*
Pub: WindStar Wildlife Institute
Contact: Thomas D. Patrick, Editor & Publisher
Released: Weekly. **Price:** Included in membership; $25, nonmembers. **Description:** Communicates how to attract wildlife to one's property and improve wildlife habitat at the same time, including personal experiences. Includes profiles of wildlife and plants, and what to plant and feed. Recurring features include interviews, news of research, reports of meetings, news of educational opportunities, book reviews, and notices of publications available. Also includes a column titled From the President.

7336 ■ *Worm Digest*
Pub: Worm Digest
Ed: Steven Zorba Frankel, Editor. **Released:** Quarterly. **Price:** $69.95; $109 two years. **Description:** Magazine reporting on worms and worm composting for organic waste utilization and soil enrichment.

VIDEOCASSETTES/ AUDIOCASSETTES

7337 ■ *How to Build a Profitable Consulting Practice 1 & 2*
Chesney Communications
2302 Martin St., Ste. 125
Irvine, CA 92612
Ph:(949)263-5500
Free: 800-223-8878
Fax:(949)263-5506
Co. E-mail: videocc@aol.com
URL: http://www.videocc.com
Released: 1987. **Price:** $59.95. **Description:** An entire Howard Shenson seminar about setting up a consulting practice, condensed into two hours. **Availability:** VHS; 3/4U.

7338 ■ *Recycle Rex*
Buena Vista Home Entertainment
500 S. Buena Vista St.
Burbank, CA 91521-1120
Free: 800-723-4763
URL: http://www.bvhe.com
Released: 1997. **Price:** $199.00. **Description:** Discusses renewable and non-renewable natural resources, recycling, reducing and reusing trash, and how items are made.

TRADE SHOWS AND CONVENTIONS

7339 ■ GLOBE - International Environmental Industry Trade Fair and Conference
GLOBE Foundation of Canada
World Trade Centre
578 999 Canada Pl.
Vancouver, BC, Canada V6C 3E1
Ph:(604)775-7300
Free: 800-274-6097
Fax:(604)666-8123
Co. E-mail: info@globe.ca
URL: http://www.globe.ca
Released: Biennial. **Audience:** Trade professionals. **Principal Exhibits:** Environmental equipment, supplies, and services.

CONSULTANTS

7340 ■ ardea consulting
10 1st St.
Woodland, CA 95695
Ph:(530)669-1645
Fax:(530)669-1674
Co. E-mail: birdtox1@ardeacon.com
URL: http://www.ardeacon.com
Contact: Michael Getz, Mgr
Scope: Provides avian and wildlife toxicology and eco toxicology guidance to engineering and environmental firms, government agencies, businesses and non-governmental organizations. Provides ecological risk assessments; assesses contaminant effects on birds and other wildlife; evaluates impacts of pesticides on birds and other wildlife; reviews and compiles scientific field research and data/literature; plans and document pesticide effects studies; collects wildlife specimens or other environmental samples, prepares samples for chemical analysis, and interpret analytical results; drafts project reports and research proposals and reviews ecotoxicology data and reports. **Publications:** "Estimating the response of ring-necked pheasants to the Conservation Reserve Program," 2008; "Identifying and handling contaminant-related wildlife mortality/morbidity," The Wildlife Society, 2005; "Productivity of American robins exposed to polychlorinated biphenyls," 2003; "Assessing impacts of environmental contaminants on wildlife". **Seminars:** Pheasant breeding bird survey response to the conservation reserve program, 2006; Society of Environmental Toxicology and Chemistry; Niov, 2006; Introduction and Demonstration of the Terrestrial Wildlife Exposure Model (TWEM), Nov, 2004; Society of Environmental Toxicology and Chemistry, Nov, 2004.

7341 ■ Chester Engineers Inc.
1555 Coraopolis Heights Rd.
Moon Township, PA 15108
Ph:(412)809-6600
Free: 877-967-1901
Fax:(412)809-6611
Co. E-mail: info@chesterengineers.com
URL: http://www.chester-engineers.com
Contact: Tom Johnson, CFO
E-mail: rkhosah@atschester.com
Scope: Provides water and wastewater engineering solutions to public and industrial clients across the United States and internationally. Specializes in

environmental data management and modeling, water resources engineering, chemical problem solving, environmental investigations, and air quality measurement.

7342 ■ EnviroBusiness Inc.
21 B St.
Burlington, MA 01803
Ph:(781)273-2500
Free: 800-786-2346
Fax:(781)273-3311
Co. E-mail: info@ebiconsulting.com
URL: http://www.ebiconsulting.com
Contact: Jeffrey T. Smith, Vice President
E-mail: skmiotek@atsebiconsultants.com
Scope: Provides environmental, civil, and structural engineering support to national and international telecommunications companies. Specializes in providing environmental health and safety management consulting and training, occupational health and safety, industrial hygiene, air quality, semiconductor safety, bio-safety, and safety engineering services. Provides environmental health and safety services to renowned institutions in the biotechnology, pharmaceutical, education, energy, education, manufacturing, and marine industries. **Seminars:** Marina Industry Regulatory Compliance Assistance, Mar, 2007; The Business of Boating in MA, Jan, 2007.

7343 ■ Groupe DGE International Inc.
2586 ch. Hamel
Sherbrooke, QC, Canada J1R 0P8
Ph:(819)820-8881
Fax:(819)820-8808
Co. E-mail: info@dgeinternational.ca
URL: http://www.dgeinternational.ca
Contact: Yves Lepine, Principle
E-mail: ylepine@atsdgeinternational.ca
Scope: Firm specializes in performing environmental management projects like the implementation of ISO 14000 environmental management system, the completion of studies and verifications as well as financial assistance requests for viability studies and implementation of international projects.

7344 ■ Immedia Technologies
107 Sierra Woods Dr.
Ottawa, ON, Canada K0A 1L0
Ph:(613)236-4419
Co. E-mail: info@immtech.com
URL: http://www.immtech.com
Contact: Dan Frederiksen, Tech Dir
Scope: Specializing in environmental information solutions.

7345 ■ J.L. Meaher & Associates Inc.
107 St. Francis St.
PO Box 2672
Mobile, AL 36602-3334
Ph:(251)433-2676
Fax:(251)433-0708
Co. E-mail: meaherasso@aol.com
Contact: Joseph L. Meaher, President
E-mail: meaheroffice@atsbellsouth.net
Scope: Offers general forestry consulting, including advice on timber and timberland taxation, estate taxation, planning, timberland sales and purchases.

7346 ■ Monte G. Cole & Associates
4915 Bay St. NE
Purcellville, VA 20132-3214
Ph:(540)338-1122
Fax:(540)338-5041
Co. E-mail: montecole@aol.com
Contact: Monte Cole, President
E-mail: montecole@friendsofdusty.org
Scope: Firm provides risk management information, software systems, education and insurance consultation, specializing in environmental health and safety issues.

7347 ■ Social Venture Partners
1601 2nd Ave., Ste. 615
Seattle, WA 98101-1539
Ph:(206)374-8757
Fax:(206)728-0552
Co. E-mail: info@svpseattle.org
URL: http://www.svpseattle.org
Contact: Sofia Michelakis, Director
E-mail: sofiam@atssvpseattle.org
Scope: Organization addresses social and environmental issues in the region. Offers consultation and grants to nonprofits. It seeks to develop philanthropy and volunteerism to achieve positive social change. Using the venture capital approach as a model, committed to giving time, money and expertise to create partnerships with not-for-profit organizations. **Publications:** "Voices That Matter: Paul Shoemaker, on Becoming a Social Entrepreneur," Oct, 2009; "Immerse Your Donors In You," The Nonprofit Times, Sep, 2009; "New Ideas Shouldn't Necessarily Spawn New Nonprofit Groups," Jan, 2009; "Inside Entrepreneurship: Nonprofit boards will welcome your talents," Dec, 2008; "Charity begins in the office," Nov, 2008.

7348 ■ Stelle & Associates Inc.
4137 S 87th E Ave.
PO Box 470071
Tulsa, OK 74145
Ph:(918)425-4277
Fax:(918)622-2206
Co. E-mail: scott@stelleassociates.com
URL: http://www.stelleassociates.com
Contact: J. Scott Stelle, President
E-mail: scott@stelleassociates.com
Scope: Consulting consortium which allows highly qualified and experienced specialists an opportunity to function singly or in conjunction with others on projects of any size or duration. Has developed several levels of environmental due diligence to fulfill the need of clients in the most cost effective manner.

FRANCHISES AND BUSINESS OPPORTUNITIES

7349 ■ Lord & Partners
9-741 Muskoka Rd., Ste. 3 N
Huntsville, ON, Canada P1H 2L3
Ph:(705)788-1966
Free: 877-490-6660
Fax:(705)788-1969
Co. E-mail: busadmin@lordandpartners.com
URL: http://www.lordandpartners.com
No. of Franchise Units: 4. **No. of Company-Owned Units:** 2. **Founded:** 1990. **Franchised:** 2005. **Description:** Unique business to business franchise network serving a growing $30 billion market in representing Canadian manufactured environmentally responsible solutions that replace hazardous traditional chemicals in the workplace and reduce environmental aspects and impacts on the community. **Equity Capital Needed:** $200,000. **Franchise Fee:** $50,000. **Training:** Provides 29 days training on the proven proprietary business, marketing systems, a demo "showroom on wheels," with ongoing support for a protected territory.

COMPUTERIZED DATABASES

7350 ■ *BioQUEST Library*
Beloit College
700 College St.
Beloit, WI 53511
Ph:(608)363-2012
Fax:(608)363-2052
Co. E-mail: bioquest@beloit.edu
URL: http://www.bioquest.org
Description: An ongoing peer-reviewed community publication of software simulations, tools, datasets, and other supporting materials from educators and developers engaged in education and research in science. Modules are downloadable and freely accessible for educational use. **Availability:** Online: Beloit College. **Type:** Full text; Image.

7351 ■ *Earthquake Intensity Database Search 1638-1985*
U.S. National Oceanic and Atmospheric Administration
325 Broadway E/GC3
Boulder, CO 80305-3328
Ph:(303)497-6345
Fax:(303)497-6513
Co. E-mail: kimberly.k.nye@noaa.gov
URL: http://www.ngdc.noaa.gov/mgg
Description: Contains more than 157,000 damage and felt reports on more than 23,000 earthquakes in the United States from 1638 to 1985. Information covers magnitudes, epicentral coordinates, focal depths, names and coordinates of reporting cities or areas, distance from city or area to epicenter, and reported intensities. **Availability:** Online: U.S. National Oceanic and Atmospheric Administration. **Type:** Properties; Time series.

7352 ■ *Energy Detente*
Lundberg Survey Inc.
PO Box 6002
Camarillo, CA 93011
Ph:(805)383-2400
Fax:(805)383-2424
Co. E-mail: lsi@lundbergsurvey.com
URL: http://www.lundbergsurvey.com
Description: Contains information on developments in the energy field worldwide. Topics include consumer prices and taxes of fuels worldwide, refining margins, international and domestic policies, refining technology and changing practices, company mergers, alternative fuels, international trade, marketing and consumer issues and environmental protection. Also includes a consumer fuel price and tax series, with national averages by country updated monthly and coverage by product. Enables users to search by date, keyword, and current issues. **Availability:** Online: Lundberg Survey Inc. **Type:** Full text.

7353 ■ *Environment & Safety Library*
The Bureau of National Affairs Inc.
1801 S Bell St.
Arlington, VA 22202
Free: 800-372-1033
Co. E-mail: customercare@bna.com
URL: http://www.bna.com
Description: Contains reports on current laws and regulations, news, and developments in the environment and safety field worldwide. Covers air pollution; ANSI standards scopes; Canadian laws and regulations; chemical manufacturing and regulation; compliance deadlines; environmental due diligence; European Union directives and regulations; federal statutes; regulations; guidance/agency documents and executive orders; food and drug regulation; food safety; hazmat transport; international treaties; bilateral agreements; conventions; environmental laws and regulations; contacts; Mexican laws and regulations; mines and mining safety; NAFTA; occupational safety and health; OSWER directives; pesticides; right-to-know; solid, hazardous, and radioactive waste; state environmental statutes and regulations; state safety statutes and regulations for OSHA-approved states; test methods; toxic substances; waste management, disposal, and cleanup; and water pollution. Includes the full text of federal statutes, codified regulations, and the *Federal Register*, the full text of state statutes and regulations; full text of international treaties, Canadian and Mexican laws, country profiles, and European Union directives; legal decisions; BNA analysis; BNA reports; more than 3,000 federal and state forms; and data on more than 80,000 regulated chemical substances. Also contains an index of more than 275,000 cross-referenced entries. **Availability:** Online: The Bureau of National Affairs Inc; CD-ROM: The Bureau of National Affairs Inc. **Type:** Full text.

7354 ■ *Environmental Law Reporter*
Environmental Law Institute
2000 L St. NW, Ste. 620
Washington, DC 20036
Ph:(202)939-3800
Fax:(202)939-3868
Co. E-mail: law@eli.org
URL: http://www.eli.org
Description: Contains information on U.S. environmental law. Corresponds to the complete text of *Environmental Law Reporter*, covering international agreements, administrative materials, and pending litigation relating to environmental and natural resource issues. Comprises the following 8 files: ELR Administrative Materials (ELR-ADMIN)—contains the complete text of environmental law documents from

federal agencies. Includes enforcement policy guides from the Environmental Protection Agency (EPA); EPA Administrative Law Judge decisions; and citations from the *Code of Federal Regulations, Federal Register*, and *Federal Executive Orders.* Covers 1971 to date. ELR Indexes, Tables & Bibliographies—contains the Cumulative Table of Cases, with citations, procedure histories, and citations to other appropriate reporting services; Subject Matter Index, with concise breakdowns of all ELR subject matter into individual subject categories; Annual Bibliographies, with citations to pertinent journal articles; ELR Cite Conversion Table; and Briefs and Pleadings Index. ELR News & Analysis (ELR-NEWS)—contains the complete text of commentaries on developments in federal and state courts, U.S. Congress, and federal administrative agencies. Corresponds to *News & Analysis.* Covers 1983 to date, with earlier materials from 1971. ELR Litigation (ELR-LIT)—contains the complete text of federal and some state case decisions that relate to environmental issues. Covers 1971 to date. ELR State News and Analysis—contains detailed state-level information on developments in environmental, land use, natural resources, and toxic tort law. Includes summaries of relevant agency developments. Provides links to sources of agency information. ELR International News and Analysis—contains comprehensive reporting and analysis of international legal developments in environmental law and related areas. Covers topics such as trade and the environment, climate change, biodiversity, sustainable development, laws in developing and developed nations, and more ELR Health and Safety News and Analysis—contains detailed information on issues surrounding occupational health and safety, cost-benefit analysis, risk regulation, ISO 1401 implementation, ergonomics, reporting requirements, and associated topics. Includes listings of articles and links to both governmental and nongovernmental sources of additional information. ELR Update (ELR-UPDATE)—contains the complete text of weekly ELR newsletters. Includes current information on cases, legislation, and other congressional activities. Also includes citations to recent administrative actions and settlements. Covers 1985 to date. **Availability:** Online: Thomson Reuters, LexisNexis Group, Environmental Law Institute. **Type:** Full text.

7355 ■ *Environmental Sciences & Pollution Management*
ProQuest LLC
789 E Eisenhower Pky.
Ann Arbor, MI 48103
Ph:(734)761-4700
Fax:(734)997-4222
Co. E-mail: info@proquest.com
URL: http://www.csa.com
Description: Provides complete, multidisciplinary coverage of the environmental sciences. Contains more than 2 million abstracts from approximately 6000 sources, including journal articles, conference proceedings, monographs, Technology reports, and books. Includes abstracts of all U.S. federal environmental impact statements indexed by subject, geographic area, statute, and agency. Abstracts include a description of the project, associated positive and negative consequences, and legal mandates. Cover such subjects as air quality, industrial and hazardous waste, water pollution, waste management, risk assessment, and much more. Also includes 13 abstract databases: Agricultural and Environmental Biotechnology Abstracts, ASFA 3: Aquatic Pollution and Environmental Quality, Bacteriology Abstracts (Microbiology B), Ecology Abstracts, Environmental Engineering Abstracts, Health and Safety Science Abstracts, Human Population & Natural Resource Management, Industrial and Applied Microbiology Abstracts (Microbiology A), Pollution Abstracts Risk Abstracts, Sustainability Science Abstracts, Toxicology Abstracts, Water Resources Abstracts. **Availability:** Online: EBSCO Publishing, Wolters Kluwer Health. **Type:** Bibliographic.

7356 ■ *The Environmentalist*
Springer Science Business Media L.L.C.
233 Spring St.
New York, NY 10013
Ph:(212)460-1500
Free: 800-777-4643
Fax:(212)461-1575
Co. E-mail: service-ny@springer.com
URL: http://www.springer.com
Description: Contains critical articles and reviews on environmental issues worldwide. Covers such issues as energy production, pollution and toxic wastes, renewable and non-renewable energy sources, agricultural land and food production, and more. Contains guest editorials, in-depth articles and features, interviews, and reports on the latest news. Stresses general environmental education and responsible environmental management by industry, government, and environmental professionals. **Availability:** Online: Springer Science Business Media L.L.C. **Type:** Full text.

7357 ■ *Jane's Merchant Ships*
IHS Global Ltd.
Sentinel House
163 Brighton Rd.
Surrey
Coulsdon CR5 2YH, United Kingdom
Ph:44 20 8700 3700
Fax:44 20 8763 1006
Co. E-mail: info.uk@janes.com
URL: http://www.janes.com
Description: Contains the complete text of *Jane's Merchant Ships*, covering almost every merchant ship in the world. Includes more than 1200 photographs of merchant ships currently sailing the seas and more than 3500 drawings of ship classes. Entries contain information such as date built, displacement, dimensions, engines, and sister ships. Highlights the key recognition characteristics, enabling identification of the class, flag, and main specifications. **Availability:** Online: IHS Global Ltd. **Type:** Full text; Directory; Image.

7358 ■ *NGDC Geologic Hazards Photos*
U.S. National Oceanic and Atmospheric Administration
325 Broadway E/GC3
Boulder, CO 80305-3328
Ph:(303)497-6345
Fax:(303)497-6513
Co. E-mail: kimberly.k.nye@noaa.gov
URL: http://www.ngdc.noaa.gov/mgg
Description: Contains geologic hazards photographs. Includes color and black and white photographs of earthquakes, volcanoes, tsunamis, and landslides, accompanied by captions. **Availability:** Online: U.S. National Oceanic and Atmospheric Administration; CD-ROM: U.S. National Oceanic and Atmospheric Administration. **Type:** Image.

7359 ■ *Significant Earthquakes Database*
U.S. National Oceanic and Atmospheric Administration
325 Broadway E/GC3
Boulder, CO 80305-3328
Ph:(303)497-6345
Fax:(303)497-6513
Co. E-mail: kimberly.k.nye@noaa.gov
URL: http://www.ngdc.noaa.gov/mgg
Description: Contains information on more than 6500 destructive earthquakes worldwide, each having a magnitude of 7.5 or greater, and/or resulting in $1 million in damages, and/or 10 or more deaths. Enables users to search by earthquake event year, latitude and longitude coordinates, and by event region. **Availability:** Online: U.S. National Oceanic and Atmospheric Administration. **Type:** Full text.

LIBRARIES

7360 ■ Andrews & Kurth L.L.P. Library
1350 I St. NW, Ste. 1100
Washington, DC 20005
Ph:(202)662-2700
Fax:(202)662-2739
URL: http://www.andrewskurth.com
Contact: Martha L. Birdseye, Libn.
Scope: Law - civil, environmental, public utilities. **Services:** Interlibrary loan; Library not open to the public. **Holdings:** 3500 volumes.

7361 ■ Appalachia-Science in the Public Interest Library
50 Lair St.
Mount Vernon, KY 40456-9806
Ph:(606)256-0077
Fax:(606)256-2779
Co. E-mail: aspi@a-spi.org
URL: http://www.a-spi.org
Scope: Appropriate technology, environmental science, solar energy, water and air environments, organic gardening, forest, nature. **Services:** Copying; Library open to the public by appointment. **Holdings:** 7000 books; 8000 periodical volumes; 3000 reports; 3000 microfiche. **Subscriptions:** 100 journals and other serials; 3 newspapers.

7362 ■ Beveridge & Diamond, P.C. Library
1350 I St. NW, Ste. 700
Washington, DC 20005-3311
Ph:(202)789-6000
Fax:(202)789-6190
Co. E-mail: slarson@bdlaw.com
URL: http://www.bdlaw.com
Scope: Law - environmental, pollution, waste disposal, water. **Services:** Interlibrary loan; Library open to the public by appointment with restrictions. **Holdings:** 10,000 volumes. **Subscriptions:** 300 journals and other serials.

7363 ■ Bracewell & Patterson Library
2000 K St. NW, Ste. 500
Washington, DC 20006-1872
Ph:(202)828-5876
Fax:(202)223-1225
Contact: Ruth Mendelson, Libn.
Scope: Law - banking, environmental, taxation. **Services:** Interlibrary loan; Library open to the public by appointment with restrictions. **Holdings:** 10,000 volumes; technical reports; videocassettes; audiocassettes.

7364 ■ Bryan Cave LLP Law Library
1155 F St., NW
Washington, DC 20004
Ph:(202)508-6000
Fax:(202)508-6200
Co. E-mail: laura.green@bryancave.com
URL: http://www.bryancave.com
Contact: Laurie Green, Mgr., Lib. & Res.Svcs.
Scope: Government and politics; law - commercial, corporate, environmental, intellectual property, taxation. **Services:** Interlibrary loan; copying; faxing; Library open to the public with restrictions. **Holdings:** 11,000 volumes. **Subscriptions:** 200 journals and other serials.

7365 ■ Cadwalader, Wickersham & Taft Library
700 6th St., N.W.
Washington, DC 20001
Ph:(202)862-2200
Fax:(202)862-2400
Co. E-mail: jane.platt-brown@cwt.com
URL: http://www.cadwalader.com
Contact: Jane Platt-Brown, Lib.Hd.
Scope: Law - antitrust, corporate, securities, taxation, business fraud. **Services:** Interlibrary loan; Library open to the public by appointment (with restrictions). **Holdings:** 15,000 volumes; microforms; CD-ROM.

7366 ■ Canada - Forest Alliance of British Columbia Library
1055 Dunsmuir St.
PO Box 49312
Vancouver, BC, Canada V7X 1L3
Ph:(604)685-7507
Fax:(604)685-5373
URL: http://www.forest.ca
Contact: Elizabeth Steele
Scope: Forestry, environment. **Services:** Library open to the public.

7367 ■ Church World Service–Video Library
28606 Phillips St.
PO Box 968
Elkhart, IN 46515
Ph:(574)264-3102
Free: 800-297-1516

Fax:(574)262-0966
Co. E-mail: videos@churchworldservice.org
URL: http://www.churchworldservice.org
Contact: Gary Arnold, Film Libn.
Scope: World hunger, the environment, poverty, development, human rights, refugees. **Services:** Library open to the public. **Holdings:** 400 videocassettes.

7368 ■ DLA Piper LLP US Library
500 8th St., NW
Washington, DC 20004
Ph:(202)799-4496
Fax:(202)799-5000
Co. E-mail: pat.mitchell@dlapiper.com
Contact: Patricia Mitchell, Hd.Libn.
Scope: Law - environmental; government contracts, communications, franchising. **Services:** Interlibrary loan; Library not open to the public. **Holdings:** 6000 books.

7369 ■ Energy & Environmental Management, Inc. E2M Library
Box 71
Murrysville, PA 15668
Ph:(412)733-0022
Fax:(412)733-0018
Contact: Larry L. Simmons, Pres.
Scope: Environmental compliance in the electric utility, metals production, mining, chemical, petroleum, sanitation, and manufacturing industries. **Services:** Library not open to the public. **Holdings:** 1000 books. **Subscriptions:** 12 journals and other serials.

7370 ■ ERM - West, Inc. Library
1777 Botelho Dr., Ste. 260
Walnut Creek, CA 94596
Ph:(925)946-0455
Fax:(925)946-9968
Co. E-mail: mike_quillin@ermwest.com
URL: http://www.erm.com/erm/main.nsf/pages/homepage
Contact: Mike Quillin
Scope: Environmental issues, groundwater, soils, air, regulations. **Services:** Interlibrary loan; Library not open to the public. **Holdings:** Government documents. **Subscriptions:** 65 journals and other serials.

7371 ■ Farmington River Watershed Association–Environmental Research Center
749 Hopmeadow St.
Simsbury, CT 06070
Ph:(860)658-4442
Fax:(860)651-7519
Co. E-mail: info@frwa.org
URL: http://www.frwa.org
Contact: Eileen Fielding, Exec.Dir.
Scope: Farmington River watershed, environmental resources. **Services:** Copying; Library open to the public with restrictions. **Holdings:** 500 books; 500 reports.

7372 ■ General Engineering Laboratories, Inc. Library
PO Box 30712
Charleston, SC 29417
Ph:(843)556-8171
Fax:(843)766-1178
Co. E-mail: bob.pullano@gel.com
URL: http://www.gel.net
Contact: Bob Pullano
Scope: Environmental analysis, environmental consulting, environmental regulations. **Holdings:** Figures not available.

7373 ■ Georgia Wildlife Federation Education Library
11600 Hazelbrand Rd.
Covington, GA 30014
Ph:(770)787-7887
Fax:(770)787-9229
Co. E-mail: dharris@gwf.org
URL: http://www.gwf.org
Contact: DeAnna Harris
Scope: Wildlife, conservation. **Services:** Library open to the public by appointment. **Holdings:** 1100 books.

7374 ■ Great Plains RC & D–Environmental Education Library
1505 N. Glenn L. English St.
Cordell, OK 73632-1405
Ph:(580)832-3661
Co. E-mail: larry.wright@ok.usda.gov
URL: http://www.greatplainsrcd.org
Contact: Alfred Miller, Chm.
Scope: Conservation education, grant researching, agriculture, solid waste and recycling, non-profit Organization, rural development. **Services:** Library open to the public with restrictions. **Holdings:** 200 books/binders; 100 videos; 15 CD-ROMs; 50 teacher guides. **Subscriptions:** 4 magazines; 30 newsletters.

7375 ■ Heartland Institute
19 S. LaSalle St., No. 903
Chicago, IL 60603
Ph:(312)377-4000
Fax:(312)377-5000
Co. E-mail: think@heartland.org
URL: http://www.heartland.org
Contact: Cheryl Parker, Adm.Asst.
Scope: Privatization, deregulation, education reform, healthcare reform, environment, libertarian thought, environmental play, economics. **Services:** Library open to the public by appointment. **Holdings:** 2500 books; 300 reports; 200 audiocassettes; 100 videotapes. **Subscriptions:** 200 journals and other serials.

7376 ■ Hudson County Improvement Authority Library
Environmental Resource Center
574 Summit Ave., 5th Fl.
Jersey City, NJ 07306
Ph:(201)795-4555
Free: 800-540-0987
Fax:(201)795-0240
Co. E-mail: recycle@hcia.org
URL: http://www.hcia.org
Contact: MaryEllen Gilpin, Dir.
Scope: Environment. **Services:** Library not open to the public. **Holdings:** Books; manuals; videocassettes; catalogs; DVDs. **Subscriptions:** 20 journals and other serials; 3 newspapers.

7377 ■ Illinois Sustainable Technology Center
1 Hazelwood Dr.
Champaign, IL 61820
Ph:(217)333-8957
Fax:(217)333-8944
Co. E-mail: library@istc.illinois.edu
URL: http://www.istc.illinois.edu
Contact: Laura L. Barnes, Libn.
Scope: Pollution prevention, hazardous waste, industrial process engineering, industrial audits, analytical chemistry, waste reduction, household hazardous waste, energy efficiency, renewable energy, alternative fuels, biodiesel. **Services:** Interlibrary loan; Library open to the public for reference use only. **Holdings:** 8000 books; 75 videotapes. **Subscriptions:** 250 journals and other serials; 1 newspaper.

7378 ■ Karpeles Manuscript Library–Duluth Museum
902 E. 1st St.
Duluth, MN 55805
Ph:(218)728-0630
URL: http://www.rain.org/lAtkarpeles/dul.html
Contact: Lee R. Fadden, Dir.
Scope: Rare manuscripts. **Services:** Library open to the public. **Holdings:** Manuscripts.

7379 ■ Keller and Heckman LLP–Law Firm Library
1001 G St. NW, Ste. 500 W.
Washington, DC 20001
Ph:(202)434-4100
Fax:(202)434-4646
Co. E-mail: khlibrary@khlaw.com
URL: http://www.khlaw.com
Contact: Abigail Ross, Lib.Mgr.
Scope: Food and drug, the environment, telecommunications, transportation, intellectual property, International trade. **Services:** Interlibrary loan; Library not open to the public. **Holdings:** 8000 books. **Subscriptions:** 140 journals and other serials; 8 newspapers.

7380 ■ Lille D'Easum Library–SPEC Library
2150 Maple St.
Vancouver, BC, Canada V6J 3T3
Ph:(604)736-7732
Fax:(604)736-7115
Scope: Environmental conservation. **Services:** Library open to the public. **Holdings:** 5000 books and reports.

7381 ■ Maritime College of Forest Technology Library
1350 Regent St.
Fredericton, NB, Canada E3C 2G6
Ph:(506)458-0653
Free: (866)619-9900
Fax:(506)458-0652
Co. E-mail: info@mcft.ca
URL: http://www.mcft.ca
Contact: Gerald Redmond, Libn.
Scope: Forestry, natural resources, environment, conservation. **Services:** Library not open to the public. **Holdings:** Figures not available. **Subscriptions:** 20 journals and other serials.

7382 ■ McKenna Long & Aldridge LLP Law Library
1900 K St. NW, Lower Level
Washington, DC 20006-1108
Ph:(202)496-7752
Fax:(202)496-7756
Co. E-mail: kmartin@mckennalong.com
URL: http://www.mckennalong.com
Contact: Kate Martin, Dir. of Lib.Svcs.
Scope: Law - government contracts, environmental, litigation, food and drug, International, health care, labor, insurance, energy. **Services:** Interlibrary loan; Library not open to the public. **Holdings:** 15,000 books; 5000 bound periodical volumes. **Subscriptions:** 400 journals and other serials.

7383 ■ M.H. Chew & Associates Corporate Library
7275 National Dr., Ste. C
Livermore, CA 94550
Ph:(925)443-5071
Fax:(510)373-0624
Co. E-mail: patricia.shannon@mhchew.com
URL: http://www.mhchew.com/
Contact: Patricia Shannon
Scope: Nuclear safety, environmental safety, health physics, radiation protection, risk analysis. **Services:** Interlibrary loan; copying; Library not open to the public. **Holdings:** 1500 books; 2000 bound periodical volumes; 5000 reports. **Subscriptions:** 100 journals and other serials.

7384 ■ Northcoast Environmental Center Library
791 8th St., Ste. 6
Arcata, CA 95521
Ph:(707)822-6918
Fax:(707)822-0827
Co. E-mail: nec@yournec.org
URL: http://www.yournec.org
Contact: Greg King, Exec.Dir.
Scope: Logging, mining, fish and wildlife, habitat protection, air and water quality, toxic hazards, recycling, sustainability. **Services:** Interlibrary loan; copying; Library open to the public with restrictions. **Holdings:** 8000 books; 5500 reports; 200 videos; 400 maps. **Subscriptions:** 70 journals and other serials; 10 newspapers.

7385 ■ O'Connor Associates Environmental Inc. Library
318 11th Ave. SE, Ste. 200
Calgary, AB, Canada T2G 0Y2
Ph:(403)294-4200

Free: 800-661-8141
Fax:(403)294-4240
Co. E-mail: info@oconnor-associates.com
URL: http://www.oconnor-associates.com/
Scope: Engineering - environmental, geotechnical; soil, air, and groundwater cleanup; environmental impact statements; risk assessment; toxicology. **Services:** Interlibrary loan; copying; Library open to the public with restrictions. **Holdings:** 4500 books. **Subscriptions:** 30 journals and other serials.

7386 ■ PA Consulting Group Library
4601 N. Fairfax Dr., Ste. 600
Arlington, VA 22203
Ph:(571)227-9000
Fax:(571)227-9001
Co. E-mail: info@paconsulting.com
URL: http://www.paconsulting.com
Contact: Michelle Reaux, Info.Mgr.
Scope: Environment, electricity, economics, coal, petroleum, developing countries. **Services:** Interlibrary loan; SDI; Library not open to the public. **Holdings:** 2000 books; 170 reports. **Subscriptions:** 118 journals and other serials; 4 newspapers.

7387 ■ Petroleum Communication Foundation Library
100-4 Avenue S.W., 409
Calgary, AB, Canada T2P 3N2
Ph:(403)264-6064
Fax:(403)237-6286
Co. E-mail: info@pcf.ca
URL: http://www.pcf.ca
Contact: Tony Laramee, Info.Svcs.
Scope: Petroleum, gasoline, oil, environment, natural gas, sour gas, flaring, benzene. **Services:** Copying; Library open to the public. **Holdings:** 570 books; 10 bound periodical volumes; 400 reports. **Subscriptions:** 26 journals and other serials; 3 newspapers.

7388 ■ S L Ross Environmental Research Ltd. Library
200-717 Belfast Rd., Ste. 200
Ottawa, ON, Canada K1G 0Z4
Ph:(613)232-1564
Fax:(613)232-6660
Co. E-mail: info@slross.com
URL: http://www.slross.com/
Scope: Oil spill research, spill risk assessment, environmental impact. **Services:** Library not open to the public. **Holdings:** Figures not available.

7389 ■ San Francisco Public Library–Wallace Stegner Environmental Center
100 Larkin St., 5th Fl.
San Francisco, CA 94102
Ph:(415)557-4500
Co. E-mail: citylibrarian@sfpl.org
URL: http://sfpl.org
Contact: Luis Herrera, City Libn.
Scope: Environmental literature. **Services:** Center open to the public. **Holdings:** 1000 books; audiocassettes; videocassettes.

7390 ■ Saskatchewan Research Council–Information Services
125-15 Innovation Blvd.
Saskatoon, SK, Canada S7N 2X8
Ph:(306)933-5400
Fax:(306)933-7446
Co. E-mail: library@src.sk.ca
URL: http://www.src.sk.ca
Contact: Colleen Marshall, Info.Mgt.Coord.
Scope: Agriculture, biotechnology and food, alternative energy and manufacturing, energy, the environment and forestry, mining and minerals. **Services:** Interlibrary loan (with other libraries) **Holdings:** 8600 monographs; 3300 SRC-authored publications. **Subscriptions:** 55 periodicals.

7391 ■ SCS Engineers Library
3900 Kilroy Airport Way, Ste. 100
Long Beach, CA 90806-6816
Ph:(562)426-9544
Fax:(562)427-0805
Co. E-mail: lbures@scsengineers.com
Contact: Loran Bures, Libn.
Scope: Environmental and civil engineering, hazardous waste control, landfills, landfill gas, environmental protection. **Services:** Copying; Library not open to the public. **Holdings:** 50,000 volumes; government reports; trade journals. **Subscriptions:** 115 journals and other serials; 3 newspapers.

7392 ■ Sedgwick County Zoo Library
5555 Zoo Blvd.
Wichita, KS 67212-1698
Ph:(316)660-9453
Fax:(316)942-3781
Co. E-mail: ask@scz.org
URL: http://www.scz.org/
Contact: Mark C. Reed, Exec.Dir.
Scope: Zoology, wildlife conservation. **Services:** Interlibrary loan; copying; Library open to the public. **Holdings:** 1000 books; 100 reports. **Subscriptions:** 10 journals and other serials.

7393 ■ Tetra Tech NUS, Inc.–Technical Information Center
900 Trail Ridge Rd.
Aiken, SC 29803
Ph:(803)649-7963
Fax:(803)642-8454
Co. E-mail: james.oliver@tetratech.com
URL: http://intranet.ttnus.com/
Contact: Debbie Pyron, Mgr.
Scope: Environment, nuclear energy. **Services:** Library not open to the public. **Holdings:** Reports. **Subscriptions:** 2 newspapers.

7394 ■ United Nations Association of Southern Arizona–Education Resource Center
United Nations Center
6242 E. Speedway Blvd.
Tucson, AZ 85712
Ph:(520)881-7060
Fax:(520)327-0314
Co. E-mail: education@untucson.org
URL: http://untucson.org
Contact: Blake Gentry, Educ.Coord.
Scope: United Nations, war and peace, International relations, world environment. **Services:** Copying; Center open to the public. **Holdings:** 2000 books; 50 bound periodical volumes. **Subscriptions:** 80 journals and other serials; 2 newspapers.

7395 ■ U.S. Environmental Protection Agency Headquarters Library
1200 Pennsylvania Ave., NW
Rm. 3340
Mailcode 3404T
Washington, DC 20460-0001
Ph:(202)566-0556
Fax:(202)566-0574
Co. E-mail: hqchemlibraries@epa.gov
URL: http://www.epa.gov/libraries/hqrepository.html
Scope: Water - pollution, quality, supply; air pollution; noise abatement; radiation; hazardous wastes; solid waste management; resource recovery; pesticides; chemistry and toxicology; social, economic, legislative, legal, administrative, and management aspects of environmental policy. **Services:** Interlibrary loan; SDI; Library open to the public with restrictions. **Holdings:** 16,000 books; 7000 hardcopy documents and technical reports; 400,000 documents and reports from the EPA and its predecessor agencies on microfiche; newspapers, abstracts and indexes, periodicals on microfilm. **Subscriptions:** 20 journals and other serials.

7396 ■ U.S. Environmental Protection Agency Library
Mail Code 3404T
1200 Pennsylvania Ave., NW
Washington, DC 20460
Ph:(202)566-0556
URL: http://www.epa.gov
Contact: Margaret Esser, Lib.Techn.
Scope: Water pollution, water quality, environmental quality, air pollution, toxic substances, hazardous wastes. **Services:** Interlibrary loan; copying; Library open to the public. **Holdings:** 3500 books; 10,000 federal and state reports; 200,000 microfiche. **Subscriptions:** 60 journals and other serials.

7397 ■ The Weinberg Group–Washington Information Resources Library
1220 19th St. NW, Ste. 300
Washington, DC 20036
Ph:(202)833-8077
Fax:(202)833-7057
Co. E-mail: library@weinberggrroup.com
URL: http://www.weinberggroup.com
Contact: Ruth Bridges, Mgr. of Res.Svcs.
Scope: Environment, medicine, chemistry. **Services:** Interlibrary loan; Library not open to the public. **Holdings:** 2000 books. **Subscriptions:** 108 journals and other serials; 4 newspapers.

7398 ■ Williams College Center for Environmental Studies–Matt Cole Memorial Library
Harper House
PO Box 632
Williamstown, MA 01267
Ph:(413)597-2346
Fax:(413)597-3489
Co. E-mail: nparker@williams.edu
URL: http://www.williams.edu/CES/mattcole.htm
Contact: Norm Parker, Info.Spec.
Scope: Agriculture, air pollution, biodiversity, climate, regional planning, coastal, ecology, energy, environmental health, environmental law and policy, forestry, hazardous substances, land use and planning, solid waste, water quality, wildlife management habitat. **Services:** Interlibrary loan; Library open to the public. **Holdings:** 7500 books; 2900 bound periodical volumes; 5000 other documents. **Subscriptions:** 250 journals and other serials.

RESEARCH CENTERS

7399 ■ Center for Environmental Research
2210 S FM 973
Austin, TX 78725
Ph:(512)972-1960
Fax:(512)972-9876
Co. E-mail: kevin.anderson@ci.austin.tx.us
URL: http://www.ci.austin.tx.us/water/cer2.htm
Contact: Kevin M. Anderson PhD, Coord.
E-mail: kevin.anderson@ci.austin.tx.us
Scope: Urban ecology and sustainability, soil ecology and biosolids recycling, sustainable agriculture, riparian ecology and restoration, avian ecology and citizen science, urban biodiversity conservation, and environmental health education. **Publications:** Discovering the Colorado: a vision for the Austin-Bastrop river corridor. **Educational Activities:** Educational tours and workshops; NGO partnerships.

7400 ■ Harvard University–Belfer Center for Science and International Affairs–Environment and Natural Resources Program
John F. Kennedy School of Government, Box 84
79 JFK St.
Cambridge, MA 02138
Ph:(617)495-1351
Fax:(617)495-1635
Co. E-mail: henry_lee@harvard.edu
URL: http://belfercenter.ksg.harvard.edu/project/43/environment_and_natural_resources. html
Contact: Henry Lee, Dir.
E-mail: henry_lee@harvard.edu
Scope: Environmental and energy issues and policies. **Publications:** Discussion Papers.

7401 ■ Holistic Management International
1010 Tijeras Ave. NW
Albuquerque, NM 87102
Ph:(505)842-5252
Fax:(505)843-7900
Co. E-mail: hmi@holisticmanagement.org
URL: http://www.holisticmanagement.org
Contact: Peter Holter, CEO
E-mail: hmi@holisticmanagement.org
Scope: Holistic approach to the management of land, human, and financial resources, with emphasis on teaching decision-making skills that effectively identify

and address the interdependent causes of social, biological, and financial deterioration, as well as the need to set goals consistent with a community's vision of the future. Evaluates effective policy analysis for planning and development to increase biodiversity and productivity of the land and communities. **Publications:** Holistic Management Newsletter: In practice. **Educational Activities:** Conferences; Holistic Management Courses; Training Program.

7402 ■ SUNY College of Environmental Science and Forestry–Randolph G. Pack Environmental Institute
106 Marshall Hall
1 Forestry Dr.
Syracuse, NY 13210-2787
Ph:(315)470-6636
Fax:(315)470-6915
Co. E-mail: vluzadis@esf.edu
URL: http://www.esf.edu/es/pack
Contact: Valerie A. Luzadis PhD, Dir.
E-mail: vluzadis@esf.edu
Scope: Cultural environmental values, environmental communication, land information systems, water resources, sustainable development, and urban environmental systems. **Services:** Assistance (annually), to local groups on environmental equity projects. **Publications:** Monographs (annually); Papers. **Educational Activities:** Day and half day trips (annually); Workshops, conferences, forums (3/year). **Awards:** Support awards (annually).

7403 ■ Texas Center for Policy Studies
707 Rio Grande St., Ste. 200
Austin, TX 78701
Ph:(512)740-4086
Fax:(512)479-8302
Co. E-mail: tcps@texascenter.org
URL: http://www.texascenter.org
Contact: David Hall, Ch.
E-mail: tcps@texascenter.org
Scope: Environmental policy studies, including water quality, water supply, pollution, forestry development, habitat destruction, waste disposal, and rural economic development. **Publications:** Newsletter (biennially); Project Review.

7404 ■ University of New Brunswick–New Brunswick Cooperative Fish and Wildlife Research Unit
Faculty of Forestry & Environmental Management
PO Box 44555
Fredericton, NB, Canada E3B 6C2
Ph:(506)453-4929
Fax:(506)453-3538
Co. E-mail: forbes@unb.ca
URL: http://www.unbf.ca/forestry/centers/cwru.htm
Contact: Graham Forbes PhD, Dir.
E-mail: forbes@unb.ca
Scope: Management and conservation of wildlife and fisheries resources and their habitats within New Brunswick and Atlantic Canada.

Environmental Store

START-UP INFORMATION

7405 ■ "EDCO Doling Out Capital Along Border" in *Austin Business JournalInc.* (Vol. 28, August 1, 2008, No. 20, pp. 1)
Pub: American City Business Journals
Ed: Sandra Zaragoza. **Description:** Non-profit business incubator Economic Development Catalyst Organization Ventures is searching for promising startup companies. The company is targeting startups in green energy, technology and consumer markets. EDCO has partnered with consumer electronics repair company CherryFusion and technology firm MiniDonations.

7406 ■ *Starting Green: An Ecopreneur's Guide to Starting a Green Business from Business Plans to Profits*
Pub: Entrepreneur Press
Ed: Glenn E. Croston. **Released:** September 9, 2010. **Price:** $21.95. **Description:** Entrepreneur and scientist outlines green business essentials and helps uncover eco-friendly business opportunities, build a sustainable business plan, and gain the competitive advantage.

ASSOCIATIONS AND OTHER ORGANIZATIONS

7407 ■ Center for Environmental Information
249 Highland Ave.
Rochester, NY 14620
Ph:(585)262-2870
Fax:(585)262-4156
Co. E-mail: cei@ceinfo.org
URL: http://www.ceinfo.org
Contact: George Thomas, Exec. Dir.
Description: Disseminates information on environmental issues. Conducts annual climate issues conference. **Publications:** *CEI Sphere* (quarterly); *Directory of Environmental Organizations in the Rochester Area* (annual).

7408 ■ EarthSave International
20555 Devonshire St., Ste. 105
Chatsworth, CA 91311
Ph:(818)407-0289
Co. E-mail: info@earthsave.org
URL: http://www.earthsave.org
Contact: Jeff Nelson, CEO
Description: Promotes food choices that are healthy for the planet. Seeks to educate, inspire and empower people to take positive action for all life on Earth. **Publications:** *EarthSave* (quarterly); *EarthSave Educational Series* .

7409 ■ Environmental Business Council of New England
375 Harvard St., Ste. 2
Brookline, MA 02446
Ph:(617)505-1818
Co. E-mail: ebc@ebcne.org
URL: http://www.ebcne.org
Contact: Daniel K. Moon, Pres./Exec. Dir.
Description: Firms that manufacture environmental and/or energy products and provide environmental and/or energy services. Fosters the development of an effective and competitive envirotech industry for the purpose of enhancing and maintaining a clean and productive environment. Provides a forum for environmental and energy company executives to network with each other and to meet leading members of the academic, nonprofit, and government communities to discuss issues of concern to the environmental industry. Provides business development and educational services. **Publications:** Newsletter (monthly).

7410 ■ Natural Products Marketing Council
PO Box 550
Truro, NS, Canada B2N 5E3
Ph:(902)893-6511
Co. E-mail: crouseea@gov.ns.ca
URL: http://www.gov.ns.ca/agri/npmc
Contact: Dave Davies, Chm.
Description: Producers and processors of natural food products and wool. Promotes growth and development of the natural products industries. Supervises natural product marketing boards.

7411 ■ Organic Trade Association
28 Vernon St., Ste. 413
Brattleboro, VT 05301
Ph:(802)275-3800
Fax:(802)275-3801
Co. E-mail: info@ota.com
URL: http://www.ota.com
Contact: Julia Sabin, Pres.
Description: Producers, processors, distributors, retailers, individuals and others involved in the organic products industry. Promotes the industry; heightens production and marketing standards. Provides certification guidelines. **Publications:** *The American Organic Standards*; *Guide to the U.S. Organic Foods Production Act of 1990*; *How to Harvest the Profits of Organic Produce*; *The Organic Report* (quarterly).

REFERENCE WORKS

7412 ■ "Burner Handles Everything From 2 to B100" in *Indoor Comfort Marketing* (Vol. 70, May 2011, No. 5, pp. 24)
Pub: Industry Publications Inc.
Description: A new oil burner being offered by AMERIgreen Energy is profiled.

7413 ■ "21st Century Filling Station" in *Austin Business JournalInc.* (Vol. 29, December 11, 2009, No. 40, pp. 1)
Pub: American City Business Journals
Ed: Jacob Dirr. **Description:** Clean Energy Fuels Corporation announced plans for the construction of a $1 million, 17,000 square foot compressed natural gas fueling station at or near the Austin-Bergstrom International Airport (ABIA). Clean Energy Fuels hopes to encourage cab and shuttle companies in the ABIA to switch from gasoline to natural gas.

7414 ■ "$40M Fund Created for Big Energy Project" in *Austin Business JournalInc.* (Vol. 29, November 27, 2009, No. 38, pp. 1)
Pub: American City Business Journals
Ed: Christopher Calnan. **Description:** A group of Texas businessmen, called Republic Power Partners LP, is planning to raise $40 million in order to launch an alternative energy project. The 6,000-megawatt initiative would generate solar, biomass and wind power in West Texas and could cost as much as $10 billion.

7415 ■ "2010: Important Year Ahead for Waterfront" in *Bellingham Business Journal* (Vol. March 2010, pp. 2)
Pub: Sound Publishing Inc.
Ed: Isaac Bonnell. **Description:** A tentative timeline has been established for the environmental impact statement (EIS) slated for completion in May 2010. The plan for the Waterfront District includes detailed economic and architectural analysis of the feasibility of reusing remaining structures and retaining some industrial icons.

7416 ■ "2011 FinOvation Awards" in *Farm Industry News* (January 19, 2011)
Pub: Penton Business Media Inc.
Ed: Jodie Wehrspann. **Description:** The 2011 FinOvation Award winners are announced, covering new products that growers need for corn and soybean crops. Winners range from small turbines and a fuel-efficient pickup to a Class 10 combine and drought-tolerant hybrids.

7417 ■ "2011 a Record Year for New Wind Energy Installations in Canada" in *CNW Group* (September 26, 2011)
Pub: CNW Group
Description: Canada reports a record for new wind energy projects in 2011 with about 1,338 MW of newly installed wind energy capacity expected to come on line, compared to 690 MW installed in 2010. Statistical data included.

7418 ■ "2011 U.S. Smart Grid – Saving Energy/Saving Money" in *Ecology,Environment & Conservation Business* (October 8, 2011, pp. 3)
Pub: HighBeam Research
Description: Highlights of the '2011 U.S. Smart Grid –Saving Energy/Saving Money Customers' Prospective Demand-Response assesses residential energy consumers' willingness to decrease their power consumption in order to mitigate power issues. Statistical details included.

7419 ■ "A Quick Guide to NATE" in *Indoor Comfort Marketing* (Vol. 70, February 2011, No. 2, pp. 12)
Pub: Industry Publications Inc.
Description: Guide for training and certification in the North American Technician Excellence award.

7420 ■ "The ABCs of a Good Show" in *Playthings* (Vol. 106, October 1, 2008, No. 9, pp. 18)
Pub: Reed Business Information
Ed: Karyn M. Peterson. **Description:** ABC Kids Expo 2008 made a strong showing with products for

babies, kids and new/expecting parents. The new Naturally Kids section promoting eco-friendly products was the highlight of the show.

7421 ■ "Acing the Test" in *Contractor* (Vol. 57, January 2010, No. 1, pp. 32)
Pub: Penton Media, Inc.
Ed: Robert P. Mader. **Description:** A ward winning mechanical system retrofitting of a middle school in Ohio is discussed. The school now operates at 37,800 Btu/sq. ft and reduced a significant amount of pollutants from being emitted into the environment.

7422 ■ "Actiontec and Verizon Team Up for a Smarter Home" in *Ecology,Environment & Conservation Business* (November 5, 2011, pp. 3)
Pub: HighBeam Research
Description: Verizon is implementing Actiontec Electronics' SG200 Service Gateway as a basic component of its Home Monitoring and Control service. This new smart home service allows customers to remotely check their homes, control locks and appliances, view home-energy use and more using a smartphone, PC, or FiOS TV.

7423 ■ "Adventures at Hydronicahh" in *Contractor* (Vol. 56, October 2009, No. 10, pp. 42)
Pub: Penton Media, Inc.
Ed: Mark Eatherton. **Description:** Design and installation of a solar thermal system for a hydronic heating project is described. This portion has two 32-square feet of flat plate glazed solar collectors that are tied to a 120-gallon reverse indirect DHW heater.

7424 ■ "AF Expands in New Green Building in Gothenburg" in *Ecology,Environment & Conservation Business* (September 24, 2011, pp. 2)
Pub: HighBeam Research
Description: AF signed a ten-year tenancy contract with Skanska for the premises of its new green building in Gothenburg, Sweden. AF offers qualified services and solutions for industrial processes, infrastructure projects and the development of products and IT systems.

7425 ■ "Agricultural Community Implements Green Technologies, Building Team" in *Contractor* (Vol. 56, September 2009, No. 9, pp. 5)
Pub: Penton Media, Inc.
Ed: Candace Ruolo. **Description:** John DeWald and Associates has initiated a residential development project which uses green technologies in Illinois. The community features a community center, organic farm and recreational trails. Comments from executives are also provided.

7426 ■ "Ahead of the Pack" in *Small Business Opportunities* (Fall 2010)
Pub: Harris Publications Inc.
Description: Profile of an organic fast-food business that is carving out a niche that is gaining favor. Elevation Burger is a unique concept offering healthier burgers in sustainable buildings.

7427 ■ "Allowing Ethanol Tax Incentive to Expire Would Risk Jobs, RFAas Dinneen Says" in *Farm Industry News* (November 3, 2010)
Pub: Penton Business Media Inc.
Description: Jobs would be at risk if the ethanol tax incentive expires.

7428 ■ "Alstom Launches te ECO 122 – 2.7MW Wind Turbine for Low Wind Sites" in *CNW Group* (September 28, 2011)
Pub: CNW Group
Description: Alstom is launching its new ECO 122, a 2.7MW onshore wind turbine that combines high power and high capacity factor (1) to boost energy yield in low wind regions around the world. The ECO 122 will produce about 25 percent increased wind farm yield that current turbines and fewer turbines would be installed in areas.

7429 ■ "Alternative Energy Calls for Alternative Marketing" in *Indoor Comfort Marketing* (Vol. 70, June 2011, No. 6, pp. 8)
Pub: Industry Publications Inc.
Ed: Richard Rutigliano. **Description:** Advice for marketing solar energy products and services is given.

7430 ■ "Alternative Energy is a Major Topic at Agritechnica 2011" in *Farm Industry News* (November 16, 2011)
Pub: Penton Business Media Inc.
Ed: Mark Moore. **Description:** Sustainable agricultural systems were a hot topic at this year's Agritechnia 2011, held in Germany. Germany is a leader in the development of on-farm biogas systems.

7431 ■ "American Chemistry Council Launches Flagship Blog" in *Ecology,Environment & Conservation Business* (October 29, 2011, pp. 5)
Pub: HighBeam Research
Description: American Chemistry Council (ACC) launched its blog, American Chemistry Matters, where interactive space allows bloggers to respond to news coverage and to discuss policy issues and their impact on innovation, competitiveness, job creation and safety.

7432 ■ "ANATURALCONCEPT" in *Crain's Cleveland Business* (Vol. 30, June 22, 2009, No. 24, pp. 1)
Pub: Crain Communications, Inc.
Ed: Dan Shingler. **Description:** Cleveland-based Biomimicry Institute, led by Cleveland's Entrepreneurs for Sustainability and the Cuyahoga County Planning Commission, are using biomimicry to incorporate eco-friendliness with industry. Biomimicry studies nature's best ideas then imitates these designs and processes to solve human problems.

7433 ■ "Answers About Commercial Wind Farms Could Come from Downstate" in *Erie Times-News* (September 27, 2011)
Pub: Erie Times-News
Ed: Valerie Myers. **Description:** Texas-based Pioneer Green Energy is measuring wind and leasing land in North East Township, Pennsylvania. The firm plans to build a 7,000-acre wind farm along wine-country ridges. About 70 turbines would harness wind in order to generate electricity that would be sold into the eastern power grid.

7434 ■ "Aquarium's Solar Demonstration Project Exceeds Expectations" in *Contractor* (Vol. 57, February 2010, No. 2, pp. 1)
Pub: Penton Media, Inc.
Ed: Candace Roulo. **Description:** Seattle Aquarium cafe installed flat-plate solar collectors to preheat water and data has shown that the system has allowed them to off-set almost double their expected consumption of natural gas. It is estimated that rthe solar panels will shrink the aquarium's carbon footprint by 2.5 tons of carbon dioxide each year.

7435 ■ "Are You Looking for an Environmentally Friendly Dry Cleaner?" in *Inc.* (Vol. 30, December 2008, No. 12, pp. 34)
Pub: Mansueto Ventures LLC
Ed: Shivani Vora. **Description:** Greenopia rates the greenness of 52 various kinds of businesses, including restaurants, nail salons, dry cleaners, and clothing stores. The guidebooks are sold through various retailers including Barnes & Noble and Amazon.com.

7436 ■ "Areva Diversifies Further Into Wind" in *Wall Street Journal Eastern Edition* (November 29, 2011, pp. B7)
Pub: Dow Jones & Company Inc.
Ed: Max Colchester, Noemie Bisserbe. **Description:** French engineering company Areva SA is diversifying and moving away from nuclear energy projects. One sign of that is its recent discussion to construct 120 wind turbines to be located at two German wind farms. Such a deal, if signed, would be worth about US$1.59 billion.

7437 ■ "Art Institute of Chicago Goes Green" in *Contractor* (Vol. 56, July 2009, No. 7, pp. 1)
Pub: Penton Media, Inc.
Ed: Candace Roulo. **Description:** Art Institute of Chicago's Modern Wing museum addition will receive a certification that makes them one of the most environmentally sound museum expansions in the U.S. A modified variable-air-volume system is being used to meet temperature and humidity requirements in the building and it also has a double curtain wall to capture summer heat.

7438 ■ "Attorney Covers Climate in Copenhagen" in *Houston Business Journal* (Vol. 40, December 25, 2009, No. 33, pp. 1)
Pub: American City Business Journals
Ed: Ford Gunter. **Description:** Houston environmental attorney Richard Faulk talks to the United Nations Climate Change Conference in Copenhagen, Denmark. Faulk believes the conference failed due to political differences between countries like US and China. Faulk believed the discussion of developed and developing countries on verification and limits on carbon emissions is something good that came from the conference.

7439 ■ "Austin to Buy $1.1B of Wind Power from Two" in *Austin Business Journal* (Vol. 31, August 19, 2011, No. 24, pp. A1)
Pub: American City Business Journals Inc.
Ed: Vicky Garza. **Description:** Austin City Council is set to approve contracts to purchase wind energy from Duke Energy Corporation and MAP Royalty Inc. The city will get 200MW from Duke and 91MW from MAP and the total contract is estimated to be worth $1.1 million.

7440 ■ "Austin Energy May Build $2.3B Biomass Plant" in *Austin Business JournalInc.* (Vol. 28, July 25, 2008, No. 19, pp. A1)
Pub: American City Business Journals
Ed: Kate Harrington. **Description:** An approval from the Austin City Council is being sought by Austin Energy for a 20-year supply contract with Nacogdoches Power LLC to build a $2.3 billion biomass plant in East Texas. The 100-megawatt biomass plant, which is to run on waste wood, will have Austin Energy as its sole buyer.

7441 ■ "Award Win Highlights Slingsby's Green Credentials" in *Ecology,Environment & Conservation Business* (August 20, 2011, pp. 3)
Pub: HighBeam Research
Description: Slingsby, an industrial and commercial equipment supplier, was joint winner with Hallmark Cards of the Baildon Business in the Community's Yorkshire and Humber Long Term Environmental Improvement Award. The firm cites its commitment to reducing environmental impact.

7442 ■ "Babynut.com to Shut Down" in *Bellingham Business Journal* (Vol. February 2010, pp. 3)
Pub: Sound Publishing Inc.
Description: Saralee Sky and Jerry Kilgore, owners of Babynut.com will close their online store. The site offered a free online and email newsletter to help mothers through pregnancy and the first three years of their child's life. Products being sold at clearance prices include organic and natural maternity and nursing clothing, baby and toddler clothes, books on pregnancy, and more.

7443 ■ "Ben & Jerry's Introduces 'Green' Freezer" in *Ice Cream Reporter* (Vol. 21, October 20, 2008, No. 11, pp. 1)
Pub: Ice Cream Reporter
Description: Ben & Jerry's describes its latest concept as a cleaner, greener freezer. The hydrocarbon-based freezer provides great environmental benefits by minimizing the freezer's impact on global warming.

7444 ■ "BETC Backers Plot Future" in *Business Journal Portland* (Vol. 27, December 10, 2010, No. 41, pp. 1)
Pub: Portland Business Journal
Ed: Erik Siemers. **Description:** A coalition of clean energy groups and industrial manufacturers have spearheaded a campaign aimed at persuading

Oregon legislators that the state's Business Energy Tax Credit (BETC) is vital in job creation. Oregon's BETC grants tax credits for 50 percent of an eligible renewable or clean energy project's cost. However, some legislators propose BETC's abolition.

7445 ■ "Beware of E15" in *Rental Product News* (Vol. 33, October 2011)
Pub: Cygnus Business Media
Ed: Curt Bennink. **Description:** Environmental Protection Agency (EPA) set a new regulation that grants partial waivers to allow gasoline containing up to 15 percent ethanol (E15) to be introduced into commerce for use in model year 2001 and newer light-duty motor vehicles, subject to certain conditions.

7446 ■ "Big Energy Ideas for Our Times" in *Canadian Business* (Vol. 83, August 17, 2010, No. 13-14, pp. 49)
Pub: Rogers Media Ltd.
Description: Five ideas Canada must consider in the production of energy are explored. These ideas are run-off-river hydroelectric projects, the tapping of natural gas inside shale formation, the water's role in creating energy, the development of a smart grid, and the reduction of energy consumption.

7447 ■ "Bigger is Definitely Not Better When It Comes to Cooling" in *Indoor Comfort Marketing* (Vol. 70, May 2011, No. 5, pp. 49)
Pub: Industry Publications Inc.
Ed: Eugene Silberstein. **Description:** Efficiency is more important when installing air conditioning equipment over size of the unit. Details are provided.

7448 ■ "Biodiesel Poised to Regain Growth" in *Farm Industry News* (January 21, 2011)
Pub: Penton Business Media Inc.
Description: According to Gary Haer, vice president of sales and marketing for Renewable Energy Group, the biodiesel industry is positioned to regain growth in 2011 with the reinstatement of the biodiesel blenders a tax credt of $1 per gallon.

7449 ■ "Bioheat – Alternative for Fueling Equipment" in *Indoor Comfort Marketing* (Vol. 70, May 2011, No. 5, pp. 14)
Pub: Industry Publications Inc.
Ed: Gary Hess. **Description:** Profile of Worley and Obetz, supplier of biofuels used as an alternative for fueling industry equipment.

7450 ■ "Blackwater is LEED Golden for Port of Portland Building" in *Contractor* (Vol. 56, October 2009, No. 10, pp. 3)
Pub: Penton Media, Inc.
Ed: Robert P. Mader. **Description:** Worrel Water Technologies' Tidal Wetlands Living Machine recycles blackwater from the toilets and sends it right back to flush the toilets. The Technology is being installed in the new headquarters of the Port of Portland which aims to get awarded a gold certificate from the Leadership in Energy and Environmental Design.

7451 ■ "Bold Goals Will Require Time" in *Contractor* (Vol. 56, October 2009, No. 10, pp. S2)
Pub: Penton Media, Inc.
Ed: Ted Lower. **Description:** Offering a broad range of courses is the Radiant Panel Association (RPA), an organization that holds education as its top priority. The RPA must lead the industry by raising the educational bar for future installers.

7452 ■ "Brown At Center of Local CleanTech Lobbying Efforts" in *Boston Business Journal* (Vol. 30, October 15, 2010, No. 36, pp. 1)
Pub: Boston Business Journal
Ed: Kyle Alspach. **Description:** U.S. Senator Scott Brown has been active in lobbying for energy reform in Massachusetts. Brown has been meeting with business groups seeking the reforms.

7453 ■ "Burning Issues: Four of Today's Hottest Energy Topics" in *Canadian Business* (Vol. 83, August 17, 2010, No. 13-14, pp. 45)
Pub: Rogers Media Ltd.
Description: A look at four issues dominating Canada's energy industry is presented. These issues are lack of transmission capacity and difficulty in transferring power across provincial boundaries, the management of intermittency of renewable generation, techniques that would clean up the Alberta's oil sands, and the impending massive use of electric cars in North America.

7454 ■ "The Business of Activism" in *Entrepreneur* (Vol. 37, September 2009, No. 9, pp. 43)
Pub: Entrepreneur Media, Inc.
Ed: Mary Catherine O'Connor. **Description:** San Francisco, California-based business incubator Virgance has been promoting sustainable projects by partnering with businesses. The company has launched campaigns which include organizing homeowners in negotiating with solar installers. The company is also planning to expand its workforce.

7455 ■ "Caber Engineering Helps to Reduce Canada's Carbon Footprint" in *Ecology,Environment & Conservation Business* (July 16, 2011, pp. 7)
Pub: HighBeam Research
Description: Calgary-based Caber Engineering Inc. will assist in the engineering design of the Alberta Carbon Trunk Line (ACTL). The ACTL is Alberta's first sizable commercial carbon capture and storage project focusing on the reduction of environmental impacts while being economically beneficial.

7456 ■ "Campaign Not Stirred by Wind Issue in Roanoke County" in *Roanoke Times* (September 18, 2011)
Pub: Roanoke Times
Ed: Katelyn Polantz. **Description:** Wind energy has brought citizens of the Roanoke area into activism this year. Comments from citizen on both sides of the issue are provided.

7457 ■ "Can HOAs Stop You From Going Green?" in *Contractor* (Vol. 56, July 2009, No. 7, pp. 39)
Pub: Penton Media, Inc.
Ed: Susan Linden McGreevy. **Description:** There have been cases concerning homeowners' associations objections to the installation of wind turbines and solar panels. Precedence with the courts show that they will look at several factors when deciding to uphold restrictions on property use including whether the item encroaches on the rights of others, is likely to adversely affect property values, and also the state of enforcement.

7458 ■ "Canada's Clean Energy Advantages Offer a Bright Future" in *Canadian Business* (Vol. 83, August 17, 2010, No. 13-14, pp. 38)
Pub: Rogers Media Ltd.
Ed: Don McKinnon. **Description:** Canada has clean energy advantages in the greenhouse gas emission-free CANada Deuterium Uranium reactor technology and carbon neutral biomass fuels that were continuously ignored by policy makers. Both are proven to significantly reduce emissions while providing reliable, affordable and secure electricity.

7459 ■ "Canada's Largest Bakery Officially Opened Today" in *Ecology,Environment & Conservation Business* (October 15, 2011, pp. 7)
Pub: HighBeam Research
Description: Maple Leaf Foods opened Canada's largest commercial bakery in Hamilton, Ontario. The firm's 385,000 square foot Trillium bakery benefits from efficient design flow and best-in-class technologies.

7460 ■ "Canadian Hydronics Businesses Promote 'Beautiful Heat'" in *Indoor Comfort Marketing* (Vol. 70, September 2011, No. 9, pp. 20)
Pub: Industry Publications Inc.
Description: Canadian hydronics companies are promoting their systems as beautiful heat. Hydronics is the use of water as the heat-transfer medium in heating and cooling system.

7461 ■ "Canadian Wind Farm Sued Due to Negative Health Effects" in *PC Magazine Online* (September 22, 2011)
Pub: PC Magazine
Description: Suncor Energy is being sued by a family in Ontario, Canada. The family claims that Suncor's wind turbines have created health problems for them, ranging from vertigo and sleep disturbance to depression and suicidal thoughts. The family's home is over 1,000 meters from the eight wind turbines, and according to Ontario officials, wind turbines must be a minimum of 550 meters from existing homes.

7462 ■ "Candidates Differ On State's Green Streak" in *Business Journal Portland* (Vol. 27, October 22, 2010, No. 34, pp. 1)
Pub: Portland Business Journal
Ed: Andy Giegerich. **Description:** The views of Oregon gubernatorial candidates Chris Dudley and John Kitzhaber on the state's economy and on environmental policies are presented. Both Dudley, who is a Republican, and his Democratic challenger believe that biomass could help drive the state's economy. Both candidates also pledged changes in Oregon's business energy tax credit (BETC) program.

7463 ■ "CanWEA Unveils WindVision for BC: 5,250 MW of Wind Energy by 2025" in *CNW Group* (October 4, 2011)
Pub: CNW Group
Description: Wind industry leaders are asking British Columbia, Canada policy makers to created conditions to further develop and integrate wind energy in accordance with greenhouse gas emission targets and projected economic growth. Statistical data included.

7464 ■ "The Carbon Equation" in *Canadian Business* (Vol. 81, October 27, 2008, No. 18, pp. 109)
Pub: Rogers Media Ltd.
Ed: Jack M. Mintz. **Description:** Economic and environmental impacts of the likely rejection of a carbon tax for the cap-and-trade system in Canada are discussed. The Conservative Party is expected tow in the 2008 elections and would likely pursue the cap-and-trade system.

7465 ■ "Carbon Trading: Current Schemes and Future Developments" in *Energy Policy* (Vol. 39, October 2011, No. 10, pp. 6040-6054)
Pub: Reed Elsevier Reference Publishing
Ed: Slobodan Perdan, Adisa Azapagic. **Description:** Current and future developments regarding carbon trading is highlighted.

7466 ■ "Case IH Announces Strategy to Meet 2014 Clean Air Standards" in *Farm Industry News* (September 15, 2011)
Pub: Penton Business Media Inc.
Ed: Jodie Wehrspann. **Description:** Case IH will meet EPA's stringent engine emissions limits imposed in 2014, called Tier 4. The limits call for a 90 percent reduction in particulate matter and nitrogen oxides (NOx) over the Tier 3 requirements from a few years ago.

7467 ■ "Cash for Appliances Targets HVAC Products, Water Heaters" in *Contractor* (Vol. 56, October 2009, No. 10, pp. 1)
Pub: Penton Media, Inc.
Ed: Candace Roulo. **Description:** States and territories would need to submit a full application that specifies their implementation plans if they are interested in joining the Cash for Appliances program funded by the American Recovery and Reinvestment Act. The Department of Energy urges states to focus on heating and cooling equipment, appliances and water heaters since these offer the greatest energy savings potential.

7468 ■ "Catch the Wind Announces Filing of Injunction Against Air Data Systems LLC and Philip Rogers" in *CNW Group* (September 30, 2011)
Pub: CNW Group
Description: Catch the Wind, providers of laser-based wind sensor products and technology, filed an injunction against Optical Air Data Systems (OADS) LLC and its former President and CEO Philip L. Rogers. The complaint seeks to have OADS and Rogers return tangible and intangible property owned by Catch the Wind, which the firm believes to be critical to the operations of their business.

7469 ■ "Catch the Wind to Hold Investor Update Conference Call on October 18, 2011" in *CNW Group* (October 4, 2011)
Pub: CNW Group
Description: Catch the Wind Ltd., providers of laser-based wind sensor products and technology, held a conference call for analysts and institutional investors. The high-growth technology firm is headquartered in Manassas, Virginia.

7470 ■ "CE2 Carbon Capital and Dogwood Carbon Solutions Partner With Missouri Landowners" in *Nanotechnolgy Business Journal* (Jan. 25, 2010)
Pub: Investment Weekly News
Description: Dogwood Carbon Solutions, a developer of agriculture and forestry based conservation projects, has partnered with CE2 Carbon Capital, one of the largest investors and owners of U.S. carbon commodities and carbon emissions reduction projects, to develop high-quality carbon offsets from over 30,000 acres of privately-owned non-industrial forest in the Ozark mountain region of Arkansas and Missouri.

7471 ■ "CEO Forecast" in *Hispanic Business* (January-February 2009, pp. 34, 36)
Pub: Hispanic Business
Ed: Jessica Haro, Richard Kaplan. **Description:** As economic uncertainty fogs the future, executives turn to government contracts in order to boost business. Revenue sources, health care challenges, environmental consulting and remediation services, as well as technological strides are discussed.

7472 ■ "Changing Fuel Compositions: What It Means To You and Your Business" in *Indoor Comfort Marketing* (Vol. 70, June 2011, No. 6, pp. 30)
Pub: Industry Publications Inc.
Ed: Paul Nazzaro. **Description:** Biofuels are outlined and the way it is changing the HVAC/R industry are discussed.

7473 ■ "Charged Up for Sales" in *Charlotte Business Journal* (Vol. 25, October 15, 2010, No. 30, pp. 1)
Pub: Charlotte Business Journal
Ed: Susan Stabley. **Description:** Li-Ion Motors Corporation is set to expand its production lines of electric cars in Sacramento, California. The plan is seen to create up to 600 jobs. The company's total investment is seen to reach $500 million.

7474 ■ "Chicago Botanic Garden Builds Green Research Facility" in *Contractor* (Vol. 56, December 2009, No. 12, pp. 5)
Pub: Penton Media, Inc.
Ed: Candace Roulo. **Description:** Chicago Botanic Garden has built a laboratory and research facility in Illinois. The facility is set to receive a United States Green Building Council LEED Gold certification. The building features a solar photovoltaic array, radiant flooring and water-conserving plumbing products.

7475 ■ "China Wind Power Generates Stronger First Quarter Results" in *Marketwire Canada* (September 28, 2011)
Pub: MarketWire Canada
Description: China Wind Power International Corporation, an independent wind power producer in China reported strong growth for the first quarter 2011. Details of the company and its future developments are highlighted.

7476 ■ "China's Transition to Green Energy Systems" in *Energy Policy* (Vol. 39, October 2011, No. 10, pp. 5909-5919)
Pub: Reed Elsevier Reference Publishing
Ed: Wei Li, Guojun Song, Melanie Beresford, Ben Ma. **Description:** The economics of home solar water heaters and their growing popularity in Dezhous City, China is discussed.

7477 ■ "Chinese Solar Panel Manufacturer Scopes Out Austin" in *Austin Business JournalInc.* (Vol. 29, October 30, 2009, No. 34, pp. 1)
Pub: American City Business Journals
Ed: Jacob Dirr. **Description:** China's Yingli Green Energy Holding Company Ltd. is looking for a site in order to construct a $20 million photovoltaic panel plant. Both Austin and San Antonio are vying to house the manufacturing hub. The project could create about 300 jobs and give Austin a chance to become a player in the solar energy market. Other solar companies are also considering Central Texas as an option to set up shop.

7478 ■ "City's New Energy Audits to Spawn 'Fantastic' Market" in *Austin Business JournalInc.* (Vol. 28, November 14, 2008, No. 35, pp. 1)
Pub: American City Business Journals
Ed: Jean Kwon. **Description:** A new law requiring older homes to undergo energy use audits is seen to provide new business for some companies in the Austin, Texas area. The new law is seen to create a new industry of performance testers. Details of the new ordinance are also given.

7479 ■ "Clean-Tech Focus Sparks Growth" in *Philadelphia Business Journal* (Vol. 28, January 15, 2010, No. 48, pp. 1)
Pub: American City Business Journals
Ed: Peter Key. **Description:** Keystone Redevelopment Group and economic development organization Ben Franklin Technology Partners of Southeastern Pennsylvania have partnered in supporting the growth of new alternative energy and clean technology companies. Keystone has also been developing the Bridge Business Center.

7480 ■ "Clean Wind Energy Tower Transitions from R&D Stage Company" in *Professional Services Close-Up* (September 30, 2011)
Pub: Close-Up Media
Description: Clean Wind Energy designed and is developing large downdraft towers that use benevolent, non-toxic natural elements to generate electricity and clean water. The firm is closing its internally staffed engineering office in Warrenton, Virginia and transitioning a development team to oversee and coordinate industry consultants and advisors to construct their first dual renewable energy tower.

7481 ■ "Climate Law Could Dig into our Coal-Dusted Pockets" in *Business Courier* (Vol. 26, November 20, 2009, No. 30, pp. 1)
Pub: American City Business Journals, Inc.
Ed: Lucy May. **Description:** Passage of federal climate legislation into law is set to increase household cost for Greater Cincinnati, according to the calculation by the Brookings Institute. The increase for residents of the area will amount to $244 in 2020 and the city was ranked the sixth-highest rate in the nation, behind Indianapolis.

7482 ■ "Cloudy Skies" in *Canadian Business* (Vol. 81, October 27, 2008, No. 18, pp. 101)
Pub: Rogers Media Ltd.
Ed: Andrew Wahl. **Description:** Canada's federal government is expected to implement its regulations on greenhouse-gas emissions by January 1, 2010, but companies are worried because the plan took so long and some details are yet to be revealed. Corporate Canada wants a firm, long-range plan similar to the European Union Emissions Trading Scheme in dealing with greenhouse-gas emissions.

7483 ■ "CO2 Emissions Embodied in China-US Trade" in *Energy Policy* (Vol. 39, October 2011, No. 10, pp. 5980-5987)
Pub: Reed Elsevier Reference Publishing
Ed: Huibin Du, Guozhu Mao, Alexander M. Smith, Xuxu Wang, Yuan Wang, Jianghong Guo. **Description:** Input and output analysis based on the energy per dollar ratio for carbon dioxide emissions involved in China-United States trade is outlined.

7484 ■ "Coming Soon: Electric Tractors" in *Farm Industry News* (November 21, 2011)
Pub: Penton Business Media Inc.
Ed: Jodie Wehrspann. **Description:** The agricultural industry is taking another look at electric farm vehicles. John Deere Product Engineering Center said that farmers can expect to see more diesel-electric systems in farm tractors, sprayers, and implements.

7485 ■ "Community Food Co-op Creates Revolving Loan Program for Local Farmers" in *Bellingham Business Journal* (Vol. February 2010, pp. 3)
Pub: Sound Publishing Inc.
Description: Community Food Co-op's Farm Fund received a $12,000 matching grant from the Sustainable Whatcom Fund of the Whatcom Community Foundation. The Farm Fund will create a new revolving loan program for local farmers committed to using sustainable practices.

7486 ■ "Consumers Like Green, But Not Mandates" in *Business Journal-Milwaukee* (Vol. 28, December 10, 2010, No. 10, pp. A1)
Pub: Milwaukee Business Journal
Ed: Sean Ryan. **Description:** Milwaukee, Wisconsin consumers are willing to spend more on green energy, a survey has revealed. Respondents also said they will pay more for efficient cars and appliances. Support for public incentives for homeowners and businesses that reduce energy use has also increased.

7487 ■ "Convert New Customers to Long Term Accounts" in *Indoor Comfort Marketing* (Vol. 70, February 2011, No. 2, pp. 22)
Pub: Industry Publications Inc.
Description: Marketing to new customers and suggestions for retaining them is covered.

7488 ■ "Corporate Responsibility" in *Professional Services Close-Up* (July 2, 2010)
Pub: Close-Up Media
Description: List of firms awarded the inaugural Best Corporate Citizens in Government Contracting by the Corporate Responsibility Magazine is presented. The list is based on the methodology of the Magazine's Best Corporate Citizen's List, with 324 data points of publicly-available information in seven categories which include: environment, climate change, human rights, philanthropy, employee relations, financial performance, and governance.

7489 ■ "The Cost of Energy" in *Canadian Business* (Vol. 83, August 17, 2010, No. 13-14, pp. 39)
Pub: Rogers Media Ltd.
Description: Canada's cheap energy has bred complacency among Canadian companies and most have not strived to conserve or develop other forms of energy. However, even costs of traditional energy such as oil are set to rise, fueled by recent events in Saudi Arabia and the Gulf of Mexico.

7490 ■ "Cost Remains Top Factor In Considering Green Technology" in *Canadian Sailings* (June 30, 2008)
Pub: Commonwealth Business Media
Ed: Julie Gedeon. **Description:** Improving its environmental performance remains a priority in the shipping industry; however, testing new technologies can prove difficult due to the harsh conditions that ships endure as well as installation which usually requires a dry dock.

7491 ■ "Could This Be Your Next Office Building?" in *Austin Business Journal* (Vol. 31, May 13, 2011, No. 10, pp. A1)
Pub: American City Business Journals Inc.
Ed: Cody Lyon. **Description:** Falcon Containers moved to a 51-acre site in Far East Austin, Texas and started construction of a 2,500-square-foot headquarters made from eight 40-foot shipping containers. Falcon's CEO Stephen Shang plans to use his headquarters building as a showroom to attract upscale, urban hipsters. Insights on the construction's environmental and social impact are shared.

7492 ■ "Council Power Shift Could Benefit Business" in *Business Courier* (Vol. 26, November 6, 2009, No. 28, pp. 1)
Pub: American City Business Journals, Inc.
Ed: Lucy May. **Description:** A majority in the Cincinnati City Council, which is comprised of reelected members, might be created by Charlie Winburn's impending return to the council. It would be empow-

ered to decide on public safety, stock options taxes, and environmental justice. How the presumed majority would affect the city's economic progress is discussed.

7493 ■ "Crude Awakening" in *Canadian Business* (Vol. 81, October 27, 2008, No. 18, pp. 14)
Pub: Rogers Media Ltd.
Ed: Jeff Sanford. **Description:** Jim Grays believes that a global liquid fuels crisis is coming and hopes the expected transition from oil dependence will be smooth. Charles Maxwell, on the other hand, predicts that a new world economy will arrive in three waves. Views of both experts are examined.

7494 ■ "Customized Before Custom Was Cool" in *Green Industry Pro* (July 2011)
Pub: Cygnus Business Media
Ed: Gregg Wartgow. **Description:** Profile of Turf Care Enterprises and owner Kevin Vogeler, who discusses his desire to use more natural programs using little or no chemicals in 1986. At that time, that sector represented 20 percent of his business, today it shares 80 percent.

7495 ■ "Cut Energy Waste" in *Inc.* (Vol. 31, January-February 2009, No. 1, pp. 42)
Pub: Mansueto Ventures LLC
Description: Carbon Control, Edison, and Saver software programs help companies cut carbon emissions by reducing the amount of energy consumed by computers while they are idle.

7496 ■ "David Robinson Column" in *Buffalo News* (October 2, 2011)
Pub: Buffalo News
Ed: David Robinson. **Description:** New York Power Authority ceased development of an offshore wind farm project. Wind farming in the waters of Lake Erie or Lake Ontario would be too costly. Details of the project are discussed.

7497 ■ "A Day Late and a Dollar Short" in *Indoor Comfort Marketing* (Vol. 70, March 2011, No. 3, pp. 30)
Pub: Industry Publications Inc.
Ed: Philip J. Baratz. **Description:** A discussion involving futures options and fuel oil prices is presented.

7498 ■ "Despite Economic Upheaval Generation Y is Still Feeling Green: RSA Canada Survey" in *CNW Group* (October 28, 2010)
Pub: CNW Group
Description: Canadian Generation Y individuals believe it is important for their company to be environmentally-friendly and one-third of those surveyed would quit their job if they found their employer was environmentally irresponsible, despite the economy.

7499 ■ "Detroit Hosts Conferences on Green Building, IT, Finance" in *Crain's Detroit Business* (Vol. 25, June 1, 2009, No. 22, pp. 9)
Pub: Crain Communications Inc. - Detroit
Ed: Tom Henderson. **Description:** Detroit will host three conferences in June 2009, one features green technology, one information technology and the third will gather black bankers and financial experts from across the nation.

7500 ■ "DeWind Delivering Turbines to Texas Wind Farm" in *Professional Services Close-Up* (September 25, 2011)
Pub: Close-Up Media
Description: DeWind Company has begun shipment of turbines to the 20 MW Frisco Wind Farm located in Hansford County, Texas. DeWind is a subsidiary of Daewoo Shipbuilding and Marine Engineering Company. Details of the project are discussed.

7501 ■ "Doing the Right Thing" in *Black Enterprise* (Vol. 38, July 2008, No. 12, pp. 50)
Pub: Earl G. Graves Publishing Co. Inc.
Ed: Tamara E. Holmes. **Description:** More business owners are trying to become more environmentally friendly, either due to their belief in social responsibility or for financial incentives or for both reasons. Tips for making one's business more environmentally responsible are included as well as a listing of resources that may be available to help owners in their efforts.

7502 ■ "Dow Champions Innovative Energy Solutions for Auto Industry at NAIAS" in *Business of Global Warming* (January 25, 2010, pp. 7)
Pub: Investment Weekly News
Description: This year's North American International Auto Show in Detroit will host the "Electric Avenue" exhibit sponsored by the Dow Chemical Company. The display will showcase the latest in innovative energy solutions from Dow as well as electric vehicles and the technology supporting them. This marks the first time a non-automotive manufacturer is part of the main floor of the show.

7503 ■ "Earth Angels" in *Playthings* (Vol. 106, September 1, 2008, No. 8, pp. 10)
Pub: Reed Business Information
Ed: Karyn M. Peterson. **Description:** ImagiPlay toy company has partnered with Whole Foods Market to distribute the company's wooden playthings across the country. The company's Earth-friendly business model is outlined.

7504 ■ "East Coast Solar" in *Contractor* (Vol. 57, February 2010, No. 2, pp. 17)
Pub: Penton Media, Inc.
Ed: Dave Yates. **Description:** U.S. Department of Energy's Solar Decathlon lets 20 college student-led teams from around the world compete to design and build a solar-powered home. A mechanical contractor discusses his work as an advisor during the competition.

7505 ■ *Eco Barons: The New Heroes of Environmental Activism*
Pub: Ecco/HarperCollins
Ed: Edward Humes. **Released:** January 19, 2010. **Price:** $14.99. **Description:** Profiles of business leaders who have dedicated their lives to saving the planet from ecological devastation.

7506 ■ "Eco-Preneuring" in *Small Business Opportunities* (July 2008)
Pub: Entrepreneur Media Inc.
Ed: Mary C. Pearl. **Description:** Profile of Wildlife Trust, a rapidly growing global organization dedicated to innovative conservation science linking health and ecology. With partners in nearly twenty countries, Wildlife Trust draws on global strengths in order to respond to well-defined local needs. In the Dominican Republic, they are working with the community and local biologists in order to restore fishing and create jobs in the field of ecotourism.

7507 ■ "Eco Smart Home Will Showcase Green Technology" in *Contractor* (Vol. 56, September 2009, No. 9, pp. 3)
Pub: Penton Media, Inc.
Ed: Steve Spaulding. **Description:** Eco Smart World Wide is building the Eco Smart Demonstration House to promote the latest in sustainable, renewable and high-efficiency practices and products. The company will use insulated concrete forms in the construction of the building. Features and dimensions of the structure are also presented.

7508 ■ "Electronic Design and a Greener Environment" in *Canadian Electronics* (Vol. 23, June-July 2008, No. 4, pp. 6)
Pub: Action Communication Inc.
Ed: Nicholas Deeble. **Description:** Companies seeking to minimize their environmental impact are using Design methodologies of Cadence Design Systems Ltd. The company's Low Power Format and Low Power Design Flow help reduce carbon dioxide emissions.

7509 ■ "EMC Greens Its Machines" in *Boston Business Journal* (Vol. 31, July 15, 2011, No. 25, pp. 3)
Pub: Boston Business Journal
Ed: Kyle Alspach. **Description:** Hopkinton, Massachusetts-based EMC Corporation has been pursuing a sustainability strategy even though it would not directly pay back money to the company or customers who use the products. EMC has been increasingly requiring sustainable practices from its suppliers and evaluating the full lifecycle impacts of its products.

7510 ■ "Energy Consulting Company to Expand" in *Austin Business JournalInc.* (Vol. 28, November 7, 2008, No. 34, pp. A1)
Pub: American City Business Journals
Ed: Kate Harrington. **Description:** CLEAResult Consulting Inc. is planning to increase its workforce and move its headquarters to a larger office. The company has posted 1,000 percent increase in revenues. The company's adoption of best practices and setting of benchmark goals are seen as the reason for its growth.

7511 ■ "Energy Efficiency Ordinance Softened" in *Austin Business JournalInc.* (Vol. 28, October 3, 2008, No. 29)
Pub: American City Business Journals
Ed: Jean Kwon. **Description:** City of Austin has eliminated mandatory energy efficiency upgrades to single-family housing as a condition for selling or renting homes or buildings. The new law proposes that an energy performance audit be conducted on single-family homes before being sold and the results of the audit disclosed to perspectives buyers.

7512 ■ *Environmental Guide to the Internet*
Pub: Government Institutes
Ed: Carol Briggs-Erickson, Editor. **Price:** $83, individuals. **Covers:** 1,200 resources covering the environment on the Internet, including organizations, products, and resources, including discussion groups, electronic journals, newsgroups, and discussion groups. **Entries Include:** Name, online address, description, e-mail address. **Arrangement:** Categories.

7513 ■ "EPA 'Finalizes' WaterSense for Homes" in *Contractor* (Vol. 57, January 2010, No. 1, pp. 70)
Pub: Penton Media, Inc.
Ed: Bob Mader. **Description:** U.S. Environmental Protection Agency released its "final" version of the WaterSense for Homes standard. The standard's provisions that affect plumbing contractors includes the specification that everything has to be leak tested and final service pressure cannot exceed 60 psi.

7514 ■ "EPA Grants E15 Waiver for 2001-2006 Vehicles" in *Farm Industry News* (January 21, 2011)
Pub: Penton Business Media Inc.
Description: U.S. Environmental Protection Agency waived a limitation on selling gasoline that contains more than 10 percent ethanol for model year 2001-2006 cars and light trucks, allowing fuel to contain up to 15 percent ethanol (E15) for these vehicles.

7515 ■ "ESolar Partners With Penglai on Landmark Solar Thermal Agreement for China" in *Business of Global Warming* (January 25, 2010, pp. 8)
Pub: Investment Weekly News
Description: Penglai Electric, a privately-owned Chinese electrical power equipment manufacturer, and eSolar, a global provider of cost-effective and reliable solar power plants, announced a master licensing agreement in which eSolar will build at least 2 gigawatts of solar thermal power plants in China over the next 10 years.

7516 ■ "Family Takes Wind Turbine Companies to Court Over Gag Clauses on Health Effects of Turbines" in *CNW Group* (September 12, 2011)
Pub: CNW Group
Description: Shawn and Trisha Drennan are concerned about the negative experiences other have had with wind turbines close to their homes, including adverse health effects. The couple's home will be approximately 650 meters from the Kingsbridge II wind farm project in Ontario, Canada.

7517 ■ "Find Private Money for FutureGen Plant" in *Crain's Chicago Business* (Vol. 34, September 12, 2011, No. 37, pp. 18)
Pub: Crain Communications Inc.
Description: FutureGen is a clean-coal power plant being developed in Southern Illinois. The need for further funding is discussed.

7518 ■ "First Suzlon S97 Turbines Arrive in North America for Installation" in *PR Newswire* (September 28, 2011)
Pub: United Business Media
Description: Suzlon Energy Ltd., the world's fifth largest manufacturer of wind turbines, will install its first S97 turbine at the Amherst Wind Farm Project. These turbines will be installed on 90-meter hub height towers and at full capacity, will generate enough electricity to power over 10,000 Canadian homes.

7519 ■ *The Flaw of Averages: Why We Underestimate Risk in the Face of Uncertainty*
Pub: John Wiley & Sons, Inc.
Ed: Sam L. Savage. **Released:** June 3, 2009. **Price:** $22.95. **Description:** Personal and business plans are based on uncertainties on a daily basis. The common avoidable mistake individuals make in assessing risk in the face of uncertainty is defined. The explains why plans based on average assumptions are wrong, on average, in areas as diverse as finance, healthcare, accounting, the war on terror, and climate change.

7520 ■ "Florida's Bright Upside" in *Tampa Bay Business Journal* (Vol. 29, November 6, 2009, No. 46, pp. 1)
Pub: American City Business Journals
Ed: Michael Hinman. **Description:** Florida's Public Service Commission (PSC) decision on a power purchase agreement that could add 25 megawatts of solar energy on Tampa Electric Company's offerings is presented. The decision could support the growing market for suppliers and marketers of renewable energy such as Jabil Circuit Inc., which manufactures photovoltaic modules. Details of the agreement are discussed.

7521 ■ "Floyd County Considers Wind Farms" in *Roanoke Times* (September 19, 2011)
Pub: Roanoke Times
Ed: Jeff Sturgeon. **Description:** German firm, Nordex USA Inc. is proposing a $100 million, 30-50 megawatt wind farm atop Wills Ridge, Virginia within the next four years. This project is one of several large wind project considered in the Roanoke and New River valleys of Virginia.

7522 ■ "Flue Vaccines are Going Green" in *Canadian Business* (Vol. 83, September 14, 2010, No. 15, pp. 24)
Pub: Rogers Media Ltd.
Ed: Angelia Chapman. **Description:** Quebec-based Medicago has found a solution to the bottleneck in the production of influenza vaccines by using plant-based processes instead of egg-based systems. Medicago's US Department of Defense funded research has produced the technology that speeds up the production time for vaccines by almost two-thirds. Insights into Medicago's patented process are also given.

7523 ■ "For Giving Us a Way To Say Yes To Solar: Lynn Jurich and Edward Fenster" in *Inc.* (Volume 32, December 2010, No. 10, pp. 110)
Pub: Inc. Magazine
Description: Profile of entrepreneurs Lynn Jurich and Edward Fenster, cofounders of SunRun. The firm installs solar panels at little or no cost and homeowners sign 20-year contracts to buy power at a fixed price.

7524 ■ "For Putting Down Roots in Business: Amy Norquist: Greensulate, New York City" in *Inc.* (Volume 32, December 2010, No. 10, pp. 106)
Pub: Inc. Magazine
Ed: Christine Lagorio. **Description:** Profile of Amy Norquist who left her position at an environmental nonprofit organization to found Greensulate. Her firm insulates rooftops with lavender, native grasses and succulents called sedum in order to eliminate carbon from the atmosphere.

7525 ■ "Forum at UNCW to Explore Offshore Wind Farming" in *Star-News* (October 4, 2011)
Pub: Star-News
Ed: Kate Elizabeth Queram. **Description:** North Carolina is poised to profit from offshore wind farming, according to regional environmental experts. The Sierra Club, in conjunction with the University of North Carolina Wilmington and Oceana are hosting an offshore wind forum featuring five panelists, focusing on potential impacts on birds and sea life, tourism and cost, as well as other pertinent issues.

7526 ■ "Fossil Fuel, Renewable Fuel Shares Expected to Flip Flop" in *Farm Industry News* (April 29, 2011)
Pub: Penton Business Media Inc.
Description: Total energy use of fossil fuels is predicted to fall 5 percent by the year 2035, with renewable fuel picking it up.

7527 ■ "Franchising's Green Scene" in *Entrepreneur* (Vol. 37, August 2009, No. 8, pp. 85)
Pub: Entrepreneur Media, Inc.
Ed: Gwen Moran. **Description:** Trends in favor of environmentally friendly franchises have been growing for about 25 years but have now become mainstream. The challenges for a prospective green franchisee is that these companies may be tricky to evaluate and they need to ask franchisors a lot of questions to weed out ones that falsely claim to be green.

7528 ■ "FSU's OGZEB Is Test Bed for Sustainable Technology" in *Contractor* (Vol. 56, October 2009, No. 10, pp. 1)
Pub: Penton Media, Inc.
Ed: Candace Roulo. **Description:** Florida State University has one of 14 off-grid zero emissions buildings (OGZEB) in the U.S. ; it was built to research sustainable and alternative energy systems. The building produces electricity from 30 photovoltaic panels and it also has three AET water heating solar panels on the roof.

7529 ■ "Fuel King: The Most Fuel-Efficient Tractor of the Decade is the John Deere 8295R" in *Farm Industry News* (November 10, 2011)
Pub: Penton Business Media Inc.
Description: Farm Industry News compiled a list of the most fuel-efficient tractors with help from the Nebraska Tractor Test Lab, with the John Deere 8295R PTO winner of the most fuel-efficient tractor of the decade.

7530 ■ "Fuel for Thought; Canadian Business Leaders on Energy Policy" in *Canadian Business* (Vol. 81, September 15, 2008, No. 14-15, pp. 12)
Pub: Rogers Media Ltd.
Ed: Joe Castaldo. **Description:** Most Canadian business leaders worry about the unreliability of the oil supply but feel that Canada is in a better position to benefit from the energy supply crisis than other countries. Many respondents also highlighted the need to invest in renewable energy sources.

7531 ■ "GE Milestone: 1,000th Wind Turbine Installed in Canada" in *CNW Group* (October 4, 2011)
Pub: CNW Group
Description: GE installed its 1,000th wind turbine in Canada at Cartier Wind Energy's Gros Morne project in the Gaspesie Region of Quebec, Canada. As Canada continues to expand its use of wind energy, GE plans to have over 1,100 wind turbines installed in the nation by the end of 2011.

7532 ■ "Germans Win Solar Decathlon - Again" in *Contractor* (Vol. 56, November 2009, No. 11, pp. 1)
Pub: Penton Media, Inc.
Ed: Robert P. Mader. **Description:** Students from Technische Universtat Darmstadt won the U.S. Department of Energy's Solar Decathlon by designing and building the most attractive and efficient solar-powered home. The winner's design produced a surplus of power even during three days of rain and photovoltaic panels covered nearly every exterior surface.

7533 ■ "Getting the Bioheat Word Out" in *Indoor Comfort Marketing* (Vol. 70, September 2011, No. 9, pp. 32)
Pub: Industry Publications Inc.
Description: Ways to market advanced liquid fuels to the public are outlined.

7534 ■ "Getting Going on Going Green" in *HRMagazine* (Vol. 53, August 2008, No. 8, pp. 8)
Pub: Society for Human Resource Management
Ed: Rita Zeidner. **Description:** Being eco-friendly can help recruit and retain workers. Resources to help firms create green initiatives are presented.

7535 ■ "Getting NORA reauthorized is high priority" in *Indoor Comfort Marketing* (Vol. 70, February 2011, No. 2, pp. 14)
Pub: Industry Publications Inc.
Description: The importance of reauthorizing the National Oilheat Research Alliance is stressed.

7536 ■ "The Global Environment Movement is Bjorn Again" in *Canadian Business* (Vol. 83, September 14, 2010, No. 15, pp. 11)
Pub: Rogers Media Ltd.
Ed: Steve Maich. **Description:** Danish academic Bjorn Lomborg is in favor of decisive action to combat climate change in his new book and was given front page treatment by a London newspaper. Environmentalist groups see this as a victory since Lomborg had not previously considered climate change an immediate issue.

7537 ■ "GM's Volt Woes Cast Shadow on E-Cars" in *Wall Street Journal Eastern Edition* (November 28, 2011, pp. B1)
Pub: Dow Jones & Company Inc.
Ed: Sharon Terlep. **Description:** The future of electric cars is darkened with the government investigation by the National Highway Traffic Safety Administration into General Motor Company's Chevy Volt after two instances of the car's battery packs catching fire during crash tests conducted by the Agency.

7538 ■ "Go Green Or Go Home" in *Black Enterprise* (Vol. 41, August 2010, No. 1, pp. 53)
Pub: Earl G. Graves Publishing Co. Inc.
Ed: Tennille M. Robinson. **Description:** The green economy has become an essential part of every business, however, small business owners need to learn how to participate, including minority owned entrepreneurs.

7539 ■ "Going Green, Going Slowly" in *Playthings* (Vol. 106, September 1, 2008, No. 8, pp. 17)
Pub: Reed Business Information
Ed: Nancy Zwiers. **Description:** Sustainability and greener materials for both product and packaging in the toy industry has become important for protecting our environment. However, in a recent survey nearly 60 percent of responders stated environmental issues did not play a part in purchasing a toy or game for their children.

7540 ■ "Golden Valley, Fling Hills Plan LNG Plant" in *Alaska Business Monthly* (Vol. 27, October 2011, No. 10, pp. 9)
Pub: Alaska Business Publishing Company
Ed: Nancy Pounds. **Description:** Golden Valley Electric Association and Flint Hills Resources have partnered on a natural gas liquefaction facility on the North Slope. The deal will deliver gas at cost to GVEA and Flint Hills and Flint Hills will become more competitive and efficient by burning LNG instead of refined crude oil at the refinery.

7541 ■ *Good Green Guide for Small Businesses: How to Change the Way Your Business Works for the Better*
Pub: A & C Black
Ed: Impetus Consulting Ltd. Staff. **Released:** September 1, 2009. **Price:** $19.95. **Description:** Guide for small businesses to take an environmental audit

of their company and shows how to minimize the impact of office essentials such as utilities, insulation, recycling and waste, electrical equipment, water systems, lighting options, food and drink, and office cleaning arrangements and products.

7542 ■ "Got to be Smarter than the Average Bear" in *Contractor* (Vol. 56, September 2009, No. 9, pp. 82)
Pub: Penton Media, Inc.
Ed: Bob Mader. **Description:** International Association of Plumbing and Mechanical Officials Green Technical Committee has debated the need for contractors to have certifications in installing green plumbing. Some have argued that qualifications would discourage homeowners from improving their properties. Comments from executives are also included.

7543 ■ "Gov. Kasich to Put DOD On Short Leash" in *Business Courier* (Vol. 27, November 26, 2010, No. 30, pp. 1)
Pub: Business Courier
Ed: Dan Monk. **Description:** Ohio Governor-elect John Kasich proposed the privatization of the Ohio Department of Development in favor of a nonprofit corporation called JobsOhio. Kasich believes that the department has lost its focus by adding to its mission issues such as energy efficiency and tourism.

7544 ■ "Grainger Show Highlights Building Green, Economy" in *Contractor* (Vol. 57, February 2010, No. 2, pp. 3)
Pub: Penton Media, Inc.
Ed: Candace Roulo. **Description:** chief U.S. economist told attendees of the Grainger's 2010 Total MRO Solutions National Customer Show that the economic recovery would be subdued. Mechanical contractors who attended the event also learned about building sustainable, green products, and technologies, and economic and business challenges.

7545 ■ "Green Acre$ Tope 10 Green Biz To Start Right Now" in *Small Business Opportunities* (September 2010)
Pub: Harris Publications Inc.
Description: A list of the top ten green businesses to start in 2010 is provided.

7546 ■ "Green Acres" in *Hawaii Business* (Vol. 54, September 2008, No. 3, pp. 48)
Pub: Hawaii Business Publishing
Ed: Jan Tenbruggencate. **Description:** Bill Cowern's Hawaiian Mahogany is a forestry business that processes low-value trees to be sold as wood chips, which can be burned to create biodiesel. Cowern is planning to obtain certification to market carbon credits and is also working with Green Energy Hawaii for the permit of a biomass-fueled power plant. Other details about Cowern's business are discussed.

7547 ■ "Green and Clean" in *Retail Merchandiser* (Vol. 51, July-August 2011, No. 4, pp. 56)
Pub: Phoenix Media Corporation
Description: Green Valley Grocery partnered with Paragon Solutions consulting firm to make their stores environmentally green.

7548 ■ "'Green' Cleaner Buys Local Firm" in *Puget Sound Business Journal* (Vol. 29, December 19, 2008, No. 35, pp. 3)
Pub: American City Business Journals
Ed: Greg Lamm. **Description:** Washington-based Blue Sky Cleaners has purchased Four Seasons Cleaners. The green company also purchased Queen Anne store and Four Seasons' routes fro Snohomish County through Seattle.

7549 ■ *The Green Collar Economy: How One Solution Can Fix Our Two Biggest Problems*
Pub: HarperCollins Publishers
Ed: Van Jones. **Released:** November 1, 2009. **Price:** $14.99. **Description:** This book offers insight into rebuilding the nation's infrastructure and creating alternative energy sources that could boost the economy through increased employment and higher wages while decreasing our dependence on fossil fuels.

7550 ■ "The Green Conversation" in *Harvard Business Review* (Vol. 86, September 2008, No. 9, pp. 58)
Pub: Harvard Business School Press
Description: Six guidelines are presented for addressing and benefiting from environmentally conscious corporate decision making and practices. Topics covered include marketing, supply chain, and leadership.

7551 ■ "Green Counting" in *Canadian Business* (Vol. 81, October 13, 2008, No. 17, pp. 27)
Pub: Rogers Media Ltd.
Ed: Joe Castaldo. **Description:** Procter and Gamble research revealed that only 10 percent of North American consumers are willing to accept trade-offs for a greener product. Three out of four North American consumers will not accept a higher price or a decrease in a product's performance for an environmental benefit. Details on green marketing are also discussed.

7552 ■ "Green Energy Exec Hits State Policy" in *Boston Business Journal* (Vol. 30, December 3, 2010, No. 45, pp. 1)
Pub: Boston Business Journal
Ed: Kyle Alspach. **Description:** American Superconductor Corporation President Dan McGahn believes that the state government of Massachusetts is not proactive enough to develop the state into a manufacturing hub for wind power technology. McGahn believes that while Governor Deval Patrick campaigned for wind turbines in the state, his administration does not have the focus required to build the turbines in the state.

7553 ■ "Green Firm Scouts Sites in Tri-State" in *Business Courier* (Vol. 27, July 23, 2010, No. 12, pp. 1)
Pub: Business Courier
Ed: Dan Monk. **Description:** CresaPartners is searching for a manufacturing facility in Cincinnati, Ohio. The company is set to tour about ten sites in the area.

7554 ■ *The Green Guide for Business: The Ultimate Environment for Businesses of All Sizes*
Pub: Profile Books Limited
Ed: Roger East, Hannah Bullock, Chris Goodall. **Released:** May 10, 2010. **Description:** Everyone wants to go green these days, but for small businesses that's easier said than done. How do you measure a company's carbon footprint? Are dryers or hand towels more eco-friendly? Recycled paper or FSC-certified? All these questions and more are explored.

7555 ■ "Green It Like You Mean It" in *Special Events Magazine* (Vol. 28, February 1, 2009, No. 2)
Pub: Special Events Magazine
Ed: Christine Landry. **Description:** Eco-friendly party planners offer advice for planning and hosting green parties or events. Tips include information for using recycled paper products, organic food and drinks. The Eco Nouveau Fashion Show held by Serene Star Productions reused old garments to create new fashions as well as art pieces from discarded doors and window frames for the show; eco-friendly treats and gift bags were highlighted at the event.

7556 ■ "Green Light" in *The Business Journal-Portland* (Vol. 25, July 11, 2008, No. 18, pp. 1)
Pub: American City Business Journals, Inc.
Ed: Erik Siemers. **Description:** Ecos Consulting, a sustainability consulting company based in Portland, Oregon, is seeing a boost in revenue as more businesses turn to sustainable practices. The company's revenue rose by 50 percent in 2007 and employees increased from 57 to 150. Other details about Ecos' growth are discussed.

7557 ■ "Green Shift Sees Red" in *Canadian Business* (Vol. 81, September 29, 2008, No. 16)
Pub: Rogers Media Ltd.
Ed: Jeff Sanford. **Description:** Green Shift Inc. is suing the Liberal Party of Canada in an $8.5 million lawsuit for using the phrase "green shift" when they rolled out their carbon tax and climate change policy. The company has come to be recognized as a consultant and provider of green products such as non-toxic, biodegradable cups, plates, and utensils for events.

7558 ■ "Greenhouse Announces Merger With Custom Q, Inc." in *Investment Weekly* (January 30, 2010, pp. 338)
Pub: Investment Weekly News
Description: In accordance with an Agreement and Plan of Share Exchange, GreenHouse Holdings, Inc., an innovative green solutions provider, has gone public via a reverse merger with Custom Q, Inc.

7559 ■ "Greening the Auto Industry" in *Business Journal-Serving Phoenix & the Valley of the Sun* (Vol. 30, July 23, 2010, No. 46, pp. 1)
Pub: Phoenix Business Journal
Ed: Patrick O'Grady. **Description:** Thermo Fluids Inc. has been recycling used oil products since 1993 and could become Arizona's first home for oil filter recycling after retrofitting its Phoenix facility to include a compaction machine. The new service could help establish Thermo Fluids as a recycling hub for nearby states.

7560 ■ "The Greening of Lunch" in *Entrepreneur* (Vol. 37, October 2009, No. 10, pp. 44)
Pub: Entrepreneur Media, Inc.
Ed: Deborah Song. **Description:** Kids Konserve is a self-funded online business selling reusable and recycled lunch kits for kids. The company also aims to increase awareness about waste reduction.

7561 ■ "Greening the Manscape" in *Canadian Business* (Vol. 81, October 13, 2008, No. 17, pp. S19)
Pub: Rogers Media Ltd.
Ed: David Lackie. **Description:** Buyer's guide of environmentally friendly grooming products for men is provided. Improved formulations have solved the problems of having synthetic ingredients in grooming products. Details about a face scrub, after shave conditioner, and a nourishing cream made of 91 percent organic ingredients are given, including prices.

7562 ■ *Greening Your Small Business: How to Improve Your Bottom Line, Grow Your Brand, Satisfy Your Customers and Save the Planet*
Pub: Prentice Hall Press
Ed: Jennifer Kaplan. **Released:** November 3, 2009. **Price:** $19.95. **Description:** A definitive resource for anyone who wants their small business to be cutting-edge, competitive, profitable, and eco-conscious. Stories from small business owners address every aspect of going green, from basics such as recycling waste, energy efficiency, and reducing information technology footprint, to more in-depth concerns such as green marketing and communications, green business travel, and green employee benefits.

7563 ■ *Guerrilla Marketing Goes Green: Winning Strategies to Improve Your Profits and Your Planet*
Pub: John Wiley & Sons, Inc.
Ed: Jay Conrad Levinson, Shel Horowitz. **Released:** January 10, 2010. **Price:** $21.95. **Description:** The latest tips on green marketing and sustainable business strategies are shared.

7564 ■ "Guide to Carbon Footprinting" in *American Printer* (Vol. 128, June 1, 2011, No. 6)
Pub: Penton Media Inc.
Description: PrintCity Alliance published its new report, 'Carbon Footprint & Energy Reduction for Graphic Industry Value Chain.' The report aims to help improve the environmental performance of printers, converters, publishers, brand owners and their suppliers.

7565 ■ "Hey, You Can't Do That" in *Green Industry Pro* (Vol. 23, September 2011)
Pub: Cygnus Business Media
Ed: Rod Dickens. **Description:** Manufacturers of landscape equipment are making better use of energy resources, such as the use of fuel-injection

systems instead of carburetors, lightweight materials, better lubricants, advanced battery technology, and innovative engine designs.

7566 ■ "Hot Air" in *Canadian Business* (Vol. 81, July 22, 2008, No. 12-13, pp. 16)
Pub: Rogers Media Ltd.
Ed: Joe Castaldo. **Description:** Over half of 101 business leaders who were recently surveyed oppose Liberal leader Stephane Dion's carbon-tax proposal, saying that manufacturers in Canada are likely to suffer from the plan. Additional key results of the survey are presented.

7567 ■ "Hot Air: On Global Warming and Carbon Tax" in *Canadian Business* (Vol. 81, October 13, 2008, No. 17, pp. 12)
Pub: Rogers Media Ltd.
Ed: Joe Castaldo. **Description:** Survey of Canadian business leaders revealed that the environment is a key issue in Canada's federal elections. Respondents believe that Prime Minister Stephen Harper's views on global warming and climate change are closer to their own views. Other key information on the survey is presented.

7568 ■ *Hot, Flat and Crowded: Why We Need a Green Revolution - and How It Can Renew America*
Pub: Farrar, Straus and Giroux
Ed: Thomas L. Friedman. **Released:** September 8, 2008. **Price:** $27.95. **Description:** Author explains how global warming, rapidly growing populations, and the expansion of the world's middle class through globalization have impacted the environment.

7569 ■ *Housecleaning Business: Organize Your Business - Get Clients and Referrals - Set Rates and Services*
Pub: The Globe Pequot Press
Ed: Laura Jorstad, Melinda Morse. **Released:** June 1, 2009. **Price:** $18.95. **Description:** This book shares insight into starting a housecleaning businesses. It shows how to develop a service manual, screen clients, serve customers, select cleaning products, competition, how to up a home office, using the Internet to grow the business and offering green cleaning options to clients.

7570 ■ "How Green Is The Valley?" in *Barron's* (Vol. 88, July 4, 2008, No. 28, pp. 13)
Pub: Dow Jones & Co., Inc.
Description: San Jose, California has made a good start towards becoming a leader in alternative energy technology through the establishment of United Laboratories' own lab in the city. The certification process for photovoltaic cells will be dramatically shortened with this endeavor.

7571 ■ "How to Keep Your Cool and Your Friends in a Heat Wave" in *Canadian Business* (Vol. 83, August 17, 2010, No. 13-14, pp. 79)
Pub: Rogers Media Ltd.
Ed: Angelina Chapin. **Description:** A buyer's guide of menswear clothing for businessmen is presented. The products include an antiperspirant and deodorant, men's dress shorts, shoes and bamboo fabric undershirt.

7572 ■ "Hydronicahh - Everything in Modulation" in *Contractor* (Vol. 56, December 2009, No. 12, pp. 24)
Pub: Penton Media, Inc.
Ed: Mark Eatherton. **Description:** Management and the environmental impact of a home hydronic system are discussed. Radiant windows have the potential to reduce energy consumption. A variable speed delta T pump is required for the construction of a hydronic wood pit.

7573 ■ "IAPMO GTC Finalizes Green Supplement" in *Contractor* (Vol. 57, January 2010, No. 1, pp. 1)
Pub: Penton Media, Inc.
Description: International Association of Plumbing and Mechanical Officials' Green Technical Committee finalized the Green Plumbing & Mechanical Code Supplement. The supplement was created to provide a set of provisions that encourage sustainable practices and work towards the design and construction of plumbing and mechanical systems.

7574 ■ "Indoor Air Quality – a Tribute to Efficiency" in *Indoor Comfort Marketing* (Vol. 70, August 2011, No. 8, pp. 8)
Pub: Industry Publications Inc.
Ed: Matthew Maleske. **Description:** Efficiency of new HVAC/R equipment has helped improve indoor air quality.

7575 ■ "Industry Escalates Lobbying Efforts For Loan Program" in *Crain's Detroit Business* (Vol. 24, September 22, 2008, No. 38, pp. 22)
Pub: Crain Communications, Inc.
Ed: Jay Greene; Ryan Beene; Harry Stoffer. **Description:** Auto suppliers such as Lear Corp., which is best known for vehicle seating, also supplies high-voltage wiring for Ford hybrids and is developing other hybrid components. These suppliers are joining automakers in lobbying for the loan program which would promote the accelerated development of fuel-efficient vehicles.

7576 ■ "Info Junkie" in *Crain's Chicago Business* (Vol. 34, October 24, 2011, No. 42, pp. 35)
Pub: Crain Communications Inc.
Ed: Christina Le Beau. **Description:** Greg Colando, president of Flor Inc., an eco-friendly carpet company located I Chicago discusses his marketing program to increase sales.

7577 ■ "Interested in 12 Billion Dollars?" in *Indoor Comfort Marketing* (Vol. 70, March 2011, No. 3, pp. 18)
Pub: Industry Publications Inc.
Ed: Matthew Maleske. **Description:** Trends in the indoor quality industry are cited, with insight into expanding an existing indoor heating and cooling business.

7578 ■ "It's Always 55 Degrees F" in *Contractor* (Vol. 56, September 2009, No. 9, pp. 38)
Pub: Penton Media, Inc.
Ed: Carol Fey. **Description:** Geothermal-exchange heating and cooling systems can save businesses up to 60 percent on energy costs for heating and cooling. Geothermal systems get heat from the earth during winter. Design, features and installation of geothermal systems are also discussed.

7579 ■ "It's Not Easy Investing Green" in *Entrepreneur* (Vol. 37, August 2009, No. 8, pp. 64)
Pub: Entrepreneur Media, Inc.
Ed: Rosalind Resnick. **Description:** Some venture capitalists remain bullish on green investing despite signs of stagnation. One way for an investor to cash in on green investing is to invest in large public companies that are investing big in green initiatives. Being an angel investor to a local clean-tech company is another avenue.

7580 ■ "KC Sewer Solutions May Overflow With Green Ideas" in *The Business Journal-Serving Metropolitan Kansas City* (August 22, 2008)
Pub: American City Business Journals, Inc.
Ed: Suzanna Stagemeyer. **Description:** Adding green solutions such as small, dispersed basins to catch runoffs and the use of deep rooted natural plants to fix the sewer system of Kansas could probably justify the $2.3 billion worth of funds needed for the project. The city has been ordered by the EPA and the Missouri Department of Natural Resources to fix their sewer systems that are overwhelmed by significant rains.

7581 ■ "Know the Facts About Natural Gas!" in *Indoor Comfort Marketing* (Vol. 70, August 2011, No. 8, pp. 26)
Pub: Industry Publications Inc.
Description: AEC Activity Update is presented on the American Energy Coalition's Website.

7582 ■ "The Lap of Eco-Luxury" in *Entrepreneur* (Vol. 37, August 2009, No. 8, pp. 38)
Pub: Entrepreneur Media, Inc.
Ed: Dina Mishev. **Description:** Founder Rob DesLauriers of the Terra Resort Group says that the natural world has taken very good care of him and that he wants to do his part to take care of it. The mattresses that their hotel uses are made from recycled steel springs and their TVs are Energy Star-approved. Their linens are made from organically grown cottons and their walls use by-products from coal burning.

7583 ■ "Large Homes can be Energy Efficient Too" in *Contractor* (Vol. 56, October 2009, No. 10, pp. 5)
Pub: Penton Media, Inc.
Ed: Candace Roulo. **Description:** Eco Estate at Briggs Chaney subdivision in Silver Spring, Maryland has model houses that use sustainable technologies and products and the homes that will be built on the subdivision will feature some of the technologies featured on the model home. The energy efficient HVAC system of the model homes are discussed.

7584 ■ "Legislation Introduced" in *Indoor Comfort Marketing* (Vol. 70, July 2011, No. 7, pp. 6)
Pub: Industry Publications Inc.
Description: New industry legislation is examined by the National Oilheat Research Alliance.

7585 ■ "Lincoln Electric Installs Large Wind Tower" in *Modern Machine Shop* (Vol. 84, October 2011, No. 5, pp. 42)
Pub: Gardner Publications
Description: Lincoln Electric, a welding product manufacturer, constructed a 443-foot-tall wind tower at its plant in Euclid, Ohio. The tower is expected to generate as much as 10 percent of the facility's energy and save as much as $500,000 annually in energy costs.

7586 ■ "The Lithium Deficit" in *Canadian Business* (Vol. 82, April 27, 2009, No. 7, pp. 17)
Pub: Rogers Media
Ed: Joe Castaldo. **Description:** Experts are concerned that there may not be enough lithium available to support the expected rise in demand for the natural resource. Lithium is used in lithium ion batteries, the standard power source for electric and hybrid vehicles. Experts believe that the demand for lithium can only be measured once the technology is out in the market.

7587 ■ "Loan Dollars Sit Idle for Energy Plan" in *Baltimore Business Journal* (Vol. 28, September 10, 2010, No. 18, pp. 1)
Pub: Baltimore Business Journal
Ed: Scott Dance. **Description:** The Maryland Energy Administration has millions of dollars in Federal stimulus and state energy efficiency cash sitting idle and might be lost once the window for stimulus spending is gone. However, businesses have no interest in betting on renewable energy because some cannot afford to take out more loans. Other challenges faced by these businesses are presented.

7588 ■ "The Long View: Roberta Bondar on Science and the Need for Education" in *Canadian Business* (Vol. 81, October 27, 2008, No. 18)
Pub: Rogers Media Ltd.
Ed: Alex Mlynek. **Description:** Roberta Bondar believes that energy and renewable energy is a critical environmental issue faced by Canada today. Bondar is the first Canadian woman and neurologist in space.

7589 ■ "A Look At Three Gas-Less Cars" in *Hispanic Business* (Vol. 30, September 2008, No. 9, pp. 90)
Pub: Hispanic Business, Inc.
Ed: Daniel Soussa. **Description:** Three major car manufacturers, Chevrolet, BMW, and Honda, are giving market leader Toyota competition for the next generation of eco-friendly car. The latest and most

advanced of the gasoline-less cars designed by the three firms, namely, the Chevrolet Volt, BMW's Hydrogen 7, and the Honda FCX Clarity, are reviewed.

7590 ■ "Lunch Box Maker Gives Back" in *Marketing to Women* (Vol. 23, November 2010, No. 11, pp. 5)
Pub: EPM Communications, Inc.
Description: Female entrepreneurs launched a new program called, "Share Your Lunch Project" that encourages mothers to give back and replace their child's lunchbox with their eco-friendly lunch boxes, which are available at select retailers. All proceeds from the project will benefit the World Food Program USA, which feeds children in developing countries.

7591 ■ "Magpower May Build Solar Panels Here" in *Austin Business Journal* (Vol. 31, May 13, 2011, No. 10, pp. A1)
Pub: American City Business Journals Inc.
Ed: Christopher Calnan. **Description:** RRE Austin Solar LLC CEO Doven Mehta has revealed plans to partner with Portugal-based Magpower SA, only if Austin energy buys electricity from planned solar energy farm in Pflugerville. Austin Energy has received 100 bids from 35 companies to supply 200 megawatts of solar- and wind-generated electricity.

7592 ■ "Making Waves" in *Business Journal Portland* (Vol. 27, November 26, 2010, No. 39, pp. 1)
Pub: Portland Business Journal
Ed: Erik Siemers. **Description:** Corvallis, Oregon-based Columbia Power Technologies LLC is about to close a $2 million Series A round of investment initiated by $750,000 from Oregon Angel Fund. The wave energy startup company was formed to commercialize the wave buoy technology developed by Oregon State University researchers.

7593 ■ "Mixing Business and Pleasure On the Green" in *Black Enterprise* (Vol. 41, October 2010, No. 3, pp. 65)
Pub: Earl G. Graves Publishing Co. Inc.
Ed: Annya M. Lott. **Description:** Glow Golf, sponsored by Glow Sports, will offer instruction to 150 female corporate executives and entrepreneurs to learn the fundamentals of the game of golf.

7594 ■ "Molycorp Funds Wind Energy Technology Company" in *Manufacturing Close-Up* (September 19, 2011)
Pub: Close-Up Media
Description: Molycorp Inc., producer of rare earth oxides (REO) and a REO producer outside of China, announced it will invest in Boulder Wind Power, which has designed a rare earth magnet powered wind turbine generator. This new generator can produce electricity as low as $0.04 per Kilowatt Hour. Boulder Wind Power's patented wind turbine technology allows for use of rare earth permanent magnets that do not require dysprosium, which is relatively scarce.

7595 ■ "Mr. Clean" in *Canadian Business* (Vol. 81, October 27, 2008, No. 18, pp. 74)
Pub: Rogers Media Ltd.
Ed: Rachel Pulfer. **Description:** Profile of Nicholas Parker, co-founder of Cleantech Group LLC, a pioneer in clean technology investing. Cleantech, now a global industry, accounts for 10 percent of all venture capital investments made by U.S. companies in 2007.

7596 ■ *The Necessary Revolution: Working Together to Create a Sustainable World*
Pub: Broadway Books
Ed: Peter M. Senge, Bryan Smith, Nina Kruschwitz, Joe Laur, Sara Schley. **Released:** April 6, 2010. **Price:** $18.00. **Description:** The book outlines various examples for companies to implement sustainable change and go green in the process.

7597 ■ "N.E.'s Largest Solar Site Set for Scituate Landfill" in *Boston Business Journal* (Vol. 30, December 17, 2010, No. 47, pp. 1)
Pub: Boston Business Journal
Ed: Kyle Alspach. **Description:** A closed 12-acre landfill in Scituate, Massachusetts is the proposed site for a 2.4-megawatt solar power plant. The town government will buy the power at a discounted rate, saving it $200,000 annually.

7598 ■ "The New Alchemists" in *Canadian Business* (Vol. 81, October 27, 2008, No. 18, pp. 22)
Pub: Rogers Media Ltd.
Ed: Joe Castaldo. **Description:** Ethanol industry expects second-generation ethanol or cellulosic biofuels to provide ecologically friendly technologies than the ethanol made from food crops. Government and industries are investing on producing cellulosic biofuels.

7599 ■ "A New Alliance For Global Change" in *Harvard Business Review* (Vol. 88, September 2010, No. 9, pp. 56)
Pub: Harvard Business School Publishing
Ed: Bill Drayton, Valeria Budinich. **Description:** Collaboration between social organizations and for-profit firms through the development of hybrid value chains to target complex global issues is promoted. While social organizations offer links to communities and consumers, firms provide financing and scale expertise.

7600 ■ "New Book Takes Alternate View on Ontario's Wind Industry" in *CNW Group* (September 19, 2011)
Pub: CNW Group
Description: Dirty Business: The Reality Behind Ontario's Rush to Wind Power, was written by editor and health care writer Jane Wilson of Ottawa, Ontario, Canada along with contributing editor Parker Gallant. The book contains articles and papers on the wind business, including information on illnesses caused from the environmental noise.

7601 ■ "A New Day is Dawning" in *Indoor Comfort Marketing* (Vol. 70, August 2011, No. 8, pp. 18)
Pub: Industry Publications Inc.
Ed: Paul Nazzaro. **Description:** New trends in the HVAC/R industry regarding biofuels and bioheat are explored.

7602 ■ "N.H. Near the LEED in Green Space" in *New Hampshire Business Review* (Vol. 33, March 25, 2011, No. 6, pp. 30)
Pub: Business Publications Inc.
Description: New Hamphire's architects, contractors and suppliers are among the leaders with LEED-certified space per capita.

7603 ■ "A Nice Consistency" in *Inc.* (Vol. 31, January-February 2009, No. 1, pp. 94)
Pub: Mansueto Ventures LLC
Ed: Jason Del Rey. **Description:** PJ Madison spent almost a quarter of its revenue promoting its latest product, organic ice cream. The Texas-based firm saw sales increase dramatically.

7604 ■ "NStar Feels the Heat" in *Cape Cod Times* (September 30, 2011)
Pub: Cape Cod Media Group
Ed: Patrick Cassidy. **Description:** Massachusetts energy officials wish to delay a merger between NStar and Northeast Utilities until it is clear how the partnership would meet the state's green energy goals. Governor Deval Patrick supports the proposed Nantucket Sound wind farm.

7605 ■ "Nuclear Renaissance" in *Canadian Business* (Vol. 83, August 17, 2010, No. 13-14, pp. 46)
Pub: Rogers Media Ltd.
Description: Nuclear energy has come back into the public's favor in Canada because it has virtually no emissions and is always available anytime of the day. Canada's nuclear industry has also achieved an incomparable record of safe, economic and reliable power generation in three provinces for 48 years.

7606 ■ "On Growth Path of Rising Star" in *Boston Business Journal* (Vol. 31, June 24, 2011, No. 22, pp. 3)
Pub: Boston Business Journal
Ed: Kyle Alspach. **Description:** 1366 Technologies Inc. of Lexington, Massachusetts is considered a rising solar power technology company. The firm secured $150 million loan guarantee from the US Department of Energy that could go to the construction of a 1,000 megawatt solar power plant.

7607 ■ "One on One With SEIA's President, CEO" in *Contractor* (Vol. 57, January 2010, No. 1, pp. 40)
Pub: Penton Media, Inc.
Ed: Dave Yates. **Description:** Solar Energy Industries Association President and CEO Rhone Resch says that the deployment of solar systems in the U.S. has exploded since 2005 and that there is a need to make inroads for shaping the U.S. energy policy. Resch says one of the hurdles they face is that there are no universal standards.

7608 ■ "OPEC Exposed" in *Hawaii Business* (Vol. 54, September 2008, No. 3, pp. 2)
Pub: Hawaii Business Publishing
Ed: Serena Lim. **Description:** Organization of the Petroleum Exporting Countries (OPEC) has said that their effort in developing an alternative energy source has driven prices up. The biofuel sector is criticizing the statement, saying that a research study found that biofuels push petroleum prices down by 15 percent. Details on the effect of rising petroleum prices are discussed.

7609 ■ "Out of Juice?" in *Canadian Business* (Vol. 81, October 27, 2008, No. 18, pp. 32)
Pub: Rogers Media Ltd.
Ed: Joe Castaldo. **Description:** Alternative energy experts suggest Canada should be more aggressive and should make major policy changes on energy alternatives despite an Ernst & Young research that rated the country high on renewable energy.

7610 ■ "Overheating Taking Place? Pay Attention to Details..." in *Indoor Comfort Marketing* (Vol. 70, March 2011, No. 3, pp.)
Pub: Industry Publications Inc.
Ed: George R. Carey. **Description:** Boiler facts are outlined to help the small HVAC company when servicing customers.

7611 ■ "An Overview of Energy Consumption of the Globalized World Economy" in *Energy Policy* (Vol. 39, October 2011, No. 10, pp. 5920-2928)
Pub: Reed Elsevier Reference Publishing
Ed: Z.M. Chen, G.Q. Chen. **Description:** Energy consumption and its impact on the global world economy is examined.

7612 ■ "Phoenix Conference Reveals Opportunities are Coming" in *Indoor Comfort Marketing* (Vol. 70, March 2011, No. 3, pp. 24)
Pub: Industry Publications Inc.
Ed: Paul J. Nazzaro. **Description:** Advanced liquid fuels were spotlighted at the Phoenix conference revealing the opportunities for using liquid fuels.

7613 ■ "Positive Transformational Change" in *Indoor Comfort Marketing* (Vol. 70, April 2011, No. 4, pp. 30)
Pub: Industry Publications Inc.
Ed: Blaine Fox. **Description:** Management changes taking place at Shark Bites HVAC firm are discussed.

7614 ■ "PPC's Major Commitment to Biofuel Infrastructure" in *Indoor Comfort Marketing* (Vol. 70, April 2011, No. 4, pp. 6)
Pub: Industry Publications Inc.
Description: Petroleum Products Corporation's commitment to the biofuel infrastructure is outlined.

7615 ■ "Provinces Tackle E-Waste Problem" in *Canadian Electronics* (Vol. 23, June-July 2008, No. 4, pp. 1)
Pub: Action Communication Inc.
Ed: Ken Manchen. **Description:** Canadian provinces are implementing measures concerning the safe and environmentally friendly disposal of electronic waste. Alberta, British Columbia, Nova Scotia, and Saskatchewan impose an e-waste recycling fee on electronic equipment purchases.

7616 ■ "PSC Approves $130M TECO Solar Project" in *Tampa Bay Business Journal* (Vol. 30, December 18, 2009, No. 52, pp. 1)
Pub: American City Business Journals
Ed: Michael Hinman. **Description:** Florida's Public Service Commission has endorsed Tampa Electric Company's plan to add 25 megawatts of solar energy to its portfolio. TECO's plan needed the approval by PSC to defray additional costs for the project through ratepayers.

7617 ■ "Radiant – the Hottest Topic in ... Cooling" in *Indoor Comfort Marketing* (Vol. 70, February 2011, No. 2, pp. 8)
Pub: Industry Publications Inc.
Description: Examination of radiant cooling systems, a new trend in cooling homes and buildings.

7618 ■ "Recycling 202: How to Take Your Recycling Practices to the Next Level" in *Black Enterprise* (Vol. 41, September 2010, No. 2, pp. 38)
Pub: Earl G. Graves Publishing Co. Inc.
Ed: Tamara E. Holmes. **Description:** Consumer Electronics Association and other organizations, manufacturers and retailers list ways to recycle all household items.

7619 ■ "Reducing the Book's Carbon Footpring" in *American Printer* (Vol. 128, July 1, 2011, No. 7)
Pub: Penton Media Inc.
Description: Green Press Initiative's Book Industry Environmental Council is working to achieve a 20 percent reduction in the book industry's carbon footprint by 2020. The Council is made up of publishers, printers, paper suppliers, and non-governmental organizations.

7620 ■ "Reinventing Marketing to Manage the Environmental Imperative" in *Journal of Marketing* (Vol. 75, July 2011, No. 4, pp. 132)
Pub: American Marketing Association
Ed: Philip Kotler. **Description:** Marketers must now examine their theory and practices due to the growing recognition of finite resources and high environmental costs. Companies also need to balance more carefully their growth goals with the need to purse sustainability. Insights on the rise of demarketing and social marketing are also given.

7621 ■ "Renewable Energy Adoption in an Aging Population" in *Energy Policy* (Vol. 39, October 2011, No. 10, pp. 6021-6029)
Pub: Reed Elsevier Reference Publishing
Ed: Ken Willis, Riccardo Scarpa, Rose Gilroy, Neveen Hamza. **Description:** Attitudes and impacts of renewable energy adoption on an aging population is examined.

7622 ■ "Renewable Energy Market Opportunities: Wind Testing" in *PR Newswire* (September 22, 2011)
Pub: United Business Media
Description: Global wind energy test systems markets are discussed. Research conducted covers both non-destructive test equipment and condition monitoring equipment product segments.

7623 ■ "ReVenture Plan Appears Close to Landing Key Legislative Deal" in *Charlotte Business Journal* (Vol. 25, July 9, 2010, No. 16, pp. 1)
Pub: Charlotte Business Journal
Ed: John Downey. **Description:** North Carolina lawmakers acted on special legislation that would boost development of Forsite Development 667-acre ReVenture Energy Park. The legislation could also improve chances that Duke Energy Carolinas will contract to purchase the power from the planned 50-megawatt biomass power plant located at the park. How utilities would benefit from the legislation is also discussed.

7624 ■ "Rivals Blow In" in *Crain's Cleveland Business* (Vol. 30, June 1, 2009, No. 21, pp. 1)
Pub: Crain Communications, Inc.
Ed: Chuck Soder. **Description:** U.S. and Canadian competitors are hoping to start construction of offshore wind farm project proposed by Cuyahoga County's Great Lakes Energy Development Task Force. Details of the project are included.

7625 ■ "Rosewood Site Faces Big Cleanup" in *Baltimore Business Journal* (Vol. 27, February 6, 2010, No. 40, pp. 1)
Pub: American City Business Journals
Ed: Daniel J. Sernovitz. **Description:** Environmental assessment report states that Maryland's Rosewood Center for the Developmentally Disabled has significant amounts of toxic chemicals, which could impact Stevenson University's decision to purchase the property. Senator Robert A. Zirkin believes that the state should pay for the cleanup, which is expected to cost millions.

7626 ■ "Rough Headwinds" in *Boston Business Journal* (Vol. 30, November 12, 2010, No. 42, pp. 1)
Pub: Boston Business Journal
Ed: Kyle Alspach. **Description:** Views of residents, as well as key information on First Wind's plan to install wind power turbines in Brimfield, Massachusetts are presented. Residents believe that First Wind's project will devalue properties, compromise quality of life, and ruin the rural quality of Brimfield. First Wind expects to produce 2,000 megawatts of power from wind by 2020.

7627 ■ "San Diego Museum Receives LEED Certification" in *Contractor* (Vol. 57, January 2010, No. 1, pp. 14)
Pub: Penton Media, Inc.
Description: San Diego Natural History Museum received an LEED certification for existing buildings. The certification process began when they committed to displaying the Dead Sea Scrolls in 2007 and they had to upgrade their buildings' air quality and to control for air moisture, temperature, and volume. They reduced their energy consumption by upwards of 20 percent.

7628 ■ "Sandvik Expands Energy-Saving Program" in *Modern Machine Shop* (Vol. 84, September 2011, No. 4, pp. 48)
Pub: Gardner Publications
Description: Sandvik Coromant, based in Fair Lawn, New Jersey, expanded its Sustainable Manufacturing Program that originally was developed to help Japanese-based firms reduce electricity consumption by 15 percent after the recent earthquake that cause loss of electrical power. The program now provides energy reduction through the Sandvick cutting tool technology, application techniques and productivity increases.

7629 ■ "Saudi Overtures" in *The Business Journal-Portland* (Vol. 25, August 15, 2008, No. 23, pp. 1)
Pub: American City Business Journals, Inc.
Ed: Aliza Earnshaw. **Description:** Saudi Arabia's huge revenue from oil is creating opportunities for Oregon companies as the country develops new cities, industrial zones, and tourism centers. Oregon exported only $46.8 million worth of goods to Saudi Arabia in 2007 but the kingdom is interested in green building materials and methods, renewable energy and water quality control, and nanotechnology all of which Oregon has expertise in.

7630 ■ "The Second Most Fuel-Efficient Tractor of the Decade: John Deere 8320R" in *Farm Industry News* (November 10, 2011)
Pub: Penton Business Media Inc.
Description: John Deere's 8320R Tractor was ranked second in the Farm Industry News listing of the top 40 most fuel-efficient tractors of the decade, following the winner, John Deere's 8295R PTO tractor.

7631 ■ "Seeing Green in Going Green" in *The Business Journal-Serving Greater Tampa Bay* (Vol. 28, July 4, 2008, No. 28, pp. 1)
Pub: American City Business Journals, Inc.
Ed: Janet Leiser. **Description:** Atlanta, Georgia-based developer IDI Corp. is pushing for Leadership in Energy and Environmental Design certification for the warehouse that is currently under construction at Madison Business Center along Port Sutton and U.S. 41. The industrial building is the first in Tampa Bay to seek certification for LEED as set by the U.S. Green Building Council.

7632 ■ "Shaw Joins Green Institute Launch" in *Home Textiles Today* (Vol. 31, May 24, 2011, No. 13, pp. 4)
Pub: Reed Business Information
Description: Shaw Industries Group joined the Green Products Innovation Institute, the first nonprofit institute of its kind in America. The institute promotes the concepts of reverse engineering, elimination of waste, safe chemistries, and closed loop technical nutrients.

7633 ■ "Shifting Gears" in *Business Journal-Serving Phoenix & the Valley of the Sun* (Vol. 31, November 12, 2010, No. 10, pp. 1)
Pub: Phoenix Business Journal
Ed: Patrick O'Grady. **Description:** Automotive parts recyclers in Arizona are benefiting from the challenging national economic conditions as well as from the green movement. Recyclers revealed that customers prefer recycled parts more because they are cheaper and are more environmentally friendly. Other information about the automotive parts recycling industry is presented.

7634 ■ "Should I or Shouldn't I?" in *Indoor Comfort Marketing* (Vol. 70, February 2011, No. 2, pp. 30)
Pub: Industry Publications Inc.
Ed: Philip J. Baratz. **Description:** Investment tips are shared for investing in futures options.

7635 ■ "Slick Science" in *Canadian Business* (Vol. 81, September 15, 2008, No. 14-15, pp. 55)
Pub: Rogers Media Ltd.
Ed: Andrew Nikiforuk. **Description:** N-Solv Corp's John Nenniger has discovered a better alternative to steam-assisted gravity drainage methods for extracting bitumen. Nenniger's technique also relies on gravity but replaces steam with propane, which leaves behind impurities like asphaltenes and heavy metals that are too dirty to burn.

7636 ■ "Small Wind Power Market to Double by 2015 at $634 Million" in *Western Farm Press* (September 30, 2011)
Pub: Penton Media Inc.
Description: Small wind power provides cost-effective electricity on a highly localized level, in both remote settings as well as in conjunction with power from the utility grid. Government incentives are spurring new growth in the industry.

7637 ■ "Smart Car Sales Take Big Hit in Recession" in *Business Journal-Milwaukee* (Vol. 28, December 10, 2010, No. 10, pp. A1)
Pub: Milwaukee Business Journal
Ed: Stacey Vogel Davis. **Description:** Sales of smart cars in Milwaukee declined in 2010. Smart Center Milwaukee sold only 52 new cars through October 2010. Increased competition is seen as a reason for the decline in sales.

7638 ■ "Snow Melt Systems Offer Practical Solutions" in *Contractor* (Vol. 56, October 2009, No. 10, pp. S6)
Pub: Penton Media, Inc.
Ed: Lisa Murton Beets. **Description:** Cases are discussed in which the installation of a snow melt system becomes a necessity. One example describes how limited space means there would be no place to put plowed snow; snow melt systems can also resolve problems that arise due to an excess of melting snow.

7639 ■ "Solar Credit Lapse Spur Late Demand" in *The Business Journal - Serving Phoenix and the Valley of the Sun* (Vol. 28, July 18, 2008)
Pub: American City Business Journals, Inc.
Ed: Patrick O'Grady. **Description:** Businesses looking to engage in the solar energy industry are facing the problems of taxation and limited solar panel supply. Solar panels manufacturers are focusing more on the European market. Political issues surrounding the federal tax credit policy on solar energy users are also discussed.

7640 ■ "Solar Hot Water Sales Are Hot, Hot, Hot" in *Contractor* (Vol. 56, December 2009, No. 12, pp. 22)
Pub: Penton Media, Inc.
Ed: Dave Yates. **Description:** Plumbing contractors in the United States can benefit from the increased sales of solar thermal water systems. Licensed plumbers have the base knowledge on the risks associated from heating and storing water. Safety issues associated with solar water heaters are also included.

7641 ■ "Something Different in the Air? The Collapse of the Schwarzenegger Health Plan in Calfornia" in *WorkingUSA* (June 2008)
Pub: Blackwell Publishers Ltd.
Ed: Daniel J.B. Mitchell. **Description:** In January 2007, California Governor Arnold Schwarzenegger proposed a state universal health care plan modeled after the Massachusetts individual mandate program. A year later, the plan was dead. Although some key interest groups eventually backed the plan, it was overwhelmed by a looming state budget crisis and a lack of gubernatorial focus. Although much acclaimed for his stance on greenhouse gases, stem cells, hydrogen highways, and other Big Ideas, diffused gubernatorial priorities and a failure to resolve California's chronic fiscal difficulties let the clock run out on universal health care.

7642 ■ "Start Connecting Today" in *Indoor Comfort Marketing* (Vol. 70, May 2011, No. 5, pp. 34)
Pub: Industry Publications Inc.
Ed: Paul Nazzaro. **Description:** An in-depth discussion regarding the use of biofuels on bioheat use and dealership.

7643 ■ "Start Moving Toward Advanced Fuels" in *Indoor Comfort Marketing* (Vol. 70, March 2011, No. 3, pp. 4)
Pub: Industry Publications Inc.
Ed: Michael L. SanGiovanni. **Description:** Commentary on advanced fuels is presented.

7644 ■ "Start Thinking About Carbon Assets - Now" in *Harvard Business Review* (Vol. 86, September 2008, No. 9, pp. 28)
Pub: Harvard Business School Press
Ed: Alex Rau; Robert Toker. **Description:** Economic and strategic benefits of adopting a corporate carbon assets policy are discussed. Topics include renewable energy and capturing waste energy.

7645 ■ "State Investment Goes Sour" in *Business Journal Portland* (Vol. 26, December 4, 2009, No. 39, pp. 1)
Pub: American City Business Journals Inc.
Ed: Erik Siemers. **Description:** Oregon might recoup only $500,000 of a $20 million loan to Vancouver-based Cascade Grain Products LLC. Cascade Grain's ethanol plant in Clatskanie, OR will be put into auction under the supervision of a bankruptcy court.

7646 ■ "Stimulus 'Loser' Won't Build Plant in Mass." in *Boston Business Journal* (Vol. 30, November 5, 2010, No. 41, pp. 1)
Pub: Boston Business Journal
Ed: Kyle Alspach. **Description:** Boston-Power Inc. no longer plans to build an electric vehicle battery plant in Massachusetts after it failed to obtain stimulus funds from the federal government. The company is instead looking to build a lithium-ion battery plant in China and possibly Europe.

7647 ■ "The Superpower Dilemma" in *Canadian Business* (Vol. 83, August 17, 2010, No. 13-14, pp. 42)
Pub: Rogers Media Ltd.
Description: Canada has been an energy superpower partly because it controls the energy source and the production means, particularly of fossil fuels. However, Canada's status as superpower could diminish if it replaces petroleum exports with renewable technology for using sources of energy available globally.

7648 ■ "Survey Finds State Execs Cool On Climate Change" in *The Business Journal-Milwaukee* (Vol. 25, August 8, 2008, No. 46, pp. A1)
Pub: American City Business Journals, Inc.
Ed: David Doege. **Description:** According to a survey of business executives in Wisconsin, business leaders do not see climate change as a pressing concern, but businesses are moving toward more energy-efficient operations. The survey also revealed that executives believe that financial incentives can promote energy conservation. Other survey results are provided.

7649 ■ "Sustainability Is Top Priority for GreenTown Chicago" in *Contractor* (Vol. 56, November 2009, No. 11, pp. 1)
Pub: Penton Media, Inc.
Ed: Candace Roulo. **Description:** GreenTown Chicago 2009 conference tackled energy-efficient practices and technologies, green design and building, and sustainable policies. Water conservation was also a topic at the conference and one mayor who made a presentation said that reducing the water loss in the system is a priority in the city's endeavor.

7650 ■ "Suzlon S88-Powered Wind Farm in Minnesota Secures Long-Term Financing" in *PR Newswire* (September 21, 2011)
Pub: United Business Media
Description: Suzlon Energy Limited is the world's fifth largest manufacturer of wind turbines. Owners of the Grant County Wind Farm in Minnesota have secured a long-term financing deal for the ten Suzlon S88 2.1 MW wind turbines that generate enough electricity to power 7,000 homes.

7651 ■ "Taxis Are Set to Go Hybrid" in *Philadelphia Business Journal* (Vol. 30, September 16, 2011, No. 31, pp. 1)
Pub: American City Business Journals Inc.
Ed: Natalie Kostelni. **Description:** Taxis are going hybrid in several major states such as New York, California and Maryland where it is mandated, but it is yet to happen in Philadelphia, Pennsylvania with the exception of one taxi company. Freedom Taxi is awaiting Philadelphia Parking Authority's sign off.

7652 ■ "Think the Oilsands Are an Environmental Disaster?" in *Canadian Business* (Vol. 83, October 12, 2010, No. 17, pp. 52)
Pub: Rogers Media Ltd.
Ed: Michael McCullough. **Description:** Studies which were commissioned by the Alberta Energy Research Institute in 2008 found that the life-cycle carbon emissions of oil derived from oilsands was 10 percent greater than the average from all sources. Synthetic crude from the oilsands is 38 percent less carbon-intensive than it was 20 years ago due to productivity improvements.

7653 ■ "Thirsty? Now There's a Water Cooler to Suit Every Taste" in *Inc.* (Vol. 33, October 2011, No. 8, pp. 43)
Pub: Inc. Magazine
Ed: John Brandon. **Description:** Brita's Hydration Station is a wall-mounted unit with a touch-free sensor for dispensing water. This water cooler cuts down on landfill waste and offers special features.

7654 ■ *The Three Secrets of Green Business: Unlocking Competitive Advantage in a Low Carbon Economy*
Pub: Earthscan
Ed: Gareth Kane. **Released:** February 10, 2010. **Price:** $96.00. **Description:** Small business is coming under increasing pressure from government, customers and campaigning groups to improve environmental performance. Soaring utility and compliance costs are critical financial burdens on small companies.

7655 ■ "Timberland's CEO On Standing Up to 65,000 Angry Activists" in *Harvard Business Review* (Vol. 88, September 2010, No. 9, pp. 39)
Pub: Harvard Business School Publishing
Ed: Jeff Swartz. **Description:** Timberland Company avoided a potential boycott by taking a two-way approach. It addressed a supplier issue that posed a threat to the environment, and launched an email campaign to keep Greenpeace activists informed of the development of a new supplier agreement.

7656 ■ "Time to Green Your Business" in *Gallup Management Journal* (April 22, 2011)
Pub: Gallup
Ed: Bryant Ott. **Description:** It's Earth Day, so expect to hear companies touting their commitment to the environment. However, according to Gallup, more companies are finding it more interested to talk about being green than actually taking the steps to become a green business.

7657 ■ "Toolmakers' New Tack" in *Crain's Detroit Business* (Vol. 25, June 8, 2009,)
Pub: Crain Communications Inc. - Detroit
Ed: Ryan Beene, Amy Lane. **Description:** MAG Industrial Automation Systems LLC and Dowding Machining Inc. have partnered to advance wind-turbine technology. The goal is to cut costs of wind energy to the same level as carbon-based fuel.

7658 ■ "Top 50 Exporters" in *Hispanic Business* (Vol. 30, July-August 2008, No. 7-8, pp. 42)
Pub: Hispanic Business, Inc.
Ed: Hildy Medina. **Description:** Increases in exports revenues reported by food exporters and green companies in a time of economic slowdown in the U.S are described. Food exporters have benefited from the growth of high-volume grocery stores in underdeveloped countries and the German governments' promotion of solar energy has benefited the U.S. solar heating equipment and solar panel manufactures.

7659 ■ "Toward a Better Future" in *Canadian Business* (Vol. 83, August 17, 2010, No. 13-14, pp. 51)
Pub: Rogers Media Ltd.
Description: A look at certain realities in order to build a better future for Canada's energy industry is presented. Canada must focus on making the oil cleaner, instead of replacing it with another source since dependency on oil will remain in this lifetime. Canada must also develop solutions toward clean technology power sources.

7660 ■ "Traer Turning to Wind Power to Meet Long-Term Energy Needs" in *Waterloo Courier* (September 20, 2011)
Pub: Lee Enterprises
Ed: Josh Nelson. **Description:** Traer Municipal Utilities is working with Clark Thompson, a Story City wind turbine developer, to erect a wind turbine to supply electrical energy to the city. Details are included.

7661 ■ "Tucson Tech Column" in *AZ Daily Star* (September 27, 2011)
Pub: Arizona Daily Star
Ed: David Wichner. **Description:** Western Wind Energy, based in Vancouver, British Columbia, Canada is able to harness energy from the sun when the wind is not blowing at the Kingman I Project wind farm. Details of this technology are outlined.

7662 ■ "Turning Green Ink to Black" in *The Business Journal-Serving Metropolitan Kansas City* (Vol. 26, August 8, 2008, No. 48, pp. 1)
Pub: American City Business Journals, Inc.
Ed: James Dornbrook. **Description:** InkCycle has introduced grenk, a line of environmentally-friendly printer toner and ink cartridges. The cartridges are collected and recycled after use by the company, which separates them into their metal, cardboard, and plastic components.

7663 ■ "Tweaking On-Board Activities, Equipment Saves Fuel, Reduces CO2" in *Canadian Sailings* (June 30, 2008)
Pub: Commonwealth Business Media
Description: Optimizing ship activities and equipment uses less fuel and therefore reduces greenhouse gas emissions. Ways in which companies are

implementing research and development techniques in order to monitor ship performance and analyze data in an attempt to become more efficient are examined.

7664 ■ "UA Turns Ann Arbor Green" in *Contractor* (Vol. 56, September 2009, No. 9, pp. 5)
Pub: Penton Media, Inc.
Ed: Robert P. Mader. **Description:** Instructors at the United Association of Plumbers and Steamfitters have studied the latest in green and sustainable construction and service at the Washtenaw Community College in Michigan. Classes included building information modeling, hydronic heating and cooling and advanced HVACR troubleshooting. The UA is currently focusing on green training.

7665 ■ "Ultra Green Energy Services Opens NJ Biodiesel Transload Facility" in *Indoor Comfort Marketing* (Vol. 70, June 2011, No. 6, pp. 35)
Pub: Industry Publications Inc.
Description: Profile of Ultra Green Energy Services and the opening of their new biodiesel facility in New Jersey is discussed.

7666 ■ "Ultra Low Sulfur Diesel: The Promise and the Reality" in *Indoor Comfort Marketing* (Vol. 70, July 2011, No. 7, pp. 22)
Pub: Industry Publications Inc.
Ed: Ed Kitchen. **Description:** Impacts of ultra low sulfur diesel are examined.

7667 ■ "Unilever to Sustainably Source All Paper and Board Packaging" in *Ice Cream Reporter* (Vol. 23, July 20, 2010, No. 8, pp. 1)
Pub: Ice Cream Reporter
Description: Unilever, a leader in the frozen dessert market, has developed a new sustainable paper and board packaging sourcing policy that will reduce environmental impact by working with suppliers to source 75 percent of paper and board packaging from sustainably managed forests or from recycled material. Unilever is parent company to Breyers, Haagen-Dazs, Klondike, Popsicle and other ice cream brands.

7668 ■ "University Data Center Goes Off-Grid, Is Test Bed" in *Contractor* (Vol. 57, February 2010, No. 2, pp. 1)
Pub: Penton Media, Inc.
Ed: Candace Roulo. **Description:** Syracuse University's Green Data Center has gone off-grid through the use of natural gas fired turbines. It is expected to use 50 percent less energy than a typical computer center. The center's heating and cooling system setup is also discussed.

7669 ■ "Valener Announces that Gaz Metro has Achieved a Key Step in Acquiring CVPS" in *CNW Group* (September 30, 2011)
Pub: CNW Group
Description: Valener Inc., which owns about 29 percent of Gaz Metro Ltd. Partnership, announced that Gaz Metro welcomes the sale of Central Vermont Public Service Corporation (CVPS). Valener owns an indirect interest of 24.5 percent in the wind power projects jointly developed by Beaupre Eole General Partnership and Boralex Inc. on private lands in Quebec. Details of the deal are included.

7670 ■ "Voices: Climategate Leads Nowhere" in *Business Strategy Review* (Vol. 21, Summer 2010, No. 2, pp. 76)
Pub: Wiley-Blackwell
Ed: Mick Blowfield. **Description:** Examination of the recent Climategate scandal and an exploration of the damage it can cause managers who are too easily mystified or misled.

7671 ■ "Volunteers Needed" in *Canadian Business* (Vol. 81, October 27, 2008, No. 18, pp. 60)
Pub: Rogers Media Ltd.
Ed: Megan Harman. **Description:** Emissions-targeting regulations focus on the biggest polluters, missing out on other companies that leave carbon footprints in things such as shipping and travel. Some companies in Canada have initiated programs to offset their carbon emissions. Critics claim that offsetting does not reduce emissions and the programs merely justify pollution.

7672 ■ "Warm Floors Make Warm Homes" in *Contractor* (Vol. 56, October 2009, No. 10, pp. S18)
Pub: Penton Media, Inc.
Ed: Lisa Murton Beets. **Description:** Three award winning radiant floor-heating installations are presented. The design and the equipment used for these systems are discussed.

7673 ■ "Was Mandating Solar Power Water Heaters For New Homes Good Policy?" in *Hawaii Business* (Vol. 54, August 2008, No. 2, pp. 28)
Pub: Hawaii Business Publishing
Description: Senator Gary L. Kooser of District 7 Kauai-Niihau believes that the mandating of energy-efficient water heaters for new single-family homes starting in 2010 will help cut Hawaii's oil consumption. Ron Richmond of the Hawaii Solar Energy Association says that the content of SB 644 has negative consequences as it allows for choice of energy and not just solar, and it also eliminates tax credits for new homebuyers.

7674 ■ "Water Conservation Helps GC's Building Attain LEED Gold Status" in *Contractor* (Vol. 56, September 2009, No. 9, pp. 5)
Pub: Penton Media, Inc.
Description: Green contractor Marshall Erdman has built a new office building using green design. The facility is seen to become a prime Leadership in Energy and Environmental Design (LEED) building model. Details of the building's design and features are also provided.

7675 ■ "Water Distiller" in *Canadian Business* (Vol. 81, September 29, 2008, No. 16, pp. 52)
Pub: Rogers Media Ltd.
Ed: Matthew McClearn. **Description:** Les Fairn's invention of a water distiller called a Solarsphere was recognized in the Great Canadian Invention Competition. Fairn's invention resembles a buoy that uses the sun's energy to vaporize dirty water then leaves the impurities behind in a sump. The invention has an application for producing potable water in impoverished countries.

7676 ■ "Western Wind Energy Corporation" in *CNW Group* (October 4, 2011)
Pub: CNW Group
Description: Profile of Western Wind Energy Corporation will complete the installation of 60 wind turbines by the end of 2011. The first 106MW are ready for pre-commissioning with the ability to sell power in November when the site is interconnected.

7677 ■ "What Are Canada's Industrial Polluters Doing to Reduce Emissions?" in *Canadian Business* (Vol. , pp.)
Pub: Rogers Media Ltd.
Ed: Matthew McClearn. **Description:** Efforts by Canada's industrial polluters to reduce emissions are examined. Syncrude Canada plans to reduce sulphur emissions by 60 percent in 2011, while TransAlta invests in emission reduction programs. Environmental groups, however, claim that companies are not doing enough to protect the environment.

7678 ■ "What Is a Geothermal Heat Pump" in *Indoor Comfort Marketing* (Vol. 70, August 2011, No. 8, pp. 14)
Pub: Industry Publications Inc.
Ed: George Carey. **Description:** Examination of geothermal heat pumps is provided, citing new trends in the industry.

7679 ■ "Where the Future is Made" in *Indoor Comfort Marketing* (Vol. 70, May 2011, No. 5, pp. 48)
Pub: Industry Publications Inc.
Description: Research being performed at Brookhaven National Laboratory, located in Upton, New York, is discussed, focusing on new energy sources for our nation.

7680 ■ "A Whiff of TV Reality" in *Houston Business Journal* (Vol. 40, January 22, 2010, No. 37, pp. A1)
Pub: American City Business Journals
Ed: Christine Hall. **Description:** Houston, Texas-based Waste Management Inc.'s president and chief operation officer, Larry O'Donnell shares some of his experience as CBS Television Network reality show 'Undercover Boss' participant. O'Donnell believes the show was a great way to show the customers how tough their jobs are and reveals that the most difficult job was being a sorter at the recycling center.

7681 ■ "Wind Gets Knocked Out of Energy Farm Plan" in *Buffalo News* (September 28, 2011)
Pub: Buffalo News
Ed: David Robinson. **Description:** New York Power Authority formally killed the proposal for a wind energy farm off the shores of Lake Erie and Lake Ontario. The Authority cited high subsidy costs would be required to make the wind farm economically feasible. Details of the proposal are outlined.

7682 ■ "Winning Gold" in *The Business Journal-Milwaukee* (Vol. 25, August 8, 2008, No. 46, pp. A1)
Pub: American City Business Journals, Inc.
Ed: Rich Rovito. **Description:** Johnson Controls Inc. of Milwaukee, Wisconsin is taking part in the 2008 Beijing Olympics with the installation of its sustainable control equipment and technology that monitor over 58,000 points in 18 Olympic venues. Details of Johnson Controls' green products and sustainable operations in China are discussed.

7683 ■ "Yates Helps Turn Log Home Green" in *Contractor* (Vol. 56, December 2009, No. 12, pp. 40)
Pub: Penton Media, Inc.
Description: Upgrading and greening of a log home's HVAC system in Pennsylvania is discussed. F. W. Behler Inc. president Dave Yates was chosen to manage the project. A large coil of R-flex was used to connect the buffer tank to the garage's radiant heat system.

7684 ■ "Yates Turns Log Home Green - Part Three" in *Contractor* (Vol. 57, January 2010, No. 1, pp. 5)
Pub: Penton Media, Inc.
Description: Dave Yates of F.W. Behler Inc. discusses remodeling a log home's HVAC system with geo-to-radiant heat and thermal-solar systems. The solar heater's installation is discussed.

7685 ■ "You're a What? Wind Turbine Service Technician" in *Occupational Outlook Quarterly* (Vol. 54, Fall 2010, No. 3, pp. 34)
Pub: U.S. Bureau of Labor Statistics
Ed: Drew Liming. **Description:** Profile of Brandon Johnson, former member of the Air Force, found a career as a wind turbine service technician.

7686 ■ "Yudelson Challenges San Antonio Groups" in *Contractor* (Vol. 56, October 2009, No. 10, pp. 6)
Pub: Penton Media, Inc.
Description: Green building consultant and author Jerry Yudelson made a presentation for the Central Texas Green Building Council and Leadership San Antonio where he discussed the European approach to sustainability and how it can be used for designing green buildings. Yudelson also discussed how to use sustainable practices for planning 25 years into the future.

TRADE PERIODICALS

7687 ■ *Fifth Estate*
Pub: Fifth Estate
Released: Quarterly. **Price:** $14; $20 Canada and Mexico; $20 libraries & institutions. **Description:** Magazine covering anarchism and radical environmentalism.

7688 ■ *Greenpeace Magazine*
Pub: Greenpeace USA
Contact: John Passacantando, Exec. Dir.
Released: Quarterly. **Description:** Magazine covering environmental issues and the activities of Greenpeace.

TRADE SHOWS AND CONVENTIONS

7689 ■ GLOBE - International Environmental Industry Trade Fair and Conference
GLOBE Foundation of Canada
World Trade Centre
578 999 Canada Pl.
Vancouver, BC, Canada V6C 3E1
Ph:(604)775-7300
Free: 800-274-6097
Fax:(604)666-8123
Co. E-mail: info@globe.ca
URL: http://www.globe.ca
Released: Biennial. **Audience:** Trade professionals. **Principal Exhibits:** Environmental equipment, supplies, and services.

7690 ■ Natural Products Expo East
New Hope Natural Media
1401 Pearl St.
Boulder, CO 80302-5346
Ph:(303)939-8440
Fax:(303)998-9020
Co. E-mail: info@newhope.com
URL: http://www.newhope.com
Released: Annual. **Audience:** Retailers, wholesalers, distributors, and brokers from the natural products industry. **Principal Exhibits:** Natural, organic and environmentally sound products, including: alternative health care, vegetarian and allergy-free personal care recycled/recyclable products, biodegradable products, and organic meats. **Dates and Locations:** 2011 Sep 21-24, Baltimore, MD.

7691 ■ Natural Products Expo West
New Hope Natural Media
1401 Pearl St.
Boulder, CO 80302-5346
Ph:(303)939-8440
Fax:(303)998-9020
Co. E-mail: info@newhope.com
URL: http://www.newhope.com
Released: Annual. **Audience:** Retailers, wholesalers, distributors, and brokers. **Principal Exhibits:** Natural, organic, and environmentally sound products, including: alternative healthcare, vegetarian and allergy-free items, cruelty-free personal care, recycled/recyclable products, biodegradable products, and organic meats.

FRANCHISES AND BUSINESS OPPORTUNITIES

7692 ■ Enviro-Tech Pest Services
Enviro-Tech Pest Franchises, Inc.
PO Box 567
Kearneysville, WV 25430
Ph:(304)728-5090
Free: 800-434-7360
Fax:(304)724-5499
No. of Franchise Units: 5. NCU 2. **Founded:** 1985. **Franchised:** 2004. **Description:** Residential and commercial pest management. **Equity Capital Needed:** $37,500-$56,900. **Franchise Fee:** $24,500. **Royalty Fee:** 5-7
%. **Financial Assistance:** No. **Training:** Yes.

7693 ■ EnviroSpect, Inc.
426 Pine St.
Williamsport, PA 17701
Ph:(570)326-4677
Free: (866)773-2881
Fax:(570)326-4672
No. of Franchise Units: 4. **Founded:** 2004. **Franchised:** 2004. **Description:** Residential and commercial environmental inspections **Equity Capital Needed:** $26,600-$39,200. **Franchise Fee:** $25,000. **Royalty Fee:** $400/month. **Financial Assistance:** No. **Training:** Yes.

LIBRARIES

7694 ■ Center for Environmental Information–CEI Library
55 Saint Paul St.
Rochester, NY 14604-1314
Ph:(585)262-2870
Fax:(585)262-4156
Co. E-mail: cei@ceinfo.org
URL: http://www.ceinfo.org
Contact: George Thomas, Exec.Dir.
Scope: Natural resources, conservation, acid rain, greenhouse effect, environment, energy, environmental education. **Services:** Library open to the public by appointment.

7695 ■ General Engineering Laboratories, Inc. Library
PO Box 30712
Charleston, SC 29417
Ph:(843)556-8171
Fax:(843)766-1178
Co. E-mail: bob.pullano@gel.com
URL: http://www.gel.net
Contact: Bob Pullano
Scope: Environmental analysis, environmental consulting, environmental regulations. **Holdings:** Figures not available.

7696 ■ Gradient Corporation–Information Resource Center
20 University Rd.
Cambridge, MA 02138
Ph:(617)395-5000
Fax:(617)395-5001
Co. E-mail: info@gradientcorp.com
URL: http://www.gradientcorp.com
Contact: Marcia A. Olson, Mgr., Info.Rsrc.Ctr.
Scope: Environmental protection, pollution, environmental chemistry, toxicology, risk assessment. **Services:** Interlibrary loan; Center not open to the public. **Holdings:** 100,000 books and reports. **Subscriptions:** 60 journals and other serials.

7697 ■ M.H. Chew & Associates Corporate Library
7275 National Dr., Ste. C
Livermore, CA 94550
Ph:(925)443-5071
Fax:(510)373-0624
Co. E-mail: patricia.shannon@mhchew.com
URL: http://www.mhchew.com/
Contact: Patricia Shannon
Scope: Nuclear safety, environmental safety, health physics, radiation protection, risk analysis. **Services:** Interlibrary loan; copying; Library not open to the public. **Holdings:** 1500 books; 2000 bound periodical volumes; 5000 reports. **Subscriptions:** 100 journals and other serials.

7698 ■ National Audubon Society–Aullwood Audubon Center and Farm Library
1000 Aullwood Rd.
Dayton, OH 45414
Ph:(937)890-7360
Fax:(937)890-2382
Co. E-mail: aullwood@gemair.com
URL: http://aullwood.center.audubon.org
Contact: Barbara Trick, Off.Mgr.
Scope: Natural history, environmental education, agriculture, protection of birds. **Services:** Copying; Library open to the public for reference use only. **Holdings:** 2000 books. **Subscriptions:** 4 journals and other serials.

7699 ■ National Environmental Health Association Library
720 S. Colorado Blvd., Ste. 1000-N
Denver, CO 80246-1926
Ph:(303)756-9090
Free: (866)956-2258
Fax:(303)691-9490
Co. E-mail: staff@neha.org
URL: http://www.neha.org
Contact: Nelson Fabian, Exec.Dir.
Scope: Environmental health concerns, environmental protection. **Services:** Library not open to the public. **Holdings:** 1000 volumes. **Subscriptions:** 10,055 journals and other serials.

7700 ■ Native Americans for a Clean Environment–Resource Office Native Americans for a Clean Environment
Box 1671
Tahlequah, OK 74465
Ph:(918)458-4322
Contact: Lance Hughes, Exec.Dir.
Scope: Nuclear energy - waste and waste routes, facilities, health effects; national environmental issues; area issues. **Services:** Copying; office will respond to telephone and written inquiries. **Holdings:** Figures not available.

7701 ■ Renew America Library
PO Box 77636
Washington, DC 20013
Ph:(202)721-1545
Fax:(202)232-2617
Co. E-mail: editor@renewamerica.us
URL: http://www.renewamerica.us/
Contact: Anna Slafer, Exec.Dir.
Scope: The environment, natural resources. **Services:** Library not open to the public. **Holdings:** 1400 case studies.

7702 ■ Stantec Consulting Services, Inc. Library
4875 Riverside Dr.
Macon, GA 31210-1117
Ph:(478)474-6100
Fax:(478)474-8933
Co. E-mail: macon@stantec.com
URL: http://www.stantec.com
Contact: Faye Adams, Libn.
Scope: Engineers, environmental professionals, architects, surveyors, transportation. **Services:** Library not open to the public. **Holdings:** 2000 books; 500 bound periodical volumes; 1100 reports; 25,000 archives; 5000 microfilms. **Subscriptions:** 250 journals and other serials; 7 newspapers.

7703 ■ Tetra Tech NUS, Inc.–Technical Information Center
900 Trail Ridge Rd.
Aiken, SC 29803
Ph:(803)649-7963
Fax:(803)642-8454
Co. E-mail: james.oliver@tetratech.com
URL: http://intranet.ttnus.com/
Contact: Debbie Pyron, Mgr.
Scope: Environment, nuclear energy. **Services:** Library not open to the public. **Holdings:** Reports. **Subscriptions:** 2 newspapers.

7704 ■ U.S. Environmental Protection Agency Headquarters Library
1200 Pennsylvania Ave., NW
Rm. 3340
Mailcode 3404T
Washington, DC 20460-0001
Ph:(202)566-0556
Fax:(202)566-0574
Co. E-mail: hqchemlibraries@epa.gov
URL: http://www.epa.gov/libraries/hqrepository.html
Scope: Water - pollution, quality, supply; air pollution; noise abatement; radiation; hazardous wastes; solid waste management; resource recovery; pesticides; chemistry and toxicology; social, economic, legislative, legal, administrative, and management aspects of environmental policy. **Services:** Interlibrary loan; SDI; Library open to the public with restrictions. **Holdings:** 16,000 books; 7000 hardcopy documents and technical reports; 400,000 documents and reports from the EPA and its predecessor agencies on microfiche; newspapers, abstracts and indexes, periodicals on microfilm. **Subscriptions:** 20 journals and other serials.

7705 ■ U.S. Environmental Protection Agency Library
Mail Code 3404T
1200 Pennsylvania Ave., NW
Washington, DC 20460
Ph:(202)566-0556
URL: http://www.epa.gov
Contact: Margaret Esser, Lib.Techn.
Scope: Water pollution, water quality, environmental quality, air pollution, toxic substances, hazardous wastes. **Services:** Interlibrary loan; copying; Library open to the public. **Holdings:** 3500 books; 10,000 federal and state reports; 200,000 microfiche. **Subscriptions:** 60 journals and other serials.

7706 ■ URS Library
Crown Corporate Center
2870 Gateway Oaks Dr., Ste. 150
Sacramento, CA 95833-4324
Ph:(916)679-2000
Fax:(916)679-2900
URL: http://www.urscorp.com
Scope: Environment, air quality, hazardous waste. **Services:** Interlibrary loan; Library not open to the public. **Holdings:** 5000 books; technical and government reports; government agency rules and regulations. **Subscriptions:** 75 journals and other serials.

7707 ■ Williams College Center for Environmental Studies–Matt Cole Memorial Library
Harper House
PO Box 632
Williamstown, MA 01267
Ph:(413)597-2346
Fax:(413)597-3489
Co. E-mail: nparker@williams.edu
URL: http://www.williams.edu/CES/mattcole.htm
Contact: Norm Parker, Info.Spec.
Scope: Agriculture, air pollution, biodiversity, climate, regional planning, coastal, ecology, energy, environmental health, environmental law and policy, forestry, hazardous substances, land use and planning, solid waste, water quality, wildlife management habitat. **Services:** Interlibrary loan; Library open to the public. **Holdings:** 7500 books; 2900 bound periodical volumes; 5000 other documents. **Subscriptions:** 250 journals and other serials.

RESEARCH CENTERS

7708 ■ Clark University–George Perkins Marsh Institute–Center for Technology, Environment, and Development
950 Main St.
Worcester, MA 01610-1477
Ph:(508)751-4622
Fax:(508)751-4600
Co. E-mail: rjohnston@clarku.edu
URL: http://www.clarku.edu/departments/marsh/centers/cented.cfm
Contact: Prof. Robert J. Johnston PhD, Dir.
E-mail: rjohnston@clarku.edu
Scope: Risk analysis, global environmental change, environment and development, and technological hazards. **Publications:** Research reports; Working papers. **Educational Activities:** Distinguished Lecture Series.

7709 ■ Green Seal
1001 Connecticut Ave. NW, Ste. 827
Washington, DC 20036-5525
Ph:(202)872-6400
Fax:(202)872-4324
Co. E-mail: greenseal@greenseal.org
URL: http://www.greenseal.org
Contact: Dr. Arthur B. Weissman, Pres./CEO
E-mail: greenseal@greenseal.org
Scope: Analyzes effects of various consumer products on the environment, including toxic chemical pollution, energy consumption, depletion and pollution of water resources, waste of natural resources, destruction of the Earth's atmosphere, global warming, and harm to fish, wildlife, and natural areas. Tests products such as toilet and facial tissue, re-refined motor oil, light bulbs for home use, water conservation devices, fine paper, coffee filters, house paints, household cleaners, paper towels, and napkins. **Services:** Awards seals of approval to products deemed to be environmentally responsible. **Publications:** Campus Green Buying Guide; Choose Green Report; Hotel Green Buying Guide; Office Green Buying Guide.

7710 ■ Tellus Institute
11 Arlington St.
Boston, MA 02116-3411
Ph:(617)266-5400
Fax:(617)266-8303
Co. E-mail: info@tellus.org
URL: http://www.tellus.org
Contact: Paul D. Raskin PhD, Pres.
E-mail: info@tellus.org
Scope: Policy and planning issues in such areas as energy, water, waste, and land use. Analyzes evolving problems and evaluates options for technological and institutional change, develops and disseminates decision-support tools to strengthen capacity to develop effective resource and environmental strategies. **Services:** Consulting, on-going, on a fee basis.

7711 ■ University of Colorado at Boulder–Environmental Program
214 UCB
Boulder, CO 80309
Ph:(303)492-7943
Fax:(303)492-1414
Co. E-mail: bob.sievers@colorado.edu
URL: http://cires.colorado.edu/env_prog/index.html
Contact: Prof. Bob Sievers, Dir.
E-mail: bob.sievers@colorado.edu
Scope: Global change and environmental quality research, including global climate change, local and regional environmental quality, and sustainable development.

Estate Planning

REFERENCE WORKS

7712 ■ "Eliminating All of Your Estate Tax Burden" in *Contractor* (Vol. 57, January 2010, No. 1, pp. 48)
Pub: Penton Media, Inc.
Ed: Irv Blackman. **Description:** Suggestions on how family owned businesses can minimize their estate tax burdens are discussed. One of these includes not using life insurance in a business succession plan to move stocks to the children and to never use Section 6166 as part of the overall estate tax plan.

7713 ■ "Estate Tax Problems may Soon Disappear" in *Contractor* (Vol. 56, September 2009, No. 9, pp. 60)
Pub: Penton Media, Inc.
Ed: Irv Blackman. **Description:** Advice on how to effectively plan estate tax in the United States. Pending changes to US estate tax laws are seen to resolve inheritance problems. Captive insurance firms can lower property and casualty insurance costs to transfer businesses to children.

7714 ■ "Expect Action on Health Care and the Economy" in *Contractor* (Vol. 57, January 2010, No. 1, pp. 30)
Pub: Penton Media, Inc.
Ed: Kevin Schwalb. **Description:** The Plumbing-Heating-Cooling Contractors National Association is working to solidify its standing in the public policy arena as the legislative agenda will focus on health care reform, estate tax and immigration reform, all of which will impact the industries.

7715 ■ "For All It's Worth" in *Entrepreneur* (Vol. 36, April 2008, No. 4, pp. 46)
Pub: Entrepreneur Media, Inc.
Ed: Farnoosh Torabi. **Description:** Discusses the federal estate tax system requires that 45 percent of the money beyond $2 million be given to the government. Ways on how to minimize the effects of estate tax on assets include: creating bypass trusts for married couples; setting up an irrevocable life insurance trust to avoid taxation of estate for insurance benefactors; and having annual gift tax exclusion.

7716 ■ "New Year, New Estate Plan" in *Hawaii Business* (Vol. 53, February 2008, No. 8, pp. 54)
Pub: Hawaii Business Publishing
Ed: Antony M. Orme. **Description:** Discusses the start of the new year which can be a time to revise wills and estate plans as failure to do so may create problems of unequal inheritance and increase in estate tax exemption, which could disinherit beneficiaries. Other circumstances that can prompt changes in wills and estate plans are presented.

7717 ■ "Retailers, Your Will, and More" in *Agency Sales Magazine* (Vol. 39, July 2009, No. 7, pp. 46)
Pub: MANA
Ed: Melvin H. Daskal. **Description:** IRS audit guide for small retail businesses is presented. Tips on how to make a will with multiple beneficiaries are discussed together with medical expenses that can not be deducted.

7718 ■ "Solutions to Family Business Problems" in *Contractor* (Vol. 56, October 2009, No. 10, pp. 51)
Pub: Penton Media, Inc.
Ed: Irv Blackman. **Description:** Several common business problems that family owned firms face are presented together with their solutions. These problems include giving the children stock bonus options while another discusses the tax burden when a father wants to transfer the business to his son.

7719 ■ *Stealing MySpace: The Battle to Control the Most Popular Website in America*
Pub: Random House
Ed: Julia Angwin. **Released:** 2009. **Price:** $27.00. **Description:** Information regarding Rupert Murdoch's outwitting Viacom's Tom Freston and details of the deal are presented.

TRADE PERIODICALS

7720 ■ *Estate Planners Alert*
Pub: Research Institute of America
Contact: Arthur Sabatini
Released: Monthly. **Price:** $210. **Description:** Spotlights critical developments in estate and financial planning.

7721 ■ *Estate Planning Review*
Pub: CCH Inc.
Released: Monthly. **Price:** $275. **Description:** Monthly newsletter covering estate and financial planning issues for individuals. Includes coverage of retirement planning, insurance planning and investments.

7722 ■ *Tax Management Estates, Gifts, and Trusts Journal*
Pub: BNA Tax and Accounting
Contact: Glenn B. Davis, Managing Editor
E-mail: gdavis@bna.com
Released: Bimonthly. **Price:** $261. **Description:** Provides practical guidance on and reviews recent developments in estates, gifts, and trusts. Recurring features include sections titled Detailed Analysis, Working Papers, and Bibliography and Reference. Remarks: Subscription includes Tax Management Memorandum.

FRANCHISES AND BUSINESS OPPORTUNITIES

7723 ■ American Prosperity Group
3 Sunny Knolls Ct.
Wayne, NJ 07470
Ph:(973)831-4424
Free: 877-885-1274
Fax:(973)831-6384
No. of Franchise Units: 14. **No. of Company-Owned Units:** 1. **Founded:** 1991. **Franchised:** 2006. **Description:** Retirement & estate planning products and services. **Equity Capital Needed:** $78,300-$121,000. **Franchise Fee:** $50,000. **Royalty Fee:** Varies. **Financial Assistance:** Limited third party financing available. **Training:** Offers 4 weeks at headquarters, 1 week onsite and ongoing support.

COMPUTERIZED DATABASES

7724 ■ *Estate Planning*
Thomson Reuters
395 Hudson St., 4th Fl.
New York, NY 10014
Ph:(212)367-6300
Free: 800-431-9025
Co. E-mail: ria@thomson.com
URL: http://ria.thomsonreuters.com
Description: Contains the complete text of *Estate Planning*, a professional journal for lawyers, accountants, insurance specialists, and others involved in estate planning, family asset management, and trust and estate administration. Covers tax planning, retirement planning, investments, closely held businesses, elder law, software, and literature. **Availability:** Online: Thomson Reuters. **Type:** Full text.

7725 ■ *Estates, Gifts, and Trust Journal*
The Bureau of National Affairs Inc.
1801 S Bell St.
Arlington, VA 22202
Free: 800-372-1033
Co. E-mail: customercare@bna.com
URL: http://www.bna.com/tax-accounting-t5000
Description: Reviews new developments which affect estate planning and planning opportunities. Includes professional practitioners' commentary. **Availability:** Online: The Bureau of National Affairs Inc. **Type:** Full text.

7726 ■ *Tax Management Portfolio Series: Estates, Gifts, and Trusts*
The Bureau of National Affairs Inc.
1801 S Bell St.
Arlington, VA 22202
Free: 800-372-1033
Co. E-mail: customercare@bna.com
URL: http://www.bna.com/tax-accounting-t5000
Description: Contains analyses of U.S. estate, gift, and trust tax issues prepared by tax attorneys and accountants. Analyses include bibliographies and recommended lists of forms and other relevant documents, including worksheets and checklists. Includes interactive Federal Tax Forms. **Availability:** Online: The Bureau of National Affairs Inc. **Type:** Full text.

LIBRARIES

7727 ■ Adler Pollock & Sheehan, P.C. Law Library
One Citizens Plaza, 8th Fl.
Providence, RI 02903
Ph:(401)274-7200
Fax:(401)751-4604
Co. E-mail: pdumaine@apslaw.com
URL: http://www.apslaw.com
Contact: Paul R. Dumaine, Mgr., Lib. & Info.Rsrcs.
Scope: Law - business, corporate, commercial, labor, tax, securities, environmental; estate planning; litigation; public utilities; telecommunications; energy;

insurance. **Services:** Interlibrary loan (limited); Library not open to the public. **Holdings:** 5000 books; 500 bound periodical volumes. **Subscriptions:** 40 journals and other serials.

7728 ■ Connecticut Judicial Branch–Putnam Law Library
Putnam Courthouse
155 Church St.
Putnam, CT 06260
Ph:(860)928-3716
Fax:(860)963-7531
Co. E-mail: donna.izbicki@jud.ct.gov
URL: http://www.jud.ct.gov/lawlib/
Contact: Donna R. Izbicki, Libn.
Scope: Law. **Services:** Copying; Library open to the public. **Holdings:** 17,000 books. **Subscriptions:** 140 journals and other serials.

7729 ■ Dewey Ballantine LLP Library
1301 Ave. of the Americas
New York, NY 10019-6092
Ph:(212)259-8000
Fax:(212)259-6333
Co. E-mail: gseer@deweyballentine.com
URL: http://www.deweyballantine.com
Contact: Gitelle Seer, Dir., Lib.Svc.
Scope: Law - antitrust, securities, taxation, real property, trusts and estates, corporate, bankruptcy, intellectual property. **Services:** Interlibrary loan; Library open to members of SLA by appointment. **Holdings:** 50,000 volumes. **Subscriptions:** 300 journals and other serials.

7730 ■ Fasken Martineau DuMoulin LLP Toronto Library
333 Bay St., Ste. 2400
Bay Adelaide Centre, Box 20
Toronto, ON, Canada M5H 2T6
Ph:(416)366-8381
Fax:(416)364-7813
Co. E-mail: mmiles@tor.fasken.com
URL: http://www.fasken.com
Contact: Michele L. Miles, Libn.
Scope: Law - corporate, administrative, real estate, estate; taxation; litigation. **Services:** Interlibrary loan. **Holdings:** 14,000 books; 50 bound periodical volumes; federal and provincial legislation. **Subscriptions:** 500 journals and other serials.

7731 ■ Goodmans Library
250 Yonge St., Ste. 2400
Toronto, ON, Canada M5B 2M6
Ph:(416)979-2211
Fax:(416)979-1234
Co. E-mail: msaulig@goodmans.ca
URL: http://www.goodmans.ca
Contact: Mary Saulig, Dir., Lib.Svcs.
Scope: Law - commercial, corporate, securities, bankruptcy, entertainment, planning, administrative; litigation; real estate; estates and trusts; taxation, e-commerce. **Services:** Interlibrary loan. **Holdings:** 12,000 volumes. **Subscriptions:** 250 journals and other serials.

7732 ■ Hancock & Estabrook Law Library
1500 AXA Tower 1
100 Madison St.
Syracuse, NY 13202
Ph:(315)471-3151
Fax:(315)471-3167
Co. E-mail: dbyrne@hancocklaw.com
URL: http://hancocklaw.com
Contact: Donna J. Byrne, Law Libn.
Scope: New York state and federal law; labor relations; taxes; securities; estates and trusts; negligence; products liability; malpractice; municipalities; real property; the environment; healthcare. **Services:** Library not open to the public. **Holdings:** 20,000 books. **Subscriptions:** 200 journals and other serials.

7733 ■ Hinckley, Allen, & Snyder LLP–Library Services
50 Kennedy Plaza, Ste. 1500
Providence, RI 02903
Ph:(401)274-2000
Fax:(401)277-9600
Co. E-mail: ctrask@haslaw.com
URL: http://www.haslaw.com/
Contact: Carolyn J. Trask, Dir., Lib.Svcs.
Scope: Law: business litigation; construction litigation; tax; commercial/business; labor; health; trusts; estates; financial planning; real estate; intellectual property. **Services:** Interlibrary loan (limited); Library not open to the public. **Holdings:** 8000 books. **Subscriptions:** 125 journals and other serials.

7734 ■ Irell & Manella Library
1800 Ave. of the Stars, Ste. 900
Los Angeles, CA 90067
Ph:(310)277-1010
Fax:(310)203-7199
Co. E-mail: info@irell.com
URL: http://www.irell.com
Contact: Louise L. Lieb
Scope: Law - intellectual property transactional, intellectual property litigation, federal and state litigation, tax, corporate, corporate securities, entertainment, antitrust, trusts and estates, probate, real estate, insurance, computer law, art law, aviation law. **Services:** Library not open to the public. **Holdings:** 70,000 volumes; microfiche; audio- and videotapes; CD-ROMs.

7735 ■ Kelley, Drye & Warren LLP Law Library
101 Park Ave.
New York, NY 10178
Ph:(212)808-7800
Fax:(212)808-7897
Co. E-mail: jkirk@kelleydrye.com
URL: http://www.kelleydrye.com
Contact: James J. Kirk
Scope: Law - banking, corporate, securities, trusts and estates, labor, tax; employee benefits. **Services:** Interlibrary loan (limited); Library not open to the public. **Holdings:** 40,000 books. **Subscriptions:** 247 journals and other serials; 28 newspapers.

7736 ■ Loeb & Loeb LLP Law Library
10100 Santa Monica Blvd., Ste. 2200
Los Angeles, CA 90067
Ph:(310)282-2000
Fax:(310)282-2200
Co. E-mail: mmayerson@loeb.com
URL: http://www.loeb.com
Contact: Mickey Mayerson, Off.Mng. Partner
Scope: Law taxation, litigation, insolvency and workout, entertainment, labor, real estate, corporate, estates and trusts, intellectual property. **Services:** Library not open to the public. **Holdings:** 34,000 volumes. **Subscriptions:** 200 journals and other serials; 12 newspapers.

7737 ■ Lum, Danzis, Drasco, Positan, & Kleinberg Law Library
103 Eisenhower Pkwy.
Roseland, NJ 07068-1049
Ph:(973)403-9000
Fax:(973)403-9021
URL: http://www.lumlaw.com
Contact: Steven J. Eisenstein
Scope: Law - taxation, labor and employment, corporate, banking, trust and estates, litigation. **Services:** Interlibrary loan; Library not open to the public. **Holdings:** 20,000 volumes. **Subscriptions:** 25 journals and other serials; 5 newspapers.

7738 ■ Mackenzie Hughes LLP Law Library
101 S. Salina St., Ste. 600
Syracuse, NY 13202
Ph:(315)474-7571
Fax:(315)474-6409
Co. E-mail: info@mackenziehughes.com
URL: http://www.mackenziehughes.com
Contact: Cheryl L. Wolfe, Law Libn.
Scope: Law - general, civil practice, tax, corporation, labor, estate, real estate. **Services:** Interlibrary loan; Library open to the public with permission of librarian. **Holdings:** 10,000 books; 50 cassettes; 800 law briefs; 300 memoranda of law. **Subscriptions:** 100 journals and other serials.

7739 ■ National Trust Company Reference Library
1 Adelaide St., E., 3rd Fl.
Toronto, ON, Canada M5C 2W8
Ph:(416)361-3611
Fax:(416)361-5551
Scope: Law; trusts and estates. **Services:** Library not open to the public. **Holdings:** 3200 books; 3500 annual reports of outside companies. **Subscriptions:** 150 journals and other serials; 8 newspapers.

7740 ■ Nixon Peabody LLP Law Library
1300 Clinton Sq.
Rochester, NY 14604
Ph:(585)263-1000
Fax:(585)263-1600
Co. E-mail: glusk@nixonpeabody.com
URL: http://www.nixonpeabody.com
Contact: Glenda Lusk, Off.Adm.
Scope: Law - corporate, tax, estates, real estate, labor, environmental, litigation. **Services:** Interlibrary loan; Library not open to the public. **Holdings:** 35,000 books. **Subscriptions:** 320 journals and other serials.

7741 ■ Ober, Kaler, Grimes & Shriver Library
120 E. Baltimore St., Ste. 800
Baltimore, MD 21202-1643
Ph:(410)685-1120
Fax:(410)547-0699
Co. E-mail: info@ober.com
URL: http://www.ober.com
Contact: Ginger J. Gerton, Libn.
Scope: Law - admiralty, hospital/healthcare, corporate, tax; litigation; estates and trusts. **Services:** Library not open to the public. **Holdings:** 15,000 books.

7742 ■ Putney, Twombly, Hall & Hirson LLP Law Library
521 5th Ave., Fl. 10
New York, NY 10175
Ph:(212)682-0020
Fax:(212)682-9380
Co. E-mail: info@putneylaw.com
URL: http://www.putneylaw.com
Scope: Law - labor, corporate, trust, estate, tax. **Services:** Library not open to the public. **Holdings:** 8000 books. **Subscriptions:** 12 journals and other serials.

7743 ■ Venable LLP Library
750 E. Pratt St., Ste. 900
Baltimore, MD 21201
Ph:(410)244-7400
Fax:(410)244-7742
Co. E-mail: lib01@venable.com
URL: http://www.venable.com
Contact: John S. Nixdorff, Libn.
Scope: Law - tax, labor, corporate, securities, environmental, trusts and estates, government contracts, healthcare, real estate; litigation; International trade; intellectual property; trade regulation; bankruptcy; employee benefits; banking. **Services:** Interlibrary loan; Library not open to the public. **Holdings:** 25,000 books; 500 bound periodical volumes. **Subscriptions:** 50 journals and other serials; 5 newspapers.

7744 ■ Willkie Farr & Gallagher Library
787 7th Ave.
New York, NY 10019-6099
Ph:(212)728-8000
Fax:(212)728-8111
URL: http://www.willkie.com
Contact: Debra Glessner, Dir., Lib.Svc.
Scope: Law - corporate, tax, real estate, trusts and estates, litigation. **Services:** Interlibrary loan; Library not open to the public. **Holdings:** 40,000 books; 400 bound periodical volumes; 7 cabinets of microforms; 45 videotapes. **Subscriptions:** 350 journals and other serials.

Estate Sales Business

ASSOCIATIONS AND OTHER ORGANIZATIONS

7745 ■ National Auctioneers Association
8880 Ballentine St.
Overland Park, KS 66214
Ph:(913)541-8084
Fax:(913)894-5281
Co. E-mail: support@auctioneers.org
URL: http://www.auctioneers.org
Contact: Hannes Combest, CEO

Description: Professional auctioneers. Provides continuing education classes for auctioneers, promotes use of the auction method of marketing in both the private and public sectors. Encourages the highest ethical standards for the profession. .

FRANCHISES AND BUSINESS OPPORTUNITIES

7746 ■ Caring Transitions
10700 Montgomery Rd., Ste. 300
Cincinnati, OH 45242
Free: 800-647-0766
Fax:(513)563-2691

No. of Franchise Units: 31. **Founded:** 2006. **Franchised:** 2006. **Description:** Sales of estates & household goods. **Equity Capital Needed:** $42,480-$70,680. **Franchise Fee:** $27,900. **Royalty Fee:** 6%. **Financial Assistance:** Limited in-house financing available. **Training:** Provides 5 days at headquarters, regional/national meetings, sales boot camps and ongoing support.

7747 ■ Estate Group
666 High St., Ste. 203
Worthington, OH 43085
Ph:(614)844-4406
Fax:(614)985-0169

No. of Franchise Units: 2. **No. of Company-Owned Units:** 1. **Founded:** 2004. **Franchised:** 2007. **Description:** Estate settlement & downsizing services. **Equity Capital Needed:** $45,700-$90,600. **Franchise Fee:** $29,000. **Royalty Fee:** Varies. **Financial Assistance:** Limited third party financing available.

ASSOCIATIONS AND OTHER ORGANIZATIONS

7748 ■ Association of Professional Recruiters of Canada
1081 Ambleside Dr., Ste. 2210
Ottawa, ON, Canada K2B 8C8
Ph:(613)721-5957
Free: 888-441-0000
Fax:(613)721-5850
Co. E-mail: info@workplace.ca
URL: http://www.workplace.ca
Contact: Ms. Nathaly Pinchuk, Exec. Dir.
Description: Employment recruiters. Seeks to advance the practice of employment recruiting; promotes ongoing professional development of members. Serves as a forum for the exchange of information among members; sponsors educational programs.

7749 ■ National Association of Executive Recruiters
1 E Wacker Dr., Ste. 2600
Chicago, IL 60601
Ph:(847)885-1453
Co. E-mail: naerinfo@naer.org
URL: http://www.naer.org
Contact: Jim Schneider, Pres. of Chase Hunter Group, Inc.
Description: Executive recruitment and search specialist firms providing counsel and assistance in identifying and hiring candidates for middle- and senior-level management positions. Promotes and enhances the public image, awareness, and understanding of the executive search profession. Serves as a forum for exchange of ideas among members; conducts educational programs and owners' roundtable. Maintains code of ethics and professional practice guidelines. .

REFERENCE WORKS

7750 ■ "Akron Community Foundation Hires Help for CEO Search" in *Crain's Cleveland Business* (Vol. 28, October 29, 2007, No. 43, pp. 6)
Pub: Crain Communications, Inc.
Ed: Shannon Mortland. **Description:** Waverly Partners LLC, an executive search firm, has been hired by the Akron Community Foundation to search for its next president and CEO as Jody Bacon, the company's current CEO, will retire on July 31, 2008.

7751 ■ "AT&T To Acquire Black Telecom Firm" in *Black Enterprise* (Vol. 38, January 2008, No. 6, pp. 24)
Pub: Earl G. Graves Publishing Co. Inc.
Ed: Alan Hughes. **Description:** Details of AT&T's acquisition of ChaseCom LP, a telecommunications company based in Houston, Texas, are covered.

7752 ■ "Calling All Recruiters: Agent HR Puts Staffing Agents In Charge" in *Black Enterprise* (Vol. 38, December 2007, No. 5, pp. 72)
Pub: Earl G. Graves Publishing Co. Inc.
Ed: Chana Garcia. **Description:** Recruiting and staffing agencies are seeing a drop in services due to slow economic growth. AgentHR partners with full-service recruiters who have three to five year's experience-specialists soliciting their own clients, provide staffing services, and manage their own accounts, thus combining the roles of recruiter and salesperson.

7753 ■ "DHR Hires Carr for Sports Group" in *Crain's Detroit Business* (Vol. 25, June 8, 2009, No. 23, pp. 5)
Pub: Crain Communications Inc. - Detroit
Ed: Sherri Begin Welch. **Description:** Lloyd Carr, former head football coach for University of Michigan, has taken a position with DHR International in order to expand its searches for collegiate and professional sports organizations, recruit athletic directors, head coaches and other executives.

7754 ■ *Directory of Executive and Professional Recruiters*
Pub: Kennedy Information
Released: Annual, latest edition 2009-2010. **Price:** $59.95, individuals. **Covers:** More than 13,000 key recruiters in 5,700 executive search firms with 7,575 executive search offices in North America; firms operating on a contingent fee basis are listed in separate section. **Entries Include:** Firm name, address, phone number and e-mail and web addresses when available, names of contact and other key personnel, brief description of firm's specialties, salary minimum; members of the Association of Executive Search Consultants are identified. For commercial use requests, please contact publisher. **Arrangement:** Alphabetical in separate retainer and contingency sections. **Indexes:** Geography, industry, job function, recruiter specialty, firm.

7755 ■ *The Directory of Toronto Recruiters*
Pub: Continental Records Company Ltd.
Contact: Neil Patte
Released: Annual, latest edition 2008. **Price:** $49. 95, individuals plus express post shipping cost and GST. **Covers:** More than 1,200 recruiting firms in the Toronto, Canada area. **Entries Include:** Firm name, address, phone, fax, e-mail, URL, name and title of contact, and industry and professional specialties.

7756 ■ "Growing Strong" in *Entrepreneur* (Vol. 35, November 2007, No. 11, pp. 36)
Pub: Entrepreneur Media Inc.
Ed: Nichole L. Torres. **Description:** Amy Langer founded Salo LL with partner John Folkestad. The company is growing fast since its 2002 launch, with over $40 million in projections for 2007. The finance and accounting staffing company tops the list of the fastest-growing women-led companies in North America.

7757 ■ "Impressive Numbers: Companies Experience Substantial Increases in Dollars, Employment" in *Hispanic Business* (July-August 2007)
Pub: Hispanic Business
Ed: Derek Reveron. **Description:** Profiles of five fastest growing Hispanic companies reporting increases in revenue and employment include Brightstar, distributor of wireless products; Greenway Ford Inc., a car dealership; Fred Loya Insurance, auto insurance carrier; and Group O, packaging company; and Diverse Staffing, Inc., an employment and staffing firm.

7758 ■ "iSymmetry's Technological Makeover Or, How a Tech Company Finally Grew Up and Discovered the World Wide Web" in *Inc.* (October 2007)
Pub: Gruner & Jahr USA Publishing
Description: Profile of iSymmetry, an Atlanta, Georgia-based IT recruiting firm, covering the issues the company faces keeping its technology equipment up-to-date. The firm has devised a program that will replace its old server-based software systems with on-demand software delivered via the Internet, known as software-as-a-service. Statistical information included.

7759 ■ "Job Search Made Easy" in *Black Enterprise* (Vol. 38, January 2008, No. 6, pp. 54)
Pub: Earl G. Graves Publishing Co. Inc.
Description: Profile of The Marquin Group's job portal called DiversityTalent.com. Marquin considered the challenges faced by corporations when recruiting senior executives; salaries, mortgage and relocation calculators for particular cities are provided.

7760 ■ "The Jobs Man" in *Business Courier* (Vol. 26, December 25, 2009, No. 35, pp. 1)
Pub: American City Business Journals, Inc.
Ed: Lucy May. **Description:** Entrepreneur Bob Messer, a volunteer for Jobs Plus Employment Network in Cincinnati's Over-the-Rhine neighborhood, regularly conducts a seminar that aims to help attendees prepare for employment. Jobs Plus founder Burr Robinson asked Messer to create the seminar in order to help unemployed jobseekers. So far, the program has helped 144 individuals with full time jobs in 2009.

7761 ■ "Matchmakers Anticipating Tech Valley Boom" in *Business Review, Albany New York* (Vol. 34, November 2, 2007, No. 31, pp. 1)
Pub: American City Business Journals, Inc.
Ed: Adam Sichko. **Description:** Qualified candidates are coming to permanent placement companies after being downsized elsewhere. The top five projected fastest-growing and top five projected fasted-decreasing jobs in the Capital Region are presented.

7762 ■ "On the Clock" in *Canadian Business* (Vol. 82, April 27, 2009, No. 7, pp. 28)
Pub: Rogers Media
Ed: Sarka Halas. **Description:** Survey of 100 Canadian executives found that senior managers can be out of a job for about nine months before their careers are adversely affected. The nine month mark can be avoided if job seekers build networks even before they lose their jobs. Job seekers should also take volunteer work and training opportunities to increase their changes of landing a job.

7763 ■ "Overseas Overtures" in *Business Journal-Portland* (Vol. 24, October 26, 2007, No. 35, pp. 1)
Pub: American City Business Journals, Inc.
Ed: Robin J. Moody. **Description:** Oregon has a workforce shortage, specifically for the health care industry. Recruiting agencies, such as the International Recruiting Network Inc., answers the high demand for workforce by recruiting foreign employees. The difficulties recruiting companies experience with regards to foreign labor laws are investigated.

7764 ■ "Regional Talent Network Unveils Jobs Web Site" in *Crain's Cleveland Business* (Vol. 30, June 1, 2009, No. 21, pp. 11)
Pub: Crain Communications, Inc.
Description: Regional Talent Network launched WhereToFindHelp.org, a Website designed to act as a directory of all Northeast Ohio resources that can help employers recruit and job seekers look for positions. The site also lists organizations offering employment and training services.

7765 ■ "Sign of the Times: Temp-To-Perm Attorneys" in *HRMagazine* (Vol. 54, January 2009, No. 1, pp. 24)
Pub: Society for Human Resource Management
Ed: Bill Leonard. **Description:** A growing number of law firms are hiring professional staff on a temp-to-perm basis according to the president of Professional Placement Services in Florida. Firms can save money while testing potential employees on a temporary basis.

7766 ■ "Staffing Firms are Picking Up the Pieces, Seeing Signs of Life" in *Milwaukee Business Journal* (Vol. 27, February 5, 2010, No. 19)
Pub: American City Business Journals
Ed: Rich Rovito. **Description:** Milwaukee, Wisconsin-based staffing firms are seeing signs of economic rebound as many businesses turned to temporary employees to fill the demands for goods and services. Economic observers believe the growth in temporary staffing is one of the early indicators of economic recovery.

7767 ■ "Talent Scout: How This Exec Finds and Develops Leaders Internally" in *Black Enterprise* (Vol. 38, November 2007, No. 4, pp. 63)
Pub: Earl G. Graves Publishing Co. Inc.
Ed: Faith Chukwudi. **Description:** Profile of Bernard Bedon, director at Public Group Media. Bedon helps attract, develop, retain, and reward talent in his media group of 10,000 employees worldwide.

7768 ■ "Wanted: African American Professional for Hire" in *Black Enterprise* (Vol. 37, November 2006, No. 4, pp. 93)
Pub: Earl G. Graves Publishing Co. Inc.
Ed: Joe Watson. **Description:** Excerpt from the book, Without Excuses: Unleash the Power of Diversity to Build Your Business, speaks to the lack of diversity in the corporate arena and why executives, recruiters, and HR professionals claim they are unable to find qualified individuals of different races when hiring.

7769 ■ "What You Look Like Online" in *Black Enterprise* (Vol. 37, January 2007, No. 6, pp. 56)
Pub: Earl G. Graves Publishing Co. Inc.
Ed: Marcia A. Reed-Woodard. **Description:** Of 100 executive recruiters 77 percent stated that they use search engines to check the backgrounds of potential job candidates, according to a survey conducted by ExecuNet. Of those surveyed 35 percent stated that they eliminate potential candidates based on information they find online so it is important to create a positive Web presence which highlights professional image qualities.

7770 ■ "Winner: Private Company, $100M-$1B" in *Crain's Detroit Business* (Vol. 25, June 22, 2009, No. 25, pp. E004)
Pub: Crain Communications Inc. - Detroit
Ed: Sherri Begin Welch. **Description:** Profile of Strategic Staffing Solutions Inc. is presented.

TRADE PERIODICALS

7771 ■ *Executive Recruiter News*
Pub: Kennedy Information Inc.
Ed: Joseph Daniel McCool, Editor, ern-editor@kennedyinfo.com. **Released:** Monthly. **Price:** $229. **Description:** The authoritative voice of the recruiting industry, covering news, analysis, practice advice, proprietary data and opinion.

VIDEOCASSETTES/ AUDIOCASSETTES

7772 ■ *From Law School to Law Practice: What Every Associate Needs to Know—The Set*
American Law Institute
American Bar Association Committee on Continuing Education
4025 Chestnut St.
Philadelphia, PA 19104
Ph:(215)243-1600
Free: 800-CLE-NEWS
Fax:(215)243-1636
Co. E-mail: custserv@ali-aba.org
URL: http://www.ali.org
Released: 1989. **Price:** $190. **Description:** Uses brief dramatizations to outline various skills and strategies for law firm success. Complete with study guide. **Availability:** VHS.

FRANCHISES AND BUSINESS OPPORTUNITIES

7773 ■ Express Employment Professionals
8516 NW Expy.
Oklahoma City, OK 73162
Free: 877-652-6400
Co. E-mail: franchising@expresspersonnel.com
URL: http://www.franchising.expresspersonnel.com
No. of Franchise Units: 550. **Founded:** 1983. **Franchised:** 1985. **Description:** Is an international fullservice staffing corporation with three distinct divisions available in one franchise agreement. The franchised offices provide clients with temporary help, full-time placements, and executive recruitment. **Equity Capital Needed:** $153,750-$242,500 depending on the market. Can be a combo of cash and equity. **Franchise Fee:** $35,000. **Financial Assistance:** Express finances temporary associate payroll. **Managerial Assistance:** Continuous follow-up training in the field and in regular seminars and workshops. **Training:** 2 week initial training at headquarters, 1 week in certified training office and ongoing field training and support. Followed by additional time in new office with assigned field representative.

7774 ■ FPC/F-O-R-T-U-N-E Personnel Consultants
145 West 45th St., 8th Fl.
New York, NY 10036
Ph:(212)302-1141
Free: 800-886-7839
Co. E-mail: rherzog@fpcnational.com
URL: http://www.fpcnational.com
No. of Franchise Units: 71. **Founded:** 1959. **Franchised:** 1973. **Description:** Executive recruiting firm. Franchise owners enjoy all of today's technologies, including a national computerized exchange program. **Equity Capital Needed:** $93,070-$138,550, excluding franchise fee. **Franchise Fee:** $50,000. **Financial Assistance:** No. **Training:** Comprehensive training and continued support by industry experienced professionals. Initial 2 weeks at national headquarters focusing on management, operations, sales, technology and industry specific topics. 1 week of training at franchise office. Continued support and ongoing training that includes: 800 line, onsite, seminars and conferences.

7775 ■ FPC (FORTUNE Personnel Consultants)
1140 Avenue of the Americas, 5th Fl.
New York, NY 10036-2711
Ph:(212)302-1141
Free: 800-886-7839
Fax:(212)302-2422
Co. E-mail: rherzoq@fpcnational.com
URL: http://www.fpcnational.com
No. of Franchise Units: 70. **Founded:** 1959. **Franchised:** 1973. **Description:** Executive recruiting firm. **Equity Capital Needed:** $93,100-$138,600. **Franchise Fee:** $40,000. **Royalty Fee:** 7%. **Financial Assistance:** Direct financial assistance available. **Training:** Offers 2 weeks training at headquarters, 5 days at franchise location with ongoing training, mentoring and coaching.

7776 ■ Management Recruiters International Inc.
CDI Corp.
75 Erieview Plc., Ste. 100
Cleveland, OH 44114
Ph:(216)416-8467
Free: 800-875-4000
Fax:(216)696-6612
No. of Franchise Units: 1,128. **No. of Company-Owned Units:** 32. **Founded:** 1957. **Franchised:** 1965. **Description:** Management level and general personnel placement, search and recruiting service on an employer-paid, contingency fee basis. **Equity Capital Needed:** $112,855-$154,345. **Franchise Fee:** $100,000. **Financial Assistance:** Yes. **Training:** Initial training program of approximately 3 weeks at headquarters, plus an additional on-the-job training program of approximately 3 weeks in licensee's first office. Training thereafter as needed. Also assists in securing suitable office space, lease negotiations, design and layout, office furniture, equipment, telephone systems, etc.

7777 ■ Pridestaff
7535 N Palm Ave., Ste. 101
Fresno, CA 93711-1393
Ph:(559)449-5804
No. of Franchise Units: 35. **No. of Company-Owned Units:** 3. **Founded:** 1978. **Franchised:** 1995. **Description:** Recruiting Agency. **Equity Capital Needed:** $162,000-$237,000. **Franchise Fee:** $32,000. **Financial Assistance:** No. **Training:** Yes.

7778 ■ Sanford Rose Associates
SRA International, Inc.
1305 Mall of Georgia Blvd., Ste. 160
Buford, GA 30519
Ph:(678)833-9305
Free: 800-731-7724
Fax:(770)904-0359
No. of Franchise Units: 64. **Founded:** 1959. **Franchised:** 1970. **Description:** Employee search service that uses a database of candidates and custom computer software to allow each office to match employees with client openings. **Equity Capital Needed:** $91,350-$129,680. **Franchise Fee:** $65,000. **Financial Assistance:** Yes. **Managerial Assistance:** The first 6-9 months, franchisee works with staff in strategic planning. **Training:** Provides a minimum of 10 days of training at corporate headquarters and an additional 5 days of training in franchisees office.

COMPUTERIZED DATABASES

7779 ■ *SkillSearch*
SkillSearch Ltd.
22-23 Kensington St.
East Sussex
Brighton BN1 4AJ, United Kingdom
Ph:44 1273 64 7280
Fax:44 1273 64 7290
Co. E-mail: mail@skillsearch.com
URL: http://www.skillsearch.com
Description: Provides information on new employment opportunities for individuals in the United Kingdom and Europe. Searchable by product area, location, and position. **Availability:** Online: SkillSearch Ltd. **Type:** Directory.

COMPUTER SYSTEMS/ SOFTWARE

7780 ■ PcHunter
Micro J. Systems, Inc.
200 East Del Mar Blvd., Ste. 91105
Pasadena, CA 91105

Ph:(310)458-1997
Free: 800-995-4868
Fax:(310)458-2177
Co. E-mail: sales@microj.com
URL: http://www.microj.com
Price: Contact MicroJ Systems. **Description:** Available for PC Computers. System provides a recruitment-management program for employment agencies.